NATIONAL CENTER FOR EDUCATION STATISTICS

Digest of Education Statistics 1997

Thomas D. Snyder
Project Director

Charlene M. Hoffman
Production Manager

Claire M. Geddes
Program Analyst

370.973
D572
1997

U.S. Department of Education
Office of Educational Research and Improvement   NCES 98–015

U.S. Department of Education
Richard W. Riley
Secretary

Office of Educational Research and Improvement
Ricky T. Takai
Acting Assistant Secretary

National Center for Education Statistics
Pascal D. Forgione, Jr.
Commissioner

The National Center for Education Statistics (NCES) is the primary federal entity for collecting, analyzing, and reporting data related to education in the United States and other nations. It fulfills a congressional mandate to collect, collate, analyze, and report full and complete statistics on the condition of education in the United States; conduct and publish reports and specialized analyses of the meaning and significance of such statistics; assist state and local education agencies in improving their statistical systems; and review and report on education activities in foreign countries.

NCES activities are designed to address high priority education data needs; provide consistent, reliable, complete, and accurate indicators of education status and trends; and report timely, useful, and high quality data to the U.S. Department of Education, the Congress, the states, other education policymakers, practitioners, data users, and the general public.

We strive to make our products available in a variety of formats and in language that is appropriate to a variety of audiences. You, as our customer, are the best judge of our success in communicating information effectively. If you have any comments or suggestions about this or any other NCES product or report, we would like to hear from you. Please direct your comments to:

> National Center for Education Statistics
> Office of Educational Research and Improvement
> U.S. Department of Education
> 555 New Jersey Avenue NW
> Washington, DC 20208–5574

December 1997

The NCES World Wide Web Home Page is
http://nces.ed.gov

Suggested Citation
U.S. Department of Education. National Center for Education Statistics. *Digest of Education Statistics, 1997*, NCES 98–015, by Thomas D. Snyder. Production Manager, Charlene M. Hoffman. Program Analyst, Claire M. Geddes. Washington, DC: 1997.

For sale by the U.S. Government Printing Office
Superintendent of Documents, Mail Stop: SSOP, Washington, DC 20402-9328
ISBN 0-16-049343-9

FOREWORD

This 1997 edition of the *Digest of Education Statistics* is the 33rd in a series of publications initiated in 1962. (The *Digest* has been issued annually except for combined editions for the years 1977-78, 1983-84, and 1985-86.) Its primary purpose is to provide a compilation of statistical information covering the broad field of American education from kindergarten through graduate school. The *Digest* includes a selection of data from many sources, both government and private, and draws especially on the results of surveys and activities carried out by the National Center for Education Statistics (NCES). The publication contains information on a variety of subjects in the field of education statistics, including the number of schools and colleges, teachers, enrollments, and graduates, in addition to educational attainment, finances, federal funds for education, employment and income of graduates, libraries, and international education. Supplemental information on population trends, attitudes on education, education characteristics of the labor force, government finances, and economic trends provides background for evaluating education data. Although the *Digest* contains important information on federal education funding, more detailed information on federal activities is available from federal education program offices. For example, the Office of Bilingual Education and Minority Languages Affairs supports the National Clearinghouse on Bilingual Education, which compiles information on students and teachers involved in bilingual education.

The *Digest* is divided into seven chapters: "All Levels of Education," "Elementary and Secondary Education," "Postsecondary Education," "Federal Programs for Education and Related Activities," "Outcomes of Education," "International Comparisons of Education," and "Learning Resources and Technology." To qualify for inclusion, material must be nationwide in scope and of current interest and value. The introduction includes a brief overview of current trends in American education, which supplements the tabular materials in chapters 1 through 7. Information on the structure of the statistical tables is contained in the "Guide to Tabular Presentation." The "Guide to Sources" provides a brief synopsis of the surveys used to generate the tabulations for the *Digest*. Also, a "Definitions" section is included to help readers understand terms. To make analyses more convenient for researchers, many new *Digest* tables include standard errors. In addition to updating many of the statistics that have appeared in previous years, this edition contains a significant amount of new material, including:

- Findings from the Third International Math and Science Study, the largest comparison of international achievement ever undertaken, tables 395 to 402;

- Percent of students in grades 4, 8, and 12 at various math and science proficiency levels in 1996, tables 119 and 124;

- Percent of public schools and school classrooms with Internet access, table 415.

Martin E. Orland
Associate Commissioner,
Data Development and Longitudinal Studies
  Group
National Center for Education Statistics
December 1997

ACKNOWLEDGMENTS

Many people have contributed in one way or another to the development of the *Digest*. Thomas D. Snyder was responsible for the overall development and preparation of this *Digest* which was prepared under the general direction of Mary Frase.

Charlene M. Hoffman provided technical assistance in all phases of its preparation and was responsible for Chapter 4, "Federal Programs for Education and Related Activities," and for tables on degrees conferred. Claire Geddes developed the text for chapter introductions and was responsible for materials dealing with higher education enrollment, finance, and faculty characteristics. William Sonnenberg provided statistical computing consultation on all phases of the report. Celestine Davis provided statistical assistance on materials dealing with educational attainment and student assessment. Debra Gerald and William Hussar prepared projections of school enrollment and finance statistics.

A number of individuals outside the Center also expended large amounts of time and effort on the *Digest*. Sherrie Aitken, Irma Alemar, Judy Blake, Ismail Iro, Michael Neimat, William Scarbrough, Linda Shafer, and Patricia Thomson of CSR, Inc., provided research and statistical assistance. In the Office of Information Services, Robert LeGrand provided editorial assistance and Phil Carr designed the cover. Jerry Fairbanks of the U.S. Government Printing Office managed the typesetting.

This year's edition of the *Digest* has received extensive reviews by individuals within and outside the Department of Education. We wish to thank them for their time and expert advice. In the Office of Educational Research and Improvement (OERI), W. Vance Grant and Duc-Le To reviewed the entire manuscript. Rosemary Clark (U.S. Bureau of the Census) also reviewed the entire document. Ellen Bradburn of the Education Statistics Services Institute reviewed substantial portions of the document. OERI staff who reviewed portions of the manuscript were: Sam Barbett, Jonaki Bose, Patricia Q. Brown, Shelley Burns, Adrienne Chute, Mike Cohen, Mary Frase, Debra Gerald, Steven Gorman, Kerry Gruber, Frank Johnson, Andrew Malizio, Marilyn McMillen, Frank Morgan, Shi-Chang Wu, and Linda Zimbler. Agency reviews were conducted by the Office of Bilingual Education and Minority Languages Affairs, the Office of Vocational Adult Education, Planning and Evaluation Service, and Budget Service.

Contents

	Page
Foreword	iii
Acknowledgments	v
Introduction	1
Chapter 1. All Levels of Education	5
Chapter 2. Elementary and Secondary Education	43
Chapter 3. Postsecondary Education	173
College and University Education	180
Vocational and Adult Education	369
Chapter 4. Federal Programs for Education and Related Activities	375
Chapter 5. Outcomes of Education	415
Chapter 6. International Comparisons of Education	433
Chapter 7. Learning Resources and Technology	457
Appendix	
Guide to Tabular Presentation	469
Guide to Sources	471
Definitions	503
Index of Table Numbers	517

Figures

1. The structure of education in the United States 7
2. Enrollment and total expenditures in current and constant dollars, by level of education: 1960–61 to 1996–97 8
3. Years of school completed by persons 25 years old and over: 1940 to 1996 9
4. Years of school completed by persons 25 to 29 years of age: 1940 to 1996 9
5. Highest level of education attained by persons 25 years and older: March 1996 10
6. Items most frequently cited by the public as a major problem facing the local public schools: 1980 to 1996 10
7. Preprimary enrollment of 3- to 5-year-olds, by attendance status: October 1970 to October 1996 46
8. Enrollment, number of teachers, pupil/teacher ratios, and expenditures in public schools: 1960–61 to 1996–97 47
9. Percentage change in public elementary and secondary enrollment, by state: Fall 1991 to fall 1996 48
10. Average annual salary for public elementary and secondary school teachers: 1969–70 to 1996–97 48
11. Sources of revenue for public elementary and secondary schools: 1970–71 to 1994–95 49
12. Current expenditure per pupil in average daily attendance in public elementary and secondary schools: 1970–71 to 1996–97 49
13. Enrollment, degrees conferred, and expenditures in institutions of higher education: 1960–61 to 1996–97 176
14. Percentage change in total enrollment of institutions of higher education, by state: Fall 1990 to fall 1995 177
15. Enrollment in institutions of higher education, by age: Fall 1970 to fall 2007 177
16. Full-time-equivalent students per staff member in public and private institutions of higher education: 1976 and 1993 178
17. Trends in bachelor's degrees conferred in selected fields of study: 1984–85, 1989–90, and 1994–95 178
18. Sources of current-fund revenue for public institutions of higher education: 1994–95 . 179
19. Sources of current-fund revenue for private institutions of higher education: 1994–95 179
20. Federal on-budget funds for education, by agency: Fiscal year 1997 385
21. Federal on-budget funds for education, by level or other educational purpose: 1965 to 1997 386
22. Department of Education outlays, by type of recipient: Fiscal year 1997 386
23. Labor force participation of persons 16 years old and over, by age and highest level of education: 1996 416

24. Unemployment rates of persons 25 years old and over, by highest degree attained: 1996 417

25. Labor force status of 1995–96 high school dropouts and graduates not enrolled in college: October 1996 417

26. Median annual income of persons with income 25 years old and over, by highest degree attained and sex: 1995 418

27. Salaries of recent bachelor's degree recipients 1 year after graduation, by field: 1987, 1991, and 1994 418

28. Percentage change in enrollment, by area of the world and level of education: 1980 to 1994 435

29. Public expenditures for education as a percentage of gross national product: Selected countries, 1993 436

30. Bachelor's degree recipients as a percent of population for selected countries, by sex: 1994 436

31. Nations' average mathematics performance compared to the United States: 1995 437

32. Nations' average science performance compared to the United States: 1995 437

33. Percent of all public schools having or expecting Internet access between fall 1994 and 2000 458

Tables

1. All Levels of Education

Enrollment, Teachers, and Schools

1. Estimated number of participants in elementary and secondary education and in higher education: Fall 1997 11

2. Enrollment in educational institutions, by level and control of institution: Fall 1980 to fall 2005 11

3. Enrollment in educational institutions, by level and by control of institution: 1869–70 to fall 2007 12

4. Teachers in elementary and secondary schools, and senior instructional staff in institutions of higher education, by control of institution: Fall 1970 to fall 2007 13

5. Educational institutions, by level and control of institution: 1978–79 to 1995–96 14

Enrollment Rates

6. Percent of the population 3 to 34 years old enrolled in school, by age: April 1940 to October 1996 15

7. Percent of the population 3 to 34 years old enrolled in school, by race/ethnicity, sex, and age: October 1975 to October 1996 16

Educational Attainment

8. Years of school completed by persons age 25 and over and 25 to 29, by race/ethnicity and sex: 1910 to 1996 17

9. Highest level of education attained by persons age 18 and over, by age, sex, and race/ethnicity: March 1996 18

10.	Number of persons age 18 and over who hold a bachelor's or higher degree, by field of study, sex, race, and age: Spring 1993	19
11.	Educational attainment of persons 25 years old and over, by state: April 1990	20
12.	Educational attainment of persons 25 years old and over, by state and race/ethnicity: April 1990	21
13.	Educational attainment of persons 25 years old and over, for the 25 largest states: March 1995	22
14.	Educational attainment of persons 25 years old and over, for the 15 largest metropolitan areas: March 1995	22

Population

15.	Estimates of resident population, by age group: July 1, 1970 to July 1, 1996	23
16.	Estimates of school-age resident population, by race and sex: July 1, 1970 to July 1, 1996	23
17.	Estimated total and school-age resident populations, by state: 1970 to 1996	24

Characteristics of Families with Children

18.	Families, by family status and presence of own children under 18: 1970 to 1995	25
19.	Characteristics of families with own children under 18, by family status and race/ethnicity: 1995	26
20.	Household income and poverty rates, by state: 1990, 1994, and 1995	27
21.	Poverty status of persons, families, and children under 18, by race/ethnicity: 1959 to 1995	28

Opinions on Education

22.	Average grade that the public would give the schools in their community and in the nation at large: 1974 to 1995	29
23.	Items most frequently cited by the general public as a major problem facing the local public schools: 1970 to 1996	29
24.	Public opinion of public and private school choice: 1989 to 1996	30
25.	Parental involvement in 8th graders' school-related activities, by selected parental characteristics: 1988	30
26.	Teachers' opinions about the most important goals for education, by type and control of school: 1990–91	31
27.	Teachers' perceptions about serious problems in their schools, by type and control of school: 1990–91 and 1993–94	31
28.	Teachers' perceptions about teaching and school conditions, by type and control of school: 1993–94	32
29.	Public's level of confidence in various institutions: 1994 and 1996	33

Charitable Contributions

30.	Percentage of households contributing to education and other charitable organizations and average annual donation, by type of charity: 1989, 1991, 1993, and 1995	33

Finances

31. Total expenditures of educational institutions related to the gross domestic product, by level of institution: 1959–60 to 1996–97 34

32. Total expenditures of educational institutions, by level and control of institution: 1899–1900 to 1996–97 35

33. Estimated total expenditures of educational institutions, by level, control of institution, and source of funds: 1979–80 to 1994–95 36

34. Governmental expenditures, by level of government and function: 1970–71 to 1992–93 37

35. Direct general expenditures of state and local governments for all functions and for education, by level and state: 1992–93 38

36. Direct general expenditures per capita of state and local governments for all functions and for education, by level and state: 1992–93 39

37. Gross domestic product, state and local expenditures, personal income, disposable personal income, median family income, and population: 1929 to 1996 40

38. Gross domestic product deflator, Consumer Price Index, education price indexes, and federal budget composite deflator: 1919 to 1997 41

2. Elementary and Secondary Education

Enrollment

39. Historical summary of public elementary and secondary school statistics: 1869–70 to 1994–95 50

40. Enrollment in public elementary and secondary schools, by level and state: Fall 1981 to fall 1996 52

41. Enrollment in public elementary and secondary schools, by grade and state: Fall 1995 54

42. Enrollment in public elementary and secondary schools, by grade and state: Fall 1994 56

43. Enrollment in public elementary and secondary schools, by grade: Fall 1981 to fall 1995 58

44. Average daily attendance in public elementary and secondary schools, by state: 1969–70 to 1994–95 59

45. Enrollment in public elementary and secondary schools, by race or ethnicity and state: Fall 1986 and fall 1995 60

46. Enrollment of 3-, 4-, and 5-year-old children in preprimary programs, by level and control of program and by attendance status: October 1965 to October 1996 61

47. Children of prekindergarten through second grade age, by enrollment status, maternal characteristics, and household income: 1991, 1993, and 1995 62

48. Percent of public school kindergarten teachers indicating the importance of various factors for kindergarten readiness: Spring 1993 62

49. Child care arrangements of preschool children, by age and household characteristics: 1991 and 1995 63

50. Participation of public kindergarten children in selected activities 5 days a week, by length and size of class and teacher preparation: Spring 1993 63

51. Public school pupils transported at public expense and current expenditures for transportation: 1929–30 to 1994–95 64

52. Children 0 to 21 years old served in federally supported programs for the disabled, by type of disability: 1976–77 to 1995–96 65

53. Percentage distribution of disabled persons 3 to 21 years old receiving education services for the disabled, by age group and educational environment: 1994–95 66

54. State legislation on gifted and talented programs and number and percent of students receiving services in public elementary and secondary schools, by state: 1993–94 and 1995–96 66

55. Number of children served under Individuals with Disabilities Education Act and Chapter 1 of the Education Consolidation and Improvement Act, State Operated Programs, by age group and state: 1990–91 to 1995–96 67

56. Enrollment in grades 9 to 12 in public and private schools compared with population 14 to 17 years of age: 1889–90 to fall 1996 68

57. Enrollment in foreign language courses compared with enrollment in grades 9 to 12 in public secondary schools: Fall 1948 to fall 1994 69

58. Student participation in school programs and services, by control, level of school, and type of community: 1993–94 70

Private Elementary and Secondary Schools

59. Private elementary and secondary enrollment and schools, by selected characteristics: 1993–94 70

60. Private elementary and secondary staff and student-staff ratios, by level and orientation of school: 1993–94 71

61. Private elementary and secondary enrollment and schools, by amount of tuition, level, and orientation of school: 1993–94 72

62. Summary statistics on Catholic elementary and secondary schools, by level: 1919–20 to 1996–97 72

63. Private elementary and secondary schools, enrollment, teachers, and high school graduates, by state: Fall 1993 73

Teachers and Other Instructional Staff

64. Public and private elementary and secondary teachers and pupil-teacher ratios, by level: Fall 1955 to fall 1997 74

65. Public elementary and secondary teachers, by level and state: Fall 1991 to fall 1996 75

66. Teachers, enrollment, and pupil-teacher ratios in public elementary and secondary schools, by state: Fall 1990 to fall 1995 76

67. Teachers in public and private elementary and secondary schools, by selected characteristics: 1993–94 77

68. Highest degree earned and number of years teaching experience for teachers in public elementary and secondary schools, by state: 1993–94 78

69.	Selected characteristics of public school teachers: Spring 1961 to spring 1996	79
70.	Public secondary school teachers, by subject taught: Spring 1966 to spring 1996	80
71.	Percent of vocational and nonvocational public school teachers of grades 9 to 12, by selected demographic and educational characteristics: 1993–94	80
72.	Mobility of public and private elementary and secondary teachers, by selected school and teacher characteristics: 1987–88 to 1993–94	81
73.	Average salaries for full-time teachers in public and private elementary and secondary schools, by selected characteristics: 1993–94	82
74.	Public school students' ratings of the quality of teachers and parental and community support for their schools, by school location and students' race/ethnicity (in percent): 1996	83
75.	Percent of students who give the teachers in their school grades "A" or "B" for their teaching skills, by school location and students' race/ethnicity: 1996	83
76.	Percent of public school students' interest in a career in education, by student characteristics: 1996	83
77.	Estimated average annual salary of teachers in public elementary and secondary schools: 1959–60 to 1996–97	84
78.	Estimated average annual salary of teachers in public elementary and secondary schools, by state: 1969–70 to 1996–97	85
79.	Minimum and average teacher salaries, by state: 1990–91, 1993–94, and 1995–96 ..	86
80.	Average annual salary of instructional staff in public elementary and secondary schools, by state: 1939–40 to 1996–97	87
81.	Estimated average annual salary of instructional staff in public elementary and secondary schools and average annual earnings of full-time employees in all industries: 1929–30 to 1996–97	88
82.	Staff employed in public elementary and secondary school systems, by functional area: 1949–50 to fall 1995	89
83.	Staff employed in public school systems, by type of assignment and state: Fall 1995	90
84.	Staff employed in public school systems, by type of assignment and state: Fall 1994	91
85.	Staff and teachers in public elementary and secondary schools, by state: Fall 1989 to fall 1995	92
86.	Staff, enrollment, and pupil-staff ratios in public elementary and secondary schools, by state: Fall 1989 to fall 1995	93
87.	Principals in public and private elementary and secondary schools, by selected characteristics: 1993–94	94

Schools and School Districts

88.	Public elementary and secondary students, schools, pupil-teacher ratios, and finances, by type of locale: 1995	95
89.	Public school districts and public and private elementary and secondary schools: 1929–30 to 1995–96	96

90.	Public school districts and enrollment, by size of district: 1988–89 to 1995–96	96
91.	Number and percentage of public elementary and secondary education agencies, by state and type of agency: 1995–96	97
92.	Selected statistics for public school districts enrolling more than 20,000 pupils, by state: 1995–96	98
93.	Enrollment of the 130 largest public school districts: Fall 1995	103
94.	Public elementary and secondary schools, by type of school: 1967–68 to 1995–96	104
95.	Public elementary and secondary schools, by type and size of school: 1995–96	104
96.	Public elementary and secondary schools, by type and state: 1990–91 to 1995–96	105
97.	Public elementary schools, by grade span and average school size, by state: 1993–94	106
98.	Public secondary schools, by grade span and average school size, by state: 1995–96	107

High School Seniors, Completions, and Dropouts

99.	High school graduates compared with population 17 years of age, by sex and control of school: 1869–70 to 1996–97	108
100.	Public high school graduates, by state: 1969–70 to 1996–97	109
101.	High school graduates and dropouts in public elementary and secondary schools, by race or ethnicity and state: 1994–95	110
102.	General Educational Development (GED) credentials issued, and number and age of test takers: United States and outlying areas, 1971 to 1995	111
103.	Percent of high school dropouts among persons 16 to 24 years old, by sex and race/ethnicity: April 1960 to October 1996	111
104.	Percent of high school dropouts among persons 16 to 34 years old, by age, sex, and race/ethnicity: October 1970 to October 1996	112
105.	Students with disabilities exiting the educational system, by age, type of disability, and basis of exit: United States and outlying areas, 1991–92 and 1993–94	113
106.	Postsecondary education and employment status, wages earned, and living arrangements of special education students out of secondary school up to 3 years, by type of disability: 1990	113

Educational Achievement

107.	Average student proficiency in reading, by age and selected characteristics of students: 1971 to 1996	114
108.	Student proficiency in reading, by percentile and age: 1971 to 1996	115
109.	Student proficiency in reading, by age, amount of time spent on homework, and reading habits: 1984, 1994, and 1996	116
110.	Percent of students at or above selected reading proficiency levels, by sex, race/ethnicity, and age: 1971 to 1996	117
111.	Average proficiency in reading for 4th graders in public schools, by selected characteristics, region, and state: 1994	118

112. Percentage distribution of 4th graders in public schools, by time spent on homework and television viewing each day: 1992 and 1996 119

113. Average writing performance of 4th, 8th, and 11th graders, by selected characteristics of students: 1984 to 1996 120

114. Student values and attitudes toward writing, by grade level: 1984, 1990, 1992, and 1994 121

115. Percent of students at or above selected history proficiency levels, by selected characteristics and grade level: 1994 121

116. Average student proficiency in geography and U.S. history, by student characteristics: 1994 122

117. Percent of students at or above selected geography proficiency levels, by selected characteristics and grade level: 1994 122

118. Average mathematics proficiency, by age and by selected characteristics of students: 1973 to 1996 123

119. Percent of students at or above selected mathematics proficiency levels, by sex, race/ethnicity, control of school, and age: 1978 to 1996 124

120. Average proficiency in mathematics content areas for 8th graders in public schools, by region and state: 1996 125

121. Average proficiency in mathematics content areas for 4th graders in public schools, by region and state: 1996 126

122. Selected characteristics of 8th grade students in public schools, by region and state: 1992 127

123. Mathematics proficiency of 17-year-olds, by highest mathematics course taken, sex, and race/ethnicity: 1978, 1990, 1992, 1994, and 1996 128

124. Percent of students at or above selected science proficiency levels, by sex, race/ethnicity, control of school, and age: 1977 to 1996 129

125. Average proficiency in science for 8th graders in public schools, by selected characteristics and state: 1996 130

126. Average science proficiency, by age and by selected characteristics of students: 1970 to 1996 131

127. Twelfth graders' achievement on history, mathematics, reading, and science tests: 1992 132

128. Scholastic Assessment Test score averages, by race/ethnicity: 1975–76 to 1994–95 132

129. Scholastic Assessment Test score averages for college-bound high school seniors, by sex: 1966–67 to 1996–97 133

130. Distribution of Scholastic Assessment Test scores, by sex of student: 1975–76 to 1994–95 134

131. Scholastic Assessment Test score averages, by intended area of study: 1977–78 to 1994–95 135

132. Scholastic Assessment Test score averages, by class rank: 1976–77 to 1994–95 135

133. Scholastic Assessment Test score averages, by state: 1974–75 to 1994–95 136

134. American College Testing (ACT) score averages, by sex: 1967 to 1996 137

135. Percent of high school seniors reporting they were in general, college preparatory, and vocational programs, by student characteristics: 1982 and 1992 137

136. Average number of Carnegie units earned by public high school graduates in various subject fields, by student characteristics: 1982 to 1994 138

137. Average number of Carnegie units earned by public school graduates in vocational education courses, by student characteristics: 1982 to 1994 139

138. Percentage of high school graduates taking selected, mathematics and science courses in high school, by sex and race/ethnicity: 1982 to 1994 140

139. Percent of high school graduates earning minimum credits in selected combinations of academic courses, by sex and race/ethnicity: 1982 to 1994 140

Student Activities and Behavior

140. Reasons given by twelfth graders for taking current mathematics and science classes, by selected student and school characteristics: 1992 141

141. Expected occupations of 8th, 10th, and 12th graders at age 30, by selected student and school characteristics: 1988, 1990, and 1992 141

142. Eighth, tenth, and twelfth graders' attitudes about school climate, by student and school characteristics: 1988, 1990, and 1992 142

143. Percentage of 3- to 5-year-olds who were read to every day in the last week by a family member: 1993, 1995, and 1996 142

144. Participation of 10th and 12th graders in extracurricular activities, by selected student characteristics: 1990 and 1992 143

145. Percent of high school seniors who plan to go to college after graduation, by student characteristics: 1982 and 1992 143

146. Percent of high school seniors who say they engage in various activities, by student characteristics: 1982 and 1992 144

147. Percent of high school seniors who participate in selected school-sponsored extracurricular activities, by student characteristics: 1980 and 1992 144

148. Percent of high school students in grades 9 through 12 who reported experience with drugs and violence on school property, by race/ethnicity, grade, and sex: 1993 and 1995 145

149. Percent of 12- to 17-year-olds reporting drug use during the past 30 days and the past year: 1979 to 1995 145

150. Percent of high school seniors reporting drug use, by type of drug and frequency of use: 1975 to 1996 146

151. Percent of students (grades 7 to 12) who feel that certain problems are very serious: 1996 146

State Regulations

152. Ages for compulsory school attendance, special education services for students, policies for kindergarten programs, and year-round schools, by state: 1997 and 1995 147

153. Tenth and twelfth graders' attendance patterns, by selected student and school characteristics: 1990 and 1992 148

154. Twelfth graders who agree or strongly agree with statements about their school: 1992 148

155. State requirements for high school graduation, in Carnegie units: 1993 and 1996 149

156. States using minimum-competency testing, by government level setting standards, grade levels assessed, and expected uses of standards: 1995–96 155

157. States requiring testing for initial certification of teachers, by authorization, year enacted, year effective, and test used: 1987 and 1990 and 1996 156

Revenues and Expenditures

158. Revenues for public elementary and secondary schools, by source of funds: 1919–20 to 1994–95 157

159. Revenues for public elementary and secondary schools, by source and state: 1994–95 158

160. Revenues for public elementary and secondary schools, by source and state: 1993–94 159

161. Funds and staff for state education agencies, by source of funding and state: 1992–93 160

162. Summary of expenditures for public elementary and secondary education, by purpose: 1919–20 to 1994–95 161

163. Total expenditures for public elementary and secondary education, by function and subfunction: 1989–90 to 1994–95 162

164. Expenditures for instruction in public elementary and secondary schools, by subfunction and state: 1993–94 and 1994–95 163

165. Current expenditures for public elementary and secondary education, by state: 1969–70 to 1996–97 164

166. Total expenditures for public elementary and secondary education, by function and state: 1994–95 166

167. Total expenditures for public elementary and secondary education, by function and state: 1993–94 168

168. Current expenditure per pupil in average daily attendance in public elementary and secondary schools, by state: 1959–60 to 1994–95 170

169. Total and current expenditure per pupil in public elementary and secondary schools: 1919–20 to 1996–97 172

3–A. Postsecondary Education: College and University Education

Enrollment

170. Enrollment and staff in, and degrees conferred by, institutions of higher education and noncollegiate postsecondary institutions: 1994–95 and fall 1993 and 1995 180

171. Historical summary of faculty, students, degrees, and finances in institutions of higher education: 1869–70 to 1994–95 181

172. Total fall enrollment in institutions of higher education, by attendance status, sex of student, and control of institution: 1947 to 1995 182

173. Total fall enrollment in institutions of higher education, by control and type of institution: 1965 to 1995 183

174. Total fall enrollment in institutions of higher education, by attendance status, sex, and age: 1970 to 2007 184

175. Total fall enrollment in institutions of higher education, by level, sex, age, and attendance status of student: 1995 185

176. Total fall enrollment in institutions of higher education, by type and control of institution, and age and attendance status of student: 1995 186

177. Total fall enrollment in institutions of higher education, by level of enrollment, sex, attendance status, and type and control of institution: 1994 and 1995 187

178. Total fall enrollment in institutions of higher education, by type and control of institution, attendance status, and sex of student: 1970 to 1995 188

179. Fall enrollment and number of institutions of higher education, by affiliation of institution: 1980 to 1995 189

180. Total fall enrollment in institutions of higher education, by type and control of institution, and attendance status and level of student: 1992 to 1995 191

181. Total first-time freshmen enrolled in institutions of higher education, by sex of student, attendance status, and type and control of institution: Fall 1955 to fall 1995 192

182. Total first-time freshmen enrolled in institutions of higher education, by attendance status, sex, control of institution, and state: Fall 1992 to fall 1995 ... 193

183. College enrollment rates of high school graduates, by race/ethnicity: 1960 to 1996 ... 194

184. College enrollment rates of high school graduates, by sex: 1960 to 1996 195

185. Graduation, college preparation, and college application rates of high school students, by selected school characteristics: 1993–94 195

186. Enrollment rates of 18- to 24-year-olds in institutions of higher education, by race/ethnicity: 1967 to 1996 196

187. Total undergraduate fall enrollment in institutions of higher education, by sex of student, attendance status, and control of institution: 1969 to 1995 196

188. Total graduate fall enrollment in institutions of higher education, by attendance status, sex of student, and control of institution: 1969 to 1995 197

189. Total first-professional fall enrollment in institutions of higher education, by attendance status, sex of student, and control of institution: 1969 to 1995 197

190. Total fall enrollment in institutions of higher education, by state: 1970 to 1995 198

191. Total fall enrollment in public institutions of higher education, by state: 1970 to 1995 199

192.	Total fall enrollment in private institutions of higher education, by state: 1970 to 1995	200
193.	Total fall enrollment in all institutions of higher education, by attendance status, sex, and state: 1994 and 1995	201
194.	Total fall enrollment in public institutions of higher education, by attendance status, sex, and state: 1994 and 1995	202
195.	Total fall enrollment in private institutions of higher education, by attendance status, sex, and state: 1994 and 1995	203
196.	Total fall enrollment in institutions of higher education, by control, type of institution, and state: 1994 and 1995	204
197.	Total fall enrollment in institutions of higher education, by level of enrollment and state: 1993 to 1995	205
198.	Total fall enrollment in institutions of higher education, by control, level of enrollment, and state: 1995	206
199.	Total fall enrollment in institutions of higher education, by control, level of enrollment, and state: 1994	207
200.	Full-time-equivalent fall enrollment in institutions of higher education, by control and type of institution: 1969 to 1995	208
201.	Full-time-equivalent fall enrollment in institutions of higher education, by control, type of institution, and state: 1993 to 1995	209
202.	Full-time-equivalent fall enrollment in institutions of higher education, by control and state: 1980 to 1995	210
203.	Residence and migration of all freshmen students in institutions of higher education, by state: Fall 1994	211
204.	Residence and migration of all freshmen students in institutions of higher education graduating from high school in the past 12 months, by state: Fall 1994	212
205.	Residence and migration of all freshmen students in 4-year colleges graduating from high school in the past 12 months, by state: Fall 1994	213
206.	Total fall enrollment in institutions of higher education, by type and control of institution and race/ethnicity of student: 1976 to 1995	214
207.	Total fall enrollment in institutions of higher education, by level of study, sex, and race/ethnicity of student: 1976 to 1995	215
208.	Total fall enrollment in institutions of higher education, by level, attendance status, sex, and race/ethnicity of student: 1994 and 1995	217
209.	Total number of institutions and fall enrollment in institutions of higher education, by percentage minority enrollment: 1995	218
210.	Total fall enrollment in institutions of higher education, by race/ethnicity of student and by state: 1992 to 1995	219
211.	Number and percent of students enrolled in postsecondary institutions, by disability status and selected student characteristics: 1995–96	220
212.	Enrollment of persons 14 to 34 years of age in institutions of higher education, by race/ethnicity, sex, and year of college: October 1965 to October 1996	221

213. Enrollment in postsecondary education, by major field of study, age, and level of student: 1992–93 222

214. Graduate enrollment in science and engineering programs in institutions of higher education, by field of study: United States and outlying areas, fall 1984 to fall 1995 223

215. Institutions of higher education and branches, by type, control, and size of enrollment: Fall 1994 and fall 1995 224

216. Enrollment of the 120 largest college and university campuses: Fall 1995 225

217. Selected statistics for college and university campuses enrolling more than 14,600 students in 1995 226

218. Fall enrollment, degrees conferred, and expenditures in historically black colleges and universities, by institution: 1995 232

219. Selected statistics on historically black colleges and universities: 1980, 1990, and 1995 234

220. Fall enrollment in historically black colleges and universities, by type and control of institution: 1976 to 1995 235

Staff

221. Employees in institutions of higher education, by primary occupation, employment status, and control of institution: Fall 1976, fall 1991, and fall 1993 235

222. Employees in institutions of higher education by race/ethnicity, primary occupation, control of institution, sex, and employment status: Fall 1993 236

223. Employees in institutions of higher education, by primary occupation, sex, employment status, and by type and control of institution: Fall 1993 237

224. Staff and student/staff ratios in institutions of higher education, by type and control of institution and by state: Fall 1993 238

Faculty

225. Full-time and part-time senior instructional faculty in institutions of higher education, by employment status, control, and type of institution: Fall 1970 to fall 1993 239

226. Full-time instructional faculty in institutions of higher education, by race/ethnicity, academic rank, and sex: Fall 1993 239

227. Full-time and part-time instructional faculty and staff in institutions of higher education, by selected characteristics and type and control of institution: Fall 1992 240

228. Full-time instructional faculty and staff in institutions of higher education, by instruction activities and type and control of institution: Fall 1992 242

229. Part-time instructional faculty and staff in institutions of higher education, by instruction activities and type and control of institution: Fall 1992 243

230. Full-time and part-time instructional faculty and staff in institutions of higher education, by type and control, academic rank, age, salary, race/ethnicity, and sex: Fall 1992 244

231. Full-time and part-time instructional faculty and staff in institutions of higher education, by faculty characterisics and field: Fall 1992 246

232. Percentage distribution of full-time and part-time instructional faculty and staff in institutions of higher education, by program area, race/ethnicity, and sex: Fall 1992 248

233. Average base salaries of full-time instructional faculty and staff in institutions of higher education, by type and control of institution and by field of instruction: 1987–88 and 1992–93 249

234. Average salary of full-time instructional faculty on 9-month contracts in institutions of higher education, by academic rank, sex, and control and type of institution: 1970–71 to 1995–96 250

235. Average salary of full-time instructional faculty on 9-month contracts in institutions of higher education, by academic rank, sex, and by type and control of institution: 1980–81, 1990–91, 1994–95, and 1995–96 252

236. Average salary of full-time instructional faculty on 9-month contracts in institutions of higher education, by type and control of institution and by state: 1995–96 253

237. Average salary of full-time instructional faculty on 9-month contracts in institutions of higher education, by type and control of institution and by state: 1994–95 254

238. Average salary of full-time instructional faculty on 9-month contracts in 4-year institutions of higher education, by type and control of institution and rank of faculty and by state: 1995–96 255

239. Average salary of full-time instructional faculty on 9-month contracts in 4-year institutions of higher education, by type and control of institution and rank of faculty and by state: 1994–95 256

240. Full-time instructional faculty with tenure for institutions reporting tenure status, by academic rank, sex, and type and control of institution: 1980–81, 1990–91, 1994–95, and 1995–96 257

Institutions

241. Institutions of higher education, by control and type of institution: 1949–50 to 1995–96 258

242. Institutions of higher education and branches, by type, control of institution, and state: 1995–96 259

243. Institutions of higher education that have closed their doors, by control and type of institution: 1960–61 to 1995–96 260

Degrees

244. Earned degrees conferred by institutions of higher education, by level of degree and sex of student: 1869–70 to 2006–07 261

245. Degrees awarded by institutions of higher education, by control, level of degree, and state: 1994–95 262

246. Earned degrees conferred by institutions of higher education, by level of degree and by state: 1993–94 and 1994–95 263

247. Associate degrees conferred by institutions of higher education, by sex of student and field of study: 1988–89 to 1992–93 264

248. Associate degrees and other subbaccalaureate awards conferred by institutions of higher education, by length of curriculum, sex of student, and field of study: 1994–95 265

249. Associate degrees and other subbaccalaureate awards conferred by institutions of higher education, by length of curriculum, sex of student, and field of study: 1993–94 266

250. Bachelor's degrees conferred by institutions of higher education, by discipline division: 1970–71 to 1994–95 267

251. Master's degrees conferred by institutions of higher education, by discipline division: 1970–71 to 1994–95 268

252. Doctor's degrees conferred by institutions of higher education, by discipline division: 1970–71 to 1994–95 269

253. Bachelor's, master's, and doctor's degrees conferred by institutions of higher education, by sex of student and field of study: 1994–95 270

254. Bachelor's, master's, and doctor's degrees conferred by institutions of higher education, by sex of student and field of study: 1993–94 278

255. Degrees conferred by institutions of higher education, by control of institution: 1969–70 to 1994–95 286

256. Degrees conferred by institutions of higher education, by control of institution, level of degree, and discipline division: 1994–95 286

257. Degrees conferred by institutions of higher education, by control of institution, level of degree, and discipline division: 1993–94 287

258. Number of institutions of higher education conferring degrees, by level of degree and discipline division: 1994–95 288

259. Number of institutions of higher education conferring degrees, by level of degree and discipline division: 1993–94 289

260. First-professional degrees conferred by institutions of higher education in dentistry, medicine, and law, by sex, and number of institutions conferring degrees: 1949–50 to 1994–95 290

261. First-professional degrees conferred by institutions of higher education, by sex of student, control of institution, and field of study: 1983–84 to 1994–95 291

262. Associate degrees conferred by institutions of higher education, by racial/ethnic group and sex of student: 1976–77 to 1994–95 292

263. Associate degrees conferred by institutions of higher education, by racial/ethnic group, major field of study, and sex of student: 1994–95 293

264. Associate degrees conferred by institutions of higher education, by racial/ethnic group, major field of study, and sex of student: 1993–94 294

265. Bachelor's degrees conferred by institutions of higher education, by racial/ethnic group and sex of student: 1976–77 to 1994–95 295

266. Bachelor's degrees conferred by institutions of higher education, by racial/ethnic group, major field of study, and sex of student: 1994–95 296

267. Bachelor's degrees conferred by institutions of higher education, by racial/ethnic group, major field of study, and sex of student: 1993–94 297

268. Master's degrees conferred by institutions of higher education, by racial/ethnic group and sex of student: 1976–77 to 1994–95 298

269.	Master's degrees conferred by institutions of higher education, by racial/ethnic group, major field of study, and sex of student: 1994–95	299
270.	Master's degrees conferred by institutions of higher education, by racial/ethnic group, major field of study, and sex of student: 1993–94	300
271.	Doctor's degrees conferred by institutions of higher education, by racial/ethnic group and sex of student: 1976–77 to 1994–95	301
272.	Doctor's degrees conferred by institutions of higher education, by racial/ethnic group, major field of study, and sex of student: 1994–95	302
273.	Doctor's degrees conferred by institutions of higher education, by racial/ethnic group, major field of study, and sex of student: 1993–94	303
274.	First-professional degrees conferred by institutions of higher education, by racial/ethnic group and sex of student: 1976–77 to 1994–95	304
275.	First-professional degrees conferred by institutions of higher education, by racial/ethnic group, major field of study, and sex of student: 1994–95	305
276.	First-professional degrees conferred by institutions of higher education, by racial/ethnic group, major field of study, and sex of student: 1993–94	305
277.	Earned degrees in agriculture and natural resources conferred by institutions of higher education, by level of degree and sex of student: 1970–71 to 1994–95	306
278.	Earned degrees in architecture and related programs conferred by institutions of higher education, by level of degree and sex of student: 1949–50 to 1994–95	306
279.	Earned degrees in the biological/life sciences conferred by institutions of higher education, by level of degree and sex of student: 1951–52 to 1994–95	307
280.	Earned degrees in biology, microbiology, and zoology conferred by institutions of higher education, by level of degree: 1970–71 to 1994–95	307
281.	Earned degrees in business conferred by institutions of higher education, by level of degree and sex of student: 1955–56 to 1994–95	308
282.	Earned degrees in communications conferred by institutions of higher education, by level of degree and sex of student: 1970–71 to 1994–95	308
283.	Earned degrees in computer and information sciences conferred by institutions of higher education, by level of degree and sex of student: 1970–71 to 1994–95	309
284.	Earned degrees in education conferred by institutions of higher education, by level of degree and sex of student: 1949–50 to 1994–95	309
285.	Earned degrees in engineering conferred by institutions of higher education, by level of degree and sex of student: 1949–50 to 1994–95	310
286.	Earned degrees in chemical, civil, electrical, and mechanical engineering conferred by institutions of higher education, by level of degree: 1970–71 to 1994–95	310
287.	Earned degrees in English language and literature/letters conferred by institutions of higher education, by level of degree and sex of student: 1949–50 to 1994–95	311
288.	Earned degrees in modern foreign languages and literatures conferred by institutions of higher education, by level of degree and sex of student: 1949–50 to 1994–95	311

289. Earned degrees in French, German, and Spanish conferred by institutions of higher education, by level of degree: 1949–50 to 1994–95 312

290. Earned degrees in the health professions and related sciences conferred by institutions of higher education, by level of degree and sex of student: 1970–71 to 1994–95 312

291. Earned degrees in mathematics conferred by institutions of higher education, by level of degree and sex of student: 1949–50 to 1994–95 313

292. Earned degrees in the physical sciences conferred by institutions of higher education, by level of degree and sex of student: 1959–60 to 1994–95 313

293. Earned degrees in chemistry, geology, and physics conferred by institutions of higher education, by level of degree: 1970–71 to 1994–95 314

294. Earned degrees in psychology conferred by institutions of higher education, by level of degree and by sex of student: 1949–50 to 1994–95 314

295. Earned degrees in public administration and services conferred by institutions of higher education, by level of degree and sex of student: 1970–71 to 1994–95 ... 315

296. Earned degrees in the social sciences and history conferred by institutions of higher education, by level of degree and sex of student: 1970–71 to 1994–95 315

297. Earned degrees in economics, history, political science and government, and sociology conferred by institutions of higher education, by level of degree: 1949–50 to 1994–95 316

298. Earned degrees in visual and performing arts conferred by institutions of higher education, by level of degree and sex of student: 1970–71 to 1994–95 316

299. Statistical profile of persons receiving doctor's degrees, by field of study: 1994–95 ... 317

300. Statistical profile of persons receiving doctor's degrees in education: 1979–80 to 1994–95 318

301. Statistical profile of persons receiving doctor's degrees in engineering: 1979–80 to 1994–95 318

302. Statistical profile of persons receiving doctor's degrees in the humanities: 1979–80 to 1994–95 319

303. Statistical profile of persons receiving doctor's degrees in the life sciences: 1979–80 to 1994–95 319

304. Statistical profile of persons receiving doctor's degrees in the physical sciences: 1979–80 to 1994–95 320

305. Statistical profile of persons receiving doctor's degrees in the social sciences: 1979–80 to 1994–95 320

306. Doctor's degrees conferred by 60 large institutions of higher education: 1985–86 to 1994–95 321

Outcomes

307. Percentage distribution of 1980 high school sophomores, by highest level of education completed through 1992, by selected student characteristics: 1980 to 1992 322

308. Mean number of semester credits completed by bachelor's degree recipients, by major and course area: 1972 to 1976 and 1980 to 1984 323

309. Colleges and universities offering remedial services, by type and control of institution: 1987–88 to 1995–96 323

310. Percent distribution of enrollment and completion status of first-time postsecondary students starting during the 1989–90 academic year, by degree objective and other student characteristics: 1994 324

311. Scores on Graduate Record Examination (GRE) and subject matter tests: 1965 to 1996 325

Student Charges and Student Financial Assistance

312. Average undergraduate tuition and fees and room and board rates paid by students in institutions of higher education, by type and control of institution: 1964–65 to 1996–97 326

313. Average undergraduate tuition and fees and room and board rates paid by students in institutions of higher education, by control of institution and by state: 1995–96 and 1996–97 328

314. Average graduate and first-professional tuition paid by students in institutions of higher education: 1987–88 to 1996–97 329

315. Percent of undergraduates receiving aid and average amount awarded in 1995–96 per student, by type and source of aid and selected student characteristics 330

316. Undergraduates enrolled full-time and part-time, by aid status and source of aid during 1995–96, and control and level of institution 332

317. Percent of undergraduates receiving aid, by type and source of aid received, and by control and level of institution: 1992–93 and 1995–96 333

318. Undergraduates enrolled full-time and part-time, by federal aid program and by control and level of institution: 1995–96 334

319. Postbaccalaureate students enrolled full-time and part-time, by aid status, source of aid, and by level of study and control and level of institution: 1992–93 and 1995–96 335

320. Postbaccalaureate students enrolled full-time and part-time, by type of aid and by level of study, control, and level of institution: 1992–93 and 1995–96 336

321. Scholarship and fellowship awards of institutions of higher education, by control of institution: 1959–60 to 1994–95 337

322. Pell Grant revenue of institutions of higher education compared to current-fund revenue and tuition, by type and control of institution: 1985–86 to 1994–95 338

323. State awards for need-based undergraduate scholarship and grant programs, by state: 1983–84 to 1995–96 339

Income

324. Current-fund revenue of institutions of higher education, by source: 1980–81 to 1994–95 340

325. Current-fund revenue of public institutions of higher education, by source: 1980–81 to 1994–95 341

326. Current-fund revenue of private institutions of higher education, by source: 1980–81 to 1994–95 342

327. Revenue of institutions of higher education, by source of funds: 1919–20 to 1994–95 343

328. Revenue of institutions of higher education, by source of funds, and by control and type of institution: 1994–95 344

329. Current-fund revenue of public institutions of higher education, by state: 1980–81 to 1994–95 345

330. Current-fund revenue of public institutions of higher education, by source of funds and state: 1994–95 346

331. Current-fund revenue of public institutions of higher education, by source of funds and state: 1993–94 347

332. Current-fund revenue from state and local governments of institutions of higher education, by state: 1985–86 to 1994–95 348

333. Current-fund revenue received from the federal government by the 120 institutions of higher education receiving the largest amounts: 1994–95 349

Expenditures

334. Current-fund expenditures and educational and general expenditures of institutions of higher education, by purpose and per student: 1929–30 to 1994–95 350

335. Expenditures of institutions of higher education, by purpose and by control and type of institution: 1994–95 352

336. Current-fund expenditures and expenditures per full-time-equivalent student in institutions of higher education, by type and control of institution: 1970–71 to 1994–95 354

337. Current-fund expenditures of institutions of higher education, by purpose: 1980–81 to 1994–95 355

338. Current-fund expenditures of public institutions of higher education, by purpose: 1980–81 to 1994–95 356

339. Current-fund expenditures of private institutions of higher education, by purpose: 1980–81 to 1994–95 357

340. Voluntary support for institutions of higher education, by source and purpose of support: 1949–50 to 1994–95 357

341. Educational and general expenditures of public universities, by purpose: 1976–77 to 1994–95 358

342. Educational and general expenditures of public 4-year colleges, by purpose: 1976–77 to 1994–95 359

343. Educational and general expenditures of public 2-year colleges, by purpose: 1976–77 to 1994–95 360

344. Educational and general expenditures of private (nonprofit) universities, by purpose: 1976–77 to 1994–95 361

345. Educational and general expenditures of private (nonprofit) 4-year colleges, by purpose: 1976–77 to 1994–95 362

346. Current-fund expenditures of public institutions of higher education, by state: 1980–81 to 1994–95 363

347. Educational and general expenditures of public institutions of higher education, by state: 1980–81 to 1994–95 364

348. Current-fund expenditures and educational and general expenditures of private institutions of higher education, by state: 1985–86 to 1994–95 365

349. Current-fund expenditures per full-time-equivalent student in institutions of higher education, by control and type of institution and purpose of expenditure: 1994–95 366

Property

350. Additions to physical plant value of institutions of higher education, by type of addition and control of institution: 1969–70 to 1994–95 366

351. Value of property and liabilities of institutions of higher education: 1899–1900 to 1994–95 367

352. Endowment funds of the 120 institutions of higher education with the largest amounts: Fiscal year 1995 368

3–B. Postsecondary Education: Vocational and Adult Education

Adult Education

353. Participation of employed persons, 17 years old and over, in adult education during the previous 12 months, by selected characteristics of participants: 1995 369

354. Participation in adult education during the previous 12 months by adults 17 years old and older, by selected characteristics of participants: 1991 and 1995 371

355. Participants in adult basic and secondary education programs, by level of enrollment and state: Fiscal years 1980, 1990, and 1995 373

Vocational Education

356. Number of noncollegiate institutions offering postsecondary education, by control and state: 1993–94, 1994–95, and 1995–96 374

4. Federal Programs for Education and Related Activities

357. Federal support and estimated federal tax expenditures for education, by category: Fiscal years 1965 to 1997 387

358. Federal on-budget funds for education, by agency: Fiscal years 1965 to 1997 388

359. Federal on-budget funds for education, by level or other educational purpose, by agency and program: Fiscal years 1965 to 1997 390

360. Estimated federal support for education, by agency and type of ultimate recipient: Fiscal year 1997 402

361. Federal on-budget funds obligated for programs administered by the Department of Education: Fiscal years 1980 to 1997 403

362. U.S. Department of Education outlays, by level of education and type of recipient: Fiscal years 1980 to 1997 404

363. U.S. Department of Education obligations for major programs, by state or other area: Fiscal year 1996 405

364. U.S. Department of Education obligations for major programs, by state or other area: Fiscal year 1995 406

365. Appropriations for Title I and Title VI, Elementary and Secondary Education Act (ESEA) of 1994, by state or other area: 1995–96 and 1996–97 407

366. Federal science and engineering obligations to colleges and universities, by agency and state: Fiscal year 1995 408

367. Summary of federal funds for research, development, and R & D plant: Fiscal years 1989 to 1997 409

368. Federal obligations to colleges and universities for research and development, by field: United States and outlying areas, 1980 to 1994 411

369. U.S. Department of Agriculture obligations for child nutrition programs, by state or other area: Fiscal years 1995 and 1996 412

370. U.S. Department of Health and Human Services allocations for Head Start and enrollment in Head Start, by state or other area: Fiscal years 1993 to 1996 413

371. Public school students receiving federally funded free or reduced price lunches, by selected school characteristics: School year 1993–94 414

372. Public and private school students receiving federally funded Chapter I services, by selected school characteristics: School year 1993–94 414

5. Outcomes of Education

Educational Characteristics of the Workforce

373. Percent of 18- to 25-year-olds reporting drug use during the past 30 days and the past year: 1979 to 1995 419

374. Percent of 1972, 1982, and 1992 high school seniors who felt that certain life values were "very important," by sex: 1972 to 1994 419

375. Labor force participation of persons 16 years old and over, by age, sex, race/ethnicity, and highest level of education: 1996 420

376. Occupation of employed persons 25 years old and over, by educational attainment and sex: 1996 420

377. Unemployment rate of persons 16 years old and over, by age, sex, race/ethnicity, and highest degree attained: 1994, 1995 and 1996 421

378. Median annual income of year-round full-time workers 25 years old and over, by level of education completed and sex: 1989 to 1995 422

379. Total annual money income and median income of persons 25 years old and over, by educational attainment and sex: 1995 423

380. College enrollment and labor force status of 1995 and 1996 high school graduates 16 to 24 years old, by sex and race/ethnicity: October 1995 and October 1996 424

Recent High School and College Graduates

381. Labor force status of 1979–80 to 1995–96 high school dropouts 16 to 24 years old, by sex and race/ethnicity: October 1980 to October 1996 425

382. Employment of 12th graders, by selected student characteristics: 1992 426

383. Full-time employment status of bachelor's degree recipients 1 year after graduation, by field of study: 1976 to 1991 427

384. Employment status of 1992–93 bachelor's degree recipients 1 year after graduation, by field of study and occupational area: 1994 428

385. Percentage of 1992–93 bachelor's degree recipients pursuing further education within one year after graduation, by type of enrollment and undergraduate major: April 1994 429

386. Average annual salary of bachelor's degree recipients employed full-time 1 year after graduation, by field of study: 1976 to 1994 429

387. Participation of young adults in voluntary or community service activities, by selected characteristics: 1992 to 1994 430

388. Literacy skills of adults, 16 years old and over, by selected characteristics: 1992 431

6. International Comparisons of Education

389. School-age populations as a percent of total population: Selected countries, 1985, 1990 and 1995 438

390. Percent of population enrolled in secondary and postsecondary institutions, by age group: Selected countries, 1985, 1990, and 1994 438

391. Estimated population, school enrollment, teachers, and public expenditures for education in major areas of the world: 1980, 1990, 1993, and 1994 439

392. Selected statistics for countries with populations over 10 million, by continent: 1980, 1990, and 1994 440

393. Pupils per teacher in public and private elementary and secondary schools, by level of education: Selected countries, 1985 to 1994 442

394. Geography proficiency of 13-year-olds in educational systems participating in the International Assessment of Educational Progress: 1991 442

395. Average eighth grade mathematics scores by content areas, and average time spent studying out of school, by country: 1994–95 443

396. Instructional practices and time spent teaching mathematics in eighth grade, by country: 1994–95 444

397. Average eighth grade science scores by content areas, and average time spent studying out of school, by country: 1994–95 445

398. Instructional practices and time spent teaching science in eighth grade, by country: 1994–95 446

399. Average size of eighth grade mathematics class, and frequency teachers assign mathematics homework, by country: 1994–95 447

400. Eighth grade students' perceptions about mathematics achievement and hours spent on leisure activities, by country: 1994–95 448

401. Average fourth grade mathematics scores, by content areas, and average time spent studying mathematics out of school, by country: 1994–95 449

402. Average fourth grade science scores, by content areas, and average time spent teaching science in school, by country: 1994–95 450

403. Reading literacy test scores of 9-year-olds: Selected countries, 1992 451

404. Reading literacy test scores of 14-year-olds: Selected countries, 1992 452

405. Number of bachelor's degree recipients per 100 persons of the theoretical age of graduation, by sex: Selected countries, 1989 to 1994 453

406.	Percent of bachelor's degrees awarded in science: Selected countries, 1985 to 1994	453
407.	Percent of graduate degrees awarded in science: Selected countries, 1985, 1990, and 1991	454
408.	Public education expenditures per student, by level of student: Selected countries, 1985 to 1993	454
409.	Public expenditures for education as a percentage of gross domestic product, by level of education: Selected countries, 1985 to 1993	455
410.	Foreign students enrolled in institutions of higher education in the United States and outlying areas, by continent, region, and selected countries of origin: 1980–81 to 1995–96	456

7. Learning Resources and Technology

Libraries

411.	Percentage of school library/media centers that offered selected services and equipment, and library/media center expenditures, by control and level of school: 1993–94	459
412.	Selected statistics on of public school library/media centers, by level and enrollment size of school: 1993–94	460
413.	Selected statistics on public school library/media centers, by state: 1993–94	461
414.	Percent of public and private schools having access to selected telecommunication capabilities, by location of access site and level of school: 1995	462
415.	Percent of public schools and school classrooms having access to the Internet, by school charecteristics: 1994, 1995 and 1996	462
416.	General statistics of college and university libraries: 1974–75 to 1994–95	463
417.	Selected statistics on the collections, staff, and operating expenditures of 60 large college and university libraries: 1994	464
418.	General statistics of public libraries, by population of legal service area: 1994	465
419.	Public libraries, books and serial volumes, library visits, and reference transactions, by state: 1994	465

Computers and Technology

420.	Percent of workers, 18 years old and over, using computers on the job, by selected characteristics and computer activities: October 1993	466
421.	Access to and use of home computers, by selected characteristics of students and other users: October 1993	467
422.	Student use of computers, by level of instruction and selected characteristics: October 1984, 1989, and 1993	468

Guide to Sources

Appendix Tables

A1.	Standard errors for enrollment and completion status of first-time postsecondary students starting during the 1989–90 academic year, by degree objective and other student characteristics: 1994	496

A2.	Respondent counts for selected High School and Beyond surveys	497
A3.	Design effects (DEFF) and root design effects (DEFT) for selected High School and Beyond surveys and subsamples	498
A4.	Respondent counts for the National Educational Longitudinal Study: 1988, 1990, and 1992	498
A5.	Design effects (DEFF) and root design effects (DEFT) for selected National Educational Longitudinal Survey samples	499
A6.	Respondent counts of full-time workers from the Recent College Graduate survey: 1976 to 1991	499
A7.	Estimated enrollment rates and standard errors in the October Current Population Survey	500
A8.	Estimated educational attainment rates and standard errors in the March Current Population Survey	500
A9.	Percent of seniors who had ever used selected drugs and 95 percent confidence limits: 1986	500
A10.	Sampling errors (95 percent confidence level) for percentages estimated from the Gallup Poll: 1992 and 1993	501
A11.	Sampling errors (95 percent confidence level) for the difference in two percentages estimated from the Gallup Poll: 1992 and 1993	501
A12.	Maximum differences required for significance (90 percent confidence level) between sample subgroups of the "Status of the American Public School Teacher" survey	501

INTRODUCTION

In the fall of 1997, about 66.3 million persons were enrolled in American schools and colleges (table 1). About 4.0 million were employed as elementary and secondary school teachers and as college faculty. Other professional, administrative, and support staff of educational institutions numbered 4.4 million. Thus about 75 million people were involved, directly or indirectly, in providing or receiving formal education. In a nation with a population of about 268 million, more than 1 out of every 4 persons participated in formal education.

Elementary/Secondary Enrollment

Since the enrollment rates of kindergarten and elementary school age children have not changed much in recent years, increases in elementary school enrollment have been driven primarily by increases in the number of young people. Enrollment in public elementary and secondary schools rose 18 percent between 1985 and 1997. The fastest growth occurred in the elementary grades, where enrollment rose 23 percent over the same period, from 27.0 million to a record high of 33.2 million in 1997 (table 2). Secondary enrollments declined 8 percent from 1985 to 1990, but then rose by 16 percent from 1990 to 1997, for a net increase of 6 percent.

Private school enrollment grew more slowly than public school enrollment over this period, rising 6 percent, from 5.6 million in 1985 to 5.9 million in 1997. As a result, the percentage of students enrolled in private schools declined from 12 percent in 1985 to 11 percent in 1996.

The National Center for Education Statistics (NCES) forecasts record levels of public school enrollment during the late 1990s. The fall 1997 public school enrollment marks a new record and new records are expected every year through the early 2000s (table 3). Between fall 1997 and fall 2007, public elementary enrollment is projected to grow by one half of one percent, while public secondary school enrollment is expected to rise by 13 percent.

Higher Education

College enrollment rose to a record level of 14.5 million in fall 1992 and is expected to increase in 1997, after falling slightly between 1993 and 1996 (table 3). Despite decreases in the traditional college-age population during the 1980s and early 1990s, total enrollment has remained relatively high because of the increased participation of older women students and a high rate of college attendance for recent high school graduates (tables 171 and 180). The number of part-time students has generally increased at a faster rate than full-time students (table 169).

Teachers

An estimated 3.1 million elementary and secondary school teachers will be engaged in classroom instruction in the fall of 1997 (table 4). This number has risen in recent years, up about 17 percent since 1987. The number of public school teachers in 1997 will be about 2.7 million and the number in private schools will be about 0.4 million. About 1.9 million teachers are expected to teach in elementary schools, while about 1.2 million will teach at the secondary level (table 4).

The number of public school teachers has risen at a slightly faster rate than the number of students over the past 10 years, resulting in a small decrease in the pupil/teacher ratio. In the fall of 1997, there were 17.3 public school pupils per teacher compared with 17.6 public school pupils per teacher 10 years earlier. During the same time period, the pupil/teacher ratio in private schools fell from 15.5 to 15.0 (table 64). Despite the historical trend towards lower pupil/teacher ratios, the fluctuations since 1990 suggest stability in the pupil/teacher ratio.

The salaries of public school teachers, which lost purchasing power to inflation during the 1970s, rose faster than the inflation rate in the 1980s. The rising salaries reflect an interest by state and local education agencies in boosting teacher salary schedules and, to some extent, an increase in teachers' experience and education levels (tables 68, 69, and 77). The value of teachers' salaries, after adjustment for inflation, rose one and a half percent between 1986–87 and 1996–97. Since 1990–91, the average salary for teachers actually fell slightly after adjusting for inflation, offsetting increases in the 1980s. The average salary for teachers in 1996–97 was $38,509 (table 77).

Public Perception

Public perception about problems facing the local public schools has shifted in the past several years.

Between 1985 and 1990, an increasing proportion of people believed that drug use was a major problem facing schools. Then, the proportion of people who felt drug use was a major problem facing schools fell, from 38 percent in 1990 to 7 percent in 1995, before rising again to 16 percent in 1996. Lack of discipline was cited by 15 percent of the population; fighting, gangs, and violence was cited by 14 percent; and the lack of financial support was cited as a major problem by 13 percent of the population (table 23).

Faculty and Staff

During the fall of 1993, there were 915,000 faculty in higher education institutions. Making up this figure were 546,000 full-time, and 370,000 part-time faculty (table 223). In 1992, full-time instructors generally taught more hours and more students than part-time instructors, with 61 percent of full-time instructors teaching eight or more hours per week and two-thirds teaching 50 or more students. About 30 percent of part-time instructors taught eight or more hours per week and 30 percent taught 50 or more students (tables 228 and 229).

White males constitute a disproportionate share of college instructional faculty and staff. Overall, about 58 percent of full-time faculty and 49 percent of part-time faculty are white males. However, this distribution varies substantially by age of faculty. Among full-time faculty under 30, the balance between male and female faculty is even and 21 percent of the faculty are minorities. Among full-time faculty between 60 and 64 years of age, 79 percent of faculty are males and minorities amount to 12 percent (table 230).

Student Performance

Reading

Overall, the reading achievement scores for the country's 9-, 13- and 17-year-old students are mixed. Reading scores for 9- and 13-year-olds were somewhat higher in 1996 than they were in 1971. However, there has been little change since the mid 1980s. The reading performance of 17-year-olds was about the same in 1996 as it was in 1971. Many of the advancements in performance that had been made in earlier years among black students have not continued or have reversed. Black 13- and 17-year-olds exhibited higher reading performance in 1996 than in 1971. Black 9-year-olds' performance improved significantly between 1971 and 1980, but it has not improved further. The performance levels of white 9- and 13-year olds also rose between 1971 and 1996. Separate data for Hispanics were not gathered in 1971, but changes between 1975 and 1996 indicate an increase among 9-year-olds. There was no significant difference between the 1975 and 1996 reading performance among 13- and 17-year-old Hispanics (table 107).

Mathematics

Results from assessments of mathematics proficiency indicate that 9- and 13-year-old students improved their performance between 1973 and 1996. However, there has been little change for 9-year-olds since 1990, and the performance of older students on advanced mathematical operations has been stable (table 118). The proportion of 17-year-olds who demonstrated skill with moderately complex procedures and reasoning rose from 52 percent in 1978 to 60 percent in 1996. During the same time period, the proportion of 17-year-olds with skill in multi-step problem solving and algebra remained unchanged (table 119).

White, black, and Hispanic students improved their mathematics performance between 1973 and 1996, among all three age groups. In contrast to some of the declines noted in reading since the mid 1980s, mathematics scores for white, black, and Hispanic 9-, 13-, and 17-year-olds improved or remained stable between 1986 and 1996 (table 118).

A 1996 voluntary assessment of the states found that mathematics proficiency varied widely among eighth graders in the 42 jurisdictions (40 states, 1 territory, and the District of Columbia) that participated in the program (table 120). Overall, 62 percent of eighth grade students performed at or above the basic level in mathematics. Only four states and the District of Columbia had fewer than 50 percent of students performing at least at the basic level in math. Ten states had 70 percent or more of their students performing at or above the basic level.

Science

Long-term changes in science performance have been mixed, though changes over the past 10 years have been generally positive. In 1996, science performance among 17-year-olds was lower than in 1970, but higher than in 1986. The science performance level of 13-year-olds was higher in 1996 than in 1986, recouping the earlier declines. The science performance of 9-year-olds increased between 1986 and 1996, after showing no significant change between 1970 and 1986 (table 126).

The science performance of white 9- and 13-year-olds was about the same in 1996 as it was in 1970, and the performance of 17-year-olds was lower in 1996. However, the performance at each of the 3 age groups was higher in 1996 than in 1986. Black and Hispanic 9- and 13-year-olds had higher science performance in 1996 than in the 1970s. Black 17-year-olds showed a pattern consistent with white 13-year-olds with a decline through 1982 and an increase by 1996. Despite significant gains by younger black and Hispanic students, their average performance remains lower than for white students. Although the performance gap between black and white students has narrowed, the science performance for black 13-year-olds was slightly lower than the average for white 9-year-olds in 1996 (table 126).

International Comparisons

The results of a 1995 international assessment in math and science show that U.S. fourth and eighth graders compare more favorably with other countries in science than in mathematics. In mathematics, U.S. eighth graders scored below the international average, falling below 20 of the 41 countries tested. Fourth graders performed above the international average of 26 countries tested, scoring below 7 countries, including Singapore, Korea, and Japan. U.S. students at both the fourth and eighth grade levels scored above the international average in science. Eighth grade students in the U.S. were outperformed by four out of 41 countries. Fourth grade students once again compared more favorably with their international counterparts than eighth grade students. Only one country outperformed the U.S. students in science out of 26 countries who participated in the fourth grade assessment (tables 395, 397, 401, and 402).

Graduates and Degrees

The number of high school graduates in 1996–97 totaled about 2.6 million. Approximately 2.4 million graduated from public schools and less than 0.3 million graduated from private schools. The number of high school graduates has declined from its peak in 1976–77 when 3.2 million people earned their diplomas. The dropout rate declined over this period, from 14 percent of all 16- to 24-year-olds in 1977 to 11 percent in 1996 (tables 99 and 103).

The number of degrees conferred by institutions of higher education during the 1995–96 school year by degree level has been estimated: 532,000 associate degrees; 1,186,000 bachelor's degrees; 406,000 master's degrees; 79,000 first-professional degrees; and 44,000 doctor's degrees (table 244).

The Bureau of the Census has collected annual statistics on the educational attainment of the population in terms of years of school completed. These data indicate that, between 1980 and 1996, the proportion of the adult population 25 years of age and over with 4 years of high school or more rose from 69 percent to 82 percent and the proportion of adults with at least 4 years of college increased from 17 percent to 24 percent. In contrast, the proportion of young adults (25- to 29-year-olds) completing high school remained virtually unchanged (table 8).

Expenditures

Expenditures for public and private education, from preprimary through graduate school, are estimated at $564 billion for 1996–97. The expenditures of elementary and secondary schools are expected to total about $340 billion for 1996–97, while those for institutions of higher education will be about $225 billion. Viewed in another context, the total expenditures for education are expected to amount to about 7.4 percent of the gross domestic product in 1996–97, about the same percentage as in the recent past (table 31).

Summary

The statistical highlights in this section of the report provide a quantitative description of the current American education scene. Assessment data indicate that there have been improvements in mathematics and science performance between 1986 and 1996. A higher proportion of high school graduates are going on to college. Yet, wide variations in student proficiency from state to state and mediocre mathematics scores of American students in international assessments pose challenges.

NOTE: Readers should be aware of the limitations of statistics. These limitations vary with the exact nature of a particular survey. For example, estimates based on a sample of institutions will differ somewhat from the figures that would have been obtained if a complete census had been taken using the same survey procedures. Although some of the surveys conducted by the National Center for Education Statistics are complete, census-type surveys, all surveys are subject to design, reporting, and processing errors and errors due to nonresponse. More information on survey methodologies can be found in the "Guide to Sources" in the appendix. Price indexes for inflation adjustments can be found in table 38.

CHAPTER 1
All Levels of Education

This chapter provides a broad overview of education in the United States. It brings together material from preprimary, elementary, secondary, and postsecondary education and from the general population to present a composite picture of the American educational system. Tables illustrate the total number of persons enrolled in school, the number of teachers, the number of schools, and total expenditures for education at all levels. This chapter also includes statistics on education-related topics such as educational attainment, family characteristics, population, and opinions about schools. Economic indicators and price indexes have been added to assist researchers in preparing comparative analyses.

Figure 1 shows the structure of education in the United States. It presents the three levels of education (elementary, secondary, and postsecondary) and gives the approximate age range of persons at each level. Pupils ordinarily spend from 6 to 8 years in the elementary grades, which may be preceded by 1 or 2 years in nursery school and kindergarten. The elementary school program is followed by a 4- to 6-year program in secondary school. Pupils normally complete the entire program through grade 12 by age 17 or 18.

High school graduates who decide to continue their education may enter a technical or vocational institution, a 2-year college, or a 4-year college or university. A 2-year college normally offers the first 2 years of a standard 4-year college curriculum and a selection of terminal-vocational programs. Academic courses completed at a 2-year college are usually transferable for credit at a 4-year college or university. A technical or vocational institution offers postsecondary technical training leading to a specific career.

An associate degree requires at least 2 years of college-level work, and a bachelor's degree normally can be earned in 4 years. At least 1 year beyond the bachelor's is necessary for a master's degree, while a doctor's degree usually requires a minimum of 3 or 4 years beyond the bachelor's.

Professional schools differ widely in admission requirements and in program length. Medical students, for example, generally complete a 4-year program of premedical studies at a college or university before they can enter the 4-year program at a medical school. Law programs normally require 3 years of coursework beyond the bachelor's degree level.

Many of the statistics in this chapter are derived from the statistical activities of the National Center for Education Statistics. In addition, substantial contributions have been drawn from the work of other groups, both government and nongovernment, as shown in the source notes of the appropriate tables. Information on survey methodologies is in the "Guide to Sources" in the appendix and in the publications cited in the source notes.

Enrollment, Teachers, and Schools

Enrollment in elementary and secondary schools grew rapidly during the 1950s and 1960s and reached a peak in 1971 (table 3). This enrollment rise was caused by what is known as the "baby boom," a dramatic increase in births following World War II. From 1971 to 1984, total elementary and secondary school enrollment decreased every year, reflecting the decline in the school-age population over that period. After these years of decline, enrollment in elementary and secondary schools started to rise, hitting an all-time high in fall 1997 (table 3).

Public school enrollment in kindergarten through grade eight rose from 27.9 million in fall 1987 to an estimated 33.2 million in fall 1997. Enrollment in the upper grades declined from 12.1 million in 1987 to 11.3 million in 1990, before showing increases in the early 1990s. The net result of these trends was an overall increase in both the secondary and elementary levels.

The increase from 1987 to 1997 was concentrated in the elementary grades, but this pattern is expected to change. The growing numbers of young pupils that have been filling the elementary schools will cause significant increases at the secondary school level during the next decade. Between fall 1997 and fall 2007, public elementary enrollment is projected to grow by less than 1 percent, while public secondary school enrollment is expected to rise by 13 percent. Public school enrollment is projected to set new records every year until 2006.

The proportion of students in private schools and colleges has changed little over the past 10 years. The percentage of private elementary and secondary students decreased slightly, from 12 percent in 1987 to 11 percent in 1997, and the percentage of college students who attended private colleges and universities remained at 22 percent. In 1997, about 5.9 million students were enrolled in private schools at the elementary and secondary levels and 3.1 million students in institutions of higher education (table 3).

College enrollment fell from 14.5 million in fall 1992 to 14.3 million in fall 1995, and projections indicate that enrollment also dropped slightly in 1996. However, total college enrollment is expected to increase during the remainder of the 1990s, as increasing numbers of high school graduates pursue higher education.

Although school attendance rates among 5- to 17-year-olds have remained relatively steady over the past 10 years, the proportion of 18- and 19-year-olds attending high school or college rose from 55 percent in 1986 to 62 percent in 1996. The proportion of 20- to 24-year-olds enrolled in school rose from 24 percent to 33 percent during the same time period (table 6).

An estimated 3.1 million elementary and secondary school teachers were engaged in classroom instruction in the fall of 1997 (table 4). This number has risen about 17 percent since 1987. The number of public school teachers in 1997 was about 2.7 million and the number in private schools was estimated at 0.4 million. About 1.9 million teachers were teaching in elementary schools, while about 1.2 million were employed at the secondary level (table 4).

Educational Attainment

Americans have become more educated. In 1996, 82 percent of the population 25 years old and over had completed high school and 24 percent had completed 4 or more years of college. This represents an increase from 1980, when 69 percent had completed high school and 17 percent had 4 years of college (table 8). In 1996, about 5 percent of persons, 25 years old or over, held a master's degree as their highest degree, slightly more than 1 percent held a professional degree (e.g., medicine or law), and 1 percent held a doctor's degree (table 9).

Expenditures

Education expenditures rose to an estimated high of $564 billion in the 1996–97 school year. Elementary and secondary schools spent about 60 percent of this total, and colleges and universities accounted for the remaining 40 percent (table 31). An estimated 7.4 percent of the gross domestic product was spent by elementary and secondary schools and colleges and universities in 1996–97 (table 30).

The proportion of total state and local government funds spent on education declined during the 1980s, at least partly as a result of the drop in elementary and secondary enrollment in the early part of the decade, and the expansion of other governmental services. During this same time period, the proportion of federal funds spent on education rose (table 34). Of the 1992–93 state and local funds spent on education, about 70 percent went to elementary and secondary schools, 26 percent to colleges and universities, and 4 percent to other education programs (table 35).

ALL LEVELS OF EDUCATION 7

Figure 1.—The structure of education in the United States

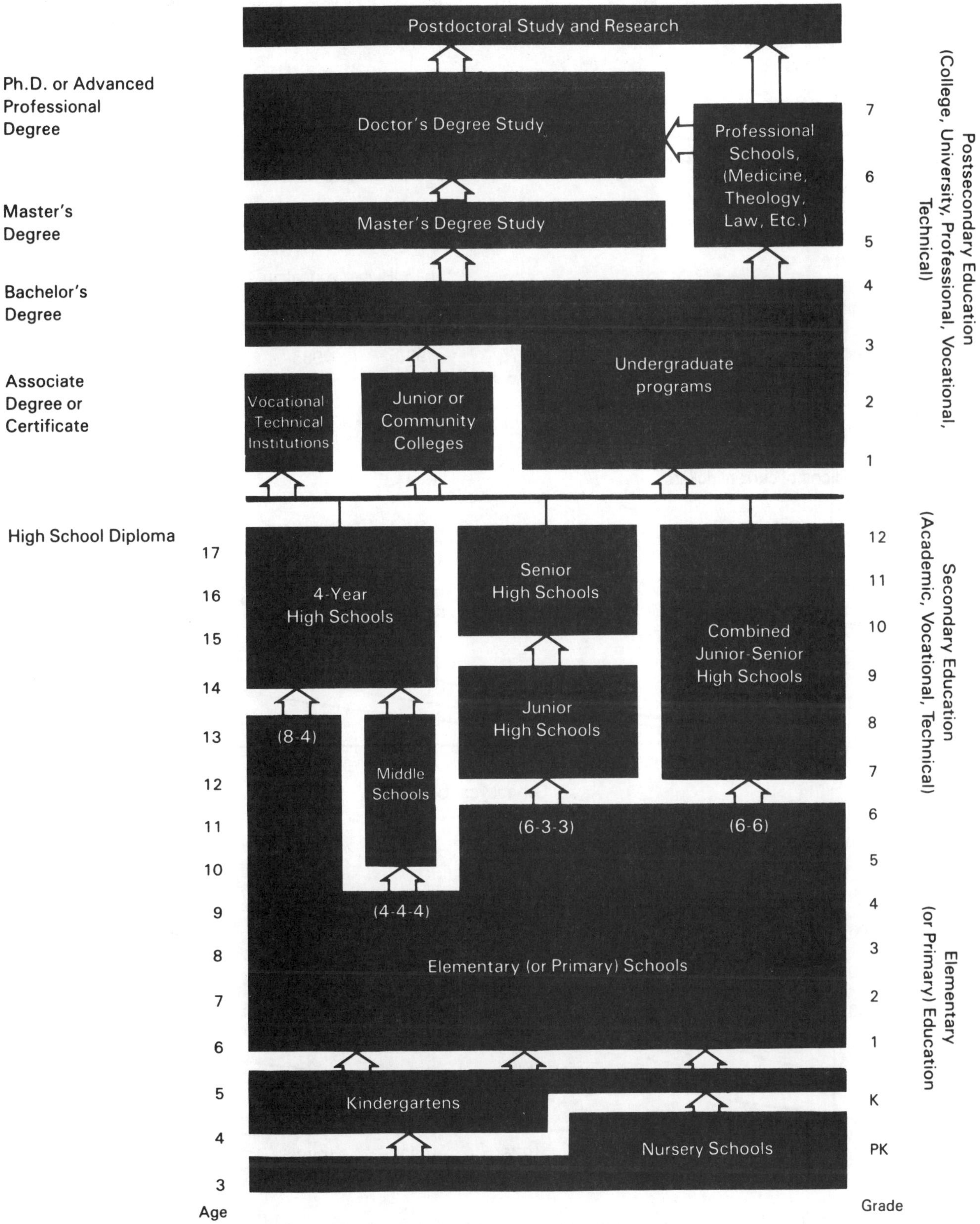

NOTE—Adult education programs, while not separately delineated above, may provide instruction at the elementary, secondary, or higher education level. Chart reflects typical patterns of progression rather than all possible variations.

SOURCE: U.S. Department of Education, National Center for Education Statistics.

Figure 2.—Enrollment and total expenditures in current and constant dollars, by level of education: 1960–61 to 1996–97

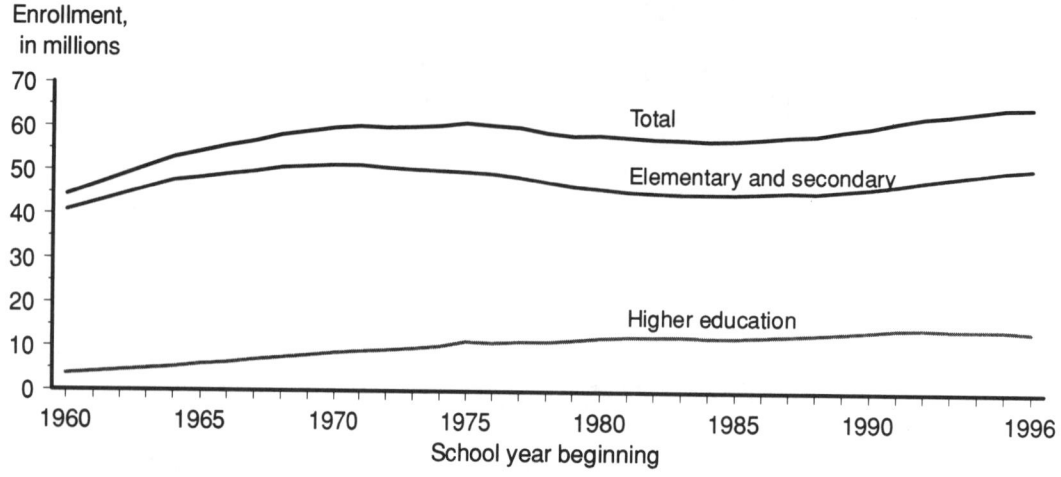

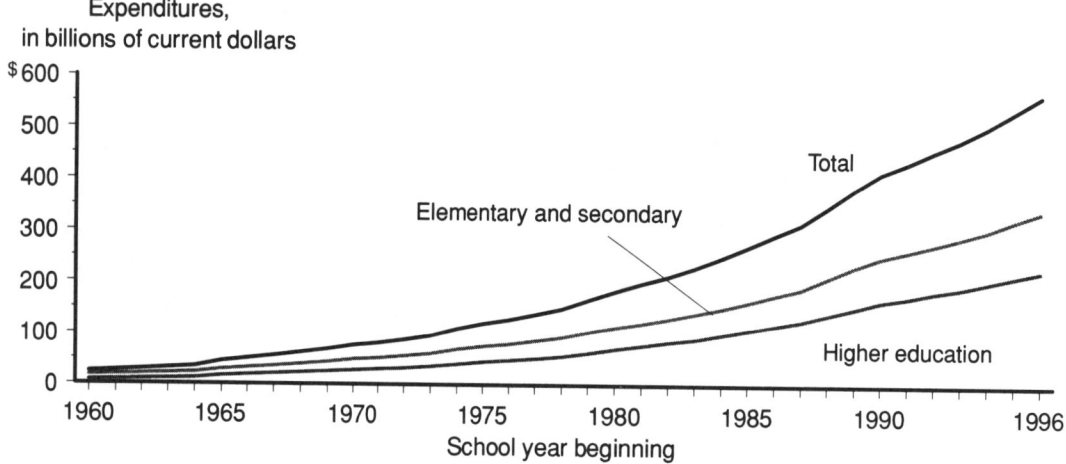

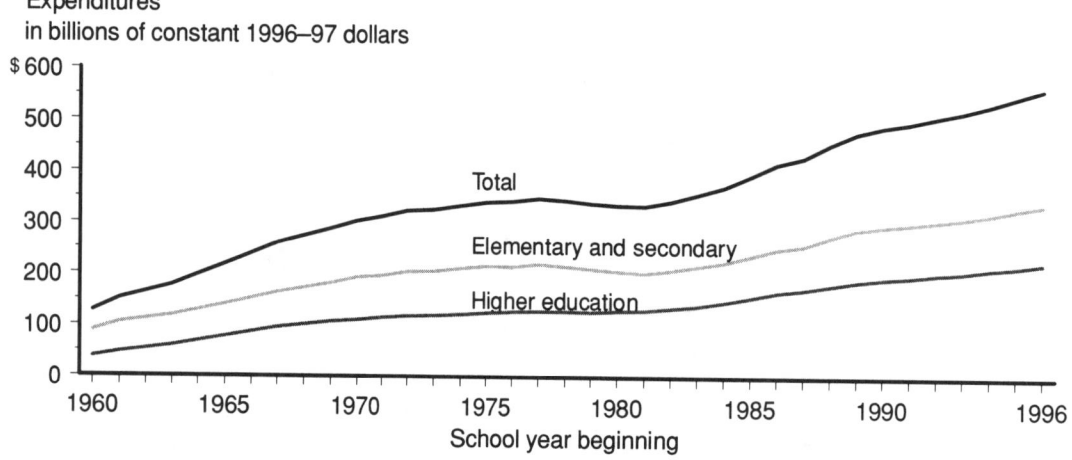

SOURCE: U.S. Department of Education, National Center for Education Statistics, *Statistics of State School Systems; Statistics of Public Elementary and Secondary School Systems; Statistics of Nonpublic Secondary Schools; Statistics of Nonpublic Elementary and Secondary Schools; Revenues and Expenditures for Public Elementary and Secondary Education; Fall Enrollment in Institutions of Higher Education; Financial Statistics of Institutions of Higher Education;* Common Core of Data surveys; and Integrated Postsecondary Education Data System surveys.

ALL LEVELS OF EDUCATION 9

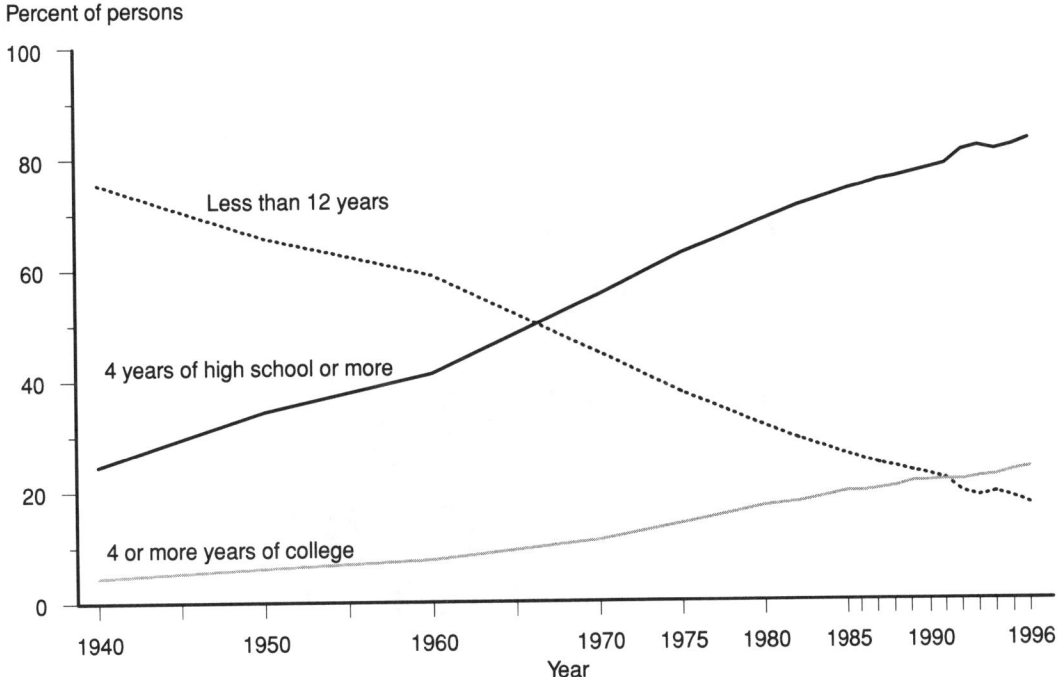

Figure 3.- Years of school completed by persons 25 years old and over: 1940 to 1996

SOURCE: U.S. Department of Commerce, Bureau of the Census, *1960 Census of Population*, Vol. 1, part 1; and *Current Population Reports*, Series P-20; and Current Population Survey, unpublished data.

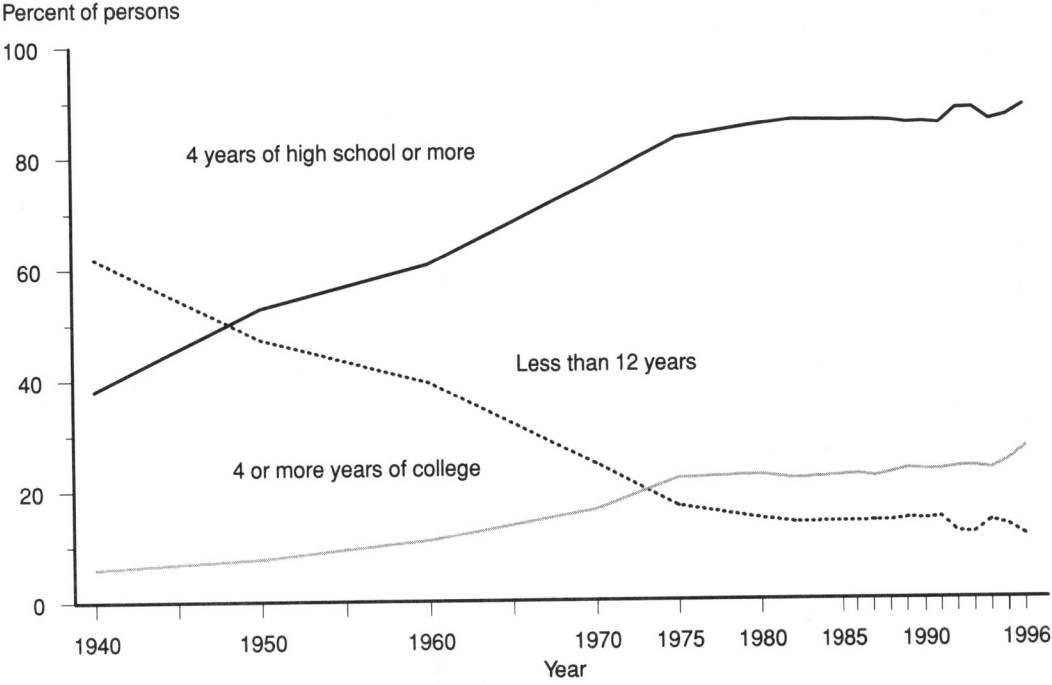

Figure 4.-Years of school completed by persons 25 to 29 years of age: 1940 to 1996

SOURCE: U.S. Department of Commerce, Bureau of the Census, *1960 Census of Population*, Vol. 1, part 1; and *Current Population Reports*, Series P-20; and Current Population Survey, unpublished data.

10 ALL LEVELS OF EDUCATION

Figure 5.–Highest level of education attained by persons 25 years and older: March 1996

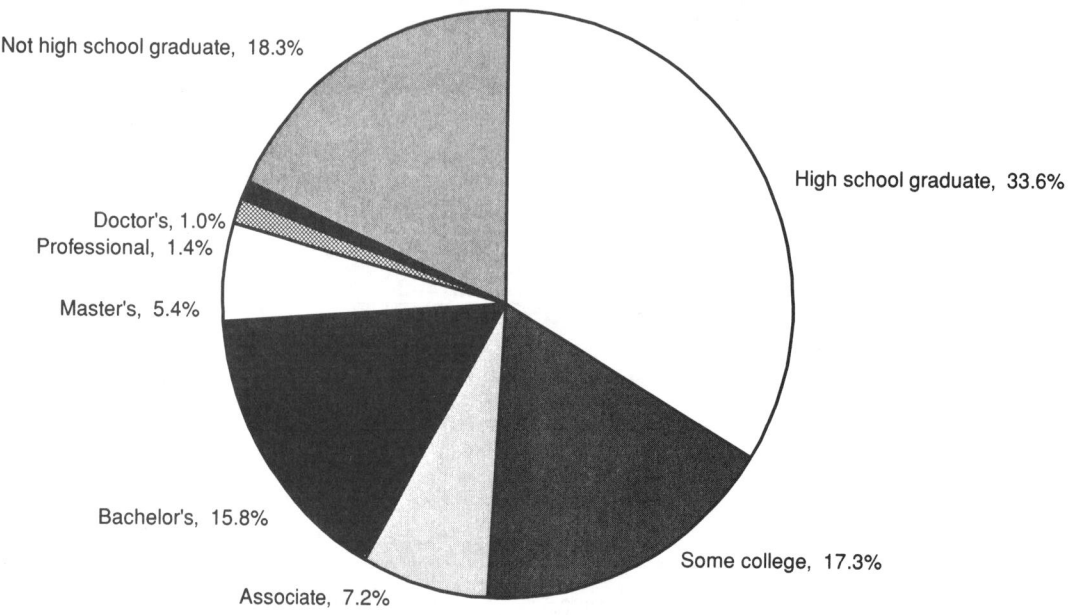

Total persons age 25 and over = 168.3 million

SOURCE: U.S. Department of Commerce, Bureau of the Census, Current Population Survey, unpublished data.

Figure 6.–Items most frequently cited by the public as a major problem facing the local public schools: 1980 to 1996

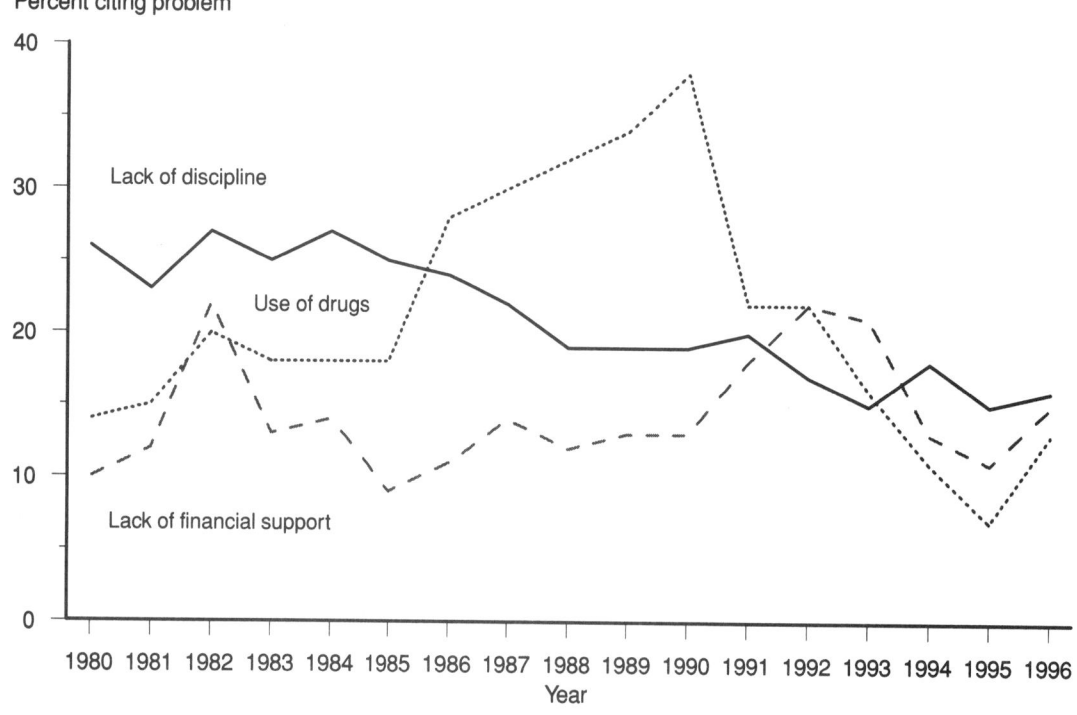

SOURCE: "The Annual Gallup Poll of the Public's Attitudes Toward the Public Schools," *Phi Delta Kappan*, various years.

ALL LEVELS: ENROLLMENT 11

Table 1.—Estimated number of participants in elementary and secondary education and in higher education: Fall 1997

[In millions]

Participants	All levels (elementary, secondary, and higher education)	Elementary and secondary schools			Institutions of higher education		
		Total	Public	Private	Total	Public	Private
1	2	3	4	5	6	7	8
Total	**74.1**	**58.0**	**51.5**	**6.5**	**16.1**	**12.4**	**3.7**
Enrollment [1]	66.3	52.2	46.4	5.9	14.1	11.0	3.1
Teachers and faculty	3.7	3.1	2.7	0.4	0.7	0.5	0.2
Other professional, administrative, and support staff	4.1	2.7	2.5	0.2	1.4	0.9	0.5

[1] Includes enrollments in local public school systems and in most private schools (religiously affiliated and nonsectarian). Excludes subcollegiate departments of institutions of higher education, residential schools for exceptional children, and federal schools. Elementary and secondary includes most kindergarten and some nursery school enrollment. Excludes preprimary enrollment in schools that do not offer first grade or above. Higher education comprises full-time and part-time students enrolled in degree-credit and nondegree-credit programs in universities, other 4-year colleges, and 2-year colleges.

NOTE.—The enrollment figures include all students in elementary and secondary schools and colleges and universities. However, the data for teachers and other staff in public and private elementary and secondary schools and colleges and universities are reported in terms of full-time equivalents. Because of rounding, details may not add to totals.

SOURCE: U.S. Department of Education, National Center for Education Statistics, unpublished projections and estimates. (This table was prepared November 1997.)

Table 2.—Enrollment in educational institutions, by level and control of institution: Fall 1980 to fall 2005

[In thousands]

Level of instruction and type of control	Fall 1980	Fall 1985	Fall 1990	Fall 1991	Fall 1992	Fall 1993	Fall 1994	Fall 1995 [1]	Projected fall 1996	Projected fall 1997	Projected fall 1998	Projected fall 1999	Projected fall 2000	Projected fall 2005
1	2	3	4	5	6	7	8	9	10	11	12	13	14	15
All levels	58,305	57,226	60,267	61,605	62,686	63,241	63,986	64,791	65,400	66,301	67,036	67,665	68,265	70,054
Public	50,335	48,901	52,061	53,356	54,208	54,654	55,245	55,933	56,594	57,381	58,011	58,548	59,050	60,544
Private	7,971	8,325	8,206	8,248	8,478	8,587	8,741	8,857	8,807	8,920	9,025	9,117	9,215	9,510
Elementary and secondary education [2]	46,208	44,979	46,448	47,246	48,198	48,936	49,707	50,528	51,484	52,217	52,725	53,132	53,465	54,349
Public	40,877	39,422	41,217	42,047	42,823	43,465	44,111	44,840	45,700	46,353	46,806	47,170	47,467	48,276
Private	5,331	5,557	5,232	5,199	5,375	5,471	[3] 5,596	[3] 5,688	5,784	5,863	5,920	5,963	5,998	6,073
Grades K–8 [4]	31,639	31,229	33,973	34,580	35,300	35,784	36,258	36,768	37,316	37,759	38,096	38,309	38,490	38,264
Public	27,647	27,034	29,878	30,506	31,088	31,504	31,898	32,341	32,826	33,216	33,512	33,699	33,858	33,660
Private	3,992	4,195	4,095	[3] 4,074	[3] 4,212	[3] 4,280	[3] 4,360	[3] 4,427	4,490	4,544	4,584	4,610	4,631	4,604
Grades 9–12	14,570	13,750	12,475	12,666	12,898	13,152	13,449	13,760	14,167	14,457	14,629	14,823	14,976	16,085
Public	13,231	12,388	11,338	11,541	11,735	11,961	12,213	12,500	12,874	13,138	13,294	13,470	13,609	14,617
Private	1,339	1,362	1,137	[3] 1,125	[3] 1,163	[3] 1,191	[3] 1,236	[3] 1,260	1,293	1,320	1,335	1,353	1,367	1,468
Higher education [5]	12,097	12,247	13,819	14,359	14,487	14,305	14,279	14,262	13,917	14,085	14,310	14,532	14,800	15,705
Public	9,457	9,479	10,845	11,310	11,385	11,189	11,134	11,092	10,894	11,028	11,205	11,378	11,583	12,268
Undergraduate [6]	8,442	8,477	9,710	10,148	10,216	10,012	9,945	9,904	9,737	9,866	10,042	10,210	10,406	11,039
First-professional	114	112	112	111	111	114	114	115	107	106	106	106	107	117
Graduate [7]	901	890	1,023	1,050	1,058	1,064	1,075	1,074	1,050	1,056	1,058	1,062	1,070	1,112
Private	2,640	2,768	2,974	3,049	3,103	3,116	3,145	3,169	3,023	3,057	3,105	3,154	3,217	3,437
Undergraduate [6]	2,033	2,120	2,250	2,291	2,321	2,312	2,317	2,328	2,243	2,275	2,323	2,368	2,425	2,608
First-professional	163	162	162	169	170	179	181	183	167	166	165	165	167	180
Graduate [7]	443	486	563	589	611	625	647	659	613	616	617	620	625	650

[1] Higher education data are preliminary.
[2] Includes enrollments in local public school systems and in most private schools (religiously affiliated and nonsectarian). Excludes subcollegiate departments of institutions of higher education, residential schools for exceptional children, and federal schools. Excludes preprimary pupils in schools that do not offer first grade or above.
[3] Estimated.
[4] Includes kindergarten and some nursery school pupils.
[5] Includes full-time and part-time students enrolled in degree-credit and nondegree-credit programs in universities and 2-year and 4-year colleges.
[6] Includes unclassified students below the baccalaureate level.
[7] Includes unclassified postbaccalaureate students.

NOTE.—Higher education enrollment projections are based on the middle alternative projections published by the National Center for Education Statistics. Because of rounding, details may not add to totals. Some data have been revised from previously published figures.

SOURCE: U.S. Department of Education, National Center for Education Statistics, Common Core of Data and Higher Education General Information Survey (HEGIS), "Fall Enrollment in Institutions of Higher Education" surveys; Integrated Postsecondary Education Data System (IPEDS), "Fall Enrollment" surveys, and *Projections of Education Statistics to 2007*. (This table was prepared August 1997.)

12 ALL LEVELS: ENROLLMENT

Table 3.—Enrollment in educational institutions, by level and by control of institution: 1869–70 to fall 2007

[In thousands]

Year	Total enrollment, all levels	Elementary and secondary, total	Public elementary and secondary schools			Private elementary and secondary schools[1]			Higher education[2]		
			Total	Pre-kindergarten through grade 8	Grades 9 through 12	Total	Kindergarten through grade 8	Grades 9 through 12	Total	Public	Private
1	2	3	4	5	6	7	8	9	10	11	12
1869–70	—	—	6,872	6,792	80	—	—	—	52	—	—
1879–80	—	—	9,868	9,757	110	—	—	—	116	—	—
1889–90	14,491	14,334	12,723	12,520	203	1,611	1,516	95	157	—	—
1899–1900	17,092	16,855	15,503	14,984	519	1,352	1,241	111	238	—	—
1909–10	19,728	19,372	17,814	16,899	915	1,558	1,441	117	355	—	—
1919–20	23,876	23,278	21,578	19,378	2,200	1,699	1,486	214	598	—	—
1929–30	29,430	28,329	25,678	21,279	4,399	2,651	2,310	341	1,101	—	—
1939–40	29,539	28,045	25,434	18,832	6,601	2,611	2,153	458	1,494	797	698
1949–50	31,151	28,492	25,111	19,387	5,725	3,380	2,708	672	2,659	1,355	1,304
Fall 1959	44,497	40,857	35,182	26,911	8,271	5,675	4,640	1,035	3,640	2,181	1,459
Fall 1964	52,996	47,716	41,416	30,025	11,391	[3]6,300	[3]5,000	1,300	5,280	3,468	1,812
Fall 1965	54,394	48,473	42,173	30,563	11,610	6,300	4,900	1,400	5,921	3,970	1,951
Fall 1966	55,629	49,239	43,039	31,145	11,894	[3]6,200	[3]4,800	[3]1,400	6,390	4,349	2,041
Fall 1967	56,803	49,891	43,891	31,641	12,250	[3]6,000	[3]4,600	[3]1,400	6,912	4,816	2,096
Fall 1968	58,257	50,744	44,944	32,226	12,718	5,800	4,400	1,400	7,513	5,431	2,082
Fall 1969	59,055	51,050	45,550	32,513	13,037	[3]5,500	[3]4,200	[3]1,300	8,005	5,897	2,108
Fall 1970	59,838	51,257	45,894	32,558	13,336	5,363	4,052	1,311	8,581	6,428	2,153
Fall 1971	60,220	51,271	46,071	32,318	13,753	[3]5,200	[3]3,900	[3]1,300	8,949	6,804	2,144
Fall 1972	59,941	50,726	45,726	31,879	13,848	[3]5,000	[3]3,700	[3]1,300	9,215	7,071	2,144
Fall 1973	60,047	50,445	45,445	31,401	14,044	[3]5,000	[3]3,700	[3]1,300	9,602	7,420	2,183
Fall 1974	60,297	50,073	45,073	30,971	14,103	[3]5,000	[3]3,700	[3]1,300	10,224	7,989	2,235
Fall 1975	61,004	49,819	44,819	30,515	14,304	[3]5,000	[3]3,700	[3]1,300	11,185	8,835	2,350
Fall 1976	60,490	49,478	44,311	29,997	14,314	5,167	3,825	1,342	11,012	8,653	2,359
Fall 1977	60,003	48,717	43,577	29,375	14,203	5,140	3,797	1,343	11,286	8,847	2,439
Fall 1978	58,897	47,637	42,551	28,463	14,088	5,086	3,732	1,353	11,260	8,786	2,474
Fall 1979	58,221	46,651	41,651	28,034	13,616	[3]5,000	[3]3,700	[3]1,300	11,570	9,037	2,533
Fall 1980	58,305	46,208	40,877	27,647	13,231	5,331	3,992	1,339	12,097	9,457	2,640
Fall 1981	57,916	45,544	40,044	27,280	12,764	[3]5,500	[3]4,100	[3]1,400	12,372	9,647	2,725
Fall 1982	57,591	45,166	39,566	27,161	12,405	[3]5,600	[3]4,200	[3]1,400	12,426	9,696	2,730
Fall 1983	57,432	44,967	39,252	26,981	12,271	5,715	4,315	1,400	12,465	9,683	2,782
Fall 1984	57,150	44,908	39,208	26,905	12,304	[3]5,700	[3]4,300	[3]1,400	12,242	9,477	2,765
Fall 1985	57,226	44,979	39,422	27,034	12,388	5,557	4,195	1,362	12,247	9,479	2,768
Fall 1986	57,709	45,205	39,753	27,420	12,333	[3]5,452	[3]4,116	[3]1,336	12,504	9,714	2,790
Fall 1987	58,254	45,488	40,008	27,933	12,076	5,479	4,232	1,247	12,767	9,973	2,793
Fall 1988	58,485	45,430	40,189	28,501	11,687	5,241	[3]4,036	[3]1,206	13,055	10,161	2,894
Fall 1989	59,436	45,898	40,543	29,152	11,390	5,355	[3]4,162	[3]1,193	13,539	10,578	2,961
Fall 1990	60,267	46,448	41,217	29,878	11,338	5,232	4,095	1,137	13,819	10,845	2,974
Fall 1991	61,605	47,246	42,047	30,506	11,541	5,199	[3]4,074	[3]1,125	14,359	11,310	3,049
Fall 1992	62,686	48,198	42,823	31,088	11,735	5,375	[3]4,212	[3]1,163	14,487	11,385	3,103
Fall 1993	63,241	48,936	43,465	31,504	11,961	5,471	[3]4,280	[3]1,191	14,305	11,189	3,116
Fall 1994	63,986	49,707	44,111	31,898	12,213	5,596	4,360	1,236	14,279	11,134	3,145
Fall 1995[4]	64,791	50,528	44,840	32,341	12,500	5,688	4,427	1,260	14,262	11,092	3,169
Fall 1996[5]	65,400	51,484	45,700	32,826	12,874	5,784	4,490	1,293	13,917	10,894	3,023
Fall 1997[5]	66,301	52,217	46,353	33,216	13,138	5,863	4,544	1,320	14,085	11,028	3,057
Fall 1998[5]	67,036	52,725	46,806	33,512	13,294	5,920	4,584	1,335	14,310	11,205	3,105
Fall 1999[5]	67,665	53,132	47,170	33,699	13,470	5,963	4,610	1,353	14,532	11,378	3,154
Fall 2000[5]	68,265	53,465	47,467	33,858	13,609	5,998	4,631	1,367	14,800	11,583	3,217
Fall 2001[5]	68,786	53,735	47,707	33,994	13,713	6,028	4,650	1,377	15,051	11,774	3,277
Fall 2002[5]	69,168	53,962	47,911	34,078	13,832	6,051	4,662	1,389	15,206	11,889	3,316
Fall 2003[5]	69,489	54,117	48,053	34,044	14,010	6,064	4,657	1,407	15,372	12,015	3,357
Fall 2004[5]	69,793	54,250	48,180	33,861	14,319	6,070	4,632	1,438	15,543	12,145	3,398
Fall 2005[5]	70,054	54,349	48,276	33,660	14,617	6,073	4,604	1,468	15,705	12,268	3,437
Fall 2006[5]	70,284	54,388	48,318	33,488	14,830	6,070	4,581	1,490	15,896	12,414	3,483
Fall 2007[5]	70,435	54,324	48,262	33,393	14,870	6,061	4,568	1,494	16,111	12,578	3,533

[1] Beginning in fall 1980, data include estimates for an expanded universe of private schools. Therefore, these totals may differ from figures shown in other tables, and direct comparisons with earlier years should be avoided.

[2] Data for 1869–70 through 1949–50 include resident degree-credit students enrolled at any time during the academic year. Beginning in 1959, data include all resident and extension students enrolled at the beginning of the fall term.

[3] Estimated.

[4] Preliminary data.

[5] Projected.

—Data not available.

NOTE.—Elementary and secondary enrollment includes pupils in local public school systems and in most private schools (religiously affiliated and nonsectarian), but generally excludes pupils in subcollegiate departments of institutions of higher education, residential schools for exceptional children, and federal schools. Public elementary enrollment includes most preprimary school pupils. Private elementary enrollment includes some preprimary students. Higher education enrollment includes students in colleges, universities, professional schools, teachers colleges, and 2-year colleges. Higher education enrollment projections are based on the middle alternative projections published by the National Center for Education Statistics. Some data have been revised from previously published figures. Because of rounding, details may not add to totals.

SOURCE: U.S. Department of Education, National Center for Education Statistics, *Statistics of State School Systems; Statistics of Public Elementary and Secondary School Systems; Statistics of Nonpublic Elementary and Secondary Schools; Projections of Education Statistics to 2007;* Common Core of Data; Higher Education General Information Survey (HEGIS), "Fall Enrollment in Institutions of Higher Education" surveys; and Integrated Postsecondary Education Data System (IPEDS), "Fall Enrollment" surveys. (This table was prepared August 1997.)

Table 4.—Teachers in elementary and secondary schools, and senior instructional staff in institutions of higher education, by control of institution: Fall 1970 to fall 2007

[In thousands]

Fall	All levels			Elementary and secondary teachers [1]									Higher education senior instructional staff [2]		
	Total	Public	Private	Total			Elementary teachers			Secondary teachers			Total	Public	Private
				Total	Public	Private	Total	Public	Private	Total	Public	Private			
1	2	3	4	5	6	7	8	9	10	11	12	13	14	15	16
1970	2,766	2,373	393	2,292	2,059	233	1,283	1,130	153	1,009	929	80	474	314	160
1975	3,081	2,641	440	2,453	2,198	[3]255	1,353	1,181	[3]172	1,100	1,017	[3]83	628	443	185
1980	3,171	2,679	492	2,485	2,184	301	1,401	1,189	212	1,084	995	89	[3]686	[3]495	[3]191
1981	3,145	2,636	509	2,440	2,127	[3]313	1,404	1,183	[3]221	1,037	945	[3]92	705	509	196
1982	3,168	2,639	529	2,458	2,133	[3]325	1,413	1,182	[3]231	1,045	951	[3]94	[3]710	[3]506	[3]204
1983	3,200	2,651	549	2,476	2,139	337	1,426	1,186	240	1,050	953	97	724	512	212
1984	3,225	2,673	552	2,508	2,168	[3]340	1,451	1,208	[3]243	1,057	960	[3]97	[3]717	[3]505	[3]212
1985	3,264	2,709	555	2,549	2,206	343	1,483	1,237	246	1,066	969	97	[3]715	[3]503	[3]212
1986	3,314	2,754	560	2,592	2,244	[3]348	1,521	1,271	[3]250	1,071	973	[3]98	[3]722	[3]510	[3]212
1987	3,425	2,832	593	2,632	2,279	[3]353	1,564	1,307	[3]257	1,068	973	[3]95	[4]793	[4]553	[4]240
1988	3,472	2,882	590	2,668	2,323	[3]345	1,604	1,353	[3]251	1,064	970	[3]94	[3]804	[3]559	[3]245
1989	3,558	2,934	624	2,734	2,357	[3]377	1,662	1,387	[3]275	1,072	970	[3]102	[4]824	[4]577	[4]247
1990	3,570	2,972	599	2,753	2,398	[3]355	1,680	1,426	[3]254	1,073	972	[3]101	[3]817	[3]574	[3]244
1991	3,613	3,013	600	2,787	2,432	[3]355	1,713	1,459	[3]254	1,074	973	[3]101	[4]826	[4]581	[4]245
1992	3,699	3,080	620	2,822	2,459	[3]363	1,752	1,492	[3]260	1,070	967	[3]103	[3]877	[3]621	[3]257
1993	3,785	3,154	631	2,870	2,504	[3]366	1,775	1,513	[3]262	1,095	991	[3]104	[4]915	[4]650	[4]265
1994	3,840	3,199	641	2,926	2,552	[3]373	1,794	1,528	[3]266	1,132	1,024	[3]108	[3]915	[3]647	[3]268
1995	3,892	3,243	650	2,978	2,598	[3]380	1,814	1,546	[3]269	1,164	1,053	[3]111	914	645	270
1996[5]	3,913	3,271	642	3,023	2,638	385	1,836	1,564	272	1,186	1,073	113	890	633	257
1997[5]	3,973	3,323	650	3,071	2,682	390	1,861	1,586	275	1,211	1,096	115	901	641	260
1998[5]	4,021	3,363	658	3,106	2,712	394	1,879	1,601	277	1,228	1,111	117	915	651	264
1999[5]	4,072	3,405	666	3,143	2,744	398	1,898	1,618	280	1,245	1,127	118	930	661	268
2000[5]	4,119	3,443	676	3,172	2,770	402	1,912	1,630	282	1,259	1,140	120	947	673	274
2001[5]	—	—	—	3,194	2,790	405	1,922	1,638	284	1,273	1,152	121	—	—	—
2002[5]	—	—	—	3,221	2,813	407	1,929	1,645	285	1,291	1,169	123	—	—	—
2003[5]	—	—	—	3,248	2,837	410	1,936	1,651	286	1,311	1,187	125	—	—	—
2004[5]	—	—	—	3,275	2,862	413	1,942	1,656	287	1,333	1,207	127	—	—	—
2005[5]	—	—	—	3,303	2,887	416	1,950	1,662	288	1,353	1,225	129	—	—	—
2006[5]	—	—	—	3,326	2,907	419	1,957	1,668	289	1,369	1,239	130	—	—	—
2007[5]	—	—	—	3,339	2,918	420	1,963	1,674	290	1,375	1,244	131	—	—	—

[1] Includes teachers in local public school systems and in most private schools (religiously affiliated and nonsectarian). Excludes subcollegiate departments of institutions of higher education, residential schools for exceptional children, and federal schools. Teachers are reported in terms of full-time equivalents.

[2] Includes full-time and part-time faculty with the rank of instructor or above in colleges, universities, professional schools, teachers colleges, and 2-year colleges. Excludes teaching assistants.

[3] Estimated.

[4] Based on actual survey data. Methodology for this year and later years is not consistent with figures for earlier years.

[5] Projected.

—Data not available.

NOTE.—Because of rounding, details may not add to totals. Some data have been revised from previously published figures.

SOURCE: U.S. Department of Education, National Center for Education Statistics, Common Core of Data; *Projections of Education Statistics*, various years; Integrated Postsecondary Education Data System (IPEDS), "Fall Staff" survey; and U.S. Equal Employment Opportunity Commission, Higher Education General Information (EEO-6) Survey (HEGIS), unpublished data. (This table was prepared June 1997.)

Table 5.—Educational institutions, by level and control of institution: 1978–79 to 1995–96

Level and control of institution	1980–81	1984–85	1986–87	1987–88	1988–89	1989–90	1990–91	1991–92	1992–93	1993–94	1994–95	1995–96
1	2	3	4	5	6	7	8	9	10	11	12	13
All institutions	**117,707**	—	**121,433**	**122,111**	—	—	**119,242**	—	—	**121,855**	—	—
Elementary and secondary schools	106,746	—	109,071	110,055	—	—	109,228	—	—	111,486	—	—
Elementary	72,659	—	74,104	74,511	—	—	74,716	—	—	75,591	—	—
Secondary	24,856	—	23,844	24,057	—	—	23,602	—	—	23,256	—	—
Combined	5,202	—	6,932	8,202	—	—	8,847	—	—	10,678	—	—
Other [1]	4,029	—	4,191	3,285	—	—	2,063	—	—	1,962	—	—
Public schools	85,982	84,007	83,455	83,248	83,165	83,425	84,538	84,578	84,497	85,393	86,221	87,125
Elementary	59,326	57,231	58,801	57,575	57,941	58,419	59,015	59,258	59,676	60,052	60,808	61,165
Secondary	22,619	22,320	21,406	21,662	21,403	21,181	21,135	20,767	20,671	20,705	20,904	20,997
Combined	1,743	1,596	1,983	2,179	2,235	2,280	2,325	2,481	2,549	2,674	2,764	2,796
Other [1]	2,294	2,860	1,265	1,832	1,586	1,545	2,063	2,072	1,601	1,962	1,745	2,167
Private schools	20,764	—	[2]25,616	26,807	—	—	24,690	25,998	—	26,093	—	—
Elementary	13,333	—	[2]15,303	16,936	—	—	15,701	15,716	—	15,539	—	—
Secondary	2,237	—	[2]2,438	2,395	—	—	2,467	2,475	—	2,551	—	—
Combined	3,459	—	[2]4,949	6,023	—	—	6,522	7,807	—	8,004	—	—
Other [1]	1,735	—	[2]2,926	1,453	—	—	([3])	([3])	—	([3])	—	—
Postsecondary institutions	[4]10,961	—	12,362	12,056	11,389	10,606	10,014	9,983	10,601	10,369	10,246	9,962
Public	[4]2,393	—	2,363	2,250	2,169	2,120	2,096	2,129	2,146	2,152	2,179	2,189
Private nonprofit	[4]2,359	—	3,432	3,254	3,092	2,942	2,808	2,810	2,926	2,890	2,916	2,877
Proprietary	[4]6,209	—	6,567	6,552	6,128	5,544	5,110	5,044	5,529	5,327	5,151	4,896
Noncollegiate institutions	[4]7,730	—	8,956	8,469	7,824	7,071	6,455	6,382	6,963	6,737	6,558	6,256
Public	[4]896	—	830	659	587	557	529	531	522	527	538	534
Private nonprofit	[4]790	—	1,797	1,581	1,434	1,286	1,159	1,148	1,254	1,203	1,214	1,171
Proprietary	[4]6,044	—	6,329	6,229	5,803	5,228	4,767	4,703	5,187	5,007	4,806	4,551
Institutions of higher education [5]	3,231	3,331	3,406	3,587	3,565	3,535	3,559	3,601	3,638	3,632	3,688	3,706
2-year colleges	1,274	1,306	1,336	1,452	1,436	1,408	1,418	1,444	1,469	1,442	1,473	1,462
Public	945	935	960	992	984	968	972	999	1,024	1,021	1,036	1,047
Private nonprofit	182	186	173	186	180	177	167	176	179	181	192	187
Proprietary	147	185	203	274	272	263	279	269	266	240	245	228
4-year colleges	1,957	2,025	2,070	2,135	2,129	2,127	2,141	2,157	2,169	2,190	2,215	2,244
Public	552	566	573	599	598	595	595	599	600	604	605	608
Private nonprofit	1,387	1,430	1,462	1,487	1,478	1,479	1,482	1,486	1,493	1,506	1,510	1,519
Proprietary	18	29	35	49	53	53	64	72	76	80	100	117

[1] Includes special education, alternative, and other schools not classified by grade span. Because of changes in survey definitions, figures for "other" schools are not comparable from year to year.
[2] Data are for 1985–86. Data were collected from a sample survey that differed significantly from earlier surveys. The sample survey was designed to correct an undercount of about 10 percent that was known to have occurred in earlier surveys.
[3] Included in other categories.
[4] Because of changes in survey procedures, figures are not directly comparable with data for later years.
[5] Includes those colleges designated as institutions of higher education by the Higher Education General Information Survey system, even if they have a less than 2-year program. Includes branch campuses. Beginning in 1980, total includes some schools accredited by the Accrediting Commission of Career Schools and Colleges of Technology.
—Data not available.

NOTE.—Some data revised from previously published figures.

SOURCE: U.S. Department of Education, National Center for Education Statistics, Common Core of Data and Private School surveys; Higher Education General Information Survey (HEGIS), "Institutional Characteristics of Colleges and Universities"; and Integrated Postsecondary Education Data System (IPEDS), "Institutional Characteristics" surveys. (This table was prepared October 1997.)

Table 6.—Percent of the population 3 to 34 years old enrolled in school,[1] by age: April 1940 to October 1996

Year	Total, 3 to 34 years	3 and 4 years	5 and 6 years	7 to 13 years	14 to 17 years	18 and 19 years	20 to 24 years			25 to 29 years	30 to 34 years
							Total	20 and 21 years	22 to 24 years		
1	2	3	4	5	6	7	8	9	10	11	12
1940[2]	—	—	—	95.0	79.3	28.9	6.6	—	—	—	—
1945	—	—	—	98.1	78.4	20.7	3.9	—	—	—	—
1947	—	—	73.8	98.5	79.3	24.3	10.2	—	—	3.0	—
1948	—	—	74.7	98.1	81.8	26.9	9.7	—	—	2.6	—
1949	—	—	76.2	98.6	81.6	25.3	9.2	—	—	3.8	—
1950	—	—	74.4	98.7	83.7	29.4	9.0	—	—	3.0	0.9
1951	—	—	73.6	99.1	85.2	26.2	8.6	—	—	2.5	—
1952	—	—	75.2	98.8	85.2	28.8	9.7	—	—	2.6	1.2
1953	—	—	78.6	99.4	85.9	31.2	11.1	—	—	2.9	1.7
1954	—	—	77.3	99.4	87.1	32.4	11.2	—	—	4.1	1.5
1955	—	—	78.1	99.2	86.9	31.5	11.1	—	—	4.2	1.6
1956	—	—	77.6	99.3	88.2	35.4	12.8	—	—	5.1	1.9
1957	—	—	78.6	99.5	89.5	34.9	14.0	—	—	—	—
1958	—	—	80.4	99.5	89.2	37.6	13.4	—	—	—	—
1959	—	—	80.0	99.4	90.2	36.8	12.7	—	—	—	—
1960	—	—	80.7	99.5	90.3	38.4	13.1	—	—	4.9	2.4
1961	—	—	81.7	99.3	91.4	38.0	13.7	—	—	—	—
1962	—	—	82.2	99.3	92.0	41.8	15.6	—	—	—	—
1963	—	—	82.7	99.3	92.9	40.9	17.3	—	—	—	—
1964	—	—	83.3	99.0	93.1	41.6	16.8	—	—	5.2	2.6
1965	55.5	10.6	84.9	99.4	93.2	46.3	19.0	27.6	13.2	6.1	3.2
1966	56.1	12.5	85.8	99.3	93.7	47.2	19.9	29.9	13.2	6.5	2.7
1967	56.6	14.2	87.4	99.3	93.7	47.6	22.0	33.3	13.6	6.6	4.0
1968	56.7	15.7	87.6	99.1	94.2	50.4	21.4	31.2	13.8	7.0	3.9
1969	57.0	16.1	88.4	99.2	94.0	50.2	23.0	34.1	15.4	7.9	4.8
1970	56.4	20.5	89.5	99.2	94.1	47.7	21.5	31.9	14.9	7.5	4.2
1971	56.2	21.2	91.6	99.1	94.5	49.2	21.9	32.2	15.4	8.0	4.9
1972	54.9	24.4	91.9	99.2	93.3	46.3	21.6	31.4	14.8	8.6	4.6
1973	53.5	24.2	92.5	99.2	92.9	42.9	20.8	30.1	14.5	8.5	4.5
1974	53.6	28.8	94.2	99.3	92.9	43.1	21.4	30.2	15.1	9.6	5.7
1975	53.7	31.5	94.7	99.3	93.6	46.9	22.4	31.2	16.2	10.1	6.6
1976	53.1	31.3	95.5	99.2	93.7	46.2	23.3	32.0	17.1	10.0	6.0
1977	52.5	32.0	95.8	99.4	93.6	46.2	22.9	31.8	16.5	10.8	6.9
1978	51.2	34.2	95.3	99.1	93.7	45.4	21.8	29.5	16.3	9.4	6.4
1979	50.3	35.1	95.8	99.2	93.6	45.0	21.7	30.2	15.8	9.6	6.4
1980	49.7	36.7	95.7	99.3	93.4	46.4	22.3	31.0	16.3	9.3	6.4
1981	48.9	36.0	94.0	99.2	94.1	49.0	22.5	31.6	16.5	9.0	6.9
1982	48.6	36.4	95.0	99.2	94.4	47.8	23.5	34.0	16.8	9.6	6.3
1983	48.4	37.5	95.4	99.2	95.0	50.4	22.7	32.5	16.6	9.6	6.4
1984	47.9	36.3	94.5	99.2	94.7	50.1	23.7	33.9	17.3	9.1	6.3
1985	48.3	38.9	96.1	99.2	94.9	51.6	24.0	35.3	16.9	9.2	6.1
1986	48.2	38.9	95.3	99.2	94.9	54.6	23.6	33.0	17.9	8.8	6.0
1987	48.6	38.3	95.1	99.5	95.0	55.6	25.5	38.7	17.5	9.0	5.8
1988	48.7	38.2	96.0	99.7	95.1	55.6	26.1	39.1	18.2	8.3	5.9
1989	49.1	39.1	95.2	99.3	95.7	56.0	27.0	38.5	19.9	9.3	5.7
1990	50.2	44.4	96.5	99.6	95.8	57.2	28.6	39.7	21.0	9.7	5.8
1991	50.7	40.5	95.4	99.6	96.0	59.6	30.2	42.0	22.2	10.2	6.2
1992	51.4	39.7	95.5	99.4	96.7	61.4	31.6	44.0	23.7	9.8	6.1
1993	51.8	40.4	95.4	99.5	96.5	61.6	30.8	42.7	23.6	10.2	5.9
1994	53.3	[3]47.3	96.7	99.4	96.6	60.2	32.0	44.9	24.0	10.8	6.7
1995	53.7	[3]48.7	96.0	98.9	96.3	59.4	31.5	44.9	23.2	11.6	5.9
1996	54.1	[3]48.3	94.0	97.7	95.4	61.5	32.5	44.4	24.8	11.9	6.1

[1] Includes enrollment in any type of graded public, parochial, or other private schools. Includes nursery schools, kindergartens, elementary schools, high schools, colleges, universities, and professional schools. Attendance may be on either a full-time or part-time basis and during the day or night. Enrollments in "special" schools, such as trade schools, business colleges, or correspondence schools, are not included.

[2] Data are as of April 1940. Data for all other years are as of October.

[3] Preprimary enrollment collected using new procedures. May not be comparable to figures for earlier years.

—Data not available.

NOTE.—Data are based upon sample surveys of the civilian noninstitutional population.

SOURCE: U.S. Department of Commerce, Bureau of the Census, *Historical Statistics of the United States, Colonial Times to 1970; Current Population Reports*, Series P-20, various years; and Current Population Survey, unpublished data. (This table was prepared August 1997.)

16 ALL LEVELS: ENROLLMENT RATES

Table 7.—Percent of the population 3 to 34 years old enrolled in school,[1] by race/ethnicity, sex, and age: October 1975 to October 1996

Year and age	Total				Male				Female			
	All races	White, non-Hispanic	Black, non-Hispanic	Hispanic origin	All races	White, non-Hispanic	Black, non-Hispanic	Hispanic origin	All races	White, non-Hispanic	Black, non-Hispanic	Hispanic origin
1	2	3	4	5	6	7	8	9	10	11	12	13
1975												
Total, 3 to 34 years	53.7	53.0	57.7	54.8	56.1	55.2	60.4	58.1	51.5	50.8	55.3	51.7
3 and 4 years	31.5	31.0	34.4	27.3	30.9	31.1	31.4	26.7	32.1	30.9	37.5	27.9
5 and 6 years	94.7	95.1	94.4	92.1	94.4	94.8	94.8	89.7	95.1	95.4	94.0	94.4
7 to 9 years	99.3	99.4	99.3	99.6	99.2	99.2	99.4	99.6	99.5	99.6	99.2	99.5
10 to 13 years	99.3	99.3	99.1	99.2	98.9	99.0	98.9	98.8	99.6	99.6	99.3	99.7
14 and 15 years	98.2	98.5	97.4	95.6	98.4	98.6	97.6	97.4	98.0	98.4	97.2	93.8
16 and 17 years	89.0	89.5	86.8	86.2	90.7	91.2	88.1	88.3	87.2	87.8	85.5	84.0
18 and 19 years	46.9	46.8	46.9	44.0	49.9	49.4	49.6	51.9	44.2	44.2	44.6	37.1
20 and 21 years	31.2	32.1	26.7	27.5	35.3	36.7	28.4	31.3	27.4	27.8	25.3	24.3
22 to 24 years	16.2	16.4	13.9	14.1	20.0	20.8	14.5	15.9	12.6	12.2	13.4	12.5
25 to 29 years	10.1	10.1	9.4	8.3	13.1	13.2	11.6	11.9	7.2	7.2	7.6	5.3
30 to 34 years	6.6	6.6	7.1	5.5	7.7	7.5	8.7	7.2	5.6	5.8	5.9	4.1
1980												
Total, 3 to 34 years	49.7	48.8	54.0	49.8	50.9	50.0	56.2	49.9	48.5	47.7	52.1	49.8
3 and 4 years	36.7	37.4	38.2	28.5	37.8	39.2	36.4	30.1	35.5	35.5	40.0	26.6
5 and 6 years	95.7	95.9	95.5	94.5	95.0	95.4	94.1	94.0	96.4	96.5	97.0	94.9
7 to 9 years	99.1	99.1	99.4	98.4	99.0	99.0	99.5	97.7	99.2	99.2	99.3	99.0
10 to 13 years	99.4	99.4	99.4	99.7	99.4	99.4	99.4	99.4	99.4	99.3	99.3	99.9
14 and 15 years	98.2	98.7	97.9	94.3	98.7	98.9	98.4	96.7	97.7	98.5	97.3	92.1
16 and 17 years	89.0	89.2	90.7	81.8	89.1	89.4	90.7	81.5	88.8	89.0	90.6	82.2
18 and 19 years	46.4	47.0	45.8	37.8	47.0	48.5	42.9	36.9	45.8	45.7	48.3	38.8
20 and 21 years	31.0	33.0	23.3	19.5	32.6	34.8	22.8	21.4	29.5	31.3	23.7	17.6
22 to 24 years	16.3	16.8	13.6	11.7	17.8	18.7	13.4	10.7	14.9	15.0	13.7	12.6
25 to 29 years	9.3	9.4	8.8	6.9	9.8	9.8	10.6	6.8	8.8	9.1	7.5	6.9
30 to 34 years	6.4	6.4	6.9	5.1	5.9	5.6	7.2	6.2	7.0	7.2	6.6	4.1
1985												
Total, 3 to 34 years	48.3	47.8	50.8	47.7	49.2	48.7	52.6	47.5	47.4	46.9	49.2	47.9
3 and 4 years	38.9	40.3	42.8	27.0	36.7	39.1	34.6	26.4	41.2	41.6	50.3	27.7
5 and 6 years	96.1	96.6	95.7	94.5	95.3	95.6	94.5	95.3	97.0	97.6	97.1	93.7
7 to 9 years	99.1	99.4	98.6	98.4	99.0	99.3	98.4	98.9	99.2	99.4	98.9	98.0
10 to 13 years	99.3	99.3	99.5	99.4	99.2	99.2	99.1	99.1	99.4	99.3	99.9	99.7
14 and 15 years	98.1	98.3	98.1	96.1	98.3	98.4	98.5	96.2	97.9	98.1	97.6	96.0
16 and 17 years	91.7	92.5	91.8	84.5	92.4	92.9	92.0	88.9	90.9	92.2	91.6	80.0
18 and 19 years	51.6	53.7	43.5	41.8	52.2	53.4	49.4	38.6	51.0	54.0	37.8	44.7
20 and 21 years	35.3	37.2	27.7	24.0	36.5	38.8	29.9	20.3	34.1	35.7	25.8	27.4
22 to 24 years	16.9	17.5	13.8	11.6	18.8	19.8	13.5	12.6	15.1	15.4	14.0	10.4
25 to 29 years	9.2	9.6	7.4	6.6	9.4	9.7	5.8	8.2	9.1	9.4	8.7	4.9
30 to 34 years	6.1	6.2	5.2	5.7	5.4	5.6	3.9	4.0	6.8	6.9	6.2	7.5
1990												
Total, 3 to 34 years	50.2	49.8	52.2	47.2	50.9	50.4	54.3	46.8	49.5	49.2	50.3	47.7
3 and 4 years	44.4	47.2	41.8	30.7	43.9	47.9	38.1	28.0	44.9	46.6	45.5	33.6
5 and 6 years	96.5	96.7	96.5	94.9	96.5	96.8	96.2	95.8	96.4	96.7	96.9	93.9
7 to 9 years	99.7	99.7	99.8	99.5	99.7	99.7	99.9	99.5	99.6	99.7	99.8	99.4
10 to 13 years	99.6	99.7	99.9	99.1	99.6	99.6	99.9	99.0	99.7	99.7	99.8	99.1
14 and 15 years	99.0	99.0	99.4	99.0	99.1	99.2	99.7	99.1	98.9	98.9	99.1	98.8
16 and 17 years	92.5	93.5	91.7	85.4	92.6	93.4	93.0	85.5	92.4	93.7	90.5	85.3
18 and 19 years	57.2	59.1	55.0	44.0	58.2	59.7	60.4	40.7	56.3	58.5	49.8	47.2
20 and 21 years	39.7	43.1	28.3	27.2	40.3	44.2	31.0	21.7	39.2	42.0	25.8	33.1
22 to 24 years	21.0	21.9	19.7	9.9	22.3	23.7	19.3	11.2	19.9	20.3	20.0	8.4
25 to 29 years	9.7	10.4	6.1	6.3	9.2	10.0	4.7	4.6	10.2	10.7	7.3	8.1
30 to 34 years	5.8	6.2	4.5	3.6	4.8	5.0	2.3	4.0	6.9	7.4	6.3	3.1
1996												
Total, 3 to 34 years	54.1	54.0	56.3	50.3	54.4	54.2	57.8	49.2	53.8	53.8	54.9	51.4
3 and 4 years[2]	48.3	50.3	49.9	38.1	46.9	48.0	47.7	39.5	49.8	52.9	52.1	36.8
5 and 6 years	94.0	96.1	90.5	89.5	93.8	95.5	89.8	91.0	94.3	96.7	91.2	87.8
7 to 9 years	97.2	97.3	97.4	96.6	97.2	97.2	98.0	95.4	97.3	97.3	96.7	97.9
10 to 13 years	98.1	98.3	97.3	97.6	98.0	98.1	97.1	97.9	98.2	98.6	97.6	97.4
14 and 15 years	98.0	98.2	99.0	96.6	98.5	98.8	98.1	98.0	97.5	97.7	100.0	95.0
16 and 17 years	92.8	93.6	92.1	88.7	93.2	93.5	93.5	90.4	92.4	93.7	90.6	86.9
18 and 19 years	61.5	65.5	53.2	47.0	60.8	63.7	55.4	46.8	62.2	67.3	51.1	47.2
20 and 21 years	44.4	48.9	37.5	25.3	43.9	48.7	39.7	19.5	44.8	49.0	35.8	31.1
22 to 24 years	24.8	25.9	21.2	17.6	25.2	27.3	19.2	16.2	24.5	24.5	22.9	19.3
25 to 29 years	11.9	11.8	13.7	8.6	11.4	11.4	12.4	6.8	12.5	12.1	14.7	10.5
30 to 34 years	6.1	5.8	7.0	5.0	4.9	4.3	5.5	4.3	7.3	7.3	8.3	5.7

[1] Includes enrollment in any type of graded public, parochial, or other private schools. Includes nursery schools, kindergartens, elementary schools, high schools, colleges, universities, and professional schools. Attendance may be on either a full-time or part-time basis and during the day or night. Enrollments in "special" schools, such as trade schools, business colleges, or correspondence schools, are not included.

[2] Preprimary enrollment collected using new procedures. May not be comparable to figures for earlier years.

NOTE.—Data are based upon sample surveys of the civilian noninstitutional population.

SOURCE: U.S. Department of Commerce, Bureau of the Census, Current Population Survey, unpublished data. (This table was prepared August 1997.)

Table 8.—Years of school completed by persons age 25 and over and 25 to 29, by race/ethnicity and sex: 1910 to 1996

Age and year	Percent, by years of school completed											
	All races			White, non-Hispanic[1]			Black, non-Hispanic[1]			Hispanic		
	Less than 5 years of elementary school	4 years of high school or more	4 or more years of college[2]	Less than 5 years of elementary school	4 years of high school or more	4 or more years of college[2]	Less than 5 years of elementary school	4 years of high school or more	4 or more years of college[2]	Less than 5 years of elementary school	4 years of high school or more	4 or more years of college[2]
1	2	3	4	5	6	7	8	9	10	11	12	13
Males and females												
25 and over												
1910[3]	23.8	13.5	2.7	—	—	—	—	—	—	—	—	—
1920[3]	22.0	16.4	3.3	—	—	—	—	—	—	—	—	—
1930[3]	17.5	19.1	3.9	—	—	—	—	—	—	—	—	—
April 1940	13.7	24.5	4.6	10.9	26.1	4.9	41.8	7.7	1.3	—	—	—
April 1950	11.1	34.3	6.2	8.9	36.4	6.6	32.6	13.7	2.2	—	—	—
April 1960	8.3	41.1	7.7	6.7	43.2	8.1	23.5	21.7	3.5	—	—	—
March 1970	5.3	55.2	11.0	4.2	57.4	11.6	14.7	36.1	6.1	—	—	—
March 1975	4.2	62.5	13.9	2.6	65.8	14.9	12.3	42.6	6.4	18.2	38.5	6.6
March 1980	3.4	68.6	17.0	1.9	71.9	18.4	9.1	51.4	7.9	15.8	44.5	7.6
March 1982	3.0	71.0	17.7	1.7	74.3	19.1	7.3	54.9	8.7	14.7	46.0	7.8
March 1985	2.7	73.9	19.4	1.4	77.5	20.8	6.1	59.9	11.1	13.5	47.9	8.5
March 1986	2.7	74.7	19.4	1.4	78.2	20.1	5.3	62.5	10.9	12.9	48.5	8.4
March 1987	2.4	75.6	19.9	1.3	79.0	20.5	4.9	63.6	10.8	11.9	50.9	8.6
March 1988	2.5	76.2	20.3	1.2	79.8	21.8	4.8	63.5	11.2	12.2	51.0	10.0
March 1989	2.5	76.9	21.1	1.2	80.7	22.8	5.2	64.7	11.7	12.2	50.9	9.9
March 1990	2.5	77.6	21.3	1.1	81.4	23.1	5.1	66.2	11.3	12.3	50.8	9.2
March 1991	2.4	78.4	21.4	1.1	82.4	23.3	4.7	66.8	11.5	12.5	51.3	9.7
March 1992	2.1	79.4	21.4	0.9	83.4	23.2	3.9	67.7	11.9	11.8	52.6	9.3
March 1993	2.1	80.2	21.9	0.8	84.1	23.8	3.7	70.5	12.2	11.8	53.1	9.0
March 1994	1.9	80.9	22.2	0.8	84.9	24.3	2.7	73.0	12.9	10.8	53.3	9.1
March 1995	1.9	81.7	23.0	0.7	85.9	23.4	2.5	73.8	13.3	10.6	53.4	9.3
March 1996	1.8	81.8	23.6	0.6	86.0	25.9	2.2	74.6	13.8	10.4	53.1	9.3
25 to 29												
1920[3]	—	—	—	12.9	22.0	4.5	44.6	6.3	1.2	—	—	—
April 1940	5.9	38.1	5.9	3.4	41.2	6.4	27.0	12.3	1.6	—	—	—
April 1950	4.6	52.8	7.7	3.3	56.3	8.2	16.1	23.6	2.8	—	—	—
April 1960	2.8	60.7	11.0	2.2	63.7	11.8	7.2	38.6	5.4	—	—	—
March 1970	1.1	75.4	16.4	0.9	77.8	17.3	2.2	58.4	10.0	—	—	—
March 1975	1.0	83.1	21.9	0.6	86.6	23.8	0.5	71.1	10.5	8.0	53.1	8.8
March 1980	0.8	85.4	22.5	0.3	89.2	25.0	0.7	76.7	11.6	6.7	58.0	7.7
March 1982	0.8	86.2	21.7	0.3	89.1	23.8	0.7	81.0	12.6	6.6	61.0	9.7
March 1985	0.7	86.1	22.2	0.2	89.5	24.4	0.4	80.5	11.6	6.0	60.9	11.1
March 1986	0.9	86.1	22.4	0.4	89.6	25.2	0.5	83.5	11.8	5.6	59.1	9.0
March 1987	0.9	86.0	22.0	0.4	89.4	24.7	0.4	83.5	11.5	4.8	59.8	8.7
March 1988	1.0	85.9	22.7	0.3	89.7	25.1	0.3	80.9	12.0	6.0	62.3	11.3
March 1989	1.0	85.5	23.4	0.3	89.3	26.3	0.5	82.3	12.7	5.4	61.0	10.1
March 1990	1.2	85.7	23.2	0.3	90.1	26.4	1.0	81.7	13.4	7.3	58.2	8.2
March 1991	1.0	85.4	23.2	0.3	89.8	26.7	0.5	81.8	11.0	5.8	56.7	9.2
March 1992	0.9	86.3	23.6	0.3	90.7	27.2	0.8	80.9	11.1	5.2	60.9	9.5
March 1993	0.7	86.7	23.7	0.3	91.2	27.2	0.2	82.7	13.3	4.0	60.9	8.3
March 1994	0.8	86.1	23.3	0.3	91.1	27.1	0.6	84.1	13.6	3.6	60.3	8.0
March 1995	1.0	86.9	24.7	0.3	92.5	28.8	0.2	86.7	15.4	4.9	57.2	8.9
March 1996	0.8	87.3	27.1	0.2	92.6	31.6	0.4	86.0	14.6	4.3	61.1	10.0
Males												
25 and over												
April 1940	15.1	22.7	5.5	12.0	24.2	5.9	46.2	6.9	1.4	—	—	—
April 1950	12.2	32.6	7.3	9.8	34.6	7.9	36.9	12.6	2.1	—	—	—
April 1960	9.4	39.5	9.7	7.4	41.6	10.3	27.7	20.0	3.5	—	—	—
March 1970	5.9	55.0	14.1	4.5	57.2	15.0	17.9	35.4	6.8	—	—	—
March 1980	3.6	69.2	20.9	2.0	72.4	22.8	11.3	51.2	7.7	16.5	44.9	9.2
March 1990	2.7	77.7	24.4	1.3	81.6	26.7	6.4	65.8	11.9	12.9	50.3	9.8
March 1994	2.1	81.1	25.1	0.8	85.1	27.8	3.9	71.8	12.7	11.4	53.4	9.6
March 1995	2.0	81.7	26.0	0.8	86.0	28.9	3.4	73.5	13.7	10.8	52.9	10.1
March 1996	1.9	81.9	26.0	0.7	86.1	28.8	2.9	74.6	12.5	10.2	53.0	10.3
Females												
25 and over												
April 1940	12.4	26.3	3.8	9.8	28.1	4.0	37.5	8.4	1.2	—	—	—
April 1950	10.0	36.0	5.2	8.1	38.2	5.4	28.6	14.7	2.4	—	—	—
April 1960	7.4	42.5	5.8	6.0	44.7	6.0	19.7	23.1	3.6	—	—	—
March 1970	4.7	55.4	8.2	3.9	57.7	8.6	11.9	36.6	5.6	—	—	—
March 1980	3.2	68.1	13.6	1.8	71.5	14.4	7.4	51.5	8.1	15.3	44.2	6.2
March 1990	2.2	77.5	18.4	1.0	81.3	19.8	4.1	66.5	10.8	11.7	51.3	8.7
March 1994	1.7	80.8	19.6	0.7	84.7	21.1	1.8	73.9	13.1	10.3	53.2	8.6
March 1995	1.7	81.6	20.2	0.6	85.8	22.2	1.8	74.1	13.0	10.4	53.8	8.4
March 1996	1.7	81.6	21.4	0.5	85.9	23.2	1.6	74.6	14.8	10.6	53.3	8.3

[1] Includes persons of Hispanic origin for years prior to 1975.
[2] Data for 1993 to 1996 are for persons with a bachelor's degree or higher.
[3] Estimates based on Bureau of the Census retrojection of 1940 Census data on education by age.
—Data not available.

NOTE.—Data for 1975 and subsequent years are for the noninstitutional population.

SOURCE: U.S. Department of Commerce, Bureau of the Census, *U.S. Census of Population, 1960*, Vol. 1, part 1; *Current Population Reports*, Series P-20; Series P-19, No. 4; *1960 Census Monograph*, "Education of the American Population," by John K. Folger and Charles B. Nam; and unpublished data from the Current Population Survey; and U.S. Department of Labor, Bureau of Labor Statistics, Office of Employment and Unemployment Statistics, "Educational Attainment of Workers, March 1991," and unpublished data. (This table was prepared October 1997.)

Table 9.—Highest level of education attained by persons age 18 and over, by age, sex, and race/ethnicity: March 1996

[In thousands]

Age, sex, and race	Total population[1]	Elementary level		High school			College					
		Less than 7 years	7 or 8 years	1 to 3 years	4 years	Graduate	Some college	Associate	Bachelor's	Master's	First-professional	Doctorate
1	2	3	4	5	6	7	8	9	10	11	12	13
Total												
18 and over	193,166	6,880	7,550	19,396	2,649	64,118	37,840	13,159	28,366	9,166	2,427	1,617
18 and 19 years old	7,190	82	154	2,569	432	1,993	1,925	29	2	—	2	2
20 to 24 years old	17,653	292	279	1,601	342	5,566	6,714	959	1,823	65	8	3
25 years old and over	168,323	6,506	7,116	15,226	1,875	56,559	29,201	12,171	26,540	9,101	2,416	1,611
25 to 29 years old	19,462	418	274	1,518	262	5,995	4,099	1,615	4,318	716	194	53
30 to 34 years old	21,457	572	323	1,752	248	7,092	3,980	1,931	4,074	1,012	326	148
35 to 39 years old	22,479	602	404	1,550	235	7,610	4,346	1,944	4,041	1,217	319	212
40 to 49 years old	38,819	996	732	2,462	348	12,662	7,090	3,554	6,906	2,894	695	482
50 to 59 years old	24,664	988	1,008	2,258	253	8,884	3,969	1,575	3,306	1,707	360	356
60 to 64 years old	9,784	576	586	1,136	98	3,570	1,419	477	1,081	579	140	122
65 years old and over	31,658	2,354	3,788	4,551	432	10,747	4,298	1,076	2,816	977	382	238
Men												
18 and over	92,741	3,458	3,574	9,176	1,393	29,603	18,063	5,748	14,062	4,838	1,675	1,152
18 and 19 years old	3,610	48	92	1,441	219	976	822	8	2	—	2	—
20 to 24 years old	8,792	148	141	803	174	2,978	3,243	437	840	26	2	—
25 years old and over	80,339	3,263	3,341	6,931	1,000	25,649	13,998	5,303	13,219	4,812	1,671	1,152
25 to 29 years old	9,752	226	116	823	154	3,113	2,056	718	2,056	355	105	29
30 to 34 years old	10,638	320	162	924	154	3,588	1,893	869	1,890	552	189	98
35 to 39 years old	11,091	324	188	803	138	3,850	2,097	845	1,847	650	194	154
40 to 49 years old	19,104	540	383	1,215	202	5,868	3,477	1,618	3,585	1,401	480	333
50 to 59 years old	11,915	517	541	1,008	115	3,899	1,865	706	1,790	929	281	262
60 to 64 years old	4,579	301	298	446	45	1,433	723	166	621	333	106	107
65 years old and over	13,260	1,034	1,653	1,712	190	3,897	1,887	381	1,430	593	315	169
Women												
18 and over	100,425	3,422	3,976	10,220	1,256	34,515	19,777	7,412	14,304	4,328	752	464
18 and 19 years old	3,580	34	62	1,128	213	1,017	1,103	21	—	—	—	2
20 to 24 years old	8,861	144	139	797	167	2,587	3,471	522	983	40	7	3
25 years old and over	87,984	3,243	3,775	8,295	876	30,911	15,203	6,868	13,321	4,288	745	459
25 to 29 years old	9,709	192	158	695	107	2,882	2,043	897	2,262	361	89	24
30 to 34 years old	10,819	252	161	828	94	3,504	2,087	1,062	2,184	460	138	50
35 to 39 years old	11,388	279	217	747	97	3,759	2,249	1,098	2,193	567	124	58
40 to 49 years old	19,715	455	349	1,246	146	6,794	3,612	1,935	3,320	1,493	214	148
50 to 59 years old	12,749	470	467	1,250	137	4,985	2,105	868	1,515	778	79	94
60 to 64 years old	5,205	275	288	690	52	2,137	695	312	460	247	34	15
65 years old and over	18,398	1,320	2,135	2,840	241	6,849	2,411	695	1,386	384	67	69
White, non-Hispanic												
18 and over	145,261	1,888	5,214	12,461	1,467	49,808	29,026	10,522	23,611	7,819	2,119	1,327
18 and 19 years old	4,807	7	76	1,654	230	1,369	1,442	26	2	—	—	—
20 to 24 years old	11,644	20	113	744	150	3,691	4,653	712	1,498	56	7	—
25 years old and over	128,810	1,862	5,025	10,063	1,087	44,748	22,930	9,783	22,110	7,764	2,112	1,327
25 to 29 years old	13,307	41	121	713	115	4,070	2,829	1,216	3,450	565	152	35
30 to 34 years old	15,051	44	136	1,000	111	4,997	2,800	1,479	3,310	792	265	117
35 to 39 years old	16,345	67	181	907	123	5,656	3,221	1,507	3,261	977	292	153
40 to 49 years old	29,759	186	352	1,372	172	9,907	5,591	2,881	5,722	2,563	615	396
50 to 59 years old	19,479	211	645	1,521	141	7,306	3,359	1,332	2,834	1,491	329	309
60 to 64 years old	7,837	171	441	821	59	3,060	1,209	402	930	509	129	107
65 years old and over	27,034	1,141	3,149	3,729	366	9,753	3,920	965	2,603	868	330	210
Black, non-Hispanic												
18 and over	21,857	848	877	3,427	540	7,618	4,582	1,341	1,943	530	78	75
18 and 19 years old	1,097	10	37	448	102	298	200	3	—	—	—	—
20 to 24 years old	2,443	8	32	317	82	862	930	111	95	3	—	3
25 years old and over	18,317	830	808	2,662	355	6,458	3,452	1,227	1,848	527	78	72
25 to 29 years old	2,545	15	21	280	39	966	669	183	326	31	15	—
30 to 34 years old	2,667	25	29	297	70	1,064	620	215	290	44	14	—
35 to 39 years old	2,757	33	37	238	31	1,093	597	236	386	85	8	11
40 to 49 years old	4,446	70	111	611	92	1,572	894	387	508	147	21	33
50 to 59 years old	2,501	143	167	462	59	901	344	115	167	130	2	10
60 to 64 years old	958	112	59	197	25	287	122	40	75	32	—	9
65 years old and over	2,445	433	385	576	39	575	206	52	97	57	18	9
Hispanic												
18 and over	18,131	3,646	1,253	2,890	522	4,837	2,761	774	1,061	259	73	54
18 and 19 years old	984	64	41	373	84	247	175	—	—	—	—	—
20 to 24 years old	2,606	253	133	459	88	811	663	101	94	1	2	—
25 years old and over	14,541	3,328	1,079	2,059	350	3,780	1,923	673	967	258	71	54
25 to 29 years old	2,612	343	127	459	88	783	429	122	229	19	10	4
30 to 34 years old	2,743	459	149	402	61	809	424	151	224	49	11	3
35 to 39 years old	2,343	443	163	358	62	627	354	103	163	39	15	16
40 to 49 years old	2,916	627	226	363	68	767	392	172	201	68	17	14
50 to 59 years old	1,784	573	156	219	36	419	173	79	70	46	4	10
60 to 64 years old	686	243	69	98	8	138	65	12	32	15	5	—
65 years old and over	1,458	639	190	160	26	236	85	34	48	22	10	7

[1] Civilian noninstitutional population.
— Data not applicable or not available.

NOTE.—Data are based on a sample survey of the noninstitutional population. Although cells with fewer than 75,000 people are subject to relatively wide sampling variation, they are included in the table to permit various types of aggregations. Because of rounding, details may not add to totals.

SOURCE: U.S. Department of Commerce, Bureau of the Census, Current Population Survey, unpublished data. (This table was prepared July 1997.)

Table 10.—Number of persons age 18 and over who hold a bachelor's or higher degree, by field of study, sex, race, and age: Spring 1993

[Numbers in thousands]

Field of study	Total	Sex		Race		Age					
		Men	Women	White [1]	Black [1]	18 to 24 years old	25 to 34 years old	35 to 44 years old	45 to 54 years old	55 to 64 years old	65 years old and over
1	2	3	4	5	6	7	8	9	10	11	12
Total population, 18 and over	188,683	90,555	98,128	159,940	21,391	25,507	42,162	41,094	28,657	20,524	30,739
Number of persons with bachelor's or higher degree	36,786	19,352	17,436	32,280	2,314	2,456	9,635	10,691	6,869	3,470	3,664
Percent of population	19.5	21.4	17.8	20.2	10.8	9.6	22.9	26.0	24.0	16.9	11.9
Agriculture and forestry	543	437	107	517	11	39	94	198	103	56	53
Biology	827	525	302	674	59	102	190	283	156	65	30
Business and management	6,739	4,524	2,215	5,947	458	472	2,091	1,839	1,250	595	490
Economics	815	551	263	695	42	58	236	213	144	96	67
Education	6,078	1,482	4,597	5,493	409	268	965	1,764	1,438	798	845
Engineering	3,425	2,986	439	2,874	164	197	1,165	906	489	353	315
English and journalism	1,356	519	837	1,163	97	109	363	383	285	86	130
Home economics	375	17	358	329	27	6	61	113	49	60	86
Law	1,167	865	301	1,045	53	56	279	372	226	110	124
Liberal arts and humanities	2,855	1,228	1,629	2,570	132	242	690	855	518	236	315
Mathematics and statistics	754	477	276	637	80	44	223	188	146	54	99
Medicine and dentistry	1,119	825	294	900	27	22	253	413	187	85	159
Nursing, pharmacy, and health technologies	2,166	352	1,814	1,845	137	156	649	665	329	180	186
Physical and earth sciences	918	650	270	837	31	48	270	198	192	77	133
Police science and law enforcement	363	251	112	309	30	19	149	114	57	14	9
Psychology	1,342	531	811	1,216	63	138	364	415	243	75	107
Religion and theology	577	484	93	525	48	9	112	172	95	88	101
Social sciences	2,341	1,023	1,318	2,028	232	226	576	689	440	210	200
Vocational and technical studies	202	140	62	165	17	20	82	38	29	20	13
Other fields	2,825	1,487	1,338	2,507	198	226	824	872	492	213	199
	Percentage distribution of degree holders, by field										
Total	100.0	100.0	100.0	100.0	100.0	100.0	100.0	100.0	100.0	100.0	100.0
Agriculture and forestry	1.5	2.3	0.6	1.6	0.5	1.6	1.0	1.9	1.5	1.6	1.4
Biology	2.2	2.7	1.7	2.1	2.5	4.2	2.0	2.6	2.3	1.9	0.8
Business and management	18.3	23.4	12.7	18.4	19.8	19.2	21.7	17.2	18.2	17.1	13.4
Economics	2.2	2.8	1.5	2.2	1.8	2.4	2.4	2.0	2.1	2.8	1.8
Education	16.5	7.7	26.4	17.0	17.7	10.9	10.0	16.5	20.9	23.0	23.1
Engineering	9.3	15.4	2.5	8.9	7.1	8.0	12.1	8.5	7.1	10.2	8.6
English and journalism	3.7	2.7	4.8	3.6	4.2	4.4	3.8	3.6	4.1	2.5	3.5
Home economics	1.0	0.1	2.1	1.0	1.2	0.2	0.6	1.1	0.7	1.7	2.3
Law	3.2	4.5	1.7	3.2	2.3	2.3	2.9	3.5	3.3	3.2	3.4
Liberal arts and humanities	7.8	6.3	9.3	8.0	5.7	9.9	7.2	8.0	7.5	6.8	8.6
Mathematics and statistics	2.0	2.5	1.6	2.0	3.5	1.8	2.3	1.8	2.1	1.6	2.7
Medicine and dentistry	3.0	4.3	1.7	2.8	1.2	0.9	2.6	3.9	2.7	2.4	4.3
Nursing, pharmacy, and health technologies	5.9	1.8	10.4	5.7	5.9	6.4	6.7	6.2	4.8	5.2	5.1
Physical and earth sciences	2.5	3.4	1.5	2.6	1.3	2.0	2.8	1.9	2.8	2.2	3.6
Police science and law enforcement	1.0	1.3	0.6	1.0	1.3	0.8	1.5	1.1	0.8	0.4	0.2
Psychology	3.6	2.7	4.7	3.8	2.7	5.6	3.8	3.9	3.5	2.2	2.9
Religion and theology	1.6	2.5	0.5	1.6	2.1	0.4	1.2	1.6	1.4	2.5	2.8
Social sciences	6.4	5.3	7.6	6.3	10.0	9.2	6.0	6.4	6.4	6.1	5.5
Vocational and technical studies	0.5	0.7	0.4	0.5	0.7	0.8	0.9	0.4	0.4	0.6	0.4
Other fields	7.7	7.7	7.7	7.8	8.6	9.2	8.6	8.2	7.2	6.1	5.4

[1] Includes persons of Hispanic origin.

NOTE.—Data are based on a sample survey of the civilian noninstitutional population. Because of rounding, details may not add to totals.

SOURCE: U.S. Department of Commerce, Bureau of the Census, *Current Population Reports*, Series P-70, No. 51, "What's It Worth? Educational Background and Economic Status: Spring 1993." (This table was prepared April 1996.)

Table 11.—Educational attainment of persons 25 years old and over, by state: April 1990

State	Number of persons 25 years old and over	Distribution of population, by highest level of education attained						
		Less than 9th grade	9th to 12th grade, no diploma	High school graduate	Some college, no degree	Associate degree	Bachelor's degree	Graduate or professional degree
1	2	3	4	5	6	7	8	9
United States	158,868,436	10.4	14.4	30.0	18.7	6.2	13.1	7.2
Alabama	2,545,969	13.7	19.4	29.4	16.8	5.0	10.1	5.5
Alaska	323,429	5.1	8.2	28.7	27.6	7.2	15.0	8.0
Arizona	2,301,177	9.0	12.3	26.1	25.4	6.8	13.3	7.0
Arkansas	1,496,150	15.2	18.4	32.7	16.6	3.7	8.9	4.5
California	18,695,499	11.2	12.6	22.3	22.6	7.9	15.3	8.1
Colorado	2,107,072	5.6	10.0	26.5	24.0	6.9	18.0	9.0
Connecticut	2,198,963	8.4	12.4	29.5	15.9	6.6	16.2	11.0
Delaware	428,499	7.2	15.3	32.7	16.9	6.5	13.7	7.7
District of Columbia	409,131	9.6	17.3	21.2	15.6	3.1	16.1	17.2
Florida	8,887,168	9.5	16.1	30.1	19.4	6.6	12.0	6.3
Georgia	4,023,420	12.0	17.1	29.6	17.0	5.0	12.9	6.4
Hawaii	709,820	10.1	9.8	28.7	20.1	8.3	15.8	7.1
Idaho	601,292	7.4	12.9	30.4	24.2	7.5	12.4	5.3
Illinois	7,293,930	10.3	13.5	30.0	19.4	5.8	13.6	7.5
Indiana	3,489,470	8.5	15.8	38.2	16.6	5.3	9.2	6.4
Iowa	1,776,798	9.2	10.7	38.5	17.0	7.7	11.7	5.2
Kansas	1,565,936	7.7	11.0	32.8	21.9	5.4	14.1	7.0
Kentucky	2,333,833	19.0	16.4	31.8	15.2	4.1	8.1	5.5
Louisiana	2,536,994	14.7	17.0	31.7	17.2	3.3	10.5	5.6
Maine	795,613	8.8	12.4	37.1	16.1	6.9	12.7	6.1
Maryland	3,122,665	7.9	13.7	28.1	18.6	5.2	15.6	10.9
Massachusetts	3,962,223	8.0	12.0	29.7	15.8	7.2	16.6	10.6
Michigan	5,842,642	7.8	15.5	32.3	20.4	6.7	10.9	6.4
Minnesota	2,770,562	8.6	9.0	33.0	19.0	8.6	15.6	6.3
Mississippi	1,538,997	15.6	20.1	27.5	16.9	5.2	9.7	5.1
Missouri	3,291,579	11.6	14.5	33.1	18.4	4.5	11.7	6.1
Montana	507,851	8.1	10.9	33.5	22.1	5.6	14.1	5.7
Nebraska	996,049	8.0	10.2	34.7	21.1	7.1	13.1	5.9
Nevada	789,638	6.0	15.2	31.5	25.8	6.2	10.1	5.2
New Hampshire	713,894	6.7	11.2	31.7	18.0	8.1	16.4	7.9
New Jersey	5,166,233	9.4	13.9	31.1	15.5	5.2	16.0	8.8
New Mexico	922,590	11.4	13.5	28.7	20.9	5.0	12.1	8.3
New York	11,818,569	10.2	15.0	29.5	15.7	6.5	13.2	9.9
North Carolina	4,253,494	12.7	17.3	29.0	16.8	6.8	12.0	5.4
North Dakota	396,550	15.0	8.3	28.0	20.5	10.0	13.5	4.5
Ohio	6,924,764	7.9	16.4	36.3	17.0	5.3	11.1	5.9
Oklahoma	1,995,424	9.8	15.6	30.5	21.3	5.0	11.8	6.0
Oregon	1,855,369	6.2	12.3	28.9	25.0	6.9	13.6	7.0
Pennsylvania	7,872,932	9.4	15.9	38.6	12.9	5.2	11.3	6.6
Rhode Island	658,956	11.1	16.9	29.5	15.0	6.3	13.5	7.8
South Carolina	2,167,590	13.6	18.1	29.5	15.8	6.3	11.2	5.4
South Dakota	430,500	13.4	9.5	33.7	18.8	7.4	12.3	4.9
Tennessee	3,139,066	16.0	17.0	30.0	16.9	4.2	10.5	5.4
Texas	10,310,605	13.5	14.4	25.6	21.1	5.2	13.9	6.5
Utah	897,321	3.4	11.5	27.2	27.9	7.8	15.4	6.8
Vermont	357,245	8.7	10.6	34.6	14.7	7.2	15.4	8.9
Virginia	3,974,814	11.2	13.7	26.6	18.5	5.5	15.4	9.1
Washington	3,126,390	5.5	10.7	27.9	25.0	7.9	15.9	7.0
West Virginia	1,171,766	16.8	17.3	36.6	13.2	3.8	7.5	4.8
Wisconsin	3,094,226	9.5	11.9	37.1	16.7	7.1	12.1	5.6
Wyoming	277,769	5.7	11.2	33.2	24.2	6.9	13.1	5.7

NOTE.—Because of rounding, details may not add to 100.0 percent.

SOURCE: U.S. Department of Commerce, Bureau of the Census, Decennial Census, Minority Economic Profiles, unpublished data. (This table was prepared June 1993.)

Table 12.—Educational attainment of persons 25 years old and over, by state and race/ethnicity: April 1990

State	Percent with high school diploma or higher						Percent with bachelor's degree or higher					
	Total	White[1]	Black[1]	Hispanic[2]	Asian/Pacific Islander[1]	American Indian or Alaskan Native[1]	Total	White[1]	Black[1]	Hispanic[2]	Asian/Pacific Islander[1]	American Indian or Alaskan Native[1]
1	2	3	4	5	6	7	8	9	10	11	12	13
United States	75.2	77.9	63.1	49.8	77.5	65.5	20.3	21.5	11.4	9.2	36.6	9.3
Alabama	66.9	70.3	54.6	73.8	78.9	64.9	15.7	17.3	9.3	20.1	43.7	11.6
Alaska	86.6	91.1	88.2	80.4	75.4	63.1	23.0	26.8	14.1	14.6	20.5	4.1
Arizona	78.7	82.4	75.1	51.7	80.2	52.1	20.3	22.2	14.3	6.9	37.5	4.6
Arkansas	66.3	68.6	51.5	59.1	66.4	65.4	13.3	14.1	8.4	11.1	24.6	9.8
California	76.2	81.1	75.6	45.0	77.2	71.4	23.4	25.4	14.8	7.1	34.1	11.1
Colorado	84.4	86.1	80.8	58.3	78.3	73.9	27.0	28.3	17.1	8.6	32.1	12.1
Connecticut	79.2	80.9	67.0	53.5	81.9	68.9	27.2	28.5	12.3	12.1	50.8	12.5
Delaware	77.5	80.3	63.2	60.1	86.1	62.0	21.4	23.0	10.6	16.5	55.9	10.2
District of Columbia	73.1	93.1	63.8	52.6	80.2	66.3	33.3	69.0	15.3	24.0	50.9	17.7
Florida	74.4	77.0	56.4	57.2	77.8	68.2	18.3	19.3	9.8	14.2	33.6	11.5
Georgia	70.9	74.9	58.6	66.2	77.5	71.6	19.3	21.8	11.0	20.5	38.6	12.5
Hawaii	80.1	89.3	94.2	73.9	74.7	84.4	22.9	30.2	15.2	10.3	19.4	17.7
Idaho	79.7	80.9	82.8	43.4	80.3	68.1	17.7	18.0	15.8	6.6	27.6	7.2
Illinois	76.2	79.1	65.2	45.0	83.9	71.4	21.0	22.4	11.4	8.0	49.8	13.4
Indiana	75.6	76.5	65.4	62.6	85.8	65.0	15.6	17.6	9.3	10.8	53.1	8.4
Iowa	80.1	80.3	70.1	64.2	76.4	67.6	16.9	16.7	12.8	13.7	47.3	9.7
Kansas	81.3	82.4	71.0	58.1	73.6	75.4	21.1	21.7	11.6	10.1	39.9	10.8
Kentucky	64.6	64.7	61.7	74.0	77.9	59.8	13.6	13.9	7.7	18.9	44.2	8.0
Louisiana	68.3	74.2	53.1	67.6	68.1	49.1	16.1	18.7	9.1	16.6	31.4	5.5
Maine	78.8	78.9	87.6	83.8	74.3	69.9	18.8	18.8	22.3	23.6	44.9	7.7
Maryland	78.4	80.8	70.6	70.3	84.8	73.4	26.5	28.9	16.1	25.2	50.3	19.7
Massachusetts	80.0	81.2	70.0	52.0	74.1	71.1	27.2	27.7	17.0	13.6	44.9	14.9
Michigan	76.8	78.6	64.9	60.9	83.3	67.8	17.4	18.1	10.1	11.6	54.1	7.6
Minnesota	82.4	82.8	76.2	71.1	69.7	68.2	21.8	21.9	17.5	17.2	33.5	7.7
Mississippi	64.3	71.7	47.3	67.7	68.2	57.4	14.7	17.2	8.8	17.1	35.1	8.1
Missouri	73.9	74.9	65.1	71.0	81.5	65.1	17.8	18.3	11.2	18.0	47.3	11.0
Montana	81.0	81.7	80.9	66.4	78.5	68.1	19.8	20.3	18.4	10.9	32.1	7.9
Nebraska	81.8	82.4	73.2	60.0	80.0	69.0	18.9	19.2	12.4	9.4	39.5	8.8
Nevada	78.8	80.9	70.8	53.7	74.1	69.8	15.3	15.9	9.0	7.0	21.9	8.0
New Hampshire	82.2	82.2	86.1	78.2	82.7	65.9	24.4	24.2	25.7	25.5	26.1	16.0
New Jersey	76.7	78.6	67.0	53.9	86.8	66.9	24.9	25.8	13.6	10.8	57.1	14.8
New Mexico	75.1	78.6	74.7	59.6	80.8	58.2	20.4	23.4	14.2	8.7	38.7	5.8
New York	76.7	78.5	64.7	50.4	72.4	65.2	23.1	25.3	12.6	9.3	38.7	13.4
North Carolina	70.0	73.1	58.1	71.0	77.9	51.5	17.4	19.3	9.5	17.9	39.3	7.9
North Dakota	76.7	76.9	95.9	75.2	83.7	64.3	18.1	18.3	17.1	15.9	37.8	8.3
Ohio	75.7	76.9	64.6	63.3	83.5	65.3	17.0	17.6	9.1	14.2	53.2	8.3
Oklahoma	74.6	75.7	70.1	55.9	76.1	68.1	17.8	18.7	12.0	10.5	34.7	10.8
Oregon	81.5	82.3	75.0	53.0	79.4	71.0	20.6	20.8	9.1	10.1	32.3	8.3
Pennsylvania	74.7	75.9	63.5	52.2	77.1	67.8	17.9	18.5	10.0	11.8	45.2	12.0
Rhode Island	72.0	73.0	65.9	46.8	59.6	64.5	21.3	21.8	12.7	8.9	30.6	8.3
South Carolina	68.3	73.6	53.3	71.8	77.4	62.5	16.6	19.8	7.6	19.8	34.4	10.9
South Dakota	77.1	77.8	82.2	71.3	74.3	62.5	17.2	17.6	24.1	13.4	33.1	6.8
Tennessee	67.1	68.2	59.4	71.5	79.3	63.1	16.0	16.7	10.2	21.9	42.6	10.5
Texas	72.1	76.2	66.1	44.6	79.1	70.9	20.3	22.6	12.0	7.3	41.3	13.9
Utah	85.1	86.2	77.0	61.0	80.7	59.3	22.3	22.7	15.9	9.1	29.4	6.4
Vermont	80.8	80.8	82.9	84.7	87.1	66.8	24.3	24.2	30.5	28.2	52.1	11.1
Virginia	75.2	78.3	60.3	70.5	82.1	70.7	24.5	27.0	11.1	22.4	40.2	14.7
Washington	83.8	85.0	81.2	56.7	77.3	72.3	22.9	23.3	15.4	11.0	30.2	9.1
West Virginia	66.0	66.0	64.7	70.3	88.8	57.9	12.3	12.2	10.9	17.6	63.3	6.5
Wisconsin	78.6	79.6	61.3	54.1	71.5	66.8	17.7	18.1	8.3	10.0	40.4	5.5
Wyoming	83.0	83.9	81.2	59.3	77.5	68.2	18.8	19.3	9.5	4.8	28.6	6.2

[1] Includes persons of Hispanic origin.
[2] Persons of Hispanic origin may be of any race.

SOURCE: U.S. Department of Commerce, Bureau of the Census, Decennial Census, Minority Economic Profiles, unpublished data. (This table was prepared June 1993.)

Table 13.—Educational attainment of persons 25 years old and over, for the 25 largest states: March 1995

State	Number of persons 25 years old and over (in thousands)			Percent high school graduate or more			Percent completed bachelor's or more		
	Total	Male	Female	Total	Male	Female	Total	Male	Female
1	2	3	4	5	6	7	8	9	10
Alabama	2,701	1,277	1,424	74.4 (2.4)	75.2 (3.4)	73.7 (3.3)	28.3 (2.0)	21.0 (3.2)	13.9 (2.6)
Arizona	2,584	1,268	1,315	82.3 (2.0)	81.2 (3.0)	83.4 (2.8)	30.4 (2.1)	22.3 (3.2)	15.9 (2.7)
California	19,887	9,716	10,171	79.6 (0.8)	80.6 (1.2)	78.6 (1.2)	38.3 (0.9)	27.6 (1.3)	21.0 (1.2)
Florida	9,497	4,430	5,066	82.8 (1.0)	83.5 (1.4)	82.2 (1.3)	36.0 (1.1)	26.0 (1.6)	18.7 (1.4)
Georgia	4,583	2,174	2,408	78.1 (2.1)	77.9 (3.1)	78.4 (2.9)	35.7 (2.2)	24.7 (3.2)	20.9 (2.9)
Illinois	7,423	3,476	3,947	82.3 (1.1)	82.7 (1.6)	82.0 (1.5)	39.4 (1.3)	27.9 (1.9)	21.7 (1.7)
Indiana	3,589	1,667	1,921	81.6 (2.2)	81.2 (3.3)	82.0 (3.0)	27.5 (2.1)	19.7 (3.3)	14.6 (2.7)
Kentucky	2,447	1,157	1,290	76.7 (2.3)	78.5 (3.3)	75.1 (3.2)	31.4 (2.2)	22.8 (3.3)	16.3 (2.8)
Louisiana	2,614	1,257	1,357	75.8 (2.5)	76.0 (3.6)	75.6 (3.5)	32.1 (2.3)	23.1 (3.5)	17.3 (3.1)
Maryland	3,368	1,622	1,746	82.0 (2.1)	82.4 (3.1)	81.7 (3.0)	41.4 (2.5)	29.0 (3.6)	23.9 (3.3)
Massachusetts	3,961	1,878	2,083	85.8 (1.0)	86.4 (1.5)	85.3 (1.4)	51.2 (1.4)	35.4 (2.0)	30.0 (1.8)
Michigan	6,000	2,824	3,176	83.7 (1.1)	83.4 (1.6)	84.0 (1.5)	33.3 (1.2)	23.7 (1.8)	18.1 (1.5)
Minnesota	2,867	1,428	1,439	88.4 (1.8)	89.2 (2.5)	87.6 (2.6)	40.8 (2.5)	28.6 (3.6)	24.4 (3.4)
Missouri	3,367	1,637	1,730	82.2 (2.2)	82.3 (3.1)	82.2 (3.0)	34.4 (2.3)	24.3 (3.5)	19.7 (3.1)
New Jersey	5,168	2,485	2,683	85.4 (1.0)	86.5 (1.4)	84.4 (1.4)	43.9 (1.3)	30.9 (1.9)	25.1 (1.7)
New York	11,818	5,414	6,404	82.5 (0.8)	82.7 (1.2)	82.3 (1.1)	42.5 (0.9)	29.9 (1.5)	23.3 (1.2)
North Carolina	4,604	2,139	2,465	76.3 (1.1)	74.2 (1.7)	78.2 (1.5)	33.0 (1.1)	23.0 (1.7)	18.6 (1.4)
Ohio	6,980	3,219	3,761	83.4 (1.1)	83.3 (1.6)	83.4 (1.4)	31.7 (1.1)	22.3 (1.7)	17.4 (1.5)
Pennsylvania	7,916	3,776	4,140	81.5 (1.1)	80.3 (1.6)	82.5 (1.5)	32.5 (1.1)	23.0 (1.7)	18.2 (1.5)
South Carolina	2,300	1,096	1,204	74.3 (2.1)	73.3 (3.1)	75.2 (2.9)	28.5 (1.9)	19.7 (2.8)	16.9 (2.5)
Tennessee	3,337	1,508	1,829	77.4 (2.1)	75.3 (3.3)	79.1 (2.8)	28.6 (2.0)	19.7 (3.0)	16.3 (2.6)
Texas	11,262	5,464	5,798	76.2 (1.2)	76.4 (1.7)	76.0 (1.6)	34.9 (1.1)	25.1 (1.7)	19.0 (1.5)
Virginia	4,320	2,103	2,217	82.7 (1.8)	81.7 (2.6)	83.7 (2.4)	41.0 (2.1)	29.3 (3.1)	22.8 (2.8)
Washington	3,329	1,627	1,702	91.4 (1.5)	91.5 (2.1)	91.3 (2.1)	42.8 (2.3)	31.9 (3.5)	21.3 (3.0)
Wisconsin	3,182	1,545	1,638	86.6 (1.8)	86.8 (2.5)	86.3 (2.5)	31.7 (2.1)	21.6 (3.0)	19.7 (2.9)

NOTE.—Because of rounding, details may not add to totals. Standard errors appear in parentheses.

SOURCE: U.S. Department of Commerce, Bureau of the Census, Current Population Reports, "Educational Attainment in the United States: March 1995." (This table was prepared November 1997.)

Table 14.—Educational attainment of persons 25 years old and over, for the 15 largest metropolitan areas: March 1995

Metropolitan area	Number of persons 25 years old and over (in thousands)			Percent High school graduate or more		Percent Completed bachelor's degree or more	
	Total	Male	Female	Male	Female	Male	Female
1	2	3	4	5	6	7	8
Atlanta, GA	1,883	899	984	87.6 (3.7)	88.4 (3.5)	37.4 (5.5)	31.5 (5.1)
Boston-Lawrence-Salem, MA/NH	3,254	1,548	1,706	88.2 (1.5)	87.1 (1.5)	38.8 (2.3)	32.5 (2.1)
Chicago-Gary-Lake County, IL/IN/WI	5,306	2,506	2,800	83.7 (1.8)	83.8 (1.7)	31.4 (2.3)	25.6 (2.1)
Cleveland-Akron-Lorain, OH	2,016	925	1,091	81.0 (3.1)	79.3 (2.9)	24.9 (3.4)	16.4 (2.7)
Dallas-Fort Worth, TX	2,595	1,260	1,336	79.3 (3.3)	79.1 (3.2)	27.3 (3.6)	20.7 (3.2)
Detroit-Ann Arbor, MI	3,472	1,652	1,820	80.9 (2.1)	80.7 (2.1)	27.2 (2.4)	18.8 (2.0)
Houston-Galveston-Brazoria, TX	3,077	1,475	1,602	83.7 (2.8)	83.4 (2.7)	31.4 (3.5)	22.1 (3.0)
Los Angeles-Anaheim-Riverside, CA	9,467	4,605	4,862	77.5 (1.5)	75.2 (1.5)	28.4 (1.6)	19.7 (1.4)
Miami-Fort Lauderdale, FL	2,232	1,055	1,177	85.7 (2.7)	81.9 (2.8)	27.3 (3.4)	20.4 (2.9)
New York-Northern New Jersey-Long Island, NY/NJ/CT	12,525	5,770	6,754	84.4 (1.1)	82.5 (1.1)	32.8 (1.4)	25.3 (1.2)
Philadelphia-Wilmington-Trenton, PA/NJ/DE/MD	4,248	2,025	2,223	83.6 (2.0)	83.8 (1.9)	34.3 (2.6)	25.8 (2.3)
Pittsburgh-Beaver Valley, PA	1,911	926	985	81.1 (3.2)	81.4 (3.1)	26.6 (3.6)	19.8 (3.1)
San Francisco-Oakland-San Jose, CA	4,298	2,136	2,162	89.2 (2.1)	87.9 (2.2)	35.8 (3.2)	29.1 (3.0)
St. Louis, MO/IL	1,641	775	866	81.1 (4.9)	83.2 (4.4)	27.5 (5.6)	20.8 (4.8)
Washington, DC/MD/VA	2,872	1,460	1,411	85.5 (3.0)	85.8 (3.0)	38.6 (4.2)	28.1 (3.9)

NOTE.—Because of rounding, details may not add to totals. Standard errors appear in parentheses.

SOURCE: U.S. Department of Commerce, Bureau of the Census, Current Population Reports, "Educational Attainment in the United States: March 1995." (This table was prepared July 1997.)

ALL LEVELS: POPULATION

Table 15.-Estimates of resident population, by age group: July 1, 1970 to July 1, 1996

[In thousands]

Year	Total, all ages	Total, 3 to 34 years	3 and 4 years	5 and 6 years	7 to 13 years	14 to 17 years	18 and 19 years	20 and 21 years	22 to 24 years	25 to 29 years	30 to 34 years
1	2	3	4	5	6	7	8	9	10	11	12
1970	203,984	108,653	6,962	7,703	28,969	15,921	7,410	6,850	9,728	13,604	11,505
1971	206,827	110,482	6,805	7,344	28,892	16,326	7,644	7,106	10,596	13,927	11,842
1972	209,284	112,287	6,789	7,051	28,628	16,637	7,854	7,447	10,418	15,142	12,321
1973	211,357	113,954	6,938	6,888	28,159	16,864	8,044	7,658	10,615	15,694	13,094
1974	213,342	115,641	7,117	6,864	27,599	17,033	8,196	7,893	10,864	16,428	13,644
1975	215,465	117,006	6,912	7,014	26,904	17,125	8,418	8,089	11,228	17,183	14,131
1976	217,563	118,073	6,437	7,194	26,321	17,117	8,604	8,240	11,554	18,177	14,428
1977	219,760	118,853	6,190	6,978	25,878	17,042	8,613	8,456	11,856	18,180	15,661
1978	222,095	119,414	6,208	6,499	25,593	16,944	8,617	8,628	12,120	18,585	16,218
1979	224,567	120,126	6,252	6,256	25,174	16,610	8,698	8,653	12,443	19,077	16,961
1980	227,225	121,132	6,366	6,291	24,800	16,143	8,718	8,669	12,716	19,686	17,743
1981	229,466	121,999	6,535	6,315	24,396	15,609	8,582	8,759	12,903	20,169	18,731
1982	231,664	121,823	6,658	6,407	24,121	15,057	8,480	8,768	12,914	20,704	18,714
1983	233,792	122,302	6,877	6,572	23,709	14,740	8,290	8,652	12,981	21,414	19,067
1984	235,825	122,254	7,045	6,694	23,367	14,725	7,932	8,567	12,962	21,459	19,503
1985	237,924	122,512	7,134	6,916	22,976	14,888	7,637	8,370	12,895	21,671	20,025
1986	240,133	122,688	7,187	7,086	22,992	14,824	7,483	8,024	12,720	21,893	20,479
1987	242,289	122,672	7,132	7,178	23,325	14,502	7,502	7,742	12,450	21,857	20,984
1988	244,499	122,713	7,176	7,238	23,791	14,023	7,701	7,606	12,048	21,739	21,391
1989	246,819	122,655	7,315	7,184	24,228	13,536	7,898	7,651	11,607	21,560	21,676
1990	249,402	122,627	7,355	7,240	24,756	13,310	7,693	7,883	11,251	21,232	21,907
1991	252,131	122,580	7,434	7,383	25,113	13,418	7,173	8,013	11,156	20,732	22,158
1992	255,028	122,622	7,591	7,429	25,579	13,653	6,889	7,756	11,295	20,179	22,251
1993	257,783	122,801	7,844	7,518	25,973	13,928	6,899	7,265	11,498	19,625	22,251
1994	260,372	122,935	8,011	7,644	26,059	14,453	7,009	7,059	11,395	19,150	22,156
1995	262,890	123,001	8,009	7,894	26,295	14,785	7,127	7,082	10,972	18,972	21,863
1996	265,284	122,916	7,904	8,066	26,525	15,170	7,322	7,116	10,443	19,007	21,361

NOTE.—Some data have been revised from previously published figures. Because of rounding, details may not add to totals.

SOURCE: U.S. Department of Commerce, Bureau of the Census, *Current Population Reports*, Series P-25, Nos. 1000, 1022, 1045, 1057, 1059, 1092, 1095, and *U.S. Population Estimates, by Age, Sex, Race, and Hispanic Origin: 1990–1996*, PPL-41, PPL-57; and unpublished data. (This table was prepared April 1997.)

Table 16.—Estimates of school-age[1] resident population, by race and sex: July 1, 1970 to July 1, 1996

[In thousands]

Year	Total			White[2]			Black[2]			Other races[2]		
	Total	Male	Female	Total	Male	Female	Total	Male	Female	Total	Male	Female
1	2	3	4	5	6	7	8	9	10	11	12	13
1970	52,593	26,793	25,801	44,783	22,877	21,906	7,108	3,561	3,547	703	355	349
1971	52,562	26,780	25,782	44,644	22,809	21,834	7,182	3,600	3,583	737	371	365
1972	52,316	26,658	25,658	44,336	22,655	21,681	7,211	3,615	3,596	768	388	380
1973	51,910	26,456	25,455	43,898	22,434	21,464	7,213	3,617	3,596	799	405	394
1974	51,498	26,249	25,249	43,454	22,210	21,244	7,213	3,618	3,596	830	420	409
1975	51,044	26,022	25,022	42,950	21,956	20,994	7,199	3,611	3,588	895	456	440
1976	50,633	25,822	24,811	42,477	21,721	20,755	7,208	3,617	3,591	948	483	465
1977	49,897	25,456	24,441	41,737	21,350	20,386	7,167	3,600	3,568	994	506	487
1978	49,038	25,024	24,013	40,883	20,919	19,964	7,116	3,576	3,540	1,039	530	509
1979	48,041	24,524	23,517	39,910	20,427	19,484	7,037	3,538	3,498	1,094	560	536
1980	47,232	24,135	23,097	39,002	19,982	19,020	6,989	3,520	3,469	1,241	633	608
1981	46,319	23,676	22,643	38,105	19,527	18,578	6,872	3,474	3,398	1,342	675	667
1982	45,585	23,309	22,276	37,365	19,153	18,212	6,826	3,442	3,384	1,394	714	680
1983	45,020	23,031	21,989	36,800	18,873	17,927	6,762	3,412	3,350	1,458	746	712
1984	44,788	22,920	21,868	36,509	18,731	17,778	6,743	3,404	3,339	1,536	785	751
1985	44,782	22,927	21,855	36,393	18,679	17,714	6,729	3,400	3,329	1,660	848	812
1986	44,903	22,996	21,907	36,408	18,701	17,707	6,802	3,438	3,364	1,693	857	836
1987	45,005	23,056	21,949	36,361	18,674	17,687	6,841	3,460	3,381	1,803	922	881
1988	45,051	23,086	21,965	36,279	18,637	17,642	6,881	3,482	3,399	1,891	967	924
1989	44,947	23,036	21,911	36,122	18,550	17,572	6,867	3,475	3,392	1,958	1,011	947
1990	45,306	23,224	22,082	36,320	18,667	17,653	6,916	3,501	3,415	2,070	1,056	1,014
1991	45,917	23,536	22,381	36,759	18,892	17,867	7,012	3,552	3,460	2,143	1,090	1,053
1992	46,662	23,918	22,744	37,288	19,162	18,126	7,147	3,624	3,523	2,226	1,133	1,093
1993	47,419	24,303	23,116	37,802	19,422	18,380	7,297	3,702	3,595	2,319	1,178	1,141
1994	48,155	24,706	23,449	38,318	19,705	18,611	7,468	3,793	3,676	2,369	1,209	1,161
1995	48,974	25,130	23,844	38,891	20,001	18,890	7,621	3,873	3,751	2,464	1,256	1,207
1996	49,762	25,534	24,229	39,431	20,276	19,154	7,770	3,949	3,820	2,562	1,308	1,253

[1] Includes persons 5 to 17 years of age.
[2] Includes persons of Hispanic origin.

NOTE.—Some data have been revised from previously published figures. Because of rounding, details may not add to totals.

SOURCE: U.S. Department of Commerce, Bureau of the Census, *Current Population Reports*, Series P-25, Nos. 1000, 1022, 1045, 1057, 1092, and *U.S. Population Estimates, by Age, Sex, Race, and Hispanic Origin: 1990–1996*, PPL-41 and PPL-57; and unpublished data. (This table was prepared April 1997.)

24   ALL LEVELS: POPULATION

Table 17.—Estimated total and school-age resident populations, by state:[1] 1970 to 1996
[In thousands]

State	1970[2]		1980[2]		1985[3]		1990[2]		1994[3]		1995[3]		1996[3]	
	Total, all ages	5- to 17-year-olds	Total, all ages	5- to 17-year-olds	Total, all ages	5- to 17-year-olds	Total, all ages	5- to 17-year-olds	Total, all ages	5- to 17-year-olds	Total, all ages	5- to 17-year-olds	Total, all ages	5- to 17-year-olds
1	2	3	4	5	6	7	8	9	10	11	12	13	14	15
United States	203,302	52,540	226,546	47,407	237,924	44,782	248,710	45,166	260,372	48,155	262,890	48,974	265,284	49,762
Alabama	3,444	934	3,894	866	3,973	798	4,041	774	4,215	774	4,246	778	4,273	780
Alaska	303	88	402	92	532	112	550	117	601	134	603	135	607	135
Arizona	1,775	486	2,718	578	3,184	601	3,665	686	4,092	781	4,305	795	4,428	807
Arkansas	1,923	498	2,286	496	2,327	461	2,351	455	2,455	469	2,485	478	2,510	484
California	19,971	4,999	23,668	4,681	26,441	4,752	29,760	5,337	31,362	5,831	31,565	5,969	31,878	6,132
Colorado	2,210	589	2,890	592	3,209	599	3,294	607	3,663	692	3,748	709	3,823	728
Connecticut	3,032	768	3,108	638	3,201	549	3,287	520	3,273	555	3,271	565	3,274	575
Delaware	548	148	594	125	618	113	666	114	708	124	717	125	725	126
District of Columbia	757	164	638	109	635	88	607	80	568	74	555	76	543	75
Florida	6,791	1,609	9,746	1,789	11,351	1,792	12,938	2,011	13,965	2,319	14,184	2,392	14,400	2,467
Georgia	4,588	1,223	5,463	1,231	5,963	1,195	6,478	1,230	7,063	1,335	7,209	1,370	7,353	1,401
Hawaii	770	204	965	198	1,040	194	1,108	196	1,173	209	1,179	212	1,184	215
Idaho	713	200	944	213	994	223	1,007	228	1,136	252	1,166	255	1,189	258
Illinois	11,110	2,859	11,427	2,401	11,400	2,192	11,431	2,095	11,734	2,168	11,790	2,206	11,847	2,241
Indiana	5,195	1,386	5,490	1,200	5,459	1,087	5,544	1,056	5,750	1,066	5,797	1,079	5,841	1,089
Iowa	2,825	743	2,914	604	2,830	543	2,777	525	2,832	538	2,843	539	2,852	537
Kansas	2,249	573	2,364	468	2,427	452	2,478	472	2,550	503	2,564	505	2,572	507
Kentucky	3,221	844	3,661	800	3,695	745	3,685	703	3,826	708	3,857	710	3,884	710
Louisiana	3,645	1,041	4,206	969	4,408	937	4,220	890	4,315	896	4,338	901	4,351	906
Maine	994	260	1,125	243	1,163	222	1,228	223	1,238	228	1,239	228	1,243	228
Maryland	3,924	1,038	4,217	895	4,413	788	4,781	803	5,000	882	5,039	905	5,072	927
Massachusetts	5,689	1,407	5,737	1,153	5,881	989	6,016	940	6,042	995	6,071	1,015	6,092	1,031
Michigan	8,882	2,450	9,262	2,067	9,076	1,824	9,295	1,754	9,486	1,812	9,538	1,845	9,594	1,865
Minnesota	3,806	1,051	4,076	865	4,184	796	4,375	828	4,572	907	4,615	920	4,658	931
Mississippi	2,217	635	2,521	599	2,588	576	2,573	550	2,668	548	2,696	551	2,716	552
Missouri	4,678	1,183	4,917	1,008	5,000	941	5,117	944	5,275	996	5,319	1,013	5,359	1,027
Montana	694	197	787	167	822	167	799	163	857	176	870	177	879	177
Nebraska	1,485	389	1,570	324	1,585	305	1,578	309	1,626	324	1,639	327	1,652	329
Nevada	489	127	800	160	951	166	1,202	204	1,464	262	1,533	277	1,603	293
New Hampshire	738	189	921	196	997	182	1,109	194	1,135	212	1,148	217	1,162	220
New Jersey	7,171	1,797	7,365	1,528	7,566	1,340	7,730	1,265	7,906	1,354	7,950	1,385	7,988	1,415
New Mexico	1,017	311	1,303	303	1,438	304	1,515	320	1,659	353	1,690	359	1,713	365
New York	18,241	4,358	17,558	3,552	17,792	3,173	17,990	3,000	18,197	3,131	18,191	3,174	18,185	3,220
North Carolina	5,084	1,323	5,882	1,254	6,254	1,175	6,629	1,147	7,079	1,249	7,202	1,285	7,323	1,321
North Dakota	618	175	653	136	677	133	639	127	640	128	642	128	644	127
Ohio	10,657	2,820	10,798	2,307	10,735	2,090	10,847	2,012	11,097	2,064	11,134	2,078	11,173	2,089
Oklahoma	2,559	640	3,025	622	3,271	635	3,146	609	3,254	639	3,275	646	3,301	653
Oregon	2,092	534	2,633	525	2,673	504	2,842	521	3,094	575	3,149	586	3,204	597
Pennsylvania	11,801	2,925	11,864	2,376	11,771	2,079	11,882	1,996	12,058	2,093	12,060	2,114	12,056	2,133
Rhode Island	950	225	947	186	969	163	1,003	159	996	167	992	170	990	172
South Carolina	2,591	720	3,122	703	3,303	663	3,487	663	3,643	674	3,667	680	3,699	684
South Dakota	666	187	691	147	698	139	696	144	724	153	730	153	732	153
Tennessee	3,926	1,002	4,591	972	4,715	903	4,877	882	5,175	928	5,247	944	5,320	958
Texas	11,199	3,002	14,229	3,137	16,273	3,318	16,987	3,437	18,434	3,725	18,801	3,792	19,128	3,870
Utah	1,059	312	1,461	350	1,643	418	1,723	457	1,910	487	1,958	490	2,000	490
Vermont	445	118	511	109	530	100	563	102	581	109	585	110	589	111
Virginia	4,651	1,197	5,347	1,114	5,715	1,039	6,187	1,060	6,550	1,133	6,615	1,156	6,675	1,177
Washington	3,413	881	4,132	826	4,400	816	4,867	893	5,351	1,008	5,448	1,030	5,533	1,051
West Virginia	1,744	442	1,950	414	1,907	383	1,793	337	1,822	320	1,825	318	1,826	315
Wisconsin	4,418	1,203	4,706	1,011	4,748	908	4,892	927	5,084	992	5,122	1,001	5,160	1,006
Wyoming	332	92	470	101	500	108	454	101	476	103	479	103	481	102

[1] Includes Armed Forces residing in each state.
[2] As of April 1.
[3] Estimates as of July 1.

NOTE.—Some data have been revised from previously published figures. Because of rounding, details may not add to totals.

SOURCE: U.S. Department of Commerce, Bureau of the Census, *Current Population Reports*, Series P-25, No. 1095 at the national level, CPH-L-74 (1990 data); and forthcoming state level P-25 Reports. (This table was prepared May 1997.)

Table 18.—Families, by family status and presence of own children under 18: 1970 to 1995

Family status	1970	1980	1985	1988	1989	1990	1991	1992	1993	1994	1995	Change, 1970 to 1980	Change, 1980 to 1995
1	2	3	4	5	6	7	8	9	10	11	12	13	14
	In thousands											Percent change	
All families	51,456	59,550	62,706	65,133	65,837	66,090	66,322	67,173	68,144	68,490	69,305	15.7	16.4
Married-couple family	44,728	49,112	50,350	51,809	52,100	52,317	52,147	52,457	53,171	53,171	53,858	9.8	9.7
No own children under 18	19,196	24,151	26,140	27,209	27,365	27,780	27,750	28,037	28,464	28,113	28,617	25.8	18.5
With own children under 18	25,532	24,961	24,210	24,600	24,735	24,537	24,397	24,420	24,707	25,058	25,241	-2.2	1.1
One own child under 18	8,163	9,671	9,640	9,904	9,829	9,583	9,319	9,520	9,466	9,452	9,564	18.5	-1.1
Two own children under 18	8,045	9,488	9,456	9,576	9,870	9,784	9,721	9,728	10,007	10,188	10,358	17.9	9.2
Three or more own children under 18	9,325	5,802	5,115	5,120	5,035	5,170	5,357	5,173	5,234	5,418	5,319	-37.8	-8.3
Other family, male householder, no spouse present	1,228	1,733	2,228	2,715	2,847	2,884	2,907	3,025	3,026	2,913	3,226	41.1	86.2
No own children under 18	887	1,117	1,331	1,669	1,779	1,731	1,725	1,742	1,702	1,599	1,786	25.9	59.9
With own children under 18	341	616	896	1,047	1,068	1,153	1,181	1,283	1,324	1,314	1,440	80.6	133.8
One own child under 18	179	374	584	657	619	723	701	768	799	805	891	108.9	138.2
Two own children under 18	87	165	213	296	326	307	363	391	397	368	405	89.7	145.5
Three or more own children under 18	75	77	100	94	121	123	117	123	128	141	144	2.7	87.0
Other family, female householder, no spouse present	5,500	8,705	10,129	10,608	10,890	10,890	11,268	11,692	11,947	12,406	12,220	58.3	40.4
No own children under 18	2,642	3,261	4,123	4,335	4,371	4,290	4,445	4,648	4,721	4,759	4,606	23.4	41.2
With own children under 18	2,858	5,445	6,006	6,273	6,519	6,599	6,823	7,043	7,226	7,647	7,615	90.5	39.9
One own child under 18	1,008	2,398	2,885	3,017	3,164	3,225	3,283	3,327	3,425	3,566	3,633	137.9	51.5
Two own children under 18	810	1,817	1,977	2,039	2,095	2,173	2,203	2,244	2,400	2,531	2,450	124.3	34.8
Three or more own children under 18	1,040	1,230	1,144	1,217	1,260	1,202	1,335	1,472	1,400	1,550	1,531	18.3	24.5
	Percent of all families											Change in percentage points	
All families	100.0	100.0	100.0	100.0	100.0	100.0	100.0	100.0	100.0	100.0	100.0	—	—
Married-couple family	86.9	82.5	80.3	79.5	79.1	79.2	78.6	78.1	78.0	77.6	77.7	-4.5	-4.8
No own children under 18	37.3	40.6	41.7	41.8	41.6	42.0	41.8	41.7	41.8	41.0	41.3	3.3	0.7
With own children under 18	49.6	41.9	38.6	37.8	37.6	37.1	36.8	36.4	36.3	36.6	36.4	-7.7	-5.5
One own child under 18	15.9	16.2	15.4	15.2	14.9	14.5	14.1	14.2	13.9	13.8	13.8	0.4	-2.4
Two own children under 18	15.6	15.9	15.1	14.7	15.0	14.8	14.7	14.5	14.7	14.9	14.9	0.3	-1.0
Three or more own children under 18	18.1	9.7	8.2	7.9	7.6	7.8	8.1	7.7	7.7	7.9	7.7	-8.4	-2.0
Other family, male householder, no spouse present	2.4	2.9	3.6	4.2	4.3	4.4	4.4	4.5	4.4	4.3	4.7	0.5	1.8
No own children under 18	1.7	1.9	2.1	2.6	2.7	2.6	2.6	2.6	2.5	2.3	2.6	0.2	0.7
With own children under 18	0.7	1.0	1.4	1.6	1.6	1.7	1.8	1.9	1.9	1.9	2.1	0.4	1.1
One own child under 18	0.3	0.6	0.9	1.0	0.9	1.1	1.1	1.1	1.2	1.2	1.3	0.3	0.7
Two own children under 18	0.2	0.3	0.3	0.5	0.5	0.5	0.5	0.6	0.6	0.5	0.6	0.1	0.3
Three or more own children under 18	0.1	0.1	0.2	0.1	0.2	0.2	0.2	0.2	0.2	0.2	0.2	([1])	0.1
Other family, female householder, no spouse present	10.7	14.6	16.2	16.3	16.5	16.5	17.0	17.4	17.5	18.1	17.6	3.9	3.0
No own children under 18	5.1	5.5	6.6	6.7	6.6	6.5	6.7	6.9	6.9	6.9	6.6	0.3	1.1
With own children under 18	5.6	9.1	9.6	9.6	9.9	10.0	10.3	10.5	10.6	11.2	11.0	3.6	1.9
One own child under 18	2.0	4.0	4.6	4.6	4.8	4.9	5.0	5.0	5.0	5.2	5.2	2.1	1.2
Two own children under 18	1.6	3.1	3.2	3.1	3.2	3.3	3.3	3.3	3.5	3.7	3.5	1.5	0.4
Three or more own children under 18	2.0	2.1	1.8	1.9	1.9	1.8	2.0	2.2	2.1	2.3	2.2	([1])	0.1

[1] Less than .05 percent.
—Not applicable.

NOTE.—Because of rounding, details may not add to totals.

SOURCE: U.S. Department of Commerce, Bureau of the Census, *Current Population Reports*, Series P-20, *Household and Family Characteristics*, various years; and unpublished data. (This table was prepared April 1997.)

Table 19.—Characteristics of families with own children under 18, by family status and race/ethnicity:[1] 1995

[Numbers in thousands]

Family characteristics	All races				White[2]				Black[2]				Hispanic origin[3]			
	Total	Married-couple families	Other families		Total	Married-couple families	Other families		Total	Married-couple families	Other families		Total	Married-couple families	Other families	
			Male householder, no spouse present	Female householder, no spouse present			Male householder, no spouse present	Female householder, no spouse present			Male householder, no spouse present	Female householder, no spouse present			Male householder, no spouse present	Female householder, no spouse present
	2	3	4	5	6	7	8	9	10	11	12	13	14	15	16	17
Total families	**69,305**	**53,858**	**3,226**	**12,220**	**58,437**	**47,899**	**2,507**	**8,013**	**8,093**	**3,843**	**536**	**3,716**	**6,200**	**4,235**	**479**	**1,485**
Total families with own children under 18	34,296	25,241	1,440	7,615	27,951	22,005	1,105	4,841	4,682	1,926	267	2,489	3,984	2,743	192	1,048
Percent of all families	49.5	46.9	44.6	62.3	47.8	45.9	44.1	60.4	57.9	50.1	49.8	67.0	64.3	64.8	40.1	70.6
Percent distribution	100.0	73.6	4.2	22.2	100.0	78.7	4.0	17.3	100.0	41.1	5.7	53.2	100.0	68.9	4.8	26.3
Families with—																
1 child under 18	14,088	9,564	891	3,633	11,491	8,340	680	2,470	1,971	769	174	1,028	1,408	885	108	415
2 children under 18	13,213	10,358	405	2,450	10,983	9,094	317	1,571	1,593	732	63	797	1,406	1,022	55	328
3 children under 18	5,004	3,905	105	1,033	4,046	3,380	75	591	722	297	24	401	753	542	17	193
4 children under 18	1,377	998	28	351	1,033	852	22	158	263	82	5	176	280	195	8	76
5 children under 18	371	261	10	100	256	216	9	31	84	21	—	64	90	67	2	21
6 or more under 18	203	155	1	47	143	123	1	19	48	25	—	23	48	32	1	15
Total own children under 18	63,253	47,690	2,145	13,419	51,444	41,604	1,663	8,177	8,713	3,633	379	4,701	8,668	6,102	335	2,230
Average number of children per family with children	1.84	1.89	1.49	1.76	1.84	1.89	1.50	1.69	1.86	1.89	1.42	1.89	2.18	2.22	1.75	2.13
Total families with own children under 6	15,609	11,950	567	3,092	12,745	10,465	425	1,854	2,033	829	108	1,096	2,174	1,550	102	522
Percent of all families	22.5	22.2	17.6	25.3	21.8	21.8	17.0	23.1	25.1	21.6	20.1	29.5	35.1	36.6	21.3	35.2
Percent distribution	100.0	76.6	3.6	19.8	100.0	82.1	3.3	14.5	100.0	40.8	5.3	53.9	100.0	71.3	4.7	24.0
Families with—																
1 child under 6	10,733	8,115	452	2,167	8,766	7,074	339	1,353	1,388	594	85	709	1,441	1,014	84	342
2 children under 6	4,172	3,356	103	714	3,477	2,973	77	427	487	207	22	258	606	457	13	137
3 children under 6	622	431	11	180	451	379	7	65	130	22	1	107	109	68	5	36
4 or more under 6	82	48	2	32	51	39	2	10	28	6	—	21	17	11	—	6
Total own children under 6	21,245	16,361	695	4,190	17,333	14,380	518	2,434	2,821	1,118	135	1,568	3,282	2,340	136	806
Average number of children per family with children	1.36	1.37	1.22	1.36	1.36	1.37	1.22	1.31	1.39	1.35	1.25	1.43	1.51	1.51	1.34	1.54
Total families with own children under 3	8,827	6,923	309	1,595	7,231	6,053	237	941	1,126	487	56	583	1,278	923	70	285
Percent of all families	12.7	12.9	9.6	13.1	12.4	12.6	9.5	11.7	13.9	12.7	10.4	15.7	20.6	21.8	14.6	19.2
Percent distribution	100.0	78.4	3.5	18.1	100.0	83.7	3.3	13.0	100.0	43.3	5.0	51.8	100.0	72.2	5.5	22.3
Families with—																
1 child under 3	7,821	6,137	285	1,398	6,430	5,348	224	858	964	444	46	474	1,134	807	68	259
2 or more under 3	1,007	786	23	198	801	705	13	83	161	43	10	109	144	116	2	26
Total own children under 3	10,168	8,009	346	1,813	8,363	7,044	262	1,056	1,302	557	66	679	1,595	1,163	83	349
Average number of children per family with children	1.15	1.16	1.12	1.14	1.16	1.16	1.11	1.12	1.16	1.14	([4])	1.16	1.25	1.26	([4])	1.23

[1] Race of family is defined as race of head of household.
[2] Includes persons of Hispanic origin.
[3] Persons of Hispanic origin may be of any race.
[4] Averages and percents are shown only when the base is 75,000 or greater.
—Less than 500.

NOTE.—Because of rounding, details may not add to totals.

SOURCE: U.S. Department of Commerce, Bureau of the Census, *Current Population Reports*, Series P20-488, *Household and Family Characteristics: March 1995*. (This table was prepared April 1997.)

Table 20.—Household income and poverty rates, by state: 1990, 1994, and 1995

| State | Median household income[1] | | | Percent of persons below the poverty level | | | | | | | | | | Poverty status of 5- to 17-year-olds, 1995 | | | |
| | | | | 1990[2] | | | | | | | | 1995 | | Number in poverty | | Percent in poverty | |
	1990[2]	1994	1995	Total	Under 5 years	5 years	6 to 11 years	12 to 17 years	18 to 64 years	65 to 74 years	75 years and over	Total	Standard error	Number (in thousands)	Standard error	Percent	Standard error
1	2	3	4	5	6	7	8	9	10	11	12	13	14	15	16	17	18
United States	$35,046	$33,178	$34,076	13.1	20.1	19.7	18.3	16.3	11.0	10.4	16.5	13.8	0.22	9,583	259	19.0	0.50
Alabama	27,515	27,967	25,991	18.3	26.1	25.8	24.3	22.3	14.6	19.2	31.1	20.1	1.96	198	39	22.6	4.01
Alaska	48,283	46,653	47,954	9.0	13.6	10.6	10.9	9.8	7.9	6.4	10.6	7.1	1.28	10	3	6.7	2.20
Arizona	32,112	32,180	30,863	15.7	24.9	24.2	21.8	19.1	14.0	9.3	13.2	16.1	1.77	199	38	24.2	4.16
Arkansas	24,658	26,290	25,814	19.1	28.5	26.6	25.2	22.7	15.3	18.0	29.9	14.9	1.75	108	22	21.7	4.02
California	41,742	36,332	37,009	12.5	19.0	19.3	18.3	17.1	10.9	6.5	9.5	16.7	0.76	1,456	120	23.4	1.73
Colorado	35,144	38,905	40,706	11.7	17.9	16.5	15.3	12.5	9.3	8.5	15.1	8.8	1.43	82	24	10.7	3.03
Connecticut	48,648	42,262	40,243	6.8	11.7	11.9	11.2	8.9	5.3	5.6	9.7	9.7	1.67	120	30	17.8	4.16
Delaware	40,665	36,890	34,928	8.7	13.3	12.7	11.8	10.8	7.2	8.2	13.5	10.3	1.72	23	6	16.6	4.18
District of Columbia	35,829	30,969	30,748	16.9	27.0	25.5	25.0	24.4	14.3	15.5	19.7	22.2	2.28	27	6	31.5	5.63
Florida	32,046	30,124	29,745	12.7	20.3	20.1	18.8	16.8	11.0	9.0	13.5	16.2	0.98	540	63	22.1	2.34
Georgia	33,839	32,359	34,099	14.7	22.1	21.3	20.1	18.1	11.4	16.5	26.7	12.1	1.46	218	49	15.6	3.24
Hawaii	45,276	43,453	42,851	8.3	12.6	12.6	11.2	10.8	6.9	6.7	10.4	10.3	1.68	31	9	14.2	3.94
Idaho	29,450	32,430	32,676	13.3	19.6	18.9	15.9	13.3	12.0	8.7	15.6	14.5	1.73	39	9	16.7	3.57
Illinois	37,607	36,075	38,071	11.9	18.9	18.7	17.0	15.0	10.0	8.9	13.4	12.4	0.98	467	60	20.3	2.38
Indiana	33,578	28,647	33,385	10.7	16.8	15.8	14.1	11.8	9.1	8.7	14.0	9.6	1.48	153	41	14.5	3.61
Iowa	30,584	34,016	35,519	11.5	17.5	15.4	14.1	11.7	10.3	8.1	15.3	12.2	1.65	98	23	15.5	3.44
Kansas	31,822	29,125	30,341	11.5	16.8	16.5	14.1	11.6	10.1	8.5	16.8	10.8	1.60	51	16	10.7	3.21
Kentucky	26,275	27,349	29,810	19.0	27.9	26.5	24.6	22.4	16.2	17.5	25.3	14.7	1.76	139	31	19.3	4.00
Louisiana	25,593	26,404	27,949	23.6	33.4	33.0	31.1	29.7	19.6	20.5	30.1	19.7	1.90	205	39	24.4	4.09
Maine	32,479	31,175	33,858	10.8	15.7	15.9	14.0	11.5	8.9	11.0	18.3	11.2	1.77	31	9	14.3	4.11
Maryland	45,925	40,309	41,041	8.3	11.9	11.9	11.5	10.2	6.8	8.8	13.6	10.1	1.59	119	36	13.3	3.77
Massachusetts	43,087	41,648	38,574	8.9	14.5	14.8	13.8	11.0	7.3	7.3	12.6	11.0	1.16	170	33	16.8	2.99
Michigan	36,170	36,284	36,426	13.1	22.1	20.4	18.1	15.7	11.2	8.7	14.3	12.2	1.04	292	46	14.8	2.18
Minnesota	36,041	34,597	37,933	10.2	14.8	14.6	12.5	10.6	8.8	8.4	17.2	9.2	1.44	101	30	10.4	2.91
Mississippi	23,479	26,120	26,538	25.2	35.8	35.1	33.5	31.9	20.0	24.0	37.1	23.5	2.11	212	32	36.4	4.51
Missouri	30,739	31,046	34,825	13.3	20.4	19.2	17.8	15.1	11.1	11.3	19.7	9.4	1.54	89	31	9.8	3.25
Montana	26,805	28,414	27,757	16.1	24.3	23.0	20.3	17.1	14.7	9.9	16.6	15.3	1.76	31	7	19.0	3.90
Nebraska	30,335	32,695	32,929	11.1	17.3	15.4	13.4	10.8	9.7	8.6	16.8	9.6	1.52	41	12	11.9	3.19
Nevada	36,160	36,888	36,084	10.2	15.1	14.4	12.6	11.9	9.1	8.4	12.3	11.1	1.70	33	11	11.1	3.41
New Hampshire	42,361	36,244	39,171	6.4	8.5	8.7	7.3	6.2	5.4	7.7	13.9	5.3	1.32	8	5	4.3	2.53
New Jersey	47,722	43,478	43,924	7.6	11.7	12.6	11.7	10.4	6.0	6.8	11.3	7.8	0.88	127	29	9.5	2.06
New Mexico	28,086	27,667	25,991	20.6	30.3	30.6	27.6	25.2	17.8	13.7	21.2	25.3	2.08	150	21	34.9	4.11
New York	38,438	32,803	33,028	13.0	20.6	21.2	19.6	17.0	11.0	10.0	14.7	16.5	0.84	805	74	23.6	1.94
North Carolina	31,071	30,967	31,979	13.0	19.2	18.5	17.2	15.3	10.1	15.7	25.9	12.6	1.25	233	41	20.2	3.24
North Dakota	27,067	29,079	29,089	14.4	19.6	18.4	17.2	14.7	13.0	10.8	19.5	12.0	1.66	17	5	13.2	3.36
Ohio	33,472	32,758	34,941	12.5	21.1	19.9	17.8	14.6	10.7	8.7	13.8	11.5	0.98	380	55	17.1	2.28
Oklahoma	27,491	27,756	26,311	16.7	25.3	23.4	21.7	18.5	14.2	13.5	24.1	17.1	1.83	151	29	24.2	4.14
Oregon	31,774	32,347	36,374	12.4	19.7	16.1	14.8	13.3	11.5	8.1	13.1	11.2	1.66	92	25	16.2	4.05
Pennsylvania	33,895	32,975	34,524	11.1	17.5	17.0	15.7	13.8	9.5	8.7	13.5	12.2	0.94	369	52	16.5	2.17
Rhode Island	37,524	32,833	35,359	9.6	16.3	16.1	13.8	11.0	7.6	8.9	15.6	10.6	1.75	27	8	16.4	4.51
South Carolina	30,615	30,692	29,071	15.4	22.8	21.8	21.2	19.1	12.0	17.3	26.5	19.9	2.11	249	43	31.7	4.73
South Dakota	26,239	30,576	29,578	15.9	23.6	22.2	20.2	17.3	13.6	11.1	21.3	14.5	1.75	25	6	17.3	3.68
Tennessee	28,926	29,451	29,015	15.7	23.9	22.5	20.8	18.5	12.5	17.2	26.7	15.5	1.83	204	46	19.6	4.03
Texas	31,501	31,627	32,039	18.1	25.6	25.5	24.2	23.0	15.2	14.9	23.8	17.4	0.98	887	90	23.1	2.11
Utah	34,363	36,728	36,480	11.4	15.8	14.4	12.0	10.0	11.0	6.4	12.5	8.4	1.31	43	12	8.4	2.28
Vermont	34,738	36,817	33,824	9.9	13.5	13.7	12.5	9.8	8.5	9.7	16.3	10.3	1.70	16	5	13.0	3.69
Virginia	38,861	38,714	36,222	10.2	14.5	14.5	13.5	11.9	8.4	11.6	18.5	10.2	1.48	154	42	14.5	3.71
Washington	36,360	34,483	35,568	10.9	17.0	16.4	14.3	12.2	9.8	7.0	12.4	12.5	1.75	156	42	16.6	4.17
West Virginia	24,248	24,232	24,880	19.7	31.7	30.3	25.9	22.4	17.7	14.1	20.8	16.7	1.77	71	15	25.8	4.67
Wisconsin	34,330	36,391	40,955	10.7	17.7	16.4	15.0	11.9	9.2	6.6	12.6	8.5	1.37	123	34	11.2	3.00
Wyoming	31,595	34,079	31,529	11.9	18.3	16.2	14.1	11.2	10.8	8.4	14.3	12.2	1.66	11	3	10.6	3.03

[1] In 1995 dollars adjusted by the Consumer Price Index for all urban consumers.
[2] Based on 1989 incomes collected in the 1990 Census. May differ from data derived from the Current Population Survey.

SOURCE: U.S. Department of Commerce, Bureau of the Census, *Decennial Census, Minority Economic Profiles,* unpublished data; and *Current Population Reports,* Series P-60, "Poverty in the United States," "Money Income of Households, Families, and Persons in the United States," and "Income, Poverty, and Valuation of Noncash Benefits," various years, and "Money Income in the U.S.: 1995," P60–193. (This table was prepared April 1997.)

28 ALL LEVELS: FAMILY CHARACTERISTICS

Table 21.—Poverty status of persons, families, and children under 18, by race/ethnicity: 1959 to 1995

Year and race/ethnicity	Number below the poverty level, in thousands						Percent below the poverty level					
	All persons	In all families			In families with female householder, no husband present		All persons	In all families			In families with female householder, no husband present	
		Total	House-holder	Related children under 18	Total	Related children under 18		Total	House-holder	Related children under 18	Total	Related children under 18
1	2	3	4	5	6	7	8	9	10	11	12	13
All races												
1959	39,490	34,562	8,320	17,208	7,014	4,145	22.4	20.8	18.5	26.9	49.4	72.2
1960	39,851	34,925	8,243	17,288	7,247	4,095	22.2	20.7	18.1	26.5	48.9	68.4
1965	33,185	28,358	6,721	14,388	7,524	4,562	17.3	15.8	13.9	20.7	46.0	64.2
1970	25,420	20,330	5,260	10,235	7,503	4,689	12.6	10.9	10.1	14.9	38.1	53.0
1971	25,559	20,405	5,303	10,344	7,797	4,850	12.5	10.8	10.0	15.1	38.7	53.1
1972	24,460	19,577	5,075	10,082	8,114	5,094	11.9	10.3	9.3	14.9	38.2	53.1
1973	22,973	18,299	4,828	9,453	8,178	5,171	11.1	9.7	8.8	14.2	37.5	52.1
1974	23,370	18,817	4,922	9,967	8,462	5,361	11.2	9.9	8.8	15.1	36.5	51.5
1975	25,877	20,789	5,450	10,882	8,846	5,597	12.3	10.9	9.7	16.8	37.5	52.7
1976	24,975	19,632	5,311	10,081	9,029	5,583	11.8	10.3	9.4	15.8	37.3	52.0
1977	24,720	19,505	5,311	10,028	9,205	5,658	11.6	10.2	9.3	16.0	36.2	50.3
1978	24,497	19,062	5,280	9,722	9,269	5,687	11.4	10.0	9.1	15.7	35.6	50.6
1979	26,072	19,964	5,461	9,993	9,400	5,635	11.7	10.2	9.2	16.0	34.9	48.6
1980	29,272	22,601	6,217	11,114	10,120	5,866	13.0	11.5	10.3	17.9	36.7	50.8
1981	31,822	24,850	6,851	12,068	11,051	6,305	14.0	12.5	11.2	19.5	38.7	52.3
1982	34,398	27,349	7,512	13,139	11,701	6,696	15.0	13.6	12.2	21.3	40.6	56.0
1983	35,303	27,933	7,647	13,427	12,072	6,747	15.2	13.9	12.3	21.8	40.2	55.4
1984	33,700	26,458	7,277	12,929	11,831	6,772	14.4	13.1	11.6	21.0	38.4	54.0
1985	33,064	25,729	7,223	12,483	11,600	6,716	14.0	12.6	11.4	20.1	37.6	53.6
1986	32,370	24,754	7,023	12,257	11,944	6,943	13.6	12.0	10.9	19.8	38.3	54.4
1987	32,221	24,725	7,005	12,275	12,148	7,074	13.4	12.0	10.7	19.7	38.1	54.7
1988	31,745	24,048	6,876	11,935	11,972	6,742	13.0	11.6	10.4	19.0	37.2	50.6
1989	31,528	24,066	6,784	12,001	11,668	6,808	12.8	11.5	10.3	19.0	35.9	51.1
1990	33,585	25,232	7,098	12,715	12,578	7,363	13.5	12.0	10.7	19.9	37.2	53.4
1991	35,708	27,143	7,712	13,658	13,824	8,065	14.2	12.8	11.5	21.1	39.7	55.5
1992	36,880	27,947	7,960	13,876	13,716	8,032	14.8	13.3	11.7	21.1	39.0	54.3
1993	39,265	29,927	8,393	14,961	14,636	8,503	15.1	13.6	12.3	22.0	38.7	53.7
1994	38,059	28,985	8,053	14,610	14,380	8,427	14.5	13.1	11.6	21.2	38.6	52.9
1995	36,425	27,501	7,532	13,999	14,205	8,364	13.8	12.3	10.8	20.2	36.5	50.3
White[1]												
1960	28,309	24,262	6,115	11,229	4,296	2,357	17.8	16.2	14.9	20.0	39.0	59.9
1965	22,496	18,508	4,824	8,595	4,092	2,321	13.3	11.7	11.1	14.4	35.4	52.9
1970	17,484	13,323	3,708	6,138	3,761	2,247	9.9	8.1	8.0	10.5	28.4	43.1
1975	17,770	13,799	3,838	6,748	4,577	2,813	9.7	8.3	7.7	12.5	29.4	44.2
1980	19,699	14,587	4,195	6,817	4,940	2,813	10.2	8.6	8.0	13.4	28.0	41.6
1985	22,860	17,125	4,983	7,838	5,990	3,372	11.4	9.9	9.1	15.6	29.8	45.2
1987	21,195	15,593	4,567	7,398	5,989	3,474	10.4	8.9	8.1	14.7	29.6	45.8
1988	20,715	15,001	4,471	7,095	5,950	3,385	10.1	8.6	7.9	14.0	29.2	43.0
1989	20,785	15,179	4,409	7,164	5,723	3,320	10.0	8.6	7.8	14.1	28.1	42.8
1990	22,326	15,916	4,622	7,696	6,210	3,597	10.7	9.0	8.1	15.1	29.8	45.9
1991	23,747	17,268	5,022	8,316	6,806	3,941	11.3	9.7	8.8	16.1	31.5	47.1
1992	25,259	18,294	5,160	8,333	6,907	3,783	11.9	10.1	8.9	16.0	30.8	45.3
1993	26,226	18,958	5,452	9,123	7,199	4,102	12.2	10.5	9.4	17.0	31.0	45.6
1994	25,379	18,474	5,312	8,826	7,228	4,099	11.7	10.1	9.1	16.3	31.8	45.7
1995	24,423	17,593	4,994	8,474	7,047	4,051	11.2	9.6	8.5	15.5	29.7	42.5
Black[1]												
1959	9,927	9,112	1,860	5,022	2,416	1,475	55.1	54.9	48.1	65.5	70.6	81.6
1966	8,867	8,090	1,620	4,774	3,160	2,107	41.8	40.9	35.5	50.6	65.3	76.6
1970	7,548	6,683	1,481	3,922	3,656	2,383	33.5	32.2	29.5	41.5	58.7	67.7
1975	7,545	6,533	1,513	3,884	4,168	2,724	31.3	30.1	27.1	41.4	54.3	66.0
1980	8,579	7,190	1,826	3,906	4,984	2,944	32.5	31.1	28.9	42.1	53.4	64.8
1985	8,926	7,504	1,983	4,057	5,342	3,181	31.3	30.5	28.7	43.1	53.2	66.9
1987	9,520	7,848	2,117	4,234	5,789	3,394	32.4	31.2	29.4	44.4	54.1	68.3
1988	9,356	7,650	2,090	4,148	5,601	3,130	31.3	30.0	28.2	42.8	51.9	61.8
1989	9,302	7,704	2,077	4,257	5,530	3,256	30.7	29.7	27.8	43.2	49.4	62.9
1990	9,837	8,160	2,193	4,412	6,005	3,543	31.9	31.0	29.3	44.2	50.6	64.7
1991	10,242	8,504	2,343	4,637	6,557	3,853	32.7	32.0	30.4	45.6	54.8	68.2
1992	10,827	9,134	2,435	4,850	6,799	3,967	33.4	32.9	30.9	46.3	54.0	67.1
1993	10,877	9,242	2,499	5,030	6,955	4,104	33.1	32.9	31.3	45.9	53.0	65.9
1994	10,196	8,447	2,212	4,787	6,489	3,935	30.6	29.6	27.3	43.3	50.2	63.2
1995	9,872	8,189	2,127	4,644	6,553	3,954	29.3	28.5	26.4	41.5	48.2	61.6
Hispanic origin[2]												
1975	2,991	2,755	627	1,619	1,053	694	26.9	26.3	25.1	33.1	57.2	68.4
1980	3,491	3,143	751	1,718	1,319	809	25.7	25.1	23.2	33.0	54.5	65.0
1985	5,236	4,605	1,074	2,512	1,983	1,247	29.0	28.3	25.5	39.6	55.7	72.4
1987	5,422	4,761	1,168	2,606	2,045	1,241	28.0	27.5	25.5	38.9	55.6	70.1
1988	5,357	4,700	1,141	2,576	2,052	1,208	26.7	26.0	23.7	37.3	55.0	65.5
1989	5,430	4,659	1,133	2,496	1,902	1,163	26.2	25.2	23.4	35.5	50.6	65.0
1990	6,006	5,091	1,244	2,750	2,115	1,314	28.1	26.9	25.0	37.7	53.0	68.4
1991	6,339	5,541	1,372	2,977	2,282	1,398	28.7	28.2	26.5	39.8	52.7	68.6
1992	7,592	6,455	1,395	2,946	2,474	1,289	29.6	28.4	26.2	38.8	51.5	65.7
1993	8,126	6,876	1,625	3,666	2,837	1,673	30.6	29.3	27.3	39.9	53.2	66.1
1994	8,416	7,357	1,724	3,956	2,920	1,804	30.7	30.2	27.8	41.1	54.8	68.3
1995	8,574	7,341	1,695	3,938	3,053	1,872	30.3	29.2	27.0	39.3	52.8	65.7

[1] Includes persons of Hispanic origin.
[2] Persons of Hispanic origin may be of any race.

SOURCE: U.S. Department of Commerce, Bureau of the Census, Current Population Reports, Series P-60-194, "Poverty in the United States" and "Income, Poverty, and Valuation of Noncash Benefits," various years. (This table was prepared April 1997.)

Table 22.—Average grade that the public would give the schools in their community and in the nation at large: 1974 to 1995

Year	All adults			No children in school			Public school parents			Private school parents		
	Nation	Local community	Local neighborhood	Nation	Local community	Local neighborhood	Nation	Local community	Local neighborhood	Nation	Local community	Local neighborhood
1	2	3	4	5	6	7	8	9	10	11	12	13
1974	—	2.63	—	—	2.57	—	—	2.80	—	—	2.15	—
1975	—	2.38	—	—	2.31	—	—	2.49	—	—	1.81	—
1976	—	2.38	—	—	2.34	—	—	2.48	—	—	2.22	—
1977	—	2.33	—	—	2.25	—	—	2.59	—	—	2.05	—
1978	—	2.21	—	—	2.11	—	—	2.47	—	—	1.69	—
1979	—	2.21	—	—	2.15	—	—	2.38	—	—	1.88	—
1980	—	2.26	—	—	—	—	—	—	—	—	—	—
1981	1.94	2.20	—	—	2.12	—	—	2.36	—	—	1.88	—
1982	2.01	2.24	—	2.04	2.18	—	2.01	2.35	—	2.02	2.20	—
1983	1.91	2.12	—	1.92	2.10	—	1.92	2.31	—	1.82	1.89	—
1984	2.09	2.36	—	2.11	2.30	—	2.11	2.49	—	2.04	2.17	—
1985	2.14	2.39	—	2.16	2.36	—	2.20	2.44	—	1.93	2.00	—
1986	2.13	2.36	—	—	2.29	—	—	2.55	—	—	2.14	—
1987	2.18	2.44	—	2.20	2.38	—	2.22	2.61	—	2.03	2.01	—
1988	2.08	2.35	—	2.02	2.32	—	2.13	2.48	—	2.00	2.13	—
1989	2.01	2.35	—	1.99	2.27	—	2.06	2.56	—	1.93	2.12	—
1990	1.99	2.29	—	1.98	2.27	—	2.03	2.44	—	1.85	2.09	—
1991	2.00	2.36	—	—	—	—	—	—	—	—	—	—
1992	1.93	2.30	—	1.92	—	—	1.94	2.73	—	1.85	—	—
1993	1.95	2.41	—	1.97	2.40	—	1.97	2.48	—	1.80	2.11	—
1994	1.95	2.26	2.43	1.95	2.16	2.34	1.90	2.55	2.64	1.86	1.90	2.23
1995	1.97	2.28	2.47	1.98	2.25	2.43	1.93	2.41	2.56	1.81	1.85	2.09

—Data not available.

NOTE.—Average based on a scale where A=4, B=3, C=2, D=1, and F=0.

SOURCE: "The Annual Gallup Poll of the Public's Attitudes Toward the Public Schools," *Phi Delta Kappan*, various years. (This table was prepared April 1996.)

Table 23.—Items most frequently cited by the general public as a major problem facing the local public schools: 1970 to 1996

Problems	Percent																	
	1970	1975	1980	1982	1983	1984	1985	1986	1987	1988	1989	1990	1991	1992	1993	1994	1995	1996
1	2	3	4	5	6	7	8	9	10	11	12	13	14	15	16	17	18	19
Lack of discipline	18	23	26	27	25	27	25	24	22	19	19	19	20	17	15	18	15	15
Lack of financial support	17	14	10	22	13	14	9	11	14	12	13	13	18	22	21	13	11	13
Fighting/violence/gangs	—	—	—	—	—	—	—	—	—	—	—	—	—	9	13	18	9	14
Use of drugs	11	9	14	20	18	18	18	28	30	32	34	38	22	22	16	11	7	16
Standards/quality of education	—	—	—	—	—	—	—	—	—	—	—	—	—	—	—	8	4	—
Large schools/overcrowding	—	10	7	4	3	4	5	5	8	6	8	7	9	9	8	7	3	8
Lack of respect	—	—	—	—	—	—	—	—	—	—	—	—	—	—	—	3	3	2
Lack of family structure/problems of home life	—	—	—	—	—	—	—	—	—	—	—	—	—	—	—	5	3	4
Crime/vandalism	—	—	—	—	—	—	—	—	—	—	—	—	—	—	—	4	2	3
Getting good teachers	12	11	6	10	8	14	10	6	9	11	7	7	11	5	5	3	2	3
Parents' lack of interest	3	2	6	5	6	5	3	4	6	7	6	4	7	5	4	3	2	—
Poor curriculum/standards	6	5	11	11	14	15	11	8	8	11	8	8	10	9	9	3	2	3
Pupils' lack of interest/truancy	—	3	5	5	5	4	5	3	6	5	3	6	5	3	4	3	2	5
Integration/segregation/racial discrimination	17	15	10	6	5	6	4	3	4	4	4	5	5	4	4	3	2	2
Management of funds/programs	—	—	—	—	—	—	—	—	—	—	—	—	—	—	—	(1)	2	—
Moral standards	—	—	—	2	4	1	2	5	7	6	3	3	3	4	3	—	—	—
Low teacher pay	—	—	—	—	—	4	2	3	5	4	4	6	4	3	3	—	—	—
Teachers' lack of interest	—	—	6	7	8	5	4	4	5	3	4	4	2	2	—	—	—	—
Drinking/alcoholism	—	—	2	3	3	4	3	5	6	5	4	4	2	—	2	—	—	—
Lack of proper facilities	11	3	2	2	1	2	1	1	2	1	1	2	—	—	—	—	—	—

—Data not available.

[1] Less than .05 percent.

SOURCE: "The Annual Gallup Poll of the Public's Attitudes Toward the Public Schools," *Phi Delta Kappan*, various years. (This table was prepared March 1997.)

Table 24.—Public opinion of public and private school choice: 1989 to 1996

Question	Percent who favor position								
	1989	1990	1991	1993	1995	1996			
						Total	No children in school	Public school parents	Nonpublic school parents
1	2	3	4	5	6	7	8	9	10
Do you favor or oppose allowing students and their parents to choose which public schools in the community the students attend regardless of where they live?	60	62	62	65	69	—	—	—	—
Do you favor or oppose allowing students and parents to choose a private school to attend at public expense?	—	—	26	24	33	36	33	39	60
Do you think private schools that accept government tuition payments for these students should be accountable to public authorities or not?									
Yes, should be accountable	—	—	—	63	73	—	—	—	—
No, should not be accountable	—	—	—	34	24	—	—	—	—
Don't know	—	—	—	3	3	—	—	—	—

—Not applicable.

SOURCE: *Phi Delta Kappan*, "The Annual Gallup Poll of the Public's Attitudes Toward the Public Schools," September 1996. (This table was prepared April 1997.)

Table 25.—Parental involvement in 8th graders' school-related activities, by selected parental characteristics: 1988

Characteristics of parents	Percent of parents[1] who talk with child regularly about			Percent of parents[1] who report family rules about			Percent of parents[1] who report that they			Percent of parents[1] who have contacted school about child's	
	Current school experiences	High school plans	Plans after high school	Number of hours of television watched on school days	Doing homework	Maintaining certain grade average	Never or seldom help with homework	Belong to a parent-teacher organization	Attend the parent-teacher organization meeting	Academic performance	Academic program
1	2	3	4	5	6	7	8	9	10	11	12
Total	79.4	47.1	38.3	61.7	92.0	72.7	29.4	31.9	36.2	52.5	34.8
Race/ethnicity											
Asian/Pacific Islander	59.8	41.7	36.5	67.1	89.3	74.7	42.8	29.4	41.2	36.0	29.4
Hispanic	67.1	52.7	44.8	68.7	92.3	79.8	44.7	15.5	43.0	48.3	34.5
Black, non-Hispanic	75.0	57.8	51.4	75.3	95.5	82.3	31.4	30.4	47.8	52.1	34.2
White, non-Hispanic	82.3	45.0	35.4	58.5	91.4	70.1	26.8	34.3	33.3	53.7	35.1
American Indian/Alaskan Native	72.5	44.6	39.9	62.9	95.9	75.7	35.5	16.6	35.0	52.5	42.5
Socioeconomic status[2]											
Lower quartile	66.3	43.0	33.5	64.0	92.2	74.2	41.7	12.2	29.2	38.1	24.2
Middle two quartiles	80.7	46.5	38.4	60.8	93.0	74.9	27.5	29.8	35.2	54.1	34.8
Highest quartile	89.0	52.7	42.9	61.6	89.9	66.9	21.9	54.0	44.4	61.9	44.1
Highest education level of parents											
Two-parent families											
Neither completed high school	60.0	40.7	29.6	64.0	92.6	75.2	47.6	10.6	32.7	32.3	21.2
One did not complete high school	72.9	45.7	34.7	61.6	92.6	74.8	33.7	15.4	28.7	42.8	28.6
Both completed high school	81.9	46.0	37.7	61.3	93.3	75.5	26.6	30.8	35.8	53.6	35.1
One graduated college[3]	87.2	51.8	42.4	61.1	91.5	69.9	21.8	48.6	42.7	60.9	41.1
Both graduated college	89.5	52.3	40.8	63.0	88.1	61.1	20.5	60.7	46.9	61.5	46.4
Single-parent families (female)											
Did not complete high school	61.0	47.1	34.6	64.3	91.2	73.2	50.3	9.7	25.1	33.9	19.0
Completed high school	77.0	48.1	42.1	62.5	92.7	75.1	33.8	24.6	33.0	53.5	32.7
Graduated college	84.0	51.8	44.8	60.1	87.0	66.3	28.3	46.7	43.9	67.8	45.6
Family composition											
Two-parent family	81.0	47.4	38.0	61.7	92.2	72.6	27.6	34.2	37.3	52.9	35.7
One-parent family	74.2	47.0	40.2	62.1	91.2	73.3	36.2	23.6	32.0	52.0	31.6

[1] The respondent was the parent most knowledgeable about the child's education. The responding parents reported on their own and their spouses' activities.
[2] Socioeconomic status was measured by a composite score on parental education and occupations, and family income.
[3] Includes a small number of cases where one parent was a high school dropout.

NOTE.—Because of rounding, details may not add to totals.

SOURCE: U.S. Department of Education, National Center for Education Statistics, National Education Longitudinal Study of 1988, "Base Year Parent Survey." (This table was prepared July 1990.)

Table 26.—Teachers' opinions about the most important goals for education, by type and control of school: 1990–91

Goal	Percent of teachers indicating item is the most important goal							
	Public school teachers				Private school teachers			
	Total	Elementary schools	Secondary schools	Combined schools	Total	Elementary schools	Secondary schools	Combined schools
1	2	3	4	5	6	7	8	9
Building basic literacy skills	49.9	52.4	45.7	49.1	32.4	34.6	26.6	32.6
Encouraging academic excellence	11.1	8.8	15.5	8.9	13.0	8.9	20.4	14.3
Promoting occupational or vocational skills	1.9	0.7	3.6	4.7	0.2	0.2	0.5	0.2
Promoting good work habits and self-discipline	13.2	11.8	15.7	12.2	8.9	8.6	10.1	8.7
Promoting personal growth	20.4	23.3	15.2	20.4	19.7	21.1	19.3	18.5
Promoting human relations	1.6	1.6	1.7	2.0	1.4	0.7	2.0	1.8
Promoting specific moral values	1.4	1.2	1.6	2.4	3.1	3.1	4.9	2.3
Promoting multicultural awareness or understanding	0.5	0.3	0.9	0.4	—	—	—	—
Fostering religious or spiritual development	—	—	—	—	21.2	22.8	16.1	21.7

—Data not available.

SOURCE: U.S. Department of Education, National Center for Education Statistics, "Schools and Staffing Survey, 1990–91." (This table was prepared May 1993.)

Table 27.—Teachers' perceptions about serious problems in their schools, by type and control of school: 1990–91 and 1993–94

Problem area	Percent of teachers indicating item is a serious problem									
	Public school teachers					Private school teachers				
	1990–91	1993–94				1990–91	1993–94			
	Total	Total	Elementary schools	Secondary schools	Combined schools	Total	Total	Elementary schools	Secondary schools	Combined schools
1	2	3	4	5	6	7	8	9	10	11
Student tardiness	11.2	10.5	6.3	18.3	7.8	3.4	2.6	1.8	4.3	2.6
Student absenteeism	14.1	14.4	7.2	27.1	15.0	2.6	2.2	0.8	5.2	2.7
Teacher absenteeism	1.6	1.5	1.3	1.9	2.0	0.7	0.8	0.7	1.2	0.9
Students cutting class	4.6	5.1	1.3	11.9	4.6	0.7	0.7	0.2	2.4	0.7
Physical conflicts among students	6.5	8.2	7.8	8.6	8.1	1.1	1.5	0.9	2.1	2.1
Robbery or theft	3.4	4.1	3.0	5.8	3.6	0.8	0.8	0.4	1.4	1.1
Vandalism of school property	5.4	6.7	5.2	9.0	5.9	0.9	1.2	0.9	2.0	1.2
Student pregnancy	6.4	7.3	1.1	18.4	10.1	0.3	0.4	0.2	1.1	0.4
Student use of alcohol	8.2	9.3	1.6	23.1	14.2	2.4	3.1	0.3	11.0	2.7
Student drug abuse	4.2	5.7	1.0	14.2	7.1	0.5	1.3	0.2	4.0	1.4
Student possession of weapons	1.2	2.8	1.2	5.6	2.7	0.1	0.3	0.2	0.6	0.3
Verbal abuse of teachers	7.5	11.1	8.6	14.8	14.3	1.7	2.3	0.7	2.8	4.4
Student disrespect for teachers	13.0	18.5	15.3	23.6	20.3	2.9	3.4	2.2	4.2	4.7
Students dropping out	6.3	5.8	1.2	14.1	7.7	0.2	0.6	0.3	1.3	0.7
Student apathy	20.6	23.6	15.6	38.0	28.9	4.1	4.5	2.2	9.7	5.1
Lack of academic challenge	5.7	6.5	4.2	10.4	9.9	1.3	1.5	1.0	2.5	1.6
Lack of parental involvement	25.4	27.6	23.0	34.5	35.5	4.3	4.0	2.8	7.1	4.7
Parental alcoholism/drug abuse	12.0	13.1	12.9	12.3	18.7	2.2	2.6	1.6	4.2	3.4
Poverty	17.1	19.5	20.8	15.9	26.8	2.0	2.7	2.2	3.2	3.0
Racial tension	3.8	5.1	4.0	6.7	5.5	0.7	0.9	0.6	1.7	0.8
Students come unprepared to learn	—	28.8	24.3	36.0	30.9	—	4.1	2.6	7.6	4.6

—Data not available.

SOURCE: U.S. Department of Education, National Center for Education Statistics, "Schools and Staffing Survey," 1990–91 and 1993–94. (This table was prepared September 1996.)

Table 28.—Teachers' perceptions about teaching and school conditions, by type and control of school: 1993–94

Statement	Percent of teachers somewhat agreeing or strongly agreeing with statement							
	Public school teachers				Private school teachers			
	Total	Elementary schools	Secondary schools	Combined schools	Total	Elementary schools	Secondary schools	Combined schools
1	2	3	4	5	6	7	8	9
The school administration's behavior toward the staff is supportive	79.2	80.7	76.8	77.0	88.2	89.4	83.3	88.7
My principal enforces school rules for student conduct and backs me up when I need it	80.8	82.0	78.6	81.4	88.4	89.3	84.4	88.5
The principal lets staff members know what is expected of them	85.6	86.9	83.5	82.1	88.2	89.1	86.6	88.2
Principal talks to me frequently about my instructional practices	44.3	49.0	35.6	45.7	54.0	58.3	41.2	53.7
Goals and priorities for the school are clear	82.8	85.4	78.1	79.3	90.2	90.9	88.3	90.2
Teachers in this school are evaluated fairly	87.9	88.6	86.6	85.3	89.8	90.4	87.3	90.3
In this school, staff members are recognized for a job well done	67.9	71.7	61.7	62.6	81.1	82.4	74.7	82.1
Principal knows what kind of school he/she wants and has communicated it to the staff	80.5	82.8	76.7	77.1	88.6	89.1	85.5	89.9
Principal does a poor job in getting resources for this school	16.1	15.1	18.1	19.6	10.5	10.6	12.9	8.7
Most of my colleagues share my beliefs and values about what the central mission of the school should be	84.2	87.3	79.1	81.4	93.2	95.0	88.4	93.7
Teachers participate in making most of the important education decisions in this school	58.3	62.8	50.3	58.4	74.0	75.1	66.1	75.3
There is a great deal of cooperative effort among staff	77.5	80.9	71.8	76.3	90.5	90.3	86.2	93.0
I receive a great deal of support from parents for the work I do	52.5	58.4	43.2	47.4	84.6	87.3	77.7	83.1
I make a conscious effort to coordinate the content of my courses with that of other teachers	85.0	88.0	79.8	82.9	85.2	86.6	78.5	86.1
Routine duties and paperwork interfere with my job of teaching	70.8	70.9	71.4	65.7	40.1	40.5	45.2	36.2
I have to follow rules in this school that conflict with my best professional judgement	24.2	22.0	27.4	26.4	15.0	15.1	19.1	13.0
Level of student misbehavior in this school interferes with my teaching	44.1	42.9	45.5	43.9	22.4	22.7	20.2	25.1
Amount of student tardiness and class cutting in this school interferes with my teaching	27.9	18.4	45.3	24.6	8.6	6.4	13.4	9.2
Rules for student behavior are consistently enforced by teachers in this school, even for students who are not in their classes	61.8	70.9	45.8	59.5	77.6	83.1	63.6	77.0
I am satisfied with my class sizes	64.9	62.9	68.2	78.1	84.4	82.2	84.0	89.3
I am satisfied with my teaching salary	44.9	44.1	47.2	43.1	41.6	35.5	43.6	49.5
I sometimes feel it is a waste of time to try to do my best as a teacher	26.8	23.4	32.6	30.8	13.4	12.1	16.5	13.7
I plan with the librarian/media specialist for the integration of services into my teaching	66.9	67.8	65.8	64.5	60.6	58.6	65.4	61.2
Library/media materials are adequate to support my instructional objectives	65.6	64.9	67.7	59.9	61.0	56.4	67.2	63.4
Necessary materials are available as needed by staff	73.1	73.7	73.0	72.3	85.7	84.5	85.3	87.3

SOURCE: U.S. Department of Education, National Center for Education Statistics, "Schools and Staffing Survey, 1993–94." (This table was prepared September 1996.)

Table 29.—Public's level of confidence in various institutions: 1994 and 1996

Institution	Percent of respondents by levels of confidence									
	1994					1996				
	A great deal	Quite a lot	Some	Very little	Can't say	A great deal	Quite a lot	Some	Very little	Can't say
1	2	3	4	5	6	7	8	9	10	11
Private higher education	14.4	33.9	30.9	12.4	8.4	18.3	38.7	28.3	7.5	7.1
Small businesses	16.2	36.7	36.8	7.2	3.2	15.3	40.8	32.6	7.6	3.6
Religious organizations	21.3	28.3	30.9	16.7	2.8	23.6	31.1	31.3	12.3	1.7
The military	15.8	32.8	34.0	14.1	3.2	16.9	37.0	31.0	12.1	3.1
Public higher education	11.4	33.9	39.2	10.7	4.8	15.0	36.4	34.2	11.6	2.8
Private elementary or secondary education	13.4	31.9	34.7	13.9	6.2	15.1	35.3	33.4	9.7	6.5
Youth development and recreation	13.8	33.0	35.6	12.1	5.5	14.8	35.2	32.7	11.6	5.7
Public elementary or secondary education	11.3	30.7	40.6	14.7	2.7	13.3	31.7	37.2	15.3	2.4
Health organizations	11.2	24.4	43.0	16.6	4.7	10.8	28.2	42.0	15.9	3.1
Federated charitable appeals, e.g., United Way	11.3	26.1	36.1	21.2	5.3	12.6	26.3	34.9	21.6	4.5
Human services organizations	10.3	22.9	45.0	15.4	6.5	9.1	28.1	42.6	15.1	5.0
Arts, culture, and humanities organizations	8.1	21.2	40.5	18.7	11.6	9.3	26.7	39.8	14.3	9.9
Recreation for adults	8.6	21.7	43.4	15.0	11.3	7.8	27.5	41.9	13.4	9.4
Environmental organizations	10.7	22.9	40.3	20.5	5.6	9.4	23.1	41.0	20.3	6.2
Private and community foundations	8.0	22.5	43.9	16.7	8.9	7.6	24.0	42.3	13.5	12.6
Local government	3.8	19.4	45.6	29.0	2.1	5.4	25.9	43.3	23.1	2.3
Public/society benefit, e.g., civil rights, social justice, community improvement organizations	6.0	17.9	45.5	24.4	6.1	7.5	22.7	43.4	20.8	5.6
Media, e.g., newspapers, TV, radio	6.1	19.8	40.5	32.0	1.6	6.3	22.7	39.5	29.7	1.8
Work-related organizations	5.5	22.6	48.8	14.6	8.6	6.1	21.5	47.2	17.4	7.9
State government	4.4	16.4	46.0	31.2	1.9	4.1	22.2	44.9	26.4	2.5
International/foreign, e.g., culture exchange, relief organizations	3.7	14.9	38.3	30.7	12.5	6.3	19.1	37.5	24.2	12.8
Organized labor	6.7	15.9	43.9	29.1	4.4	6.6	17.7	40.9	29.3	5.6
Major corporations	5.1	17.2	50.6	22.7	4.4	4.9	18.7	44.2	27.4	4.8
Federal government	3.5	15.5	44.2	34.8	1.9	5.2	17.5	43.9	31.1	2.2
Organizations that advocate a particular cause	3.9	12.5	39.5	37.6	6.6	4.0	15.7	42.7	29.5	8.1
Congress	3.2	12.0	40.9	41.3	2.6	3.4	12.4	41.7	39.0	3.5
Political organizations, e.g., Republican or Democratic parties	3.9	12.7	40.3	39.7	3.4	3.8	10.8	39.2	42.6	3.7

NOTE.—Institutions are listed in rank order as determined by the combined responses of "a great deal" and "quite a lot" of confidence.

SOURCE: Independent Sector, The Gallup Organization, *Giving and Volunteering in the United States, 1994* and *1996*. (This table was prepared April 1997.)

Table 30.—Percentage of households contributing to education and other charitable organizations and average annual donation, by type of charity: 1989, 1991, 1993, and 1995

Type of charity	1989			1991			1993			1995		
	Percentage of total households[1]	Average annual contribution		Percentage of total households[1]	Average annual contribution		Percentage of total households[1]	Average annual contribution		Percentage of total households[1]	Average annual contribution	
		Per contributing household	Per total household		Per contributing household	Per total household		Per contributing household	Per total household		Per contributing household	Per total household
1	2	3	4	5	6	7	8	9	10	11	12	13
Total	75.1	$978	$734	72.2	$899	$649	73.4	$880	$646	68.5	$1,017	$696
Religious	53.2	896	477	51.3	800	410	49.2	817	402	48.0	868	417
Health	32.4	143	46	32.9	154	51	25.7	139	36	27.3	214	58
Human services	23.0	263	60	27.5	260	71	26.7	208	56	25.1	271	68
Youth development	21.6	129	28	22.1	114	25	17.9	106	19	20.9	137	29
Education	19.1	291	56	21.1	225	47	17.5	424	74	20.3	318	65
Environment	13.4	88	12	16.3	99	16	11.6	89	10	11.5	106	12
Arts, culture, and humanities	9.6	193	19	9.4	194	18	8.1	139	11	9.4	216	20
Public and societal benefit	11.2	120	13	11.2	132	15	11.2	160	18	10.3	122	13
Private and community foundations	6.4	116	7	6.0	113	7	5.3	144	8	6.1	181	11
Recreation, adults	6.2	135	8	6.3	164	10	4.6	193	9	7.0	161	11
International, foreign	4.2	202	8	3.5	198	7	2.8	(²)	(²)	6.1	283	17
Other	3.0	195	6	2.8	233	7	4.7	81	4	2.1	160	3

[1] Percents do not add to total because of respondents giving to more than one type of charity.

[2] Sample size too small for reliable data.

NOTE.—Details for total households do not add to total because details only include households which reported a donation amount for the particular type of charity. The percentage of total includes households who reported giving donations, but did not specify amount.

SOURCE: Independent Sector, The Gallup Organization, *Giving and Volunteering in the United States*, 1989, 1991, 1993, and 1996. (This table was prepared April 1997.)

Table 31.—Total expenditures of educational institutions related to the gross domestic product, by level of institution: 1959–60 to 1996–97

Year	Gross domestic product (in billions)	School year	Total expenditures for education (amounts in millions of current dollars)					
			All educational institutions		All elementary and secondary schools		All colleges and universities	
			Amount	As a percent of gross domestic product	Amount	As a percent of gross domestic product	Amount	As a percent of gross domestic product
1	2	3	4	5	6	7	8	9
1959	$507.2	1959–60	$23,860	4.7	$16,713	3.3	$7,147	1.4
1961	544.8	1961–62	28,503	5.2	19,673	3.6	8,830	1.6
1963	617.4	1963–64	34,440	5.6	22,825	3.7	11,615	1.9
1965	719.1	1965–66	43,682	6.1	28,048	3.9	15,634	2.2
1967	833.6	1967–68	55,652	6.7	35,077	4.2	20,575	2.5
1969	982.2	1969–70	68,459	7.0	43,183	4.4	25,276	2.6
1970	1,035.6	1970–71	75,741	7.3	48,200	4.7	27,541	2.7
1971	1,125.4	1971–72	80,672	7.2	50,950	4.5	29,722	2.6
1972	1,237.3	1972–73	86,875	7.0	54,952	4.4	31,923	2.6
1973	1,382.6	1973–74	95,396	6.9	60,370	4.4	35,026	2.5
1974	1,496.9	1974–75	108,664	7.3	68,846	4.6	39,818	2.7
1975	1,630.6	1975–76	118,706	7.3	75,101	4.6	43,605	2.7
1976	1,819.0	1976–77	126,417	6.9	79,194	4.4	47,223	2.6
1977	2,026.9	1977–78	137,042	6.8	86,544	4.3	50,498	2.5
1978	2,291.4	1978–79	148,308	6.5	93,012	4.1	55,296	2.4
1979	2,557.5	1979–80	165,627	6.5	103,162	4.0	62,465	2.4
1980	2,784.2	1980–81	182,849	6.6	112,325	4.0	70,524	2.5
1981	3,115.9	1981–82	197,801	6.3	120,486	3.9	77,315	2.5
1982	3,242.1	1982–83	212,081	6.5	128,725	4.0	83,356	2.6
1983	3,514.5	1983–84	228,597	6.5	139,000	4.0	89,597	2.5
1984	3,902.4	1984–85	247,657	6.3	149,400	3.8	98,257	2.5
1985	4,180.7	1985–86	269,485	6.4	161,800	3.9	107,685	2.6
1986	4,422.2	1986–87	291,974	6.6	175,200	4.0	116,774	2.6
1987	4,692.3	1987–88	313,375	6.7	187,999	4.0	125,376	2.7
1988	5,049.6	1988–89	346,883	6.9	209,377	4.1	137,506	2.7
1989	5,438.7	1989–90	381,525	7.0	230,970	4.2	150,555	2.8
1990	5,743.8	1990–91	412,652	7.2	248,930	4.3	163,722	2.9
1991	5,916.7	1991–92	432,987	7.3	261,255	4.4	171,732	2.9
1992	6,244.4	1992–93	456,070	7.3	274,335	4.4	181,735	2.9
1993	6,553.0	1993–94	477,237	7.3	287,507	4.4	189,730	2.9
1994	6,935.7	1994–95[1]	503,891	7.3	302,366	4.4	201,525	2.9
1995	7,253.8	1995–96[2]	533,400	7.4	321,000	4.4	212,400	2.9
1996	7,576.1	1996–97[2]	564,200	7.4	339,700	4.5	224,500	3.0

[1] Preliminary.
[2] Estimated.

NOTE.—Total expenditures for public elementary and secondary schools include current expenditures, interest on school debt, and capital outlay. Data for private elementary and secondary schools are estimated. Total expenditures for colleges and universities include current-fund expenditures and additions to plant value. Excludes expenditures of noncollegiate postsecondary institutions. Some data revised from previously published figures. Because of rounding, details may not add to totals.

SOURCE: U.S. Department of Education, National Center for Education Statistics, *Statistics of State School Systems; Revenues and Expenditures for Public Elementary and Secondary Education; Financial Statistics of Institutions of Higher Education;* Common Core of Data survey; Higher Education General Information Survey (HEGIS), "Financial Statistics of Institutions of Higher Education" survey, Integrated Postsecondary Education Data System (IPEDS) "Finance" survey, and unpublished data; Council of Economic Advisers, *Economic Indicators;* and National Education Association, *Estimates of School Statistics*, various years. (This table was prepared September 1997.)

Table 32.—Total expenditures of educational institutions, by level and control of institution: 1899–1900 to 1996–97

[In millions of current dollars]

School year	Total	Elementary and secondary schools			Colleges and universities		
		Total	Public	Private [1]	Total	Public	Private
1	2	3	4	5	6	7	8
1899–1900	—	—	$215	—	—	—	—
1909–10	—	—	426	—	—	—	—
1919–20	—	—	1,036	—	—	—	—
1929–30	—	—	2,317	—	$632	$292	$341
1939–40	—	—	2,344	—	758	392	367
1949–50	$8,911	$6,249	5,838	$411	2,662	1,430	1,233
1951–52	10,735	7,861	7,344	517	2,874	1,565	1,309
1953–54	13,147	9,733	9,092	641	3,414	1,912	1,502
1955–56	15,907	11,727	10,955	772	4,180	2,348	1,832
1957–58	20,055	14,525	13,569	956	5,530	3,237	2,293
1959–60	23,860	16,713	15,613	1,100	7,147	3,904	3,244
1961–62	28,503	19,673	18,373	1,300	8,830	4,919	3,911
1963–64	34,440	22,825	21,325	1,500	11,615	6,558	5,057
1965–66	43,682	28,048	26,248	1,800	15,634	9,047	6,588
1967–68	55,652	35,077	32,977	2,100	20,575	12,750	7,824
1969–70	68,459	43,183	40,683	2,500	25,276	16,234	9,041
1970–71	75,741	48,200	45,500	2,700	27,541	18,028	9,513
1971–72	80,672	50,950	48,050	2,900	29,722	19,538	10,184
1972–73	86,875	54,952	51,852	3,100	31,923	21,144	10,779
1973–74	95,396	60,370	56,970	3,400	35,026	23,542	11,484
1974–75	108,664	68,846	64,846	4,000	39,818	26,966	12,852
1975–76	118,706	75,101	70,601	4,500	43,605	29,736	13,869
1976–77	126,417	79,194	74,194	5,000	47,223	31,997	15,226
1977–78	137,042	86,544	80,844	5,700	50,498	34,031	16,467
1978–79	148,308	93,012	86,712	6,300	55,296	37,110	18,187
1979–80	165,627	103,162	95,962	7,200	62,465	41,434	21,031
1980–81	182,849	112,325	104,125	8,200	70,524	46,559	23,965
1981–82	197,801	120,486	111,186	9,300	77,315	50,813	26,502
1982–83	212,081	128,725	118,425	10,300	83,356	54,338	29,018
1983–84	228,597	139,000	127,500	11,500	89,597	58,124	31,473
1984–85	247,657	149,400	137,000	12,400	98,257	63,705	34,553
1985–86	269,485	161,800	148,600	13,200	107,685	70,069	37,616
1986–87	291,974	175,200	160,900	14,300	116,774	74,552	42,222
1987–88	313,375	187,999	172,699	15,300	125,376	79,859	45,516
1988–89	346,883	209,377	192,977	16,400	137,506	87,107	50,398
1989–90	381,525	230,970	212,770	18,200	150,555	96,387	54,169
1990–91	412,652	248,930	229,430	19,500	163,722	104,433	59,288
1991–92	432,987	261,255	241,055	20,200	171,732	108,667	63,065
1992–93	456,070	274,335	252,935	21,400	181,735	115,169	66,566
1993–94	477,237	287,507	265,307	22,200	189,730	119,573	70,157
1994–95 [2]	503,891	302,366	278,966	23,400	201,525	127,594	73,930
1995–96 [1]	533,400	321,000	296,200	24,800	212,400	134,600	77,800
1996–97 [1]	564,200	339,700	313,500	26,200	224,500	142,600	81,900

[1] Estimated.
[2] Preliminary.
—Data not available.

NOTE.—Total expenditures for public elementary and secondary schools include current expenditures, interest on school debt, and capital outlay. Data for private elementary and secondary schools are estimated. Total expenditures for colleges and universities include current-fund expenditures and additions to plant value. Excludes expenditures of noncollegiate postsecondary institutions. Some data have been revised from previously published figures. Because of rounding, details may not add to totals.

SOURCE: U.S. Department of Education, National Center for Education Statistics, Statistics of State School Systems; Revenues and Expenditures for Public Elementary and Secondary Education; Financial Statistics of Institutions of Higher Education; Common Core of Data survey; Higher Education General Information Survey (HEGIS), "Financial Statistics of Institutions of Higher Education" survey; Integrated Postsecondary Education Data System (IPEDS) "Finance" survey; and National Education Association, Estimates of School Statistics, various years. (This table was prepared September 1997.)

Table 33.—Estimated total expenditures of educational institutions, by level, control of institution, and source of funds: 1979–80 to 1994–95

[In billions of current dollars]

Level and control of institution and source of funds	1979–80 Amount	1979–80 Percent	1984–85 Amount	1984–85 Percent	1989–90[1] Amount	1989–90[1] Percent	1990–91 Amount	1990–91 Percent	1993–94[1] Amount	1993–94[1] Percent	1994–95[2] Amount	1994–95[2] Percent
1	2	3	4	5	6	7	8	9	10	11	12	13
All levels												
Total public and private	$165.6	100.0	$247.7	100.0	$381.5	100.0	$412.7	100.0	$477.2	100.0	$503.9	100.0
Federal	18.9	11.4	21.3	8.6	31.6	8.3	34.1	8.3	42.1	8.8	43.7	8.7
State	64.3	38.8	96.1	38.8	142.2	37.3	151.6	36.7	164.2	34.4	177.9	35.3
Local	43.3	26.1	63.3	25.6	97.9	25.7	105.5	25.6	125.0	26.2	127.6	25.3
All other	39.1	23.6	66.9	27.0	109.8	28.8	121.5	29.4	146.0	30.6	154.7	30.7
Total public	137.4	100.0	200.7	100.0	309.2	100.0	333.9	100.0	384.9	100.0	406.6	100.0
Federal	14.8	10.8	15.8	7.9	23.0	7.4	24.9	7.5	31.9	8.3	33.1	8.1
State	63.9	46.5	95.5	47.6	140.8	45.5	150.3	45.0	162.7	42.3	176.3	43.4
Local	43.1	31.4	63.1	31.4	97.5	31.6	105.0	31.5	124.5	32.4	127.2	31.3
All other	15.6	11.3	26.3	13.1	47.9	15.5	53.7	16.1	65.8	17.1	70.0	17.2
Total private	28.2	100.0	47.0	100.0	72.4	100.0	78.8	100.0	92.5	100.0	97.3	100.0
Federal	4.1	14.5	5.5	11.7	8.6	11.9	9.2	11.6	10.2	11.0	10.6	10.9
State	0.4	1.6	0.7	1.4	1.4	1.9	1.3	1.7	1.5	1.6	1.6	1.6
Local	0.2	0.6	0.2	0.5	0.4	0.6	0.4	0.5	0.5	0.6	0.4	0.4
All other	23.5	83.4	40.6	86.4	62.0	85.6	67.9	86.1	80.2	86.8	84.7	87.0
Elementary and secondary schools												
Total public and private	103.2	100.0	149.4	100.0	231.0	100.0	248.9	100.0	287.5	100.0	302.4	100.0
Federal	9.4	9.1	9.1	6.1	13.0	5.6	14.2	5.7	18.7	6.5	19.0	6.3
State	44.7	43.3	66.8	44.7	100.6	43.6	108.2	43.5	119.8	41.7	130.4	43.1
Local	41.6	40.3	60.8	40.7	94.0	40.7	101.2	40.6	119.7	41.7	122.1	40.4
All other	7.5	7.3	12.8	8.6	23.3	10.1	25.4	10.2	29.3	10.2	30.9	10.2
Total public	96.0	100.0	137.0	100.0	212.8	100.0	229.4	100.0	265.3	100.0	279.0	100.0
Federal	9.4	9.8	9.1	6.6	13.0	6.1	14.2	6.2	18.7	7.1	19.0	6.8
State	44.7	46.6	66.8	48.7	100.6	47.3	108.2	47.2	119.8	45.2	130.4	46.8
Local	41.6	43.3	60.8	44.3	94.0	44.2	101.2	44.1	119.7	45.1	122.1	43.8
All other	0.3	0.3	0.4	0.3	[3]5.1	[3]2.4	[3]5.9	[3]2.6	[3]7.1	[3]2.7	[3]7.5	[3]2.7
Total private[4]	7.2	100.0	12.4	100.0	18.2	100.0	19.5	100.0	22.2	100.0	23.4	100.0
All other	7.2	100.0	12.4	100.0	18.2	100.0	19.5	100.0	22.2	100.0	23.4	100.0
Institutions of higher education												
Total public and private	62.5	100.0	98.3	100.0	150.6	100.0	163.7	100.0	189.7	100.0	201.5	100.0
Federal	9.5	15.2	12.2	12.4	18.6	12.3	19.9	12.2	23.4	12.3	24.8	12.3
State	19.6	31.4	29.4	29.9	41.6	27.6	43.4	26.5	44.4	23.4	47.4	23.5
Local	1.7	2.7	2.5	2.6	3.9	2.6	4.3	2.6	5.3	2.8	5.5	2.7
All other	31.6	50.6	54.1	55.1	86.5	57.4	96.1	58.7	116.7	61.5	123.8	61.5
Total public	41.4	100.0	63.7	100.0	96.4	100.0	104.4	100.0	119.6	100.0	127.6	100.0
Federal	5.4	13.1	6.7	10.6	9.9	10.3	10.7	10.3	13.2	11.0	14.1	11.1
State	19.2	46.3	28.7	45.1	40.2	41.7	42.1	40.3	42.9	35.9	45.8	35.9
Local	1.5	3.7	2.3	3.6	3.5	3.7	3.9	3.7	4.8	4.0	5.1	4.0
All other	15.3	36.9	25.9	40.7	42.7	44.3	47.7	45.7	58.7	49.1	62.6	49.0
Total private	21.0	100.0	34.6	100.0	54.2	100.0	59.3	100.0	70.2	100.0	73.9	100.0
Federal	4.1	19.4	5.5	15.9	8.6	15.9	9.2	15.4	10.2	14.5	10.6	14.4
State	0.4	2.1	0.7	1.9	1.4	2.6	1.3	2.3	1.5	2.1	1.6	2.1
Local	0.2	0.8	0.2	0.6	0.4	0.7	0.4	0.7	0.5	0.7	0.4	0.6
All other	16.3	77.7	28.2	81.6	43.8	80.8	48.4	81.6	58.0	82.7	61.3	82.9

[1] Revised from previously published data.
[2] Preliminary data.
[3] Revenues from individuals including fees for transportation and books and food service receipts. This expenditure includes only the individual contributions for these categories and excludes contributions from public sources.
[4] Some private elementary and secondary school revenues come from federal, state, and local sources. However, comprehensive data are not available to delineate the sources of revenues for private schools.

NOTE.—Estimated distribution of expenditures by source of funds are obtained from distribution of revenue sources for current funds. Federally-supported student aid that goes to higher education institutions through students' tuition payments is shown under "All other" rather than "federal." Such payments would add substantial amounts and several percentage points to the federal share. Other federal programs, not included in this table because they do not support regular educational institutions, would increase the federal share even further. Typical examples of these payments would be federal support for libraries and museums. Additionally, the federal contribution to education through tax expenditures is not reflected in this table. Because of rounding, details may not add to totals.

SOURCE: U.S. Department of Education, National Center for Education Statistics, Common Core of Data; Higher Education General Information Survey (HEGIS), "Financial Statistics of Institutions of Higher Education" survey; Integrated Postsecondary Education Data System (IPEDS) "Finance" survey, unpublished data. (This table was prepared July 1997.)

Table 34.—Governmental expenditures, by level of government and function: 1970–71 to 1992–93

Expenditure, by function	All governments¹								Federal government				State and local governments²			
	1970–71	1980–81	1988–89	1989–90	1990–91	1991–92	1992–93		1970–71	1980–81	1990–91	1992–93	1970–71	1980–81	1990–91	1992–93
1	2	3	4	5	6	7	8		9	10	11	12	13	14	15	16
	In millions															
General expenditures²	$301,096	$827,877	$1,542,620	$1,686,807	$1,804,005	$1,858,760	$1,904,746		$150,422	$422,301	$1,059,508	$1,083,257	$150,674	$407,449	$908,108	$1,026,806
Selected federal programs																
National defense and international relations	80,910	174,564	346,338	344,069	366,112	351,684	344,008		80,910	174,564	366,112	344,008	—	—	—	—
Postal service	8,683	20,466	36,472	39,065	43,102	44,890	44,528		8,683	20,466	43,102	44,528	—	—	—	—
Space research and technology	3,334	5,523	10,806	12,063	13,514	13,550	13,873		3,334	5,523	13,514	13,873	—	—	—	—
Education and libraries	64,042	158,012	284,963	310,080	334,333	353,399	373,125		4,629	12,408	45,256	55,521	60,174	147,649	313,744	346,950
Social services and income maintenance																
Public welfare	20,446	74,643	126,132	140,734	167,681	202,364	218,707		2,220	22,395	119,135	157,130	18,226	54,121	130,402	167,098
Hospitals and health	14,835	47,378	85,091	92,487	102,817	108,166	119,172		3,630	11,277	28,207	32,654	11,205	36,101	81,110	94,884
Social insurance administration	2,031	5,075	7,352	7,716	8,193	9,172	9,587		1,086	2,799	7,995	9,309	945	2,276	3,250	3,945
Transportation	23,722	46,578	74,289	78,539	84,048	87,360	90,672		4,062	7,724	24,768	28,560	19,819	39,231	75,410	80,878
Public safety																
Police protection	5,706	16,851	32,723	35,921	38,942	41,248	43,763		478	1,904	6,725	8,080	5,228	14,947	32,772	36,407
Correction	1,979	7,806	22,500	26,229	29,297	31,112	32,053		94	413	2,122	2,690	1,885	7,393	27,356	29,631
Environment and housing																
Natural resources	13,740	43,599	64,353	80,915	56,949	64,550	64,599		10,658	38,896	46,549	53,859	3,082	6,175	12,575	13,236
Housing and community development	4,467	13,884	28,230	32,430	33,346	32,549	31,357		1,913	6,808	30,199	31,321	2,554	7,086	16,648	18,775
Governmental administration																
Financial administration	3,612	10,944	22,125	24,200	27,204	28,852	29,971		1,341	3,714	10,308	11,762	2,271	7,230	16,995	19,324
General control³	3,567	11,514	30,088	33,346	36,977	38,327	42,740		540	1,973	7,900	9,527	4,432	12,771	31,466	33,213
Interest on general debt	21,688	97,641	220,883	237,691	247,376	254,968	253,895		16,599	80,510	195,142	198,795	5,089	17,131	52,234	55,100
Other and unallocable	28,334	93,389	150,274	191,322	214,115	196,570	192,699		10,245	30,927	112,474	81,640	15,764	55,338	114,147	127,398
	Percentage distribution															
General expenditures²	100.0	100.0	100.0	100.0	100.0	100.0	100.0		100.0	100.0	100.0	100.0	100.0	100.0	100.0	100.0
Selected federal programs																
National defense and international relations	26.9	21.1	22.5	20.4	20.3	18.9	18.1		53.8	41.3	34.6	31.8	—	—	—	—
Postal service	2.9	2.5	2.4	2.3	2.4	2.4	2.3		5.8	4.8	4.1	4.1	—	—	—	—
Space research and technology	1.1	0.7	0.7	0.7	0.7	0.7	0.7		2.2	1.3	1.3	1.3	—	—	—	—
Education and libraries	21.3	19.1	18.5	18.4	18.5	19.0	19.6		3.1	2.9	4.3	5.1	39.9	36.2	34.5	33.8
Social services and income maintenance																
Public welfare	6.8	9.0	8.2	8.3	9.3	10.9	11.5		1.5	5.3	11.2	14.5	12.1	13.3	14.4	16.3
Hospitals and health	4.9	5.7	5.5	5.5	5.7	5.8	6.3		2.4	2.7	2.7	3.0	7.4	8.9	8.9	9.2
Social insurance administration	0.7	0.6	0.5	0.5	0.5	0.5	0.5		0.7	0.7	0.8	0.9	0.6	0.6	0.4	0.4
Transportation	7.9	5.6	4.8	4.7	4.7	4.7	4.8		2.7	1.8	2.3	2.6	13.2	9.6	8.3	7.9
Public safety																
Police protection	1.9	2.0	2.1	2.1	2.2	2.2	2.3		0.3	0.5	0.6	0.7	3.5	3.7	3.6	3.5
Correction	0.7	0.9	1.5	1.6	1.6	1.7	1.7		0.1	0.1	0.2	0.2	1.3	1.8	3.0	2.9
Environment and housing																
Natural resources	4.6	5.3	4.2	4.8	3.2	3.5	3.4		7.1	9.2	4.4	5.0	2.0	1.5	1.4	1.3
Housing and community development	1.5	1.7	1.8	1.9	1.8	1.8	1.6		1.3	1.6	2.9	2.9	1.7	1.7	1.8	1.8
Governmental administration																
Financial administration	1.2	1.3	1.4	1.4	1.5	1.6	1.6		0.9	0.9	1.0	1.1	1.5	1.8	1.9	1.9
General control³	1.2	1.4	2.0	2.0	2.0	2.1	2.2		0.4	0.5	0.7	0.9	2.9	3.1	3.5	3.2
Interest on general debt	7.2	11.8	14.3	14.1	13.7	13.7	13.3		11.0	19.1	18.4	18.4	3.4	4.2	5.8	5.4
Other and unallocable	9.4	11.3	9.7	11.3	11.9	10.6	10.1		6.8	7.3	10.6	7.5	10.5	13.6	12.6	12.4

—Not applicable.

¹Excludes duplicative intergovernmental transactions.
²General expenditures include monies paid by states to the federal government ($3,626,834 in 1992–93), which are excluded from direct general expenditures.
³Includes judicial and legal expenditures and expenditures on general and public buildings and other governmental administration.

SOURCE: U.S. Department of Commerce, Bureau of the Census, unpublished data. (This table was prepared November 1997.)

Table 35.—Direct general expenditures of state and local governments for all functions and for education, by level and state: 1992-93

[In millions]

State	Total direct general expenditures [1]	Education expenditures							
		Total	Elementary and secondary education			Higher education			Other education [3]
			Total	Current expenditure	Capital outlay [2]	Total	Current expenditure	Capital outlay	
1	2	3	4	5	6	7	8	9	10
United States	$1,026,806.5	$342,287.1	$240,310.0	$218,208.1	$22,101.9	$88,108.6	$79,159.8	$8,948.8	$13,868.5
Alabama	13,754.0	4,441.1	2,530.3	2,319.8	210.5	1,576.6	1,416.4	160.2	334.2
Alaska	6,021.5	1,463.9	1,088.9	957.4	131.5	323.8	269.0	54.8	51.2
Arizona	14,195.4	5,129.3	3,462.9	2,702.5	760.4	1,503.3	1,371.3	132.0	163.1
Arkansas	7,208.9	2,792.3	1,714.3	1,583.3	131.1	859.5	733.0	126.5	218.5
California	134,571.3	39,425.3	26,530.1	24,891.6	1,638.5	11,494.3	10,353.1	1,141.2	1,400.9
Colorado	14,460.5	4,935.1	3,291.1	2,934.0	357.1	1,527.2	1,405.8	121.4	116.9
Connecticut	15,770.9	4,745.8	3,776.5	3,538.8	237.6	777.7	753.9	23.8	191.6
Delaware	3,062.6	1,159.8	680.8	632.4	48.3	395.7	381.6	14.1	83.3
District of Columbia	4,472.1	720.3	620.5	581.9	38.6	99.8	95.4	4.5	—
Florida	50,431.3	14,878.7	11,159.9	9,754.4	1,405.5	3,193.1	2,699.1	494.0	525.7
Georgia	24,241.0	8,004.6	5,941.9	5,350.2	591.7	1,712.6	1,558.8	153.8	350.1
Hawaii	6,370.3	1,447.0	834.1	744.1	90.0	591.4	502.8	88.6	21.5
Idaho	3,457.7	1,281.0	837.4	755.6	81.8	389.8	348.5	41.3	53.9
Illinois	42,974.6	14,521.6	10,243.1	9,340.8	902.3	3,588.5	3,245.6	342.9	690.0
Indiana	19,965.7	7,478.2	4,922.8	4,390.7	532.1	2,247.6	2,000.5	247.1	307.8
Iowa	10,772.2	4,075.8	2,551.6	2,326.6	225.0	1,351.1	1,250.0	101.1	173.1
Kansas	9,017.2	3,614.9	2,391.9	2,193.8	198.0	1,098.4	1,003.2	95.2	124.7
Kentucky	12,398.5	4,169.6	2,595.3	2,430.0	165.4	1,243.2	1,076.8	166.4	331.1
Louisiana	16,533.0	4,941.0	3,371.8	3,189.2	182.6	1,301.9	1,222.6	79.3	267.3
Maine	4,789.5	1,615.2	1,186.5	1,094.2	92.3	368.6	330.2	38.4	60.1
Maryland	18,451.9	6,629.1	4,496.6	4,162.6	334.0	1,814.7	1,575.0	239.8	317.8
Massachusetts	25,821.8	6,654.8	4,971.9	4,818.9	153.0	1,330.6	1,260.1	70.6	352.3
Michigan	37,642.0	14,813.6	10,254.3	9,254.9	999.5	4,173.6	3,845.2	328.4	385.7
Minnesota	21,692.6	7,193.1	5,064.6	4,567.4	497.2	1,818.1	1,655.6	162.5	310.5
Mississippi	7,945.8	2,782.5	1,801.8	1,673.2	128.6	830.7	742.2	88.5	150.0
Missouri	15,230.0	5,510.3	4,104.0	3,688.2	415.8	1,204.7	1,129.7	75.0	201.6
Montana	3,104.2	1,146.1	810.0	769.9	40.1	263.8	248.0	15.8	72.3
Nebraska	5,803.5	2,367.8	1,605.7	1,463.5	142.2	686.5	637.3	49.2	75.6
Nevada	5,587.8	1,626.1	1,190.6	999.2	191.4	399.3	336.8	62.4	36.2
New Hampshire	4,257.9	1,380.9	1,015.6	973.2	42.4	319.2	299.0	20.1	46.1
New Jersey	36,406.0	12,667.2	10,020.4	9,414.1	606.3	2,305.0	2,093.9	211.1	341.7
New Mexico	6,548.2	2,295.2	1,402.6	1,248.0	154.7	810.8	744.8	66.0	81.8
New York	107,595.1	30,300.3	23,470.7	21,812.1	1,658.6	5,589.1	4,863.9	725.2	1,240.5
North Carolina	23,107.6	8,583.4	5,381.8	4,889.9	491.9	2,865.6	2,556.4	309.2	336.0
North Dakota	2,556.8	962.7	547.5	506.1	41.4	365.9	333.5	32.4	49.3
Ohio	39,442.6	13,901.7	9,841.9	9,371.4	470.5	3,497.1	2,858.2	638.9	562.8
Oklahoma	10,268.8	3,955.0	2,720.8	2,527.5	193.3	1,084.2	1,013.7	70.5	150.0
Oregon	12,417.4	4,483.9	3,098.0	2,892.5	205.5	1,231.5	1,129.2	102.3	154.3
Pennsylvania	45,941.8	16,902.5	12,448.1	11,440.5	1,007.7	3,420.8	3,132.7	288.1	1,033.6
Rhode Island	4,494.4	1,337.9	929.0	895.3	33.7	308.9	287.8	21.0	100.1
South Carolina	12,492.9	4,343.5	2,900.1	2,675.0	225.1	1,257.9	1,127.9	130.0	185.4
South Dakota	2,430.4	868.3	613.0	554.0	59.0	210.6	191.4	19.2	44.7
Tennessee	15,657.1	4,873.9	3,171.7	2,931.9	239.8	1,511.7	1,341.6	170.1	190.5
Texas	61,780.0	24,138.3	17,153.1	14,130.7	3,022.4	6,419.7	5,899.7	520.0	565.5
Utah	6,320.0	2,659.2	1,626.2	1,421.5	204.7	932.2	829.6	102.6	100.8
Vermont	2,257.5	887.3	550.3	536.9	13.4	277.6	256.8	20.8	59.4
Virginia	21,991.1	8,310.7	5,713.1	5,234.8	478.3	2,192.2	2,020.0	172.2	405.4
Washington	24,989.3	8,569.7	5,951.0	4,647.2	1,303.8	2,249.5	1,937.4	312.1	369.2
West Virginia	6,348.6	2,409.0	1,698.5	1,518.9	179.6	572.3	530.2	42.0	138.2
Wisconsin	21,352.6	8,011.7	5,431.1	4,929.7	501.4	2,268.4	2,041.6	226.8	312.2
Wyoming	2,402.5	880.7	594.4	547.7	46.7	252.3	223.1	29.2	34.0

[1] Includes state and local government expenditures for education services, social services and income maintenance, transportation, public safety, environment and housing, governmental administration, interest on general debt, and other general expenditures. Includes intergovernmental expenditure to the federal government.

[2] Includes outlays for "other education."

[3] Includes assistance and subsidies to individuals and private institutions for elementary, secondary, and higher education, as well as miscellaneous education expenditures.

—Not applicable.

NOTE.—Current expenditure data in this table differ from figures appearing in other tables because of slightly varying definitions used in the *Governmental Finances* and *Common Core of Data* surveys. Because of rounding, details may not add to totals.

SOURCE: U.S. Department of Commerce, Bureau of the Census, unpublished data. (This table was prepared May 1997.)

Table 36.—Direct general expenditures per capita of state and local governments for all functions and for education, by level and state: 1992–93

State	Total, all direct general expenditures per capita [1]	Education expenditures							
		Total		Elementary and secondary education		Higher education		Other education [2]	
		Amount per capita	As a percent of all functions	Amount per capita	As a percent of all functions	Amount per capita	As a percent of all functions	Amount per capita	As a percent of all functions
1	2	3	4	5	6	7	8	9	10
United States	$3,981.27	$1,327.16	33.3	$931.76	23.4	$341.63	8.6	$53.77	1.4
Alabama	3,284.93	1,060.70	32.3	604.32	18.4	376.55	11.5	79.82	2.4
Alaska	10,052.55	2,443.96	24.3	1,817.84	18.1	540.58	5.4	85.54	0.9
Arizona	3,606.56	1,303.18	36.1	879.81	24.4	381.93	10.6	41.44	1.1
Arkansas	2,973.96	1,151.93	38.7	707.23	23.8	354.57	11.9	90.13	3.0
California	4,311.66	1,263.19	29.3	850.02	19.7	368.28	8.5	44.88	1.0
Colorado	4,055.10	1,383.94	34.1	922.90	22.8	428.27	10.6	32.77	0.8
Connecticut	4,812.61	1,448.21	30.1	1,152.41	23.9	237.33	4.9	58.47	1.2
Delaware	4,375.10	1,656.86	37.9	972.53	22.2	565.35	12.9	118.98	2.7
District of Columbia	7,723.83	1,244.05	16.1	1,071.63	13.9	172.42	2.2	—	—
Florida	3,686.77	1,087.70	29.5	815.84	22.1	233.43	6.3	38.43	1.0
Georgia	3,504.56	1,157.24	33.0	859.03	24.5	247.59	7.1	50.62	1.4
Hawaii	5,435.44	1,234.67	22.7	711.69	13.1	504.60	9.3	18.39	0.3
Idaho	3,146.25	1,165.61	37.0	761.93	24.2	354.66	11.3	49.02	1.6
Illinois	3,673.99	1,241.48	33.8	875.70	23.8	306.79	8.4	58.99	1.6
Indiana	3,494.79	1,308.98	37.5	861.68	24.7	393.42	11.3	53.88	1.5
Iowa	3,828.09	1,448.41	37.8	906.75	23.7	480.13	12.5	61.53	1.6
Kansas	3,562.68	1,428.26	40.1	945.03	26.5	433.98	12.2	49.25	1.4
Kentucky	3,272.24	1,100.46	33.6	684.97	20.9	328.11	10.0	87.38	2.7
Louisiana	3,849.36	1,150.41	29.9	785.06	20.4	303.11	7.9	62.24	1.6
Maine	3,865.65	1,303.65	33.7	957.67	24.8	297.50	7.7	48.49	1.3
Maryland	3,716.39	1,335.17	35.9	905.65	24.4	365.50	9.8	64.02	1.7
Massachusetts	4,295.04	1,106.92	25.8	826.99	19.3	221.33	5.2	58.60	1.4
Michigan	3,971.51	1,562.94	39.4	1,081.91	27.2	440.34	11.1	40.69	1.0
Minnesota	4,802.45	1,592.45	33.2	1,121.22	23.3	402.49	8.4	68.74	1.4
Mississippi	3,006.35	1,052.79	35.0	681.73	22.7	314.30	10.5	56.76	1.9
Missouri	2,909.83	1,052.79	36.2	784.10	26.9	230.18	7.9	38.51	1.3
Montana	3,699.85	1,366.02	36.9	965.42	26.1	314.42	8.5	86.17	2.3
Nebraska	3,611.38	1,473.44	40.8	999.19	27.7	427.18	11.8	47.07	1.3
Nevada	4,022.88	1,170.67	29.1	857.19	21.3	287.44	7.1	26.05	0.6
New Hampshire	3,784.82	1,227.49	32.4	902.77	23.9	283.70	7.5	41.02	1.1
New Jersey	4,620.64	1,607.71	34.8	1,271.79	27.5	292.55	6.3	43.37	0.9
New Mexico	4,052.10	1,420.30	35.1	867.96	21.4	501.75	12.4	50.59	1.2
New York	5,912.79	1,665.12	28.2	1,289.81	21.8	307.14	5.2	68.17	1.2
North Carolina	3,327.22	1,235.90	37.1	774.92	23.3	412.61	12.4	48.38	1.5
North Dakota	4,026.44	1,516.13	37.7	862.27	21.4	576.24	14.3	77.62	1.9
Ohio	3,556.27	1,253.43	35.2	887.37	25.0	315.31	8.9	50.74	1.4
Oklahoma	3,178.20	1,224.08	38.5	842.09	26.5	335.55	10.6	46.44	1.5
Oregon	4,095.46	1,478.85	36.1	1,021.77	24.9	406.17	9.9	50.90	1.2
Pennsylvania	3,813.23	1,402.93	36.8	1,033.21	27.1	283.93	7.4	85.79	2.2
Rhode Island	4,494.39	1,337.95	29.8	928.98	20.7	308.88	6.9	100.09	2.2
South Carolina	3,429.30	1,192.27	34.8	796.08	23.2	345.30	10.1	50.90	1.5
South Dakota	3,399.18	1,214.45	35.7	857.34	25.2	294.60	8.7	62.51	1.8
Tennessee	3,070.62	955.86	31.1	622.02	20.3	296.47	9.7	37.37	1.2
Texas	3,426.32	1,338.71	39.1	951.31	27.8	356.04	10.4	31.36	0.9
Utah	3,397.84	1,429.69	42.1	874.29	25.7	501.20	14.8	54.22	1.6
Vermont	3,919.23	1,540.41	39.3	955.41	24.4	481.92	12.3	103.07	2.6
Virginia	3,387.94	1,280.34	37.8	880.16	26.0	337.73	10.0	62.46	1.8
Washington	4,755.34	1,630.78	34.3	1,132.45	23.8	428.07	9.0	70.26	1.5
West Virginia	3,488.25	1,323.61	37.9	933.24	26.8	314.43	9.0	75.94	2.2
Wisconsin	4,238.31	1,590.24	37.5	1,078.02	25.4	450.25	10.6	61.97	1.5
Wyoming	5,111.67	1,873.80	36.7	1,264.73	24.7	536.72	10.5	72.34	1.4

[1] Includes state and local government expenditures for education services, social services and income maintenance, transportation, public safety, environment and housing, governmental administration, interest on general debt, and other general expenditures. Includes intergovernmental expenditure to the federal government.

[2] Includes assistance and subsidies to individuals and private institutions for elementary, secondary, and higher education, as well as miscellaneous education expenditures.

—Not applicable.

NOTE.—Per capita amounts are based on population figures as of July 1, 1993, and are computed on the basis of amounts rounded to the nearest thousand. Because of rounding, details may not add to totals.

SOURCE: U.S. Department of Commerce, Bureau of the Census, unpublished data. (This table was prepared May 1997.)

Table 37.—Gross domestic product, state and local expenditures, personal income, disposable personal income, median family income, and population: 1929 to 1996

Year	Gross domestic product, in billions		State and local expenditures,[1] in millions		Personal income, in billions	Disposable personal income, in billions of chained 1992 dollars	Disposable personal income per capita		Median family income	Total population in thousands	
	Current dollars	Chained 1992 dollars	All general expenditures	Education expenditures			Current dollars	Chained 1992 dollars		Annual averages of quarterly data[2]	As of July 1[3]
1	2	3	4	5	6	7	8	9	10	11	12
1929	$103.8	790.9	—	—	$85.2	$635.3	$680	$5,213	—	—	121,878
1933	56.2	577.3	—	—	46.8	481.6	363	3,831	—	—	125,690
1939	91.9	866.5	—	—	72.8	687.9	539	5,250	—	—	131,028
1940	101.2	941.2	$9,229	$2,638	78.3	734.3	575	5,558	—	—	132,122
1941	126.7	1,101.8	—	—	96.0	845.6	697	6,339	—	—	133,402
1942	161.6	1,308.9	9,190	2,586	123.3	952.8	872	7,065	—	—	134,860
1943	198.3	1,523.0	—	—	151.8	995.8	982	7,282	—	—	136,739
1944	219.7	1,644.7	8,863	2,793	165.7	1,031.3	1,062	7,452	—	—	138,397
1945	223.2	1,626.7	—	—	171.3	1,016.8	1,077	7,267	—	—	139,928
1946	222.6	1,447.7	11,028	3,356	179.0	1,011.0	1,136	7,150	—	—	141,389
1947	244.6	1,430.7	—	—	191.8	974.1	1,185	6,759	$3,031	—	144,126
1948	269.7	1,491.0	17,684	5,379	210.7	1,025.6	1,297	6,994	3,187	—	146,631
1949	267.8	1,479.8	—	—	207.8	1,031.6	1,272	6,915	3,107	—	149,188
1950	294.6	1,611.3	22,787	7,177	229.7	1,124.7	1,382	7,415	3,319	—	151,684
1951	339.7	1,734.0	—	—	258.6	1,157.3	1,492	7,501	3,709	—	154,287
1952	358.6	1,798.7	26,098	8,318	276.0	1,194.8	1,545	7,613	3,890	—	156,954
1953	379.7	1,881.4	27,910	9,390	292.9	1,254.3	1,617	7,861	4,242	—	159,565
1954	381.3	1,868.2	30,701	10,557	255.7	1,270.2	1,625	7,822	4,167	—	162,391
1955	415.1	2,001.1	33,724	11,907	317.3	1,355.6	1,710	8,202	4,418	—	165,275
1956	438.0	2,040.2	36,711	13,220	340.5	1,418.5	1,794	8,432	4,780	—	168,221
1957	461.0	2,078.5	40,375	14,134	359.6	1,452.6	1,859	8,481	4,966	—	171,274
1958	467.3	2,057.5	44,851	15,919	370.3	1,466.4	1,892	8,421	5,087	—	174,882
1959	507.2	2,210.2	48,887	17,283	394.4	1,533.9	1,975	8,660	5,417	177,073	177,830
1960	526.6	2,262.9	51,876	18,719	412.5	1,569.2	2,013	8,681	5,620	180,760	180,671
1961	544.8	2,314.3	56,201	20,574	430.0	1,619.4	2,066	8,814	5,735	183,742	183,691
1962	585.2	2,454.8	60,206	22,216	457.0	1,697.5	2,156	9,098	5,956	186,590	186,538
1963	617.4	2,559.4	63,977	23,729	480.0	1,759.3	2,229	9,294	6,249	189,300	189,242
1964	663.0	2,708.4	69,302	26,286	514.5	1,885.8	2,389	9,825	6,569	191,927	191,889
1965	719.1	2,881.1	74,678	28,563	556.7	2,003.9	2,546	10,311	6,957	194,347	194,303
1966	787.8	3,069.2	82,843	33,287	605.7	2,110.6	2,720	10,735	7,532	196,599	196,560
1967	833.6	3,147.2	93,350	37,919	650.7	2,202.3	2,882	11,081	7,933	198,752	198,712
1968	910.6	3,293.9	102,411	41,158	714.5	2,302.1	3,101	11,468	8,632	200,745	200,706
1969	982.2	3,393.6	116,728	47,238	779.3	2,377.2	3,302	11,726	9,433	202,736	202,677
1970	1,035.6	3,397.6	131,332	52,718	837.1	2,469.0	3,550	12,039	9,867	205,089	205,052
1971	1,125.4	3,510.0	150,674	59,413	900.2	2,568.3	3,811	12,366	10,285	207,692	207,661
1972	1,237.3	3,702.3	168,550	65,814	988.8	2,685.7	4,082	12,794	11,116	209,924	209,896
1973	1,382.6	3,916.3	181,357	69,714	1,107.5	2,875.2	4,562	13,566	12,051	211,939	211,909
1974	1,496.9	3,891.2	198,959	75,833	1,215.9	2,854.2	4,941	13,344	12,902	213,898	213,854
1975	1,630.6	3,873.9	230,721	87,858	1,319.0	2,903.6	5,383	13,444	13,719	215,981	215,973
1976	1,819.0	4,082.9	256,731	97,216	1,459.4	3,017.6	5,856	13,837	14,958	218,086	218,035
1977	2,026.9	4,273.6	274,215	102,780	1,616.1	3,115.4	6,383	14,142	16,009	220,289	220,239
1978	2,291.4	4,503.0	296,983	110,758	1,825.9	3,276.0	7,123	14,715	17,640	222,629	222,585
1979	2,557.5	4,630.6	327,517	119,448	2,055.8	3,365.5	7,888	14,951	19,587	225,106	225,055
1980	2,784.2	4,615.0	369,086	133,211	2,293.0	3,385.7	8,697	14,867	21,023	227,726	227,726
1981	3,115.9	4,720.7	407,449	145,784	2,568.5	3,464.9	9,601	15,064	22,388	230,008	229,966
1982	3,242.1	4,620.3	436,896	154,282	2,727.2	3,495.6	10,145	15,053	23,433	232,218	232,188
1983	3,514.5	4,803.7	466,421	163,876	2,900.8	3,592.8	10,803	15,332	24,674	234,332	234,307
1984	3,902.4	5,140.1	505,008	176,108	3,215.3	3,855.4	11,929	16,309	26,433	236,394	236,348
1985	4,180.7	5,323.5	553,899	192,686	3,449.8	3,972.0	12,629	16,654	27,735	238,506	238,466
1986	4,422.2	5,487.7	605,623	210,819	3,658.4	4,101.0	13,289	17,039	29,458	240,682	240,651
1987	4,692.3	5,649.5	657,134	226,619	3,888.7	4,168.2	13,896	17,164	[4]30,970	242,842	242,804
1988	5,049.6	5,865.2	704,921	242,683	4,184.6	4,332.1	14,905	17,678	[4]32,191	245,061	245,021
1989	5,438.7	6,062.0	762,360	263,898	4,501.0	4,416.8	15,790	17,854	[4]34,213	247,387	247,342
1990	5,743.8	6,136.3	834,818	288,148	4,804.2	4,498.2	16,721	17,996	[4]35,353	249,956	249,913
1991	5,916.7	6,079.4	908,108	309,302	4,981.6	4,500.0	17,242	17,809	[4]35,939	252,680	252,650
1992	6,244.4	6,244.4	981,253	324,652	5,277.2	4,626.7	18,113	18,113	[4]36,573	255,432	255,419
1993	6,553.0	6,386.1	1,027,488	342,595	5,495.6	4,682.0	18,615	18,136	[4]36,959	258,159	258,137
1994	6,935.7	6,608.4	—	—	5,762.0	4,786.7	19,298	18,362	[4]38,782	260,681	260,660
1995	7,253.8	6,742.2	—	—	6,112.4	4,943.3	20,214	18,789	[4]40,611	263,090	263,034
1996	7,576.1	6,906.8	—	—	6,449.5	5,086.0	21,040	19,158	—	265,482	265,455

[1] Data for years prior to 1963 include expenditures for government fiscal years ending during that particular calendar year. Data for 1963 and later years are the aggregations of expenditures for government fiscal years which ended on June 30 of the stated year. General expenditures exclude expenditures of publicly owned utilities and liquor stores, and of insurance-trust activities. Intergovernmental payments between state and local governments are excluded. Payments to the federal government are included.
[2] Population of the United States including Armed Forces overseas; includes Alaska and Hawaii beginning 1960. Quarterly data are averages for the period.
[3] Population of the United States including Armed Forces overseas; includes Alaska and Hawaii beginning 1958. Includes revisions based on the 1990 Census.
[4] Revised methodology.
—Data not available.

NOTE.—Gross domestic product data are adjusted by the GDP chained weight price deflator. Personal income data are adjusted by the personal consumption deflator. Some data have been revised from previously published figures.

SOURCE: Executive Office of the President, Economic Report of the President, February 1997, and Economic Indicators, May 1997; and U.S. Department of Commerce, Bureau of the Census, Consumer Income, Series P-60, No. 174; and Bureau of Economic Analysis, Survey of Current Business. (This table was prepared July 1997.)

ALL LEVELS: FINANCES 41

Table 38.—Gross domestic product deflator, Consumer Price Index, education price indexes, and federal budget composite deflator: 1919 to 1997

Calendar year			School year						Federal fiscal year	
Year	Gross domestic product chain weight deflator	Consumer Price Index [1]	Year	Consumer Price Index [2]	Elementary/ Secondary Price Index	Higher Education Price Index	Research and Development Index	Academic Library Operations Index	Year	Federal budget composite deflator
1	2	3	4	5	6	7	8	9	10	11
1919	—	17.3	1919–20	19.1	—	—	—	—	1919	—
1929	—	17.1	1929–30	17.1	—	—	—	—	1929	—
1934	—	13.4	1934–35	13.6	—	—	—	—	1934	—
1939	—	13.9	1939–40	14.0	—	—	—	—	1939	—
1940	—	14.0	1940–41	14.2	—	—	—	—	1940	0.0867
1941	—	14.7	1941–42	15.6	—	—	—	—	1941	0.0909
1942	—	16.3	1942–43	16.9	—	—	—	—	1942	0.1052
1943	—	17.3	1943–44	17.4	—	—	—	—	1943	0.1174
1944	—	17.6	1944–45	17.8	—	—	—	—	1944	0.1106
1945	—	18.0	1945–46	18.2	—	—	—	—	1945	0.1075
1946	—	19.5	1946–47	21.2	—	—	—	—	1946	0.1044
1947	—	22.3	1947–48	23.3	—	—	—	—	1947	0.1249
1948	—	24.1	1948–49	24.1	—	—	—	—	1948	0.1280
1949	—	23.8	1949–50	23.7	—	—	—	—	1949	0.1286
1950	—	24.1	1950–51	25.1	—	—	—	—	1950	0.1333
1951	—	26.0	1951–52	26.3	—	—	—	—	1951	0.1298
1952	—	26.5	1952–53	26.7	—	—	—	—	1952	0.1335
1953	—	26.7	1953–54	26.9	—	—	—	—	1953	0.1440
1954	—	26.9	1954–55	26.8	—	—	—	—	1954	0.1493
1955	—	26.8	1955–56	26.9	—	—	—	—	1955	0.1518
1956	—	27.2	1956–57	27.7	—	—	—	—	1956	0.1602
1957	—	28.1	1957–58	28.6	—	—	—	—	1957	0.1702
1958	—	28.9	1958–59	29.0	—	—	—	—	1958	0.1799
1959	23.0	29.1	1959–60	29.4	—	—	—	—	1959	0.1917
1960	23.3	29.6	1960–61	29.8	—	25.6	26.7	—	1960	0.2012
1961	23.6	29.9	1961–62	30.1	—	26.5	27.5	—	1961	0.2062
1962	23.9	30.2	1962–63	30.4	—	27.6	28.5	—	1962	0.2087
1963	24.2	30.6	1963–64	30.8	—	28.6	29.5	—	1963	0.2164
1964	24.6	31.0	1964–65	31.2	—	29.8	30.7	—	1964	0.2199
1965	25.0	31.5	1965–66	31.9	—	31.3	32.0	—	1965	0.2227
1966	25.7	32.4	1966–67	32.9	—	32.9	33.8	—	1966	0.2295
1967	26.6	33.4	1967–68	34.0	—	34.9	35.7	—	1967	0.2368
1968	27.7	34.8	1968–69	35.7	—	37.1	38.0	—	1968	0.2469
1969	29.0	36.7	1969–70	37.8	—	39.5	40.3	—	1969	0.2606
1970	30.6	38.8	1970–71	39.7	—	42.1	42.7	—	1970	0.2765
1971	32.1	40.5	1971–72	41.2	—	44.3	45.0	—	1971	0.2939
1972	33.5	41.8	1972–73	42.8	—	46.7	47.1	—	1972	0.3123
1973	35.4	44.4	1973–74	46.6	—	49.9	50.1	—	1973	0.3280
1974	38.5	49.3	1974–75	51.8	52.7	54.3	54.8	—	1974	0.3547
1975	42.2	53.8	1975–76	55.5	57.3	57.8	59.0	57.3	1975	0.4199
1976	44.6	56.9	1976–77	58.7	60.9	61.5	62.7	61.6	1976	0.4199
1977	47.5	60.6	1977–78	62.6	64.8	65.7	66.8	65.8	1977	0.4540
1978	50.9	65.2	1978–79	68.5	70.5	70.5	71.7	71.4	1978	0.4857
1979	55.3	72.6	1979–80	77.6	76.6	77.5	78.3	78.5	1979	0.5267
1980	60.4	82.4	1980–81	86.6	85.9	85.8	86.6	86.1	1980	0.5819
1981	66.1	90.9	1981–82	94.1	93.7	93.9	94.0	94.0	1981	0.6421
1982	70.2	96.5	1982–83	98.2	100.0	100.0	100.0	100.0	1982	0.6865
1983	73.2	99.6	1983–84	101.8	105.0	104.8	104.3	105.1	1983	0.7195
1984	75.9	103.9	1984–85	105.8	112.0	110.8	109.8	111.2	1984	0.7545
1985	78.6	107.6	1985–86	108.8	118.5	116.3	115.2	117.6	1985	0.7829
1986	80.6	109.6	1986–87	111.2	123.3	120.9	120.0	124.2	1986	0.8050
1987	83.1	113.6	1987–88	115.8	129.8	126.1	126.8	130.0	1987	0.8273
1988	86.1	118.3	1988–89	121.2	136.3	132.8	132.1	138.6	1988	0.8546
1989	89.7	124.0	1989–90	127.0	144.3	140.8	139.0	147.4	1989	0.8902
1990	93.6	130.7	1990–91	133.9	152.3	148.2	145.8	155.7	1990	0.9257
1991	97.3	136.2	1991–92	138.2	158.5	153.4	150.5	163.3	1991	0.9695
1992	100.0	140.3	1992–93	142.5	162.2	157.9	155.2	169.7	1992	1.0000
1993	102.6	144.5	1993–94	146.2	167.1	163.3	160.2	176.0	1993	1.0252
1994	105.0	148.2	1994–95	150.4	170.6	168.2	165.4	183.3	1994	1.0492
1995	107.6	152.4	1995–96	154.5	—	—	—	—	1995	1.0745
1996	109.7	156.9	1996–97	158.9	—	—	—	—	1996	1.0991
1997	—	—	1997–98	—	—	—	—	—	1997	1.1283

[1] Index for urban wage earners and clerical workers through 1977; 1978 and later figures are for all urban consumers.
[2] Consumer Price Index adjusted to a school-year basis (July through June).
—Data not available.

NOTE.—Some data have been revised from previously published figures.

SOURCE: Council of Economic Advisers, *Economic Indicators*, February 1991 and April 1997, and *Economic Report of the President*, February 1996; U.S. Department of Labor, Bureau of Labor Statistics, Consumer Price Index; Research Associates of Washington, "Inflation Measures for Schools and Colleges, 1990 Update," and unpublished data; and U.S. Office of Management and Budget, *Budget of the U.S. Government, Fiscal Year 1997*. (This table was prepared June 1997.)

CHAPTER 2
Elementary and Secondary Education

This chapter contains a variety of statistics on public and private elementary and secondary education. Data are presented for enrollments, teachers, schools, student performance, graduates, and expenditures. These data are derived from surveys conducted by the National Center for Education Statistics (NCES) and other public and private organizations. The variety of information provided ranges from simple counts of students and schools, to opinions of teachers and students concerning the state of education today.

Enrollments

Combined public elementary and secondary school enrollments increased by 14 percent from 1986 to 1996, but examined separately, enrollment at the elementary and secondary levels exhibited different patterns. Between 1986 and 1996, public elementary enrollment rose by 20 percent, while secondary enrollment increased by 4 percent. Secondary enrollment declined in most years during this period (tables 3 and 40).

Preprimary education enrollment has grown substantially. Between 1986 and 1996, preprimary enrollment of 3- to 5-year-olds rose by 27 percent. An important feature of the increasing participation of young children in preprimary schools is the increasing proportion in full-day programs. In 1996 about 47 percent of the children attended school all day compared with 38 percent in 1986 (table 46).

Slightly increasing numbers and proportions of children are being served in programs for the disabled. During the 1980–81 school year, 10 percent of students were served in these programs compared with 12 percent in 1995–96. Much of the rise since 1980–81 may be attributed to the increasing proportion of children identified as learning disabled, which rose from 4 percent of enrollment in 1980–81 to 6 percent of enrollment in 1995–96 (table 52).

Tuition at Private Schools

The average full tuition (highest tuition charged) for private schools was $3,116 in 1993–94. Schools with religious orientation charged significantly lower tuition than nonsectarian schools. Students at Catholic schools paid $2,178 on average and students at schools with other religious orientations paid $2,915 on average, compared with the average tuition of $6,631 for nonsectarian private schools. Mean tuition paid for private elementary school students was lower than that paid by secondary and combined elementary/secondary schools' students, with Catholic school students paying $1,628. Students at elementary schools with other religious orientations paid $2,606, and students at nonsectarian schools paid $4,693. Mean tuition paid for private secondary school students was substantially higher than that for private elementary school students, averaging $3,643 at Catholic schools, $5,261 at other religiously oriented schools, and $9,525 at nonsectarian schools (table 61).

Teachers and Other School Staff

During the 1970s and early 1980s, public school enrollment decreased, while the number of teachers rose. As a result, the pupil/teacher ratio fell from 22.3 in 1970 to 17.9 in 1985. After 1985, the number of pupils per teacher continued downward, reaching 17.2 in 1990. Between 1990 and 1997, enrollment rose at about the same rate as the number of teachers, and the pupil-teacher ratio was estimated at 17.3 in fall 1997 (table 64).

In 1993–94, 73 percent of public school teachers were women, 33 percent were under 40, and more than 47 percent had a master's degree or above. By comparison, about 75 percent of the 378,000 full-time and part-time private school teachers were women. About 42 percent of the private school teachers were under age 40, and 34 percent had a master's or higher degree (table 67).

Principals tended to be older and have higher level credentials than teachers. Also, they were more likely to be male. About 7 percent of public school principals in 1993–94 were under age 40 and 99 percent had a master's degree or above. About 35 percent of the principals were women (table 87).

In general, public school teachers have higher salaries than private school teachers. In 1993–94, the average base salary for public school teachers was $34,153, compared with $21,968 for private school teachers (table 73). The average salary for public school teachers grew slowly during the 1990s, reaching $38,509 in 1996–97. After adjustment for inflation, teachers' salaries rose 1.5 percent between 1986–87 and 1996–97 (table 77).

The number of nonteaching staff employed by public schools grew at a faster rate than the number of pupils and teachers in the 1970s. During the 1970s, the proportion of the total staff who were teachers declined from 60 percent to 52 percent in fall 1980. In the 1980s and early 1990s, the number of teachers grew at about the same rate as other public school staff. In 1980, there were 9.8 pupils per staff member (total staff) compared with 9.0 pupils per staff member in 1995. In 1993–94, the number of pupils per staff member at private schools was 9.3 (tables 60 and 82).

Schools

Over the past decades, the trend to consolidate small schools has brought a large decline in the total number of public schools in the United States. In 1930, there were more than 262,000 public schools, compared with around 87,000 today. But this number has grown in recent years, with an increase of more than 2,600 schools between 1992–93 and 1995–96 (table 89).

The shift in structure of public school systems toward middle schools (grades 4, 5, or 6 to 6, 7, or 8) is continuing. The number of elementary schools rose by 7 percent to 61,000 between 1984–85 and 1995–96, but middle schools accounted for a disproportionate share of this increase, rising by 48 percent. Meanwhile, the number of junior high schools (grades 7 to 8 and 7 to 9) declined by 37 percent (table 94).

Elementary enrollment has risen faster than the number of schools, with the average elementary school size increasing as a result. Schools tend to be smaller in predominantly rural states, such as Nebraska, South Dakota, Montana, and North Dakota, and larger in states with large urban populations, such as California, Hawaii, Georgia, and Florida (tables 94, 96, 97, and 98).

Completions and Achievement

The dropout rate among 16- to 24-year-olds (which counts GED recipients and special program completers as graduates) suggests some improvements have been made over the past quarter century. Between 1968 and 1990, the dropout rate for 16- to 24-year-olds fell from 16.2 percent to 12.1 percent. The dropout rate for 1996 was 11.1, which is slightly lower than the 1990 figure. The dropout rate statistic is based on the civilian noninstitutionalized population, which excludes persons in prisons and persons not living in households (table 103). Comparisons of the number of public and private high school graduates with the 17-year-old population suggest that the proportion of young people earning regular high school diplomas has not increased over the past 20 years. At its highest point in 1968–69, there were 77 graduates for every 100 persons 17 years of age. This ratio declined during the 1970s, falling to 71 in 1979–80. The ratio has fluctuated since then, reaching 70 in 1996–97. This indicator is not a graduation rate, however, because many students complete their high school education through alternative programs, such as night schools and the General Educational Development (GED) program (table 99).

Student achievement has improved in a number of areas. An overall increase was seen in reading proficiency scores for 9- and 13-year-olds since 1971, with 17-year-olds scoring about the same in 1996 as in 1971. After significant gains during the 1970s, 9-year-old reading proficiency fell during the 1980s, but the 1996 score remained above the 1971 level. The increase in reading ability was reflected by higher average proficiencies in other subjects for 9- and 13-year-old students. Significant gaps in performance continue to exist between racial/ethnic subgroups and between male and female students. Gender gaps favoring female students in reading were essentially the same in 1996 as in the 1971 (table 107).

The results of assessments in average writing achievement from 1984 to 1996 reveal a shift at grades 4 and 8. After declining between 1984 and 1990, average performance at grade 8 increased, and by 1996 had again returned to the earlier level. Also, at grade 4 there was an increase in performance between 1990 and 1996, countering downward fluctuations in the 1980s, so that performance was essentially unchanged between 1984 and 1996. Overall grade 11 writing performance declined between 1984 and 1996 (table 113).

Results from national assessments of mathematics achievement indicated a significant improvement at ages 9 and 13, between 1973 and 1996. Performance of 17-year-olds declined between 1973 and 1982, but an upturn during the following decade returned average performance back up to 1973 levels. For 9-, 13-, and 17-year-olds, there were increases in average mathematics proficiency between 1986 and 1996, including increases among black and Hispanic 9- and 17-year-olds. Gender gaps in mathematics among 17-year-olds narrowed between 1973 and 1996. However, the gap among 9- and 13-year-olds favoring females in 1973 reversed, and in 1996 the gap favored males (table 118).

Average science proficiency increased for 9-, 13-, and 17-year-old black students between 1970 and 1996. Although the average science proficiency of white students at all three age groups (ages 9, 13, and 17) remained significantly higher than the average proficiencies of black and Hispanic students, there was some evidence of gaps narrowing between 1970 and 1996. The performance gap between white and black students decreased for 9-year-olds and 13-year-olds between 1970 and 1996, but the gaps for 17-year-olds remained about the same. The performance gaps between white and Hispanic 9- and 17-year-olds remained about the same in 1996 as they were in 1977 (table 126). Gender gaps favoring 9-year-old and 13-year-old males in science did not narrow significantly between 1970 and 1996, but there was a narrowing of the gap between 17-year-old males and females (table 126).

The Scholastic Assessment Test (SAT, formerly known as the Scholastic Aptitude Test) was not designed as an indicator of student achievement, but rather to help predict how well students will do in college. Between 1986–87 and 1996–97, mathematics SAT scores increased by 10 points, while verbal scores fell by 2 points (table 129).

Over the past 12 years, the average number of science and mathematics courses completed by public high school graduates increased substantially. The mean number of mathematics courses (Carnegie units) completed in high school rose from 2.6 in 1982 to 3.4 in 1994, and the number of science courses rose from 2.2 to 3.0. The average number of courses in vocational-technical areas completed by all high school graduates dropped gradually, from 4.7 units in 1982 to 3.9 units in 1994. As a result of the increased academic course load, the proportion of students completing the recommendations of the National Commission on Excellence (4 units of English, 3 units of social studies, 3 units of science, 3 units of mathematics, and .5 units of computer science) rose from 3 percent in 1982 to 32 percent in 1994 (tables 133, 136, and 139).

Drugs and Violence

Twelfth-grade students at public schools were less likely to feel safe at school and were more likely to report fights between racial/ethnic groups and gangs at school than students at Catholic and other private schools. About 10 percent of all 1992 high school seniors reported that they did not feel safe at school and 23 percent reported that there were often fights between different racial/ethnic groups (table 142). The proportion of public and private high school seniors who reported ever using an illicit drug rose from 55 percent in 1975 to 66 percent in 1981. After 1981, the proportion of seniors who had ever used drugs fell. After reaching 41 percent in 1992, the proportion rose again to 51 percent in 1996. Also, the proportion of high school seniors who had ever used cocaine fell from 17 percent in 1985 to 7 percent in 1996. Alcohol remained the most often used drug. The proportion of seniors who had used alcohol within the previous 30 days declined from 72 percent in 1980 to 51 percent in 1996 (table 150).

Resources and Expenditures

The state share of revenues for public elementary and secondary schools had grown steadily for many decades, but this trend began to reverse in the late 1980s. Between 1986–87 and 1994–95, the state share declined from 49.7 percent of all revenues to 46.8 percent, while the local share rose from 43.9 percent to 46.4 percent. The federal share also rose slightly over this period, from 6.4 percent to 6.8 percent (table 158).

The expenditure per student in public schools rose significantly during the late 1980s, but increased more slowly during the first part of the 1990s. Between 1985–86 and 1990–91, current expenditures per student in average daily attendance grew 14 percent, after adjustment for inflation. From 1990–91 to 1996–97, expenditures per student grew by 5 percent. In 1996–97, the estimated current expenditure per student in average daily attendance was $6,564 (table 169).

Figure 7.-Preprimary enrollment of 3- to 5-year-olds, by attendance status: October 1970 to October 1996

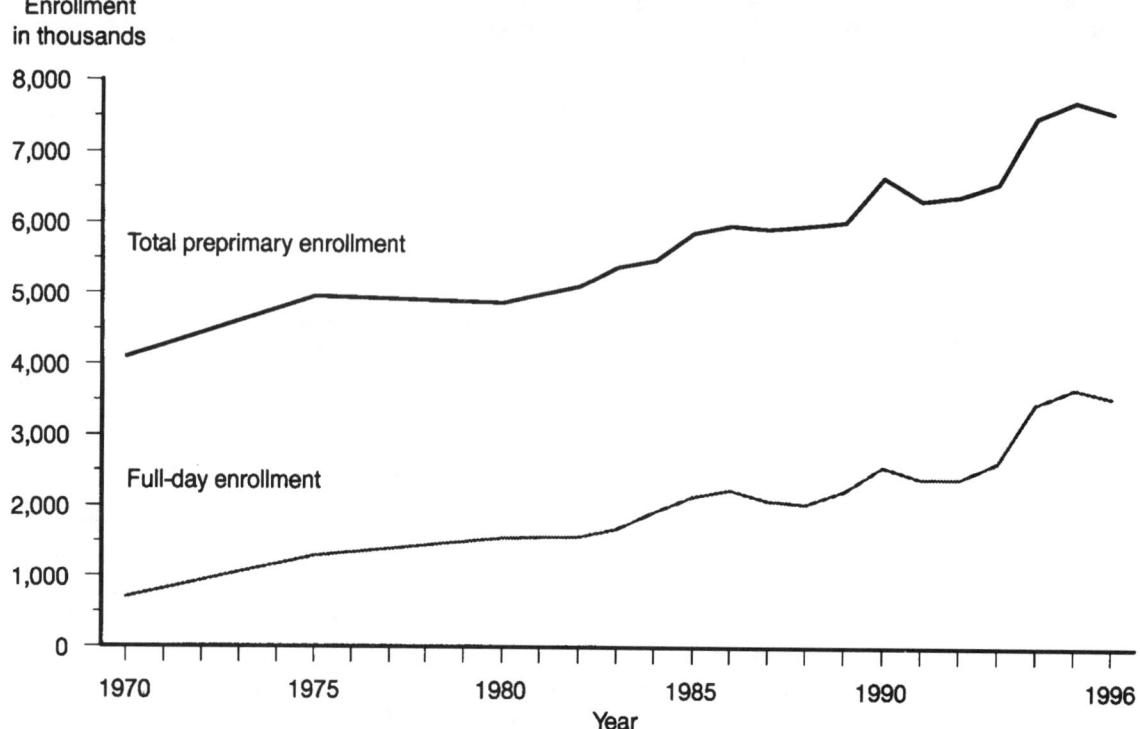

NOTE.—Data for 1994, 1995, and 1996 were collected using new procedures and may not be comparable with figures for earlier years.

SOURCE: U.S. Department of Education, National Center for Education Statistics, *Preprimary Enrollment*, various years; and U.S. Department of Commerce, Bureau of the Census, Current Population Survey, unpublished data.

ELEMENTARY AND SECONDARY EDUCATION 47

Figure 8.—Enrollment, number of teachers, pupil/teacher ratios, and expenditures in public schools: 1960–61 to 1996–97

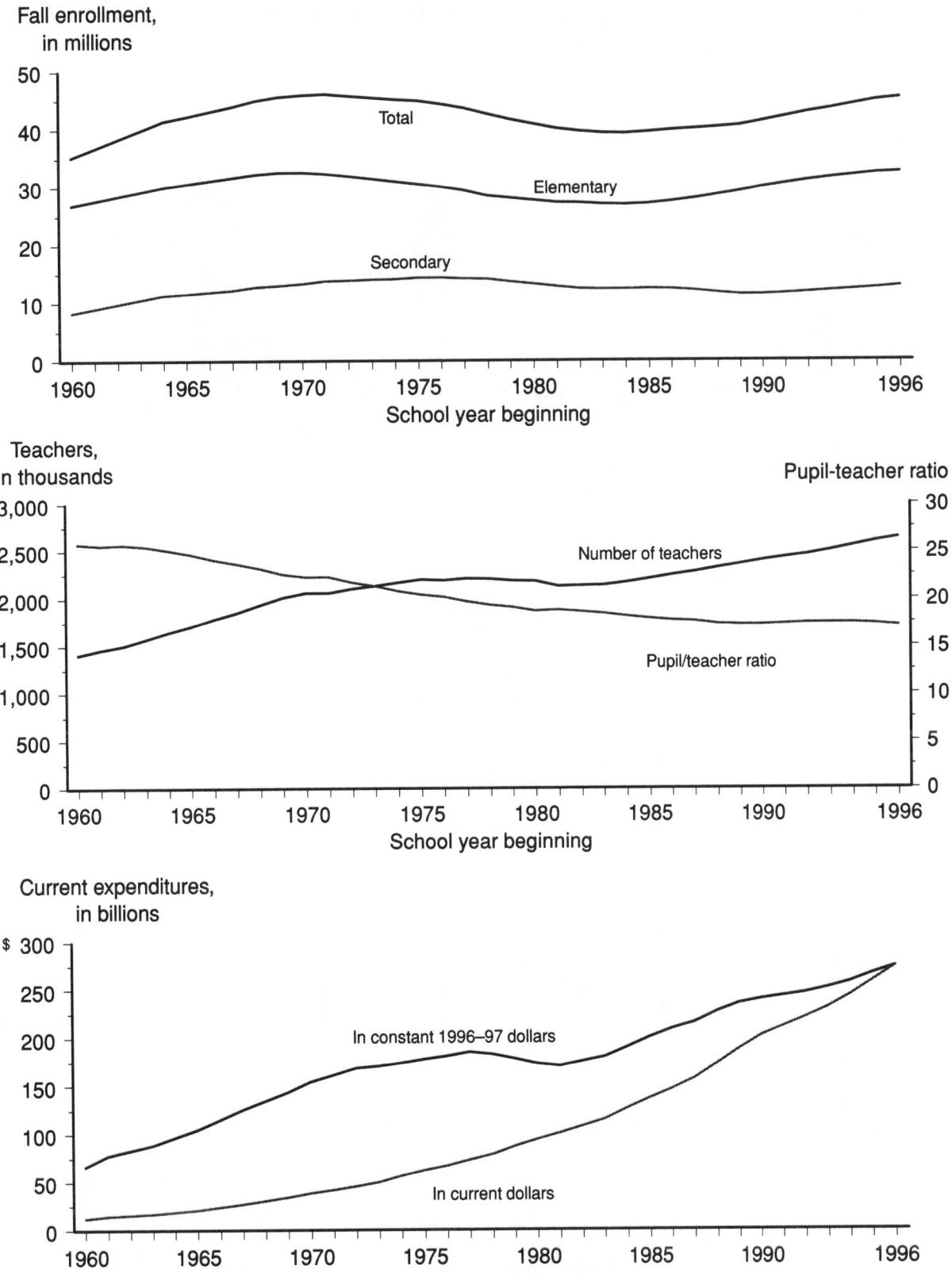

SOURCE: U.S. Department of Education, National Center for Education Statistics, *Statistics of State School Systems; Statistics of Public Elementary and Secondary School Systems; Revenues and Expenditures for Public Elementary and Secondary Education;* and Common Core of Data surveys.

48 ELEMENTARY AND SECONDARY EDUCATION

Figure 9.–Percentage change in public elementary and secondary enrollment, by state: Fall 1991 to fall 1996

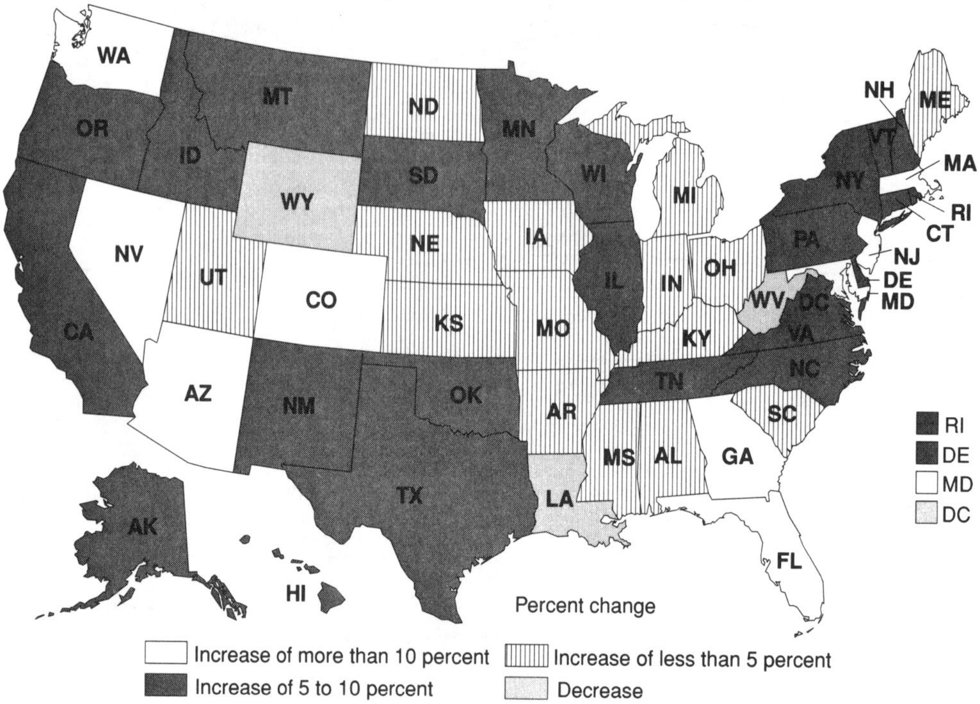

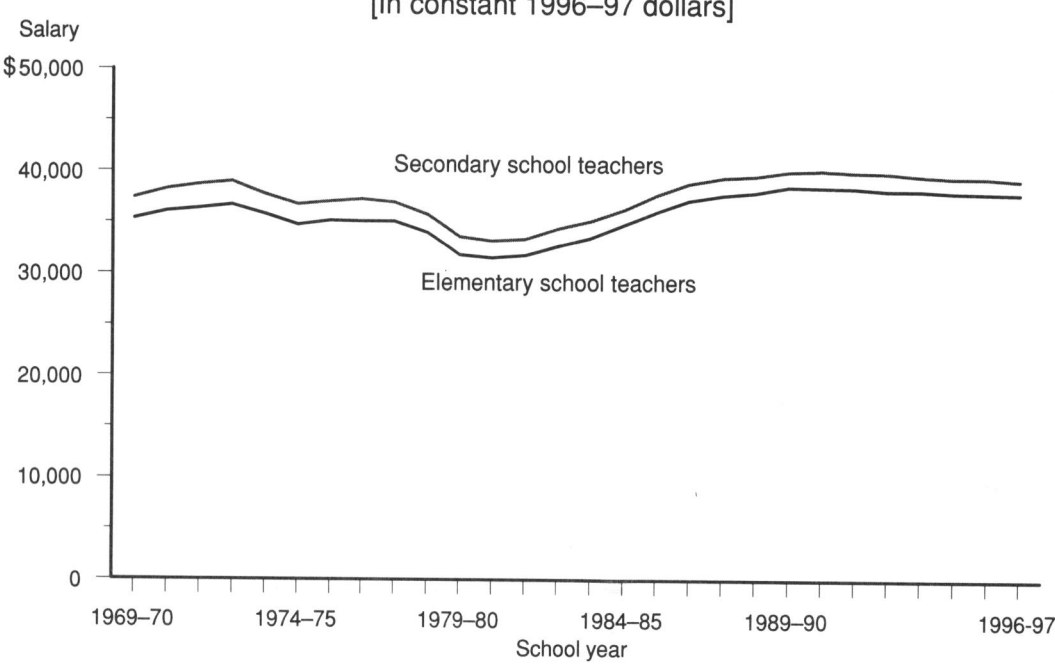

Percent change

☐ Increase of more than 10 percent   ⦀ Increase of less than 5 percent
■ Increase of 5 to 10 percent   ▧ Decrease

SOURCE: U.S. Department of Education, National Center for Education Statistics, Common Core of Data surveys.

Figure 10.–Average annual salary for public elementary and secondary school teachers: 1969–70 to 1996–97
[In constant 1996–97 dollars]

SOURCE: National Education Association, *Estimates of School Statistics*, latest edition 1996-97. Copyright 1997 by the National Education Association. (All rights reserved.)

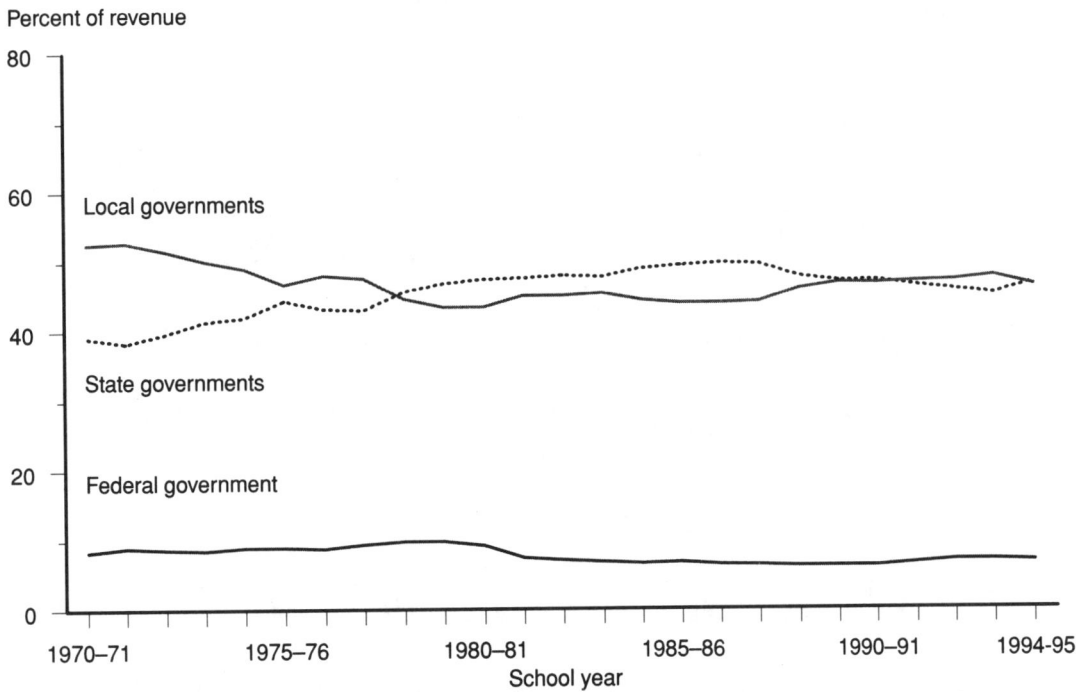

Figure 11.-Sources of revenue for public elementary and secondary schools: 1970–71 to 1994-95

SOURCE: U.S. Department of Education, National Center for Education Statistics, *Statistics of State School Systems; Revenues and Expenditures for Public Elementary and Secondary Education;* and Common Core of Data surveys.

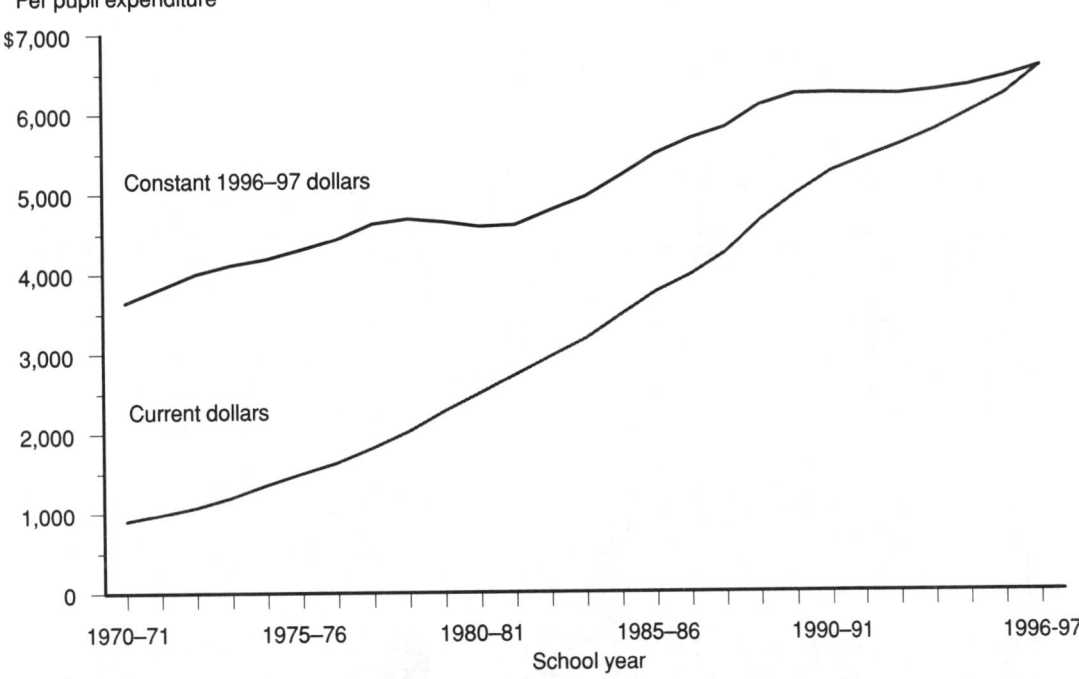

Figure 12.-Current expenditure per pupil in average daily attendance in public elementary and secondary schools: 1970-71 to 1996–97

SOURCE: U.S. Department of Education, National Center for Education Statistics, *Statistics of State School Systems; Revenues and Expenditures for Public Elementary and Secondary Education;* and Common Core of Data surveys.

Table 39.—Historical summary of public elementary and secondary school statistics: 1869–70 to 1994–95

Item	1869–70	1879–80	1889–90	1899–1900	1909–10	1919–20	1929–30	1939–40	1949–50	1959–60	1969–70	1979–80	1989–90	1990–91	1993–94	1994–95
1	2	3	4	5	6	7	8	9	10	11	12	13	14	15	16	17
Population, pupils, and instructional staff																
Total population,[1] in thousands	38,558	50,156	62,622	75,995	90,490	104,514	121,878	131,028	149,188	177,830	201,385	224,567	246,819	249,402	257,783	260,372
Population aged 5–17 years,[1] in thousands	11,683	15,066	18,473	21,573	24,011	27,571	31,414	30,151	30,223	43,881	52,386	48,041	44,947	45,306	47,419	48,155
Percent of total population 5–17	30.3	30.0	29.5	28.4	26.5	26.4	25.8	23.0	20.3	24.7	26.0	21.4	18.2	18.2	18.4	18.5
Total enrollment in elementary and secondary schools, in thousands[2]	[3]7,562	9,867	12,723	15,503	17,814	21,578	25,678	25,434	25,112	36,087	45,550	41,651	40,543	41,217	43,465	44,111
Kindergarten and grades 1–8, in thousands	[3]7,481	9,757	12,520	14,984	16,899	19,378	21,279	18,833	19,387	27,602	32,513	28,034	29,152	29,878	31,504	31,898
Grades 9–12, in thousands	80	110	203	519	915	2,200	4,399	6,601	5,725	8,485	13,037	13,616	11,390	11,338	11,961	12,213
Enrollment as a percent of total population	[3]19.6	19.7	20.3	20.4	19.7	20.6	21.1	19.4	16.8	20.3	22.6	18.5	16.4	16.5	16.9	16.9
Enrollment as a percent of 5- to 17-year-olds	[3]64.7	65.5	68.9	71.9	74.2	78.3	81.7	84.4	83.1	82.2	87.0	86.7	90.2	91.0	91.7	91.6
Percent of total enrollment in high schools (grades 9–12 and postgraduate)	[3]1.1	1.1	1.6	3.3	5.1	10.2	17.1	26.0	22.8	23.5	28.6	32.7	28.1	27.5	27.5	27.7
High school graduates, in thousands	—	—	22	62	111	231	592	1,143	1,063	1,627	2,589	2,748	2,320	2,235	2,221	2,274
Average daily attendance, in thousands	4,077	6,144	8,154	10,633	12,827	16,150	21,265	22,042	22,284	32,477	41,934	38,289	37,799	38,427	40,146	40,721
Total number of days attended by pupils enrolled, in millions	539	801	1,098	1,535	2,011	2,615	3,673	3,858	3,964	5,782	7,501	[4]6,835	—	—	—	—
Percent of enrolled pupils attending daily	59.3	62.3	64.1	68.6	72.1	74.8	82.8	86.7	88.7	90.0	90.4	[4]90.1	—	—	—	—
Average length of school term, in days	132.2	130.3	134.7	144.3	157.5	161.9	172.7	175.0	177.9	178.0	178.9	[4]178.5	—	—	—	—
Average number of days attended per pupil	78.4	81.1	86.3	99.0	113	121.2	143	151.7	157.9	160.2	161.7	[4]160.8	—	—	—	—
Total instructional staff, in thousands	—	—	—	—	—	—	—	—	963	1,457	2,286	2,406	2,986	3,051	3,209	3,281
Supervisors, in thousands	—	—	—	—	—	—	7	5	—	—	—	—	—	—	—	—
Principals, in thousands	—	—	—	—	—	—	31	32	43	64	91	106	126	127	121	120
Teachers, librarians, and other nonsupervisory instructional staff,[5] in thousands	201	287	364	423	523	657	843	875	920	1,393	2,195	2,300	2,860	2,924	3,088	3,161
Men, in thousands	78	123	126	127	110	93	140	195	196	404	[4]711	[4]782	—	—	—	—
Women, in thousands	123	164	238	296	413	585	703	681	724	989	[4]1,484	[4]1,518	—	—	—	—
Percent men	38.7	42.8	34.5	29.9	21.1	14.1	16.6	22.2	21.3	29.0	[4]32.4	[4]34.0	—	—	—	—
Finance												Amounts in millions of current dollars				
Total revenue receipts	—	—	$143	$220	$433	$970	$2,089	$2,261	$5,437	$14,747	$40,267	$96,881	$208,548	$223,341	$260,159	$273,138
Federal government	—	—	—	—	—	2	7	40	156	652	3,220	9,504	12,701	13,776	18,341	18,582
State governments	—	—	—	—	—	160	354	684	2,166	5,768	16,063	45,349	98,239	105,325	117,474	127,720
Local sources, including intermediate	—	—	—	—	—	808	1,728	1,536	3,116	8,327	20,985	42,029	97,608	104,240	124,344	126,837
Percent of revenue receipts from																
Federal government	—	—	—	—	—	0.3	0.4	1.8	2.9	4.4	8.0	9.8	6.1	6.2	7.1	6.8
State governments	—	—	—	—	—	16.5	16.9	30.3	39.8	39.1	39.9	46.8	47.1	47.2	45.2	46.8
Local sources, including intermediate	—	—	—	—	—	83.2	82.7	68.0	57.3	56.5	52.1	43.4	46.8	46.7	47.8	46.4
Total expenditures for public schools	$63	$78	$141	$215	$426	$1,036	$2,317	$2,344	$5,838	$15,613	$40,683	$95,962	$212,770	$229,430	$265,307	$278,966
Current expenditures[6]	—	—	114	180	356	861	1,844	1,942	4,687	12,329	34,218	[7]86,984	[7]188,229	[7]202,038	[7]231,543	[7]243,845
Capital outlay[8]	—	—	26	35	70	154	371	258	1,014	2,662	4,659	6,506	19,771	19,771	23,747	24,454
Interest on school debt	—	—	—	—	—	18	93	131	101	490	1,171	1,874	3,776	4,325	5,335	5,519
Other current expenditures[9]	—	—	—	—	—	3	10	13	36	133	636	[10]598	2,983	3,296	4,682	5,149
Percent of total expenditures devoted to:																
Current expenditures[6]	—	—	81.3	83.5	83.6	83.1	79.6	82.8	80.3	[7]79.0	[7]84.1	[7]90.6	[7]88.5	[7]88.1	[7]87.3	[7]87.4
Capital outlay[8]	—	—	18.7	16.5	16.4	14.8	16.0	11.0	17.4	17.0	11.5	6.8	8.4	8.6	9.0	8.8
Interest on school debt	—	—	—	—	—	4.0	4.0	5.6	1.7	3.1	2.9	2.0	1.8	1.9	2.0	2.0
Other current expenditures[9]	—	—	—	—	—	0.3	0.4	0.6	0.6	0.8	1.6	[10]0.6	1.4	1.4	1.8	1.8

ELEMENTARY AND SECONDARY EDUCATION: ENROLLMENT 51

Table 39.—Historical summary of public elementary and secondary school statistics: 1869–70 to 1994–95—Continued

Item	1869–70	1879–80	1889–90	1899–1900	1909–10	1919–20	1929–30	1939–40	1949–50	1959–60	1969–70	1979–80	1989–90	1990–91	1993–94	1994–95
1	2	3	4	5	6	7	8	9	10	11	12	13	14	15	16	17
Amounts in current dollars																
Annual salary of instructional staff [11]	$189	$195	$252	$325	$485	$871	$1,420	$1,441	$3,010	$5,174	$9,047	[12] $16,715	[12] $34,401	[12] $37,441	[12] $38,441	[12] $38,501
Personal income per member of labor force [1]	—	—	—	—	—	—	1,732	1,318	3,391	5,769	9,653	19,586	36,337	38,177	42,536	43,966
Total school expenditures per capita of total population	1.59	1.56	2.23	2.83	4.71	9.91	19.01	17.89	39	88	202	427	862	920	1,029	1,071
National income [1] per capita	—	—	—	—	—	—	710	556	1,456	2,328	3,999	9,256	17,816	18,653	20,321	21,259
Current expenditure [6,13] per pupil in A.D.A. [14]	—	—	13.99	16.67	27.85	53.32	86.70	88.09	210	375	816	2,272	4,980	5,258	5,767	5,988
Total expenditure [15] per pupil in A.D.A.	15.55	12.71	17.23	20.21	33.23	64.16	108.49	105.74	260	471	955	2,491	5,550	5,885	6,492	6,724
National income per pupil in A.D.A.	—	—	—	—	—	—	4,068	3,303	9,747	12,744	19,206	54,285	116,333	121,065	130,485	135,931
Current expenditure per day [16] per pupil in A.D.A. [6]	—	—	0.10	0.12	0.18	0.33	0.50	0.50	1.17	2.11	4.56	12.73	—	—	—	—
Total expenditure per day per pupil in A.D.A.	0.12	0.10	0.13	0.14	0.21	0.40	0.63	0.60	1.46	2.65	5.34	13.95	—	—	—	—
Amounts in constant 1994–95 dollars																
Annual salary of instructional staff [11]	—	—	—	—	—	$6,874	$12,478	$15,509	$19,116	$26,485	$36,022	[12] $32,384	[12] $38,661	[12] $38,637	[12] $38,514	[12] $38,441
Personal income per member of labor force [1]	—	—	—	—	—	—	15,223	14,187	21,534	29,529	38,434	37,947	43,043	42,878	43,755	43,966
Total school expenditures per capita of total population	—	—	—	—	—	78	167	193	249	449	804	828	1,021	1,033	1,059	1,071
National income [1] per capita	—	—	—	—	—	—	6,236	5,980	9,246	11,914	15,924	17,932	21,104	20,950	20,904	21,259
Current expenditure [6,13] per pupil in A.D.A.	—	—	—	—	—	421	762	948	1,334	1,920	3,249	4,401	5,899	5,905	5,933	5,988
Total expenditure [15] per pupil in A.D.A.	—	—	—	—	—	506	953	1,138	1,654	2,411	3,803	4,826	6,574	6,610	6,678	6,724
National income per pupil in A.D.A.	—	—	—	—	—	—	35,743	35,547	61,901	65,237	76,474	105,172	137,802	135,973	134,225	135,931
Current expenditure per day [16] per pupil in A.D.A. [6]	—	—	—	—	—	2.60	4.39	5.38	7.43	10.80	18.16	24.66	—	—	—	—
Total expenditure per day per pupil in A.D.A.	—	—	—	—	—	2.81	4.93	5.75	8.26	12.08	18.93	24.06	—	—	—	—

[1] Data on population and labor force are from the Bureau of the Census, and data on personal income and national income are from the Bureau of Economic Analysis, U.S. Department of Commerce. Population data through 1900 are based on total population from the decennial census. From 1909–10 to 1959–60, population data are total population, including armed forces overseas, as of July 1. Data for later years are for resident population that excludes armed forces overseas.
[2] Data for 1869–70 through 1959–60 are school year enrollment. Data for later years are fall enrollment.
[3] Data for 1870–71.
[4] Estimated by the National Center for Education Statistics.
[5] Prior to 1919–20, data are for the number of different persons employed rather than number of positions.
[6] Prior to 1919–20, includes interest on school debt.
[7] Because of the modification of the scope of "current expenditures for elementary and secondary schools," data for 1959–60 and later years are not entirely comparable with prior years.
[8] Beginning in 1969–70, includes capital outlay by state and local school building authorities.
[9] Includes summer schools, community colleges, and adult education. Beginning in 1959–60, also includes community services, formerly classified with "current expenditures for elementary and secondary schools."
[10] Excludes community colleges and adult education.
[11] Average includes supervisors, principals, teachers, and other nonsupervisory instructional staff.
[12] Estimated by the National Education Association.
[13] Excludes current expenditures not allocable to pupil costs.
[14] "A.D.A." means average daily attendance in elementary and secondary schools.
[15] The expenditure figure used here is the sum of current expenditures allocable to pupil costs, capital outlay, and interest on school debt.
[16] Per-day rates derived by dividing annual rates by average length of term.
—Data not collected.

NOTE.—Kindergarten enrollment includes a relatively small number of nursery school pupils. Because of rounding, details may not add to totals. Some data have been revised from previously published figures. Beginning in 1959–60, data include Alaska and Hawaii.

SOURCE: U.S. Department of Education, National Center for Education Statistics, *Statistics of State School Systems*; *Statistics of Public Elementary and Secondary School Systems*; *Revenues and Expenditures for Public Elementary and Secondary Education, FY 1980*; Common Core of Data surveys; and Council of Economic Advisers, *Economic Report of the President*. (This table was prepared July 1997.)

Table 40.—Enrollment in public elementary and secondary schools, by level and state: Fall 1981 to fall 1996

State or other area	Fall 1981 Total	Fall 1982 Total	Fall 1983 Total	Fall 1984 Total	Fall 1985 Total	Fall 1986 Total	Fall 1987 Total	Fall 1988 Total	Fall 1989 Total	Fall 1990 Total	Fall 1991 Total
1	2	3	4	5	6	7	8	9	10	11	12
United States	40,044,093	39,565,610	39,252,308	39,208,252	39,421,961	39,753,172	40,008,213	40,188,690	40,542,707	41,216,683	42,046,878
Alabama	743,448	724,037	721,901	712,586	730,460	733,735	729,234	724,751	723,743	721,806	722,004
Alaska[3]	90,858	89,413	98,206	104,599	107,345	107,848	106,869	106,481	109,280	113,903	118,680
Arizona	507,199	510,296	506,682	530,062	548,252	534,538	572,421	574,890	607,615	639,853	656,980
Arkansas	437,121	432,565	432,120	432,668	433,410	437,438	437,036	436,387	434,960	436,286	438,518
California	4,046,156	4,065,486	4,089,017	4,151,110	4,255,554	4,377,989	4,488,398	4,618,120	4,771,978	4,950,474	5,107,145
Colorado	544,174	545,209	542,196	545,427	550,642	558,415	560,236	560,081	562,755	574,213	593,030
Connecticut[5]	505,386	486,470	477,585	468,145	462,026	468,847	465,465	460,637	461,560	469,123	481,050
Delaware	95,072	92,646	91,406	91,767	92,901	94,410	95,659	96,678	97,808	99,658	102,196
District of Columbia	94,975	91,105	88,843	87,397	87,092	85,612	86,435	84,792	81,301	80,694	80,618
Florida	1,487,721	1,484,734	1,495,543	1,524,107	1,562,283	1,607,320	1,664,774	1,720,930	1,789,925	1,861,592	1,932,131
Georgia	1,056,117	1,053,689	1,050,859	1,062,315	1,079,594	1,096,425	1,110,947	1,107,994	1,126,535	1,151,687	1,177,569
Hawaii	162,805	162,024	162,241	163,860	164,169	164,640	166,120	167,488	169,493	171,708	174,747
Idaho	204,524	202,973	206,352	208,080	208,669	208,391	212,444	214,615	214,932	220,840	225,680
Illinois	1,924,084	1,880,289	1,853,316	1,834,355	1,826,478	1,825,185	1,811,446	1,794,916	1,797,355	1,821,407	1,848,166
Indiana	1,025,172	999,542	984,384	972,659	966,106	966,780	964,129	960,994	954,165	954,525	956,988
Iowa	516,216	504,983	497,287	491,011	485,332	481,286	480,826	478,200	478,486	483,652	491,363
Kansas	409,909	407,074	405,222	405,347	410,229	416,091	421,112	426,596	430,864	437,034	445,390
Kentucky	658,350	651,084	647,414	644,421	643,833	642,778	642,696	637,627	630,688	636,401	646,024
Louisiana	782,053	784,027	800,193	800,941	788,349	795,188	793,093	786,683	783,025	784,757	794,128
Maine	216,293	211,986	209,753	207,537	206,101	211,752	211,817	212,902	213,775	215,149	216,400
Maryland	721,841	699,201	683,491	673,840	671,560	675,747	683,797	688,947	698,806	715,176	736,238
Massachusetts	947,037	908,984	878,844	859,391	844,330	833,918	825,320	823,428	825,588	834,314	846,155
Michigan	1,724,787	1,674,697	1,635,963	1,609,448	1,602,747	1,597,154	1,589,287	1,582,785	1,576,785	1,584,431	1,593,561
Minnesota	733,741	715,190	705,236	701,697	705,140	711,134	721,481	726,950	739,553	756,374	773,571
Mississippi	471,615	468,294	467,744	466,058	471,195	498,639	505,550	503,326	502,020	502,417	504,127
Missouri	818,705	802,535	795,453	793,793	795,107	800,606	802,060	806,639	807,934	816,558	842,965
Montana	153,435	152,335	153,646	154,412	153,869	153,327	152,207	152,191	151,265	152,974	155,779
Nebraska	273,340	269,009	266,998	265,599	265,819	267,139	268,100	269,434	270,920	274,081	279,552
Nevada	151,339	151,104	150,442	151,633	154,948	161,239	168,353	176,474	186,834	201,316	211,810
New Hampshire	163,827	160,197	159,030	158,614	160,974	163,717	166,045	169,413	171,696	172,785	177,138
New Jersey	1,199,643	1,172,520	1,147,841	1,129,223	1,116,194	1,107,467	1,092,982	1,080,871	1,076,005	1,089,646	1,109,796
New Mexico	268,091	268,632	269,711	272,478	277,551	281,943	287,229	292,425	296,057	301,881	308,667
New York	2,783,017	2,718,678	2,674,818	2,645,811	2,621,378	2,607,719	2,594,070	2,573,715	2,565,841	2,598,337	2,643,993
North Carolina	1,108,960	1,096,815	1,089,606	1,088,724	1,086,165	1,085,248	1,085,976	1,083,156	1,080,744	1,086,871	1,097,598
North Dakota	117,708	117,078	117,213	118,711	118,570	118,703	119,004	118,809	117,816	117,825	118,376
Ohio	1,898,501	1,860,245	1,827,300	1,805,440	1,793,965	1,793,508	1,793,431	1,778,544	1,764,410	1,771,089	1,783,767
Oklahoma	582,572	593,825	591,389	589,690	592,327	593,183	584,212	580,426	578,580	579,087	588,263
Oregon	457,165	448,184	447,109	446,884	447,527	449,307	455,895	461,752	472,394	472,394	498,614
Pennsylvania	1,839,015	1,783,969	1,737,952	1,701,880	1,683,221	1,674,161	1,668,542	1,659,714	1,655,279	1,667,834	1,692,797
Rhode Island	143,414	139,959	136,412	134,610	133,949	134,690	134,800	133,585	135,729	138,813	142,144
South Carolina	609,158	608,518	604,553	602,718	606,643	611,629	614,921	615,774	616,177	622,112	627,470
South Dakota	125,657	123,897	123,060	123,314	124,291	125,458	126,817	126,910	127,329	129,164	131,576
Tennessee	838,297	828,264	822,057	817,212	813,753	818,073	823,783	821,580	819,660	824,595	833,651
Texas	2,935,547	2,985,659	2,989,796	3,040,305	3,131,705	3,209,515	3,236,787	3,283,707	3,328,514	3,382,887	3,464,371
Utah	355,554	370,183	378,208	390,141	403,305	415,994	423,386	431,119	438,554	446,652	456,430
Vermont	93,183	91,454	90,416	90,089	90,157	92,112	92,755	93,381	94,779	95,762	97,137
Virginia	989,548	975,727	966,110	965,222	968,104	975,135	979,417	982,393	985,346	998,601	1,016,204
Washington	750,188	739,215	736,239	741,177	749,706	761,428	775,755	790,918	810,232	839,709	869,327
West Virginia	377,772	375,115	371,251	362,941	357,923	351,837	344,236	335,912	327,540	322,389	320,249
Wisconsin	804,262	784,830	774,646	767,542	768,234	767,819	772,363	774,857	782,905	797,621	814,671
Wyoming	99,541	101,665	99,254	101,261	102,779	100,955	98,455	97,793	97,172	98,226	102,074
Outlying areas											
American Samoa	9,896	—	10,124	—	—	11,055	11,248	11,764	12,258	12,463	13,365
Guam	25,084	25,676	26,249	—	26,043	25,676	25,936	26,041	26,493	26,391	28,334
Northern Marianas	5,300	—	4,499	4,841	—	—	5,819	6,079	6,101	6,449	7,096
Puerto Rico	721,419	708,794	701,925	692,923	686,914	679,489	672,837	661,693	651,225	644,734	642,392
Virgin Islands	25,525	25,699	26,126	26,122	25,448	24,435	24,020	23,492	21,193	21,750	22,346

ELEMENTARY AND SECONDARY: ENROLLMENT 53

Table 40.—Enrollment in public elementary and secondary schools, by level and state: Fall 1981 to fall 1996—Continued

State or other areas	Fall 1992 Total	Fall 1993 Total	Fall 1993 Kindergarten through grade 8[2]	Fall 1993 Grades 9 to 12	Fall 1994 Total	Fall 1994 Kindergarten through grade 8[2]	Fall 1994 Grades 9 to 12	Fall 1995 Total	Fall 1995 Kindergarten through grade 8[2]	Fall 1995 Grades 9 to 12	Estimated fall 1996[1] Total
1	13	14	15	16	17	18	19	20	21	22	23
United States	42,823,312	43,464,916	31,504,032	11,960,884	44,111,482	31,898,249	12,213,233	44,840,481	32,340,501	12,499,980	45,228,526
Alabama	731,634	734,288	535,637	198,651	736,531	535,246	201,285	746,149	539,309	206,840	741,933
Alaska[3]	122,487	125,948	93,601	32,347	127,057	93,719	33,338	127,618	93,434	34,184	126,015
Arizona	673,477	709,453	526,412	183,041	737,424	542,904	194,520	743,566	548,526	195,040	[4]749,759
Arkansas	441,490	444,271	317,713	126,558	447,565	319,282	128,283	453,257	322,440	130,817	457,076
California	5,254,844	5,327,231	3,903,137	1,424,094	5,407,475	3,955,868	1,451,607	5,536,406	4,041,224	1,495,182	5,535,312
Colorado	612,635	625,062	459,930	165,132	640,521	469,755	170,766	656,279	478,881	177,398	673,438
Connecticut[5]	488,476	496,298	368,632	127,666	506,824	375,638	131,186	517,935	384,274	133,661	523,054
Delaware	104,321	105,547	76,617	28,930	106,813	76,819	29,994	108,461	77,028	31,433	[6]110,549
District of Columbia	80,937	80,678	61,434	19,244	80,450	62,126	18,324	79,802	61,836	17,966	[4]79,159
Florida	1,981,407	2,040,763	1,515,194	525,569	2,111,188	1,569,666	541,522	2,176,222	1,613,510	562,712	[6]2,240,283
Georgia	1,207,186	1,235,304	910,425	324,879	1,270,948	934,650	336,298	1,311,126	965,707	345,419	1,321,239
Hawaii	177,448	180,410	131,638	48,772	183,795	133,675	50,120	187,180	135,671	51,509	188,485
Idaho	231,668	236,774	166,999	69,775	240,448	168,887	71,561	243,097	169,556	73,541	[6]245,252
Illinois	1,873,567	1,893,078	1,356,329	536,749	1,916,172	1,368,041	548,131	1,943,623	1,390,475	553,148	1,961,299
Indiana	960,630	965,633	679,066	286,567	969,022	678,970	290,052	977,263	684,348	292,915	984,610
Iowa	494,839	498,519	348,006	150,513	500,440	345,865	154,575	502,343	343,997	158,346	504,511
Kansas	451,536	457,614	329,708	127,906	460,838	329,211	131,627	463,008	328,701	134,307	465,140
Kentucky	655,041	655,265	467,315	187,950	657,642	467,005	190,637	659,821	468,242	191,579	663,071
Louisiana	797,985	800,560	587,490	213,070	797,933	583,892	214,041	797,366	580,348	217,018	[6]777,570
Maine	216,453	216,995	156,528	60,467	212,601	155,903	56,698	213,569	156,016	57,553	[6]218,560
Maryland	751,850	772,638	569,497	203,141	790,938	580,903	210,035	805,544	590,155	215,389	818,947
Massachusetts	859,948	877,726	645,518	232,208	893,727	658,507	235,220	915,007	674,588	240,419	[4]936,794
Michigan	1,603,610	1,599,377	1,159,968	439,409	1,614,784	1,170,251	444,533	1,641,456	1,191,671	449,785	1,662,100
Minnesota	793,724	810,233	576,980	233,253	821,693	581,426	240,267	835,166	586,080	249,086	836,700
Mississippi	506,668	505,907	368,688	137,219	505,962	366,846	139,116	506,272	366,186	140,086	[6]504,168
Missouri	859,357	866,378	622,171	244,207	878,541	628,286	250,255	889,881	635,771	254,110	883,327
Montana	160,011	163,009	116,668	46,341	164,341	116,748	47,593	165,547	116,403	49,144	166,909
Nebraska	282,414	285,097	203,426	81,671	287,100	203,055	84,045	289,744	203,022	86,722	292,121
Nevada	222,974	235,800	175,054	60,746	250,747	185,336	65,411	265,041	195,892	69,149	[6]282,131
New Hampshire	181,247	185,360	136,211	49,149	189,319	138,851	50,468	194,171	141,721	52,450	[6]194,581
New Jersey	1,130,560	1,151,307	843,526	307,781	1,174,206	862,331	311,875	1,197,381	880,350	317,031	[4]1,221,013
New Mexico	315,668	322,292	226,287	96,005	327,248	229,168	98,080	329,640	229,239	100,401	330,522
New York	2,689,686	2,733,813	1,920,609	813,204	2,766,208	1,949,245	816,963	2,813,230	1,980,208	833,022	2,825,000
North Carolina	1,114,083	1,133,231	828,171	305,060	1,156,767	847,463	309,304	1,183,090	871,320	311,770	[6]1,199,962
North Dakota	118,734	119,127	84,127	35,000	119,288	83,419	35,869	119,100	82,333	36,767	[6]118,427
Ohio	1,795,199	1,807,319	1,290,197	517,122	1,814,290	1,295,289	519,001	1,836,015	1,297,313	538,702	1,841,095
Oklahoma	597,096	604,076	441,094	162,982	609,718	442,607	167,111	616,393	445,780	170,613	620,379
Oregon	510,122	516,611	368,141	148,470	521,945	371,967	149,978	527,914	375,966	151,948	[6]537,783
Pennsylvania	1,717,613	1,744,082	1,233,113	510,969	1,764,946	1,243,983	520,963	1,787,533	1,256,621	530,912	1,807,250
Rhode Island	143,798	145,676	107,047	38,629	147,487	107,913	39,574	149,799	109,815	39,984	151,181
South Carolina	640,464	643,696	466,951	176,745	648,725	468,850	179,875	645,586	463,305	182,281	648,980
South Dakota	134,573	142,825	102,281	40,544	143,482	101,805	41,677	144,685	101,491	43,194	[6]142,910
Tennessee	855,231	866,557	630,015	236,542	881,425	640,604	240,821	893,770	650,601	243,169	891,101
Texas	3,541,769	3,608,262	2,681,053	927,209	3,677,171	2,720,623	956,548	3,748,167	2,757,273	990,894	3,809,186
Utah	463,870	471,365	329,926	141,439	474,675	328,482	146,193	477,121	327,790	149,331	[6]478,085
Vermont	98,558	102,755	74,828	27,927	104,533	75,590	28,943	105,565	75,227	30,338	106,607
Virginia	1,031,925	1,045,471	767,347	278,124	1,060,809	774,319	286,490	1,079,854	787,945	291,909	[6]1,096,093
Washington	896,475	915,952	660,424	255,528	938,314	673,107	265,207	956,572	680,009	276,563	[6]971,903
West Virginia	318,296	314,383	215,784	98,599	310,511	212,808	97,703	307,112	211,008	96,104	[6]303,441
Wisconsin	829,415	844,001	595,717	248,284	860,581	601,215	259,366	870,175	602,964	267,211	[6]884,738
Wyoming	100,313	100,899	71,402	29,497	100,314	70,130	30,184	99,859	68,931	30,928	[6]98,777
Outlying areas											
American Samoa	13,994	14,484	10,974	3,510	14,445	11,054	3,391	14,576	11,207	3,369	[4]14,708
Guam	30,077	30,920	23,153	7,767	32,185	24,189	7,996	32,960	24,877	8,083	[4]33,754
Northern Marianas	8,086	8,188	6,380	1,808	8,429	6,559	1,870	8,809	6,825	1,984	[6]8,253
Puerto Rico	637,034	631,460	464,117	167,343	621,121	455,653	165,468	627,620	460,585	167,035	613,009
Virgin Islands	22,887	22,752	16,706	6,046	23,126	16,659	6,467	22,737	16,342	6,395	22,146

[1] Data estimated by state education agencies.
[2] Includes a relatively small number of prekindergarten students.
[3] Beginning in 1983, data include students enrolled in public schools on federal bases and other special arrangements.
[4] Data estimated by the National Center for Education Statistics.
[5] Beginning in 1986, data include state vocational/technical schools.
[6] Actual data.
—Data not available.

NOTE.—Some data have been revised from previously published figures.

SOURCE: U.S. Department of Education, National Center for Education Statistics, Common Core of Data surveys. (This table was prepared April 1997.)

ELEMENTARY AND SECONDARY: ENROLLMENT

Table 41.—Enrollment in public elementary and secondary schools, by grade and state: Fall 1995

State or other area	Total, all levels	Prekindergarten through grade 8 and elementary unclassified							
		Total	Prekindergarten [1]	Kindergarten	Grade 1	Grade 2	Grade 3	Grade 4	Grade 5
1	2	3	4	5	6	7	8	9	10
United States	44,840,481	32,340,501	636,846	3,536,227	3,670,903	3,507,022	3,444,740	3,430,583	3,437,943
Alabama	746,149	539,309	[2] 9,324	59,739	61,694	57,452	57,732	56,486	57,142
Alaska	127,618	93,434	2,419	10,567	10,444	10,352	10,030	10,222	10,112
Arizona	743,566	548,526	4,027	61,420	64,215	61,418	59,828	60,202	59,894
Arkansas	453,257	322,440	1,525	36,731	36,369	34,257	33,621	33,955	34,875
California	5,536,406	4,041,224	[2] 69,182	472,334	466,167	453,020	435,380	428,553	424,838
Colorado	656,279	478,881	10,472	50,316	52,767	51,786	52,030	52,783	52,646
Connecticut	517,935	384,274	8,093	44,148	45,969	43,030	42,010	41,365	40,650
Delaware	108,461	77,028	670	7,775	8,579	8,721	8,425	8,527	8,362
District of Columbia	79,802	61,836	5,387	7,736	7,931	6,533	6,063	5,852	5,332
Florida	2,176,222	1,613,510	51,123	176,767	180,182	175,891	172,039	173,169	175,358
Georgia	1,311,126	965,707	22,621	111,462	110,955	105,752	103,936	103,072	102,516
Hawaii	187,180	135,671	609	16,562	16,013	15,546	15,106	14,867	14,489
Idaho	243,097	169,556	1,665	17,750	18,260	18,285	17,952	17,640	18,626
Illinois	1,943,623	1,390,475	45,947	151,485	154,534	149,128	142,500	142,660	142,836
Indiana	977,263	684,348	4,901	73,833	80,279	74,964	71,585	72,356	73,101
Iowa	502,343	343,997	5,957	37,629	36,107	35,029	34,884	36,431	37,204
Kansas	463,008	328,701	3,209	33,925	35,538	35,037	35,100	36,004	36,596
Kentucky	659,821	468,242	20,290	45,038	47,250	45,845	56,613	46,834	48,572
Louisiana	797,366	580,348	19,440	61,323	63,719	59,414	59,552	61,315	61,232
Maine	213,569	156,016	821	16,826	17,250	17,003	16,568	17,419	17,397
Maryland	805,544	590,155	19,092	63,232	67,348	65,055	63,940	62,207	61,814
Massachusetts	915,007	674,588	14,792	79,163	79,565	75,647	73,380	71,800	71,606
Michigan	1,641,456	1,191,671	8,870	141,238	134,513	125,809	124,197	122,266	123,894
Minnesota	835,166	586,080	8,340	63,896	63,268	62,511	62,564	64,545	65,191
Mississippi	506,272	366,186	1,083	39,632	42,510	39,015	37,304	38,004	38,332
Missouri	889,881	635,771	16,225	68,513	69,659	67,080	66,928	68,159	68,889
Montana	165,547	116,403	519	12,214	12,519	12,279	12,535	12,899	13,200
Nebraska	289,744	203,022	3,853	22,282	21,748	21,082	21,210	21,886	22,351
Nevada	265,041	195,892	1,631	22,074	23,301	22,368	21,752	21,784	21,253
New Hampshire	194,171	141,721	1,357	8,859	17,973	16,601	16,566	16,275	16,480
New Jersey	1,197,381	880,350	9,301	93,978	102,521	95,581	91,352	88,686	86,889
New Mexico	329,640	229,239	3,426	24,329	26,152	24,703	24,395	24,200	24,407
New York	2,813,230	1,980,208	32,087	216,112	231,136	218,744	209,174	203,089	200,446
North Carolina	1,183,090	871,320	9,013	100,525	101,945	96,229	92,552	90,795	90,445
North Dakota	119,100	82,333	551	8,573	8,824	8,678	8,590	9,017	9,201
Ohio	1,836,015	1,297,313	18,997	141,589	148,354	140,090	138,135	138,942	140,465
Oklahoma	616,393	445,780	5,470	48,635	54,178	46,642	46,456	47,407	48,073
Oregon	527,914	375,966	855	39,875	41,952	40,802	40,790	41,721	42,083
Pennsylvania	1,787,533	1,256,621	3,502	134,584	146,077	139,562	136,887	137,850	135,565
Rhode Island	149,799	109,815	531	10,947	13,868	12,343	12,053	11,596	11,439
South Carolina	645,586	463,305	[2] 8,067	39,964	55,944	51,837	50,451	50,860	51,338
South Dakota	144,685	101,491	1,475	10,609	10,700	10,365	10,675	10,937	11,234
Tennessee	893,770	650,601	[2] 11,168	73,962	76,015	69,266	67,326	67,705	67,859
Texas	3,748,167	2,757,273	133,754	281,708	303,928	294,298	291,993	292,191	293,834
Utah	477,121	327,790	3,455	34,645	34,857	34,782	33,937	34,598	34,976
Vermont	105,565	75,227	1,111	7,953	8,371	8,067	8,200	8,287	8,327
Virginia	1,079,854	787,945	3,111	87,618	89,183	83,414	82,713	82,797	83,955
Washington	956,572	680,009	5,984	73,581	75,721	73,810	73,888	75,186	75,599
West Virginia	307,112	211,008	3,499	22,577	22,875	21,610	21,991	22,178	22,478
Wisconsin	870,175	602,964	18,045	62,859	64,574	63,141	64,541	65,427	66,577
Wyoming	99,859	68,931	—	7,135	7,102	7,148	7,311	7,577	7,965
Outlying areas									
American Samoa	14,576	11,207	1,458	1,162	1,189	1,142	1,181	1,089	1,052
Guam	32,960	24,877	962	2,961	2,994	2,856	2,739	2,722	2,549
Northern Marianas	8,809	6,825	560	598	781	781	805	683	667
Puerto Rico	627,620	460,585	255	44,566	54,545	50,423	49,531	49,762	49,863
Virgin Islands	22,737	16,342	—	1,638	1,647	1,654	1,717	1,655	1,712

Table 41.—Enrollment in public elementary and secondary schools, by grade and state: Fall 1995—Continued

State or other area	Prekindergarten through grade 8 and elementary unclassified				Grades 9 through 12 and secondary unclassified					
	Grade 6	Grade 7	Grade 8	Elementary unclassified	Total	Grade 9	Grade 10	Grade 11	Grade 12	Secondary unclassified
1	11	12	13	14	15	16	17	18	19	20
United States	3,395,307	3,422,290	3,356,338	502,302	12,499,980	3,704,455	3,237,391	2,826,023	2,487,135	244,976
Alabama	58,704	61,122	59,914	—	206,840	65,299	53,780	46,780	40,981	—
Alaska	9,870	9,845	9,573	—	34,184	10,263	9,045	7,765	7,111	—
Arizona	58,281	58,829	56,407	4,005	195,040	59,346	52,654	43,547	39,197	296
Arkansas	35,104	37,023	36,696	2,284	130,817	37,005	35,209	30,566	27,083	954
California	413,776	409,978	399,039	68,957	1,495,182	437,974	396,020	343,419	287,428	30,341
Colorado	51,856	52,282	51,180	763	177,398	52,472	47,128	41,751	35,480	567
Connecticut	39,468	38,253	37,320	3,968	133,661	39,380	34,797	31,198	28,282	4
Delaware	8,520	8,883	8,566	—	31,433	10,112	8,325	6,785	6,211	—
District of Columbia	4,980	5,052	4,749	2,221	17,966	5,159	4,896	3,700	2,972	1,239
Florida	174,079	171,381	163,521	—	562,712	182,980	154,030	126,183	99,519	—
Georgia	103,015	102,287	100,091	—	345,419	117,429	90,117	74,137	63,736	—
Hawaii	14,617	14,022	13,793	47	51,509	16,277	13,274	11,442	10,478	38
Idaho	19,392	19,857	20,129	—	73,541	20,195	19,349	17,904	16,093	—
Illinois	138,679	133,484	132,678	56,544	553,148	149,289	139,115	122,384	107,244	35,116
Indiana	74,734	77,279	78,278	3,038	292,915	83,436	76,232	67,902	62,659	2,686
Iowa	37,117	38,833	38,715	6,091	158,346	41,385	39,680	36,861	34,565	5,855
Kansas	36,534	37,317	36,782	2,659	134,307	38,484	35,290	31,064	28,491	978
Kentucky	49,131	51,000	50,091	7,578	191,579	56,572	49,429	43,614	38,797	3,167
Louisiana	60,647	62,873	57,918	12,915	217,018	68,655	55,225	47,422	40,663	5,053
Maine	17,280	17,206	16,771	1,475	57,553	16,007	14,636	13,773	12,670	467
Maryland	61,099	60,747	58,835	6,786	215,389	64,468	54,286	47,345	42,974	6,316
Massachusetts	69,122	67,176	65,724	6,613	240,419	68,623	62,856	57,029	51,911	—
Michigan	120,347	120,121	118,996	51,420	449,785	129,820	112,588	99,551	87,840	19,986
Minnesota	64,439	65,677	65,649	—	249,086	67,226	64,478	59,589	57,793	—
Mississippi	38,737	41,223	39,809	10,537	140,086	43,241	35,552	28,587	25,741	6,965
Missouri	67,847	69,368	66,493	6,610	254,110	72,575	66,804	59,378	52,939	2,414
Montana	13,153	13,407	13,342	336	49,144	13,921	12,569	11,635	10,897	122
Nebraska	22,777	22,817	23,016	—	86,722	23,813	23,184	20,450	19,275	—
Nevada	20,616	20,449	19,970	694	69,149	19,661	18,773	16,553	14,143	19
New Hampshire	15,805	15,798	15,487	520	52,450	15,420	13,597	12,387	10,996	50
New Jersey	84,950	83,920	81,997	61,175	317,031	84,649	76,042	70,493	65,647	20,200
New Mexico	25,300	26,434	25,893	—	100,401	29,164	24,981	20,195	17,078	8,983
New York	197,470	199,440	194,347	78,163	833,022	235,320	205,305	178,043	142,841	71,513
North Carolina	88,925	89,747	88,056	23,088	311,770	100,505	82,512	69,100	59,653	—
North Dakota	9,270	9,770	9,859	—	36,767	9,927	9,377	8,950	8,513	—
Ohio	137,737	141,979	142,469	8,556	538,702	159,777	138,771	125,275	114,879	—
Oklahoma	48,683	49,709	49,012	1,515	170,613	49,992	45,289	38,997	35,733	602
Oregon	41,735	42,449	42,141	1,563	151,948	42,438	39,326	36,420	33,202	562
Pennsylvania	133,770	137,376	136,069	15,379	530,912	150,460	134,653	121,885	111,050	12,864
Rhode Island	11,586	11,515	11,032	2,905	39,984	11,922	10,530	9,113	8,263	156
South Carolina	51,322	52,214	51,308	—	182,281	60,808	48,165	38,508	34,800	—
South Dakota	11,143	11,583	11,654	1,116	43,194	12,176	11,388	10,090	9,116	424
Tennessee	66,227	68,309	66,513	16,251	243,169	74,398	64,144	55,308	49,319	—
Texas	288,502	292,190	284,875	—	990,894	335,819	255,132	213,714	186,229	—
Utah	35,877	36,693	38,090	5,880	149,331	37,941	38,485	36,487	32,006	4,412
Vermont	8,553	8,352	8,006	—	30,338	8,125	7,465	6,909	6,507	1,332
Virginia	82,996	81,619	81,254	29,285	291,909	86,779	76,045	66,764	62,204	117
Washington	75,313	75,875	75,052	—	276,563	78,514	73,402	65,035	59,612	—
West Virginia	22,825	24,521	25,089	1,365	96,104	26,261	24,769	22,052	21,844	1,178
Wisconsin	65,289	66,723	65,788	—	267,211	74,700	70,262	64,458	57,791	—
Wyoming	8,108	8,283	8,302	—	30,928	8,293	8,430	7,526	6,679	—
Outlying areas										
American Samoa	1,042	941	951	—	3,369	915	837	796	756	65
Guam	2,384	2,342	2,368	—	8,083	2,862	2,122	1,666	1,433	—
Northern Marianas	642	712	596	—	1,984	575	536	406	467	—
Puerto Rico	47,978	51,731	48,934	12,997	167,035	45,673	44,939	38,184	32,535	5,704
Virgin Islands	1,577	2,285	1,607	850	6,395	1,774	1,629	1,251	1,102	639

[1] Data include imputations for nonrespondents.
[2] Includes imputations for underreporting.
—Data not reported or not applicable.

SOURCE: U.S. Department of Education, National Center for Education Statistics, Common Core of Data survey. (This table was prepared April 1997.)

56 ELEMENTARY AND SECONDARY: ENROLLMENT

Table 42.—Enrollment in public elementary and secondary schools, by grade and state: Fall 1994

State or other area	Total, all levels	Prekindergarten through grade 8 and elementary unclassified							
		Total	Prekindergarten[1]	Kindergarten	Grade 1	Grade 2	Grade 3	Grade 4	Grade 5
1	2	3	4	5	6	7	8	9	10
United States	44,111,482	31,898,249	602,535	3,444,276	3,593,382	3,439,828	3,439,042	3,425,951	3,371,884
Alabama	736,531	535,246	[2]9,051	57,723	60,366	56,502	57,259	56,773	57,923
Alaska	127,057	93,719	2,593	10,309	10,679	10,194	10,420	10,318	10,086
Arizona	737,424	542,904	3,540	59,545	63,198	60,274	60,591	60,032	58,579
Arkansas	447,565	319,282	1,652	35,620	35,359	33,615	33,626	34,488	34,620
California	5,407,475	3,955,868	[2]66,450	448,237	457,886	438,672	431,169	426,919	416,333
Colorado	640,521	469,755	9,853	48,673	51,634	51,229	52,191	51,877	51,311
Connecticut	506,824	375,638	7,601	43,511	44,869	42,023	41,225	40,737	39,693
Delaware	106,813	76,819	618	7,523	9,097	8,450	8,595	8,367	8,402
District of Columbia	80,450	62,126	5,508	7,628	7,184	6,515	6,365	5,783	5,457
Florida	2,111,188	1,569,666	47,993	172,135	175,106	169,651	170,632	173,297	170,397
Georgia	1,270,948	934,650	12,859	108,398	105,961	102,495	101,656	101,054	100,813
Hawaii	183,795	133,675	631	15,678	15,696	15,208	15,052	14,572	14,828
Idaho	240,448	168,887	1,501	17,260	18,324	17,665	17,326	18,361	19,116
Illinois	1,916,172	1,368,041	42,938	146,314	152,229	143,486	143,029	143,030	138,902
Indiana	969,022	678,970	4,660	71,594	78,458	71,276	71,895	72,408	73,176
Iowa	500,440	345,865	5,901	37,402	35,301	34,775	36,326	36,960	36,540
Kansas	460,838	329,211	2,640	33,445	36,070	35,191	35,915	36,488	36,115
Kentucky	657,642	467,005	17,934	44,191	45,866	46,173	55,697	48,233	48,778
Louisiana	797,933	583,892	19,292	60,705	63,448	60,476	61,849	62,461	60,139
Maine	212,601	155,903	1,006	16,569	17,524	16,583	17,351	17,397	17,154
Maryland	790,938	580,903	18,834	62,341	65,377	64,160	62,270	61,982	61,010
Massachusetts	893,727	658,507	13,982	77,777	77,583	73,836	71,606	71,131	68,837
Michigan	1,614,784	1,170,251	4,409	136,353	129,951	125,664	123,321	123,829	119,821
Minnesota	821,693	581,426	8,060	62,908	62,446	61,956	63,873	64,605	63,660
Mississippi	505,962	366,846	1,146	38,528	41,762	37,940	38,135	38,606	39,004
Missouri	878,541	628,286	16,002	66,607	67,874	66,607	67,802	68,457	67,020
Montana	164,341	116,748	483	11,820	12,852	12,391	12,845	13,009	13,113
Nebraska	287,100	203,055	3,985	21,752	21,275	21,223	21,705	22,144	22,496
Nevada	250,747	185,336	1,424	20,462	21,827	21,062	20,941	20,573	20,048
New Hampshire	189,319	138,851	1,210	8,325	18,014	16,411	16,185	16,352	15,678
New Jersey	1,174,206	862,331	10,283	92,316	99,907	92,142	89,159	87,374	85,007
New Mexico	327,248	229,168	4,174	24,055	25,770	24,912	24,554	24,294	24,033
New York	2,766,208	1,949,245	32,227	212,239	225,269	212,486	205,740	202,024	196,405
North Carolina	1,156,767	847,463	8,949	97,508	97,339	91,560	90,471	89,492	87,139
North Dakota	119,288	83,419	639	8,677	8,893	8,634	8,966	9,236	9,292
Ohio	1,814,290	1,295,289	17,505	141,284	144,280	141,064	141,329	136,834	138,552
Oklahoma	609,718	442,607	5,367	46,355	53,654	46,476	47,234	47,929	48,221
Oregon	521,945	371,967	1,069	38,930	40,710	40,348	41,248	41,739	41,623
Pennsylvania	1,764,946	1,243,983	3,583	132,132	146,636	137,635	137,533	135,061	131,944
Rhode Island	147,487	107,913	469	10,701	13,721	12,154	11,707	11,549	11,504
South Carolina	648,725	468,850	[2]7,972	46,859	54,602	50,731	51,139	51,268	50,585
South Dakota	143,482	101,805	1,244	10,618	10,615	10,649	10,917	11,116	11,138
Tennessee	881,425	640,604	[2]10,831	71,413	73,170	66,964	67,349	67,339	65,872
Texas	3,677,171	2,720,623	128,736	272,065	300,731	290,911	289,548	291,604	286,219
Utah	474,675	328,482	3,273	33,750	34,790	33,734	34,515	34,837	35,668
Vermont	104,533	75,590	1,903	8,040	8,176	8,183	8,224	8,396	8,430
Virginia	1,060,809	774,319	3,115	85,160	84,678	82,663	82,990	84,103	81,212
Washington	938,314	673,107	6,155	71,637	73,594	73,187	74,642	75,299	74,861
West Virginia	310,511	212,808	2,754	22,377	22,186	22,123	22,210	22,236	22,651
Wisconsin	860,581	601,215	18,531	61,898	64,040	64,247	65,127	65,996	64,380
Wyoming	100,314	70,130	—	6,929	7,405	7,322	7,588	7,982	8,099
Outlying areas									
American Samoa	14,445	11,054	1,570	1,126	1,173	1,184	1,094	1,071	1,045
Guam	32,185	24,189	465	2,931	2,981	2,835	2,753	2,587	2,531
Northern Marianas	8,429	6,559	510	556	793	805	695	681	630
Puerto Rico	621,121	455,653	143	39,962	53,773	49,955	48,958	50,311	49,778
Virgin Islands	23,126	16,659	—	1,487	1,816	1,837	1,732	1,745	1,702

Table 42.—Enrollment in public elementary and secondary schools, by grade and state: Fall 1994—Continued

State or other area	Prekindergarten through grade 8 and elementary unclassified				Grades 9 through 12 and secondary unclassified					
	Grade 6	Grade 7	Grade 8	Elementary unclassified	Total	Grade 9	Grade 10	Grade 11	Grade 12	Secondary unclassified
1	11	12	13	14	15	16	17	18	19	20
United States	3,381,439	3,403,550	3,302,297	494,065	12,213,233	3,604,115	3,131,234	2,748,189	2,487,552	242,143
Alabama	58,719	61,765	59,165	—	201,285	63,656	50,929	44,970	41,730	—
Alaska	9,674	9,943	9,503	—	33,338	9,947	8,692	7,642	7,057	—
Arizona	58,791	58,676	55,334	4,344	194,520	59,150	51,564	43,363	40,119	324
Arkansas	35,024	36,795	36,437	2,046	128,283	36,689	34,158	29,429	27,161	846
California	409,387	403,367	388,561	68,887	1,451,607	420,643	381,364	334,408	285,132	30,060
Colorado	51,775	51,103	49,332	777	170,766	50,078	44,702	39,956	35,464	566
Connecticut	38,110	37,577	35,665	4,627	131,186	38,001	33,780	30,760	28,640	5
Delaware	8,416	8,788	8,563	—	29,994	9,469	7,979	6,681	5,865	—
District of Columbia	4,978	5,244	5,031	2,433	18,324	4,923	4,904	3,920	3,203	1,374
Florida	169,061	165,542	155,852	—	541,522	172,947	147,942	119,913	100,720	—
Georgia	101,974	100,458	98,982	—	336,298	114,176	85,636	71,880	64,606	—
Hawaii	14,540	13,832	13,592	46	50,120	15,597	11,979	12,034	10,473	37
Idaho	19,478	20,176	19,680	—	71,561	19,777	19,098	16,906	15,780	—
Illinois	133,142	134,518	135,134	55,319	548,131	148,944	135,955	119,266	109,360	34,606
Indiana	75,453	78,378	77,799	3,873	290,052	83,147	73,567	67,198	62,727	3,413
Iowa	38,036	38,459	39,039	7,126	154,575	40,593	37,874	35,400	34,078	6,630
Kansas	36,981	37,116	36,757	2,493	131,627	38,007	33,574	30,338	28,811	897
Kentucky	49,973	51,190	50,562	8,408	190,637	55,758	48,521	43,371	39,482	3,505
Louisiana	62,011	63,214	57,747	12,550	214,041	68,599	54,796	45,167	40,666	4,813
Maine	17,112	16,867	16,571	1,769	56,698	15,503	14,674	13,434	12,534	553
Maryland	60,953	60,049	57,222	6,705	210,035	63,067	51,978	45,585	43,223	6,182
Massachusetts	66,869	66,447	64,097	6,342	235,220	66,707	60,669	56,226	51,618	—
Michigan	118,795	120,642	117,380	50,086	444,533	128,383	109,751	98,671	88,136	19,592
Minnesota	63,918	65,393	64,607	—	240,267	65,149	61,728	57,408	55,982	—
Mississippi	39,174	42,294	39,970	10,287	139,116	43,434	33,918	28,584	26,436	6,744
Missouri	68,357	66,705	66,025	6,830	250,255	72,584	65,084	57,447	52,654	2,486
Montana	13,194	13,329	13,229	483	47,593	13,309	12,148	11,286	10,681	169
Nebraska	22,511	22,927	23,037	—	84,045	23,281	21,958	19,662	19,144	—
Nevada	19,920	19,524	18,881	674	65,411	18,685	17,463	15,586	13,659	18
New Hampshire	15,732	15,473	14,926	545	50,468	14,564	12,969	11,965	10,919	51
New Jersey	83,410	83,350	80,901	58,482	311,875	83,256	74,858	68,708	65,662	19,391
New Mexico	25,831	26,102	25,443	—	98,080	28,547	23,885	20,114	16,925	8,609
New York	197,222	197,519	191,181	76,933	816,963	227,040	202,906	172,751	144,139	70,127
North Carolina	87,733	88,336	86,344	22,592	309,304	97,534	81,618	67,828	62,324	—
North Dakota	9,526	9,862	9,694	—	35,869	9,564	9,091	8,796	8,418	—
Ohio	141,349	146,443	142,132	4,517	519,001	151,879	132,103	122,753	112,266	—
Oklahoma	49,524	49,377	47,149	1,321	167,111	48,838	43,273	38,583	35,899	518
Oregon	42,276	41,973	40,473	1,578	149,978	41,301	39,088	35,667	33,356	566
Pennsylvania	134,201	136,184	132,994	16,080	520,963	147,352	131,606	119,008	109,673	13,324
Rhode Island	11,114	11,324	10,747	2,923	39,574	11,534	10,318	9,124	8,440	158
South Carolina	51,743	53,152	50,799	—	179,875	60,058	46,796	37,645	35,376	—
South Dakota	11,226	11,800	11,604	878	41,677	12,077	10,794	9,560	8,925	321
Tennessee	66,194	68,508	65,598	17,366	240,821	72,593	63,757	55,070	49,401	—
Texas	288,987	290,713	281,109	—	956,548	323,162	243,914	205,735	183,737	—
Utah	36,499	38,163	37,519	5,734	146,193	38,356	37,318	32,978	33,337	4,204
Vermont	8,349	8,063	7,826	—	28,943	7,993	7,311	6,669	6,458	512
Virginia	81,313	81,795	79,929	27,361	286,490	84,447	73,958	65,077	62,899	109
Washington	75,442	75,308	72,982	—	265,207	75,684	69,532	61,841	58,150	—
West Virginia	23,904	25,517	25,200	1,650	97,703	26,766	24,415	23,031	22,058	1,433
Wisconsin	65,362	65,844	65,790	—	259,366	73,063	67,229	61,667	57,407	—
Wyoming	8,176	8,426	8,203	—	30,184	8,304	8,110	7,128	6,642	—
Outlying areas										
American Samoa	945	943	903	—	3,391	885	869	829	746	62
Guam	2,396	2,433	2,275	2	7,996	2,795	2,266	1,666	1,262	7
Northern Marianas	647	692	550	—	1,870	625	429	410	406	—
Puerto Rico	49,129	54,180	49,774	9,690	165,468	45,789	44,240	38,239	32,935	4,265
Virgin Islands	1,715	2,197	1,585	843	6,467	1,935	1,553	1,210	1,140	629

[1] Data include imputations for nonrespondents.
[2] Includes imputations for underreporting.
—Data not reported or not applicable.

NOTE.—Some data have been revised from previously published figures.

SOURCE: U.S. Department of Education, National Center for Education Statistics, Common Core of Data survey. (This table was prepared April 1997.)

Table 43.—Enrollment in public elementary and secondary schools, by grade: Fall 1981 to fall 1995

Grade	Fall 1981	Fall 1982	Fall 1983	Fall 1984	Fall 1985	Fall 1986	Fall 1987	Fall 1988	Fall 1989	Fall 1990	Fall 1991	Fall 1992	Fall 1993	Fall 1994	Fall 1995
1	2	3	4	5	6	7	8	9	10	11	12	13	14	15	16
	In thousands														
All grades	40,044	39,566	39,252	39,208	39,422	39,753	40,008	40,189	40,543	41,217	42,047	42,823	43,465	44,111	44,840
Elementary	27,280	27,161	26,981	26,905	27,034	27,420	27,933	28,501	29,152	29,878	30,506	31,088	31,504	31,898	32,341
Prekindergarten	100	106	105	109	151	183	193	225	262	303	375	505	545	603	637
Kindergarten	2,588	2,740	2,754	2,900	3,041	3,127	3,196	3,208	3,225	3,306	3,311	3,313	3,377	3,444	3,536
1st grade	2,951	2,937	3,080	3,113	3,239	3,358	3,407	3,460	3,485	3,499	3,556	3,542	3,529	3,593	3,671
2nd grade	2,782	2,790	2,781	2,904	2,941	3,054	3,173	3,223	3,289	3,327	3,360	3,431	3,429	3,440	3,507
3rd grade	2,806	2,763	2,772	2,765	2,895	2,933	3,046	3,167	3,235	3,297	3,334	3,361	3,437	3,439	3,445
4th grade	2,918	2,798	2,758	2,772	2,771	2,896	2,938	3,051	3,182	3,248	3,315	3,342	3,361	3,426	3,431
5th grade	3,127	2,912	2,798	2,761	2,776	2,775	2,901	2,945	3,067	3,197	3,268	3,325	3,350	3,372	3,438
6th grade	3,180	3,142	2,928	2,831	2,789	2,806	2,811	2,937	2,987	3,110	3,239	3,303	3,356	3,381	3,395
7th grade	3,183	3,288	3,247	3,036	2,938	2,899	2,910	2,905	3,027	3,067	3,181	3,299	3,355	3,404	3,422
8th grade	3,059	3,123	3,222	3,186	2,982	2,870	2,839	2,853	2,853	2,979	3,020	3,129	3,249	3,302	3,356
Elementary ungraded	587	563	535	528	511	520	520	527	540	543	545	539	515	494	502
Secondary	12,764	12,405	12,271	12,304	12,388	12,333	12,076	11,687	11,390	11,338	11,541	11,735	11,961	12,213	12,500
9th grade	3,286	3,248	3,330	3,440	3,439	3,256	3,143	3,106	3,141	3,169	3,313	3,352	3,487	3,604	3,704
10th grade	3,218	3,137	3,103	3,145	3,230	3,215	3,020	2,895	2,868	2,896	2,915	3,027	3,050	3,131	3,237
11th grade	3,039	2,917	2,861	2,819	2,866	2,954	2,936	2,749	2,629	2,612	2,645	2,656	2,751	2,748	2,826
12th grade	2,907	2,787	2,678	2,599	2,550	2,601	2,681	2,650	2,473	2,381	2,392	2,431	2,424	2,488	2,487
Secondary ungraded	314	315	299	300	303	308	296	288	279	282	275	269	248	242	245
	Percent														
All grades	100.0	100.0	100.0	100.0	100.0	100.0	100.0	100.0	100.0	100.0	100.0	100.0	100.0	100.0	100.0
Elementary	68.1	68.6	68.7	68.6	68.6	69.0	69.8	70.9	71.9	72.5	72.6	72.6	72.5	72.3	72.1
Prekindergarten	0.2	0.3	0.3	0.3	0.4	0.5	0.5	0.6	0.6	0.7	0.9	1.2	1.3	1.4	1.4
Kindergarten	6.5	6.9	7.0	7.4	7.7	7.9	8.0	8.0	8.0	8.0	7.9	7.7	7.8	7.8	7.9
1st grade	7.4	7.4	7.8	7.9	8.2	8.4	8.5	8.6	8.6	8.5	8.5	8.3	8.1	8.1	8.2
2nd grade	6.9	7.1	7.1	7.4	7.5	7.7	7.9	8.0	8.1	8.1	8.0	8.0	7.9	7.8	7.8
3rd grade	7.0	7.0	7.1	7.1	7.3	7.4	7.6	7.9	8.0	8.0	7.9	7.8	7.9	7.8	7.7
4th grade	7.3	7.1	7.0	7.1	7.0	7.3	7.3	7.6	7.8	7.9	7.9	7.8	7.7	7.8	7.7
5th grade	7.8	7.4	7.1	7.0	7.0	7.0	7.2	7.3	7.6	7.8	7.8	7.8	7.7	7.6	7.7
6th grade	7.9	7.9	7.5	7.2	7.1	7.1	7.0	7.3	7.4	7.5	7.7	7.7	7.7	7.7	7.6
7th grade	7.9	8.3	8.3	7.7	7.5	7.3	7.3	7.2	7.5	7.4	7.6	7.7	7.7	7.7	7.6
8th grade	7.6	7.9	8.2	8.1	7.6	7.2	7.1	7.1	7.0	7.2	7.2	7.3	7.5	7.5	7.5
Elementary ungraded	1.5	1.4	1.4	1.3	1.3	1.3	1.3	1.3	1.3	1.3	1.3	1.3	1.2	1.1	1.1
Secondary	31.9	31.4	31.3	31.4	31.4	31.0	30.2	29.1	28.1	27.5	27.4	27.4	27.5	27.7	27.9
9th grade	8.2	8.2	8.5	8.8	8.7	8.2	7.9	7.7	7.7	7.7	7.9	7.8	8.0	8.2	8.3
10th grade	8.0	7.9	7.9	8.0	8.2	8.1	7.5	7.2	7.1	7.0	6.9	7.1	7.0	7.1	7.2
11th grade	7.6	7.4	7.3	7.2	7.3	7.4	7.3	6.8	6.5	6.3	6.3	6.2	6.3	6.2	6.3
12th grade	7.3	7.0	6.8	6.6	6.5	6.5	6.7	6.6	6.1	5.8	5.7	5.7	5.6	5.6	5.5
Secondary ungraded	0.8	0.8	0.8	0.8	0.8	0.8	0.7	0.7	0.7	0.7	0.7	0.6	0.6	0.5	0.5

NOTE.—Because of changes in reporting practices and imputation of data for nonrespondents in later years, data for prekindergarten enrollment are not comparable over time. Some data have been revised from previously published figures. Because of rounding, details may not add to totals.

SOURCE: U.S. Department of Education, National Center for Education Statistics, *Statistics of Public Elementary and Secondary School Systems;* and Common Core of Data surveys. (This table was prepared April 1997.)

Table 44.—Average daily attendance in public elementary and secondary schools, by state: 1969–70 to 1994–95

State or other area	1969–70	1979–80	1980–81	1985–86	1989–90	1990–91	1992–93	1993–94	1994–95
1	2	3	4	5	6	7	8	9	10
United States	41,934,376	38,288,911	37,703,744	36,523,103	37,799,296	38,426,543	39,570,462	40,146,393	40,720,763
Alabama	777,123	711,432	701,925	686,716	683,833	682,524	694,078	696,071	687,047
Alaska	72,489	79,945	83,745	98,535	98,213	102,585	110,797	112,869	113,874
Arizona	391,526	481,905	476,149	494,504	557,252	573,140	610,558	631,450	658,084
Arkansas	414,158	423,610	417,080	408,601	403,025	408,145	413,076	416,479	420,229
California [1]	4,418,423	4,044,736	4,014,917	4,245,090	4,893,341	5,065,647	5,066,708	5,108,907	5,198,308
Colorado	500,388	513,475	508,750	507,876	519,419	521,899	568,158	579,682	594,019
Connecticut	618,881	507,362	501,085	452,058	439,524	450,808	468,992	465,487	481,742
Delaware	120,819	94,058	89,609	84,936	89,838	91,052	95,660	97,247	98,793
District of Columbia	138,600	91,576	85,773	76,241	71,468	69,092	71,201	70,079	71,446
Florida	1,312,693	1,464,461	1,389,487	1,442,921	1,646,583	1,714,394	1,818,011	1,873,199	1,927,172
Georgia	1,019,427	989,433	988,612	1,004,799	1,054,097	1,075,728	1,125,385	1,148,319	1,181,724
Hawaii	168,140	151,563	151,713	151,174	157,360	160,193	165,851	169,779	169,254
Idaho	170,920	189,199	190,144	198,141	203,987	209,085	217,933	223,489	225,986
Illinois	2,084,844	1,770,435	1,765,357	1,604,265	1,587,733	1,618,101	1,685,678	1,709,915	1,734,175
Indiana	1,111,043	983,444	944,424	870,463	884,568	888,177	897,799	899,585	900,017
Iowa	624,403	510,081	501,403	454,341	450,224	456,614	467,788	477,916	478,285
Kansas	470,296	382,019	374,451	371,655	388,986	397,609	408,689	410,862	413,699
Kentucky	647,970	619,868	614,676	577,190	569,795	569,713	579,446	578,020	572,952
Louisiana	776,555	727,601	715,844	732,230	727,125	720,551	722,626	732,202	730,148
Maine	225,146	211,400	207,554	198,358	195,089	196,229	200,462	199,125	199,387
Maryland	785,989	686,336	664,866	592,383	620,617	637,370	668,778	687,455	701,594
Massachusetts	1,056,207	935,960	950,675	745,991	763,231	770,802	796,897	810,028	831,918
Michigan	1,991,235	1,758,427	1,711,139	1,481,068	1,446,996	1,452,700	1,467,900	1,474,413	1,492,653
Minnesota	864,595	748,606	710,836	669,385	699,001	714,072	744,567	756,725	770,549
Mississippi	524,623	454,401	446,515	448,117	476,048	474,029	473,262	471,367	470,974
Missouri	906,132	777,269	756,536	714,230	729,693	733,680	759,529	778,605	794,177
Montana	162,664	144,608	141,641	138,829	135,406	138,341	144,718	146,849	148,325
Nebraska	314,516	270,524	263,797	250,975	254,754	257,587	267,975	267,931	268,732
Nevada	113,421	134,995	138,481	143,941	173,149	185,755	204,440	217,681	229,862
New Hampshire	140,203	154,187	150,316	147,561	154,915	156,579	172,376	175,968	179,892
New Jersey	1,322,124	1,140,111	1,121,272	1,029,797	997,561	1,016,159	1,053,135	1,079,653	1,102,565
New Mexico	259,997	253,453	240,496	252,892	290,245	291,215	304,661	310,610	314,822
New York	3,099,192	2,530,289	2,475,055	2,276,842	2,244,110	2,278,531	2,347,468	2,404,426	2,388,973
North Carolina	1,104,295	1,072,150	1,055,651	1,014,795	1,012,274	1,012,613	1,035,258	1,051,295	1,071,640
North Dakota	141,961	118,986	111,759	108,947	109,659	109,691	111,174	111,770	111,502
Ohio	2,246,282	1,849,283	1,801,914	1,660,718	1,584,735	1,603,025	1,594,191	1,609,855	1,627,984
Oklahoma	560,993	548,065	542,800	553,370	543,170	548,387	560,744	566,155	570,381
Oregon	436,736	418,593	417,009	401,476	419,771	431,806	452,509	455,492	458,107
Pennsylvania	2,169,225	1,808,630	1,754,782	1,560,746	1,524,839	1,542,077	1,588,514	1,609,125	1,629,877
Rhode Island	163,205	139,195	135,096	122,109	125,934	129,856	134,736	135,016	136,229
South Carolina	600,292	569,612	580,132	558,716	569,029	573,138	581,775	586,178	608,699
South Dakota	158,543	124,934	121,663	118,269	119,823	121,403	126,916	127,550	128,335
Tennessee	836,010	806,696	797,237	762,225	761,766	767,738	786,146	796,744	806,895
Texas	2,432,420	2,608,817	2,647,288	2,923,741	3,075,333	3,085,648	3,237,958	3,306,297	3,364,830
Utah	287,405	312,813	323,048	379,249	408,917	417,609	432,781	439,484	442,617
Vermont	97,772	95,045	90,884	85,875	87,832	88,901	96,121	97,550	98,608
Virginia	995,580	955,105	938,794	904,347	989,197	1,011,513	1,049,901	1,065,071	1,079,496
Washington	764,735	710,929	704,655	696,372	755,141	781,371	833,641	850,813	870,163
West Virginia	372,278	353,264	351,823	330,145	301,947	300,067	294,202	291,238	287,937
Wisconsin	880,609	770,554	743,505	694,351	711,466	731,088	765,184	769,717	782,395
Wyoming	81,293	89,471	91,381	95,547	91,277	92,506	94,109	94,650	93,691
Outlying areas									
American Samoa	—	—	—	10,816	11,448	12,272	14,150	14,094	14,000
Guam	20,315	—	22,343	23,220	23,883	25,330	30,417	31,711	31,779
Northern Marianas	—	—	—	4,921	6,809	6,062	7,334	7,278	7,351
Puerto Rico	—	656,709	671,661	636,268	597,436	597,418	548,067	588,484	547,561
Virgin Islands	—	—	23,312	23,811	18,924	19,984	20,624	20,381	20,339

[1] Data for California are not strictly comparable with those for other states because California's attendance figures through 1990–91 include excused absences.
—Data not available.

SOURCE: U.S. Department of Education, National Center for Education Statistics, *Revenues and Expenditures for Public Elementary and Secondary Education; Statistics of State School Systems;* and Common Core of Data survey. (This table was prepared April 1997.)

Table 45.—Enrollment in public elementary and secondary schools, by race or ethnicity and state: Fall 1986 and fall 1995

State or other area	Percent distribution, fall 1986						Percent distribution, fall 1995					
	Total	White [1]	Black [1]	Hispanic	Asian or Pacific Islander	American Indian/ Alaskan Native	Total	White [1]	Black [1]	Hispanic	Asian or Pacific Islander	American Indian/ Alaskan Native
1	2	3	4	5	6	7	8	9	10	11	12	13
United States	100.0	70.4	16.1	9.9	2.8	0.9	100.0	64.8	16.8	13.5	3.7	1.1
Alabama	100.0	62.0	37.0	0.1	0.4	0.5	100.0	62.1	36.0	0.5	0.6	0.7
Alaska	100.0	65.7	4.3	1.7	3.3	25.1	100.0	63.7	4.6	2.7	4.4	24.5
Arizona	100.0	62.2	4.0	26.4	1.3	6.1	100.0	56.9	4.3	30.0	1.7	7.2
Arkansas	100.0	74.7	24.2	0.4	0.6	0.2	100.0	73.9	23.6	1.5	0.7	0.4
California	100.0	53.7	9.0	27.5	9.1	0.7	100.0	40.4	8.8	38.7	11.2	0.9
Colorado	100.0	78.7	4.5	13.7	2.0	1.0	100.0	72.5	5.5	18.4	2.5	1.1
Connecticut	100.0	77.2	12.1	8.9	1.5	0.2	100.0	72.0	13.5	11.8	2.4	0.3
Delaware	100.0	68.3	27.7	2.5	1.4	0.2	100.0	64.7	29.4	4.0	1.7	0.2
District of Columbia	100.0	4.0	91.1	3.9	0.9	0.1	100.0	4.0	87.6	7.0	1.4	([2])
Florida	100.0	65.4	23.7	9.5	1.2	0.2	100.0	57.5	25.3	15.3	1.8	0.2
Georgia	100.0	60.7	37.9	0.6	0.8	([2])	100.0	58.2	37.8	2.2	1.6	0.1
Hawaii	100.0	23.5	2.3	2.2	71.7	0.3	100.0	22.9	2.6	4.9	69.3	0.4
Idaho	100.0	92.6	0.3	4.9	0.8	1.3	100.0	88.4	0.6	8.4	1.2	1.3
Illinois	100.0	69.8	18.7	9.2	2.3	0.1	100.0	63.6	21.1	12.2	3.0	0.1
Indiana	100.0	88.7	9.0	1.7	0.5	0.1	100.0	85.6	11.1	2.3	0.8	0.2
Iowa	100.0	94.6	3.0	0.9	1.2	0.3	100.0	92.7	3.3	2.1	1.5	0.4
Kansas	100.0	85.6	7.6	4.4	1.9	0.6	100.0	82.6	8.5	6.0	1.8	1.1
Kentucky	100.0	89.2	10.2	0.1	0.5	([2])	100.0	89.1	9.8	0.4	0.6	0.1
Louisiana	100.0	56.5	41.3	0.8	1.1	0.3	100.0	51.0	46.0	1.1	1.3	0.5
Maine	100.0	98.3	0.5	0.2	0.8	0.2	100.0	97.3	0.8	0.4	0.9	0.6
Maryland	100.0	59.7	35.3	1.7	3.1	0.2	100.0	57.5	35.0	3.3	3.8	0.3
Massachusetts	100.0	83.7	7.4	6.0	2.8	0.1	100.0	78.5	8.2	9.3	3.8	0.2
Michigan	100.0	76.4	19.8	1.8	1.2	0.8	100.0	76.4	18.4	2.7	1.5	1.0
Minnesota	100.0	93.9	2.1	0.9	1.7	1.5	100.0	87.4	4.8	2.0	3.9	1.9
Mississippi	100.0	43.9	55.5	0.1	0.4	0.1	100.0	47.7	51.0	0.3	0.6	0.4
Missouri	100.0	83.4	14.9	0.7	0.8	0.2	100.0	81.7	16.1	1.0	1.0	0.2
Montana	100.0	92.7	0.3	0.9	0.5	5.5	100.0	87.5	0.5	1.4	0.8	9.8
Nebraska	100.0	91.4	4.4	2.4	0.8	1.0	100.0	87.2	5.9	4.4	1.3	1.4
Nevada	100.0	77.4	9.6	7.5	3.2	2.3	100.0	66.5	9.8	17.2	4.5	1.9
New Hampshire	100.0	98.0	0.7	0.5	0.8	0.1	100.0	96.7	0.9	1.2	1.1	0.2
New Jersey	100.0	69.1	17.4	10.7	2.7	0.1	100.0	62.5	18.5	13.5	5.4	0.2
New Mexico	100.0	43.1	2.3	45.1	0.8	8.7	100.0	39.5	2.4	46.8	1.0	10.4
New York	100.0	68.4	16.5	12.3	2.7	0.2	100.0	56.9	20.2	17.4	5.0	0.4
North Carolina	100.0	68.4	28.9	0.4	0.6	1.7	100.0	64.6	30.7	1.9	1.3	1.5
North Dakota	100.0	92.4	0.6	1.1	0.8	5.0	100.0	90.8	0.8	1.1	0.8	6.6
Ohio	100.0	83.1	15.0	1.0	0.7	0.1	100.0	82.2	15.3	1.4	1.0	0.1
Oklahoma	100.0	79.0	7.8	1.6	1.0	10.6	100.0	69.4	10.5	3.9	1.3	15.0
Oregon	100.0	89.8	2.2	3.9	2.4	1.7	100.0	85.3	2.6	6.8	3.4	2.0
Pennsylvania	100.0	84.4	12.6	1.8	1.2	0.1	100.0	80.6	14.0	3.5	1.8	0.1
Rhode Island	100.0	87.9	5.6	3.7	2.4	0.3	100.0	78.9	7.0	10.3	3.3	0.5
South Carolina	100.0	54.6	44.5	0.2	0.6	0.1	100.0	56.3	42.1	0.7	0.8	0.2
South Dakota	100.0	90.6	0.5	0.6	0.7	7.6	100.0	83.7	0.9	0.7	0.7	13.9
Tennessee	100.0	76.5	22.6	0.2	0.6	([2])	100.0	75.3	23.1	0.7	0.8	0.1
Texas	100.0	51.0	14.4	32.5	2.0	0.2	100.0	46.4	14.3	36.7	2.3	0.3
Utah	100.0	93.7	0.4	3.0	1.5	1.5	100.0	90.4	0.7	5.3	2.2	1.4
Vermont	100.0	98.4	0.3	0.2	0.6	0.6	100.0	97.3	0.7	0.4	1.0	0.6
Virginia	100.0	72.6	23.7	1.0	2.6	0.1	100.0	66.6	26.5	3.2	3.5	0.2
Washington	100.0	84.5	4.2	3.8	5.1	2.3	100.0	78.3	4.7	7.8	6.5	2.6
West Virginia	100.0	95.9	3.7	0.1	0.3	([2])	100.0	95.2	4.0	0.3	0.4	0.1
Wisconsin	100.0	86.6	8.9	1.9	1.7	1.0	100.0	83.2	9.4	3.3	2.8	1.3
Wyoming	100.0	90.7	0.9	5.9	0.6	1.9	100.0	89.3	1.0	6.1	0.8	2.7
Outlying areas												
American Samoa	—	—	—	—	—	—	100.0	—	—	—	100.0	—
Guam	—	—	—	—	—	—	100.0	6.7	1.3	0.5	91.5	—
Northern Marianas	—	—	—	—	—	—	100.0	0.7	—	—	99.3	—
Puerto Rico	—	—	—	—	—	—	100.0	—	—	100.0	—	—
Virgin Islands	—	—	—	—	—	—	100.0	0.9	84.5	14.3	0.4	—

[1] Excludes persons of Hispanic origin.
[2] Less than 0.05 percent.
—Data not available.

NOTE.—The 1986–87 data were derived from the 1986 Elementary and Secondary School Civil Rights sample survey of public school districts. Because of rounding, details may not add to totals.

SOURCE: U.S. Department of Education, Office for Civil Rights, *1986 State Summaries of Elementary and Secondary School Civil Rights Survey*; and National Center for Education Statistics, Common Core of Data survey. (This table was prepared April 1997.)

ELEMENTARY AND SECONDARY: ENROLLMENT 61

Table 46.—Enrollment of 3-, 4-, and 5-year-old children in preprimary programs, by level and control of program and by attendance status: October 1965 to October 1996

[In thousands]

Year and age	Total population, 3 to 5 years old	Enrollment by level and control						Enrollment by attendance		
		Total	Percent enrolled	Nursery school		Kindergarten		Full-day	Part-day	Percent full-day
				Public	Private	Public	Private			
1	2	3	4	5	6	7	8	9	10	11
Total, 3 to 5 years old										
1965	12,549	3,407	27.1	127	393	2,291	596	—	3,405	—
1970	10,949	4,104	37.5	332	762	2,498	511	698	3,405	17.0
1975	10,185	4,955	48.7	570	1,174	2,682	528	1,295	3,659	26.1
1980	9,284	4,878	52.5	628	1,353	2,438	459	1,551	3,327	31.8
1983	10,254	5,384	52.5	809	1,538	2,416	623	1,686	3,700	31.3
1984	10,612	5,480	51.6	742	1,593	2,668	476	1,929	3,550	35.2
1985	10,733	5,865	54.6	846	1,631	2,847	541	2,144	3,722	36.6
1986	10,866	5,971	55.0	829	1,715	2,859	567	2,241	3,730	37.5
1987	10,872	5,931	54.6	819	1,736	2,842	534	2,090	3,841	35.2
1988	10,993	5,978	54.4	851	1,770	2,875	481	2,044	3,935	34.2
1989	11,039	6,026	54.6	930	1,894	2,704	497	2,238	3,789	37.1
1990	11,207	6,659	59.4	1,199	2,180	2,772	509	2,577	4,082	38.7
1991	11,370	6,334	55.7	996	1,828	2,967	543	2,408	3,926	38.0
1992	11,545	6,402	55.5	1,073	1,783	2,995	550	2,410	3,992	37.6
1993	11,954	6,581	55.1	1,205	1,779	3,020	577	2,642	3,939	40.1
1994[1]	12,328	7,514	61.0	1,848	2,314	2,819	534	3,468	4,046	46.2
1995[1]	12,518	7,739	61.8	1,950	2,381	2,800	608	3,689	4,051	47.7
1996[1]	12,378	7,580	61.2	1,830	2,317	2,853	580	3,562	4,019	47.0
3 years old										
1965	4,149	203	4.9	41	153	5	4	—	—	—
1970	3,516	454	12.9	110	322	12	10	142	312	31.3
1975	3,177	683	21.5	179	474	11	18	259	423	37.9
1980	3,143	857	27.3	221	604	16	17	321	536	37.5
1983	3,574	1,004	28.1	314	631	21	39	357	648	35.5
1984	3,609	1,004	27.8	295	658	30	22	401	603	39.9
1985	3,594	1,035	28.8	278	679	52	26	350	685	33.8
1986	3,607	1,041	28.9	257	737	26	21	399	642	38.3
1987	3,569	1,022	28.6	264	703	24	31	378	644	37.0
1988	3,719	1,027	27.6	298	678	24	26	369	658	35.9
1989	3,713	1,005	27.1	277	707	3	18	390	615	38.8
1990	3,692	1,205	32.6	347	840	11	7	447	758	37.1
1991	3,811	1,074	28.2	313	702	38	22	388	687	36.1
1992	3,905	1,081	27.7	336	685	26	34	371	711	34.3
1993	4,053	1,097	27.1	369	687	20	20	426	670	38.9
1994[1]	4,081	1,385	33.9	469	887	19	9	670	715	48.4
1995[1]	4,148	1,489	35.9	511	947	15	17	754	736	50.6
1996[1]	4,045	1,506	37.2	511	947	22	26	657	848	43.7
4 years old										
1965	4,238	683	16.1	68	213	284	118	—	—	—
1970	3,620	1,007	27.8	176	395	318	117	230	776	22.8
1975	3,499	1,418	40.5	332	644	313	129	411	1,008	29.0
1980	3,072	1,423	46.3	363	701	239	120	467	956	32.8
1983	3,414	1,619	47.4	402	813	231	173	442	1,177	27.3
1984	3,579	1,603	44.8	376	860	257	110	521	1,082	32.5
1985	3,598	1,766	49.1	496	859	276	135	643	1,123	36.4
1986	3,616	1,772	49.0	498	903	257	115	622	1,150	35.1
1987	3,597	1,717	47.7	431	881	280	125	548	1,169	31.9
1988	3,598	1,768	49.1	481	922	261	104	519	1,249	29.4
1989	3,692	1,882	51.0	524	1,055	202	100	592	1,290	31.4
1990	3,723	2,087	56.1	695	1,144	157	91	716	1,371	34.3
1991	3,763	1,994	53.0	584	982	287	140	667	1,326	33.5
1992	3,807	1,982	52.1	602	971	282	126	632	1,350	31.9
1993	4,044	2,178	53.9	719	957	349	154	765	1,413	35.1
1994[1]	4,202	2,532	60.3	1,020	1,232	198	82	1,095	1,438	43.2
1995[1]	4,145	2,553	61.6	1,054	1,208	207	84	1,104	1,449	43.3
1996[1]	4,148	2,454	59.2	1,029	1,168	180	77	1,034	1,420	42.1
5 years old										
1965	4,162	2,521	60.6	18	27	2,002	474	—	—	—
1970	3,814	2,643	69.3	45	45	2,168	384	326	2,317	12.3
1975	3,509	2,854	81.3	59	57	2,358	381	625	2,228	21.9
1980	3,069	2,598	84.7	44	48	2,183	322	763	1,835	29.4
1983	3,266	2,761	84.5	93	94	2,164	410	887	1,875	32.1
1984	3,423	2,872	83.9	72	76	2,381	344	1,007	1,865	35.1
1985	3,542	3,065	86.5	73	94	2,519	379	1,151	1,914	37.6
1986	3,643	3,157	86.7	75	75	2,576	432	1,220	1,937	38.6
1987	3,706	3,192	86.1	124	152	2,538	378	1,163	2,028	36.4
1988	3,676	3,184	86.6	72	170	2,590	351	1,155	2,028	36.3
1989	3,633	3,139	86.4	129	132	2,499	378	1,255	1,883	40.0
1990	3,792	3,367	88.8	157	196	2,604	411	1,414	1,953	42.0
1991	3,796	3,267	86.0	100	143	2,642	382	1,354	1,913	41.4
1992	3,832	3,339	87.1	135	127	2,688	390	1,408	1,931	42.2
1993	3,857	3,306	85.7	116	136	2,651	403	1,451	1,856	43.9
1994[1]	4,044	3,597	88.9	359	194	2,601	442	1,704	1,893	47.4
1995[1]	4,224	3,697	87.5	385	226	2,578	507	1,830	1,867	49.5
1996[1]	4,185	3,621	86.5	290	202	2,652	477	1,870	1,750	51.7

[1] Data collected using new procedures. May not be comparable with figures for earlier years.
—Data not available.

NOTE.—Data are based on sample surveys of the civilian noninstitutional population. Although cells with fewer than 75,000 children are subject to wide sampling variation, they are included in the table to permit various types of aggregations. Enrollment data for 5-year-olds include only those students in preprimary programs. Because of rounding, details may not add to totals.

SOURCE: U.S. Department of Education, National Center for Education Statistics, *Preprimary Enrollment*, various years; and U.S. Department of Commerce, Bureau of the Census, Current Population Survey, unpublished data. (This table was prepared June 1997.)

Table 47.—Children of prekindergarten through second grade age, by enrollment status, maternal characteristics, and household income: 1991, 1993, and 1995

Maternal characteristics and household income	3- to 5-year-olds, not enrolled in school[1]			Enrolled in nursery school or prekindergarten			Enrolled in kindergarten			Enrolled in 1st grade			Enrolled in 2nd grade		
	1991	1993	1995	1991	1993	1995	1991	1993	1995	1991	1993	1995	1991	1993	1995
1	2	3	4	5	6	7	8	9	10	11	12	13	14	15	16
Total children, in thousands	4,853	4,670	4,595	3,571	3,938	4,655	4,022	4,027	4,149	4,001	3,988	4,025	3,724	3,436	3,777
	Percent distribution														
Mother's highest education[2]	100	100	100	100	100	100	100	100	100	100	100	100	100	100	100
Less than high school	18	19	22	8	11	10	16	14	17	16	14	16	16	16	20
High school diploma[3]	43	42	35	32	29	28	40	38	33	38	38	31	38	35	31
Some postsecondary	23	24	21	29	31	23	24	27	22	24	26	24	26	27	21
Associate degree	4	3	7	5	5	9	4	5	7	4	5	7	4	4	8
Bachelor's degree	9	8	10	17	14	19	11	10	14	12	11	14	10	10	13
Graduate/professional school	4	4	5	10	11	12	5	6	8	7	7	8	6	8	8
Mother's employment status[2]	100	100	100	100	100	100	100	100	100	100	100	100	100	100	100
Working 35 hours/week or more	34	30	33	34	35	38	35	38	36	38	38	39	39	37	41
Working less than 35 hours/week	21	19	18	27	23	24	22	20	21	24	22	21	22	22	21
Looking for work	7	8	7	5	6	6	6	6	6	6	7	5	7	6	5
Not in labor force	39	43	42	34	35	32	37	36	38	32	34	36	32	34	33
Household income	100	100	100	100	100	100	100	100	100	100	100	100	100	100	100
$10,000 or less	20	19	23	15	17	16	18	19	19	19	18	17	18	17	19
$10,001 to $20,000	19	22	16	14	14	10	17	18	13	17	18	13	17	17	12
$20,001 to $30,000	23	21	19	17	14	13	21	17	16	20	17	17	19	18	16
$30,001 to $40,000	16	17	16	16	15	12	15	15	15	15	15	14	15	15	16
$40,001 to $50,000	10	9	11	12	11	12	11	10	12	11	11	11	12	11	11
$50,000 to $75,000	8	8	11	16	16	19	12	13	14	11	12	16	12	14	15
More than $75,000	3	4	5	11	13	17	7	8	11	7	8	12	7	8	10

[1] Includes a very small number of older children of first and second grade age.
[2] Excludes data for households with no mother present.
[3] Includes equivalency certificates.

SOURCE: U.S. Department of Education, National Center for Education Statistics, *National Household Survey (NHES)*, 1991, 1993, and 1995. (This table was prepared October 1997.)

Table 48.—Percent of public school kindergarten teachers indicating the importance of various factors for kindergarten readiness: Spring 1993

Kindergarten readiness factors	Not at all important	Not very important	Somewhat important	Very important	Essential	Percent rating readiness factor as "Very important" or "Essential," by percentage of school's students eligible for free or reduced-price lunches		
						Less than 20 percent	20 to 49 percent	50 percent or more
1	2	3	4	5	6	7	8	9
Is physically healthy, rested, and well nourished	0	([1])	4	24	72	97	95	95
Finishes tasks	3	11	47	31	9	43	40	37
Can count to 20 or more	33	34	26	5	3	8	6	9
Takes turns and shares	2	8	34	37	19	64	55	52
Has good problem-solving skills	8	23	44	20	5	29	23	23
Is enthusiastic and curious in approaching new activities	1	3	19	43	33	83	76	73
Is able to use pencils or paint brushes	15	27	38	16	5	23	21	19
Is not disruptive of the class	2	8	30	36	24	61	58	61
Knows the English language	13	12	33	24	17	40	45	39
Is sensitive to other children's feelings	1	6	35	41	17	61	58	56
Sits still and pays attention	3	12	43	30	12	46	37	43
Knows the letters of the alphabet	27	30	33	6	4	7	9	13
Can follow directions	2	7	31	41	19	61	61	58
Identifies primary colors and basic shapes	13	24	40	17	7	22	21	27
Communicates needs, wants, and thoughts verbally in child's primary language	1	1	15	41	43	85	84	83

[1] Less than 0.5 percent.

SOURCE: U.S. Department of Education, National Center for Education Statistics, Kindergarten Teacher Survey on Student Readiness. (This table was prepared April 1994.)

Table 49.—Child care arrangements of preschool children, by age and household characteristics: 1991 and 1995

Characteristics	Children[1]		Percent in nonparental arrangements[2]			Percent with parental care only
	Number, in thousands	Percent	Relative care	Nonrelative care	Center based program[3]	
1	2	3	4	5	6	7
1991						
Age, total	8,428	100.0	16.9	14.8	52.8	31.0
3 years old	3,749	44.5	16.1	14.8	42.3	37.8
4 years old	3,636	43.1	18.1	14.8	60.4	25.9
5 years old	1,044	12.4	15.6	15.0	63.9	24.3
Race/ethnicity						
White, non-hispanic	5,867	69.6	14.8	17.3	54.0	30.6
Black, non-hispanic	1,239	14.7	24.1	7.9	58.2	25.0
Hispanic	1,002	11.9	19.5	9.7	38.9	40.6
Other	319	3.8	19.3	12.1	53.2	32.6
Household income						
$10,000 or less	1,495	17.7	16.8	6.3	44.9	42.4
10,001 to 20,000	1,437	17.0	19.3	11.8	44.5	35.9
20,001 to 30,000	1,711	20.3	18.9	12.9	44.5	38.5
30,001 to 40,000	1,319	15.7	15.9	15.7	53.2	29.7
40,001 to 50,000	936	11.1	16.6	21.4	60.0	23.1
50,001 to 75,000	974	11.6	15.6	21.9	68.4	15.2
More than 75,000	556	6.6	9.6	25.9	80.4	8.8
1995						
Age, total	9,232	100.0	19.4	16.9	55.1	25.9
3 years old	4,126	44.7	21.4	18.5	40.7	32.0
4 years old	4,065	44.0	18.3	15.3	64.7	22.2
5 years old	1,041	11.3	15.1	17.2	74.5	16.2
Race/ethnicity						
White, non-hispanic	6,337	68.6	16.5	19.4	56.9	25.2
Black, non-hispanic	1,396	15.1	28.6	11.3	59.5	20.3
Hispanic	1,042	11.3	22.8	12.5	37.4	38.4
Other	457	5.0	22.6	10.5	56.7	24.2
Household income						
$10,000 or less	1,795	19.4	18.1	10.5	48.8	34.4
10,001 to 20,000	1,204	13.0	25.2	15.1	44.6	32.7
20,001 to 30,000	1,484	16.1	20.7	13.5	45.5	34.2
30,001 to 40,000	1,319	14.3	20.0	20.3	46.1	29.7
40,001 to 50,000	1,037	11.2	18.1	19.8	55.5	23.1
50,001 to 75,000	1,381	15.0	18.8	19.1	71.1	11.8
More than 75,000	1,012	11.0	13.7	25.2	82.2	7.8

[1] Estimates are based only on children 3 to 5 years old who have not entered kindergarten.
[2] Columns do not add up to total because some children participated in more than one type of nonparental arrangement.
[3] Center based programs include day care centers, nursery schools, prekindergarten, preschools and Head Start programs.

SOURCE: U.S. Department of Education, National Center for Education Statistics, National Household Education Survey (NHES), 1991 and 1995. (This table was prepared July 1996.)

Table 50.—Participation of public kindergarten children in selected activities 5 days a week, by length and size of class and teacher preparation: Spring 1993

Activity	Total	Percent of kindergarten classes participating in activity every day						
		Length of kindergarten class		Size of kindergarten class			Teacher majored in early childhood education	
		Full-day	Half-day	Less than 20	20 to 25	More than 25	Yes	No
1	2	3	4	5	6	7	8	9
Listening to stories read aloud	90	91	90	87	92	91	91	89
Running, climbing, jumping, and other gross motor activities	58	72	48	55	57	64	60	56
Free play	66	72	62	64	67	67	67	66
Choosing from a set of specific options (like building blocks, objects, or books)	69	72	67	69	71	65	72	66
Using objects for math or science	49	61	41	48	51	48	53	45
Dramatic play, arts and crafts, music (creative activities)	64	66	63	62	65	66	68	60
Using worksheets for literary skills	14	25	13	21	18	17	19	18
Using worksheets for math or science	18	20	9	17	12	15	16	12

SOURCE: U.S. Department of Education, National Center for Education Statistics, Kindergarten Teacher Survey on Student Readiness. (This table was prepared April 1994.)

Table 51.—Public school pupils transported at public expense and current expenditures for transportation: 1929–30 to 1994–95

School year	Average daily attendance, all students	Pupils transported at public expense		Expenditures for transportation (in current dollars)		Expenditures for transportation (in constant 1994–95 dollars)	
		Number	Percent of total	Total[1] (in thousands)	Average per pupil transported	Total[1] (in thousands)	Average per pupil transported
1	2	3	4	5	6	7	8
1929–30	21,265,000	1,902,826	8.9	$54,823	$29	$481,733	$253
1931–32	22,245,000	2,419,173	10.9	58,078	24	605,909	250
1933–34	22,458,000	2,794,724	12.4	53,908	19	612,309	219
1935–36	22,299,000	3,250,658	14.6	62,653	19	685,745	211
1937–38	22,298,000	3,769,242	16.9	75,637	20	794,165	211
1939–40	22,042,000	4,144,161	18.8	83,283	20	896,346	216
1941–42	21,031,000	4,503,081	21.4	92,922	21	896,371	199
1943–44	19,603,000	4,512,412	23.0	107,754	24	930,104	206
1945–46	19,849,000	5,056,966	25.5	129,756	26	1,069,857	212
1947–48	20,910,000	5,854,041	28.0	176,265	30	1,137,840	194
1949–50	22,284,000	6,947,384	31.2	214,504	31	1,362,290	196
1951–52	23,257,000	7,697,130	33.1	268,827	35	1,538,399	200
1953–54	25,643,871	8,411,719	32.8	307,437	37	1,719,507	204
1955–56	27,740,149	9,695,819	35.0	353,972	37	1,980,442	204
1957–58	29,722,275	10,861,689	36.5	416,491	38	2,193,556	202
1959–60	32,477,440	12,225,142	37.6	486,338	40	2,489,505	204
1961–62	34,682,340	13,222,667	38.1	576,361	44	2,884,068	218
1963–64	37,405,058	14,475,778	38.7	673,845	47	3,286,158	227
1965–66	39,154,497	15,536,567	39.7	787,358	51	3,711,450	239
1967–68	40,827,965	17,130,873	42.0	981,006	57	4,338,719	253
1969–70	41,934,376	18,198,577	43.4	1,218,557	67	4,851,905	267
1971–72	42,254,272	19,474,355	46.1	1,507,830	77	5,511,293	283
1973–74	41,438,054	21,347,039	51.5	1,858,141	87	5,994,193	281
1975–76	41,269,720	21,772,483	52.8	2,377,313	109	6,447,526	296
1977–78	40,079,590	[2]21,800,000	54.4	2,731,041	125	6,558,370	[2]301
1979–80	38,288,911	21,713,515	56.7	3,833,145	177	7,426,425	342
1980–81	37,703,744	[2]22,272,000	59.1	[2]4,408,000	198	[2]7,654,000	[2]344
1981–82	37,094,652	[2]22,246,000	60.0	[2]4,793,000	215	[2]7,660,000	[2]344
1982–83	36,635,868	[2]22,199,000	60.6	[2]5,000,000	225	[2]7,662,000	[2]345
1983–84	36,362,978	[2]22,031,000	60.6	[2]5,284,000	240	[2]7,808,000	[2]354
1984–85	36,404,261	[2]22,320,000	61.3	[2]5,722,000	256	[2]8,137,000	[2]365
1985–86	36,523,103	[2]22,041,000	60.3	[2]6,123,000	278	[2]8,463,000	[2]384
1986–87	36,863,867	[2]22,397,000	60.8	[2]6,551,000	292	[2]8,858,000	[2]396
1987–88	37,050,707	[2]22,158,000	59.8	[2]6,888,000	311	[2]8,943,000	[2]404
1988–89	37,268,072	[2]22,635,000	60.7	[2]7,550,000	334	[2]9,370,000	[2]414
1989–90	37,799,296	[2]22,459,000	59.4	8,030,990	358	9,513,094	[2]424
1990–91	38,426,543	[2]22,000,000	57.3	8,678,954	394	9,747,711	[2]443
1991–92	38,960,783	[2]23,165,000	59.5	8,769,754	379	9,543,884	[2]412
1992–93	39,570,462	[2]23,439,000	59.2	9,252,300	395	9,764,041	[2]417
1993–94	40,146,393	[2]23,857,752	59.4	9,627,155	404	9,903,097	[2]415
1994–95	40,720,763	[2]23,693,000	58.2	9,889,137	417	9,889,137	[2]417

[1] Excludes capital outlay for years through 1979–80, and 1989–90 to 1994–95. From 1980–81 to 1988–89 total transportation figures include capital outlay.
[2] Estimate based on data appearing in January issues of *School Bus Fleet*.

NOTE.—Constant dollars are adjusted for inflation using the Consumer Price Index computed on a school year basis. Some data have been revised from previously published figures.

SOURCE: U.S. Department of Education, National Center for Education Statistics, *Statistics of State School Systems; Revenues and Expenditures for Public Elementary and Secondary Education*, and unpublished data; and Bobbit Publishing Co., *School Bus Fleet*, January issues. (This table was prepared September 1997.)

Table 52.—Children 0 to 21 years old served in federally supported programs for the disabled, by type of disability: 1976–77 to 1995–96

Type of disability	1976–77	1980–81	1983–84	1984–85	1985–86	1986–87	1987–88	1988–89	1989–90	1990–91	1991–92	1992–93	1993–94	1994–95	1995–96
1	2	3	4	5	6	7	8	9	10	11	12	13	14	15	16
Number served,[1] in thousands															
All disabilities	3,692	4,142	4,298	4,315	4,317	4,374	4,447	4,544	4,641	4,762	4,949	5,125	5,309	5,378	5,573
Specific learning disabilities	796	1,462	1,806	1,832	1,862	1,914	1,928	1,987	2,050	2,130	2,234	2,354	2,408	2,489	2,579
Speech or language impairments	1,302	1,168	1,128	1,126	1,125	1,136	953	967	973	985	997	996	1,014	1,015	1,022
Mental retardation	959	829	727	694	660	643	582	564	548	534	538	519	536	555	570
Serious emotional disturbance	283	346	361	372	375	383	373	376	381	390	399	401	414	427	438
Hearing impairments	87	79	72	69	66	65	56	56	57	58	60	60	64	64	67
Orthopedic impairments	87	58	56	56	57	57	47	47	48	49	51	52	56	60	63
Other health impairments	141	98	53	68	57	52	45	43	52	55	58	65	82	106	133
Visual impairments	38	31	29	28	27	26	22	23	22	23	24	23	24	24	25
Multiple disabilities	—	68	65	69	86	97	77	85	86	96	97	102	108	88	93
Deaf-blindness	—	3	2	2	2	2	1	2	2	1	1	1	1	1	1
Autism and other	—	—	—	—	—	—	—	—	—	—	5	19	24	29	39
Preschool disabled[2]	([3])	([3])	([3])	([3])	([3])	([3])	363	394	422	441	484	531	578	519	544
Percentage distribution of children served															
All disabilities	100.0	100.0	100.0	100.0	100.0	100.0	100.0	100.0	100.0	100.0	100.0	100.0	100.0	100.0	100.0
Specific learning disabilities	21.6	35.3	42.0	42.4	43.1	43.8	43.4	43.6	44.2	44.7	45.1	45.9	45.4	46.3	46.3
Speech or language impairments	35.3	28.2	26.2	26.1	26.1	26.0	21.4	21.1	21.0	20.7	20.2	19.4	19.1	18.9	18.3
Mental retardation	26.0	20.0	16.9	16.1	15.3	14.7	13.1	12.7	11.8	11.2	10.9	10.1	10.1	10.3	10.2
Serious emotional disturbance	7.7	8.4	8.4	8.6	8.7	8.8	8.4	8.3	8.2	8.2	8.1	7.8	7.8	7.9	7.9
Hearing impairments	2.4	1.9	1.7	1.6	1.5	1.5	1.3	1.3	1.2	1.2	1.2	1.2	1.2	1.2	1.2
Orthopedic impairments	2.4	1.4	1.3	1.3	1.3	1.3	1.1	1.1	1.0	1.0	1.0	1.0	1.1	1.1	1.1
Other health impairments	3.8	2.4	1.2	1.6	1.3	1.2	1.0	1.0	1.1	1.2	1.2	1.3	1.5	2.0	2.4
Visual impairments	1.0	0.7	0.7	0.7	0.6	0.6	0.5	0.5	0.5	0.5	0.5	0.5	0.5	0.4	0.4
Multiple disabilities	—	1.6	1.5	1.6	2.0	2.2	1.7	1.8	1.9	2.0	2.0	2.0	2.0	1.6	1.7
Deaf-blindness	—	0.1	0.1	([4])	([4])	([4])	([4])	([4])	([4])	([4])	([4])	([4])	([4])	([4])	([4])
Autism and other	—	—	—	—	—	—	—	—	—	—	0.1	0.4	0.4	0.5	0.7
Preschool disabled[2]	([3])	([3])	([3])	([3])	([3])	([3])	8.2	8.7	9.1	9.3	9.8	10.4	10.9	9.6	9.8
Number served as a percent of total enrollment[5]															
All disabilities	8.33	10.13	10.95	11.00	10.95	11.00	11.11	11.30	11.44	11.55	11.77	11.96	12.21	12.19	12.43
Specific learning disabilities	1.80	3.58	4.60	4.67	4.72	4.81	4.82	4.94	5.06	5.17	5.31	5.50	5.54	5.64	5.75
Speech or language impairments	2.94	2.86	2.87	2.87	2.85	2.86	2.38	2.41	2.40	2.39	2.37	2.33	2.33	2.30	2.28
Mental retardation	2.16	2.03	1.85	1.77	1.68	1.62	1.45	1.40	1.35	1.30	1.28	1.21	1.23	1.26	1.27
Serious emotional disturbance	0.64	0.85	0.92	0.95	0.95	0.96	0.93	0.94	0.94	0.95	0.95	0.94	0.95	0.97	0.98
Hearing impairments	0.20	0.19	0.18	0.18	0.17	0.16	0.14	0.14	0.14	0.14	0.14	0.14	0.15	0.15	0.15
Orthopedic impairments	0.20	0.14	0.14	0.14	0.14	0.14	0.12	0.12	0.12	0.12	0.12	0.12	0.13	0.14	0.14
Other health impairments	0.32	0.24	0.13	0.17	0.14	0.13	0.11	0.11	0.13	0.13	0.14	0.15	0.19	0.24	0.30
Visual impairments	0.09	0.08	0.07	0.07	0.07	0.07	0.05	0.06	0.06	0.06	0.06	0.05	0.06	0.05	0.06
Multiple disabilities	—	0.17	0.17	0.17	0.22	0.24	0.19	0.21	0.21	0.23	0.23	0.24	0.25	0.20	0.21
Deaf-blindness	—	0.01	0.01	([6])	0.01	([6])	([6])	([6])	([6])	([6])	([6])	([6])	([6])	([6])	([6])
Autism and other	—	—	—	—	—	—	—	—	—	—	0.01	0.04	0.05	0.07	0.09
Preschool disabled[2]	([3])	([3])	([3])	([3])	([3])	([3])	0.91	0.98	1.04	1.07	1.15	1.24	1.33	1.18	1.21

[1] Includes students served under Chapter I and Individuals with Disabilities Education Act (IDEA), formerly the Education of the Handicapped Act.
[2] Includes preschool children 3–5 years and 0–5 years served under Chapter I and IDEA, respectively.
[3] Prior to 1987–88, these students were included in the counts by handicapping condition. Beginning in 1987–88, states were no longer required to report preschool handicapped students (0–5 years) by handicapping condition.
[4] Less than .05 percent.
[5] Based on the enrollment in public schools, kindergarten through 12th grade, including a relatively small number of prekindergarten students.
[6] Less than .005 percent.
—Data not available.

NOTE.—Counts are based on reports from the 50 states and District of Columbia only (i.e., figures from U.S. territories are not included). Increases since 1987–88 are due in part to new legislation enacted fall 1986, which mandates public school special education services for all handicapped children ages 3 through 5. Some data have been revised from previously published figures. Because of rounding, details may not add to totals.

SOURCE: U.S. Department of Education, Office of Special Education and Rehabilitative Services, *Annual Report to Congress on the Implementation of The Individuals with Disabilities Education Act*, various years, and unpublished tabulations; and National Center for Education Statistics, Common Core of Data survey. (This table was prepared May 1997.)

Table 53.—Percentage distribution of disabled persons 3 to 21 years old receiving education services for the disabled, by age group and educational environment: 1994–95

Type of disability	All environments	Regular class	Resource room	Separate class	Public separate school facility	Private separate school facility	Public residential facility	Private residential facility	Homebound/hospital environment
1	2	3	4	5	6	7	8	9	10
All persons, 3 to 21 years old	100.0	50.7	9.3	31.7	4.1	1.5	0.1	0.1	2.5
3 to 5 years old	100.0	45.4	26.8	23.2	2.2	1.0	0.4	0.2	0.7
6 to 21 years old	100.0	44.8	28.5	22.4	2.0	1.0	0.5	0.3	0.6
Mental retardation	100.0	9.9	26.9	56.0	5.2	1.0	0.4	0.2	0.5
Speech or language impairments	100.0	87.6	7.5	4.5	0.2	0.1	(1)	(1)	0.1
Visual impairments	100.0	46.8	20.1	17.4	2.9	1.9	9.4	0.9	0.5
Serious emotional disturbance	100.0	22.1	24.0	35.2	8.3	5.4	1.7	1.6	1.8
Orthopedic impairments	100.0	39.3	20.4	31.9	4.4	1.1	0.3	0.1	2.5
Other health impairments	100.0	42.8	28.8	18.5	1.1	0.6	0.1	0.2	7.9
Specific learning disabilities	100.0	41.3	39.3	18.4	0.3	0.3	0.1	(1)	0.2
Deaf-blindness	100.0	9.7	8.7	37.2	17.7	3.8	17.8	2.7	2.3
Multiple disabilities	100.0	9.1	11.9	51.5	15.4	6.7	2.0	1.5	1.9
Hearing impairments	100.0	35.4	19.1	28.5	3.8	2.7	9.3	1.0	0.2
Autism	100.0	10.8	9.4	54.7	15.2	6.6	0.7	2.2	0.5
Traumatic brain injury	100.0	26.1	24.2	30.3	3.1	11.3	0.3	2.0	2.7

[1] Less than 0.05 percent.

NOTE.—There are some reporting variations, e.g., estimated or incomplete data and nonstandard definitions, from state to state. Data for 3- to 5-year-old children are no longer collected by type of disability. Because of rounding, details may not add to totals.

SOURCE: U.S. Department of Education, Office of Special Education and Rehabilitative Services, *Annual Report to Congress on the Implementation of The Individuals with Disabilities Education Act.* (This table was prepared May 1997.)

Table 54.—State legislation on gifted and talented programs and number and percent of students receiving services in public elementary and secondary schools, by state: 1993–94 and 1995–96

State	State-mandated gifted and talented programs, 1995–96[1]	Discretionary state-supported gifted and talented, 1995–96[2]	Gifted and talented students receiving services, 1993–94	Gifted and talented students as a percent of enrollment, 1993–94	State	State-mandated gifted and talented programs, 1995–96[1]	Discretionary state-supported gifted and talented, 1995–96[2]	Gifted and talented students receiving services, 1993–94	Gifted and talented students as a percent of enrollment, 1993–94
1	2	3	4	5	1	2	3	4	5
Alabama	X		16,522	2.4	Montana	X		—	—
Alaska	X		4,696	4.0	Nebraska	X		18,600	10.0
Arizona	X		39,200	—	Nevada		X	8,343	2.0
Arkansas	X		34,710	8.0	New Hampshire		X	—	—
California		X	290,000	5.0	New Jersey	—	—	—	—
Colorado		X	—	—	New Mexico	X		—	—
Connecticut	X		16,871	[3]3.5	New York	X		135,000	6.0
Delaware		X	—	5.0	North Carolina	X		88,450	8.0
District of Columbia	—	—	—	9.0	North Dakota		X	1,107	1.0
Florida	X		74,572	3.5	Ohio		X	244,670	13.0
Georgia	—	—	—	5.0	Oklahoma	X		61,082	10.0
Hawaii	X		18,000	11.0	Oregon	X		—	8.5
Idaho	X		—	1.3	Pennsylvania	X		79,756	4.6
Illinois	X		[4]166,234	5.0	Rhode Island		X	—	3.5–5.0
Indiana		X	85,192	8.9	South Carolina	X		52,000	10.0
Iowa	X		—	4.0	South Dakota		X	6,515	4.4
Kansas	X		—	3.1	Tennessee	X		18,626	2.0
Kentucky	X		52,600	5.0	Texas	X		248,769	7.0
Louisiana	X		24,000	3.2	Utah	X		—	—
Maine	X		10,100	5.0	Vermont	—	—	—	—
Maryland		X	90,222	12.0	Virginia	X		121,598	9.2
Massachusetts		X	—	—	Washington		X	38,781	1.5
Michigan		X	225,154	14.0	West Virginia	X		—	3.5
Minnesota		X	55,467	7.2	Wisconsin	X		—	15.0
Mississippi	X		21,678	4.3	Wyoming		X	—	3.0
Missouri		X	24,877	5.0	Guam	X		—	—

[1] Mandate requiring identification of and/or services for gifted/talented students.
[2] No mandate requiring identification of or services for gifted/talented students.
[3] Grades 2 through 6 only.
[4] Data for 1991–92.
—Data not available.

SOURCE: Council of State Directors of Programs for the Gifted, *The 1994 and 1996 State of the States Gifted and Talented Education Reports.* (This table was prepared July 1997.)

Table 55.—Number of children served under Individuals with Disabilities Education Act and Chapter 1 of the Education Consolidation and Improvement Act, State Operated Programs, by age group and state: 1990–91 to 1995–96

State	Birth to age 21				Percent of students that are disabled 1995–96[1]	Ages 0 to 5				Percent change, birth to 21, 1990–91 to 1995–96
	1990–91	1993–94	1994–95	1995–96		1990–91	1993–94	1994–95	1995–96	
1	2	3	4	5	6	7	8	9	10	11
United States	4,761,742	5,308,660	5,377,868	5,573,350	12.4	440,661	578,225	518,746	544,436	17.0
Alabama	94,945	99,760	99,171	98,266	13.2	7,498	9,161	8,498	8,594	3.5
Alaska	14,745	18,006	17,552	17,604	13.8	1,813	2,633	2,068	2,015	19.4
Arizona	57,235	69,530	72,443	76,089	10.2	4,936	7,685	7,277	7,880	32.9
Arkansas	47,835	53,187	52,637	53,880	11.9	5,274	6,972	6,901	7,520	12.6
California	469,282	533,807	544,018	565,670	10.2	40,489	52,061	51,990	54,795	20.5
Colorado	57,102	66,343	68,037	69,850	10.6	4,894	6,985	6,753	7,153	22.3
Connecticut	64,562	71,863	73,792	76,123	14.7	6,142	7,875	6,961	7,338	17.9
Delaware	14,294	15,196	15,424	15,624	14.4	1,579	1,953	2,010	1,905	9.3
District of Columbia	6,290	6,994	6,627	7,058	8.8	411	600	338	387	12.2
Florida	236,013	286,772	294,608	310,184	14.3	16,387	29,879	25,177	27,080	31.4
Georgia	101,997	123,143	129,212	135,042	10.3	7,333	11,869	12,789	13,314	32.4
Hawaii	13,169	15,348	15,137	16,029	8.6	1,273	1,890	1,199	1,306	21.7
Idaho	22,017	23,571	22,868	23,826	9.8	3,129	3,657	2,980	3,091	8.2
Illinois	239,185	250,829	250,524	257,427	13.2	26,122	27,985	24,258	25,432	7.6
Indiana	114,643	127,961	128,576	133,962	13.7	8,937	12,874	11,065	12,261	16.9
Iowa	60,695	63,373	64,028	65,952	13.1	6,329	6,633	5,673	5,838	8.7
Kansas	45,212	50,438	51,661	53,602	11.6	4,308	6,421	5,856	6,135	18.6
Kentucky	79,421	80,539	80,687	82,887	12.6	11,008	13,668	14,009	14,683	4.4
Louisiana	73,663	86,931	88,711	91,059	11.4	7,541	11,083	9,658	9,588	23.6
Maine	27,987	29,350	30,562	31,870	14.9	2,895	2,873	3,220	3,553	13.9
Maryland	91,940	97,998	96,771	100,863	12.5	10,409	12,018	9,052	9,486	9.7
Massachusetts	154,616	160,275	156,670	157,196	17.2	17,014	21,163	14,267	14,241	1.7
Michigan	166,927	181,251	182,833	188,768	11.5	14,963	19,748	17,664	18,241	13.1
Minnesota	80,896	90,850	93,975	98,311	11.8	10,529	12,725	10,758	10,781	21.5
Mississippi	60,934	64,153	65,490	66,804	13.2	5,704	5,896	6,449	6,607	9.6
Missouri	101,955	114,008	116,826	121,407	13.6	4,889	9,108	7,975	8,395	19.1
Montana	17,204	18,401	17,679	18,364	11.1	1,934	2,131	1,635	1,766	6.7
Nebraska	32,761	37,203	38,026	39,201	13.5	2,961	3,728	3,311	3,304	19.7
Nevada	18,440	25,242	26,363	28,202	10.6	1,742	3,215	2,900	3,166	52.9
New Hampshire	19,658	23,354	23,754	25,150	13.0	2,077	2,561	1,996	2,165	27.9
New Jersey	181,319	190,003	191,912	197,062	16.5	17,190	18,025	15,942	16,639	8.7
New Mexico	36,037	43,474	45,364	47,578	14.4	2,247	3,631	4,116	4,563	32.0
New York	307,458	365,697	374,361	394,104	14.0	26,353	46,243	45,009	47,972	28.2
North Carolina	123,126	136,513	139,513	147,078	12.4	10,700	15,042	15,133	16,671	19.5
North Dakota	12,504	12,440	12,176	12,355	10.4	1,374	1,336	1,119	1,169	-1.2
Ohio	205,440	219,875	223,640	227,529	12.4	12,487	16,347	18,193	18,204	10.8
Oklahoma	65,653	73,130	70,809	71,728	11.6	5,359	6,627	4,970	5,312	9.3
Oregon	55,149	63,212	59,363	65,022	12.3	3,581	5,859	4,774	6,097	17.9
Pennsylvania	219,428	211,422	207,436	211,711	11.8	23,156	24,312	19,715	20,680	-3.5
Rhode Island	21,076	23,582	23,693	25,072	16.7	2,112	2,798	2,131	2,333	19.0
South Carolina	77,765	81,930	82,626	86,522	13.4	8,346	10,571	9,904	10,319	11.3
South Dakota	14,987	15,907	15,755	15,512	10.7	2,366	2,518	2,227	2,176	3.5
Tennessee	104,898	119,146	123,753	126,461	14.1	7,536	11,799	9,825	10,151	20.6
Texas	350,636	411,917	420,540	441,543	11.8	30,955	38,059	30,647	32,262	25.9
Utah	47,747	51,950	51,218	52,463	11.0	4,565	5,256	4,568	4,861	9.9
Vermont	12,263	10,513	10,718	11,242	10.6	1,200	1,232	1,184	1,215	-8.3
Virginia	113,971	131,599	136,166	141,759	13.1	11,791	14,271	12,746	13,284	24.4
Washington	85,395	101,254	104,483	106,890	11.2	11,409	14,392	12,830	12,565	25.2
West Virginia	43,135	44,528	45,315	46,487	15.1	3,630	5,298	4,461	4,842	7.8
Wisconsin	86,930	102,412	102,215	106,413	12.2	12,213	15,648	13,070	13,545	22.4
Wyoming	11,202	12,480	12,150	12,549	12.6	1,571	1,911	1,495	1,556	12.0

[1] Percent based on the enrollment in public schools, prekindergarten through 12th grade.

NOTE.—Individuals with Disabilities Education Act (IDEA), formerly known as the Education of the Handicapped Act, now extends the right to a free and appropriate education to 3- to 5-year-old disabled children.

SOURCE: U.S. Department of Education, Office of Special Education and Rehabilitative Services, *Annual Report to Congress on the Implementation of The Individuals with Disabilities Education Act*, various years, and unpublished tabulations. (This table was prepared May 1997.)

Table 56.—Enrollment in grades 9 to 12 in public and private schools compared with population 14 to 17 years of age: 1889–90 to fall 1996

[Numbers in thousands]

Year	Enrollment, grades 9 to 12 [1]			Population 14 to 17 years of age [3]	Enrollment as a percent of population 14 to 17 years of age [4]
	All schools	Public schools	Private schools [2]		
1	2	3	4	5	6
1889–90	298	203	95	5,355	5.6
1899–1900	630	519	111	6,152	10.2
1909–10	1,032	915	117	7,220	14.3
1919–20	2,414	2,200	214	7,736	31.2
1929–30	4,741	4,399	[5] 341	9,341	50.7
1939–40	7,059	6,601	[6] 458	9,720	72.6
1949–50	6,397	5,725	672	8,405	76.1
1951–52	6,538	5,882	656	8,516	76.8
1953–54	7,038	6,290	747	8,861	79.4
1955–56	7,696	6,873	823	9,207	83.6
1957–58	8,790	7,860	931	10,139	86.7
Fall 1959	9,306	8,271	1,035	11,155	83.4
Fall 1961	10,489	9,369	1,120	12,046	87.1
Fall 1963	12,170	10,883	1,287	13,492	90.2
Fall 1965	13,010	11,610	1,400	14,146	92.0
Fall 1966	13,294	11,894	1,400	14,398	92.3
Fall 1967	13,650	12,250	1,400	14,727	92.7
Fall 1968	14,118	12,718	1,400	15,170	93.1
Fall 1969	14,337	13,037	1,300	15,549	92.2
Fall 1970	14,647	13,336	1,311	15,921	92.0
Fall 1971	15,053	13,753	[7] 1,300	16,326	92.2
Fall 1972	15,148	13,848	[7] 1,300	16,637	91.0
Fall 1973	15,344	14,044	[7] 1,300	16,864	91.0
Fall 1974	15,403	14,103	[7] 1,300	17,033	90.4
Fall 1975	15,604	14,304	[7] 1,300	17,125	91.1
Fall 1976	15,656	14,314	1,342	17,117	91.5
Fall 1977	15,546	14,203	1,343	17,042	91.2
Fall 1978	15,441	14,088	1,353	16,944	91.1
Fall 1979	14,916	13,616	[7] 1,300	16,610	89.8
Fall 1980	14,570	13,231	1,339	16,143	90.3
Fall 1981	14,164	12,764	[7] 1,400	15,609	90.7
Fall 1982	13,805	12,405	[7] 1,400	15,057	91.7
Fall 1983	13,671	12,271	[7] 1,400	14,740	92.7
Fall 1984	13,704	12,304	[7] 1,400	14,725	93.1
Fall 1985	13,750	12,388	1,362	14,888	92.4
Fall 1986	13,669	12,333	[7] 1,336	14,824	92.2
Fall 1987	13,323	12,076	1,247	14,502	91.9
Fall 1988	12,893	11,687	[7] 1,206	14,023	91.9
Fall 1989	12,583	11,390	[7] 1,193	13,536	93.0
Fall 1990	12,475	11,338	[7] 1,137	13,310	93.7
Fall 1991	12,666	11,541	[7] 1,125	13,418	94.4
Fall 1992	12,898	11,735	[7] 1,163	13,653	94.5
Fall 1993	13,152	11,961	[7] 1,191	13,928	94.4
Fall 1994	13,449	12,213	[7] 1,236	14,427	93.2
Fall 1995	13,769	12,500	[7] 1,269	14,765	93.3
Fall 1996	14,167	[7] 12,874	[7] 1,293	15,170	93.4

[1] Includes a relatively small number of secondary ungraded and postgraduate students.
[2] Data for most years are partly estimated.
[3] Data for 1890 through 1950 and for 1960 are from the decennial censuses of population. The other figures are Bureau of the Census estimates as of July 1 preceding the opening of the school year.
[4] Gross enrollment ratio based on school enrollment of all ages in grades 9 to 12 divided by the 14- to 17-year-old population. Differs from enrollment rates in other tables which are based on the enrollment of persons in the given age group only.
[5] Data are for 1927–28.
[6] Data are for 1940–41.
[7] Estimated.

NOTE.—Includes enrollment in public schools that are a part of state and local school systems and also in most private schools, both religiously affiliated and nonsectarian. Excludes enrollment in subcollegiate departments of institutions of higher education, residential schools for exceptional children, and federal schools. Because of rounding, details may not add to totals. Some data have been revised from previously published figures.

SOURCE: U.S. Department of Education, National Center for Education Statistics, *Statistics of State School Systems; Statistics of Public Elementary and Secondary School Systems; Statistics of Nonpublic Elementary and Secondary Schools;* Common Core of Data survey; and *Projections of Education Statistics to 2007.* (This table was prepared May 1997.)

Table 57.—Enrollment in foreign language courses compared with enrollment in grades 9 to 12 in public secondary schools: Fall 1948 to fall 1994

[In thousands]

Language	Fall 1948	Fall 1960	Fall 1965	Fall 1968	Fall 1970	Fall 1974	Fall 1976	Fall 1978	Fall 1982	Fall 1985	Fall 1990	Fall 1994	Percent change in enrollment 1976 to 1990	Percent change in enrollment 1990 to 1994
1	2	3	4	5	6	7	8	9	10	11	12	13	14	15
Total enrollment, grades 9 to 12	[1]5,602	8,589	11,610	12,718	13,336	14,103	14,314	14,088	12,405	12,388	11,338	12,214	−20.8	7.7
All foreign languages [2]														
Number enrolled	1,170	2,522	3,659	3,890	3,779	3,295	3,174	3,200	2,910	4,029	4,257	5,002	34.1	17.5
Percent of all students	20.9	29.4	31.5	30.6	28.3	23.3	22.2	22.7	23.3	32.2	37.5	41.0	—	—
Modern foreign languages														
Number enrolled	741	1,867	3,068	3,518	3,514	3,127	3,023	3,048	2,740	3,852	4,093	4,813	35.4	17.6
Percent of all students	13.2	21.7	26.4	27.7	26.4	22.1	21.1	21.6	21.9	31.1	36.1	42.4	—	—
Spanish														
Number enrolled	443	933	1,427	1,698	1,811	1,678	1,717	1,631	1,563	2,334	2,611	3,220	52.1	23.3
Percent of all students	7.9	10.9	12.3	13.4	13.6	11.9	12.0	11.6	12.5	18.8	23.0	28.4	—	—
French														
Number enrolled	254	744	1,251	1,328	1,231	978	888	856	858	1,134	1,089	1,106	22.6	1.5
Percent of all students	4.5	8.7	10.8	10.4	9.2	6.9	6.2	6.1	6.9	9.2	9.6	9.8	—	—
German														
Number enrolled	43	151	328	423	411	393	353	331	267	312	295	326	−16.2	10.3
Percent of all students	0.8	1.8	2.8	3.3	3.1	2.8	2.5	2.3	2.1	2.5	2.6	2.9	—	—
Russian														
Number enrolled	—	10	27	24	20	15	11	9	6	6	16	16	46.6	−0.4
Percent of all students	—	0.1	0.2	0.2	0.2	0.1	0.1	0.1	[3]	[3]	0.1	0.1	—	—
Italian														
Number enrolled	—	20	25	27	27	40	46	46	44	47	40	44	−11.4	8.5
Percent of all students	—	0.2	0.2	0.2	0.2	0.3	0.3	0.3	0.4	0.4	0.4	0.4	—	—
Japanese [4]														
Number enrolled	—	—	—	—	—	—	—	—	—	—	25	42	—	68.3
Percent of all students	—	—	—	—	—	—	—	—	—	—	0.2	0.3	—	—
Other modern foreign languages [5]														
Number enrolled	1	9	9	18	15	23	9	176	3	18	15	59	73.0	296.1
Percent of all students	[3]	0.1	0.1	0.1	0.1	0.2	0.1	1.2	[3]	0.1	0.1	0.5	—	—
Latin														
Number enrolled	429	655	591	372	265	167	150	152	170	177	164	189	8.9	15.2
Percent of all students	7.7	7.6	5.1	2.9	2.0	1.2	1.1	1.1	1.4	1.4	1.4	1.7	—	—

[1] Estimated.
[2] Includes enrollment in ancient Greek (not shown separately). Fewer than 1,000 students were enrolled in this language in each of the years shown.
[3] Less than 0.05 percent.
[4] Until 1990, student enrollment in Japanese courses was included in the Other modern foreign languages category.
[5] Includes students enrolled in unspecified modern foreign languages. In 1978, a relatively large number of students were not identified by field of study. Since 1990, enrollment in Japanese courses is reported as a separate category.

—Data not reported, not available, or not applicable.

SOURCE: U.S. Department of Education, National Center for Education Statistics, Common Core of Data survey; and American Council on the Teaching of Foreign Languages, *Foreign Language Enrollments in Public Secondary Schools, Fall 1989, Fall 1990,* and *Fall 1994.* (This table was prepared April 1997.)

Table 58.—Student participation in school programs and services, by control, level of school, and type of community: 1993–94

Control, level, and community type	Total students		Percent of students participating in program or service							
	Number	Percent distribution	Bilingual education	English as a second language	Remedial reading	Remedial mathematics	Programs for the disabled	Programs for the gifted and talented	Diagnostic and prescriptive	Extended day
1	2	3	4	5	6	7	8	9	10	11
Public total	**41,621,660**	**100.0**	**3.07**	**3.97**	**10.88**	**6.90**	**6.88**	**6.43**	**0.27**	**2.50**
School level[1]										
Elementary	26,886,026	64.6	3.98	4.75	13.46	7.77	6.76	6.25	0.31	3.58
Secondary	13,757,801	33.1	1.39	2.58	5.63	5.03	6.54	6.90	0.20	0.48
Combined	977,833	2.3	1.80	1.88	13.70	9.39	14.84	4.72	0.44	1.31
Community type										
Central city	12,163,036	29.2	6.30	7.13	12.86	8.34	7.05	6.55	0.23	3.82
Urban fringe/large town	13,559,662	32.6	2.04	3.90	8.84	5.60	6.34	7.26	0.23	2.69
Rural/small town	15,898,962	38.2	1.48	1.60	11.09	6.90	7.20	5.63	0.35	1.33
Private total	**4,970,548**	**100.0**	**0.81**	**0.58**	**6.35**	**4.16**	**2.98**	**4.93**	**0.89**	**9.20**
School level[1]										
Elementary	2,803,359	56.4	0.77	0.45	7.22	4.33	0.93	3.34	0.94	12.48
Secondary	811,087	16.3	0.19	0.62	4.24	3.06	3.43	8.56	0.47	0.23
Combined	1,356,102	27.3	1.25	0.83	5.82	4.46	6.95	6.05	1.03	7.76
Community type										
Central city	2,261,125	45.5	0.83	0.71	7.33	4.77	2.68	5.56	0.72	11.36
Urban fringe/large town	1,810,230	36.4	0.97	0.57	5.98	4.15	3.58	5.24	0.85	8.89
Rural/small town	899,193	18.1	0.42	0.27	4.63	2.62	2.50	2.75	1.48	4.39

[1] Elementary schools have grade 6 or lower or a low grade of ungraded and no grade higher than 8. Secondary schools have no grade lower than 7. Combined schools have grades lower than 7 and higher than 8.

NOTE.—Students may participate in more than one program or service. Includes only kindergarten pupils who attend schools that offer first grade or above. Excludes prekindergarten students. Totals differ from data appearing in other tables because of varying survey processing procedures and time period coverages.

SOURCE: U.S. Department of Education, National Center for Education Statistics, "Schools and Staffing Survey, 1993–94." (This table was prepared September 1996.)

Table 59.—Private elementary and secondary enrollment and schools, by selected characteristics: 1993–94

Selected characteristics	Kindergarten through 12th grade enrollment[1]				Schools			
	Total	Catholic	Other religious	Non-sectarian	Total	Catholic	Other religious	Non-sectarian
1	2	3	4	5	6	7	8	9
Total	**4,970,646**	**2,516,130**	**1,686,064**	**768,451**	**26,093**	**8,351**	**12,180**	**5,563**
School enrollment								
Less than 150	890,343	168,200	509,028	213,115	14,155	1,572	8,499	4,084
150 to 299	1,482,210	853,139	467,749	161,322	6,820	3,815	2,232	773
300 to 499	1,243,578	719,037	359,278	165,263	3,272	1,885	973	414
500 to 749	736,057	432,557	196,751	106,749	1,228	729	327	172
750 or more	618,457	343,197	153,257	122,003	619	350	149	120
Percent minority students								
Less than 5%	1,855,365	876,589	774,050	204,726	10,750	3,152	6,137	1,461
5%, but less than 20%	1,620,369	761,747	502,822	355,800	7,482	2,376	3,070	2,036
20%, but less than 50%	704,432	375,825	189,615	138,992	3,785	1,095	1,395	1,295
50% or more	790,479	501,969	219,577	68,933	4,076	1,727	1,578	771
Community type								
Central city	2,261,124	1,179,765	754,308	327,051	9,707	3,543	4,061	2,103
Urban fringe/large town	1,810,231	995,081	529,918	285,232	8,583	2,963	3,399	2,221
Rural/small town	899,192	341,182	401,843	156,168	7,803	1,844	4,720	1,239

[1] Includes only kindergarten pupils who attend schools that offer first grade.

NOTE.—Data are based upon a sample survey and may not be strictly comparable with data reported elsewhere. Includes only schools that offer first grade or above. Excludes prekindergarten students. Because of rounding, details may not add to totals.

SOURCE: U.S. Department of Education, National Center for Education Statistics, "Schools and Staffing Survey, 1993–94." (This table was prepared September 1996.)

ELEMENTARY AND SECONDARY: PRIVATE SCHOOLS

Table 60.—Private elementary and secondary staff and student-staff ratios, by level and orientation of school: 1993–94

Orientation and type of staff	Full-time equivalent staff				Students per full-time equivalent staff member			
	Total	Elementary[1]	Secondary[2]	Combined[3]	Total	Elementary[1]	Secondary[2]	Combined[3]
1	2	3	4	5	6	7	8	9
Total	534,636	240,894	104,213	189,529	9.3	11.6	7.8	7.2
Principals	23,589	13,180	2,459	7,950	210.7	212.7	329.8	170.6
Assistant principals	8,361	3,094	2,113	3,154	594.5	906.1	383.9	430.0
Other managers	7,801	1,510	3,483	2,808	637.2	1,856.5	232.9	483.0
Instruction coordinators	6,063	1,837	1,293	2,933	819.8	1,526.1	627.3	462.4
Teachers	330,838	155,220	60,644	114,974	15.0	18.1	13.4	11.8
Teacher aides	33,905	16,516	2,566	14,823	146.6	169.7	316.1	91.5
Guidance counselors	8,640	1,713	3,758	3,169	575.3	1,636.5	215.8	428.0
Librarians/media specialists	8,946	4,320	1,950	2,676	555.6	648.9	415.9	506.8
Library/media center aides	3,768	1,942	588	1,238	1,319.2	1,443.5	1,379.4	1,095.5
Student support staff[4]	11,003	2,207	2,684	6,112	451.8	1,270.2	302.2	221.9
Secretaries/clerical staff	37,634	15,170	9,061	13,403	132.1	184.8	89.5	101.2
Other employees[5]	54,092	24,187	13,615	16,290	91.9	115.9	59.6	83.3
Catholic								
Total	206,094	135,831	59,239	11,024	12.2	13.6	10.0	6.9
Principals	8,186	6,702	1,177	307	307.4	275.8	503.0	247.1
Assistant principals	2,854	1,210	1,475	169	881.6	1,527.5	401.4	448.9
Other managers	3,139	717	2,168	254	801.6	2,577.8	273.1	298.7
Instruction coordinators	1,138	619	477	42	2,211.0	2,985.9	1,241.1	1,806.2
Teachers	132,240	88,524	37,132	6,584	19.0	20.9	15.9	11.5
Teacher aides	9,078	8,144	176	758	277.2	226.9	3,363.7	100.1
Guidance counselors	3,843	1,144	2,341	358	654.7	1,615.6	252.9	211.9
Librarians/media specialists	4,291	2,836	1,230	225	586.4	651.7	481.3	337.2
Library/media center aides	1,969	1,489	363	117	1,277.9	1,241.3	1,630.9	648.4
Student support staff[4]	2,287	1,418	568	301	1,100.2	1,303.4	1,042.3	252.0
Secretaries/clerical staff	13,731	8,139	4,841	751	183.2	227.1	122.3	101.0
Other employees[5]	23,338	14,889	7,291	1,158	107.8	124.1	81.2	65.5
Other religious orientation								
Total	184,521	72,798	16,970	94,753	9.1	9.9	7.3	8.9
Principals	9,917	4,535	573	4,809	170.0	158.4	217.2	175.4
Assistant principals	3,184	1,102	278	1,804	529.5	651.7	447.7	467.5
Other managers	1,932	584	340	1,008	872.7	1,229.7	366.0	836.8
Instruction coordinators	2,298	775	153	1,370	733.7	926.7	813.4	615.7
Teachers	120,253	46,973	10,366	62,914	14.0	15.3	12.0	13.4
Teacher aides	10,021	4,827	171	5,023	168.3	148.8	727.8	167.9
Guidance counselors	2,001	473	403	1,125	842.6	1,518.3	308.8	749.7
Librarians/media specialists	2,596	977	349	1,270	649.5	735.1	356.6	664.1
Library/media center aides	990	330	112	548	1,703.1	2,176.3	1,111.1	1,539.1
Student support staff[4]	1,318	489	231	598	1,279.3	1,468.7	538.7	1,410.4
Secretaries/clerical staff	13,551	5,033	1,637	6,881	124.4	142.7	76.0	122.6
Other employees[5]	16,460	6,700	2,357	7,403	102.4	107.2	52.8	113.9
Non-sectarian								
Total	144,025	32,267	28,005	83,753	5.3	7.3	3.4	5.2
Principals	5,486	1,943	709	2,834	140.1	121.9	133.5	154.2
Assistant principals	2,323	782	360	1,181	330.8	303.0	262.9	369.9
Other managers	2,730	209	975	1,546	281.5	1,133.6	97.1	282.6
Instruction coordinators	2,627	443	663	1,521	292.5	534.8	142.7	287.2
Teachers	78,345	19,723	13,146	45,476	9.8	12.0	7.2	9.6
Teacher aides	14,806	3,545	2,219	9,042	51.9	66.8	42.6	48.3
Guidance counselors	2,796	96	1,014	1,686	274.8	2,468.0	93.3	259.1
Librarians/media specialists	2,059	507	371	1,181	373.2	467.3	255.1	369.9
Library/media center aides	809	123	113	573	949.9	1,926.3	837.4	762.5
Student support staff[4]	7,398	300	1,885	5,213	103.9	789.8	50.2	83.8
Secretaries/clerical staff	10,352	1,998	2,583	5,771	74.2	118.6	36.6	75.7
Other employees[5]	14,294	2,598	3,967	7,729	53.8	91.2	23.9	56.5

[1] Includes schools beginning with grade 6 or below and with no grade higher than 8.
[2] Schools have no grade lower than 7.
[3] Schools have grades lower than 7 and higher than 8.
[4] Includes student support services professional staff, such as school psychologists, social workers, occupational therapists, speech therapists, and nurses.
[5] Includes cafeteria workers and maintenance staff.

NOTE.—Data are based upon a sample survey and may not be strictly comparable with data reported elsewhere. Includes only schools that offer first grade or above.

SOURCE: U.S. Department of Education, National Center for Education Statistics, "Schools and Staffing Survey, 1993–94." (This table was prepared August 1995.)

Table 61.—Private elementary and secondary enrollment and schools, by amount of tuition, level, and orientation of school: 1993–94

Orientation and tuition	Kindergarten through 12th grade enrollment[1]				Schools				Average tuition paid by students[2]			
	Total	Elementary	Secondary	Combined	Total	Elementary	Secondary	Combined	Total	Elementary	Secondary	Combined
1	2	3	4	5	6	7	8	9	10	11	12	13
Total	4,970,646	2,803,359	811,087	1,356,199	26,093	15,538	2,551	8,004	$3,116	$2,138	$4,578	$4,266
Catholic	2,516,130	1,848,257	592,011	75,862	8,351	6,924	1,161	266	2,178	1,628	3,643	4,153
Less than $1,000	393,901	378,724	([3])	([3])	1,786	1,706	([3])	([3])	—	—	—	—
$1,000 to $2,499	1,368,046	1,274,601	81,955	([3])	4,834	4,542	235	([3])	—	—	—	—
$2,500 to $4,999	675,708	188,123	452,901	([3])	1,533	642	782	([3])	—	—	—	—
$5,000 or more	71,929	([3])	([3])	([3])	([3])	([3])	([3])	([3])	—	—	—	—
Other religious	1,686,064	718,170	124,447	843,448	12,180	6,328	612	5,240	2,915	2,606	5,261	2,831
Less than $1,000	113,382	66,259	([3])	45,878	2,435	1,386	([3])	1,044	—	—	—	—
$1,000 to $2,499	839,447	387,917	([3])	435,788	6,759	3,645	([3])	3,012	—	—	—	—
$2,500 to $4,999	513,773	187,164	62,993	263,615	2,198	970	316	913	—	—	—	—
$5,000 or more	203,014	68,255	38,655	96,104	738	303	172	263	—	—	—	—
Non-sectarian	768,451	236,932	94,629	436,890	5,563	2,287	778	2,498	6,631	4,693	9,525	7,056
Less than $1,000	49,128	([3])	([3])	([3])	912	([3])	([3])	([3])	—	—	—	—
$1,000 to $2,499	121,869	([3])	([3])	([3])	666	([3])	([3])	([3])	—	—	—	—
$2,500 to $4,999	200,857	119,326	([3])	74,395	1,810	1,301	([3])	465	—	—	—	—
$5,000 or more	396,244	82,596	74,283	239,364	2,166	456	408	1,302	—	—	—	—

[1] Only includes kindergarten students who attend schools that offer first grade or above.
[2] Tuition weighted by the number of students enrolled in schools.
[3] Too few sample cases (fewer than 30 schools) for reliable estimates.
—Data not applicable.

NOTE.—Data are based upon a sample survey and may not be strictly comparable with data reported elsewhere. Elementary schools have grade 6 or lower and no grade higher than 8. Secondary schools have no grade lower than 7. Combined schools have grades lower than 7 and higher than 8. Excludes prekindergarten students. Because of rounding and missing values in cells with too few sample cases, details may not add to totals.

SOURCE: U.S. Department of Education, National Center for Education Statistics, "Schools and Staffing Survey, 1993–94." (This table was prepared August 1995.)

Table 62.—Summary statistics on Catholic elementary and secondary schools, by level: 1919–20 to 1996–97

School year	Number of schools			Enrollment			Instructional staff		
	Total	Elementary	Secondary	Total	Elementary	Secondary	Total	Elementary	Secondary
1	2	3	4	5	6	7	8	9	10
1919–20	8,103	6,551	1,552	1,925,521	1,795,673	129,848	[1]49,516	[1]41,592	[1]7,924
1929–30	10,046	7,923	2,123	2,464,467	2,222,598	241,869	[1]72,552	[1]58,245	[1]14,307
1939–40	10,049	7,944	2,105	2,396,305	2,035,182	361,123	[1]81,057	[1]60,081	[1]20,976
1949–50	10,778	8,589	2,189	3,066,387	2,560,815	505,572	[1]94,295	[1]66,525	[1]27,770
Fall 1960	12,893	10,501	2,392	5,253,791	4,373,422	880,369	[1]151,902	[1]108,169	[1]43,733
1969–70	11,771	9,695	2,076	4,658,098	3,607,168	1,050,930	[2]195,400	[2]133,200	[2]62,200
1970–71	11,350	9,370	1,980	4,363,566	3,355,478	1,008,088	166,208	112,750	53,458
1974–75	10,127	8,437	1,690	3,504,000	2,602,000	902,000	150,179	100,011	50,168
1975–76	9,993	8,340	1,653	3,415,000	2,525,000	890,000	149,276	99,319	49,957
1979–80	9,640	8,100	1,540	3,139,000	2,293,000	846,000	147,294	97,724	49,570
1980–81	9,559	8,043	1,516	3,106,000	2,269,000	837,000	145,777	96,739	49,038
1981–82	9,494	7,996	1,498	3,094,000	2,266,000	828,000	146,172	96,847	49,325
1982–83	9,432	7,950	1,482	3,007,189	2,211,412	795,777	146,460	97,337	49,123
1983–84	9,401	7,937	1,464	2,969,000	2,179,000	790,000	146,913	98,591	48,322
1984–85	9,325	7,876	1,449	2,903,000	2,119,000	784,000	149,888	99,820	50,068
1985–86	9,220	7,790	1,430	2,821,000	2,061,000	760,000	146,594	96,741	49,853
1986–87	9,102	7,693	1,409	2,726,000	1,998,000	728,000	141,930	93,554	48,376
1987–88	8,992	7,601	1,391	2,623,000	1,942,000	681,000	139,887	93,199	46,688
1988–89	8,867	7,505	1,362	2,551,000	1,912,000	639,000	137,700	93,154	44,546
1989–90	8,719	7,395	1,324	2,499,000	1,894,000	606,000	136,900	94,197	42,703
1990–91	8,587	7,291	1,296	2,475,439	1,883,906	591,533	131,198	91,039	40,159
1991–92	8,508	7,239	1,269	2,442,924	1,856,302	586,622	153,334	109,084	44,250
1992–93	8,423	7,174	1,249	2,444,842	1,860,937	583,905	154,816	109,825	44,991
1993–94	8,345	7,114	1,231	2,444,609	1,859,947	584,662	157,201	112,199	45,002
1994–95	8,293	7,055	1,238	2,475,207	1,877,782	597,425	[3]164,219	[3]117,620	[3]46,599
1995–96[4]	8,250	7,022	1,228	2,491,111	1,884,461	606,650	[3]166,759	[3]118,753	[3]48,006
1996–97	8,231	7,005	1,226	2,497,198	1,885,037	612,161	[3]153,276	[3]107,548	[3]45,728

[1] Includes part-time teachers.
[2] Includes estimates for the nonreporting schools.
[3] Full-time equivalent.
[4] Revised from previously published figures.

NOTE.—Data reported by the National Catholic Educational Association and data reported by the National Center for Education Statistics are not directly comparable because survey procedures and definitions differ. Excludes prekindergarten enrollment.

SOURCE: National Catholic Educational Association, *A Statistical Report on Catholic Elementary and Secondary Schools for the Years 1967–68 to 1969–70*, as compiled from the Official Catholic Directory (Copyright © 1970 by the National Catholic Educational Association); *Catholic Schools in America* (1978 edition, Copyright © 1978 by the Franklin Press); and *United States Catholic Elementary and Secondary Schools, 1989–90, 1990–91, 1991–92, 1992–93, 1993–94, 1994–95, 1995–96,* and *1996–97* (Copyright © 1990, 1991, 1992, 1993, 1994, 1995, 1996, and 1997 by the National Catholic Educational Association. All rights reserved.) (This table was prepared July 1997.)

ELEMENTARY AND SECONDARY: PRIVATE SCHOOLS

Table 63.—Private elementary and secondary schools, enrollment, teachers, and high school graduates, by state:[1] Fall 1993

State	Number of schools		Enrollment		Teachers		High school graduates, 1992–93	
	Total	Standard error	Total	Standard error	Total	Standard error	Total	Standard error
1	2	3	4	5	6	7	8	9
United States[2]	26,093	205	4,836,442	12,875	338,162	1,319	247,278	697
Alabama	410	79	72,630	4,724	5,424	456	4,174	348
Alaska	66	—	5,884	0	476	—	213	—
Arizona	263	—	41,957	—	2,796	—	2,415	—
Arkansas	179	30	29,011	3,995	2,023	335	1,023	—
California	3,145	65	569,062	1,987	35,170	248	24,436	65
Colorado	391	68	53,732	7,798	4,115	632	1,826	283
Connecticut	360	22	70,198	1,875	6,345	125	6,291	46
Delaware	90	—	22,308	—	1,780	—	1,446	—
District of Columbia	80	—	15,854	—	1,544	—	1,054	—
Florida	1,262	83	233,743	3,789	16,842	424	9,820	54
Georgia	580	81	97,726	3,586	8,283	300	5,630	127
Hawaii	121	—	30,537	—	2,144	—	1,886	—
Idaho	78	—	8,019	—	552	—	341	—
Illinois	1,347	12	293,038	794	17,550	70	14,724	98
Indiana	619	—	91,986	—	6,139	—	4,061	—
Iowa	290	30	50,602	211	3,291	34	2,495	—
Kansas	206	—	37,045	—	2,382	—	1,668	—
Kentucky	296	—	58,058	—	3,815	—	2,949	—
Louisiana	458	19	145,512	4,036	9,286	301	7,844	—
Maine	140	—	16,999	—	1,535	—	1,914	—
Maryland	522	—	112,481	—	8,646	—	5,648	—
Massachusetts	648	29	126,744	1,362	11,329	168	10,281	—
Michigan	1,075	—	187,741	—	11,322	—	8,925	—
Minnesota	542	—	86,051	—	5,595	—	3,453	—
Mississippi	221	30	58,655	1,564	3,995	150	3,901	180
Missouri	719	69	117,466	616	7,973	85	5,839	212
Montana	82	—	9,111	—	684	—	355	—
Nebraska	223	—	39,564	—	2,575	—	1,904	—
Nevada	58	—	10,723	—	654	—	646	—
New Hampshire	130	—	18,386	—	1,742	—	1,730	—
New Jersey	878	—	195,921	—	14,281	—	11,025	—
New Mexico	166	—	20,007	—	1,569	—	1,029	—
New York	1,985	59	473,119	4,776	34,771	482	26,625	125
North Carolina	463	18	69,000	1,803	5,746	147	2,983	—
North Dakota	59	—	7,577	—	529	—	332	—
Ohio	1,016	58	246,805	3,480	14,872	306	12,398	172
Oklahoma	190	62	25,837	3,584	2,250	450	1,536	288
Oregon	250	—	34,092	—	2,254	—	1,700	—
Pennsylvania	1,846	54	342,298	4,260	21,880	235	18,532	304
Rhode Island	112	—	23,153	—	1,835	—	1,408	—
South Carolina	297	21	51,600	1,819	3,989	155	2,383	—
South Dakota	96	—	9,575	—	707	—	254	—
Tennessee	496	54	84,538	2,909	6,684	162	4,970	—
Texas	1,353	98	211,337	7,591	16,726	708	8,447	469
Utah	66	—	9,793	—	749	—	590	—
Vermont	85	—	9,107	—	945	—	1,120	—
Virginia	515	55	84,438	4,584	7,391	621	4,580	—
Washington	486	53	70,205	1,858	4,798	348	2,644	—
West Virginia	145	—	13,539	—	1,085	—	672	—
Wisconsin	954	—	141,762	—	8,927	—	5,129	—
Wyoming	35	—	1,919	—	167	—	31	—

[1] Includes special education, vocational/technical education, and alternative schools. Excludes prekindergarten enrollment.

[2] The National Center for Education Statistics employed an area frame sample to account for noninclusion of schools at the national level. However, caution should be exercised in interpreting state by state characteristics since the samples were not designed to produce such numbers.

—Insufficient data to compute a standard error.

NOTE.—Tabulation includes only schools that offer first grade or above.

SOURCE: U.S. Department of Education, National Center for Education Statistics, "Private School Survey, 1993–94." (This table was prepared August 1995.)

Table 64.—Public and private elementary and secondary teachers and pupil-teacher ratios, by level: Fall 1955 to fall 1997

Year	Public and private elementary and secondary			Public elementary and secondary			Private elementary and secondary		
	Kindergarten to grade 12	Elementary	Secondary	Kindergarten to grade 12	Elementary	Secondary	Kindergarten to grade 12	Elementary	Secondary
1	2	3	4	5	6	7	8	9	10
Number of teachers, in thousands									
1955	1,286	827	459	1,141	733	408	[1] 145	[1] 94	[1] 51
1960	1,600	991	609	1,408	858	550	[1] 192	[1] 133	[1] 59
1965	1,933	1,112	822	1,710	965	746	223	147	76
1966	2,012	1,153	859	1,789	1,006	783	[1] 223	[1] 147	[1] 76
1967	2,079	1,188	891	1,855	1,040	815	[1] 224	[1] 148	[1] 76
1968	2,161	1,223	938	1,936	1,076	860	225	147	78
1969	2,245	1,260	986	2,016	1,109	908	[1] 229	[1] 151	[1] 78
1970	2,292	1,283	1,009	2,059	1,130	929	233	153	80
1971	2,293	1,263	1,030	2,063	1,111	952	[1] 230	[1] 152	[1] 78
1972	2,337	1,296	1,041	2,106	1,142	964	[1] 231	[1] 154	[1] 77
1973	2,372	1,308	1,064	2,136	1,151	985	[1] 236	[1] 157	[1] 79
1974	2,410	1,330	1,079	2,165	1,166	998	[1] 245	[1] 164	[1] 81
1975	2,453	1,353	1,100	2,198	1,181	1,017	[1] 255	[1] 172	[1] 83
1976	2,457	1,351	1,106	2,189	1,168	1,021	268	183	85
1977	2,488	1,375	1,113	2,209	1,185	1,024	279	190	89
1978	2,479	1,376	1,103	2,207	1,191	1,016	272	185	87
1979	2,461	1,379	1,082	2,185	1,191	994	[1] 276	[1] 188	[1] 88
1980	2,485	1,401	1,084	2,184	1,189	995	301	212	89
1981	2,440	1,404	1,037	2,127	1,183	945	[1] 313	[1] 221	[1] 92
1982	2,458	1,413	1,045	2,133	1,182	951	[1] 325	[1] 231	[1] 94
1983	2,476	1,426	1,050	2,139	1,186	953	337	240	97
1984	2,508	1,451	1,057	2,168	1,208	960	[1] 340	[1] 243	[1] 97
1985	2,549	1,483	1,066	2,206	1,237	969	343	246	97
1986	2,592	1,521	1,071	2,244	1,271	973	[1] 348	[1] 250	[1] 98
1987	2,632	1,564	1,068	2,279	1,307	973	[1] 353	[1] 257	[1] 95
1988	2,668	1,604	1,064	2,323	1,353	970	[1] 345	[1] 251	[1] 94
1989	2,734	1,662	1,072	2,357	1,387	970	[1] 377	[1] 275	[1] 102
1990	2,753	1,680	1,073	2,398	1,426	972	[1] 355	[1] 254	[1] 101
1991	2,787	1,713	1,074	2,432	1,459	973	[1] 355	[1] 254	[1] 101
1992	2,822	1,752	1,070	2,459	1,492	967	[1] 363	[1] 260	[1] 103
1993	2,870	1,775	1,095	2,504	1,513	991	[1] 366	[1] 262	[1] 104
1994	2,926	1,794	1,132	2,552	1,528	1,024	[1] 373	[1] 266	[1] 108
1995	2,978	1,814	1,164	2,598	1,546	1,053	[1] 380	[1] 269	[1] 111
1996 [2]	3,023	1,836	1,186	2,638	1,564	1,073	[1] 385	[1] 272	[1] 113
1997 [3]	3,071	1,861	1,211	2,682	1,586	1,096	390	275	115
Pupil-teacher ratios									
1955	27.4	31.4	20.3	26.9	30.2	20.9	[1] 31.7	[1] 40.4	[1] 15.7
1960	26.4	29.4	21.4	25.8	28.4	21.7	[1] 30.7	[1] 36.1	[1] 18.6
1965	25.1	28.4	20.6	24.7	27.6	20.8	28.3	33.3	18.4
1966	24.5	27.7	20.2	24.1	26.9	20.3	[1] 27.8	[1] 32.7	[1] 18.4
1967	24.0	26.9	20.1	23.7	26.3	20.3	[1] 26.8	[1] 31.1	[1] 18.4
1968	23.5	26.0	20.2	23.2	25.4	20.4	25.8	29.9	17.9
1969	22.7	25.1	19.7	22.6	24.7	20.0	[1] 24.0	[1] 27.8	[1] 16.7
1970	22.4	24.6	19.5	22.3	24.3	19.8	23.0	26.5	16.4
1971	22.4	25.0	19.1	22.3	24.9	19.3	[1] 22.6	[1] 25.7	[1] 16.7
1972	21.7	23.9	18.9	21.7	23.9	19.1	[1] 21.6	[1] 24.0	[1] 16.9
1973	21.3	23.0	19.1	21.3	23.0	19.3	[1] 21.2	[1] 23.6	[1] 16.5
1974	20.8	22.6	18.5	20.8	22.6	18.7	[1] 20.4	[1] 22.6	[1] 16.0
1975	20.3	21.7	18.6	20.4	21.7	18.8	[1] 19.6	[1] 21.5	[1] 15.7
1976	20.1	21.7	18.3	20.2	21.8	18.5	19.3	20.9	15.8
1977	19.6	20.9	17.9	19.7	21.1	18.2	18.4	20.0	15.1
1978	19.2	20.9	17.1	19.3	21.0	17.3	18.7	20.2	15.6
1979	19.0	20.5	17.0	19.1	20.6	17.2	[1] 18.1	[1] 19.7	[1] 14.8
1980	18.6	20.1	16.6	18.7	20.4	16.8	17.7	18.8	15.0
1981	18.7	20.0	16.8	18.8	20.3	16.9	[1] 17.6	[1] 18.6	[1] 15.2
1982	18.4	19.8	16.4	18.6	20.2	16.6	[1] 17.2	[1] 18.2	[1] 14.9
1983	18.2	19.6	16.2	18.4	19.9	16.4	17.0	18.0	14.4
1984	17.9	19.3	16.0	18.1	19.7	16.1	[1] 16.8	[1] 17.7	[1] 14.4
1985	17.6	19.1	15.6	17.9	19.5	15.8	16.2	17.1	14.0
1986	17.4	18.8	15.5	17.7	19.3	15.7	[1] 15.7	[1] 16.5	[1] 13.6
1987	17.3	18.8	15.0	17.6	19.3	15.2	[1] 15.5	[1] 16.4	[1] 13.1
1988	17.0	18.6	14.7	17.3	19.0	14.9	[1] 15.2	[1] 16.1	[1] 12.8
1989	16.8	18.4	14.3	17.2	19.0	14.6	[1] 14.2	[1] 15.1	[1] 11.7
1990	16.9	18.5	14.3	17.2	19.0	14.6	[1] 14.7	[1] 16.1	[1] 11.3
1991	17.0	18.5	14.5	17.3	18.9	14.9	[1] 14.6	[1] 16.0	[1] 11.1
1992	17.1	18.4	14.8	17.4	18.8	15.2	[1] 14.8	[1] 16.2	[1] 11.3
1993	17.1	18.5	14.7	17.4	18.9	15.1	[1] 14.9	[1] 16.3	[1] 11.5
1994	17.1	18.6	14.7	17.3	18.9	15.1	[1] 15.0	[1] 16.4	[1] 11.4
1995	17.0	18.6	14.5	17.3	18.9	14.8	[1] 15.0	[1] 16.5	[1] 11.4
1996 [2]	16.9	18.5	14.4	17.1	18.8	14.7	[1] 15.0	[1] 16.5	[1] 11.4
1997 [3]	17.0	18.6	14.5	17.3	19.0	14.9	15.0	16.5	11.5

[1] Estimated.
[2] Preliminary data.
[3] Projected.

NOTE.—Data for teachers are expressed in full-time equivalents. Distribution of unclassified teachers by level is estimated. Distribution of elementary and secondary school teachers by level is determined by reporting units. Kindergarten includes a relatively small number of nursery school teachers and students. Some data have been revised from previously published figures. Because of rounding, details may not add to totals.

SOURCE: U.S. Department of Education, National Center for Education Statistics, *Statistics of Public Elementary and Secondary Day Schools;* Common Core of Data surveys; and *Projections of Education Statistics to 2007.* (This table was prepared June 1997.)

ELEMENTARY AND SECONDARY: TEACHERS 75

Table 65.—Public elementary and secondary teachers, by level and state: Fall 1991 to fall 1996
[In full-time equivalents]

State or other area	Fall 1991	Fall 1992	Fall 1993	Fall 1994[1]				Fall 1995[1]				Estimated, 1996[2]
				Total	Elementary	Secondary	Unclassified	Total	Elementary	Secondary	Unclassified	
1	2	3	4	5	6	7	8	9	10	11	12	13
United States	2,432,243	2,458,956	2,503,901	2,551,875	1,419,749	911,671	220,455	2,598,220	1,428,852	952,189	217,179	[3]2,637,846
Alabama	40,480	41,961	43,003	42,791	24,170	18,423	198	44,056	24,935	19,121	—	[4]42,492
Alaska	7,118	7,282	7,193	7,205	4,666	2,539	—	7,379	4,780	2,599	—	7,644
Arizona	33,978	36,076	37,493	38,132	27,595	10,537	—	38,017	27,518	10,499	—	[3]39,315
Arkansas	25,785	26,017	26,014	26,181	13,884	12,160	137	26,449	13,882	12,370	197	29,194
California	224,000	218,566	221,787	225,016	142,810	58,586	23,620	230,849	145,601	60,743	24,505	228,028
Colorado	33,093	33,419	33,661	34,894	18,008	16,886	—	35,388	17,998	17,390	—	35,900
Connecticut	34,383	34,193	34,526	35,316	20,745	9,340	5,231	36,070	21,230	9,445	5,395	36,800
Delaware	6,095	6,252	6,380	6,416	3,215	3,201	—	6,463	3,205	3,258	—	6,642
District of Columbia	6,346	6,064	6,056	6,110	3,497	2,173	440	5,305	3,083	1,815	407	[3]5,398
Florida	109,939	107,590	110,653	110,674	48,150	40,893	21,631	114,938	50,660	42,745	21,533	[4]120,450
Georgia	63,816	66,942	74,172	77,914	56,211	21,703	—	79,480	40,888	38,592	—	81,683
Hawaii	9,451	10,083	10,111	10,240	5,770	4,425	45	10,500	5,843	4,616	41	10,675
Idaho	11,626	11,827	12,007	12,582	6,388	6,018	176	12,784	6,505	6,122	157	13,059
Illinois	110,153	111,461	110,874	110,830	66,462	28,619	15,749	113,538	67,972	29,208	16,358	115,859
Indiana	54,509	54,552	55,107	55,496	27,527	25,251	2,718	55,821	28,257	24,881	2,683	56,412
Iowa	31,395	31,403	31,616	31,726	18,662	11,973	1,091	32,318	19,151	12,063	1,104	32,549
Kansas	29,324	29,753	30,283	30,579	14,823	12,763	2,993	30,729	14,752	12,878	3,099	30,750
Kentucky	37,571	37,868	37,324	38,784	27,054	11,730	—	39,120	27,422	11,698	—	39,235
Louisiana	46,170	46,904	46,913	47,599	26,916	12,176	8,507	46,980	27,691	19,289	—	48,047
Maine	15,416	15,375	15,344	15,404	10,524	4,880	—	15,392	10,553	4,839	—	14,458
Maryland	43,616	44,495	44,171	46,565	25,792	20,773	—	47,819	24,999	22,820	—	47,005
Massachusetts	55,963	57,225	58,766	60,489	22,342	29,922	8,225	62,710	23,121	30,891	8,698	[3]65,863
Michigan	82,967	82,301	80,267	80,522	34,846	36,701	8,975	83,179	36,406	38,200	8,573	84,200
Minnesota	44,903	45,050	46,956	46,958	23,980	22,948	30	46,971	23,979	22,983	9	47,600
Mississippi	28,111	27,829	28,376	28,866	15,071	8,864	4,931	28,997	15,047	9,070	4,880	29,237
Missouri	52,643	52,984	54,860	56,606	29,054	26,782	770	57,951	29,386	27,817	748	59,222
Montana	9,883	10,135	9,949	10,079	7,009	3,070	—	10,076	6,974	3,102	—	10,110
Nebraska	19,069	19,323	19,616	19,774	11,368	8,406	—	20,028	11,452	8,506	70	[4]20,109
Nevada	11,409	11,953	12,579	13,414	6,784	5,058	1,572	13,878	7,057	5,210	1,611	[4]14,723
New Hampshire	11,464	11,654	11,972	12,109	8,158	3,951	—	12,346	8,447	3,899	—	12,394
New Jersey	80,515	83,057	84,564	85,258	47,280	26,439	11,539	86,706	48,359	26,362	11,985	[3]90,703
New Mexico	17,498	17,912	18,404	19,025	11,265	4,342	3,418	19,398	11,311	4,518	3,569	[4]19,608
New York	171,914	176,375	179,413	182,273	91,408	63,928	26,937	181,559	92,550	62,355	26,654	185,063
North Carolina	65,326	66,630	69,421	71,592	42,480	24,700	4,412	73,201	42,990	25,795	4,416	73,839
North Dakota	7,733	7,794	7,755	7,796	5,223	2,573	—	7,501	5,061	2,440	—	7,706
Ohio	103,372	106,233	107,444	109,085	72,005	36,912	168	107,347	71,376	35,718	253	104,583
Oklahoma	37,650	38,433	39,031	39,406	18,735	16,517	4,154	39,364	18,582	16,601	4,181	39,350
Oregon	26,745	26,634	26,488	26,208	14,128	8,484	3,596	26,680	13,889	8,981	3,810	26,757
Pennsylvania	100,475	100,912	101,302	102,988	46,918	43,798	12,272	104,921	47,975	44,455	12,491	106,400
Rhode Island	9,709	10,069	9,823	10,066	4,597	4,090	1,379	10,482	4,540	4,477	1,465	10,586
South Carolina	37,115	37,295	38,620	39,437	26,820	12,617	—	39,922	27,122	12,800	—	40,640
South Dakota	8,868	8,767	9,557	9,985	6,098	2,738	1,149	9,641	5,889	2,676	1,076	9,474
Tennessee	43,062	43,566	46,066	47,406	33,039	12,795	1,572	53,403	37,969	13,939	1,495	51,369
Texas	219,192	219,385	224,830	234,213	116,999	85,987	31,227	240,371	118,881	88,843	32,647	247,526
Utah	18,305	19,191	19,053	19,524	9,041	8,056	2,427	20,039	9,162	8,390	2,487	[4]20,224
Vermont	7,031	7,521	7,330	7,566	3,131	2,952	1,483	7,676	3,129	2,969	1,578	7,952
Virginia	64,537	68,181	70,859	72,505	44,246	28,259	—	74,731	46,225	28,506	—	80,896
Washington	42,931	44,295	45,524	46,439	24,077	18,247	4,115	46,907	24,423	18,501	3,983	[4]47,479
West Virginia	20,997	20,961	21,029	21,024	10,212	7,244	3,568	21,073	10,600	6,788	3,685	20,642
Wisconsin	52,028	53,387	52,822	54,054	37,235	16,819	—	55,033	36,808	17,015	1,210	55,296
Wyoming	6,564	5,821	6,537	6,754	3,331	3,423	—	6,734	3,217	3,391	126	6,700
Outlying areas												
American Samoa	671	725	656	698	484	196	18	728	521	192	15	[3]754
Guam	1,499	1,628	1,644	1,826	870	784	172	1,802	801	825	176	[3]1,893
Northern Marianas	430	425	431	406	224	182	—	422	240	182	—	[4]421
Puerto Rico	37,291	38,381	39,816	39,933	22,001	14,617	3,315	39,328	21,680	14,386	3,262	39,748
Virgin Islands	1,581	1,595	1,570	1,528	757	703	68	1,622	731	814	77	1,636

[1] Data have been revised from previously published figures.
[2] Data estimated by state education agencies.
[3] Data imputed by the National Center for Education Statistics based on previous year's data.
[4] Actual preliminary count by state.
— Data not available, not reported, or not applicable.

NOTE.—Distribution of elementary and secondary teachers determined by reporting units. Teachers reported in full-time equivalents.

SOURCE: U.S. Department of Education, National Center for Education Statistics, Common Core of Data surveys. (This table was prepared April 1997.)

Table 66.—Teachers, enrollment, and pupil-teacher ratios in public elementary and secondary schools, by state: Fall 1990 to fall 1995

State or other area	Pupil-teacher ratio, fall 1990	Pupil-teacher ratio, fall 1991	Pupil-teacher ratio, fall 1992	Fall 1993			Fall 1994			Fall 1995		
				Teachers	Enrollment	Pupil-teacher ratio	Teachers	Enrollment	Pupil-teacher ratio	Teachers	Enrollment	Pupil-teacher ratio
1	2	3	4	5	6	7	8	9	10	11	12	13
United States	17.2	17.3	17.4	2,503,901	43,464,916	17.4	2,551,875	44,111,482	17.3	2,598,220	44,840,481	17.3
Alabama	19.9	17.8	17.4	43,003	734,288	17.1	42,791	736,531	17.2	44,056	746,149	16.9
Alaska	17.0	16.7	16.8	7,193	125,948	17.5	7,205	127,057	17.6	7,379	127,618	17.3
Arizona	19.4	19.3	18.7	37,493	709,453	18.9	38,132	737,424	19.3	38,017	743,566	19.6
Arkansas	16.8	17.0	17.0	26,014	444,271	17.1	26,181	447,565	17.1	26,449	453,257	17.1
California	22.8	22.8	24.0	221,787	5,327,231	24.0	225,016	5,407,475	24.0	230,849	5,536,406	24.0
Colorado	17.8	17.9	18.3	33,661	625,062	18.6	34,894	640,521	18.4	35,388	656,279	18.5
Connecticut	13.5	14.0	14.3	34,526	496,298	14.4	35,316	506,824	14.4	36,070	517,935	14.4
Delaware	16.7	16.8	16.7	6,380	105,547	16.5	6,416	106,813	16.6	6,463	108,461	16.8
District of Columbia	13.6	12.7	13.3	6,056	80,678	13.3	6,110	80,450	13.2	5,305	79,802	15.0
Florida	17.2	17.6	18.4	110,653	2,040,763	18.4	110,674	2,111,188	19.1	114,938	2,176,222	18.9
Georgia	18.3	18.5	18.0	74,172	1,235,304	16.7	77,914	1,270,948	16.3	79,480	1,311,126	16.5
Hawaii	18.9	18.5	17.6	10,111	180,410	17.8	10,240	183,795	17.9	10,500	187,180	17.8
Idaho	19.6	19.4	19.6	12,007	236,774	19.7	12,582	240,448	19.1	12,784	243,097	19.0
Illinois	16.7	16.8	16.8	110,814	1,893,078	17.1	110,830	1,916,172	17.3	113,538	1,943,623	17.1
Indiana	17.4	17.6	17.6	55,107	965,633	17.5	55,496	969,022	17.5	55,821	977,263	17.5
Iowa	15.6	15.7	15.8	31,616	498,519	15.8	31,726	500,440	15.8	32,318	502,343	15.5
Kansas	15.0	15.2	15.2	30,283	457,614	15.1	30,579	460,838	15.1	30,729	463,008	15.1
Kentucky	17.3	17.2	17.3	37,324	655,265	17.6	38,784	657,642	17.0	39,120	659,821	16.9
Louisiana	17.3	16.6	17.0	46,913	800,560	17.1	47,599	797,933	16.8	46,980	797,366	16.6
Maine	13.9	14.0	14.1	15,344	216,995	14.1	15,404	212,601	13.8	15,392	213,569	13.9
Maryland	16.8	16.9	16.9	44,171	772,638	17.5	46,565	790,938	17.0	47,819	805,544	16.8
Massachusetts	15.4	15.1	15.0	58,766	877,726	14.9	60,489	893,727	14.8	62,710	915,007	14.6
Michigan	19.8	19.2	19.5	80,267	1,599,377	19.9	80,522	1,614,784	20.1	83,179	1,641,456	19.7
Minnesota	17.4	17.2	17.6	46,956	810,233	17.3	46,958	821,693	17.5	46,971	835,166	17.8
Mississippi	17.9	17.9	18.2	28,376	505,907	17.8	28,866	505,962	17.5	28,997	506,272	17.5
Missouri	15.6	16.0	16.2	54,860	866,378	15.8	56,606	878,541	15.5	57,951	889,881	15.4
Montana	15.9	15.8	15.8	9,949	163,009	16.4	10,079	164,341	16.3	10,076	165,547	16.4
Nebraska	14.6	14.7	14.6	19,616	285,097	14.5	19,774	287,100	14.5	20,028	289,744	14.5
Nevada	19.4	18.6	18.7	12,579	235,800	18.7	13,414	250,747	18.7	13,878	265,041	19.1
New Hampshire	16.2	15.5	15.6	11,972	185,360	15.5	12,109	189,319	15.6	12,346	194,171	15.7
New Jersey	13.6	13.8	13.6	84,564	1,151,307	13.6	85,258	1,174,206	13.8	86,706	1,197,381	13.8
New Mexico	18.1	17.6	17.6	18,404	322,242	17.5	19,025	327,248	17.2	19,398	329,640	17.0
New York	14.7	15.4	15.2	179,413	2,733,813	15.2	182,273	2,766,208	15.2	181,559	2,813,230	15.5
North Carolina	16.9	16.8	16.7	69,421	1,133,231	16.3	71,592	1,156,767	16.2	73,201	1,183,090	16.2
North Dakota	15.5	15.3	15.2	7,755	119,127	15.4	7,796	119,288	15.3	7,501	119,100	15.9
Ohio	17.2	17.3	16.9	107,444	1,807,319	16.8	109,085	1,814,290	16.6	107,347	1,836,015	17.1
Oklahoma	15.6	15.6	15.5	39,031	604,076	15.5	39,406	609,718	15.5	39,364	616,393	15.7
Oregon	18.0	18.6	19.2	26,488	516,611	19.5	26,208	521,945	19.9	26,680	527,914	19.8
Pennsylvania	16.6	16.8	17.0	101,302	1,744,082	17.2	102,988	1,764,946	17.1	104,921	1,787,533	17.0
Rhode Island	14.6	14.6	14.3	9,823	145,676	14.8	10,066	147,487	14.7	10,482	149,799	14.3
South Carolina	16.8	16.9	17.2	38,620	643,696	16.7	39,437	648,725	16.4	39,922	645,586	16.2
South Dakota	15.2	14.8	15.3	9,557	142,825	14.9	9,985	143,482	14.4	9,641	144,685	15.0
Tennessee	19.2	19.4	19.6	46,066	866,557	18.8	47,406	881,425	18.6	53,403	893,770	16.7
Texas	15.4	15.8	16.1	224,830	3,608,262	16.0	234,213	3,677,171	15.7	240,371	3,748,167	15.6
Utah	25.0	24.9	24.2	19,053	471,365	24.7	19,524	474,675	24.3	20,039	477,121	23.8
Vermont	13.2	13.8	13.1	7,330	102,755	14.0	7,566	104,533	13.8	7,676	105,565	13.8
Virginia	15.7	15.7	15.1	70,859	1,045,471	14.8	72,505	1,060,809	14.6	74,731	1,079,854	14.4
Washington	20.1	20.2	20.2	45,524	915,952	20.1	46,439	938,314	20.2	46,907	956,572	20.4
West Virginia	15.0	15.3	15.2	21,029	314,383	14.9	21,024	310,511	14.8	21,073	307,112	14.6
Wisconsin	16.2	15.7	15.5	52,822	844,001	16.0	54,054	860,581	15.9	55,033	870,175	15.8
Wyoming	14.5	15.6	17.2	6,537	100,899	15.4	6,754	100,314	14.9	6,734	99,859	14.8
Outlying areas												
American Samoa	18.8	19.9	19.3	656	14,484	22.1	698	14,445	20.7	728	14,576	20.0
Guam	17.1	18.9	18.5	1,644	30,920	18.8	1,826	32,185	17.6	1,802	32,960	18.3
Northern Marianas	15.5	16.5	19.0	431	8,188	19.0	406	8,429	20.8	422	8,809	20.9
Puerto Rico	18.8	17.2	16.6	39,816	631,460	15.9	39,933	621,121	15.6	39,328	627,620	16.0
Virgin Islands	13.8	14.1	14.3	1,570	22,752	14.5	1,528	23,126	15.1	1,622	22,737	14.0

NOTE.—Some data have been revised from previously published figures. Teachers reported in full-time equivalents.

SOURCE: U.S. Department of Education, National Center for Education Statistics, Common Core of Data surveys. (This table was prepared April 1997.)

ELEMENTARY AND SECONDARY: TEACHERS

Table 67.—Teachers in public and private elementary and secondary schools, by selected characteristics: 1993–94

Selected characteristics	Total[1]	Percent of teachers, by highest degree earned						Percent of teachers, by years of full-time teaching experience			
		No degree	Associate	Bachelor's	Master's	Education specialist	Doctor's	Less than 3	3 to 9	10 to 20	Over 20
1	2	3	4	5	6	7	8	9	10	11	12
Public schools											
Total	2,561,294	0.6	0.2	52.0	42.0	4.6	0.7	9.7	25.5	35.0	29.8
Men	694,098	1.3	0.4	46.2	45.7	5.1	1.3	8.9	21.6	29.9	39.6
Women	1,867,195	0.3	0.1	54.1	40.6	4.4	0.5	10.0	26.9	37.0	26.1
Race/ethnicity											
White	2,216,605	0.5	0.1	51.8	42.5	4.4	0.7	9.4	25.5	35.1	30.0
Black	188,371	0.5	0.2	48.4	44.6	5.4	0.9	8.5	20.8	35.5	35.2
Hispanic	108,744	0.9	0.5	62.8	29.8	4.6	1.4	16.7	32.1	34.1	17.1
Asian or Pacific Islander	27,510	0.9	0.4	49.3	34.7	13.1	1.7	14.9	29.7	29.2	26.2
American Indian or Alaskan	20,064	0.8	0.3	54.9	39.1	4.3	0.6	11.3	27.6	34.5	26.6
Age											
Less than 30	280,342	0.5	0.1	83.9	14.5	1.0	0.1	47.8	52.2	([2])	([2])
30 to 39	573,444	0.5	0.2	59.4	36.6	3.0	0.3	10.5	48.7	40.8	([2])
40 to 49	1,070,459	0.4	0.1	46.3	47.0	5.4	0.7	4.3	16.9	47.5	31.3
50 to 59	540,491	0.7	0.2	40.6	51.2	6.1	1.2	1.4	7.8	25.0	65.7
60 or more	96,557	1.5	0.1	43.1	46.2	6.6	2.5	0.8	4.4	19.9	74.9
Level											
Elementary	1,331,281	0.2	([2])	55.5	39.7	4.1	0.4	9.7	27.1	35.5	27.7
General	938,636	0.3	([2])	58.0	38.0	3.5	0.3	9.2	26.5	34.9	29.4
English	2,093	([2])	([2])	46.0	52.3	1.0	0.8	12.5	11.2	17.9	58.4
Mathematics	3,372	([2])	([2])	74.6	24.4	([2])	1.0	11.6	13.1	40.9	34.3
Special education	127,877	([2])	([2])	45.1	46.9	7.2	0.9	11.1	34.1	39.9	15.0
Other elementary	259,304	0.3	0.1	51.3	42.6	4.9	0.8	11.1	25.8	35.6	27.5
Secondary	1,230,013	0.9	0.3	48.2	44.4	5.1	1.1	9.7	23.8	34.5	32.0
English	172,603	0.1	([2])	48.3	44.8	5.5	1.3	9.2	22.9	33.6	34.3
Mathematics	141,051	0.1	([2])	50.2	45.5	3.4	0.8	9.4	24.3	31.7	34.5
Science	132,179	0.2	([2])	47.9	45.8	4.8	1.2	9.5	26.1	31.2	33.2
Social studies	130,045	0.1	([2])	47.8	46.0	4.9	1.2	10.3	20.5	28.7	40.5
Special education	111,215	0.1	0.1	42.1	49.1	7.2	1.3	9.3	28.8	45.1	16.8
Vocational/technical	113,269	7.3	2.3	45.2	39.9	4.7	0.5	6.8	23.0	35.7	34.5
Other secondary	429,653	0.5	0.2	50.1	43.0	5.1	1.1	10.7	23.1	35.6	30.7
Private schools											
Total	378,365	5.2	1.5	59.0	29.8	2.9	1.7	20.9	33.9	29.6	15.6
Men	93,130	4.4	0.9	47.3	40.6	2.6	4.3	21.7	28.2	28.7	21.4
Women	285,235	5.4	1.7	62.8	26.3	3.0	0.8	20.6	35.8	29.9	13.7
Race/ethnicity											
White	347,811	4.8	1.3	59.4	30.2	2.6	1.6	20.4	33.6	30.0	16.0
Black	11,664	8.3	3.7	55.8	26.4	4.8	1.0	26.9	34.9	27.9	10.3
Hispanic	12,221	11.1	4.9	57.4	19.9	4.4	2.3	25.5	41.8	21.6	11.1
Asian or Pacific Islander	5,167	6.8	0.9	46.1	36.8	5.7	3.6	26.1	34.6	26.6	12.7
American Indian or Alaskan	1,502	3.4	6.0	49.4	16.1	25.1	([2])	29.4	42.8	17.9	9.9
Age											
Less than 30	65,168	7.7	1.6	78.8	10.8	1.0	0.2	54.9	44.9	0.1	([2])
30 to 39	93,999	5.9	1.2	63.1	25.7	2.6	1.4	21.7	51.2	27.1	([2])
40 to 49	131,492	3.9	1.6	54.0	35.1	3.4	2.0	12.6	29.8	45.5	12.1
50 to 59	65,691	4.0	1.8	49.7	38.4	3.5	2.5	7.4	15.7	35.7	41.2
60 or more	22,015	5.6	0.9	39.4	46.6	4.4	2.9	6.6	6.5	13.8	73.1
Level											
Elementary	221,036	7.0	1.7	65.9	21.8	2.8	0.8	21.9	36.0	29.0	13.1
General	153,691	6.1	1.3	69.4	19.5	3.2	0.4	17.7	37.4	31.0	14.0
Special education	7,652	5.0	0.2	46.4	45.0	3.4	0.0	18.2	46.8	26.5	8.5
Other elementary	59,692	9.3	2.9	59.3	24.7	1.6	2.0	33.3	31.2	24.2	11.3
Secondary	157,329	2.6	1.2	49.2	41.1	3.0	2.8	19.5	30.9	30.4	19.2
English	24,335	1.6	([2])	51.3	43.1	1.5	2.5	16.3	30.8	31.3	21.7
Mathematics	23,238	1.3	0.9	50.1	42.6	3.0	2.2	14.7	31.1	29.3	24.8
Science	18,399	0.1	([2])	49.5	42.3	4.2	4.0	21.3	27.7	31.2	19.9
Social studies	20,059	0.2	0.4	53.5	38.7	4.1	3.1	21.0	27.8	30.8	20.4
Special education	6,048	0.1	3.7	56.5	33.7	5.1	0.9	17.8	42.8	29.0	10.4
Vocational/technical	2,834	14.0	4.6	40.8	40.6	([2])	([2])	12.7	22.6	42.1	22.6
Other secondary	62,415	4.8	2.0	46.3	40.9	2.9	3.1	22.0	32.1	29.7	16.2

[1] Data are based upon a sample survey and may not be strictly comparable with data reported elsewhere.
[2] Less than .05 percent.

NOTE.—Excludes prekindergarten teachers. Some data revised from previously published figures. Details may not add to totals because of survey item nonresponse and rounding.

SOURCE: U.S. Department of Education, National Center for Education Statistics, "Schools and Staffing Survey, 1993–94." (This table was prepared June 1997.)

Table 68.—Highest degree earned and number of years teaching experience for teachers in public elementary and secondary schools, by state: 1993–94

State	Total[1]	Percent of teachers, by highest degree[2]				Percent of teachers, by years of full-time teaching experience			
		Bachelor's	Master's	Education specialist	Doctor's	Less than 3	3 to 9	10 to 20	Over 20
1	2	3	4	5	6	7	8	9	10
United States	2,561,294	52.0	42.0	4.6	0.7	9.7	25.5	35.0	29.8
Alabama	44,791	38.5	52.6	7.8	0.7	11.1	22.0	42.2	24.7
Alaska	8,152	59.0	35.3	4.2	(3)	8.0	29.3	42.7	20.0
Arizona	37,600	51.4	43.3	4.0	0.7	13.1	29.1	38.1	19.8
Arkansas	30,621	64.9	32.5	1.8	0.5	9.2	27.3	40.2	23.3
California	209,032	58.6	32.6	6.8	1.0	9.8	27.8	31.8	30.7
Colorado	35,723	46.5	49.4	2.5	0.5	9.4	26.1	38.7	25.7
Connecticut	35,465	19.6	62.4	15.7	1.4	6.4	19.8	35.5	38.3
Delaware	7,027	46.0	48.3	5.1	—	7.7	24.1	36.2	32.0
District of Columbia	5,185	41.2	54.4	2.4	2.0	10.8	14.7	30.6	43.9
Florida	106,535	57.2	37.0	3.3	1.4	8.7	29.4	37.8	24.0
Georgia	74,907	48.9	42.5	7.7	(3)	13.3	28.3	35.6	22.8
Hawaii	11,137	47.8	21.7	27.5	1.0	16.2	28.1	22.0	33.7
Idaho	12,166	74.4	21.7	2.6	0.6	12.4	33.3	33.7	20.6
Illinois	111,511	49.7	46.1	3.4	0.5	9.0	25.1	30.8	35.1
Indiana	57,732	21.4	72.9	4.9	—	5.6	24.7	37.1	32.6
Iowa	35,861	67.3	31.3	1.2	(3)	10.1	23.3	32.1	34.5
Kansas	31,164	53.5	42.8	2.3	1.1	12.3	28.2	35.2	24.3
Kentucky	41,571	23.4	56.8	18.7	0.8	9.5	26.8	32.9	30.8
Louisiana	48,948	60.5	31.2	6.9	0.5	9.7	29.8	35.1	25.5
Maine	15,658	68.4	28.4	1.6	(3)	7.0	28.7	37.4	26.9
Maryland	43,862	43.3	49.6	6.2	0.6	11.7	23.6	32.4	32.4
Massachusetts	58,416	38.8	54.8	3.9	0.9	8.4	17.1	33.6	41.0
Michigan	83,288	46.6	48.1	4.7	0.6	7.4	21.5	29.4	41.9
Minnesota	44,150	63.4	33.6	2.6	(3)	13.0	20.0	33.0	34.0
Mississippi	29,851	56.3	37.5	4.3	(3)	10.5	22.8	39.8	26.9
Missouri	62,454	54.3	42.4	2.2	0.6	10.6	26.9	37.2	25.3
Montana	12,851	71.3	26.0	1.8	0.5	11.1	27.5	39.0	22.5
Nebraska	20,411	61.5	36.0	1.9	(3)	10.1	24.4	39.0	26.5
Nevada	12,822	50.5	42.8	5.7	0.6	12.0	33.2	35.0	19.8
New Hampshire	12,299	60.2	35.9	2.6	0.7	10.6	26.8	38.2	24.4
New Jersey	83,935	56.2	37.4	4.8	1.0	5.8	21.1	34.6	38.5
New Mexico	19,265	53.2	43.6	2.2	(3)	12.5	32.5	33.9	21.1
New York	178,701	25.0	68.1	5.3	1.5	10.3	23.9	29.7	36.1
North Carolina	72,305	61.8	35.0	1.2	0.5	9.7	26.6	38.8	25.0
North Dakota	8,404	79.3	18.0	1.6	—	12.1	27.2	37.7	23.0
Ohio	111,518	53.2	41.8	3.1	(3)	6.8	23.2	38.6	31.4
Oklahoma	42,220	56.9	39.5	3.2	(3)	10.4	27.0	41.2	21.5
Oregon	25,706	51.5	43.1	4.0	0.8	7.4	27.0	39.6	26.0
Pennsylvania	114,571	46.7	45.6	6.9	(3)	6.9	18.3	33.0	41.8
Rhode Island	9,217	40.1	53.3	5.7	1.0	7.2	21.9	28.6	42.3
South Carolina	39,623	48.8	43.4	5.6	0.7	10.5	25.1	42.3	22.1
South Dakota	10,579	75.1	23.2	1.5	—	10.4	28.6	37.3	23.8
Tennessee	47,662	51.2	42.0	4.8	1.2	12.4	22.9	35.5	29.2
Texas	223,800	69.7	26.8	1.8	0.9	12.1	30.1	37.5	20.4
Utah	19,884	70.6	23.5	4.2	(3)	12.7	32.8	36.1	18.3
Vermont	7,327	49.4	47.5	2.1	—	12.3	25.3	34.4	28.0
Virginia	64,937	64.4	31.3	2.4	0.5	10.5	26.0	37.5	26.1
Washington	48,452	56.3	37.5	3.6	1.0	10.8	30.1	32.2	26.9
West Virginia	21,473	41.7	53.1	4.3	—	4.4	21.6	42.7	31.4
Wisconsin	62,958	59.3	38.1	1.7	0.6	9.1	24.7	29.5	36.7
Wyoming	7,567	71.3	26.5	1.4	(3)	9.4	22.6	41.6	26.5

[1] Data are based on a head count of all teachers rather than on the number of full-time equivalent teachers appearing in other tables.
[2] Teachers with less than a bachelor's degree are not shown.
[3] Less than 0.05 percent.
— Data not available.

NOTE.—Excludes prekindergarten teachers. Details may not add to totals due to rounding or item nonresponse.

SOURCE: U.S. Department of Education, National Center for Education Statistics, "Schools and Staffing Survey, 1993–94." (This table was prepared June 1995.)

Table 69.—Selected characteristics of public school teachers: Spring 1961 to spring 1996

Item	1961	1966	1971	1976	1981	1986	1991	1996
1	2	3	4	5	6	7	8	9
Number of teachers, in thousands	1,408	1,710	2,055	2,196	2,185	2,206	2,398	2,164
Sex (percent)								
Men	31.3	31.1	34.3	32.9	33.1	31.2	27.9	25.6
Women	68.7	68.9	65.7	67.1	66.9	68.8	72.1	74.4
Median age (years)								
All teachers	41	36	35	33	37	41	42	44
Men	34	33	33	33	38	42	43	46
Women	46	40	37	33	36	41	42	44
Race (percent)								
White	—	—	88.3	90.8	91.6	89.6	86.8	90.7
Black	—	—	8.1	8.0	7.8	6.9	8.0	7.3
Other	—	—	3.6	1.2	0.7	3.4	5.2	2.0
Marital status (percent)								
Single	22.3	22.0	19.5	20.1	18.5	12.9	11.7	12.4
Married	68.0	69.1	71.9	71.3	73.0	75.7	75.7	75.9
Widowed, divorced, or separated	9.7	9.0	8.6	8.6	8.5	11.4	12.6	11.8
Highest degree held (percent) [1]								
Less than bachelor's	14.6	7.0	2.9	0.9	0.4	0.3	0.6	0.3
Bachelor's	61.9	69.6	69.6	61.6	50.1	48.3	46.3	43.6
Master's or specialist degree	23.1	23.2	27.1	37.1	49.3	50.7	52.6	54.5
Doctor's	0.4	0.1	0.4	0.4	0.3	0.7	0.5	1.7
College credits earned in last 3 years								
Percent who earned credits	—	—	60.7	63.2	56.1	53.1	50.3	50.2
Mean number of credits earned [2]	—	—	14	—	9	4	4	—
Median years of teaching experience	11	8	8	8	12	15	15	15
Teaching for first year (percent)	8.0	9.1	9.1	5.5	2.4	3.1	3.0	2.1
Average number of pupils per class								
Elementary teachers, not departmentalized	29	28	27	25	25	24	24	24
Elementary teachers, departmentalized	—	—	25	23	22	—	—	—
Secondary teachers	28	26	27	25	23	25	26	31
Mean number of students taught per day by secondary teachers	138	132	134	126	118	94	93	97
Average number of hours in required school day	7.4	7.3	7.3	7.3	7.3	7.3	7.2	7.3
Average number of hours per week spent on all teaching duties								
All teachers	47	47	47	46	46	49	47	49
Elementary teachers	49	47	46	44	44	47	44	47
Secondary teachers	46	48	48	48	48	51	50	52
Average number of days of classroom teaching in school year	—	181	181	180	180	180	180	180
Average number of nonteaching days in school year	—	5	4	5	6	5	5	6
Average annual salary as classroom teacher	[3] $5,264	$6,253	$9,261	$12,005	$17,209	$24,504	$31,790	$35,549
Total income, including spouse's (if married)	—	—	$15,021	$19,957	$29,831	$43,413	$55,491	$63,171
Willingness to teach again (percent)								
Certainly would	49.9	52.6	44.9	37.5	21.8	22.7	28.6	32.1
Probably would	26.9	25.4	29.5	26.1	24.6	26.3	30.5	30.5
Chances about even	12.5	12.9	13.0	17.5	17.6	19.8	18.5	17.3
Probably would not	7.9	7.1	8.9	13.4	24.0	22.0	17.0	15.8
Certainly would not	2.8	2.0	3.7	5.6	12.0	9.3	5.4	4.3

[1] Figures for curriculum specialist or professional diploma based on six years of college study are not included.
[2] Measured in semester hours.
[3] Includes extra pay for extra duties.
—Data not available.

NOTE.—Data are based upon sample surveys of public school teachers. Data differ from figures appearing in other tables because of varying processing procedures and time period coverages. Because of rounding, percents may not add to 100.0.

SOURCE: National Education Association, "Status of the American Public School Teacher, 1995–96." (Copyright © 1997 by the National Education Association. All rights reserved.) (This table was prepared October 1997.)

Table 70.—Public secondary school teachers, by subject taught: Spring 1966 to spring 1996

[Percentage distribution]

Teaching field in which largest portion of time was spent	1966	1971	1976	1981	1986	1991	1996
1	2	3	4	5	6	7	8
Total secondary school teachers, in thousands	746	927	1,016	995	970	1,012	1,049
All fields	100.0	100.0	100.0	100.0	100.0	100.0	100.0
Agriculture	1.6	0.6	0.6	1.1	0.6	0.3	0.5
Art	2.0	3.7	2.4	3.1	1.5	2.6	3.3
Business education	7.0	5.9	4.6	6.2	6.5	3.5	4.1
English	18.1	20.4	19.9	23.8	21.8	25.0	23.9
Foreign language	6.4	4.8	4.2	2.8	3.7	3.8	5.2
Health and physical education	6.9	8.3	7.9	6.5	5.6	7.5	5.9
Home economics	5.9	5.1	2.8	3.6	2.6	3.1	2.2
Industrial arts	5.1	4.1	3.9	5.2	2.2	2.1	0.5
Mathematics	13.9	14.4	18.2	15.3	19.2	14.5	17.2
Music	4.7	3.8	3.0	3.7	4.8	4.2	4.3
Science	10.8	10.6	13.1	12.1	11.0	13.3	12.6
Social studies	15.3	14.0	12.4	11.2	13.6	11.0	13.4
Special education	0.4	1.1	3.0	2.1	3.5	5.2	1.7
Other	1.9	3.1	4.0	3.3	3.4	3.9	5.2

NOTE.—Because of rounding, percents may not add to 100.0. Data are based upon sample surveys of public school teachers.

SOURCE: National Education Association, *Status of the American Public School Teacher, 1995–96*. (Copyright © 1997 by the National Education Association. All rights reserved.) (This table was prepared October 1997.)

Table 71.—Percent of vocational and nonvocational public school teachers of grades 9 to 12, by selected demographic and educational characteristics: 1993–94

Characteristics of teachers	Total	Teacher type		Characteristics of teachers	Total	Teacher type	
		Nonvocational	Vocational			Nonvocational	Vocational
1	2	3	4	1	2	3	4
Total	100.0	100.0	100.0				
Sex				**Major field of study**			
Male	48.3	46.2	63.2	Business and management	1.1	0.7	6.5
Female	51.7	53.8	36.8	Education	52.4	50.3	75.2
				Academic area	26.7	28.6	5.3
				English education	5.2	5.7	0.3
Race/ethnicity				Music education	3.4	3.7	0.2
White	88.8	88.9	88.5	Physical education	9.1	9.5	3.8
Black	6.0	5.9	7.1	Other academic area	9.0	9.7	1.0
Hispanic	3.4	3.5	2.8	Administration	5.3	5.1	7.0
Asian	0.9	0.9	0.8	General	4.5	4.6	3.3
American Indian or Alaskan Native	0.8	0.8	0.8	Special education	6.8	7.3	1.3
				Vocational education	6.5	3.7	37.2
				Other education	7.9	6.7	21.5
Age				English	4.1	4.4	0.3
Under 30 years	9.8	10.3	6.4	Foreign language	4.7	5.1	0.1
30 to 39 years	22.1	22.3	20.8	Mathematics	3.2	3.5	0.6
40 to 49 years	40.7	40.7	40.6	Sciences	7.8	8.1	4.3
50 years and over	27.5	26.8	32.2	Social sciences and history	10.0	10.7	1.8
				Visual and performing arts	2.6	2.7	1.0
				Other	6.1	6.2	5.5
Highest college degree				**Age at which first began to teach full-time or part-time**			
Less than a bachelor's degree	1.7	0.5	10.3	25 or under	75.7	75.6	76.5
Bachelor's degree	46.6	47.0	43.5	26 to 35	22.1	22.1	21.7
Master's degree	45.4	46.2	39.8	36 to 45	2.2	2.2	1.9
Education specialist[1]	5.3	5.2	5.6	46 to 55	0.1	0.1	0.0
Doctorate or first professional	1.1	1.1	0.7				

[1] Education specialist degrees or certificates are generally awarded for one year's work beyond the master's level.

SOURCE: U.S. Department of Education, National Center for Education Statistics, "Schools and Staffing Survey, 1993–94." (This table was prepared September 1996.)

ELEMENTARY AND SECONDARY: TEACHERS 81

Table 72.—Mobility of public and private elementary and secondary teachers, by selected school and teacher characteristics: 1987–88 to 1994–95

Characteristic	Percentage distribution of public school teachers									Percentage distribution of private school teachers				
	1987–88 to 1988–89			1990–91 to 1991–92			1993–94 to 1994–95			1987–88 to 1988–89	1990–91 to 1991–92	1993–94 to 1994–95		
	Remained teaching in the same school	Remained in teaching but changed schools	Left teaching	Remained teaching in the same school	Remained in teaching but changed schools	Left teaching	Remained teaching in the same school	Remained in teaching but changed schools	Left teaching	Left teaching	Left teaching	Remained teaching in the same school	Remained in teaching but changed schools	Left teaching
1	2	3	4	5	6	7	8	9	10	11	12	13	14	15
Total	86.5	7.9	5.6	87.6	7.3	5.1	86.3	7.2	6.6	12.7	12.3	82.3	5.8	11.9
Sex														
Male	87.7	7.3	5.1	89.1	6.4	4.5	88.2	6.6	5.2	10.2	12.1	82.1	4.8	13.1
Female	86.1	8.1	5.8	87.1	7.6	5.3	85.6	7.4	7.1	13.4	12.3	82.4	6.1	11.6
Race/ethnicity														
White, non-Hispanic	86.5	7.8	5.7	87.6	7.3	5.1	86.7	6.8	6.5	12.1	12.0	82.5	5.7	11.7
Total minority	87.0	8.6	4.4	87.5	7.1	5.3	83.7	9.5	6.8	21.4	15.4	79.2	—	14.8
Black, non-Hispanic	86.2	8.8	5.1	85.5	8.3	6.1	84.9	8.5	6.6	34.7	19.3	82.3	—	12.6
Hispanic	88.9	8.2	2.9	89.6	6.0	4.4	79.4	11.5	9.1	21.3	13.6	77.2	—	14.6
Age														
Less than 25	78.7	17.0	4.3	73.8	17.2	9.1	81.1	15.2	3.8	19.0	23.8	67.4	12.6	20.0
25 to 29	75.0	16.1	9.0	76.6	14.3	9.0	76.3	13.7	10.0	17.6	17.8	76.1	10.8	13.1
30 to 39	85.2	9.0	5.8	85.9	9.9	4.2	84.8	8.6	6.7	12.4	13.7	77.6	7.5	14.9
40 to 49	91.2	6.4	2.4	92.5	5.5	2.0	89.9	6.1	3.9	10.5	7.7	87.2	4.1	8.7
50 to 59	90.4	3.9	5.7	89.3	4.0	6.7	88.9	4.8	6.3	11.3	9.6	89.3	2.4	8.2
60 to 64	72.0	4.5	23.4	71.0	2.2	26.8	68.0	1.5	30.5	16.9	17.8	84.9	2.0	13.1
65 and over	83.3	0.0	16.7	48.9	10.3	40.9	63.2	—	34.1	7.9	20.7	56.6	—	41.9
Full-time teaching experience														
Less than 1 year	76.9	11.5	11.6	51.5	31.3	17.2	79.7	11.1	9.3	27.4	28.4	70.3	7.6	22.1
1 to 3 years	77.4	14.3	8.3	79.7	13.1	7.2	79.6	12.7	7.8	15.9	16.7	72.3	10.3	17.3
1 year	77.3	14.2	8.5	79.0	12.6	8.4	81.2	12.4	6.4	18.8	18.8	66.7	11.6	21.7
2 years	78.8	13.6	7.6	78.7	14.1	7.1	76.4	14.6	9.1	14.6	15.8	71.9	11.2	17.0
3 years	76.0	15.2	8.8	81.6	12.4	5.9	81.4	10.8	7.8	14.3	14.7	79.8	7.8	12.4
4 to 9 years	82.9	11.1	6.0	84.8	9.9	5.3	83.0	9.9	7.1	12.8	12.7	81.2	7.0	11.9
10 to 19 years	89.3	6.7	4.0	91.0	6.5	2.4	89.1	6.6	4.4	11.4	6.2	89.7	2.4	7.9
20 to 24 years	93.6	4.1	2.2	93.3	3.3	3.4	92.5	2.8	4.6	7.4	4.7	92.3	2.5	5.2
25 years or more	84.9	4.1	11.0	85.9	3.1	11.0	84.9	4.1	11.1	7.4	14.6	85.5	2.9	11.6
Level taught														
Elementary	85.0	9.5	5.5	87.1	8.1	4.8	86.0	7.6	6.4	12.5	11.3	82.4	6.1	11.5
Secondary	88.1	6.2	5.6	88.2	6.4	5.5	86.6	6.7	6.7	12.9	13.3	82.2	5.2	12.6
School size														
Less than 150	85.6	9.8	4.5	86.6	8.1	5.3	78.6	10.3	11.1	19.4	17.0	76.0	7.9	16.2
150 to 299	84.6	9.9	5.4	88.0	7.7	4.3	85.8	7.0	7.1	12.1	13.8	79.6	8.0	12.4
300 to 499	86.9	7.5	5.6	85.8	8.5	5.7	86.2	7.3	6.5	10.2	7.7	84.3	3.2	12.5
500 to 749	86.8	7.5	5.7	87.7	7.6	4.7	85.3	7.1	7.6	9.2	9.8	89.6	3.3	7.1
750 or more	87.7	7.4	4.9	88.6	6.1	5.4	87.7	6.6	5.7	12.8	6.7	89.6	4.2	6.2
Percent minority enrollment														
Less than 5%	88.0	6.9	5.1	89.6	5.7	4.6	87.1	4.9	8.0	13.2	11.5	83.9	5.1	11.0
5 to 19%	86.6	7.6	5.8	88.1	6.4	5.5	87.3	6.7	6.0	10.3	12.2	84.8	4.2	11.1
20 to 49%	87.3	7.6	5.2	85.6	8.6	5.9	86.6	7.2	6.2	18.9	12.2	77.0	7.4	15.6
50% or more	85.0	9.7	5.3	86.2	8.9	4.9	83.6	9.6	6.8	13.6	13.1	75.8	10.9	13.2
Community type														
Central city	—	—	—	86.3	8.6	5.2	86.1	7.6	6.3	—	12.7	83.4	5.7	10.9
Urban fringe/small town	—	—	—	87.2	7.3	5.5	86.3	7.2	6.5	—	10.6	81.9	5.5	12.6
Rural/small town	—	—	—	88.8	6.4	4.8	86.4	6.8	6.8	—	13.9	80.0	6.4	13.6

—Data not available or not applicable.

NOTE.—Details may not add to 100 percent due to rounding.

SOURCE: U.S. Department of Education, National Center for Education Statistics, *Characteristics of Stayers, Movers, and Leavers: Results from the Teacher Followup Survey: 1994–95*. (This table was prepared April 1997.)

Table 73.—Average salaries for full-time teachers in public and private elementary and secondary schools, by selected characteristics: 1993–94

Selected characteristics	Total earned income	Base salary	Number of full-time teachers	School year supplemental contract		Supplemental contract during summer		Number of teachers with nonschool employment		
				Number of teachers	Supplemental salary	Number of teachers	Supplemental salary	Teaching or tutor	Education related	Not education related
1	2	3	4	5	6	7	8	9	10	11
	\multicolumn{10}{c}{Public schools}									
Total	$36,498	$34,153	2,340,443	815,827	$2,075	401,516	$2,070	118,603	80,014	237,177
Men	41,031	36,182	642,807	348,855	2,923	147,299	2,530	37,297	39,150	124,487
Women	34,781	33,384	1,697,636	466,972	1,442	254,218	1,803	81,305	40,863	112,689
Race/ethnicity										
White, non-Hispanic	36,576	34,221	2,012,142	722,694	2,067	328,492	2,015	100,017	68,991	208,306
Black, non-Hispanic	36,200	33,889	181,896	48,968	2,325	40,819	2,221	10,734	5,490	16,336
Hispanic	35,197	32,996	102,965	31,653	1,930	24,122	2,477	5,817	3,644	7,337
Asian or Pacific Islander	38,292	36,134	25,383	6,391	1,873	5,381	2,285	1,298	910	2,327
American Indian or Alaskan Native	35,635	32,994	18,057	6,121	2,068	2,703	2,305	737	979	2,871
Age										
Less than 30	27,151	24,737	258,692	113,918	1,777	51,862	1,819	11,924	8,078	28,228
30 to 39	31,596	29,270	517,638	204,607	2,163	102,314	1,942	24,860	19,623	49,690
40 to 49	38,106	35,751	974,299	328,974	2,107	161,320	2,053	50,193	34,480	100,528
50 or more	42,243	39,931	589,815	168,328	2,109	86,021	2,404	31,625	17,833	58,730
Years of teaching experience										
First year	26,641	23,544	99,833	35,238	1,573	16,007	2,516	4,554	2,463	13,210
2 to 4 years	27,217	25,089	272,905	109,127	1,660	54,192	1,806	10,991	9,575	30,150
5 to 9 years	30,709	28,451	388,370	145,326	1,998	79,198	2,046	23,195	11,272	36,451
10 to 14 years	33,805	31,792	355,460	114,950	2,110	58,360	2,003	16,150	12,281	30,036
15 to 19 years	37,984	35,809	380,168	131,094	2,177	65,105	1,842	19,878	14,175	35,835
20 or more years	43,796	41,215	843,707	280,091	2,279	128,653	2,285	43,835	30,248	91,495
Level										
Elementary	34,944	33,517	1,193,257	254,890	1,503	170,059	1,801	47,820	27,084	90,749
Secondary	38,114	34,815	1,147,186	560,937	2,335	231,457	2,267	70,783	52,930	146,427
	\multicolumn{10}{c}{Private schools}									
Total	$24,053	$21,968	302,431	64,063	$1,894	62,847	$2,122	20,237	11,424	34,099
Men	30,215	26,120	72,264	27,418	2,408	21,317	2,584	3,993	4,969	14,283
Women	22,118	20,669	230,167	36,645	1,509	41,530	1,885	16,244	6,456	19,816
Race/ethnicity										
White, non-Hispanic	24,084	22,000	278,749	59,475	1,903	55,950	2,109	18,461	10,677	31,724
Black, non-Hispanic	23,043	20,796	8,946	1,350	2,451	3,024	2,173	(¹)	(¹)	(¹)
Hispanic	22,256	20,672	9,862	2,013	1,209	2,269	2,298	(¹)	(¹)	(¹)
Asian or Pacific Islander	28,505	25,861	3,786	997	2,054	1,185	2,643	(¹)	(¹)	(¹)
American Indian or Alaskan Native	25,082	21,625	1,088	(¹)	(¹)	(¹)	(¹)	(¹)	(¹)	(¹)
Age										
Less than 30	19,438	17,010	56,709	14,802	1,572	15,865	1,781	4,600	2,373	8,982
30 to 39	23,334	20,925	73,855	16,590	1,947	17,227	2,161	4,636	3,247	10,087
40 to 49	25,230	23,224	102,226	21,284	1,915	20,355	2,196	6,965	3,794	9,580
50 or more	26,845	25,273	69,641	11,388	2,193	9,400	2,467	4,035	2,010	5,449
Years of teaching experience										
First year	19,408	16,318	22,922	4,832	1,539	4,545	1,973	1,798	(¹)	3,395
2 to 4 years	19,858	17,719	54,831	12,001	1,580	15,974	1,899	3,970	1,924	8,207
5 to 9 years	21,764	19,748	66,567	13,905	1,816	14,111	2,112	4,625	3,184	8,044
10 to 14 years	24,266	22,424	49,880	10,007	1,741	9,171	2,032	2,369	1,404	5,133
15 to 19 years	27,238	25,351	42,209	8,985	2,129	8,460	2,257	3,601	1,812	3,452
20 or more years	29,258	27,178	66,022	14,334	2,310	10,585	2,508	3,874	2,320	5,867
Level										
Elementary	21,485	19,977	179,936	23,015	1,514	33,338	1,846	11,805	5,645	18,137
Secondary	27,824	24,896	122,496	41,048	2,106	29,509	2,435	8,432	5,780	15,962

¹Too few sample cases (fewer than 30) for a reliable estimate.

NOTE.—Some data have been revised from previously published figures. Details may not add to totals because of rounding or missing values in cells with too few cases, or survey item nonresponse.

SOURCE: U.S. Department of Education, National Center for Education Statistics, "Schools and Staffing Survey, 1993–94," unpublished data. (This table was prepared November 1997.)

Table 74.—Public school students' ratings of the quality of teachers and parental and community support for their schools, by school location and students' race/ethnicity (in percent): 1996

Item	Total	School location			Race/ethnicity		
		Urban	Suburban	Rural	White	Black	Hispanic
1	2	3	4	5	6	7	8
Quality of teachers							
Excellent	16	18	17	11	15	19	16
Pretty good	57	51	56	68	62	47	51
Only fair	20	23	20	16	17	25	24
Poor	5	7	5	5	5	6	5
Don't know	1	2	2	0	1	3	4
Parental and community support for your school							
Excellent	13	10	13	16	14	12	11
Pretty good	38	34	38	43	41	32	34
Only fair	26	27	26	26	26	30	22
Poor	14	18	14	9	12	17	21
Don't know	9	11	9	6	8	11	12

SOURCE: Metropolitan Life/Louis Harris Associates, Inc., *The Metropolitan Life Survey of The American Teacher, 1996,* Part II. "Students Voice Their Opinions on: Their Education, Teachers and Schools." (This table was prepared July 1997).

Table 75.—Percent of students who give the teachers in their school grades "A" or "B" for their teaching skills, by school location and students' race/ethnicity: 1996

Teaching skill	Total	School location			Race/ethnicity		
		Urban	Suburban	Rural	White	Black	Hispanic
1	2	3	4	5	6	7	8
Understanding the subjects they teach	77	71	80	83	81	68	73
Helping students who are having problems with their studies	70	67	70	74	72	67	63
Treating students with respect	65	63	63	70	67	59	61
Keeping control and discipline in their classrooms	65	59	66	71	68	59	56
Caring about their students' futures	62	60	65	62	63	62	61
Encouraging students' academic interests	58	51	64	59	61	49	47
Making learning interesting for everyone	39	41	38	38	38	42	44
Taking an interest in students' home and personal lives	27	26	25	31	26	31	28

SOURCE: Metropolitan Life/Louis Harris Associates, Inc., *The Metropolitan Life Survey of The American Teacher, 1996,* Part II. "Students Voice Their Opinions on: Their Education, Teachers and Schools." (This table was prepared July 1997).

Table 76.—Percent of public school students' interest in a career in education, by student characteristics: 1996

Item	Total	School level		Sex	
		Grades 7 and 8	Grades 9 through 12	Male	Female
1	2	3	4	5	6
Interest in becoming a teacher					
Very interested	8	8	8	5	11
Somewhat interested	24	23	25	22	27
Not very interested	25	23	27	24	27
Not at all interested	41	45	39	48	34
Don't know	1	1	1	2	1
Ever talked to a teacher about becoming a teacher					
Yes	12	9	14	9	15
No	87	90	85	89	84
Don't know	1	1	1	2	1
A teacher has told you they thought you would make a good teacher					
Yes	22	20	24	17	28
No	73	75	71	77	68
Don't know	5	5	5	5	4

SOURCE: Metropolitan Life/Louis Harris Associates, Inc., *The Metropolitan Life Survey of The American Teacher, 1996,* Part II. "Students Voice Their Opinions on: Their Education, Teachers and Schools." (This table was prepared July 1997).

Table 77.—Estimated average annual salary of teachers in public elementary and secondary schools: 1959–60 to 1996–97

School year	Current dollars			Constant 1996–97 dollars[1]		
	All teachers	Elementary teachers	Secondary teachers	All teachers	Elementary teachers	Secondary teachers
1	2	3	4	5	6	7
1959–60	$4,995	$4,815	$5,276	$27,014	$26,040	$28,533
1961–62	5,515	5,340	5,775	29,156	28,231	30,531
1963–64	5,995	5,805	6,266	30,888	29,909	32,284
1965–66	6,485	6,279	6,761	32,297	31,271	33,671
1967–68	7,423	7,208	7,692	34,685	33,681	35,942
1969–70	8,626	8,412	8,891	36,287	35,387	37,402
1970–71	9,268	9,021	9,568	37,074	36,086	38,274
1971–72	9,705	9,424	10,031	37,478	36,392	38,736
1972–73	10,174	9,893	10,507	37,767	36,724	39,003
1973–74	10,770	10,507	11,077	36,706	35,810	37,753
1974–75	11,641	11,334	12,000	35,717	34,775	36,818
1975–76	12,600	12,280	12,937	36,104	35,187	37,069
1976–77	13,354	12,989	13,776	36,156	35,168	37,298
1977–78	14,198	13,845	14,602	36,022	35,127	37,047
1978–79	15,032	14,681	15,450	34,872	34,057	35,841
1979–80	15,970	15,569	16,459	32,689	31,868	33,690
1980–81	17,644	17,230	18,142	32,367	31,607	33,280
1981–82	19,274	18,853	19,805	32,546	31,835	33,442
1982–83	20,695	20,227	21,291	33,506	32,748	34,471
1983–84	21,935	21,487	22,554	34,246	33,546	35,212
1984–85	23,600	23,200	24,187	35,457	34,856	36,339
1985–86	25,199	24,718	25,846	36,799	36,096	37,744
1986–87	26,569	26,057	27,244	37,957	37,225	38,921
1987–88	28,034	27,519	28,798	38,456	37,750	39,504
1988–89	29,564	29,022	30,218	38,765	38,054	39,622
1989–90	31,367	30,832	32,049	39,256	38,586	40,109
1990–91	33,084	32,490	33,896	39,258	38,553	40,222
1991–92	34,063	33,479	34,827	39,165	38,493	40,043
1992–93	35,029	34,350	35,880	39,056	38,298	40,004
1993–94	35,733	35,233	36,555	38,834	38,291	39,728
1994–95	36,609	36,084	37,404	38,678	38,123	39,518
1995–96	37,560	36,976	38,423	38,632	38,031	39,519
1996–97	38,509	37,969	39,310	38,509	37,969	39,310

[1] Based on the Consumer Price Index, prepared by the Bureau of Labor Statistics, U.S. Department of Labor.

NOTE.—Some data have been revised from previously published figures.

SOURCE: National Education Association, *Estimates of School Statistics;* and unpublished data. (Latest edition 1996–97. Copyright © 1997 by the National Education Association. All rights reserved.) (This table was prepared August 1997.)

ELEMENTARY AND SECONDARY: TEACHERS 85

Table 78.—Estimated average annual salary of teachers in public elementary and secondary schools, by state: 1969–70 to 1996–97

State	Current dollars							Constant 1996–97 dollars [1]							Percent change, 1979–80 to 1996–97 in constant dollars
	1969–70	1979–80	1989–90	1993–94	1994–95	1995–96	1996–97	1969–70	1979–80	1989–90	1993–94	1994–95	1995–96	
1	2	3	4	5	6	7	8	9	10	11	12	13	14	15
United States	$8,626	$15,970	$31,367	[2]$35,733	$36,609	[2]$37,560	[2]$38,509	$36,287	$32,689	$39,256	$38,834	$38,678	$38,632	17.8
Alabama	6,818	13,060	24,828	28,705	31,144	31,313	32,549	28,681	26,733	31,072	31,196	32,904	32,206	21.8
Alaska	10,560	27,210	43,153	47,512	47,951	[2]49,620	[2]50,647	44,423	55,697	54,006	51,636	50,661	51,036	–9.1
Arizona	8,711	15,054	29,402	31,800	32,175	[2]32,484	[2]33,350	36,645	30,814	36,796	34,560	33,993	33,411	8.2
Arkansas	6,307	12,299	22,352	28,098	28,934	29,322	[2]29,975	26,532	25,175	27,973	30,537	30,569	30,159	19.1
California	10,315	18,020	37,998	40,264	41,078	42,259	[2]43,474	43,392	36,885	47,554	43,759	43,399	43,465	17.9
Colorado	7,761	16,205	30,758	33,826	34,571	35,364	[2]36,175	32,648	33,170	38,493	36,762	36,525	36,373	9.1
Connecticut	9,262	16,229	40,461	49,769	50,045	50,254	50,426	38,962	33,219	50,637	54,089	52,873	51,688	51.8
Delaware	9,015	16,148	33,377	37,469	39,076	40,533	41,436	37,923	33,054	41,771	40,721	41,284	41,689	25.4
District of Columbia	10,285	22,190	38,402	42,543	43,700	43,700	[2]45,012	43,266	45,421	48,060	46,236	46,170	44,947	–0.9
Florida	8,412	14,149	28,803	31,944	32,588	33,330	33,881	35,387	28,962	36,047	34,717	34,430	34,281	17.0
Georgia	7,276	13,853	28,006	30,712	32,291	34,002	36,042	30,608	28,356	35,049	33,378	34,116	34,972	27.1
Hawaii	9,453	19,920	32,047	36,564	38,518	35,807	35,842	39,766	40,775	40,107	39,738	40,695	36,829	–12.1
Idaho	6,890	13,611	23,861	27,756	29,783	30,891	31,818	28,984	27,861	29,862	30,165	31,466	31,772	14.2
Illinois	9,569	17,601	32,794	39,387	39,431	40,919	42,679	40,254	36,028	41,041	42,806	41,659	42,086	18.5
Indiana	8,833	15,599	30,902	35,712	36,785	37,675	38,575	37,158	31,930	38,674	38,812	38,864	38,750	20.8
Iowa	8,355	15,203	26,747	30,760	31,511	32,372	33,275	35,147	31,119	33,474	33,430	33,292	33,296	6.9
Kansas	7,612	13,690	28,744	33,914	34,652	35,134	35,837	32,021	28,022	35,973	36,858	36,610	36,136	27.9
Kentucky	6,953	14,520	26,292	31,625	32,257	33,080	[2]33,950	29,249	29,721	32,904	34,370	34,080	34,024	14.2
Louisiana	7,028	13,760	24,300	26,095	26,461	26,800	28,347	29,565	28,166	30,411	28,360	27,956	27,565	0.6
Maine	7,572	13,071	26,881	30,996	31,972	32,869	[2]33,800	31,853	26,755	33,641	33,686	33,779	33,807	26.3
Maryland	9,383	17,558	36,319	39,453	40,661	41,160	41,148	39,471	35,940	45,453	42,877	42,959	42,334	14.5
Massachusetts	8,764	17,253	34,712	39,023	40,795	42,264	43,806	36,867	35,315	43,442	42,410	43,100	43,470	24.0
Michigan	9,826	19,663	37,072	44,856	41,895	[2]44,796	[2]44,251	41,335	40,248	46,395	48,749	44,263	46,074	9.9
Minnesota	8,658	15,912	32,190	[2]35,440	35,948	[2]36,937	[2]37,975	36,422	32,570	40,285	38,516	37,980	37,991	16.6
Mississippi	5,798	11,850	24,292	25,153	26,818	27,692	27,720	24,390	24,256	30,401	27,336	28,334	28,482	14.3
Missouri	7,799	13,682	27,094	30,319	31,189	33,341	[2]34,342	32,808	28,006	33,908	32,951	32,952	34,292	22.6
Montana	7,606	14,537	25,081	28,200	28,785	29,364	[2]29,950	31,996	29,756	31,389	30,648	30,412	30,202	0.7
Nebraska	7,375	13,516	25,522	29,564	30,922	31,496	31,768	31,024	27,666	31,941	32,130	32,669	32,395	14.8
Nevada	9,215	16,295	30,590	33,955	34,836	36,167	37,340	38,765	33,354	38,283	36,902	36,805	37,199	11.9
New Hampshire	7,771	13,017	28,986	34,121	34,720	35,792	[2]36,867	32,690	26,645	36,276	37,083	36,682	36,813	38.4
New Jersey	9,130	17,161	35,676	44,693	46,087	47,910	[2]49,349	38,407	35,127	44,648	48,572	48,692	49,277	40.5
New Mexico	7,796	14,887	24,756	27,202	28,493	29,074	29,715	32,795	30,472	30,982	29,563	30,103	29,904	–2.5
New York	10,336	19,812	38,925	45,772	47,612	48,115	49,560	43,480	40,553	48,714	49,745	50,303	49,488	22.2
North Carolina	7,494	14,117	27,883	29,728	30,793	30,411	[2]31,225	31,525	28,896	34,895	32,308	32,533	31,279	8.1
North Dakota	6,696	13,263	23,016	25,506	26,327	26,969	27,711	28,168	27,148	28,804	27,720	27,815	27,738	2.1
Ohio	8,300	15,269	31,218	35,673	36,802	37,835	38,831	34,916	31,254	39,069	38,769	38,882	38,914	24.2
Oklahoma	6,882	13,107	23,070	27,009	28,172	28,404	29,270	28,950	26,829	28,872	29,353	29,764	29,214	9.1
Oregon	8,818	16,266	30,840	37,713	38,555	39,706	40,900	37,095	33,295	38,596	40,986	40,734	40,839	22.8
Pennsylvania	8,858	16,515	33,338	42,411	44,510	46,087	47,429	37,263	33,805	41,722	46,092	47,025	47,402	40.3
Rhode Island	8,776	18,002	36,057	39,261	40,729	[2]42,160	[2]43,019	36,918	36,849	45,125	42,669	43,031	43,363	16.7
South Carolina	6,927	13,063	27,217	29,566	30,279	31,622	32,659	29,140	26,739	34,062	32,132	31,990	32,524	22.1
South Dakota	6,403	12,348	21,300	25,259	25,994	26,346	26,764	26,935	25,275	26,657	27,451	27,463	27,098	5.9
Tennessee	7,050	13,972	27,052	30,514	32,477	33,126	33,789	29,657	28,599	33,855	33,162	34,312	34,071	18.1
Texas	7,255	14,132	27,496	30,529	31,223	32,000	32,644	30,520	28,927	34,411	33,179	32,988	32,913	12.8
Utah	7,644	14,909	23,686	27,706	29,082	30,588	31,750	32,156	30,517	29,643	30,111	30,726	31,461	4.0
Vermont	7,968	12,484	29,012	34,517	35,406	36,295	[2]37,200	33,519	25,554	36,308	37,513	37,407	37,331	45.6
Virginia	8,070	14,060	30,938	33,009	33,987	34,792	[2]35,837	33,948	28,780	38,719	35,874	35,908	35,785	24.5
Washington	9,225	18,820	30,457	35,863	36,151	37,853	37,860	38,807	38,523	38,117	38,976	38,194	38,933	–1.7
West Virginia	7,650	13,710	22,842	30,549	31,944	32,155	33,159	32,181	28,063	28,587	33,201	33,749	33,072	18.2
Wisconsin	8,963	16,006	31,921	35,990	37,746	38,182	[2]38,950	37,705	32,763	39,949	39,114	39,879	39,271	18.9
Wyoming	8,232	16,012	28,141	30,952	31,285	31,571	31,721	34,630	32,775	35,218	33,638	33,053	32,472	–3.2

[1] Based on the Consumer Price Index prepared by the Bureau of Labor Statistics, U.S. Department of Labor. Price index does not account for different rates of change in the cost of living among states.
[2] Estimated by the National Education Association.

NOTE.—Some data have been revised from previously published figures.

SOURCE: National Education Association, Estimates of School Statistics; and unpublished data. (Latest edition 1996–97. Copyright © 1997 by the National Education Association. All rights reserved.) (This table was prepared August 1997.)

86 ELEMENTARY AND SECONDARY: TEACHERS

Table 79.—Minimum and average teacher salaries, by state: 1990–91, 1993–94, and 1995–96

State	1990–91				1993–94				1995–96			Percent change, 1990–91 to 1995–96 (constant dollars)[1]	
	Minimum (beginning) salary	Average salary	Minimum (beginning) salary (in 1995–96 dollars)[1]	Average salary (in 1995–96 dollars)[1]	Minimum (beginning) salary	Average salary	Minimum (beginning) salary (in 1995–96 dollars)[1]	Average salary (in 1995–96 dollars)[1]	Minimum (beginning) salary	Average salary	Minimum (beginning) salary as a percent of average salary	Minimum salary	Average salary
1	2	3	4	5	6	7	8	9	10	11	12	13	14
United States	$21,542	$32,880	$24,853	$36,929	$23,258	$35,813	$24,576	$37,842	$24,507	$37,643	65.1	–1.4	1.9
Alabama	22,114	26,846	25,513	30,972	[2]22,500	28,659	[2]23,775	30,282	24,824	31,323	79.3	–2.7	1.1
Alaska	[3]29,950	43,406	[3]34,553	50,077	[3]31,800	[2]47,902	[3]33,601	[2]50,616	[3]34,800	47,349	73.5	0.7	–5.4
Arizona	[3]21,375	30,773	[3]24,660	35,503	21,825	31,825	23,061	33,628	[3]24,042	32,843	73.2	–2.5	–7.5
Arkansas	[4]17,458	[2]23,735	[4]20,141	[2]27,383	[2]19,694	[2]28,312	[2]20,810	[2]29,916	[2]21,189	[2]29,845	71.0	5.2	9.0
California	[3]24,570	[3]39,118	[3]28,346	[3]45,130	[3]25,500	[3]40,636	[3]26,945	[3]42,938	[3]25,762	[3]42,161	61.1	–9.1	–6.6
Colorado	19,786	31,819	22,827	36,710	20,091	33,826	21,229	35,742	21,472	36,364	59.0	–5.9	–0.9
Connecticut	25,312	43,398	29,202	50,068	28,052	50,389	29,641	53,243	28,840	50,938	56.6	–1.2	1.7
Delaware	21,112	35,246	24,357	40,663	22,795	37,469	24,086	39,592	24,300	40,533	60.0	–0.2	–0.3
District of Columbia	23,327	[3]39,362	26,912	[3]45,412	25,825	43,014	27,288	45,451	25,937	42,424	61.1	–3.6	–6.6
Florida	21,368	30,555	24,652	35,251	23,171	31,944	24,484	33,754	23,508	33,330	70.5	–4.6	–5.5
Georgia	20,471	[2]28,950	23,617	[2]33,400	21,885	[5]29,214	23,125	[5]30,869	24,693	[5]34,130	72.3	4.6	2.2
Hawaii	23,792	33,548	27,449	38,704	25,100	36,564	26,522	38,635	25,436	37,044	68.7	–7.3	–4.3
Idaho	15,685	25,510	18,096	29,431	[2]18,700	27,756	[2]19,759	29,328	19,667	30,894	63.7	8.7	5.0
Illinois	[2]21,954	[2]34,642	[2]25,328	[2]39,966	[6]25,171	[6]39,416	[6]26,597	[6]41,649	[6]26,753	[6]40,513	66.0	5.6	1.4
Indiana	[2]20,247	[2]32,931	[2]23,359	[2]37,992	22,021	[2]35,741	23,268	[2]37,766	[2]24,216	[2]37,677	64.3	3.7	–0.8
Iowa	19,404	27,949	22,386	32,245	20,709	30,760	21,882	32,503	21,338	32,376	65.9	–4.7	0.4
Kansas	[7]18,954	[7]28,188	[7]21,867	[7]32,520	[2]22,624	[7]31,700	[2]23,906	[7]33,496	[7]21,607	[7]32,531	66.4	–1.2	0.0
Kentucky	19,311	29,115	22,279	33,590	21,257	31,639	22,461	33,431	[3]22,457	33,079	67.9	0.8	–1.5
Louisiana	17,486	26,170	20,174	30,192	18,195	26,243	19,226	27,730	19,406	[3]26,800	72.4	–3.8	–11.2
Maine	18,878	28,531	21,780	32,916	19,840	30,996	20,964	32,752	20,725	32,869	63.1	–4.8	–0.1
Maryland	23,548	[2]38,312	27,167	[2]44,201	24,703	39,475	26,102	41,711	[6]26,846	41,229	65.1	–1.2	–6.7
Massachusetts	[3]21,800	36,090	[3]25,151	41,637	[3]23,000	38,960	[3]24,303	41,167	[3]25,815	43,025	60.0	2.6	3.3
Michigan	[3]22,400	[3]37,800	[3]25,843	[3]43,610	24,400	[3]45,218	25,782	[3]47,780	[3]25,635	[3]47,430	54.0	–0.8	8.8
Minnesota	[2]21,029	33,128	[2]24,261	38,220	[5]23,408	[2]36,146	[5]24,734	[2]38,194	23,998	36,847	65.1	–1.1	–3.6
Mississippi	[3]18,950	[3]24,609	[3]21,863	[3]28,391	18,833	25,153	19,900	26,578	20,150	27,692	72.8	–7.8	–2.5
Missouri	[3]20,293	[3]27,636	[3]23,412	[3]31,884	21,078	30,324	22,272	32,042	21,996	32,369	68.0	–6.0	1.5
Montana	[3]18,400	26,696	[3]21,228	30,799	[3]18,750	28,200	[3]19,812	29,797	[3]19,992	29,364	68.1	–5.8	–4.7
Nebraska	18,344	26,592	21,163	30,679	19,283	29,564	[3]21,983	31,239	21,299	31,496	67.6	0.6	2.7
Nevada	[8]24,358	[8]35,269	[8]28,102	[8]40,690	[8]24,155	[8]37,181	[8]25,523	[8]39,287	25,576	[8]39,535	64.7	–9.0	–2.8
New Hampshire	[3]20,635	31,273	[3]23,807	36,080	[3]22,400	34,121	[3]23,669	36,054	[3]23,510	35,792	65.7	–1.2	–0.8
New Jersey	24,500	38,411	28,266	44,315	29,346	45,582	31,008	48,164	[3]31,435	48,920	64.3	11.2	10.4
New Mexico	19,124	[2]25,800	22,063	[2]29,765	22,057	27,922	23,306	29,504	22,634	29,118	77.7	2.6	–2.2
New York	[9]26,375	[9]42,080	[9]30,429	[9]48,548	[9]26,903	[9]45,772	[9]28,427	[9]48,365	28,749	48,115	59.8	–5.5	–0.9
North Carolina	19,810	29,165	22,855	33,648	20,002	29,727	21,135	31,411	[3,9]20,620	[2]30,411	67.8	–9.8	–9.6
North Dakota	16,274	23,574	18,775	27,197	17,453	25,506	18,442	26,951	18,225	26,966	67.6	–2.9	–0.9
Ohio	18,452	31,964	21,288	36,877	19,553	35,912	20,661	37,946	[2]20,355	[2]38,075	53.5	–4.4	3.2
Oklahoma	[7]18,575	[7]24,378	[7]21,430	[7]28,125	22,181	27,612	23,438	29,176	24,187	[7]29,177	82.9	12.9	3.7
Oregon	[8]20,357	[8]32,295	[8]23,486	[8]37,259	[8]23,186	[8]37,589	[8]24,499	[8]39,718	[8]24,592	[8]39,311	62.6	4.7	5.5
Pennsylvania	[3]23,250	[2]36,057	[3]26,824	[2]41,599	28,231	42,411	29,830	44,814	29,514	46,087	64.0	10.0	10.8
Rhode Island	20,887	[3]38,220	24,097	[3]44,094	23,365	39,261	24,689	41,485	24,754	41,829	59.2	2.7	–5.1
South Carolina	[2]19,757	[2]28,174	[2]22,794	[2]32,504	20,533	[2]29,414	21,696	[2]31,080	21,791	[2]31,397	69.4	–4.4	–3.4
South Dakota	16,676	22,363	19,239	25,800	18,935	25,259	20,008	26,690	19,609	26,369	74.4	1.9	2.2
Tennessee	20,150	28,248	23,247	32,590	19,625	30,514	20,737	32,243	21,537	[2]33,126	65.0	–7.4	1.6
Texas	[3]20,150	[3]28,100	[3]23,247	[3]32,419	21,806	[10]30,519	23,041	[10]32,248	22,642	[10]31,633	71.6	–2.6	–2.4
Utah	17,234	[2]25,415	19,883	[2]29,321	18,787	[2]28,056	19,851	[2]29,645	20,544	30,390	67.6	3.3	3.6
Vermont	[3]18,509	[3]29,714	[3]21,354	[3]34,281	22,982	34,517	24,284	36,472	[3]24,445	[3]36,263	67.4	14.5	5.8
Virginia	[2]22,206	[2]32,692	[2]25,619	[2]37,717	23,273	33,472	24,591	35,368	[3]25,500	34,687	73.5	–0.5	–8.0
Washington	[2]20,612	[2]32,975	[2]23,780	[2]38,043	[5]23,183	35,860	[5]24,496	37,891	[2]24,590	[2]38,001	64.7	3.4	–0.1
West Virginia	18,728	25,966	21,606	29,957	21,450	30,549	22,665	32,280	22,011	32,155	68.5	1.9	7.3
Wisconsin	20,689	33,077	23,869	38,161	23,677	36,644	25,018	38,720	24,560	[3]37,586	65.3	2.9	–1.5
Wyoming	19,238	28,996	22,195	33,453	[3]20,416	30,954	[3]21,573	32,708	[3]21,900	31,571	69.4	–1.3	–5.6

[1] Based on the Consumer Price Index prepared by the Bureau of Labor Statistics, U.S. Department of Labor. Price index does not account for different rates of change in the cost of living among states.
[2] Preliminary or state estimate.
[3] Estimated by the American Federation of Teachers. See NOTE.
[4] Excludes state-paid health insurance.
[5] Reflects the redefinition of classroom teacher.
[6] Preliminary or state estimate. Includes pay for extra duties.
[7] Estimated to exclude fringe benefits.
[8] Includes 6 percent pension pick-up in Oregon and 9.5 percent in Nevada.
[9] Median salary.
[10] Including incentive pay or career ladder stipends and revision of classroom teacher definition.

NOTE.—Data in this table reflect results of surveys conducted by the American Federation of Teachers. Because of differing survey and estimation methods, these data are not entirely comparable with figures appearing in other tables.

SOURCE: American Federation of Teachers, *Survey and Analysis of Salary Trends*, various years. (This table was prepared April 1997.)

ELEMENTARY AND SECONDARY: TEACHERS 87

Table 80.—Average annual salary of instructional staff [1] in public elementary and secondary schools, by state: 1939–40 to 1996–97

State or other area	Current dollars									Constant 1996–97 dollars [2]				
	1939–40	1949–50	1959–60	1969–70	1979–80	1989–90	1994–95	1995–96	1996–97	1969–70	1979–80	1989–90	1994–95	1995–96
1	2	3	4	5	6	7	8	9	10	11	12	13	14	15
United States	$1,441	$3,010	$5,174	$9,047	$16,715	$32,638	[3]$38,441	[3]$39,451	[3]$40,580	$38,058	$34,214	$40,846	$40,613	$40,577
Alabama	744	2,111	4,002	6,954	13,338	26,200	32,597	32,459	33,744	29,253	27,302	32,789	34,439	33,385
Alaska	—	—	6,859	10,993	27,697	[3]43,161	[3]48,929	[3]50,516	[3]52,033	46,244	56,693	54,016	51,694	51,957
Arizona	1,544	3,556	5,590	8,975	16,180	33,592	[3]41,325	[3]42,870	[3]44,157	37,755	33,119	42,040	43,660	44,093
Arkansas	584	1,801	3,295	6,461	12,704	23,296	30,103	30,607	[3]31,526	27,179	26,004	29,155	31,804	31,480
California	2,351	—	[3]6,600	10,950	18,626	[3]39,309	[3]42,538	[3]44,027	[3]45,349	46,063	38,126	49,195	44,942	45,283
Colorado	1,393	2,821	4,997	8,105	16,840	31,832	35,712	36,353	[3]37,445	34,095	34,470	39,837	37,730	37,390
Connecticut	1,861	3,558	6,008	9,597	16,989	41,888	51,770	51,951	52,067	40,372	34,775	52,422	54,696	53,433
Delaware	1,684	3,273	[3]5,800	9,387	16,845	34,620	40,668	42,177	43,085	39,488	34,480	43,327	42,966	43,380
District of Columbia	2,350	3,920	6,280	10,700	23,027	43,637	39,663	39,663	[3]40,854	45,012	47,134	54,611	41,904	40,795
Florida	1,012	2,958	5,080	8,785	14,875	30,275	33,617	34,411	34,983	36,956	30,448	37,889	35,517	35,393
Georgia	770	1,963	[4]3,904	7,520	14,547	29,541	33,963	35,786	37,933	31,634	29,776	36,970	35,882	36,807
Hawaii	—	—	5,390	9,600	20,436	32,956	37,319	37,057	36,986	40,384	41,831	41,244	39,428	38,114
Idaho	1,057	2,481	4,216	7,081	14,110	24,758	31,063	32,285	33,277	29,788	28,882	30,984	32,818	33,206
Illinois	1,700	3,458	[5]5,814	9,789	18,271	33,912	40,855	42,411	44,235	41,179	37,399	42,441	43,164	43,621
Indiana	1,433	3,401	5,542	9,239	16,256	31,905	37,922	38,832	39,998	38,866	33,275	39,929	40,065	39,940
Iowa	1,017	2,420	[3]4,030	8,779	15,776	27,619	32,622	33,529	34,480	36,931	32,292	34,565	34,466	34,486
Kansas	1,014	2,628	[3]4,450	7,811	14,513	30,154	36,709	37,626	38,379	32,859	29,707	37,737	38,784	38,699
Kentucky	826	1,936	3,327	7,325	15,350	27,482	34,232	33,115	[3]34,109	30,814	31,420	34,393	36,167	34,060
Louisiana	1,006	2,983	4,978	7,264	14,020	25,036	27,631	28,167	[3]29,013	30,557	28,698	31,332	29,193	28,971
Maine	894	2,115	3,694	8,059	13,743	27,831	33,050	33,994	[3]35,015	33,902	28,131	34,830	34,918	34,964
Maryland	1,642	3,594	5,557	9,885	18,308	37,520	42,300	42,958	42,988	41,583	37,475	46,956	44,690	44,184
Massachusetts	2,037	3,338	[6]5,545	9,347	18,900	40,175	49,860	52,663	[3]54,244	39,320	38,687	50,279	52,678	54,166
Michigan	1,576	3,420	5,654	10,125	20,682	[3]37,286	[3]48,507	[3]50,764	[3]52,288	42,593	42,334	46,663	51,248	52,212
Minnesota	1,276	3,013	5,275	9,250	16,654	33,340	37,145	[3]37,680	[3]38,811	38,912	34,089	41,725	39,244	38,755
Mississippi	559	1,416	3,314	5,959	12,274	25,079	27,764	28,712	28,648	25,068	25,124	31,386	29,333	29,531
Missouri	1,159	2,581	4,536	8,064	14,543	28,166	32,725	33,870	[3]34,887	33,923	29,768	35,249	34,574	34,836
Montana	1,184	2,962	[3]4,425	7,875	15,080	29,526	30,052	30,908	[3]31,836	33,128	30,867	36,952	31,750	31,790
Nebraska	829	2,292	3,876	7,633	14,236	27,024	32,803	34,023	35,045	32,110	29,140	33,820	34,657	34,994
Nevada	1,557	3,209	5,693	9,615	17,290	31,970	36,553	37,879	39,179	40,447	35,391	40,010	38,619	38,960
New Hampshire	1,258	2,712	4,455	8,016	13,508	[3]29,798	[3]39,564	42,188	[3]43,455	33,721	27,650	37,292	41,800	43,392
New Jersey	2,093	3,511	5,871	9,650	18,851	37,485	48,463	50,435	[3]51,949	40,595	38,586	46,912	51,202	51,874
New Mexico	1,144	3,215	5,382	10,021	15,406	25,790	28,866	[3]29,389	[3]30,271	42,155	31,535	32,276	30,497	30,227
New York	2,604	3,706	6,537	11,240	20,400	40,000	48,500	48,754	50,218	47,283	41,757	50,060	51,241	50,145
North Carolina	946	2,688	4,178	7,762	14,445	28,952	32,070	31,622	[3]32,571	32,652	29,568	36,233	33,882	32,524
North Dakota	745	2,324	3,695	6,840	13,684	23,788	26,515	27,153	27,905	28,774	28,010	29,770	28,013	27,928
Ohio	1,587	3,088	5,124	8,594	16,100	32,467	37,988	39,038	40,087	36,152	32,955	40,632	40,135	40,152
Oklahoma	1,014	2,736	4,659	7,257	13,500	23,944	29,129	30,584	31,000	30,528	27,633	29,966	30,775	31,457
Oregon	1,333	3,323	5,535	9,200	16,996	32,100	39,800	40,980	[3]42,210	38,702	34,789	40,173	42,049	42,149
Pennsylvania	1,640	3,006	5,308	8,899	17,060	34,110	45,456	47,087	48,500	37,435	34,920	42,688	48,025	48,430
Rhode Island	1,809	3,294	[7]5,499	9,030	18,425	36,704	41,464	[3]42,900	[3]44,188	37,986	37,714	45,935	43,807	44,124
South Carolina	743	1,891	3,450	7,069	13,670	28,453	31,748	33,155	34,219	29,737	27,981	35,609	33,542	34,101
South Dakota	807	2,064	3,725	7,200	13,010	22,120	26,037	27,354	27,767	30,288	26,630	27,683	27,508	28,134
Tennessee	862	2,302	3,929	7,187	14,193	27,949	33,724	34,412	35,093	30,234	29,052	34,978	35,630	35,394
Texas	1,079	3,122	4,708	7,598	14,729	28,549	33,164	33,861	35,217	31,962	30,149	35,729	35,038	34,827
Utah	1,394	3,103	5,096	8,049	17,403	24,591	30,145	31,780	33,000	33,860	35,622	30,775	31,849	32,687
Vermont	981	2,348	4,466	8,225	13,300	29,012	36,375	37,054	[3]38,167	34,600	27,224	36,308	38,431	38,111
Virginia	899	2,328	4,312	8,364	14,655	31,656	34,828	35,535	[3]36,602	35,185	29,998	39,617	36,796	36,549
Washington	1,706	3,487	[7]5,643	9,792	19,735	31,828	37,807	39,594	39,591	41,192	40,396	39,832	39,944	40,724
West Virginia	1,170	2,425	3,971	7,954	14,395	23,842	33,070	33,296	34,360	33,460	29,465	29,838	34,925	34,246
Wisconsin	1,379	3,007	[8]4,870	9,150	16,335	32,445	38,952	39,212	[3]40,389	38,491	33,436	40,605	41,153	40,331
Wyoming	1,169	2,798	4,937	8,496	16,830	29,047	32,181	32,493	32,626	35,740	34,450	36,352	34,000	33,420
Outlying areas														
American Samoa	—	—	852	5,130	—	—	—	—	—	21,580	—	—	—	—
Guam	—	—	4,107	7,800	—	—	—	—	—	32,812	—	—	—	—
Puerto Rico	—	—	[9]2,360	—	—	—	—	—	—	—	—	—	—	—
Virgin Islands	—	—	—	3,407	—	—	—	—	—	—	—	—	—	—

[1] Includes supervisors, principals, classroom teachers, and other instructional staff.
[2] Based on the Consumer Price Index prepared by the Bureau of Labor Statistics, U.S. Department of Labor. Price index does not account for different rates of change in the cost of living among states.
[3] Estimated by National Education Association.
[4] Excludes kindergarten teachers.
[5] Includes administrators.
[6] Includes clerical assistants to instructional personnel.
[7] Includes attendance personnel.
[8] Excludes vocational schools not operated as part of the regular public school system.
[9] Median salary.
—Data not available.

NOTE.—Some data have been revised from previously published figures.

SOURCE: U.S. Department of Education, National Center for Education Statistics, *Statistics of State School Systems*; National Education Association, *Estimates of School Statistics*; (Latest edition 1996–97. Copyright © 1997 by the National Education Association. All rights reserved.) and unpublished data. (This table was prepared August 1997.)

Table 81.—Estimated average annual salary of instructional staff[1] in public elementary and secondary schools and average annual earnings of full-time employees in all industries: 1929–30 to 1996–97

School year	Current dollars		Constant 1996–97 dollars[2]		
	Average salary of instructional staff	Earnings per full-time employee working for wages or salary[3]	Average salary of instructional staff	Earnings per full-time employee working for wages or salary[3]	Ratio of instructional staff salary to salary for all full-time employees
1	2	3	4	5	6
1929–30	$1,420	$1,386	$13,183	$12,867	1.02
1931–32	1,417	1,198	15,619	13,205	1.18
1933–34	1,227	1,070	14,724	12,840	1.15
1935–36	1,283	1,160	14,836	13,414	1.11
1937–38	1,374	1,224	15,242	13,578	1.12
1939–40	1,441	1,282	16,385	14,577	1.12
1941–42	1,507	1,576	15,359	16,062	0.96
1943–44	1,728	2,030	15,759	18,513	0.85
1945–46	1,995	2,272	17,379	19,792	0.88
1947–48	2,639	2,692	17,998	18,360	0.98
1949–50	3,010	2,930	20,196	19,660	1.03
1951–52	3,450	3,322	20,859	20,085	1.04
1953–54	3,825	3,628	22,602	21,438	1.05
1955–56	4,156	3,924	24,567	23,195	1.06
1957–58	4,702	4,276	26,164	23,793	1.10
1959–60	5,174	4,632	27,982	25,051	1.12
1961–62	5,700	4,928	30,134	26,053	1.16
1963–64	6,240	5,373	32,151	27,683	1.16
1965–66	6,935	5,838	34,538	29,074	1.19
1967–68	7,630	6,444	35,652	30,111	1.18
1969–70	9,047	7,334	38,058	30,852	1.23
1970–71	9,698	7,815	38,794	31,262	1.24
1971–72	10,213	8,334	39,439	32,183	1.23
1972–73	10,634	8,858	39,475	32,882	1.20
1973–74	11,254	9,647	38,356	32,879	1.17
1974–75	12,167	10,420	37,331	31,971	1.17
1975–76	13,124	11,218	37,605	32,144	1.17
1976–77	13,840	11,991	37,472	32,466	1.15
1977–78	14,698	12,829	37,291	32,548	1.15
1978–79	15,764	13,851	36,570	32,132	1.14
1979–80	16,715	15,095	34,214	30,897	1.11
1980–81	18,404	16,495	33,761	30,259	1.12
1981–82	20,327	17,818	34,324	30,087	1.14
1982–83	21,641	18,883	35,037	30,571	1.15
1983–84	23,005	19,749	35,916	30,833	1.16
1984–85	24,666	20,626	37,059	30,989	1.20
1985–86	26,362	21,518	38,497	31,423	1.23
1986–87	27,706	22,432	39,581	32,046	1.24
1987–88	29,219	23,467	40,082	32,191	1.25
1988–89	30,850	24,502	40,451	32,127	1.26
1989–90	32,638	25,555	40,846	31,982	1.28
1990–91	34,401	26,668	40,821	31,645	1.29
1991–92	35,556	27,829	40,881	31,998	1.28
1992–93	36,460	29,060	40,651	32,400	1.25
1993–94	37,441	29,781	40,691	32,365	1.26
1994–95	38,441	30,582	40,613	32,310	1.26
1995–96	39,451	31,577	40,577	32,477	1.25
1996–97	40,580	—	40,580	—	—

[1] Includes supervisors, principals, classroom teachers, and other instructional staff.
[2] Based on the Consumer Price Index prepared by the Bureau of Labor Statistics, U.S. Department of Labor.
[3] Calendar-year data from the U.S. Department of Commerce have been converted to a school-year basis by averaging the two appropriate calendar years in each case. Beginning in 1992–93, data are wage and salary accruals per full-time equivalent employee.
—Data not available.

NOTE.—Some data have been revised from previously published figures.

SOURCE: U.S. Department of Education, National Center for Education Statistics, *Statistics of State School Systems*, and unpublished data; National Education Association, *Estimates of School Statistics, 1996–97*, (Copyright © 1997 by the National Education Association. All rights reserved.), unpublished data; and U.S. Department of Commerce, *Survey of Current Business*, July and August issues. (This table was prepared August 1997.)

ELEMENTARY AND SECONDARY: STAFF 89

Table 82.—Staff employed in public elementary and secondary school systems, by functional area: 1949–50 to fall 1995

[In full-time equivalents]

School year	Total	School district administrative staff						Instructional staff								Support staff						
		Total	Intermediate district staff	School district superintendents	Officials and administrators	Instruction coordinators	Total	Principals and assistant principals	Teachers	Instructional aides	Librarians	Guidance counselors	Psychological personnel	Other instructional staff	Total	Secretarial and clerical personnel	Transportation staff	Food service	Plant operation and maintenance	Health	Recreational and other staff
1	2	3	4	5	6	7	8	9	10	11	12	13	14	15	16	17	18	19	20	21	22
1949–50	1,300,031	33,642	5,843	18,025	(1)	9,774	963,110	43,137	913,671	(2)	17,363	(2)	(2)	6,302	303,280	31,824	81,626	68,814	105,874	9,412	5,730
1959–60	2,089,283	42,423	9,901	13,361	5,386	13,775	1,457,329	63,554	1,353,372	(2)	42,689	14,643	2,121	6,277	589,531	75,930	113,111	161,925	132,655	16,104	29,807
1969–70	3,360,763	65,282	7,113	13,014	13,618	31,537	2,285,568	90,593	2,016,244	57,418	42,763	48,763	6,168	23,693	1,009,913	164,476	175,351	270,338	273,395	26,562	99,791
Fall 1980	4,168,286	78,784	—	13,269	44,961	20,554	2,859,573	107,061	2,184,216	325,755	48,018	63,973	14,033	116,517	1,229,929	223,647	(4)	(4)	(4)	(4)	1,006,282
Fall 1985	4,159,624	67,404	—	(3)	45,712	32,702	2,756,232	129,297	2,205,987	306,860	47,442	66,646	—	(5)	1,335,988	(5)	(5)	(5)	(5)	(5)	(5)
Fall 1986	4,232,805	67,404	—	(3)	—	—	2,756,232	129,297	2,205,987	306,860	47,442	66,646	—	(5)	1,335,988	(5)	(5)	(5)	(5)	(5)	(5)
Fall 1987	4,311,941	374,191	—	—	—	—	2,822,059	131,564	2,243,579	330,398	47,938	68,580	—	70,282	1,336,205	(5)	(5)	(5)	(5)	(5)	(5)
Fall 1988	4,319,356	369,334	—	—	—	—	2,859,626	125,927	2,279,241	335,991	48,185	70,282	—	(5)	1,378,124	(5)	(5)	(5)	(5)	(5)	(5)
Fall 1989	4,431,033	370,302	—	—	—	—	2,930,547	126,609	2,323,213	356,682	48,980	75,063	—	(5)	1,319,475	(5)	(5)	(5)	(5)	(5)	(5)
Fall 1990	4,494,076	375,868	—	—	—	—	2,985,851	125,594	2,356,702	356,702	48,763	79,614	—	(5)	1,374,880	(5)	(5)	(5)	(5)	(5)	(5)
Fall 1991	4,559,359	376,084	—	—	45,712	—	3,051,404	127,417	2,398,169	374,172	49,769	79,950	—	(5)	1,366,804	(5)	(5)	(5)	(5)	(5)	(5)
Fall 1992	4,708,286	678,414	—	—	47,614	33,248	3,103,939	129,304	2,432,243	395,959	49,917	81,937	—	(5)	1,379,336	(5)	(5)	(5)	(5)	(5)	(5)
Fall 1993	4,808,080	680,862	—	—	47,614	33,248	3,139,544	121,936	2,458,956	427,279	50,324	81,049	—	(5)	1,490,328	(5)	(5)	(5)	(5)	(5)	(5)
Fall 1994	4,904,757	681,867	—	—	48,827	33,040	3,209,381	121,486	2,503,901	450,519	50,511	82,964	—	(5)	1,517,837	(5)	(5)	(5)	(5)	(5)	(5)
Fall 1995	4,994,358	682,998	—	—	49,315	33,683	3,351,528	120,629	2,598,220	494,289	50,862	87,528	—	(5)	1,559,832	(5)	(5)	(5)	(5)	(5)	(5)

Percentage distribution

1949–50	100.0	2.6	0.4	1.4	(1)	0.8	74.1	3.3	70.3	(2)	(2)	(2)	(2)	0.5	23.3	2.4	6.3	5.3	8.1	0.7	0.4
1959–60	100.0	2.0	0.5	0.6	0.3	0.7	69.8	3.0	64.8	(2)	0.8	0.7	0.1	0.3	28.2	3.6	5.4	7.8	9.2	0.8	1.4
1969–70	100.0	1.9	0.2	0.4	0.4	0.9	68.0	2.7	60.0	1.7	1.3	1.5	0.2	0.7	30.1	4.9	5.2	8.0	8.1	0.8	3.0
Fall 1980	100.0	1.9	—	0.3	1.1	0.5	68.6	2.6	52.4	7.8	1.2	1.5	0.3	2.8	29.5	5.4	(4)	(4)	(4)	(4)	24.1
Fall 1985	100.0	1.6	—	(3)	—	—	66.7	3.1	53.0	7.4	1.1	1.6	—	(5)	32.1	(5)	(5)	(5)	(5)	(5)	(5)
Fall 1986	100.0	1.8	—	(3)	—	—	66.7	3.1	53.0	7.8	1.1	1.6	—	(5)	31.6	(5)	(5)	(5)	(5)	(5)	(5)
Fall 1987	100.0	1.6	—	—	—	—	67.8	2.9	52.9	7.8	1.1	1.6	—	(5)	32.0	(5)	(5)	(5)	(5)	(5)	(5)
Fall 1988	100.0	1.7	—	—	—	—	67.8	2.9	53.8	8.3	1.1	1.7	—	(5)	30.5	(5)	(5)	(5)	(5)	(5)	(5)
Fall 1989	100.0	1.6	—	—	—	—	67.4	2.9	53.2	8.4	1.1	1.8	—	(5)	31.0	(5)	(5)	(5)	(5)	(5)	(5)
Fall 1990	100.0	1.7	—	—	—	—	67.9	2.8	53.4	8.8	1.1	1.8	—	(5)	30.4	(5)	(5)	(5)	(5)	(5)	(5)
Fall 1991	100.0	1.7	—	—	1.0	0.7	68.1	2.8	53.3	9.0	1.1	1.8	—	(5)	30.3	(5)	(5)	(5)	(5)	(5)	(5)
Fall 1992	100.0	61.7	—	—	1.0	0.7	66.7	2.6	52.1	9.1	1.1	1.7	—	(5)	31.7	(5)	(5)	(5)	(5)	(5)	(5)
Fall 1993	100.0	61.7	—	—	1.0	0.7	66.3	2.5	52.1	9.4	1.1	1.7	—	(5)	31.6	(5)	(5)	(5)	(5)	(5)	(5)
Fall 1994	100.0	61.7	—	—	1.0	0.7	66.9	2.4	52.0	9.7	1.0	1.7	—	(5)	31.4	(5)	(5)	(5)	(5)	(5)	(5)
Fall 1995	100.0	61.7	—	—	1.0	0.7	67.1	2.4	52.0	9.9	1.0	1.8	—	(5)	31.2	(5)	(5)	(5)	(5)	(5)	(5)

Pupils per staff member

1949–50	19.3	746.4	4,297.7	1,393.1	—	2,569.2	26.1	582.1	27.5	(2)	(2)	(2)	(2)	3,984.7	82.8	789.1	307.6	364.9	237.2	2,668.0	4,382.4
1959–60	16.8	829.3	3,553.4	2,633.2	6,532.2	2,554.1	24.1	553.6	26.0	(2)	2,026.3	2,402.7	16,589.1	5,605.1	59.7	463.4	311.0	217.3	182.6	2,184.7	1,180.3
1969–70	13.6	697.7	6,403.8	3,500.1	3,344.9	1,444.3	19.9	502.8	22.6	793.3	1,067.0	934.1	7,384.9	1,922.5	45.1	276.9	259.8	168.5	166.6	1,714.9	456.5
Fall 1980	9.8	518.9	—	3,080.7	909.2	1,988.8	14.3	381.8	18.7	125.5	851.3	639.0	2,913.0	350.8	33.2	182.8	(4)	(4)	(4)	(4)	40.6
Fall 1985	9.5	3,584.9	—	(3)	—	—	314.3	304.9	17.9	128.5	831.0	591.5	—	(5)	329.5	(5)	(5)	(5)	(5)	(5)	(5)
Fall 1986	9.4	3,533.3	—	(3)	—	—	314.1	302.2	17.7	120.3	829.3	579.7	—	(5)	329.8	(5)	(5)	(5)	(5)	(5)	(5)
Fall 1987	9.3	3,539.3	—	—	—	—	313.7	317.7	17.6	119.1	830.3	569.3	—	(5)	329.0	(5)	(5)	(5)	(5)	(5)	(5)
Fall 1988	9.3	3,579.6	—	—	—	—	313.7	314.7	17.3	112.7	820.5	535.4	—	(5)	330.5	(5)	(5)	(5)	(5)	(5)	(5)
Fall 1989	9.1	3,576.7	—	—	—	—	313.6	322.8	17.2	108.4	814.6	509.2	—	(5)	329.5	(5)	(5)	(5)	(5)	(5)	(5)
Fall 1990	9.2	3,543.3	—	—	—	—	313.5	323.5	17.2	104.1	825.8	515.5	—	(5)	330.2	(5)	(5)	(5)	(5)	(5)	(5)
Fall 1991	9.2	3,552.6	—	—	936.8	1,309.5	313.5	325.2	17.3	102.4	842.3	513.2	—	(5)	330.5	(5)	(5)	(5)	(5)	(5)	(5)
Fall 1992	9.1	6,546.1	—	—	936.8	1,309.5	313.6	351.2	17.4	100.2	851.0	528.4	—	(5)	328.7	(5)	(5)	(5)	(5)	(5)	(5)
Fall 1993	9.1	6,537.5	—	—	912.9	1,307.3	313.5	357.8	17.4	96.5	860.5	523.9	—	(5)	328.6	(5)	(5)	(5)	(5)	(5)	(5)
Fall 1994	9.0	6,538.8	—	—	903.4	1,335.1	313.4	367.5	17.3	93.2	870.6	519.9	—	(5)	328.7	(5)	(5)	(5)	(5)	(5)	(5)
Fall 1995	9.0	6,540.3	—	—	909.3	1,331.2	313.4	371.7	17.3	90.7	881.6	512.3	—	(5)	328.7	(5)	(5)	(5)	(5)	(5)	(5)

[1] Data included in column 5.
[2] Data included in column 10.
[3] Data not comparable with figures for years prior to 1984.
[4] Data included in column 22.
[5] Data included in column 16.
[6] Because of classification revisions, data are not directly comparable with figures for prior years.
[7] Data included in column 6.
—Data not available.

NOTE.—Some data have been revised from previously published figures. Because of variations in data collection instruments, some categories are only roughly comparable over time. Because of rounding, details may not add to totals.

SOURCE: U.S. Department of Education, National Center for Education Statistics, *Statistics of State School Systems*, Common Core of Data surveys, and unpublished estimates. (This table was prepared April 1997.)

Table 83.—Staff employed in public school systems, by type of assignment and state: Fall 1995
[In full-time equivalents]

State or other area	Total	School district staff			School staff						Student support staff	Other support services staff
		Officials and administrators	Administrative support staff	Instruction coordinators	Principals and assistant principals	School and library support staff	Teachers	Instructional aides	Guidance counselors	Librarians		
1	2	3	4	5	6	7	8	9	10	11	12	13
United States [1]	4,994,358	49,315	144,842	33,683	120,629	237,389	2,598,220	494,289	87,528	50,862	142,655	1,034,946
Alabama	83,256	428	1,039	980	2,221	2,768	44,056	6,657	1,684	1,259	468	21,696
Alaska [2]	15,022	294	549	112	436	886	7,379	1,751	225	147	819	2,424
Arizona	75,931	428	641	182	1,611	6,123	38,017	9,613	1,050	737	7,312	10,217
Arkansas	49,178	554	583	179	1,460	1,646	26,449	3,523	1,223	952	387	12,222
California [3]	444,014	2,155	19,920	4,685	10,335	28,571	230,849	56,822	5,115	896	9,989	74,677
Colorado	67,447	846	2,211	775	1,749	4,749	35,388	5,919	1,080	700	1,608	12,422
Connecticut	66,133	955	1,611	453	1,823	3,246	36,070	7,520	1,116	672	3,239	9,428
Delaware	11,869	87	388	58	399	472	6,463	861	215	122	498	2,306
District of Columbia	9,410	402	290	144	305	442	5,305	327	217	143	53	1,782
Florida	237,721	1,739	12,267	812	5,964	12,110	114,938	24,111	4,794	2,560	7,147	51,279
Georgia [4]	165,058	2,127	3,488	691	3,754	6,423	79,480	21,709	2,476	1,987	2,699	40,224
Hawaii	16,841	141	263	438	483	704	10,500	937	540	287	512	2,036
Idaho	21,814	114	443	210	661	876	12,784	1,914	520	185	381	3,726
Illinois	209,036	3,292	5,114	1,656	5,132	9,984	113,538	21,137	2,823	1,941	6,503	37,916
Indiana	116,363	928	496	1,368	2,818	7,872	55,821	14,421	1,720	1,021	1,650	28,248
Iowa	62,075	519	756	382	1,762	4,465	32,318	6,083	1,331	662	2,192	11,605
Kansas	57,265	1,253	961	74	1,671	2,487	30,729	4,760	1,087	972	2,298	10,973
Kentucky	84,425	1,170	2,188	434	1,906	3,147	39,120	10,916	1,282	1,173	2,093	20,996
Louisiana	93,070	265	689	1,026	2,379	2,907	46,980	10,026	2,610	1,172	2,248	22,768
Maine	29,413	448	660	113	853	1,393	15,392	3,776	600	238	1,049	4,891
Maryland	87,868	720	719	701	2,647	3,765	47,819	7,318	1,830	1,043	1,443	19,863
Massachusetts	113,154	991	5,788	1,065	2,166	3,073	62,710	12,867	2,090	611	1,860	19,933
Michigan	177,495	2,250	3,264	497	5,079	7,890	83,179	14,318	2,871	1,450	6,704	49,993
Minnesota	74,891	1,288	1,735	487	1,589	3,316	46,971	6,088	902	986	2,863	8,666
Mississippi	60,855	906	1,433	418	1,493	2,110	28,997	8,758	824	750	2,221	12,945
Missouri	120,621	638	4,578	1,244	2,579	8,189	57,951	7,228	2,593	1,368	1,758	32,495
Montana [4,5]	18,586	156	469	155	489	907	10,076	1,938	403	348	68	3,577
Nebraska	37,894	612	684	236	953	1,479	20,028	3,578	755	575	996	7,998
Nevada	23,742	184	489	101	680	1,340	13,878	1,489	498	241	605	4,237
New Hampshire	23,143	360	455	144	479	812	12,346	3,519	620	281	447	3,680
New Jersey	163,069	1,680	6,826	1,305	4,383	8,393	86,706	13,936	3,150	1,781	8,767	26,142
New Mexico	40,124	435	1,887	553	859	2,694	19,398	4,574	645	259	1,039	7,781
New York	355,723	2,737	23,774	1,263	6,878	7,110	181,559	28,001	5,456	2,998	8,720	87,227
North Carolina [4]	140,204	1,285	2,977	720	3,993	5,794	73,201	22,287	2,976	2,176	2,720	22,075
North Dakota	13,804	435	164	54	394	475	7,501	1,471	248	183	364	2,515
Ohio	194,579	5,242	9,467	353	971	12,597	107,347	10,092	3,219	1,628	1,252	42,411
Oklahoma [4]	83,802	533	94	590	1,456	5,754	39,364	7,186	1,390	902	12,589	13,944
Oregon	51,458	874	1,315	341	1,622	3,410	26,680	6,381	1,229	612	997	7,997
Pennsylvania	198,087	1,344	7,175	1,594	4,087	9,840	104,921	14,831	3,676	2,202	9,904	38,513
Rhode Island	16,517	148	426	78	361	804	10,482	1,458	309	75	378	1,998
South Carolina [4,5]	74,859	264	1,830	467	2,224	3,537	39,922	7,558	1,517	1,097	2,494	13,949
South Dakota [4]	18,126	268	400	148	473	878	9,641	2,302	354	202	269	3,191
Tennessee	98,948	918	2,297	761	4,654	4,572	53,403	9,992	1,456	1,386	2,927	16,582
Texas	462,661	2,580	2,451	1,100	11,251	18,644	240,371	43,046	8,219	4,252	3,679	127,068
Utah	37,385	109	715	465	926	2,098	20,039	5,037	596	291	369	6,740
Vermont	15,640	152	278	294	411	719	7,676	2,931	332	216	1,668	963
Virginia [2]	137,546	1,760	1,739	1,483	3,535	5,627	74,731	12,072	3,111	1,950	3,147	28,391
Washington [2,4]	91,322	1,015	2,540	841	2,501	4,760	46,907	8,582	1,758	1,263	3,695	17,460
West Virginia	38,645	279	1,896	322	1,095	366	21,073	2,957	611	357	886	8,803
Wisconsin	95,105	842	2,276	1,090	2,353	4,463	55,033	8,361	1,925	1,416	4,005	13,341
Wyoming	13,164	165	144	41	326	702	6,734	1,350	257	137	676	2,632
Outlying areas												
American Samoa	1,417	30	38	26	60	81	728	15	19	6	48	366
Guam	3,728	15	288	18	62	40	1,802	476	80	30	146	771
Northern Marianas	1,054	9	88	17	30	54	422	216	28	4	75	111
Puerto Rico	69,731	314	111	618	1,382	4,738	39,328	—	886	865	1,995	19,494
Virgin Islands	3,421	36	322	21	86	106	1,622	298	86	46	431	367

[1] Includes imputations for undercounts in designated states.
[2] Includes imputation for instruction coordinators.
[3] Includes imputation for prekindergarten teachers.
[4] Includes imputation for support staff.
[5] Includes imputation for instruction aides.

—Data not available or not applicable.

SOURCE: U.S. Department of Education, National Center for Education Statistics, Common Core of Data survey; and unpublished estimates. (This table was prepared April 1997.)

ELEMENTARY AND SECONDARY: STAFF 91

Table 84.—Staff employed in public school systems, by type of assignment and state: Fall 1994
[In full-time equivalents]

State or other area	Total	School district staff			School staff						Student support staff	Other support services staff
		Officials and administrators	Administrative support staff	Instruction coordinators	Principals and assistant principals	School and library support staff	Teachers	Instructional aides	Guidance counselors	Librarians		
1	2	3	4	5	6	7	8	9	10	11	12	13
United States[1]	4,904,757	48,827	147,609	33,040	120,017	235,720	2,551,875	473,348	84,844	50,668	138,102	1,020,707
Alabama[2]	81,544	406	1,085	957	2,163	2,651	42,791	6,678	1,643	1,215	455	21,500
Alaska[3]	15,150	194	533	113	428	891	7,205	1,842	229	148	560	3,007
Arizona	74,540	420	681	198	1,689	5,877	38,132	9,049	1,009	771	7,036	9,678
Arkansas	50,201	563	993	754	1,435	1,747	26,181	2,572	1,212	949	1,286	12,509
California[2]	436,140	2,048	20,256	4,314	10,352	27,764	225,016	56,391	4,999	850	9,600	74,550
Colorado	64,985	812	2,180	729	1,772	4,382	34,894	5,440	1,066	709	1,503	11,498
Connecticut	64,742	1,160	1,753	451	1,531	3,217	35,316	6,822	1,115	653	3,182	9,542
Delaware	11,759	90	381	55	406	473	6,416	829	214	120	477	2,298
District of Columbia	10,507	438	331	161	305	442	6,110	359	264	176	61	1,860
Florida	226,975	1,673	11,666	801	5,768	11,588	110,674	22,243	4,585	2,512	6,523	48,942
Georgia[4]	161,390	2,136	3,771	649	3,777	7,391	77,914	21,172	2,338	1,986	1,494	38,762
Hawaii	16,567	152	296	456	471	678	10,240	790	532	288	494	2,170
Idaho	21,194	121	433	202	633	830	12,582	1,805	478	180	375	3,555
Illinois	204,413	3,274	5,473	1,624	4,980	9,967	110,830	19,470	2,757	1,910	6,270	37,858
Indiana	115,441	874	513	1,307	2,719	7,814	55,496	14,372	1,650	1,028	1,585	28,083
Iowa	60,469	507	763	377	1,735	4,365	31,726	5,346	1,300	652	2,160	11,538
Kansas	56,790	473	2,399	163	1,659	2,449	30,579	4,451	1,073	968	1,839	10,737
Kentucky	81,720	1,197	1,658	622	1,728	3,110	38,784	9,784	1,254	1,136	2,854	19,593
Louisiana	96,124	1,531	1,903	97	2,391	3,011	47,599	10,177	1,068	1,206	2,072	25,069
Maine	29,264	449	703	117	844	1,314	15,404	3,726	591	235	1,015	4,866
Maryland	84,699	789	759	677	2,607	3,568	46,565	7,255	1,719	1,055	1,533	18,172
Massachusetts	108,281	954	5,626	1,010	2,126	3,059	60,489	11,714	2,004	579	1,792	18,928
Michigan	164,766	1,331	2,602	579	4,995	7,466	80,522	13,412	2,876	1,445	6,014	43,524
Minnesota	74,914	1,278	1,730	487	1,593	3,372	46,958	6,088	901	984	2,859	8,664
Mississippi	60,708	900	1,390	450	1,492	2,161	28,866	8,930	794	704	2,079	12,942
Missouri	116,974	650	4,537	1,288	2,516	7,782	56,606	6,909	2,483	1,317	1,635	31,251
Montana[4,5]	18,452	161	500	149	484	903	10,079	1,841	398	341	66	3,530
Nebraska	37,144	616	703	217	938	1,414	19,774	3,370	728	567	975	7,842
Nevada	23,098	178	505	110	660	1,375	13,414	1,643	452	241	557	3,963
New Hampshire	22,336	353	453	142	474	793	12,109	3,098	617	261	441	3,595
New Jersey	161,586	1,691	7,029	1,336	4,427	8,212	85,258	13,274	3,130	1,785	8,632	26,812
New Mexico	39,016	441	1,726	543	851	2,774	19,025	4,269	641	249	849	7,648
New York	356,386	2,813	23,618	1,399	6,944	7,467	182,273	27,390	5,770	3,061	8,642	87,009
North Carolina[4]	137,791	1,281	3,148	725	3,967	5,714	71,592	21,766	2,926	2,154	2,743	21,775
North Dakota	13,919	268	330	58	392	467	7,796	1,343	246	179	350	2,490
Ohio	200,141	5,497	9,513	434	1,001	14,277	109,085	9,884	3,510	1,753	1,304	43,883
Oklahoma[4]	78,270	548	186	625	2,375	5,572	39,406	7,205	1,368	899	11,801	8,285
Oregon	50,377	710	1,359	344	1,565	3,378	26,208	5,501	1,278	658	1,468	7,908
Pennsylvania	193,696	1,335	6,575	1,580	4,021	9,953	102,988	13,680	3,626	2,190	9,639	38,109
Rhode Island	15,438	157	315	79	370	791	10,066	1,272	306	76	185	1,821
South Carolina[4,5]	74,196	260	1,974	502	2,182	3,565	39,437	7,268	1,514	1,103	2,457	13,934
South Dakota[4]	17,989	337	765	23	654	758	9,985	1,905	394	213	271	2,684
Tennessee	96,281	960	2,840	730	4,560	4,495	47,406	9,574	1,389	1,363	3,402	19,562
Texas	450,462	2,554	2,393	1,168	11,010	18,044	234,213	41,317	8,026	4,201	3,520	124,016
Utah	36,186	107	677	449	885	1,998	19,524	4,665	529	279	386	6,687
Vermont	15,337	146	245	337	428	720	7,566	2,776	353	224	1,556	986
Virginia[2]	133,485	1,771	1,740	1,264	3,458	5,538	72,505	11,632	3,074	1,948	3,080	27,475
Washington[3,4]	90,438	1,053	2,535	838	2,469	4,721	46,439	8,480	1,735	1,259	3,554	17,355
West Virginia	38,481	271	1,883	327	1,100	371	21,024	2,867	596	364	940	8,738
Wisconsin	100,996	782	2,023	977	2,359	4,337	54,054	8,442	1,914	1,387	3,836	20,885
Wyoming	12,999	117	159	46	328	714	6,754	1,260	170	137	695	2,619
Outlying areas												
American Samoa	1,340	26	38	38	59	84	698	13	24	7	43	310
Guam	4,730	20	115	26	65	47	1,826	499	79	34	181	1,838
Northern Marianas	1,051	9	99	18	28	57	406	231	23	3	88	89
Puerto Rico	68,868	286	144	629	1,339	4,394	39,933	[6]	954	897	2,050	18,242
Virgin Islands	3,193	101	300	[6]	78	126	1,528	314	76	35	285	350

[1] Includes imputations for undercounts in designated states.
[2] Includes imputation for prekindergarten teachers.
[3] Includes imputation for instruction coordinators.
[4] Includes imputation for support staff.
[5] Includes imputation for instruction aides.
[6] Data not reported.

NOTE.—Some data have been revised from previously published figures.

SOURCE: U.S. Department of Education, National Center for Education Statistics, Common Core of Data survey; and unpublished estimates. (This table was prepared April 1997.)

Table 85.—Staff and teachers in public elementary and secondary schools, by state: Fall 1989 to fall 1995

State or other area	Teachers as a percent of staff				Fall 1993			Fall 1994[1]			Fall 1995		
	Fall 1989	Fall 1990	Fall 1991	Fall 1992	Staff	Teachers	Teachers as a percent of staff	Staff	Teachers	Teachers as a percent of staff	Staff	Teachers	Teachers as a percent of staff
1	2	3	4	5	6	7	8	9	10	11	12	13	14
United States[2]	53.2	53.4	53.3	52.2	4,808,080	2,503,901	52.1	4,904,757	2,551,875	52.0	4,994,358	2,598,220	52.0
Alabama	50.0	48.7	49.4	[3]53.2	[3]80,923	[3]43,003	[3]53.1	81,544	[3]42,791	[3]52.5	83,256	44,056	52.9
Alaska	48.3	50.3	50.9	49.2	15,689	7,193	45.8	[3]15,150	7,205	[3]47.6	[3]15,022	7,379	[3]49.1
Arizona	52.7	52.0	51.9	50.4	74,679	37,493	50.2	74,540	38,132	51.2	75,931	38,017	50.1
Arkansas	51.8	52.2	49.9	53.2	50,502	26,014	51.5	50,201	26,181	52.2	49,178	26,449	53.8
California	50.7	51.7	52.2	[3]51.1	[3]431,093	[3]221,787	[3]51.4	436,140	[3]225,016	[3]51.6	444,014	[3]230,849	[3]52.0
Colorado	52.7	52.6	52.9	53.2	62,927	33,661	53.5	64,985	34,894	53.7	67,447	35,388	52.5
Connecticut	55.5	56.3	56.8	53.7	62,014	34,526	55.7	64,742	35,316	54.5	66,133	36,070	54.5
Delaware	54.8	55.2	55.5	54.9	11,640	6,380	54.8	11,759	6,416	54.6	11,869	6,463	54.5
District of Columbia	57.0	58.3	57.0	57.4	10,591	6,056	57.2	10,507	6,110	58.2	9,410	5,305	56.4
Florida	50.5	49.8	50.0	49.5	226,911	110,653	48.8	226,975	110,674	48.8	237,721	114,938	48.3
Georgia	48.8	48.9	48.0	[3]46.9	[3]156,005	74,172	[3]47.5	[3]161,390	77,914	[3]48.3	[3]165,058	79,480	[3]48.2
Hawaii	60.2	59.9	60.7	56.9	18,292	10,111	55.3	16,567	10,240	61.8	16,841	10,500	62.3
Idaho	62.4	62.3	62.4	60.4	19,983	12,007	60.1	21,194	12,582	59.4	21,814	12,784	58.6
Illinois	56.6	56.7	55.9	55.9	198,862	110,874	55.8	204,413	110,830	54.2	209,036	113,538	54.3
Indiana	50.9	50.7	50.1	48.7	113,892	55,107	48.4	115,441	55,496	48.1	116,363	55,821	48.0
Iowa	53.4	53.0	52.1	52.2	60,267	31,616	52.5	60,469	31,726	52.5	62,075	32,318	52.1
Kansas	57.3	56.8	56.8	54.9	55,783	30,283	54.3	56,790	30,579	53.8	57,265	30,729	53.7
Kentucky	50.1	49.5	48.7	47.8	81,279	37,324	45.9	81,720	38,784	47.5	84,425	39,120	46.3
Louisiana	49.9	49.8	69.6	50.9	93,197	46,913	50.3	96,124	47,599	49.5	93,070	46,980	50.5
Maine	57.8	57.3	56.9	53.1	28,865	15,344	53.2	29,264	15,404	52.6	29,413	15,392	52.3
Maryland	54.4	53.9	54.6	55.0	82,753	44,171	53.4	84,699	46,565	55.0	87,868	47,819	54.4
Massachusetts	56.7	57.2	56.5	56.5	104,196	58,766	56.4	108,281	60,489	55.9	113,154	62,710	55.4
Michigan	46.9	46.4	46.6	47.3	169,283	80,267	47.4	164,766	80,522	48.9	177,495	83,179	46.9
Minnesota	56.5	56.2	57.4	56.9	74,859	46,956	62.7	74,914	46,958	62.7	74,891	46,971	62.7
Mississippi	49.0	48.3	47.5	48.1	59,853	28,376	47.4	60,708	28,866	47.5	60,855	28,997	47.6
Missouri	50.6	50.6	52.3	[3]48.4	112,810	54,860	48.6	116,974	56,606	48.4	120,621	57,951	48.0
Montana	[4]76.8	[4]76.4	[4]75.6	[3]54.0	[3]18,717	9,949	[3]53.2	[3]18,452	10,079	[3]54.6	[3]18,586	10,076	[3]54.2
Nebraska	55.4	53.4	55.0	[3]54.2	[3]36,832	19,616	[3]53.3	37,144	19,774	53.2	37,894	20,028	52.9
Nevada	[4]89.0	[4]89.4	[4]86.8	[3]55.7	22,418	12,579	56.1	23,098	13,414	58.1	23,742	13,878	58.5
New Hampshire	51.4	51.8	56.0	54.8	21,913	11,972	54.6	22,336	12,109	54.2	23,143	12,346	53.3
New Jersey	54.3	54.2	54.2	54.8	160,202	84,564	52.8	161,586	85,258	52.8	163,069	86,706	53.2
New Mexico	50.2	50.3	50.7	51.5	36,694	18,404	50.2	39,016	19,025	48.8	40,124	19,398	48.3
New York	50.6	50.9	50.8	51.3	353,603	179,413	50.7	356,386	182,273	51.1	355,723	181,559	51.0
North Carolina	51.6	51.2	51.7	[3]51.5	133,059	69,421	52.2	[3]137,791	71,592	[3]52.0	[3]140,204	73,201	[3]52.2
North Dakota	55.3	54.5	56.9	56.5	13,780	7,755	56.3	13,919	7,796	56.0	13,804	7,501	54.3
Ohio	54.0	54.0	53.1	52.9	201,828	107,444	53.2	200,141	109,085	54.5	194,579	107,347	55.2
Oklahoma	54.2	54.2	54.0	53.3	73,067	39,031	53.4	[3]78,270	39,406	[3]50.3	[3]83,802	39,364	[3]47.0
Oregon	53.1	53.2	53.0	51.5	50,392	26,488	52.6	50,377	26,208	52.0	51,458	26,680	51.8
Pennsylvania	55.4	52.5	52.7	52.7	190,885	101,302	53.1	193,696	102,988	53.2	198,087	104,921	53.0
Rhode Island	61.7	60.2	62.8	63.6	15,442	9,823	63.6	15,438	10,066	65.2	16,517	10,482	63.5
South Carolina	57.4	56.0	55.7	55.6	[3]71,433	38,620	[3]54.1	[3]74,196	39,437	[3]53.2	[3]74,859	39,922	[3]53.3
South Dakota	58.0	56.3	60.1	55.9	17,201	9,557	55.6	[3]17,989	9,985	[3]55.5	[3]18,126	9,641	[3]53.2
Tennessee	49.8	49.4	51.0	50.2	[3]92,349	46,066	[3]49.9	96,281	47,406	49.2	98,948	53,403	54.0
Texas	59.9	66.0	65.0	52.2	433,102	224,830	51.9	450,462	234,213	52.0	462,661	240,371	52.0
Utah	56.2	55.2	55.0	55.1	35,301	19,053	54.0	36,186	19,524	54.0	37,385	20,039	53.6
Vermont	57.3	53.6	50.5	50.2	[3]14,928	7,330	[3]49.1	15,337	7,566	49.3	15,640	7,676	49.1
Virginia	51.7	49.0	[5]49.4	[5]53.8	130,033	70,859	54.5	133,485	[3]72,505	[3]54.3	137,546	[3]74,731	[3]54.3
Washington	55.5	55.1	55.0	54.4	87,734	45,524	51.9	[3]90,438	46,439	[3]51.3	[3]91,322	46,907	[3]51.4
West Virginia	54.9	54.9	54.5	54.5	38,486	21,029	54.6	38,481	21,024	54.6	38,645	21,073	54.5
Wisconsin	59.0	58.1	59.0	57.9	88,640	52,822	59.6	100,996	54,054	53.5	95,105	55,033	57.9
Wyoming	49.9	53.1	50.0	50.6	12,893	6,537	50.7	12,999	6,754	52.0	13,164	6,734	51.2
Outlying areas													
American Samoa	53.1	52.6	52.5	53.7	1,339	656	49.0	1,340	698	52.1	1,417	728	51.4
Guam	54.3	52.6	50.6	46.3	3,839	1,644	42.8	4,730	1,826	38.6	3,728	1,802	48.3
Northern Marianas	52.0	51.1	47.5	38.8	1,101	431	39.1	1,051	406	38.6	1,054	422	40.0
Puerto Rico	53.5	55.4	54.9	56.7	68,005	39,816	58.5	68,868	39,933	58.0	69,731	39,328	56.4
Virgin Islands	48.0	48.0	48.1	47.6	3,324	1,570	47.2	[4]3,193	1,528	47.9	3,421	1,622	47.4

[1] Some data have been revised from previously published figures.
[2] U.S. totals include imputations for underreporting and nonreporting states.
[3] Includes imputations for underreporting.
[4] Support staff underreported.
[5] Data estimated by the National Center for Education Statistics.

SOURCE: U.S. Department of Education, National Center for Education Statistics, Common Core of Data survey; and unpublished estimates. (This table was prepared April 1997.)

Table 86.—Staff, enrollment, and pupil-staff ratios in public elementary and secondary schools, by state: Fall 1989 to fall 1995

State or other area	Pupil-staff ratio				Fall 1993			Fall 1994 [1]			Fall 1995		
	Fall 1989	Fall 1990	Fall 1991	Fall 1992	Staff	Enrollment	Pupil-staff ratio	Staff	Enrollment	Pupil-staff ratio	Staff	Enrollment	Pupil-staff ratio
1	2	3	4	5	6	7	8	9	10	11	12	13	14
United States	[2]9.1	[2]9.2	[2]9.2	[2]9.1	[2]4,808,080	43,464,916	[2]9.0	[2]4,904,757	[2]44,111,482	[2]9.0	[2]4,994,358	[2]44,840,481	[2]9.0
Alabama	9.1	9.7	8.8	[3]9.3	[3]80,923	734,288	[3]9.1	[3]81,544	736,531	[3]9.0	83,256	746,149	[3]9.0
Alaska	8.1	8.5	8.5	8.3	15,689	125,948	8.0	[3]15,150	127,057	[3]8.4	[3]15,022	127,618	[3]8.5
Arizona	10.0	10.1	10.0	9.4	74,679	709,453	9.5	74,540	737,424	9.9	75,931	743,566	9.8
Arkansas	8.8	8.8	8.5	9.0	50,502	444,271	8.8	50,201	447,565	8.9	49,178	453,257	9.2
California	11.4	11.8	11.9	[3]12.3	[3]431,093	5,327,231	[3]12.4	[3]436,140	5,407,475	[3]12.4	[3]444,014	5,536,406	[3]12.5
Colorado	9.3	9.3	9.5	9.8	62,927	625,062	9.9	64,985	640,521	9.9	67,447	656,279	9.7
Connecticut	7.4	7.6	8.0	7.7	62,014	496,298	8.0	64,742	506,824	7.8	66,133	517,935	7.8
Delaware	9.0	9.2	9.3	9.2	11,640	105,547	9.1	11,759	106,813	9.1	11,869	108,461	9.1
District of Columbia	7.7	7.9	7.2	7.7	10,591	80,678	7.6	10,507	80,450	7.7	9,410	79,802	8.5
Florida	8.7	8.6	8.8	9.1	226,911	2,040,763	9.0	226,975	2,111,188	9.3	237,721	2,176,222	9.2
Georgia	8.9	8.9	8.9	[3]8.5	[3]156,005	1,235,304	[3]7.9	[3]161,390	1,270,948	[3]7.9	[3]165,058	1,311,126	[3]7.9
Hawaii	11.5	11.3	11.2	10.0	18,292	180,410	9.9	16,567	183,795	11.1	16,841	187,180	11.1
Idaho	12.5	12.2	12.1	11.8	19,983	236,774	11.8	21,194	240,448	11.3	21,814	243,097	11.1
Illinois	9.6	9.5	9.4	9.4	198,862	1,893,078	9.5	204,413	1,916,172	9.4	209,036	1,943,623	9.3
Indiana	8.9	8.8	8.8	8.6	113,892	965,633	8.5	115,441	969,022	8.4	116,363	977,263	8.4
Iowa	8.4	8.3	8.1	8.2	60,267	498,519	8.3	60,469	500,440	8.3	62,075	502,343	8.1
Kansas	8.6	8.5	8.6	8.3	55,783	457,614	8.2	56,790	460,838	8.1	57,265	463,008	8.1
Kentucky	8.8	8.6	8.4	8.3	81,279	655,265	8.1	81,720	657,642	8.0	84,425	659,821	7.8
Louisiana	8.8	8.6	[4]12.0	8.7	93,197	800,560	8.6	96,124	797,933	8.3	93,070	797,366	8.6
Maine	8.1	8.0	8.0	7.5	28,865	216,995	7.5	29,264	212,601	7.3	29,413	213,569	7.3
Maryland	9.1	9.1	9.2	9.3	82,753	772,638	9.3	84,699	790,938	9.3	87,868	805,544	9.2
Massachusetts	7.9	8.8	8.5	8.5	104,196	877,726	8.4	108,281	893,727	8.3	113,154	915,007	8.1
Michigan	9.2	9.2	8.9	9.2	169,283	1,599,377	9.4	164,766	1,614,784	9.8	177,495	1,641,456	9.2
Minnesota	9.7	9.8	9.9	10.0	74,859	810,233	10.8	74,914	821,693	11.0	74,891	835,166	11.2
Mississippi	8.9	8.6	8.5	8.8	59,853	505,907	8.5	60,708	505,962	8.3	60,855	506,272	8.3
Missouri	8.0	7.9	8.4	[3]7.9	112,810	866,378	7.7	116,974	878,541	7.5	120,621	889,881	7.4
Montana	[4]12.1	[4]12.2	[4]11.9	[3]8.5	[3]18,717	163,009	[3]8.7	[3]18,452	164,341	[3]8.9	[3]18,586	165,547	[3]8.9
Nebraska	8.1	7.8	8.1	[3]7.9	[3]36,832	285,097	[3]7.7	37,144	287,100	7.7	37,894	289,744	7.6
Nevada	[4]18.1	[4]17.3	[4]16.1	[3]10.4	22,418	235,800	10.5	23,098	250,747	10.9	23,742	265,041	11.2
New Hampshire	8.4	8.4	8.6	8.5	21,913	185,360	8.5	22,336	189,319	8.5	23,143	194,171	8.4
New Jersey	7.3	7.4	7.5	7.5	160,202	1,151,307	7.2	161,586	1,174,206	7.3	163,069	1,197,381	7.3
New Mexico	9.2	9.1	8.9	9.1	36,694	322,292	8.8	39,016	327,248	8.4	40,124	329,640	8.2
New York	7.4	7.5	7.8	7.8	353,603	2,733,813	7.7	356,386	2,766,208	7.8	355,723	2,813,230	7.9
North Carolina	8.8	8.7	8.7	[3]8.6	133,059	1,133,231	8.5	[3]137,791	1,156,767	[3]8.4	[3]140,204	1,183,090	[3]8.4
North Dakota	8.3	8.5	8.7	8.6	13,780	119,127	8.6	13,919	119,288	8.6	13,804	119,100	8.6
Ohio	9.4	9.3	9.2	8.9	201,828	1,807,319	9.0	200,141	1,814,290	9.1	194,579	1,836,015	9.4
Oklahoma	8.8	8.4	8.4	8.3	73,067	604,076	8.3	[3]78,270	609,718	[3]7.8	[3]83,802	616,393	[3]7.4
Oregon	9.8	9.6	9.9	9.9	50,392	516,611	10.3	50,377	521,945	10.4	51,458	527,914	10.3
Pennsylvania	8.7	8.7	8.9	9.0	190,885	1,744,082	9.1	193,696	1,764,946	9.1	198,087	1,787,533	9.0
Rhode Island	8.9	8.8	9.2	9.1	15,442	145,676	9.4	15,438	147,487	9.6	16,517	149,799	9.1
South Carolina	9.7	9.4	9.4	9.5	[3]71,433	643,696	[3]9.0	[3]74,196	648,725	[3]8.7	[3]74,859	645,586	[3]8.6
South Dakota	9.0	8.5	8.9	8.6	17,201	142,825	8.3	[3]17,989	143,482	[3]8.0	[3]18,126	144,685	[3]8.0
Tennessee	9.5	9.5	9.9	9.9	[3]92,349	866,557	[3]9.4	96,281	881,425	[3]9.2	98,948	893,770	[3]9.0
Texas	10.0	10.2	10.3	8.4	433,102	3,608,262	8.3	450,462	3,677,171	8.2	462,661	3,748,167	8.1
Utah	14.0	13.8	13.7	13.3	35,301	471,365	13.4	36,186	474,675	13.1	37,385	477,121	12.8
Vermont	7.9	7.1	7.0	6.6	[3]14,928	102,755	[3]6.9	15,337	104,533	6.8	15,640	105,565	6.7
Virginia	8.2	7.7	[5]7.8	8.1	130,033	1,045,471	8.0	[3]133,485	1,060,809	[3]7.9	[3]137,546	1,079,854	[3]7.9
Washington	11.2	11.1	11.1	11.0	87,734	915,952	10.4	[3]90,438	938,314	[3]10.4	[3]91,322	956,572	[3]10.5
West Virginia	8.3	8.2	8.3	8.3	38,486	314,383	8.2	38,481	310,511	8.1	38,645	307,112	7.9
Wisconsin	9.4	9.4	9.2	9.0	88,640	844,001	9.5	100,996	860,581	8.5	95,105	870,175	9.1
Wyoming	7.2	7.7	7.8	8.7	12,893	100,899	7.8	12,999	100,314	7.7	13,164	99,859	7.6
Outlying areas													
American Samoa	9.9	9.9	10.5	10.4	1,339	14,484	10.8	1,340	14,445	10.8	1,417	14,576	10.3
Guam	8.9	9.0	9.6	8.6	3,839	30,920	8.1	4,730	32,185	6.8	3,728	32,960	8.8
Northern Marianas	8.9	7.9	7.8	7.4	1,101	8,188	7.4	1,051	8,429	8.0	1,054	8,809	8.4
Puerto Rico	10.4	10.4	9.5	9.4	68,005	631,460	9.3	[4]68,868	621,121	[4]9.0	69,731	627,620	9.0
Virgin Islands	6.4	6.6	6.8	6.8	3,324	22,752	6.8	[4]3,193	23,126	[4]7.2	3,421	22,737	6.6

[1] Some data have been revised from previously published figures.
[2] U.S. totals include imputations for underreporting and nonreporting states.
[3] Includes imputations for underreporting.
[4] Support staff underreported.
[5] Estimated by the National Center for Education Statistics.

SOURCE: U.S. Department of Education, National Center for Education Statistics, Common Core of Data survey; and unpublished estimates. (This table was prepared April 1997.)

Table 87.—Principals in public and private elementary and secondary schools, by selected characteristics: 1993–94

Selected characteristics	Total[1]	Percent of principals, by highest degree earned[2]				Average years of experience		Average annual salary of principals, by length of school year[3]			
		Bachelor's	Master's	Education specialist	Doctor's and first-professional	As a principal	Prior teaching experience	Total	10 months or less	11 months	12 months
1	2	3	4	5	6	7	8	9	10	11	12

Public schools

Selected characteristics	Total	Bachelor's	Master's	Ed. spec.	Doct.	As principal	Prior teach.	Total	10 mo	11 mo	12 mo
Total	79,618	1.4	63.4	25.8	9.3	8.7	11.0	$54,858	$50,103	$53,117	$58,399
Men	52,114	1.1	65.1	24.7	9.1	10.3	10.0	54,922	49,545	52,946	58,492
Women	27,505	2.0	60.2	27.9	9.8	5.6	13.0	54,736	50,908	53,439	58,195
Race/ethnicity											
White, non-Hispanic	67,081	1.5	62.8	26.5	9.2	9.0	10.8	54,466	48,797	52,893	58,311
Black, non-Hispanic	8,018	0.0	64.3	23.7	11.9	7.1	12.7	57,669	58,346	54,061	58,836
Hispanic	3,269	2.7	74.5	17.3	5.5	6.3	11.3	55,862	50,035	54,898	59,597
Asian or Pacific Islander	620	6.7	50.9	25.4	17.0	5.6	11.7	59,447	56,916	(4)	(4)
American Indian or Alaskan Native	631	1.1	65.8	24.8	8.2	8.2	9.9	51,117	46,401	49,121	55,337
Age											
Under 40	5,936	4.5	71.2	18.9	5.3	2.8	7.8	46,542	41,817	46,877	49,779
40 to 44	14,571	1.6	65.4	26.2	6.7	5.0	10.3	52,038	48,033	49,581	55,443
45 to 49	25,427	0.9	59.8	30.0	9.3	7.1	11.4	55,423	50,663	53,705	58,872
50 to 54	18,868	1.0	63.9	24.9	10.3	10.3	11.8	56,559	52,464	54,279	59,643
55 or over	14,817	1.4	63.8	22.4	12.4	15.1	11.6	57,826	52,414	56,355	62,148
Type of school											
Elementary	53,684	1.5	64.1	25.7	8.6	8.9	11.2	54,161	50,306	52,930	57,620
Secondary	18,262	1.2	63.1	25.4	10.3	8.0	10.6	56,601	47,100	53,982	60,204
Combined	2,747	2.6	60.2	27.8	9.4	7.5	10.9	52,825	50,729	51,879	54,040

Private schools

Selected characteristics	Total	Bachelor's	Master's	Ed. spec.	Doct.	As principal	Prior teach.	Total	10 mo	11 mo	12 mo
Total	25,015	25.9	51.6	8.2	5.9	8.8	9.4	32,075	21,994	32,215	35,295
Men	11,606	23.1	49.6	6.8	9.2	9.0	7.6	35,597	21,144	41,663	38,350
Women	13,410	28.3	53.3	9.4	3.0	8.6	11.1	29,185	22,537	27,818	32,231
Race/ethnicity											
White, non-Hispanic	23,133	25.6	52.1	8.1	5.8	8.7	9.5	31,969	21,289	32,071	35,283
Black, non-Hispanic	1,060	26.5	43.6	11.0	4.6	8.3	7.4	34,383	(4)	(4)	35,801
Hispanic	524	34.5	44.0	9.2	12.1	10.1	12.1	31,350	(4)	(4)	(4)
Age											
Under 40	4,794	38.1	36.6	8.2	1.4	3.5	5.0	26,308	17,903	33,527	29,420
40 to 44	4,403	35.9	45.5	8.5	5.3	5.3	7.9	30,486	20,004	30,127	33,044
45 to 49	5,144	22.2	59.0	8.1	5.5	8.3	9.9	34,641	23,945	31,812	38,932
50 to 54	4,120	15.1	59.1	7.7	11.0	9.6	11.1	37,727	27,338	35,421	40,097
55 or over	6,553	20.0	56.0	8.3	6.8	14.8	12.4	31,781	23,679	31,308	35,144
Type of school											
Elementary	13,354	26.1	54.2	8.0	4.7	9.4	10.4	28,779	23,427	30,050	30,687
Secondary	2,304	6.0	67.4	14.0	12.4	7.8	10.5	43,683	(4)	40,018	45,195
Combined	6,772	29.4	44.2	6.6	5.5	8.0	7.5	33,634	17,957	39,884	37,490

[1] Total differs from data appearing in other tables because of varying survey processing procedures and time period coverages.
[2] Percentages for those with less than a bachelor's degree are not shown.
[3] Excludes principals reporting a salary of $0. About 7.4 percent of private school principals had $0 salary. If these principals are included in the average annual salary calculations, the average for all private school principals is $29,714.
[4] Too few cases for reliable estimate.

NOTE.—Details may not add to 100.0 percent because of rounding and survey item nonresponse. Data revised from previously published figures.

SOURCE: U.S. Department of Education, National Center for Education Statistics, "Schools and Staffing Survey, 1993–94." (This table was prepared November 1996.)

Table 88.—Public elementary and secondary students, schools, pupil-teacher ratios, and finances, by type of locale: 1995

Characteristic	Total	Large central city[1]	Mid-size central city[2]	Urban fringe of large city[3]	Urban fringe of mid-size city[4]	Large town[5]	Small town[6]	Rural[7]
1	2	3	4	5	6	7	8	9
Schools, enrollment, and teachers, 1995–96								
Enrollment, in thousands	44,709	8,069	7,546	13,076	4,255	792	5,237	5,734
Schools	87,125	11,754	12,983	21,073	7,753	1,582	12,483	19,497
Average school size[8]	513	686	581	621	549	500	420	294
Pupil-teacher ratio[9]	17.7	19.0	17.7	18.5	17.7	17.3	16.7	15.8
Enrollment (percent distribution)	100.0	18.0	16.9	29.2	9.5	1.8	11.7	12.8
Schools (percent distribution)	100.0	13.5	14.9	24.2	8.9	1.8	14.3	22.4
Revenues and expenditures, 1993–94 (in millions)								
Total revenue	$232,578	$47,538	$39,767	$69,514	$20,733	$3,545	$23,642	$27,839
Federal	21,963	6,024	4,045	4,784	1,626	354	2,555	2,575
Impact aid	691	71	113	141	47	17	132	170
Bilingual education	415	186	58	102	37	3	18	12
Indian education	30	3	2	2	1	1	11	10
Children with disabilites	1,654	326	343	430	151	32	203	169
Eisenhower science awards	145	42	28	31	11	3	16	14
Drug Free schools	366	109	70	75	27	6	42	38
Chapter 2 (block grants)	356	102	67	73	26	8	41	39
Vocational education	547	180	109	88	40	10	71	49
Chapter 1	5,984	1,980	1,144	875	410	100	747	728
Other and unclassified	11,774	3,025	2,110	2,968	876	174	1,274	1,346
State	105,758	21,959	19,370	26,242	9,622	1,936	12,442	14,186
State school lunch programs	290	75	51	68	24	4	33	35
Local	104,858	19,555	16,352	38,488	9,485	1,255	8,645	11,079
Property tax[10]	75,441	12,043	11,693	28,993	6,458	966	6,834	8,453
Parent government contribution[10]	20,564	5,839	3,220	6,985	2,045	158	833	1,483
Lunch sales	3,798	467	615	1,251	409	66	452	539
Transportation	45	4	9	19	4	1	4	4
Other and unclassified	5,010	1,202	815	1,239	569	63	522	600
Total revenue (percent distribution)	100.0	100.0	100.0	100.0	100.0	100.0	100.0	100.0
Federal	9.4	12.7	10.2	6.9	7.8	10.0	10.8	9.2
State	45.5	46.2	48.7	37.8	46.4	54.6	52.6	51.0
Local	45.1	41.1	41.1	55.4	45.7	35.4	36.6	39.8
Total expenditures	240,654	49,523	41,383	72,799	21,156	3,667	24,118	28,008
Current expenditures	219,723	45,460	37,742	66,198	19,200	3,384	22,106	25,633
Instruction	132,384	27,161	22,606	39,604	11,861	2,070	13,503	15,579
Operation and maintenance	22,396	4,886	3,857	6,923	1,860	344	2,108	2,418
Food service	9,042	1,929	1,587	2,146	834	154	1,149	1,244
Other	55,901	11,485	9,692	17,525	4,645	816	5,346	6,391
Capital outlay	16,423	3,230	2,894	5,115	1,514	218	1,621	1,831
Interest on debt	4,508	833	748	1,486	442	64	391	544
Current expenditures (percent distribution)	100.0	100.0	100.0	100.0	100.0	100.0	100.0	100.0
Instruction	60.3	59.7	59.9	59.8	61.8	61.2	61.1	60.8
Operation and maintenance	10.2	10.7	10.2	10.5	9.7	10.2	9.5	9.4
Food service	4.1	4.2	4.2	3.2	4.3	4.6	5.2	4.9
Other	25.4	25.3	25.7	26.5	24.2	24.1	24.2	24.9
Current expenditure per student	5,386	5,818	5,272	5,815	4,944	4,526	4,642	5,081
Instruction expenditure per student	3,245	3,476	3,158	3,479	3,055	2,768	2,835	3,088

[1] Central city of metropolitan statistical area (MSA) with population of 400,000 or more or a population density of 6,000 or more persons per square mile.
[2] Central city of an MSA but not designated as a large central city.
[3] Place within the MSA of a large central city.
[4] Place within the MSA of a mid-size central city.
[5] Place not within an MSA but with population of 25,000 or more and defined as urban.
[6] Place not within an MSA with a population of at least 2,500 but less than 25,000.
[7] Place with a population of less than 2,500.
[8] Average for schools reporting enrollment.
[9] Ratio for schools reporting both FTE teachers and fall enrollment data.
[10] Property tax and parent government contributions are determined on the basis of independence or dependence of the local school system and are mutually exclusive.

NOTE.—Locale classification procedures not comparable with previous years. Enrollments by locale were used to distribute school district revenue and expenditure amounts by locale classification.

SOURCE: U.S. Department of Education, National Center for Education Statistics, Common Core of Data survey; and U.S. Department of Commerce, Bureau of the Census, *Survey of Local Government Finances*, unpublished data. (This table was prepared October 1997.)

Table 89.—Public school districts and public and private elementary and secondary schools: 1929–30 to 1995–96

School year	Public school districts [1]	Public schools [2]					Private schools [2,3]		
		Total, all schools [4]	Total, regular schools [5]	Elementary schools		Secondary schools	Total [4]	Elementary schools	Secondary schools
				Total	One-teacher				
1	2	3	4	5	6	7	8	9	10
1929–30	—	—	—	238,306	149,282	23,930	—	9,275	3,258
1937–38	119,001	—	—	221,660	121,178	25,467	—	9,992	3,327
1939–40	117,108	—	—	—	113,600	—	—	11,306	3,568
1945–46	101,382	—	—	160,227	86,563	24,314	—	9,863	3,294
1947–48	94,926	—	—	146,760	75,096	25,484	—	10,071	3,292
1949–50	83,718	—	—	128,225	59,652	24,542	—	10,375	3,331
1951–52	71,094	—	—	123,763	50,742	23,746	—	10,666	3,322
1953–54	63,057	—	—	110,875	42,865	25,637	—	11,739	3,913
1955–56	54,859	—	—	104,427	34,964	26,046	—	12,372	3,887
1957–58	47,594	—	—	95,446	25,341	25,507	—	13,065	3,994
1959–60	40,520	—	—	91,853	20,213	25,784	—	13,574	4,061
1961–62	35,676	—	—	81,910	13,333	25,350	—	14,762	4,129
1963–64	31,705	—	—	77,584	9,895	26,431	—	—	4,451
1965–66	26,983	—	—	73,216	6,491	26,597	17,849	15,340	4,606
1967–68	22,010	—	94,197	70,879	4,146	27,011	—	—	—
1970–71	17,995	—	89,372	65,800	1,815	25,352	—	14,372	3,770
1973–74	16,730	—	88,655	65,070	1,365	25,906	—	—	—
1975–76	16,376	88,597	87,034	63,242	1,166	25,330	—	—	—
1976–77	16,271	—	86,501	62,644	1,111	25,378	19,910	16,385	5,904
1978–79	16,014	—	84,816	61,982	1,056	24,504	19,489	16,097	5,766
1980–81	15,912	85,982	83,688	61,069	921	24,362	20,764	16,792	5,678
1982–83	15,824	84,740	82,039	59,656	798	23,988	—	—	—
1983–84	15,747	84,178	81,418	59,082	838	23,947	[6]27,694	[6]20,872	[6]7,862
1984–85	—	84,007	81,147	58,827	825	23,916	—	—	—
1985–86	—	—	—	—	—	—	[6]25,616	[6]20,252	[6]7,387
1986–87	[7]15,713	83,455	82,190	60,784	763	23,389	—	—	—
1987–88	[7]15,577	83,248	81,416	59,754	729	23,841	[6]26,807	[6]22,959	[6]8,418
1988–89	[7]15,376	83,165	81,579	60,176	583	23,638	—	—	—
1989–90	[7]15,367	83,425	81,880	60,699	630	23,461	—	—	—
1990–91	[7]15,358	84,538	82,475	61,340	617	23,460	[6]24,690	[6]22,223	[6]8,989
1991–92	[7]15,173	84,578	82,506	61,739	569	23,248	[6]25,998	[6]23,523	[6]9,282
1992–93	[7]15,025	84,497	82,896	62,225	430	23,220	—	—	—
1993–94	[7]14,881	85,393	83,431	62,726	442	23,379	[6]26,093	[6]23,543	[6]10,555
1994–95	[7]14,772	86,221	84,476	63,572	458	23,668	—	—	—
1995–96	[7]14,883	87,125	84,958	63,961	474	23,793	—	—	—

[1] Includes operating and nonoperating districts.
[2] Schools with both elementary and secondary programs are included under elementary schools and also under secondary schools.
[3] Data for most years are partly estimated.
[4] Includes regular schools and special schools not classified by grade span.
[5] Includes elementary, secondary, and combined elementary/secondary schools.
[6] These data are from sample surveys and should not be compared directly with the data for earlier years.
[7] Because of expanded survey coverage, data are not directly comparable with figures for earlier years.
—Data not available.

SOURCE: U.S. Department of Education, National Center for Education Statistics, *Statistics of State School Systems; Statistics of Public Elementary and Secondary School Systems; Statistics of Nonpublic Elementary and Secondary Schools; Private Schools in American Education;* and Common Core of Data surveys. (This table was prepared September 1997.)

Table 90.—Public school districts and enrollment, by size of district: 1988–89 to 1995–96

Enrollment size of district	1988–89	1989–90	1990–91	1991–92	1992–93	1993–94	1994–95			1995–96		
	Number of districts	Number of districts	Number of districts	Number of districts	Number of districts	Number of districts	Number of districts	Percent of districts	Percent of students	Number of districts	Percent of districts	Percent of students
1	2	3	4	5	6	7	8	9	10	11	12	13
Total	15,376	15,367	15,358	15,173	15,025	14,881	14,772	100.0	100.0	14,883	100.0	100.0
25,000 or more	177	179	190	195	202	206	207	1.4	29.9	216	1.5	30.5
10,000 to 24,999	473	479	489	502	510	525	542	3.7	18.6	553	3.7	18.6
5,000 to 9,999	924	913	937	941	955	973	996	6.7	15.7	1,013	6.8	15.7
2,500 to 4,999	1,907	1,937	1,940	1,981	2,002	2,008	2,013	13.6	16.1	2,027	13.6	16.0
1,000 to 2,499	3,529	3,547	3,542	3,525	3,530	3,570	3,579	24.2	13.4	3,554	23.9	13.1
600 to 999	1,813	1,801	1,799	1,793	1,798	1,785	1,777	12.0	3.2	1,777	11.9	3.2
300 to 599	2,266	2,283	2,275	2,222	2,200	2,162	2,113	14.3	2.1	2,104	14.1	2.1
1 to 299	3,984	3,910	3,816	3,648	3,465	3,294	3,173	21.5	1.0	3,123	21.0	1.0
Size not reported [1]	303	318	370	366	363	358	372	2.5	—	516	3.5	—

[1] Includes school districts reporting enrollment of 0.
—Data not reported.

NOTE.—Because of rounding, details may not add to totals.

SOURCE: U.S. Department of Education, National Center for Education Statistics, Common Core of Data surveys. (This table was prepared September 1997.)

Table 91.—Number and percentage of public elementary and secondary education agencies, by state and type of agency: 1995–96

State or other area	Total agencies	Regular school districts, including supervisory union components		Regional education service agencies and supervisory union administrative centers		State-operated agencies		Federally operated and other agencies	
		Number	Percent	Number	Percent	Number	Percent	Number	Percent
1	2	3	4	5	6	7	8	9	10
United States	16,410	14,883	90.7	1,185	7.2	197	1.2	145	0.9
Alabama	131	127	96.9	0	0.0	1	0.8	3	2.3
Alaska	56	56	100.0	0	0.0	0	0.0	0	0.0
Arizona	242	227	93.8	5	2.1	1	0.4	9	3.7
Arkansas	335	314	93.7	17	5.1	4	1.2	0	0.0
California	1,067	1,006	94.3	58	5.4	3	0.3	0	0.0
Colorado	194	176	90.7	18	9.3	0	0.0	0	0.0
Connecticut	179	166	92.7	6	3.4	4	2.2	3	1.7
Delaware	22	19	86.4	0	0.0	3	13.6	0	0.0
District of Columbia	1	1	100.0	0	0.0	0	0.0	0	0.0
Florida	74	67	90.5	0	0.0	1	1.4	6	8.1
Georgia	184	181	98.4	0	0.0	0	0.0	3	1.6
Hawaii	1	1	100.0	0	0.0	0	0.0	0	0.0
Idaho	113	112	99.1	0	0.0	1	0.9	0	0.0
Illinois	1,038	916	88.2	86	8.3	5	0.5	31	3.0
Indiana	327	295	90.2	28	8.6	3	0.9	1	0.3
Iowa	421	390	92.6	15	3.6	15	3.6	1	0.2
Kansas	304	304	100.0	0	0.0	0	0.0	0	0.0
Kentucky	258	176	68.2	0	0.0	80	31.0	2	0.8
Louisiana	72	66	91.7	0	0.0	5	6.9	1	1.4
Maine	329	285	86.6	42	12.8	1	0.3	1	0.3
Maryland	24	24	100.0	0	0.0	0	0.0	0	0.0
Massachusetts	464	353	76.1	85	18.3	1	0.2	25	5.4
Michigan	695	633	91.1	57	8.2	4	0.6	1	0.1
Minnesota	489	419	85.7	67	13.7	3	0.6	0	0.0
Mississippi	165	153	92.7	0	0.0	11	6.7	1	0.6
Missouri	542	536	98.9	0	0.0	2	0.4	4	0.7
Montana	561	481	85.7	77	13.7	3	0.5	0	0.0
Nebraska	799	680	85.1	112	14.0	7	0.9	0	0.0
Nevada	18	17	94.4	0	0.0	1	5.6	0	0.0
New Hampshire	247	178	72.1	69	27.9	0	0.0	0	0.0
New Jersey	620	608	98.1	12	1.9	0	0.0	0	0.0
New Mexico	89	89	100.0	0	0.0	0	0.0	0	0.0
New York	757	719	95.0	38	5.0	0	0.0	0	0.0
North Carolina	123	119	96.7	0	0.0	2	1.6	2	1.6
North Dakota	289	243	84.1	38	13.1	3	1.0	5	1.7
Ohio	790	661	83.7	102	12.9	3	0.4	24	3.0
Oklahoma	551	551	100.0	0	0.0	0	0.0	0	0.0
Oregon	258	248	96.1	7	2.7	2	0.8	1	0.4
Pennsylvania	614	501	81.6	101	16.4	12	2.0	0	0.0
Rhode Island	37	36	97.3	0	0.0	1	2.7	0	0.0
South Carolina	106	95	89.6	11	10.4	0	0.0	0	0.0
South Dakota	218	177	81.2	17	7.8	5	2.3	19	8.7
Tennessee	140	140	100.0	0	0.0	0	0.0	0	0.0
Texas	1,044	1,044	100.0	0	0.0	0	0.0	0	0.0
Utah	47	40	85.1	5	10.6	2	4.3	0	0.0
Vermont	344	284	82.6	60	17.4	0	0.0	0	0.0
Virginia	165	141	85.5	22	13.3	0	0.0	2	1.2
Washington	305	296	97.0	9	3.0	0	0.0	0	0.0
West Virginia	57	55	96.5	0	0.0	2	3.5	0	0.0
Wisconsin	446	428	96.0	16	3.6	2	0.4	0	0.0
Wyoming	58	49	84.5	5	8.6	4	6.9	0	0.0
Department of Defense dependents schools	12	0	0.0	0	0.0	0	0.0	12	100.0
Outlying areas									
American Samoa	1	1	100.0	0	0.0	0	0.0	0	0.0
Guam	1	1	100.0	0	0.0	0	0.0	0	0.0
Northern Marianas	1	1	100.0	0	0.0	0	0.0	0	0.0
Puerto Rico	1	1	100.0	0	0.0	0	0.0	0	0.0
Virgin Islands	1	1	100.0	0	0.0	0	0.0	0	0.0

SOURCE: U.S. Department of Education, National Center for Education Statistics, Common Core of Data survey. (This table was prepared September 1997.)

98 ELEMENTARY AND SECONDARY: SCHOOLS AND SCHOOL DISTRICTS

Table 92.—Selected statistics for public school districts enrolling more than 20,000 pupils, by state: 1995–96

Name of district, by state	State	Enrollment, fall 1995	Classroom teachers,[1] fall 1995	Pupils per teacher, fall 1995	Percent minority pupils, fall 1995	Number of schools, 1995–96	Number of 1994–95 graduates[2]	Revenue and expenditures,[3] 1993–94 (in thousands of dollars)							Current expenditure per pupil 1993–94[4]
								Revenue receipts				Total expenditures	Current expenditures			Interest on school debt	
								Total	Federal	State	Local		Total	Instruction	Capital outlay		
1	2	3	4	5	6	7	8	9	10	11	12	13	14	15	16	17	18
Districts with more than 20,000 students[5]	—	15,274,273	827,721	18.5	56.8	21,525	683,216	$86,759,726	$7,143,815	$41,617,895	$37,998,016	$85,435,239	$77,601,940	$47,051,356	$6,231,968	$1,601,331	$5,249
Baldwin County	AL	20,699	1,218	17.0	18.8	35	1,025	80,088	6,562	47,095	26,431	78,278	69,981	42,789	5,640	2,657	3,610
Birmingham City	AL	41,824	2,578	16.2	93.1	92	1,886	178,600	27,605	104,517	46,478	185,114	180,833	104,211	4,281	0	4,220
Huntsville City	AL	24,163	1,660	14.6	43.1	43	1,351	124,134	9,054	64,618	50,462	126,236	118,394	69,933	7,842	0	4,722
Jefferson County	AL	41,054	2,425	16.9	16.7	58	2,493	167,458	11,217	104,365	51,876	174,284	161,385	100,011	9,425	3,474	3,962
Mobile County	AL	65,602	3,560	18.4	50.8	88	3,333	242,187	35,041	155,416	51,730	234,376	221,128	138,937	12,569	679	3,321
Montgomery County	AL	35,065	2,099	16.7	68.7	55	1,501	126,336	16,950	85,887	23,499	130,674	129,382	78,747	1,198	94	3,671
Anchorage	AK	47,318	2,368	20.0	31.1	84	2,158	308,432	26,373	204,982	77,077	344,793	294,399	152,851	39,098	11,296	6,219
Deer Valley	AZ	20,420	1,008	20.3	12.0	20	771	97,507	3,125	34,387	59,995	93,260	67,983	41,496	17,446	7,831	3,766
Mesa Unified	AZ	70,035		24.0	24.0	71	3,270	296,606	15,697	154,141	126,768	293,332	249,137	158,869	36,247	7,948	3,683
Paradise Valley	AZ	32,099	1,533	20.9	12.5	33	1,502	138,204	4,432	60,215	73,557	144,173	114,853	72,609	17,107	12,213	3,823
Peoria Unified	AZ	27,052	1,217	22.2	22.6	25	1,301	100,615	3,665	56,579	40,371	102,945	86,063	53,818	9,753	7,129	3,477
Phoenix Union High	AZ	21,083		22.5	72.5	15	3,042	152,941	12,559	13,269	127,113	166,535	127,340	68,694	28,783	10,412	6,314
Scottsdale	AZ	24,467	1,202	20.4	12.8	26	1,235	110,959	2,804	22,999	85,156	127,133	89,232	50,817	28,134	9,767	4,038
Tucson Unified	AZ	62,317		18.1	53.5	110	2,497	281,811	26,505	132,988	122,318	339,579	244,373	139,539	73,648	21,558	4,037
Washington School District 6	AZ	24,587	1,358	18.1	77.0	32	0	100,639	6,244	56,622	37,773	97,430	88,689	57,709	7,085	1,656	3,693
Little Rock	AR	24,901	1,613	15.4	68.7	48	1,445	138,930	10,095	62,961	65,874	150,129	139,891	86,253	5,992	4,246	5,477
Pulaski County Special	AR	20,534	1,192	17.2	33.4	37	1,005	107,376	6,960	65,980	34,436	106,795	97,756	59,522	7,820	1,219	4,786
ABC Unified	CA	21,819	863	25.3	80.1	30	1,367	101,740	6,044	69,862	25,834	93,258	91,571	58,699	1,630	57	4,311
Anaheim Union High	CA	24,412	895	27.3	64.9	20	2,658	127,265	8,416	70,950	47,899	121,207	110,514	65,427	10,693	0	4,710
Bakersfield City Elementary	CA	26,232	1,100	23.8	74.9	37	0	128,497	16,302	85,990	26,205	128,453	112,421	69,281	13,465	2,567	4,264
Capistrano Unified	CA	34,929	1,378	25.3	23.4	36	1,659	169,882	4,299	64,051	101,532	179,971	132,371	85,584	47,375	225	4,234
Chino Unified	CA	28,514	1,117	25.5	49.5	30	1,308	146,151	3,988	101,924	40,239	137,908	111,493	74,267	25,935	480	4,190
Clovis Unified	CA	29,522	1,175	25.1	35.2	31	1,621	150,664	31,778	82,897	35,989	152,835	114,814	68,136	39,816	4,205	4,188
Compton Unified	CA	28,133	944	29.8	99.8	38	810	150,338	18,506	104,658	27,174	158,535	128,824	78,550	4,175	0	4,523
Corona Norco Unified	CA	28,014	1,071	26.2	49.8	34	1,335	117,626	6,011	74,684	36,931	114,770	105,900	65,672	8,870	0	4,128
East Side Union High	CA	22,082	954	23.1	79.7	14	4,235	123,968	8,821	65,892	49,255	116,495	114,256	74,454	1,536	703	5,186
Elk Grove Unified	CA	35,936	1,471	24.4	56.0	41	1,527	178,633	9,266	117,065	52,302	189,164	137,599	85,971	51,502	63	4,295
Fairfield-Suisun Joint Unified	CA	20,999	901	23.3	51.9	27	958	90,662	3,773	64,558	22,331	83,516	77,247	54,332	6,269	0	3,722
Fontana Unified	CA	30,979	1,185	26.1	75.0	31	1,416	139,134	12,942	102,144	24,048	135,790	123,824	75,956	10,851	1,115	4,160
Fremont Unified	CA	29,587	1,178	25.1	48.1	40	1,585	144,589	4,938	76,850	62,801	133,217	119,737	82,879	11,817	1,717	4,139
Fresno Unified	CA	77,880	3,195	24.4	76.1	92	2,974	400,967	46,528	262,058	92,381	386,577	342,501	215,724	44,076	0	4,486
Garden Grove Unified	CA	43,413	1,659	26.2	74.4	63	2,246	191,895	17,776	101,325	72,794	186,672	185,610	117,821	1,060	2	4,455
Glendale Unified	CA	29,747	1,120	26.6	40.9	29	1,645	130,431	12,298	74,602	43,531	125,655	122,271	79,906	3,384	0	4,254
Grossmont Union High	CA	21,431	860	24.9	29.4	13	3,599	105,105	5,866	47,458	51,781	98,106	93,764	54,979	4,342	126	4,686
Hacienda La Puente Unified	CA	21,943	816	26.9	59.6	34	1,454	136,914	8,828	103,278	24,806	136,134	91,825	53,103	2,824	6	4,206
Hayward Unified	CA	20,511	854	24.0	88.1	35	1,930	159,955	7,405	90,660	75,109	150,539	91,775	53,954	4,414	8	4,284
Irvine Unified	CA	21,975	829	26.6	74.0	26	1,224	107,141	1,072	69,367	30,204	95,908	78,749	49,708	4,133	0	4,601
Kern High	CA	24,714	911	23.7	35.0	31	877	101,963	7,570	62,735	64,569	146,111	96,349	62,259	1,670	0	4,477
Lodi Unified	CA	25,500	1,070	27.1	51.1	37	1,579	100,092	8,539	30,378	65,992	146,111	116,303	60,997	25,462	4,346	5,136
Long Beach Unified	CA	80,520	3,187	23.8	53.4	82	4,298	148,411	8,501	73,918	65,992	111,592	106,811	67,255	4,619	162	4,246
Los Angeles Unified	CA	647,612	25,788	25.3	79.4	644	3,217	117,697	9,244	73,935	34,518	116,401	346,643	220,597	39,072	0	4,515
Montebello Unified	CA	32,801	1,074	25.1	88.7	30	24,887	411,024	48,448	269,591	92,985	3,291,789	3,166,510	1,979,635	125,227	52	4,954
Moreno Valley Unified	CA	31,503	1,267	30.5	95.9	34	1,546	3,777,164	475,847	2,428,837	872,480	137,982	135,056	85,869	2,926	0	4,179
Mt. Diablo Unified	CA	35,258	1,511	24.9	59.6	55	1,454	163,503	15,887	112,521	35,095	136,134	133,184	82,994	2,824	126	4,212
Norwalk La Mirada Unified	CA	20,885	785	26.6	31.1	26	1,930	136,914	8,828	103,278	24,806	150,539	146,117	93,357	4,414	8	4,284
Oakland Unified	CA	52,452	2,211	23.7	93.2	90	1,647	159,955	7,405	77,441	75,109	95,908	91,775	53,954	4,133	0	4,601
Ontario Montclair Elementary	CA	23,682	898	26.4	81.0	31	0	107,141	7,570	69,367	30,204	285,160	278,765	162,656	5,630	765	5,387
Orange Unified	CA	27,432	1,060	25.9	49.7	37	1,458	101,327	5,859	72,615	19,275	102,006	93,498	61,631	8,506	2	4,128
Pasadena Unified	CA	22,136	855	25.9	82.8	31	1,244	115,100	12,324	65,310	34,518	108,669	107,418	64,197	1,251	162	4,071
Placentia-Yorba Linda Unified	CA	23,632	915	25.8	35.7	29	1,093	120,455	19,366	49,369	48,396	116,401	113,905	66,256	2,496	0	5,170
Pomona Unified	CA	30,625	1,153	26.6	89.4	36	1,183	101,484	19,366	49,369	33,499	103,308	101,074	63,825	2,137	97	4,496
Poway Unified	CA	30,043	1,211	24.8	27.2	28	1,024	165,304	3,124	112,439	33,499	162,615	134,611	80,393	26,038	1,966	4,505
Rialto Unified	CA	23,830	911	26.2	79.6	24	1,711	147,883	6,086	67,743	77,016	146,434	122,233	75,920	23,769	432	4,349
Richmond Unified	CA	31,894	1,292	24.7	76.3	57	1,043	119,512	13,531	95,241	18,185	122,092	92,764	56,168	29,287	41	4,136
Riverside Unified	CA	35,055	1,386	25.3	54.1	42	1,469	150,916	11,113	84,646	52,739	151,018	142,463	90,584	8,555	8	4,547
Sacramento City Unified	CA	50,104	1,904	26.3	71.5	75	1,560	156,687	27,417	99,381	46,193	149,883	141,797	87,506	8,078	0	4,213
Saddleback Valley Unified	CA	30,116	1,232	24.4	26.3	36	1,883	247,546	27,417	155,558	64,571	235,993	225,055	150,710	1,251	97	4,501
San Bernardino City Unified	CA	45,091	1,824	24.7	73.4	58	1,723	120,739	21,392	41,549	75,808	120,764	116,539	74,324	3,883	16	4,204
San Diego City Unified	CA	130,360	5,527	23.6	70.0	164	1,565	224,717	21,392	168,344	34,981	214,132	201,161	116,000	12,971	342	4,579
San Francisco Unified	CA	61,889	2,849	21.7	86.9	112	5,731	711,190	59,809	297,470	353,911	691,795	654,705	381,526	37,028	62	5,145
							3,398	331,392	32,087	107,343	191,962	313,151	301,899	193,801	11,252	0	4,898

ELEMENTARY AND SECONDARY: SCHOOLS AND SCHOOL DISTRICTS 99

Table 92.—Selected statistics for public school districts enrolling more than 20,000 pupils, by state: 1995–96—Continued

Name of district, by state	State	Enrollment, fall 1995	Class-room teachers,[1] fall 1995	Pupils per teacher, fall 1995	Percent minority pupils, fall 1995	Number of schools, 1995–96	Number of 1994–95 graduates[2]	Revenue and expenditures,[3] 1993–94 (in thousands of dollars)								Current expenditure per pupil 1993–94[4]
								Revenue receipts				Total expenditures	Current expenditures			
								Total	Federal	State	Local	Total	Total	Instruction	Capital outlay	Interest on school debt	
1	2	3	4	5	6	7	8	9	10	11	12	13	14	15	16	17	18
San Jose Unified	CA	32,160	1,375	23.4	67.2	49	1,617	173,684	13,677	75,258	84,749	168,170	161,599	92,459	6,391	180	5,229
San Juan Unified	CA	47,581	1,879	25.3	21.6	87	2,730	230,820	15,503	143,965	71,352	221,270	210,352	136,620	10,915	3	4,415
Santa Ana Unified	CA	50,268	1,805	27.8	96.1	47	1,759	236,327	20,604	130,953	84,770	211,509	199,258	129,524	12,056	195	4,116
Stockton City Unified	CA	34,637	1,460	23.7	82.8	41	1,048	176,559	22,853	115,863	37,843	173,026	164,935	102,014	8,065	26	4,803
Sweetwater Union High	CA	29,567	1,222	24.2	81.2	19	3,389	151,747	11,232	105,826	34,689	145,759	136,689	80,366	9,070	0	4,751
Torrance Unified	CA	22,619	924	24.5	49.7	30	1,451	96,134	3,159	52,934	40,041	86,994	85,596	52,267	1,393	5	4,031
Visalia Unified	CA	24,232	951	25.5	52.1	31	1,062	113,532	8,468	81,170	23,894	99,800	92,919	61,517	6,881	0	3,976
Vista Unified	CA	24,094	953	25.3	47.7	25	1,010	102,482	5,710	59,503	37,269	99,057	94,565	59,242	4,489	3	4,309
Adams-Arapahoe	CO	27,825	1,480	18.8	42.4	44	1,227	154,119	7,136	82,275	64,708	146,987	135,157	81,405	6,022	5,808	4,927
Boulder Valley	CO	25,230	1,353	18.6	16.6	51	1,365	137,958	4,477	27,866	105,615	136,481	131,022	76,405	2,480	2,979	5,440
Cherry Creek	CO	35,761	1,921	18.6	16.1	46	2,034	210,434	3,320	68,169	138,945	197,919	176,831	111,066	9,040	12,048	5,303
Colorado Springs	CO	32,960	1,688	19.5	26.5	60	1,610	139,899	7,574	72,551	59,774	145,880	143,904	81,214	1,976	0	4,525
Denver	CO	64,322	3,271	19.7	72.9	113	2,721	396,687	33,918	105,457	257,312	407,820	352,966	195,000	42,204	12,650	5,632
Douglas County	CO	22,032	1,214	18.1	6.5	35	972	103,391	1,363	40,606	61,422	95,736	81,955	44,799	7,393	6,388	4,603
Jefferson County	CO	85,495	4,005	21.3	13.4	143	4,411	440,930	11,709	206,516	222,705	501,561	383,419	225,064	88,416	29,726	4,633
Northglenn-Thornton	CO	24,603	1,238	19.9	23.9	40	1,164	116,518	5,300	65,270	45,948	117,827	102,782	63,524	6,662	8,383	4,510
Poudre	CO	21,283	1,004	21.2	14.5	44	1,156	106,226	4,726	42,085	59,415	137,248	92,430	59,085	35,522	9,296	4,512
Bridgeport City Schools	CT	21,519	1,355	15.9	88.4	40	615	173,898	15,356	121,331	37,211	166,024	157,978	104,191	4,753	3,293	7,708
Hartford Public Schools	CT	23,791			95.2	35	746	245,254	19,278	154,356	71,620	229,702	226,518	150,949	342	2,842	8,956
D.C. Public Schools	DC	79,802	5,305	15.0	96.0	188	3,061	735,661	79,432	0	656,229	751,933	741,205	351,028	10,728	0	9,187
Alachua County	FL	29,166	1,652	17.7	42.3	42	1,177	162,933	16,526	96,819	49,588	164,582	130,740	69,861	27,170	6,672	4,599
Bay County	FL	25,228	1,463	17.2	19.1	35	1,084	127,748	10,340	80,625	36,783	118,953	113,745	70,347	5,043	165	4,765
Brevard County	FL	65,621	3,724	17.6	20.1	89	3,012	329,645	19,451	175,034	135,160	354,749	285,417	170,102	63,744	5,588	4,563
Broward County	FL	208,359	9,870	21.1	51.0	192	8,222	1,196,522	73,252	617,046	506,224	1,158,259	967,779	536,199	157,157	33,323	5,097
Clay County	FL	24,875	1,306	19.0	13.4	27	1,216	173,410	5,607	77,171	29,877	108,722	94,034	54,198	14,488	200	4,063
Collier County	FL	26,376	1,494	17.7	35.6	40	968	173,431	12,523	28,938	131,970	182,298	138,145	82,779	38,764	5,389	5,774
Dade County	FL	333,817	16,692	20.0	85.8	327	14,587	2,010,957	165,583	1,148,158	697,216	1,932,111	1,711,914	995,411	196,291	23,906	5,550
Duval County	FL	123,916	6,096	20.3	45.2	155	4,607	615,055	51,462	355,647	207,946	599,153	529,277	299,452	58,744	11,132	4,419
Escambia County	FL	45,215	2,621	17.3	38.9	72	2,225	244,755	25,674	157,914	61,167	245,422	219,764	123,241	21,870	3,788	4,923
Hillsborough County	FL	143,192	8,652	16.6	43.0	173	5,886	802,571	77,539	455,171	269,861	784,042	697,501	391,537	76,361	10,180	5,163
Lake County	FL	24,827	1,328	18.7	24.3	41	1,059	125,452	9,125	70,772	45,555	111,611	100,064	54,734	9,875	1,672	4,414
Lee County	FL	50,945	2,700	18.9	27.8	71	2,142	293,158	18,261	88,876	186,021	350,447	245,531	128,408	93,441	11,475	4,414
Leon County	FL	31,335	1,771	17.7	41.0	47	1,295	188,084	12,464	112,895	62,725	163,032	141,585	77,266	15,816	5,631	5,181
Manatee County	FL	31,805	1,678	19.0	29.0	61	1,125	173,410	12,103	78,771	82,536	168,787	140,219	81,171	28,194	374	4,745
Marion County	FL	35,526	1,936	18.4	28.1	47	1,462	173,860	14,306	104,384	55,170	169,680	148,961	85,928	16,784	3,935	4,555
Okaloosa County	FL	29,454	1,598	18.5	19.5	36	1,724	142,749	11,793	91,760	39,196	128,072	120,579	69,913	5,961	1,532	4,179
Orange County School Board	FL	123,165	6,647	18.5	47.7	157	5,323	671,458	43,890	296,455	331,113	627,217	547,836	287,996	64,844	14,537	4,363
Osceola County	FL	25,670	1,266	20.3	39.4	31	1,205	130,812	6,311	71,637	52,864	113,582	100,886	54,923	8,582	17,916	5,330
Palm Beach County	FL	132,215	7,356	18.0	45.0	133	5,645	842,551	47,933	242,004	552,614	763,878	649,860	407,459	96,102	5,882	4,683
Pasco County School Board	FL	41,791	2,318	18.0	11.0	45	1,778	218,481	15,554	122,328	80,549	208,986	179,200	98,583	23,904	591	4,814
Pinellas County	FL	104,335	5,748	18.2	24.6	148	4,668	580,123	36,905	254,575	288,643	552,254	482,004	281,724	69,659	5,019	4,599
Polk County	FL	72,807	4,122	17.7	31.8	119	3,096	362,607	32,147	222,263	108,197	344,478	320,649	179,727	18,810	5,120	5,532
Sarasota County	FL	31,035	1,716	18.1	16.2	38	1,531	212,876	9,759	105,644	97,473	212,589	167,097	89,491	20,672	6,837	5,125
Seminole County	FL	54,603	2,823	19.3	27.6	55	2,570	268,497	10,924	142,008	115,070	247,056	219,272	129,559	20,947	2,105	4,230
St. Lucie County	FL	27,044	1,913	14.1	39.4	35	962	142,897	11,419	60,076	70,972	138,116	120,610	66,102	8,329	11,390	4,162
Volusia County	FL	56,788	3,417	16.6	24.1	72	2,585	296,797	11,849	145,706	132,778	303,147	248,183	139,569	39,601	9,177	4,777
Atlanta Public Schools	GA	60,209			93.4	109	2,175	493,486	18,313	145,476	307,943	461,734	410,211	234,432	51,523	15,363	4,598
Bibb County	GA	25,066			67.1	40	917	121,249	40,067	71,401	37,348	124,762	111,879	67,908	10,670	0	6,924
Chatham County	GA	35,860	2,072	17.3	64.6	44	1,630	212,876	12,500	105,644	97,473	212,589	181,221	111,935	26,670	2,213	4,447
Cherokee County	GA	20,893	1,205	17.4	4.5	27	867	90,450	9,759	50,529	36,887	89,188	79,382	48,776	7,570	4,698	5,125
Clayton County	GA	40,562	2,329	17.4	54.8	44	1,619	274,773	15,084	94,381	165,308	182,320	171,038	99,862	9,177	2,236	4,230
Cobb County	GA	82,870	4,910	16.9	22.4	86	4,055	376,423	6,363	184,754	185,306	377,192	224,938	155,007	15,315	11,390	4,506
DeKalb County	GA	87,291	5,205	16.8	82.5	106	4,228	528,942	21,722	194,029	313,191	465,628	295,497	155,007	9,516	3,257	4,519
Fulton County	GA	56,338	3,567	15.8	49.3	55	2,527	333,274	12,099	103,278	217,897	329,245	277,130	212,645	44,182	7,933	5,559
Gwinnett County	GA	84,555	4,852	17.4	19.5	71	3,957	385,120	8,245	184,980	191,895	395,008	331,086	212,645	52,848	11,074	5,522
Muscogee County	GA	33,117	1,911	17.4	61.0	50	1,532	230,800	16,330	120,972	58,771	163,151	156,645	90,928	5,709	797	4,329
Richmond County	GA	36,359	2,065	17.6	67.0	56	1,622	164,579	15,765	93,498	58,771	155,660	149,941	91,014	4,046	1,673	4,898
Hawaii Public Schools	HI	187,104	10,500	17.8	77.1	246	9,980	1,133,949	77,993	1,025,813	30,143	1,095,317	998,144	615,270	97,173	0	4,233
Boise City ISD	ID	26,714	1,396	19.1	—	47	1,524	117,735	6,123	55,635	55,977	114,406	106,655	69,326	5,534	2,217	5,508
City of Chicago	IL	412,921	22,918	18.0	89.2	606	14,818	2,546,064	318,382	815,400	1,412,282	2,343,099	2,298,318	1,367,781	43,930	851	5,613
Rockford	IL	27,637	1,646	16.8	37.5	50	1,265	144,273	8,965	55,087	80,221	162,729	154,362	91,950	2,161	6,206	5,575

100 ELEMENTARY AND SECONDARY: SCHOOLS AND SCHOOL DISTRICTS

Table 92.—Selected statistics for public school districts enrolling more than 20,000 pupils, by state: 1995–96—Continued

Name of district, by state	State	Enrollment, fall 1995	Class-room teach-ers,[1] fall 1995	Pupils per teacher, fall 1995	Percent minority pupils, fall 1995	Number of schools, 1995–96	Number of 1994–95 graduates[2]	Revenue and expenditures,[3] 1993–94 (in thousands of dollars)									Current expenditure per pupil 1993–94[4]
								Revenue receipts				Total expenditures	Current expenditures		Capital outlay	Interest on school debt	
								Total	Federal	State	Local		Total	Instruction			
1	2	3	4	5	6	7	8	9	10	11	12	13	14	15	16	17	18
School District U-46 (Elgin Area)	IL	31,168	1,404	22.2	38.1	51	1,471	162,881	5,296	45,974	111,611	146,892	141,366	93,389	1,661	3,865	4,767
Evansville-Vanderburgh	IN	23,713	1,408	16.8	15.3	40	1,280	155,440	9,608	61,345	84,487	154,224	142,349	83,549	11,267	608	5,975
Fort Wayne Community Schools	IN	31,748	1,708	18.6	29.9	53	1,664	190,534	11,414	80,888	98,232	187,083	174,498	107,847	11,839	746	5,500
Gary Community Schools	IN	22,489	1,173	19.2	98.9	43	1,289	149,193	14,804	86,850	47,539	156,565	145,636	73,900	10,158	771	6,030
Indianapolis Public Schools	IN	44,896	2,491	18.0	59.4	97	1,461	352,861	26,620	180,621	145,620	330,211	295,045	162,955	33,497	1,669	6,324
South Bend Community Schools	IN	21,136	1,222	17.3	40.7	36	1,085	131,725	5,841	66,215	59,669	126,124	110,892	68,450	14,602	630	5,165
Des Moines Independent Community	IA	32,414	2,106	15.4	23.7	65	1,598	186,527	11,911	93,940	80,676	175,080	169,753	109,530	4,747	580	5,363
Kansas City Unified	KS	21,670	1,286	16.9	68.1	48	961	132,783	13,314	84,115	35,354	131,487	125,709	70,939	5,778	0	5,689
Shawnee Mission Unified	KS	31,844	2,016	15.8	9.4	58	2,073	176,792	4,420	65,895	106,477	171,297	163,560	99,608	5,216	2,521	5,139
Wichita Unified	KS	45,626	2,707	16.9	39.3	108	2,537	259,538	15,538	135,546	108,454	256,099	247,620	140,083	8,479	0	5,254
Fayette County	KY	32,880	2,116	15.5	26.2	57	1,666	180,072	10,053	86,581	83,438	167,651	160,364	94,903	4,048	3,239	4,847
Jefferson County	KY	93,070	5,526	16.8	33.2	151	5,279	544,001	61,551	271,943	210,507	519,155	491,608	305,808	18,313	9,234	5,256
Caddo Parish	LA	49,578	2,858	17.3	61.6	75	2,314	220,234	23,145	118,757	78,332	217,027	207,981	125,507	7,368	1,678	4,058
Calcasieu Parish	LA	34,163	2,031	16.8	31.9	59	1,785	149,137	13,610	74,112	61,415	143,310	134,278	81,038	5,240	3,792	3,906
East Baton Rouge Parish	LA	60,761	3,736	16.3	63.6	105	3,016	284,358	31,602	153,481	99,275	279,956	275,400	164,609	4,556	0	4,359
Jefferson Parish	LA	56,021	3,326	16.8	52.7	83	2,276	300,883	26,809	132,443	141,631	290,013	264,728	163,411	7,866	0	4,622
Lafayette Parish School Board	LA	32,011	1,763	18.2	35.9	41	1,433	127,922	13,339	67,305	47,278	118,945	112,561	71,827	3,629	17,419	3,618
Orleans Parish	LA	85,596	3,855	22.2	94.4	122	3,267	385,883	65,498	191,817	128,568	391,250	364,746	229,224	17,499	9,005	4,242
Rapides Parish	LA	24,792	1,540	16.1	42.9	54	1,224	118,205	14,847	63,670	39,688	114,332	107,787	63,615	1,844	4,701	4,402
St. Tammany Parish	LA	31,984	1,990	16.1	16.2	48	1,203	140,936	9,471	74,733	56,732	143,994	126,126	77,502	13,417	4,451	4,137
Terrebonne Parish	LA	22,194	1,101	20.2	35.3	42	1,890	74,773	10,225	45,692	18,856	74,122	72,112	43,822	1,091	919	3,273
Anne Arundel County	MD	71,383	3,839	18.6	21.3	111	4,020	430,606	16,818	157,891	255,897	435,404	408,382	240,348	23,106	3,916	5,917
Baltimore City	MD	109,980	6,047	18.2	85.7	180	3,569	682,723	75,897	392,173	214,653	639,683	620,177	390,699	15,139	4,367	5,471
Baltimore County	MD	101,564	6,048	16.8	29.5	158	5,459	628,437	25,374	201,882	401,181	624,849	587,062	321,961	34,412	3,375	6,090
Carroll County	MD	25,408	1,359	18.7	3.9	34	1,478	142,609	4,525	64,423	73,661	144,071	131,034	79,051	11,429	1,608	5,522
Charles County	MD	20,966	1,084	19.3	29.8	32	1,173	129,373	5,468	56,019	67,886	126,636	119,188	66,904	7,448	0	5,929
Frederick County	MD	32,766	1,877	17.5	10.7	49	1,807	178,499	5,727	76,016	96,756	179,534	167,052	100,847	10,317	2,165	5,486
Harford County	MD	36,820	2,193	16.8	13.9	51	1,849	202,617	8,629	94,218	99,770	205,826	187,927	115,441	17,070	829	5,404
Howard County	MD	37,547	2,257	16.6	25.1	56	2,088	316,464	4,779	135,109	176,576	270,695	227,315	136,683	39,064	4,316	6,605
Montgomery County	MD	120,291	6,812	17.7	44.2	181	6,825	942,395	26,022	172,800	743,573	940,930	851,258	531,406	67,350	22,322	7,505
Prince George's County	MD	122,415	6,675	18.3	81.5	179	6,788	745,094	39,824	315,700	389,570	764,927	730,798	420,081	33,876	253	6,304
Boston City	MA	63,293	—	—	82.2	123	2,813	537,817	54,276	159,520	324,021	506,291	496,021	296,902	0	10,270	7,782
Springfield City	MA	23,584	—	—	71.1	44	848	178,482	19,725	124,621	34,136	162,088	156,097	96,711	0	5,991	6,474
Worcester Public Schools	MA	23,419	—	—	42.1	49	741	153,975	13,889	73,878	66,208	147,718	143,259	89,212	1,542	2,917	6,534
Detroit Public Schools	MI	173,750	7,545	23.0	94.3	268	6,075	1,214,533	139,622	778,021	296,890	1,179,281	1,143,871	635,172	16,139	19,271	6,601
Flint City	MI	26,390	1,264	20.9	74.3	48	906	193,634	19,723	100,237	73,674	182,744	182,039	87,696	705	0	6,946
Grand Rapids Public Schools	MI	27,087	1,337	20.3	56.2	97	726	187,234	15,304	64,584	107,346	203,286	189,006	102,732	10,915	3,365	6,976
Lansing City	MI	20,103	1,057	19.0	51.5	45	818	151,122	9,197	56,530	85,395	148,418	145,703	78,455	1,051	1,664	7,106
Utica Community	MI	24,949	1,203	20.7	4.1	39	1,549	151,891	2,221	12,373	137,297	149,271	143,358	86,776	1,908	4,005	6,140
Anoka Junction	MN	39,152	—	—	6.5	50	2,048	222,798	5,875	139,040	77,883	209,412	195,594	120,680	9,201	4,617	5,178
Minneapolis Special	MN	46,612	—	—	63.4	146	1,549	368,786	27,109	159,628	182,049	344,136	321,559	200,195	15,494	7,083	7,223
Osseo Independent	MN	21,479	1,093	19.7	14.9	33	1,165	122,404	2,961	73,983	45,460	122,538	107,722	71,590	7,198	7,618	5,130
Rosemount	MN	25,816	1,387	18.6	8.3	36	1,200	127,689	2,375	77,962	47,352	127,506	103,137	70,500	13,460	10,909	4,270
St. Paul Independent	MN	42,520	—	—	54.1	143	1,533	281,781	23,308	153,897	104,576	274,306	242,108	153,573	27,325	4,873	6,170
Jackson Municipal Schools	MS	32,719	1,774	18.4	87.1	59	1,367	153,156	19,830	60,402	72,924	152,876	137,010	81,504	11,057	4,809	4,097
Kansas City	MO	36,515	2,841	12.9	78.1	85	1,050	359,485	23,450	193,156	142,879	361,075	321,640	151,150	39,435	0	8,788
Parkway	MO	21,841	1,281	17.0	25.3	32	1,547	114,588	1,697	29,180	83,711	131,912	125,897	80,358	3,387	2,628	5,549
Springfield	MO	24,740	1,479	16.7	7.2	57	1,360	93,974	7,037	33,958	52,979	114,197	96,539	59,849	13,952	3,706	3,919
St. Louis City Board of Education	MO	41,720	3,152	13.2	81.5	112	1,151	317,735	39,554	151,502	126,679	358,782	300,788	154,560	45,277	12,717	7,298
Lincoln	NE	30,693	2,070	14.8	11.7	54	1,633	184,944	10,385	52,010	122,549	189,990	170,521	116,924	13,726	5,743	5,681
Omaha City	NE	44,247	2,774	16.0	39.1	83	2,132	250,389	19,999	83,241	147,149	250,478	230,091	139,077	14,836	5,551	5,276
Clark County	NV	166,788	8,095	20.6	39.3	198	6,541	488,426	34,054	230,882	223,490	778,251	660,590	388,136	85,023	32,638	4,546
Washoe County	NV	47,572	2,487	19.1	26.0	81	2,000	130,759	9,465	52,665	68,629	241,531	193,201	119,931	38,130	10,200	4,420
Jersey City	NJ	31,666	2,034	15.6	90.8	37	1,047	286,615	23,681	180,996	81,938	275,324	258,606	155,554	16,718	0	8,424
Newark	NJ	45,805	3,360	13.6	91.4	80	1,413	558,484	50,265	419,990	88,229	534,849	500,357	282,276	31,379	3,113	10,683
Paterson City	NJ	23,408	1,595	14.7	93.4	35	632	253,021	18,026	179,456	55,539	214,314	203,430	130,910	10,735	149	8,995
Albuquerque	NM	89,019	5,495	16.2	55.2	127	4,273	438,049	32,203	336,165	69,681	390,112	358,572	220,106	30,833	707	3,868
Las Cruces	NM	22,112	1,224	18.1	64.5	35	817	92,627	9,580	71,191	11,856	87,457	80,417	44,902	4,523	2,517	3,679
Buffalo City	NY	48,540	3,191	15.2	65.8	76	2,013	404,766	45,162	258,188	101,416	394,645	350,504	222,298	41,119	3,022	7,283

ELEMENTARY AND SECONDARY: SCHOOLS AND SCHOOL DISTRICTS 101

Table 92.—Selected statistics for public school districts enrolling more than 20,000 pupils, by state: 1995–96—Continued

Name of district, by state	State	Enrollment, fall 1995	Class-room teachers, fall 1995	Pupils per teacher, fall 1995	Percent minority pupils, fall 1995	Number of schools, 1995–96	Number of 1994–95 graduates[2]	Revenue receipts				Total expenditures,[3] 1993–94	Current expenditures		Capital outlay	Interest on school debt	Current expenditure per pupil 1993–94[4]
								Total	Federal	State	Local		Total	Instruction			
1	2	3	4	5	6	7	8	9	10	11	12	13	14	15	16	17	18
New York City	NY	1,049,039	54,591	19.2	83.5	1,115	35,026	7,972,476	909,697	3,026,968	4,035,811	8,667,299	7,545,292	5,267,063	871,202	250,805	7,504
Rochester City	NY	36,962	2,475	14.9	79.5	60	879	350,402	36,234	177,901	136,267	370,329	319,101	201,311	48,536	2,692	8,972
Syracuse City	NY	23,573	1,619	14.6	49.1	36	770	195,219	15,773	118,440	61,006	201,078	185,906	121,344	11,007	4,165	7,966
Yonkers City	NY	22,741	1,392	16.3	74.0	35	763	214,251	12,593	67,779	133,879	204,758	198,296	126,354	3,296	3,166	9,322
Buncombe County	NC	24,207	1,447	16.7	7.9	35	1,298	129,181	6,524	74,160	48,497	124,241	108,065	67,334	11,961	4,215	4,621
Charlotte-Mecklenburg	NC	89,544	5,248	17.1	46.6	126	4,055	428,961	29,255	249,635	150,071	454,644	410,120	248,592	33,193	11,331	4,951
Cumberland County	NC	51,148	3,086	16.6	52.4	72	2,621	214,529	30,460	139,921	44,148	238,208	204,467	127,545	31,182	2,559	4,152
Durham County	NC	28,472	2,005	14.2	60.3	46	1,318	158,838	9,217	81,298	68,323	185,769	144,075	83,716	31,506	10,188	5,231
Forsyth County-Winston-Salem	NC	40,895	2,939	13.9	41.2	58	2,163	200,275	11,438	116,109	72,728	205,338	192,723	120,172	8,268	4,347	4,992
Gaston County	NC	29,334	1,808	16.2	21.2	53	1,460	133,485	8,920	88,256	36,346	131,398	120,429	78,471	10,370	599	4,173
Guilford County	NC	57,211	3,585	16.0	42.8	93	3,078	298,767	17,160	168,256	113,351	293,406	284,389	172,395	7,649	1,368	5,223
New Hanover County	NC	21,180	1,361	15.6	31.7	30	1,168	95,059	7,299	60,921	26,839	94,627	91,272	55,644	2,673	682	4,482
Onslow County	NC	20,489	1,169	17.5	31.4	29	1,024	85,212	8,096	61,090	16,026	82,901	73,044	45,398	9,092	765	4,219
Robeson County	NC	23,482	1,443	16.3	76.7	41	1,185	102,191	15,806	71,171	15,214	102,174	98,788	62,309	2,971	415	3,703
Wake County	NC	81,438	5,166	15.8	31.5	98	3,798	387,615	18,888	212,525	156,202	381,516	331,682	206,158	38,380	11,454	4,527
Akron City	OH	32,095	2,146	15.0	46.9	62	1,382	174,663	15,917	86,253	72,493	176,728	171,469	102,636	4,998	261	5,119
Cincinnati City[6]	OH	52,172	3,050	17.1	68.9	83	1,848	350,704	29,200	125,721	195,783	346,137	337,233	203,525	3,922	4,982	6,438
Cleveland City	OH	74,380	4,326	17.2	79.3	131	27	496,060	58,394	264,993	172,673	478,059	462,435	264,942	1,999	13,625	6,280
Columbus City	OH	63,082	3,579	17.6	57.2	144	2,096	422,780	35,369	150,478	236,933	438,508	418,353	230,963	13,853	6,302	6,549
Dayton City	OH	27,942	1,748	16.0	67.3	50	796	185,057	20,181	80,294	84,582	169,194	167,603	97,518	1,576	15	5,802
Toledo City	OH	39,193	2,512	15.6	49.5	64	1,632	233,040	21,139	112,641	99,260	231,075	228,631	131,198	1,915	529	5,827
Oklahoma City	OK	39,829	2,402	16.6	62.0	86	1,508	167,343	19,459	99,543	48,341	175,232	167,236	95,543	5,254	2,742	4,395
Tulsa	OK	41,125	2,457	16.7	46.3	80	1,659	191,382	16,530	98,567	76,285	190,521	177,376	81,863	8,347	4,798	4,291
Beaverton	OR	29,025	1,292	22.5	18.1	42	1,538	136,994	4,388	34,321	98,285	168,353	135,828	81,863	27,443	5,082	4,941
Portland	OR	55,130	2,785	19.8	32.3	101	2,757	341,872	27,640	118,959	195,273	366,560	356,238	205,442	1,009	9,313	6,588
Salem Keizer	OR	31,364	1,290	24.3	15.9	52	1,756	165,649	8,973	78,775	77,901	197,251	157,550	97,286	36,072	3,629	5,094
Philadelphia	PA	210,503	10,973	19.2	79.6	258	8,446	1,407,413	163,776	715,157	528,480	1,216,731	1,133,083	667,970	59,978	23,670	5,456
Pittsburgh City	PA	39,761	2,477	16.1	57.1	86	2,177	395,101	28,495	153,610	212,996	359,415	336,331	185,715	18,345	4,739	8,386
Providence City	RI	24,069	1,377	17.5	74.9	42	834	160,318	13,046	77,925	69,347	153,856	143,715	93,437	5,904	4,237	6,294
Aiken County	SC	24,367	1,313	18.6	35.0	37	1,237	106,733	9,007	56,059	41,667	108,569	94,691	58,104	12,596	1,282	3,818
Berkley County	SC	26,062	1,453	17.9	37.2	38	1,303	116,587	13,226	65,546	37,815	111,051	106,873	58,834	2,571	1,607	3,792
Charleston County	SC	43,480	2,694	16.1	60.4	71	1,756	209,064	22,918	88,745	97,401	205,984	189,491	113,898	11,668	4,825	4,222
Greenville County	SC	54,619	3,292	16.6	28.8	92	2,804	248,481	16,381	109,630	122,470	240,547	222,113	134,208	13,576	4,858	4,169
Horry County	SC	25,470	1,688	15.1	30.3	36	1,258	132,389	11,687	43,585	77,117	125,625	116,582	68,814	3,992	5,051	4,711
Richland	SC	27,139	1,929	14.1	77.9	51	1,182	152,638	15,168	57,178	80,292	150,910	139,507	78,665	8,929	2,474	5,164
Chattanooga City	TN	20,491	1,188	17.2	64.0	38	872	99,301	11,683	38,564	49,054	106,889	96,425	57,467	8,763	1,701	4,754
Hamilton County	TN	23,866	1,383	17.3	5.1	43	1,340	91,653	4,750	42,987	43,916	98,116	93,235	62,512	2,807	2,074	3,903
Knox County	TN	52,627			15.4	90	2,774	233,635	17,313	92,376	123,946	237,523	213,449	135,484	20,687	3,387	4,125
Memphis City	TN	109,286	5,853	18.7	84.3	164	4,555	483,740	62,513	202,984	218,243	481,231	459,193	279,466	10,966	3,836	4,333
Montgomery County	TN	21,492	1,233	17.4	29.4	25	974	71,301	8,207	37,262	25,832	79,939	65,137	41,772	9,479	5,292	3,349
Nashville-Davidson County	TN	70,913			47.1	122	2,840	332,214	26,846	122,091	183,277	342,408	327,637	201,974	2,147	2,091	4,520
Rutherford County	TN	21,965	1,098	20.0	11.5	34	945	103,730	5,681	38,796	34,172	79,113	74,875	47,969	12,830	3,059	3,770
Shelby County	TN	40,270	2,389	19.1	18.1	42	1,299	94,552	3,994	74,160	67,029	207,499	138,475	91,616	10,423	1,353	4,906
Sumner County	TN	20,343	1,562	17.0	22.4	27	2,422	240,907	6,227	19,360	102,449	100,946	92,326	49,869	4,133	4,487	4,909
Aldine ISD	TX	26,563	1,922	14.9	43.3	44	975	128,722	3,474	15,372	30,449	142,156	115,359	64,375	20,888	5,909	4,709
Alief ISD	TX	28,573	2,416	20.4	25.4	29	1,382	126,388	4,579	72,759	88,849	174,519	135,399	75,849	30,817	8,303	5,180
Amarillo ISD	TX	45,139	2,950	15.3	20.4	30	1,312	150,709	5,558	128,268	92,009	209,113	189,183	112,675	13,340	6,590	4,465
Arlington ISD	TX	36,587	2,219	16.5	14.9	37	1,587	239,092	17,239	133,004	52,392	173,444	152,346	85,102	12,739	8,359	4,573
Austin ISD	TX	29,958	1,852	16.2	17.2	32	1,827	196,333	7,993	96,331	145,464	127,915	120,227	73,070	5,002	2,686	4,165
Birdville ISD	TX	51,960	3,036	16.2	74.6	50	2,529	137,828	10,100	75,334	218,243	215,613	192,724	113,857	11,963	10,926	3,960
Brownsville ISD	TX	74,772	4,502	16.6	40.5	61	2,406	211,879	8,753	57,662	272,904	379,935	362,731	205,067	2,009	15,195	5,062
Carrollton-Farmers	TX	20,129	3,102	16.6	38.5	106	1,187	424,792	26,457	125,431	183,277	124,984	84,029	54,435	7,464	3,059	4,274
Clear Creek ISD	TX	20,129	1,223	16.5	61.1	34	2,887	103,730	5,681	45,359	52,690	207,499	193,316	126,129	12,830	1,353	4,906
Conroe ISD	TX	40,270	2,682	15.0	18.1	42	945	240,907	30,313	189,193	109,876	100,946	92,326	49,869	4,133	4,487	4,909
Corpus Christi	TX	26,563	1,280	15.9	97.1	29	1,667	128,722	3,474	15,372	102,449	142,156	115,359	64,375	20,888	5,909	4,709
Cypress-Fairbanks ISD	TX	28,573	1,562	17.0	43.3	30	1,382	126,388	4,579	19,360	72,759	174,519	135,399	75,849	30,817	8,303	5,180
Dallas ISD	TX	41,624	1,922	17.2	25.4	37	1,312	150,709	20,609	128,268	79,727	209,113	189,183	112,675	13,340	6,590	4,465
Ector County	TX	50,817	2,416	17.2	14.9	63	1,827	228,604	6,726	91,550	156,070	271,017	247,316	138,963	11,286	12,415	5,126
El Paso ISD	TX	148,839	8,881	16.8	32.8	49	2,418	254,346	72,886	205,959	496,055	742,418	704,889	413,290	21,081	16,448	4,941
Fort Bend ISD	TX	28,528	1,676	17.0	88.1	205	4,677	774,900	10,953	66,053	58,734	124,984	118,010	64,209	6,548	426	4,187
Fort Worth ISD	TX	64,260	4,023	16.0	54.9	45	1,101	135,740	35,736	197,662	99,760	338,971	297,345	179,882	33,219	8,407	4,636
	TX	40,223	2,026	19.9	81.3	81	2,921	333,158	6,048	99,249	103,654	226,031	188,078	102,637	29,119	8,834	4,480
	TX	74,021	4,150	17.8	55.4	42	2,340	208,951	30,757	195,441	171,096	345,691	337,893	189,597	735	7,063	4,686

102 ELEMENTARY AND SECONDARY: SCHOOLS AND SCHOOL DISTRICTS

Table 92.—Selected statistics for public school districts enrolling more than 20,000 pupils, by state: 1995–96—Continued

Name of district, by state	State	Enrollment, fall 1995	Class-room teachers, fall 1995	Pupils per teacher, fall 1995	Percent minority pupils, fall 1995	Number of schools, 1995–96	Number of 1994–95 graduates[2]	Revenue and expenditures,[3] 1993–94 (in thousands of dollars)					Current expenditures			Interest on school debt	Current expenditure per pupil 1993–94[4]
								Total	Revenue receipts			Total expenditures	Total	Instruction	Capital outlay		
									Federal	State	Local						
1	2	3	4	5	6	7	8	9	10	11	12	13	14	15	16	17	18
Garland ISD	TX	43,553	2,462	17.7	40.2	60	1,750	196,858	8,784	95,880	92,194	195,816	166,500	93,972	19,222	10,094	4,048
Houston ISD	TX	206,704	11,922	17.3	88.5	273	6,786	1,121,988	111,541	382,291	628,156	983,089	913,544	519,047	48,630	20,915	4,558
Humble ISD	TX	22,159	1,468	15.1	19.4	28	1,194	116,292	3,170	51,812	61,310	116,307	98,430	53,781	10,571	7,306	4,620
Irving ISD	TX	26,459	1,570	16.9	53.6	31	1,048	130,395	6,105	36,701	87,589	134,010	113,982	68,088	13,049	6,979	4,481
Katy ISD	TX	25,231	1,469	17.2	20.4	24	1,124	115,328	2,733	40,717	71,878	110,409	100,165	56,694	3,488	6,756	4,444
Killeen ISD	TX	27,892	1,714	16.3	58.1	41	962	139,395	24,901	92,031	22,463	122,395	104,806	60,066	14,748	2,841	3,912
Klein ISD	TX	29,324	1,781	16.5	31.2	27	1,689	152,310	4,151	77,140	71,019	157,161	142,973	80,928	9,378	4,810	5,096
Laredo ISD	TX	23,434	1,391	16.8	98.3	28	1,214	128,832	11,105	103,398	14,329	110,228	102,771	58,947	6,353	1,104	4,305
Lewisville ISD	TX	28,320	1,865	15.2	16.6	40	1,224	119,810	3,830	44,311	71,669	135,631	106,848	63,698	20,606	8,177	4,308
Lubbock ISD	TX	30,317	2,052	14.8	54.3	60	1,546	175,240	14,208	93,673	67,359	151,250	145,055	86,367	2,628	3,567	4,745
McAllen ISD	TX	21,830	1,419	15.4	88.5	31	1,142	140,988	12,418	96,187	32,383	112,928	110,397	68,257	428	2,103	5,090
Mesquite ISD	TX	29,242	1,626	18.0	27.3	38	1,270	131,314	4,539	71,411	55,364	134,665	113,273	62,168	11,933	9,459	4,019
Midland ISD	TX	23,159	1,333	17.4	47.0	35	981	109,167	8,376	52,916	47,875	99,135	97,123	58,966	145	1,867	4,260
North East ISD	TX	44,447	2,844	15.6	44.2	53	2,376	243,294	10,987	95,082	137,225	183,548	181,032	111,557	884	1,632	4,198
Northside ISD	TX	57,409	3,652	15.7	59.0	75	2,993	303,575	15,982	166,513	121,080	267,522	248,755	149,848	6,346	12,421	4,523
Pasadena ISD	TX	40,053	2,308	17.4	60.6	52	1,623	176,755	12,997	82,859	80,899	185,051	175,885	100,819	5,676	3,490	4,479
Pharr San Juan-Alamo ISD	TX	20,299	1,241	16.4	98.3	29	882	123,031	16,040	93,644	13,347	93,785	88,638	51,690	3,982	1,165	4,527
Plano ISD	TX	38,429	2,392	16.1	21.4	47	2,013	213,708	5,350	24,750	183,608	208,912	186,944	104,283	11,668	10,300	5,348
Richardson ISD	TX	33,984	2,070	16.4	40.6	52	1,911	188,427	4,830	26,094	157,503	179,575	171,911	92,631	2,180	5,484	5,132
Round Rock ISD	TX	25,087	1,673	15.0	24.9	31	1,301	130,309	3,944	61,367	64,998	125,345	114,130	67,717	3,990	7,225	4,987
San Antonio ISD	TX	60,794	3,667	16.6	94.4	111	1,949	384,441	43,957	249,700	90,784	322,665	314,093	189,654	6,107	2,465	5,275
Socorro ISD	TX	20,115	1,192	16.9	90.0	19	889	101,524	6,700	76,427	18,397	90,057	84,492	48,534	1,355	4,210	4,797
Spring Branch ISD	TX	29,543	1,883	15.7	58.7	36	1,264	177,000	10,313	27,617	139,070	161,131	153,392	88,755	1,600	6,139	5,545
Spring ISD	TX	20,246	1,249	16.2	43.9	22	885	104,639	3,630	43,378	57,631	102,979	97,751	55,097	2,916	2,312	5,047
Ysleta ISD	TX	47,144	2,945	16.0	88.4	67	2,495	267,397	24,083	184,925	58,389	252,360	235,606	132,684	13,040	3,714	4,771
Alpine	UT	42,763	1,911	22.4	5.0	48	2,709	141,542	8,061	93,257	40,224	144,308	127,866	85,649	12,357	4,085	3,074
Davis County	UT	58,782	2,558	23.0	5.5	75	3,738	199,512	13,873	126,044	59,595	205,538	176,011	109,907	22,721	6,806	3,038
Granite	UT	77,106	3,496	22.1	13.0	99	4,657	285,149	19,166	160,221	105,762	267,580	255,857	166,951	10,003	1,720	3,208
Jordan	UT	71,702	3,143	22.8	5.6	72	4,361	261,290	11,260	147,199	102,831	271,975	225,099	153,253	39,034	7,842	3,204
Salt Lake City	UT	25,712	1,294	19.9	32.5	40	1,168	119,469	13,505	39,312	66,652	120,936	105,215	63,530	15,721	0	4,035
Weber County	UT	27,731	1,253	22.1	6.3	39	1,840	94,163	6,270	61,057	26,836	91,132	85,332	55,711	2,560	3,240	3,162
Chesapeake City	VA	34,980	—	—	36.3	41	1,902	148,537	9,027	64,886	74,624	181,918	157,025	98,584	22,198	2,695	4,732
Chesterfield County	VA	49,057	—	—	22.7	56	2,652	219,808	7,562	86,785	125,461	239,889	207,383	131,323	20,671	11,835	4,328
Fairfax County	VA	140,820	—	—	34.4	210	8,850	879,461	28,737	108,342	742,382	968,704	857,039	512,064	88,105	23,560	6,329
Hampton City	VA	23,611	—	—	56.5	35	1,278	97,972	8,911	45,084	43,977	106,413	104,618	66,769	1,249	546	4,550
Henrico County	VA	37,112	—	—	35.3	57	2,013	175,781	8,713	54,577	112,491	189,628	171,595	105,989	12,829	5,204	4,909
Newport News City Schools	VA	32,574	—	—	57.0	41	1,411	145,421	14,273	65,338	65,810	155,797	144,544	87,975	8,597	2,656	4,532
Norfolk City Schools	VA	36,771	—	—	68.0	58	1,111	195,878	25,454	76,562	93,862	201,697	190,456	111,851	9,809	1,432	5,225
Prince William County	VA	47,072	—	—	30.9	68	2,591	253,765	9,314	85,532	158,919	266,127	246,382	146,120	14,512	5,233	5,490
Richmond City Schools	VA	27,708	—	—	91.6	61	1,024	190,522	17,908	48,992	123,622	197,395	188,290	105,244	5,793	3,312	6,856
Virginia Beach City	VA	76,508	—	—	31.0	82	3,613	343,897	26,910	141,112	175,875	391,033	329,879	215,672	51,915	9,239	4,405
Edmonds	WA	20,868	1,003	20.8	19.0	39	937	121,173	4,282	83,858	33,033	116,558	106,523	63,332	6,322	3,713	5,218
Federal Way	WA	20,579	954	21.6	26.9	36	1,029	120,076	3,877	84,520	31,679	128,394	99,684	59,516	23,409	5,301	5,089
Kent	WA	24,492	1,175	20.8	20.4	38	1,345	146,771	4,643	100,271	41,857	149,726	118,464	71,081	22,994	8,268	4,974
Lake Washington	WA	24,332	1,120	21.7	14.4	45	1,405	152,760	3,145	96,509	53,106	135,238	119,220	73,153	8,494	7,524	5,099
Seattle	WA	46,757	2,417	19.3	58.9	116	2,463	296,709	24,124	193,124	79,461	305,236	291,005	157,323	14,182	49	6,444
Spokane	WA	32,341	1,592	20.3	12.8	66	1,884	186,530	10,706	136,982	38,842	191,992	163,596	101,834	24,857	3,539	5,256
Tacoma	WA	31,596	1,710	18.5	39.3	71	1,234	213,697	16,661	138,201	58,835	207,275	191,552	115,540	14,384	1,339	6,163
Kanawha County	WV	32,026	2,080	15.4	10.9	88	2,185	187,067	12,595	108,651	65,821	174,188	171,719	111,155	2,469	0	5,104
Madison Metropolitan	WI	25,046	—	—	28.4	52	1,373	190,499	5,798	33,058	151,643	197,505	176,040	113,763	16,322	5,143	5,218
Milwaukee City	WI	98,378	—	—	76.4	155	2,934	711,478	68,330	393,840	249,308	688,111	664,738	418,186	23,373	0	7,199
Racine Unified	WI	22,303	1,382	16.1	36.0	37	1,096	144,896	6,383	67,549	70,964	147,907	138,654	89,239	6,255	2,998	6,229

[1] Data exclude teachers reported as working in school district offices rather than in schools.
[2] Includes all categories of high school completers such as GEDs.
[3] Expenditures by local school districts only. Excludes expenditures by state education agencies for local school districts.
[4] Current expenditure per pupil based on fall enrollment collected by the Bureau of the Census, not the enrollment figure shown in column 3.
[5] Includes estimates of teachers for nonreporting school districts.
[6] High school graduate figure for 1993–94.
ISD=Independent school district.
—=Data not available or not applicable.

NOTE.—Data on finances and per pupil expenditures prepared by the Bureau of the Census.

SOURCE: U.S. Department of Education, National Center for Education Statistics, Common Core of Data survey; and U.S. Department of Commerce, "Survey of Local Government Finances." (This table was prepared September 1997.)

Table 93.—Enrollment of the 130 largest public school districts: Fall 1995

Name of school district	State	Rank order[1]	Enrollment, fall 1995	Name of school district	State	Rank order[1]	Enrollment, fall 1995
1	2	3	4	1	2	3	4
New York City	NY	1	1,049,039	Seminole County	FL	66	54,603
Los Angeles Unified	CA	2	647,612	Knox County	TN	67	52,627
City of Chicago	IL	3	412,921	Oakland Unified	CA	68	52,452
Dade County	FL	4	333,817	Cincinnati City	OH	69	52,172
Philadelphia	PA	5	210,503	Arlington ISD	TX	70	51,960
Broward County	FL	6	208,359	Cumberland County	NC	71	51,148
Houston ISD	TX	7	206,704	Lee County	FL	72	50,945
Hawaii Public Schools	HI	8	187,104	Cypress-Fairbanks ISD	TX	73	50,817
Detroit Public Schools	MI	9	173,750	Santa Ana Unified	CA	74	50,268
Clark County	NV	10	166,788	Sacramento City Unified	CA	75	50,104
Dallas ISD	TX	11	148,839	Caddo Parish	LA	76	49,578
Hillsborough County	FL	12	143,192	Chesterfield County	VA	77	49,057
Fairfax County	VA	13	140,820	Buffalo City	NY	78	48,540
Palm Beach County	FL	14	132,215	San Juan Unified	CA	79	47,581
San Diego City Unified	CA	15	130,360	Washoe County	NV	80	47,572
Duval County	FL	16	123,910	Anchorage	AK	81	47,318
Orange County School Board	FL	17	123,165	Ysleta ISD	TX	82	47,144
Prince George's County	MD	18	122,415	Prince William County	VA	83	47,072
Montgomery County	MD	19	120,291	Seattle	WA	84	46,757
Baltimore City	MD	20	109,980	Minneapolis Special	MN	85	46,612
Memphis City	TN	21	109,286	Newark	NJ	86	45,805
Pinellas County	FL	22	104,335	Shelby County	TN	87	45,686
Baltimore County	MD	23	101,564	Wichita Unified	KS	88	45,626
Milwaukee City	WI	24	98,378	Escambia County	FL	89	45,215
Jefferson County	KY	25	93,070	Aldine ISD	TX	90	45,139
Charlotte-Mecklenburg	NC	26	89,544	San Bernardino City Unified	CA	91	45,091
Albuquerque	NM	27	89,019	Indianapolis Public Schools	IN	92	44,896
DeKalb County	GA	28	87,291	North East ISD	TX	93	44,447
Orleans Parish	LA	29	85,596	Omaha City	NE	94	44,247
Jefferson County	CO	30	85,495	Garland ISD	TX	95	43,553
Gwinnett County	GA	31	84,555	Charleston County	SC	96	43,480
Cobb County	GA	32	82,870	Garden Grove Unified	CA	97	43,413
Wake County	NC	33	81,438	Alpine	UT	98	42,763
Long Beach Unified	CA	34	80,520	St. Paul Independent	MN	99	42,520
D.C. Public Schools	DC	35	79,802	Birmingham City	AL	100	41,824
Fresno Unified	CA	36	77,880	Pasco County School Board	FL	101	41,791
Granite	UT	37	77,106	St. Louis City Board of Education	MO	102	41,720
Virginia Beach City	VA	38	76,508	Corpus Christi	TX	103	41,624
Austin ISD	TX	39	74,772	Tulsa	OK	104	41,125
Cleveland City	OH	40	74,380	Jefferson County	AL	105	41,054
Fort Worth ISD	TX	41	74,021	Forsyth County-Winston-Salem	NC	106	40,895
Polk County	FL	42	72,807	Clayton County	GA	107	40,562
Jordan	UT	43	71,702	Brownsville ISD	TX	108	40,270
Anne Arundel County	MD	44	71,383	Fort Bend ISD	TX	109	40,223
Nashville-Davidson County	TN	45	70,913	Pasadena ISD	TX	110	40,053
Mesa Unified	AZ	46	70,035	Oklahoma City	OK	111	39,829
Brevard County	FL	47	65,621	Pittsburgh City	PA	112	39,761
Mobile County	AL	48	65,602	Toledo City	OH	113	39,193
Denver	CO	49	64,322	Anoka Junction	MN	114	39,152
El Paso ISD	TX	50	64,260	Plano ISD	TX	115	38,429
Boston City	MA	51	63,293	Howard County	MD	116	37,547
Columbus City	OH	52	63,082	Henrico County	VA	117	37,112
Tucson Unified	AZ	53	62,317	Rochester City	NY	118	36,962
San Francisco Unified	CA	54	61,889	Harford County	MD	119	36,820
San Antonio ISD	TX	55	60,794	Norfolk City Schools	VA	120	36,771
East Baton Rouge Parish	LA	56	60,761	Alief ISD	TX	121	36,587
Atlanta Public Schools	GA	57	60,209	Kansas City	MO	122	36,515
Davis County	UT	58	58,782	Richmond County	GA	123	36,359
Northside ISD	TX	59	57,409	Elk Grove Unified	CA	124	35,936
Guilford County	NC	60	57,211	Chatham County	GA	125	35,860
Volusia County	FL	61	56,788	Cherry Creek	CO	126	35,761
Fulton County	GA	62	56,338	Marion County	FL	127	35,526
Jefferson Parish	LA	63	56,021	Mt. Diablo Unified	CA	128	35,258
Portland	OR	64	55,130	Montgomery County	AL	129	35,065
Greenville County	SC	65	54,619	Riverside Unified	CA	130	35,055

[1] Public school districts ranked by size of enrollment in fall 1995.
ISD=Independent School District.

SOURCE: U.S. Department of Education, National Center for Education Statistics, Common Core of Data survey. (This table was prepared September 1997.)

104 ELEMENTARY AND SECONDARY: SCHOOLS

Table 94.—Public elementary and secondary schools, by type of school: 1967–68 to 1995–96

Year	Total, all public schools	Regular schools										Combined elementary/ secondary schools[6]	Other schools[7]
		Total[1]	Elementary schools				Secondary schools						
			Total[2]	Middle schools[3]	One-teacher schools	Other elementary schools	Total[4]	Junior high[5]	3-year or 4-year high schools	5-year or 6-year high schools	Other secondary schools		
1	2	3	4	5	6	7	8	9	10	11	12	13	14
1967–68	—	94,197	67,186	—	4,146	63,040	23,318	7,437	10,751	4,650	480	3,693	—
1970–71	—	89,372	64,020	2,080	1,815	60,125	23,572	7,750	11,265	3,887	670	1,780	—
1972–73	—	88,864	62,942	2,308	1,475	59,159	23,919	7,878	11,550	3,962	529	2,003	—
1974–75	—	87,456	61,759	3,224	1,247	57,288	23,837	7,690	11,480	4,122	545	1,860	—
1975–76	88,597	87,034	61,704	3,916	1,166	56,622	23,792	7,521	11,572	4,113	586	1,538	1,563
1976–77	—	86,501	61,123	4,180	1,111	55,832	23,857	7,434	11,658	4,130	635	1,521	—
1978–79	—	84,816	60,312	5,879	1,056	53,377	22,834	6,282	11,410	4,429	713	1,670	—
1980–81	85,982	83,688	59,326	6,003	921	52,402	22,619	5,890	10,758	4,193	1,778	1,743	2,294
1982–83	84,740	82,039	58,051	6,875	798	50,378	22,383	5,948	11,678	4,067	690	1,605	2,701
1983–84	84,178	81,418	57,471	6,885	838	49,748	22,336	5,936	11,670	4,046	684	1,611	2,760
1984–85	84,007	81,147	57,231	6,893	825	49,513	22,320	5,916	11,671	4,021	712	1,596	2,860
1986–87	83,455	82,190	58,801	7,452	763	50,586	21,406	5,142	11,453	4,197	614	1,983	[8]1,265
1987–88	83,248	81,416	57,575	7,641	729	49,205	21,662	4,900	11,279	4,048	1,435	2,179	[8]1,832
1988–89	83,165	81,579	57,941	7,957	583	49,401	21,403	4,687	11,350	3,994	1,372	2,235	[8]1,586
1989–90	83,425	81,880	58,419	8,272	630	49,517	21,181	4,512	11,492	3,812	1,365	2,280	[8]1,545
1990–91	84,538	82,475	59,015	8,545	617	49,853	21,135	4,561	11,537	3,723	1,314	2,325	2,063
1991–92	84,578	82,506	59,258	8,829	569	49,860	20,767	4,298	11,528	3,699	1,242	2,481	2,072
1992–93	84,497	82,896	59,676	9,152	430	50,094	20,671	4,115	11,651	3,613	1,292	2,549	1,601
1993–94	85,393	83,431	60,052	9,573	442	50,037	20,705	3,970	11,858	3,595	1,282	2,674	1,962
1994–95	86,221	84,476	60,808	9,954	458	50,396	20,904	3,859	12,058	3,628	1,359	2,764	1,745
1995–96	87,125	84,958	61,165	10,205	474	50,486	20,997	3,743	12,168	3,621	1,465	2,796	2,167

[1] Excludes special education, alternative, and other schools not classified by grade span.
[2] Includes schools beginning with grade 6 or below and with no grade higher than 8.
[3] Includes schools with grade spans beginning with 4, 5, or 6 and ending with grade 6, 7, or 8.
[4] Includes schools with no grade lower than 7.
[5] Includes schools with grades 7 and 8 or grades 7 through 9.
[6] Includes schools beginning with grade 6 or lower and ending with grade 9 or above.
[7] Includes special education, alternative, and other schools not classified by grade span.
[8] Because of revision in data collection procedures, figures not comparable to data for other years.
—Data not available.

SOURCE: U.S. Department of Education, National Center for Education Statistics, *Statistics of State School Systems*; and Common Core of Data surveys. (This table was prepared September 1997.)

Table 95.—Public elementary and secondary schools, by type and size of school: 1995–96

Enrollment size of school	Number of schools, by type						Enrollment, by type of school[1]					
	Total[2]	Elementary[3]	Secondary[4]		Combined elementary/secondary[5]	Other[2]	Total[2]	Elementary[3]	Secondary[4]		Combined elementary/secondary[5]	Other[2]
			All schools	Regular schools[6]					All schools	Regular schools[6]		
1	2	3	4	5	6	7	8	9	10	11	12	13
Total	87,125	61,165	20,997	18,090	2,796	2,167	44,681,987	29,119,541	14,342,507	13,940,501	1,121,512	98,427
Percent[7]	100.00	100.00	100.00	100.00	100.00	100.00	100.00	100.00	100.00	100.00	100.00	100.00
Under 100	8.92	5.82	13.45	7.55	30.36	59.94	0.81	0.60	0.92	0.58	3.27	18.90
100 to 199	9.53	8.85	10.53	9.72	14.70	18.51	2.72	2.82	2.21	1.86	5.30	18.85
200 to 299	11.23	12.16	8.58	8.64	10.16	10.77	5.38	6.46	3.04	2.80	6.23	19.61
300 to 399	13.50	15.77	7.75	8.11	7.94	5.11	8.99	11.59	3.84	3.67	6.88	13.18
400 to 499	13.41	15.97	7.07	7.66	6.72	2.49	11.47	15.06	4.51	4.45	7.47	8.09
500 to 599	11.76	13.77	6.75	7.39	7.12	1.10	12.27	15.85	5.27	5.26	9.70	4.33
600 to 699	8.78	9.84	6.39	7.01	5.08	0.28	10.81	13.37	5.90	5.90	8.17	1.37
700 to 799	6.24	6.69	5.36	5.95	4.26	0.28	8.88	10.50	5.73	5.79	7.94	1.45
800 to 999	7.20	6.78	8.95	9.92	5.29	0.69	12.19	12.60	11.42	11.54	11.90	4.65
1,000 to 1,499	6.26	3.89	13.73	15.29	5.08	0.69	14.25	9.47	23.90	24.28	15.36	6.38
1,500 to 1,999	1.98	0.38	6.82	7.60	2.11	0.00	6.45	1.32	16.72	16.98	8.91	0.00
2,000 to 2,999	1.03	0.07	3.97	4.45	0.79	0.00	4.60	0.33	13.31	13.60	4.48	0.00
3,000 or more	0.17	0.00	0.64	0.71	0.39	0.14	1.18	0.04	3.23	3.30	4.37	3.19
Average enrollment[7]	525	476	703	771	401	136	525	476	703	771	401	136

[1] These enrollment data should be regarded as approximations only. Totals differ from those reported in other tables because this table represents data reported by schools rather than by states or school districts. Percent distribution and average enrollment calculations excludes data for schools not reporting enrollment.
[2] Includes special education, alternative, and other schools not classified by grade span.
[3] Includes schools beginning with grade 6 or below and with no grade higher than 8.
[4] Includes schools with no grade lower than 7.
[5] Includes schools beginning with grade 6 or below and ending with grade 9 or above.
[6] Excludes special education schools, vocational schools, and alternative schools.
[7] Data are for schools reporting their enrollment size.

NOTE.—Because of rounding, details may not add to totals.

SOURCE: U.S. Department of Education, National Center for Education Statistics, Common Core of Data survey. (This table was prepared September 1997.)

Table 96.—Public elementary and secondary schools, by type and state: 1990–91 to 1995–96

State or other area	Total, all schools, 1990–91	Total, all schools, 1993–94	Total, all schools, 1994–95	Number of schools, 1995–96								
				Total	Elementary[1]	Secondary[2]	Combined elementary/secondary[3]					Alternative[5]	Special education[5]
							Total	Prekindergarten, kindergarten, or 1st grade to grade 12	Other schools ending with grade 12	Other combined schools	Other[4]		
1	2	3	4	5	6	7	8	9	10	11	12	13	14
United States	84,538	85,393	86,221	87,125	61,165	20,997	2,796	1,505	662	629	2,167	3,243	1,992
Alabama	1,297	1,294	1,309	1,319	864	298	154	119	15	20	3	18	17
Alaska	498	496	498	495	186	87	208	161	4	43	14	36	3
Arizona	1,049	1,133	1,136	1,133	817	240	15	4	9	2	61	43	16
Arkansas	1,098	1,070	1,073	1,098	674	414	7	6	0	1	3	0	0
California	7,913	7,734	7,821	7,876	5,750	1,866	182	110	41	31	78	756	127
Colorado	1,344	1,419	1,460	1,486	1,034	356	22	5	7	10	74	102	9
Connecticut	985	1,000	1,045	1,045	763	188	26	2	3	21	68	54	18
Delaware	173	177	182	181	120	42	19	14	1	4	0	2	28
District of Columbia	181	173	175	186	126	41	2	0	0	2	17	7	11
Florida	2,516	2,615	2,733	2,760	1,914	443	346	194	77	75	57	262	104
Georgia	1,734	1,755	1,767	1,763	1,383	307	73	17	43	13	0	19	8
Hawaii	235	241	242	246	186	44	16	5	5	6	0	1	4
Idaho	582	603	608	618	384	209	18	10	2	6	7	45	14
Illinois	4,239	4,195	4,195	4,142	3,061	898	32	24	4	4	151	44	240
Indiana	1,915	1,912	1,912	1,924	1,406	448	34	13	15	6	36	33	44
Iowa	1,588	1,556	1,554	1,556	1,075	443	28	6	21	1	10	26	18
Kansas	1,477	1,482	1,491	1,487	1,048	426	9	2	4	3	4	18	1
Kentucky	1,400	1,372	1,374	1,402	1,002	360	3	0	1	2	37	49	8
Louisiana	1,533	1,459	1,459	1,470	1,006	319	119	91	16	12	26	56	39
Maine	747	706	733	726	550	158	14	9	3	2	4	0	2
Maryland	1,220	1,271	1,263	1,276	1,038	213	20	9	5	6	5	27	47
Massachusetts	1,842	1,791	1,831	1,850	1,465	336	27	18	6	3	22	29	7
Michigan	3,313	3,356	3,432	3,748	2,514	811	92	40	34	18	331	135	159
Minnesota	1,590	2,083	2,100	2,157	1,190	686	92	26	27	39	189	513	108
Mississippi	972	1,009	1,018	1,011	571	314	75	62	10	3	51	35	0
Missouri	2,199	2,217	2,234	2,256	1,447	627	30	4	18	8	152	61	67
Montana	900	900	899	894	532	361	0	0	0	0	1	3	2
Nebraska	1,506	1,427	1,419	1,411	1,010	354	26	11	7	8	21	0	63
Nevada	354	407	421	423	313	96	9	2	6	1	5	23	12
New Hampshire	439	461	458	460	357	98	5	3	0	2	0	0	0
New Jersey	2,272	2,287	2,295	2,279	1,770	427	7	1	4	2	75	0	79
New Mexico	681	709	715	721	536	178	3	1	2	0	4	25	14
New York	4,010	4,082	4,130	4,149	2,972	940	145	85	37	23	92	65	83
North Carolina	1,955	1,958	1,968	1,985	1,538	393	44	20	9	15	10	48	27
North Dakota	663	640	623	613	352	224	4	1	2	1	33	0	31
Ohio	3,731	3,818	3,812	3,865	2,694	948	130	49	24	57	93	10	34
Oklahoma	1,880	1,820	1,824	1,830	1,216	604	0	0	0	0	10	0	15
Oregon	1,199	1,219	1,213	1,216	913	252	46	31	8	7	5	35	15
Pennsylvania	3,260	3,193	3,190	3,182	2,350	788	30	9	12	9	14	10	11
Rhode Island	309	311	308	310	249	57	2	2	0	0	2	3	4
South Carolina	1,097	1,094	1,094	1,095	795	289	11	4	5	2	0	18	11
South Dakota	802	777	827	824	506	301	2	1	1	0	15	11	15
Tennessee	1,543	1,523	1,554	1,563	1,133	338	53	36	6	11	39	14	17
Texas	5,991	6,324	6,465	6,638	4,515	1,721	402	208	101	93	0	345	221
Utah	714	718	728	735	476	227	10	5	2	3	22	40	24
Vermont	397	400	394	384	271	55	17	12	5	0	41	1	60
Virginia	1,811	1,828	1,851	1,889	1,384	394	20	3	13	4	91	60	48
Washington	1,936	2,030	2,064	2,124	1,315	534	105	49	30	26	170	122	81
West Virginia	1,015	907	883	877	624	209	29	11	2	16	15	12	12
Wisconsin	2,018	2,032	2,030	2,037	1,486	518	33	10	15	8	0	18	9
Wyoming	415	409	411	410	284	117	0	0	0	0	9	9	5
Department of Defense dependents schools	—	—	—	171	116	41	14	11	2	1	0	0	0
Outlying areas													
American Samoa	30	31	31	31	24	6	0	0	0	0	1	0	1
Guam	35	35	35	35	30	5	0	0	0	0	0	0	1
Northern Marianas	26	25	25	24	20	4	0	0	0	0	0	0	0
Puerto Rico	1,619	1,584	1,566	1,561	972	359	191	2	1	188	39	10	22
Virgin Islands	33	32	32	34	23	10	1	0	0	1	0	0	0

[1] Includes schools beginning with grade 6 or below and with no grade higher than 8.
[2] Includes schools with no grade lower than 7.
[3] Includes schools beginning with grade 6 or below and ending with grade 9 or above.
[4] Includes special education, alternative, and other schools not classified by grade span.
[5] Schools are included under elementary, secondary, combined, or other as appropriate.
—Data not available.

SOURCE: U.S. Department of Education, National Center for Education Statistics, Common Core of Data survey. (This table was prepared September 1997.)

Table 97.—Public elementary schools, by grade span and average school size, by state: 1995–96

State or other area	Total, all elementary schools	Total, all regular elementary schools [1]	Schools, by grade span						Average number of students per school [2]	
			Prekindergarten, kindergarten, or 1st grade to grades 3 or 4	Prekindergarten, kindergarten, or 1st grade to grade 5	Prekindergarten, kindergarten, or 1st grade to grade 6	Prekindergarten, kindergarten, or 1st grade to grade 8	Grades 4, 5, or 6 to 6, 7, or 8	Other grade spans	All elementary schools	Regular elementary schools [1]
1	2	3	4	5	6	7	8	9	10	11
United States	61,165	56,695	4,944	19,885	15,996	4,503	10,205	5,632	476	481
Alabama	864	853	87	244	199	74	173	87	490	496
Alaska	186	184	4	28	100	17	19	18	371	374
Arizona	817	800	45	182	267	153	111	59	587	593
Arkansas	674	673	89	64	361	6	87	67	394	391
California	5,750	5,708	176	1,769	2,331	547	715	212	620	623
Colorado	1,034	1,034	34	470	250	15	195	70	431	431
Connecticut	763	761	83	297	140	40	141	62	469	469
Delaware	120	112	40	14	8	1	29	28	560	593
District of Columbia	126	125	8	11	89	5	8	5	419	420
Florida	1,914	1,861	24	1,174	222	32	356	106	782	798
Georgia	1,383	1,381	33	736	115	23	279	197	657	658
Hawaii	186	185	1	32	123	8	17	5	627	630
Idaho	384	382	32	76	172	17	52	35	370	371
Illinois	3,061	2,963	344	539	628	714	454	382	423	433
Indiana	1,406	1,395	63	584	421	36	229	73	442	445
Iowa	1,075	1,066	130	311	264	20	212	138	288	290
Kansas	1,048	1,041	77	311	260	134	167	99	287	288
Kentucky	1,002	992	58	404	225	104	181	30	418	422
Louisiana	1,006	982	113	288	212	75	207	111	498	501
Maine	550	550	82	89	87	107	89	96	261	261
Maryland	1,038	998	19	580	168	18	193	60	547	562
Massachusetts	1,465	1,456	217	450	275	76	242	205	430	431
Michigan	2,514	2,475	224	947	574	66	442	261	434	436
Minnesota	1,190	1,044	144	231	462	34	157	162	426	474
Mississippi	571	571	78	83	156	52	112	90	518	518
Missouri	1,447	1,446	98	475	375	108	258	133	388	389
Montana	532	531	29	76	252	63	44	68	188	189
Nebraska	1,010	972	61	107	492	164	55	131	168	174
Nevada	313	306	11	128	87	19	43	25	586	597
New Hampshire	357	357	57	74	78	47	66	35	373	373
New Jersey	1,770	1,764	270	432	297	261	306	204	456	457
New Mexico	536	525	27	192	158	4	98	57	404	409
New York	2,972	2,970	278	932	793	75	521	373	611	611
North Carolina	1,538	1,519	81	696	198	112	334	117	537	542
North Dakota	352	352	15	26	227	42	20	22	192	192
Ohio	2,694	2,682	329	773	784	86	480	242	428	429
Oklahoma	1,216	1,207	53	346	215	297	203	102	338	339
Oregon	913	894	56	372	189	87	160	49	377	383
Pennsylvania	2,350	2,350	296	817	624	61	393	159	483	483
Rhode Island	249	248	34	75	70	4	36	30	406	406
South Carolina	795	791	89	333	89	21	197	66	540	542
South Dakota	506	502	31	108	137	87	77	66	183	184
Tennessee	1,133	1,132	108	322	227	226	177	73	511	511
Texas	4,515	4,414	473	1,667	770	96	979	530	551	559
Utah	476	474	8	90	325	2	36	15	547	548
Vermont	271	252	21	20	122	61	18	29	240	254
Virginia	1,384	1,380	80	697	178	2	270	157	528	529
Washington	1,315	1,276	64	422	478	58	190	103	451	461
West Virginia	624	622	58	186	234	36	83	27	294	295
Wisconsin	1,486	1,477	97	535	363	105	252	134	373	374
Wyoming	284	283	15	70	125	5	42	27	209	209
Department of Defense dependents schools	116	116	6	25	59	11	14	1	488	488
Outlying areas										
American Samoa	24	24	0	1	0	21	1	1	467	467
Guam	30	29	0	21	0	0	6	3	843	849
Northern Marianas	20	20	0	0	10	0	0	10	274	274
Puerto Rico	972	971	98	27	755	5	39	48	304	305
Virgin Islands	23	23	0	0	23	0	0	0	505	505

[1] Excludes special education and alternative schools.
[2] Average for schools reporting enrollment data.

NOTE.—Includes schools beginning with grade 6 or below and with no grade higher than 8. Excludes schools not reported by grade level, such as some special education schools for the disabled.

SOURCE: U.S. Department of Education, National Center for Education Statistics, Common Core of Data survey. (This table was prepared September 1997.)

Table 98.—Public secondary schools, by grade span and average school size, by state: 1995-96

State or other area	Total, all secondary schools	Total, all regular secondary schools[1]	Schools, by grade span							Vocational schools[2]	Average number of students per school[3]	
			Grades 7 to 8 and 7 to 9	Grades 7 to 12	Grades 8 to 12	Grades 9 to 12	Grades 10 to 12	Other spans ending with grade 12	Other grade spans		All secondary schools	Regular secondary schools[1]
1	2	3	4	5	6	7	8	9	10	11	12	13
United States	20,997	18,090	3,743	3,158	463	11,321	847	141	1,324	890	703	771
Alabama	298	284	34	78	10	154	11	1	10	3	708	736
Alaska	87	72	14	22	3	40	2	0	6	5	453	520
Arizona	240	218	67	8	2	152	8	0	3	6	1,008	1,067
Arkansas	414	414	77	214	1	47	59	0	16	0	447	447
California	1,866	1,256	426	99	44	1,117	103	10	67	0	960	1,352
Colorado	356	306	55	66	2	205	13	2	13	7	588	657
Connecticut	188	166	30	7	1	147	1	0	2	18	778	819
Delaware	42	34	10	2	0	30	0	0	0	5	930	989
District of Columbia	41	39	18	0	0	22	1	0	0	1	569	580
Florida	443	314	28	44	16	258	24	18	55	40	1,159	1,561
Georgia	307	288	22	9	26	244	2	0	4	1	1,146	1,204
Hawaii	44	41	10	9	2	20	0	0	3	0	1,367	1,462
Idaho	209	164	46	37	1	92	20	1	12	0	470	583
Illinois	898	836	219	33	9	588	9	3	37	27	701	730
Indiana	448	408	70	105	2	231	8	1	31	26	809	833
Iowa	443	418	70	103	2	249	16	0	3	0	408	425
Kansas	426	420	67	64	3	274	12	3	3	0	377	381
Kentucky	360	316	41	56	7	208	9	1	38	12	625	689
Louisiana	319	282	62	50	12	181	6	2	6	10	764	821
Maine	158	131	22	13	1	91	2	0	29	27	506	506
Maryland	213	185	27	5	3	167	2	2	7	11	1,080	1,176
Massachusetts	336	275	41	45	16	223	4	2	5	45	789	842
Michigan	811	706	113	120	18	473	21	6	60	48	671	724
Minnesota	686	446	87	241	39	199	59	24	37	12	457	670
Mississippi	314	229	44	42	9	106	15	3	95	85	672	672
Missouri	627	557	60	205	9	262	18	1	72	59	527	535
Montana	361	357	185	0	0	173	2	0	1	0	181	183
Nebraska	354	353	40	219	2	81	11	0	1	0	334	335
Nevada	96	74	16	17	4	53	1	0	5	3	845	1,023
New Hampshire	98	98	24	0	0	72	2	0	0	0	581	581
New Jersey	427	382	70	37	10	254	3	2	51	44	887	936
New Mexico	178	156	41	27	2	93	7	0	8	0	624	695
New York	940	858	134	195	14	499	26	1	71	24	946	968
North Carolina	393	360	53	23	3	282	16	1	15	8	882	941
North Dakota	224	217	19	150	5	32	7	1	10	7	242	242
Ohio	948	854	172	143	31	498	16	3	85	83	724	739
Oklahoma	604	601	123	0	0	377	82	4	18	0	333	335
Oregon	252	237	43	25	6	171	4	0	3	0	684	718
Pennsylvania	788	701	113	176	18	346	47	8	80	83	855	860
Rhode Island	57	52	14	3	0	38	1	0	1	2	850	907
South Carolina	289	230	35	23	9	159	6	1	56	43	836	892
South Dakota	301	293	112	0	0	182	3	0	4	3	173	174
Tennessee	338	301	57	38	4	200	11	0	28	27	876	918
Texas	1,721	1,393	309	198	34	977	36	31	136	21	679	821
Utah	227	190	80	30	11	45	50	2	9	2	917	1,073
Vermont	55	54	6	24	0	25	0	0	0	0	611	621
Virginia	394	322	39	15	43	227	9	0	61	49	981	1,041
Washington	534	415	121	54	18	271	40	5	25	8	640	786
West Virginia	209	170	47	23	3	81	17	0	38	34	622	650
Wisconsin	518	506	89	61	6	342	15	2	3	0	580	592
Wyoming	117	111	41	0	2	63	10	0	1	1	347	360
Department of Defense dependents schools	41	41	3	26	0	12	0	0	0	0	475	475
Outlying areas												
American Samoa	6	5	0	0	0	6	0	0	0	1	551	600
Guam	5	5	0	0	0	5	0	0	0	0	1,617	1,617
Northern Marianas	4	4	1	2	0	1	0	0	0	0	803	803
Puerto Rico	359	332	168	29	0	3	136	0	23	27	643	656
Virgin Islands	10	9	5	0	0	4	0	0	1	1	1,136	1,136

[1] Excludes vocational, special education, and alternative schools.
[2] Vocational schools are included under appropriate grade span.
[3] Average for schools reporting enrollment data.

NOTE.—Includes schools with no grade lower than 7. Excludes schools not reported by grade level, such as some special education schools for the disabled.

SOURCE: U.S. Department of Education, National Center for Education Statistics, Common Core of Data survey. (This table was prepared September 1997.)

Table 99.—High school graduates compared with population 17 years of age, by sex and control of school: 1869–70 to 1996–97

[Numbers in thousands]

School year	Population 17 years old [1]	High school graduates					Graduates as a percent of 17-year-old population
		Total [2]	Sex		Control		
			Male	Female	Public [3]	Private [4]	
1	2	3	4	5	6	7	8
1869–70	815	16	7	9	—	—	2.0
1879–80	946	24	11	13	—	—	2.5
1889–90	1,259	44	19	25	22	22	3.5
1899–1900	1,489	95	38	57	62	33	6.4
1909–10	1,786	156	64	93	111	45	8.8
1919–20	1,855	311	124	188	231	80	16.8
1929–30	2,296	667	300	367	592	75	29.0
1939–40	2,403	1,221	579	643	1,143	78	50.8
1947–48	2,261	1,190	563	627	1,073	117	52.6
1949–50	2,034	1,200	571	629	1,063	136	59.0
1951–52	2,086	1,197	569	627	1,056	141	57.4
1953–54	2,135	1,276	613	664	1,129	147	59.8
1955–56	2,242	1,415	680	735	1,252	163	63.1
1956–57	2,272	1,434	690	744	1,270	164	63.1
1957–58	2,325	1,506	725	781	1,332	174	64.8
1958–59	2,458	1,627	784	843	1,435	192	66.2
1959–60	2,672	1,858	895	963	1,627	231	69.5
1960–61	2,892	1,964	955	1,009	1,725	239	67.9
1961–62	2,768	1,918	938	980	1,678	240	69.3
1962–63	2,740	1,943	956	987	1,710	233	70.9
1963–64	2,978	2,283	1,120	1,163	2,008	275	76.7
1964–65	3,684	2,658	1,311	1,347	2,360	298	72.1
1965–66	3,489	2,665	1,323	1,342	2,367	298	76.4
1966–67	3,500	2,672	1,328	1,344	2,374	298	76.3
1967–68	3,532	2,695	1,338	1,357	2,395	300	76.3
1968–69	3,659	2,822	1,399	1,423	2,522	300	77.1
1969–70	3,757	2,889	1,430	1,459	2,589	300	76.9
1970–71	3,872	2,938	1,454	1,484	2,638	300	75.9
1971–72	3,973	3,002	1,487	1,515	2,700	302	75.6
1972–73	4,049	3,035	1,500	1,535	2,729	306	75.0
1973–74	4,132	3,073	1,512	1,561	2,763	310	74.4
1974–75	4,256	3,133	1,542	1,591	2,823	310	73.6
1975–76	4,272	3,148	1,552	1,596	2,837	311	73.7
1976–77	4,272	3,152	1,548	1,604	2,837	315	73.8
1977–78	4,286	3,127	1,531	1,596	2,825	302	73.0
1978–79	4,327	3,101	1,517	1,584	2,801	300	71.7
1979–80	4,262	3,043	1,491	1,552	2,748	295	71.4
1980–81	4,212	3,020	1,483	1,537	2,725	295	71.7
1981–82	4,134	2,995	1,471	1,524	2,705	290	72.4
1982–83	3,962	2,888	1,437	1,451	2,598	290	72.9
1983–84	3,784	2,767	—	—	2,495	272	73.1
1984–85	3,699	2,677	—	—	2,414	263	72.4
1985–86	3,670	2,643	—	—	2,383	260	72.0
1986–87	3,754	2,694	—	—	2,429	265	71.8
1987–88	3,849	2,773	—	—	2,500	273	72.1
1988–89	3,842	2,727	—	—	2,459	268	71.0
1989–90	3,574	2,586	—	—	2,320	266	72.4
1990–91	3,417	2,503	—	—	2,235	268	73.2
1991–92	3,381	2,482	—	—	2,226	256	73.4
1992–93	3,433	2,490	—	—	2,233	257	72.5
1993–94	3,442	2,479	—	—	2,221	258	72.0
1994–95	3,571	2,531	—	—	2,274	257	70.9
1995–96 [5]	3,629	2,557	—	—	2,293	264	70.4
1996–97 [5]	3,762	2,623	—	—	2,358	265	69.7

[1] Derived from *Current Population Reports*, Series P-25. 17-year-old population adjusted to reflect October 17-year-old population.
[2] Includes graduates of public and private schools.
[3] Data for 1929–30 and preceding years are from *Statistics of Public High Schools* and exclude graduates of high schools which failed to report to the Office of Education.
[4] For most years, private school data have been estimated based on periodic private school surveys. For years through 1957–58, private includes data for subcollegiate departments of institutions of higher education and residential schools for exceptional children.
[5] Public high school graduates based on state estimates.
—Data not available.

NOTE.—Includes graduates of regular day school programs. Excludes graduates of other programs, when separately reported, and recipients of high school equivalency certificates. Some data have been revised from previously published figures. Because of rounding, details may not add to totals.

SOURCE: U.S. Department of Education, National Center for Education Statistics, *Statistics of Public High Schools; Biennial Survey of Education in the United States; Statistics of State School Systems; Statistics of Nonpublic Elementary and Secondary Schools;* Common Core of Data surveys; and U.S. Department of Commerce, Bureau of the Census, *Current Population Reports*, Series P-25. (This table was prepared April 1997.)

ELEMENTARY AND SECONDARY: GRADUATES 109

Table 100.—Public high school graduates, by state: 1969–70 to 1996–97

State	1969–70	1979–80	1980–81	1985–86	1990–91	1992–93	1993–94[1]	1994–95	Estimated 1995–96	Estimated 1996–97	Percent change, 1990–91 to 1996–97
1	2	3	4	5	6	7	8	9	10	11	12
United States	2,588,639	2,747,678	2,725,285	2,382,616	2,234,893	2,233,241	2,220,849	2,273,541	[2]2,292,626	[2]2,357,649	5.5
Alabama	45,286	45,190	44,894	39,620	39,042	36,007	34,447	36,268	[3]35,043	35,253	-9.7
Alaska	3,297	5,223	5,343	5,464	5,458	5,535	5,747	5,765	5,709	6,376	16.8
Arizona	22,040	28,633	28,416	27,533	31,282	31,747	31,799	30,989	[4]31,014	[4]31,826	1.7
Arkansas	26,068	29,052	29,577	26,227	25,668	25,655	24,990	24,636	24,628	24,874	-3.1
California	260,908	249,217	242,172	229,026	234,164	249,320	253,083	255,200	262,441	265,400	13.3
Colorado	30,312	36,804	35,897	32,621	31,293	31,839	31,867	32,409	[3]32,607	34,688	10.8
Connecticut	34,755	37,683	38,369	33,571	27,290	26,799	26,330	26,445	[3]26,445	26,560	-2.7
Delaware	6,985	7,582	7,349	5,791	5,223	5,492	5,230	5,234	[3]5,609	5,822	11.5
District of Columbia[5]	4,980	4,959	4,848	3,875	3,369	3,136	3,207	2,974	[4]2,928	[4]2,956	-12.3
Florida	70,478	87,324	88,755	83,029	87,419	89,428	88,032	89,827	89,242	96,070	9.9
Georgia	56,859	61,621	62,963	59,082	60,088	57,602	56,356	56,660	[3]57,797	59,421	-1.1
Hawaii	10,407	11,493	11,472	9,958	8,974	8,854	9,369	9,407	9,993	10,143	13.0
Idaho	12,296	13,187	12,679	12,059	11,961	12,974	13,281	14,198	[3]14,667	15,562	30.1
Illinois	126,864	135,579	136,795	114,319	103,329	103,628	102,126	105,164	[3]104,626	107,766	4.3
Indiana	69,984	73,143	73,381	59,817	57,892	57,559	54,650	56,058	56,575	57,720	-0.3
Iowa	44,063	43,445	42,635	34,279	28,593	30,677	30,247	31,268	[3]31,689	32,479	13.6
Kansas	33,394	30,890	29,397	25,587	24,414	24,720	25,319	26,125	[3]25,803	26,450	8.3
Kentucky	37,473	41,203	41,714	37,288	35,835	36,361	38,454	37,626	37,245	37,453	4.5
Louisiana	43,641	46,297	46,199	39,965	33,489	33,682	34,822	36,480	[3]36,881	[4]36,128	7.9
Maine	14,003	15,445	15,554	13,006	13,151	12,103	11,384	11,501	[3]13,470	13,250	0.8
Maryland	46,462	54,270	54,050	46,700	39,014	39,523	39,091	41,387	[3]41,785	42,482	8.9
Massachusetts	63,865	73,802	74,831	60,360	50,216	48,321	47,453	47,679	[4]48,451	[4]50,482	0.5
Michigan	121,000	124,316	124,372	101,042	88,234	85,302	83,385	84,628	84,300	90,600	2.7
Minnesota	60,480	64,908	64,166	51,988	46,474	48,002	47,514	49,354	50,300	52,500	13.0
Mississippi	29,653	27,586	28,083	25,134	23,665	23,597	23,379	23,837	23,040	23,185	-2.0
Missouri	55,315	62,265	60,359	49,204	46,928	46,864	46,566	48,862	48,870	49,986	6.5
Montana	11,520	12,135	11,634	9,761	9,013	9,389	9,601	10,134	10,224	10,645	18.1
Nebraska	21,280	22,410	21,411	17,845	16,500	17,569	17,072	17,969	[3]18,591	20,682	25.3
Nevada	5,449	8,473	9,069	8,784	9,370	9,042	9,485	10,038	10,374	11,257	20.1
New Hampshire	8,516	11,722	11,552	10,648	10,059	10,065	9,933	10,145	9,478	9,353	-7.0
New Jersey	86,498	94,564	93,168	78,781	67,003	67,134	66,125	67,403	[4]68,222	[4]70,798	5.7
New Mexico	16,060	18,424	17,915	15,468	15,157	15,172	14,892	14,928	[3]15,446	15,871	4.7
New York	190,000	204,064	198,465	162,165	133,562	132,963	132,708	132,401	134,500	137,420	2.9
North Carolina	68,886	70,862	69,395	65,865	62,792	60,460	57,738	59,540	[3]56,770	58,000	-7.6
North Dakota	11,150	9,928	9,924	7,610	7,573	7,310	7,522	7,811	[3]7,967	8,063	6.5
Ohio	142,248	144,169	143,503	119,561	107,484	109,200	107,700	109,418	102,755	103,755	-3.5
Oklahoma	36,293	39,305	38,875	34,452	33,007	30,542	31,872	33,319	32,843	30,628	-7.2
Oregon	32,236	29,939	28,729	26,286	24,597	26,301	26,338	26,713	[3]27,093	27,200	10.6
Pennsylvania	151,014	146,458	144,645	122,871	104,770	103,715	101,958	104,146	108,520	112,920	7.8
Rhode Island	10,146	10,864	10,719	8,908	7,744	7,640	7,450	7,826	7,693	7,695	-0.6
South Carolina	34,940	38,697	38,347	34,500	32,999	31,297	30,603	30,680	34,300	35,800	8.5
South Dakota	11,757	10,689	10,385	7,870	7,127	7,952	8,442	8,355	[3]8,671	9,385	31.7
Tennessee	49,000	49,845	50,648	43,263	44,847	44,166	40,643	43,556	[3]43,556	43,902	-2.1
Texas	139,046	171,449	171,665	161,150	174,306	160,546	163,191	170,322	171,321	175,996	1.0
Utah	18,395	20,035	19,886	19,774	22,219	24,197	26,407	27,670	27,819	30,248	36.1
Vermont	6,095	6,733	6,424	5,794	5,212	5,215	5,414	5,871	[4]5,885	[4]6,048	16.0
Virginia	58,562	66,621	67,126	63,113	58,441	56,948	56,140	58,260	[3]59,633	61,388	5.0
Washington	50,425	50,402	50,046	45,805	42,514	45,262	47,235	49,294	50,670	53,843	26.6
West Virginia	26,139	23,369	23,580	21,870	21,064	20,228	19,884	20,131	[3]20,531	19,947	-5.3
Wisconsin	66,753	69,332	67,743	58,340	49,340	50,027	48,371	51,735	52,710	55,473	12.4
Wyoming	5,363	6,072	6,161	5,587	5,728	6,174	5,997	5,889	[3]5,886	5,900	3.0
Outlying areas											
American Samoa	[6]367	—	—	608	597	712	738	695	[4]696	[4]702	17.6
Guam	972	—	—	840	1,014	912	985	987	[4]1,003	[4]1,027	1.3
Northern Marianas	—	—	—	—	273	245	328	319	[3]322	288	5.5
Puerto Rico	24,917	—	—	31,597	29,329	29,064	27,718	29,747	[3]29,875	30,003	2.3
Virgin Islands	[6]432	—	—	1,044	981	927	886	995	940	935	-4.7

[1] Revised from previously published data.
[2] National total includes estimates for nonreporting states.
[3] Actual count.
[4] Data imputed by the National Center for Education Statistics based on previous year's data.
[5] Beginning in 1985–86, graduates from adult programs are excluded.
[6] Data are for 1970–71.
—Data not reported.

NOTE.—Data include graduates of regular day school programs, but exclude graduates of other programs and persons receiving high school equivalency certificates. They also exclude graduates of subcollegiate departments of institutions of higher education, federal schools for American Indians and on federal installations, and residential schools for disabled children. Some data have been revised from previously published figures. All 1995–96 and 1996–97 data are state estimates unless otherwise indicated.

SOURCE: U.S. Department of Education, National Center for Education Statistics, Common Core of Data surveys. (This table was prepared April 1997.)

110 ELEMENTARY AND SECONDARY: GRADUATES

Table 101.—High school graduates and dropouts in public elementary and secondary schools, by race or ethnicity and state: 1994–95

State	High school graduates, by race						Percent of 9th to 12th graders who dropped out during 1994–95, by race/ethnicity					
	Total	White[1]	Black[1]	Hispanic	Asian or Pacific Islander	American Indian/ Alaskan Native	Total	White[1]	Black[1]	Hispanic	Asian or Pacific Islander	American Indian/ Alaskan Native
1	2	3	4	5	6	7	8	9	10	11	12	13
United States	2,252,064	1,637,556	288,032	212,101	92,659	21,716	—	—	—	—	—	—
Alabama	36,268	24,816	10,637	131	251	433	6.2	5.8	7.1	6.6	3.0	1.6
Alaska	5,765	4,054	230	123	248	1,110	—	—	—	—	—	—
Arizona	30,989	20,094	1,135	7,047	769	1,944	—	—	—	—	—	—
Arkansas[2]	24,636	18,883	5,279	194	206	74	4.9	4.0	7.8	9.5	4.8	4.5
California	255,200	120,488	18,864	76,557	37,029	2,262	4.4	2.8	7.9	6.5	2.4	4.8
Colorado	32,409	25,584	1,396	4,195	990	244	—	—	—	—	—	—
Connecticut	26,445	20,965	2,774	1,940	707	59	4.9	3.3	8.8	12.9	2.8	2.6
Delaware	5,234	3,712	1,247	135	128	12	4.6	4.0	5.8	7.5	3.0	1.2
District of Columbia	2,946	94	2,646	152	54	0	10.6	10.9	10.6	15.4	10.0	0.0
Florida	89,827	55,815	18,501	12,882	2,458	171	—	—	—	—	—	—
Georgia	56,660	36,600	18,273	658	1,063	66	9.0	8.2	10.3	13.1	5.6	9.4
Hawaii	3,162	1,811	171	456	693	31	4.9	3.7	5.1	5.6	4.2	8.3
Idaho	14,198	13,323	41	548	169	117	—	—	—	—	—	—
Illinois	105,164	77,181	15,411	8,263	4,089	220	—	—	—	—	—	—
Indiana	56,058	50,011	4,597	991	421	38	4.6	4.3	6.9	6.8	1.3	5.8
Iowa	31,268	29,654	580	403	562	69	3.4	3.3	7.0	9.2	3.0	10.6
Kansas	26,125	22,648	1,587	1,096	594	200	5.0	4.3	9.4	12.1	4.7	7.4
Kentucky[2]	37,588	33,795	2,923	146	249	475	—	—	—	—	—	—
Louisiana	36,766	21,788	13,803	404	644	127	3.5	2.3	5.0	8.1	3.1	2.4
Maine	11,501	11,253	65	41	93	49	3.3	3.4	3.8	4.8	2.4	5.9
Maryland	41,387	25,662	12,354	1,223	2,068	80	—	—	—	—	—	—
Massachusetts	47,679	39,844	3,278	2,699	1,804	54	3.5	2.6	7.2	9.2	3.0	5.2
Michigan	84,628	70,216	10,558	1,634	1,454	766	—	—	—	—	—	—
Minnesota	49,354	45,539	1,051	690	1,571	503	5.2	4.0	20.6	15.8	7.6	20.4
Mississippi	23,837	12,513	11,033	35	182	74	6.4	6.1	7.1	5.4	6.3	9.9
Missouri	48,862	42,386	5,420	404	564	88	7.1	6.1	13.3	9.9	4.6	9.0
Montana	10,134	9,250	33	145	74	632	—	—	—	—	—	—
Nebraska	17,969	16,574	608	445	236	106	4.5	3.5	12.8	13.2	8.2	16.1
Nevada	10,038	7,590	761	1,035	521	131	10.3	8.8	11.8	17.2	9.0	12.8
New Hampshire[3]	10,145	9,794	87	113	132	19	—	—	—	—	—	—
New Jersey	67,403	46,742	9,868	6,766	3,932	95	—	—	—	—	—	—
New Mexico	14,928	6,611	313	6,235	232	1,537	8.5	6.4	9.5	10.9	6.7	8.6
New York	132,401	92,226	18,885	12,910	7,949	431	4.1	2.5	6.8	8.1	3.3	5.3
North Carolina	59,540	41,076	16,266	496	914	788	—	—	—	—	—	—
North Dakota	7,817	7,345	66	53	67	286	2.5	—	—	—	—	—
Ohio	96,992	87,263	7,475	1,043	1,112	99	5.3	4.5	9.8	11.6	3.9	9.9
Oklahoma	33,804	24,644	2,852	852	551	4,905	—	—	—	—	—	—
Oregon	26,483	23,777	274	1,081	941	410	7.1	6.4	10.9	17.6	5.4	10.7
Pennsylvania	104,146	89,993	9,860	1,966	2,271	56	4.1	2.9	10.2	12.2	3.3	8.8
Rhode Island	7,826	6,759	428	348	259	32	4.6	4.0	7.4	9.5	4.1	2.7
South Carolina[3]	30,680	18,424	11,748	147	312	49	—	—	—	—	—	—
South Dakota	8,355	7,646	34	43	69	563	—	—	—	—	—	—
Tennessee	41,319	33,490	7,165	178	463	23	—	—	—	—	—	—
Texas	170,322	95,072	20,286	49,375	5,189	400	2.7	1.8	3.5	3.6	4.2	3.6
Utah	27,670	26,053	90	736	560	231	3.5	—	—	—	—	—
Vermont	5,867	5,730	24	30	53	30	—	—	—	—	—	—
Virginia	58,260	41,640	12,469	1,407	2,654	90	—	—	—	—	—	—
Washington[2]	48,254	39,188	1,816	2,319	3,959	972	—	—	—	—	—	—
West Virginia	20,131	19,221	698	60	124	28	4.2	4.2	5.3	1.1	1.0	7.5
Wisconsin	51,735	47,354	2,030	942	967	442	—	—	—	—	—	—
Wyoming	5,889	5,365	42	329	58	95	6.7	5.9	19.0	13.0	2.7	17.4
Other areas												
American Samoa	695	0	0	0	695	0	—	—	—	—	—	—
Guam	—	—	—	—	—	—	—	—	—	—	—	—
Northern Marianas	319	0	0	0	319	0	—	—	—	—	—	—
Puerto Rico	29,747	0	0	29,747	0	0	—	—	—	2.2	—	—
Virgin Islands	—	—	—	—	—	—	—	—	—	—	—	—

[1] Excludes persons of Hispanic origin.
[2] Estimates provided by state education agencies.
[3] Racial/ethnic distribution estimated by NCES based on 12th grade racial/ethnic distribution reported by state.
—Data not available.

NOTE.—Because data for some graduates are not available by race, totals differ from figures reported elsewhere.

SOURCE: U.S. Department of Education, National Center for Education Statistics, Common Core of Data survey; and unpublished data. (This table was prepared November 1997.)

Table 102.—General Educational Development (GED) credentials issued, and number and age of test takers: United States and outlying areas, 1971 to 1995

Year	Number of credentials issued, in thousands[1]	Number completing test battery, in thousands[2]	Number of test takers, in thousands[3]	Percentage distribution of test takers, by age				
				19 years old or less	20- to 24-year-olds	25- to 29-year-olds	30- to 34-year-olds	35 years old or over
1	2	3	4	5	6	7	8	9
1971	227	—	377	—	—	—	—	—
1972	245	—	419	—	—	—	—	—
1973	249	—	423	—	—	—	—	—
1974	295	412	540	35	27	13	9	17
1975	342	507	652	33	26	14	9	18
1976	337	507	656	31	28	14	10	17
1977	331	488	680	40	24	13	9	14
1978	381	467	641	31	27	13	10	19
1979	435	583	744	35	27	13	8	16
1980	488	708	779	37	27	13	8	15
1981	500	701	770	37	27	13	8	15
1982	494	692	756	37	28	13	8	15
1983	477	678	740	34	29	14	9	15
1984	437	613	676	32	28	15	9	16
1985	427	622	685	33	26	15	10	16
1986	439	648	713	33	26	15	10	16
1987	458	662	729	33	24	15	10	18
1988	421	617	701	36	23	14	10	17
1989	364	554	645	36	24	13	10	16
1990	419	628	727	35	25	14	10	17
1991	471	672	770	33	27	14	10	17
1992	465	653	754	32	28	13	11	16
1993	476	652	757	33	27	14	11	16
1994	499	684	793	34	26	13	10	16
1995	513	698	803	37	25	13	10	15

[1] Number of people receiving high school equivalency credentials based on the GED tests.
[2] Number of people completing the entire GED battery of five tests.
[3] Number of people taking the GED tests (one or more subtests).
—Data not available.

NOTE.—Because of rounding, percentages may not add to 100. Some data have been revised from previously published figures.

SOURCE: American Council on Education, General Educational Development Testing Service. (This table was prepared April 1997.)

Table 103.—Percent of high school dropouts among persons 16 to 24 years old,[1] by sex and race/ethnicity: April 1960 to October 1996

Year	Total				Men				Women			
	All races	White, non-Hispanic	Black, non-Hispanic	Hispanic origin	All races	White, non-Hispanic	Black, non-Hispanic	Hispanic origin	All races	White, non-Hispanic	Black, non-Hispanic	Hispanic origin
1	2	3	4	5	6	7	8	9	10	11	12	13
1960[2]	27.2	—	—	—	27.8	—	—	—	26.7	—	—	—
1967[3]	17.0	15.4	28.6	—	16.5	14.7	30.6	—	17.3	16.1	26.9	—
1968[3]	16.2	14.7	27.4	—	15.8	14.4	27.1	—	16.5	15.0	27.6	—
1969[3]	15.2	13.6	26.7	—	14.3	12.6	26.9	—	16.0	14.6	26.7	—
1970[3]	15.0	13.2	27.9	—	14.2	12.2	29.4	—	15.7	14.1	26.6	—
1971[3]	14.7	13.4	23.7	—	14.2	12.6	25.5	—	15.2	14.2	22.1	—
1972	14.6	12.3	21.3	34.3	14.1	11.7	22.3	33.7	15.1	12.8	20.5	34.9
1973	14.1	11.6	22.2	33.5	13.7	11.5	21.5	30.4	14.5	11.8	22.8	36.4
1974	14.3	11.9	21.2	33.0	14.2	12.0	20.1	33.8	14.4	11.8	22.1	32.2
1975	13.9	11.4	22.9	29.2	13.3	11.0	23.0	26.7	14.5	11.8	22.9	31.6
1976	14.1	12.0	20.5	31.4	14.1	12.1	21.2	30.3	14.2	11.8	19.9	32.3
1977	14.1	11.9	19.8	33.0	14.5	12.6	19.5	31.6	13.8	11.2	20.0	34.3
1978	14.2	11.9	20.2	33.3	14.6	12.2	22.5	33.6	13.9	11.6	18.3	33.1
1979	14.6	12.0	21.1	33.8	15.0	12.6	22.4	33.0	14.2	11.5	20.0	34.5
1980	14.1	11.4	19.1	35.2	15.1	12.3	20.8	37.2	13.1	10.5	17.7	33.2
1981	13.9	11.4	18.4	33.2	15.1	12.5	19.9	36.0	12.8	10.2	17.1	30.4
1982	13.9	11.4	18.4	31.7	14.5	12.1	21.2	30.5	13.3	10.9	15.9	32.8
1983	13.7	11.2	18.0	31.6	14.9	12.2	19.9	34.3	12.5	10.1	16.2	29.1
1984	13.1	11.0	15.5	29.8	14.0	12.0	16.8	30.6	12.3	10.1	14.3	29.0
1985	12.6	10.4	15.2	27.6	13.4	11.1	16.1	29.9	11.8	9.8	14.3	25.2
1986	12.2	9.7	14.2	30.1	13.1	10.3	15.0	32.8	11.4	9.1	13.5	27.2
1987	12.7	10.4	14.1	28.6	13.2	10.8	15.0	29.1	12.1	10.0	13.3	28.1
1988	12.9	9.6	14.5	35.8	13.5	10.4	15.0	36.0	12.2	8.9	14.1	35.4
1989	12.6	9.4	13.9	33.0	13.6	10.3	14.9	34.4	11.7	8.5	13.0	31.6
1990	12.1	9.0	13.2	32.4	12.3	9.3	11.9	34.3	11.8	8.7	14.4	30.3
1991	12.5	8.9	13.6	35.3	13.0	8.9	13.5	39.2	11.9	8.9	13.7	31.1
1992[4]	11.0	7.7	13.7	29.4	11.3	8.0	12.5	32.1	10.7	7.5	14.8	26.6
1993[4]	11.0	7.9	13.6	27.5	11.2	8.2	12.6	28.1	10.9	7.7	14.4	26.9
1994[4]	11.5	7.7	12.6	30.0	12.3	8.0	14.1	31.6	10.6	7.5	11.3	28.1
1995[4]	12.0	8.6	12.1	30.0	12.2	9.0	11.1	30.0	11.7	8.2	12.9	30.0
1996[4]	11.1	7.3	13.0	29.4	11.4	7.3	13.5	30.3	10.9	7.3	12.5	28.3

[1] "Status" dropouts.
[2] Based on the April 1960 decennial census.
[3] White and black include persons of Hispanic origin.
[4] Because of changes in data collection procedures, data may not be comparable with figures for earlier years.
—Data not available.

NOTE.—"Status" dropouts are persons who are not enrolled in school and who are not high school graduates. People who have received GED credentials are counted as graduates. Data are based upon sample surveys of the civilian noninstitutional population.

SOURCE: U.S. Department of Commerce, Bureau of the Census, Current Population Survey, unpublished tabulations; and U.S. Department of Education, National Center for Education Statistics, Dropout Rates in the United States. (This table was prepared September 1997.)

Table 104.—Percent of high school dropouts among persons 16 to 34 years old,[1] by age, sex, and race/ethnicity: October 1970 to October 1996

Year, race/ethnicity, and sex	16 and 17 years	18 and 19 years	20 and 21 years	22 to 24 years	25 to 29 years	30 to 34 years
1	2	3	4	5	6	7
October 1970						
All races	8.0	16.2	16.6	18.7	22.5	26.5
Male	7.1	16.0	16.1	17.9	21.4	26.2
Female	8.9	16.3	16.9	19.4	23.6	26.8
White[2]	7.3	14.1	14.6	16.3	19.9	24.6
Male	6.3	13.3	14.1	15.3	19.0	24.2
Female	8.4	14.8	15.1	17.2	20.7	24.9
Black[2]	12.8	31.2	29.6	37.8	44.4	43.5
Male	13.3	36.4	29.6	39.5	43.1	45.9
Female	12.4	26.6	29.6	36.4	45.6	41.5
October 1980						
All races	8.9	15.7	16.0	15.2	13.9	14.6
Male	8.9	16.9	17.8	16.4	13.8	14.0
Female	8.8	14.7	14.3	14.0	14.0	15.2
White, non-Hispanic	8.6	12.7	12.1	11.8	10.4	11.0
Male	8.5	13.6	13.5	13.2	10.6	10.7
Female	8.6	11.9	10.9	10.4	10.3	11.3
Black, non-Hispanic	7.0	21.0	24.6	23.6	22.4	23.1
Male	7.2	22.2	30.8	24.6	22.2	21.9
Female	6.8	19.8	19.6	22.8	22.6	24.0
Hispanic origin	16.5	39.0	41.6	40.6	40.9	45.4
Male	18.1	43.1	41.4	42.9	40.1	43.9
Female	15.0	34.6	41.9	38.6	41.7	47.0
October 1990						
All races	6.3	14.2	12.8	13.8	13.9	12.9
Male	6.6	14.6	13.2	14.0	14.5	13.3
Female	6.1	13.8	12.4	13.6	13.4	12.5
White, non-Hispanic	5.4	11.1	9.4	9.5	9.2	8.7
Male	5.9	11.4	9.6	9.8	9.8	9.4
Female	5.0	10.8	9.1	9.1	8.5	8.0
Black, non-Hispanic	6.9	16.6	15.6	13.6	19.3	16.7
Male	6.3	15.5	12.4	13.2	18.9	16.4
Female	7.5	17.6	18.6	13.9	19.6	16.9
Hispanic origin	12.9	34.2	31.6	42.8	41.7	42.4
Male	13.1	39.4	37.9	41.4	42.6	41.4
Female	12.5	29.4	25.0	44.4	40.7	43.5
October 1995[3]						
All races	5.4	14.6	13.8	13.6	12.4	11.7
Male	4.8	14.7	13.6	14.9	13.9	12.0
Female	6.1	14.5	13.9	12.3	10.9	11.4
White, non-Hispanic	4.7	11.4	9.4	8.9	7.8	7.7
Male	4.2	11.7	9.3	10.4	9.0	7.9
Female	5.2	11.0	9.5	7.4	6.7	7.5
Black, non-Hispanic	5.6	15.7	15.1	12.6	11.6	11.6
Male	4.1	18.1	16.2	9.4	11.3	12.1
Female	7.3	13.7	14.2	15.4	11.8	11.1
Hispanic origin	10.7	30.8	34.4	37.4	39.0	36.6
Male	11.2	27.0	33.4	39.0	42.1	35.5
Female	10.2	35.0	35.4	35.3	35.6	37.8
October 1996[3]						
All races	6.0	12.7	13.2	12.4	11.8	12.0
Male	5.7	13.1	14.0	12.9	12.3	12.9
Female	6.3	12.3	12.5	12.0	11.3	11.2
White, non-Hispanic	5.1	9.3	7.2	7.5	7.5	7.8
Male	5.3	9.6	7.0	7.4	8.0	8.5
Female	4.9	9.0	7.4	7.6	7.0	7.2
Black, non-Hispanic	6.2	14.4	17.6	14.4	10.7	11.6
Male	5.0	15.2	19.5	16.0	8.3	12.8
Female	7.4	13.6	16.0	13.0	12.7	10.7
Hispanic origin	10.8	29.5	38.4	35.3	35.7	38.6
Male	9.0	30.5	42.3	36.0	37.5	37.9
Female	12.7	28.4	34.5	34.5	33.8	39.5

[1] "Status" dropouts.
[2] Includes persons of Hispanic origin.
[3] Because of changes in data collection procedures, data may not be comparable with figures for earlier years.

NOTE.—"Status" dropouts are persons who are not enrolled in school and who are not high school graduates. People who have received GED credentials are counted as graduates. Data are based upon sample surveys of the civilian noninstitutional population.

SOURCE: U.S. Department of Commerce, Bureau of the Census, Current Population Survey, unpublished data. (This table was prepared September 1997.)

ELEMENTARY AND SECONDARY: GRADUATES 113

Table 105.—Students with disabilities exiting the educational system, by age, type of disability, and basis of exit: United States and outlying areas, 1991–92 and 1993–94

Student characteristics	Number						Percent					
	Graduated with diploma		Graduated with certificate		Reached maximum age[1]		Graduated with diploma		Graduated with certificate		Reached maximum age[1]	
	1991–92	1993–94[2]	1991–92	1993–94[2]	1991–92	1993–94[2]	1991–92	1993–94[2]	1991–92	1993–94[2]	1991–92	1993–94[2]
1	2	3	4	5	6	7	8	9	10	11	12	13
Age group												
14 to 21 (and over)	100,742	113,945	30,839	23,948	4,337	4,594	43.9	28.1	13.4	5.9	1.9	1.1
14	138	91	223	130	8	7	1.2	0.2	2.0	0.3	0.1	0.0
15	171	169	158	71	16	9	1.3	0.4	1.2	0.1	0.1	0.0
16	505	532	217	178	44	39	2.4	1.0	1.1	0.3	0.2	0.1
17	14,356	15,417	1,929	2,016	70	106	39.2	22.7	5.3	3.0	0.2	0.2
18	45,063	47,854	7,263	7,759	115	110	65.2	51.9	10.5	8.4	0.2	0.1
19	29,325	35,735	7,593	6,996	68	91	65.1	59.8	16.8	11.7	0.2	0.2
20	7,444	9,371	7,190	3,398	588	525	41.1	48.0	39.7	17.4	3.2	2.7
21 (and over)	3,740	4,776	6,266	3,400	3,428	3,707	24.2	31.0	40.6	22.0	22.2	24.0
Type of disability												
All disabilities, 14 to 21 and over	100,742	113,945	30,839	23,948	4,337	4,594	43.9	28.1	13.4	5.9	1.9	1.1
Specific learning disabilities	65,851	76,735	14,318	10,871	662	891	49.7	32.5	10.8	4.6	0.5	0.4
Mental retardation	14,088	13,900	10,797	9,117	2,359	2,307	36.1	26.3	27.7	17.2	6.0	4.4
Serious emotional disturbance	9,557	11,251	2,217	1,649	338	331	28.1	16.1	6.5	2.4	1.0	0.5
Speech or language impairments	3,562	3,423	596	473	87	121	43.9	18.3	7.4	2.5	1.1	0.6
Multiple disabilities	1,560	1,254	977	675	529	553	38.7	25.1	24.3	13.5	13.1	11.1
Other health impairments	1,771	2,250	614	191	67	44	48.6	21.7	16.9	1.8	1.8	0.4
Hearing impairments	1,900	2,209	587	391	69	48	55.8	44.1	17.2	7.8	2.0	1.0
Orthopedic impairments	1,379	1,557	439	285	123	133	50.2	33.5	16.0	6.1	4.5	2.9
Visual impairments	879	931	172	105	55	53	60.7	46.3	11.9	5.2	3.8	2.6
Autism	82	169	75	120	29	80	28.2	24.1	25.8	17.1	10.0	11.4
Deaf-blindness	72	34	42	26	15	8	50.3	23.9	29.4	18.3	10.5	5.6
Traumatic brain injury	41	232	5	45	4	25	64.1	35.4	7.8	6.9	6.3	3.8

[1] These figures reflect an estimate of those who were actually known to have dropped out and do not include youth who simply stopped coming to school or whose status was unknown.
[2] Upper age limits for service eligibility vary by state.

SOURCE: U.S. Department of Education, Office of Special Education and Rehabilitative Services, Sixteenth and Seventeenth Annual Report to Congress on the Implementation of The Individuals with Disabilities Education Act, 1995 and 1996. (This table was prepared April 1997.)

Table 106.—Postsecondary education and employment status, wages earned, and living arrangements of special education students out of secondary school up to 3 years, by type of disability: 1990

Type of disability	Percent in postsecondary education		Percent currently competitively employed	Average annual total compensation	Percent living independently[1]
	Academic	Vocational			
1	2	3	4	5	6
All disabilities[2]	16.5	14.7	55.0	$5,524	27.8
Learning disabled	18.7	17.8	63.1	6,932	33.9
Serious emotional disturbance	15.3	13.3	52.0	5,310	21.1
Speech/language impairments	37.0	17.9	58.5	4,389	36.4
Mental retardation	2.5	5.7	40.8	3,078	14.8
Visual impairment	53.9	14.9	30.3	2,027	39.3
Hard of hearing	35.0	20.0	43.6	2,773	25.9
Deaf	28.3	19.9	24.8	1,689	32.3
Orthopedic impairments	30.9	13.4	26.4	1,636	16.6
Other health impairments	35.1	23.5	47.5	4,388	17.2
Multiple disabilities	8.0	4.0	15.8	778	8.0

[1] Living independently includes living alone, with a spouse or roommate, in a college dormitory, or in military housing not as a dependent.
[2] All conditions includes youth in each of the 11 Federal special education disability categories. Percentages are reported separately only for categories with at least 25 youth in the sample.

NOTE.—Data based on students who had been out of school up to three years and had attended special and regular schools in the 1985–86 or 1986–87 school years.

SOURCE: U.S. Department of Education, Office of Special Education and Rehabilitative Services, The Seventeenth Annual Report to Congress on the Implementation of The Individuals with Disabilities Education Act, The National Longitudinal Transition Study, 1995. (This table was prepared April 1996.)

Table 107.—Average student proficiency in reading, by age and selected characteristics of students: 1971 to 1996

Selected characteristics of students	1971	1975	1980	1984	1988	1990	1992	1994	1996
1	2	3	4	5	6	7	8	9	10
9-year-olds									
Total	207.6	210.0	215.0	210.9	211.8	209.2	210.5	211.0	212.4
Male	201.2	204.3	210.0	207.5	207.5	204.0	205.9	207.3	206.8
Female	213.9	215.8	220.1	214.2	216.3	214.5	215.4	214.7	218.0
Race/ethnicity									
White, non-Hispanic	214.0	216.6	221.3	218.2	217.7	217.0	217.9	218.0	219.9
Black, non-Hispanic	170.1	181.2	189.3	185.7	188.5	181.8	184.5	185.4	190.0
Hispanic	(1)	182.7	190.2	187.2	193.7	189.4	191.7	185.9	194.1
Parental education									
Not high school graduate	188.6	189.9	194.3	195.1	192.5	192.6	194.9	189.1	197.0
Graduated high school	207.8	211.3	213.0	208.9	210.8	209.1	207.4	207.1	207.0
Post high school	223.9	221.5	226.0	222.9	220.0	217.7	219.5	221.0	220.0
Control of school									
Public	—	—	213.5	209.4	210.2	207.5	208.6	209.4	210.0
Private	—	—	227.0	222.8	223.4	228.3	224.7	225.0	227.0
Region									
Northeast	213.0	214.8	221.1	215.7	215.2	217.4	217.6	217.4	220.0
Southeast	193.9	201.1	210.3	204.3	207.2	197.4	199.3	208.4	206.0
Central	214.9	215.5	216.7	215.3	218.2	212.7	215.8	214.3	215.0
West	205.0	207.0	212.8	207.8	207.9	209.6	209.3	205.1	210.0
13-year-olds [2]									
Total	255.2	255.9	258.5	257.1	257.5	256.8	259.8	257.9	259.1
Male	249.6	249.6	254.3	252.6	251.8	250.5	254.1	250.6	252.5
Female	260.8	262.3	262.6	261.7	263.0	263.1	265.3	265.7	265.4
Race/ethnicity									
White, non-Hispanic	260.9	262.1	264.4	262.6	261.3	262.3	266.4	265.1	267.0
Black, non-Hispanic	222.4	225.7	232.8	236.3	242.9	241.5	237.6	234.3	235.6
Hispanic	(1)	232.5	237.2	239.6	240.1	237.8	239.2	235.1	239.9
Parental education									
Not high school graduate	238.4	238.7	238.5	240.0	246.5	240.8	239.2	236.7	241.0
Graduated high school	255.5	254.6	253.5	253.4	252.7	251.4	252.1	251.4	252.0
Post high school	270.2	269.8	270.9	267.6	265.3	266.9	269.9	268.5	270.0
Control of school									
Public	—	—	256.9	255.2	256.1	255.0	257.2	255.6	257.0
Private	—	—	270.6	271.2	268.3	269.7	276.3	275.8	274.0
Region									
Northeast	261.1	258.5	260.0	260.4	258.6	258.9	264.6	269.0	261.0
Southeast	244.7	249.3	252.6	256.4	257.6	255.5	253.8	252.7	252.0
Central	260.1	261.5	264.5	258.8	255.9	257.4	263.5	259.3	268.0
West	253.6	253.2	256.4	253.8	257.9	255.6	257.5	252.9	258.0
17-year-olds [2]									
Total	285.2	285.6	285.5	288.8	290.1	290.2	289.7	288.1	286.9
Male	278.9	279.7	281.8	283.8	286.0	284.0	284.2	281.7	279.9
Female	291.3	291.2	289.2	293.9	293.8	296.5	295.7	294.7	294.4
Race/ethnicity									
White, non-Hispanic	291.4	293.0	292.8	295.2	294.7	296.6	297.4	295.7	294.4
Black, non-Hispanic	238.7	240.6	243.1	264.3	274.4	267.3	260.6	266.2	265.4
Hispanic	(1)	252.4	261.4	268.1	270.8	274.8	271.2	263.2	264.7
Parental education									
Not high school graduate	261.3	262.5	262.1	269.4	267.4	269.7	270.8	267.9	267.0
Graduated high school	283.0	281.4	277.5	281.2	282.0	282.9	280.5	276.1	273.0
Post high school	302.2	300.6	298.9	301.2	299.5	299.9	298.6	298.5	297.0
Control of school									
Public	—	—	284.4	287.2	288.7	288.6	287.8	286.0	286.0
Private	—	—	298.4	303.0	299.6	311.0	309.6	306.1	294.0
Region									
Northeast	291.3	289.1	285.9	292.2	294.8	295.7	297.3	296.8	291.0
Southeast	270.5	276.5	280.1	284.7	285.5	285.1	278.4	283.5	279.0
Central	290.7	291.8	287.4	290.0	291.2	293.5	293.8	285.7	292.0
West	283.7	281.6	287.3	288.4	289.0	286.8	290.4	287.8	286.0

[1] Test scores of Hispanics were not tabulated separately.
[2] All participants of this age were in school.
—Data not available.

NOTE.—These test scores are from the National Assessment of Educational Progress (NAEP). The NAEP scores have been evaluated at certain performance levels. A score of 300 implies an ability to find, understand, summarize, and explain relatively complicated literary and informational material. A score of 250 implies an ability to search for specific information, interrelate ideas, and make generalizations about literature, science, and social studies materials. A score of 200 implies an ability to understand, combine ideas, and make inferences based on short uncomplicated passages about specific or sequentially related information. A score of 150 implies an ability to follow brief written directions and carry out simple, discrete reading tasks. Scale ranges from 0 to 500.

SOURCE: U.S. Department of Education, National Center for Education Statistics, National Assessment of Educational Progress, *NAEP 1996 Trends in Academic Progress*, by Educational Testing Service. (This table was prepared September 1997).

Table 108.—Student proficiency in reading, by percentile and age: 1971 to 1996

Percentile	1971	1975	1980	1984	1988	1990	1992	1994	1996
1	2	3	4	5	6	7	8	9	10
9-year-olds									
Average	**207.6**	**210.0**	**215.0**	**210.9**	**211.8**	**209.2**	**210.5**	**211.0**	**212.4**
Standard deviation	42.1	38.6	37.9	41.1	41.2	44.7	40.3	40.5	40.5
Percentiles									
5th	134.8	143.2	148.5	140.5	141.9	134.8	140.7	140.1	141.8
10th	151.6	159.2	165.1	156.7	156.7	150.1	156.0	155.6	157.6
25th	180.0	185.2	191.1	183.7	184.3	178.7	183.1	184.1	185.0
50th	209.3	211.9	217.2	212.6	213.7	210.3	213.6	214.8	215.5
75th	236.7	236.9	241.3	239.6	240.1	240.3	239.3	240.0	241.4
90th	260.5	258.1	261.7	262.8	263.0	265.7	259.9	260.1	261.5
95th	274.1	270.6	273.3	276.5	277.5	280.4	272.1	271.7	274.1
13-year-olds									
Average	**255.2**	**255.9**	**258.5**	**257.1**	**257.5**	**256.8**	**259.8**	**257.9**	**259.1**
Standard deviation	35.7	35.8	34.9	35.5	34.7	36.0	39.4	39.8	38.4
Percentiles									
5th	192.8	193.5	199.1	196.7	199.5	195.7	190.9	188.2	191.5
10th	207.8	208.7	212.8	210.2	212.9	209.8	207.9	205.1	208.5
25th	232.3	232.9	235.3	233.9	234.2	233.2	234.7	232.5	234.8
50th	257.0	257.7	259.6	258.2	257.9	257.2	261.6	260.1	261.2
75th	279.9	280.6	282.8	281.6	281.4	281.5	287.0	285.2	285.5
90th	299.6	300.5	302.3	301.7	301.6	302.0	309.2	307.4	306.5
95th	310.8	311.8	313.9	313.7	313.7	314.4	321.9	320.3	319.4
17-year-olds[1]									
Average	**285.2**	**285.6**	**285.5**	**288.8**	**290.1**	**290.2**	**289.7**	**288.1**	**286.9**
Standard deviation	45.8	44.0	41.8	40.3	37.1	41.3	43.0	44.4	42.3
Percentiles									
5th	206.1	209.3	213.0	219.9	226.1	220.0	214.3	210.8	213.2
10th	225.3	228.4	230.6	236.0	241.5	236.9	232.7	230.0	231.4
25th	255.9	257.8	258.7	262.5	265.7	263.5	262.6	259.8	259.1
50th	287.7	287.9	287.5	290.3	291.1	291.1	293.0	289.9	288.2
75th	316.7	315.7	314.6	316.8	316.0	318.6	319.4	318.7	315.8
90th	341.7	340.0	337.5	339.6	336.9	342.7	342.7	343.0	340.4
95th	356.5	354.3	350.9	352.6	348.7	356.0	355.8	357.7	354.4

[1] All participants of this age were in school.

NOTE.—These test scores are from the National Assessment of Educational Progress (NAEP). The NAEP scores have been evaluated at certain performance levels. A score of 300 implies an ability to find, understand, summarize, and explain relatively complicated literary and informational material. A score of 250 implies an ability to search for specific information, interrelate ideas, and make generalizations about literature, science, and social studies materials. A score of 200 implies an ability to understand, combine ideas, and make inferences based on short uncomplicated passages about specific or sequentially related information. A score of 150 implies an ability to follow brief written directions and carry out simple, discrete reading tasks. Scale ranges from 0 to 500.

SOURCE: U.S. Department of Education, National Center for Education Statistics, National Assessment of Educational Progress, *NAEP 1996 Trends in Academic Progress*, by Educational Testing Service. (This table was prepared September 1997.)

Table 109.—Student proficiency in reading, by age, amount of time spent on homework, and reading habits: 1984, 1994, and 1996

Time spent on homework and reading habits	9-year-olds			13-year-olds			17-year-olds[1]		
	1984	1994	1996	1984	1994	1996	1984	1994	1996
1	2	3	4	5	6	7	8	9	10
	Average proficiency								
Materials read a few times a year or more									
Poems	211	210	—	260	261	—	290	293	—
Plays	211	207	—	260	263	—	290	294	—
Biographies	213	210	—	261	261	—	292	293	—
Science books	212	211	—	259	260	—	289	293	—
Books about other places	211	211	—	259	260	—	289	293	—
Frequency of reading for fun									
Daily	214	215	213	264	272	270	297	302	301
Weekly	212	214	212	255	255	259	290	286	292
Monthly	204	213	210	255	255	260	290	286	290
Yearly	197	—	—	252	252	—	280	281	285
Never	198	193	199	239	237	238	269	258	269
Time spent on homework each day									
None	213	213	210	254	250	256	276	273	273
Didn't do assignment	199	200	195	247	243	251	287	285	281
Less than 1 hour	218	212	215	261	261	259	290	288	288
1 to 2 hours	216	214	220	266	268	267	296	297	295
More than 2 hours	201	193	198	265	270	269	303	306	307
	Percent								
Materials read a few times a year or more									
Poems	70	62	60	68	79	80	76	85	80
Plays	56	45	42	59	63	67	63	70	67
Biographies	45	47	46	62	68	65	59	69	66
Science books	84	87	83	90	92	90	70	84	82
Books about other places	79	79	78	83	83	84	81	82	81
Frequency of reading for fun									
Daily	53	58	54	35	32	32	31	30	23
Weekly	28	25	27	35	32	31	34	31	32
Monthly	7	5	8	14	14	15	17	15	17
Yearly	3	3	3	7	10	9	10	12	12
Never	9	9	8	9	12	13	9	12	16
Time spent on homework each day									
None	36	32	26	23	23	22	22	23	23
Didn't do assignment	4	5	4	4	6	5	11	11	13
Less than 1 hour	42	48	53	36	34	37	26	27	28
1 to 2 hours	13	12	13	29	28	27	27	26	24
More than 2 hours	6	4	4	9	9	8	13	13	11

[1] Excludes persons not enrolled in school.

NOTE.—These test scores are from the National Assessment of Educational Progress (NAEP). The NAEP scores have been evaluated at certain performance levels. A score of 300 implies an ability to find, understand, summarize and explain relatively complicated literary and informational material. A score of 250 implies an ability to search for specific information, interrelate ideas, and make generalizations about literature, science, and social studies materials. A score of 200 implies an ability to understand, combine ideas, and make inferences based on short uncomplicated passages about specific or sequentially related information. A score of 150 implies an ability to follow brief written directions and carry out simple, discrete reading tasks. Scale ranges from 0 to 500.

SOURCE: U.S. Department of Education, National Center for Education Statistics, National Assessment of Educational Progress, *NAEP 1996 Trends in Academic Progress*, by Educational Testing Service. (This table was prepared September 1997.)

Table 110.—Percent of students at or above selected reading proficiency levels,[1] by sex, race/ethnicity, and age: 1971 to 1996

Sex, race/ethnicity, and level	1971	1975	1980	1984	1988	1990	1992	1994	1996
1	2	3	4	5	6	7	8	9	10
9-year-olds[2]									
Total									
Level 150[3]	90.6	93.1	94.6	92.3	92.7	90.1	92.3	92.1	92.7
Level 200[4]	58.7	62.1	67.7	61.5	62.6	58.9	62.0	63.3	63.7
Level 250[5]	15.6	14.6	17.7	17.2	17.5	18.4	16.2	16.5	17.7
Male									
Level 150[3]	87.9	91.0	92.9	90.4	90.4	87.9	90.2	90.2	90.7
Level 200[4]	52.7	56.2	62.7	58.0	58.4	53.8	56.9	59.2	57.8
Level 250[5]	12.0	11.5	14.6	15.9	15.8	16.1	14.2	15.2	15.0
Female									
Level 150[3]	93.2	95.3	96.4	94.2	94.9	92.4	94.4	94.0	94.6
Level 200[4]	64.6	68.1	72.7	65.2	66.9	64.2	67.3	67.3	69.5
Level 250[5]	19.2	17.7	20.7	18.4	19.1	20.8	18.2	17.8	20.4
White[6]									
Level 150[3]	94.0	96.0	97.1	95.4	95.1	93.5	95.8	95.7	95.9
Level 200[4]	65.0	69.0	74.2	68.6	68.4	66.0	69.3	70.1	70.9
Level 250[5]	18.0	17.4	21.0	20.9	20.3	22.6	19.6	19.7	21.6
Black[6]									
Level 150[3]	69.7	80.7	84.9	81.3	83.2	76.9	79.6	78.7	83.1
Level 200[4]	22.0	31.6	41.3	36.6	39.4	33.9	36.6	38.3	41.3
Level 250[5]	1.6	2.0	4.1	4.5	5.6	5.2	4.6	4.4	6.6
Hispanic									
Level 150[3]	—	80.8	84.5	82.0	85.6	83.7	83.4	80.4	84.2
Level 200[4]	—	34.6	41.6	39.6	45.9	40.9	43.1	37.1	47.5
Level 250[5]	—	2.6	5.0	4.3	8.6	5.8	7.2	6.4	7.5
13-year-olds[2]									
Total									
Level 150[3]	99.8	99.7	99.9	99.8	99.9	99.8	99.5	99.3	99.6
Level 200[4]	93.0	93.2	94.8	93.9	94.9	93.8	92.7	91.7	92.8
Level 250[5]	57.8	58.6	60.7	59.0	58.7	58.7	61.6	60.4	61.3
Level 300[7]	9.8	10.2	11.3	11.0	10.9	11.0	15.3	14.1	13.8
Male									
Level 150[3]	99.6	99.6	99.8	99.7	99.7	99.7	99.2	99.1	99.5
Level 200[4]	90.7	90.9	93.4	92.2	92.8	91.4	90.4	88.8	90.1
Level 250[5]	51.6	51.7	55.9	54.0	52.3	52.4	55.5	53.3	54.8
Level 300[7]	7.3	7.0	9.1	9.0	8.6	7.6	12.8	10.1	10.3
Female									
Level 150[3]	99.9	99.9	99.9	99.9	100.0	99.9	99.8	99.6	99.8
Level 200[4]	95.2	95.5	96.1	95.8	96.9	96.3	95.0	94.9	95.3
Level 250[5]	64.0	65.5	65.4	64.0	65.0	65.0	67.5	67.9	67.5
Level 300[7]	12.3	13.5	13.5	13.2	13.2	14.5	17.7	18.4	17.1
White[6]									
Level 150[3]	99.9	99.9	100.0	99.9	99.9	99.9	99.8	99.6	99.8
Level 200[4]	96.2	96.4	97.1	96.2	96.0	96.0	95.9	95.0	95.9
Level 250[5]	64.2	65.5	67.8	65.3	63.7	64.8	68.5	68.1	70.1
Level 300[7]	11.3	12.1	13.6	13.1	12.4	13.3	18.1	17.2	17.2
Black[6]									
Level 150[3]	98.6	98.4	99.3	99.4	99.8	99.4	98.7	98.6	99.4
Level 200[4]	74.2	76.9	84.1	85.5	91.3	87.7	82.0	80.6	82.7
Level 250[5]	21.1	24.8	30.1	34.6	40.2	41.7	38.4	35.6	35.1
Level 300[7]	0.8	1.5	1.8	2.8	4.6	4.6	5.7	3.9	3.1
Hispanic									
Level 150[3]	—	99.6	99.7	99.5	99.2	99.1	98.1	98.7	98.7
Level 200[4]	—	81.3	86.8	86.7	87.4	85.8	83.4	82.4	86.1
Level 250[5]	—	32.0	35.4	39.0	38.0	37.2	40.9	33.9	39.8
Level 300[7]	—	2.2	2.3	4.1	4.4	3.9	6.0	4.3	5.5
17-year-olds[2]									
Total									
Level 150[3]	99.6	99.7	99.9	100.0	100.0	99.9	99.8	99.8	100.0
Level 200[4]	96.0	96.4	97.2	98.3	98.9	98.1	97.1	96.8	97.4
Level 250[5]	78.6	80.1	80.7	83.1	85.7	84.1	82.5	80.8	81.4
Level 300[7]	39.0	38.7	37.8	40.3	40.9	41.4	43.2	41.0	38.6
Male									
Level 150[3]	99.4	99.5	99.8	99.9	100.0	99.8	99.7	99.7	99.9
Level 200[4]	94.7	95.3	96.3	97.6	98.5	97.0	96.3	95.5	96.3
Level 250[5]	74.4	75.6	77.9	79.6	82.9	79.7	78.4	76.2	76.7
Level 300[7]	33.9	33.7	35.0	35.4	37.1	36.1	38.4	35.6	32.8
Female									
Level 150[3]	99.8	99.8	99.9	99.9	100.0	100.0	99.9	99.9	100.0
Level 200[4]	97.3	97.5	98.1	99.0	99.3	99.2	97.9	98.0	98.6
Level 250[5]	82.6	84.3	83.6	86.8	88.2	88.6	86.8	85.6	86.4
Level 300[7]	44.0	43.6	40.7	45.0	44.4	46.8	48.5	46.5	44.7
White[6]									
Level 150[3]	99.9	99.9	100.0	100.0	100.0	100.0	99.9	100.0	100.0
Level 200[4]	97.9	98.6	99.1	99.0	99.3	99.3	98.8	98.1	98.5
Level 250[5]	83.7	86.2	86.9	88.0	88.7	88.3	88.0	86.2	86.8
Level 300[7]	43.2	43.9	43.3	46.3	45.4	47.5	50.1	47.7	45.1
Black[6]									
Level 150[3]	97.6	97.7	99.0	99.9	100.0	99.6	99.1	99.5	99.8
Level 200[4]	81.9	82.0	85.6	95.9	98.0	95.7	91.6	93.4	94.8
Level 250[5]	40.1	43.0	44.0	65.7	75.8	69.1	61.4	65.7	67.2
Level 300[7]	7.7	8.1	7.1	16.2	24.9	19.7	16.9	21.5	18.0
Hispanic									
Level 150[3]	—	99.3	99.8	99.8	99.9	99.7	99.8	99.0	99.9
Level 200[4]	—	88.7	93.3	95.6	96.3	95.9	93.4	91.1	94.0
Level 250[5]	—	52.9	62.2	68.3	71.5	75.2	69.2	63.0	64.2
Level 300[7]	—	12.6	16.5	21.2	23.3	27.1	27.3	20.1	20.0

[1] As measured by the National Assessment of Educational Progress (NAEP).
[2] All participants of this age were in school.
[3] Able to follow brief written directions and carry out simple, discrete reading tasks.
[4] Able to understand, combine ideas, and make inferences based on short uncomplicated passages about specific or sequentially related information.
[5] Able to search for specific information, interrelate ideas, and make generalizations about literature, science, and social studies materials.
[6] Data for 1971 include persons of Hispanic origin.
[7] Able to find, understand, summarize, and explain relatively complicated literary and informational material.
—Data not available.

SOURCE: U.S. Department of Education, National Center for Education Statistics, National Assessment of Educational Progress, *NAEP 1996 Trends in Academic Progress*, by Educational Testing Service. (This table was prepared September 1997.)

Table 111.—Average proficiency in reading for 4th graders in public schools,[1] by selected characteristics, region, and state: 1994

Region and state	Average	Race/ethnicity						Sex		Parental education[2]			
		White	Black	Hispanic	Asian	Pacific Islander	American Indian	Male	Female	Did not finish high school	Graduated high school	Some education after high school	Graduated college
1	2	3	4	5	6	7	8	9	10	11	12	13	14
United States	212	223	186	188	231	216	200	207	218	188	206	222	222
Region													
Northeast	212	224	184	191	(3)	(3)	(3)	207	216	(3)	202	222	221
Southeast	208	219	188	184	(3)	(3)	(3)	202	215	186	207	222	216
Central	218	225	182	199	(3)	(3)	(3)	212	225	(3)	215	221	226
West	212	222	186	186	5 226	(3)	(3)	207	217	188	201	221	223
State													
Alabama	208	220	188	178	(3)	(3)	(3)	203	213	197	201	217	217
Arizona	206	220	183	188	(3)	(3)	181	201	211	189	200	219	218
Arkansas	209	218	183	192	(3)	(3)	(3)	204	213	196	203	221	215
California	197	211	182	174	211	5 213	(3)	194	200	166	191	207	207
Colorado	213	222	191	193	(3)	(3)	204	209	218	192	213	220	222
Connecticut	222	234	190	190	(3)	(3)	(3)	218	226	204	209	234	231
Delaware	206	215	188	190	(3)	(3)	(3)	200	212	185	202	217	214
Florida	205	218	183	189	(3)	(3)	(3)	199	210	187	195	219	212
Georgia	207	222	185	184	(3)	(3)	(3)	201	212	185	199	219	217
Hawaii	201	219	189	185	219	191	(3)	194	208	192	194	215	208
Indiana	220	225	193	201	(3)	(3)	(3)	216	223	198	216	230	229
Iowa	223	225	5 186	204	(3)	(3)	(3)	219	227	211	219	232	229
Kentucky	212	215	190	196	(3)	(3)	(3)	206	217	195	212	222	218
Louisiana	197	213	180	175	(3)	(3)	(3)	193	200	188	196	209	200
Maine	228	229	(3)	218	(3)	(3)	(3)	225	231	214	225	237	236
Maryland	210	223	185	197	232	(3)	(3)	205	214	195	202	215	217
Massachusetts	223	231	199	194	5 201	(3)	(3)	221	226	206	212	230	232
Minnesota	218	222	173	202	(3)	(3)	196	214	223	(3)	212	220	229
Mississippi	202	220	187	181	(3)	(3)	(3)	196	207	192	199	213	207
Missouri	217	223	192	200	(3)	(3)	212	213	221	199	216	227	225
Montana[4]	222	226	(3)	208	—	—	203	218	227	211	219	227	230
Nebraska[4]	220	224	5 190	205	(3)	(3)	202	216	224	(3)	215	232	231
New Hampshire[4]	223	224	(3)	213	(3)	(3)	(3)	218	229	207	220	236	231
New Jersey	219	231	193	200	237	(3)	(3)	216	222	193	209	225	230
New Mexico	205	219	196	196	(3)	(3)	185	201	208	188	200	220	215
New York	212	226	191	193	230	(3)	(3)	207	216	196	208	224	220
North Carolina	214	225	193	189	(3)	(3)	5 201	209	220	195	204	226	223
North Dakota	225	228	(3)	212	(3)	(3)	5 197	221	230	(3)	217	232	233
Pennsylvania[4]	215	224	180	187	(3)	(3)	(3)	211	220	187	210	221	224
Rhode Island[4]	220	226	197	195	203	(3)	(3)	215	225	203	217	230	228
South Carolina	203	219	184	182	(3)	(3)	(3)	199	208	189	193	216	213
Tennessee[4]	213	220	188	196	(3)	(3)	(3)	208	217	200	213	225	219
Texas	212	227	191	198	(3)	(3)	(3)	210	214	195	207	224	222
Utah	217	221	(3)	199	(3)	(3)	195	213	222	(3)	211	225	226
Virginia	213	224	192	206	(3)	(3)	(3)	208	219	196	207	220	221
Washington	213	217	198	190	220	208	207	209	217	197	209	216	223
West Virginia	213	215	202	192	(3)	(3)	(3)	208	218	196	213	226	221
Wisconsin[4]	224	228	197	203	(3)	(3)	(3)	221	227	212	223	228	233
Wyoming	221	224	(3)	209	(3)	(3)	5 210	218	224	203	215	230	228
Department of Defense Overseas Schools	218	224	205	211	222	215	210	213	223	(3)	209	226	223
Guam	181	192	171	171	180	183	(3)	172	190	164	176	189	185

[1] As measured by the National Assessment of Educational Progress (NAEP). Forty-one states and Guam participated in the test, but the sample size in two states was insufficient to permit a reliable estimate.
[2] Parents' highest level of education. Data not shown for students who did not know parents' level of education.
[3] Sample size is insufficient to permit a reliable estimate.
[4] Did not satisfy one or more of the guidelines for school sample participation rates. Data are subject to appreciable nonresponse bias.
[5] The nature of the sample does not allow accurate determination of the variability of this value.
—Data not available.

NOTE.—These test scores are from the National Assessment of Educational Progress (NAEP). The NAEP scores have been evaluated at certain performance levels. A score of 300 implies an ability to find, understand, summarize, and explain relatively complicated literary and informational material. A score of 250 implies an ability to search for specific information, interrelate ideas, and make generalizations about literature, science, and social studies materials. A score of 200 implies an ability to understand, combine ideas, and make inferences based on short uncomplicated passages about specific or sequentially related information. A score of 150 implies an ability to follow brief written directions and carry out simple, discrete reading tasks. Scale ranges from 0 to 500. Excludes states not participating in the survey. Some data have been revised from previously published figures.

SOURCE: U.S. Department of Education, National Center for Education Statistics, National Assessment of Educational Progress, *1994 NAEP Reading, Revised Edition: A First Look,* prepared by Educational Testing Service. (This table was prepared November 1995).

Table 112.— Percentage distribution of 4th graders in public schools, by time spent on homework and television viewing each day: 1992 and 1996

Selected characteristics of students	Time spent on homework each day					Amount of television watched each day			
	Don't have	Don't do	Half hour or less	One hour	More than one hour	Six hours or more	Four to five hours	Two to three hours	One hour or less
1	2	3	4	5	6	7	8	9	10
1992									
All students	15.1 (1.2)	3.0 (0.3)	39.4 (1.3)	26.7 (0.9)	15.8 (0.7)	21.2 (0.7)	21.6 (0.7)	35.9 (0.7)	21.3 (0.7)
Male	16.6 (1.5)	4.6 (0.4)	38.8 (1.4)	25.0 (1.1)	15.0 (0.9)	25.3 (1.1)	21.8 (0.9)	34.3 (1.2)	18.5 (0.9)
Female	13.5 (1.1)	1.4 (0.3)	40.1 (1.5)	28.4 (1.0)	16.6 (0.8)	17.1 (0.8)	21.3 (0.9)	37.4 (1.0)	24.1 (0.9)
Race/ethnicity									
White	16.9 (1.4)	2.4 (0.3)	38.9 (1.6)	27.7 (1.1)	14.1 (0.7)	15.1 (0.8)	22.3 (0.9)	39.8 (0.8)	22.9 (0.9)
Black	9.5 (1.4)	5.3 (0.9)	42.7 (1.5)	22.2 (1.4)	20.2 (1.3)	44.0 (2.0)	18.8 (1.5)	22.6 (1.6)	14.5 (1.0)
Hispanic	11.6 (1.5)	3.6 (0.7)	38.3 (1.8)	27.1 (1.4)	19.4 (1.6)	28.6 (1.6)	20.7 (1.2)	31.4 (1.7)	19.2 (1.6)
Asian/Pacific Islander	8.9 (2.6)	2.2 (1.1)	35.2 (2.9)	34.1 (3.4)	19.5 (2.7)	19.2 (2.4)	21.7 (2.9)	33.4 (3.5)	25.7 (3.0)
American Indian	16.4 (3.1)	1.8 (0.9)	43.8 (4.3)	15.8 (2.7)	22.1 (3.4)	28.1 (3.7)	23.4 (3.9)	25.1 (3.5)	23.3 (3.0)
Parents' highest level of education									
Less than high school	17.6 (3.1)	5.1 (1.6)	37.6 (2.8)	24.2 (2.3)	15.4 (2.1)	28.2 (3.9)	20.8 (2.1)	32.3 (4.1)	18.8 (3.4)
Graduated high school	14.3 (2.0)	3.2 (0.6)	39.9 (2.6)	23.2 (1.9)	19.4 (1.6)	24.5 (1.9)	25.2 (2.4)	36.1 (1.7)	14.3 (1.2)
Some education after high school	16.9 (2.4)	2.8 (0.8)	40.9 (2.3)	25.8 (2.3)	13.6 (1.7)	20.8 (1.8)	24.9 (1.9)	35.9 (2.2)	18.4 (1.7)
Graduated college	14.4 (1.5)	2.2 (0.3)	40.0 (1.5)	28.7 (1.3)	14.7 (0.9)	17.5 (1.1)	19.4 (0.9)	37.0 (1.1)	26.2 (1.2)
Region									
Northeast	2.9 (0.4)	2.4 (0.5)	42.8 (1.7)	33.6 (1.6)	18.2 (1.3)	21.9 (2.4)	21.5 (2.2)	36.6 (1.6)	20.0 (1.8)
Southeast	11.4 (1.5)	4.8 (0.7)	38.0 (1.9)	27.4 (1.7)	18.5 (1.2)	27.0 (1.7)	18.3 (1.0)	35.0 (1.4)	19.7 (1.5)
Central	27.0 (3.4)	2.0 (0.5)	34.6 (2.8)	22.7 (1.6)	13.7 (1.1)	17.8 (1.2)	24.7 (0.9)	38.2 (1.3)	19.2 (1.0)
West	15.9 (2.5)	2.8 (0.3)	42.7 (3.1)	24.8 (1.9)	13.8 (1.6)	19.0 (1.4)	21.4 (1.5)	33.9 (1.5)	25.7 (1.3)
Type of location									
Central city	13.1 (2.5)	4.2 (0.6)	43.2 (2.4)	23.7 (1.7)	15.7 (1.3)	26.8 (1.5)	21.2 (0.6)	30.8 (1.1)	21.2 (1.3)
Urban fringe/large town	16.0 (1.9)	2.4 (0.3)	41.2 (2.1)	27.1 (1.3)	13.4 (1.1)	17.2 (1.1)	21.0 (1.4)	38.5 (1.3)	23.3 (1.3)
Rural/small town	18.2 (2.8)	3.4 (0.6)	35.7 (2.5)	27.0 (2.3)	15.8 (1.3)	20.4 (1.5)	23.2 (1.2)	38.3 (1.5)	18.1 (1.2)
1996									
All students	11.0 (1.0)	3.0 (0.3)	40.3 (1.1)	29.3 (0.8)	16.4 (0.6)	19.0 (0.7)	19.5 (0.7)	36.4 (0.7)	25.1 (1.1)
Male	11.8 (1.1)	4.4 (0.5)	40.0 (1.4)	27.7 (1.0)	16.1 (0.7)	22.4 (0.9)	21.4 (1.0)	34.8 (1.0)	21.4 (1.3)
Female	10.2 (1.1)	1.6 (0.2)	40.7 (1.3)	30.9 (1.2)	16.6 (1.0)	15.5 (0.9)	17.6 (1.0)	38.0 (0.8)	28.9 (1.2)
Race/ethnicity									
White	12.6 (1.4)	2.5 (0.4)	39.0 (1.3)	30.7 (1.0)	15.1 (0.8)	13.3 (0.7)	19.9 (0.9)	40.5 (0.8)	26.3 (1.3)
Black	7.4 (1.6)	5.2 (0.7)	43.5 (1.7)	24.5 (1.6)	19.4 (1.5)	42.1 (2.0)	19.0 (1.4)	22.1 (1.5)	16.8 (1.6)
Hispanic	7.8 (1.2)	3.8 (0.8)	42.3 (2.1)	28.1 (2.0)	18.1 (1.7)	21.5 (1.8)	18.2 (1.2)	33.8 (1.7)	26.6 (1.8)
Asian/Pacific Islander	4.8 (1.8)	1.7 (0.9)	41.5 (4.3)	28.8 (2.5)	23.1 (3.4)	18.9 (3.1)	18.8 (3.3)	29.2 (3.8)	33.1 (5.2)
American Indian	14.4 (3.2)	3.0 (1.6)	44.7 (3.7)	24.2 (4.2)	13.6 (2.8)	25.1 (4.2)	16.2 (3.3)	29.1 (4.1)	29.6 (4.7)
Parents' highest level of education									
Less than high school	6.8 (2.1)	6.4 (1.7)	42.1 (4.6)	21.7 (3.4)	23.0 (3.8)	27.3 (3.6)	24.9 (3.0)	24.4 (3.3)	23.4 (2.8)
Graduated high school	12.2 (2.0)	3.5 (0.8)	42.7 (2.1)	26.8 (1.9)	14.8 (1.3)	22.1 (1.8)	19.8 (1.5)	38.6 (1.8)	19.6 (1.9)
Some education after high school	11.0 (2.4)	1.9 (0.7)	39.7 (2.7)	35.5 (2.7)	11.9 (1.6)	15.8 (2.1)	24.5 (2.3)	39.6 (2.2)	20.1 (2.1)
Graduated college	10.5 (1.2)	1.9 (0.3)	39.5 (1.6)	31.5 (1.2)	16.6 (0.9)	16.8 (1.1)	17.3 (1.2)	38.9 (1.1)	27.0 (1.7)
Region									
Northeast	2.5 (0.8)	2.9 (0.5)	39.2 (2.8)	36.3 (1.6)	19.1 (1.4)	17.2 (1.7)	21.7 (1.2)	36.2 (1.8)	24.9 (1.9)
Southeast	4.8 (1.0)	3.4 (0.5)	44.2 (1.9)	29.5 (0.8)	18.1 (1.4)	27.8 (1.9)	18.8 (1.8)	31.9 (1.5)	21.5 (1.6)
Central	23.2 (3.1)	3.0 (0.6)	35.2 (1.6)	24.6 (1.6)	13.9 (1.2)	16.4 (1.4)	20.0 (1.6)	40.0 (0.8)	23.6 (2.2)
West	11.5 (1.9)	2.8 (0.5)	42.6 (2.1)	27.8 (1.8)	15.3 (1.2)	16.4 (1.3)	18.1 (1.2)	36.7 (1.4)	28.8 (2.3)
Type of location									
Central city	9.1 (1.7)	4.0 (0.6)	42.7 (1.6)	26.9 (1.5)	17.3 (1.3)	23.9 (1.2)	18.6 (1.0)	34.5 (1.0)	23.1 (1.3)
Urban fringe/large town	9.4 (1.5)	2.6 (0.3)	42.2 (1.6)	30.8 (1.2)	15.0 (1.1)	15.1 (1.1)	19.6 (1.1)	38.8 (1.0)	26.5 (1.6)
Rural/small town	18.2 (2.8)	3.7 (0.7)	38.8 (2.4)	24.7 (2.5)	14.7 (1.5)	20.4 (1.3)	20.6 (1.4)	34.2 (1.6)	24.9 (2.1)

NOTE.—Standard errors appear in parentheses.

SOURCE: U.S. Department of Education, National Center for Education Statistics, National Assessment of Educational Progress, *National Mathematics Results, 1992* and *1996*. (This table was prepared September 1997).

Table 113.—Average writing performance of 4th, 8th, and 11th graders, by selected characteristics of students: 1984 to 1996

Selected characteristics of students	1984	1988	1990	1992	1994	1996
1	2	3	4	5	6	7
4th graders						
Total	204 (1.5)	206 (1.6)	202 (1.5)	207 (1.5)	205 (1.6)	207 (1.2)
Male	201 (2.8)	199 (2.3)	195 (1.9)	198 (1.7)	196 (1.7)	200 (1.8)
Female	208 (3.1)	213 (2.0)	209 (2.2)	216 (1.7)	214 (2.2)	214 (1.9)
Race/ethnicity						
White	211 (1.9)	215 (1.9)	211 (2.0)	217 (1.7)	214 (1.5)	216 (1.6)
Black	182 (5.0)	173 (4.7)	171 (5.4)	175 (3.8)	173 (3.2)	182 (2.3)
Hispanic	189 (5.8)	190 (3.5)	184 (4.1)	189 (3.6)	189 (3.1)	191 (3.2)
Parental education						
Not high school graduate	179 (4.6)	194 (5.4)	186 (3.9)	191 (3.2)	188 (7.8)	190 (5.5)
Graduated high school	192 (3.4)	199 (3.0)	197 (3.0)	202 (3.2)	202 (2.3)	203 (2.3)
Post high school	208 (6.5)	211 (6.3)	214 (4.0)	201 (4.5)	212 (4.0)	205 (5.2)
Graduated college	218 (3.0)	212 (2.2)	209 (1.6)	214 (1.4)	212 (2.1)	214 (1.7)
Control of school						
Public	202 (1.8)	204 (2.0)	200 (1.4)	205 (1.6)	204 (1.8)	206 (1.5)
Private	215 (4.6)	216 (4.1)	216 (5.7)	222 (3.3)	213 (4.3)	218 (3.2)
Region						
Northeast	212 (4.0)	204 (4.9)	211 (3.6)	216 (4.0)	210 (4.0)	213 (2.8)
Southeast	204 (3.3)	200 (2.3)	192 (4.0)	193 (2.4)	198 (3.4)	200 (3.4)
Central	201 (2.6)	212 (3.0)	203 (3.1)	214 (3.1)	209 (3.3)	212 (3.1)
West	201 (4.9)	207 (3.4)	201 (2.7)	206 (2.2)	203 (2.7)	205 (2.5)
8th graders						
Total	267 (2.0)	264 (1.3)	257 (1.2)	274 (1.3)	265 (1.3)	264 (1.0)
Male	258 (2.3)	254 (1.5)	246 (1.5)	264 (1.9)	254 (1.8)	251 (1.1)
Female	276 (2.4)	274 (1.7)	268 (1.3)	285 (1.3)	278 (1.4)	276 (1.2)
Race/ethnicity						
White	272 (2.1)	269 (1.3)	262 (1.6)	279 (1.3)	272 (1.4)	271 (1.0)
Black	247 (5.7)	246 (3.5)	239 (2.3)	258 (4.0)	245 (3.4)	242 (2.6)
Hispanic	247 (6.4)	250 (2.5)	246 (2.8)	265 (2.2)	252 (3.3)	246 (2.3)
Parental education						
Not high school graduate	258 (4.8)	254 (3.9)	246 (3.7)	258 (5.3)	250 (4.1)	245 (4.5)
Graduated high school	261 (1.6)	258 (2.1)	253 (1.4)	268 (1.6)	259 (2.2)	258 (1.9)
Post high school	271 (3.9)	275 (3.3)	267 (3.0)	280 (2.2)	270 (3.1)	270 (2.4)
Graduated college	278 (1.8)	271 (1.8)	265 (1.8)	284 (1.9)	275 (1.3)	274 (1.3)
Control of school						
Public	264 (2.0)	262 (1.5)	254 (1.2)	272 (1.3)	264 (1.6)	263 (1.2)
Private	282 (5.5)	276 (3.0)	277 (4.4)	288 (3.2)	279 (3.8)	272 (3.3)
Region						
Northeast	273 (3.6)	265 (2.7)	261 (3.3)	285 (3.3)	277 (2.2)	264 (2.4)
Southeast	267 (3.6)	268 (2.3)	252 (2.8)	266 (2.2)	259 (2.1)	260 (3.5)
Central	264 (2.3)	258 (2.2)	259 (3.9)	277 (2.0)	270 (4.1)	268 (2.3)
West	264 (3.0)	264 (2.1)	255 (2.6)	271 (2.3)	259 (1.6)	263 (1.3)
11th graders						
Total	290 (1.6)	291 (1.3)	287 (1.0)	287 (1.4)	285 (1.2)	283 (1.2)
Male	281 (1.4)	282 (2.0)	276 (1.6)	279 (1.2)	276 (1.5)	275 (1.4)
Female	299 (2.5)	299 (1.2)	298 (1.5)	296 (2.0)	293 (1.5)	292 (1.4)
Race/ethnicity						
White	297 (1.8)	296 (1.3)	293 (1.2)	294 (1.2)	291 (1.4)	289 (1.5)
Black	270 (3.6)	275 (2.9)	268 (2.3)	263 (3.2)	267 (2.2)	267 (3.0)
Hispanic	259 (6.6)	274 (4.4)	277 (2.6)	274 (3.8)	271 (4.0)	269 (2.5)
Parental education						
Not high school graduate	274 (5.2)	276 (3.5)	268 (4.0)	271 (3.7)	269 (4.7)	260 (3.0)
Graduated high school	284 (3.0)	285 (2.2)	278 (1.9)	278 (2.2)	279 (1.7)	275 (1.6)
Post high school	298 (2.5)	296 (2.6)	292 (2.7)	292 (2.0)	286 (1.7)	287 (2.1)
Graduated college	300 (2.4)	299 (2.0)	298 (2.0)	296 (1.4)	293 (1.5)	291 (1.9)
Control of school						
Public	288 (1.6)	290 (1.2)	286 (1.1)	287 (1.6)	284 (1.4)	283 (1.4)
Private	305 (3.7)	300 (3.6)	306 (5.2)	295 (4.4)	291 (3.8)	287 (6.6)
Region						
Northeast	291 (3.0)	295 (2.8)	295 (2.5)	290 (2.3)	291 (2.4)	290 (2.2)
Southeast	287 (4.9)	289 (2.2)	280 (2.3)	278 (3.3)	277 (2.5)	273 (2.2)
Central	291 (2.7)	292 (4.0)	289 (2.7)	291 (2.2)	284 (2.3)	285 (2.5)
West	289 (3.7)	289 (2.3)	285 (2.1)	289 (2.1)	287 (2.7)	284 (2.2)

NOTE.—These test scores are from the National Assessment of Educational Progress (NAEP). The writing scale score ranges from 0 to 500 and is defined as the average of a respondent's estimated scores on specific writing tasks. The average response method is used to estimate average writing achievement for each participant as if each had performed all 11 writing tasks. Standard errors appear in parentheses.

SOURCE: U.S. Department of Education, National Center for Education Statistics, National Assessment of Educational Progress, NAEP 1996 Trends in Academic Progress, by Educational Testing Service. (This table was prepared September 1997.)

Table 114.—Student values and attitudes toward writing, by grade level: 1984, 1990, 1992, and 1994

Statements about writing	Percent of students reporting the statement is true more than half the time, by grade level											
	Grade 4				Grade 8				Grade 11			
	1984	1990	1992	1994	1984	1990	1992	1994	1984	1990	1992	1994
1	2	3	4	5	6	7	8	9	10	11	12	13
Writing helps me think more clearly	—	—	—	—	44	46	42	42	52	47	50	54
Writing helps me tell others what I think	—	—	—	—	52	56	52	54	55	58	57	58
Writing helps tell others how I feel	—	—	—	—	50	56	52	52	55	60	60	60
Writing helps me understand my own feelings	—	—	—	—	40	47	44	45	47	50	49	54
People who write well have a better chance of getting good jobs	—	—	—	—	47	53	51	51	54	58	59	58
People who write well are more influential	—	—	—	—	49	55	52	51	54	60	60	57
I like to write	56	57	54	56	39	42	43	42	40	39	43	42
I am a good writer	60	62	63	64	42	44	44	49	39	44	49	46
People like what I write	53	56	55	58	38	39	44	44	36	42	46	44
I write on my own outside of school	48	42	46	45	36	35	37	36	31	28	33	32
I don't like to write things that will be graded	38	33	32	33	31	36	37	38	27	30	30	33
If I didn't have to write for school, I wouldn't write anything	33	27	28	27	17	19	18	21	15	16	17	17

—Data not available.

SOURCE: U.S. Department of Education, National Center for Education Statistics, *NAEP 1994 Trends in Academic Progress,* by Educational Testing Service. (This table was prepared March 1997.)

Table 115.—Percent of students at or above selected history proficiency levels, by selected characteristics and grade level: 1994

Selected characteristics of students	Percentage of 4th graders				Percentage of 8th graders				Percentage of 12th graders			
	Below basic	At or above basic	At or above proficient	At or above advanced	Below basic	At or above basic	At or above proficient	At or above advanced	Below basic	At or above basic	At or above proficient	At or above advanced
1	2	3	4	5	6	7	8	9	10	11	12	13
All students	**36**	**64**	**17**	**2**	**39**	**61**	**14**	**1**	**57**	**43**	**11**	**1**
Sex												
Male	38	62	18	2	39	61	15	1	55	45	12	1
Female	35	65	16	2	39	61	13	1	60	40	9	1
Race/ethnicity												
White	26	74	22	3	29	71	17	1	50	50	13	1
Black	64	36	4	0	67	33	4	0	83	17	2	0
Hispanic	59	41	6	1	59	41	5	0	78	22	4	0
Asian	36	64	22	4	28	72	23	2	54	46	16	2
Pacific Islander	41	59	16	3	48	52	11	1	67	33	7	1
American Indian	49	51	9	0	58	42	5	0	70	30	5	0
Region												
Northeast	37	63	18	3	31	69	19	1	54	46	13	1
Southeast	39	61	15	2	49	51	9	0	63	37	8	0
Central	29	71	20	3	31	69	17	1	55	45	11	1
West	39	61	16	1	42	58	11	1	57	43	10	1
Parents' level of education												
Not high school graduate	63	37	2	0	63	37	3	0	85	15	1	0
Graduated high school	43	57	10	1	50	50	7	0	71	29	4	0
Some college	26	74	21	3	32	68	14	0	58	42	8	1
Graduated college	26	74	25	4	26	74	22	1	44	56	17	1

SOURCE: U.S. Department of Education, National Center for Education Statistics, National Assessment of Educational Progress, *NAEP 1994 U.S. History Report Card.* (This table was prepared November 1995.)

Table 116.—Average student proficiency in geography and U.S. history, by student characteristics: 1994

Characteristic	Percentage distribution of 12th graders in geography	Geography scores			History scores			Characteristic	Percentage distribution of 12th graders in geography	Geography scores			History scores		
		4th graders	8th graders	12th graders	4th graders	8th graders	12th graders			4th graders	8th graders	12th graders	4th graders	8th graders	12th graders
1	2	3	4	5	6	7	8	1	2	3	4	5	6	7	8
United States	100	206	260	285	205	259	286								
Sex															
Male	50	208	262	288	203	259	288	Type of school							
Female	50	203	258	281	206	259	285	Public	89	204	258	283	203	257	284
								Nonpublic schools	11	221	276	294	222	278	299
Race								Catholic schools	6	222	276	291	221	279	298
White	74	218	270	291	215	267	292	Other nonpublic	4	220	276	298	224	277	299
Black	12	168	229	258	177	239	265								
Hispanic	8	183	239	268	180	243	267								
								Parents' level of education							
Region								Not high school graduate	7	186	238	263	177	241	263
Northeast	21	203	266	284	204	266	289	Graduated high school	22	197	250	274	197	251	276
Southeast	23	200	252	278	201	251	282	Some college	25	216	265	286	214	264	287
Central	28	215	268	289	212	266	288	Graduated college	44	216	272	294	216	270	296
West	29	205	255	286	202	256	286								

NOTE.—These test scores are from the National Assessment of Educational Progress (NAEP). As with the NAEP reading scale, these scales range from 0 to 500. However, the distribution of scores varies by subject. Therefore, direct score comparisons among the subjects should be avoided.

SOURCE: U.S. Department of Education, National Center for Education Statistics, National Assessment of Educational Progress, *NAEP 1994 U.S. History Report Card,* and *The Geography Report Card,* prepared by Educational Testing Service. (This table was prepared November 1995.)

Table 117.—Percent of students at or above selected geography proficiency levels, by selected characteristics and grade level: 1994

Selected characteristics of students	Percentage of 4th graders				Percentage of 8th graders				Percentage of 12th graders			
	Below basic	At or above basic	At or above proficient	At or above advanced	Below basic	At or above basic	At or above proficient	At or above advanced	Below basic	At or above basic	At or above proficient	At or above advanced
1	2	3	4	5	6	7	8	9	10	11	12	13
All students	30	70	22	3	29	71	28	4	30	70	27	2
Sex												
Male	29	71	26	4	28	72	30	5	27	73	32	2
Female	32	68	19	2	31	69	25	3	33	67	22	1
Race/ethnicity												
White	19	81	29	4	18	82	36	5	22	78	33	2
Black	66	34	3	0	66	34	5	0	68	32	5	0
Hispanic	51	49	10	1	50	50	10	1	52	48	10	0
Asian	21	79	32	5	21	79	40	8	31	69	32	3
Region												
Northeast	33	67	22	3	24	76	33	6	31	69	25	2
Southeast	36	64	17	2	38	62	21	3	40	60	20	1
Central	22	78	28	4	20	80	36	6	25	75	32	2
West	30	70	21	3	33	67	23	3	28	72	29	2
Parents' level of education												
Not high school graduate	48	52	8	0	53	47	8	1	59	41	7	0
Graduated high school	37	63	15	1	38	62	15	1	44	56	14	0
Some college	20	80	30	3	21	79	29	3	25	75	24	1
Graduated college	22	78	31	5	18	82	41	7	19	81	40	3

SOURCE: U.S. Department of Education, National Center for Education Statistics, National Assessment of Educational Progress, *NAEP 1994 Geography Report Card.* (This table was prepared November 1995.)

Table 118.—Average mathematics proficiency, by age and by selected characteristics of students: 1973 to 1996

Selected characteristics of students	1973	1978	1982	1986	1990	1992	1994	1996
1	2	3	4	5	6	7	8	9
	9-year-olds							
Total	219 (0.8)	219 (0.8)	219 (1.1)	222 (1.0)	230 (0.8)	230 (0.8)	231 (0.8)	231 (0.8)
Male	218 (0.7)	217 (0.7)	217 (1.2)	222 (1.1)	229 (0.9)	231 (1.0)	232 (1.0)	233 (1.2)
Female	220 (1.1)	220 (1.0)	221 (1.2)	222 (1.2)	230 (1.1)	228 (1.0)	230 (0.9)	229 (0.7)
Race/ethnicity								
White	225 (1.0)	224 (0.9)	224 (1.1)	227 (1.1)	235 (0.8)	235 (0.8)	237 (1.0)	237 (1.0)
Black	190 (1.8)	192 (1.1)	195 (1.6)	202 (1.6)	208 (2.2)	208 (2.0)	212 (1.6)	212 (1.4)
Hispanic	202 (2.4)	203 (2.2)	204 (1.3)	205 (2.1)	214 (2.1)	212 (2.3)	210 (2.3)	215 (1.7)
Parental education								
Not high school graduate	— —	200 (1.5)	199 (1.7)	201 (2.5)	210 (2.3)	217 (2.2)	210 (3.0)	220 (3.3)
Graduated high school	— —	219 (1.1)	218 (1.1)	218 (1.6)	226 (1.2)	222 (1.5)	225 (1.3)	221 (1.7)
Some education after high school	— —	230 (1.7)	225 (2.1)	229 (2.1)	236 (2.0)	237 (1.9)	239 (2.1)	238 (2.5)
Graduated college	— —	231 (1.1)	229 (1.5)	231 (1.1)	238 (1.3)	236 (1.0)	238 (0.8)	240 (1.4)
Control of school								
Public	— —	217 (0.8)	217 (1.1)	220 (1.2)	229 (0.9)	228 (0.9)	229 (0.9)	230 (0.8)
Private	— —	231 (1.7)	232 (2.1)	230 (2.5)	238 (2.3)	242 (1.7)	245 (2.3)	239 (2.1)
Region								
Northeast	227 (1.9)	227 (1.9)	226 (1.8)	226 (2.7)	236 (2.1)	235 (1.9)	238 (2.2)	236 (2.0)
Southeast	208 (1.3)	209 (1.2)	210 (2.5)	218 (2.5)	224 (2.4)	221 (1.7)	229 (1.4)	227 (2.0)
Central	224 (1.5)	224 (1.5)	221 (2.7)	226 (2.3)	231 (1.3)	234 (1.6)	233 (1.8)	233 (2.3)
West	216 (2.2)	214 (1.3)	219 (1.8)	217 (2.4)	229 (1.8)	229 (2.3)	226 (1.6)	229 (1.3)
	13-year-olds [1]							
Total	266 (1.1)	264 (1.1)	269 (1.1)	269 (1.2)	270 (0.9)	273 (0.9)	274 (1.0)	274 (0.8)
Male	265 (1.3)	264 (1.3)	269 (1.4)	270 (1.1)	271 (1.2)	274 (1.1)	276 (1.3)	276 (0.9)
Female	267 (1.1)	265 (1.1)	268 (1.1)	268 (1.5)	270 (0.9)	272 (1.0)	273 (1.0)	272 (1.0)
Race/ethnicity								
White	274 (0.9)	272 (0.8)	274 (1.0)	274 (1.3)	276 (1.1)	279 (0.9)	281 (0.9)	281 (0.9)
Black	228 (1.9)	230 (1.9)	240 (1.6)	249 (2.3)	249 (2.3)	250 (1.9)	252 (3.5)	252 (1.3)
Hispanic	239 (2.2)	238 (2.0)	252 (1.7)	254 (2.9)	255 (1.8)	259 (1.8)	256 (1.9)	256 (1.6)
Parental education								
Not high school graduate	— —	245 (1.2)	251 (1.4)	252 (2.3)	253 (1.8)	256 (1.0)	255 (2.1)	254 (2.4)
Graduated high school	— —	263 (1.0)	263 (0.8)	263 (1.2)	263 (1.2)	263 (1.2)	266 (1.1)	267 (1.1)
Some education after high school	— —	273 (1.2)	275 (0.9)	274 (0.8)	277 (1.0)	278 (1.0)	277 (1.6)	278 (1.4)
Graduated college	— —	284 (1.2)	282 (1.5)	280 (1.4)	280 (1.0)	283 (1.0)	285 (1.2)	283 (1.2)
Control of school								
Public	— —	263 (1.2)	267 (1.3)	269 (1.2)	269 (1.0)	272 (1.0)	273 (1.1)	273 (0.9)
Private	— —	279 (1.4)	281 (2.1)	276 (4.9)	280 (1.7)	283 (2.5)	285 (2.4)	286 (3.6)
Region								
Northeast	275 (2.4)	273 (2.4)	277 (2.0)	277 (2.2)	275 (2.3)	274 (2.2)	284 (1.5)	275 (2.1)
Southeast	255 (3.2)	253 (3.3)	258 (2.2)	264 (1.4)	266 (1.9)	271 (2.5)	269 (2.0)	270 (1.8)
Central	271 (1.8)	269 (1.8)	273 (2.1)	266 (4.5)	272 (2.4)	275 (1.5)	275 (3.4)	280 (1.3)
West	262 (1.9)	260 (1.9)	266 (2.4)	270 (2.1)	269 (1.6)	272 (1.4)	272 (1.7)	273 (1.9)
	17-year-olds [1]							
Total	304 (1.1)	300 (1.0)	299 (0.9)	302 (0.9)	305 (0.9)	307 (0.9)	306 (1.0)	307 (1.2)
Male	309 (1.2)	304 (1.0)	302 (1.0)	305 (1.2)	306 (1.1)	309 (1.1)	309 (1.4)	310 (1.3)
Female	301 (1.1)	297 (1.0)	296 (1.0)	299 (1.0)	303 (1.1)	305 (1.1)	304 (1.1)	305 (1.4)
Race/ethnicity								
White	310 (1.1)	306 (0.9)	304 (0.9)	308 (1.0)	310 (1.0)	312 (0.8)	312 (1.1)	313 (1.4)
Black	270 (1.3)	268 (1.3)	272 (1.2)	279 (2.1)	289 (2.8)	286 (2.2)	286 (1.8)	286 (1.7)
Hispanic	277 (2.2)	276 (2.3)	277 (1.8)	283 (2.9)	284 (2.9)	292 (2.6)	291 (3.7)	292 (2.1)
Parental education								
Not high school graduate	— —	280 (1.2)	279 (1.0)	279 (2.3)	285 (2.2)	286 (2.3)	284 (2.4)	281 (2.4)
Graduated high school	— —	294 (0.8)	293 (0.8)	293 (1.0)	294 (0.9)	298 (1.7)	295 (1.1)	297 (2.4)
Some education after high school	— —	305 (0.9)	304 (0.9)	305 (1.2)	308 (1.0)	308 (1.1)	305 (1.3)	307 (1.5)
Graduated college	— —	317 (1.0)	312 (1.0)	314 (1.4)	316 (1.3)	316 (1.0)	318 (1.4)	317 (1.3)
Control of school								
Public	— —	300 (1.0)	297 (0.9)	301 (1.0)	304 (0.8)	305 (0.9)	304 (0.9)	306 (1.1)
Private	— —	314 (3.2)	311 (1.7)	320 (9.8)	318 (6.6)	320 (3.0)	319 (4.0)	316 (4.5)
Region								
Northeast	312 (1.8)	307 (1.8)	304 (2.0)	307 (1.9)	304 (2.1)	311 (2.0)	313 (2.9)	309 (3.0)
Southeast	296 (1.8)	292 (1.7)	292 (2.1)	297 (1.4)	301 (2.3)	301 (1.9)	301 (1.6)	303 (2.1)
Central	306 (1.8)	305 (1.9)	302 (1.4)	304 (1.9)	311 (2.1)	312 (2.0)	307 (2.2)	314 (2.0)
West	303 (2.0)	296 (1.8)	294 (1.9)	299 (2.7)	302 (1.5)	303 (1.5)	305 (2.4)	304 (2.3)

[1] All participants of this age were in school.
—Data not available.

NOTE.—These test scores are from the National Assessment of Educational Progress (NAEP). Performers at the 150 level know some basic addition and subtraction facts, and most can add two-digit numbers without regrouping. They recognize simple situations in which addition and subtraction apply. Performers at the 200 level have considerable understanding of two-digit numbers and know some basic multiplication and division facts. Performers at the 250 level have an initial understanding of the four basic operations. They can also compare information from graphs and charts, and are developing an ability to analyze simple logical relations. Performers at the 300 level can compute decimals, simple fractions and percents. They can identify geometric figures, measure lengths and angles, and calculate areas of rectangles. They are developing the skills to operate with signed numbers, exponents, and square roots. Performers at the 350 level can apply a range of reasoning skills to solve multi-step problems. They can solve routine problems involving fractions and percents, recognize properties of basic geometric figures, and work with exponents and square roots. Scale ranges from 0 to 500. Standard errors appear in parentheses.

SOURCE: U.S. Department of Education, National Center for Education Statistics, National Assessment of Educational Progress, NAEP 1996 Trends in Academic Progress, prepared by Educational Testing Service. (This table was prepared August 1997.)

Table 119.—Percent of students at or above selected mathematics proficiency levels,[1] by sex, race/ethnicity, control of school, and age: 1978 to 1996

Sex, race/ethnicity, control, and year	9-year-olds[2]				13-year-olds[3]				17-year-olds[3]			
	Simple arithmetic facts[4]	Beginning skills and understanding[5]	Numerical operations and beginning problem solving[6]	Moderately complex procedures and reasoning[7]	Beginning skills and understanding[5]	Numerical operations and beginning problem solving[6]	Moderately complex procedures and reasoning[7]	Multi-step problem solving and algebra[8]	Beginning skills and understanding[5]	Numerical operations and beginning problem solving[6]	Moderately complex procedures and reasoning[7]	Multi-step problem solving and algebra[8]
1	2	3	4	5	6	7	8	9	10	11	12	13
Total												
1978	96.7 (0.3)	70.4 (0.9)	19.6 (0.7)	0.8 (0.1)	94.6 (0.5)	64.9 (1.2)	18.0 (0.7)	1.0 (0.2)	99.8 (0.1)	92.0 (0.5)	51.5 (1.1)	7.3 (0.4)
1982	97.1 (0.3)	71.4 (1.2)	18.8 (1.0)	0.6 (0.1)	97.7 (0.4)	71.4 (1.2)	17.4 (0.9)	0.5 (0.1)	99.9 (0.0)	93.0 (0.5)	48.5 (1.3)	5.5 (0.4)
1986	97.9 (0.3)	74.1 (1.2)	20.7 (0.9)	0.6 (0.2)	98.6 (0.2)	73.3 (1.6)	15.8 (1.0)	0.4 (0.1)	99.9 —	95.6 (0.5)	51.7 (1.4)	6.5 (0.5)
1990	99.1 (0.2)	81.5 (1.0)	27.7 (0.9)	1.2 (0.3)	98.5 (0.2)	74.7 (1.0)	17.3 (1.0)	0.4 (0.1)	100.0 —	96.0 (0.5)	56.1 (1.4)	7.2 (0.6)
1992	99.0 (0.2)	81.4 (0.8)	27.8 (0.9)	1.2 (0.3)	98.7 (0.3)	77.9 (1.1)	18.9 (1.0)	0.4 (0.2)	100.0 —	96.6 (0.5)	59.1 (1.3)	7.2 (0.6)
1994	99.0 (0.2)	82.0 (0.7)	29.9 (1.1)	1.3 (0.4)	98.5 (0.3)	78.1 (1.1)	21.3 (1.4)	0.6 (0.2)	100.0 —	96.5 (0.5)	58.6 (1.4)	7.4 (0.8)
1996	99.1 (0.2)	81.5 (0.8)	29.7 (1.0)	1.6 (0.3)	98.8 (0.2)	78.6 (0.9)	20.6 (1.2)	0.6 (0.1)	100.0 —	96.8 (0.4)	60.1 (1.7)	7.4 (0.8)
Male												
1978	96.2 (0.5)	68.9 (1.0)	19.2 (0.6)	0.7 (0.2)	93.9 (0.5)	63.9 (1.3)	18.4 (0.9)	1.1 (0.2)	99.9 (0.1)	93.0 (0.5)	55.1 (1.2)	9.5 (0.6)
1982	96.5 (0.5)	68.8 (1.3)	18.1 (1.1)	0.6 (0.1)	97.5 (0.6)	71.3 (1.4)	18.9 (1.2)	0.7 (0.2)	100.0 —	93.9 (0.6)	51.9 (1.5)	6.9 (0.7)
1986	98.0 (0.5)	74.0 (1.4)	20.9 (1.0)	0.7 (0.3)	98.5 (0.3)	73.8 (1.8)	17.6 (1.1)	0.5 (0.2)	99.9 —	96.1 (0.6)	54.6 (1.8)	8.4 (0.9)
1990	99.0 (0.3)	80.6 (1.4)	27.5 (1.0)	1.3 (0.4)	98.2 (0.3)	75.1 (1.8)	19.0 (1.2)	0.5 (0.2)	99.9 —	95.8 (0.8)	57.6 (1.4)	8.8 (0.8)
1992	99.0 (0.3)	81.9 (1.0)	29.4 (1.2)	1.4 (0.3)	98.8 (0.4)	78.1 (1.6)	20.7 (1.1)	0.5 (0.2)	100.0 —	96.9 (0.6)	60.5 (1.8)	9.1 (0.7)
1994	99.1 (0.3)	82.3 (0.9)	31.5 (1.6)	1.4 (0.4)	98.3 (0.4)	78.9 (1.5)	23.9 (1.6)	0.8 (0.3)	100.0 —	97.3 (0.6)	60.2 (2.1)	9.3 (1.0)
1996	99.1 (0.2)	82.5 (1.1)	32.7 (1.7)	2.0 (0.5)	98.7 (0.3)	79.8 (1.4)	23.0 (1.6)	0.8 (0.2)	100.0 —	97.0 (0.7)	62.7 (1.8)	9.5 (1.3)
Female												
1978	97.2 (0.3)	72.0 (1.1)	19.9 (1.0)	0.8 (0.2)	95.2 (0.5)	65.9 (1.2)	17.5 (0.7)	0.9 (0.2)	99.7 (0.1)	91.0 (0.6)	48.2 (1.3)	5.2 (0.7)
1982	97.6 (0.3)	74.0 (1.3)	19.6 (1.1)	0.5 (0.1)	98.0 (0.3)	71.4 (1.3)	15.9 (1.0)	0.4 (0.2)	99.9 (0.0)	92.1 (0.6)	45.3 (1.4)	4.1 (0.4)
1986	97.8 (0.4)	74.3 (1.3)	20.6 (1.3)	0.6 (0.3)	98.6 (0.3)	72.7 (1.9)	14.1 (1.3)	0.3 (0.1)	100.0 —	95.1 (0.7)	48.9 (1.7)	4.7 (0.6)
1990	99.1 (0.3)	82.3 (1.3)	27.9 (1.1)	1.0 (0.3)	98.9 (0.2)	74.4 (1.3)	15.7 (1.0)	0.2 (0.1)	100.0 —	96.2 (0.8)	54.7 (1.8)	5.6 (0.8)
1992	99.0 (0.3)	80.9 (1.1)	26.3 (1.5)	1.0 (0.4)	98.6 (0.2)	77.7 (1.1)	17.2 (1.4)	0.3 —	100.0 —	96.3 (0.7)	57.7 (1.6)	5.2 (0.8)
1994	98.9 (0.3)	81.7 (0.9)	28.3 (1.3)	1.1 (0.4)	98.7 (0.3)	77.3 (1.0)	18.7 (1.4)	0.5 (0.3)	100.0 —	96.0 (0.6)	57.2 (1.4)	5.5 (0.9)
1996	99.1 (0.4)	80.7 (0.9)	26.7 (1.1)	1.2 (0.4)	98.8 (0.3)	77.4 (1.1)	18.4 (1.5)	0.5 (0.3)	100.0 —	96.7 (0.6)	57.6 (2.2)	5.3 (0.8)
White, non-Hispanic												
1978	98.3 (0.2)	76.3 (1.0)	22.9 (0.9)	0.9 (0.2)	97.6 (0.3)	72.9 (0.9)	21.4 (0.7)	1.2 (0.2)	100.0 —	95.6 (0.3)	57.6 (1.1)	8.5 (0.5)
1982	98.5 (0.3)	76.8 (1.2)	21.8 (1.1)	0.6 (0.1)	99.1 (0.1)	78.3 (0.9)	20.5 (1.0)	0.6 (0.1)	100.0 —	96.2 (0.3)	54.7 (1.4)	6.4 (0.5)
1986	98.8 (0.2)	79.6 (1.3)	24.6 (1.0)	0.8 (0.3)	99.3 (0.3)	78.9 (1.7)	18.6 (1.2)	0.4 (0.1)	100.0 —	98.0 (0.4)	59.1 (1.7)	7.9 (0.7)
1990	99.6 (0.2)	86.9 (0.9)	32.7 (1.0)	1.5 (0.4)	99.4 (0.1)	82.0 (1.0)	21.0 (1.2)	0.4 (0.2)	100.0 —	97.6 (0.3)	63.2 (1.6)	8.3 (0.7)
1992	99.6 (0.1)	86.9 (0.7)	32.4 (1.0)	1.4 (0.3)	99.6 (0.2)	84.9 (1.1)	22.8 (1.3)	0.4 (0.1)	100.0 —	98.3 (0.4)	66.4 (1.4)	8.7 (0.9)
1994	99.6 (0.2)	87.0 (0.8)	35.3 (1.3)	1.5 (0.4)	99.0 (0.2)	85.5 (0.9)	25.6 (1.6)	0.7 (0.3)	100.0 —	98.4 (0.4)	67.0 (1.4)	9.4 (1.1)
1996	99.6 (0.1)	86.6 (0.8)	35.7 (1.4)	2.0 (0.4)	99.6 (0.2)	86.4 (1.0)	25.4 (1.5)	0.8 (0.2)	100.0 —	98.7 (0.4)	68.7 (2.2)	9.2 (1.0)
Black, non-Hispanic												
1978	88.4 (1.0)	42.0 (1.4)	4.1 (0.6)	0.0 —	79.7 (1.5)	28.7 (2.1)	2.3 (0.5)	0.0 —	98.8 (0.3)	70.7 (1.7)	16.8 (1.6)	0.5 (0.2)
1982	90.2 (1.0)	46.1 (2.4)	4.4 (0.8)	0.0 —	90.2 (1.6)	37.9 (2.5)	2.9 (1.0)	0.0 —	99.7 (0.2)	76.4 (1.5)	17.1 (1.5)	0.5 (0.3)
1986	93.9 (1.4)	53.4 (2.5)	5.6 (0.9)	0.1 —	95.4 (0.9)	49.0 (3.7)	4.0 (1.4)	0.1 —	100.0 —	85.6 (2.5)	20.8 (2.8)	0.2 —
1990	96.9 (0.9)	60.0 (2.8)	9.4 (1.7)	0.1 —	95.4 (1.1)	48.7 (3.6)	3.9 (1.6)	0.1 —	99.9 —	92.4 (2.2)	32.8 (4.5)	2.0 (1.0)
1992	96.6 (1.1)	59.8 (2.8)	9.6 (1.4)	0.1 —	95.0 (1.4)	51.0 (2.7)	4.0 (0.7)	0.1 —	100.0 —	89.6 (2.5)	29.8 (3.9)	0.9 —
1994	97.4 (1.0)	65.9 (2.6)	11.1 (1.7)	0.0 —	95.6 (1.6)	51.0 (3.9)	6.4 (2.4)	0.3 —	100.0 —	90.6 (1.8)	29.8 (3.4)	0.4 —
1996	97.3 (0.8)	65.3 (2.4)	10.0 (1.2)	0.1 —	96.2 (1.3)	53.7 (2.6)	4.8 (1.1)	0.1 —	100.0 —	90.6 (1.3)	31.2 (2.5)	0.9 —
Hispanic												
1978	93.0 (1.2)	54.2 (2.8)	9.2 (2.5)	0.2 —	86.4 (0.9)	36.0 (2.9)	4.0 (1.0)	0.1 —	99.3 (0.4)	78.3 (2.3)	23.4 (2.7)	1.4 (0.6)
1982	94.3 (1.2)	55.7 (2.3)	7.8 (1.7)	0.0 —	95.9 (0.9)	52.2 (2.5)	6.3 (1.0)	0.0 —	99.8 —	81.4 (1.9)	21.6 (2.2)	0.7 (0.4)
1986	96.4 (1.3)	57.6 (2.9)	7.3 (2.8)	0.1 —	96.9 (1.4)	56.0 (5.0)	5.5 (1.1)	0.2 —	99.4 —	89.3 (2.5)	26.5 (4.5)	1.1 —
1990	98.0 (0.8)	68.4 (3.0)	11.3 (3.5)	0.2 —	96.8 (1.1)	56.7 (3.3)	6.4 (1.7)	0.1 —	99.6 —	85.8 (4.2)	30.1 (3.1)	1.9 (0.8)
1992	97.2 (1.3)	65.0 (2.9)	11.7 (2.5)	0.1 —	98.1 (0.7)	63.3 (2.7)	7.0 (1.2)	0.0 —	100.0 —	94.1 (2.2)	39.2 (4.9)	1.2 —
1994	97.2 (1.2)	63.5 (3.1)	9.7 (1.8)	0.0 —	97.1 (1.3)	59.2 (2.2)	6.4 (1.8)	0.0 —	100.0 —	91.8 (3.6)	38.3 (5.5)	1.4 —
1996	98.1 (0.7)	67.1 (2.1)	13.8 (2.3)	0.2 —	96.2 (0.8)	58.3 (2.3)	6.7 (1.2)	0.0 —	99.9 —	92.2 (2.2)	40.1 (3.5)	1.8 —
Public												
1978	96.4 (0.3)	68.8 (0.9)	18.5 (0.7)	0.7 (0.2)	94.1 (0.5)	63.3 (1.2)	17.0 (0.8)	0.9 (0.2)	99.8 (0.1)	91.7 (0.5)	50.6 (1.2)	7.0 (0.4)
1982	96.8 (0.4)	69.4 (1.2)	17.3 (0.9)	0.5 (0.1)	97.5 (0.4)	69.7 (1.3)	16.4 (1.0)	0.5 (0.1)	99.9 (0.0)	92.5 (0.6)	46.9 (1.4)	5.2 (0.4)
1986	97.7 (0.3)	72.7 (1.4)	19.1 (1.1)	0.6 (0.2)	98.5 (0.3)	72.9 (1.7)	15.6 (1.0)	0.4 (0.1)	99.9 —	95.5 (0.5)	50.7 (1.6)	6.1 (0.5)
1990	99.0 (0.2)	80.5 (1.1)	26.8 (1.0)	1.1 (0.3)	98.4 (0.2)	73.3 (1.2)	16.7 (1.1)	0.3 (0.1)	100.0 —	95.8 (0.6)	55.0 (1.3)	6.5 (0.5)
1992	98.8 (0.2)	79.7 (0.9)	26.1 (0.9)	1.1 (0.3)	98.5 (0.3)	76.3 (1.2)	18.0 (1.0)	0.3 (0.2)	100.0 —	96.3 (0.6)	56.9 (1.2)	6.7 (0.7)
1994	98.9 (0.3)	80.6 (0.8)	27.9 (1.2)	1.1 (0.4)	98.5 (0.3)	76.7 (1.2)	20.0 (1.4)	0.6 (0.2)	100.0 —	96.2 (0.5)	56.2 (1.3)	6.4 (0.7)
1996	99.0 (0.2)	80.7 (0.8)	28.3 (1.1)	1.5 (0.3)	98.6 (0.2)	77.2 (0.9)	19.2 (1.3)	0.6 (0.1)	100.0 —	96.7 (0.5)	59.0 (1.8)	7.1 (0.7)
Private												
1978	99.0 —	83.3 (1.9)	28.4 (2.0)	1.2 (0.4)	99.0 (0.4)	80.8 (1.7)	26.9 (1.8)	1.4 (0.4)	100.0 —	97.1 (0.6)	67.7 (3.3)	12.9 (2.7)
1982	99.0 (0.4)	84.3 (2.1)	28.6 (2.6)	1.0 (0.6)	99.5 (0.3)	85.1 (1.6)	26.3 (3.1)	1.0 (0.3)	100.0 —	98.1 (0.5)	66.3 (2.4)	8.2 (1.4)
1986	98.7 (0.8)	81.8 (2.3)	28.9 (2.7)	1.1 (0.6)	98.9 (0.6)	81.9 (3.3)	22.0 (6.8)	0.1 —	100.0 —	99.4 —	75.1 (10.6)	16.3 (9.1)
1990	99.7 —	89.3 (1.8)	35.2 (3.3)	1.8 (1.2)	99.7 —	87.0 (2.0)	23.2 (2.5)	0.7 (0.4)	100.0 —	98.2 (1.2)	71.0 (7.9)	15.7 (5.3)
1992	99.8 (0.1)	92.2 (1.2)	38.6 (2.7)	1.9 (0.7)	99.9 —	89.7 (2.1)	25.9 (3.7)	0.7 (0.4)	100.0 —	99.5 —	79.5 (3.7)	12.2 (2.7)
1994	99.8 —	92.3 (1.3)	44.4 (4.0)	2.2 (0.8)	98.7 —	88.5 (2.6)	30.7 (3.7)	1.0 —	100.0 —	98.8 (0.6)	75.7 (4.3)	14.5 (3.5)
1996	99.6 —	87.1 (1.5)	38.7 (3.0)	2.1 (1.1)	99.6 —	89.3 (3.5)	31.6 (4.8)	1.0 (0.6)	100.0 —	98.5 (0.8)	71.5 (6.4)	10.4 (1.0)

[1] As measured by the National Assessment of Educational Progress (NAEP).
[2] Virtually no students were able to perform multi-step problems and algebra.
[3] Virtually all students knew simple arithmetic facts. Data are only for students enrolled in school.
[4] Scale score of 150 or above.
[5] Scale score of 200 or above.
[6] Scale score of 250 or above.
[7] Scale score of 300 or above.
[8] Scale score of 350 or above.
—Data not available or not applicable.

NOTE.—Standard errors appear in parentheses.

SOURCE: U.S. Department of Education, National Assessment of Educational Progress, NAEP 1996 Trends in Academic Progress, prepared by Educational Testing Service. (This table was prepared September 1997.)

Table 120.—Average proficiency in mathematics content areas for 8th graders in public schools, by region and state: 1996

Region and state	Average proficiency	Percent attaining mathematics achievement levels [1]				Percent of students by highest level of education attained by parents [2]			
		Below basic	Basic or above [3]	Proficient or above [4]	Advanced or above [5]	Did not finish high school	Graduated high school	Some education after high school	Graduated college
1	2	3	4	5	6	7	8	9	10
United States	271 (1.1)	38 (1.1)	62 (1.1)	24 (1.1)	4 (0.5)	8 (0.5)	23 (0.8)	19 (0.8)	39 (1.4)
Region									
Northeast	277 (3.1)	33 (3.1)	67 (3.1)	27 (3.7)	5 (1.9)	—	—	—	—
Southeast	266 (2.6)	44 (3.2)	56 (3.2)	18 (1.8)	3 (0.6)	—	—	—	—
Central	277 (3.1)	31 (3.4)	69 (3.4)	29 (2.5)	5 (1.0)	—	—	—	—
West	269 (2.2)	41 (2.2)	59 (2.2)	22 (1.9)	3 (0.6)	—	—	—	—
State									
Alabama	257 (2.1)	55 (2.6)	45 (2.6)	12 (1.8)	1 (0.4)	10 (0.8)	30 (1.5)	15 (0.8)	37 (2.1)
Alaska	278 (1.8)	32 (2.3)	68 (2.3)	30 (1.6)	7 (1.1)	4 (0.7)	19 (1.1)	20 (1.1)	43 (1.5)
Arizona	268 (1.6)	43 (1.9)	57 (1.9)	18 (1.2)	2 (0.3)	9 (0.9)	18 (1.1)	21 (1.0)	38 (1.8)
Arkansas	262 (1.5)	48 (1.8)	52 (1.8)	13 (1.0)	2 (0.4)	10 (0.8)	30 (1.6)	19 (1.0)	30 (1.4)
California	263 (1.9)	49 (2.1)	51 (2.1)	17 (1.5)	3 (0.5)	10 (0.8)	17 (0.8)	16 (1.0)	38 (1.7)
Colorado	276 (1.1)	33 (1.3)	67 (1.3)	25 (1.3)	3 (0.5)	6 (0.6)	19 (0.9)	20 (0.8)	45 (1.5)
Connecticut	280 (1.1)	30 (1.4)	70 (1.4)	31 (1.5)	5 (0.6)	5 (0.6)	19 (0.9)	17 (0.9)	51 (1.3)
Delaware	267 (0.9)	45 (1.3)	55 (1.3)	19 (1.0)	3 (0.6)	5 (0.5)	27 (1.2)	19 (0.9)	38 (1.2)
District of Columbia	233 (1.3)	80 (1.2)	20 (1.2)	5 (0.8)	1 (0.3)	7 (0.6)	28 (1.1)	18 (0.9)	33 (1.3)
Florida	264 (1.8)	46 (2.1)	54 (2.1)	17 (1.3)	2 (0.4)	8 (0.7)	23 (1.1)	18 (0.9)	40 (1.6)
Georgia	262 (1.6)	49 (2.0)	51 (2.0)	16 (1.8)	2 (0.5)	8 (0.7)	27 (1.4)	18 (1.0)	39 (2.0)
Hawaii	262 (1.0)	49 (1.5)	51 (1.5)	16 (0.9)	2 (0.4)	4 (0.5)	26 (1.1)	16 (0.8)	38 (1.0)
Indiana	276 (1.4)	32 (2.0)	68 (2.0)	24 (1.7)	3 (0.5)	7 (0.7)	30 (1.2)	21 (1.1)	36 (1.4)
Iowa	284 (1.3)	22 (1.4)	78 (1.4)	31 (1.8)	4 (0.6)	5 (0.5)	24 (1.6)	19 (0.9)	46 (1.7)
Kentucky	267 (1.1)	44 (1.6)	56 (1.6)	16 (1.2)	1 (0.3)	13 (0.8)	31 (0.9)	17 (0.8)	30 (1.3)
Louisiana	252 (1.6)	62 (2.0)	38 (2.0)	7 (1.1)	0 (0.2)	9 (0.7)	33 (1.0)	19 (0.8)	30 (1.3)
Maine	284 (1.3)	23 (1.5)	77 (1.5)	31 (1.7)	6 (0.7)	5 (0.5)	23 (0.9)	21 (1.1)	44 (1.6)
Maryland	270 (2.1)	43 (2.2)	57 (2.2)	24 (2.3)	5 (1.0)	5 (0.6)	24 (1.3)	17 (1.0)	45 (1.6)
Massachusetts	278 (1.7)	32 (2.3)	68 (2.3)	28 (1.8)	5 (0.8)	6 (0.6)	18 (1.0)	15 (0.8)	51 (1.7)
Michigan	277 (1.8)	33 (2.1)	67 (2.1)	28 (1.8)	4 (0.8)	5 (0.5)	22 (1.5)	21 (0.9)	42 (1.6)
Minnesota	284 (1.3)	25 (1.5)	75 (1.5)	34 (1.8)	6 (0.8)	3 (0.3)	21 (1.1)	19 (1.1)	50 (1.6)
Mississippi	250 (1.2)	64 (1.3)	36 (1.3)	7 (0.8)	0 (0.2)	11 (0.6)	29 (1.1)	15 (0.7)	36 (1.2)
Missouri	273 (1.4)	36 (2.0)	64 (2.0)	22 (1.4)	2 (0.5)	8 (0.6)	27 (1.0)	19 (0.9)	37 (1.6)
Montana	283 (1.3)	25 (1.7)	75 (1.7)	32 (1.5)	5 (0.5)	6 (0.8)	21 (1.1)	20 (1.2)	48 (1.5)
Nebraska	283 (1.0)	24 (1.1)	76 (1.1)	31 (1.5)	5 (0.7)	6 (0.7)	19 (1.5)	18 (1.2)	49 (2.4)
New Mexico	262 (1.2)	49 (1.6)	51 (1.6)	14 (1.1)	2 (0.3)	11 (0.9)	25 (1.1)	19 (1.0)	34 (1.3)
New York	270 (1.7)	39 (2.0)	61 (2.0)	22 (1.5)	3 (0.5)	6 (0.6)	20 (1.1)	17 (1.0)	45 (1.5)
North Carolina	268 (1.4)	44 (1.8)	56 (1.8)	20 (1.3)	3 (0.6)	7 (0.5)	24 (1.1)	20 (0.9)	40 (1.5)
North Dakota	284 (0.9)	23 (1.2)	77 (1.2)	33 (1.5)	4 (0.7)	3 (0.4)	19 (1.0)	16 (0.7)	55 (1.2)
Oregon	276 (1.5)	33 (1.7)	67 (1.7)	26 (1.6)	4 (0.7)	7 (0.6)	18 (0.9)	20 (1.0)	44 (1.7)
Rhode Island	269 (0.9)	40 (1.6)	60 (1.6)	20 (1.3)	3 (0.4)	8 (0.5)	22 (0.9)	17 (0.7)	40 (0.9)
South Carolina	261 (1.5)	52 (1.7)	48 (1.7)	14 (1.2)	2 (0.4)	9 (0.7)	28 (1.1)	17 (0.9)	37 (1.4)
Tennessee	263 (1.4)	47 (1.8)	53 (1.8)	15 (1.3)	2 (0.3)	10 (0.7)	32 (1.4)	19 (0.8)	31 (1.6)
Texas	270 (1.4)	41 (1.8)	59 (1.8)	21 (1.5)	3 (0.4)	13 (1.1)	21 (1.0)	15 (1.0)	38 (2.0)
Utah	277 (1.0)	30 (1.5)	70 (1.5)	24 (1.3)	3 (0.4)	3 (0.4)	17 (0.8)	18 (0.8)	53 (1.3)
Vermont	279 (1.0)	28 (1.7)	72 (1.7)	27 (1.4)	4 (0.6)	5 (0.5)	25 (1.1)	16 (0.9)	49 (1.4)
Virginia	270 (1.6)	42 (2.0)	58 (2.0)	21 (1.2)	3 (0.4)	8 (0.8)	26 (1.1)	16 (0.9)	42 (1.7)
Washington	276 (1.3)	33 (1.6)	67 (1.6)	26 (1.2)	4 (0.7)	6 (0.6)	16 (0.9)	21 (0.8)	46 (1.4)
West Virginia	265 (1.0)	46 (1.6)	54 (1.6)	14 (0.9)	1 (0.4)	11 (0.8)	33 (0.9)	19 (0.8)	30 (1.1)
Wisconsin	283 (1.5)	25 (2.0)	75 (2.0)	32 (2.0)	5 (0.8)	5 (0.7)	26 (1.1)	21 (0.9)	40 (1.6)
Wyoming	275 (0.9)	32 (1.2)	68 (1.2)	22 (1.0)	2 (0.6)	5 (0.5)	21 (0.9)	20 (0.8)	44 (1.2)
Outlying area									
Guam	239 (1.7)	71 (1.6)	29 (1.6)	6 (0.8)	0 —	2 (0.6)	21 (1.5)	22 (1.7)	43 (2.1)

[1] Achievement levels are in developmental status.
[2] Excludes students who responded "I don't know" to the question about education level of parents.
[3] This level denotes partial mastery of prerequisite knowledge and skills that are fundamental for proficient work at the 8th grade.
[4] This level represents solid academic performance for 8th graders. Students reaching this level have demonstrated competency over challenging subject matter, including subject-matter knowledge, application of such knowledge to real-world situations, and analytical skills appropriate to the subject matter.
[5] This level signifies superior performance.
—Data not available.

NOTE.—These test scores are from the National Assessment of Educational Progress (NAEP). Forty-four states, the District of Columbia, and one outlying area participated in the 1996 Trial State Assessment of 8th graders. Scale ranges from 0 to 500. Results are not shown for states with a school participation rate of less than 70 percent. Standard errors appear in parentheses.

SOURCE: U.S. Department of Education, National Center for Education Statistics, National Assessment of Educational Progress, *NAEP 1996 Mathematics Report Card for the Nation and the States,* prepared by Educational Testing Service. (This table was prepared August 1997.)

Table 121.—Average proficiency in mathematics content areas for 4th graders in public schools, by region and state: 1996

Region and state	Average proficiency	Percent attaining mathematics achievement levels [1]				Percent of students by highest level of education attained by parents [2]			
		Below basic	Basic or above [3]	Proficient or above [4]	Advanced or above [5]	Did not finish high school	Graduated high school	Some education after high school	Graduated college
1	2	3	4	5	6	7	8	9	10
United States	224 (1.0)	36 (1.4)	64 (1.4)	21 (1.0)	2 (0.3)	4 (0.4)	13 (0.7)	7 (0.4)	37 (1.3)
Region									
Northeast	228 (2.0)	30 (2.9)	70 (2.9)	26 (1.6)	3 (0.9)	—	—	—	—
Southeast	218 (1.9)	45 (2.9)	55 (2.9)	16 (2.4)	2 (0.8)	—	—	—	—
Central	231 (2.9)	25 (2.6)	75 (2.6)	27 (2.1)	2 (0.6)	—	—	—	—
West	220 (1.7)	42 (2.8)	58 (2.8)	18 (1.7)	2 (0.5)	—	—	—	—
State									
Alabama	212 (1.2)	52 (2.0)	48 (2.0)	11 (1.1)	1 (0.2)	7 (0.8)	19 (1.0)	9 (0.7)	35 (1.6)
Alaska	224 (1.3)	35 (2.0)	65 (2.0)	21 (1.2)	2 (0.5)	3 (0.5)	10 (0.9)	8 (0.7)	34 (1.5)
Arizona	218 (1.7)	43 (2.4)	57 (2.4)	15 (1.6)	1 (0.4)	5 (0.5)	11 (0.9)	9 (0.6)	34 (1.7)
Arkansas	216 (1.5)	46 (2.2)	54 (2.2)	13 (1.4)	1 (0.3)	6 (0.6)	20 (1.0)	9 (0.7)	31 (1.3)
California	209 (1.8)	54 (2.4)	46 (2.4)	11 (1.5)	1 (0.4)	4 (0.6)	9 (0.7)	7 (0.6)	32 (1.4)
Colorado	226 (1.0)	33 (1.6)	67 (1.6)	22 (1.3)	2 (0.3)	3 (0.4)	10 (0.7)	10 (0.6)	42 (1.6)
Connecticut	232 (1.1)	25 (1.5)	75 (1.5)	31 (1.7)	3 (0.5)	3 (0.4)	9 (0.6)	8 (0.6)	47 (1.3)
Delaware	215 (0.6)	46 (1.1)	54 (1.1)	16 (1.2)	1 (0.4)	3 (0.4)	13 (0.8)	8 (0.7)	37 (1.0)
District of Columbia	187 (1.1)	80 (0.8)	20 (0.8)	5 (0.5)	1 (0.4)	4 (0.4)	15 (0.6)	6 (0.4)	42 (1.0)
Florida	216 (1.2)	45 (1.7)	55 (1.7)	15 (1.1)	1 (0.2)	4 (0.6)	12 (1.0)	7 (0.6)	38 (1.5)
Georgia	215 (1.5)	47 (2.1)	53 (2.1)	13 (1.3)	1 (0.3)	6 (0.6)	17 (0.9)	7 (0.6)	36 (1.6)
Hawaii	215 (1.1)	47 (1.6)	53 (1.6)	16 (1.1)	2 (0.4)	2 (0.3)	12 (0.7)	6 (0.5)	39 (1.2)
Indiana	229 (1.0)	28 (1.7)	72 (1.7)	24 (1.6)	2 (0.5)	4 (0.4)	19 (1.0)	9 (0.9)	37 (1.8)
Iowa	229 (1.1)	26 (1.4)	74 (1.4)	22 (1.4)	1 (0.4)	3 (0.4)	16 (0.9)	9 (0.7)	36 (1.7)
Kentucky	220 (1.1)	40 (1.8)	60 (1.8)	16 (1.1)	1 (0.3)	9 (0.9)	19 (1.1)	8 (0.7)	31 (1.2)
Louisiana	209 (1.1)	56 (1.8)	44 (1.8)	8 (0.9)	0 (0.2)	6 (0.6)	19 (1.1)	9 (0.7)	35 (1.4)
Maine	232 (1.0)	25 (1.4)	75 (1.4)	27 (1.4)	3 (0.6)	3 (0.4)	13 (0.9)	9 (0.6)	39 (1.8)
Maryland	221 (1.6)	41 (1.8)	59 (1.8)	22 (1.7)	3 (0.7)	3 (0.4)	13 (0.9)	7 (0.6)	45 (1.6)
Massachusetts	229 (1.4)	29 (1.8)	71 (1.8)	24 (1.9)	2 (0.5)	2 (0.3)	10 (0.7)	8 (0.6)	48 (1.9)
Michigan	226 (1.3)	32 (1.8)	68 (1.8)	23 (1.5)	2 (0.5)	4 (0.5)	14 (1.0)	8 (0.7)	38 (1.5)
Minnesota	232 (1.1)	24 (1.5)	76 (1.5)	29 (1.5)	3 (0.5)	2 (0.3)	11 (0.8)	7 (0.6)	42 (1.5)
Mississippi	208 (1.2)	58 (1.9)	42 (1.9)	8 (0.9)	0 (0.2)	7 (0.6)	19 (1.0)	7 (0.5)	35 (1.3)
Missouri	225 (1.1)	34 (1.7)	66 (1.7)	20 (1.3)	1 (0.3)	4 (0.5)	16 (0.9)	9 (0.7)	36 (1.6)
Montana	228 (1.2)	29 (1.9)	71 (1.9)	22 (1.6)	1 (0.4)	3 (0.4)	11 (0.8)	11 (0.8)	40 (1.5)
Nebraska	228 (1.2)	30 (1.6)	70 (1.6)	24 (1.4)	2 (0.3)	3 (0.4)	13 (0.9)	9 (0.7)	41 (1.2)
Nevada	218 (1.3)	43 (1.8)	57 (1.8)	14 (1.2)	1 (0.3)	4 (0.6)	12 (0.7)	8 (0.6)	34 (1.2)
New Jersey	227 (1.5)	32 (2.1)	68 (2.1)	25 (1.7)	3 (0.7)	3 (0.5)	12 (1.1)	7 (0.6)	46 (2.0)
New Mexico	214 (1.4)	49 (2.4)	51 (2.4)	13 (1.2)	1 (0.3)	6 (0.6)	15 (1.0)	11 (0.9)	35 (1.3)
New York	223 (1.2)	36 (1.8)	64 (1.8)	20 (1.2)	2 (0.4)	4 (0.4)	10 (0.8)	6 (0.6)	43 (1.6)
North Carolina	224 (1.2)	36 (1.6)	64 (1.6)	21 (1.3)	2 (0.4)	5 (0.6)	12 (0.8)	7 (0.6)	42 (1.7)
North Dakota	231 (1.2)	25 (1.9)	75 (1.9)	24 (1.3)	2 (0.5)	2 (0.3)	11 (0.7)	8 (0.8)	47 (1.4)
Oregon	223 (1.4)	35 (2.2)	65 (2.2)	21 (1.3)	2 (0.5)	4 (0.5)	11 (0.8)	7 (0.5)	38 (1.5)
Pennsylvania	226 (1.2)	32 (1.8)	68 (1.8)	20 (1.5)	1 (0.3)	—	—	—	—
Rhode Island	220 (1.4)	39 (2.0)	61 (2.0)	17 (1.3)	1 (0.3)	5 (0.4)	12 (0.9)	7 (0.5)	40 (1.3)
South Carolina	213 (1.3)	52 (1.8)	48 (2.0)	12 (1.3)	1 (0.3)	5 (0.5)	16 (1.0)	7 (0.8)	38 (1.2)
Tennessee	219 (1.4)	42 (2.0)	58 (2.0)	17 (1.5)	1 (0.3)	6 (0.6)	19 (0.9)	8 (0.7)	36 (1.6)
Texas	229 (1.4)	31 (1.9)	69 (1.9)	25 (1.5)	3 (0.5)	6 (0.5)	11 (0.8)	7 (0.5)	38 (1.6)
Utah	227 (1.2)	31 (1.6)	69 (1.6)	23 (1.3)	2 (0.4)	2 (0.3)	10 (0.7)	8 (0.6)	41 (1.7)
Vermont	225 (1.2)	33 (2.1)	67 (2.1)	23 (1.1)	3 (0.5)	3 (0.4)	12 (0.9)	7 (0.7)	44 (1.4)
Virginia	223 (1.4)	38 (2.2)	62 (2.2)	19 (1.5)	2 (0.5)	5 (0.7)	15 (1.0)	7 (0.7)	41 (1.8)
Washington	225 (1.2)	33 (1.8)	67 (1.8)	21 (1.2)	1 (0.2)	2 (0.3)	9 (0.7)	8 (0.6)	38 (1.5)
West Virginia	223 (1.0)	37 (1.6)	63 (1.6)	19 (1.2)	2 (0.5)	7 (0.7)	21 (0.9)	9 (0.7)	35 (1.4)
Wisconsin	231 (1.0)	26 (1.2)	74 (1.2)	27 (1.3)	3 (0.6)	2 (0.5)	13 (1.0)	8 (0.8)	38 (1.6)
Wyoming	223 (1.4)	36 (1.7)	64 (1.7)	19 (1.2)	1 (0.3)	4 (0.5)	12 (0.7)	8 (0.5)	38 (1.2)
Outlying area									
Guam	188 (1.3)	77 (1.4)	23 (1.4)	3 (0.5)	0 —	5 (0.7)	14 (1.0)	5 (0.6)	36 (1.4)

[1] Achievement levels are in developmental status.
[2] Excludes students who responded "I don't know" to the question about educational level of parents.
[3] This level denotes partial mastery of prerequisite knowledge and skills that are fundamental for proficient work at the 4th grade.
[4] This level represents solid academic mastery for 4th graders. Students reaching this level have demonstrated competency over challenging subject matter, including subject-matter knowledge, application of such knowledge to real-world situations, and analytical skills appropriate to the subject matter.
[5] This level signifies superior performance.
—Data not available.

NOTE.—These test scores are from the National Assessment of Educational Progress (NAEP). Forty-seven states, the District of Columbia, and Guam participated in the 1996 Trial State Assessment of 4th graders. Scale ranges from 0 to 500. Results are not shown for states with a school participation rate of less than 70 percent. Standard errors appear in parentheses.

SOURCE: U.S. Department of Education, National Center for Education Statistics, National Assessment of Educational Progress, *NAEP 1996 Mathematics Report Card for the Nation and the States,* prepared by Educational Testing Service. (This table was prepared August 1997.)

Table 122.—Selected characteristics of 8th grade students in public schools, by region and state: 1992[1]

Region and state	Math units required for graduation	Year of revision of state guides with NCTM standards[2]	Length of school year		Passing test in math required for graduation in 1993	Percent of students with 4 or more hours of math instruction each week	Percent of students reporting					
			1989	1992			Spending 30 minutes or more on math homework each day	Spending 1 or 2 hours on all homework each day	Spending more than 2 hours on all homework each day	Positive attitudes towards math[3]	Both parents living at home	Watching 6 or more hours of television each day
1	2	3	4	5	6	7	8	9	10	11	12	13
United States	—	—	—	—	—	32	64	59	8	59	75	13
Region												
Northeast	—	—	—	—	—	35	59	62	8	56	75	14
Southeast	—	—	—	—	—	37	65	56	7	59	71	17
Central	—	—	—	—	—	24	63	65	6	63	79	11
West	—	—	—	—	—	30	68	56	10	56	75	12
State												
Alabama	2	1989	175	175	Yes	60	65	59	7	62	72	20
Alaska	2	Devel.,1994	—	180	No	—	—	—	—	—	—	—
Arizona	2	1992	175	175	No	34	65	56	5	54	76	9
Arkansas	3	1993	178	178	No	42	61	56	7	60	75	20
California	2	1991	180	180	No	43	67	63	10	56	74	10
Colorado	([4])	1994	180	([5])	No	27	65	61	7	58	77	7
Connecticut	3	Devel.,1995	180	180	No	21	61	70	9	59	79	11
Delaware	2	Devel.,1994	180	180	No	30	57	62	5	63	73	17
District of Columbia	3	1993	190	180	No	52	63	63	10	73	45	31
Florida	3	Devel.,1994	180	180	Yes	40	62	57	7	61	71	15
Georgia	3	1992	180	180	Yes	56	65	59	7	66	71	18
Hawaii	3	Devel.,1994	183	180	Yes	34	68	55	11	54	75	22
Idaho	2	1994	180	180	No	28	63	57	5	56	83	7
Illinois	2	Devel.,1994	180	180	No	—	—	—	—	—	—	—
Indiana	2	1991	180	180	No	32	62	60	6	61	78	9
Iowa	([4])	1987	180	180	No	20	61	63	4	63	83	7
Kansas	2	1991	—	180	No	—	—	—	—	—	—	—
Kentucky	3	1993	175	175	No	47	61	54	6	57	78	13
Louisiana	3	Devel.,1994	180	180	Yes	54	62	61	10	63	71	20
Maine	2	Devel.,1994	—	175	No	12	66	70	8	61	81	8
Maryland	3	1985	180	180	Yes	45	60	65	7	61	73	17
Massachusetts	([4])	1994	—	180	No	28	67	70	9	57	77	8
Michigan	3	Devel.,1994	180	180	Yes	39	67	61	7	60	75	13
Minnesota	1	Devel.,1994	175	175	No	41	64	59	5	57	85	5
Mississippi	2	1993	—	180	Yes	60	68	60	8	67	70	21
Missouri	2	1990	—	174	No	44	66	60	6	60	77	12
Montana	2	Devel.,1995	180	180	No	—	—	—	—	—	—	—
Nebraska	([4])	Devel.,1994	([5])	([5])	No	25	69	61	5	60	81	8
Nevada	2	1993	—	180	Yes	—	—	—	—	—	—	—
New Hampshire	2	1993	180	180	No	38	62	68	9	58	81	7
New Jersey	3	1993	180	180	Yes	28	62	68	10	62	78	13
New Mexico	3	1992	180	180	Yes	26	65	56	7	56	75	11
New York	2	Devel.,1994	180	180	Yes	20	54	66	9	62	75	15
North Carolina	2	1992	180	180	Yes	52	64	64	7	65	73	16
North Dakota	2	1993	180	180	No	44	70	63	6	55	85	5
Ohio	2	1990	182	182	Yes	26	62	62	6	62	74	12
Oklahoma	2	1993	175	175	No	37	69	59	7	58	78	11
Oregon	2	Devel.,1994	175	([5])	No	—	—	—	—	—	—	—
Pennsylvania	3	none	180	180	No	24	58	63	4	59	79	9
Rhode Island	2	Devel.,1994	180	180	No	43	62	67	7	56	78	9
South Carolina	3	1993	—	180	Yes	59	61	61	7	70	73	17
South Dakota	2	Devel.,1995	—	175	No	—	—	—	—	—	—	—
Tennessee	2	1991	—	180	Yes	60	67	62	6	58	73	14
Texas	3	1991	175	175	Yes	38	67	57	8	61	75	12
Utah	2	1993	—	180	No	28	62	56	5	55	85	5
Vermont	([6])	Devel.,1994	—	175	No	—	—	—	—	—	—	—
Virginia	2	1988	180	180	Yes	38	65	63	7	63	77	15
Washington	2	Devel.,1994	—	180	No	—	—	—	—	—	—	—
West Virginia	2	1992	180	180	Yes	40	57	55	5	58	78	13
Wisconsin	2	Devel.,1995	180	180	No	32	59	61	5	59	80	8
Wyoming	([4])	1990	175	175	No	24	60	55	5	58	81	8
Outlying areas												
Guam	—	—	—	—	—	28	68	47	12	50	79	20
Virgin Islands	—	—	—	180	—	31	61	47	11	75	56	32

[1] Data are for 1992 unless otherwise specified.
[2] Standards recommended by the National Council of Teachers of Mathematics.
[3] Percent of students agreeing or strongly agreeing with positive statements about mathematics.
[4] Local board determines.
[5] No statewide policy.
[6] 5 units of math and science combined.

—Data not available or not applicable.

SOURCE: U.S. Department of Education, National Center for Education Statistics, National Assessment of Educational Progress, *The State of Mathematics Achievement*, by Educational Testing Service; and Council of Chief State School Officers, *State Education Indicators*. (This table was prepared June 1994.)

Table 123.— Mathematics proficiency of 17-year-olds, by highest mathematics course taken, sex, and race/ethnicity: 1978, 1990, 1992, 1994, and 1996

Year, sex, and race/ethnicity	Percent of students	Average proficiency by highest mathematics course taken						Percent of students at or above			
		All areas	Prealgebra or general mathematics	Algebra I	Geometry	Algebra II	Precalculus or calculus	200[1]	250[2]	300[3]	350[4]
1	2	3	4	5	6	7	8	9	10	11	12
1978											
Total	100.0	300.4	267	286	307	321	334	99.8	92.0	51.5	7.3
Male	48.7	303.8	269	289	310	325	337	99.9	93.0	55.1	9.5
Female	51.3	297.1	265	284	304	318	329	99.7	91.0	48.2	5.2
White	83.1	305.9	272	291	310	325	338	100.0	95.6	57.6	8.5
Black	11.8	268.4	247	264	281	292	297	98.8	70.7	16.8	0.5
Hispanic	4.0	276.3	256	273	294	303	306	99.3	78.3	23.4	1.4
Other[5]	1.1	312.9	—	—	—	—	—	100.0	94.5	64.7	15.4
1990											
Total	100.0	304.6	273	288	299	319	344	100.0	96.0	56.1	7.2
Male	48.6	306.3	274	291	302	323	347	99.9	95.8	57.6	8.8
Female	51.4	302.9	271	285	296	316	341	100.0	96.2	54.7	5.6
White	73.3	309.5	277	292	304	323	347	100.0	97.6	63.2	8.3
Black	15.6	288.5	264	278	285	302	329	99.9	92.4	32.8	2.0
Hispanic	6.9	283.5	259	278	286	306	323	99.6	85.8	30.1	1.9
Other[5]	4.2	312.5	—	—	—	—	—	100.0	97.9	61.6	15.9
1992											
Total	100.0	306.7	271	289	302	320	343	100.0	96.6	59.1	7.2
Male	50.7	308.9	275	291	306	323	344	100.0	96.9	60.5	9.1
Female	49.3	304.5	267	287	297	317	341	100.0	96.3	57.7	5.2
White	74.7	311.9	276	293	306	323	347	100.0	98.3	66.4	8.7
Black	14.8	285.8	256	279	283	301	313	100.0	89.6	29.8	0.9
Hispanic	7.4	292.2	269	285	297	312	320	100.0	94.1	39.2	1.2
Other[5]	3.1	317.1	—	—	—	—	—	100.0	96.5	69.8	16.9
1994											
Total	100.0	306.2	272	288	297	316	340	100.0	96.5	58.6	7.4
Male	49.5	308.5	274	289	301	320	343	100.0	97.3	60.2	9.3
Female	50.5	304.1	268	286	293	313	337	100.0	96.0	57.2	5.5
White	72.5	312.3	275	292	301	320	344	100.0	98.4	67.0	9.4
Black	15.5	285.5	—	275	283	297	—	100.0	90.6	29.8	0.4
Hispanic	8.8	290.8	—	—	—	304	—	100.0	91.8	38.3	1.4
Other[5]	3.2	312.7	—	—	—	—	—	100.0	97.0	66.4	12.1
1996											
Total	100.0	307.2	269	283	298	316	339	100.0	96.8	60.4	7.4
Male	49.5	309.5	272	287	302	320	342	100.0	97.0	62.7	9.5
Female	50.5	304.9	265	278	294	313	335	100.0	96.7	57.6	5.3
White	71.0	313.4	273	287	304	320	342	100.0	98.7	68.7	9.2
Black	15.0	286.4	—	273	280	299	—	100.0	90.6	31.2	0.9
Hispanic	9.0	292.0	—	—	—	306	—	99.9	92.2	40.1	1.8
Other[5]	5.0	—	—	—	—	—	—	100.0	97.4	63.5	13.7

[1] Indicates ability to perform simple additive reasoning and problem solving.
[2] Indicates ability to perform simple multiplicative reasoning and 2-step problem solving.
[3] Indicates ability to perform reasoning and problem solving involving fractions, decimals, percents, elementary geometry, and simple algebra.
[4] Indicates ability to perform reasoning and problem solving involving geometry, algebra, and beginning statistics and probability.
[5] Includes Asian/Pacific Islanders and American Indians/Alaskan Natives.

—Data not available.

NOTE.—These test scores are from the National Assessment of Educational Progress (NAEP). Scale ranges from 0 to 500.

SOURCE: U.S. Department of Education, National Center for Education Statistics, National Assessment of Educational Progress, *NAEP 1996 Trends in Academic Progress*, prepared by Educational Testing Service. (This table was prepared September 1997.)

Table 124.—Percent of students at or above selected science proficiency levels,[1] by sex, race/ethnicity, control of school, and age: 1977 to 1996

Sex, race/ethnicity, control, and year	9-year-olds[2]				13-year-olds[3]				17-year-olds[3]			
	Know everyday science facts[4]	Understand simple scientific principles[5]	Apply general scientific information[6]	Analyze scientific procedures and data[7]	Understand simple scientific principles[5]	Apply general scientific information[6]	Analyze scientific procedures and data[7]	Integrate specialized scientific information[8]	Understand simple scientific principles[5]	Apply general scientific information[6]	Analyze scientific procedures and data[7]	Integrate specialized scientific information[8]
1	2	3	4	5	6	7	8	9	10	11	12	13
Total												
1977	93.5 (0.6)	68.0 (1.1)	25.7 (0.7)	3.2 (0.3)	86.0 (0.7)	48.8 (1.1)	11.1 (0.5)	0.7 (0.1)	97.1 (0.2)	81.6 (0.7)	41.7 (0.9)	8.5 (0.4)
1982	95.2 (0.7)	70.7 (1.9)	24.3 (1.8)	2.3 (0.7)	89.8 (0.8)	50.9 (1.6)	9.6 (0.7)	0.4 (0.1)	95.7 (0.5)	76.6 (1.0)	37.3 (0.9)	7.1 (0.4)
1986	96.2 (0.5)	72.0 (1.1)	27.5 (1.4)	3.0 (0.5)	91.6 (1.0)	52.5 (1.6)	9.1 (0.9)	0.2 (0.1)	97.1 (0.5)	80.7 (1.3)	41.3 (1.4)	7.9 (0.7)
1990	97.0 (0.3)	76.4 (0.9)	31.1 (0.8)	3.1 (0.3)	92.3 (0.7)	56.5 (1.0)	11.2 (0.6)	0.4 (0.1)	96.7 (0.3)	81.2 (0.9)	43.3 (1.3)	9.2 (0.5)
1992	97.4 (0.3)	78.0 (1.2)	32.8 (1.0)	3.4 (0.3)	93.1 (0.5)	61.3 (1.1)	12.0 (0.8)	0.2 (0.1)	97.8 (0.5)	83.3 (1.2)	46.6 (1.5)	10.1 (0.7)
1994	97.2 (0.4)	77.4 (1.0)	33.7 (1.2)	3.8 (0.4)	92.4 (0.6)	59.5 (1.1)	11.8 (0.9)	0.2 (0.1)	97.1 (0.7)	83.1 (1.2)	47.5 (1.3)	10.0 (0.8)
1996	96.8 (0.5)	76.0 (1.0)	32.4 (1.2)	4.4 (0.5)	92.2 (0.6)	57.7 (1.2)	12.3 (0.8)	0.4 (0.2)	97.8 (0.3)	83.6 (0.9)	48.5 (1.3)	10.8 (0.9)
Male												
1977	94.3 (0.5)	69.5 (1.2)	27.4 (0.9)	3.7 (0.3)	87.2 (0.8)	52.3 (1.3)	13.1 (0.6)	0.9 (0.2)	97.8 (0.2)	85.2 (0.7)	48.8 (1.1)	11.8 (0.6)
1982	95.0 (1.0)	69.7 (2.0)	25.6 (2.6)	2.5 (1.0)	91.9 (0.8)	56.2 (1.8)	12.6 (1.1)	0.5 (0.2)	96.8 (0.5)	81.2 (1.2)	45.2 (1.2)	10.4 (0.8)
1986	96.8 (0.5)	74.1 (1.4)	29.9 (2.0)	3.8 (0.6)	92.9 (1.0)	57.3 (2.1)	11.9 (1.3)	0.3 (0.2)	97.4 (0.7)	82.4 (1.4)	48.8 (2.1)	11.4 (1.3)
1990	96.8 (0.5)	76.3 (1.2)	33.1 (1.1)	4.2 (0.6)	92.7 (0.8)	59.8 (1.3)	14.0 (0.9)	0.6 (0.2)	96.8 (0.5)	82.5 (1.2)	48.2 (1.6)	13.0 (0.8)
1992	97.7 (0.3)	80.4 (1.4)	37.2 (1.7)	4.6 (0.6)	93.1 (0.8)	62.9 (1.4)	14.2 (1.1)	0.3 (0.1)	98.0 (0.6)	85.0 (1.4)	50.9 (2.0)	13.6 (1.0)
1994	97.1 (0.4)	77.6 (0.9)	35.3 (1.4)	4.5 (0.7)	92.2 (0.8)	62.0 (1.3)	14.8 (1.1)	0.3 (0.2)	97.1 (0.6)	84.9 (1.3)	52.9 (1.8)	13.8 (1.2)
1996	96.9 (0.5)	77.0 (1.7)	34.4 (1.8)	5.4 (0.8)	93.2 (0.9)	61.9 (1.4)	15.7 (0.8)	0.7 (0.3)	97.6 (0.5)	83.9 (1.1)	53.3 (1.7)	14.3 (1.5)
Female												
1977	92.8 (0.7)	66.5 (1.1)	24.0 (0.9)	2.6 (0.3)	84.7 (0.8)	45.4 (1.2)	9.0 (0.5)	0.4 (0.1)	96.4 (0.3)	78.0 (1.0)	34.8 (1.0)	5.3 (0.4)
1982	95.5 (1.2)	71.8 (2.2)	23.0 (2.0)	2.1 (0.6)	87.9 (1.0)	46.0 (1.6)	6.9 (0.7)	0.2 (0.1)	94.6 (0.8)	72.2 (1.3)	29.9 (1.2)	3.9 (0.4)
1986	95.6 (0.6)	70.0 (1.3)	25.1 (1.4)	2.2 (0.5)	90.3 (1.2)	47.7 (1.7)	6.3 (1.1)	0.1 (0.1)	96.9 (0.5)	79.1 (1.7)	34.1 (1.5)	4.5 (0.8)
1990	97.1 (0.4)	76.4 (1.1)	29.1 (1.0)	2.0 (0.3)	92.0 (0.8)	53.3 (1.4)	8.5 (0.6)	0.2 —	96.6 (0.6)	79.9 (1.4)	38.7 (1.7)	5.5 (0.5)
1992	97.1 (0.4)	75.7 (1.2)	28.6 (1.1)	2.2 (0.3)	93.1 (0.7)	59.6 (1.4)	9.9 (0.8)	0.1 —	97.5 (0.7)	81.6 (1.4)	42.0 (1.7)	6.6 (1.0)
1994	97.3 (0.5)	77.2 (1.4)	32.2 (1.5)	3.2 (0.4)	92.6 (0.6)	57.1 (1.4)	8.8 (1.0)	0.1 —	97.2 (1.0)	81.6 (1.6)	42.4 (1.8)	6.4 (0.6)
1996	96.6 (0.6)	75.0 (0.9)	30.5 (1.8)	3.5 (0.6)	91.1 (0.9)	53.8 (1.7)	9.1 (0.8)	0.2 —	98.0 (0.5)	83.4 (1.2)	43.9 (1.9)	7.4 (0.9)
White, non-Hispanic												
1977	97.7 (0.3)	76.8 (0.7)	30.8 (0.7)	3.9 (0.3)	92.2 (0.5)	56.5 (0.9)	13.4 (0.5)	0.8 (0.1)	99.2 (0.1)	88.2 (0.4)	47.5 (0.7)	10.0 (0.4)
1982	98.3 (0.4)	78.4 (2.0)	29.4 (2.1)	2.9 (0.9)	94.4 (0.6)	58.3 (1.4)	11.5 (0.8)	0.4 (0.1)	98.6 (0.2)	84.9 (0.9)	43.9 (1.1)	8.6 (0.6)
1986	98.2 (0.3)	78.9 (1.0)	32.7 (1.5)	3.8 (0.6)	96.1 (0.8)	61.0 (1.7)	11.3 (1.2)	0.3 (0.1)	98.8 (0.3)	87.8 (1.4)	48.7 (1.7)	9.6 (0.9)
1990	99.2 (0.2)	84.4 (0.7)	37.5 (1.1)	3.9 (0.4)	96.9 (0.4)	66.5 (1.2)	14.2 (0.8)	0.5 (0.1)	99.0 (0.2)	89.6 (0.8)	51.2 (1.5)	11.4 (0.7)
1992	99.2 (0.1)	85.5 (0.9)	39.4 (1.1)	4.3 (0.4)	97.9 (0.4)	71.1 (1.3)	15.0 (1.0)	0.3 (0.1)	99.3 (0.3)	90.5 (1.0)	55.4 (1.7)	12.8 (0.9)
1994	99.1 (0.3)	85.6 (1.0)	40.8 (1.5)	4.9 (0.6)	97.6 (0.4)	70.5 (1.1)	14.8 (1.0)	0.3 (0.1)	99.3 (0.3)	91.5 (0.9)	57.5 (1.6)	13.2 (1.1)
1996	98.7 (0.4)	83.9 (1.1)	39.9 (1.5)	6.0 (0.7)	97.2 (0.5)	68.7 (1.4)	15.9 (0.9)	0.6 (0.3)	99.4 (0.3)	91.3 (0.6)	58.7 (1.6)	14.0 (1.3)
Black, non-Hispanic												
1977	72.4 (1.8)	27.2 (1.5)	3.5 (0.6)	0.2 —	57.3 (2.4)	14.9 (1.7)	1.2 (0.4)	0.0 —	83.6 (1.3)	40.5 (1.5)	7.7 (1.0)	0.4 (0.2)
1982	82.1 (3.0)	38.9 (2.7)	3.9 (1.3)	0.1 —	68.6 (2.4)	17.1 (1.9)	0.8 (0.3)	0.0 —	79.7 (1.9)	35.0 (2.1)	6.5 (1.1)	0.2 (0.2)
1986	88.6 (1.4)	46.2 (2.3)	8.3 (1.5)	0.3 —	73.6 (3.0)	19.6 (2.8)	1.1 (0.4)	0.0 —	90.9 (2.1)	52.2 (3.2)	12.5 (2.2)	0.9 (0.6)
1990	88.0 (1.3)	46.4 (3.1)	8.5 (1.1)	0.1 —	77.6 (3.6)	24.3 (3.3)	1.5 (0.5)	0.1 —	88.3 (1.9)	51.4 (3.7)	15.7 (4.0)	1.5 (0.8)
1992	90.7 (1.8)	51.3 (3.5)	9.2 (1.4)	0.3 —	73.8 (2.8)	26.2 (2.8)	1.8 (0.8)	0.0 —	92.1 (1.8)	55.7 (3.7)	14.1 (2.5)	0.8 —
1994	91.0 (1.5)	51.6 (2.3)	11.1 (1.4)	0.2 —	73.5 (3.2)	22.4 (4.3)	2.2 —	0.0 —	91.1 (1.9)	58.1 (3.7)	15.4 (2.3)	0.5 (0.3)
1996	90.7 (1.5)	51.3 (3.0)	10.6 (1.9)	0.3 —	76.3 (2.7)	25.3 (2.1)	2.0 (0.9)	0.0 —	92.7 (1.4)	59.0 (3.4)	17.2 (2.1)	0.9 (0.5)
Hispanic												
1977	84.6 (1.8)	42.0 (3.1)	8.8 (1.7)	0.3 —	62.2 (2.4)	18.1 (1.8)	1.8 (0.8)	0.0 —	93.1 (1.7)	61.5 (1.7)	18.5 (2.1)	1.8 (0.6)
1982	85.1 (3.1)	40.2 (6.1)	4.2 (2.7)	0.0 —	75.5 (3.3)	24.1 (5.1)	2.4 (0.9)	0.0 —	86.9 (2.9)	48.0 (2.7)	11.1 (2.0)	1.4 (0.9)
1986	89.6 (2.4)	50.1 (3.7)	10.7 (2.4)	0.2 —	76.7 (3.2)	24.9 (4.3)	1.5 (0.7)	0.0 —	93.3 (2.4)	60.0 (7.2)	14.8 (2.9)	1.1 (0.7)
1990	93.6 (1.5)	56.3 (3.7)	11.6 (2.1)	0.4 —	80.2 (2.9)	30.0 (2.8)	3.3 (0.8)	0.1 —	91.9 (2.2)	59.9 (5.0)	21.1 (3.3)	2.1 —
1992	92.4 (1.7)	55.5 (4.3)	11.7 (1.8)	0.4 —	86.2 (2.6)	36.5 (2.9)	3.3 (1.3)	0.0 —	94.6 (2.6)	68.3 (6.6)	23.0 (3.8)	2.5 (1.2)
1994	91.1 (2.3)	49.9 (3.1)	10.8 (2.5)	0.7 (0.5)	81.2 (2.5)	31.6 (3.3)	2.4 (0.9)	0.0 —	89.9 (3.3)	58.6 (7.4)	21.7 (4.1)	1.5 (0.7)
1996	92.5 (1.8)	57.1 (2.5)	12.7 (2.9)	0.3 —	80.9 (2.3)	30.7 (3.3)	3.2 (0.8)	0.0 —	93.8 (2.1)	66.2 (4.0)	24.0 (3.1)	2.8 (1.3)
Public												
1977	93.0 (0.7)	66.4 (1.3)	24.5 (0.9)	2.9 (0.3)	84.9 (0.8)	46.7 (1.2)	10.2 (0.5)	0.6 (0.1)	97.0 (0.2)	80.8 (0.7)	40.5 (0.8)	8.1 (0.4)
1982	94.9 (0.8)	69.5 (2.1)	23.9 (2.1)	2.3 (0.7)	89.2 (0.9)	49.2 (1.8)	8.9 (0.8)	0.3 (0.1)	95.4 (0.6)	75.8 (1.0)	36.6 (0.9)	6.9 (0.4)
1986	95.8 (0.4)	70.5 (1.3)	26.3 (1.5)	2.8 (0.6)	91.3 (1.0)	51.9 (1.7)	8.9 (0.9)	0.2 (0.1)	97.0 (0.5)	80.1 (1.4)	39.9 (1.5)	7.2 (0.7)
1990	96.7 (0.4)	75.5 (1.0)	30.3 (0.8)	3.0 (0.4)	91.6 (0.8)	54.7 (1.2)	10.7 (0.7)	0.4 (0.1)	96.5 (0.4)	80.4 (0.9)	42.0 (1.3)	8.7 (0.5)
1992	97.1 (0.4)	76.7 (1.3)	31.5 (1.0)	3.2 (0.3)	92.7 (0.5)	60.2 (1.2)	11.9 (0.9)	0.3 (0.1)	97.5 (0.5)	82.0 (1.2)	44.8 (1.5)	9.6 (0.8)
1994	96.9 (0.4)	76.1 (1.2)	32.5 (1.4)	3.6 (0.5)	91.9 (0.6)	57.8 (1.2)	11.3 (0.9)	0.2 (0.1)	96.8 (0.7)	81.7 (1.3)	45.3 (1.1)	9.4 (0.5)
1996	96.7 (0.5)	75.1 (1.2)	31.1 (1.3)	4.2 (0.4)	91.6 (0.7)	56.1 (1.3)	11.5 (0.8)	0.4 (0.2)	97.7 (0.3)	83.1 (1.1)	47.8 (1.4)	10.7 (1.0)
Private												
1977	98.1 (0.6)	80.3 (1.7)	35.6 (1.9)	5.1 (1.1)	95.7 (1.0)	68.8 (2.6)	19.6 (1.9)	1.6 (0.3)	99.5 (0.2)	92.9 (1.2)	58.9 (2.8)	14.8 (1.9)
1982	98.9 —	82.6 (3.5)	28.2 (5.6)	2.1 (1.2)	95.0 (1.5)	65.8 (4.1)	16.0 (2.4)	0.8 (0.5)	97.9 (0.7)	83.5 (2.8)	44.2 (2.6)	8.5 (2.3)
1986	98.2 (0.7)	79.7 (2.3)	33.8 (2.8)	4.0 (0.7)	97.3 (1.8)	66.8 (8.2)	12.8 (3.6)	0.3 —	99.8 —	96.5 (2.2)	74.6 (10.9)	23.1 (7.7)
1990	98.7 —	83.6 (2.4)	37.2 (3.0)	3.9 (1.0)	98.4 (0.8)	72.0 (2.6)	16.2 (1.5)	0.5 —	99.5 —	90.6 (4.1)	59.8 (6.7)	15.8 (3.2)
1992	99.2 —	86.2 (2.0)	40.6 (3.4)	4.6 (1.3)	96.4 (1.1)	68.9 (3.1)	13.2 (2.0)	0.1 —	100.0 —	95.5 (2.0)	63.1 (5.3)	14.1 (2.7)
1994	99.3 (0.4)	87.1 (2.4)	42.7 (2.8)	5.6 (1.0)	96.5 (1.4)	72.7 (3.2)	15.5 (2.6)	0.1 —	99.3 (0.4)	93.1 (2.3)	62.7 (5.2)	14.8 (4.0)
1996	97.2 (1.3)	81.3 (3.2)	40.6 (3.6)	6.4 (1.9)	96.2 (2.1)	70.9 (5.2)	18.5 (3.2)	1.0 —	98.8 —	89.6 (3.2)	56.5 (6.4)	12.6 (3.2)

[1] As measured by the National Assessment of Educational Progress (NAEP).
[2] Virtually no students were able to integrate specialized scientific information.
[3] Virtually all students knew everyday science facts. Data exclude persons not enrolled in school.
[4] Scale score of 150 or above.
[5] Scale score of 200 or above.
[6] Scale score of 250 or above.
[7] Scale score of 300 or above.
[8] Scale score of 350 or above.
—Data not available or not applicable.

NOTE.—Standard errors appear in parentheses.

SOURCE: U.S. Department of Education, National Assessment of Educational Progress, *NAEP 1996 Trends in Academic Progress*, prepared by Educational Testing Service. (This table was prepared September 1997.)

Table 125.—Average proficiency in science for 8th graders in public schools, by selected characteristics and state: 1996

State	Average	Race/ethnicity					Sex		Parental education[1]			
		White	Black	Hispanic	Asian	American Indian	Male	Female	Did not finish high school	Graduated high school	Some education after high school	Graduated college
1	2	3	4	5	6	7	8	9	10	11	12	13
United States	148	159	120	127	150	148	149	148	131	140	155	157
State												
Alabama	139	151	117	107	(2)	(2)	138	139	130	129	145	147
Alaska[3]	153	162	(2)	137	152	129	155	150	(2)	141	155	163
Arizona	145	157	124	129	(2)	121	147	143	121	136	151	158
Arkansas[3]	144	154	116	122	(2)	(2)	147	142	129	136	150	154
California	138	156	121	121	148	(2)	140	136	118	129	144	153
Colorado	155	162	142	135	155	142	156	153	133	142	157	163
Connecticut	155	165	121	122	163	(2)	156	155	129	140	155	167
Delaware	142	152	122	116	(2)	(2)	143	140	121	135	146	151
District of Columbia	113	(2)	112	98	(2)	(2)	113	113	106	107	120	121
Florida	142	155	119	129	(2)	(2)	144	140	127	132	148	150
Georgia	142	155	122	128	(2)	(2)	144	139	127	129	145	153
Hawaii	135	146	128	121	138	(2)	135	135	119	120	139	147
Indiana	153	158	125	139	(2)	(2)	154	152	139	144	156	162
Iowa[3]	158	160	131	140	(2)	(2)	159	157	141	150	160	165
Kentucky	147	151	127	113	(2)	(2)	148	147	130	143	151	158
Louisiana	132	148	113	104	(2)	(2)	136	129	123	128	141	136
Maine	163	164	(2)	141	(2)	(2)	165	161	141	153	164	171
Maryland[3]	145	160	124	121	161	(2)	146	145	126	136	147	153
Massachusetts	157	163	126	126	152	(2)	159	154	134	145	156	166
Michigan[3]	153	161	122	134	(2)	(2)	156	150	137	144	156	161
Minnesota	159	162	130	134	152	(2)	161	157	137	151	161	165
Mississippi	133	149	119	105	(2)	(2)	134	132	125	126	142	138
Missouri	151	158	120	130	(2)	(2)	152	150	136	144	156	159
Montana[3]	162	166	(2)	147	(2)	139	164	160	139	155	164	168
Nebraska	157	161	130	134	(2)	(2)	160	155	133	148	161	165
New Mexico	141	159	(2)	130	(2)	126	143	139	119	131	147	154
New York[3]	146	161	120	116	155	(2)	148	143	123	138	147	157
North Carolina	147	157	126	123	(2)	136	149	145	126	134	150	158
North Dakota	162	164	(2)	137	(2)	137	163	161	148	157	160	167
Oregon	155	158	(2)	133	157	142	157	153	137	143	157	164
Rhode Island	149	155	130	118	142	(2)	150	148	123	141	154	160
South Carolina[3]	139	153	122	122	(2)	(2)	141	136	125	127	145	148
Tennessee	143	151	117	104	(2)	(2)	144	142	127	135	149	154
Texas	145	161	127	129	157	(2)	147	143	128	137	152	157
Utah	156	159	(2)	133	143	(2)	159	154	129	147	156	162
Vermont[3]	157	159	(2)	136	(2)	(2)	158	156	132	146	157	167
Virginia	149	158	126	132	165	(2)	150	148	127	136	152	161
Washington	150	156	127	125	149	130	152	147	128	141	154	158
West Virginia	147	149	127	122	(2)	(2)	148	147	130	142	152	156
Wisconsin[3]	160	165	115	141	(2)	(2)	161	158	140	155	161	169
Wyoming	158	161	(2)	140	(2)	138	159	156	139	150	159	165
Department of Defense Overseas Schools	155	164	140	146	156	(2)	157	154	(2)	144	159	158
Guam	120	138	(2)	106	122	(2)	120	120	106	113	130	128

[1] Parents' highest level of education. Data not shown for students who did not know parents' level of education.
[2] Sample size is insufficient to permit a reliable estimate.
[3] Did not satisfy one or more of the guidelines for school sample participation rates. Data are subject to appreciable nonresponse bias.

NOTE.—These test scores are from the National Assessment of Educational Progress (NAEP). The NAEP scores have been evaluated at certain performance levels. A score of 300 implies an ability to find, understand, summarize, and explain relatively complicated literary and informational material. A score of 250 implies an ability to search for specific information, interrelate ideas, and make generalizations about literature, science, and social studies materials. A score of 200 implies an ability to understand, combine ideas, and make inferences based on short uncomplicated passages about specific or sequentially related information. A score of 150 implies an ability to follow brief written directions and carry out simple, discrete reading tasks. Scale ranges from 0 to 500. Excludes states not participating in the survey. Some data have been revised from previously published figures.

SOURCE: U.S. Department of Education, National Center for Education Statistics, National Assessment of Educational Progress, *NAEP 1996 Science Report Card for the Nation and the States*, prepared by Educational Testing Service. (This table was prepared June 1997).

Table 126.—Average science proficiency, by age and by selected characteristics of students: 1970 to 1996

Selected characteristics of students	1970	1973	1977	1982	1986	1990	1992	1994	1996
1	2	3	4	5	6	7	8	9	10
9-year-olds									
Total	225 (1.2)	220 (1.2)	220 (1.2)	221 (1.8)	224 (1.2)	229 (0.8)	231 (1.0)	231 (1.2)	230 (1.2)
Male	228 (1.3)	223 (1.3)	222 (1.3)	221 (2.3)	227 (1.4)	230 (1.1)	235 (1.2)	232 (1.3)	232 (1.8)
Female	223 (1.2)	218 (1.2)	218 (1.2)	221 (2.0)	221 (1.4)	227 (1.0)	227 (1.0)	230 (1.4)	228 (1.4)
Race/ethnicity									
White, non-Hispanic	236 (0.9)	231 (0.9)	230 (0.9)	229 (1.9)	232 (1.2)	238 (0.8)	239 (1.0)	240 (1.3)	239 (1.4)
Black, non-Hispanic	179 (1.9)	177 (1.9)	175 (1.8)	187 (3.0)	196 (1.9)	196 (2.0)	200 (2.7)	201 (1.7)	201 (2.6)
Hispanic	— —	— —	192 (2.7)	189 (4.2)	199 (3.1)	206 (2.2)	205 (2.8)	201 (2.7)	207 (2.5)
Parental education									
Not high school graduate	— —	— —	199 (2.2)	198 (6.0)	204 (2.9)	210 (2.7)	217 (2.6)	211 (3.4)	215 (4.0)
Graduated high school	— —	— —	223 (1.4)	218 (3.3)	220 (1.5)	226 (1.7)	222 (1.9)	225 (1.4)	222 (2.5)
Some college	— —	— —	237 (1.5)	229 (3.2)	236 (2.6)	238 (2.1)	237 (2.4)	239 (2.8)	242 (3.9)
Graduated college	— —	— —	232 (1.4)	231 (2.3)	235 (1.4)	236 (1.3)	239 (1.2)	239 (1.4)	240 (1.5)
Type of school									
Public	— —	— —	218 (1.4)	220 (2.0)	223 (1.4)	228 (0.9)	229 (1.0)	230 (1.4)	229 (1.3)
Private	— —	— —	235 (2.2)	232 (3.2)	233 (2.9)	237 (2.4)	240 (2.7)	242 (2.8)	238 (3.8)
Region									
Northeast	230 (2.9)	222 (2.9)	224 (1.6)	222 (2.9)	228 (3.5)	231 (2.4)	234 (2.8)	235 (2.5)	235 (2.5)
Southeast	206 (1.6)	207 (1.6)	205 (2.9)	214 (3.6)	219 (3.1)	220 (1.9)	223 (1.7)	227 (2.2)	223 (3.4)
Central	233 (3.0)	228 (3.0)	225 (2.2)	226 (3.5)	228 (2.2)	234 (1.7)	238 (1.8)	236 (2.7)	234 (2.1)
West	226 (2.2)	221 (2.2)	221 (2.2)	220 (4.1)	222 (3.2)	230 (1.8)	227 (2.2)	226 (2.7)	228 (2.1)
13-year-olds									
Total	255 (1.1)	250 (1.1)	247 (1.1)	250 (1.3)	251 (1.4)	255 (0.9)	258 (0.8)	257 (1.0)	256 (1.0)
Male	257 (1.3)	252 (1.3)	251 (1.3)	256 (1.5)	256 (1.6)	259 (1.1)	260 (1.2)	259 (1.2)	261 (1.1)
Female	253 (1.2)	247 (1.2)	244 (1.2)	245 (1.3)	247 (1.5)	252 (1.1)	256 (1.0)	254 (1.2)	252 (1.3)
Race/ethnicity									
White, non-Hispanic	263 (0.8)	259 (0.8)	256 (0.8)	257 (1.1)	259 (1.4)	264 (0.9)	267 (1.0)	267 (1.0)	266 (1.2)
Black, non-Hispanic	215 (2.4)	205 (2.4)	208 (2.4)	217 (1.3)	222 (2.5)	226 (3.1)	224 (2.7)	224 (4.2)	226 (2.2)
Hispanic	— —	— —	213 (1.9)	226 (3.9)	226 (3.1)	232 (2.6)	238 (2.6)	232 (2.4)	232 (2.5)
Parental education									
Not high school graduate	— —	— —	224 (1.3)	225 (1.9)	229 (2.7)	233 (2.1)	234 (2.9)	234 (2.5)	232 (3.2)
Graduated high school	— —	— —	245 (1.1)	243 (1.3)	245 (1.4)	247 (1.3)	246 (1.4)	247 (1.2)	248 (1.6)
Some college	— —	— —	260 (1.3)	259 (1.5)	258 (1.4)	263 (1.2)	266 (1.1)	260 (2.0)	260 (1.3)
Graduated college	— —	— —	266 (1.0)	264 (1.5)	264 (1.9)	268 (1.1)	269 (1.0)	269 (1.3)	266 (1.2)
Type of school									
Public	— —	— —	245 (1.2)	249 (1.4)	251 (1.4)	254 (1.1)	257 (1.0)	255 (1.1)	255 (1.1)
Private	— —	— —	268 (2.1)	264 (3.2)	263 (6.4)	269 (1.8)	265 (2.4)	268 (2.6)	268 (5.0)
Region									
Northeast	261 (2.2)	256 (2.2)	255 (2.3)	254 (2.1)	258 (3.1)	257 (2.7)	257 (2.2)	263 (1.7)	256 (2.9)
Southeast	239 (2.4)	237 (2.4)	235 (1.8)	239 (2.3)	247 (2.2)	251 (1.9)	254 (2.8)	253 (2.6)	250 (2.7)
Central	262 (1.8)	256 (1.8)	254 (1.8)	254 (2.6)	249 (5.3)	260 (2.8)	263 (2.1)	261 (3.5)	266 (1.8)
West	255 (1.8)	248 (1.8)	243 (2.3)	252 (2.8)	252 (2.7)	253 (2.1)	258 (1.6)	252 (2.1)	254 (1.9)
17-year-olds[1]									
Total	305 (1.0)	296 (1.0)	290 (1.0)	283 (1.2)	289 (1.4)	290 (1.1)	294 (1.3)	294 (1.6)	296 (1.2)
Male	314 (1.2)	304 (1.2)	297 (1.2)	292 (1.4)	295 (1.9)	296 (1.3)	299 (1.7)	300 (2.0)	300 (1.7)
Female	297 (1.1)	288 (1.1)	282 (1.1)	275 (1.3)	282 (1.5)	285 (1.6)	289 (1.5)	289 (1.7)	292 (1.4)
Race/ethnicity									
White, non-Hispanic	312 (0.8)	304 (0.8)	298 (0.7)	293 (1.0)	298 (1.7)	301 (1.1)	304 (1.3)	306 (1.5)	307 (1.2)
Black, non-Hispanic	258 (1.5)	250 (1.5)	240 (1.5)	235 (1.7)	253 (2.9)	253 (4.5)	256 (3.2)	257 (3.1)	260 (2.3)
Hispanic	— —	— —	262 (2.2)	249 (2.3)	259 (3.8)	262 (4.4)	270 (5.6)	261 (6.7)	269 (3.0)
Parental education									
Not high school graduate	— —	— —	265 (1.3)	259 (2.4)	258 (3.1)	261 (2.8)	262 (3.8)	256 (4.2)	261 (3.9)
Graduated high school	— —	— —	284 (0.8)	275 (1.6)	277 (2.0)	276 (1.4)	280 (2.4)	279 (1.7)	282 (2.7)
Some college	— —	— —	296 (1.1)	290 (1.7)	295 (2.5)	297 (1.6)	296 (1.7)	295 (1.9)	297 (1.9)
Graduated college	— —	— —	309 (1.0)	300 (1.7)	304 (2.1)	306 (1.7)	308 (1.3)	311 (1.6)	308 (1.5)
Type of school									
Public	— —	— —	288 (1.0)	282 (1.1)	287 (1.6)	289 (1.1)	292 (1.3)	292 (1.5)	295 (1.2)
Private	— —	— —	308 (2.4)	292 (2.9)	321 (10.1)	308 (6.6)	312 (3.7)	310 (4.8)	303 (5.5)
Region									
Northeast	308 (2.5)	298 (2.5)	296 (2.2)	284 (2.0)	292 (4.3)	293 (3.2)	300 (2.4)	299 (4.2)	297 (3.3)
Southeast	287 (2.3)	283 (2.3)	276 (1.9)	276 (2.7)	284 (2.0)	284 (2.4)	283 (2.5)	288 (2.8)	287 (3.1)
Central	308 (1.9)	300 (1.9)	294 (1.5)	289 (2.6)	294 (2.3)	300 (3.0)	304 (2.7)	298 (3.7)	307 (2.5)
West	308 (1.7)	295 (1.7)	287 (1.5)	281 (2.7)	283 (3.8)	286 (2.3)	290 (3.8)	292 (4.1)	292 (2.2)

[1] Excludes persons not enrolled in school.
—Data not available.

NOTE.—These test scores are from the National Assessment of Educational Progress (NAEP). Performers at the 150 level know some general scientific facts of the type that could be learned from everyday experiences. Performers at the 200 level are developing some understanding of simple scientific principles, particularly in the life sciences. Performers at the 250 level can interpret data from simple tables and make inferences about the outcomes of experimental procedures. They exhibit knowledge and understanding of the life sciences and also demonstrate some knowledge of basic information from the physical sciences. Performers at the 300 level can evaluate the appropriateness of the design of an experiment and have the skill to apply their scientific knowledge in interpreting information from text and graphs. These students also exhibit a growing understanding of principles from the physical sciences. Performers at the 350 level can infer relationships and draw conclusions using detailed scientific knowledge from the physical sciences, particularly chemistry. They also can apply basic principles of genetics and interpret the societal implications of research in this field. Scale ranges from 0 to 500. Standard errors appear in parentheses.

SOURCE: U.S. Department of Education, National Center for Education Statistics, National Assessment of Educational Progress, NAEP 1996 Trends in Academic Progress, prepared by Educational Testing Service. (This table was prepared September 1997.)

Table 127.—Twelfth graders' achievement on history, mathematics, reading, and science tests: 1992

Achievement test	Total	Sex		Race/ethnicity					Socioeconomic status [1]			Control of school		
		Male	Female	White	Black	Hispanic	Asian	American Indian	Low	Middle	High	Public	Catholic	Other private
1	2	3	4	5	6	7	8	9	10	11	12	13	14	15
Twelfth graders' achievement, standardized score [2]														
History	51.2	51.9	50.5	52.5	45.9	47.4	52.1	44.5	45.8	50.5	55.9	50.8	55.1	54.9
Mathematics	51.4	51.8	51.0	52.9	44.8	47.3	54.3	45.2	45.5	50.6	56.7	50.9	55.1	56.1
Reading	51.0	49.9	52.2	52.4	45.5	47.2	51.4	45.2	45.9	50.4	55.5	50.6	54.7	55.0
Science	51.1	52.4	49.7	52.9	43.3	46.5	51.8	44.8	45.4	50.5	55.9	50.7	53.9	55.0
Distribution of twelfth graders' achievement, by score quartile [3]														
History	100.0	100.0	100.0	100.0	100.0	100.0	100.0	100.0	100.0	100.0	100.0	100.0	100.0	100.0
Lower quartile	20.2	19.6	20.9	15.5	39.6	32.4	16.8	41.1	37.6	20.5	7.9	21.4	7.1	13.8
Lower middle quartile	24.6	21.5	27.9	23.4	28.1	28.9	25.6	32.5	30.9	26.9	16.5	25.2	21.0	17.2
Upper middle quartile	26.9	26.3	27.4	28.4	21.5	23.5	25.5	13.6	21.1	27.7	29.2	26.8	31.2	22.1
Upper quartile	28.3	32.5	23.8	32.7	10.8	15.3	32.2	12.7	10.3	24.8	46.5	26.6	40.7	46.9
Mathematics	100.0	100.0	100.0	100.0	100.0	100.0	100.0	100.0	100.0	100.0	100.0	100.0	100.0	100.0
Lower quartile	19.7	20.1	19.2	14.8	41.2	31.6	11.9	42.8	37.0	20.4	6.5	20.9	8.2	7.6
Lower middle quartile	24.2	22.4	26.0	22.5	30.0	30.6	21.1	29.8	32.4	26.3	15.2	24.9	17.0	17.3
Upper middle quartile	27.6	26.9	28.4	29.5	20.3	22.9	28.4	18.5	22.4	29.3	28.4	27.2	34.3	28.5
Upper quartile	28.5	30.6	26.3	33.2	8.5	14.9	38.7	8.9	8.3	23.9	50.0	27.0	40.5	46.6
Reading	100.0	100.0	100.0	100.0	100.0	100.0	100.0	100.0	100.0	100.0	100.0	100.0	100.0	100.0
Lower quartile	21.1	25.6	16.4	16.6	38.2	31.6	23.2	41.2	36.3	21.6	9.8	22.3	8.1	14.0
Lower middle quartile	24.6	24.5	24.7	22.6	31.3	32.9	20.0	31.1	32.4	26.8	15.8	25.5	18.1	13.6
Upper middle quartile	26.4	25.0	27.9	28.3	20.7	21.2	24.9	15.5	20.8	27.4	28.6	25.8	36.3	25.2
Upper quartile	27.8	24.9	30.9	32.5	9.8	14.3	31.9	12.2	10.5	24.3	45.9	26.4	37.5	47.2
Science	100.0	100.0	100.0	100.0	100.0	100.0	100.0	100.0	100.0	100.0	100.0	100.0	100.0	100.0
Lower quartile	20.9	18.2	23.6	14.0	52.6	34.3	17.7	37.6	39.0	20.9	8.4	21.9	11.7	10.5
Lower middle quartile	24.5	21.1	28.1	23.0	25.2	33.8	25.2	35.8	31.9	26.8	16.0	25.0	22.0	17.4
Upper middle quartile	26.3	27.1	25.5	29.0	16.0	18.9	26.5	20.9	19.8	28.3	27.4	26.3	27.3	26.1
Upper quartile	28.3	33.6	22.7	33.9	6.2	13.1	30.5	5.7	9.3	24.1	48.3	26.8	39.0	46.0

[1] Socioeconomic status was measured by a composite score on parental education and occupations, and family income. The "Low" SES group is the lowest quartile; the "Middle" SES group is the middle two quartiles; and the "High" SES group is the upper quartile.

[2] In the full data file, the standardized scores have a mean of 50 and a standard deviation of 10. Because dropouts and students who were retained in grades between 8 and 11 were excluded from this tabulation, the scores are slightly higher.

[3] In the full data file, twenty-five percent of all students fall into each one of the quartile groupings. Because dropouts and students who were retained in grades between 8 and 11 were excluded from this tabulation, the scores are slightly higher.

NOTE.—Because of rounding, details may not add to totals.

SOURCE: U.S. Department of Education, National Center for Education Statistics, "National Education Longitudinal Study of 1988, Second Followup" survey. (This table was prepared July 1995.)

Table 128.—Scholastic Assessment Test [1] score averages, by race/ethnicity: 1975–76 to 1994–95

Racial/ethnic background	1975–76	1977–78	1978–79	1979–80	1980–81	1981–82	1982–83	1983–84	1984–85	1986–87	1987–88	1988–89	1989–90	1990–91	1991–92	1992–93	1993–94	1994–95
1	2	3	4	5	6	7	8	9	10	11	12	13	14	15	16	17	18	19
SAT-Verbal																		
All students	431	429	427	424	424	426	425	426	431	430	428	427	424	422	423	424	423	428
White	451	446	444	442	442	444	443	445	449	447	445	446	442	441	442	444	443	448
Black	332	332	330	330	332	341	339	342	346	351	353	351	352	351	352	353	352	356
Mexican-American	371	370	370	372	373	377	375	376	382	379	382	381	380	377	372	374	372	376
Puerto Rican	364	349	345	350	353	360	358	358	368	360	355	360	359	361	366	367	367	372
Asian-American	414	401	396	396	397	398	395	398	404	405	408	409	410	411	413	415	416	418
American Indian	388	387	386	390	391	388	388	390	392	393	393	384	388	393	395	400	396	403
Other	410	399	393	394	388	392	386	388	391	405	410	414	410	411	417	422	425	432
SAT-Mathematical																		
All students	472	468	467	466	466	467	468	471	475	476	476	476	476	474	476	478	479	482
White	493	485	483	482	483	483	484	487	490	489	490	491	491	489	491	494	495	498
Black	354	354	358	360	362	366	369	373	376	377	384	386	385	385	385	388	388	388
Mexican-American	410	402	410	413	415	416	417	420	426	424	428	430	429	427	425	428	427	426
Puerto Rican	401	388	388	394	398	403	403	405	409	400	402	406	405	406	409	411	411	411
Asian-American	518	510	511	509	513	513	514	519	518	521	522	525	528	530	532	535	535	538
American Indian	420	419	421	426	425	424	425	427	428	432	435	428	437	437	442	447	441	447
Other	458	450	447	449	447	449	446	450	448	455	460	467	467	466	473	477	480	486

[1] Formerly known as the Scholastic Aptitude Test.

NOTE.—Possible scores on each part of the SAT range from 200 to 800. No racial/ethnic group data are available prior to 1975–76. No data are available for 1985–86 due to changes in the Student Descriptive Questionnaire completed when students registered for the test.

SOURCE: College Entrance Examination Board, *National Report on College-Bound Seniors*, various years. (Copyright ©1995 by the College Entrance Examination Board. All rights reserved.) (This table was prepared November 1995.)

Table 129.—Scholastic Assessment Test[1] score averages for college-bound high school seniors, by sex: 1966–67 to 1996–97

School year	Scholastic Assessment Test I (recentered scale)[2]						Scholastic Aptitude Test (old scale)					
	Verbal score			Mathematical score			Verbal score			Mathematical score		
	Total	Male	Female	Total	Male	Female	Total	Male	Female	Total	Male	Female
1	2	3	4	5	6	7	8	9	10	11	12	13
1966–67	—	—	—	—	—	—	466	463	468	492	514	467
1967–68	—	—	—	—	—	—	466	464	466	492	512	470
1968–69	—	—	—	—	—	—	463	459	466	493	513	470
1969–70	—	—	—	—	—	—	460	459	461	488	509	465
1970–71	—	—	—	—	—	—	455	454	457	488	507	466
1971–72	530	531	529	509	527	489	453	454	452	484	505	461
1972–73	523	523	521	506	525	489	445	446	443	481	502	460
1973–74	521	524	520	505	524	488	444	447	442	480	501	459
1974–75	512	515	509	498	518	479	434	437	431	472	495	449
1975–76	509	511	508	497	520	475	431	433	430	472	497	446
1976–77	507	509	505	496	520	474	429	431	427	470	497	445
1977–78	507	511	503	494	517	474	429	433	425	468	494	444
1978–79	505	509	501	493	516	473	427	431	423	467	493	443
1979–80	502	506	498	492	515	473	424	428	420	466	491	443
1980–81	502	508	496	492	516	473	424	430	418	466	492	443
1981–82	504	509	499	493	516	473	426	431	421	467	493	443
1982–83	503	508	498	494	516	474	425	430	420	468	493	445
1983–84	504	511	498	497	518	478	426	433	420	471	495	449
1984–85	509	514	503	500	522	480	431	437	425	475	499	452
1985–86	509	515	504	500	523	479	431	437	426	475	501	451
1986–87	507	512	502	501	523	481	430	435	425	476	500	453
1987–88	505	512	499	501	521	483	428	435	422	476	498	455
1988–89	504	510	498	502	523	482	427	434	421	476	500	454
1989–90	500	505	496	501	521	483	424	429	419	476	499	455
1990–91	499	503	495	500	520	482	422	426	418	474	497	453
1991–92	500	504	496	501	521	484	423	428	419	476	499	456
1992–93	500	504	497	503	524	484	424	428	420	478	502	457
1993–94	499	501	497	504	523	487	423	425	421	479	501	460
1994–95	504	505	502	506	525	490	428	429	426	482	503	463
1995–96	505	507	503	508	527	492	—	—	—	—	—	—
1996–97	505	507	503	511	530	494	—	—	—	—	—	—

[1] Formerly known as the Scholastic Aptitude Test.
[2] Data for 1972 to 1986 were converted to the recentered scale by using a formula applied to the original mean and standard deviation. For 1987 to 1995, individual student scores were converted to the recentered scale and recomputed.
—Data not available.

NOTE.—Possible scores on each part of the SAT range from 200 to 800. Data for the years 1966–67 through 1970–71 are estimates derived from the test scores of all participants.

SOURCE: College Entrance Examination Board, *National Report on College-Bound Seniors*, various years. (Copyright ©1997 by the College Entrance Examination Board. All rights reserved.) (This table was prepared August 1997.)

Table 130.—Distribution of Scholastic Assessment Test[1] scores, by sex of student: 1975–76 to 1994–95

Year	Number of test takers	Percent of students with specified scores											
		200 or higher	250 or higher	300 or higher	350 or higher	400 or higher	450 or higher	500 or higher	550 or higher	600 or higher	650 or higher	700 or higher	750 or higher
1	2	3	4	5	6	7	8	9	10	11	12	13	14
Verbal													
Total													
1975–76	999,809	100.00	96.26	89.26	77.47	60.27	43.01	28.11	15.58	8.20	3.55	1.23	0.25
1980–81	994,046	100.00	95.46	87.32	75.34	58.44	40.64	25.76	13.87	7.00	3.01	1.03	0.21
1985–86	1,000,748	100.00	95.81	88.92	77.55	61.77	43.17	28.03	15.75	7.87	3.25	0.99	0.14
1986–87	1,080,426	100.00	96.08	88.57	76.62	60.18	43.02	27.85	15.44	8.14	3.42	1.07	0.13
1987–88	1,134,364	100.00	95.81	88.62	76.44	60.53	42.38	26.91	14.94	7.32	3.22	0.92	0.09
1988–89	1,088,223	100.00	95.72	88.21	75.39	59.55	42.17	26.77	14.85	7.76	3.16	0.87	0.10
1989–90	1,025,523	100.00	95.20	87.44	74.97	58.70	40.67	25.11	14.41	7.43	3.13	1.00	0.12
1990–91	1,032,685	100.00	94.89	86.96	74.38	57.58	40.38	25.22	14.08	7.25	3.15	1.03	0.13
1991–92	1,034,131	100.00	94.70	86.95	74.29	58.68	40.96	25.42	14.02	7.28	3.18	0.98	0.13
1992–93	1,044,465	100.00	94.85	87.20	74.71	58.70	40.85	25.77	14.87	7.77	3.37	1.00	0.12
1993–94	1,050,386	100.00	94.76	86.97	74.58	57.72	40.26	25.95	14.76	7.58	3.32	1.11	0.14
1994–95	1,067,993	100.00	95.24	87.96	75.60	59.81	41.83	26.52	15.98	8.25	3.65	1.20	0.13
Male													
1975–76	494,626	100.00	96.39	89.54	77.90	60.90	43.65	28.69	16.04	8.49	3.69	1.29	0.26
1980–81	478,448	100.00	95.97	88.50	77.16	60.73	42.89	27.53	15.03	7.67	3.30	1.13	0.23
1985–86	481,477	100.00	96.19	89.87	79.10	63.74	45.17	29.71	17.02	8.71	3.68	1.11	0.15
1986–87	520,326	100.00	96.23	89.12	77.72	61.79	44.91	29.71	16.93	9.22	4.02	1.26	0.15
1987–88	544,065	100.00	96.14	89.54	78.21	62.92	45.04	29.25	16.70	8.44	3.82	1.13	0.11
1988–89	521,229	100.00	96.00	89.06	77.04	61.86	44.81	29.15	16.63	8.93	3.75	1.07	0.12
1989–90	490,420	100.00	95.40	88.00	76.04	60.19	42.62	27.05	15.91	8.40	3.60	1.15	0.14
1990–91	493,252	100.00	95.08	87.45	75.29	58.94	41.99	26.71	15.18	7.98	3.51	1.16	0.14
1991–92	491,748	100.00	94.89	87.46	75.34	60.23	42.68	26.98	15.16	8.00	3.55	1.10	0.15
1992–93	495,086	100.00	94.98	87.55	75.35	59.75	42.21	27.18	16.01	8.60	3.83	1.18	0.15
1993–94	493,063	100.00	94.67	86.93	74.71	58.21	41.15	26.90	15.54	8.10	3.61	1.23	0.15
1994–95	496,016	100.00	95.18	87.98	75.83	60.28	42.47	27.32	16.68	8.78	3.94	1.31	0.15
Female													
1975–76	505,183	100.00	96.14	88.97	77.05	59.65	42.38	27.55	15.13	7.92	3.42	1.17	0.24
1980–81	515,598	100.00	94.99	86.23	73.66	56.32	38.56	24.11	12.80	6.39	2.73	0.94	0.18
1985–86	519,271	100.00	95.46	88.04	76.11	59.95	41.31	26.42	14.57	7.09	2.85	0.88	0.12
1986–87	560,100	100.00	95.93	88.07	75.60	58.67	41.26	26.13	14.05	7.14	2.87	0.90	0.11
1987–88	590,299	100.00	95.50	87.76	74.82	58.33	39.93	24.76	13.32	6.29	2.66	0.74	0.06
1988–89	566,994	100.00	95.45	87.42	73.88	57.42	39.75	24.58	13.21	6.68	2.61	0.69	0.08
1989–90	535,103	100.00	95.01	86.93	73.98	57.34	38.88	23.34	13.04	6.53	2.70	0.86	0.10
1990–91	539,433	100.00	94.71	86.52	73.55	56.33	38.90	23.85	13.08	6.58	2.81	0.92	0.12
1991–92	542,383	100.00	94.53	86.49	73.34	57.28	39.40	24.00	12.98	6.62	2.84	0.87	0.12
1992–93	549,379	100.00	94.74	86.88	74.13	57.76	39.62	24.50	13.84	7.01	2.95	0.83	0.09
1993–94	557,323	100.00	94.84	87.01	74.47	57.28	39.49	25.10	14.06	7.12	3.06	1.00	0.12
1994–95	571,977	100.00	95.29	87.95	75.39	59.40	41.28	25.83	15.38	7.80	3.40	1.10	0.11
Mathematical													
Total													
1975–76	999,776	100.00	98.78	93.65	83.55	70.87	57.16	41.82	26.94	16.34	8.49	3.75	1.16
1980–81	993,672	100.00	98.85	92.99	82.77	70.48	55.57	40.59	25.98	14.45	7.08	2.71	0.66
1985–86	1,000,747	100.00	98.91	93.63	84.64	71.98	57.41	42.32	29.29	17.95	9.56	4.08	1.01
1986–87	1,080,426	100.00	98.91	93.30	84.22	71.61	57.40	42.32	29.67	18.32	9.94	3.86	1.02
1987–88	1,134,364	100.00	99.08	93.93	84.62	72.17	57.43	43.03	29.55	17.60	9.26	3.78	0.91
1988–89	1,088,223	100.00	99.08	94.04	84.57	71.97	57.94	42.81	29.33	18.01	10.07	4.27	1.11
1989–90	1,025,523	100.00	98.89	93.77	84.21	71.57	57.71	43.20	29.59	18.41	10.14	4.23	1.18
1990–91	1,032,685	100.00	98.83	93.63	83.49	70.80	56.63	42.68	29.27	17.85	9.70	4.51	1.32
1991–92	1,034,131	100.00	98.70	93.65	84.25	71.81	57.96	43.36	28.83	18.12	10.10	4.60	1.37
1992–93	1,044,465	100.00	98.49	93.34	84.28	72.33	58.55	44.39	29.78	18.80	10.63	5.11	1.62
1993–94	1,050,386	100.00	98.51	93.75	84.49	72.99	59.13	44.48	30.21	18.90	10.56	4.85	1.42
1994–95	1,067,993	100.00	98.95	94.49	83.96	71.65	57.65	44.37	31.58	21.51	12.44	5.65	1.49
Male													
1975–76	494,619	100.00	99.13	95.37	87.63	77.29	65.30	50.65	34.93	22.71	12.70	6.02	1.99
1980–81	478,301	100.00	99.20	94.98	87.17	77.17	63.99	49.45	33.92	20.38	10.75	4.46	1.17
1985–86	481,477	100.00	99.24	95.38	88.49	78.26	65.53	51.16	37.47	24.49	14.00	6.44	1.73
1986–87	520,326	100.00	99.16	94.91	87.75	77.36	64.90	50.74	37.66	24.82	14.47	6.15	1.75
1987–88	544,065	100.00	99.31	95.37	87.91	77.48	64.40	50.71	36.91	23.63	13.43	5.96	1.57
1988–89	521,229	100.00	99.30	95.45	88.00	77.62	65.19	50.91	37.13	24.43	14.42	6.70	1.89
1989–90	490,420	100.00	99.16	95.17	87.70	77.13	64.71	50.81	36.85	24.40	14.41	6.53	2.00
1990–91	493,252	100.00	99.08	94.91	86.79	76.22	63.65	50.40	36.59	23.82	13.93	6.96	2.23
1991–92	491,748	100.00	98.99	95.05	87.50	77.03	64.73	50.88	36.01	24.05	14.28	6.96	2.24
1992–93	495,086	100.00	98.83	94.73	87.55	77.69	65.50	52.10	37.18	25.00	15.09	7.77	2.69
1993–94	493,063	100.00	98.86	94.97	87.55	77.92	65.65	51.91	37.27	24.78	14.75	7.28	2.29
1994–95	496,016	100.00	99.16	95.56	87.03	76.62	63.97	51.17	38.13	27.22	16.75	8.12	2.34
Female													
1975–76	505,157	100.00	98.45	91.96	79.56	64.59	49.20	33.17	19.12	10.11	4.37	1.53	0.34
1980–81	515,371	100.00	98.53	91.14	78.69	64.27	47.76	32.37	18.60	8.94	3.66	1.09	0.19
1985–86	519,270	100.00	98.61	92.01	81.07	66.16	49.87	34.12	21.70	11.88	5.45	1.89	0.34
1986–87	560,100	100.00	98.67	91.80	80.93	66.26	50.44	34.59	22.25	12.29	5.74	1.73	0.33
1987–88	590,299	100.00	98.87	92.60	81.58	67.28	51.00	35.94	22.78	12.05	5.42	1.77	0.30
1988–89	566,994	100.00	98.87	92.75	81.42	66.77	51.27	35.37	22.15	12.11	5.90	2.03	0.39
1989–90	535,103	100.00	98.65	92.50	81.01	66.47	51.30	36.22	22.94	12.92	6.22	2.12	0.44
1990–91	539,433	100.00	98.60	92.45	80.48	65.85	50.22	35.52	22.57	12.40	5.83	2.26	0.49
1991–92	542,383	100.00	98.45	92.37	81.31	67.07	51.82	36.54	22.32	12.74	6.30	2.45	0.57
1992–93	549,379	100.00	98.18	92.09	81.34	67.50	52.28	37.45	23.11	13.21	6.61	2.72	0.65
1993–94	557,323	100.00	98.25	92.72	81.79	68.64	53.36	37.92	23.96	13.69	6.86	2.69	0.65
1994–95	571,977	100.00	98.76	93.55	81.30	67.34	52.18	38.46	25.89	16.56	8.70	3.50	0.75

[1] Formerly known as the Scholastic Aptitude Test.

NOTE.—Possible scores on each part of the SAT range from 200 to 800. In some years, mathematics and verbal test results were not available for every student.

SOURCE: College Entrance Examination Board, *National Report on College-Bound Seniors*, various years. (Copyright ©1995 by the College Entrance Examination Board. All rights reserved.) (This table was prepared November 1995.)

Table 131.—Scholastic Assessment Test[1] score averages, by intended area of study:[2] 1977–78 to 1994–95

Test and year	Intended area of study[3]									
	Arts and humanities	Biological sciences and related areas	Business, commerce, and communications	Computer and information sciences	Education	Engineering	Mathematics	Physical sciences	Social sciences and related areas	Miscellaneous[4]
1	2	3	4	5	6	7	8	9	10	11
Verbal										
1977–78	439	436	409	420	396	448	464	499	448	422
1978–79	436	435	408	419	392	445	459	498	446	420
1979–80	434	433	406	417	389	444	455	495	448	419
1980–81	434	433	406	416	391	446	456	498	446	420
1981–82	436	434	409	417	394	449	455	496	450	424
1982–83	438	432	409	413	394	448	453	496	451	421
1983–84	440	434	410	411	398	453	457	501	451	423
1984–85	445	439	414	413	404	453	459	506	454	429
1986–87	447	438	415	403	408	456	475	507	452	410
1987–88	444	434	414	400	407	453	468	500	447	409
1988–89	445	433	414	396	406	452	473	504	447	410
1989–90	441	430	410	392	406	449	473	503	441	408
1990–91	440	428	407	390	406	446	469	497	437	410
1991–92	442	428	407	394	407	447	467	497	435	414
1992–93	444	427	407	400	409	448	468	497	435	415
1993–94	441	427	407	406	407	446	471	496	435	414
1994–95	452	431	413	416	409	451	480	500	438	418
Change, 1984–85 to 1994–95	7	–8	–1	3	5	–2	21	–6	–16	–11
Mathematical										
1977–78	454	474	448	499	422	540	585	566	464	461
1978–79	452	472	448	498	420	536	580	561	463	458
1979–80	452	472	446	496	418	535	577	560	463	459
1980–81	453	472	446	492	418	534	572	558	463	459
1981–82	452	470	446	489	419	537	569	558	464	461
1982–83	454	470	445	484	418	539	572	560	466	460
1983–84	456	475	449	483	425	543	578	564	467	463
1984–85	462	480	455	488	432	545	578	569	471	469
1986–87	469	482	459	476	437	554	602	576	472	453
1987–88	471	482	462	470	442	547	596	568	472	455
1988–89	473	481	465	472	440	551	606	577	473	459
1989–90	475	481	465	468	442	550	609	577	471	460
1990–91	473	478	462	467	441	548	605	572	466	463
1991–92	475	479	463	472	443	550	606	573	465	472
1992–93	478	480	465	479	446	553	607	574	464	481
1993–94	480	482	468	488	447	553	611	574	467	472
1994–95	476	486	471	495	446	556	619	580	468	474
Change, 1984–85 to 1994–95	14	6	16	7	14	11	41	11	–3	5

[1] Formerly known as the Scholastic Aptitude Test.
[2] Students indicated their first and second choices of fields of study. Only their first choices are reported here.
[3] Based on classifications reported by College Entrance Examination Board.
[4] Includes "trade and vocational," "other," and "undecided" through 1984–85. Data for 1985–86 to 1994–95 exclude "other."

NOTE.—Possible scores on each part of the SAT range from 200 to 800. No data are available for 1985–86 due to changes in the Student Descriptive Questionnaire completed when students registered for the test.

SOURCE: College Entrance Examination Board, *National Report on College-Bound Seniors*, various years. (Copyright ©1995 by the College Entrance Examination Board. All rights reserved.) (This table was prepared November 1995.)

Table 132.—Scholastic Assessment Test[1] score averages, by class rank:[2] 1976–77 to 1994–95

Year	Top tenth		Second tenth		Second fifth		Third fifth		Fourth fifth		Lowest fifth	
	Verbal	Mathematics	Verbal	Mathematics	Verbal	Mathematics	Verbal	Mathematics	Verbal	Mathematics	Verbal	Mathematics
1	2	3	4	5	6	7	8	9	10	11	12	13
1976–77	518	574	452	499	415	453	372	401	347	374	339	364
1977–78	515	570	450	494	414	451	372	400	349	374	339	364
1978–79	514	568	448	494	413	451	371	400	347	372	337	364
1979–80	510	568	446	494	411	451	370	401	346	373	339	366
1980–81	511	567	447	496	412	453	371	402	348	374	339	368
1981–82	511	568	449	497	415	454	374	404	349	375	343	368
1982–83	508	570	447	498	414	455	374	403	351	375	343	369
1983–84	511	575	450	503	417	459	377	406	353	377	341	365
1984–85	516	577	455	508	421	463	381	411	357	380	346	369
1986–87	518	585	456	511	418	461	380	409	358	380	353	374
1987–88	515	585	454	511	417	463	379	411	358	382	352	373
1988–89	515	585	453	512	416	463	376	410	354	381	346	373
1989–90	512	585	449	512	412	463	373	410	351	381	342	370
1990–91	512	584	448	511	411	462	372	409	350	379	340	368
1991–92	512	585	448	511	412	464	373	411	350	379	338	363
1992–93	513	586	449	513	412	466	373	413	350	380	336	363
1993–94	512	586	447	514	410	467	373	415	349	382	332	363
1994–95	518	594	452	518	414	467	375	413	349	379	334	362

[1] Formerly known as the Scholastic Aptitude Test.
[2] Self-reported class rank.

NOTE.—Possible scores on each part of the SAT range from 200 to 800.

SOURCE: College Entrance Examination Board, *National Report on College-Bound Seniors*, various years. (Copyright ©1995 by the College Entrance Examination Board. All rights reserved.) (This table was prepared November 1995.)

Table 133.—Scholastic Assessment Test[1] score averages, by state: 1974–75 to 1994–95

State	1974–75		1980–81		1985–86		1990–91		1992–93		1993–94		1994–95		Percent of graduates taking SAT, 1994–95[2]
	Verbal	Mathematical	Verbal	Mathematical	Verbal	Mathematical	Verbal	Mathematical	Verbal	Mathematical	Verbal	Mathematical	Verbal	Mathematical	
1	2	3	4	5	6	7	8	9	10	11	12	13	14	15	16
United States	434	472	424	466	431	475	422	474	424	478	423	479	428	482	41
Alabama	426	457	457	488	476	514	476	515	480	526	482	529	491	538	8
Alaska	461	481	449	486	445	479	439	481	438	477	434	477	445	489	47
Arizona	496	525	476	514	466	509	442	490	444	497	443	496	448	496	27
Arkansas	482	510	477	510	482	519	482	523	478	519	477	518	482	523	6
California	435	473	426	475	423	481	415	482	415	484	413	482	417	485	45
Colorado	479	515	467	513	466	514	453	506	454	509	456	513	462	518	29
Connecticut	442	471	430	463	440	474	429	468	430	474	426	472	431	477	81
Delaware	439	476	429	470	442	475	428	464	429	465	428	464	429	468	68
District of Columbia	—	—	—	—	413	439	405	435	405	441	406	443	412	445	53
Florida	441	474	424	463	426	469	416	466	416	466	413	466	420	469	48
Georgia	397	427	390	426	402	440	400	444	399	445	398	446	406	448	65
Hawaii	414	478	390	464	403	477	405	478	401	478	401	480	407	482	57
Idaho	493	524	486	523	475	512	463	505	465	507	461	508	468	511	15
Illinois	460	510	459	508	466	519	471	535	475	541	478	546	488	560	13
Indiana	418	463	406	451	415	459	408	457	409	460	410	466	415	467	58
Iowa	523	568	515	566	519	576	515	578	520	583	506	574	516	583	5
Kansas	503	540	502	542	498	544	493	546	494	548	494	550	503	557	9
Kentucky	470	507	474	509	483	519	473	520	476	522	474	523	477	522	11
Louisiana	456	491	461	494	474	507	476	518	481	527	481	530	486	535	9
Maine	437	471	426	465	434	466	421	458	422	463	420	463	427	469	68
Maryland	436	471	423	461	436	475	429	475	431	478	429	479	430	479	64
Massachusetts	434	469	422	462	436	473	426	470	427	476	426	475	430	477	80
Michigan	451	498	456	508	462	514	461	519	469	528	472	537	484	549	11
Minnesota	506	552	486	539	482	540	480	543	489	556	495	562	506	579	9
Mississippi	477	503	473	502	485	516	477	520	481	521	485	528	496	540	4
Missouri	465	500	462	504	476	519	476	526	481	532	485	537	495	550	9
Montana	500	547	485	539	485	541	464	518	459	516	463	523	473	536	21
Nebraska	459	507	489	537	493	549	481	543	479	544	482	543	494	556	9
Nevada	465	497	445	487	445	485	435	484	432	488	429	484	434	483	30
New Hampshire	449	485	439	479	450	485	440	481	442	487	438	486	444	491	70
New Jersey	424	454	414	450	424	465	417	469	419	473	418	475	420	478	70
New Mexico	486	516	474	510	489	527	474	522	478	525	475	528	485	530	11
New York	441	484	427	471	427	471	413	468	416	471	416	472	419	473	74
North Carolina	399	428	391	427	399	436	400	444	406	453	405	455	411	454	60
North Dakota	510	554	494	544	508	556	502	571	518	583	497	559	515	592	5
Ohio	456	499	457	500	460	503	450	496	454	505	456	510	460	515	23
Oklahoma	480	514	485	526	487	521	476	521	482	530	482	537	491	536	9
Oregon	440	468	431	469	444	486	439	483	441	492	436	491	448	499	51
Pennsylvania	430	470	421	459	429	465	417	459	418	460	417	462	419	461	70
Rhode Island	432	469	415	452	432	466	421	459	419	464	420	462	425	463	70
South Carolina	382	412	374	406	395	431	395	437	396	442	395	443	401	443	58
South Dakota	523	561	519	561	531	567	496	551	502	558	483	548	505	563	5
Tennessee	477	511	475	514	486	521	487	528	486	531	488	535	497	543	12
Texas	431	467	415	455	419	458	411	463	413	472	412	474	419	474	47
Utah	516	553	511	548	506	541	494	537	500	549	509	558	513	563	4
Vermont	439	476	427	467	442	474	424	466	426	467	427	472	429	472	68
Virginia	431	463	424	461	435	473	424	466	425	469	424	469	428	468	65
Washington	489	522	472	517	461	502	433	480	435	486	434	488	443	494	48
West Virginia	462	502	458	495	462	502	441	485	439	485	439	482	448	484	17
Wisconsin	492	544	477	533	478	536	481	542	485	551	487	557	501	572	9
Wyoming	506	548	478	528	484	534	466	514	463	507	459	521	476	525	10

[1] Formerly known as the Scholastic Aptitude Test.
[2] Based on the number of high school graduates in 1995 as projected by the Western Interstate Commission for Higher Education and the number of 1995 seniors who took the SAT.
—Data not available.

NOTE.—Possible scores on each part of the SAT range from 200 to 800. Rankings of states based on SAT scores alone are invalid because of the varying proportions of students in each state taking the tests.

SOURCE: College Entrance Examination Board, "College-Bound Seniors: 1995 Profile of SAT Program Test Takers," Copyright 1995 by the College Entrance Examination Board. All rights reserved.) (This table was prepared November 1995.)

Table 134.—American College Testing (ACT) score[1] averages, by sex: 1967 to 1996

Type of test and sex	1967	1970	1975	1980	1983	1984	1985	1986	1987	1988	1989	1990	1991	1992	1993	1994	1995	1996
1	2	3	4	5	6	7	8	9	10	11	12	13	14	15	16	17	18	19
Participants:[2]																		
Total (in thousands)	788	714	822	836	835	849	739	730	777	842	855	817	796	832	876	892	945	924
								Test scores[3]										
Composite, total	19.9	18.6	18.5	18.5	18.3	18.5	18.6	18.8	18.7	18.8	18.6	20.6	20.6	20.6	20.7	20.8	20.8	20.9
Male	20.3	19.5	19.3	19.3	19.1	19.3	19.4	19.6	19.5	19.6	19.3	21.0	20.9	20.9	21.0	20.9	21.0	21.0
Female	19.4	17.8	17.8	17.8	17.6	17.9	17.9	18.1	18.1	18.1	18.0	20.3	20.4	20.5	20.5	20.7	20.7	20.8
English, total	18.5	17.7	17.9	17.8	17.8	18.1	18.1	18.5	18.4	18.5	18.4	20.5	20.3	20.2	20.3	20.3	20.2	20.3
Male	17.6	17.1	17.3	17.3	17.3	17.5	17.6	17.9	17.9	18.0	17.8	20.1	19.8	19.8	19.8	19.8	19.8	19.8
Female	19.4	18.3	18.3	18.2	18.2	18.6	18.6	18.9	19.0	18.9	18.9	20.9	20.7	20.6	20.6	20.7	20.6	20.7
Math, total	20.0	17.6	17.4	17.3	16.9	17.3	17.2	17.3	17.2	17.2	17.1	19.9	20.0	20.0	20.1	20.2	21.3	20.2
Male	21.1	19.3	18.9	18.9	18.4	18.6	18.6	18.8	18.6	18.4	18.3	20.7	20.6	20.7	20.8	20.8	20.9	20.9
Female	18.8	16.2	16.2	16.0	15.7	16.1	16.0	16.0	16.1	16.1	16.1	19.3	19.4	19.5	19.6	19.6	19.7	19.7
Social studies, total[4]	19.7	17.4	17.2	17.2	17.1	17.3	17.4	17.6	17.5	17.4	17.2	—	21.2	21.1	21.2	21.2	21.3	21.3
Male	20.3	18.7	18.2	18.3	18.0	18.1	18.3	18.6	18.4	18.4	18.1	—	21.3	21.1	21.2	21.1	21.1	21.0
Female	19.0	16.4	16.4	16.4	16.4	16.5	16.6	16.9	16.7	16.6	16.4	—	21.1	21.1	21.2	21.4	21.4	21.6
Natural science, total[5]	20.8	21.1	21.1	21.0	20.9	21.0	21.2	21.4	21.4	21.4	21.2	—	20.7	20.7	20.8	20.9	21.0	21.1
Male	21.6	22.4	22.4	22.3	22.4	22.4	22.6	22.7	22.8	22.8	22.6	—	21.3	21.4	21.5	21.6	21.6	21.7
Female	20.0	20.0	20.0	20.0	19.6	19.9	20.0	20.2	20.2	20.2	20.0	—	20.1	20.1	20.3	20.4	20.5	20.5
								Percent										
Obtaining composite scores of—																		
26 or above[6]	14	14	13	13	13	13	14	14	14	14	14	12	11	12	12	13	13	13
15 or below[7]	21	33	33	33	35	33	32	31	31	31	32	35	35	35	35	34	34	34
Planned major field of study																		
Business[8]	18	21	20	19	18	19	21	22	23	23	22	20	18	15	13	12	12	12
Engineering[9]	8	6	8	10	10	9	9	9	8	9	9	9	10	10	9	9	8	8
Social science[10]	10	9	6	6	6	7	7	8	9	10	11	10	10	10	9	9	8	8
Education[11]	16	12	9	7	8	6	6	7	8	9	8	8	10	5	8	8	8	9

[1] Test scores for 1990 and later years are not comparable with previous years because a new version of the ACT was introduced. Estimated average composite scores for the new version for prior years were: 1989, 20.6; 1988, 1987, and 1986, 20.8; and 1982, 20.3.
[2] Beginning in 1985, data are for seniors who graduated in year shown and had taken the ACT in their junior or senior years.
[3] Minimum score, 1; maximum score, 36.
[4] Beginning in 1990, the test was changed to "reading".
[5] Beginning in 1990, the test was changed to "science reasoning".
[6] Beginning in 1990, scores were 27 or above.
[7] As of 1990, scores were 18 or below.
[8] Includes political and persuasive (e.g., sales) fields through 1975; thereafter, business and commerce.
[9] Beginning in 1993, includes engineering and engineering related technologies.
[10] Includes religion through 1975.
[11] Includes education and teacher education.
—Not available.

SOURCE: The American College Testing program, *High School Profile Report*, annual. (This table prepared April 1997.)

Table 135.—Percent of high school seniors reporting they were in general, college preparatory, and vocational programs, by student characteristics: 1982 and 1992

Student characteristics	General[1]		College preparatory or academic		Vocational	
	1982	1992	1982	1992	1982	1992
1	2	3	4	5	6	7
All seniors	35.2	45.3	37.9	43.0	26.9	11.7
Males	38.1	46.3	36.8	41.8	25.1	11.9
Females	32.4	44.2	38.9	44.2	28.7	11.6
Race/ethnicity						
White	34.8	43.3	40.6	45.7	24.6	11.0
Black	35.1	48.9	33.3	35.6	31.6	15.4
Hispanic	37.4	56.4	24.9	30.6	37.7	13.1
Asian	27.5	40.3	55.9	50.9	16.6	8.8
American Indian	55.3	60.8	19.1	22.6	25.6	16.7
Test performance quartile						
Lowest test quartile	42.0	61.5	12.3	15.2	45.6	23.3
Second test quartile	44.6	53.9	20.5	30.0	34.9	16.1
Third test quartile	37.9	39.7	37.6	50.0	24.5	10.4
Highest test quartile	18.9	25.4	73.1	72.0	8.0	2.6
Socioeconomic status[2]						
Low quartile	40.3	55.6	20.5	23.2	39.2	21.2
Middle 2 quartiles	36.2	46.0	36.4	40.9	27.4	13.1
High quartile	27.4	36.2	60.1	60.8	12.5	3.0
Control of school						
Public	36.7	47.1	34.5	40.0	28.8	12.9
Catholic	21.9	24.4	67.4	73.5	10.7	2.2
Other private	22.1	33.1	67.6	65.9	10.3	1.0
Location of school						
Urban	32.2	43.3	37.4	45.5	30.4	11.2
Suburban	33.6	45.5	41.4	44.6	25.0	9.8
Rural/nonmetropolitan area	39.6	46.5	32.6	38.6	27.9	14.9

[1] Includes special education, "other," and "don't know."
[2] Socioeconomic status was measured by a composite score on parental education and occupations, and family income. The "Low" SES group is the lowest quartile; the "Middle" SES group is the middle two quartiles; and the "High" SES group is the upper quartile.

SOURCE: U.S. Department of Education, National Center for Education Statistics, "High School and Beyond," First Followup survey; and "National Education Longitudinal Study of 1988," Second Followup Student survey. (This table was prepared April 1995.)

Table 136.—Average number of Carnegie units earned by public high school graduates in various subject fields, by student characteristics: 1982 to 1994

Student characteristics	Total	English	History/social studies	Mathematics			Science					Foreign languages	Arts	Vocational education [1]	Personal use [2]	Computer science [3]
				Total	Less than algebra	Algebra or higher	Total	General science	Biology	Chemistry	Physics					
1	2	3	4	5	6	7	8	9	10	11	12	13	14	15	16	17
1982 graduates	21.64	3.90	3.19	2.57	0.92	1.65	2.17	0.74	0.93	0.34	0.17	0.97	1.46	4.68	2.69	0.14
Male	21.44	3.86	3.19	2.65	0.99	1.66	2.24	0.77	0.89	0.35	0.22	0.78	1.29	4.63	2.80	0.16
Female	21.82	3.93	3.20	2.49	0.85	1.64	2.11	0.71	0.97	0.32	0.12	1.14	1.63	4.72	2.60	0.13
Race/ethnicity																
White	21.75	3.88	3.23	2.61	0.79	1.82	2.25	0.73	0.96	0.37	0.19	1.03	1.52	4.58	2.63	0.15
Black	21.25	4.06	3.11	2.55	1.39	1.16	2.04	0.81	0.89	0.25	0.09	0.71	1.25	4.84	2.68	0.16
Hispanic	21.30	3.89	3.03	2.26	1.23	1.03	1.78	0.77	0.79	0.16	0.06	0.76	1.31	5.26	3.02	0.09
Asian	22.43	3.82	3.18	3.16	0.71	2.44	2.59	0.50	1.09	0.60	0.40	1.96	1.31	3.23	3.17	0.23
American Indian	21.51	3.94	3.25	2.12	1.12	1.00	2.00	0.71	0.80	0.38	0.11	0.48	1.69	5.09	2.96	0.09
Academic track																
Academic [4]	22.41	4.25	3.53	3.34	0.77	2.57	2.98	0.77	1.21	0.66	0.34	1.62	1.51	2.54	2.66	0.15
Vocational [5]	20.99	3.52	2.79	1.81	1.03	0.78	1.44	0.71	0.63	0.07	0.03	0.35	1.02	7.55	2.48	0.16
Both [6]	24.21	4.34	3.75	3.04	1.16	1.88	2.53	0.92	1.04	0.39	0.19	0.57	0.88	6.47	2.61	0.22
Neither [7]	20.21	3.60	2.89	1.98	0.94	1.05	1.57	0.66	0.77	0.11	0.03	0.75	2.02	4.39	2.98	0.09
1987 graduates	23.06	4.06	3.37	3.05	0.95	2.10	2.53	0.75	1.09	0.48	0.21	1.38	1.43	4.48	2.94	0.49
Male	22.92	4.03	3.35	3.10	1.01	2.09	2.58	0.78	1.05	0.49	0.26	1.18	1.23	4.58	3.13	0.49
Female	23.18	4.09	3.39	3.00	0.89	2.11	2.49	0.73	1.13	0.47	0.16	1.57	1.63	4.38	2.75	0.49
Race/ethnicity																
White	23.14	4.06	3.33	3.06	0.84	2.22	2.59	0.74	1.12	0.51	0.23	1.38	1.49	4.55	2.86	0.50
Black	22.43	4.17	3.37	2.97	1.45	1.52	2.29	0.87	1.02	0.30	0.10	1.07	1.17	4.64	3.08	0.41
Hispanic	23.00	4.03	3.30	2.91	1.40	1.50	2.31	0.82	1.06	0.32	0.11	1.61	1.36	4.20	3.49	0.45
Asian	24.77	4.01	3.75	3.89	0.64	3.24	3.20	0.59	1.17	0.92	0.53	2.48	1.09	2.95	3.45	0.63
American Indian	23.26	4.22	3.22	3.05	1.53	1.52	2.48	0.83	1.25	0.30	0.10	0.73	1.60	4.82	3.43	0.44
Academic track																
Academic [4]	23.65	4.28	3.67	3.56	0.72	2.84	3.07	0.73	1.26	0.74	0.34	1.92	1.61	2.77	2.88	0.50
Vocational [5]	21.95	3.64	2.76	2.07	1.23	0.85	1.60	0.75	0.77	0.07	0.02	0.48	0.96	7.86	2.86	0.47
Both [6]	23.92	4.20	3.50	3.17	1.19	1.98	2.50	0.88	1.11	0.38	0.14	0.89	0.83	6.38	2.65	0.64
Neither [7]	21.16	3.62	2.86	2.19	1.22	0.97	1.71	0.71	0.86	0.12	0.02	1.03	2.11	4.42	3.61	0.31
1990 graduates	23.54	4.09	3.50	3.20	0.99	2.21	2.75	0.84	1.14	0.54	0.23	1.59	1.55	4.10	2.95	0.55
Male	23.36	4.04	3.47	3.22	1.06	2.16	2.78	0.87	1.11	0.53	0.28	1.39	1.31	4.23	3.17	0.52
Female	23.70	4.13	3.52	3.18	0.93	2.25	2.72	0.82	1.17	0.54	0.19	1.78	1.77	3.99	2.74	0.57
Race/ethnicity																
White	23.55	4.08	3.48	3.17	0.89	2.28	2.79	0.83	1.15	0.56	0.25	1.58	1.61	4.13	2.87	0.53
Black	23.41	4.25	3.51	3.25	1.33	1.92	2.68	0.97	1.11	0.44	0.16	1.23	1.34	4.39	3.02	0.61
Hispanic	23.85	4.05	3.46	3.22	1.41	1.81	2.49	0.83	1.11	0.42	0.14	1.99	1.48	3.99	3.43	0.59
Asian	24.08	4.02	3.70	3.64	0.83	2.81	2.97	0.68	1.12	0.74	0.42	2.52	1.30	2.89	3.12	0.55
American Indian	22.64	4.01	3.36	3.17	1.25	1.93	2.48	0.83	1.09	0.42	0.15	1.15	1.11	4.43	3.14	0.60
Academic track																
Academic [4]	23.84	4.26	3.72	3.54	0.78	2.76	3.12	0.82	1.25	0.73	0.33	2.02	1.74	2.64	2.92	0.53
Vocational [5]	22.53	3.58	2.75	2.18	1.46	0.72	1.77	0.88	0.80	0.07	0.02	0.55	1.01	8.15	2.93	0.53
Both [6]	24.29	4.16	3.50	3.18	1.30	1.88	2.58	0.96	1.12	0.37	0.13	0.99	0.93	6.47	2.70	0.70
Neither [7]	21.45	3.51	2.97	2.25	1.24	1.01	1.85	0.77	0.88	0.16	0.05	1.19	2.08	4.39	3.55	0.41
1994 graduates	24.16	4.20	3.57	3.37	0.85	2.53	3.04	0.87	1.26	0.62	0.28	1.76	1.66	3.87	2.92	0.65
Male	23.98	4.16	3.54	3.36	0.93	2.44	3.02	0.90	1.20	0.60	0.32	1.54	1.43	4.07	3.18	0.65
Female	24.33	4.23	3.61	3.38	0.77	2.62	3.05	0.85	1.31	0.65	0.25	1.97	1.87	3.69	2.68	0.65
Race/ethnicity																
White	24.31	4.19	3.58	3.39	0.78	2.62	3.12	0.88	1.29	0.66	0.30	1.75	1.74	3.87	2.87	0.64
Black	23.60	4.31	3.54	3.26	1.15	2.12	2.80	0.91	1.21	0.50	0.18	1.37	1.36	4.24	3.00	0.65
Hispanic	24.07	4.22	3.49	3.39	1.09	2.30	2.69	0.83	1.19	0.50	0.18	2.10	1.51	3.70	3.36	0.76
Asian	24.50	4.04	3.68	3.76	0.81	2.95	3.35	0.79	1.22	0.82	0.52	2.62	1.31	2.88	2.92	0.73
American Indian	24.25	4.22	3.79	3.15	1.05	2.10	2.82	0.92	1.29	0.46	0.14	1.26	1.96	4.06	3.19	0.74
Academic track																
Academic [4]	24.30	4.30	3.75	3.62	0.69	2.93	3.33	0.84	1.34	0.78	0.37	2.11	1.88	2.56	2.89	0.61
Vocational [5]	22.77	3.67	2.77	2.19	1.38	0.81	1.87	0.87	0.91	0.06	0.02	0.54	0.97	8.33	2.97	0.65
Both [6]	24.95	4.22	3.50	3.27	1.07	2.20	2.80	1.00	1.20	0.45	0.16	1.16	1.08	6.49	2.67	0.84
Neither [7]	21.52	3.53	2.84	2.35	1.26	1.09	1.92	0.79	0.93	0.15	0.05	1.23	1.89	4.54	4.18	0.45

[1] Includes nonoccupational vocational education, vocational general introduction, agriculture, business, marketing, health, occupational home economics, trade and industry, and technical courses.

[2] Includes personal and social courses, religion and theology, and courses not included in the other subject fields.

[3] Computer courses are included in mathematics and vocational categories.

[4] Includes students who complete at least 12 Carnegie units in academic courses, but less than 3 Carnegie units in any specific labor market preparation field.

[5] Includes students who complete at least 3 Carnegie units in a specific labor market preparation field, but less than 12 Carnegie units in academic courses.

[6] Includes students who complete at least 12 Carnegie units in academic courses and at least 3 Carnegie units in a specific labor market preparation field.

[7] Includes students who complete less than 12 Carnegie units in academic courses and less than 3 Carnegie units in a specific labor market preparation field.

NOTE.—The Carnegie unit is a standard of measurement that represents one credit for the completion of a 1-year course.

SOURCE: U.S. Department of Education, National Center for Education Statistics, "High School and Beyond," First Followup survey; "1990 High School Transcript Study," "National Education Longitudinal Study of 1988," Second Followup survey, and the "1994 High School Transcript Study." (This table was prepared June 1997.)

Table 137.—Average number of Carnegie units earned by public school graduates in vocational education courses, by student characteristics: 1982 to 1994

Student characteristics	Total	General labor market preparation	Consumer and home-making education	Specific labor market preparation								
				Total	Agri-culture	Business	Marketing	Health	Occupational home economics	Trade and industrial	Technical/ communications	Other
1	2	3	4	5	6	7	8	9	10	11	12	13
1982 graduates	4.68	1.08	0.69	2.91	0.22	1.05	0.16	0.05	0.18	1.06	0.12	0.09
Male	4.63	1.03	0.31	3.29	0.37	0.49	0.14	0.02	0.05	1.97	0.14	0.11
Female	4.72	1.12	1.05	2.55	0.08	1.57	0.17	0.08	0.29	0.20	0.09	0.07
Race/ethnicity												
White	4.58	1.05	0.64	2.88	0.24	1.08	0.15	0.04	0.17	1.01	0.12	0.08
Black	4.84	1.10	0.90	2.84	0.09	0.98	0.22	0.13	0.23	0.97	0.11	0.10
Hispanic	5.26	1.21	0.86	3.19	0.24	1.00	0.15	0.07	0.20	1.34	0.07	0.12
Asian	3.23	1.06	0.29	1.89	0.05	0.59	0.04	0.03	0.05	0.88	0.17	0.08
American Indian	5.09	1.22	0.52	3.35	0.27	0.74	0.14	0.07	0.10	1.86	0.05	0.12
Academic track												
Academic[1]	2.54	0.87	0.48	1.19	0.06	0.51	0.05	0.03	0.05	0.36	0.12	0.02
Vocational[2]	7.55	1.11	0.64	5.80	0.51	1.85	0.29	0.09	0.35	2.40	0.11	0.20
Both[3]	6.47	0.94	0.56	4.97	0.43	1.66	0.26	0.10	0.28	1.97	0.14	0.11
Neither[4]	4.39	1.38	1.10	1.91	0.10	0.84	0.14	0.04	0.15	0.46	0.10	0.07
1987 graduates	4.48	0.92	0.59	2.96	0.21	0.98	0.17	0.07	0.19	0.98	0.24	0.12
Male	4.58	0.89	0.32	3.37	0.35	0.58	0.13	0.02	0.08	1.78	0.30	0.13
Female	4.38	0.94	0.86	2.58	0.07	1.37	0.20	0.11	0.30	0.23	0.19	0.11
Race/ethnicity												
White	4.55	0.93	0.59	3.03	0.25	0.99	0.16	0.06	0.18	1.02	0.26	0.10
Black	4.64	1.01	0.74	2.89	0.10	1.00	0.18	0.12	0.29	0.80	0.18	0.21
Hispanic	4.20	0.93	0.55	2.72	0.07	0.92	0.17	0.06	0.17	1.05	0.14	0.14
Asian	2.95	0.62	0.31	2.02	0.13	0.68	0.10	0.04	0.09	0.50	0.37	0.10
American Indian	4.82	0.89	0.66	3.27	0.21	1.11	0.09	0.08	0.09	1.39	0.19	0.11
Academic track												
Academic[1]	2.77	0.81	0.49	1.46	0.05	0.61	0.06	0.03	0.06	0.33	0.27	0.04
Vocational[2]	7.86	1.07	0.66	6.14	0.52	1.68	0.39	0.15	0.52	2.45	0.17	0.26
Both[3]	6.38	0.90	0.47	5.02	0.47	1.60	0.25	0.12	0.27	1.86	0.27	0.18
Neither[4]	4.42	1.19	1.06	2.17	0.10	0.79	0.18	0.05	0.19	0.54	0.17	0.15
1990 graduates	4.10	0.83	0.57	2.70	0.20	0.90	0.16	0.04	0.17	0.87	0.22	0.14
Male	4.23	0.78	0.33	3.12	0.32	0.58	0.13	0.02	0.06	1.58	0.27	0.15
Female	3.99	0.87	0.79	2.32	0.09	1.19	0.18	0.06	0.27	0.22	0.18	0.12
Race/ethnicity												
White	4.13	0.80	0.55	2.78	0.24	0.87	0.16	0.04	0.15	0.94	0.22	0.15
Black	4.39	0.96	0.81	2.62	0.06	1.08	0.17	0.04	0.28	0.64	0.23	0.11
Hispanic	3.99	0.85	0.54	2.61	0.15	0.95	0.19	0.02	0.27	0.75	0.17	0.10
Asian	2.89	0.73	0.32	1.85	0.04	0.66	0.05	0.01	0.05	0.73	0.26	0.05
American Indian	4.43	0.84	0.72	2.87	0.36	0.96	0.15	0.02	0.08	0.95	0.16	0.19
Academic track												
Academic[1]	2.64	0.73	0.52	1.39	0.05	0.60	0.07	0.02	0.07	0.32	0.24	0.04
Vocational[2]	8.15	1.02	0.62	6.50	0.69	1.60	0.32	0.11	0.51	2.73	0.16	0.37
Both[3]	6.47	0.81	0.50	5.16	0.44	1.60	0.38	0.09	0.33	1.81	0.22	0.29
Neither[4]	4.39	1.24	0.99	2.16	0.13	0.77	0.17	0.04	0.14	0.56	0.17	0.19
1994 graduates	3.87	0.70	0.53	2.65	0.24	0.89	0.18	0.08	0.19	0.70	0.22	0.15
Male	4.07	0.74	0.35	2.99	0.38	0.67	0.14	0.03	0.08	1.25	0.28	0.16
Female	3.69	0.66	0.70	2.33	0.11	1.10	0.22	0.12	0.30	0.17	0.16	0.14
Race/ethnicity												
White	3.87	0.69	0.52	2.66	0.28	0.88	0.19	0.08	0.16	0.72	0.22	0.15
Black	4.24	0.77	0.62	2.84	0.13	1.02	0.20	0.11	0.38	0.60	0.21	0.19
Hispanic	3.70	0.67	0.48	2.55	0.13	0.94	0.15	0.07	0.26	0.65	0.20	0.16
Asian	2.88	0.56	0.37	1.96	0.14	0.71	0.11	0.06	0.12	0.50	0.28	0.05
American Indian	4.06	0.81	0.62	2.63	0.36	0.92	0.05	0.15	0.13	0.57	0.26	0.19
Academic track												
Academic[1]	2.56	0.60	0.48	1.48	0.08	0.65	0.09	0.05	0.08	0.29	0.21	0.04
Vocational[2]	8.33	1.01	0.70	6.62	0.80	1.44	0.37	0.17	0.55	2.46	0.25	0.59
Both[3]	6.49	0.72	0.50	5.28	0.63	1.54	0.42	0.17	0.42	1.50	0.26	0.34
Neither[4]	4.54	1.35	0.94	2.25	0.18	0.73	0.20	0.06	0.20	0.53	0.16	0.18

[1] Includes students who complete at least 12 Carnegie units in academic courses, but less than 3 Carnegie units in any specific labor market preparation field.
[2] Includes students who complete at least 3 Carnegie units in a specific labor market preparation field, but less than 12 Carnegie units in academic courses.
[3] Includes students who complete at least 12 Carnegie units in academic courses and at least 3 Carnegie units in a specific labor market preparation field.
[4] Includes students who complete less than 12 Carnegie units in academic courses and less than 3 Carnegie units in a specific labor market preparation field.

NOTE.—The Carnegie unit is a standard of measurement that represents one credit for the completion of a 1-year course.

SOURCE: U.S. Department of Education, National Center for Education Statistics, "High School and Beyond," First Followup survey; "1990 High School Transcript Study," "National Education Longitudinal Study of 1988," Second Followup survey, and the "1994 High School Transcript Study." (This table was prepared June 1997.)

Table 138.—Percentage of high school graduates taking selected mathematics and science courses in high school, by sex and race/ethnicity: 1982 to 1994

Courses (credits)	1982	1987	1990	1994 Total	Sex Men	Sex Women	White	Black	Hispanic	Asian/Pacific Islander	American Indian/Alaskan Native
1	2	3	4	5	6	7	8	9	10	11	12
Mathematics[1]											
Any mathematics (1.0)	98.5	98.9	99.6	99.6	99.5	99.6	99.6	99.3	99.2	100.0	98.9
Algebra I (1.0)	53.9	64.0	64.2	66.4	64.7	68.1	67.5	65.0	70.7	61.7	58.7
Geometry (1.0)	45.5	59.7	63.4	70.4	68.3	72.4	72.7	58.1	69.4	75.8	60.0
Algebra II (0.5)	32.2	48.6	51.7	58.6	55.4	61.6	61.6	43.7	51.0	66.6	39.2
Trigonometry (0.5)	12.1	18.6	18.2	17.2	16.6	17.8	18.6	13.6	9.8	25.3	6.7
Analysis/pre-calculus (0.5)	5.9	12.6	13.4	17.3	16.3	18.2	18.2	9.8	13.9	33.9	8.7
Statistics/probability (0.5)	1.0	1.3	1.0	2.0	2.0	2.1	2.3	1.7	1.0	1.1	1.2
Calculus (1.0)	4.6	6.0	6.5	9.2	9.4	9.1	9.6	3.8	6.0	23.4	3.8
AP calculus (1.0)	1.5	3.2	4.1	7.0	7.2	6.8	7.3	2.0	4.6	21.0	2.2
Science											
Any science (1.0)	96.6	98.7	99.4	99.5	99.3	99.8	99.7	99.5	99.3	99.3	99.7
Biology (1.0)	76.4	87.8	91.3	93.5	92.3	94.7	94.4	91.3	94.0	90.9	91.2
AP/honors biology (1.0)	6.6	2.7	4.9	4.6	4.0	5.1	4.6	2.7	3.3	8.3	1.7
Chemistry (1.0)	30.9	43.7	49.0	56.0	53.2	58.7	58.5	43.8	46.5	69.3	41.3
AP/honors chemistry (1.0)	2.9	3.3	3.5	3.9	4.1	3.7	4.3	2.1	2.5	7.7	0.6
Physics (1.0)	14.2	19.2	21.5	24.4	26.9	22.0	26.1	14.7	16.0	42.3	10.3
AP/honors physics (1.0)	1.0	1.6	2.0	2.4	3.0	1.8	2.5	1.4	1.8	6.0	0.3
Engineering (1.0)	0.1	0.1	0.1	0.3	0.4	0.2	0.2	0.4	0.1	1.0	—
Astronomy (0.5)	1.1	1.0	1.2	1.7	2.0	1.5	2.0	0.6	0.4	0.8	2.2
Geology/earth science (0.5)	13.2	14.5	24.8	23.0	22.8	23.2	23.8	23.3	15.3	16.7	23.2
Biology and chemistry (2.0)	28.1	42.1	47.6	53.8	50.9	56.6	56.4	42.2	45.1	64.8	39.6
Biology, chemistry, and physics (3.0)	10.6	16.4	18.8	21.3	23.1	19.6	22.7	13.0	13.4	37.2	8.0

[1] These data only report the percentage of students who earned credit in each mathematics course while in high school and does not count those students who took these courses prior to entering high school. In 1992, approximately 93 percent of graduates had taken algebra I before or during high school, and 70 percent had taken geometry.
—Less than 0.05 percent.

SOURCE: U.S. Department of Education, National Center for Education Statistics, National Assessment of Educational Progress, *The 1994 High School Transcript Study Tabulations: Comparative Data on Credits Earned and Demographics for 1994, 1990, 1987, and 1982 High School Graduates*, 1996. (This table was prepared September 1996.)

Table 139.—Percent of high school graduates earning minimum credits in selected combinations of academic courses, by sex and race/ethnicity: 1982 to 1994

Year of graduation and course combinations taken[1]	All students	Sex Male	Sex Female	White	Black	Hispanic	Asian	American Indian/Alaskan Native
1	2	3	4	5	6	7	8	9
1982 graduates								
4 Eng., 3 S.S., 3 Sci., 3 Math, .5 Comp., & 2 F.L.[2]	2.0	2.2	1.8	2.4	0.9	0.6	5.6	0.1
4 Eng., 3 S.S., 3 Sci., 3 Math, & .5 Comp.[3]	2.9	3.6	2.3	3.4	1.3	0.9	6.6	0.1
4 Eng., 3 S.S., 3 Sci., 3 Math, & 2 F.L.	9.2	8.8	9.6	10.5	5.3	3.7	17.1	5.7
4 Eng., 3 S.S., 3 Sci., 3 Math	14.0	14.8	13.3	15.5	11.6	6.5	21.3	6.5
4 Eng., 3 S.S., 2 Sci., 2 Math	31.5	31.6	31.5	32.5	31.7	25.2	34.3	35.7
1987 graduates								
4 Eng., 3 S.S., 3 Sci., 3 Math, .5 Comp., & 2 F.L.[2]	12.1	13.0	11.4	12.8	7.8	6.4	25.6	2.8
4 Eng., 3 S.S., 3 Sci., 3 Math, & .5 Comp.[3]	16.6	18.1	15.1	17.6	11.3	9.0	28.8	15.2
4 Eng., 3 S.S., 3 Sci., 3 Math, & 2 F.L.	20.6	20.2	20.9	21.4	15.0	12.9	42.6	5.8
4 Eng., 3 S.S., 3 Sci., 3 Math	27.9	28.8	27.1	29.2	22.0	17.6	48.8	26.6
4 Eng., 3 S.S., 2 Sci., 2 Math	54.0	53.5	54.7	53.4	56.0	51.6	68.9	66.7
1990 graduates								
4 Eng., 3 S.S., 3 Sci., 3 Math, .5 Comp., & 2 F.L.[2]	18.3	18.1	18.4	18.9	15.5	18.2	23.9	7.8
4 Eng., 3 S.S., 3 Sci., 3 Math, & .5 Comp.[3]	23.3	23.9	22.8	23.5	25.3	20.5	27.2	14.6
4 Eng., 3 S.S., 3 Sci., 3 Math, & 2 F.L.	30.3	29.2	31.3	32.0	23.3	25.8	43.7	9.9
4 Eng., 3 S.S., 3 Sci., 3 Math	38.8	39.2	38.4	39.8	39.5	30.3	48.8	20.9
4 Eng., 3 S.S., 2 Sci., 2 Math	66.5	65.9	67.1	65.8	73.3	64.6	70.6	47.9
1994 graduates								
4 Eng., 3 S.S., 3 Sci., 3 Math, .5 Comp., & 2 F.L.[2]	25.3	23.5	26.9	26.5	19.5	27.7	36.3	12.9
4 Eng., 3 S.S., 3 Sci., 3 Math, & .5 Comp.[3]	32.0	31.1	32.9	33.5	28.2	31.1	40.2	25.5
4 Eng., 3 S.S., 3 Sci., 3 Math, & 2 F.L.	39.1	35.1	42.9	41.6	30.2	36.3	51.2	22.5
4 Eng., 3 S.S., 3 Sci., 3 Math	49.8	47.5	51.9	52.7	45.0	41.2	56.1	46.0
4 Eng., 3 S.S., 2 Sci., 2 Math	74.6	72.2	76.9	75.5	76.7	77.5	73.1	77.0

[1] Eng. = English; S.S. = social studies; Sci. = science; Comp. = computer science; and F.L. = foreign language.
[2] The National Commission on Excellence in Education recommended that all college-bound high school students take these courses as a minimum.
[3] The National Commission on Excellence in Education recommended that all high school students take these courses as a minimum.

SOURCE: U.S. Department of Education, National Center for Education Statistics, *The 1994 High School Transcript Study Tabulations: Comparative Data on Credits Earned and Demographics for 1994, 1990, 1987, and 1982 High School Graduates*, 1996. (This table was prepared October 1996.)

Table 140.—Reasons given by twelfth graders for taking current mathematics and science classes, by selected student and school characteristics: 1992

Class subject and opinion	All 12th graders	Sex		Race/ethnicity					Socioeconomic status quartile [1]				Control of school attended		
		Male	Female	White	Black	Hispanic	Asian	American Indian	Lowest	Second	Third	Highest	Public	Catholic	Other private
1	2	3	4	5	6	7	8	9	10	11	12	13	14	15	16
Mathematics class															
I am interested in mathematics	74.5	77.4	71.3	72.9	74.6	80.4	81.9	87.7	78.0	74.6	73.1	74.2	73.8	78.4	81.7
I do well in mathematics	77.1	80.2	73.7	76.4	76.1	79.7	83.6	76.8	79.5	77.8	76.3	76.1	76.7	78.4	82.1
I need it for college or trade school	87.2	86.6	87.8	86.5	89.8	86.5	90.8	90.5	83.3	85.4	88.9	88.6	87.1	87.9	87.5
I need it for a job after high school	64.7	65.9	63.4	62.5	69.7	70.9	66.3	83.9	71.2	68.5	65.5	57.8	65.9	58.1	51.9
I need it for advanced placement	53.6	53.3	54.0	49.6	58.4	62.5	72.6	56.9	59.8	46.7	52.2	55.7	54.1	47.2	53.9
Advised to take class by:															
Teacher	65.9	63.3	68.8	63.6	74.8	71.1	66.7	70.6	69.2	65.1	66.3	64.7	65.7	66.2	70.0
Guidance counselor	64.8	62.9	66.8	60.7	77.8	76.2	64.2	83.0	76.4	67.5	62.6	58.6	65.8	55.1	59.6
Parent	71.6	69.1	74.2	70.5	74.6	74.4	73.3	79.8	66.3	67.2	70.3	76.6	71.8	68.4	71.4
Friend	42.2	41.4	43.2	39.8	51.2	43.7	50.8	56.2	46.1	43.2	41.7	40.7	42.5	40.6	39.1
Sibling	30.9	29.5	32.5	26.3	37.2	43.1	46.2	51.5	40.4	29.7	27.7	29.4	31.8	21.9	28.9
Science class															
I am interested in science	78.8	82.7	74.4	78.5	77.4	78.9	83.6	74.9	74.5	76.7	76.9	82.7	77.9	81.1	89.9
I do well in science	80.6	83.9	77.0	80.1	76.7	86.1	84.2	86.6	78.1	80.1	77.1	84.0	80.1	79.8	90.2
I need it for college or trade school	83.3	81.7	85.0	82.4	86.4	83.5	88.4	88.8	78.5	81.9	84.6	84.8	83.3	85.3	80.7
I need it for a job after high school	47.0	47.9	45.9	44.5	53.2	57.6	51.3	55.9	53.4	47.6	50.4	41.6	47.8	45.7	35.7
I need it for advanced placement	50.2	49.7	50.9	47.1	51.6	59.0	66.8	59.6	48.9	47.9	46.8	53.9	49.2	53.5	60.3
Advised to take class by:															
Teacher	58.9	56.2	61.9	57.6	61.7	63.7	61.0	67.2	61.3	57.7	58.3	59.0	57.8	60.3	74.1
Guidance counselor	59.4	57.8	61.2	56.2	71.4	70.9	59.7	57.9	74.0	59.5	55.8	55.5	60.3	44.1	67.3
Parent	66.3	63.4	69.4	65.7	69.1	70.5	64.1	73.8	61.9	59.9	66.4	70.6	67.0	58.7	67.4
Friend	43.5	43.4	43.6	42.9	40.9	44.6	49.7	62.9	45.6	41.6	41.0	45.0	43.6	36.6	52.5
Sibling	28.7	26.8	31.0	25.3	35.0	35.5	44.3	57.6	36.1	25.2	25.2	29.6	29.4	21.0	30.5

[1] Socioeconomic status was measured by a composite score on parental education and occupations, and family income.

SOURCE: U.S. Department of Education, National Center for Education Statistics, "National Education Longitudinal Study of 1988," Second Followup survey. (This table was prepared February 1994.)

Table 141.—Expected occupations of 8th, 10th, and 12th graders at age 30, by selected student and school characteristics: 1988, 1990, and 1992

[Percentage distribution]

Expected occupation at age 30	8th graders in 1988	10th graders in 1990	12th graders in 1992													
			Total	Sex		Race/ethnicity						Socioeconomic status [1]			Control of school attended		
				Male	Female	White	Black	Hispanic	Asian	American Indian	Low	Middle	High	Public	Catholic	Other private
1	2	3	4	5	6	7	8	9	10	11	12	13	14	15	16	17
Total	100.0	100.0	100.0	100.0	100.0	100.0	100.0	100.0	100.0	100.0	100.0	100.0	100.0	100.0	100.0	100.0
Craftsperson or operator	4.2	5.6	3.5	6.6	0.5	3.7	3.4	2.7	2.4	2.7	6.8	3.9	0.7	3.9	0.9	0.3
Farmer or farm manager	1.0	1.1	0.9	1.4	0.3	1.0	0.6	0.7	0.1	([2])	1.4	1.0	0.5	0.9	0.6	0.6
Housewife/homemaker	2.3	2.0	1.0	0.1	2.0	1.2	0.4	0.7	0.8	([2])	0.9	1.1	1.2	1.1	0.7	1.5
Laborer or farm worker	0.6	0.8	0.7	1.3	0.1	0.7	0.3	0.6	1.2	1.9	1.2	0.8	0.2	0.7	0.4	0.8
Military, police, or security officer	9.6	5.7	6.6	11.2	2.0	6.4	7.7	7.4	5.1	10.0	9.3	7.4	3.6	7.0	3.3	1.7
Professional, business, or managerial	34.5	45.7	50.8	45.9	55.7	50.0	55.1	47.1	61.3	43.3	38.7	48.1	63.0	49.4	66.3	59.2
Teacher	([3])	4.1	7.5	4.1	10.8	8.4	3.7	6.7	3.4	4.8	6.2	7.6	8.2	7.3	8.1	11.1
Business owner	6.2	5.3	6.0	7.8	4.3	5.6	6.8	7.7	7.0	6.4	6.7	6.4	4.9	6.3	3.8	3.3
Technical	6.2	4.7	5.4	7.5	3.4	5.0	5.5	7.5	6.0	8.2	7.1	5.9	3.5	5.7	2.4	3.6
Salesperson, clerical, or office worker	2.8	4.9	4.8	3.1	6.5	4.6	5.3	6.4	4.1	5.2	8.0	4.7	3.1	4.9	2.6	5.8
Service worker	4.9	1.8	2.4	0.5	4.2	2.3	3.1	2.5	0.6	5.8	4.6	2.3	0.9	2.5	1.5	0.8
Other employment	17.0	7.7	10.2	10.3	10.2	10.8	8.0	9.6	8.0	10.6	8.8	10.8	10.2	10.3	9.6	11.3
Don't know or no plans	10.5	10.5	0.2	0.2	0.2	0.2	0.2	0.5	0.2	1.0	0.4	0.2	0.1	0.2	([2])	0.1

[1] Socioeconomic status was measured by a composite score on parental education and occupations, and family income. The "Low" SES group is the lowest quartile; the "Middle" SES group is the middle two quartiles; and the "High" SES group is the upper quartile.
[2] Less than .05 percent.
[3] Included under "Professional, business, or managerial."

SOURCE: U.S. Department of Education, National Center for Education Statistics, "National Education Longitudinal Study of 1988," First and Second Followup surveys. (This table was prepared March 1994.)

Table 142.—Eighth, tenth, and twelfth graders' attitudes about school climate, by student and school characteristics: 1988, 1990, and 1992

Statements about school climate	Eighth graders in 1988	Tenth graders in 1990	Percent who strongly agree or agree with statement — Twelfth graders in 1992														
			Total	Sex		Race/ethnicity					Socioeconomic status quartile[1]				Control of school attended		
				Male	Female	White	Black	Hispanic	Asian	American Indian	Lowest	Second	Third	Highest	Public	Catholic	Other private
1	2	3	4	5	6	7	8	9	10	11	12	13	14	15	16	17	18
There is real school spirit	68.6	70.4	71.4	72.9	69.8	72.1	67.4	71.0	70.7	62.0	73.4	71.3	72.0	69.5	70.4	82.2	76.0
Discipline is fair	69.1	70.2	68.0	67.0	69.0	68.0	58.6	74.7	75.6	73.0	66.3	66.2	68.1	69.7	67.3	69.9	77.0
Teaching is good	80.2	81.9	85.4	84.8	86.0	85.1	84.1	88.5	85.5	88.3	85.6	84.2	84.3	87.2	84.7	90.4	93.7
Teachers are interested in students	75.2	76.0	81.6	81.5	81.8	81.9	78.4	83.7	80.1	83.0	80.3	80.5	80.1	84.8	80.4	91.1	95.4
I don't feel safe at this school	11.8	8.0	10.4	10.8	10.1	8.6	16.1	14.7	15.8	13.0	13.1	11.2	10.5	7.5	11.1	4.9	3.5
Disruptions by other students interfere with my learning	39.6	39.9	33.1	31.6	34.7	30.8	38.1	39.8	41.4	40.5	37.0	35.9	34.6	26.3	34.2	25.4	21.8
Fights often occur between different racial/ethnic groups	—	—	22.7	22.2	23.2	20.9	22.2	31.9	30.5	29.9	25.1	23.9	23.5	18.6	24.5	8.3	3.0
There are many gangs in school	—	—	16.3	16.4	16.2	12.5	17.5	36.4	27.2	23.2	21.9	15.8	16.7	12.1	17.7	4.5	1.5
Students are graded fairly	—	—	78.3	78.6	78.0	79.5	71.6	77.6	77.3	74.7	74.8	76.3	78.3	82.4	77.3	84.1	91.8
There is a lot of cheating on tests and assignments	—	—	58.8	56.0	61.7	59.7	57.1	53.8	63.5	59.8	55.8	59.1	61.8	58.6	60.2	56.9	32.6
Some teachers ignore cheating when they see it	—	—	30.9	29.3	32.6	32.7	25.4	26.0	30.7	24.8	26.9	31.4	32.7	31.9	31.9	26.5	16.9

[1] Socioeconomic status was measured by a composite score on parental education and occupations, and family income.

SOURCE: U.S. Department of Education, National Center for Education Statistics, "National Education Longitudinal Study of 1988," Base Year and First and Second Followup surveys. (This table was prepared February 1994.)

Table 143.—Percentage of 3- to 5-year-olds who were read to every day in the last week by a family member: 1993, 1995, and 1996

Characteristic	1993	1995	1996
1	2	3	4
Percent of all 3- to 5-year-olds	53	58	57
Sex			
Male	51	57	56
Female	54	59	57
Race/ethnicity			
White, non-Hispanic	59	65	64
Black, non-Hispanic	39	43	44
Hispanic	37	38	39
Poverty status			
Above poverty threshold	56	62	61
At or below poverty threshold	44	48	46
Family composition of household			
Two parents	55	61	61
One or no parent	46	49	46
Mother's education			
Less than high school	37	40	37
High school/high school equivalent	48	48	49
Vocational/technical or some college	57	64	62
College graduate	71	76	77
Mother's employment status			
35 hours or more per week	52	55	54
Less than 35 hours per week	56	63	59
Not in labor force	55	60	59

SOURCE: U.S. Department of Education, National Center for Education Statistics, National Household Education Survey, 1993, 1995, and 1996. (This table was prepared July 1997).

Table 144.—Participation of 10th and 12th graders in extracurricular activities, by selected student characteristics: 1990 and 1992

Extracurricular activities	Total 1990 10th graders	1992 12th graders													
		Total	Sex		Race/ethnicity						Socioeconomic status [1]			Control of school attended		
			Male	Female	White	Black	Hispanic	Asian	American Indian	Low	Middle	High	Public	Catholic	Other private
1	2	3	4	5	6	7	8	9	10	11	12	13	14	15	16
Athletics															
Interscholastic team sport	—	30.4	41.2	19.7	30.8	32.3	25.8	28.3	30.4	25.3	30.1	34.4	29.6	31.2	48.9
Interscholastic individual sport	—	20.3	26.8	13.9	20.9	21.2	14.9	21.6	20.7	13.6	18.7	27.7	20.0	24.6	21.8
Intramural team sport	—	22.7	31.8	13.8	22.3	25.8	20.8	24.9	27.9	20.4	22.9	24.1	22.0	29.7	29.6
Intramural individual sport	—	13.3	16.7	10.0	12.5	16.7	14.0	14.7	18.2	10.8	12.5	15.9	13.5	13.3	10.7
Performing arts															
Cheerleading	5.9	7.6	2.0	13.0	7.4	10.6	6.7	5.1	11.9	6.5	7.9	7.8	7.6	8.3	5.9
School band or orchestra	20.9	19.8	15.1	24.5	19.6	24.4	16.9	17.7	16.8	17.6	19.6	22.0	19.8	12.0	31.3
School play or musical	11.0	15.4	14.1	16.7	16.1	15.9	10.6	13.7	14.0	11.4	14.8	19.4	15.0	14.2	26.2
School government/clubs															
Student government	7.3	15.4	13.1	17.7	15.4	16.7	14.7	14.6	14.3	11.0	14.7	19.8	15.0	14.5	27.9
Academic honor society	7.7	18.5	14.4	22.7	19.6	14.0	12.5	27.2	13.6	9.6	15.9	29.5	17.7	28.0	22.9
School yearbook/newspaper	8.8	18.8	14.0	23.5	19.7	14.3	16.8	18.9	21.2	14.3	16.9	25.1	17.0	28.0	46.7
School service clubs	11.5	13.9	10.3	17.4	13.6	13.6	14.4	19.3	11.6	8.4	12.5	19.6	13.6	17.3	15.4
School academic clubs	30.7	25.1	22.9	27.4	25.8	20.7	22.6	32.3	17.7	18.8	24.1	31.1	25.1	26.4	24.5
School hobby clubs	7.3	7.7	8.1	7.4	7.4	6.6	9.1	11.3	10.8	6.7	7.0	9.3	7.4	9.8	11.0
School FTA, FHA, and FFA	11.7	17.7	14.7	20.7	17.6	22.5	16.4	8.8	22.1	24.8	19.7	9.9	19.4	2.4	2.9

[1] Socioeconomic status was measured by a composite score on parental education and occupations, and family income. The "Low" SES group is the lowest quartile; the "Middle" SES group is the middle two quartiles; and the "High" SES group is the upper quartile.

SOURCE: U.S. Department of Education, National Center for Education Statistics, "National Education Longitudinal Study of 1988," First and Second Followup surveys. (This table was prepared March 1994.)

Table 145.—Percent of high school seniors who plan to go to college after graduation, by student characteristics: 1982 and 1992

Student characteristics	No college		Right after high school		After a year		After more than a year		Don't know	
	1982	1992	1982	1992	1982	1992	1982	1992	1982	1992
1	2	3	4	5	6	7	8	9	10	11
All seniors	18.3	4.0	58.3	76.6	7.1	10.7	3.9	4.1	12.3	4.6
Male	22.8	5.7	53.4	73.0	6.6	10.2	4.0	5.6	13.1	5.5
Female	14.0	2.3	63.0	80.1	7.6	11.1	3.8	2.7	11.6	3.8
Race/ethnicity										
White	18.2	3.9	60.2	76.6	7.0	10.6	3.4	4.4	11.3	4.5
Black	14.6	5.4	57.5	75.2	8.2	11.2	5.7	3.2	14.1	5.2
Hispanic	24.1	3.5	45.6	75.4	7.5	11.6	5.8	3.6	17.0	5.9
Asian	5.6	2.6	81.7	83.4	5.6	8.6	2.1	2.4	5.1	3.1
American Indian	22.2	5.8	48.5	65.7	9.0	15.5	3.3	5.3	17.1	7.7
Test performance quartile										
Lowest test quartile	32.3	11.4	32.8	59.3	9.1	15.1	4.5	3.4	21.3	10.9
Second test quartile	26.5	3.9	45.2	71.2	7.8	14.3	4.8	4.4	15.8	6.3
Third test quartile	15.6	2.0	61.9	81.2	7.9	9.9	3.8	4.1	10.8	2.8
Highest test quartile	3.8	0.6	85.4	90.9	4.7	4.8	2.4	2.6	3.8	1.2
Socioeconomic status [1]										
Low quartile	29.1	8.1	38.3	60.3	7.6	16.5	5.8	5.8	19.2	9.4
Middle 2 quartiles	18.3	4.1	56.6	74.6	8.1	11.8	4.1	4.7	12.9	4.8
High quartile	6.6	1.1	82.8	91.1	5.0	4.6	1.5	1.7	4.1	1.5
Control of school										
Public	19.4	4.4	56.0	74.8	7.3	11.4	4.1	4.5	13.1	4.9
Catholic	8.2	0.5	80.0	93.0	5.1	4.3	1.4	0.7	5.4	1.6
Other private	9.9	0.7	77.3	92.0	6.4	3.0	2.5	0.6	3.9	3.7
Location of school										
Urban	16.6	3.0	59.3	79.5	8.2	10.1	4.0	3.0	11.8	4.4
Suburban	15.5	3.3	62.3	78.6	6.8	9.7	4.1	4.4	11.3	4.0
Rural/nonmetropolitan area	24.0	5.9	51.4	71.2	6.9	12.3	3.6	4.9	14.2	5.8

[1] Socioeconomic status was measured by a composite score on parental education and occupations, and family income. The "Low" SES group is the lowest quartile; the "Middle" SES group is the middle two quartiles; and the "High" SES group is the upper quartile.

SOURCE: U.S. Department of Education, National Center for Education Statistics, "High School and Beyond," First Followup survey; and "National Education Longitudinal Study of 1988," Second Followup Student survey. (This table was prepared April 1995.)

Table 146.—Percent of high school seniors who say they engage in various activities, by student characteristics: 1982 and 1992

Activity	Total	Sex		Race/ethnicity					Socioeconomic status [1]			Control of school attended		
		Male	Female	White	Black	Hispanic	Asian	American Indian	Low	Middle	High	Public	Catholic	Other private
1	2	3	4	5	6	7	8	9	10	11	12	13	14	15
Percent of 12th graders, 1982														
At least once a week														
Talking with friends	92.7	92.5	93.0	94.2	89.1	88.9	86.7	91.3	88.6	93.7	95.6	92.3	96.4	97.2
Reading for pleasure	50.4	43.4	57.1	51.0	53.9	43.1	56.4	50.3	45.2	50.1	56.8	50.1	51.4	56.2
Going on dates	61.3	60.6	62.0	63.9	51.9	58.1	40.3	54.5	55.8	63.4	62.8	61.4	60.7	60.7
Driving or riding around	62.4	65.9	59.1	65.2	48.9	60.7	42.4	62.3	56.2	65.0	65.1	62.6	64.6	55.0
Thinking or daydreaming	68.5	61.8	74.8	71.1	64.6	58.0	62.4	53.9	63.3	67.5	75.9	67.7	75.2	76.5
Talking with parents	83.9	79.9	87.6	85.6	80.1	78.0	79.8	76.0	78.5	84.7	87.8	83.4	87.7	87.9
Reading front page of newspaper	69.1	70.8	67.5	69.7	71.9	63.3	73.5	61.8	61.5	69.1	77.0	68.5	75.7	72.0
Five or more hours on weekdays														
Watches television	11.5	11.9	11.2	9.4	22.2	13.8	8.1	20.9	16.5	11.5	6.4	12.1	8.0	3.9
Percent of 12th graders, 1992														
At least once a week														
Use personal computer	23.7	28.1	19.3	23.9	23.6	20.9	27.0	23.8	18.9	23.3	27.7	23.4	25.2	28.0
Work on hobbies	40.9	44.4	37.4	42.0	34.8	39.9	37.8	49.8	36.3	41.1	43.5	40.6	43.4	43.2
Attend religious activities	31.0	28.1	33.8	31.4	33.7	26.9	30.4	14.6	22.2	29.4	39.9	29.4	38.8	54.9
Attend youth groups	22.4	24.6	20.1	22.5	23.3	18.5	26.4	22.1	16.6	21.3	28.1	21.8	22.9	33.3
Perform community service	11.3	10.7	11.9	11.1	12.1	10.9	14.0	9.2	7.7	9.5	16.7	9.7	22.3	31.2
Driving or riding around	73.3	74.3	72.3	75.7	67.8	66.2	66.7	71.0	69.6	75.3	72.4	73.4	77.8	63.0
Do things with friends	88.1	88.2	88.0	90.7	79.8	82.4	85.9	77.2	80.8	88.1	93.2	87.5	94.5	91.9
Do things with parent	66.7	61.2	72.1	68.2	62.0	63.8	63.4	61.2	59.6	66.3	71.7	66.0	73.6	72.8
Talk with other adult	47.7	45.4	49.9	48.8	44.3	46.2	43.0	44.0	47.6	49.0	45.0	47.3	46.4	58.8
Take music, art, or dance class	10.1	7.9	12.2	9.9	9.7	9.8	14.0	10.6	7.1	8.8	14.0	9.7	13.4	12.4
Take sports lessons	7.3	9.7	5.0	7.0	7.4	8.2	9.4	11.6	5.6	6.6	9.5	7.1	11.1	7.8
Play ball or other sport	26.3	38.8	14.0	27.1	22.9	23.6	28.7	29.4	20.7	24.5	33.1	25.6	34.0	31.4
More than an hour a day														
Reading for pleasure	55.4	53.1	57.7	56.3	51.0	53.5	54.4	59.3	51.6	55.0	58.6	55.0	56.0	62.9
Plays video games	13.0	19.2	6.8	11.7	19.9	13.0	13.5	21.1	16.9	13.7	9.4	13.3	10.4	8.9
Five or more hours on weekdays														
Watches television	8.4	8.5	8.4	6.4	21.3	9.3	6.4	12.7	12.0	9.4	4.1	8.7	7.9	4.1

[1] Socioeconomic status was measured by a composite score on parental education and occupations, and family income. The "Low" SES group is the lowest quartile; the "Middle" SES group is the middle two quartiles; and the "High" SES group is the upper quartile.

SOURCE: U.S. Department of Education, National Center for Education Statistics, "National Education Longitudinal Study of 1988," Second Followup survey, and "High School and Beyond," First Followup survey. (This table was prepared March 1994.)

Table 147.—Percent of high school seniors who participate in selected school-sponsored extracurricular activities, by student characteristics: 1980 and 1992

Student characteristics	Academic clubs		Athletics		Cheerleading and drill team		Newspaper or yearbook		Music, drama, debate		Vocational clubs	
	1980	1992	1980	1992	1980	1992	1980	1992	1980	1992	1980	1992
1	2	3	4	5	6	7	8	9	10	11	12	13
All seniors	25.6	25.1	51.8	42.9	15.1	7.5	19.9	18.8	36.5	27.9	23.1	17.7
Male	20.3	22.8	64.0	55.3	4.5	2.0	15.4	14.0	28.4	23.0	19.1	14.7
Female	30.9	27.4	40.6	30.3	24.8	13.0	24.0	23.5	44.0	32.7	26.7	20.6
Race/ethnicity												
White	25.0	25.8	51.6	44.1	14.9	7.4	20.1	19.7	35.8	28.1	22.3	17.6
Black	33.1	20.6	54.4	41.4	17.6	10.6	17.8	14.3	43.2	32.2	30.1	22.5
Hispanic	24.2	22.6	49.4	35.3	12.3	6.6	15.8	16.8	31.1	22.3	27.3	16.4
Asian	26.6	32.3	48.8	45.2	14.6	5.1	21.4	18.9	36.6	25.8	9.6	8.8
Test performance quartile												
Lowest test quartile	24.6	18.1	46.3	40.3	15.0	8.5	14.6	12.0	31.8	23.3	33.0	25.0
Middle 2 test quartiles	24.3	23.3	49.4	42.3	16.0	7.6	18.7	17.1	35.6	26.5	24.2	20.0
Highest test quartile	29.0	37.1	54.0	49.0	13.5	7.9	27.1	27.9	43.4	35.2	12.4	11.4
Socioeconomic status [1]												
Low quartile	24.6	19.4	43.2	33.9	13.0	6.7	15.7	14.2	31.0	24.1	30.6	24.8
Middle 2 quartiles	24.3	24.5	52.1	41.7	15.9	8.0	19.2	17.5	35.8	27.8	24.1	18.5
High quartile	29.0	31.7	61.7	53.9	15.6	7.7	25.3	25.5	43.8	31.6	13.4	9.3
Region												
Northwest	19.6	23.1	54.5	48.6	11.5	6.9	24.6	28.3	34.5	28.4	10.6	8.1
Midwest	21.4	25.4	52.8	45.8	15.3	8.0	18.4	18.2	37.1	32.0	20.0	18.4
South	30.8	28.2	48.2	38.8	18.0	8.5	18.8	15.0	37.9	25.6	40.0	27.2
West	21.9	21.6	52.9	40.6	14.0	6.0	16.8	16.5	35.2	25.6	15.8	10.0
High school program [2]												
General	19.6	18.3	49.9	37.8	14.0	7.1	16.7	14.6	34.5	26.3	22.6	16.7
Academic	28.7	34.2	60.1	50.8	17.2	8.8	26.9	24.9	44.1	32.8	13.1	12.6
Vocational	23.1	14.7	42.4	30.1	13.3	4.9	13.2	11.2	27.7	16.2	39.3	41.2

[1] Socioeconomic status was measured by a composite score on parental education and occupations, and family income. The "low" SES group is the lowest quartile; the middle SES group is the middle two quartiles; and the "high" SES group is the upper quartile.

[2] Program as reported by student.

SOURCE: U.S. Department of Education, National Center for Education Statistics, "High School and Beyond," Senior Cohort; and "National Education Longitudinal Study of 1988," Second Followup survey. (This table was prepared February 1996.)

Table 148.—Percent of students in grades 9 through 12 who reported experience with drugs and violence on school property, by race/ethnicity, grade, and sex: 1993 and 1995

Type of violence or drug-related behavior	1993 Total	1995 Total	1995 Race/ethnicity			1995 Grade			
			White	Black	Hispanic	9	10	11	12
1	2	3	4	5	6	7	8	9	10
Felt too unsafe to go to school [1]									
Total	4.4	4.5	2.8	7.7	8.4	5.6	5.0	4.1	3.3
Male	4.3	4.7	3.4	7.1	8.6	5.9	4.6	4.2	3.9
Female	4.4	4.3	2.2	8.2	8.3	5.1	5.5	4.1	2.8
Carried a weapon on school property [1,2]									
Total	11.8	9.8	9.0	10.3	14.1	10.7	10.4	10.2	7.6
Male	17.9	14.3	14.1	12.2	19.4	14.9	14.8	15.4	12.0
Female	5.1	4.9	3.1	8.8	8.9	5.6	5.7	4.5	3.1
Threatened or injured with a weapon on school property [3]									
Total	7.3	8.4	7.0	11.0	12.4	9.6	9.6	7.7	6.7
Male	9.2	10.9	9.2	15.2	15.2	11.9	12.0	10.6	9.0
Female	5.4	5.8	4.5	7.7	9.6	6.8	7.0	4.6	4.5
In a physical fight on school property [3]									
Total	16.2	15.5	12.9	20.3	21.1	21.6	16.5	13.6	10.6
Male	23.5	21.0	18.4	27.9	25.7	29.4	20.8	18.6	15.5
Female	8.6	9.6	6.5	14.3	16.6	12.1	11.9	8.4	5.6
Property stolen or deliberately damaged on school property [3]									
Total	32.7	34.9	34.9	33.6	34.0	39.0	36.2	35.2	29.4
Male	37.0	41.4	42.2	39.6	35.6	46.3	40.5	41.4	37.5
Female	28.1	28.0	26.6	29.0	32.4	30.2	31.6	28.6	21.5
Cigarette use on school property [1]									
Total	13.2	16.0	17.6	7.6	14.9	13.9	15.4	16.7	17.5
Male	13.5	16.8	17.5	11.6	16.2	15.3	15.3	16.4	20.0
Female	12.9	15.1	17.7	4.5	13.6	12.4	15.5	17.0	14.9
Smokeless tobacco use on school property [4]									
Total	6.8	6.3	8.0	1.3	3.0	5.3	6.2	7.2	5.9
Male	12.5	11.2	14.2	2.7	3.9	8.8	11.2	13.7	11.2
Female	0.8	0.9	0.8	0.2	2.2	1.1	1.0	0.3	0.6
Alcohol use on school property [1]									
Total	5.2	6.3	5.6	7.6	9.7	7.5	6.0	5.7	6.2
Male	6.2	7.2	6.5	9.6	10.0	7.9	6.3	6.1	8.4
Female	4.2	5.3	4.6	5.2	9.4	6.5	5.6	5.2	4.0
Marijuana use on school property [1]									
Total	5.6	8.8	7.0	12.3	12.9	8.7	9.8	8.6	8.0
Male	7.8	11.9	9.7	17.6	17.6	11.2	12.9	12.0	11.2
Female	3.3	5.5	4.0	8.1	8.3	5.8	6.6	4.9	4.7
Offered, sold, or given an illegal drug on school property [3]									
Total	24.0	32.1	31.7	28.5	40.7	31.1	35.0	32.8	29.1
Male	28.5	38.8	38.8	35.3	46.7	35.8	43.0	39.8	36.2
Female	19.1	24.8	23.5	22.5	34.9	24.9	26.4	25.3	22.0

[1] On one or more of the 30 days preceding the survey.
[2] Such as a gun, knife, or club.
[3] One or more times during the 12 months preceding the survey.
[4] Used chewing tobacco or snuff during the 30 days preceding the survey.

SOURCE: U.S. Department of Health and Human Services, Centers for Disease Control and Prevention, National Center for Chronic Disease, Prevention and Health Promotion, Division of Adolescent and School Health, The Youth Risk Behavior Surveillance System: 1995. (This table was prepared April 1997.)

Table 149.—Percent of 12- to 17-year olds reporting drug use during the past 30 days and the past year: 1979 to 1995

Type of drug and frequency of use	1979	1982	1985	1988	1990	1991	1992	1993	1994	1995
1	2	3	4	5	6	7	8	9	10	11
Percent reporting drug use during past 30 days										
Any illicit use	16.3	—	13.2	8.1	7.1	5.8	5.3	5.7	8.2	10.9
Marijuana	14.2	9.9	10.2	5.4	4.4	3.6	3.4	4.0	6.0	8.2
Cocaine	1.5	1.9	1.5	1.2	0.6	0.4	0.3	0.4	0.3	0.8
Alcohol	49.6	34.9	41.2	33.4	32.5	27.0	20.9	23.9	21.6	21.1
Cigarettes	—	—	29.4	22.7	22.4	20.9	18.4	18.5	18.9	20.2
Percent reporting drug use during past year										
Any illicit use	24.3	—	20.7	14.9	14.1	13.1	10.4	11.9	15.5	18.0
Marijuana	21.3	17.7	16.7	10.7	9.6	8.5	6.9	8.5	11.4	14.2
Cocaine	3.6	3.7	3.4	2.5	1.9	1.3	1.0	0.7	1.1	1.7
Alcohol	55.9	46.1	52.7	45.5	41.8	41.2	33.3	35.9	36.2	35.1
Cigarettes	—	—	29.9	26.8	26.2	23.7	21.4	22.5	24.5	26.6

—Data not available, or low precision; no estimate reported.
NOTE.—Due to changes in the survey instrument and administration and to improve comparability with new data, estimates for 1979 through 1993 have been adjusted and may differ from those reported in previous years.

SOURCE: U.S. Department of Health and Human Services, Substance Abuse and Mental Health Services Administration, "Preliminary Estimates from the 1995 National Household Survey on Drug Abuse," 1996. (This table was prepared April 1997.)

Table 150.—Percent of high school seniors reporting drug use, by type of drug and frequency of use: 1975 to 1996

Type of drug and frequency of use	Class of 1975	Class of 1980	Class of 1981	Class of 1982	Class of 1983	Class of 1984	Class of 1985	Class of 1986	Class of 1987	Class of 1988	Class of 1989	Class of 1990	Class of 1991	Class of 1992	Class of 1993	Class of 1994	Class of 1995	Class of 1996
1	2	3	4	5	6	7	8	9	10	11	12	13	14	15	16	17	18	19
Percent reporting having ever used drugs																		
Alcohol[1]	90.4	93.2	92.6	92.8	92.6	92.6	92.2	91.3	92.2	92.0	90.7	89.5	88.0	87.5	80.0	80.4	80.7	79.2
Any illicit drug	55.2	65.4	65.6	64.4	62.9	61.6	60.6	57.6	56.6	53.9	50.9	47.9	44.1	40.7	42.9	45.6	48.4	50.8
Marijuana only	19.0	26.7	22.8	23.3	22.5	21.3	20.9	19.9	20.8	21.4	19.5	18.5	17.2	15.6	16.2	18.0	20.3	22.3
Any illicit drug other than marijuana[2]	36.2	38.7	42.8	41.1	40.4	40.3	39.7	37.7	35.8	32.5	31.4	29.4	26.9	25.1	26.7	27.6	28.1	28.5
Use of selected drugs																		
Cocaine	9.0	15.7	16.5	16.0	16.2	16.1	17.3	16.9	15.2	12.1	10.3	9.4	7.8	6.1	6.1	5.9	6.0	7.1
Heroin	2.2	1.1	1.1	1.2	1.2	1.3	1.2	1.1	1.2	1.1	1.3	1.3	0.9	1.2	1.1	1.2	1.6	1.8
LSD	11.3	9.3	9.8	9.6	8.9	8.0	7.5	7.2	8.4	7.7	8.3	8.7	8.8	8.6	10.3	10.5	11.7	12.6
Marijuana/hashish	47.3	60.3	59.5	58.7	57.0	54.9	54.2	50.9	50.2	47.2	43.7	40.7	36.7	32.6	35.3	38.2	41.7	44.9
PCP	—	9.6	7.8	6.0	5.6	5.0	4.9	4.8	3.0	2.9	3.9	2.8	2.9	2.4	2.9	2.8	2.7	4.0
Percent reporting use of drugs in the past 12 months																		
Alcohol[1]	84.8	87.9	87.0	86.8	87.3	86.0	85.6	84.5	85.7	85.3	82.7	80.6	77.7	76.8	72.7	73.0	73.7	72.5
Any illicit drug	45.0	53.1	52.1	49.4	47.4	45.8	46.3	44.3	41.7	38.5	35.4	32.5	29.4	27.1	31.0	35.8	39.0	40.2
Marijuana only	18.8	22.7	18.1	19.3	19.0	17.8	18.9	18.4	17.6	17.4	15.4	14.6	13.2	12.2	13.9	17.8	19.6	20.4
Any illicit drug other than marijuana[2]	26.2	30.4	34.0	30.1	28.4	28.0	27.4	25.9	24.1	21.1	20.0	17.9	16.2	14.9	17.1	18.0	19.4	19.8
Use of selected drugs																		
Cocaine	5.6	12.3	12.4	11.5	11.4	11.6	13.1	12.7	10.3	7.9	6.5	5.3	3.5	3.1	3.3	3.6	4.0	4.9
Heroin	1.0	0.5	0.5	0.6	0.6	0.5	0.6	0.5	0.5	0.5	0.6	0.5	0.4	0.6	0.5	0.6	1.1	1.0
LSD	7.2	6.5	6.5	6.1	5.4	4.7	4.4	4.5	5.2	4.8	4.9	5.4	5.2	5.6	6.8	6.9	8.4	8.8
Marijuana/hashish	40.0	48.8	46.1	44.3	42.3	40.0	40.6	38.8	36.3	33.1	29.6	27.0	23.9	21.9	26.0	30.7	34.7	35.8
PCP	—	4.4	3.2	2.2	2.6	2.3	2.9	2.4	1.3	1.2	2.4	1.2	1.4	1.4	1.4	1.6	1.8	2.6
Percent reporting use of drugs in the past 30 days																		
Alcohol[1]	68.2	72.0	70.7	69.7	69.4	67.2	65.9	65.3	66.4	63.9	60.0	57.1	54.0	51.3	48.6	50.1	51.3	50.8
Any illicit drug	30.7	37.2	36.9	32.5	30.5	29.2	29.7	27.1	24.7	21.3	19.7	17.2	16.4	14.4	18.3	21.9	23.8	24.6
Marijuana only	15.3	18.8	15.2	15.5	15.1	14.1	14.8	13.9	13.1	11.3	10.6	9.2	9.3	8.1	10.4	13.1	13.8	15.1
Any illicit drug other than marijuana[2]	15.4	18.4	21.7	17.0	15.4	15.1	14.9	13.2	11.6	10.0	9.1	8.0	7.1	6.3	7.9	8.8	10.0	9.5
Use of selected drugs																		
Cocaine	1.9	5.2	5.8	5.0	4.9	5.8	6.7	6.2	4.3	3.4	2.8	1.9	1.4	1.3	1.3	1.5	1.8	2.0
Heroin	0.4	0.2	0.2	0.2	0.2	0.3	0.3	0.2	0.2	0.2	0.3	0.2	0.2	0.3	0.2	0.3	0.6	0.5
LSD	2.3	2.3	2.5	2.4	1.9	1.5	1.6	1.7	1.8	1.8	1.8	1.9	1.9	2.0	2.4	2.6	4.0	2.5
Marijuana/hashish	27.1	33.7	31.6	28.5	27.0	25.2	25.7	23.4	21.0	18.0	16.7	14.0	13.8	11.9	15.5	19.0	21.2	21.9
PCP	—	1.4	1.4	1.0	1.3	1.0	1.6	1.3	0.6	0.3	1.4	0.4	0.5	0.6	1.0	0.7	0.6	1.3

[1] Survey question changed in 1993; data are not comparable to figures for earlier years.
[2] Other illicit drugs include any use of hallucinogens, cocaine, and heroin, or any use of other opiates, stimulants, sedatives, or tranquilizers not under a doctor's orders.
—Data not available.

NOTE.—A revised questionnaire was used in 1982 and later years to reduce the inappropriate reporting of nonprescription stimulants. This slightly reduced the positive responses for some types of drug abuse.

SOURCE: U.S. Department of Health and Human Services, Alcohol, Drug Abuse, and Mental Health Administration, *Drug Use Among American High School Students and Other Young Adults, National Trends Through 1988*; and press releases dated January 1992, April 1993, and January 1994; and University of Michigan, Institute for Social Research, *Monitoring the Future*, unpublished data. (This table was prepared April 1997.)

Table 151.—Percent of students (grades 7 to 12) who feel that certain problems are very serious: 1996

Student characteristics	Tight groups of friends that do not talk to one another	Hostile or threatening remarks between groups of students	Threats or destructive acts, other than physical fights	Turf battles between different groups of students	Physical fights between members of different groups of friends	Gang violence
1	2	3	4	5	6	7
All students	10	25	24	21	26	26
Location						
Urban	11	32	33	30	33	36
Suburban	11	22	20	18	24	21
Rural	8	20	19	13	20	17
Sex						
Male	10	24	23	21	26	25
Female	10	27	26	21	27	26
School level						
7th and 8th grades	9	32	28	24	32	31
9th through 12th grades	11	22	22	20	23	23
Race/ethnicity						
White	9	22	21	16	22	19
African American	12	36	33	32	37	40
Hispanic	13	33	32	33	34	41

SOURCE: Metropolitan Life/Louis Harris Associates, Inc., *The Metropolitan Life Survey of The American Teacher, 1996. Part I. "Students Voice Their Opinions On: Violence, Social Tension and Equality Among Teens."* (This table was prepared July 1997.)

Table 152.—Ages for compulsory school attendance, special education services for students, policies for kindergarten programs, and year-round schools, by state: 1997 and 1995

State	Compulsory attendance, 1997	Compulsory special education services, 1997[1]	Year-round schools, 1995		Provision of kindergarten education, 1995			
			Has policy on year-round schools	Has districts with year-round schools	School districts required to offer		Attendance required	
					Half day	Full day	Half day	Full day
1	2	3	4	5	6	7	8	9
Alabama	7 to 16	3 to 21		X		X		
Alaska	[2]7 to 16	3 to 21		X				
Arizona	[3]6 to 16	3 to 21	X	X	X		X	
Arkansas	5 to 17	3 to 21	X	X		X		X
California	6 to 18	3 to 21	X	X	X			
Colorado	7 to 16	[4]3 to 20		X				
Connecticut	7 to 16	3 to 20			X			
Delaware	5 to 16	3 to 20			X			
District of Columbia	5 to 18	[5]3 to 21				X		X
Florida	6 to 16	3 to 20		X		X		
Georgia	7 to 16	3 to 21		X		X		
Hawaii	[6]6 to 18	3 to 20		X				
Idaho	7 to 16	3 to 20	X	X				
Illinois	7 to 16	3 to 20	X	X	X			
Indiana	[7]7 to 18	3 to 21		X				
Iowa	6 to 16	Birth to 20						
Kansas	7 to 16	3 to 20						
Kentucky	[8]6 to 16	3 to 20		X	X			
Louisiana	7 to 17	3 to 21	—	—	—	—	—	—
Maine	7 to 17	3 to 19						
Maryland	5 to 16	Birth to 20			X			
Massachusetts	6 to 16	3 to 21			X			
Michigan	6 to 16	Birth to 25						
Minnesota	[9]7 to 16	Birth to 20	X	X	X			
Mississippi	6 to 17	3 to 20		X		X		
Missouri	7 to 16	3 to 20		X	X		X	
Montana	[10]7 to 16	3 to 18			X			
Nebraska	7 to 16	Birth to 20	X					
Nevada	7 to 17	3 to 21			X	X		
New Hampshire	6 to 16	3 to 20						
New Jersey	6 to 16	3 to 21						
New Mexico	5 to 18	3 to 21			X	X	X	
New York	[11]6 to 16	3 to 21	X	X				
North Carolina	7 to 16	3 to 20	X	X				
North Dakota	7 to 16	3 to 20			X	X	X	X
Ohio	6 to 18	3 to 21		X	X		X	
Oklahoma	5 to 18	3 to 21	X	X	X			
Oregon	7 to 18	3 to 21		X	X			
Pennsylvania	8 to 17	3 to 20			X			
Rhode Island	6 to 16	3 to 20			X		X	
South Carolina	[12]5 to 17	[4]3 to 21		X	X		X	
South Dakota	[10]6 to 16	3 to 21	X		X	X	X	
Tennessee	7 to 17	3 to 21			X		X	
Texas	6 to 17	3 to 21	X	X	X	X	X	
Utah	6 to 18	3 to 21	X	X	X		X	
Vermont	7 to 16	3 to 21			X			
Virginia	5 to 18	2 to 21		X	X	X	X	X
Washington	[13]8 to 18	3 to 20		X				
West Virginia	6 to 16	3 to 20	X		X			
Wisconsin	[14]6 to 18	[4]3 to 20						
Wyoming	7 to 16	[4]3 to 20			X			

[1] Most states have an upper age limit whereby education is provided up to a certain age or completion of secondary school, whichever comes first.
[2] Ages 7 to 16 or high school graduation.
[3] Ages 6 to 16 or tenth grade completion.
[4] Upper age limit for eligibility has been updated for 1997.
[5] State has established two points in the program year by which children must be 3 years of age to be eligible for services.
[6] Students over the age of 16 may withdraw with the approval of a principal and student's guardians, and if an alternative education program exists.
[7] From age 7 until student (1) graduates; (2) between age 16 to 18 and meets requirements for exit interview before graduation; or (3) reaches 18. Withdrawal before 18 requires parent/guardian and principal written permission.
[8] Must have parental signature for leaving school between ages 16 to 18.
[9] Age 18 takes effect in 2000.
[10] Age 16 or completion of eighth grade.
[11] Ages 6 to 17 for New York City and Buffalo.
[12] Permits parental waiver of kindergarten at age 5.
[13] Or can exit if age 16 or older, has a useful occupation, has met graduation requirements or has a certificate of education competency.
[14] Ages 6 to 18 or high school graduation.
—Data not available.

NOTE.—The Education of the Handicapped Act (EHA) Amendments of 1986 make it mandatory for all states receiving EHA funds to serve all 3- to 18-year-old disabled children.

SOURCE: U.S. Department of Education, Office of Special Education and Rehabilitative Services, *The Eighteenth Annual Report to Congress on the Implementation of The Individuals with Disabilities Education Act, 1996*; National Association of State Directors of Special Education, Inc., unpublished data; Education Commission of the States, "Clearinghouse Notes," March 1997; and Council of Chief State School Officers, *State Education Policies on Student Attendance and Use of Time: 1995*. (This table was prepared May 1997.)

Table 153.—Tenth and twelfth graders' attendance patterns, by selected student and school characteristics: 1990 and 1992

Attendance pattern	All students	Sex		Race/ethnicity					Socioeconomic status [1]			Control of school attended		
		Male	Female	White	Black	Hispanic	Asian	American Indian	Low	Middle	High	Public	Catholic	Other private
1	2	3	4	5	6	7	8	9	10	11	12	13	14	15
Percent of 10th graders in 1990														
Number of days missed first half of current school year														
None	14.3	17.1	11.6	13.0	21.2	12.5	23.1	12.0	13.1	15.0	14.9	14.0	18.3	15.1
1 or 2 days	23.2	24.9	21.5	22.8	27.2	20.6	28.6	12.5	20.0	23.0	26.6	22.6	26.4	33.6
3 or 4 days	27.7	27.1	28.3	28.8	24.5	25.0	23.9	33.7	25.3	27.6	29.5	27.9	26.6	27.7
5 or more days	34.8	30.9	38.7	35.4	27.1	41.9	24.4	41.9	41.6	34.3	29.0	35.4	28.8	23.5
Number of times late first half of current school year														
None	25.2	25.4	24.9	27.8	17.8	17.8	22.0	18.6	23.9	25.7	26.6	25.3	27.7	17.9
1 or 2 days	38.2	38.1	38.3	38.0	41.1	36.7	39.7	31.3	37.4	38.6	38.2	37.8	39.8	44.6
3 or more days	36.7	36.6	36.8	34.2	41.1	45.5	38.3	50.1	38.7	35.7	35.2	36.9	32.4	37.5
Cut classes														
Never or almost never	84.8	83.5	86.2	85.8	86.5	75.8	87.1	81.4	82.3	84.5	89.0	84.0	95.2	90.9
At least sometimes	15.2	16.5	13.8	14.2	13.5	24.2	12.9	18.6	17.7	15.5	11.0	16.0	4.8	9.1
Percent of 12th graders in 1992														
Number of days missed first half of current school year														
None	8.7	10.5	6.9	7.4	15.8	6.9	15.6	11.3	8.7	8.6	8.8	8.6	10.2	9.1
1 or 2 days	30.3	30.8	29.9	29.9	31.0	31.6	34.3	22.4	27.5	30.8	31.7	30.2	31.2	32.7
3 to 6 days	35.0	35.0	35.1	36.2	31.2	34.4	27.4	37.8	34.0	34.0	37.7	34.8	37.5	37.8
7 or more days	25.9	23.7	28.2	26.5	22.1	27.1	22.7	28.6	29.8	26.6	21.8	26.4	21.1	20.5
Number of times late first half of current school year														
None	19.0	17.7	20.3	20.6	14.0	14.7	16.2	19.1	19.7	19.0	18.7	19.2	19.5	12.3
1 or 2 days	33.5	32.4	34.5	34.4	32.1	28.7	33.8	25.3	32.8	34.2	33.1	33.0	36.4	37.6
3 or more days	47.6	49.9	45.2	45.0	53.9	56.6	50.0	55.6	47.5	46.8	48.2	47.8	44.1	50.1
Cut classes														
Never or almost never	75.6	72.8	78.4	76.5	77.7	67.9	72.7	73.7	76.2	75.6	75.4	74.3	87.1	86.3
At least sometimes	24.4	27.2	21.6	23.5	22.3	32.1	27.3	26.3	23.8	24.4	24.6	25.7	12.9	13.7

[1] Socioeconomic status was measured by a composite score on parental education and occupations, and family income. The "Low" SES group is the lowest quartile; the "Middle" SES group is the middle two quartiles; and the "High" SES group is the upper quartile.

SOURCE: U.S. Department of Education, National Center for Education Statistics, "National Education Longitudinal Study of 1988," First and Second Followup surveys. (This table was prepared March 1994.)

Table 154.—Twelfth graders who agree or strongly agree with statements about their school: 1992

Students' response	Percent of 12th graders													
	All 12th graders	Sex		Race/ethnicity					Socioeconomic status [1]			Control of school attended		
		Male	Female	White	Black	Hispanic	Asian	American Indian	Low	Middle	High	Public	Catholic	Other private
1	2	3	4	5	6	7	8	9	10	11	12	13	14	15
Teaching is good at school	83.5	82.5	84.6	83.5	81.7	85.7	85.1	84.9	84.6	82.1	85.5	83.1	88.9	92.5
Teachers are interested in students	79.7	78.8	80.7	80.2	75.8	81.1	80.3	81.2	78.9	78.4	82.7	79.0	89.9	93.9
Do not feel safe at school	10.7	11.1	10.2	8.8	16.0	14.7	15.8	11.7	12.5	10.9	8.3	10.8	5.1	4.4
Disruptions impede learning	33.6	32.2	35.2	31.5	37.5	40.1	40.9	45.9	39.2	35.2	26.2	34.4	25.4	23.0
Grading is fair	76.8	76.7	76.8	77.9	71.1	76.4	76.7	73.3	74.0	75.4	81.2	75.8	82.9	90.1
There is cheating at school	57.8	54.9	60.7	58.6	56.6	51.9	63.2	59.8	55.4	58.7	58.1	59.4	56.9	29.5
Discipline is fair	66.5	64.7	68.4	66.2	58.9	73.5	74.5	74.3	65.7	65.5	68.5	65.6	68.8	74.7

[1] Socioeconomic status was measured by a composite score on parental education and occupations and family income. The "Low" SES group is the lowest quartile; the "Middle" SES group is the middle two quartiles; and the "High" SES group is the upper quartile.

SOURCE: U.S. Department of Education, National Center for Education Statistics, "National Education Longitudinal Study of 1988, Second Followup" survey. (This table was prepared July 1996.)

ELEMENTARY AND SECONDARY: REGULATIONS 149

Table 155.—State requirements for high school graduation, in Carnegie units: 1993 and 1996

State	1993 All courses	1996 All courses	1996 Subject areas						Other courses	First graduating class to which these requirements apply	Notes
			English/ language arts	Social studies	Mathematics	Science	Physical education/ health	Electives			
1	2	3	4	5	6	7	8	9	10	11	12
Alabama Standard	22	24	4	4	4	4	1.5	5.5	1 (.5 fine arts; .5 computer applications).	2000	Students must become computer literate through related coursework.
Alaska	21	21	4	3	2	2	1	9		—	
Arizona	20	20	4	2.5	2	2	0	8	1.5 (.5 free enterprise, 1 fine arts).	1996	State board is required to adopt competency tests for graduation in reading, writing and mathematics (1996). Social studies requirement includes 1 unit in world history and geography; 1.5 units in U.S. and Arizona Constitutions and Arizona history.[1]
Arkansas Technical postsecondary preparatory	20	21	4	2	3	3	1	3	5 (.5 oral communications; 1 vocational/technical; .5 fine arts; seniors take at least 3 academic courses).	1997	Science requirements include 1 unit in life science and 1 unit in physical science. Physical education requirement includes .5 unit in health and safety and .5 unit in physical education. Physical education cannot exceed 1 unit.[2]
College preparatory	—	21	4	3	3	3	1	3	4 (.5 oral communication; .5 fine arts; seniors take at least 3 academic courses).	1988	Science requirements include 1 unit in life science and 1 unit in physical science. Physical education requirement includes .5 unit in health and safety and .5 unit in physical education. Physical education cannot exceed 1 unit.[1,2]
California Standard	13	13	3	3	2	2	2	—	1 (includes foreign language or American Sign Language or visual and performing arts).	1989	Social studies requirement includes 1 unit in U.S. history and geography, 1 unit in world history, culture and geography, .5 unit American government, and .5 unit economics. Science requirement includes 1 unit in biological and 1 unit in physical science.[3]
Colorado	—	—	([1])	([1])	([1])	([1])	([1])	([1])		—	([1,3])
Connecticut	20	20	4	3	3	2	1	1	6	1988	Electives could be in arts or vocational education.
Delaware Standard (1997, 1998)	19	19	4	3	2	2	1.5	6.5	—	1997	Physical education requirement includes .5 unit in health and 1 unit in physical education.
Standard (1999)	—	20	4	3	2	2	1.5	6.5	1 (computer literacy); students must become computer literate through formal class or related coursework.	1999	Physical education requirement includes .5 unit in health and 1 unit in physical education.
Standard (2000)	—	22	4	3	3	3	1.5	—	7.5 (1 computer literacy; students must become computer literate through formal class or related coursework; 3 Career Pathway[4]; 3.5 additional academic coursework).	2000	Physical education requirement includes .5 unit in health and 1 unit in physical education.
District of Columbia	23.5	23.5	4	3.5	3	3	1.5	3.5	5 (2 foreign language; 1 life skills; 1 career/vocational; .5 fine arts; .5 music).	1996	D.C. requires 100 hours of community service without credit.
Florida	24	24	4	2.5	3	3	1	9	1.5 (.5 economics; 1 practical arts or exploratory career education).	—	Social studies requirement includes 1 unit in American history, 1 unit in world history and .5 unit in American government. Two science units must have a laboratory component. The physical education requirement includes .5 unit in life management skills and .5 units in physical education.[1,2]
Georgia Standard	21	21	4	3	3	3	1	6	1 (computer technology and/or fine arts and/or vocational education and/or junior ROTC).	1997	Students who completed 4 units of vocational education in addition to requirements receive a state seal of endorsement. Mathematics requirement includes 1 unit in algebra.[1,2]

150 ELEMENTARY AND SECONDARY: REGULATIONS

Table 155.—State requirements for high school graduation, in Carnegie units: 1993 and 1996—Continued

State	1993 All courses	1996 All courses	English/ language arts	Social studies	Mathematics	Science	Physical education/ health	Electives	Other courses	First graduating class to which these requirements apply	Notes
1	2	3	4	5	6	7	8	9	10	11	12
Advanced	21	21	4	3	3	3	1	4	3 (2 foreign language; 1 fine arts, vocational education, computer technology, or ROTC).	—	([1,2])
Hawaii Standard	22	22	4	4	3	3	2	6	—	1997	Physical education includes 1 unit in health and guidance and 1 unit in physical education. 10th grade students take the Hawaii State Test of Essential Competencies (HSTEC).
Recognition diploma	—	24	4	4	3	3	2	6	2 (foreign language, performing/fine arts, or vocational education).	1997	Physical education requirement includes 1 unit in health and guidance and 1 unit in physical education. 10th grade students take Hawaii State of Essential Competencies (HSTEC).
Idaho	21	21	4	2	2	2	1.5	6	3.5 (.5 reading; .5 speech; .5 consumer education; 2 humanities. Practical arts may substitute for 1 of the 2 units in the humanities).	1997	State requires a C average, demonstrated competency in core curriculum on a junior class competency test or adherence to a local district's achievement plan for graduation. History requirement includes 1 unit in U.S. history and 1 unit in American government. Both science units must include a laboratory component. The physical education requirement includes .5 unit in health and 1 unit in physical education.
Illinois	16	16	3	2	2	1	4.5	2.25	1.25 (1 from music, art, foreign language which includes American Sign Language, or vocational education; .25 from consumer education).	1995	1 year of mathematics may be computer technology. Social studies requirement includes 1 unit in U.S. history or .5 unit in U.S. history and .5 unit in American government. Physical education requirement includes .5 unit in health education.[2]
Indiana Standard	19.5	19.5	4	2	2	2	1.5	8	—	1989	State does not use standard Carnegie units. Tenth grade exit exam begins with the class of 1999–2000.[1]
Academic honors	24	24	4	3	4	4	1	4 or 5	3 or 4 in foreign language (3 years of 1 language or 2 years in 2 languages)	1990	State does not use standard Carnegie units. Tenth grade exit exam begins with the class of 1999–2000.[1]
Iowa	—	—	—	1.5	—	—	—	—	—	—	All students must participate in physical education unless they qualify under certain exceptions. Social studies requirement includes 1 unit in U.S. history and .5 unit in American government.[1,3]
Kansas	21	21	4	3	2	2	1	9	—	—	Students are required to take a course in Kansas history or government (consisting of a minimum of 9 weeks and 1,800 minutes) in grades 7–12. English/language arts requirement includes 3 units in English. Social studies requirement includes 1 unit in American history and .5 unit in American government.[1]
Kentucky Standard	20	20	4	2	3	2	1	8	—	1987	Social studies requirement includes 1 unit in U.S. history. The physical education requirement includes .5 unit in health and .5 unit in physical education.
Commonwealth	22	22	5	2	3	2	1	8	1 foreign language in advanced placement.	1993	Completion of 1 exam in at least 3 of the advanced placement classes (science or mathematics, foreign language and English) is required. Physical education requirement includes .5 unit in health and .5 unit in physical education.

ELEMENTARY AND SECONDARY: REGULATIONS 151

Table 155.—State requirements for high school graduation, in Carnegie units: 1993 and 1996—Continued

State	1993 All courses	1996 All courses	English/ language arts	Social studies	Mathe- matics	Science	Physical education/ health	Electives	Other courses	First graduating class to which these requirements apply	Notes
1	2	3	4	5	6	7	8	9	10	11	12
Louisiana Standard	23	23	4	3	3	3	2	7.5	.5 computer literacy	1987	With an ACT score of 29 or above, 3.5 GPA or above with no semester grade lower than a B, and no un-excused absences or suspensions, students may receive a Scholar Program Seal on their di-ploma.[1,2]
Regents program	24	24	4	3.5	3	3	2	4.5	4 (3 foreign language; 1 fine arts).	1983	(1,2)
Maine	16	16	4	2	2	2	1.5	3.5	1 fine arts	1989	Social studies requirement includes 1 unit in Amer-ican history and 1 unit in American government. One science unit must include a laboratory compo-nent. Students must pass computer proficiency standards.[1]
Maryland	21	21	4	3	3	2	1	5	3 (1 fine arts; 1 industrial arts/ technology education, home economics, vocational edu-cation, or computer studies; and 1 community service).	1997	(2)
Massachusetts	—	—	—	1	—	—	4	—	—	—	American history is required.[1,2,3]
Michigan	—	—	—	—	—	—	—	—	—	1993	A competency exam is optional for students wanting an endorsed diploma. Students must receive in-struction on U.S. and Michigan history and take a semester of civics.[3]
Minnesota	20	—	—	—	—	—	—	—	—	2000	(1,2)
Mississippi	18	18	4	2	2	2	—	8	—	1989	One science unit must include a laboratory compo-nent.[2]
Missouri Standard	22	22	3	2	2	2	1	10	2 (1 practical arts; 1 fine arts).	1988	Local districts may add to the requirements.
College preparatory certificate	24	24	4	3	3	2	1	9	2 (1 practical arts; 1 fine arts).	1988	Social studies requirement includes 1 unit in Amer-ican history. One science unit must include a lab-oratory component. Of the 9 elective units, 3 core electives are selected from foreign language, Eng-lish, social studies, mathematics, science or fine arts. A GPA of 3.0 and SAT of 1014 or enhanced ACT of 21 is required.
Montana	20	20	4	2	2	2	1	7	2 (1 fine arts; 1 vocational/prac-tical arts).	1989	The state does not use standard Carnegie units.[3]
Nebraska	—	—	—	—	—	—	—	—	—	1991	
Nevada	22.5	22.5	4	2	2	2	2.5	8.5	1.5 (1 arts and humanities; .5 computer literacy).	1992	Computer literacy course requirement may be waived by demonstration of competency. Social studies re-quirement includes 1 unit in American government and 1 unit American history. Physical education re-quirement includes .5 unit in health and 2 units in physical education.[1,2]
New Hampshire	19.75	19.75	4	2	2	2	1.25	7	1.5 (.5 arts; .5 computer edu-cation; .5 basic business and economics).	1989	The social studies requirement includes 1 unit in U.S. and New Hampshire history and 1 elective unit. Science requirement includes 1 unit in physical and 1 unit in biological science. Physical education re-quirement includes .25 unit in health and 1 unit in physical education.[3]
New Jersey	21.5	21.5	4	3	3	2	4	4	1.5 (1 fine, practical, or perform-ing arts; .5 career education).	1990	110 credit hours are required for graduation. (The state does not use standard Carnegie units.) Social studies requirement includes 2 units in U.S. history and 1 unit in world history/cultures. Science unit may be either natural or physical science. The state allows credit for college coursework.[1,2]

Table 155.—State requirements for high school graduation, in Carnegie units: 1993 and 1996—Continued

State	1993 All courses	1996 All courses	English/ language arts	Social studies	Mathematics	Science	Physical education/ health	Electives	Other courses	First graduating class to which these requirements apply	Notes
1	2	3	4	5	6	7	8	9	10	11	12
New Mexico	23	23	4	3	3	2	1	9	1 communication skills	1990	One science unit must have a laboratory component. Social studies requirement includes government and economics, world history and geography, and U.S. history and geography.[2]
New York											
Standard	18.5	20.5	—	4	—	—	2.5	2	4 (1 art and/or music; 3 second language).	1989	Social studies requirement includes U.S. history and government.[2]
Regents diploma	18.5	18.5	4	4	2	2	2.5	3 to 5	1 (foreign language, art and/or music, occupational, technical or home economics education).	2000	Physical education requirement includes .5 unit in health and 2 physical education. Physical education courses may not be included toward the 18.5 units required for graduation. One science credit must include a laboratory component. The 3 to 5 elective units are chosen from a specified sequence of courses.[2]
North Carolina											
Standard	20	20	4	2	2	2	1	9	—	1987	One science class must include a laboratory component.[2]
Scholars program	22	22	4	3	3	3	1	4	4 (2 foreign language; 2 additional credits from English, mathematics, science, social science, or foreign language).	1994	One science class must include a laboratory component.[2]
North Dakota	17	17	4	3	2	2	1	5	—	1994	The social studies requirement includes 1 unit in world history and geography and 1 unit in U.S. history and geography. A unit of higher level foreign language may be substituted for the fourth unit of English.[3]
Ohio	18	18	3	2	2	1	1	9	3 (total units in a subject area other than language arts/English must be taken to complete a "minor").	1988	([1,2])
Oklahoma											
Standard	20	21	4	2	3	2	0	8	2 (1 fine/performing arts; 1 citizenship skills).	2000	([1])
College preparatory	15	15	4	2	3	2	0	—	4 (3 units chosen from foreign language, computer science, English, mathematics, history, sociology, science, speech, or psychology; 1 unit from economics, geography, government or non-Western culture.	1996	([1])
Oregon	22	22	3	3.5	2	2	2	8	1 (.5 career development; 1 applied arts, or foreign language).	1988	Students receive an honors diploma for a GPA of 3.5 or higher.
Pennsylvania	21	21	4	3	3	3	1	5	2 credits in arts, humanities or computer science	1989	Students must achieve 52 state academic performances and locally developed outcomes.
Rhode Island											
Standard	16	16	4	2	2	2	—	6	—	1989	
College preparatory	18	18	4	2	3	2	—	4	3 (2 credits in foreign language; .5 computer, .5 arts).	—	

ELEMENTARY AND SECONDARY: REGULATIONS 153

Table 155.—State requirements for high school graduation, in Carnegie units: 1993 and 1996—Continued

State	1993 All courses	1996 All courses	English/ language arts	Social studies	Mathematics	Science	Physical education/ health	Electives	Other courses	First graduating class to which these requirements apply	Notes
1	2	3	4	5	6	7	8	9	10	11	12
South Carolina Technical preparatory	20	24	4	3	4	3	1	3	6 (4 credits in occupational specialty; 2 in foreign language).	2000	Students must complete an occupational specialty program consisting of four sequential units of instruction in a career major. Students must demonstrate keyboarding proficiency and computer literacy before high school graduation. The social studies requirement includes 1 world history or geography; 1 unit in U.S. history; .5 unit in U.S. government and .5 unit in economics.[2]
Dual Path	22	24	4	4	4	4	1	1	6 (4 occupational specialty; 2 foreign language).	2000	Social studies requirement includes 1 unit in world history; 1 unit in world geography; 1 unit in U.S. history; .5 unit in U.S. government; and .5 unit in economics.[2]
College preparatory	—	24	4	4	4	4	1	4	3 credits in foreign language	—	Proficiency in computer keyboarding/computer literacy is required for graduation. Social studies requirement includes 1 unit in world history; 1 unit in world geography; 1 unit in U.S. history; .5 unit in U.S. government; and .5 unit in economics.[2]
South Dakota	20	20	4	3	2	2	—	8	1 (.5 computer studies; .5 fine arts).	1989	Language arts/English requirement includes 1.5 units in writing, .5 unit in American literature, .5 unit in literature and .5 unit in speech. Social studies requirement includes 1 unit in U.S. history, .5 unit in U.S. government and .5 unit in geography. Both science units must include a laboratory.
Tennessee Technical preparatory	20	20	4	3	3	3	1	2	4 (program of study focusing on a particular technical area).	1989	Exit exam with no passing standards is required before graduation; it is used to assess readiness for workplace or higher education.
University preparatory	20.5	20	4	3	3	3	1	3	3 (2 in foreign language; 1 fine art)	1989	Exit exam with no passing standards is required before graduation; it is used to assess readiness for workplace or higher education.
Texas Standard (1998)	21	22	4	2	3	2	2	7	2 (.5 economics/free enterprise; .5 speech; 1 technology application).	1998	Physical education requirement includes .5 unit in health and 1.5 units in physical education.[2]
Standard (2000)	22	24	4	4	3	3	2	5	3 (3 foreign language; 1 technology application; 1 fine arts).	2000	Students must choose one of the three-credit additional options for electives. College Board advanced placement and International Baccalaureate courses may be substituted for requirements in appropriate proficiency areas to receive dual credits for college coursework. Physical education requirement includes .5 unit in health and 1.5 units in physical education. Social studies requirement includes economics.
Utah	24	24	3	3	2	2	2	9.5	2.5 (1.5 arts; 1 applied technical education or occupational preparation).	1988	Students may accumulate credits more quickly than peers and be eligible to receive a Centennial Scholarship for Early Graduation to be applied to college tuition.[1,3]
Vermont	14.5	14.5	4	3	0 to 5	0 to 5	1.5	—	1 arts	1989	A total of 5 credits are required in mathematics and science.
Virginia Standard	21	21	4	3	2	2	2	6	2 (1 additional mathematics or science; 1 fine or practical arts).	1989	[2]
Advanced studies	23	23	4	3	3	3	2	4	4 (3 foreign language; 1 fine or practical arts).	—	[2]

154 ELEMENTARY AND SECONDARY: REGULATIONS

Table 155.—State requirements for high school graduation, in Carnegie units: 1993 and 1996—Continued

State	1993 All courses	1996								First graduating class to which these requirements apply	Notes
		All courses	Subject areas								
			English/ language arts	Social studies	Mathematics	Science	Physical education/ health	Electives	Other courses		
1	2	3	4	5	6	7	8	9	10	11	12
Washington	19	19	3	2.5	2	2	2	5.5	2 (1 occupational education; 1 fine/visual or performing arts).	1991	(1)
West Virginia Standard (1989)	21	21	4	3	2	2	2	8	—	1989	Electives must be from applied arts, fine or performing arts, or a foreign language.
Standard (2002)	21	21.5	4	3	2	2	2	7	1 art, music, theater or dance	2002	
Wisconsin	13	13	4	3	2	2	2	—	—	1989	Grades 9–12 need 1.5 units of physical education and grades 7–12 need .5 unit of health.[1,3]
Wyoming	18	18	4	3	2	2	—	5	—	1997	(3)

[1] State allows dual credit for college coursework.
[2] Minimum competency test is required.
[3] Local boards determine at least some requirements.

[2] A Career Pathway is a planned program of sequenced or specialized courses designed to develop knowledge and skills in a particular career area. Students may use the Additional Academic Coursework (visual and performing arts,

foreign language and/or vocational technical education coursework, including Junior ROTC) as an option, to pursue individual academic interests. The credits in these two categories will eventually replace the elective credits.

—Data not available or not applicable.

NOTE.—Local school districts frequently have other graduation requirements in addition to state requirements.

SOURCE: Education Commission of the States, Clearinghouse Notes, "Minimum High School Graduation Requirements," November 1996. (This table was prepared July 1997.)

Table 156.—States using minimum-competency testing, by government level setting standards, grade levels assessed, and expected uses of standards: 1995–96

State	Grade levels assessed	Student diagnosis or placement[1]	Improvement of instruction[1]	Program evaluation[1]	Student diagnosis or placement[2]	Student promotion[2]	High school graduation[2]	Student awards or recognition[3]	Public school performance reporting[3]	Accreditation[3]	Other
1	2	3	4	5	6	7	8	9	10	11	12
Alabama	3–12	X	X	X			X		X		
Alaska	4,8,11		X						X		
Arizona	4,7,10	X	X	X					X		
Arkansas	4,5,7,10,11	X	X	X					X		
California	9–12[4]	X			X						
Colorado[5]											
Connecticut	4,6,8,10	X	X	X	X			X	X		
Delaware	3,5,8,10	X	X	X							
Florida	4,8,10,11		X	X			X				
Georgia	K,3,5,8,11,12	X	X	X			X		X		
Hawaii	3,6,8,10–12	X	X	X			X	X	X		
Idaho	3–11		X						X		
Illinois	3,4,6–8,10,11									X	
Indiana	3,6,10	X	X	X				X	X	X	
Iowa[5]											
Kansas	3–5,7,8,10	X	X	X					X	X	
Kentucky	4,8,11,12		X	X			X		X		
Louisiana	K,3–7,10,11	X	X	X		X	X	X	X		
Maine	4,8,11		X	X	X						
Maryland	3,5,7–12	X	X	X			X		X	X	(6)
Massachusetts	4,8,10		X						X		
Michigan	4,5,7,8,11		X	X	X			X	X	X	(7)
Minnesota[5]											
Mississippi	4–9,11	X	X	X			X		X	X	(6)
Missouri	3,5,6,8,10,11[8]		X	X					X	X	
Montana	4,8,11		X	X							
Nebraska[5]											
Nevada	4,8,11,12	X	X	X			X		X		
New Hampshire	3,6,10		X	X							
New Jersey	8,11,12	X	X				X		X	X	
New Mexico	1–6,8,10–12	X	X	X			X		X		(6)
New York	3–6,8–12		X	X	X	X	X		X		(7,9)
North Carolina	3–10		X	X	X	X	X				
North Dakota	3,6,8,11	X	X	X	X						
Ohio	4,6,8–12		X	X			X	X	X		
Oklahoma	3,5–9,11,12	X	X	X					X	X	
Oregon	3,5,8,11		X	X					X		
Pennsylvania	5,6,8,9,11[8]	X	X						X		
Rhode Island	4,8,10		X	X					X		
South Carolina	3–11	X	X	X		X	X	X	X		(6)
South Dakota	4,8,11		X	X							
Tennessee	2–9,11	X	X	X			X		X		(7)
Texas	3–8,10–12	X	X	X	X		X		X	X	
Utah	1–12[4]	X	X	X	X				X		
Vermont	4,8,10[4]	X	X	X					X		
Virginia	4,6–12	X	X	X	X	X	X		X		
Washington	4,8,11	X	X	X					X		
West Virginia	1–11		X							X	(6)
Wisconsin	3,4,8,10			X					X		
Wyoming	9–12[8]		X	X							

[1] Testing program is for instructional purposes.
[2] Testing program is for the purpose of student accountability.
[3] Testing program is for school accountability.
[4] Inclusion is voluntary for students, schools or school districts for one or more grades.
[5] States did not administer any statewide assessments for the 1995–96 school year.
[6] High school skills guarantee.
[7] Endorced diploma.
[8] A sample of students is tested for one or more grades.
[9] Honors diploma.

SOURCE: Council of Chief State School Officers/North Central Regional Educational Laboratory, "Annual Survey of State Student Assessment Programs, Fall 1996." (This table was prepared July 1997.)

Table 157.—States requiring testing for initial certification of teachers, by authorization, year enacted, year effective, and test used: 1987, 1990, and 1996

State	1987				Assessment for certification 1990				Assessment for certification 1996		
	Authority[1]	Enacted	Effective	Test used[2]	Basic skills	Professional skills	Content knowledge	In-class observation	Basic skills	Other exam(s)	In-class observation
1	2	3	4	5	6	7	8	9	10	11	12
Alabama	St. Bd.	1980	1981	State					X	[3]X	X
Alaska	—	—	—	—							
Arizona	Leg.	1980	1980	State	X	X			X		
Arkansas	Leg.	1979	1983	NTE		X	X		X	[4]X	X
California	Leg.	1981	1982	State	X		X		X	[5]X	X
Colorado	Leg.	1981	1983	California Achievement	X			X	X	X	X
Connecticut	St. Bd.	1982	1985	State	X		X	X	X		X
Delaware	St. Bd.	1982	1983	P-P.S.T	X				X		X
District of Columbia	—	—	—	—	X		X		X	[6]X	X
Florida	Leg.	1978	1980	State		X	X	X	X	X	
Georgia	St. Bd.	1975	1980	State			X	X		[7]X	X
Hawaii	St. Bd.	1986	1986	NTE	X	X	X		X	[4,6]X	X
Idaho	Leg.	1987	1988	NTE		X	X				X
Illinois	Leg.	1985	1988	State		X	X		X	[7]X	X
Indiana	Leg.	1984	1985	NTE	X	X	X		X	[4]X	
Iowa	—	—	—	—	X	X	X	X			X
Kansas	Leg.	1984	1986	To be determined	X	X			X		X
Kentucky	Leg.	1984	1985	NTE				X	X	[4,6]X	X
Louisiana	Leg.	1977	1978	NTE	X	X	X		X	[4]X	X
Maine	Leg.	1984	1988	NTE	X	X	X	X		[8,9]X	
Maryland	St. Bd.	1986	1986	NTE	X	X	X			[4]X	
Massachusetts	Leg.	1985	([10])	To be determined	([11])				X	[11]X	X
Michigan	Leg.	1986	1991	To be determined[12]					X	X	X
Minnesota	—	—	—	—	X				X		X
Mississippi	Leg.	1975	1977	NTE		X	X	X	X	[4]X	X
Missouri	Leg.	1985	1988	To be determined			X		X	[4]X	X
Montana	B.P.E.	1985	1986	NTE	X	X			X	[4]X	X
Nebraska	Leg.	1984	1989	To be determined[12]	X				X		X
Nevada	St. Bd.	1984	([10])	To be determined	X	X	X		X		X
New Hampshire	St. Bd.	1984	1985	NTE	X				X		X
New Jersey	St. Bd.	1984	1985	NTE			X			X	X
New Mexico	St. Bd.	1981	1983	NTE	X	X		X	X	X	X
New York	St. Bd.	1980	1984	NTE	X	X				X	X
North Carolina	St. Bd.	1964	1964	NTE				X	X	[4]X	X
North Dakota	—	—	—	—					X		X
Ohio[13]	St. Bd.	1986	1987	NTE		X	X		X	[4]X	X
Oklahoma	Leg.	1980	1982	State				X	X	[5]X	X
Oregon	O.T.S.P.C.	1984	1985	C.B.E.S.T.	X	X	X		X	[5,9]X	X
Pennsylvania	St. Bd.	1985	1987	State	X	X	X		X	[5]X	
Rhode Island	St. Bd.	1985	1986	NTE	X	X		X	X		X
South Carolina	Leg.	1979	1982	NTE and State		X		X	X	[5,9]X	X
South Dakota	St. Bd.	1985	1986	NTE							X
Tennessee	St. Bd.	1980	1981	NTE				X	X	[4]X	X
Texas	Leg.	1981	1986	State	X	X	X		X	X	X
Utah	—	—	—	—			X				X
Vermont	—	—	—	—							X
Virginia	Leg.	1979	1980	NTE	X	X	X	X	X	[4]X	X
Washington	St. Bd.	1984	([10])	To be determined[7]					X		X
West Virginia[14]	St. Bd.	1982	1985	State	X		X	X	X	[5]X	X
Wisconsin	S.P.I.	1986	1990	To be determined	X				X		X
Wyoming	—	—	—	—							X

[1] St. Bd. = State Board of Education; Leg. = Legislature; B.P.E. = Board of Public Education; O.T.S.P.C. = Oregon Teacher Standards and Practice Commission; S.P.I. = Superintendent of Public Instruction.
[2] NTE = National Teacher Examination; State = State developed test; C.B.E.S.T. = California Basic Education Skills Test; P-P.S.T. = Preprofessional Skills Test (Praxis).
[3] Institution's Exit Exam.
[4] NTE.
[5] Speciality area exams.
[6] Praxis.
[7] State and undetermined tests will be used.
[8] General knowledge.
[9] Pedagogical exams.
[10] Effective year is yet to be determined.
[11] Test required for foreign language, bilingual, and English as a Second Language.
[12] For basic skills and subject-matter competencies.
[13] Test requirements set by local school districts.
[14] Required for individuals entering West Virginia-approved education programs as of fall 1985.
—Data not available or not applicable.

SOURCE: Education Commission of the States, Clearinghouse Notes, "States Requiring Testing for Initial Certification of Teachers, April 1987;" "State Education Leader, Winter 1989;" "State Education Indicators, 1990;" and National Association of State Directors of Teacher Education and Certification, "The NASDTEC Manual, 1996–1997: Manual on Certification & Preparation of Educational Personnel in the United States & Canada." (This table was prepared May 1996.)

Table 158.—Revenues for public elementary and secondary schools, by source of funds: 1919–20 to 1994–95

School year	In thousands				Percentage distribution			
	Total	Federal	State	Local (including intermediate)[1]	Total	Federal	State	Local (including intermediate)[1]
1	2	3	4	5	6	7	8	9
1919–20	$970,121	$2,475	$160,085	$807,561	100.0	0.3	16.5	83.2
1929–30	2,088,557	7,334	353,670	1,727,553	100.0	0.4	16.9	82.7
1939–40	2,260,527	39,810	684,354	1,536,363	100.0	1.8	30.3	68.0
1941–42	2,416,580	34,305	759,993	1,622,281	100.0	1.4	31.4	67.1
1943–44	2,604,322	35,886	859,183	1,709,253	100.0	1.4	33.0	65.6
1945–46	3,059,845	41,378	1,062,057	1,956,409	100.0	1.4	34.7	63.9
1947–48	4,311,534	120,270	1,676,362	2,514,902	100.0	2.8	38.9	58.3
1949–50	5,437,044	155,848	2,165,689	3,115,507	100.0	2.9	39.8	57.3
1951–52	6,423,816	227,711	2,478,596	3,717,507	100.0	3.5	38.6	57.9
1953–54	7,866,852	355,237	2,944,103	4,567,512	100.0	4.5	37.4	58.1
1955–56	9,686,677	441,442	3,828,886	5,416,350	100.0	4.6	39.5	55.9
1957–58	12,181,513	486,484	4,800,368	6,894,661	100.0	4.0	39.4	56.6
1959–60	14,746,618	651,639	5,768,047	8,326,932	100.0	4.4	39.1	56.5
1961–62	17,527,707	760,975	6,789,190	9,977,542	100.0	4.3	38.7	56.9
1963–64	20,544,182	896,956	8,078,014	11,569,213	100.0	4.4	39.3	56.3
1965–66	25,356,858	1,996,954	9,920,219	13,439,686	100.0	7.9	39.1	53.0
1967–68	31,903,064	2,806,469	12,275,536	16,821,063	100.0	8.8	38.5	52.7
1969–70	40,266,923	3,219,557	16,062,776	20,984,589	100.0	8.0	39.9	52.1
1970–71	44,511,292	3,753,461	17,409,086	23,348,745	100.0	8.4	39.1	52.5
1971–72	50,003,645	4,467,969	19,133,256	26,402,420	100.0	8.9	38.3	52.8
1972–73[2]	52,117,930	4,525,000	20,699,752	26,893,180	100.0	8.7	39.7	51.6
1973–74	58,230,892	4,930,351	24,113,409	29,187,132	100.0	8.5	41.4	50.1
1974–75[2]	64,445,239	5,811,595	27,060,563	31,573,079	100.0	9.0	42.0	49.0
1975–76[2]	71,206,073	6,318,345	31,602,885	33,284,840	100.0	8.9	44.4	46.7
1976–77	75,322,532	6,629,498	32,526,018	36,137,018	100.0	8.8	43.2	48.0
1977–78	81,443,160	7,694,194	35,013,266	38,735,700	100.0	9.4	43.0	47.6
1978–79	87,994,143	8,600,116	40,132,136	39,261,891	100.0	9.8	45.6	44.6
1979–80	96,881,165	9,503,537	45,348,814	42,028,813	100.0	9.8	46.8	43.4
1980–81	105,949,087	9,768,262	50,182,659	45,998,166	100.0	9.2	47.4	43.4
1981–82	110,191,257	8,186,466	52,436,435	49,568,356	100.0	7.4	47.6	45.0
1982–83	117,497,502	8,339,990	56,282,157	52,875,354	100.0	7.1	47.9	45.0
1983–84	126,055,419	8,576,547	60,232,981	57,245,892	100.0	6.8	47.8	45.4
1984–85	137,294,678	9,105,569	67,168,684	61,020,425	100.0	6.6	48.9	44.4
1985–86	149,127,779	9,975,622	73,619,575	65,532,582	100.0	6.7	49.4	43.9
1986–87	158,523,693	10,146,013	78,830,437	69,547,243	100.0	6.4	49.7	43.9
1987–88	169,561,974	10,716,687	84,004,415	74,840,873	100.0	6.3	49.5	44.1
1988–89	192,016,374	11,902,001	91,768,911	88,345,462	100.0	6.2	47.8	46.0
1989–90	208,547,573	12,700,784	98,238,633	97,608,157	100.0	6.1	47.1	46.8
1990–91	223,340,537	13,776,066	105,324,533	104,239,939	100.0	6.2	47.2	46.7
1991–92	234,581,384	15,493,330	108,783,449	110,304,605	100.0	6.6	46.4	47.0
1992–93	247,626,168	17,261,252	113,403,436	116,961,481	100.0	7.0	45.8	47.2
1993–94[2]	260,159,468	18,341,483	117,474,209	124,343,776	100.0	7.1	45.2	47.8
1994–95	273,137,899	18,581,511	127,719,673	126,836,715	100.0	6.8	46.8	46.4

[1] Includes a relatively small amount from nongovernmental private sources (gifts and tuition and transportation fees from patrons). These sources accounted for 2.7 percent of total revenues in 1994–95.
[2] Revised from previously published figures.

NOTE.—Beginning in 1980–81, revenues for state education agencies are excluded. Beginning in 1988–89, data reflect new survey collection procedures and may not be entirely comparable with figures for earlier years. Because of rounding, details may not add to totals.

SOURCE: U.S. Department of Education, National Center for Education Statistics, *Statistics of State School Systems; Revenues and Expenditures for Public Elementary and Secondary Education;* and Common Core of Data surveys. (This table was prepared September 1997.)

Table 159.—Revenues for public elementary and secondary schools, by source and state: 1994–95

[Amounts in thousands of dollars]

State or other area	Total	Federal		State		Local and intermediate		Private [1]	
		Amount	Percent of total	Amount	Percent of total	Amount	Percent of total	Amount	Percent of total
1	2	3	4	5	6	7	8	9	10
United States	$273,137,899	$18,581,511	6.8	$127,719,673	46.8	$119,538,243	43.8	$7,298,472	2.7
Alabama	3,541,876	343,927	9.7	2,161,685	61.0	766,020	21.6	270,244	7.6
Alaska	1,207,000	129,911	10.8	815,286	67.5	234,263	19.4	27,541	2.3
Arizona	3,783,285	354,242	9.4	1,664,966	44.0	1,673,192	44.2	90,886	2.4
Arkansas	2,175,109	199,163	9.2	1,266,778	58.2	605,499	27.8	103,669	4.8
California	28,891,301	2,751,519	9.5	15,670,329	54.2	10,127,054	35.1	342,399	1.2
Colorado	3,679,162	193,865	5.3	1,578,428	42.9	1,788,285	48.6	118,585	3.2
Connecticut	4,431,602	177,446	4.0	1,748,802	39.5	2,375,694	53.6	129,660	2.9
Delaware	745,036	53,885	7.2	479,319	64.3	199,689	26.8	12,143	1.6
District of Columbia	701,300	66,716	9.5	0	—	631,028	90.0	3,556	0.5
Florida	12,805,853	971,277	7.6	6,286,323	49.1	5,067,892	39.6	480,362	3.8
Georgia	6,965,472	512,456	7.4	3,530,615	50.7	2,785,137	40.0	137,265	2.0
Hawaii	1,177,915	86,882	7.4	1,062,296	90.2	6,307	0.5	22,429	1.9
Idaho	1,088,596	84,012	7.7	666,387	61.2	318,671	29.3	19,527	1.8
Illinois	12,016,320	780,212	6.5	3,361,268	28.0	7,605,409	63.3	269,431	2.2
Indiana	6,362,528	306,971	4.8	3,391,558	53.3	2,472,119	38.9	191,880	3.0
Iowa	2,881,176	151,225	5.2	1,381,238	47.9	1,182,483	41.0	166,230	5.8
Kansas	2,883,345	152,757	5.3	1,655,905	57.4	1,002,034	34.8	72,648	2.5
Kentucky	3,240,926	301,243	9.3	2,132,169	65.8	782,230	24.1	25,283	0.8
Louisiana	3,837,862	458,344	11.9	1,999,368	52.1	1,281,012	33.4	99,138	2.6
Maine	1,400,439	79,403	5.7	670,517	47.9	635,247	45.4	15,272	1.1
Maryland	5,559,604	279,464	5.0	2,059,241	37.0	3,049,831	54.9	171,068	3.1
Massachusetts	6,549,468	352,760	5.4	2,376,538	36.3	3,668,716	56.0	151,453	2.3
Michigan	11,925,311	734,290	6.2	8,023,133	67.3	2,937,025	24.6	230,863	1.9
Minnesota	5,606,567	247,964	4.4	2,939,545	52.4	2,210,175	39.4	208,884	3.7
Mississippi	2,099,795	310,249	14.8	1,185,185	56.4	532,021	25.3	72,340	3.4
Missouri	4,891,384	317,002	6.5	1,892,112	38.7	2,481,121	50.7	201,149	4.1
Montana	915,392	91,912	10.0	453,778	49.6	331,846	36.3	37,857	4.1
Nebraska	1,797,785	104,608	5.8	582,430	32.4	1,002,900	55.8	107,847	6.0
Nevada	1,370,529	67,369	4.9	412,904	30.1	837,374	61.1	52,883	3.9
New Hampshire	1,149,673	35,169	3.1	83,611	7.3	1,004,110	87.3	26,782	2.3
New Jersey	11,485,382	383,016	3.3	4,361,977	38.0	6,433,765	56.0	306,623	2.7
New Mexico	1,695,358	199,231	11.8	1,261,807	74.4	196,841	11.6	37,480	2.2
New York	24,889,904	1,196,994	4.8	10,127,462	40.7	13,330,601	53.6	234,847	0.9
North Carolina	5,940,519	443,701	7.5	3,867,413	65.1	1,463,703	24.6	165,702	2.8
North Dakota	592,481	73,400	12.4	249,273	42.1	238,440	40.2	31,367	5.3
Ohio	11,024,539	714,840	6.5	4,410,699	40.0	5,433,715	49.3	465,286	4.2
Oklahoma	2,767,709	260,760	9.4	1,644,176	59.4	715,199	25.8	147,575	5.3
Oregon	3,294,014	224,139	6.8	1,521,760	46.2	1,442,103	43.8	106,011	3.2
Pennsylvania	13,271,164	746,601	5.6	5,325,072	40.1	6,943,281	52.3	256,210	1.9
Rhode Island	1,080,260	59,458	5.5	437,494	40.5	571,698	52.9	11,609	1.1
South Carolina	3,450,203	299,232	8.7	1,598,971	46.3	1,399,989	40.6	152,010	4.4
South Dakota	691,685	69,162	10.0	183,552	26.5	418,328	60.5	20,643	3.0
Tennessee	3,908,306	348,729	8.9	1,855,784	47.5	1,443,757	36.9	260,036	6.7
Texas	19,678,883	1,511,000	7.7	7,908,524	40.2	9,712,168	49.4	547,191	2.8
Utah	1,940,247	133,543	6.9	1,054,222	54.3	645,245	33.3	107,237	5.5
Vermont	753,905	34,424	4.6	224,941	29.8	476,096	63.2	18,445	2.4
Virginia	6,456,380	368,102	5.7	2,052,415	31.8	3,813,487	59.1	222,376	3.4
Washington	5,976,441	357,615	6.0	4,103,287	68.7	1,330,433	22.3	185,106	3.1
West Virginia	1,940,425	156,555	8.1	1,234,701	63.6	520,036	26.8	29,134	1.5
Wisconsin	5,985,761	262,315	4.4	2,460,520	41.1	3,139,562	52.5	123,364	2.1
Wyoming	632,720	42,453	6.7	303,908	48.0	275,412	43.5	10,947	1.7
Outlying areas									
American Samoa	45,151	37,858	83.8	6,987	15.5	190	0.4	116	0.3
Guam	171,866	17,132	10.0	0	—	153,269	89.2	1,465	0.9
Northern Marianas	44,122	11,663	26.4	32,321	73.3	54	0.1	85	0.2
Puerto Rico	1,641,580	474,419	28.9	1,166,632	71.1	218	(2)	311	(2)
Virgin Islands	142,961	25,435	17.8	0	—	117,441	82.1	85	0.1

[1] Includes revenues from gifts, and tuition and fees from patrons.
[2] Less than .05 percent.
—Data not available or not applicable.

NOTE.—Excludes revenues for state education agencies. Because of rounding, details may not add to totals.

SOURCE: U.S. Department of Education, National Center for Education Statistics, Common Core of Data survey. (This table was prepared April 1997.)

Table 160.—Revenues for public elementary and secondary schools, by source and state: 1993–94

[Amounts in thousands of dollars]

State or other area	Total	Federal		State		Local and intermediate		Private[1]	
		Amount	Percent of total	Amount	Percent of total	Amount	Percent of total	Amount	Percent of total
1	2	3	4	5	6	7	8	9	10
United States	**$260,159,468**	**$18,341,483**	**7.1**	**$117,474,209**	**45.2**	**$117,424,118**	**45.1**	**$6,919,657**	**2.7**
Alabama	3,121,320	346,246	11.1	1,850,898	59.3	667,382	21.4	256,794	8.2
Alaska	1,159,259	138,061	11.9	777,478	67.1	217,973	18.8	25,747	2.2
Arizona	3,550,177	332,091	9.4	1,474,316	41.5	1,661,537	46.8	82,232	2.3
Arkansas	2,014,900	176,931	8.8	1,164,432	57.8	577,017	28.6	96,521	4.8
California	29,050,409	2,572,258	8.9	16,324,953	56.2	9,824,487	33.8	328,711	1.1
Colorado	3,368,596	185,835	5.5	1,466,584	43.5	1,599,758	47.5	116,419	3.5
Connecticut	4,103,215	163,091	4.0	1,653,755	40.3	2,176,137	53.0	110,231	2.7
Delaware	684,411	53,531	7.8	441,043	64.4	178,558	26.1	11,278	1.6
District of Columbia	735,722	79,433	10.8	0	—	652,754	88.7	3,535	0.5
Florida	11,927,112	921,140	7.7	5,945,110	49.8	4,610,243	38.7	450,619	3.8
Georgia	6,630,693	518,047	7.8	3,360,515	50.7	2,617,848	39.5	134,283	2.0
Hawaii	1,140,173	84,217	7.4	1,025,813	90.0	8,862	0.8	21,281	1.9
Idaho	955,081	80,589	8.4	576,967	60.4	279,049	29.2	18,476	1.9
Illinois	11,322,719	743,760	6.6	3,196,325	28.2	7,116,481	62.9	266,153	2.4
Indiana	5,918,601	299,738	5.1	3,097,205	52.3	2,337,103	39.5	184,554	3.1
Iowa	2,782,621	147,123	5.3	1,339,923	48.2	1,141,428	41.0	154,147	5.5
Kansas	2,695,033	148,303	5.5	1,558,260	57.8	920,280	34.1	68,191	2.5
Kentucky	3,194,404	329,830	10.3	2,105,658	65.9	733,116	23.0	25,800	0.8
Louisiana	3,608,433	439,492	12.2	1,912,880	53.0	1,160,708	32.2	95,353	2.6
Maine	1,327,946	78,641	5.9	641,322	48.3	592,856	44.6	15,127	1.1
Maryland	5,145,236	268,305	5.2	2,002,376	38.9	2,715,108	52.8	159,447	3.1
Massachusetts	6,227,191	334,600	5.4	2,125,314	34.1	3,652,395	58.7	114,882	1.8
Michigan	11,134,083	714,960	6.4	3,200,682	28.7	7,007,174	62.9	211,267	1.9
Minnesota	5,160,259	236,773	4.6	2,840,930	55.1	1,887,199	36.6	195,358	3.8
Mississippi	1,879,377	307,241	16.3	1,024,792	54.5	478,941	25.5	68,404	3.6
Missouri	4,526,828	297,101	6.6	1,733,542	38.3	2,307,866	51.0	188,319	4.2
Montana	877,807	84,632	9.6	451,223	51.4	306,411	34.9	35,542	4.0
Nebraska	1,674,836	106,686	6.4	547,921	32.7	917,262	54.8	102,966	6.1
Nevada	1,269,131	58,827	4.6	416,469	32.8	746,914	58.9	46,920	3.7
New Hampshire	1,097,159	35,284	3.2	89,552	8.2	945,881	86.2	26,442	2.4
New Jersey	11,301,907	406,261	3.6	4,564,512	40.4	6,048,625	53.5	282,510	2.5
New Mexico	1,567,823	193,924	12.4	1,153,974	73.6	184,483	11.8	35,441	2.3
New York	23,775,186	1,472,573	6.2	9,090,191	38.2	12,979,174	54.6	233,248	1.0
North Carolina	5,560,310	454,606	8.2	3,559,792	64.0	1,320,661	23.8	225,252	4.1
North Dakota	563,352	67,042	11.9	240,860	42.8	225,514	40.0	29,936	5.3
Ohio	10,499,236	668,428	6.4	4,280,781	40.8	5,121,069	48.8	428,958	4.1
Oklahoma	3,077,910	263,440	8.6	1,811,319	58.8	870,556	28.3	132,595	4.3
Oregon	3,074,679	212,437	6.9	1,215,454	39.5	1,550,028	50.4	96,760	3.1
Pennsylvania	12,601,361	724,185	5.7	5,075,591	40.3	6,558,357	52.0	243,228	1.9
Rhode Island	1,022,861	60,415	5.9	399,395	39.0	552,150	54.0	10,901	1.1
South Carolina	3,200,412	294,566	9.2	1,478,065	46.2	1,285,545	40.2	142,237	4.4
South Dakota	647,026	69,536	10.7	168,964	26.1	390,003	60.3	18,523	2.9
Tennessee	3,649,630	347,887	9.5	1,707,740	46.8	1,344,658	36.8	249,345	6.8
Texas	18,744,302	1,516,708	8.1	7,542,112	40.2	9,174,217	48.9	511,265	2.7
Utah	1,785,758	126,294	7.1	981,014	54.9	581,418	32.6	97,032	5.4
Vermont	703,939	35,655	5.1	220,614	31.3	432,877	61.5	14,793	2.1
Virginia	6,162,830	370,560	6.0	1,895,429	30.8	3,671,851	59.6	224,990	3.7
Washington	5,723,616	334,306	5.8	3,988,235	69.7	1,224,521	21.4	176,554	3.1
West Virginia	1,879,452	151,207	8.0	1,214,154	64.6	486,196	25.9	27,895	1.5
Wisconsin	5,661,241	249,844	4.4	2,188,298	38.7	3,110,476	54.9	112,622	2.0
Wyoming	673,906	38,846	5.8	351,479	52.2	273,010	40.5	10,571	1.6
Outlying areas									
American Samoa	41,683	34,722	83.3	6,699	16.1	99	0.2	164	0.4
Guam	168,461	16,765	10.0	0	—	150,067	89.1	1,629	1.0
Northern Marianas	41,406	11,042	26.7	30,215	73.0	64	0.2	85	0.2
Puerto Rico	1,510,847	473,394	31.3	1,036,657	68.6	387	([2])	408	([2])
Virgin Islands	132,711	25,169	19.0	0	—	107,467	81.0	75	0.1

[1] Includes revenues from gifts, and tuition and fees from patrons.
[2] Less than .05 percent.
—Data not available or not applicable.

NOTE.—Excludes revenues for state education agencies. Because of rounding, details may not add to totals.

SOURCE: U.S. Department of Education, National Center for Education Statistics, Common Core of Data survey. (This table was prepared April 1997.)

Table 161.—Funds and staff for state education agencies,[1] by source of funding and state: 1992–93

State	Funds retained for state administration, by source, in thousands				Total state administration funds per student	State education agency (FTE) staff, by source of funds for position			Students per state FTE staff
	Total	Federal (core activities)[2]	Percent federal	State and local		Total FTE staff	Federally supported (core activities)[2]	State and local supported	
1	2	3	4	5	6	7	8	9	10
United States[3]	$1,966,453	$526,847	26.8	$1,439,606	$46	28,626	7,054	21,572	1,496
Alabama	52,111	13,007	25.0	39,103	71	1,006	127	879	727
Alaska	38,461	5,046	13.1	33,414	314	503	44	460	244
Arizona	19,315	7,460	38.6	11,856	29	362	175	187	1,862
Arkansas	17,561	4,204	23.9	13,356	40	290	74	216	1,522
California	148,989	52,316	35.1	96,673	28	1,898	419	1,479	2,768
Colorado	21,361	5,991	28.0	15,370	35	223	90	133	2,750
Connecticut	139,733	11,433	8.2	128,300	286	2,005	196	1,809	244
Delaware	10,949	2,578	23.5	8,371	105	128	44	84	817
District of Columbia	—	—	—	—	—	—	—	—	—
Florida	56,310	25,470	45.2	30,840	28	688	323	366	2,878
Georgia	58,632	9,918	16.9	48,714	49	935	147	788	1,291
Hawaii	—	—	—	—	—	—	—	—	—
Idaho	7,346	2,938	40.0	4,408	32	104	45	59	2,224
Illinois	42,854	22,092	51.6	20,762	23	746	317	429	2,511
Indiana	29,220	7,339	25.1	21,880	30	309	132	177	3,109
Iowa	20,589	9,582	46.5	11,007	42	226	106	120	2,192
Kansas	12,701	5,422	42.7	7,279	28	199	83	116	2,269
Kentucky	49,745	6,202	12.5	43,542	76	859	105	754	763
Louisiana	35,978	13,015	36.2	22,963	45	573	254	320	1,393
Maine[4]	17,356	4,248	24.5	13,109	80	207	90	117	1,046
Maryland	42,343	8,737	20.6	33,606	56	556	126	430	1,351
Massachusetts	30,191	13,557	44.9	16,633	35	368	173	195	2,337
Michigan	53,743	15,656	29.1	38,088	34	844	256	588	1,899
Minnesota	23,730	9,072	38.2	14,658	30	416	129	287	1,908
Mississippi	40,892	5,703	13.9	35,190	81	724	144	580	700
Missouri	42,860	8,708	20.3	34,152	50	1,448	132	1,317	593
Montana	8,070	3,490	43.2	4,581	50	137	52	85	1,168
Nebraska	20,624	5,018	24.3	15,607	73	398	75	323	710
Nevada	5,305	2,643	49.8	2,662	24	90	47	42	2,491
New Hampshire	7,889	2,662	33.7	5,226	44	157	60	97	1,154
New Jersey	65,111	25,857	39.7	39,254	58	1,001	326	675	1,129
New Mexico	10,398	3,753	36.1	6,645	33	216	67	149	1,461
New York	181,649	47,866	26.4	133,783	68	2,565	567	1,998	1,049
North Carolina	49,298	13,990	28.4	35,308	44	796	144	652	1,399
North Dakota	5,683	3,187	56.1	2,496	48	93	52	41	1,277
Ohio	32,879	14,741	44.8	18,139	18	511	242	269	3,513
Oklahoma	32,178	8,347	25.9	23,831	54	499	98	401	1,196
Oregon	61,178	15,822	25.9	45,357	120	418	58	360	1,221
Pennsylvania	72,979	19,746	27.1	53,233	42	1,134	237	897	1,515
Rhode Island	13,705	4,347	31.7	9,358	95	152	59	93	948
South Carolina	87,109	9,130	10.5	77,979	136	946	105	841	677
South Dakota	7,419	3,988	53.8	3,430	55	102	42	60	1,324
Tennessee	36,778	10,525	28.6	26,253	43	456	100	356	1,876
Texas	59,560	18,321	30.8	41,238	17	1,013	358	654	3,498
Utah	25,763	6,092	23.6	19,671	56	364	62	302	1,273
Vermont	7,348	2,672	36.4	4,675	75	143	65	78	689
Virginia	29,236	9,830	33.6	19,406	28	371	102	270	2,781
Washington	19,472	6,843	35.1	12,629	22	253	88	165	3,542
West Virginia	21,188	5,069	23.9	16,119	67	403	113	289	790
Wisconsin	87,883	11,377	12.9	76,506	106	692	179	512	1,199
Wyoming	4,782	1,837	38.4	2,945	48	100	25	75	1,003

[1] Excludes funds for schools and school districts.
[2] Core education activities include: Chapter 1; Chapter 2; Special Education; Child Nutrition; Vocational Education; Adult Education; AIDS Education; Civil Rights Act; and Homeless Education Programs.
[3] Excludes District of Columbia and Hawaii.
[4] Excludes State Teacher Retirement Program.
—Data not available.

FTE=full-time equivalent.

NOTE.—Because of rounding, details may not add to totals.

SOURCE: U.S. General Accounting Office, *Education Finance, Extent of Federal Funding in State Education Agencies,* and U.S. Department of Education, National Center for Education Statistics, Common Core of Data survey. (This table was prepared September 1996.)

Table 162.—Summary of expenditures for public elementary and secondary education, by purpose: 1919–20 to 1994–95

Purpose of expenditures	1919–20	1929–30	1939–40	1949–50	1959–60	1969–70	1979–80	1989–90[1]	1993–94[1]	1994–95
1	2	3	4	5	6	7	8	9	10	11
	Amounts in thousands of dollars									
Total expenditures, all schools	$1,036,151	$2,316,790	$2,344,049	$5,837,643	$15,613,255	$40,683,429	$95,961,561	$212,769,564	$265,306,634	$278,965,657
Current expenditures, all schools	864,396	1,853,377	1,955,166	4,722,887	12,461,955	34,853,578	87,581,727	191,211,902	236,224,562	248,993,151
Public elementary and secondary schools	861,120	1,843,552	1,941,799	4,687,274	12,329,389	34,217,773	86,984,142	188,229,359	231,542,764	243,844,646
Administration	36,752	78,680	91,571	220,050	528,408	1,606,646	4,263,757	—	—	—
Instruction	632,556	1,317,727	1,403,285	3,112,340	8,350,738	23,270,158	53,257,937	—	—	—
Plant operation	115,707	216,072	194,365	427,587	1,085,036	2,537,257	[2]9,744,785	—	—	—
Plant maintenance	30,432	78,810	73,321	214,164	422,586	974,941	([2])	—	—	—
Fixed charges	9,286	50,270	50,116	261,469	909,323	3,266,920	11,793,934	—	—	—
Other school services[3]	36,387	101,993	129,141	451,663	1,033,297	2,561,856	7,923,729	—	—	—
Other current expenditures										
Summer schools	([4])	([4])	([4])	([4])	13,263	106,481	24,753	2,982,543	4,681,798	5,148,505
Adult education[4]	3,277	9,825	13,367	35,614	26,858	128,778	—	([5])	([5])	([5])
Community colleges	([4])	([4])	([4])	([4])	34,492	138,813	—	([5])	([5])	([5])
Community services	([3])	([3])	([3])	([3])	57,953	261,731	572,832	([5])	([5])	([5])
Capital outlay[6]	153,543	370,878	257,974	1,014,176	2,661,786	4,659,072	6,506,167	17,781,342	23,747,021	24,453,851
Interest on school debt	18,212	92,536	130,909	100,578	489,514	1,170,782	1,873,666	3,776,321	5,335,050	5,518,655
	Percentage distribution									
Total expenditures, all schools	100.0	100.0	100.0	100.0	100.0	100.0	100.0	100.0	100.0	100.0
Current expenditures, all schools	83.4	80.0	83.4	80.9	79.8	85.7	91.2	89.9	89.0	89.3
Public elementary and secondary schools	83.1	79.6	82.8	80.3	79.0	84.1	90.6	88.5	87.3	87.4
Administration	3.5	3.4	3.9	3.8	3.4	3.9	4.4	—	—	—
Instruction	61.0	56.9	59.9	53.3	53.5	57.2	55.5	—	—	—
Plant operation	11.2	9.3	8.3	7.3	6.9	6.2	[2]10.2	—	—	—
Plant maintenance	2.9	3.4	3.1	3.7	2.7	2.4	([2])	—	—	—
Fixed charges	0.9	2.2	2.1	4.5	5.8	8.0	12.3	—	—	—
Other school services[3]	3.5	4.4	5.5	7.7	6.6	6.3	8.3	—	—	—
Other current expenditures										
Summer schools	([4])	([4])	([4])	([4])	0.1	0.3	([7])	1.4	1.8	1.8
Adult education[4]	0.3	0.4	0.6	0.6	0.2	0.3	—	([5])	([5])	([5])
Community colleges	([4])	([4])	([4])	([4])	0.2	0.3	—	([5])	([5])	([5])
Community services	([3])	([3])	([3])	([3])	0.4	0.6	0.6	([5])	([5])	([5])
Capital outlay[6]	14.8	16.0	11.0	17.4	17.0	11.5	6.8	8.4	9.0	8.8
Interest on school debt	1.8	4.0	5.6	1.7	3.1	2.9	2.0	1.8	2.0	2.0

[1] Revised from previously published data.
[2] Plant operation also includes plant maintenance.
[3] Prior to 1959–60, items included under "other school services" were listed under "auxiliary services," a more comprehensive classification that also included community services.
[4] Prior to 1959–60, data shown for adult education represent combined expenditures for adult education, summer schools, and community colleges.
[5] Included under summer schools.
[6] Prior to 1969–70, excludes capital outlay by state and local schoolhousing authorities.
[7] Less than 0.05 percent.

—Data not available.

NOTE.—Beginning in 1959–60, includes Alaska and Hawaii. Beginning in 1980–81, state administration expenditures were excluded from both "total" and "current" expenditures. Beginning in 1988–89, extensive changes were made in the data collection procedures. Because of rounding, details may not add to totals.

SOURCE: U.S. Department of Education, National Center for Education Statistics, *Statistics of State School Systems;* and Common Core of Data surveys. (This table was prepared May 1997.)

Table 163.—Total expenditures for public elementary and secondary education, by function and subfunction: 1989–90 to 1994–95

Items	Expenditures (in thousands)						Percentage distribution				
	1989–90	1990–91	1991–92	1992–93	1993–94	1994–95	1990–91	1991–92	1992–93	1993–94	1994–95
1	2	3	4	5	6	7	8	9	10	11	12
Total expenditures	$212,769,564	$229,429,715	$241,054,784	$252,934,872	$265,306,634	$278,965,657	—	—	—	—	—
Current expenditures	188,229,359	202,037,752	211,210,190	220,948,052	231,542,764	243,844,646	100.00	100.00	100.00	100.00	100.00
Salaries	[1]123,467,492	[1]132,730,931	138,279,377	144,276,674	150,545,401	158,893,370	65.70	65.47	65.30	65.02	65.16
Employee benefits	[1]31,414,347	[1]33,954,456	36,062,813	39,267,087	41,181,982	43,102,187	16.81	17.07	17.77	17.79	17.68
Purchased services	[1]15,540,414	[1]16,380,643	17,790,523	17,933,497	19,232,698	20,639,818	8.11	8.42	8.12	8.31	8.46
Tuition	[1]1,012,623	[1]1,192,505	939,322	967,884	1,231,076	1,476,701	0.59	0.44	0.44	0.53	0.61
Supplies	[1]14,051,890	[1]14,805,956	14,944,495	16,370,100	17,249,817	17,359,679	7.33	7.08	7.41	7.45	7.12
Other	[1]2,742,592	[1]2,973,261	3,193,661	2,132,810	2,101,790	2,372,891	1.47	1.51	0.97	0.91	0.97
Instruction	113,550,405	122,223,362	128,475,859	134,971,088	141,620,474	150,521,920	60.50	60.83	61.09	61.16	61.73
Salaries	84,350,068	90,742,284	95,018,405	99,089,718	103,506,419	109,680,814	44.91	44.99	44.85	44.70	44.98
Employee benefits	20,702,032	22,347,524	23,683,606	26,075,723	27,456,084	29,184,690	11.06	11.21	11.80	11.86	11.97
Purchased services	2,558,153	2,722,639	3,348,142	3,357,323	3,421,355	3,819,015	1.35	1.59	1.52	1.48	1.57
Tuition	1,012,623	1,192,505	939,322	967,884	1,231,076	1,476,701	0.59	0.44	0.44	0.53	0.61
Supplies	4,275,002	4,584,754	4,703,762	5,052,972	5,507,720	5,762,374	2.27	2.23	2.29	2.38	2.36
Other	652,526	633,656	782,620	427,468	497,820	598,326	0.31	0.37	0.19	0.22	0.25
Students [2]	8,265,657	8,926,010	9,226,247	9,760,087	10,946,191	11,679,338	4.42	4.37	4.42	4.73	4.79
Salaries	6,073,265	6,565,965	6,791,228	7,134,434	7,998,204	8,519,853	3.25	3.22	3.23	3.45	3.49
Employee benefits	1,528,864	1,660,082	1,751,537	1,904,341	2,110,012	2,212,875	0.82	0.83	0.86	0.91	0.91
Purchased services	431,976	455,996	441,946	489,215	593,522	657,273	0.23	0.21	0.22	0.26	0.27
Supplies	173,526	191,482	181,261	195,240	206,352	238,868	0.09	0.09	0.09	0.09	0.10
Other	58,025	52,485	60,275	36,857	38,101	50,469	0.03	0.03	0.02	0.02	0.02
Instructional services [3]	7,806,238	8,467,142	8,827,800	9,241,929	9,236,588	9,654,714	4.19	4.18	4.18	3.99	3.96
Salaries	5,123,186	5,560,129	5,808,305	6,014,671	5,933,810	6,162,682	2.75	2.75	2.72	2.56	2.53
Employee benefits	1,266,016	1,408,217	1,463,736	1,601,713	1,583,597	1,638,315	0.70	0.69	0.72	0.68	0.67
Purchased services	547,862	622,487	685,654	741,983	785,841	898,506	0.31	0.32	0.34	0.34	0.37
Supplies	759,207	776,863	772,096	820,919	860,224	872,369	0.38	0.37	0.37	0.37	0.36
Other	109,965	99,445	98,009	62,644	73,116	82,842	0.05	0.05	0.03	0.03	0.03
General administration	5,455,371	5,791,253	6,039,397	5,851,983	5,909,692	5,731,462	2.87	2.86	2.65	2.55	2.35
Salaries	2,486,406	2,603,562	2,688,515	2,787,145	2,688,481	2,808,098	1.29	1.27	1.26	1.16	1.15
Employee benefits	770,967	777,381	815,581	846,638	888,209	844,290	0.38	0.39	0.38	0.38	0.35
Purchased services	1,393,617	1,482,427	1,540,476	1,592,937	1,856,065	1,563,570	0.73	0.73	0.72	0.80	0.64
Supplies	166,495	172,898	158,193	211,727	168,785	177,448	0.09	0.07	0.10	0.07	0.07
Other	637,886	754,985	836,633	413,535	308,151	338,055	0.37	0.40	0.19	0.13	0.14
School administration	10,891,620	11,695,344	12,280,680	12,777,815	13,492,502	14,149,344	5.79	5.81	5.78	5.83	5.80
Salaries	8,310,370	8,935,903	9,293,958	9,593,613	10,144,727	10,680,028	4.42	4.40	4.34	4.38	4.38
Employee benefits	2,089,463	2,257,783	2,410,404	2,615,351	2,738,216	2,796,511	1.12	1.14	1.18	1.18	1.15
Purchased services	241,248	247,750	277,904	300,288	320,442	359,827	0.12	0.13	0.14	0.14	0.15
Supplies	188,393	189,711	196,485	207,078	223,794	245,354	0.09	0.09	0.09	0.10	0.10
Other	62,146	64,197	101,929	61,485	65,323	67,623	0.03	0.05	0.03	0.03	0.03
Operation and maintenance	20,261,415	21,290,655	21,889,514	22,823,758	23,875,871	24,543,091	10.54	10.36	10.33	10.31	10.07
Salaries	8,395,005	8,849,559	9,143,832	9,384,209	9,768,777	10,117,085	4.38	4.33	4.25	4.22	4.15
Employee benefits	2,423,326	2,633,075	2,788,592	2,970,466	3,048,615	3,027,382	1.30	1.32	1.34	1.32	1.24
Purchased services	5,554,610	5,721,125	5,830,363	6,013,075	6,451,727	7,261,824	2.83	2.76	2.72	2.79	2.98
Supplies	3,579,084	3,761,738	3,807,024	4,262,006	4,399,064	3,927,676	1.86	1.80	1.93	1.90	1.61
Other	309,391	325,157	319,703	194,002	207,688	209,124	0.16	0.15	0.09	0.09	0.09
Student transportation	8,030,990	8,678,954	8,769,754	9,252,300	9,627,155	9,889,113	4.30	4.15	4.19	4.16	4.06
Salaries	3,045,942	3,285,127	3,268,689	3,407,602	3,567,556	3,775,220	1.63	1.55	1.54	1.54	1.55
Employee benefits	808,635	892,985	965,731	1,063,064	1,107,878	1,138,506	0.44	0.46	0.48	0.48	0.47
Purchased services	3,094,099	3,345,232	3,548,716	3,758,313	3,946,935	4,016,478	1.66	1.68	1.70	1.70	1.65
Supplies	897,799	961,447	811,781	877,077	854,940	800,345	0.48	0.38	0.40	0.37	0.33
Other	184,516	194,163	174,837	146,243	149,847	158,588	0.10	0.08	0.07	0.06	0.07
Other student support services	4,989,078	5,587,837	6,088,305	6,207,775	6,318,312	6,708,268	2.77	2.88	2.81	2.73	2.75
Salaries	2,533,744	2,900,394	2,890,746	3,192,790	3,164,490	3,286,068	1.44	1.37	1.45	1.37	1.35
Employee benefits	868,792	980,859	1,153,683	1,088,011	1,109,764	1,136,298	0.49	0.55	0.49	0.48	0.47
Purchased services	786,814	798,922	1,149,930	1,045,655	1,141,643	1,262,457	0.40	0.54	0.47	0.49	0.52
Supplies	295,241	294,527	306,701	327,377	362,838	372,847	0.15	0.15	0.15	0.16	0.15
Other	504,488	613,135	587,245	553,942	539,576	650,597	0.30	0.28	0.25	0.23	0.27
Food services	8,116,277	8,430,490	8,821,308	9,263,181	9,774,315	10,266,321	4.17	4.18	4.19	4.22	4.21
Salaries			3,118,637	3,398,599	3,532,183	3,697,981		1.48	1.54	1.53	1.52
Employee benefits	—	—	979,089	1,042,743	1,095,686	1,081,325	—	0.46	0.47	0.47	0.44
Purchased services			720,018	497,100	556,251	629,336		0.34	0.22	0.24	0.26
Supplies			3,829,025	4,186,945	4,445,897	4,715,841		1.81	1.89	1.92	1.93
Other			174,539	137,793	144,298	141,838		0.08	0.06	0.06	0.06
Enterprise operations [4]	862,308	946,705	791,326	798,136	741,665	701,051	0.47	0.37	0.36	0.32	0.29
Salaries			257,063	273,893	240,754	165,540		0.12	0.12	0.10	0.07
Employee benefits			50,854	59,038	43,921	41,995		0.02	0.03	0.02	0.02
Purchased services			247,373	137,608	158,917	171,532		0.12	0.06	0.07	0.07
Supplies			178,166	228,758	220,203	246,554		0.08	0.10	0.10	0.10
Other			57,869	98,840	77,870	75,429		0.03	0.04	0.03	0.03
Other current expenditures	2,982,543	3,295,717	4,393,698	4,378,506	4,681,798	5,148,505	—	—	—	—	—
Community services	872,531	964,370	1,177,742	1,331,004	1,485,670	1,933,565	—	—	—	—	—
Nonpublic school programs	493,252	527,609	652,403	644,150	689,888	569,851	—	—	—	—	—
Adult education	1,229,456	1,365,523	1,498,962	1,484,057	1,489,405	1,460,149	—	—	—	—	—
Community colleges	11,555	5,356	5,136	5,454	7,432	83,573	—	—	—	—	—
Other	375,750	432,858	1,059,455	913,841	1,009,402	1,101,367	—	—	—	—	—
Capital outlay [5]	17,781,342	19,771,478	20,286,977	22,171,768	23,747,021	24,453,851	—	—	—	—	—
Interest on school debt	3,776,321	4,324,768	5,163,919	5,436,547	5,335,050	5,518,655	—	—	—	—	—

[1] Includes estimated data for subfunctions of food services and enterprise operations.
[2] Includes expenditures for guidance, health, attendance, and speech pathology services.
[3] Includes expenditures for curriculum development, staff training, libraries, and media and computer centers.
[4] Includes expenditures for operations funded by sales of products or services (e.g., school bookstore or computer time).
[5] Includes expenditures for property, and for buildings and alterations completed by school district staff or contractors.

—Data not available or not applicable.

NOTE.—Excludes expenditures for state education agencies. Some data have been revised from previously published figures. Because of rounding, details may not add to totals.

SOURCE: U.S. Department of Education, National Center for Education Statistics, Common Core of Data survey. (This table was prepared September 1997.)

ELEMENTARY AND SECONDARY: FINANCES 163

Table 164.—Expenditures for instruction in public elementary and secondary schools, by subfunction and state: 1993–94 and 1994–95

[In thousands of dollars]

State or other area	1993–94							1994–95 [1]					
	Total	Salaries	Employee benefits	Purchased services [2]	Supplies	Tuition and other		Total	Salaries	Employee benefits	Purchased services [2]	Supplies	Tuition and other
1	2	3	4	5	6	7		8	9	10	11	12	13
United States	$141,620,474	$103,506,419	$27,456,084	$3,421,355	$5,507,720	$1,728,895		$150,521,920	$109,680,814	$29,184,690	$3,819,015	$5,762,374	$2,075,027
Alabama	1,757,077	1,329,103	317,861	5,505	87,994	16,613		1,906,471	1,446,029	335,738	5,645	99,824	19,236
Alaska	517,200	370,381	84,893	20,562	21,311	20,053		574,167	413,346	100,477	18,210	21,512	20,622
Arizona	1,680,405	1,404,486	207,938	13,704	28,531	25,745		1,811,054	1,500,416	238,820	16,435	31,128	24,256
Arkansas	1,116,796	862,527	194,647	17,569	32,663	9,390		1,144,389	868,482	206,954	16,435	35,930	9,793
California	15,028,418	10,535,742	3,275,864	417,732	534,495	264,585		15,549,692	11,038,093	3,262,337	424,379	536,517	288,366
Colorado	1,815,426	1,403,567	280,586	54,564	69,799	6,909		1,970,908	1,508,701	306,238	67,936	80,563	7,470
Connecticut	2,501,019	1,949,504	435,277	37,744	64,920	13,574		2,721,552	2,004,391	463,152	50,246	64,845	138,919
Delaware	399,147	279,411	94,677	6,374	14,897	3,788		431,618	297,607	103,254	7,194	15,843	7,719
District of Columbia	351,028	251,437	73,230	7,967	5,558	12,835		336,543	239,594	65,979	5,251	3,556	22,163
Florida	5,970,755	4,016,237	1,336,262	361,131	196,670	60,455		6,395,934	4,283,275	1,422,087	408,034	209,508	73,030
Georgia	3,473,765	2,571,602	712,847	33,534	151,782	4,000		3,779,713	2,799,934	770,839	39,991	164,184	4,763
Hawaii	615,270	443,179	123,385	19,218	27,938	1,551		636,952	457,861	127,015	18,255	32,471	1,352
Idaho	543,377	389,041	120,933	8,960	23,999	444		602,232	430,919	130,741	11,204	28,940	428
Illinois	6,064,603	4,697,555	905,583	105,297	235,412	120,755		6,367,082	4,797,408	1,061,451	120,542	265,284	122,397
Indiana	3,121,188	2,309,246	673,493	32,707	100,174	5,569		3,262,523	2,417,230	697,094	35,344	107,345	5,510
Iowa	1,558,177	1,115,162	263,334	62,452	107,452	9,777		1,623,942	1,160,673	277,271	56,959	116,398	12,641
Kansas	1,345,121	1,069,472	187,192	11,579	71,444	5,434		1,387,198	1,108,730	193,070	12,294	67,297	5,807
Kentucky	1,768,270	1,427,161	269,831	88	71,170	20		1,787,624	1,423,656	291,715	94	72,140	19
Louisiana	1,967,293	1,459,276	403,272	16,167	84,227	4,352		2,071,476	1,544,288	415,405	19,349	87,321	5,113
Maine	808,608	550,050	166,324	22,399	26,660	43,175		859,560	570,803	190,981	24,493	27,895	45,388
Maryland	2,890,997	1,992,747	658,207	73,927	80,822	85,295		3,127,996	2,130,372	729,842	86,737	88,971	92,074
Massachusetts	3,398,730	2,461,875	385,677	267,298	98,610	185,269		3,994,523	2,691,297	728,275	254,433	111,466	209,053
Michigan	5,691,574	4,139,256	1,259,843	77,832	193,110	21,533		6,228,315	4,328,190	1,569,832	84,022	210,776	35,495
Minnesota	2,757,594	2,033,003	538,195	68,805	98,115	19,476		2,946,240	2,160,089	579,243	78,764	105,214	22,929
Mississippi	1,066,080	821,115	166,575	16,477	56,697	5,215		1,197,868	891,328	216,101	18,628	65,880	5,931
Missouri	2,415,629	1,840,689	329,085	43,996	191,915	9,945		2,597,027	1,969,708	355,700	53,142	207,753	10,724
Montana	514,036	369,489	97,938	13,156	31,205	2,247		525,617	379,161	101,394	11,080	31,900	2,082
Nebraska	941,392	700,536	159,735	21,827	37,875	21,419		997,580	732,361	178,023	24,370	40,341	22,484
Nevada	654,996	491,876	132,187	4,662	25,270	1,000		706,132	528,908	144,432	4,552	27,143	1,097
New Hampshire	646,681	467,975	100,808	13,691	21,158	43,050		679,046	498,773	97,439	16,606	21,773	44,455
New Jersey	6,260,952	4,527,397	1,183,042	45,473	212,716	292,324		6,467,203	4,715,340	1,128,758	51,960	232,132	339,014
New Mexico	775,050	570,209	148,257	7,981	43,549	5,054		837,029	618,787	158,931	8,022	45,294	5,995
New York	14,884,460	10,895,343	3,302,335	340,172	344,180	2,429		15,636,396	11,525,744	3,387,241	358,939	361,933	2,539
North Carolina	3,161,009	2,383,123	588,767	45,782	140,203	3,134		3,387,680	2,556,856	623,633	48,461	155,787	2,942
North Dakota	320,294	234,827	58,894	8,274	15,493	2,806		328,461	240,567	60,009	8,896	16,378	2,610
Ohio	5,717,214	4,170,324	1,158,036	94,873	224,924	69,057		5,960,083	4,362,651	1,182,673	103,167	235,248	76,343
Oklahoma	1,572,751	1,199,978	269,447	19,719	81,967	1,641		1,662,373	1,266,325	261,121	56,993	97,571	11,190
Oregon	1,708,679	1,133,552	427,436	50,290	88,577	8,823		1,776,148	1,193,420	412,583	59,993	99,712	10,441
Pennsylvania	7,144,739	4,753,300	1,609,574	479,975	212,470	89,420		7,460,973	5,049,611	1,591,109	512,608	224,403	83,241
Rhode Island	659,748	461,270	147,798	16,235	13,146	21,300		669,274	470,133	150,373	11,784	14,302	22,683
South Carolina	1,651,858	1,251,017	312,363	22,422	64,858	1,197		1,727,214	1,298,160	320,509	27,097	80,175	1,274
South Dakota	360,621	262,590	57,153	10,549	20,787	9,542		376,116	272,643	59,785	11,243	22,634	9,811
Tennessee	2,125,274	1,635,375	372,014	39,428	72,376	6,080		2,285,884	1,740,065	395,947	38,603	104,857	6,413
Texas	9,602,153	7,492,386	1,197,000	156,463	719,546	36,758		10,753,150	8,517,213	1,268,868	294,413	606,632	66,025
Utah	1,013,630	662,696	230,024	14,387	47,072	59,451		1,089,195	706,401	250,913	16,429	46,339	69,112
Vermont	419,909	295,898	79,058	14,198	12,934	17,822		434,933	306,881	77,637	15,984	13,596	20,835
Virginia	3,275,030	2,487,274	621,527	43,510	117,838	4,881		3,483,576	2,640,491	671,729	48,638	118,633	9,811
Washington	2,921,122	2,066,990	639,335	85,052	109,654	20,091		3,075,785	2,156,923	670,680	101,440	104,857	22,096
West Virginia	1,034,956	723,919	262,282	10,065	38,524	166		1,090,056	766,359	280,057	11,134	32,343	163
Wisconsin	3,285,249	2,300,226	768,388	49,266	115,175	52,194		3,441,286	2,400,781	800,389	55,545	129,411	55,160
Wyoming	345,120	246,023	67,675	10,316	19,854	1,252		358,131	253,841	70,846	11,073	20,630	1,741
Outlying areas													
American Samoa	11,582	8,612	1,336	316	1,090	229		11,796	8,900	1,386	236	1,065	211
Guam	86,713	72,705	13,292	75	385	255		79,336	65,432	13,237	83	424	161
Northern Marianas	29,959	19,199	4,620	2,234	3,660	247		35,613	21,718	6,259	3,678	3,551	407
Puerto Rico	972,817	798,483	114,161	9,683	20,961	29,529		1,093,038	903,531	127,031	11,148	20,234	31,094
Virgin Islands	68,548	55,140	10,763	525	604	1,515		69,349	55,563	11,042	572	652	1,520

[1] Preliminary data.
[2] Includes purchased professional services of teachers or others who provide instruction for students and travel for instructional staff.

NOTE.—Excludes expenditures for state education agencies. Because of rounding, details may not add to totals. Some 1993–94 data have been revised from previously published figures.

SOURCE: U.S. Department of Education, National Center for Education Statistics, Common Core of Data surveys. (This table was prepared May 1997.)

Table 165.—Current expenditures for public elementary and secondary education, by state: 1969–70 to 1996–97

[In thousands of dollars]

State or other area	1969–70	1979–80	1980–81	1984–85	1985–86	1986–87	1987–88	1988–89
1	2	3	4	5	6	7	8	9
United States	$34,217,773	$86,984,142	$94,321,093	$126,337,491	$137,164,965	$146,364,922	$157,097,951	$173,098,906
Alabama	422,730	1,146,713	1,393,137	1,590,856	1,761,154	1,775,997	1,873,390	2,188,020
Alaska	81,374	377,947	476,368	754,967	818,219	769,015	756,577	739,020
Arizona	281,941	949,753	1,075,362	1,436,844	1,649,832	1,836,908	2,002,395	2,143,148
Arkansas	235,083	666,949	709,394	1,005,347	1,085,943	1,118,904	1,211,156	1,319,370
California	3,831,595	9,172,158	9,936,642	13,477,768	15,040,898	16,512,668	17,402,063	19,417,178
Colorado	369,218	1,243,049	1,369,883	1,868,058	2,018,579	2,129,964	2,172,563	2,324,625
Connecticut	588,710	1,227,892	1,440,881	2,117,798	2,144,094	2,414,708	2,748,567	2,984,542
Delaware	108,747	269,108	270,439	353,191	391,558	418,116	440,631	479,327
District of Columbia	141,138	298,448	295,155	387,918	406,910	441,135	489,357	584,035
Florida	961,273	2,766,468	3,336,657	4,589,068	5,092,668	5,650,083	6,288,977	7,245,515
Georgia	599,371	1,608,028	1,688,714	2,629,681	2,979,980	3,254,786	3,549,038	4,006,069
Hawaii	141,324	351,889	395,038	521,692	575,456	576,749	608,264	643,319
Idaho	103,107	313,927	352,912	467,532	492,092	513,011	532,274	570,013
Illinois	1,896,067	4,579,355	4,773,179	5,662,354	6,066,390	6,463,564	6,923,298	7,655,153
Indiana	809,105	1,851,292	1,898,194	2,696,072	2,851,080	3,106,616	3,330,525	3,779,468
Iowa	527,086	1,186,659	1,337,504	1,599,674	1,644,359	1,708,440	1,859,173	1,925,623
Kansas	362,593	830,133	958,281	1,315,469	1,423,225	1,486,814	1,568,041	1,712,260
Kentucky	353,265	1,054,459	1,096,472	1,384,722	1,434,962	1,583,158	1,741,799	1,918,741
Louisiana	503,217	1,303,902	1,767,692	2,191,478	2,333,748	2,260,393	2,289,241	2,468,307
Maine	155,907	385,492	401,355	599,189	688,673	760,446	839,860	921,931
Maryland	721,794	1,783,056	1,937,159	2,446,771	2,634,209	2,845,404	3,128,165	3,505,018
Massachusetts	907,341	2,638,734	2,794,762	3,139,486	3,403,505	3,744,131	4,098,062	4,516,604
Michigan	1,799,945	4,642,847	5,196,249	5,735,303	6,184,767	6,427,556	6,913,261	7,492,267
Minnesota	781,243	1,786,768	1,900,322	2,461,571	2,637,722	2,818,390	2,981,209	3,282,296
Mississippi	262,760	756,018	716,878	1,023,720	1,058,301	1,112,535	1,221,560	1,365,846
Missouri	642,030	1,504,988	1,643,258	2,106,539	2,277,576	2,515,846	2,747,234	3,096,666
Montana	127,176	358,118	380,092	538,245	567,901	583,861	590,226	592,454
Nebraska	231,612	581,615	629,017	870,019	911,983	948,149	995,235	1,105,009
Nevada	87,273	281,901	287,752	397,254	495,147	513,014	555,272	628,657
New Hampshire	101,370	295,400	340,518	473,151	522,604	589,850	677,507	733,240
New Jersey	1,343,564	3,638,533	3,648,914	4,697,534	5,735,895	6,099,473	6,621,860	7,309,147
New Mexico	183,736	515,451	560,213	784,442	808,036	865,789	916,305	975,552
New York	4,111,839	8,760,500	9,259,948	12,681,301	13,686,039	14,724,687	16,073,392	17,127,596
North Carolina	676,193	1,880,862	2,112,417	2,674,774	2,991,747	3,193,337	3,424,194	3,892,971
North Dakota	97,895	228,483	254,197	365,341	379,470	374,941	385,427	431,814
Ohio	1,639,805	3,836,576	4,149,858	5,504,161	5,856,999	6,114,426	6,446,903	7,484,434
Oklahoma	339,105	1,055,844	1,193,373	1,575,467	1,740,981	1,707,396	1,692,283	1,833,743
Oregon	403,844	1,126,812	1,292,624	1,560,242	1,662,372	1,747,125	1,944,657	2,123,241
Pennsylvania	1,912,644	4,584,320	4,955,115	6,660,369	6,750,520	7,176,886	7,679,986	8,579,546
Rhode Island	145,443	362,046	395,389	525,824	569,935	608,318	663,800	747,852
South Carolina	367,689	997,984	1,006,088	1,556,552	1,708,603	1,814,160	1,932,502	2,118,732
South Dakota	109,375	238,332	242,215	338,800	360,832	368,266	389,436	428,014
Tennessee	473,226	1,319,303	1,429,938	1,836,012	1,990,889	2,167,026	2,352,183	2,668,341
Texas	1,518,181	4,997,689	5,310,181	8,996,476	9,642,812	10,152,521	10,791,854	11,761,447
Utah	179,981	518,251	587,648	813,817	906,484	932,740	974,666	1,043,759
Vermont	78,921	189,811	224,901	313,026	346,164	378,264	456,992	485,226
Virginia	704,677	1,881,519	2,045,412	2,845,540	3,183,707	3,444,952	3,793,475	4,151,050
Washington	699,984	1,825,782	1,791,477	2,565,957	2,702,652	2,808,636	3,005,980	3,209,992
West Virginia	249,404	678,386	754,889	1,090,514	1,164,882	1,229,069	1,231,966	1,202,486
Wisconsin	777,288	1,908,523	2,035,879	2,655,729	2,893,797	3,086,878	3,318,247	3,688,311
Wyoming	69,584	226,067	271,153	453,874	488,616	489,825	466,921	491,930
Outlying areas								
American Samoa	—	—	—	13,348	14,997	19,497	20,186	22,314
Guam	16,652	—	—	58,815	78,545	78,278	76,359	94,368
Northern Marianas	—	—	—	9,394	12,556	15,714	19,694	16,118
Puerto Rico	—	—	713,000	856,743	842,827	872,050	935,392	1,030,387
Virgin Islands	—	—	—	—	76,751	97,585	89,217	111,750

ELEMENTARY AND SECONDARY: FINANCES 165

Table 165.—Current expenditures for public elementary and secondary education, by state: 1969–70 to 1996–97—Continued

[In thousands of dollars]

State or other area	1989–90[1]	1990–91	1991–92	1992–93	1993–94[1]	1994–95	Estimated 1995–96[2]	Estimated 1996–97[2]
1	10	11	12	13	14	15	16	17
United States	$188,229,359	$202,037,752	$211,210,190	$220,948,052	$231,542,764	$243,844,646	[3]$258,922,087	[3]$274,065,348
Alabama	2,275,233	2,475,216	2,465,523	2,610,514	2,809,713	3,026,287	3,169,728	3,459,903
Alaska	828,051	854,499	931,869	967,765	1,002,515	1,020,675	1,051,296	1,082,834
Arizona	2,258,660	2,469,543	2,599,586	2,753,504	2,911,304	3,144,540	[4]3,331,835	[4]3,549,233
Arkansas	1,404,545	1,510,092	1,656,201	1,703,621	1,782,645	1,873,595	[5]1,496,991	1,541,900
California	21,485,782	22,748,218	23,696,863	24,219,792	25,140,639	25,949,033	27,521,544	30,273,699
Colorado	2,451,833	2,642,850	2,754,087	2,919,916	2,954,793	3,232,976	3,315,190	[4]3,593,903
Connecticut	3,444,520	3,540,411	3,665,505	3,739,497	3,943,891	4,247,327	4,321,000	4,471,000
Delaware	520,953	543,933	572,152	600,161	643,915	694,473	[5]748,655	[4]783,317
District of Columbia	639,983	647,901	677,422	670,677	713,427	666,938	[4]695,279	[4]728,611
Florida	8,228,531	9,045,710	9,314,079	9,661,012	10,331,896	11,019,735	11,469,259	12,019,783
Georgia	4,505,962	4,804,225	4,856,583	5,273,143	5,643,843	6,136,689	[5]7,781,018	8,247,879
Hawaii	700,012	827,579	884,591	946,074	998,143	1,028,729	960,400	982,000
Idaho	627,794	708,045	760,440	804,231	859,088	951,350	[5]1,042,161	1,090,031
Illinois	8,125,493	8,932,538	9,244,655	9,942,737	10,076,889	10,640,279	12,181,620	12,547,068
Indiana	4,074,578	4,379,142	4,544,829	4,797,946	5,064,685	5,243,761	5,559,000	5,837,000
Iowa	2,004,742	2,136,561	2,356,196	2,459,141	2,527,434	2,622,510	2,743,145	2,873,445
Kansas	1,848,302	1,938,012	2,028,440	2,224,080	2,325,247	2,406,580	[5]2,492,762	2,567,544
Kentucky	2,134,011	2,480,363	2,709,623	2,823,134	2,952,119	2,988,892	3,460,737	3,557,638
Louisiana	2,838,283	3,023,690	3,188,024	3,199,919	3,309,018	3,475,926	[5]3,461,971	3,531,211
Maine	1,048,195	1,070,965	1,121,360	1,217,418	1,208,411	1,281,706	1,271,792	1,322,663
Maryland	3,894,644	4,240,862	4,362,679	4,556,266	4,783,023	5,083,380	4,926,216	5,323,364
Massachusetts	4,760,390	4,906,828	5,035,973	5,281,067	5,637,337	6,062,303	[4]6,522,008	[4]7,054,231
Michigan	8,025,621	8,545,805	9,156,501	9,532,994	9,816,830	10,440,206	[5]10,735,664	11,039,483
Minnesota	3,474,398	3,740,820	3,936,695	4,135,284	4,328,093	4,622,930	4,857,100	4,975,400
Mississippi	1,472,710	1,510,552	1,536,295	1,600,752	1,725,386	1,921,480	[5]1,998,743	2,098,680
Missouri	3,288,738	3,487,786	3,611,613	3,710,426	3,981,614	4,275,217	[5]4,172,801	4,405,644
Montana	641,345	719,963	751,710	785,159	822,015	844,257	861,142	878,365
Nebraska	1,233,431	1,297,643	1,381,290	1,430,039	1,513,971	1,594,928	1,658,725	1,749,955
Nevada	712,898	864,379	962,800	1,035,623	1,099,685	1,186,132	1,286,767	1,415,231
New Hampshire	821,671	890,116	927,625	972,963	1,007,129	1,053,966	1,184,025	1,251,854
New Jersey	8,119,336	8,897,612	9,660,899	9,915,482	10,448,096	10,776,982	[4]11,548,068	[4]12,440,741
New Mexico	1,020,148	1,134,156	1,212,189	1,240,310	1,323,459	1,443,789	[5]1,823,809	2,125,111
New York	18,090,978	19,514,583	19,781,384	20,898,267	22,059,949	22,989,629	23,748,287	24,531,980
North Carolina	4,342,826	4,605,384	4,660,027	4,930,823	5,145,416	5,440,426	5,845,439	6,169,266
North Dakota	459,391	460,581	491,293	511,095	522,377	532,398	[5]561,849	578,704
Ohio	7,994,379	8,407,428	9,124,731	9,173,393	9,612,678	10,030,956	[5]10,396,689	11,000,000
Oklahoma	1,905,332	2,107,513	2,268,958	2,442,320	2,680,113	2,763,721	[5]2,951,191	3,039,727
Oregon	2,297,944	2,453,934	2,626,803	2,849,009	2,852,723	2,948,539	3,028,000	3,247,000
Pennsylvania	9,496,788	10,087,322	10,371,796	10,944,392	11,236,417	11,587,027	12,300,000	13,020,000
Rhode Island	801,908	823,655	865,898	934,815	990,094	1,017,554	[5]1,071,151	1,103,286
South Carolina	2,322,618	2,494,254	2,564,949	2,690,009	2,790,878	2,920,230	2,920,230	3,173,705
South Dakota	447,074	481,304	518,156	553,005	584,894	612,825	[5]624,379	665,026
Tennessee	2,790,808	2,903,209	2,859,755	3,139,223	3,305,579	3,540,682	4,264,551	4,570,746
Texas	12,763,954	13,695,327	14,709,628	15,121,655	16,193,722	17,572,269	[5]19,658,698	20,944,470
Utah	1,130,135	1,235,916	1,296,723	1,376,319	1,511,205	1,618,047	[5]1,739,255	[5]1,833,122
Vermont	546,901	599,018	606,410	616,212	643,828	665,559	[4]706,280	753,516
Virginia	4,621,071	4,958,213	4,993,480	5,228,326	5,441,384	5,750,318	[4]6,062,752	6,672,808
Washington	3,550,819	3,906,471	4,259,048	4,679,698	4,892,690	5,138,931	[5]5,613,481	[5]5,790,558
West Virginia	1,316,637	1,473,640	1,503,980	1,626,005	1,663,868	1,758,557	1,763,439	1,825,159
Wisconsin	3,929,920	4,292,434	4,597,004	4,954,900	5,170,343	5,422,264	5,435,968	5,732,554
Wyoming	509,084	521,549	545,870	547,938	558,353	577,144	[5]580,000	595,000
Outlying areas								
American Samoa	21,838	24,946	26,972	23,636	25,161	28,643	[4]30,372	[4]32,377
Guam	101,130	116,406	132,494	161,477	160,797	157,913	[4]173,721	[4]187,947
Northern Marianas	20,476	26,822	32,498	38,784	32,824	38,427	[5]42,499	[5]50,953
Puerto Rico	1,045,407	1,142,863	1,207,235	1,295,452	1,360,762	1,501,485	1,646,313	1,658,302
Virgin Islands	128,065	119,950	121,660	120,510	120,556	122,094	135,291	140,299

[1] Data revised from previously published figures.
[2] Data estimated by state education agencies.
[3] U.S. total includes National Center for Education Statistics estimates for nonreporting states.
[4] Estimated by the National Center for Education Statistics.
[5] Actual preliminary count.

NOTE.—Beginning in 1980–81, expenditures for state administration are excluded. Because of rounding, details may not add to totals.

SOURCE: U.S. Department of Education, National Center for Education Statistics, *Statistics of State School Systems;* and Common Core of Data surveys. (This table was prepared September 1997.)

Table 166.—Total expenditures for public elementary and secondary education, by function and state: 1994–95

[In thousands]

State or other area	Total expenditures							
	Total	Current expenditures for public schools	Current expenditures for elementary and secondary programs					
			Instruction	Student services			General administration	School administration
				Total	Students [3]	Instructional [4]		
1	2	3	4	5	6	7	8	9
United States	$278,965,657	$243,844,646	$150,521,920	$82,355,354	$11,679,338	$9,654,714	$5,731,462	$14,149,344
Alabama	3,372,114	3,026,287	1,906,471	887,965	95,915	101,461	67,361	178,661
Alaska	1,208,525	1,020,675	574,167	414,601	46,112	59,776	59,146	62,651
Arizona	4,071,643	3,144,540	1,811,054	1,122,492	136,819	101,247	127,861	172,402
Arkansas	2,094,833	1,873,595	1,144,389	601,518	80,417	81,129	69,890	108,937
California	29,070,435	25,949,033	15,549,692	9,299,207	1,389,412	1,184,061	157,603	1,988,240
Colorado	3,867,788	3,232,976	1,970,908	1,138,810	134,882	105,180	95,407	212,746
Connecticut	4,501,537	4,247,327	2,721,552	1,308,873	205,801	125,781	85,815	230,445
Delaware	776,034	694,473	431,618	234,509	35,208	10,054	8,607	39,851
District of Columbia	706,728	666,938	336,543	301,372	68,249	35,583	24,128	35,772
Florida	13,756,867	11,019,735	6,395,934	4,085,932	493,124	621,024	124,221	751,327
Georgia	7,394,767	6,136,689	3,779,713	1,980,428	243,585	308,258	92,699	390,256
Hawaii	1,185,571	1,028,729	636,952	328,578	56,477	47,903	8,317	61,235
Idaho	1,110,948	951,350	602,232	304,596	47,883	27,869	22,736	57,616
Illinois	12,102,804	10,640,279	6,367,082	3,913,546	598,430	414,320	346,332	567,303
Indiana	6,297,458	5,243,761	3,262,523	1,746,052	220,704	150,548	97,521	286,489
Iowa	2,876,604	2,622,510	1,623,942	869,366	151,650	111,906	93,466	136,484
Kansas	2,651,153	2,406,580	1,387,198	901,603	122,448	96,919	97,200	163,849
Kentucky	3,228,465	2,988,892	1,787,624	1,048,826	114,995	94,131	116,323	192,833
Louisiana	3,811,767	3,475,926	2,071,476	1,092,851	129,617	134,672	79,512	191,691
Maine	1,402,024	1,281,706	859,560	375,712	37,206	35,897	25,281	71,727
Maryland	5,616,288	5,083,380	3,127,996	1,714,032	204,542	205,561	28,724	407,145
Massachusetts	6,255,672	6,062,303	3,994,523	1,867,028	280,004	193,981	154,586	262,665
Michigan	11,864,469	10,440,206	6,228,315	3,905,033	646,546	440,927	216,139	621,034
Minnesota	5,829,727	4,622,930	2,946,240	1,490,265	150,969	244,948	120,037	211,671
Mississippi	2,158,879	1,921,480	1,197,868	573,685	67,952	75,608	57,872	104,056
Missouri	4,970,915	4,275,217	2,597,027	1,491,719	177,983	172,595	135,644	250,535
Montana	917,118	844,257	525,617	283,019	38,085	28,041	28,878	44,106
Nebraska	1,858,791	1,594,928	997,580	464,411	61,438	52,704	59,617	80,733
Nevada	1,382,856	1,186,132	706,132	439,092	44,003	34,017	19,791	85,859
New Hampshire	1,165,598	1,053,966	679,046	337,455	57,185	29,372	37,333	59,972
New Jersey	11,785,829	10,776,982	6,467,203	3,962,515	711,455	343,400	333,877	616,362
New Mexico	1,675,685	1,443,789	837,029	527,597	109,502	62,194	38,770	73,534
New York	26,273,275	22,989,629	15,636,396	6,716,673	920,036	515,478	532,921	967,188
North Carolina	6,206,915	5,440,426	3,387,680	1,700,284	275,299	203,004	109,618	360,519
North Dakota	585,046	532,398	328,461	158,320	15,055	11,342	26,664	24,667
Ohio	11,711,711	10,030,956	5,960,083	3,696,226	494,237	491,446	256,871	600,742
Oklahoma	3,064,964	2,763,721	1,662,373	932,702	146,932	80,318	111,885	153,770
Oregon	3,327,032	2,948,539	1,776,148	1,071,438	144,181	140,178	64,919	186,509
Pennsylvania	13,135,222	11,587,027	7,460,973	3,674,151	520,141	360,427	323,749	531,342
Rhode Island	1,059,316	1,017,554	669,274	319,313	63,298	35,542	23,123	51,408
South Carolina	3,353,682	2,920,230	1,727,214	1,007,017	188,416	164,710	50,323	185,744
South Dakota	695,692	612,825	376,116	203,434	25,030	20,853	18,149	34,923
Tennessee	4,027,607	3,540,682	2,285,884	1,063,138	107,096	184,306	77,382	193,446
Texas	20,352,717	17,572,269	10,753,150	5,793,863	818,794	756,747	657,189	983,347
Utah	2,050,021	1,618,047	1,089,195	433,062	46,035	59,045	16,309	91,455
Vermont	727,870	665,559	434,933	209,344	39,133	20,037	19,726	43,535
Virginia	6,637,550	5,750,318	3,483,576	1,959,196	276,456	310,885	63,440	343,478
Washington	6,172,350	5,138,931	3,075,785	1,824,722	324,226	248,340	137,716	258,070
West Virginia	1,945,379	1,758,557	1,090,056	564,738	56,646	47,696	45,205	103,189
Wisconsin	6,030,769	5,422,264	3,441,286	1,816,370	227,651	255,756	152,683	282,766
Wyoming	638,647	577,144	358,131	198,676	32,069	17,539	12,896	35,055
Outlying areas								
American Samoa	34,511	28,643	11,796	11,453	3,314	2,397	471	1,568
Guam	158,302	157,913	79,336	68,478	19,120	4,585	2,207	9,681
Northern Marianas	41,546	38,427	35,613	0	0	0	0	0
Puerto Rico	1,551,369	1,501,485	1,093,038	219,007	34,985	0	94,633	15,904
Virgin Islands	137,020	122,094	69,349	45,951	6,171	7,677	9,289	6,801

Table 166.—Total expenditures for public elementary and secondary education, by function and state: 1994–95—Continued

[In thousands]

State or other area	Total expenditures							
	Current expenditures for elementary and secondary programs					Other current expenditures[1]	Capital outlay[2]	Interest on school debt
	Student services			Food services	Enterprise operations[5]			
	Operation and maintenance	Student transportation	Other support services					
1	10	11	12	13	14	15	16	17
United States	**$24,543,091**	**$9,889,137**	**$6,708,268**	**$10,266,321**	**$701,051**	**$5,148,505**	**$24,453,851**	**$5,518,655**
Alabama	257,876	125,387	61,304	231,851	0	55,454	247,086	43,287
Alaska	149,321	35,338	2,258	27,454	4,453	5,636	157,651	24,563
Arizona	355,175	121,234	107,755	169,981	41,012	26,014	725,588	175,501
Arkansas	160,194	71,079	29,872	112,852	14,837	11,060	165,941	44,237
California	2,703,051	728,475	1,148,364	1,096,200	3,934	493,215	2,529,013	99,174
Colorado	288,364	91,328	210,903	112,961	10,297	8,237	458,354	168,220
Connecticut	390,086	180,164	90,782	124,397	92,505	66,132	86,860	101,217
Delaware	66,400	40,603	33,785	28,347	0	20,661	52,594	8,306
District of Columbia	100,787	14,673	22,179	26,953	2,071	9,183	27,400	3,206
Florida	1,284,882	461,045	350,308	537,869	0	398,246	2,077,463	261,424
Georgia	541,410	236,703	167,517	372,965	3,583	245,749	899,069	113,260
Hawaii	109,945	20,932	23,769	63,199	0	33,858	94,706	28,277
Idaho	88,963	44,129	15,399	44,522	0	1,699	134,626	23,273
Illinois	1,176,403	488,953	321,805	359,650	0	387,113	835,313	240,099
Indiana	571,228	296,455	123,106	235,186	0	40,278	644,345	369,075
Iowa	230,119	83,499	62,242	118,903	10,299	15,714	209,806	28,574
Kansas	267,158	99,645	54,384	117,778	0	3,238	186,381	54,954
Kentucky	310,055	178,019	42,470	152,442	0	7,540	167,857	64,176
Louisiana	301,605	198,378	57,375	262,485	49,114	22,939	219,307	93,594
Maine	124,030	59,747	21,824	46,432	3	15,461	69,977	34,880
Maryland	508,935	258,942	100,184	161,657	79,695	20,811	458,718	53,379
Massachusetts	607,195	260,916	107,680	200,752	0	22,046	56,327	114,995
Michigan	1,106,729	443,303	430,355	306,858	0	396,602	779,103	248,558
Minnesota	374,231	246,818	141,593	186,425	0	206,489	832,894	167,414
Mississippi	161,563	79,374	27,260	149,321	606	12,975	189,219	35,206
Missouri	414,091	252,573	88,297	186,472	0	72,886	527,098	95,714
Montana	88,928	36,971	18,010	35,335	286	3,446	58,245	11,170
Nebraska	137,977	45,967	25,975	61,069	71,868	1,895	234,277	27,691
Nevada	124,105	52,440	78,878	40,907	0	7,831	126,517	62,377
New Hampshire	95,545	47,868	10,180	37,465	0	3,853	80,403	27,376
New Jersey	1,187,881	542,987	226,552	305,128	42,136	155,678	713,452	139,717
New Mexico	151,975	72,478	19,144	69,589	9,575	9,795	199,753	22,348
New York	2,112,752	1,135,476	532,822	636,560	0	891,267	1,911,244	481,135
North Carolina	452,060	202,679	97,104	352,461	0	34,895	602,044	129,550
North Dakota	47,023	24,086	9,483	26,159	19,459	4,271	41,158	7,218
Ohio	976,449	267,937	608,545	372,258	2,390	693,248	709,604	277,903
Oklahoma	281,658	89,730	68,410	146,101	22,545	10,678	271,306	19,259
Oregon	283,418	117,678	134,554	98,931	2,023	9,784	304,585	64,124
Pennsylvania	1,191,240	464,772	282,480	442,456	9,448	284,200	994,217	269,779
Rhode Island	86,956	47,007	11,979	28,967	0	6,645	17,978	17,140
South Carolina	265,137	91,002	61,685	175,774	10,225	61,754	293,549	78,150
South Dakota	59,110	24,625	20,743	31,867	1,408	1,194	69,492	12,181
Tennessee	326,088	128,713	46,107	191,660	0	16,785	395,526	74,614
Texas	1,956,723	485,709	135,354	993,076	32,180	87,311	2,148,179	544,958
Utah	147,363	45,359	27,497	91,662	4,128	48,035	337,844	46,095
Vermont	53,494	22,184	11,236	19,129	2,154	3,502	49,269	9,540
Virginia	604,534	253,327	107,077	221,934	85,611	110,016	631,622	145,594
Washington	530,680	206,454	119,226	165,327	73,097	24,984	785,663	222,772
West Virginia	174,973	113,597	23,432	103,652	111	28,917	141,023	16,882
Wisconsin	493,584	229,896	174,034	164,608	0	47,641	455,293	105,571
Wyoming	63,640	22,485	14,992	20,336	0	1,643	48,913	10,947
Outlying areas								
American Samoa	1,614	834	1,254	5,394	0	2,901	2,967	0
Guam	16,199	10,608	6,078	10,099	0	169	219	0
Northern Marianas	0	0	0	2,814	0	261	2,858	0
Puerto Rico	38,081	34,259	1,144	189,440	0	20,351	28,709	824
Virgin Islands	7,020	3,214	5,780	6,731	64	1,485	13,441	0

[1] Includes expenditures for adult education, community colleges, private school programs funded by local and state education agencies, and community services.
[2] Includes expenditures for property and for building and alterations completed by school district staff or contractors.
[3] Includes expenditures for health, attendance, and speech pathology services.
[4] Includes expenditures for curriculum development, staff training, libraries, and media and computer centers.
[5] Includes expenditures for operations funded by sales of products or services (e.g., school bookstore or computer time).

NOTE.—Excludes expenditures for state education agencies. Because of rounding, details may not add to totals.

SOURCE: U.S. Department of Education, National Center for Education Statistics, Common Core of Data survey. (This table was prepared May 1997.)

Table 167.—Total expenditures for public elementary and secondary education, by function and state: 1993–94

[In thousands]

State or other area	Total expenditures							
	Total	Current expenditures for public schools	Current expenditures for elementary and secondary programs					
			Instruction	Student services			General administration	School administration
				Total	Students[3]	Instructional[4]		
1	2	3	4	5	6	7	8	9
United States	$265,306,634	$231,542,764	$141,620,474	$79,406,310	$10,946,191	$9,236,588	$5,909,692	$13,492,502
Alabama	3,140,345	2,809,713	1,757,077	830,470	92,628	93,780	63,555	163,638
Alaska	1,136,211	1,002,515	517,200	454,317	102,311	54,248	58,091	60,274
Arizona	3,820,218	2,911,304	1,680,405	1,040,553	125,023	96,951	117,957	157,366
Arkansas	1,990,699	1,782,645	1,116,796	544,703	71,860	69,270	56,068	101,813
California	28,680,918	25,140,639	15,028,418	9,061,351	1,313,791	1,119,247	153,833	1,955,639
Colorado	3,648,423	2,954,793	1,815,426	1,028,399	129,829	96,792	92,901	196,540
Connecticut	4,224,269	3,943,891	2,501,019	1,253,016	198,821	116,173	80,424	211,033
Delaware	725,346	643,915	399,147	217,672	31,874	9,269	7,770	37,608
District of Columbia	748,227	713,427	351,028	332,951	66,083	35,503	29,120	37,893
Florida	12,724,793	10,331,896	5,970,755	3,856,344	458,470	579,523	116,306	704,821
Georgia	6,685,598	5,643,843	3,473,765	1,823,252	209,112	287,043	89,073	356,813
Hawaii	1,174,178	998,143	615,270	322,735	56,024	46,622	8,321	59,276
Idaho	977,726	859,088	543,377	273,726	40,615	25,725	20,973	50,263
Illinois	11,116,627	10,076,889	6,064,603	3,670,213	554,917	390,663	327,040	536,535
Indiana	6,010,771	5,064,685	3,121,188	1,721,595	208,933	144,927	95,039	276,985
Iowa	2,768,958	2,527,434	1,558,177	855,845	81,997	196,920	92,303	129,257
Kansas	2,553,527	2,325,247	1,345,121	865,968	116,836	91,872	90,459	154,565
Kentucky	3,189,586	2,952,119	1,768,270	1,029,675	112,570	93,476	113,005	189,656
Louisiana	3,610,624	3,309,018	1,967,293	1,044,538	119,028	128,684	75,256	181,027
Maine	1,327,718	1,208,411	808,608	355,651	34,478	33,285	23,648	67,802
Maryland	5,240,358	4,783,023	2,890,997	1,649,604	179,302	207,282	27,162	359,987
Massachusetts	5,822,837	5,637,337	3,398,730	2,042,430	252,617	173,536	451,396	243,151
Michigan	11,410,269	9,816,830	5,691,574	3,839,812	641,895	435,048	207,455	622,566
Minnesota	5,352,068	4,328,093	2,757,594	1,395,507	131,930	202,263	104,434	201,957
Mississippi	1,928,072	1,725,386	1,066,080	521,331	60,017	63,291	59,269	93,119
Missouri	4,601,996	3,981,614	2,415,629	1,389,998	158,051	160,103	126,432	233,880
Montana	898,790	822,015	514,036	273,001	35,340	26,517	28,945	43,460
Nebraska	1,709,853	1,513,971	941,392	443,860	57,153	49,708	56,920	76,189
Nevada	1,346,021	1,099,685	654,996	407,307	39,699	34,083	18,682	78,997
New Hampshire	1,071,273	1,007,129	646,681	324,847	53,290	28,760	36,193	57,490
New Jersey	11,324,207	10,448,096	6,260,952	3,852,523	681,251	344,008	321,334	603,959
New Mexico	1,515,025	1,323,459	775,050	471,933	93,399	64,781	34,966	47,405
New York	24,980,871	22,059,949	14,884,460	6,549,494	875,668	477,834	518,700	929,531
North Carolina	5,844,294	5,145,416	3,161,009	1,592,366	244,921	196,158	104,393	336,188
North Dakota	585,115	522,377	320,294	157,071	15,435	10,396	26,899	23,781
Ohio	11,067,854	9,612,678	5,717,214	3,540,689	461,622	451,671	273,479	574,627
Oklahoma	2,895,353	2,680,113	1,572,751	884,117	118,982	79,133	110,176	149,472
Oregon	3,160,049	2,852,723	1,708,679	1,047,136	143,722	137,178	61,734	185,260
Pennsylvania	12,679,566	11,236,417	7,144,739	3,664,768	500,757	345,105	313,539	522,116
Rhode Island	1,028,196	990,094	659,748	304,999	56,472	36,676	21,883	48,212
South Carolina	3,182,916	2,790,878	1,651,858	963,310	187,650	150,825	51,899	177,589
South Dakota	665,531	584,894	360,621	191,974	23,651	19,941	17,913	33,804
Tennessee	3,686,856	3,305,579	2,125,274	998,576	94,205	166,326	79,312	183,930
Texas	19,918,597	16,193,722	9,602,153	5,620,902	765,429	769,606	706,820	929,964
Utah	1,848,240	1,511,205	1,013,630	405,340	41,501	55,714	15,212	84,626
Vermont	717,553	643,828	419,909	202,607	37,508	19,656	19,195	42,195
Virginia	6,276,202	5,441,384	3,275,030	1,883,594	263,523	281,134	67,118	330,525
Washington	5,960,965	4,892,690	2,921,122	1,745,781	303,844	235,649	131,373	245,833
West Virginia	1,864,725	1,663,868	1,034,956	534,640	52,898	45,415	43,133	98,841
Wisconsin	5,848,843	5,170,343	3,285,249	1,730,242	217,354	242,137	150,022	270,778
Wyoming	619,376	558,353	345,120	193,577	31,903	16,681	12,561	34,263
Outlying areas								
American Samoa	31,145	25,161	11,582	10,792	3,416	2,084	440	1,523
Guam	161,708	160,797	86,713	65,406	14,999	4,509	2,494	7,453
Northern Marianas	34,662	32,824	29,959	0	0	0	0	0
Puerto Rico	1,396,575	1,360,762	972,817	203,994	26,763	0	88,311	12,653
Virgin Islands	146,950	120,556	68,548	45,795	6,143	7,653	9,204	6,797

Table 167.—Total expenditures for public elementary and secondary education, by function and state: 1993–94—Continued

[In thousands]

State or other area	Total expenditures							
	Current expenditures for elementary and secondary programs					Other current expenditures [1]	Capital outlay [2]	Interest on school debt
	Student services			Food services	Enterprise operations [5]			
	Operation and maintenance	Student transportation	Other support services					
1	10	11	12	13	14	15	16	17
United States	$23,875,871	$9,627,155	$6,318,312	$9,774,315	$741,665	$4,681,798	$23,747,021	$5,335,050
Alabama	247,788	113,563	55,519	222,166	0	49,200	239,011	42,422
Alaska	143,230	33,915	2,247	26,588	4,409	5,572	97,445	30,679
Arizona	333,866	114,758	94,632	156,046	34,299	19,447	710,338	179,130
Arkansas	156,121	67,042	22,529	108,229	12,917	10,176	155,652	42,226
California	2,658,782	727,000	1,133,059	1,047,490	3,380	476,340	2,978,644	85,294
Colorado	275,311	87,611	149,415	106,200	4,769	10,271	383,288	300,070
Connecticut	385,815	173,332	87,419	108,541	81,315	122,648	60,726	97,004
Delaware	61,115	38,241	31,796	27,095	0	18,496	55,794	7,140
District of Columbia	122,422	15,810	26,120	27,735	1,713	6,045	22,589	6,167
Florida	1,239,701	427,224	330,297	504,797	0	381,405	1,775,752	235,740
Georgia	514,002	217,646	149,563	343,116	3,710	234,256	722,879	84,621
Hawaii	107,415	20,557	24,521	60,138	0	33,528	114,779	27,728
Idaho	81,687	41,006	13,457	41,985	0	1,489	99,974	17,174
Illinois	1,116,712	464,380	279,965	342,073	0	93,801	692,578	253,360
Indiana	568,362	284,551	142,797	221,901	0	38,286	563,058	344,742
Iowa	226,133	80,523	48,712	105,535	7,877	14,607	195,171	31,746
Kansas	271,427	96,045	44,764	114,158	0	3,117	181,352	43,811
Kentucky	307,320	174,751	38,896	154,173	0	6,761	170,264	60,442
Louisiana	295,414	191,596	53,533	253,175	44,011	20,720	197,619	83,268
Maine	116,695	58,810	20,933	44,101	51	13,973	72,127	33,207
Maryland	524,648	258,431	92,792	161,420	81,002	26,751	382,831	47,752
Massachusetts	569,361	237,490	114,879	181,654	14,523	45,279	42,055	98,166
Michigan	1,099,403	429,437	404,009	285,444	0	402,149	865,393	325,897
Minnesota	360,097	232,303	162,521	174,993	0	187,876	699,746	136,353
Mississippi	150,559	69,814	25,261	137,010	966	10,673	161,552	30,461
Missouri	388,138	243,243	80,151	175,987	0	65,905	444,127	110,349
Montana	85,088	36,323	17,328	34,687	291	4,026	59,778	12,972
Nebraska	134,511	44,734	24,645	57,910	70,809	2,381	165,295	28,207
Nevada	117,104	46,788	71,954	37,382	0	7,653	184,464	54,219
New Hampshire	92,694	47,086	9,334	35,601	0	5,016	34,262	24,866
New Jersey	1,177,387	508,433	216,150	301,037	33,584	153,411	604,357	118,343
New Mexico	145,044	69,160	17,179	68,610	7,865	6,045	165,597	19,925
New York	2,053,189	1,186,347	508,224	625,996	0	861,366	1,598,019	461,537
North Carolina	438,048	183,532	89,125	332,545	59,496	30,251	535,060	133,566
North Dakota	46,234	23,862	10,464	27,015	17,997	2,638	51,684	8,416
Ohio	958,447	255,039	565,803	352,451	2,326	642,813	662,350	150,013
Oklahoma	282,760	88,921	54,673	141,204	82,040	7,353	189,791	18,095
Oregon	274,914	115,801	128,527	94,822	2,087	9,189	243,419	54,719
Pennsylvania	1,185,990	519,714	277,546	421,528	5,382	268,369	941,072	233,708
Rhode Island	86,555	43,882	11,319	25,346	0	6,324	15,285	16,493
South Carolina	251,875	82,780	60,692	167,239	8,471	51,268	258,683	82,086
South Dakota	58,480	24,295	13,889	31,071	1,228	1,134	64,254	15,249
Tennessee	316,043	122,434	36,324	181,729	0	13,993	287,270	80,015
Texas	1,841,570	480,076	127,437	967,578	3,088	65,937	3,123,644	535,294
Utah	139,647	42,932	25,707	88,117	4,117	44,324	247,982	44,729
Vermont	53,629	20,491	9,932	18,734	2,578	3,515	61,388	8,823
Virginia	597,978	239,101	104,216	207,043	75,716	100,079	606,991	127,749
Washington	510,994	200,251	117,836	156,434	69,353	22,535	844,008	201,731
West Virginia	167,345	105,943	21,064	93,977	294	26,439	160,754	13,664
Wisconsin	476,128	218,358	155,466	154,852	0	45,467	508,229	124,803
Wyoming	62,690	21,791	13,687	19,655	0	1,501	48,644	10,878
Outlying areas								
American Samoa	1,405	849	1,075	2,787	0	2,362	3,622	0
Guam	16,935	10,903	8,113	8,677	0	912	0	0
Northern Marianas	0	0	0	2,865	0	498	1,340	0
Puerto Rico	39,147	36,582	538	183,890	61	15,744	20,069	0
Virgin Islands	7,014	3,209	5,774	6,213	0	1,481	24,914	0

[1] Includes expenditures for adult education, community colleges, private school programs funded by local and state education agencies, and community services.
[2] Includes expenditures for property and for building and alterations completed by school district staff or contractors.
[3] Includes expenditures for health, attendance, and speech pathology services.
[4] Includes expenditures for curriculum development, staff training, libraries, and media and computer centers.
[5] Includes expenditures for operations funded by sales of products or services (e.g., school bookstore or computer time).

NOTE.—Excludes expenditures for state education agencies. Some data have been revised from previously published figures. Because of rounding, details may not add to totals.

SOURCE: U.S. Department of Education, National Center for Education Statistics, Common Core of Data survey. (This table was prepared May 1997.)

Table 168.—Current expenditure per pupil in average daily attendance in public elementary and secondary schools, by state: 1959–60 to 1994–95

State or other area	Unadjusted dollars													
	1959–60	1969–70	1979–80	1980–81	1985–86	1986–87	1987–88	1988–89	1989–90	1990–91	1991–92	1992–93	1993–94	1994–95
1	2	3	4	5	6	7	8	9	10	11	12	13	14	15
United States	$375	$816	$2,272	$2,502	$3,756	$3,970	$4,240	$4,645	$4,980	$5,258	$5,421	$5,584	$5,767	$5,988
Alabama	241	544	1,612	1,985	2,565	2,573	2,718	3,197	3,327	3,627	3,616	3,761	4,037	4,405
Alaska	546	1,123	4,728	5,688	8,304	8,010	7,971	7,716	8,431	8,330	8,450	8,735	8,882	8,963
Arizona	404	720	1,971	2,258	3,336	3,544	3,744	3,902	4,053	4,309	4,381	4,510	4,611	4,778
Arkansas	225	568	1,574	1,701	2,658	2,733	2,989	3,273	3,485	3,700	4,031	4,124	4,280	4,459
California	[2]424	867	2,268	2,475	3,543	3,728	3,840	4,135	4,391	4,491	4,746	4,780	4,921	4,992
Colorado	396	738	2,421	2,693	3,975	4,147	4,220	4,521	4,720	5,064	5,172	5,139	5,097	5,443
Connecticut	436	951	2,420	2,876	4,743	5,435	6,230	6,857	7,837	7,853	8,016	7,973	8,473	8,817
Delaware	456	900	2,861	3,018	4,610	4,825	5,017	5,422	5,799	5,974	6,093	6,274	6,621	7,030
District of Columbia	431	1,018	3,259	3,441	5,337	5,742	6,132	7,850	8,955	9,377	9,549	9,419	10,180	9,335
Florida	318	732	1,889	2,401	3,529	3,794	4,092	4,563	4,997	5,276	5,243	5,314	5,516	5,718
Georgia	253	588	1,625	1,708	2,966	3,181	3,434	3,852	4,275	4,466	4,419	4,686	4,915	5,193
Hawaii	325	841	2,322	2,604	3,807	3,787	3,919	4,121	4,448	5,166	5,420	5,704	5,879	6,078
Idaho	290	603	1,659	1,856	2,484	2,585	2,667	2,833	3,078	3,386	3,556	3,690	3,844	4,210
Illinois	438	909	2,587	2,704	3,781	4,106	4,369	4,906	5,118	5,520	5,670	5,898	5,893	6,136
Indiana	369	728	1,882	2,010	3,275	3,556	3,794	4,284	4,606	4,930	5,074	5,344	5,630	5,826
Iowa	368	844	2,326	2,668	3,619	3,770	4,124	4,285	4,453	4,679	5,096	5,257	5,288	5,483
Kansas	348	771	2,173	2,559	3,829	3,933	4,076	4,443	4,752	4,874	5,007	5,442	5,659	5,817
Kentucky	233	545	1,701	1,784	2,486	2,733	3,011	3,347	3,745	4,354	4,719	4,872	5,107	5,217
Louisiana	372	648	1,792	2,469	3,187	3,069	3,138	3,317	3,903	4,196	4,354	4,428	4,519	4,761
Maine	283	692	1,824	1,934	3,472	3,850	4,258	4,744	5,373	5,458	5,652	6,073	6,069	6,428
Maryland	393	918	2,598	2,914	4,447	4,777	5,201	5,758	6,275	6,654	6,679	6,813	6,958	7,245
Massachusetts	409	859	2,819	2,940	4,562	5,145	5,471	5,972	6,237	6,366	6,408	6,627	6,959	7,287
Michigan	415	904	2,640	3,037	4,176	4,353	4,692	5,150	5,546	5,883	6,268	6,494	6,658	6,994
Minnesota	425	904	2,387	2,673	3,941	4,180	4,386	4,755	4,971	5,239	5,409	5,554	5,720	6,000
Mississippi	206	501	1,664	1,605	2,362	2,350	2,548	2,861	3,094	3,187	3,245	3,382	3,660	4,080
Missouri	344	709	1,936	2,172	3,189	3,472	3,786	4,263	4,507	4,754	4,830	4,885	5,114	5,383
Montana	411	782	2,476	2,683	4,091	4,194	4,246	4,293	4,736	5,204	5,319	5,425	5,598	5,692
Nebraska	337	736	2,150	2,384	3,634	3,756	3,943	4,360	4,842	5,038	5,263	5,336	5,651	5,935
Nevada	430	769	2,088	2,078	3,440	3,440	3,623	3,871	4,117	4,653	4,926	5,066	5,052	5,160
New Hampshire	347	723	1,916	2,265	3,542	3,933	4,457	4,807	5,304	5,685	5,790	5,644	5,723	5,859
New Jersey	388	1,016	3,191	3,254	5,570	5,953	6,564	7,549	8,139	8,756	9,321	9,415	9,677	9,774
New Mexico	363	707	2,034	2,329	3,195	3,558	3,691	3,473	3,515	3,895	3,765	4,071	4,261	4,586
New York	562	1,327	3,462	3,741	6,011	6,497	7,151	7,663	8,062	8,565	8,527	8,902	9,175	9,623
North Carolina	237	612	1,754	2,001	2,948	3,129	3,368	3,874	4,290	4,548	4,556	4,763	4,894	5,077
North Dakota	367	690	1,920	2,275	3,483	3,437	3,519	3,952	4,189	4,199	4,441	4,597	4,674	4,775
Ohio	365	730	2,075	2,303	3,527	3,673	3,998	4,686	5,045	5,245	5,694	5,754	5,971	6,162
Oklahoma	311	604	1,926	2,199	3,146	3,099	3,093	3,379	3,508	3,843	4,078	4,355	4,734	4,845
Oregon	448	925	2,692	3,100	4,141	4,337	4,789	5,182	5,474	5,683	5,913	6,296	6,263	6,436
Pennsylvania	409	882	2,535	2,824	4,325	4,616	4,989	5,597	6,228	6,541	6,613	6,890	6,983	7,109
Rhode Island	413	891	2,601	2,927	4,667	4,985	5,329	6,064	6,368	6,343	6,546	6,938	7,333	7,469
South Carolina	220	613	1,752	1,734	3,058	3,214	3,408	3,736	4,082	4,352	4,436	4,624	4,761	4,797
South Dakota	347	690	1,908	1,991	3,051	3,097	3,249	3,585	3,731	3,965	4,173	4,357	4,586	4,775
Tennessee	238	566	1,635	1,794	2,612	2,827	3,068	3,491	3,664	3,782	3,692	3,993	4,149	4,388
Texas	332	624	1,916	2,006	3,298	3,409	3,608	3,877	4,150	4,438	4,632	4,670	4,898	5,222
Utah	322	626	1,657	1,819	2,390	2,415	2,454	2,588	2,764	2,960	3,040	3,180	3,439	3,656
Vermont	344	807	1,997	2,475	4,031	4,399	5,207	5,481	6,227	6,738	6,671	6,411	6,600	6,750
Virginia	274	708	1,970	2,179	3,520	3,780	4,149	4,539	4,672	4,902	4,880	4,980	5,109	5,327
Washington	420	915	2,568	2,542	3,881	3,964	4,164	4,359	4,702	5,000	5,270	5,614	5,751	5,906
West Virginia	258	670	1,920	2,146	3,528	3,784	3,858	3,883	4,360	4,911	5,078	5,527	5,713	6,107
Wisconsin	413	883	2,477	2,738	4,168	4,523	4,747	5,266	5,524	5,871	6,139	6,475	6,717	6,930
Wyoming	450	856	2,527	2,967	5,114	5,201	5,051	5,375	5,577	5,638	5,812	5,822	5,899	6,160
Outlying areas														
American Samoa	—	—	—	—	1,387	1,846	1,908	1,988	1,908	2,033	2,085	1,670	1,785	2,046
Guam	236	820	—	—	3,383	3,344	3,295	4,067	4,234	4,596	5,231	5,309	5,071	4,969
Northern Marianas	—	—	—	—	2,552	3,099	3,366	2,414	3,007	4,425	5,247	5,288	4,510	5,227
Puerto Rico	106	—	—	—	1,325	1,384	1,504	1,692	1,750	1,913	2,162	2,364	2,312	2,742
Virgin Islands	271	—	—	—	3,223	4,277	4,036	5,281	6,767	6,002	5,935	5,843	5,915	6,003

ELEMENTARY AND SECONDARY: FINANCES 171

Table 168.—Current expenditure per pupil in average daily attendance in public elementary and secondary schools, by state: 1959–60 to 1994–95—Continued

State or other area	Constant 1994–95 dollars [1]													
	1959–60	1969–70	1979–80	1980–81	1985–86	1986–87	1987–88	1988–89	1989–90	1990–91	1991–92	1992–93	1993–94	1994–95
1	16	17	18	19	20	21	22	23	24	25	26	27	28	29
United States	$1,920	$3,249	$4,401	$4,344	$5,191	$5,369	$5,505	$5,764	$5,899	$5,905	$5,900	$5,892	$5,933	$5,988
Alabama	1,234	2,166	3,123	3,446	3,545	3,479	3,529	3,967	3,941	4,073	3,935	3,969	4,152	4,405
Alaska	2,797	4,470	9,159	9,877	11,478	10,831	10,349	9,576	9,987	9,355	9,196	9,218	9,137	8,963
Arizona	2,066	2,867	3,818	3,921	4,612	4,793	4,861	4,843	4,801	4,839	4,767	4,759	4,743	4,778
Arkansas	1,153	2,260	3,050	2,953	3,674	3,696	3,881	4,062	4,128	4,156	4,386	4,352	4,403	4,459
California	[2]2,170	3,453	4,393	4,297	4,897	5,040	4,986	5,132	5,201	5,044	5,165	5,045	5,062	4,992
Colorado	2,028	2,938	4,690	4,675	5,494	5,608	5,479	5,610	5,591	5,687	5,628	5,424	5,243	5,443
Connecticut	2,232	3,788	4,689	4,993	6,556	7,349	8,090	8,511	9,283	8,821	8,724	8,414	8,715	8,817
Delaware	2,333	3,584	5,543	5,240	6,372	6,524	6,515	6,730	6,869	6,710	6,631	6,621	6,811	7,030
District of Columbia	2,207	4,055	6,314	5,975	7,377	7,765	7,962	9,743	10,607	10,532	10,392	9,940	10,472	9,335
Florida	1,626	2,916	3,660	4,170	4,878	5,130	5,313	5,663	5,920	5,926	5,706	5,608	5,674	5,718
Georgia	1,297	2,341	3,149	2,966	4,099	4,302	4,459	4,781	5,064	5,016	4,809	4,945	5,056	5,193
Hawaii	1,661	3,347	4,498	4,521	5,261	5,121	5,088	5,114	5,269	5,802	5,898	6,020	6,048	6,078
Idaho	1,483	2,402	3,215	3,223	3,433	3,496	3,463	3,516	3,646	3,803	3,870	3,894	3,954	4,210
Illinois	2,244	3,621	5,011	4,695	5,227	5,552	5,672	6,088	6,062	6,200	6,170	6,225	6,062	6,136
Indiana	1,887	2,899	3,647	3,490	4,527	4,808	4,926	5,317	5,456	5,538	5,521	5,640	5,791	5,826
Iowa	1,882	3,361	4,507	4,632	5,003	5,098	5,354	5,318	5,275	5,255	5,546	5,548	5,440	5,483
Kansas	1,780	3,070	4,210	4,444	5,293	5,318	5,293	5,514	5,628	5,474	5,449	5,743	5,822	5,817
Kentucky	1,193	2,171	3,296	3,097	3,436	3,696	3,909	4,154	4,436	4,890	5,135	5,142	5,254	5,217
Louisiana	1,904	2,580	3,472	4,288	4,405	4,150	4,075	4,117	4,624	4,713	4,738	4,673	4,649	4,761
Maine	1,447	2,757	3,533	3,358	4,799	5,205	5,529	5,887	6,364	6,130	6,151	6,409	6,243	6,428
Maryland	2,010	3,656	5,033	5,059	6,146	6,460	6,753	7,146	7,434	7,473	7,268	7,190	7,157	7,245
Massachusetts	2,093	3,421	5,462	5,104	6,306	6,957	7,104	7,412	7,388	7,150	6,974	6,994	7,159	7,287
Michigan	2,125	3,599	5,115	5,273	5,772	5,887	6,092	6,391	6,570	6,607	6,821	6,854	6,849	6,994
Minnesota	2,177	3,598	4,624	4,642	5,447	5,652	5,695	5,901	5,888	5,884	5,886	5,861	5,883	6,000
Mississippi	1,054	1,994	3,223	2,788	3,264	3,178	3,308	3,550	3,665	3,579	3,532	3,569	3,765	4,080
Missouri	1,761	2,821	3,751	3,771	4,408	4,694	4,915	5,290	5,339	5,339	5,256	5,155	5,260	5,383
Montana	2,103	3,113	4,798	4,659	5,654	5,672	5,513	5,327	5,611	5,845	5,789	5,726	5,758	5,692
Nebraska	1,725	2,932	4,165	4,140	5,023	5,078	5,120	5,411	5,735	5,658	5,728	5,632	5,813	5,935
Nevada	2,203	3,064	4,046	3,608	4,755	4,651	4,704	4,804	4,877	5,226	5,361	5,346	5,197	5,160
New Hampshire	1,777	2,879	3,712	3,933	4,895	5,319	5,787	5,966	6,283	6,385	6,301	5,957	5,887	5,859
New Jersey	1,984	4,046	6,183	5,650	7,699	8,050	8,523	9,369	9,641	9,834	10,144	9,936	9,955	9,774
New Mexico	1,856	2,815	3,940	4,045	4,416	4,811	4,793	4,310	4,163	4,374	4,097	4,296	4,383	4,586
New York	2,875	5,283	6,708	6,496	8,308	8,786	9,285	9,511	9,549	9,619	9,280	9,395	9,438	9,623
North Carolina	1,214	2,438	3,399	3,474	4,075	4,230	4,373	4,808	5,082	5,108	4,958	5,026	5,035	5,077
North Dakota	1,877	2,746	3,720	3,949	4,814	4,648	4,570	4,904	4,962	4,716	4,833	4,852	4,808	4,775
Ohio	1,869	2,907	4,019	3,999	4,875	4,967	5,191	5,816	5,976	5,891	6,197	6,073	6,142	6,162
Oklahoma	1,594	2,407	3,732	3,817	4,349	4,190	4,016	4,194	4,155	4,316	4,438	4,596	4,870	4,845
Oregon	2,295	3,682	5,215	5,382	5,723	5,864	6,218	6,432	6,485	6,383	6,435	6,644	6,442	6,436
Pennsylvania	2,096	3,511	4,911	4,903	5,978	6,242	6,478	6,947	7,377	7,347	7,197	7,271	7,183	7,109
Rhode Island	2,116	3,548	5,039	5,082	6,451	6,741	6,919	7,526	7,543	7,124	7,124	7,322	7,543	7,469
South Carolina	1,126	2,439	3,394	3,011	4,227	4,346	4,425	4,636	4,835	4,888	4,827	4,880	4,898	4,797
South Dakota	1,775	2,747	3,696	3,457	4,217	4,188	4,218	4,449	4,420	4,453	4,541	4,598	4,717	4,775
Tennessee	1,219	2,254	3,169	3,114	3,610	3,823	3,984	4,333	4,340	4,247	4,018	4,214	4,268	4,388
Texas	1,701	2,485	3,712	3,483	4,559	4,610	4,684	4,812	4,916	4,985	5,041	4,928	5,038	5,222
Utah	1,651	2,493	3,210	3,158	3,304	3,265	3,186	3,212	3,274	3,324	3,309	3,356	3,537	3,656
Vermont	1,761	3,214	3,869	4,297	5,572	5,949	6,761	6,802	7,376	7,568	7,259	6,765	6,789	6,750
Virginia	1,404	2,818	3,817	3,783	4,866	5,112	5,387	5,634	5,534	5,505	5,310	5,255	5,255	5,327
Washington	2,152	3,645	4,976	4,414	5,364	5,360	5,406	5,410	5,570	5,615	5,736	5,924	5,915	5,906
West Virginia	1,323	2,667	3,721	3,726	4,877	5,117	5,009	4,819	5,165	5,516	5,526	5,833	5,877	6,107
Wisconsin	2,114	3,515	4,799	4,754	5,761	6,115	6,164	6,536	6,543	6,594	6,681	6,834	6,910	6,930
Wyoming	2,305	3,408	4,895	5,152	7,068	7,033	6,559	6,671	6,607	6,332	6,325	6,144	6,068	6,160
Outlying areas														
American Samoa	—	—	—	—	1,916	2,497	2,478	2,468	2,260	2,283	2,269	1,763	1,836	2,046
Guam	1,210	3,264	—	—	4,676	4,522	4,279	5,048	5,016	5,161	5,692	5,602	5,216	4,969
Northern Marianas	—	—	—	—	3,527	4,190	4,370	—	3,562	4,969	5,710	5,581	4,639	5,227
Puerto Rico	544	—	—	—	1,831	1,872	1,953	2,100	2,073	2,149	2,352	2,494	2,379	2,742
Virgin Islands	1,385	—	—	—	4,455	5,784	5,241	6,555	8,016	6,741	6,459	6,166	6,085	6,003

[1] Based on the Consumer Price Index, prepared by the Bureau of Labor Statistics, U.S. Department of Labor, adjusted to a school-year basis. These data do not reflect differences in inflation rates from state to state.
[2] Estimated by the National Center for Education Statistics.
—Data not available or not applicable.

NOTE.—Beginning in 1980–81, state administration expenditures are excluded. Beginning in 1988–89, extensive changes were made in the data collection procedures. Some data have been revised from previously published figures.

SOURCE: U.S. Department of Education, National Center for Education Statistics, *Statistics of State School Systems;* and Common Core of Data surveys. (This table was prepared April 1997.)

Table 169.—Total and current expenditure per pupil in public elementary and secondary schools: 1919–20 to 1996–97

School year	Expenditure per pupil in average daily attendance				Expenditure per pupil in fall enrollment [1]			
	Unadjusted dollars		Constant 1996–97 [2] dollars		Unadjusted dollars		Constant 1996–97 dollars [2]	
	Total expenditure	Current expenditure	Total expenditure	Current expenditure	Total expenditure	Current expenditure	Total expenditure	Current expenditure
1	2	3	4	5	6	7	8	9
1919–20	$64	$53	$533	$445	$48	$40	$399	$333
1929–30	108	87	1,007	805	90	72	834	667
1931–32	97	81	1,068	894	82	69	904	757
1933–34	76	67	915	810	65	57	777	688
1935–36	88	74	1,017	859	74	63	860	727
1937–38	100	84	1,106	930	86	72	949	799
1939–40	106	88	1,202	1,002	92	76	1,042	868
1941–42	110	98	1,121	1,002	94	84	960	858
1943–44	125	117	1,137	1,067	105	99	958	899
1945–46	146	136	1,271	1,188	124	116	1,083	1,012
1947–48	205	181	1,397	1,238	179	158	1,220	1,081
1949–50	260	210	1,747	1,411	231	187	1,550	1,252
1951–52	314	246	1,901	1,488	275	215	1,665	1,302
1953–54	351	265	2,074	1,565	312	236	1,844	1,392
1955–56	387	294	2,288	1,739	354	269	2,091	1,590
1957–58	447	341	2,490	1,898	408	311	2,271	1,731
1959–60	471	375	2,547	2,029	440	350	2,380	1,895
1961–62	517	419	2,734	2,215	485	393	2,565	2,079
1963–64	559	460	2,879	2,372	520	428	2,679	2,208
1965–66	654	538	3,256	2,678	607	499	3,023	2,486
1967–68	786	658	3,675	3,076	732	612	3,418	2,861
1969–70	955	816	4,017	3,433	878	750	3,693	3,155
1970–71	1,049	911	4,198	3,645	970	842	3,880	3,368
1971–72	1,128	990	4,355	3,822	1,034	907	3,994	3,504
1972–73	1,211	1,077	4,494	3,998	1,116	993	4,144	3,686
1973–74	1,364	1,207	4,648	4,114	1,244	1,101	4,240	3,753
1974–75	1,545	1,365	4,740	4,187	1,424	1,258	4,368	3,859
1975–76	1,697	1,504	4,863	4,308	1,564	1,385	4,481	3,970
1976–77	1,816	1,638	4,917	4,434	1,673	1,509	4,531	4,085
1977–78	2,002	1,823	5,080	4,625	1,842	1,677	4,673	4,254
1978–79	2,210	2,020	5,127	4,687	2,029	1,855	4,708	4,304
1979–80	2,491	2,272	5,098	4,650	2,290	2,089	4,687	4,275
1980–81	[3]2,742	2,502	[3]5,031	4,589	[3]2,529	2,307	[3]4,640	4,233
1981–82	[3]2,973	2,726	[3]5,021	4,603	[3]2,754	2,525	[3]4,651	4,264
1982–83	[3]3,203	2,955	[3]5,186	4,785	[3]2,966	2,736	[3]4,802	4,430
1983–84	[3]3,471	3,173	[3]5,419	4,954	[3]3,216	2,940	[3]5,021	4,590
1984–85	[3]3,722	3,470	[3]5,592	5,214	[3]3,456	3,222	[3]5,192	4,841
1985–86	[3]4,020	3,756	[3]5,870	5,484	[3]3,724	3,479	[3]5,439	5,081
1986–87	[3]4,308	3,970	[3]6,154	5,672	[3]3,995	3,682	[3]5,707	5,260
1987–88	[3]4,654	4,240	[3]6,384	5,816	[3]4,310	3,927	[3]5,912	5,386
1988–89	5,109	4,645	6,699	6,090	4,738	4,307	6,212	5,648
1989–90	5,550	4,980	6,946	6,232	5,174	4,643	6,476	5,810
1990–91	5,885	5,258	6,983	6,239	5,486	4,902	6,510	5,817
1991–92	6,075	5,421	6,984	6,233	5,629	5,023	6,472	5,776
1992–93	6,281	5,584	7,003	6,225	5,804	5,160	6,471	5,753
1993–94	6,492	5,767	7,055	6,268	5,996	5,327	6,517	5,789
1994–95 [3]	6,724	5,988	7,104	6,327	6,207	5,528	6,558	5,840
1995–96 [3]	7,024	6,255	7,224	6,434	6,484	5,774	6,669	5,939
1996–97 [3]	7,371	6,564	7,371	6,564	6,804	6,060	6,804	6,060

[1] Data for 1919–20 to 1953–54 are based on school-year enrollment.
[2] Based on the Consumer Price Index, prepared by the Bureau of Labor Statistics, U.S. Department of Labor, adjusted to a school-year basis.
[3] Estimated.

NOTE.—Beginning in 1980–81, state administration expenditures are excluded from both "total" and "current" expenditures. Beginning in 1988–89, extensive changes were made in the data collection procedures. Some data have been revised from previously published figures.

SOURCE: U.S. Department of Education, National Center for Education Statistics, Statistics of State School Systems; Revenues and Expenditures for Public Elementary and Secondary Education; and Common Core of Data surveys. (This table was prepared July 1997.)

CHAPTER 3
Postsecondary Education

Postsecondary education includes an array of diverse educational experiences, including a wide range of programs offered by American colleges and universities. For example, a community college may offer vocational training or the first 2 years of training at the college level. A university typically offers a full undergraduate course of study leading to a bachelor's degree as well as first-professional and graduate programs leading to advanced degrees. Vocational and technical institutions offer training programs which are designed to prepare students for specific careers. Other types of educational opportunities for adults include community groups, churches, libraries, and businesses.

This chapter provides an overview of the latest statistics on postsecondary education, which includes academic, vocational and continuing professional education programs after high school. However, to maintain comparability over time, most of the data in the Digest are for higher education institutions, which include 2- and 4-year colleges and universities and exclude most vocational and continuing education programs. This chapter highlights historical data that enable the reader to observe long-range trends in American higher education.

Other chapters provide related information on postsecondary education. Data on price indexes and on the number of degrees held by the general population are in chapter 1. Chapter 4 contains tabulations on federal funding for postsecondary education. Information on employment outcomes for college graduates is in chapter 5. Chapter 7 contains data on college libraries and use of computers by young adults. Further information on survey methodologies is in the "Guide to Sources" in the appendix and in the publications cited in the source notes.

Enrollment

Higher education enrollment increased by 9 percent between 1975 and 1985. Between 1985 and 1995, enrollment increased at a faster rate (16 percent), from 12.2 million to 14.3 million. There was a slight decline in enrollment in the later part of the period from 1992 to 1995, but it was overshadowed by large increases in the late 1980s. Much of this growth was in part-time and female enrollment (table 172). Between 1985 and 1995, the number of men enrolled rose 9 percent, while the number of women increased by 23 percent. Part-time enrollment rose by 19 percent compared to an increase of 15 percent in full-time enrollment. In addition to the enrollment in 2-year colleges, 4-year colleges, and universities, about 850,000 students attended noncollegiate postsecondary institutions in fall 1995 (table 170). The number of older students has been growing more rapidly than the number of younger students, though this pattern is beginning to change. Between 1985 and 1995, the enrollment of students under age 25 increased by 13 percent. During the same period, enrollment of persons 25 and over rose by 22 percent. From 1995 to 2007, NCES projects a rise of 20 percent in enrollments of persons under 25 and an increase of 4 percent in the number 25 and over (table 176).

Enrollment trends have differed at the undergraduate, graduate, and first-professional levels. Undergraduate enrollment generally increased during the 1970s, but dipped between 1983 and 1985. From 1985 to 1992, undergraduate enrollment increased each year, rising 18 percent before declining slightly between 1993 and 1995. Graduate enrollment had been steady at about 1.3 million in the late 1970s and early 1980s, but rose about 26 percent between 1985 and 1995. After rising very rapidly during the 1970s, enrollment in first-professional programs stabilized in the 1980s. There was a 9 percent increase in first-professional enrollment between 1985 and 1995 (tables 187, 188, and 189).

Since 1984, the number of women in graduate schools has exceeded the number of men. Between 1985 and 1995, the number of male full-time graduate students increased by 23 percent, compared to 64 percent for full-time women. Among part-time graduate students, the number of men increased by 6 percent compared to a 26 percent increase for women (table 188).

The proportion of American college students who are minorities has been increasing. In 1976, 16 percent were minorities, compared with 25 percent in 1995. Much of the change can be attributed to rising numbers of Hispanic and Asian students. The proportion of Asian and Pacific Islander students rose from 2 percent to 6 percent, and the Hispanic proportion rose from 4 percent to 8 percent during that time period. The proportion of black students has fluctuated over the previous 19 years, before rising to 11 percent in 1995. These percentages exclude foreign students enrolled in U.S. colleges and universities (table 206).

Despite the sizable numbers of small colleges, most students attend the larger colleges and universities. In fall 1995, 36 percent of higher education campuses had fewer than 1,000 students; however, these campuses enrolled only 4 percent of college students. While 11 percent of the campuses enrolled 10,000 or more students, they accounted for 50 percent of total college enrollment (table 215).

Faculty, Staff, and Salaries

The student/staff ratio at colleges and universities dropped from 5.4 in 1976 to 4.9 in 1993. During the same time period, the student/faculty ratio dropped from 16.6 to 15.5. The proportion of administrative staff and other non-teaching professional staff rose from 15 percent in 1976 to 22 percent in 1993, while the proportion of nonprofessional staff declined from 42 percent to 35 percent (table 221).

Approximately 2.6 million people were employed in colleges and universities in the fall of 1993, including 1.7 million professional and .9 million nonprofessional staff. About 43 percent of the staff were faculty or teaching assistants, 6 percent were managerial, 16 percent were other non-teaching professionals, and 35 percent were nonprofessional staff (table 223).

Colleges differ widely in their practices of employing part-time and full-time staff. In fall 1993, 51 percent of the employees at public 2-year colleges were employed full-time compared with 72 percent at public 4-year colleges and 73 percent at private 4-year colleges. A higher proportion of the faculty at public 4-year colleges were employed full-time (76 percent) than at private 4-year colleges (62 percent) or public 2-year colleges (35 percent) (table 223).

Full-time and part-time faculty and instructional staff also differ by the number and types of students that they teach. In 1992, 67 percent of full-time faculty taught 50 students or more, while only 30 percent of part-time faculty taught that many students. Part-time faculty also taught fewer hours per week. About 46 percent of full-time faculty taught for 10 or more hours per week, compared to 18 percent of part-time faculty. Of the full-time faculty teaching only undergraduate students, 61 percent taught three or more classes, compared to 18 percent of part-time faculty (tables 228 and 229).

The proportion of time that full-time faculty spent teaching was 55 percent in 1992. For the remaining faculty time, research and scholarship accounted for 18 percent of the time; professional growth, 5 percent; administration, 13 percent; outside consulting, 3 percent; service and non-teaching activities, 7 percent (table 228).

About 12 percent of U.S. faculty in colleges and universities were minorities in 1993. Five percent of the faculty were black; 4 percent, Asian/Pacific Islanders; 3 percent, Hispanic; and .4 percent, American Indian/Alaskan Native. The majority of college faculty were white males. Fifty-two percent of faculty fell in this category, while 33 percent were white females. About 14 percent of executive, managerial, and administrative staff were minorities in 1993, compared to about 29 percent of the nonprofessional staff. The distribution of minority staff was similar at public and private institutions. About 19 percent of all staff at public institutions were minorities compared to 20 percent at private institutions (table 222).

College faculty generally suffered losses in the purchasing power of their salaries from 1972–73 to 1980–81, when average salaries fell 17 percent after adjustment for inflation. During the 1980s, average salaries rose and recouped most of the losses. Between 1992–93 and 1995–96, there was a slight rise in average faculty salaries. Average salaries for men in 1995–96 ($52,814) were considerably higher than the average for women ($42,871), but women's salaries have increased at a slightly faster rate since 1990–91 (table 234).

The proportion of faculty with tenure has remained relatively stable in recent years. About 65 percent of full-time faculty had tenure in 1995–96, but a large difference existed between the proportion of men and women with tenure. Seventy-two percent of men compared with 51 percent of women had tenure in 1995–96. About 68 percent of the faculty at public institutions had tenure, compared with 58 percent of faculty at private institutions (table 240).

The age distribution of full-time faculty was concentrated in the middle age brackets in 1992. Faculty under the age of thirty composed one percent of the total, but 36 percent were ages 30 to 44, and 37 percent were 45 to 54 years old. Thirteen percent were 55 to 59; 8 percent, 60 to 64; and 5 percent, 65 or older (table 231).

Degrees

During the 1995–96 academic year, 9,962 institutions offered postsecondary education. This included 2,244 4-year colleges, 1,462 2-year colleges, and 6,256 vocational and technical institutions (tables 242 and 356). Institutions awarding various higher education degrees in 1994–95 numbered 2,184 for associate degrees, 1,855 for bachelor's degrees, 1,351 for master's degrees, and 482 for doctor's degrees (tables 258).

More people are completing college. Between 1984–85 and 1994–95, the number of associate, bachelor's, master's, and doctor's degrees rose. Associate degrees increased 19 percent, bachelor's degrees increased 18 percent, master's degrees increased 39 percent, and doctor's degrees increased 35 percent during this period. The number of first-professional degrees was slightly higher in 1994–95 than it was in 1984–85. The number of first-professional degrees declined in the mid 1980s before increasing in the early 1990s (table 244).

The total number of bachelor's degrees increased slowly during the early 1980s and more rapidly towards the end of that decade, especially for women. Between 1984–85 and 1994–95, the number of bachelor's degrees awarded to men increased by 9 percent, while those awarded to women rose by 28 percent (table 244).

Of the 1,160,000 bachelor's degrees conferred in 1994–95, the largest numbers of degrees were conferred in the fields of business (234,000), social sciences (128,000), and education (106,000). At the master's degree level, the largest fields were education (101,000) and business (94,000). The largest fields at the doctor's degree level were education (6,900), engineering (6,100), biological sciences (4,600) and physical sciences (4,500) (tables 250, 251, and 252).

The pattern of bachelor's degrees by field of study has shifted significantly in recent years. Declines are significant in some male majority fields such as engineering and computer and information sciences. Engineering and engineering technologies declined 15 percent between 1984–85 and 1989–90, and then posted a further 4 percent decline between 1989–90 and 1994–95 (table 285). Computer and information sciences grew rapidly during the 1970s and mid 1980s, but dropped 42 percent between 1985–86 and 1994–95 (table 283). Other technical fields have been driven upwards in recent years, in part, by increasing numbers of female graduates. For example, biological science degrees declined by 3 percent between 1984–85 and 1989–90, and then rose 50 percent between 1989–90 and 1994–95. During the later period, the number of male graduates grew 46 percent, while the number of female graduates grew 55 percent (table 279). After declining by 32 percent overall between 1984–85 and 1989–90, the number of male graduates in the physical sciences grew by 13 percent, while the number of female graduates grew 33 percent between 1989–90 and 1994–95 (table 292). After declining by 29 percent between 1984–85 and 1989–90, the number of male graduates in agriculture and natural resources grew by 44 percent between 1989–90 and 1994–95, while the number of female graduates grew 75 percent (table 277).

Some fields that had been increasing grew at a more rapid pace between 1989–90 and 1994–95. For example, the number of degrees conferred in visual and performing arts increased by 5 percent between 1984–85 and 1989–90, but increased 22 percent between 1989–90 and 1994–95 (table 298). Public administration rose by 18 percent during the first period and by 34 percent in the second 5 year period (table 295). Some fields, such as psychology, increased rapidly in both of the 5 year periods, rising 35 percent between 1984–85 and 1989–90, and then a further 34 percent between 1989–90 and 1994–95 (table 294).

Less than half (46 percent) of the bachelor's degree seeking students who enrolled in college in 1989–90 had completed their degree by spring 1994. About 8 percent of students had completed an associate degree or other certificate below the bachelor's degree, 18 percent of the students were still enrolled toward a bachelor's degree, and 28 percent were no longer working towards a bachelor's degree (table 310).

Finances

For the 1996–97 academic year, annual undergraduate charges for tuition, room, and board were estimated to be $6,534 at public colleges and $18,071 at private colleges. Between 1986–87 and 1996–97, charges at public colleges have risen by 20 percent, and charges at private colleges have increased by 31 percent, after adjustment for inflation (tables 38 and 312).

Trend data show increases in the expenditures per student at institutions of higher education through the late 1980s and further increases after 1992. After an adjustment for inflation at colleges and universities, current-fund expenditures per student rose about 8 percent between 1984–85 and 1989–90, and another 8 percent between 1989–90 and 1994–95 (table 336).

Scholarships and fellowships have been rising more rapidly than most other types of college expenditures in recent years. At public universities, between 1984–85 and 1994–95, inflation adjusted scholarships and fellowships expenditures per full-time-equivalent student rose 91 percent compared with 11 percent for instruction expenditures per student. At private universities during the same period, scholarships and fellowships costs per student rose 78 percent, and the instruction costs rose by 38 percent (tables 341 and 344). Another rapidly rising expenditure for public colleges during the decade was research, which rose by 38 percent per full-time-equivalent student at public universities, and by 47 percent at other public 4-year colleges (tables 341 and 342).

Figure 13.–Enrollment, degrees conferred, and expenditures in institutions of higher education: 1960–61 to 1996–97

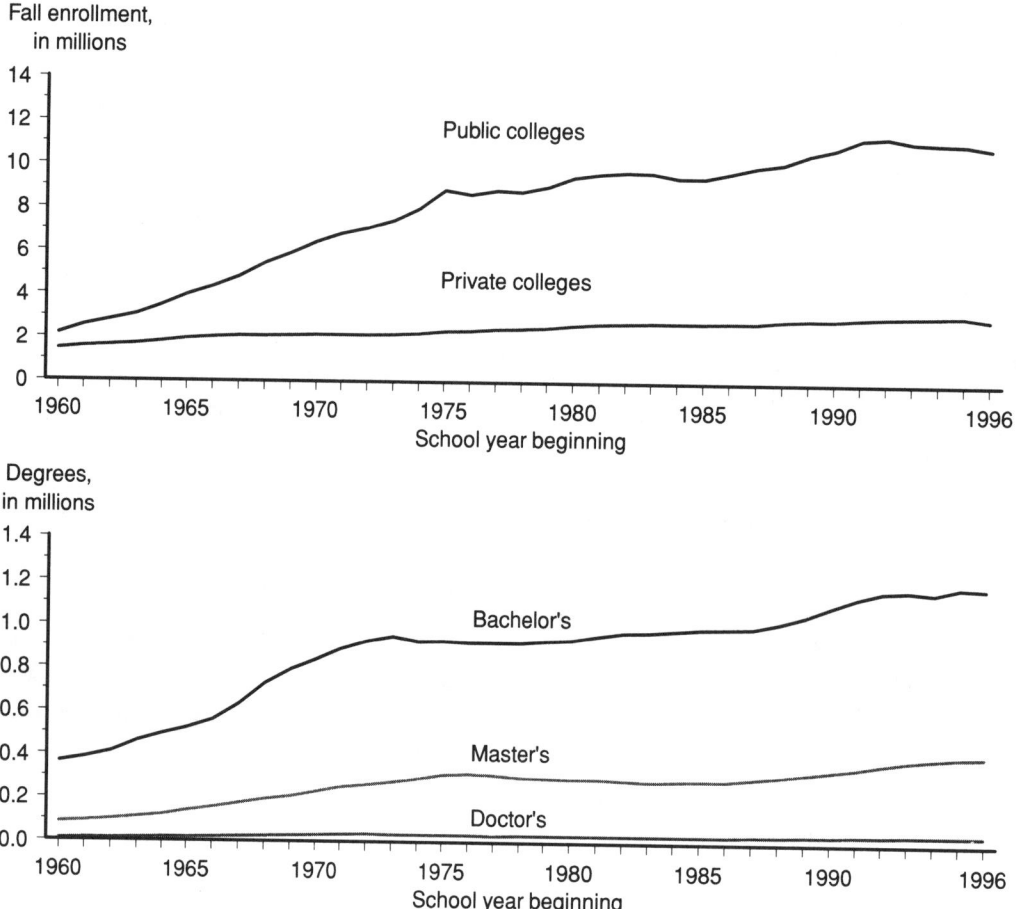

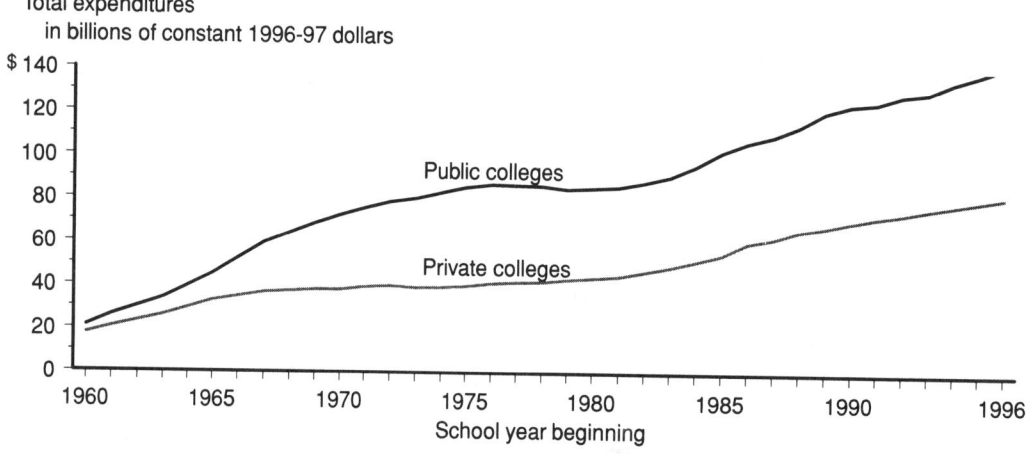

NOTE: Degree and finance data for 1995–96 and 1996–97 and enrollment data for fall 1996 are estimated.

SOURCE: U.S. Department of Education, National Center for Education Statistics, Higher Education General Information Survey (HEGIS), "Fall Enrollment in Institutions of Higher Education," "Degrees and Other Formal Awards Conferred," and "Financial Statistics of Institutions of Higher Education" surveys; and Integrated Postsecondary Education Data System (IPEDS), "Fall Enrollment," "Completions," and "Finance" surveys.

POSTSECONDARY EDUCATION 177

Figure 14.–Percentage change in total enrollment of institutions of higher education, by state: Fall 1990 to fall 1995

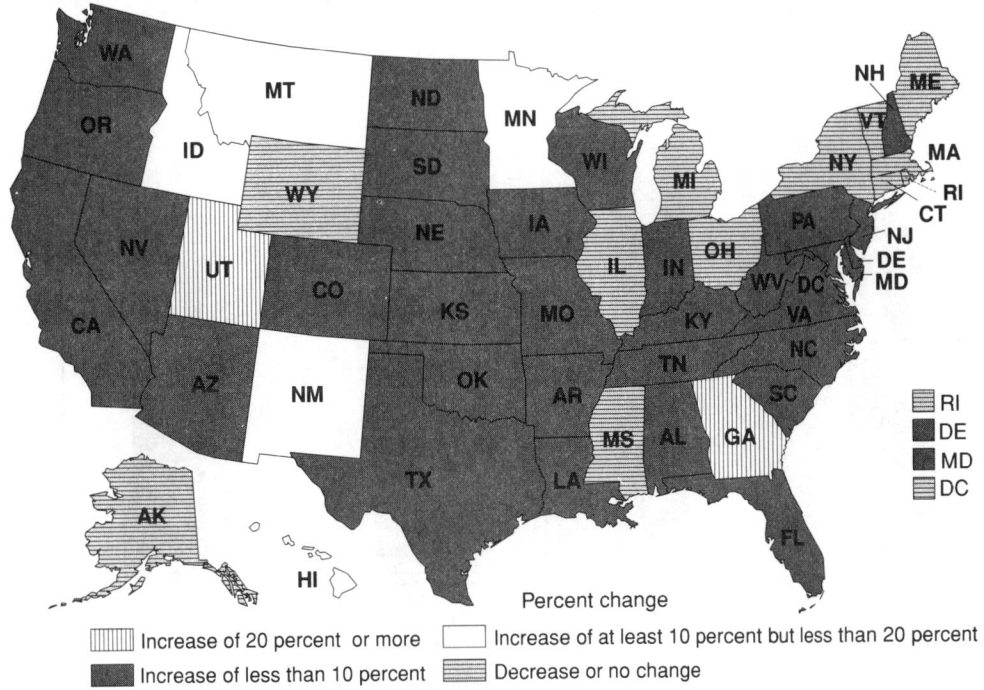

SOURCE: U.S. Department of Education, National Center for Education Statistics, Integrated Postsecondary Education Data System (IPEDS), "Fall Enrollment" surveys.

Figure 15.–Enrollment in institutions of higher education, by age: Fall 1970 to fall 2007

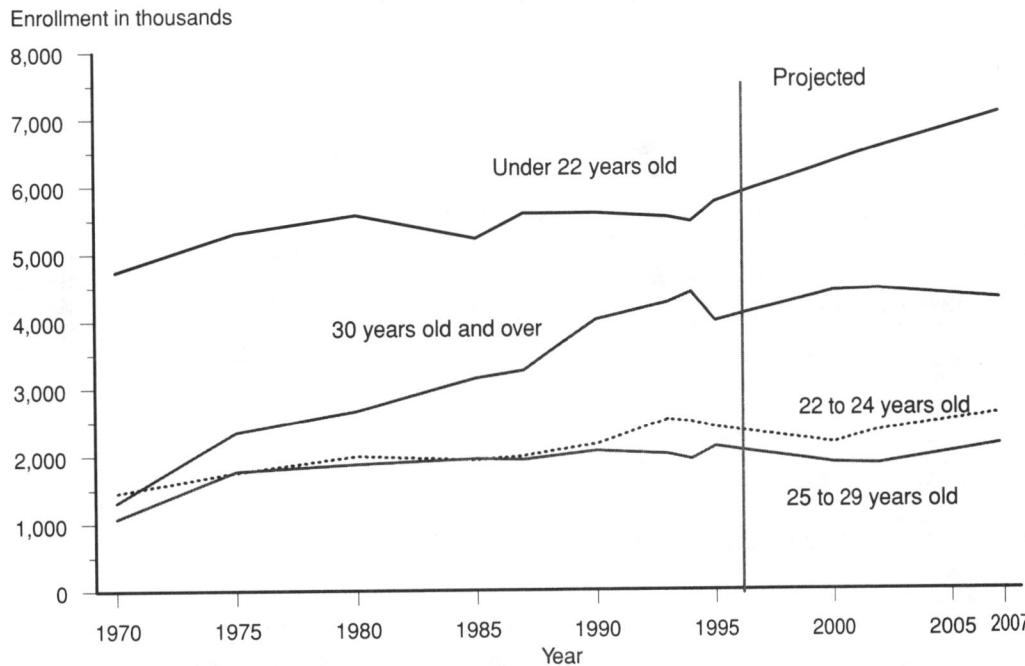

SOURCE: U.S. Department of Education, National Center for Education Statistics, Higher Education General Information Survey (HEGIS), "Fall Enrollment in Institutions of Higher Education" survey; Integrated Postsecondary Education Data System (IPEDS), "Fall Enrollment" surveys; Projections of Education Statistics to 2007; and U.S. Department of Commerce, Bureau of the Census, Current Population Reports, Series P-20, "Social and Economic Characteristics of Students," various years.

Figure 16.-Full-time-equivalent students per staff member in public and private institutions of higher education: 1976 and 1993

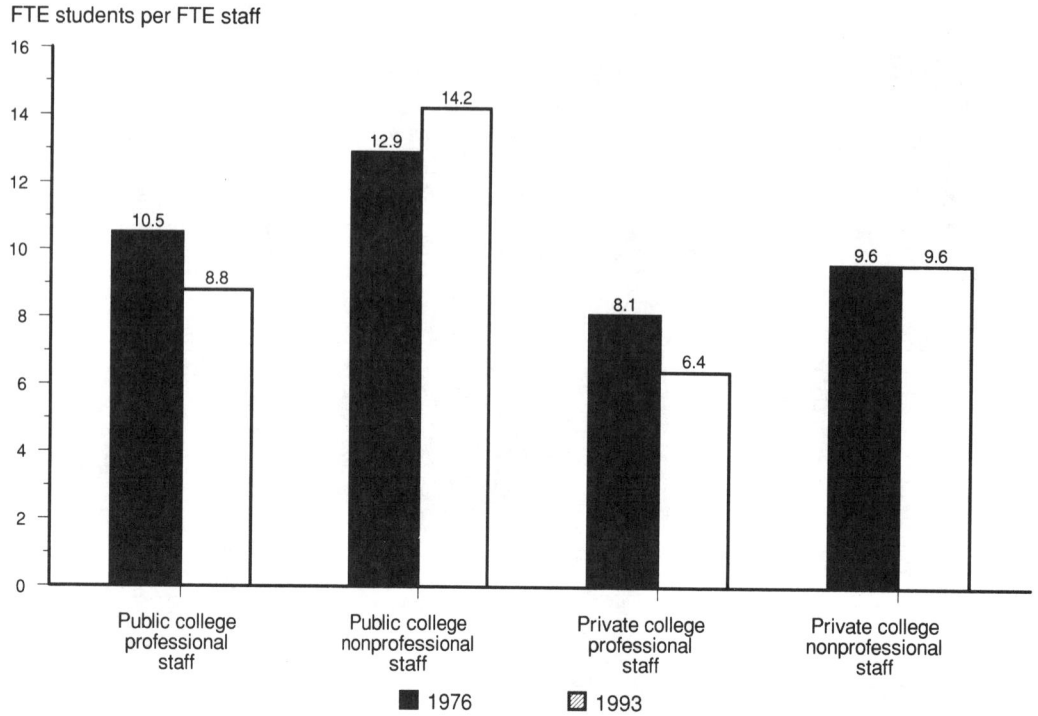

SOURCE: U.S. Department of Education, National Center for Education Statistics, Higher Education General Information Survey (HEGIS), "Staff" survey, and Integrated Postsecondary Education Data System (IPEDS), "Staff" surveys.

Figure 17.-Trends in bachelor's degrees conferred in selected fields of study: 1984-85, 1989-90, and 1994-95

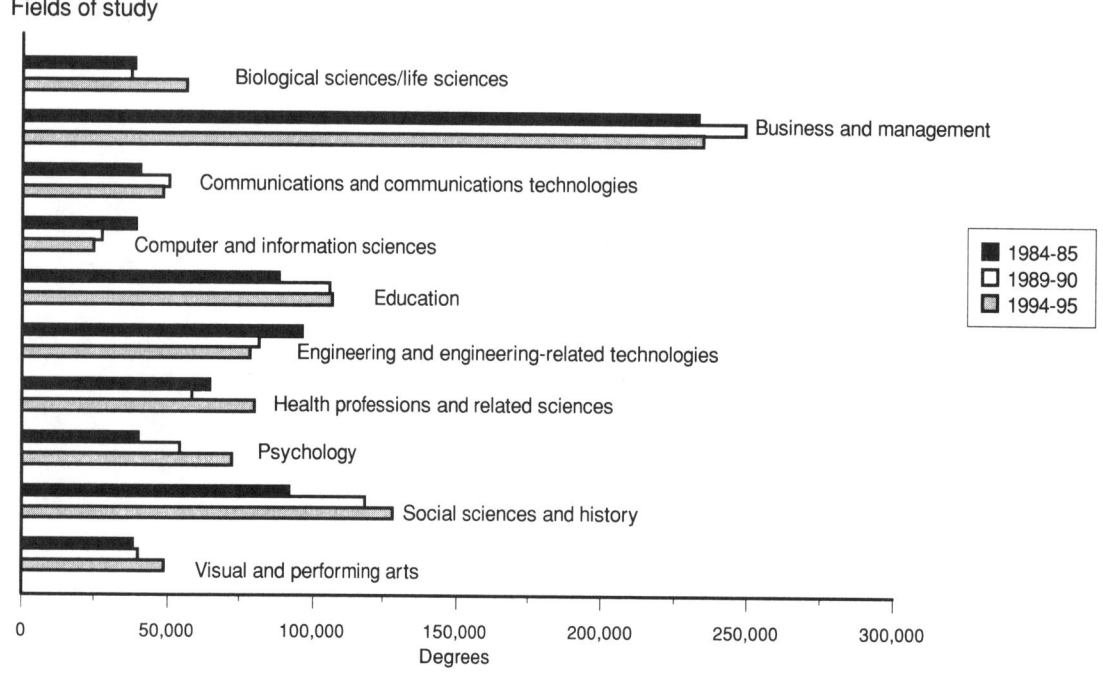

SOURCE: U.S. Department of Education, National Center for Education Statistics, Higher Education General Information Survey (HEGIS), "Degrees and Other Formal Awards Conferred" survey, and Integrated Postsecondary Education Data System (IPEDS), "Completions" surveys.

Figure 18.-Sources of current-fund revenue for public institutions of higher education: 1994–95

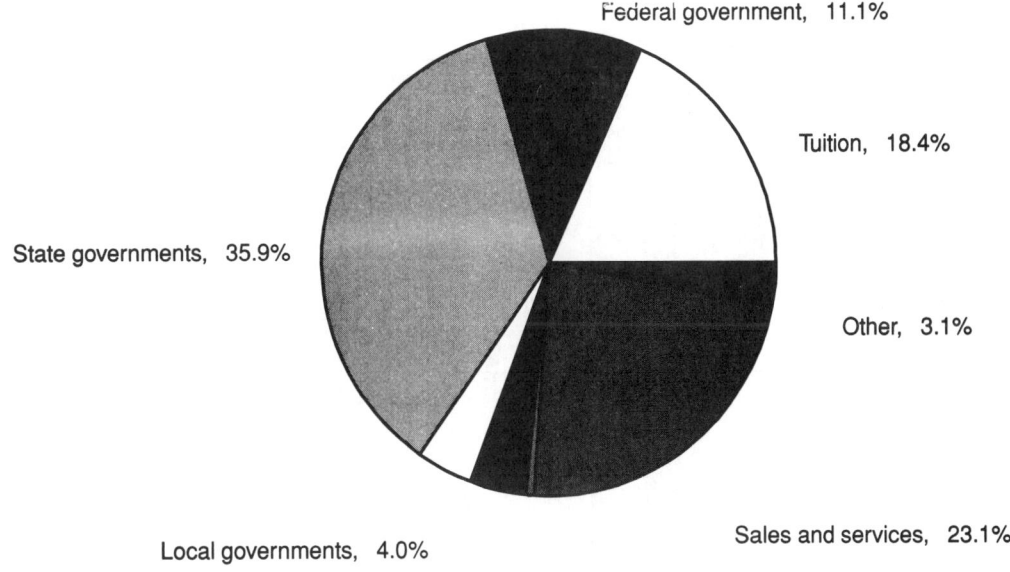

Total revenues=$119.3 billion

SOURCE: U.S. Department of Education, National Center for Education Statistics, Integrated Postsecondary Education Data System (IPEDS), "Finance FY95" survey.

Figure 19.-Sources of current-fund revenue for private institutions of higher education: 1994–95

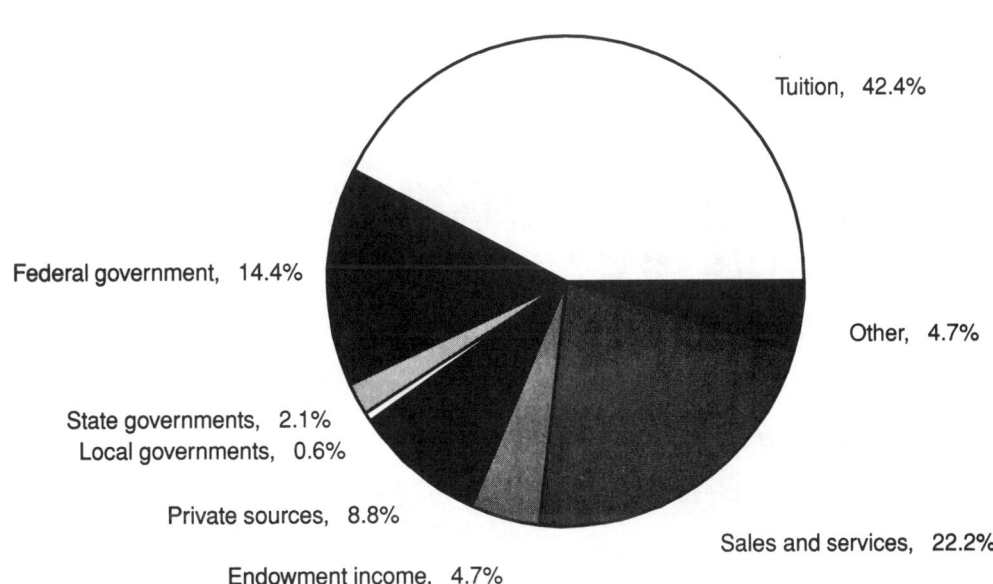

Total revenues = $69.8 billion

SOURCE: U.S. Department of Education, National Center for Education Statistics, Integrated Postsecondary Education Data System (IPEDS), "Finance, FY95" survey.

Table 170.—Enrollment and staff in, and degrees conferred by, institutions of higher education and noncollegiate postsecondary institutions: 1994–95 and fall 1993 and 1995

Level of institution, type of degree, and sex of student	All post-secondary	Institutions of higher education					Noncollegiate postsecondary institutions				
		Total	Public	Private			Total	Public	Private		
				Total	Nonprofit	Proprietary			Total	Nonprofit	Proprietary
1	2	3	4	5	6	7	8	9	10	11	12
Enrollment, fall 1995											
Total [1]	15,112,043	14,261,781	11,092,374	3,169,407	2,929,044	240,363	850,262	279,291	570,971	181,015	389,956
4-year institutions [1]	8,879,390	8,769,252	5,814,545	2,954,707	2,853,890	100,817	110,138	423	109,715	90,830	18,885
Men	4,076,416	4,013,930	2,671,542	1,342,388	1,283,830	58,558	62,486	194	62,292	52,190	10,102
Women	4,755,790	4,755,322	3,143,003	1,612,319	1,570,060	42,259	468	229	239	38,640	8,783
2-year institutions [1]	5,747,991	5,457,563	5,277,255	180,308	74,920	105,388	290,428	139,404	151,024	43,208	107,816
Men	2,437,905	2,313,624	2,235,862	77,762	29,184	48,578	124,281	69,319	54,962	14,791	40,171
Women	3,310,086	3,143,939	3,041,393	102,546	45,736	56,810	166,147	70,085	96,062	28,417	67,645
Less than 2-year	484,662	34,966	574	34,392	234	34,158	449,696	139,464	310,232	46,977	263,255
Men	172,874	14,985	231	14,754	161	14,593	157,889	63,406	94,483	20,500	73,983
Women	311,788	19,981	343	19,638	73	19,565	291,807	76,058	215,749	26,477	189,272
Staff, fall 1993											
Total	2,727,504	2,602,612	1,812,513	790,099	766,723	23,376	124,892	31,554	93,338	34,348	58,990
Professional staff	1,777,843	1,687,287	1,193,284	494,003	476,257	17,746	90,556	23,076	67,480	22,408	45,072
Administrative	160,638	143,675	81,209	62,466	59,867	2,599	16,963	1,652	15,311	4,041	11,270
Faculty	973,289	915,474	650,434	265,040	254,130	10,910	57,815	18,142	39,673	12,485	27,188
Faculty assistants	203,049	202,819	173,678	29,141	28,065	1,076	230	22	208	189	19
Other professionals	440,867	425,319	287,963	137,356	134,195	3,161	15,548	3,260	12,288	5,693	6,595
Nonprofessional staff	949,661	915,325	619,229	296,096	290,466	5,630	34,336	8,478	25,858	11,940	13,918
Student/staff ratio	5.6	5.5	6.2	3.9	3.7	9.9	7.4	9.0	6.9	4.5	8.3
Degrees conferred, 1994–95											
Less than 1-year awards and 1- to 4-year awards	725,177	237,232	177,339	59,893	12,280	47,613	487,945	146,140	341,805	43,832	297,973
4-year institutions	25,638	20,039	10,690	9,349	7,706	1,643	5,599	—	5,599	5,420	179
Men	13,050	9,397	5,463	3,934	3,116	818	3,653	—	3,653	3,607	46
Women	12,588	10,642	5,227	5,415	4,590	825	1,946	—	1,946	1,813	133
2-year institutions	319,651	185,388	165,955	19,433	4,218	15,215	134,263	68,197	66,066	14,946	51,120
Men	141,551	80,903	72,264	8,639	1,516	7,123	60,648	34,244	26,404	4,707	21,697
Women	178,100	104,485	93,691	10,794	2,702	8,092	73,615	33,953	39,662	10,239	29,423
Less than 2-year	379,888	31,805	694	31,111	356	30,755	348,083	77,943	270,140	23,466	246,674
Men	137,864	14,982	255	14,727	253	14,474	122,882	35,287	87,595	10,213	77,382
Women	242,024	16,823	439	16,384	103	16,281	225,201	42,656	182,545	13,253	169,292
Associate [1]	559,086	539,691	451,539	88,152	48,643	39,509	19,395	2,159	17,236	2,457	14,779
4-year	80,080	78,745	37,845	40,900	31,029	9,871	1,335	—	1,335	624	711
Men	34,871	34,144	15,557	18,587	11,889	6,698	727	—	727	317	410
Women	45,209	44,601	22,288	22,313	19,140	3,173	608	—	608	307	301
2-year	478,996	460,946	413,694	47,252	17,614	29,638	18,050	2,150	15,900	1,833	14,067
Men	191,458	184,208	163,291	20,917	6,886	14,031	7,250	1,051	6,199	750	5,449
Women	287,538	276,738	250,403	26,335	10,728	15,607	10,800	1,099	9,701	1,083	8,618
Less than 2-year	10	—	—	—	—	—	10	9	1	—	1
Men	10	—	—	—	—	—	10	9	1	—	1
Women	—	—	—	—	—	—	—	—	—	—	—
Bachelor's [1]	1,168,475	1,160,134	776,670	383,464	373,454	10,010	8,341	7	8,334	6,757	1,577
Men	530,352	526,131	354,675	171,456	165,598	5,858	4,221	3	4,218	3,259	959
Women	638,123	634,003	421,995	212,008	207,856	4,152	4,120	4	4,116	3,498	618
Master's [1]	400,771	397,629	224,152	173,477	170,505	2,972	3,142	6	3,136	2,155	981
Men	180,453	178,598	97,094	81,504	79,780	1,724	1,855	1	1,854	1,279	575
Women	220,318	219,031	127,058	91,973	90,725	1,248	1,287	5	1,282	876	406
Doctor's [1]	45,292	44,446	28,917	15,529	15,265	264	846	6	840	537	303
Men	27,483	26,916	17,623	9,293	9,169	124	567	1	566	373	193
Women	17,809	17,530	11,294	6,236	6,096	140	279	5	274	164	110
First-professional [1]	77,480	75,800	29,871	45,929	45,390	539	1,680	86	1,594	1,372	222
Men	45,962	44,853	16,898	27,955	27,635	320	1,109	43	1,066	910	156
Women	31,518	30,947	12,973	17,974	17,755	219	571	43	528	462	66

[1] Includes noncollegiate institutions that offer non-accredited degree programs.
—Not applicable.
NOTE.—Enrollment data are preliminary.

SOURCE: U.S. Department of Education, National Center for Education Statistics, Integrated Postsecondary Education Data System (IPEDS), "Fall Enrollment," "Staff," and "Completions" surveys. (This table was prepared May 1997.)

HIGHER EDUCATION: SUMMARY 181

Table 171.—Historical summary of faculty, students, degrees, and finances in institutions of higher education: 1869–70 to 1994–95

Item	1869–70	1879–80	1889–90	1899–1900	1909–10	1919–20	1929–30	1939–40	1949–50	1959–60	1969–70	1979–80	1989–90	1993–94	1994–95
1	2	3	4	5	6	7	8	9	10	11	12	13	14	15	16
Total institutions[1]	563	811	998	977	951	1,041	1,409	1,708	1,851	2,008	2,525	3,152	3,535	3,632	3,688
Total faculty[2]	[3]5,553	[3]11,522	[3]15,809	23,868	36,480	48,615	82,386	146,929	246,722	380,554	[4]450,000	[4]675,000	[5]824,220	[5]915,474	[3,5]915,000
Men	[3]4,887	[3]7,328	[3]12,704	19,151	29,132	35,807	60,017	106,328	186,189	296,773	[4]346,000	[4]479,000	[5]577,298	[5]561,123	—
Women	[3]666	[3]4,194	[3]3,105	4,717	7,348	12,808	22,369	40,601	60,533	83,781	[4]104,000	[4]196,000	[5]246,922	[5]354,351	—
Total fall enrollment[6]	[3]52,286	[3]115,817	[3]156,756	237,592	[3]355,213	597,880	1,100,737	1,494,203	2,659,021	3,639,847	8,004,660	11,569,899	13,538,560	14,304,803	14,278,790
Men	[3]41,160	[3]77,972	[3]100,453	152,254	[3]214,648	314,938	619,935	893,250	1,853,068	2,332,617	4,746,201	5,682,877	6,190,015	6,427,450	6,371,898
Women	[3]11,126	[3]37,845	[3]56,303	85,338	[3]140,565	282,942	480,802	600,953	805,953	1,307,230	3,258,459	5,887,022	7,348,545	7,877,353	7,906,892
Earned degrees conferred															
Associate, total	—	—	—	—	—	—	—	—	—	—	206,023	400,910	455,102	530,632	539,691
Men	—	—	—	—	—	—	—	—	—	—	117,432	183,737	191,195	215,261	[7]218,352
Women	—	—	—	—	—	—	—	—	—	—	88,591	217,173	263,907	315,371	[7]321,339
Bachelor's,[8] total	9,371	12,896	15,539	27,410	37,199	48,622	122,484	186,500	432,058	392,440	792,656	929,417	1,051,344	1,169,275	[7]1,160,134
Men	7,993	10,411	12,857	22,173	28,762	31,980	73,615	109,546	328,841	254,063	451,380	473,611	491,696	532,422	[7]526,131
Women	1,378	2,485	2,682	5,237	8,437	16,642	48,869	76,954	103,217	138,377	341,276	455,806	559,648	636,853	[7]634,003
Master's,[9] total	0	879	1,015	1,583	2,113	4,279	14,969	26,731	58,183	74,435	208,291	298,081	324,301	387,070	[7]397,629
Men	0	868	821	1,280	1,555	2,985	8,925	16,508	41,220	50,898	125,624	150,749	153,653	176,085	[7]178,598
Women	0	11	194	303	558	1,294	6,044	10,223	16,963	23,537	82,667	147,332	170,648	210,985	[7]219,031
First-professional,[8] total	([8])	([8])	([8])	([8])	([8])	([8])	([8])	([8])	([8])	([8])	34,578	70,131	70,988	75,418	775,800
Men	([8])	([8])	([8])	([8])	([8])	([8])	([8])	([8])	([8])	([8])	32,794	52,716	43,961	44,707	[7]44,853
Women	([8])	([8])	([8])	([8])	([8])	([8])	([8])	([8])	([8])	([8])	1,784	17,415	27,027	30,711	[7]30,947
Doctor's, total	1	54	149	382	443	615	2,299	3,290	6,420	9,829	29,866	32,615	38,371	43,185	[7]44,446
Men	1	51	147	359	399	522	1,946	2,861	5,804	8,801	25,890	22,943	24,401	26,552	[7]26,916
Women	0	3	2	23	44	93	353	429	616	1,028	3,976	9,672	13,970	16,633	[7]17,530
Finances, in thousands															
Current-fund revenue Educational and general income	—	—	$21,464	$35,084	$76,883	$199,922	$554,511	$715,211	$2,374,645	$5,785,537	$21,515,242	$58,519,982	$139,635,477	$179,226,601	[7]$189,120,570
Current-fund expenditures Educational and general expenditures	—	—	—	—	67,917	172,929	483,065 507,142	571,288 674,688	1,833,845 2,245,661	4,688,352 5,601,376	16,486,177 21,043,113	56,913,588	134,655,571	173,350,617	[7]182,968,610
Value of physical property	—	—	95,426	253,599	457,594	747,333	377,903 2,065,049	521,990 [10]2,753,780	1,706,444 4,799,964	4,685,258 13,548,548	16,845,210 42,093,580	44,542,843 83,733,387	105,585,076 164,635,000	136,024,350 199,463,715	[7]144,158,002 [7]212,201,113
Market value of endowment funds	—	[11]78,788	[11]194,998	[11]323,661	[11]569,071	[11]1,372,068	[11]1,686,283	[11]2,601,223	[11]5,322,080	11,206,632	20,743,045	67,978,726	96,012,591	[7]109,706,704

[1] Prior to 1979–80, excludes branch campuses.
[2] Total number of different individuals (not reduced to full-time equivalent). Beginning in 1959–60, data are for the first term of the academic year. Beginning in 1969–70, data include only instructional faculty with the rank of instructor or above.
[3] Estimated.
[4] Estimated number of senior instructional staff. Excludes graduate assistants.
[5] Because of revised survey procedures, data may not be directly comparable with figures prior to 1989–90.
[6] Data for 1869–70 to 1949–50 are for resident degree-credit students who enrolled at any time during the academic year.
[7] Preliminary data.
[8] From 1869–70 to 1959–60, first-professional degrees included under bachelor's degrees.
[9] Figures for years prior to 1969–70 are not precisely comparable with later data.
[10] Includes unexpended plant funds.
[11] Book value. Includes other nonexpendable funds.
— Data not available.

NOTE.—Some data have been revised from previously published figures.

SOURCE: U.S. Department of Education, National Center for Education Statistics. *Biennial Survey of Education in the United States; Education Directory, Colleges and Universities; Faculty and Other Professional Staff in Institutions of Higher Education; Fall Enrollment in Colleges and Universities; Earned Degrees Conferred; Financial Statistics of Institutions of Higher Education;* and Higher Education General Information Survey (HEGIS), "Fall Enrollment in Institutions of Higher Education," "Degrees and Other Formal Awards Conferred," and "Financial Statistics of Institutions of Higher Education" surveys; and Integrated Postsecondary Education Data System (IPEDS), "Fall Enrollment," "Completions," and "Finance" surveys. (This table was prepared July 1997.)

Table 172.—Total fall enrollment in institutions of higher education, by attendance status, sex of student, and control of institution: 1947 to 1995

Year	Total enrollment	Attendance status		Sex of student		Control of institution			
		Full-time	Part-time	Men	Women	Public	Private		
							Total	Nonprofit	Proprietary
1	2	3	4	5	6	7	8	9	10
1947[1]	2,338,226	—	—	1,659,249	678,977	1,152,377	1,185,849	—	—
1948[1]	2,403,396	—	—	1,709,367	694,029	1,185,588	1,217,808	—	—
1949[1]	2,444,900	—	—	1,721,572	723,328	1,207,151	1,237,749	—	—
1950[1]	2,281,298	—	—	1,560,392	720,906	1,139,699	1,141,599	—	—
1951[1]	2,101,962	—	—	1,390,740	711,222	1,037,938	1,064,024	—	—
1952[1]	2,134,242	—	—	1,380,357	753,885	1,101,240	1,033,002	—	—
1953[1]	2,231,054	—	—	1,422,598	808,456	1,185,876	1,045,178	—	—
1954[1]	2,446,693	—	—	1,563,382	883,311	1,353,531	1,093,162	—	—
1955[1]	2,653,034	—	—	1,733,184	919,850	1,476,282	1,176,752	—	—
1956[1]	2,918,212	—	—	1,911,458	1,006,754	1,656,402	1,261,810	—	—
1957	3,323,783	—	—	2,170,765	1,153,018	1,972,673	1,351,110	—	—
1959	3,639,847	2,421,016	[2]1,218,831	2,332,617	1,307,230	2,180,982	1,458,865	—	—
1961	4,145,065	2,785,133	[2]1,359,932	2,585,821	1,559,244	2,561,447	1,583,618	—	—
1963	4,779,609	3,183,833	[2]1,595,776	2,961,540	1,818,069	3,081,279	1,698,330	—	—
1964	5,280,020	3,573,238	[2]1,706,782	3,248,713	2,031,307	3,467,708	1,812,312	—	—
1965	5,920,864	4,095,728	[2]1,825,136	3,630,020	2,290,844	3,969,596	1,951,268	—	—
1966	6,389,872	4,438,606	[2]1,951,266	3,856,216	2,533,656	4,348,917	2,040,955	—	—
1967	6,911,748	4,793,128	[2]2,118,620	4,132,800	2,778,948	4,816,028	2,095,720	—	—
1968	7,513,091	5,210,155	2,302,936	4,477,649	3,035,442	5,430,652	2,082,439	—	—
1969	8,004,660	5,498,883	2,505,777	4,746,201	3,258,459	5,896,868	2,107,792	—	—
1970	8,580,887	5,816,290	2,764,597	5,043,642	3,537,245	6,428,134	2,152,753	—	—
1971	8,948,644	6,077,232	2,871,412	5,207,004	3,741,640	6,804,309	2,144,335	—	—
1972	9,214,820	6,072,389	3,142,471	5,238,757	3,976,103	7,070,635	2,144,185	—	—
1973	9,602,123	6,189,493	3,412,630	5,371,052	4,231,071	7,419,516	2,182,607	—	—
1974	10,223,729	6,370,273	3,853,456	5,622,429	4,601,300	7,988,500	2,235,229	—	—
1975	11,184,859	6,841,334	4,343,525	6,148,997	5,035,862	8,834,508	2,350,351	—	—
1976	11,012,137	6,717,058	4,295,079	5,810,828	5,201,309	8,653,477	2,358,660	2,314,298	44,362
1977	11,285,787	6,792,925	4,492,862	5,789,016	5,496,771	8,846,993	2,438,794	2,386,652	52,142
1978	11,260,092	6,667,657	4,592,435	5,640,998	5,619,094	8,785,893	2,474,199	2,408,331	65,868
1979	11,569,899	6,794,039	4,775,860	5,682,877	5,887,022	9,036,822	2,533,077	2,461,773	71,304
1980	12,096,895	7,097,958	4,998,937	5,874,374	6,222,521	9,457,394	2,639,501	2,527,787	[3]111,714
1981	12,371,672	7,181,250	5,190,422	5,975,056	6,396,616	9,647,032	2,724,640	2,572,405	[3]152,235
1982	12,425,780	7,220,618	5,205,162	6,031,384	6,394,396	9,696,087	2,729,693	2,552,739	[3]176,954
1983	12,464,661	7,261,050	5,203,611	6,023,725	6,440,936	9,682,734	2,781,927	2,589,187	192,740
1984	12,241,940	7,098,388	5,143,552	5,863,574	6,378,366	9,477,370	2,764,570	2,574,419	190,151
1985	12,247,055	7,075,221	5,171,834	5,818,450	6,428,605	9,479,273	2,767,782	2,571,791	195,991
1986	12,503,511	7,119,550	5,383,961	5,884,515	6,618,996	9,713,893	2,789,618	2,572,479	[4]217,139
1987	12,766,642	7,231,085	5,535,557	5,932,056	6,834,586	9,973,254	2,793,388	2,602,350	[4]191,038
1988	13,055,337	7,436,768	5,618,569	6,001,896	7,053,441	10,161,388	2,893,949	2,673,567	220,382
1989	13,538,560	7,660,950	5,877,610	6,190,015	7,348,545	10,577,963	2,960,597	2,731,174	229,423
1990	13,818,637	7,820,985	5,997,652	6,283,909	7,534,728	10,844,717	2,973,920	2,760,227	213,693
1991	14,358,953	8,115,329	6,243,624	6,501,844	7,857,109	11,309,563	3,049,390	2,819,041	230,349
1992	14,487,359	8,162,118	6,325,241	6,523,989	7,963,370	11,384,567	3,102,792	2,872,523	230,269
1993	14,304,803	8,127,618	6,177,185	6,427,450	7,877,353	11,189,088	3,115,715	2,888,897	226,818
1994	14,278,790	8,137,776	6,141,014	6,371,898	7,906,892	11,133,680	3,145,110	2,910,107	235,003
1995[5]	14,261,781	8,128,802	6,132,979	6,342,539	7,919,242	11,092,374	3,169,407	2,929,044	240,363

[1] Degree-credit enrollment only.
[2] Includes part-time resident students and all extension students.
[3] Large increases are due to the addition of schools accredited by the Accrediting Commission of Career Schools and Colleges of Technology.
[4] Because of imputation techniques, data are not consistent with figures for other years.
[5] Preliminary data.

—Data not available.

SOURCE: U.S. Department of Education, National Center for Education Statistics, Higher Education General Information Survey (HEGIS), "Fall Enrollment in Colleges and Universities" surveys; and Integrated Postsecondary Education Data System (IPEDS), "Fall Enrollment" surveys. (This table was prepared January 1997.)

Table 173.—Total fall enrollment in institutions of higher education, by control and type of institution: 1965 to 1995

Year	All institutions						Public institutions						Private institutions				
	Total	4-year			2-year	Total	Total	4-year			2-year	Total	Total	4-year			2-year
		Total	University	Other 4-year				Total	University	Other 4-year				Total	University	Other 4-year	
1	2	3	4	5	6	7	8	9	10	11	12	13	14	15	16
1965[1]	5,920,864	4,747,912	—	—	1,172,952	3,969,596	2,928,332	—	—	1,041,264	1,951,268	1,819,580	—	—	131,688
1966[1]	6,389,872	5,063,902	—	—	1,325,970	4,348,917	3,159,748	—	—	1,189,169	2,040,955	1,904,154	—	—	136,801
1967[1]	6,911,748	5,398,986	—	—	1,512,762	4,816,028	3,443,975	—	—	1,372,053	2,095,720	1,955,011	—	—	140,709
1968[1]	7,513,091	5,720,795	—	—	1,792,296	5,430,652	3,784,178	—	—	1,646,474	2,082,439	1,936,617	—	—	145,822
1969	8,004,660	5,937,127	—	—	2,067,533	5,896,868	3,962,522	—	—	1,934,346	2,107,792	1,974,605	—	—	133,187
1970	8,580,887	6,261,502	—	—	2,319,385	6,428,134	4,232,722	—	—	2,195,412	2,152,753	2,028,780	—	—	123,973
1971	8,948,644	6,369,355	—	—	2,579,289	6,804,309	4,346,990	—	—	2,457,319	2,144,335	2,022,365	—	—	121,970
1972	9,214,820	6,458,634	—	—	2,756,186	7,070,635	4,429,696	—	—	2,640,939	2,144,185	2,028,938	—	—	115,247
1973	9,602,123	6,590,023	—	—	3,012,100	7,419,516	4,529,895	—	—	2,889,621	2,182,607	2,060,128	—	—	122,479
1974	10,223,729	6,819,735	—	—	3,403,994	7,988,500	4,703,018	—	—	3,285,482	2,235,229	2,116,717	—	—	118,512
1975	11,184,859	7,214,740	2,838,266	4,376,474	3,970,119	8,834,508	4,998,142	2,124,221	2,873,921	3,836,366	2,350,351	2,216,598	714,045	1,502,553	133,753
1976	11,012,137	7,128,816	2,780,289	4,348,527	3,883,321	8,653,477	4,901,691	2,079,929	2,821,762	3,751,786	2,358,660	2,227,125	700,360	1,526,765	131,535
1977	11,285,787	7,242,845	2,793,418	4,449,427	4,042,942	8,846,993	4,945,224	2,070,032	2,875,192	3,901,769	2,438,794	2,297,621	723,386	1,574,235	141,173
1978	11,260,092	7,231,625	2,780,729	4,451,222	4,028,467	8,785,893	4,912,203	2,062,295	2,849,908	3,873,690	2,474,199	2,319,422	718,434	1,601,314	154,777
1979	11,569,899	7,353,233	2,839,582	4,513,651	4,216,666	9,036,822	4,980,012	2,099,525	2,880,487	4,056,810	2,533,077	2,373,221	740,057	1,633,164	159,856
1980	12,096,895	7,570,608	2,902,014	4,668,594	4,526,287	9,457,394	5,128,612	2,154,283	2,974,329	4,328,782	2,639,501	2,441,996	747,731	1,694,265	[2]197,505
1981	12,371,672	7,655,461	2,901,344	4,754,117	4,716,211	9,647,032	5,166,324	2,152,474	3,013,850	4,480,708	2,724,640	2,489,137	748,870	1,740,267	[2]235,503
1982	12,425,780	7,654,074	2,883,735	4,770,339	4,771,706	9,696,087	5,176,434	2,152,547	3,023,887	4,519,653	2,729,693	2,477,640	731,188	1,746,452	252,053
1983	12,464,661	7,741,195	2,888,813	4,852,382	4,723,466	9,682,734	5,223,404	2,154,790	3,068,614	4,459,330	2,781,927	2,517,791	734,023	1,783,768	264,136
1984	12,241,940	7,711,167	2,870,329	4,840,838	4,530,773	9,477,370	5,198,273	2,138,621	3,059,652	4,279,097	2,764,570	2,512,894	731,708	1,781,186	251,676
1985	12,247,055	7,715,978	2,870,692	4,845,286	4,531,077	9,479,273	5,209,540	2,141,112	3,068,428	4,269,733	2,767,782	2,506,438	729,580	1,776,858	261,344
1986	12,503,511	7,823,963	2,897,207	4,926,756	4,679,548	9,713,893	5,300,202	2,160,646	3,139,556	4,413,691	2,789,618	2,523,761	736,561	1,787,200	[3]265,857
1987	12,766,642	7,990,420	2,929,327	5,061,093	4,776,222	9,973,254	5,432,200	2,188,008	3,244,192	4,541,054	2,793,388	2,558,220	741,319	1,816,901	[3]235,168
1988	13,055,337	8,180,182	2,978,593	5,201,589	4,875,155	10,161,388	5,545,901	2,229,868	3,316,033	4,615,487	2,893,949	2,634,281	748,725	1,885,556	259,668
1989	13,538,560	8,387,671	3,019,115	5,368,556	5,150,889	10,577,963	5,694,303	2,266,056	3,428,247	4,883,660	2,960,597	2,693,368	753,059	1,940,309	267,229
1990	13,818,637	8,578,554	3,044,670	5,533,884	5,240,083	10,844,717	5,848,242	2,290,464	3,557,778	4,996,475	2,973,920	2,730,312	754,206	1,976,106	243,608
1991	14,358,953	8,707,053	3,065,429	5,641,624	5,651,900	11,309,563	5,904,748	2,301,222	3,603,526	5,404,815	3,049,390	2,802,305	764,207	2,038,098	247,085
1992	14,487,359	8,764,969	3,050,345	5,714,624	5,722,390	11,384,567	5,900,012	2,283,834	3,616,178	5,484,555	3,102,792	2,864,957	766,511	2,098,446	237,835
1993	14,304,803	8,738,936	3,022,728	5,716,208	5,565,867	11,189,088	5,851,760	2,259,692	3,592,068	5,337,328	3,115,715	2,887,176	763,036	2,124,140	228,539
1994	14,278,790	8,749,080	3,009,072	5,740,008	5,529,710	11,133,680	5,825,213	2,244,636	3,580,577	5,308,467	3,145,110	2,923,867	764,436	2,159,431	221,243
1995[4]	14,261,781	8,769,252	2,999,641	5,769,611	5,492,529	11,092,374	5,814,545	2,235,939	3,578,606	5,277,829	3,169,407	2,954,707	763,702	2,191,005	214,700

—Data not available.

[1] Data for 2-year branch campuses of 4-year institutions are included with the 4-year institutions.
[2] Large increases are due to the addition of schools accredited by the Accrediting Commission of Career Schools and Colleges of Technology.
[3] Because of imputation techniques, data are not consistent with figures for other years.
[4] Preliminary data.

SOURCE: U.S. Department of Education, National Center for Education Statistics, Higher Education General Information Survey (HEGIS), "Fall Enrollment in Colleges and Universities" surveys; and Integrated Postsecondary Education Data System (IPEDS), "Fall Enrollment" surveys. (This table was prepared January 1997.)

Table 174.—Total fall enrollment in institutions of higher education, by attendance status, sex, and age: 1970 to 2007

[In thousands]

Sex and age	1970	1975	1980	1985	1987	1990	1991	1993	1994	1995	Projected		
											2000	2002	2007
1	2	3	4	5	6	7	8	9	10	11	12	13	14
Men and women, total	8,581	11,185	12,097	12,247	12,767	13,819	14,359	14,305	14,279	14,262	14,800	15,206	16,111
14 to 17 years old	259	278	247	235	237	167	120	176	163	148	229	244	290
18 and 19 years old	2,600	2,786	2,901	2,600	2,847	2,800	2,714	2,640	2,756	2,894	3,265	3,321	3,597
20 and 21 years old	1,880	2,243	2,423	2,383	2,504	2,619	2,769	2,708	2,538	2,705	2,840	2,983	3,174
22 to 24 years old	1,457	1,754	1,989	1,933	1,989	2,166	2,287	2,523	2,483	2,411	2,170	2,351	2,604
25 to 29 years old	1,074	1,774	1,871	1,953	1,930	2,063	2,134	2,008	1,935	2,120	1,874	1,856	2,143
30 to 34 years old	487	967	1,243	1,261	1,266	1,360	1,467	1,472	1,409	1,236	1,386	1,412	1,348
35 years old and over	823	1,383	1,422	1,885	1,993	2,644	2,867	2,779	2,995	2,747	3,036	3,039	2,954
Men	5,044	6,149	5,874	5,818	5,932	6,284	6,502	6,427	6,372	6,343	6,459	6,605	6,939
14 to 17 years old	130	126	99	121	114	82	46	83	66	61	99	103	115
18 and 19 years old	1,349	1,397	1,375	1,230	1,363	1,351	1,217	1,224	1,251	1,338	1,484	1,505	1,620
20 and 21 years old	1,095	1,245	1,259	1,216	1,258	1,304	1,306	1,294	1,185	1,282	1,319	1,380	1,454
22 to 24 years old	964	1,047	1,064	1,048	1,003	1,107	1,214	1,260	1,280	1,153	1,069	1,148	1,245
25 to 29 years old	783	1,122	993	991	964	976	1,082	950	890	962	900	884	1,003
30 to 34 years old	308	557	576	574	541	564	664	661	608	561	579	586	550
35 years old and over	415	654	507	639	690	901	972	955	1,092	986	1,008	999	953
Women	3,537	5,036	6,223	6,429	6,835	7,535	7,857	7,877	7,907	7,919	8,341	8,601	9,172
14 to 17 years old	129	152	148	113	123	85	75	93	96	87	129	141	175
18 and 19 years old	1,250	1,389	1,526	1,370	1,484	1,450	1,497	1,416	1,504	1,557	1,781	1,816	1,977
20 and 21 years old	786	998	1,165	1,166	1,246	1,315	1,463	1,414	1,353	1,424	1,521	1,603	1,721
22 to 24 years old	493	706	925	885	986	1,059	1,072	1,263	1,204	1,258	1,101	1,202	1,359
25 to 29 years old	291	652	878	962	966	1,087	1,053	1,058	1,045	1,159	974	972	1,141
30 to 34 years old	179	410	667	687	725	796	803	811	801	675	807	826	799
35 years old and over	409	729	914	1,246	1,303	1,743	1,895	1,824	1,903	1,760	2,028	2,040	2,001
Full-time	5,816	6,841	7,098	7,075	7,231	7,821	8,115	8,128	8,138	8,129	8,469	8,811	9,555
14 to 17 years old	242	242	216	203	142	141	114	159	140	123	198	212	254
18 and 19 years old	2,406	2,510	2,580	2,322	2,488	2,479	2,407	2,330	2,418	2,387	2,797	2,845	3,077
20 and 21 years old	1,647	1,854	2,060	1,975	2,024	2,121	2,299	2,219	2,086	2,109	2,287	2,404	2,557
22 to 24 years old	881	1,008	1,174	1,227	1,223	1,387	1,497	1,639	1,597	1,517	1,382	1,505	1,680
25 to 29 years old	407	692	610	695	693	802	868	755	782	908	765	769	907
30 to 34 years old	100	279	264	310	293	403	401	413	426	430	410	427	421
35 years old and over	134	256	193	345	367	487	528	613	689	653	630	648	659
Men	3,505	3,926	3,689	3,608	3,611	3,808	3,929	3,891	3,855	3,807	3,829	3,940	4,181
14 to 17 years old	124	109	84	102	69	70	39	72	53	54	82	85	95
18 and 19 years old	1,265	1,269	1,229	1,108	1,190	1,198	1,096	1,086	1,098	1,091	1,273	1,290	1,385
20 and 21 years old	990	1,053	1,104	1,027	1,029	1,055	1,077	1,084	964	999	1,052	1,100	1,155
22 to 24 years old	650	686	687	730	669	757	836	868	867	789	696	747	806
25 to 29 years old	327	474	379	395	371	413	494	386	406	454	379	372	418
30 to 34 years old	72	184	129	149	146	162	190	177	178	183	165	167	155
35 years old and over	75	152	77	97	138	154	197	216	290	238	183	179	168
Women	2,311	2,915	3,409	3,468	3,620	4,013	4,186	4,237	4,283	4,321	4,640	4,871	5,373
14 to 17 years old	117	133	132	101	73	71	75	87	88	69	115	127	159
18 and 19 years old	1,140	1,241	1,352	1,214	1,298	1,281	1,311	1,244	1,319	1,296	1,524	1,555	1,693
20 and 21 years old	657	800	955	948	995	1,067	1,223	1,135	1,123	1,111	1,235	1,304	1,403
22 to 24 years old	231	322	487	497	554	630	661	770	731	729	687	758	874
25 to 29 years old	80	218	232	299	323	389	374	369	375	455	387	398	488
30 to 34 years old	28	95	135	161	147	242	211	236	248	247	245	260	266
35 years old and over	59	105	115	248	229	333	331	397	399	415	447	469	491
Part-time	2,765	4,344	4,999	5,172	5,536	5,998	6,244	6,177	6,141	6,133	6,331	6,394	6,556
14 to 17 years old	17	36	31	32	95	26	6	16	22	25	31	32	36
18 and 19 years old	194	276	320	278	359	321	307	310	338	507	468	476	519
20 and 21 years old	233	390	364	408	480	498	470	488	452	596	553	579	617
22 to 24 years old	576	746	815	705	766	779	790	885	886	894	788	845	925
25 to 29 years old	668	1,082	1,261	1,258	1,237	1,261	1,266	1,253	1,153	1,212	1,109	1,087	1,237
30 to 34 years old	388	687	979	951	972	957	1,066	1,059	983	805	977	985	927
35 years old and over	689	1,127	1,229	1,540	1,626	2,157	2,339	2,167	2,307	2,093	2,406	2,390	2,295
Men	1,540	2,222	2,185	2,211	2,321	2,476	2,572	2,537	2,517	2,535	2,630	2,665	2,758
14 to 17 years old	5	17	15	19	46	12	6	10	13	7	17	18	20
18 and 19 years old	84	128	146	122	173	153	121	138	153	246	211	215	235
20 and 21 years old	105	192	154	189	229	250	230	209	221	283	267	280	299
22 to 24 years old	314	362	377	318	334	350	378	392	413	365	374	402	440
25 to 29 years old	456	649	615	596	593	563	587	564	483	508	521	513	584
30 to 34 years old	236	373	447	424	395	402	475	484	430	378	415	419	394
35 years old and over	340	502	430	542	552	747	775	739	803	748	825	820	785
Women	1,225	2,120	2,814	2,961	3,214	3,521	3,671	3,640	3,624	3,598	3,701	3,729	3,798
14 to 17 years old	12	19	17	12	50	13	0	6	9	18	14	14	16
18 and 19 years old	110	147	174	156	186	168	186	172	185	261	257	261	284
20 and 21 years old	128	198	209	218	251	248	240	279	231	313	286	299	318
22 to 24 years old	262	384	438	388	432	429	411	493	473	529	414	444	485
25 to 29 years old	212	433	646	662	643	699	679	689	670	704	587	575	653
30 to 34 years old	151	315	531	527	578	555	591	575	553	427	562	566	533
35 years old and over	349	625	799	998	1,074	1,410	1,563	1,427	1,504	1,345	1,581	1,570	1,510

NOTE.—Distributions by age are estimates based on samples of the civilian noninstitutional population. Because of rounding, details may not add to totals.

SOURCE: U.S. Department of Education, National Center for Education Statistics, *Fall Enrollment in Institutions of Higher Education*; Integrated Postsecondary Education Data System (IPEDS), "Fall Enrollment" surveys; *Projections of Education Statistics to 2007*; and U.S. Department of Commerce, Bureau of the Census, *Current Population Reports*, "Social and Economic Characteristics of Students," various years. (This table was prepared November 1997.)

HIGHER EDUCATION: ENROLLMENT 185

Table 175.—Total fall enrollment in institutions of higher education, by level, sex, age, and attendance status of student: 1995

Attendance status and age of student	All levels			Undergraduate			First-professional			Graduate		
	Total	Men	Women	Total	Men	Women	Total	Men	Women	Total	Men	Women
1	2	3	4	5	6	7	8	9	10	11	12	13
All students	14,261,781	6,342,539	7,919,242	12,231,719	5,401,130	6,830,589	297,592	173,897	123,695	1,732,470	767,512	964,958
Under 18	285,383	114,735	170,648	284,759	114,456	170,303	77	40	37	547	239	308
18 and 19	2,796,149	1,256,770	1,539,379	2,794,635	1,256,001	1,538,634	352	179	173	1,162	590	572
20 and 21	2,617,440	1,220,653	1,396,787	2,597,107	1,211,777	1,385,330	7,366	3,249	4,117	12,967	5,627	7,340
22 to 24	2,356,678	1,157,227	1,199,451	1,991,784	991,364	1,000,420	107,149	58,389	48,760	257,745	107,474	150,271
25 to 29	2,113,799	1,008,579	1,105,220	1,484,742	690,986	793,756	110,853	68,846	42,007	518,204	248,747	269,457
30 to 34	1,295,176	561,110	734,066	954,866	380,067	574,799	33,729	21,577	12,152	306,581	159,466	147,115
35 to 39	980,171	376,083	604,088	757,416	272,998	484,418	16,661	10,089	6,572	206,094	92,996	113,098
40 to 49	1,234,660	427,681	806,979	910,307	309,117	601,190	15,529	8,496	7,033	308,824	110,068	198,756
50 to 64	356,036	123,342	232,694	269,524	94,144	175,380	3,408	1,696	1,712	83,104	27,502	55,602
65 and over	80,950	33,454	47,496	75,125	30,799	44,326	336	192	144	5,489	2,463	3,026
Age unknown	145,339	62,905	82,434	111,454	49,421	62,033	2,132	1,144	988	31,753	12,340	19,413
Full-time	8,128,802	3,807,392	4,321,410	7,145,268	3,296,610	3,848,658	266,414	155,056	111,358	717,120	355,726	361,394
Under 18	115,479	45,123	70,356	115,193	44,988	70,205	61	30	31	225	105	120
18 and 19	2,395,257	1,072,206	1,323,051	2,394,042	1,071,549	1,322,493	345	176	169	870	481	389
20 and 21	2,088,263	977,094	1,111,169	2,070,547	969,175	1,101,372	7,260	3,199	4,061	10,456	4,720	5,736
22 to 24	1,501,692	771,189	730,503	1,224,186	637,463	586,723	104,110	56,754	47,356	173,396	76,972	96,424
25 to 29	951,825	493,254	458,571	597,685	295,896	301,789	101,168	62,741	38,427	252,972	134,617	118,355
30 to 34	423,324	191,737	231,587	280,133	108,369	171,764	27,121	17,307	9,814	116,070	66,061	50,009
35 to 39	265,514	104,568	160,946	191,114	66,111	125,003	12,180	7,296	4,884	62,220	31,161	31,059
40 to 49	279,755	106,129	173,626	194,854	70,101	124,753	10,284	5,580	4,704	74,617	30,448	44,169
50 to 64	57,402	22,360	35,042	38,184	14,816	23,368	2,068	1,025	1,043	17,150	6,519	10,631
65 and over	6,615	3,282	3,333	5,481	2,679	2,802	236	139	97	898	464	434
Age unknown	43,676	20,450	23,226	33,849	15,463	18,386	1,581	809	772	8,246	4,178	4,068
Part-time	6,132,979	2,535,147	3,597,832	5,086,451	2,104,520	2,981,931	31,178	18,841	12,337	1,015,350	411,786	603,564
Under 18	169,904	69,612	100,292	169,566	69,468	100,098	16	10	6	322	134	188
18 and 19	400,892	184,564	216,328	400,593	184,452	216,141	7	3	4	292	109	183
20 and 21	529,177	243,559	285,618	526,560	242,602	283,958	106	50	56	2,511	907	1,604
22 to 24	854,986	386,038	468,948	767,598	353,901	413,697	3,039	1,635	1,404	84,349	30,502	53,847
25 to 29	1,161,974	515,325	646,649	887,057	395,090	491,967	9,685	6,105	3,580	265,232	114,130	151,102
30 to 34	871,852	369,373	502,479	674,733	271,698	403,035	6,608	4,270	2,338	190,511	93,405	97,106
35 to 39	714,657	271,515	443,142	566,302	206,887	359,415	4,481	2,793	1,688	143,874	61,835	82,039
40 to 49	954,905	321,552	633,353	715,453	239,016	476,437	5,245	2,916	2,329	234,207	79,620	154,587
50 to 64	298,634	100,982	197,652	231,340	79,328	152,012	1,340	671	669	65,954	20,983	44,971
65 and over	74,335	30,172	44,163	69,644	28,120	41,524	100	53	47	4,591	1,999	2,592
Age unknown	101,663	42,455	59,208	77,605	33,958	43,647	551	335	216	23,507	8,162	15,345
	Percentage distribution											
All students	100.0	100.0	100.0	100.0	100.0	100.0	100.0	100.0	100.0	100.0	100.0	100.0
Under 18	2.0	1.8	2.2	2.3	2.1	2.5	(1)	(1)	(1)	(1)	(1)	(1)
18 and 19	19.6	19.8	19.4	22.8	23.3	22.5	0.1	0.1	0.1	0.1	0.1	0.1
20 and 21	18.4	19.2	17.6	21.2	22.4	20.3	2.5	1.9	3.3	0.7	0.7	0.8
22 to 24	16.5	18.2	15.1	16.3	18.4	14.6	36.0	33.6	39.4	14.9	14.0	15.6
25 to 29	14.8	15.9	14.0	12.1	12.8	11.6	37.2	39.6	34.0	29.9	32.4	27.9
30 to 34	9.1	8.8	9.3	7.8	7.0	8.4	11.3	12.4	9.8	17.7	20.8	15.2
35 to 39	6.9	5.9	7.6	6.2	5.1	7.1	5.6	5.8	5.3	11.9	12.1	11.7
40 to 49	8.7	6.7	10.2	7.4	5.7	8.8	5.2	4.9	5.7	17.8	14.3	20.6
50 to 64	2.5	1.9	2.9	2.2	1.7	2.6	1.1	1.0	1.4	4.8	3.6	5.8
65 and over	0.6	0.5	0.6	0.6	0.6	0.6	0.1	0.1	0.1	0.3	0.3	0.3
Age unknown	1.0	1.0	1.0	0.9	0.9	0.9	0.7	0.7	0.8	1.8	1.6	2.0
Full-time	100.0	100.0	100.0	100.0	100.0	100.0	100.0	100.0	100.0	100.0	100.0	100.0
Under 18	1.4	1.2	1.6	1.6	1.4	1.8	(1)	(1)	(1)	(1)	(1)	(1)
18 and 19	29.5	28.2	30.6	33.5	32.5	34.4	0.1	0.1	0.2	0.1	0.1	0.1
20 and 21	25.7	25.7	25.7	29.0	29.4	28.6	2.7	2.1	3.6	1.5	1.3	1.6
22 to 24	18.5	20.3	16.9	17.1	19.3	15.2	39.1	36.6	42.5	24.2	21.6	26.7
25 to 29	11.7	13.0	10.6	8.4	9.0	7.8	38.0	40.5	34.5	35.3	37.8	32.7
30 to 34	5.2	5.0	5.4	3.9	3.3	4.5	10.2	11.2	8.8	16.2	18.6	13.8
35 to 39	3.3	2.7	3.7	2.7	2.0	3.2	4.6	4.7	4.4	8.7	8.8	8.6
40 to 49	3.4	2.8	4.0	2.7	2.1	3.2	3.9	3.6	4.2	10.4	8.6	12.2
50 to 64	0.7	0.6	0.8	0.5	0.4	0.6	0.8	0.7	0.9	2.4	1.8	2.9
65 and over	0.1	0.1	0.1	0.1	0.1	0.1	0.1	0.1	0.1	0.1	0.1	0.1
Age unknown	0.5	0.5	0.5	0.5	0.5	0.5	0.6	0.5	0.7	1.1	1.2	1.1
Part-time	100.0	100.0	100.0	100.0	100.0	100.0	100.0	100.0	100.0	100.0	100.0	100.0
Under 18	2.8	2.7	2.8	3.3	3.3	3.4	0.1	0.1	(1)	(1)	(1)	(1)
18 and 19	6.5	7.3	6.0	7.9	8.8	7.2	(1)	(1)	(1)	(1)	(1)	(1)
20 and 21	8.6	9.6	7.9	10.4	11.5	9.5	0.3	0.3	0.5	0.2	0.2	0.3
22 to 24	13.9	15.2	13.0	15.1	16.8	13.9	9.7	8.7	11.4	8.3	7.4	8.9
25 to 29	18.9	20.3	18.0	17.4	18.8	16.5	31.1	32.4	29.0	26.1	27.7	25.0
30 to 34	14.2	14.6	14.0	13.3	12.9	13.5	21.2	22.7	19.0	18.8	22.7	16.1
35 to 39	11.7	10.7	12.3	11.1	9.8	12.1	14.4	14.8	13.7	14.2	15.0	13.6
40 to 49	15.6	12.7	17.6	14.1	11.4	16.0	16.8	15.5	18.9	23.1	19.3	25.6
50 to 64	4.9	4.0	5.5	4.5	3.8	5.1	4.3	3.6	5.4	6.5	5.1	7.5
65 and over	1.2	1.2	1.2	1.4	1.3	1.4	0.3	0.3	0.4	0.5	0.5	0.4
Age unknown	1.7	1.7	1.6	1.5	1.6	1.5	1.8	1.8	1.8	2.3	2.0	2.5

[1] Less than 0.05 percent.

NOTE.—Because of rounding, details may not add to 100.0 percent.

SOURCE: U.S. Department of Education, National Center for Education Statistics, Integrated Postsecondary Education Data System, "Fall Enrollment, 1995" survey. (This table was prepared January 1997.)

Table 176.—Total fall enrollment in institutions of higher education, by type and control of institution, and age and attendance status of student: 1995

Attendance status and age of student	All institutions			Public institutions			Private institutions		
	Total	4-year	2-year	Total	4-year	2-year	Total	4-year	2-year
1	2	3	4	5	6	7	8	9	10
All students	14,261,781	8,769,252	5,492,529	11,092,374	5,814,545	5,277,829	3,169,407	2,954,707	214,700
Under 18	285,383	120,128	165,255	232,944	71,696	161,248	52,439	48,432	4,007
18 and 19	2,796,149	1,771,315	1,024,834	2,149,691	1,171,170	978,521	646,458	600,145	46,313
20 and 21	2,617,440	1,803,281	814,159	2,006,878	1,225,544	781,334	610,562	577,737	32,825
22 to 24	2,356,678	1,619,883	736,795	1,888,417	1,183,191	705,226	468,261	436,692	31,569
25 to 29	2,113,799	1,323,542	790,257	1,629,437	872,668	756,769	484,362	450,874	33,488
30 to 34	1,295,176	710,029	585,147	1,009,461	446,471	562,990	285,715	263,558	22,157
35 to 39	980,171	500,210	479,961	769,045	306,134	462,911	211,126	194,076	17,050
40 to 49	1,234,660	650,510	584,150	967,950	401,321	566,629	266,710	249,189	17,521
50 to 64	356,036	159,542	196,494	286,672	94,425	192,247	69,364	65,117	4,247
65 and over	80,950	19,877	61,073	74,103	13,424	60,679	6,847	6,453	394
Age unknown	145,339	90,935	54,404	77,776	28,501	49,275	67,563	62,434	5,129
Full-time	8,128,802	6,151,755	1,977,047	5,925,301	4,084,711	1,840,590	2,203,501	2,067,044	136,457
Under 18	115,479	74,749	40,730	80,738	42,529	38,209	34,741	32,220	2,521
18 and 19	2,395,257	1,697,545	697,712	1,766,874	1,111,423	655,451	628,383	586,122	42,261
20 and 21	2,088,263	1,665,857	422,406	1,512,500	1,115,658	396,842	575,763	550,199	25,564
22 to 24	1,501,692	1,243,540	258,152	1,136,955	899,614	237,341	364,737	343,926	20,811
25 to 29	951,825	741,706	210,119	675,068	483,407	191,661	276,757	258,299	18,458
30 to 34	423,324	296,556	126,768	303,791	187,311	116,480	119,533	109,245	10,288
35 to 39	265,514	174,137	91,377	189,805	105,424	84,381	75,709	68,713	6,996
40 to 49	279,755	185,797	93,958	196,730	109,114	87,616	83,025	76,683	6,342
50 to 64	57,402	36,010	21,392	38,404	18,391	20,013	18,998	17,619	1,379
65 and over	6,615	3,115	3,500	4,637	1,238	3,399	1,978	1,877	101
Age unknown	43,676	32,743	10,933	19,799	10,602	9,197	23,877	22,141	1,736
Part-time	6,132,979	2,617,497	3,515,482	5,167,073	1,729,834	3,437,239	965,906	887,663	78,243
Under 18	169,904	45,379	124,525	152,206	29,167	123,039	17,698	16,212	1,486
18 and 19	400,892	73,770	327,122	382,817	59,747	323,070	18,075	14,023	4,052
20 and 21	529,177	137,424	391,753	494,378	109,886	384,492	34,799	27,538	7,261
22 to 24	854,986	376,343	478,643	751,462	283,577	467,885	103,524	92,766	10,758
25 to 29	1,161,974	581,836	580,138	954,369	389,261	565,108	207,605	192,575	15,030
30 to 34	871,852	413,473	458,379	705,670	259,160	446,510	166,182	154,313	11,869
35 to 39	714,657	326,073	388,584	579,240	200,710	378,530	135,417	125,363	10,054
40 to 49	954,905	464,713	490,192	771,220	292,207	479,013	183,685	172,506	11,179
50 to 64	298,634	123,532	175,102	248,268	76,034	172,234	50,366	47,498	2,868
65 and over	74,335	16,762	57,573	69,466	12,186	57,280	4,869	4,576	293
Age unknown	101,663	58,192	43,471	57,977	17,899	40,078	43,686	40,293	3,393
	Percentage distribution								
All students	100.0	100.0	100.0	100.0	100.0	100.0	100.0	100.0	100.0
Under 18	2.0	1.4	3.0	2.1	1.2	3.1	1.7	1.6	1.9
18 and 19	19.6	20.2	18.7	19.4	20.1	18.5	20.4	20.3	21.6
20 and 21	18.4	20.6	14.8	18.1	21.1	14.8	19.3	19.6	15.3
22 to 24	16.5	18.5	13.4	17.0	20.3	13.4	14.8	14.8	14.7
25 to 29	14.8	15.1	14.4	14.7	15.0	14.3	15.3	15.3	15.6
30 to 34	9.1	8.1	10.7	9.1	7.7	10.7	9.0	8.9	10.3
35 to 39	6.9	5.7	8.7	6.9	5.3	8.8	6.7	6.6	7.9
40 to 49	8.7	7.4	10.6	8.7	6.9	10.7	8.4	8.4	8.2
50 to 64	2.5	1.8	3.6	2.6	1.6	3.6	2.2	2.2	2.0
65 and over	0.6	0.2	1.1	0.7	0.2	1.1	0.2	0.2	0.2
Age unknown	1.0	1.0	1.0	0.7	0.5	0.9	2.1	2.1	2.4
Full-time	100.0	100.0	100.0	100.0	100.0	100.0	100.0	100.0	100.0
Under 18	1.4	1.2	2.1	1.4	1.0	2.1	1.6	1.6	1.8
18 and 19	29.5	27.6	35.3	29.8	27.2	35.6	28.5	28.4	31.0
20 and 21	25.7	27.1	21.4	25.5	27.3	21.6	26.1	26.6	18.7
22 to 24	18.5	20.2	13.1	19.2	22.0	12.9	16.6	16.6	15.3
25 to 29	11.7	12.1	10.6	11.4	11.8	10.4	12.6	12.5	13.5
30 to 34	5.2	4.8	6.4	5.1	4.6	6.3	5.4	5.3	7.5
35 to 39	3.3	2.8	4.6	3.2	2.6	4.6	3.4	3.3	5.1
40 to 49	3.4	3.0	4.8	3.3	2.7	4.8	3.8	3.7	4.6
50 to 64	0.7	0.6	1.1	0.6	0.5	1.1	0.9	0.9	1.0
65 and over	0.1	0.1	0.2	0.1	0.0	0.2	0.1	0.1	0.2
Age unknown	0.5	0.5	0.6	0.3	0.3	0.5	1.1	1.1	1.3
Part-time	100.0	100.0	100.0	100.0	100.0	100.0	100.0	100.0	100.0
Under 18	2.8	1.7	3.5	2.9	1.7	3.6	1.8	1.8	1.9
18 and 19	6.5	2.8	9.3	7.4	3.5	9.4	1.9	1.6	5.2
20 and 21	8.6	5.3	11.1	9.6	6.4	11.2	3.6	3.1	9.3
22 to 24	13.9	14.4	13.6	14.5	16.4	13.6	10.7	10.5	13.7
25 to 29	18.9	22.2	16.5	18.5	22.5	16.4	21.5	21.7	19.2
30 to 34	14.2	15.8	13.0	13.7	15.0	13.0	17.2	17.4	15.2
35 to 39	11.7	12.5	11.1	11.2	11.6	11.0	14.0	14.1	12.8
40 to 49	15.6	17.8	13.9	14.9	16.9	13.9	19.0	19.4	14.3
50 to 64	4.9	4.7	5.0	4.8	4.4	5.0	5.2	5.4	3.7
65 and over	1.2	0.6	1.6	1.3	0.7	1.7	0.5	0.5	0.4
Age unknown	1.7	2.2	1.2	1.1	1.0	1.2	4.5	4.5	4.3

NOTE.—Because of rounding, details may not add to 100.0 percent.

SOURCE: U.S. Department of Education, National Center for Education Statistics, Integrated Postsecondary Education Data System, "Fall Enrollment, 1995" survey. (This table was prepared January 1997.)

Table 177.—Total fall enrollment in institutions of higher education, by level of enrollment, sex, attendance status, and type and control of institution: 1994 and 1995

Attendance status, and type and control of institution	Total			Undergraduate			First-professional			Graduate		
	Total	Men	Women	Total	Men	Women	Total	Men	Women	Total	Men	Women
1	2	3	4	5	6	7	8	9	10	11	12	13
1994												
Total	14,278,790	6,371,898	7,906,892	12,262,608	5,422,113	6,840,495	294,713	173,956	120,757	1,721,469	775,829	945,640
Full-time	8,137,776	3,855,183	4,282,593	7,168,706	3,341,591	3,827,115	263,311	155,018	108,293	705,759	358,574	347,185
Part-time	6,141,014	2,516,715	3,624,299	5,093,902	2,080,522	3,013,380	31,402	18,938	12,464	1,015,710	417,255	598,455
Total 4-year	8,749,080	4,048,695	4,700,385	6,732,999	3,098,952	3,634,047	294,711	173,955	120,756	1,721,370	775,788	945,582
Full-time	6,106,062	2,943,593	3,162,469	5,136,993	2,430,002	2,706,991	263,311	155,018	108,293	705,758	358,573	347,185
Part-time	2,643,018	1,105,102	1,537,916	1,596,006	668,950	927,056	31,400	18,937	12,463	1,015,612	417,215	598,397
Total 2-year	5,529,710	2,323,203	3,206,507	5,529,609	2,323,161	3,206,448	2	1	1	99	41	58
Full-time	2,031,714	911,590	1,120,124	2,031,713	911,589	1,120,124	—	—	—	1	1	—
Part-time	3,497,996	1,411,613	2,086,383	3,497,896	1,411,572	2,086,324	2	1	1	98	40	58
Public, total	11,133,680	4,930,068	6,203,612	9,945,128	4,394,309	5,550,819	113,997	63,844	50,153	1,074,555	471,915	602,640
Full-time	5,950,820	2,813,226	3,137,594	5,406,741	2,531,506	2,875,235	109,245	61,225	48,020	434,834	220,495	214,339
Part-time	5,182,860	2,116,842	3,066,018	4,538,387	1,862,803	2,675,584	4,752	2,619	2,133	639,721	251,420	388,301
Public 4-year	5,825,213	2,703,415	3,121,798	4,636,762	2,167,698	2,469,064	113,995	63,843	50,152	1,074,456	471,874	602,582
Full-time	4,065,067	1,965,524	2,099,543	3,520,989	1,683,805	1,837,184	109,245	61,225	48,020	434,833	220,494	214,339
Part-time	1,760,146	737,891	1,022,255	1,115,773	483,893	631,880	4,750	2,618	2,132	639,623	251,380	388,243
Public 2-year	5,308,467	2,226,653	3,081,814	5,308,366	2,226,611	3,081,755	2	1	1	99	41	58
Full-time	1,885,753	847,702	1,038,051	1,885,752	847,701	1,038,051	—	—	—	1	1	—
Part-time	3,422,714	1,378,951	2,043,763	3,422,614	1,378,910	2,043,704	2	1	1	98	40	58
Private, total	3,145,110	1,441,830	1,703,280	2,317,480	1,027,804	1,289,676	180,716	110,112	70,604	646,914	303,914	343,000
Full-time	2,186,956	1,041,957	1,144,999	1,761,965	810,085	951,880	154,066	93,793	60,273	270,925	138,079	132,846
Part-time	958,154	399,873	558,281	555,515	217,719	337,796	26,650	16,319	10,331	375,989	165,835	210,154
Private 4-year	2,923,867	1,345,280	1,578,587	2,096,237	931,254	1,164,983	180,716	110,112	70,604	646,914	303,914	343,000
Full-time	2,040,995	978,069	1,062,926	1,616,004	746,197	869,807	154,066	93,793	60,273	270,925	138,079	132,846
Part-time	882,872	367,211	515,661	480,233	185,057	295,176	26,650	16,319	10,331	375,989	165,835	210,154
Private 2-year	221,243	96,550	124,693	221,243	96,550	124,693	—	—	—	—	—	—
Full-time	145,961	63,888	82,073	145,961	63,888	82,073	—	—	—	—	—	—
Part-time	75,282	32,662	42,620	75,282	32,662	42,620	—	—	—	—	—	—
1995[1]												
Total	14,261,781	6,342,539	7,919,242	12,231,719	5,401,130	6,830,589	297,592	173,897	123,695	1,732,470	767,512	964,958
Full-time	8,128,802	3,807,392	4,321,410	7,145,268	3,296,610	3,848,658	266,414	155,056	111,358	717,120	355,726	361,394
Part-time	6,132,979	2,535,147	3,597,832	5,086,451	2,104,520	2,981,931	31,178	18,841	12,337	1,015,350	411,786	603,564
Total 4-year	8,769,252	4,013,930	4,755,322	6,739,621	3,072,630	3,666,991	297,592	173,897	123,695	1,732,039	767,403	964,636
Full-time	6,151,755	2,929,177	3,222,578	5,168,222	2,418,395	2,749,827	266,414	155,056	111,358	717,119	355,726	361,393
Part-time	2,617,497	1,084,753	1,532,744	1,571,399	654,235	917,164	31,178	18,841	12,337	1,014,920	411,677	603,243
Total 2-year	5,492,529	2,328,609	3,163,920	5,492,098	2,328,500	3,163,598	—	—	—	431	109	322
Full-time	1,977,047	878,215	1,098,832	1,977,046	878,215	1,098,831	—	—	—	1	0	1
Part-time	3,515,482	1,450,394	2,065,088	3,515,052	1,450,285	2,064,767	—	—	—	430	109	321
Public, total	11,092,374	4,907,635	6,184,739	9,903,626	4,380,030	5,523,596	115,072	63,594	51,478	1,073,676	464,011	609,665
Full-time	5,925,301	2,769,745	3,155,556	5,376,259	2,491,091	2,885,168	110,160	60,890	49,270	438,882	217,764	221,118
Part-time	5,167,073	2,137,890	3,029,183	4,527,367	1,888,939	2,638,428	4,912	2,704	2,208	634,794	246,247	388,547
Public 4-year	5,814,545	2,671,542	3,143,003	4,626,228	2,144,046	2,482,182	115,072	63,594	51,478	1,073,245	463,902	609,343
Full-time	4,084,711	1,951,140	2,133,571	3,535,670	1,672,486	1,863,184	110,160	60,890	49,270	438,881	217,764	221,117
Part-time	1,729,834	720,402	1,009,432	1,090,558	471,560	618,998	4,912	2,704	2,208	634,364	246,138	388,226
Public 2-year	5,277,829	2,236,093	3,041,736	5,277,398	2,235,984	3,041,414	—	—	—	431	109	322
Full-time	1,840,590	818,605	1,021,985	1,840,589	818,605	1,021,984	—	—	—	1	0	1
Part-time	3,437,239	1,417,488	2,019,751	3,436,809	1,417,379	2,019,430	—	—	—	430	109	321
Private, total	3,169,407	1,434,904	1,734,503	2,328,093	1,021,100	1,306,993	182,520	110,303	72,217	658,794	303,501	355,293
Full-time	2,203,501	1,037,647	1,165,854	1,769,009	805,519	963,490	156,254	94,166	62,088	278,238	137,962	140,276
Part-time	965,906	397,257	568,649	559,084	215,581	343,503	26,266	16,137	10,129	380,556	165,539	215,017
Private 4-year	2,954,707	1,342,388	1,612,319	2,113,393	928,584	1,184,809	182,520	110,303	72,217	658,794	303,501	355,293
Full-time	2,067,044	978,037	1,089,007	1,632,552	745,909	886,643	156,254	94,166	62,088	278,238	137,962	140,276
Part-time	887,663	364,351	523,312	480,841	182,675	298,166	26,266	16,137	10,129	380,556	165,539	215,017
Private 2-year	214,700	92,516	122,184	214,700	92,516	122,184	—	—	—	—	—	—
Full-time	136,457	59,610	76,847	136,457	59,610	76,847	—	—	—	—	—	—
Part-time	78,243	32,906	45,337	78,243	32,906	45,337	—	—	—	—	—	—

[1] Preliminary data.
—Not applicable.

SOURCE: U.S. Department of Education, National Center for Education Statistics, Integrated Postsecondary Education Data System (IPEDS), "Fall Enrollment" surveys. (This table was prepared March 1997.)

Table 178.—Total fall enrollment in institutions of higher education, by type and control of institution, attendance status, and sex of student: 1970 to 1995

Type and control of institution, sex and attendance status of student	1970	1975	1980	1985	1988	1989	1990	1991	1992	1993	1994	1995[1]
1	2	3	4	5	6	7	8	9	10	11	12	13
Total	**8,580,887**	**11,184,859**	**12,096,895**	**12,247,055**	**13,055,337**	**13,538,560**	**13,818,637**	**14,358,953**	**14,487,359**	**14,304,803**	**14,278,790**	**14,261,781**
Full-time	5,816,290	6,841,334	7,097,958	7,075,221	7,436,768	7,660,950	7,820,985	8,115,329	8,162,118	8,127,618	8,137,776	8,128,802
Men	3,504,095	3,926,753	3,689,244	3,607,720	3,661,779	3,740,243	3,807,752	3,929,375	3,926,905	3,890,571	3,855,183	3,807,392
Women	2,312,195	2,914,581	3,408,714	3,467,501	3,774,989	3,920,707	4,013,233	4,185,954	4,235,213	4,237,047	4,282,593	4,321,410
Part-time	2,764,597	4,343,525	4,998,937	5,171,834	5,618,569	5,877,610	5,997,652	6,243,624	6,325,241	6,177,185	6,141,014	6,132,979
Men	1,539,547	2,222,244	2,185,130	2,210,730	2,340,117	2,449,772	2,476,157	2,572,469	2,597,084	2,536,879	2,516,715	2,535,147
Women	1,225,050	2,121,281	2,813,807	2,961,104	3,278,452	3,427,838	3,521,495	3,671,155	3,728,157	3,640,306	3,624,299	3,597,832
4-year, total	6,261,502	7,214,740	7,570,608	7,715,978	8,180,182	8,387,671	8,578,554	8,707,053	8,764,969	8,738,936	8,749,080	8,769,252
Full-time	4,587,379	5,080,256	5,344,163	5,384,614	5,693,176	5,805,249	5,937,023	6,040,799	6,082,112	6,084,299	6,106,062	6,151,755
Men	2,732,796	2,891,192	2,809,528	2,781,412	2,843,186	2,870,555	2,926,360	2,967,978	2,975,089	2,962,355	2,943,593	2,929,177
Women	1,854,583	2,189,064	2,534,635	2,603,202	2,849,990	2,934,694	3,010,663	3,072,821	3,107,023	3,121,944	3,162,469	3,222,578
Part-time	1,674,123	2,134,484	2,226,445	2,331,364	2,487,006	2,582,422	2,641,531	2,666,254	2,682,857	2,654,637	2,643,018	2,617,497
Men	936,189	1,092,461	1,017,813	1,034,804	1,069,021	1,102,660	1,124,780	1,131,956	1,135,624	1,119,636	1,105,102	1,084,753
Women	737,934	1,042,023	1,208,632	1,296,560	1,417,985	1,479,762	1,516,751	1,534,298	1,547,233	1,535,001	1,537,916	1,532,744
Public 4-year	4,232,722	4,998,142	5,128,612	5,209,540	5,545,901	5,694,303	5,848,242	5,904,748	5,900,012	5,851,760	5,825,213	5,814,545
Full-time	3,086,491	3,469,821	3,592,193	3,623,341	3,842,375	3,934,437	4,033,654	4,088,970	4,095,310	4,074,055	4,065,067	4,084,711
Men	1,813,584	1,947,823	1,873,397	1,863,689	1,910,326	1,937,888	1,982,369	2,005,941	2,005,043	1,989,410	1,965,524	1,951,140
Women	1,272,907	1,521,998	1,718,796	1,759,652	1,932,049	1,996,549	2,051,285	2,083,029	2,090,267	2,084,645	2,099,543	2,133,571
Part-time	1,146,231	1,528,321	1,536,419	1,586,199	1,703,526	1,759,866	1,814,588	1,815,778	1,804,702	1,777,705	1,760,146	1,729,834
Men	609,422	760,469	685,051	693,115	721,832	743,137	764,248	764,969	760,186	750,409	737,891	720,402
Women	536,809	767,852	851,368	893,084	981,694	1,016,729	1,050,340	1,050,809	1,044,516	1,027,296	1,022,255	1,009,432
Private 4-year	2,028,780	2,216,598	2,441,996	2,506,438	2,634,281	2,693,368	2,730,312	2,802,305	2,864,957	2,887,176	2,923,867	2,954,707
Full-time	1,500,888	1,610,435	1,751,970	1,761,273	1,850,801	1,870,812	1,903,369	1,951,829	1,986,802	2,010,244	2,040,995	2,067,044
Men	919,212	943,369	936,131	917,723	932,860	932,667	943,991	962,037	970,046	972,945	978,069	978,037
Women	581,676	667,066	815,839	843,550	917,941	938,145	959,378	989,792	1,016,756	1,037,299	1,062,926	1,089,007
Part-time	527,892	606,163	690,026	745,165	783,480	822,556	826,943	850,476	878,155	876,932	882,872	887,663
Men	326,767	331,992	332,762	341,689	347,189	359,523	360,532	366,987	375,438	369,227	367,211	364,351
Women	201,125	274,171	357,264	403,476	436,291	463,033	466,411	483,489	502,717	507,705	515,661	523,312
2-year, total	2,319,385	3,970,119	4,526,287	4,531,077	4,875,155	5,150,889	5,240,083	5,651,900	5,722,390	5,565,867	5,529,710	5,492,529
Full-time	1,228,911	1,761,078	1,753,795	1,690,607	1,743,592	1,855,701	1,883,962	2,074,530	2,080,006	2,043,319	2,031,714	1,977,047
Men	771,299	1,035,561	879,716	826,308	818,593	869,688	881,392	961,397	951,816	928,216	911,590	878,215
Women	457,612	725,517	874,079	864,299	924,999	986,013	1,002,570	1,113,133	1,128,190	1,115,103	1,120,124	1,098,832
Part-time	1,090,474	2,209,041	2,772,492	2,840,470	3,131,563	3,295,188	3,356,121	3,577,370	3,642,384	3,522,548	3,497,996	3,515,482
Men	603,358	1,129,783	1,167,317	1,175,926	1,271,096	1,347,112	1,351,377	1,440,513	1,461,460	1,417,243	1,411,613	1,450,394
Women	487,116	1,079,258	1,605,175	1,664,544	1,860,467	1,948,076	2,004,744	2,136,857	2,180,924	2,105,305	2,086,383	2,065,088
Public 2-year	2,195,412	3,836,366	4,328,782	4,269,733	4,615,487	4,883,660	4,996,475	5,404,815	5,484,555	5,337,328	5,308,467	5,277,829
Full-time	1,129,165	1,662,621	1,595,493	1,496,905	1,567,973	1,674,249	1,716,843	1,885,607	1,915,565	1,888,507	1,885,753	1,840,590
Men	720,440	988,701	811,871	742,673	745,912	793,251	810,664	881,576	878,076	858,600	847,702	818,605
Women	408,725	673,920	783,622	754,232	822,061	880,998	906,179	1,004,031	1,037,489	1,029,907	1,038,051	1,021,985
Part-time	1,066,247	2,173,745	2,733,289	2,772,828	3,047,514	3,209,411	3,279,632	3,519,208	3,568,990	3,448,821	3,422,714	3,437,239
Men	589,439	1,107,680	1,152,268	1,138,011	1,230,888	1,302,074	1,317,730	1,413,870	1,431,091	1,386,092	1,378,951	1,417,488
Women	476,808	1,066,065	1,581,021	1,634,817	1,816,626	1,907,337	1,961,902	2,105,338	2,137,899	2,062,729	2,043,763	2,019,751
Private 2-year	123,973	133,753	[2]197,505	261,344	259,668	267,229	243,608	247,085	237,835	228,539	221,243	214,700
Full-time	99,746	98,457	[2]158,302	193,702	175,619	181,452	167,119	188,923	164,441	154,812	145,961	136,457
Men	50,859	46,860	[2]67,845	83,635	72,681	76,437	70,728	79,821	73,740	69,616	63,888	59,610
Women	48,887	51,597	[2]90,457	110,067	102,938	105,015	96,391	109,102	90,701	85,196	82,073	76,847
Part-time	24,227	35,296	[2]39,203	67,642	84,049	85,777	76,489	58,162	73,394	73,727	75,282	78,243
Men	13,919	22,103	[2]15,049	37,915	40,208	45,038	33,647	26,643	30,369	31,151	32,662	32,906
Women	10,308	13,193	[2]24,154	29,727	43,841	40,739	42,842	31,519	43,025	42,576	42,620	45,337

[1] Preliminary data.
[2] Large increase is due to the addition of schools accredited by the Accrediting Commission of Career Schools and Colleges of Technology.

SOURCE: U.S. Department of Education, National Center for Education Statistics, Higher Education General Information Survey (HEGIS), "Fall Enrollment in Colleges and Universities" surveys; and Integrated Postsecondary Education Data Systems (IPEDS), "Fall Enrollment" surveys. (This table was prepared December 1996.)

HIGHER EDUCATION: ENROLLMENT 189

Table 179.—Fall enrollment and number of institutions of higher education, by affiliation[1] of institution: 1980 to 1995

Affiliation	Enrollment									Number of institutions[2]	
	Total, fall 1980	Total, fall 1990	Total, fall 1994	Fall 1995[3]						Fall 1980	Fall 1995
				Total	Full-time		Part-time				
					Men	Women	Men	Women			
1	2	3	4	5	6	7	8	9		10	11
All institutions	12,096,895	13,818,637	14,278,790	14,261,781	3,807,392	4,321,410	2,535,147	3,597,832		3,226	3,545
Public institutions	9,457,394	10,844,717	11,133,680	11,092,374	2,769,745	3,155,556	2,137,890	3,029,183		1,493	1,603
Federal	50,989	—	53,548	90,046	16,614	3,320	58,795	11,317		12	14
State	5,879,057	—	7,869,965	7,842,782	2,276,015	2,567,455	1,224,037	1,775,275		881	1,123
Local	1,011,412	—	3,064,925	3,023,723	452,797	556,030	821,753	1,193,143		190	429
Public other	2,515,936	—	145,242	135,823	24,319	28,751	33,305	49,448		410	37
Private institutions	2,639,501	2,973,920	3,145,110	3,169,407	1,037,647	1,165,854	397,257	568,649		1,733	1,942
Independent nonprofit	1,521,614	1,471,446	1,506,994	1,511,151	513,081	538,683	196,650	262,737		795	716
Proprietary	111,714	213,693	235,003	240,363	82,426	77,585	39,303	41,049		164	298
Religiously affiliated	1,006,173	1,288,781	1,403,113	1,417,893	442,140	549,586	161,304	264,863		774	928
Advent Christian Church	143	—	—	—	—	—	—	—		1	—
African Methodist Episcopal Zion Church	1,091	88	—	—	—	—	—	—		3	—
African Methodist Episcopal	4,541	3,220	3,799	3,503	1,452	1,779	120	152		6	6
American Baptist	6,131	10,800	12,221	11,394	2,743	3,780	1,660	3,211		11	12
American Evangelical Lutheran Church	—	—	814	779	388	248	54	89		—	1
American Lutheran and Lutheran Church in America	3,092	—	1,335	1,304	308	496	225	275		3	1
American Lutheran	21,608	—	10,163	10,459	3,804	4,652	449	1,554		13	9
Assemblies of God Church	7,814	8,307	9,493	9,652	4,138	4,351	586	577		10	13
Baptist	38,231	99,314	100,991	105,802	36,805	44,195	10,759	14,043		33	64
Brethren Church	3,925	958	1,447	1,456	576	599	170	111		3	3
Brethren in Christ Church	1,301	2,239	2,344	2,416	945	1,417	21	33		1	1
Christian and Missionary Alliance Church	1,705	2,519	3,386	3,723	1,435	1,730	217	341		3	4
Christian Church (Disciples of Christ)	14,913	30,397	32,629	33,029	6,850	10,237	6,479	9,463		12	16
Christian Churches and Churches of Christ	1,342	2,263	3,394	3,494	1,490	1,427	354	223		7	11
Christian Methodist Episcopal	2,486	2,174	2,456	2,598	1,040	1,297	98	163		4	3
Christian Reformed Church	5,408	4,488	4,075	4,205	1,833	2,057	154	161		3	2
Church of Christ (Scientist)	2,773	2,557	4,222	4,320	1,786	1,904	403	227		6	5
Church of God of Prophecy	—	249	—	—	—	—	—	—		—	—
Church of God	6,082	5,627	4,534	4,410	1,657	1,935	348	470		9	7
Church of New Jerusalem	170	—	—	—	—	—	—	—		1	—
Church of the Brethren	8,482	4,463	2,870	2,812	1,010	1,521	113	168		6	3
Church of the Nazarene	11,716	10,779	14,450	14,466	5,204	6,582	1,097	1,583		10	10
Churches of Christ	9,343	14,331	22,495	22,807	7,691	8,331	3,171	3,614		9	15
Cumberland Presbyterian	594	746	715	799	349	236	90	124		2	2
Evangelical Congregational Church	80	88	95	65	7	3	44	11		1	1
Evangelical Convent Church of America	1,401	1,035	1,650	1,745	480	681	219	365		1	1
Evangelical Free Church of America	833	2,355	3,840	3,778	1,461	1,068	865	384		1	4
Evangelical Lutheran Church	743	49,210	38,218	39,089	14,125	18,812	2,261	3,891		3	26
Free Methodist	5,543	5,902	8,375	8,696	2,948	3,970	701	1,077		5	5
Free Will Baptist Church	1,132	1,177	1,312	1,467	471	500	259	237		4	2
Friends United Meeting	1,109	—	—	—	—	—	—	—		1	—
Friends	5,157	5,844	6,586	6,600	2,470	3,260	337	533		5	6
General Conference Mennonite Church	820	1,243	899	1,046	383	545	32	86		2	1
Greek Orthodox	204	148	197	168	125	31	7	5		1	1

Table 179.—Fall enrollment and number of institutions of higher education, by affiliation[1] of institution: 1980 to 1995—Continued

Affiliation	Total, fall 1980	Total, fall 1990	Total, fall 1994	Enrollment Fall 1995[3] Total	Full-time Men	Full-time Women	Part-time Men	Part-time Women	Number of institutions[2] Fall 1980	Number of institutions[2] Fall 1995
1	2	3	4	5	6	7	8	9	10	11
Interdenominational	1,254	11,103	6,342	5,571	2,580	2,241	489	261	4	10
Jewish	5,738	15,628	13,038	11,481	9,770	737	737	237	24	58
Latter-Day Saints	39,172	42,274	40,296	40,086	17,277	19,461	1,637	1,711	4	3
Lutheran Church—Missouri Synod	11,727	13,827	10,614	11,315	3,947	4,809	906	1,653	15	8
Lutheran Church in America	23,877	5,796	4,338	4,321	1,587	2,216	146	372	20	3
Mennonite Brethren Church	1,344	1,864	2,161	2,269	586	772	310	601	3	3
Mennonite Church	4,008	2,859	3,462	3,502	1,297	1,649	213	343	6	5
Missionary Church Inc.	487	699	1,201	1,352	338	495	147	372	1	1
Moravian Church	2,434	2,511	2,741	2,804	634	1,294	308	568	2	2
Multiple Protestant Denominations	5,526	211	167	164	21	35	50	58	8	1
North American Baptist	155	—	170	186	77	44	40	25	1	1
Pentecostal Holiness Church	767	566	968	1,002	364	383	107	148	3	3
Presbyterian U.S. and United Presbyterian	47,144	76,625	69,790	70,357	26,544	32,098	4,659	7,056	57	65
Presbyterian Church in America	—	1,877	3,745	3,809	1,637	1,683	313	176	—	3
Protestant Episcopal	5,396	4,559	4,514	4,603	1,794	2,222	243	344	12	11
Protestant, other	4,072	38,136	59,870	60,386	21,215	24,567	6,449	8,155	11	67
Reformed Church in America	2,713	5,525	5,419	5,582	2,268	2,963	163	188	4	4
Reformed Episcopal Church	67	—	—	—	—	—	—	—	1	—
Reformed Presbyterian Church	2,014	1,556	1,767	1,771	727	729	169	146	4	2
Reorganized Latter-Day Saints Church	4,274	4,793	10,508	11,063	2,250	2,046	2,144	4,623	2	2
Roman Catholic	422,842	530,742	592,119	594,464	151,512	208,376	80,897	153,679	229	249
Russian Orthodox	47	—	24	32	30	0	2	0	1	1
Seventh-Day Adventists	19,168	15,771	17,110	17,519	6,367	7,411	1,320	2,421	11	11
Southern Baptist	85,281	49,493	45,165	46,042	14,113	16,087	7,844	7,998	54	30
Undenominational	—	1,714	17,330	18,729	6,364	7,459	2,743	2,163	—	17
Unitarian Universalist	87	82	106	126	46	67	3	10	2	2
United Brethren Church	545	601	635	721	285	338	65	33	1	1
United Church of Christ	14,169	19,219	24,305	24,013	6,630	9,999	2,438	4,946	16	21
United Methodist	127,099	148,851	146,935	148,091	50,556	62,557	13,802	21,176	91	90
Wesleyan Church	3,583	5,311	7,497	7,734	2,770	4,216	262	486	5	3
Wisconsin Evangelical Lutheran Synod	808	931	1,142	1,165	545	585	17	18	1	2
Other religiously affiliated	462	13,136	10,629	11,551	4,035	4,403	1,388	1,725	1	14

[1] Religious affiliation as reported by institutions of higher education.
[2] Because data are derived from the "Fall Enrollment" survey, counts of institutions may differ from counts on other tables.
[3] Preliminary data.
—Data not applicable or not reported.

SOURCE: U.S. Department of Education, National Center for Education Statistics, Higher Education General Information Survey (HEGIS), "Fall Enrollment in Institutions of Higher Education" and "Institutional Characteristics" surveys; and Integrated Postsecondary Education Data System (IPEDS), "Fall Enrollment" and "Institutional Characteristics" surveys. (This table was prepared January 1997).

Table 180.—Total fall enrollment in institutions of higher education, by type and control of institution, and attendance status and level of student: 1992 to 1995

Level of student and enrollment status	Total, fall 1992	Total, fall 1993	1994					1995[1]				
			Total	Public 4-year	Private 4-year	Public 2-year	Private 2-year	Total	Public 4-year	Private 4-year	Public 2-year	Private 2-year
1	2	3	4	5	6	7	8	9	10	11	12	13
All students	14,487,359	14,304,803	14,278,790	5,825,213	2,923,867	5,308,467	221,243	14,261,781	5,814,545	2,954,707	5,277,829	214,700
Undergraduate, full-time and part-time	12,537,700	12,323,959	12,262,608	4,636,762	2,096,237	5,308,366	221,243	12,231,719	4,626,228	2,113,393	5,277,398	214,700
Degree seeking	10,898,144	10,712,921	10,728,256	4,411,471	1,989,928	4,122,092	204,765	10,621,283	4,412,318	2,006,457	4,035,413	167,095
First-time freshmen	2,184,113	2,160,710	2,133,205	709,042	405,917	952,468	65,778	2,168,831	731,836	419,025	954,595	63,375
Other first-year	2,647,813	2,553,478	2,501,937	500,205	196,349	1,762,250	43,133	2,433,434	499,031	195,269	1,696,556	42,578
Second year	2,772,163	2,735,854	2,807,591	875,944	430,270	1,405,557	95,820	2,767,344	893,859	429,464	1,382,879	61,142
Third year	1,427,952	1,412,478	1,410,544	992,510	417,298	702	34	1,394,845	972,297	421,858	690	—
Fourth year and beyond	1,695,711	1,714,421	1,722,393	1,265,038	456,805	550	—	1,714,665	1,250,630	463,453	582	—
Unclassified by level	170,392	135,980	152,586	68,732	83,289	565	—	142,164	64,665	77,388	111	—
Others in credit courses	1,639,556	1,611,038	1,534,352	225,291	106,309	1,186,274	16,478	1,610,436	213,910	106,936	1,241,985	47,605
Full-time	7,244,442	7,179,482	7,168,706	3,520,989	1,616,004	1,885,752	145,961	7,145,268	3,535,670	1,632,552	1,840,589	136,457
Degree seeking	6,966,414	6,890,412	6,903,775	3,483,650	1,599,517	1,680,016	140,592	6,883,159	3,501,697	1,614,871	1,636,391	130,200
First-time freshmen	1,603,737	1,608,274	1,603,106	658,234	380,411	507,774	56,687	1,646,812	686,103	392,234	511,680	56,795
Other first-year	1,220,062	1,172,662	1,165,709	371,002	131,259	631,079	32,369	1,136,399	373,267	129,941	602,460	30,731
Second year	1,700,615	1,676,199	1,695,721	731,518	371,903	540,797	51,503	1,688,726	752,561	371,486	522,005	42,674
Third year	1,152,753	1,138,661	1,138,336	792,583	345,545	175	33	1,126,949	777,039	349,747	163	—
Fourth year and beyond	1,258,925	1,266,046	1,267,625	916,392	351,161	72	—	1,259,327	902,766	356,481	80	—
Unclassified by level	30,322	28,570	33,278	13,921	19,238	119	—	24,946	9,961	14,982	3	—
Others in credit courses	278,028	289,070	264,931	37,339	16,487	205,736	5,369	262,109	33,973	17,681	204,198	6,257
Part-time	5,293,258	5,144,477	5,093,902	1,115,773	480,233	3,422,614	75,282	5,086,451	1,090,558	480,841	3,436,809	78,243
Degree seeking	3,931,730	3,822,509	3,824,481	927,821	390,411	2,442,076	64,173	3,738,124	910,621	391,586	2,399,022	36,895
First-time freshmen	580,376	552,436	530,099	50,808	25,506	444,694	9,091	522,019	45,733	26,791	442,915	6,580
Other first-year	1,427,751	1,380,816	1,336,228	129,203	65,090	1,131,171	10,764	1,297,035	125,764	65,328	1,094,096	11,847
Second year	1,071,548	1,059,655	1,111,870	144,426	58,367	864,760	44,317	1,078,618	141,298	57,978	860,874	18,468
Third year	275,199	273,817	272,208	199,927	71,753	527	1	267,896	195,258	72,111	527	—
Fourth year and beyond	436,786	448,375	454,768	348,646	105,644	478	—	455,338	347,864	106,972	502	—
Unclassified by level	140,070	107,410	119,308	54,811	64,051	446	—	117,218	54,704	62,406	108	—
Others in credit courses	1,361,528	1,321,968	1,269,421	187,952	89,822	980,538	11,109	1,348,327	179,937	89,255	1,037,787	41,348
Postbaccalaureate	1,949,659	1,980,844	2,016,182	1,188,451	827,630	101	—	2,030,062	1,188,317	841,314	431	—
First-professional	280,922	292,431	294,713	113,995	180,716	2	—	297,592	115,072	182,520	—	—
Full-time	252,138	259,764	263,311	109,245	154,066	—	—	266,414	110,160	156,254	—	—
First-time	74,825	80,654	80,286	30,789	49,497	—	—	78,890	30,252	48,638	—	—
Other	177,313	179,110	183,025	78,456	104,569	—	—	187,524	79,908	107,616	—	—
Part-time	28,784	32,667	31,402	4,750	26,650	2	—	31,178	4,912	26,266	—	—
First-time	7,469	10,826	9,872	1,087	8,783	2	—	10,760	966	9,794	—	—
Other	21,315	21,841	21,530	3,663	17,867	—	—	20,418	3,946	16,472	—	—
Graduate students	1,668,737	1,688,413	1,721,469	1,074,456	646,914	99	—	1,732,470	1,073,245	658,794	431	—
Full-time	665,538	688,372	705,759	434,833	270,925	1	—	717,120	438,881	278,238	1	—
Degree seeking	623,538	646,956	665,966	403,881	262,084	1	—	670,222	401,660	268,561	1	—
First-time	208,802	216,198	224,412	124,145	100,267	—	—	222,196	123,761	98,435	—	—
Other degree seeking	414,736	430,758	441,554	279,736	161,817	1	—	448,026	277,899	170,126	1	—
Others in credit courses	42,000	41,416	39,793	30,952	8,841	—	—	46,898	37,221	9,677	—	—
Part-time	1,003,199	1,000,041	1,015,710	639,623	375,989	98	—	1,015,350	634,364	380,556	430	—
Degree seeking	770,066	770,271	774,962	462,541	312,358	63	—	775,811	457,090	318,598	123	—
First-time	153,148	146,325	147,236	78,637	68,579	20	—	148,220	79,687	68,499	34	—
Other degree seeking	616,918	623,946	627,726	383,904	243,779	43	—	627,591	377,403	250,099	89	—
Others in credit courses	233,133	229,770	240,748	177,082	63,631	35	—	239,539	177,274	61,958	307	—

[1] Preliminary data.
—Data not available or not applicable.

SOURCE: U.S. Department of Education, National Center for Education Statistics, Integrated Postsecondary Education Data System, "Fall Enrollment" surveys. (This table was prepared March 1997.)

Table 181.—Total first-time freshmen enrolled in institutions of higher education, by sex of student, attendance status, and type and control of institution: Fall 1955 to fall 1995

[In thousands]

Year	Total, all freshmen	Men			Women			Type of institution, by control			
		Total	Full-time	Part-time	Total	Full-time	Part-time	4-year Public	4-year Private	2-year Public	2-year Private
1	2	3	4	5	6	7	8	9	10	11	12
1955[1]	670	416	—	—	254	—	—	[2]283	[2]247	[2]117	[2]23
1956[1]	718	443	—	—	275	—	—	[2]293	[2]262	[2]137	[2]25
1957[1]	724	442	—	—	282	—	—	[2]294	[2]263	[2]141	[2]27
1958[1]	775	465	—	—	310	—	—	[2]328	[2]272	[2]146	[2]29
1959[1]	822	488	—	—	334	—	—	[2]348	[2]292	[2]153	[2]28
1960[1]	923	540	—	—	384	—	—	[2]396	[2]313	[2]182	[2]32
1961[1]	1,018	592	—	—	426	—	—	[2]438	[2]336	[2]210	[2]34
1962[1]	1,031	598	—	—	432	—	—	[2]445	[2]325	[2]225	[2]36
1963[1]	1,046	604	—	—	442	—	—	—	—	—	—
1964[1]	1,225	702	—	—	523	—	—	[2]539	[2]363	[2]275	[2]47
1965[1]	1,442	829	—	—	613	—	—	[2]642	[2]399	[2]348	[2]53
1966	1,554	890	—	—	665	—	—	[2]626	[2]383	[2]478	[2]67
1967	1,641	931	761	170	710	574	136	[2]645	[2]368	[2]561	[2]67
1968	1,893	1,082	847	235	810	624	187	[2]725	[2]378	[2]718	[2]72
1969	1,967	1,118	876	242	849	649	200	[2]737	[2]393	[2]776	[2]61
1970	2,063	1,152	896	256	911	691	221	[2]754	[2]397	[2]854	[2]58
1971	2,119	1,171	896	275	949	710	238	[2]738	[2]386	[2]937	[2]58
1972	2,153	1,158	858	299	995	716	279	680	381	1,037	55
1973	2,226	1,182	867	315	1,044	740	304	699	379	1,089	59
1974	2,366	1,244	896	348	1,122	777	345	746	386	1,176	58
1975	2,515	1,328	942	386	1,187	821	366	772	395	1,284	64
1976	2,347	1,170	855	316	1,177	808	369	717	414	1,153	63
1977	2,394	1,156	840	316	1,239	841	398	737	405	1,186	67
1978	2,390	1,142	817	324	1,248	834	414	737	407	1,174	73
1979	2,503	1,180	840	340	1,323	866	457	760	415	1,254	74
1980	2,588	1,219	862	357	1,369	887	481	765	418	1,314	91
1981	2,595	1,218	852	366	1,378	886	492	754	419	1,318	104
1982	2,505	1,199	837	362	1,306	851	455	731	404	1,254	116
1983	2,444	1,159	825	334	1,285	853	431	728	404	1,190	122
1984	2,357	1,112	786	326	1,245	827	418	714	403	1,130	110
1985	2,292	1,076	775	301	1,216	827	389	717	399	1,060	116
1986	2,219	1,047	769	278	1,173	821	352	720	392	991	[3]117
1987	2,246	1,047	779	267	1,200	847	352	758	405	980	[3]104
1988	2,379	1,100	807	293	1,279	892	387	783	426	1,049	121
1989	2,341	1,095	791	303	1,246	865	381	762	414	1,049	116
1990	2,257	1,045	771	274	1,211	846	366	727	400	1,041	[4]88
1991	2,278	1,068	798	270	1,209	855	355	718	393	1,070	[4]97
1992	2,184	1,013	760	253	1,171	843	328	697	408	993	[4]85
1993	2,161	1,008	762	245	1,153	846	307	702	411	974	[4]74
1994	2,133	985	751	233	1,149	852	297	709	406	952	[4]66
1995[5]	2,169	1,001	767	234	1,168	880	288	732	419	955	[4]63

[1] Excludes first-time freshmen in occupational programs not creditable towards a bachelor's degree.
[2] Data for 2-year branches of 4-year college systems are aggregated with the 4-year institutions.
[3] Because of imputation techniques, data are not consistent with figures for other years.
[4] Data not comparable with pre-1990 figures because of a change in reporting procedures.
[5] Preliminary data.

—Data not available.

NOTE.—Alaska and Hawaii are included in all years. Because of rounding, details may not add to totals.

SOURCE: U.S. Department of Education, National Center for Education Statistics, *Fall Enrollment in Higher Education*, various years; "Fall Enrollment in Colleges and Universities" survey; and Integrated Postsecondary Education Data System (IPEDS), "Fall Enrollment" surveys. (This table was prepared January 1997.)

HIGHER EDUCATION: ENROLLMENT

Table 182.—Total first-time freshmen enrolled in institutions of higher education, by attendance status, sex, control of institution, and state: Fall 1992 to fall 1995

State or other area	Fall 1992	Fall 1993	Fall 1994	Fall 1995[1]							Public institutions	Private institutions
				Total	Full-time			Part-time				
					Total	Men	Women	Total	Men	Women		
1	2	3	4	5	6	7	8	9	10	11	12	13
United States	2,184,113	2,160,710	2,133,205	2,168,831	1,646,812	767,185	879,627	522,019	233,867	288,152	1,686,431	482,400
Alabama	42,604	41,812	41,542	37,166	31,562	14,198	17,364	5,604	2,406	3,198	32,879	4,287
Alaska	2,584	2,700	1,835	1,880	1,564	740	824	316	116	200	1,770	110
Arizona	31,358	36,671	32,753	37,049	22,769	11,167	11,602	14,280	5,992	8,288	33,317	3,732
Arkansas	18,680	17,406	16,378	16,924	14,838	6,515	8,323	2,086	848	1,238	14,268	2,656
California	252,762	250,810	258,687	272,715	149,633	70,140	79,493	123,082	58,678	64,404	242,622	30,093
Colorado	33,359	31,353	31,001	32,775	24,070	11,989	12,081	8,705	4,049	4,656	28,597	4,178
Connecticut	22,490	21,489	21,259	21,268	16,611	7,718	8,893	4,657	1,749	2,908	12,846	8,422
Delaware	7,227	7,361	6,921	8,092	5,915	2,502	3,413	2,177	849	1,328	6,354	1,738
District of Columbia	8,427	8,954	9,706	9,077	7,921	3,150	4,771	1,156	423	733	666	8,411
Florida	72,311	71,351	71,318	72,722	53,386	24,941	28,445	19,336	8,282	11,054	57,040	15,682
Georgia	56,389	59,784	58,991	59,829	47,798	20,923	26,875	12,031	4,608	7,423	47,808	12,021
Hawaii	9,461	9,752	10,309	9,524	6,493	2,949	3,544	3,031	1,394	1,637	7,659	1,865
Idaho	10,960	11,069	10,646	10,103	8,663	4,060	4,603	1,440	606	834	7,061	3,042
Illinois	116,967	112,542	111,309	109,483	73,639	35,197	38,442	35,844	16,194	19,650	86,201	23,282
Indiana	50,147	49,111	48,059	51,071	42,687	20,316	22,371	8,384	3,542	4,842	36,654	14,417
Iowa	36,730	35,922	35,229	35,097	29,377	14,200	15,177	5,720	2,220	3,500	26,574	8,523
Kansas	25,453	25,304	24,641	29,083	19,544	9,823	9,721	9,539	3,989	5,550	26,466	2,617
Kentucky	29,738	31,334	28,983	29,024	25,575	11,205	14,370	3,449	1,483	1,966	23,022	6,002
Louisiana	31,810	30,160	30,951	31,412	28,400	12,358	16,042	3,012	1,264	1,748	26,809	4,603
Maine	8,765	8,751	8,149	8,273	7,371	3,540	3,831	902	289	613	5,271	3,002
Maryland	32,133	31,675	31,647	32,993	23,809	10,749	13,060	9,184	3,716	5,468	28,362	4,631
Massachusetts	64,751	68,316	65,768	64,892	55,057	25,029	30,028	9,835	3,646	6,189	30,325	34,567
Michigan	88,744	87,025	83,697	76,360	55,364	25,375	29,989	20,996	9,095	11,901	61,438	14,922
Minnesota	50,869	43,794	43,783	46,794	35,920	17,413	18,507	10,874	4,613	6,261	37,165	9,629
Mississippi	25,960	26,223	25,862	26,602	23,001	10,488	12,513	3,601	1,294	2,307	24,857	1,745
Missouri	39,886	40,868	38,544	39,610	32,820	14,827	17,993	6,790	2,982	3,808	26,585	13,025
Montana	6,413	6,950	6,819	7,473	6,599	3,264	3,335	874	361	513	6,516	957
Nebraska	17,362	15,943	16,616	16,147	13,769	6,677	7,092	2,378	1,016	1,362	12,991	3,156
Nevada	4,620	5,367	6,939	6,799	3,563	1,617	1,946	3,236	1,427	1,809	6,673	126
New Hampshire	11,316	11,659	11,373	11,789	9,889	4,418	5,471	1,900	746	1,154	6,219	5,570
New Jersey	44,932	44,971	43,063	45,308	37,835	17,771	20,064	7,473	3,190	4,283	36,209	9,099
New Mexico	11,818	13,358	13,864	12,104	7,431	3,456	3,975	4,673	2,028	2,645	11,474	630
New York	158,380	157,350	155,922	151,682	135,432	62,009	73,423	16,250	6,980	9,270	92,134	59,548
North Carolina	55,075	52,857	51,346	51,706	45,432	20,218	25,214	6,274	2,879	3,395	38,634	13,072
North Dakota	8,813	8,322	8,122	8,386	7,556	4,042	3,514	830	359	471	7,468	918
Ohio	92,902	90,190	88,585	89,510	72,960	33,783	39,177	16,550	7,210	9,340	66,140	23,370
Oklahoma	30,296	30,252	29,627	28,474	19,948	9,498	10,450	8,526	3,611	4,915	25,458	3,016
Oregon	22,930	23,293	23,321	20,562	15,977	7,615	8,362	4,585	2,297	2,288	17,032	3,530
Pennsylvania	113,070	100,372	98,488	101,053	86,253	40,778	45,475	14,800	5,998	8,802	60,478	40,575
Rhode Island	12,813	13,106	12,645	12,745	11,258	5,465	5,793	1,487	601	886	5,571	7,174
South Carolina	30,185	30,070	28,577	29,036	24,775	10,951	13,824	4,261	1,838	2,423	22,947	6,089
South Dakota	6,513	6,691	6,607	6,378	5,759	2,674	3,085	619	227	392	5,076	1,302.00
Tennessee	35,721	35,341	34,180	36,628	32,542	14,824	17,718	4,086	1,635	2,451	25,592	11,036
Texas	127,584	129,921	127,586	131,905	95,676	45,706	49,970	36,229	16,528	19,701	112,347	19,558
Utah	23,536	24,465	24,383	24,041	19,223	8,882	10,341	4,818	2,532	2,286	18,683	5,358
Vermont	6,274	6,347	6,132	6,506	5,658	2,706	2,952	848	266	582	3,784	2,722
Virginia	45,011	43,820	45,272	46,533	40,174	18,098	22,076	6,359	2,795	3,564	35,162	11,371
Washington	68,649	70,476	68,613	73,255	44,022	20,968	23,054	29,233	13,866	15,367	67,822	5,433
West Virginia	17,029	15,727	15,928	15,880	13,900	6,597	7,303	1,980	720	1,260	13,087	2,793
Wisconsin	47,271	47,351	46,479	49,201	39,420	18,328	21,092	9,781	4,102	5,679	40,597	8,604
Wyoming	4,686	4,858	4,814	4,626	3,914	1,900	2,014	712	253	459	4,435	191
U.S. Service Schools	10,349	10,116	9,936	11,286	4,060	3,428	632	7,226	6,075	1,151	11,286	—
Outlying areas	35,409	41,759	30,573	38,692	35,379	14,296	21,083	3,313	1,411	1,902	17,390	21,302
American Samoa	989	967	948	943	702	360	342	241	134	107	943	—
Federated States of Micronesia	409	235	410	354	314	163	151	40	22	18	354	—
Guam	709	1,490	956	478	303	104	199	175	77	98	478	—
Marshall Islands	139	166	22	—	—	—	—	—	—	—	—	—
Northern Marianas	173	455	440	153	101	40	61	52	24	28	153	—
Palau	24	24	13	14	13	3	10	1	0	1	14	—
Puerto Rico	32,664	38,057	27,408	36,343	33,593	13,540	20,053	2,750	1,139	1,611	15,041	21,302
Virgin Islands	302	365	376	407	353	86	267	54	15	39	407	—

[1] Preliminary data.
—Data not available or not applicable.

SOURCE: U.S. Department of Education, National Center for Education Statistics, Integrated Postsecondary Education Data System, "Fall Enrollment" surveys. (This table was prepared January 1997.)

Table 183.—College enrollment rates of high school graduates, by race/ethnicity: 1960 to 1996

[Numbers in thousands]

Year	High school graduates[1]				Enrolled in college[2]								
	Total	White[3]	Black[3,4]	Hispanic[4]	Total		White[3]		Black[3,4]		Hispanic[4]		
											Number	Percent	
					Number	Percent	Number	Percent	Number	Percent		Annual	3-year moving average
1	2	3	4	5	6	7	8	9	10	11	12	13	14
1960	1,679	1,565	—	—	758	45.1	717	45.8	—	—	—	—	—
1961	1,763	1,612	—	—	847	48.0	798	49.5	—	—	—	—	—
1962	1,838	1,660	—	—	900	49.0	840	50.6	—	—	—	—	—
1963	1,741	1,615	—	—	784	45.0	736	45.6	—	—	—	—	—
1964	2,145	1,964	—	—	1,037	48.3	967	49.2	—	—	—	—	—
1965	2,659	2,417	—	—	1,354	50.9	1,249	51.7	—	—	—	—	—
1966	2,612	2,403	—	—	1,309	50.1	1,243	51.7	—	—	—	—	—
1967	2,525	2,267	—	—	1,311	51.9	1,202	53.0	—	—	—	—	—
1968	2,606	2,303	—	—	1,444	55.4	1,304	56.6	—	—	—	—	—
1969	2,842	2,538	—	—	1,516	53.3	1,402	55.2	—	—	—	—	—
1970	2,757	2,461	—	—	1,427	51.8	1,280	52.0	—	—	—	—	—
1971	2,872	2,596	—	—	1,535	53.4	1,402	54.0	—	—	—	—	—
1972	2,961	2,614	—	—	1,457	49.2	1,292	49.4	—	—	—	—	—
1973	3,059	2,707	—	—	1,425	46.6	1,302	48.1	—	—	—	—	—
1974	3,101	2,736	—	—	1,474	47.5	1,288	47.1	—	—	—	—	—
1975	3,186	2,825	—	—	1,615	50.7	1,446	51.2	—	—	—	—	—
1976	2,987	2,640	320	152	1,458	48.8	1,291	48.9	134	41.9	80	52.6	—
1977	3,140	2,768	335	156	1,590	50.6	1,403	50.7	166	49.6	80	51.3	48.9
1978	3,161	2,750	352	133	1,584	50.1	1,378	50.1	161	45.7	57	42.9	46.3
1979	3,160	2,776	324	154	1,559	49.3	1,376	49.6	147	45.4	69	44.8	46.8
1980	3,089	2,682	361	129	1,524	49.3	1,339	49.9	151	41.8	68	52.7	49.9
1981	3,053	2,626	359	146	1,646	53.9	1,434	54.6	154	42.9	76	52.1	49.3
1982	3,100	2,644	384	174	1,568	50.6	1,376	52.0	140	36.5	75	43.1	49.8
1983	2,964	2,496	392	138	1,562	52.7	1,372	55.0	151	38.5	75	54.3	47.3
1984	3,012	2,514	438	185	1,662	55.2	1,455	57.9	176	40.2	82	44.3	49.9
1985	2,666	2,241	333	141	1,539	57.7	1,332	59.4	141	42.3	72	51.1	46.6
1986	2,786	2,307	386	169	1,499	53.8	1,292	56.0	141	36.5	75	44.4	43.0
1987	2,647	2,207	337	176	1,503	56.8	1,249	56.6	175	51.9	59	33.5	45.0
1988	2,673	2,187	382	179	1,575	58.9	1,328	60.7	172	45.0	102	57.0	48.6
1989	2,454	2,051	337	168	1,463	59.6	1,238	60.4	178	52.8	93	55.4	53.2
1990	2,355	1,921	341	112	1,410	59.9	1,182	61.5	158	46.3	53	47.3	53.3
1991	2,276	1,867	320	154	1,420	62.4	1,207	64.6	146	45.6	88	57.1	53.1
1992	2,398	1,900	353	199	1,479	61.7	1,204	63.4	169	47.9	109	54.8	58.1
1993	2,338	1,910	302	200	1,464	62.6	1,200	62.8	168	55.6	125	62.5	55.4
1994	2,517	2,065	318	178	1,559	61.9	1,313	63.6	162	50.9	87	48.9	55.1
1995	2,599	2,088	356	288	1,610	61.9	1,308	62.6	183	51.4	155	53.8	51.1
1996	2,660	2,092	416	227	1,729	65.0	1,377	65.8	230	55.3	115	50.7	—

[1] Individuals age 16 to 24 who graduated from high school during the preceding 12 months.

[2] Enrollment in college as of October of each year for individuals age 16 to 24 who graduated from high school during the preceding 12 months.

[3] Includes persons of Hispanic origin.

[4] Due to the small sample size, data are subject to relatively large sampling errors.

—Data not available.

NOTE.—Data are based upon sample surveys of the civilian population. High school graduate data in this table differ from figures appearing in other tables because of varying survey procedures and coverage. High school graduates include GED recipients.

SOURCE: American College Testing Program, unpublished tabulations, 1987, derived from statistics collected by the U.S. Bureau of the Census; and U.S. Department of Labor, *College Enrollment of High School Graduates*, various years. (This table was prepared July 1997.)

Table 184.—College enrollment rates of high school graduates, by sex: 1960 to 1996

[Numbers in thousands]

Year	Total high school graduates[1]			Enrolled in college[2]					
	Total	Males	Females	Total		Males		Females	
				Number	Percent	Number	Percent	Number	Percent
1	2	3	4	5	6	7	8	9	10
1960	1,679	756	923	758	45.1	408	54.0	350	37.9
1961	1,763	790	973	847	48.0	445	56.3	402	41.3
1962	1,838	872	966	900	49.0	480	55.0	420	43.5
1963	1,741	794	947	784	45.0	415	52.3	369	39.0
1964	2,145	997	1,148	1,037	48.3	570	57.2	467	40.7
1965	2,659	1,254	1,405	1,354	50.9	718	57.3	636	45.3
1966	2,612	1,207	1,405	1,309	50.1	709	58.7	600	42.7
1967	2,525	1,142	1,383	1,311	51.9	658	57.6	653	47.2
1968	2,606	1,184	1,422	1,444	55.4	748	63.2	696	48.9
1969	2,842	1,352	1,490	1,516	53.3	812	60.1	704	47.2
1970	2,757	1,343	1,414	1,427	51.8	741	55.2	686	48.5
1971	2,872	1,369	1,503	1,535	53.4	788	57.6	747	49.7
1972	2,961	1,420	1,541	1,457	49.2	749	52.7	708	45.9
1973	3,059	1,458	1,601	1,425	46.6	730	50.1	695	43.4
1974	3,101	1,491	1,610	1,474	47.5	736	49.4	738	45.8
1975	3,186	1,513	1,673	1,615	50.7	796	52.6	819	49.0
1976	2,987	1,450	1,537	1,458	48.8	685	47.2	773	50.3
1977	3,140	1,482	1,658	1,590	50.6	773	52.2	817	49.3
1978	3,161	1,485	1,676	1,584	50.1	758	51.0	826	49.3
1979	3,160	1,474	1,686	1,559	49.3	743	50.4	816	48.4
1980	3,089	1,500	1,589	1,524	49.3	701	46.7	823	51.8
1981	3,053	1,490	1,563	1,646	53.9	816	54.8	830	53.1
1982	3,100	1,508	1,592	1,568	50.6	739	49.0	829	52.1
1983	2,964	1,390	1,574	1,562	52.7	721	51.9	841	53.4
1984	3,012	1,429	1,583	1,662	55.2	800	56.0	862	54.5
1985	2,666	1,286	1,380	1,539	57.7	754	58.6	785	56.9
1986	2,786	1,331	1,455	1,499	53.8	744	55.9	755	51.9
1987	2,647	1,278	1,369	1,503	56.8	746	58.4	757	55.3
1988	2,673	1,334	1,339	1,575	58.9	761	57.0	814	60.8
1989	2,454	1,208	1,245	1,463	59.6	696	57.6	767	61.6
1990	2,355	1,169	1,185	1,410	59.9	676	57.8	735	62.0
1991	2,276	1,139	1,137	1,420	62.4	656	57.6	763	67.1
1992	2,398	1,216	1,182	1,479	61.7	725	59.6	754	63.8
1993	2,338	1,118	1,219	1,464	62.6	668	59.7	797	65.4
1994	2,517	1,244	1,273	1,559	61.9	754	60.6	805	63.2
1995	2,599	1,238	1,361	1,610	61.9	775	62.6	835	61.4
1996	2,660	1,297	1,363	1,729	65.0	779	60.1	950	69.7

[1] Individuals age 16 to 24 who graduated from high school during the preceding 12 months.
[2] Enrollment in college as of October of each year for individuals age 16 to 24 who graduated from high school during the preceding 12 months.
NOTE.—Data are based upon sample surveys of the civilian population. High school graduate data in this table differ from figures appearing in other tables because of varying survey procedures and coverage. High school graduates include GED recipients.

SOURCE: American College Testing Program, unpublished tabulations, 1987, derived from statistics collected by the U.S. Bureau of the Census; and U.S. Department of Labor, *College Enrollment of High School Graduates*, various years. (This table was prepared July 1997.)

Table 185.—Graduation, college preparation, and college application rates of high school students, by selected school characteristics: 1993–94

Selected school characteristics	Public schools			Private schools		
	Number of schools with 12th graders	1993 graduation rate of fall 1992 12th graders	Average college application rate of 12th graders	Number of schools with 12th graders	1993 graduation rate of fall 1992 12th graders	Average college application rate of 12th graders
1	2	3	4	5	6	7
Total	17,838	92.6	57.4	7,875	98.2	87.5
Percent minority students						
Less than 5%	6,843	94.1	56.4	2,926	98.9	84.8
5% to 19%	3,784	93.7	60.2	2,735	98.5	90.0
20% to 49%	3,850	92.1	58.5	1,439	97.7	90.2
50% or more	3,360	90.1	54.2	775	96.5	79.9
Community type						
Central city	2,949	89.7	56.5	2,808	98.3	89.0
Suburban/large town	3,798	92.5	61.6	2,486	98.4	88.1
Small town/rural	11,091	94.6	54.3	2,581	97.6	81.5

NOTE.—Data are based upon a sample survey and may not be strictly comparable with data reported elsewhere. Only includes schools with students enrolled in 12th grade. Some data have been revised from previously published figures. Because of rounding, details may not add to totals.

SOURCE: U.S. Department of Education, National Center for Education Statistics, "Schools and Staffing Survey, 1993–94." (This table was prepared September 1996.)

Table 186.—Enrollment rates of 18- to 24-year-olds in institutions of higher education, by race/ethnicity: 1967 to 1996

Year	Total		White, non-Hispanic		Black, non-Hispanic		Hispanic origin	
	Enrollment as a percent of 18- to 24-year-olds	Enrollment as a percent of high school graduates[1]	Enrollment as a percent of 18- to 24-year-olds	Enrollment as a percent of high school graduates[1]	Enrollment as a percent of 18- to 24-year-olds	Enrollment as a percent of high school graduates[1]	Enrollment as a percent of 18- to 24-year-olds	Enrollment as a percent of high school graduates[1]
1	2	3	4	5	6	7	8	9
1967[2]	25.5	33.7	26.9	34.5	13.0	23.3	—	—
1968[2]	26.0	34.2	27.5	34.9	14.5	25.2	—	—
1969[2]	27.3	35.0	28.7	35.6	16.0	27.2	—	—
1970[2]	25.7	32.7	27.1	33.2	15.5	26.0	—	—
1971[2]	26.2	33.2	27.2	33.5	18.2	29.2	—	—
1972	25.5	31.1	27.2	31.9	18.3	25.2	13.4	24.1
1973	24.0	28.9	25.5	29.5	15.9	22.5	16.1	27.6
1974	24.6	29.8	25.8	29.9	17.6	24.6	18.0	30.7
1975	26.3	31.4	27.4	31.3	20.4	30.1	20.4	33.0
1976	26.7	32.3	27.6	32.1	22.5	32.1	20.0	34.7
1977	26.1	31.4	27.2	31.3	21.1	29.1	17.2	30.5
1978	25.3	30.0	26.5	30.1	20.1	27.9	15.2	25.9
1979	25.0	29.9	26.3	30.2	19.8	27.5	16.7	27.8
1980	25.7	30.5	27.3	31.0	19.4	26.0	16.1	27.6
1981	26.2	31.3	27.7	31.6	19.9	26.6	16.6	28.5
1982	26.6	31.6	28.1	32.0	19.9	26.5	16.8	27.6
1983	26.2	31.3	28.0	31.8	19.2	25.3	17.3	29.9
1984	27.1	31.8	28.9	32.6	20.3	25.6	17.9	28.8
1985	27.8	32.5	30.0	33.9	19.6	24.5	16.9	25.0
1986	27.9	32.7	29.7	33.3	21.9	26.9	17.6	28.3
1987	29.7	35.4	31.9	36.6	23.0	28.2	17.7	26.6
1988	30.2	36.0	33.1	37.4	21.1	26.8	17.1	29.1
1989	30.9	36.5	34.2	38.3	23.4	28.5	16.0	26.6
1990	32.1	37.7	35.2	39.2	25.3	30.4	16.2	26.8
1991	33.3	39.3	36.8	41.0	23.4	28.2	17.8	31.4
1992	34.4	42.0	37.3	42.8	25.2	33.9	21.3	37.5
1993	34.0	41.6	36.8	42.6	24.5	32.8	21.7	36.1
1994	34.6	42.3	38.1	43.7	27.7	35.6	18.8	33.1
1995	34.3	42.3	37.9	44.0	27.5	35.4	20.7	35.2
1996	35.5	43.4	39.5	45.1	27.4	35.9	20.1	34.5

[1] Includes students who were enrolled in college, but did not report high school completion.
[2] Data for white and black enrollment include persons of Hispanic origin.
—Data not available.
NOTE.—Data are based upon sample surveys of the civilian noninstitutional population. Percents based on 18- to 24-year-old high school graduates for 1992 and later years, use a slightly different definition of graduation and may not be directly comparable with figures for other years. All college students are counted as high school graduates.
SOURCE: U.S. Department of Commerce, Bureau of the Census, Current Population Survey, unpublished data. (This table was prepared June 1997.)

Table 187.—Total undergraduate fall enrollment[1] in institutions of higher education, by sex of student, attendance status, and control of institution: 1969 to 1995

[In thousands]

Year	Total	Full-time	Part-time	Men	Women	Men		Women		Men		Women	
						Full-time	Part-time	Full-time	Part-time	Public	Private	Public	Private
1	2	3	4	5	6	7	8	9	10	11	12	13	14
1969	6,884	4,991	1,893	4,008	2,876	2,952	1,056	2,039	837	2,997	1,011	2,162	714
1970	7,376	5,280	2,096	4,254	3,122	3,097	1,157	2,183	939	3,241	1,013	2,387	735
1971	7,743	5,512	2,231	4,418	3,325	3,201	1,217	2,311	1,014	3,427	991	2,580	745
1972	7,941	5,488	2,453	4,429	3,512	3,121	1,308	2,367	1,145	3,467	962	2,756	756
1973	8,261	5,580	2,681	4,538	3,723	3,135	1,403	2,445	1,278	3,579	959	2,943	780
1974	8,798	5,726	3,072	4,765	4,033	3,191	1,574	2,535	1,498	3,799	966	3,232	801
1975	9,679	6,169	3,510	5,257	4,422	3,459	1,798	2,710	1,712	4,245	1,012	3,581	841
1976	9,429	6,030	3,399	4,902	4,527	3,242	1,660	2,788	1,739	3,949	953	3,668	859
1977	9,717	6,094	3,623	4,897	4,820	3,188	1,709	2,906	1,914	3,937	960	3,906	914
1978	9,691	5,967	3,724	4,766	4,925	3,072	1,694	2,895	2,030	3,812	954	3,974	951
1979	9,998	6,080	3,919	4,821	5,178	3,087	1,734	2,993	2,185	3,865	956	4,181	995
1980	10,475	6,362	4,113	5,000	5,475	3,227	1,773	3,135	2,340	4,014	985	4,427	1,048
1981	10,755	6,449	4,306	5,109	5,646	3,261	1,848	3,188	2,458	4,090	1,018	4,558	1,088
1982	10,825	6,484	4,341	5,170	5,655	3,299	1,871	3,184	2,470	4,140	1,031	4,573	1,081
1983	10,846	6,514	4,332	5,158	5,688	3,304	1,854	3,210	2,478	4,117	1,042	4,580	1,107
1984	10,618	6,348	4,270	5,007	5,611	3,195	1,812	3,153	2,459	3,990	1,017	4,504	1,107
1985	10,597	6,320	4,277	4,962	5,635	3,156	1,806	3,163	2,471	3,953	1,010	4,525	1,110
1986	10,798	6,352	4,446	5,018	5,780	3,146	1,871	3,206	2,575	4,002	1,015	4,658	1,122
1987	11,046	6,463	4,584	5,068	5,978	3,164	1,905	3,299	2,679	4,076	992	4,842	1,136
1988	11,317	6,642	4,674	5,138	6,179	3,206	1,931	3,436	2,743	4,113	1,024	4,990	1,189
1989	11,743	6,841	4,902	5,311	6,432	3,279	2,032	3,562	2,869	4,272	1,039	5,216	1,216
1990	11,959	6,976	4,983	5,380	6,579	3,337	2,043	3,639	2,940	4,353	1,027	5,357	1,223
1991	12,439	7,221	5,218	5,571	6,868	3,436	2,135	3,786	3,082	4,531	1,040	5,617	1,251
1992	12,538	7,244	5,293	5,583	6,955	3,425	2,158	3,820	3,135	4,537	1,046	5,679	1,275
1993	12,324	7,179	5,144	5,484	6,840	3,382	2,102	3,797	3,043	4,447	1,036	5,565	1,276
1994	12,263	7,169	5,094	5,422	6,840	3,342	2,081	3,827	3,013	4,394	1,028	5,551	1,290
1995[2]	12,232	7,145	5,086	5,401	6,831	3,297	2,105	3,849	2,982	4,380	1,021	5,524	1,307

[1] Includes unclassified undergraduate students.
[2] Preliminary data.
NOTE.—Because of rounding, details may not add to totals.
SOURCE: U.S. Department of Education, National Center for Education Statistics, Higher Education General Information Survey (HEGIS), "Fall Enrollment in Colleges and Universities" surveys; and Integrated Postsecondary Education Data System, "Fall Enrollment" surveys. (This table was prepared December 1996.)

Table 188.—Total graduate fall enrollment[1] in institutions of higher education, by attendance status, sex of student, and control of institution: 1969 to 1995

[In thousands]

Year	Total	Full-time	Part-time	Men	Women	Men		Women		Men		Women	
						Full-time	Part-time	Full-time	Part-time	Public	Private	Public	Private
1	2	3	4	5	6	7	8	9	10	11	12	13	14
1969	955	363	593	590	366	252	338	111	255	393	197	273	93
1970	1,031	379	651	630	400	264	366	115	285	423	207	301	99
1971	1,012	388	621	615	394	269	346	119	275	415	200	296	100
1972	1,066	394	671	626	439	268	358	126	313	427	199	330	109
1973	1,123	410	715	648	477	273	375	137	340	442	206	358	119
1974	1,190	427	762	663	526	276	387	151	375	454	209	398	128
1975	1,263	453	810	700	563	290	410	163	400	481	219	425	138
1976	1,333	463	870	714	619	287	427	176	443	477	237	454	165
1977	1,319	473	845	700	617	289	411	184	434	458	243	443	174
1978	1,312	468	844	682	630	280	402	188	442	441	241	453	177
1979	1,309	476	833	669	640	280	389	196	444	427	242	457	182
1980	1,343	485	860	675	670	281	394	204	466	426	247	474	195
1981	1,343	484	859	674	669	277	397	207	462	419	255	468	201
1982	1,322	485	838	670	653	280	390	205	447	417	253	453	200
1983	1,340	497	843	677	663	286	391	211	452	418	259	454	209
1984	1,345	501	844	672	673	286	386	215	459	411	261	459	215
1985	1,376	509	867	677	700	289	388	220	479	414	263	477	223
1986	1,435	522	913	693	742	294	399	228	514	433	260	508	234
1987	1,452	527	925	693	759	294	400	233	525	429	264	516	243
1988	1,472	553	919	697	774	304	393	249	526	429	268	520	254
1989	1,522	572	949	710	811	309	401	263	548	437	273	541	271
1990	1,586	599	987	737	849	321	416	278	571	456	281	567	282
1991	1,639	642	997	761	878	341	419	300	578	471	290	580	299
1992	1,669	666	1,003	772	896	351	421	314	582	474	298	584	313
1993	1,688	688	1,000	771	917	355	416	334	584	473	298	590	327
1994	1,721	706	1,016	776	946	359	417	347	598	472	304	603	343
1995[2]	1,732	717	1,015	768	965	356	412	361	604	464	304	610	355

[1] Includes unclassified postbaccalaureate students.
[2] Preliminary data.

NOTE.—Because of rounding, details may not add to totals.

SOURCE: U.S. Department of Education, National Center for Education Statistics, Higher Education General Information Survey (HEGIS) "Fall Enrollment in Colleges and Universities" surveys; and Integrated Postsecondary Education Data System (IPEDS), "Fall Enrollment" surveys. (This table was prepared January 1997.)

Table 189.—Total first-professional fall enrollment in institutions of higher education, by attendance status, sex of student, and control of institution: 1969 to 1995

Year	Total	Full-time	Part-time	Men	Women	Men		Women		Men		Women	
						Full-time	Part-time	Full-time	Part-time	Public	Private	Public	Private
1	2	3	4	5	6	7	8	9	10	11	12	13	14
1969	164,737	143,081	21,656	148,926	15,811	131,368	17,558	11,713	4,098	64,241	84,685	8,354	7,457
1970	173,411	157,384	16,027	158,649	14,762	144,270	14,379	13,114	1,648	68,956	89,693	6,501	8,261
1971	192,668	176,224	16,444	174,058	18,610	159,386	14,672	16,838	1,772	98,233	75,825	9,430	9,180
1972	206,659	190,039	16,620	183,443	23,216	168,990	14,453	21,049	2,167	79,723	103,720	10,842	12,374
1973	218,990	201,663	17,327	186,297	32,693	171,731	14,566	29,932	2,761	81,811	104,486	16,138	16,555
1974	235,452	216,329	19,123	194,079	41,373	178,926	15,153	37,403	3,970	84,271	109,808	20,085	21,288
1975	242,267	219,886	22,381	192,100	50,167	177,117	14,983	42,769	7,398	79,240	112,860	23,557	26,610
1976	244,292	220,124	24,168	189,810	54,482	171,967	17,843	48,157	6,325	77,873	111,937	23,468	31,014
1977	251,357	226,318	25,039	191,451	59,906	173,165	18,286	53,153	6,753	78,189	113,262	24,901	35,005
1978	256,904	232,540	24,364	192,221	64,683	174,906	17,315	57,634	7,049	77,748	114,473	26,839	37,844
1979	263,404	238,949	24,455	193,363	70,041	176,394	16,969	62,555	7,486	77,122	116,241	29,026	41,015
1980	277,767	251,359	26,408	199,344	78,423	181,448	17,896	69,911	8,512	81,022	118,322	33,415	45,008
1981	274,595	248,328	26,267	192,936	81,659	175,414	17,522	72,914	8,745	77,562	115,374	34,177	47,482
1982	278,425	252,108	26,317	191,200	87,225	173,941	17,259	78,167	9,058	76,273	114,927	37,183	50,042
1983	278,529	249,636	28,893	188,096	90,433	169,071	19,025	80,565	9,868	74,938	113,158	38,484	51,949
1984	278,598	249,708	28,890	184,949	93,649	166,286	18,663	83,422	10,227	73,722	111,227	40,186	53,463
1985	274,200	246,619	27,581	179,792	94,408	162,368	17,424	84,251	10,157	71,373	108,419	40,435	53,973
1986	270,401	245,647	24,754	173,851	96,550	158,557	15,294	87,090	9,460	70,326	103,525	41,699	54,851
1987	268,332	241,807	26,525	170,129	98,203	153,668	16,461	88,139	10,064	68,089	102,040	41,947	56,256
1988	267,109	241,228	25,881	166,912	100,197	151,045	15,867	90,183	10,014	66,196	100,716	42,743	57,454
1989	274,451	247,812	26,639	168,773	105,678	152,511	16,262	95,301	10,377	67,548	101,225	45,090	60,588
1990	273,366	245,854	27,512	166,798	106,568	149,805	16,993	96,049	10,519	66,071	100,727	45,674	60,894
1991	280,531	252,012	28,519	169,875	110,656	152,356	17,519	99,656	11,000	64,821	105,054	46,661	63,995
1992	280,922	252,138	28,784	168,620	112,302	151,025	17,595	101,113	11,189	63,511	105,109	47,178	65,124
1993	292,431	259,764	32,667	172,788	119,643	153,873	18,915	105,891	13,752	63,973	108,815	49,681	69,962
1994	294,713	263,311	31,402	173,956	120,757	155,018	18,938	108,293	12,464	63,844	110,112	50,153	70,604
1995[1]	297,592	266,414	31,178	173,897	123,695	155,056	18,841	111,358	12,337	63,594	110,303	51,478	72,217

[1] Preliminary data.

SOURCE: U.S. Department of Education, National Center for Education Statistics, Higher Education General Information Survey (HEGIS), "Fall Enrollment in Colleges and Universities" surveys; and Integrated Postsecondary Education Data System (IPEDS), "Fall Enrollment" surveys. (This table was prepared December 1996.)

Table 190.—Total fall enrollment in institutions of higher education, by state: 1970 to 1995

State or other area	Fall 1970	Fall 1975	Fall 1980	Fall 1985	Fall 1990	Fall 1991	Fall 1992	Fall 1993	Fall 1994	Fall 1995[1]	Percent change, 1990 to 1995
1	2	3	4	5	6	7	8	9	10	11	12
United States	8,580,887	11,184,859	12,096,895	12,247,055	13,818,637	14,358,953	14,487,359	14,304,803	14,278,790	14,261,781	3.2
Alabama	103,936	164,700	164,306	179,343	218,589	224,331	230,537	233,525	229,511	225,612	3.2
Alaska	9,471	13,998	21,296	27,479	29,833	30,793	30,902	30,638	28,798	29,348	-1.6
Arizona	109,619	173,542	202,716	216,854	264,148	272,971	274,671	272,300	274,932	273,981	3.7
Arkansas	52,039	65,547	77,607	77,958	90,425	94,340	97,578	99,262	96,294	98,180	8.6
California	1,257,245	1,787,932	1,790,993	1,650,439	1,808,740	2,024,274	1,978,003	1,836,349	1,835,791	1,817,042	0.5
Colorado	123,395	149,814	162,916	161,314	227,131	235,108	241,352	239,805	241,295	242,739	6.9
Connecticut	124,700	148,491	159,632	159,348	168,604	165,824	165,874	162,300	159,990	157,695	-6.5
Delaware	25,260	32,389	32,939	31,883	42,004	42,988	42,763	43,528	44,197	44,307	5.5
District of Columbia[2]	77,158	84,190	86,675	78,201	79,551	77,353	81,202	81,565	77,256	77,277	-2.9
Florida	235,525	344,267	411,891	451,392	588,086	611,781	618,285	623,403	634,237	637,303	8.4
Georgia	126,511	173,585	184,159	196,826	251,786	277,023	293,606	302,844	308,587	314,712	25.0
Hawaii	36,562	46,671	47,181	49,937	56,436	57,302	61,162	62,871	64,322	63,198	12.0
Idaho	34,567	39,075	43,018	42,668	51,881	55,397	57,798	58,768	60,393	59,566	14.8
Illinois	452,146	584,089	644,245	678,689	729,246	753,297	748,805	734,089	731,420	717,854	-1.6
Indiana	192,668	213,820	247,253	250,567	284,832	290,301	296,912	294,685	292,276	289,615	1.7
Iowa	108,902	121,678	140,449	152,897	170,515	171,024	172,805	172,797	172,450	173,835	1.9
Kansas	102,485	120,833	136,605	141,359	163,733	167,699	169,419	170,135	170,603	177,643	8.5
Kentucky	98,591	125,253	143,066	141,724	177,852	187,958	188,322	187,332	182,577	178,858	0.6
Louisiana	120,728	153,213	160,058	177,176	186,840	197,438	204,379	201,987	203,567	203,935	9.1
Maine	34,134	40,443	43,264	52,201	57,186	57,178	57,977	56,294	56,724	56,547	-1.1
Maryland	149,607	205,570	225,526	231,649	259,700	267,931	268,399	268,005	266,214	266,310	2.5
Massachusetts	303,809	384,485	418,415	421,175	417,833	419,381	422,976	420,127	416,505	413,794	-1.0
Michigan	392,726	496,405	520,131	507,293	569,803	568,491	560,773	568,210	551,307	548,339	-3.8
Minnesota	160,788	184,756	206,691	221,162	253,789	255,054	272,920	268,118	289,300	280,816	10.6
Mississippi	73,967	99,962	102,364	101,180	122,883	125,350	123,754	122,408	120,884	122,690	-0.2
Missouri	183,930	223,115	234,421	241,146	289,899	297,154	296,617	297,062	293,810	291,536	0.6
Montana	30,062	30,843	35,177	35,958	35,876	37,821	39,644	39,557	40,095	42,674	18.9
Nebraska	66,915	74,705	89,488	97,769	112,831	113,648	122,603	115,523	116,000	115,718	2.6
Nevada	13,669	30,187	40,455	43,656	61,728	62,664	63,877	63,947	64,085	67,826	9.9
New Hampshire	29,400	41,030	46,794	52,283	59,510	63,718	63,924	64,043	62,847	64,327	8.1
New Jersey	216,121	297,114	321,610	297,658	324,286	334,641	343,232	343,029	335,480	333,831	2.9
New Mexico	44,461	51,944	58,283	68,295	85,500	93,507	99,276	101,460	101,881	102,405	19.8
New York	806,479	1,005,063	992,237	1,000,098	1,048,286	1,056,487	1,064,822	1,062,924	1,057,841	1,041,566	-0.6
North Carolina	171,925	251,786	287,537	327,288	352,138	371,968	383,453	371,280	369,386	372,003	5.6
North Dakota	31,495	29,743	34,069	37,939	37,878	38,739	40,470	40,316	40,184	40,399	6.7
Ohio	376,267	436,052	489,145	514,745	557,690	569,326	573,183	562,402	549,304	540,275	-3.1
Oklahoma	110,155	146,613	160,295	169,173	173,221	183,536	187,846	183,342	185,174	180,676	4.3
Oregon	122,177	145,281	157,458	137,967	165,741	167,107	167,415	165,834	164,447	167,145	0.8
Pennsylvania	411,044	470,536	507,716	533,198	604,060	620,036	626,904	621,228	611,174	617,759	2.3
Rhode Island	45,898	64,479	66,869	69,927	78,273	79,112	79,165	77,407	74,718	74,100	-5.3
South Carolina	69,518	133,023	132,476	131,902	159,302	164,907	171,443	174,302	173,070	174,125	9.3
South Dakota	30,639	30,260	32,761	32,772	34,208	36,332	37,596	38,166	37,764	36,695	7.3
Tennessee	135,103	181,435	204,581	194,845	226,238	238,042	242,970	244,936	242,966	245,962	8.7
Texas	442,225	624,390	701,391	769,692	901,437	917,443	938,526	942,178	954,495	952,525	5.7
Utah	81,687	87,323	93,987	103,994	121,303	130,419	133,083	138,139	146,196	147,324	21.5
Vermont	22,209	29,095	30,628	31,416	36,398	37,436	37,377	36,415	35,409	35,065	-3.7
Virginia	151,915	244,671	280,504	292,416	353,442	356,325	354,172	348,535	354,149	355,919	0.7
Washington	183,544	227,168	303,603	231,553	263,384	274,740	275,556	279,845	284,662	285,819	8.5
West Virginia	63,153	78,619	81,973	76,659	84,790	88,602	90,252	88,852	87,741	86,034	1.5
Wisconsin	202,058	240,701	269,086	275,069	299,774	308,986	307,902	309,036	303,861	300,223	0.1
Wyoming	15,220	18,078	21,147	24,204	31,326	32,118	31,548	30,702	30,682	30,176	-3.7
U.S. Service Schools[2]	17,079	36,897	49,808	54,719	48,692	53,532	53,329	52,998	51,939	88,451	81.7
Outlying areas	67,237	104,270	137,749	164,890	164,618	168,771	169,759	172,989	170,686	183,657	11.6
American Samoa	—	689	976	758	1,219	1,267	1,295	1,264	1,249	1,232	1.1
Federated States of Micronesia	—	—	—	—	975	837	1,028	1,148	1,374	1,296	32.9
Guam	2,719	3,800	3,217	4,601	4,741	5,016	4,845	5,843	6,449	6,010	26.8
Marshall Islands	—	—	—	—	—	—	374	386	424	418	
Northern Marianas	—	—	—	318	661	847	796	1,261	1,253	959	45.1
Palau	—	—	—	—	491	355	445	436	403	351	-28.5
Puerto Rico	63,073	97,517	131,184	155,917	154,065	157,733	158,120	159,709	156,439	170,337	10.6
Trust Territory of the Pacific	—	185	224	724	—	—	—	—	—	—	
Virgin Islands	1,445	2,079	2,148	2,572	2,466	2,716	2,856	2,942	3,095	3,054	23.8

[1] Preliminary data.
[2] Some data revised from previously published figures.
— Data not reported or not applicable.

SOURCE: U.S. Department of Education, National Center for Education Statistics, Higher Education General Information Survey (HEGIS), "Fall Enrollment in Colleges and Universities" surveys; and Integrated Postsecondary Education Data System (IPEDS), "Fall Enrollment" surveys. (This table was prepared January 1997.)

Table 191.—Total fall enrollment in public institutions of higher education, by state: 1970 to 1995

State or other area	Fall 1970	Fall 1975	Fall 1980	Fall 1985	Fall 1990	Fall 1991	Fall 1992	Fall 1993	Fall 1994	Fall 1995[1]	Percent change, 1990 to 1995
1	2	3	4	5	6	7	8	9	10	11	12
United States	6,428,134	8,834,508	9,457,394	9,479,273	10,844,717	11,309,563	11,384,567	11,189,088	11,133,680	11,092,374	2.3
Alabama	87,884	145,698	143,674	158,688	195,939	202,311	206,287	210,094	206,546	203,165	3.7
Alaska	8,563	13,218	20,561	26,510	27,792	29,019	29,037	28,708	27,631	28,368	2.1
Arizona	107,315	168,666	194,034	202,036	248,213	253,631	255,907	246,754	252,184	254,530	2.5
Arkansas	43,599	56,127	66,068	66,123	78,645	82,152	85,829	87,942	85,601	87,067	10.7
California	1,123,529	1,617,558	1,599,838	1,444,207	1,594,710	1,804,654	1,748,649	1,604,158	1,582,837	1,564,230	−1.9
Colorado	108,562	136,370	145,598	142,031	200,653	206,645	212,427	209,932	209,717	210,312	4.8
Connecticut	73,391	93,567	97,788	98,616	109,556	107,321	107,786	105,446	102,450	100,539	−8.2
Delaware	21,151	27,082	28,325	27,933	34,252	35,311	35,313	35,771	36,322	36,204	5.7
District of Columbia[2]	12,194	15,159	13,900	12,080	11,990	11,422	11,578	10,608	10,599	9,663	−19.4
Florida	189,450	287,745	334,349	362,241	489,081	506,342	511,226	518,480	528,024	530,607	8.5
Georgia	101,900	142,593	140,158	148,956	196,413	218,924	233,078	239,755	243,855	248,682	26.6
Hawaii	32,963	43,278	43,269	43,246	45,728	45,682	49,605	50,618	51,646	50,198	9.8
Idaho	27,072	31,298	34,491	33,666	41,315	44,149	46,607	47,524	48,994	48,986	18.6
Illinois	315,634	444,458	491,274	520,224	551,333	571,249	566,614	549,745	545,958	530,248	−3.8
Indiana	136,739	159,453	189,224	193,833	223,953	228,378	234,624	231,259	228,270	224,795	0.4
Iowa	68,390	83,572	97,454	109,765	117,834	120,360	122,841	122,267	122,017	122,396	3.9
Kansas	88,215	107,761	121,987	127,220	149,117	152,349	153,399	154,016	152,798	160,449	7.6
Kentucky	77,240	105,265	114,884	110,836	147,095	155,773	157,838	156,160	151,575	148,808	1.2
Louisiana	101,127	132,054	136,703	153,173	158,290	168,822	177,373	173,950	175,112	174,873	10.5
Maine	25,405	31,092	31,878	33,188	41,500	40,928	40,846	39,819	39,188	38,195	−8.0
Maryland	118,988	176,544	195,051	198,992	220,783	228,638	227,987	226,666	223,692	222,857	0.9
Massachusetts	116,127	173,564	183,765	185,602	186,035	180,559	183,119	181,461	179,799	176,777	−5.0
Michigan	339,625	436,655	454,147	434,270	487,359	486,301	473,322	483,145	466,758	462,390	−5.1
Minnesota	130,567	148,630	162,379	173,984	199,211	199,753	212,158	207,131	227,015	217,249	9.1
Mississippi	64,968	89,919	90,661	90,704	109,038	111,386	109,911	109,373	108,398	110,600	1.4
Missouri	132,540	158,196	165,179	168,829	200,093	203,125	198,610	197,821	191,859	189,993	−5.0
Montana	27,287	27,798	31,178	32,032	31,865	33,453	33,765	34,326	34,927	37,435	17.5
Nebraska	51,454	61,240	73,509	81,202	94,614	94,692	103,196	95,782	95,877	95,599	1.0
Nevada	13,576	30,010	40,280	43,368	61,242	61,985	63,192	63,229	63,271	66,683	8.9
New Hampshire	15,979	24,205	24,119	26,669	32,163	34,518	35,255	35,571	34,988	36,069	12.1
New Jersey	145,373	227,764	247,028	237,297	261,601	270,728	278,385	278,361	272,420	271,069	3.6
New Mexico	40,795	47,605	55,077	66,059	83,403	89,853	94,901	98,093	97,073	97,220	16.6
New York	449,437	613,842	563,251	563,251	616,884	605,898	606,308	604,989	604,433	588,491	−4.6
North Carolina	123,761	201,288	228,154	267,044	285,405	305,473	315,518	303,556	303,649	303,099	6.2
North Dakota	30,192	27,954	31,709	34,802	34,690	35,218	36,783	36,644	36,639	36,810	6.1
Ohio	281,099	336,931	381,765	379,164	427,613	436,292	437,027	429,756	417,566	409,818	−4.2
Oklahoma	91,438	124,372	137,188	146,827	151,073	160,166	164,728	160,901	161,748	158,026	4.6
Oregon	108,483	129,785	140,102	119,612	144,427	144,451	144,902	143,352	141,027	143,617	−0.6
Pennsylvania	232,982	287,436	292,499	300,523	343,478	354,435	359,856	351,747	342,565	339,928	−1.0
Rhode Island	25,527	32,311	35,052	35,389	42,350	42,503	43,264	40,833	39,376	38,653	−8.7
South Carolina	47,101	107,690	107,683	105,854	131,134	137,012	145,580	148,933	148,514	148,706	13.4
South Dakota	23,936	21,925	24,328	23,339	26,596	28,888	30,346	31,427	30,980	29,693	11.6
Tennessee	98,897	139,526	156,835	147,951	175,049	186,441	192,302	194,225	191,425	193,136	10.3
Texas	365,522	542,212	613,552	677,192	802,314	816,554	832,458	834,696	843,002	836,851	4.3
Utah	49,588	56,536	59,598	69,426	86,108	94,802	96,958	100,271	108,593	110,560	28.4
Vermont	12,536	17,145	17,984	18,844	20,910	21,485	21,397	21,001	20,505	20,470	−2.1
Virginia	123,279	215,253	246,500	250,754	291,286	298,107	297,522	293,810	293,165	293,127	0.6
Washington	162,718	202,531	276,028	201,532	227,632	238,345	238,763	241,813	244,772	246,635	8.3
West Virginia	51,363	68,117	71,228	66,531	74,108	78,215	79,284	77,500	76,120	74,857	1.0
Wisconsin	170,374	210,535	235,179	238,735	253,529	260,082	256,890	256,669	250,246	245,770	−3.1
Wyoming	15,220	18,078	21,121	24,204	30,623	31,251	30,687	30,002	30,015	29,420	−3.9
U.S. Service Schools[2]	17,079	36,897	49,808	54,719	48,692	53,532	53,329	52,998	51,939	88,451	81.7
Outlying areas	46,680	59,923	60,692	65,411	66,244	66,074	66,702	69,115	70,917	77,050	16.3
American Samoa	—	689	976	758	1,219	1,267	1,295	1,264	1,249	1,232	1.1
Federated States of Micronesia	—	—	—	—	975	837	1,028	1,148	1,374	1,296	32.9
Guam	2,719	3,800	3,217	4,601	4,741	5,016	4,845	5,843	6,449	6,010	26.8
Marshall Islands	—	—	—	—	—	—	374	386	424	418	—
Northern Marianas	—	—	—	318	661	847	796	1,261	1,253	959	45.1
Palau	—	—	—	—	491	355	445	436	403	351	−28.5
Puerto Rico	42,516	53,170	54,127	56,438	55,691	55,036	55,063	55,835	56,670	63,730	14.4
Trust Territory of the Pacific	—	185	224	724	—	—	—	—	—	—	—
Virgin Islands	1,445	2,079	2,148	2,572	2,466	2,716	2,856	2,942	3,095	3,054	23.8

[1] Preliminary data.
[2] Some data revised from previously published figures.
—Data not reported or not applicable.

SOURCE: U.S. Department of Education, National Center for Education Statistics, Higher Education General Information Survey (HEGIS), "Fall Enrollment in Colleges and Universities" surveys; and Integrated Postsecondary Education Data System (IPEDS), "Fall Enrollment" surveys. (This table was prepared December 1996).

Table 192.—Total fall enrollment in private institutions of higher education, by state: 1970 to 1995

State or other area	Fall 1970	Fall 1975	Fall 1980	Fall 1985	Fall 1990	Fall 1991	Fall 1992	Fall 1993	Fall 1994	1995[1]	Percent change, 1990 to 1995
1	2	3	4	5	6	7	8	9	10	11	12
United States	2,152,753	2,350,351	2,639,501	2,767,782	2,973,920	3,049,390	3,102,792	3,115,715	3,145,110	3,169,407	6.6
Alabama	16,052	19,002	20,632	20,655	22,650	22,020	24,250	23,431	22,965	22,447	-0.9
Alaska	908	780	735	969	2,041	1,774	1,865	1,930	1,167	980	-52.0
Arizona	2,304	4,876	8,682	14,818	15,935	19,340	18,764	25,546	22,748	19,451	22.1
Arkansas	8,440	9,420	11,539	11,835	11,780	12,188	11,749	11,320	10,693	11,113	-5.7
California	133,716	170,374	191,155	206,232	214,030	219,620	229,354	232,191	252,954	252,812	18.1
Colorado	14,833	13,444	17,318	19,283	26,478	28,463	28,925	29,873	31,578	32,427	22.5
Connecticut	51,309	54,924	61,844	60,732	59,048	58,503	58,088	56,854	57,540	57,156	-3.2
Delaware	4,109	5,307	4,614	3,950	7,752	7,677	7,450	7,757	7,875	8,103	4.5
District of Columbia	64,964	69,031	72,775	66,121	67,561	65,931	69,624	70,957	66,657	67,614	0.1
Florida	46,075	56,522	77,542	89,151	99,005	105,439	107,059	104,923	106,213	106,696	7.8
Georgia	24,611	30,992	44,001	47,870	55,373	58,099	60,528	63,089	64,732	66,030	19.2
Hawaii	3,599	3,393	3,912	6,691	10,708	11,620	11,557	12,253	12,676	13,000	21.4
Idaho	7,495	7,777	8,527	9,002	10,566	11,248	11,191	11,244	11,399	10,580	0.1
Illinois	136,512	139,631	152,971	158,465	177,913	182,048	182,191	184,344	185,462	187,606	5.4
Indiana	55,929	54,367	58,029	56,734	60,879	61,923	62,288	63,426	64,006	64,820	6.5
Iowa	40,512	38,106	42,995	43,132	52,681	50,664	49,964	50,530	50,433	51,439	-2.4
Kansas	14,270	13,072	14,618	14,139	14,616	15,350	16,020	16,119	17,805	17,194	17.6
Kentucky	21,351	19,988	28,182	30,888	30,757	32,185	30,484	31,172	31,002	30,050	-2.3
Louisiana	19,601	21,159	23,355	24,003	28,550	28,616	27,006	28,037	28,455	29,062	1.8
Maine	8,729	9,351	11,386	19,013	15,686	16,250	17,131	16,475	17,536	18,352	17.0
Maryland	30,619	29,026	30,475	32,657	38,917	39,293	40,412	41,339	42,522	43,453	11.7
Massachusetts	187,682	210,921	234,650	235,573	231,798	238,822	239,857	238,666	236,706	237,017	2.3
Michigan	53,101	59,750	65,984	73,023	82,444	82,190	87,451	85,065	84,549	85,949	4.3
Minnesota	30,221	36,126	44,312	47,178	54,578	55,301	60,762	60,987	62,285	63,567	16.5
Mississippi	8,999	10,043	11,703	10,476	13,845	13,964	13,843	13,035	12,486	12,090	-12.7
Missouri	51,390	64,919	69,242	72,317	89,806	94,029	98,007	99,241	101,951	101,543	13.1
Montana	2,775	3,045	3,999	3,926	4,011	4,368	5,879	5,231	5,168	5,239	30.6
Nebraska	15,461	13,465	15,979	16,567	18,217	18,956	19,407	19,741	20,123	20,119	10.4
Nevada	93	177	175	288	486	679	685	718	814	1,143	135.2
New Hampshire	13,421	16,825	22,675	25,614	27,347	29,200	28,669	28,472	27,859	28,258	3.3
New Jersey	70,748	69,350	74,582	60,361	62,685	63,913	64,847	64,668	63,060	62,762	0.1
New Mexico	3,666	4,339	3,206	2,236	2,097	3,654	4,375	3,367	4,808	5,185	147.3
New York	357,042	391,221	428,986	436,847	431,402	450,589	458,514	457,935	453,408	453,075	5.0
North Carolina	48,164	50,498	59,383	60,244	66,733	66,495	67,935	67,724	65,747	68,931	3.3
North Dakota	1,303	1,789	2,360	3,137	3,188	3,521	3,687	3,672	3,545	3,589	12.6
Ohio	95,168	99,121	107,380	135,581	130,077	133,034	136,156	132,646	131,738	130,457	0.3
Oklahoma	18,717	22,241	23,107	22,346	22,148	23,370	23,118	22,441	23,426	22,650	2.3
Oregon	13,694	15,496	17,356	18,355	21,314	22,656	22,513	22,482	23,420	23,528	10.4
Pennsylvania	178,062	183,100	215,217	232,675	260,582	265,601	267,048	269,481	268,609	277,831	6.6
Rhode Island	20,371	32,168	31,817	34,538	35,923	36,609	35,901	36,574	35,342	35,447	-1.3
South Carolina	22,417	25,333	24,793	26,048	28,168	27,895	25,863	25,369	24,556	25,419	-9.8
South Dakota	6,703	8,335	8,433	9,433	7,612	7,444	7,250	6,739	6,784	7,002	-8.0
Tennessee	36,206	41,909	47,746	46,894	51,189	51,601	50,668	50,711	51,541	52,826	3.2
Texas	76,703	82,178	87,839	92,500	99,123	100,889	106,068	107,482	111,493	115,674	16.7
Utah	32,099	30,787	34,389	34,568	35,195	35,617	36,125	37,868	37,603	36,764	4.5
Vermont	9,673	11,950	12,644	12,572	15,488	15,951	15,980	15,414	14,904	14,595	-5.8
Virginia	28,636	29,418	34,004	41,662	62,156	58,218	56,650	54,725	60,984	62,792	1.0
Washington	20,826	24,637	27,575	30,021	35,752	36,415	36,793	38,032	39,890	39,184	9.6
West Virginia	11,790	10,502	10,745	10,128	10,682	10,387	10,968	11,352	11,621	11,177	4.6
Wisconsin	31,684	30,166	33,907	36,334	46,245	48,904	51,012	52,367	53,615	54,453	17.7
Wyoming	—	—	26	—	703	867	861	700	667	756	7.5
Outlying areas	20,557	44,347	77,057	99,479	98,374	102,697	103,057	103,874	99,769	106,607	8.4
American Samoa	—	—	—	—	—	—	—	—	—	—	—
Federated States of Micronesia	—	—	—	—	—	—	—	—	—	—	—
Guam	—	—	—	—	—	—	—	—	—	—	—
Marshall Islands	—	—	—	—	—	—	—	—	—	—	—
Northern Marianas	—	—	—	—	—	—	—	—	—	—	—
Palau	—	—	—	—	—	—	—	—	—	—	—
Puerto Rico	20,557	44,347	77,057	99,479	98,374	102,697	103,057	103,874	99,769	106,607	8.4
Trust Territory of the Pacific	—	—	—	—	—	—	—	—	—	—	—
Virgin Islands	—	—	—	—	—	—	—	—	—	—	—

[1] Preliminary data.

—Data not reported or not applicable.

SOURCE: U.S. Department of Education, National Center for Education Statistics, Higher Education General Information Survey (HEGIS), "Fall Enrollment in Colleges and Universities" surveys; and Integrated Postsecondary Education Data System (IPEDS), "Fall Enrollment" surveys. (This table was prepared December 1996.)

Table 193.—Total fall enrollment in all institutions of higher education, by attendance status, sex, and state: 1994 and 1995

State or other area	Fall 1994[1]					Fall 1995[2]				
	Total	Full-time		Part-time		Total	Full-time		Part-time	
		Men	Women	Men	Women		Men	Women	Men	Women
1	2	3	4	5	6	7	8	9	10	11
United States	14,278,790	3,855,183	4,282,593	2,516,715	3,624,299	14,261,781	3,807,392	4,321,410	2,535,147	3,597,832
Alabama	229,511	69,230	82,660	33,045	44,576	225,612	68,713	83,031	31,064	42,804
Alaska	28,798	5,668	6,788	6,161	10,181	29,348	5,424	6,559	6,444	10,921
Arizona	274,932	63,697	64,013	60,773	86,449	273,981	61,685	64,369	61,226	86,701
Arkansas	96,294	30,261	36,712	11,093	18,228	98,180	30,077	37,101	11,626	19,376
California	1,835,791	412,716	450,914	421,148	551,013	1,817,042	408,376	458,540	410,267	539,859
Colorado	241,295	63,265	65,091	48,463	64,476	242,739	62,892	65,994	48,117	65,736
Connecticut	159,990	39,144	42,766	30,283	47,797	157,695	38,877	43,222	29,623	45,973
Delaware	44,197	11,521	14,411	7,533	10,732	44,307	11,287	14,252	7,576	11,192
District of Columbia	77,256	22,470	26,610	12,646	15,530	77,277	22,706	27,643	11,807	15,121
Florida	634,237	142,547	159,592	136,851	195,247	637,303	142,368	162,172	135,424	197,339
Georgia	308,587	92,709	110,110	42,371	63,397	314,712	93,962	115,663	40,920	64,167
Hawaii	64,322	16,061	19,169	12,871	16,221	63,198	16,175	19,166	12,030	15,827
Idaho	60,393	19,255	21,103	7,908	12,127	59,566	19,013	21,136	7,706	11,711
Illinois	731,420	178,957	193,474	145,279	213,710	717,854	174,969	193,430	141,323	208,132
Indiana	292,276	92,089	97,935	41,063	61,189	289,615	90,941	98,818	41,298	58,558
Iowa	172,450	58,901	61,720	19,478	32,351	173,835	58,553	62,170	19,478	33,634
Kansas	170,603	48,013	49,915	28,114	44,561	177,643	47,394	50,144	31,446	48,659
Kentucky	182,577	53,533	65,836	22,407	40,801	178,858	52,229	65,429	22,025	39,175
Louisiana	203,567	64,832	79,536	21,798	37,401	203,935	64,292	79,971	21,820	37,852
Maine	56,724	15,014	17,035	8,032	16,643	56,547	14,632	16,920	7,978	17,017
Maryland	266,214	57,746	66,913	54,678	86,877	266,310	57,822	68,689	54,075	85,724
Massachusetts	416,505	123,189	138,072	60,797	94,447	413,794	121,670	140,343	59,062	92,719
Michigan	551,307	130,298	148,247	112,668	160,094	548,339	127,404	146,846	113,756	160,333
Minnesota	289,300	77,477	84,168	53,571	74,084	280,816	74,919	83,181	51,380	71,336
Mississippi	120,884	40,937	49,527	11,282	19,138	122,690	41,390	50,577	11,219	19,504
Missouri	293,810	79,571	87,509	50,435	76,295	291,536	77,858	88,270	49,402	76,006
Montana	40,095	15,246	15,508	3,798	5,543	42,674	15,967	16,789	3,991	5,927
Nebraska	116,000	32,353	34,308	19,706	29,633	115,718	32,125	34,529	19,787	28,737
Nevada	64,085	10,186	11,011	18,044	24,844	67,826	10,196	11,524	19,787	26,319
New Hampshire	62,847	18,376	21,513	8,470	14,488	64,327	18,307	21,598	9,070	15,352
New Jersey	335,480	81,351	91,263	65,599	97,267	333,831	81,944	92,990	63,695	95,202
New Mexico	101,881	23,684	27,696	20,075	30,426	102,405	23,306	28,210	19,900	30,989
New York	1,057,841	311,858	363,375	144,142	238,466	1,041,566	301,712	363,252	142,426	234,176
North Carolina	369,386	104,943	130,290	54,140	80,013	372,030	105,756	132,332	54,248	79,694
North Dakota	40,184	16,426	15,439	3,585	4,734	40,399	16,462	15,756	3,480	4,701
Ohio	549,304	160,869	181,175	87,286	119,974	540,275	157,392	180,152	84,648	118,083
Oklahoma	185,174	52,979	57,218	30,890	44,087	180,676	51,848	56,218	30,422	42,188
Oregon	164,447	45,748	46,680	31,295	40,724	167,145	43,214	46,067	33,792	44,072
Pennsylvania	611,174	186,827	199,592	91,629	133,126	617,759	186,435	201,884	91,493	137,947
Rhode Island	74,718	22,796	24,221	10,770	16,931	74,100	22,522	24,308	10,642	16,628
South Carolina	173,070	49,154	58,332	24,356	41,228	174,125	48,980	60,159	23,666	41,320
South Dakota	37,764	12,950	14,538	3,717	6,559	36,695	12,586	14,021	3,610	6,478
Tennessee	242,966	72,240	83,777	35,384	51,565	245,962	73,010	86,590	35,318	51,044
Texas	954,495	250,851	263,609	192,609	247,426	952,525	248,597	267,274	189,578	247,076
Utah	146,196	48,699	47,148	24,669	25,680	147,324	49,018	48,685	24,854	24,767
Vermont	35,409	11,434	12,461	3,684	7,830	35,065	11,238	12,739	3,599	7,489
Virginia	354,149	92,054	107,374	63,443	91,278	355,919	91,570	108,894	63,394	92,061
Washington	284,662	81,419	90,980	45,744	66,519	285,819	81,914	93,836	44,585	65,484
West Virginia	87,741	29,373	31,215	9,381	17,772	86,034	28,848	30,935	9,191	17,060
Wisconsin	303,861	85,012	95,951	49,305	73,593	300,223	84,279	97,288	48,088	70,568
Wyoming	30,682	8,669	8,886	4,793	8,334	30,176	8,532	9,068	4,543	8,033
U.S. Service Schools	51,939	20,585	9,207	9,453	12,694	88,451	16,006	2,676	58,708	11,061
Outlying areas	170,686	49,427	76,346	19,016	25,897	183,657	53,526	83,879	18,544	27,708
American Samoa	1,249	433	438	222	156	1,232	428	436	217	151
Federated States of Micronesia	1,374	449	422	316	187	1,296	518	447	150	181
Guam	6,449	1,174	1,770	1,645	1,860	6,010	989	1,597	1,567	1,857
Marshall Islands	424	92	76	147	109	418	89	75	146	108
Northern Marianas	1,253	148	202	425	478	959	203	253	188	315
Palau	403	198	136	34	35	351	143	125	31	52
Puerto Rico	156,439	46,580	72,315	15,769	21,775	170,337	50,834	79,876	15,798	23,829
Virgin Islands	3,095	353	987	458	1,297	3,054	322	1,070	447	1,215

[1] Revised from previously published data.
[2] Preliminary data.

SOURCE: U.S. Department of Education, National Center for Education Statistics, Integrated Postsecondary Education Data System (IPEDS), "Fall Enrollment" survey. (This table was prepared April 1997.)

Table 194.—Total fall enrollment in public institutions of higher education, by attendance status, sex, and state: 1994 and 1995

State or other area	Fall 1994[1]					Fall 1995[2]				
	Total	Full-time		Part-time		Total	Full-time		Part-time	
		Men	Women	Men	Women		Men	Women	Men	Women
1	2	3	4	5	6	7	8	9	10	11
United States	11,133,680	2,813,226	3,137,594	2,116,842	3,066,018	11,092,374	2,769,745	3,155,556	2,137,890	3,029,183
Alabama	206,546	60,804	71,839	31,510	42,393	203,165	60,666	72,704	29,366	40,429
Alaska	27,631	5,367	6,318	5,995	9,951	28,368	5,171	6,201	6,290	10,706
Arizona	252,184	53,487	55,865	58,995	83,837	254,530	52,572	57,142	59,849	84,967
Arkansas	85,601	25,767	31,632	10,681	17,521	87,067	25,493	31,866	11,145	18,563
California	1,582,837	323,244	356,573	388,424	514,596	1,564,230	319,499	362,281	378,663	503,787
Colorado	209,717	52,922	55,323	42,777	58,695	210,312	52,690	55,717	42,163	59,742
Connecticut	102,450	21,556	24,035	21,546	35,313	100,539	21,063	23,818	21,226	34,432
Delaware	36,322	9,961	12,534	5,874	7,953	36,204	9,713	12,429	5,897	8,165
District of Columbia	10,599	1,651	2,093	2,804	4,051	9,663	1,444	2,015	2,482	3,722
Florida	528,024	105,949	124,501	119,118	178,456	530,607	105,794	126,880	118,165	179,768
Georgia	243,855	68,164	81,927	36,659	57,105	248,682	68,441	86,296	36,366	57,579
Hawaii	51,646	12,600	15,202	9,809	14,035	50,198	12,419	14,997	9,392	13,390
Idaho	48,994	14,930	15,440	7,481	11,143	48,986	14,759	15,562	7,443	11,222
Illinois	545,958	120,292	130,610	117,878	177,178	530,248	116,061	128,965	114,352	170,870
Indiana	228,270	66,120	72,001	37,294	52,855	224,795	65,085	71,868	37,579	50,263
Iowa	122,017	41,780	42,084	14,724	23,429	122,396	41,636	42,672	14,870	23,218
Kansas	152,798	41,950	42,874	26,354	41,620	160,449	41,551	43,254	29,814	45,830
Kentucky	151,575	42,852	52,976	19,789	35,958	148,808	42,192	53,218	19,316	34,082
Louisiana	175,112	55,288	67,727	18,522	33,575	174,873	54,727	68,616	18,188	33,342
Maine	39,188	10,588	10,479	6,748	11,373	38,195	10,024	10,288	6,646	11,237
Maryland	223,692	47,252	54,760	47,011	74,669	222,857	46,869	56,092	46,512	73,384
Massachusetts	179,799	44,675	50,704	32,804	51,616	176,777	43,528	50,097	32,004	51,148
Michigan	466,758	109,531	120,876	98,338	138,013	462,390	106,872	119,925	98,467	137,126
Minnesota	227,015	58,482	59,576	46,968	61,989	217,249	55,886	58,199	43,815	59,349
Mississippi	108,398	37,258	44,200	10,041	16,899	110,600	37,592	45,524	9,988	17,496
Missouri	191,859	49,912	56,907	32,007	53,033	189,993	48,618	56,455	31,883	53,037
Montana	34,927	13,835	13,378	3,191	4,523	37,435	14,596	14,638	3,320	4,881
Nebraska	95,877	25,633	26,008	18,119	26,117	95,599	25,462	26,147	18,694	25,296
Nevada	63,271	9,938	10,756	17,939	24,638	66,683	9,790	11,031	19,698	26,164
New Hampshire	34,988	10,169	12,204	4,715	7,900	36,069	10,016	11,947	5,461	8,645
New Jersey	272,420	62,691	72,201	55,501	82,027	271,069	63,116	73,508	53,991	80,454
New Mexico	97,073	21,890	25,679	19,779	29,725	97,220	21,459	25,789	19,618	30,334
New York	604,433	165,600	200,641	88,732	149,460	588,491	158,869	197,894	87,647	144,081
North Carolina	303,649	79,562	101,016	50,051	73,020	303,099	79,417	101,777	49,422	72,483
North Dakota	36,639	15,137	13,620	3,447	4,435	36,810	15,101	13,936	3,371	4,402
Ohio	417,566	117,887	135,467	67,350	96,862	409,818	115,135	133,907	65,403	95,373
Oklahoma	161,748	43,443	47,988	28,561	41,756	158,026	42,828	47,622	27,747	39,829
Oregon	141,027	37,290	37,211	29,039	37,487	143,617	34,837	36,319	31,503	40,958
Pennsylvania	342,565	104,923	112,304	49,492	75,846	339,928	104,724	113,496	47,661	74,047
Rhode Island	39,376	8,302	11,100	7,127	12,847	38,653	8,123	11,040	6,919	12,571
South Carolina	148,514	39,912	46,905	22,928	38,769	148,706	39,600	48,272	22,148	38,686
South Dakota	30,980	11,139	11,643	3,045	5,153	29,693	10,710	11,159	2,858	4,966
Tennessee	191,425	51,302	61,486	32,341	46,296	193,136	51,586	63,275	32,233	46,042
Texas	843,002	208,779	223,409	178,286	232,528	836,851	205,744	225,376	174,241	231,490
Utah	108,593	32,052	30,885	22,471	23,185	110,560	32,939	32,010	22,957	22,654
Vermont	20,505	6,216	6,614	2,478	5,197	20,470	6,094	6,749	2,464	5,163
Virginia	293,165	73,308	82,383	55,892	81,582	293,127	73,170	83,865	55,091	81,001
Washington	244,772	68,791	75,747	40,628	59,606	246,635	69,018	78,010	40,335	59,272
West Virginia	76,120	25,514	25,794	8,620	16,192	74,857	25,009	25,724	8,542	15,582
Wisconsin	250,246	68,941	76,009	42,713	62,583	245,770	68,248	77,247	41,414	58,861
Wyoming	30,015	8,005	8,883	4,793	8,334	29,420	7,783	9,061	4,543	8,033
U.S. Service Schools	51,939	20,585	9,207	9,453	12,694	88,451	16,006	2,676	58,708	11,061
Outlying areas	70,917	20,386	32,001	7,297	11,233	77,050	22,397	36,464	6,978	11,211
American Samoa	1,249	433	438	222	156	1,232	428	436	217	151
Federated States of Micronesia	1,374	449	422	316	187	1,296	518	447	150	181
Guam	6,449	1,174	1,770	1,645	1,860	6,010	989	1,597	1,567	1,857
Marshall Islands	424	92	76	147	109	418	89	75	146	108
Northern Marianas	1,253	148	202	425	478	959	203	253	188	315
Palau	403	198	136	34	35	351	143	125	31	52
Puerto Rico	56,670	17,539	27,970	4,050	7,111	63,730	19,705	32,461	4,232	7,332
Virgin Islands	3,095	353	987	458	1,297	3,054	322	1,070	447	1,215

[1] Revised from previously published data.
[2] Preliminary data.

SOURCE: U.S. Department of Education, National Center for Education Statistics, Integrated Postsecondary Education Data System (IPEDS), "Fall Enrollment" surveys. (This table was prepared April 1997.)

HIGHER EDUCATION: ENROLLMENT 203

Table 195.—Total fall enrollment in private institutions of higher education, by attendance status, sex, and state: 1994 and 1995

State or other area	Fall 1994					Fall 1995[1]				
	Total	Full-time		Part-time		Total	Full-time		Part-time	
		Men	Women	Men	Women		Men	Women	Men	Women
1	2	3	4	5	6	7	8	9	10	11
United States	3,145,110	1,041,957	1,144,999	399,873	558,281	3,169,407	1,037,647	1,165,854	397,257	568,649
Alabama	22,965	8,426	10,821	1,535	2,183	22,447	8,047	10,327	1,698	2,375
Alaska	1,167	301	470	166	230	980	253	358	154	215
Arizona	22,748	10,210	8,148	1,778	2,612	19,451	9,113	7,227	1,377	1,734
Arkansas	10,693	4,494	5,080	412	707	11,113	4,584	5,235	481	813
California	252,954	89,472	94,341	32,724	36,417	252,812	88,877	96,259	31,604	36,072
Colorado	31,578	10,343	9,768	5,686	5,781	32,427	10,202	10,277	5,954	5,994
Connecticut	57,540	17,588	18,731	8,737	12,484	57,156	17,814	19,404	8,397	11,541
Delaware	7,875	1,560	1,877	1,659	2,779	8,103	1,574	1,823	1,679	3,027
District of Columbia	66,657	20,819	24,517	9,842	11,479	67,614	21,262	25,628	9,325	11,399
Florida	106,213	36,598	35,091	17,733	16,791	106,696	36,574	35,292	17,259	17,571
Georgia	64,732	24,545	28,183	5,712	6,292	66,030	25,521	29,367	4,554	6,588
Hawaii	12,676	3,461	3,967	3,062	2,186	13,000	3,756	4,169	2,638	2,437
Idaho	11,399	4,325	5,663	427	984	10,580	4,254	5,574	263	489
Illinois	185,462	58,665	62,864	27,401	36,532	187,606	58,908	64,465	26,971	37,262
Indiana	64,006	25,969	25,934	3,769	8,334	64,820	25,856	26,950	3,719	8,295
Iowa	50,433	17,121	19,636	4,754	8,922	51,439	16,917	19,498	4,608	10,416
Kansas	17,805	6,063	7,041	1,760	2,941	17,194	5,843	6,890	1,632	2,829
Kentucky	31,002	10,681	12,860	2,618	4,843	30,050	10,037	12,211	2,709	5,093
Louisiana	28,455	9,544	11,809	3,276	3,826	29,062	9,565	11,355	3,632	4,510
Maine	17,536	4,426	6,556	1,284	5,270	18,352	4,608	6,632	1,332	5,780
Maryland	42,522	10,494	12,153	7,667	12,208	43,453	10,953	12,597	7,563	12,340
Massachusetts	236,706	78,514	87,368	27,993	42,831	237,017	78,142	90,246	27,058	41,571
Michigan	84,549	20,767	27,371	14,330	22,081	85,949	20,532	26,921	15,289	23,207
Minnesota	62,285	18,995	24,592	6,603	12,095	63,567	19,033	24,982	7,565	11,987
Mississippi	12,486	3,679	5,327	1,241	2,239	12,090	3,798	5,053	1,231	2,008
Missouri	101,951	29,659	30,602	18,428	23,262	101,543	29,240	31,815	17,519	22,969
Montana	5,168	1,411	2,130	607	1,020	5,239	1,371	2,151	671	1,046
Nebraska	20,123	6,720	8,300	1,587	3,516	20,119	6,663	8,382	1,633	3,441
Nevada	814	248	255	105	206	1,143	406	493	89	155
New Hampshire	27,859	8,207	9,309	3,755	6,588	28,258	8,291	9,651	3,609	6,707
New Jersey	63,060	18,660	19,062	10,098	15,240	62,762	18,828	19,482	9,704	14,748
New Mexico	4,808	1,794	2,017	296	701	5,185	1,847	2,421	262	655
New York	453,408	146,258	162,734	55,410	89,006	453,075	142,843	165,358	54,779	90,095
North Carolina	65,737	25,381	29,274	4,089	6,993	68,931	26,339	30,555	4,826	7,211
North Dakota	3,545	1,289	1,819	138	299	3,589	1,361	1,820	109	299
Ohio	131,738	42,982	45,708	19,936	23,112	130,457	42,257	46,245	19,245	22,710
Oklahoma	23,426	9,536	9,230	2,329	2,331	22,650	9,020	8,596	2,675	2,359
Oregon	23,420	8,458	9,469	2,256	3,237	23,528	8,377	9,748	2,289	3,114
Pennsylvania	268,609	81,904	87,288	42,137	57,280	277,831	81,711	88,388	43,832	63,900
Rhode Island	35,342	14,494	13,121	3,643	4,084	35,447	14,399	13,268	3,723	4,057
South Carolina	24,556	9,242	11,427	1,428	2,459	25,419	9,380	11,887	1,518	2,634
South Dakota	6,784	1,811	2,895	672	1,406	7,002	1,876	2,862	752	1,512
Tennessee	51,541	20,938	22,291	3,043	5,269	52,826	21,424	23,315	3,085	5,002
Texas	111,493	42,072	40,200	14,323	14,898	115,674	42,853	41,898	15,337	15,586
Utah	37,603	16,647	16,263	2,198	2,495	36,764	16,079	16,675	1,897	2,113
Vermont	14,904	5,218	5,847	1,206	2,633	14,595	5,144	5,990	1,135	2,326
Virginia	60,984	18,746	24,991	7,551	9,696	62,792	18,400	25,029	8,303	11,060
Washington	39,890	12,628	15,233	5,116	6,913	39,184	12,896	15,826	4,250	6,212
West Virginia	11,621	3,859	5,421	761	1,580	11,177	3,839	5,211	649	1,478
Wisconsin	53,615	16,071	19,942	6,592	11,010	54,453	16,031	20,041	6,674	11,707
Wyoming	667	664	3	—	—	756	749	7	—	—
Outlying areas	99,769	29,041	44,345	11,719	14,664	106,607	31,129	47,415	11,566	16,497
American Samoa	—	—	—	—	—	—	—	—	—	—
Federated States of Micronesia	—	—	—	—	—	—	—	—	—	—
Guam	—	—	—	—	—	—	—	—	—	—
Marshall Islands	—	—	—	—	—	—	—	—	—	—
Northern Marianas	—	—	—	—	—	—	—	—	—	—
Palau	—	—	—	—	—	—	—	—	—	—
Puerto Rico	99,769	29,041	44,345	11,719	14,664	106,607	31,129	47,415	11,566	16,497
Virgin Islands	—	—	—	—	—	—	—	—	—	—

[1] Preliminary data.
—Data not reported or not applicable.

SOURCE: U.S. Department of Education, National Center for Education Statistics, Integrated Postsecondary Education Data System (IPEDS), "Fall Enrollment" surveys. (This table was prepared December 1996.)

HIGHER EDUCATION: ENROLLMENT

Table 196.—Total fall enrollment in institutions of higher education, by control, type of institution, and state: 1994 and 1995

State or other area	Fall 1994[1]				Fall 1995[2]			
	Public 4-year	Public 2-year	Private 4-year	Private 2-year	Public 4-year	Public 2-year	Private 4-year	Private 2-year
1	2	3	4	5	6	7	8	9
United States	5,825,213	5,308,467	2,923,867	221,243	5,814,545	5,277,829	2,954,707	214,700
Alabama	126,079	80,467	21,609	1,356	126,508	76,657	21,949	498
Alaska	27,037	594	828	339	27,556	812	776	204
Arizona	101,418	150,766	21,819	929	101,718	152,812	18,562	889
Arkansas	64,540	21,061	10,347	346	62,809	24,258	10,667	446
California	483,332	1,099,505	239,288	13,666	490,231	1,073,999	238,755	14,057
Colorado	132,748	76,969	28,224	3,354	132,616	77,696	28,804	3,623
Connecticut	57,867	44,583	55,767	1,773	57,711	42,828	55,594	1,562
Delaware	24,966	11,356	7,875	—	24,540	11,664	8,103	—
District of Columbia	10,599	—	66,657	—	9,663	—	67,614	—
Florida	201,242	326,782	101,233	4,980	206,961	323,646	101,265	5,431
Georgia	157,391	86,464	58,559	6,173	160,425	88,257	61,480	4,550
Hawaii	23,741	27,905	12,676	—	23,345	26,853	13,000	—
Idaho	41,629	7,365	2,988	8,411	41,449	7,537	2,308	8,272
Illinois	194,489	351,469	179,359	6,103	192,532	337,716	183,336	4,270
Indiana	186,586	41,684	60,357	3,649	184,184	40,611	61,331	3,489
Iowa	65,617	56,400	49,042	1,391	65,841	56,555	50,324	1,115
Kansas	86,285	66,513	16,888	917	86,770	73,679	16,316	878
Kentucky	106,259	45,316	26,496	4,506	105,529	43,279	27,382	2,668
Louisiana	147,110	28,002	27,251	1,204	147,920	26,953	27,884	1,178
Maine	31,899	7,289	15,664	1,872	31,275	6,920	16,437	1,915
Maryland	112,250	111,442	41,381	1,141	113,738	109,119	42,267	1,186
Massachusetts	101,796	78,003	222,237	14,469	101,814	74,963	228,964	8,053
Michigan	258,107	208,651	82,086	2,463	258,996	203,394	83,304	2,645
Minnesota	119,233	107,782	57,897	4,388	117,188	100,061	59,410	4,157
Mississippi	57,507	50,891	11,431	1,055	58,847	51,753	11,278	812
Missouri	117,361	74,498	96,085	5,866	117,871	72,122	96,946	4,597
Montana	30,604	4,323	4,395	773	31,412	6,023	4,319	920
Nebraska	58,007	37,870	19,698	425	58,081	37,518	19,575	544
Nevada	31,333	31,938	787	27	30,831	35,852	1,116	27
New Hampshire	26,315	8,673	24,011	3,848	26,497	9,572	24,227	4,031
New Jersey	136,654	135,766	59,079	3,981	137,829	133,240	58,045	4,717
New Mexico	50,800	46,273	4,157	651	49,819	47,401	4,231	954
New York	345,202	259,231	424,708	28,700	335,728	252,763	425,065	28,010
North Carolina	156,445	147,204	63,203	2,534	157,414	145,685	67,448	1,483
North Dakota	28,301	8,338	3,299	246	28,396	8,414	3,334	255
Ohio	267,719	149,847	117,273	14,465	262,036	147,782	117,115	13,342
Oklahoma	97,271	64,477	20,768	2,658	95,387	62,639	20,621	2,029
Oregon	62,651	78,376	23,252	168	63,056	80,561	23,359	169
Pennsylvania	231,347	111,218	220,321	48,288	233,433	106,495	220,269	57,562
Rhode Island	23,375	16,001	33,211	2,131	22,764	15,889	33,021	2,426
South Carolina	87,374	61,140	23,070	1,486	87,813	60,893	24,124	1,295
South Dakota	30,783	197	6,573	211	29,484	209	6,769	233
Tennessee	114,151	77,274	48,722	2,819	115,042	78,094	50,388	2,438
Texas	423,647	419,355	105,376	6,117	417,431	419,420	109,724	5,950
Utah	79,554	29,039	36,405	1,198	80,088	30,472	35,505	1,259
Vermont	15,873	4,632	14,717	187	15,835	4,635	14,394	201
Virginia	162,432	130,733	56,440	4,544	164,782	128,345	57,917	4,875
Washington	85,523	159,249	37,781	2,109	86,080	160,555	36,950	2,234
West Virginia	68,912	7,208	10,768	853	67,877	6,980	10,391	786
Wisconsin	142,998	107,248	51,809	1,806	139,192	106,578	52,744	1,709
Wyoming	12,022	17,993	—	667	11,361	18,059	—	756
U.S. Service Schools	18,832	33,107	—	—	18,840	69,611	—	—
Outlying areas	57,588	13,329	87,311	12,458	62,568	14,482	97,712	8,895
American Samoa	—	1,249	—	—	—	1,232	—	—
Federated States of Micronesia	—	1,374	—	—	—	1,296	—	—
Guam	4,064	2,385	—	—	3,654	2,356	—	—
Marshall Islands	—	424	—	—	—	418	—	—
Northern Marianas	—	1,253	—	—	—	959	—	—
Palau	—	403	—	—	—	351	—	—
Puerto Rico	50,429	6,241	87,311	12,458	55,860	7,870	97,712	8,895
Virgin Islands	3,095	—	—	—	3,054	—	—	—

[1] Revised from previously published data.
[2] Preliminary data.
—Data not reported or not applicable.

SOURCE: U.S. Department of Education, National Center for Education Statistics, Integrated Postsecondary Education Data System (IPEDS), "Fall Enrollment" surveys. (This table was prepared April 1997.)

Table 197.—Total fall enrollment in institutions of higher education, by level of enrollment and state: 1993 to 1995

State or other area	Fall 1993[1]				Fall 1994[1]				Fall 1995[2]		
	Total	Under-graduate	First-professional	Graduate	Total	Under-graduate	First-professional	Graduate	Under-graduate	First-professional	Graduate
1	2	3	4	5	6	7	8	9	10	11	12
United States	**14,304,803**	**12,323,959**	**292,431**	**1,688,413**	**14,278,790**	**12,262,608**	**294,713**	**1,721,469**	**12,231,719**	**297,592**	**1,732,470**
Alabama	233,525	208,019	3,520	21,986	229,511	202,408	3,834	23,269	198,050	4,139	23,423
Alaska	30,638	29,047	—	1,591	28,798	27,189	—	1,609	27,657	—	1,691
Arizona	272,300	239,657	2,720	29,923	274,932	241,290	1,549	32,093	242,113	1,561	30,307
Arkansas	99,262	90,123	1,705	7,434	96,294	87,197	1,705	7,392	88,460	1,702	8,018
California	1,836,349	1,628,210	35,331	172,808	1,835,791	1,624,924	35,340	175,527	1,605,825	35,547	175,670
Colorado	239,805	200,368	3,183	36,254	241,295	201,110	3,206	36,979	201,005	3,130	38,604
Connecticut	162,300	128,063	3,309	30,928	159,990	125,939	3,394	30,657	124,063	3,416	30,216
Delaware	43,528	37,913	1,403	4,212	44,197	38,296	1,333	4,568	38,177	1,289	4,841
District of Columbia	81,565	47,666	8,732	25,167	77,726	43,623	8,819	24,814	43,365	9,068	24,844
Florida	623,403	554,662	8,693	60,048	634,237	562,961	8,653	62,623	564,635	9,284	63,384
Georgia	302,844	259,718	8,970	34,156	308,587	263,604	9,595	35,388	267,900	10,060	36,752
Hawaii	62,871	54,512	516	7,843	64,322	55,850	495	7,977	54,901	498	7,799
Idaho	58,768	51,651	509	6,608	60,393	51,783	559	8,051	51,978	529	7,059
Illinois	734,089	621,576	16,817	95,696	731,420	617,549	17,173	96,698	601,745	17,368	98,741
Indiana	294,685	255,747	5,470	33,468	292,276	252,801	5,513	33,962	249,847	5,339	34,429
Iowa	172,797	149,762	6,580	16,455	172,450	149,331	6,650	16,469	151,082	6,568	16,185
Kansas	170,135	148,164	2,129	19,842	170,603	148,046	2,075	20,482	155,852	2,074	19,717
Kentucky	187,332	163,460	4,946	18,926	182,577	158,177	4,512	19,888	153,840	4,647	20,371
Louisiana	201,987	171,195	6,071	24,721	203,567	172,561	6,102	24,904	171,941	6,129	25,865
Maine	56,294	50,391	663	5,240	56,724	50,274	667	5,783	49,730	681	6,136
Maryland	268,005	223,272	3,900	40,833	266,214	220,535	4,173	41,506	218,536	4,410	43,364
Massachusetts	420,127	329,593	13,421	77,113	416,505	323,868	13,283	79,354	319,541	13,450	80,803
Michigan	568,210	490,372	11,361	66,477	551,307	474,357	10,681	66,269	470,493	10,719	67,127
Minnesota	268,118	231,090	7,082	29,946	289,300	251,649	5,838	31,813	242,048	6,085	32,683
Mississippi	122,408	109,959	1,779	10,670	120,884	108,003	1,895	10,986	109,298	1,759	11,633
Missouri	297,062	251,661	10,050	35,351	293,810	247,484	10,208	36,118	242,876	9,370	39,290
Montana	39,557	35,945	223	3,389	40,095	36,414	235	3,446	39,113	236	3,325
Nebraska	115,523	101,048	3,159	11,316	116,000	100,482	3,219	12,299	100,107	3,165	12,446
Nevada	63,947	57,227	202	6,518	64,085	57,103	218	6,764	60,398	211	7,217
New Hampshire	64,043	54,884	484	8,675	62,847	53,154	724	8,969	54,114	702	9,511
New Jersey	343,029	293,162	6,512	43,355	335,480	286,020	6,588	42,872	284,552	6,611	42,668
New Mexico	101,460	88,301	649	12,510	101,881	88,643	625	12,613	88,793	635	12,977
New York	1,062,924	865,052	27,393	170,479	1,057,841	856,719	27,707	173,415	841,352	27,783	172,431
North Carolina	371,280	331,937	6,196	33,147	369,386	327,812	6,525	35,049	329,893	6,663	35,474
North Dakota	40,316	37,226	497	2,593	40,184	37,016	483	2,685	37,183	447	2,769
Ohio	562,402	484,422	12,304	65,676	549,304	471,266	12,321	65,717	461,524	12,500	66,251
Oklahoma	183,342	157,413	3,349	22,580	185,174	159,288	3,582	22,304	154,949	3,481	22,246
Oregon	165,834	146,370	4,013	15,451	164,447	144,583	3,559	16,305	147,444	3,653	16,048
Pennsylvania	621,228	524,312	15,190	81,726	611,174	513,257	15,462	82,455	520,371	15,626	81,762
Rhode Island	77,407	67,598	324	9,485	74,718	64,743	655	9,320	64,072	820	9,208
South Carolina	174,302	149,183	2,470	22,649	173,070	148,120	2,369	22,581	148,808	2,423	22,894
South Dakota	38,166	33,573	516	4,077	37,764	33,281	512	3,971	32,160	637	3,898
Tennessee	244,936	214,249	5,451	25,236	242,966	211,374	5,766	25,826	213,842	5,619	26,501
Texas	942,178	822,359	17,017	102,802	954,495	832,145	19,194	103,156	830,381	19,463	102,681
Utah	138,139	125,984	1,247	10,908	146,196	132,211	1,250	12,735	134,213	1,253	11,752
Vermont	36,415	31,228	885	4,302	35,409	30,459	898	4,052	30,488	890	3,687
Virginia	348,535	296,858	6,396	45,281	354,149	300,598	6,419	47,132	300,612	6,461	48,846
Washington	279,845	254,630	3,285	21,930	284,662	257,746	3,307	23,609	259,928	3,596	22,295
West Virginia	88,852	75,138	1,413	12,301	87,741	74,844	1,384	11,513	73,845	1,397	10,792
Wisconsin	309,036	274,280	3,509	31,247	303,861	269,548	3,568	30,745	267,273	3,605	29,345
Wyoming	30,702	27,713	224	2,765	30,682	27,771	232	2,679	27,620	225	2,331
U.S. Service Schools	52,998	48,016	663	4,319	51,939	47,202	659	4,078	83,620	668	4,163
Outlying areas	172,989	158,854	3,256	10,879	170,686	155,093	2,691	12,902	168,107	2,890	12,660
American Samoa	1,264	1,264	—	—	1,249	1,249	—	—	1,232	—	—
Federated States of Micronesia	1,148	1,148	—	—	1,374	1,374	—	—	1,296	—	—
Guam	5,843	5,522	—	321	6,449	6,052	—	397	5,644	—	366
Marshall Islands	386	386	—	—	424	424	—	—	418	—	—
Northern Marianas	1,261	1,261	—	—	1,253	1,253	—	—	959	—	—
Palau	436	436	—	—	403	403	—	—	351	—	—
Puerto Rico	159,709	146,164	3,256	10,289	156,439	141,543	2,691	12,205	155,430	2,890	12,017
Virgin Islands	2,942	2,673	—	269	3,095	2,795	—	300	2,777	—	277

[1] Revised from previously published data.
[2] Preliminary data.
—Data not reported or not applicable.

SOURCE: U.S. Department of Education, National Center for Education Statistics, Integrated Postsecondary Education Data System (IPEDS), "Fall Enrollment" survey. (This table was prepared April 1997.)

Table 198.—Total fall enrollment in institutions of higher education, by control, level of enrollment, and state: 1995[1]

State or other area	Public					Private				
	Undergraduate			First-pro-fessional	Graduate	Undergraduate			First-pro-fessional	Graduate
	Total	4-year	2-year			Total	4-year	2-year		
1	2	3	4	5	6	7	8	9	10	11
United States	9,903,626	4,626,228	5,277,398	115,072	1,073,676	2,328,093	2,113,393	214,700	182,520	658,794
Alabama	179,073	102,416	76,657	2,282	21,810	18,977	18,479	498	1,857	1,613
Alaska	26,878	26,066	812	—	1,490	779	575	204	—	201
Arizona	228,108	75,296	152,812	1,561	24,861	14,005	13,116	889	—	5,446
Arkansas	77,654	53,396	24,258	1,702	7,711	10,806	10,360	446	—	307
California	1,461,528	387,529	1,073,999	7,866	94,836	144,297	130,240	14,057	27,681	80,834
Colorado	179,961	102,265	77,696	1,784	28,567	21,044	17,421	3,623	1,346	10,037
Connecticut	84,780	41,952	42,828	1,161	14,598	39,283	37,721	1,562	2,255	15,618
Delaware	32,707	21,043	11,664	—	3,497	5,470	5,470	—	1,289	1,344
District of Columbia	9,179	9,179	—	—	484	34,186	34,186	—	9,068	24,360
Florida	486,639	162,993	323,646	3,411	40,557	77,996	72,565	5,431	5,873	22,827
Georgia	217,773	129,516	88,257	3,076	27,833	50,127	45,577	4,550	6,984	8,919
Hawaii	43,651	16,798	26,853	453	6,094	11,250	11,250	—	45	1,705
Idaho	41,777	34,240	7,537	529	6,680	10,201	1,929	8,272	—	379
Illinois	479,731	142,015	337,716	4,397	46,120	122,014	117,744	4,270	12,971	52,621
Indiana	193,364	152,753	40,611	3,529	27,902	56,483	52,994	3,489	1,810	6,527
Iowa	106,854	50,299	56,555	2,811	12,731	44,228	43,113	1,115	3,757	3,454
Kansas	140,376	66,697	73,679	2,005	18,068	15,476	14,598	878	69	1,649
Kentucky	128,633	85,354	43,279	2,990	17,185	25,207	22,539	2,668	1,657	3,186
Louisiana	151,350	124,397	26,953	2,631	20,892	20,591	19,413	1,178	3,498	4,973
Maine	34,057	27,137	6,920	286	3,852	15,673	13,758	1,915	395	2,284
Maryland	194,618	85,499	109,119	3,593	24,646	23,918	22,732	1,186	817	18,718
Massachusetts	157,775	82,812	74,963	423	18,579	161,766	153,713	8,053	13,027	62,224
Michigan	397,593	194,199	203,394	6,615	58,182	72,900	70,255	2,645	4,104	8,945
Minnesota	198,113	98,052	100,061	2,612	16,524	43,935	39,778	4,157	3,473	16,159
Mississippi	99,430	47,677	51,753	1,212	9,958	9,868	9,056	812	547	1,675
Missouri	169,460	97,338	72,122	2,441	18,092	73,416	68,819	4,597	6,929	21,198
Montana	34,020	27,997	6,023	236	3,179	5,093	4,173	920	—	146
Nebraska	83,346	45,828	37,518	1,345	10,908	16,761	16,217	544	1,820	1,538
Nevada	59,581	23,729	35,852	211	6,891	817	790	27	—	326
New Hampshire	32,122	22,550	9,572	—	3,947	21,992	17,961	4,031	702	5,564
New Jersey	240,280	107,040	133,240	3,593	27,196	44,272	39,555	4,717	3,018	15,472
New Mexico	84,537	37,136	47,401	635	12,048	4,256	3,302	954	—	929
New York	523,666	270,903	252,763	4,760	60,065	317,686	289,676	28,010	23,023	112,366
North Carolina	272,390	126,705	145,685	2,604	28,105	57,503	56,020	1,483	4,059	7,369
North Dakota	33,726	25,312	8,414	447	2,637	3,457	3,202	255	—	132
Ohio	355,683	208,332	147,351	7,722	46,413	105,841	92,499	13,342	4,778	19,838
Oklahoma	137,601	74,962	62,639	2,045	18,380	17,348	15,319	2,029	1,436	3,866
Oregon	130,049	49,488	80,561	1,200	12,368	17,395	17,226	169	2,453	3,680
Pennsylvania	297,548	191,053	106,495	4,416	37,964	222,823	165,261	57,562	11,210	43,798
Rhode Island	33,619	17,730	15,889	15	5,019	30,453	28,027	2,426	805	4,189
South Carolina	125,825	64,932	60,893	1,876	21,005	22,983	21,688	1,295	547	1,889
South Dakota	25,660	25,451	209	533	3,500	6,500	6,267	233	104	398
Tennessee	170,622	92,528	78,094	2,749	19,765	43,220	40,782	2,438	2,870	6,736
Texas	744,492	325,072	419,420	9,829	82,530	85,889	79,939	5,950	9,634	20,151
Utah	101,576	71,104	30,472	785	8,199	32,743	31,484	1,259	468	3,553
Vermont	18,559	13,924	4,635	377	1,534	11,929	11,728	201	513	2,153
Virginia	248,866	120,521	128,345	4,376	39,885	51,746	46,871	4,875	2,085	8,961
Washington	231,917	71,362	160,555	1,831	12,887	28,011	25,777	2,234	1,765	9,408
West Virginia	63,108	56,128	6,980	1,397	10,352	10,737	9,951	786	—	440
Wisconsin	223,287	116,709	106,578	1,827	20,656	43,986	42,277	1,709	1,778	8,689
Wyoming	26,864	8,805	18,059	225	2,331	756	—	756	—	—
U.S. Service Schools	83,620	14,009	69,611	668	4,163	—	—	—	—	—
Outlying areas	70,515	56,033	14,482	1,114	5,421	97,592	88,697	8,895	1,776	7,239
American Samoa	1,232	—	1,232	—	—	—	—	—	—	—
Federated States of Micronesia	1,296	—	1,296	—	—	—	—	—	—	—
Guam	5,644	3,288	2,356	—	366	—	—	—	—	—
Marshall Islands	418	—	418	—	—	—	—	—	—	—
Northern Marianas	959	—	959	—	—	—	—	—	—	—
Palau	351	—	351	—	—	—	—	—	—	—
Puerto Rico	57,838	49,968	7,870	1,114	4,778	97,592	88,697	8,895	1,776	7,239
Virgin Islands	2,777	2,777	—	—	277	—	—	—	—	—

[1] Preliminary data.
—Data not reported or not applicable.

SOURCE: U.S. Department of Education, National Center for Education Statistics, Integrated Postsecondary Education Data System (IPEDS), "Fall Enrollment, 1995" survey. (This table was prepared April 1997.)

Table 199.—Total fall enrollment in institutions of higher education, by control, level of enrollment, and state: 1994[1]

State or other area	Public					Private				
	Undergraduate			First-pro-fessional	Graduate	Undergraduate			First-pro-fessional	Graduate
	Total	4-year	2-year			Total	4-year	2-year		
1	2	3	4	5	6	7	8	9	10	11
United States	9,945,128	4,636,762	5,308,366	113,997	1,074,555	2,317,480	2,096,237	221,243	180,716	646,914
Alabama	182,503	102,036	80,467	2,315	21,728	19,905	18,549	1,356	1,519	1,541
Alaska	26,239	25,645	594	—	1,392	950	611	339	—	217
Arizona	225,991	75,225	150,766	1,549	24,644	15,299	14,370	929	—	7,449
Arkansas	76,743	55,682	21,061	1,705	7,153	10,454	10,108	346	—	239
California	1,480,506	381,001	1,099,505	7,879	94,452	144,418	130,752	13,666	27,461	81,075
Colorado	180,120	103,151	76,969	1,773	27,824	20,990	17,636	3,354	1,433	9,155
Connecticut	86,884	42,301	44,583	1,172	14,394	39,055	37,282	1,773	2,222	16,263
Delaware	32,839	21,483	11,356	—	3,483	5,457	5,457	—	1,333	1,085
District of Columbia	10,004	10,004	—	—	595	33,619	33,619	—	8,819	24,219
Florida	484,380	157,598	326,782	3,296	40,348	78,581	73,601	4,980	5,357	22,275
Georgia	213,503	127,041	86,462	3,029	27,323	50,101	43,928	6,173	6,566	8,065
Hawaii	44,678	16,773	27,905	450	6,518	11,172	11,172	—	45	1,459
Idaho	41,484	34,119	7,365	559	6,951	10,299	1,888	8,411	—	1,100
Illinois	495,208	143,739	351,469	4,364	46,386	122,341	116,238	6,103	12,809	50,312
Indiana	196,811	155,127	41,684	3,530	27,929	55,990	52,341	3,649	1,983	6,033
Iowa	106,200	49,800	56,400	2,808	13,009	43,131	41,740	1,391	3,842	3,460
Kansas	132,289	65,776	66,513	2,023	18,486	15,757	14,840	917	52	1,996
Kentucky	131,985	86,669	45,316	2,852	16,738	26,192	21,686	4,506	1,660	3,150
Louisiana	152,312	124,310	28,002	2,645	20,155	20,249	19,045	1,204	3,457	4,749
Maine	35,102	27,813	7,289	268	3,818	15,172	13,300	1,872	399	1,965
Maryland	196,203	84,761	111,442	3,355	24,134	24,332	23,191	1,141	818	17,372
Massachusetts	160,901	82,898	78,003	422	18,476	162,967	148,498	14,469	12,861	60,878
Michigan	401,826	193,175	208,651	6,608	58,324	72,531	70,068	2,463	4,073	7,945
Minnesota	207,720	99,938	107,782	2,520	16,775	43,929	39,541	4,388	3,318	15,038
Mississippi	97,507	46,616	50,891	1,200	9,691	10,496	9,441	1,055	695	1,295
Missouri	172,048	97,550	74,498	2,466	17,345	75,436	69,570	5,866	7,742	18,773
Montana	31,361	27,038	4,323	235	3,331	5,053	4,280	773	—	115
Nebraska	83,460	45,590	37,870	1,421	10,996	17,022	16,597	425	1,798	1,303
Nevada	56,459	24,521	31,938	218	6,594	644	617	27	—	170
New Hampshire	31,486	22,813	8,673	—	3,502	21,668	17,820	3,848	724	5,467
New Jersey	241,849	106,083	135,766	3,536	27,035	44,171	40,190	3,981	3,052	15,837
New Mexico	84,582	38,309	46,273	625	11,866	4,061	3,410	651	—	747
New York	538,260	279,029	259,231	4,733	61,440	318,459	289,759	28,700	22,974	111,975
North Carolina	273,034	125,830	147,204	2,645	27,970	54,778	52,244	2,534	3,880	7,079
North Dakota	33,576	25,238	8,338	483	2,580	3,440	3,194	246	—	105
Ohio	363,892	214,144	149,748	7,554	46,120	107,374	92,909	14,465	4,767	19,597
Oklahoma	140,615	76,138	64,477	2,118	19,015	18,673	16,015	2,658	1,464	3,289
Oregon	127,125	48,749	78,376	1,135	12,767	17,458	17,290	168	2,424	3,538
Pennsylvania	300,209	188,991	111,218	4,449	37,907	213,048	164,760	48,288	11,013	44,548
Rhode Island	34,077	18,076	16,001	5	5,294	30,666	28,535	2,131	650	4,026
South Carolina	125,742	64,602	61,140	1,888	20,884	22,378	20,892	1,486	481	1,697
South Dakota	26,849	26,652	197	418	3,713	6,432	6,221	211	94	258
Tennessee	168,981	91,707	77,274	2,888	19,556	42,393	39,574	2,819	2,878	6,270
Texas	749,620	330,265	419,355	9,800	83,582	82,525	76,408	6,117	9,394	19,574
Utah	99,180	70,141	29,039	762	8,651	33,031	31,833	1,198	488	4,084
Vermont	18,529	13,897	4,632	374	1,602	11,930	11,743	187	524	2,450
Virginia	250,242	119,509	130,733	4,227	38,696	50,356	45,812	4,544	2,192	8,436
Washington	230,132	70,883	159,249	1,632	13,008	27,614	25,505	2,109	1,675	10,601
West Virginia	63,636	56,428	7,208	1,384	11,100	11,208	10,355	853	—	413
Wisconsin	225,940	118,692	107,248	1,788	22,518	43,608	41,802	1,806	1,780	8,227
Wyoming	27,104	9,111	17,993	232	2,679	667	—	667	—	—
U.S. Service Schools	47,202	14,095	33,107	659	4,078	—	—	—	—	—
Outlying areas	64,849	51,520	13,329	1,124	4,944	90,244	77,786	12,458	1,567	7,958
American Samoa	1,249	—	1,249	—	—	—	—	—	—	—
Federated States of Micronesia	1,374	—	1,374	—	—	—	—	—	—	—
Guam	6,052	3,667	2,385	—	397	—	—	—	—	—
Marshall Islands	424	—	424	—	—	—	—	—	—	—
Northern Marianas	1,253	—	1,253	—	—	—	—	—	—	—
Palau	403	—	403	—	—	—	—	—	—	—
Puerto Rico	51,299	45,058	6,241	1,124	4,247	90,244	77,786	12,458	1,567	7,958
Virgin Islands	2,795	2,795	—	—	300	—	—	—	—	—

[1] Revised from previously published data.
—Data not reported or not applicable.

SOURCE: U.S. Department of Education, National Center for Education Statistics, Integrated Postsecondary Education Data System (IPEDS), "Fall Enrollment, 1994" survey. (This table was prepared April 1997.)

208 HIGHER EDUCATION: ENROLLMENT

Table 200.—Full-time-equivalent fall enrollment in institutions of higher education, by control and type of institution: 1969 to 1995

Year	All institutions			Public institutions			Private institutions		
	Total	4-year	2-year	Total	4-year	2-year	Total	4-year	2-year
1	2	3	4	5	6	7	8	9	10
1969	6,334,139	4,899,526	1,434,612	4,577,985	3,259,676	1,318,309	1,756,153	1,639,850	116,303
1970	6,737,817	5,145,410	1,592,404	4,953,149	3,468,572	1,484,577	1,784,665	1,676,838	107,827
1971	7,148,575	5,357,708	1,790,867	5,344,356	3,660,624	1,683,732	1,804,219	1,697,084	107,135
1972	7,253,712	5,406,792	1,846,921	5,452,851	3,706,238	1,746,613	1,800,862	1,700,554	100,308
1973	7,453,467	5,439,226	2,014,241	5,629,568	3,721,035	1,908,533	1,823,899	1,718,191	105,708
1974	7,805,454	5,606,248	2,199,206	5,944,799	3,847,542	2,097,257	1,860,655	1,758,706	101,949
1975	8,479,688	5,900,403	2,579,285	6,522,310	4,056,500	2,465,810	1,957,378	1,843,903	113,475
1976	8,312,502	5,848,001	2,464,501	6,349,903	3,998,450	2,351,453	1,962,599	1,849,551	113,048
1977	8,415,339	5,935,076	2,480,263	6,396,476	4,039,071	2,357,405	2,018,863	1,896,005	122,858
1978	8,348,482	5,932,357	2,416,125	6,279,199	3,996,126	2,283,073	2,069,283	1,936,231	133,052
1979	8,487,317	6,016,072	2,471,245	6,392,617	4,059,304	2,333,313	2,094,700	1,956,768	137,932
1980	8,819,013	6,161,372	2,657,641	6,642,294	4,158,267	2,484,027	2,176,719	2,003,105	[1]173,614
1981	9,014,521	6,249,847	2,764,674	6,781,300	4,208,506	2,572,794	2,233,221	2,041,341	[1]191,880
1982	9,091,648	6,248,923	2,842,725	6,850,589	4,220,648	2,629,941	2,241,059	2,028,275	212,784
1983	9,166,398	6,325,222	2,841,176	6,881,479	4,265,807	2,615,672	2,284,919	2,059,415	225,504
1984	8,951,695	6,292,711	2,658,984	6,684,664	4,237,895	2,446,769	2,267,031	2,054,816	212,215
1985	8,943,433	6,294,339	2,649,094	6,667,781	4,239,622	2,428,159	2,275,652	2,054,717	220,935
1986	9,064,165	6,360,325	2,703,842	6,778,045	4,295,494	2,482,551	2,286,122	2,064,831	[2]221,291
1987	9,229,736	6,486,504	2,743,230	6,937,690	4,395,728	2,541,961	2,292,045	2,090,776	201,269
1988	9,464,271	6,664,146	2,800,125	7,096,905	4,505,774	2,591,131	2,367,366	2,158,372	208,994
1989	9,780,881	6,813,602	2,967,279	7,371,590	4,619,828	2,751,762	2,409,291	2,193,774	215,517
1990	9,983,436	6,968,008	3,015,428	7,557,982	4,740,049	2,817,933	2,425,454	2,227,959	197,495
1991	10,360,606	7,081,454	3,279,152	7,862,845	4,795,704	3,067,141	2,497,761	2,285,750	212,011
1992	10,436,776	7,129,379	3,307,397	7,911,701	4,797,884	3,113,817	2,525,075	2,331,495	193,580
1993	10,351,415	7,120,921	3,230,494	7,812,394	4,765,983	3,046,411	2,539,021	2,354,938	184,083
1994	10,348,072	7,137,341	3,210,731	7,784,396	4,749,524	3,034,872	2,563,676	2,387,817	175,859
1995[3]	10,334,956	7,172,844	3,162,112	7,751,815	4,757,223	2,994,592	2,583,141	2,415,621	167,520

[1] Large increases are due to the addition of schools accredited by the Accrediting Commission of Career Schools and Colleges of Technology in 1980 and 1981.
[2] Because of imputation techniques, data are not consistent with figures for other years.
[3] Preliminary data.

NOTE.—Because of a revision in data compilation procedures, figures for 1986 and later years are not directly comparable with data for earlier years.

SOURCE: U.S. Department of Education, National Center for Education Statistics, Higher Education General Information Survey (HEGIS), "Fall Enrollment in Colleges and Universities" surveys; and Integrated Postsecondary Education Data System (IPEDS), "Fall Enrollment" surveys. (This table was prepared January 1997.)

Table 201.—Full-time-equivalent fall enrollment in institutions of higher education, by control, type of institution, and state: 1993 to 1995

State or other area	Public 4-year			Public 2-year			Private 4-year			Private 2-year		
	1993[1]	1994[1]	1995[2]	1993	1994	1995[2]	1993	1994	1995[2]	1993	1994	1995[2]
1	2	3	4	5	6	7	8	9	10	11	12	13
United States	4,765,983	4,749,524	4,757,223	3,046,411	3,034,872	2,994,592	2,354,938	2,387,817	2,415,621	184,083	175,859	167,520
Alabama	105,089	103,200	104,189	56,950	56,255	54,564	19,224	19,485	19,533	1,750	1,231	450
Alaska	18,072	17,810	17,823	253	244	326	1,004	622	588	238	303	167
Arizona	78,324	82,558	83,010	76,627	76,262	76,822	22,320	19,129	16,658	1,077	929	889
Arkansas	55,685	54,540	53,057	14,074	13,281	15,177	9,599	9,666	9,975	951	346	349
California	417,202	413,527	421,100	577,405	575,613	563,047	178,651	199,213	199,346	13,271	12,344	12,886
Colorado	104,399	104,474	104,521	40,444	40,104	40,332	18,942	21,477	21,702	3,867	3,121	3,442
Connecticut	45,083	43,582	43,441	22,805	22,303	21,322	42,414	43,398	43,831	1,163	1,188	1,157
Delaware	20,946	20,982	20,533	6,349	6,529	6,705	5,182	5,232	5,298	—	—	—
District of Columbia	6,583	6,495	5,950	—	—	—	56,151	53,802	55,068	—	—	—
Florida	147,729	155,232	160,046	180,327	179,177	176,817	79,769	80,234	80,301	4,454	4,884	5,123
Georgia	126,594	128,563	132,111	54,825	55,739	56,843	50,329	52,189	55,179	5,685	5,319	4,132
Hawaii	19,311	19,437	19,158	16,025	16,692	16,222	9,287	9,485	9,916	—	—	—
Idaho	31,449	32,237	32,161	5,007	5,218	5,265	2,141	2,252	1,998	8,522	8,280	8,122
Illinois	163,884	161,500	159,900	191,411	190,946	183,337	139,625	141,160	144,744	5,819	5,421	3,784
Indiana	151,282	147,844	146,709	23,954	24,279	23,310	53,004	53,673	54,658	2,953	2,997	2,866
Iowa	58,156	57,556	57,870	39,833	39,735	39,829	40,644	40,905	41,377	1,930	1,212	926
Kansas	73,783	71,257	71,592	36,132	37,568	39,813	12,663	14,166	13,756	819	784	735
Kentucky	88,286	87,211	86,774	30,565	29,039	28,227	22,256	22,331	22,965	4,618	4,153	2,361
Louisiana	123,798	124,883	125,563	17,155	17,595	17,057	23,050	23,195	23,442	602	985	754
Maine	24,035	23,461	22,812	4,593	4,549	4,369	11,545	11,945	12,364	1,506	1,602	1,655
Maryland	85,869	86,578	87,997	59,917	58,471	57,419	28,575	29,393	30,193	870	937	1,032
Massachusetts	79,000	78,686	78,616	48,436	47,035	44,938	184,779	184,199	189,336	9,592	9,506	5,997
Michigan	209,703	205,800	206,495	114,289	108,182	103,720	62,076	61,100	61,116	1,971	1,614	1,728
Minnesota	91,811	89,990	88,696	55,659	67,471	62,765	46,201	47,395	48,406	3,833	3,521	3,263
Mississippi	51,147	50,417	51,561	41,568	40,669	41,384	9,928	9,425	9,400	1,107	960	722
Missouri	97,160	95,401	94,930	44,231	41,935	40,677	69,802	71,773	73,005	5,150	4,934	3,939
Montana	26,678	26,857	27,724	2,992	3,294	4,607	3,556	3,652	3,597	571	529	600
Nebraska	48,511	47,248	47,537	18,634	20,129	19,711	16,285	16,682	16,627	443	338	403
Nevada	21,318	21,963	21,806	13,807	13,855	15,191	559	598	967	25	27	27
New Hampshire	21,763	21,962	21,960	5,316	5,025	5,136	18,876	18,603	18,845	3,108	2,952	3,122
New Jersey	103,462	102,204	103,590	83,472	81,903	81,176	45,114	44,368	44,052	3,435	3,295	3,851
New Mexico	41,227	39,973	39,186	25,099	25,126	25,717	2,214	3,550	3,671	566	651	954
New York	268,270	272,066	265,171	182,769	180,543	175,517	343,641	339,369	339,528	27,827	26,016	25,311
North Carolina	131,718	132,091	132,949	91,489	91,727	91,106	58,064	56,789	60,326	2,538	2,241	1,327
North Dakota	25,257	25,055	25,147	6,592	6,642	6,792	3,094	3,038	3,091	264	242	249
Ohio	228,303	223,580	219,518	92,358	88,888	87,324	95,266	95,994	96,059	10,381	9,586	8,909
Oklahoma	77,877	78,501	77,450	38,250	38,063	37,142	17,652	18,138	17,675	1,948	2,459	1,909
Oregon	52,787	52,916	53,445	46,522	44,748	42,866	19,345	19,949	20,115	182	163	158
Pennsylvania	200,053	198,056	200,590	67,024	64,045	61,233	179,371	179,269	179,812	29,184	28,926	32,634
Rhode Island	18,836	18,015	17,634	8,696	8,524	8,490	29,658	28,720	28,583	2,025	1,930	2,149
South Carolina	71,698	71,132	71,984	37,219	37,571	37,475	21,103	20,849	21,694	1,748	1,343	1,200
South Dakota	26,215	25,822	24,753	171	158	172	5,336	5,384	5,487	128	143	143
Tennessee	94,910	93,976	95,789	47,353	46,958	46,996	43,144	44,083	45,903	2,846	2,425	2,018
Texas	339,313	339,801	337,321	233,900	237,787	237,117	86,388	87,907	91,399	4,875	5,987	5,641
Utah	58,244	61,636	62,683	17,260	18,453	19,369	33,985	33,661	33,170	1,085	1,079	1,146
Vermont	13,415	13,765	13,715	2,479	1,834	1,885	12,729	12,390	12,301	161	163	178
Virginia	136,339	136,115	138,030	68,650	67,688	66,674	42,023	46,742	46,992	3,698	3,744	4,016
Washington	76,501	77,461	78,111	96,449	101,499	103,132	29,432	30,620	30,744	1,988	1,938	2,063
West Virginia	56,628	55,841	55,159	4,840	4,930	4,792	8,860	9,349	9,104	944	846	776
Wisconsin	123,700	122,297	121,755	65,297	59,860	58,958	40,082	41,269	41,724	1,665	1,598	1,501
Wyoming	9,976	10,116	9,752	11,364	11,318	11,430	—	—	—	700	667	756
U.S. Service Schools	18,604	17,854	17,849	19,575	19,413	24,297	—	—	—	—	—	—
Outlying areas	48,931	49,518	54,519	9,021	9,886	11,238	77,146	73,595	81,801	11,393	10,161	7,806
American Samoa	—	—	—	1,007	998	988	—	—	—	—	—	—
Federated States of Micronesia	—	—	—	743	1,040	1,076	—	—	—	—	—	—
Guam	2,908	3,159	2,787	912	1,049	1,032	—	—	—	—	—	—
Marshall Islands	—	—	—	374	254	249	—	—	—	—	—	—
Northern Marianas	—	—	—	653	653	625	—	—	—	—	—	—
Palau	—	—	—	377	357	296	—	—	—	—	—	—
Puerto Rico	44,107	44,321	49,679	4,955	5,535	6,972	77,146	73,595	81,801	11,393	10,161	7,806
Virgin Islands	1,916	2,038	2,053	—	—	—	—	—	—	—	—	—

[1] Revised from previously published data.
[2] Preliminary data.
—Data not reported or not applicable.

SOURCE: U.S. Department of Education, National Center for Education Statistics, Integrated Postsecondary Education Data System (IPEDS), "Fall Enrollment" surveys. (This table was prepared April 1997.)

Table 202.—Full-time-equivalent fall enrollment in institutions of higher education, by control and state: 1980 to 1995

State or other area	Total					Public			Private		
	1980	1985	1990	1994	1995[1]	1990	1994	1995[1]	1990	1994	1995[1]
1	2	3	4	5	6	7	8	9	10	11	12
United States	8,819,013	8,943,433	9,983,436	10,348,072	10,334,956	7,557,982	7,784,396	7,751,815	2,425,454	2,563,676	2,583,141
Alabama	138,910	149,895	174,610	180,171	178,736	154,343	159,455	158,753	20,267	20,716	19,983
Alaska	10,073	14,098	18,496	18,979	18,904	17,087	18,054	18,149	1,409	925	755
Arizona	127,114	134,954	167,617	178,878	177,379	153,500	158,820	159,832	14,117	20,058	17,547
Arkansas	64,307	63,230	74,449	77,833	78,558	63,472	67,821	68,234	10,977	10,012	10,324
California	1,099,559	1,062,439	1,156,288	1,200,697	1,196,379	979,663	989,140	984,147	176,625	211,557	212,232
Colorado	123,589	121,804	159,032	169,176	169,997	138,350	144,578	144,853	20,682	24,598	25,144
Connecticut	112,612	107,803	115,791	110,471	109,751	70,870	65,885	64,763	44,921	44,586	44,988
Delaware	26,284	25,750	31,612	32,743	32,536	26,059	27,511	27,238	5,553	5,232	5,298
District of Columbia	62,126	58,945	61,549	60,297	61,018	7,294	6,495	5,950	54,255	53,802	55,068
Florida	290,647	308,315	383,385	419,527	422,287	302,579	334,409	336,863	80,806	85,118	85,424
Georgia	152,369	161,952	198,549	241,810	248,265	149,115	184,302	188,954	49,434	57,508	59,311
Hawaii	35,859	36,986	41,097	45,614	45,296	32,496	36,129	35,380	8,601	9,485	9,916
Idaho	33,938	32,649	41,275	47,987	47,546	31,408	37,455	37,426	9,867	10,532	10,120
Illinois	432,365	450,504	493,364	499,027	491,765	353,247	352,446	343,237	140,117	146,581	148,528
Indiana	193,445	195,630	222,835	228,793	227,543	168,984	172,123	170,019	53,851	56,670	57,524
Iowa	120,083	128,492	138,565	139,408	140,002	95,772	97,291	97,699	42,793	42,117	42,303
Kansas	101,147	100,807	118,969	123,775	125,896	106,570	108,825	111,405	12,399	14,950	14,491
Kentucky	113,709	110,539	137,651	142,734	140,327	111,858	116,250	115,001	25,793	26,484	25,326
Louisiana	132,780	148,983	154,132	166,658	166,816	129,357	142,478	142,620	24,775	24,180	24,196
Maine	34,471	37,993	42,021	41,557	41,200	29,876	28,010	27,181	12,145	13,547	14,019
Maryland	149,202	148,091	169,972	175,379	176,641	141,950	145,049	145,416	28,022	30,330	31,225
Massachusetts	315,937	321,022	320,299	319,426	318,887	130,962	125,721	123,554	189,337	193,705	195,333
Michigan	366,058	354,690	389,814	376,696	373,059	326,952	313,982	310,215	62,862	62,714	62,844
Minnesota	162,559	170,958	190,608	208,377	203,130	143,424	157,461	151,461	47,184	50,916	51,669
Mississippi	85,621	86,846	103,957	101,471	103,067	92,269	91,086	92,945	11,688	10,385	10,122
Missouri	180,156	178,090	210,104	214,043	212,551	142,953	137,336	135,607	67,151	76,707	76,944
Montana	29,428	29,992	29,905	34,332	36,528	26,835	30,151	32,331	3,070	4,181	4,197
Nebraska	68,505	70,778	80,989	84,397	84,278	65,739	67,377	67,248	15,250	17,020	17,030
Nevada	22,467	23,093	33,814	36,443	37,991	33,392	35,818	36,997	422	625	994
New Hampshire	39,456	41,733	45,762	48,542	49,063	24,948	26,987	27,096	20,814	21,555	21,967
New Jersey	218,838	201,270	221,468	231,770	232,669	174,324	184,107	184,766	47,144	47,663	47,903
New Mexico	43,722	47,169	59,517	69,300	69,528	57,870	65,099	64,903	1,647	4,201	4,625
New York	760,305	763,596	798,696	817,994	805,527	446,379	452,609	440,688	352,317	365,385	364,839
North Carolina	235,266	249,901	269,025	282,848	285,708	208,321	223,818	224,055	60,704	59,030	61,653
North Dakota	30,188	32,456	33,118	34,977	35,279	30,276	31,697	31,939	2,842	3,280	3,340
Ohio	369,342	383,898	420,499	418,048	411,810	317,837	312,468	306,842	102,662	105,580	104,968
Oklahoma	115,701	126,691	128,203	137,161	134,176	108,933	116,564	114,592	19,270	20,597	19,584
Oregon	110,649	102,247	120,176	117,776	116,584	101,424	97,664	96,311	18,752	20,112	20,273
Pennsylvania	404,192	422,349	464,179	470,296	474,269	261,305	262,101	261,823	202,874	208,195	212,446
Rhode Island	50,628	53,016	60,168	57,189	56,856	28,804	26,539	26,124	31,364	30,650	30,732
South Carolina	109,346	109,303	127,225	130,895	132,353	101,918	108,703	109,459	25,307	22,192	22,894
South Dakota	27,873	26,988	28,256	31,507	30,555	22,128	25,980	24,925	6,128	5,527	5,630
Tennessee	161,058	152,967	175,961	187,442	190,706	130,184	140,934	142,785	45,777	46,508	47,921
Texas	527,724	566,736	637,742	671,482	671,478	553,436	577,588	574,438	84,306	93,894	97,040
Utah	78,199	84,095	94,012	114,829	116,368	63,495	80,089	82,052	30,517	34,740	34,316
Vermont	25,572	25,649	29,072	28,152	28,079	16,048	15,599	15,600	13,024	12,553	12,479
Virginia	199,549	204,928	251,708	254,289	255,712	202,285	203,803	204,704	49,423	50,486	51,008
Washington	194,440	171,668	189,521	211,518	214,050	160,889	178,960	181,243	28,632	32,558	32,807
West Virginia	60,394	58,438	68,235	70,966	69,831	59,229	60,771	59,951	9,006	10,195	9,880
Wisconsin	206,790	211,749	229,975	225,024	223,938	192,107	182,157	180,713	37,868	42,867	43,225
Wyoming	14,725	17,037	21,888	22,101	21,938	21,185	21,434	21,182	703	667	756
U.S. Service Schools	49,736	54,221	48,281	37,267	42,146	48,281	37,267	42,146	—	—	—
Outlying areas	117,637	145,530	140,954	143,160	155,115	55,908	59,404	65,757	85,046	83,756	89,607
American Samoa	824	497	952	998	988	952	998	988	—	—	—
Federated States of Micronesia	—	—	549	1,040	1,076	549	1,040	1,076	—	—	—
Guam	2,115	3,049	2,956	4,208	3,819	2,956	4,208	3,819	—	—	—
Marshall Islands	—	—	—	254	249	—	254	249	—	—	—
Northern Marianas	—	183	376	653	625	376	653	625	—	—	—
Palau	—	—	—	423	357	296	423	357	296	—	—
Puerto Rico	113,285	139,627	134,193	133,612	146,258	49,147	49,856	56,651	85,046	83,756	89,607
Trust Territory of the Pacific	195	680	—	—	—	—	—	—	—	—	—
Virgin Islands	1,218	1,494	1,505	2,038	2,053	1,505	2,038	2,053	—	—	—

[1] Preliminary data.
— Data not reported or not applicable.

SOURCE: U.S. Department of Education, National Center for Education Statistics, Integrated Postsecondary Education Data System (IPEDS), "Fall Enrollment" surveys. (This table was prepared January 1997.)

Table 203.—Residence and migration of all freshmen students [1] in institutions of higher education, by state: Fall 1994

State or other area	Students enrolled in institutions located in the state [2]	Student residents of state		Ratio of students remaining to—		Migration of students		
		Attending college in any state [3]	Attending college in home state [4]	Students enrolled (col.4 ÷ col.2)	Student residents (col.4 ÷ col.3)	Out of (col.3 − col.4)	Into (col.2 − col.4)	Net (col.8 − col.7)
1	2	3	4	5	6	7	8	9
United States	2,111,310	2,074,870	1,746,637	0.83	0.84	328,233	364,673	[5] 36,440
Alabama	41,542	36,857	34,230	0.82	0.93	2,627	7,312	4,685
Alaska	1,761	2,988	1,487	0.84	0.50	1,501	274	−1,227
Arizona	32,753	28,930	26,320	0.80	0.91	2,610	6,433	3,823
Arkansas	16,178	15,728	13,454	0.83	0.86	2,274	2,724	450
California	255,308	254,428	235,856	0.92	0.93	18,572	19,452	880
Colorado	32,113	29,359	24,109	0.75	0.82	5,250	8,004	2,754
Connecticut	21,524	25,887	14,699	0.68	0.57	11,188	6,825	−4,363
Delaware	6,921	5,523	4,074	0.59	0.74	1,449	2,847	1,398
District of Columbia	9,706	3,873	2,339	0.24	0.60	1,534	7,367	5,833
Florida	70,212	67,826	57,316	0.82	0.85	10,510	12,896	2,386
Georgia	58,991	56,829	49,857	0.85	0.88	6,972	9,134	2,162
Hawaii	10,279	10,314	8,320	0.81	0.81	1,994	1,959	−35
Idaho	10,646	9,770	7,738	0.73	0.79	2,032	2,908	876
Illinois	110,396	120,051	102,114	0.92	0.85	17,937	8,282	−9,655
Indiana	48,059	42,524	37,023	0.77	0.87	5,501	11,036	5,535
Iowa	35,229	31,425	27,737	0.79	0.88	3,688	7,492	3,804
Kansas	24,641	22,760	20,340	0.83	0.89	2,420	4,301	1,881
Kentucky	28,604	27,210	24,091	0.84	0.89	3,119	4,513	1,394
Louisiana	30,897	29,129	25,413	0.82	0.87	3,716	5,484	1,768
Maine	8,102	9,325	5,893	0.73	0.63	3,432	2,209	−1,223
Maryland	32,734	35,441	24,962	0.76	0.70	10,479	7,772	−2,707
Massachusetts	65,768	55,975	42,892	0.65	0.77	13,083	22,876	9,793
Michigan	83,446	84,143	76,823	0.92	0.91	7,320	6,623	−697
Minnesota	37,991	38,095	29,384	0.77	0.77	8,711	8,607	−104
Mississippi	25,862	24,510	22,349	0.86	0.91	2,161	3,513	1,352
Missouri	38,302	35,660	29,961	0.78	0.84	5,699	8,341	2,642
Montana	6,819	7,218	5,225	0.77	0.72	1,993	1,594	−399
Nebraska	16,616	16,499	13,883	0.84	0.84	2,616	2,733	117
Nevada	6,939	6,403	4,746	0.68	0.74	1,657	2,193	536
New Hampshire	11,373	9,306	5,569	0.49	0.60	3,737	5,804	2,067
New Jersey	43,063	63,725	39,376	0.91	0.62	24,349	3,687	−20,662
New Mexico	13,864	14,298	12,059	0.87	0.84	2,239	1,805	−434
New York	155,799	157,630	131,641	0.84	0.84	25,989	24,158	−1,831
North Carolina	51,346	42,659	39,256	0.76	0.92	3,403	12,090	8,687
North Dakota	8,122	7,048	5,544	0.68	0.79	1,504	2,578	1,074
Ohio	88,460	86,809	75,746	0.86	0.87	11,063	12,714	1,651
Oklahoma	29,345	28,797	26,032	0.89	0.90	2,765	3,313	548
Oregon	23,321	21,992	18,209	0.78	0.83	3,783	5,112	1,329
Pennsylvania	97,982	91,568	76,826	0.78	0.84	14,742	21,156	6,414
Rhode Island	12,645	7,958	5,524	0.44	0.69	2,434	7,121	4,687
South Carolina	28,532	26,626	23,547	0.83	0.88	3,079	4,985	1,906
South Dakota	6,600	6,038	4,543	0.69	0.75	1,495	2,057	562
Tennessee	33,870	31,499	26,715	0.79	0.85	4,784	7,155	2,371
Texas	127,166	124,774	114,927	0.90	0.92	9,847	12,239	2,392
Utah	24,383	19,396	18,096	0.74	0.93	1,300	6,287	4,987
Vermont	6,132	4,628	2,603	0.42	0.56	2,025	3,529	1,504
Virginia	45,272	41,227	33,012	0.73	0.80	8,215	12,260	4,045
Washington	68,604	65,507	60,346	0.88	0.92	5,161	8,258	3,097
West Virginia	15,799	13,816	11,725	0.74	0.85	2,091	4,074	1,983
Wisconsin	46,479	45,339	39,109	0.84	0.86	6,230	7,370	1,140
Wyoming	4,814	4,646	3,597	0.75	0.77	1,049	1,217	168
State unknown [6]	—	24,904	—	—	—	24,904	—	−24,904
Outlying areas	29,493	30,958	28,474	0.97	0.92	2,484	1,019	−1,465
American Samoa	—	53	—	—	—	53	—	−53
Federated States of Micronesia	410	1,322	409	1.00	0.31	913	1	−912
Guam	956	191	14	0.01	0.07	177	942	765
Marshall Islands	22	34	18	0.82	0.53	16	4	−12
Northern Marianas	440	450	440	1.00	0.98	10	—	−10
Palau	13	19	13	1.00	0.68	6	—	−6
Puerto Rico	27,276	28,121	27,221	1.00	0.97	900	55	−845
Virgin Islands	376	768	359	0.95	0.47	409	17	−392
Foreign countries	—	34,975	—	—	—	34,975	—	−34,975

[1] Students who are enrolled at the reporting institution for the first time.
[2] All of the new students reported by the institutions in that state; i.e., all in-migrants and "remaining" students.
[3] All students living in a particular state when admitted to an institution in any state. Students may be enrolled in any state.
[4] Students who attend institutions in their home state.
[5] Includes students coming to U.S. colleges from foreign countries and the outlying areas.
[6] Students are reported in "state unknown" when an institution is unable to determine the student's home state.
—Data not available or not applicable.

NOTE.—Data for U.S. Service Schools are included in state totals. Some data revised from previously published figures.

SOURCE: U.S. Department of Education, National Center for Education Statistics, Integrated Postsecondary Education Data System (IPEDS), "Residence of First-Time Students" survey, 1994. (This table was prepared October 1997.)

Table 204.—Residence and migration of all freshmen students[1] in institutions of higher education graduating from high school in the past 12 months, by state: Fall 1994

State or other area	Students enrolled in institutions located in the state[2]	Student residents of state		Ratio of students remaining to—		Migration of students		
		Attending college in any state[3]	Attending college in home state[4]	Students enrolled (col.4 ÷ col.2)	Student residents (col.4 ÷ col.3)	Out of (col.3 − col.4)	Into (col.2 − col.4)	Net (col.8 − col.7)
1	2	3	4	5	6	7	8	9
UNITED STATES	1,441,705	1,418,343	1,145,673	0.79	0.81	272,670	296,032	[5]23,362
Alabama	28,927	24,757	22,554	0.78	0.91	2,203	6,373	4,170
Alaska	1,198	2,227	997	0.83	0.45	1,230	201	−1,029
Arizona	17,850	15,160	13,002	0.73	0.86	2,158	4,848	2,690
Arkansas	12,734	12,535	10,689	0.84	0.85	1,846	2,045	199
California	167,374	168,806	153,097	0.91	0.91	15,709	14,277	−1,432
Colorado	18,410	17,432	12,773	0.69	0.73	4,659	5,637	978
Connecticut	15,055	19,343	9,011	0.60	0.47	10,332	6,044	−4,288
Delaware	5,504	4,124	2,818	0.51	0.68	1,306	2,686	1,380
District of Columbia	8,476	3,035	1,758	0.21	0.58	1,277	6,718	5,441
Florida	48,583	48,197	39,134	0.81	0.81	9,063	9,449	386
Georgia	38,246	36,792	30,746	0.80	0.84	6,046	7,500	1,454
Hawaii	5,944	6,943	5,188	0.87	0.75	1,755	756	−999
Idaho	7,316	6,545	4,860	0.66	0.74	1,685	2,456	771
Illinois	64,861	74,366	58,504	0.90	0.79	15,862	6,357	−9,505
Indiana	37,514	32,312	27,758	0.74	0.86	4,554	9,756	5,202
Iowa	24,063	20,980	17,769	0.74	0.85	3,211	6,294	3,083
Kansas	16,910	15,427	13,397	0.79	0.87	2,030	3,513	1,483
Kentucky	21,823	20,454	17,985	0.82	0.88	2,469	3,838	1,369
Louisiana	24,550	22,766	19,584	0.80	0.86	3,182	4,966	1,784
Maine	5,913	6,872	3,863	0.65	0.56	3,009	2,050	−959
Maryland	21,803	24,670	15,285	0.70	0.62	9,385	6,518	−2,867
Massachusetts	46,209	37,994	26,154	0.57	0.69	11,840	20,055	8,215
Michigan	54,817	55,230	49,170	0.90	0.89	6,060	5,647	−413
Minnesota	25,651	26,790	19,359	0.75	0.72	7,431	6,292	−1,139
Mississippi	19,922	18,711	16,821	0.84	0.90	1,890	3,101	1,211
Missouri	28,430	26,645	21,875	0.77	0.82	4,770	6,555	1,785
Montana	5,031	5,398	3,707	0.74	0.69	1,691	1,324	−367
Nebraska	11,532	11,464	9,234	0.80	0.81	2,230	2,298	68
Nevada	3,282	3,806	2,425	0.74	0.64	1,381	857	−524
New Hampshire	8,148	6,509	3,464	0.43	0.53	3,045	4,684	1,639
New Jersey	30,524	49,881	27,486	0.90	0.55	22,395	3,038	−19,357
New Mexico	7,693	8,191	6,379	0.83	0.78	1,812	1,314	−498
New York	106,847	110,852	87,271	0.82	0.79	23,581	19,576	−4,005
North Carolina	39,418	30,961	28,285	0.72	0.91	2,676	11,133	8,457
North Dakota	6,609	5,353	4,309	0.65	0.80	1,044	2,300	1,256
Ohio	61,777	61,673	51,983	0.84	0.84	9,690	9,794	104
Oklahoma	16,516	16,482	14,221	0.86	0.86	2,261	2,295	34
Oregon	16,487	16,103	12,766	0.77	0.79	3,337	3,721	384
Pennsylvania	74,938	68,581	55,543	0.74	0.81	13,038	19,395	6,357
Rhode Island	10,344	5,795	3,644	0.35	0.63	2,151	6,700	4,549
South Carolina	20,994	19,271	16,594	0.79	0.86	2,677	4,400	1,723
South Dakota	4,786	4,342	3,067	0.64	0.71	1,275	1,719	444
Tennessee	26,527	24,407	20,227	0.76	0.83	4,180	6,300	2,120
Texas	86,748	86,587	78,262	0.90	0.90	8,325	8,486	161
Utah	19,420	15,071	13,994	0.72	0.93	1,077	5,426	4,349
Vermont	4,802	3,318	1,573	0.33	0.47	1,745	3,229	1,484
Virginia	35,769	32,378	25,141	0.70	0.78	7,237	10,628	3,391
Washington	28,578	28,619	24,425	0.85	0.85	4,194	4,153	−41
West Virginia	12,162	10,181	8,561	0.70	0.84	1,620	3,601	1,981
Wisconsin	31,404	32,013	26,627	0.85	0.83	5,386	4,777	−609
Wyoming	3,286	3,173	2,334	0.71	0.74	839	952	113
State unknown[6]	—	8,821	—	—	—	8,821	—	−8,821
Outlying areas	26,091	27,376	25,873	0.99	0.95	1,503	218	−1,285
American Samoa	—	38	—	—	—	38	—	−38
Federated States of Micronesia	212	462	212	1.00	0.46	250	—	−250
Guam	177	166	7	0.04	0.04	159	170	11
Marshall Islands	11	22	9	0.82	0.41	13	2	−11
Northern Marianas	440	445	440	1.00	0.99	5	—	−5
Palau	13	17	13	1.00	0.76	4	—	−4
Puerto Rico	24,956	25,677	24,916	1.00	0.97	761	40	−721
Virgin Islands	282	549	276	0.98	0.50	273	6	−267
Foreign countries	—	22,077	—	—	—	22,077	—	−22,077

[1] Students who are enrolled at the reporting institution for the first time.
[2] All of the new students reported by the institutions in that state; i.e., all in-migrants and "remaining" students.
[3] All students living in a particular state when first admitted to an institution in any state. Students may be enrolled in any state.
[4] Students who attend institutions in their home state.
[5] Includes students coming to U.S. colleges from foreign countries and the outlying areas.
[6] Students are reported in "state unknown" when an institution is unable to determine the student's home state.
—Data not available or not applicable.

NOTE.—Data for U.S. Service Schools are included in state totals. Some data revised from previously published figures.

SOURCE: U.S. Department of Education, National Center for Education Statistics, Integrated Postsecondary Education Data System (IPEDS), "Residence of First-Time Students" survey, 1994. (This table was prepared October 1997.)

HIGHER EDUCATION: ENROLLMENT 213

Table 205.—Residence and migration of all freshmen students [1] in 4-year colleges graduating from high school in the past 12 months, by state: Fall 1994

State or other area	Students enrolled in institutions located in the state [2]	Student residents of state		Ratio of students remaining to—		Migration of students		
		Attending college in any state [3]	Attending college in home state [4]	Students enrolled (col.4 ÷ col.2)	Student residents (col.4 ÷ col.3)	Out of (col.3 − col.4)	Into (col.2 − col.4)	Net (col.8 − col.7)
1	2	3	4	5	6	7	8	9
United States	963,335	942,240	691,313	0.72	0.73	250,927	272,022	[5] 21,095
Alabama	16,883	13,016	11,044	0.65	0.85	1,972	5,839	3,867
Alaska	1,193	2,117	992	0.83	0.47	1,125	201	−924
Arizona	10,937	8,563	6,668	0.61	0.78	1,895	4,269	2,374
Arkansas	10,423	9,957	8,570	0.82	0.86	1,387	1,853	466
California	63,217	67,247	52,260	0.83	0.78	14,987	10,957	−4,030
Colorado	15,068	14,204	9,943	0.66	0.70	4,261	5,125	864
Connecticut	12,193	16,205	6,286	0.52	0.39	9,919	5,907	−4,012
Delaware	4,581	3,227	1,961	0.43	0.61	1,266	2,620	1,354
District of Columbia	8,476	2,979	1,758	0.21	0.59	1,221	6,718	5,497
Florida	26,950	27,526	19,007	0.71	0.69	8,519	7,943	−576
Georgia	26,954	25,554	19,945	0.74	0.78	5,609	7,009	1,400
Hawaii	2,877	3,792	2,177	0.76	0.57	1,615	700	−915
Idaho	3,747	4,440	2,971	0.79	0.67	1,469	776	−693
Illinois	35,655	44,602	29,500	0.83	0.66	15,102	6,155	−8,947
Indiana	33,419	28,056	24,061	0.72	0.86	3,995	9,358	5,363
Iowa	15,336	12,580	9,576	0.62	0.76	3,004	5,760	2,756
Kansas	10,997	10,276	8,359	0.76	0.81	1,917	2,638	721
Kentucky	15,811	14,411	12,222	0.77	0.85	2,189	3,589	1,400
Louisiana	21,760	19,651	16,828	0.77	0.86	2,823	4,932	2,109
Maine	5,003	5,847	3,004	0.60	0.51	2,843	1,999	−844
Maryland	14,022	17,114	7,937	0.57	0.46	9,177	6,085	−3,092
Massachusetts	36,548	28,893	17,493	0.48	0.61	11,400	19,055	7,655
Michigan	37,214	37,394	31,792	0.85	0.85	5,602	5,422	−180
Minnesota	18,162	19,542	12,517	0.69	0.64	7,025	5,645	−1,380
Mississippi	8,416	7,543	5,789	0.69	0.77	1,754	2,627	873
Missouri	22,449	20,591	16,264	0.72	0.79	4,327	6,185	1,858
Montana	4,402	4,342	3,116	0.71	0.72	1,226	1,286	60
Nebraska	9,035	8,898	6,900	0.76	0.78	1,998	2,135	137
Nevada	2,552	2,927	1,811	0.71	0.62	1,116	741	−375
New Hampshire	6,713	5,203	2,440	0.36	0.47	2,763	4,273	1,510
New Jersey	17,446	36,512	14,695	0.84	0.40	21,817	2,751	−19,066
New Mexico	4,520	5,120	3,596	0.80	0.70	1,524	924	−600
New York	75,455	79,606	56,756	0.75	0.71	22,850	18,699	−4,151
North Carolina	32,053	23,766	21,358	0.67	0.90	2,408	10,695	8,287
North Dakota	4,588	3,628	2,669	0.58	0.74	959	1,919	960
Ohio	48,165	48,105	38,967	0.81	0.81	9,138	9,198	60
Oklahoma	10,638	10,517	8,679	0.82	0.83	1,838	1,959	121
Oregon	9,892	9,594	6,509	0.66	0.68	3,085	3,383	298
Pennsylvania	61,040	54,695	42,322	0.69	0.77	12,373	18,718	6,345
Rhode Island	8,598	4,135	2,138	0.25	0.52	1,997	6,460	4,463
South Carolina	14,733	12,981	10,514	0.71	0.81	2,467	4,219	1,752
South Dakota	4,773	4,145	3,056	0.64	0.74	1,089	1,717	628
Tennessee	18,803	16,587	12,709	0.68	0.77	3,878	6,094	2,216
Texas	55,610	56,431	48,543	0.87	0.86	7,888	7,067	−821
Utah	14,476	9,965	9,390	0.65	0.94	575	5,086	4,511
Vermont	4,688	3,076	1,484	0.32	0.48	1,592	3,204	1,612
Virginia	28,864	25,405	18,525	0.64	0.73	6,880	10,339	3,459
Washington	13,371	13,789	10,031	0.75	0.73	3,758	3,340	−418
West Virginia	11,040	9,001	7,642	0.69	0.85	1,359	3,398	2,039
Wisconsin	22,343	22,676	17,770	0.80	0.78	4,906	4,573	−333
Wyoming	1,246	1,478	769	0.62	0.52	709	477	−232
State unknown [6]	—	4,331	—	—	—	4,331	—	−4,331
Outlying areas	20,456	21,510	20,241	0.99	0.94	1,269	215	−1,054
American Samoa	—	30	—	—	—	30	—	−30
Federated States of Micronesia	—	109	—	—	—	109	—	−109
Guam	169	146	—	—	—	146	169	23
Marshall Islands	—	10	—	—	—	10	—	−10
Northern Marianas	—	3	—	—	—	3	—	−3
Palau	—	2	—	—	—	2	—	−2
Puerto Rico	20,005	20,682	19,965	1.00	0.97	717	40	−677
Virgin Islands	282	528	276	0.98	0.52	252	6	−246
Foreign countries	—	20,041	—	—	—	20,041	—	−20,041

[1] Students who are enrolled at the reporting institution for the first time.
[2] All of the new students reported by the institutions in that state; i.e., all in-migrants and "remaining" students.
[3] All students living in a particular state when first admitted to an institution in any state. Students may be enrolled in any state.
[4] Students who attend institutions in their home state.
[5] Includes students coming to U.S. colleges from foreign countries and the outlying areas.
[6] Students are reported in "state unknown" when an institution is unable to determine the student's home state.
—Data not available or not applicable.

NOTE.—Data for U.S. Service Schools are included in state totals. Some data revised from previously published figures.

SOURCE: U.S. Department of Education, National Center for Education Statistics, Integrated Postsecondary Education Data System (IPEDS), "Residence of First-Time Students" survey, 1994. (This table was prepared October 1997.)

Table 206.—Total fall enrollment in institutions of higher education, by type and control of institution and race/ethnicity of student: 1976 to 1995

Type and control of institution and race/ethnicity of student	Number, in thousands								Percentage distribution by type and control[1]						
	1976	1980	1990	1991	1992	1993	1994	1995[2]	1976	1980	1990	1992	1993	1994	1995[2]
1	2	3	4	5	6	7	8	9	10	11	12	13	14	15	16
All students															
Total	10,985.6	12,086.8	13,818.6	14,359.0	14,487.4	14,304.8	14,278.8	14,261.8	100.0	100.0	100.0	100.0	100.0	100.0	100.0
White, non-Hispanic	9,076.1	9,833.0	10,722.5	10,989.8	10,875.4	10,600.0	10,427.0	10,311.2	84.3	83.5	79.9	77.5	76.5	75.4	74.7
Total minority	1,690.8	1,948.6	2,704.7	2,952.0	3,164.2	3,247.6	3,395.9	3,496.2	15.7	16.5	20.1	22.5	23.5	24.6	25.3
Black, non-Hispanic	1,033.0	1,106.8	1,247.0	1,335.4	1,392.9	1,412.8	1,448.6	1,473.7	9.6	9.4	9.3	9.9	10.2	10.5	10.7
Hispanic	383.8	471.7	782.4	866.6	955.0	988.8	1,045.6	1,093.8	3.6	4.0	5.8	6.8	7.1	7.6	7.9
Asian or Pacific Islander	197.9	286.4	572.4	637.2	697.0	724.4	774.3	797.4	1.8	2.4	4.3	5.0	5.2	5.6	5.8
American Indian/Alaskan Native	76.1	83.9	102.8	113.7	119.3	121.7	127.4	131.3	0.7	0.7	0.8	0.8	0.9	0.9	1.0
Nonresident alien	218.7	305.0	391.5	416.4	447.7	457.1	455.9	454.4	—	—	—	—	—	—	—
4-year															
Total	7,106.5	7,565.4	8,578.6	8,707.1	8,765.0	8,738.9	8,749.1	8,769.3	100.0	100.0	100.0	100.0	100.0	100.0	100.0
White, non-Hispanic	5,999.0	6,274.5	6,768.1	6,791.0	6,744.3	6,639.5	6,565.3	6,517.2	86.6	85.7	82.0	80.2	79.3	78.3	77.6
Total minority	931.0	1,049.9	1,486.1	1,573.3	1,663.7	1,733.6	1,819.2	1,885.8	13.4	14.3	18.0	19.8	20.7	21.7	22.4
Black, non-Hispanic	603.7	634.3	722.8	757.8	791.2	813.7	833.6	852.2	8.7	8.7	8.8	9.4	9.7	9.9	10.1
Hispanic	173.6	216.6	358.2	382.9	410.0	432.0	462.7	485.5	2.5	3.0	4.3	4.9	5.2	5.5	5.8
Asian or Pacific Islander	118.7	162.1	357.2	381.5	407.5	429.4	461.8	482.4	1.7	2.2	4.3	4.8	5.1	5.5	5.7
American Indian/Alaskan Native	35.0	36.9	47.9	51.1	54.9	58.5	61.2	65.7	0.5	0.5	0.6	0.7	0.7	0.7	0.8
Nonresident alien	176.5	240.9	324.3	342.8	357.0	365.9	364.5	366.2	—	—	—	—	—	—	—
Public	4,892.9	5,127.6	5,848.2	5,904.7	5,900.4	5,851.8	5,825.2	5,814.5	100.0	100.0	100.0	100.0	100.0	100.0	100.0
White, non-Hispanic	4,120.2	4,243.0	4,605.6	4,597.4	4,531.6	4,432.9	4,355.0	4,303.3	86.1	85.1	81.5	79.7	78.7	77.6	76.8
Total minority	666.7	740.8	1,046.2	1,101.7	1,155.8	1,202.1	1,256.7	1,299.3	13.9	14.9	18.5	20.3	21.3	22.4	23.2
Black, non-Hispanic	421.8	438.2	495.1	516.2	535.5	548.2	561.4	572.5	8.8	8.8	8.8	9.4	9.7	10.0	10.2
Hispanic	129.3	156.4	262.5	278.7	295.2	311.5	332.6	346.8	2.7	3.1	4.6	5.2	5.5	5.9	6.2
Asian or Pacific Islander	87.5	117.2	250.6	266.2	281.9	296.6	315.3	329.3	1.8	2.4	4.4	5.0	5.3	5.6	5.9
American Indian/Alaskan Native	28.2	29.0	38.0	40.6	43.0	45.9	47.5	50.8	0.6	0.6	0.7	0.8	0.8	0.8	0.9
Nonresident alien	106.0	143.8	196.4	205.6	212.6	216.7	213.4	211.9	—	—	—	—	—	—	—
Private	2,213.6	2,437.8	2,730.3	2,802.3	2,865.0	2,887.2	2,923.9	2,954.7	100.0	100.0	100.0	100.0	100.0	100.0	100.0
White, non-Hispanic	1,878.8	2,031.5	2,162.5	2,193.5	2,212.6	2,206.6	2,210.3	2,213.9	87.7	86.8	83.1	81.3	80.6	79.7	79.1
Total minority	264.3	309.2	439.8	471.5	507.9	531.5	562.5	586.5	12.3	13.2	16.9	18.7	19.4	20.3	20.9
Black, non-Hispanic	182.0	196.1	227.7	241.5	255.7	265.6	272.2	279.7	8.5	8.4	8.7	9.4	9.7	9.8	10.0
Hispanic	44.3	60.2	95.7	104.2	114.8	120.4	130.1	138.7	2.1	2.6	3.7	4.2	4.4	4.7	5.0
Asian or Pacific Islander	31.2	44.9	106.6	115.3	125.6	132.8	146.5	153.2	1.5	1.9	4.1	4.6	4.9	5.3	5.5
American Indian/Alaskan Native	6.8	7.9	9.9	10.6	11.8	12.6	13.6	14.9	0.3	0.3	0.4	0.4	0.5	0.5	0.5
Nonresident alien	70.5	97.1	127.9	137.2	144.4	149.1	151.1	154.3	—	—	—	—	—	—	—
2-year															
Total	3,879.1	4,521.4	5,240.1	5,651.9	5,722.4	5,565.9	5,529.7	5,492.5	100.0	100.0	100.0	100.0	100.0	100.0	100.0
White, non-Hispanic	3,077.1	3,558.5	3,954.3	4,198.8	4,131.2	3,960.6	3,861.7	3,794.0	80.2	79.8	76.4	73.4	72.3	71.0	70.2
Total minority	759.8	898.9	1,218.6	1,379.6	1,500.6	1,514.1	1,576.6	1,610.4	19.8	20.2	23.6	26.6	27.7	29.0	29.8
Black, non-Hispanic	429.3	472.5	524.3	577.6	601.6	599.0	615.0	621.5	11.2	10.6	10.1	10.7	10.9	11.3	11.5
Hispanic	210.2	255.1	424.2	483.7	545.0	556.8	582.9	608.4	5.5	5.7	8.2	9.7	10.2	10.7	11.3
Asian or Pacific Islander	79.2	124.3	215.2	255.7	289.5	295.0	312.5	314.9	2.1	2.8	4.2	5.1	5.4	5.7	5.8
American Indian/Alaskan Native	41.2	47.0	54.9	62.6	64.4	63.2	66.2	65.6	1.1	1.1	1.1	1.1	1.2	1.2	1.2
Nonresident alien	42.2	64.1	67.1	73.5	90.6	91.2	91.4	88.1	—	—	—	—	—	—	—
Public	3,748.1	4,328.8	4,996.5	5,404.8	5,484.6	5,337.3	5,308.5	5,277.8	100.0	100.0	100.0	100.0	100.0	100.0	100.0
White, non-Hispanic	2,974.3	3,413.1	3,779.8	4,024.8	3,961.2	3,793.7	3,701.3	3,642.1	80.2	80.0	76.6	73.4	72.3	70.9	70.1
Total minority	734.5	855.4	1,153.0	1,310.3	1,436.4	1,456.0	1,519.3	1,550.2	19.8	20.0	23.4	26.6	27.7	29.1	29.9
Black, non-Hispanic	409.5	437.9	481.4	537.2	565.0	566.1	583.2	588.2	11.0	10.3	9.8	10.5	10.8	11.2	11.3
Hispanic	207.5	249.8	408.9	463.4	527.1	539.8	566.1	590.3	5.6	5.9	8.3	9.8	10.3	10.8	11.4
Asian or Pacific Islander	78.2	122.5	210.3	250.1	284.0	289.7	306.8	308.7	2.1	2.9	4.3	5.3	5.5	5.9	5.9
American Indian/Alaskan Native	39.3	45.2	52.4	59.6	60.3	60.5	63.2	63.0	1.1	1.1	1.1	1.1	1.2	1.2	1.2
Nonresident alien	39.2	60.3	63.6	69.7	86.9	87.6	87.8	85.6	—	—	—	—	—	—	—
Private	131.0	192.6	243.6	247.1	237.8	228.5	221.2	214.7	100.0	100.0	100.0	100.0	100.0	100.0	100.0
White, non-Hispanic	102.8	145.4	174.5	174.0	170.0	166.9	160.3	152.0	80.3	77.0	72.7	72.6	74.2	73.7	71.6
Total minority	25.3	43.5	65.6	69.2	64.1	58.1	57.3	60.2	19.7	23.0	27.3	27.4	25.8	26.3	28.4
Black, non-Hispanic	19.8	34.6	42.9	40.4	36.6	32.9	31.9	33.3	15.5	18.3	17.9	15.6	14.6	14.6	15.7
Hispanic	2.6	5.3	15.3	20.3	17.9	17.1	16.7	18.1	2.1	2.8	6.4	7.6	7.6	7.7	8.5
Asian or Pacific Islander	0.9	1.8	4.9	5.6	5.5	5.4	5.7	6.2	0.7	1.0	2.0	2.4	2.4	2.6	2.9
American Indian/Alaskan Native	1.8	1.8	2.5	3.0	4.1	2.7	3.0	2.6	1.4	1.0	1.1	1.8	1.2	1.4	1.2
Nonresident alien	3.0	3.7	3.5	3.8	3.7	3.6	3.6	2.6	—	—	—	—	—	—	—

[1] Distribution for U.S. citizens only.
[2] Preliminary data.
—Not applicable.

NOTE.—Because of underreporting and nonreporting of racial/ethnic data, some figures are slightly lower than corresponding data in other tables. Because of rounding, details may not add to totals.

SOURCE: U.S. Department of Education, National Center for Education Statistics, Higher Education General Information Survey (HEGIS), "Fall Enrollment in Colleges and Universities" surveys; and Integrated Postsecondary Education Data System (IPEDS), "Fall Enrollment" surveys. (This table was prepared January 1997.)

Table 207.—Total fall enrollment in institutions of higher education, by level of study, sex, and race/ethnicity of student: 1976 to 1995

Level of study, sex, and race/ethnicity of student	Number, in thousands								Percent distribution by level of study [1]						
	1976	1980	1990	1991	1992	1993	1994	1995[2]	1976	1980	1990	1992	1993	1994	1995[2]
1	2	3	4	5	6	7	8	9	10	11	12	13	14	15	16
All students															
Total	10,985.6	12,086.8	13,818.6	14,359.0	14,487.4	14,304.8	14,278.8	14,261.8	100.0	100.0	100.0	100.0	100.0	100.0	100.0
White, non-Hispanic	9,076.1	9,833.0	10,722.5	10,989.8	10,875.4	10,600.0	10,427.0	10,311.2	84.3	83.5	79.9	77.5	76.5	75.4	74.7
Total minority	1,690.8	1,948.8	2,704.7	2,952.8	3,164.2	3,247.7	3,395.9	3,496.2	15.7	16.5	20.1	22.5	23.5	24.6	25.3
Black, non-Hispanic	1,033.0	1,106.8	1,247.0	1,335.4	1,392.9	1,412.8	1,448.6	1,473.7	9.6	9.4	9.3	9.9	10.2	10.5	10.7
Hispanic	383.8	471.7	782.4	866.6	955.0	988.1	1,045.6	1,093.8	3.6	4.0	5.8	6.8	7.1	7.6	7.9
Asian or Pacific Islander	197.9	286.4	572.4	637.2	697.0	724.4	774.3	797.4	1.8	2.4	4.3	5.0	5.2	5.6	5.8
American Indian/Alaskan Native	76.1	83.9	102.8	113.7	119.3	121.7	127.4	131.3	0.7	0.7	0.8	0.8	0.9	0.9	1.0
Nonresident alien	218.7	305.0	391.5	416.4	447.7	457.1	455.9	454.4	—	—	—	—	—	—	—
Men	5,794.4	5,868.1	6,283.9	6,501.8	6,524.0	6,427.5	6,371.9	6,342.5	52.4	48.0	45.0	44.5	44.4	44.1	44.0
White, non-Hispanic	4,813.7	4,772.9	4,861.0	4,962.2	4,884.6	4,755.0	4,650.7	4,594.1	44.7	40.5	36.2	34.8	34.3	33.6	33.3
Total minority	826.6	884.4	1,176.6	1,280.3	1,366.3	1,399.1	1,451.7	1,484.2	7.7	7.5	8.8	9.7	10.1	10.5	10.7
Black, non-Hispanic	469.9	463.7	484.7	517.0	536.9	543.7	549.7	555.9	4.4	3.9	3.6	3.8	3.9	4.0	4.0
Hispanic	209.7	231.6	353.9	390.5	427.1	441.2	464.0	480.2	1.9	2.0	2.6	3.0	3.2	3.4	3.5
Asian or Pacific Islander	108.4	151.3	294.9	325.1	351.5	363.1	385.0	393.3	1.0	1.3	2.2	2.5	2.6	2.8	2.8
American Indian/Alaskan Native	38.5	37.8	43.1	47.6	50.2	51.2	53.0	54.8	0.4	0.3	0.3	0.4	0.4	0.4	0.4
Nonresident alien	154.1	210.8	246.3	259.4	273.1	273.4	269.5	264.3	—	—	—	—	—	—	—
Women	5,191.2	6,218.7	7,534.7	7,857.1	7,963.4	7,877.4	7,906.9	7,919.2	47.6	52.0	55.0	55.5	55.6	55.9	56.0
White, non-Hispanic	4,262.4	5,060.1	5,861.5	6,027.6	5,990.8	5,845.1	5,776.3	5,717.2	39.6	42.9	43.7	42.7	42.2	41.8	41.4
Total minority	864.2	1,064.4	1,528.1	1,672.5	1,797.9	1,848.6	1,944.2	2,012.0	8.0	9.0	11.4	12.8	13.3	14.1	14.6
Black, non-Hispanic	563.1	643.0	762.3	818.4	856.0	869.1	898.9	917.8	5.2	5.5	5.7	6.1	6.3	6.5	6.6
Hispanic	174.1	240.1	428.5	476.0	527.3	547.6	581.6	613.7	1.6	2.0	3.2	3.8	4.0	4.2	4.4
Asian or Pacific Islander	89.4	135.2	277.5	312.0	345.6	361.3	389.3	404.1	0.8	1.1	2.1	2.5	2.6	2.8	2.9
American Indian/Alaskan Native	37.6	46.1	59.7	66.1	69.1	70.5	74.4	76.5	0.3	0.4	0.4	0.5	0.5	0.5	0.6
Nonresident alien	64.6	94.2	145.2	157.0	174.6	183.7	186.4	190.1	—	—	—	—	—	—	—
Undergraduate															
Total	9,419.0	10,469.1	11,959.1	12,439.3	12,537.7	12,324.0	12,262.6	12,231.7	100.0	100.0	100.0	100.0	100.0	100.0	100.0
White, non-Hispanic	7,740.5	8,480.7	9,272.6	9,507.7	9,387.6	9,100.4	8,916.0	8,805.6	83.4	82.7	79.0	76.4	75.5	74.3	73.6
Total minority	1,535.3	1,778.5	2,467.7	2,697.9	2,892.2	2,955.4	3,077.2	3,158.5	16.6	17.3	21.0	23.6	24.5	25.7	26.4
Black, non-Hispanic	943.4	1,018.8	1,147.2	1,229.3	1,280.6	1,290.4	1,317.3	1,333.6	10.2	9.9	9.8	10.4	10.7	11.0	11.1
Hispanic	352.9	433.1	724.6	804.2	887.8	918.1	968.3	1,012.0	3.8	4.2	6.2	7.2	7.6	8.1	8.5
Asian or Pacific Islander	169.3	248.7	500.5	558.7	613.0	634.2	674.1	692.2	1.8	2.4	4.3	5.0	5.3	5.6	5.8
American Indian/Alaskan Native	69.7	77.9	95.5	105.8	110.9	112.7	117.4	120.7	0.8	0.8	0.8	0.9	0.9	1.0	1.0
Nonresident alien	143.2	209.9	218.7	233.6	257.9	268.2	269.4	267.6	—	—	—	—	—	—	—
Men	4,896.8	4,997.4	5,379.8	5,571.0	5,582.9	5,483.7	5,422.1	5,401.1	51.8	47.3	44.7	44.3	44.3	44.0	43.9
White, non-Hispanic	4,052.2	4,054.9	4,184.4	4,273.0	4,195.5	4,067.0	3,963.1	3,918.1	43.7	39.5	35.6	34.2	33.7	33.0	32.7
Total minority	748.2	802.7	1,069.5	1,165.2	1,244.2	1,270.1	1,312.4	1,339.3	8.1	7.8	9.1	10.1	10.5	10.9	11.2
Black, non-Hispanic	430.7	428.2	448.0	478.1	495.6	499.6	502.9	506.8	4.6	4.2	3.8	4.0	4.1	4.2	4.2
Hispanic	191.7	211.2	326.9	361.4	397.1	409.2	429.4	444.2	2.1	2.1	2.8	3.2	3.4	3.6	3.7
Asian or Pacific Islander	91.1	128.5	254.5	281.5	305.0	314.1	331.4	338.1	1.0	1.3	2.2	2.5	2.6	2.8	2.8
American Indian/Alaskan Native	34.8	34.8	39.9	44.2	46.6	47.2	48.6	50.2	0.4	0.3	0.3	0.4	0.4	0.4	0.4
Nonresident alien	96.4	139.8	126.1	132.8	143.3	146.6	146.6	143.8	—	—	—	—	—	—	—
Women	4,522.1	5,471.7	6,579.3	6,868.3	6,954.8	6,840.3	6,840.5	6,830.6	48.2	52.7	55.3	55.7	55.7	56.0	56.1
White, non-Hispanic	3,688.3	4,425.8	5,088.2	5,234.6	5,192.1	5,033.4	4,953.0	4,887.5	39.8	43.1	43.3	42.2	41.8	41.3	40.9
Total minority	787.0	975.8	1,398.5	1,532.7	1,648.0	1,685.2	1,764.8	1,819.2	8.5	9.5	11.9	13.4	14.0	14.7	15.2
Black, non-Hispanic	512.7	590.6	699.2	751.1	785.0	790.8	814.4	826.9	5.5	5.8	6.0	6.4	6.6	6.8	6.9
Hispanic	161.2	221.8	397.6	442.7	490.7	508.9	538.9	567.8	1.7	2.2	3.4	4.0	4.2	4.5	4.7
Asian or Pacific Islander	78.2	120.2	246.0	277.2	308.0	320.0	342.7	354.1	0.8	1.2	2.1	2.5	2.7	2.9	3.0
American Indian/Alaskan Native	34.9	43.1	55.5	61.6	64.3	65.5	68.8	70.5	0.4	0.4	0.5	0.5	0.5	0.6	0.6
Nonresident alien	46.8	70.1	92.6	100.8	114.6	121.7	122.8	123.8	—	—	—	—	—	—	—
Graduate															
Total	1,322.5	1,340.9	1,586.2	1,639.1	1,668.7	1,688.4	1,721.5	1,732.5	100.0	100.0	100.0	100.0	100.0	100.0	100.0
White, non-Hispanic	1,115.6	1,104.7	1228.4	1258.0	1,267.2	1,273.8	1,286.8	1,282.3	89.2	88.5	86.6	85.3	84.6	83.5	82.6
Total minority	134.5	144.0	190.5	204.1	217.9	232.7	255.2	270.7	10.8	11.5	13.4	14.7	15.4	16.5	17.4
Black, non-Hispanic	78.5	75.1	83.9	88.9	94.1	102.2	110.6	118.6	6.3	6.0	5.9	6.3	6.8	7.2	7.6
Hispanic	26.4	32.1	47.2	50.9	55.3	57.9	63.9	68.0	2.1	2.6	3.3	3.7	3.8	4.1	4.4
Asian or Pacific Islander	24.5	31.6	53.2	57.6	61.5	65.2	72.6	75.6	2.0	2.5	3.8	4.1	4.3	4.7	4.9
American Indian/Alaskan Native	5.1	5.2	6.2	6.6	7.0	7.3	8.1	8.5	0.4	0.4	0.4	0.5	0.5	0.5	0.5
Nonresident alien	72.4	92.2	167.3	177.0	183.6	182.0	179.5	179.5	—	—	—	—	—	—	—
Men	707.9	672.2	737.4	761.0	772.4	771.0	775.8	767.5	52.2	48.3	43.8	43.6	43.1	42.7	42.0
White, non-Hispanic	589.1	538.5	538.8	550.7	553.7	550.9	551.4	541.6	47.1	43.1	38.0	37.3	36.6	35.8	34.9
Total minority	63.7	65.0	82.1	87.8	93.3	98.1	106.3	110.4	5.1	5.2	5.8	6.3	6.5	6.9	7.1
Black, non-Hispanic	32.0	28.2	29.3	31.0	33.1	35.3	37.7	39.8	2.6	2.3	2.1	2.2	2.3	2.4	2.6
Hispanic	14.6	15.7	20.6	22.4	23.6	24.8	27.0	28.2	1.2	1.3	1.5	1.6	1.6	1.8	1.8
Asian or Pacific Islander	14.4	18.6	29.7	31.8	33.8	35.1	38.3	39.0	1.2	1.5	2.1	2.3	2.3	2.5	2.5
American Indian/Alaskan Native	2.7	2.5	2.6	2.7	2.9	3.0	3.3	3.4	0.2	0.2	0.2	0.2	0.2	0.2	0.2
Nonresident alien	55.1	68.7	116.4	122.4	125.4	122.0	118.1	115.6	—	—	—	—	—	—	—
Women	614.6	668.7	848.8	878.2	896.3	917.4	945.6	965.0	47.8	51.7	56.2	56.4	56.9	57.3	58.0
White, non-Hispanic	526.5	566.2	689.5	707.3	713.6	722.9	735.4	740.7	42.1	45.3	48.6	48.0	48.0	47.7	47.7
Total minority	70.8	79.0	108.3	116.3	124.6	134.6	148.9	160.3	5.7	6.3	7.6	8.4	8.9	9.7	10.3
Black, non-Hispanic	46.5	46.9	54.6	57.9	61.0	66.9	72.9	78.8	3.7	3.8	3.8	4.1	4.4	4.7	5.1
Hispanic	11.8	16.4	26.6	28.6	31.7	33.1	36.9	39.9	0.9	1.3	1.9	2.1	2.2	2.4	2.6
Asian or Pacific Islander	10.1	13.0	23.6	25.9	27.8	30.2	34.3	36.6	0.8	1.0	1.7	1.9	2.0	2.2	2.4
American Indian/Alaskan Native	2.4	2.7	3.6	3.9	4.1	4.3	4.8	5.0	0.2	0.2	0.3	0.3	0.3	0.3	0.3
Nonresident alien	17.3	23.5	50.9	54.6	58.2	59.9	61.4	63.9	—	—	—	—	—	—	—

Table 207.—Total fall enrollment in institutions of higher education, by level of study, sex, and race/ethnicity of student: 1976 to 1995—Continued

Level of study, sex, and race/ethnicity of student	Number, in thousands								Percent distribution by level of study [1]						
	1976	1980	1990	1991	1992	1993	1994	1995[2]	1976	1980	1990	1992	1993	1994	1995[2]
1	2	3	4	5	6	7	8	9	10	11	12	13	14	15	16
First-professional															
Total	244.1	276.8	273.4	280.5	280.9	292.4	294.7	297.6	100.0	100.0	100.0	100.0	100.0	100.0	100.0
White, non-Hispanic	220.0	247.7	221.5	224.0	220.6	225.9	224.2	223.3	91.3	90.4	82.6	80.3	79.1	77.9	76.9
Total minority	21.1	26.3	46.5	50.8	54.1	59.6	63.5	67.0	8.7	9.6	17.4	19.7	20.9	22.1	23.1
Black, non-Hispanic	11.2	12.8	15.9	17.2	18.2	20.2	20.7	21.4	4.6	4.7	5.9	6.6	7.1	7.2	7.4
Hispanic	4.5	6.5	10.7	11.4	12.0	12.8	13.4	13.8	1.9	2.4	4.0	4.4	4.5	4.7	4.8
Asian or Pacific Islander	4.1	6.1	18.7	20.8	22.5	25.0	27.6	29.6	1.7	2.2	7.0	8.2	8.8	9.6	10.2
American Indian/Alaskan Native	1.3	0.8	1.1	1.3	1.5	1.7	1.8	2.1	0.5	0.3	0.4	0.5	0.6	0.6	0.7
Nonresident alien	3.1	2.9	5.4	5.8	6.2	6.9	7.0	7.3	—	—	—	—	—	—	—
Men	189.6	198.5	166.8	169.9	168.6	172.8	174.0	173.9	77.6	71.6	60.8	59.8	58.8	58.8	58.2
White, non-Hispanic	172.4	179.5	137.8	138.6	135.5	137.2	136.2	134.4	71.5	65.5	51.4	49.3	48.0	47.3	46.3
Total minority	14.7	16.7	25.3	27.2	28.8	30.9	33.0	34.6	6.1	6.1	9.4	10.5	10.8	11.5	11.9
Black, non-Hispanic	7.2	7.4	7.4	7.9	8.2	8.8	9.1	9.4	3.0	2.7	2.8	3.0	3.1	3.2	3.2
Hispanic	3.5	4.6	6.4	6.7	7.0	7.2	7.5	7.8	1.5	1.7	2.4	2.6	2.5	2.6	2.7
Asian or Pacific Islander	2.9	4.1	10.8	11.9	12.7	13.9	15.3	16.2	1.2	1.5	4.0	4.6	4.9	5.3	5.6
American Indian/Alaskan Native	1.0	0.5	0.6	0.7	0.8	0.9	1.0	1.2	0.4	0.2	0.2	0.3	0.3	0.4	0.4
Nonresident alien	2.5	2.3	3.8	4.1	4.4	4.8	4.8	4.9	—	—	—	—	—	—	—
Women	54.5	78.4	106.6	110.7	112.3	119.6	120.8	123.7	22.4	28.4	39.2	40.2	41.2	41.2	41.8
White, non-Hispanic	47.6	68.1	83.7	85.4	85.1	88.8	88.0	88.9	19.7	24.9	31.2	31.0	31.1	30.6	30.6
Total minority	6.4	9.6	21.3	23.5	25.3	28.8	30.5	32.4	2.6	3.5	7.9	9.2	10.1	10.6	11.2
Black, non-Hispanic	3.9	5.5	8.5	9.3	10.0	11.4	11.5	12.1	1.6	2.0	3.2	3.6	4.0	4.0	4.2
Hispanic	1.0	1.9	4.3	4.7	4.9	5.5	5.9	6.0	0.4	0.7	1.6	1.8	1.9	2.0	2.1
Asian or Pacific Islander	1.1	2.0	7.9	8.9	9.8	11.1	12.3	13.4	0.5	0.7	3.0	3.6	3.9	4.3	4.6
American Indian/Alaskan Native	0.2	0.3	0.5	0.6	0.7	0.7	0.8	0.9	0.1	0.1	0.2	0.2	0.3	0.3	0.3
Nonresident alien	0.5	0.6	1.6	1.7	1.8	2.1	2.3	2.4	—	—	—	—	—	—	—

[1] Distribution for U.S. citizens only.
[2] Preliminary data.
—Not applicable.

NOTE.—Because of underreporting and nonreporting of racial/ethnic data, some figures are slightly lower than corresponding data in other tables. Because of rounding, details may not add to totals.

SOURCE: U.S. Department of Education, National Center for Education Statistics, Higher Education General Information Survey (HEGIS), "Fall Enrollment in Colleges and Universities" surveys; and Integrated Postsecondary Education Data System (IPEDS), "Fall Enrollment" surveys. (This table was prepared January 1997.)

Table 208.—Total fall enrollment in institutions of higher education, by level, attendance status, sex, and race/ethnicity of student: 1994 and 1995

Level and enrollment status	1995[1]											Percent minority, fall 1994[2]
	Total	Enrollment, by sex		Enrollment, by race/ethnicity							Non-resident alien	
		Male	Female	White	Total, minority[2]	Percent minority[2]	Black, non-Hispanic	Hispanic	Asian/Pacific Islander	American Indian/Alaskan Native		
1	2	3	4	5	6	7	8	9	10	11	12	13
All students	14,261,781	6,342,539	7,919,242	10,311,243	3,496,174	25.3	1,473,672	1,093,839	797,359	131,304	454,364	24.6
Undergraduate, full-time and part-time	12,231,719	5,401,130	6,830,589	8,805,607	3,158,507	26.4	1,333,641	1,011,969	692,182	120,715	267,605	25.7
Degree seeking	10,621,283	4,708,420	5,912,863	7,619,193	2,763,827	26.6	1,181,433	874,517	604,490	103,387	238,263	25.8
First-time freshmen	2,168,831	1,001,052	1,167,779	1,541,387	586,401	27.6	252,076	190,120	121,007	23,198	41,043	27.4
Other first-year	2,433,434	1,046,475	1,386,959	1,603,129	781,101	32.8	332,827	274,063	145,885	28,326	49,204	32.0
Second year	2,767,344	1,174,985	1,592,359	2,022,764	688,827	25.4	299,393	218,006	143,819	27,609	55,753	24.4
Third year	1,394,845	631,360	763,485	1,042,087	314,541	23.2	133,205	86,913	83,950	10,473	38,217	22.2
Fourth year and beyond	1,714,665	795,243	919,422	1,296,067	368,722	22.1	150,973	100,559	104,634	12,556	49,876	20.9
Unclassified by level	142,164	59,305	82,859	113,759	24,235	17.6	12,959	4,856	5,195	1,225	4,170	17.2
Others in credit courses	1,610,436	692,710	917,726	1,186,414	394,680	25.0	152,208	137,452	87,692	17,328	29,342	24.4
Full-time	7,145,268	3,296,610	3,848,658	5,163,439	1,780,446	25.6	777,506	512,237	423,336	67,367	201,383	25.1
Degree seeking	6,883,159	3,174,144	3,709,015	4,990,474	1,704,056	25.5	747,102	486,088	406,441	64,425	188,629	24.9
First-time freshmen	1,646,812	767,185	879,627	1,194,389	419,413	26.0	190,520	122,990	89,968	15,935	33,010	25.9
Other first-year	1,136,399	520,469	615,930	745,014	358,966	32.5	167,473	112,564	64,825	14,104	32,419	32.0
Second year	1,688,726	758,647	930,079	1,241,020	402,968	24.5	175,593	113,866	97,037	16,472	44,738	23.9
Third year	1,126,949	525,848	601,101	842,865	248,911	22.8	102,648	65,766	72,167	8,330	35,173	21.9
Fourth year and beyond	1,259,327	590,948	668,379	950,057	268,061	22.0	107,420	69,893	81,366	9,382	41,209	20.8
Unclassified by level	24,946	11,047	13,899	17,129	5,737	25.1	3,448	1,009	1,078	202	2,080	24.5
Others in credit courses	262,109	122,466	139,643	172,965	76,390	30.6	30,404	26,149	16,895	2,942	12,754	30.7
Part-time	5,086,451	2,104,520	2,981,931	3,642,168	1,378,061	27.5	556,135	499,732	268,846	53,348	66,222	26.5
Degree seeking	3,738,124	1,534,276	2,203,848	2,628,719	1,059,771	28.7	434,331	388,429	198,049	38,962	49,634	27.6
First-time freshmen	522,019	233,867	288,152	346,998	166,988	32.5	61,556	67,130	31,039	7,263	8,033	31.9
Other first-year	1,297,035	526,006	771,029	858,115	422,135	33.0	165,354	161,499	81,060	14,222	16,785	32.0
Second year	1,078,618	416,338	662,280	781,744	285,859	26.8	123,800	104,140	46,782	11,137	11,015	25.1
Third year	267,896	105,512	162,384	199,222	65,630	24.8	30,557	21,147	11,783	2,143	3,044	23.5
Fourth year and beyond	455,338	204,295	251,043	346,010	100,661	22.5	43,553	30,666	23,268	3,174	8,667	21.2
Unclassified by level	117,218	48,258	68,960	96,630	18,498	16.1	9,511	3,847	4,117	1,023	2,090	15.3
Others in credit courses	1,348,327	570,244	778,083	1,013,449	318,290	23.9	121,804	111,303	70,797	14,386	16,588	23.1
Postbaccalaureate	2,030,062	941,409	1,088,653	1,505,636	337,667	18.3	140,031	81,870	105,177	10,589	186,759	17.4
First-professional	297,592	173,897	123,695	223,301	66,989	23.1	21,444	13,835	29,571	2,139	7,302	22.1
Full-time	266,414	155,056	111,358	198,934	60,712	23.4	18,497	12,489	27,844	1,882	6,768	22.4
First-time	78,890	45,285	33,605	57,585	19,233	25.0	6,048	3,974	8,560	651	2,072	24.2
Other	187,524	109,771	77,753	141,349	41,479	22.7	12,449	8,515	19,284	1,231	4,696	21.6
Part-time	31,178	18,841	12,337	24,367	6,277	20.5	2,947	1,346	1,727	257	534	19.3
First-time	10,760	6,487	4,273	8,266	2,327	22.0	1,026	539	689	73	167	22.3
Other	20,418	12,354	8,064	16,101	3,950	19.7	1,921	807	1,038	184	367	18.0
Graduate students	1,732,470	767,512	964,958	1,282,335	270,678	17.4	118,587	68,035	75,606	8,450	179,457	16.5
Full-time	717,120	355,726	361,394	471,443	114,164	19.5	44,389	28,446	37,561	3,768	131,513	18.5
Degree seeking	670,222	335,639	334,583	439,479	103,049	19.0	41,107	24,971	33,543	3,428	127,694	18.2
First-time	222,196	108,606	113,590	146,572	35,298	19.4	13,603	8,874	11,658	1,163	40,326	18.6
Other degree seeking	448,026	227,033	220,993	292,907	67,751	18.8	27,504	16,097	21,885	2,265	87,368	17.9
Others in credit courses	46,898	20,087	26,811	31,964	11,115	25.8	3,282	3,475	4,018	340	3,819	23.1
Part-time	1,015,350	411,786	603,564	810,892	156,514	16.2	74,198	39,589	38,045	4,682	47,944	15.4
Degree seeking	775,811	329,521	446,290	615,570	117,017	16.0	54,973	28,948	29,601	3,495	43,224	15.1
First-time	148,220	60,322	87,898	115,825	25,896	18.3	12,415	6,850	5,984	647	6,499	17.0
Other degree seeking	627,591	269,199	358,392	499,745	91,121	15.4	42,558	22,098	23,617	2,848	36,725	14.6
Others in credit courses	239,539	82,265	157,274	195,322	39,497	16.8	19,225	10,641	8,444	1,187	4,720	16.4

[1] Preliminary data.
[2] Percentage based on U.S. citizens only.

SOURCE: U.S. Department of Education, National Center for Education Statistics, Integrated Postsecondary Education Data System (IPEDS), "Fall Enrollment" surveys. (This table was prepared March 1997.)

218 HIGHER EDUCATION: ENROLLMENT

Table 209.—Total number of institutions and fall enrollment in institutions of higher education, by percentage minority enrollment: 1995 [1]

Minority percentage of U.S. citizen enrollment	Total enrollment	Public institutions					Private institutions			
		Total	4-year institutions			2-year	Total	4-year institutions		2-year
			Total	University	Other 4-year			Total	University	Other 4-year	
1	2	3	4	5	6	7	8	9	10	11	12
All institutions											
Number of institutions	3,545	1,603	602	94	508	1,001	1,942	1,572	62	1,510	370
Total enrollment	14,261,781	11,092,374	5,814,545	2,235,939	3,578,606	5,277,829	3,169,407	2,954,707	763,702	2,191,005	214,700
U.S. citizens	13,807,417	10,794,917	5,602,655	2,116,669	3,485,986	5,192,262	3,012,500	2,800,361	695,271	2,105,090	212,139
Minority	3,496,174	2,849,526	1,299,343	377,112	922,231	1,550,183	646,648	586,474	168,995	417,479	60,174
90.0 percent or more minority enrollment											
Number of institutions	125	50	25	0	25	25	75	63	1	62	12
Total enrollment	309,665	229,158	128,231	0	128,231	100,927	80,507	73,246	10,332	62,914	7,261
U.S. citizens	301,358	223,353	124,986	0	124,986	98,367	78,005	70,837	9,784	61,053	7,168
Minority	288,410	212,089	117,995	0	117,995	94,094	76,321	69,492	9,636	59,856	6,829
75.0 to 89.9 percent minority enrollment											
Number of institutions	80	55	20	0	20	35	25	12	0	12	13
Total enrollment	445,047	423,304	134,292	0	134,292	289,012	21,743	12,530	0	12,530	9,213
U.S. citizens	427,829	406,502	129,021	0	129,021	277,481	21,327	12,212	0	12,212	9,115
Minority	351,813	333,948	107,055	0	107,055	226,893	17,865	10,343	0	10,343	7,522
50.0 to 74.9 percent minority enrollment											
Number of institutions	197	107	30	3	27	77	90	41	0	41	49
Total enrollment	1,083,289	989,399	384,786	84,112	300,674	604,613	93,890	72,475	0	72,475	21,415
U.S. citizens	1,042,747	951,962	367,721	78,761	288,960	584,241	90,785	69,929	0	69,929	20,856
Minority	636,548	580,708	224,100	48,617	175,483	356,608	55,840	42,809	0	42,809	13,031
25.0 to 49.9 percent minority enrollment											
Number of institutions	640	314	83	11	72	231	326	246	22	224	80
Total enrollment	3,163,014	2,443,738	975,904	338,293	637,611	1,467,834	719,276	679,973	311,336	368,637	39,303
U.S. citizens	3,035,188	2,374,061	935,909	318,083	617,826	1,438,152	661,127	622,488	278,138	344,350	38,639
Minority	1,052,637	830,097	325,583	100,181	225,402	504,514	222,540	209,006	90,458	118,548	13,534
10.0 to 24.9 percent minority enrollment											
Number of institutions	1,226	554	235	53	182	319	672	579	35	544	93
Total enrollment	6,028,744	4,652,184	2,794,930	1,340,298	1,454,632	1,857,254	1,376,560	1,290,774	385,345	905,429	85,786
U.S. citizens	5,830,763	4,524,300	2,684,689	1,266,587	1,418,102	1,839,611	1,306,463	1,221,020	353,154	867,866	85,443
Minority	973,229	751,235	438,014	196,338	241,676	313,221	221,994	205,589	65,526	140,063	16,405
Less than 10.0 percent minority enrollment											
Number of institutions	1,277	523	209	27	182	314	754	631	4	627	123
Total enrollment	3,232,022	2,354,591	1,396,402	473,236	923,166	958,189	877,431	825,709	56,689	769,020	51,722
U.S. citizens	3,169,532	2,314,739	1,360,329	453,238	907,091	954,410	854,793	803,875	54,195	749,680	50,918
Minority	193,537	141,449	86,596	31,976	54,620	54,853	52,088	49,235	3,375	45,860	2,853

[1] Preliminary data. Minority includes black, Hispanic, Asian or Pacific Islander, and American Indian/Alaskan Native students.

NOTE.—Some institutions do not report separate enrollment data for each branch campus. For this reason, counts of institutions in this table are somewhat lower than figures appearing in other tables.

SOURCE: U.S. Department of Education, National Center for Education Statistics, Integrated Postsecondary Education Data System (IPEDS), "Fall Enrollment" survey. (This table was prepared January 1997.)

Table 210.—Total fall enrollment in institutions of higher education, by race/ethnicity of student and by state: 1992 to 1995

State or other area	1995[1]								Percent minority[2]			
	Total	White, non-Hispanic	Minority enrollment, by race/ethnicity					Non-resident alien	1992[3]	1993[3]	1994[3]	1995
			Total	Black, non-Hispanic	Hispanic	Asian/ Pacific Islander	American Indian/ Alaskan Native					
1	2	3	4	5	6	7	8	9	10	11	12	13
United States	14,261,781	10,311,243	3,496,174	1,473,672	1,093,839	797,359	131,304	454,364	22.5	23.5	24.6	25.3
Alabama	225,612	163,372	57,663	52,311	1,718	2,326	1,308	4,577	23.7	24.8	25.5	26.1
Alaska	29,348	23,211	5,534	1,004	796	879	2,855	603	18.3	18.6	18.7	19.3
Arizona	273,981	200,052	66,658	8,776	38,691	8,578	10,613	7,271	22.2	23.8	24.0	25.0
Arkansas	98,180	78,663	17,163	14,432	737	1,121	873	2,354	16.8	17.2	17.1	17.9
California	1,817,042	905,116	832,127	138,218	357,893	314,877	21,139	79,799	40.5	44.0	46.3	47.9
Colorado	242,739	195,023	42,071	8,421	22,483	8,146	3,021	5,645	15.8	16.4	16.9	17.7
Connecticut	157,695	126,335	25,763	11,879	7,735	5,610	539	5,597	14.2	15.1	16.3	16.9
Delaware	44,307	35,299	8,071	6,018	793	1,064	196	937	16.0	16.9	18.0	18.6
District of Columbia	77,277	37,346	31,906	24,429	3,015	4,248	214	8,025	44.0	44.0	45.4	46.1
Florida	637,303	426,419	191,314	83,432	86,064	18,927	2,891	19,570	27.5	28.4	29.5	31.0
Georgia	314,712	215,506	91,064	77,418	4,659	8,143	844	8,142	26.4	27.9	29.0	29.7
Hawaii	63,198	16,781	40,643	1,238	1,362	37,787	256	5,774	69.6	69.9	70.6	70.8
Idaho	59,566	54,535	3,740	390	1,683	874	793	1,291	5.5	6.1	6.1	6.4
Illinois	717,854	509,044	190,803	90,674	58,244	39,477	2,408	18,007	25.6	26.1	26.9	27.3
Indiana	289,615	250,483	30,578	17,980	6,277	5,233	1,088	8,554	9.8	10.2	10.5	10.9
Iowa	173,835	154,375	12,419	4,878	2,792	4,034	715	7,041	6.2	6.6	7.2	7.4
Kansas	177,643	149,727	21,926	9,419	5,856	4,043	2,608	5,990	10.7	11.0	11.5	12.8
Kentucky	178,858	159,762	15,977	12,089	1,150	2,083	655	3,119	8.2	8.6	8.9	9.1
Louisiana	203,935	135,074	62,880	53,002	4,634	4,120	1,124	5,981	29.7	30.2	31.4	31.8
Maine	56,547	53,241	2,712	620	359	875	858	594	4.4	3.3	3.7	4.8
Maryland	266,310	177,612	79,438	57,579	6,209	14,590	1,060	9,260	27.3	28.5	30.0	30.9
Massachusetts	413,794	322,092	67,405	23,079	18,102	24,513	1,711	24,297	14.4	15.2	16.5	17.3
Michigan	548,339	440,026	91,310	59,893	11,593	15,320	4,504	17,003	15.3	16.2	16.8	17.2
Minnesota	280,816	250,123	24,305	7,975	3,985	9,514	2,831	6,388	6.8	7.5	8.0	8.9
Mississippi	122,690	82,685	38,027	35,884	654	1,051	438	1,978	29.8	30.6	31.2	31.5
Missouri	291,536	246,071	38,051	25,493	4,653	6,405	1,500	7,414	12.6	12.9	13.2	13.4
Montana	42,674	36,924	4,729	146	484	337	3,762	1,021	12.9	11.5	11.5	11.4
Nebraska	115,718	104,352	8,784	3,408	2,268	2,216	892	2,582	7.2	7.0	7.4	7.8
Nevada	67,826	51,988	13,929	3,715	5,135	4,004	1,075	1,909	18.7	18.0	19.5	21.1
New Hampshire	64,327	59,885	3,280	1,056	950	1,017	257	1,162	5.4	4.9	4.6	5.2
New Jersey	333,831	230,349	92,089	39,273	30,764	21,105	947	11,393	24.8	25.6	27.4	28.6
New Mexico	102,405	57,229	43,383	2,593	32,067	1,694	7,029	1,793	39.8	40.9	41.8	43.1
New York	1,041,566	690,917	306,102	135,813	99,972	66,543	3,774	44,547	26.9	28.1	29.8	30.7
North Carolina	372,030	277,844	88,486	73,185	4,438	7,074	3,789	5,700	22.6	23.2	24.1	24.2
North Dakota	40,399	35,871	2,968	343	247	302	2,076	1,560	7.3	7.5	7.8	7.6
Ohio	540,275	452,802	71,511	50,853	7,831	10,782	2,045	15,962	12.1	12.7	13.2	13.6
Oklahoma	180,676	137,276	35,256	13,147	4,180	4,092	13,837	8,144	17.7	18.7	19.9	20.4
Oregon	167,145	139,202	21,555	2,980	6,306	9,683	2,586	6,388	10.6	11.6	12.2	13.4
Pennsylvania	617,759	516,552	84,254	51,269	11,171	20,463	1,351	16,953	12.5	12.5	13.2	14.0
Rhode Island	74,100	62,824	8,773	3,200	2,709	2,593	271	2,503	10.2	11.0	11.4	12.3
South Carolina	174,125	127,856	43,352	39,088	1,550	2,232	482	2,917	23.7	23.8	24.7	25.3
South Dakota	36,695	32,509	3,189	293	178	264	2,454	997	7.5	6.8	8.6	8.9
Tennessee	245,962	198,271	42,824	36,165	2,346	3,563	750	4,867	17.1	17.3	17.7	17.8
Texas	952,525	590,137	336,140	93,660	195,377	42,311	4,792	26,248	32.4	33.4	35.1	36.3
Utah	147,324	132,566	9,416	904	3,821	3,088	1,603	5,342	5.9	6.6	6.5	6.6
Vermont	35,065	32,242	2,033	477	481	676	399	790	4.0	3.9	4.8	5.9
Virginia	355,919	264,430	83,662	56,981	8,080	17,231	1,370	7,827	21.3	22.4	23.6	24.0
Washington	285,819	228,386	48,472	10,599	10,197	22,451	5,225	8,961	14.8	15.7	16.9	17.5
West Virginia	86,034	79,347	4,961	3,395	469	900	197	1,726	5.4	5.6	5.9	5.9
Wisconsin	300,223	265,457	27,864	12,670	6,283	6,452	2,459	6,902	8.7	9.1	9.4	9.5
Wyoming	30,176	27,517	2,212	254	1,269	236	453	447	7.3	6.7	6.9	7.4
U.S. Service Schools	88,451	70,537	17,402	11,674	3,129	2,212	387	512	21.1	21.6	22.0	19.8
Outlying areas	183,657	764	181,939	2,647	170,385	8,889	18	954	99.5	99.4	99.5	99.6
American Samoa	1,232	0	1,232	0	0	1,232	0	0	100.0	100.0	100.0	100.0
Federated States of Micronesia	1,296	0	1,295	0	0	1,295	0	1	100.0	100.0	100.0	100.0
Guam	6,010	527	4,978	38	41	4,890	9	505	89.5	89.3	90.0	90.4
Marshall Islands	418	0	407	0	0	407	0	11	100.0	99.7	100.0	100.0
Northern Marianas	959	58	673	0	2	671	0	228	89.5	92.1	92.3	92.1
Palau	351	0	351	0	0	351	0	0	100.0	100.0	100.0	100.0
Puerto Rico	170,337	20	170,252	12	170,224	11	5	65	100.0	99.9	100.0	100.0
Virgin Islands	3,054	159	2,751	2,597	118	32	4	144	91.3	91.7	92.5	94.5

[1] Preliminary data.
[2] Percent minority based on U.S. citizen enrollment (total enrollment less enrollment of nonresident aliens).
[3] Some data revised from previously published figures.

NOTE.—Because of adjustments to underreported and nonreported racial/ethnic data, figures are slightly different from corresponding data in other tables.

SOURCE: U.S. Department of Education, National Center for Education Statistics, Integrated Postsecondary Education Data System (IPEDS), "Fall Enrollment" surveys. (This table was prepared April 1997.)

Table 211.—Number and percent of students enrolled in postsecondary institutions, by disability status and selected student characteristics: 1995–96

Selected student characteristics	Undergraduate			Graduate and first-professional[1]		
	All students	Disabled students[2]	Nondisabled students	All students	Disabled students[2]	Nondisabled students
1	2	3	4	5	6	7
Total (in thousands)	16,678	892	15,786	2,784	89	2,695
Sex	100.0	100.0	100.0	100.0	100.0	100.0
Male	44.1	50.0	43.8	45.7	31.3	46.2
Female	55.9	50.0	56.2	54.3	68.7	53.8
Race/ethnicity of student	100.0	100.0	100.0	100.0	100.0	100.0
White, non-Hispanic	71.4	80.9	70.8	80.6	73.9	80.9
Black, non-Hispanic	11.6	7.1	11.9	6.4	10.7	6.2
Hispanic	10.3	7.7	10.5	4.9	9.8	4.7
Asian/Pacific Islander	5.3	1.8	5.5	8.1	5.6	8.2
American Indian/Alaskan Native	0.9	2.1	0.8	—	—	—
Other	0.5	0.4	0.5	—	—	—
Age	100.0	100.0	100.0	100.0	100.0	100.0
15 to 23	54.9	46.0	55.5	9.2	7.6	9.3
24 to 29	17.9	13.6	18.1	42.7	32.3	43.0
30 or older	27.2	40.4	26.4	48.1	60.0	47.7
Attendance status	100.0	100.0	100.0	100.0	100.0	100.0
Full time	40.5	38.7	40.6	32.5	34.2	32.5
Part time	59.5	61.3	59.4	67.5	65.8	67.5
Student housing status	100.0	100.0	100.0	100.0	100.0	100.0
On-campus	14.6	12.0	14.8	6.5	6.6	6.5
Off-campus	58.0	62.7	57.7	86.9	82.3	87.1
With parents or relatives	27.4	25.3	27.5	6.6	11.1	6.4
Dependency status	100.0	100.0	100.0	100.0	100.0	100.0
Dependent	49.3	40.7	49.8	50.5	48.8	50.5
Independent, unmarried	16.7	21.5	16.4	20.7	21.5	20.7
Independent, married	9.8	8.0	9.9	28.8	29.7	28.8
Independent with dependents	24.2	29.8	23.9	—	—	—
Veteran status	100.0	100.0	100.0	100.0	100.0	100.0
Veteran	5.2	9.7	5.0	5.2	10.6	5.0
Not veteran	94.8	90.3	95.0	94.8	89.4	95.0
Field of study	100.0	100.0	100.0	100.0	100.0	100.0
Business/management	15.7	13.8	15.8	17.1	14.8	17.1
Education	6.8	6.6	6.8	26.1	23.8	26.2
Engineering/computer science	9.6	10.9	9.6	8.3	3.7	8.4
Health	10.1	9.0	10.2	13.0	28.6	12.5
Humanities	11.6	13.9	11.5	9.7	6.2	9.8
Law	0.0	0.0	0.0	5.2	4.1	5.2
Life/physical sciences	5.3	3.2	5.4	6.3	2.1	6.5
Social/Behavioral sciences	7.6	7.5	7.6	7.8	5.8	7.9
Vocational/technical	2.1	3.0	2.1	0.0	0.0	0.0
Undeclared	20.3	20.9	20.3	3.5	7.1	3.4
Other	10.8	11.3	10.7	2.9	3.8	2.9

[1] Includes chiropractic medicine, medicine, dentistry, optometry, osteopathic medicine, pharmacy, podiatry, and veterinary medicine.
[2] Disabled students are those who reported that they had one or more of the following conditions: a specific learning disability, a visual handicap, hard of hearing, deafness, a speech disability, an orthopedic handicap, or a health impairment.
—Sample size too small for a reliable estimate.

NOTE.—Because of rounding and survey item nonresponse, details may not add to totals.

SOURCE: U.S. Department of Education, National Center for Education Statistics, "The 1995–96 National Postsecondary Student Aid Study." (This table was prepared October 1997).

Table 212.—Enrollment of persons 14 to 34 years of age[1] in institutions of higher education, by race/ethnicity, sex, and year of college: October 1965 to October 1996

Characteristic	1965	1970	1975	1980	1985[2]	1986	1987	1988	1989	1990	1991	1992	1993	1994[3]	1995	1996
1	2	3	4	5	6	7	8	9	10	11	12	13	14	15	16	17
	Numbers in thousands															
All students	5,675	7,413	9,697	10,181	10,863	10,605	10,915	10,937	11,066	11,303	11,589	11,671	11,409	12,298	12,046	12,448
White, non-Hispanic[4]																
Total	5,317	6,759	8,141	8,453	8,781	8,284	8,519	8,616	8,786	8,892	8,916	8,883	8,592	9,076	8,973	8,943
Men	3,326	4,066	4,566	4,225	4,361	4,158	4,221	4,155	4,220	4,298	4,323	4,207	4,168	4,313	4,319	4,222
Women	1,991	2,693	3,576	4,228	4,420	4,126	4,299	4,461	4,565	4,594	4,594	4,676	4,424	4,764	4,654	4,721
Black, non-Hispanic[4]																
Total	274	522	927	996	1,036	1,126	1,162	1,096	1,116	1,167	1,190	1,205	1,227	1,469	1,415	1,513
Men	126	253	433	431	458	484	505	423	425	508	523	467	515	641	579	633
Women	148	269	494	565	578	642	657	674	690	659	667	738	713	828	837	879
Hispanic origin																
Total	—	—	411	443	579	677	667	654	640	617	721	816	867	982	1,014	1,039
Men	—	—	219	222	280	331	369	313	311	297	310	349	391	443	495	440
Women	—	—	192	221	299	346	298	341	330	321	411	468	475	539	519	599
Year of college																
First	1,861	2,212	2,886	2,958	2,956	2,965	2,915	3,131	2,983	3,109	2,995	3,274	3,139	3,357	3,236	3,295
Second	1,256	1,739	2,376	2,411	2,585	2,564	2,745	2,598	2,680	2,798	2,959	3,002	2,964	3,075	3,068	3,060
Third	896	1,248	1,491	1,716	1,931	1,803	2,011	1,979	2,017	1,958	2,009	2,136	2,080	2,244	2,239	2,235
Fourth	803	1,074	1,354	1,403	1,642	1,640	1,556	1,631	1,676	1,817	1,877	1,681	1,692	1,902	1,772	2,033
Fifth or higher	859	1,140	1,590	1,692	1,749	1,633	1,690	1,598	1,711	1,620	1,749	1,578	1,535	1,719	1,731	1,823
	Percentage distribution															
All students	100.0	100.0	100.0	100.0	100.0	100.0	100.0	100.0	100.0	100.0	100.0	100.0	100.0	100.0	100.0	100.0
White, non-Hispanic[4]																
Total	93.7	91.2	84.0	83.0	80.8	78.1	78.1	78.8	79.4	78.7	76.9	76.1	75.3	73.8	74.5	71.8
Men	58.6	54.8	47.1	41.5	40.1	39.2	38.7	38.0	38.1	38.0	37.3	36.0	36.5	35.1	35.9	33.9
Women	35.1	36.3	36.9	41.5	40.7	38.9	39.4	40.8	41.3	40.6	39.6	40.1	38.8	38.7	38.6	37.9
Black, non-Hispanic[4]																
Total	4.8	7.0	9.6	9.8	9.5	10.6	10.6	10.0	10.1	10.3	10.3	10.3	10.8	11.9	11.7	12.2
Men	2.2	3.4	4.5	4.2	4.2	4.6	4.6	3.9	3.8	4.5	4.5	4.0	4.5	5.2	4.8	5.1
Women	2.6	3.6	5.1	5.5	5.3	6.1	6.0	6.2	6.2	5.8	5.8	6.3	6.2	6.7	6.9	7.1
Hispanic origin																
Total	—	—	4.2	4.4	5.3	6.4	6.1	6.0	5.8	5.5	6.2	7.0	7.6	8.0	8.4	8.3
Men	—	—	2.3	2.2	2.6	3.1	3.4	2.9	2.8	2.6	2.7	3.0	3.4	3.6	4.1	3.5
Women	—	—	2.0	2.2	2.8	3.3	2.7	3.1	3.0	2.8	3.5	4.0	4.2	4.4	4.3	4.8
Year of college																
First	32.8	29.8	29.8	29.1	27.2	28.0	26.7	28.6	27.0	27.5	25.8	28.1	27.5	27.3	26.9	26.5
Second	22.1	23.5	24.5	23.7	23.8	24.2	25.1	23.8	24.2	24.8	25.5	25.7	26.0	25.0	25.5	24.6
Third	15.8	16.8	15.4	16.9	17.8	17.0	18.4	18.1	18.2	17.3	17.3	18.3	18.2	18.3	18.6	18.0
Fourth	14.1	14.5	14.0	13.8	15.1	15.5	14.3	14.9	15.1	16.1	16.2	14.4	14.8	15.5	14.7	16.3
Fifth or higher	15.1	15.4	16.4	16.6	16.1	15.4	15.5	14.6	15.5	14.3	15.1	13.5	13.5	14.0	14.4	14.6

[1] Totals differ from those shown in other tables. This table presents data collected in sample surveys of households rather than surveys of institutions. Excludes persons age 35 and over.

[2] Data for 1985 to 1993 are controlled to 1980 census base.

[3] Data are controlled to 1990 census base. Large increase in 1994 is partly due to the change in census base and change in survey form administration procedures.

[4] Data for 1965 and 1970 include persons of Hispanic origin.

—Data not available.

NOTE.—Data are based upon sample surveys of the civilian noninstitutional population. Because of rounding, details may not add to totals.

SOURCE: U.S. Department of Commerce, Bureau of the Census, *Current Population Reports*, Series P-20, No. 403, and unpublished data. (This table was prepared June 1997.)

Table 213.—Enrollment in postsecondary education, by major field of study, age, and level of student: 1995–96

Field of study	All students					Undergraduate									Graduate and first-professional				
	Total, in thousands	Percentage distribution, by age				2-year institutions[1]					4-year institutions								
						Total, in thousands	Percentage distribution, by age			Total, in thousands	Percentage distribution, by age			Total, in thousands	Percentage distribution, by age			
		Under 25	25 to 34	Over 35			Under 25	25 to 34	Over 35		Under 25	25 to 34	Over 35		Under 25	25 to 34	Over 35	
1	2	3	4	5	6	7	8	9	10	11	12	13	14	15	16	17			
Total	19,444	53.0	26.3	20.7	8,887	48.1	27.0	24.9	7,791	71.4	17.1	11.5	2,767	17.4	49.5	33.1			
Agriculture	204	65.8	21.1	13.1	71	60.5	21.0	18.5	109	80.5	12.0	7.5	24	13.7	63.8	22.5			
Architecture/city planning	82	62.8	32.5	4.6	(²)	(²)	(²)	(²)	50	89.0	8.8	2.2	22	16.3	73.5	10.2			
Area studies	—	—	—	—	(²)	(²)	(²)	(²)	24	76.2	11.5	12.3	(²)	(²)	(²)	(²)			
Business	2,949	48.7	29.7	21.6	1,295	45.2	29.0	25.8	1,233	64.2	20.8	15.0	420	13.9	58.0	28.1			
Communications/journalism	335	71.5	17.5	11.0	89	57.3	23.1	19.6	224	82.0	11.8	6.2	22	21.3	52.9	25.8			
Computer science	554	42.7	31.6	25.7	275	34.4	31.1	34.5	219	62.4	23.4	14.2	60	9.2	63.3	27.6			
Education	1,590	45.0	27.0	28.0	337	63.0	22.2	14.8	649	67.0	17.5	15.5	604	11.3	39.9	48.9			
Engineering	1,002	58.6	28.9	12.5	403	48.2	30.4	21.5	477	77.6	18.5	3.8	122	18.7	64.4	16.9			
Foreign language	—	—	—	—	(²)	(²)	(²)	(²)	55	78.2	16.1	5.7	(²)	(²)	(²)	(²)			
Health	2,157	47.4	31.4	21.2	1,273	42.7	34.4	22.9	637	65.9	19.8	14.3	247	23.6	46.1	30.3			
Medicine/dentistry	83	43.3	49.9	6.8	(²)	(²)	(²)	(²)	(²)	(²)	(²)	(²)	83	9.2	49.9	6.8			
Home economics	473	55.8	27.7	16.5	375	53.0	30.5	16.6	81	77.8	13.0	9.2	17	15.0	36.1	48.9			
Industrial arts	210	53.2	30.0	16.8	181	41.9	33.5	24.7	28	81.9	11.0	7.1	(²)	(²)	(²)	(²)			
Interdisciplinary science	153	62.8	22.4	14.9	37	73.8	11.7	14.6	89	72.8	17.0	10.2	27	14.0	55.1	30.9			
Law	636	53.2	30.0	16.8	352	52.2	27.1	20.6	142	69.0	21.0	10.0	142	39.6	46.3	14.1			
Letters/liberal studies	1,340	60.6	21.9	17.5	908	59.1	22.3	18.6	383	69.9	17.4	12.7	48	15.8	50.9	33.3			
Library science	24	5.8	57.6	36.6	(²)	(²)	(²)	(²)	(²)	(²)	(²)	(²)	24	5.8	57.6	36.6			
Life sciences	558	77.2	19.1	3.7	118	72.0	23.2	4.8	380	87.4	10.3	2.3	60	22.5	67.1	10.4			
Mathematics	113	56.7	28.8	14.5	(²)	(²)	(²)	(²)	63	76.5	17.6	6.0	25	20.6	61.1	18.4			
Mechanics/transportation	230	39.4	29.3	31.3	208	34.8	30.9	34.3	22	82.1	15.0	3.0	(²)	(²)	(²)	(²)			
Philosophy and religion	90	44.6	33.9	21.5	(²)	(²)	(²)	(²)	46	71.5	15.0	13.5	42	12.5	56.1	31.4			
Physical science	178	63.4	29.1	7.5	(²)	(²)	(²)	(²)	106	81.4	17.0	1.6	44	20.9	59.5	19.6			
Psychology	495	67.4	21.1	11.5	84	69.8	20.8	9.4	347	75.3	15.7	9.1	65	21.9	50.8	27.3			
Public administration/social work	241	38.7	34.5	26.8	59	39.1	33.5	27.4	90	55.0	20.7	24.2	93	22.7	48.4	29.0			
Social sciences	713	67.3	21.4	11.3	122	65.2	22.0	12.8	492	76.9	15.0	8.2	99	22.7	52.4	24.9			
Visual and performing arts	603	66.0	20.7	13.3	169	57.1	19.4	23.5	357	79.4	14.7	5.9	78	23.6	51.2	25.2			
Other[3]	181	53.0	23.4	23.5	27	35.1	27.0	37.9	115	71.3	16.2	12.6	38	10.3	43.1	46.5			
Undeclared	3,523	54.0	21.2	24.9	2,196	45.5	23.4	31.1	1,248	71.7	15.5	12.8	78	9.8	49.0	41.2			

[1] Includes less-than-2-year schools.
[2] Too few sample cases for a reliable estimate.
[3] Includes students whose classification is unknown.
—Data not available.

NOTE.—Because of different survey editing and processing procedures, enrollment data in this table may differ from those appearing in other tables. Because of rounding, details may not add to totals. Includes students who enrolled at any time during the 1995–96 academic year.

SOURCE: U.S. Department of Education, National Center for Education Statistics, "The 1995–96 National Postsecondary Student Aid Study," unpublished data. (This table was prepared November 1997).

Table 214.—Graduate enrollment in science and engineering programs in institutions of higher education, by field of study: United States and outlying areas, fall 1984 to fall 1995

Field of engineering or science	1984[1]	1985[1]	1986[1]	1987[1]	1988	1989	1990	1991	1992	1993	1994	1995	Percent change, 1990 to 1995
1	2	3	4	5	6	7	8	9	10	11	12	13	14
Total, all fields	394,718	404,088	415,557	421,526	424,671	434,637	452,250	471,314	493,826	504,838	505,259	501,510	10.9
Engineering, total	92,712	95,991	101,874	103,953	102,829	104,043	107,625	113,576	118,035	116,881	113,060	107,529	−0.1
Aerospace	2,340	2,538	2,804	3,015	3,223	3,524	3,934	4,120	4,036	3,940	3,715	3,343	−15.0
Agricultural	961	948	1,071	1,080	1,052	1,043	946	983	1,008	1,018	1,061	1,054	11.4
Biomedical	1,343	1,370	1,534	1,674	1,752	1,916	2,136	2,239	2,537	2,675	2,750	2,687	25.8
Chemical	7,373	7,150	7,012	7,111	6,618	6,460	6,735	7,127	7,397	7,516	7,608	7,432	10.3
Civil	15,192	14,902	14,976	14,682	14,811	14,909	15,542	17,398	19,572	19,583	19,925	19,218	23.7
Electrical	26,388	28,203	29,969	31,399	32,035	33,257	33,722	35,182	36,460	35,337	33,052	31,060	−7.9
Engineering science	2,153	2,098	2,362	2,343	2,386	2,077	2,020	2,154	2,218	2,180	2,089	1,955	−3.2
Industrial	9,282	10,499	11,529	12,220	11,393	11,094	11,248	12,676	13,525	13,596	13,696	13,182	17.2
Mechanical	13,855	14,157	15,713	16,366	16,151	16,265	16,879	17,730	18,637	18,477	17,761	16,360	−3.1
Metallurgical/materials	3,657	3,943	4,208	4,366	4,337	4,594	4,941	5,160	5,512	5,363	5,191	4,920	−0.4
Mining	502	489	512	513	489	418	437	489	437	427	424	373	−14.6
Nuclear	1,234	1,220	1,265	1,279	1,303	1,323	1,278	1,282	1,286	1,306	1,246	1,154	−9.7
Petroleum	744	782	747	818	742	665	670	705	737	725	624	610	−9.0
Other engineering	7,688	7,692	8,172	7,087	6,537	6,498	7,137	6,331	4,673	4,738	3,918	4,181	−41.4
All sciences, total	302,006	308,097	313,683	317,573	321,842	330,594	344,625	357,738	375,791	387,957	392,199	393,981	14.3
Physical sciences, total	30,056	30,981	32,246	32,727	32,962	33,616	34,075	34,710	35,348	35,318	34,449	33,470	−1.8
Astronomy	639	671	689	719	731	789	810	829	869	880	973	912	12.6
Chemistry	17,755	18,305	18,744	18,827	18,579	18,828	19,118	19,407	19,929	20,131	19,797	19,645	2.8
Physics	11,331	11,672	12,437	12,807	13,308	13,657	13,813	14,081	14,122	13,841	13,162	12,427	−10.0
Other physical sciences	331	333	376	374	344	342	334	393	428	466	517	486	45.5
Earth, atmospheric, and ocean sciences	15,505	15,420	15,066	14,371	13,867	13,643	13,984	14,480	15,347	15,805	16,042	15,802	13.0
Atmospheric sciences	907	964	961	952	940	912	929	968	1,089	1,112	1,109	1,072	15.4
Geosciences	10,370	10,294	9,819	8,998	8,463	8,052	7,692	7,567	7,744	7,785	7,741	7,602	−1.2
Oceanography	2,102	2,081	2,128	2,127	2,033	2,207	2,333	2,386	2,530	2,611	2,853	2,703	15.9
Other environmental sciences	2,126	2,081	2,158	2,294	2,431	2,472	3,030	3,559	3,984	4,297	4,339	4,425	46.0
Mathematical sciences, total	17,443	17,563	17,949	18,508	19,077	19,247	19,774	19,952	20,355	20,000	19,579	18,509	−6.4
Mathematics and applied mathematics	15,278	15,437	15,615	16,015	16,490	16,723	17,096	17,206	17,404	16,945	16,463	15,400	−9.9
Statistics	2,165	2,126	2,334	2,493	2,587	2,524	2,678	2,746	2,951	3,055	3,116	3,109	16.1
Computer sciences, total	25,526	29,769	31,349	32,051	32,227	32,482	34,257	34,610	36,320	36,298	34,278	33,509	−2.2
Life sciences, total	102,961	103,635	105,661	106,036	108,084	111,910	116,396	121,890	129,033	136,971	143,843	148,767	27.8
Agricultural sciences, total	12,226	11,561	11,458	11,118	11,135	11,190	11,316	11,506	11,827	11,914	12,199	12,426	9.8
Biological sciences, total	45,763	46,112	46,765	46,747	47,565	48,852	49,989	51,778	54,177	56,452	58,143	58,753	17.5
Anatomy	1,029	993	973	1,016	1,056	1,078	1,000	1,051	1,030	1,027	1,079	1,056	5.6
Biochemistry	4,449	4,654	4,873	4,813	4,921	5,082	5,039	5,201	5,376	5,513	5,632	5,550	10.1
Biology	12,890	12,710	12,678	12,331	12,393	12,761	13,027	13,292	13,874	14,327	14,220	14,211	9.1
Biometry/epidemiology	1,004	1,360	1,434	1,556	1,682	1,722	1,871	2,032	2,365	2,658	2,710	2,812	50.3
Biophysics	433	441	547	591	592	655	642	697	751	780	794	855	33.2
Botany	3,212	3,157	3,123	2,979	2,912	2,826	2,733	2,694	2,689	2,714	2,748	2,609	−4.5
Cell biology	1,256	1,429	1,716	1,964	2,078	2,234	2,555	2,809	3,093	3,374	3,768	3,859	51.0
Ecology	1,088	1,028	1,022	963	999	1,084	1,136	1,180	1,301	1,410	1,566	1,717	51.1
Entomology/parasitology	1,438	1,342	1,306	1,244	1,240	1,181	1,173	1,171	1,193	1,247	1,263	1,241	5.8
Genetics	1,059	1,120	1,262	1,314	1,289	1,365	1,408	1,520	1,639	1,785	1,699	1,700	20.7
Microbiology	4,324	4,445	4,371	4,452	4,773	4,827	4,873	4,928	4,972	5,068	5,141	5,095	4.6
Nutrition	4,220	4,241	4,259	4,158	4,132	4,164	4,172	4,164	4,159	4,388	4,747	5,012	20.1
Pathology	1,413	1,305	1,323	1,369	1,333	1,369	1,354	1,449	1,456	1,575	1,707	1,670	23.3
Pharmacology	2,060	2,103	2,078	2,072	2,124	2,267	2,353	2,432	2,529	2,645	2,830	2,703	14.9
Physiology	2,158	2,211	2,220	2,213	2,220	2,206	2,236	2,332	2,317	2,372	2,378	2,540	13.6
Zoology	2,293	2,127	2,075	2,104	2,029	2,083	2,104	2,191	2,139	2,120	2,092	2,073	−1.5
Other biosciences	1,437	1,446	1,505	1,608	1,792	1,948	2,313	2,635	3,294	3,449	3,769	4,050	75.1
Health fields, total	44,972	45,962	47,438	48,171	49,384	51,868	55,091	58,606	63,029	68,605	73,501	77,588	40.8
Medical fields	8,655	9,221	9,244	9,809	10,101	10,232	10,950	11,707	12,594	14,184	15,065	15,795	44.2
Other health fields	36,317	36,741	38,194	38,362	39,283	41,636	44,141	46,899	50,435	54,421	58,436	61,793	40.0
Dentistry	817	797	908	1,022	1,048	1,004	956	1,016	1,121	1,135	1,199	1,251	30.9
Nursing	17,987	17,965	18,398	18,444	18,862	19,689	21,194	22,012	23,213	24,781	27,042	28,441	34.2
Pharmaceutical sciences	2,519	2,553	2,682	2,607	2,613	2,787	2,889	2,968	2,804	2,871	2,901	2,948	2.0
Speech pathology/audiology	7,665	7,761	7,774	7,314	7,479	7,911	8,354	8,945	9,791	10,740	11,473	12,098	44.8
Veterinary sciences	557	637	630	731	752	801	900	894	942	877	875	929	3.2
Other health related	6,772	7,028	7,802	8,244	8,529	9,444	9,848	11,064	12,564	14,017	14,946	16,126	63.7
Psychology, total	40,931	40,721	41,241	42,612	43,963	45,528	48,168	51,343	53,599	54,680	54,726	54,243	12.6
Psychology, general	104	104	118	267	15,443	16,822	18,144	20,954	22,707	23,263	23,895	23,915	31.8
Clinical psychology	40,173	39,919	40,361	41,566	20,548	19,408	20,108	19,555	18,819	18,920	18,179	17,675	−12.1
Other psychology	654	698	762	779	7,972	9,298	9,916	10,834	12,073	12,497	12,652	12,653	27.6
Social sciences, total	69,584	70,008	70,171	71,268	71,662	74,168	77,971	80,753	85,789	88,885	89,282	89,681	15.0
Agricultural economics	2,279	2,268	2,248	2,203	2,259	2,276	2,273	2,364	2,522	2,415	2,289	2,321	2.1
Anthropology	5,590	5,631	5,805	5,835	5,945	6,128	6,479	6,731	7,123	7,361	7,665	7,694	18.8
Economics (except agricultural)	12,507	12,430	12,103	11,998	12,036	12,139	12,326	12,707	13,252	13,214	12,978	12,790	3.8
Geography	3,035	2,936	3,055	3,223	3,208	3,479	3,530	3,760	4,102	4,378	4,502	4,402	24.7
History and philosophy of science	274	272	266	294	288	304	331	337	360	369	387	401	21.1
Linguistics	3,160	3,055	3,109	3,282	3,243	3,286	3,404	3,425	3,277	3,321	3,279	3,194	−6.2
Political science	25,570	26,621	27,091	27,429	27,723	29,194	30,582	31,707	33,797	35,151	34,383	34,374	12.4
Sociology	6,812	6,637	6,565	7,026	7,117	7,405	7,801	8,393	9,011	9,425	9,498	9,575	22.7
Sociology/anthropology	1,024	983	988	942	960	988	1,164	899	979	935	987	941	−19.2
Other social sciences	9,333	9,175	8,941	9,036	8,883	8,969	10,081	10,430	11,366	12,316	13,314	13,989	38.8

[1] Includes estimates for master's degree granting institutions which were surveyed on a sample basis from 1985 through 1987.
—Data not available.

NOTE.—Some data have been revised from previously published figures. Because of rounding, details may not add to totals.

SOURCE: National Science Foundation, Division of Science Resources Studies, Survey of Graduate Students and Postdoctorates in Science and Engineering, 1995. (This table was prepared April 1997.)

Table 215.—Institutions of higher education and branches, by type, control, and size of enrollment: Fall 1994 and fall 1995 [1]

Control of institution branch and size of total enrollment	All institutions		Universities		All other 4-year institutions		2-year institutions	
	Number [2]	Enrollment	Number [2]	Enrollment	Number [2]	Enrollment	Number [2]	Enrollment
1	2	3	4	5	6	7	8	9
Fall 1994								
Total	3,561	14,278,790	156	3,009,072	2,008	5,740,008	1,397	5,529,710
Under 200	377	41,590	0	0	252	26,625	125	14,965
200 to 499	417	140,028	0	0	219	74,393	198	65,635
500 to 999	507	371,102	0	0	357	263,286	150	107,816
1,000 to 2,499	864	1,438,335	0	0	567	924,194	297	514,141
2,500 to 4,999	536	1,851,721	4	15,975	272	941,366	260	894,380
5,000 to 9,999	459	3,247,731	26	198,321	208	1,446,400	225	1,603,010
10,000 to 19,999	281	3,889,296	57	793,929	112	1,540,219	112	1,555,148
20,000 to 29,999	92	2,230,957	47	1,163,390	20	487,482	25	580,085
30,000 or more	28	1,068,030	22	837,457	1	36,043	5	194,530
Fall 1995 [1]								
Total	3,545	14,261,781	156	2,999,641	2,018	5,769,611	1,371	5,492,529
Under 200	365	39,723	0	0	252	26,934	113	12,789
200 to 499	416	141,479	0	0	230	79,531	186	61,948
500 to 999	489	356,483	0	0	341	250,182	148	106,301
1,000 to 2,499	865	1,429,095	0	0	571	923,841	294	505,254
2,500 to 4,999	552	1,898,147	4	16,038	281	967,151	267	914,958
5,000 to 9,999	466	3,286,555	29	227,500	211	1,460,970	226	1,598,085
10,000 to 19,999	271	3,767,108	56	802,280	110	1,509,517	105	1,455,311
20,000 to 29,999	92	2,216,009	43	1,056,139	21	515,343	28	644,527
30,000 or more	29	1,127,182	24	897,684	1	36,142	4	193,356
Public institutions	1,603	11,092,374	94	2,235,939	508	3,578,606	1,001	5,277,829
Under 200	5	677	0	0	0	0	5	677
200 to 499	33	11,107	0	0	9	3,273	24	7,834
500 to 999	117	89,641	0	0	30	23,186	87	66,455
1,000 to 2,499	347	603,450	0	0	84	143,019	263	460,431
2,500 to 4,999	378	1,314,767	0	0	115	412,276	263	902,491
5,000 to 9,999	375	2,669,414	6	54,577	146	1,035,530	223	1,579,307
10,000 to 19,999	234	3,255,805	28	423,217	102	1,409,837	104	1,422,751
20,000 to 29,999	87	2,087,466	38	927,596	21	515,343	28	644,527
30,000 or more	27	1,060,047	22	830,549	1	36,142	4	193,356
Private institutions	1,942	3,169,407	62	763,702	1,510	2,191,005	370	214,700
Under 200	360	39,046	0	0	252	26,934	108	12,112
200 to 499	383	130,372	0	0	221	76,258	162	54,114
500 to 999	372	266,842	0	0	311	226,996	61	39,846
1,000 to 2,499	518	825,645	0	0	487	780,822	31	44,823
2,500 to 4,999	174	583,380	4	16,038	166	554,875	4	12,467
5,000 to 9,999	91	617,141	23	172,923	65	425,440	3	18,778
10,000 to 19,999	37	511,303	28	379,063	8	99,680	1	32,560
20,000 to 29,999	5	128,543	5	128,543	0	0	0	0
30,000 or more	2	67,135	2	67,135	0	0	0	0

[1] These preliminary data represent the institution branches and enrollments reported in the "Fall Enrollment" survey.

[2] Some institutions do not report separate enrollment data for each branch campus. For this reason, counts of institutions in this table are somewhat lower than figures appearing in other tables.

SOURCE: U.S. Department of Education, National Center for Education Statistics, Integrated Postsecondary Education Data System (IPEDS), "Fall Enrollment" surveys. (This table was prepared January 1997.)

Table 216.—Enrollment of the 120 largest college and university campuses:[1] Fall 1995

Institution	State	Rank	Control[2]	Type[3]	Total enrollment, fall 1995	Institution	State	Rank	Control[2]	Type[3]	Total enrollment, fall 1995
1	2	3	4	5	6	1	2	3	4	5	6
Community College of the Air Force[4]	Ala.	1	1	2	69,611	Virginia Polytechnic Inst. and State Univ.	Va.	61	1	1	25,492
University of Minnesota, Twin Cities	Minn.	2	1	1	51,445	University of Massachusetts, Amherst	Mass.	62	1	1	25,267
Ohio State University, Main Campus	Ohio	3	1	1	48,676	Macomb Community College	Mich.	63	1	2	25,176
University of Texas, Austin	Tex.	4	1	1	47,905	University of North Texas	Tex.	64	1	1	25,114
Miami-Dade Community College	Fla.	5	1	2	47,060	University of Kansas, Main Campus	Kans.	65	1	1	25,036
Arizona State University	Ariz.	6	1	1	42,040	California State University, Northridge	Calif.	66	1	1	25,015
Texas A&M University	Tex.	7	1	1	41,790	University of Illinois at Chicago	Ill.	67	1	1	24,870
Michigan State University	Mich.	8	1	1	40,647	Harvard University	Mass.	68	2	1	24,687
Pennsylvania State U., Main Campus	Pa.	9	1	1	39,646	Iowa State University	Iowa	69	1	1	24,673
Houston Community College System	Tex.	10	1	2	39,541	Northeastern University	Mass.	70	2	1	24,605
University of Florida	Fla.	11	1	1	39,412	University of New Mexico, Main Campus	N.Mex.	71	1	1	24,605
University of Wisconsin, Madison	Wisc.	12	1	1	39,005	SUNY at Buffalo	N.Y.	72	1	1	24,493
University of Illinois, Urbana Campus	Ill.	13	1	1	38,420	University of North Carolina, Chapel Hill	N.C.	73	1	1	24,439
Northern Virginia Community College	Va.	14	1	2	37,144	University of Nebraska, Lincoln	Nebr.	74	1	1	24,320
University of Michigan, Ann Arbor	Mich.	15	1	1	36,687	Georgia State University	Ga.	75	1	1	24,274
Purdue University, Main Campus	Ind.	16	1	1	36,427	Texas Tech University	Tex.	76	1	1	24,185
University of South Florida	Fla.	17	1	1	36,142	George Mason University	Va.	77	1	1	24,172
New York University	N.Y.	18	2	1	35,835	University of Kentucky	Ky.	78	1	1	23,794
Indiana University, Bloomington	Ind.	19	1	1	35,063	University of Akron, Main Campus	Ohio	79	1	1	23,640
University of Arizona	Ariz.	20	1	1	34,777	Central Michigan University	Mich.	80	1	1	23,575
University of California, Los Angeles	Calif.	21	1	1	34,713	Valencia Community College	Fla.	81	1	2	23,569
University of Washington	Wash.	22	1	1	33,996	Eastern Michigan University	Mich.	82	1	1	23,142
Rutgers University, New Brunswick	N.J.	23	1	1	33,773	University of California, Davis	Calif.	83	1	1	23,091
U. of Maryland, College Park Campus	Md.	24	1	1	32,908	California State University, Sacramento	Calif.	84	1	1	22,796
International Correspondence Schools	Pa.	25	3	2	32,560	Cuyahoga Community College District	Ohio	85	1	2	22,785
Wayne State University	Mich.	26	1	1	32,149	California State University, Fullerton	Calif.	86	1	1	22,604
Brigham Young University	Utah	27	2	1	31,300	De Anza College	Calif.	87	1	2	22,545
University of Houston, University Park	Tex.	28	1	1	30,766	University of Connecticut	Conn.	88	1	1	22,471
Florida State University	Fla.	29	1	1	30,155	Southern Illinois University, Carbondale	Ill.	89	1	1	22,418
University of Georgia	Ga.	30	1	1	30,149	University of Missouri, Columbia	Mo.	90	1	1	22,356
College of Du Page	Ill.	31	1	2	29,888	University of Oklahoma, Norman Campus	Okla.	91	1	1	22,299
University of California, Berkeley	Calif.	32	1	1	29,630	Northern Illinois University	Ill.	92	1	1	22,218
San Diego State University	Calif.	33	1	1	29,350	Mount San Antonio College	Calif.	93	1	2	22,202
Boston University	Mass.	34	2	1	29,132	University of Pennsylvania	Pa.	94	2	1	22,148
Temple University	Pa.	35	1	1	29,028	Auburn University, Main Campus	Ala.	95	1	1	22,122
University of Cincinnati, Main Campus	Ohio	36	1	1	28,373	University of Texas, Arlington	Tex.	96	1	1	22,121
North Carolina State University, Raleigh	N.C.	37	1	1	28,250	University of Toledo	Ohio	97	1	1	21,991
Florida International University	Fla.	38	1	1	28,171	Milwaukee Area Technical College	Wisc.	98	1	2	21,903
University of Iowa	Iowa	39	1	1	28,052	University of Wisconsin, Milwaukee	Wisc.	99	1	1	21,891
University of Southern California	Calif.	40	2	1	27,971	El Paso Community College	Tex.	100	1	2	21,856
Pima Community College	Ariz.	41	1	2	27,866	Nassau Community College	N.Y.	101	1	2	21,737
University of Colorado, Boulder	Colo.	42	1	1	27,624	University of Virginia, Main Campus	Va.	102	1	1	21,728
University of Utah	Utah	43	1	1	27,137	El Camino College	Calif.	103	1	2	21,540
Indiana U. - Purdue U. at Indianapolis	Ind.	44	1	1	26,939	West Virginia University	W.Va.	104	1	1	21,517
San Francisco State University	Calif.	45	1	1	26,791	University of Delaware	Del.	105	1	1	21,365
La. St. U. & A&M & Hebert Laws Center	La.	46	1	1	26,573	Virginia Commonwealth University	Va.	106	1	1	21,349
University of Central Florida	Fla.	47	1	1	26,556	Mesa Community College	Ariz.	107	1	2	21,244
Portland Community College	Oreg.	48	1	2	26,540	Florida Community College, Jacksonville	Fla.	108	1	2	21,237
Western Michigan University	Mich.	49	1	1	26,537	Saint Petersburg Junior College	Fla.	109	1	2	21,176
California State University, Long Beach	Calif.	50	1	1	26,403	Orange Coast College	Calif.	110	1	2	21,135
University of South Carolina, Columbia	S.C.	51	1	1	26,346	Pasadena City College	Calif.	111	1	2	21,101
Colorado State University	Colo.	52	1	1	26,340	Kent State University, Main Campus	Ohio	112	1	1	20,972
University of Pittsburgh, Main Campus	Pa.	53	1	1	26,083	Southwest Texas State University	Tex.	113	1	1	20,917
City College of San Francisco	Calif.	54	1	2	26,019	University of Louisville	Ky.	114	1	1	20,559
San Jose State University	Calif.	55	1	1	25,997	Community College of Southern Nevada	Nev.	115	1	2	20,417
Tarrant County Junior College District	Tex.	56	1	2	25,953	Santa Monica College	Calif.	116	1	2	20,392
Oakland Community College	Mich.	57	1	2	25,913	Rancho Santiago College	Calif.	117	1	2	20,392
Broward Community College	Fla.	58	1	2	25,738	Hillsborough Community College	Fla.	118	1	2	20,311
University of Tennessee, Knoxville	Tenn.	59	1	1	25,723	American River College	Calif.	119	1	2	20,170
Austin Community College	Tex.	60	1	2	25,620	Northern Arizona University	Ariz.	120	1	1	20,131

[1] College and university campuses ranked by fall 1995 preliminary enrollment data.
[2] Publicly controlled institutions are identified by a "1," private, nonprofit, by a "2," and private, proprietary, by a "3."
[3] The types of institutions are identified as follows: "1" for 4-year institutions and "2" for 2-year institutions.
[4] Estimated.

SOURCE: U.S. Department of Education, National Center for Education Statistics, Integrated Postsecondary Education Data System (IPEDS), "Fall Enrollment, 1995" survey. (This table was prepared May 1997.)

HIGHER EDUCATION: ENROLLMENT

Table 217.—Selected statistics for college and university campuses enrolling more than 14,600 students in 1995

Line no.	Institution	State	Control[1]	Type[2]	Total enrollment, fall 1990	Total enrollment, fall 1993	Total enrollment, fall 1994	Total enrollment, fall 1995	Enrollment, by sex, fall 1995		Enrollment, by attendance status, fall 1995	
									Men	Women	Full-time	Part-time
1	2	3	4	5	6	7	8	9	10	11	12	13
—	United States, all institutions	—	—	—	13,818,637	14,304,803	14,278,790	14,261,781	6,342,539	7,919,242	8,128,802	6,132,979
—	Colleges with enrollment over 14,600	—	—	—	5,009,716	5,034,690	5,007,466	5,046,294	2,381,059	2,665,235	2,953,422	2,092,872
1	Auburn University, Main Campus	Ala.	1	1	21,537	21,363	21,226	22,122	11,771	10,351	18,800	3,322
2	University of Alabama	Ala.	1	1	19,794	19,480	19,306	18,985	9,112	9,873	15,556	3,429
3	University of Alabama, Birmingham	Ala.	1	1	15,356	15,913	15,362	15,502	6,905	8,597	9,872	5,630
4	University of Alaska, Anchorage	Alaska	1	1	17,490	17,275	16,189	16,206	6,314	9,892	6,286	9,920
5	Arizona State University	Ariz.	1	1	42,936	41,250	42,189	42,040	20,865	21,175	29,130	12,910
6	Glendale Community College	Ariz.	1	2	18,512	17,520	18,033	17,699	7,808	9,891	5,229	12,470
7	Mesa Community College	Ariz.	1	2	19,818	19,508	20,110	21,244	10,063	11,181	6,842	14,402
8	Northern Arizona University	Ariz.	1	1	16,992	18,817	19,242	20,131	8,208	11,923	13,469	6,662
9	Pima Community College	Ariz.	1	2	28,766	28,268	27,960	27,866	12,230	15,636	7,104	20,762
10	University of Arizona	Ariz.	1	1	35,729	35,279	35,306	34,777	17,161	17,616	27,004	7,773
11	University of Arkansas, Fayetteville	Ark.	1	1	14,732	14,280	14,495	14,692	7,836	6,856	11,649	3,043
12	American River College	Calif.	1	2	18,716	20,377	19,766	20,170	8,847	11,323	4,845	15,325
13	Calif. Polytechnic State U., San Luis Obispo	Calif.	1	1	17,751	15,449	15,440	16,023	9,162	6,861	14,320	1,703
14	California State Polytechnic U., Pomona	Calif.	1	1	19,468	17,050	16,304	16,605	9,476	7,129	11,666	4,939
15	California State University, Fresno	Calif.	1	1	19,960	17,956	17,293	17,461	7,966	9,495	13,781	3,680
16	California State University, Fullerton	Calif.	1	1	25,592	22,565	22,097	22,604	9,786	12,818	14,098	8,506
17	California State University, Long Beach	Calif.	1	1	33,987	27,073	26,277	26,403	11,793	14,610	17,294	9,109
18	California State University, Los Angeles	Calif.	1	1	21,597	17,788	18,224	18,385	7,479	10,906	10,918	7,467
19	California State University, Northridge	Calif.	1	1	31,167	27,282	24,310	25,015	10,699	14,316	15,903	9,112
20	California State University, Sacramento	Calif.	1	1	26,336	23,316	22,726	22,796	10,000	12,796	15,426	7,370
21	Cerritos College	Calif.	1	2	15,886	19,653	19,571	19,981	8,829	11,152	4,296	15,685
22	City College of San Francisco	Calif.	1	2	24,408	26,630	26,356	26,019	11,706	14,313	7,029	18,990
23	De Anza College	Calif.	1	2	21,948	22,701	22,634	22,545	10,399	12,146	7,229	15,316
24	Diablo Valley College	Calif.	1	2	20,255	18,888	18,075	18,192	8,370	9,822	6,493	11,699
25	East Los Angeles College	Calif.	1	2	12,447	14,470	15,257	15,289	6,373	8,916	4,508	10,781
26	El Camino College	Calif.	1	2	25,789	22,953	21,763	21,540	9,770	11,770	5,820	15,720
27	Fresno City College	Calif.	1	2	14,710	16,554	16,952	16,287	7,617	8,670	5,272	11,015
28	Fullerton College	Calif.	1	2	17,548	18,387	18,141	17,748	8,557	9,191	5,498	12,250
29	Long Beach City College	Calif.	1	2	18,378	18,745	18,438	18,137	8,011	10,126	4,361	13,776
30	Los Angeles Valley College	Calif.	1	2	16,457	16,684	16,290	15,362	6,659	8,703	3,673	11,689
31	Mount San Antonio College	Calif.	1	2	20,563	22,438	22,274	22,202	10,204	11,998	6,773	15,429
32	Orange Coast College	Calif.	1	2	22,365	21,928	21,662	21,135	10,420	10,715	6,066	15,069
33	Palomar College	Calif.	1	2	16,707	18,983	18,659	18,894	8,946	9,948	4,877	14,017
34	Pasadena City College	Calif.	1	2	19,581	22,248	21,787	21,101	9,412	11,689	6,436	14,665
35	Rancho Santiago College	Calif.	1	2	20,532	20,920	20,875	20,392	10,831	9,561	4,992	15,400
36	Riverside Community College	Calif.	1	2	15,683	20,293	19,263	18,633	7,555	11,078	5,027	13,606
37	Sacramento City College	Calif.	1	2	14,474	16,052	16,154	16,098	6,834	9,264	5,056	11,042
38	San Diego Mesa College	Calif.	1	2	23,410	20,217	19,284	19,904	9,416	10,488	5,255	14,649
39	San Diego State University	Calif.	1	1	35,493	28,131	28,372	29,350	13,199	16,151	20,616	8,734
40	San Francisco State University	Calif.	1	1	29,343	25,713	26,260	26,791	11,104	15,687	17,626	9,165
41	San Joaquin Delta College	Calif.	1	2	14,792	15,806	14,895	14,640	6,153	8,487	4,920	9,720
42	San Jose State University	Calif.	1	1	30,334	27,057	26,299	25,997	12,304	13,693	16,369	9,628
43	Santa Monica College	Calif.	1	2	18,108	21,768	20,102	20,392	8,853	11,539	6,539	13,853
44	Santa Rosa Junior College	Calif.	1	2	20,475	20,428	20,869	20,102	8,500	11,602	5,723	14,379
45	Southwestern College	Calif.	1	2	13,010	15,384	15,116	15,037	6,956	8,081	4,856	10,181
46	Stanford University	Calif.	2	1	14,724	15,980	16,049	16,003	9,339	6,664	12,691	3,312
47	University of California, Berkeley	Calif.	1	1	30,634	30,341	29,634	29,630	15,810	13,820	27,026	2,604
48	University of California, Davis	Calif.	1	1	23,890	22,476	22,442	23,091	11,313	11,778	20,697	2,394
49	University of California, Irvine	Calif.	1	1	16,808	16,815	17,073	17,256	8,678	8,578	16,184	1,072
50	University of California, Los Angeles	Calif.	1	1	36,420	34,446	35,110	34,713	17,624	17,089	32,672	2,041
51	University of California, San Diego	Calif.	1	1	17,790	17,851	17,774	18,315	9,654	8,661	17,430	885
52	University of California, Santa Barbara	Calif.	1	1	18,385	18,581	17,834	18,224	8,900	9,324	17,467	757
53	University of Southern California	Calif.	2	1	28,374	27,658	28,185	27,971	15,220	12,751	21,016	6,955
54	Colorado State University	Colo.	1	1	26,828	27,384	27,130	26,340	13,014	13,326	19,462	6,878
55	Metropolitan State College of Denver	Colo.	1	1	17,400	17,721	17,624	16,932	7,470	9,462	9,145	7,787
56	University of Colorado, Boulder	Colo.	1	1	28,600	28,352	27,862	27,624	14,761	12,863	20,931	6,693
57	University of Connecticut	Conn.	1	1	25,497	23,182	22,466	22,471	10,980	11,491	15,910	6,561
58	University of Delaware	Del.	1	1	20,818	21,735	21,585	21,365	9,610	11,755	15,594	5,771
59	George Washington University	D.C.	2	1	19,103	18,992	19,298	19,670	10,126	9,544	11,428	8,242
60	Broward Community College	Fla.	1	2	24,365	25,714	26,151	25,738	9,961	15,777	7,193	18,545
61	Florida Atlantic University	Fla.	1	1	12,767	15,769	17,487	17,704	7,316	10,388	7,836	9,868
62	Florida Community College, Jacksonville	Fla.	1	2	20,974	21,228	21,840	21,237	8,631	12,606	5,508	15,729
63	Florida International University	Fla.	1	1	22,466	24,321	26,547	28,171	11,991	16,180	13,558	14,613
64	Florida State University	Fla.	1	1	28,170	28,575	29,527	30,155	13,702	16,453	23,912	6,243
65	Hillsborough Community College	Fla.	1	2	19,134	21,497	20,084	20,311	8,485	11,826	4,318	15,993
66	Miami-Dade Community College	Fla.	1	2	50,078	48,232	47,069	47,060	19,379	27,681	15,631	31,429
67	Palm Beach Community College	Fla.	1	2	18,392	18,586	19,022	18,310	7,028	11,282	4,897	13,413
68	Saint Petersburg Junior College	Fla.	1	2	20,012	22,799	22,112	21,176	8,299	12,877	6,533	14,643
69	University of Central Florida	Fla.	1	1	21,541	23,692	25,592	26,556	12,366	14,190	15,191	11,365
70	University of Florida	Fla.	1	1	35,477	37,324	38,277	39,412	20,938	18,474	33,466	5,946
71	University of South Florida	Fla.	1	1	32,326	34,768	36,043	36,142	15,215	20,927	18,138	18,004
72	Valencia Community College	Fla.	1	2	18,438	22,593	22,727	23,569	9,863	13,706	7,907	15,662

HIGHER EDUCATION: ENROLLMENT 227

Table 217.—Selected statistics for college and university campuses enrolling more than 14,600 students in 1995—Continued

Enrollment, by level, fall 1995		Earned degrees conferred, 1994–95					Financial statistics, 1994–95, in thousands			Full-time-equivalent enrollment, fall 1994	Full-time-equivalent enrollment, fall 1995	Line no.
Undergraduate	Postbaccalaureate	Associate	Bachelor's	Master's	Doctor's	First professional	Current-fund revenues	Current-fund expenditures	Educational and general expenditures			
14	15	16	17	18	19	20	21	22	23	24	25	26
12,231,719	2,030,062	539,691	1,160,134	397,629	44,446	75,800	$189,120,570	$182,968,610	$144,158,002	10,348,072	10,334,956	—
4,134,343	911,951	111,221	483,662	181,591	29,672	26,935	[3]$77,895,311	[3]$75,682,399	[3]$58,163,668	3,699,900	3,710,606	—
18,615	3,507	—	3,527	675	137	96	366,723	352,785	308,502	19,206	20,074	1
14,838	4,147	—	2,785	993	162	180	292,554	274,539	226,187	17,037	16,871	2
10,747	4,755	—	1,610	869	97	255	967,893	881,172	445,222	11,864	12,077	3
15,613	593	612	885	159	—	—	114,781	112,826	105,248	10,411	10,274	4
31,212	10,828	—	5,808	2,047	305	160	495,639	475,990	419,020	34,128	34,122	5
17,699	—	582	—	—	—	—	41,532	36,768	33,709	9,592	9,416	6
21,244	—	967	—	—	—	—	56,882	47,735	42,732	11,113	11,677	7
14,368	5,763	—	2,554	1,371	86	—	190,116	183,223	156,050	15,343	15,978	8
27,866	—	1,060	—	—	—	—	73,661	72,627	71,815	14,207	14,075	9
26,153	8,624	—	4,807	1,357	396	285	751,130	725,654	642,406	30,327	30,013	10
11,937	2,755	4	1,712	611	132	118	257,684	251,738	215,544	12,700	12,820	11
20,170	—	948	—	—	—	—	—	—	—	9,730	9,990	12
14,944	1,079	—	3,080	275	—	—	158,356	154,148	138,609	14,384	14,991	13
14,765	1,840	—	2,685	303	—	—	134,553	138,719	131,409	13,141	13,607	14
14,462	2,999	—	2,985	575	3	—	144,695	145,901	139,586	15,055	15,203	15
18,869	3,735	—	3,963	776	—	—	140,817	146,945	132,001	16,918	17,432	16
21,264	5,139	—	4,232	1,022	—	—	191,472	189,052	172,869	20,454	20,835	17
13,828	4,557	—	2,391	696	5	—	132,993	132,220	125,719	13,639	13,801	18
20,028	4,987	—	3,961	722	—	—	221,490	223,819	208,787	18,800	19,452	19
18,320	4,476	—	4,030	940	—	—	169,584	168,821	157,621	18,259	18,301	20
19,981	—	1,082	—	—	—	—	59,258	53,369	48,868	9,473	9,562	21
26,019	—	1,755	—	—	—	—	—	—	—	13,700	13,405	22
22,545	—	1,297	—	—	—	—	—	—	—	12,388	12,371	23
18,192	—	822	—	—	—	—	47,828	47,981	43,731	10,171	10,421	24
15,289	—	470	—	—	—	—	44,083	43,551	43,551	8,042	8,128	25
21,540	—	1,216	—	—	—	—	—	—	—	11,166	11,098	26
16,287	—	1,205	—	—	—	—	49,993	47,705	42,876	9,333	8,970	27
17,748	—	1,029	—	—	—	—	—	—	—	9,458	9,611	28
18,137	—	839	—	—	—	—	58,611	56,610	56,114	9,170	8,986	29
15,362	—	453	—	—	—	—	45,879	43,192	43,192	8,056	7,597	30
22,202	—	1,076	—	—	—	—	—	—	—	11,939	11,953	31
21,135	—	799	—	—	—	—	—	—	—	11,555	11,125	32
18,894	—	834	—	—	—	—	58,927	58,131	52,701	9,569	9,583	33
21,101	—	957	—	—	—	—	—	—	—	11,651	11,360	34
20,392	—	1,269	—	—	—	—	80,521	68,175	63,926	10,372	10,162	35
18,633	—	915	—	—	—	—	—	—	—	9,338	9,595	36
16,098	—	806	—	—	—	—	—	—	—	8,755	8,763	37
19,904	—	617	—	—	—	—	44,742	37,694	31,733	10,020	10,173	38
23,554	5,796	—	4,752	1,501	18	—	229,400	218,379	198,113	23,068	24,008	39
20,404	6,387	—	3,659	1,234	7	—	198,803	194,270	180,732	20,448	21,190	40
14,640	—	813	—	—	—	—	53,339	51,814	47,151	8,331	8,183	41
20,453	5,544	—	3,975	1,279	—	—	200,164	200,213	176,014	20,315	20,120	42
20,392	—	1,113	—	—	—	—	—	—	—	10,845	11,190	43
20,102	—	988	—	—	—	—	65,964	64,265	58,830	11,168	10,551	44
15,037	—	772	—	—	—	—	41,812	44,531	39,722	8,350	8,274	45
6,946	9,057	—	1,615	1,964	574	249	1,783,758	1,766,806	1,093,213	13,974	13,980	46
21,048	8,582	—	5,536	1,643	828	339	893,815	903,369	839,112	27,910	28,037	47
18,053	5,038	—	3,990	506	341	356	1,136,663	1,064,185	648,551	21,105	21,652	48
13,716	3,540	—	3,183	580	188	85	642,923	633,419	424,664	16,391	16,606	49
23,769	10,944	—	5,494	1,957	663	568	1,798,045	1,756,492	1,156,541	33,700	33,472	50
14,846	3,469	—	3,248	392	274	106	1,101,232	1,070,344	724,593	17,213	17,783	51
15,934	2,290	—	4,030	394	202	—	344,437	343,644	293,018	17,379	17,766	52
15,166	12,805	—	3,388	2,716	539	595	1,021,606	1,003,501	782,704	23,811	23,690	53
20,058	6,282	—	3,139	798	209	131	390,371	379,549	322,294	22,385	22,088	54
16,932	—	—	2,109	—	—	—	70,291	69,624	67,706	12,716	12,287	55
21,315	6,309	—	4,441	1,001	299	160	474,649	460,040	377,079	23,606	23,465	56
14,667	7,804	10	2,941	1,253	265	197	448,245	446,469	386,840	18,400	18,444	57
18,141	3,224	8	3,250	643	139	—	384,945	361,677	313,578	18,035	17,859	58
7,392	12,278	34	1,279	2,581	157	606	784,575	744,951	354,944	14,235	14,629	59
25,738	—	1,955	—	—	—	—	75,161	74,248	67,637	13,796	13,419	60
14,218	3,486	29	2,403	634	37	—	139,885	136,108	123,152	11,451	11,708	61
21,237	—	2,155	—	—	—	—	86,319	86,303	84,223	10,876	10,789	62
22,478	5,693	—	3,466	991	43	—	191,509	184,665	164,398	18,071	19,290	63
23,411	6,744	768	5,225	1,280	295	86	394,268	384,944	326,886	25,913	26,309	64
20,311	—	1,924	—	—	—	—	53,790	56,481	52,621	9,694	9,687	65
47,060	—	4,350	—	—	—	—	205,370	210,085	197,868	26,170	26,183	66
18,310	—	1,566	—	—	—	—	45,653	45,635	45,300	9,585	9,400	67
21,176	—	2,586	—	—	—	—	59,902	58,051	57,804	11,949	11,449	68
21,714	4,842	199	4,629	1,045	67	—	185,374	177,458	158,207	18,801	19,619	69
29,859	9,553	887	5,707	1,842	400	725	878,378	878,083	805,255	34,620	35,760	70
26,878	9,264	285	5,417	1,731	104	96	421,615	418,763	366,981	25,043	25,136	71
23,569	—	2,102	—	—	—	—	64,494	61,922	56,543	12,616	13,165	72

228 HIGHER EDUCATION: ENROLLMENT

Table 217.—Selected statistics for college and university campuses enrolling more than 14,600 students in 1995—Continued

Line no.	Institution	State	Control[1]	Type[2]	Total enrollment, fall 1990	Total enrollment, fall 1993	Total enrollment, fall 1994	Total enrollment, fall 1995	Enrollment, by sex, fall 1995		Enrollment, by attendance status, fall 1995	
									Men	Women	Full-time	Part-time
1	2	3	4	5	6	7	8	9	10	11	12	13
73	DeKalb College	Ga.	1	2	13,944	16,349	16,099	16,073	6,248	9,825	5,706	10,367
74	Georgia State University	Ga.	1	1	23,336	23,605	23,730	24,274	9,922	14,352	12,422	11,852
75	University of Georgia	Ga.	1	1	28,395	28,753	29,469	30,149	13,845	16,304	25,924	4,225
76	University of Hawaii at Manoa	Hi.	1	1	18,799	20,061	20,010	19,769	8,973	10,796	14,185	5,584
77	City Colleges of Chicago-Harry S Truman College	Ill.	1	2	16,460	15,566	15,405	14,883	6,588	8,295	3,589	11,294
78	College of Du Page	Ill.	1	2	29,185	31,132	30,806	29,888	12,860	17,028	8,442	21,446
79	De Paul University	Ill.	2	1	15,711	16,479	16,747	17,133	7,759	9,374	9,681	7,452
80	Illinois State University	Ill.	1	1	22,662	20,610	19,595	19,756	8,470	11,286	16,076	3,680
81	Northern Illinois University	Ill.	1	1	24,509	23,177	22,881	22,218	9,929	12,289	16,042	6,176
82	Northwestern University	Ill.	2	1	17,041	17,551	17,781	17,780	9,175	8,605	13,995	3,785
83	Southern Illinois University, Carbondale	Ill.	1	1	24,078	23,881	23,162	22,418	12,915	9,503	18,436	3,982
84	Triton College	Ill.	1	2	16,759	15,308	15,150	15,362	7,310	8,052	3,899	11,463
85	University of Illinois at Chicago	Ill.	1	1	24,959	25,445	25,040	24,870	11,610	13,260	18,748	6,122
86	University of Illinois, Urbana Campus	Ill.	1	1	38,163	38,912	38,545	38,420	21,093	17,327	33,613	4,807
87	William Rainey Harper College	Ill.	1	2	16,509	16,212	16,051	15,106	6,362	8,744	4,478	10,628
88	Ball State University	Ind.	1	1	20,343	21,626	20,390	20,014	9,301	10,713	16,231	3,783
89	Indiana University, Bloomington	Ind.	1	1	35,451	35,551	35,594	35,063	16,409	18,654	29,301	5,762
90	Indiana U. - Purdue U. at Indianapolis	Ind.	1	1	27,517	27,552	26,766	26,939	11,318	15,621	12,722	14,217
91	Purdue University, Main Campus	Ind.	1	1	37,588	37,094	36,172	36,427	21,323	15,104	30,652	5,775
92	Iowa State University	Iowa	1	1	25,737	25,413	24,990	24,673	14,111	10,562	20,910	3,763
93	University of Iowa	Iowa	1	1	28,785	27,688	27,671	28,052	13,596	14,456	21,418	6,634
94	Johnson County Community College	Kans.	1	2	13,740	15,353	15,035	15,477	6,846	8,631	4,619	10,858
95	Kansas State U. of Agr. and App. Sci.	Kans.	1	1	21,137	20,050	19,883	19,681	10,394	9,287	16,088	3,593
96	University of Kansas, Main Campus	Kans.	1	1	26,434	26,127	25,336	25,036	12,308	12,728	19,428	5,608
97	Eastern Kentucky University	Ky.	1	1	15,290	16,343	16,038	15,703	6,587	9,116	11,504	4,199
98	University of Kentucky	Ky.	1	1	22,538	23,670	23,622	23,794	11,662	12,132	18,543	5,251
99	University of Louisville	Ky.	1	1	22,979	21,172	20,721	20,559	9,483	11,076	12,624	7,935
100	Western Kentucky University	Ky.	1	1	15,170	15,271	14,728	14,675	5,898	8,777	10,510	4,165
101	La. St. U. & A&M & Hebert Laws Center	La.	1	1	26,112	26,085	26,010	26,573	13,186	13,387	20,784	5,789
102	University of New Orleans	La.	1	1	15,322	15,570	15,239	15,483	6,803	8,680	9,164	6,319
103	University of Southwestern Louisiana	La.	1	1	15,764	16,573	16,789	16,902	7,362	9,540	12,718	4,184
104	Johns Hopkins University	Md.	2	1	13,363	15,074	15,548	15,765	8,241	7,524	7,397	8,368
105	Towson State University	Md.	1	1	15,035	14,696	14,551	14,643	5,691	8,952	9,875	4,768
106	U. of Maryland, College Park Campus	Md.	1	1	34,829	32,441	32,493	32,908	17,145	15,763	25,180	7,728
107	Boston College	Mass.	2	1	14,502	14,586	14,713	14,729	6,755	7,974	11,521	3,208
108	Boston University	Mass.	2	1	27,996	28,653	29,072	29,132	13,365	15,767	23,135	5,997
109	Harvard University	Mass.	2	1	22,851	26,007	24,806	24,687	12,955	11,732	18,272	6,415
110	Northeastern University	Mass.	2	1	30,510	26,554	25,086	24,605	12,639	11,966	13,824	10,781
111	University of Massachusetts, Amherst	Mass.	1	1	26,025	24,234	24,825	25,267	12,818	12,449	19,616	5,651
112	Central Michigan University	Mich.	1	1	18,286	23,998	23,390	23,575	10,372	13,203	14,886	8,689
113	Eastern Michigan University	Mich.	1	1	25,011	24,600	23,321	23,142	9,288	13,854	12,841	10,301
114	Lansing Community College	Mich.	1	2	22,343	18,419	16,816	16,404	6,968	9,436	4,276	12,128
115	Macomb Community College	Mich.	1	2	31,538	27,391	25,809	25,176	12,245	12,931	5,512	19,664
116	Michigan State University	Mich.	1	1	44,307	39,743	40,254	40,647	19,442	21,205	32,470	8,177
117	Oakland Community College	Mich.	1	2	28,069	28,232	26,324	25,913	10,468	15,445	5,119	20,794
118	University of Michigan, Ann Arbor	Mich.	1	1	36,391	36,845	36,543	36,687	19,602	17,085	33,234	3,453
119	Wayne State University	Mich.	1	1	33,872	34,280	32,906	32,149	14,105	18,044	14,619	17,530
120	Western Michigan University	Mich.	1	1	26,989	26,555	25,673	26,537	11,921	14,616	16,691	9,846
121	University of Minnesota, Twin Cities	Minn.	1	1	57,168	51,880	51,478	51,445	24,477	26,968	23,316	28,129
122	Southwest Missouri State University	Minn.	1	1	19,480	18,160	17,310	16,439	7,268	9,171	11,962	4,477
123	University of Missouri, Columbia	Mo.	1	1	25,058	22,225	22,175	22,356	10,836	11,520	18,339	4,017
124	University of Missouri, Saint Louis	Mo.	1	1	15,393	15,411	15,588	15,972	5,999	9,973	5,540	10,432
125	University of Nebraska, Lincoln	Nebr.	1	1	24,453	24,491	23,854	24,320	13,024	11,296	19,094	5,226
126	University of Nebraska, Omaha	Nebr.	1	1	15,804	15,897	15,051	14,691	6,648	8,043	7,801	6,890
127	Community College of Southern Nevada	Nev.	1	2	14,161	17,118	16,718	20,417	9,243	11,174	2,553	17,864
128	University of Nevada, Las Vegas	Nev.	1	1	17,937	18,534	18,954	18,842	8,577	10,265	9,014	9,828
129	University of New Hampshire, Main Campus	N.H.	1	1	13,260	13,942	15,394	15,466	6,540	8,926	11,795	3,671
130	Rutgers University, New Brunswick	N.J.	1	1	33,016	33,568	33,464	33,773	15,406	18,367	24,754	9,019
131	Albuquerque Technical Vocational Institute	N.Mex.	1	2	9,739	14,841	14,552	15,225	6,407	8,818	4,210	11,015
132	New Mexico State University, Main Campus	N.Mex.	1	1	14,812	15,788	15,643	15,127	7,479	7,648	10,652	4,475
133	University of New Mexico, Main Campus	N.Mex.	1	1	23,950	25,663	24,572	24,605	10,824	13,781	14,608	9,997
134	Columbia University, New York	N.Y.	2	1	18,242	19,023	19,051	19,302	9,870	9,432	15,402	3,900
135	CUNY, Bernard Baruch College	N.Y.	1	1	15,849	15,064	15,091	15,433	6,736	8,697	9,344	6,089
136	CUNY, Borough of Manhattan Community College	N.Y.	1	2	14,819	16,702	16,728	16,334	5,624	10,710	9,729	6,605
137	CUNY, Brooklyn College	N.Y.	1	1	16,605	15,580	15,984	16,282	6,111	10,171	8,247	8,035
138	CUNY, Hunter College	N.Y.	1	1	19,639	18,657	19,663	18,250	4,823	13,427	8,849	9,401
139	Monroe Community College	N.Y.	1	2	13,545	13,949	13,731	14,633	6,988	7,645	6,871	7,762
140	Nassau Community College	N.Y.	1	2	21,537	22,215	21,955	21,737	9,920	11,817	11,108	10,629
141	New York University	N.Y.	2	1	32,813	33,309	35,425	35,835	15,360	20,475	22,977	12,858
142	Queens College	N.Y.	1	1	18,072	17,753	17,958	17,522	6,537	10,985	9,141	8,381
143	Regents College-U. of the State of N.Y.	N.Y.	2	1	13,303	15,628	17,259	19,433	7,226	12,207	—	19,433
144	Saint John's University of New York	N.Y.	2	1	19,105	18,188	17,820	17,393	7,982	9,411	12,528	4,865
145	SUNY at Albany	N.Y.	1	1	17,400	16,759	16,622	15,996	7,778	8,218	11,757	4,239
146	SUNY at Buffalo	N.Y.	1	1	27,638	25,635	24,943	24,493	13,162	11,331	18,320	6,173
147	SUNY at Stony Brook	N.Y.	1	1	17,624	17,205	17,621	17,665	8,429	9,236	13,294	4,371
148	Syracuse University, Main Campus	N.Y.	2	1	21,900	19,353	18,971	18,804	8,783	10,021	13,557	5,247

HIGHER EDUCATION: ENROLLMENT   229

Table 217.—Selected statistics for college and university campuses enrolling more than 14,600 students in 1995—Continued

Enrollment, by level, fall 1995		Earned degrees conferred, 1994–95					Financial statistics, 1994–95, in thousands			Full-time-equivalent enrollment, fall 1994	Full-time-equivalent enrollment, fall 1995	Line no.
Undergraduate	Postbaccalaureate	Associate	Bachelor's	Master's	Doctor's	First professional	Current-fund revenues	Current-fund expenditures	Educational and general expenditures			
14	15	16	17	18	19	20	21	22	23	24	25	26
16,073	—	973	—	—	—	—	56,265	55,943	52,390	9,195	9,187	73
16,807	7,467	10	2,638	1,574	170	168	204,352	202,440	199,886	16,393	17,112	74
23,572	6,577	—	4,714	1,260	342	303	653,368	640,002	587,681	26,813	27,567	75
13,401	6,368	—	2,603	1,070	155	121	455,055	455,617	408,157	16,480	16,300	76
14,883	—	437	—	—	—	—	45,351	45,485	45,485	8,038	7,381	77
29,888	—	1,672	—	—	—	—	85,519	78,355	71,372	16,047	15,642	78
10,450	6,683	—	1,648	1,430	13	289	178,666	172,728	154,427	12,215	12,623	79
16,665	3,091	—	3,989	633	58	—	196,089	180,413	144,462	17,373	17,477	80
15,760	6,458	—	3,312	1,195	117	103	231,916	233,093	181,641	19,008	18,358	81
9,765	8,015	—	1,968	2,155	375	434	726,404	709,469	672,724	15,481	15,463	82
18,172	4,246	552	4,572	786	168	173	317,357	325,344	292,199	20,479	19,966	83
15,362	—	820	—	—	—	—	47,611	44,462	40,682	7,554	7,748	84
16,154	8,716	—	2,879	1,495	245	511	938,576	922,233	596,261	21,200	21,110	85
27,843	10,577	—	6,169	2,505	761	269	879,244	870,159	761,858	35,456	35,455	86
15,106	—	1,209	—	—	—	—	70,668	71,071	66,633	8,535	8,046	87
17,456	2,558	256	3,424	738	56	—	241,359	233,583	195,086	17,983	17,691	88
27,094	7,969	62	5,076	1,825	383	265	678,911	660,288	479,621	31,968	31,520	89
19,667	7,272	531	2,129	608	31	583	828,247	803,236	412,338	17,887	18,352	90
29,629	6,798	633	5,185	1,273	509	100	689,675	655,103	565,189	32,626	32,887	91
19,941	4,732	—	3,795	785	318	86	556,030	534,911	434,148	22,666	22,350	92
18,824	9,228	—	3,301	1,416	340	468	1,061,550	1,035,559	540,385	23,496	23,946	93
15,477	—	803	—	—	—	—	71,064	63,809	57,976	8,155	8,264	94
16,219	3,462	47	3,024	719	166	84	270,439	269,818	251,076	17,556	17,466	95
18,087	6,949	—	3,308	1,192	250	177	340,959	328,956	281,090	21,793	21,527	96
13,639	2,064	261	1,771	357	—	—	125,790	121,639	105,966	13,534	13,131	97
17,384	6,410	—	2,836	1,065	223	290	800,570	738,057	501,054	20,422	20,567	98
15,152	5,407	142	1,766	874	61	332	340,721	305,044	265,319	15,765	15,726	99
12,608	2,067	301	1,856	575	—	—	114,434	111,019	98,767	12,126	12,125	100
20,363	6,210	—	3,149	1,040	222	277	443,806	439,168	368,055	22,574	23,035	101
11,694	3,789	—	1,430	548	37	—	109,022	106,152	95,898	11,443	11,600	102
15,291	1,611	69	1,643	326	31	—	112,903	108,479	92,139	14,224	14,364	103
4,488	11,277	3	986	2,566	271	119	1,459,703	1,441,459	996,310	10,464	10,602	104
12,770	1,873	—	2,664	423	—	—	122,664	119,548	88,786	11,581	11,738	105
24,373	8,535	—	4,537	1,521	480	—	640,324	604,417	514,864	27,521	28,116	106
10,136	4,593	—	2,422	1,064	108	288	337,472	304,040	235,225	12,769	12,757	107
18,555	10,577	8	3,249	2,977	315	624	822,592	785,477	696,898	25,145	25,458	108
10,515	14,172	5	1,771	2,767	556	771	1,466,218	1,468,763	1,340,479	20,817	20,764	109
19,737	4,868	356	2,357	1,368	80	181	296,857	294,367	278,183	18,075	18,037	110
19,164	6,103	102	3,311	929	307	—	485,627	471,327	376,093	21,304	21,741	111
16,058	7,517	—	2,868	2,427	12	—	179,501	166,903	135,249	17,730	18,144	112
18,176	4,966	—	3,023	1,218	—	—	178,001	170,957	144,384	16,905	16,824	113
16,404	—	1,335	—	—	—	—	71,121	62,384	61,803	8,612	8,348	114
25,176	—	2,611	—	—	—	—	84,956	78,086	72,011	12,646	12,114	115
31,329	9,318	—	6,071	1,487	419	275	893,165	851,114	704,616	35,413	35,613	116
25,913	—	1,945	—	—	—	—	78,291	86,991	81,388	12,461	12,100	117
23,575	13,112	—	4,981	2,840	714	723	2,245,047	2,029,683	1,095,896	34,294	34,548	118
18,638	13,511	—	2,856	2,366	220	455	459,272	434,339	420,990	22,073	21,413	119
20,187	6,350	—	3,867	1,441	74	—	260,451	252,947	198,049	20,028	20,447	120
37,711	13,734	3	5,162	2,271	685	682	1,618,588	1,604,896	1,164,166	34,103	34,376	121
14,566	1,873	3	2,382	342	—	—	124,998	117,989	99,949	14,521	13,710	122
16,784	5,572	—	3,447	1,036	219	302	742,333	677,926	418,552	19,567	19,866	123
13,002	2,970	—	1,680	524	24	35	100,151	95,103	86,630	10,061	9,648	124
19,186	5,134	18	2,890	757	229	147	398,428	387,827	307,625	20,661	21,097	125
11,921	2,770	—	1,586	595	—	—	89,135	86,235	79,083	10,695	10,492	126
20,417	—	562	—	—	—	—	33,819	31,660	31,400	7,082	8,551	127
14,907	3,935	—	2,076	523	10	—	167,766	157,007	135,906	12,727	12,844	128
12,530	2,936	256	2,395	490	51	—	254,562	240,558	195,492	13,128	13,207	129
25,464	8,309	—	5,028	1,360	405	17	—	—	—	27,630	28,172	130
15,225	—	621	—	—	—	—	54,514	49,497	45,997	7,387	7,908	131
12,572	2,555	210	1,918	660	75	—	251,399	243,124	204,654	12,915	12,413	132
16,367	8,238	62	2,489	1,153	201	172	735,259	720,506	411,944	18,394	18,441	133
6,853	12,449	—	1,365	4,630	660	576	1,159,571	1,119,131	1,075,507	16,678	16,911	134
13,122	2,311	—	1,920	669	—	—	109,969	113,020	113,020	11,392	11,734	135
16,334	—	1,625	—	—	—	—	82,278	85,177	84,664	12,179	11,947	136
11,339	4,943	—	1,385	778	—	—	113,534	116,270	115,954	11,220	11,295	137
13,980	4,270	—	1,612	1,121	—	—	134,532	139,305	137,914	13,592	12,495	138
14,633	—	1,935	—	—	—	—	78,695	79,435	74,077	9,504	9,477	139
21,737	—	3,136	—	—	—	—	120,315	120,315	120,315	14,705	14,677	140
16,391	19,444	394	3,007	4,855	380	941	1,532,142	1,509,166	989,462	27,339	27,933	141
14,143	3,379	—	1,942	844	—	—	130,569	134,698	130,900	12,671	12,394	142
19,433	—	2,071	2,130	—	—	—	14,559	13,390	13,390	6,780	7,634	143
12,395	4,998	404	2,458	996	20	386	204,960	199,093	193,976	14,950	14,452	144
10,911	5,085	—	2,536	1,266	168	—	237,419	239,868	210,982	13,892	13,340	145
16,150	8,343	51	3,079	1,505	318	451	492,542	506,631	471,500	20,875	20,665	146
11,485	6,180	—	2,338	1,184	241	145	793,842	766,115	407,047	14,969	14,934	147
11,965	6,839	8	2,524	1,666	202	248	409,309	400,690	331,498	15,727	15,580	148

Table 217.—Selected statistics for college and university campuses enrolling more than 14,600 students in 1995—Continued

Line no.	Institution	State	Control[1]	Type[2]	Total enrollment, fall 1990	Total enrollment, fall 1993	Total enrollment, fall 1994	Total enrollment, fall 1995	Enrollment, by sex, fall 1995		Enrollment, by attendance status, fall 1995	
									Men	Women	Full-time	Part-time
1	2	3	4	5	6	7	8	9	10	11	12	13
149	Central Piedmont Community College	N.C.	1	2	16,311	16,575	16,056	15,176	6,423	8,753	4,640	10,536
150	East Carolina University	N.C.	1	1	17,564	18,186	18,076	17,923	7,422	10,501	14,304	3,619
151	North Carolina State Universitiy, Raleigh	N.C.	1	1	27,199	27,810	28,223	28,250	16,652	11,598	18,729	9,521
152	University of North Carolina, Chapel Hill	N.C.	1	1	23,878	24,334	24,565	24,439	10,330	14,109	19,814	4,625
153	University of North Carolina, Charlotte	N.C.	1	1	14,699	15,942	15,648	16,069	7,696	8,373	10,577	5,492
154	Bowling Green State U., Main Campus	Ohio	1	1	18,657	17,767	17,669	17,554	7,472	10,082	15,012	2,542
155	Cleveland State University	Ohio	1	1	19,214	16,881	16,377	15,566	7,306	8,260	8,869	6,697
156	Columbus State Community College	Ohio	1	2	13,290	17,042	16,795	16,013	6,609	9,404	5,597	10,416
157	Cuyahoga Community College District	Ohio	1	2	23,157	25,913	24,079	22,785	8,077	14,708	7,614	15,171
158	Kent State University, Main Campus	Ohio	1	1	24,434	22,700	21,413	20,972	8,566	12,406	15,334	5,638
159	Miami University, Oxford Campus	Ohio	1	1	15,835	16,281	15,624	15,745	7,193	8,552	14,252	1,493
160	Ohio State University, Main Campus	Ohio	1	1	54,087	50,623	49,542	48,676	25,202	23,474	39,198	9,478
161	Ohio University, Main Campus	Ohio	1	1	18,505	19,086	19,461	19,727	9,313	10,414	17,838	1,889
162	Sinclair Community College	Ohio	1	2	16,367	18,751	17,783	17,344	6,636	10,708	5,979	11,365
163	University of Akron, Main Campus	Ohio	1	1	28,801	26,032	24,488	23,640	11,153	12,487	13,316	10,324
164	University of Cincinnati, Main Campus	Ohio	1	1	31,013	28,662	28,758	28,373	14,673	13,700	19,712	8,661
165	University of Toledo	Ohio	1	1	24,691	24,188	23,107	21,991	10,521	11,470	15,426	6,565
166	Wright State University, Main Campus	Ohio	1	1	16,393	16,460	16,029	15,710	7,100	8,610	10,134	5,576
167	Oklahoma State University, Main Campus	Okla.	1	1	19,827	19,153	18,807	19,196	10,416	8,780	14,708	4,488
168	Tulsa Junior College	Okla.	1	2	17,955	19,098	18,604	18,632	7,448	11,184	4,995	13,637
169	University of Central Oklahoma	Okla.	1	1	14,232	15,043	16,076	15,480	6,444	9,036	8,913	6,567
170	University of Oklahoma, Norman Campus	Okla.	1	1	20,774	21,696	22,043	22,299	11,955	10,344	15,607	6,692
171	Portland Community College	Oreg.	1	2	21,888	22,527	23,158	26,540	11,485	15,055	3,595	22,945
172	Portland State University	Oreg.	1	1	16,921	16,243	15,818	15,600	7,035	8,565	7,880	7,720
173	University of Oregon	Oreg.	1	1	18,840	16,877	16,962	17,470	8,506	8,964	15,119	2,351
174	Community College of Allegheny County	Pa.	1	2	20,553	20,721	18,859	17,723	7,383	10,340	7,323	10,400
175	Community College of Philadelphia	Pa.	1	2	15,151	19,786	18,305	17,865	6,087	11,778	5,329	12,536
176	International Correspondence Schools	Pa.	3	2	20,727	23,552	24,911	32,560	13,871	18,689	—	32,560
177	Pennsylvania State U., Main Campus	Pa.	1	1	38,864	37,658	38,294	39,646	22,105	17,541	35,025	4,621
178	Temple University	Pa.	1	1	29,714	30,040	29,616	29,028	13,388	15,640	18,831	10,197
179	University of Pennsylvania	Pa.	2	1	21,868	22,469	22,720	22,148	11,466	10,682	18,139	4,009
180	University of Pittsburgh, Main Campus	Pa.	1	1	28,120	27,528	26,328	26,083	12,767	13,316	18,835	7,248
181	Community College of Rhode Island	R.I.	1	2	16,620	16,399	16,001	15,889	5,925	9,964	4,750	11,139
182	Clemson University	S.C.	1	1	15,714	16,609	16,290	16,318	8,785	7,533	13,632	2,686
183	University of South Carolina, Columbia	S.C.	1	1	25,613	26,710	26,754	26,346	11,332	15,014	17,242	9,104
184	Middle Tennessee State University	Tenn.	1	1	14,865	17,383	17,120	17,424	7,840	9,584	12,923	4,501
185	University of Memphis	Tenn.	1	1	20,681	20,373	19,849	19,975	8,746	11,229	13,048	6,927
186	University of Tennessee, Knoxville	Tenn.	1	1	26,055	26,397	25,914	25,723	12,780	12,943	19,673	6,050
187	Austin Community College	Tex.	1	2	24,251	24,564	25,276	25,620	11,818	13,802	6,610	19,010
188	Central Texas College	Tex.	1	2	4,815	7,814	14,547	14,746	9,292	5,454	2,427	12,319
189	El Paso Community College	Tex.	1	2	17,081	18,843	18,656	21,856	8,713	13,143	7,019	14,837
190	Houston Community College System	Tex.	1	2	36,437	39,321	45,893	39,541	17,163	22,378	10,557	28,984
191	North Harris-Montgomery Community College	Tex.	1	2	15,653	17,587	17,850	19,251	7,619	11,632	6,600	12,651
192	San Antonio College	Tex.	1	2	20,083	18,944	18,558	19,319	8,139	11,180	6,927	12,392
193	Southwest Texas State University	Tex.	1	1	20,940	20,879	20,889	20,917	9,538	11,379	14,812	6,105
194	Tarrant County Junior College District	Tex.	1	2	28,161	27,353	26,257	25,953	11,118	14,835	7,578	18,375
195	Texas A&M University	Tex.	1	1	41,171	42,524	42,018	41,790	23,373	18,417	37,211	4,579
196	Texas Tech University	Tex.	1	1	25,363	24,007	24,083	24,185	13,109	11,076	20,361	3,824
197	University of Texas, Arlington	Tex.	1	1	24,782	23,763	23,373	22,121	11,246	10,875	12,256	9,865
198	University of Texas, Austin	Tex.	1	1	49,617	48,555	47,957	47,905	24,898	23,007	41,382	6,523
199	University of Texas, El Paso	Tex.	1	1	16,524	17,006	17,196	16,275	7,454	8,821	9,710	6,565
200	University of Texas, San Antonio	Tex.	1	1	15,489	17,097	17,579	17,389	8,040	9,349	10,087	7,302
201	University of Houston, University Park	Tex.	1	1	33,115	32,124	31,299	30,766	15,016	15,750	19,042	11,724
202	University of North Texas	Tex.	1	1	27,160	25,759	25,605	25,114	11,919	13,195	16,342	8,772
203	Brigham Young University	Utah	2	1	31,662	31,706	31,511	31,300	15,342	15,958	28,388	2,912
204	Salt Lake Community College	Utah	1	2	13,344	17,437	18,534	19,568	10,287	9,281	7,204	12,364
205	University of Utah	Utah	1	1	24,922	27,113	26,906	27,137	14,341	12,796	17,978	9,159
206	Utah State University	Utah	1	1	15,155	17,556	20,371	19,861	9,579	10,282	12,120	7,741
207	George Mason University	Va.	1	1	20,308	21,300	21,774	24,172	10,496	13,676	11,934	12,238
208	Northern Virginia Community College	Va.	1	2	35,194	37,477	37,655	37,144	16,774	20,370	9,128	28,016
209	Old Dominion University	Va.	1	1	16,729	15,974	16,490	17,077	7,924	9,153	9,880	7,197
210	Tidewater Community College	Va.	1	2	17,726	17,511	17,749	16,780	7,104	9,676	4,630	12,150
211	University of Virginia, Main Campus	Va.	1	1	21,110	21,394	21,421	21,728	10,116	11,612	17,738	3,990
212	Virginia Commonwealth University	Va.	1	1	21,764	21,854	21,523	21,349	8,616	12,733	13,640	7,709
213	Virginia Polytechnic Inst. and State Univ.	Va.	1	1	25,568	26,030	25,842	25,492	14,960	10,532	22,471	3,021
214	University of Washington	Wash.	1	1	33,854	34,000	33,719	33,996	17,076	16,920	27,992	6,004
215	Washington State University	Wash.	1	1	18,412	18,822	19,314	19,571	10,223	9,348	16,963	2,608
216	West Virginia University	W.Va.	1	1	20,854	23,080	22,500	21,517	10,740	10,777	17,325	4,192
217	Milwaukee Area Technical College	Wisc.	1	2	21,600	24,072	23,010	21,903	9,205	12,698	5,268	16,635
218	University of Wisconsin, Madison	Wisc.	1	1	43,209	39,999	39,361	39,005	19,474	19,531	33,534	5,471
219	University of Wisconsin, Milwaukee	Wisc.	1	1	26,020	23,806	22,604	21,891	9,849	12,042	13,077	8,814
220	Community College of the Air Force	Ala.	1	2	29,567	33,447	[4]33,107	[4]69,611	58,535	11,076	1,394	68,217

Table 217.—Selected statistics for college and university campuses enrolling more than 14,600 students in 1995—Continued

Enrollment, by level, fall 1995		Earned degrees conferred, 1994–95					Financial statistics, 1994–95, in thousands			Full-time-equivalent enrollment, fall 1994	Full-time-equivalent enrollment, fall 1995	Line no.
Undergraduate	Postbaccalaureate	Associate	Bachelor's	Master's	Doctor's	First professional	Current-fund revenues	Current-fund expenditures	Educational and general expenditures			
14	15	16	17	18	19	20	21	22	23	24	25	26
15,176	—	906	—	—	—	—	54,401	54,367	48,068	8,637	8,177	149
14,399	3,524	—	2,682	688	5	74	293,616	282,224	237,918	15,765	15,677	150
21,637	6,613	159	3,866	963	304	70	571,071	560,918	487,605	22,327	22,380	151
15,702	8,737	—	3,506	1,460	369	480	940,220	914,714	702,074	21,535	21,532	152
13,337	2,732	—	2,491	555	—	—	138,848	134,267	106,090	12,356	12,704	153
14,630	2,924	3	2,806	710	74	—	205,147	207,296	159,546	16,057	15,979	154
10,593	4,973	—	1,630	1,034	29	265	142,202	135,403	125,113	11,980	11,506	155
16,013	—	1,360	—	—	—	—	56,610	53,617	49,197	9,694	9,094	156
22,785	—	1,509	—	—	—	—	122,863	111,692	104,754	13,482	12,707	157
16,222	4,750	—	2,977	1,068	188	—	218,914	212,723	168,013	17,868	17,491	158
14,117	1,628	205	3,460	514	44	—	215,183	215,325	159,490	14,820	14,830	159
35,475	13,201	245	7,017	2,353	699	668	1,490,371	1,424,888	932,647	43,382	42,850	160
16,737	2,990	191	3,535	965	116	85	263,357	255,941	212,706	18,309	18,579	161
17,344	—	1,304	—	—	—	—	73,854	63,833	58,376	10,042	9,795	162
19,268	4,372	651	2,258	802	109	145	203,153	195,269	170,129	18,141	17,400	163
20,926	7,447	532	2,937	1,222	264	265	696,107	759,549	452,220	23,332	23,092	164
18,522	3,469	547	2,399	638	71	152	206,579	207,455	169,431	18,923	18,018	165
11,507	4,203	—	1,940	780	36	88	171,100	172,406	160,562	12,637	12,270	166
14,528	4,668	—	2,560	747	157	64	294,536	278,922	223,987	15,957	16,399	167
18,632	—	1,550	—	—	—	—	51,807	48,913	43,409	9,482	9,573	168
12,114	3,366	—	2,126	696	—	—	63,938	60,347	52,381	11,702	11,469	169
15,375	6,924	—	2,328	1,161	172	238	272,066	269,805	215,156	17,785	18,124	170
26,540	—	1,032	—	—	—	—	93,717	91,811	84,567	12,473	11,298	171
10,773	4,827	—	1,752	855	30	—	122,876	118,825	106,231	11,000	10,858	172
13,826	3,644	—	2,871	796	192	133	260,521	248,482	198,126	15,536	16,029	173
17,723	—	2,080	—	—	—	—	92,618	88,241	83,915	11,466	10,815	174
17,865	—	1,135	—	—	—	—	69,962	72,167	71,530	9,825	9,538	175
32,560	—	—	—	—	—	—	—	—	—	9,891	12,928	176
32,790	6,856	73	7,884	1,222	563	—	856,685	834,272	726,161	35,422	36,786	177
18,903	10,125	22	3,202	1,590	315	651	885,774	863,270	408,707	23,194	22,789	178
11,504	10,644	23	2,468	2,276	539	587	1,730,945	1,748,903	907,774	20,090	19,699	179
16,447	9,636	—	3,159	2,347	324	448	707,002	675,835	626,685	21,682	21,606	180
15,889	—	1,579	—	—	—	—	57,334	56,704	52,961	8,524	8,490	181
12,542	3,776	—	2,537	1,217	99	—	334,685	322,475	263,543	14,444	14,640	182
15,915	10,431	17	2,904	1,877	237	348	369,673	354,581	316,901	20,549	20,690	183
15,415	2,009	4	2,106	383	15	—	113,916	111,430	99,199	14,199	14,681	184
15,071	4,904	—	1,846	860	98	137	179,424	180,318	157,788	15,466	15,737	185
18,750	6,973	—	3,433	1,718	257	213	497,337	498,422	420,020	22,168	21,988	186
25,620	—	773	—	—	—	—	71,274	71,767	71,085	12,866	12,992	187
14,746	—	1,473	—	—	—	—	53,656	48,682	44,540	6,509	6,563	188
21,856	—	782	—	—	—	—	73,672	73,656	73,453	11,868	12,000	189
39,541	—	1,095	—	—	—	—	131,692	125,587	125,330	23,006	20,288	190
19,251	—	688	—	—	—	—	58,762	56,233	54,080	10,200	10,847	191
19,319	—	658	—	—	—	—	55,810	56,275	55,954	10,612	11,087	192
17,886	3,031	7	3,033	590	—	—	152,174	150,227	110,641	17,190	17,188	193
25,953	—	1,526	—	—	—	—	80,917	80,714	74,393	13,936	13,747	194
34,371	7,419	—	7,081	1,352	564	157	806,619	826,659	733,101	39,084	38,981	195
19,796	4,389	—	3,095	785	142	202	257,521	237,483	194,298	21,474	21,840	196
17,897	4,224	—	2,982	1,080	94	—	162,090	160,254	135,737	16,946	16,141	197
35,086	12,819	—	7,189	2,698	727	500	865,961	826,781	736,392	43,931	43,953	198
13,915	2,360	—	1,660	444	6	—	129,875	126,481	103,412	13,075	12,291	199
14,935	2,454	—	2,061	535	—	—	97,160	94,076	88,219	13,028	12,959	200
22,853	7,913	—	3,447	1,344	192	395	295,450	307,936	270,664	23,783	23,702	201
18,654	6,460	—	3,454	1,201	189	—	196,615	189,709	158,350	20,074	19,716	202
28,417	2,883	5	6,088	1,138	86	155	529,329	460,951	303,141	29,569	29,521	203
19,568	—	1,523	—	—	—	—	75,621	70,222	61,537	10,901	11,355	204
22,083	5,054	—	3,354	876	208	218	832,174	801,781	502,181	21,343	21,631	205
16,197	3,664	69	2,200	701	64	—	254,684	249,407	223,204	15,201	15,125	206
13,774	10,398	—	2,666	1,618	147	165	206,205	200,614	155,343	15,378	16,607	207
37,144	—	2,318	—	—	—	—	84,347	83,258	82,396	18,780	18,534	208
11,463	5,614	—	1,926	1,126	78	—	150,378	136,091	114,562	12,294	12,619	209
16,780	—	1,145	—	—	—	—	45,059	44,144	43,664	9,043	8,709	210
13,108	8,620	—	2,857	1,475	312	504	919,486	872,875	459,826	18,681	19,224	211
14,532	6,817	20	2,349	1,202	109	259	725,665	728,844	317,371	16,522	16,610	212
19,498	5,994	37	4,336	1,467	361	77	508,984	510,997	433,403	23,736	23,588	213
24,838	9,158	—	6,156	1,890	482	370	1,402,648	1,371,980	975,042	30,070	30,370	214
16,237	3,334	—	3,433	640	169	83	408,283	399,987	340,985	17,827	17,972	215
15,042	6,475	—	3,041	1,378	156	249	364,961	357,723	315,601	19,501	18,886	216
21,903	—	1,338	—	—	—	—	122,660	117,903	108,580	11,531	10,853	217
27,615	11,390	—	5,569	2,068	758	526	1,448,810	1,373,929	1,016,872	35,761	35,683	218
17,234	4,657	—	2,617	1,067	75	—	231,316	230,525	211,106	16,524	16,506	219
69,611	—	11,977	—	—	—	—	—	—	—	19,413	24,297	220

[1] Publicly controlled institutions are identified by a "1;" private, nonprofit by a "2;" and private, proprietary, by a "3."
[2] The types of institutions are identified as follows: "1" 4-year institutions; "2" 2-year institutions.
[3] Includes estimates for nonreporting institutions.
[4] Estimated.
—Data not available or not applicable.

SOURCE: U.S. Department of Education, National Center for Education Statistics, Integrated Postsecondary Education Data System (IPEDS), "Completions," "Finance," and "Fall Enrollment" surveys. (This table was prepared July 1997.)

Table 218.—Fall enrollment, degrees conferred, and expenditures in historically black colleges and universities, by institution: 1995

Institution	Type and control [1]	Enrollment, 1995		Degrees conferred, 1994–95					Expenditures, 1994–95 (In thousands)	
		Total	Black	Associate	Bachelor's	Master's	Doctor's	First-professional	Current-fund expenditures	Educational and general expenditures
1	2	3	4	5	6	7	8	9	10	11
Total	—	278,725	229,418	2,883	28,327	5,560	230	1,147	$3,598,223	$2,976,538
** Alabama A&M University, AL	1	5,400	4,123	—	576	366	6	—	64,833	58,968
Alabama State University, AL	1	5,416	5,020	2	399	109	—	—	49,282	39,904
Bishop State Community College, AL	2	4,127	2,248	434	—	—	—	—	21,106	19,976
C. A. Fredd State Technical College, AL [2]	2	134	103	—	—	—	—	—	—	—
Concordia College, AL	4	472	464	39	5	—	—	—	3,403	3,082
J.F. Drake Technical College, AL	2	683	295	59	—	—	—	—	4,703	4,585
Lawson State Community College, AL	2	1,892	1,809	139	—	—	—	—	10,192	9,787
Miles College, AL	3	1,122	1,121	—	115	—	—	—	9,022	8,177
Oakwood College, AL	3	1,626	1,430	26	187	—	—	—	20,310	16,090
Selma University, AL	3	207	206	10	18	—	—	—	[3] 4,713	[3] 4,353
Stillman College, AL	3	842	827	—	161	—	—	—	11,811	10,294
Talladega College, AL	3	786	784	—	134	—	—	—	13,711	12,278
Trenholm State Technical College, AL	2	707	540	67	—	—	—	—	7,477	7,267
** Tuskegee University, AL	3	3,100	2,846	—	494	59	—	53	71,071	62,519
Arkansas Baptist College, AR	3	203	202	1	29	—	—	—	1,995	1,888
Philander Smith College, AR	3	956	903	—	63	—	—	—	5,943	5,587
Shorter College, AR	4	261	184	18	—	—	—	—	1,077	1,007
** University of Arkansas, Pine Bluff, AR	1	3,242	2,889	—	385	12	—	—	34,561	30,526
** Delaware State College, DE	1	3,175	2,164	—	302	95	—	—	44,179	37,457
Howard University, DC	3	10,332	9,370	—	1,333	369	79	304	568,132	311,189
** University of the District of Columbia, DC	1	9,663	8,081	73	542	120	—	—	[3] 99,351	[3] 98,041
Bethune-Cookman College, FL	3	2,402	2,255	—	292	—	—	—	28,131	24,010
Edward Waters College, FL	3	524	470	—	78	—	—	—	7,216	6,811
** Florida A&M University, FL	1	10,306	9,095	32	1,409	217	9	35	128,698	116,935
Florida Memorial College, FL	3	1,457	1,290	—	202	—	—	—	14,375	13,236
Albany State College, GA	1	3,151	2,784	—	306	81	—	—	32,727	28,036
Clark Atlanta University, GA	3	5,311	5,122	—	483	346	23	—	118,018	111,800
** Fort Valley State College, GA	1	2,978	2,757	3	248	104	—	—	32,834	28,486
Interdenominational Theological Center, GA	3	419	390	—	—	6	3	70	6,071	6,038
Morehouse College, GA	3	2,889	2,871	—	501	—	—	—	[3] 46,713	[3] 40,566
Morehouse School of Medicine, GA	3	163	139	—	—	—	—	29	[3] 48,646	[3] 48,646
Morris Brown College, GA	3	2,065	1,976	—	179	—	—	—	23,137	20,279
Paine College, GA	3	812	790	—	64	—	—	—	8,433	7,357
Savannah State College, GA	1	3,211	2,853	—	299	—	—	—	28,419	23,551
Spelman College, GA	3	1,961	1,905	—	421	—	—	—	37,177	31,807
** Kentucky State University, KY	1	2,579	1,272	73	212	24	—	—	36,395	32,719
Dillard University, LA	3	1,562	1,534	—	212	—	—	—	19,791	18,121
Grambling State University, LA	1	6,800	6,496	49	849	194	13	—	61,671	45,288
** Southern University and A&M College, Baton Rouge, LA	1	10,359	9,807	35	836	192	1	100	92,852	80,625
Southern University, New Orleans, LA	1	4,325	3,977	33	421	96	—	—	21,077	19,608
Southern University, Shreveport-Bossier City Campus, LA	2	1,212	1,115	131	—	—	—	—	7,530	7,261
Xavier University of Louisiana, LA	3	3,463	3,115	—	419	102	—	105	51,216	47,451
Bowie State University, MD	1	5,258	3,879	—	505	474	—	—	34,636	29,609
Coppin State College, MD	1	3,540	3,294	—	313	88	—	—	25,268	22,760
Morgan State University, MD	1	6,016	5,655	—	619	125	5	—	75,953	64,207
** University of Maryland, Eastern Shore, MD	1	2,878	2,023	—	346	39	3	—	38,513	33,900
Lewis College of Business, MI	4	232	231	17	—	—	—	—	1,984	1,977
** Alcorn State University, MS	1	3,033	2,836	38	388	44	—	—	36,585	32,017
Coahoma Community College, MS	2	934	908	96	—	—	—	—	7,845	7,186
Hinds Community College, Utica Campus, MS [4]	2	1,410	1,160	78	—	—	—	—	—	—
Jackson State University, MS	1	6,313	5,932	—	697	176	4	—	73,209	62,468
Mary Holmes College, MS	4	375	360	48	—	—	—	—	6,304	6,063
Mississippi Valley State University, MS	1	2,153	2,132	—	222	4	—	—	25,985	22,672
Rust College, MS	3	994	932	—	149	—	—	—	11,281	9,624
Tougaloo College, MS	3	1,017	1,017	—	152	—	—	—	14,272	13,466
Harris-Stowe State College, MO	1	1,674	1,263	—	137	—	—	—	11,159	11,159
** Lincoln University, MO	1	3,454	863	101	280	85	—	—	26,698	24,851
Barber-Scotia College, NC	3	436	422	—	60	—	—	—	5,689	5,371
Bennett College, NC	3	620	611	—	61	—	—	—	11,853	10,812
Elizabeth City State University, NC	1	1,981	1,484	—	315	—	—	—	29,517	25,402
Fayetteville State University, NC	1	4,009	2,610	43	585	122	—	—	38,689	33,487
Johnson C. Smith University, NC	3	1,398	1,390	—	154	—	—	—	20,808	17,910

Table 218.—Fall enrollment, degrees conferred, and expenditures in historically black colleges and universities, by institution: 1995—Continued

Institution	Type and control [1]	Enrollment, 1995		Degrees conferred, 1994–95					Expenditures, 1994–95 (In thousands)	
		Total	Black	Associate	Bachelor's	Master's	Doctor's	First-professional	Current-fund expenditures	Educational and general expenditures
1	2	3	4	5	6	7	8	9	10	11
Livingstone College, NC	3	750	729	—	68	2	—	10	12,480	11,033
**North Carolina Agricultural and Technical State University, NC	1	7,947	6,878	—	977	256	—	—	106,338	91,762
North Carolina Central University, NC	1	5,555	4,604	—	596	244	—	85	59,628	50,059
St. Augustine's College, NC	3	1,639	1,630	—	197	—	—	—	25,429	21,403
Shaw University, NC	3	2,485	2,372	—	321	—	—	—	24,588	22,227
Winston-Salem State University, NC	1	2,890	2,183	—	475	—	—	—	32,365	26,909
Central State University, OH	1	2,579	2,386	1	351	4	—	—	[3]38,486	[3]31,889
Wilberforce University, OH	3	920	894	—	79	—	—	—	13,467	10,757
**Langston University, OK	1	3,468	1,949	—	463	12	—	—	23,190	19,561
Cheyney University of Pennsylvania, PA	1	1,386	1,311	—	175	86	—	—	25,202	22,670
Lincoln University, PA	1	1,553	1,427	—	264	83	—	—	27,908	24,259
Allen University, SC	3	249	249	—	25	—	—	—	3,583	3,231
Benedict College, SC	3	1,861	1,858	—	179	—	—	—	17,761	15,575
Claflin College, SC	3	1,002	988	—	126	—	—	—	10,983	9,150
Clinton Junior College, SC [5]	4	—	—	—	—	—	—	—	—	—
Denmark Technical College, SC	2	842	763	93	—	—	—	—	[3]5,278	[3]4,418
Morris College, SC	3	850	850	—	95	—	—	—	10,361	9,148
**South Carolina State College, SC	1	4,993	4,595	—	651	129	14	—	50,572	39,576
Voorhees College, SC	3	786	765	—	99	—	—	—	8,374	6,972
Fisk University, TN	3	879	876	—	122	16	—	—	14,841	12,902
Knoxville College, TN	3	730	717	5	61	—	—	—	[3]7,835	[3]6,841
Lane College, TN	3	664	663	—	83	—	—	—	7,691	6,273
Le Moyne-Owen College, TN	3	1,267	1,251	—	177	35	—	—	14,797	14,610
Meharry Medical College, TN	3	721	605	—	—	21	6	110	76,339	62,939
**Tennessee State University, TN	1	8,464	5,508	176	718	195	29	—	74,364	68,841
Huston-Tillotson College, TX	3	641	522	—	67	—	—	—	8,231	7,379
Jarvis Christian College, TX	3	533	522	—	88	—	—	--	7,476	6,911
Paul Quinn College, TX	3	799	744	—	71	—	—	—	8,394	8,149
**Prairie View A&M University, TX	1	5,999	5,158	—	572	240	—	—	68,833	54,611
St. Philip's College, TX	2	6,507	1,323	438	—	—	—	—	27,189	27,120
Southwestern Christian College, TX	3	174	151	48	—	—	—	—	2,927	2,619
Texas College, TX	3	328	317	—	43	—	—	—	4,573	4,261
Texas Southern University, TX	1	9,510	7,684	—	563	188	30	200	78,389	72,504
Wiley College, TX	3	608	550	—	88	—	—	—	7,349	6,716
Hampton University, VA	3	6,035	5,086	—	845	103	—	—	83,521	74,651
Norfolk State University, VA	1	8,129	6,782	62	920	172	—	—	66,464	55,032
St. Paul's College, VA	3	666	614	—	110	—	—	—	10,319	8,950
**Virginia State University, VA	1	3,993	3,552	—	523	88	—	—	51,081	41,361
Virginia Union University, VA	3	1,405	1,383	—	175	—	5	46	18,976	16,252
Bluefield State College, WV	1	2,496	169	200	252	—	—	—	12,151	11,312
West Virginia State College, WV	1	4,486	552	179	401	—	—	—	22,584	18,268
**University of the Virgin Islands, St. Thomas Campus, VI	1	1,916	1,634	36	150	37	—	—	33,656	30,889

[1] 1=public 4-year; 2=public 2-year; 3=private 4-year; and 4=private 2-year.
[2] School merged with Sheldon State Community College. Enrollment is for C.A. Fredd State Technical College only. School reported data.
[3] School did not report. Data imputed.
[4] School reported data.
[5] School lost accreditation.
—Data not reported or not applicable.

**Land-grant institution.

SOURCE: U.S. Department of Education, National Center for Education Statistics, Integrated Postsecondary Education Data System (IPEDS), "Fall Enrollment, 1995," "Completions, 1994–95," and "Finance, 1994–95" surveys. (This table was prepared July 1997.)

Table 219.—Selected statistics on historically black colleges and universities:[1] 1980, 1990, and 1995

Item	Total	Public 4-year	Public 2-year	Private 4-year	Private 2-year
1	2	3	4	5	6
Number of institutions, fall 1995	103	40	10	49	4
Total enrollment, fall 1980	233,557	155,085	13,132	62,924	2,416
Men	106,387	70,236	6,758	28,352	1,041
Men, black	81,818	53,654	2,781	24,412	971
Women	127,170	84,849	6,374	34,572	1,375
Women, black	109,171	70,582	4,644	32,589	1,356
Total enrollment, fall 1990	257,152	171,969	15,077	68,528	1,578
Men	105,157	70,220	6,321	28,054	562
Men, black	82,897	54,041	3,214	25,198	444
Women	151,995	101,749	8,756	40,474	1,016
Women, black	125,785	80,883	6,066	38,115	721
Total enrollment, fall 1995	278,725	186,278	18,448	73,131	868
Men	112,637	75,194	7,839	29,239	365
Men, black	91,132	60,007	3,733	27,113	279
Women	166,088	111,084	10,609	43,892	503
Women, black	138,286	89,654	6,531	41,605	496
Full-time enrollment, fall 1995	214,091	138,159	10,056	65,253	623
Men	88,711	58,049	4,131	26,254	277
Women	125,380	80,110	5,925	38,999	346
Part-time enrollment, fall 1995	64,634	48,119	8,392	7,878	245
Men	23,926	17,145	3,708	2,985	88
Women	40,708	30,974	4,684	4,893	157
Earned degrees conferred, 1994–95					
Associate	2,883	1,136	1,535	129	83
Men	1,009	389	555	39	26
Men, black	376	120	207	23	26
Women	1,874	747	980	90	57
Women, black	1,021	238	643	83	57
Bachelor's	28,327	19,242	—	9,085	—
Men	10,469	7,209	—	3,260	—
Men, black	8,583	5,598	—	2,985	—
Women	17,858	12,033	—	5,825	—
Women, black	15,370	9,842	—	5,528	—
Master's	5,560	4,501	—	1,059	—
Men	1,840	1,507	—	333	—
Men, black	970	756	—	214	—
Women	3,720	2,994	—	726	—
Women, black	2,492	1,903	—	589	—
Doctor's	230	114	—	116	—
Men	116	47	—	69	—
Men, black	67	21	—	46	—
Women	114	67	—	47	—
Women, black	75	40	—	35	—
First-professional	1,147	420	—	727	—
Men	568	208	—	360	—
Men, black	375	102	—	273	—
Women	579	212	—	367	—
Women, black	436	147	—	289	—
Financial statistics, 1994–95, in thousands of dollars					
Current-fund revenues	$3,681,616	$1,941,454	$94,438	$1,637,253	$8,470
Tuition and fees	902,850	398,497	17,382	484,186	2,786
Federal government[2]	797,728	299,360	16,698	479,022	2,648
State governments[2]	914,357	818,856	47,363	47,613	525
Local governments[2]	98,223	83,230	7,193	7,762	38
Private gifts, grants, and contracts	212,557	36,370	234	175,131	822
Endowment income	29,818	2,173	63	27,573	9
Sales and services	657,171	260,668	4,501	390,814	1,188
Other sources	68,913	42,301	1,005	25,153	454
Current-fund expenditures	3,598,223	1,914,303	91,321	1,583,234	9,365
Educational and general expenditures	2,976,538	1,662,182	87,599	1,217,710	9,047
Auxiliary enterprises	367,846	252,121	3,722	111,686	318
Hospitals	234,877	0	0	234,877	0
Independent operations	18,962	0	0	18,962	0

[1] Historically black colleges and universities are accredited institutions of higher education established prior to 1964 with the principal mission of educating black Americans. Federal regulations, 20 U.S. Code, Section 1061 (2), allow for certain exceptions to the founding date. Most institutions are in the southern and border states and were established prior to 1954.

[2] Includes appropriations, grants, contracts, and independent operations.

—Not applicable.

NOTE.—Because of rounding, details may not add to totals.

SOURCE: U.S. Department of Education, National Center for Education Statistics, Higher Education General Information Survey (HEGIS), "Fall Enrollment in Institutions of Higher Education"; and Integrated Postsecondary Education Data System (IPEDS), "Fall Enrollment," "Completions," and "Finance" surveys. (This table was prepared July 1997.)

Table 220.—Fall enrollment in historically black colleges and universities, by type and control of institution: 1976 to 1995

Year	Total enrollment	Type of institution		Public institutions			Private institutions		
		4-year	2-year	Total	4-year	2-year	Total	4-year	2-year
1	2	3	4	5	6	7	8	9	10
1976	222,613	206,676	15,937	156,836	143,528	13,308	65,777	63,148	2,629
1977	226,062	209,898	16,164	158,823	145,450	13,373	67,239	64,448	2,791
1978	227,797	211,651	16,146	163,237	150,168	13,069	64,560	61,483	3,077
1979	230,124	214,147	15,977	166,315	153,139	13,176	63,809	61,008	2,801
1980	233,557	218,009	15,548	168,217	155,085	13,132	65,340	62,924	2,416
1981	232,460	217,152	15,308	166,991	154,269	12,722	65,469	62,883	2,586
1982	228,371	212,017	16,354	165,871	151,472	14,399	62,500	60,545	1,955
1983	234,446	217,909	16,537	170,051	155,665	14,386	64,395	62,244	2,151
1984	227,519	212,844	14,675	164,116	151,289	12,827	63,403	61,555	1,848
1985	225,801	210,648	15,153	163,677	150,002	13,675	62,124	60,646	1,478
1986	223,275	207,231	16,044	162,048	147,631	14,417	61,227	59,600	1,627
1987	227,994	211,654	16,340	165,486	150,560	14,926	62,508	61,094	1,414
1988	239,755	223,250	16,505	173,672	158,606	15,066	66,083	64,644	1,439
1989	249,096	232,890	16,206	181,151	166,481	14,670	67,945	66,409	1,536
1990	257,152	240,497	16,655	187,046	171,969	15,077	70,106	68,528	1,578
1991	269,335	252,093	17,242	197,847	182,204	15,643	71,488	69,889	1,599
1992	279,541	261,089	18,452	204,966	188,143	16,823	74,575	72,946	1,629
1993	282,856	262,430	20,426	208,197	189,032	19,165	74,659	73,398	1,261
1994	280,071	259,997	20,074	206,520	187,735	18,785	73,551	72,262	1,289
1995	278,725	259,409	19,316	204,726	186,278	18,448	73,999	73,131	868

SOURCE: U.S. Department of Education, National Center for Education Statistics, Higher Education General Information Survey (HEGIS), "Fall Enrollment in Colleges and Universities" surveys; and Integrated Postsecondary Education Data System (IPEDS), "Fall Enrollment" survey. (This table was prepared May 1997.)

Table 221.—Employees in institutions of higher education, by primary occupation, employment status, and control of institution: Fall 1976, fall 1991, and fall 1993

Primary occupation and control of institution	Fall 1976					Fall 1991					Fall 1993				
	Total staff			Full-time equivalent staff		Total staff			Full-time equivalent staff		Total staff			Full-time equivalent staff	
	Number	Percent	Full-time	Total	FTE students per FTE staff	Number	Percent		Total	FTE students per FTE staff	Number	Percent		Total	FTE students per FTE staff
1	2	3	4	5	6	7	8		9	10	11	12		13	14
Total, all institutions	1,863,790	100.0	1,339,911	1,541,339	5.4	2,545,235	100.0		2,094,628	4.9	2,602,612	100.0		2,094,681	4.9
Professional staff	1,073,119	57.6	709,400	845,456	9.8	1,595,460	62.7		1,244,588	8.3	1,687,287	64.8		1,280,382	8.1
Executive/administrative/managerial	101,263	5.4	97,003	98,972	84.0	144,755	5.7		141,718	73.1	143,675	5.5		140,522	73.7
Faculty (instruction and research)	633,210	34.0	434,071	500,533	16.6	826,252	32.5		632,565	16.4	915,474	35.2		668,819	15.5
Instruction and research assistants	160,086	8.6	28,007	82,684	100.5	197,751	7.8		81,467	127.2	202,819	7.8		83,717	123.6
Non-faculty professionals	178,560	9.6	150,319	163,267	50.9	426,702	16.8		388,838	26.6	425,319	16.3		387,323	26.7
Nonprofessional staff	790,671	42.4	630,511	695,883	11.9	949,775	37.3		850,040	12.2	915,325	35.2		814,299	12.7
Public, total	1,329,122	100.0	946,354	1,092,558	5.8	1,783,328	100.0		1,449,398	5.4	1,812,513	100.0		1,434,747	5.4
Professional staff	769,836	57.9	502,325	601,942	10.5	1,133,264	63.5		868,112	9.1	1,193,284	65.8		883,579	8.8
Executive/administrative/managerial	60,733	4.6	58,649	59,579	106.6	84,446	4.7		82,835	94.9	81,209	4.5		79,426	98.4
Faculty (instruction and research)	448,733	33.8	313,367	357,761	17.7	580,908	32.6		446,113	17.6	650,434	35.9		470,537	16.6
Instruction and research assistants	127,925	9.6	19,076	63,420	100.1	173,560	9.7		70,707	111.2	173,678	9.6		70,755	110.4
Non-faculty professionals	132,445	10.0	111,233	121,182	52.4	294,350	16.5		268,458	29.3	287,963	15.9		262,862	29.7
Nonprofessional staff	559,286	42.1	444,029	490,616	12.9	650,064	36.5		581,286	13.5	619,229	34.2		551,168	14.2
Private, total	534,668	100.0	393,557	448,781	4.4	761,907	100.0		645,231	3.9	790,099	100.0		659,934	3.8
Professional staff	303,283	56.7	207,075	243,514	8.1	462,196	60.7		376,476	6.6	494,003	62.5		396,802	6.4
Executive/administrative/managerial	40,530	7.6	38,354	39,393	49.8	60,309	7.9		58,883	42.4	62,466	7.9		61,096	41.6
Faculty (instruction and research)	184,477	34.5	120,704	142,772	13.7	245,344	32.2		186,452	13.4	265,040	33.5		198,282	12.8
Instruction and research assistants	32,161	6.0	8,931	19,264	101.9	24,191	3.2		10,760	232.1	29,141	3.7		12,962	195.9
Non-faculty professionals	46,115	8.6	39,086	42,085	46.6	132,352	17.4		120,380	20.7	137,356	17.4		124,461	20.4
Nonprofessional staff	231,385	43.3	186,482	205,267	9.6	299,711	39.3		268,755	9.3	296,096	37.5		263,131	9.6

NOTE.—Because of rounding, details may not add to totals.

SOURCE: U.S. Department of Education, National Center for Education Statistics, Higher Education General Information Survey (HEGIS), "Staff, 1976" survey; and Integrated Postsecondary Education Data System (IPEDS), "Fall Staff" surveys. (This table was prepared January 1996.)

Table 222.—Employees in institutions of higher education by race/ethnicity, primary occupation, control of institution, sex, and employment status: Fall 1993

Primary occupation, control of institution, sex, and employment status	Total	White, non-Hispanic	Black, non-Hispanic	Hispanic	Asian/Pacific Islander	American Indian/Alaskan Native	Non-resident alien	Race/ethnicity unknown
1	2	3	4	5	6	7	8	9
Total, all institutions	2,602,612	2,021,998	274,555	100,990	95,831	12,615	70,359	26,264
Professional staff	1,687,287	1,375,939	103,327	44,085	70,518	6,829	64,097	22,492
Executive/administrative/managerial	143,675	123,737	12,619	3,715	2,395	745	279	185
Faculty (instruction and research)	915,474	779,041	45,172	22,312	35,289	3,407	14,878	15,375
Instruction and research assistants	202,819	131,242	7,487	5,245	14,832	677	37,751	5,585
Non-faculty professionals	425,319	341,919	38,049	12,813	18,002	2,000	11,189	1,347
Nonprofessional staff	915,325	646,059	171,228	56,905	25,313	5,786	6,262	3,772
Public, total	1,812,513	1,408,756	183,885	71,862	65,685	10,495	54,921	16,909
Professional staff	1,193,284	966,121	72,658	33,120	49,711	5,679	51,820	14,175
Executive/administrative/managerial	81,209	69,596	7,268	2,206	1,340	559	147	93
Faculty (instruction and research)	650,434	551,205	33,895	17,217	24,308	2,870	11,179	9,760
Instruction and research assistants	173,678	113,600	5,966	4,547	12,616	610	32,966	3,373
Non-faculty professionals	287,963	231,720	25,529	9,150	11,447	1,640	7,528	949
Nonprofessional staff	619,229	442,635	111,227	38,742	15,974	4,816	3,101	2,734
Private, total	790,099	613,242	90,670	29,128	30,146	2,120	15,438	9,355
Professional staff	494,003	409,818	30,669	10,965	20,807	1,150	12,277	8,317
Executive/administrative/managerial	62,466	54,141	5,351	1,509	1,055	186	132	92
Faculty (instruction and research)	265,040	227,836	11,277	5,095	10,981	537	3,699	5,615
Instruction and research assistants	29,141	17,642	1,521	698	2,216	67	4,785	2,212
Non-faculty professionals	137,356	110,199	12,520	3,663	6,555	360	3,661	398
Nonprofessional staff	296,096	203,424	60,001	18,163	9,339	970	3,161	1,038
Men, total	1,256,037	980,640	106,290	46,953	53,029	5,827	48,411	14,887
Professional staff	930,933	758,678	44,270	22,778	43,072	3,534	45,347	13,254
Executive/administrative/managerial	82,748	72,585	6,097	2,026	1,314	421	185	120
Faculty (instruction and research)	561,123	478,654	22,660	12,966	24,695	1,955	11,122	9,071
Instruction and research assistants	120,384	73,979	3,415	2,767	9,627	354	26,836	3,406
Non-faculty professionals	166,678	133,460	12,098	5,019	7,436	804	7,204	657
Nonprofessional staff	325,104	221,962	62,020	24,175	9,957	2,293	3,064	1,633
Women, total	1,346,575	1,041,358	168,265	54,037	42,802	6,788	21,948	11,377
Professional staff	756,354	617,261	59,057	21,307	27,446	3,295	18,750	9,238
Executive/administrative/managerial	60,927	51,152	6,522	1,689	1,081	324	94	65
Faculty (instruction and research)	354,351	300,387	22,512	9,346	10,594	1,452	3,756	6,304
Instruction and research assistants	82,435	57,263	4,072	2,478	5,205	323	10,915	2,179
Non-faculty professionals	258,641	208,459	25,951	7,794	10,566	1,196	3,985	690
Nonprofessional staff	590,221	424,097	109,208	32,730	15,356	3,493	3,198	2,139
Full-time, total	1,783,510	1,392,311	219,074	73,960	62,034	9,229	23,912	2,990
Professional staff	1,039,094	871,647	71,263	26,700	42,946	4,446	20,284	1,808
Executive/administrative/managerial	137,834	118,651	12,232	3,580	2,243	726	246	156
Faculty (instruction and research)	545,706	468,770	25,658	12,076	25,269	1,997	10,829	1,107
Non-faculty professionals	355,554	284,226	33,373	11,044	15,434	1,723	9,209	545
Nonprofessional staff	744,416	520,664	147,811	47,260	19,088	4,783	3,628	1,182
Part-time, total	819,102	629,687	55,481	27,030	33,797	3,386	46,447	23,274
Professional staff	648,193	504,292	32,064	17,385	27,572	2,383	43,813	20,684
Executive/administrative/managerial	5,841	5,086	387	135	152	19	33	29
Faculty (instruction and research)	369,768	310,271	19,514	10,236	10,020	1,410	4,049	14,268
Instruction and research assistants	202,819	131,242	7,487	5,245	14,832	677	37,751	5,585
Non-faculty professionals	69,765	57,693	4,676	1,769	2,568	277	1,980	802
Nonprofessional staff	170,909	125,395	23,417	9,645	6,225	1,003	2,634	2,590

SOURCE: U.S. Department of Education, National Center for Education Statistics, Integrated Postsecondary Education Data System (IPEDS), "Fall Staff" survey. (This table was prepared January 1996.)

Table 223.—Employees in institutions of higher education, by primary occupation, sex, employment status, and by type and control of institution: Fall 1993

Primary occupation and type and control of institution	Full-time and part-time					Full-time				Part-time		
	Total		Men	Women		Total		Men	Women	Total	Men	Women
	Number	Percent		Number	Percent of all employees	Number	Percent of all employees					
1	2	3	4	5	6	7	8	9	10	11	12	13
Total, all employees	2,602,612	100.0	1,256,037	1,346,575	51.7	1,783,510	68.5	854,308	929,202	819,102	401,729	417,373
Professional staff	1,687,287	64.8	930,933	756,354	44.8	1,039,094	61.6	586,228	452,866	648,193	344,705	303,488
Executive/administrative/managerial	143,675	5.5	82,748	60,927	42.4	137,834	95.9	80,098	57,736	5,841	2,650	3,191
Faculty (instruction and research)	915,474	35.2	561,123	354,351	38.7	545,706	59.6	363,430	182,276	369,768	197,693	172,075
Instruction and research assistants	202,819	7.8	120,384	82,435	40.6	—	—	—	—	202,819	120,384	82,435
Non-faculty professionals	425,319	16.3	166,678	258,641	60.8	355,554	83.6	142,700	212,854	69,765	23,978	45,787
Nonprofessional staff	915,325	35.2	325,104	590,221	64.5	744,416	81.3	268,080	476,336	170,909	57,024	113,885
Technical and paraprofessionals	183,987	7.1	73,241	110,746	60.2	142,846	77.6	59,070	83,776	41,141	14,171	26,970
Clerical and secretarial	438,041	16.8	50,898	387,143	88.4	351,962	80.3	32,801	319,161	86,079	18,097	67,982
Skilled crafts	64,065	2.5	59,901	4,164	6.5	60,926	95.1	57,736	3,190	3,139	2,165	974
Service and maintenance	229,232	8.8	141,064	88,168	38.5	188,682	82.3	118,473	70,209	40,550	22,591	17,959
Public 4-year, total	1,333,533	100.0	659,112	674,421	50.6	964,028	72.3	472,776	491,252	369,505	186,336	183,169
Professional staff	855,913	64.2	487,132	368,781	43.1	555,457	64.9	322,992	232,465	300,456	164,140	136,316
Executive/administrative/managerial	59,678	4.5	37,238	22,440	37.6	57,847	96.9	36,332	21,515	1,831	906	925
Faculty (instruction and research)	374,021	28.0	248,397	125,624	33.6	285,457	76.3	199,899	85,558	88,564	48,498	40,066
Instruction and research assistants	170,916	12.8	101,836	69,080	40.4	—	—	—	—	170,916	101,836	69,080
Non-faculty professionals	251,298	18.8	99,661	151,637	60.3	212,153	84.4	86,761	125,392	39,145	12,900	26,245
Nonprofessional staff	477,620	35.8	171,980	305,640	64.0	408,571	85.5	149,784	258,787	69,049	22,196	46,853
Technical and paraprofessionals	99,950	7.5	39,707	60,243	60.3	80,053	80.1	33,099	46,954	19,897	6,608	13,289
Clerical and secretarial	217,581	16.3	23,465	194,116	89.2	185,414	85.2	17,061	168,353	32,167	6,404	25,763
Skilled crafts	40,299	3.0	37,989	2,310	5.7	38,865	96.4	36,917	1,948	1,434	1,072	362
Service and maintenance	119,790	9.0	70,819	48,971	40.9	104,239	87.0	62,707	41,532	15,551	8,112	7,439
Public 2-year, total	478,980	100.0	219,672	259,308	54.1	242,392	50.6	109,938	132,454	236,588	109,734	126,854
Professional staff	337,371	70.4	171,764	165,607	49.1	145,969	43.3	76,762	69,207	191,402	95,002	96,400
Executive/administrative/managerial	21,531	4.5	12,813	8,718	40.5	20,142	93.5	12,174	7,968	1,389	639	750
Faculty (instruction and research)	276,413	57.7	143,650	132,763	48.0	97,291	35.2	53,288	44,003	179,122	90,362	88,760
Instruction and research assistants	2,762	0.6	1,145	1,617	58.5	—	—	—	—	2,762	1,145	1,617
Non-faculty professionals	36,665	7.7	14,156	22,509	61.4	28,536	77.8	11,300	17,236	8,129	2,856	5,273
Nonprofessional staff	141,609	29.6	47,908	93,701	66.2	96,423	68.1	33,176	63,247	45,186	14,732	30,454
Technical and paraprofessionals	31,701	6.6	11,939	19,762	62.3	19,536	61.6	7,752	11,784	12,165	4,187	7,978
Clerical and secretarial	72,571	15.2	8,160	64,411	88.8	48,176	66.4	2,903	45,273	24,395	5,257	19,138
Skilled crafts	6,363	1.3	5,589	774	12.2	5,635	88.6	5,173	462	728	416	312
Service and maintenance	30,974	6.5	22,220	8,754	28.3	23,076	74.5	17,348	5,728	7,898	4,872	3,026
Private 4-year, total	762,034	100.0	364,978	397,056	52.1	558,179	73.2	263,311	294,868	203,855	101,667	102,188
Professional staff	473,372	62.1	262,106	211,266	44.6	324,189	68.5	179,871	144,318	149,183	82,235	66,948
Executive/administrative/managerial	59,230	7.8	30,988	28,242	47.7	56,701	95.7	29,919	26,782	2,529	1,069	1,460
Faculty (instruction and research)	251,948	33.1	162,287	89,661	35.6	156,039	61.9	106,428	49,611	95,909	55,859	40,050
Instruction and research assistants	28,880	3.8	17,254	11,626	40.3	—	—	—	—	28,880	17,254	11,626
Non-faculty professionals	133,314	17.5	51,577	81,737	61.3	111,449	83.6	43,524	67,925	21,865	8,053	13,812
Nonprofessional staff	288,662	37.9	102,872	185,790	64.4	233,990	81.1	83,440	150,550	54,672	19,432	35,240
Technical and paraprofessionals	51,111	6.7	21,211	29,900	58.5	42,367	82.9	17,915	24,452	8,744	3,296	5,448
Clerical and secretarial	144,047	18.9	18,943	125,104	86.8	115,493	80.2	12,654	102,839	28,554	6,289	22,265
Skilled crafts	17,072	2.2	16,071	1,001	5.9	16,158	94.6	15,415	743	914	656	258
Service and maintenance	76,432	10.0	46,647	29,785	39.0	59,972	78.5	37,456	22,516	16,460	9,191	7,269
Private 2-year, total	28,065	100.0	12,275	15,790	56.3	18,911	67.4	8,283	10,628	9,154	3,992	5,162
Professional staff	20,631	73.5	9,931	10,700	51.9	13,479	65.3	6,603	6,876	7,152	3,328	3,824
Executive/administrative/managerial	3,236	11.5	1,709	1,527	47.2	3,144	97.2	1,673	1,471	92	36	56
Faculty (instruction and research)	13,092	46.6	6,789	6,303	48.1	6,919	52.8	3,815	3,104	6,173	2,974	3,199
Instruction and research assistants	261	0.9	149	112	42.9	—	—	—	—	261	149	112
Non-faculty professionals	4,042	14.4	1,284	2,758	68.2	3,416	84.5	1,115	2,301	626	169	457
Nonprofessional staff	7,434	26.5	2,344	5,090	68.5	5,432	73.1	1,680	3,752	2,002	664	1,338
Technical and paraprofessionals	1,225	4.4	384	841	68.7	890	72.7	304	586	335	80	255
Clerical and secretarial	3,842	13.7	330	3,512	91.4	2,879	74.9	183	2,696	963	147	816
Skilled crafts	331	1.2	252	79	23.9	268	81.0	231	37	63	21	42
Service and maintenance	2,036	7.3	1,378	658	32.3	1,395	68.5	962	433	641	416	225

—Not applicable.

NOTE.—Because of rounding, details may not add to totals.

SOURCE: U.S. Department of Education, National Center for Education Statistics, Integrated Postsecondary Education Data System (IPEDS), "Fall Staff" survey. (This table was prepared December 1995.)

Table 224.—Staff and student/staff ratios in institutions of higher education, by type and control of institution and by state: Fall 1993

State or other area	Full-time-equivalent staff				Full-time-equivalent faculty				Full-time-equivalent students per FTE staff				Full-time-equivalent students per FTE faculty				Full-time-equivalent faculty as a percent of FTE staff			
	Public		Private		Public		Private		Public		Private		Public		Private		Public		Private	
	4-year	2-year	4-year	2-year	4-year	2-year	4-year	2-year	4-year	2-year	4-year	2-year	4-year	2-year	4-year	2-year	4-year	2-year	4-year	2-year
1	2	3	4	5	6	7	8	9	10	11	12	13	14	15	16	17	18	19	20	21
United States	1,109,789	324,958	637,622	22,312	314,502	156,035	189,227	9,055	4.3	9.4	3.7	8.3	15.2	19.5	12.4	20.3	28.3	48.0	29.7	40.6
Alabama	32,656	5,338	3,947	267	6,878	2,856	1,377	105	3.2	10.7	4.9	6.5	15.3	19.9	14.0	16.7	21.1	53.5	34.9	39.3
Alaska	3,122	29	209	31	991	9	77	11	5.8	—	4.8	7.8	18.2	—	13.1	20.8	31.7	—	36.7	37.5
Arizona	17,912	6,376	1,540	128	4,352	2,820	703	48	4.4	12.0	14.5	8.4	18.0	27.2	31.7	22.3	24.3	44.2	45.7	37.7
Arkansas	14,197	1,520	1,886	70	3,791	717	635	36	3.9	9.3	5.1	13.6	14.7	19.6	15.1	26.4	26.7	47.1	33.7	51.5
California	91,480	46,908	44,282	1,983	29,363	23,003	13,960	731	4.6	12.3	4.0	6.7	14.2	25.1	12.8	18.1	32.1	49.0	31.5	36.9
Colorado	20,415	4,260	3,720	406	7,633	2,184	1,326	176	5.1	9.5	5.1	9.5	13.7	18.5	14.3	22.0	37.4	51.3	35.6	43.2
Connecticut	10,598	2,723	14,722	238	3,092	1,482	4,920	89	4.3	8.4	2.9	4.9	14.6	15.4	8.6	13.1	29.2	54.4	33.4	37.3
Delaware	4,340	786	609	—	992	297	236	—	4.8	8.1	8.5	—	21.1	21.3	21.9	—	22.9	37.9	38.8	—
District of Columbia	1,509	—	26,456	—	601	—	5,605	—	4.5	—	2.1	—	11.4	—	10.0	—	39.8	—	21.2	—
Florida	31,694	22,487	18,174	712	9,067	9,602	5,811	334	4.7	8.0	4.4	6.3	16.3	18.8	13.7	13.3	28.6	42.7	32.0	46.9
Georgia	30,490	7,542	14,352	673	7,593	3,735	4,103	300	4.2	7.3	3.5	8.5	16.7	14.7	12.3	19.0	24.9	49.5	28.6	44.6
Hawaii	4,903	1,505	1,216	—	1,787	771	489	—	3.9	10.6	7.6	—	10.8	20.8	19.0	—	36.5	51.2	40.3	—
Idaho	5,681	640	374	874	2,082	281	171	372	5.5	7.8	5.7	9.7	15.1	17.8	12.5	22.9	36.7	44.0	45.8	42.5
Illinois	43,829	19,673	38,784	703	11,200	9,219	11,439	316	3.7	9.7	3.6	8.3	14.6	20.8	12.2	18.4	25.6	46.9	29.5	44.9
Indiana	33,476	3,711	12,212	240	9,940	1,828	3,749	102	4.5	6.5	4.3	12.3	15.2	13.1	14.1	29.0	29.7	49.3	30.7	42.4
Iowa	16,981	4,645	7,852	270	3,926	1,995	2,772	88	3.4	8.6	5.2	7.2	14.8	20.0	14.7	21.9	23.1	42.9	35.3	32.7
Kansas	15,759	4,739	2,407	185	4,705	2,198	955	73	4.7	7.6	5.3	4.4	15.7	16.4	13.3	11.2	29.9	46.4	39.7	39.6
Kentucky	20,157	2,677	4,457	413	5,833	1,570	1,598	161	4.4	11.4	5.0	11.2	15.1	19.5	13.9	28.7	28.9	58.7	35.8	39.0
Louisiana	16,702	1,509	6,259	66	5,674	853	1,906	31	7.4	11.4	3.7	9.1	21.8	20.1	12.1	19.3	34.0	56.5	30.5	47.1
Maine	5,097	600	2,860	113	1,475	296	822	58	4.7	7.7	4.0	13.3	16.3	15.5	14.1	26.2	28.9	49.4	28.7	51.0
Maryland	19,968	7,671	12,572	155	6,678	3,305	3,524	52	4.3	7.8	2.3	5.6	12.9	18.1	8.1	16.7	33.4	43.1	28.0	33.6
Massachusetts	18,285	5,486	55,034	1,247	5,165	2,617	14,103	495	4.3	8.8	3.4	7.7	15.3	18.5	13.1	19.4	28.2	47.7	25.6	39.7
Michigan	50,871	10,844	10,245	316	13,805	5,212	3,593	118	4.1	10.5	6.1	6.2	15.2	21.9	17.3	16.7	27.1	48.1	35.1	37.4
Minnesota	22,409	5,474	8,693	410	5,527	3,089	3,247	203	4.1	10.2	5.3	9.3	16.6	18.0	14.2	18.9	24.7	56.4	37.4	49.4
Mississippi	14,675	4,682	1,525	168	3,389	2,461	533	60	3.5	8.9	6.5	6.6	15.1	16.9	18.6	18.4	23.1	52.6	35.0	35.8
Missouri	22,494	4,723	18,095	721	7,531	2,211	5,588	321	4.3	9.4	3.9	7.1	12.9	20.0	12.5	16.0	33.5	46.8	30.9	44.5
Montana	4,790	444	668	92	1,550	201	227	33	5.6	6.7	5.3	6.2	17.2	14.9	15.7	17.3	32.4	45.2	34.0	36.0
Nebraska	12,424	2,158	3,904	139	3,291	887	1,421	45	3.9	8.6	4.2	3.2	14.7	21.0	11.5	9.8	26.5	41.1	36.4	32.7
Nevada	3,999	1,598	74	13	1,329	973	21	5	5.3	8.6	7.6	1.9	16.0	14.2	27.3	5.0	33.2	60.9	27.8	38.8
New Hampshire	3,879	834	5,145	265	1,233	548	1,530	102	5.6	6.4	3.7	11.7	17.6	9.7	12.3	30.5	31.8	65.7	29.7	38.4
New Jersey	27,779	8,188	11,854	371	6,914	3,373	3,442	139	3.7	10.2	3.8	9.3	15.0	24.7	13.1	24.6	24.9	41.2	29.0	37.6
New Mexico	12,122	2,992	405	43	2,817	1,309	166	20	3.4	8.4	5.5	13.0	14.6	19.2	13.3	27.7	23.2	43.7	41.0	47.0
New York	53,411	20,521	112,837	2,741	17,549	9,667	30,835	1,142	5.0	8.9	3.0	10.2	15.3	18.9	11.2	24.4	32.9	47.1	27.3	41.7
North Carolina	32,803	14,468	26,042	510	8,428	7,983	5,292	211	4.0	6.3	2.2	5.0	15.6	11.5	11.0	12.0	25.7	55.2	20.3	41.4
North Dakota	5,752	916	373	175	1,911	395	172	36	4.4	7.2	8.3	1.5	13.2	16.7	18.0	7.3	33.2	43.1	46.1	20.6
Ohio	49,726	9,961	19,099	889	13,916	4,847	6,978	432	4.6	9.3	5.0	11.7	16.4	19.1	13.7	24.0	28.0	48.7	36.5	48.6
Oklahoma	15,388	4,367	3,491	635	4,619	1,757	1,260	168	5.1	8.8	5.1	3.1	16.9	21.8	14.0	11.6	30.0	40.2	36.1	26.5
Oregon	15,169	6,836	3,909	23	4,894	3,098	1,533	8	3.5	6.8	4.9	7.9	10.8	15.0	12.6	2.8	32.3	45.3	39.2	34.6
Pennsylvania	51,345	7,583	51,886	3,207	15,180	4,034	16,216	1,131	3.9	8.8	3.5	9.1	13.2	16.6	11.1	25.8	29.6	53.2	31.3	35.3
Rhode Island	3,522	666	7,078	197	1,091	285	1,970	100	5.3	13.0	4.2	—	17.3	30.5	15.1	—	31.0	42.8	27.8	—
South Carolina	19,962	4,985	4,103	217	5,369	2,278	1,362	80	3.6	7.5	5.1	8.1	13.4	16.3	15.5	21.8	26.9	45.7	33.2	37.0
South Dakota	4,181	30	997	24	1,482	13	382	14	6.3	5.8	5.3	5.2	17.7	13.5	14.0	8.9	35.4	42.6	38.3	59.1
Tennessee	22,325	4,728	17,842	348	6,428	2,240	4,330	166	4.3	10.0	2.4	8.2	14.8	21.1	10.0	17.2	28.8	47.4	24.3	47.5
Texas	80,362	28,794	21,879	535	19,876	13,895	6,801	234	4.2	8.1	3.9	9.1	17.1	16.8	12.7	20.8	24.7	48.3	31.1	43.7
Utah	11,894	1,506	4,351	131	3,343	556	1,647	69	4.9	11.5	7.8	8.3	17.4	31.0	20.6	15.7	28.1	36.9	37.9	52.9
Vermont	3,437	459	3,069	151	1,131	235	954	99	3.9	5.4	4.1	1.1	11.9	10.5	13.3	1.6	32.9	51.3	31.1	65.0
Virginia	35,868	4,759	10,123	664	9,025	2,015	3,347	322	3.8	14.4	4.2	5.6	15.1	34.1	12.6	11.5	25.2	42.3	33.1	48.5
Washington	24,149	8,823	5,645	215	6,066	4,074	2,374	95	3.2	10.9	5.2	9.2	12.6	23.7	12.4	20.9	25.1	46.2	42.0	44.3
West Virginia	10,454	530	1,623	56	3,744	233	576	17	5.4	9.1	5.5	16.8	15.1	20.8	15.4	54.4	35.8	43.9	35.5	30.8
Wisconsin	26,118	10,643	8,744	130	7,798	5,826	3,153	62	4.7	6.1	4.6	12.8	15.9	11.2	12.7	26.7	29.9	54.7	36.1	48.0
Wyoming	2,848	1,533	—	150	805	700	—	43	3.5	7.4	—	4.7	12.4	16.2	—	16.3	28.3	45.7	—	28.7
U.S. Service Schools	6,383	88	—	—	1,643	—	—	—	2.9	222.4	—	—	11.2	—	—	—	25.7	—	—	—
Outlying areas	11,297	1,680	6,926	1,206	3,740	684	2,711	438	4.3	5.1	11.1	9.5	13.1	12.6	28.5	26.0	33.1	40.7	39.1	36.3
American Samoa	—	180	—	—	—	98	—	—	—	5.6	—	—	—	10.3	—	—	—	54.4	—	—
Federated States of Micronesia	—	83	—	—	—	42	—	—	—	9.0	—	—	—	17.7	—	—	—	50.6	—	—
Guam	591	325	—	—	222	152	—	—	4.9	2.8	—	—	13.1	6.0	—	—	37.6	46.8	—	—
Marshall Islands	—	31	—	—	—	8	—	—	—	—	—	—	—	—	—	—	—	25.7	—	—
Northern Marianas	—	181	—	—	—	73	—	—	—	3.6	—	—	—	8.9	—	—	—	40.4	—	—
Palau	—	116	—	—	—	43	—	—	—	3.2	—	—	—	8.7	—	—	—	37.2	—	—
Puerto Rico	10,222	764	6,926	1,206	3,397	268	2,711	438	4.3	6.5	11.1	9.5	13.0	18.5	28.5	26.0	33.2	35.0	39.1	36.3
Virgin Islands	484	—	—	—	121	—	—	—	4.0	—	—	—	15.8	—	—	—	25.0	—	—	—

—Data not reported or not applicable.

NOTE.—Data include imputations for nonrespondent institutions.

SOURCE: U.S. Department of Education, National Center for Education Statistics, Integrated Postsecondary Education Data System (IPEDS), "Fall Staff, 1993" and "Fall Enrollment" surveys. (This table was prepared January 1996.)

Table 225.—Full-time and part-time senior instructional faculty [1] in institutions of higher education, by employment status, control, and type of institution: Fall 1970 to fall 1993

[In thousands]

Year	Total	Employment status		Control		Type	
		Full-time	Part-time	Public	Private	4-year	2-year
1	2	3	4	5	6	7	8
1970	474	369	104	314	160	382	92
1971 [2]	492	379	113	333	159	387	105
1972	500	380	120	343	157	384	116
1973 [2]	527	389	138	365	162	401	126
1974 [2]	567	406	161	397	170	427	140
1975 [2]	628	440	188	443	185	467	161
1976	633	434	199	449	184	467	166
1977	678	448	230	492	186	485	193
1979 [2]	675	445	230	488	187	494	182
1980 [2]	686	450	236	495	191	494	192
1981	705	461	244	509	196	493	212
1982 [2]	710	462	248	506	204	493	217
1983	724	471	254	512	212	504	220
1984 [2]	717	462	255	505	212	504	213
1985 [2]	715	459	256	503	212	504	211
1986 [2]	722	459	263	510	212	506	216
1987 [3]	793	523	270	553	240	548	246
1989	824	524	300	577	247	584	241
1991	826	536	291	581	245	591	235
1993	915	546	370	650	265	626	290

[1] Includes faculty members with the title of professor, associate professor, assistant professor, instructor, lecturer, assisting professor, adjunct professor, or interim professor (or the equivalent). Excluded are graduate students with titles such as graduate or teaching fellow who assist senior faculty.
[2] Estimated on the basis of enrollment.
[3] Because of revised survey methods, data are not directly comparable with figures for years prior to 1987.

NOTE.—Data exclude faculty employed by system offices. Some data have been revised from previously published figures. For methodological details on estimates, see *Projections of Education Statistics to 2000*. Because of rounding, details may not add to totals.

SOURCE: U.S. Department of Education, National Center for Education Statistics, *Employees in Institutions of Higher Education*, various years; *Projections of Education Statistics to 2000*; Integrated Postsecondary Education Data System (IPEDS), "Fall Staff" survey; and U.S. Equal Employment Opportunity Commission, Higher Education Staff Information (EEO-6) Survey, 1977, 1981, and 1983. (This table was prepared April 1996.)

Table 226.—Full-time instructional faculty in institutions of higher education, by race/ethnicity, academic rank, and sex: Fall 1993

Academic rank and sex	Total	Race/ethnicity						
		White, non-Hispanic	Black, non-Hispanic	Hispanic	Asian or Pacific Islander	American Indian/ Alaskan Native	Nonresident alien	Race/ ethnicity unknown
1	2	3	4	5	6	7	8	9
Men and women, all ranks	545,706	468,770	25,658	12,076	25,269	1,997	10,829	1,107
Professors	157,253	141,848	4,526	2,387	7,033	352	942	165
Associate professors	120,696	106,017	5,326	2,291	5,471	283	1,139	169
Assistant professors	129,159	105,091	7,686	3,387	7,586	431	4,602	376
Instructors	67,700	56,900	4,712	2,260	2,143	610	852	223
Lecturers	13,714	11,292	839	418	557	56	527	25
Other faculty	57,184	47,622	2,569	1,333	2,479	265	2,767	149
Men, all ranks	363,430	313,278	13,385	7,459	18,943	1,237	8,355	773
Professors	130,574	118,308	2,982	1,776	6,245	283	848	132
Associate professors	84,506	74,191	3,089	1,590	4,367	193	942	134
Assistant professors	74,822	59,709	3,801	1,951	5,277	208	3,628	248
Instructors	34,343	28,768	2,094	1,214	1,136	394	582	155
Lecturers	6,689	5,503	377	190	254	29	321	15
Other faculty	32,496	26,799	1,042	738	1,664	130	2,034	89
Women, all ranks	182,276	155,492	12,273	4,617	6,326	760	2,474	334
Professors	26,679	23,540	1,544	611	788	69	94	33
Associate professors	36,190	31,826	2,237	701	1,104	90	197	35
Assistant professors	54,337	45,382	3,885	1,436	2,309	223	974	128
Instructors	33,357	28,132	2,618	1,046	1,007	216	270	68
Lecturers	7,025	5,789	462	228	303	27	206	10
Other faculty	24,688	20,823	1,527	595	815	135	733	60

NOTE.—Data exclude faculty employed by system offices. Totals may differ from figures reported in other tables because of varying survey methodologies.

SOURCE: U.S. Department of Education, National Center for Education Statistics, Integrated Postsecondary Education Data System (IPEDS), "Fall Staff" survey. (This table was prepared June 1996.)

Table 227.—Full-time and part-time instructional faculty and staff in institutions of higher education, by selected characteristics and type and control of institution: Fall 1992

Selected characteristics	Number in thousands	Percent total	Public research	Private research	Public doctoral	Private doctoral	Public comprehensive	Private comprehensive	Private liberal arts	Public 2-year	Other
1	2	3	4	5	6	7	8	9	10	11	12
					Full-time instructional faculty						
Total (in thousands)	528	—	107	32	53	29	94	39	38	110	26
Percent	—	100.0	20.3	6.1	10.0	5.4	17.9	7.3	7.2	20.8	5.0
					Percentage distribution						
Total	—	100.0	100.0	100.0	100.0	100.0	100.0	100.0	100.0	100.0	100.0
Sex											
Male	353	66.8	76.7	69.1	69.9	76.4	66.1	64.9	61.1	54.7	70.5
Female	176	33.2	23.3	30.9	30.1	23.6	33.9	35.2	38.9	45.3	29.5
Race											
White, non-Hispanic	457	86.5	88.0	83.7	87.5	84.1	82.7	91.3	90.0	85.5	89.2
Black, non-Hispanic	27	5.2	2.8	5.0	3.1	4.9	9.1	3.5	5.4	6.2	3.7
Hispanic	14	2.6	2.2	2.1	2.5	3.7	2.6	1.6	1.3	4.1	1.4
Asian/Pacific Islander	28	5.2	6.9	9.0	6.1	7.1	5.1	3.3	2.8	3.3	5.2
American Indian/Alaskan Native	3	0.5	0.1	0.2	0.8	0.2	0.5	0.2	0.5	1.0	0.5
Age											
29 or younger	8	1.4	1.0	1.8	1.2	0.6	1.5	1.4	2.1	1.7	2.0
30 to 34	35	6.7	7.2	7.8	8.4	9.2	5.9	7.0	7.0	5.3	5.1
35 to 39	67	12.6	14.3	20.4	14.4	15.4	10.6	10.4	13.9	9.8	10.8
40 to 44	90	17.1	18.1	19.9	17.4	17.9	15.1	16.4	17.4	16.8	16.5
45 to 49	98	18.5	17.0	15.3	16.8	19.7	18.8	18.9	19.7	20.8	17.8
50 to 54	95	18.0	15.9	11.5	17.4	12.8	21.5	16.7	14.7	21.9	18.2
55 to 59	67	12.7	12.8	9.1	11.7	10.0	14.4	12.8	11.9	13.5	14.4
60 to 64	45	8.4	8.9	8.3	8.2	8.0	8.2	11.3	8.5	7.1	9.6
65 or older	24	4.5	4.8	5.9	4.5	6.5	3.9	5.1	4.8	3.2	5.8
Highest degree											
Doctoral	284	54.0	70.8	63.7	62.6	58.2	68.1	60.8	58.4	16.6	40.7
Professional	58	11.1	17.0	24.9	20.1	29.4	4.3	7.7	3.2	2.3	9.7
Master's	156	29.7	10.6	10.2	16.0	10.5	26.4	29.3	35.3	63.9	42.1
Bachelor's	21	4.0	1.6	1.1	1.3	1.9	1.1	2.1	3.1	11.9	6.6
Less than bachelor's	6	1.2	0.1	0.1	(¹)	(¹)	0.2	0.1	(¹)	5.4	0.9
Academic rank											
Full professor	161	30.4	39.8	33.3	31.3	30.5	34.3	26.8	28.7	19.1	27.8
Associate professor	124	23.4	26.4	22.7	26.3	26.8	26.9	29.0	25.3	12.9	23.4
Assistant professor	124	23.5	22.7	27.0	31.2	29.1	26.1	31.9	29.9	11.3	21.8
Instructor	74	14.0	4.0	4.6	7.6	9.1	8.6	8.0	9.2	39.7	12.5
Lecturer	12	2.2	3.9	6.7	1.7	1.8	2.6	1.2	1.6	0.4	0.7
Other	17	3.2	3.2	4.8	1.8	2.6	1.4	1.9	3.7	5.7	2.9
No rank	17	3.2	0.2	1.0	0.2	0.1	0.2	1.3	1.7	11.0	10.9
Base salary											
Under $10,000	14	2.6	2.0	3.0	2.1	2.7	2.1	2.7	2.5	3.5	3.6
$10,000 to 24,999	29	5.6	3.6	5.1	4.7	2.8	5.5	5.3	10.0	6.2	10.7
$25,000 to 39,999	182	34.4	19.5	14.4	29.0	24.5	37.1	44.0	53.5	47.2	36.9
$40,000 to 54,999	164	31.0	29.4	28.5	29.8	24.9	34.0	32.1	24.6	33.8	35.5
$55,000 to 69,999	77	14.5	22.7	15.7	17.0	19.8	16.9	10.0	6.0	8.0	6.5
$70,000 to 84,999	32	6.1	12.1	13.0	9.0	9.9	3.3	3.6	2.2	0.8	4.0
$85,000 to 99,999	11	2.1	4.4	3.7	2.3	7.7	0.7	1.0	0.6	0.1	1.6
$100,000 or more	20	3.7	6.5	16.6	6.2	7.7	0.4	1.4	0.5	0.4	1.2

Table 227.—Full-time and part-time instructional faculty and staff in institutions of higher education, by selected characteristics and type and control of institution: Fall 1992—Continued

Selected characteristics	Number in thousands	Percent total	Public research	Private research	Public doctoral	Private doctoral	Public comprehensive	Private comprehensive	Private liberal arts	Public 2-year	Other
1	2	3	4	5	6	7	8	9	10	11	12
	Part-time instructional faculty										
Total (in thousands)	377	—	25	17	21	18	47	37	21	166	24
Percent	—	100.0	6.7	4.6	5.5	4.8	12.5	9.7	5.6	44.2	6.5
	Percentage distribution										
Total	—	100.0	100.0	100.0	100.0	100.0	100.0	100.0	100.0	100.0	100.0
Sex											
Male	209	55.4	56.8	58.7	55.4	63.1	49.1	56.4	46.6	56.6	56.1
Female	168	44.6	43.3	41.3	44.6	36.9	51.0	43.7	53.4	43.4	44.0
Race											
White, non-Hispanic	333	88.3	87.8	89.5	91.4	87.7	85.0	90.8	89.6	87.9	90.8
Black, non-Hispanic	18	4.8	2.5	4.4	3.3	7.1	7.2	5.0	5.9	4.6	3.2
Hispanic	11	3.0	3.2	2.7	1.6	1.5	3.0	1.1	2.9	4.0	1.1
Asian/Pacific Islander	12	3.2	6.6	3.0	3.3	3.5	4.1	2.5	1.6	2.7	3.8
American Indian/Alaskan Native	2	0.6	[1]	0.4	0.4	0.2	0.7	0.5	0.1	0.8	1.1
Age											
29 or younger	20	5.4	4.0	2.7	8.3	1.9	7.7	4.0	2.7	6.1	5.0
30 to 34	36	9.5	6.5	18.5	6.5	7.4	10.1	6.9	8.0	10.0	11.7
35 to 39	59	15.6	15.7	13.8	16.8	27.3	15.0	14.6	19.3	14.6	14.5
40 to 44	70	18.6	20.1	11.8	19.4	16.0	17.9	18.4	21.4	19.5	16.1
45 to 49	68	18.0	19.0	19.0	17.1	18.9	16.1	20.9	21.8	17.5	16.7
50 to 54	45	12.0	12.9	12.1	10.5	9.9	11.0	11.8	9.3	12.7	13.4
55 to 59	29	7.6	8.1	11.1	6.2	3.8	10.0	9.3	6.1	7.2	6.3
60 to 64	23	6.1	5.0	8.1	5.4	6.5	5.9	6.5	4.2	6.5	4.9
65 or older	27	7.1	8.9	2.8	10.0	8.4	6.4	7.6	7.2	6.1	11.6
Highest degree											
Doctoral	59	16.0	30.4	26.3	17.5	26.0	19.0	21.5	21.8	8.1	17.6
Professional	40	10.7	18.5	23.7	29.2	34.4	5.2	10.5	3.2	5.1	15.0
Master's	190	51.6	39.1	43.2	41.4	31.5	61.1	58.4	58.7	53.0	50.3
Bachelor's	63	17.0	12.1	6.8	11.7	7.9	14.0	9.3	15.7	24.0	13.3
Less than bachelor's	17	4.7	[1]	[1]	0.2	0.2	0.7	0.2	0.6	9.8	3.8
Academic rank											
Full professor	32	8.6	11.6	18.6	9.5	14.0	6.6	15.2	11.5	4.1	15.1
Associate professor	23	6.0	17.3	15.5	13.5	11.6	3.2	6.4	4.7	2.4	7.0
Assistant professor	24	6.4	14.2	12.6	11.6	19.9	4.1	7.5	11.3	2.4	5.8
Instructor	215	57.2	24.7	27.8	40.1	27.4	51.3	43.5	53.6	76.4	52.7
Lecturer	45	12.0	24.2	18.1	12.9	18.9	23.1	17.6	10.4	5.2	7.4
Other	28	7.3	7.8	5.9	10.9	7.3	11.0	7.9	7.8	5.7	7.7
No rank	9	2.5	0.3	1.6	1.4	0.8	0.8	1.9	0.7	3.8	4.3
Base salary											
Under $10,000	281	74.5	51.8	70.9	65.1	66.3	69.2	79.4	70.0	81.7	72.2
$10,000 to 24,999	68	18.1	30.8	19.3	21.8	23.3	23.0	16.4	23.1	13.2	19.3
$25,000 to 39,999	16	4.2	8.8	5.0	8.1	4.2	5.1	2.9	4.4	2.9	4.7
$40,000 to 54,999	5	1.4	2.6	1.9	2.8	2.2	1.0	0.7	1.1	1.1	2.1
$55,000 to 69,999	2	0.6	3.5	0.9	0.5	0.5	0.3	0.5	0.1	0.3	[1]
$70,000 to 84,999	1	0.3	0.2	[1]	0.6	1.4	0.2	[1]	0.1	0.2	0.9
$85,000 to 99,999	1	0.3	1.7	1.6	0.1	0.2	[1]	[1]	0.1	0.1	[1]
$100,000 or more	3	0.7	0.6	0.4	1.0	1.9	1.1	0.1	1.1	0.5	0.9

[1] Less than 0.05 percent.
—Data not applicable.

NOTE.—Data may not add to totals because of rounding or missing data.

SOURCE: U.S. Department of Education, National Center for Education Statistics, National Study of Postsecondary Faculty (NSOPF), 1993. (This table was prepared September 1996.)

Table 228.—Full-time instructional faculty and staff in institutions of higher education, by instruction activities and type and control of institution: Fall 1992

Instruction activities	All institutions	Public research	Private research	Public doctoral	Private doctoral	Public comprehensive	Private comprehensive	Private liberal arts	Public 2-year	Other
1	2	3	4	5	6	7	8	9	10	11
Number of full-time instructional faculty and staff (in thousands)	528	107	32	53	29	94	39	38	110	26
Percentage distribution	100.0	20.3	6.1	10.0	5.4	17.9	7.3	7.2	20.8	5.0
Hours worked per week										
Average hours worked per week	52.5	56.4	57.6	55.1	53.4	52.4	51.8	52.5	46.9	49.0
Paid activities within institution	42.6	48.0	48.6	46.2	44.6	41.3	40.9	42.4	36.0	39.5
Unpaid activities within institution	5.1	4.3	4.1	4.3	3.4	5.9	5.8	5.8	6.0	5.1
Outside paid activities	2.8	2.4	2.6	2.5	3.6	2.8	3.0	2.6	3.1	2.8
Unpaid activities outside institution	2.0	1.8	2.2	2.1	1.8	2.3	2.1	1.6	1.9	1.7
Work time distribution (percent)										
Total	100.0	100.0	100.0	100.0	100.0	100.0	100.0	100.0	100.0	100.0
Teaching	54.5	40.4	34.7	46.9	44.5	60.3	59.7	63.7	68.8	60.8
Research/scholarship	17.7	31.6	35.5	23.8	21.7	14.0	11.8	9.7	4.5	10.7
Professional growth	4.6	3.7	3.3	4.1	4.3	5.0	4.9	4.7	5.8	5.1
Administration	13.0	12.9	12.9	13.2	15.7	12.0	14.6	14.7	12.0	14.9
Outside consulting	2.7	2.5	3.0	2.5	2.8	2.7	3.1	2.3	2.7	2.8
Service/non-teaching	7.4	8.9	10.6	9.6	11.0	6.1	5.9	4.9	6.1	5.6
Preferred work time distribution (percent)										
Total	100.0	100.0	100.0	100.0	100.0	100.0	100.0	100.0	100.0	100.0
Teaching	49.0	36.6	33.2	41.8	39.4	52.4	52.9	56.1	64.1	54.1
Research/scholarship	24.7	38.5	41.7	31.1	30.1	22.4	19.8	18.8	9.2	17.6
Professional growth	8.1	6.5	6.2	7.2	6.9	8.5	8.6	8.8	9.8	9.3
Administration	8.2	7.8	7.1	8.0	10.2	7.7	9.2	8.6	8.1	9.6
Outside consulting	3.3	3.1	3.4	3.3	3.6	3.5	3.9	2.9	3.1	3.7
Service/non-teaching	6.6	7.4	8.4	8.6	9.9	5.6	5.7	4.8	5.7	5.6
Distribution of hours taught per week (percent)										
Total	100.0	100.0	100.0	100.0	100.0	100.0	100.0	100.0	100.0	100.0
Less than 4.0	15.0	30.4	36.7	18.9	21.5	8.2	8.2	6.3	6.2	10.5
4.0 to 5.9	8.0	15.0	18.9	10.4	9.1	4.9	5.2	5.8	3.3	5.9
6.0 to 7.9	15.9	26.5	21.0	21.2	24.9	12.6	14.7	13.1	6.0	14.6
8.0 to 9.9	14.6	11.9	7.0	19.0	18.9	19.9	21.9	22.2	6.5	12.3
10.0 to 14.9	22.5	8.9	8.4	16.9	15.1	36.5	34.6	34.1	19.8	28.6
15.0 or more	23.9	7.3	8.1	13.6	10.6	17.9	15.4	18.5	58.2	28.0
Distribution of number of students taught (percent)										
Total	100.0	100.0	100.0	100.0	100.0	100.0	100.0	100.0	100.0	100.0
Less than 25	13.1	21.7	33.3	15.9	18.5	7.3	8.3	11.7	5.9	13.2
25 to 49	19.9	23.1	24.3	22.2	22.4	15.1	20.4	29.8	14.3	23.0
50 to 74	19.5	18.7	11.6	16.7	13.0	20.2	27.8	26.7	17.4	24.7
75 to 99	15.8	11.0	8.9	13.7	11.1	19.4	21.2	15.8	18.8	15.1
100 to 149	18.9	10.9	10.2	15.5	17.6	25.1	17.4	12.0	27.6	16.3
150 or more	12.8	14.7	11.7	16.1	17.5	13.0	5.0	4.0	16.0	7.7
Distribution of student classroom contact hours per week[1] (percent)										
Total	100.0	100.0	100.0	100.0	100.0	100.0	100.0	100.0	100.0	100.0
Less than 50	8.4	16.6	25.7	10.3	13.2	3.3	4.6	6.1	2.4	6.6
50 to 99	10.6	16.2	18.2	13.5	12.7	7.6	9.9	11.8	4.6	12.1
100 to 199	21.9	25.8	21.9	22.5	25.3	20.0	27.6	34.8	11.8	25.7
200 to 349	27.6	20.1	18.4	25.9	18.1	34.0	38.4	30.2	28.2	28.7
350 to 499	15.7	8.3	4.8	11.3	13.6	20.4	11.8	10.4	26.5	14.8
500 or more	15.8	13.0	11.0	16.6	17.1	14.8	7.8	6.9	26.6	12.1
Distribution of total classroom credit hours (percent)										
Total	100.0	100.0	100.0	100.0	100.0	100.0	100.0	100.0	100.0	100.0
Less than 4.0	14.1	26.2	28.6	15.4	19.4	8.0	8.5	11.8	7.2	12.1
4.0 to 5.9	8.6	14.7	14.8	12.5	10.8	5.8	6.0	5.9	4.2	7.8
6.0 to 7.9	18.3	31.0	25.0	26.0	26.5	15.0	13.6	13.2	8.0	15.3
8.0 to 9.9	18.6	15.0	16.1	22.6	18.8	23.6	28.2	24.4	10.7	18.8
10.0 to 14.9	24.9	9.5	7.4	17.9	17.0	37.3	34.6	34.9	28.4	29.1
15.0 or more	15.5	3.7	8.0	5.6	7.5	10.3	9.2	9.9	41.5	17.0
Number of classes taught for credit										
Faculty with undergraduate classes only (percent)										
Total	100.0	100.0	100.0	100.0	100.0	100.0	100.0	100.0	100.0	100.0
1	16.0	34.4	40.9	20.6	22.1	11.5	11.3	9.9	12.3	13.1
2	23.2	42.9	37.2	34.0	40.8	20.8	21.2	21.6	13.9	19.6
3	23.6	14.5	7.9	27.6	25.0	31.9	31.2	35.0	15.3	27.1
4	20.0	6.1	7.4	13.3	6.5	26.7	26.1	20.7	21.9	25.4
5 or more	17.2	2.1	6.5	4.5	5.5	9.2	10.2	12.9	36.6	14.8
Faculty with graduate classes only (percent)										
Total	100.0	100.0	100.0	100.0	100.0	100.0	100.0	—	—	100.0
1	47.9	57.1	53.2	45.4	46.4	30.3	21.0	—	—	32.6
2	33.4	33.7	38.4	35.0	31.3	23.0	36.3	—	—	36.0
3	12.6	6.8	4.7	13.4	17.4	28.2	30.1	—	—	18.1
4	4.1	1.9	1.6	3.5	3.5	13.3	9.9	—	—	9.3
5 or more	2.0	0.6	2.1	2.7	1.4	5.2	2.8	—	—	4.1
Faculty with both undergraduate and graduate classes (percent)										
Total	100.0	100.0	100.0	100.0	100.0	100.0	100.0	100.0	—	—
2	42.3	58.9	67.6	48.3	40.5	25.0	17.6	22.1	—	—
3	32.2	29.9	22.8	31.3	36.6	34.0	45.7	21.7	—	—
4	16.1	5.5	7.4	14.6	12.1	25.7	27.6	37.0	—	—
5 or more	9.5	5.7	2.2	5.8	10.8	15.3	9.1	19.3	—	—

[1] Hours that faculty and instructional staff spend each week with students during classroom instruction multiplied by the number of students taught.
—Data not available or not applicable.

NOTE.—Because of rounding, details may not add to totals.

SOURCE: U.S. Department of Education, National Center for Education Statistics, National Study of Postsecondary Faculty (NSOPF), 1993. (This table was prepared September 1996.)

Table 229.—Part-time instructional faculty and staff in institutions of higher education, by instruction activities and type and control of institution: Fall 1992

Instruction activities	All institutions	Public research	Private research	Public doctoral	Private doctoral	Public comprehensive	Private comprehensive	Private liberal arts	Public 2-year	Other
1	2	3	4	5	6	7	8	9	10	11
Number of part-time instructional faculty and staff (in thousands)	377	25	17	21	18	47	37	21	166	24
Percentage distribution	100.0	6.7	4.6	5.5	4.8	12.5	9.7	5.6	44.2	6.5
Hours worked per week										
Average hours worked per week	33.8	38.9	40.3	34.6	37.0	34.7	35.6	33.4	31.5	32.6
Paid activities within institution	11.7	19.9	11.6	14.3	10.7	13.5	10.3	12.8	10.1	10.4
Unpaid activities within institution	3.2	4.2	4.3	3.9	3.6	3.5	2.3	2.5	3.1	2.8
Outside paid activities	16.9	12.5	22.7	14.5	20.6	15.5	20.9	16.2	16.5	17.1
Unpaid activities outside institution	1.9	2.3	1.7	2.0	2.0	2.2	2.1	1.9	1.8	2.3
Work time distribution (percent)										
Total	100.0	100.0	100.0	100.0	100.0	100.0	100.0	100.0	100.0	100.0
Teaching	59.8	52.1	38.7	60.7	42.7	61.6	56.6	61.4	64.9	59.3
Research/scholarship	7.1	15.7	17.7	8.7	8.9	8.2	5.9	6.6	4.4	7.0
Professional growth	5.8	5.2	8.2	7.5	5.8	6.0	5.8	6.1	5.5	5.1
Administration	5.8	5.4	12.7	5.1	4.6	6.2	6.3	7.0	5.0	5.2
Outside consulting	10.4	10.4	11.0	8.6	17.0	8.2	12.4	10.6	9.9	11.0
Service/non-teaching	11.1	11.2	11.6	9.2	21.0	9.7	12.9	8.3	10.3	12.5
Preferred work time distribution (percent)										
Total	100.0	100.0	100.0	100.0	100.0	100.0	100.0	100.0	100.0	100.0
Teaching	57.7	51.9	37.5	58.2	40.6	57.0	56.2	58.8	63.1	56.4
Research/scholarship	11.2	18.8	21.2	13.2	12.6	13.3	10.1	11.4	8.1	11.4
Professional growth	9.0	7.6	9.4	9.7	8.6	9.3	8.4	9.0	9.1	8.6
Administration	4.3	3.8	9.6	3.2	4.0	5.0	5.1	4.8	3.6	3.8
Outside consulting	8.6	7.6	9.9	7.2	16.8	7.2	9.4	8.8	8.0	9.2
Service/non-teaching	9.3	10.3	12.3	8.5	17.4	8.3	10.8	7.3	8.0	10.6
Distribution of hours taught per week (percent)										
Total hours taught per week	100.0	100.0	100.0	100.0	100.0	100.0	100.0	100.0	100.0	100.0
Less than 4.0	34.6	44.3	60.5	36.2	52.5	36.0	42.0	36.7	26.7	37.2
4.0 to 5.9	15.3	11.1	14.8	15.3	16.4	15.7	13.2	16.7	15.9	16.1
6.0 to 7.9	20.0	15.7	14.5	19.5	13.8	20.9	18.0	20.2	22.9	12.9
8.0 to 9.9	12.4	13.0	4.6	14.9	6.9	11.6	9.7	8.8	14.6	12.8
10.0 to 14.9	9.7	5.7	3.4	8.5	4.0	9.7	8.5	9.2	11.6	10.9
15.0 or more	7.9	10.2	2.2	5.8	6.4	6.2	8.6	8.5	8.4	10.2
Distribution of number of students taught (percent)										
Total students taught	100.0	100.0	100.0	100.0	100.0	100.0	100.0	100.0	100.0	100.0
Less than 25	36.5	36.0	57.4	27.1	48.2	26.2	47.2	50.1	31.8	49.2
25 to 49	33.5	22.9	25.5	29.4	31.8	33.7	28.9	32.7	38.7	23.4
50 to 74	16.2	15.6	11.1	20.2	9.9	21.1	13.2	10.1	16.9	15.7
75 to 99	6.2	5.9	3.1	8.7	2.4	8.0	5.4	3.5	6.7	5.3
100 to 149	5.1	8.5	2.7	8.3	0.5	8.4	4.0	3.1	4.4	5.7
150 or more	2.5	11.1	0.2	6.2	7.2	2.7	1.4	0.6	1.5	0.7
Distribution of student classroom contact hours per week[1] (percent)										
Total contact hours	100.0	100.0	100.0	100.0	100.0	100.0	100.0	100.0	100.0	100.0
Less than 50	18.6	23.8	45.3	13.2	35.4	12.4	27.6	27.2	11.6	30.3
50 to 99	26.8	18.9	34.6	21.8	28.5	24.0	30.0	33.3	27.8	20.2
100 to 199	30.3	25.0	9.5	35.7	22.1	36.9	25.5	25.6	33.6	24.7
200 to 349	15.4	14.4	7.7	17.6	4.5	14.8	9.6	8.9	18.8	18.0
350 to 499	4.6	6.7	2.7	5.0	2.1	6.7	2.7	4.0	4.6	4.5
500 or more	4.4	11.1	0.2	6.6	7.5	5.2	4.7	1.1	3.7	2.3
Distribution of total classroom credit hours (percent)										
Total credit hours	100.0	100.0	100.0	100.0	100.0	100.0	100.0	100.0	100.0	100.0
Less than 4.0	40.3	48.7	51.5	36.9	54.6	39.9	48.5	47.8	35.1	37.3
4.0 to 5.9	15.7	12.8	27.8	17.2	10.9	13.7	9.6	14.2	16.4	21.9
6.0 to 7.9	21.5	16.8	8.9	21.6	16.8	24.9	20.9	18.8	23.8	17.2
8.0 to 9.9	12.4	16.9	5.5	9.3	11.5	13.9	8.9	9.5	13.4	13.7
10.0 to 14.9	6.9	3.2	6.3	8.1	4.3	5.4	7.9	7.3	8.0	5.2
15.0 or more	3.2	1.6	([2])	7.0	2.0	2.3	4.4	2.5	3.3	4.7
Number of classes taught for credit										
Faculty with undergraduate classes only (percent)										
Total undergraduate credit courses	100.0	100.0	100.0	100.0	100.0	100.0	100.0	100.0	100.0	100.0
1	50.2	49.4	69.1	48.6	61.6	49.6	54.5	50.7	48.1	52.4
2	32.0	26.7	26.1	34.8	27.0	32.6	28.0	30.8	33.8	28.3
3	11.2	12.8	0.8	11.0	8.5	12.5	10.7	9.3	11.6	12.1
4	4.0	6.6	4.0	4.6	1.5	3.6	4.0	4.1	3.8	5.6
5 or more	2.6	4.5	([2])	1.1	1.5	1.7	3.0	5.2	2.8	1.6
Faculty with graduate classes only (percent)										
Total graduate credit courses	100.0	100.0	100.0	100.0	100.0	100.0	100.0	—	—	100.0
1	72.4	70.5	77.6	62.7	72.9	57.6	74.5	—	—	84.1
2	18.0	13.1	14.5	33.0	16.1	33.2	18.9	—	—	6.3
3	7.1	12.8	5.9	4.1	8.7	8.1	3.1	—	—	5.7
4	1.3	0.9	2.0	([2])	1.4	1.0	1.4	—	—	1.8
5 or more	1.2	2.7	([2])	0.2	1.0	([2])	2.1	—	—	2.2
Faculty with both undergraduate and graduate classes (percent)										
Total graduate and undergraduate courses	100.0	—	—	—	—	—	—	—	—	—
2	48.0	—	—	—	—	—	—	—	—	—
3	35.7	—	—	—	—	—	—	—	—	—
4	10.6	—	—	—	—	—	—	—	—	—
5 or more	5.7	—	—	—	—	—	—	—	—	—

[1] Hours that faculty and instructional staff spend each week with students during classroom instruction multiplied by the number of students taught.
[2] Less than .05 percent.
—Data not available or not applicable.

NOTE.—Because of rounding, details may not add to totals.

SOURCE: U.S. Department of Education, National Center for Education Statistics, National Study of Postsecondary Faculty (NSOPF), 1993. (This table was prepared September 1996.)

Table 230.—Full-time and part-time instructional faculty and staff in institutions of higher education, by type and control, academic rank, age, salary, race/ethnicity, and sex: Fall 1992

Selected characteristics	Number	Percent	White, non-Hispanic		Black, non-Hispanic		Hispanic		Asian/Pacific Islander		American Indian/Alaskan Native	
			Male	Female	Male	Female	Male	Female	Male	Female	Male	Female
1	2	3	4	5	6	7	8	9	10	11	12	13
	Full-time instructional faculty and staff											
All institutions	528,260	—	306,477	150,265	14,457	12,941	9,289	4,564	20,858	6,851	1,638	920
Percentage distribution	—	100.0	58.0	28.4	2.7	2.4	1.8	0.9	3.9	1.3	0.3	0.2
Type and control												
Public research	107,358	100.0	67.8	20.2	1.5	1.2	1.6	0.6	5.6	1.3	0.1	0.1
Private research	32,164	100.0	58.0	25.7	3.0	2.0	1.3	0.8	6.6	2.4	0.2	—
Public doctoral	52,808	100.0	61.0	26.5	1.7	1.4	1.8	0.7	4.7	1.4	0.6	0.2
Private doctoral	28,684	100.0	64.8	19.4	3.4	1.5	2.6	1.1	5.6	1.6	0.1	0.1
Public comprehensive	94,477	100.0	55.0	27.7	5.0	4.1	1.8	0.8	4.1	1.0	0.2	0.3
Private comprehensive	38,561	100.0	59.7	31.6	1.7	1.9	1.0	0.6	2.5	0.9	(¹)	0.1
Private liberal arts	38,052	100.0	54.4	35.6	3.7	1.7	0.8	0.5	1.9	0.9	0.3	0.2
Public 2-year	109,957	100.0	47.2	38.3	2.5	3.7	2.5	1.6	1.9	1.4	0.7	0.3
Other	26,200	100.0	63.6	25.5	1.7	2.1	1.1	0.4	3.8	1.4	0.3	0.2
Academic rank												
Full professor	160,559	100.0	75.0	14.7	2.2	1.1	1.5	0.4	4.4	0.4	0.2	0.1
Associate professor	123,708	100.0	62.3	25.2	2.9	2.3	1.5	0.8	3.6	1.0	0.3	0.1
Assistant professor	124,293	100.0	46.8	36.3	2.9	3.2	2.1	1.2	4.9	2.2	0.2	0.2
Instructor	73,897	100.0	43.2	41.3	3.2	4.0	2.2	1.1	2.4	1.8	0.6	0.3
Lecturer	11,869	100.0	28.7	54.5	2.6	3.7	2.0	1.2	3.8	2.5	—	1.1
Other	17,072	100.0	40.3	40.6	4.2	4.8	2.2	1.8	4.1	1.7	0.2	0.1
No rank	16,862	100.0	50.9	39.0	1.3	1.3	1.8	0.9	1.9	1.7	0.9	0.3
Age												
Under 30	7,636	100.0	39.5	39.5	2.4	5.3	2.0	1.9	6.1	3.0	0.3	0.1
30 to 34	35,418	100.0	45.6	33.3	4.1	3.6	3.1	1.2	6.4	2.4	0.2	—
35 to 39	66,757	100.0	49.9	33.9	2.7	2.5	1.8	1.0	5.5	2.1	0.4	0.2
40 to 44	90,175	100.0	51.1	33.3	2.5	3.1	2.1	1.5	4.2	1.6	0.2	0.5
45 to 49	97,705	100.0	56.2	31.5	2.5	2.9	2.0	0.9	2.7	1.2	0.3	0.1
50 to 54	94,852	100.0	63.3	26.2	2.5	1.9	1.3	0.6	3.1	0.8	0.3	0.2
55 to 59	67,332	100.0	67.2	21.2	2.8	1.7	1.3	0.3	4.0	0.8	0.7	0.1
60 to 64	44,609	100.0	70.2	18.2	2.8	1.8	1.3	0.5	4.2	0.8	0.2	0.1
65 or older	23,778	100.0	69.5	20.0	3.9	1.1	1.6	0.7	2.3	0.5	0.1	0.3
Base salary												
Under $10,000	13,771	100.0	53.2	30.4	7.1	4.9	0.9	0.3	1.9	1.0	0.3	0.1
10,000 to 24,999	29,384	100.0	35.7	50.6	1.8	3.9	1.3	1.3	2.5	2.3	0.1	0.6
25,000 to 39,999	181,830	100.0	45.4	40.7	2.8	3.4	1.8	1.2	2.5	1.6	0.4	0.2
40,000 to 54,999	163,774	100.0	61.8	23.7	2.8	2.1	1.9	1.0	5.1	1.2	0.3	0.1
55,000 to 69,999	76,716	100.0	73.3	15.2	2.4	1.3	2.3	0.4	4.0	0.9	0.2	0.1
70,000 to 84,999	32,096	100.0	78.9	11.2	2.1	0.9	1.7	(¹)	4.5	0.6	0.2	—
85,000 to 99,999	11,068	100.0	71.2	12.7	4.7	0.4	0.7	—	9.6	0.8	—	—
100,000 or more	19,622	100.0	78.5	9.4	1.4	0.6	0.7	0.1	7.1	1.5	0.6	0.2
Total income												
Under $10,000	6,825	100.0	47.4	39.1	3.0	4.9	0.6	0.5	2.3	1.9	—	0.3
10,000 to 24,999	17,522	100.0	32.5	50.3	3.4	4.6	1.6	1.5	2.8	1.8	0.4	1.0
25,000 to 39,999	129,649	100.0	40.2	46.2	2.6	3.6	1.1	1.3	2.7	1.8	0.2	0.3
40,000 to 54,999	158,575	100.0	55.1	30.2	3.0	2.7	2.2	1.1	3.9	1.3	0.4	0.1
55,000 to 69,999	94,903	100.0	69.6	17.6	2.7	1.9	1.7	0.7	4.4	0.9	0.4	0.2
70,000 to 84,999	49,484	100.0	75.3	13.0	2.1	1.4	1.8	0.4	4.7	1.0	0.3	(¹)
85,000 to 99,999	23,811	100.0	76.4	11.1	4.0	0.6	1.8	0.1	5.3	0.4	0.3	—
100,000 or more	47,490	100.0	77.1	10.9	1.9	0.7	2.3	0.1	5.8	1.0	0.2	0.1

Table 230.—Full-time and part-time instructional faculty and staff in institutions of higher education, by type and control, academic rank, age, salary, race/ethnicity, and sex: Fall 1992—Continued

Selected characteristics	Number	Percent	White, non-Hispanic		Black, non-Hispanic		Hispanic		Asian/Pacific Islander		American Indian/Alaskan Native	
			Male	Female	Male	Female	Male	Female	Male	Female	Male	Female
1	2	3	4	5	6	7	8	9	10	11	12	13
			Part-time instructional faculty and staff									
All institutions	376,675	—	182,976	149,814	10,274	7,987	6,965	4,232	7,016	5,135	1,478	797
Percentage distribution	—	100.0	48.6	39.8	2.7	2.1	1.8	1.1	1.9	1.4	0.4	0.2
Type and control												
Public research	25,360	100.0	49.0	38.7	0.8	1.7	2.1	1.1	4.8	1.7	—	—
Private research	17,259	100.0	50.6	39.0	3.3	1.2	2.7	—	1.8	1.2	0.4	—
Public doctoral	20,761	100.0	50.6	40.8	1.7	1.6	1.0	0.5	1.8	1.5	0.2	0.3
Private doctoral	18,014	100.0	54.6	33.1	6.0	1.2	1.3	0.2	1.0	2.5	0.2	—
Public comprehensive	47,056	100.0	40.4	44.6	4.3	2.9	1.1	1.9	2.7	1.4	0.5	0.2
Private comprehensive	36,525	100.0	51.4	39.5	2.1	2.8	0.8	0.3	1.6	0.9	0.4	0.1
Private liberal arts	20,909	100.0	40.5	49.1	3.9	2.0	1.4	1.5	0.8	0.8	0.1	—
Public 2-year	166,335	100.0	49.6	38.3	2.6	2.0	2.6	1.4	1.5	1.2	0.4	0.3
Other	24,454	100.0	52.4	38.4	0.7	2.5	0.6	0.5	1.6	2.2	0.8	0.3
Academic rank												
Full professor	32,269	100.0	63.2	25.0	3.5	1.7	1.7	0.4	2.9	0.7	0.8	0.2
Associate professor	22,518	100.0	59.4	30.1	1.6	1.2	1.5	0.4	3.7	1.3	0.4	0.4
Assistant professor	24,237	100.0	49.1	37.4	5.7	2.5	0.6	0.4	2.4	1.9	—	0.1
Instructor	215,442	100.0	46.1	42.4	2.5	2.2	2.4	1.2	1.4	1.2	0.5	0.2
Lecturer	45,328	100.0	48.5	39.8	2.1	2.0	1.3	1.6	2.5	1.8	0.2	0.2
Other	27,553	100.0	43.7	44.8	3.6	2.3	0.8	1.2	1.2	2.0	—	0.5
No rank	9,328	100.0	42.4	45.9	2.1	2.8	—	2.0	2.9	1.3	0.6	—
Age												
Under 30	20,483	100.0	41.2	46.3	2.1	2.1	1.5	1.9	1.5	2.5	0.3	0.5
30 to 34	35,908	100.0	41.6	44.6	2.0	2.1	2.6	1.5	2.1	2.7	0.5	0.2
35 to 39	58,923	100.0	42.8	43.8	4.1	2.2	2.1	1.0	2.0	1.1	0.6	0.2
40 to 44	70,025	100.0	47.5	41.8	2.2	1.9	1.8	1.4	1.6	1.5	0.2	0.2
45 to 49	67,969	100.0	48.2	41.8	2.1	1.7	1.5	1.3	2.2	1.0	(1)	0.3
50 to 54	45,093	100.0	49.2	36.5	3.6	2.8	2.2	0.6	2.3	1.6	0.9	0.3
55 to 59	28,764	100.0	55.3	34.6	3.3	1.6	1.4	0.6	2.0	1.0	0.2	—
60 to 64	22,943	100.0	56.2	33.6	2.1	2.3	2.2	0.5	1.2	0.9	1.1	0.1
65 or older	26,565	100.0	65.6	25.4	2.4	2.8	1.1	0.9	1.3	0.4	—	—
Base salary												
Under $10,000	280,526	100.0	49.6	39.1	2.7	2.3	1.7	1.1	1.6	1.3	0.3	0.2
10,000 to 24,999	68,117	100.0	43.1	44.9	2.2	1.4	2.8	1.3	2.5	1.5	0.3	0.2
25,000 to 39,999	15,840	100.0	49.4	38.1	4.1	2.0	1.6	0.3	2.5	1.2	0.8	—
40,000 to 54,999	5,307	100.0	55.2	32.8	2.1	1.9	1.5	2.7	0.1	1.8	1.9	—
55,000 to 69,999	2,157	—	—	—	3.5	—	0.6	—	22.0	8.6	—	—
70,000 to 84,999	1,127	—	—	—	7.7	4.2	—	—	2.7	—	8.0	—
85,000 to 99,999	942	—	—	—	—	—	—	—	—	—	—	—
100,000 or more	2,657	100.0	46.9	39.0	10.5	0.5	1.2	—	—	2.0	—	—
Total income												
Under $10,000	70,693	100.0	35.4	52.6	2.3	2.9	1.9	1.3	1.6	1.6	(1)	0.4
10,000 to 24,999	84,803	100.0	33.2	57.1	1.3	1.8	1.3	1.7	1.3	1.9	0.4	0.1
25,000 to 39,999	74,809	100.0	48.5	39.6	2.5	2.9	2.0	1.2	1.6	1.4	0.2	0.3
40,000 to 54,999	58,057	100.0	55.8	32.1	3.4	1.9	1.5	1.2	1.8	0.7	1.3	0.4
55,000 to 69,999	32,386	100.0	69.3	17.5	3.4	1.6	3.2	0.5	3.0	1.2	0.3	—
70,000 to 84,999	17,199	100.0	69.4	17.8	4.7	0.7	2.9	0.7	2.8	0.5	0.5	—
85,000 to 99,999	8,231	100.0	70.2	18.1	4.7	0.8	4.7	—	1.4	—	—	—
100,000 or more	30,497	100.0	68.9	19.0	4.7	1.5	1.0	—	3.3	1.6	0.1	—

[1] Less than 0.05 percent.
—Data not available or applicable.
NOTE.—Because of rounding, details may not add to totals.

SOURCE: U.S. Department of Education, National Center for Education Statistics, National Study of Postsecondary Faculty (NSOPF), 1993. (This table was prepared September 1996.)

Table 231.—Full-time and part-time instructional faculty and staff in institutions of higher education, by faculty characteristics and field: Fall 1992

Faculty characteristics	Number in thousands	All fields	Agriculture and home economics	Business	Education	Engineering	Fine arts	Health	Humanities	Natural sciences	Social sciences	Other and not reported
1	2	3	4	5	6	7	8	9	10	11	12	13
Full-time instructional faculty and staff												
Full-time, in thousands	528	—	11	40	37	24	32	79	74	102	58	62
Percent	—	100.0	2.2	7.7	7.1	4.7	6.1	15.3	14.2	19.5	11.2	11.9
Percentage distribution of full-time faculty												
Total	528	100.0	100.0	100.0	100.0	100.0	100.0	100.0	100.0	100.0	100.0	100.0
Sex												
Male	353	66.8	75.3	68.9	48.9	93.9	67.0	49.9	58.6	79.9	72.5	69.6
Female	176	33.2	24.7	31.2	51.1	6.1	33.0	50.1	41.4	20.1	27.5	30.4
Race/ethnicity												
White, non-Hispanic	457	86.5	90.8	88.5	84.7	76.6	88.6	85.9	88.1	85.8	87.3	88.1
Black, non-Hispanic	27	5.2	3.9	4.1	9.4	2.8	5.8	5.6	4.2	3.6	6.2	6.0
Hispanic	14	2.6	1.8	1.6	3.3	3.1	2.5	2.3	4.1	1.9	2.8	2.5
Asian/Pacific Islander	28	5.2	2.9	4.8	1.6	16.8	2.7	6.0	3.2	8.3	3.3	2.9
American Indian/Alaskan Native	3	0.5	0.7	1.0	1.0	0.7	0.5	0.2	0.5	0.3	0.5	0.4
Age												
Under 30	8	1.4	0.4	1.2	1.1	1.3	1.3	1.1	1.7	1.5	0.8	2.4
30 to 34	35	6.7	7.3	6.3	3.5	11.0	6.2	8.4	4.7	6.7	7.3	6.8
35 to 39	67	12.6	9.1	13.5	7.7	13.1	13.1	16.2	9.6	13.9	13.0	12.3
40 to 44	90	17.1	15.7	16.6	17.6	16.9	17.7	21.8	13.4	15.8	16.4	17.9
45 to 49	98	18.5	17.7	20.9	19.7	14.8	18.5	19.2	19.9	17.2	17.9	17.7
50 to 54	95	18.0	18.4	16.2	21.1	12.2	17.2	13.3	21.4	19.3	19.2	18.4
55 to 59	67	12.7	14.4	11.7	14.1	15.0	14.1	9.6	14.7	13.5	12.2	12.4
60 to 64	45	8.4	11.4	7.9	10.5	10.6	7.9	7.6	9.9	7.4	9.2	7.3
65 or older	24	4.5	5.7	5.7	4.7	5.0	4.1	2.8	4.8	4.7	4.1	5.0
Degree												
Less than bachelor's	6	1.2	0.2	0.5	0.3	2.0	0.7	1.2	(1)	0.2	0.1	6.2
Bachelor's	21	4.0	5.7	4.5	2.9	5.2	5.4	5.8	1.3	2.8	0.7	8.2
Master's	156	29.7	22.0	38.4	30.8	18.7	56.2	30.1	31.7	22.2	19.3	33.6
Professional	58	11.1	4.4	4.5	2.9	2.3	4.3	42.9	2.4	4.5	3.5	17.1
Doctoral	284	54.0	67.8	52.0	63.2	71.8	33.4	20.0	64.6	70.3	76.4	35.0
Rank												
Full professor	161	30.4	41.4	24.7	24.3	36.8	32.0	21.2	33.1	37.0	36.8	26.9
Associate professor	124	23.4	22.6	25.5	29.5	28.0	25.4	23.0	22.4	22.5	24.8	19.3
Assistant professor	124	23.5	19.3	25.6	22.9	22.5	21.4	32.9	19.3	20.7	24.3	23.0
Instructor	74	14.0	10.8	16.7	13.2	10.4	10.3	16.9	14.9	11.7	7.9	21.7
Lecturer	12	2.2	1.0	1.3	2.5	0.9	2.8	2.3	3.9	1.7	1.7	2.7
Other	17	3.2	3.2	2.2	5.5	0.5	3.3	2.5	1.9	2.4	2.0	3.6
No rank	17	3.2	1.7	4.0	1.9	1.0	4.8	1.4	4.7	3.9	2.5	3.0

Table 231.—Full-time and part-time instructional faculty and staff in institutions of higher education, by faculty characteristics and field: Fall 1992—Continued

Faculty characteristics	Number in thousands	All fields	Agriculture and home economics	Business	Education	Engineering	Fine arts	Health	Humanities	Natural sciences	Social sciences	Other and not reported
1	2	3	4	5	6	7	8	9	10	11	12	13
		Part-time instructional faculty and staff										
Part-time, in thousands	377	—	3	35	31	12	33	45	60	60	34	60
Percent	—	100.0	0.7	9.3	8.3	3.1	8.8	12.0	16.2	16.2	9.1	16.2
		Percentage distribution of part-time faculty										
Total	377	100.0	100.0	100.0	100.0	100.0	100.0	100.0	100.0	100.0	100.0	100.0
Sex												
Male	209	55.4	48.0	70.0	32.7	92.0	51.7	43.5	41.0	67.8	56.9	63.9
Female	168	44.6	52.0	30.0	67.3	8.0	48.3	56.5	59.0	32.2	43.2	36.1
Race/ethnicity												
White, non-Hispanic	333	88.3	98.9	89.6	87.7	86.5	89.3	88.2	87.4	87.5	87.2	90.2
Black, non-Hispanic	18	4.8	0.0	5.1	8.0	1.9	5.1	5.7	3.3	4.1	6.6	4.6
Hispanic	11	3.0	1.1	2.7	2.0	2.0	2.6	1.6	5.8	2.5	2.7	2.9
Asian/Pacific Islander	12	3.2	(1)	2.1	1.5	7.6	2.3	4.0	2.8	5.2	3.1	2.3
American Indian/Alaskan Native	2	0.6	(1)	0.6	0.9	1.9	0.6	0.5	0.8	0.7	0.5	0.1
Age												
Under 30	20	5.4	8.4	2.2	2.4	7.9	4.3	4.6	6.6	6.8	7.6	5.4
30 to 34	36	9.5	5.9	7.3	3.6	8.9	11.1	11.1	10.6	11.2	8.3	9.7
35 to 39	59	15.6	18.9	13.3	7.3	21.9	18.6	22.8	11.5	13.1	16.2	19.8
40 to 44	70	18.6	22.1	17.1	26.7	16.0	21.0	20.4	15.6	15.2	16.7	21.1
45 to 49	68	18.0	16.2	23.1	18.8	12.8	14.3	14.1	20.6	16.8	16.6	19.8
50 to 54	45	12.0	6.9	15.4	13.3	9.2	10.2	11.1	13.5	13.0	12.8	9.4
55 to 59	29	7.6	7.5	7.7	8.6	6.3	8.7	4.9	8.9	8.4	8.8	6.5
60 to 64	23	6.1	10.0	6.0	8.6	7.2	5.7	2.9	6.1	8.7	6.7	4.1
65 or older	27	7.1	4.2	7.8	10.7	9.9	6.2	8.1	6.7	6.7	6.4	4.3
Degree												
Less than bachelor's	17	4.7	1.8	2.2	0.7	13.4	3.6	9.6	0.3	1.9	0.1	13.0
Bachelor's	63	17.0	30.2	21.3	14.0	27.5	21.8	17.5	7.3	22.2	6.0	21.4
Master's	190	51.6	52.8	59.6	61.3	32.5	66.3	26.4	71.9	53.0	53.3	34.1
Professional	40	10.7	8.6	8.1	0.7	(1)	1.6	38.2	2.0	4.7	6.2	21.5
Doctoral	59	16.0	6.6	8.8	23.4	26.6	6.7	8.4	18.5	18.2	34.3	9.9
Rank												
Full professor	32	8.6	8.8	8.5	7.4	15.7	9.8	6.7	6.9	6.7	8.5	12.0
Associate professor	23	6.0	11.6	4.6	5.2	5.4	4.2	17.4	3.2	4.3	6.3	4.2
Assistant professor	24	6.4	(1)	6.4	4.9	7.4	6.9	16.9	3.5	4.3	8.8	3.4
Instructor	215	57.2	55.1	60.2	57.4	50.4	56.3	45.6	60.0	62.5	51.9	61.8
Lecturer	45	12.0	19.9	11.3	10.8	13.0	12.3	6.5	17.5	10.6	16.4	10.0
Other	28	7.3	4.5	6.3	10.8	7.2	6.8	6.0	5.8	8.2	6.7	7.1
No rank	9	2.5	(1)	2.8	3.6	0.8	3.9	0.9	3.0	3.5	1.4	1.5

[1] Less than 0.05 percent.
—Not applicable.

NOTE.—Because of rounding and survey item nonresponse, details may not add to totals.

SOURCE: U.S. Department of Education, National Center for Education Statistics, National Study of Postsecondary Faculty (NSOPF), 1993. (This table was prepared September 1996.)

Table 232.—Percentage distribution of full-time and part-time instructional faculty and staff in institutions of higher education, by program area, race/ethnicity, and sex: Fall 1992

Program area	Number	Percent	White, non-Hispanic		Black, non-Hispanic		Hispanic		Asian/Pacific Islander		American Indian/Alaskan Native	
			Male	Female	Male	Female	Male	Female	Male	Female	Male	Female
1	2	3	4	5	6	7	8	9	10	11	12	13
Full-time instructional faculty and staff												
Total	528,260	100.0	58.0	28.4	2.7	2.4	1.8	0.9	3.9	1.3	0.3	0.2
Agriculture and home economics	11,366	100.0	70.4	20.3	2.3	1.6	1.6	0.2	1.0	1.9	—	0.7
Business	39,928	100.0	61.3	27.2	2.0	2.2	1.0	0.6	3.9	0.8	0.6	0.3
Communications	10,296	100.0	55.9	30.4	2.9	2.7	1.5	—	4.3	1.2	0.8	0.3
Education	37,066	100.0	42.8	41.9	4.0	5.4	1.0	2.4	0.5	1.1	0.7	0.3
Teacher education	12,490	100.0	39.8	50.3	2.1	4.9	0.1	0.7	0.3	1.0	0.5	0.2
Other education	24,576	100.0	44.4	37.6	4.9	5.7	1.4	3.3	0.6	1.1	0.8	0.3
Engineering	24,431	100.0	72.7	3.9	2.1	0.7	2.9	0.2	15.5	1.3	0.7	—
Fine arts	31,659	100.0	59.6	29.0	3.8	1.9	2.1	0.3	1.2	1.5	0.3	0.2
Health sciences	79,422	100.0	42.1	43.8	2.3	3.4	1.5	0.7	3.9	2.2	0.1	0.1
First-professional	36,867	100.0	63.3	19.0	3.6	1.0	2.8	0.9	7.2	2.1	0.2	—
Nursing	21,776	100.0	0.9	87.5	0.5	7.1	—	0.9	0.1	2.9	—	0.2
Other health sciences	20,779	100.0	47.5	42.0	1.8	3.7	0.9	0.3	2.0	1.5	0.2	0.2
Humanities	73,923	100.0	52.8	35.2	2.1	2.1	2.1	2.0	1.2	1.9	0.3	0.1
English and literature	37,432	100.0	44.5	45.5	2.2	2.9	1.3	1.0	0.8	1.2	0.5	0.1
Foreign languages	13,722	100.0	39.5	36.8	1.2	0.6	5.7	7.5	1.8	6.4	—	0.4
History	14,574	100.0	70.2	20.2	3.0	2.3	1.3	0.4	1.7	0.4	0.3	—
Philosophy	8,195	100.0	82.1	12.5	1.7	0.2	1.2	0.3	1.5	0.2	0.2	—
Law	8,524	100.0	57.6	30.1	5.4	3.0	1.2	1.0	0.2	1.4	—	—
Natural sciences	101,505	100.0	68.2	17.6	2.6	1.0	1.6	0.4	7.3	1.0	0.2	0.1
Biological sciences	34,289	100.0	67.1	20.8	3.2	1.5	1.1	0.5	4.5	0.9	0.3	0.1
Physical sciences	28,313	100.0	76.7	10.2	2.2	0.3	2.0	0.1	7.7	0.9	—	—
Mathematics	25,325	100.0	61.3	21.6	2.7	1.0	1.7	0.6	9.1	1.2	0.5	0.4
Computer sciences	13,578	100.0	65.8	17.8	2.1	1.3	1.7	0.1	10.3	0.8	—	—
Social sciences	58,232	100.0	64.6	22.7	3.1	3.1	1.9	0.8	2.6	0.7	0.3	0.2
Economics	9,778	100.0	69.8	12.3	3.9	0.3	3.0	1.1	7.8	1.7	—	—
Political science	9,324	100.0	75.0	14.8	3.6	1.9	2.7	0.5	1.1	0.2	0.1	—
Psychology	17,784	100.0	56.9	32.3	2.3	4.3	1.5	0.8	1.1	0.3	0.1	0.2
Sociology	9,511	100.0	67.4	20.6	2.7	3.3	2.3	0.5	1.3	0.8	0.9	—
Other social sciences	11,835	100.0	61.3	25.0	3.4	4.3	0.8	1.1	2.7	0.6	0.3	0.6
Occupationally specific programs	15,268	100.0	75.7	13.8	3.6	0.9	2.9	0.3	1.9	0.2	0.5	0.2
All other programs	27,717	100.0	57.4	30.7	2.8	3.4	2.0	0.6	2.2	0.6	—	0.1
Part-time instructional faculty and staff												
Total	376,675	100.0	48.6	39.8	2.7	2.1	1.8	1.1	1.9	1.4	0.4	0.2
Agriculture and home economics	2,758	100.0	46.9	52.0	—	—	1.1	—	—	—	—	—
Business	34,679	100.0	63.6	25.9	3.3	1.9	2.0	0.7	1.0	1.1	0.2	0.4
Communications	10,307	100.0	43.2	49.9	4.0	0.9	—	0.6	0.5	0.3	0.3	0.1
Education	30,758	100.0	28.9	58.8	2.5	5.5	0.7	1.3	0.4	1.1	0.3	0.6
Teacher education	12,390	100.0	20.0	68.5	2.3	6.6	0.6	0.8	0.5	0.8	—	—
Other education	18,368	100.0	34.9	52.2	2.7	4.8	0.7	1.6	0.3	1.3	0.5	1.0
Engineering	11,632	100.0	79.3	7.2	1.9	—	2.0	—	6.8	0.8	1.9	—
Fine arts	32,814	100.0	46.2	43.1	3.4	1.8	1.3	1.3	0.4	1.9	0.5	0.2
Health sciences	44,763	100.0	36.8	51.4	3.0	2.6	1.0	0.7	2.3	1.7	0.4	0.1
First-professional	17,710	100.0	57.6	27.7	6.1	1.1	0.6	0.3	4.9	1.8	—	—
Nursing	10,498	100.0	5.4	84.0	—	6.6	—	0.9	—	2.4	—	0.6
Other health sciences	16,555	100.0	34.5	56.0	1.7	1.8	2.0	0.9	0.9	1.2	1.1	—
Humanities	60,041	100.0	35.8	51.5	1.1	2.2	2.7	3.1	1.1	1.7	0.3	0.5
English and literature	37,395	100.0	29.4	60.9	0.6	2.9	2.0	1.5	0.6	1.2	0.4	0.6
Foreign languages	10,566	100.0	27.0	44.7	1.1	1.7	5.9	12.1	2.2	4.9	—	0.5
History	7,812	100.0	61.9	30.7	2.9	0.7	1.7	0.2	1.5	—	0.3	—
Philosophy	4,268	100.0	66.3	24.6	2.6	0.3	2.7	—	2.3	1.2	—	—
Law	13,552	100.0	68.2	23.6	3.7	2.7	0.3	0.2	1.3	—	—	—
Natural sciences	60,242	100.0	58.3	29.2	3.1	1.0	2.1	0.4	3.6	1.6	0.7	(1)
Biological sciences	11,747	100.0	50.3	37.4	3.2	1.1	2.1	0.6	1.8	3.5	—	—
Physical sciences	10,626	100.0	67.6	21.2	1.5	0.4	1.1	0.9	5.5	1.9	—	—
Mathematics	24,559	100.0	52.8	34.5	4.6	0.9	2.4	0.2	3.4	0.7	0.4	0.1
Computer sciences	13,310	100.0	68.2	18.4	1.7	1.4	2.3	0.3	4.0	1.2	2.4	—
Social sciences	33,854	100.0	48.8	38.3	3.7	2.9	1.8	0.9	2.2	0.9	0.4	0.1
Economics	3,038	100.0	69.0	13.8	1.7	1.0	2.7	—	9.1	2.5	—	—
Political science	3,055	100.0	72.4	18.6	4.6	0.4	3.4	0.5	—	—	—	—
Psychology	15,617	100.0	45.6	45.7	2.5	1.5	1.5	0.5	2.0	0.3	0.2	0.3
Sociology	4,384	100.0	33.2	52.5	6.3	4.0	1.2	0.2	1.5	1.0	—	—
Other social sciences	7,760	100.0	47.0	32.8	4.9	7.0	1.7	2.4	1.0	1.9	1.2	—
Occupationally specific programs	16,490	100.0	71.2	18.0	3.5	0.8	5.1	—	1.3	—	0.1	—
All other programs	19,769	100.0	44.7	43.5	1.9	1.5	2.3	1.6	2.4	2.1	—	—

[1] Less than 0.05 percent.
—Data not available or not applicable.

NOTE.—Because of rounding and nonresponse to program area question, details may not add to totals.

SOURCE: U.S. Department of Education, National Center for Education Statistics, National Study of Postsecondary Faculty (NSOPF), 1993. (This table was prepared September 1996.)

HIGHER EDUCATION: FACULTY 249

Table 233.—Average base salaries of full-time instructional faculty and staff in institutions of higher education, by type and control of institution and by field of instruction: 1987–88 and 1992–93

Field of instruction	All institutions	Total public	Total private	Public research	Private research	Public doctoral	Private doctoral	Public comprehensive	Private comprehensive	Private liberal arts	Public 2-year	Other
1	2	3	4	5	6	7	8	9	10	11	12	13
					1987–88 salaries in 1992–93 dollars							
Instructional faculty, in thousands	515	356	159	102	42	56	25	97	37	38	96	22
All fields	$48,381	$48,826	$47,386	$58,118	$63,669	$54,028	$57,215	$45,342	$39,564	$35,462	$39,847	$37,698
Agriculture and home economics	48,452	48,713	—	54,431	—	43,501	—	46,934	45,319	—	—	—
Business	45,243	45,785	44,078	58,218	—	49,161	—	43,413	33,499	29,400	40,707	35,292
Education	40,498	42,517	33,529	45,861	—	43,315	—	41,766	51,481	—	41,133	—
Engineering	52,213	51,412	55,095	61,363	—	53,133	—	50,316	33,170	34,484	36,794	—
Fine arts	37,840	39,547	34,368	40,297	—	38,155	—	39,367	47,683	—	40,216	—
Health	64,860	64,447	65,689	73,454	77,144	71,065	67,278	57,124	37,089	38,127	37,017	—
Humanities	42,420	44,092	39,867	46,326	48,988	39,327	46,313	44,601	38,763	37,760	43,461	34,783
Natural sciences	47,811	48,399	46,495	57,947	61,731	49,917	46,912	46,684	38,613	35,728	39,692	37,499
Social sciences	46,234	46,506	45,730	52,842	61,043	47,938	—	44,933	38,613	35,728	41,052	—
Other	44,712	44,239	45,834	52,646	—	45,427	—	41,853	35,733	—	37,762	44,331
					1992–93							
Instructional faculty, in thousands	478	339	140	89	25	46	23	91	37	37	105	25
All fields	$46,833	$46,767	$46,993	$56,443	$63,967	$51,497	$56,011	$43,487	$43,255	$37,623	$39,351	$40,458
Agriculture and home economics	47,809	48,488	—	54,735	—	44,480	—	43,377	—	—	39,788	—
Business	49,223	49,955	47,318	65,209	—	58,808	54,369	47,739	53,786	32,322	42,017	33,587
Education	42,046	43,259	37,618	49,822	61,084	42,202	49,254	41,456	37,961	32,419	41,224	—
Engineering	55,569	55,923	54,190	66,781	86,221	53,577	55,040	48,703	45,855	—	38,648	56,036
Fine arts	40,574	39,285	42,526	41,337	73,080	39,379	37,874	39,144	35,812	37,764	37,524	34,100
Health	55,624	54,097	59,720	73,467	44,695	63,839	66,120	38,311	45,678	42,363	35,790	41,900
Humanities	40,972	41,601	39,634	44,018	67,170	39,661	42,928	40,735	41,043	37,667	41,183	36,547
Natural sciences	48,192	47,500	49,933	55,432	59,296	51,691	56,665	45,922	46,666	37,534	39,651	42,143
Social sciences	45,960	46,103	45,667	53,139	65,685	48,709	49,505	43,686	39,838	40,492	40,312	44,389
Other	44,594	43,431	47,030	51,007	—	43,777	61,854	45,357	41,722	36,436	37,668	39,199

—Too few sample cases (fewer than 30) for a reliable estimate.

NOTE.—Data for 1992–93 differ from other tables because of adjustments to maintain consistency with the 1987–88 data. Data have been revised from previously published figures. Because of rounding, details may not add to totals.

SOURCE: U.S. Department of Education, National Center for Education Statistics, National Study of Postsecondary Faculty (NSOPF), 1987–88 and 1992–93. (This table was prepared September 1996.)

Table 234.—Average salary of full-time instructional faculty on 9-month contracts in institutions of higher education, by academic rank, sex, and control and type of institution: 1970–71 to 1995–96

Academic year and sex	All faculty	Academic rank						Public institutions			Private institutions		
		Professor	Associate professor	Assistant professor	Instructor	Lecturer	No rank	Total	4-year	2-year	Total	4-year	2-year
1	2	3	4	5	6	7	8	9	10	11	12	13	14
						Current dollars							
Total													
1970–71	$12,710	$17,958	$13,563	$11,176	$9,360	$11,196	$12,333	$12,953	$13,121	$12,644	$11,619	$11,824	$8,664
1972–73	13,856	19,191	14,580	12,032	10,737	11,637	12,676	14,016	14,417	12,919	13,452	13,622	9,288
1974–75	15,622	21,277	16,146	13,295	12,691	12,575	13,532	15,879	16,271	14,897	14,912	15,092	10,242
1975–76	16,659	22,649	17,065	13,986	13,672	12,906	15,196	16,942	17,400	15,820	15,921	16,116	10,901
1976–77	17,560	23,792	17,905	14,662	11,835	13,431	16,634	17,845	18,313	16,685	16,787	16,977	11,637
1977–78	18,709	25,133	18,987	15,530	12,504	14,528	17,831	19,045	19,517	17,895	17,773	17,966	12,191
1978–79	19,820	26,470	20,047	16,374	13,193	15,281	18,725	20,179	20,722	18,844	18,807	19,010	12,496
1979–80	21,348	28,388	21,451	17,465	14,023	16,122	20,262	21,798	22,349	20,429	20,105	20,318	13,250
1980–81	23,302	30,753	23,214	18,901	15,178	17,301	22,334	23,745	24,373	22,177	22,093	22,325	15,065
1981–82	25,449	33,437	25,278	20,608	16,450	18,756	24,331	25,886	26,591	24,193	24,255	24,509	15,926
1982–83	27,196	35,540	26,921	22,056	17,601	20,072	25,557	27,488	28,293	25,567	26,393	26,691	16,595
1984–85	30,447	39,743	29,945	24,668	20,230	22,334	27,683	30,646	31,764	27,864	29,910	30,247	18,510
1985–86	32,392	42,268	31,787	26,277	20,918	23,770	29,088	32,750	34,033	29,590	31,402	31,732	19,436
1987–88	35,897	47,040	35,231	29,110	22,728	25,977	31,532	36,231	37,840	32,209	35,049	35,346	21,867
1989–90	40,133	52,810	39,392	32,689	25,030	28,990	34,559	40,416	42,365	35,516	39,464	39,817	24,601
1990–91	42,165	55,540	41,414	34,434	26,332	30,097	36,395	42,510	44,510	37,055	41,788	42,224	24,088
1991–92	43,851	57,433	42,929	35,745	30,916	30,456	37,783	43,641	45,638	38,959	44,376	44,793	25,673
1992–93	44,714	58,788	43,945	36,625	28,499	30,543	37,771	44,197	46,515	38,935	45,985	46,427	26,105
1993–94	46,364	60,649	45,278	37,630	28,828	32,729	40,584	45,920	48,019	41,040	47,465	47,880	28,435
1994–95	47,811	62,709	46,713	38,756	29,665	33,198	41,227	47,432	49,738	42,101	48,741	49,379	25,613
1995–96	49,309	64,540	47,966	39,696	30,344	34,136	42,996	48,837	51,172	43,295	50,466	50,819	31,915
Men													
1972–73	14,422	19,414	14,723	12,193	11,147	12,106	13,047	14,545	14,944	13,268	14,116	14,253	9,571
1974–75	16,303	21,532	16,282	13,458	13,350	13,232	14,008	16,522	16,918	15,350	15,709	15,852	10,633
1975–76	17,414	22,902	17,209	14,174	14,430	13,579	15,761	17,661	18,121	16,339	16,784	16,946	11,378
1976–77	18,378	24,029	18,055	14,851	12,085	14,147	17,253	18,620	19,091	17,235	17,736	17,891	12,193
1977–78	19,575	25,370	19,133	15,726	12,729	15,181	18,459	19,867	20,347	18,479	18,783	18,935	12,759
1978–79	20,777	26,727	20,221	16,602	13,441	15,927	19,400	21,080	21,628	19,475	19,935	20,086	13,048
1979–80	22,394	28,672	21,651	17,720	14,323	16,932	20,901	22,789	23,350	21,131	21,317	21,472	13,938
1980–81	24,499	31,082	23,451	19,227	15,545	18,281	23,170	24,873	25,509	22,965	23,493	23,669	16,075
1981–82	26,796	33,799	25,553	21,025	16,906	19,721	25,276	27,149	27,864	25,085	25,849	26,037	16,834
1982–83	28,664	35,956	27,262	22,586	18,160	21,225	26,541	28,851	29,661	26,524	28,159	28,380	17,346
1984–85	32,182	40,269	30,392	25,330	21,159	23,557	28,670	32,240	33,344	28,891	32,028	32,278	19,460
1985–86	34,294	42,833	32,273	27,094	21,693	25,238	30,267	34,528	35,786	30,758	33,656	33,900	20,412
1987–88	38,112	47,735	35,823	30,086	23,645	27,652	32,747	38,314	39,898	33,477	37,603	37,817	22,641
1989–90	42,763	53,650	40,131	33,781	25,933	31,162	35,980	42,959	44,834	37,081	42,312	42,595	25,218
1990–91	45,065	56,549	42,239	35,636	27,388	32,398	38,036	45,084	47,168	38,787	45,019	45,319	25,937
1991–92	46,848	58,494	43,814	36,969	33,359	32,843	39,422	46,483	48,401	40,811	47,733	48,042	26,825
1992–93	47,866	59,972	44,855	37,842	29,583	32,512	39,365	47,175	49,392	40,725	49,518	49,837	27,402
1993–94	49,579	61,857	46,229	38,794	29,815	34,796	42,251	48,956	50,989	42,938	51,076	51,397	30,783
1994–95	51,228	64,046	47,705	39,923	30,528	35,082	43,103	50,629	52,874	44,020	52,653	53,036	29,639
1995–96	52,814	65,949	49,037	40,858	30,940	36,135	44,624	52,163	54,448	45,209	54,364	54,649	33,301
Women													
1972–73	11,925	17,123	13,827	11,510	10,098	10,775	11,913	12,250	12,300	12,165	11,044	11,219	8,888
1974–75	13,471	19,012	15,481	12,858	11,740	11,543	12,619	13,892	13,831	13,987	12,233	12,423	9,735
1975–76	14,308	20,308	16,364	13,522	12,572	11,901	14,094	14,762	14,758	14,769	13,030	13,231	10,201
1976–77	15,100	21,536	17,189	14,225	11,589	12,397	15,467	15,573	15,539	15,628	13,709	13,899	10,850
1977–78	16,159	22,943	18,325	15,109	12,288	13,688	16,637	16,684	16,619	16,785	14,597	14,799	11,470
1978–79	17,080	24,143	19,300	15,914	12,966	14,465	17,482	17,646	17,627	17,676	15,388	15,611	11,898
1979–80	18,396	25,910	20,642	16,974	13,750	15,142	19,069	19,042	18,985	19,134	16,539	16,787	12,541
1980–81	19,996	27,959	22,295	18,302	14,854	16,168	20,843	20,673	20,608	20,778	18,073	18,326	13,892
1981–82	21,802	30,438	24,271	19,866	16,054	17,676	22,672	22,524	22,454	22,632	19,743	20,024	14,984
1982–83	23,261	32,221	25,738	21,130	17,102	18,830	23,855	23,892	23,876	23,917	21,451	21,785	15,845
1984–85	25,941	35,824	28,517	23,575	19,362	21,004	26,050	26,566	26,813	26,172	24,186	24,560	17,575
1985–86	27,576	38,252	30,300	24,966	20,237	22,273	27,171	28,299	28,680	27,693	25,523	25,889	18,504
1987–88	30,499	42,371	33,528	27,600	21,962	24,370	29,605	31,215	31,820	30,228	28,621	28,946	21,215
1989–90	34,183	47,663	37,469	31,090	24,320	26,995	32,528	34,796	35,704	33,307	32,650	33,010	24,002
1990–91	35,881	49,728	39,329	32,724	25,534	28,111	34,179	36,459	37,573	34,720	34,359	34,898	22,585
1991–92	37,534	51,621	40,766	34,063	28,873	28,550	35,622	37,800	38,634	36,517	36,828	37,309	24,683
1992–93	38,385	52,755	41,861	35,032	27,700	28,922	35,792	38,356	39,470	36,710	38,460	38,987	25,068
1993–94	40,058	54,746	43,178	36,169	28,136	31,048	38,474	40,118	41,031	38,707	39,902	40,378	26,142
1994–95	41,369	56,555	44,626	37,352	29,072	31,677	38,967	41,548	42,663	39,812	40,908	41,815	22,851
1995–96	42,871	58,318	45,803	38,345	29,940	32,584	41,085	42,871	43,986	41,086	42,871	43,236	30,671

Table 234.—Average salary of full-time instructional faculty on 9-month contracts in institutions of higher education, by academic rank, sex, and control and type of institution: 1970-71 to 1995-96—Continued

Academic year and sex	All faculty	Academic rank						Public institutions			Private institutions		
		Professor	Associate professor	Assistant professor	Instructor	Lecturer	No rank	Total	4-year	2-year	Total	4-year	2-year
1	2	3	4	5	6	7	8	9	10	11	12	13	14
	Constant dollars 1995-96 dollars [1]												
Total													
1970-71	$49,431	$69,841	$52,751	$43,466	$36,402	$43,544	$47,967	$50,379	$51,033	$49,176	$45,187	$45,987	$33,696
1972-73	50,009	69,261	52,622	43,424	38,750	41,998	45,749	50,585	52,032	46,625	48,550	49,163	33,523
1974-75	46,601	63,471	48,166	39,659	37,857	37,514	40,368	47,368	48,539	44,440	44,482	45,021	30,552
1975-76	46,409	63,098	47,542	38,964	38,090	35,954	42,334	47,199	48,475	44,072	44,353	44,899	30,368
1976-77	46,226	62,630	47,133	38,597	31,154	35,356	43,786	46,974	48,208	43,921	44,189	44,689	30,633
1977-78	46,149	61,998	46,836	38,309	30,843	35,836	43,985	46,979	48,144	44,142	43,843	44,317	30,071
1978-79	44,704	59,703	45,217	36,932	29,756	34,465	42,233	45,513	46,738	42,502	42,419	42,876	28,184
1979-80	42,486	56,497	42,690	34,758	27,907	32,084	40,323	43,382	44,477	40,657	40,011	40,435	26,369
1980-81	41,560	54,850	41,403	33,711	27,071	30,857	39,834	42,350	43,470	39,554	39,404	39,818	26,869
1981-82	41,780	54,895	41,500	33,833	27,006	30,792	39,945	42,498	43,655	39,718	39,821	40,238	26,146
1982-83	42,810	55,944	42,377	34,719	27,706	31,596	40,230	43,269	44,537	40,246	41,546	42,015	26,123
1984-85	44,476	58,055	43,742	36,034	29,551	32,625	40,438	44,766	46,400	40,703	43,691	44,184	27,039
1985-86	45,991	60,013	45,132	37,308	29,700	33,749	41,300	46,499	48,321	42,012	44,585	45,054	27,596
1987-88	47,876	62,738	46,988	38,824	30,312	34,645	42,055	48,322	50,468	42,958	46,745	47,141	29,164
1989-90	48,833	64,257	47,931	39,775	30,456	35,275	42,050	49,177	51,548	43,215	48,018	48,449	29,934
1990-91	48,646	64,077	47,779	39,727	30,379	34,723	41,989	48,822	51,351	42,750	48,211	48,714	27,791
1991-92	49,021	64,203	47,989	39,959	34,560	34,046	42,237	48,786	51,017	43,552	49,607	50,073	28,699
1992-93	48,471	63,727	47,637	39,702	30,894	33,109	40,944	47,910	50,423	42,206	49,849	50,328	28,298
1993-94	48,991	64,085	47,842	39,762	30,461	34,583	42,883	48,522	50,739	43,364	50,154	50,592	30,046
1994-95	49,112	64,415	47,984	39,810	30,472	34,101	42,349	48,722	51,091	43,246	50,067	50,722	26,310
1995-96	49,309	64,540	47,966	39,696	30,344	34,136	42,996	48,837	51,172	43,295	50,466	50,819	31,915
Men													
1972-73	52,051	70,068	53,138	44,007	40,232	43,690	47,089	52,496	53,934	47,886	50,946	51,441	34,543
1974-75	48,632	64,231	48,570	40,147	39,823	39,472	41,786	49,286	50,468	45,790	46,862	47,286	31,719
1975-76	48,513	63,802	47,941	39,488	40,200	37,829	43,908	49,202	50,482	45,520	46,759	47,209	31,697
1976-77	48,378	63,253	47,529	39,095	31,813	37,239	45,417	49,014	50,255	45,369	46,687	47,096	32,097
1977-78	48,287	62,581	47,197	38,793	31,400	37,447	45,533	49,006	50,190	45,583	46,334	46,707	31,472
1978-79	46,861	60,283	45,607	37,445	30,315	35,924	43,755	47,546	48,782	43,926	44,962	45,303	29,429
1979-80	44,567	57,061	43,088	35,265	28,505	33,696	41,596	45,353	46,470	42,053	42,425	42,732	27,739
1980-81	43,695	55,436	41,826	34,292	27,725	32,605	41,325	44,362	45,497	40,959	41,901	42,215	28,671
1981-82	43,992	55,489	41,951	34,517	27,755	32,377	41,496	44,571	45,745	41,183	42,437	42,745	27,637
1982-83	45,121	56,599	42,914	35,553	28,586	33,411	41,779	45,415	46,690	41,752	44,326	44,674	27,305
1984-85	47,010	58,823	44,395	37,001	30,908	34,411	41,880	47,095	48,708	42,203	46,785	47,150	28,426
1985-86	48,691	60,815	45,822	38,468	30,800	35,833	42,974	49,023	50,809	43,671	47,785	48,132	28,981
1987-88	50,830	63,664	47,778	40,127	31,535	36,880	43,675	51,100	53,212	44,649	50,152	50,437	30,197
1989-90	52,033	65,280	48,830	41,104	31,554	37,917	43,706	52,271	54,553	45,120	51,485	51,828	30,685
1990-91	51,992	65,241	48,731	41,113	31,598	37,377	43,882	52,014	54,417	44,749	51,939	52,285	29,923
1991-92	52,370	65,389	48,979	41,326	37,291	36,715	44,069	51,962	54,107	45,622	53,359	53,705	29,987
1992-93	51,887	65,011	48,624	41,021	32,069	35,244	42,673	51,138	53,542	44,146	53,679	54,025	29,704
1993-94	52,387	65,361	48,848	40,991	31,504	36,767	44,644	51,729	53,877	45,370	53,970	54,309	32,527
1994-95	52,622	65,789	49,003	41,009	31,359	36,036	44,276	52,007	54,312	45,218	54,085	54,479	30,446
1995-96	52,814	65,949	49,037	40,858	30,940	36,135	44,624	52,163	54,448	45,209	54,364	54,649	33,301
Women													
1972-73	43,038	61,798	49,902	41,540	36,446	38,887	42,997	44,213	44,393	43,903	39,860	40,490	32,076
1974-75	40,184	56,714	46,183	38,356	35,022	34,433	37,642	41,440	41,259	41,724	36,493	37,059	29,040
1975-76	39,859	56,576	45,588	37,611	35,024	33,154	39,264	41,177	41,124	41,144	36,301	36,859	28,418
1976-77	39,748	56,690	45,249	37,446	30,506	32,633	40,714	40,994	40,903	41,138	36,087	36,588	28,560
1977-78	39,860	56,595	45,203	37,270	30,311	33,766	41,041	41,155	40,996	41,405	36,007	36,507	28,295
1978-79	38,524	54,454	43,531	35,893	29,244	32,625	39,431	39,800	39,758	39,867	34,708	35,211	26,835
1979-80	36,611	51,565	41,080	33,780	27,365	30,135	37,951	37,896	37,782	38,080	32,914	33,408	24,957
1980-81	35,664	49,866	39,764	32,643	26,493	28,836	37,175	36,871	36,755	37,059	32,234	32,685	24,777
1981-82	35,793	49,971	39,846	32,615	26,356	29,019	37,221	36,978	36,863	37,156	32,412	32,873	24,600
1982-83	36,616	50,720	40,515	33,261	26,921	29,641	37,551	37,609	37,584	37,648	33,766	34,292	24,942
1984-85	37,894	52,330	41,656	34,437	28,283	30,682	38,053	38,806	39,167	38,231	35,330	35,876	25,673
1985-86	39,153	54,311	43,020	35,447	28,733	31,624	38,578	40,179	40,720	39,319	36,238	36,758	26,272
1987-88	40,677	56,511	44,717	36,811	29,291	32,502	39,485	41,632	42,439	40,315	38,172	38,606	28,295
1989-90	41,593	57,995	45,591	37,829	29,591	32,847	39,580	42,339	43,444	40,527	39,727	40,166	29,205
1990-91	41,395	57,372	45,374	37,754	29,459	32,432	39,432	42,063	43,348	40,057	39,640	40,262	26,057
1991-92	41,958	57,706	45,571	38,078	32,277	31,915	39,822	42,256	43,188	40,822	41,169	41,707	27,593
1992-93	41,610	57,188	45,378	37,976	30,028	31,352	38,799	41,578	42,786	39,795	41,691	42,262	27,174
1993-94	42,328	57,847	45,624	38,218	29,730	32,807	40,653	42,390	43,355	40,900	42,163	42,665	27,623
1994-95	42,495	58,093	45,840	38,368	29,863	32,538	40,027	42,678	43,823	40,895	42,021	42,952	23,473
1995-96	42,871	58,318	45,803	38,345	29,940	32,584	41,085	42,871	43,986	41,086	42,871	43,236	30,671

[1] Data adjusted by the Consumer Price Index prepared by the Bureau of Labor Statistics, averaged on an academic year time frame.

NOTE.—Data for 1987-88 to 1995-96 include imputations for nonrespondent institutions.

SOURCE: U.S. Department of Education, National Center for Education Statistics, Higher Education General Information Survey (HEGIS), "Faculty Salaries, Tenure, and Fringe Benefits" surveys; and Integrated Postsecondary Education Data System (IPEDS), "Salaries, Tenure, and Fringe Benefits of Full-Time Instructional Faculty" surveys. (This table was prepared January 1997.)

Table 235.—Average salary of full-time instructional faculty on 9-month contracts in institutions of higher education, by academic rank, sex, and by type and control of institution: 1980–81, 1990–91, 1994–95, and 1995–96

Academic year, control, and type of institution	All faculty	Academic rank						Sex	
		Professor	Associate professor	Assistant professor	Instructor	Lecturer	No academic rank	Men	Women
1	2	3	4	5	6	7	8	9	10
1980–81									
All institutions	$23,302	$30,753	$23,214	$18,901	$15,178	$17,301	$22,334	$24,499	$19,996
4-year	23,693	31,016	23,265	18,867	15,056	17,375	17,380	24,909	19,809
University	25,949	33,622	24,392	19,684	15,530	17,327	17,856	27,206	20,736
Other 4-year	22,230	28,798	22,558	18,398	14,887	17,425	17,334	23,271	19,372
2-year	21,898	26,528	22,750	19,166	15,621	16,222	22,615	22,736	20,434
Public institutions	23,745	31,077	23,772	19,431	15,613	17,620	22,820	24,873	20,673
4-year	24,373	31,442	23,898	19,442	15,486	17,712	19,240	25,509	20,608
University	25,571	32,945	24,268	19,637	15,305	17,426	17,358	26,788	20,564
Other 4-year	23,500	30,097	23,639	19,315	15,567	17,797	19,798	24,499	20,633
2-year	22,177	26,880	22,947	19,370	15,928	16,458	22,875	22,965	20,778
Private institutions	22,093	29,994	21,833	17,767	14,192	15,899	15,946	23,493	18,073
4-year	22,325	30,089	21,887	17,816	14,316	15,971	16,706	23,669	18,326
University	26,897	35,227	24,730	19,792	16,197	16,956	18,933	28,251	21,176
Other 4-year	19,996	26,173	20,502	16,939	13,905	14,741	16,617	21,040	17,342
2-year	15,065	18,645	17,685	14,663	12,155	12,441	14,993	16,075	13,892
1990–91									
All institutions	42,165	55,540	41,414	34,434	26,332	30,097	36,395	45,065	35,881
4-year	43,693	56,485	41,811	34,657	25,772	30,209	31,494	46,519	36,574
University	49,430	63,437	44,877	37,838	27,105	31,748	31,533	52,426	39,788
Other 4-year	40,313	51,467	39,994	33,020	25,370	29,009	31,488	42,660	35,135
2-year	36,642	44,916	37,650	32,253	27,933	28,048	36,752	38,465	34,224
Public institutions	42,317	55,371	42,101	35,137	26,907	29,881	36,990	45,084	36,459
4-year	44,510	56,668	42,742	35,520	26,134	29,956	32,349	47,168	37,573
University	47,499	60,536	43,851	36,889	25,647	30,429	30,412	50,405	38,363
Other 4-year	42,499	53,704	41,969	34,680	26,316	29,664	33,507	44,804	37,147
2-year	37,055	45,411	38,051	32,673	28,389	28,780	37,096	38,787	34,720
Private institutions	41,788	55,911	39,983	33,116	24,928	30,864	28,523	45,019	34,359
4-year	42,224	56,127	40,122	33,235	25,159	31,053	31,122	45,319	34,898
University	53,875	69,732	47,405	40,013	31,239	34,444	36,211	56,989	43,273
Other 4-year	36,888	47,405	36,965	30,688	23,973	25,416	30,915	39,162	32,251
2-year	24,088	29,520	26,353	24,587	20,911	—	23,187	25,937	22,585
1994–95									
All institutions	47,811	62,709	46,713	38,756	29,665	33,198	41,227	51,228	41,369
4-year	49,608	64,027	47,141	39,048	29,193	33,104	35,324	52,932	42,343
University	56,455	72,476	50,560	42,634	30,277	34,722	36,104	60,104	46,342
Other 4-year	45,674	57,989	45,154	37,350	28,857	31,899	35,208	48,330	40,563
2-year	41,523	50,412	42,531	36,080	30,815	35,298	41,635	43,640	39,046
Public institutions	47,432	61,366	46,955	39,147	29,877	32,761	42,186	50,629	41,548
4-year	49,738	63,091	47,581	39,605	29,058	32,606	35,523	52,874	42,663
University	53,444	67,853	48,855	41,219	28,632	33,328	32,627	56,881	44,153
Other 4-year	47,294	59,451	46,696	38,681	29,222	32,206	36,563	49,988	41,863
2-year	42,101	50,656	42,925	36,434	31,211	35,339	42,334	44,020	39,812
Private institutions	48,741	65,633	46,228	38,025	29,089	34,597	30,095	52,653	40,908
4-year	49,379	65,791	46,369	38,146	29,433	34,605	35,235	53,036	41,815
University	63,280	82,279	54,734	45,941	35,254	37,085	42,030	67,250	51,617
Other 4-year	43,196	55,446	42,892	35,516	28,302	30,261	34,726	45,690	38,722
2-year	25,613	37,096	30,861	28,315	22,140	21,132	23,473	29,639	22,851
1995–96									
All institutions	49,309	64,540	47,966	39,696	30,344	34,136	42,996	52,814	42,871
4-year	51,044	65,866	48,432	39,991	29,941	34,082	35,657	54,520	43,702
University	58,173	74,650	51,993	43,838	30,689	35,272	36,818	61,972	48,011
Other 4-year	46,946	59,599	46,356	38,179	29,718	33,140	35,470	49,726	41,773
2-year	43,009	51,454	43,107	36,927	31,421	35,165	43,537	44,944	40,791
Public institutions	48,837	63,189	48,122	40,092	30,581	33,634	43,590	52,163	42,871
4-year	51,172	64,946	48,815	40,562	29,907	33,525	36,829	54,448	43,986
University	55,068	69,924	50,186	42,335	29,186	34,139	35,532	58,648	45,676
Other 4-year	48,566	61,076	47,850	39,544	30,178	33,134	37,266	51,375	43,063
2-year	43,295	51,679	43,389	37,241	31,805	35,244	43,754	45,209	41,086
Private institutions	50,466	67,457	47,654	38,964	29,701	35,792	34,599	54,364	42,871
4-year	50,819	67,598	47,760	39,071	30,002	35,810	35,098	54,649	43,236
University	65,405	84,970	56,517	47,387	35,782	37,516	38,649	69,579	53,717
Other 4-year	44,504	57,089	44,186	36,325	28,993	33,170	34,771	47,126	39,982
2-year	31,915	37,929	33,283	29,887	23,895	—	33,410	33,301	30,671

—Data not available.

NOTE.—Data for 1990–91 through 1995–96 include imputations for nonrespondent institutions.

SOURCE: U.S. Department of Education, National Center for Education Statistics, Higher Education General Information Survey (HEGIS), "Faculty Salaries, Tenure, and Fringe Benefits, 1980–81"; and Integrated Postsecondary Education Data System (IPEDS), "Salaries, Tenure, and Fringe Benefits of Full-Time Instructional Faculty" surveys. (This table was prepared January 1997.)

Table 236.—Average salary of full-time instructional faculty on 9-month contracts in institutions of higher education, by type and control of institution and by state: 1995–96

State or other area	All institutions	Public institutions					Private institutions				
		Total	4-year institutions			2-year	Total	4-year institutions			2-year
			Total	University	Other 4-year			Total	University	Other 4-year	
1	2	3	4	5	6	7	8	9	10	11	12
United States	$49,309	$48,837	$51,172	$55,068	$48,566	$43,295	$50,466	$50,819	$65,405	$44,504	$31,915
Alabama	40,505	41,450	43,580	47,854	40,872	36,364	35,431	35,594	—	35,594	24,809
Alaska	49,036	49,646	49,594	49,685	49,531	56,164	37,489	37,489	—	37,489	—
Arizona	50,841	51,255	52,809	55,301	44,966	48,231	39,682	39,682	—	39,682	—
Arkansas	38,782	39,378	41,299	47,001	39,502	31,125	36,037	36,748	—	36,748	16,052
California	57,716	57,320	60,674	70,350	58,876	52,789	59,328	59,716	74,410	52,233	33,405
Colorado	47,874	47,745	50,262	56,009	45,562	35,652	48,763	48,763	53,584	43,665	—
Connecticut	59,253	59,018	61,635	67,363	56,188	51,143	59,524	60,090	77,086	53,141	33,576
Delaware	55,148	55,378	57,693	59,944	45,399	42,950	53,092	53,092	—	53,092	—
District of Columbia	56,994	51,610	51,610	—	51,610	—	57,758	57,758	59,352	44,266	—
Florida	45,677	45,609	50,487	54,649	47,864	39,594	45,944	46,125	57,361	42,076	27,245
Georgia	45,188	45,297	47,318	52,580	46,014	36,167	44,883	45,385	67,915	39,120	29,695
Hawaii	51,470	51,937	56,477	57,741	48,292	44,244	46,540	46,540	—	46,540	—
Idaho	42,271	42,604	43,446	47,733	41,495	36,646	41,196	37,910	—	37,910	42,721
Illinois	51,065	49,527	49,976	53,824	46,548	48,796	53,818	54,091	71,189	43,184	30,610
Indiana	47,351	47,006	49,176	51,805	43,809	34,662	48,101	48,324	68,842	42,239	29,925
Iowa	46,113	49,686	55,947	58,998	47,591	35,726	40,149	40,109	51,045	38,644	45,578
Kansas	41,497	43,372	46,436	48,886	41,003	35,716	30,603	31,003	—	31,003	24,510
Kentucky	41,791	43,418	46,269	52,345	42,650	33,107	35,949	36,106	—	36,106	27,036
Louisiana	40,689	39,037	39,929	46,288	38,298	31,745	48,104	48,133	54,380	37,270	46,619
Maine	43,075	41,823	43,946	47,438	41,987	33,378	46,393	46,966	—	46,966	28,818
Maryland	49,835	48,994	51,395	57,592	48,264	44,772	52,861	52,923	68,457	45,004	24,267
Massachusetts	56,498	48,720	52,530	60,364	49,430	39,963	60,944	61,270	69,753	52,094	35,083
Michigan	52,555	54,677	55,244	61,133	50,274	52,722	41,843	42,067	44,205	41,805	26,714
Minnesota	46,617	47,873	52,284	62,922	46,711	41,664	43,613	43,803	—	43,803	36,427
Mississippi	39,565	40,004	43,367	45,722	41,882	35,808	36,152	37,077	—	37,077	22,701
Missouri	44,993	45,438	47,125	55,872	45,419	39,479	44,113	44,424	58,456	36,649	33,675
Montana	38,784	39,737	41,120	42,742	37,603	30,952	32,029	31,834	—	31,834	34,981
Nebraska	43,443	44,599	48,000	54,734	43,255	33,692	39,726	39,726	46,658	35,985	—
Nevada	49,235	49,338	52,010	55,724	49,758	43,284	29,688	29,688	—	29,688	—
New Hampshire	48,438	46,856	49,817	52,205	45,604	34,956	50,547	51,242	—	51,242	24,508
New Jersey	60,408	60,796	64,539	73,263	61,394	52,283	59,408	59,540	71,701	49,817	39,947
New Mexico	42,565	42,715	46,635	49,071	39,650	31,257	39,443	39,443	—	39,443	—
New York	55,764	55,594	58,182	62,285	57,527	50,933	55,938	56,393	66,589	49,800	29,601
North Carolina	45,065	46,299	48,732	56,948	45,296	30,638	42,206	42,516	60,020	35,977	32,711
North Dakota	35,303	36,104	37,259	37,983	35,580	31,232	29,709	31,298	—	31,298	22,297
Ohio	48,468	50,008	52,784	54,168	47,857	40,886	45,025	45,134	64,920	42,989	24,138
Oklahoma	40,798	41,046	42,958	48,109	38,836	35,038	39,807	40,286	51,464	35,457	25,039
Oregon	44,272	44,002	45,646	47,983	42,832	42,091	45,278	45,278	—	45,278	—
Pennsylvania	53,987	55,481	56,830	60,944	54,526	48,206	52,196	52,742	69,693	47,251	28,934
Rhode Island	52,805	50,493	53,509	57,683	46,702	41,379	54,585	54,585	—	54,585	—
South Carolina	40,820	41,813	46,655	52,582	40,494	31,510	36,544	36,682	—	36,682	30,294
South Dakota	35,982	37,139	37,274	38,096	36,101	24,834	31,858	31,943	—	31,943	24,000
Tennessee	44,431	44,940	48,112	54,072	46,011	34,743	43,278	43,586	66,150	35,055	27,747
Texas	45,164	44,294	46,992	53,063	41,883	39,331	48,938	49,130	58,942	41,439	24,942
Utah	45,437	43,796	45,919	50,097	39,301	35,147	49,268	49,540	50,420	38,275	33,089
Vermont	43,171	45,068	45,068	48,168	37,379	—	41,430	42,640	—	42,640	20,024
Virginia	47,365	48,405	51,675	56,288	48,691	38,142	43,894	44,204	—	44,204	26,614
Washington	45,703	45,774	51,202	54,727	45,381	38,753	45,421	45,421	—	45,421	—
West Virginia	39,793	40,667	41,323	47,507	38,401	31,816	35,038	35,038	—	35,038	—
Wisconsin	48,332	49,578	51,246	62,321	47,325	47,064	42,805	42,805	54,746	39,066	—
Wyoming	39,998	39,998	47,216	47,216	—	32,766	—	—	—	—	—
U.S. Service Schools	61,758	61,758	61,758	—	61,758	—	—	—	—	—	—
Outlying areas	31,663	33,248	33,796	34,217	33,495	31,026	19,633	19,633	—	19,633	—
American Samoa	32,522	32,522	—	—	—	32,522	—	—	—	—	—
Federated States of Micronesia	26,884	26,884	—	—	—	26,884	—	—	—	—	—
Guam	47,021	47,021	51,273	—	51,273	42,964	—	—	—	—	—
Marshall Islands	14,722	14,722	—	—	—	14,722	—	—	—	—	—
Northern Marianas	32,321	32,321	—	—	—	32,321	—	—	—	—	—
Palau	15,143	15,143	—	—	—	15,143	—	—	—	—	—
Puerto Rico	30,321	32,059	32,334	34,217	30,743	29,577	19,633	19,633	—	19,633	—
Virgin Islands	45,452	45,452	45,452	—	45,452	—	—	—	—	—	—

—Data not reported or not applicable.

NOTE.—Data include imputations for nonrespondent institutions.

SOURCE: U.S. Department of Education, National Center for Education Statistics, Integrated Postsecondary Education Data System (IPEDS), "Salaries, Tenure, and Fringe Benefits of Full-Time Instructional Faculty, 1995–96" survey. (This table was prepared January 1997).

Table 237.—Average salary of full-time instructional faculty on 9-month contracts in institutions of higher education, by type and control of institution and by state: 1994–95

State or other area	All institutions	Public institutions					Private institutions				
		Total	4-year institutions			2-year	Total	4-year institutions			2-year
			Total	University	Other 4-year			Total	University	Other 4-year	
1	2	3	4	5	6	7	8	9	10	11	12
United States	$47,811	$47,432	$49,738	$53,444	$47,294	$42,101	$48,741	$49,379	$63,280	$43,196	$25,613
Alabama	40,576	41,681	43,457	47,655	40,731	37,442	34,517	34,685	—	34,685	22,073
Alaska	49,023	49,601	49,554	50,160	49,150	53,813	37,514	37,514	—	37,514	—
Arizona	48,863	49,089	51,903	54,269	44,433	43,935	42,552	42,552	—	42,552	—
Arkansas	37,655	38,262	40,073	45,026	38,541	30,003	34,907	35,939	—	35,939	10,730
California	55,247	54,814	58,335	65,800	56,978	50,541	57,006	57,249	72,275	50,026	35,504
Colorado	46,350	46,290	49,137	55,186	44,131	33,320	46,757	46,757	51,759	41,755	—
Connecticut	56,559	55,421	58,443	64,088	52,883	46,344	57,914	58,711	73,973	52,239	29,119
Delaware	52,773	52,741	54,684	57,443	40,198	41,883	53,041	53,041	—	53,041	—
District of Columbia	54,560	50,764	50,764	—	50,764	—	55,078	55,078	56,708	42,353	—
Florida	43,078	42,837	48,581	52,611	45,957	36,463	44,045	44,106	55,494	40,263	22,510
Georgia	42,852	42,848	44,833	49,712	43,660	34,010	42,861	43,434	65,210	37,493	28,538
Hawaii	51,978	52,545	57,481	58,714	49,137	44,501	45,581	45,581	—	45,581	—
Idaho	40,248	40,670	41,418	45,199	39,685	35,349	38,655	34,275	—	34,275	39,771
Illinois	49,511	47,960	48,312	51,818	45,157	47,391	52,289	52,627	68,938	41,972	29,281
Indiana	45,395	45,140	47,206	49,624	42,304	33,648	45,953	46,140	66,026	40,515	29,320
Iowa	44,571	47,658	53,226	55,522	46,385	34,634	39,299	39,343	48,205	38,107	33,420
Kansas	40,538	42,292	45,166	47,224	40,033	35,848	29,763	30,063	—	30,063	24,757
Kentucky	40,463	42,080	44,860	50,737	41,424	32,157	34,652	34,821	—	34,821	25,968
Louisiana	39,725	38,105	39,029	46,090	37,181	30,406	47,775	47,775	55,151	35,816	—
Maine	41,499	40,293	42,268	44,564	40,712	32,483	44,756	45,383	—	45,383	28,987
Maryland	48,051	47,428	49,333	55,476	46,410	44,174	50,292	50,350	66,638	42,373	23,500
Massachusetts	55,110	48,814	52,787	60,658	49,688	39,945	58,669	59,076	67,018	50,342	33,712
Michigan	50,804	53,038	53,641	59,084	49,086	51,134	39,929	40,488	43,039	40,161	26,727
Minnesota	46,147	47,716	50,685	60,309	45,887	42,743	42,366	42,619	—	42,619	34,277
Mississippi	37,250	37,641	41,109	41,505	40,850	33,359	34,340	35,202	—	35,202	21,442
Missouri	43,280	43,639	45,199	52,406	43,796	38,175	42,579	43,032	57,276	35,653	30,849
Montana	36,728	37,436	38,522	39,784	35,796	29,390	31,986	32,081	—	32,081	30,943
Nebraska	42,293	43,598	46,341	52,393	42,002	32,167	38,278	38,278	44,885	34,675	—
Nevada	46,820	47,042	48,957	52,147	46,928	41,863	29,877	31,773	—	31,773	21,658
New Hampshire	47,424	46,402	49,267	53,432	42,944	34,543	48,747	49,433	—	49,433	22,709
New Jersey	59,200	60,174	64,540	73,731	61,189	50,457	56,822	56,952	69,320	47,640	24,900
New Mexico	41,898	42,129	45,575	48,154	38,232	31,153	37,362	37,362	—	37,362	—
New York	53,915	54,815	57,273	60,991	56,709	50,274	52,980	55,295	64,679	48,539	16,233
North Carolina	44,472	45,525	47,844	55,701	44,593	30,454	42,053	42,600	60,048	34,841	29,536
North Dakota	35,213	36,001	37,229	37,923	35,714	31,311	29,413	30,866	—	30,866	20,917
Ohio	47,164	48,768	51,520	52,924	46,614	39,750	43,484	43,714	62,449	41,655	19,224
Oklahoma	39,686	39,677	41,622	46,235	37,849	33,648	39,723	40,545	50,579	35,385	25,693
Oregon	42,639	42,490	44,533	46,776	41,794	40,213	43,193	43,193	—	43,193	—
Pennsylvania	52,303	53,446	54,748	59,074	52,288	46,963	50,920	51,528	67,414	46,261	28,248
Rhode Island	51,818	51,032	54,102	57,853	47,610	41,758	52,440	52,440	—	52,440	—
South Carolina	39,333	40,182	44,821	50,699	38,961	30,336	35,696	35,825	—	35,825	30,217
South Dakota	35,269	36,298	36,324	37,170	35,090	27,514	31,386	31,386	—	31,386	—
Tennessee	43,721	44,595	47,601	54,147	45,244	34,736	41,730	42,132	64,035	34,009	28,159
Texas	43,892	43,202	45,785	52,241	41,442	38,624	46,952	47,108	56,044	40,056	23,613
Utah	43,744	42,037	44,454	48,611	38,008	32,854	47,542	47,822	48,675	37,074	31,537
Vermont	42,053	43,336	43,336	46,851	34,877	—	40,804	41,730	—	41,730	—
Virginia	45,710	46,557	49,811	54,497	46,596	36,766	42,797	43,081	—	43,081	20,729
Washington	44,107	44,044	49,086	52,271	43,796	37,453	44,353	44,353	—	44,353	26,726
West Virginia	37,812	38,644	39,226	44,861	36,513	30,492	33,101	33,341	—	33,341	—
Wisconsin	47,633	48,955	51,171	61,756	47,271	45,511	41,455	41,455	53,411	37,682	24,538
Wyoming	39,291	39,291	46,418	46,418	—	31,622	—	—	—	—	—
U.S. Service Schools	56,032	56,032	56,032	—	56,032	—	—	—	—	—	—
Outlying areas	32,230	33,696	33,886	31,962	33,886	32,519	19,796	19,796	—	19,796	—
American Samoa	33,334	33,334	—	—	—	33,334	—	—	—	—	—
Federated States of Micronesia	18,681	18,681	—	—	—	18,681	—	—	—	—	—
Guam	46,839	46,839	50,586	—	50,586	42,171	—	—	—	—	—
Marshall Islands	16,032	16,032	—	—	—	16,032	—	—	—	—	—
Northern Marianas	33,706	33,706	—	—	—	33,706	—	—	—	—	—
Palau	15,143	15,143	—	—	—	15,143	—	—	—	—	—
Puerto Rico	30,626	32,232	32,175	31,962	32,392	33,641	19,796	19,796	—	19,796	—
Virgin Islands	42,821	42,821	42,821	—	42,821	—	—	—	—	—	—

—Data not reported or not applicable.

NOTE.—Data include imputations for nonrespondent institutions.

SOURCE: U.S. Department of Education, National Center for Education Statistics, Integrated Postsecondary Education Data System (IPEDS), "Salaries, Tenure, and Fringe Benefits of Full-Time Instructional Faculty, 1994–95" survey. (This table was prepared November 1995.)

Table 238.—Average salary of full-time instructional faculty on 9-month contracts in 4-year institutions of higher education, by type and control of institution and rank of faculty and by state: 1995–96

State or other area	Public university			Public other 4-year			Private university			Private other 4-year		
	Professor	Associate professor	Assistant professor	Professor	Associate professor	Assistant professor	Professor	Associate professor	Assistant professor	Professor	Associate professor	Assistant professor
1	2	3	4	5	6	7	8	9	10	11	12	13
United States	$69,924	$50,186	$42,335	$61,076	$47,850	$39,544	$84,970	$56,517	$47,387	$57,089	$44,186	$36,325
Alabama	62,390	46,175	39,248	53,010	42,698	36,375	—	—	—	45,566	37,175	31,028
Alaska	65,161	54,047	43,848	61,135	50,717	41,174	—	—	—	41,498	41,676	34,410
Arizona	68,888	49,492	43,066	58,775	47,539	38,981	—	—	—	47,956	44,806	31,343
Arkansas	61,336	47,575	41,002	50,980	41,391	35,689	—	—	—	43,878	37,204	31,116
California	85,413	56,794	49,216	67,003	51,564	42,685	93,239	61,898	51,850	66,408	49,750	40,383
Colorado	67,322	50,431	43,378	56,309	45,183	38,142	67,217	50,895	44,940	56,859	42,967	33,621
Connecticut	82,383	61,187	47,683	68,680	55,361	42,014	100,780	56,269	47,455	67,060	50,438	42,412
Delaware	78,998	57,324	45,542	60,902	47,905	41,092	—	—	—	63,372	57,739	40,078
District of Columbia	—	—	—	60,588	48,285	39,443	77,980	53,007	43,517	55,920	44,624	36,383
Florida	65,827	46,252	42,734	60,336	46,483	40,759	75,661	53,277	43,032	54,865	41,324	35,065
Georgia	69,549	49,500	41,710	59,802	47,848	39,414	88,656	57,909	48,878	49,438	40,894	33,869
Hawaii	72,025	54,713	47,058	58,252	47,664	42,804	—	—	—	54,152	46,456	41,138
Idaho	55,463	45,181	41,217	49,845	41,736	36,822	—	—	—	45,725	37,299	33,190
Illinois	70,074	49,458	42,042	57,942	46,799	39,292	90,944	59,938	50,859	53,928	43,650	36,943
Indiana	67,151	48,838	40,835	59,107	45,465	39,201	86,818	60,580	49,998	51,722	42,292	35,328
Iowa	72,891	53,185	44,020	62,052	48,729	41,629	63,809	47,234	40,652	48,518	39,040	32,773
Kansas	61,279	45,374	39,387	51,778	41,733	35,815	—	—	—	36,583	32,111	28,159
Kentucky	66,430	47,686	40,938	53,759	43,728	36,265	—	—	—	44,955	36,242	31,722
Louisiana	61,130	44,254	37,898	49,829	40,080	34,664	72,166	53,193	42,826	46,697	38,563	34,696
Maine	58,275	45,694	38,353	51,474	41,513	34,135	—	—	—	65,027	47,161	36,588
Maryland	73,989	52,297	46,196	63,003	49,311	41,577	84,580	58,834	47,902	54,772	44,139	36,306
Massachusetts	70,319	53,098	43,258	56,565	47,801	39,336	90,651	58,456	50,289	67,374	49,051	41,314
Michigan	75,895	56,450	47,456	60,929	49,253	40,987	55,356	44,226	37,182	50,041	41,451	36,109
Minnesota	74,328	51,463	45,611	54,485	44,753	37,897	—	—	—	55,776	43,256	36,024
Mississippi	58,615	46,386	40,649	53,495	43,670	37,733	—	—	—	45,818	37,042	32,997
Missouri	68,773	51,557	45,108	57,140	46,356	38,212	76,800	52,602	45,574	45,663	37,430	32,730
Montana	50,728	41,570	36,430	46,558	37,626	32,732	—	—	—	35,697	31,047	31,518
Nebraska	71,391	49,411	42,735	53,718	44,698	37,161	69,771	48,644	35,633	43,626	36,600	32,035
Nevada	70,672	52,609	42,054	65,586	51,336	42,708	—	—	—	43,691	29,914	13,273
New Hampshire	64,240	48,104	40,127	55,694	44,153	37,049	—	—	—	68,903	45,483	38,183
New Jersey	92,584	65,547	50,285	77,607	61,134	47,872	97,220	58,733	45,208	61,080	49,684	39,914
New Mexico	61,962	47,364	39,341	51,348	40,084	34,460	—	—	—	43,296	36,506	30,930
New York	78,428	55,887	43,915	70,935	54,347	43,701	83,612	58,311	48,607	64,002	49,809	39,691
North Carolina	72,682	51,440	45,144	57,847	46,052	39,827	76,066	54,509	44,586	44,847	36,641	31,727
North Dakota	48,084	39,786	35,827	45,131	36,887	33,415	—	—	—	41,017	34,158	31,044
Ohio	68,621	50,523	41,440	62,596	48,037	38,718	79,893	57,359	49,829	54,807	42,356	35,267
Oklahoma	60,434	44,890	37,858	47,875	40,570	36,880	68,185	49,088	39,205	45,394	38,630	29,639
Oregon	61,149	46,138	40,124	51,820	40,855	35,929	—	—	—	56,483	43,361	35,767
Pennsylvania	79,229	56,381	44,953	71,512	55,784	44,542	89,077	59,000	49,988	60,123	47,137	38,447
Rhode Island	65,870	49,774	43,346	52,979	46,045	38,662	—	—	—	69,683	50,282	43,466
South Carolina	65,998	48,591	41,654	49,727	42,142	35,537	—	—	—	47,102	36,172	31,038
South Dakota	47,974	38,615	35,270	47,079	38,980	32,553	—	—	—	40,347	32,752	30,257
Tennessee	63,839	49,636	42,613	56,843	45,508	37,704	86,111	57,222	45,353	44,141	35,691	31,378
Texas	69,440	46,850	41,170	53,810	43,590	36,831	77,482	53,540	46,490	52,668	41,411	33,416
Utah	63,886	46,098	39,541	48,595	39,511	35,211	63,292	47,942	40,652	46,967	39,284	33,638
Vermont	62,301	47,018	38,208	44,854	36,723	30,548	—	—	—	55,337	41,376	35,455
Virginia	71,669	50,956	43,504	61,642	47,985	39,168	—	—	—	55,891	43,744	35,576
Washington	67,725	48,179	42,880	53,051	43,707	37,650	—	—	—	57,791	45,041	38,287
West Virginia	58,545	46,249	38,084	46,150	38,404	32,697	—	—	—	42,483	36,147	30,821
Wisconsin	70,851	52,938	46,561	56,095	46,069	39,377	71,423	53,621	43,878	49,252	39,352	33,800
Wyoming	58,722	45,679	41,098	—	—	—	—	—	—	—	—	—
U.S. Service Schools	—	—	—	73,712	57,491	52,214	—	—	—	—	—	—
Outlying areas	41,404	34,589	28,640	40,061	35,275	30,408	—	—	—	15,790	23,472	22,720
American Samoa	—	—	—	—	—	—	—	—	—	—	—	—
Federated States of Micronesia	—	—	—	—	—	—	—	—	—	—	—	—
Guam	—	—	—	70,692	57,425	44,197	—	—	—	—	—	—
Northern Marianas	—	—	—	—	—	—	—	—	—	—	—	—
Palau	—	—	—	—	—	—	—	—	—	—	—	—
Puerto Rico	41,404	34,589	28,640	37,870	31,559	27,202	—	—	—	15,790	23,472	22,720
Virgin Islands	—	—	—	55,827	46,009	39,102	—	—	—	—	—	—

—Data not reported or not applicable.

NOTE.—Data include imputations for nonrespondent institutions.

SOURCE: U.S. Department of Education, National Center for Education Statistics, Integrated Postsecondary Education Data System (IPEDS), "Salaries, Tenure, and Fringe Benefits of Full-Time Instructional Faculty, 1995–96" survey. (This table was prepared January 1997.)

Table 239.—Average salary of full-time instructional faculty on 9-month contracts in 4-year institutions of higher education, by type and control of institution and rank of faculty and by state: 1994–95

State or other area	Public university			Public other 4-year			Private university			Private other 4-year		
	Professor	Associate professor	Assistant professor	Professor	Associate professor	Assistant professor	Professor	Associate professor	Assistant professor	Professor	Associate professor	Assistant professor
1	2	3	4	5	6	7	8	9	10	11	12	13
United States	$67,853	$48,855	$41,219	$59,451	$46,696	$38,681	$82,279	$54,734	$45,941	$55,446	$42,892	$35,516
Alabama	62,540	46,441	39,699	52,368	42,775	36,478	—	—	—	45,677	35,456	30,448
Alaska	64,525	55,389	44,724	61,380	50,783	40,956	—	—	—	43,902	44,831	34,143
Arizona	66,703	48,332	42,454	57,867	46,968	39,287	—	—	—	47,370	52,471	29,441
Arkansas	57,623	45,635	39,789	49,959	40,278	34,625	—	—	—	42,414	36,160	30,352
California	79,866	53,573	45,808	64,815	50,052	41,566	90,140	60,209	50,580	63,724	47,687	39,186
Colorado	66,061	49,869	42,991	54,041	43,755	37,459	64,122	49,224	44,356	55,084	40,814	32,995
Connecticut	78,326	58,895	46,685	64,742	51,848	39,817	96,821	54,891	46,489	64,872	49,086	41,781
Delaware	75,506	55,059	43,639	53,035	44,171	37,381	—	—	—	62,256	56,355	39,203
District of Columbia	—	—	—	59,630	47,628	38,645	75,358	52,147	42,549	58,903	43,501	37,036
Florida	63,138	44,275	41,079	57,320	44,624	39,903	73,275	51,445	42,657	51,332	39,957	34,121
Georgia	65,381	47,086	39,590	56,441	45,138	37,681	84,710	55,042	47,675	46,615	38,596	33,145
Hawaii	73,450	55,002	47,472	58,359	48,120	43,375	—	—	—	54,179	45,446	40,613
Idaho	52,388	43,004	39,357	46,858	39,135	35,099	—	—	—	30,559	—	33,000
Illinois	67,068	48,004	40,283	55,782	44,733	38,428	88,131	58,382	48,988	52,221	42,641	35,998
Indiana	64,414	46,766	39,160	57,392	44,596	37,659	82,747	58,258	48,250	49,470	40,086	34,273
Iowa	71,033	50,892	42,389	60,088	47,642	40,464	60,759	44,986	40,338	47,272	37,883	33,027
Kansas	59,503	44,079	37,821	50,340	40,148	34,886	—	—	—	35,110	31,183	27,462
Kentucky	63,819	46,364	39,875	51,655	42,217	35,577	—	—	—	43,521	34,892	30,951
Louisiana	61,197	44,139	38,230	48,008	38,855	33,929	69,891	50,247	42,618	45,068	36,356	33,083
Maine	56,652	43,363	36,143	50,518	40,398	33,152	—	—	—	62,332	45,123	35,672
Maryland	71,645	50,090	43,312	60,306	48,017	40,345	82,202	55,415	46,644	53,065	42,853	35,663
Massachusetts	70,551	53,505	44,080	56,898	48,101	39,441	87,864	55,904	48,648	65,493	47,649	39,926
Michigan	73,515	54,845	45,950	59,353	48,067	40,508	53,982	43,961	36,430	48,520	39,532	34,773
Minnesota	71,786	50,028	44,136	54,387	44,452	37,443	—	—	—	54,852	41,997	34,881
Mississippi	52,972	41,639	37,685	52,287	42,827	36,959	—	—	—	44,232	34,682	31,042
Missouri	64,582	48,262	42,597	55,177	44,523	37,374	74,667	50,369	44,576	44,234	36,449	32,402
Montana	47,208	38,688	34,265	43,388	35,920	30,700	—	—	—	38,745	34,016	29,073
Nebraska	68,242	47,898	41,750	51,522	43,602	36,993	67,860	47,072	34,420	42,264	35,479	30,773
Nevada	66,395	49,162	39,915	61,642	49,365	40,879	—	—	—	41,910	35,685	25,166
New Hampshire	65,286	49,609	40,680	52,849	42,436	35,150	—	—	—	66,783	44,158	37,607
New Jersey	92,907	65,637	51,099	77,490	61,168	47,585	93,741	57,396	43,567	58,284	47,485	39,030
New Mexico	60,566	46,084	39,017	49,834	39,316	32,976	—	—	—	35,229	35,598	28,858
New York	77,256	54,667	43,508	70,357	54,093	43,273	81,561	56,321	46,700	62,143	48,247	38,869
North Carolina	71,748	50,951	43,676	56,675	45,737	39,595	76,174	53,636	44,645	43,945	35,475	30,831
North Dakota	47,360	39,905	35,483	44,507	37,224	34,254	—	—	—	39,746	33,463	30,245
Ohio	67,041	49,016	40,581	61,206	46,156	38,387	78,434	54,957	48,710	53,079	41,331	34,379
Oklahoma	57,936	43,599	37,520	46,647	39,700	35,975	68,621	49,807	38,992	46,127	36,877	31,438
Oregon	58,766	45,315	38,860	50,637	40,143	34,646	—	—	—	54,656	41,096	34,987
Pennsylvania	76,390	55,337	44,463	68,726	53,966	42,837	85,880	58,021	48,499	59,152	45,996	37,860
Rhode Island	66,974	50,053	44,619	54,208	46,341	39,600	—	—	—	70,527	48,844	41,572
South Carolina	63,596	46,740	40,733	48,678	40,692	34,114	—	—	—	46,147	36,105	30,180
South Dakota	46,861	37,730	34,298	45,999	37,878	32,040	—	—	—	40,943	33,823	29,077
Tennessee	64,114	49,245	43,373	55,842	45,000	37,303	83,129	54,647	44,451	42,161	35,027	30,416
Texas	68,359	45,910	40,232	53,265	42,791	36,098	73,682	51,097	44,475	49,986	40,575	33,058
Utah	61,493	44,315	38,788	46,511	37,526	34,040	61,136	46,634	38,932	45,760	38,127	33,352
Vermont	60,942	46,076	37,216	42,544	34,612	29,550	—	—	—	54,825	40,165	35,429
Virginia	69,653	49,472	42,481	59,680	46,390	38,086	—	—	—	55,538	42,286	34,464
Washington	65,346	46,514	40,845	50,193	41,866	35,651	—	—	—	56,015	43,474	36,952
West Virginia	54,984	44,217	37,145	45,616	36,460	30,526	—	—	—	41,156	35,379	29,616
Wisconsin	70,553	52,223	46,433	56,142	45,887	39,514	69,974	51,928	42,844	46,613	38,534	32,479
Wyoming	57,025	44,608	40,052	—	—	—	—	—	—	—	—	—
U.S. Service Schools	—	—	—	67,164	53,236	44,774	—	—	—	—	—	—
Outlying areas	39,392	32,646	27,406	41,364	35,082	29,623	—	—	—	16,282	26,029	22,141
American Samoa	—	—	—	—	—	—	—	—	—	—	—	—
Federated States of Micronesia	—	—	—	—	—	—	—	—	—	—	—	—
Guam	—	—	—	69,087	54,807	43,628	—	—	—	—	—	—
Northern Marianas	—	—	—	—	—	—	—	—	—	—	—	—
Palau	—	—	—	—	—	—	—	—	—	—	—	—
Puerto Rico	39,392	32,646	27,406	40,570	32,895	27,771	—	—	—	16,282	26,029	22,141
Virgin Islands	—	—	—	53,747	44,580	37,691	—	—	—	—	—	—

—Data not reported or not applicable.

NOTE.—Data include imputations for nonrespondent institutions.

SOURCE: U.S. Department of Education, National Center for Education Statistics, Integrated Postsecondary Education Data System (IPEDS), "Salaries, Tenure, and Fringe Benefits of Full-Time Instructional Faculty, 1994–95" survey. (This table was prepared January 1997.)

Table 240.—Full-time instructional faculty with tenure for institutions reporting tenure status, by academic rank, sex, and type and control of institution: 1980–81, 1990–91, 1994–95, and 1995–96

Academic year, type, and control of institution	Percent with tenure, by rank							Percent with tenure, by sex	
	All ranks	Professor	Associate professor	Assistant professor	Instructor	Lecturer	No academic rank	Men	Women
1	2	3	4	5	6	7	8	9	10
1980–81									
All institutions	64.8	95.8	82.9	27.9	9.2	11.9	77.4	70.0	49.7
4-year	62.7	95.8	82.2	24.1	6.6	10.7	24.7	68.3	44.0
University	64.5	96.7	83.7	15.3	5.4	4.3	3.5	70.0	41.0
Other 4-year	61.3	94.9	81.2	29.7	7.1	17.8	32.4	67.0	45.5
2-year	74.5	95.6	89.2	58.9	19.8	34.8	81.1	78.8	66.6
Public institutions	68.0	96.6	85.9	32.5	11.8	14.3	79.4	72.8	54.0
4-year	65.7	96.6	85.3	27.6	8.7	12.8	12.2	71.1	47.5
University	66.0	96.9	86.5	16.8	6.1	4.9	4.5	71.3	42.8
Other 4-year	65.5	96.3	84.4	35.5	10.0	21.4	17.2	70.9	50.2
2-year	75.2	95.9	89.5	59.5	20.3	35.8	81.8	79.3	67.5
Private institutions	55.9	93.8	75.2	17.5	3.0	1.5	43.4	62.2	37.2
4-year	56.0	93.8	75.2	17.4	2.8	1.5	37.5	62.2	37.2
University	60.4	96.3	75.8	11.5	3.5	1.8	0.6	66.3	36.5
Other 4-year	53.6	92.0	74.9	20.2	2.6	1.2	43.4	59.8	37.4
2-year	49.5	84.7	77.3	35.2	8.8	—	52.2	57.3	39.5
1990–91									
All institutions	61.2	95.6	80.8	18.6	6.8	6.9	36.3	67.8	45.3
4-year	61.7	95.7	80.4	15.8	4.1	6.0	19.1	68.6	43.9
University	65.2	97.2	85.4	9.0	3.5	2.1	1.4	71.6	43.6
Other 4-year	59.4	94.6	77.1	19.7	4.3	9.2	30.2	66.3	44.0
2-year	57.1	93.7	85.3	50.7	16.3	26.6	39.8	60.9	51.9
Public institutions	62.9	96.3	83.7	21.7	8.6	8.4	36.6	69.4	47.4
4-year	64.0	96.5	83.5	18.0	5.3	7.3	11.3	70.8	45.9
University	66.3	97.3	88.3	9.7	4.2	2.4	0.4	72.8	44.5
Other 4-year	62.3	95.9	79.9	23.4	5.7	10.6	23.5	69.1	46.7
2-year	57.3	93.7	85.6	51.4	16.7	26.7	39.7	61.0	52.2
Private institutions	56.7	93.9	73.8	11.8	1.5	1.0	33.3	63.7	39.8
4-year	56.8	93.9	73.8	11.6	1.4	1.0	31.2	63.7	39.8
University	62.2	96.9	77.4	7.3	1.4	1.4	6.5	68.5	41.3
Other 4-year	53.9	91.9	72.0	13.5	1.5	0.5	36.3	60.9	39.2
2-year	45.7	90.2	70.9	29.0	4.3	—	49.7	53.1	39.3
1994–95									
All institutions	64.3	96.0	82.2	16.8	7.4	1.5	75.9	71.3	50.3
4-year	62.5	96.2	82.1	13.9	3.9	1.5	22.8	70.2	45.3
University	66.6	97.4	87.0	7.5	2.7	1.3	3.7	74.0	45.7
Other 4-year	59.9	95.3	78.9	17.2	4.2	1.7	31.2	67.5	45.1
2-year	73.3	93.4	84.0	48.5	18.4	0.3	79.9	78.2	67.1
Public institutions	67.2	97.0	86.1	20.0	9.3	1.6	77.1	74.0	53.6
4-year	65.3	97.4	86.3	15.9	5.0	1.6	13.0	73.0	47.4
University	68.7	98.1	90.7	8.5	3.4	1.5	1.3	76.0	47.6
Other 4-year	62.8	96.9	83.0	20.3	5.6	1.7	19.2	70.6	47.3
2-year	73.4	93.4	84.3	49.1	18.1	0.3	79.9	78.2	67.3
Private institutions	57.3	93.7	73.8	10.6	2.2	1.2	56.1	64.8	41.7
4-year	57.2	93.7	73.8	10.5	1.7	1.2	34.9	64.6	41.4
University	61.6	95.9	77.1	5.4	0.9	0.7	7.6	68.9	41.3
Other 4-year	55.0	92.3	72.3	12.5	1.9	2.0	44.4	62.2	41.5
2-year	68.2	89.7	66.4	27.2	29.9	—	80.4	75.8	57.3
1995–96									
All institutions	64.8	96.1	83.3	16.7	7.1	1.3	75.1	71.8	51.0
4-year	63.1	96.3	83.1	13.7	3.9	1.3	21.1	70.8	46.2
University	66.9	97.4	87.9	6.7	2.5	1.0	5.5	74.3	46.3
Other 4-year	60.6	95.4	80.0	17.4	4.3	1.6	29.2	68.3	46.1
2-year	73.7	93.4	85.0	50.0	18.1	0.0	79.8	78.0	68.3
Public institutions	67.7	97.3	87.1	19.8	9.1	1.4	76.6	74.6	54.3
4-year	65.9	97.7	87.3	15.5	5.2	1.5	12.5	73.8	48.2
University	69.1	98.2	91.4	7.3	3.0	1.1	5.9	76.7	47.9
Other 4-year	63.5	97.3	84.1	20.6	6.1	1.7	16.2	71.3	48.3
2-year	73.8	93.4	85.4	50.7	18.0	0.0	79.7	78.1	68.5
Private institutions	57.8	93.4	75.2	10.7	1.4	0.9	51.1	65.2	42.9
4-year	57.7	93.4	75.2	10.6	1.1	0.9	32.2	65.1	42.6
University	61.5	95.5	78.8	5.5	1.1	0.9	5.1	68.5	42.7
Other 4-year	55.7	92.0	73.6	12.8	1.1	1.0	45.9	63.1	42.6
2-year	66.9	95.0	59.2	25.1	21.3	—	80.5	73.0	59.1

—Data not available or not applicable.

SOURCE: U.S. Department of Education, National Center for Education Statistics, Higher Education General Information Survey (HEGIS), "Faculty Salaries, Tenure, and Fringe Benefits"; and Integrated Postsecondary Education Data System (IPEDS), "Salaries, Tenure, and Fringe Benefits of Full-Time Instructional Faculty" surveys. (This table was prepared January 1997.)

Table 241.—Institutions of higher education, by control and type of institution: 1949–50 to 1995–96

Year	All institutions			Public			Private		
	Total	4-year	2-year	Total	4-year	2-year	Total	4-year	2-year
1	2	3	4	5	6	7	8	9	10
Excluding branch campuses									
1949–50	1,851	1,327	524	641	344	297	1,210	983	227
1950–51	1,852	1,312	540	636	341	295	1,216	971	245
1951–52	1,832	1,326	506	641	350	291	1,191	976	215
1952–53	1,882	1,355	527	639	349	290	1,243	1,006	237
1953–54	1,863	1,345	518	662	369	293	1,201	976	225
1954–55	1,849	1,333	516	648	353	295	1,201	980	221
1955–56	1,850	1,347	503	650	360	290	1,200	987	213
1956–57	1,878	1,355	523	656	359	297	1,222	996	226
1957–58	1,930	1,390	540	666	366	300	1,264	1,024	240
1958–59	1,947	1,394	553	673	366	307	1,274	1,028	246
1959–60	2,004	1,422	582	695	367	328	1,309	1,055	254
1960–61	2,021	1,431	590	700	368	332	1,321	1,063	258
1961–62	2,033	1,443	590	718	374	344	1,315	1,069	246
1962–63	2,093	1,468	625	740	376	364	1,353	1,092	261
1963–64	2,132	1,499	633	760	386	374	1,372	1,113	259
1964–65	2,175	1,521	654	799	393	406	1,376	1,128	248
1965–66	2,230	1,551	679	821	401	420	1,409	1,150	259
1966–67	2,329	1,577	752	880	403	477	1,449	1,174	275
1967–68	2,374	1,588	786	934	414	520	1,440	1,174	266
1968–69	2,483	1,619	864	1,011	417	594	1,472	1,202	270
1969–70	2,525	1,639	886	1,060	426	634	1,465	1,213	252
1970–71	2,556	1,665	891	1,089	435	654	1,467	1,230	237
1971–72	2,606	1,675	931	1,137	440	697	1,469	1,235	234
1972–73	2,665	1,701	964	1,182	449	733	1,483	1,252	231
1973–74	2,720	1,717	1,003	1,200	440	760	1,520	1,277	243
1974–75	2,747	1,744	1,003	1,214	447	767	1,533	1,297	236
1975–76	2,765	1,767	998	1,219	447	772	1,546	1,320	226
1976–77	2,785	1,783	1,002	1,231	452	779	1,554	1,331	223
1977–78	2,826	1,808	1,018	1,241	454	787	1,585	1,354	231
1978–79	2,954	1,843	1,111	1,308	463	845	1,646	1,380	266
1979–80	2,975	1,863	1,112	1,310	464	846	1,665	1,399	266
1980–81	3,056	1,861	1,195	1,334	465	869	1,722	1,396	[1]326
1981–82	3,083	1,883	1,200	1,340	471	869	1,743	1,412	[1]331
1982–83	3,111	1,887	1,224	1,336	472	864	1,775	1,415	[1]360
1983–84	3,117	1,914	1,203	1,325	474	851	1,792	1,440	352
1984–85	3,146	1,911	1,235	1,329	461	868	1,817	1,450	367
1985–86	3,155	1,915	1,240	1,326	461	865	1,829	1,454	375
Including branch campuses									
1974–75	3,004	1,866	1,138	1,433	537	896	1,571	1,329	242
1975–76	3,026	1,898	1,128	1,442	545	897	1,584	1,353	231
1976–77	3,046	1,913	1,133	1,455	550	905	1,591	1,363	228
1977–78	3,095	1,938	1,157	1,473	552	921	1,622	1,386	236
1978–79	3,134	1,941	1,193	1,474	550	924	1,660	1,391	269
1979–80	3,152	1,957	1,195	1,475	549	926	1,677	1,408	269
1980–81	3,231	1,957	1,274	1,497	552	945	1,734	1,405	[1]329
1981–82	3,253	1,979	1,274	1,498	558	940	1,755	1,421	[1]334
1982–83	3,280	1,984	1,296	1,493	560	933	1,787	1,424	[1]363
1983–84	3,284	2,013	1,271	1,481	565	916	1,803	1,448	355
1984–85	3,331	2,025	1,306	1,501	566	935	1,830	1,459	371
1985–86	3,340	2,029	1,311	1,498	566	932	1,842	1,463	379
1986–87[2]	3,406	2,070	1,336	1,533	573	960	1,873	1,497	376
1987–88[2]	3,587	2,135	1,452	1,591	599	992	1,996	1,536	460
1988–89[2]	3,565	2,129	1,436	1,582	598	984	1,983	1,531	452
1989–90[2]	3,535	2,127	1,408	1,563	595	968	1,972	1,532	440
1990–91[2]	3,559	2,141	1,418	1,567	595	972	1,992	1,546	446
1991–92[2]	3,601	2,157	1,444	1,598	599	999	2,003	1,558	445
1992–93[2]	3,638	2,169	1,469	1,624	600	1,024	2,014	1,569	445
1993–94[2]	3,632	2,190	1,442	1,625	604	1,021	2,007	1,586	421
1994–95[2]	3,688	2,215	1,473	1,641	605	1,036	2,047	1,610	437
1995–96[2]	3,706	2,244	1,462	1,655	608	1,047	2,051	1,636	415

[1] Large increases are due to the addition of schools accredited by the Accrediting Commission of Career Schools and Colleges of Technology.
[2] Because of revised survey procedures, data are not entirely comparable with figures for earlier years. The number of branch campuses reporting separately has increased since 1986–87.

NOTE.—Includes those colleges designated as institutions of higher education by the Integrated Postsecondary Education Data System, even if they have a less than 2-year program.

SOURCE: U.S. Department of Education, National Center for Education Statistics, *Education Directory, Colleges and Universities;* Higher Education General Information Survey (HEGIS), "Fall Enrollment in Higher Education" and "Institutional Characteristics of Colleges and Universities" surveys; and Integrated Postsecondary Education Data System (IPEDS), "Institutional Characteristics" surveys. (This table was prepared September 1996.)

Table 242.—Institutions of higher education and branches, by type, control of institution, and state: 1995–96

State or other area	Total	Public, 4-year institutions							Public 2-year	Private 4-year institutions						Private 2-year
		Total	Research[1]	Doctoral[2]	Master[3]	Baccalaureate[4]	Other 4-year[5]			Total	Research[1]	Doctoral[2]	Master[3]	Baccalaureate[4]	Other 4-year[5]	
1	2	3	4	5	6	7	8		9	10	11	12	13	14	15	16
United States	3,706	608	85	66	278	114	65		1,047	1,636	40	49	293	633	621	415
Alabama	82	18	2	2	13	1	0		35	18	0	0	4	10	4	11
Alaska	9	3	0	1	2	0	0		1	3	0	0	1	1	1	2
Arizona	45	5	2	1	1	0	1		18	18	0	0	2	6	10	4
Arkansas	38	10	1	0	6	2	1		16	10	0	0	1	8	1	2
California	349	31	9	1	19	0	2		107	169	3	9	35	26	96	42
Colorado	59	14	2	3	2	5	2		16	20	0	1	3	4	12	9
Connecticut	42	7	1	0	4	1	1		12	19	1	0	7	6	5	4
Delaware	9	2	1	0	1	0	0		3	4	0	0	2	1	1	0
District of Columbia	18	1	0	0	1	0	0		0	17	3	2	3	1	8	0
Florida	114	9	3	3	3	0	0		29	59	1	2	11	22	23	17
Georgia	120	19	2	1	12	1	3		54	37	1	2	2	21	11	10
Hawaii	17	3	1	0	0	2	0		7	7	0	0	2	1	4	0
Idaho	12	4	1	1	1	1	0		2	4	0	0	0	3	1	2
Illinois	169	12	3	2	7	0	0		49	95	2	3	15	28	47	13
Indiana	78	14	2	3	7	2	0		14	40	1	0	6	22	11	10
Iowa	59	3	2	0	1	0	0		17	36	0	0	5	25	6	3
Kansas	54	10	2	1	4	1	2		21	21	0	0	5	13	3	2
Kentucky	61	8	1	1	6	0	0		14	29	0	0	4	17	8	10
Louisiana	36	14	1	3	9	0	1		6	13	1	0	3	4	5	3
Maine	33	8	0	1	1	5	1		6	13	0	1	1	7	4	6
Maryland	57	13	1	1	9	1	1		20	21	1	0	4	6	10	3
Massachusetts	116	15	1	1	8	2	3		17	73	6	3	12	25	27	11
Michigan	109	15	3	2	10	0	0		30	56	0	2	6	22	26	8
Minnesota	106	11	1	0	6	4	0		51	36	0	1	4	16	15	8
Mississippi	46	9	2	1	3	2	1		22	12	0	0	2	5	5	3
Missouri	101	13	1	3	6	2	1		17	57	2	0	9	18	28	14
Montana	28	6	0	2	3	1	0		13	7	0	0	0	4	3	2
Nebraska	35	7	1	0	4	1	1		11	15	0	0	2	9	4	2
Nevada	10	2	0	1	1	0	0		4	3	0	0	0	1	2	1
New Hampshire	30	5	0	1	2	2	0		7	14	0	2	2	6	4	4
New Jersey	61	14	1	2	7	3	1		19	21	1	2	5	7	6	7
New Mexico	35	6	2	0	3	0	1		18	9	0	0	1	5	3	2
New York	310	42	3	3	19	8	9		47	169	8	9	29	44	79	52
North Carolina	121	16	2	1	9	3	1		58	42	1	1	7	26	7	5
North Dakota	21	6	0	2	1	3	0		9	5	0	0	1	1	3	1
Ohio	156	24	4	6	1	11	2		37	68	1	1	11	32	23	27
Oklahoma	45	14	2	0	6	4	2		15	11	0	1	4	3	3	5
Oregon	45	8	2	1	2	1	2		14	22	0	0	4	9	9	1
Pennsylvania	217	45	3	2	16	21	3		20	101	3	3	19	45	31	51
Rhode Island	12	2	1	0	1	0	0		1	8	1	0	1	2	4	1
South Carolina	59	12	2	0	6	3	1		21	22	0	0	2	17	3	4
South Dakota	21	8	0	1	2	2	3		1	10	0	0	0	8	2	2
Tennessee	76	10	1	3	5	0	1		14	42	1	0	5	24	12	10
Texas	179	40	4	6	22	2	6		67	58	1	3	14	21	19	14
Utah	17	5	2	0	1	2	0		5	4	1	0	2	1	0	3
Vermont	22	5	1	0	2	2	0		1	14	0	0	3	9	2	2
Virginia	89	15	3	3	6	3	0		24	39	0	0	13	19	7	11
Washington	64	8	2	0	5	1	0		29	24	0	0	11	2	11	3
West Virginia	28	13	1	0	1	9	2		3	10	0	0	3	6	1	2
Wisconsin	66	13	2	0	11	0	0		17	31	0	1	5	14	11	5
Wyoming	9	1	1	0	0	0	0		7	0	0	0	0	0	0	1
U.S. Service Schools	11	10	0	0	0	0	10		1	0	0	0	0	0	0	0
Outlying areas	74	13	0	1	4	4	4		14	37	0	0	6	19	12	10
American Samoa	1	0	0	0	0	0	0		1	0	0	0	0	0	0	0
Guam	2	1	0	0	1	0	0		1	0	0	0	0	0	0	0
Marshall Islands	1	0	0	0	0	0	0		1	0	0	0	0	0	0	0
Micronesia	5	0	0	0	0	0	0		5	0	0	0	0	0	0	0
Northern Marianas	1	0	0	0	0	0	0		1	0	0	0	0	0	0	0
Palau	1	0	0	0	0	0	0		1	0	0	0	0	0	0	0
Puerto Rico	61	10	0	1	1	4	4		4	37	0	0	6	19	12	10
Virgin Islands	2	2	0	0	2	0	0		0	0	0	0	0	0	0	0

[1] Research institutions are commited to graduate education through the doctorate, give high priority to research and receive more than $15.5 million in federal research funds annual.

[2] Offer a full range of baccalaureate programs and are committed to eduation through the doctorate. They award at least 40 doctoral degrees annually in 5 or more disciplines.

[3] Offer a full range of baccalaureate programs and are commited to education through the master's degree. The award at least 20 masters degrees per year.

[4] Primarily undergraduate colleges with major emphasis on baccalaureate degrees.

[5] Other specialized 4-year institutions awarding degrees primarily in single fields of study, such as medicine, business, fine arts, theology and engineering. Also, includes some institutions which have 4–year programs, but have not reported sufficient data to identify program category.

NOTE.—New institutions which do not have sufficient data to report by detailed level are included under "other 4-year" or 2-year depending on level reported by institution.

SOURCE: U.S. Department of Education, National Center for Education Statistics, Integrated Postsecondary Education Data System (IPEDS), "Institutional Characteristics, 1995–96" survey. (This table was prepared October 1997.)

Table 243.—Institutions of higher education that have closed their doors, by control and type of institution: 1960–61 to 1995–96

Year	All institutions			Public			Private		
	Total	4-year	2-year	Total	4-year	2-year	Total	4-year	2-year
1	2	3	4	5	6	7	8	9	10
Excluding branch campuses:									
Total, 1960–61 to 1991–92	343	179	164	38	1	37	305	178	127
1960–61	8	1	7	1	—	1	7	1	6
1961–62	2	1	1	—	—	—	2	1	1
1962–63	—	—	—	—	—	—	—	—	—
1963–64	7	1	6	1	—	1	6	1	5
1964–65	8	1	7	4	—	4	4	1	3
1965–66	8	2	6	4	—	4	4	2	2
1966–67	9	2	7	3	—	3	6	2	4
1967–68	14	6	8	—	—	—	14	6	8
1968–69	21	11	10	1	—	1	20	11	9
1969–70	18	8	10	3	—	3	15	8	7
1970–71	32	9	23	9	—	9	23	9	14
1971–72	12	3	9	3	—	3	9	3	6
1972–73	19	12	7	2	—	2	17	12	5
1973–74	18	11	7	—	—	—	18	11	7
1974–75	17	13	4	3	—	3	14	13	1
1975–76	8	6	2	2	1	1	6	5	1
1976–77	8	5	3	—	—	—	8	5	3
1977–78	12	9	3	—	—	—	12	9	3
1978–79	9	4	5	—	—	—	9	4	5
1979–80	6	5	1	—	—	—	6	5	1
1980–81	4	3	1	—	—	—	4	3	1
1981–82	7	6	1	—	—	—	7	6	1
1982–83	7	4	3	—	—	—	7	4	3
1983–84	4	4	—	—	—	—	4	4	—
1984–85	4	4	—	—	—	—	4	4	—
1985–86	10	6	4	1	—	1	9	6	3
1986–87 and 1987–88	25	19	6	1	—	1	24	19	5
1988–89	14	6	8	—	—	—	14	6	8
1989–90	12	6	6	—	—	—	12	6	6
1990–91	10	4	6	—	—	—	10	4	6
1991–92	10	7	3	—	—	—	10	7	3
Including branch campuses:									
Total, 1969–70 to 1995–96	419	204	215	38	5	33	381	199	182
1969–70	24	10	14	5	1	4	19	9	10
1970–71	35	10	25	11	—	11	24	10	14
1971–72	14	5	9	3	—	3	11	5	6
1972–73	21	12	9	4	—	4	17	12	5
1973–74	20	12	8	1	—	1	19	12	7
1974–75	18	13	5	4	—	4	14	13	1
1975–76	9	7	2	2	1	1	7	6	1
1976–77	9	6	3	—	—	—	9	6	3
1977–78	12	9	3	—	—	—	12	9	3
1978–79	9	4	5	—	—	—	9	4	5
1979–80	6	5	1	—	—	—	6	5	1
1980–81	4	3	1	—	—	—	4	3	1
1981–82	7	6	1	—	—	—	7	6	1
1982–83	7	4	3	—	—	—	7	4	3
1983–84	5	5	—	1	1	—	4	4	—
1984–85	4	4	—	—	—	—	4	4	—
1985–86	12	8	4	1	1	—	11	7	4
1986–87 and 1987–88	26	19	7	1	—	1	25	19	6
1988–89	14	6	8	—	—	—	14	6	8
1989–90	19	8	11	—	—	—	19	8	11
1990–91	18	6	12	—	—	—	18	6	12
1991–92	26	8	18	1	—	1	25	8	17
1992–93	24	6	18	—	—	—	24	6	18
1993–94	38	10	28	1	—	1	37	10	27
1994–95	15	8	7	2	—	2	13	8	5
1995–96	23	10	13	1	1	—	22	9	13

—Data not applicable or not available.

NOTE.—This table indicates the year in which the institution closed. Some data revised from previously published figures.

SOURCE:: U.S. Department of Education, National Center for Education Statistics, *Education Directory, Higher Education*, 1960–61 to 1974–75; *Education Directory, Colleges and Universities*, 1975–76 to 1983–84; *1982–83 Supplement to the Education Directory, Colleges and Universities*; and Integrated Postsecondary Education Data System, "Institutional Characteristics" surveys, unpublished data. (This table was prepared February 1997.)

Table 244.—Earned degrees conferred by institutions of higher education, by level of degree and sex of student: 1869–70 to 2006–07

Year	Associate degrees			Bachelor's degrees			Master's degrees			First-professional degrees			Doctor's degrees		
	Total	Men	Women	Total	Men	Women	Total	Men	Women	Total	Men	Women	Total	Men	Women
1	2	3	4	5	6	7	8	9	10	11	12	13	14	15	16
1869–70	—	—	—	¹9,371	¹7,993	¹1,378	0	0	0	(²)	(²)	(²)	1	1	0
1879–80	—	—	—	¹12,896	¹10,411	¹2,485	879	868	11	(²)	(²)	(²)	54	51	3
1889–90	—	—	—	¹15,539	¹12,857	¹2,682	1,015	821	194	(²)	(²)	(²)	149	147	2
1899–1900	—	—	—	¹27,410	¹22,173	¹5,237	1,583	1,280	303	(²)	(²)	(²)	382	359	23
1909–10	—	—	—	¹37,199	¹28,762	¹8,437	2,113	1,555	558	(²)	(²)	(²)	443	399	44
1919–20	—	—	—	¹48,622	¹31,980	¹16,642	4,279	2,985	1,294	(²)	(²)	(²)	615	522	93
1929–30	—	—	—	¹122,484	¹73,615	¹48,869	14,969	8,925	6,044	(²)	(²)	(²)	2,299	1,946	353
1939–40	—	—	—	¹186,500	¹109,546	¹76,954	26,731	16,508	10,223	(²)	(²)	(²)	3,290	2,861	429
1949–50	—	—	—	¹432,058	¹328,841	¹103,217	58,183	41,220	16,963	(²)	(²)	(²)	6,420	5,804	616
1959–60	—	—	—	¹392,440	¹254,063	¹138,377	74,435	50,898	23,537	(²)	(²)	(²)	9,829	8,801	1,028
1960–61	—	—	—	365,174	224,538	140,636	84,609	57,830	26,779	25,253	24,577	676	10,575	9,463	1,112
1961–62	—	—	—	383,961	230,456	153,505	91,418	62,603	28,815	25,607	24,836	771	11,622	10,377	1,245
1962–63	—	—	—	411,420	241,309	170,111	98,684	67,302	31,382	26,590	25,753	837	12,822	11,448	1,374
1963–64	—	—	—	461,266	265,349	195,917	109,183	73,850	35,333	27,209	26,357	852	14,490	12,955	1,535
1964–65	—	—	—	493,757	282,173	211,584	121,167	81,319	39,848	28,290	27,283	1,007	16,467	14,692	1,775
1965–66	111,607	63,779	47,828	520,115	299,287	220,828	140,602	93,081	47,521	30,124	28,982	1,142	18,237	16,121	2,116
1966–67	139,183	78,356	60,827	558,534	322,711	235,823	157,726	103,109	54,617	31,695	30,401	1,294	20,617	18,163	2,454
1967–68	159,441	90,317	69,124	632,289	357,682	274,607	176,749	113,552	63,197	33,939	32,402	1,537	23,089	20,183	2,906
1968–69	183,279	105,661	77,618	728,845	410,595	318,250	193,756	121,531	72,225	35,114	33,595	1,519	26,158	22,722	3,436
1969–70	206,023	117,432	88,591	792,316	451,097	341,219	208,291	125,624	82,667	34,918	33,077	1,841	29,866	25,890	3,976
1970–71	252,311	144,144	108,167	839,730	475,594	364,136	230,509	138,146	92,363	37,946	35,544	2,402	32,107	27,530	4,577
1971–72	292,014	166,227	125,787	887,273	500,590	386,683	251,633	149,550	102,083	43,411	40,723	2,688	33,363	28,090	5,273
1972–73	316,174	175,413	140,761	922,362	518,191	404,171	263,371	154,468	108,903	50,018	46,489	3,529	34,777	28,571	6,206
1973–74	343,924	188,591	155,333	945,776	527,313	418,463	277,033	157,842	119,191	53,816	48,530	5,286	33,816	27,365	6,451
1974–75	360,171	191,017	169,154	922,933	504,841	418,092	292,450	161,570	130,880	55,916	48,956	6,960	34,083	26,817	7,266
1975–76	391,454	209,996	181,458	925,746	504,925	420,821	311,771	167,248	144,523	62,649	52,892	9,757	34,064	26,267	7,797
1976–77	406,377	210,842	195,535	919,549	495,545	424,004	317,164	167,783	149,381	64,359	52,374	11,985	33,232	25,142	8,090
1977–78	412,246	204,718	207,528	921,204	487,347	433,857	311,620	161,212	150,408	66,581	52,270	14,311	32,131	23,658	8,473
1978–79	402,702	192,091	210,611	921,390	477,344	444,046	301,079	153,370	147,709	68,848	52,652	16,196	32,730	23,541	9,189
1979–80	400,910	183,737	217,173	929,417	473,611	455,806	298,081	150,749	147,332	70,131	52,716	17,415	32,615	22,943	9,672
1980–81	416,377	188,638	227,739	935,140	469,883	465,257	295,739	147,043	148,696	71,956	52,792	19,164	32,958	22,711	10,247
1981–82	434,526	196,944	237,582	952,998	473,364	479,634	295,546	145,532	150,014	72,032	52,223	19,809	32,707	22,224	10,483
1982–83	449,620	203,991	245,629	969,510	479,140	490,370	289,921	144,697	145,224	73,054	51,250	21,804	32,775	21,902	10,873
1983–84	452,240	202,704	249,536	974,309	482,319	491,990	284,263	143,595	140,668	74,468	51,378	23,090	33,209	22,064	11,145
1984–85	454,712	202,932	251,780	979,477	482,528	496,949	286,251	143,390	142,861	75,063	50,455	24,608	32,943	21,700	11,243
1985–86	446,047	196,166	249,881	987,823	485,923	501,900	288,567	143,508	145,059	73,910	49,261	24,649	33,653	21,819	11,834
1986–87	436,304	190,839	245,465	991,264	480,782	510,482	289,349	141,269	148,080	71,617	46,523	25,094	34,041	22,061	11,980
1987–88	435,085	190,047	245,038	994,829	477,203	517,626	299,317	145,163	154,154	70,735	45,484	25,251	34,870	22,615	12,255
1988–89	436,764	186,316	250,448	1,018,755	483,346	535,409	310,621	149,354	161,267	70,856	45,046	25,810	35,720	22,648	13,072
1989–90	455,102	191,195	263,907	1,051,344	491,696	559,648	324,301	153,653	170,648	70,988	43,961	27,027	38,371	24,401	13,970
1990–91	481,720	198,634	283,086	1,094,538	504,045	590,493	337,168	156,482	180,686	71,948	43,846	28,102	39,294	24,756	14,538
1991–92	504,231	207,481	296,750	1,136,553	520,811	615,742	352,838	161,842	190,996	74,146	45,071	29,075	40,659	25,557	15,102
1992–93	514,756	211,964	302,792	1,165,178	532,881	632,297	369,585	169,258	200,327	75,387	45,153	30,234	42,132	26,073	16,059
1993–94	530,632	215,261	315,371	1,169,275	532,422	636,853	387,070	176,085	210,985	75,418	44,707	30,711	43,185	26,552	16,633
1994–95	539,691	218,352	321,339	1,160,134	526,131	634,003	397,629	178,598	219,031	75,800	44,853	30,947	44,446	26,916	17,530
1995–96³	532,000	214,000	318,000	1,186,000	531,000	655,000	406,000	192,000	214,000	78,700	45,600	33,100	43,600	26,700	16,900
1996–97³	529,000	211,000	318,000	1,183,000	528,000	655,000	410,000	194,000	216,000	76,900	46,200	30,700	44,200	26,800	17,400
1997–98³	514,000	208,000	307,000	1,169,000	509,000	660,000	414,000	196,000	218,000	74,900	44,300	30,600	44,500	26,700	17,800
1998–99³	517,000	207,000	310,000	1,140,000	501,000	640,000	418,000	198,000	220,000	73,500	42,400	31,100	44,900	26,600	18,300
1999–2000³	525,000	208,000	317,000	1,138,000	500,000	637,000	422,000	200,000	222,000	73,100	41,700	31,400	45,300	26,500	18,800
2000–01³	535,000	210,000	326,000	1,151,000	504,000	647,000	426,000	202,000	224,000	72,900	41,000	31,900	45,700	26,400	19,300
2001–02³	545,000	211,000	333,000	1,169,000	508,000	660,000	430,000	204,000	226,000	73,400	40,700	32,700	46,000	26,300	19,700
2002–03³	556,000	213,000	343,000	1,191,000	516,000	675,000	434,000	206,000	228,000	74,400	40,700	33,700	46,400	26,200	20,200
2003–04³	566,000	214,000	352,000	1,216,000	522,000	694,000	438,000	208,000	230,000	75,500	40,900	34,600	46,800	26,100	20,700
2004–05³	572,000	215,000	357,000	1,237,000	524,000	713,000	442,000	210,000	232,000	76,700	41,300	35,400	47,200	26,000	21,200
2005–06³	579,000	216,000	363,000	1,253,000	529,000	724,000	446,000	212,000	234,000	78,000	41,700	36,300	47,500	25,900	21,600
2006–07³	587,000	217,000	369,000	1,268,000	532,000	735,000	450,000	214,000	236,000	79,300	42,100	37,200	47,900	25,800	22,100

¹ Includes first-professional degrees.
² First-professional degrees are included with bachelor's degrees.
³ Projected.
— Data not available.

NOTE.—Some data have been revised from previously published figures. Because of rounding, details may not add to totals.

SOURCE: U.S. Department of Education, National Center for Education Statistics, *Earned Degrees Conferred; Projections of Education Statistics to 2007;* Higher Education General Information Survey (HEGIS), "Degrees and Other Formal Awards Conferred" surveys; and Integrated Postsecondary Education Data System (IPEDS), "Completions" surveys. (This table was prepared April 1997.)

Table 245.—Degrees awarded by institutions of higher education, by control, level of degree, and state: 1994–95

State or other area	Public					Private				
	Associate degrees	Bachelor's degrees	First-professional degrees[1]	Master's degrees	Doctor's degrees (Ph.D., Ed.D., etc.)	Associate degrees	Bachelor's degrees	First-professional degrees[1]	Master's degrees	Doctor's degrees (Ph.D., Ed.D., etc.)
1	2	3	4	5	6	7	8	9	10	11
United States	451,539	776,670	29,871	224,152	28,917	88,152	383,464	45,929	173,477	15,529
Alabama	7,176	16,821	591	5,540	435	659	3,103	372	443	3
Alaska	834	1,428	—	386	19	126	98	—	77	—
Arizona	5,886	13,877	445	4,850	787	923	2,298	—	1,648	—
Arkansas	2,416	7,141	482	1,982	155	76	1,482	—	59	—
California	53,982	83,300	2,200	18,187	2,847	6,521	26,414	6,583	19,878	2,520
Colorado	5,126	16,054	463	4,531	666	1,858	3,875	370	2,580	122
Connecticut	4,009	7,368	310	2,384	265	791	6,604	610	4,035	442
Delaware	934	3,552	—	738	139	207	914	418	364	30
District of Columbia	73	542	—	120	—	132	6,485	2,467	6,487	474
Florida	34,286	30,885	942	8,449	961	6,447	14,039	1,552	6,344	692
Georgia	7,193	19,302	692	6,705	712	1,950	7,010	1,369	1,939	222
Hawaii	2,109	3,156	121	1,070	155	278	1,344	39	450	11
Idaho	1,140	3,870	167	934	80	3,041	365	—	143	—
Illinois	24,273	30,170	1,103	9,858	1,358	2,853	22,100	3,257	13,629	1,492
Indiana	7,918	20,941	948	5,648	1,013	2,145	9,312	537	1,949	139
Iowa	7,608	9,429	554	2,540	667	583	7,992	981	938	19
Kansas	6,482	11,522	572	3,748	450	479	3,072	19	602	—
Kentucky	4,937	11,576	739	3,676	284	1,509	2,994	388	543	113
Louisiana	2,879	14,880	711	3,933	373	490	3,040	969	1,413	126
Maine	1,710	3,491	79	730	40	735	2,402	101	223	2
Maryland	8,186	15,864	808	4,658	587	446	4,044	193	4,333	290
Massachusetts	8,333	12,510	99	3,264	379	4,475	27,769	3,557	18,012	1,904
Michigan	19,578	33,837	1,493	13,720	1,493	3,118	10,480	1,003	1,740	55
Minnesota	8,623	15,996	682	3,508	685	3,593	8,072	856	2,252	204
Mississippi	5,340	8,602	346	2,227	340	179	1,733	146	394	59
Missouri	6,075	15,656	663	3,805	341	2,853	12,275	1,633	6,550	378
Montana	1,162	3,880	78	836	66	167	474	—	21	—
Nebraska	3,014	6,961	368	1,839	249	351	3,144	457	413	6
Nevada	1,379	3,291	54	895	77	32	80	—	2	—
New Hampshire	2,000	3,839	—	684	51	1,530	3,556	193	1,578	61
New Jersey	12,012	18,138	906	4,846	584	843	6,489	764	3,415	469
New Mexico	3,199	5,582	172	2,218	285	78	781	—	220	—
New York	41,340	41,447	1,171	13,560	1,375	13,331	52,102	6,465	31,166	2,599
North Carolina	13,195	22,583	709	5,645	750	912	9,738	987	1,785	272
North Dakota	1,682	3,812	187	595	84	56	628	—	33	—
Ohio	17,030	32,988	1,901	10,421	1,644	3,153	16,600	1,168	4,966	547
Oklahoma	6,568	12,480	602	3,595	347	443	2,827	353	1,333	67
Oregon	5,488	9,219	321	2,705	430	325	3,698	583	1,209	63
Pennsylvania	12,801	31,872	1,200	8,742	1,283	7,768	31,155	2,742	10,895	1,119
Rhode Island	1,579	3,334	4	898	108	2,311	5,644	72	1,143	187
South Carolina	5,435	11,573	539	4,102	365	730	3,603	75	423	26
South Dakota	488	3,474	124	931	58	346	819	13	76	5
Tennessee	5,658	13,209	704	4,366	452	1,063	7,254	732	1,827	213
Texas	23,210	54,752	2,577	17,075	2,355	2,590	15,296	2,198	5,665	372
Utah	5,390	7,757	218	1,663	272	422	6,784	155	1,382	86
Vermont	664	2,323	90	384	53	647	2,268	—	707	1
Virginia	8,941	23,265	1,172	8,381	1,048	1,941	7,841	645	2,325	29
Washington	18,210	16,843	453	3,610	651	892	4,985	456	4,337	36
West Virginia	2,124	7,349	358	2,140	159	716	1,307	—	128	—
Wisconsin	8,396	19,868	526	5,043	833	866	7,075	451	1,403	74
Wyoming	1,491	1,777	70	396	63	172	—	—	—	—
U.S. Service Schools	11,977	3,284	157	1,391	44	—	—	—	—	—
Outlying areas	2,075	6,417	267	737	32	2,328	7,885	390	1,062	35
American Samoa	419	—	—	—	—	—	—	—	—	—
Federated States of Micronesia	163	—	—	—	—	—	—	—	—	—
Guam	48	295	—	45	—	—	—	—	—	—
Marshall Islands	40	—	—	—	—	—	—	—	—	—
Northern Marianas	180	—	—	—	—	—	—	—	—	—
Palau	21	—	—	—	—	—	—	—	—	—
Puerto Rico	1,148	5,927	267	628	32	2,328	7,885	390	1,062	35
Virgin Islands	56	195	—	64	—	—	—	—	—	—

[1] Includes degrees which require at least 6 years of college work for completion (including at least 2 years of preprofessional training). See Definitions for details.
—Data not available or not applicable.

SOURCE: U.S. Department of Education, National Center for Education Statistics, Integrated Postsecondary Education Data System (IPEDS), "Completions" survey. (This table was prepared April 1997.)

HIGHER EDUCATION: DEGREES 263

Table 246.—Earned degrees conferred by institutions of higher education, by level of degree and by state: 1993–94 and 1994–95

State or other area	1993–94					1994–95				
	Associate degrees[1]	Bachelor's degrees	First-professional degrees[2]	Master's degrees	Doctor's degrees (Ph.D., Ed.D., etc.)	Associate degrees	Bachelor's degrees	First-professional degrees[2]	Master's degrees	Doctor's degrees (Ph.D., Ed.D., etc.)
1	2	3	4	5	6	7	8	9	10	11
United States	530,632	1,169,275	75,418	387,070	43,185	539,691	1,160,134	75,800	397,629	44,446
Alabama	7,781	21,150	908	5,763	476	7,835	19,924	963	5,983	438
Alaska	1,002	1,396	—	422	24	960	1,526	0	463	19
Arizona	6,796	16,093	462	6,399	754	6,809	16,175	445	6,498	787
Arkansas	2,808	8,549	441	1,995	146	2,492	8,623	482	2,041	155
California	56,417	111,848	9,228	38,708	5,034	60,503	109,714	8,783	38,065	5,367
Colorado	6,746	18,954	809	6,859	765	6,984	19,929	833	7,111	788
Connecticut	5,081	13,929	769	6,649	646	4,800	13,972	920	6,419	707
Delaware	1,191	4,187	461	955	121	1,141	4,466	418	1,102	169
District of Columbia	305	7,184	2,420	6,176	489	205	7,027	2,467	6,607	474
Florida	40,620	44,075	2,382	14,056	1,644	40,733	44,924	2,494	14,793	1,653
Georgia	9,419	26,283	2,015	8,326	813	9,143	26,312	2,061	8,644	934
Hawaii	2,391	4,314	172	1,369	175	2,387	4,500	160	1,520	166
Idaho	4,068	4,203	148	1,017	88	4,181	4,235	167	1,077	80
Illinois	27,022	52,330	4,321	23,689	2,592	27,126	52,270	4,360	23,487	2,850
Indiana	9,589	30,769	1,454	6,962	1,103	10,063	30,253	1,485	7,597	1,152
Iowa	8,314	17,846	1,442	3,488	689	8,191	17,421	1,535	3,478	686
Kansas	6,716	14,599	619	4,618	415	6,961	14,594	591	4,350	450
Kentucky	6,416	14,629	1,118	4,028	401	6,446	14,570	1,127	4,219	397
Louisiana	3,303	17,787	1,582	5,205	447	3,369	17,920	1,680	5,346	499
Maine	2,463	5,953	173	896	53	2,445	5,893	180	953	42
Maryland	8,292	20,720	972	8,182	934	8,632	19,908	1,001	8,991	877
Massachusetts	13,084	42,351	3,771	20,745	2,228	12,808	40,279	3,656	21,276	2,283
Michigan	24,215	44,925	2,746	15,474	1,483	22,696	44,317	2,496	15,460	1,548
Minnesota	9,708	24,746	1,536	5,678	917	12,216	24,068	1,538	5,760	889
Mississippi	5,538	10,524	478	2,630	352	5,519	10,335	492	2,621	399
Missouri	8,424	27,494	2,206	10,130	778	8,928	27,931	2,296	10,355	719
Montana	1,031	4,357	70	803	57	1,329	4,354	78	857	66
Nebraska	3,189	10,087	811	2,201	244	3,365	10,105	825	2,252	255
Nevada	1,295	3,276	39	922	52	1,411	3,371	54	897	77
New Hampshire	3,350	7,546	182	2,228	136	3,530	7,395	193	2,262	112
New Jersey	12,625	25,234	1,709	8,274	1,032	12,855	24,627	1,670	8,261	1,053
New Mexico	3,065	6,118	192	2,348	243	3,277	6,363	172	2,438	285
New York	53,784	93,134	7,442	42,903	4,025	54,671	93,549	7,636	44,726	3,974
North Carolina	13,621	32,730	1,673	7,276	988	14,107	32,321	1,696	7,430	1,022
North Dakota	1,718	4,558	189	675	74	1,738	4,440	187	628	84
Ohio	20,117	50,982	3,251	14,992	2,127	20,183	49,588	3,069	15,387	2,191
Oklahoma	6,689	15,734	846	4,954	387	7,011	15,307	955	4,928	414
Oregon	5,986	13,272	946	3,617	531	5,813	12,917	904	3,914	493
Pennsylvania	21,172	64,326	3,745	18,906	2,247	20,569	63,027	3,942	19,637	2,402
Rhode Island	3,941	9,145	87	2,019	255	3,890	8,978	76	2,041	295
South Carolina	6,218	15,318	627	4,452	459	6,165	15,176	614	4,525	391
South Dakota	873	4,164	141	1,038	60	834	4,293	137	1,007	63
Tennessee	6,894	19,992	1,296	5,740	672	6,721	20,463	1,436	6,193	665
Texas	25,787	69,298	4,768	21,838	2,732	25,800	70,048	4,775	22,740	2,727
Utah	5,318	14,191	367	2,837	338	5,812	14,541	373	3,045	358
Vermont	1,268	4,671	93	1,174	62	1,311	4,591	90	1,091	54
Virginia	11,339	31,226	1,839	9,980	1,006	10,882	31,106	1,817	10,706	1,077
Washington	18,365	21,321	918	7,268	696	19,102	21,828	909	7,947	687
West Virginia	3,012	9,045	367	2,032	127	2,840	8,656	358	2,268	159
Wisconsin	9,394	27,484	966	6,267	956	9,262	26,943	977	6,446	907
Wyoming	1,862	1,794	66	457	73	1,663	1,777	70	396	63
U.S. Service Schools	11,010	3,434	155	1,450	39	11,977	3,284	157	1,391	44
Outlying areas	4,125	13,866	582	1,938	76	4,403	14,302	657	1,799	67
American Samoa	44	—	—	—	—	419	—	—	—	—
Federated States of Micronesia	105	—	—	—	—	163	—	—	—	—
Guam	25	208	—	26	—	48	295	—	45	—
Marshall Islands	40	—	—	—	—	40	—	—	—	—
Northern Marianas	69	—	—	—	—	180	—	—	—	—
Palau	13	—	—	—	—	21	—	—	—	—
Puerto Rico	3,769	13,486	582	1,858	76	3,476	13,812	657	1,690	67
Virgin Islands	60	172	—	54	—	56	195	—	64	—

[1] Data revised from previously published figures.
[2] Includes degrees which require at least 6 years of college work for completion (including at least 2 years of preprofessional training). See Definitions for details.
—Data not available or not applicable.

SOURCE: U.S. Department of Education, National Center for Education Statistics, Integrated Postsecondary Education Data System (IPEDS), "Completions" survey. (This table was prepared April 1997.)

Table 247.—Associate degrees conferred by institutions of higher education, by sex of student and field of study: 1988–89 to 1992–93

Field of study	Total					Women				
	1988–89	1989–90	1990–91	1991–92	1992–93	1988–89	1989–90	1990–91	1991–92	1992–93
1	2	3	4	5	6	7	8	9	10	11
Total	436,764	455,102	481,720	504,231	514,756	250,448	263,907	283,086	296,750	302,792
Agriculture and natural resources, total	4,725	4,832	4,910	5,251	5,398	1,655	1,600	1,588	1,675	1,648
Agricultural business and production	2,884	2,894	2,905	3,046	3,222	969	930	962	1,011	1,018
Agricultural sciences	963	925	879	951	837	543	507	444	432	372
Conservation and renewable natural resources	878	1,013	1,126	1,254	1,339	143	163	182	232	258
Architecture and related programs	1,815	2,013	2,031	443	372	1,559	1,745	1,741	337	253
Area, ethnic, and cultural studies	16	68	19	29	33	8	56	13	20	23
Biological/life sciences	982	1,023	1,119	1,361	1,435	568	593	667	797	847
Business management and administrative services	92,481	92,390	89,537	93,762	91,719	62,703	63,163	62,109	65,459	63,364
Accounting	14,266	14,858	14,577	15,687	15,115	10,690	11,275	11,111	11,888	11,587
Business, general	11,929	11,878	11,618	11,823	11,190	6,940	7,095	7,188	7,293	7,046
Business administration and management	27,252	28,292	26,625	31,185	29,556	15,782	16,753	15,863	18,902	17,932
Business and management, other	11,162	11,691	11,663	11,089	12,285	6,130	6,480	6,655	6,769	6,645
Business data processing	9,831	8,532	8,182	6,394	6,405	5,501	4,733	4,775	3,679	3,693
Secretarial and related programs	18,041	17,139	16,872	17,584	17,168	17,660	16,827	16,517	16,928	16,461
Communications	1,777	1,657	1,847	1,886	1,904	955	910	966	996	959
Communications technologies	1,993	2,027	2,032	1,794	1,828	681	678	681	649	632
Computer and information sciences	7,900	7,574	7,677	9,290	9,196	3,908	3,768	3,770	4,725	4,655
Construction trades	1,731	1,765	1,793	1,560	1,653	75	68	78	69	72
Consumer and personal services	2,815	2,121	2,494	4,420	4,692	1,028	843	887	1,519	1,572
Education	7,445	8,061	7,842	10,267	9,315	5,285	5,731	5,640	6,559	6,284
Engineering	2,676	2,345	2,451	2,685	2,478	310	279	268	344	309
Engineering-related technologies	42,593	40,033	37,890	35,861	36,321	4,237	4,006	3,724	3,757	3,690
English language and literature/letters	468	527	426	1,019	1,320	330	358	302	671	851
Foreign languages and literatures	324	329	327	433	511	214	251	210	305	358
Health professions and related sciences	59,535	64,113	70,833	79,453	86,237	52,495	56,125	61,495	68,648	73,266
Dental assisting	3,650	3,697	3,810	4,013	4,165	3,427	3,502	3,612	3,822	3,929
Emergency medical technician-ambulance and paramedic	354	332	371	378	442	99	100	116	114	139
Medical lab technician	1,724	1,627	1,731	1,874	2,172	1,339	1,284	1,311	1,425	1,601
Medical assisting	1,786	1,404	1,496	1,960	2,130	1,695	1,375	1,451	1,741	1,907
Nursing assisting	12	0	5	19	86	11	0	4	13	70
Practical nursing	591	589	797	795	890	539	535	692	742	804
Nursing, R.N. and other	36,475	40,212	45,317	51,193	54,085	33,904	36,915	41,261	46,217	48,289
Health sciences, other	14,943	16,252	17,306	19,221	22,267	11,481	12,414	13,048	14,574	16,527
Home economics and vocational home economics	7,559	7,798	8,067	6,436	6,914	5,745	6,080	6,243	5,749	6,259
Law and legal studies	3,742	4,552	5,484	7,053	8,028	3,271	3,967	4,892	6,146	7,069
Liberal arts and sciences, general studies, and humanities	121,988	133,466	142,722	154,594	158,040	71,588	78,768	84,977	91,777	94,173
Library science	101	107	111	103	85	90	95	102	85	76
Marketing operations/marketing and distribution	14,338	14,015	12,713	8,465	7,445	11,003	10,829	9,510	6,494	5,646
Mathematics	654	756	670	744	743	239	270	264	280	315
Mechanics and repairers	7,769	7,704	7,640	10,264	10,966	427	431	445	671	686
Multi/interdisciplinary studies	7,737	8,176	7,454	7,841	8,486	3,888	4,156	3,998	4,059	4,411
Parks, recreation, leisure, and fitness studies	641	485	425	620	717	329	200	177	251	288
Philosophy and religion	81	93	89	60	111	23	34	28	17	35
Physical sciences	1,838	2,021	2,091	2,066	2,241	806	811	901	861	945
Physical sciences, other	1,090	1,279	1,281	1,228	1,390	487	539	562	522	598
Science technologies	748	742	810	838	851	319	272	339	339	347
Precision production trades	7,414	8,616	9,093	9,005	9,204	1,584	1,898	1,975	1,872	1,811
Protective services	11,682	12,855	13,564	15,117	16,834	3,292	3,402	3,599	3,876	4,545
Criminal justice and corrections	9,663	10,658	11,358	12,649	14,295	3,079	3,137	3,367	3,628	4,265
Fire control and safety	1,493	1,621	1,634	1,989	2,020	78	91	92	116	137
Protective services, other	526	576	572	479	519	135	174	140	132	143
Psychology	1,090	1,115	997	1,209	1,237	811	829	740	871	955
Public administration and services	2,493	2,613	2,779	3,162	3,301	1,959	2,076	2,243	2,523	2,653
R.O.T.C. and military technologies	164	129	85	172	52	31	15	8	16	8
Social sciences and history	2,741	2,872	2,505	3,160	3,930	1,544	1,611	1,494	1,760	2,252
Theological studies/religious vocations	568	653	578	496	508	248	264	243	216	227
Transportation and material moving workers	2,090	2,619	2,609	2,418	2,210	340	395	469	440	360
Visual and performing arts	8,178	8,740	9,126	11,888	12,690	4,952	5,327	5,362	7,085	7,606
Fine arts, general	1,091	1,150	1,166	1,159	1,346	719	729	766	767	886
Design and music	5,340	5,900	5,986	9,142	9,699	3,218	3,588	3,499	5,536	5,866
Visual and performing arts, other	1,747	1,690	1,974	1,587	1,645	1,015	1,010	1,097	782	854
Not classified by field of study	4,620	4,839	19,690	9,844	6,602	2,267	2,275	11,277	5,171	3,689

SOURCE: U.S. Department of Education, National Center for Education Statistics, Integrated Postsecondary Education Data System (IPEDS), "Completions" surveys. (This table was prepared March 1997.)

Table 248.—Associate degrees and other subbaccalaureate awards conferred by institutions of higher education, by length of curriculum, sex of student, and field of study: 1994–95

Field of study	Less than 1-year awards			1- to less than 4-year awards			Associate degrees		
	Total	Men	Women	Total	Men	Women	Total	Men	Women
1	2	3	4	5	6	7	8	9	10
Total	85,195	42,636	42,559	152,037	62,646	89,391	539,691	218,352	321,339
Agriculture and natural resources, total	1,705	1,320	385	4,067	2,242	1,825	5,730	4,001	1,729
Agricultural business and production	1,311	997	314	1,344	913	431	3,564	2,458	1,106
Agricultural sciences	334	274	60	1,548	427	1,121	829	465	364
Conservation and renewable natural resources	60	49	11	1,175	902	273	1,337	1,078	259
Architecture and related programs	15	4	11	10	2	8	277	70	207
Area, ethnic, and cultural studies	118	28	90	136	10	126	68	17	51
Biological/life sciences	297	152	145	62	32	30	1,879	752	1,127
Business management and administrative services	12,446	3,451	8,995	27,005	4,835	22,170	90,113	26,629	63,484
Accounting	1,019	215	804	4,470	796	3,674	14,970	3,313	11,657
Business, general	447	209	238	906	318	588	11,622	4,368	7,254
Business administration and management	1,687	674	1,013	2,367	834	1,533	28,968	11,076	17,892
Business and management, other	1,913	832	1,081	3,336	1,429	1,907	10,233	4,072	6,161
Business data processing	1,401	508	893	2,067	696	1,371	6,962	3,275	3,687
Secretarial and related programs	5,979	1,013	4,966	13,859	762	13,097	17,358	525	16,833
Communications	1,712	1,182	530	348	134	214	3,160	1,624	1,536
Communications technologies	90	63	27	327	198	129	1,984	1,298	686
Computer and information sciences	2,154	1,120	1,034	5,295	2,473	2,822	9,152	4,743	4,409
Construction trades	2,310	2,133	177	4,582	4,328	254	1,728	1,598	130
Consumer and personal services	1,518	425	1,093	6,120	1,371	4,749	5,626	3,747	1,879
Education	355	37	318	1,461	152	1,309	9,658	3,058	6,600
Engineering	209	181	28	309	293	16	2,232	1,931	301
Engineering-related technologies	2,050	1,618	432	7,491	6,638	853	34,732	30,820	3,912
English language and literature/letters	98	28	70	50	14	36	1,548	505	1,043
Foreign languages and literatures	248	86	162	196	118	78	616	177	439
Health professions and related sciences	25,428	6,785	18,643	42,467	6,590	35,877	98,474	16,530	81,944
Dental assisting	298	14	284	2,673	92	2,581	4,312	282	4,030
Emergency medical technician-ambulance and paramedic	6,215	4,022	2,193	1,619	1,149	470	771	536	235
Medical lab technician	98	13	85	154	59	95	2,769	742	2,027
Medical assisting	1,069	97	972	3,886	115	3,771	3,544	135	3,409
Nursing assisting	8,794	1,019	7,775	187	19	168	2	0	2
Practical nursing	571	57	514	19,976	2,287	17,689	772	86	686
Nursing, R.N. and other	2,156	251	1,905	2,897	364	2,533	57,456	7,142	50,314
Health sciences, other	6,227	1,312	4,915	11,075	2,505	8,570	28,848	7,607	21,241
Home economics and vocational home economics	5,218	2,129	3,089	8,582	1,638	6,944	7,821	815	7,006
Law and legal studies	902	130	772	1,686	281	1,405	9,140	1,163	7,977
Liberal arts and sciences, general studies, and humanities	334	249	85	1,273	423	850	170,817	67,834	102,983
Library science	73	5	68	53	8	45	101	9	92
Marketing operations/marketing and distribution	2,152	710	1,442	2,444	579	1,865	6,187	1,526	4,661
Mathematics	5	4	1	1	0	1	782	438	344
Mechanics and repairers	4,850	4,355	495	20,835	19,127	1,708	11,497	10,754	743
Multi/interdisciplinary studies	181	17	164	130	56	74	8,692	4,228	4,464
Parks, recreation, leisure, and fitness studies	86	43	43	145	73	72	864	501	363
Philosophy and religion	46	19	27	483	192	291	81	52	29
Physical sciences	32	16	16	79	47	32	2,456	1,424	1,032
Physical sciences, other	16	8	8	29	21	8	1,645	921	724
Science technologies	16	8	8	50	26	24	811	503	308
Precision production trades	2,956	2,424	532	7,179	5,845	1,334	9,344	7,453	1,891
Protective services	8,678	6,796	1,882	3,536	2,628	908	19,709	14,202	5,507
Criminal justice and corrections	7,499	5,737	1,762	2,943	2,108	835	16,584	11,408	5,176
Fire control and safety	1,117	1,007	110	500	466	34	2,447	2,294	153
Protective services, other	62	52	10	93	54	39	678	500	178
Psychology	33	9	24	69	19	50	1,600	446	1,154
Public administration and services	608	235	373	732	230	502	3,882	783	3,099
R.O.T.C. and military technologies	1	1	0	0	0	0	364	331	33
Social sciences and history	136	114	22	96	41	55	3,634	1,461	2,173
Theological studies/religious vocations	65	33	32	617	332	285	607	309	298
Transportation and material moving workers	7,759	6,601	1,158	668	466	202	1,446	1,226	220
Visual and performing arts	324	131	193	3,401	1,191	2,210	12,544	5,275	7,269
Fine arts, general	19	4	15	469	190	279	1,420	483	937
Design and music	276	113	163	2,234	671	1,563	9,805	4,176	5,629
Visual and performing arts, other	29	14	15	698	330	368	1,319	616	703
Not classified by field of study	3	2	1	102	40	62	1,146	622	524

SOURCE: U.S. Department of Education, National Center for Education Statistics, Integrated Postsecondary Education Data System (IPEDS), "Completions" survey. (This table was prepared March 1997.)

Table 249.—Associate degrees and other subbaccalaureate awards conferred by institutions of higher education, by length of curriculum, sex of student, and field of study: 1993–94[1]

Field of study	Less than 1-year awards			1- to less than 4-year awards			Associate degrees		
	Total	Men	Women	Total	Men	Women	Total	Men	Women
1	2	3	4	5	6	7	8	9	10
Total	71,640	34,655	36,985	151,590	63,292	88,298	530,632	215,261	315,371
Agriculture and natural resources, total	1,430	1,108	322	4,157	2,290	1,867	5,636	3,822	1,814
Agricultural business and production	1,224	947	277	1,339	920	419	3,434	2,353	1,081
Agricultural sciences	155	116	39	1,596	430	1,166	871	483	388
Conservation and renewable natural resources	51	45	6	1,222	940	282	1,331	986	345
Architecture and related programs	10	0	10	44	16	28	353	115	238
Area, ethnic, and cultural studies	133	32	101	505	141	364	75	25	50
Biological/life sciences	43	34	9	83	41	42	1,771	707	1,064
Business management and administrative services	10,471	2,819	7,652	28,263	5,267	22,996	92,284	27,427	64,857
Accounting	1,088	217	871	4,272	788	3,484	15,307	3,440	11,867
Business, general	245	104	141	1,463	463	1,000	11,452	4,215	7,237
Business administration and management	1,914	796	1,118	2,125	751	1,374	29,691	11,601	18,090
Business and management, other	2,101	1,015	1,086	4,099	1,687	2,412	11,114	4,621	6,493
Business data processing	901	361	540	2,297	803	1,494	6,883	3,030	3,853
Secretarial and related programs	4,222	326	3,896	14,007	775	13,232	17,837	520	17,317
Communications	426	246	180	350	135	215	2,052	953	1,099
Communications technologies	82	53	29	331	192	139	2,469	1,635	834
Computer and information sciences	1,793	878	915	3,918	1,956	1,962	9,301	4,624	4,677
Construction trades	1,495	1,393	102	4,512	4,270	242	1,695	1,618	77
Consumer and personal services	1,229	296	933	6,098	1,460	4,638	5,175	3,484	1,691
Education	499	135	364	1,292	133	1,159	9,271	2,952	6,319
Engineering	222	199	23	104	84	20	2,445	2,145	300
Engineering-related technologies	2,351	2,027	324	8,909	7,937	972	35,618	31,819	3,799
English language and literature/letters	92	28	64	120	39	81	1,289	467	822
Foreign languages and literatures	324	132	192	77	35	42	492	147	345
Health professions and related sciences	24,907	7,140	17,767	42,230	6,695	35,535	94,601	15,152	79,449
Dental assisting	283	16	267	2,535	125	2,410	4,259	282	3,977
Emergency medical technician-ambulance and paramedic	6,551	4,293	2,258	1,834	1,307	527	510	355	155
Medical lab technician	39	5	34	152	50	102	2,570	665	1,905
Medical assisting	1,684	205	1,479	3,374	102	3,272	2,785	113	2,672
Nursing assisting	8,046	1,010	7,036	295	35	260	6	1	5
Practical nursing	519	63	456	19,395	2,118	17,277	740	68	672
Nursing, R.N. and other	2,187	249	1,938	3,176	337	2,839	57,405	6,665	50,740
Health sciences, other	5,598	1,299	4,299	11,469	2,621	8,848	26,326	7,003	19,323
Home economics and vocational home economics	3,428	974	2,454	8,491	1,790	6,701	7,463	642	6,821
Law and legal studies	962	167	795	2,092	376	1,716	8,681	1,029	7,652
Liberal arts and sciences, general studies, and humanities	149	57	92	635	270	365	165,106	66,081	99,025
Library science	97	4	93	53	5	48	118	16	102
Marketing operations/marketing and distribution	2,040	712	1,328	2,255	555	1,700	6,736	1,687	5,049
Mathematics	17	11	6	0	0	0	704	395	309
Mechanics and repairers	3,505	3,373	132	20,409	18,897	1,512	11,332	10,594	738
Multi/interdisciplinary studies	379	128	251	119	47	72	8,436	4,054	4,382
Parks, recreation, leisure, and fitness studies	47	34	13	129	53	76	755	454	301
Philosophy and religion	53	22	31	514	212	302	82	46	36
Physical sciences	38	22	16	58	33	25	2,546	1,477	1,069
Physical sciences, other	17	9	8	18	12	6	1,567	896	671
Science technologies	21	13	8	40	21	19	979	581	398
Precision production trades	2,374	1,996	378	7,585	6,303	1,282	9,357	7,511	1,846
Protective services	6,660	5,377	1,283	2,398	1,667	731	18,199	13,068	5,131
Criminal justice and corrections	5,634	4,458	1,176	1,916	1,262	654	15,262	10,439	4,823
Fire control and safety	939	842	97	375	342	33	2,243	2,111	132
Protective services, other	87	77	10	107	63	44	694	518	176
Psychology	30	7	23	6	1	5	1,377	337	1,040
Public administration and services	249	72	177	500	143	357	3,696	758	2,938
R.O.T.C. and military technologies	0	0	0	0	0	0	265	245	20
Social sciences and history	40	32	8	93	25	68	3,936	1,536	2,400
Theological studies/religious vocations	126	69	57	590	288	302	641	342	299
Transportation and material moving workers	5,567	4,942	625	447	370	77	1,922	1,602	320
Visual and performing arts	329	121	208	3,910	1,442	2,468	13,227	5,496	7,731
Fine arts, general	7	4	3	646	259	387	1,473	566	907
Design and music	311	112	199	2,423	765	1,658	10,173	4,133	6,040
Visual and performing arts, other	11	5	6	841	418	423	1,581	797	784
Not classified by field of study	43	15	28	313	124	189	1,526	799	727

[1] Data revised from previously published data.

SOURCE: U.S. Department of Education, National Center for Education Statistics, Integrated Postsecondary Education Data System (IPEDS), "Completions" survey. (This table was prepared April 1997.)

HIGHER EDUCATION: DEGREES 267

Table 250.—Bachelor's degrees conferred by institutions of higher education, by discipline division: 1970–71 to 1994–95

Discipline division	1970–71	1975–76	1980–81	1982–83	1983–84	1984–85	1985–86	1986–87	1987–88	1988–89	1989–90	1990–91	1991–92	1992–93	1993–94	1994–95
1	2	3	4	5	6	7	8	9	10	11	12	13	14	15	16	17
Total	839,730	925,746	935,140	969,510	974,309	979,477	987,823	991,264	994,829	1,018,755	1,051,344	1,094,538	1,136,553	1,165,178	1,169,275	1,160,134
Agriculture and natural resources	12,672	19,402	21,886	20,909	19,317	18,107	16,823	14,991	14,222	13,492	12,900	13,124	15,124	16,778	18,070	19,841
Architecture and related programs	5,570	9,146	9,455	9,823	9,186	9,325	9,119	8,950	8,603	9,150	9,364	9,781	8,753	9,167	8,975	8,756
Area, ethnic and cultural studies	2,582	3,577	2,887	3,068	3,005	2,985	3,178	3,427	3,601	4,102	4,613	4,884	5,342	5,481	5,573	5,706
Biological sciences/life sciences	35,743	54,275	43,216	39,982	38,640	38,445	38,524	38,121	36,755	36,059	37,204	39,530	42,941	47,038	51,383	55,984
Business	114,729	142,034	198,983	226,627	229,478	232,636	237,319	240,546	243,021	246,399	248,698	249,311	256,603	256,842	246,654	234,323
Communications	10,324	20,045	29,428	36,954	38,586	40,358	41,666	43,953	45,410	47,405	50,114	51,650	54,257	53,874	51,164	48,104
Communications technologies	478	1,237	1,854	1,613	1,527	1,644	1,410	1,384	1,239	1,204	1,194	1,123	720	832	663	699
Computer and information sciences	2,388	5,652	15,121	24,510	32,172	38,878	41,889	39,589	34,523	30,454	27,257	25,083	24,557	24,200	24,200	24,404
Education	176,307	154,437	108,074	97,895	92,299	88,072	87,114	86,936	91,112	96,913	105,112	110,807	108,006	107,781	107,600	106,079
Engineering	44,898	38,388	63,287	72,163	75,638	77,066	76,225	73,747	69,380	66,099	63,609	61,531	61,206	61,973	62,220	62,342
Engineering-related technologies	5,148	7,943	11,713	16,855	18,547	18,762	19,435	19,069	19,126	18,903	17,713	17,119	16,335	16,078	16,005	15,812
English language and literature/letters	64,342	42,006	32,254	31,829	32,834	33,218	34,552	36,284	38,661	42,470	47,519	51,841	54,951	56,133	53,924	51,901
Foreign languages and literatures	20,536	16,484	11,273	10,599	10,384	10,827	10,984	11,034	10,926	11,693	12,386	13,133	13,903	14,387	14,378	13,775
Health professions and related sciences	25,226	53,958	63,649	64,685	64,288	64,422	64,396	63,103	60,644	59,005	58,302	59,070	61,720	67,089	74,421	79,855
Home economics and vocational home economics	11,167	17,409	18,370	16,296	15,948	15,157	14,889	14,417	14,320	14,160	14,491	14,892	14,898	15,100	15,522	15,345
Law and legal studies	545	531	776	1,099	1,272	1,157	1,197	1,178	1,303	1,976	1,592	1,758	2,144	2,056	2,171	2,032
Liberal arts and sciences, general studies, and humanities	7,481	18,855	21,643	21,603	21,479	21,818	21,336	23,717	24,274	26,388	27,985	30,526	32,174	33,456	33,397	33,356
Library science	1,013	843	375	254	252	197	155	136	119	121	77	90	97	83	62	50
Mathematics	24,937	16,329	11,433	12,719	13,764	15,861	17,147	16,999	16,608	15,994	15,176	15,310	14,783	14,812	14,396	13,723
Multi/interdisciplinary studies	6,286	13,588	12,848	14,107	13,940	12,978	13,489	13,933	14,723	15,168	16,267	17,561	20,647	23,955	25,167	26,033
Parks, recreation, leisure and fitness studies	1,621	5,182	5,729	5,214	4,850	4,725	4,620	4,264	4,235	4,376	4,582	4,315	8,446	9,859	11,470	12,889
Philosophy and religion	8,146	8,447	6,776	6,483	6,435	6,400	6,239	5,984	5,963	6,425	6,868	7,315	7,526	7,781	7,546	7,276
Physical sciences and science technologies	21,412	21,465	23,952	23,381	23,651	23,704	21,717	20,070	17,806	17,186	16,066	16,344	16,960	17,545	18,400	19,177
Precision production trades	—	—	—	384	371	553	400	455	481	482	528	460	378	388	420	353
Protective services	2,045	12,507	13,707	12,579	12,654	12,510	12,704	12,930	13,367	14,698	15,354	16,806	18,855	20,902	23,009	24,157
Psychology	38,187	50,278	41,068	40,460	39,955	39,900	40,628	42,994	45,187	48,910	53,952	58,655	63,513	66,728	69,259	72,083
Public administration and services	5,466	15,440	16,707	14,414	12,570	11,754	11,887	12,328	12,385	13,162	13,908	14,350	15,987	16,775	17,815	18,586
R.O.T.C. and military technologies	357	952	42	195	256	82	384	82	198	184	11	19	27
Social sciences and history	155,324	126,396	100,513	95,228	93,323	91,570	93,840	96,342	100,460	108,151	118,083	125,107	133,974	135,703	133,680	128,154
Theological studies/religious vocations	3,744	5,520	5,841	6,054	5,920	6,047	5,607	5,730	5,565	5,318	5,200	4,813	4,729	5,433	5,434	5,578
Transportation and material moving workers	662	1,282	1,801	1,662	1,698	1,962	1,837	1,654	1,983	2,062	2,387	2,622	3,598	3,930	3,923	3,698
Visual and performing arts	30,394	42,138	40,479	39,794	40,131	38,140	37,241	36,615	36,944	38,227	39,934	42,186	46,522	47,761	49,053	48,690
Not classified by field of study	0	0	0	0	0	0	0	0	1,801	2,405	2,713	13,258	6,720	5,247	3,302	1,346

—Data not available or not applicable.

NOTE.—The new Classification of Instructional Programs was initiated in 1991–92. The figures for earlier years have been reclassified when necessary to make them conform to the new taxonomy. To facilitate trend comparisons, certain aggregations have been made of the degree fields as reported in the IPEDS "Completions" survey: "Agriculture and natural resources" includes Agricultural business and production, Agricultural sciences, and Conservation and renewable natural resources; "Business" includes Business management and administrative services, Marketing operations/marketing and distribution, and Consumer and personal services; and "Engineering-related technologies" includes Engineering-related technologies, Mechanics and repairers, and Construction trades.

SOURCE: U.S. Department of Education, National Center for Education Statistics, Higher Education General Information Survey (HEGIS), "Degrees and Other Formal Awards Conferred" surveys, and Integrated Postsecondary Education Data System (IPEDS), "Completions" surveys. (This table was prepared March 1997.)

268 HIGHER EDUCATION: DEGREES

Table 251.—Master's degrees conferred by institutions of higher education, by discipline division: 1970–71 to 1994–95

Discipline division	1970–71	1975–76	1980–81	1982–83	1983–84	1984–85	1985–86	1986–87	1987–88	1988–89	1989–90	1990–91	1991–92	1992–93	1993–94	1994–95
1	2	3	4	5	6	7	8	9	10	11	12	13	14	15	16	17
Total	230,509	311,771	295,739	289,921	284,263	286,251	288,567	289,349	299,317	310,621	324,301	337,168	352,838	369,585	387,070	397,629
Agriculture and natural resources	2,457	3,340	4,003	4,254	4,178	3,928	3,801	3,522	3,479	3,245	3,382	3,295	3,735	3,965	4,119	4,252
Architecture and related programs	1,705	3,215	3,153	3,357	3,223	3,275	3,260	3,163	3,159	3,383	3,499	3,490	3,640	3,808	3,943	3,923
Area, ethnic, and cultural studies	1,032	995	804	845	897	904	945	864	911	1,016	1,212	1,263	1,385	1,523	1,633	1,639
Biological sciences/life sciences	5,728	6,582	5,978	5,696	5,406	5,059	5,013	4,952	4,784	4,961	4,869	4,765	4,785	4,756	5,196	5,393
Business	25,977	42,054	57,391	64,758	66,150	66,996	66,689	67,093	69,230	73,065	76,676	78,255	84,642	89,615	93,437	93,809
Communications	1,770	2,961	2,896	3,502	3,513	3,460	3,500	3,622	3,678	3,940	4,063	4,123	4,180	4,754	5,005	5,142
Communications technologies	86	165	209	102	143	209	323	271	247	317	299	213	284	455	414	467
Computer and information sciences	1,588	2,603	4,218	5,321	6,190	7,101	8,070	8,481	9,197	9,414	9,677	9,324	9,530	10,163	10,416	10,326
Education	87,666	126,061	96,713	83,250	75,664	74,654	74,801	74,045	76,566	81,174	84,881	87,343	92,668	96,028	98,938	101,242
Engineering	16,309	16,014	16,386	18,807	20,078	20,905	21,040	22,015	22,627	23,740	23,863	23,962	24,983	27,626	28,621	28,553
Engineering-related technologies	134	328	323	537	577	650	617	639	758	828	909	996	994	1,100	1,133	1,117
English language and literature/letters	10,686	8,809	5,929	5,048	5,010	5,187	5,518	5,483	5,562	5,950	6,567	7,026	7,450	7,790	7,885	7,845
Foreign languages and literatures	5,217	4,190	2,690	2,478	2,581	2,471	2,494	2,379	2,469	2,595	2,760	2,800	2,926	3,198	3,288	3,136
Health professions and related sciences	5,749	12,556	16,515	17,047	17,411	17,385	18,573	18,394	18,657	19,268	20,321	21,200	23,065	25,718	28,025	31,243
Home economics and vocational home economics	1,452	2,179	2,570	2,385	2,416	2,375	2,294	2,064	2,047	2,164	2,100	2,019	2,412	2,479	2,421	2,864
Law and legal studies	955	1,442	1,832	2,091	1,802	1,796	1,924	1,943	1,880	2,013	1,888	2,057	2,369	2,197	2,432	2,511
Liberal arts and sciences, general studies, and humanities	885	2,633	2,375	1,286	1,796	1,696	1,586	1,581	1,814	1,850	1,999	2,213	2,394	2,416	2,496	2,565
Library science	7,001	8,037	4,859	3,904	3,782	3,870	3,564	3,783	3,674	3,906	4,341	4,763	4,893	4,871	5,116	5,057
Mathematics	5,695	4,315	3,074	3,398	3,244	3,413	3,607	3,730	3,867	3,903	4,146	4,041	4,011	4,067	4,100	4,181
Multi/interdisciplinary studies	821	1,158	2,144	2,499	2,431	2,583	2,625	2,482	2,575	2,762	2,834	1,796	2,126	2,498	2,464	2,457
Parks, recreation, leisure and fitness studies	218	571	643	608	603	596	570	560	544	535	529	483	1,358	1,434	1,625	1,755
Philosophy and religion	1,326	1,356	1,229	1,091	1,153	1,167	1,163	1,109	1,099	1,280	1,306	1,441	1,146	1,425	1,350	1,380
Physical sciences and science technologies	6,367	5,466	5,284	5,290	5,576	5,796	5,902	5,629	5,733	5,723	5,449	5,309	5,374	5,366	5,679	5,753
Precision production trades	—	—	—	—	—	—	0	4	0	0	3	0	0	2	2	5
Protective services	194	1,197	1,538	1,300	1,219	1,235	1,074	1,019	1,024	1,047	1,151	1,108	1,249	1,357	1,437	1,706
Psychology	5,717	10,167	10,223	9,981	9,525	9,891	9,845	9,562	9,180	9,940	10,730	11,349	10,215	10,957	12,181	13,921
Public administration and services	7,785	15,209	17,803	16,046	15,060	15,575	15,692	16,432	16,424	17,020	17,399	17,905	19,243	20,634	21,833	23,501
R.O.T.C. and military technologies	2	0	43	110	127	119	83	119	49	0	0	0	0	108	124	124
Social sciences and history	16,539	15,953	11,945	11,205	10,577	10,503	10,564	10,506	10,412	11,023	11,634	12,233	12,702	13,471	14,561	14,845
Theological studies/religious vocations	2,710	3,290	4,220	4,871	5,211	4,435	4,556	4,966	4,905	4,749	4,959	4,810	5,185	4,985	4,956	5,240
Transportation and material moving workers	63	108	120	91	194	295	454	433	679	692	538	406	385	495	664	823
Visual and performing arts	6,675	8,817	8,629	8,763	8,526	8,718	8,420	8,508	7,939	8,267	8,481	8,657	9,353	9,440	9,925	10,277
Not classified by field of study	0	0	0	0	0	0	0	0	4,144	851	1,836	8,523	4,156	884	1,651	577

—Data not available or not applicable.

NOTE.—The new Classification of Instructional Programs was initiated in 1991–92. The figures for earlier years have been reclassified when necessary to make them conform to the new taxonomy. To facilitate trend comparisons, certain aggregations have been made of the degree fields as reported in the IPEDS "Completions" survey: "Agriculture and natural resources" includes Agricultural business and production, Agricultural sciences, and Conservation and renewable natural resources; "Business" includes Business management and administrative services, Marketing operations/marketing and distribution, and Consumer and personal services; and "Engineering-related technologies" includes Engineering-related technologies, Mechanics and repairers, and Construction trades.

SOURCE: U.S. Department of Education, National Center for Education Statistics, Higher Education General Information Survey (HEGIS), "Degrees and Other Formal Awards Conferred" surveys, and Integrated Postsecondary Education Data System (IPEDS), "Completions" surveys. (This table was prepared March 1997.)

HIGHER EDUCATION: DEGREES 269

Table 252.—Doctor's degrees conferred by institutions of higher education, by discipline division: 1970–71 to 1994–95

Discipline division	1970–71	1975–76	1980–81	1982–83	1983–84	1984–85	1985–86	1986–87	1987–88	1988–89	1989–90	1990–91	1991–92	1992–93	1993–94	1994–95
1	2	3	4	5	6	7	8	9	10	11	12	13	14	15	16	17
Total	32,107	34,064	32,958	32,775	33,209	32,943	33,653	34,041	34,870	35,720	38,371	39,294	40,659	42,132	43,185	44,446
Agriculture and natural resources	1,086	928	1,067	1,149	1,172	1,213	1,158	1,049	1,142	1,183	1,295	1,185	1,214	1,173	1,278	1,264
Architecture and related programs	36	82	93	97	84	89	73	92	98	86	103	135	132	148	161	141
Area, ethnic, and cultural studies	144	188	162	155	141	140	159	134	142	114	131	167	155	178	155	186
Biological sciences/life sciences	3,645	3,392	3,718	3,341	3,437	3,432	3,358	3,419	3,629	3,520	3,844	4,093	4,243	4,435	4,534	4,645
Business	757	900	795	776	929	831	934	1,062	1,063	1,100	1,093	1,185	1,242	1,346	1,364	1,394
Communications	145	196	171	205	215	228	212	273	230	247	267	259	252	293	337	320
Communications technologies	0	8	11	9	4	6	11	2	4	6	6	15	3	8	8	1
Computer and information sciences	128	244	252	262	251	248	344	374	428	551	627	676	772	805	810	884
Education	6,041	7,202	7,279	7,057	6,911	6,612	6,605	6,407	6,060	6,337	6,502	6,187	6,864	7,030	6,908	6,905
Engineering	3,637	2,819	2,551	2,818	2,979	3,221	3,398	3,801	4,174	4,506	4,967	5,258	5,488	5,823	5,963	6,110
Engineering-related technologies	1	2	10	13	2	9	12	17	17	17	14	14	11	20	16	18
English language and literature/letters	1,650	1,672	1,164	991	1,018	1,041	991	961	981	1,022	1,078	1,184	1,273	1,341	1,344	1,561
Foreign languages and literatures	988	1,076	804	673	659	635	672	661	602	632	724	758	850	830	886	905
Health professions and related sciences	466	577	842	1,155	1,164	1,199	1,241	1,213	1,261	1,437	1,536	1,613	1,661	1,767	1,902	2,069
Home economics and vocational home economics	123	178	247	255	277	273	311	296	307	264	301	253	293	345	365	388
Law and legal studies	20	76	60	72	121	105	54	120	89	76	111	90	68	86	79	88
Liberal arts and sciences, general studies, and humanities	32	162	121	215	173	112	90	56	66	72	63	70	67	81	80	90
Library science	39	71	71	52	74	87	62	57	46	61	42	56	50	77	45	55
Mathematics	1,249	909	775	731	743	734	777	759	796	915	966	1,036	1,082	1,189	1,157	1,226
Multi/interdisciplinary studies	59	111	158	225	249	219	263	247	224	212	272	220	231	196	227	238
Parks, recreation, leisure, and fitness studies	2	15	42	33	27	36	39	32	29	35	35	28	61	108	116	149
Philosophy and religion	554	554	410	404	442	468	477	421	405	465	439	456	475	448	528	507
Physical sciences and science technologies	4,390	3,431	3,141	3,269	3,306	3,403	3,551	3,673	3,809	3,858	4,164	4,290	4,391	4,393	4,650	4,483
Precision production trades	—	—	—	0	0	0	0	0	0	0	0	0	0	0	0	0
Protective services	1	9	21	38	31	33	21	18	32	26	38	28	24	32	25	26
Psychology	2,144	3,157	3,576	3,602	3,535	3,447	3,593	3,560	3,480	3,685	3,811	3,932	3,373	3,651	3,563	3,822
Public administration and services	174	292	362	347	420	431	382	398	470	428	508	430	432	459	519	556
R.O.T.C. and military technologies	0	0	0	0	0	0	0	0	0	0	0	0	0	0	0	0
Social sciences and history	3,660	4,157	3,122	2,931	2,911	2,851	2,955	2,916	2,781	2,885	3,010	3,012	3,218	3,460	3,627	3,725
Theological studies/religious vocations	312	1,033	1,276	1,208	1,204	1,144	1,185	1,230	1,199	1,166	1,317	1,079	1,259	1,417	1,448	1,591
Transportation and material moving workers	3	3	3	0	0	0	3	0	0	0	0	0	0	0	0	0
Visual and performing arts	621	620	654	692	730	696	722	793	727	753	849	838	906	882	1,054	1,080
Not classified by field of study	0	0	0	0	0	0	0	0	579	61	258	747	569	111	36	19

—Data not available or not applicable.

NOTE.—The new Classification of Instructional Programs was initiated in 1991–92. The figures for earlier years have been reclassified when necessary to make them conform to the new taxonomy. To facilitate trend comparisons, certain aggregations have been made of the degree fields as reported in the IPEDS "Completions" survey: "Agriculture and natural resources" includes Agricultural business and production, Agricultural sciences, and Conservation and renewable natural resources; "Business" includes Business management and administrative services, Marketing operations/marketing and distribution, and Consumer and personal services; and "Engineering-related technologies" includes Engineering-related technologies, Mechanics and repairers, and Construction trades.

SOURCE: U.S. Department of Education, National Center for Education Statistics, Higher Education General Information Survey (HEGIS), "Degrees and Other Formal Awards Conferred" surveys, and Integrated Postsecondary Education Data System (IPEDS), "Completions" surveys. (This table was prepared March 1997.)

Table 253.—Bachelor's, master's, and doctor's degrees conferred by institutions of higher education, by sex of student and field of study: 1994–95

Field of study	Bachelor's degrees requiring 4 or 5 years			Master's degrees			Doctor's degrees (Ph.D., Ed.D., etc.)		
	Total	Men	Women	Total	Men	Women	Total	Men	Women
1	2	3	4	5	6	7	8	9	10
All fields	1,160,134	526,131	634,003	397,629	178,598	219,031	44,446	26,916	17,530
Agriculture and natural resources, total	19,841	12,692	7,149	4,252	2,551	1,701	1,264	962	302
Agricultural business and production, total	5,046	3,593	1,453	660	434	226	218	162	56
Agricultural business and management, total	3,420	2,472	948	519	339	180	180	139	41
Agricultural business and management, general	875	619	256	48	29	19	0	0	0
Agricultural business/agribusiness operations	1,032	757	275	29	16	13	11	10	1
Agricultural economics	1,346	958	388	433	288	145	169	129	40
Agricultural business and management, other	167	138	29	9	6	3	0	0	0
Agricultural mechanization	253	229	24	6	5	1	0	0	0
Agricultural production workers and managers	160	118	42	50	42	8	16	12	4
Horticulture service operations and management	492	340	152	31	17	14	9	3	6
International agriculture	21	13	8	10	5	5	0	0	0
Agricultural business and production, other	700	421	279	44	26	18	13	8	5
Agricultural sciences, total	6,818	3,928	2,890	1,541	888	653	712	541	171
Agriculture/agricultural sciences, general	1,045	730	315	154	98	56	4	4	0
Animal sciences, total	3,207	1,556	1,651	396	226	170	196	158	38
Animal sciences, general	2,696	1,269	1,427	270	150	120	141	110	31
Agricultural animal breeding and genetics	19	7	12	5	2	3	13	12	1
Agricultural animal health	14	5	9	8	4	4	0	0	0
Agricultural animal nutrition	0	0	0	9	1	8	9	8	1
Dairy science	81	54	27	32	23	9	9	8	1
Poultry science	141	115	26	26	15	11	7	6	1
Animal sciences, other	256	106	150	46	31	15	17	14	3
Food sciences and technology	498	186	312	322	136	186	128	74	54
Plant sciences, total	1,771	1,251	520	526	341	185	312	251	61
Plant sciences, general	280	187	93	74	44	30	36	26	10
Agronomy and crop science	588	504	84	185	137	48	160	134	26
Horticulture science	532	313	219	146	77	69	65	46	19
Plant breeding and genetics	0	0	0	13	9	4	15	14	1
Agricultural plant pathology	9	6	3	9	5	4	4	4	0
Plant protection (pest management)	26	22	4	19	14	5	5	4	1
Range science and management	243	157	86	44	31	13	17	14	3
Plant sciences, other	93	62	31	36	24	12	10	9	1
Soil sciences	155	113	42	101	64	37	63	46	17
Agriculture/agricultural sciences, other	142	92	50	42	23	19	9	8	1
Conservation and renewable natural resources, total	7,977	5,171	2,806	2,051	1,229	822	334	259	75
Natural resources conservation, general	4,310	2,531	1,779	1,158	638	520	95	75	20
Natural resources management and policy	438	280	158	84	50	34	4	4	0
Fishing and fisheries sciences and management	206	161	45	106	83	23	24	22	2
Forest harvesting and production technology/technician	267	189	78	38	28	10	22	18	4
Forestry, general	1,289	1,012	277	468	293	175	154	114	40
Wildlife and wildlands management	1,084	758	326	152	109	43	25	20	5
Conservation and renewable natural resources, other	383	240	143	45	28	17	10	6	4
Architecture and related programs, total	8,756	5,741	3,015	3,923	2,310	1,613	141	95	46
Architecture	5,122	3,675	1,447	1,969	1,282	687	37	26	11
City/urban, community, and regional planning	521	381	140	1,285	696	589	76	47	29
Architectural environmental design	727	455	272	63	19	44	5	4	1
Interior architecture	771	111	660	7	0	7	0	0	0
Landscape architecture	1,016	727	289	359	167	192	3	2	1
Architectural urban design and planning	0	0	0	79	57	22	3	2	1
Architecture and related programs, other	599	392	207	161	89	72	17	14	3
Area, ethnic, and cultural studies, total	5,706	2,092	3,614	1,639	765	874	186	80	106
Area studies, total	3,827	1,539	2,288	1,173	542	631	138	68	70
African studies	40	15	25	18	12	6	2	1	1
American studies/civilization	1,591	614	977	247	89	158	73	34	39
Latin American studies	400	148	252	233	113	120	10	5	5
Middle Eastern studies	98	55	43	81	38	43	20	13	7
Russian and Slavic studies	214	80	134	118	53	65	0	0	0
Asian studies	813	401	412	295	135	160	22	10	12
European studies	230	87	143	79	39	40	3	1	2
Area studies, other	441	139	302	102	63	39	8	4	4
Ethnic and cultural studies, total	1,659	475	1,184	276	97	179	40	11	29
Afro-American (black) studies	516	191	325	71	28	43	10	4	6
Hispanic-American studies	142	57	85	14	6	8	0	0	0
Women's studies	533	10	523	62	2	60	11	0	11
Ethnic studies, other	468	217	251	129	61	68	19	7	12
Area, ethnic and cultural studies, other	220	78	142	190	126	64	8	1	7
Biological sciences/life sciences, total	55,984	26,687	29,297	5,393	2,602	2,791	4,645	2,771	1,874
Biology, general	41,658	19,499	22,159	2,350	1,155	1,195	729	436	293

HIGHER EDUCATION: DEGREES

Table 253.—Bachelor's, master's, and doctor's degrees conferred by institutions of higher education, by sex of student and field of study: 1994–95—Continued

Field of study	Bachelor's degrees requiring 4 or 5 years			Master's degrees			Doctor's degrees (Ph.D., Ed.D., etc.)		
	Total	Men	Women	Total	Men	Women	Total	Men	Women
1	2	3	4	5	6	7	8	9	10
Biochemistry and biophysics	2,889	1,570	1,319	339	175	164	703	422	281
Botany, total	315	154	161	224	114	110	244	169	75
Botany, general	293	142	151	139	70	69	126	83	43
Plant pathology	5	3	2	71	38	33	74	59	15
Botany, other	17	9	8	14	6	8	44	27	17
Cell and molecular biology, total	1,759	938	821	157	73	84	521	290	231
Cell biology	202	108	94	51	23	28	142	78	64
Molecular biology	631	345	286	74	32	42	245	139	106
Cell and molecular biology, other	926	485	441	32	18	14	134	73	61
Microbiology/bacteriology	1,908	925	983	295	132	163	443	253	190
Miscellaneous biological specializations, total	2,717	1,267	1,450	1,202	494	708	1,046	605	441
Anatomy	81	48	33	63	34	29	92	48	44
Ecology	732	372	360	205	106	99	95	66	29
Marine/aquatic biology	687	338	349	88	48	40	39	29	10
Neurosciences	193	106	87	49	35	14	188	111	77
Nutritional sciences	372	94	278	266	36	230	104	40	64
Toxicology	56	27	29	74	35	39	83	49	34
Genetics, plant and animal	179	74	105	131	43	88	223	133	90
Biometrics	15	9	6	38	18	20	15	9	6
Miscellaneous specialized areas, other	402	199	203	288	139	149	207	120	87
Zoology, total	3,206	1,572	1,634	689	392	297	767	478	289
Zoology, general	2,667	1,286	1,381	198	99	99	164	104	60
Entomology	61	41	20	137	94	43	122	95	27
Pathology, human and animal	8	0	8	52	18	34	89	55	34
Pharmacology, human and animal	49	28	21	53	22	31	192	105	87
Physiology, human and animal	412	211	201	249	159	90	200	119	81
Zoology, other	9	6	3	0	0	0	0	0	0
Biological sciences/life sciences, other	1,532	762	770	137	67	70	192	118	74
Business management, administrative services and marketing operations/marketing and distribution, total	234,323	121,898	112,425	93,809	59,109	34,700	1,394	1,014	380
Business management and administrative services, total	229,286	119,878	109,408	93,050	58,670	34,380	1,385	1,012	373
Business, general	23,603	12,506	11,097	11,150	7,433	3,717	228	164	64
Business administration and management, total	85,641	45,105	40,536	52,990	33,890	19,100	738	542	196
Office supervision and management	847	97	750	0	0	0	0	0	0
Operations management and supervision	1,902	1,310	592	461	351	110	6	6	0
Business administration and management, other	82,892	43,698	39,194	52,529	33,539	18,990	732	536	196
Accounting	43,940	19,235	24,705	4,494	2,377	2,117	54	35	19
Secretarial and related programs	334	58	276	0	0	0	0	0	0
Business/managerial economics	2,988	1,845	1,143	228	164	64	57	44	13
Small business management and ownership	415	277	138	56	36	20	0	0	0
Finance, general and banking and financial support services	20,427	13,741	6,686	5,267	3,788	1,479	56	52	4
Actuarial sciences	285	169	116	73	44	29	0	0	0
Insurance and risk management	555	336	219	83	52	31	7	6	1
Investments and securities and financial planning	296	168	128	307	222	85	0	0	0
Hospitality services management	5,553	2,542	3,011	457	217	240	1	1	0
Human resources management	5,129	2,028	3,101	1,943	800	1,143	25	16	9
Labor/personnel relations and studies	905	456	449	736	298	438	22	15	7
Organizational behavior studies	1,102	490	612	308	118	190	35	12	23
International business	2,988	1,517	1,471	2,956	1,817	1,139	10	8	2
Business information systems, total	6,166	3,707	2,459	2,406	1,673	733	29	20	9
Management information systems and data processing, general	5,788	3,462	2,326	2,012	1,408	604	26	17	9
Business information systems, other	378	245	133	394	265	129	3	3	0
Quantitative methods and management science, total	1,759	978	781	1,308	882	426	31	24	7
Business statistics	32	11	21	30	14	16	4	2	2
Management science, other	1,727	967	760	1,278	868	410	27	22	5
Marketing management and research	22,062	11,862	10,200	1,893	985	908	40	32	8
Real estate	484	347	137	275	197	78	0	0	0
Taxation	0	0	0	1,607	929	678	0	0	0
Consumer and personal services	253	160	93	0	0	0	0	0	0
Business management and administrative services, other	4,401	2,351	2,050	4,513	2,748	1,765	52	41	11
Marketing operations/marketing and distribution, total	5,037	2,020	3,017	759	439	320	9	2	7
Apparel and accessories marketing operations	1,223	48	1,175	0	0	3	4	0	4
Business and personal services marketing operations	340	158	182	8	4	4	0	0	0
General/retailing and wholesaling operations and skills	2,660	1,331	1,329	514	272	242	5	2	3
Transportation and travel marketing	188	56	132	15	6	9	0	0	0
Marketing and distribution, other	626	427	199	219	157	62	0	0	0
Communications and communications technologies, total	48,803	20,404	28,399	5,609	2,108	3,501	321	162	159
Communications, total	48,104	20,028	28,076	5,142	1,869	3,273	320	162	158
Communications, general	22,894	9,176	13,718	1,927	656	1,271	222	105	117
Advertising	2,791	1,175	1,616	244	87	157	1	1	0
Journalism	9,501	3,532	5,969	1,438	514	924	21	14	7
Broadcast journalism	554	217	337	8	0	8	0	0	0

272 HIGHER EDUCATION: DEGREES

Table 253.—Bachelor's, master's, and doctor's degrees conferred by institutions of higher education, by sex of student and field of study: 1994–95—Continued

Field of study	Bachelor's degrees requiring 4 or 5 years			Master's degrees			Doctor's degrees (Ph.D., Ed.D., etc.)		
	Total	Men	Women	Total	Men	Women	Total	Men	Women
1	2	3	4	5	6	7	8	9	10
Public relations and organizational communications	2,190	689	1,501	277	62	215	0	0	0
Radio and television broadcasting	5,438	3,065	2,373	335	160	175	12	9	3
Communications, other	4,736	2,174	2,562	913	390	523	64	33	31
Communications technologies, total	699	376	323	467	239	228	1	0	1
Photographic technology	18	6	12	0	0	0	0	0	0
Radio and television technology	567	307	260	349	170	179	1	0	1
Communications technologies, other	114	63	51	118	69	49	0	0	0
Computer and information sciences, total	24,404	17,463	6,941	10,326	7,627	2,699	884	723	161
Computer and information sciences, general	15,606	11,558	4,048	7,402	5,610	1,792	723	601	122
Computer programming	239	172	67	10	7	3	0	0	0
Data processing technology/technician	196	108	88	0	0	0	0	0	0
Information science and systems	4,042	2,435	1,607	1,349	856	493	28	19	9
Computer systems analysis	222	153	69	56	39	17	6	6	0
Computer and information sciences, other	4,099	3,037	1,062	1,509	1,115	394	127	97	30
Education, total	106,079	25,641	80,438	101,242	23,806	77,436	6,905	2,621	4,284
Education, general	1,801	322	1,479	10,995	2,631	8,364	1,262	451	811
Bilingual/bicultural education	74	11	63	286	51	235	12	3	9
Curriculum and instruction	17	14	3	8,898	1,679	7,219	778	243	535
Education administration and supervision, total	117	23	94	10,957	4,233	6,724	2,179	951	1,228
Education administration and supervision, general	5	0	5	7,488	2,953	4,535	1,585	701	884
Administration of special education	0	0	0	8	2	6	4	1	3
Adult and continuing education administration	0	0	0	126	33	93	54	16	38
Educational supervision	0	0	0	613	167	446	21	6	15
Elementary, middle, and secondary education administration	111	23	88	1,440	579	861	46	25	21
Higher education administration	0	0	0	480	183	297	337	147	190
Community and junior college education administration	0	0	0	68	20	48	1	1	0
Education administration and supervision, other	1	0	1	734	296	438	131	54	77
Educational/instructional media design	30	15	15	1,058	288	770	60	31	29
Educational evaluation and research, general	41	10	31	34	16	18	11	5	6
Educational statistics and research methods	1	0	1	30	14	16	21	7	14
Educational assessment, testing and measurement	0	0	0	132	25	107	23	9	14
Social and philosophical foundations of education	8	2	6	286	80	206	96	42	54
Special education, total	9,780	925	8,855	10,698	1,525	9,173	214	51	163
Special education, general	6,677	710	5,967	8,688	1,283	7,405	193	47	146
Education of the deaf and hearing impaired	259	6	253	217	25	192	0	0	0
Education of the gifted and talented	1	0	1	138	19	119	7	1	6
Education of the emotionally handicapped	312	38	274	231	47	184	2	0	2
Education of the mentally handicapped	578	36	542	123	13	110	1	0	1
Education of the multiple handicapped	142	13	129	214	25	189	4	1	3
Education of the physically handicapped	38	6	32	60	6	54	0	0	0
Education of the blind and visually handicapped	40	6	34	11	1	10	0	0	0
Education of the specific learning disabled	633	48	585	549	50	499	5	2	3
Education of the speech impaired	798	36	762	218	12	206	0	0	0
Special education, other	302	26	276	249	44	205	2	0	2
Counselor education/counseling and guidance services	26	5	21	12,621	2,727	9,894	344	113	231
General teacher education, total	59,210	7,483	51,727	23,494	4,210	19,284	441	136	305
Adult and continuing education	46	17	29	951	277	674	198	77	121
Elementary education	46,840	5,106	41,734	13,256	1,598	11,658	71	8	63
Junior high/intermediate/middle school education	1,397	295	1,102	615	112	503	0	0	0
Pre-elementary/early childhood/kindergarten education	6,236	178	6,058	2,021	47	1,974	29	0	29
Secondary education	4,150	1,828	2,322	4,123	1,557	2,566	66	22	44
Teacher education, general programs, other	541	59	482	2,528	619	1,909	77	29	48
Teacher education, academic and vocational programs	33,711	16,301	17,410	16,209	5,093	11,116	839	373	466
Agricultural education (vocational)	424	290	134	247	150	97	39	22	17
Art education	1,484	350	1,134	731	130	601	23	8	15
Business education (vocational)	1,237	317	920	430	139	291	12	8	4
Driver and safety education	56	46	10	62	44	18	1	1	0
English education	2,812	623	2,189	901	202	699	26	10	16
Foreign languages education	284	43	241	255	48	207	19	8	11
Health education	1,746	484	1,262	868	198	670	95	22	73
Home economics education (vocational)	262	8	254	125	5	120	12	0	12
Technology/industrial arts education	1,447	1,233	214	413	284	129	15	9	6
Marketing operations/marketing and distribution education	108	48	60	19	7	12	0	0	0
Mathematics education	1,756	667	1,089	837	291	546	50	23	27
Music education	2,747	1,129	1,618	749	319	430	103	54	49
Physical education and coaching	11,829	7,096	4,733	2,961	1,557	1,404	162	94	68
Reading education	158	16	142	3,723	230	3,493	61	6	55
Science education	1,126	506	620	730	304	426	44	18	26
Social science education	875	492	383	103	44	59	4	2	2
Social studies education	2,192	1,298	894	499	281	218	4	1	3
Technical education (vocational)	192	139	53	309	125	184	41	21	20
Trade and industrial education (vocational)	971	702	269	435	198	237	70	39	31

Table 253.—Bachelor's, master's, and doctor's degrees conferred by institutions of higher education, by sex of student and field of study: 1994–95—Continued

Field of study	Bachelor's degrees requiring 4 or 5 years			Master's degrees			Doctor's degrees (Ph.D., Ed.D., etc.)		
	Total	Men	Women	Total	Men	Women	Total	Men	Women
1	2	3	4	5	6	7	8	9	10
Teacher education, academic and vocational programs, other	2,005	814	1,191	1,812	537	1,275	58	27	31
Teaching English as a second language/foreign language	45	11	34	1,634	314	1,320	16	7	9
Education, other	1,218	519	699	3,910	920	2,990	609	199	410
Engineering and engineering-related technologies, total	78,154	65,933	12,221	29,670	24,836	4,834	6,128	5,399	729
Engineering, total	62,342	51,646	10,696	28,553	23,935	4,618	6,110	5,383	727
Engineering, general	2,041	1,711	330	1,401	1,145	256	238	205	33
Aerospace, aeronautical, and astronautical engineering	1,771	1,541	230	821	722	99	229	217	12
Agricultural engineering	591	486	105	160	132	28	86	78	8
Architectural engineering	558	438	120	25	23	2	4	4	0
Bioengineering and biomedical engineering	913	618	295	480	362	118	175	133	42
Ceramic sciences and engineering	191	151	40	88	64	24	57	48	9
Chemical engineering	5,901	3,988	1,913	1,085	822	263	571	475	96
Civil engineering	9,927	8,007	1,920	4,077	3,315	762	625	554	71
Computer engineering	2,345	2,057	288	1,040	838	202	140	125	15
Electrical, electronics, and communications engineering	14,929	13,089	1,840	7,693	6,694	999	1,543	1,380	163
Engineering mechanics	131	109	22	151	130	21	75	72	3
Engineering physics	263	222	41	63	50	13	44	40	4
Engineering science	279	215	64	326	259	67	48	43	5
Environmental/environmental health engineering	641	432	209	1,056	776	280	45	32	13
Geological engineering	125	97	28	40	31	9	13	12	1
Geophysical engineering	19	16	3	6	6	0	2	2	0
Industrial/manufacturing engineering	3,147	2,222	925	2,061	1,664	397	296	243	53
Material engineering	501	371	130	506	388	118	363	299	64
Mechanical engineering	14,794	13,141	1,653	4,213	3,784	429	890	833	57
Metallurgical engineering	268	211	57	165	144	21	92	80	12
Mining and mineral engineering	121	108	13	72	63	9	15	15	0
Naval architecture and marine engineering	278	265	13	30	24	6	6	5	1
Nuclear engineering	247	222	25	264	236	28	111	100	11
Ocean engineering	152	125	27	109	96	13	28	25	3
Petroleum engineering	303	265	38	200	177	23	51	50	1
Systems engineering	349	278	71	404	325	79	34	32	2
Textile sciences and engineering	68	39	29	28	19	9	6	2	4
Engineering, other	1,489	1,222	267	1,989	1,646	343	323	279	44
Engineering-related technologies, total	15,812	14,287	1,525	1,117	901	216	18	16	2
Architectural engineering technologies	574	498	76	0	0	0	0	0	0
Civil technologies	474	434	40	0	0	0	0	0	0
Electrical and electronic technologies	4,272	3,966	306	29	26	3	0	0	0
Electromechanical instrumentation and maintenance technologies	179	167	12	17	16	1	4	4	0
Environmental control technologies	268	207	61	110	77	33	0	0	0
Industrial production technologies	4,011	3,542	469	224	196	28	8	6	2
Quality control and safety technologies	554	451	103	352	268	84	0	0	0
Mechanical and related technologies	1,729	1,620	109	0	0	0	0	0	0
Mining and petroleum technologies	14	14	0	0	0	0	0	0	0
Surveying	165	149	16	21	18	3	6	6	0
Mechanics and repairers	66	63	3	0	0	0	0	0	0
Construction trades	113	91	22	7	4	3	0	0	0
Engineering and related technologies, other	3,393	3,085	308	357	296	61	0	0	0
English language and literature/letters, total	51,901	17,810	34,091	7,845	2,764	5,081	1,561	665	896
English language and literature, general	39,170	13,094	26,076	5,439	1,906	3,533	1,100	458	642
Comparative literature	731	229	502	233	92	141	168	76	92
English composition	301	118	183	24	10	14	6	1	5
English creative writing	947	396	551	898	365	533	9	6	3
American literature (United States)	38	13	25	18	8	10	9	5	4
English literature (British and Commonwealth)	1,059	374	685	258	98	160	93	41	52
Speech and rhetorical studies	8,045	2,999	5,046	731	209	522	132	60	72
English technical and business writing	166	59	107	137	44	93	0	0	0
English language and literature/letters, other	1,444	528	916	107	32	75	44	18	26
Foreign languages and literatures, total	13,775	4,243	9,532	3,136	995	2,141	905	395	510
Foreign languages and literatures, total	1,504	430	1,074	935	286	649	251	127	124
Foreign languages and literatures, general	940	277	663	333	100	233	57	26	31
Linguistics	564	153	411	602	186	416	194	101	93
East and Southeast Asian languages and literatures, total	536	303	233	118	34	84	25	15	10
Chinese	107	65	42	63	16	47	16	9	7
Japanese	314	169	145	33	8	25	1	0	1
East and Southeast Asian languages, other	115	69	46	22	10	12	8	6	2
East European languages and literatures, total	629	277	352	155	61	94	41	26	15
Russian languages	572	252	320	66	30	36	3	3	0
Slavic languages (other than Russian)	55	23	32	78	26	52	36	21	15
East European languages, other	2	2	0	11	5	6	2	2	0
Germanic languages and literatures, total	1,395	577	818	305	113	192	92	33	59

Table 253.—Bachelor's, master's, and doctor's degrees conferred by institutions of higher education, by sex of student and field of study: 1994–95—Continued

Field of study	Bachelor's degrees requiring 4 or 5 years			Master's degrees			Doctor's degrees (Ph.D., Ed.D., etc.)		
	Total	Men	Women	Total	Men	Women	Total	Men	Women
1	2	3	4	5	6	7	8	9	10
German	1,352	561	791	278	100	178	83	29	54
Scandinavian languages	27	9	18	7	4	3	4	1	3
Germanic languages, other	16	7	9	20	9	11	5	3	2
South Asian languages and literatures	3	1	2	2	1	1	5	3	2
Romance languages and literatures, total	8,718	2,199	6,519	1,344	352	992	387	135	252
French	2,764	555	2,209	470	119	351	118	40	78
Italian	271	70	201	69	14	55	31	9	22
Portuguese	25	18	7	8	5	3	3	0	3
Spanish	5,602	1,543	4,059	709	188	521	161	64	97
Romance languages, other	56	13	43	88	26	62	74	22	52
Middle Eastern languages and literatures, total	88	32	56	49	27	22	19	12	7
Arabic	10	4	6	1	0	1	1	0	1
Hebrew	57	18	39	30	17	13	7	5	2
Middle East languages, other	21	10	11	18	10	8	11	7	4
Classical and ancient Near East languages and literatures, total	722	357	365	169	100	69	54	28	26
Classics	595	292	303	151	91	60	50	26	24
Greek (ancient and medieval)	35	20	15	6	2	4	2	0	2
Latin (ancient and medieval)	92	45	47	12	7	5	2	2	0
Foreign languages, other	180	67	113	59	21	38	31	16	15
Health professions and related sciences, total	79,855	14,443	65,412	31,243	6,754	24,489	2,069	867	1,202
Communication disorders sciences and services	5,940	308	5,632	4,655	233	4,422	105	27	78
Community health liaison	731	147	584	162	37	125	0	0	0
Dentistry	24	16	8	389	259	130	51	20	31
Dental services	909	23	886	50	24	26	1	0	1
Epidemiology	0	0	0	299	129	170	94	34	60
Health services administration, total	3,872	964	2,908	3,871	1,377	2,494	60	33	27
Health services administration	1,948	523	1,425	2,163	825	1,338	38	21	17
Medical records administration	756	94	662	0	0	0	0	0	0
Medical records technology/technician	0	0	0	1	1	0	4	3	1
Health and medical administrative services, other	1,168	347	821	1,707	551	1,156	18	9	9
Health and medical assistants, total	1,305	612	693	375	139	236	0	0	0
Medical assistant	1	0	1	0	0	0	0	0	0
Physician assistant	1,163	565	598	341	124	217	0	0	0
Health and medical assistants, other	141	47	94	34	15	19	0	0	0
Health and medical diagnostic and treatment services, total	1,499	580	919	60	34	26	1	1	0
Respiratory therapy technology/technician	386	153	233	0	0	0	0	0	0
Health and medical diagnostic and treatment services, other	1,113	427	686	60	34	26	1	1	0
Medical laboratory technologies, total	3,033	910	2,123	430	160	270	79	34	45
Medical technology	2,632	776	1,856	63	18	45	1	1	0
Health and medical laboratory technologies/technicians, other	401	134	267	367	142	225	78	33	45
Pre-dentistry studies	161	107	54	0	0	0	0	0	0
Pre-medicine studies	639	365	274	0	0	0	0	0	0
Pre-pharmacy studies	2	1	1	0	0	0	0	0	0
Pre-veterinary studies	142	47	95	0	0	0	0	0	0
Medical basic sciences	361	134	227	427	209	218	422	237	185
Mental health services, total	603	115	488	347	71	276	8	1	7
Alcohol/drug abuse counseling	153	43	110	61	23	38	0	0	0
Psychiatric/mental health services technician	112	24	88	37	9	28	0	0	0
Clinical and medical social work	87	12	75	49	12	37	8	1	7
Mental health services, other	251	36	215	200	27	173	0	0	0
Nursing	42,186	4,457	37,729	9,629	666	8,963	397	16	381
Optometry	193	75	118	11	5	6	6	6	0
Pharmacy	6,025	2,290	3,735	309	131	178	275	154	121
Rehabilitation/therapeutic services, total	7,678	1,647	6,031	5,198	1,312	3,886	25	9	16
Art therapy	74	7	67	216	19	197	0	0	0
Dance therapy	2	0	2	22	1	21	0	0	0
Music therapy	157	15	142	47	9	38	0	0	0
Occupational therapy	2,850	329	2,521	762	91	671	0	0	0
Orthotics/prosthetics	36	26	10	0	0	0	0	0	0
Physical therapy	3,355	1,004	2,351	2,942	843	2,099	3	0	3
Recreational therapy	183	34	149	18	1	17	1	0	1
Vocational rehabilitation counseling	193	44	149	685	174	511	4	4	0
Rehabilitative services, other	828	188	640	506	174	332	17	5	12
Veterinary medicine	48	20	28	144	76	68	96	66	30
Miscellaneous health professions	433	217	216	780	453	327	59	37	22
Health professions and related sciences, other	4,071	1,408	2,663	4,107	1,439	2,668	390	192	198
Home economics and vocational home economics, total	15,345	1,808	13,537	2,864	492	2,372	388	99	289
Home economics, total	14,771	1,560	13,211	2,820	491	2,329	382	97	285
Home economics, general	2,752	216	2,536	345	31	314	44	14	30
Home economics business services	153	16	137	2	0	2	0	0	0
Family and community studies	212	18	194	54	11	43	10	5	5
Family and consumer resource management	1,215	388	827	64	7	57	28	4	24
Food and nutrition studies	3,272	418	2,854	584	73	511	61	20	41
Housing studies	479	64	415	20	5	15	4	1	3

Table 253.—Bachelor's, master's, and doctor's degrees conferred by institutions of higher education, by sex of student and field of study: 1994–95—Continued

Field of study	Bachelor's degrees requiring 4 or 5 years			Master's degrees			Doctor's degrees (Ph.D., Ed.D., etc.)		
	Total	Men	Women	Total	Men	Women	Total	Men	Women
1	2	3	4	5	6	7	8	9	10
Individual and family development studies	5,172	367	4,805	1,637	348	1,289	212	47	165
Clothing/apparel and textile studies	1,405	64	1,341	96	14	82	15	4	11
Home economics, other	111	9	102	18	2	16	8	2	6
Vocational home economics, total	574	248	326	44	1	43	6	2	4
Child care and guidance management	144	3	141	32	0	32	1	0	1
Custodial, housekeeping and home services workers and managers	1	0	1	0	0	0	0	0	0
Vocational home economics, other	429	245	184	12	1	11	5	2	3
Law and legal studies, total	2,032	595	1,437	2,511	1,680	831	88	62	26
Pre-law studies	214	105	109	0	0	0	0	0	0
Paralegal/legal assistant	1,031	172	859	29	10	19	0	0	0
Law and legal studies, other	787	318	469	2,482	1,670	812	88	62	26
Liberal arts and sciences, general studies, and humanities, total	33,356	13,157	20,199	2,565	924	1,641	90	41	49
Liberal arts and sciences/liberal studies	21,113	7,622	13,491	1,738	625	1,113	30	10	20
Humanities/humanistic studies	2,820	962	1,858	472	185	287	45	25	20
Liberal arts and sciences, general studies, other	9,423	4,573	4,850	355	114	241	15	6	9
Library science, total	50	2	48	5,057	1,054	4,003	55	20	35
Library science/librarianship	49	2	47	4,938	1,034	3,904	54	20	34
Library science, other	1	0	1	119	20	99	1	0	1
Mathematics, total	13,723	7,295	6,428	4,181	2,543	1,638	1,226	955	271
Mathematics	11,988	6,260	5,728	2,440	1,468	972	845	660	185
Applied mathematics, total	930	553	377	747	495	252	155	123	32
Applied mathematics, general and other	701	412	289	386	241	145	110	87	23
Operations research (quantitative methods)	229	141	88	361	254	107	45	36	9
Mathematical statistics	467	279	188	909	528	381	202	155	47
Mathematics, other	338	203	135	85	52	33	24	17	7
Multi/interdisciplinary studies, total	26,033	9,158	16,875	2,457	1,093	1,364	238	129	109
Biological and physical sciences	2,404	1,219	1,185	230	108	122	28	18	10
Systems science and theory	107	63	44	214	109	105	16	9	7
Museology/museum studies	2	0	2	110	20	90	0	0	0
Multi/interdisciplinary studies, other	23,520	7,876	15,644	1,903	856	1,047	194	102	92
Parks, recreation, leisure, and fitness studies, total	12,889	6,724	6,165	1,755	892	863	149	87	62
Parks, recreation and leisure studies	2,187	1,014	1,173	229	97	132	32	20	12
Parks, recreation and leisure facilities management	2,758	1,321	1,437	270	115	155	44	14	30
Health and physical education/fitness	7,679	4,247	3,432	1,243	671	572	67	51	16
Parks, recreation, leisure and fitness studies, other	265	142	123	13	9	4	6	2	4
Philosophy and religion, total	7,276	4,670	2,606	1,380	875	505	507	365	142
Philosophy	4,442	3,019	1,423	654	485	169	289	219	70
Religion/religious studies	2,494	1,455	1,039	639	362	277	212	140	72
Philosophy and religion, other	340	196	144	87	28	59	6	6	0
Physical sciences and science technologies, total	19,177	12,497	6,680	5,753	4,013	1,740	4,483	3,428	1,055
Physical sciences, total	19,057	12,424	6,633	5,718	3,986	1,732	4,478	3,423	1,055
Physical sciences, general	413	268	145	36	27	9	1	1	0
Astronomy	121	83	38	86	60	26	96	77	19
Astrophysics	48	34	14	33	28	5	16	12	4
Atmospheric science and meteorology	444	362	82	203	152	51	83	69	14
Chemistry, total	9,722	5,666	4,056	2,099	1,216	883	2,273	1,561	712
Chemistry, general	9,457	5,500	3,957	1,956	1,140	816	2,080	1,421	659
Analytical chemistry	6	2	4	16	10	6	14	12	2
Inorganic chemistry	0	0	0	3	2	1	4	1	3
Organic chemistry	11	5	6	22	12	10	13	11	2
Medicinal/pharmaceutical chemistry	16	7	9	37	17	20	62	42	20
Chemistry, other	232	152	80	65	35	30	100	74	26
Geological and related sciences, total	3,118	1,993	1,125	993	697	296	398	312	86
Geology	2,856	1,821	1,035	853	600	253	325	255	70
Geochemistry	14	6	8	4	3	1	2	1	1
Geophysics and seismology	65	46	19	75	55	20	51	41	10
Geological and related sciences, other	183	120	63	61	39	22	20	15	5
Miscellaneous physical sciences, total	1,020	652	368	397	249	148	150	114	36
Metallurgy	0	0	0	11	10	1	2	2	0
Oceanography	214	136	78	138	91	47	79	59	20
Earth and planetary sciences	700	462	238	149	92	57	62	48	14
Miscellaneous physical sciences, other	106	54	52	99	56	43	7	5	2
Physics, total	3,823	3,151	672	1,817	1,527	290	1,424	1,251	173

Table 253.—Bachelor's, master's, and doctor's degrees conferred by institutions of higher education, by sex of student and field of study: 1994–95—Continued

Field of study	Bachelor's degrees requiring 4 or 5 years			Master's degrees			Doctor's degrees (Ph.D., Ed.D., etc.)		
	Total	Men	Women	Total	Men	Women	Total	Men	Women
1	2	3	4	5	6	7	8	9	10
Physics, general	3,669	3,018	651	1,677	1,410	267	1,338	1,179	159
Physics, other	154	133	21	140	117	23	86	72	14
Physical sciences, other	348	215	133	54	30	24	37	26	11
Science technologies, total	120	73	47	35	27	8	5	5	0
Precision production trades, total	353	247	106	5	4	1	0	0	0
Drafting, general	121	94	27	0	0	0	0	0	0
Precision production trades, other	232	153	79	5	4	1	0	0	0
Protective services, total	24,157	15,049	9,108	1,706	912	794	26	14	12
Criminal justice and corrections, total	23,828	14,759	9,069	1,672	882	790	26	14	12
Corrections/correctional administration	609	301	308	85	53	32	0	0	0
Criminal justice/law enforcement administration	8,062	5,075	2,987	673	400	273	0	0	0
Criminal justice studies	12,393	7,513	4,880	788	359	429	26	14	12
Forensic studies	28	11	17	51	29	22	0	0	0
Law enforcement/police science	1,719	1,283	436	67	35	32	0	0	0
Criminal justice, other	1,017	576	441	8	6	2	0	0	0
Fire control and safety	224	214	10	29	26	3	0	0	0
Protective services, other	105	76	29	5	4	1	0	0	0
Psychology, total	72,083	19,548	52,535	13,921	3,893	10,028	3,822	1,431	2,391
Psychology, general	67,954	18,469	49,485	4,788	1,453	3,335	1,616	642	974
Clinical psychology	66	12	54	1,477	350	1,127	1,413	493	920
Counseling psychology	256	60	196	4,221	1,087	3,134	296	107	189
Developmental and child psychology	712	77	635	113	14	99	46	9	37
Experimental psychology	219	65	154	88	40	48	57	24	33
Industrial and organizational psychology	109	29	80	952	421	531	65	33	32
Physiological psychology/psychobiology	184	60	124	3	1	2	24	12	12
Social psychology	500	136	364	120	31	89	48	18	30
School psychology	0	0	0	886	174	712	107	38	69
Psychology, other	2,083	640	1,443	1,273	322	951	150	55	95
Public administration and services, total	18,586	3,935	14,651	23,501	6,870	16,631	556	274	282
Public administration	2,429	1,258	1,171	7,288	3,710	3,578	166	117	49
Community organization, resources and services	1,615	371	1,244	261	92	169	9	3	6
Public policy analysis	375	169	206	846	421	425	110	60	50
Social work	13,720	1,954	11,766	14,658	2,469	12,189	258	86	172
Public affairs, other	447	183	264	448	178	270	13	8	5
R.O.T.C. and military technologies, total	27	24	3	124	117	7	0	0	0
Social sciences and history, total	128,154	68,139	60,015	14,845	8,207	6,638	3,725	2,319	1,406
Social sciences, general	7,185	2,959	4,226	594	263	331	70	28	42
Anthropology	5,675	2,071	3,604	1,024	373	651	373	157	216
Archeology	123	43	80	29	12	17	15	6	9
Criminology	2,384	1,406	978	103	65	38	9	5	4
Demography and population studies	2	0	2	38	12	26	9	6	3
Economics	17,673	12,244	5,429	2,400	1,653	747	910	684	226
Geography, total	4,295	2,930	1,365	807	524	283	152	109	43
Geography	4,254	2,898	1,356	805	522	283	152	109	43
Cartography	41	32	9	2	2	0	0	0	0
History	26,598	16,596	10,002	3,091	1,905	1,186	816	513	303
International relations and affairs	5,486	2,373	3,113	2,138	1,139	999	46	30	16
Political science and government, general	33,013	18,941	14,072	2,019	1,216	803	637	455	182
Sociology	22,886	7,406	15,480	1,748	664	1,084	546	259	287
Urban affairs/studies	648	323	325	303	146	157	56	26	30
Social sciences and history, other	2,186	847	1,339	551	235	316	86	41	45
Theological studies/religious vocations, total	5,578	4,201	1,377	5,240	3,178	2,062	1,591	1,375	216
Biblical and other theological languages and literatures	23	22	1	70	37	33	8	8	0
Bible/biblical studies	1,713	1,332	381	316	258	58	40	38	2
Missions/missionary studies and misology	275	171	104	230	139	91	52	52	0
Religious education	928	538	390	1,015	545	470	55	42	13
Religious/sacred music	179	91	88	142	85	57	13	11	2
Theology/theological studies	2,038	1,746	292	2,572	1,659	913	960	848	112
Pastoral counseling and specialized ministries	167	128	39	595	264	331	257	200	57
Theological studies and religious vocations, other	255	173	82	300	191	109	206	176	30
Transportation and material moving workers, total	3,698	3,297	401	823	775	48	0	0	0
Air transportation workers	3,595	3,205	390	819	771	48	0	0	0
Water transportation workers	88	81	7	0	0	0	0	0	0
Transportation and material moving, other	15	11	4	4	4	0	0	0	0

Table 253.—Bachelor's, master's, and doctor's degrees conferred by institutions of higher education, by sex of student and field of study: 1994–95—Continued

Field of study	Bachelor's degrees requiring 4 or 5 years			Master's degrees			Doctor's degrees (Ph.D., Ed.D., etc.)		
	Total	Men	Women	Total	Men	Women	Total	Men	Women
1	2	3	4	5	6	7	8	9	10
Visual and performing arts, total	48,690	19,781	28,909	10,277	4,374	5,903	1,080	545	535
Visual and performing arts, general	1,327	499	828	130	50	80	17	7	10
Crafts, folk art, and artisanry	116	33	83	10	3	7	0	0	0
Dance	864	73	791	182	31	151	10	0	10
Design and applied art	7,893	3,145	4,748	536	225	311	1	1	0
Dramatic/theater arts and stagecraft	6,212	2,547	3,665	1,422	680	742	95	47	48
Film/video and photographic arts, total	2,715	1,679	1,036	632	350	282	10	7	3
Film-video making/cinematography and production	1,036	694	342	248	137	111	4	3	1
Photography	907	472	435	183	90	93	1	1	0
Film arts, other	772	513	259	201	123	78	5	3	2
Fine arts and art studies, total	20,428	7,226	13,202	3,284	1,178	2,106	185	66	119
Art, general	11,522	4,278	7,244	1,019	414	605	35	14	21
Art history, criticism and conservation	4,642	1,289	3,353	1,097	318	779	149	52	97
Arts management	83	19	64	131	28	103	1	0	1
Painting	734	315	419	207	90	117	0	0	0
Ceramic arts and ceramics	200	69	131	43	18	25	0	0	0
Fiber, textile and weaving arts	99	5	94	45	6	39	0	0	0
Metal and jewelry arts	73	15	58	12	3	9	0	0	0
Fine arts and art studies, other	3,075	1,236	1,839	730	301	429	0	0	0
Music, total	8,510	4,337	4,173	3,565	1,677	1,888	738	409	329
Music, general	4,372	2,064	2,308	1,173	534	639	326	184	142
Music history and literature	53	17	36	41	16	25	28	13	15
Music, general performance	2,674	1,310	1,364	1,787	847	940	257	135	122
Music theory and composition	362	292	70	162	114	48	65	48	17
Music, other	1,049	654	395	402	166	236	62	29	33
Visual and performing arts, other	625	242	383	516	180	336	24	8	16
Not classified by field of study	1,346	957	389	577	475	102	19	18	1

NOTE.—Aggregations by field of study derived from the *Classification of Instructional Programs* developed by the National Center for Education Statistics.

SOURCE: U.S. Department of Education, National Center for Education Statistics, Integrated Postsecondary Education Data System (IPEDS), "Completions" survey. (This table was prepared March 1997.)

Table 254.—Bachelor's, master's, and doctor's degrees conferred by institutions of higher education, by sex of student and field of study: 1993–94

Field of study	Bachelor's degrees requiring 4 or 5 years			Master's degrees			Doctor's degrees (Ph.D., Ed.D., etc.)		
	Total	Men	Women	Total	Men	Women	Total	Men	Women
1	2	3	4	5	6	7	8	9	10
All fields	1,169,275	532,422	636,853	387,070	176,085	210,985	43,185	26,552	16,633
Agriculture and natural resources, total	18,070	11,748	6,322	4,119	2,515	1,604	1,278	982	296
Agricultural business and production, total	4,959	3,611	1,348	703	487	216	206	170	36
Agricultural business and management, total	3,370	2,505	865	543	376	167	166	143	23
Agricultural business and management, general	816	556	260	54	35	19	0	0	0
Agricultural business/agribusiness operations	1,005	779	226	21	11	10	0	0	0
Agricultural economics	1,368	1,018	350	454	321	133	166	143	23
Agricultural business and management, other	181	152	29	14	9	5	0	0	0
Agricultural mechanization	244	229	15	9	7	2	1	1	0
Agricultural production workers and managers	140	106	34	59	51	8	12	8	4
Horticulture service operations and management	466	335	131	23	10	13	16	12	4
International agriculture	18	11	7	19	7	12	0	0	0
Agricultural business and production, other	721	425	296	50	36	14	13	6	5
Agricultural sciences, total	6,432	3,750	2,682	1,595	951	644	789	594	195
Agriculture/agricultural sciences, general	936	696	240	151	108	43	2	0	2
Animal sciences, total	3,165	1,511	1,654	441	268	173	226	168	58
Animal sciences, general	2,641	1,251	1,390	339	203	136	159	118	41
Agricultural animal breeding and genetics	32	12	20	10	7	3	15	14	1
Agricultural animal health	14	4	10	4	2	2	0	0	0
Agricultural animal nutrition	0	0	0	9	6	3	10	8	2
Dairy science	109	71	38	22	13	9	3	2	1
Poultry science	121	92	29	20	15	5	17	14	3
Animal sciences, other	248	81	167	37	22	15	22	12	10
Food sciences and technology	448	187	261	329	122	207	148	81	67
Plant sciences, total	1,557	1,158	399	519	355	164	344	289	55
Plant sciences, general	242	180	62	61	42	19	34	29	5
Agronomy and crop science	526	458	68	234	167	67	195	171	24
Horticulture science	552	347	205	129	77	52	62	49	13
Plant breeding and genetics	0	0	0	10	7	3	8	7	1
Agricultural plant pathology	0	0	0	2	0	2	8	6	2
Plant protection (pest management)	16	13	3	16	12	4	1	1	0
Range science and management	162	116	46	49	38	11	20	12	8
Plant sciences, other	59	44	15	18	12	6	16	14	2
Soil sciences	129	95	34	71	47	24	57	48	9
Agriculture/agricultural sciences, other	197	103	94	84	51	33	12	8	4
Conservation and renewable natural resources, total	6,679	4,387	2,292	1,821	1,077	744	283	218	65
Natural resources conservation, general	3,333	1,955	1,378	925	514	411	80	57	23
Natural resources management and policy	375	256	119	89	54	35	1	1	0
Fishing and fisheries sciences and management	215	171	44	90	53	37	27	22	5
Forest harvesting and production technology/technician	218	163	55	25	21	4	15	14	1
Forestry, general	1,187	955	232	522	326	196	123	97	26
Wildlife and wildlands management	957	654	303	123	86	37	18	14	4
Conservation and renewable natural resources, other	394	233	161	47	23	24	19	13	6
Architecture and related programs, total	8,975	5,764	3,211	3,943	2,428	1,515	161	111	50
Architecture	5,141	3,617	1,524	2,031	1,376	655	53	42	11
City/urban, community, and regional planning	567	402	165	1,240	710	530	86	55	31
Architectural environmental design	717	458	259	49	17	32	2	2	0
Interior architecture	902	129	773	11	2	9	0	0	0
Landscape architecture	1,045	748	297	378	181	197	2	2	0
Architectural urban design and planning	29	18	11	62	43	19	3	1	2
Architecture and related programs, other	574	392	182	172	99	73	15	9	6
Area, ethnic, and cultural studies, total	5,573	1,958	3,615	1,633	768	865	155	75	80
Area studies, total	3,931	1,513	2,418	1,207	565	642	123	60	63
African studies	24	5	19	14	4	10	2	1	1
American studies/civilization	1,587	569	1,018	244	95	149	76	35	41
Latin American studies	406	153	253	252	116	136	7	1	6
Middle Eastern studies	96	40	56	94	51	43	18	10	8
Russian and Slavic studies	264	107	157	119	58	61	0	0	0
Asian studies	842	388	454	292	149	143	11	9	2
European studies	266	86	180	80	35	45	3	0	3
Area studies, other	446	165	281	112	57	55	6	4	2
Ethnic and cultural studies, total	1,435	369	1,066	264	96	168	26	13	13
Afro-American (black) studies	492	175	317	79	36	43	6	3	3
Hispanic-American studies	128	42	86	12	3	9	0	0	0
Women's studies	479	11	468	52	0	52	5	0	5
Ethnic studies, other	336	141	195	121	57	64	15	10	5
Area, ethnic and cultural studies, other	207	76	131	162	107	55	6	2	4
Biological sciences/life sciences, total	51,383	25,050	26,333	5,196	2,465	2,731	4,534	2,690	1,844
Biology, general	38,103	18,252	19,851	2,178	1,033	1,145	665	392	273

Table 254.—Bachelor's, master's, and doctor's degrees conferred by institutions of higher education, by sex of student and field of study: 1993–94—Continued

Field of study	Bachelor's degrees requiring 4 or 5 years			Master's degrees			Doctor's degrees (Ph.D., Ed.D., etc.)		
	Total	Men	Women	Total	Men	Women	Total	Men	Women
1	2	3	4	5	6	7	8	9	10
Biochemistry and biophysics	2,570	1,420	1,150	276	147	129	659	392	267
Botany, total	303	138	165	220	122	98	264	173	91
Botany, general	283	128	155	129	69	60	136	85	51
Plant pathology	6	3	3	73	46	27	80	56	24
Botany, other	14	7	7	18	7	11	48	32	16
Cell and molecular biology, total	1,574	839	735	170	72	98	444	250	194
Cell biology	170	77	93	60	23	37	127	68	59
Molecular biology	544	296	248	64	30	34	205	113	92
Cell and molecular biology, other	860	466	394	46	19	27	112	69	43
Microbiology/bacteriology	1,841	916	925	332	139	193	478	273	205
Miscellaneous biological specializations, total	2,444	1,143	1,301	1,149	473	676	1,036	586	450
Anatomy	20	13	7	72	34	38	111	59	52
Ecology	659	354	305	185	102	83	90	57	33
Marine/aquatic biology	613	289	324	89	50	39	41	30	11
Neurosciences	139	69	70	72	37	35	167	101	66
Nutritional sciences	346	75	271	266	32	234	111	40	71
Toxicology	63	35	28	64	33	31	67	32	35
Genetics, plant and animal	203	99	104	136	54	82	241	153	88
Biometrics	18	10	8	25	14	11	19	13	6
Miscellaneous specialized areas, other	383	199	184	240	117	123	189	101	88
Zoology, total	3,207	1,688	1,519	749	420	329	805	515	290
Zoology, general	2,592	1,354	1,238	278	158	120	156	109	47
Entomology	83	59	24	135	82	53	123	95	28
Pathology, human and animal	15	2	13	36	15	21	93	55	38
Pharmacology, human and animal	44	24	20	59	30	29	211	116	95
Physiology, human and animal	465	244	221	241	135	106	222	140	82
Zoology, other	8	5	3	0	0	0	0	0	0
Biological sciences/life sciences, other	1,341	654	687	122	59	63	183	109	74
Business management, administrative services and marketing operations/marketing and distribution, total	246,654	129,161	117,493	93,437	59,335	34,102	1,364	980	384
Business management and administrative services, total	240,864	126,891	113,973	92,759	58,950	33,809	1,356	979	377
Business, general	25,572	13,746	11,826	13,191	8,594	4,597	232	174	58
Business administration and management, total	87,395	46,166	41,229	51,833	33,574	18,259	714	535	179
Office supervision and management	1,040	122	918	0	0	0	0	0	0
Operations management and supervision	1,993	1,428	565	506	370	136	16	11	5
Business administration and management, other	84,362	44,616	39,746	51,327	33,204	18,123	698	524	174
Accounting	47,804	21,446	26,358	4,162	2,258	1,904	63	34	29
Secretarial and related programs	594	152	442	1	0	1	0	0	0
Business/managerial economics	3,454	2,274	1,180	251	159	92	47	34	13
Small business management and ownership	399	258	141	57	40	17	0	0	0
Finance, general and banking and financial support services	21,465	14,593	6,872	4,903	3,470	1,433	64	53	11
Actuarial sciences	371	227	144	82	53	29	0	0	0
Insurance and risk management	600	382	218	66	41	25	7	4	3
Investments and securities and financial planning	353	212	141	260	198	62	0	0	0
Hospitality services management	5,910	2,662	3,248	421	211	210	2	1	1
Human resources management	4,960	1,953	3,007	2,195	980	1,215	29	17	12
Labor/personnel relations and studies	1,061	544	517	810	333	477	23	14	9
Organizational behavior studies	989	464	525	302	116	186	29	12	17
International business	2,875	1,325	1,550	3,000	1,878	1,122	21	18	3
Business information systems, total	5,839	3,474	2,365	2,140	1,429	711	13	7	6
Management information systems and data processing, general	5,434	3,221	2,213	1,877	1,239	638	13	7	6
Business information systems, other	405	253	152	263	190	73	0	0	0
Quantitative methods and management science, total	1,846	1,031	815	990	634	356	36	31	5
Business statistics	51	23	28	30	15	15	5	4	1
Management science, other	1,795	1,008	787	960	619	341	31	27	4
Marketing management and research	24,692	13,312	11,380	1,891	1,026	865	38	17	21
Real estate	558	416	142	317	261	56	1	1	0
Taxation	0	0	0	1,396	873	523	0	0	0
Consumer and personal services	155	98	57	0	0	0	0	0	0
Business management and administrative services, other	3,972	2,156	1,816	4,491	2,822	1,669	37	27	10
Marketing operations/marketing and distribution, total	5,790	2,270	3,520	678	385	293	8	1	7
Apparel and accessories marketing operations	1,383	59	1,324	0	1	2	6	0	6
Business and personal services marketing operations	456	247	209	9	2	7	0	0	0
General/retailing and wholesaling operations and skills	3,132	1,506	1,626	440	226	214	2	1	1
Transportation and travel marketing	173	44	129	12	3	9	0	0	0
Marketing and distribution, other	646	414	232	214	153	61	0	0	0
Communications and communications technologies, total	51,827	21,359	30,468	5,419	2,098	3,321	345	174	171
Communications, total	51,164	21,023	30,141	5,005	1,870	3,135	337	172	165
Communications, general	24,496	9,783	14,713	1,822	636	1,186	215	108	107
Advertising	2,773	1,095	1,678	256	90	166	4	2	2
Journalism	10,214	3,718	6,496	1,432	517	915	28	19	9
Broadcast journalism	630	258	372	16	7	9	0	0	0

280 HIGHER EDUCATION: DEGREES

Table 254.—Bachelor's, master's, and doctor's degrees conferred by institutions of higher education, by sex of student and field of study: 1993–94—Continued

Field of study	Bachelor's degrees requiring 4 or 5 years			Master's degrees			Doctor's degrees (Ph.D., Ed.D., etc.)		
	Total	Men	Women	Total	Men	Women	Total	Men	Women
1	2	3	4	5	6	7	8	9	10
Public relations and organizational communications	2,393	779	1,614	240	58	182	0	0	0
Radio and television broadcasting	5,883	3,246	2,637	383	183	200	10	6	4
Communications, other	4,775	2,144	2,631	856	379	477	80	37	43
Communications technologies, total	663	336	327	414	228	186	8	2	6
Photographic technology	11	5	6	0	0	0	0	0	0
Radio and television technology	575	292	283	317	165	152	8	2	6
Communications technologies, other	77	39	38	97	63	34	0	0	0
Computer and information sciences, total	24,200	17,317	6,883	10,416	7,724	2,692	810	685	125
Computer and information sciences, general	15,411	11,302	4,109	7,533	5,687	1,846	652	555	97
Computer programming	175	122	53	23	19	4	0	0	0
Data processing technology/technician	222	139	83	0	0	0	1	1	0
Information science and systems	3,947	2,500	1,447	1,305	832	473	23	13	10
Computer systems analysis	301	206	95	51	43	8	12	10	2
Computer and information sciences, other	4,144	3,048	1,096	1,504	1,143	361	122	106	16
Education, total	107,600	24,450	83,150	98,938	23,008	75,930	6,908	2,706	4,202
Education, general	1,617	266	1,351	10,553	2,537	8,016	1,232	440	792
Bilingual/bicultural education	54	6	48	264	46	218	13	2	11
Curriculum and instruction	7	2	5	8,246	1,552	6,694	775	253	522
Education administration and supervision, total	9	3	6	10,892	4,290	6,602	2,187	988	1,199
Education administration and supervision, general	2	0	2	7,339	2,947	4,392	1,562	733	829
Administration of special education	0	0	0	5	1	4	8	0	8
Adult and continuing education administration	3	1	2	133	32	101	72	29	43
Educational supervision	0	0	0	683	200	483	30	6	24
Elementary, middle, and secondary education administration	3	1	2	1,498	626	872	44	23	21
Higher education administration	1	1	0	544	196	348	340	141	199
Community and junior college education administration	0	0	0	86	38	48	6	4	2
Education administration and supervision, other	0	0	0	604	250	354	125	52	73
Educational/instructional media design	35	20	15	957	261	696	60	26	34
Educational evaluation and research, general	30	8	22	38	11	27	14	4	10
Educational statistics and research methods	2	0	2	54	37	17	28	14	14
Educational assessment, testing and measurement	0	0	0	98	21	77	28	12	16
Social and philosophical foundations of education	3	3	0	262	54	208	131	55	76
Special education, total	9,099	729	8,370	10,497	1,423	9,074	194	34	160
Special education, general	6,085	528	5,557	8,284	1,158	7,126	184	31	153
Education of the deaf and hearing impaired	222	8	214	238	25	213	0	0	0
Education of the gifted and talented	4	0	4	135	14	121	0	0	0
Education of the emotionally handicapped	329	43	286	239	47	192	0	0	0
Education of the mentally handicapped	691	37	654	154	24	130	0	0	0
Education of the multiple handicapped	125	7	118	187	20	167	1	0	1
Education of the physically handicapped	21	2	19	62	5	57	0	0	0
Education of the blind and visually handicapped	32	0	32	40	5	35	0	0	0
Education of the specific learning disabled	649	58	591	602	66	536	3	1	2
Education of the speech impaired	673	19	654	224	4	220	0	0	0
Special education, other	268	27	241	332	55	277	6	2	4
Counselor education/counseling and guidance services	36	7	29	12,217	2,664	9,553	364	129	235
General teacher education, total	61,017	6,699	54,318	22,877	3,808	19,069	402	129	273
Adult and continuing education	89	20	69	880	224	656	134	55	79
Elementary education	48,733	4,642	44,091	12,958	1,444	11,514	91	19	72
Junior high/intermediate/middle school education	1,378	298	1,080	653	98	555	0	0	0
Pre-elementary/early childhood/kindergarten education	6,474	164	6,310	1,996	41	1,955	31	1	30
Secondary education	3,746	1,537	2,209	3,986	1,467	2,519	56	21	35
Teacher education, general programs, other	597	38	559	2,404	534	1,870	90	33	57
Teacher education, academic and vocational programs	34,428	16,229	18,199	16,106	4,935	11,171	832	397	435
Agricultural education (vocational)	470	312	158	222	131	91	50	38	12
Art education	1,535	336	1,199	650	118	532	20	5	15
Business education (vocational)	1,434	360	1,074	456	122	334	11	5	6
Driver and safety education	46	38	8	56	42	14	0	0	0
English education	2,904	609	2,295	683	144	539	15	7	8
Foreign languages education	361	64	297	279	55	224	24	8	16
Health education	1,547	413	1,134	808	151	657	116	42	74
Home economics education (vocational)	318	6	312	112	4	108	8	0	8
Technology/industrial arts education	1,502	1,252	250	493	343	150	30	20	10
Marketing operations/marketing and distribution education	92	32	60	16	6	10	1	0	1
Mathematics education	1,914	741	1,173	846	272	574	31	14	17
Music education	2,771	1,172	1,599	838	322	516	74	31	43
Physical education and coaching	11,888	6,998	4,890	2,994	1,544	1,450	154	92	62
Reading education	161	13	148	3,869	179	3,690	78	12	66
Science education	1,102	469	633	720	289	431	48	27	21
Social science education	850	426	424	132	65	67	1	1	0
Social studies education	2,088	1,229	859	501	282	219	3	1	2
Technical education (vocational)	209	134	75	267	106	161	42	24	18
Trade and industrial education (vocational)	1,014	714	300	391	172	219	74	44	30
Teacher education, academic and vocational programs, other	2,222	911	1,311	1,773	588	1,185	52	26	26

Table 254.—Bachelor's, master's, and doctor's degrees conferred by institutions of higher education, by sex of student and field of study: 1993–94—Continued

Field of study	Bachelor's degrees requiring 4 or 5 years			Master's degrees			Doctor's degrees (Ph.D., Ed.D., etc.)		
	Total	Men	Women	Total	Men	Women	Total	Men	Women
1	2	3	4	5	6	7	8	9	10
Teaching English as a second language/foreign language	45	15	30	1,548	334	1,214	6	1	5
Education, other	1,218	463	755	4,329	1,035	3,294	642	222	420
Engineering and engineering-related technologies, total	78,225	66,597	11,628	29,754	25,154	4,600	5,979	5,315	664
Engineering, total	62,220	52,035	10,185	28,621	24,218	4,403	5,963	5,299	664
Engineering, general	2,015	1,670	345	1,391	1,171	220	233	204	29
Aerospace, aeronautical, and astronautical engineering	2,330	2,035	295	1,038	938	100	220	209	11
Agricultural engineering	519	440	79	150	121	29	87	77	10
Architectural engineering	525	418	107	36	31	5	1	1	0
Bioengineering and biomedical engineering	719	481	238	489	349	140	168	128	40
Ceramic sciences and engineering	240	188	52	92	67	25	57	51	6
Chemical engineering	5,163	3,588	1,575	1,032	785	247	604	510	94
Civil engineering	9,479	7,776	1,703	3,873	3,199	674	651	582	69
Computer engineering	2,237	1,944	293	1,071	893	178	123	109	14
Electrical, electronics, and communications engineering	15,823	13,892	1,931	7,791	6,820	971	1,470	1,331	139
Engineering mechanics	128	111	17	172	155	17	92	87	5
Engineering physics	293	260	33	70	63	7	38	34	4
Engineering science	268	218	50	295	257	38	50	45	5
Environmental/environmental health engineering	434	296	138	985	716	269	46	34	12
Geological engineering	143	100	43	57	45	12	12	11	1
Geophysical engineering	11	7	4	9	7	2	4	4	0
Industrial/manufacturing engineering	3,122	2,207	915	2,096	1,701	395	253	215	38
Material engineering	532	416	116	569	452	117	347	289	58
Mechanical engineering	15,030	13,327	1,703	4,099	3,700	399	887	825	62
Metallurgical engineering	250	209	41	172	139	33	83	73	10
Mining and mineral engineering	118	107	11	57	49	8	21	20	1
Naval architecture and marine engineering	307	287	20	23	22	1	5	5	0
Nuclear engineering	256	228	28	255	220	35	94	84	10
Ocean engineering	127	97	30	125	108	17	31	29	2
Petroleum engineering	316	275	41	167	155	12	45	38	7
Systems engineering	420	336	84	404	328	76	39	33	6
Textile sciences and engineering	72	45	27	32	24	8	1	1	0
Engineering, other	1,343	1,077	266	2,071	1,703	368	301	270	31
Engineering-related technologies, total	16,005	14,562	1,443	1,133	936	197	16	16	0
Architectural engineering technologies	670	603	67	0	0	0	0	0	0
Civil technologies	482	443	39	0	0	0	0	0	0
Electrical and electronic technologies	4,142	3,869	273	77	65	12	0	0	0
Electromechanical instrumentation and maintenance technologies	202	188	14	6	6	0	8	8	0
Environmental control technologies	263	212	51	53	35	18	0	0	0
Industrial production technologies	4,134	3,651	483	304	248	56	5	5	0
Quality control and safety technologies	554	464	90	301	246	55	0	0	0
Mechanical and related technologies	1,750	1,656	94	2	2	0	0	0	0
Mining and petroleum technologies	20	20	0	0	0	0	0	0	0
Surveying	131	118	13	25	22	3	3	3	0
Mechanics and repairers	107	106	1	0	0	0	0	0	0
Construction trades	75	70	5	0	0	0	0	0	0
Engineering and related technologies, other	3,475	3,162	313	365	312	53	0	0	0
English language and literature/letters, total	53,924	18,425	35,499	7,885	2,712	5,173	1,344	568	776
English language and literature, general	40,497	13,426	27,071	5,375	1,842	3,533	946	406	540
Comparative literature	774	211	563	274	92	182	139	56	83
English composition	331	138	193	21	4	17	4	0	4
English creative writing	903	424	479	835	360	475	7	4	3
American literature (United States)	59	18	41	16	6	10	4	2	2
English literature (British and Commonwealth)	1,368	483	885	372	110	262	74	32	42
Speech and rhetorical studies	8,637	3,272	5,365	725	210	515	128	54	74
English technical and business writing	156	52	104	142	44	98	0	0	0
English language and literature/letters, other	1,199	401	798	125	44	81	42	14	28
Foreign languages and literatures, total	14,378	4,304	10,074	3,288	1,087	2,201	886	355	531
Foreign languages and literatures, total	1,463	398	1,065	970	316	654	252	108	144
Foreign languages and literatures, general	852	225	627	321	85	236	63	22	41
Linguistics	611	173	438	649	231	418	189	86	103
East and Southeast Asian languages and literatures, total	546	276	270	138	46	92	32	18	14
Chinese	112	59	53	48	16	32	18	11	7
Japanese	311	149	162	48	10	38	2	0	2
East and Southeast Asian languages, other	123	68	55	42	20	22	12	7	5
East European languages and literatures, total	702	297	405	179	56	123	38	16	22
Russian languages	611	259	352	71	22	49	3	0	3
Slavic languages (other than Russian)	83	36	47	98	30	68	33	15	18
East European languages, other	8	2	6	10	4	6	2	1	1
Germanic languages and literatures, total	1,626	628	998	338	126	212	64	30	34
German	1,580	610	970	298	114	184	61	28	33

Table 254.—Bachelor's, master's, and doctor's degrees conferred by institutions of higher education, by sex of student and field of study: 1993–94—Continued

Field of study	Bachelor's degrees requiring 4 or 5 years			Master's degrees			Doctor's degrees (Ph.D., Ed.D., etc.)		
	Total	Men	Women	Total	Men	Women	Total	Men	Women
1	2	3	4	5	6	7	8	9	10
Scandinavian languages	31	9	22	11	1	10	1	0	1
Germanic languages, other	15	9	6	29	11	18	2	2	0
South Asian languages and literatures	6	2	4	4	1	3	8	6	2
Romance languages and literatures, total	8,981	2,215	6,766	1,307	363	944	358	105	253
French	3,094	587	2,507	479	116	363	104	31	73
Italian	264	67	197	47	13	34	24	10	14
Portuguese	37	18	19	8	3	5	0	0	0
Spanish	5,505	1,516	3,989	691	206	485	160	46	114
Romance languages, other	81	27	54	82	25	57	70	18	52
Middle Eastern languages and literatures, total	72	29	43	56	35	21	15	11	4
Arabic	8	3	5	2	1	1	0	0	0
Hebrew	49	18	31	35	25	10	3	2	1
Middle East languages, other	15	8	7	19	9	10	12	9	3
Classical and ancient Near East languages and literatures, total	756	371	385	193	107	86	77	43	34
Classics	617	298	319	169	98	71	74	40	34
Greek (ancient and medieval)	34	17	17	10	7	3	1	1	0
Latin (ancient and medieval)	105	56	49	14	2	12	2	2	0
Foreign languages, other	226	88	138	103	37	66	42	18	24
Health professions and related sciences, total	74,421	13,062	61,359	28,025	5,814	22,211	1,902	789	1,113
Communication disorders sciences and services	5,405	270	5,135	4,176	211	3,965	94	21	73
Community health liaison	586	120	466	176	41	135	0	0	0
Dentistry	0	0	0	346	251	95	42	32	10
Dental services	915	27	888	42	20	22	0	0	0
Epidemiology	0	0	0	271	106	165	111	43	68
Health services administration, total	3,635	899	2,736	3,525	1,219	2,306	80	30	50
Health services administration	1,815	474	1,341	1,807	683	1,124	47	18	29
Medical records administration	699	93	606	0	0	0	0	0	0
Medical records technology/technician	1	0	1	3	2	1	2	2	0
Health and medical administrative services, other	1,120	332	788	1,715	534	1,181	31	10	21
Health and medical assistants, total	1,015	497	518	178	54	124	0	0	0
Medical assistant	1	0	1	0	0	0	0	0	0
Physician assistant	924	479	445	160	49	111	0	0	0
Health and medical assistants, other	90	18	72	18	5	13	0	0	0
Health and medical diagnostic and treatment services, total	1,459	553	906	95	68	27	2	2	0
Respiratory therapy technology/technician	417	184	233	0	0	0	0	0	0
Health and medical diagnostic and treatment services, other	1,042	369	673	95	68	27	2	2	0
Medical laboratory technologies, total	2,763	856	1,907	481	185	296	80	33	47
Medical technology	2,393	725	1,668	75	26	49	4	3	1
Health and medical laboratory technologies/technicians, other	370	131	239	406	159	247	76	30	46
Pre-dentistry studies	70	46	24	0	0	0	0	0	0
Pre-medicine studies	756	438	318	23	5	18	0	0	0
Pre-pharmacy studies	52	25	27	0	0	0	0	0	0
Pre-veterinary studies	314	101	213	3	1	2	0	0	0
Medical basic sciences	245	94	151	261	136	125	335	201	134
Mental health services, total	546	103	443	384	89	295	31	7	24
Alcohol/drug abuse counseling	69	22	47	62	18	44	1	0	1
Psychiatric/mental health services technician	127	26	101	36	11	25	0	0	0
Clinical and medical social work	119	22	97	103	31	72	30	7	23
Mental health services, other	231	33	198	183	29	154	0	0	0
Nursing	39,076	3,735	35,341	8,991	599	8,392	382	24	358
Optometry	221	95	126	18	4	14	1	1	0
Pharmacy	6,044	2,235	3,809	243	134	109	278	144	134
Rehabilitation/therapeutic services, total	7,169	1,531	5,638	4,433	1,084	3,349	34	15	19
Art therapy	74	1	73	164	9	155	0	0	0
Dance therapy	2	0	2	30	1	29	0	0	0
Music therapy	144	21	123	18	4	14	0	0	0
Occupational therapy	2,652	305	2,347	619	58	561	4	0	4
Orthotics/prosthetics	58	46	12	0	0	0	0	0	0
Physical therapy	3,265	903	2,362	2,583	734	1,849	4	1	3
Recreational therapy	137	28	109	22	2	20	1	0	1
Vocational rehabilitation counseling	155	45	110	640	175	465	8	6	2
Rehabilitative services, other	682	182	500	357	101	256	17	8	9
Veterinary medicine	87	33	54	178	95	83	117	75	42
Miscellaneous health professions	436	205	231	249	122	127	35	23	12
Health professions and related sciences, other	3,627	1,199	2,428	3,952	1,390	2,562	280	138	142
Home economics and vocational home economics, total	15,522	1,933	13,589	2,421	405	2,016	365	93	272
Home economics, total	14,874	1,616	13,258	2,379	401	1,978	361	93	268
Home economics, general	2,801	206	2,595	284	22	262	28	4	24
Home economics business services	155	14	141	1	0	1	0	0	0
Family and community studies	179	23	156	58	10	48	3	1	2
Family and consumer resource management	1,327	437	890	60	5	55	21	3	18
Food and nutrition studies	2,967	391	2,576	519	65	454	55	23	32
Housing studies	583	97	486	18	3	15	2	1	1
Individual and family development studies	5,051	362	4,689	1,295	274	1,021	225	56	169

Table 254.—Bachelor's, master's, and doctor's degrees conferred by institutions of higher education, by sex of student and field of study: 1993–94—Continued

Field of study	Bachelor's degrees requiring 4 or 5 years			Master's degrees			Doctor's degrees (Ph.D., Ed.D., etc.)		
	Total	Men	Women	Total	Men	Women	Total	Men	Women
1	2	3	4	5	6	7	8	9	10
Clothing/apparel and textile studies	1,699	81	1,618	107	19	88	24	4	20
Home economics, other	112	5	107	37	3	34	3	1	2
Vocational home economics, total	648	317	331	42	4	38	4	0	4
Child care and guidance management	148	8	140	40	4	36	3	0	3
Custodial, housekeeping and home services workers and managers	2	1	1	0	0	0	0	0	0
Vocational home economics, other	498	308	190	2	0	2	1	0	1
Law and legal studies, total	2,171	648	1,523	2,432	1,608	824	79	63	16
Pre-law studies	239	120	119	0	0	0	0	0	0
Paralegal/legal assistant	1,028	154	874	97	70	27	36	31	5
Law and legal studies, other	904	374	530	2,335	1,538	797	43	32	11
Liberal arts and sciences, general studies, and humanities, total	33,397	13,117	20,280	2,496	913	1,583	80	46	34
Liberal arts and sciences/liberal studies	20,963	7,597	13,366	1,633	589	1,044	25	12	13
Humanities/humanistic studies	2,796	949	1,847	504	203	301	44	24	20
Liberal arts and sciences, general studies, other	9,638	4,571	5,067	359	121	238	11	10	1
Library science, total	62	5	57	5,116	1,040	4,076	45	14	31
Library science/librarianship	61	5	56	4,995	1,013	3,982	45	14	31
Library science, other	1	0	1	121	27	94	0	0	0
Mathematics, total	14,396	7,735	6,661	4,100	2,536	1,564	1,157	904	253
Mathematics	12,517	6,539	5,978	2,400	1,446	954	818	648	170
Applied mathematics, total	1,012	622	390	770	556	214	147	115	32
Applied mathematics, general and other	787	481	306	352	257	95	115	91	24
Operations research (quantitative methods)	225	141	84	418	299	119	32	24	8
Mathematical statistics	534	343	191	829	480	349	178	131	47
Mathematics, other	333	231	102	101	54	47	14	10	4
Multi/interdisciplinary studies, total	25,167	9,058	16,109	2,464	1,194	1,270	227	151	76
Biological and physical sciences	2,191	1,141	1,050	231	136	95	24	15	9
Systems science and theory	112	72	40	226	150	76	11	10	1
Museology/museum studies	4	1	3	107	21	86	0	0	0
Multi/interdisciplinary studies, other	22,860	7,844	15,016	1,900	887	1,013	192	126	66
Parks, recreation, leisure, and fitness studies, total	11,470	5,823	5,647	1,625	845	780	116	70	46
Parks, recreation and leisure studies	2,197	966	1,231	244	110	134	21	11	10
Parks, recreation and leisure facilities management	2,709	1,287	1,422	234	113	121	18	9	9
Health and physical education/fitness	6,242	3,385	2,857	1,130	612	518	75	48	27
Parks, recreation, leisure and fitness studies, other	322	185	137	17	10	7	2	2	0
Philosophy and religion, total	7,546	4,844	2,702	1,350	837	513	528	383	145
Philosophy	4,691	3,218	1,473	727	508	219	301	217	84
Religion/religious studies	2,486	1,425	1,061	563	315	248	221	162	59
Philosophy and religion, other	369	201	168	60	14	46	6	4	2
Physical sciences and science technologies, total	18,400	12,223	6,177	5,679	4,018	1,661	4,650	3,642	1,008
Physical sciences, total	18,295	12,164	6,131	5,670	4,015	1,655	4,634	3,626	1,008
Physical sciences, general	353	236	117	47	35	12	0	0	0
Astronomy	88	62	26	93	68	25	74	63	11
Astrophysics	75	55	20	36	30	6	26	20	6
Atmospheric science and meteorology	405	329	76	197	150	47	91	74	17
Chemistry, total	9,425	5,591	3,834	1,999	1,173	826	2,353	1,691	662
Chemistry, general	9,138	5,409	3,729	1,850	1,089	761	2,149	1,531	618
Analytical chemistry	0	0	0	26	16	10	14	12	2
Inorganic chemistry	0	0	0	3	3	0	10	8	2
Organic chemistry	8	3	5	17	8	9	16	14	2
Medicinal/pharmaceutical chemistry	8	5	3	31	8	23	55	36	19
Chemistry, other	271	174	97	72	49	23	109	90	19
Geological and related sciences, total	2,677	1,766	911	937	645	292	422	345	77
Geology	2,482	1,639	843	798	549	249	344	283	61
Geochemistry	8	5	3	3	3	0	5	5	0
Geophysics and seismology	50	35	15	62	45	17	53	44	9
Geological and related sciences, other	137	87	50	74	48	26	20	13	7
Miscellaneous physical sciences, total	852	596	256	357	246	111	166	121	45
Metallurgy	2	0	2	7	6	1	1	1	0
Oceanography	197	142	55	148	99	49	77	58	19
Earth and planetary sciences	582	425	157	136	100	36	78	59	19
Miscellaneous physical sciences, other	71	29	42	66	41	25	10	3	7
Physics, total	4,001	3,292	709	1,945	1,650	295	1,465	1,285	180
Physics, general	3,717	3,063	654	1,791	1,518	273	1,321	1,156	165

Table 254.—Bachelor's, master's, and doctor's degrees conferred by institutions of higher education, by sex of student and field of study: 1993–94—Continued

Field of study	Bachelor's degrees requiring 4 or 5 years			Master's degrees			Doctor's degrees (Ph.D., Ed.D., etc.)		
	Total	Men	Women	Total	Men	Women	Total	Men	Women
1	2	3	4	5	6	7	8	9	10
Physics, other	284	229	55	154	132	22	144	129	15
Physical sciences, other	419	237	182	59	18	41	37	27	10
Science technologies, total	105	59	46	9	3	6	16	16	0
Precision production trades, total	420	308	112	2	0	2	0	0	0
Drafting, general	145	125	20	0	0	0	0	0	0
Precision production trades, other	275	183	92	2	0	2	0	0	0
Protective services, total	23,009	14,169	8,840	1,437	902	535	25	14	11
Criminal justice and corrections, total	22,745	13,920	8,825	1,405	871	534	25	14	11
Corrections/correctional administration	705	388	317	50	36	14	0	0	0
Criminal justice/law enforcement administration	7,267	4,490	2,777	539	340	199	0	0	0
Criminal justice studies	11,702	6,959	4,743	678	426	252	25	14	11
Forensic studies	158	96	62	56	30	26	0	0	0
Law enforcement/police science	1,799	1,317	482	53	28	25	0	0	0
Criminal justice, other	1,114	670	444	29	11	18	0	0	0
Fire control and safety	229	221	8	22	21	1	0	0	0
Protective services, other	35	28	7	10	10	0	0	0	0
Psychology, total	69,259	18,642	50,617	12,181	3,401	8,780	3,563	1,346	2,217
Psychology, general	65,559	17,662	47,897	4,644	1,432	3,212	1,618	652	966
Clinical psychology	48	10	38	1,368	366	1,002	1,206	413	793
Counseling psychology	261	58	203	3,560	871	2,689	296	111	185
Developmental and child psychology	755	77	678	116	25	91	56	12	44
Experimental psychology	227	61	166	97	41	56	65	30	35
Industrial and organizational psychology	134	33	101	352	116	236	45	18	27
Physiological psychology/psychobiology	189	70	119	2	0	2	22	6	16
Social psychology	240	54	186	99	31	68	35	15	20
School psychology	0	0	0	702	130	572	87	37	50
Psychology, other	1,846	617	1,229	1,241	389	852	133	52	81
Public administration and services, total	17,815	3,919	13,896	21,833	6,406	15,427	519	238	281
Public administration	2,600	1,335	1,265	6,698	3,421	3,277	148	98	50
Community organization, resources and services	1,339	314	1,025	265	91	174	5	0	5
Public policy analysis	424	211	213	777	402	375	80	51	29
Social work	13,016	1,853	11,163	13,738	2,353	11,385	259	79	180
Public affairs, other	436	206	230	355	139	216	27	10	17
R.O.T.C. and military technologies, total	19	16	3	124	117	7	0	0	0
Social sciences and history, total	133,680	72,006	61,674	14,561	8,152	6,409	3,627	2,317	1,310
Social sciences, general	7,375	3,122	4,253	527	226	301	69	37	32
Anthropology	5,502	2,009	3,493	962	371	591	383	179	204
Archeology	120	43	77	27	8	19	21	8	13
Criminology	2,181	1,272	909	102	61	41	12	8	4
Demography and population studies	2	1	1	34	15	19	12	9	3
Economics	19,496	13,747	5,749	2,521	1,697	824	869	660	209
Geography, total	4,449	3,011	1,438	723	481	242	141	105	36
Geography	4,401	2,971	1,430	720	479	241	141	105	36
Cartography	48	40	8	3	2	1	0	0	0
History	27,503	17,260	10,243	3,009	1,824	1,185	752	472	280
International relations and affairs	5,860	2,547	3,313	1,995	1,089	906	85	67	18
Political science and government, general	36,097	20,741	15,356	2,147	1,348	799	616	438	178
Sociology	22,368	7,114	15,254	1,639	636	1,003	530	261	269
Urban affairs/studies	709	366	343	377	183	194	58	30	28
Social sciences and history, other	2,018	773	1,245	498	213	285	79	43	36
Theological studies/religious vocations, total	5,434	4,125	1,309	4,956	3,034	1,922	1,448	1,235	213
Biblical and other theological languages and literatures	57	53	4	50	20	30	8	7	1
Bible/biblical studies	1,390	1,086	304	285	239	46	34	31	3
Missions/missionary studies and misology	323	190	133	189	126	63	37	37	0
Religious education	923	546	377	964	550	414	52	36	16
Religious/sacred music	156	88	68	138	88	50	9	7	2
Theology/theological studies	2,121	1,826	295	2,396	1,521	875	921	797	124
Pastoral counseling and specialized ministries	163	124	39	560	236	324	205	172	33
Theological studies and religious vocations, other	301	212	89	374	254	120	182	148	34
Transportation and material moving workers, total	3,923	3,500	423	664	610	54	0	0	0
Air transportation workers	3,594	3,202	392	657	603	54	0	0	0
Water transportation workers	305	278	27	0	0	0	0	0	0
Transportation and material moving, other	24	20	4	7	7	0	0	0	0
Visual and performing arts, total	49,053	19,538	29,515	9,925	4,229	5,696	1,054	585	469

Table 254.—Bachelor's, master's, and doctor's degrees conferred by institutions of higher education, by sex of student and field of study: 1993–94—Continued

Field of study	Bachelor's degrees requiring 4 or 5 years			Master's degrees			Doctor's degrees (Ph.D., Ed.D., etc.)		
	Total	Men	Women	Total	Men	Women	Total	Men	Women
1	2	3	4	5	6	7	8	9	10
Visual and performing arts, general	1,571	676	895	114	45	69	9	5	4
Crafts, folk art, and artisanry	108	32	76	8	5	3	0	0	0
Dance	813	75	738	184	24	160	14	2	12
Design and applied art	8,077	3,148	4,929	462	188	274	1	0	1
Dramatic/theater arts and stagecraft	6,117	2,452	3,665	1,283	607	676	104	55	49
Film/video and photographic arts, total	2,652	1,641	1,011	583	331	252	12	8	4
Film-video making/cinematography and production	918	634	284	244	133	111	4	2	2
Photography	961	495	466	151	86	65	1	1	0
Film arts, other	773	512	261	188	112	76	7	5	2
Fine arts and art studies, total	20,865	7,136	13,729	3,363	1,240	2,123	177	67	110
Art, general	11,422	4,152	7,270	1,020	429	591	27	11	16
Art history, criticism and conservation	3,006	609	2,397	645	138	507	141	55	86
Arts management	117	23	94	119	26	93	0	0	0
Painting	811	335	476	202	93	109	0	0	0
Ceramic arts and ceramics	181	69	112	48	25	23	0	0	0
Fiber, textile and weaving arts	109	8	101	34	3	31	1	0	1
Metal and jewelry arts	84	14	70	25	9	16	0	0	0
Fine arts and art studies, other	5,135	1,926	3,209	1,270	517	753	8	1	7
Music, total	8,268	4,151	4,117	3,619	1,697	1,922	708	438	270
Music, general	4,149	2,003	2,146	1,209	585	624	308	191	117
Music history and literature	70	32	38	41	16	25	26	14	12
Music, general performance	2,728	1,282	1,446	1,849	850	999	232	135	97
Music theory and composition	244	190	54	161	105	56	71	52	19
Music, other	1,077	644	433	359	141	218	71	46	25
Visual and performing arts, other	582	227	355	309	92	217	29	10	19
Not classified by field of study	3,302	1,618	1,684	1,651	730	921	36	21	15

NOTE.—Aggregations by field of study derived from the *Classification of Instructional Programs* developed by the National Center for Education Statistics.

SOURCE: U.S. Department of Education, National Center for Education Statistics, Integrated Postsecondary Education Data System (IPEDS), "Completions" survey. (This table was prepared February 1996.)

Table 255.—Degrees conferred by institutions of higher education, by control of institution: 1969–70 to 1994–95

Year	Public institutions					Private institutions				
	Associate	Bachelor's	Master's	Doctor's	First-professional [1]	Associate	Bachelor's	Master's	Doctor's	First-professional [1]
1	2	3	4	5	6	7	8	9	10	11
1969–70	170,966	519,550	134,545	19,183	14,542	35,057	272,766	73,746	10,683	20,376
1970–71	215,645	557,996	151,603	20,788	16,139	36,666	281,734	78,906	11,319	21,807
1971–72	255,218	599,615	167,075	21,776	18,521	36,796	287,658	84,558	11,587	24,890
1972–73	278,132	630,899	174,405	22,357	21,872	38,042	291,463	88,966	12,420	28,146
1973–74	303,188	651,544	184,632	21,810	23,208	40,736	294,232	92,401	12,006	30,608
1974–75	318,474	634,785	193,804	22,176	23,612	41,697	288,148	98,646	11,907	32,304
1975–76	345,006	635,161	206,298	21,751	25,766	46,448	290,585	105,473	12,313	36,883
1976–77	355,650	630,463	208,901	21,229	26,344	50,727	289,086	108,263	12,003	38,015
1977–78	358,874	627,903	202,099	20,456	27,097	53,372	293,301	109,521	11,675	39,484
1978–79	346,808	621,666	192,016	20,817	27,785	55,894	299,724	109,063	11,913	41,063
1979–80	344,536	624,084	187,499	20,608	27,942	56,374	305,233	110,582	12,007	42,189
1980–81	352,391	626,452	184,384	20,895	29,128	63,986	308,688	111,355	12,063	42,828
1981–82	[2] 366,732	636,475	182,295	20,889	29,611	[2] 67,794	316,523	113,251	11,818	42,421
1982–83	377,817	646,317	176,246	21,186	29,757	71,803	323,193	113,675	11,589	43,297
1983–84	[2] 379,249	646,013	170,693	21,141	29,586	[2] 72,991	328,296	113,570	12,068	44,882
1984–85	377,625	652,246	170,000	21,337	30,152	77,087	327,231	116,251	11,606	44,911
1985–86	369,052	658,586	169,903	21,433	29,568	76,995	329,237	118,664	12,220	44,342
1986–87	358,811	659,260	167,797	21,870	29,346	77,493	332,004	121,552	12,171	42,271
1987–88	354,180	658,491	173,778	22,488	29,153	80,905	336,338	125,539	12,382	41,582
1988–89	357,001	675,675	179,109	22,970	28,993	79,763	343,080	131,512	12,750	41,863
1989–90	375,635	700,015	186,104	24,641	28,810	79,467	351,329	138,197	13,730	42,178
1990–91	398,055	724,062	193,057	25,681	29,554	83,665	370,476	144,111	13,613	42,394
1991–92	420,265	759,475	203,398	26,820	29,366	83,966	377,078	149,440	13,839	44,780
1992–93	430,321	785,112	213,843	27,392	29,628	84,435	380,066	155,742	14,740	45,759
1993–94	[3] 444,373	789,148	221,428	28,524	29,842	86,259	380,127	165,642	14,661	45,576
1994–95	451,539	776,670	224,152	28,917	29,871	88,152	383,464	173,477	15,529	45,929

[1] Includes degrees which require at least 6 years of college work for completion (including at least 2 years of preprofessional training).
[2] Data are approximations.
[3] Revised from previously published figures.

SOURCE: U.S. Department of Education, National Center for Education Statistics, Higher Education General Information Survey (HEGIS), "Degrees and Other Formal Awards Conferred" surveys, and Integrated Postsecondary Education Data System (IPEDS), "Completions" surveys. (This table was prepared April 1997.)

Table 256.—Degrees conferred by institutions of higher education, by control of institution, level of degree, and discipline division: 1994–95

Discipline division	Public institutions				Private institutions			
	Associate degrees	Bachelor's degrees	Master's degrees	Doctor's degrees	Associate degrees	Bachelor's degrees	Master's degrees	Doctor's degrees
1	2	3	4	5	6	7	8	9
Total	451,539	776,670	224,152	28,917	88,152	383,464	173,477	15,529
Agriculture and natural resources [1]	5,418	18,471	3,778	1,246	312	1,370	474	18
Architecture and related programs	253	6,532	2,708	81	24	2,224	1,215	60
Area, ethnic, and cultural studies	52	2,980	963	87	16	2,726	676	99
Biological sciences/life sciences	1,802	36,640	3,904	3,274	77	19,344	1,489	1,371
Business [2]	75,415	142,206	37,114	970	26,511	92,117	56,695	424
Communications	1,340	33,847	2,773	266	1,820	14,257	2,369	54
Communications technologies	1,659	471	82	0	325	228	385	1
Computer and information sciences	6,716	14,793	5,661	594	2,436	9,611	4,665	290
Construction trades	1,345	38	0	0	383	7	7	0
Education	8,414	79,536	65,265	5,139	1,244	26,543	35,977	1,766
Engineering	1,908	47,026	19,314	4,277	324	15,316	9,239	1,833
Engineering-related technologies	22,521	11,550	954	18	12,211	4,083	156	0
English language and literature/letters	1,491	34,848	5,900	1,098	57	17,053	1,945	463
Foreign languages and literatures	349	8,896	2,301	563	267	4,879	835	342
Health professions and related sciences	84,962	53,101	18,049	1,468	13,512	26,754	13,194	601
Home economics and vocational home economics	7,476	13,223	1,586	248	345	2,122	1,278	140
Law and legal studies	6,208	1,242	550	10	2,932	790	1,961	78
Liberal arts and sciences, general studies, and humanities	159,722	20,906	1,096	32	11,095	12,450	1,469	58
Library science	98	45	4,176	49	3	5	881	6
Mathematics	748	8,939	3,190	867	34	4,784	991	359
Mechanics and repairers	9,880	32	0	0	1,617	34	0	0
Multi/interdisciplinary studies	8,575	20,157	1,609	171	117	5,876	848	67
Parks, recreation, leisure, and fitness studies	730	10,234	1,375	120	134	2,655	380	29
Philosophy and religion	45	2,931	496	203	36	4,345	884	304
Physical sciences and science technologies	2,397	12,505	4,251	3,052	59	6,672	1,502	1,431
Precision production trades	6,413	336	0	0	2,931	17	5	0
Protective services	19,007	19,347	1,047	26	702	4,810	659	0
Psychology	1,437	48,255	5,985	1,766	163	23,828	7,936	2,056
Public administration and services	3,499	13,349	14,206	291	383	5,237	9,295	265
R.O.T.C. and military technologies	349	6	124	0	15	21	0	0
Social sciences and history	3,251	84,021	9,596	2,303	383	44,133	5,249	1,422
Theological studies/religious vocations	35	2	2	0	572	5,576	5,238	1,591
Transportation and material moving workers	1,174	1,693	75	0	272	2,005	748	0
Visual and performing arts	6,402	28,227	5,664	679	6,142	20,463	4,613	401
Not classified by field of study	448	285	358	19	698	1,061	219	0

[1] Includes "Agricultural business and production," "Agricultural sciences," and "Conservation and renewable natural resources."
[2] Includes "Business management and administrative services," "Marketing operations/marketing and distribution" and "Consumer and personal services."

SOURCE: U.S. Department of Education, National Center for Education Statistics, Integrated Postsecondary Education Data System, "Completions" survey, 1994–95 and "Consolidated" survey 1995. (This table was prepared March 1997.)

Table 257.—Degrees conferred by institutions of higher education, by control of institution, level of degree, and discipline division: 1993–94[1]

Discipline division	Public institutions				Private institutions			
	Associate degrees	Bachelor's degrees	Master's degrees	Doctor's degrees	Associate degrees	Bachelor's degrees	Master's degrees	Doctor's degrees
1	2	3	4	5	6	7	8	9
Total	444,373	789,148	221,428	28,524	86,259	380,127	165,642	14,661
Agriculture and natural resources[2]	5,301	17,080	3,745	1,255	335	990	374	23
Architecture and related programs	314	6,585	2,711	97	39	2,390	1,232	64
Area, ethnic, and cultural studies	48	2,956	1,007	79	27	2,617	626	76
Biological sciences/life sciences	1,690	33,747	3,847	3,240	81	17,636	1,349	1,294
Business[3]	77,003	153,288	37,578	987	27,192	93,366	55,859	377
Communications	1,432	36,024	2,827	297	620	15,140	2,178	40
Communications technologies	2,072	438	61	0	397	225	353	8
Computer and information sciences	6,926	15,231	5,748	553	2,375	8,969	4,668	257
Construction trades	1,293	34	0	0	402	41	0	0
Education	8,067	81,577	64,753	5,112	1,204	26,023	34,185	1,796
Engineering	1,997	46,690	19,297	4,156	446	15,530	9,324	1,807
Engineering-related technologies	23,574	11,641	1,017	16	12,044	4,182	116	0
English language and literature/letters	1,231	36,379	5,905	981	58	17,545	1,980	363
Foreign languages and literatures	303	9,181	2,419	529	189	5,197	869	357
Health professions and related sciences	82,658	50,641	17,009	1,356	11,943	23,780	11,016	546
Home economics and vocational home economics	7,029	13,457	1,410	245	434	2,065	1,011	120
Law and legal studies	5,957	1,429	546	6	2,724	742	1,886	73
Liberal arts and sciences, general studies, and humanities	154,147	21,298	1,182	26	10,959	12,099	1,314	54
Library science	109	52	4,298	43	9	10	818	2
Mathematics	685	9,394	3,159	819	19	5,002	941	338
Mechanics and repairers	9,765	45	0	0	1,567	62	0	0
Multi/interdisciplinary studies	8,344	19,392	1,588	176	92	5,775	876	51
Parks, recreation, leisure, and fitness studies	640	9,246	1,313	110	115	2,224	312	6
Philosophy and religion	35	3,009	540	207	47	4,537	810	321
Physical sciences and science technologies	2,473	12,133	4,271	3,344	73	6,267	1,408	1,306
Precision production trades	6,563	364	0	0	2,794	56	2	0
Protective services	17,560	18,693	964	24	639	4,316	473	1
Psychology	1,229	47,005	5,554	1,727	148	22,254	6,627	1,836
Public administration and services	3,270	12,824	13,403	310	426	4,991	8,430	209
R.O.T.C. and military technologies	253	3	124	0	12	16	0	0
Social sciences and history	3,545	88,111	9,479	2,172	391	45,569	5,082	1,455
Theological studies/religious vocations	0	1	0	0	641	5,433	4,956	1,448
Transportation and material moving workers	1,644	1,826	70	0	278	2,097	594	0
Visual and performing arts	6,779	28,906	5,526	657	6,448	20,147	4,399	397
Not classified by field of study	437	468	77	0	1,089	2,834	1,574	36

[1] Data revised from previously published data.
[2] Includes "Agricultural business and production," "Agricultural sciences," and "Conservation and renewable natural resources."
[3] Includes "Business management and administrative services," "Marketing operations/marketing and distribution," and "Consumer and personal services."

SOURCE: U.S. Department of Education, National Center for Education Statistics, Integrated Postsecondary Education Data System, "Completions" survey, 1993–94 and "Consolidated" survey 1994. (This table was prepared April 1997.)

Table 258.—Number of institutions of higher education conferring degrees, by level of degree and discipline division: 1994–95

Discipline division	Total number of institutions awarding degrees				Number of public institutions awarding degrees				Number of private institutions awarding degrees			
	Associate degrees	Bachelor's degrees	Master's degrees	Doctor's degrees	Associate degrees	Bachelor's degrees	Master's degrees	Doctor's degrees	Associate degrees	Bachelor's degrees	Master's degrees	Doctor's degrees
1	2	3	4	5	6	7	8	9	10	11	12	13
Total	**2,184**	**1,855**	**1,351**	**482**	**1,252**	**557**	**488**	**217**	**932**	**1,298**	**863**	**265**
Agricultural business and production	306	129	60	32	292	98	57	31	14	31	3	1
Agricultural sciences	94	129	75	52	85	114	72	52	9	15	3	0
Architecture and related programs	44	171	119	26	36	107	92	18	8	64	27	8
Area, ethnic, and cultural studies	24	372	105	35	21	165	64	19	3	207	41	16
Biological sciences/life sciences	186	1,236	422	216	172	474	307	142	14	762	115	74
Business management and administrative services	1,577	1,383	729	118	1,097	497	352	80	480	886	377	38
Communications	227	900	226	46	187	369	156	36	40	531	70	10
Communications technologies	165	34	11	1	148	16	2	0	17	18	9	1
Computer and information sciences	727	1,068	339	119	529	437	209	83	198	631	130	36
Conservation and renewable natural resources	116	257	100	45	108	141	85	42	8	116	15	3
Consumer and personal services	218	12	0	0	187	7	0	0	31	5	0	0
Construction trades	179	7	1	0	166	3	0	0	13	4	1	0
Education	382	1,152	840	213	289	428	419	145	93	724	421	68
Engineering	267	393	264	171	237	214	171	122	30	179	93	49
Engineering-related technologies	969	315	70	3	801	224	55	3	168	91	15	0
English language and literature/letters	139	1,248	417	133	128	477	294	88	11	771	123	45
Foreign languages and literatures	73	841	194	85	68	367	141	52	5	474	53	33
Health professions and related sciences	1,247	937	547	148	962	423	297	107	285	514	250	41
Home economics	70	324	184	42	53	210	119	32	17	114	65	10
Law and legal studies	434	132	62	14	295	45	26	3	139	87	36	11
Liberal arts and sciences, general studies, and humanities	1,316	714	140	21	1,001	297	68	10	315	417	72	11
Library science	30	11	69	16	28	10	58	13	2	1	11	3
Marketing operations/marketing and distribution	502	177	23	3	393	66	4	2	109	111	19	1
Mathematics	139	1,145	343	157	129	472	256	108	10	673	87	49
Mechanics and repairers	529	9	0	0	495	4	0	0	34	5	0	0
Multi/interdisciplinary studies	176	612	180	59	156	257	123	40	20	355	57	19
Parks, recreation, leisure, and fitness studies	131	500	121	24	118	243	102	22	13	257	19	2
Philosophy and religion	29	839	187	90	20	286	86	49	9	553	101	41
Physical sciences	152	1,064	341	201	146	459	245	132	6	605	96	69
Precision production trades	631	26	1	0	554	21	0	0	77	5	1	0
Protective services	788	439	103	6	720	243	76	6	68	196	27	0
Psychology	155	1,241	529	233	134	460	307	128	21	781	222	105
Public administration and services	260	635	349	79	224	293	230	45	36	342	119	34
R.O.T.C. and military technologies	4	4	1	0	3	3	1	0	1	1	0	0
Science technologies	103	19	4	3	95	9	3	3	8	10	1	0
Social sciences and history	216	1,290	418	174	178	486	297	114	38	804	121	60
Theological studies/religious vocations	82	337	269	111	1	1	1	0	81	336	268	111
Transportation and material moving workers	107	66	6	0	91	33	2	0	16	33	4	0
Visual and performing arts	540	1,207	377	97	410	443	236	62	130	764	141	35
Vocational home economics	505	42	9	2	479	21	6	1	26	21	3	1
Not classified by field of study	10	14	6	1	2	2	1	1	8	12	5	0

NOTE.—Data represent programs, not organizational units within institutions.

SOURCE: U.S. Department of Education, National Center for Education Statistics, Integrated Postsecondary Education Data System, "Completions" survey, 1994–95 and "Consolidated" survey, 1995. (This table was prepared March 1997.)

Table 259.—Number of institutions of higher education conferring degrees, by level of degree and discipline division: 1993–94[1]

Discipline division	Total number of institutions awarding degrees				Number of public institutions awarding degrees				Number of private institutions awarding degrees			
	Associate degrees	Bachelor's degrees	Master's degrees	Doctor's degrees	Associate degrees	Bachelor's degrees	Master's degrees	Doctor's degrees	Associate degrees	Bachelor's degrees	Master's degrees	Doctor's degrees
1	2	3	4	5	6	7	8	9	10	11	12	13
Total	2,182	1,853	1,347	473	1,242	552	487	214	940	1,301	860	259
Agricultural business and production	304	127	63	33	293	99	60	32	11	28	3	1
Agricultural sciences	94	133	76	51	86	115	73	50	8	18	3	1
Architecture and related programs	42	171	120	24	36	109	92	16	6	62	28	8
Area, ethnic, and cultural studies	23	348	106	34	21	164	65	20	2	184	41	14
Biological sciences/life sciences	176	1,230	418	223	164	471	303	148	12	759	115	75
Business management and administrative services	1,584	1,369	714	113	1,094	491	353	79	490	878	361	34
Communications	238	886	223	47	194	362	156	38	44	524	67	9
Communications technologies	161	30	10	2	140	14	1	0	21	16	9	2
Computer and information sciences	709	1,042	325	117	514	432	208	81	195	610	117	36
Conservation and renewable natural resources	111	208	96	43	100	129	85	38	11	79	11	5
Consumer and personal services	198	8	0	0	169	5	0	0	29	3	0	0
Construction trades	172	4	0	0	161	2	0	0	11	2	0	0
Education	379	1,146	829	207	288	428	414	141	91	718	415	66
Engineering	268	390	268	167	239	214	174	119	29	176	94	48
Engineering-related technologies	980	315	62	3	809	219	52	3	171	96	10	0
English language and literature/letters	136	1,248	414	134	123	478	290	91	13	770	124	43
Foreign languages and literatures	78	833	198	86	73	364	142	54	5	469	56	32
Health professions and related sciences	1,224	929	520	151	954	419	291	111	270	510	229	40
Home economics	85	327	177	38	66	212	119	29	19	115	58	9
Law and legal studies	401	121	60	14	277	41	26	2	124	80	34	12
Liberal arts and sciences, general studies, and humanities	1,284	711	146	17	983	291	69	6	301	420	77	11
Library science	35	13	73	14	33	11	61	12	2	2	12	2
Marketing operations/marketing and distribution	501	190	21	3	391	67	4	2	110	123	17	1
Mathematics	133	1,147	338	151	127	473	254	106	6	674	84	45
Mechanics and repairers	522	10	0	0	489	4	0	0	33	6	0	0
Multi/interdisciplinary studies	158	602	177	53	143	265	118	38	15	337	59	15
Parks, recreation, leisure, and fitness studies	118	461	110	25	107	231	92	23	11	230	18	2
Philosophy and religion	29	845	186	92	20	284	88	49	9	561	98	43
Physical sciences	141	1,057	334	200	131	456	238	133	10	601	96	67
Precision production trades	613	32	1	0	540	23	0	0	73	9	1	0
Protective services	781	429	105	7	721	242	79	6	60	187	26	1
Psychology	150	1,228	517	225	127	457	301	127	23	771	216	98
Public administration and services	255	627	337	72	218	292	227	43	37	335	110	29
R.O.T.C. and military technologies	6	4	1	0	5	3	1	0	1	1	0	0
Science technologies	110	16	3	2	103	8	2	2	7	8	1	0
Social sciences and history	222	1,289	425	171	182	485	297	114	40	804	128	57
Theological studies/religious vocations	86	343	271	107	0	1	0	0	86	342	271	107
Transportation and material moving workers	121	58	5	0	107	31	2	0	14	27	3	0
Visual and performing arts	547	1,194	376	98	404	434	238	63	143	760	138	35
Vocational home economics	512	38	7	2	480	21	5	1	32	17	2	1
Not classified by field of study	15	20	18	4	1	1	1	0	14	19	17	4

[1] Data revised from previously published data.

NOTE.—Data represent programs, not organizational units within institutions.

SOURCE: U.S. Department of Education, National Center for Education Statistics, Integrated Postsecondary Education Data System, "Completions" survey, 1993–94 and "Consolidated" survey, 1994. (This table was prepared April 1997.)

Table 260.—First-professional degrees conferred by institutions of higher education in dentistry, medicine, and law, by sex, and number of institutions conferring degrees: 1949–50 to 1994–95

Year	Dentistry (D.D.S. or D.M.D.)				Medicine (M.D.)				Law (LL.B. or J.D.)			
	Number of institutions conferring degrees	Degrees conferred			Number of institutions conferring degrees	Degrees conferred			Number of institutions conferring degrees	Degrees conferred		
		Total	Men	Women		Total	Men	Women		Total	Men	Women
1	2	3	4	5	6	7	8	9	10	11	12	13
1949–50	40	2,579	2,561	18	72	5,612	5,028	584	(1)	(1)	(1)	(1)
1951–52	41	2,918	2,895	23	72	6,201	5,871	330	(1)	(1)	(1)	(1)
1953–54	42	3,102	3,063	39	73	6,712	6,377	335	(1)	(1)	(1)	(1)
1955–56	42	3,009	2,975	34	73	6,810	6,464	346	131	8,262	7,974	288
1957–58	43	3,065	3,031	34	75	6,816	6,469	347	131	9,394	9,122	272
1959–60	45	3,247	3,221	26	79	7,032	6,645	387	134	9,240	9,010	230
1961–62	46	3,183	3,166	17	81	7,138	6,749	389	134	9,364	9,091	273
1963–64	46	3,180	3,168	12	82	7,303	6,878	425	133	10,679	10,372	307
1965–66	47	3,178	3,146	32	84	7,673	7,170	503	136	13,246	12,776	470
1967–68	48	3,422	3,375	47	85	7,944	7,318	626	138	16,454	15,805	649
1969–70	48	3,718	3,684	34	86	8,314	7,615	699	145	14,916	14,115	801
1970–71	48	3,745	3,703	42	89	8,919	8,110	809	147	17,421	16,181	1,240
1971–72	48	3,862	3,819	43	92	9,253	8,423	830	147	21,764	20,266	1,498
1972–73	51	4,047	3,992	55	97	10,307	9,388	919	152	27,205	25,037	2,168
1973–74	52	4,440	4,355	85	99	11,356	10,093	1,263	151	29,326	25,986	3,340
1974–75	52	4,773	4,627	146	104	12,447	10,818	1,629	154	29,296	24,881	4,415
1975–76	56	5,425	5,187	238	107	13,426	11,252	2,174	166	32,293	26,085	6,208
1976–77	57	5,138	4,764	374	109	13,461	10,891	2,570	169	34,104	26,447	7,657
1977–78	57	5,189	4,623	566	109	14,279	11,210	3,069	169	34,402	25,457	8,945
1978–79	58	5,434	4,794	640	109	14,786	11,381	3,405	175	35,206	25,180	10,026
1979–80	58	5,258	4,558	700	112	14,902	11,416	3,486	179	35,647	24,893	10,754
1980–81	58	5,460	4,672	788	116	15,505	11,672	3,833	176	36,331	24,563	11,768
1981–82	59	5,282	4,467	815	119	15,814	11,867	3,947	180	35,991	23,965	12,026
1982–83	59	5,585	4,631	954	118	15,484	11,350	4,134	177	36,853	23,550	13,303
1983–84	60	5,353	4,302	1,051	119	15,813	11,359	4,454	179	37,012	23,382	13,630
1984–85	59	5,339	4,233	1,106	120	16,041	11,167	4,874	181	37,491	23,070	14,421
1985–86	59	5,046	3,907	1,139	120	15,938	11,022	4,916	181	35,844	21,874	13,970
1986–87	58	4,741	3,603	1,138	121	15,428	10,431	4,997	179	36,056	21,561	14,495
1987–88	57	4,477	3,300	1,177	122	15,358	10,278	5,080	180	35,397	21,067	14,330
1988–89	58	4,265	3,124	1,141	124	15,460	10,310	5,150	182	35,634	21,069	14,565
1989–90	57	4,100	2,834	1,266	124	15,075	9,923	5,152	182	36,485	21,079	15,406
1990–91	55	3,699	2,510	1,189	121	15,043	9,629	5,414	179	37,945	21,643	16,302
1991–92	52	3,593	2,431	1,162	120	15,243	9,796	5,447	177	38,848	22,260	16,588
1992–93	55	3,605	2,383	1,222	122	15,531	9,679	5,852	184	40,302	23,182	17,120
1993–94	53	3,787	2,330	1,457	121	15,368	9,544	5,824	185	40,044	22,826	17,218
1994–95	53	3,897	2,480	1,417	119	15,537	9,507	6,030	183	39,349	22,592	16,757

[1] Data prior to 1955–56 are not shown because they lack comparability with the figures for subsequent years.

SOURCE: U.S. Department of Education, National Center for Education Statistics, Higher Education General Information Survey (HEGIS), "Degrees and Other Formal Awards Conferred" surveys, and Integrated Postsecondary Education Data System (IPEDS), "Completions" surveys. (This table was prepared March 1997.)

HIGHER EDUCATION: DEGREES 291

Table 261.—First-professional degrees[1] conferred by institutions of higher education, by sex of student, control of institution, and field of study: 1983–84 to 1994–95

Control of institution and field of study	1983–84[2] Total	1984–85 Total	1985–86 Total	1986–87 Total	1987–88 Total	1988–89 Total	1989–90 Total	1990–91 Total	1991–92 Total	1992–93 Total			1993–94			1994–95		
										Total	Men	Women	Total	Men	Women	Total	Men	Women
1	2	3	4	5	6	7	8	9	10	11	12	13	14	15	16	17	18	19
Total, all institutions	74,468	75,063	73,910	71,617	70,735	70,856	70,988	71,948	74,146	75,387	45,153	30,234	75,418	44,707	30,711	75,800	44,853	30,947
Dentistry (D.D.S. or D.M.D.)	5,353	5,339	5,046	4,741	4,477	4,265	4,100	3,699	3,593	3,605	2,383	1,222	3,787	2,330	1,457	3,897	2,480	1,417
Medicine (M.D.)	15,813	16,041	15,938	15,428	15,358	15,460	15,075	15,043	15,243	15,531	9,679	5,852	15,368	9,544	5,824	15,537	9,507	6,030
Optometry (O.D.)	1,086	1,115	1,029	1,082	1,023	1,093	1,072	1,115	1,232	1,148	584	564	1,103	554	549	1,185	538	647
Osteopathic medicine (D.O.)	1,515	1,489	1,547	1,618	1,544	1,635	1,555	1,459	1,326	1,627	1,091	536	1,798	1,165	633	1,854	1,249	605
Pharmacy (Pharm. D.)	709	861	903	861	962	1,074	1,199	1,244	1,339	1,904	673	1,231	1,936	643	1,293	2,264	785	1,479
Podiatry (Pod. D. or D.P.) or podiatric medicine (D.P.M.)	607	582	612	590	645	636	675	589	504	476	350	126	465	330	135	545	370	175
Veterinary medicine (D.V.M.)	2,269	2,178	2,270	2,230	2,235	2,157	2,151	2,032	2,044	2,057	766	1,291	2,089	798	1,291	2,148	762	1,386
Chiropractic (D.C. or D.C.M.)	3,105	2,661	3,395	2,493	2,628	2,890	2,581	2,640	2,694	2,799	1,991	808	2,806	2,010	796	2,968	2,094	874
Law (LL.B. or J.D.)	37,012	37,491	35,844	36,056	35,397	35,634	36,485	37,945	38,848	40,302	23,182	17,120	40,044	22,826	17,218	39,349	22,592	16,757
Theology (M. Div., M.H.L., B.D., or Ord. and M.H.L./Rav.)	6,878	7,221	7,283	6,518	6,466	6,012	5,851	5,695	5,251	5,447	4,096	1,351	5,967	4,486	1,481	5,978	4,443	1,535
Other	121	85	43	0	0	0	244	487	2,072	491	358	133	55	21	34	75	33	42
Total, public institutions	29,586	30,152	29,568	29,346	29,153	28,993	28,810	29,554	29,366	29,628	17,126	12,502	29,842	17,040	12,802	29,871	16,898	12,973
Dentistry (D.D.S. or D.M.D.)	3,174	3,051	2,827	2,655	2,524	2,512	2,353	2,308	2,200	2,167	1,462	705	2,189	1,377	812	2,236	1,477	759
Medicine (M.D.)	9,674	10,071	9,991	9,711	9,557	9,491	9,108	9,364	9,259	9,370	5,843	3,527	9,506	5,977	3,529	9,599	5,905	3,694
Optometry (O.D.)	384	456	441	454	429	451	444	477	595	460	221	239	471	219	252	461	203	258
Osteopathic medicine (D.O.)	537	455	486	480	434	500	458	493	416	490	336	154	531	349	182	492	322	170
Pharmacy (Pharm. D.)	356	416	473	475	615	679	727	808	852	1,171	405	766	1,185	390	795	1,344	489	855
Podiatry (Pod. D. or D.P.) or podiatric medicine (D.P.M.)	0	0	0	0	0	0	0	0	0	0	0	0	0	0	0	0	0	0
Veterinary medicine (D.V.M.)	2,060	1,963	1,931	2,003	2,014	1,943	1,943	1,814	1,831	1,840	701	1,139	1,895	744	1,151	1,927	689	1,238
Chiropractic (D.C. or D.C.M.)	0	0	0	0	0	0	0	0	0	0	0	0	0	0	0	0	0	0
Law (LL.B. or J.D.)	13,380	13,695	13,419	13,568	13,580	13,417	13,585	14,290	14,097	14,130	8,158	5,972	14,065	7,984	6,081	13,812	7,813	5,999
Theology (M. Div., M.H.L., B.D., or Ord. and M.H.L./Rav.)	0	0	0	0	0	0	0	0	0	0	0	0	0	0	0	0	0	0
Other	21	43	0	0	0	0	192	0	116	0	0	0	0	0	0	0	0	0
Total, private institutions	44,882	44,911	44,342	42,271	41,582	41,863	42,178	42,394	44,780	45,759	28,027	17,732	45,576	27,667	17,909	45,929	27,955	17,974
Dentistry (D.D.S. or D.M.D.)	2,179	2,288	2,219	2,086	1,953	1,753	1,747	1,391	1,393	1,438	921	517	1,598	953	645	1,661	1,003	658
Medicine (M.D.)	6,139	5,970	5,947	5,717	5,801	5,969	5,967	5,679	5,984	6,161	3,836	2,325	5,862	3,567	2,295	5,938	3,602	2,336
Optometry (O.D.)	702	659	588	628	594	642	628	638	637	688	363	325	632	335	297	724	335	389
Osteopathic medicine (D.O.)	978	1,034	1,061	1,138	1,110	1,135	1,097	966	910	1,137	755	382	1,267	816	451	1,362	927	435
Pharmacy (Pharm. D.)	353	445	430	386	347	395	472	436	487	733	268	465	751	253	498	920	296	624
Podiatry (Pod. D. or D.P.) or podiatric medicine (D.P.M.)	607	582	612	590	645	636	675	589	504	476	350	126	465	330	135	545	370	175
Veterinary medicine (D.V.M.)	209	215	339	227	221	214	208	218	213	217	65	152	194	54	140	221	73	148
Chiropractic (D.C. or D.C.M.)	3,105	2,661	3,395	2,493	2,628	2,890	2,581	2,640	2,694	2,799	1,991	808	2,806	2,010	796	2,968	2,094	874
Law (LL.B. or J.D.)	23,632	23,796	22,425	22,488	21,817	22,217	22,900	23,655	24,751	26,172	15,024	11,148	25,979	14,842	11,137	25,537	14,779	10,758
Theology (M. Div., M.H.L., B.D., or Ord. and M.H.L./Rav.)	6,878	7,219	7,283	6,518	6,466	6,012	5,851	5,695	5,251	5,447	4,096	1,351	5,967	4,486	1,481	5,978	4,443	1,535
Other	100	42	43	0	0	0	52	487	1,956	491	358	133	55	21	34	75	33	42

[1] Includes degrees which require at least 6 years of college work for completion (including at least 2 years of preprofessional training).
[2] Revised from previously published figures.

SOURCE: U.S. Department of Education, National Center for Education Statistics, Higher Education General Information Survey (HEGIS), "Degrees and Other Formal Awards Conferred" surveys, and Integrated Postsecondary Education Data System (IPEDS), "Completions" survey. (This table was prepared March 1997.)

Table 262.—Associate degrees conferred by institutions of higher education, by racial/ethnic group and sex of student: 1976–77 to 1994–95

Year and sex of student	Total	White, non-Hispanic	Black, non-Hispanic	Hispanic	Asian or Pacific Islander	American Indian/Alaskan Native	Nonresident alien
1	2	3	4	5	6	7	8
	Number of degrees conferred						
1976–77, total[1]	404,956	342,290	33,159	16,636	7,044	2,498	3,329
Men	209,672	178,236	15,330	9,105	3,630	1,216	2,155
Women	195,284	164,054	17,829	7,531	3,414	1,282	1,174
1978–79, total[2]	396,745	331,092	34,979	16,269	7,518	2,336	4,551
Men	187,284	156,671	14,425	8,135	4,058	1,069	2,926
Women	209,461	174,421	20,554	8,134	3,460	1,267	1,625
1980–81, total[3]	410,174	339,167	35,330	17,800	8,650	2,584	6,643
Men	183,819	151,242	14,290	8,327	4,557	1,108	4,295
Women	226,355	187,925	21,040	9,473	4,093	1,476	2,348
1984–85, total[4]	429,815	355,343	35,791	19,407	9,914	2,953	6,407
Men	190,409	157,278	14,184	8,561	5,492	1,198	3,696
Women	239,406	198,065	21,607	10,846	4,422	1,755	2,711
1986–87, total	436,304	361,861	35,447	19,334	11,779	3,195	4,688
Men	190,839	158,132	13,959	8,760	6,169	1,263	2,556
Women	245,465	203,729	21,488	10,574	5,610	1,932	2,132
1988–89, total[5,6]	432,144	354,865	34,664	20,384	12,519	3,331	6,381
Men	183,963	150,978	12,884	9,217	6,366	1,323	3,195
Women	248,181	203,887	21,780	11,167	6,153	2,008	3,186
1989–90, total[5,7]	450,263	369,580	35,327	22,195	13,482	3,530	6,149
Men	188,631	154,748	13,147	9,859	6,477	1,433	2,967
Women	261,632	214,832	22,180	12,336	7,005	2,097	3,182
1990–91, total[5,8]	462,030	376,081	37,657	24,251	13,725	3,672	6,644
Men	190,221	155,330	13,718	10,210	6,440	1,373	3,150
Women	271,809	220,751	23,939	14,041	7,285	2,299	3,494
1991–92, total[5,9]	494,387	400,530	39,411	26,905	15,596	4,008	7,937
Men	202,808	164,799	14,294	11,536	7,254	1,531	3,394
Women	291,579	235,731	25,117	15,369	8,342	2,477	4,543
1992–93, total[5,10]	508,154	405,883	42,340	29,991	16,632	4,379	8,929
Men	209,051	167,312	15,497	12,924	7,877	1,663	3,778
Women	299,103	238,571	26,843	17,067	8,755	2,716	5,151
1993–94, total[5,11]	529,106	418,301	45,461	32,074	18,433	4,871	9,966
Men	214,462	170,137	16,917	13,204	8,288	1,836	4,080
Women	314,644	248,164	28,544	18,870	10,145	3,035	5,886
1994–95, total[5,12]	538,545	419,323	47,142	36,013	20,717	5,492	9,858
Men	217,730	169,475	16,786	15,717	9,283	2,106	4,363
Women	320,815	249,848	30,356	20,296	11,434	3,386	5,495
	Percentage distribution of degrees conferred						
1976–77, total[1]	100.0	84.5	8.2	4.1	1.7	0.6	0.8
Men	100.0	85.0	7.3	4.3	1.7	0.6	1.0
Women	100.0	84.0	9.1	3.9	1.7	0.7	0.6
1980–81, total[3]	100.0	82.7	8.6	4.3	2.1	0.6	1.6
Men	100.0	82.3	7.8	4.5	2.5	0.6	2.3
Women	100.0	83.0	9.3	4.2	1.8	0.7	1.0
1984–85, total[4]	100.0	82.7	8.3	4.5	2.3	0.7	1.5
Men	100.0	82.6	7.4	4.5	2.9	0.6	1.9
Women	100.0	82.7	9.0	4.5	1.8	0.7	1.1
1988–89, total[5,6]	100.0	82.1	8.0	4.7	2.9	0.8	1.5
Men	100.0	82.1	7.0	5.0	3.5	0.7	1.7
Women	100.0	82.2	8.8	4.5	2.5	0.8	1.3
1989–90, total[5,7]	100.0	82.1	7.8	4.9	3.0	0.8	1.4
Men	100.0	82.0	7.0	5.2	3.4	0.8	1.6
Women	100.0	82.1	8.5	4.7	2.7	0.8	1.2
1990–91, total[5,8]	100.0	81.4	8.2	5.2	3.0	0.8	1.4
Men	100.0	81.7	7.2	5.4	3.4	0.7	1.7
Women	100.0	81.2	8.8	5.2	2.7	0.8	1.3
1991–92, total[5,9]	100.0	81.0	8.0	5.4	3.2	0.8	1.6
Men	100.0	81.3	7.0	5.7	3.6	0.8	1.7
Women	100.0	80.8	8.6	5.3	2.9	0.8	1.6
1992–93, total[5,10]	100.0	79.9	8.3	5.9	3.3	0.9	1.8
Men	100.0	80.0	7.4	6.2	3.8	0.8	1.8
Women	100.0	79.8	9.0	5.7	2.9	0.9	1.7
1993–94, total[5,11]	100.0	79.1	8.6	6.1	3.5	0.9	1.9
Men	100.0	79.3	7.9	6.2	3.9	0.9	1.9
Women	100.0	78.9	9.1	6.0	3.2	1.0	1.9
1994–95, total[5,12]	100.0	77.9	8.8	6.7	3.8	1.0	1.8
Men	100.0	77.8	7.7	7.2	4.3	1.0	2.0
Women	100.0	77.9	9.5	6.3	3.6	1.1	1.7

[1] Excludes 1,170 men and 251 women whose racial/ethnic group was not available.
[2] Excludes 4,807 men and 1,150 women whose racial/ethnic group was not available.
[3] Excludes 4,819 men and 1,384 women whose racial/ethnic group was not available.
[4] Racial/ethnic data were imputed for approximately 45,400 men and 55,400 women. This tabulation excludes 11,490 men and 10,862 women whose racial/ethnic group could not be imputed. In addition, data for 1,033 men and 1,512 women were not available by field of study and were not imputed by race.
[5] Reported racial/ethnic distributions of students by level of degree, field of degree, and sex were used to estimate race/ethnicity for students whose race/ethnicity was not reported.
[6] Excludes 2,353 men and 2,267 women whose racial/ethnic group and field of study were not available.
[7] Excludes 2,564 men and 2,275 women whose racial/ethnic group and field of study were not available.
[8] Excludes 8,413 men and 11,277 women whose racial/ethnic group and field of study were not available.
[9] Excludes 4,673 men and 5,171 women whose racial/ethnic group and field of study were not available.
[10] Excludes 2,913 men and 3,689 women whose racial/ethnic group and field of study were not available.
[11] Excludes 799 men and 727 women whose racial/ethnic group and field of study were not available. Data revised from previously published data.
[12] Excludes 622 men and 524 women whose racial/ethnic group and field of study were not available.

NOTE.—Because of rounding, percents may not add to 100.0.

SOURCE: U.S. Department of Education, National Center for Education Statistics, Higher Education General Information Survey (HEGIS), "Degrees and Other Formal Awards Conferred" surveys, and Integrated Postsecondary Education Data System (IPEDS), "Completions" surveys. (This table was prepared April 1997.)

HIGHER EDUCATION: DEGREES 293

Table 263.—Associate degrees conferred by institutions of higher education, by racial/ethnic group, major field of study, and sex of student: 1994–95

Major field of study	Total								Men							Women						
	Total	White, non-Hispanic	Black, non-Hispanic	Hispanic	Asian/Pacific Islander	American Indian/Alaskan Native	Non-resident alien	Total	White, non-Hispanic	Black, non-Hispanic	Hispanic	Asian/Pacific Islander	American Indian/Alaskan Native	Non-resident alien	Total	White, non-Hispanic	Black, non-Hispanic	Hispanic	Asian/Pacific Islander	American Indian/Alaskan Native	Non-resident alien
1	2	3	4	5	6	7	8	9	10	11	12	13	14	15	16	17	18	19	20	21	22
All fields, total[1]	538,545	419,323	47,142	36,013	20,717	5,492	9,858	217,730	169,475	16,786	15,717	9,283	2,106	4,363	320,815	249,848	30,356	20,296	11,434	3,386	5,495
Agriculture and natural resources	5,730	5,380	57	118	37	82	56	4,001	3,772	39	78	25	50	37	1,729	1,608	18	40	12	32	19
Architecture and related programs	277	243	4	17	4	1	8	70	58	2	7	2	0	1	207	185	3	10	2	0	7
Area, ethnic, and cultural studies	68	19	9	8	2	16	14	17	3	1	3	0	6	3	51	16	7	5	2	10	11
Biological sciences/life sciences	1,879	1,225	150	191	195	41	77	752	503	53	70	82	11	33	1,127	722	97	121	113	30	44
Business	101,926	76,068	11,366	6,972	4,089	987	2,444	31,902	24,098	3,120	2,146	1,328	260	950	70,024	51,970	8,246	4,826	2,761	727	1,494
Communications	3,160	2,687	216	135	53	24	45	1,624	1,429	90	60	22	10	13	1,536	1,258	126	75	31	14	32
Communications technologies	1,984	1,512	194	155	56	13	54	1,298	1,010	110	103	34	10	31	686	502	84	52	22	3	23
Computer and information sciences	9,152	6,470	1,037	757	517	113	258	4,743	3,500	418	371	266	46	142	4,409	2,970	619	386	251	67	116
Construction trades	1,728	1,456	81	68	81	29	13	1,598	1,336	78	66	79	27	12	130	120	3	2	2	2	1
Education	9,658	7,350	915	855	221	223	94	3,058	2,252	311	268	104	76	47	6,600	5,098	604	587	117	147	47
Engineering	2,232	1,703	153	121	157	22	76	1,931	1,489	124	97	132	19	70	301	214	29	24	25	3	6
Engineering-related technologies	34,732	27,453	2,866	2,405	1,391	257	360	30,820	24,466	2,383	2,176	1,266	226	303	3,912	2,987	483	229	125	31	57
English language and literature/letters	1,548	756	103	194	149	25	321	505	227	38	68	47	3	122	1,043	529	65	126	102	22	199
Foreign languages and literatures	616	466	10	78	28	1	33	177	130	6	23	10	1	7	439	336	4	55	18	0	26
Health professions and related sciences	98,474	83,473	7,211	3,654	2,701	812	623	16,530	13,598	1,081	846	688	164	153	81,944	69,875	6,130	2,808	2,013	648	470
Home economics and vocational home economics	7,821	5,580	1,005	667	300	89	180	815	496	116	69	86	10	38	7,006	5,084	889	598	214	79	142
Law and legal studies	9,140	7,278	986	637	145	73	21	1,163	857	157	94	33	17	5	7,977	6,421	829	543	112	56	16
Liberal arts and sciences, general studies, and humanities	170,817	130,736	14,545	12,574	7,434	1,765	3,763	67,834	51,870	5,413	5,033	3,159	624	1,735	102,983	78,866	9,132	7,541	4,275	1,141	2,028
Library science	101	91	4	0	6	0	0	9	8	0	0	1	0	0	92	83	4	0	5	0	0
Mathematics	782	488	46	101	95	13	39	438	253	26	57	62	8	32	344	235	20	44	33	5	7
Mechanics and repairers	11,497	9,089	745	755	593	143	172	10,754	8,553	663	691	550	132	165	743	536	82	64	43	11	7
Multi/interdisciplinary studies	8,692	6,863	884	434	372	45	94	4,228	3,334	422	236	166	24	46	4,464	3,529	462	198	206	21	48
Parks, recreation, leisure and fitness studies	864	680	81	50	19	6	28	501	381	51	34	13	2	20	363	299	30	16	6	4	8
Philosophy and religion	81	66	3	9	2	0	1	52	43	2	4	2	0	1	29	23	1	5	0	0	0
Physical sciences and science technologies	2,456	1,840	173	132	187	33	91	1,424	1,099	86	79	94	20	46	1,032	741	87	53	93	13	45
Precision production trades	9,344	7,605	373	734	449	92	91	7,453	6,108	280	601	337	67	60	1,891	1,497	93	133	112	25	31
Protective services	19,709	15,395	1,601	2,078	347	219	69	14,202	11,399	801	1,525	288	145	44	5,507	3,996	800	553	59	74	25
Psychology	1,600	1,163	128	196	59	35	19	446	308	48	53	19	13	5	1,154	855	80	143	40	22	14
Public administration and services	3,882	2,484	859	360	83	82	14	783	489	164	74	28	25	3	3,099	1,995	695	286	55	57	11
R.O.T.C. and military technologies	364	279	36	28	13	3	5	331	253	32	25	13	3	5	33	26	4	3	0	0	0
Social sciences and history	3,634	2,418	425	361	213	94	123	1,461	977	183	143	75	31	52	2,173	1,441	242	218	138	63	71
Theological studies and religious vocations	607	521	34	21	11	5	15	309	263	19	12	8	1	6	298	258	15	9	3	4	9
Transportation and material moving workers	1,446	1,154	88	103	45	18	38	1,226	982	77	88	38	15	26	220	172	11	15	7	3	12
Visual and performing arts	12,544	9,332	754	1,045	663	131	619	5,275	3,931	392	517	226	59	150	7,269	5,401	362	528	437	72	469

[1] Reported racial/ethnic distributions of students by level of degree, field of degree, and sex were used to estimate race/ethnicity for students whose race/ethnicity was not reported. Excludes 622 men and 524 women whose racial/ethnic group and field of study were not available.

NOTE.—To facilitate trend comparisons, certain aggregations have been made of the degree fields as reported in the IPEDS "Completions" survey: "Agriculture and natural resources" includes Agricultural business and production, Agricultural sciences, and Conservation and renewable natural resources; and "Business" includes Business management and administrative services, Marketing operations/marketing and distribution, and Consumer and personal services.

SOURCE: U.S. Department of Education, National Center for Education Statistics, Integrated Postsecondary Education Data System (IPEDS), "Completions" survey. (This table was prepared April 1997.)

Table 264.—Associate degrees conferred by institutions of higher education, by racial/ethnic group, major field of study, and sex of student: 1993–94

Major field of study	Total								Men								Women						
	Total	White, non-Hispanic	Black, non-His-panic	His-panic	Asian/Pacific Islander	American Indian/Alaskan Native	Non-resident alien		Total	White, non-His-panic	Black, non-His-panic	His-panic	Asian/Pacific Is-lander	American Indian/Alaskan Native	Non-resident alien		Total	White, non-His-panic	Black, non-His-panic	His-panic	Asian/Pacific Is-lander	American Indian/Alaskan Native	Non-resident alien
1	2	3	4	5	6	7	8		9	10	11	12	13	14	15		16	17	18	19	20	21	22
All fields, total[1]	529,106	418,301	45,461	32,074	18,433	4,871	9,966		214,462	170,137	16,917	13,204	8,288	1,836	4,080		314,644	248,164	28,544	18,870	10,145	3,035	5,886
Agriculture and natural resources	5,636	5,290	49	106	31	86	74		3,822	3,584	32	74	25	59	48		1,814	1,706	17	32	6	27	26
Architecture and related programs	353	260	8	42	31	0	12		115	66	6	26	12	0	5		238	194	2	16	19	0	7
Area, ethnic, and cultural studies	75	12	10	9	0	20	24		25	5	6	3	0	10	1		50	7	4	6	0	10	23
Biological sciences/life sciences	1,771	1,263	97	151	171	36	53		707	496	31	67	77	16	20		1,064	767	66	84	94	20	33
Business	104,195	78,507	11,521	6,655	3,956	871	2,685		32,598	24,782	3,374	1,944	1,337	216	945		71,597	53,725	8,147	4,711	2,619	655	1,740
Communications	2,052	1,649	174	101	54	15	59		953	797	63	48	16	6	23		1,099	852	111	53	38	9	36
Communications technologies	2,469	1,967	324	104	31	8	35		1,635	1,327	209	65	21	3	10		834	640	115	39	10	5	25
Computer and information sciences	9,301	6,684	1,089	695	489	107	237		4,624	3,411	423	352	272	36	130		4,677	3,273	666	343	217	71	107
Construction trades	1,695	1,422	89	62	74	36	12		1,618	1,360	81	61	72	34	10		77	62	8	1	2	2	2
Education	9,271	7,407	845	647	102	187	83		2,952	2,385	322	147	22	53	23		6,319	5,022	523	500	80	134	60
Engineering	2,445	1,903	161	112	171	17	81		2,145	1,690	137	97	136	16	69		300	213	24	15	35	1	12
Engineering-related technologies	35,618	28,772	2,848	2,153	1,234	243	368		31,819	25,834	2,407	1,947	1,112	210	309		3,799	2,938	441	206	122	33	59
English language and literature/letters	1,289	735	67	172	92	12	211		467	250	25	69	27	4	92		822	485	42	103	65	8	119
Foreign languages and literatures	492	346	7	61	26	8	44		147	102	3	21	10	2	9		345	244	4	40	16	6	35
Health professions and related sciences	94,601	80,720	6,641	3,433	2,267	751	789		15,152	12,370	1,086	817	564	152	163		79,449	68,350	5,555	2,616	1,703	599	626
Home economics and vocational home economics	7,463	5,547	879	551	255	78	153		642	475	55	31	58	12	11		6,821	5,072	824	520	197	66	142
Law and legal studies	8,681	6,927	919	577	125	81	52		1,029	735	155	85	30	14	10		7,652	6,192	764	492	95	67	42
Liberal arts and sciences, general studies, and humanities	165,106	128,357	13,739	11,399	6,504	1,506	3,601		66,081	51,385	5,256	4,430	2,852	536	1,622		99,025	76,972	8,483	6,969	3,652	970	1,979
Library science	118	103	8	3	4	0	0		16	11	1	1	3	0	0		102	92	7	2	1	0	0
Mathematics	704	460	32	85	79	10	38		395	244	24	45	50	7	25		309	216	8	40	29	3	13
Mechanics and repairers	11,332	9,328	799	546	451	100	108		10,594	8,779	716	493	411	93	102		738	549	83	53	40	7	6
Multi/interdisciplinary studies	8,436	6,857	727	396	357	46	53		4,054	3,275	360	192	182	24	21		4,382	3,582	367	204	175	22	32
Parks, recreation, leisure and fitness studies	755	603	73	39	18	11	11		454	349	55	23	13	9	5		301	254	18	16	5	2	6
Philosophy and religion	82	68	4	7	3	0	0		46	37	4	2	3	0	0		36	31	0	5	0	0	0
Physical sciences and science technologies	2,546	1,999	182	120	160	26	59		1,477	1,196	74	67	94	13	33		1,069	803	108	53	66	13	26
Precision production trades	9,357	7,722	369	698	407	81	80		7,511	6,227	282	582	297	67	56		1,846	1,495	87	116	110	14	24
Protective services	18,199	15,050	1,536	1,092	249	156	116		13,068	11,202	788	725	185	102	66		5,131	3,848	748	367	64	54	50
Psychology	1,377	1,038	111	143	30	34	21		337	244	33	38	8	8	6		1,040	794	78	105	22	26	15
Public administration and services	3,696	2,440	721	328	78	78	51		758	477	150	69	27	17	18		2,938	1,963	571	259	51	61	33
R.O.T.C. and military technologies	265	221	40	4	0	0	0		245	207	35	3	0	0	0		20	14	5	1	0	0	0
Social sciences and history	3,936	2,638	401	476	194	105	122		1,536	1,050	158	161	82	32	53		2,400	1,588	243	315	112	73	69
Theological studies and religious vocations	641	510	71	18	19	5	18		342	267	39	12	16	2	6		299	243	32	6	3	3	12
Transportation and material moving workers	1,922	1,605	141	73	36	14	53		1,602	1,353	122	65	28	10	24		320	252	19	8	8	4	29
Visual and performing arts	13,227	9,891	779	1,016	735	143	663		5,496	4,165	405	442	246	73	165		7,731	5,726	374	574	489	70	498

[1] Reported racial/ethnic distributions of students by level of degree, field of degree, and sex were used to estimate race/ethnicity for students whose race/ethnicity was not reported. Excludes 799 men and 727 women whose racial/ethnic group and field of study were not available.

NOTE.—To facilitate trend comparisons, certain aggregations have been made of the degree fields as reported in the IPEDS "Completions" survey. "Agriculture and natural resources" includes Agricultural business and production, Agricultural sciences, and Conservation and renewable natural resources; and "Business" includes Business management and administrative services, Marketing operations/marketing and distribution, and Consumer and personal services. Data revised from previously published data.

SOURCE: U.S. Department of Education, National Center for Education Statistics, Integrated Postsecondary Education Data System (IPEDS), "Completions" survey. (This table was prepared April 1997.)

HIGHER EDUCATION: DEGREES 295

Table 265.—Bachelor's degrees conferred by institutions of higher education, by racial/ethnic group and sex of student: 1976–77 to 1994–95

Year and sex of student	Total	White, non-Hispanic	Black, non-Hispanic	Hispanic	Asian or Pacific Islander	American Indian/Alaskan Native	Nonresident alien
1	2	3	4	5	6	7	8
Number of degrees conferred							
1976–77, total [1]	917,900	807,688	58,636	18,743	13,793	3,326	15,714
Men	494,424	438,161	25,147	10,318	7,638	1,804	11,356
Women	423,476	369,527	33,489	8,425	6,155	1,522	4,358
1978–79, total [2]	919,540	802,542	60,246	20,096	15,407	3,410	17,839
Men	476,065	418,215	24,659	10,418	8,261	1,736	12,776
Women	443,475	384,327	35,587	9,678	7,146	1,674	5,063
1980–81, total [3]	934,800	807,319	60,673	21,832	18,794	3,593	22,589
Men	469,625	406,173	24,511	10,810	10,107	1,700	16,324
Women	465,175	401,146	36,162	11,022	8,687	1,893	6,265
1984–85, total [4]	968,311	826,106	57,473	25,874	25,395	4,246	29,217
Men	476,148	405,085	23,018	12,402	13,554	1,998	20,091
Women	492,163	421,021	34,455	13,472	11,841	2,248	9,126
1986–87, total [5]	991,264	841,818	56,560	26,988	32,624	3,968	29,306
Men	480,782	406,749	22,501	12,865	17,253	1,817	19,597
Women	510,482	435,069	34,059	14,123	15,371	2,151	9,709
1988–89, total [5,6]	1,016,350	859,703	58,078	29,918	37,674	3,951	27,026
Men	481,946	407,154	22,370	13,950	19,260	1,730	17,482
Women	534,404	452,549	35,708	15,968	18,414	2,221	9,544
1989–90, total [5,7]	1,048,631	884,376	61,063	32,844	39,248	4,392	26,708
Men	490,317	413,573	23,262	14,941	19,721	1,859	16,961
Women	558,314	470,803	37,801	17,903	19,527	2,533	9,747
1990–91, total [5,8]	1,081,280	904,062	65,341	36,612	41,618	4,513	29,134
Men	496,424	415,505	24,328	16,158	20,678	1,901	17,854
Women	584,856	488,557	41,013	20,454	20,940	2,612	11,280
1991–92, total [5,9]	1,129,833	936,771	72,326	40,761	46,720	5,176	28,079
Men	516,976	429,842	26,956	17,976	23,248	2,182	16,772
Women	612,857	506,929	45,370	22,785	23,472	2,994	11,307
1992–93, total [5,10]	1,159,931	947,309	77,872	45,376	51,463	5,671	32,240
Men	530,541	435,084	28,883	19,865	25,293	2,449	18,967
Women	629,390	512,225	48,989	25,511	26,170	3,222	13,273
1993–94, total [5,11]	1,165,973	936,227	83,576	50,241	55,660	6,189	34,080
Men	530,804	429,121	30,648	21,807	26,938	2,616	19,674
Women	635,169	507,106	52,928	28,434	28,722	3,573	14,406
1994–95, total [5,12]	1,158,788	913,377	87,203	54,201	60,478	6,606	36,923
Men	525,174	417,006	31,775	23,600	28,973	2,736	21,084
Women	633,614	496,371	55,428	30,601	31,505	3,870	15,839
Percentage distribution of degrees conferred							
1976–77, total [1]	100.0	88.0	6.4	2.0	1.5	0.4	1.7
Men	100.0	88.6	5.1	2.1	1.5	0.4	2.3
Women	100.0	87.3	7.9	2.0	1.5	0.4	1.0
1980–81, total [3]	100.0	86.4	6.5	2.3	2.0	0.4	2.4
Men	100.0	86.5	5.2	2.3	2.2	0.4	3.5
Women	100.0	86.2	7.8	2.4	1.9	0.4	1.3
1984–85, total [4]	100.0	85.3	5.9	2.7	2.6	0.4	3.0
Men	100.0	85.1	4.8	2.6	2.8	0.4	4.2
Women	100.0	85.5	7.0	2.7	2.4	0.5	1.9
1988–89, total [5,6]	100.0	84.6	5.7	2.9	3.7	0.4	2.7
Men	100.0	84.5	4.6	2.9	4.0	0.4	3.6
Women	100.0	84.7	6.7	3.0	3.4	0.4	1.8
1989–90, total [5,7]	100.0	84.3	5.8	3.1	3.7	0.4	2.5
Men	100.0	84.3	4.7	3.0	4.0	0.4	3.5
Women	100.0	84.3	6.8	3.2	3.5	0.5	1.7
1990–91, total [5,8]	100.0	83.6	6.0	3.4	3.8	0.4	2.7
Men	100.0	83.7	4.9	3.3	4.2	0.4	3.6
Women	100.0	83.5	7.0	3.5	3.6	0.4	1.9
1991–92, total [5,9]	100.0	82.9	6.4	3.6	4.1	0.5	2.5
Men	100.0	83.1	5.2	3.5	4.5	0.4	3.2
Women	100.0	82.7	7.4	3.7	3.8	0.5	1.8
1992–93, total [5,10]	100.0	81.7	6.7	3.9	4.4	0.5	2.8
Men	100.0	82.0	5.4	3.7	4.8	0.5	3.6
Women	100.0	81.4	7.8	4.1	4.2	0.5	2.1
1993–94, total [5,11]	100.0	80.3	7.2	4.3	4.8	0.5	2.9
Men	100.0	80.8	5.8	4.1	5.1	0.5	3.7
Women	100.0	79.8	8.3	4.5	4.5	0.6	2.3
1994–95, total [5,12]	100.0	78.8	7.5	4.7	5.2	0.6	3.2
Men	100.0	79.4	6.1	4.5	5.5	0.5	4.0
Women	100.0	78.3	8.7	4.8	5.0	0.6	2.5

[1] Excludes 1,121 men and 528 women whose racial/ethnic group was not available.
[2] Excludes 1,279 men and 571 women whose racial/ethnic group was not available.
[3] Excludes 258 men and 82 women whose racial/ethnic group was not available.
[4] Excludes 6,380 men and 4,786 women whose racial/ethnic group was not available.
[5] Reported racial/ethnic distributions of students by level of degree, field of degree, and sex were used to estimate race/ethnicity for students whose race/ethnicity was not reported.
[6] Excludes 1,400 men and 1,005 women whose racial/ethnic group and field of study were not available.
[7] Excludes 1,379 men and 1,334 women whose racial/ethnic group and field of study were not available.
[8] Excludes 7,621 men and 5,637 women whose racial/ethnic group and field of study were not available.
[9] Excludes 3,835 men and 2,885 women whose racial/ethnic group and field of study were not available.
[10] Excludes 2,340 men and 2,907 women whose racial/ethnic group and field of study were not available.
[11] Excludes 1,618 men and 1,684 women whose racial/ethnic group and field of study were not available.
[12] Excludes 957 men and 389 women whose racial/ethnic group and field of study were not available.

NOTE.—Because of rounding, percents may not add to 100.0.

SOURCE: U.S. Department of Education, National Center for Education Statistics, Higher Education General Information Survey (HEGIS), "Degrees and Other Formal Awards Conferred" surveys, and Integrated Postsecondary Education Data System (IPEDS), "Completions" surveys. (This table was prepared April 1997.)

Table 266.—Bachelor's degrees conferred by institutions of higher education, by racial/ethnic group, major field of study, and sex of student: 1994–95

Major field of study	Total								Men								Women						
	Total	White, non-Hispanic	Black, non-Hispanic	Hispanic	Asian/Pacific Islander	American Indian/Alaskan Native	Non-resident alien		Total	White, non-Hispanic	Black, non-Hispanic	Hispanic	Asian/Pacific Islander	American Indian/Alaskan Native	Non-resident alien	Total	White, non-Hispanic	Black, non-Hispanic	Hispanic	Asian/Pacific Islander	American Indian/Alaskan Native	Non-resident alien
1	2	3	4	5	6	7	8		9	10	11	12	13	14	15	16	17	18	19	20	21	22
All fields, total[1]	1,158,788	913,377	87,203	54,201	60,478	6,606	36,923		525,174	417,006	31,775	23,600	28,973	2,736	21,084	633,614	496,371	55,428	30,601	31,505	3,870	15,839
Agriculture and natural resources	19,841	17,986	472	460	424	163	336		12,692	11,645	233	280	204	99	231	7,149	6,341	239	180	220	64	105
Architecture and related programs	8,756	6,716	345	544	704	28	419		5,741	4,470	213	366	404	17	271	3,015	2,246	132	178	300	11	148
Area, ethnic, and cultural studies	5,706	3,704	650	519	558	47	228		2,092	1,321	221	102	196	25	140	3,614	2,383	429	330	362	22	88
Biological sciences/life sciences	55,984	41,573	3,303	2,331	7,208	291	1,278		26,687	20,276	1,004	1,102	3,553	131	621	29,297	21,297	2,299	1,229	3,655	160	657
Business	234,323	176,471	20,286	10,753	13,174	999	12,640		121,898	95,039	7,991	5,258	6,029	478	7,103	112,425	81,432	12,295	5,495	7,145	521	5,537
Communications	48,104	39,240	4,036	2,014	1,378	204	1,232		20,028	16,808	1,389	773	490	79	489	28,076	22,432	2,647	1,241	888	125	743
Communications technologies	699	553	86	14	16	4	28		376	318	30	8	8	1	11	323	235	56	6	8	3	17
Computer and information sciences	24,404	15,932	2,563	1,077	2,425	113	2,294		17,463	12,095	1,273	730	1,623	75	1,667	6,941	3,837	1,290	347	802	38	627
Construction trades	113	95	8	0	2	1	7		91	75	6	0	2	1	7	22	20	2	0	0	0	0
Education	106,079	93,033	6,658	3,430	1,381	846	731		25,641	22,347	1,640	823	382	214	235	80,438	70,686	5,018	2,607	999	632	496
Engineering	62,342	44,735	2,908	2,724	6,939	226	4,810		51,646	37,662	1,890	2,203	5,467	180	4,244	10,696	7,073	1,018	521	1,472	46	566
Engineering-related technologies	15,633	12,332	1,262	688	714	115	522		14,133	11,253	1,035	610	639	99	497	1,500	1,079	227	78	75	16	25
English language and literature/letters	51,901	43,881	3,303	2,101	1,755	288	573		17,810	15,495	816	686	524	99	190	34,091	28,386	2,487	1,415	1,231	189	383
Foreign languages and literatures	13,775	10,251	498	1,903	591	55	477		4,243	3,284	134	526	154	12	133	9,532	6,967	364	1,377	437	43	344
Health professions and related sciences	79,855	66,402	5,806	2,601	3,563	467	1,016		14,443	11,757	869	543	910	95	269	65,412	54,645	4,937	2,058	2,653	372	747
Home economics and vocational home economics	15,345	13,103	1,051	395	459	93	244		1,808	1,487	154	47	71	8	41	13,537	11,616	897	348	388	85	203
Law and legal studies	2,032	1,646	211	88	66	14	7		595	467	67	26	28	5	2	1,437	1,179	144	62	38	9	5
Liberal arts and sciences, general studies, and humanities	33,356	25,842	3,155	2,413	1,091	298	557		13,157	10,557	1,077	791	380	100	252	20,199	15,285	2,078	1,622	711	198	305
Library science	50	46	2	0	0	1	1		2	2	0	0	0	0	0	48	44	2	0	0	1	1
Mathematics	13,723	10,559	1,011	520	984	59	590		7,295	5,589	485	306	530	30	355	6,428	4,970	526	214	454	29	235
Mechanics and repairers	66	57	2	0	2	0	5		63	56	2	0	1	0	4	3	1	0	0	1	0	1
Multi/interdisciplinary studies	26,033	20,006	1,893	2,088	1,478	147	421		9,158	7,081	649	557	608	56	207	16,875	12,925	1,244	1,531	870	91	214
Parks, recreation, leisure and fitness studies	12,889	11,245	715	499	183	74	173		6,724	5,769	439	310	87	34	85	6,165	5,476	276	189	96	40	88
Philosophy and religion	7,276	6,102	326	315	346	42	145		4,670	3,911	194	238	199	24	104	2,606	2,191	132	77	147	18	41
Physical sciences and science technologies	19,177	15,398	1,056	507	1,387	102	727		12,497	10,319	505	320	809	69	475	6,680	5,079	551	187	578	33	252
Precision production trades	353	281	43	11	12	1	5		247	200	29	8	7	1	2	106	81	14	3	5	0	3
Protective services	24,157	17,980	3,702	1,701	420	203	151		15,049	11,845	1,726	983	287	107	101	9,108	6,135	1,976	718	133	96	50
Psychology	72,083	57,297	5,878	4,149	3,404	417	938		19,548	15,653	1,439	1,111	990	123	232	52,535	41,644	4,439	3,038	2,414	294	706
Public administration and services	18,586	13,533	3,026	1,170	467	205	185		3,935	2,833	640	253	134	36	39	14,651	10,700	2,386	917	333	169	146
R.O.T.C. and military sciences	27	26	0	0	1	0	0		24	23	0	0	1	0	0	3	3	0	0	0	0	0
Social sciences and history	128,154	99,544	10,562	7,002	6,626	798	3,622		68,139	54,659	4,466	3,462	3,136	389	2,027	60,015	44,885	6,096	3,540	3,490	409	1,595
Theological studies and religious vocations	5,578	4,830	243	136	151	24	194		4,201	3,707	160	99	96	16	123	1,377	1,123	83	37	55	8	71
Transportation and material moving workers	3,698	3,213	168	120	101	24	72		3,297	2,880	139	105	90	21	62	401	333	29	15	11	3	10
Visual and performing arts	48,690	39,765	1,975	1,928	2,468	259	2,295		19,781	16,123	860	887	934	112	865	28,909	23,642	1,115	1,041	1,534	147	1,430

[1] Reported racial/ethnic distributions of students by level of degree, field of degree, and sex were used to estimate race/ethnicity for students whose race/ethnicity was not reported. Excludes 957 men and 389 women whose racial/ethnic group and field of study were not available.

NOTE.—To facilitate trend comparisons, certain aggregations have been made of the degree fields as reported in the IPEDS "Completions" survey. "Agriculture and natural resources" includes Agricultural business and production, Agricultural sciences, and Conservation and renewable natural resources; and "Business" includes Business management and administrative services, Marketing operations/marketing and distribution, and Consumer and personal services.

SOURCE: U.S. Department of Education, National Center for Education Statistics, Integrated Postsecondary Education Data System (IPEDS), "Completions" survey. (This table was prepared April 1997.)

HIGHER EDUCATION: DEGREES 297

Table 267.—Bachelor's degrees conferred by institutions of higher education, by racial/ethnic group, major field of study, and sex of student: 1993–94

Major field of study	Total								Men							Women						
	Total	White, non-Hispanic	Black, non-Hispanic	Hispanic	Asian/Pacific Islander	American Indian/Alaskan Native	Non-resident alien	Total	White, non-Hispanic	Black, non-Hispanic	Hispanic	Asian/Pacific Islander	American Indian/Alaskan Native	Non-resident alien	Total	White, non-Hispanic	Black, non-Hispanic	Hispanic	Asian/Pacific Islander	American Indian/Alaskan Native	Non-resident alien
1	2	3	4	5	6	7	8	9	10	11	12	13	14	15	16	17	18	19	20	21	22
All fields, total[1]	1,165,973	936,227	83,576	50,241	55,660	6,189	34,080	530,804	429,121	30,648	21,807	26,938	2,616	19,674	635,169	507,106	52,928	28,434	28,722	3,573	14,406
Agriculture and natural resources	18,070	16,404	502	386	309	128	341	11,748	10,801	266	223	148	78	232	6,322	5,603	236	163	161	50	109
Architecture and related programs	8,975	6,961	348	479	717	36	434	5,764	4,495	233	305	424	22	285	3,211	2,466	115	174	293	14	149
Area, ethnic, and cultural studies	5,573	3,737	636	484	479	53	184	1,958	1,318	215	161	148	19	97	3,615	2,419	421	323	331	34	87
Biological/life sciences	51,383	38,736	3,022	2,137	6,083	252	1,153	25,050	19,298	944	1,063	3,057	115	573	26,333	19,438	2,078	1,074	3,026	137	580
Business	246,654	191,111	20,366	10,264	12,486	1,036	11,391	129,161	103,573	7,966	4,997	5,619	474	6,532	117,493	87,538	12,400	5,267	6,867	562	4,859
Communications	51,164	42,453	4,122	1,942	1,301	223	1,123	21,023	17,854	1,427	765	450	95	432	30,141	24,599	2,695	1,177	851	128	691
Communications technologies	663	535	88	10	6		17	336	284	32	6	4		10	327	251	56	4	2		7
Computer and information sciences	24,200	16,191	2,455	899	2,301	79	2,275	17,317	12,305	1,188	584	1,511	60	1,669	6,883	3,886	1,267	315	790	19	606
Construction trades	75	57	11	1	2	1	3	70	55	8	2		1	3	5	2	3				0
Education	107,600	95,482	6,316	3,295	1,122	739	646	24,450	21,549	1,477	746	270	199	209	83,150	73,933	4,839	2,549	852	540	437
Engineering	62,220	45,639	2,712	2,452	6,652	223	4,542	52,035	38,677	1,824	2,005	5,352	183	3,994	10,185	6,962	888	447	1,300	40	548
Engineering-related technologies	15,823	12,682	1,190	651	726	98	476	14,386	11,693	950	582	652	85	424	1,437	989	240	69	74	13	52
English language and literature/letters	53,924	46,166	3,250	1,980	1,738	262	528	18,425	16,150	829	639	548	93	166	35,499	30,016	2,421	1,341	1,190	169	362
Foreign languages and literatures	14,378	10,963	510	1,798	588	55	464	4,304	3,374	113	515	162	18	122	10,074	7,589	397	1,283	426	37	342
Health professions and related sciences	74,421	62,756	4,896	2,274	3,070	398	1,027	13,062	10,861	674	469	709	82	267	61,359	51,895	4,222	1,805	2,361	316	760
Home economics and vocational home economics	15,522	13,369	959	394	476	87	237	1,933	1,618	148	53	64	11	39	13,589	11,751	811	341	412	76	198
Law and legal studies	2,171	1,735	208	121	87	14	6	648	503	52	46	37	8	2	1,523	1,232	156	75	50	6	4
Liberal arts and sciences, general studies, and humanities	33,397	26,450	2,968	2,084	1,072	302	521	13,117	10,715	995	671	396	105	235	20,280	15,735	1,973	1,413	676	197	286
Library science	62	54	4	0	0	0	4	5	4	0	0	0	0	1	57	50	4	0	0	0	3
Mathematics	14,396	11,300	1,004	526	944	61	561	7,735	6,051	465	291	535	30	363	6,661	5,249	539	235	409	31	198
Mechanics and repairers	107	88	3	2	9	2	11	106	88	3	2	9	2	11	1	0	0	0	1	0	0
Multi/interdisciplinary studies	25,167	19,778	1,687	1,884	1,340	141	337	9,058	7,264	557	451	561	57	168	16,109	12,514	1,130	1,433	779	84	169
Parks, recreation, leisure and fitness studies	11,470	10,190	556	424	118	75	107	5,823	5,085	320	257	66	32	63	5,647	5,105	236	167	52	43	44
Philosophy and religion	7,546	6,416	319	305	336	35	135	4,844	4,136	207	202	200	20	79	2,702	2,280	112	103	136	15	56
Physical sciences and science technologies	18,400	15,007	946	523	1,126	85	713	12,223	10,220	475	342	666	53	467	6,177	4,787	471	181	460	32	246
Precision production trades	420	355	41	6	9	1	8	308	264	31	3	5	0	5	112	91	10	3	4	1	3
Protective services	23,009	17,393	3,482	1,412	403	160	159	14,169	11,254	1,634	798	280	96	107	8,840	6,139	1,848	614	123	64	52
Psychology	69,259	56,220	5,359	3,581	2,841	404	854	18,642	15,307	1,266	917	829	116	207	50,617	40,913	4,093	2,664	2,012	288	647
Public administration and services	17,815	13,253	2,717	1,067	396	188	194	3,919	2,879	593	258	115	35	39	13,896	10,374	2,124	809	281	153	155
R.O.T.C. and military sciences	19	18	0	0	1	0	0	16	15	0	0	1	0	0	3	3	0	0	0	0	0
Social sciences and history	133,680	105,776	10,460	6,851	6,408	783	3,402	72,006	58,555	4,543	3,453	3,133	385	1,937	61,674	47,221	5,917	3,398	3,275	398	1,465
Theological studies/religious vocations	5,434	4,770	188	121	159	20	176	4,125	3,649	144	85	99	16	132	1,309	1,121	44	36	60	4	44
Transportation and material moving workers	3,923	3,425	183	134	84	18	79	3,500	3,057	156	119	71	16	81	423	368	27	15	8	2	3
Visual and performing arts	49,053	40,757	2,068	1,754	2,279	228	1,967	19,538	16,170	913	798	824	110	723	29,515	24,587	1,155	956	1,455	118	1,244

[1] Reported racial/ethnic distributions of students by level of degree, field of degree, and sex were used to estimate race/ethnicity for students whose race/ethnicity was not reported. Excludes 1,618 men and 1,684 women whose racial/ethnic group and field of study were not available.

NOTE.—To facilitate trend comparisons, certain aggregations have been made of the degree fields as reported in the IPEDS "Completions" survey: "Agriculture and natural resources" includes Agricultural business and production, Agricultural sciences, and Conservation and renewable natural resources; and "Business" includes Business management and administrative services, Marketing operations/marketing and distribution, and Consumer and personal services.

SOURCE: U.S. Department of Education, National Center for Education Statistics, Integrated Postsecondary Education Data System (IPEDS), "Completions" survey. (This table was prepared February 1996.)

Table 268.—Master's degrees conferred by institutions of higher education, by racial/ethnic group and sex of student: 1976–77 to 1994–95

Year and sex of student	Total	White, non-Hispanic	Black, non-Hispanic	Hispanic	Asian or Pacific Islander	American Indian/Alaskan Native	Nonresident alien
1	2	3	4	5	6	7	8
	Number of degrees conferred						
1976–77, total[1]	316,602	266,061	21,037	6,071	5,122	967	17,344
Men	167,396	139,210	7,781	3,268	3,123	521	13,493
Women	149,206	126,851	13,256	2,803	1,999	446	3,851
1978–79, total[2]	300,255	249,360	19,418	5,555	5,496	999	19,427
Men	152,637	124,058	7,070	2,786	3,325	495	14,903
Women	147,618	125,302	12,348	2,769	2,171	504	4,524
1980–81, total[3]	294,183	241,216	17,133	6,461	6,282	1,034	22,057
Men	145,666	115,562	6,158	3,085	3,773	501	16,587
Women	148,517	125,654	10,975	3,376	2,509	533	5,470
1984–85, total[4]	280,421	223,628	13,939	6,864	7,782	1,256	26,952
Men	139,417	106,059	5,200	3,059	4,842	583	19,674
Women	141,004	117,569	8,739	3,805	2,940	673	7,278
1986–87, total[5]	289,349	228,874	13,873	7,044	8,559	1,103	29,896
Men	141,269	105,572	5,153	3,331	5,239	518	21,456
Women	148,080	123,302	8,720	3,713	3,320	585	8,440
1988–89, total[5,6]	309,770	242,764	14,095	7,277	10,335	1,086	34,213
Men	148,872	109,715	5,175	3,325	6,048	476	24,133
Women	160,898	133,049	8,920	3,952	4,287	610	10,080
1989–90, total[5,7]	322,465	251,690	15,446	7,950	10,577	1,101	35,701
Men	152,926	112,877	5,539	3,586	6,002	463	24,459
Women	169,539	138,813	9,907	4,364	4,575	638	11,242
1990–91, total[5,8]	328,645	255,281	16,139	8,386	11,180	1,136	36,523
Men	151,796	111,224	5,709	3,670	6,319	459	24,415
Women	176,849	144,057	10,430	4,716	4,861	677	12,108
1991–92, total[5,9]	348,682	268,371	18,116	9,358	12,658	1,273	38,906
Men	159,543	116,096	6,054	4,132	7,062	523	25,676
Women	189,139	152,275	12,062	5,226	5,596	750	13,230
1992–93, total[5,10]	368,701	278,829	19,780	10,665	13,866	1,407	44,154
Men	168,754	120,225	6,821	4,735	7,544	586	28,843
Women	199,947	158,604	12,959	5,930	6,322	821	15,311
1993–94, total[5,11]	385,419	288,288	21,937	11,913	15,267	1,697	46,317
Men	175,355	123,854	7,413	5,113	8,225	691	30,059
Women	210,064	164,434	14,524	6,800	7,042	1,006	16,258
1994–95, total[5,12]	397,052	292,784	24,171	12,907	16,842	1,621	48,727
Men	178,123	123,809	8,103	5,490	8,920	659	31,142
Women	218,929	168,975	16,068	7,417	7,922	962	17,585
	Percentage distribution of degrees conferred						
1976–77, total[1]	100.0	84.0	6.6	1.9	1.6	0.3	5.5
Men	100.0	83.2	4.6	2.0	1.9	0.3	8.1
Women	100.0	85.0	8.9	1.9	1.3	0.3	2.6
1980–81, total[3]	100.0	82.0	5.8	2.2	2.1	0.4	7.5
Men	100.0	79.3	4.2	2.1	2.6	0.3	11.4
Women	100.0	84.6	7.4	2.3	1.7	0.4	3.7
1984–85, total[4]	100.0	79.7	5.0	2.4	2.8	0.4	9.6
Men	100.0	76.1	3.7	2.2	3.5	0.4	14.1
Women	100.0	83.4	6.2	2.7	2.1	0.5	5.2
1988–89, total[5,6]	100.0	78.4	4.6	2.3	3.3	0.4	11.0
Men	100.0	73.7	3.5	2.2	4.1	0.3	16.2
Women	100.0	82.7	5.5	2.5	2.7	0.4	6.3
1989–90, total[5,7]	100.0	78.1	4.8	2.5	3.3	0.3	11.1
Men	100.0	73.8	3.6	2.3	3.9	0.3	16.0
Women	100.0	81.9	5.8	2.6	2.7	0.4	6.6
1990–91, total[5,8]	100.0	77.7	4.9	2.6	3.4	0.3	11.1
Men	100.0	73.3	3.8	2.4	4.2	0.3	16.1
Women	100.0	81.5	5.9	2.7	2.7	0.4	6.8
1991–92, total[5,9]	100.0	77.0	5.2	2.7	3.6	0.4	11.2
Men	100.0	72.8	3.8	2.6	4.4	0.3	16.1
Women	100.0	80.5	6.4	2.8	3.0	0.4	7.0
1992–93, total[5,10]	100.0	75.6	5.4	2.9	3.8	0.4	12.0
Men	100.0	71.2	4.0	2.8	4.5	0.3	17.1
Women	100.0	79.3	6.5	3.0	3.2	0.4	7.7
1993–94, total[5,11]	100.0	74.8	5.7	3.1	4.0	0.4	12.0
Men	100.0	70.6	4.2	2.9	4.7	0.4	17.1
Women	100.0	78.3	6.9	3.2	3.4	0.5	7.7
1994–95, total[5,12]	100.0	73.7	6.1	3.3	4.2	0.4	12.3
Men	100.0	69.5	4.5	3.1	5.0	0.4	17.5
Women	100.0	77.2	7.3	3.4	3.6	0.4	8.0

[1] Excludes 387 men and 175 women whose racial/ethnic group was not available.
[2] Excludes 733 men and 91 women whose racial/ethnic group was not available.
[3] Excludes 1,377 men and 179 women whose racial/ethnic group was not available.
[4] Excludes 3,973 men and 1,857 women whose racial/ethnic group was not available.
[5] Reported racial/ethnic distributions of students by level of degree, field of degree, and sex were used to estimate race/ethnicity for students whose race/ethnicity was not reported.
[6] Excludes 482 men and 369 women whose racial/ethnic group and field of study were not available.
[7] Excludes 727 men and 1,109 women whose racial/ethnic group and field of study were not available.
[8] Excludes 4,686 men and 3,837 women whose racial/ethnic group and field of study were not available.
[9] Excludes 2,299 men and 1,857 women whose racial/ethnic group and field of study were not available.
[10] Excludes 504 men and 380 women whose racial/ethnic group and field of study were not available.
[11] Excludes 730 men and 921 women whose racial/ethnic group and field of study were not available.
[12] Excludes 475 men and 102 women whose racial/ethnic group and field of study were not available.

NOTE.—Because of rounding, percents may not add to 100.0.

SOURCE: U.S. Department of Education, National Center for Education Statistics, Higher Education General Information Survey (HEGIS), "Degrees and Other Formal Awards Conferred" surveys, and Integrated Postsecondary Education Data System (IPEDS), "Completions" surveys. (This table was prepared April 1997.)

Table 269.—Master's degrees conferred by institutions of higher education, by racial/ethnic group, major field of study, and sex of student: 1994–95

Major field of study	Total								Men							Women						
	Total	White, non-Hispanic	Black, non-Hispanic	Hispanic	Asian/Pacific Islander	American Indian/Alaskan Native	Non-resident alien	Total	White, non-Hispanic	Black, non-Hispanic	Hispanic	Asian/Pacific Islander	American Indian/Alaskan Native	Non-resident alien	Total	White, non-Hispanic	Black, non-Hispanic	Hispanic	Asian/Pacific Islander	American Indian/Alaskan Native	Non-resident alien
1	2	3	4	5	6	7	8	9	10	11	12	13	14	15	16	17	18	19	20	21	22
All fields, total[1]	397,052	292,784	24,171	12,907	16,842	1,621	48,727	178,123	123,809	8,103	5,490	8,920	659	31,142	218,929	168,975	16,068	7,417	7,922	962	17,585
Agriculture and natural resources	4,252	3,007	116	98	129	15	887	2,551	1,787	57	54	59	11	583	1,701	1,220	59	44	70	4	304
Architecture and related programs	3,923	2,628	142	155	282	9	707	2,310	1,557	73	93	134	4	449	1,613	1,071	69	62	148	5	258
Area, ethnic, and cultural studies	1,639	1,138	121	93	86	12	189	765	542	47	49	39	4	84	874	596	74	44	47	8	105
Biological sciences/life sciences	5,393	3,741	169	154	431	21	877	2,602	1,805	52	68	215	11	451	2,791	1,936	117	86	216	10	426
Business	93,809	66,553	5,165	2,590	4,924	311	14,266	59,109	42,711	2,427	1,621	2,902	199	9,249	34,700	23,842	2,738	969	2,022	112	5,017
Communications	5,142	3,597	376	131	171	21	846	1,869	1,358	105	45	46	7	308	3,273	2,239	271	86	125	14	538
Communications technologies	467	259	34	12	14	0	148	239	149	16	8	5	0	61	228	110	18	4	9	0	87
Computer and information sciences	10,326	4,521	372	207	1,329	17	3,880	7,627	3,488	215	160	847	12	2,905	2,699	1,033	157	47	482	5	975
Construction trades	7	3	0	1	0	0	3	4	1	0	0	0	0	2	3	2	0	0	0	0	1
Education	101,242	83,646	8,163	4,048	1,706	514	3,165	23,806	19,303	1,875	1,032	411	133	1,052	77,436	64,343	6,288	3,016	1,295	381	2,113
Engineering	28,553	14,686	706	688	2,732	45	9,696	23,935	12,323	494	561	2,153	42	8,362	4,618	2,363	212	127	579	3	1,334
Engineering-related technologies	1,110	808	58	31	46	6	161	897	649	42	27	40	4	135	213	159	16	4	6	2	26
English language and literature/letters	7,845	6,758	300	198	192	38	359	2,764	2,418	74	73	63	15	121	5,081	4,340	226	125	129	23	238
Foreign languages and literatures	3,136	2,071	75	288	112	5	585	995	690	27	83	28	3	164	2,141	1,381	48	205	84	2	421
Health professions and related sciences	31,243	25,244	1,682	849	1,590	131	1,747	6,754	4,879	293	233	606	28	715	24,489	20,365	1,389	616	984	103	1,032
Home economics and vocational home economics	2,864	2,176	238	92	76	12	270	492	359	26	25	13	3	66	2,372	1,817	212	67	63	9	204
Law and legal studies	2,511	1,228	89	65	59	6	1,064	1,680	818	43	47	38	3	731	831	410	46	18	21	3	333
Liberal arts and sciences, general studies, and humanities	2,565	2,114	158	70	39	14	170	924	747	60	24	8	7	78	1,641	1,367	98	46	31	7	92
Library science	5,057	4,384	227	114	146	12	174	1,054	925	30	27	26	3	43	4,003	3,459	197	87	120	9	131
Mathematics	4,181	2,523	162	72	257	11	1,156	2,543	1,485	70	52	147	5	784	1,638	1,038	92	20	110	6	372
Multi/interdisciplinary studies	2,457	2,001	131	65	75	13	172	1,093	860	54	28	42	7	102	1,364	1,141	77	37	33	6	70
Parks, recreation, leisure and fitness studies	1,755	1,519	64	33	20	7	112	892	769	36	20	10	4	53	863	750	28	13	10	3	59
Philosophy and religion	1,380	1,128	44	51	27	9	121	875	704	31	28	18	4	90	505	424	13	23	9	5	31
Physical sciences and science technologies	5,753	3,385	156	119	307	23	1,763	4,013	2,401	91	79	199	15	1,228	1,740	984	65	40	108	8	535
Precision production trades	5	5	0	0	0	0	0	4	4	0	0	0	0	0	1	1	0	0	0	0	0
Protective services	1,706	1,321	252	54	33	3	43	912	705	117	34	20	3	33	794	616	135	20	13	0	10
Psychology	13,921	11,562	898	579	310	88	484	3,893	3,240	228	164	82	31	148	10,028	8,322	670	415	228	57	336
Public administration and services	23,501	18,056	2,702	1,128	593	137	885	6,870	5,030	739	357	205	38	501	16,631	13,026	1,963	771	388	99	384
R.O.T.C. and military technologies	124	105	7	4	7	1	0	117	99	6	4	7	1	0	7	6	1	0	0	0	0
Social sciences and history	14,845	10,299	874	483	485	87	2,617	8,207	5,636	403	248	255	32	1,633	6,638	4,663	471	235	230	55	984
Theological studies and religious vocations	5,240	3,949	274	120	230	4	663	3,178	2,322	177	84	157	2	436	2,062	1,627	97	36	73	2	227
Transportation and material moving workers	823	741	30	19	18	6	9	775	703	26	18	16	4	8	48	38	4	1	2	2	1
Visual and performing arts	10,277	7,631	383	296	416	43	1,508	4,374	3,343	168	143	129	24	567	5,903	4,288	215	153	287	19	941

[1] Reported racial/ethnic distributions of students by level of degree, field of degree, and sex were used to estimate race/ethnicity for students whose race/ethnicity was not reported. Excludes 475 men and 102 women whose racial/ethnic group and field of study were not available.

NOTE.—To facilitate trend comparisons, certain aggregations have been made of the degree fields as reported in the IPEDS "Completions" survey: "Agriculture and natural resources" includes Agricultural business and production,

Agricultural sciences, and Conservation and renewable natural resources; and "Business" includes Business management and administrative services, Marketing operations/marketing and distribution, and Consumer and personal services.

SOURCE: U.S. Department of Education, National Center for Education Statistics, Integrated Postsecondary Education Data System (IPEDS), "Completions" survey. (This table was prepared April 1997.)

300 HIGHER EDUCATION: DEGREES

Table 270.—Master's degrees conferred by institutions of higher education, by racial/ethnic group, major field of study, and sex of student: 1993–94

Major field of study	Total									Men							Women						
	Total	White, non-His-panic	Black, non-His-panic	His-panic	Asian/Pacific Islander	Amer-ican Indian/Alas-kan Native	Non-resi-dent alien	Total	White, non-His-panic	Black, non-His-panic	His-panic	Asian/Pacific Is-lander	Amer-ican Indian/Alas-kan Native	Non-resi-dent alien	Total	White, non-His-panic	Black, non-His-panic	His-panic	Asian/Pacific Is-lander	Amer-ican Indian/Alas-kan Native	Non-resi-dent alien
1	2	3	4	5	6	7	8	9	10	11	12	13	14	15	16	17	18	19	20	21	22
All fields, total[1]	385,419	288,288	21,937	11,913	15,267	1,697	46,317	175,355	123,854	7,413	5,113	8,225	691	30,059	210,064	164,434	14,524	6,800	7,042	1,006	16,258
Agriculture and natural resources	4,119	2,767	116	190	96	12	938	2,515	1,670	72	109	43	9	612	1,604	1,097	44	81	53	3	326
Architecture and related programs	3,943	2,676	144	135	221	12	755	2,428	1,640	87	78	115	6	502	1,515	1,036	57	57	106	6	253
Area, ethnic, and cultural studies	1,633	1,129	113	96	103	17	175	768	542	46	48	50	9	73	865	587	67	48	53	8	102
Biological sciences/life sciences	5,196	3,621	149	126	347	18	935	2,465	1,722	50	60	157	13	463	2,731	1,899	99	66	190	5	472
Business	93,437	67,669	5,213	2,568	4,625	299	13,063	59,335	43,591	2,519	1,590	2,752	175	8,708	34,102	24,078	2,694	978	1,873	124	4,355
Communications	5,005	3,609	243	107	136	21	789	1,870	1,378	92	35	41	18	306	3,135	2,231	251	72	95	3	483
Communications technologies	414	263	21	10	13	2	105	228	158	9	3	4	0	54	186	105	12	7	9	2	51
Computer and information sciences	10,416	4,605	391	176	1,317	19	3,908	7,724	3,570	221	126	847	13	2,947	2,692	1,035	170	50	470	6	961
Education	98,938	83,065	7,199	3,601	1,534	605	2,934	23,008	19,031	1,574	918	405	166	914	75,930	64,034	5,625	2,683	1,129	439	2,020
Engineering	28,621	15,327	623	670	2,586	64	9,351	24,218	12,980	448	545	2,050	51	8,144	4,403	2,347	175	125	536	13	1,207
Engineering-related technologies	1,133	820	59	30	37	1	186	936	671	45	27	32	0	161	197	149	14	3	5	1	25
English language and literature/letters	7,885	6,781	248	195	202	39	420	2,712	2,369	53	70	64	15	141	5,173	4,412	195	125	138	24	279
Foreign languages and literatures	3,288	2,158	49	307	137	9	628	1,087	737	16	99	34	7	194	2,201	1,421	33	208	103	2	434
Health professions and related sciences	28,025	23,175	1,496	710	1,007	137	1,500	5,814	4,446	232	200	311	27	598	22,211	18,729	1,264	510	696	110	902
Home economics and vocational home eco-nomics	2,421	1,928	139	56	70	7	221	405	308	20	10	11	3	53	2,016	1,620	119	46	59	4	168
Law and legal studies	2,432	1,218	47	76	61	7	1,023	1,608	787	24	52	43	5	697	824	431	23	24	18	2	326
Liberal arts and sciences, general studies, and humanities	2,496	2,125	125	48	34	14	150	913	767	44	14	15	7	66	1,583	1,358	81	34	19	7	84
Library science	5,116	4,409	244	92	150	14	207	1,040	871	53	26	32	2	56	4,076	3,538	191	66	118	12	151
Mathematics	4,100	2,559	118	71	250	6	1,096	2,536	1,546	68	42	137	5	738	1,564	1,013	50	29	113	1	358
Multi/interdisciplinary studies	2,464	2,024	111	95	62	14	158	1,194	968	39	46	40	3	98	1,270	1,056	72	49	22	11	60
Parks, recreation, leisure and fitness studies	1,625	1,361	78	22	28	8	128	845	696	38	14	17	2	78	780	665	40	8	11	6	50
Philosophy and religion	1,350	1,102	38	53	38	3	116	837	683	19	28	24	3	80	513	419	19	25	14	0	36
Physical sciences and science technologies	5,679	3,354	136	102	301	17	1,769	4,018	2,419	80	70	195	14	1,240	1,661	935	56	32	106	3	529
Precision production trades	2	2	0	0	0	0	0	0	0	0	0	0	0	0	2	2	0	0	0	0	0
Protective services	1,437	1,092	220	48	23	7	47	902	706	110	33	16	3	34	535	386	110	15	7	4	13
Psychology	12,181	10,333	659	483	280	65	361	3,401	2,877	167	130	77	20	130	8,780	7,456	492	353	203	45	231
Public administration and services	21,833	16,891	2,506	990	495	143	808	6,406	4,848	612	300	161	42	443	15,427	12,043	1,894	690	334	101	365
R.O.T.C. and military technologies	124	111	4	4	4	1	0	117	106	3	3	4	1	0	7	5	1	1	0	0	0
Social sciences and history	14,561	10,247	737	459	481	71	2,566	8,152	5,712	336	237	246	38	1,583	6,409	4,535	401	222	235	33	983
Theological studies/religious vocations	4,956	3,773	259	125	226	10	563	3,034	2,256	182	63	150	4	379	1,922	1,517	77	62	76	6	184
Transportation and material moving workers	664	598	25	15	15	4	7	610	551	21	15	13	4	6	54	47	4	0	2	0	1
Visual and performing arts	9,925	7,496	327	253	388	51	1,410	4,229	3,248	133	122	139	26	561	5,696	4,248	194	131	249	25	849

[1] Reported racial/ethnic distributions of students by level of degree, field of degree, and sex were used to estimate race/ethnicity for students whose race/ethnicity was not reported. Excludes 730 men and 921 women whose racial/ethnic group and field of study were not available.

NOTE.—To facilitate trend comparisons, certain aggregations have been made of the degree fields as reported in the IPEDS "Completions" survey: "Agriculture and natural resources" includes Agricultural business and production, Agricultural sciences, and Conservation and renewable natural resources; and "Business" includes Business management and administrative services, Marketing operations/marketing and distribution, and Consumer and personal services.

SOURCE: U.S. Department of Education, National Center for Education Statistics, Integrated Postsecondary Education Data System (IPEDS), "Completions" survey. (This table was prepared February 1996.)

HIGHER EDUCATION: DEGREES 301

Table 271.—Doctor's degrees [1] conferred by institutions of higher education, by racial/ethnic group and sex of student: 1976–77 to 1994–95

Year and sex of student	Total	White, non-Hispanic	Black, non-Hispanic	Hispanic	Asian or Pacific Islander	American Indian/Alaskan Native	Nonresident alien
1	2	3	4	5	6	7	8
			Number of degrees conferred				
1976–77, total [2]	33,126	26,851	1,253	522	658	95	3,747
Men	25,036	20,032	766	383	540	67	3,248
Women	8,090	6,819	487	139	118	28	499
1978–79, total [3]	32,675	26,138	1,268	439	811	104	3,915
Men	23,488	18,433	734	294	646	69	3,312
Women	9,187	7,705	534	145	165	35	603
1980–81, total [4]	32,839	25,908	1,265	456	877	130	4,203
Men	22,595	17,310	694	277	655	95	3,564
Women	10,244	8,598	571	179	222	35	639
1984–85, total [5]	32,307	23,934	1,154	677	1,106	119	5,317
Men	21,296	15,017	561	431	802	64	4,421
Women	11,011	8,917	593	246	304	55	896
1986–87, total [6]	34,041	24,434	1,057	751	1,098	105	6,596
Men	22,061	14,812	485	441	794	57	5,472
Women	11,980	9,622	572	310	304	48	1,124
1988–89, total [6,7]	35,659	24,884	1,066	629	1,323	85	7,672
Men	22,597	14,541	491	350	945	50	6,220
Women	13,062	10,343	575	279	378	35	1,452
1989–90, total [6,8]	38,113	25,880	1,153	788	1,235	99	8,958
Men	24,248	15,105	533	423	871	49	7,267
Women	13,865	10,775	620	365	364	50	1,691
1990–91, total [6,9]	38,547	25,328	1,211	732	1,459	102	9,715
Men	24,333	14,565	581	387	987	58	7,755
Women	14,214	10,763	630	345	472	44	1,960
1991–92, total [6,10]	40,090	25,813	1,223	811	1,559	118	10,566
Men	25,168	14,674	576	458	1,062	65	8,333
Women	14,922	11,139	647	353	497	53	2,233
1992–93, total [6,11]	42,021	26,700	1,352	827	1,582	106	11,454
Men	25,980	14,902	615	439	1,041	51	8,932
Women	16,041	11,798	737	388	541	55	2,522
1993–94, total [6,12]	43,149	27,156	1,393	903	2,025	134	11,538
Men	26,531	15,126	631	465	1,373	66	8,870
Women	16,618	12,030	762	438	652	68	2,668
1994–95, total [6,13]	44,427	27,826	1,667	984	2,690	130	11,130
Men	26,898	15,354	731	488	1,758	58	8,509
Women	17,529	12,472	936	496	932	72	2,621
			Percentage distribution of degrees conferred				
1976–77, total [2]	100.0	81.1	3.8	1.6	2.0	0.3	11.3
Men	100.0	80.0	3.1	1.5	2.2	0.3	13.0
Women	100.0	84.3	6.0	1.7	1.5	0.3	6.2
1980–81, total [4]	100.0	78.9	3.9	1.4	2.7	0.4	12.8
Men	100.0	76.6	3.1	1.2	2.9	0.4	15.8
Women	100.0	83.9	5.6	1.7	2.2	0.3	6.2
1984–85, total [5]	100.0	74.1	3.6	2.1	3.4	0.4	16.5
Men	100.0	70.5	2.6	2.0	3.8	0.3	20.8
Women	100.0	81.0	5.4	2.2	2.8	0.5	8.1
1988–89, total [6,7]	100.0	69.8	3.0	1.8	3.7	0.2	21.5
Men	100.0	64.3	2.2	1.5	4.2	0.2	27.5
Women	100.0	79.2	4.4	2.1	2.9	0.3	11.1
1989–90, total [6,8]	100.0	67.9	3.0	2.1	3.2	0.3	23.5
Men	100.0	62.3	2.2	1.7	3.6	0.2	30.0
Women	100.0	77.7	4.5	2.6	2.6	0.4	12.2
1990–91, total [6,9]	100.0	65.7	3.1	1.9	3.8	0.3	25.2
Men	100.0	59.9	2.4	1.6	4.1	0.2	31.9
Women	100.0	75.7	4.4	2.4	3.3	0.3	13.8
1991–92, total [6,10]	100.0	64.4	3.1	2.0	3.9	0.3	26.4
Men	100.0	58.3	2.3	1.8	4.2	0.3	33.1
Women	100.0	74.6	4.3	2.4	3.3	0.4	15.0
1992–93, total [6,11]	100.0	63.5	3.2	2.0	3.8	0.3	27.3
Men	100.0	57.4	2.4	1.7	4.0	0.2	34.4
Women	100.0	73.5	4.6	2.4	3.4	0.3	15.7
1993–94, total [6,12]	100.0	62.9	3.2	2.1	4.7	0.3	26.7
Men	100.0	57.0	2.4	1.8	5.2	0.2	33.4
Women	100.0	72.4	4.6	2.6	3.9	0.4	16.1
1994–95, total [6,13]	100.0	62.6	3.8	2.2	6.1	0.3	25.1
Men	100.0	57.1	2.7	1.8	6.5	0.2	31.6
Women	100.0	71.2	5.3	2.8	5.3	0.4	15.0

[1] Includes Ph.D., Ed.D, and comparable degrees at the doctoral level. Excludes first-professional degrees.
[2] Excludes 106 men whose racial/ethnic group was not available.
[3] Excludes 53 men and 2 women whose racial/ethnic group was not available.
[4] Excludes 116 men and 3 women whose racial/ethnic group was not available.
[5] Excludes 404 men and 232 women whose racial/ethnic group was not available.
[6] Reported racial/ethnic distributions of students by level of degree, field of degree, and sex were used to estimate race/ethnicity for students whose race/ethnicity was not reported.
[7] Excludes 51 men and 10 women whose racial/ethnic group and field of study were not available.
[8] Excludes 153 men and 105 women whose racial/ethnic group and field of study were not available.
[9] Excludes 423 men and 324 women whose racial/ethnic group and field of study were not available.
[10] Excludes 389 men and 180 women whose racial/ethnic group and field of study were not available.
[11] Excludes 93 men and 18 women whose racial/ethnic group and field of study were not available.
[12] Excludes 21 men and 15 women whose racial/ethnic group and field of study were not available.
[13] Excludes 18 men and 1 woman whose racial/ethnic group and field of study were not available.

NOTE.—Because of rounding, percents may not add to 100.0.

SOURCE: U.S. Department of Education, National Center for Education Statistics, Higher Education General Information Survey (HEGIS), "Degrees and Other Formal Awards Conferred" surveys, and Integrated Postsecondary Education Data System (IPEDS), "Completions" surveys. (This table was prepared April 1997.)

Table 272.—Doctor's degrees conferred by institutions of higher education, by racial/ethnic group, major field of study, and sex of student: 1994–95

Major field of study	Total								Men								Women					
	Total	White, non-His-panic	Black, non-His-panic	His-panic	Asian/ Pacific Islander	Amer-ican Indian/ Alas-kan Native	Non-resi-dent alien	Total	White, non-His-panic	Black, non-His-panic	His-panic	Asian/ Pacific Is-lander	Amer-ican Indian/ Alas-kan Native	Non-resi-dent alien	Total	White, non-His-panic	Black, non-His-panic	His-panic	Asian/ Pacific Is-lander	Amer-ican Indian/ Alas-kan Native	Non-resi-dent alien
1	2	3	4	5	6	7	8	9	10	11	12	13	14	15	16	17	18	19	20	21	22
All fields, total[1]	44,427	27,826	1,667	984	2,690	130	11,130	26,898	15,354	731	488	1,758	58	8,509	17,529	12,472	936	496	932	72	2,621
Agriculture and natural resources	1,264	601	13	19	71	2	558	962	446	9	12	52	1	442	302	155	4	7	19	1	116
Architecture and related programs	141	69	6	6	4	0	56	95	43	4	5	3	0	40	46	26	2	1	1	0	16
Area, ethnic, and cultural studies	186	121	22	6	5	4	28	80	53	8	1	3	1	14	106	68	14	5	2	3	14
Biological sciences/life sciences	4,645	2,883	87	98	407	4	1,166	2,771	1,687	52	63	228	0	741	1,874	1,196	35	35	179	4	425
Business	1,394	848	41	16	82	5	402	1,014	568	25	11	58	5	347	380	280	16	5	24	0	55
Communications	320	234	14	6	15	1	51	162	116	3	0	7	0	33	158	118	11	3	8	0	18
Communications technologies	1	1	0	0	0	0	0	0	0	0	0	0	0	0	1	0	1	0	0	0	0
Computer and information sciences	884	401	9	6	92	0	376	723	311	8	2	73	0	329	161	90	1	4	19	0	47
Education	6,905	5,205	620	252	151	40	637	2,621	1,964	191	88	52	15	311	4,284	3,241	429	164	99	25	326
Engineering	6,110	2,333	76	60	635	5	3,001	5,383	1,972	59	51	525	3	2,773	727	361	17	9	110	2	228
Engineering-related technologies	18	7	0	0	2	1	8	16	7	0	0	2	1	6	2	0	0	0	0	0	2
English language and literature/letters	1,561	1,268	37	26	35	7	188	665	525	9	8	8	3	112	896	743	28	18	27	4	76
Foreign languages and literatures	905	536	8	71	33	3	254	395	221	5	27	13	3	126	510	315	3	44	20	0	128
Health professions and related sciences	2,069	1,311	90	38	153	9	468	867	444	32	17	86	2	286	1,202	867	58	21	67	7	182
Home economics and vocational home economics	388	279	28	7	9	0	65	99	67	6	1	2	0	23	289	212	22	6	7	0	42
Law and legal studies	88	32	1	0	1	0	54	62	20	1	0	0	0	41	26	12	0	0	1	0	13
Liberal arts and sciences, general studies, and humanities	90	71	8	0	2	0	9	41	31	1	0	2	0	7	49	40	7	0	0	0	2
Library science	55	29	7	2	5	0	12	20	10	1	0	2	0	6	35	19	6	2	3	0	6
Mathematics	1,226	562	5	14	95	1	549	955	433	3	11	75	1	433	271	129	2	3	20	1	116
Multi/interdisciplinary studies	238	155	13	8	14	2	46	129	79	5	4	8	0	33	109	76	8	4	6	1	13
Parks, recreation, leisure and fitness studies	149	110	5	7	6	0	21	87	61	4	4	2	0	16	62	49	1	3	4	0	5
Philosophy and religion	507	401	14	9	13	2	68	365	281	10	6	9	1	58	142	120	4	3	4	1	10
Physical sciences and science technologies	4,483	2,455	45	62	438	9	1,474	3,428	1,865	30	45	312	5	1,171	1,055	590	15	17	126	4	303
Precision production trades	0	0	0	0	0	0	0	0	0	0	0	0	0	0	0	0	0	0	0	0	0
Protective services	26	17	4	0	3	0	2	14	8	3	0	2	0	1	12	9	1	0	1	0	1
Psychology	3,822	3,231	154	129	104	18	186	1,431	1,213	35	44	41	5	93	2,391	2,018	119	85	63	13	93
Public administration and services	556	381	59	13	16	2	85	274	172	23	7	12	1	59	282	209	36	6	4	1	26
R.O.T.C. and military technologies	0	0	0	0	0	0	0	0	0	0	0	0	0	0	0	0	0	0	0	0	0
Social sciences and history	3,725	2,360	119	86	196	10	954	2,319	1,378	60	58	120	7	696	1,406	982	59	28	76	3	258
Theological studies and religious vocations	1,591	1,108	150	30	51	4	248	1,375	955	125	12	45	4	234	216	153	25	18	6	0	14
Transportation and material moving workers	0	0	0	0	0	0	0	0	0	0	0	0	0	0	0	0	0	0	0	0	0
Visual and performing arts	1,080	817	32	13	52	2	164	545	424	19	7	16	1	78	535	393	13	6	36	1	86

[1] Reported racial/ethnic distributions of students by level of degree, field of degree, and sex were used to estimate race/ethnicity for students whose race/ethnicity was not reported. Excludes 18 men and 1 woman whose racial/ethnic group and field of study were not available.

NOTE.—To facilitate trend comparisons, certain aggregations have been made of the degree fields as reported in the IPEDS "Completions" survey: "Agriculture and natural resources" includes Agricultural business and production, Agricultural sciences, and Conservation and renewable natural resources; and "Business" includes Business management and administrative services, Marketing operations/marketing and distribution, and Consumer and personal services.

SOURCE: U.S. Department of Education, National Center for Education Statistics, Integrated Postsecondary Education Data System (IPEDS), "Completions" survey. (This table was prepared April 1997.)

HIGHER EDUCATION: DEGREES 303

Table 273.—Doctor's degrees conferred by institutions of higher education, by racial/ethnic group, major field of study, and sex of student: 1993–94

Major field of study	Total								Men							Women						
	Total	White, non-Hispanic	Black, non-Hispanic	Hispanic	Asian/Pacific Islander	American Indian/Alaskan Native	Non-resident alien	Total	White, non-Hispanic	Black, non-Hispanic	Hispanic	Asian/Pacific Islander	American Indian/Alaskan Native	Non-resident alien	Total	White, non-Hispanic	Black, non-Hispanic	Hispanic	Asian/Pacific Islander	American Indian/Alaskan Native	Non-resident alien
1	2	3	4	5	6	7	8	9	10	11	12	13	14	15	16	17	18	19	20	21	22
All fields, total[1]	43,149	27,156	1,393	903	2,025	134	11,538	26,531	15,126	631	465	1,373	66	8,870	16,618	12,030	762	438	652	68	2,668
Agriculture and natural resources	1,278	596	16	18	34	2	612	982	429	13	13	25	1	501	296	167	3	5	9	1	111
Architecture and related programs	161	65	4	4	6	1	85	111	44	1	0	4	0	62	50	21	3	0	2	1	23
Area, ethnic, and cultural studies	155	99	16	0	8	4	26	75	43	8	0	4	4	16	80	56	8	0	4	0	10
Biological sciences/life sciences	4,534	2,828	64	96	291	9	1,246	2,690	1,625	31	51	172	5	806	1,844	1,203	33	45	119	4	440
Business	1,364	847	38	13	66	7	393	980	561	22	10	52	5	330	384	286	16	3	14	2	63
Communications	337	221	23	7	6	2	78	172	110	9	3	3	1	46	165	111	14	4	3	1	32
Communications technologies	8	4	0	0	0	1	3	2	1	0	0	0	0	1	6	3	0	0	0	1	2
Computer and information sciences	810	366	11	5	64	1	363	685	295	9	5	56	1	320	125	71	2	0	8	0	43
Education	6,908	5,393	523	201	152	42	597	2,706	2,101	160	69	67	16	293	4,202	3,292	363	132	85	26	304
Engineering	5,963	2,209	60	51	461	5	3,177	5,299	1,886	45	44	403	4	2,917	664	323	15	7	58	1	260
Engineering-related technologies	16	1	0	1	3	0	11	16	0	0	1	3	0	11	0	0	0	0	0	0	0
English language and literature/letters	1,344	1,088	32	26	24	9	165	568	448	6	16	7	2	89	776	640	26	10	17	7	76
Foreign languages and literatures	886	514	8	73	24	0	267	355	198	5	23	12	0	117	531	316	3	50	12	0	150
Health professions and related sciences	1,902	1,282	59	26	104	7	424	789	465	14	10	58	1	241	1,113	817	45	16	46	6	183
Home economics and vocational home economics	365	279	10	5	9	1	61	93	70	2	1	1	1	18	272	209	8	4	8	0	43
Law and legal studies	79	16	1	7	3	0	52	63	12	1	7	3	0	40	16	4	0	0	0	0	12
Liberal arts and sciences, general studies, and humanities	80	59	7	2	5	0	7	46	34	2	2	2	0	6	34	25	5	0	3	0	1
Library science	45	31	3	1	2	0	8	14	9	1	1	0	0	3	31	22	2	0	2	0	5
Mathematics	1,157	494	7	11	83	1	561	904	373	6	9	61	1	454	253	121	1	2	22	0	107
Multi/interdisciplinary studies	227	140	10	6	5	4	62	151	83	5	3	3	2	55	76	57	5	3	2	2	7
Parks, recreation, leisure and fitness studies	116	78	3	1	2	1	31	70	43	1	0	1	1	24	46	35	2	1	1	0	7
Philosophy and religion	528	417	22	5	16	0	68	383	296	17	4	13	0	53	145	121	5	1	3	0	15
Physical sciences and science technologies	4,650	2,536	46	83	323	6	1,656	3,642	2,006	35	63	225	6	1,307	1,008	530	11	20	98	0	349
Precision production trades	0	0	0	0	0	0	0	0	0	0	0	0	0	0	0	0	0	0	0	0	0
Protective services	25	19	2	1	0	0	3	14	10	1	1	0	0	2	11	9	1	0	0	0	1
Psychology	3,563	3,027	126	140	93	11	166	1,346	1,137	46	49	33	5	76	2,217	1,890	80	91	60	6	90
Public administration and services	519	356	44	14	14	4	87	238	135	19	11	9	2	62	281	221	25	3	5	2	25
R.O.T.C. and military technologies	0	0	0	0	0	0	0	0	0	0	0	0	0	0	0	0	0	0	0	0	0
Social sciences and history	3,627	2,318	123	73	130	12	971	2,317	1,362	68	41	84	6	756	1,310	956	55	32	46	6	215
Theological studies/religious vocations	1,448	1,058	113	17	66	2	192	1,235	892	89	13	64	2	175	213	166	24	4	2	0	17
Transportation and material moving workers	0	0	0	0	0	0	0	0	0	0	0	0	0	0	0	0	0	0	0	0	0
Visual and performing arts	1,054	815	22	18	31	2	166	585	457	15	14	8	2	89	469	358	7	4	23	0	77

[1] Reported racial/ethnic distributions of students by level of degree, field of degree, and sex were used to estimate race/ethnicity for students whose race/ethnicity was not reported. Excludes 21 men and 15 women whose racial/ethnic group and field of study were not available.

NOTE.—To facilitate trend comparisons, certain aggregations have been made of the degree fields as reported in the IPEDS "Completions" survey: "Agriculture and natural resources" includes Agricultural business and production, Agricultural sciences, and Conservation and renewable natural resources; and "Business" includes Business management and administrative services, Marketing operations/marketing and distribution, and Consumer and personal services.

SOURCE: U.S. Department of Education, National Center for Education Statistics, Integrated Postsecondary Education Data System (IPEDS), "Completions" survey. (This table was prepared February 1996.)

304 HIGHER EDUCATION: DEGREES

Table 274.—First-professional degrees conferred by institutions of higher education, by racial/ethnic group and sex of student: 1976–77 to 1994–95

Year and sex of student	Total	White, non-Hispanic	Black, non-Hispanic	Hispanic	Asian or Pacific Islander	American Indian/Alaskan Native	Nonresident alien
1	2	3	4	5	6	7	8
Number of degrees conferred							
1976–77, total[1]	63,953	58,422	2,537	1,076	1,021	196	701
Men	51,980	47,777	1,761	893	776	159	614
Women	11,973	10,645	776	183	245	37	87
1978–79, total[2]	68,611	62,430	2,836	1,283	1,205	216	641
Men	52,425	48,123	1,783	989	860	150	520
Women	16,186	14,307	1,053	294	345	66	121
1980–81, total[3]	71,340	64,551	2,931	1,541	1,456	192	669
Men	52,194	47,629	1,772	1,131	991	134	537
Women	19,146	16,922	1,159	410	465	58	132
1984–85, total[4]	71,057	63,219	3,029	1,884	1,816	248	861
Men	47,501	42,630	1,623	1,239	1,152	176	681
Women	23,556	20,589	1,406	645	664	72	180
1986–87, total	71,617	62,688	3,420	2,051	2,270	304	884
Men	46,523	41,149	1,835	1,303	1,420	183	633
Women	25,094	21,539	1,585	748	850	121	251
1988–89, total	70,856	61,214	3,148	2,269	2,976	264	985
Men	45,046	39,399	1,618	1,374	1,819	148	688
Women	25,810	21,815	1,530	895	1,157	116	297
1989–90, total[5]	70,744	60,240	3,410	2,427	3,362	257	1,048
Men	43,778	37,850	1,672	1,450	1,963	135	708
Women	26,966	22,390	1,738	977	1,399	122	340
1990–91, total[6]	71,515	60,327	3,575	2,527	3,755	261	1,070
Men	43,601	37,348	1,672	1,506	2,178	144	753
Women	27,914	22,979	1,903	1,021	1,577	117	317
1991–92, total[7]	72,129	59,800	3,560	2,766	4,455	296	1,252
Men	43,812	36,939	1,603	1,635	2,593	157	885
Women	28,317	22,861	1,957	1,131	1,862	139	367
1992–93, total[8]	74,960	60,830	4,100	2,984	5,160	368	1,518
Men	44,821	37,157	1,777	1,762	2,858	190	1,077
Women	30,139	23,673	2,323	1,222	2,302	178	441
1993–94, total	75,418	60,140	4,444	3,134	5,892	371	1,437
Men	44,707	36,573	1,902	1,781	3,214	222	1,015
Women	30,711	23,567	2,542	1,353	2,678	149	422
1994–95, total	75,800	59,402	4,747	3,231	6,397	412	1,611
Men	44,853	36,146	2,077	1,836	3,491	222	1,081
Women	30,947	23,256	2,670	1,395	2,906	190	530
Percentage distribution of degrees conferred							
1976–77, total[1]	100.0	91.4	4.0	1.7	1.6	0.3	1.1
Men	100.0	91.9	3.4	1.7	1.5	0.3	1.2
Women	100.0	88.9	6.5	1.5	2.0	0.3	0.7
1980–81, total[3]	100.0	90.5	4.1	2.2	2.0	0.3	0.9
Men	100.0	91.3	3.4	2.2	1.9	0.3	1.0
Women	100.0	88.4	6.1	2.1	2.4	0.3	0.7
1984–85, total[4]	100.0	89.0	4.3	2.7	2.6	0.3	1.2
Men	100.0	89.7	3.4	2.6	2.4	0.4	1.4
Women	100.0	87.4	6.0	2.7	2.8	0.3	0.8
1986–87, total	100.0	87.5	4.8	2.9	3.2	0.4	1.2
Men	100.0	88.4	3.9	2.8	3.1	0.4	1.4
Women	100.0	85.8	6.3	3.0	3.4	0.5	1.0
1988–89, total	100.0	86.4	4.4	3.2	4.2	0.4	1.4
Men	100.0	87.5	3.6	3.1	4.0	0.3	1.5
Women	100.0	84.5	5.9	3.5	4.5	0.4	1.2
1989–90, total[5]	100.0	85.2	4.8	3.4	4.8	0.4	1.5
Men	100.0	86.5	3.8	3.3	4.5	0.3	1.6
Women	100.0	83.0	6.4	3.6	5.2	0.5	1.3
1990–91, total[6]	100.0	84.4	5.0	3.5	5.3	0.4	1.5
Men	100.0	85.7	3.8	3.5	5.0	0.3	1.7
Women	100.0	82.3	6.8	3.7	5.6	0.4	1.1
1991–92, total[7]	100.0	82.9	4.9	3.8	6.2	0.4	1.7
Men	100.0	84.3	3.7	3.7	5.9	0.4	2.0
Women	100.0	80.7	6.9	4.0	6.6	0.5	1.3
1992–93, total[8]	100.0	81.1	5.5	4.0	6.9	0.5	2.0
Men	100.0	82.9	4.0	3.9	6.4	0.4	2.4
Women	100.0	78.5	7.7	4.1	7.6	0.6	1.5
1993–94, total	100.0	79.7	5.9	4.2	7.8	0.5	1.9
Men	100.0	81.8	4.3	4.0	7.2	0.5	2.3
Women	100.0	76.7	8.3	4.4	8.7	0.5	1.4
1994–95, total	100.0	78.4	6.3	4.3	8.4	0.5	2.1
Men	100.0	80.6	4.6	4.1	7.8	0.5	2.4
Women	100.0	75.1	8.6	4.5	9.4	0.6	1.7

[1] Excludes 394 men and 12 women whose racial/ethnic group was not available.
[2] Excludes 227 men and 10 women whose racial/ethnic group was not available.
[3] Excludes 598 men and 18 women whose racial/ethnic group was not available.
[4] Excludes 2,954 men and 1,052 women whose racial/ethnic group and field of study were not available.
[5] Excludes 183 men and 61 women whose racial/ethnic group and field of study were not available.
[6] Excludes 245 men and 188 women whose racial/ethnic group and field of study were not available.
[7] Excludes 1,259 men and 758 women whose racial/ethnic group and field of study were not available.
[8] Excludes 332 men and 95 women whose racial/ethnic group and field of study were not available.

NOTE.—For years 1984–85 to 1994–95, reported racial/ethnic distributions of students by level of degree, field of degree, and sex were used to estimate race/ethnicity for students whose race/ethnicity was not reported. Because of rounding, percents may not add to 100.0.

SOURCE: U.S. Department of Education, National Center for Education Statistics, Higher Education General Information Survey (HEGIS), "Degrees and Other Formal Awards Conferred" surveys, and Integrated Postsecondary Education Data System (IPEDS), "Completions" surveys. (This table was prepared April 1997.)

HIGHER EDUCATION: DEGREES 305

Table 275.—First-professional degrees conferred by institutions of higher education, by racial/ethnic group, major field of study, and sex of student: 1994–95

Major field of study	Total									Men							Women						
	Total	White, non-Hispanic	Black, non-Hispanic	Hispanic	Asian/Pacific Islander	American Indian/Alaskan Native	Non-resident alien	Total	White, non-Hispanic	Black, non-Hispanic	Hispanic	Asian/Pacific Islander	American Indian/Alaskan Native	Non-resident alien	Total	White, non-Hispanic	Black, non-Hispanic	Hispanic	Asian/Pacific Islander	American Indian/Alaskan Native	Non-resident alien
1	2	3	4	5	6	7	8	9	10	11	12	13	14	15	16	17	18	19	20	21	22
All fields[1]	75,800	59,402	4,747	3,231	6,397	412	1,611	44,853	36,146	2,077	1,836	3,491	222	1,081	30,947	23,256	2,670	1,395	2,906	190	530
Dentistry (D.D.S. or D.M.D.)	3,897	2,616	180	233	589	12	267	2,480	1,774	83	128	313	9	173	1,417	842	97	105	276	3	94
Medicine (M.D.)	15,537	11,215	929	648	2,485	65	195	9,507	7,058	409	399	1,490	28	123	6,030	4,157	520	249	995	37	72
Optometry (O.D.)	1,185	899	27	36	157	5	61	538	439	5	16	48	2	28	647	460	22	20	109	3	33
Osteopathic medicine (D.O.)	1,854	1,524	51	67	185	9	18	1,249	1,040	32	49	109	6	13	605	484	19	18	76	3	5
Pharmacy (Pharm. D.)	2,264	1,444	233	50	434	7	96	785	522	66	20	134	1	42	1,479	922	167	30	300	6	54
Podiatry (Pod. D. or D.P.) or podiatric medicine (D.P.M.)	545	416	28	32	57	1	11	370	290	15	19	38	1	7	175	126	13	13	19	0	4
Veterinary medicine (D.V.M.)	2,148	1,983	52	53	37	12	11	762	694	22	27	9	5	5	1,386	1,289	30	26	28	7	6
Chiropractic medicine (D.C. or D.C.M.)	2,968	2,477	50	81	125	14	221	2,094	1,750	28	56	91	13	156	874	727	22	25	34	1	65
Law (LL.B. or J.D.)	39,349	32,126	2,699	1,897	2,011	272	344	22,592	19,108	1,118	1,016	987	146	217	16,757	13,018	1,581	881	1,024	126	127
Theology (M. Div., M.H.L., B.D., or Ord.)	5,978	4,641	496	132	317	15	377	4,443	3,443	298	106	272	11	313	1,535	1,198	198	26	45	4	64
Other	75	61	2	2	0	0	10	33	28	0	0	0	0	5	42	33	2	1	0	0	6

[1] Reported racial/ethnic distributions of students by level of degree, field of degree, and sex were used to estimate race/ethnicity for students whose race/ethnicity was not reported.

SOURCE: U.S. Department of Education, National Center for Education Statistics, Integrated Postsecondary Education Data System (IPEDS), "Completions" survey. (This table was prepared April 1997.)

Table 276.—First-professional degrees conferred by institutions of higher education, by racial/ethnic group, major field of study, and sex of student: 1993–94

Major field of study	Total									Men							Women						
	Total	White, non-Hispanic	Black, non-Hispanic	Hispanic	Asian/Pacific Islander	American Indian/Alaskan Native	Non-resident alien	Total	White, non-Hispanic	Black, non-Hispanic	Hispanic	Asian/Pacific Islander	American Indian/Alaskan Native	Non-resident alien	Total	White, non-Hispanic	Black, non-Hispanic	Hispanic	Asian/Pacific Islander	American Indian/Alaskan Native	Non-resident alien
1	2	3	4	5	6	7	8	9	10	11	12	13	14	15	16	17	18	19	20	21	22
All fields[1]	75,418	60,140	4,444	3,134	5,892	371	1,437	44,707	36,573	1,902	1,781	3,214	222	1,015	30,711	23,567	2,542	1,353	2,678	149	422
Dentistry (D.D.S. or D.M.D.)	3,787	2,559	171	218	538	17	284	2,330	1,672	73	117	272	10	186	1,457	887	98	101	266	7	98
Medicine (M.D.)	15,368	11,287	937	613	2,282	68	181	9,544	7,223	398	363	1,398	41	121	5,824	4,064	539	250	884	27	60
Optometry (O.D.)	1,103	818	36	38	153	3	55	554	448	9	14	51	1	31	549	370	27	24	102	2	24
Osteopathic medicine (D.O.)	1,798	1,478	48	70	182	8	12	1,165	975	29	41	104	7	9	633	503	19	29	78	1	3
Pharmacy (Pharm.D.)	1,936	1,297	155	54	347	1	82	643	464	39	30	74	0	36	1,293	833	116	24	273	1	46
Podiatry (Pod.D. or D.P.) or podiatric medicine (D.P.M.)	465	339	32	41	43	2	8	330	248	13	33	26	6	0	135	91	19	8	17	0	0
Veterinary medicine (D.V.M.)	2,089	1,923	39	66	40	14	7	798	740	11	30	8	3	6	1,291	1,183	28	36	32	8	4
Chiropractic medicine (D.C. or D.C.M.)	2,806	2,370	40	80	115	19	182	2,010	1,710	21	55	77	16	131	796	660	19	25	38	3	51
Law (LL.B. or J.D.)	40,044	33,420	2,472	1,842	1,816	223	271	22,826	19,624	988	1,002	890	130	192	17,218	13,796	1,484	840	926	93	79
Theology (M.Div., M.H.L., B.D., or Ord.)	5,967	4,607	513	109	375	16	347	4,486	3,455	321	95	314	9	292	1,481	1,152	192	14	61	7	55
Other	55	42	1	3	1	0	8	21	14	0	1	0	0	0	34	28	1	2	1	0	2

[1] Reported racial/ethnic distributions of students by level of degree, field of degree, and sex were used to estimate race/ethnicity for students whose race/ethnicity was not reported.

SOURCE: U.S. Department of Education, National Center for Education Statistics, Integrated Postsecondary Education Data System (IPEDS), "Completions" survey. (This table was prepared November 1995.)

Table 277.—Earned degrees in agriculture and natural resources[1] conferred by institutions of higher education, by level of degree and sex of student: 1970–71 to 1994–95

Year	Bachelor's degrees			Master's degrees			Doctor's degrees		
	Total	Men	Women	Total	Men	Women	Total	Men	Women
1	2	3	4	5	6	7	8	9	10
1970–71	12,672	12,136	536	2,457	2,313	144	1,086	1,055	31
1971–72	13,516	12,779	737	2,680	2,490	190	971	945	26
1972–73	14,756	13,661	1,095	2,807	2,588	219	1,059	1,031	28
1973–74	16,253	14,684	1,569	2,928	2,640	288	930	897	33
1974–75	17,528	15,061	2,467	3,067	2,703	364	991	958	33
1975–76	19,402	15,845	3,557	3,340	2,862	478	928	867	61
1976–77	21,467	16,690	4,777	3,724	3,177	547	893	831	62
1977–78	22,650	17,069	5,581	4,023	3,268	755	971	909	62
1978–79	23,134	16,854	6,280	3,994	3,187	807	950	877	73
1979–80	22,802	16,045	6,757	3,976	3,082	894	991	879	112
1980–81	21,886	15,154	6,732	4,003	3,061	942	1,067	940	127
1981–82	21,029	14,443	6,586	4,163	3,114	1,049	1,079	925	154
1982–83	20,909	14,085	6,824	4,254	3,129	1,125	1,149	1,004	145
1983–84	19,317	13,206	6,111	4,178	2,989	1,189	1,172	1,001	171
1984–85	18,107	12,477	5,630	3,928	2,846	1,082	1,213	1,036	177
1985–86	16,823	11,544	5,279	3,801	2,701	1,100	1,158	966	192
1986–87	14,991	10,314	4,677	3,522	2,460	1,062	1,049	871	178
1987–88	14,222	9,744	4,478	3,479	2,427	1,052	1,142	926	216
1988–89	13,492	9,298	4,194	3,245	2,231	1,014	1,183	950	233
1989–90	12,900	8,822	4,078	3,382	2,239	1,143	1,295	1,038	257
1990–91	13,124	8,832	4,292	3,295	2,160	1,135	1,185	953	232
1991–92	15,124	9,869	5,255	3,735	2,413	1,322	1,214	963	251
1992–93	16,778	11,080	5,698	3,965	2,477	1,488	1,173	879	294
1993–94	18,070	11,748	6,322	4,119	2,515	1,604	1,278	982	296
1994–95	19,841	12,692	7,149	4,252	2,551	1,701	1,264	962	302

[1] Includes degrees in agricultural business and production; agricultural sciences; and conservation and renewable natural resources.

SOURCE: U.S. Department of Education, National Center for Education Statistics, Higher Education General Information Survey (HEGIS), "Degrees and Other Formal Awards Conferred" surveys, and Integrated Postsecondary Education Data System (IPEDS), "Completions" surveys. (This table was prepared March 1997.)

Table 278.—Earned degrees in architecture and related programs[1] conferred by institutions of higher education, by level of degree and sex of student: 1949–50 to 1994–95

Year	Bachelor's degrees			Master's degrees			Doctor's degrees		
	Total	Men	Women	Total	Men	Women	Total	Men	Women
1	2	3	4	5	6	7	8	9	10
1949–50	2,563	2,441	122	166	159	7	1	1	0
1959–60	1,801	1,744	57	319	305	14	17	17	0
1967–68	3,057	2,931	126	1,021	953	68	15	15	0
1969–70	4,105	3,888	217	1,427	1,260	167	35	33	2
1970–71	5,570	4,906	664	1,705	1,469	236	36	33	3
1971–72	6,440	5,667	773	1,899	1,626	273	50	43	7
1972–73	6,962	6,042	920	2,307	1,943	364	58	54	4
1973–74	7,822	6,665	1,157	2,702	2,208	494	69	65	4
1974–75	8,226	6,791	1,435	2,938	2,343	595	69	58	11
1975–76	9,146	7,396	1,750	3,215	2,545	670	82	69	13
1976–77	9,222	7,249	1,973	3,213	2,489	724	73	62	11
1977–78	9,250	7,054	2,196	3,115	2,304	811	73	57	16
1978–79	9,273	6,876	2,397	3,113	2,226	887	96	74	22
1979–80	9,132	6,596	2,536	3,139	2,245	894	79	66	13
1980–81	9,455	6,800	2,655	3,153	2,234	919	93	73	20
1981–82	9,728	6,825	2,903	3,327	2,242	1,085	80	58	22
1982–83	9,823	6,403	3,420	3,357	2,224	1,133	97	74	23
1983–84	9,186	5,895	3,291	3,223	2,197	1,026	84	62	22
1984–85	9,325	6,019	3,306	3,275	2,148	1,127	89	66	23
1985–86	9,119	5,824	3,295	3,260	2,129	1,131	73	56	17
1986–87	8,950	5,617	3,333	3,163	2,086	1,077	92	66	26
1987–88	8,603	5,271	3,332	3,159	2,042	1,117	98	66	32
1988–89	9,150	5,545	3,605	3,383	2,192	1,191	86	63	23
1989–90	9,364	5,703	3,661	3,499	2,228	1,271	103	73	30
1990–91	9,781	5,788	3,993	3,490	2,244	1,246	135	101	34
1991–92	8,753	5,805	2,948	3,640	2,271	1,369	132	93	39
1992–93	9,167	5,940	3,227	3,808	2,376	1,432	148	105	43
1993–94	8,975	5,764	3,211	3,943	2,428	1,515	161	111	50
1994–95	8,756	5,741	3,015	3,923	2,310	1,613	141	95	46

[1] Prior to 1967–68, includes degrees in architecture. From 1967–68, includes degrees in architecture; city/urban, community, and regional planning; architectural environmental design; interior architecture; landscape architecture; architectural urban design and planning; and architecture and related programs, other.

SOURCE: U.S. Department of Education, National Center for Education Statistics, Higher Education General Information Survey (HEGIS), "Degrees and Other Formal Awards Conferred" surveys, and Integrated Postsecondary Education Data System (IPEDS), "Completions" surveys. (This table was prepared March 1997.)

HIGHER EDUCATION: DEGREES 307

Table 279.—Earned degrees in the biological/life sciences [1] conferred by institutions of higher education, by level of degree and sex of student: 1951-52 to 1994-95

Year	Bachelor's degrees			Master's degrees			Doctor's degrees		
	Total	Men	Women	Total	Men	Women	Total	Men	Women
1	2	3	4	5	6	7	8	9	10
1951-52	11,094	8,212	2,882	2,307	1,908	399	764	680	84
1955-56	12,423	9,515	2,908	1,759	1,379	380	1,025	908	117
1959-60	15,576	11,654	3,922	2,154	1,668	486	1,205	1,086	119
1961-62	16,915	12,136	4,779	2,642	1,982	660	1,338	1,179	159
1963-64	22,723	16,321	6,402	3,296	2,348	948	1,625	1,432	193
1965-66	26,916	19,368	7,548	4,232	3,085	1,147	2,097	1,792	305
1967-68	31,826	22,986	8,840	5,506	3,959	1,547	2,784	2,345	439
1969-70	34,034	23,919	10,115	5,800	3,975	1,825	3,289	2,820	469
1970-71	35,743	25,333	10,410	5,728	3,805	1,923	3,645	3,050	595
1971-72	37,293	26,323	10,970	6,101	4,087	2,014	3,653	3,031	622
1972-73	42,233	29,636	12,597	6,263	4,354	1,909	3,636	2,926	710
1973-74	48,340	33,245	15,095	6,552	4,555	1,997	3,439	2,740	699
1974-75	51,741	34,612	17,129	6,550	4,587	1,963	3,384	2,641	743
1975-76	54,275	35,520	18,755	6,582	4,497	2,085	3,392	2,663	729
1976-77	53,605	34,218	19,387	7,114	4,718	2,396	3,397	2,671	726
1977-78	51,502	31,705	19,797	6,806	4,400	2,406	3,309	2,511	798
1978-79	48,846	29,191	19,655	6,831	4,265	2,566	3,542	2,636	906
1979-80	46,370	26,828	19,542	6,510	4,098	2,412	3,636	2,690	946
1980-81	43,216	24,149	19,067	5,978	3,654	2,324	3,718	2,666	1,052
1981-82	41,639	22,754	18,885	5,874	3,426	2,448	3,743	2,654	1,089
1982-83	39,982	21,564	18,418	5,696	3,214	2,482	3,341	2,266	1,075
1983-84	38,640	20,558	18,082	5,406	2,996	2,410	3,437	2,381	1,056
1984-85	38,445	20,064	18,381	5,059	2,647	2,412	3,432	2,307	1,125
1985-86	38,524	19,993	18,531	5,013	2,616	2,397	3,358	2,229	1,129
1986-87	38,121	19,657	18,464	4,952	2,538	2,414	3,419	2,225	1,194
1987-88	36,755	18,245	18,510	4,784	2,423	2,361	3,629	2,349	1,280
1988-89	36,059	17,953	18,106	4,961	2,492	2,469	3,520	2,234	1,286
1989-90	37,204	18,312	18,892	4,869	2,395	2,474	3,844	2,394	1,450
1990-91	39,530	19,412	20,118	4,765	2,302	2,463	4,093	2,577	1,516
1991-92	42,941	20,798	22,143	4,785	2,301	2,484	4,243	2,620	1,623
1992-93	47,038	22,842	24,196	4,756	2,343	2,413	4,435	2,664	1,771
1993-94	51,383	25,050	26,333	5,196	2,465	2,731	4,534	2,690	1,844
1994-95	55,984	26,687	29,297	5,393	2,602	2,791	4,645	2,771	1,874

[1] Includes degrees in biology; biochemistry and biophysics; botany; cell and molecular biology; microbiology/bacteriology; zoology; and other biological sciences.

SOURCE: U.S. Department of Education, National Center for Education Statistics, Higher Education General Information Survey (HEGIS), "Degrees and Other Formal Awards Conferred" surveys, and Integrated Postsecondary Education Data System (IPEDS), "Completions" surveys. (This table was prepared March 1997.)

Table 280.—Earned degrees in biology, microbiology, and zoology conferred by institutions of higher education, by level of degree: 1970-71 to 1994-95

Year	Biology, general			Microbiology [1]			Zoology [2]		
	Bachelor's	Master's	Doctor's	Bachelor's	Master's	Doctor's	Bachelor's	Master's	Doctor's
1	2	3	4	5	6	7	8	9	10
1970-71	26,294	2,665	536	1,475	456	365	5,722	1,167	1,107
1971-72	27,473	2,943	580	1,548	470	351	5,522	1,189	1,094
1972-73	31,185	2,959	627	1,940	517	344	5,770	1,191	1,008
1973-74	36,188	3,186	657	2,311	505	384	6,192	1,250	919
1974-75	38,748	3,109	637	2,767	552	345	6,116	1,216	920
1975-76	40,163	3,177	624	2,927	585	364	6,105	1,153	909
1976-77	39,530	3,322	608	2,884	659	325	5,608	1,168	950
1977-78	37,598	3,094	664	2,695	615	353	5,139	1,160	885
1978-79	35,962	3,093	663	2,670	597	395	4,913	1,109	938
1979-80	33,523	2,911	718	2,631	596	376	4,374	1,078	955
1980-81	31,323	2,598	734	2,414	482	370	3,946	1,090	946
1981-82	29,651	2,579	678	2,377	470	350	3,664	1,028	936
1982-83	28,022	2,354	521	2,306	446	331	3,453	918	809
1983-84	27,379	2,313	617	2,329	447	360	3,294	867	826
1984-85	27,593	2,130	658	2,180	413	302	3,128	778	802
1985-86	27,618	2,173	574	2,217	353	336	2,940	723	844
1986-87	27,465	2,022	537	2,098	390	337	2,858	740	787
1987-88	26,838	1,981	576	2,014	357	386	2,580	725	786
1988-89	26,229	2,097	527	1,780	411	356	2,582	736	744
1989-90	27,213	1,998	551	1,814	366	409	2,501	638	810
1990-91	29,285	1,956	632	1,757	324	419	2,673	640	833
1991-92	31,909	1,995	657	1,722	336	454	2,840	620	818
1992-93	34,932	2,000	671	1,769	328	520	3,071	637	786
1993-94	38,103	2,178	665	1,841	332	478	3,207	749	805
1994-95	41,658	2,350	729	1,908	295	443	3,206	689	767

[1] Includes bacteriology.
[2] Includes general zoology; entomology; pathology; pharmacology; physiology; and zoology, other.

SOURCE: U.S. Department of Education, National Center for Education Statistics, Higher Education General Information Survey (HEGIS), "Degrees and Other Formal Awards Conferred" surveys, and Integrated Postsecondary Education Data System (IPEDS), "Completions" surveys. (This table was prepared March 1997.)

Table 281.—Earned degrees in business[1] conferred by institutions of higher education, by level of degree and sex of student: 1955–56 to 1994–95

Year	Bachelor's degrees			Master's degrees			Doctor's degrees		
	Total	Men	Women	Total	Men	Women	Total	Men	Women
1	2	3	4	5	6	7	8	9	10
1955–56	42,813	38,706	4,107	3,280	3,118	162	129	127	2
1957–58	51,991	48,063	3,928	4,223	4,072	151	110	105	5
1959–60	51,076	47,262	3,814	4,643	4,476	167	135	133	2
1961–62	49,017	45,184	3,833	7,691	7,484	207	226	221	5
1963–64	55,474	51,056	4,418	9,251	9,008	243	275	268	7
1965–66	62,721	57,516	5,205	12,959	12,628	331	387	370	17
1967–68	79,074	72,126	6,948	17,795	17,186	609	441	427	14
1969–70	105,580	96,346	9,234	21,561	20,792	769	620	610	10
1970–71	114,729	104,275	10,454	25,977	24,967	1,010	757	736	21
1971–72	121,266	109,688	11,578	30,028	28,845	1,183	859	840	19
1972–73	126,144	112,783	13,361	30,638	29,128	1,510	902	850	52
1973–74	131,640	114,729	16,911	32,172	30,044	2,128	919	870	49
1974–75	132,731	111,144	21,587	35,758	32,732	3,026	936	897	39
1975–76	142,034	113,954	28,080	42,054	37,145	4,909	900	851	49
1976–77	150,765	115,353	35,412	46,006	39,400	6,606	827	775	52
1977–78	159,691	116,171	43,520	47,837	39,743	8,094	823	753	70
1978–79	171,241	118,825	52,416	49,855	40,274	9,581	821	724	97
1979–80	184,867	122,508	62,359	54,484	42,288	12,196	753	642	111
1980–81	198,983	125,523	73,460	57,391	42,980	14,411	795	675	120
1981–82	213,374	129,262	84,112	60,763	43,807	16,956	815	668	147
1982–83	226,627	131,538	95,089	64,758	45,999	18,759	776	644	132
1983–84	229,478	129,559	99,919	66,150	46,178	19,972	929	730	199
1984–85	232,636	127,659	104,977	66,996	46,209	20,787	831	688	143
1985–86	237,319	128,780	108,539	66,689	45,938	20,751	934	729	205
1986–87	240,546	128,603	111,943	67,093	44,913	22,180	1,062	808	254
1987–88	243,021	129,552	113,469	69,230	45,980	23,250	1,063	810	253
1988–89	246,399	131,157	115,242	73,065	48,540	24,525	1,100	800	300
1989–90	248,698	132,329	116,369	76,676	50,585	26,091	1,093	818	275
1990–91	249,311	131,624	117,687	78,255	50,883	27,372	1,185	876	309
1991–92	256,603	135,440	121,163	84,642	54,705	29,937	1,242	953	289
1992–93	256,842	135,573	121,269	89,615	57,651	31,964	1,346	969	377
1993–94	246,654	129,161	117,493	93,437	59,335	34,102	1,364	980	384
1994–95	234,323	121,898	112,425	93,809	59,109	34,700	1,394	1,014	380

[1] Includes degrees in business management/administrative services; marketing operations/marketing and distribution; and consumer and personal services.

SOURCE: U.S. Department of Education, National Center for Education Statistics, Higher Education General Information Survey (HEGIS), "Degrees and Other Formal Awards Conferred" surveys, and Integrated Postsecondary Education Data System (IPEDS), "Completions" surveys. (This table was prepared March 1997.)

Table 282.—Earned degrees in communications[1] conferred by institutions of higher education, by level of degree and sex of student: 1970–71 to 1994–95

Year	Bachelor's degrees			Master's degrees			Doctor's degrees		
	Total	Men	Women	Total	Men	Women	Total	Men	Women
1	2	3	4	5	6	7	8	9	10
1970–71	10,802	6,989	3,813	1,856	1,214	642	145	126	19
1971–72	12,340	7,964	4,376	2,200	1,443	757	111	96	15
1972–73	14,317	9,074	5,243	2,406	1,546	860	139	114	25
1973–74	17,096	10,536	6,560	2,640	1,668	972	175	146	29
1974–75	19,248	11,455	7,793	2,794	1,618	1,176	165	119	46
1975–76	21,282	12,458	8,824	3,126	1,818	1,308	204	154	50
1976–77	23,214	12,932	10,282	3,091	1,719	1,372	171	130	41
1977–78	25,400	13,480	11,920	3,296	1,673	1,623	191	138	53
1978–79	26,457	13,266	13,191	2,882	1,483	1,399	192	138	54
1979–80	28,616	13,656	14,960	3,082	1,527	1,555	193	121	72
1980–81	31,282	14,179	17,103	3,105	1,448	1,657	182	107	75
1981–82	34,222	14,917	19,305	3,327	1,578	1,749	200	136	64
1982–83	38,567	16,161	22,406	3,604	1,661	1,943	214	126	88
1983–84	40,113	16,604	23,509	3,656	1,600	2,056	219	131	88
1984–85	42,002	17,175	24,827	3,669	1,576	2,093	234	143	91
1985–86	43,076	17,639	25,437	3,823	1,610	2,213	223	116	107
1986–87	45,337	18,110	27,227	3,893	1,590	2,303	275	158	117
1987–88	46,649	18,527	28,122	3,925	1,568	2,357	234	134	100
1988–89	48,609	19,215	29,394	4,257	1,737	2,520	253	138	115
1989–90	51,308	20,218	31,090	4,362	1,707	2,655	273	145	128
1990–91	52,773	20,645	32,128	4,336	1,711	2,625	274	151	123
1991–92	54,977	21,497	33,480	4,464	1,692	2,772	255	132	123
1992–93	54,706	22,028	32,678	5,209	1,980	3,229	301	146	155
1993–94	51,827	21,359	30,468	5,419	2,098	3,321	345	174	171
1994–95	48,803	20,404	28,399	5,609	2,108	3,501	321	162	159

[1] Includes degrees in communications, general; advertising; journalism; broadcast journalism; public relations and organizational communications; radio and television broadcasting; other communications; and communications technologies.

SOURCE: U.S. Department of Education, National Center for Education Statistics, Higher Education General Information Survey (HEGIS), "Degrees and Other Formal Awards Conferred" surveys, and Integrated Postsecondary Education Data System (IPEDS), "Completions" surveys. (This table was prepared March 1997.)

HIGHER EDUCATION: DEGREES 309

Table 283.—Earned degrees in computer and information sciences[1] conferred by institutions of higher education, by level of degree and sex of student: 1970–71 to 1994–95

Year	Bachelor's degrees			Master's degrees			Doctor's degrees		
	Total	Men	Women	Total	Men	Women	Total	Men	Women
1	2	3	4	5	6	7	8	9	10
1970–71	2,388	2,064	324	1,588	1,424	164	128	125	3
1971–72	3,402	2,941	461	1,977	1,752	225	167	155	12
1972–73	4,304	3,664	640	2,113	1,888	225	196	181	15
1973–74	4,756	3,976	780	2,276	1,983	293	198	189	9
1974–75	5,033	4,080	953	2,299	1,961	338	213	199	14
1975–76	5,652	4,534	1,118	2,603	2,226	377	244	221	23
1976–77	6,407	4,876	1,531	2,798	2,332	466	216	197	19
1977–78	7,201	5,349	1,852	3,038	2,471	567	196	181	15
1978–79	8,719	6,272	2,447	3,055	2,480	575	236	206	30
1979–80	11,154	7,782	3,372	3,647	2,883	764	240	213	27
1980–81	15,121	10,202	4,919	4,218	3,247	971	252	227	25
1981–82	20,267	13,218	7,049	4,935	3,625	1,310	251	230	21
1982–83	24,510	15,606	8,904	5,321	3,813	1,508	262	228	34
1983–84	32,172	20,246	11,926	6,190	4,379	1,811	251	225	26
1984–85	38,878	24,579	14,299	7,101	5,064	2,037	248	223	25
1985–86	41,889	26,923	14,966	8,070	5,658	2,412	344	299	45
1986–87	39,589	25,865	13,724	8,481	5,985	2,496	374	322	52
1987–88	34,523	23,331	11,192	9,197	6,726	2,471	428	380	48
1988–89	30,454	21,087	9,367	9,414	6,775	2,639	551	466	85
1989–90	27,257	19,117	8,140	9,677	6,960	2,717	627	534	93
1990–91	25,083	17,726	7,357	9,324	6,563	2,761	676	584	92
1991–92	24,557	17,510	7,047	9,530	6,884	2,646	772	669	103
1992–93	24,200	17,403	6,797	10,163	7,410	2,753	805	689	116
1993–94	24,200	17,317	6,883	10,416	7,724	2,692	810	685	125
1994–95	24,404	17,463	6,941	10,326	7,627	2,699	884	723	161

[1] Includes degrees in computer and information sciences, general; computer programming; data processing technology/technician; information science and systems; computer systems analysis; and other computer and information sciences.

SOURCE: U.S. Department of Education, National Center for Education Statistics, Higher Education General Information Survey (HEGIS), "Degrees and Other Formal Awards Conferred" surveys, and Integrated Postsecondary Education Data System (IPEDS), "Completions" surveys. (This table was prepared March 1997.)

Table 284.—Earned degrees in education conferred by institutions of higher education, by level of degree and sex of student: 1949–50 to 1994–95

Year	Bachelor's degrees			Master's degrees			Doctor's degrees		
	Total	Men	Women	Total	Men	Women	Total	Men	Women
1	2	3	4	5	6	7	8	9	10
1949–50	61,472	31,398	30,074	20,069	12,025	8,044	953	797	156
1959–60	89,002	25,556	63,446	33,433	18,057	15,376	1,591	1,279	312
1967–68	133,965	31,926	102,039	63,399	30,672	32,727	4,078	3,250	828
1969–70	163,964	40,420	123,544	78,020	34,832	43,188	5,588	4,479	1,109
1970–71	176,307	44,896	131,411	87,666	38,365	49,301	6,041	4,771	1,270
1971–72	190,880	49,344	141,536	96,668	41,141	55,527	6,648	5,104	1,544
1972–73	193,984	51,300	142,684	103,777	43,298	60,479	6,857	5,191	1,666
1973–74	184,907	48,997	135,910	110,402	44,112	66,290	6,757	4,974	1,783
1974–75	166,758	44,463	122,295	117,841	44,430	73,411	6,975	4,856	2,119
1975–76	154,437	42,004	112,433	126,061	44,831	81,230	7,202	4,826	2,376
1976–77	143,234	39,867	103,367	124,267	42,308	81,959	7,338	4,832	2,506
1977–78	135,821	37,410	98,411	116,916	37,662	79,254	7,018	4,281	2,737
1978–79	125,873	33,743	92,130	109,866	34,410	75,456	7,170	4,174	2,996
1979–80	118,038	30,901	87,137	101,819	30,300	71,519	7,314	4,100	3,214
1980–81	108,074	27,039	81,035	96,713	27,548	69,165	7,279	3,843	3,436
1981–82	100,932	24,380	76,552	91,601	25,339	66,262	6,999	3,612	3,387
1982–83	97,895	23,644	74,251	83,250	22,823	60,427	7,057	3,547	3,510
1983–84	92,299	22,195	70,104	75,664	21,142	54,522	6,911	3,446	3,465
1984–85	88,072	21,252	66,820	74,654	20,537	54,117	6,612	3,172	3,440
1985–86	87,114	20,959	66,155	74,801	20,295	54,506	6,605	3,088	3,517
1986–87	86,936	20,729	66,207	74,045	19,293	54,752	6,407	2,931	3,476
1987–88	91,112	20,988	70,124	76,566	19,108	57,458	6,060	2,739	3,321
1988–89	96,913	21,662	75,251	81,174	19,956	61,218	6,337	2,704	3,633
1989–90	105,112	23,007	82,105	84,881	20,467	64,414	6,502	2,776	3,726
1990–91	110,807	23,417	87,390	87,343	20,448	66,895	6,187	2,613	3,574
1991–92	108,006	22,686	85,320	92,668	21,244	71,424	6,864	2,783	4,081
1992–93	107,781	23,233	84,548	96,028	22,197	73,831	7,030	2,867	4,163
1993–94	107,600	24,450	83,150	98,938	23,008	75,930	6,908	2,706	4,202
1994–95	106,079	25,641	80,438	101,242	23,806	77,436	6,905	2,621	4,284

SOURCE: U.S. Department of Education, National Center for Education Statistics, Higher Education General Information Survey (HEGIS), "Degrees and Other Formal Awards Conferred" surveys, and Integrated Postsecondary Education Data System (IPEDS), "Completions" surveys. (This table was prepared March 1997.)

Table 285.—Earned degrees in engineering [1] conferred by institutions of higher education, by level of degree and sex of student: 1949–50 to 1994–95

Year	Bachelor's degrees			Master's degrees			Doctor's degrees		
	Total	Men	Women	Total	Men	Women	Total	Men	Women
1	2	3	4	5	6	7	8	9	10
1949–50	52,246	52,071	175	4,496	4,481	15	417	416	1
1959–60	37,679	37,537	142	7,159	7,133	26	786	783	3
1969–70	44,479	44,149	330	15,593	15,421	172	3,681	3,657	24
1970–71	50,046	49,646	400	16,443	16,258	185	3,638	3,615	23
1971–72	51,164	50,638	526	16,960	16,688	272	3,671	3,649	22
1972–73	51,265	50,652	613	16,619	16,341	278	3,492	3,438	54
1973–74	50,286	49,490	796	15,379	15,023	356	3,312	3,257	55
1974–75	46,852	45,838	1,014	15,348	14,973	375	3,108	3,042	66
1975–76	46,331	44,871	1,460	16,342	15,760	582	2,821	2,755	66
1976–77	49,283	47,065	2,218	16,245	15,525	720	2,586	2,513	73
1977–78	55,654	51,945	3,709	16,398	15,533	865	2,440	2,383	57
1978–79	62,375	57,201	5,174	15,495	14,544	951	2,506	2,423	83
1979–80	68,893	62,488	6,405	16,243	15,101	1,142	2,507	2,412	95
1980–81	75,000	67,301	7,699	16,709	15,347	1,362	2,561	2,457	104
1981–82	80,005	70,899	9,106	17,939	16,311	1,628	2,636	2,496	140
1982–83	89,018	78,096	10,922	19,344	17,548	1,796	2,831	2,706	125
1983–84	94,185	82,092	12,093	20,655	18,500	2,155	2,981	2,816	165
1984–85	95,828	83,232	12,596	21,555	19,247	2,308	3,230	3,022	208
1985–86	95,660	83,117	12,543	21,657	19,165	2,492	3,410	3,181	229
1986–87	92,816	80,104	12,712	22,654	19,804	2,850	3,818	3,555	263
1987–88	88,506	76,372	12,134	23,385	20,476	2,909	4,191	3,898	293
1988–89	85,002	73,436	11,566	24,568	21,374	3,194	4,523	4,123	400
1989–90	81,322	70,071	11,251	24,772	21,357	3,415	4,981	4,536	445
1990–91	78,650	67,738	10,912	24,958	21,430	3,528	5,272	4,787	485
1991–92	77,541	66,716	10,825	25,977	22,143	3,834	5,499	4,972	527
1992–93	78,051	66,836	11,215	28,726	24,454	4,272	5,843	5,283	560
1993–94	78,225	66,597	11,628	29,754	25,154	4,600	5,979	5,315	664
1994–95	78,154	65,933	12,221	29,670	24,836	4,834	6,128	5,399	729

[1] Includes degrees in engineering, engineering-related technologies, construction trades, and mechanics and repairers from 1969–70 through 1994–95.

SOURCE: U.S. Department of Education, National Center for Education Statistics, Higher Education General Information Survey (HEGIS), "Degrees and Other Formal Awards Conferred" surveys, and Integrated Postsecondary Education Data System (IPEDS), "Completions" surveys. (This table was prepared March 1997.)

Table 286.—Earned degrees in chemical, civil, electrical, and mechanical engineering conferred by institutions of higher education, by level of degree: 1970–71 to 1994–95

Year	Chemical engineering			Civil engineering [1]			Electrical, electronics, and communications engineering			Mechanical engineering		
	Bachelor's	Master's	Doctor's	Bachelor's	Master's	Doctor's	Bachelor's	Master's	Doctor's	Bachelor's	Master's	Doctor's
1	2	3	4	5	6	7	8	9	10	11	12	13
1970–71	3,579	1,100	406	6,526	2,425	446	12,198	4,282	879	8,858	2,237	438
1971–72	3,625	1,154	394	6,803	2,487	415	12,101	4,206	824	8,530	2,282	411
1972–73	3,578	1,051	397	7,390	2,627	397	12,313	3,895	791	8,523	2,141	370
1973–74	3,399	1,044	400	8,017	2,652	368	11,316	3,499	705	7,677	1,843	385
1974–75	3,070	990	346	7,651	2,769	356	10,161	3,469	701	6,890	1,858	340
1975–76	3,140	1,031	308	7,923	2,999	370	9,791	3,774	649	6,800	1,907	305
1976–77	3,524	1,086	291	8,228	2,964	309	9,936	3,788	566	7,703	1,952	283
1977–78	4,569	1,235	259	9,135	2,685	277	11,133	3,740	503	8,875	1,942	279
1978–79	5,568	1,149	304	9,809	2,646	253	12,338	3,591	586	10,107	1,877	271
1979–80	6,320	1,270	284	10,326	2,683	270	13,821	3,836	525	11,808	2,060	281
1980–81	6,527	1,267	300	10,678	2,891	325	14,938	3,901	535	13,329	2,291	276
1981–82	6,740	1,285	311	10,524	2,995	329	16,455	4,462	526	13,922	2,399	333
1982–83	7,185	1,368	319	9,989	3,074	340	18,049	4,531	550	15,675	2,511	299
1983–84	7,475	1,514	330	9,693	3,146	369	19,943	5,078	585	16,629	2,797	319
1984–85	7,146	1,544	418	9,162	3,172	377	21,691	5,153	660	16,794	3,053	409
1985–86	5,877	1,361	446	8,679	2,926	395	23,742	5,534	722	16,194	3,075	426
1986–87	4,991	1,184	497	8,147	2,901	451	24,547	6,183	724	15,450	3,198	528
1987–88	3,917	1,088	579	7,488	2,836	481	23,597	6,688	860	14,900	3,329	596
1988–89	3,663	1,093	602	7,312	2,903	505	21,908	7,028	998	14,843	3,498	633
1989–90	3,430	1,035	562	7,252	2,812	516	20,711	7,225	1,162	14,336	3,424	742
1990–91	3,444	903	611	7,314	2,927	536	19,320	7,095	1,220	13,977	3,516	757
1991–92	3,754	956	590	8,034	3,113	540	17,958	7,360	1,282	14,067	3,653	851
1992–93	4,459	990	595	8,868	3,610	577	17,281	7,870	1,413	14,464	3,982	871
1993–94	5,163	1,032	604	9,479	3,873	651	15,823	7,791	1,470	15,030	4,099	887
1994–95	5,901	1,085	571	9,927	4,077	625	14,929	7,693	1,543	14,794	4,213	890

[1] From 1970–71 to 1981–82 includes "construction and transportation engineering."

NOTE.—Degrees in engineering-related technologies are not included in this tabulation.

SOURCE: U.S. Department of Education, National Center for Education Statistics, Higher Education General Information Survey (HEGIS), "Degrees and Other Formal Awards Conferred" surveys, and Integrated Postsecondary Education Data System (IPEDS), "Completions" surveys. (This table was prepared March 1997.)

Table 287.—Earned degrees in English language and literature/letters [1] conferred by institutions of higher education, by level of degree and sex of student: 1949–50 to 1994–95

Year	Bachelor's degrees			Master's degrees			Doctor's degrees		
	Total	Men	Women	Total	Men	Women	Total	Men	Women
1	2	3	4	5	6	7	8	9	10
1949–50	17,240	8,221	9,019	2,259	1,320	939	230	181	49
1959–60	20,128	7,580	12,548	2,931	1,458	1,473	397	314	83
1969–70	56,410	18,650	37,760	8,517	3,326	5,191	1,213	837	376
1970–71	64,342	22,155	42,187	10,686	4,211	6,475	1,650	1,175	475
1971–72	63,976	22,657	41,319	10,579	4,123	6,456	1,826	1,233	593
1972–73	61,003	22,156	38,847	10,239	4,063	6,176	1,935	1,258	677
1973–74	54,590	20,214	34,376	9,803	3,917	5,886	1,885	1,208	677
1974–75	47,619	17,880	29,739	9,444	3,569	5,875	1,711	1,025	686
1975–76	42,006	16,073	25,933	8,809	3,383	5,426	1,672	967	705
1976–77	37,794	14,295	23,499	8,016	2,985	5,031	1,508	841	667
1977–78	35,328	13,137	22,191	7,655	2,706	4,949	1,400	758	642
1978–79	33,561	12,198	21,363	6,684	2,369	4,315	1,314	708	606
1979–80	32,541	11,380	21,161	6,189	2,233	3,956	1,294	686	608
1980–81	32,254	11,198	21,056	5,929	2,092	3,837	1,164	553	611
1981–82	33,419	11,414	22,005	5,772	1,983	3,789	1,101	511	590
1982–83	31,829	10,859	20,970	5,048	1,710	3,338	991	471	520
1983–84	32,834	11,170	21,664	5,010	1,736	3,274	1,018	459	559
1984–85	33,218	11,334	21,884	5,187	1,786	3,401	1,041	470	571
1985–86	34,552	11,819	22,733	5,518	1,881	3,637	991	428	563
1986–87	36,284	12,353	23,931	5,483	1,891	3,592	961	415	546
1987–88	38,661	12,836	25,825	5,562	1,870	3,692	981	428	553
1988–89	42,470	13,927	28,543	5,950	2,002	3,948	1,022	458	564
1989–90	47,519	15,662	31,857	6,567	2,205	4,362	1,078	480	598
1990–91	51,841	17,146	34,695	7,026	2,296	4,730	1,184	517	667
1991–92	54,951	18,536	36,415	7,450	2,513	4,937	1,273	537	736
1992–93	56,133	19,247	36,886	7,790	2,667	5,123	1,341	550	791
1993–94	53,924	18,425	35,499	7,885	2,712	5,173	1,344	568	776
1994–95	51,901	17,810	34,091	7,845	2,764	5,081	1,561	665	896

[1] Includes degrees conferred in English language and literature, general; comparative literature; English composition; English creative writing; American literature; English literature; speech and rhetorical studies; English technical and business writing; and English language and literature/letters, other.

SOURCE: U.S. Department of Education, National Center for Education Statistics, Higher Education General Information Survey (HEGIS), "Degrees and Other Formal Awards Conferred" surveys, and Integrated Postsecondary Education Data System (IPEDS), "Completions" surveys. (This table was prepared March 1997.)

Table 288.—Earned degrees in modern foreign languages and literatures [1] conferred by institutions of higher education, by level of degree and sex of student: 1949–50 to 1994–95

Year	Bachelor's degrees			Master's degrees			Doctor's degrees		
	Total	Men	Women	Total	Men	Women	Total	Men	Women
1	2	3	4	5	6	7	8	9	10
1949–50	4,477	1,746	2,731	919	456	463	168	135	33
1959–60	4,527	1,548	2,979	832	392	440	150	100	50
1969–70	19,457	4,921	14,536	4,154	1,476	2,678	590	369	221
1970–71	19,055	4,734	14,321	4,407	1,492	2,915	703	425	278
1971–72	18,137	4,445	13,692	4,277	1,449	2,828	753	466	287
1972–73	18,232	4,347	13,885	3,992	1,407	2,585	889	519	370
1973–74	18,252	4,276	13,976	3,793	1,252	2,541	875	487	388
1974–75	17,115	3,912	13,203	3,672	1,179	2,493	829	442	387
1975–76	15,079	3,495	11,584	3,359	1,095	2,264	830	429	401
1976–77	13,626	3,225	10,401	2,986	886	2,100	728	347	381
1977–78	12,448	2,938	9,510	2,653	768	1,885	626	282	344
1978–79	11,531	2,705	8,826	2,338	685	1,653	625	287	338
1979–80	10,816	2,583	8,233	2,152	628	1,524	522	217	305
1980–81	10,050	2,402	7,648	2,018	657	1,361	556	259	297
1981–82	9,576	2,278	7,298	1,913	571	1,342	495	220	275
1982–83	9,334	2,343	6,991	1,597	528	1,069	451	183	268
1983–84	9,152	2,399	6,753	1,640	512	1,128	424	191	233
1984–85	9,675	2,529	7,146	1,611	503	1,108	387	156	231
1985–86	9,808	2,685	7,123	1,655	482	1,173	426	173	253
1986–87	9,858	2,655	7,203	1,692	491	1,201	403	162	241
1987–88	9,790	2,628	7,162	1,795	564	1,231	380	159	221
1988–89	10,498	2,767	7,731	1,821	552	1,269	389	145	244
1989–90	11,092	2,902	8,190	1,931	584	1,347	475	183	292
1990–91	11,724	3,207	8,517	1,973	595	1,378	477	200	277
1991–92	12,367	3,390	8,977	2,119	652	1,467	537	222	315
1992–93	12,819	3,537	9,282	2,353	744	1,609	535	210	325
1993–94	12,785	3,672	9,113	2,343	712	1,631	578	208	370
1994–95	12,309	3,666	8,643	2,306	688	1,618	626	250	376

[1] Includes degrees conferred in a single language or a combination of modern foreign languages. Excludes degrees in linguistics, Latin, classical Greek, and "other" foreign languages.

SOURCE: U.S. Department of Education, National Center for Education Statistics, Higher Education General Information Survey (HEGIS), "Degrees and Other Formal Awards Conferred" surveys, and Integrated Postsecondary Education Data System (IPEDS), "Completions" surveys. (This table was prepared March 1997.)

312 HIGHER EDUCATION: DEGREES

Table 289.—Earned degrees in French, German, and Spanish conferred by institutions of higher education, by level of degree: 1949–50 to 1994–95

Year	French			German			Spanish		
	Bachelor's	Master's	Doctor's	Bachelor's	Master's	Doctor's	Bachelor's	Master's	Doctor's
1	2	3	4	5	6	7	8	9	10
1949–50	1,471	299	53	540	121	40	2,122	373	34
1959–60	1,927	316	58	659	126	21	1,610	261	31
1967–68	7,068	1,301	152	2,368	771	117	6,381	1,188	123
1969–70	7,624	1,409	181	2,652	669	118	7,226	1,372	139
1970–71	7,306	1,437	192	2,601	690	144	7,068	1,456	168
1971–72	6,822	1,421	193	2,477	608	167	6,847	1,421	152
1972–73	6,705	1,277	203	2,520	598	176	7,209	1,298	206
1973–74	6,263	1,195	213	2,425	550	149	7,250	1,217	203
1974–75	5,745	1,077	200	2,289	480	147	6,719	1,228	202
1975–76	4,783	914	190	1,983	471	164	5,984	1,080	176
1976–77	4,228	875	177	1,820	394	126	5,359	930	153
1977–78	3,708	692	155	1,647	357	101	4,832	822	113
1978–79	3,558	576	143	1,524	344	106	4,563	720	118
1979–80	3,285	513	128	1,466	309	94	4,331	685	103
1980–81	3,178	460	115	1,286	294	79	3,870	592	131
1981–82	3,054	485	92	1,327	324	76	3,633	568	140
1982–83	2,871	360	106	1,367	281	68	3,349	506	129
1983–84	2,876	418	86	1,292	241	63	3,254	537	102
1984–85	2,991	385	74	1,411	240	58	3,415	505	115
1985–86	3,015	409	86	1,396	249	73	3,385	521	95
1986–87	3,062	421	85	1,366	234	70	3,450	504	104
1987–88	3,082	437	89	1,350	244	71	3,416	553	93
1988–89	3,297	444	83	1,428	263	59	3,748	552	101
1989–90	3,259	478	115	1,437	253	67	4,176	573	108
1990–91	3,355	480	98	1,543	242	58	4,480	609	125
1991–92	3,371	465	112	1,616	273	85	4,768	647	143
1992–93	3,280	513	98	1,572	317	86	5,233	667	145
1993–94	3,094	479	104	1,580	298	61	5,505	691	160
1994–95	2,764	470	118	1,352	278	83	5,602	709	161

SOURCE: U.S. Department of Education, National Center for Education Statistics, Higher Education General Information Survey (HEGIS), "Degrees and Other Formal Awards Conferred" surveys, and Integrated Postsecondary Education Data System (IPEDS), "Completions" surveys. (This table was prepared March 1997.)

Table 290.—Earned degrees in the health professions and related sciences [1] conferred by institutions of higher education, by level of degree and sex of student: 1970–71 to 1994–95

Year	Bachelor's degrees			Master's degrees			Doctor's degrees		
	Total	Men	Women	Total	Men	Women	Total	Men	Women
1	2	3	4	5	6	7	8	9	10
1970–71	25,226	5,788	19,438	5,749	2,567	3,182	466	389	77
1971–72	28,611	7,005	21,606	7,207	3,141	4,066	442	362	80
1972–73	33,564	7,754	25,810	8,362	3,567	4,795	646	485	161
1973–74	41,459	9,388	32,071	9,599	3,819	5,780	578	447	131
1974–75	49,090	10,930	38,160	10,692	4,092	6,600	618	441	177
1975–76	53,958	11,456	42,502	12,556	4,217	8,339	577	411	166
1976–77	57,328	11,947	45,381	12,951	4,163	8,788	538	366	172
1977–78	59,434	11,593	47,841	14,325	4,265	10,060	654	402	252
1978–79	62,085	11,205	50,880	15,485	4,494	10,991	718	454	264
1979–80	63,920	11,391	52,529	15,704	4,357	11,347	786	435	351
1980–81	63,649	10,519	53,130	16,515	4,316	12,199	842	475	367
1981–82	63,653	10,105	53,548	16,503	4,006	12,497	925	503	422
1982–83	64,685	10,218	54,467	17,047	4,235	12,812	1,155	649	506
1983–84	64,288	10,040	54,248	17,411	4,251	13,160	1,164	574	590
1984–85	64,422	9,741	54,681	17,385	4,119	13,266	1,199	565	634
1985–86	64,396	9,630	54,766	18,573	4,428	14,145	1,241	604	637
1986–87	63,103	9,134	53,969	18,394	3,874	14,520	1,213	564	649
1987–88	60,644	8,929	51,715	18,657	4,047	14,610	1,261	548	713
1988–89	59,005	8,872	50,133	19,268	4,226	15,042	1,437	609	828
1989–90	58,302	9,118	49,184	20,321	4,534	15,787	1,536	704	832
1990–91	59,070	9,596	49,474	21,200	4,444	16,756	1,613	694	919
1991–92	61,720	10,189	51,531	23,065	4,691	18,374	1,661	698	963
1992–93	67,089	11,347	55,742	25,718	5,227	20,491	1,767	753	1,014
1993–94	74,421	13,062	61,359	28,025	5,814	22,211	1,902	789	1,113
1994–95	79,855	14,443	65,412	31,243	6,754	24,489	2,069	867	1,202

[1] Includes degrees in chiropractic; communication disorders sciences; community health liaison; dentistry; dental services; health services administration; health and medical assistants; health and medical diagnostic and treatment services; medical laboratory technologies; predentistry; premedicine; prepharmacy; preveterinary; medical basic sciences; mental health services; nursing; optometry; pharmacy; epidemiology; rehabilitation and therapeutic services; veterinary medicine; and other health professions.

SOURCE: U.S. Department of Education, National Center for Education Statistics, Higher Education General Information Survey (HEGIS), "Degrees and Other Formal Awards Conferred" surveys, and Integrated Postsecondary Education Data System (IPEDS), "Completions" surveys. (This table was prepared March 1997.)

HIGHER EDUCATION: DEGREES 313

Table 291.—Earned degrees in mathematics[1] conferred by institutions of higher education, by level of degree and sex of student: 1949–50 to 1994–95

Year	Bachelor's degrees			Master's degrees			Doctor's degrees		
	Total	Men	Women	Total	Men	Women	Total	Men	Women
1	2	3	4	5	6	7	8	9	10
1949–50	6,382	4,942	1,440	974	784	190	160	151	9
1959–60	11,399	8,293	3,106	1,757	1,422	335	303	285	18
1967–68	23,513	14,782	8,731	5,527	4,199	1,328	947	895	52
1969–70	27,442	17,177	10,265	5,636	3,966	1,670	1,236	1,140	96
1970–71	24,937	15,498	9,439	5,695	4,149	1,546	1,249	1,154	95
1971–72	23,807	14,542	9,265	5,537	3,976	1,561	1,165	1,075	90
1972–73	23,186	13,910	9,276	5,397	3,878	1,519	1,089	987	102
1973–74	21,761	12,912	8,849	5,306	3,784	1,522	1,093	992	101
1974–75	18,460	10,853	7,607	4,816	3,358	1,458	1,048	936	112
1975–76	16,329	9,788	6,541	4,315	2,961	1,354	909	812	97
1976–77	14,395	8,476	5,919	4,109	2,762	1,347	859	748	111
1977–78	13,065	7,806	5,259	3,862	2,635	1,227	848	722	126
1978–79	12,329	7,301	5,028	3,553	2,412	1,141	769	644	125
1979–80	11,872	6,951	4,921	3,382	2,262	1,120	763	659	104
1980–81	11,433	6,614	4,819	3,074	2,106	968	775	656	119
1981–82	12,226	6,999	5,227	3,263	2,257	1,006	721	623	98
1982–83	12,719	7,175	5,544	3,398	2,316	1,082	731	611	120
1983–84	13,764	7,716	6,048	3,244	2,178	1,066	743	614	129
1984–85	15,861	8,537	7,324	3,413	2,289	1,124	734	620	114
1985–86	17,147	9,216	7,931	3,607	2,397	1,210	777	648	129
1986–87	16,999	9,110	7,889	3,730	2,328	1,402	759	628	131
1987–88	16,608	8,919	7,689	3,867	2,391	1,476	796	668	128
1988–89	15,994	8,662	7,332	3,903	2,418	1,485	915	737	178
1989–90	15,176	8,236	6,940	4,146	2,568	1,578	966	794	172
1990–91	15,310	8,178	7,132	4,041	2,446	1,595	1,036	837	199
1991–92	14,783	7,888	6,895	4,011	2,452	1,559	1,082	851	231
1992–93	14,812	7,827	6,985	4,067	2,455	1,612	1,139	906	283
1993–94	14,396	7,735	6,661	4,100	2,536	1,564	1,157	904	253
1994–95	13,723	7,295	6,428	4,181	2,543	1,638	1,226	955	271

[1] Includes degrees conferred in statistics.

SOURCE: U.S. Department of Education, National Center for Education Statistics, Higher Education General Information Survey (HEGIS), "Degrees and Other Formal Awards Conferred" surveys, and Integrated Postsecondary Education Data System (IPEDS), "Completions" surveys. (This table was prepared March 1997.)

Table 292.—Earned degrees in the physical sciences[1] conferred by institutions of higher education, by level of degree and sex of student: 1959–60 to 1994–95

Year	Bachelor's degrees			Master's degrees			Doctor's degrees		
	Total	Men	Women	Total	Men	Women	Total	Men	Women
1	2	3	4	5	6	7	8	9	10
1959–60	16,007	14,013	1,994	3,376	3,049	327	1,838	1,776	62
1967–68	19,380	16,739	2,641	5,499	4,869	630	3,593	3,405	188
1969–70	21,439	18,522	2,917	5,935	5,093	842	4,312	4,077	235
1970–71	21,412	18,459	2,953	6,367	5,521	846	4,390	4,144	246
1971–72	20,745	17,663	3,082	6,287	5,404	883	4,103	3,830	273
1972–73	20,696	17,626	3,070	6,257	5,414	843	4,006	3,738	268
1973–74	21,178	17,674	3,504	6,062	5,186	876	3,626	3,373	253
1974–75	20,778	16,992	3,786	5,807	4,969	838	3,626	3,325	301
1975–76	21,465	17,353	4,112	5,466	4,648	818	3,431	3,132	299
1976–77	22,497	17,996	4,501	5,331	4,450	881	3,341	3,022	319
1977–78	22,986	18,090	4,896	5,561	4,620	941	3,133	2,821	312
1978–79	23,207	17,985	5,222	5,451	4,461	990	3,102	2,752	350
1979–80	23,410	17,864	5,546	5,219	4,248	971	3,089	2,705	384
1980–81	23,952	18,064	5,888	5,284	4,200	1,084	3,141	2,765	376
1981–82	24,052	17,866	6,186	5,514	4,318	1,196	3,286	2,835	451
1982–83	23,381	16,993	6,388	5,290	4,157	1,133	3,269	2,811	458
1983–84	23,651	17,116	6,535	5,576	4,268	1,308	3,306	2,815	491
1984–85	23,704	17,069	6,635	5,796	4,452	1,344	3,403	2,851	552
1985–86	21,717	15,755	5,962	5,902	4,470	1,432	3,551	2,963	588
1986–87	20,070	14,372	5,698	5,629	4,219	1,410	3,673	3,039	634
1987–88	17,806	12,389	5,417	5,733	4,324	1,409	3,809	3,123	686
1988–89	17,186	12,077	5,109	5,723	4,199	1,524	3,858	3,088	770
1989–90	16,066	11,031	5,035	5,449	4,010	1,439	4,164	3,356	808
1990–91	16,344	11,176	5,168	5,309	3,837	1,472	4,290	3,447	843
1991–92	16,960	11,431	5,529	5,374	3,909	1,465	4,391	3,429	962
1992–93	17,545	11,825	5,720	5,366	3,808	1,558	4,393	3,432	961
1993–94	18,400	12,223	6,177	5,679	4,018	1,661	4,650	3,642	1,008
1994–95	19,177	12,497	6,680	5,753	4,013	1,740	4,483	3,428	1,055

[1] Includes degrees in physical sciences, general; astronomy; astrophysics; atmospheric science and meteorology; chemistry; geology; miscellaneous physical sciences; physics; science technologies; and other physical sciences.

SOURCE: U.S. Department of Education, National Center for Education Statistics, Higher Education General Information Survey (HEGIS), "Degrees and Other Formal Awards Conferred" surveys, and Integrated Postsecondary Education Data System (IPEDS), "Completions" surveys. (This table was prepared March 1997.)

Table 293.—Earned degrees in chemistry, geology, and physics conferred by institutions of higher education, by level of degree: 1970–71 to 1994–95

Year	Chemistry			Geology [1]			Physics		
	Bachelor's	Master's	Doctor's	Bachelor's	Master's	Doctor's	Bachelor's	Master's	Doctor's
1	2	3	4	5	6	7	8	9	10
1970–71	11,063	2,275	2,159	2,414	651	324	5,071	2,188	1,482
1971–72	10,590	2,248	1,971	2,573	841	310	4,634	2,033	1,344
1972–73	10,128	2,225	1,872	2,923	827	305	4,259	1,747	1,338
1973–74	10,438	2,125	1,823	3,253	938	315	3,952	1,655	1,115
1974–75	10,549	1,986	1,822	3,319	932	292	3,706	1,574	1,080
1975–76	11,022	1,783	1,621	3,358	1,003	313	3,544	1,451	997
1976–77	11,215	1,767	1,568	3,879	1,047	325	3,420	1,319	945
1977–78	11,315	1,886	1,521	4,342	1,239	268	3,330	1,294	873
1978–79	11,509	1,757	1,516	4,502	1,300	286	3,337	1,319	918
1979–80	11,232	1,723	1,545	4,597	1,295	313	3,396	1,192	830
1980–81	11,347	1,654	1,622	5,202	1,396	294	3,441	1,294	866
1981–82	11,062	1,751	1,722	5,538	1,540	282	3,472	1,284	873
1982–83	10,796	1,622	1,746	6,102	1,552	295	3,793	1,369	873
1983–84	10,704	1,667	1,744	6,549	1,514	315	3,907	1,532	953
1984–85	10,482	1,719	1,789	6,308	1,692	289	4,097	1,523	951
1985–86	10,116	1,754	1,908	4,974	1,767	271	4,180	1,501	1,010
1986–87	9,670	1,738	1,976	3,665	1,603	280	4,318	1,543	1,074
1987–88	9,052	1,708	1,995	2,551	1,523	350	4,100	1,675	1,093
1988–89	8,625	1,774	2,037	2,252	1,404	358	4,352	1,736	1,112
1989–90	8,132	1,682	2,183	1,767	1,200	414	4,155	1,831	1,192
1990–91	8,321	1,665	2,238	1,784	1,089	446	4,236	1,725	1,209
1991–92	8,641	1,780	2,280	2,078	990	413	4,098	1,834	1,337
1992–93	8,914	1,842	2,261	2,299	925	406	4,063	1,777	1,277
1993–94	9,425	1,999	2,353	2,677	937	422	4,001	1,945	1,465
1994–95	9,722	2,099	2,273	3,118	993	398	3,823	1,817	1,424

[1] Includes geology, geochemistry, and geophysics and seismology. Beginning in 1982–83, also includes other geological sciences.

SOURCE: U.S. Department of Education, National Center for Education Statistics, Higher Education General Information Survey (HEGIS), "Degrees and Other Formal Awards Conferred" surveys, and Integrated Postsecondary Education Data System (IPEDS), "Completions" surveys. (This table was prepared March 1997.)

Table 294.—Earned degrees in psychology conferred by institutions of higher education, by level of degree and by sex of student: 1949–50 to 1994–95

Year	Bachelor's degrees			Master's degrees			Doctor's degrees		
	Total	Men	Women	Total	Men	Women	Total	Men	Women
1	2	3	4	5	6	7	8	9	10
1949–50	9,569	6,055	3,514	1,316	948	368	283	241	42
1959–60	8,061	4,773	3,288	1,406	981	425	641	544	97
1967–68	23,819	13,792	10,027	3,479	2,321	1,158	1,268	982	286
1969–70	33,679	19,077	14,602	5,158	2,975	2,183	1,962	1,505	457
1970–71	38,187	21,227	16,960	5,717	3,395	2,322	2,144	1,629	515
1971–72	43,433	23,352	20,081	6,764	3,934	2,830	2,277	1,694	583
1972–73	47,940	25,117	22,823	7,619	4,325	3,294	2,550	1,797	753
1973–74	52,139	25,868	26,271	8,796	4,983	3,813	2,872	1,987	885
1974–75	51,245	24,284	26,961	9,394	5,035	4,359	2,913	1,979	934
1975–76	50,278	22,898	27,380	10,167	5,136	5,031	3,157	2,115	1,042
1976–77	47,861	20,627	27,234	10,859	5,293	5,566	3,386	2,127	1,259
1977–78	44,879	18,422	26,457	10,282	4,670	5,612	3,164	1,974	1,190
1978–79	42,697	16,540	26,157	10,132	4,405	5,727	3,228	1,895	1,333
1979–80	42,093	15,440	26,653	9,938	4,096	5,842	3,395	1,921	1,474
1980–81	41,068	14,332	26,736	10,223	4,066	6,157	3,576	2,002	1,574
1981–82	41,212	13,645	27,567	9,947	3,823	6,124	3,461	1,856	1,605
1982–83	40,460	13,131	27,329	9,981	3,647	6,334	3,602	1,838	1,764
1983–84	39,955	12,812	27,143	9,525	3,400	6,125	3,535	1,774	1,761
1984–85	39,900	12,706	27,194	9,891	3,452	6,439	3,447	1,739	1,708
1985–86	40,628	12,605	28,023	9,845	3,347	6,498	3,593	1,724	1,869
1986–87	42,994	13,362	29,632	9,562	3,172	6,390	3,560	1,615	1,945
1987–88	45,187	13,538	31,649	9,180	2,923	6,257	3,480	1,573	1,907
1988–89	48,910	14,246	34,664	9,940	3,122	6,818	3,685	1,590	2,095
1989–90	53,952	15,336	38,616	10,730	3,377	7,353	3,811	1,566	2,245
1990–91	58,655	16,067	42,588	11,349	3,329	8,020	3,932	1,520	2,412
1991–92	63,513	17,031	46,482	10,215	2,988	7,227	3,373	1,359	2,014
1992–93	66,728	17,908	48,820	10,957	3,029	7,928	3,651	1,415	2,236
1993–94	69,259	18,642	50,617	12,181	3,401	8,780	3,563	1,346	2,217
1994–95	72,083	19,548	52,535	13,921	3,893	10,028	3,822	1,431	2,391

SOURCE: U.S. Department of Education, National Center for Education Statistics, Higher Education General Information Survey (HEGIS), "Degrees and Other Formal Awards Conferred" surveys, and Integrated Postsecondary Education Data System (IPEDS), "Completions" surveys. (This table was prepared March 1997.)

Table 295.—Earned degrees in public administration and services [1] conferred by institutions of higher education, by level of degree and sex of student: 1970–71 to 1994–95

Year	Bachelor's degrees			Master's degrees			Doctor's degrees		
	Total	Men	Women	Total	Men	Women	Total	Men	Women
1	2	3	4	5	6	7	8	9	10
1970–71	5,466	1,726	3,740	7,785	3,893	3,892	174	132	42
1971–72	7,508	2,588	4,920	8,756	4,537	4,219	193	150	43
1972–73	10,690	3,998	6,692	10,068	5,271	4,797	198	160	38
1973–74	11,966	4,266	7,700	11,415	6,028	5,387	201	154	47
1974–75	13,661	4,630	9,031	13,617	7,200	6,417	257	192	65
1975–76	15,440	5,706	9,734	15,209	7,969	7,240	292	192	100
1976–77	16,136	5,544	10,592	17,026	8,810	8,216	292	197	95
1977–78	16,607	5,096	11,511	17,337	8,513	8,824	357	237	120
1978–79	17,328	4,938	12,390	17,306	8,051	9,255	315	215	100
1979–80	16,644	4,451	12,193	17,560	7,866	9,694	342	216	126
1980–81	16,707	4,248	12,459	17,803	7,460	10,343	362	212	150
1981–82	16,495	4,176	12,319	17,416	6,975	10,441	372	205	167
1982–83	14,414	3,343	11,071	16,046	5,961	10,085	347	184	163
1983–84	12,570	2,998	9,572	15,060	5,634	9,426	420	230	190
1984–85	11,754	2,829	8,925	15,575	5,573	10,002	431	213	218
1985–86	11,887	2,966	8,921	15,692	5,594	10,098	382	171	211
1986–87	12,328	2,993	9,335	16,432	5,673	10,759	398	216	182
1987–88	12,385	2,923	9,462	16,424	5,631	10,793	470	238	232
1988–89	13,162	3,214	9,948	17,020	5,615	11,405	428	210	218
1989–90	13,908	3,334	10,574	17,399	5,634	11,765	508	235	273
1990–91	14,350	3,215	11,135	17,905	5,679	12,226	430	190	240
1991–92	15,987	3,479	12,508	19,243	5,769	13,474	432	204	228
1992–93	16,775	3,801	12,974	20,634	6,105	14,529	459	215	244
1993–94	17,815	3,919	13,896	21,833	6,406	15,427	519	238	281
1994–95	18,586	3,935	14,651	23,501	6,870	16,631	556	274	282

[1] Includes degrees in public administration; community organization, resources and services; public policy analysis; social work; and public affairs, other.

SOURCE: U.S. Department of Education, National Center for Education Statistics, Higher Education General Information Survey (HEGIS), "Degrees and Other Formal Awards Conferred" surveys, and Integrated Postsecondary Education Data System (IPEDS), "Completions" surveys. (This table was prepared March 1997.)

Table 296.—Earned degrees in the social sciences and history [1] conferred by institutions of higher education, by level of degree and sex of student: 1970–71 to 1994–95

Year	Bachelor's degrees			Master's degrees			Doctor's degrees		
	Total	Men	Women	Total	Men	Women	Total	Men	Women
1	2	3	4	5	6	7	8	9	10
1970–71	155,324	98,173	57,151	16,539	11,833	4,706	3,660	3,153	507
1971–72	158,060	100,895	57,165	17,445	12,540	4,905	4,081	3,483	598
1972–73	155,970	99,735	56,235	17,477	12,605	4,872	4,234	3,573	661
1973–74	150,320	95,650	54,670	17,293	12,321	4,972	4,124	3,383	741
1974–75	135,190	84,826	50,364	16,977	11,875	5,102	4,212	3,334	878
1975–76	126,396	78,691	47,705	15,953	10,918	5,035	4,157	3,262	895
1976–77	117,040	71,128	45,912	15,533	10,413	5,120	3,802	2,957	845
1977–78	112,952	67,217	45,735	14,718	9,845	4,873	3,594	2,722	872
1978–79	108,059	62,852	45,207	12,963	8,395	4,568	3,371	2,501	870
1979–80	103,662	58,511	45,151	12,176	7,794	4,382	3,230	2,357	873
1980–81	100,513	56,131	44,382	11,945	7,457	4,488	3,122	2,274	848
1981–82	99,705	55,196	44,509	12,002	7,468	4,534	3,061	2,237	824
1982–83	95,228	52,771	42,457	11,205	6,974	4,231	2,931	2,042	889
1983–84	93,323	52,154	41,169	10,577	6,551	4,026	2,911	2,030	881
1984–85	91,570	51,226	40,344	10,503	6,475	4,028	2,851	1,933	918
1985–86	93,840	52,724	41,116	10,564	6,419	4,145	2,955	1,970	985
1986–87	96,342	53,949	42,393	10,506	6,373	4,133	2,916	2,026	890
1987–88	100,460	56,377	44,083	10,412	6,310	4,102	2,781	1,849	932
1988–89	108,151	60,121	48,030	11,023	6,599	4,424	2,885	1,949	936
1989–90	118,083	65,887	52,196	11,634	6,898	4,736	3,010	2,019	991
1990–91	125,107	68,701	56,406	12,233	7,016	5,217	3,012	1,956	1,056
1991–92	133,974	73,001	60,973	12,702	7,237	5,465	3,218	2,126	1,092
1992–93	135,703	73,589	62,114	13,471	7,671	5,800	3,460	2,203	1,257
1993–94	133,680	72,006	61,674	14,561	8,152	6,409	3,627	2,317	1,310
1994–95	128,154	68,139	60,015	14,845	8,207	6,638	3,725	2,319	1,406

[1] Includes degrees in social sciences, general; anthropology; archeology; criminology; demography and population studies; economics; geography; history; international relations and affairs; political science and government; sociology; urban affairs/studies; and social sciences and history, other.

SOURCE: U.S. Department of Education, National Center for Education Statistics, Higher Education General Information Survey (HEGIS), "Degrees and Other Formal Awards Conferred" surveys, and Integrated Postsecondary Education Data System (IPEDS), "Completions" surveys. (This table was prepared March 1997.)

316 HIGHER EDUCATION: DEGREES

Table 297.—Earned degrees in economics, history, political science and government, and sociology conferred by institutions of higher education, by level of degree: 1949–50 to 1994–95

Year	Economics			History			Political science and government [1]			Sociology		
	Bachelor's	Master's	Doctor's	Bachelor's	Master's	Doctor's	Bachelor's	Master's	Doctor's	Bachelor's	Master's	Doctor's
1	2	3	4	5	6	7	8	9	10	11	12	13
1949–50	14,568	921	200	13,542	1,801	275	6,336	710	127	7,870	552	98
1951–52	8,593	695	239	10,187	1,445	317	4,911	525	147	6,648	517	141
1953–54	6,719	609	245	9,363	1,220	355	5,314	534	153	5,692	440	184
1955–56	6,555	581	232	10,510	1,114	259	5,633	509	203	5,878	402	170
1957–58	7,457	669	239	12,840	1,397	297	6,116	665	170	6,568	397	150
1959–60	7,453	708	237	14,737	1,794	342	6,596	722	201	7,147	440	161
1961–62	8,366	853	268	17,340	2,163	343	8,326	839	214	8,120	578	173
1963–64	10,583	1,104	385	23,668	2,705	507	12,126	1,163	263	10,943	646	198
1965–66	11,555	1,522	458	28,612	3,883	599	15,242	1,429	336	15,038	981	244
1967–68	15,193	1,916	600	35,291	4,845	688	20,387	1,937	457	21,710	1,193	367
1969–70	17,197	1,988	794	43,386	5,049	1,038	25,713	2,105	525	30,436	1,813	534
1970–71	15,758	1,995	721	44,663	5,157	991	27,482	2,318	700	33,263	1,808	574
1971–72	15,231	2,224	794	43,695	5,217	1,133	28,135	2,451	758	35,216	1,944	636
1972–73	14,770	2,225	845	40,943	5,030	1,140	30,100	2,398	747	35,436	1,923	583
1973–74	14,285	2,141	788	37,049	4,533	1,114	30,744	2,448	766	35,491	2,196	632
1974–75	14,046	2,127	815	31,470	4,226	1,117	29,126	2,333	680	31,488	2,112	693
1975–76	14,741	2,087	763	28,400	3,658	1,014	28,302	2,191	723	27,634	2,009	729
1976–77	15,296	2,158	758	25,433	3,393	921	26,411	2,222	641	24,713	1,830	714
1977–78	15,661	1,995	706	23,004	3,033	813	26,069	2,069	636	22,750	1,611	599
1978–79	16,409	1,955	712	21,019	2,536	756	25,628	2,037	563	20,285	1,415	612
1979–80	17,863	1,821	677	19,301	2,367	712	25,457	1,938	535	18,881	1,341	583
1980–81	18,753	1,911	727	18,301	2,237	643	24,977	1,875	484	17,272	1,240	610
1981–82	19,876	1,964	677	17,146	2,210	636	25,658	1,954	513	16,042	1,145	558
1982–83	20,517	1,972	734	16,467	2,041	575	25,791	1,829	435	14,105	1,112	522
1983–84	20,719	1,891	729	16,643	1,940	561	25,719	1,769	457	13,145	1,008	520
1984–85	20,711	1,992	749	16,049	1,921	468	25,834	1,500	441	11,968	1,022	480
1985–86	21,602	1,937	789	16,415	1,961	497	26,439	1,704	439	12,271	965	504
1986–87	22,378	1,855	750	16,997	2,021	534	26,817	1,618	435	12,239	950	451
1987–88	22,911	1,847	770	18,207	2,093	517	27,207	1,579	391	13,024	984	452
1988–89	23,454	1,886	827	20,159	2,121	487	30,450	1,598	452	14,435	1,135	451
1989–90	23,923	1,950	806	22,476	2,369	570	33,560	1,580	480	16,035	1,198	432
1990–91	23,488	1,951	802	24,541	2,591	606	35,737	1,772	468	17,550	1,260	465
1991–92	23,423	2,106	866	26,966	2,754	644	37,805	1,908	535	19,568	1,347	501
1992–93	21,321	2,292	879	27,774	2,952	690	37,931	1,943	529	20,896	1,521	536
1993–94	19,496	2,521	869	27,503	3,009	752	36,097	2,147	616	22,368	1,639	530
1994–95	17,673	2,400	910	26,598	3,091	816	33,013	2,019	637	22,886	1,748	546

[1] Excludes degrees in public administration and international relations.

SOURCE: U.S. Department of Education, National Center for Education Statistics, Higher Education General Information Survey (HEGIS), "Degrees and Other Formal Awards Conferred" surveys, and Integrated Postsecondary Education Data System (IPEDS), "Completions" surveys. (This table was prepared March 1997.)

Table 298.—Earned degrees in visual and performing arts [1] conferred by institutions of higher education, by level of degree and sex of student: 1970–71 to 1994–95

Year	Bachelor's degrees			Master's degrees			Doctor's degrees		
	Total	Men	Women	Total	Men	Women	Total	Men	Women
1	2	3	4	5	6	7	8	9	10
1970–71	30,394	12,256	18,138	6,675	3,510	3,165	621	483	138
1971–72	33,831	13,580	20,251	7,537	4,049	3,488	572	428	144
1972–73	36,017	14,267	21,750	7,254	4,005	3,249	616	449	167
1973–74	39,730	15,821	23,909	8,001	4,325	3,676	585	440	145
1974–75	40,782	15,532	25,250	8,362	4,448	3,914	649	446	203
1975–76	42,138	16,491	25,647	8,817	4,507	4,310	620	447	173
1976–77	41,793	16,166	25,627	8,636	4,211	4,425	662	447	215
1977–78	40,951	15,572	25,379	9,036	4,327	4,709	708	448	260
1978–79	40,969	15,380	25,589	8,524	3,933	4,591	700	454	246
1979–80	40,892	15,065	25,827	8,708	4,067	4,641	655	413	242
1980–81	40,479	14,798	25,681	8,629	4,056	4,573	654	396	258
1981–82	40,422	14,819	25,603	8,746	3,866	4,880	670	380	290
1982–83	39,794	14,690	25,104	8,763	4,013	4,750	692	404	288
1983–84	40,131	15,089	25,042	8,526	3,897	4,629	730	406	324
1984–85	38,140	14,462	23,678	8,718	3,894	4,824	696	407	289
1985–86	37,241	14,236	23,005	8,420	3,775	4,645	722	396	326
1986–87	36,615	13,751	22,864	8,508	3,756	4,752	793	447	346
1987–88	36,944	14,068	22,876	7,939	3,442	4,497	727	424	303
1988–89	38,227	14,539	23,688	8,267	3,611	4,656	753	446	307
1989–90	39,934	15,189	24,745	8,481	3,706	4,775	849	472	377
1990–91	42,186	15,761	26,425	8,657	3,830	4,827	838	466	372
1991–92	46,522	17,616	28,906	9,353	4,078	5,275	906	504	402
1992–93	47,761	18,610	29,151	9,440	4,099	5,341	882	478	404
1993–94	49,053	19,538	29,515	9,925	4,229	5,696	1,054	585	469
1994–95	48,690	19,781	28,909	10,277	4,374	5,903	1,080	545	535

[1] Prior to 1982–83: Includes visual and performing arts, general; crafts, folk art, and artisanry; dance; design and applied art; theatre arts; film and photographic arts; fine arts; graphic arts technology; music; and precision production. From 1982–83: Includes visual and performing arts, general; crafts, folk art, and artisanry; dance; design and applied art; theatre arts and stagecraft; film/video and photographic arts; fine arts and art studies; music; and visual and performing arts, other.

SOURCE: U.S. Department of Education, National Center for Education Statistics, Higher Education General Information Survey (HEGIS), "Degrees and Other Formal Awards Conferred" surveys, and Integrated Postsecondary Education Data System (IPEDS), "Completions" surveys. (This table was prepared March 1997.)

Table 299.—Statistical profile of persons receiving doctor's degrees,[1] by field of study: 1994–95

Item	All fields	Field of study								
		Education	Engineering	Humanities	Life sciences	Physical sciences[2]		Business and management	Social sciences and psychology	Other professional fields
						Total	Mathematics			
1	2	3	4	5	6	7	8	9	10	11
Doctor's degrees conferred (number)	41,610	6,546	6,007	5,061	7,913	6,806	1,190	1,323	6,623	1,305
Sex (percent)										
Men	60.7	38.4	88.4	51.7	57.9	78.0	77.7	71.6	49.2	54.9
Women	39.3	61.6	11.6	48.3	42.1	22.0	22.3	28.4	50.8	45.1
Racial/ethnic group (percent)[3]										
American Indian	0.5	0.7	0.3	0.4	0.5	0.2	0.3	0.7	0.5	0.5
Asian	13.6	3.0	31.5	5.1	18.5	25.3	27.2	11.9	7.3	4.9
Black	4.6	10.4	2.2	2.9	3.1	1.3	0.7	3.3	5.2	8.5
Hispanic	3.3	4.4	2.4	3.8	3.0	2.2	2.0	1.8	4.2	3.1
White	78.0	81.6	63.7	87.8	74.9	71.0	69.9	82.3	82.8	83.0
Citizenship (percent)										
United States	66.3	86.8	39.7	78.6	63.1	53.7	46.6	64.9	76.0	77.0
Non-U.S., permanent visa	10.4	3.3	15.9	6.6	13.4	17.2	18.2	7.8	6.0	5.4
Non-U.S., temporary visa	21.2	7.7	42.0	12.8	21.8	27.2	32.1	25.5	15.4	14.8
Unknown	2.1	2.3	2.5	1.9	1.7	2.0	3.1	1.8	2.6	2.8
Median age at doctorate (years)	33.9	43.8	31.7	35.4	32.4	31.0	31.1	35.7	34.1	39.6
Percent with bachelor's degree in same field as doctorate	55.0	37.0	79.1	56.6	50.8	66.7	72.1	35.3	52.2	26.9
Median time lapse from bachelor's to doctorate (years)										
Total time	10.9	19.9	9.1	12.0	9.5	8.4	8.6	12.1	10.5	15.3
Registered time	7.2	8.2	6.4	8.4	7.0	6.9	6.9	7.2	7.5	8.2
Postdoctoral plans (percent)										
Postdoctoral study plans	26.7	4.5	23.4	8.3	57.9	44.6	26.3	2.9	19.1	4.7
Fellowship	13.7	1.5	8.1	4.3	33.8	19.9	12.5	1.4	12.7	2.0
Research associateship	10.1	1.2	13.4	1.3	17.8	22.7	10.5	0.8	3.7	1.5
Traineeship	0.9	0.4	0.9	0.5	1.6	0.4	0.7	0.2	1.5	0.2
Other	2.0	1.5	1.0	2.1	4.7	1.5	2.6	0.6	1.1	1.0
Postdoctoral employment	65.1	86.6	67.9	83.5	35.3	47.3	64.8	90.2	72.0	86.4
Educational institution[4]	38.4	68.3	17.2	68.9	17.8	19.7	45.1	70.3	38.5	57.0
Industry, business	14.1	4.9	39.1	4.5	7.8	19.8	12.9	13.2	10.8	6.7
Government	4.7	5.0	6.0	1.2	4.6	3.3	2.2	2.3	7.7	5.4
Nonprofit organization	3.4	3.9	1.1	3.8	2.1	0.7	0.7	1.1	7.7	13.2
Other and unknown	4.6	4.5	4.5	5.1	3.0	3.8	3.9	3.3	7.3	4.1
Postdoctoral plans unknown	8.2	8.9	8.7	8.2	6.7	8.2	8.9	6.9	8.9	8.9
Definite postdoctoral study	17.7	2.5	12.6	4.3	41.5	30.1	16.5	2.0	12.6	2.5
Seeking postdoctoral study	9.0	2.0	10.8	4.0	16.4	14.4	9.8	1.0	6.5	2.2
Definite employment	41.6	62.5	38.3	48.8	22.6	28.4	38.4	67.4	46.0	60.9
Seeking employment	23.5	24.0	29.6	34.7	12.7	18.8	26.4	22.8	26.1	25.5
Primary postdoctoral activity (percent)[5]										
Research and development	28.1	5.8	67.2	8.1	39.8	53.5	37.5	29.6	26.2	10.2
Teaching	35.7	35.7	12.4	67.4	29.6	26.7	44.3	48.4	30.0	49.0
Administration	11.6	33.6	2.1	4.7	7.0	2.0	1.1	5.8	5.6	10.1
Professional services	10.8	9.6	5.8	4.4	10.1	6.0	4.8	5.4	25.6	13.7
Other	3.0	2.4	3.5	3.5	3.3	3.0	2.0	2.2	2.6	5.3
Activity unknown	10.7	13.0	9.0	11.9	10.1	8.8	10.3	8.6	10.0	11.7
Region of employment after doctorate (percent)[5]										
New England	5.8	5.1	5.1	7.5	4.6	6.1	7.0	6.1	6.7	3.9
Middle Atlantic	12.8	11.6	11.3	14.6	9.4	16.3	13.6	13.2	13.3	13.1
East North Central	12.9	14.1	12.7	14.1	12.0	13.3	16.4	12.3	11.3	10.8
West North Central	6.7	9.2	4.0	6.7	7.5	5.3	6.6	5.4	6.0	7.5
South Atlantic	15.0	17.0	10.7	14.5	13.4	12.5	11.4	16.0	18.1	14.2
East South Central	4.4	5.7	2.4	4.9	3.9	2.3	2.8	5.7	4.2	7.9
West South Central	8.1	9.3	7.8	7.4	8.4	7.1	5.9	10.2	6.6	11.1
Mountain	5.5	6.4	6.3	4.8	5.1	6.2	7.7	4.7	4.7	4.8
Pacific and insular	11.9	9.8	17.6	11.0	11.0	14.8	11.8	8.5	11.6	9.6
U.S., region unknown	4.5	5.7	3.8	4.5	3.7	3.6	3.1	2.5	4.8	4.2
Foreign	12.3	6.0	17.8	9.7	20.6	12.2	13.6	15.2	12.7	12.8
Region unknown	0.1	0.1	0.4	0.0	0.2	0.3	0.2	0.1	0.0	0.1

[1] Includes Ph.D., Ed.D., and comparable degrees at the doctoral level. Excludes first-professional degrees, such as M.D., D.D.S., and D.V.M.
[2] Includes mathematics, computer science, physics, astronomy, chemistry, and earth, atmospheric, and marine sciences.
[3] Distribution by race/ethnicity based on U.S. citizens and those with permanent visas only.
[4] Includes 2-year, 4-year, and foreign colleges and universities, medical schools, and elementary/secondary schools.
[5] Includes only recipients with definite employment plans.

NOTE.—The above classification of degrees by field differs somewhat from that in most publications of the National Center for Education Statistics (NCES). The major differences are that history is included under humanities rather than social sciences and that psychology is included under social sciences. The number of degrees also differs slightly from that reported in the NCES "Completions" survey. The above tabulation excludes some non-research doctorate degrees such as doctor's degrees in theology. Total includes a small number of graduates not reported by field of study. Because of rounding, percents may not add to 100.0.

SOURCE: National Academy of Sciences, National Research Council, Office of Scientific and Engineering Personnel, *Summary Report 1995: Doctorate Recipients from United States Universities*. (This table was prepared April 1997.)

318 HIGHER EDUCATION: DEGREES

Table 300.—Statistical profile of persons receiving doctor's degrees in education: 1979–80 to 1994–95

Item	1979–80	1980–81	1982–83	1983–84	1984–85	1985–86	1986–87	1987–88	1988–89	1989–90	1990–91	1991–92	1992–93	1993–94	1994–95
1	2	3	4	5	6	7	8	9	10	11	12	13	14	15	16
Number of doctorates	**7,576**	**7,489**	**7,147**	**6,780**	**6,717**	**6,602**	**6,447**	**6,349**	**6,265**	**6,484**	**6,397**	**6,622**	**6,647**	**6,683**	**6,546**
Sex (percent)															
Men	55.5	52.8	49.6	49.0	48.2	45.6	44.9	44.8	42.5	42.4	41.9	40.5	41.3	39.1	38.4
Women	44.5	47.2	50.4	51.0	51.8	54.4	55.1	55.2	57.5	57.6	58.1	59.5	58.7	60.9	61.6
Racial/ethnic group (percent)[1]															
American Indian	0.8	0.6	0.7	0.5	0.7	0.5	0.7	0.6	0.4	0.6	1.0	0.8	0.8	0.6	0.7
Asian	1.3	1.9	1.9	1.5	1.7	1.6	1.7	2.4	1.9	1.8	2.2	2.4	2.4	2.9	3.0
Black	9.1	9.1	8.2	8.7	8.7	8.1	7.4	7.6	8.1	8.2	7.9	8.4	9.4	8.6	10.4
Hispanic	2.4	2.5	2.9	2.6	3.2	3.7	3.6	2.9	3.1	3.3	3.3	3.5	3.7	4.0	4.4
White	86.3	85.9	86.2	86.7	85.6	86.1	86.6	86.4	86.5	86.0	85.6	84.8	83.7	83.9	81.6
Citizenship (percent)															
United States	88.7	87.7	87.1	86.8	85.5	84.7	84.9	83.1	82.9	84.4	84.8	86.8	86.4	87.4	86.8
Foreign	8.2	8.8	9.8	9.8	10.4	9.6	9.2	10.2	9.7	9.7	10.2	10.7	10.8	11.0	11.0
Unknown	3.1	3.6	3.1	3.4	4.1	5.6	6.0	6.7	7.4	5.8	5.0	2.4	2.7	1.6	2.3
Median age at doctorate (years)	37.0	37.3	37.8	38.4	38.7	39.4	39.8	40.5	41.1	41.6	42.1	42.7	43.0	43.6	43.8
Percent with bachelor's degree in same field as doctorate	39.0	38.9	39.5	39.6	38.7	39.0	37.8	36.9	38.5	37.5	39.3	38.7	37.4	36.9	37.0
Median time lapse from bachelor's to doctorate (years)															
Total time	13.1	13.5	14.1	14.6	15.1	15.7	16.2	16.9	17.3	17.9	18.4	18.9	19.2	19.7	19.9
Registered time	6.9	7.0	7.4	7.6	7.6	7.8	7.9	8.1	8.2	8.1	8.1	8.2	8.2	8.1	8.2

[1] Longitudinal comparisons by race/ethnicity should be done with extreme care, due to periodic changes in the survey. Distribution by race/ethnicity based on U.S. citizens and those with permanent visas only.

NOTE.—The National Research Council's classification of degrees by field differs somewhat from that in most publications of the National Center for Education Statistics (NCES). The number of degrees also differs slightly from that reported in the NCES "Completions" survey. Because of rounding, percents may not add to 100.0.

SOURCE: National Academy of Sciences, National Research Council, Office of Scientific and Engineering Personnel, *Doctorate Records File*. (This table was prepared April 1997.)

Table 301.—Statistical profile of persons receiving doctor's degrees in engineering: 1979–80 to 1994–95

Item	1979–80	1980–81	1982–83	1983–84	1984–85	1985–86	1986–87	1987–88	1988–89	1989–90	1990–91	1991–92	1992–93	1993–94	1994–95
1	2	3	4	5	6	7	8	9	10	11	12	13	14	15	16
Number of doctorates	**2,479**	**2,528**	**2,780**	**2,915**	**3,165**	**3,376**	**3,716**	**4,190**	**4,536**	**4,892**	**5,212**	**5,437**	**5,696**	**5,826**	**6,007**
Sex (percent)															
Men	96.4	96.1	95.5	94.8	93.7	93.3	93.5	93.2	91.8	91.5	91.3	90.7	90.9	89.1	88.4
Women	3.6	3.9	4.5	5.2	6.3	6.7	6.6	6.8	8.2	8.5	8.7	9.3	9.1	10.9	11.6
Racial/ethnic group (percent)[1]															
American Indian	0.2	0.3	0.1	0.2	0.1	0.3	0.4	0.2	0.3	0.2	0.3	0.4	0.1	0.2	0.3
Asian	18.9	20.0	17.3	17.1	18.4	15.6	17.7	16.0	16.6	15.3	17.4	18.2	19.7	28.8	31.5
Black	1.2	1.4	2.0	1.0	2.2	1.4	1.3	1.4	1.4	1.8	2.4	1.9	1.9	1.8	2.2
Hispanic	1.9	1.0	2.1	2.4	1.5	2.1	1.8	3.0	2.2	2.4	2.6	3.0	2.4	2.2	2.4
White	77.8	77.3	78.6	79.3	77.8	80.6	78.8	79.4	79.5	80.4	77.4	76.5	75.9	67.0	63.7
Citizenship (percent)															
United States	50.6	46.2	41.8	42.5	40.4	40.8	41.8	42.4	40.9	39.4	37.9	38.7	39.1	38.0	39.7
Foreign	46.3	49.1	53.5	52.9	54.6	50.8	50.7	49.8	50.4	52.5	54.7	57.8	57.1	60.0	57.9
Unknown	3.1	4.7	4.7	4.6	5.0	8.4	7.4	7.7	8.8	8.1	7.3	3.5	3.9	2.1	2.5
Median age at doctorate (years)	30.3	30.5	30.8	30.7	30.9	31.0	31.0	31.0	31.1	31.2	31.4	31.5	31.6	31.7	31.7
Percent with bachelor's degree in same field as doctorate	75.2	74.1	74.0	74.3	74.2	73.0	75.2	76.4	76.2	76.9	79.0	81.8	80.1	80.4	79.1
Median time lapse from bachelor's to doctorate (years)															
Total time	7.6	7.9	8.0	8.0	8.1	8.1	8.1	8.1	8.1	8.2	8.5	8.7	8.8	9.0	9.1
Registered time	5.6	5.6	5.7	5.8	5.8	5.9	5.9	5.9	6.0	6.0	6.1	6.2	6.3	6.4	6.4

[1] Longitudinal comparisons by race/ethnicity should be done with extreme care, due to periodic changes in the survey. Distribution by race/ethnicity based on U.S. citizens and those with permanent visas only.

NOTE.—The National Research Council's classification of degrees by field differs somewhat from that in most publications of the National Center for Education Statistics (NCES). The number of degrees also differs slightly from that reported in the NCES "Completions" survey. Because of rounding, percents may not add to 100.0.

SOURCE: National Academy of Sciences, National Research Council, Office of Scientific and Engineering Personnel, *Doctorate Records File*. (This table was prepared April 1997.)

HIGHER EDUCATION: DEGREES 319

Table 302.—Statistical profile of persons receiving doctor's degrees in the humanities:[1] 1979–80 to 1994–95

Item	1979–80	1980–81	1982–83	1983–84	1984–85	1985–86	1986–87	1987–88	1988–89	1989–90	1990–91	1991–92	1992–93	1993–94	1994–95
1	2	3	4	5	6	7	8	9	10	11	12	13	14	15	16
Number of doctorates	3,863	3,745	3,494	3,528	3,428	3,461	3,504	3,553	3,558	3,820	4,094	4,444	4,481	4,743	5,061
Sex (percent)															
Men	60.4	58.7	56.2	55.0	56.6	54.8	55.1	55.7	54.5	54.4	53.5	53.7	52.5	52.3	51.7
Women	39.6	41.3	43.8	45.0	43.4	45.2	44.9	44.3	45.5	45.6	46.5	46.3	47.5	47.7	48.3
Racial/ethnic group (percent)[2]															
American Indian	0.3	0.4	0.2	0.2	0.3	0.2	0.4	0.2	0.2	0.3	0.3	0.5	0.3	0.6	0.4
Asian	2.0	1.8	1.5	1.8	2.3	1.8	2.1	2.3	3.0	2.4	2.5	3.0	3.6	4.6	5.1
Black	3.0	2.9	2.6	3.4	2.6	2.9	2.9	3.0	2.9	2.3	3.0	2.7	3.0	2.9	2.9
Hispanic	3.0	3.2	3.7	3.7	3.8	3.5	4.3	3.9	3.8	4.2	4.3	3.9	4.2	4.4	3.8
White	91.6	91.7	92.0	90.9	91.1	91.6	90.3	90.5	90.2	90.9	89.9	89.9	88.9	87.5	87.8
Citizenship (percent)															
United States	87.3	85.7	85.3	83.7	83.1	78.8	78.0	78.4	76.4	78.3	77.0	77.7	78.3	78.3	78.6
Foreign	8.8	10.2	10.7	11.2	12.1	13.7	14.3	14.4	15.5	15.2	18.3	19.2	18.7	19.9	19.4
Unknown	3.9	4.1	4.0	5.2	4.8	7.4	7.7	7.1	8.1	6.5	4.7	3.2	3.0	1.8	1.9
Median age at doctorate (years)	33.4	33.5	34.0	34.5	34.7	35.0	35.0	35.4	35.7	35.7	35.8	35.6	35.6	35.7	35.4
Percent with bachelor's degree in same field as doctorate	64.2	61.0	58.4	60.2	58.8	58.2	58.5	56.7	55.5	57.1	57.7	56.5	56.4	57.4	56.6
Median time lapse from bachelor's to doctorate (years)															
Total time	10.6	10.8	11.1	11.5	11.7	12.1	12.0	12.2	12.5	12.2	12.3	12.0	11.9	12.0	12.0
Registered time	7.7	7.7	8.0	8.2	8.3	8.2	8.4	8.5	8.4	8.3	8.4	8.3	8.3	8.5	8.4

[1] Includes American studies, archeology, art history, classics, history, letters, literature, music, philosophy, religion, and theatre.
[2] Longitudinal comparisons by race/ethnicity should be done with extreme care, due to periodic changes in the survey. Distribution by race/ethnicity based on U.S. citizens and those with permanent visas only.

NOTE.—The National Research Council's classification of degrees by field differs somewhat from that in most publications of the National Center for Education Statistics (NCES). The major differences are that history is included under humanities rather than social sciences and that psychology is included under social sciences. The number of degrees also differs slightly from that reported in the NCES "Completions" survey. Because of rounding, percents may not add to 100.0.

SOURCE: National Academy of Sciences, National Research Council, Office of Scientific and Engineering Personnel, *Doctorate Records File*. (This table was prepared April 1997.)

Table 303.—Statistical profile of persons receiving doctor's degrees in the life sciences:[1] 1979–80 to 1994–95

Item	1979–80	1980–81	1982–83	1983–84	1984–85	1985–86	1986–87	1987–88	1988–89	1989–90	1990–91	1991–92	1992–93	1993–94	1994–95
1	2	3	4	5	6	7	8	9	10	11	12	13	14	15	16
Number of doctorates	5,325	5,461	5,540	5,745	5,748	5,720	5,742	6,143	6,343	6,613	6,928	7,108	7,397	7,734	7,913
Sex (percent)															
Men	74.8	73.6	69.0	68.9	67.7	66.0	64.8	63.2	61.8	62.6	61.4	60.7	58.3	58.4	57.9
Women	25.2	26.4	31.0	31.1	32.3	34.0	35.2	36.8	38.2	37.4	38.6	39.3	41.7	41.6	42.1
Racial/ethnic group (percent)[2]															
American Indian	0.2	0.2	0.2	0.3	0.4	0.5	0.4	0.4	0.3	0.2	0.4	0.4	0.3	0.4	0.5
Asian	5.3	4.8	5.3	4.7	4.7	4.9	5.7	5.0	5.3	5.6	6.6	7.1	8.7	15.7	18.5
Black	1.6	1.9	1.6	2.1	2.1	1.9	2.5	2.2	2.1	1.9	2.4	2.3	2.9	2.6	3.1
Hispanic	1.1	1.4	1.2	1.4	1.9	2.1	2.0	2.3	2.1	2.7	2.6	2.8	3.0	3.2	3.0
White	91.8	91.7	91.6	91.5	90.8	90.5	89.4	90.0	90.1	89.6	88.0	87.3	85.1	78.2	74.9
Citizenship (percent)															
United States	80.4	80.3	79.9	79.4	77.1	75.9	73.5	71.3	71.1	68.0	66.8	65.7	65.3	64.0	63.1
Foreign	17.6	17.1	17.4	17.6	19.3	18.8	20.5	22.2	22.1	26.3	29.1	31.8	32.6	34.9	35.2
Unknown	2.0	2.6	2.6	3.0	3.6	5.3	6.1	6.4	6.9	5.6	4.0	2.5	2.2	1.1	1.7
Median age at doctorate (years)	30.0	30.1	30.6	31.0	31.3	31.6	31.7	31.9	32.2	32.3	32.4	32.7	32.5	32.7	32.4
Percent with bachelor's degree in same field as doctorate	40.9	40.7	56.3	58.1	58.3	57.1	55.6	55.4	53.4	53.8	54.1	53.5	51.9	51.0	50.8
Median time lapse from bachelor's to doctorate (years)															
Total time	7.3	7.3	7.9	8.2	8.4	8.7	8.7	8.9	9.1	9.1	9.1	9.4	9.4	9.5	9.5
Registered time	5.8	5.9	6.1	6.3	6.3	6.4	6.5	6.5	6.5	6.7	6.7	6.7	6.8	7.0	7.0

[1] Includes agricultural, biological, and health sciences.
[2] Longitudinal comparisons by race/ethnicity should be done with extreme care, due to periodic changes in the survey. Distribution by race/ethnicity based on U.S. citizens and those with permanent visas only.

NOTE.—The National Research Council's classification of degrees by field differs somewhat from that in most publications of the National Center for Education Statistics (NCES). The number of degrees also differs slightly from that reported in the NCES "Completions" survey. Because of rounding, percents may not add to 100.0.

SOURCE: National Academy of Sciences, National Research Council, Office of Scientific and Engineering Personnel, *Doctorate Records File*. (This table was prepared April 1997.)

Table 304.—Statistical profile of persons receiving doctor's degrees in the physical sciences:[1] 1979–80 to 1994–95

Item	1979–80	1980–81	1982–83	1983–84	1984–85	1985–86	1986–87	1987–88	1988–89	1989–90	1990–91	1991–92	1992–93	1993–94	1994–95
1	2	3	4	5	6	7	8	9	10	11	12	13	14	15	16
Number of doctorates	3,151	3,208	3,438	3,459	3,531	3,679	3,837	4,046	3,987	4,263	4,439	4,573	4,472	4,799	4,618
Sex (percent)															
Men	87.7	88.7	86.4	85.4	83.7	83.6	83.3	82.6	80.9	81.2	81.0	79.1	78.9	79.0	77.3
Women	12.3	11.3	13.6	14.6	16.3	16.4	16.7	17.4	19.1	18.8	19.0	20.9	21.1	21.0	22.7
Racial/ethnic group (percent)[2]															
American Indian	0.2	0.1	0.3	0.2	0.1	0.2	0.3	0.3	0.6	0.1	0.5	0.5	0.3	0.2	0.3
Asian	7.7	6.9	6.6	6.6	6.9	7.1	7.0	5.7	6.7	6.6	6.6	8.9	10.2	20.8	25.3
Black	1.0	1.3	1.0	1.3	1.2	1.0	1.0	1.3	1.3	1.0	1.2	1.1	1.6	1.6	1.4
Hispanic	1.1	1.3	1.3	2.0	1.7	2.1	2.4	2.6	2.6	3.1	2.9	3.2	3.4	2.6	2.5
White	90.0	90.5	90.7	89.9	90.1	89.5	89.3	90.1	88.8	89.3	88.8	86.4	84.5	74.8	70.6
Citizenship (percent)															
United States	75.9	75.4	74.0	73.6	70.3	66.1	65.1	64.3	62.5	61.0	59.3	57.9	57.1	56.3	56.7
Foreign	21.6	21.3	23.1	23.5	25.5	27.8	28.5	28.8	29.8	32.4	35.9	39.6	39.7	41.7	41.7
Unknown	2.4	3.3	2.9	2.9	4.1	6.1	6.4	6.9	7.8	6.7	4.8	2.5	3.2	2.1	1.8
Median age at doctorate (years)	29.1	29.0	29.3	29.5	29.5	29.9	29.8	30.1	30.0	30.7	30.2	30.3	30.6	30.7	30.7
Percent with bachelor's degree in same field as doctorate	76.5	76.6	75.4	77.7	75.0	73.4	72.6	72.6	72.6	80.0	76.9	74.5	72.9	73.0	70.8
Median time lapse from bachelor's to doctorate (years)															
Total time	6.8	6.7	7.0	7.0	7.1	7.1	7.1	7.2	7.2	7.8	7.5	7.8	8.0	8.2	8.1
Registered time	5.7	5.7	5.9	6.0	6.0	6.0	5.9	6.1	6.0	6.3	6.2	6.4	6.4	6.6	6.8

[1] Includes physics, astronomy, chemistry, and earth, atmospheric, and marine sciences. Excludes mathematics and computer science.
[2] Longitudinal comparisons by race/ethnicity should be done with extreme care, due to periodic changes in the survey. Distribution by race/ethnicity based on U.S. citizens and those with permanent visas only.

NOTE.—The National Research Council's classification of degrees by field differs somewhat from that in most publications of the National Center for Education Statistics (NCES). The number of degrees also differs slightly from that reported in the NCES "Completions" survey. Because of rounding, percents may not add to 100.0.

SOURCE: National Academy of Sciences, National Research Council, Office of Scientific and Engineering Personnel, Doctorate Records File. (This table was prepared April 1997.)

Table 305.—Statistical profile of persons receiving doctor's degrees in the social sciences:[1] 1979–80 to 1994–95

Item	1979–80	1980–81	1982–83	1983–84	1984–85	1985–86	1986–87	1987–88	1988–89	1989–90	1990–91	1991–92	1992–93	1993–94	1994–95
1	2	3	4	5	6	7	8	9	10	11	12	13	14	15	16
Number of doctorates	6,253	6,505	6,055	5,895	5,720	5,841	5,718	5,769	5,955	6,076	6,127	6,205	6,545	6,624	6,623
Sex (percent)															
Men	65.4	64.4	60.7	59.2	58.9	57.6	57.2	55.0	54.8	53.7	50.6	52.6	50.7	50.6	49.2
Women	34.6	35.6	39.3	40.8	41.1	42.4	42.8	45.0	45.2	46.3	49.4	47.4	49.3	49.4	50.8
Racial/ethnic group (percent)[2]															
American Indian	0.3	0.2	0.2	0.2	0.4	0.4	0.5	0.3	0.4	0.5	0.4	0.5	0.4	0.5	0.5
Asian	2.8	2.5	2.2	2.5	2.6	2.6	3.2	3.3	3.1	3.0	3.3	3.6	4.0	6.1	7.3
Black	4.2	4.0	3.9	4.6	4.4	4.1	3.8	4.4	4.4	4.4	4.9	4.5	4.7	4.7	5.2
Hispanic	2.0	2.3	3.0	2.8	2.9	3.3	3.6	3.3	3.3	3.9	4.2	3.8	4.1	3.6	4.2
White	90.7	91.0	90.7	90.0	89.8	89.7	89.0	88.8	88.7	88.2	87.2	87.7	86.9	85.0	82.8
Citizenship (percent)															
United States	84.7	84.0	82.9	80.6	79.3	77.9	76.1	74.8	70.4	73.8	73.4	74.3	75.5	75.5	76.0
Foreign	11.6	11.9	12.5	14.1	15.3	15.3	15.7	16.1	17.3	18.0	19.8	21.2	21.3	21.7	21.4
Unknown	3.7	4.2	4.5	5.4	5.4	6.9	8.3	9.1	12.2	8.2	6.8	4.4	3.1	2.8	2.6
Median age at doctorate (years)	31.6	32.0	32.4	32.7	33.0	33.4	33.5	34.1	33.9	34.2	34.1	34.3	34.3	34.1	34.1
Percent with bachelor's degree in same field as doctorate	58.6	59.1	58.9	59.3	58.5	57.0	56.4	54.5	52.3	55.4	54.2	53.1	53.7	53.2	52.2
Median time lapse from bachelor's to doctorate (years)															
Total time	8.7	9.0	9.3	9.7	9.9	10.0	10.3	10.5	10.3	10.6	10.5	10.6	10.4	10.5	10.5
Registered time	6.4	6.5	6.8	7.1	7.1	7.2	7.4	7.4	7.4	7.5	7.5	7.5	7.5	7.5	7.5

[1] Includes anthropology, area studies, criminology, economics, geography, political science, public policy, psychology, and sociology.
[2] Longitudinal comparisons by race/ethnicity should be done with extreme care, due to periodic changes in the survey. Distribution by race/ethnicity based on U.S. citizens and those with permanent visas only.

NOTE.—The National Research Council's classification of degrees by field differs somewhat from that in most publications of the National Center for Education Statistics (NCES). The major differences are that history is included under humanities rather than social sciences and that psychology is included under social sciences. The number of degrees also differs slightly from that reported in the NCES "Completions" survey. Because of rounding, percents may not add to 100.0.

SOURCE: National Academy of Sciences, National Research Council, Office of Scientific and Engineering Personnel, Doctorate Records File. (This table was prepared April 1997.)

Table 306.—Doctor's degrees[1] conferred by 60 large institutions of higher education: 1985–86 to 1994–95

Institution	Rank order[2]	Total, 1985–86 to 1994–95	1985–86	1986–87	1987–88	1988–89	1989–90	1990–91	1991–92	1992–93	1993–94	1994–95
1	2	3	4	5	6	7	8	9	10	11	12	13
United States, all institutions	—	386,371	33,653	34,041	34,870	35,720	38,371	39,294	40,659	42,132	43,185	44,446
Total, 60 large institutions	—	223,527	19,666	20,135	20,506	21,099	22,252	22,888	23,518	24,057	24,631	24,775
University of California, Berkeley	1	7,992	753	727	742	838	800	800	798	810	896	828
University of Wisconsin, Madison	2	6,946	606	667	684	667	717	708	680	676	783	758
University of Illinois, Urbana Campus	3	6,820	560	616	646	647	707	737	775	705	666	761
Columbia University in the City of New York	4	6,531	610	593	567	615	723	802	630	687	644	660
University of Texas at Austin	5	6,483	545	612	588	583	647	710	671	686	714	727
Ohio State University, Main Campus	6	6,245	512	570	542	608	604	644	671	685	710	699
University of Michigan, Ann Arbor	7	6,215	598	589	564	527	583	661	676	654	649	714
University of Minnesota, Twin Cities	8	6,143	556	508	527	543	633	706	651	627	707	685
University of California, Los Angeles	9	5,517	433	448	508	459	558	558	613	657	620	663
Stanford University (Calif.)	10	5,495	530	562	560	540	532	487	569	581	560	574
Massachusetts Institute of Technology	11	4,986	455	458	516	492	509	497	514	516	508	521
Harvard University (Mass.)	12	4,957	452	434	465	461	505	505	501	540	538	556
Cornell University (N.Y.)[3]	13	4,899	456	445	454	481	555	531	540	520	593	324
Pennsylvania State University, Main Campus	14	4,476	350	341	379	417	420	463	541	495	507	563
Texas A & M University	15	4,475	336	369	382	420	411	446	472	496	579	564
University of Maryland, College Park Campus	16	4,430	370	378	364	393	468	453	506	490	528	480
Purdue University, Main Campus (Ind.)	17	4,416	379	370	366	420	467	430	478	504	493	509
University of Pennsylvania	18	4,348	341	307	319	414	462	495	477	506	488	539
Michigan State University	19	4,317	438	464	427	434	432	397	476	401	429	419
University of Washington	20	4,216	345	411	392	403	457	459	396	416	455	482
University of Southern California	21	4,012	363	354	354	429	429	359	355	415	415	539
New York University	22	3,929	377	392	421	376	392	392	404	404	391	380
University of Florida	23	3,574	290	313	315	342	366	370	364	372	442	400
University of Pittsburgh, Main Campus	24	3,556	390	394	390	367	337	344	343	333	334	324
Rutgers University, New Brunswick (N.J.)	25	3,529	320	320	311	327	342	326	402	376	400	405
Indiana University, Bloomington	26	3,499	353	374	319	313	321	342	398	348	348	383
Nova Southeastern University (Fla.)	27	3,442	263	271	292	306	316	290	336	433	485	450
University of Arizona	28	3,430	260	298	290	326	311	382	352	373	442	396
University of Massachusetts at Amherst	29	3,397	290	311	281	329	362	400	409	370	338	307
University of Chicago (Ill.)	30	3,357	329	319	318	310	335	317	322	346	395	366
University of North Carolina at Chapel Hill	31	3,335	283	311	301	299	337	336	338	388	373	369
Northwestern University (Ill.)	32	3,331	312	319	313	358	327	308	351	363	305	375
Virginia Polytechnic Institute and State University	33	3,308	274	295	287	303	342	332	366	369	379	361
Yale University (Conn.)	34	3,257	259	305	290	317	312	344	347	369	348	366
University of Georgia	35	3,219	309	275	316	340	313	332	331	352	309	342
University of Iowa	36	3,196	258	287	312	287	299	360	380	331	342	340
Iowa State University	37	2,921	256	296	309	257	282	297	277	322	307	318
Boston University (Mass.)	38	2,845	307	299	245	304	277	258	280	271	289	315
Temple University (Pa.)	39	2,795	277	290	277	285	249	251	282	282	287	315
State University of New York at Buffalo	40	2,716	206	209	240	274	249	265	290	320	345	318
University of California, Davis	41	2,702	245	228	238	221	258	258	284	306	323	341
City University of New York Graduate School and University Center	42	2,681	232	232	258	225	259	320	257	318	286	294
University of Virginia, Main Campus	43	2,662	217	218	229	242	253	291	291	315	294	312
Johns Hopkins University (Md.)	44	2,602	220	213	267	229	240	285	297	318	262	271
North Carolina State University at Raleigh	45	2,598	219	200	239	224	294	256	279	283	300	304
Florida State University	46	2,569	224	226	250	246	249	257	286	262	274	295
University of Colorado at Boulder	47	2,543	198	229	231	221	248	263	249	299	306	299
Princeton University (N.J.)	48	2,485	216	218	269	227	240	244	255	249	267	300
University of Tennessee, Knoxville	49	2,285	233	206	217	209	214	214	260	249	226	257
University of Missouri, Columbia	50	2,284	202	181	227	236	236	212	258	260	253	219
University of South Carolina at Columbia	51	2,208	168	169	191	169	215	248	242	281	288	237
Vanderbilt University (Tenn.)	52	2,185	259	252	196	218	229	222	220	215	193	181
University of Nebraska, Lincoln	53	2,181	201	203	233	236	217	202	212	221	227	229
University of Cincinnati, Main Campus (Ohio)	54	2,166	187	182	188	182	213	231	220	226	273	264
University of Kansas, Main Campus	55	2,161	211	221	213	224	180	209	235	193	225	250
State University of New York at Stony Brook	56	2,151	144	156	196	190	200	248	225	283	268	241
University of California, San Diego	57	2,137	163	163	186	189	185	185	227	280	285	274
Arizona State University, Main Campus	58	2,128	157	146	158	194	191	227	222	270	258	305
University of Connecticut	59	2,123	174	193	180	198	217	228	206	216	246	265
University of Rochester (N.Y.)	60	2,121	195	198	167	208	226	194	231	224	236	242

[1] Includes Ph.D., Ed.D., and comparable degrees at the doctoral level. Excludes first-professional degrees (e.g., M.D., D.D.S., and D.V.M.).
[2] Institutions are ranked by the total number of doctor's degrees conferred during the 10-year period ending June 30, 1995.
[3] Includes degrees conferred by the Endowed and Statutory Colleges.
—Not applicable.

SOURCE: U.S. Department of Education, National Center for Education Statistics, Higher Education General Information Survey (HEGIS), "Degrees and Other Formal Awards Conferred" surveys, and Integrated Postsecondary Education Data System (IPEDS), "Completions" surveys. (This table was prepared May 1997.)

Table 307.—Percentage distribution of 1980 high school sophomores, by highest level of education completed through 1992, by selected student characteristics: 1980 to 1992

Student characteristics	All 1980 sopho-mores	Less than high school	High school	Certificate	Associate degree	Bachelor's degree	Master's degree	Professional degree	Doctor's degree
1	2	3	4	5	6	7	8	9	10
Total	100.0	5.8	51.5	11.0	7.9	20.0	2.7	0.9	0.2
Sex									
Male	100.0	6.5	53.5	9.7	6.7	19.5	2.6	1.3	0.2
Female	100.0	5.0	49.5	12.4	9.1	20.5	2.8	0.5	0.1
Race/ethnicity									
White, non-Hispanic	100.0	4.9	49.1	10.1	8.4	23.1	3.2	1.0	0.2
Black, non-Hispanic	100.0	6.9	59.6	16.3	5.2	10.0	1.5	0.5	0.2
Hispanic	100.0	11.9	59.6	11.2	7.3	9.0	0.6	0.3	—
Asian/Pacific Islander	100.0	0.6	40.9	6.9	6.2	32.7	4.7	7.5	0.7
American Indian/Alaskan Native	100.0	17.8	58.2	11.8	5.0	6.7	0.5	—	—
Socioeconomic status (1980)									
Low quartile	100.0	9.0	64.6	12.3	6.9	6.4	0.7	0.1	—
Middle two quartiles	100.0	3.9	53.8	11.5	9.1	19.0	2.0	0.5	0.1
High quartile	100.0	1.4	32.7	7.0	7.6	41.2	6.9	2.7	0.5
Test score composite (1982)									
Low quartile	100.0	15.6	64.0	13.0	4.1	3.0	0.2	—	0.1
Middle two quartiles	100.0	3.1	56.2	12.8	10.1	16.1	1.5	0.3	—
High quartile	100.0	0.1	26.5	4.8	7.2	49.2	8.7	3.0	0.6
Parents' educational attainment in 1980									
No high school diploma	100.0	6.5	59.8	12.8	8.6	10.8	1.2	0.3	0.1
High school graduate	100.0	5.2	59.1	12.4	6.0	16.6	0.3	0.4	—
Vocational/technical	100.0	3.0	49.2	15.4	10.2	19.1	2.4	0.5	0.1
Some college	100.0	2.1	43.7	8.4	8.4	32.0	4.3	1.0	0.2
Bachelor's degree	100.0	1.4	32.6	4.9	8.1	42.4	6.9	3.1	0.5
Advanced degree	100.0	3.5	23.9	8.6	4.9	44.1	10.0	4.3	0.7
High school diploma status									
Regular diploma in 1982	100.0	0.3	51.9	10.8	8.7	23.9	3.2	1.1	0.2
Returned for diploma	100.0	6.8	68.3	14.4	7.0	3.4	0.1	0.1	—
Returned but no diploma	100.0	27.1	47.7	19.9	3.4	1.9	—	—	—
Never returned	100.0	51.5	35.7	9.5	2.1	0.9	0.3	—	—
Postsecondary expectations in 1982									
None	100.0	15.5	71.1	9.3	3.0	1.0	0.1	—	0.1
Vocational/technical	100.0	4.6	61.6	19.8	10.7	3.3	0.1	—	—
Less-than-4-year degree	100.0	1.6	53.2	13.3	15.6	15.0	1.1	0.2	—
Bachelor's degree	100.0	0.9	35.3	6.8	6.3	44.9	5.0	0.8	0.1
Advanced degree	100.0	0.8	28.9	5.2	5.7	45.1	9.0	4.4	0.8
Type of start in postsecondary education									
Fall 1982 full-time 4-year	100.0	—	21.2	3.5	4.6	57.8	9.0	3.4	0.5
Fall 1982 full-time public 2-year	100.0	0.3	36.5	11.9	24.4	24.6	2.1	0.2	—
Fall 1982 part-time 4-year	100.0	—	52.2	6.7	10.0	27.2	3.5	0.1	0.4
Fall 1982 part-time public 2-year	100.0	1.6	59.5	13.4	9.4	14.4	0.9	0.8	—
Fall 1982 other	100.0	0.2	23.0	34.3	24.5	15.7	1.9	0.4	—
Delayed 4-year	100.0	0.4	55.6	8.1	7.4	24.0	3.7	0.4	0.4
Delayed public 2-year	100.0	1.7	63.0	16.9	12.0	6.2	0.2	—	—
Delayed other	100.0	1.9	31.4	48.4	14.4	3.8	0.1	0.1	—
Other enrollment	100.0	—	—	86.5	5.1	6.0	1.1	0.4	0.8
Never enrolled	100.0	16.1	83.9	—	—	—	—	—	—

—Data not applicable or not available.

NOTE.—Because of rounding, details may not add to 100.0 percent.

SOURCE: National Center for Education Statistics, *High School and Beyond, Educational Attainment of High School Sophomores by 1992.* (This table was prepared May 1995.)

Table 308.—Mean number of semester credits completed by bachelor's degree recipients, by major and course area: 1972 to 1976 and 1980 to 1984

Selected college majors	Course areas									
	Total	Business	Computer science	Education	Engineering	Mathematics	Biological sciences	Physical sciences	Social sciences	Other
1	2	3	4	5	6	7	8	9	10	11
1972–76[1]										
Mean, all majors	124.0	7.8	1.0	9.7	2.3	7.4	7.6	9.0	30.3	48.8
Business and management	124.4	41.2	2.3	0.5	0.4	10.2	2.5	4.8	30.4	32.0
Computer science	133.3	6.6	33.5	0.4	5.3	22.4	1.9	7.8	20.6	34.8
Education	126.4	0.9	0.3	40.2	—	5.0	5.5	4.3	23.9	46.4
Engineering	134.8	1.6	2.0	0.1	50.0	18.2	1.3	20.5	14.0	27.1
English	117.8	0.5	0.1	7.8	0.1	3.2	3.4	3.4	24.2	75.2
Fine arts	124.9	0.3	0.1	6.6	—	1.3	2.5	2.1	13.6	98.4
Life sciences	122.2	0.4	0.8	1.7	—	8.4	35.6	26.2	17.8	31.3
Physical sciences	122.7	0.8	1.4	0.9	1.9	16.2	9.6	49.5	13.1	29.2
Psychology	119.1	2.0	0.5	5.9	0.3	5.5	6.2	5.9	56.0	36.9
Social sciences	120.6	3.4	0.4	3.3	0.4	5.3	3.2	4.3	60.3	40.1
1980–84[2]										
Mean, all majors	123.5	12.8	3.3	6.2	4.6	8.4	5.3	8.1	27.5	47.2
Business and management	122.8	41.2	4.5	0.6	1.1	8.9	2.2	3.9	27.5	32.7
Computer science	129.3	11.8	27.9	0.3	4.7	21.3	1.8	8.5	19.0	33.9
Education	127.4	0.7	0.3	45.5	0.1	4.4	4.4	3.8	20.8	47.3
Engineering	132.3	1.0	2.3	0.8	52.5	16.2	1.1	20.2	12.3	25.9
English	114.8	1.7	1.5	6.9	—	2.2	2.1	4.7	21.4	74.4
Fine arts	120.5	1.7	0.6	5.1	—	1.7	2.7	1.5	14.1	93.1
Life sciences	121.9	0.7	1.5	1.9	0.2	10.1	33.5	22.6	18.1	33.3
Physical sciences	124.3	0.2	4.9	0.1	2.0	14.1	12.9	48.7	11.6	30.0
Psychology	120.7	3.0	2.7	2.1	—	6.5	5.8	4.2	55.2	41.2
Social sciences	119.2	6.0	1.4	1.0	0.5	5.4	4.4	5.1	52.0	43.3

[1] Sample survey based on 1972 high school seniors who completed bachelor's degrees by 1976.
[2] Sample survey based on 1980 high school seniors who completed bachelor's degrees by 1984.
—Data not available.

NOTE.—Because of rounding, details may not add to totals.

SOURCE: U.S. Department of Education, National Center for Education Statistics, National Longitudinal Study of 1972 and High School and Beyond survey. (This table was prepared April 1986.)

Table 309.—Colleges and universities offering remedial services, by type and control of institution: 1987–88 to 1995–96

Type and control of institution	Percent of colleges offering remedial instruction or tutoring									Change in percentage points	
	1987–88	1988–89	1989–90	1990–91	1991–92	1992–93	1993–94	1994–95	1995–96	1987–88 to 1995–96	1990–91 to 1995–96
1	2	3	4	5	6	7	8	9	10	11	12
Total	72.7	74.9	76.6	77.7	78.6	76.6	77.1	78.0	77.8	5.1	0.1
All 4-year colleges	66.0	68.2	69.6	70.6	71.4	69.7	70.4	71.9	71.6	5.6	1.0
All 2-year colleges	82.7	84.7	87.2	88.4	89.2	86.6	87.2	87.1	87.4	4.7	1.0
Public institutions											
4-year colleges	80.5	81.8	82.9	83.5	84.5	78.4	78.4	79.4	80.0	0.5	3.6
2-year colleges	96.4	96.6	98.2	98.9	99.6	95.6	95.5	95.5	95.5	0.9	3.4
Private institutions											
4-year colleges	60.3	63.0	64.5	65.6	66.4	66.2	67.2	68.9	68.2	7.9	2.6
2-year colleges	53.0	58.6	63.0	65.5	65.8	65.4	66.7	66.6	66.3	13.2	0.8

SOURCE: U.S. Department of Education, National Center for Education Statistics, Integrated Postsecondary Education Data System (IPEDS), "Institutional Characteristics" surveys. (This table was prepared September 1996.)

Table 310.—Percent distribution of enrollment and completion status of first-time postsecondary students starting during the 1989–90 academic year, by degree objective and other student characteristics: 1994

Student characteristics	2-year college students starting in 1989–90						Students seeking bachelor's degrees in 1989–90					
	Attained by 1994[1]				No degree by 1994		Highest degree completed, not enrolled for bachelor's degree[2]				Still enrolled for bachelor's[3]	No degree, not enrolled[4]
	Total	Certificate	Associate	Bachelor's	Enrolled	Not enrolled	Total, any degree	Certificate	Associate	Bachelor's		
1	2	3	4	5	6	7	8	9	10	11	12	13
Total	**36.7**	**12.9**	**17.5**	**6.3**	**14.7**	**48.6**	**54.3**	**3.3**	**5.1**	**45.8**	**17.5**	**28.3**
Male	33.8	12.7	15.5	5.6	17.1	49.1	48.8	2.7	4.8	41.3	20.3	30.9
Female	39.6	13.2	19.5	7.0	12.4	48.1	59.7	4.0	5.4	50.3	14.6	25.7
Race												
White, non-Hispanic	37.3	12.3	18.4	6.6	13.0	49.7	56.4	3.3	4.9	48.1	16.6	27.0
Black, non-Hispanic	31.8	16.1	12.5	3.1	13.2	55.1	45.2	3.6	7.3	34.3	18.0	36.8
Hispanic	38.0	15.2	15.6	7.2	22.2	39.8	41.3	5.4	3.5	32.4	22.1	36.6
Asian/Pacific Islander	—	—	—	—	—	—	52.8	0.6	5.3	46.8	21.8	25.5
Socioeconomic status in 1989–90												
Low (25 percent)	30.2	17.7	10.6	1.9	10.3	59.5	31.7	3.8	5.7	22.1	16.5	51.8
Middle (50 percent)	34.3	13.7	15.0	5.7	16.4	49.3	47.1	3.5	4.8	38.9	19.4	33.5
High (25 percent)	44.8	8.7	26.1	10.1	14.5	40.7	61.5	3.2	5.3	52.9	16.3	22.3
Dependent student family income in 1989–90												
Less than $20,000	39.4	12.0	21.4	5.9	15.5	45.2	43.2	1.4	4.9	36.9	19.2	37.6
$20,000 to $39,999	43.4	12.8	20.5	10.0	13.8	42.9	52.6	4.1	5.3	43.2	18.2	29.2
$40,000 to $59,999	42.4	11.2	21.9	9.3	13.1	44.6	57.0	4.4	4.1	48.5	16.1	26.9
$60,000 or more	46.9	5.4	31.5	10.0	24.6	28.5	68.1	1.5	6.0	60.6	16.0	15.9
Diploma/delayed entry status[5]												
Diploma, did not delay	45.5	10.6	24.9	10.0	16.3	38.3	58.2	2.9	4.9	50.3	17.0	24.8
Diploma, delayed entry	26.4	16.3	8.6	1.5	14.5	59.1	30.9	6.6	7.1	17.3	21.5	47.6
No diploma	21.8	14.2	5.9	1.7	4.5	73.7	21.0	3.7	2.4	15.0	14.1	64.8
Age (as of 12/31/89)												
18 years or younger	47.4	9.4	26.1	11.9	14.9	37.7	59.2	2.9	4.9	51.4	16.4	24.5
19 years	31.9	12.7	17.1	2.2	20.8	47.3	45.8	3.4	4.2	38.3	21.1	33.0
20 to 29 years	27.3	16.4	8.3	2.5	13.0	59.8	36.3	7.9	9.4	19.0	19.6	44.1
30 years or over	25.7	18.2	6.9	0.6	9.2	65.1	19.1	3.3	6.0	9.8	17.3	63.5
Marital status												
Never married	41.1	11.8	21.1	8.1	16.2	42.7	56.8	3.4	5.3	48.1	17.4	25.8
Married	26.3	15.4	8.7	2.2	9.2	64.5	26.7	4.2	2.4	20.1	17.8	55.5
Divorced, widowed, separated	29.9	25.6	3.3	1.0	8.8	61.2	21.7	0.6	9.5	11.6	18.4	59.9
Expected degree level for 2-year students												
Less than 2 years	23.9	19.8	4.1	0.0	12.3	63.8	—	—	—	—	—	—
2 to 4 years	30.2	18.3	10.5	1.4	11.8	58.0	—	—	—	—	—	—
Bachelor's or higher	40.6	9.9	21.7	9.0	16.1	43.3	—	—	—	—	—	—
Average hours worked per week while enrolled												
None	40.5	21.2	13.8	5.6	11.1	48.4	56.2	2.0	4.4	49.8	17.8	26.0
1 to 20 hours	45.4	12.2	23.7	9.6	14.6	40.0	59.0	2.5	5.2	51.3	16.4	24.5
More than 20 hours	33.3	10.9	16.8	5.6	15.7	51.0	50.3	4.5	5.4	40.4	17.9	31.7
Received financial aid during 1989–90												
Yes	39.9	13.1	17.3	9.6	8.6	51.5	60.4	2.2	3.2	55.1	13.8	25.8
No	35.5	12.9	17.6	5.0	17.0	47.5	48.4	4.5	7.0	36.9	21.0	30.7

—Data not available or not applicable.

[1] Highest degree attained at any institution. Students who have attained may also be enrolled.
[2] Status as of 1994. Includes those students who are no longer working towards a bachelor's degree, but who had completed another type of degree or award.
[3] Status as of 1994. Includes students who had completed another type of degree or award (associate degree: 11.8 percent, certificate: 2.7 percent) but are still working toward a bachelor's degree.
[4] Status as of 1994. Enrollment can be full-time or part-time. Includes students who are still enrolled, but are no longer working toward a bachelor's degree.
[5] Students were considered to have a diploma only if they had a regular high school diploma. Students with a GED or other high school credentials were considered to have no diploma.

NOTE.—Data reflect completion and enrollment status by spring 1994 of first-time postsecondary students starting academic year 1989–90. Some cells in this table have relatively large sampling errors. See sampling error table in appendix.

SOURCE: U.S. Department of Education, National Center for Education Statistics, Beginning Postsecondary Student Longitudinal Survey, 1994. (This table was prepared September 1996.)

HIGHER EDUCATION: OUTCOMES 325

Table 311.—Scores on Graduate Record Examination (GRE) and subject matter tests: 1965 to 1996

Academic year ending	Number of GRE takers	GRE takers as a percent of bachelor's degrees	Verbal		Quantitative		Analytical		Subject matter tests											
									Biology		Chemistry		Education		Engineering		Literature		Psychology	
			Mean	Standard deviation	Mean	Standard deviation	Mean	Standard deviation	Mean	Standard deviation	Mean	Standard deviation	Mean	Standard deviation	Mean	Standard deviation	Mean	Standard deviation	Mean	Standard deviation
1	2	3	4	5	6	7	8	9	10	11	12	13	14	15	16	17	18	19	20	21
1965	93,792	18.7	530	124	533	137	—	—	617	117	628	114	481	86	618	108	591	95	556	91
1966	123,960	23.8	520	124	528	133	—	—	610	115	618	110	474	87	609	106	588	94	552	91
1967	151,134	27.0	519	125	528	134	—	—	613	114	615	104	476	90	603	104	582	91	553	93
1968	182,432	28.8	520	124	527	135	—	—	614	114	617	104	478	87	601	105	572	91	547	93
1969	206,113	28.3	515	124	524	132	—	—	613	112	613	104	477	88	591	103	569	89	543	89
1970	265,359	33.5	503	123	516	132	—	—	603	111	613	113	462	92	586	110	556	90	532	91
1971	293,600	35.0	497	125	512	134	—	—	603	114	618	117	457	95	587	115	546	91	530	92
1972	293,506	33.1	494	126	508	136	—	—	606	115	624	124	446	93	594	119	544	96	528	92
1973	290,104	31.5	497	125	512	135	—	—	619	110	630	114	459	96	593	114	545	96	529	92
1974	301,070	31.8	492	126	509	137	—	—	624	110	634	115	452	93	591	121	547	99	530	95
1975	298,335	32.3	493	125	508	137	—	—	—	—	—	—	—	—	—	—	—	—	—	—
1976	299,292	32.3	492	127	510	138	—	—	627	112	627	107	454	93	594	119	539	101	531	93
1977	287,715	31.3	490	129	514	139	—	—	625	113	630	109	453	93	592	115	532	101	532	95
1978	286,383	31.1	484	128	518	135	—	—	622	113	624	108	452	91	594	114	530	102	529	97
1979	282,482	30.7	476	130	517	135	—	—	621	117	623	104	451	89	592	115	525	102	530	97
1980	272,281	29.3	474	131	522	136	—	—	619	115	618	105	449	90	590	116	521	105	534	98
1981	262,855	28.1	473	128	523	136	—	—	617	115	615	103	453	90	590	116	520	99	532	97
1982	256,381	26.9	469	130	533	137	498	126	616	114	616	105	456	89	593	115	521	100	532	97
1983	263,674	27.2	473	131	541	138	504	128	623	115	620	105	459	90	599	114	527	98	542	95
1984	265,221	27.2	475	130	541	139	512	129	622	115	619	102	461	90	604	114	530	97	543	96
1985	271,972	27.8	474	126	545	140	516	129	619	114	621	101	459	89	615	120	531	95	541	95
1986	279,428	28.3	475	126	552	140	520	129	612	113	628	106	464	87	616	119	527	96	542	97
1987	293,560	29.6	477	126	550	140	521	128	616	116	629	104	465	86	619	119	526	95	536	95
1988	303,703	30.5	483	123	557	140	528	128	615	114	631	108	467	85	622	120	525	94	537	94
1989	326,096	32.0	484	125	560	142	530	129	612	114	642	117	465	87	626	116	528	91	538	95
1990	344,572	32.8	486	123	562	143	534	128	612	114	662	123	461	84	617	111	523	92	537	95
1991	379,882	34.7	485	122	562	141	536	129	609	113	660	123	457	85	611	111	523	93	535	95
1992	411,528	36.2	483	120	561	140	537	129	605	113	654	128	462	82	610	117	525	92	536	95
1993	400,246	34.4	481	117	557	140	541	129	606	114	662	133	467	80	602	115	516	94	536	97
1994	[1]399,395	34.3	479	116	553	139	545	129	620	116	627	113	465	104	601	115	517	95	538	96
1995	[1]389,539	33.0	477	115	553	140	544	131	622	116	675	138	[2]488	102	596	113	513	96	544	98
1996	[1]376,013	31.9	473	114	558	139	549	131	614	114	678	135	[2]489	104	604	119	512	97	547	99

[1] Total includes examinees who received no score on one or more General Test measures.
[2] Data reported for 1994, 1995, and 1996 are from the revised education test.
—Data not reported or not applicable.

NOTE.—GRE scores for the verbal, quantitative, and analytical sections range from 200 to 800. Subject matter test scores range from 200 to 990.

SOURCE: Graduate Record Examination Board, Examinee and Score Trends for the GRE General Test, various years; and A Summary of Data Collected From Graduate Record Examinations Test-Takers During 1986–87; unpublished data; and U.S. Department of Education, National Center for Education Statistics, Higher Education General Information Survey (HEGIS), "Degrees and Other Formal Awards Conferred" surveys, and Integrated Postsecondary Education Data System (IPEDS), "Completions" surveys. (This table was prepared April 1997.)

Table 312.—Average undergraduate tuition and fees and room and board rates paid by students in institutions of higher education, by type and control of institution: 1964–65 to 1996–97

Year and control of institution	All institutions	Total tuition, room, and board					All institutions	Tuition and required fees (in-state)					All institutions	Dormitory rooms					All institutions	Board (7-day basis)[1]			
		4-year institutions				2-year		4-year institutions				2-year		4-year institutions				2-year		4-year institutions			
		All 4-year	Universities	Other 4-year				All 4-year	Universities	Other 4-year				All 4-year	Universities	Other 4-year				All 4-year	Universities	Other 4-year	
1	2	3	4	5		6	7	8	9	10		11	12	13	14	15		16	17	18	19	20	21
All institutions																								
1976–77	$2,275	$2,577	$2,647	$2,527		$1,598	$924	$1,218	$1,210	$1,223		$346	$603	$611	$649	$584		$503	$748	$748	$788	$719	$750
1977–78	2,411	2,725	2,777	2,685		1,703	984	1,291	1,269	1,305		378	645	654	691	628		525	781	780	818	752	801
1978–79	2,587	2,917	2,967	2,879		1,828	1,073	1,397	1,370	1,413		411	688	696	737	667		575	826	825	860	800	842
1979–80	2,809	3,167	3,223	3,124		1,979	1,163	1,513	1,484	1,530		451	751	759	803	729		628	895	895	936	865	900
1980–81	3,101	3,499	3,535	3,469		2,230	1,289	1,679	1,634	1,705		526	836	846	881	821		705	976	975	1,020	943	1,000
1981–82	3,489	3,951	4,005	3,908		2,476	1,457	1,907	1,860	1,935		590	950	961	1,023	919		793	1,083	1,082	1,121	1,055	1,094
1982–83	3,877	4,406	4,466	4,356		2,713	1,626	2,139	2,081	2,173		675	1,064	1,078	1,150	1,028		873	1,187	1,189	1,235	1,155	1,165
1983–84	4,167	4,747	4,793	4,712		2,854	1,783	2,344	2,300	2,368		730	1,145	1,162	1,211	1,130		916	1,239	1,242	1,282	1,214	1,208
1984–85	4,563	5,160	5,236	5,107		3,179	1,985	2,567	2,539	2,583		821	1,267	1,282	1,343	1,242		1,058	1,310	1,311	1,353	1,282	1,301
1985–86[2]	4,885	5,504	5,597	5,441		3,367	2,181	2,784	2,770	2,793		888	1,338	1,355	1,424	1,309		1,107	1,365	1,365	1,403	1,339	1,372
1986–87[3]	5,206	5,964	6,124	5,857		3,295	2,312	3,042	3,042	3,042		897	1,405	1,427	1,501	1,376		1,034	1,489	1,495	1,581	1,439	1,364
1987–88	5,494	6,272	6,339	6,226		3,263	2,458	3,201	3,168	3,220		809	1,488	1,516	1,576	1,478		1,017	1,549	1,555	1,596	1,529	1,437
1988–89	5,869	6,725	6,801	6,673		3,573	2,658	3,472	3,422	3,499		979	1,575	1,609	1,665	1,573		1,085	1,636	1,644	1,715	1,601	1,509
1989–90	6,207	7,212	7,347	7,120		3,705	2,839	3,800	3,765	3,819		978	1,638	1,675	1,732	1,638		1,105	1,730	1,737	1,850	1,663	1,622
1990–91	6,562	7,602	7,709	7,528		3,930	3,016	4,009	3,958	4,036		1,087	1,743	1,782	1,848	1,740		1,182	1,802	1,811	1,903	1,751	1,660
1991–92	7,074	8,252	8,389	8,164		4,089	3,282	4,399	4,366	4,417		1,186	1,874	1,921	1,998	1,874		1,210	1,918	1,931	2,026	1,873	1,692
1992–93	7,452	8,758	8,934	8,648		4,207	3,517	4,752	4,665	4,795		1,276	1,939	1,991	2,104	1,926		1,240	1,996	2,015	2,165	1,927	1,692
1993–94	7,931	9,296	9,495	9,186		4,449	3,827	5,119	5,104	5,127		1,399	2,057	2,111	2,190	2,068		1,332	2,047	2,067	2,201	1,992	1,718
1994–95	8,306	9,728	9,863	9,646		4,633	4,044	5,391	5,287	5,441		1,488	2,145	2,200	2,281	2,155		1,396	2,116	2,138	2,295	2,049	1,750
1995–96	8,800	10,330	10,560	10,195		4,725	4,338	5,786	5,733	5,812		1,522	2,264	2,318	2,423	2,260		1,473	2,199	2,226	2,404	2,123	1,730
1996–97[4]	9,199	10,825	11,027	10,704		4,896	4,561	6,107	6,050	6,135		1,543	2,364	2,419	2,518	2,363		1,527	2,275	2,299	2,460	2,206	1,826
Public institutions																								
1964–65	950	—	1,051	867		638	243	—	298	224		99	271	—	291	241		178	436	—	462	402	361
1965–66	983	—	1,105	904		670	257	—	327	241		109	281	—	304	255		194	445	—	474	408	367
1966–67	1,026	—	1,171	947		710	275	—	360	259		121	294	—	321	271		213	457	—	490	417	376
1967–68	1,064	—	1,199	997		789	283	—	366	268		144	313	—	337	292		243	468	—	496	437	402
1968–69	1,117	—	1,245	1,063		883	295	—	377	281		170	337	—	359	318		278	485	—	509	464	435
1969–70	1,203	—	1,362	1,135		951	323	—	427	306		178	369	—	395	346		308	511	—	540	483	465
1970–71	1,287	—	1,477	1,206		998	351	—	478	332		187	401	—	431	375		338	535	—	568	499	473
1971–72	1,357	—	1,579	1,263		1,073	376	—	526	354		192	430	—	463	400		366	551	—	590	509	515
1972–73	1,458	—	1,668	1,460		1,197	407	—	566	455		233	476	—	500	455		398	575	—	602	550	566
1973–74	1,517	—	1,707	1,506		1,274	438	—	581	463		274	480	—	505	464		409	599	—	621	579	591
1974–75	1,563	—	1,760	1,558		1,339	432	—	599	448		277	506	—	527	497		424	625	—	634	613	638
1975–76	1,666	—	1,935	1,657		1,386	433	—	642	469		245	544	—	573	533		442	689	—	720	655	699
1976–77	1,789	1,935	2,067	1,827		1,491	479	617	689	564		283	582	592	614	572		465	728	727	763	692	742
1977–78	1,888	2,038	2,170	1,931		1,590	512	655	736	596		306	621	631	649	616		486	755	752	785	720	797
1978–79	1,994	2,145	2,289	2,027		1,691	543	688	777	622		327	655	664	689	641		527	796	793	823	764	837
1979–80	2,165	2,327	2,487	2,198		1,822	583	738	840	662		355	715	725	750	703		574	867	865	898	833	893
1980–81	2,373	2,550	2,712	2,421		2,027	635	804	915	722		391	799	811	827	796		642	940	936	969	904	994
1981–82	2,663	2,871	3,079	2,705		2,224	714	909	1,042	813		434	909	925	970	885		703	1,039	1,036	1,067	1,006	1,086
1982–83	2,945	3,196	3,403	3,032		2,390	798	1,031	1,164	936		473	1,010	1,030	1,072	993		755	1,136	1,134	1,167	1,103	1,162
1983–84	3,156	3,433	3,628	3,285		2,534	891	1,148	1,284	1,052		528	1,087	1,110	1,131	1,092		801	1,178	1,175	1,213	1,141	1,205
1984–85	3,408	3,682	3,899	3,518		2,807	971	1,228	1,386	1,117		584	1,196	1,217	1,237	1,200		921	1,241	1,237	1,276	1,201	1,302
1985–86[2]	3,571	3,859	4,146	3,637		2,981	1,045	1,318	1,536	1,157		641	1,242	1,263	1,290	1,240		960	1,285	1,278	1,320	1,240	1,380
1986–87[3]	3,805	4,138	4,469	3,891		2,989	1,106	1,414	1,651	1,248		660	1,301	1,323	1,355	1,295		979	1,398	1,401	1,464	1,348	1,349
1987–88	4,050	4,403	4,619	4,250		3,066	1,218	1,537	1,726	1,407		706	1,378	1,410	1,410	1,409		943	1,454	1,456	1,482	1,434	1,417
1988–89	4,274	4,678	4,905	4,526		3,183	1,285	1,646	1,846	1,515		730	1,457	1,496	1,483	1,506		965	1,533	1,536	1,576	1,504	1,488
1989–90	4,504	4,975	5,324	4,723		3,299	1,356	1,780	2,035	1,608		756	1,513	1,557	1,561	1,554		962	1,635	1,638	1,728	1,561	1,581
1990–91	4,757	5,243	5,585	5,004		3,467	1,454	1,888	2,159	1,707		824	1,612	1,657	1,658	1,655		1,050	1,691	1,698	1,767	1,641	1,594

HIGHER EDUCATION: STUDENT CHARGES 327

Table 312.—Average undergraduate tuition and fees and room and board rates paid by students in institutions of higher education, by type and control of institution: 1964–65 to 1996–97—Continued

Year and control of institution	Total tuition, room, and board						Tuition and required fees (in-state)						Dormitory rooms						Board (7-day basis)[1]			
	All institutions	4-year institutions				2-year	All institutions	4-year institutions				2-year	All institutions	4-year institutions				2-year	All institutions	4-year institutions			2-year
		All 4-year	Universities	Other 4-year				All 4-year	Universities	Other 4-year				All 4-year	Universities	Other 4-year				All 4-year	Universities	Other 4-year	
1	2	3	4	5	6	7	8	9	10	11	12	13	14	15	16	17	18	19	20	21
1991–92	5,135	5,695	6,051	5,459	3,623	1,624	2,119	2,410	1,933	937	1,731	1,785	1,789	1,782	1,074	1,780	1,792	1,852	1,745	1,612
1992–93	5,379	6,020	6,442	5,740	3,799	1,782	2,349	2,604	2,192	1,025	1,756	1,816	1,856	1,787	1,106	1,841	1,854	1,982	1,761	1,668
1993–94	5,694	6,365	6,710	6,146	3,996	1,942	2,537	2,820	2,360	1,125	1,873	1,934	1,897	1,958	1,190	1,880	1,895	1,993	1,828	1,681
1994–95	5,965	6,670	7,077	6,409	4,137	2,057	2,681	2,977	2,499	1,192	1,959	2,023	1,992	2,044	1,232	1,949	1,967	2,108	1,866	1,712
1995–96	6,256	7,014	7,448	6,730	4,217	2,179	2,848	3,151	2,660	1,239	2,057	2,121	2,104	2,133	1,297	2,020	2,045	2,192	1,937	1,681
1996–97[4]	6,534	7,331	7,793	7,028	4,412	2,277	2,986	3,321	2,778	1,283	2,148	2,212	2,189	2,228	1,346	2,110	2,133	2,283	2,023	1,782
Private institutions																				
1964–65	1,907	—	2,202	1,810	1,455	1,088	—	1,297	1,023	702	331	—	390	308	289	488	—	515	479	464
1965–66	2,005	—	2,316	1,899	1,557	1,154	—	1,369	1,086	768	356	—	418	330	316	495	—	529	483	473
1966–67	2,124	—	2,456	2,007	1,679	1,233	—	1,456	1,162	845	385	—	452	355	347	506	—	548	490	487
1967–68	2,205	—	2,545	2,104	1,762	1,297	—	1,534	1,237	892	392	—	455	366	366	516	—	556	501	504
1968–69	2,321	—	2,673	2,237	1,876	1,383	—	1,638	1,335	956	404	—	463	382	391	534	—	572	520	529
1969–70	2,530	—	2,920	2,420	1,993	1,533	—	1,809	1,468	1,034	436	—	503	409	413	561	—	608	543	546
1970–71	2,738	—	3,163	2,599	2,103	1,684	—	1,980	1,603	1,109	468	—	542	434	434	586	—	641	562	560
1971–72	2,917	—	3,375	2,748	2,186	1,820	—	2,133	1,721	1,172	494	—	576	454	449	603	—	666	573	565
1972–73	3,038	—	3,512	2,934	2,273	1,898	—	2,226	1,846	1,221	524	—	622	490	457	616	—	664	598	595
1973–74	3,164	—	3,717	3,040	2,410	1,989	—	2,375	1,925	1,303	533	—	622	502	483	642	—	720	613	624
1974–75	3,403	—	4,076	3,156	2,591	2,117	—	2,614	1,954	1,367	586	—	691	536	564	700	—	771	666	660
1975–76	3,663	—	4,467	3,385	2,711	2,272	—	2,881	2,084	1,427	636	—	753	583	572	755	—	833	718	712
1976–77	3,906	3,977	4,715	3,714	2,971	2,467	2,534	3,051	2,351	1,592	649	651	783	604	607	790	791	882	759	772
1977–78	4,158	4,240	5,033	3,967	3,148	2,624	2,700	3,240	2,520	1,706	698	702	850	648	631	836	838	943	800	811
1978–79	4,514	4,609	5,403	4,327	3,389	2,867	2,958	3,487	2,771	1,831	758	761	916	704	700	889	890	1,000	851	858
1979–80	4,912	5,013	5,891	4,700	3,751	3,130	3,225	3,811	3,020	2,062	827	831	1,001	768	766	955	957	1,078	912	923
1980–81	5,470	5,594	6,569	5,249	4,303	3,498	3,617	4,275	3,390	2,413	918	921	1,086	859	871	1,054	1,056	1,209	1,000	1,019
1981–82	6,166	6,330	7,443	5,947	4,746	3,953	4,113	4,887	3,853	2,605	1,038	1,039	1,229	970	1,022	1,175	1,178	1,327	1,124	1,119
1982–83	6,920	7,126	8,536	6,646	5,364	4,439	4,639	5,583	4,329	3,008	1,181	1,181	1,453	1,083	1,177	1,300	1,306	1,501	1,234	1,179
1983–84	7,508	7,759	9,308	7,244	5,571	4,851	5,093	6,217	4,726	3,099	1,278	1,279	1,531	1,191	1,253	1,380	1,387	1,559	1,327	1,219
1984–85	8,202	8,451	10,243	7,849	6,203	5,315	5,556	6,843	5,135	3,485	1,426	1,426	1,753	1,309	1,424	1,462	1,469	1,647	1,405	1,294
1985–86[2]	8,885	9,228	11,034	8,551	6,512	5,789	6,121	7,374	5,641	3,672	1,553	1,557	1,940	1,420	1,500	1,542	1,551	1,720	1,490	1,340
1986–87[3]	9,676	10,039	12,278	9,276	6,384	6,316	6,658	8,118	6,171	3,684	1,658	1,673	2,097	1,518	1,266	1,702	1,708	2,063	1,587	1,434
1987–88	10,512	10,659	13,075	9,854	7,078	6,988	7,116	8,771	6,574	4,161	1,748	1,760	2,244	1,593	1,380	1,775	1,783	2,060	1,687	1,537
1988–89	11,189	11,474	14,073	10,620	7,967	7,461	7,722	9,451	7,172	4,817	1,849	1,863	2,353	1,686	1,540	1,880	1,889	2,269	1,762	1,609
1989–90	12,018	12,284	15,098	11,374	8,670	8,147	8,396	10,348	7,778	5,196	1,923	1,935	2,411	1,774	1,663	1,948	1,953	2,339	1,823	1,811
1990–91	12,910	13,237	16,503	12,220	9,330	8,772	9,083	11,379	8,389	5,570	2,063	2,077	2,654	1,889	1,744	2,074	2,077	2,470	1,943	1,989
1991–92	13,907	14,273	17,779	13,189	9,631	9,434	9,775	12,192	9,053	5,752	2,221	2,241	2,860	2,038	1,789	2,252	2,257	2,727	2,098	2,090
1992–93	14,634	15,009	18,898	13,882	9,903	9,942	10,294	13,055	9,533	6,059	2,348	2,362	3,018	2,151	1,970	2,344	2,354	2,825	2,197	1,875
1993–94	15,496	15,904	20,097	14,640	10,406	10,572	10,952	13,874	10,100	6,370	2,490	2,506	3,277	2,261	2,067	2,434	2,445	2,946	2,278	1,970
1994–95	16,207	16,602	21,041	15,363	11,170	11,111	11,481	14,537	10,653	6,914	2,587	2,601	3,460	2,347	2,233	2,509	2,520	3,035	2,362	2,023
1995–96	17,208	17,612	22,502	16,198	11,563	11,864	12,243	15,605	11,297	7,094	2,738	2,751	3,680	2,473	2,371	2,606	2,617	3,218	2,429	2,098
1996–97[4]	18,071	18,476	23,491	17,027	11,889	12,537	12,920	16,531	11,911	7,190	2,873	2,885	3,820	2,597	2,513	2,661	2,670	3,140	2,518	2,186

[1] Data for 1986–87 and later years reflect 20 meals per week rather than meals 7 days per week.
[2] Room and board data are estimated.
[3] Because of revisions in data collection procedures, figures are not entirely comparable with those for previous years. In particular, data on board rates are somewhat higher than earlier years because they reflect a basis of 20 meals per week rather than meals served 7 days per week. Since many institutions serve fewer than 3 meals each day, the 1986–87 and later data reflect a more accurate accounting of total board costs. Because of their low response rate, data for private 2-year colleges must be interpreted with caution.
[4] Preliminary data based on fall 1995 enrollment weights.
—Data not available.

NOTE.—Data are for the entire academic year and are average charges paid by students. Tuition and fees were weighted by the number of full-time-equivalent undergraduates but were not adjusted to reflect student residency. Room and board were based on full-time students. The data have not been adjusted for changes in the purchasing power of the dollar. Some data have been revised from previously published figures. Because of rounding, details may not add to totals.

SOURCE: U.S. Department of Education, National Center for Education Statistics, Higher Education General Information Survey (HEGIS), "Institutional Characteristics of Colleges and Universities" and "Fall Enrollment in Institutions of Higher Education" surveys; Integrated Postsecondary Education Data System (IPEDS), "Fall Enrollment" and "Institutional Characteristics" surveys. (This table was prepared October 1997.)

Table 313.—Average undergraduate tuition and fees and room and board rates paid by students in institutions of higher education, by control of institution and by state: 1995–96 and 1996–97

State or other area	Public 4-year, 1995–96		Public 4-year, 1996–97[1]				Private 4-year, 1995–96		Private 4-year, 1996–97[1]				Public 2-year, tuition only (in-state)	
	Total	Tuition (in-state)	Total	Tuition (in-state)	Room	Board	Total	Tuition	Total	Tuition (in-state)	Room	Board	1995–96	1996–97[1]
1	2	3	4	5	6	7	8	9	10	11	12	13	14	15
United States	$7,014	$2,848	$7,331	$2,986	$2,212	$2,133	$17,612	$12,243	$18,476	$12,920	$2,885	$2,670	$1,239	$1,283
Alabama	5,735	2,239	6,008	2,363	1,811	1,834	11,636	7,580	12,182	8,023	1,852	2,307	1,316	1,358
Alaska	6,663	2,488	6,896	2,552	2,407	1,937	12,568	7,996	12,681	8,108	1,843	2,729	2,120	1,850
Arizona	5,996	1,926	6,307	2,009	2,361	1,937	11,290	7,008	12,122	7,811	2,077	2,234	764	782
Arkansas	5,055	2,028	5,398	2,255	1,669	1,474	10,157	6,553	10,764	7,012	1,560	2,193	912	941
California	8,209	2,664	8,324	2,731	3,038	2,556	20,040	13,905	20,987	14,650	3,287	3,050	361	371
Colorado	7,030	2,472	7,319	2,562	2,124	2,632	17,188	11,899	18,329	12,189	2,649	3,491	1,340	1,403
Connecticut	8,755	3,850	9,251	4,105	2,741	2,405	22,954	16,601	23,956	17,495	3,751	2,710	1,646	1,722
Delaware	8,512	4,003	8,896	4,180	2,530	2,185	11,450	7,285	12,800	7,674	2,785	2,341	1,266	1,330
District of Columbia	—	1,118	—	1,502	—	—	21,406	14,734	22,432	15,457	4,140	2,834	—	—
Florida	6,251	1,766	6,574	1,789	2,455	2,330	15,130	10,447	16,020	11,099	2,517	2,403	1,103	1,151
Georgia	5,690	2,104	6,499	2,244	2,138	2,117	15,215	10,221	16,459	10,973	3,060	2,427	1,060	1,110
Hawaii	—	1,578	—	2,298	—	—	11,610	6,230	14,102	6,492	2,950	4,660	524	789
Idaho	5,306	1,678	5,673	1,973	1,585	2,115	15,258	11,806	15,760	12,256	1,374	2,131	991	1,045
Illinois	7,841	3,355	8,192	3,525	2,130	2,538	16,671	11,649	17,649	12,424	2,814	2,412	1,232	1,290
Indiana	7,388	3,038	8,120	3,200	1,993	2,926	16,853	12,621	17,707	13,268	2,052	2,386	1,928	2,331
Iowa	5,945	2,564	6,174	2,655	1,771	1,748	15,878	11,894	16,559	12,394	1,913	2,252	1,785	1,840
Kansas	5,688	2,116	5,898	2,223	1,780	1,894	12,345	8,605	13,052	9,180	1,622	2,250	1,133	1,244
Kentucky	5,454	2,162	5,455	2,241	1,437	1,777	11,267	7,564	12,063	8,134	1,824	2,105	1,124	1,211
Louisiana	5,503	2,221	5,623	2,230	1,506	1,887	17,313	12,081	18,509	13,002	2,778	2,729	1,026	1,054
Maine	7,899	3,424	8,252	3,639	2,286	2,328	22,003	16,338	22,469	16,802	2,780	2,887	2,376	2,558
Maryland	8,731	3,575	9,177	3,848	2,826	2,503	21,076	14,561	22,014	15,365	3,622	3,028	1,969	2,103
Massachusetts	8,770	4,262	9,039	4,266	2,526	2,248	23,353	16,430	24,391	17,248	3,919	3,224	2,361	2,342
Michigan	8,189	3,895	8,648	3,986	2,115	2,546	13,425	9,259	14,037	9,683	2,157	2,196	1,527	1,578
Minnesota	6,734	3,229	7,131	3,539	2,063	1,530	17,177	12,864	17,980	13,633	2,122	2,225	2,050	2,219
Mississippi	5,416	2,459	5,528	2,497	1,482	1,549	9,965	6,835	10,480	7,226	1,656	1,599	941	952
Missouri	6,768	3,024	7,179	3,230	2,152	1,798	14,160	9,611	14,937	10,169	2,303	2,464	1,252	1,283
Montana	7,803	2,369	6,497	2,488	1,856	2,152	11,049	7,540	11,862	8,022	1,661	2,179	1,516	1,600
Nebraska	5,503	2,189	5,722	2,269	1,477	1,976	13,201	9,409	13,808	9,859	1,860	2,089	1,132	1,224
Nevada	7,400	1,686	7,690	1,814	3,191	2,684	—	7,388	13,380	7,780	3,300	2,300	974	1,002
New Hampshire	8,730	4,445	9,126	4,644	2,711	1,770	20,984	14,965	21,447	15,863	3,178	2,406	2,419	2,784
New Jersey	9,118	3,972	9,668	4,269	3,228	2,171	19,753	13,579	20,998	14,388	3,437	3,174	1,880	1,947
New Mexico	5,299	1,940	5,427	2,016	1,528	1,883	14,251	9,717	15,256	10,356	2,322	2,578	674	689
New York	8,971	3,715	9,298	3,797	3,053	2,448	20,910	13,909	21,538	14,559	3,889	3,090	2,426	2,519
North Carolina	5,119	1,641	5,437	1,841	1,802	1,794	15,334	10,916	16,357	11,682	2,221	2,455	581	581
North Dakota	5,641	2,247	5,921	2,381	1,058	2,483	9,924	7,020	10,429	7,419	1,294	1,715	1,697	1,783
Ohio	8,157	3,606	8,480	3,834	2,535	2,111	17,186	12,425	17,914	12,989	2,429	2,496	2,266	2,323
Oklahoma	4,296	1,848	5,079	1,936	1,284	1,859	11,615	7,700	11,525	7,579	1,709	2,237	1,253	1,262
Oregon	7,395	3,246	7,986	3,407	1,890	2,689	18,841	13,856	19,878	14,766	2,387	2,725	1,342	1,524
Pennsylvania	9,138	4,731	9,509	4,994	2,314	2,201	19,894	14,131	20,860	14,908	3,068	2,883	1,906	2,012
Rhode Island	9,453	3,861	9,652	3,907	3,044	2,700	22,015	15,340	22,465	15,644	3,751	3,071	1,726	1,736
South Carolina	6,964	3,096	7,235	3,206	2,109	1,921	13,464	9,669	14,177	10,253	1,900	2,024	1,066	1,114
South Dakota	5,613	2,644	5,831	2,727	1,293	1,811	13,111	9,184	13,749	9,624	1,628	2,497	3,430	3,430
Tennessee	5,373	1,989	5,498	2,051	1,728	1,719	13,953	9,745	14,885	10,387	2,314	2,184	1,022	1,046
Texas	5,471	1,824	5,904	2,022	1,979	1,902	13,022	8,848	13,686	9,385	2,044	2,258	768	788
Utah	5,389	2,006	5,557	2,010	1,527	2,020	7,366	2,940	7,677	3,073	1,436	3,167	1,390	1,392
Vermont	10,657	5,922	11,366	6,538	3,161	1,667	21,589	15,646	22,748	16,378	3,554	2,816	2,370	2,516
Virginia	8,207	3,917	8,451	3,962	2,302	2,187	15,032	10,614	15,761	11,149	2,159	2,453	1,433	1,465
Washington	7,129	2,792	7,313	2,928	2,234	2,151	17,956	13,147	18,597	13,794	2,543	2,261	1,370	1,445
West Virginia	6,119	2,020	6,348	2,088	2,086	2,174	14,412	10,185	15,213	10,805	1,965	2,444	1,319	1,376
Wisconsin	5,839	2,614	6,072	2,747	1,775	1,550	15,732	11,629	16,888	12,492	1,940	2,457	1,835	1,942
Wyoming	5,429	2,005	6,016	2,144	1,596	2,276	—	—	—	—	—	—	948	1,046

[1] Preliminary data based on fall 1995 enrollments.
—Data not reported or not applicable.

NOTE.—Data are for the entire academic year and are average charges. Tuition and fees were weighted by the number of full-time-equivalent undergraduates in 1995, but are not adjusted to reflect student residency. Room and board are based on full-time students. Because of rounding, details may not add to totals.

SOURCE: U.S. Department of Education, National Center for Education Statistics, Integrated Postsecondary Education Data System (IPEDS), "Fall Enrollment" and "Institutional Characteristics" surveys. (This table was prepared October 1997.)

Table 314.—Average graduate and first-professional tuition paid by students in institutions of higher education: 1987–88 to 1996–97

Year	Average full-time graduate tuition	Average full-time first-professional tuition									
		Chiropractic	Dentistry	Medicine	Optometry	Osteopathic medicine	Pharmacy	Podiatry	Veterinary medicine	Law	Theology
1	2	3	4	5	6	7	8	9	10	11	12
All institutions											
1987–88	$3,599	$6,996	$9,399	$9,034	$7,926	$10,674	$5,201	$12,736	$4,503	$6,636	$3,572
1988–89	3,728	7,972	9,324	9,439	8,503	11,462	4,952	13,232	4,856	7,099	3,911
1989–90	4,135	8,315	10,515	10,597	9,469	11,888	5,890	14,611	5,470	8,059	4,079
1990–91	4,488	9,108	10,270	10,571	9,512	12,830	5,889	15,143	5,396	8,708	4,569
1991–92	5,116	10,226	12,049	11,646	9,610	13,004	6,731	16,257	6,367	9,469	4,876
1992–93	5,475	11,117	12,710	12,265	10,858	14,297	6,635	17,426	6,771	10,463	5,331
1993–94	5,973	11,503	14,403	13,074	10,385	15,038	7,960	17,621	7,159	11,552	5,253
1994–95	6,247	12,324	15,164	13,834	11,053	15,913	8,315	18,138	7,741	12,374	5,648
1995–96[1]	6,741	12,495	16,171	14,703	11,784	16,853	8,908	18,444	8,161	13,227	6,031
1996–97[2]	7,100	12,927	16,950	15,448	12,471	17,564	9,628	19,083	8,623	14,163	6,425
Public[3]											
1987–88	1,827	—	4,614	5,245	2,789	5,125	2,462	—	3,523	2,810	—
1988–89	1,913	—	5,286	5,669	3,455	6,269	2,218	—	3,889	2,766	—
1989–90	1,999	—	5,728	6,259	3,569	6,521	2,816	—	4,505	3,196	—
1990–91	2,206	—	5,927	6,437	3,821	7,188	2,697	—	4,840	3,430	—
1991–92	2,524	—	6,595	7,106	4,161	7,699	2,871	—	5,231	3,933	—
1992–93	2,791	—	7,006	7,867	5,106	8,404	2,987	—	5,553	4,261	—
1993–94	3,050	—	7,525	8,329	5,325	8,640	3,567	—	6,107	4,835	—
1994–95	3,250	—	8,125	8,812	5,643	8,954	3,793	—	6,571	5,307	—
1995–96[1]	3,449	—	8,727	9,514	6,242	9,315	4,186	—	6,952	5,836	—
1996–97[2]	3,613	—	9,394	10,133	6,687	9,812	4,749	—	7,373	6,588	—
Private											
1987–88	6,769	6,996	16,201	14,945	11,635	13,311	8,834	12,736	12,544	9,048	3,572
1988–89	6,945	7,972	16,127	15,610	12,050	13,536	9,692	13,232	13,285	9,892	3,911
1989–90	7,881	8,315	16,800	16,826	13,640	14,117	10,656	14,611	14,184	10,901	4,079
1990–91	8,507	9,108	18,270	17,899	13,767	15,009	11,546	15,143	14,159	12,247	4,569
1991–92	9,592	10,226	20,318	19,225	14,366	16,098	12,937	16,257	15,816	12,946	4,876
1992–93	10,008	11,117	21,309	19,585	14,459	17,098	13,373	17,426	17,103	13,975	5,331
1993–94	10,790	11,503	23,824	20,769	14,156	17,720	14,838	17,621	17,433	15,193	5,253
1994–95	11,338	12,324	24,641	21,819	14,497	18,422	14,894	18,138	17,940	16,201	5,648
1995–96[1]	12,083	12,495	26,191	22,955	15,312	19,570	15,778	18,444	18,699	17,228	6,031
1996–97[2]	12,702	12,927	27,122	24,131	16,153	20,656	16,727	19,083	19,521	18,320	6,425

[1] Preliminary first-professional figures based on 1994–95 graduates.
[2] Preliminary graduate figures based on fall 1995 data and first-professional figures based on 1994–95 graduates.
[3] Data are based on in-state tuition only.
—Data not available or not applicable.

NOTE.—Average graduate student tuition weighted by fall full-time-equivalent graduate enrollment. Average first-professional tuition weighted by number of degrees conferred during the academic year. Some year-to-year fluctuations in tuition data may reflect non-reporting by individual institutions. Excludes institutions not reporting degrees conferred and institutions not reporting tuition. Some data have been revised from previously published figures.

SOURCE: U.S. Department of Education, National Center for Education Statistics, Integrated Postsecondary Education Data System (IPEDS), "Institutional Characteristics," "Fall Enrollment," and "Degrees Conferred" surveys. (This table was prepared October 1997.)

Table 315.—Percent of undergraduates receiving aid and average amount awarded in 1995–96 per student, by type and source of aid and selected student characteristics

Selected student characteristics	Enrollment of under-graduates,[1] in thousands	Any aid			Grants			Loans			Work study	Other		
		Total[2]	Federal	Non-federal	Total	Federal	Non-federal	Total	Federal	Non-federal	Total[3]	Total	Federal	Non-federal
1	2	3	4	5	6	7	8	9	10	11	12	13	14	15
Percent of all undergraduates receiving aid														
All undergraduates	16,677	49.7	36.6	32.0	39.0	21.9	27.6	25.6	25.3	1.1	5.0	7.4	2.4	4.8
Sex														
Men	7,197	46.7	33.1	31.4	35.8	18.2	26.4	24.4	23.9	1.3	4.3	8.7	2.7	5.8
Women	9,481	51.9	39.2	32.5	41.4	24.8	28.5	26.5	26.2	0.9	5.6	6.5	2.2	4.2
Race/ethnicity														
White, non-Hispanic	11,681	47.1	33.2	31.1	35.4	16.6	26.9	25.6	25.2	1.0	4.6	7.5	2.5	4.8
Black, non-Hispanic	2,030	62.9	50.0	38.3	52.8	38.1	31.7	30.9	30.4	1.3	6.1	9.8	2.6	7.0
Hispanic	1,723	54.2	44.6	30.6	47.3	36.1	27.2	22.3	22.0	0.9	5.8	5.2	1.5	3.6
Asian American/ Pacific Islander	967	42.9	33.1	30.8	35.7	22.9	27.5	21.3	20.7	1.3	6.6	5.7	2.2	3.5
American Indian/ Alaskan Native	163	59.4	47.8	37.1	48.4	37.3	27.3	25.2	25.2	0.2	3.9	12.0	1.5	7.7
Age														
23 years old or younger	9,116	53.5	42.1	34.0	41.7	22.7	30.9	31.1	30.7	1.2	7.7	7.7	4.4	3.4
24 to 29 years old	3,049	49.0	37.8	29.2	38.5	25.5	23.3	25.8	25.5	1.0	2.5	7.1	0.0	6.9
30 years old or over	4,513	42.5	24.8	29.9	33.9	18.0	23.8	14.5	14.1	0.8	1.4	7.1	0.0	6.4
Marital status														
Married	3,494	45.2	27.6	30.5	35.4	18.7	24.2	16.8	16.5	0.7	1.4	7.3	0.0	6.8
Not married[4]	12,861	50.4	38.4	32.2	39.4	22.0	28.5	27.9	27.5	1.2	6.1	7.3	3.1	4.1
Separated	322	70.9	61.6	38.7	62.0	54.3	29.1	30.0	30.0	0.8	3.3	13.4	0.1	12.5
Attendance status[5]														
Full-time	6,306	68.4	55.6	45.7	54.1	30.6	41.0	43.7	43.2	1.7	11.0	10.9	5.0	5.9
Part-time	10,157	44.1	29.4	28.1	34.6	19.2	24.0	18.2	17.8	0.5	2.2	5.5	0.8	4.4
Dependency status														
Dependent	8,201	50.9	39.2	33.4	38.8	18.9	30.7	30.5	30.1	1.3	7.8	7.7	4.9	3.0
Less than $20,000	1,543	70.2	62.9	43.0	66.3	57.0	40.4	35.4	35.2	1.1	10.9	6.5	3.0	3.6
$20,000–$39,999	1,873	60.3	49.2	40.5	51.0	31.7	38.1	38.2	37.4	2.0	10.4	7.5	4.4	3.2
$40,000–$59,999	1,865	47.4	34.6	31.8	30.4	3.7	29.2	32.4	32.2	1.1	7.8	9.0	6.3	2.9
$60,000–$79,999	1,366	42.5	28.4	28.1	25.3	0.5	25.3	27.0	26.6	1.1	5.8	8.1	5.6	2.6
$80,000–$99,999	681	37.6	24.4	24.4	50.4	0.2	20.3	23.3	23.1	0.6	4.9	9.0	6.0	3.2
$100,000 or more	873	27.5	13.9	19.7	17.3	0.3	17.1	12.6	12.2	1.0	2.7	6.0	4.1	1.9
Independent	8,476	48.5	34.1	30.7	39.2	24.8	24.6	20.9	20.5	0.9	2.3	7.1	0.0	6.7
Less than $9,999	2,470	67.4	59.0	37.5	60.5	52.3	30.8	34.0	33.7	1.1	5.7	8.4	0.0	8.2
$10,000–$19,999	1,923	50.6	38.6	29.8	38.4	24.4	23.2	23.7	23.1	1.3	1.6	7.7	0.0	7.2
$20,000–$29,999	1,382	41.9	26.0	28.3	34.0	18.3	22.9	15.7	15.4	0.9	0.9	6.3	0.0	5.9
$30,000–$49,999	1,502	36.3	16.4	27.3	24.7	6.0	21.0	12.3	12.1	0.4	0.6	6.9	0.0	6.2
$50,000 or more	1,201	29.3	7.0	25.1	20.7	0.1	20.7	5.9	5.8	0.2	0.1	4.9	0.0	4.3
Housing status														
School-owned	2,292	73.6	60.0	54.6	59.5	26.6	51.6	53.1	52.5	2.4	18.9	13.7	9.3	4.7
Off-campus, not with parents	10,188	46.1	32.5	29.0	35.5	20.6	23.8	22.2	21.8	0.9	2.8	7.0	1.1	5.5
With parents	4,197	45.3	33.7	26.9	36.4	22.6	23.8	19.0	18.7	0.7	2.9	5.1	1.6	3.3
Average 1995–96 award for full-time, full-year undergraduates enrolled in fall 1995 (Award averages are computed for students participating in the designated program.)														
All full-time, full-year undergraduates	6,306	$6,832	$5,362	$3,883	$3,864	$2,001	$3,599	$4,345	$4,288	$2,747	$1,371	$4,904	$6,334	$3,463
Sex														
Men	2,843	6,847	5,553	3,952	3,759	1,961	3,532	4,396	4,339	2,729	1,350	4,983	6,261	3,788
Women	3,462	6,821	5,225	3,831	3,939	2,027	3,648	4,308	4,251	2,762	1,384	4,818	6,400	3,053
Race/ethnicity														
White, non-Hispanic	4,500	6,836	5,549	3,848	3,762	1,894	3,541	4,437	4,366	2,912	1,367	5,070	6,426	3,550
Black, non-Hispanic	674	6,945	5,262	3,739	3,904	2,122	3,533	4,070	4,046	2,197	1,370	4,147	5,717	3,000
Hispanic	588	5,999	4,644	3,328	3,486	2,113	3,017	4,168	4,137	2,235	1,152	4,527	6,047	3,475
Asian American/ Pacific Islander	423	8,099	5,106	5,200	5,477	2,164	5,028	4,073	4,053	2,414	1,618	5,364	6,625	4,050
American Indian/ Alaskan Native	59	6,591	5,046	3,792	3,961	2,301	3,658	4,278	4,244	—	—	—	—	—
Age														
23 years old or younger	4,989	6,903	5,172	4,154	4,172	1,997	3,924	4,003	3,927	3,036	1,346	5,362	6,334	3,543
24 to 29 years old	686	6,909	6,165	2,814	2,829	1,992	2,087	5,471	5,471	1,668	1,569	3,652	—	3,364
30 years old or over	631	6,255	5,628	2,941	2,887	2,033	2,247	5,391	5,389	1,611	1,516	3,633	—	3,380
Marital status														
Married	600	6,143	5,587	2,926	2,744	1,914	2,225	5,296	5,284	2,826	1,576	3,729	—	3,318
Not married[4]	5,626	6,944	5,342	4,008	4,022	2,013	3,748	4,230	4,168	2,749	1,360	5,116	6,334	3,540
Separated	80	5,378	4,877	2,473	2,650	2,061	1,850	4,532	4,519	—	—	2,675	—	2,703
Dependency status														
Dependent	4,659	6,938	5,137	4,253	4,279	1,969	4,027	3,900	3,820	3,015	1,348	5,475	6,334	3,590
Less than $20,000	808	7,198	4,921	4,063	4,682	2,329	3,896	3,778	3,737	1,844	1,317	3,616	4,534	2,858
$20,000–$39,999	1,042	7,258	4,930	4,388	4,296	1,619	4,208	3,975	3,924	2,441	1,360	4,212	5,207	2,608
$40,000–$59,999	1,043	6,913	5,090	4,436	4,176	1,147	4,180	3,908	3,819	3,044	1,387	5,277	5,643	3,807
$60,000–$79,999	798	6,455	5,338	4,236	3,992	1,370	3,972	3,904	3,815	3,340	1,278	6,337	6,779	4,766
$80,000–$99,999	399	6,758	6,008	4,207	3,839	—	3,843	3,793	3,731	—	1,288	7,756	7,936	6,671
$100,000 or more	568	6,051	6,319	3,816	3,481	—	3,465	4,082	3,707	6,051	1,523	7,990	9,705	3,668
Independent	1,647	6,587	5,822	2,872	2,939	2,043	2,234	5,368	5,362	1,936	1,474	3,606	—	3,355
Less than $9,999	754	7,051	5,920	2,800	3,151	2,111	2,256	5,251	5,263	1,573	1,473	3,448	—	3,248

Table 315.—Percent of undergraduates receiving aid and average amount awarded in 1995–96 per student, by type and source of aid and selected student characteristics—Continued

Selected student characteristics	Enrollment of under-graduates,[1] in thousands	Any aid			Grants			Loans			Work study	Other		
		Total[2]	Federal	Non-federal	Total	Federal	Non-federal	Total	Federal	Non-federal	Total[3]	Total	Federal	Non-federal
1	2	3	4	5	6	7	8	9	10	11	12	13	14	15
$10,000–$19,999	377	6,310	5,695	2,653	2,756	2,115	2,060	5,526	5,516	1,678	1,708	3,174	—	3,061
$20,000–$29,999	213	6,065	5,789	2,812	2,386	1,805	1,790	5,245	5,254	—	—	4,544	—	4,254
$30,000–$49,999	187	6,420	5,857	3,770	2,687	1,147	2,951	5,949	5,856	—	—	4,247	—	3,797
$50,000 or more	117	4,597	5,095	3,186	2,647	—	2,647	4,984	4,933	—	—	3,087	—	2,387
Housing status														
School-owned	1,802	8,907	5,931	5,370	5,409	2,118	5,039	3,996	3,887	3,235	1,408	5,929	6,728	3,772
Off-campus, not with parents	2,731	6,466	5,630	3,178	3,192	1,975	2,777	4,889	4,861	2,458	1,390	4,294	6,035	3,412
With parents	1,772	4,629	3,980	2,613	2,856	1,935	2,405	3,693	3,672	2,105	1,163	4,014	5,166	3,197
		Average 1995–96 award for other undergraduates enrolled in fall 1995 (Award averages are computed for students participating in the designated program.)												
All other undergraduates[6]	10,372	$2,859	$3,276	$1,327	$1,452	$1,296	$1,119	$3,583	$3,588	$1,411	$1,524	$2,187	$4,327	$1,726
Sex														
Men	4,353	2,999	3,570	1,525	1,442	1,274	1,195	3,625	3,647	1,285	1,564	2,521	4,009	2,136
Women	6,019	2,772	3,115	1,188	1,458	1,306	1,069	3,556	3,551	1,592	1,502	1,875	4,674	1,355
Race/ethnicity														
White, non-Hispanic	7,181	2,869	3,436	1,347	1,378	1,238	1,132	3,620	3,629	1,362	1,537	2,175	4,488	1,695
Black, non-Hispanic	1,356	2,889	3,166	1,320	1,524	1,315	1,119	3,491	3,500	1,259	1,570	2,081	3,879	1,817
Hispanic	1,135	2,526	2,740	985	1,431	1,352	829	3,434	3,437	1,646	1,372	2,040	3,325	1,735
Asian American/ Pacific Islander	544	3,563	3,592	1,817	2,038	1,526	1,549	3,842	3,777	—	1,612	3,356	5,212	2,150
American Indian/ Alaskan Native	105	2,552	2,459	1,296	1,772	1,553	1,166	2,938	2,938	—	—	—	—	—
Age														
23 years old or younger	4,127	3,159	3,118	1,556	1,683	1,316	1,403	3,097	3,069	1,973	1,442	2,828	4,336	1,742
24 to 29 years old	2,363	3,062	3,612	1,265	1,308	1,254	944	4,053	4,067	1,071	1,564	2,098	—	1,985
30 years old or over	3,882	2,395	3,233	1,181	1,308	1,302	977	4,023	4,097	1,086	1,763	1,669	—	1,562
Marital status														
Married	2,894	2,365	3,201	1,208	1,259	1,245	987	3,979	3,984	1,155	1,994	1,721	—	1,650
Not married[4]	7,236	3,047	3,318	1,381	1,530	1,312	1,199	3,483	3,490	1,501	1,498	2,406	4,336	1,695
Separated	242	3,123	3,021	1,430	1,515	1,301	768	3,517	3,481	—	—	2,411	—	2,514
Dependency status														
Dependent	3,542	3,278	3,241	1,675	1,766	1,320	1,555	2,978	2,941	2,029	1,415	3,053	4,336	1,595
Less than $20,000	736	3,260	2,892	1,567	1,967	1,480	1,504	2,879	2,847	—	1,451	2,250	3,059	1,322
$20,000–$39,999	820	3,163	3,149	1,478	1,510	1,042	1,367	2,923	2,934	—	1,296	2,807	3,766	1,659
$40,000–$59,999	822	3,347	3,467	1,788	1,658	608	1,692	2,886	2,843	—	1,407	3,333	4,447	1,571
$60,000–$79,999	568	3,590	3,962	2,110	1,797	—	1,775	3,363	3,251	—	1,533	3,634	5,190	—
$80,000–$99,999	283	3,012	3,787	1,697	1,865	—	1,865	3,139	3,118	—	—	2,602	—	—
$100,000 or more	305	3,315	4,881	1,849	1,674	—	1,674	3,244	3,053	—	—	4,390	—	—
Independent	6,829	2,686	3,294	1,208	1,337	1,287	958	3,962	3,996	1,093	1,648	1,841	—	1,752
Less than $9,999	1,716	3,239	3,251	1,229	1,590	1,362	950	3,812	3,821	1,110	1,579	1,916	—	1,861
$10,000–$19,999	1,546	2,870	3,325	1,200	1,326	1,366	836	3,970	4,059	883	1,735	1,941	—	1,936
$20,000–$29,999	1,169	2,357	3,144	1,101	1,042	1,008	802	4,151	4,209	823	—	2,106	—	1,969
$30,000–$49,999	1,315	2,091	3,496	1,224	1,020	737	1,007	4,162	4,139	—	—	1,740	—	1,511
$50,000 or more	1,083	1,705	3,814	1,273	1,263	—	1,262	4,350	4,392	—	—	1,250	—	1,135
Housing status														
School-owned	490	2,782	3,362	1,267	1,371	1,273	1,045	3,815	3,828	1,461	1,669	1,960	4,356	1,696
Off-campus, not with parents	7,456	4,827	4,218	2,513	2,481	1,460	2,305	3,303	3,284	1,583	1,208	4,071	4,961	2,474
With parents	2,425	2,497	2,713	1,160	1,406	1,316	960	2,994	2,991	1,163	1,467	2,373	3,690	1,722

[1] Numbers of undergraduates may not equal figures reported in other tables, since these data are based on a sample survey. Includes all postsecondary institutions.
[2] Includes students who reported they were awarded aid, but did not specify the source or type of aid.
[3] Details on federal and nonfederal work study participants are not available.
[4] Includes students who were single, divorced, or widowed.
[5] Excludes persons whose attendance status was not reported.
[6] Enrollment data include persons whose attendance status was not reported.

NOTE.—Because of rounding and/or the fact that some students receive aid from multiple sources, row details may not add to totals. Because of rounding and survey item nonresponse, enrollment data may not add to totals. Data include undergraduates in noncollegiate and collegiate institutions.
—Data not applicable.

SOURCE: U.S. Department of Education, National Center for Education Statistics, National Postsecondary Student Aid Study, 1995–96. (This table was prepared September 1997.)

Table 316.—Undergraduates enrolled full-time and part-time, by aid status and source of aid during 1995–96, and control and level of institution

Control and level of institution	Number of undergraduates, 1995,[1] in thousands	Cumulative amount borrowed for undergraduate education	Aid status, 1995–96, in percents					
			Nonaided	Receiving aid, by source				
				Any aid[2]	Federal	State	Institutional	Other[2]
1	2	3	4	5	6	7	8	9
	Full-time students[3]							
All institutions	6,306	$7,747	31.6	68.4	55.6	19.8	27.7	10.9
Public	4,413	7,082	37.2	62.8	50.8	17.4	18.8	9.3
4-year doctoral	1,859	8,699	34.7	65.4	51.9	17.6	22.9	11.0
Other 4-year	1,070	7,168	30.7	69.3	59.8	22.8	19.1	8.6
2-year	1,397	4,120	44.1	55.9	44.5	13.5	13.9	7.4
Less than 2-year	88	3,111	60.5	39.5	20.6	9.6	7.2	12.6
Private, nonprofit	1,555	9,460	19.7	80.3	64.0	28.1	56.3	14.0
4-year doctoral	508	10,415	29.4	70.6	55.4	19.5	52.3	13.3
Other 4-year	958	9,243	14.4	85.6	68.3	33.1	60.5	14.6
2-year or less	89	6,867	20.8	79.2	67.5	24.0	33.9	11.4
Private, proprietary	337	6,942	13.8	86.2	79.7	12.8	11.5	17.2
2-year and above	167	9,026	14.3	85.8	79.1	18.1	5.9	15.3
Less than 2-year	170	4,745	13.4	86.6	80.3	7.6	17.0	19.1
	Part-time students[3]							
All institutions	10,157	$5,672	61.8	38.3	24.8	6.5	8.9	5.4
Public	8,519	5,265	66.3	33.7	20.8	5.5	7.4	4.7
4-year doctoral	1,211	8,210	41.8	41.8	31.2	7.5	10.1	5.8
Other 4-year	1,030	6,581	41.9	41.9	30.9	8.1	6.1	4.8
2-year	6,174	3,833	30.7	30.7	17.2	4.5	7.1	4.4
Less than 2-year	105	3,274	34.3	34.3	13.9	13.9	4.4	8.6
Private, nonprofit	1,070	8,302	44.4	55.6	34.9	12.8	21.2	8.6
4-year doctoral	280	9,474	51.0	51.0	27.7	10.2	22.5	8.4
Other 4-year	668	8,305	58.4	58.4	37.0	14.6	22.0	8.9
2-year or less	123	5,529	50.8	50.8	39.7	9.0	14.5	7.8
Private, proprietary	567	5,194	25.9	74.1	66.4	9.5	8.9	10.4
2-year and above	269	6,395	74.5	74.5	66.9	11.2	6.7	12.2
Less than 2-year	298	4,055	73.8	73.8	66.1	7.9	10.9	8.7

[1] Numbers of undergraduates may not equal figures reported in other tables, since these data are based on a sample survey. Includes students who enrolled at any time during the academic year.

[2] Includes students who reported that they were awarded aid but did not specify the source of the aid.

[3] Full-time students are students who attend full-time for the entire academic year. All other students, including those who attend full-time for part of the academic year, are counted as part-time students.

NOTE.—Because some students receive aid from multiple sources, percents do not add to totals. Excludes students whose attendance status was not reported.

SOURCE: U.S. Department of Education, National Center for Education Statistics, National Postsecondary Student Aid Study, 1992–93 and 1995–96. (This table was prepared September 1997.)

Table 317.—Percent of undergraduates receiving aid, by type and source of aid received, and by control and level of institution: 1992–93 and 1995–96

Control and level of institution	Number of undergraduates,[1] in thousands	Any aid			Grants			Loans			Work-study			Other		
		Total[2]	Federal	Non-federal	Total	Federal	Non-federal	Total	Federal	Non-federal	Total	Federal[3]	Total	Federal	Non-federal
1	2	3	4	5	6	7	8	9	10	11	12	13	14	15	16
Full-time students,[4] 1992–93															
All institutions	6,000	57.9	45.6	37.9	48.1	29.4	34.0	33.6	32.7	2.7	10.2	6.8	9.5	5.2	4.6
Public	4,110	51.9	40.0	33.0	42.3	27.8	29.1	26.9	26.1	2.0	6.8	4.2	7.9	3.7	4.4
4-year doctoral	1,772	53.7	39.3	34.8	41.9	23.8	30.8	33.0	32.2	2.4	7.1	4.3	8.6	5.0	3.9
Other 4-year	1,087	56.4	46.1	37.4	45.5	32.1	32.4	33.7	32.7	2.8	9.5	5.5	7.9	4.2	3.8
2-year	1,196	45.9	36.0	27.0	40.6	29.9	24.3	12.7	12.3	0.7	4.1	3.0	7.0	1.3	5.7
Less than 2-year	55	35.0	31.6	15.7	29.9	26.6	12.8	3.0	3.0	0.6	1.5	1.4	5.1	0.8	4.4
Private, nonprofit	1,469	69.5	53.4	58.0	62.1	27.7	54.1	46.5	44.9	4.9	22.2	15.9	12.1	7.7	5.0
4-year doctoral	681	62.7	44.5	54.8	55.2	17.3	51.8	41.6	39.7	6.1	18.9	13.2	11.6	7.4	4.5
Other 4-year	719	75.5	60.8	62.7	68.7	35.6	58.1	51.7	50.3	4.1	27.0	19.7	12.2	7.9	5.3
2-year or less	70	73.9	63.9	42.0	61.3	47.3	35.4	41.1	39.5	2.5	4.6	3.0	17.2	9.4	7.8
Private, proprietary	421	76.1	72.4	16.4	55.3	50.9	11.4	54.1	53.8	2.1	1.9	0.7	15.6	11.3	4.5
2-year and above	182	80.6	77.4	22.7	49.5	43.4	16.4	65.2	65.2	3.0	3.5	1.4	24.6	18.8	6.5
Less than 2-year	238	72.7	68.6	11.5	59.7	56.7	7.5	45.6	45.1	1.5	0.7	0.2	8.7	5.6	3.1
Full-time students,[4] 1995–96															
All institutions	6,306	68.4	55.6	45.7	54.1	30.6	41.0	43.7	43.2	1.7	11.0	9.0	10.9	5.0	5.9
Public	4,413	62.8	50.8	39.0	47.5	29.6	34.2	37.2	36.9	0.8	7.0	5.4	9.3	3.7	5.5
4-year doctoral	1,859	65.4	51.9	42.2	47.6	26.1	37.2	44.5	44.1	1.4	7.4	5.3	11.0	5.6	5.4
Other 4-year	1,070	69.3	59.8	44.5	52.3	34.4	40.0	47.4	47.2	0.4	9.2	6.7	8.6	3.7	4.8
2-year	1,397	55.9	44.5	31.3	44.6	31.1	26.9	21.8	21.3	0.4	5.1	4.7	7.4	1.3	6.0
Less than 2-year	88	39.5	20.6	27.5	30.9	18.5	16.0	4.4	4.4	0.0	0.1	0.1	12.6	0.1	12.0
Private, nonprofit	1,555	80.3	64.0	67.6	71.3	28.6	64.8	56.9	56.2	3.4	24.6	21.0	14.0	8.2	6.1
4-year doctoral	508	70.6	55.4	61.2	61.6	19.3	58.7	50.9	49.9	3.9	22.6	20.2	13.3	8.6	4.9
Other 4-year	958	85.6	68.3	72.5	77.3	32.5	70.1	60.4	60.0	2.6	27.6	23.0	14.6	8.2	6.7
2-year or less	89	79.2	67.5	52.0	61.9	40.0	42.0	52.9	51.7	9.3	5.3	4.6	11.4	5.0	6.3
Private, proprietary	337	86.2	79.7	32.7	61.3	53.9	20.2	67.7	65.5	5.1	0.5	0.5	17.2	7.6	8.9
2-year and above	167	85.8	80.3	33.0	60.0	49.1	26.0	70.9	70.9	1.4	0.7	0.7	15.3	7.8	6.9
Less than 2-year	170	86.6	79.1	32.5	62.5	58.6	14.5	64.6	60.3	8.7	0.3	0.2	19.1	7.4	10.9
Part-time students,[4] 1995–96															
All institutions	10,157	38.3	24.8	24.0	29.9	16.6	19.7	14.4	14.1	0.7	1.4	1.1	5.4	0.8	4.3
Public	8,519	33.7	20.8	21.7	26.5	14.4	17.9	10.5	10.3	0.3	1.2	0.9	4.7	0.4	3.9
4-year doctoral	1,211	41.8	31.2	23.7	28.9	16.9	19.0	25.9	25.6	0.7	2.4	1.4	5.8	1.7	3.9
Other 4-year	1,030	41.9	30.9	22.8	30.2	18.2	19.3	22.3	22.1	0.4	2.3	2.0	4.8	0.8	3.7
2-year	6,174	30.7	17.2	21.1	25.4	13.4	17.5	5.7	5.5	0.3	0.8	0.7	4.4	0.2	3.9
Less than 2-year	105	34.3	13.9	26.0	27.8	12.3	17.4	2.2	2.2	0.0	0.0	0.0	8.6	0.0	8.3
Private, nonprofit	1,070	55.6	34.9	41.5	44.1	17.9	36.1	26.4	26.1	1.3	4.0	3.1	8.6	2.0	6.6
4-year doctoral	280	51.0	27.7	39.7	39.3	12.0	34.3	24.4	23.6	1.4	4.6	3.7	8.4	2.1	5.9
Other 4-year	668	58.4	37.0	44.6	47.5	19.1	39.7	27.3	27.2	0.8	4.5	3.3	8.9	1.7	7.1
2-year or less	123	50.8	39.7	28.3	36.8	24.6	20.5	26.2	25.9	4.3	0.4	0.3	7.8	2.9	5.1
Private, proprietary	567	74.1	66.4	24.3	53.4	46.4	15.3	50.3	49.3	4.6	0.4	0.4	10.4	4.2	5.7
2-year and above	269	74.5	66.9	25.5	53.4	44.8	17.9	50.2	49.8	1.7	0.8	0.7	12.2	4.9	6.9
Less than 2-year	298	73.8	66.1	23.2	53.5	47.9	13.0	50.5	48.8	7.2	0.1	0.1	8.7	3.5	4.7

[1] Numbers of undergraduates may not equal figures reported in other tables, since these data are based on a sample survey. Includes students who enrolled at any time during the academic year.
[2] Includes students who reported they were awarded aid but did not specify the source of aid.
[3] Details on nonfederal work study participants are not available.
[4] Full-time students are students who attend full-time for the entire academic year. All other students, including those who attend full-time for part of the academic year, are counted as part-time students.

NOTE.—Excludes students whose attendance status was not reported. Because some students receive multiple types and sources of aid and rounding, details may not add to totals.

SOURCE: U.S. Department of Education, National Center for Education Statistics, National Postsecondary Student Aid Study, 1992–93 and 1995–96. (This table was prepared September 1997.)

Table 318.—Undergraduates enrolled full-time and part-time, by federal aid program and by control and level of institution: 1995–96

Control and level of institution	Number of undergraduates, 1995,[1] in thousands	Percent receiving federal aid in 1995–96, by type							
		Any federal aid	Selected Title IV programs[2]						
			Any Title IV aid	Pell	SEOG[3]	CWS[4]	Perkins[5]	Stafford[6]	Plus[7]
1	2	3	4	5	6	7	8	9	10
Full-time students[8]									
All institutions	6,306	55.6	54.7	30.1	9.1	9.0	7.6	42.2	5.0
Public	4,413	50.8	49.9	29.2	7.2	5.4	5.4	36.0	3.7
4-year doctoral	1,859	51.9	50.9	25.5	6.9	5.3	8.5	43.2	5.6
Other 4-year	1,070	59.8	59.1	34.0	8.4	6.7	6.0	45.8	3.7
2-year	1,397	44.5	43.3	31.1	7.3	4.7	1.4	20.7	1.3
Less than 2-year	88	20.6	20.2	18.5	0.3	0.1	—	4.4	0.1
Private, nonprofit	1,555	64.0	63.2	27.4	13.0	21.0	14.4	55.1	8.2
4-year doctoral	508	55.4	54.5	17.8	9.7	20.2	17.0	48.9	8.6
Other 4-year	958	68.3	67.6	31.4	15.2	23.0	14.3	58.8	8.2
2-year or less	89	67.5	66.8	39.5	8.3	4.6	1.4	51.2	5.0
Private, proprietary	337	79.7	79.4	53.6	16.1	0.5	4.9	64.6	7.6
2-year and above	167	80.3	80.0	48.8	16.1	0.7	8.0	70.5	7.8
Less than 2-year	170	79.1	78.8	58.3	16.1	0.2	1.8	58.8	7.4
Part-time students[8]									
All institutions	10,157	24.8	23.8	16.4	3.3	1.1	1.4	13.8	0.8
Public	8,519	20.8	19.7	14.4	2.5	0.9	1.0	10.0	0.4
4-year doctoral	1,211	31.2	30.4	16.7	3.3	1.4	3.5	25.1	1.7
Other 4-year	1,030	30.9	30.0	18.1	3.4	2.0	2.2	21.5	0.8
2-year	6,174	17.2	16.0	13.3	2.3	0.7	0.3	5.3	0.1
Less than 2-year	105	13.9	13.0	12.3	—	—	—	2.2	—
Private, nonprofit	1,070	34.9	33.5	17.1	4.7	3.1	3.4	25.3	2.0
4-year doctoral	280	27.7	27.5	11.6	3.9	3.7	5.2	23.2	2.1
Other 4-year	668	37.0	34.9	18.2	5.3	3.3	3.3	26.2	1.7
2-year or less	123	39.7	39.4	24.2	3.1	0.3	0.1	25.8	2.9
Private, proprietary	567	66.4	66.2	46.1	11.3	0.4	3.1	48.4	4.2
2-year and above	269	66.9	66.3	44.7	11.9	0.7	5.1	49.2	4.9
Less than 2-year	298	66.1	66.1	47.4	10.7	0.1	1.4	47.6	3.5

[1] Numbers of undergraduates may not equal figures reported in other tables, since these data are based on a sample survey. Includes students who enrolled at any time during the academic year.
[2] Title IV of the Higher Education Act.
[3] Supplemental Educational Opportunity Grants.
[4] College Work Study (CWS). Prior to October 17, 1986, private, proprietary institutions were prohibited by law from spending CWS funds for on-campus work. Includes persons who participated in the program, but had no earnings.
[5] Formerly National Direct Student Loans (NDSL).
[6] Formerly Guaranteed Student Loans (GSL).
[7] Parent loans for Undergraduate Students.
[8] Full-time students are students who attend full-time for the entire academic year. All other students, including those who attend full-time for part of the academic year, are counted as part-time students.
—Less than .05 percent.

NOTE.—Excludes students whose attendance status was not reported. Because some students receive aid from multiple sources and rounding, percents do not add to totals.

SOURCE: U.S. Department of Education, National Center for Education Statistics, National Postsecondary Student Aid Study, 1995–96. (This table was prepared October 1997.)

Table 319.—Postbaccalaureate students enrolled full-time and part-time, by aid status, source of aid, and by level of study and control and level of institution: 1992–93 and 1995–96

Level of degree, control and type of institution	Postbaccalaureate students,[1] in thousands	Cumulative amount borrowed for postbaccalaureate education	Aid status in percents						
			Nonaided	Receiving aid, by source					
				Any aid[2]	Federal	State	Institutional	Employer	Other[3]
1	2	3	4	5	6	7	8	9	10
Full-time students,[4] 1992–93									
All institutions	673	$18,572	31.9	68.1	44.4	7.0	40.6	5.3	14.6
Master's degree	281	11,109	37.5	62.5	33.8	5.8	42.4	8.3	12.0
Public	163	9,335	34.6	65.4	33.9	7.8	44.0	7.6	9.7
4-year doctoral	139	9,597	34.3	65.7	32.4	6.7	46.3	7.7	10.1
Other 4-year	24	7,970	36.1	63.9	42.5	14.4	30.4	6.8	7.5
Private	118	13,628	41.6	58.4	33.7	3.2	40.2	9.4	15.2
4-year doctoral	102	13,879	39.3	60.7	34.2	2.9	42.9	8.9	16.4
Other 4-year	16	—	56.5	43.5	30.5	5.1	22.8	12.1	7.4
Doctor's degree	120	16,895	30.4	69.6	28.3	4.4	51.6	3.0	13.2
Public	73	12,758	30.3	69.7	22.3	6.5	55.5	3.9	11.7
Private	46	21,742	30.4	69.6	37.8	1.1	45.5	1.7	15.7
First-professional	211	30,045	23.0	77.0	68.2	10.0	37.0	2.3	20.3
Public	101	24,469	20.7	79.3	72.5	13.4	37.7	2.3	15.8
Private	110	35,301	25.1	74.9	64.3	6.8	36.4	2.3	24.4
Other graduate	61	13,102	39.3	60.7	42.4	6.7	22.9	6.0	9.1
Full-time students,[4] 1995–96									
All institutions	861	$27,122	23.9	76.1	49.3	4.1	43.4	9.6	22.7
Master's degree	387	18,806	27.4	72.6	43.6	2.4	42.8	16.4	22.5
Public	236	15,905	25.3	74.7	40.7	3.0	45.6	16.7	31.4
4-year doctoral	195	16,910	23.5	76.5	40.5	2.6	47.9	19.2	34.1
Other 4-year	41	11,417	34.0	66.0	41.4	5.1	35.0	4.9	18.7
Private	151	22,568	30.6	69.4	48.2	1.4	38.3	15.9	8.7
4-year doctoral	104	23,816	28.8	71.2	44.6	1.5	42.2	20.2	11.5
Other 4-year	47	20,299	34.6	65.4	56.1	1.3	29.7	6.6	2.6
Doctor's degree	147	24,380	17.1	82.9	27.6	0.6	75.7	4.0	53.4
Public	94	22,687	14.1	85.9	27.6	1.0	77.8	5.1	62.1
Private	53	28,083	22.5	77.5	27.6	0.0	72.0	2.1	37.9
First-professional	253	37,540	16.8	83.2	73.9	9.4	31.6	2.2	8.7
Public	115	34,463	14.3	85.7	79.5	9.7	33.5	1.2	8.0
Private	138	40,350	19.0	81.0	69.3	9.2	30.0	3.1	9.3
Other graduate	54	12,057	43.5	56.5	34.0	2.2	31.4	7.0	14.7
Public 4-year doctoral	18	—	36.9	63.1	32.2	4.0	35.2	—	17.3
Public other 4-year	36	12,057	46.8	53.2	35.0	1.2	29.4	10.5	13.4
Part-time students,[4] 1995–96									
All institutions	1,869	$16,193	59.3	40.7	13.8	1.4	16.7	26.0	10.4
Master's degree	1,118	14,635	56.3	43.7	15.1	1.2	16.5	27.9	10.3
Public	649	12,971	57.3	42.7	13.6	1.7	18.5	24.2	13.3
4-year doctoral	432	14,443	52.8	47.2	14.8	1.2	22.6	25.7	16.5
Other 4-year	217	9,273	66.4	33.6	11.1	2.8	10.3	21.4	6.9
Private	470	16,904	54.9	45.1	17.2	0.5	13.7	33.0	6.3
4-year doctoral	255	19,948	55.3	44.7	17.7	0.6	17.2	29.0	7.6
Other 4-year	215	13,006	54.5	45.5	16.6	0.3	9.6	37.8	4.7
Doctor's degree	181	19,530	48.6	51.4	12.1	0.6	39.3	11.9	27.0
Public	119	16,288	46.1	53.9	9.5	0.9	42.5	13.2	32.5
Private	62	24,882	53.3	46.7	17.2	0.0	33.3	9.3	16.6
First-professional	60	32,803	32.2	67.8	47.4	4.3	27.0	14.2	7.0
Public	15	31,882	29.6	70.4	59.6	4.0	25.7	9.3	8.6
Private	46	33,160	33.1	66.9	43.5	4.3	27.4	15.8	6.5
Other graduate	483	13,008	74.0	26.0	7.0	1.9	8.4	26.7	5.1
Public 4-year doctoral	166	11,166	67.8	32.2	9.8	0.5	12.4	24.7	4.0
Public other 4-year	317	15,473	77.3	22.7	5.5	2.6	6.3	27.8	5.7

[1] Numbers of postbaccalaureate students may not equal figures reported in other tables, since these data are based on a sample survey of all postbaccalaureate students. Includes students who enrolled at any time during the academic year.
[2] Includes students who reported they were awarded aid but did not specify the source of aid.
[3] Includes aid provided by corporations, unions, foundations, fraternal organizations, community organizations, etc.
[4] Full-time students are students who attend full-time for the entire academic year. All other students, including those who attend full-time for part of the academic year, are counted as part-time students.

—Sample size too small to permit reliable estimate.

NOTE.—Excludes students whose attendance status was not reported. Total includes some students whose level of study was unknown. Because some students receive aid from multiple sources and rounding, percents do not add to totals.

SOURCE: U.S. Department of Education, National Center for Education Statistics, National Postsecondary Student Aid Study, 1992–93 and 1995–96. (This table was prepared October 1997.)

336 HIGHER EDUCATION: STUDENT CHARGES

Table 320.—Postbaccalaureate students enrolled full-time and part-time, by type of aid and by level of study, control, and level of institution: 1992–93 and 1995–96

Level of degree, control and type of institution	Postbaccalaureate students,[1] in thousands	Type of aid in percents							
		Any aid[2]	Fellowship grants	Tuition waivers	Assistantships[3]	Employer	Loans		
							Any loans	Stafford[4]	Perkins
1	2	3	4	5	6	7	8	9	10
Full-time students,[5] 1992–93									
All institutions	673	68.1	3.5	12.4	14.3	3.3	43.5	41.1	9.0
Master's degree	281	62.5	3.5	15.6	18.1	5.1	32.5	30.5	5.0
Public	163	65.4	2.2	20.5	22.4	4.8	32.2	30.8	4.0
4-year doctoral	139	65.7	2.4	23.3	23.5	4.7	30.6	29.6	3.3
Other 4-year	24	63.9	1.0	4.4	15.8	5.3	41.5	38.4	8.3
Private	118	58.4	5.3	8.9	12.1	5.6	32.9	30.0	6.4
4-year doctoral	102	60.7	6.2	9.5	13.6	5.7	33.6	30.8	6.8
Other 4-year	16	43.5	0.0	5.4	3.0	4.7	28.7	24.6	4.4
Doctor's degree	120	69.6	9.3	19.4	27.0	2.2	25.8	23.9	3.5
Public	73	69.7	4.2	23.1	31.6	3.1	20.6	18.9	2.9
Private	46	69.6	17.5	13.6	19.9	0.9	34.1	31.9	4.3
First-professional	211	77.0	0.9	5.6	4.4	1.2	67.8	65.5	19.3
Public	101	79.3	0.4	5.4	4.3	1.3	71.8	69.9	23.2
Private	110	74.9	1.2	5.8	4.5	1.2	64.1	61.6	15.7
Other graduate	61	60.7	1.1	7.5	6.2	3.7	44.4	39.6	2.7
Full-time students,[5] 1995–96									
All institutions	861	76.1	5.2	11.7	19.5	5.0	48.7	48.0	8.1
Master's degree	387	72.6	4.3	13.5	20.2	6.6	43.1	42.5	5.1
Public	236	74.7	4.8	17.8	28.8	7.1	39.5	38.8	3.5
4-year doctoral	195	76.5	5.2	19.5	31.1	7.6	39.2	38.6	4.0
Other 4-year	41	66.0	2.5	9.9	18.1	4.5	40.8	39.8	1.5
Private	151	69.4	3.6	6.7	6.6	5.8	48.6	48.2	7.6
4-year doctoral	104	71.2	3.6	6.4	8.8	7.1	44.6	44.6	9.6
Other 4-year	47	65.4	3.7	7.4	1.9	3.2	57.4	56.1	3.3
Doctor's degree	147	82.9	15.8	24.3	51.8	5.5	25.2	25.2	1.5
Public	94	85.9	13.7	30.9	59.9	5.9	26.7	26.7	1.4
Private	53	77.5	19.6	12.4	37.3	4.9	22.6	22.6	1.7
First-professional	253	83.2	1.4	3.0	4.0	1.3	74.4	73.0	18.4
Public	115	85.7	2.0	3.8	4.1	1.5	79.0	78.6	20.7
Private	138	81.0	0.9	2.4	3.8	1.2	70.6	68.3	16.4
Other graduate	54	56.5	2.1	9.8	6.4	6.1	31.3	30.9	1.7
Public 4-year doctoral	18	63.1	0.0	9.2	6.2	1.8	30.2	30.2	3.6
Public other 4-year	36	53.2	3.1	10.1	6.6	8.3	31.8	31.2	0.7
Part-time students,[5] 1995–96									
All institutions	1,869	40.7	0.8	6.1	7.4	16.1	13.4	13.1	0.9
Master's degree	1,118	43.7	0.8	5.6	7.4	18.4	14.5	14.2	0.7
Public	649	42.7	0.8	6.0	10.7	16.0	13.2	12.9	0.9
4-year doctoral	432	47.2	1.0	7.1	13.7	16.6	14.3	14.2	1.0
Other 4-year	217	33.6	0.4	3.9	4.9	14.8	11.0	10.5	0.6
Private	470	45.1	0.9	5.1	2.7	21.7	16.4	16.1	0.5
4-year doctoral	255	44.7	1.2	4.3	4.0	18.3	17.6	17.0	0.8
Other 4-year	215	45.5	0.5	5.9	1.2	25.9	15.0	14.9	0.1
Doctor's degree	181	51.4	2.5	12.7	26.0	9.0	12.0	12.0	0.4
Public	119	53.9	3.1	15.6	31.9	9.2	9.2	9.2	0.3
Private	62	46.7	1.4	7.4	14.7	8.6	17.2	17.2	0.7
First-professional	60	67.8	1.4	3.8	3.1	7.0	47.8	45.7	8.6
Public	15	70.4	1.6	4.8	7.9	7.5	58.1	57.4	12.2
Private	46	66.9	1.3	3.5	1.6	6.8	44.5	41.9	8.6
Other graduate	483	26.0	0.2	5.5	1.5	13.3	6.7	6.5	0.5
Public 4-year doctoral	166	32.2	0.0	8.6	0.4	14.9	9.7	9.6	0.6
Public other 4-year	317	22.7	0.2	3.8	2.1	12.4	5.2	5.0	0.4

[1] Numbers of postbaccalaureate students may not equal figures reported in other tables, since these data are based on a sample survey of all postbaccalaureate students. Includes students who enrolled at any time during the academic year.
[2] Includes students who reported they were awarded aid but did not specify the source of aid.
[3] Includes students who received teaching or research assistantships and/or participated in work-study programs.
[4] Stafford loans, formerly Graduate Student Loans (GSL).
[5] Full-time students are students who attend full-time for the entire academic year. All other students, including those who attend full-time for part of the academic year, are counted as part-time students.

—Data not applicable.

NOTE.—Excludes students whose attendance status was not reported. Total includes some students whose level of study was unknown. Because some students receive aid from multiple sources and rounding, details do not add to totals.

SOURCE: U.S. Department of Education, National Center for Education Statistics, National Postsecondary Student Aid Study, 1992–93 and 1995–96. (This table was prepared October 1997.)

Table 321.—Scholarship and fellowship awards[1] of institutions of higher education, by control of institution: 1959–60 to 1994–95

[In thousands]

Year	Total scholarship and fellowship awards			Scholarship and fellowship awards from unrestricted funds			Scholarship and fellowship awards from restricted funds		
	All institutions	Public	Private	All institutions	Public	Private	All institutions	Public	Private
1	2	3	4	5	6	7	8	9	10
1959–60	$172,051	$59,673	$112,377	—	—	—	—	—	—
1961–62	228,765	78,255	150,510	—	—	—	—	—	—
1963–64	300,370	107,767	192,603	—	—	—	—	—	—
1965–66	425,524	153,256	272,269	—	—	—	—	—	—
1966–67	583,390	248,077	335,311	—	—	—	—	—	—
1967–68	712,425	326,915	385,510	—	—	—	—	—	—
1968–69	814,755	367,433	447,322	—	—	—	—	—	—
1969–70	984,594	456,977	527,617	—	—	—	—	—	—
1970–71	1,098,198	528,243	569,955	—	—	—	—	—	—
1971–72	1,241,372	621,387	619,986	—	—	—	—	—	—
1972–73	1,322,411	656,054	666,357	—	—	—	—	—	—
1973–74	1,396,488	705,691	690,797	—	—	—	—	—	—
1974–75	1,449,542	718,780	730,762	$631,801	$267,191	$364,610	$817,741	$451,589	$366,152
1975–76	1,635,859	798,515	837,343	686,604	276,334	410,269	949,255	522,181	427,074
1976–77	1,770,215	859,011	911,204	748,763	291,073	457,690	1,021,451	567,938	453,514
1977–78	1,839,298	840,666	998,632	818,101	305,563	512,537	1,021,197	535,102	486,095
1978–79	1,944,599	861,578	1,083,021	883,213	326,201	557,012	1,061,386	535,377	526,009
1979–80	2,200,468	970,363	1,230,106	904,876	324,224	580,652	1,295,592	646,138	649,454
1980–81	2,504,525	1,064,864	1,439,661	1,080,614	367,476	713,138	1,423,911	697,388	726,523
1981–82	2,684,945	1,088,717	1,596,228	1,236,081	374,632	861,449	1,448,864	714,085	734,779
1982–83	2,922,897	1,188,383	1,734,514	1,478,762	460,291	1,018,470	1,444,136	728,092	716,044
1983–84	3,301,673	1,276,644	2,025,028	1,738,188	518,626	1,219,562	1,563,485	758,018	805,466
1984–85	3,670,355	1,374,803	2,295,551	1,961,597	569,058	1,392,539	1,708,758	805,745	903,012
1985–86	4,160,174	1,575,909	2,584,266	2,285,116	696,973	1,588,143	1,875,059	878,935	996,123
1986–87	4,776,100	1,751,671	3,024,430	2,644,615	750,931	1,893,684	2,131,486	1,000,740	1,130,746
1987–88	5,325,358	1,941,389	3,383,968	2,941,143	830,195	2,110,948	2,384,215	1,111,194	1,273,021
1988–89	5,918,666	2,150,350	3,768,316	3,282,698	944,001	2,338,697	2,635,969	1,206,349	1,429,619
1989–90	6,655,544	2,386,493	4,269,051	3,853,904	1,099,425	2,754,479	2,801,640	1,287,068	1,514,572
1990–91	7,551,184	2,688,532	4,862,651	4,445,106	1,270,158	3,174,947	3,106,078	1,418,374	1,687,704
1991–92	9,060,000	3,255,660	5,804,340	5,205,797	1,523,721	3,682,076	3,854,203	1,731,939	2,122,264
1992–93	10,148,373	3,727,838	6,420,536	5,949,037	1,745,339	4,203,697	4,199,337	1,982,498	2,216,838
1993–94	11,238,010	4,222,923	7,015,087	6,644,717	1,934,617	4,710,100	4,593,293	2,288,306	2,304,987
1994–95[2]	12,285,328	4,662,023	7,623,304	7,329,384	2,149,036	5,180,348	4,955,944	2,512,988	2,442,957

[1] Includes Supplemental Educational Opportunity Grants and State Student Incentive Grants, but excludes Pell Grants.
[2] Preliminary data.
—Data not collected.

NOTE.—Because of rounding, details may not add to totals.

SOURCE: U.S. Department of Education, National Center for Education Statistics, Higher Education General Information Survey (HEGIS), "Financial Statistics of Institutions of Higher Education" surveys; and Integrated Postsecondary Education Data System (IPEDS), "Finance" surveys. (This table was prepared July 1997.)

338 HIGHER EDUCATION: STUDENT CHARGES

Table 322.—Pell Grant revenue of institutions of higher education compared to current-fund revenue and tuition, by type and control of institution: 1985–86 to 1994–95

[Amounts in thousands]

Year and type of control of institution	Total				Public				Private			
	Current-fund revenue	Tuition	Pell Grant revenue	Pell Grants as a percent of current-fund revenue	Current-fund revenue	Tuition	Pell Grant revenue	Pell Grants as a percent of current-fund revenue	Current-fund revenue	Tuition	Pell Grant revenue	Pell Grants as a percent of current-fund revenue
1	2	3	4	5	6	7	8	9	10	11	12	13
1985–86	$100,437,616	$23,116,605	$2,565,048	2.6	$65,004,632	$9,439,177	$1,873,456	2.9	$35,432,985	$13,677,429	$691,592	2.0
4-year	88,144,386	20,498,399	1,770,042	2.0	53,746,503	7,539,717	1,214,303	2.3	34,397,882	12,958,683	555,739	1.6
2-year	12,293,231	2,618,206	795,006	6.5	11,258,128	1,899,460	659,153	5.9	1,035,102	718,746	135,853	13.1
1987–88	117,340,109	27,836,781	2,496,133	2.1	74,771,255	11,184,657	1,876,777	2.5	42,568,854	16,652,124	619,355	1.5
4-year	103,280,070	24,779,364	1,714,118	1.7	61,958,780	9,032,936	1,207,418	1.9	41,321,290	15,746,428	506,700	1.2
2-year	14,060,039	3,057,417	782,015	5.6	12,812,475	2,151,721	669,359	5.2	1,247,564	905,696	112,656	9.0
1989–90	139,635,477	33,926,060	3,348,018	2.4	88,911,433	13,820,240	2,566,209	2.9	50,724,044	20,105,820	781,809	1.5
4-year	122,858,290	30,302,689	2,253,803	1.8	73,415,696	11,090,012	1,591,684	2.2	49,442,595	19,212,677	662,119	1.3
2-year	16,777,187	3,623,371	1,094,215	6.5	15,495,738	2,730,229	974,525	6.3	1,281,449	893,143	119,690	9.3
1990–91	149,766,051	37,434,462	3,510,537	2.3	94,904,506	15,258,024	2,725,357	2.9	54,861,545	22,176,439	785,180	1.4
4-year	131,743,973	33,405,241	2,312,931	1.8	78,272,989	12,188,851	1,647,376	2.1	53,470,984	21,216,389	665,554	1.2
2-year	18,022,078	4,029,222	1,197,606	6.6	16,631,517	3,069,173	1,077,981	6.5	1,390,562	960,049	119,625	8.6
1991–92	161,395,896	41,559,037	4,238,047	2.6	102,202,890	17,460,263	3,312,386	3.2	59,193,006	24,098,774	925,661	1.6
4-year	141,700,893	36,910,390	2,710,510	1.9	83,969,040	13,827,245	1,928,623	2.3	57,731,852	23,083,145	781,887	1.4
2-year	19,695,003	4,648,647	1,527,537	7.8	18,233,850	3,633,018	1,383,763	7.6	1,461,153	1,015,629	143,774	9.8
1992–93	170,880,503	45,346,071	4,701,905	2.8	108,186,484	19,490,221	3,663,529	3.4	62,694,018	25,855,850	1,038,377	1.7
4-year	150,075,119	40,127,624	2,982,999	2.0	88,952,983	15,406,746	2,097,638	2.4	61,122,135	24,720,878	885,360	1.4
2-year	20,805,384	5,218,447	1,718,907	8.3	19,233,501	4,083,475	1,565,890	8.1	1,571,883	1,134,972	153,017	9.7
1993–94	179,226,601	48,646,538	4,564,790	2.5	112,968,097	20,825,388	3,543,643	3.1	66,258,504	27,821,149	1,021,147	1.5
4-year	157,265,446	43,052,545	2,674,392	1.7	92,747,344	16,457,225	1,860,187	2.0	64,518,102	26,595,320	814,204	1.3
2-year	21,961,155	5,593,993	1,890,399	8.6	20,220,753	4,368,164	1,683,456	8.3	1,740,402	1,225,829	206,942	11.9
1994–95[1]	189,120,570	51,506,876	4,524,313	2.4	119,312,493	21,908,104	3,594,407	3.0	69,808,077	29,598,772	929,906	1.3
4-year	166,144,023	45,863,702	2,690,643	1.6	97,963,262	17,385,587	1,890,393	1.9	68,180,761	28,478,115	800,250	1.2
2-year	22,976,547	5,643,174	1,833,670	8.0	21,349,231	4,522,517	1,704,014	8.0	1,627,317	1,120,657	129,656	8.0

[1] Preliminary data.

NOTE.—Pell Grants which are spent on campus for tuition, room, board or other college expenses are included in current-fund revenue. Because of rounding, details may not add to totals.

SOURCE: U.S. Department of Education, National Center for Education Statistics, Higher Education General Information Survey (HEGIS), "Financial Statistics of Institutions of Higher Education" surveys; and Integrated Postsecondary Education Data System (IPEDS), "Finance" surveys. (This table was prepared July 1997.)

Table 323.—State awards for need-based[1] undergraduate scholarship and grant programs, by state: 1983–84 to 1995–96:

[In millions]

State	1983–84	1985–86	1987–88	1988–89	1989–90	1990–91	1991–92	1992–93[2]	1993–94[2]	1994–95[2]	1995–96[2]	Percent change, 1983–84 to 1995–96[3]
1	2	3	4	5	6	7	8	9	10	11	12	13
United States	$1,024,206	$1,222,112	$1,377,996	$1,423,743	$1,529,421	$1,658,221	$1,781,820	$1,923,720	$2,195,993	$2,421,952	$2,435,687	137.8
Alabama	1,731	2,242	2,260	2,196	2,984	2,878	2,183	2,271	2,283	2,281	2,142	23.7
Alaska	189	241	240	234	228	464	475	470	454	444	430	127.5
Arizona	2,027	2,401	3,222	3,508	3,420	3,318	2,278	2,437	3,476	3,482	2,291	13.0
Arkansas	2,226	4,108	3,759	3,903	3,946	3,885	4,742	6,319	7,701	8,907	10,765	383.6
California	86,031	112,373	118,819	129,264	153,045	161,642	172,852	151,379	207,969	232,067	235,582	173.8
Colorado	7,341	9,282	9,327	9,395	10,349	11,276	12,380	14,812	16,480	18,252	21,076	187.1
Connecticut	9,371	11,095	14,650	21,149	19,915	20,580	20,595	20,805	20,641	20,690	20,372	117.4
Delaware	548	756	807	829	956	1,066	906	1,121	1,270	1,033	1,188	116.8
District of Columbia	759	1,106	1,106	1,075	1,069	947	978	1,015	1,022	1,022	939	23.7
Florida	12,515	14,819	15,245	16,522	20,134	24,729	29,279	29,628	31,277	36,824	34,822	178.2
Georgia	3,683	4,510	4,599	5,197	4,607	5,070	5,084	4,951	26,853	5,147	4,757	29.2
Hawaii	493	604	563	598	726	612	632	724	748	732	499	1.2
Idaho	378	509	343	348	346	350	483	580	634	779	763	101.9
Illinois	104,384	122,300	135,880	143,373	171,361	183,508	184,753	203,532	214,809	244,352	256,672	146.1
Indiana	20,380	26,448	45,408	35,692	41,874	46,756	[4]50,441	55,814	55,814	67,742	68,340	235.3
Iowa	20,263	22,379	25,960	30,050	32,467	35,586	34,654	34,067	34,718	35,642	38,953	92.2
Kansas	4,664	5,609	5,337	5,540	6,478	6,462	6,587	6,894	9,060	9,802	9,526	104.2
Kentucky	7,886	8,758	12,161	12,522	12,605	19,866	16,996	20,520	20,619	25,517	26,215	232.4
Louisiana	1,693	2,003	1,880	1,947	2,786	3,827	4,446	5,125	6,374	6,429	6,580	288.7
Maine	477	809	1,418	1,408	1,877	4,802	5,002	5,200	5,170	5,787	6,988	1,365.0
Maryland	5,459	6,859	8,737	12,841	14,800	15,607	16,253	20,828	23,713	24,571	30,350	456.0
Massachusetts	25,655	43,466	61,600	62,443	50,844	46,000	23,690	45,989	45,059	61,850	54,565	112.7
Michigan	30,753	57,645	70,099	75,467	70,721	68,918	78,116	75,469	79,735	81,340	84,154	173.6
Minnesota	46,600	45,486	63,300	68,293	58,136	74,656	81,322	83,170	102,920	97,920	92,069	97.6
Mississippi	1,015	1,288	1,230	1,251	1,243	1,136	1,131	1,244	1,255	1,248	1,175	15.8
Missouri	8,766	9,645	8,394	10,234	10,796	11,078	10,142	11,097	11,124	11,913	12,233	39.6
Montana	353	440	419	420	415	383	414	418	401	419	393	11.3
Nebraska	860	1,093	1,094	1,052	1,276	2,192	2,370	2,613	2,686	2,726	3,114	262.1
Nevada	327	414	352	352	[4]352	321	326	341	342	342	2,595	693.6
New Hampshire	536	660	810	886	918	770	825	1,253	840	1,425	765	42.7
New Jersey	47,980	65,173	70,298	76,204	84,347	87,054	100,220	118,868	135,251	159,683	132,383	175.9
New Mexico	695	1,461	4,107	5,024	5,601	6,479	[4]7,293	8,295	9,266	13,886	14,629	2,004.9
New York	327,320	363,949	372,363	355,192	382,655	428,358	504,195	554,803	618,849	636,704	625,711	91.2
North Carolina	3,974	4,440	4,559	4,489	3,046	2,519	2,908	3,163	14,436	13,774	16,659	319.2
North Dakota	635	808	490	976	1,242	1,177	1,475	2,162	2,036	1,996	1,898	198.9
Ohio	41,974	45,000	49,200	50,865	53,848	54,600	57,275	66,000	77,940	91,225	86,053	105.0
Oklahoma	6,561	8,242	10,245	9,861	11,591	11,871	12,612	13,286	13,405	13,325	13,642	107.9
Oregon	8,546	9,514	9,959	10,108	10,092	11,809	12,023	12,606	12,903	13,761	13,651	59.7
Pennsylvania	83,474	96,800	110,992	118,986	132,344	142,389	158,092	173,214	188,751	218,604	232,020	178.0
Rhode Island	6,745	7,856	8,138	8,967	9,917	9,522	9,141	9,586	6,500	6,340	5,741	-14.9
South Carolina	12,588	15,146	16,346	17,810	18,150	17,901	16,800	17,105	16,795	17,297	18,622	47.9
South Dakota	440	624	516	506	504	468	480	587	589	589	562	27.7
Tennessee	6,700	9,434	12,591	11,977	12,977	13,487	12,793	13,723	16,755	18,313	18,811	180.8
Texas	21,438	19,033	22,705	22,266	24,784	24,135	27,385	27,467	29,102	29,102	40,768	90.2
Utah	1,538	1,131	1,133	1,081	1,091	1,001	1,034	1,115	1,132	1,129	1,197	-22.2
Vermont	7,039	7,724	8,414	9,264	11,137	10,184	11,019	11,120	11,167	11,788	11,865	68.6
Virginia	4,075	4,415	4,414	8,062	7,966	7,351	4,892	6,654	6,408	53,885	59,568	1361.8
Washington	7,530	8,827	12,425	12,858	13,925	21,095	23,527	23,571	46,617	53,369	56,573	651.3
West Virginia	4,376	5,167	5,189	5,204	5,217	5,559	5,781	5,868	5,802	6,761	8,132	85.8
Wisconsin	23,011	27,816	34,653	35,842	38,072	42,365	42,324	44,216	46,592	49,511	46,470	101.9
Wyoming	204	204	240	212	[4]241	[4]212	216	225	250	225	219	7.4

[1] In 1987–88, 1988–89, 1989–90, 1990–91, 1991–92, 1992–93, 1993–94, 1994–95, and 1995–96 need-based aid to undergraduates comprised 81.0, 78.2, 76.8, 77.4, 74.7, 75.7, 75.7, 77.5, and 84.4 percent of all aid, respectively, compared with non-need-based aid or other types of aid to all undergraduate and graduate students. This table excludes loans.

[2] Estimated.

[3] Changes may reflect introduction of new programs or discontinuation of existing programs.

[4] Data are estimated based on prior year's report.

NOTE.-Some data have been revised from previously published figures. Because of rounding, details may not add to totals.

SOURCE: National Association of State Scholarship and Grant Programs, *Annual Survey Report*, (1983–84 to 1994–95) and National Association of State Student Grant and Aid Programs, Annual Survey Report (1995–96). (This table was prepared April 1997.)

Table 324.—Current-fund revenue of institutions of higher education, by source: 1980–81 to 1994–95

Source	1980–81	1985–86	1988–89	1989–90	1990–91	1991–92	1992–93	1993–94	1994–95[1]
1	2	3	4	5	6	7	8	9	10
	\multicolumn{9}{c}{In thousands}								
Total current-fund revenue	$65,584,789	$100,437,616	$128,501,638	$139,635,477	$149,766,051	$161,395,896	$170,880,503	$179,226,601	$189,120,570
Tuition and fees	13,773,259	23,116,605	30,806,566	33,926,060	37,434,462	41,559,037	45,346,071	48,646,538	51,506,876
Federal government	9,747,586	12,704,750	15,893,978	17,254,874	18,236,082	19,833,317	21,014,564	22,076,385	23,243,172
Appropriations	1,346,835	1,617,510	1,677,430	1,890,046	1,840,694	1,907,403	1,872,840	1,994,279	1,984,450
Unrestricted grants and contracts	1,126,558	1,658,636	2,150,079	2,353,119	2,504,859	2,703,590	2,913,256	3,129,307	3,297,173
Restricted grants and contracts[2]	6,005,317	7,190,345	9,009,709	9,773,266	10,443,977	11,561,444	12,589,727	13,554,435	14,421,419
Independent operations (FFRDC)[3]	1,268,877	2,238,259	3,056,760	3,238,442	3,446,552	3,660,881	3,638,741	3,398,364	3,540,129
State governments	20,106,222	29,911,500	36,031,208	38,349,239	39,480,874	40,586,907	41,247,955	41,910,288	44,343,012
Appropriations	19,266,186	28,402,288	33,287,034	35,223,174	36,255,090	36,884,957	37,314,176	37,824,061	39,638,444
Unrestricted grants and contracts	84,848	154,109	357,221	411,757	366,206	376,176	382,204	360,852	524,586
Restricted grants and contracts	755,188	1,355,102	2,386,953	2,714,309	2,859,577	3,325,774	3,551,575	3,725,375	4,179,982
Local governments	1,790,740	2,544,506	3,363,676	3,639,902	3,931,239	4,159,876	4,444,875	4,998,306	5,165,961
Appropriations	1,482,536	2,153,160	2,758,086	2,919,447	3,177,696	3,336,012	3,599,983	4,023,620	4,247,748
Unrestricted grants and contracts	29,629	56,975	98,787	122,404	116,982	140,135	139,881	134,491	134,611
Restricted grants and contracts	278,575	334,371	506,803	598,051	636,561	683,729	705,011	840,195	783,602
Private gifts, grants, and contracts	3,176,670	5,410,905	7,060,730	7,781,422	8,361,265	8,977,271	9,659,977	10,203,062	10,866,749
Unrestricted	1,210,903	2,111,972	2,429,579	2,634,974	2,720,233	2,921,997	3,229,718	3,400,457	3,556,608
Restricted	1,965,766	3,298,933	4,631,151	5,146,448	5,641,032	6,055,274	6,430,259	6,802,605	7,310,141
Endowment income	1,364,443	2,275,898	2,914,396	3,143,696	3,268,629	3,442,009	3,627,773	3,669,536	3,988,217
Unrestricted	770,358	1,285,194	1,498,703	1,614,088	1,521,940	1,549,930	1,536,511	1,557,733	1,649,296
Restricted	594,085	990,704	1,415,694	1,529,608	1,746,690	1,892,079	2,091,262	2,111,803	2,338,921
Sales and services	13,677,366	21,274,265	28,162,465	30,787,233	34,107,502	37,519,828	39,824,766	41,791,319	43,039,561
Educational activities	1,409,730	2,373,494	3,315,620	3,632,100	4,054,703	4,520,890	5,037,901	5,294,030	5,603,251
Auxiliary enterprises	7,287,290	10,674,136	12,855,580	13,938,469	14,903,127	15,758,599	16,662,850	17,537,514	18,336,094
Hospitals	4,980,346	8,226,635	11,991,265	13,216,664	15,149,672	17,240,338	18,124,015	18,959,776	19,100,217
Other sources	1,948,503	3,199,186	4,268,618	4,753,051	4,945,998	5,317,651	5,714,523	5,931,167	6,967,023
	\multicolumn{9}{c}{Percentage distribution}								
Total current-fund revenue	100.0	100.0	100.0	100.0	100.0	100.0	100.0	100.0	100.0
Tuition and fees	21.0	23.0	24.0	24.3	25.0	25.7	26.5	27.1	27.2
Federal government	14.9	12.6	12.4	12.4	12.2	12.3	12.3	12.3	12.3
Appropriations	2.1	1.6	1.3	1.4	1.2	1.2	1.1	1.1	1.0
Unrestricted grants and contracts	1.7	1.7	1.7	1.7	1.7	1.7	1.7	1.7	1.7
Restricted grants and contracts[2]	9.2	7.2	7.0	7.0	7.0	7.2	7.4	7.6	7.6
Independent operations (FFRDC)[3]	1.9	2.2	2.4	2.3	2.3	2.3	2.1	1.9	1.9
State governments	30.7	29.8	28.0	27.5	26.4	25.1	24.1	23.4	23.4
Appropriations	29.4	28.3	25.9	25.2	24.2	22.9	21.8	21.1	21.0
Unrestricted grants and contracts	0.1	0.2	0.3	0.3	0.2	0.2	0.2	0.2	0.3
Restricted grants and contracts	1.2	1.3	1.9	1.9	1.9	2.1	2.1	2.1	2.2
Local governments	2.7	2.5	2.6	2.6	2.6	2.6	2.6	2.8	2.7
Appropriations	2.3	2.1	2.1	2.1	2.1	2.1	2.1	2.2	2.2
Unrestricted grants and contracts	([4])	0.1	0.1	0.1	0.1	0.1	0.1	0.1	0.1
Restricted grants and contracts	0.4	0.3	0.4	0.4	0.4	0.4	0.4	0.5	0.4
Private gifts, grants, and contracts	4.8	5.4	5.5	5.6	5.6	5.6	5.7	5.7	5.7
Unrestricted	1.8	2.1	1.9	1.9	1.8	1.8	1.9	1.9	1.9
Restricted	3.0	3.3	3.6	3.7	3.8	3.8	3.8	3.8	3.9
Endowment income	2.1	2.3	2.3	2.3	2.2	2.1	2.1	2.0	2.1
Unrestricted	1.2	1.3	1.2	1.2	1.0	1.0	0.9	0.9	0.9
Restricted	0.9	1.0	1.1	1.1	1.2	1.2	1.2	1.2	1.2
Sales and services	20.9	21.2	21.9	22.0	22.8	23.2	23.3	23.3	22.8
Educational activities	2.1	2.4	2.6	2.6	2.7	2.8	2.9	3.0	3.0
Auxiliary enterprises	11.1	10.6	10.0	10.0	10.0	9.8	9.8	9.8	9.7
Hospitals	7.6	8.2	9.3	9.5	10.1	10.7	10.6	10.6	10.1
Other sources	3.0	3.2	3.3	3.4	3.3	3.3	3.3	3.3	3.7

[1] Preliminary data.
[2] Excludes Pell Grants. Federally supported student aid that is received through students is included under tuition and auxiliary enterprises.
[3] Generally includes only those revenues associated with major federally funded research and development centers (FFRDC).
[4] Less than 0.05 percent.

NOTE.—Because of rounding, details may not add to totals.

SOURCE: U.S. Department of Education, National Center for Education Statistics, Higher Education General Information Survey (HEGIS), "Financial Statistics of Institutions of Higher Education" surveys; and Integrated Postsecondary Education Data System (IPEDS), "Finance" surveys. (This table was prepared July 1997.)

HIGHER EDUCATION: REVENUE

Table 325.—Current-fund revenue of public institutions of higher education, by source: 1980–81 to 1994–95

Source	1980–81	1985–86	1988–89	1989–90	1990–91	1991–92	1992–93	1993–94	1994–95[1]
1	2	3	4	5	6	7	8	9	10
					In thousands				
Total current-fund revenue	$43,195,617	$65,004,632	$81,927,371	$88,911,433	$94,904,506	$102,202,890	$108,186,484	$112,968,097	$119,312,493
Tuition and fees	5,570,404	9,439,177	12,435,763	13,820,240	15,258,024	17,460,263	19,490,221	20,825,388	21,908,104
Federal government	5,540,101	6,852,370	8,412,582	9,171,488	9,763,427	10,783,842	11,655,011	12,465,038	13,191,843
Appropriations	1,128,101	1,401,367	1,443,539	1,636,047	1,604,548	1,662,229	1,658,052	1,781,837	1,766,412
Unrestricted grants and contracts	529,424	816,364	1,083,575	1,214,836	1,319,035	1,462,372	1,601,201	1,694,596	1,802,822
Restricted grants and contracts[2]	3,812,197	4,481,723	5,656,468	6,106,112	6,629,484	7,426,627	8,155,317	8,776,458	9,368,072
Independent operations (FFRDC)[3]	70,379	152,916	228,999	214,493	210,360	232,613	240,441	212,148	254,537
State governments	19,675,968	29,220,586	34,835,716	37,052,307	38,239,978	39,107,560	39,789,641	40,536,393	42,854,681
Appropriations	19,006,716	28,071,070	32,929,719	34,858,904	35,898,653	36,612,540	37,073,932	37,565,065	39,405,865
Unrestricted grants and contracts	45,390	88,779	240,028	297,338	250,168	253,184	259,046	271,298	381,165
Restricted grants and contracts	623,863	1,060,737	1,665,969	1,896,065	2,091,157	2,241,836	2,456,663	2,700,030	3,067,650
Local governments	1,622,938	2,325,844	3,025,703	3,264,303	3,531,714	3,778,615	4,040,897	4,508,604	4,756,884
Appropriations	1,478,001	2,150,459	2,751,704	2,910,444	3,159,789	3,319,119	3,594,207	4,021,421	4,243,984
Unrestricted grants and contracts	9,915	27,852	64,455	82,405	73,281	90,257	84,974	71,098	60,123
Restricted grants and contracts	135,022	147,533	209,544	271,453	298,644	369,239	361,717	416,084	452,777
Private gifts, grants, and contracts	1,100,084	2,109,782	2,948,827	3,368,635	3,651,107	4,039,212	4,330,112	4,521,452	4,737,529
Unrestricted	110,462	279,381	362,011	436,028	529,496	650,468	686,214	698,497	684,264
Restricted	989,622	1,830,401	2,586,815	2,932,607	3,121,611	3,388,743	3,643,898	3,822,955	4,053,266
Endowment income	214,561	398,603	422,252	461,701	431,235	593,998	667,711	639,343	693,313
Unrestricted	102,888	181,624	149,650	164,242	147,368	248,770	257,113	259,172	266,960
Restricted	111,673	216,979	272,602	297,459	283,867	345,228	410,598	380,172	426,354
Sales and services	8,455,449	12,990,670	17,586,819	19,330,429	21,546,202	23,738,382	25,282,113	26,404,241	27,517,662
Educational activities	943,737	1,596,946	2,186,448	2,423,779	2,700,185	2,960,980	3,236,037	3,329,681	3,616,034
Auxiliary enterprises	4,614,561	6,684,794	7,809,284	8,473,282	9,058,745	9,655,373	10,255,044	10,814,804	11,373,646
Hospitals	2,897,151	4,708,930	7,591,087	8,433,369	9,787,271	11,122,029	11,791,033	12,259,757	12,527,982
Other sources	1,016,110	1,667,600	2,259,709	2,442,330	2,482,819	2,701,019	2,930,778	3,067,638	3,652,477
					Percentage distribution				
Total current-fund revenue	100.0	100.0	100.0	100.0	100.0	100.0	100.0	100.0	100.0
Tuition and fees	12.9	14.5	15.2	15.5	16.1	17.1	18.0	18.4	18.4
Federal government	12.8	10.5	10.3	10.3	10.3	10.6	10.8	11.0	11.1
Appropriations	2.6	2.2	1.8	1.8	1.7	1.6	1.5	1.6	1.5
Unrestricted grants and contracts	1.2	1.3	1.3	1.4	1.4	1.4	1.5	1.5	1.5
Restricted grants and contracts[2]	8.8	6.9	6.9	6.9	7.0	7.3	7.5	7.8	7.9
Independent operations (FFRDC)[3]	0.2	0.2	0.3	0.2	0.2	0.2	0.2	0.2	0.2
State governments	45.6	45.0	42.5	41.7	40.3	38.3	36.8	35.9	35.9
Appropriations	44.0	43.2	40.2	39.2	37.8	35.8	34.3	33.3	33.0
Unrestricted grants and contracts	0.1	0.1	0.3	0.3	0.3	0.2	0.2	0.2	0.3
Restricted grants and contracts	1.4	1.6	2.0	2.1	2.2	2.2	2.3	2.4	2.6
Local governments	3.8	3.6	3.7	3.7	3.7	3.7	3.7	4.0	4.0
Appropriations	3.4	3.3	3.4	3.3	3.3	3.2	3.3	3.6	3.6
Unrestricted grants and contracts	([4])	([4])	0.1	0.1	0.1	0.1	0.1	0.1	0.1
Restricted grants and contracts	0.3	0.2	0.3	0.3	0.3	0.4	0.3	0.4	0.4
Private gifts, grants, and contracts	2.5	3.2	3.6	3.8	3.8	4.0	4.0	4.0	4.0
Unrestricted	0.3	0.4	0.4	0.5	0.6	0.6	0.6	0.6	0.6
Restricted	2.3	2.8	3.2	3.3	3.3	3.3	3.4	3.4	3.4
Endowment income	0.5	0.6	0.5	0.5	0.5	0.6	0.6	0.6	0.6
Unrestricted	0.2	0.3	0.2	0.2	0.2	0.2	0.2	0.2	0.2
Restricted	0.3	0.3	0.3	0.3	0.3	0.3	0.4	0.3	0.4
Sales and services	19.6	20.0	21.5	21.7	22.7	23.2	23.4	23.4	23.1
Educational activities	2.2	2.5	2.7	2.7	2.8	2.9	3.0	2.9	3.0
Auxiliary enterprises	10.7	10.3	9.5	9.5	9.5	9.4	9.5	9.6	9.5
Hospitals	6.7	7.2	9.3	9.5	10.3	10.9	10.9	10.9	10.5
Other sources	2.4	2.6	2.8	2.7	2.6	2.6	2.7	2.7	3.1

[1] Preliminary data.
[2] Excludes Pell Grants. Federally supported student aid that is received through students is included under tuition and auxiliary enterprises.
[3] Generally includes only those revenues associated with major federally funded research and development centers (FFRDC).
[4] Less than 0.05 percent.

NOTE.—Because of rounding, details may not add to totals.

SOURCE: U.S. Department of Education, National Center for Education Statistics, Higher Education General Information Survey (HEGIS), "Financial Statistics of Institutions of Higher Education" surveys; and Integrated Postsecondary Education Data System (IPEDS), "Finance" surveys. (This table was prepared July 1997.)

Table 326.—Current-fund revenue of private institutions of higher education, by source: 1980–81 to 1994–95

Source	1980–81	1985–86	1988–89	1989–90	1990–91	1991–92	1992–93	1993–94	1994–95[1]
1	2	3	4	5	6	7	8	9	10
In thousands									
Total current-fund revenue	$22,389,172	$35,432,985	$46,574,267	$50,724,044	$54,861,545	$59,193,006	$62,694,018	$66,258,504	$69,808,077
Tuition and fees	8,202,855	13,677,429	18,370,803	20,105,820	22,176,439	24,098,774	25,855,850	27,821,149	29,598,772
Federal government	4,207,485	5,852,380	7,481,396	8,083,386	8,472,654	9,049,476	9,359,554	9,611,348	10,051,329
Appropriations	218,733	216,143	233,891	254,000	236,146	245,173	214,788	212,443	218,038
Unrestricted grants and contracts	597,134	842,272	1,066,504	1,138,283	1,185,824	1,241,218	1,312,056	1,434,711	1,494,351
Restricted grants and contracts[2]	2,193,119	2,708,622	3,353,241	3,667,154	3,814,493	4,134,817	4,434,410	4,777,978	5,053,347
Independent operations (FFRDC)[3]	1,198,498	2,085,343	2,827,761	3,023,949	3,236,192	3,428,267	3,398,300	3,186,216	3,285,593
State governments	430,253	690,914	1,195,492	1,296,932	1,240,896	1,479,347	1,458,314	1,373,894	1,488,332
Appropriations	259,470	331,219	357,315	364,270	356,437	272,417	240,244	258,996	232,579
Unrestricted grants and contracts	39,458	65,330	117,193	114,419	116,038	122,992	123,158	89,554	143,421
Restricted grants and contracts	131,326	294,365	720,984	818,244	768,421	1,083,938	1,094,912	1,025,344	1,112,332
Local governments	167,801	218,662	337,973	375,599	399,525	381,261	403,977	489,703	409,077
Appropriations	4,535	2,701	6,383	9,003	17,907	16,893	5,776	2,199	3,763
Unrestricted grants and contracts	19,714	29,123	34,332	39,999	43,701	49,878	54,907	63,393	74,488
Restricted grants and contracts	143,552	186,838	297,258	326,598	337,917	314,490	343,294	424,111	330,826
Private gifts, grants, and contracts	2,076,585	3,301,124	4,111,904	4,412,787	4,710,158	4,938,060	5,329,865	5,681,610	6,129,220
Unrestricted	1,100,441	1,832,592	2,067,568	2,198,946	2,190,736	2,271,529	2,543,504	2,701,960	2,872,344
Restricted	976,144	1,468,532	2,044,336	2,213,841	2,519,421	2,666,531	2,786,361	2,979,650	3,256,876
Endowment income	1,149,883	1,877,295	2,492,144	2,681,995	2,837,394	2,848,012	2,960,062	3,030,193	3,294,904
Unrestricted	667,471	1,103,570	1,349,053	1,449,846	1,374,572	1,301,160	1,279,398	1,298,562	1,382,336
Restricted	482,412	773,725	1,143,091	1,232,149	1,462,822	1,546,851	1,680,664	1,731,631	1,912,567
Sales and services	5,221,917	8,283,595	10,575,646	11,456,804	12,561,301	13,781,446	14,542,653	15,387,078	15,521,899
Educational activities	465,993	776,548	1,129,171	1,208,322	1,354,518	1,559,910	1,801,865	1,964,349	1,987,217
Auxiliary enterprises	2,672,729	3,989,342	5,046,296	5,465,187	5,844,382	6,103,226	6,407,806	6,722,710	6,962,448
Hospitals	2,083,195	3,517,705	4,400,178	4,783,295	5,362,401	6,118,309	6,332,982	6,700,019	6,572,234
Other sources	932,392	1,531,586	2,008,909	2,310,720	2,463,178	2,616,632	2,783,744	2,863,529	3,314,546
Percentage distribution									
Total current-fund revenue	100.0	100.0	100.0	100.0	100.0	100.0	100.0	100.0	100.0
Tuition and fees	36.6	38.6	39.4	39.6	40.4	40.7	41.2	42.0	42.4
Federal government	18.8	16.5	16.1	15.9	15.4	15.3	14.9	14.5	14.4
Appropriations	1.0	0.6	0.5	0.5	0.4	0.4	0.3	0.3	0.3
Unrestricted grants and contracts	2.7	2.4	2.3	2.2	2.2	2.1	2.1	2.2	2.1
Restricted grants and contracts[2]	9.8	7.6	7.2	7.2	7.0	7.0	7.1	7.2	7.2
Independent operations (FFRDC)[3]	5.4	5.9	6.1	6.0	5.9	5.8	5.4	4.8	4.7
State governments	1.9	1.9	2.6	2.6	2.3	2.5	2.3	2.1	2.1
Appropriations	1.2	0.9	0.8	0.7	0.6	0.5	0.4	0.4	0.3
Unrestricted grants and contracts	0.2	0.2	0.3	0.2	0.2	0.2	0.2	0.1	0.2
Restricted grants and contracts	0.6	0.8	1.5	1.6	1.4	1.8	1.7	1.5	1.6
Local governments	0.7	0.6	0.7	0.7	0.7	0.6	0.6	0.7	0.6
Appropriations	([4])	([4])	([4])	([4])	([4])	([4])	([4])	([4])	([4])
Unrestricted grants and contracts	0.1	0.1	0.1	0.1	0.1	0.1	0.1	0.1	0.1
Restricted grants and contracts	0.6	0.5	0.6	0.6	0.6	0.5	0.5	0.6	0.5
Private gifts, grants, and contracts	9.3	9.3	8.8	8.7	8.6	8.3	8.5	8.6	8.8
Unrestricted	4.9	5.2	4.4	4.3	4.0	3.8	4.1	4.1	4.1
Restricted	4.4	4.1	4.4	4.4	4.6	4.5	4.4	4.5	4.7
Endowment income	5.1	5.3	5.4	5.3	5.2	4.8	4.7	4.6	4.7
Unrestricted	3.0	3.1	2.9	2.9	2.5	2.2	2.0	2.0	2.0
Restricted	2.2	2.2	2.5	2.4	2.7	2.6	2.7	2.6	2.7
Sales and services	23.3	23.4	22.7	22.6	22.9	23.3	23.2	23.2	22.2
Educational activities	2.1	2.2	2.4	2.4	2.5	2.6	2.9	3.0	2.8
Auxiliary enterprises	11.9	11.3	10.8	10.8	10.7	10.3	10.2	10.1	10.0
Hospitals	9.3	9.9	9.4	9.4	9.8	10.3	10.1	10.1	9.4
Other sources	4.2	4.3	4.3	4.6	4.5	4.4	4.4	4.3	4.7

[1] Preliminary data.
[2] Excludes Pell Grants. Federally supported student aid that is received through students is included under tuition and auxiliary enterprises.
[3] Generally includes only those revenues associated with major federally funded research and development centers (FFRDC).
[4] Less than 0.05 percent.

NOTE.—Because of rounding, details may not add to totals.

SOURCE: U.S. Department of Education, National Center for Education Statistics, Higher Education General Information Survey (HEGIS), "Financial Statistics of Institutions of Higher Education" surveys; and Integrated Postsecondary Education Data System (IPEDS), "Finance" surveys. (This table was prepared May 1997.)

HIGHER EDUCATION: REVENUE 343

Table 327.—Revenue of institutions of higher education, by source of funds: 1919–20 to 1994–95

[In thousands]

Year	Current-fund revenue	Student tuition and fees [1]	Federal government [2]	State governments [3]	Local governments	Endowment earnings	Private gifts and grants [4]	Sales and services of educational activities	Auxiliary enterprises	Hospitals [5]	Other current income
1	2	3	4	5	6	7	8	9	10	11	12
1919–20	$199,922	$42,255	$12,783	$61,690	([6])	$26,482	$7,584	—	$26,993	—	$22,135
1929–30	554,511	144,126	20,658	150,847	([6])	68,605	26,172	—	60,419	—	83,684
1939–40	715,211	200,897	38,860	151,222	$24,392	71,304	40,453	$32,777	143,923	—	11,383
1949–50	2,374,645	394,610	524,319	491,636	61,700	96,341	118,627	111,987	511,265	—	64,160
1959–60	5,785,537	1,157,482	1,036,990	1,374,476	151,715	206,619	382,569	102,525	1,004,283	$187,769	181,110
1969–70	21,515,242	4,419,845	4,130,066	5,873,626	778,162	516,038	1,129,438	612,777	2,900,390	619,578	535,323
1975–76	39,703,166	8,171,942	6,477,178	12,260,885	1,616,975	687,470	1,917,036	645,420	4,547,622	2,494,340	884,298
1976–77	43,436,827	9,024,932	7,169,031	13,285,684	1,626,908	764,788	2,105,070	779,058	4,919,602	2,859,376	902,377
1977–78	47,034,032	9,855,270	6,968,501	14,746,166	1,744,230	832,286	2,320,368	882,715	5,327,821	3,268,956	1,087,719
1978–79	51,837,789	10,704,171	7,851,326	16,363,784	1,573,018	985,242	2,489,366	1,037,130	5,741,309	3,763,453	1,328,991
1979–80	58,519,982	11,930,340	8,902,844	18,378,299	1,587,552	1,176,627	2,808,075	1,239,439	6,481,458	4,373,384	1,641,965
1980–81	65,584,789	13,773,259	9,747,586	20,106,222	1,790,740	1,364,443	3,176,670	1,409,730	7,287,290	4,980,346	1,948,503
1981–82	72,190,856	15,774,038	9,591,805	21,848,791	1,937,669	1,596,813	3,563,558	1,582,922	8,121,611	5,838,565	2,335,084
1982–83	77,595,726	17,776,041	9,631,097	23,065,636	2,031,353	1,720,677	4,052,649	1,723,484	8,769,521	6,531,562	2,293,706
1983–84	84,417,287	19,714,884	10,406,166	24,706,990	2,192,275	1,873,945	4,415,275	1,970,747	9,456,369	7,040,662	2,639,973
1984–85	92,472,694	21,283,329	11,509,125	27,583,011	2,387,212	2,096,298	4,896,325	2,126,927	10,100,410	7,474,575	3,015,483
1985–86	100,437,616	23,116,605	12,704,750	29,911,500	2,544,506	2,275,898	5,410,905	2,373,494	10,674,136	8,226,635	3,199,186
1986–87	108,809,827	25,705,827	13,904,049	31,309,303	2,799,321	2,377,958	5,952,682	2,641,906	11,364,188	9,277,834	3,476,760
1987–88	117,340,109	27,836,781	14,771,954	33,517,166	3,006,263	2,586,441	6,359,282	2,918,090	11,947,778	10,626,566	3,769,787
1988–89	128,501,638	30,806,566	15,893,978	36,031,208	3,363,676	2,914,396	7,060,730	3,315,620	12,855,580	11,991,265	4,268,618
1989–90	139,635,477	33,926,060	17,254,874	38,349,239	3,639,902	3,143,696	7,781,422	3,632,100	13,938,469	13,216,664	4,753,051
1990–91	149,766,051	37,434,462	18,236,082	39,480,874	3,931,239	3,268,629	8,361,265	4,054,703	14,903,127	15,149,672	4,945,998
1991–92	161,395,896	41,559,037	19,833,317	40,586,907	4,159,876	3,442,009	8,977,271	4,520,890	15,758,599	17,240,338	5,317,651
1992–93	170,880,503	45,346,071	21,014,564	41,247,955	4,444,875	3,627,773	9,659,977	5,037,901	16,662,850	18,124,015	5,714,523
1993–94	179,226,601	48,646,538	22,076,385	41,910,288	4,998,306	3,669,536	10,203,062	5,294,030	17,537,514	18,959,776	5,931,167
1994–95 [7]	189,120,570	51,506,876	23,243,172	44,343,012	5,165,961	3,988,217	10,866,749	5,603,251	18,336,094	19,100,217	6,967,023

[1] Tuition and fees received from veterans under Public Law 550 are reported under student fees and are not under income from the federal government.
[2] Federally supported student aid that is received through students is included under tuition and auxiliary enterprises.
[3] Includes federal aid received through state channels and regional compacts, through 1959–60.
[4] Beginning in 1969–70, the private grants represent nongovernmental revenue for sponsored research, student aid, and other sponsored programs.
[5] Prior to 1959–60, data for hospitals are included under sales and services of educational activities.
[6] Income from state and local governments tabulated under "State governments."
[7] Preliminary data.
— Data not available.

NOTE.—Data for years prior to 1969–70 are not entirely comparable with data for later years. Also, some details for 1969–70 are not directly comparable with data for later years. Because of rounding, details may not add to totals.

SOURCE: U.S. Department of Education, National Center for Education Statistics, Higher Education General Information Survey (HEGIS), "Financial Statistics of Institutions of Higher Education" surveys; and Integrated Postsecondary Education Data System (IPEDS), "Finance" surveys. (This table was prepared July 1997.)

Table 328.—Revenue of institutions of higher education, by source of funds, and by control and type of institution: 1994–95 [1]

Control and type of institution	Current-fund revenue	Student tuition and fees [2]	Federal government [3]	State governments	Local governments	Private gifts and grants	Endowment earnings	Educational activities	Auxiliary enterprises	Hospitals	Other current income
1	2	3	4	5	6	7	8	9	10	11	12
In thousands											
Total	$189,120,570	$51,506,876	$23,243,172	$44,343,012	$5,165,961	$10,866,749	$3,988,217	$5,603,251	$18,336,094	$19,100,217	$6,967,023
Public	119,312,493	21,908,104	13,191,843	42,854,681	4,756,884	4,737,529	693,313	3,616,034	11,373,646	12,527,982	3,652,477
Research I universities [4]	44,824,870	6,627,721	6,881,771	12,799,794	223,025	2,633,661	380,913	1,940,425	4,548,997	7,678,102	1,110,460
Research II universities [4]	7,181,999	1,639,760	826,969	2,875,687	20,847	373,810	52,486	227,217	968,814	0	196,409
Doctoral universities	12,666,282	2,892,565	1,055,505	5,198,571	121,637	524,425	150,095	274,302	1,454,705	370,782	623,694
Master's	19,017,225	5,049,340	975,971	8,988,919	133,938	380,028	45,871	411,899	2,435,388	212,761	383,111
Baccalaureate	2,514,859	756,407	162,796	1,127,165	21,070	58,890	5,080	30,362	301,628	0	51,461
Associate of arts	21,295,371	4,514,730	1,139,315	9,143,632	4,132,969	207,466	23,958	138,875	1,314,105	0	680,322
Specialized institutions [5]											
Health and medicine	10,042,820	283,925	1,060,103	2,456,637	75,595	535,584	32,718	588,081	227,875	4,209,355	572,945
Engineering	207,524	45,961	15,629	111,893	41	9,606	31	2,268	16,151	0	5,944
Business	25,852	6,333	915	14,400	23	343	15	1,810	1,819	0	194
Fine arts	122,410	29,556	753	38,787	22,786	1,509	13	77	12,522	0	16,406
Other specialized	1,337,055	52,415	1,024,079	96,843	2,415	6,780	354	77	88,403	56,982	8,706
Tribal colleges [6]	76,225	9,390	48,035	2,353	2,538	5,428	1,779	641	3,238	0	2,823
4-year	22,365	1,604	16,535	399	17	1,380	1,033	53	334	0	1,011
2-year	53,859	7,786	31,500	1,954	2,521	4,047	746	588	2,904	0	1,812
Private	69,808,077	29,598,772	10,051,329	1,488,332	409,077	6,129,220	3,294,904	1,987,217	6,962,448	6,572,234	3,314,546
Research I universities [4]	26,860,577	6,178,954	7,501,202	307,116	230,702	2,580,135	1,479,270	1,467,817	1,791,647	4,273,224	1,050,509
Research II universities [4]	4,070,600	1,557,387	346,604	53,278	678	411,837	208,622	99,672	556,698	613,937	221,886
Doctoral universities	6,565,928	3,579,799	457,521	169,927	8,754	412,188	230,110	119,485	625,877	420,707	541,559
Master's	10,058,313	6,694,924	510,532	299,971	4,086	563,150	242,024	136,187	1,308,824	9,045	289,570
Baccalaureate	12,608,249	7,506,456	413,518	339,147	2,814	1,086,520	819,745	33,146	2,069,587	0	337,314
Associate of arts	1,616,015	1,119,611	40,030	106,453	3,004	79,417	17,591	13,469	119,193	59,943	57,305
Specialized institutions [5]											
Religion and theology	1,068,652	329,302	16,164	4,789	1,323	369,901	117,334	33,092	148,350	0	48,397
Health and medicine	4,273,824	701,969	680,864	136,103	154,979	459,187	93,030	49,245	121,229	1,195,377	681,840
Engineering	392,267	238,497	30,028	9,220	0	42,511	28,550	3,273	28,199	0	11,988
Business	988,550	734,930	14,544	35,646	56	31,550	12,267	24,464	112,379	0	22,713
Fine arts	737,940	522,022	15,602	21,492	813	56,807	35,407	2,691	60,841	0	22,266
Other specialized	544,649	432,244	8,325	4,989	1,805	34,709	10,865	4,650	19,187	0	27,875
Tribal colleges [6]	22,513	2,677	16,394	201	62	1,308	88	25	435	0	1,324
4-year	11,413	1,630	7,665	201	0	810	0	25	220	0	861
2-year	11,100	1,046	8,728	0	62	498	88	0	214	0	463
Percentage distribution											
Total	100.00	27.23	12.29	23.45	2.73	5.75	2.11	2.96	9.70	10.10	3.68
Public	100.00	18.36	11.06	35.92	3.99	3.97	0.58	3.03	9.53	10.50	3.06
Research I universities [4]	100.00	14.79	15.35	28.56	0.50	5.88	0.85	4.33	10.15	17.13	2.48
Research II universities [4]	100.00	22.83	11.51	40.04	0.29	5.20	0.73	3.16	13.49	0.00	2.73
Doctoral universities	100.00	22.84	8.33	41.04	0.96	4.14	1.18	2.17	11.48	2.93	4.92
Master's	100.00	26.55	5.13	47.27	0.70	2.00	0.24	2.17	12.81	1.12	2.01
Baccalaureate	100.00	30.08	6.47	44.82	0.84	2.34	0.20	1.21	11.99	0.00	2.05
Associate of arts	100.00	21.20	5.35	42.94	19.41	0.97	0.11	0.65	6.17	0.00	3.19
Specialized institutions [5]											
Health and medicine	100.00	2.83	10.56	24.46	0.75	5.33	0.33	5.86	2.27	41.91	5.71
Engineering	100.00	22.15	7.53	53.92	0.02	4.63	0.01	1.09	7.78	0.00	2.86
Business	100.00	24.50	3.54	55.70	0.09	1.33	0.06	7.00	7.04	0.00	0.75
Fine arts	100.00	24.14	0.62	31.69	18.61	1.23	0.01	0.06	10.23	0.00	13.40
Other specialized	100.00	3.92	76.59	7.24	0.18	0.51	0.03	0.01	6.61	4.26	0.65
Tribal colleges [6]	100.00	12.32	63.02	3.09	3.33	7.12	2.33	0.84	4.25	0.00	3.70
4-year	100.00	7.17	73.93	1.78	0.07	6.17	4.62	0.24	1.49	0.00	4.52
2-year	100.00	14.46	58.49	3.63	4.68	7.51	1.39	1.09	5.39	0.00	3.36
Private	100.00	42.40	14.40	2.13	0.59	8.78	4.72	2.85	9.97	9.41	4.75
Research I universities [4]	100.00	23.00	27.93	1.14	0.86	9.61	5.51	5.46	6.67	15.91	3.91
Research II universities [4]	100.00	38.26	8.51	1.31	0.02	10.12	5.13	2.45	13.68	15.08	5.45
Doctoral universities	100.00	54.52	6.97	2.59	0.13	6.28	3.50	1.82	9.53	6.41	8.25
Master's	100.00	66.56	5.08	2.98	0.04	5.60	2.41	1.35	13.01	0.09	2.88
Baccalaureate	100.00	59.54	3.28	2.69	0.02	8.62	6.50	0.26	16.41	0.00	2.68
Associate of arts	100.00	69.28	2.48	6.59	0.19	4.91	1.09	0.83	7.38	3.71	3.55
Specialized institutions [5]											
Religion and theology	100.00	30.81	1.51	0.45	0.12	34.61	10.98	3.10	13.88	0.00	4.53
Health and medicine	100.00	16.42	15.93	3.18	3.63	10.74	2.18	1.15	2.84	27.97	15.95
Engineering	100.00	60.80	7.66	2.35	0.00	10.84	7.28	0.83	7.19	0.00	3.06
Business	100.00	74.34	1.47	3.61	0.01	3.19	1.24	2.47	11.37	0.00	2.30
Fine arts	100.00	70.74	2.11	2.91	0.11	7.70	4.80	0.36	8.24	0.00	3.02
Other specialized	100.00	79.36	1.53	0.92	0.33	6.37	1.99	0.85	3.52	0.00	5.12
Tribal colleges [6]	100.00	11.89	72.82	0.89	0.28	5.81	0.39	0.11	1.93	0.00	5.88
4-year	100.00	14.28	67.16	1.76	0.00	7.10	0.00	0.22	1.93	0.00	7.54
2-year	100.00	9.43	78.63	0.00	0.56	4.49	0.79	0.00	1.93	0.00	4.17

[1] Preliminary data.
[2] Includes federally supported aid received through students.
[3] Includes appropriations, grants, contracts, and revenues associated with major federally funded research and development centers (FFRDC). Excludes Pell Grants.
[4] Research institutions are committed to graduate education through the doctorate, and give high priority to research. Research I institutions receive $40 million or more annually in federal support. Research II institutions receive between $15.5 million and $40 million annually.
[5] Specialized institutions award baccalaureate or higher level degrees in specific fields of study.
[6] Tribally controlled colleges are located on reservations and are members of the American Indian Higher Education Consortium.

NOTE.—Because of rounding, details may not add to totals.

SOURCE: U.S. Department of Education, National Center for Education Statistics, Integrated Postsecondary Education Data System (IPEDS), "Finance, 1994–95" survey. (This table was prepared July 1997.)

Table 329.—Current-fund revenue of public institutions of higher education, by state: 1980–81 to 1994–95

[In thousands of dollars]

State	1980–81	1985–86	1988–89	1989–90	1990–91	1991–92	1992–93	1993–94	1994–95[1]	Percent change, 1989–90 to 1994–95
1	2	3	4	5	6	7	8	9	10	11
United States	$43,195,617	$65,004,632	$81,927,371	$88,911,433	$94,904,506	$102,202,890	$108,186,484	$112,968,097	$119,312,493	34.2
Alabama	889,121	1,401,693	1,743,168	1,926,148	2,131,005	2,296,665	2,521,938	2,614,224	2,805,154	45.6
Alaska	159,446	221,837	244,857	270,926	291,826	304,857	323,740	342,624	344,877	27.3
Arizona	719,835	1,049,493	1,353,468	1,483,996	1,596,710	1,655,873	1,677,711	1,834,035	1,931,523	30.2
Arkansas	350,597	539,185	716,105	781,375	818,079	920,699	995,482	1,036,610	1,113,954	42.6
California	5,906,729	8,739,396	11,022,341	11,776,298	12,281,700	13,628,928	14,262,239	13,868,703	14,558,144	23.6
Colorado	747,040	1,085,076	1,371,303	1,390,413	1,483,901	1,594,541	1,714,698	1,803,735	1,914,233	37.7
Connecticut	378,527	578,866	788,194	833,154	889,831	940,067	976,380	1,020,170	1,148,389	37.8
Delaware	168,522	251,677	324,853	354,322	388,635	433,186	446,768	471,017	496,696	40.2
District of Columbia[2]	66,138	84,144	98,240	96,906	95,729	100,038	98,170	99,749	103,770	7.1
Florida	1,202,788	1,810,090	2,510,894	2,812,644	2,944,935	3,049,921	3,202,499	3,411,727	3,584,085	27.4
Georgia	765,826	1,267,472	1,648,753	1,794,990	1,953,866	2,042,825	2,268,331	2,494,263	2,760,323	53.8
Hawaii	219,633	316,246	384,775	433,164	497,495	579,805	594,752	628,043	651,282	50.4
Idaho	169,274	235,507	290,303	320,119	359,710	396,173	416,359	456,107	492,918	54.0
Illinois	1,809,981	2,560,241	3,067,687	3,370,011	3,566,406	3,659,328	3,924,599	4,100,967	4,360,136	29.4
Indiana	1,094,560	1,701,421	2,083,416	2,302,583	2,494,029	2,767,477	2,882,592	3,009,908	3,080,345	33.8
Iowa	784,950	1,109,681	1,529,907	1,653,221	1,775,267	1,827,776	1,930,399	2,014,244	2,106,504	27.4
Kansas	594,104	864,119	1,047,219	1,174,759	1,219,129	1,297,129	1,350,052	1,469,872	1,553,593	32.2
Kentucky	671,414	943,068	1,194,424	1,283,778	1,450,958	1,565,021	1,576,644	1,656,119	1,778,568	38.5
Louisiana	735,374	1,055,941	1,180,464	1,301,127	1,447,772	1,553,258	1,821,190	1,844,187	1,968,669	51.3
Maine	157,370	222,624	317,636	352,024	373,770	375,512	384,730	398,639	400,426	13.7
Maryland	818,850	1,144,230	1,515,369	1,638,822	1,777,841	1,745,479	1,913,029	1,984,038	2,074,521	26.6
Massachusetts	582,873	1,075,348	1,365,350	1,429,770	1,457,142	1,525,943	1,639,854	1,491,921	1,586,319	10.9
Michigan	2,094,394	3,071,172	3,992,084	4,322,956	4,648,488	5,127,892	5,329,224	5,529,883	5,798,882	34.1
Minnesota	894,236	1,373,436	1,880,373	1,916,297	2,080,637	2,261,978	2,363,483	2,494,341	2,671,566	39.4
Mississippi	543,209	734,813	903,637	956,300	1,005,448	1,054,530	1,150,201	1,215,602	1,443,162	50.9
Missouri	717,626	1,032,685	1,289,742	1,416,556	1,517,071	1,566,480	1,698,594	1,805,266	1,978,783	39.7
Montana	123,933	181,462	197,605	227,403	258,189	334,243	349,102	362,905	385,984	69.7
Nebraska	390,372	554,814	699,859	787,282	870,289	941,062	989,156	1,033,731	1,124,836	42.9
Nevada	113,298	184,883	243,208	286,719	336,841	368,245	392,258	412,884	484,276	68.9
New Hampshire	131,990	190,462	255,948	275,121	304,315	324,186	348,839	373,498	391,619	42.3
New Jersey	917,143	1,446,098	2,065,233	2,253,830	2,413,530	2,610,949	2,745,100	2,920,767	3,106,652	37.8
New Mexico	334,392	473,716	786,667	858,989	944,248	1,056,819	1,125,366	1,190,519	1,316,934	53.3
New York	2,519,437	3,830,119	4,772,942	5,014,789	5,424,379	5,616,604	6,117,555	6,574,152	6,887,321	37.3
North Carolina	1,146,931	1,857,124	2,295,295	2,480,396	2,650,124	2,873,684	3,113,193	3,299,213	3,521,601	42.0
North Dakota	196,267	286,550	327,293	365,089	377,960	411,293	431,464	431,381	467,926	28.2
Ohio	1,828,079	2,824,411	3,561,646	3,871,477	4,184,621	4,484,576	4,628,902	4,895,812	4,976,134	28.5
Oklahoma	588,936	873,446	902,463	997,781	1,072,967	1,190,393	1,209,863	1,257,552	1,300,779	30.4
Oregon	647,391	899,709	1,128,211	1,242,595	1,358,244	1,523,505	1,615,882	1,687,205	1,816,031	46.1
Pennsylvania	1,575,104	2,473,794	3,262,178	3,511,535	3,692,745	4,153,483	4,262,533	4,423,633	4,684,460	33.4
Rhode Island	156,451	213,859	270,500	291,376	292,404	308,383	325,003	329,277	344,171	18.1
South Carolina	630,966	957,771	1,216,468	1,333,941	1,502,709	1,629,876	1,733,468	1,924,747	1,997,203	49.7
South Dakota	127,839	147,699	169,210	184,954	198,583	219,751	241,536	260,907	260,853	41.0
Tennessee	675,770	1,104,118	1,435,262	1,556,416	1,634,491	1,672,605	1,839,384	1,961,312	2,053,495	31.9
Texas	2,858,725	4,558,275	5,204,122	5,777,100	6,015,609	6,664,828	7,126,068	7,688,388	8,123,435	40.6
Utah	431,294	686,817	870,334	960,027	1,020,836	1,160,882	1,224,127	1,307,681	1,402,962	46.1
Vermont	127,337	191,559	244,836	267,178	281,526	298,524	305,477	316,905	329,679	23.4
Virginia	1,159,453	1,876,151	2,486,637	2,736,307	2,902,939	3,041,850	3,176,437	3,323,028	3,483,691	27.3
Washington	998,146	1,445,849	1,809,540	1,966,838	2,188,366	2,355,445	2,539,934	2,744,035	2,877,386	46.3
West Virginia	318,915	385,170	447,533	502,436	563,796	608,294	631,619	666,268	693,159	38.0
Wisconsin	1,228,414	1,761,927	2,191,795	2,343,203	2,487,501	2,629,388	2,775,635	2,954,564	3,033,547	29.5
Wyoming	140,520	208,595	224,602	237,093	251,760	271,290	270,515	278,270	293,209	23.7
U.S. Service Schools[2]	586,095	920,790	993,422	1,188,896	1,128,158	1,181,348	1,204,411	1,253,468	1,248,328	5.0
Outlying areas	242,380	451,734	515,558	573,106	557,655	665,323	704,076	589,470	750,676	31.0
American Samoa	1,305	2,413	3,060	3,585	3,939	4,057	4,428	4,610	4,817	34.3
Federated States of Micronesia	—	—	1,789	1,842	2,063	2,078	3,453	3,932	6,517	253.8
Guam	14,291	31,139	39,282	50,411	61,667	70,658	74,928	68,198	71,873	42.6
Marshall Islands	—	—	—	—	—	3,798	1,111	2,176	1,633	—
Northern Marianas	—	1,350	748	791	1,458	1,715	2,462	3,511	12,174	1,440.0
Palau	—	—	3,643	4,038	4,100	3,948	5,133	4,762	4,083	1.1
Puerto Rico	213,012	392,194	441,449	487,133	428,768	518,747	581,128	468,739	615,912	26.4
Trust Territory of the Pacific	1,669	5,681	—	—	—	—	—	—	—	—
Virgin Islands	12,103	18,957	25,587	25,307	55,659	60,322	31,432	33,542	33,668	33.0

[1] Preliminary data.
[2] Data revised from previously published figures.
—Data not available or not applicable.

NOTE.—Because of rounding, details may not add to totals.

SOURCE: U.S. Department of Education, National Center for Education Statistics, Higher Education General Information Survey (HEGIS), "Financial Statistics of Institutions of Higher Education" surveys; and Integrated Postsecondary Education Data System (IPEDS), "Finance" surveys. (This table was prepared July 1997.)

346 HIGHER EDUCATION: REVENUE

Table 330.—Current-fund revenue of public institutions of higher education, by source of funds and state: 1994–95 [1]

[In thousands of dollars]

State	Total	Tuition and fees	Federal appropriations, grants, and contracts [2]	State appropriations, grants, and contracts	Local appropriations, grants, and contracts	Private gifts, grants, and contracts	Endowment income	Auxiliary enterprises	Hospitals	Educational activities and other
1	2	3	4	5	6	7	8	9	10	11
United States	$119,312,493	$21,908,104	$13,191,843	$42,854,681	$4,756,884	$4,737,529	$693,313	$11,373,646	$12,527,982	$7,268,511
Alabama	2,805,154	394,846	288,564	932,269	12,827	108,873	20,115	196,402	688,581	162,677
Alaska	344,877	44,282	53,125	183,183	1,484	8,751	4,424	20,965	0	28,663
Arizona	1,931,523	417,437	289,468	677,981	207,387	94,965	4,951	172,181	0	67,154
Arkansas	1,113,954	157,945	88,617	428,995	4,836	28,841	1,561	91,823	262,342	48,995
California	14,558,144	1,925,425	1,488,730	5,136,791	1,436,249	467,666	93,966	977,893	1,786,356	1,245,068
Colorado	1,914,233	529,501	361,312	513,024	31,058	93,448	7,550	242,308	21,697	114,336
Connecticut	1,148,389	240,963	73,453	483,674	3	28,729	29	85,554	188,246	47,738
Delaware	496,696	168,566	45,589	144,038	6,404	18,424	19,594	63,401	0	30,680
District of Columbia	103,770	10,834	7,198	0	76,822	509	745	686	0	6,976
Florida	3,584,085	630,396	334,083	1,945,909	9,406	170,314	451	339,537	0	153,988
Georgia	2,760,323	421,658	259,024	1,353,550	24,990	142,696	3,383	234,879	243,834	76,310
Hawaii	651,282	49,393	118,703	400,248	866	15,809	1,907	55,564	0	8,792
Idaho	492,918	81,763	40,966	233,397	10,199	24,089	8,526	61,439	0	32,540
Illinois	4,360,136	785,264	411,547	1,526,511	415,509	128,261	4,540	439,042	290,289	359,172
Indiana	3,080,345	667,290	245,079	997,241	2,485	131,184	8,592	505,492	337,027	185,956
Iowa	2,106,504	306,259	291,733	644,529	28,206	67,431	1,189	211,661	408,107	147,390
Kansas	1,553,593	270,928	136,406	534,983	123,932	35,890	33,176	126,387	205,404	86,487
Kentucky	1,778,568	308,502	126,816	723,541	6,689	43,558	10,457	140,923	254,025	164,056
Louisiana	1,968,669	361,178	131,191	722,746	4,842	52,884	3,788	215,840	233,197	243,002
Maine	400,426	95,166	37,732	170,016	54	14,937	2,409	52,293	0	27,819
Maryland	2,074,521	533,817	231,506	746,749	135,183	84,204	5,402	245,288	0	92,372
Massachusetts	1,586,319	489,187	146,036	657,970	7,640	47,221	2,901	169,164	6,253	59,947
Michigan	5,798,882	1,324,433	576,638	1,549,814	270,342	280,757	31,474	789,543	693,849	282,031
Minnesota	2,671,566	452,163	281,445	944,191	12,140	204,456	10,967	228,265	349,949	188,079
Mississippi	1,443,162	211,749	167,756	577,021	33,999	41,484	917	154,065	193,866	62,305
Missouri	1,978,783	445,292	116,570	672,581	70,403	77,159	11,273	191,918	225,693	167,896
Montana	385,984	83,962	65,963	127,456	5,349	14,694	260	55,565	0	32,736
Nebraska	1,124,836	143,020	123,956	376,415	55,893	54,094	3,656	116,648	207,068	44,087
Nevada	484,276	74,680	52,260	245,977	6,989	27,855	1,468	46,037	0	29,010
New Hampshire	391,619	158,519	37,003	85,739	2,200	17,933	2,178	72,833	0	15,214
New Jersey	3,106,652	638,453	200,184	1,178,646	166,050	93,456	11,405	236,490	412,290	169,677
New Mexico	1,316,934	111,777	248,072	435,562	45,947	60,926	12,343	91,238	232,906	78,162
New York	6,887,321	1,353,229	511,853	2,936,415	400,559	268,175	16,413	411,486	821,039	168,152
North Carolina	3,521,601	395,357	410,645	1,719,471	80,338	160,493	24,455	568,919	0	161,922
North Dakota	467,926	90,081	69,312	152,737	10,617	9,330	2,647	84,185	13,076	35,941
Ohio	4,976,134	1,316,933	338,914	1,496,777	106,878	210,032	43,812	469,762	772,301	220,725
Oklahoma	1,300,779	212,190	182,377	588,246	16,827	46,596	2,463	206,153	0	45,927
Oregon	1,816,031	310,600	263,044	480,700	108,039	83,535	5,226	166,731	311,672	86,484
Pennsylvania	4,684,460	1,337,745	504,383	1,185,305	86,983	187,252	37,900	476,893	679,862	188,138
Rhode Island	344,171	113,798	40,573	123,733	0	4,928	0	47,155	0	13,984
South Carolina	1,997,203	349,249	177,590	632,927	25,902	73,937	2,718	182,026	492,824	60,029
South Dakota	260,853	61,618	35,396	104,922	17	8,661	1,038	31,226	0	17,974
Tennessee	2,053,495	316,665	177,565	867,689	14,391	91,514	14,222	173,029	304,376	94,043
Texas	8,123,435	1,173,143	833,823	3,444,421	337,615	343,462	140,806	548,766	269,625	1,031,775
Utah	1,402,962	185,596	178,645	414,059	26,961	39,222	10,343	111,192	256,821	180,124
Vermont	329,679	141,177	39,285	47,322	114	26,386	4,785	37,632	0	32,979
Virginia	3,483,691	759,433	304,650	920,807	27,942	169,963	30,181	445,412	755,757	69,546
Washington	2,877,386	512,285	472,037	988,475	19,136	141,288	11,783	353,953	246,295	132,135
West Virginia	693,159	175,146	66,256	326,596	2,012	18,004	0	84,271	0	20,874
Wisconsin	3,033,547	527,641	361,851	945,078	261,078	145,071	16,156	230,519	306,372	239,782
Wyoming	293,209	40,987	37,985	128,346	15,093	20,514	2,768	38,853	0	8,662
U.S. Service Schools	1,248,328	583	1,108,932	0	0	7,667	0	74,163	56,982	0
Outlying areas	750,676	75,136	65,845	548,747	19,394	8,397	750	12,892	0	19,515
American Samoa	4,817	81	2,114	2,622	0	0	0	0	0	0
Federated States of Micronesia	6,517	3,061	299	50	2,470	70	8	506	0	53
Guam	71,873	6,947	7,095	39,743	11,761	896	509	2,759	0	2,162
Marshall Islands	1,633	521	697	313	0	11	12	67	0	11
Northern Marianas	12,174	2,357	3,020	6,388	146	0	0	38	0	225
Palau	4,083	781	522	1,993	0	0	0	598	0	189
Puerto Rico	615,912	56,847	47,348	480,551	2,680	5,807	0	6,148	0	16,532
Virgin Islands	33,668	4,542	4,750	17,087	2,336	1,613	220	2,777	0	343

[1] Preliminary data.
[2] Includes independent operations (federally funded research and development centers).

NOTE.—Because of rounding, details may not add to totals.

SOURCE: U.S. Department of Education, National Center for Education Statistics, Integrated Postsecondary Education Data System (IPEDS), "Finance" survey. (This table was prepared July 1997.)

Table 331.—Current-fund revenue of public institutions of higher education, by source of funds and state: 1993–94

[In thousands of dollars]

State	Total	Tuition and fees	Federal appropriations, grants, and contracts [1]	State appropriations, grants, and contracts	Local appropriations, grants, and contracts	Private gifts, grants, and contracts	Endowment income	Auxiliary enterprises	Hospitals	Educational activities and other
1	2	3	4	5	6	7	8	9	10	11
United States	$112,968,097	$20,825,388	$12,465,038	$40,536,393	$4,508,604	$4,521,452	$639,343	$10,814,804	$12,259,757	$6,397,319
Alabama	2,614,224	388,272	273,092	829,100	11,948	106,613	18,715	190,160	669,006	127,319
Alaska	342,624	42,295	55,652	184,624	1,659	9,001	3,133	19,972	0	26,288
Arizona	1,834,035	390,731	258,662	629,532	187,605	88,315	5,425	207,411	0	66,354
Arkansas	1,036,610	152,610	80,718	411,337	2,672	27,156	1,934	83,431	232,355	44,397
California	13,868,703	1,809,463	1,402,402	5,000,654	1,362,354	408,307	87,813	862,152	1,795,767	1,139,791
Colorado	1,803,735	499,752	332,389	489,353	26,832	89,336	10,685	226,012	26,659	102,717
Connecticut	1,020,170	211,790	72,482	381,843	606	30,601	144	89,640	186,726	46,338
Delaware	471,017	161,016	43,134	134,920	5,031	17,789	17,803	62,988	0	28,336
District of Columbia [2]	99,749	10,383	6,857	0	73,622	509	745	657	0	6,976
Florida	3,411,727	617,023	308,662	1,819,205	17,718	248,458	860	320,238	0	79,562
Georgia	2,494,263	401,204	235,427	1,182,831	23,877	126,363	7,070	217,903	231,317	68,270
Hawaii	628,043	51,201	96,272	400,133	805	13,975	1,580	51,553	0	12,525
Idaho	456,107	75,347	42,389	208,662	9,556	28,052	8,931	51,482	0	31,689
Illinois	4,100,967	744,287	408,123	1,428,289	395,718	126,132	4,286	424,531	247,440	322,160
Indiana	3,009,908	633,318	230,338	990,283	3,361	120,609	9,149	492,688	348,540	181,624
Iowa	2,014,244	292,465	282,191	624,926	26,274	62,873	1,362	193,411	396,835	133,906
Kansas	1,469,872	249,485	137,299	510,409	114,791	32,329	32,100	124,624	183,014	85,821
Kentucky	1,656,119	288,258	126,789	691,122	7,658	28,520	5,309	137,165	229,556	141,743
Louisiana	1,844,187	354,362	109,635	654,322	4,921	47,689	1,342	205,454	274,383	192,079
Maine	398,639	93,104	38,512	176,310	105	13,536	2,151	52,445	0	22,476
Maryland	1,984,038	500,885	232,967	732,941	124,672	77,459	3,453	228,509	0	83,152
Massachusetts	1,491,921	476,225	133,474	601,965	4,622	49,886	1,437	160,165	6,921	57,225
Michigan	5,529,883	1,271,950	547,232	1,497,147	228,446	250,279	27,213	769,203	679,763	258,650
Minnesota	2,494,341	437,237	268,831	905,202	27,232	189,788	11,065	221,159	303,480	130,347
Mississippi	1,215,602	209,811	155,880	439,750	31,046	33,492	867	155,630	140,593	48,532
Missouri	1,805,266	411,254	112,346	614,613	64,336	62,301	10,253	175,447	220,545	134,173
Montana	362,905	71,591	64,366	130,490	5,497	12,208	312	51,737	0	26,704
Nebraska	1,033,731	136,898	83,063	366,341	52,726	52,389	2,796	109,703	191,820	37,996
Nevada	412,884	65,470	49,955	202,052	6,154	23,239	1,223	35,747	0	29,043
New Hampshire	373,498	148,366	38,582	81,998	2,006	18,379	1,717	69,869	0	12,581
New Jersey	2,920,767	602,689	181,856	1,125,800	163,761	89,946	11,668	226,609	373,822	144,616
New Mexico	1,190,519	109,788	210,991	386,814	43,131	62,178	12,737	82,049	218,631	64,202
New York	6,574,152	1,333,795	448,010	2,738,816	417,399	252,651	15,747	379,235	829,597	158,901
North Carolina	3,299,213	376,510	379,945	1,617,885	76,314	154,558	15,603	532,251	0	146,146
North Dakota	431,381	83,589	67,408	136,448	22	18,054	1,539	76,300	12,263	35,756
Ohio	4,895,812	1,274,358	337,922	1,411,337	91,256	192,273	38,321	449,627	896,400	204,320
Oklahoma	1,257,552	199,815	186,065	563,195	15,263	42,492	2,075	200,092	0	48,555
Oregon	1,687,205	280,576	239,159	447,540	120,234	74,423	5,270	160,136	281,470	78,398
Pennsylvania	4,423,633	1,295,220	470,654	1,112,965	82,127	180,238	35,330	445,913	623,567	177,618
Rhode Island	329,277	108,895	41,383	116,257	0	5,892	0	45,347	0	11,502
South Carolina	1,924,747	333,680	151,768	597,477	24,254	80,917	2,536	175,457	496,328	62,331
South Dakota	260,907	61,659	36,279	104,824	1,162	7,915	318	29,002	0	19,748
Tennessee	1,961,312	306,436	178,713	802,243	13,625	87,499	14,193	167,916	311,542	79,145
Texas	7,688,388	1,087,047	783,742	3,362,792	317,947	340,517	139,191	545,820	271,289	840,043
Utah	1,307,681	171,251	171,852	380,812	21,081	36,802	9,296	106,146	240,334	170,105
Vermont	316,905	137,912	39,812	46,882	13	23,863	3,533	36,622	0	28,268
Virginia	3,323,028	709,490	287,967	871,285	14,253	154,498	28,618	447,955	749,019	59,944
Washington	2,744,035	452,847	453,159	1,005,332	15,216	129,010	11,306	319,102	228,172	129,892
West Virginia	666,268	164,577	62,620	314,469	1,465	20,548	0	82,084	0	20,506
Wisconsin	2,954,564	501,808	362,833	948,082	252,331	149,641	8,763	213,932	287,705	229,469
Wyoming	278,270	36,821	37,159	124,785	13,899	15,259	2,425	38,841	0	9,080
U.S. Service Schools [2]	1,253,468	572	1,108,021	0	0	6,693	0	63,284	74,900	0
Outlying areas	589,470	68,487	305,741	154,796	20,036	10,295	679	13,283	0	16,153
American Samoa	4,610	78	2,024	2,509	0	0	0	0	0	0
Federated States of Micronesia	3,932	1,441	336	18	1,361	50	0	533	0	194
Guam	68,198	6,002	5,374	38,858	11,469	1,316	464	3,016	0	1,699
Marshall Islands	2,176	698	935	419	0	11	12	89	0	11
Northern Marianas	3,511	1,276	298	16	1,206	50	0	472	0	194
Palau	4,762	998	2,342	697	0	0	0	597	0	128
Puerto Rico	468,739	54,322	290,572	95,191	2,483	6,788	0	5,733	0	13,650
Virgin Islands	33,542	3,672	3,861	17,087	3,518	2,080	202	2,844	0	277

[1] Includes independent operations (federally funded research and development centers).
[2] Data revised from previously published figures.

NOTE.—Because of rounding, details may not add to totals.

SOURCE: U.S. Department of Education, National Center for Education Statistics, Integrated Postsecondary Education Data System (IPEDS), "Finance" survey. (This table was prepared May 1997.)

Table 332.—Current-fund revenue from state and local governments of institutions of higher education, by state: 1985–86 to 1994–95

[In thousands]

State	Current-fund revenue from state and local governments					Current-fund revenue from state and local governments, 1994–95 [1]					
	1985–86	1990–91	1991–92	1992–93	1993–94	Total	State appropriations for public institutions	Local appropriations for public institutions	State and local appropriations for private institutions	State and local grants and contracts for public institutions	State and local grants and contracts for private institutions
1	2	3	4	5	6	7	8	9	10	11	12
United States [2]	$32,456,006	$43,412,081	$44,746,783	$45,692,830	$46,908,594	$49,508,974	$39,405,865	$4,243,984	$236,343	$3,961,715	$1,661,066
Alabama	656,823	758,900	762,004	791,758	849,967	956,058	893,353	4,266	5,365	47,478	5,597
Alaska	159,781	175,938	181,358	180,110	186,305	184,683	172,463	713	0	11,490	17
Arizona	539,054	768,654	779,292	769,328	817,274	885,484	657,604	198,406	0	29,357	117
Arkansas	266,898	332,367	371,131	407,115	415,536	436,261	395,497	4,702	0	33,631	2,431
California	4,943,659	6,628,037	7,127,388	7,072,896	6,411,115	6,620,028	4,606,377	1,319,989	3	646,675	46,985
Colorado	391,468	510,649	508,624	508,586	521,088	550,059	460,730	27,809	5	55,543	5,972
Connecticut	280,012	406,306	390,250	379,720	411,711	517,270	451,210	0	4,875	32,467	28,719
Delaware	88,661	124,881	142,638	134,355	140,191	150,656	136,064	999	0	13,379	214
District of Columbia	71,761	84,471	83,808	79,935	77,727	81,762	0	69,337	0	7,485	4,940
Florida	1,172,112	1,863,133	1,793,785	1,808,015	1,942,724	2,071,336	1,805,882	3,751	14,696	145,682	101,325
Georgia	689,379	1,001,889	977,304	1,077,918	1,242,527	1,419,447	1,224,804	18,618	14,020	135,118	26,886
Hawaii	195,375	321,195	381,118	379,025	400,980	401,145	385,772	0	0	15,342	31
Idaho	125,338	193,188	206,819	205,370	218,399	244,514	218,578	10,102	0	14,916	919
Illinois	1,405,622	1,855,023	1,821,597	1,865,744	1,931,481	2,064,998	1,367,563	403,423	17	171,034	122,961
Indiana	645,880	984,176	999,381	1,002,215	1,019,058	1,026,788	936,630	2,382	0	60,714	27,061
Iowa	431,840	599,407	613,147	635,838	673,738	697,177	618,557	26,529	0	27,650	24,442
Kansas	422,278	556,372	571,270	587,290	630,158	662,454	500,747	115,389	0	42,778	3,539
Kentucky	483,027	665,808	707,859	684,648	705,050	737,954	672,986	5,106	0	52,139	7,724
Louisiana	562,205	634,541	670,183	676,781	683,174	756,642	610,705	3,126	2,798	113,757	26,256
Maine	103,724	189,099	171,887	176,327	178,079	171,750	153,863	0	0	16,207	1,680
Maryland	631,471	943,620	823,075	876,755	898,788	924,547	685,878	131,883	27,822	64,171	14,793
Massachusetts	589,876	545,606	507,248	580,056	639,251	700,546	606,191	93	4,450	59,326	30,486
Michigan	1,215,291	1,589,630	1,764,129	1,730,143	1,769,771	1,866,604	1,462,136	258,370	7,965	99,650	38,484
Minnesota	533,573	818,117	871,048	893,456	956,836	982,180	868,344	5,143	68	82,755	25,871
Mississippi	362,517	419,177	401,458	441,825	471,136	611,482	535,729	30,286	0	45,004	463
Missouri	506,246	651,819	613,905	655,962	685,610	751,150	624,028	69,373	0	49,583	8,166
Montana	97,672	119,813	139,753	133,037	136,263	133,066	118,848	4,104	0	9,853	262
Nebraska	248,544	374,112	387,688	402,829	419,798	432,997	361,069	49,735	0	21,503	689
Nevada	99,841	173,580	191,292	197,213	208,216	252,977	226,103	0	0	26,863	11
New Hampshire	52,393	79,979	80,343	85,033	90,950	95,768	78,490	0	0	9,449	7,829
New Jersey	837,214	1,190,657	1,280,172	1,285,916	1,359,960	1,409,358	1,030,214	159,908	1,650	154,574	63,011
New Mexico	221,094	413,558	437,925	419,182	431,098	482,860	397,463	40,643	0	43,404	1,350
New York	2,726,150	3,421,222	3,578,508	3,675,680	3,893,354	3,982,026	2,547,935	348,602	45,486	440,437	599,566
North Carolina	1,074,960	1,633,096	1,703,504	1,810,371	1,746,867	1,852,503	1,664,641	77,743	0	57,426	52,693
North Dakota	118,691	133,796	140,149	151,668	136,744	163,593	146,311	5	0	17,038	238
Ohio	1,132,678	1,541,996	1,490,804	1,448,082	1,553,389	1,659,566	1,403,112	98,374	5,022	102,168	50,889
Oklahoma	437,693	535,024	590,597	601,040	580,522	606,743	524,139	16,374	1	64,560	1,669
Oregon	394,899	544,631	580,442	616,623	571,448	592,624	437,230	95,352	0	56,157	3,885
Pennsylvania	961,089	1,276,665	1,334,311	1,298,755	1,379,619	1,508,534	1,083,273	80,330	56,774	108,684	179,473
Rhode Island	107,265	123,502	116,197	118,844	117,735	125,567	116,425	0	50	7,308	1,784
South Carolina	491,802	618,304	601,894	627,013	631,482	669,239	616,532	23,315	0	18,980	10,411
South Dakota	65,151	86,262	93,150	97,575	106,452	105,197	99,060	0	0	5,879	258
Tennessee	528,933	711,103	681,944	763,246	824,936	898,678	827,754	2,057	1,157	52,270	15,441
Texas	2,521,860	3,069,093	3,315,755	3,496,729	3,783,870	3,895,369	3,171,462	261,933	31,636	348,641	81,697
Utah	256,997	346,711	369,253	385,953	402,523	441,726	394,074	0	0	46,945	706
Vermont	35,334	48,485	49,405	49,418	49,586	49,432	40,667	114	0	6,654	1,996
Virginia	775,474	961,845	887,077	873,539	914,056	977,099	846,612	1,972	12,478	100,163	15,873
Washington	620,383	915,462	922,706	985,218	1,023,612	1,009,039	863,971	0	0	143,640	1,428
West Virginia	222,693	280,199	293,370	297,177	316,565	329,313	298,016	678	0	29,914	705
Wisconsin	825,610	1,053,246	1,094,481	1,134,317	1,213,191	1,219,284	935,211	258,949	5	11,996	13,123
Wyoming	127,714	137,727	144,360	137,201	138,684	143,439	125,560	14,005	0	3,875	0

[1] Preliminary data.
[2] Excludes U.S. Service Schools.

NOTE.—Because of rounding, details may not add to totals.

SOURCE: U.S. Department of Education, National Center for Education Statistics, Higher Education General Information Survey (HEGIS), "Financial Statistics of Institutions of Higher Education" surveys; and Integrated Postsecondary Education Data System (IPEDS), "Finance" surveys. (This table was prepared July 1997.)

Table 333.—Current-fund revenue received from the federal government by the 120 institutions of higher education receiving the largest amounts: 1994–95

[In thousands]

Institution	Rank order	Current-fund revenue from the federal government [1]	Institution	Rank order	Current-fund revenue from the federal government [1]
1	2	3	1	2	3
United States (all institutions)	—	$23,243,172			
120 institutions receiving the largest amounts	—	17,386,616			
California Institute of Technology	1	1,200,356	Rutgers University, Central Office (NJ)	61	98,735
Johns Hopkins University (MD)	2	787,850	University of Virginia, Main Campus	62	98,724
University of Chicago (IL)	3	770,553	University of Hawaii at Manoa	63	97,669
Massachusetts Institute of Technology	4	612,736	Oregon State University	64	94,730
Stanford University (CA)	5	440,102	University of Utah	65	93,253
University of Washington	6	363,126	University of Texas, Southwestern Medical Center, Dallas	66	91,075
University of Michigan, Ann Arbor	7	326,160	Uniformed Services University of the Health Sciences (MD)	67	89,699
United States Military Academy (NY)	8	282,059	University of Oklahoma, Health Sciences Center	68	86,034
University of Wisconsin, Madison	9	278,112	North Carolina State University at Raleigh	69	85,794
University of California, Los Angeles	10	266,944	Colorado State University	70	83,357
University of Miami (FL)	11	266,890	University of Georgia	71	83,140
Cornell University Medical Center (NY)	12	263,153	State University of New York at Stony Brook	72	81,374
University of California, San Diego	13	262,478	Yeshiva University (NY)	73	75,390
Harvard University (MA)	14	251,306	University of Tennessee, Knoxville	74	74,820
University of Southern California	15	250,482	University of California, Irvine	75	74,355
United States Air Force Academy (CO)	16	244,818	Tulane University of Louisiana	76	74,353
Columbia University in the City of New York	17	244,699	Virginia Polytechnic Institute and State University	77	73,563
University of Pennsylvania	18	237,571	Cornell University, Statutory Colleges (NY)	78	73,340
University of Minnesota, Twin Cities	19	235,384	State University of New York at Buffalo	79	73,310
Georgetown University (DC)	20	228,046	Wake Forest University (NC)	80	73,292
University of California, San Francisco	21	227,303	New Mexico State University, Main Campus	81	70,022
Howard University (DC)	22	219,283	University of Cincinnati, Main Campus (OH)	82	69,309
United States Naval Academy (MD)	23	217,054	University of Kentucky	83	68,010
University of North Carolina, Chapel Hill	24	205,553	Mount Sinai School of Medicine (NY)	84	66,379
Yale University (CT)	25	200,141	Utah State University	85	66,180
University of Arizona	26	193,300	Virginia Commonwealth University	86	65,082
Pennsylvania State University, Main Campus	27	189,335	University of Texas, Health Science Center, San Antonio	87	63,796
University of Pittsburgh, Main Campus (PA)	28	186,513	Washington State University	88	63,639
University of Illinois at Urbana	29	181,249	University of Maryland, Baltimore Professional Schools	89	63,379
University of California, Berkeley	30	179,213	Oregon Health Science University	90	62,873
Duke University (NC)	31	177,804	Wayne State University (MI)	91	62,117
Princeton University (NJ)	32	176,551	Indiana University-Purdue University at Indianapolis	92	61,247
Washington University (MO)	33	163,689	University of Texas Health Science Center	93	59,954
University of Texas at Austin	34	162,956	University of California, Santa Barbara	94	59,276
Ohio State University, Main Campus	35	143,294	Gallaudet University (DC)	95	58,015
Cornell University, Endowed Colleges (NY)	36	141,373	University of Medicine and Dentistry of New Jersey	96	57,299
University of New Mexico, Main Campus	37	134,730	Indiana University, Bloomington	97	57,147
University of Iowa	38	132,688	Tufts University (MA)	98	56,092
University of Alabama at Birmingham	39	125,789	City University of New York System Office	99	55,510
Carnegie Mellon University (PA)	40	124,352	Mississippi State University	100	55,414
Iowa State University	41	123,737	Arizona State University, Main Campus	101	54,841
University of Rochester (NY)	42	123,634	Florida State University	102	54,568
Naval Postgraduate School (CA)	43	122,455	Thomas Jefferson University (PA)	103	53,361
University of Colorado at Boulder	44	118,612	Clark Atlanta University (GA)	104	51,780
Case Western Reserve University (OH)	45	118,474	University of Massachusetts, Amherst	105	51,578
University of California, Davis	46	116,129	West Virginia University	106	51,257
New York University	47	114,930	Rochester Institute of Technology (NY)	107	49,991
Vanderbilt University (TN)	48	114,086	University of Nebraska at Lincoln	108	48,632
Georgia Institute of Technology, Main Campus	49	112,417	University of South Carolina at Columbia	109	48,211
Texas A & M University	50	110,857	Brown University (RI)	110	48,137
Baylor College of Medicine (TX)	51	110,278	Wheeling Jesuit College (WV)	111	46,821
University of Florida	52	110,135	Dartmouth College (NH)	112	46,618
University of Maryland, College Park Campus	53	106,791	University of Missouri, Columbia	113	44,937
Emory University (GA)	54	105,635	The University of Texas Medical Branch, Galveston	114	43,774
Northwestern University (IL)	55	105,069	Clemson University (SC)	115	43,560
Boston University (MA)	56	104,677	University of Alaska, Fairbanks	116	43,289
Purdue University, Main Campus (IN)	57	104,006	State University of New York at Albany	117	43,202
University of Colorado, Health Sciences Center	58	101,289	California State University, Northridge	118	42,817
Michigan State University	59	99,573	University of Dayton (OH)	119	42,800
University of Illinois at Chicago	60	99,444	University of Nebraska, Central Office	120	42,471

[1] Includes federal appropriations, unrestricted and restricted federal contracts and grants, and revenue for independent operations. Independent operations generally include only the revenues associated with major federally funded research and development centers. Excludes Pell Grants. Federally supported student aid that is received through students is excluded.

—Not applicable.

SOURCE: U.S. Department of Education, National Center for Education Statistics, Integrated Postsecondary Education Data System (IPEDS), "Finance, 1994–95" survey. (This table was prepared July 1997.)

Table 334.—Current-fund expenditures and educational and general expenditures of institutions of higher education, by purpose and per student: 1929–30 to 1994–95

[Columns 2 through 17 in thousands]

Year	Current-fund expenditures	Educational and general expenditures							
		Total	Administration and general expense	Instruction and departmental research	Organized research	Libraries	Plant operation and maintenance	Organized activities related to instructional departments	Other sponsored programs [1]
1	2	3	4	5	6	7	8	9	10
1929–30	$507,142	$377,903	$42,633	$221,598	[5]$18,007	$9,622	$61,061	([6])	—
1931–32	536,523	420,633	47,232	232,645	[5]21,978	11,379	56,797	[7]$21,297	—
1933–34	469,329	369,661	43,155	203,332	[5]17,064	13,387	51,046	[7]14,155	—
1935–36	541,391	419,883	48,069	225,143	[5]22,091	15,531	56,802	[7]20,241	—
1937–38	614,385	475,191	56,406	253,006	[5]25,213	17,588	62,738	[7]24,031	—
1939–40	674,688	521,990	62,827	280,248	[5]27,266	19,487	69,612	[7]27,225	—
1941–42	738,169	572,465	66,968	298,558	[5]34,287	19,763	72,594	[7]37,771	—
1943–44	974,118	753,846	69,668	334,189	[5]58,456	20,452	81,201	[7]48,415	[8]$97,044
1945–46	1,088,422	820,326	104,808	375,122	[5]86,812	26,560	110,947	[7]60,604	—
1947–48	1,883,269	1,391,594	171,829	657,945	[5]159,090	44,208	201,996	[7]85,346	—
1949–50	2,245,661	1,706,444	213,070	780,994	[5]225,341	56,147	225,110	[7]119,108	—
1951–52	2,471,008	1,960,481	233,844	823,117	[5]317,928	60,612	240,446	[7]147,854	—
1953–54	2,882,864	2,345,331	288,147	960,556	[5]372,643	72,944	277,874	[7]186,905	—
1955–56	3,499,463	2,861,858	355,207	1,140,655	[5]500,793	85,563	324,229	[7]222,007	—
1957–58	4,509,666	3,734,350	473,945	1,465,603	[5]727,776	109,715	406,226	[7]238,455	—
1959–60	5,601,376	4,685,258	583,224	1,793,320	[5]1,022,353	135,384	469,943	[7]294,255	—
1961–62	7,154,526	5,997,007	730,429	2,202,443	[5]1,474,406	177,362	564,225	[7]375,040	—
1963–64	9,177,677	7,725,433	957,512	2,801,707	[5]1,973,383	236,718	686,054	[7]458,507	—
1965–66	12,509,489	10,376,630	1,251,107	3,756,175	[5]2,448,300	346,248	844,506	[7]558,170	155,202
1966–67	14,230,341	10,724,974	1,445,074	4,356,413	1,565,102	415,903	969,275	591,848	350,950
1967–68	16,480,786	12,847,350	1,738,946	5,139,179	1,933,473	493,266	1,127,290	350,711	514,294
1968–69	18,481,583	14,718,140	2,277,585	5,941,972	2,034,074	571,572	1,337,903	535,269	668,483
1969–70	21,043,110	16,845,210	2,627,993	6,883,844	2,144,076	652,596	1,541,698	648,089	769,253
1970–71	23,375,197	18,714,642	2,983,911	7,804,410	2,209,338	716,212	1,730,664	693,011	890,507
1971–72	25,559,560	20,441,878	3,344,215	8,443,261	2,265,282	764,481	1,927,553	779,728	1,059,989
1972–73	27,955,624	22,400,379	3,713,068	9,243,641	2,394,261	840,727	2,141,162	791,290	1,284,085
1973–74	30,713,581	24,653,849	4,200,955	10,219,118	2,480,450	939,023	2,494,057	838,170	1,355,027
1974–75	35,057,563	27,547,620	4,495,391	11,797,823	3,132,132	1,001,868	2,786,768	1,253,824	—
1975–76	38,903,177	30,598,685	5,240,066	13,094,943	3,287,364	1,223,723	3,082,959	1,248,670	—
1976–77	42,599,816	33,151,681	5,590,669	14,031,145	3,600,067	1,250,314	3,436,705	1,544,646	—
1977–78	45,970,790	36,256,604	6,177,029	15,336,229	3,919,830	1,348,747	3,795,043	1,781,160	—
1978–79	50,720,984	39,833,116	6,832,004	16,662,820	4,447,760	1,426,614	4,178,574	2,044,386	—
1979–80	56,913,588	44,542,843	7,621,143	18,496,717	5,099,151	1,623,811	4,700,070	2,252,577	—
1980–81	64,052,938	50,073,805	8,681,513	20,733,166	5,657,719	1,759,784	5,350,310	2,513,502	—
1981–82	70,339,448	54,848,752	9,648,069	22,962,527	5,929,894	1,922,416	5,979,281	2,734,038	—
1982–83	75,935,749	58,929,218	10,412,233	24,673,293	6,265,280	2,039,671	6,391,596	3,047,220	—
1983–84	81,993,360	63,741,276	11,561,260	26,436,308	6,723,534	2,231,149	6,729,825	3,300,003	—
1984–85	89,951,263	70,061,324	12,765,452	28,777,183	7,551,892	2,361,793	7,345,482	3,712,460	—
1985–86	97,535,742	76,127,965	13,913,724	31,032,099	8,437,367	2,551,331	7,605,226	4,116,061	—
1986–87	105,763,557	82,955,555	15,060,576	33,711,146	9,352,309	2,441,184	7,819,032	5,134,267	—
1987–88	113,786,476	89,157,430	16,171,015	35,833,563	10,350,931	2,836,498	8,230,986	5,305,083	—
1988–89	123,867,184	96,803,377	17,309,956	38,812,690	11,432,170	3,009,870	8,739,895	5,894,409	—
1989–90	134,655,571	105,585,076	19,062,179	42,145,987	12,505,961	3,254,239	9,458,262	6,183,405	—
1990–91	146,087,836	114,139,901	20,751,966	45,496,117	13,444,040	3,343,892	10,062,581	6,706,881	—
1991–92	156,189,161	121,567,157	21,984,118	47,997,196	14,261,554	3,595,834	10,346,580	6,981,184	—
1992–93	165,241,040	128,977,968	23,414,977	50,340,914	15,291,309	3,684,852	10,783,727	7,388,118	—
1993–94	173,350,617	136,024,350	24,489,022	52,775,599	16,117,610	3,908,412	11,368,496	7,769,499	—
1994–95 [10]	182,968,610	144,158,002	25,904,821	55,719,707	17,109,541	4,165,761	11,745,905	8,112,930	—

Table 334.—Current-fund expenditures and educational and general expenditures of institutions of higher education, by purpose and per student: 1929–30 to 1994–95—Continued

[Columns 2 through 17 in thousands]

Year	Educational and general expenditures			Auxiliary enterprises	Independent operations[2]	Hospitals	Other current expenditures	Educational and general expenditures per student in fall enrollment[3]	
	Extension and public service	Scholarships and fellowships	Other general expenditures					Current dollars	Constant 1994–95 dollars[4]
1	11	12	13	14	15	16	17	18	19
1929–30	$24,982	[6]	—	$3,127	[5]	[7]	$126,112	$343	$3,017
1931–32	24,066	[6]	$5,239	90,897	[5]	[7]	24,993	364	3,802
1933–34	20,020	[6]	7,502	78,730	[5]	[7]	20,938	350	3,979
1935–36	29,426	[6]	2,580	95,332	[5]	[7]	26,176	348	3,804
1937–38	34,189	[6]	2,020	115,620	[5]	[7]	23,574	352	3,693
1939–40	35,325	[6]	—	124,184	[5]	[7]	28,514	349	3,760
1941–42	42,525	[6]	—	137,328	[5]	[7]	28,375	408	3,933
1943–44	44,421	[6]	—	199,344	[5]	[7]	20,928	653	5,632
1945–46	55,473	[6]	—	242,028	[5]	[7]	26,068	489	4,034
1947–48	71,180	[6]	—	438,988	[5]	[7]	52,687	595	3,842
1949–50	86,674	[6]	—	476,401	[5]	[7]	62,816	698	4,433
1951–52	97,408	$39,272	—	477,672	[5]	[7]	32,855	933	5,337
1953–54	112,227	74,035	—	537,533	[5]	[7]	—	1,051	5,880
1955–56	137,914	95,490	—	637,605	[5]	[7]	—	1,079	6,035
1957–58	175,256	129,935	7,439	775,316	[5]	[7]	—	1,124	5,917
1959–60	205,595	172,050	9,134	916,117	[5]	[7]	—	1,287	6,589
1961–62	244,337	228,765	—	1,157,517	[5]	[7]	—	1,447	7,240
1963–64	297,350	300,370	13,832	1,452,244	[5]	[7]	—	1,616	7,882
1965–66	438,385	425,524	153,013	1,887,744	[5]	[7]	[9] 245,115	1,753	8,261
1966–67	226,566	583,390	220,453	2,060,130	$951,668	$253,790	[9] 239,780	1,678	7,669
1967–68	597,544	712,425	240,222	2,302,419	765,495	290,000	[9] 275,523	1,859	8,221
1968–69	536,527	814,755	—	2,539,183	697,317	526,943	—	1,959	8,261
1969–70	593,067	984,594	—	2,769,276	757,388	671,236	—	2,104	8,379
1970–71	588,390	1,098,198	—	2,988,407	829,596	842,552	—	2,181	8,258
1971–72	615,997	1,241,372	—	3,178,272	940,825	998,585	—	2,284	8,350
1972–73	669,735	1,322,411	—	3,337,789	1,033,746	1,183,709	—	2,431	8,541
1973–74	730,560	1,396,488	—	3,613,256	1,014,872	1,431,604	—	2,568	8,283
1974–75	1,097,788	1,449,542	532,485	4,073,590	1,085,590	2,350,763	—	2,694	7,825
1975–76	1,238,603	1,635,859	546,498	4,476,841	1,132,016	2,695,635	—	2,736	7,420
1976–77	1,343,404	1,770,214	584,515	4,858,328	1,434,738	3,155,069	—	3,010	7,715
1977–78	1,425,294	1,839,298	633,973	5,261,477	855,054	3,597,655	—	3,213	7,715
1978–79	1,593,097	1,944,599	703,262	5,749,974	1,007,119	4,130,775	—	3,538	7,768
1979–80	1,816,521	2,200,468	732,385	6,485,608	1,127,728	4,757,409	—	3,850	7,459
1980–81	2,057,770	2,504,525	815,516	7,288,089	1,257,934	5,433,111	—	4,139	7,187
1981–82	2,203,726	2,684,945	783,854	7,997,632	1,258,777	6,234,287	—	4,433	7,086
1982–83	2,320,478	2,922,897	856,548	8,614,316	1,406,126	6,986,089	—	4,742	7,268
1983–84	2,499,203	3,301,673	958,321	9,250,196	1,622,233	7,379,654	—	5,114	7,557
1984–85	2,861,095	3,670,355	1,015,613	10,012,248	1,867,550	8,010,141	—	5,723	8,139
1985–86	3,119,533	4,160,174	1,192,449	10,528,303	2,187,361	8,692,113	—	6,216	8,592
1986–87	3,448,453	4,776,100	1,212,488	11,037,333	2,597,655	9,173,014	—	6,635	8,971
1987–88	3,786,362	5,325,358	1,317,633	11,399,953	2,822,632	10,406,461	—	6,984	9,067
1988–89	4,227,323	5,918,666	1,458,397	12,280,063	2,958,962	11,824,782	—	7,415	9,202
1989–90	4,689,758	6,655,544	1,629,742	13,203,984	3,187,225	12,679,286	—	7,799	9,238
1990–91	5,076,177	7,551,184	1,707,063	14,272,247	3,349,824	14,325,865	—	8,259	9,276
1991–92	5,489,298	9,060,000	1,851,393	14,966,100	3,551,592	16,104,313	—	8,466	9,214
1992–93	5,935,095	10,148,373	1,990,603	15,561,508	3,651,891	17,049,672	—	8,903	9,395
1993–94	6,242,414	11,238,010	2,115,288	16,429,341	3,387,323	17,509,603	—	9,509	9,782
1994–95 [10]	6,691,485	12,285,328	2,422,524	17,204,917	3,534,332	18,071,359	—	10,108	10,108

[1] Includes all separately budgeted programs, other than research, which are supported by sponsors outside the institution. Examples are training programs, workshops, and training and instructional institutes. For years not shown, most expenditures for these programs are included under "Extension and public service."
[2] Generally includes only those expenditures associated with federally funded research and development centers (FFRDCs).
[3] Data for 1929–30 to 1945–46 are based on school year enrollment.
[4] Data adjusted by the consumer price index computed on a school year basis.
[5] Expenditures for federally funded research and development centers are included under "Organized research."
[6] Included under "Other current expenditures."
[7] Expenditures for hospitals included under "Organized activities related to instructional departments."
[8] Expenditures were for federal contract courses.
[9] Includes current expenditures for physical plant assets. In later years, the educational and general expenditures for physical plant assets are included under "Other general expenditures."
[10] Preliminary data.
—Data not available.

NOTE.—The data in this table reflect limitations of data availability and comparability. Major changes in data collection forms in 1965–66 and 1974–75 cause significant data comparability problems among the three mostly consistent time periods, 1929–30 to 1963–64, 1965–66 to 1973–74, and 1974–75 to the present. The largest problems affect Hospitals, Independent operations, Organized research, Other sponsored programs, Extension and public service, and Scholarships and fellowships.

SOURCE: U.S. Department of Education, National Center for Education Statistics, *Biennial Survey of Education in the United States;* Higher Education General Information Survey (HEGIS), "Financial Statistics of Institutions of Higher Education" surveys; and Integrated Postsecondary Education Data System, "Finance" surveys. (This table was prepared July 1997.)

Table 335.—Expenditures of institutions of higher education, by purpose and by control and type of institution: 1994–95 [1]

Control and type of institution	Current-fund expenditures	Educational and general expenditures					
		Total	Instruction	Research	Public service	Academic support	
						Total	Libraries only
1	2	3	4	5	6	7	8
	In thousands						
Total	$182,968,610	$144,158,002	$55,719,707	$17,109,541	$6,691,485	$12,278,691	$4,165,761
Public	115,464,975	92,173,768	37,599,194	11,829,665	5,034,445	8,463,236	2,614,609
Research I universities [3]	43,353,284	31,701,282	10,785,597	7,917,074	2,372,673	3,036,017	871,473
Research II universities [3]	7,068,658	6,070,400	2,294,812	1,078,045	496,227	604,172	230,418
Doctoral universities	12,141,645	10,301,903	4,027,454	1,161,855	618,691	1,079,098	348,526
Master's	18,661,964	16,017,997	7,278,634	518,288	629,671	1,503,208	569,887
Baccalaureate	2,439,001	2,095,331	874,474	25,079	71,030	202,905	70,995
Associate of arts	20,519,749	19,210,525	9,424,668	29,173	442,401	1,540,092	431,890
Specialized institutions [4]							
Health and medicine	9,448,711	5,123,904	2,366,971	1,016,258	386,699	325,512	61,425
Engineering	211,703	192,636	76,454	21,109	3,159	15,825	5,697
Business	25,404	23,732	11,275	0	1,164	2,768	685
Fine arts	120,962	109,453	47,716	0	1,095	8,316	3,787
Other specialized	1,400,256	1,255,385	388,511	62,579	10,414	138,118	18,072
Tribal colleges [5]	73,636	71,220	22,630	206	1,221	7,206	1,755
4-year	23,272	22,872	6,525	66	316	2,068	546
2-year	50,364	48,347	16,105	140	905	5,138	1,208
Private	67,503,635	51,984,234	18,120,513	5,279,876	1,657,040	3,815,455	1,551,152
Research I universities [3]	26,154,592	17,562,997	6,528,294	3,858,552	539,110	1,191,276	527,363
Research II universities [3]	3,868,995	2,744,436	1,130,894	315,228	19,322	220,248	90,394
Doctoral universities	6,381,985	5,374,037	2,015,375	336,660	242,505	455,008	183,681
Master's	9,654,630	8,546,886	2,989,009	166,030	117,783	641,897	257,602
Baccalaureate	12,218,292	10,541,968	3,261,104	97,318	70,667	758,436	323,975
Associate of arts	1,497,157	1,347,130	386,193	985	3,313	124,749	28,363
Specialized institutions [4]							
Religion and theology	1,056,969	931,683	267,196	2,911	52,386	89,736	49,182
Health and medicine	4,167,296	2,612,981	773,975	467,017	580,773	119,956	32,390
Engineering	372,810	350,963	118,182	30,270	1,319	22,294	5,092
Business	916,463	830,265	236,162	186	3,089	88,576	15,150
Fine arts	702,640	646,097	228,941	301	11,772	45,659	11,531
Other specialized	490,730	474,144	180,050	4,385	11,735	55,724	26,158
Tribal colleges [5]	21,076	20,647	5,137	32	3,268	1,897	269
4-year	10,603	10,383	2,780	18	3,268	749	133
2-year	10,473	10,264	2,358	13	0	1,148	136
	Percentage distribution of current-fund expenditures						
Total	100.00	78.79	30.45	9.35	3.66	6.71	2.28
Public	100.00	79.83	32.56	10.25	4.36	7.33	2.26
Research I universities [3]	100.00	73.12	24.88	18.26	5.47	7.00	2.01
Research II universities [3]	100.00	85.88	32.46	15.25	7.02	8.55	3.26
Doctoral universities	100.00	84.85	33.17	9.57	5.10	8.89	2.87
Master's	100.00	85.83	39.00	2.78	3.37	8.05	3.05
Baccalaureate	100.00	85.91	35.85	1.03	2.91	8.32	2.91
Associate of arts	100.00	93.62	45.93	0.14	2.16	7.51	2.10
Specialized institutions [4]							
Health and medicine	100.00	54.23	25.05	10.76	4.09	3.45	0.65
Engineering	100.00	90.99	36.11	9.97	1.49	7.47	2.69
Business	100.00	93.42	44.38	0.00	4.58	10.90	2.70
Fine arts	100.00	90.49	39.45	0.00	0.91	6.87	3.13
Other specialized	100.00	89.65	27.75	4.47	0.74	9.86	1.29
Tribal colleges [5]	100.00	96.72	30.73	0.28	1.66	9.79	2.38
4-year	100.00	98.28	28.04	0.28	1.36	8.88	2.35
2-year	100.00	96.00	31.98	0.28	1.80	10.20	2.40
Private	100.00	77.01	26.84	7.82	2.45	5.65	2.30
Research I universities [3]	100.00	67.15	24.96	14.75	2.06	4.55	2.02
Research II universities [3]	100.00	70.93	29.23	8.15	0.50	5.69	2.34
Doctoral universities	100.00	84.21	31.58	5.28	3.80	7.13	2.88
Master's	100.00	88.53	30.96	1.72	1.22	6.65	2.67
Baccalaureate	100.00	86.28	26.69	0.80	0.58	6.21	2.65
Associate of arts	100.00	89.98	25.80	0.07	0.22	8.33	1.89
Specialized institutions [4]							
Religion and theology	100.00	88.15	25.28	0.28	4.96	8.49	4.65
Health and medicine	100.00	62.70	18.57	11.21	13.94	2.88	0.78
Engineering	100.00	94.14	31.70	8.12	0.35	5.98	1.37
Business	100.00	90.59	25.77	0.02	0.34	9.66	1.65
Fine arts	100.00	91.95	32.58	0.04	1.68	6.50	1.64
Other specialized	100.00	96.62	36.69	0.89	2.39	11.36	5.33
Tribal colleges [5]	100.00	97.96	24.37	0.15	15.50	9.00	1.28
4-year	100.00	97.93	26.22	0.17	30.82	7.07	1.25
2-year	100.00	98.00	22.51	0.13	0.00	10.96	1.30

Table 335.—Expenditures of institutions of higher education, by purpose and by control and type of institution: 1994–95 [1]—Continued

Control and type of institution	Educational and general expenditures					Auxiliary enterprises	Hospitals	Independent operations [2]
	Student services	Institutional support	Plant operation	Scholarships and fellowships	Mandatory transfers			
1	9	10	11	12	13	14	15	16
	In thousands							
Total	$9,059,994	$16,844,827	$11,745,905	$12,285,328	$2,422,524	$17,204,917	$18,071,359	$3,534,332
Public	5,614,011	9,929,007	7,668,919	4,662,023	1,373,267	11,235,143	11,801,589	254,474
Research I universities [3]	1,077,467	2,070,270	2,090,136	1,747,950	604,098	4,389,211	7,172,428	90,363
Research II universities [3]	279,787	478,804	438,634	320,847	79,071	996,750	0	1,508
Doctoral universities	567,702	1,292,376	781,425	602,392	170,910	1,505,659	329,784	4,300
Master's	1,268,507	2,048,939	1,511,260	981,515	277,977	2,418,978	207,804	17,185
Baccalaureate	198,568	312,080	215,542	156,544	39,110	301,488	0	42,182
Associate of arts	2,024,542	2,932,077	1,961,857	715,049	140,666	1,292,224	0	17,000
Specialized institutions [4]								
Health and medicine	47,473	515,242	357,590	61,225	46,935	211,518	4,034,544	78,745
Engineering	11,970	26,868	19,088	10,680	7,484	15,881	0	3,186
Business	1,315	3,402	2,344	1,463	0	1,673	0	0
Fine arts	6,818	26,832	12,907	5,720	49	11,509	0	0
Other specialized	119,822	207,958	269,624	52,069	6,292	87,836	57,031	4
Tribal colleges [5]	10,041	14,160	8,511	6,570	676	2,417	0	0
4-year	5,314	4,707	2,883	994	0	400	0	0
2-year	4,726	9,453	5,628	5,576	676	2,017	0	0
Private	3,445,983	6,915,821	4,076,986	7,623,304	1,049,256	5,969,773	6,269,769	3,279,859
Research I universities [3]	519,071	1,555,806	1,261,235	1,793,173	316,481	1,659,071	4,027,772	2,904,752
Research II universities [3]	118,423	280,197	193,365	419,109	47,650	494,870	618,189	11,501
Doctoral universities	330,572	722,225	395,119	752,594	123,979	580,680	382,326	44,942
Master's	823,441	1,317,772	650,462	1,607,481	233,012	1,077,155	8,864	21,724
Baccalaureate	1,113,715	1,725,900	921,781	2,390,415	202,634	1,642,386	0	33,938
Associate of arts	188,290	291,692	168,402	176,893	6,612	93,893	55,871	263
Specialized institutions [4]								
Religion and theology	66,061	223,046	102,727	114,923	12,698	118,951	0	6,335
Health and medicine	69,280	325,060	150,087	70,327	56,505	121,904	1,176,748	255,663
Engineering	28,956	66,129	37,887	37,492	8,434	21,848	0	0
Business	99,379	181,161	78,595	123,958	19,159	86,197	0	0
Fine arts	50,943	129,188	69,455	97,998	11,840	56,099	0	444
Other specialized	35,198	93,612	46,018	37,232	10,190	16,289	0	296
Tribal colleges [5]	2,654	4,031	1,853	1,710	64	429	0	0
4-year	656	1,458	322	1,132	0	220	0	0
2-year	1,998	2,574	1,531	578	64	209	0	0
	Percentage distribution of current-fund expenditures							
Total	4.95	9.21	6.42	6.71	1.32	9.40	9.88	1.93
Public	4.86	8.60	6.64	4.04	1.19	9.73	10.22	0.22
Research I universities [3]	2.49	4.78	4.82	4.03	1.39	10.12	16.54	0.21
Research II universities [3]	3.96	6.77	6.21	4.54	1.12	14.10	0.00	0.02
Doctoral universities	4.68	10.64	6.44	4.96	1.41	12.40	2.72	0.04
Master's	6.80	10.98	8.10	5.26	1.49	12.96	1.11	0.09
Baccalaureate	8.14	12.80	8.84	6.42	1.60	12.36	0.00	1.73
Associate of arts	9.87	14.29	9.56	3.48	0.69	6.30	0.00	0.08
Specialized institutions [4]								
Health and medicine	0.50	5.45	3.78	0.65	0.50	2.24	42.70	0.83
Engineering	5.65	12.69	9.02	5.04	3.53	7.50	0.00	1.50
Business	5.18	13.39	9.23	5.76	0.00	6.58	0.00	0.00
Fine arts	5.64	22.18	10.67	4.73	0.04	9.51	0.00	0.00
Other specialized	8.56	14.85	19.26	3.72	0.45	6.27	4.07	0.00
Tribal colleges [5]	13.64	19.23	11.56	8.92	0.92	3.28	0.00	0.00
4-year	22.84	20.23	12.39	4.27	0.00	1.72	0.00	0.00
2-year	9.38	18.77	11.17	11.07	1.34	4.00	0.00	0.00
Private	5.10	10.25	6.04	11.29	1.55	8.84	9.29	4.86
Research I universities [3]	1.98	5.95	4.82	6.86	1.21	6.34	15.40	11.11
Research II universities [3]	3.06	7.24	5.00	10.83	1.23	12.79	15.98	0.30
Doctoral universities	5.18	11.32	6.19	11.79	1.94	9.10	5.99	0.70
Master's	8.53	13.65	6.74	16.65	2.41	11.16	0.09	0.23
Baccalaureate	9.12	14.13	7.54	19.56	1.66	13.44	0.00	0.28
Associate of arts	12.58	19.48	11.25	11.82	0.44	6.27	3.73	0.02
Specialized institutions [4]								
Religion and theology	6.25	21.10	9.72	10.87	1.20	11.25	0.00	0.60
Health and medicine	1.66	7.80	3.60	1.69	1.36	2.93	28.24	6.13
Engineering	7.77	17.74	10.16	10.06	2.26	5.86	0.00	0.00
Business	10.84	19.77	8.58	13.53	2.09	9.41	0.00	0.00
Fine arts	7.25	18.39	9.88	13.95	1.69	7.98	0.00	0.06
Other specialized	7.17	19.08	9.38	7.59	2.08	3.32	0.00	0.06
Tribal colleges [5]	12.59	19.13	8.79	8.11	0.31	2.04	0.00	0.00
4-year	6.19	13.75	3.03	10.68	0.00	2.07	0.00	0.00
2-year	19.08	24.57	14.62	5.52	0.61	2.00	0.00	0.00

[1] Preliminary data.
[2] Generally includes only those expenditures associated with major federally funded research and development centers (FFRDC).
[3] Research institutions are committed to graduate education through the doctorate, and give high priority to research. Research I institutions receive $40 million or more annually in federal support. Research II institutions receive between $15.5 million and $40 million annually.
[4] Specialized institutions award baccalaureate or higher level degrees in specific fields of study.
[5] Tribally controlled colleges are located on reservations. They are members of the American Indian Higher Education Consortium.

SOURCE: U.S. Department of Education, National Center for Education Statistics, Integrated Postsecondary Education Data System (IPEDS), "Finance, 1994–95" survey. (This table was prepared July 1997.)

Table 336.—Current-fund expenditures and expenditures per full-time-equivalent student in institutions of higher education, by type and control of institution: 1970–71 to 1994–95

Control of institution and year	All institutions			4-year institutions			2-year institutions		
	Current-fund expenditures, in millions		Current-fund expenditures per student, in constant 1994–95 dollars[1]	Current-fund expenditures, in millions		Current-fund expenditures per student, in constant 1994–95 dollars[1]	Current-fund expenditures, in millions		Current-fund expenditures per student, in constant 1994–95 dollars[1]
	Unadjusted dollars	Constant 1994–95 dollars[1]		Unadjusted dollars	Constant 1994–95 dollars[1]		Unadjusted dollars	Constant 1994–95 dollars[1]	
1	2	3	4	5	6	7	8	9	10
All institutions									
1970–71	$23,375	$93,390	$13,861	$21,049	$84,094	$16,344	$2,327	$9,296	$5,837
1975–76	38,903	113,210	13,351	33,811	98,392	16,675	5,092	14,818	5,745
1976–77	42,600	116,509	14,016	37,052	101,335	17,328	5,548	15,174	6,157
1977–78	45,971	117,691	13,985	39,899	102,145	17,210	6,072	15,546	6,268
1978–79	50,721	121,011	14,495	44,163	105,365	17,761	6,558	15,646	6,476
1979–80	56,914	123,521	14,554	49,661	107,780	17,915	7,253	15,741	6,370
1980–81	64,053	125,568	14,238	55,840	109,468	17,767	8,212	16,100	6,058
1981–82	70,339	125,997	13,977	61,333	109,865	17,579	9,006	16,132	5,835
1982–83	75,936	127,724	14,048	66,238	111,413	17,829	9,697	16,311	5,738
1983–84	81,993	131,596	14,356	71,680	115,043	18,188	10,314	16,553	5,826
1984–85	89,951	136,551	15,254	78,744	119,537	18,996	11,207	17,013	6,398
1985–86	97,536	141,062	15,773	85,560	123,742	19,659	11,976	17,320	6,538
1986–87	105,764	147,142	16,233	92,985	129,363	20,339	12,779	17,779	6,575
1987–88	113,786	151,775	16,444	100,143	133,577	20,593	13,644	18,199	6,634
1988–89	123,867	156,886	16,577	109,141	138,234	20,743	14,726	18,652	6,661
1989–90	134,656	160,860	16,446	118,578	141,654	20,790	16,077	19,206	6,473
1990–91	146,088	165,803	16,608	128,594	145,948	20,945	17,494	19,855	6,584
1991–92	156,189	171,258	16,530	137,375	150,629	21,271	18,814	20,629	6,291
1992–93	165,241	176,020	16,865	145,300	154,778	21,710	19,941	21,242	6,423
1993–94	173,351	178,552	17,249	152,164	156,730	22,010	21,187	21,823	6,755
1994–95[2]	182,969	182,969	17,681	160,891	160,891	22,542	22,078	22,078	6,876
Public institutions									
1970–71	14,996	59,913	12,096	12,899	51,534	14,858	2,097	8,379	5,644
1975–76	26,184	76,196	11,682	21,392	62,251	15,346	4,792	13,945	5,655
1976–77	28,635	78,315	12,333	23,411	64,028	16,013	5,224	14,288	6,076
1977–78	30,725	78,660	12,297	25,013	64,037	15,854	5,712	14,624	6,203
1978–79	33,733	80,480	12,817	27,600	65,849	16,478	6,132	14,631	6,408
1979–80	37,768	81,969	12,822	30,979	67,234	16,563	6,789	14,735	6,315
1980–81	42,280	82,884	12,478	34,677	67,981	16,348	7,602	14,904	6,000
1981–82	46,219	82,791	12,209	37,890	67,870	16,127	8,330	14,921	5,799
1982–83	49,573	83,382	12,171	40,616	68,316	16,186	8,957	15,066	5,729
1983–84	53,087	85,202	12,381	43,588	69,957	16,399	9,499	15,245	5,828
1984–85	58,315	88,524	13,243	48,017	72,892	17,200	10,298	15,632	6,389
1985–86	63,194	91,395	13,707	52,184	75,472	17,802	11,010	15,923	6,558
1986–87	67,654	94,122	13,886	56,003	77,913	18,138	11,651	16,210	6,529
1987–88	72,641	96,893	13,966	60,137	80,214	18,248	12,505	16,679	6,562
1988–89	78,946	99,990	14,089	65,349	82,769	18,369	13,597	17,221	6,646
1989–90	85,771	102,462	13,900	70,865	84,655	18,324	14,906	17,806	6,471
1990–91	92,961	105,506	13,960	76,722	87,076	18,370	16,239	18,431	6,540
1991–92	98,847	108,384	13,784	81,334	89,181	18,596	17,513	19,203	6,261
1992–93	104,570	111,391	14,079	86,065	91,679	19,108	18,505	19,712	6,331
1993–94	109,310	112,589	14,412	89,697	92,389	19,385	19,612	20,201	6,631
1994–95[2]	115,465	115,465	14,833	94,895	94,895	19,980	20,570	20,570	6,778
Private institutions									
1970–71	8,379	33,477	18,758	8,150	32,560	19,417	230	917	8,505
1975–76	12,719	37,013	18,910	12,419	36,141	19,600	300	873	7,690
1976–77	13,965	38,194	19,461	13,641	37,307	20,171	324	887	7,842
1977–78	15,246	39,031	19,333	14,885	38,109	20,099	360	922	7,506
1978–79	16,988	40,531	19,587	16,563	39,515	20,408	425	1,015	7,629
1979–80	19,146	41,552	19,837	18,682	40,546	20,721	464	1,007	7,298
1980–81	21,773	42,683	19,609	21,163	41,487	20,712	610	1,196	6,889
1981–82	24,120	43,206	19,347	23,444	41,994	20,572	676	1,211	6,314
1982–83	26,363	44,342	19,786	25,623	43,097	21,248	740	1,245	5,851
1983–84	28,907	46,394	20,305	28,092	45,086	21,893	815	1,308	5,800
1984–85	31,637	48,026	21,185	30,727	46,645	22,700	910	1,381	6,508
1985–86	34,342	49,667	21,826	33,376	48,270	23,492	966	1,397	6,323
1986–87	38,110	53,019	23,192	36,982	51,450	24,918	1,128	1,569	7,090
1987–88	41,145	54,882	23,945	40,006	53,362	25,523	1,139	1,520	7,550
1988–89	44,922	56,896	24,034	43,792	55,465	25,698	1,130	1,431	6,845
1989–90	48,885	58,398	24,239	47,713	56,999	25,982	1,172	1,400	6,494
1990–91	53,127	60,296	24,860	51,872	58,872	26,424	1,255	1,424	7,210
1991–92	57,342	62,874	25,172	56,041	61,448	26,883	1,301	1,427	6,729
1992–93	60,671	64,629	25,595	59,235	63,099	27,064	1,436	1,529	7,901
1993–94	64,041	65,963	25,980	62,466	64,341	27,322	1,575	1,622	8,810
1994–95[2]	67,504	67,504	26,331	65,996	65,996	27,639	1,508	1,508	8,573

[1] Dollars adjusted by the Higher Education Price Index.
[2] Preliminary data.

NOTE.—Because of rounding, details may not add to totals.

SOURCE: U.S. Department of Education, National Center for Education Statistics, Higher Education General Information Survey (HEGIS), "Financial Statistics of Institutions of Higher Education" and "Fall Enrollment in Colleges and Universities" surveys; and Integrated Postsecondary Education Data System (IPEDS), "Fall Enrollment" and "Finance" surveys. (This table was prepared July 1997.)

Table 337.—Current-fund expenditures of institutions of higher education, by purpose: 1980–81 to 1994–95

Purpose	1980–81	1985–86	1988–89	1989–90	1990–91	1991–92	1992–93	1993–94	1994–95[1]
1	2	3	4	5	6	7	8	9	10
In thousands									
Total current-fund expenditures	**$64,052,938**	**$97,535,742**	**$123,867,184**	**$134,655,571**	**$146,087,836**	**$156,189,161**	**$165,241,040**	**$173,350,617**	**$182,968,610**
Educational and general expenditures	50,073,805	76,127,965	96,803,377	105,585,076	114,139,901	121,567,157	128,977,968	136,024,350	144,158,002
Instruction	20,733,166	31,032,099	38,812,690	42,145,987	45,496,117	47,997,196	50,340,914	52,775,599	55,719,707
Research	5,657,719	8,437,367	11,432,170	12,505,961	13,444,040	14,261,554	15,291,309	16,117,610	17,109,541
Public service	2,057,770	3,119,533	4,227,323	4,689,758	5,076,177	5,489,298	5,935,095	6,242,414	6,691,485
Academic support	4,273,286	6,667,392	8,904,279	9,437,644	10,050,773	10,577,018	11,072,970	11,677,911	12,278,691
Libraries	1,759,784	2,551,331	3,009,870	3,254,239	3,343,892	3,595,834	3,684,852	3,908,412	4,165,761
Student services	2,908,998	4,562,938	5,780,837	6,388,148	7,025,482	7,509,094	8,165,079	8,562,783	9,059,994
Institutional support	5,772,515	9,350,786	11,529,119	12,674,031	13,726,484	14,475,023	15,249,898	15,926,239	16,844,827
Operation and maintenance of plant	5,350,310	7,605,226	8,739,895	9,458,262	10,062,581	10,346,580	10,783,727	11,368,496	11,745,905
Scholarships and fellowships	2,504,525	4,160,174	5,918,666	6,655,544	7,551,184	9,060,000	10,148,373	11,238,010	12,285,328
From unrestricted funds	1,080,614	2,285,116	3,282,698	3,853,904	4,445,106	5,205,797	5,949,037	6,644,717	7,329,384
From restricted funds[2]	1,423,911	1,875,059	2,635,969	2,801,640	3,106,078	3,854,203	4,199,337	4,593,293	4,955,944
Mandatory transfers	815,516	1,192,449	1,458,397	1,629,742	1,707,063	1,851,393	1,990,603	2,115,288	2,422,524
Auxiliary enterprises	7,288,089	10,528,303	12,280,063	13,203,984	14,272,247	14,966,100	15,561,508	16,429,341	17,204,917
Mandatory transfers	508,377	617,171	774,752	836,852	936,876	1,003,299	1,109,549	1,158,848	1,228,278
Hospitals	5,433,111	8,692,113	11,824,782	12,679,286	14,325,865	16,104,313	17,049,672	17,509,603	18,071,359
Mandatory transfers	57,963	128,833	240,278	222,192	274,452	333,714	308,059	344,665	346,072
Independent operations (FFRDC)[3]	1,257,934	2,187,361	2,958,962	3,187,224	3,349,824	3,551,592	3,651,891	3,387,323	3,534,332
Mandatory transfers	643	3,432	6,987	5,812	5,645	3,396	2,271	2,354	2,373
Percentage distribution									
Total current-fund expenditures	**100.0**	**100.0**	**100.0**	**100.0**	**100.0**	**100.0**	**100.0**	**100.0**	**100.0**
Educational and general expenditures	78.2	78.1	78.2	78.4	78.1	77.8	78.1	78.5	78.8
Instruction	32.4	31.8	31.3	31.3	31.1	30.7	30.5	30.4	30.5
Research	8.8	8.7	9.2	9.3	9.2	9.1	9.3	9.3	9.4
Public service	3.2	3.2	3.4	3.5	3.5	3.5	3.6	3.6	3.7
Academic support	6.7	6.8	7.2	7.0	6.9	6.8	6.7	6.7	6.7
Libraries	2.7	2.6	2.4	2.4	2.3	2.3	2.2	2.3	2.3
Student services	4.5	4.7	4.7	4.7	4.8	4.8	4.9	4.9	5.0
Institutional support	9.0	9.6	9.3	9.4	9.4	9.3	9.2	9.2	9.2
Operation and maintenance of plant	8.4	7.8	7.1	7.0	6.9	6.6	6.5	6.6	6.4
Scholarships and fellowships	3.9	4.3	4.8	4.9	5.2	5.8	6.1	6.5	6.7
From unrestricted funds	1.7	2.3	2.7	2.9	3.0	3.3	3.6	3.8	4.0
From restricted funds[2]	2.2	1.9	2.1	2.1	2.1	2.5	2.5	2.6	2.7
Mandatory transfers	1.3	1.2	1.2	1.2	1.2	1.2	1.2	1.2	1.3
Auxiliary enterprises	11.4	10.8	9.9	9.8	9.8	9.6	9.4	9.5	9.4
Mandatory transfers	0.8	0.6	0.6	0.6	0.6	0.6	0.7	0.7	0.7
Hospitals	8.5	8.9	9.5	9.4	9.8	10.3	10.3	10.1	9.9
Mandatory transfers	0.1	0.1	0.2	0.2	0.2	0.2	0.2	0.2	0.2
Independent operations (FFRDC)[3]	2.0	2.2	2.4	2.4	2.3	2.3	2.2	2.0	1.9
Mandatory transfers	(4)	(4)	(4)	(4)	(4)	(4)	(4)	(4)	(4)

[1] Preliminary data.
[2] Excludes Pell Grants.
[3] Generally includes only those expenditures associated with major federally funded research and development centers (FFRDC).
[4] Less than 0.05 percent.

NOTE.—Because of rounding, details may not add to totals.

SOURCE: U.S. Department of Education, National Center for Education Statistics, Higher Education General Information Survey (HEGIS), "Financial Statistics of Institutions of Higher Education" surveys; and Integrated Postsecondary Education Data System (IPEDS), "Finance" surveys. (This table was prepared May 1997.)

Table 338.—Current-fund expenditures of public institutions of higher education, by purpose: 1980–81 to 1994–95

Purpose	1980–81	1985–86	1988–89	1989–90	1990–91	1991–92	1992–93	1993–94	1994–95[1]
1	2	3	4	5	6	7	8	9	10
	In thousands								
Total current-fund expenditures	$42,279,806	$63,193,853	$78,945,618	$85,770,530	$92,961,093	$98,847,180	$104,570,101	$109,309,541	$115,464,975
Educational and general expenditures	34,173,013	50,872,962	63,444,908	69,163,958	74,395,428	78,554,534	83,210,979	87,139,226	92,173,768
Instruction	14,849,822	21,880,782	26,893,691	29,257,209	31,371,394	32,828,420	34,260,177	35,688,497	37,599,194
Research	3,813,350	5,705,144	7,796,952	8,542,235	9,364,213	9,948,580	10,604,973	11,180,363	11,829,665
Public service	1,718,924	2,515,734	3,351,950	3,688,664	3,990,232	4,285,501	4,563,397	4,741,719	5,034,445
Academic support	3,029,284	4,693,543	5,941,906	6,535,076	6,933,847	7,274,159	7,613,244	8,035,556	8,463,236
Libraries	1,187,116	1,685,052	1,956,497	2,102,672	2,167,161	2,284,520	2,329,625	2,449,109	2,614,609
Student services	1,950,566	2,921,758	3,678,419	4,021,328	4,398,365	4,690,921	5,173,239	5,315,370	5,614,011
Institutional support	3,563,194	5,667,144	6,876,360	7,490,137	8,030,642	8,423,156	9,049,589	9,328,236	9,929,007
Operation and maintenance of plant	3,681,921	5,177,254	5,913,267	6,333,582	6,655,605	6,790,215	7,076,805	7,433,185	7,668,919
Scholarships and fellowships	1,064,864	1,575,909	2,150,350	2,386,493	2,688,532	3,255,660	3,727,838	4,222,923	4,662,023
From unrestricted funds	367,476	696,973	944,001	1,099,425	1,270,158	1,523,721	1,745,339	1,934,617	2,149,036
From restricted funds[2]	697,388	878,935	1,206,349	1,287,068	1,418,374	1,731,939	1,982,498	2,288,306	2,512,988
Mandatory transfers	501,087	735,695	842,012	909,234	962,598	1,057,923	1,141,717	1,193,379	1,373,267
Auxiliary enterprises	4,658,140	6,830,235	7,744,725	8,282,332	9,049,935	9,634,131	10,024,352	10,637,783	11,235,143
Mandatory transfers	344,043	410,777	512,413	551,331	623,146	655,301	758,644	784,115	835,993
Hospitals	3,377,972	5,358,699	7,533,912	8,113,989	9,315,902	10,432,773	11,100,602	11,317,674	11,801,589
Mandatory transfers	26,613	75,569	159,507	156,029	195,961	224,095	223,241	242,216	262,343
Independent operations (FFRDC)[3]	70,681	131,956	222,072	210,252	199,827	225,742	234,168	214,858	254,474
Mandatory transfers	322	846	1,787	2,276	1,201	510	462	474	465
	Percentage distribution								
Total current-fund expenditures	100.0	100.0	100.0	100.0	100.0	100.0	100.0	100.0	100.0
Educational and general expenditures	80.8	80.5	80.4	80.6	80.0	79.5	79.6	79.7	79.8
Instruction	35.1	34.6	34.1	34.1	33.7	33.2	32.8	32.6	32.6
Research	9.0	9.0	9.9	10.0	10.1	10.1	10.1	10.2	10.2
Public service	4.1	4.0	4.2	4.3	4.3	4.3	4.4	4.3	4.4
Academic support	7.2	7.4	7.5	7.6	7.5	7.4	7.3	7.4	7.3
Libraries	2.8	2.7	2.5	2.5	2.3	2.3	2.2	2.2	2.3
Student services	4.6	4.6	4.7	4.7	4.7	4.7	4.9	4.9	4.9
Institutional support	8.4	9.0	8.7	8.7	8.6	8.5	8.7	8.5	8.6
Operation and maintenance of plant	8.7	8.2	7.5	7.4	7.2	6.9	6.8	6.8	6.6
Scholarships and fellowships	2.5	2.5	2.7	2.8	2.9	3.3	3.6	3.9	4.0
From unrestricted funds	0.9	1.1	1.2	1.3	1.4	1.5	1.7	1.8	1.9
From restricted funds[2]	1.6	1.4	1.5	1.5	1.5	1.8	1.9	2.1	2.2
Mandatory transfers	1.2	1.2	1.1	1.1	1.0	1.1	1.1	1.1	1.2
Auxiliary enterprises	11.0	10.8	9.8	9.7	9.7	9.7	9.6	9.7	9.7
Mandatory transfers	0.8	0.7	0.6	0.6	0.7	0.7	0.7	0.7	0.7
Hospitals	8.0	8.5	9.5	9.5	10.0	10.6	10.6	10.4	10.2
Mandatory transfers	0.1	0.1	0.2	0.2	0.2	0.2	0.2	0.2	0.2
Independent operations (FFRDC)[3]	0.2	0.2	0.3	0.2	0.2	0.2	0.2	0.2	0.2
Mandatory transfers	([4])	([4])	([4])	([4])	([4])	([4])	([4])	([4])	([4])

[1] Preliminary data.
[2] Excludes Pell Grants.
[3] Generally includes only those expenditures associated with major federally funded research and development centers (FFRDC).
[4] Less than 0.05 percent.

NOTE.—Because of rounding, details may not add to totals.

SOURCE: U.S. Department of Education, National Center for Education Statistics, Higher Education General Information Survey (HEGIS), "Financial Statistics of Institutions of Higher Education" surveys; and Integrated Postsecondary Education Data System (IPEDS), "Finance" surveys. (This table was prepared May 1997.)

HIGHER EDUCATION: EXPENDITURES 357

Table 339.—Current-fund expenditures of private institutions of higher education, by purpose: 1980–81 to 1994–95

Purpose	1980–81	1985–86	1988–89	1989–90	1990–91	1991–92	1992–93	1993–94	1994–95[1]
1	2	3	4	5	6	7	8	9	10
	\multicolumn{9}{c}{In thousands}								
Total current-fund expenditures	$21,773,132	$34,341,889	$44,921,566	$48,885,041	$53,126,743	$57,341,982	$60,670,938	$64,041,076	$67,503,635
Educational and general expenditures	15,900,792	25,255,003	33,358,469	36,421,118	39,744,472	43,012,623	45,766,989	48,885,124	51,984,234
Instruction	5,883,343	9,151,318	11,918,999	12,888,779	14,124,723	15,168,776	16,080,736	17,087,102	18,120,513
Research	1,844,369	2,732,222	3,635,218	3,963,726	4,079,827	4,312,973	4,686,336	4,937,247	5,279,876
Public service	338,845	603,799	875,373	1,001,094	1,085,945	1,203,797	1,371,697	1,500,695	1,657,040
Academic support	1,244,002	1,973,849	2,962,374	2,902,568	3,116,927	3,302,859	3,459,726	3,642,355	3,815,455
Libraries	572,667	866,279	1,053,372	1,151,567	1,176,731	1,311,314	1,355,227	1,459,304	1,551,152
Student services	958,432	1,641,180	2,102,418	2,366,819	2,627,117	2,818,174	2,991,840	3,247,414	3,445,983
Institutional support	2,209,321	3,683,642	4,652,759	5,183,893	5,695,842	6,051,868	6,200,308	6,598,004	6,915,821
Operation and maintenance of plant	1,668,389	2,427,972	2,826,628	3,124,680	3,406,975	3,556,365	3,706,923	3,935,311	4,076,986
Scholarships and fellowships	1,439,661	2,584,266	3,768,316	4,269,051	4,862,651	5,804,340	6,420,536	7,015,087	7,623,304
From unrestricted funds	713,138	1,588,143	2,338,697	2,754,479	3,174,947	3,682,076	4,203,697	4,710,100	5,180,348
From restricted funds[2]	726,523	996,123	1,429,619	1,514,572	1,687,704	2,122,264	2,216,838	2,304,987	2,442,957
Mandatory transfers	314,429	456,754	616,385	720,508	744,465	793,471	848,886	921,908	1,049,256
Auxiliary enterprises	2,629,948	3,698,067	4,535,337	4,921,653	5,222,312	5,331,969	5,537,156	5,791,558	5,969,773
Mandatory transfers	164,335	206,394	262,339	285,521	313,730	347,999	350,905	374,733	392,285
Hospitals	2,055,139	3,333,414	4,290,869	4,565,297	5,009,963	5,671,540	5,949,070	6,191,929	6,269,769
Mandatory transfers	31,349	53,264	80,771	66,164	78,491	109,619	84,818	102,449	83,729
Independent operations (FFRDC)[3]	1,187,253	2,055,405	2,736,890	2,976,973	3,149,996	3,325,850	3,417,723	3,172,465	3,279,859
Mandatory transfers	321	2,586	5,200	3,535	4,444	2,886	1,808	1,880	1,908
	\multicolumn{9}{c}{Percentage distribution}								
Total current-fund expenditures	100.0	100.0	100.0	100.0	100.0	100.0	100.0	100.0	100.0
Educational and general expenditures	73.0	73.5	74.3	74.5	74.8	75.0	75.4	76.3	77.0
Instruction	27.0	26.6	26.5	26.4	26.6	26.5	26.5	26.7	26.8
Research	8.5	8.0	8.1	8.1	7.7	7.5	7.7	7.7	7.8
Public service	1.6	1.8	1.9	2.0	2.0	2.1	2.3	2.3	2.5
Academic support	5.7	5.7	6.6	5.9	5.9	5.8	5.7	5.7	5.7
Libraries	2.6	2.5	2.3	2.4	2.2	2.3	2.2	2.3	2.3
Student services	4.4	4.8	4.7	4.8	4.9	4.9	4.9	5.1	5.1
Institutional support	10.1	10.7	10.4	10.6	10.7	10.6	10.2	10.3	10.2
Operation and maintenance of plant	7.7	7.1	6.3	6.4	6.4	6.2	6.1	6.1	6.0
Scholarships and fellowships	6.6	7.5	8.4	8.7	9.2	10.1	10.6	11.0	11.3
From unrestricted funds	3.3	4.6	5.2	5.6	6.0	6.4	6.9	7.4	7.7
From restricted funds[2]	3.3	2.9	3.2	3.1	3.2	3.7	3.7	3.6	3.6
Mandatory transfers	1.4	1.3	1.4	1.5	1.4	1.4	1.4	1.4	1.6
Auxiliary enterprises	12.1	10.8	10.1	10.1	9.8	9.3	9.1	9.0	8.8
Mandatory transfers	0.8	0.6	0.6	0.6	0.6	0.6	0.6	0.6	0.6
Hospitals	9.4	9.7	9.6	9.3	9.4	9.9	9.8	9.7	9.3
Mandatory transfers	0.1	0.2	0.2	0.1	0.1	0.2	0.1	0.2	0.1
Independent operations (FFRDC)[3]	5.5	6.0	6.1	6.1	5.9	5.8	5.6	5.0	4.9
Mandatory transfers	([4])	([4])	([4])	([4])	([4])	([4])	([4])	([4])	([4])

[1] Preliminary data.
[2] Excludes Pell Grants.
[3] Generally includes only those expenditures associated with major federally funded research and development centers (FFRDC).
[4] Less than 0.05 percent.

NOTE.—Because of rounding, details may not add to totals.

SOURCE: U.S. Department of Education, National Center for Education Statistics, Higher Education General Information Survey (HEGIS), "Financial Statistics of Institutions of Higher Education" surveys; and Integrated Postsecondary Education Data System (IPEDS), "Finance" surveys. (This table was prepared May 1997.)

Table 340.—Voluntary support for institutions of higher education, by source and purpose of support: 1949–50 to 1994–95

[In millions]

Source and purpose of support	1949–50	1959–60	1965–66	1970–71	1975–76	1980–81	1985–86	1989–90	1990–91	1991–92	1992–93	1993–94	1994–95
1	2	3	4	5	6	7	8	9	10	11	12	13	14
Total voluntary support[1]	$240	$815	$1,440	$1,860	$2,410	$4,230	$7,400	$9,800	$10,200	$10,700	$11,200	$12,350	$12,750
Sources													
Alumni	60	191	310	458	588	1,049	1,825	2,540	2,680	2,840	2,980	3,410	3,600
Nonalumni individuals	60	194	350	495	569	1,007	1,781	2,230	2,310	2,500	2,530	2,800	2,940
Corporations	28	130	230	259	379	778	1,702	2,170	2,230	2,260	2,400	2,510	2,560
Foundations	60	163	357	418	549	922	1,363	1,920	2,030	2,090	2,200	2,540	2,460
Religious organizations	16	80	108	104	130	140	211	240	240	240	250	240	250
Other	16	57	85	126	195	334	518	700	710	770	840	850	940
Purpose													
Current operations	101	385	675	1,050	1,480	2,590	4,022	5,440	5,830	6,100	6,300	6,710	7,230
Capital purposes	139	430	765	810	930	1,640	3,378	4,360	4,370	4,600	4,900	5,640	5,520
Voluntary support as a percent of total expenditures[2]	9.0	11.4	9.2	6.8	5.5	6.0	6.9	6.5	6.2	6.2	6.1	6.4	6.3

[1] Data are based on sample surveys of institutions of higher education.
[2] Total expenditures include current-fund expenditures and additions to plant value.

SOURCE: Council for Aid to Education, Research Report, "Contributions to Colleges Drop for First Time Since 1975"; and "Voluntary Support of Education," various years. (This table was prepared June 1996.)

Table 341.—Educational and general expenditures of public universities, by purpose: 1976–77 to 1994–95

Year	Educational and general expenditures									
	Total	Instruction	Administration[1]	Student services	Research	Libraries	Public service	Operation and maintenance of plant	Scholarships and fellowships	Mandatory transfers
1	2	3	4	5	6	7	8	9	10	11
	Expenditures, in thousands of current dollars									
1976–77	$9,413,626	$3,670,554	$1,222,410	$346,906	$1,727,807	$331,614	$763,809	$857,677	$377,749	$115,099
1977–78	10,220,191	4,009,870	1,344,538	388,262	1,896,578	343,198	803,309	938,952	389,682	105,803
1978–79	11,284,191	4,408,025	1,478,568	419,231	2,136,135	363,875	920,726	1,046,740	396,356	114,533
1979–80	12,540,072	4,860,411	1,572,523	473,460	2,444,471	463,642	1,012,376	1,148,942	439,461	124,786
1980–81	13,951,029	5,374,271	1,795,504	525,891	2,743,145	451,978	1,158,512	1,270,339	492,225	139,164
1981–82	15,077,263	5,852,958	1,974,219	566,366	2,903,178	488,939	1,223,417	1,412,557	525,498	130,131
1982–83	16,089,168	6,247,358	2,107,933	604,657	3,086,846	528,470	1,300,353	1,512,947	562,903	137,702
1983–84	17,234,711	6,646,501	2,263,565	643,614	3,295,053	577,136	1,385,191	1,627,702	624,642	171,306
1984–85	18,960,810	7,257,618	2,598,784	701,451	3,682,755	609,365	1,519,324	1,745,825	677,533	168,155
1985–86	20,716,657	7,807,522	2,882,006	762,324	4,076,258	669,253	1,664,917	1,831,618	780,080	242,679
1986–87	22,023,387	8,368,187	3,088,348	819,829	4,399,405	677,531	1,725,613	1,829,880	847,328	267,266
1987–88	23,848,427	8,902,624	3,311,806	889,528	4,911,929	762,858	1,857,008	1,934,489	949,438	328,746
1988–89	26,138,665	9,623,797	3,638,424	975,801	5,476,936	813,888	2,096,267	2,069,744	1,096,447	347,362
1989–90	28,077,757	10,269,007	3,867,818	1,028,463	5,997,942	860,981	2,263,623	2,200,111	1,199,643	390,170
1990–91	30,367,325	11,012,373	4,157,677	1,103,058	6,599,209	906,506	2,479,956	2,305,115	1,367,754	435,676
1991–92	31,565,791	11,373,749	4,198,990	1,161,633	6,937,360	946,098	2,609,520	2,323,220	1,556,868	458,354
1992–93	32,836,061	11,708,500	4,317,605	1,211,143	7,330,922	959,306	2,714,785	2,365,942	1,734,530	493,328
1993–94	34,318,548	12,115,695	4,578,770	1,273,008	7,676,832	1,006,301	2,784,869	2,459,895	1,909,173	514,006
1994–95[2]	36,255,063	12,837,030	4,814,366	1,348,617	8,082,388	1,096,566	2,943,284	2,526,104	2,057,116	549,593
	Percentage distribution									
1976–77	100.0	39.0	13.0	3.7	18.4	3.5	8.1	9.1	4.0	1.2
1977–78	100.0	39.2	13.2	3.8	18.6	3.4	7.9	9.2	3.8	1.0
1978–79	100.0	39.1	13.1	3.7	18.9	3.2	8.2	9.3	3.5	1.0
1979–80	100.0	38.8	12.5	3.8	19.5	3.7	8.1	9.2	3.5	1.0
1980–81	100.0	38.5	12.9	3.8	19.7	3.2	8.3	9.1	3.5	1.0
1981–82	100.0	38.8	13.1	3.8	19.3	3.2	8.1	9.4	3.5	0.9
1982–83	100.0	38.8	13.1	3.8	19.2	3.3	8.1	9.4	3.5	0.9
1983–84	100.0	38.6	13.1	3.7	19.1	3.3	8.0	9.4	3.6	1.0
1984–85	100.0	38.3	13.7	3.7	19.4	3.2	8.0	9.2	3.6	0.9
1985–86	100.0	37.7	13.9	3.7	19.7	3.2	8.0	8.8	3.8	1.2
1986–87	100.0	38.0	14.0	3.7	20.0	3.1	7.8	8.3	3.8	1.2
1987–88	100.0	37.3	13.9	3.7	20.6	3.2	7.8	8.1	4.0	1.4
1988–89	100.0	36.8	13.9	3.7	21.0	3.1	8.0	7.9	4.2	1.3
1989–90	100.0	36.6	13.8	3.7	21.4	3.1	8.1	7.8	4.3	1.4
1990–91	100.0	36.3	13.7	3.6	21.7	3.0	8.2	7.6	4.5	1.4
1991–92	100.0	36.0	13.3	3.7	22.0	3.0	8.3	7.4	4.9	1.5
1992–93	100.0	35.7	13.1	3.7	22.3	2.9	8.3	7.2	5.3	1.5
1993–94	100.0	35.3	13.3	3.7	22.4	2.9	8.1	7.2	5.6	1.5
1994–95[2]	100.0	35.4	13.3	3.7	22.3	3.0	8.1	7.0	5.7	1.5
	Expenditure per full-time-equivalent student in constant 1994–95 dollars									
1976–77	$14,668	$5,719	$1,905	$541	$2,692	$517	$1,190	$1,336	$589	$179
1977–78	14,798	5,806	1,947	562	2,746	497	1,163	1,360	564	153
1978–79	15,336	5,991	2,009	570	2,903	495	1,251	1,423	539	156
1979–80	15,173	5,881	1,903	573	2,958	561	1,225	1,390	532	151
1980–81	14,938	5,754	1,922	563	2,937	484	1,240	1,360	527	149
1981–82	14,726	5,717	1,928	553	2,836	478	1,195	1,380	513	127
1982–83	14,693	5,705	1,925	552	2,819	483	1,188	1,382	514	126
1983–84	15,049	5,804	1,977	562	2,877	504	1,210	1,421	545	150
1984–85	15,758	6,032	2,160	583	3,061	506	1,263	1,451	563	140
1985–86	16,371	6,170	2,277	602	3,221	529	1,316	1,447	616	192
1986–87	16,657	6,329	2,336	620	3,327	512	1,305	1,384	641	202
1987–88	17,110	6,387	2,376	638	3,524	547	1,332	1,388	681	236
1988–89	17,433	6,418	2,427	651	3,653	543	1,398	1,380	731	232
1989–90	17,388	6,359	2,395	637	3,714	533	1,402	1,362	743	242
1990–91	17,700	6,419	2,423	643	3,847	528	1,446	1,344	797	254
1991–92	17,611	6,346	2,343	648	3,870	528	1,456	1,296	869	256
1992–93	18,041	6,433	2,372	665	4,028	527	1,492	1,300	953	271
1993–94	18,399	6,496	2,455	683	4,116	540	1,493	1,319	1,024	276
1994–95[2]	18,950	6,710	2,516	705	4,225	573	1,538	1,320	1,075	287

[1] Includes institutional and academic support less libraries.
[2] Preliminary data.

NOTE.—Data in this table may differ slightly from data appearing in other tables. Data for 1976–77 through 1985–86 include only institutions which provided both enrollment and finance data. The Higher Education Price Index was used to convert the per student figures to constant dollars. Because of rounding, details may not add to totals.

SOURCE: U.S. Department of Education, National Center for Education Statistics, Higher Education General Information Survey (HEGIS), "Financial Statistics of Institutions of Higher Education" surveys; Integrated Postsecondary Education Data System (IPEDS), "Finance" surveys; and Research Associates of Washington, unpublished data. (This table was prepared July 1997.)

HIGHER EDUCATION: EXPENDITURES 359

Table 342.—Educational and general expenditures of public 4-year colleges,[1] by purpose: 1976–77 to 1994–95

Year	Educational and general expenditures									
	Total	Instruction	Administration[2]	Student services	Research	Libraries	Public service	Operation and maintenance of plant	Scholarships and fellowships	Mandatory transfers
1	2	3	4	5	6	7	8	9	10	11
	Expenditures, in thousands of current dollars									
1976–77	$8,682,538	$4,027,051	$1,445,651	$500,832	$607,235	$340,002	$250,152	$1,001,848	$338,432	$171,335
1977–78	9,568,977	4,423,487	1,598,092	572,193	677,414	369,408	274,314	1,118,393	332,899	202,777
1978–79	10,455,134	4,770,598	1,789,534	651,541	786,072	395,299	301,387	1,214,996	337,588	208,119
1979–80	11,750,398	5,271,621	2,029,327	733,557	937,874	448,190	359,467	1,375,308	383,036	212,019
1980–81	13,139,618	5,890,759	2,258,987	807,249	1,043,614	511,817	407,816	1,563,514	412,972	242,890
1981–82	14,321,586	6,537,888	2,518,182	834,225	1,086,146	536,080	440,736	1,738,210	403,069	227,050
1982–83	15,286,145	6,980,269	2,660,360	904,745	1,150,011	559,353	469,841	1,857,151	450,067	254,349
1983–84	16,538,128	7,464,035	3,013,666	1,041,488	1,246,289	622,879	513,732	1,873,628	473,503	288,908
1984–85	18,333,578	8,211,171	3,370,676	1,140,312	1,420,844	669,518	603,018	2,137,225	489,188	291,626
1985–86	19,860,947	8,945,373	3,658,627	1,235,418	1,618,737	712,112	648,178	2,118,522	569,841	354,139
1986–87	21,490,078	9,608,239	4,019,850	1,318,666	1,846,712	695,692	766,865	2,226,599	660,940	346,515
1987–88	23,124,455	10,310,532	4,261,440	1,434,726	2,053,638	774,274	864,347	2,340,495	711,704	373,299
1988–89	24,639,653	10,991,086	4,496,286	1,504,869	2,305,152	813,801	941,434	2,429,103	754,412	403,508
1989–90	27,210,634	12,079,093	5,076,792	1,648,526	2,525,080	888,526	1,088,113	2,607,385	871,944	425,175
1990–91	28,903,790	12,818,677	5,374,417	1,800,723	2,745,613	888,162	1,145,892	2,728,949	963,436	437,921
1991–92	30,720,827	13,270,992	5,805,724	1,868,329	2,986,474	945,097	1,310,700	2,782,200	1,248,220	503,091
1992–93	33,119,294	13,906,211	6,416,859	2,164,309	3,246,542	979,635	1,447,684	2,960,373	1,457,901	539,779
1993–94	34,477,869	14,519,321	6,477,847	2,135,560	3,473,971	1,018,304	1,525,406	3,084,509	1,685,785	557,166
1994–95[3]	36,659,833	15,321,392	6,909,606	2,236,127	3,717,964	1,084,945	1,647,855	3,175,330	1,884,283	682,332
	Percentage distribution									
1976–77	100.0	46.4	16.7	5.8	7.0	3.9	2.9	11.5	3.9	2.0
1977–78	100.0	46.2	16.7	6.0	7.1	3.9	2.9	11.7	3.5	2.1
1978–79	100.0	45.6	17.1	6.2	7.5	3.8	2.9	11.6	3.2	2.0
1979–80	100.0	44.9	17.3	6.2	8.0	3.8	3.1	11.7	3.3	1.8
1980–81	100.0	44.8	17.2	6.1	7.9	3.9	3.1	11.9	3.1	1.8
1981–82	100.0	45.7	17.6	5.8	7.6	3.7	3.1	12.1	2.8	1.6
1982–83	100.0	45.7	17.4	5.9	7.5	3.7	3.1	12.1	2.9	1.7
1983–84	100.0	45.1	18.2	6.3	7.5	3.8	3.1	11.3	2.9	1.7
1984–85	100.0	44.8	18.4	6.2	7.7	3.7	3.3	11.7	2.7	1.6
1985–86	100.0	45.0	18.4	6.2	8.2	3.6	3.3	10.7	2.9	1.8
1986–87	100.0	44.7	18.7	6.1	8.6	3.2	3.6	10.4	3.1	1.6
1987–88	100.0	44.6	18.4	6.2	8.9	3.3	3.7	10.1	3.1	1.6
1988–89	100.0	44.6	18.2	6.1	9.4	3.3	3.8	9.9	3.1	1.6
1989–90	100.0	44.4	18.7	6.1	9.3	3.3	4.0	9.6	3.2	1.6
1990–91	100.0	44.3	18.6	6.2	9.5	3.1	4.0	9.4	3.3	1.5
1991–92	100.0	43.2	18.9	6.1	9.7	3.1	4.3	9.1	4.1	1.6
1992–93	100.0	42.0	19.4	6.5	9.8	3.0	4.4	8.9	4.4	1.6
1993–94	100.0	42.1	18.8	6.2	10.1	3.0	4.4	8.9	4.9	1.6
1994–95[3]	100.0	41.8	18.8	6.1	10.1	3.0	4.5	8.7	5.1	1.9
	Expenditure per full-time-equivalent student in constant 1994–95 dollars									
1976–77	$10,696	$4,961	$1,781	$617	$748	$419	$308	$1,234	$417	$211
1977–78	10,787	4,987	1,802	645	764	416	309	1,261	375	229
1978–79	11,133	5,080	1,905	694	837	421	321	1,294	359	222
1979–80	11,257	5,050	1,944	703	898	429	344	1,318	367	203
1980–81	11,144	4,996	1,916	685	885	434	346	1,326	350	206
1981–82	11,088	5,062	1,950	646	841	415	341	1,346	312	176
1982–83	10,820	4,941	1,883	640	814	396	333	1,315	319	180
1983–84	10,933	4,934	1,992	689	824	412	340	1,239	313	191
1984–85	11,542	5,169	2,122	718	894	421	380	1,345	308	184
1985–86	11,921	5,369	2,196	742	972	427	389	1,272	342	213
1986–87	11,917	5,328	2,229	731	1,024	386	425	1,235	367	192
1987–88	12,159	5,421	2,241	754	1,080	407	454	1,231	374	196
1988–89	11,972	5,340	2,185	731	1,120	395	457	1,180	367	196
1989–90	12,080	5,363	2,254	732	1,121	394	483	1,158	387	189
1990–91	11,746	5,209	2,184	732	1,116	361	466	1,109	392	178
1991–92	11,901	5,141	2,249	724	1,157	366	508	1,078	484	195
1992–93	12,339	5,181	2,391	806	1,210	365	539	1,103	543	201
1993–94	12,483	5,257	2,345	773	1,258	369	552	1,117	610	202
1994–95[3]	12,925	5,402	2,436	788	1,311	383	581	1,120	664	241

[1] Excludes universities. See preceding table.
[2] Includes institutional and academic support less libraries.
[3] Preliminary data.

NOTE.—Data in this table may differ slightly from data appearing in other tables. Data for 1976–77 through 1985–86 include only institutions which provided both enrollment and finance data. The Higher Education Price Index was used to convert the per student figures to constant dollars. Because of rounding, details may not add to totals.

SOURCE: U.S. Department of Education, National Center for Education Statistics, Higher Education General Information Survey (HEGIS), "Financial Statistics of Institutions of Higher Education" surveys; Integrated Postsecondary Education Data System (IPEDS), "Finance" surveys; and Research Associates of Washington, unpublished data. (This table was prepared July 1997.)

360 HIGHER EDUCATION: EXPENDITURES

Table 343.—Educational and general expenditures of public 2-year colleges, by purpose: 1976–77 to 1994–95

Year	Educational and general expenditures									
	Total	Instruction	Administration[1]	Student services	Research	Libraries	Public service	Operation and maintenance of plant	Scholarships and fellowships	Mandatory transfers
1	2	3	4	5	6	7	8	9	10	11
Expenditures, in thousands of current dollars										
1976–77	$4,875,998	$2,490,274	$882,813	$409,217	$15,698	$171,409	$97,635	$547,515	$142,827	$118,610
1977–78	5,336,153	2,700,489	1,035,206	437,060	9,333	188,201	112,944	605,464	117,996	129,458
1978–79	5,734,611	2,877,651	1,119,840	482,323	21,289	193,703	110,918	650,447	127,633	150,807
1979–80	6,334,777	3,185,815	1,204,082	547,457	26,288	202,583	141,000	743,014	147,865	136,672
1980–81	7,063,474	3,575,743	1,347,020	615,869	26,591	222,391	152,597	844,781	159,474	119,008
1981–82	7,757,435	3,947,065	1,473,733	684,650	15,632	262,697	147,385	952,691	160,109	113,473
1982–83	8,292,446	4,218,388	1,620,644	741,179	18,090	248,682	123,722	1,016,267	175,069	130,403
1983–84	8,820,575	4,481,854	1,748,535	775,084	18,189	263,485	150,109	1,076,371	178,500	128,448
1984–85	9,560,507	4,806,050	1,929,968	841,101	15,591	278,363	193,903	1,156,074	207,975	131,482
1985–86	10,252,955	5,116,884	2,122,060	920,299	10,136	295,691	202,440	1,220,646	225,979	138,820
1986–87	10,845,969	5,382,631	2,363,275	1,020,496	12,508	246,131	235,115	1,252,152	243,402	90,258
1987–88	11,666,586	5,741,049	2,479,661	1,157,858	11,358	316,278	264,809	1,326,748	280,247	88,578
1988–89	12,666,590	6,278,809	2,727,058	1,197,748	14,864	328,809	314,250	1,414,420	299,491	91,142
1989–90	13,875,566	6,909,109	2,977,932	1,344,339	19,213	353,165	336,927	1,526,086	314,906	93,889
1990–91	15,124,313	7,540,344	3,265,233	1,494,583	19,390	372,492	364,384	1,621,542	357,343	89,001
1991–92	16,267,915	8,183,678	3,408,080	1,660,958	24,747	393,325	365,281	1,684,796	450,572	96,477
1992–93	17,255,624	8,645,466	3,598,745	1,797,787	27,510	390,684	400,927	1,750,489	535,406	108,610
1993–94	18,342,808	9,053,480	3,858,066	1,906,802	29,560	424,504	431,444	1,888,780	627,964	122,207
1994–95[2]	19,258,872	9,440,773	4,053,662	2,029,268	29,313	433,098	443,306	1,967,485	720,624	141,342
Percentage distribution										
1976–77	100.0	51.1	18.1	8.4	0.3	3.5	2.0	11.2	2.9	2.4
1977–78	100.0	50.6	19.4	8.2	0.2	3.5	2.1	11.3	2.2	2.4
1978–79	100.0	50.2	19.5	8.4	0.4	3.4	1.9	11.3	2.2	2.6
1979–80	100.0	50.3	19.0	8.6	0.4	3.2	2.2	11.7	2.3	2.2
1980–81	100.0	50.6	19.1	8.7	0.4	3.1	2.2	12.0	2.3	1.7
1981–82	100.0	50.9	19.0	8.8	0.2	3.4	1.9	12.3	2.1	1.5
1982–83	100.0	50.9	19.5	8.9	0.2	3.0	1.5	12.3	2.1	1.6
1983–84	100.0	50.8	19.8	8.8	0.2	3.0	1.7	12.2	2.0	1.5
1984–85	100.0	50.3	20.2	8.8	0.2	2.9	2.0	12.1	2.2	1.4
1985–86	100.0	49.9	20.7	9.0	0.1	2.9	2.0	11.9	2.2	1.4
1986–87	100.0	49.6	21.8	9.4	0.1	2.3	2.2	11.5	2.2	0.8
1987–88	100.0	49.2	21.3	9.9	0.1	2.7	2.3	11.4	2.4	0.8
1988–89	100.0	49.6	21.5	9.5	0.1	2.6	2.5	11.2	2.4	0.7
1989–90	100.0	49.8	21.5	9.7	0.1	2.5	2.4	11.0	2.3	0.7
1990–91	100.0	49.9	21.6	9.9	0.1	2.5	2.4	10.7	2.4	0.6
1991–92	100.0	50.3	20.9	10.2	0.2	2.4	2.2	10.4	2.8	0.6
1992–93	100.0	50.1	20.9	10.4	0.2	2.3	2.3	10.1	3.1	0.6
1993–94	100.0	49.4	21.0	10.4	0.2	2.3	2.4	10.3	3.4	0.7
1994–95[2]	100.0	49.0	21.0	10.5	0.2	2.2	2.3	10.2	3.7	0.7
Expenditure per full-time-equivalent student in constant 1994–95 dollars										
1976–77	$5,765	$2,944	$1,044	$484	$19	$203	$115	$647	$169	$140
1977–78	5,795	2,933	1,124	475	10	204	123	658	128	141
1978–79	5,993	3,007	1,170	504	22	202	116	680	133	158
1979–80	5,892	2,963	1,120	509	24	188	131	691	138	127
1980–81	5,647	2,859	1,077	492	21	178	122	675	127	95
1981–82	5,641	2,870	1,072	498	11	191	107	693	116	83
1982–83	5,337	2,715	1,043	477	12	160	80	654	113	84
1983–84	5,412	2,750	1,073	476	11	162	92	660	110	79
1984–85	5,932	2,982	1,197	522	10	173	120	717	129	82
1985–86	6,107	3,048	1,264	548	6	176	121	727	135	83
1986–87	6,206	3,080	1,352	584	7	141	135	716	139	52
1987–88	6,123	3,013	1,301	608	6	166	139	696	147	46
1988–89	6,192	3,069	1,333	585	7	161	154	691	146	45
1989–90	6,024	2,999	1,293	584	8	153	146	663	137	41
1990–91	6,091	3,037	1,315	602	8	150	147	653	144	36
1991–92	5,816	2,926	1,218	594	9	141	131	602	161	34
1992–93	5,903	2,958	1,231	615	9	134	137	599	183	37
1993–94	6,202	3,061	1,304	645	10	144	146	639	212	41
1994–95[2]	6,346	3,111	1,336	669	10	143	146	648	237	47

[1] Includes institutional and academic support less libraries.
[2] Preliminary data.

NOTE.—Data in this table may differ slightly from data appearing in other tables. Data for 1976–77 through 1985–86 include only institutions which provided both enrollment and finance data. The Higher Education Price Index was used to convert the per student figures to constant dollars. Because of rounding, details may not add to totals.

SOURCE: U.S. Department of Education, National Center for Education Statistics, Higher Education General Information Survey (HEGIS), "Financial Statistics of Institutions of Higher Education" surveys; Integrated Postsecondary Education Data System (IPEDS), "Finance" surveys; and Research Associates of Washington, unpublished data. (This table was prepared July 1997.)

Table 344.—Educational and general expenditures of private (nonprofit) universities, by purpose: 1976–77 to 1994–95

Year	Educational and general expenditures									
	Total	Instruction	Administration[1]	Student services	Research	Libraries	Public service	Operation and maintenance of plant	Scholarships and fellowships	Mandatory transfers
1	2	3	4	5	6	7	8	9	10	11
	Expenditures, in thousands of current dollars									
1976–77	$4,694,593	$1,784,975	$621,733	$156,457	$988,656	$195,146	$105,011	$411,340	$380,821	$50,453
1977–78	5,120,125	1,943,031	683,988	172,261	1,063,906	215,068	108,201	447,743	427,907	58,019
1978–79	5,675,608	2,120,800	796,751	195,238	1,175,657	221,676	119,082	510,819	460,200	75,385
1979–80	6,408,288	2,426,312	908,580	215,646	1,315,469	236,184	148,028	568,806	507,257	82,006
1980–81	7,249,102	2,763,320	1,009,957	254,872	1,436,318	267,142	149,946	660,152	596,241	111,154
1981–82	7,951,934	3,105,731	1,100,088	289,398	1,505,340	294,523	160,496	752,673	650,285	93,401
1982–83	8,198,167	3,227,925	1,214,617	304,617	1,464,809	295,709	169,382	754,480	670,390	96,238
1983–84	9,491,967	3,660,650	1,445,910	350,096	1,683,020	360,238	187,615	859,065	833,108	112,266
1984–85	10,431,950	3,965,165	1,556,854	393,526	1,892,570	366,356	253,010	930,229	931,027	143,212
1985–86	11,407,571	4,308,432	1,711,155	438,678	2,108,731	397,745	271,271	981,131	1,040,677	149,751
1986–87	13,013,183	4,998,565	1,977,175	502,291	2,399,976	397,460	332,223	1,006,334	1,218,002	181,159
1987–88	13,876,586	5,209,101	2,107,206	529,261	2,597,435	484,987	340,475	1,073,880	1,328,775	205,464
1988–89	15,123,369	5,743,104	2,293,256	565,903	2,786,178	510,820	377,820	1,135,273	1,472,675	238,340
1989–90	16,363,342	6,188,447	2,411,051	607,623	3,048,455	555,752	414,916	1,231,028	1,615,096	290,974
1990–91	17,827,649	6,827,220	2,633,605	669,160	3,170,083	567,800	456,615	1,383,686	1,833,124	286,357
1991–92	19,307,030	7,367,629	2,852,739	711,041	3,364,795	624,416	484,871	1,453,365	2,142,466	305,707
1992–93	20,435,319	7,844,576	2,874,208	719,657	3,648,010	644,005	547,159	1,495,825	2,322,331	339,547
1993–94	21,702,227	8,347,500	3,009,434	772,524	3,831,668	693,223	603,658	1,578,840	2,481,742	383,638
1994–95[2]	23,059,247	8,838,806	3,158,159	820,099	4,121,604	752,683	612,464	1,632,166	2,680,828	442,438
	Percentage distribution									
1976–77	100.0	38.0	13.2	3.3	21.1	4.2	2.2	8.8	8.1	1.1
1977–78	100.0	37.9	13.4	3.4	20.8	4.2	2.1	8.7	8.4	1.1
1978–79	100.0	37.4	14.0	3.4	20.7	3.9	2.1	9.0	8.1	1.3
1979–80	100.0	37.9	14.2	3.4	20.5	3.7	2.3	8.9	7.9	1.3
1980–81	100.0	38.1	13.9	3.5	19.8	3.7	2.1	9.1	8.2	1.5
1981–82	100.0	39.1	13.8	3.6	18.9	3.7	2.0	9.5	8.2	1.2
1982–83	100.0	39.4	14.8	3.7	17.9	3.6	2.1	9.2	8.2	1.2
1983–84	100.0	38.6	15.2	3.7	17.7	3.8	2.0	9.1	8.8	1.2
1984–85	100.0	38.0	14.9	3.8	18.1	3.5	2.4	8.9	8.9	1.4
1985–86	100.0	37.8	15.0	3.8	18.5	3.5	2.4	8.6	9.1	1.3
1986–87	100.0	38.4	15.2	3.9	18.4	3.1	2.6	7.7	9.4	1.4
1987–88	100.0	37.5	15.2	3.8	18.7	3.5	2.5	7.7	9.6	1.5
1988–89	100.0	38.0	15.2	3.7	18.4	3.4	2.5	7.5	9.7	1.6
1989–90	100.0	37.8	14.7	3.7	18.6	3.4	2.5	7.5	9.9	1.8
1990–91	100.0	38.3	14.8	3.8	17.8	3.2	2.6	7.8	10.3	1.6
1991–92	100.0	38.2	14.8	3.7	17.4	3.2	2.5	7.5	11.1	1.6
1992–93	100.0	38.4	14.1	3.5	17.9	3.2	2.7	7.3	11.4	1.7
1993–94	100.0	38.5	13.9	3.6	17.7	3.2	2.8	7.3	11.4	1.8
1994–95[2]	100.0	38.3	13.7	3.6	17.9	3.3	2.7	7.1	11.6	1.9
	Expenditure per full-time-equivalent student in constant 1994–95 dollars									
1976–77	$22,706	$8,633	$3,007	$757	$4,782	$944	$508	$1,990	$1,842	$244
1977–78	22,438	8,515	2,997	755	4,662	943	474	1,962	1,875	254
1978–79	22,722	8,491	3,190	782	4,707	887	477	2,045	1,842	302
1979–80	23,051	8,728	3,268	776	4,732	850	532	2,046	1,825	295
1980–81	23,333	8,894	3,251	820	4,623	860	483	2,125	1,919	358
1981–82	23,242	9,077	3,215	846	4,400	861	469	2,200	1,901	273
1982–83	23,430	9,225	3,471	871	4,186	845	484	2,156	1,916	275
1983–84	25,147	9,698	3,831	928	4,459	954	497	2,276	2,207	297
1984–85	26,171	9,947	3,906	987	4,748	919	635	2,334	2,336	359
1985–86	27,160	10,258	4,074	1,044	5,021	947	646	2,336	2,478	357
1986–87	29,645	11,387	4,504	1,144	5,467	905	757	2,293	2,775	413
1987–88	30,023	11,270	4,559	1,145	5,620	1,049	737	2,323	2,875	445
1988–89	30,679	11,650	4,652	1,148	5,652	1,036	766	2,303	2,987	483
1989–90	31,020	11,731	4,571	1,152	5,779	1,054	787	2,334	3,062	552
1990–91	31,975	12,245	4,724	1,200	5,686	1,018	819	2,482	3,288	514
1991–92	32,924	12,564	4,865	1,213	5,738	1,065	827	2,478	3,654	521
1992–93	33,844	12,992	4,760	1,192	6,042	1,067	906	2,477	3,846	562
1993–94	34,820	13,393	4,828	1,239	6,148	1,112	969	2,533	3,982	616
1994–95[2]	35,745	13,701	4,896	1,271	6,389	1,167	949	2,530	4,156	686

[1] Includes institutional and academic support less libraries.
[2] Preliminary data.

NOTE.—Data in this table may differ slightly from data appearing in other tables. Data for 1976–77 through 1985–86 include only institutions which provided both enrollment and finance data. The Higher Education Price Index was used to convert the per student figures to constant dollars. Because of rounding, details may not add to totals.

SOURCE: U.S. Department of Education, National Center for Education Statistics, Higher Education General Information Survey (HEGIS), "Financial Statistics of Institutions of Higher Education" surveys; Integrated Postsecondary Education Data System (IPEDS), "Finance" surveys; and Research Associates of Washington, unpublished data. (This table was prepared May 1997.)

Table 345.—Educational and general expenditures of private (nonprofit) 4-year colleges,[1] by purpose: 1976–77 to 1994–95

Year	Educational and general expenditures									
	Total	Instruction	Administration[2]	Student services	Research	Libraries	Public service	Operation and maintenance of plant	Scholarships and fellowships	Mandatory transfers
1	2	3	4	5	6	7	8	9	10	11
	Expenditures, in thousands of current dollars									
1976–77	$5,139,939	$1,919,574	$1,047,932	$381,428	$259,530	$200,844	$123,717	$574,910	$511,907	$120,097
1977–78	5,637,836	2,114,043	1,160,141	428,265	271,637	221,807	123,214	638,330	550,372	130,026
1978–79	6,263,692	2,328,418	1,299,063	483,031	328,042	240,098	136,861	704,180	598,487	145,513
1979–80	7,063,953	2,589,908	1,466,556	549,639	374,520	259,969	153,056	807,943	694,791	167,570
1980–81	8,061,774	2,907,255	1,703,307	639,795	407,622	289,944	186,399	930,075	811,636	185,741
1981–82	9,061,667	3,271,255	1,938,727	727,382	419,283	322,702	228,368	1,036,118	913,999	203,834
1982–83	9,805,459	3,552,387	2,124,446	804,943	437,286	356,768	236,142	1,092,836	983,887	216,764
1983–84	10,845,622	3,900,082	2,347,962	890,707	480,459	388,153	259,932	1,184,788	1,149,813	243,726
1984–85	11,835,351	4,213,485	2,564,844	980,416	539,322	416,539	289,124	1,251,490	1,312,673	267,459
1985–86	12,855,040	4,507,505	2,790,504	1,067,717	623,050	446,766	328,827	1,317,062	1,481,954	291,654
1986–87	14,232,003	4,886,585	3,249,910	1,184,395	693,450	410,013	384,594	1,386,729	1,717,948	318,379
1987–88	15,405,503	5,248,764	3,403,279	1,293,302	776,022	485,517	456,111	1,462,345	1,966,124	313,939
1988–89	16,980,645	5,738,789	3,766,237	1,437,829	848,094	530,032	495,683	1,596,786	2,198,328	368,866
1989–90	18,717,398	6,276,102	4,097,242	1,599,951	909,862	578,520	581,730	1,712,000	2,547,600	414,432
1990–91	20,374,743	6,809,318	4,533,043	1,770,071	901,357	589,052	624,663	1,809,977	2,898,547	438,715
1991–92	22,121,380	7,320,211	4,723,853	1,919,662	942,407	659,416	714,728	1,896,424	3,478,153	466,528
1992–93	23,609,625	7,743,656	4,887,700	2,044,830	1,036,676	680,457	821,381	1,995,164	3,900,807	498,954
1993–94	25,262,199	8,169,221	5,199,838	2,205,411	1,104,561	733,711	893,500	2,112,367	4,316,138	527,451
1994–95[3]	26,999,085	8,714,437	5,438,969	2,350,717	1,157,255	764,903	1,040,959	2,195,045	4,739,447	597,354
	Percentage distribution									
1976–77	100.0	37.3	20.4	7.4	5.0	3.9	2.4	11.2	10.0	2.3
1977–78	100.0	37.5	20.6	7.6	4.8	3.9	2.2	11.3	9.8	2.3
1978–79	100.0	37.2	20.7	7.7	5.2	3.8	2.2	11.2	9.6	2.3
1979–80	100.0	36.7	20.8	7.8	5.3	3.7	2.2	11.4	9.8	2.4
1980–81	100.0	36.1	21.1	7.9	5.1	3.6	2.3	11.5	10.1	2.3
1981–82	100.0	36.1	21.4	8.0	4.6	3.6	2.5	11.4	10.1	2.2
1982–83	100.0	36.2	21.7	8.2	4.5	3.6	2.4	11.1	10.0	2.2
1983–84	100.0	36.0	21.6	8.2	4.4	3.6	2.4	10.9	10.6	2.2
1984–85	100.0	35.6	21.7	8.3	4.6	3.5	2.4	10.6	11.1	2.3
1985–86	100.0	35.1	21.7	8.3	4.8	3.5	2.6	10.2	11.5	2.3
1986–87	100.0	34.3	22.8	8.3	4.9	2.9	2.7	9.7	12.1	2.2
1987–88	100.0	34.1	22.1	8.4	5.0	3.2	3.0	9.5	12.8	2.0
1988–89	100.0	33.8	22.2	8.5	5.0	3.1	2.9	9.4	12.9	2.2
1989–90	100.0	33.5	21.9	8.5	4.9	3.1	3.1	9.1	13.6	2.2
1990–91	100.0	33.4	22.2	8.7	4.4	2.9	3.1	8.9	14.2	2.2
1991–92	100.0	33.1	21.4	8.7	4.3	3.0	3.2	8.6	15.7	2.1
1992–93	100.0	32.8	20.7	8.7	4.4	2.9	3.5	8.5	16.5	2.1
1993–94	100.0	32.3	20.6	8.7	4.4	2.9	3.5	8.4	17.1	2.1
1994–95[3]	100.0	32.3	20.1	8.7	4.3	2.8	3.9	8.1	17.6	2.2
	Expenditure per full-time-equivalent student in constant 1994–95 dollars									
1976–77	$11,194	$4,181	$2,282	$831	$565	$437	$269	$1,252	$1,115	$262
1977–78	11,144	4,179	2,293	846	537	438	244	1,262	1,088	257
1978–79	11,281	4,193	2,340	870	591	432	246	1,268	1,078	262
1979–80	11,473	4,206	2,382	893	608	422	249	1,312	1,128	272
1980–81	11,527	4,157	2,435	915	583	415	267	1,330	1,160	266
1981–82	11,674	4,214	2,498	937	540	416	294	1,335	1,177	263
1982–83	11,918	4,318	2,582	978	532	434	287	1,328	1,196	263
1983–84	12,320	4,430	2,667	1,012	546	441	295	1,346	1,306	277
1984–85	12,765	4,545	2,766	1,057	582	449	312	1,350	1,416	288
1985–86	13,205	4,630	2,866	1,097	640	459	338	1,353	1,522	300
1986–87	13,985	4,802	3,194	1,164	681	403	378	1,363	1,688	313
1987–88	14,334	4,884	3,167	1,203	722	452	424	1,361	1,829	292
1988–89	14,477	4,893	3,211	1,226	723	452	423	1,361	1,874	314
1989–90	14,720	4,936	3,222	1,258	716	455	458	1,346	2,004	326
1990–91	14,964	5,001	3,329	1,300	662	433	459	1,329	2,129	322
1991–92	15,347	5,078	3,277	1,332	654	457	496	1,316	2,413	324
1992–93	15,494	5,082	3,208	1,342	680	447	539	1,309	2,560	327
1993–94	15,859	5,129	3,264	1,385	693	461	561	1,326	2,710	331
1994–95[3]	16,304	5,262	3,284	1,420	699	462	629	1,326	2,862	361

[1] Excludes universities. See preceding table.
[2] Includes institutional and academic support less libraries.
[3] Preliminary data.

NOTE.—Data in this table may differ slightly from data appearing in other tables. Data for 1976–77 through 1985–86 include only institutions which provided both enrollment and finance data. The Higher Education Price Index was used to convert the per student figures to constant dollars. Because of rounding, details may not add to totals.

SOURCE: U.S. Department of Education, National Center for Education Statistics, Higher Education General Information Survey (HEGIS), "Financial Statistics of Institutions of Higher Education" surveys; Integrated Postsecondary Education Data System (IPEDS), "Finance" surveys; and Research Associates of Washington, unpublished data. (This table was prepared June 1997.)

Table 346.—Current-fund expenditures of public institutions of higher education, by state: 1980–81 to 1994–95

[In thousands of dollars]

State	1980–81	1985–86	1988–89	1989–90	1990–91	1991–92	1992–93	1993–94	1994–95[1]	Percent change, 1989–90 to 1994–95
1	2	3	4	5	6	7	8	9	10	11
United States	$42,279,806	$63,193,853	$78,945,618	$85,770,530	$92,961,093	$98,847,180	$104,570,101	$109,309,541	$115,464,975	34.6
Alabama	839,366	1,324,774	1,669,401	1,831,657	2,054,798	2,189,029	2,428,620	2,510,081	2,648,077	44.6
Alaska	158,700	224,042	240,913	268,057	289,606	306,218	322,620	336,405	336,584	25.6
Arizona	691,481	1,017,203	1,317,954	1,446,388	1,586,891	1,620,019	1,621,716	1,754,682	1,854,180	28.2
Arkansas	340,621	528,831	692,970	751,336	797,291	878,783	976,735	1,002,908	1,070,668	42.5
California	5,775,482	8,515,440	10,182,106	11,230,941	12,023,304	12,910,152	13,537,367	13,244,130	13,899,338	23.8
Colorado	738,363	1,057,558	1,331,091	1,374,188	1,452,137	1,546,642	1,670,921	1,760,679	1,862,438	35.5
Connecticut	367,850	562,696	774,179	811,282	886,846	957,627	981,286	1,026,593	1,134,014	39.8
Delaware	158,332	229,377	314,003	342,119	367,012	396,947	416,699	442,488	469,085	37.1
District of Columbia[2]	71,791	80,764	93,710	99,120	97,556	99,535	98,826	97,072	99,351	([3])
Florida	1,170,305	1,782,180	2,443,879	2,766,267	2,896,046	2,988,794	3,179,353	3,408,957	3,549,470	28.3
Georgia	754,060	1,255,964	1,622,707	1,769,744	1,929,993	2,015,816	2,227,608	2,453,100	2,728,682	54.2
Hawaii	222,718	312,248	379,799	424,473	498,307	575,337	602,346	613,356	653,303	53.9
Idaho	166,844	238,438	289,148	314,398	353,561	391,441	409,167	445,463	473,733	50.7
Illinois	1,780,403	2,571,409	3,015,395	3,310,763	3,528,967	3,644,740	3,877,243	4,053,858	4,293,437	29.7
Indiana	1,064,395	1,602,203	2,005,740	2,186,604	2,391,173	2,643,997	2,671,055	2,858,990	2,967,184	35.7
Iowa	767,590	1,092,542	1,491,442	1,617,626	1,734,476	1,776,217	1,899,159	1,981,068	2,051,631	26.8
Kansas	579,857	848,602	1,028,578	1,131,558	1,190,573	1,262,215	1,329,587	1,429,200	1,495,926	32.2
Kentucky	673,775	898,718	1,143,612	1,236,680	1,400,529	1,514,985	1,516,017	1,577,584	1,663,738	34.5
Louisiana	716,702	1,039,177	1,172,325	1,286,648	1,439,415	1,541,126	1,800,188	1,835,151	1,909,675	48.4
Maine	153,658	216,737	315,700	344,435	355,074	362,905	375,090	387,991	391,269	13.6
Maryland	795,100	1,064,430	1,389,900	1,522,145	1,684,341	1,674,918	1,829,812	1,940,403	1,997,636	31.2
Massachusetts	553,019	980,585	1,306,814	1,357,588	1,435,063	1,474,589	1,605,121	1,496,856	1,557,225	14.7
Michigan	2,053,795	2,946,336	3,745,488	4,076,519	4,416,914	4,741,682	4,925,759	5,095,422	5,395,757	32.4
Minnesota	876,632	1,324,691	1,809,757	1,802,133	2,012,225	2,219,016	2,286,336	2,459,437	2,624,464	45.6
Mississippi	539,222	706,380	864,611	922,574	978,366	1,012,544	1,102,806	1,200,196	1,358,795	47.3
Missouri	687,643	999,869	1,237,603	1,349,451	1,453,608	1,501,166	1,582,746	1,694,484	1,836,878	36.1
Montana	121,894	182,102	198,475	218,231	254,175	320,876	337,189	350,943	376,618	72.6
Nebraska	378,928	537,858	676,527	762,480	848,778	916,814	968,407	1,004,263	1,076,670	41.2
Nevada	111,347	180,107	240,711	281,018	330,592	363,306	377,786	415,785	447,901	59.4
New Hampshire	134,391	183,959	247,686	259,157	281,542	307,217	335,575	360,833	371,554	43.4
New Jersey	903,169	1,406,490	1,968,859	2,165,562	2,309,968	2,489,088	2,630,533	2,809,931	2,982,535	37.7
New Mexico	325,960	456,600	751,405	828,157	896,299	1,010,859	1,069,497	1,142,903	1,278,741	54.4
New York	2,519,104	3,802,602	4,732,811	5,058,750	5,605,621	5,681,964	6,096,863	6,481,594	6,922,118	36.8
North Carolina	1,128,383	1,799,173	2,238,155	2,420,825	2,581,156	2,770,977	3,002,915	3,192,215	3,406,215	40.7
North Dakota	192,046	288,214	319,583	357,832	367,959	408,219	419,268	432,190	456,730	27.6
Ohio	1,784,754	2,718,408	3,494,228	3,726,135	4,084,840	4,359,943	4,389,408	4,640,316	4,907,686	31.7
Oklahoma	583,174	844,829	887,293	973,213	1,057,248	1,158,696	1,177,061	1,214,084	1,263,002	29.8
Oregon	642,411	880,696	1,116,966	1,219,341	1,329,794	1,484,621	1,560,699	1,623,771	1,756,424	44.0
Pennsylvania	1,544,586	2,392,145	3,147,180	3,390,869	3,602,685	3,904,332	4,004,062	4,240,094	4,506,833	32.9
Rhode Island	158,365	213,253	270,411	287,194	292,199	303,606	330,038	331,359	344,457	19.9
South Carolina	617,963	951,848	1,179,216	1,324,647	1,475,074	1,595,552	1,702,419	1,766,671	1,817,631	37.2
South Dakota	124,103	149,092	169,308	184,153	197,853	217,756	240,061	259,120	252,443	37.1
Tennessee	665,885	1,081,052	1,411,226	1,519,680	1,585,614	1,621,202	1,776,066	1,911,953	2,042,171	34.4
Texas	2,736,276	4,375,082	5,166,389	5,604,164	5,959,584	6,370,847	6,982,016	7,414,174	7,817,433	39.5
Utah	405,314	669,714	835,250	914,771	993,625	1,116,845	1,174,239	1,260,797	1,354,017	48.0
Vermont	122,708	188,112	241,314	260,371	274,746	294,045	298,626	306,100	316,455	21.5
Virginia	1,143,755	1,825,156	2,431,539	2,682,902	2,812,109	2,939,683	3,072,851	3,301,020	3,414,167	27.3
Washington	993,171	1,399,780	1,779,855	1,922,673	2,157,074	2,278,549	2,486,455	2,639,504	2,807,168	46.0
West Virginia	317,482	376,293	451,503	493,825	548,802	582,453	609,447	650,642	674,664	36.6
Wisconsin	1,208,396	1,754,395	2,159,069	2,307,325	2,469,260	2,596,853	2,726,350	2,872,001	2,941,034	27.5
Wyoming	126,082	203,307	212,813	227,131	240,216	265,048	260,592	271,396	294,334	29.6
U.S. Service Schools[2]	592,454	912,393	739,019	805,430	1,150,209	1,241,392	1,267,497	1,309,330	1,313,438	63.1
Outlying areas	268,310	451,370	494,087	543,925	516,958	574,988	654,292	662,130	727,524	33.8
American Samoa	1,609	1,092	2,642	2,879	3,187	3,228	3,356	3,416	3,483	21.0
Federated States of Micronesia	—	—	1,789	1,842	3,777	3,765	3,294	3,520	5,056	174.5
Guam	16,100	31,310	38,488	48,954	57,645	67,220	71,917	66,913	81,148	65.8
Marshall Islands	—	—	—	—	—	3,588	1,298	1,527	1,237	—
Northern Marianas	—	1,350	950	1,003	2,798	3,194	2,505	3,214	12,366	1,133.5
Palau	—	—	3,513	3,870	3,837	3,687	4,485	3,476	3,667	–5.2
Puerto Rico	237,319	394,046	424,125	460,897	385,511	434,032	536,917	546,575	586,910	27.3
Trust Territory of the Pacific	1,447	5,992	—	—	—	—	—	—	—	—
Virgin Islands	11,835	17,580	22,580	24,480	60,202	56,274	30,520	33,489	33,656	37.5

[1] Preliminary data.
[2] Data revised from previously published figures.
[3] Change of less than .05 percent.
—Data not reported or not applicable.

NOTE.—Because of rounding, details may not add to totals.

SOURCE: U.S. Department of Education, National Center for Education Statistics, Higher Education General Information Survey (HEGIS), "Financial Statistics of Institutions of Higher Education" surveys; and Integrated Postsecondary Education Data System (IPEDS), "Finance" surveys. (This table was prepared July 1997.)

Table 347.—Educational and general expenditures of public institutions of higher education, by state: 1980–81 to 1994–95

[In thousands of dollars]

State	1980–81	1985–86	1988–89	1989–90	1990–91	1991–92	1992–93	1993–94	1994–95[1]	Percent change, 1989–90 to 1994–95
1	2	3	4	5	6	7	8	9	10	11
United States	$34,173,013	$50,872,962	$63,444,908	$69,163,958	$74,395,428	$78,554,534	$83,210,979	$87,139,226	$92,173,768	33.3
Alabama	611,409	979,770	1,223,329	1,305,463	1,415,440	1,456,605	1,580,484	1,710,955	1,834,533	40.5
Alaska	150,421	210,894	227,331	253,392	273,577	288,999	304,137	316,779	316,397	24.9
Arizona	554,120	862,816	1,122,890	1,236,696	1,364,060	1,407,819	1,409,122	1,523,655	1,653,840	33.7
Arkansas	266,522	415,800	530,691	573,923	633,194	604,885	676,378	707,166	746,129	30.0
California	4,847,879	7,049,635	8,352,924	9,238,960	9,615,356	10,341,888	11,000,665	10,734,842	11,280,758	22.1
Colorado	561,552	809,621	1,052,644	1,167,864	1,258,356	1,363,615	1,452,957	1,529,290	1,604,656	37.4
Connecticut	281,581	439,397	605,228	622,298	673,182	736,202	731,570	771,954	883,759	42.0
Delaware	135,164	202,331	277,543	303,220	325,838	349,369	366,801	387,810	413,692	36.4
District of Columbia[2]	71,245	79,922	92,548	97,447	96,411	98,973	97,586	95,824	98,041	0.6
Florida	1,071,754	1,638,227	2,250,014	2,546,201	2,657,553	2,710,041	2,904,932	3,101,072	3,234,938	27.0
Georgia	628,939	1,046,341	1,364,338	1,482,499	1,617,020	1,665,009	1,834,141	2,037,534	2,277,756	53.6
Hawaii	202,154	282,058	341,609	384,535	454,880	526,269	546,473	556,567	590,389	53.5
Idaho	141,296	202,736	244,969	268,690	303,224	334,762	346,932	375,289	395,733	47.3
Illinois	1,487,123	2,152,955	2,556,337	2,812,244	2,979,768	3,068,891	3,245,802	3,397,183	3,583,012	27.4
Indiana	771,564	1,183,098	1,534,653	1,671,111	1,842,610	1,935,566	2,014,834	2,105,645	2,196,013	31.4
Iowa	512,205	736,894	987,522	1,077,810	1,172,328	1,184,382	1,267,646	1,354,777	1,392,753	29.2
Kansas	461,979	660,995	801,774	884,775	928,772	994,560	1,059,683	1,134,392	1,196,211	35.2
Kentucky	527,235	737,101	916,498	992,403	1,112,190	1,208,448	1,212,211	1,254,859	1,321,523	33.2
Louisiana	557,825	810,479	908,303	1,005,278	1,135,955	1,215,771	1,275,446	1,339,408	1,449,305	44.2
Maine	127,983	183,349	271,016	297,782	308,699	316,116	324,515	338,776	343,665	15.4
Maryland	604,419	911,562	1,186,989	1,299,110	1,443,669	1,428,072	1,564,259	1,673,163	1,737,204	33.7
Massachusetts	441,068	779,341	1,051,636	1,076,241	1,122,629	1,165,598	1,295,720	1,339,199	1,400,824	30.2
Michigan	1,610,016	2,278,217	2,850,114	3,079,227	3,325,625	3,556,178	3,727,115	3,885,984	4,042,460	31.3
Minnesota	667,119	1,023,324	1,330,114	1,420,124	1,563,054	1,728,356	1,775,640	1,937,650	2,068,280	45.6
Mississippi	409,942	542,022	674,608	719,821	756,492	772,618	842,603	919,354	1,049,356	45.8
Missouri	553,793	802,936	995,472	1,083,473	1,155,531	1,184,338	1,260,304	1,339,527	1,456,516	34.4
Montana	99,990	148,099	161,543	179,510	210,813	262,480	279,323	303,495	322,880	79.9
Nebraska	286,122	397,523	489,501	543,341	600,224	639,475	672,427	706,454	727,977	34.0
Nevada	105,177	163,714	220,033	257,526	301,487	332,246	353,875	379,154	402,097	56.1
New Hampshire	104,285	143,191	195,404	206,207	229,360	252,021	275,138	295,687	304,474	47.7
New Jersey	735,097	1,140,310	1,607,786	1,765,002	1,875,481	2,002,975	2,103,355	2,237,339	2,363,439	33.9
New Mexico	278,960	393,151	561,308	626,386	671,206	724,157	769,646	806,673	899,545	43.6
New York	2,249,821	3,238,773	3,961,073	4,252,153	4,680,376	4,768,772	5,113,506	5,398,182	5,799,931	36.4
North Carolina	971,928	1,527,535	1,941,331	2,101,016	2,227,060	2,406,405	2,600,325	2,671,176	2,849,310	35.6
North Dakota	151,372	228,609	248,612	282,247	292,978	328,738	336,361	344,187	361,276	28.0
Ohio	1,327,483	2,019,351	2,630,782	2,799,829	3,046,603	3,214,612	3,185,955	3,362,837	3,616,901	29.2
Oklahoma	404,178	594,561	688,953	762,034	830,929	906,908	930,102	953,027	996,963	30.8
Oregon	497,593	672,175	839,670	911,812	996,887	1,086,673	1,142,781	1,194,805	1,281,381	40.5
Pennsylvania	1,231,502	1,814,384	2,385,349	2,596,987	2,737,817	2,963,168	3,087,186	3,280,879	3,439,340	32.4
Rhode Island	138,965	185,215	236,790	250,604	251,992	260,123	284,957	285,742	297,597	18.8
South Carolina	481,737	741,740	903,484	1,012,928	1,065,867	1,100,035	1,172,246	1,244,696	1,310,645	29.4
South Dakota	108,632	130,825	149,457	162,001	173,396	192,001	211,716	229,080	222,811	37.5
Tennessee	515,578	865,946	1,107,583	1,194,378	1,231,619	1,228,340	1,352,125	1,478,085	1,581,929	32.4
Texas	2,278,337	3,674,109	4,394,333	4,816,945	5,105,246	5,439,843	5,961,535	6,352,088	6,643,734	37.9
Utah	320,278	503,557	602,628	656,772	730,496	826,170	856,933	921,052	991,014	50.9
Vermont	101,539	157,266	204,586	222,470	238,512	258,150	263,475	271,261	279,882	25.8
Virginia	796,616	1,241,534	1,647,075	1,807,829	1,852,416	1,892,627	1,991,591	2,124,635	2,248,402	24.4
Washington	837,281	1,143,285	1,450,608	1,564,535	1,757,053	1,837,095	2,007,044	2,074,451	2,211,588	41.4
West Virginia	228,755	310,142	371,151	411,950	459,984	494,733	522,173	560,380	579,349	40.6
Wisconsin	998,862	1,438,918	1,824,067	1,931,561	2,057,786	2,158,188	2,266,312	2,394,285	2,437,859	26.2
Wyoming	111,170	171,335	181,985	194,506	204,028	225,238	222,188	231,190	254,469	30.8
U.S. Service Schools[2]	555,447	805,892	688,724	752,844	1,030,399	1,110,028	1,130,748	1,169,731	1,181,234	56.9
Outlying areas	253,820	421,500	457,344	501,855	498,958	555,054	607,730	637,164	700,528	39.6
American Samoa	1,609	1,092	2,642	2,879	3,187	3,228	3,356	3,416	3,483	21.0
Federated States of Micronesia	—	—	1,474	1,351	3,302	3,286	2,898	3,096	4,589	239.8
Guam	15,582	29,916	36,276	47,380	55,641	64,772	68,550	63,515	77,783	64.2
Marshall Islands	—	—	—	—	—	3,093	1,220	1,454	1,183	—
Northern Marianas	—	1,328	794	766	2,472	2,803	2,230	2,838	12,305	1,506.0
Palau	—	—	2,993	3,297	3,277	3,172	3,808	2,847	3,156	-4.3
Puerto Rico	224,988	367,523	392,814	426,754	378,352	427,021	497,590	529,255	567,140	32.9
Trust Territory of the Pacific	1,320	5,992	—	—	—	—	—	—	—	—
Virgin Islands	10,322	15,649	20,351	19,427	52,726	47,679	28,078	30,743	30,889	59.0

[1] Preliminary data.
[2] Data revised from previously published figures.
—Data not reported or not applicable.

NOTE.—Because of rounding, details may not add to totals.

SOURCE: U.S. Department of Education, National Center for Education Statistics, Higher Education General Information Survey (HEGIS), "Financial Statistics of Institutions of Higher Education" surveys; and Integrated Postsecondary Education Data System (IPEDS), "Finance" surveys. (This table was prepared July 1997.)

Table 348.—Current-fund expenditures and educational and general expenditures of private institutions of higher education, by state: 1985–86 to 1994–95

[In thousands of dollars]

State	Current-fund expenditures					Educational and general expenditures				
	1985–86	1991–92	1992–93	1993–94	1994–95[1]	1985–86	1991–92	1992–93	1993–94	1994–95[1]
1	2	3	4	5	6	7	8	9	10	11
United States	$34,341,889	$57,341,982	$60,670,938	$64,041,076	$67,503,635	$25,255,003	$43,012,623	$45,766,989	$48,885,124	$51,984,234
Alabama	186,596	263,052	286,584	299,982	310,329	164,093	229,670	252,259	265,046	273,268
Alaska	10,171	18,454	22,693	23,199	19,825	9,106	15,851	18,687	18,140	15,631
Arizona	52,887	94,564	106,478	118,954	130,973	48,600	86,087	100,150	111,414	122,573
Arkansas	70,755	118,373	124,091	130,253	140,758	56,492	98,442	103,347	108,969	118,323
California	3,644,031	5,957,016	6,171,590	6,419,322	6,841,207	2,275,958	3,836,270	4,051,762	4,366,131	4,630,342
Colorado	160,193	305,244	306,824	327,275	342,407	142,218	269,386	279,956	297,087	312,444
Connecticut	836,949	1,376,756	1,437,827	1,527,283	1,608,612	733,144	1,224,643	1,280,969	1,363,083	1,441,297
Delaware	29,569	27,215	29,293	31,836	32,995	26,501	24,741	26,575	29,040	30,471
District of Columbia	1,307,377	2,100,279	2,307,943	2,386,469	2,533,943	803,566	1,246,366	1,311,616	1,375,811	1,463,154
Florida	723,270	1,386,602	1,510,855	1,561,498	1,672,960	553,391	1,089,712	1,193,708	1,234,246	1,329,012
Georgia	696,734	1,371,887	1,514,055	1,683,308	1,798,384	429,639	886,314	981,355	1,122,545	1,188,358
Hawaii	32,553	41,760	91,016	95,803	100,596	25,323	36,124	72,609	76,909	81,060
Idaho	49,768	82,255	87,532	95,011	98,011	37,736	65,018	72,006	82,923	86,269
Illinois	2,729,672	4,366,966	4,694,688	4,778,173	5,103,123	1,495,654	2,544,490	2,698,324	2,936,263	3,186,567
Indiana	530,163	889,004	941,404	1,000,966	1,073,603	426,813	736,784	782,734	831,223	895,861
Iowa	353,753	595,007	634,046	676,124	701,059	292,291	501,547	534,230	573,136	595,823
Kansas	105,193	147,336	157,139	171,402	180,052	87,719	126,939	136,036	149,127	157,710
Kentucky	194,873	304,780	315,147	330,341	348,262	159,293	255,870	263,722	275,986	291,198
Louisiana	353,433	629,158	673,080	739,368	624,279	221,928	397,191	439,834	459,780	523,694
Maine	133,778	210,328	223,573	238,196	250,032	106,912	176,530	187,523	199,895	210,350
Maryland	896,251	1,550,526	1,622,871	1,729,558	1,797,362	562,773	1,048,953	1,133,491	1,217,678	1,299,953
Massachusetts	3,544,867	5,580,304	5,850,688	6,116,367	6,416,410	2,817,687	4,600,897	4,874,439	5,122,411	5,430,455
Michigan	447,436	738,699	789,175	826,746	855,969	384,533	651,408	696,518	730,458	759,066
Minnesota	521,441	776,325	812,893	800,291	859,388	443,972	654,953	678,472	679,001	732,714
Mississippi	64,054	110,325	115,789	123,506	129,945	55,252	96,217	101,895	108,547	115,582
Missouri	904,573	1,645,969	1,666,001	1,769,749	1,897,323	713,411	1,306,990	1,347,644	1,453,221	1,579,030
Montana	22,349	33,238	39,500	44,193	50,343	18,565	28,567	33,873	38,509	44,086
Nebraska	161,066	269,968	287,540	303,472	319,962	138,929	242,660	258,485	271,942	290,697
Nevada	2,448	5,971	5,490	6,768	8,194	2,448	5,127	4,666	5,998	7,294
New Hampshire	264,440	432,080	455,312	487,785	507,227	230,657	374,323	395,395	426,736	442,671
New Jersey	714,733	1,082,717	1,167,222	1,208,726	1,252,185	540,245	863,322	926,131	980,224	1,022,274
New Mexico	22,196	46,252	33,162	40,520	42,331	19,678	39,813	28,659	35,079	37,509
New York	5,596,257	9,003,453	9,536,982	10,157,945	10,653,695	4,572,405	7,401,300	7,837,705	8,315,046	8,721,147
North Carolina	837,291	1,911,631	2,008,628	2,166,337	2,329,951	592,910	1,255,073	1,313,943	1,417,518	1,515,305
North Dakota	18,853	34,323	33,758	36,380	37,350	15,860	29,719	28,821	31,776	32,912
Ohio	976,303	1,613,085	1,696,377	1,807,756	1,905,659	833,879	1,403,786	1,486,111	1,586,086	1,673,414
Oklahoma	178,905	256,332	266,152	286,118	298,275	149,565	220,403	230,661	248,299	263,719
Oregon	171,604	287,800	307,280	334,424	365,448	149,289	256,162	275,352	299,529	327,566
Pennsylvania	3,155,505	5,452,687	5,667,740	6,008,469	6,246,550	2,033,015	3,521,644	3,802,781	4,115,506	4,386,385
Rhode Island	315,651	559,922	590,911	636,510	667,901	261,616	476,062	504,274	545,057	575,255
South Carolina	196,271	274,300	293,819	318,200	333,278	154,496	225,437	245,689	268,292	282,443
South Dakota	51,675	71,462	63,406	66,315	69,866	44,726	63,351	56,780	59,358	62,863
Tennessee	686,514	1,199,755	1,226,183	1,352,769	1,410,990	440,308	785,347	827,801	894,506	955,718
Texas	993,824	1,633,787	1,716,860	1,833,288	1,955,975	855,445	1,460,510	1,540,238	1,653,269	1,764,618
Utah	183,060	317,586	454,442	458,878	492,298	110,880	257,271	313,342	317,681	333,683
Vermont	150,689	287,261	300,593	269,666	288,223	126,299	250,999	261,364	232,565	250,310
Virginia	387,455	706,344	748,902	807,849	874,960	313,055	607,724	645,752	702,430	766,327
Washington	227,211	401,261	435,993	475,565	513,782	189,575	345,756	375,031	413,941	448,823
West Virginia	73,716	114,586	129,367	143,742	172,925	60,900	98,830	112,959	126,231	153,757
Wisconsin	373,533	651,420	702,292	775,629	827,317	326,254	585,465	633,564	701,051	746,036
Wyoming	—	6,578	9,752	12,788	11,142	—	6,578	7,752	10,426	9,219
Outlying areas	198,653	284,662	306,098	337,721	360,203	189,080	267,789	290,189	320,304	343,782
Puerto Rico	198,653	284,662	306,098	337,721	360,203	189,080	267,789	290,189	320,304	343,782

[1] Preliminary data.

—Data not reported or not applicable.

NOTE.—Because of rounding, details may not add to totals.

SOURCE: U.S. Department of Education, National Center for Education Statistics, Higher Education General Information Survey (HEGIS), "Financial Statistics of Institutions of Higher Education" survey; and Integrated Postsecondary Education Data System (IPEDS), "Finance" surveys. (This table was prepared May 1997.)

Table 349.—Current-fund expenditures per full-time-equivalent student in institutions of higher education, by control and type of institution and purpose of expenditure: 1994–95 [1]

Item	Total				Public				Private		
	All institutions	Universities	Other 4-year	2-year	All institutions	Universities	Other 4-year	2-year	All institutions [2]	Universities	Other 4-year
1	2	3	4	5	6	7	8	9	10	11	12
Total current-fund expenditures [3]	$17,681	$31,045	$17,792	$6,876	$14,833	$24,531	$16,910	$6,778	$26,331	$50,363	$19,226
Educational and general expenditures	13,931	23,185	14,026	6,421	11,841	18,950	12,925	6,346	20,277	35,745	15,819
Instruction	5,385	8,473	5,288	3,061	4,830	6,710	5,402	3,111	7,068	13,701	5,103
Research	1,653	4,770	1,065	9	1,520	4,225	1,311	10	2,059	6,389	664
Public service	647	1,390	587	139	647	1,538	581	146	646	949	597
Academic support	1,187	1,994	1,203	520	1,087	1,771	1,244	509	1,488	2,652	1,135
Libraries	403	723	405	144	336	573	383	143	605	1,167	442
Student services	876	848	1,020	691	721	705	788	669	1,344	1,271	1,398
Institutional support	1,628	1,846	1,941	1,008	1,276	1,318	1,574	969	2,698	3,410	2,537
Operation and maintenance of plant	1,135	1,625	1,190	666	985	1,320	1,120	648	1,590	2,530	1,305
Scholarships and fellowships	1,187	1,852	1,452	280	599	1,075	664	237	2,974	4,156	2,734
From unrestricted funds	708	1,182	900	58	276	623	289	45	2,021	2,838	1,893
From restricted funds [4]	479	670	552	222	323	452	375	193	953	1,318	841
Mandatory transfers	234	388	280	46	176	287	241	47	409	686	344

[1] Preliminary data.
[2] Includes private 2-year colleges.
[3] Includes expenditures for auxiliary enterprises, hospitals, and independent operations which are not shown separately.
[4] Excludes Pell Grants.

NOTE.—Data for private 2-year colleges are not shown separately because of low survey response rate. Because of rounding, details may not add to totals.

SOURCE: U.S. Department of Education, National Center for Education Statistics, Integrated Postsecondary Education Data System (IPEDS), "Fall Enrollment" and "Finance" surveys. (This table was prepared July 1997.)

Table 350.—Additions to physical plant value of institutions of higher education, by type of addition and control of institution: 1969–70 to 1994–95

[In millions]

Year	Total, all institutions	Public institutions				Private institutions			
		Total	Land	Buildings	Equipment	Total	Land	Buildings	Equipment
1	2	3	4	5	6	7	8	9	10
1969–70	$4,233	$2,985	$152	$2,185	$648	$1,248	$59	$967	$221
1970–71	4,165	3,032	128	2,241	663	1,134	41	895	198
1971–72	4,163	3,054	112	2,277	665	1,109	53	860	195
1972–73	3,967	2,940	126	2,077	737	1,028	53	750	225
1973–74	4,312	3,206	205	2,188	813	1,106	55	816	235
1974–75	4,761	3,476	263	2,246	967	1,284	67	860	357
1975–76	4,702	3,552	168	2,365	1,019	1,150	58	768	325
1976–77	4,623	3,362	128	2,208	1,026	1,261	58	838	366
1977–78	4,527	3,306	102	2,117	1,087	1,221	45	777	400
1978–79	4,576	3,377	154	1,944	1,279	1,199	52	763	383
1979–80	5,551	3,666	164	2,149	1,354	1,886	98	1,220	568
1980–81	6,471	4,279	146	2,555	1,579	2,192	104	1,398	690
1981–82	6,975	4,594	170	2,679	1,744	2,382	83	1,488	811
1982–83	7,421	4,765	374	2,396	1,994	2,656	106	1,666	884
1983–84	7,604	5,038	196	2,427	2,415	2,566	110	1,507	950
1984–85	8,306	5,390	202	2,455	2,733	2,916	135	1,671	1,110
1985–86	10,149	6,875	237	3,318	3,320	3,274	128	1,922	1,225
1986–87	10,675	6,899	313	3,235	3,351	3,776	160	2,408	1,208
1987–88	11,589	7,218	272	3,520	3,426	4,371	250	2,715	1,406
1988–89	13,638	8,162	562	3,845	3,756	5,477	243	3,401	1,833
1989–90	15,900	10,616	532	5,438	4,647	5,284	408	3,277	1,599
1990–91	17,634	11,472	449	6,168	4,855	6,162	448	3,799	1,914
1991–92	15,543	9,820	412	5,272	4,136	5,723	380	3,419	1,925
1992–93	16,494	10,599	336	5,982	4,281	5,895	491	3,458	1,946
1993–94	16,379	10,263	361	5,582	4,320	6,116	259	3,840	2,017
1994–95	18,556	12,129	448	7,079	4,603	6,427	277	3,994	2,156

NOTE.—Because of rounding, details may not add to totals. Some data have been revised from previously published figures.

SOURCE: U.S. Department of Education, National Center for Education Statistics, Higher Education General Information Survey (HEGIS), "Financial Statistics of Institutions of Higher Education" surveys; and Integrated Postsecondary Education Data System (IPEDS), "Finance" surveys. (This table was prepared July 1997.)

Table 351.—Value of property and liabilities of institutions of higher education: 1899–1900 to 1994–95

[In thousands]

Academic year	Property value at end of year					Endowment (book value)[1]	Endowment (end of year market value)[1]	Liabilities of plant funds
	Total	Physical plant value						
		Total	Land	Buildings	Equipment			
1	2	3	4	5	6	7	8	9
1899–1900	$448,597	$253,599	—	—	—	[2]$194,998	—	—
1909–10	781,255	457,594	$92,359	$297,153	$68,082	[2]323,661	—	—
1919–20	1,316,404	747,333	128,922	495,920	122,491	[2]569,071	—	—
1929–30	3,437,117	2,065,049	304,114	1,490,014	270,921	[2]1,372,068	—	—
1935–36	3,913,028	2,359,418	334,085	1,636,722	388,611	[2]1,553,610	—	—
1937–38	4,208,695	2,556,075	313,665	1,811,309	431,101	1,652,620	—	—
1939–40	4,440,063	2,753,780	—	—	—	1,686,283	—	—
1941–42	4,525,925	2,759,261	—	—	—	[2]1,766,664	—	—
1947–48	6,076,212	3,691,725	—	—	—	2,384,487	—	—
1949–50	7,401,187	4,799,964	—	—	—	[2]2,601,223	—	—
1951–52	9,241,725	6,373,195	—	—	—	2,868,530	—	—
1953–54	10,717,082	7,523,193	—	—	—	3,193,889	—	—
1955–56	12,561,046	8,858,907	624,467	[3]6,697,648	1,536,792	3,702,139	—	$894,383
1957–58	15,770,197	11,124,489	733,182	[3]8,540,429	1,850,878	4,645,708	—	1,444,602
1959–60	18,870,628	13,548,548	842,664	[3]10,472,478	2,233,407	5,322,080	—	1,964,306
1961–62	22,761,193	16,681,844	1,009,294	[3]12,900,093	2,772,457	6,079,349	—	2,806,868
1963–64	28,232,362	21,279,346	1,292,691	[3]16,460,867	3,525,788	6,953,016	—	4,190,189
1965–66	35,274,597	26,851,273	1,758,901	[3]20,653,028	4,439,344	8,423,324	$11,126,831	6,071,750
1967–68	—	34,506,348	2,062,545	[3]26,673,826	5,769,977	—	—	—
1969–70	52,930,923	42,093,580	3,076,751	31,865,179	7,151,649	10,837,343	11,206,632	9,384,731
1970–71	57,394,951	46,053,585	3,117,895	35,042,590	7,893,100	11,341,366	13,714,330	9,786,240
1971–72	62,136,459	50,153,251	3,287,326	38,131,339	8,734,586	11,983,208	15,180,934	10,291,095
1972–73	66,814,103	53,814,596	3,492,611	40,808,481	9,513,503	12,999,507	15,099,840	10,823,595
1973–74	71,305,817	58,002,777	3,888,372	43,701,491	10,412,914	13,303,040	13,168,076	11,400,916
1974–75	75,585,674	62,183,078	4,210,901	46,453,642	11,518,536	13,402,596	14,364,545	12,413,420
1975–76	80,300,595	66,348,304	4,345,232	49,349,224	12,653,847	13,952,291	15,488,265	12,687,015
1976–77	85,486,550	70,739,427	4,444,927	52,384,393	13,910,107	14,747,123	16,304,553	13,068,341
1977–78	90,337,044	74,770,804	4,621,071	55,188,603	14,961,131	15,566,240	16,840,129	13,437,861
1978–79	95,442,468	78,637,991	4,824,250	57,563,005	16,250,737	16,804,477	18,158,634	13,712,648
1979–80	102,294,859	83,733,387	5,037,172	60,847,097	17,849,119	18,561,472	20,743,045	14,181,991
1980–81	109,701,242	88,760,567	5,212,453	64,158,017	19,390,097	20,940,675	23,465,001	14,794,669
1981–82	117,601,954	94,516,512	5,402,339	67,794,877	21,319,297	23,085,442	24,415,245	15,487,618
1982–83	127,345,302	100,992,841	5,889,080	71,519,718	23,584,042	26,352,461	32,691,133	16,749,900
1983–84	137,141,741	107,640,113	6,109,746	75,220,765	26,309,602	29,501,629	32,975,610	18,277,315
1984–85	148,163,096	114,763,986	6,236,159	79,133,998	29,393,829	33,399,110	39,916,361	22,105,712
1985–86	160,959,517	122,261,355	6,573,923	82,886,012	32,801,419	38,698,162	50,280,775	25,699,408
1986–87	—	126,426,171	7,165,445	84,838,657	34,422,069	—	56,585,153	—
1987–88	—	139,456,342	8,307,789	92,428,615	38,719,937	—	57,391,814	—
1988–89	—	158,693,085	9,462,095	104,743,145	44,487,845	—	64,155,247	—
1989–90	—	164,635,000	9,968,000	108,609,000	46,058,000	—	67,978,726	—
1990–91	—	178,084,000	10,028,000	117,683,000	50,373,000	—	72,048,579	—
1991–92	—	184,813,238	10,528,395	122,422,566	51,862,277	—	82,534,026	—
1992–93	—	192,760,817	11,006,451	128,436,599	53,317,767	—	92,239,311	—
1993–94	—	199,463,715	11,197,662	133,124,680	55,141,373	—	96,012,591	—
1994–95	—	212,201,113	11,710,436	142,553,837	57,936,840	—	109,706,704	—

[1] Includes funds functioning as endowment.
[2] Includes annuity funds.
[3] Includes improvements to land and equipment. These funds are included under appropriate categories after 1967–68.
—Data not available.

NOTE.—Because of rounding, details may not add to totals. Some data have been revised from previously published figures.

SOURCE: U.S. Department of Education, National Center for Education Statistics, Higher Education General Information Survey (HEGIS), "Financial Statistics of Institutions of Higher Education" surveys; and Integrated Postsecondary Education Data System (IPEDS), "Finance" surveys. (This table was prepared July 1997.)

Table 352.—Endowment funds of the 120 institutions of higher education with the largest amounts: Fiscal year 1995

Institution	Rank order[1]	Market value of endowment, in thousands of dollars (end of fiscal year)	Institution	Rank order[1]	Market value of endowment, in thousands of dollars (end of fiscal year)
1	2	3	1	2	3
United States (all institutions)	—	**$109,706,704**			
120 institutions with the largest amounts	—	78,744,171			
Harvard University (MA)	1	7,045,863	Trinity University (TX)	61	367,389
University of Texas at Austin	2	4,068,800	Pennsylvania State University, Main Campus	62	364,340
Yale University (CT)	3	3,967,756	Amherst College (MA)	63	362,407
Stanford University (CA)	4	3,295,597	University of Minnesota, Twin Cities	64	362,400
Princeton University (NJ)	5	2,872,865	Vassar College (NY)	65	350,693
Columbia University (NY)	6	2,325,383	Wesleyan University (CT)	66	345,061
University of California System	7	2,166,920	Baylor University (TX)	67	340,764
Massachusetts Institute of Technology	8	2,093,216	Tulane University of Louisiana	68	333,264
Emory University (GA)	9	2,025,681	Lafayette College (PA)	69	315,291
Washington University (MO)	10	2,014,164	Yeshiva University (NY)	70	313,887
University of Pennsylvania	11	1,675,740	Rensselaer Polytechnic Institute (NY)	71	299,453
Rice University (TX)	12	1,529,982	Purdue University, Main Campus (IN)	72	294,802
Northwestern University (IL)	13	1,367,141	Oberlin College (OH)	73	290,216
University of Chicago (IL)	14	1,317,895	The Juilliard School (NY)	74	270,017
University of Michigan, Ann Arbor	15	1,331,726	Syracuse University, Main Campus (NY)	75	268,874
Cornell University, Endowed Colleges (NY)	16	1,060,587	University of Miami (FL)	76	264,928
University of Notre Dame (IN)	17	996,895	Brigham Young University (UT)	77	259,071
Dartmouth College (NH)	18	993,735	Carleton College (MN)	78	252,556
Vanderbilt University (TN)	19	966,957	Thomas Jefferson University (PA)	79	252,056
University of Southern California	20	883,798	Agnes Scott College (GA)	80	251,560
Johns Hopkins University (MD)	21	838,220	Tufts University (MA)	81	247,191
Duke University (NC)	22	790,584	Rochester Institute of Technology (NY)	82	244,547
New York University	23	767,907	Cornell University Medical College (NY)	83	244,034
University of Rochester (NY)	24	733,833	University of Florida	84	243,733
University of Virginia, Main Campus	25	721,558	Northeastern University (MA)	85	243,459
California Institute of Technology	26	695,949	Bryn Mawr College (PA)	86	240,061
Brown University (RI)	27	676,026	University of Texas, Southwest Medical Center	87	239,895
Case Western Reserve University (OH)	28	621,344	Mount Holyoke College (MA)	88	235,339
Rockefeller University (NY)	29	613,001	Mount Sinai School of Medicine (NY)	89	224,507
University of North Carolina at Chapel Hill	30	554,816	University of South Alabama	90	224,357
Ohio State University, Main Campus	31	547,885	Bowdoin College (ME)	91	222,618
Princeton Theological Seminary (NJ)	32	536,755	Loyola University in New Orleans (LA)	92	219,923
Swarthmore College (PA)	33	536,430	Rush University (IL)	93	218,226
Wellesley College (MA)	34	525,487	Colgate University (NY)	94	212,462
University of Washington	35	504,711	Claremont McKenna College (CA)	95	212,109
Smith College (MA)	36	502,216	Brandeis University (MA)	96	210,502
Boston College (MA)	37	500,733	Trinity College (CT)	97	208,306
Southern Methodist University (TX)	38	498,192	Virginia Polytechnic Institute and State U.	98	201,459
Macalester College (MN)	39	484,427	Hamilton College (NY)	99	200,309
Baylor College of Medicine (TX)	40	484,011	University of Tennessee (Central office)	100	196,449
Texas Christian University	41	481,858	Rutgers, The State U. Central Office (NJ)	101	194,103
Grinnell College (IA)	42	479,223	University of Alabama	102	187,971
Williams College (MA)	43	460,399	Colorado College	103	186,090
Carnegie Mellon University (PA)	44	453,492	North Carolina State University at Raleigh	104	185,949
University of Richmond (VA)	45	443,885	Cornell University, Statutory Colleges (NY)	105	183,912
Loyola University of Chicago (IL)	46	442,504	College of the Holy Cross (MA)	106	182,187
Pomona College (CA)	47	438,901	Denison University (OH)	107	180,844
University of Pittsburgh, Main Campus (PA)	48	438,499	Academy of the New Church (PA)	108	180,424
University of Delaware	49	435,823	Santa Clara University (CA)	109	179,958
Wake Forest University (NC)	50	421,712	Southwestern University (TX)	110	175,405
Georgetown University (DC)	51	415,678	University of New Mexico, Main Campus	111	174,798
George Washington University (DC)	52	404,401	Earlham College (IN)	112	172,247
Washington and Lee University (VA)	53	403,576	Depauw University (IN)	113	172,037
Lehigh University (PA)	54	398,028	University of Louisville (KY)	114	169,230
University of Tulsa (OK)	55	396,547	Wabash College (IN)	115	167,848
University of Cincinnati, Main Campus (OH)	56	394,724	Bucknell University (PA)	116	167,113
Berea College (KY)	57	390,389	University of Missouri at Columbia	117	166,771
Saint Louis University, Main Campus (MO)	58	388,013	Pepperdine University (CA)	118	165,271
Boston University (MA)	59	378,605	State University of New York at Buffalo	119	164,968
Middlebury College (VT)	60	373,011	University of Wisconsin, Madison	120	164,472

[1] Institutions ranked by size of endowment. Excludes institutions which have not reported data for 1994–95.
—Not applicable. Because of rounding, details may not add to total.

SOURCE: U.S. Department of Education, National Center for Education Statistics, Integrated Postsecondary Education Data System (IPEDS), "Finance, 1994–95" survey. (This table was prepared June 1997.)

Table 353.—Participation of employed persons, 17 years old and over, in adult education during the previous 12 months, by selected characteristics of participants: 1995

Characteristics of employed persons	Employed persons, in thousands	Adult education participants, in thousands [1]	Percent of adults participating					Number of career or job-related courses taken, in thousands	Number of career or job related courses taken, per employee	Percent of career or job-related courses provided by businesses [2]	Percent of career or job-related courses payed for by businesses [2]	Percent of part-time higher education courses provided by businesses [3]	Percent of part-time higher education courses payed for by businesses [3]	Percent of employees receiving work-related computer-aided instruction
			In any program	In part-time higher education	In career or job related courses	In apprentice programs	Other personal courses							
1	2	3	4	5	6	7	8	9	10	11	12	13	14	15
Total	117,826	59,734	50.7	8.2	31.1	1.5	22.0	91,408	0.78	49.0	86.5	11.2	43.4	17.0
Sex														
Men	63,127	29,346	46.5	7.0	29.0	2.1	17.9	44,151	0.70	46.7	88.1	13.0	49.4	16.0
Women	54,699	30,387	55.6	9.7	33.4	0.8	26.8	47,257	0.86	50.9	85.1	9.6	38.3	18.1
Age														
17 to 24 years	15,104	7,653	50.7	14.2	18.6	4.1	21.8	5,924	0.39	53.8	75.7	8.8	18.7	14.7
25 to 29 years	14,207	7,746	54.5	12.5	31.2	2.8	22.2	10,855	0.76	51.3	89.9	10.1	40.6	17.4
30 to 34 years	16,291	8,323	51.1	8.9	31.6	1.4	22.8	12,765	0.78	49.7	89.7	11.3	49.2	18.3
35 to 39 years	17,595	9,361	53.2	8.4	35.1	1.3	21.8	15,927	0.91	51.8	89.1	11.6	53.6	18.3
40 to 44 years	16,049	8,906	55.5	8.0	36.6	1.0	26.0	14,957	0.93	44.9	85.9	13.4	59.7	18.6
45 to 49 years	13,743	7,586	55.2	6.3	39.6	0.6	23.0	14,127	1.03	44.8	85.3	9.3	47.8	19.2
50 to 54 years	10,408	5,222	50.2	4.9	34.4	0.3	20.9	9,041	0.87	49.2	84.5	19.5	49.3	20.2
55 to 59 years	6,698	2,667	39.8	2.3	26.7	0.3	18.0	4,432	0.66	46.8	84.8	—	—	10.3
60 to 64 years	4,435	1,394	31.4	0.6	21.1	0.2	15.3	2,175	0.49	58.6	85.5	—	—	10.3
65 and over	3,297	876	26.6	0.3	13.7	0.0	16.3	1,203	0.37	39.7	87.3	—	—	6.7
Racial/ethnic group														
White, non-Hispanic	92,333	47,967	51.9	8.0	33.2	1.2	22.7	77,096	0.83	47.9	86.8	11.9	45.1	17.5
Black, non-Hispanic	11,577	5,800	50.1	10.5	26.2	2.6	23.1	7,785	0.67	58.4	86.0	9.4	42.6	14.3
Hispanic	8,980	3,627	40.4	6.7	18.1	2.3	15.1	3,361	0.37	46.8	82.9	5.8	26.7	14.3
Asian American/Pacific Islander	2,825	1,246	44.1	8.0	25.5	2.8	15.1	1,636	0.58	48.6	87.3	15.2	—	18.1
American Indian/Alaskan Native	663	329	49.6	13.9	34.0	0.5	25.2	570	0.86	54.6	81.8	—	—	24.4
Highest level of education completed														
Less than high school diploma	9,635	2,444	25.4	0.8	8.8	1.7	9.4	1,412	0.15	56.6	76.3	—	—	4.9
High school diploma	38,071	14,639	38.5	4.9	20.9	1.9	16.5	17,072	0.45	56.7	91.0	13.9	48.9	11.8
Some vocational/technical	3,997	2,078	52.0	7.2	32.3	1.7	23.5	3,258	0.82	45.3	85.9	7.6	—	15.6
Some college	23,006	12,868	55.9	14.3	29.9	2.2	25.4	17,039	0.74	53.5	86.3	9.6	31.8	19.8
Associate degree	7,591	4,746	62.5	13.3	39.2	1.4	27.7	7,718	1.02	49.7	87.9	13.2	45.2	20.3
Bachelor's degree	20,602	12,948	62.8	8.3	44.6	0.6	26.5	24,024	1.17	47.2	86.5	8.3	48.8	22.9
Some graduate work (or study)	14,924	10,010	67.1	9.9	50.2	0.4	29.6	20,885	1.40	40.3	82.9	11.8	52.6	24.1
No degree	2,770	1,987	71.8	19.7	44.3	0.2	34.8	3,333	1.20	45.6	83.7	11.5	50.0	23.3
Master's	8,149	5,456	67.0	9.6	50.5	0.4	30.4	11,704	1.44	41.7	83.9	9.4	55.3	24.7
Doctor's	2,060	1,133	55.0	5.0	40.4	0.6	22.4	2,008	0.98	35.5	79.5	—	—	24.4
Professional	1,946	1,434	73.7	2.6	67.6	0.8	26.4	3,840	1.97	31.4	79.7	—	—	22.9
Metropolitan area														
Inside metropolitan area	89,192	46,911	52.6	8.7	32.4	1.5	22.6	72,388	0.81	48.6	86.3	11.6	41.9	17.7
Inside central city	74,367	39,519	53.1	8.8	33.3	1.5	22.5	62,033	0.83	48.3	86.4	11.1	41.6	18.5
Outside central city	14,825	7,392	49.9	8.0	27.9	1.5	23.1	10,355	0.70	50.9	86.0	14.3	43.7	13.8
Outside metropolitan area	28,634	12,823	44.8	6.9	26.9	1.4	20.2	19,020	0.66	50.2	87.2	9.4	49.1	14.7
Occupation														
Executive, administrative, or managerial	12,500	7,070	56.6	7.4	42.9	0.4	23.4	15,041	1.20	37.7	90.2	8.7	54.1	27.8
Engineers, surveyors, and architects	1,702	1,116	65.6	14.5	44.2	1.1	23.7	1,828	1.07	59.0	94.6	6.1	82.0	25.0
Natural scientists and mathematicians	1,648	1,211	73.5	10.4	59.7	0.0	25.6	2,875	1.75	44.0	94.6	—	—	30.7
Social scientists and workers, lawyers	2,438	1,873	76.8	11.7	59.5	1.5	32.4	4,307	1.77	35.6	83.1	7.1	31.3	17.5
Teachers, elementary/secondary	5,207	4,046	77.7	16.9	53.9	0.2	36.9	7,619	1.46	50.5	76.3	8.3	31.6	18.3
Teachers, postsecondary	1,175	657	55.9	4.4	41.6	0.0	26.1	1,213	1.03	53.5	79.8	—	—	26.6
Physicians, dentists, veterinarians	828	590	71.3	1.3	68.6	0.9	18.3	1,656	2.00	32.4	64.7	—	—	20.0
Registered nurses, pharmacists	2,143	1,896	88.5	11.2	72.8	0.2	34.6	4,791	2.24	45.6	74.0	9.9	43.8	13.1
Writers, artists, entertainers, and athletes	1,675	829	49.5	8.1	23.4	1.7	28.7	776	0.46	33.3	73.6	—	—	20.2
Health technologists and technicians	1,528	1,147	75.1	12.9	50.0	0.0	32.1	2,130	1.39	45.0	76.5	5.2	49.6	15.9
Technologists, except health	3,283	2,153	65.6	12.9	43.8	0.8	28.3	3,685	1.12	55.8	91.2	9.2	58.0	31.6
Marketing and sales occupations	15,666	7,131	45.5	6.6	25.2	1.1	20.2	8,619	0.55	51.2	86.5	10.2	21.6	19.6
Administrative support, including clerical	20,460	10,727	52.4	9.3	30.8	0.7	24.1	14,064	0.69	52.4	91.5	10.5	46.6	24.0
Service occupations	17,355	8,238	47.5	9.0	22.6	1.7	22.7	10,404	0.60	57.0	85.4	12.3	28.8	7.3
Agriculture, forestry, and fishing	1,908	500	26.2	1.8	12.4	0.4	14.8	493	0.26	—	—	—	—	6.6
Mechanics and repairers	4,266	2,129	49.9	7.6	29.1	3.9	16.6	3,109	0.73	57.2	90.7	19.5	60.0	9.8
Construction and extractive occupations	5,490	2,093	38.1	4.6	18.6	5.5	18.4	1,832	0.33	48.8	83.8	—	—	5.9
Precision production occupations	1,685	754	44.8	5.9	25.6	4.9	16.2	982	0.58	40.8	84.2	—	—	12.0
Production workers	8,309	2,515	30.3	5.9	14.8	2.9	10.1	2,203	0.27	58.5	97.9	16.2	57.2	8.1
Transportation, material moving	4,488	1,295	28.8	3.8	15.8	1.0	12.1	1,274	0.28	60.6	82.0	—	—	6.0
Handler, equipment, cleaners, helpers, and laborers	1,989	519	26.1	3.1	11.7	2.9	10.3	422	0.21	46.9	70.6	—	—	7.5
Miscellaneous occupations	2,022	1,194	59.0	8.5	38.8	4.0	22.1	2,088	1.03	51.8	90.4	—	—	20.9

Table 353.—Participation of employed persons, 17 years old and over, in adult education during the previous 12 months, by selected characteristics of participants: 1995—Continued

Characteristics of employed persons	Employed persons, in thousands	Adult education participants, in thousands[1]	Percent of adults participating					Number of career or job-related courses taken, in thousands	Number of career or job related courses taken, per employee	Percent of career or job-related courses provided by businesses[2]	Percent of career or job-related courses payed for by businesses[2]	Percent of part-time higher education courses provided by businesses[3]	Percent of part-time higher education courses payed for by businesses[3]	Percent of employees receiving work-related computer-aided instruction
			In any program	In part-time higher education	In career or job related courses	In apprentice programs	Other personal courses							
1	2	3	4	5	6	7	8	9	10	11	12	13	14	15
Annual family income														
$10,000 or less	9,776	3,224	33.0	6.1	12.6	1.7	15.6	2,441	0.25	50.9	75.2	19.0	18.7	9.2
$10,001 to $15,000	6,183	2,389	38.6	7.2	15.1	1.6	19.5	2,257	0.37	59.1	82.0	10.0	11.2	10.7
$15,001 to $20,000	7,321	3,040	41.5	8.0	20.1	2.4	18.2	3,110	0.42	52.8	83.0	7.5	26.0	14.6
$20,001 to $25,000	7,832	3,164	40.4	7.4	20.4	1.5	19.3	3,785	0.48	53.1	82.9	12.1	28.5	12.6
$25,001 to $30,000	10,133	4,803	47.4	8.8	24.7	2.1	21.4	5,461	0.54	55.8	86.9	8.4	40.7	14.4
$30,001 to $40,000	19,617	9,734	49.6	8.9	30.2	1.8	21.9	14,903	0.76	50.2	89.2	12.1	42.9	17.0
$40,001 to $50,000	15,115	8,127	53.8	8.0	34.7	1.3	22.9	12,430	0.82	48.3	85.3	14.0	55.3	16.8
$50,001 to $75,000	23,006	13,288	57.8	8.9	40.0	1.1	23.7	23,430	1.02	48.3	86.9	10.2	55.9	20.8
More than $75,000	18,843	11,964	63.5	8.6	45.2	0.9	26.5	23,592	1.25	45.0	87.6	9.2	49.2	22.7

[1] Adult education is defined as all education activities, except full-time enrollment in higher education credential programs. Examples of adult education activities include part-time college attendance, classes or seminars given by employers, and classes taken for adult literacy purposes, or for recreation and enjoyment. Includes adult basic education and English as a second language classes.

[2] Percentages based on the respondent's reports of the first six work-related courses taken.

[2] Percentages based on the respondent's reports of the first three part-time higher education courses taken.

NOTE.—Data are based upon a sample survey of the civilian noninstitutional population. Because of rounding and survey item nonresponse, details may not add to totals.

SOURCE: U.S. Department of Education, National Center for Education Statistics, National Household Education Survey, "Participation in Adult Education," unpublished data. (This table was prepared October 1997.)

Table 354.—Participation in adult education during the previous 12 months by adults 17 years old and older, by selected characteristics of participants: 1991 and 1995

Characteristics of participants	1991						1995								
	Population, in thousands	Adult education participants, in thousands [1]	Percent of adults participating				Population, in thousands	Adult education participants, in thousands [1]	Percent of adults participating						
			In any program	In basic education	In English as a second language	In part-time higher education			In any program	In basic education	In English as a second language	In part-time higher education	In career or job related courses	In apprentice programs	Other personal courses
1	2	3	4	5	6	7	8	9	10	11	12	13	14	15	16
Total	181,800	59,924	33.0	2.8	0.8	3.9	189,543	76,261	40.2	1.2	0.7	6.1	20.9	1.1	19.9
Sex															
Men	82,154	26,817	32.6	2.6	0.8	3.5	90,256	34,450	38.2	1.2	0.7	5.6	21.8	1.7	15.8
Women	99,646	33,108	33.2	2.9	0.9	4.2	99,287	41,811	42.1	1.2	0.6	6.5	20.2	0.6	23.5
Age															
17 to 24 years	21,688	8,197	37.8	7.4	1.9	7.9	22,407	10,539	47.0	4.6	1.4	12.6	14.7	3.2	21.5
25 to 29 years	22,603	9,049	40.0	4.1	1.7	6.7	18,988	9,420	49.6	1.4	1.4	10.9	25.5	2.5	21.0
30 to 34 years	24,641	9,275	37.6	2.9	1.0	5.0	21,338	10,088	47.3	1.1	0.8	8.0	26.1	1.3	23.3
35 to 39 years	21,000	8,839	42.1	2.8	0.9	5.5	22,494	10,737	47.7	1.2	1.0	7.5	29.1	1.3	20.9
40 to 44 years	17,565	8,650	49.2	2.7	0.6	4.4	19,810	10,078	50.9	0.9	0.8	7.1	31.2	0.9	24.9
45 to 49 years	11,303	4,523	40.0	2.0	0.3	3.2	17,463	8,499	48.7	0.6	0.4	5.7	32.5	0.5	21.1
50 to 54 years	14,072	3,767	26.8	1.7	0.6	1.3	14,344	6,093	42.5	0.5	0.1	3.9	26.3	0.3	19.7
55 to 59 years	9,564	2,770	29.0	1.7	0.1	1.0	11,096	3,577	32.2	0.4	0.2	1.7	17.8	0.3	17.3
60 to 64 years	10,403	1,808	17.4	0.6	0.1	0.5	10,728	2,540	23.7	0.1	0.3	0.6	10.6	0.3	15.2
65 to 69 years	9,920	1,409	14.2	0.5	0.0	0.3	10,215	1,850	18.1	0.1	0.0	0.2	4.0	0.0	15.3
70 years and over	19,040	1,638	8.6	0.2	0.0	0.1	20,661	2,841	13.8	0.0	0.0	0.1	1.4	0.0	12.6
Racial/ethnic group															
White, non-Hispanic	143,144	48,843	34.1	2.2	0.2	4.0	144,587	59,982	41.5	0.7	0.1	6.0	22.8	0.9	20.8
Black, non-Hispanic	20,141	5,207	25.9	4.5	0.6	3.2	20,806	7,704	37.0	2.3	0.1	7.3	16.2	1.6	18.9
Hispanic	13,804	4,339	31.4	6.0	6.6	3.6	15,689	5,281	33.7	3.6	5.7	4.8	11.8	1.8	13.8
Asian American/Pacific Islander	2,738	984	35.9	4.1	4.9	6.4	4,377	1,739	39.7	1.9	4.0	6.5	18.1	2.6	15.9
American Indian/Alaskan Native	997	293	29.3	2.3	4.2	12.5	1,155	448	38.8	3.6	0.0	9.3	20.6	0.9	21.6
Highest level of education completed															
Eighth grade or less	10,163	784	7.7	1.9	1.2	0.0	12,808	1,283	10.0	1.8	2.4	0.1	1.9	0.5	4.9
9th to 12th grade, no diploma	17,581	2,781	15.8	2.9	1.1	0.7	16,511	3,332	20.2	6.7	0.4	0.8	4.9	1.1	9.2
High school diploma	67,129	16,194	24.1	2.5	0.6	2.1	62,956	19,341	30.7	1.0	0.7	3.6	13.9	1.3	15.4
Some vocational/technical	6,994	2,392	34.2	1.8	0.9	1.3	6,327	2,648	41.9	0.6	0.6	5.4	21.9	1.5	21.1
Some college	36,823	15,260	41.4	4.4	1.3	7.7	34,433	16,978	49.3	0.5	0.5	12.1	22.3	1.8	25.3
Associate degree	5,034	2,479	49.2	3.7	1.3	7.0	9,975	5,601	56.1	0.4	0.2	10.9	32.1	1.4	27.4
Bachelor's degree	23,545	12,025	51.1	1.8	0.6	6.0	26,858	15,286	56.9	0.0	0.4	7.1	36.1	0.5	27.0
Some graduate work (or study)	14,531	8,009	55.1	2.2	0.6	5.9	19,677	11,792	59.9	0.0	0.8	8.5	40.4	0.4	29.1
No degree	—	—	—	—	—	—	4,123	2,563	62.2	0.0	0.7	15.2	32.5	0.5	33.5
Master's	—	—	—	—	—	—	10,522	6,219	59.1	0.0	0.9	8.1	41.0	0.4	29.0
Doctor's	—	—	—	—	—	—	2,564	1,384	54.0	0.0	0.4	4.7	35.0	0.5	25.1
Professional	—	—	—	—	—	—	2,467	1,626	65.9	0.0	0.9	3.0	56.6	0.6	26.0
Metropolitan area															
Inside metropolitan area	137,472	47,387	34.5	3.0	0.9	4.3	142,522	59,627	41.8	1.2	0.9	6.5	22.0	1.2	20.3
Inside central city	—	—	—	—	—	—	118,170	49,996	42.3	1.3	1.0	6.7	22.7	1.2	20.2
Outside central city	—	—	—	—	—	—	24,352	9,630	39.5	1.1	0.5	5.6	18.4	1.0	21.1
Outside metropolitan area	44,328	12,537	28.3	2.2	0.5	2.7	47,021	16,634	35.4	1.0	0.1	4.9	17.9	1.0	18.5
Labor force status															
In labor force	125,439	51,068	40.7	3.4	0.9	5.1	125,982	62,717	49.8	1.3	0.6	8.1	29.8	1.5	21.7
Employed	115,620	48,512	42.0	3.3	0.8	5.2	117,826	59,734	50.7	1.1	0.5	8.2	31.1	1.5	22.0
Unemployed	9,820	2,556	26.0	4.7	2.3	3.9	8,155	2,983	36.6	5.0	2.3	5.5	11.1	2.3	17.4
Not in labor force	56,361	8,856	15.7	1.4	0.6	1.2	63,562	13,544	21.3	0.9	0.8	2.2	3.4	0.3	16.2
Occupation															
Executive, administrative, or managerial	14,092	6,949	49.3	2.5	0.2	5.8	13,098	7,313	55.8	0.0	0.0	7.3	42.1	0.4	23.1
Engineers, surveyors, and architects	2,820	1,765	62.6	3.2	0.4	6.2	1,756	1,150	65.5	0.0	1.0	14.1	44.6	1.0	23.3
Natural scientists and mathematicians	1,009	487	48.2	0.3	0.3	5.7	1,743	1,261	72.3	0.0	0.2	9.9	58.6	0.0	24.8
Social scientists and workers, lawyers	3,206	1,781	55.6	1.2	0.1	4.4	2,530	1,938	76.6	0.0	0.2	11.5	59.4	1.5	32.3
Teachers, elementary and secondary	7,824	4,305	55.0	5.0	1.0	11.1	5,414	4,155	76.7	0.0	0.0	16.6	52.4	0.2	36.9
Teachers, postsecondary	1,247	568	45.5	1.5	0.5	9.4	1,254	687	54.8	0.0	0.3	4.1	40.8	0.0	26.0
Physicians, dentists, veterinarians	1,045	701	67.1	0.8	1.1	1.3	859	611	71.1	0.0	0.0	1.2	67.1	0.8	19.0
Registered nurses, pharmacists	4,692	2,798	59.6	2.5	0.9	6.9	2,337	2,026	86.7	0.1	0.1	10.6	71.3	0.2	33.6
Writers, artists, entertainers, and athletes	3,459	1,485	42.9	1.5	0.2	4.0	1,874	934	49.9	0.1	0.6	7.7	23.1	1.5	30.0
Health technologists and technicians	1,233	846	68.6	5.9	2.9	6.6	1,697	1,270	74.8	0.0	0.5	12.8	47.5	0.0	33.0
Technologists, except health	2,225	1,232	55.4	4.5	0.7	6.4	3,543	2,279	64.3	0.3	0.1	13.5	41.3	0.8	28.7
Marketing and sales occupations	18,787	6,470	34.4	2.3	0.6	3.1	18,174	8,038	44.2	1.1	0.4	6.8	23.2	1.0	20.4
Administrative support, including clerical	32,321	9,662	29.9	2.5	0.4	4.6	22,968	11,867	51.7	1.0	0.3	9.5	28.9	0.7	24.7
Service occupations	25,386	6,409	25.2	3.8	1.1	3.4	20,072	9,342	46.5	2.4	0.9	9.0	20.9	1.6	22.8
Agriculture, forestry, and fishing	4,800	686	14.3	0.6	0.4	0.9	2,336	616	26.4	0.4	0.5	1.6	11.5	0.3	15.6
Mechanics and repairers	6,744	2,165	32.1	3.1	0.4	2.5	4,692	2,231	47.6	2.1	0.6	7.1	27.7	4.5	15.6
Construction and extractive occupations	6,201	1,360	21.9	3.2	1.0	1.6	6,100	2,319	38.0	1.2	0.8	4.3	17.6	5.8	18.0
Precision production occupations	3,690	1,152	31.2	3.3	1.8	4.3	1,875	807	43.0	1.5	2.2	5.5	23.2	4.8	16.1
Production workers	14,368	3,029	21.1	2.9	1.2	1.6	9,483	2,908	30.7	2.5	1.1	5.8	14.7	2.8	10.7
Transportation, material moving	5,655	1,173	20.7	1.6	0.2	1.0	5,311	1,507	28.4	1.9	0.1	3.5	15.5	0.9	11.9

Table 354.—Participation in adult education during the previous 12 months by adults 17 years old and older, by selected characteristics of participants: 1991 and 1995—Continued

Characteristics of participants	1991						1995								
	Population, in thousands	Adult education participants, in thousands[1]	Percent of adults participating				Population, in thousands	Adult education participants, in thousands[1]	Percent of adults participating						
			In any program	In basic education	In English as a second language	In part-time higher education			In any program	In basic education	In English as a second language	In part-time higher education	In career or job related courses	In apprentice programs	Other personal courses
1	2	3	4	5	6	7	8	9	10	11	12	13	14	15	16
Handler, equipment, cleaners, helpers, and laborers	5,069	1,056	20.8	3.7	2.0	2.2	2,456	617	25.1	2.7	0.7	3.1	11.1	3.3	9.7
Miscellaneous occupations	—	—	—	—	—	—	2,311	1,308	56.6	0.5	1.5	7.9	35.4	4.0	22.6
Annual family income															
$5,000 or less	10,227	1,394	13.6	3.8	2.0	1.2	12,638	2,689	21.3	3.1	1.7	3.3	4.1	1.1	11.8
$5,001 to $10,000	17,277	3,024	17.5	2.3	0.8	2.2	17,560	4,194	23.9	2.5	1.5	4.0	6.7	1.0	13.2
$10,001 to $15,000	15,465	3,521	22.8	2.4	1.1	2.7	13,523	3,610	26.7	2.0	0.8	4.0	8.7	1.1	14.8
$15,001 to $20,000	16,117	3,525	21.9	2.7	1.2	3.1	13,116	4,176	31.8	1.3	1.1	5.4	13.0	1.5	15.8
$20,001 to $25,000	16,092	4,294	26.7	2.5	1.2	3.3	13,812	4,339	31.4	1.1	0.8	4.8	13.3	1.1	17.0
$25,001 to $30,000	17,973	5,772	32.1	3.4	1.1	4.5	16,386	6,208	37.9	1.2	0.4	6.5	17.1	1.3	19.2
$30,001 to $40,000	26,110	9,288	35.6	3.0	0.6	4.4	28,628	12,220	42.7	0.8	0.4	6.9	22.1	1.4	22.0
$40,001 to $50,000	21,303	9,550	44.8	3.0	0.7	5.4	20,446	9,567	46.8	0.7	0.4	6.8	27.0	1.0	22.4
$50,001 to $75,000	24,540	11,425	46.6	3.0	0.3	5.6	29,161	15,169	52.0	0.4	0.3	7.6	32.8	1.0	23.6
More than $75,000	16,695	8,130	48.7	1.9	0.3	4.0	24,274	14,089	58.0	0.5	0.3	7.7	37.3	0.8	26.8

[1] Adult education is defined as all education activities, except full-time enrollment in higher education credential programs. Examples of adult education activities include part-time college attendance, classes or seminars given by employers, and classes taken for adult literacy purposes, or for recreation and enjoyment.

NOTE.—Data are based upon a sample survey of the civilian noninstitutional population. Because of rounding and survey item nonresponse, details may not add to totals.

SOURCE: U.S. Department of Education, National Center for Education Statistics, "Participation in Adult Education," unpublished data. (This table was prepared February 1997.)

Table 355.—Participants in adult basic and secondary education programs, by level of enrollment and state: Fiscal years 1980, 1990, and 1995

State or other area	1980				1990			1995		
	Total	Level of enrollment			Total	Level of enrollment		Total	Level of enrollment	
		Adult basic education	Adult secondary education	Ungraded		Adult basic education[1]	Adult secondary education		Adult basic education[1]	Adult secondary education
1	2	3	4	5	6	7	8	9	10	11
United States	2,018,906	915,936	531,663	571,307	3,535,970	2,435,649	1,100,321	3,875,452	2,948,302	927,150
Alabama	51,599	36,726	12,372	2,501	40,177	32,984	7,193	56,488	45,193	11,295
Alaska	5,667	2,200	2,188	1,279	5,067	4,267	800	7,906	6,203	1,703
Arizona	9,996	9,968	22	6	33,805	24,915	8,890	52,656	40,002	12,654
Arkansas	8,583	7,308	1,275	—	29,065	17,103	11,962	42,457	24,344	18,113
California	267,625	60,385	—	207,240	1,021,227	753,282	267,945	1,088,044	1,057,257	30,787
Colorado	9,381	4,295	2,644	2,442	12,183	9,877	2,306	14,851	11,020	3,831
Connecticut	21,889	8,882	4,805	8,202	46,434	25,560	20,874	26,170	15,766	10,404
Delaware	1,797	1,110	503	184	2,662	2,348	314	3,884	3,391	493
District of Columbia	25,214	4,928	6,502	13,784	19,586	12,631	6,955	9,138	6,656	2,482
Florida	467,162	100,958	184,568	181,636	419,429	249,339	170,090	474,651	302,990	171,661
Georgia	50,820	26,734	17,008	7,078	69,580	49,622	19,958	92,022	64,079	27,943
Hawaii	16,457	16,457	—	—	52,012	31,766	20,246	61,664	36,988	24,676
Idaho	12,851	8,915	3,010	926	11,171	9,180	1,991	9,828	7,467	2,361
Illinois	76,456	59,314	17,142	—	87,121	69,770	17,351	94,808	80,122	14,686
Indiana	20,882	18,127	2,660	95	44,166	27,138	17,028	38,102	26,170	11,932
Iowa	25,851	16,928	5,153	3,770	41,507	30,470	11,037	40,510	28,961	11,549
Kansas	14,405	3,687	7,436	3,282	10,274	9,191	1,083	13,762	10,679	3,083
Kentucky	27,800	6,147	4,735	16,918	28,090	20,406	7,684	30,352	23,207	7,145
Louisiana	16,046	12,608	2,485	953	40,039	20,941	19,098	46,087	24,663	21,424
Maine	5,327	3,029	942	1,356	14,964	6,620	8,344	15,687	7,050	8,637
Maryland	34,572	23,421	6,043	5,108	41,230	36,244	4,986	30,677	21,692	8,985
Massachusetts	20,420	10,241	5,044	5,135	34,220	28,140	6,080	15,014	11,828	3,186
Michigan	40,973	29,945	—	11,028	194,178	80,206	113,972	164,075	69,014	95,061
Minnesota	10,826	8,627	877	1,322	45,648	33,190	12,458	36,350	26,556	9,794
Mississippi	14,317	10,340	2,918	1,059	18,957	15,834	3,123	22,857	17,660	5,197
Missouri	33,292	27,206	3,732	2,354	31,815	27,274	4,541	34,804	29,882	4,922
Montana	3,525	1,795	978	752	6,071	3,962	2,109	6,545	4,044	2,501
Nebraska	7,514	5,152	2,362	—	6,158	5,349	809	7,616	6,974	642
Nevada	3,063	845	82	2,136	17,262	7,270	9,992	16,359	4,556	11,803
New Hampshire	4,844	2,657	1,625	562	7,198	5,073	2,125	6,223	3,309	2,914
New Jersey	35,770	17,152	6,790	11,828	64,080	46,526	17,554	37,500	29,410	8,090
New Mexico	13,102	3,590	5,147	4,365	30,236	18,069	12,167	35,080	20,628	14,452
New York	94,574	57,217	20,002	17,355	156,611	125,893	30,718	209,390	165,892	43,498
North Carolina	84,252	33,854	46,679	3,719	109,740	71,698	38,042	120,945	83,673	37,272
North Dakota	2,810	1,963	538	309	3,587	2,500	1,087	3,270	2,329	941
Ohio	50,056	42,421	7,635	—	95,476	79,527	15,949	110,305	91,221	19,084
Oklahoma	14,701	6,983	5,697	2,021	24,307	19,131	5,176	32,778	26,621	6,157
Oregon	27,645	10,690	12,594	4,361	37,075	24,915	12,160	40,800	22,875	17,925
Pennsylvania	29,477	19,246	6,436	3,795	52,444	40,108	12,336	52,176	37,497	14,679
Rhode Island	5,844	2,266	1,357	2,221	7,347	5,874	1,473	6,182	4,829	1,353
South Carolina	69,659	27,959	35,165	6,535	81,200	37,117	44,083	108,041	46,644	61,397
South Dakota	4,067	2,080	1,109	878	3,184	2,458	726	4,518	3,624	894
Tennessee	26,268	17,079	3,244	5,945	41,721	39,604	2,117	51,054	39,019	12,035
Texas	157,349	94,245	51,126	11,978	218,747	145,067	73,680	207,921	159,983	47,938
Utah	18,541	3,756	14,785	—	24,841	6,003	18,838	30,302	11,147	19,155
Vermont	4,583	3,990	—	593	4,808	4,452	356	4,800	4,434	366
Virginia	21,525	10,480	3,804	7,241	31,649	30,005	1,644	33,786	24,920	8,866
Washington	16,286	7,245	3,894	5,147	31,776	25,336	6,440	44,728	39,061	5,667
West Virginia	14,628	9,743	3,672	1,213	21,186	14,227	[2]6,959	26,232	18,912	7,320
Wisconsin	16,158	14,185	1,973	—	61,081	45,116	15,965	78,544	60,162	18,382
Wyoming	2,457	857	905	695	3,578	2,071	[2]1,507	4,370	2,912	1,458
Outlying areas										
American Samoa	313	252	61	—	—	—	—	—	—	—
Northern Marianas	—	—	—	—	—	—	—	430	246	184
Guam	1,346	612	471	263	1,311	414	[2]897	2,034	632	1,402
Puerto Rico	30,164	17,844	9,010	3,310	28,436	28,436	—	68,394	32,943	35,451
Trust Territory of the Pacific	3,753	2,138	699	916	—	—	—	—	—	—
Virgin Islands	3,500	1,002	859	1,639	1,653	1,215	438	2,285	965	1,320

[1] Includes English as a second language.
[2] Estimated.
—Data not available or not applicable.

SOURCE: U.S. Department of Education, National Center for Education Statistics, "Women and Minority Groups Make Up Largest Segment of Adult Basic and Secondary Education Programs;" and Office of Vocational and Adult Education, "Adult Education Program Facts, Program Year 1990–1991," and Division of Adult Education and Literacy, "Adult Education Program Facts Program Year 1995–96." (This table was prepared April 1997).

Table 356.—Number of noncollegiate institutions offering postsecondary education, by control and state: 1993–94, 1994–95, and 1995–96

State or other area	1993–94			1994–95					1995–96				
	Total	Public	Private	Total	Public	Private			Total	Public	Private		
						Total	Nonprofit	Proprietary			Total	Nonprofit	Proprietary
1	2	3	4	5	6	7	8	9	10	11	12	13	14
United States	6,737	527	6,210	6,558	538	6,020	1,214	4,806	6,256	534	5,722	1,171	4,551
Alabama	76	10	66	71	8	63	8	55	63	7	56	7	49
Alaska	32	3	29	31	3	28	5	23	31	3	28	5	23
Arizona	125	4	121	124	4	120	16	104	113	4	109	16	93
Arkansas	82	20	62	76	19	57	9	48	69	16	53	8	45
California	1,126	32	1,094	1,041	35	1,006	230	776	997	35	962	225	737
Colorado	138	8	130	146	8	138	21	117	143	6	137	22	115
Connecticut	100	1	99	105	1	104	21	83	97	2	95	20	75
Delaware	15	1	14	14	1	13	2	11	12	1	11	2	9
District of Columbia	24	1	23	21	1	20	9	11	19	1	18	8	10
Florida	341	40	301	339	40	299	56	243	333	39	294	54	240
Georgia	102	4	98	104	4	100	15	85	101	5	96	16	80
Hawaii	29	1	28	26	1	25	4	21	22	1	21	3	18
Idaho	26	1	25	25	1	24	1	23	24	1	23	1	22
Illinois	304	12	292	285	11	274	56	218	264	10	254	56	198
Indiana	117	8	109	114	7	107	13	94	108	8	100	14	86
Iowa	72	0	72	66	0	66	17	49	62	0	62	16	46
Kansas	62	14	48	62	13	49	11	38	53	10	43	7	36
Kentucky	112	21	91	113	22	91	7	84	105	23	82	6	76
Louisiana	165	49	116	150	49	101	9	92	141	51	90	9	81
Maine	21	0	21	23	0	23	8	15	24	1	23	8	15
Maryland	135	0	135	122	0	122	21	101	112	0	112	20	92
Massachusetts	159	13	146	162	12	150	44	106	160	12	148	42	106
Michigan	247	6	241	282	6	276	44	232	264	6	258	43	215
Minnesota	89	14	75	88	5	83	18	65	79	4	75	16	59
Mississippi	52	0	52	49	0	49	4	45	38	0	38	3	35
Missouri	168	30	138	170	31	139	25	114	159	31	128	24	104
Montana	45	5	40	43	4	39	9	30	36	0	36	8	28
Nebraska	50	0	50	51	0	51	8	43	50	0	50	8	42
Nevada	46	0	46	47	0	47	1	46	57	0	57	1	56
New Hampshire	25	0	25	22	0	22	2	20	18	0	18	2	16
New Jersey	176	10	166	166	10	156	37	119	161	12	149	33	116
New Mexico	46	3	43	45	4	41	6	35	38	3	35	6	29
New York	353	15	338	337	26	311	118	193	343	31	312	115	197
North Carolina	81	4	77	81	4	77	8	69	74	4	70	7	63
North Dakota	19	0	19	19	0	19	6	13	17	0	17	5	12
Ohio	312	52	260	303	54	249	60	189	290	55	235	56	179
Oklahoma	95	34	61	111	33	78	5	73	108	33	75	4	71
Oregon	109	0	109	99	0	99	9	90	94	1	93	11	82
Pennsylvania	347	19	328	352	30	322	100	222	345	31	314	103	211
Rhode Island	28	0	28	28	0	28	9	19	29	0	29	9	20
South Carolina	60	2	58	56	2	54	11	43	57	1	56	11	45
South Dakota	17	5	12	17	5	12	5	7	16	5	11	4	7
Tennessee	143	30	113	139	29	110	20	90	135	29	106	17	89
Texas	382	6	376	360	7	353	37	316	350	6	344	38	306
Utah	43	6	37	42	6	36	2	34	39	5	34	2	32
Vermont	13	3	10	13	3	10	4	6	10	0	10	4	6
Virginia	148	11	137	144	11	133	32	101	139	12	127	31	96
Washington	111	5	106	107	5	102	13	89	104	5	99	12	87
West Virginia	70	19	51	73	18	55	14	41	71	19	52	13	39
Wisconsin	90	4	86	86	5	81	24	57	74	5	69	20	49
Wyoming	9	1	8	8	0	8	0	8	8	0	8	0	8
Outlying areas	95	5	90	84	6	78	16	62	84	6	78	14	64
American Samoa	0	0	0	0	0	0	0	0	0	0	0	0	0
Guam	1	0	1	0	0	0	0	0	0	0	0	0	0
Northern Marianas	0	0	0	0	0	0	0	0	0	0	0	0	0
Palau	0	0	0	0	0	0	0	0	0	0	0	0	0
Puerto Rico	94	5	89	84	6	78	16	62	84	6	78	14	64
Virgin Islands	0	0	0	0	0	0	0	0	0	0	0	0	0

SOURCE: U.S. Department of Education, National Center for Education Statistics, Integrated Postsecondary Education Data System (IPEDS), "Institutional Characteristics" surveys. (This table was prepared September 1996.)

CHAPTER 4
Federal Programs for Education and Related Activities

This chapter provides a summary of federal funds for education to help describe the magnitude of the federal fiscal effort and give some indication of the scope and variety of the education programs. Data in this chapter reflect outlays and obligations of federal agencies. These tabulations differ from federal receipts reported in other chapters because of numerous variations in the data collection systems. Federal dollars are not necessarily spent by recipient institutions in the same year they are appropriated. In some cases, institutions cannot identify the source of federal revenues because they flow through state agencies. Some types of revenues, such as tuition and fees, are reported as revenues from students even though they may be supported by federal student aid programs. Some institutions that receive federal education funds are not included in regular surveys conducted by the National Center for Education Statistics. Thus, the revenue data tabulated in this chapter are not comparable with figures reported in other chapters. Readers should be careful about comparing data on obligations shown in some tables with data on outlays and appropriations appearing in others.

Federal on-budget funding for education showed sizable growth between fiscal years (FYs) 1965 and 1997, after adjustment for inflation. Particularly large increases occurred between 1965 and 1975. After a period of small increases between 1975 and 1980, federal funding for education, excluding estimated federal tax expenditures for education, declined approximately 16 percent between 1980 and 1985 after adjustment for inflation. From 1985 to 1997, federal on-budget funding for education increased by 30 percent (table 357).

During the 1965 to 1975 period, after adjustment for inflation, federal funds for elementary and secondary education rose by 210 percent, postsecondary education by 263 percent, other education by 144 percent, and by 7 percent for research at educational institutions. Between 1975 and 1980, federal funding for elementary and secondary education rose by 2 percent and research by 14 percent, but postsecondary education fell slightly by 2 percent and other education fell by 35 percent. After declining 22 percent between 1980 and 1985, federal funding for elementary and secondary education programs rose by 50 percent between 1985 and 1997. Postsecondary education fell by 25 percent between 1980 and 1985 then fell 4 percent between 1985 and 1997. Between 1985 and 1997, other education rose by 69 percent, and research by 25 percent, after adjustment for inflation (table 357).

According to FY 1997 estimates, $31.1 billion or about 43 percent of the $73.1 billion spent by the federal government on education came from the U.S. Department of Education. Large amounts of money also came from the U.S. Department of Health and Human Services ($13.1 billion), the U.S. Department of Agriculture ($9.7 billion), the U.S. Department of Labor ($4.6 billion), the U.S. Department of Defense ($3.7 billion), and the U.S. Department of Energy ($2.6 billion) (table 358).

Fiscal year 1997 estimates call for federal program funds for elementary and secondary education to be $36.6 billion; for postsecondary education, $15.4 billion; for research at universities and related institutions, $15.9 billion; and for other programs, $5.1 billion (table 359).

Over 58 percent of total federal education support, excluding estimated federal tax expenditures, went to educational institutions in FY 97. Another 19 percent was used for student support. Banks and other lending agencies received 9 percent, and all other recipients, including libraries, museums, and federal institutions, received 14 percent (table 360).

Between FYs 1990 and 1997, U.S. Department of Education obligations rose 88 percent, after adjustment for inflation. Funds for student financial assistance increased to $35.8 billion in 1997, a rise of 165 percent since 1990. Funds for elementary and secondary education were an estimated $10.5 billion in 1997, an increase of 20 percent since 1990, after adjustment for inflation. Funds for the handicapped increased by 59 percent, to $6.7 billion, and funds for vocational and adult education increased 10 percent, after adjustment for inflation (tables 38 and 361).

Of the $31.1 billion spent by the U.S. Department of Education in FY 1997, about $11.8 billion went to school districts, $5.1 billion to institutions of higher education, $5.1 billion to college students, and $4.0 billion to state education agencies. A portion of the remaining $5.2 billion went to banks to subsidize student loans (table 362).

Thirty-three percent of public elementary and secondary school students in the United States received publicly funded free or reduced-price lunches in 1993–94. At public elementary schools, the participation rate was 39 percent compared with 22 percent for public secondary schools (table 371).

About 13 percent of all elementary and secondary school children received Title I services in 1993–94. Federally sponsored Title I programs are designed to compensate the link between family poverty and low student achievement, particularly for children in schools with high concentrations of poverty. Children in rural areas (13 percent) and central cities (17 percent) were more likely to receive services than those in suburban areas (9 percent) (table 372).

Federal Education Legislation

A capsule view of the history of federal education activities is provided in the following list of selected legislation:

1787 *Northwest Ordinance* authorized land grants for the establishment of educational institutions.

1802 *An Act Fixing the Military Peace Establishment of the United States* established the U.S. Military Academy. (The U.S. Naval Academy was established in 1845 by the Secretary of the Navy.)

1862 *First Morrill Act* authorized public land grants to the states for the establishment and maintenance of agricultural and mechanical colleges.

1867 *Department of Education Act* authorized the establishment of the U.S. Department of Education.*

1876 *Appropriation Act,* U.S. Department of the Treasury, established the U.S. Coast Guard Academy.

1890 *Second Morrill Act* provided for money grants for support of instruction in the agricultural and mechanical colleges.

1911 *State Marine School Act* authorized federal funds to be used for the benefit of any nautical school in any of 11 specified state seaport cities.

1917 *Smith-Hughes Act* provided for grants to states for support of vocational education.

---

*The U.S. Department of Education as established in 1867 was later known as the Office of Education. In 1980, under Public Law 96–88, it became a cabinet-level department. Therefore, for purposes of consistency, it is referred to as the "U.S. Department of Education" even in those tables covering years when it was officially the Office of Education.

1918 *Vocational Rehabilitation Act* provided for grants for rehabilitation through training of World War I veterans.

1919 *An Act to Provide for Further Educational Facilities* authorized the sale by the federal government of surplus machine tools to educational institutions at 15 percent of acquisition cost.

1920 *Smith-Bankhead Act* authorized grants to states for vocational rehabilitation programs.

1935 *Bankhead-Jones Act* (Public Law 74–182) authorized grants to states for agricultural experiment stations.

Agricultural Adjustment Act (Public Law 74–320) authorized 30 percent of the annual customs receipts to be used to encourage the exportation and domestic consumption of agricultural commodities. Commodities purchased under this authorization began to be used in school lunch programs in 1936. The National School Lunch Act of 1946 continued and expanded this assistance.

1936 *An Act to Further the Development and Maintenance of an Adequate and Well-Balanced American Merchant Marine* (Public Law 74–415) established the U.S. Merchant Marine Academy.

1937 *National Cancer Institute Act* established the Public Health Service fellowship program.

1941 *Amendment to Lanham Act of 1940* authorized federal aid for construction, maintenance, and operation of schools in federally impacted areas. Such assistance was continued under Public Law 815 and Public Law 874, 81st Congress, in 1950.

1943 *Vocational Rehabilitation Act* (Public Law 78–16) provided assistance to disabled veterans.

School Lunch Indemnity Plan (Public Law 78–129) provided funds for local lunch food purchases.

1944 *Servicemen's Readjustment Act* (Public Law 78–346) known as the GI Bill, provided assistance for the education of veterans.

Surplus Property Act (Public Law 78–457) authorized transfer of surplus property to educational institutions.

1946 *National School Lunch Act* (Public Law 79–396) authorized assistance through grants-in-aid and other means to states to assist in providing adequate foods and facilities for the establishment, maintenance, operation, and expansion of nonprofit school lunch programs.

George-Barden Act (Public Law 80–402) expanded federal support of vocational education.

1948 *United States Information and Educational Exchange Act* (Public Law 80–402) provided for the interchange of persons, knowledge, and skills between the United States and other countries.

1949 *Federal Property and Administrative Services Act* (Public Law 81–152) provided for donation of surplus property to educational institutions and for other public purposes.

1950 *Financial Assistance for Local Educational Agencies Affected by Federal Activities* (Public Law 81–815 and Public Law 81–874) provided assistance for construction (Public Law 815) and operation (Public Law 874) of schools in federally affected areas.

Housing Act (Public Law 81–475) authorized loans for construction of college housing facilities.

1954 *An Act for the Establishment of the United States Air Force Academy and Other Purposes* (Public Law 83–325) established the U.S. Air Force Academy.

Educational Research Act (Public Law 83–531) authorized cooperative arrangements with universities, colleges, and state educational agencies for educational research.

School Milk Program Act (Public Law 83–597) provided funds for purchase of milk for school lunch programs.

1956 *Library Services Act* (Public Law 84–597) provided grants to states for extension and improvement of rural public library services.

1957 *Practical Nurse Training Act* (Public Law 84–911) provided grants to states for practical nurse training.

1958 *National Defense Education Act* (Public Law 85–864) provided assistance to state and local school systems for strengthening instruction in science, mathematics, modern foreign languages, and other critical subjects; improvement of state statistical services; guidance, counseling, and testing services and training institutes; higher education student loans and fellowships; foreign language study and training provided by colleges and universities; experimentation and dissemination of information on more effective utilization of television, motion pictures, and related media for educational purposes; and vocational education for technical occupations necessary to the national defense.

Education of Mentally Retarded Children Act (Public Law 85–926) authorized federal assistance for training teachers of the handicapped.

Captioned Films for the Deaf Act (Public Law 85–905) authorized a loan service of captioned films for the deaf.

1961 *Area Redevelopment Act* (Public Law 87–27) included provisions for training or retraining of persons in redevelopment areas.

1962 *Manpower Development and Training Act* (Public Law 87–415) provided training in new and improved skills for the unemployed and underemployed.

Migration and Refugee Assistance Act of 1962 (Public Law 87–510) authorized loans, advances, and grants for education and training of refugees.

1963 *Health Professions Educational Assistance Act of 1963* (Public Law 88–129) provided funds to expand teaching facilities and for loans to students in the health professions.

Vocational Education Act of 1963 (Part of Public Law 88–210) increased federal support of vocational education schools; vocational work-study programs; and research, training, and demonstrations in vocational education.

Higher Education Facilities Act of 1963 (Public Law 88–204) authorized grants and loans for classrooms, libraries, and laboratories in public community colleges and technical institutes, as well as undergraduate and graduate facilities in other institutions of higher education.

1964 *Civil Rights Act of 1964* (Public Law 88–352) authorized the Commissioner of Education to arrange for support for institutions of higher education and school districts to provide in-service programs for assisting instructional staff in dealing with problems caused by desegregation.

Economic Opportunity Act of 1964 (Public Law 88–452) authorized grants for college work-study programs for students from low-income families; established a Job Corps program and authorized support for work-training programs to provide education and vocational training and work experience opportunities in welfare programs; authorized support of education and training activities and of community action programs, including Head Start, Follow Through, and Upward Bound; and authorized the establishment of Volunteers in Service to America (VISTA).

1965 *Elementary and Secondary Education Act of 1965* (Public Law 89–10) authorized grants for elementary and secondary school programs for children of low-income families; school library resources, textbooks, and other instructional materials for school children; supplementary educational centers and services; strengthening state education agencies; and educational research and research training.

Health Professions Educational Assistance Amendments of 1965 (Public Law 89–290) authorized scholarships to aid needy students in the health professions.

Higher Education Act of 1965 (Public Law 89–329) provided grants for university community service programs, college library assistance, library training and research, strengthening developing institutions, teacher training programs, and undergraduate instructional equipment. Authorized insured student loans, established a National Teacher Corps, and provided for graduate teacher training fellowships.

National Foundation on the Arts and the Humanities Act (Public Law 89–209) authorized grants and loans for projects in the creative and performing arts and for research, training, and scholarly publications in the humanities.

National Technical Institute for the Deaf Act (Public Law 89–36) provided for the establishment, construction, equipping, and operation of a residential school for postsecondary education and technical training of the deaf.

School Assistance in Disaster Areas Act (Public Law 89–313) provided for assistance to local education agencies to help meet exceptional costs resulting from a major disaster.

1966 *International Education Act* (Public Law 89–698) provided grants to institutions of higher education for the establishment, strengthening, and operation of centers for research and training in international studies and the international aspects of other fields of study.

National Sea Grant College and Program Act (Public Law 89–688) authorized the establishment and operation of Sea Grant Colleges and programs by initiating and supporting programs of education and research in the various fields relating to the development of marine resources.

Adult Education Act (Public Law 89–750) authorized grants to states for the encouragement and expansion of educational programs for adults, including training of teachers of adults and demonstrations in adult education (previously part of Economic Opportunity Act of 1964).

Model Secondary School for the Deaf Act (Public Law 89–694) authorized the establishment and operation, by Gallaudet College, of a model secondary school for the deaf.

1967 *Education Professions Development Act* (Public Law 90–35) amended the Higher Education Act of 1965 for the purpose of improving the quality of teaching and to help meet critical shortages of adequately trained educational personnel.

Public Broadcasting Act of 1967 (Public Law 90–129) established a Corporation for Public Broadcasting to assume major responsibility in channeling federal funds to noncommercial radio and television stations, program production groups, and ETV networks; conduct research, demonstration, or training in matters related to noncommercial broadcasting; and award grants for construction of educational radio and television facilities.

1968 *Elementary and Secondary Education Amendments of 1968* (Public Law 90–247) modified existing programs, authorized support of regional centers for education of handicapped children, model centers and services for deaf-blind children, recruitment of personnel and dissemination of information on education of the handicapped; technical assistance in education to rural areas; support of dropout prevention projects; and support of bilingual education programs.

Handicapped Children's Early Education Assistance Act (Public Law 90–538) authorized preschool and early education programs for handicapped children.

Vocational Education Amendments of 1968 (Public Law 90–576) modified existing programs and provided for a National Advisory Council on Vocational Education and collection and dissemination of information for programs administered by the Commissioner of Education.

1970 *Elementary and Secondary Education Assistance Programs, Extension* (Public Law 91–230) authorized comprehensive planning and evaluation grants to state and local education agencies; provided for the establishment of a National Commission on School Finance.

National Commission on Libraries and Information Services Act (Public Law 91–345) established a National Commission on Libraries and Information Science to effectively utilize the nation's educational resources.

Office of Education Appropriation Act (Public Law 91–380) provided emergency school assistance to desegregating local education agencies.

Environmental Education Act (Public Law 91–516) established an Office of Environmental Education to develop curriculum and initiate and maintain environmental education programs at the elementary-secondary levels; disseminate information; provide training programs for teachers and other educational, public, community, labor, and industrial leaders and employees; provide community education programs; and distribute material dealing with the environment and ecology.

Drug Abuse Education Act of 1970 (Public Law 91–527) provided for development, demonstration, and evaluation of curricula on the problems of drug abuse.

1971 *Comprehensive Health Manpower Training Act of 1971* (Public Law 92–257) amended Title VII of the Public Health Service Act, increasing and expanding provisions for health manpower training and training facilities.

1972 *Drug Abuse Office and Treatment Act of 1972* (Public Law 92–255) established a Special Action Office for Drug Abuse Prevention to provide overall planning and policy for all federal drug-abuse prevention functions; a National Advisory Council for Drug Abuse Prevention; community assistance grants for community mental health centers for treatment and rehabilitation of persons with drug-abuse problems, and, in December 1974, a National Institute on Drug Abuse.

Education Amendments of 1972 (Public Law 92–318) established the Education Division in the U.S. Department of Health, Education, and Welfare and the National Institute of Education; general aid for institutions of higher education; federal matching grants for state Student Incentive Grants; a National Commission on Financing Postsecondary Education; State Advisory Councils on Community Colleges; a Bureau of Occupational and Adult Education and State Grants for the design, establishment, and conduct of postsecondary occupational education; and a bureau-level Office of Indian Education. Amended current Office of Education programs to increase their effectiveness and better meet special needs. Prohibited sex bias in admission to vocational, professional, and graduate schools, and public institutions of undergraduate higher education.

1973 *Older Americans Comprehensive Services Amendment of 1973* (Public Law 93–29) made available to older citizens comprehensive programs of health, education, and social services.

Comprehensive Employment and Training Act of 1973 (Public Law 93–203) provided for opportunities for employment and training to unemployed and underemployed persons. Extended and expanded provisions in the Manpower Development and Training Act of 1962, Title I of the Economic Opportunity Act of 1962, Title I of the Economic Opportunity Act of 1964, and the Emergency Employment Act of 1971 as in effect prior to June 30, 1973.

1974 *Education Amendments of 1974* (Public Law 93–380) provided for the consolidation of certain programs; and established a National Center for Education Statistics.

Juvenile Justice and Delinquency Prevention Act of 1974 (Public Law 93–415) provided for technical assistance, staff training, centralized research, and resources to develop and implement programs to keep students in elementary and secondary schools; and established, in the U.S. Department of Justice, a National Institute for Juvenile Justice and Delinquency Prevention.

1975 *Indian Self-Determination and Education Assistance Act* (Public Law 93–638) provided for increased participation of Indians in the establishment and conduct of their education programs and services.

Harry S Truman Memorial Scholarship Act (Public Law 93–642) established the Harry S Truman Scholarship Foundation and created a perpetual education scholarship fund for young Americans to prepare and pursue careers in public service.

Indochina Migration and Refugee Assistance Act of 1975 (Public Law 94–23) authorized funds to be used for education and training of aliens who have fled from Cambodia or Vietnam.

Education for All Handicapped Children Act (Public Law 94–142) provided that all handicapped children have available to them a free appropriate education designed to meet their unique needs.

1976 *Educational Broadcasting Facilities and Telecommunications Demonstration Act of 1976* (Public Law 94–309) established a telecommunications demonstration program to promote the development of nonbroadcast telecommunications facilities and services for the transmission, distribution, and delivery of health, education, and public or social service information.

Education Amendments of 1976 (Public Law 94–482) extended and revised federal programs for education assistance for higher education, vocational education, and a variety of other programs.

1977 *Youth Employment and Demonstration Projects Act of 1977* (Public Law 95–93) established a youth employment training program that includes, among other activities, promoting education-to-work transition, literacy training and bilingual training, and attainment of certificates of high school equivalency.

Career Education Incentive Act (Public Law 95–207) authorized the establishment of a career education program for elementary and secondary schools.

1978 *Tribally Controlled Community College Assistance Act of 1978* (Public Law 95–471) provided federal funds for the operation and improvement of tribally controlled community colleges for Indian students.

Education Amendments of 1978 (Public Law 95–561) established a comprehensive basic skills program aimed at improving pupil achievement (replaced the existing National Reading Improvement program); and established a community schools program to provide for the use of public buildings.

Middle Income Student Assistance Act (Public Law 95–566) modified the provisions for student financial assistance programs to allow middle-income as well as low-income students attending college or other postsecondary institutions to qualify for federal education assistance.

1979 *Department of Education Organization Act* (Public Law 96–88) established a U.S. Department of Education containing functions from the Education Division of the U.S. Department of Health, Education, and Welfare along with other selected education programs from HEW, the U.S. Department of Justice, U.S. Department of Labor, and the National Science Foundation.

1980 *Asbestos School Hazard Detection and Control Act of 1980* (Public Law 96–270) established a program for inspection of schools for detection of hazardous asbestos materials and provided loans to assist educational agencies to contain or remove and replace such materials.

1981 *Education Consolidation and Improvement Act of 1981* (Part of Public Law 97–35) consolidated 42 programs into 7 programs to be funded under the elementary and secondary block grant authority.

1983 *Student Loan Consolidation and Technical Amendments Act of 1983* (Public Law 98–79) established 8 percent interest rate for Guaranteed Student Loans and extended Family Contribution Schedule.

Challenge Grant Amendments of 1983 (Public Law 98–95) amended Title III, Higher Education Act, and added authorization of Challenge Grant program. The Challenge Grant program provides funds to eligible institutions on a matching basis as incentive to seek alternative sources of funding.

Education of the Handicapped Act Amendments of 1983 (Public Law 98–199) added the Architectural Barrier amendment and clarified participation of handicapped children in private schools.

1984 *Education for Economic Security Act* (Public Law 98–377) added new science and mathematics programs for elementary, secondary, and postsecondary education. The new programs included magnet schools, excellence in education, and equal access.

Carl D. Perkins Vocational Education Act (Public Law 98–524) continued federal assistance for vocational education through FY 1989. The act replaced the Vocational Education Act of 1963. It provided aid to the states to make vocational education programs accessible to all persons, including handicapped and disadvantaged, single parents and homemakers, and the incarcerated.

Human Services Reauthorization Act (Public Law 98–558) reauthorized the Head Start and Follow Through programs through FY 1986. It also created a Carl D. Perkins scholarship program, a National Talented Teachers Fellowship program, a Federal Merit Scholarships program, and a Leadership in Educational Administration program.

1985 *Montgomery GI Bill—Active Duty* (Public Law 98–525), brought about a new GI Bill for individuals who initially entered active military duty on or after July 1, 1985.

Montgomery GI Bill—Selected Reserve (Public Law 98–525), is an education program for members of the Selected Reserve (which includes the National Guard) who enlist, reenlist, or extend an enlistment after June 30, 1985, for a 6-year period.

1986 *Handicapped Children's Protection Act of 1986* (Public Law 99–372) allowed parents of handicapped children to collect attorneys' fees in cases brought under the Education of the Handicapped Act and provided that the Education of the Handicapped Act does not preempt other laws, such as Section 504 of the Rehabilitation Act.

Drug-Free Schools and Communities Act of 1986 (Part of Public Law 99–570), part of the Anti-Drug Abuse Act of 1986, authorized funding for FYs 1987–89. Established programs for drug abuse education and prevention, coordinated with related community efforts and resources, through the use of federal financial assistance.

1987 *Higher Education Act Amendments of 1987* (Public Law 100–50) made technical corrections, clarifications, or conforming amendments related to the enactment of the Higher Education Amendments of 1986.

1988 *Augustus F. Hawkins-Robert T. Stafford Elementary and Secondary School Improvement Amendments of 1988* (Public Law 100–297) reauthorized through 1993 major elementary and secondary education programs including: Chapter 1, Chapter 2, Bilingual Education, Math-Science Education, Magnet Schools, Impact Aid, Indian Education, Adult Education, and other smaller education programs.

Technology-Related Assistance for Individuals with Disabilities Act of 1988 (Public Law 100–407) provided financial assistance to states to develop and implement consumer-responsive statewide programs of technology-related assistance for persons of all ages with disabilities.

Stewart B. McKinney Homeless Assistance Amendments Act of 1988 (Public Law 100–628) extended for 2 additional years programs providing assistance to the homeless, including literacy training for homeless adults and education for homeless youths.

Tax Reform Technical Amendments (Public Law 100–647) authorized an Education Savings Bond for the purpose of postsecondary educational expenses. The bill grants tax exclusion for interest earned on regular series EE savings bonds.

1989 *Children with Disabilities Temporary Care Reauthorization Act of 1989* (Public Law 101–127) revised and extended the programs established in the Temporary Child Care for Handicapped Children and Crises Nurseries Act of 1986.

Drug-Free Schools and Communities Act Amendments of 1989 (Public Law 101–226) amended the Drug-Free Schools and Communities Act of 1986 to revise certain requirements relating to the provision of drug abuse education and prevention programs in elementary and secondary schools.

Childhood Education and Development Act of 1989 (Part of Public Law 101–239) authorized the appropriations to expand Head Start Programs and programs carried out under the Elementary and Secondary Education Act of 1965 to include child care services.

1990 *Excellence in Mathematics, Science and Engineering Education Act of 1990* (Public Law 101–589) promotes excellence in American mathematics, science, and engineering education by creating a national mathematics and science clearinghouse, and creating several other mathematics, science, and engineering education programs.

Student Right-To-Know and Campus Security Act (Public Law 101–542) requires institutions of higher education receiving federal financial assistance to provide certain information with respect to the graduation rates of student-athletes at such institutions. The act also requires the institution to certify that it has a campus security policy and will annually submit a uniform crime report to the Federal Bureau of Investigation (FBI).

Americans with Disabilities Act of 1990 (Public Law 101–336) prohibits discrimination against persons with disabilities.

National and Community Service Act of 1990 (Public Law 101–610) increased school and college-based community service opportunities and authorized the President's Points of Light Foundation.

School Dropout Prevention and Basic Skills Improvement Act of 1990 (Public Law 101–600) improves secondary school programs for basic skills improvements and dropout reduction.

Asbestos School Hazard Abatement Reauthorization Act of 1990 (Public Law 101–637) reauthorized the Asbestos School Hazard Abatement Act of 1984, which provided financial support to elementary and secondary schools to inspect for asbestos and to develop and implement an asbestos management plan.

Eisenhower Exchange Fellowship Act of 1990 (Public Law 101–454) provided a permanent endowment for the Eisenhower Exchange Fellowship Program.

Public Service Assistance Education Act (Enacted as part of Department of Defense Authorization Act, Public Law 101–510) gave federal agencies authority to provide new educational benefits to employees by paying for an employee to obtain an academic degree for which there is an agency shortage of qualified personnel, and by repaying up to $6,000 per year of the student loan of a qualified employee in exchange for a 3-year commitment.

Omnibus Budget Reconciliation Act of 1990 (Public Law 101–508) included a set of student aid provisions that were estimated to yield a savings of $2 billion over 5 years. These provisions included delayed Guaranteed Student Loan disbursements, tightened ability-to-benefit eligibility, and expanded pro rata refund policy and the elimination of student aid eligibility at high default schools.

1991 *National Literacy Act of 1991* (Public Law 102–73) established the National Institute for Literacy, the National Institute Board, and the Interagency Task Force on Literacy. Amended various federal laws to establish and extend various literacy programs.

National Defense Authorization Act for Fiscal Years 1992 and 1993 (Public Law 102–190) authorized appropriations for military functions of the U.S. Department of Defense. Included Defense Manufacturing Education Program and planning for science, mathematics, and engineering education.

National Commission on Time and Learning Act (Public Law 102–62) established the National Education Commission on Time and Learning. Directed the Secretary of Education to: (1) make grants for research in the teaching of writing; and (2) carry out a program to educate students about the history and principles of the Constitution, including the Bill of Rights. Established the National Council on Education Standards and Testing.

High-Performance Computing Act of 1991 (Public Law 102–194) directed the President to implement a National High-Performance Computing Program. Provided for: (1) establishment of a National Research and Education Network; (2) standards and guidelines for high performance networks; and (3) the responsibility of certain federal departments and agencies with regard to the Network.

Veterans' Educational Assistance Amendments of 1991 (Public Law 102–127) restored certain educational benefits available to reserve and active-duty personnel under the Montgomery GI Bill to students whose course studies were interrupted by the Persian Gulf War.

Civil Rights Act of 1991 (Public Law 102–166) amended the Civil Rights Act of 1964, the Age Discrimination in Employment Act of 1967, and the Americans with Disabilities Act of 1990, with regard to employment discrimination. Established the Technical Assistance Training Institute.

1992 *Higher Education Amendments of 1992* (Public Law 102–325) amended the Higher Education Act of 1965 to revise and reauthorize funding for its various programs.

Ready-To-Learn Act (Public Law 102–545) amended the General Education Provisions Act to establish Ready-To-Learn Television programs to support educational programming and support materials for preschool and elementary school children and their parents, child care providers, and educators.

National Commission on Time and Learning, Extension (Public Law 102–359) amended the National Education Commission on Time and Learning Act to extend the authorization of appropriations for such Commission, amended the Elementary and Secondary Education Act of 1965 to revise provisions for (1) a specified civic education program; (2) schoolwide projects for educationally disadvantaged children, and provided for additional Assistant Secretaries of Education.

1993 *Student Loan Reform Act* (Public Law 103–66) reformed the student aid process by phasing in a system of direct lending designed to provide savings for taxpayers and students. Allows students to choose among a variety of repayment options, including income contingency.

National Service Trust Act (Public Law 103–82) amended the National and Community Service Act of 1990 to establish a Corporation for National Service and enhance opportunities for national service. In addition, the Act provided education grants up to $4,725 per year for 2 years to people age 17 years or older who perform community service before, during, or after postsecondary education.

NAEP Assessment Authorization (Public Law 103–33) authorizes the use of NAEP for state-by-state comparisons.

Migrant Student Record Transfer System Extension (Public Law 103–59) extends the operation of the migrant student record transfer system.

1994 *Goals 2000: Educate America Act* (Public Law 103–227) established a new federal partnership through a system of grants to states and local communities to reform the nation's education system. The Act formalized the national education goals and established the National Education Goals Panel. It also created a National Education Standards and Improvement Council (NESIC) to provide voluntary national certification of state and local education standards and assessments and established the National Skill Standards Board to develop voluntary national skill standards.

School-To-Work Opportunities Act of 1994 (Public Law 103–239) established a national framework within which states and communities can develop School-To-Work Opportunities systems to prepare young people for first jobs and continuing education. The Act also provided money to states and communities to develop a system of programs that include work-based learning, school-based learning, and connecting activities components. School-To-Work programs will provide students with a high school diploma (or its equivalent), a nationally recognized skill certificate, or an associate degree (if appropriate) and may lead to a first job or further education.

Safe Schools Act of 1994 (Part of Public Law 103–227) authorized the award of competitive grants to local educational agencies with serious crime to implement violence prevention activities such as conflict resolution and peer mediation.

Educational Research, Development, Dissemination, and Improvement Act of 1994 (Part of Public Law 103–227) authorized the educational research and dissemination activities of the Office of Educational Research and Improvement. The regional educational laboratories and university-based research and development centers are authorized under this act.

Student Loan Default Exemption Extension (Public Law 103–235) amended the Higher Education Act of 1965 to extend until July 1, 1998, the effective date for cohort default rate extension for Historically Black Colleges and Universities, tribally controlled community colleges, and Navajo community colleges.

Improving America's Schools Act (Public Law 103–382) reauthorized and revamps the Elementary and Secondary Education Act. The legislation includes Title I, the federal government's largest program providing educational assistance to disadvantaged children; professional development and technical assistance programs; a safe and drug-free schools and communities provision; and provisions promoting school equity.

1995

Amendment to the Elementary and Secondary Education Act of 1965 (Public Law 104–5) amended a provision of Part A of Title IX of the Elementary and Secondary Education Act of 1965 relating to Indian education, to provide a technical amendment and for other purposes.

1996 *Contract With America: Unfunded mandates* (Public Law 104–4) a bill to curb the practice of imposing unfunded federal mandates on states and local governments; to strengthen the partnership between the federal government and state, local, and tribal governments; to end the imposition, in the absence of full consideration by Congress, of federal mandates on state, local, and tribal governments without adequate funding, in a manner that may displace other essential governmental priorities and to ensure that the federal government pays the costs incurred by those governments in complying with certain requirements under federal statutes and regulations; and for other purposes.

Developmental Disabilities Assistance and Bill of Rights Act Amendments of 1996 (Public Law 104–1834) amended the Developmental Disabilities Assistance and Bill of Rights Act to extend the act, and for other purposes.

Remove grant limits on historically black colleges (Public Law 104–141) amended section 326 of the Higher Education Act of 1965 to permit continued participation by historically black graduate and professional schools in the grant program authorized by that section.

Correct impact-aid payments (Public Law 104–195) amends the Impact Aid Program to provide for a hold-harmless with respect to amounts for payments relating to the federal acquisition of real property, and for other purposes.

Human Rights, Refugee, and Other Foreign Relations Provisions Act of 1996 (Public Law 104–319) made certain provisions with respect to internationally recognized human rights, refugees, and foreign relations to revise U.S. human rights policy.

Figure 20.-Federal on-budget funds for education, by agency: Fiscal Year 1997

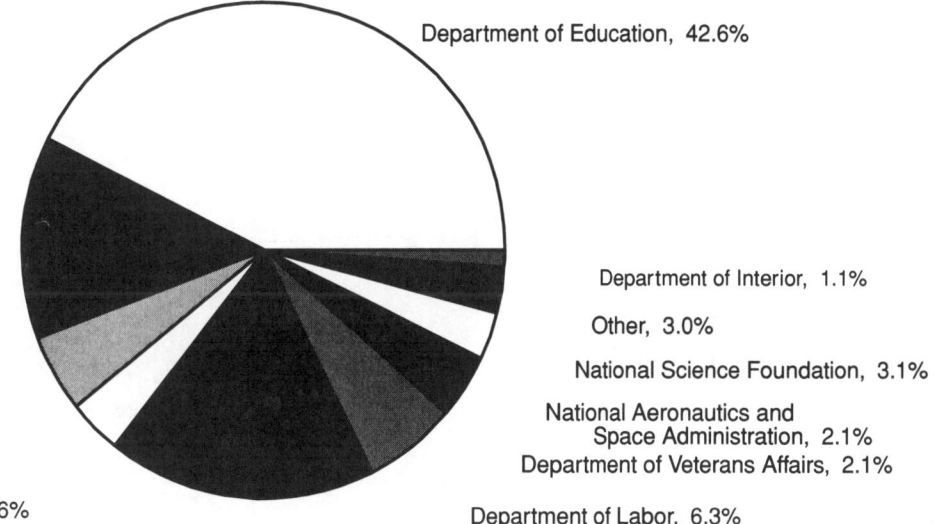

Total = $73.1 billion

SOURCE: U.S. Office of Management and Budget, *Budget of the U.S. Government, Fiscal Year 1998*; and National Science Foundation, *Federal Funds for Research and Development, Fiscal Years 1995, 1996, and 1997.*

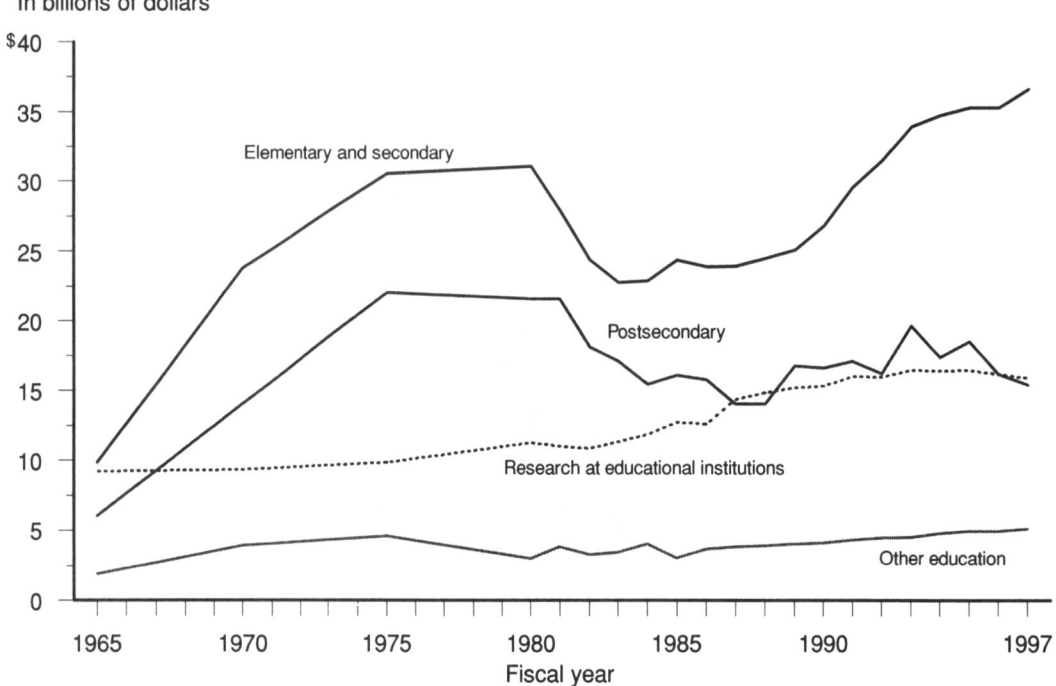

Figure 21.-Federal on-budget funds for education, by level or other educational purpose: 1965 to 1997
[In constant FY 1997 dollars]

SOURCE: U.S. Office of Management and Budget, *Budget of the U.S. Government,* fiscal years 1967 to 1998; National Science Foundation, *Federal Funds for Research and Development,* fiscal years 1967 to 1997; and unpublished data.

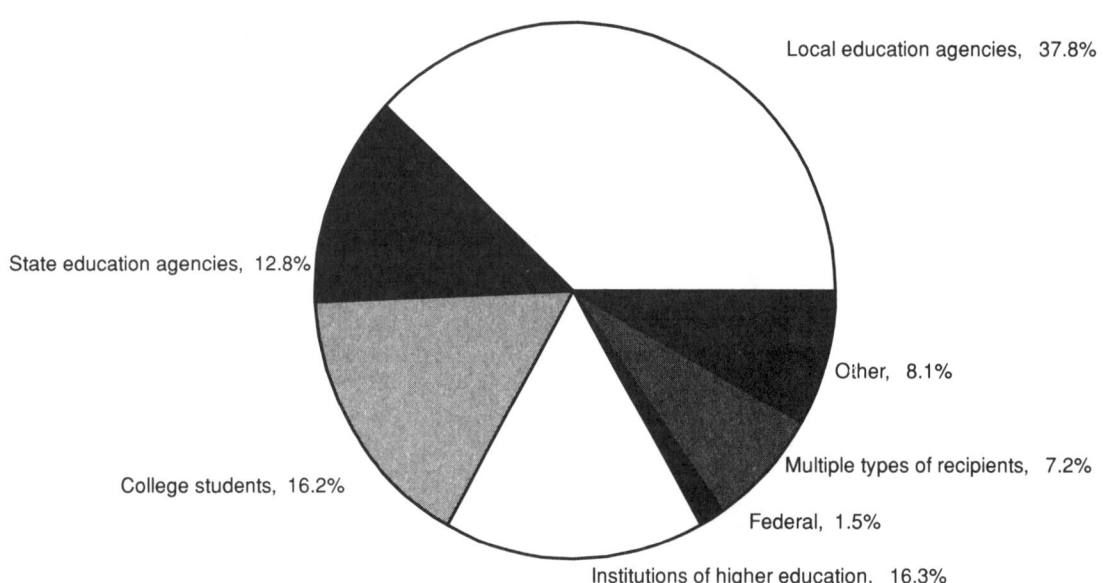

Figure 22.-Department of Education outlays, by type of recipient: Fiscal Year 1997

Total outlays=$31.1 billion

SOURCE: U.S. Office of Management and Budget, *Budget of the U.S. Government, Fiscal Year 1998; Catalog of Federal Domestic Assistance*; National Science Foundation, *Federal Funds for Research and Development , Fiscal Years 1995, 1996, and 1997*; and unpublished data obtained from various federal agencies.

FEDERAL PROGRAMS 387

Table 357.—Federal support and estimated federal tax expenditures for education, by category: Fiscal years 1965 to 1997

[In millions of dollars]

Fiscal year	Total on-budget support, off-budget support, and nonfederal funds generated by federal legislation	On-budget support [1]						Off-budget support and nonfederal funds generated by federal legislation							Estimated federal tax expenditures for education [9]
		Total	Elementary and secondary	Post-secondary	Other education	Research at educational institutions	Total	Off-budget support	Nonfederal funds						
								Federal Direct Student Loan [2]	Federal Family Education Loan Program [3]	Perkins Loans [4]	Income Contingent Loans [5]	State Student Incentive Grants [6]	Supplemental Educational Opportunity Grants [7]	Work-Study aid [8]	
1	2	3	4	5	6	7	8	9	10	11	12	13	14	15	16
Current dollars															
1965	$5,354.7	$5,331.0	$1,942.6	$1,197.5	$374.7	$1,816.3	$23.7	—	—	$16.1	—	—	—	$7.6	
1970	13,359.1	12,526.5	5,830.4	3,447.7	964.7	2,283.6	832.6	—	$770.0	21.0	—	—	—	41.6	
1975	24,691.5	23,288.1	10,617.2	7,644.0	1,608.5	3,418.4	1,403.4	—	1,233.0	35.7	—	$20.0	—	114.7	$8,605.0
1980	39,349.2	34,493.5	16,027.7	11,115.9	1,548.7	5,801.2	4,855.7	—	4,598.0	31.8	—	76.5	—	149.4	13,320.0
1981	44,296.7	36,621.3	15,903.7	12,260.0	2,182.2	6,275.5	7,675.4	—	7,433.0	20.7	—	76.5	—	145.2	16,380.0
1982	40,292.7	34,455.1	14,839.2	11,023.3	1,995.1	6,597.4	5,837.5	—	5,597.0	19.8	—	72.0	—	148.7	16,180.0
1983	41,709.4	34,883.9	14,527.8	10,918.1	2,204.1	7,233.8	6,825.5	—	6,582.0	19.8	—	60.0	—	163.7	16,725.0
1984	44,042.4	36,271.0	15,292.4	10,329.7	2,710.4	7,938.6	7,771.4	—	7,520.0	17.9	—	76.0	—	157.5	17,090.0
1985	47,753.4	39,027.9	16,901.3	11,174.4	2,107.6	8,844.6	8,725.5	—	8,467.0	21.4	—	76.0	—	161.1	18,035.0
1986	48,357.3	39,962.9	17,049.9	10,329.7	2,620.0	9,009.4	8,394.4	—	8,142.0	17.9	—	72.7	—	159.5	19,460.0
1987	50,724.6	41,194.7	17,535.7	10,300.0	2,820.4	10,538.6	9,529.8	—	9,272.0	21.4	$0.6	76.0	—	160.4	19,590.0
1988	54,078.9	43,454.4	18,564.9	10,657.5	2,981.6	10,380.0	10,624.5	—	10,380.0	20.2	0.5	72.7	—	150.4	16,190.0
1989	59,537.4	48,269.6	19,809.5	13,269.9	3,180.3	12,009.8	11,267.8	—	10,938.0	20.9	0.5	73.0	$22.0	215.0	16,890.0
1990	62,811.5	51,624.3	21,984.4	13,650.9	3,383.0	12,606.0	11,187.2	—	10,826.0	20.6	0.5	59.2	48.8	237.7	18,140.0
1991	70,371.7	57,595.7	25,418.0	14,703.6	3,698.6	13,775.4	12,776.1	—	12,372.0	20.4	0.5	63.5	87.7	235.0	
1992	74,477.9	60,479.8	27,926.9	14,384.1	3,992.0	14,176.9	13,998.0	—	13,568.0	15.0	0.5	72.0	97.2	242.9	
1993	84,741.5	67,740.6	30,834.3	17,844.6	4,107.2	14,955.1	17,000.8	—	16,524.0	17.3	—	72.4	184.6	190.5	
1994	92,778.2	68,250.9	32,304.4	16,173.8	4,483.7	15,289.1	24,527.3	$813.0	23,214.0	29.3	—	72.4	184.6	190.5	
1995	95,807.6	71,636.3	33,623.8	15,677.9	4,719.7	15,677.9	24,171.2	5,161.0	18,519.0	52.7	—	63.4	184.6	190.5	
1996	96,248.9	70,743.4	34,391.5	15,772.3	4,828.0	15,751.6	25,505.5	8,357.0	16,711.0	52.7	—	31.3	184.6	190.5	
1997[10]	100,501.2	73,070.4	36,634.8	15,417.7	5,125.2	15,892.7	27,430.8	9,938.0	16,965.0	52.7	—	50.0	184.6	240.5	
Constant fiscal year 1997 dollars [11]															
1965	$27,129.5	$27,009.4	$9,842.0	$6,067.1	$1,898.2	$9,202.1	$120.1	—	—	$81.6	—	—	—	$38.5	
1970	54,513.7	51,116.3	23,792.0	14,068.8	3,936.2	9,318.7	3,397.5	—	$3,142.1	85.6	—	—	—	169.8	
1975	71,051.8	67,013.5	30,551.9	21,996.3	4,628.5	9,836.6	4,038.3	—	3,548.1	102.6	—	$57.6	—	330.1	$24,761.6
1980	76,297.8	66,882.7	31,077.6	21,553.6	3,003.0	11,248.5	9,415.1	—	8,915.5	61.6	—	148.3	—	289.7	25,827.4
1981	77,838.3	64,351.1	27,946.0	21,543.3	3,834.5	11,027.2	13,487.2	—	13,061.3	36.3	—	134.4	—	255.1	28,783.0
1982	66,223.2	56,628.9	24,389.1	18,117.4	3,279.1	10,843.2	9,594.3	—	9,199.0	32.6	—	118.3	—	244.4	26,592.7
1983	65,407.6	54,704.0	22,782.2	17,121.5	3,456.5	11,343.9	10,703.6	—	10,321.7	31.1	—	94.1	—	256.7	26,227.1
1984	65,862.2	54,240.7	22,868.7	15,447.2	4,053.2	11,871.5	11,621.6	—	11,245.6	26.8	—	113.7	—	235.5	25,556.9
1985	68,821.2	56,246.2	24,357.9	16,104.3	3,037.4	12,746.6	12,575.0	—	12,202.5	30.8	—	109.5	—	232.2	25,991.7
1986	67,778.3	56,012.6	23,897.5	15,815.2	3,672.3	12,627.6	11,765.7	—	11,411.9	28.3	—	101.9	—	223.6	27,275.4
1987	69,179.9	56,182.8	23,915.8	14,047.5	3,846.6	14,372.9	12,997.1	—	12,645.5	28.5	$0.8	103.7	—	218.8	26,717.5
1988	71,398.6	57,371.4	24,510.2	14,047.5	3,936.5	14,853.6	14,027.2	—	13,704.4	27.2	0.6	96.4	$27.9	198.6	21,375.1
1989	75,461.8	61,180.1	25,107.9	14,819.2	4,031.0	15,222.1	14,281.6	—	13,863.6	25.8	0.7	91.1	59.5	272.5	21,407.5
1990	76,558.6	62,922.9	28,795.9	16,638.6	4,123.4	15,365.0	13,635.6	—	13,195.4	18.3	0.7	72.1	102.1	289.7	22,110.1
1991	81,898.3	67,029.6	29,581.4	17,112.0	4,304.4	16,031.8	14,868.7	—	14,398.5	20.2	0.6	73.9	109.7	273.5	
1992	84,033.4	68,239.4	31,509.9	16,229.6	4,504.1	15,995.8	15,794.0	—	15,308.8	19.6	0.6	81.2	102.1	274.1	
1993	93,263.6	74,553.0	33,935.2	19,638.5	4,520.2	16,459.1	18,710.6	—	18,185.7	32.2	—	79.7	203.2	209.7	
1994	99,772.8	73,396.4	34,739.8	17,393.1	4,821.7	16,441.8	26,376.4	$874.3	24,964.1	56.6	—	77.9	198.5	204.9	
1995	100,604.0	75,223.1	35,307.3	18,496.9	4,956.1	16,462.9	25,381.5	5,419.4	19,446.2	55.3	—	66.6	193.9	200.1	
1996	98,806.0	72,622.9	35,305.2	16,191.5	4,956.3	16,170.1	26,183.1	8,579.0	17,155.0	31.9	—	32.1	189.5	195.6	
1997[10]	100,501.2	73,070.4	36,634.8	15,417.7	5,125.2	15,892.7	27,430.8	9,938.0	16,965.0	52.7	—	50.0	184.6	240.5	

[1] On-budget support includes federal funds for education programs tied to appropriations.
[2] The Federal Direct Student Loan (FDSL) program, recently renamed the William D. Ford Direct Loan program, provides students with the same benefits they are currently eligible to receive under the Federal Family Education Loan (FFEL) program but provides loans to students through federal capital rather than through private lenders. This program is an off-budget support program.
[3] Formerly the Guaranteed Student Loan program. New student loans guaranteed by the federal government and disbursed to borrowers.
[4] Student loans created from institutional matching funds (1/3 of the federal contribution). Excludes repayments of outstanding loans.
[5] Student loans created from institutional matching funds (1/9 of the federal contribution). This was a demonstration project that involved only 10 institutions and had unsubsidized interest rates.
[6] Required state matching contributions.
[7] Institutions award grants to undergraduate students, and the federal share of such grants may not exceed 75 percent of the total grant.
[8] Employer contributions to student earnings.
[9] Losses of tax revenue attributable to provisions of the federal income tax laws that allow a special exclusion, exemption, or deduction from gross income or provide a special credit, preferential rate of tax, or a deferral of tax affecting individual or corporate income tax liabilities.
[10] Estimated.
[11] Data adjusted by the federal funds composite deflator prepared by the U.S. Office of Management and Budget.
—Data not available or not applicable.

NOTE.—To the extent possible, federal education funds data represent outlays rather than obligations. Because of rounding, details may not add to totals. Some data have been revised from previously published figures.

SOURCE: U.S. Department of Education, National Center for Education Statistics, compiled from data appearing in U.S. Office of Management and Budget, *Budget of the U.S. Government, Appendix,* fiscal years 1967 to 1998; National Science Foundation, *Federal Funds for Research and Development,* fiscal years 1965 to 1997; "Federal Tax Expenditures, FY 1980 to FY 1984," "Federal Tax Expenditures, FY 1984 to FY 1988," and "Federal Tax Expenditures, FY 1970 to FY 1990" by Stephen M. Barro, prepared for the National Center for Education Statistics; and unpublished data obtained from various federal agencies. (This table was prepared May 1997.)

Table 358.—Federal on-budget funds for education, by agency: Fiscal years 1965 to 1997
[In thousands of dollars]

Agency	1965	1970	1975	1980	1982	1983	1984	1985	1986	1987
1	2	3	4	5	6	7	8	9	10	11
Total	**$5,331,016**	**$12,526,499**	**$23,288,120**	**$34,493,502**	**$34,455,134**	**$34,883,900**	**$36,271,011**	**$39,027,876**	**$39,962,901**	**$41,194,718**
Department of Education	1,000,567	4,625,224	7,350,355	13,137,785	14,109,272	14,585,825	15,534,737	16,701,065	17,740,051	16,879,827
Department of Agriculture	768,927	960,910	2,219,352	4,562,467	4,107,473	4,340,869	4,616,372	4,782,274	5,041,317	5,189,779
Department of Commerce	9,347	13,990	38,967	135,561	60,150	55,090	55,160	55,114	64,613	38,896
Department of Defense	587,412	821,388	1,009,229	1,560,301	2,097,256	2,487,597	2,625,146	3,119,213	3,354,588	3,695,617
Department of Energy	442,434	551,527	764,676	1,605,558	1,751,803	1,933,068	2,042,881	2,247,822	2,181,391	2,256,799
Department of Health and Human Services	1,027,537	1,796,854	3,675,225	5,613,930	5,604,470	4,968,658	4,902,016	5,322,356	5,316,853	6,104,812
Department of Housing and Urban Development	221,256	114,709	−52,768	5,314	969	2,158	2,000	438	342	463
Department of the Interior	170,088	190,975	300,191	440,547	476,030	484,314	576,779	549,479	454,273	485,922
Department of Justice	10,252	15,728	61,542	60,721	57,890	68,700	62,282	66,802	72,191	79,815
Department of Labor	230,041	424,494	1,103,935	1,862,738	1,799,315	1,833,392	1,755,839	1,948,685	1,976,960	2,258,631
Department of State	64,200	59,742	89,433	25,188	21,181	23,813	23,086	23,820	23,401	24,288
Department of Transportation	—	27,534	52,290	54,712	75,404	82,139	83,931	82,035	66,214	75,360
Department of the Treasury	8,240	18	1,118,840	1,247,463	286,980	287,300	287,905	290,276	41,257	19,279
Department of Veterans Affairs	97,237	1,032,918	4,402,212	2,351,233	1,978,872	1,672,348	1,445,049	1,289,849	1,055,948	1,002,109
Other agencies and programs:										
ACTION	—	—	7,081	2,833	1,720	1,830	4,975	1,761	1,368	3,368
Agency for International Development	63,329	88,034	78,896	176,770	205,177	173,629	236,983	198,807	198,929	240,827
Appalachian Regional Commission	—	37,838	45,786	19,032	7,626	2,899	4,919	4,745	6,582	5,445
Barry Goldwater Scholarship and Excellence in Education Foundation	—	—	—	—	—	—	—	—	—	—
Corporation for National and Community Service	—	—	—	—	—	—	—	—	—	—
Environmental Protection Agency	—	19,446	33,875	41,083	67,798	43,557	43,700	60,521	69,718	67,465
Estimated education share of federal aid to the District of Columbia	11,350	33,019	55,487	81,847	91,615	97,516	97,385	107,340	101,844	126,942
Federal Emergency Management Agency	—	290	290	1,946	2,625	1,195	351	1,828	290	290
General Services Administration	4,013	14,775	22,532	34,800	37,300	44,200	50,894	—	—	—
Harry S Truman Scholarship fund	—	—	—	−1,895	1,667	1,795	1,929	1,332	2,441	2,717
Institute of American Indian and Alaskan Native Culture and Arts Development	—	—	—	—	—	—	—	—	—	—
James Madison Memorial Fellowship Foundation	—	—	—	—	—	—	—	—	—	—
Japanese-United States Friendship Commission	—	—	—	2,294	1,807	2,364	1,611	2,236	235	3,225
Library of Congress	15,111	29,478	63,766	151,871	144,911	154,198	164,080	169,310	166,130	160,835
National Aeronautics and Space Administration	208,788	258,366	197,901	255,511	369,105	367,763	354,528	487,624	490,948	787,391
National Archives and Records Administration	—	—	—	—	—	—	—	—	52,118	55,252	59,521
National Commission on Libraries and Information Science	—	—	449	2,090	638	681	733	723	781	512
National Endowment for the Arts	—	340	4,754	5,220	4,823	4,701	5,197	5,536	5,188	5,394
National Endowment for the Humanities	—	8,459	63,955	142,586	115,818	123,315	127,571	125,671	121,125	124,407
National Science Foundation	181,216	295,628	535,294	808,392	854,665	907,917	1,035,746	1,147,115	1,147,273	1,270,415
Nuclear Regulatory Commission	—	—	7,093	32,590	38,150	37,987	36,400	30,261	27,472	29,176
Office of Economic Opportunity	189,871	1,092,410	16,619	—	—	—	—	—	—	—
Smithsonian Institution	2,233	2,461	5,509	5,153	5,215	6,073	5,758	7,886	6,191	6,545
United States Arms Control Agency	—	100	—	661	184	157	—	395	276	3,244
United States Information Agency	7,512	8,423	9,405	66,210	77,185	86,556	83,768	143,007	170,514	179,653
United States Institute of Peace	—	—	—	—	—	—	—	—	230	4,083
Other agencies	10,055	1,421	5,949	990	40	296	1,300	432	715	1,666

Table 358.—Federal on-budget funds for education, by agency: Fiscal years 1965 to 1997—Continued
[In thousands of dollars]

Agency	1988	1989	1990	1991	1992	1993	1994	1995	1996	1997[1]
1	12	13	14	15	16	17	18	19	20	21
Total	$43,454,423	$48,269,575	$51,624,342	$57,595,664	$60,479,844	$67,740,618	$68,250,906	$71,636,320	$70,743,418	$73,070,374
Department of Education	18,326,916	21,671,232	23,198,575	25,391,310	26,116,013	30,478,215	29,713,408	31,403,000	29,977,805	31,104,329
Department of Agriculture	5,481,976	5,793,616	6,260,843	6,875,216	7,586,729	8,067,050	8,494,772	9,092,089	9,276,943	9,657,266
Department of Commerce	38,553	47,586	53,835	67,204	80,510	74,354	85,423	88,929	80,516	74,479
Department of Defense	3,461,345	3,746,031	3,605,509	3,707,276	3,948,471	3,958,746	3,899,582	3,879,002	3,780,805	3,735,929
Department of Energy	2,385,966	2,563,978	2,561,950	2,738,862	2,917,137	2,787,423	2,671,660	2,692,314	2,558,809	2,609,288
Department of Health and Human Services	6,505,428	6,952,995	7,956,011	9,470,027	9,362,010	10,885,245	11,921,727	12,469,563	13,115,136	13,063,049
Department of Housing and Urban Development	51	186	118	48	203	401	856	1,613	1,400	987
Department of the Interior	528,409	542,466	630,537	844,830	715,382	723,448	696,649	702,796	674,286	798,383
Department of Justice	83,405	88,129	99,775	114,653	134,235	148,381	150,398	172,350	217,247	237,718
Department of Labor	2,272,228	2,277,556	2,511,380	3,214,695	3,709,531	4,241,590	4,015,434	3,967,914	4,089,440	4,593,150
Department of State	38,671	45,848	51,225	49,086	53,343	69,051	54,414	54,671	55,394	54,116
Department of Transportation	65,134	90,840	76,186	69,887	91,485	115,925	119,806	132,616	135,120	126,924
Department of the Treasury	32,768	39,511	41,715	60,356	51,779	56,912	63,301	49,496	59,673	61,081
Department of Veterans Affairs	966,549	896,435	757,476	783,789	1,047,579	1,145,108	1,381,925	1,324,382	1,420,861	1,557,191
Other agencies and programs:										
ACTION	4,110	4,800	8,472	11,321	8,600	—	—	—	—	—
Agency for International Development	242,650	227,864	249,786	209,018	245,199	242,907	266,582	290,580	325,894	303,024
Appalachian Regional Commission	6,377	6,145	93	3,907	7,608	7,974	10,242	10,623	8,322	8,322
Barry Goldwater Scholarship and Excellence in Education Foundation	—	753	1,033	1,941	2,900	3,023	2,789	3,000	3,000	3,000
Corporation for National and Community Service	—	—	—	—	—	8,500	93,250	214,600	279,000	335,000
Environmental Protection Agency	58,053	64,517	87,481	62,753	152,012	124,500	98,241	125,721	104,200	132,434
Estimated education share of federal aid to the District of Columbia	122,366	103,764	104,940	125,835	130,371	139,755	97,752	78,796	70,427	98,479
Federal Emergency Management Agency	290	77	215	33	261	76,467	85,200	170,400	7,500	8,300
General Services Administration	—	—	—	—	—	—	—	—	—	—
Harry S Truman Scholarship fund	2,815	2,851	2,883	2,968	2,401	2,894	2,323	3,000	3,000	3,000
Institute of American Indian and Alaskan Native Culture and Arts Development	—	3,094	4,305	5,447	6,612	7,462	12,213	13,000	6,000	6,000
James Madison Memorial Fellowship Foundation	13,200	10,005	191	531	885	1,298	1,464	2,000	2,000	2,000
Japanese-United States Friendship Commission	2,274	3,004	2,299	1,377	1,610	1,503	1,585	2,000	2,000	2,000
Library of Congress	160,505	177,954	189,827	279,745	296,044	311,453	312,724	241,000	252,000	269,000
National Aeronautics and Space Administration	899,897	978,778	1,093,303	1,275,970	1,383,422	1,374,042	1,418,765	1,757,900	1,617,301	1,518,077
National Archives and Records Administration	65,153	86,266	77,397	81,462	99,412	106,975	110,411	105,172	104,536	111,277
National Commission on Libraries and Information Science	522	839	3,281	3,447	1,437	867	724	1,000	1,000	1,000
National Endowment for the Arts	5,550	5,655	5,577	6,498	8,286	7,784	7,221	9,421	4,548	9,000
National Endowment for the Humanities	125,230	137,076	141,048	149,832	159,103	160,275	157,468	151,727	93,359	93,359
National Science Foundation	1,329,520	1,472,835	1,588,891	1,738,471	1,875,072	2,080,154	2,031,024	2,086,195	2,123,217	2,241,988
Nuclear Regulatory Commission	25,676	25,690	42,328	23,860	27,418	22,934	20,227	22,188	12,958	15,890
Office of Economic Opportunity	—	—	—	—	—	—	—	—	—	—
Smithsonian Institution	5,393	5,880	5,779	5,906	6,578	7,828	10,059	9,961	9,908	9,990
United States Arms Control Agency	2,633	1,619	25	69	100	25	—	—	—	—
United States Information Agency	189,464	185,521	201,547	208,181	237,226	288,059	230,493	294,800	257,400	210,600
United States Institute of Peace	3,476	7,232	7,621	8,238	11,350	10,468	10,794	12,000	11,000	12,000
Other agencies	1,870	947	885	1,616	1,532	1,622	—	500	1,415	2,745

[1] Estimated.
—Data not available or not applicable.

NOTE.—To the extent possible, amounts reported represent outlays, rather than obligations. Some data have been revised from previously published data. Because of rounding, details may not add to totals.

SOURCE: U.S. Department of Education, National Center for Education Statistics, compiled from data appearing in U.S. Office of Management and Budget, *Budget of the U.S. Government, Appendix*, fiscal years 1982 to 1998; National Science Foundation, *Federal Funds for Research and Development*, fiscal years 1965 to 1997; and unpublished data obtained from various federal agencies. (This table was prepared May 1997.)

Table 359.—Federal on-budget funds for education, by level or other educational purpose, by agency and program: Fiscal years 1965 to 1997

[In thousands of dollars]

Level or educational purpose, by agency and program	1965	1970	1975	1980	1982	1983	1984	1985	1986	1987
1	2	3	4	5	6	7	8	9	10	11
Total, all programs	$5,331,016	$12,526,499	$23,288,120	$34,493,502	$34,455,134	$34,883,900	$36,271,011	$39,027,876	$39,962,901	$41,194,718
Elementary/secondary education programs	$1,942,577	$5,830,442	$10,617,195	$16,027,686	$14,839,241	$14,527,848	$15,292,409	$16,901,334	$17,049,940	$17,535,707
Department of Education[9]	567,343	2,719,204	4,132,742	6,629,095	6,456,322	5,986,633	6,220,820	7,296,702	7,551,973	7,554,487
Grants for the disadvantaged	—	1,339,014	1,874,353	3,204,664	2,954,438	2,645,688	3,077,304	4,206,754	3,404,687	3,209,923
Impact aid program[10]	349,671	656,372	618,711	690,170	546,299	548,205	577,676	647,402	684,311	704,197
School improvement programs	72,298	288,304	700,470	788,918	751,130	552,590	631,537	526,401	618,850	889,478
Indian education	—	—	40,036	93,365	78,353	69,603	71,588	82,328	62,067	39,638
Bilingual education	—	21,250	92,693	169,540	167,114	163,268	167,400	157,539	119,601	141,483
Education for the handicapped	13,849	79,090	151,244	821,777	1,141,444	1,289,710	952,778	1,017,964	1,627,894	1,339,241
Vocational and adult education	131,525	335,174	655,235	860,661	817,544	717,569	742,537	658,314	1,034,563	1,230,527
Education Reform - Goals 2000[11]										
Department of Agriculture	623,014	760,477	1,884,345	4,064,497	3,528,208	3,727,171	3,992,808	4,134,906	4,428,143	4,562,093
Child nutrition programs[12]	178,580	299,131	1,452,267	3,377,056	3,019,724	3,278,133	3,536,378	3,664,561	3,819,734	4,044,830
Agricultural Marketing Service— commodities[13]	340,073	341,597	248,839	388,000	363,883	362,297	338,764	336,502	344,350	350,118
Special milk program[12]	86,609	83,800	122,858	159,293	22,884	14,912	16,000	15,993	15,267	15,446
Estimated education share of Forest Service permanent appropriations	17,752	35,949	60,381	140,148	121,717	71,829	101,666	117,850	248,792	151,699
Department of Commerce	—	—	—	54,816	5,399	1,348	337	—	—	—
Local public works program— school facilities[14]	—	—	—	54,816	5,399	1,348	337	—	—	—
Department of Defense	73,000	143,100	264,500	370,846	514,993	564,885	694,946	831,625	903,493	861,393
Junior R.O.T.C.	—	12,100	12,500	32,000	42,300	50,400	44,300	55,600	58,600	57,440
Overseas dependents schools	73,000	131,000	252,000	338,846	386,693	414,485	546,072	613,437	691,437	664,941
Section VI schools[10]	—	—	—	—	86,000	100,000	104,574	162,588	153,456	139,012
Department of Energy[15]	100	200	300	77,633	19,985	40,798	22,469	23,031	21,385	12,061
Energy conservation for school buildings[16]	—	—	—	77,240	19,765	40,634	22,269	22,731	21,000	11,761
Pre-engineering program	100	200	300	393	220	164	200	300	385	300
Department of Health and Human Services[17]	79,999	167,333	683,885	1,077,000	1,385,700	1,265,000	1,472,750	1,531,059	1,455,315	1,555,542
Head Start[18]	—	—	403,900	735,000	911,700	912,000	995,750	1,075,059	1,040,315	1,130,542
Payments to states for AFDC work programs[19]										
Social Security student benefits[20]	79,999	167,333	279,985	342,000	474,000	353,000	477,000	456,000	415,000	425,000
Department of the Interior	130,096	140,705	220,392	318,170	328,584	346,242	393,529	389,810	308,089	344,183
Mineral Leasing Act and other funds:										
Payments to states—estimated education share	11,075	12,294	27,389	62,636	124,480	123,670	170,645	127,369	98,606	87,437
Payments to counties—estimated education share	10,731	16,359	29,494	48,953	49,108	20,220	24,221	59,016	5,615	36,455
Indian Education:										
Bureau of Indian Affairs schools	92,603	95,850	141,056	178,112	114,093	176,878	173,141	177,265	181,235	195,994
Johnson-O'Malley assistance[21]	15,534	16,080	22,251	28,081	40,497	25,077	25,029	25,675	22,053	22,824
Education expenses for children of employees, Yellowstone National Park	153	122	202	388	406	397	493	485	580	1,473
Department of Justice	6,402	8,237	9,822	23,890	25,620	30,462	31,759	36,117	39,684	44,531
Vocational training expenses for prisoners in federal prisons[22]	1,466	2,720	3,039	4,966	5,066	8,230	7,377	8,292	8,744	8,744
Inmate programs[23]	4,936	5,517	6,783	18,924	20,554	22,232	24,382	27,825	30,940	35,787
Department of Labor	230,041	420,927	1,097,811	1,849,800	1,790,400	1,827,000	1,751,039	1,945,268	1,976,619	2,258,199
Job Corps[24]	—	—	175,000	469,800	570,000	563,000	595,772	604,748	632,619	678,599
Training programs—estimated funds for education programs[25]	230,041	420,927	922,811	1,380,000	1,220,400	1,264,000	1,155,267	1,340,520	1,344,000	1,579,600
Department of Transportation[26]	—	45	50	60	57	65	105	60	60	55
Tuition assistance for educational accreditation— Coast Guard personnel[27]	—	45	50	60	57	65	105	60	60	55
Department of the Treasury	32	—	847,139	935,903	273,728	273,728	273,278	273,728	25,085	—
Estimated education share of general revenue sharing:[28]										
State[29]	—	—	475,224	525,019	—	—	—	—	—	—
Local	—	—	371,915	410,884	273,728	273,728	273,278	273,728	25,085	—
Tuition assistance for educational accreditation— Coast Guard personnel[27]	32	—	—	—	—	—	—	—	—	—
Department of Veterans Affairs[30]	41,250	338,910	1,371,500	545,786	427,065	378,663	351,940	344,758	251,782	235,297
Noncollegiate and job training programs[31]	14,550	281,640	1,249,410	439,993	291,818	244,060	227,991	224,035	137,805	119,702
Vocational rehabilitation for disabled veterans[32]	17,400	41,700	73,100	87,980	116,285	117,598	110,187	107,480	103,159	105,947
Dependents' education[33]	9,300	15,570	48,990	17,813	18,962	17,005	13,762	13,243	10,818	9,648
Service members occupational conversion and training act of 1992[22,34]	—	—	—	—	—	—	—	—	—	—
Other agencies										
Appalachian Regional Commission[35]	—	33,161	41,667	9,157	4,936	2,801	4,589	4,632	4,632	5,323
National Endowment for the Arts[36]	—	—	3,686	4,989	4,099	4,069	4,378	4,399	4,060	4,099
Arts in education	—	—	3,686	4,989	4,099	4,069	4,378	4,399	4,060	4,099
National Endowment for the Humanities[37]	—	20	149	330	418	510	462	321	460	352

Table 359.—Federal on-budget funds for education, by level or other educational purpose, by agency and program: Fiscal years 1965 to 1997—Continued

[In thousands of dollars]

Level or educational purpose, by agency and program	1988	1989	1990[1]	1991[2]	1992[3]	1993[4]	1994[5]	1995[6]	1996[7]	1997[8]
1	12	13	14	15	16	17	18	19	20	21
Total, all programs	$43,454,423	$48,269,575	$51,624,342	$57,595,664	$60,479,844	$67,740,618	$68,250,906	$71,636,320	$70,743,418	$73,070,374
Elementary/secondary education programs	$18,564,859	$19,809,528	$21,984,361	$25,418,031	$27,926,888	$30,834,326	$32,304,357	$33,623,809	$34,391,501	$36,634,811
Department of Education[9]	8,098,436	8,869,300	9,681,313	10,865,336	12,057,746	13,058,974	13,769,196	14,029,000	14,323,770	15,663,123
Grants for the disadvantaged	4,027,559	4,185,357	4,494,111	5,218,749	6,158,813	6,615,047	6,845,651	6,808,000	7,020,460	7,234,818
Impact aid program[10]	707,539	755,477	816,366	753,530	794,794	432,153	829,952	808,000	952,277	900,957
School improvement programs	443,468	975,237	1,189,158	1,375,910	1,514,892	2,032,552	1,469,964	1,397,000	1,247,360	1,520,613
Indian education	18,339	65,683	69,451	65,639	68,523	99,925	79,095	71,000	77,402	67,471
Bilingual education	159,746	164,759	188,919	186,748	198,332	124,778	221,681	225,000	184,529	225,430
Education for the handicapped	1,465,985	1,880,751	1,616,623	2,174,358	2,243,338	2,564,070	2,980,328	3,177,000	3,222,180	3,425,900
Vocational and adult education	1,275,800	842,036	1,306,685	1,090,402	1,079,054	1,190,449	1,340,762	1,482,000	1,348,064	1,597,391
Education Reform - Goals 2000[11]	—	—	—	—	—	—	1,763	61,000	271,498	690,543
Department of Agriculture	4,806,766	5,104,502	5,528,950	6,074,735	6,714,082	7,154,483	7,604,447	8,201,294	8,408,072	8,795,195
Child nutrition programs[12]	4,286,242	4,555,581	4,977,075	5,536,966	6,126,983	6,596,588	7,043,699	7,644,789	7,875,000	8,264,000
Agricultural Marketing Service—commodities[13]	349,670	342,071	350,441	350,859	400,000	389,900	400,000	400,000	400,000	400,000
Special milk program[12]	18,342	18,544	18,707	19,900	19,178	15,535	([12])	([12])	([12])	([12])
Estimated education share of Forest Service permanent appropriations	152,512	188,306	182,727	167,010	167,921	152,460	160,748	156,505	133,072	131,195
Department of Commerce	—	—	—	—	—	—	—	—	—	—
Local public works program—school facilities[14]	—	—	—	—	—	—	—	—	—	—
Department of Defense	988,265	1,059,259	1,097,876	1,253,105	1,197,318	1,259,374	1,210,168	1,295,547	1,313,126	1,373,115
Junior R.O.T.C.	45,300	53,930	39,300	53,174	54,746	84,100	95,500	155,600	163,800	167,800
Overseas dependents schools	773,810	821,365	864,958	960,293	912,916	895,674	849,649	855,772	813,270	856,258
Section VI schools[10]	169,155	183,964	193,618	239,638	229,656	279,600	265,019	284,175	336,056	349,057
Department of Energy[15]	12,931	12,851	15,563	15,676	15,236	6,254	11,615	12,646	—	—
Energy conservation for school buildings[16]	12,611	12,442	15,213	14,206	12,586	5,054	10,535	10,746	—	—
Pre-engineering program	320	409	350	1,470	2,650	1,200	1,080	1,900	—	—
Department of Health and Human Services[17]	1,651,324	1,789,026	2,396,793	2,997,194	3,310,200	4,114,498	4,669,181	5,116,559	5,185,871	4,946,624
Head Start[18]	1,206,324	1,234,869	1,447,758	1,951,775	2,201,800	2,776,286	3,215,946	3,534,000	3,570,000	3,981,000
Payments to states for AFDC work programs[19]	—	85,511	459,221	545,700	594,184	736,474	838,981	953,000	931,000	324,000
Social Security student benefits[20]	445,000	468,646	489,814	499,719	514,216	601,738	614,254	629,559	684,871	641,624
Department of the Interior	379,645	379,381	445,267	644,770	517,666	536,483	485,758	493,124	486,463	603,794
Mineral Leasing Act and other funds: Payments to states—estimated education share	92,227	114,414	123,811	131,683	122,045	108,924	21,693	18,750	17,940	42,320
Payments to counties—estimated education share	34,922	54,804	102,522	35,038	45,805	34,903	39,819	37,490	39,000	92,000
Indian Education: Bureau of Indian Affairs schools	231,512	186,643	192,841	452,521	325,582	368,817	399,234	411,524	408,889	450,218
Johnson-O'Malley assistance[21]	20,400	23,000	25,556	24,931	23,590	22,980	24,326	24,359	19,634	18,256
Education expenses for children of employees, Yellowstone National Park	584	520	538	597	644	859	686	1,000	1,000	1,000
Department of Justice	50,679	58,523	65,997	78,050	94,724	107,857	112,447	128,850	175,900	196,900
Vocational training expenses for prisoners in federal prisons[22]	8,679	6,933	2,066	1,748	1,944	1,725	1,240	3,000	−3,500	−11,500
Inmate programs[23]	42,000	51,590	63,931	76,302	92,780	106,132	111,207	125,850	179,400	208,400
Department of Labor	2,266,700	2,271,966	2,505,487	3,209,147	3,708,362	4,240,990	4,011,184	3,957,800	4,084,000	4,593,000
Job Corps[24]	712,218	771,966	739,376	805,270	925,826	949,287	964,234	1,029,000	1,114,000	1,146,000
Training programs—estimated funds for education programs[25]	1,554,482	1,500,000	1,766,111	2,403,877	2,782,536	3,291,703	3,046,950	2,928,800	2,970,000	3,447,000
Department of Transportation[26]	50	40	46	31	60	60	60	62	40	40
Tuition assistance for educational accreditation—Coast Guard personnel[27]	50	40	46	31	60	60	60	62	40	40
Department of the Treasury	—	—	—	—	—	—	—	—	—	—
Estimated education share of general revenue sharing:[28]										
State[29]	—	—	—	—	—	—	—	—	—	—
Local	—	—	—	—	—	—	—	—	—	—
Tuition assistance for educational accreditation—Coast Guard personnel[27]	—	—	—	—	—	—	—	—	—	—
Department of Veterans Affairs[30]	196,159	168,865	155,351	167,040	190,608	222,567	335,866	311,768	344,298	371,384
Noncollegiate and job training programs[31]	76,367	43,696	12,848	—	—	—	—	—	—	—
Vocational rehabilitation for disabled veterans[32]	112,058	118,749	136,780	161,096	184,500	216,276	265,597	298,132	349,637	377,389
Dependents' education[33]	7,734	6,420	5,723	5,944	6,108	5,840	5,740	5,961	4,493	3,998
Service members occupational conversion and training act of 1992[22,34]	—	—	—	—	—	451	64,529	7,675	−9,832	−10,003
Other agencies										
Appalachian Regional Commission[35]	5,327	5,145	93	3,790	5,182	5,382	2,529	2,173	2,862	2,862
National Endowment for the Arts[36]	4,350	4,462	4,641	4,870	5,000	5,000	5,000	7,117	4,030	2,850
Arts in education	4,350	4,462	4,641	4,870	5,000	5,000	5,000	7,117	4,030	2,850
National Endowment for the Humanities[37]	826	698	404	590	809	1,645	278	997	101	101

Table 359.—Federal on-budget funds for education, by level or other educational purpose, by agency and program: Fiscal years 1965 to 1997—Continued

[In thousands of dollars]

Level or educational purpose, by agency and program	1965	1970	1975	1980	1982	1983	1984	1985	1986	1987
1	2	3	4	5	6	7	8	9	10	11
Office of Economic Opportunity[38]	182,793	1,072,375	16,619	—	—	—	—	—	—	—
Head Start[39]	96,400	325,700	—	—	—	—	—	—	—	—
Other elementary and secondary programs[40]	20,000	42,809	16,612	—	—	—	—	—	—	—
Job Corps[41]	34,000	144,000	—	—	—	—	—	—	—	—
Youth Corps and other training programs[42]	31,000	553,368	7	—	—	—	—	—	—	—
Volunteers in Service to America (VISTA)[43]	1,393	6,498	—	—	—	—	—	—	—	—
Other programs										
Estimated education share of federal aid to the District of Columbia	8,507	25,748	42,588	65,714	73,727	78,473	77,200	84,918	79,160	98,092
Postsecondary education programs	**$1,197,511**	**$3,447,697**	**$7,644,037**	**$11,115,882**	**$11,023,323**	**$10,918,099**	**$10,329,650**	**$11,174,379**	**$11,283,589**	**$10,299,998**
Department of Education[9]	237,955	1,187,962	2,089,184	5,682,242	6,418,740	7,213,341	7,341,239	8,202,499	8,444,924	7,438,674
Student financial assistance[44]	—	—	—	3,682,789	2,732,467	4,043,597	3,743,262	4,162,695	4,585,210	4,779,817
Federal Direct Student Loan Program[45]	—	—	—	—	—	—	—	—	—	—
Federal Family Education Loan Program[46]	—	2,323	111,087	1,407,977	3,023,463	2,555,539	3,245,226	3,534,795	3,322,734	2,548,179
Higher education	218,264	1,029,131	1,838,066	399,787	379,281	364,422	419,200	404,511	402,035	419,105
Facilities—loans and insurance[22]	3,588	114,199	16,292	−19,031	25,201	21,148	−945	5,307	1,920	−84,866
College housing loans[22,47]	—	—	—	14,082	36,531	−16,510	−238,818	−164,061	−73,992	−558,178
Educational activities overseas[22]	129	774	1,881	3,561	1,322	1,243	1,259	1,838	−1,413	−8
Historically Black Colleges and Universities Capital Financing, Program Account[48]	—	—	—	—	—	—	—	—	—	—
Gallaudet College and Howard University	15,974	38,559	111,971	176,829	196,748	216,782	148,600	229,938	171,729	299,085
National Technical Institute for the Deaf[49]	—	2,976	9,887	16,248	23,727	27,120	23,455	27,476	36,701	35,540
Department of Agriculture	—	—	6,450	10,453	12,241	16,241	17,241	17,741	16,877	16,877
Agriculture Extension Service, Second Morrill Act payments to agricultural and mechanical colleges and Tuskegee Institute[50]	—	—	6,450	10,453	12,241	16,241	17,241	17,741	16,877	16,877
Department of Commerce	5,081	8,277	14,973	29,971	2,533	2,282	2,223	2,163	2,207	2,061
Sea Grant Program[51]	—	—	1,886	3,123	2,533	2,282	2,223	2,163	2,207	2,061
Merchant Marine Academy[52]	3,570	6,160	10,152	14,809	—	—	—	—	—	—
State marine schools[52]	1,511	2,117	2,935	12,039	—	—	—	—	—	—
Department of Defense[53]	77,500	322,100	379,800	545,000	692,400	810,500	857,700	1,041,700	1,068,300	1,079,768
Tuition assistance for military personnel	—	57,500	86,800	([54])	50,800	61,300	68,900	77,100	89,700	111,368
Service academies[55]	77,500	78,700	86,200	106,100	142,500	151,900	160,700	196,400	214,500	223,700
Senior R.O.T.C.	—	108,100	116,500	([54])	304,500	345,700	395,100	354,000	362,000	382,440
Professional development education[56]	—	77,800	90,300	([54])	194,600	251,600	233,000	414,200	402,100	362,260
Department of Energy[15]	3,000	3,000	3,000	57,701	16,039	31,158	19,012	19,475	18,051	19,225
University laboratory cooperative program	3,000	3,000	3,000	2,800	3,600	4,284	3,467	6,500	5,714	9,859
Teacher development projects[57]	—	—	—	1,400	1,200	—	—	—	—	—
Graduate traineeship programs[22,58]	—	—	—	—	1,000	—	—	—	52	−4
Energy conservation for buildings—higher education[16]	—	—	—	53,501	10,239	26,874	15,395	12,705	11,815	8,500
Minority honors vocational training[59]	—	—	—	—	—	—	150	150	230	390
Honors research program[59]	—	—	—	—	—	—	—	120	240	480
Students and teachers[60]	—	—	—	—	—	—	—	—	—	—
Department of Health and Human Services[17]	469,223	981,483	1,686,650	2,412,058	1,977,423	1,209,860	629,690	516,088	492,524	506,093
Health professions training programs[61]	139,795	353,029	599,350	460,736	174,887	172,004	180,715	212,200	198,004	202,710
Indian health manpower[62]	—	—	—	7,187	5,676	5,692	5,471	5,577	4,750	7,018
National Health Service Corps scholarships	—	—	1,206	70,667	59,767	32,016	14,526	2,268	2,130	2,277
National Institutes of Health training grants[63]	—	—	154,875	176,388	150,474	164,654	166,462	217,927	217,943	222,542
National Institute of Occupational Safety and Health training grants	4,327	8,088	7,182	12,899	5,760	5,760	8,760	8,760	8,383	9,900
Alcohol, drug abuse, and mental health training programs[64]	85,101	118,366	83,727	122,103	100,676	59,380	27,607	43,617	46,216	61,075
Health teaching facilities	—	—	353	3,078	4,183	40,354	6,149	739	15,098	571
Social Security postsecondary students' benefits[65]	240,000	502,000	839,957	1,559,000	1,476,000	730,000	220,000	25,000	—	—
Department of Housing and Urban Development[22]	220,744	114,199	−55,418	—	—	—	—	—	—	—
College housing loans[22,47]	220,744	114,199	−55,418	—	—	—	—	—	—	—
Department of the Interior	30,153	31,749	50,844	80,202	113,275	109,456	146,750	125,247	109,744	108,386
Shared revenues, Mineral Leasing Act and other receipts—estimated education share	6,260	6,949	15,480	35,403	70,358	69,900	96,451	71,991	55,733	49,421
Indian programs:										
Continuing education[66]	8,993	9,380	13,311	16,909	16,636	14,951	25,299	24,338	24,167	25,986
Higher education scholarships	14,900	15,420	22,053	27,890	26,281	24,605	25,000	28,918	29,844	32,979
Department of State	53,420	30,850	50,347	—	—	—	—	—	—	—
Educational exchange[67]	53,420	30,850	50,347	—	—	—	—	—	—	—
Mutual educational and cultural exchange activities	47,025	30,454	50,300	—	—	—	—	—	—	—
International educational exchange activities	6,395	396	47	—	—	—	—	—	—	—
Russian, Eurasian, and East European Research and Training[68]	—	—	—	—	—	—	—	—	—	—

Table 359.—Federal on-budget funds for education, by level or other educational purpose, by agency and program: Fiscal years 1965 to 1997—Continued

[In thousands of dollars]

Level or educational purpose, by agency and program	1988	1989	1990[1]	1991[2]	1992[3]	1993[4]	1994[5]	1995[6]	1996[7]	1997[8]
1	12	13	14	15	16	17	18	19	20	21
Office of Economic Opportunity[38]	—	—	—	—	—	—	—	—	—	—
Head Start[39]	—	—	—	—	—	—	—	—	—	—
Other elementary and secondary programs[40]	—	—	—	—	—	—	—	—	—	—
Job Corps[41]	—	—	—	—	—	—	—	—	—	—
Youth Corps and other training programs[42]	—	—	—	—	—	—	—	—	—	—
Volunteers in Service to America (VISTA)[43]	—	—	—	—	—	—	—	—	—	—
Other programs										
Estimated education share of federal aid to the District of Columbia	103,400	85,510	86,579	103,697	109,894	120,759	86,627	66,871	62,968	85,823
Postsecondary education programs	**$10,657,530**	**$13,269,888**	**$13,650,915**	**$14,703,594**	**$14,384,138**	**$17,844,015**	**$16,173,751**	**$17,614,937**	**$15,772,257**	**$15,417,707**
Department of Education[9]	8,247,103	10,640,044	11,175,978	12,002,766	11,323,584	14,660,704	12,871,390	14,234,000	12,257,553	11,735,308
Student financial assistance[44]	5,219,916	5,859,774	5,920,328	6,333,839	7,071,440	7,678,293	7,118,034	7,047,000	6,861,599	7,598,977
Federal Direct Student Loan Program[45]	—	—	—	—	—	10,000	148,247	840,000	594,761	413,105
Federal Family Education Loan Program[46]	2,779,304	3,899,387	4,372,446	4,781,918	3,253,648	5,554,920	4,509,696	5,190,000	3,663,956	2,561,178
Higher education	411,775	606,849	659,492	615,372	718,406	1,041,583	796,278	871,000	846,517	880,188
Facilities—loans and insurance[22]	−43,282	10,182	19,219	34,805	25,984	−2,976	−5,605	−6,000	8,837	−4,300
College housing loans[22,47]	−372,778	−31,299	−57,167	−33,249	−39,907	−28,355	−18,434	−46,000	−34,815	−23,337
Educational activities overseas[22]	233	374	82	−47	—	—	—	—	—	—
Historically Black Colleges and Universities Capital Financing, Program Account[48]	—	—	—	—	—	—	129	—	323	162
Gallaudet College and Howard University	224,781	258,519	230,327	233,209	263,497	353,390	280,945	292,000	273,904	268,876
National Technical Institute for the Deaf[49]	27,154	36,258	31,251	36,919	30,516	53,849	42,100	46,000	42,471	40,459
Department of Agriculture	27,799	27,799	31,273	32,302	34,238	32,730	25,472	33,373	32,872	32,639
Agriculture Extension Service, Second Morrill Act payments to agricultural and mechanical colleges and Tuskegee Institute[50]	27,799	27,799	31,273	32,302	34,238	32,730	25,472	33,373	32,872	32,639
Department of Commerce	2,420	2,765	3,312	4,334	3,270	3,549	4,000	3,487	3,384	3,500
Sea Grant Program[51]	2,420	2,765	3,312	4,334	3,270	3,549	4,000	3,487	3,384	3,500
Merchant Marine Academy[52]	—	—	—	—	—	—	—	—	—	—
State marine schools[52]	—	—	—	—	—	—	—	—	—	—
Department of Defense[53]	573,400	746,464	635,769	665,059	680,194	696,800	679,000	729,500	864,900	872,100
Tuition assistance for military personnel	134,500	236,089	95,300	92,800	102,400	123,400	130,200	127,000	260,300	258,700
Service academies[55]	109,100	115,150	120,613	132,487	125,146	128,000	141,500	163,300	171,700	176,200
Senior R.O.T.C.	179,200	198,325	193,056	198,072	193,348	184,100	195,300	219,400	218,200	231,100
Professional development education[56]	150,600	196,900	226,800	241,700	259,300	261,300	212,000	219,800	214,700	206,100
Department of Energy[15]	22,609	15,062	25,502	30,851	34,373	17,654	17,951	28,027	—	—
University laboratory cooperative program	13,571	5,929	9,402	19,330	19,100	4,000	3,600	8,552	—	—
Teacher development projects[57]	—	—	—	—	—	—	—	—	—	—
Graduate traineeship programs[22,58]	−26	—	—	—	—	—	—	—	—	—
Energy conservation for buildings— higher education[16]	7,746	6,493	7,459	7,411	9,573	6,654	8,051	7,381	—	—
Minority honors vocational training[59]	598	720	—	—	—	—	—	—	—	—
Honors research program[59]	720	820	6,472	1,000	1,000	1,000	900	2,221	—	—
Students and teachers[60]	—	1,100	2,169	3,110	4,700	6,000	5,400	9,873	—	—
Department of Health and Human Services[17]	509,927	542,796	578,542	697,385	743,456	720,911	795,914	796,035	798,596	862,299
Health professions training programs[61]	210,404	223,811	230,600	271,937	305,829	299,785	305,549	298,302	273,519	313,876
Indian health manpower[62]	5,998	5,972	9,508	13,379	19,460	26,100	26,398	27,000	26,000	28,000
National Health Service Corps scholarships	4,100	6,531	4,759	48,795	58,706	33,323	79,250	78,206	28,847	31,229
National Institutes of Health training grants[63]	238,430	255,558	241,356	268,492	348,034	350,804	372,698	380,502	457,000	476,000
National Institute of Occupational Safety and Health training grants	9,718	10,095	10,461	10,472	10,972	10,472	11,622	11,660	12,898	12,898
Alcohol, drug abuse, and mental health training programs[64]	40,726	40,301	81,353	83,829	—	—	—	—	—	—
Health teaching facilities	551	528	505	481	455	427	397	365	332	296
Social Security postsecondary students' benefits[65]	—	—	—	—	—	—	—	—	—	—
Department of Housing and Urban Development[22]	—	—	—	—	—	—	—	—	—	—
College housing loans[22,47]	—	—	—	—	—	—	—	—	—	—
Department of the Interior	113,661	123,529	135,480	141,523	140,266	132,916	156,734	159,054	132,478	146,465
Shared revenues, Mineral Leasing Act and other receipts—estimated education share	52,117	64,669	69,980	74,430	68,982	61,566	79,815	82,810	59,020	70,980
Indian programs:										
Continuing education[66]	30,822	28,424	34,911	36,875	38,970	39,840	43,184	43,907	47,173	49,631
Higher education scholarships	30,722	30,436	30,589	30,218	32,315	31,510	33,735	32,337	26,285	25,854
Department of State	4,120	4,422	2,167	6,396	9,057	10,211	7,842	3,000	2,000	—
Educational exchange[67]	—	—	—	—	—	—	—	—	—	—
Mutual educational and cultural exchange activities	—	—	—	—	—	—	—	—	—	—
International educational exchange activities	—	—	—	—	—	—	—	—	—	—
Russian, Eurasian, and East European Research and Training[68]	4,120	4,422	2,167	6,396	9,057	10,211	7,842	3,000	2,000	—

Table 359.—Federal on-budget funds for education, by level or other educational purpose, by agency and program: Fiscal years 1965 to 1997—Continued

[In thousands of dollars]

Level or educational purpose, by agency and program	1965	1970	1975	1980	1982	1983	1984	1985	1986	1987
1	2	3	4	5	6	7	8	9	10	11
Department of Transportation[26]	—	11,197	11,885	12,530	46,709	46,177	57,245	55,569	44,074	47,226
Merchant Marine Academy[52]	—	—	—	—	21,507	23,211	18,739	19,898	19,505	20,476
State marine schools[69]	—	—	—	—	12,351	9,383	23,733	19,777	8,363	12,073
Coast Guard Academy[27]	—	9,342	9,780	10,000	10,200	10,329	11,364	11,857	11,845	10,086
Postgraduate training for Coast Guard officers[70]	—	1,655	1,855	2,230	2,360	2,891	2,959	3,499	3,807	3,978
Tuition assistance to Coast Guard military personnel[27]	—	200	250	300	291	363	450	538	554	613
Department of the Treasury	8,208	—	268,605	296,750	—	—	—	—	—	—
General revenue sharing—estimated state share to higher education[28,29]	—	—	268,605	296,750	—	—	—	—	—	—
Coast Guard Academy[27]	6,815	—	—	—	—	—	—	—	—	—
Postgraduate training for Coast Guard officers[70]	1,293	—	—	—	—	—	—	—	—	—
Tuition assistance to Coast Guard military personnel[27]	100	—	—	—	—	—	—	—	—	—
Department of Veterans Affairs[30]	55,650	693,490	3,029,600	1,803,847	1,550,161	1,292,885	1,092,609	944,091	803,166	764,561
Vietnam-era veterans:[71]	33,950	638,260	2,840,600	1,579,974	1,319,081	1,077,391	861,310	694,217	514,476	411,967
College student support	—	—	—	1,560,081	1,294,698	1,052,859	839,135	679,953	504,290	403,527
Work-study	—	—	—	19,893	24,383	24,532	22,175	14,264	10,186	8,440
Service persons college support[72]	—	18,900	74,690	46,617	38,978	36,054	38,896	35,630	30,707	28,410
Post-Vietnam veterans[73]	—	—	—	922	14,438	24,871	52,241	82,554	121,929	171,752
All-volunteer-force educational assistance:[74]	—	—	—	—	—	—	—	196	24,171	45,688
Veterans[75]	—	—	—	—	—	—	—	—	2	107
Reservists[76]	—	—	—	—	—	—	—	196	24,169	45,581
Veteran dependents' education[77]	21,700	36,330	114,310	176,334	177,664	154,569	140,162	131,494	111,883	106,744
Payments to state education agencies[78]										
Other agencies.										
Appalachian Regional Commission[35]	—	4,105	2,545	1,751	1,039	—	—	—	1,950	30
National Endowment for the Humanities[37]	—	3,349	25,320	56,451	46,979	48,457	52,359	49,098	42,346	48,679
National Science Foundation	27,170	42,000	60,283	64,583	67,637	50,126	29,746	60,069	74,151	85,494
Science and engineering education programs	27,170	37,000	60,283	64,583	67,637	50,126	29,746	60,069	74,151	85,494
Sea Grant Program[51]	—	5,000	—	—	—	—	—	—	—	—
United States Information Agency[79]	7,512	8,423	9,405	51,095	60,933	69,298	64,394	124,041	148,483	162,897
Educational and cultural affairs[67]	—	—	—	49,546	59,966	68,041	17,414	21,079	23,008	24,313
Educational and cultural exchange programs[80]	—	—	—	—	—	—	45,570	101,529	125,246	138,039
Educational exchange activities, international	—	—	—	1,549	967	1,257	1,410	1,433	229	545
Information center and library activities[81]	7,512	8,423	9,405	—	—	—	—	—	—	—
Other programs										
Barry Goldwater Scholarship and Excellence in Education Foundation[82]	—	—	—	—	—	—	—	—	—	—
Estimated education share of federal aid to the District of Columbia	1,895	5,513	10,564	13,143	15,547	16,523	17,513	15,266	14,351	17,310
Harry S Truman Scholarship fund[22,83]	—	—	—	−1,895	1,667	1,795	1,929	1,332	2,441	2,717
Institute of American Indian and Alaskan Native Culture and Arts Development[84]	—	—	—	—	—	—	—	—	—	—
James Madison Memorial Fellowship Foundation[85]	—	—	—	—	—	—	—	—	—	—
Other education programs	**$374,652**	**$964,719**	**$1,608,478**	**$1,548,730**	**$1,995,147**	**$2,204,147**	**$2,710,402**	**$2,107,588**	**$2,620,021**	**$2,820,407**
Department of Education[9]	182,021	630,235	1,045,659	747,706	1,152,009	1,326,271	1,813,128	1,173,055	1,674,171	1,825,754
Administration	17,732	47,456	108,372	187,317	265,726	247,966	307,447	284,900	263,216	285,296
Libraries[86]	26,111	108,284	225,810	129,127	101,437	124,451	87,059	85,650	96,406	129,062
Rehabilitative services and disability research	137,313	473,091	709,483	426,886	779,699	948,650	1,414,396	798,298	1,311,485	1,405,357
American Printing House for the Blind	865	1,404	1,994	4,349	5,000	5,174	4,054	4,230	3,031	5,989
Trust funds and contributions[22]	—	—	—	27	147	30	172	−23	33	50
Department of Agriculture	87,551	135,637	220,395	271,112	311,949	322,430	327,123	336,375	322,599	330,866
Extension Service	85,924	131,734	215,523	263,584	303,461	312,413	317,099	325,986	311,132	322,095
National Agricultural Library	1,627	3,903	4,872	7,528	8,488	10,017	10,024	10,389	11,467	8,771
Department of Commerce	251	1,226	2,317	2,479	—	—	—	—	—	—
Maritime Administration:										
Training for private sector employees[52]	251	1,226	2,317	2,479	—	—	—	—	—	—
Department of Health and Human Services[17]	3,953	24,273	31,653	37,819	46,640	44,899	48,876	47,195	59,306	59,770
National Library of Medicine	3,953	24,273	31,653	37,819	46,640	44,899	48,876	47,195	59,306	59,770
Department of Housing and Urban Development	512	—	—	—	—	—	—	—	—	—
Urban mass transportation—managerial training grants[87]	512	—	—	—	—	—	—	—	—	—
Department of Justice	3,850	5,546	42,818	27,642	26,304	31,082	23,723	25,517	27,412	26,293
F.B.I. National Academy	1,850	2,066	5,100	7,234	4,843	8,832	4,285	4,189	3,946	4,408
F.B.I. Field Police Academy	1,450	2,500	5,254	7,715	8,332	8,792	8,069	10,220	9,756	8,984
Narcotics and dangerous drug training	550	980	1,152	2,416	1,684	1,740	63	83	68	—
National Institute of Corrections[88]	—	—	31,312	10,277	11,445	11,718	11,306	11,025	13,642	12,901
Department of State	10,780	20,672	28,113	25,000	21,174	23,784	23,086	23,791	23,371	23,856
Foreign Service Institute	6,395	15,857	20,750	25,000	21,174	23,784	23,086	23,791	23,371	23,856
Center for Cultural and Technical Interchange[67]	4,385	4,815	7,363	—	—	—	—	—	—	—

Table 359.—Federal on-budget funds for education, by level or other educational purpose, by agency and program: Fiscal years 1965 to 1997—Continued

[In thousands of dollars]

Level or educational purpose, by agency and program	1988	1989	1990[1]	1991[2]	1992[3]	1993[4]	1994[5]	1995[6]	1996[7]	1997[8]
1	12	13	14	15	16	17	18	19	20	21
Department of Transportation[26]	44,998	63,559	46,025	46,647	53,991	57,576	56,640	56,057	50,268	50,642
Merchant Marine Academy[52]	20,579	20,611	20,926	22,855	27,007	26,788	30,241	30,850	31,000	31,000
State marine schools[69]	7,961	26,062	8,269	8,829	11,072	10,320	10,270	8,980	7,000	7,000
Coast Guard Academy[27]	10,810	11,740	12,074	12,074	13,071	13,602	13,103	13,500	9,553	9,917
Postgraduate training for Coast Guard officers[70]	5,084	4,621	4,173	2,248	2,540	6,306	2,726	2,313	2,261	2,313
Tuition assistance to Coast Guard military personnel[27]	564	525	582	641	301	560	300	414	454	412
Department of the Treasury	—	—	—	—	—	—	—	—	—	—
General revenue sharing—estimated state share to higher education[28,29]	—	—	—	—	—	—	—	—	—	—
Coast Guard Academy[27]	—	—	—	—	—	—	—	—	—	—
Postgraduate training for Coast Guard officers[70]	—	—	—	—	—	—	—	—	—	—
Tuition assistance to Coast Guard military personnel[27]	—	—	—	—	—	—	—	—	—	—
Department of Veterans Affairs[30]	768,090	725,270	599,825	614,449	854,480	919,991	1,043,709	1,010,114	1,074,713	1,183,807
Vietnam-era veterans:[71]	345,242	264,702	46,998	—	—	—	—	—	—	—
College student support	337,568	258,982	39,458	—	—	—	—	—	—	—
Work-study	7,674	5,720	7,540	—	—	—	—	—	—	—
Service persons college support[72]	33,472	34,399	8,911	—	—	—	—	—	—	—
Post-Vietnam veterans[73]	203,262	195,142	161,475	118,139	88,500	65,894	48,114	33,596	44,387	59,933
All-volunteer-force educational assistance:[74]	73,731	122,222	269,947	380,720	650,540	745,786	886,951	868,394	922,807	1,017,803
Veterans[75]	8,386	43,423	183,765	303,861	530,820	626,669	769,481	760,390	809,336	907,110
Reservists[76]	65,345	78,799	86,182	76,859	119,720	119,117	117,470	108,004	113,471	110,693
Veteran dependents' education[77]	100,883	96,805	100,494	103,590	103,440	96,311	96,644	95,124	94,519	93,071
Payments to state education agencies[78]	11,500	12,000	12,000	12,000	12,000	12,000	12,000	13,000	13,000	13,000
Other agencies.										
Appalachian Regional Commission[35]	1,050	825	—	92	1,487	1,587	3,413	2,741	2,704	2,704
National Endowment for the Humanities[37]	47,601	51,449	50,938	55,861	58,512	57,804	58,404	56,481	30,896	30,896
National Science Foundation	97,466	130,187	161,884	191,661	210,375	246,591	225,168	211,800	262,000	273,000
Science and engineering education programs	97,466	130,187	161,884	191,661	210,375	246,591	225,168	211,800	262,000	273,000
Sea Grant Program[51]	—	—	—	—	—	—	—	—	—	—
United States Information Agency[79]	166,705	164,807	181,172	185,905	207,676	256,068	200,429	260,800	239,400	198,600
Educational and cultural affairs[67]	29,724	21,596	35,862	35,714	38,858	44,183	28,927	13,600	17,000	13,000
Educational and cultural exchange programs[80]	136,646	143,194	145,307	150,183	168,818	211,885	171,502	247,200	222,400	185,600
Educational exchange activities, international	335	17	3	8	—	—	—	—	—	—
Information center and library activities[81]	—	—	—	—	—	—	—	—	—	—
Other programs										
Barry Goldwater Scholarship and Excellence in Education Foundation[82]	—	753	1,033	1,941	2,900	3,023	2,789	3,000	3,000	3,000
Estimated education share of federal aid to the District of Columbia	14,566	14,207	14,637	17,477	16,382	14,247	8,896	9,468	6,494	11,747
Harry S Truman Scholarship fund[22,83]	2,815	2,851	2,883	2,968	2,401	2,894	2,323	3,000	3,000	3,000
Institute of American Indian and Alaskan Native Culture and Arts Development[84]	—	3,094	4,305	5,447	6,612	7,462	12,213	13,000	6,000	6,000
James Madison Memorial Fellowship Foundation[85]	13,200	10,005	191	531	885	1,298	1,464	2,000	2,000	2,000
Other education programs	**$2,981,571**	**$3,180,334**	**$3,383,031**	**$3,698,617**	**$3,991,955**	**$4,107,193**	**$4,483,704**	**$4,719,655**	**$4,828,038**	**$5,125,197**
Department of Education[9]	1,938,998	2,071,574	2,251,801	2,419,277	2,579,883	2,526,372	2,795,984	2,861,000	3,085,587	3,293,040
Administration	295,615	301,260	328,293	365,681	368,420	353,545	403,877	404,000	502,949	414,256
Libraries[86]	101,202	140,398	137,264	142,596	214,928	181,219	142,223	117,000	167,585	167,721
Rehabilitative services and disability research	1,536,905	1,623,255	1,780,360	1,902,338	1,991,875	1,983,848	2,244,226	2,333,000	2,410,178	2,702,207
American Printing House for the Blind	5,234	6,645	5,736	8,242	4,587	7,774	5,636	7,000	4,693	8,771
Trust funds and contributions[22]	42	16	148	420	73	−14	22	—	182	85
Department of Agriculture	342,523	347,021	352,511	382,343	400,442	443,650	426,316	422,878	412,878	408,849
Extension Service	330,164	333,571	337,907	366,176	385,087	424,928	409,110	405,371	394,878	390,849
National Agricultural Library	12,359	13,450	14,604	16,167	15,355	18,722	17,206	17,507	18,000	18,000
Department of Commerce										
Maritime Administration:										
Training for private sector employees[52]	—	—	—	—	—	—	—	—	—	—
Department of Health and Human Services[17]	62,060	71,912	77,962	89,094	97,643	96,860	107,896	138,000	117,000	145,000
National Library of Medicine	62,060	71,912	77,962	89,094	97,643	96,860	107,896	138,000	117,000	145,000
Department of Housing and Urban Development	—	—	—	—	—	—	—	—	—	—
Urban mass transportation—managerial training grants[87]	—	—	—	—	—	—	—	—	—	—
Department of Justice	26,361	23,906	26,920	30,543	34,525	37,028	34,065	36,296	35,072	33,743
F.B.I. National Academy	5,385	5,513	6,028	6,368	10,631	14,388	10,311	12,831	14,411	13,431
F.B.I. Field Police Academy	9,995	7,673	10,548	12,700	12,578	10,563	11,790	11,140	10,277	7,858
Narcotics and dangerous drug training	142	824	850	1,180	695	230	275	325	384	454
National Institute of Corrections[88]	10,839	9,896	9,494	10,295	10,621	11,847	11,689	12,000	10,000	12,000
Department of State	33,308	40,157	47,539	41,790	44,086	58,840	46,557	51,648	53,330	54,052
Foreign Service Institute	33,308	40,157	47,539	41,790	44,086	58,840	46,557	51,648	53,330	54,052
Center for Cultural and Technical Interchange[67]	—	—	—	—	—	—	—	—	—	—

Table 359.—Federal on-budget funds for education, by level or other educational purpose, by agency and program: Fiscal years 1965 to 1997—Continued

[In thousands of dollars]

Level or educational purpose, by agency and program	1965	1970	1975	1980	1982	1983	1984	1985	1986	1987
1	2	3	4	5	6	7	8	9	10	11
Department of Transportation[26]	—	3,964	11,877	10,212	6,030	6,175	4,781	3,785	1,865	2,895
Highways training and education grants[89]	—	2,418	3,250	3,412	3,545	3,527	2,050	1,500	—	1,000
Maritime Administration:										
Training for private sector employees[52]	—	—	—	—	1,305	1,448	1,381	1,135	1,143	1,291
Urban mass transportation—managerial training grants[87]	—	1,546	2,627	500	1,100	1,200	1,350	1,150	722	604
Federal Aviation Administration[90]										
Air traffic controllers second career program[91]	—	—	6,000	6,300	80	—	—	—	—	—
Department of the Treasury	—	18	3,096	14,584	13,247	13,334	14,327	16,160	15,982	19,110
Federal Law Enforcement Training Center[92]	—	18	3,096	14,584	13,247	13,334	14,327	16,160	15,982	19,110
Other agencies										
ACTION[93]	—	—	7,045	2,833	1,720	1,830	4,975	1,761	1,368	3,368
Estimated education funds[94]	—	—	7,045	2,833	1,720	1,830	4,975	1,761	1,368	3,368
Agency for International Development	63,329	88,034	78,896	99,707	135,580	130,257	127,383	141,847	154,627	186,175
Education and human resources	53,968	61,570	58,349	80,518	105,405	109,624	101,408	115,104	126,132	152,332
American schools and hospitals abroad	9,361	26,464	20,547	19,189	30,175	20,633	25,975	26,743	28,495	33,843
Appalachian Regional Commission[34]	—	572	1,574	8,124	1,651	98	330	113	—	92
Corporation for National and Community Service[93]	—	—	—	—	—	—	—	—	—	—
Estimated education funds[94]	—	—	—	—	—	—	—	—	—	—
Federal Emergency Management Agency[95]	—	290	290	281	278	390	351	405	290	290
Estimated architect/engineer student development program[96]	—	40	40	31	98	90	71	155	40	40
Estimated other training programs[97]	—	250	250	250	180	300	280	250	250	250
Estimated disaster relief[98]	—	—	—	—	—	—	—	—	—	—
General Services Administration[99]										
Libraries and other archival activities	4,013	14,775	22,532	34,800	37,300	44,200	50,894	—	—	—
Japanese-United States Friendship Commission[100]	—	—	—	2,294	1,807	2,364	1,611	2,236	235	3,225
Library of Congress	15,111	29,478	63,766	151,871	144,911	154,198	164,080	169,310	166,130	160,835
Salaries and expenses	11,421	20,700	48,798	102,364	109,235	122,823	127,935	130,354	126,747	124,878
Books for the blind and the physically handicapped	2,317	6,195	11,908	31,436	29,592	26,116	30,739	32,954	35,460	33,813
Special foreign currency program	1,187	2,273	2,333	3,492	3,364	3,578	3,745	4,621	2,372	809
Furniture and furnishings	186	310	727	14,579	2,720	1,681	1,661	1,381	1,551	1,335
National Aeronautics and Space Administration										
Aerospace education services project	100	350	600	882	956	1,323	1,628	1,800	1,900	2,250
National Archives and Records Administration[101]										
Libraries and other archival activities	—	—	—	—	—	—	—	52,118	55,252	59,521
National Commission on Libraries and Information Science[102]	—	—	449	2,090	638	681	733	723	781	512
National Endowment for the Arts[36]	—	340	1,068	231	724	632	819	1,137	1,128	1,295
National Endowment for the Humanities[37]	—	5,090	38,486	85,805	68,421	74,348	74,750	76,252	78,319	75,376
Smithsonian Institution	2,233	2,461	5,509	5,153	5,215	6,073	5,758	7,886	6,191	6,545
Museum programs and related research	2,133	2,261	4,203	3,254	2,788	3,365	2,642	4,665	2,341	2,506
National Gallery of Art extension service	100	200	300	426	524	617	692	675	662	731
Woodrow Wilson International Center for Scholars	—	—	1,006	1,473	1,903	2,091	2,424	2,546	3,188	3,308
U.S. Information Agency—Center for Cultural and Technical Interchange[67]	—	—	—	15,115	16,252	17,258	19,374	18,966	20,531	16,756
U.S. Institute of Peace[103]	—	—	—	—	—	—	—	—	230	4,083
Other programs:										
Estimated education share of federal aid for the District of Columbia	948	1,758	2,335	2,990	2,341	2,520	2,672	7,156	8,333	11,540
Research programs at universities and related institutions[104]	**$1,816,276**	**$2,283,641**	**$3,418,410**	**$5,801,204**	**$6,597,423**	**$7,233,806**	**$7,938,550**	**$8,844,575**	**$9,009,351**	**$10,538,606**
Department of Education[105]	13,248	87,823	82,770	78,742	82,201	59,580	159,550	28,809	68,983	60,912
Department of Agriculture	58,362	64,796	108,162	216,405	255,075	275,027	279,200	293,252	273,698	279,943
Department of Commerce	4,015	4,487	21,677	48,295	52,218	51,460	52,600	52,951	62,406	36,835
Department of Defense	436,912	356,188	364,929	644,455	889,863	1,112,212	1,072,500	1,245,888	1,382,795	1,754,456
Department of Energy	439,334	548,327	761,376	1,470,224	1,715,779	1,861,112	2,001,400	2,205,316	2,141,955	2,225,513
Department of Health and Human Services	474,362	623,765	1,273,037	2,087,053	2,194,707	2,448,899	2,750,700	3,228,014	3,309,708	3,983,407
Department of Housing and Urban Development	—	510	2,650	5,314	969	2,158	2,000	438	342	463
Department of the Interior	9,839	18,521	28,955	42,175	34,171	28,616	36,500	34,422	36,440	33,353
Department of Justice	—	1,945	8,902	9,189	5,966	7,156	6,800	5,168	5,095	8,991
Department of Labor	—	3,567	6,124	12,938	8,915	6,392	4,800	3,417	341	432
Department of State	—	8,220	10,973	188	7	29	—	29	30	432
Department of Transportation	—	12,328	28,478	31,910	22,608	29,722	21,800	22,621	20,215	25,184
Department of the Treasury	—	—	—	226	5	238	300	388	190	169
Department of Veterans Affairs	337	518	1,112	1,600	1,646	800	500	1,000	1,000	2,251
ACTION	—	—	36	—	—	—	—	—	—	—
Agency for International Development	—	—	—	77,063	69,597	43,372	109,600	56,960	44,302	54,652

FEDERAL PROGRAMS 397

Table 359.—Federal on-budget funds for education, by level or other educational purpose, by agency and program: Fiscal years 1965 to 1997—Continued

[In thousands of dollars]

Level or educational purpose, by agency and program	1988	1989	1990[1]	1991[2]	1992[3]	1993[4]	1994[5]	1995[6]	1996[7]	1997[8]
1	12	13	14	15	16	17	18	19	20	21
Department of Transportation[26]	3,153	4,415	1,507	2,022	2,419	500	500	650	700	650
Highways training and education grants[89]	1,416	1,416	—	1,371	1,945	—	—	—	—	—
Maritime Administration: Training for private sector employees[52]	1,517	1,499	1,507	651	474	500	500	650	700	650
Urban mass transportation—managerial training grants[87]	220	1,500	—	—	—	—	—	—	—	—
Federal Aviation Administration[90] Air traffic controllers second career program[91]	—	—	—	—	—	—	—	—	—	—
Department of the Treasury	32,768	39,100	41,488	60,127	51,694	56,779	61,992	48,000	59,000	61,000
Federal Law Enforcement Training Center[92]	32,768	39,100	41,488	60,127	51,694	56,779	61,992	48,000	59,000	61,000
Other agencies										
ACTION[93]	4,110	4,800	8,472	11,321	8,600	—	—	—	—	—
Estimated education funds[94]	4,110	4,800	8,472	11,321	8,600	—	—	—	—	—
Agency for International Development	193,115	182,839	170,371	154,021	212,220	215,248	241,948	260,408	307,000	290,000
Education and human resources	160,051	146,915	142,801	122,231	195,570	190,020	221,988	248,408	302,000	287,000
American schools and hospitals abroad	33,064	35,924	27,570	31,790	16,650	25,228	19,960	12,000	5,000	3,000
Appalachian Regional Commission[34]	—	175	—	25	938	1,005	4,299	5,709	2,756	2,756
Corporation for National and Community Service[93]	—	—	—	—	—	8,500	93,250	214,600	279,000	335,000
Estimated education funds[94]	—	—	—	—	—	8,500	93,250	214,600	279,000	335,000
Federal Emergency Management Agency[95]	290	77	215	33	261	76,467	85,200	170,400	7,500	8,300
Estimated architect/engineer student development program[96]	40	50	200	28	250	375	—	—	—	—
Estimated other training programs[97]	250	27	15	5	11	92	—	—	—	—
Estimated disaster relief[98]	—	—	—	—	—	76,000	85,200	170,400	7,500	8,300
General Services Administration[99] Libraries and other archival activities	—	—	—	—	—	—	—	—	—	—
Japanese-United States Friendship Commission[100]	2,274	3,004	2,299	1,377	1,610	1,503	1,585	2,000	2,000	2,000
Library of Congress	160,505	177,954	189,827	279,745	296,044	311,453	312,724	241,000	252,000	269,000
Salaries and expenses	122,356	137,637	148,985	239,429	252,623	260,918	261,814	198,000	201,000	215,000
Books for the blind and the physically handicapped	36,245	38,233	37,473	36,878	38,688	45,261	46,600	39,000	47,000	48,000
Special foreign currency program	405	99	10	10	10	30	—	—	—	—
Furniture and furnishings	1,499	1,985	3,359	3,428	4,723	5,244	4,310	4,000	4,000	6,000
National Aeronautics and Space Administration Aerospace education services project	2,400	2,300	3,300	5,900	6,100	6,500	6,100	5,923	5,927	6,119
National Archives and Records Administration[101] Libraries and other archival activities	65,153	86,266	77,397	81,462	99,412	106,975	110,411	105,172	104,536	111,277
National Commission on Libraries and Information Science[102]	522	839	3,281	3,447	1,437	867	724	1,000	1,000	1,000
National Endowment for the Arts[36]	1,200	1,193	936	1,628	3,286	2,784	2,221	2,304	518	6,150
National Endowment for the Humanities[37]	76,803	84,929	89,706	93,381	99,782	100,826	98,786	94,249	62,362	62,362
Smithsonian Institution	5,393	5,880	5,779	5,906	6,578	7,828	10,059	9,961	9,908	9,990
Museum programs and related research	1,223	870	690	440	93	1,165	3,060	3,190	3,180	3,240
National Gallery of Art extension service	656	650	474	641	793	763	816	771	728	750
Woodrow Wilson International Center for Scholars	3,514	4,360	4,615	4,825	5,692	5,900	6,183	6,000	6,000	6,000
U.S. Information Agency—Center for Cultural and Technical Interchange[67]	22,759	20,714	20,375	22,276	29,550	31,991	30,064	34,000	18,000	12,000
U.S. Institute of Peace[103]	3,476	7,232	7,621	8,238	11,350	10,468	10,794	12,000	11,000	12,000
Other programs: Estimated education share of federal aid for the District of Columbia	4,400	4,047	3,724	4,661	4,095	4,749	2,229	2,457	964	909
Research programs at universities and related institutions[104]	$11,250,464	$12,009,825	$12,606,035	$13,775,422	$14,176,863	$14,955,083	$15,289,094	$15,677,919	$15,751,622	$15,892,660
Department of Education[105]	42,379	90,314	89,483	103,931	154,800	232,165	276,838	279,000	310,895	412,858
Department of Agriculture	304,888	314,294	348,109	385,836	437,967	436,187	438,537	434,544	423,121	420,583
Department of Commerce	36,133	44,821	50,523	62,870	77,240	70,805	81,423	85,442	77,132	70,979
Department of Defense	1,899,680	1,940,308	1,871,864	1,789,112	2,070,959	2,002,572	2,010,414	1,853,955	1,602,779	1,490,714
Department of Energy	2,350,426	2,536,065	2,520,885	2,692,335	2,867,528	2,763,515	2,642,094	2,651,641	2,558,809	2,609,288
Department of Health and Human Services	4,282,117	4,549,261	4,902,714	5,686,354	5,210,711	5,952,976	6,348,736	6,418,969	7,013,669	7,109,126
Department of Housing and Urban Development	51	186	118	48	203	401	856	1,613	1,400	987
Department of the Interior	35,103	39,556	49,790	58,537	57,449	54,049	54,157	50,618	55,345	48,124
Department of Justice	6,365	5,700	6,858	6,060	4,986	3,496	3,886	7,204	6,275	7,075
Department of Labor	5,528	5,590	5,893	5,548	1,169	600	4,250	10,114	5,440	150
Department of State	1,243	1,269	1,519	900	200	—	15	23	64	64
Department of Transportation	16,933	22,826	28,608	21,187	35,015	57,789	62,606	75,847	84,112	75,592
Department of the Treasury	—	411	227	229	85	133	1,309	1,496	673	81
Department of Veterans Affairs	2,300	2,300	2,300	2,300	2,491	2,550	2,350	2,500	1,850	2,000
ACTION	—	—	—	—	—	—	—	—	—	—
Agency for International Development	49,535	45,025	79,415	54,997	32,979	27,659	24,634	30,172	18,894	13,024

Table 359.—Federal on-budget funds for education, by level or other educational purpose, by agency and program: Fiscal years 1965 to 1997—Continued

[In thousands of dollars]

Level or educational purpose, by agency and program	1965	1970	1975	1980	1982	1983	1984	1985	1986	1987
1	2	3	4	5	6	7	8	9	10	11
Corporation for National and Community Service	—	—	—	—	—	—	—	—	—	—
Environmental Protection Agency	—	19,446	33,875	41,083	67,798	43,557	43,700	60,521	69,718	67,465
Federal Emergency Management Agency	—	—	—	1,665	2,347	805	—	1,423	—	—
National Aeronautics and Space Administration	208,688	258,016	197,301	254,629	368,149	366,440	352,900	485,824	489,048	785,141
National Science Foundation	154,046	253,628	475,011	743,809	787,028	857,791	1,006,000	1,087,046	1,073,122	1,184,921
Nuclear Regulatory Commission	—	—	7,093	32,590	38,150	37,987	36,400	30,261	27,472	29,176
Office of Economic Opportunity	7,078	20,035	—	—	—	—	—	—	—	—
U.S. Arms Control and Disarmament Agency	—	100	—	661	184	157	—	395	276	3,244
U.S. Information Agency	—	—	—	—	—	—	—	—	1,500	—
Other agencies	10,055	1,421	5,949	990	40	296	1,300	432	715	1,666

Footnotes

[1] Excludes $4,440,000,000 for federal support for medical education benefits under Medicare in the U.S. Department of Health and Human Services. Is not included in the total because data before fiscal year 1990 are not available. This program has existed since Medicare began, but was not available as a separate budget item until FY 90.

[2] Excludes $4,900,000,000 for federal support for medical education benefits under Medicare in the U.S. Department of Health and Human Services. Is not included in the total because data before fiscal year 1990 are not available. This program has existed since Medicare began, but was not available as a separate budget item until FY 90.

[3] Excludes $5,350,000,000 for federal support for medical education benefits under Medicare in the U.S. Department of Health and Human Services. Is not included in the total because data before fiscal year 1990 are not available. This program has existed since Medicare began, but was not available as a separate budget item until FY 90.

[4] Excludes $5,710,000,000 for federal support for medical education benefits under Medicare in the U.S. Department of Health and Human Services. Is not included in the total because data before fiscal year 1990 are not available. This program has existed since Medicare began, but was not available as a separate budget item until FY 90.

[5] Excludes $6,150,000,000 for federal support for medical education benefits under Medicare in the U.S. Department of Health and Human Services. Is not included in the total because data before fiscal year 1990 are not available. This program has existed since Medicare began, but was not available as a separate budget item until FY 90.

[6] Excludes $7,510,000,000 for federal support for medical education benefits under Medicare in the U.S. Department of Health and Human Services. Is not included in the total because data before fiscal year 1990 are not available. This program has existed since Medicare began, but was not available as a separate budget item until FY 90.

[7] Excludes $8,010,000,000 for federal support for medical education benefits under Medicare in the U.S. Department of Health and Human Services. Is not included in the total because data before fiscal year 1990 are not available. This program has existed since Medicare began, but was not available as a separate budget item until FY 90.

[8] Estimated. Excludes $8,700,000,000 for federal support for medical education benefits under Medicare in the U.S. Department of Health and Human Services. Is not included in the total because data before fiscal year 1990 are not available. This program has existed since Medicare began, but was not available as a separate budget item until FY 90.

[9] The U.S. Department of Education was created in May 1980. It formerly was the Office of Education in the U.S. Department of Health, Education, and Welfare.

[10] Section VI was funded by the U.S. Department of Education in FYs 65–81 in the Impact Aid program. This program provides for the education of dependents of federal employees residing on federal property in cases where free public education is available only in the nearby community.

[11] This program creates a national framework for education reform and meeting the National Education Goals. This program includes the School-To-Work Opportunities program which will initiate a national system to be administered jointly by the U.S. Departments of Education and Labor. Both departments are to establish a national framework within which all states can create statewide systems to help youth acquire the knowledge, skills, abilities, and labor market information they need to make an effective transition from school to work or to further their education or training.

[12] Starting in FY 94, the Special Milk program was included in the Child Nutrition program.

[13] These commodities are purchased under Section 32 of the Act of August 24, 1935, for use in the child nutrition programs.

[14] This program assisted in the construction of public facilities, such as vocational schools, through grants or loans. No funds have been appropriated for this account since FY 77, and it was completely phased out in FY 84 after the monitoring of closeouts of projects was completed. Data are not available for previous years.

[15] The U.S. Department of Energy was created in 1977. It formerly was the Energy Research and Development Administration and before that the Atomic Energy Commission. No funds were designated for any of the education programs listed on this table in the U.S. Department of Energy in FYs 96 and 97, due to budget cuts.

[16] This program was established in 1979. Funds were first appropriated for this program in FY 80.

[17] The U.S. Department of Health and Human Services was part of the U.S. Department of Health, Education, and Welfare until May 1980.

[18] The Head Start program was formerly in the Office of Economic Opportunity, and funds were appropriated to the U.S. Department of Health, Education, and Welfare, Office of Child Development, beginning in 1972.

[19] This program was created by the Family Support Act of 1988. It provides funds for the Job Opportunities and Basic Skills Training program.

[20] After age 18, benefits terminate at the end of the school term or in 3 months, whichever is less.

[21] This program provides funding for supplemental programs for eligible Indian students in public schools.

[22] Negative amounts occur when program receipts exceed outlays.

[23] This program finances the cost of academic, social, and occupational education courses for inmates in federal prisons.

Table 359.—Federal on-budget funds for education, by level or other educational purpose, by agency and program: Fiscal years 1965 to 1997—Continued

[In thousands of dollars]

Level or educational purpose, by agency and program	1988	1989	1990[1]	1991[2]	1992[3]	1993[4]	1994[5]	1995[6]	1996[7]	1997[8]
1	12	13	14	15	16	17	18	19	20	21
Corporation for National and Community Service	—	—	—	—	—	—	—	—	—	—
Environmental Protection Agency	58,053	64,517	87,481	62,753	152,012	124,500	98,241	125,721	104,200	132,434
Federal Emergency Management Agency	—	—	—	—	—	—	—	—	—	—
National Aeronautics and Space Administration	897,497	976,478	1,090,003	1,270,070	1,377,322	1,367,542	1,412,665	1,751,977	1,611,374	1,511,958
National Science Foundation	1,232,054	1,342,648	1,427,007	1,546,810	1,664,697	1,833,563	1,805,856	1,874,395	1,861,217	1,968,988
Nuclear Regulatory Commission	25,676	25,690	42,328	23,860	27,418	22,934	20,227	22,188	12,958	15,890
Office of Economic Opportunity	—	—	—	—	—	—	—	—	—	—
U.S. Arms Control and Disarmament Agency	2,633	1,619	25	69	100	25	—	—	—	—
U.S. Information Agency	—	—	—	—	—	—	—	—	—	—
Other agencies	1,870	947	885	1,616	1,532	1,622	—	500	1,415	2,745

Footnotes—Continued

[24] The Job Corps program was formerly in the Office of Economic Opportunity, and funds were appropriated to the U.S. Department of Labor beginning in 1971 and 1972.

[25] Some of the work and training programs included in this program were in the Office of Economic Opportunity and were transferred to the U.S. Department of Labor in 1971 and 1972. Beginning in FY 94, the School-to-Work Opportunities program is included. This program is administered jointly by the U.S. Departments of Education and Labor.

[26] The U.S. Department of Transportation was created in 1967.

[27] This program was transferred from the U.S. Department of the Treasury to the U.S. Department of Transportation in 1967.

[28] This program was established in FY 72 and closed in FY 86.

[29] The states' share of revenue-sharing funds could not be spent on education in FYs 81–86.

[30] The U.S. Department of Veterans Affairs, formerly the Veterans Administration, was created in March 1989.

[31] This program provides educational assistance allowances in order to restore lost educational opportunities to those individuals whose careers were interrupted or impeded by reason of active military service between January 31, 1955, and January 1, 1977. Includes "Readjustment Benefits," Chapter 34, for education other than college and also includes the Veterans Job Training program for service persons and veterans. The Chapter 34 program closed December 31, 1989. The Veterans Job Training Program was put in the program Payments to State Education Agencies. Veterans who were still eligible to receive benefits under Chapter 34 were covered by Chapter 30 (The All-Volunteer-Force Educational Assistance program).

[32] This program is in "Readjustment Benefits" program, Chapter 31, and covers the costs of subsistence, tuition, books, supplies, and equipment for disabled veterans requiring vocational rehabilitation.

[33] This program is in the "Readjustment Benefits" program, Chapter 35, and provides benefits to children and spouses of veterans.

[34] The purpose of this program is to provide stable and permanent employment to those men and women who have served on active duty on or after August 2, 1990, and are unemployed.

[35] This agency was established March 9, 1965. Its first year of appropriations was 1966. The outlays were larger in the years 1970 and 1975 for elementary and secondary education because of the construction of facilities for vocational schools.

[36] This agency was established in 1965. In 1970, $900,000 was appropriated through the Office of Education, U.S. Department of Health, Education, and Welfare, for the National Endowment for the Arts, Arts in Education program.

[37] This agency was established in 1965. First year of appropriations was 1966.

[38] The Economic Opportunity Act of 1964 authorized 10 major action programs, including Job Corps, Neighborhood Youth Corps, Adult Literacy, Work Experience, College Work-Study, and Community Action programs, including Head Start, Follow Through, and Upward Bound, and authorized the establishment of Volunteers in Service to America (VISTA). These programs were transferred to the U.S. Department of Health, Education, and Welfare, U.S. Department of Labor, and the Action Agency in the 1970s. An act on January 4, 1975 established the Community Services Administration as the successor agency to the Office of Economic Opportunity.

[39] Head Start program funds were transferred to the U.S. Department of Health, Education, and Welfare, Office of Child Development, in 1972.

[40] Most of these programs were transferred to the U.S. Department of Health, Education, and Welfare, Office of Education, in 1972.

[41] The Job Corps programs were transferred to the U.S. Department of Labor in 1971 and 1972.

[42] These programs were transferred to the U.S. Department of Labor in 1971 and 1972.

[43] These programs were transferred to the Action Agency in 1972.

[44] Similar programs were included in the "higher education" program in 1965 through 1975.

[45] The Student Loan Reform Act of 1993 authorized a new Federal Direct Student Loan (FDSL) program, recently renamed the William D. Ford Direct Loan program. This program is a new streamlined lending system that simplifies the process of obtaining and repaying loans for student and parent borrowers and provides borrowers with greater choice in repayment plans. The FDSL program was phased in beginning with the 1994–95 academic year.

[46] Similar programs were included in the "higher education" program in 1965 through 1975, formerly called the "Guaranteed Student Loan" program.

[47] This program was transferred from the U.S. Department of Housing and Urban Development to the U.S. Department of Health, Education, and Welfare, Office of Education, in FY 79.

[48] The Historically Black Colleges and Universities (HBCUs) Capital Financing program was authorized by the Higher Education Act Amendments of 1992 to provide HBCUs with private funds for projects such as repairs, renovation and construction of classrooms, libraries, laboratories, dormitories, instructional equipment, and research instruments.

[49] First year of appropriations for this program was 1967.

[50] Program funds were first appropriated for Tuskegee Institute in 1972.

[51] The Sea Grant College Program Act of 1966 established a matching fund grant program that provides for the establishment of a network of programs in fields related to development and preservation of the nation's coastal and marine resources. This program was transferred from the National Science Foundation to the U.S. Department of Commerce, October 1970. Appropriations began in 1968.

Footnotes—Continued

[52] This program was transferred to the U.S. Department of Transportation in FY 81 by Public Law 97–31, from the U.S. Department of Commerce.

[53] The U.S. Department of Defense funds for FYs 90 to 96 exclude military pay and reserve accounts which were included in previous years. FY 65 data are not available except for service academies.

[54] Included in total above.

[55] Instructional costs only are included. These include academics, audiovisual, academic computing center, faculty training, military training, physical education, and libraries.

[56] Includes special education programs (military and civilian); legal education program; flight training; advanced degree program; college degree program (officers); and "Armed Forces Health Professions Scholarship" program.

[57] No funds have been appropriated for this program since FY 82.

[58] This program receives funds periodically.

[59] Appropriations began in FY 84.

[60] Appropriations began in FY 89.

[61] Does not include higher education assistance loans.

[62] Appropriations began in FY 78.

[63] Alcohol, drug abuse, and mental health training programs are included starting in fiscal year 1992.

[64] Beginning in fiscal year 1992, data were included in the National Institutes of Health training grants program.

[65] Postsecondary student benefits were ended by the Omnibus Budget Reconciliation Act of 1981 (Public Law 97–35) and were completely phased out by August 1985.

[66] Includes adult education, tribally-controlled community colleges, postsecondary instruction, and other education.

[67] This program was transferred from the U.S. Department of State to the International Communication Agency (I.C.A.) in the Reorganization Plan No. 2 of 1977, which consolidated the functions of the U.S. Information Agency (U.S.I.A.) and the U.S. Department of State's Bureau of Educational and Cultural Affairs. In FY 82 the I.C.A. became the U.S.I.A.

[68] This program provides funds for advanced study and research projects of the Russian, Eurasian, and Eastern European countries by American institutions of higher education and private research firms. Appropriations began in FY 88.

[69] This program was transferred to the U.S. Department of Transportation in FY 81 by Public Law 97–31 from the U.S. Department of Commerce.

[70] Includes flight training. This program was in the U.S. Department of the Treasury in 1965 and was transferred to the U.S. Department of Transportation in 1967.

[71] Includes benefits for Vietnam-era veterans under Chapter 34 (GI Bill) of the "Readjustment Benefits" education and training program. This program provides educational assistance allowances, primarily on a monthly basis, in order to restore lost educational opportunities to those individuals whose careers were interrupted or impeded by reason of active military service between January 31, 1955, and January 1, 1977. This program closed December 31, 1989. Some veterans who were still eligible were put in Chapter 30 (the All-Volunteer-Force Educational Assistance program).

[72] Includes service persons under Chapter 34 (GI Bill) of the "Readjustment Benefits" education and training program. Service persons with over 180 days of active duty, any part of which was before January 1, 1977, are eligible to participate in this program.

[73] Includes post-Vietnam-era veterans, under Chapter 32, of the post-Vietnam-era "Veterans Education Account." Provides education and training assistance payments to veterans and service persons with no active duty time before January 1, 1977. Funding is provided through participants' contributions while on active duty and through transfers from the U.S. Department of Defense (DOD). Participants' contributions, up to a maximum of $2,700, are deposited to the fund prior to discharge. When the participant enters training, the monthly disbursement from his or her account is matched two for one from funds provided by DOD. Additional amounts in the form of incentive bonuses may also be provided by DOD funds. The U.S. Department of Veterans Affairs funds are not appropriated for this program, so these data represent obligations, which are funded through other agencies' appropriations.

[74] Public Law 98–525, enacted October 19, 1984 (New GI Bill), established two new peacetime educational programs: an assistance program for veterans who entered active duty during the period beginning July 1, 1985, and ending on June 30, 1988, and an assistance program for certain members of the Selected Reserve.

[75] Chapter 30, also called the Montgomery Bill, and the new GI Bill are for eligible veterans who have agreed to have their military pay reduced $100 per month for their first 12 months of active duty in order to participate in this program. The "Readjustment Benefits" account under the U.S. Department of Veterans Affairs pays only the basic allowance, up to a maximum of $300 per month, for full-time training. "Supplemental Benefits" are paid by the U.S. Department of Defense (DOD).

[76] Chapter 106 is for members of the Selected Reserve. The reserve components include the Army, Navy, Air Force, Marine Corps Reserve, Army National Guard and Air National Guard under the U.S. Department of Defense (DOD), and the Coast Guard Reserve, which is under the U.S. Department of Transportation (DOT) when it is not operating as a service in the Navy. Eligible persons can receive up to $140 per month for full-time training. The DOD and DOT pay for this program, and the U.S. Department of Veterans Affairs administers it.

[77] Includes dependents of veterans under Chapter 35, the "Readjustment Benefits" education and training program. Provides education and training benefits to dependents of veterans who died of a service-connected disability or whose service-connected disability is rated permanent and total.

[78] These payments have been made to state education agencies for a number of years but were not a separate budget item until FY 88.

[79] The U.S.I.A. was called the "International Communication Agency" in FYs 80 and 81.

[80] This program was in the "Educational and Cultural Affairs" program in FYs 80–83, and became an independent program in FY 84.

[81] This program was combined with the "Educational and Cultural Affairs" program in FY 77.

[82] Public Law 99–661 established this program to operate the scholarship program in tribute to the former Senator from Arizona. The Foundation awards scholarships and fellowships to outstanding graduate and undergraduate students who intend to pursue careers or advanced degrees in science or mathematics. The Foundation may also award honoraria to outstanding individuals who have made significant contributions to improve the instruction of science and mathematics in secondary schools.

[83] Appropriations for this program began in FY 76.

[84] Public Law 99–498 established this Institute as an independent non-profit corporation administered by a Board of Trustees. The Institute provides Native Americans with an opportunity to obtain a postsecondary education in various fields of Indian art and culture.

[85] Public Laws 99–500 and 99–591 established the James Madison Memorial Fellowship Foundation to operate a fellowship program to encourage graduate study of the American Constitution. First year of appropriations was FY 88.

[86] This program will be transferred to the Institute of Museum and Library and Library Services beginning in fiscal year 1998.

[87] This program was transferred to the U.S. Department of Transportation in FY 68 from the U.S. Department of Housing and Urban Development.

Footnotes—Continued

[88] This program was established by the Juvenile Justice and Delinquency Prevention Act of 1974 to provide education and training and to provide leadership in improving correctional programs and practices in prisons. FY 75 had large outlays because of the construction of buildings and facilities.

[89] Appropriations for this program began in FY 70. This program is part of the Federal-Aid Highway Act of 1970, Public Law 91–605.

[90] The Federal Aviation Administration, originally an independent agency, was transferred to the U.S. Department of Transportation in FY 67.

[91] Appropriations began in FY 72. No funds have been appropriated since FY 82.

[92] First year of appropriations was FY 70.

[93] The National Service Trust Act of 1993 established a new agency, the Corporation for National and Community Service. On October 1, 1993, ACTION became part of the Corporation for National and Community Service—ACTION was established on July 1, 1971. This agency brings together a number of volunteer programs. Some of these funds were formerly in the Office of Economic Opportunity.

[94] These programs included the Service Learning programs, University Year for ACTION, Volunteers in Service to America, Youth Challenge program, and the National Student Volunteer program in FY 1975. In FY 80, programs included were the University Year for ACTION, Young Volunteers for ACTION, and National Service Learning programs. In fiscal year 1985, the program included was the Service Learning programs, and in FYs 89 to 94, programs included were the Literacy Corps and the Student Community Services program. In FYs 94 through 97 the AmeriCorps program was included. This program provides education grants of up to $4,725 per year, for up to 2 years, to help pay for college or to repay student loans for people age 17 years or older who perform community service before, during or after postsecondary education.

[95] The Federal Emergency Management Agency was created on March 25, 1979, representing a combination of five existing agencies. The two largest were the Defense Civil Preparedness Agency in the U.S. Department of Defense and the Federal Preparedness Agency in the General Services Administration. The funds for the Federal Emergency Management Agency in FY 70 to FY 75 were in the other agencies.

[96] First year of appropriations was FY 68.

[97] First appropriations for the "other training programs" were in the late 1960s. These programs include the Fall-Out Shelter Analysis, Blast Protection Design through 1992. Starting in FY 1993, earthquake training and safety for teachers and administrators for grades 1 through 12 are included.

[98] The disaster relief program repairs and replaces damaged and destroyed school buildings. In FY 94 and FY 95 funds were for repairs due to the Northridge Earthquake in California. In FY 94, $37.2 million was spent on school districts; $4.2 million was spent on community colleges and $43.8 million spent on universities. In FY 95, $74.4 million was spent on school districts; $8.4 million on community colleges and $87.6 million on colleges and universities.

[99] This program was transferred from the General Services Administration to the National Archives and Records Administration in April 1985.

[100] This program makes grants for the promotion of scholarly, cultural, and artistic exchanges between Japan and the United States. Appropriations began in FY 76.

[101] The National Archives and Records Administration became an independent agency in April 1985.

[102] This program was established by the act of July 20, 1970, Public Law 91–345.

[103] This program was established by Congress to conduct and support research and scholarships in the fields of peace, arms control, and conflict resolution. This program began operation in February 1986.

[104] Includes federal obligations for research and development centers administered by colleges and universities. FYs 96 and 97 are estimated.

[105] Total outlays for FYs 65 and 70 include the "Research and Training" program. FY 75 includes the "National Institute of Education" program. FYs 80 to 97 include outlays for the Office of Educational Research and Improvement.

—Data not available or not applicable.

NOTE.—Some data have been revised from previously published figures. To the extent possible, amounts reported represent outlays rather than obligations. Because of rounding, details may not add to totals.

SOURCE: U.S. Department of Education, National Center for Education Statistics, compiled from data appearing in U.S. Office of Management and Budget, *Budget of the U.S. Government,* fiscal years 1967 to 1998; National Science Foundation, *Federal Funds for Research and Development,* fiscal years 1965 to 1997; and unpublished data obtained from various federal agencies. (This table was prepared May 1997.)

Table 360.—Estimated federal support for education, by agency and type of ultimate recipient: Fiscal year 1997

[In millions of dollars]

Agency	Total	Local education agencies	State education agencies	College students	Institutions of higher education	Federal	Multiple types of recipients	Other[1]
1	2	3	4	5	6	7	8	9
Total[2]	$100,501.2	$21,241.6	$5,298.4	$19,452.2	$31,344.7	$3,247.9	$11,275.6	$8,640.7
Total program funds - on-budget	$73,070.4	$21,241.6	$4,747.8	$7,957.5	$21,379.7	$3,247.9	$11,275.6	$3,220.2
Department of Education	31,104.3	11,757.7	3,968.2	5,051.2	5,078.7	472.6	2,244.7	2,531.4
Department of Agriculture	9,657.3	8,712.6	82.6	—	453.3	18.0	—	390.8
Department of Commerce	74.5	—	—	—	74.5	—	—	—
Department of Defense	3,735.9	167.8	—	279.2	1,701.3	1,381.5	206.1	—
Department of Energy	2,609.3	—	—	—	2,609.3	—	—	—
Department of Health and Human Services	13,063.0	398.1	—	881.2	7,480.6	145.0	4,158.1	—
Department of Housing and Urban Development	1.0	—	—	—	1.0	—	—	—
Department of the Interior	798.4	111.3	42.3	25.9	119.1	450.2	49.6	—
Department of Justice	237.7	—	—	—	7.1	230.6	—	—
Department of Labor	4,593.2	—	651.7	—	0.2	—	3,941.3	—
Department of State	54.1	—	—	—	—	54.1	—	—
Department of Transportation	126.9	—	—	0.2	75.8	40.9	2.9	7.0
Department of the Treasury	61.1	—	—	—	0.1	61.0	—	—
Department of Veterans Affairs	1,557.2	—	3.0	1,552.2	2.0	—	—	—
Other agencies and programs								
Agency for International Development	303.0	—	—	—	13.0	—	—	290.0
Appalachian Regional Commission	8.3	—	—	—	2.7	—	5.6	—
Barry Goldwater Scholarship and Excellence in Education Foundation	3.0	—	—	—	—	—	3.0	—
Corporation for National and Community Service	335.0	—	—	—	—	—	335.0	—
Environmental Protection Agency	132.4	—	—	—	132.4	—	—	—
Estimated education share of federal aid to the District of Columbia	98.5	85.8	—	—	11.7	—	0.9	—
Federal Emergency Management Agency	8.3	8.3	—	—	—	—	—	—
General Services Administration	—	—	—	—	—	—	—	—
Harry S Truman scholarship fund	3.0	—	—	—	—	—	3.0	—
Institute of American Indian and Alaskan Native Culture and Arts Development	6.0	—	—	—	—	—	6.0	—
James Madison Memorial Fellowship Foundation	2.0	—	—	—	—	—	2.0	—
Japanese-United States Friendship Commission	2.0	—	—	—	—	—	2.0	—
Library of Congress	269.0	—	—	—	—	269.0	—	—
National Aeronautics and Space Administration	1,518.1	—	—	—	1,512.0	—	6.1	—
National Archives and Records Administration	111.3	—	—	—	—	111.3	—	—
National Commission on Libraries and Information Science	1.0	—	—	—	—	—	—	1.0
National Endowment for the Arts	9.0	—	—	—	—	—	9.0	—
National Endowment for the Humanities	93.4	—	—	—	—	—	93.4	—
National Science Foundation	2,242.0	—	—	155.6	2,086.4	—	—	—
Nuclear Regulatory Commission	15.9	—	—	—	15.9	—	—	—
Smithsonian Institution	10.0	—	—	—	—	0.8	9.2	—
U. S. Arms Control and Disarmament Agency	—	—	—	—	—	—	—	—
U.S. Information Agency	210.6	—	—	12.0	—	13.0	185.6	—
U.S. Institute of Peace	12.0	—	—	—	—	—	12.0	—
Other agencies	2.7	—	—	—	2.7	—	—	—
Off-budget support and nonfederal funds generated by federal legislation	27,430.8	—	550.6	11,494.7	9,965.0	—	—	5,420.5

[1] Other recipients include Indian tribes, private nonprofit agencies, and banks.
[2] Includes on-budget support, off-budget support, and nonfederal funds generated by federal legislation. Excludes federal tax expenditures.
—Data not available or not applicable.

NOTE.—Outlays by type of recipient are estimated based on obligation data. Because of rounding, details may not add to totals.

SOURCE: U.S. Department of Education, Office of the Undersecretary, unpublished tabulations; U.S. Office of Management and Budget, *Budget of the U.S. Government, Fiscal Year 1998*; National Science Foundation, *Federal Funds for Research and Development, Fiscal Years 1995, 1996, and 1997*; and unpublished data obtained from various federal agencies. (This table was prepared May 1997.)

FEDERAL PROGRAMS 403

Table 361.—Federal on-budget funds obligated for programs administered by the U.S. Department of Education: Fiscal years 1980 to 1997

[In thousands of dollars]

Program	1980	1985	1990	1992	1993	1994	1995	1996[1]	1997[2]
1	2	3	4	5	6	7	8	9	10
Total	**$14,102,165**	**$18,818,201**	**$25,214,923**	**$34,966,632**	**$33,748,670**	**$36,735,985**	**$46,433,000**	**$45,540,000**	**$57,875,000**
Elementary and secondary education	4,239,022	4,732,864	7,169,693	8,606,349	8,565,459	8,820,052	9,124,000	7,824,000	10,508,000
Grants for the disadvantaged	3,204,664	3,745,855	5,383,960	6,717,712	6,659,203	7,038,334	7,200,000	5,893,000	7,731,000
School improvement programs	788,918	748,000	1,524,001	1,587,369	1,600,013	1,368,108	1,343,000	1,220,000	1,434,000
Bilingual education	169,540	171,605	188,152	224,911	225,693	239,805	206,000	178,000	262,000
Indian education	75,900	67,404	73,580	76,357	80,550	82,762	81,000	53,000	61,000
Education Reform - Goals 2000	—	—	—	—	—	91,043	294,000	480,000	1,020,000
School assistance in federally affected areas	812,873	695,746	815,573	835,394	760,456	911,716	783,000	703,000	839,000
Maintenance and operations	690,000	665,000	717,354	744,491	713,108	787,263	715,000	689,000	790,000
Construction	110,873	23,037	22,929	43,155	5,291	8,584	2,000	13,000	22,000
Disaster assistance	12,000	7,709	75,290	47,748	42,057	115,869	66,000	1,000	27,000
Education for the handicapped	1,555,253	2,666,056	3,480,122	4,750,048	4,752,116	5,965,688	5,767,000	5,849,000	6,749,000
State grant programs	815,805	1,245,219	1,258,871	1,980,432	1,842,956	2,779,228	2,467,000	2,350,000	3,119,000
Early childhood education[3]	38,745	27,625	280,341	480,599	476,180	661,665	661,000	820,000	891,000
Special centers, projects, and research	55,075	53,430	72,966	109,976	139,265	101,605	132,000	110,000	115,000
Captioned films and media services	17,778	35,670	15,191	16,593	17,571	18,608	19,000	19,000	20,000
Personnel training	55,375	68,025	70,838	89,753	90,120	104,012	91,000	91,000	93,000
Handicapped rehabilitation service and research	572,475	1,236,087	1,781,915	2,072,695	2,186,024	2,300,570	2,397,000	2,459,000	2,511,000
Vocational education and adult programs	1,153,743	856,271	1,138,674	1,774,664	1,575,268	1,456,185	1,461,000	1,366,000	1,528,000
Basic programs[4]	744,653	725,624	858,716	1,253,148	1,049,834	950,244	1,004,000	1,083,000	1,140,000
Consumer and homemaking	63,169	33,138	34,517	48,989	35,872	33,895	1,000	—	—
Program improvement and supportive services	162,512	5,202	—	—	—	—	—	—	—
State planning and advisory councils	13,423	7,584	7,923	9,325	8,928	9,087	9,000	4,000	—
Adult education, grants to states	153,724	84,723	188,280	235,650	309,810	254,724	299,000	272,000	370,000
Other[5]	16,262	—	49,238	227,552	170,824	208,235	148,000	7,000	18,000
Postsecondary student financial assistance	5,108,534	8,534,205	11,112,068	17,008,333	16,065,617	17,400,855	26,956,000	27,705,000	35,838,000
Educational opportunity grants[6]	2,534,378	3,558,440	4,919,264	6,274,116	6,764,683	7,092,393	6,484,000	5,545,000	7,917,000
Work-study	596,065	599,467	615,269	621,139	625,043	620,878	620,000	619,000	832,000
Perkins loan program	322,749	219,850	157,415	157,518	183,262	177,413	187,000	118,000	179,000
Federal Family Education Loan program[7]	1,597,877	4,130,920	5,341,039	9,855,159	8,380,619	8,444,937	10,461,000	10,722,000	12,133,000
Other student assistance programs[8]	57,465	25,528	79,081	100,401	112,010	1,065,234	9,204,000	10,701,000	14,777,000
Direct aid to postsecondary institutions	277,068	329,714	341,634	518,380	518,908	740,677	780,000	830,000	872,000
Aid to minority and developing institutions	114,680	140,374	99,812	130,215	130,743	211,054	231,000	304,000	306,000
Special programs for the disadvantaged	147,389	174,940	241,822	388,165	388,165	529,623	549,000	526,000	566,000
Cooperative education	14,999	14,400	—	—	—	—	—	—	—
Higher education facilities	268,493	194,556	84,305	92,923	81,026	49,888	46,000	51,000	46,000
Construction loans and insurance	35,362	33,188	30,000	38,095	46,472	20,607	15,000	1,000	1,000
Interest subsidy grants	24,626	24,968	38,741	41,181	22,647	18,188	21,000	17,000	20,000
College housing loans	208,505	136,400	15,564	13,647	11,907	11,093	10,000	33,000	25,000
Other higher education programs	34,927	74,340	188,999	198,993	201,734	129,951	120,000	—	—
International education and foreign languages[9]	19,977	32,050	86,337	107,812	114,761	—	—	—	—
Funds for Improvement of Postsecondary Education[10]	12,000	12,710	99,450	87,831	86,257	129,554	116,000	([11])	([11])
Other	2,950	29,580	3,212	3,350	716	397	4,000	—	—
Public library services	101,218	116,027	132,583	148,208	144,380	149,591	150,000	128,000	147,000
Public library services	66,451	75,000	82,505	83,898	83,227	83,227	83,000	93,000	101,000
Interlibrary cooperation	—	18,000	19,551	19,908	19,749	19,749	24,000	18,000	12,000
Public library construction	—	16,027	14,837	17,179	14,871	21,074	24,000	12,000	27,000
Research libraries	5,992	6,000	6,593	5,855	5,808	5,808	—	3,000	5,000
Other	28,775	1,000	9,097	21,368	20,725	19,733	19,000	2,000	2,000
Payments to special institutions	273,860	253,622	292,736	327,521	320,455	321,753	340,000	314,000	325,000
American Printing House for the Blind	4,349	5,500	5,663	5,900	6,298	6,463	7,000	7,000	7,000
National Technical Institute for the Deaf	19,799	31,400	35,594	39,278	40,964	41,836	43,000	42,000	43,000
Gallaudet College	49,409	59,092	67,643	76,540	77,589	78,435	80,000	78,000	79,000
Howard University	200,303	157,630	183,836	205,803	195,604	195,019	210,000	187,000	196,000
Departmental accounts	277,174	364,800	458,536	705,819	763,251	789,629	906,000	770,000	1,023,000
Educational research and improvement	51,415	60,556	87,074	267,569	283,078	294,323	327,000	353,000	598,000
Departmental management account	223,857	300,885	370,844	438,246	480,166	495,249	579,000	416,000	419,000
Other	1,875	3,349	—	—	—	—	—	1,000	6,000
Trust funds	27	10	618	4	7	57	—	—	—

[1] Revised from previously published data.
[2] Estimated.
[3] Includes preschool incentive grants.
[4] Includes programs of national significance and special programs for the disadvantaged.
[5] Includes national programs for research, demonstrations, evaluation and technical assistance, literacy training for homeless adults, and some other small programs.
[6] Includes Pell Grants, Supplemental Education Opportunity Grants, State Student Incentive Grants, and Income Contingent Loans.
[7] Formerly the Guaranteed Student Loan program.
[8] Includes Federal Direct Student Loan program starting in fiscal year 1994.
[9] This program starting in fiscal year 1994 is included under the program, "Funds for Improvement of Postsecondary Education."
[10] International education and foreign languages are included under this program starting in fiscal year 1994.
[11] This program is included under the "Special programs for the disadvantaged" program.

—Data are not available or not applicable.

NOTE.—Because of rounding, details may not add to totals. Data presented in this tabulation are obligations, which differ from outlay figures reported in other tables in this chapter.

SOURCE: U.S. Office of Management and Budget, *Budget of the United States Government,* fiscal years 1982 to 1998. (This table was prepared April 1997.)

Table 362.—U.S. Department of Education outlays, by level of education and type of recipient: Fiscal years 1980 to 1997

[In millions of dollars]

Year and area of education	Total	Local education agencies	State education agencies	College students	Institutions of higher education	Federal	Multiple types of recipients	Other[1]
1	2	3	4	5	6	7	8	9
1980 total	$13,137.8	$5,313.7	$1,103.2	$2,137.4	$2,267.2	$249.8	$693.8	$1,372.7
Elementary/secondary	6,629.1	5,309.4	662.2	34.2	22.0	62.5	513.4	25.5
Postsecondary education	5,682.2	—	99.5	2,103.2	2,166.5	—	—	1,313.0
Other programs	747.7	4.3	341.5	—	—	187.3	180.4	34.2
Education research and statistics	78.7	—	—	—	78.7	—	—	—
1982 total	14,109.3	5,425.8	1,414.2	1,610.2	1,951.8	268.3	535.4	2,903.6
Elementary/secondary	6,456.3	5,420.8	593.8	48.9	21.9	2.6	340.3	27.9
Postsecondary education	6,418.8	—	196.6	1,561.3	1,847.7	—	—	2,813.2
Other programs	1,152.0	5.0	623.8	—	—	265.7	195.1	62.5
Education research and statistics	82.2	—	—	—	82.2	—	—	—
1984 total	15,534.7	5,256.5	1,879.0	2,193.4	2,167.4	330.2	516.7	3,191.4
Elementary/secondary	6,220.8	5,252.4	536.0	55.5	35.3	22.9	259.9	58.8
Postsecondary education	7,341.2	—	211.5	2,137.9	1,972.5	—	—	3,019.3
Other programs	1,813.1	4.1	1,131.5	—	—	307.3	256.8	113.3
Education research and statistics	159.6	—	—	—	159.6	—	—	—
1986 total	17,740.1	6,435.1	1,823.3	2,685.9	2,637.2	265.4	625.8	3,267.5
Elementary/secondary	7,552.0	6,432.1	558.5	68.3	45.2	2.2	372.0	73.8
Postsecondary education	8,444.9	—	215.6	2,617.6	2,523.0	—	—	3,088.7
Other programs	1,674.2	3.0	1,049.2	—	—	263.2	253.8	105.0
Education research and statistics	69.0	—	—	—	69.0	—	—	—
1988 total	18,326.9	6,614.8	2,234.6	3,103.4	2,519.5	319.4	838.8	2,696.3
Elementary/secondary	8,098.4	6,606.3	717.9	66.2	39.5	23.8	616.7	28.0
Postsecondary education	8,247.1	—	184.6	3,037.2	2,437.6	—	—	2,587.7
Other programs	1,939.0	8.5	1,332.1	—	—	295.6	222.1	80.6
Education research and statistics	42.4	—	—	—	42.4	—	—	—
1990 total	23,198.6	8,000.7	2,490.3	3,859.6	3,649.8	441.4	912.2	3,844.4
Elementary/secondary	9,681.3	7,995.0	700.3	80.5	85.4	113.1	650.7	56.3
Postsecondary education	11,176.0	—	261.6	3,779.1	3,475.0	—	—	3,660.4
Other programs	2,251.8	5.7	1,528.5	—	—	328.3	261.5	127.8
Education research and statistics	89.5	—	—	—	89.5	—	—	—
1992 total	26,116.0	9,834.7	2,883.2	4,090.7	4,107.4	418.3	1,189.4	3,592.4
Elementary/secondary	12,057.7	9,830.1	1,011.0	92.9	232.7	49.8	762.3	78.8
Postsecondary education	11,323.6	—	245.5	3,997.7	3,719.9	—	—	3,360.5
Other programs	2,579.9	4.6	1,626.6	—	—	368.5	427.0	153.1
Education research and statistics	154.8	—	—	—	154.8	—	—	—
1994 total	29,713.4	10,935.6	3,264.8	4,800.5	4,831.3	504.5	1,258.2	4,118.5
Elementary/secondary	13,769.2	10,929.2	1,354.0	159.9	275.2	60.9	902.1	87.9
Postsecondary education	12,871.4	—	53.0	4,640.6	4,279.3	—	—	3,898.5
Other programs	2,796.0	6.4	1,857.8	—	—	443.6	356.1	132.1
Education research and statistics	276.8	—	—	—	276.8	—	—	—
1995 total	31,403.0	11,210.7	3,584.0	4,964.7	5,016.1	485.4	1,349.2	4,792.9
Elementary/secondary	14,029.0	11,203.3	1,410.0	190.5	170.1	70.3	946.9	37.9
Postsecondary education	14,234.0	—	250.8	4,774.2	4,567.0	—	—	4,642.0
Other programs	2,861.0	7.4	1,923.2	—	—	415.1	402.3	113.0
Education research and statistics	279.0	—	—	—	279.0	—	—	—
1996 total	29,977.8	11,077.8	3,669.6	5,129.8	5,053.4	562.1	1,682.3	2,802.9
Elementary/secondary	14,323.8	11,073.1	1,650.7	161.1	141.5	59.2	1,201.4	36.8
Postsecondary education	12,257.6	—	90.7	4,968.7	4,601.0	—	—	2,597.2
Other programs	3,085.6	4.7	1,928.2	—	—	502.9	480.9	168.9
Education research and statistics	310.9	—	—	—	310.9	—	—	—
1997 total	31,104.3	11,757.7	3,968.2	5,051.2	5,078.7	472.6	2,244.7	2,531.4
Elementary/secondary	15,663.1	11,748.9	1,757.8	171.3	161.7	58.3	1,725.7	39.4
Postsecondary education	11,735.3	—	48.6	4,879.9	4,504.1	—	—	2,302.8
Other programs	3,293.0	8.8	2,161.8	—	—	414.3	519.0	189.2
Education research and statistics	412.9	—	—	—	412.9	—	—	—

[1] Other recipients include Indian tribes, private nonprofit agencies, and banks.
—Data are not available or not applicable.

NOTE.—Outlays by type of recipient are estimated based on obligation data. Some data have been revised from previously published figures. Because of rounding, details may not add to totals.

SOURCE: U.S. Office of Management and Budget, *Budget of the U.S. Government,* Fiscal Years 1982 to 1998, and *Catalog of Federal Domestic Assistance;* National Science Foundation, *Federal Funds for Research and Development,* Fiscal Years 1980 to 1997; and unpublished data obtained from various federal agencies. (This table was prepared May 1997.)

FEDERAL PROGRAMS 405

Table 363.—U.S. Department of Education obligations for major programs, by state or other area: Fiscal year 1996
[In thousands]

State or other area	Total	Grants for the disadvantaged [1]	Block grants to states for school improvement [2]	School assistance in federally affected areas [3]	Vocational and adult education [4]	Education for the handicapped [5]	Bilingual education [6]	Indian education	Higher and continuing education [7]	Student financial assistance [8]	Public library programs [9]	Rehabilitation services [10]	Goals 2000 [11]
1	2	3	4	5	6	7	8	9	10	11	12	13	14
Total	$23,169,044	$5,877,908	$1,014,622	$621,707	$1,324,769	$3,144,751	$186,524	$50,180	$1,037,480	$7,275,673	$122,624	$2,191,920	$320,885
Alabama	401,419	104,932	16,386	3,822	25,534	55,413	214	1,205	39,758	99,388	2,343	46,370	$6,054
Alaska	115,798	22,498	4,974	50,357	4,984	10,390	1,016	5,715	2,456	4,618	899	7,862	29
Arizona	410,975	87,262	15,136	67,929	20,932	40,807	7,185	5,864	7,282	117,446	1,982	33,596	5,554
Arkansas	221,201	64,679	9,837	889	15,057	29,434	100	101	14,102	57,400	1,328	28,204	69
California	2,517,806	691,965	111,557	52,700	140,435	344,881	66,018	3,494	74,588	765,436	13,004	210,819	42,909
Colorado	254,932	57,264	12,210	6,140	16,096	41,004	2,129	321	11,759	75,903	1,564	26,538	4,004
Connecticut	181,800	45,962	9,703	5,411	12,061	42,656	1,754	21	6,326	39,105	1,660	17,077	66
Delaware	63,584	14,308	4,974	67	5,253	9,124	160	0	4,636	15,357	562	7,874	1,267
District of Columbia	369,884	17,857	4,874	1,515	4,363	4,756	716	0	198,518	123,567	570	11,595	1,552
Florida	979,634	252,802	43,463	11,227	61,095	172,852	8,532	40	26,151	279,772	5,548	103,138	15,014
Georgia	517,636	143,475	25,677	6,058	37,781	71,144	686	0	35,486	123,752	2,796	61,652	9,129
Hawaii	86,306	16,056	4,974	17,414	6,247	10,427	1,550	0	6,736	13,863	1,007	8,005	26
Idaho	102,623	22,888	4,975	3,230	6,904	14,720	747	213	3,351	30,615	650	11,252	3,076
Illinois	864,739	266,003	44,193	9,063	51,880	133,309	5,639	68	31,564	235,991	4,497	82,230	303
Indiana	420,921	92,514	19,058	538	30,439	68,549	301	8	12,979	143,409	2,324	44,122	6,681
Iowa	225,630	42,509	9,446	124	14,669	33,610	615	88	12,268	79,920	1,440	24,582	6,359
Kansas	213,163	49,909	9,092	9,759	12,565	28,661	989	281	10,230	66,239	1,369	20,909	3,160
Kentucky	351,966	109,184	15,497	966	23,672	47,360	275	0	14,596	91,289	1,626	41,842	5,659
Louisiana	476,701	156,947	21,338	5,346	27,048	48,661	2,011	405	25,631	131,605	2,630	47,287	7,793
Maine	102,845	24,459	4,974	2,443	6,495	16,700	743	112	5,203	26,410	899	12,840	1,567
Maryland	319,999	72,257	15,573	8,962	19,462	53,545	1,116	129	18,429	90,689	2,209	32,511	5,118
Massachusetts	525,798	103,185	20,499	3,904	23,859	91,048	3,951	61	18,676	202,189	2,522	42,540	13,366
Michigan	762,383	261,032	39,009	5,025	46,088	99,024	990	2,081	24,918	189,000	4,166	77,117	13,926
Minnesota	333,882	69,899	15,731	4,632	20,569	56,709	2,158	1,880	13,750	98,648	2,490	36,874	10,541
Mississippi	316,673	102,740	13,511	3,356	17,571	34,158	100	184	18,073	86,539	1,207	34,041	5,191
Missouri	418,419	98,868	18,601	6,040	26,773	60,645	1,008	35	13,893	129,487	2,152	48,134	12,782
Montana	113,558	21,422	4,974	20,219	5,751	9,946	1,606	1,604	7,064	29,748	685	8,949	1,590
Nebraska	152,432	28,478	5,542	6,728	8,170	19,935	506	342	4,526	60,934	829	14,419	2,024
Nevada	69,984	15,994	5,026	3,047	6,515	15,190	413	409	1,777	10,214	927	9,142	1,330
New Hampshire	73,135	13,604	4,974	986	6,208	13,074	412	0	2,729	20,196	652	8,984	1,315
New Jersey	476,660	118,721	24,258	11,571	29,886	99,695	2,086	97	13,214	120,798	3,103	44,273	8,959
New Mexico	223,086	49,780	7,619	36,628	9,840	24,248	4,303	4,327	8,541	56,231	1,181	17,726	2,663
New York	1,896,975	515,108	71,682	17,716	73,572	214,036	27,341	958	39,106	810,531	7,661	118,750	513
North Carolina	486,613	111,143	22,433	7,820	38,172	77,113	875	1,785	35,211	121,617	2,801	67,496	147
North Dakota	92,451	14,559	4,974	14,665	5,278	7,230	1,464	859	4,165	28,220	597	7,813	2,626
Ohio	969,863	247,970	41,853	3,537	55,788	126,415	829	6	21,717	338,348	4,762	99,296	29,341
Oklahoma	317,729	69,293	12,460	18,309	18,847	37,096	7,715	9,493	16,285	88,959	1,600	33,192	4,480
Oregon	216,654	66,750	10,675	2,516	14,935	33,291	2,289	1,071	8,061	45,714	1,430	26,047	3,876
Pennsylvania	927,378	258,813	42,383	2,611	54,771	125,741	1,668	0	24,468	310,111	5,196	101,323	294
Rhode Island	95,837	17,931	4,974	2,492	6,416	13,187	630	0	2,681	35,950	742	7,965	2,868
South Carolina	317,256	75,967	13,344	5,562	22,092	49,661	129	21	19,326	85,433	2,027	38,894	4,800
South Dakota	149,118	16,314	4,974	13,497	5,355	9,196	1,881	1,755	3,628	82,700	513	7,866	1,439
Tennessee	401,598	100,063	18,114	2,067	28,832	63,771	283	0	22,784	106,456	2,231	50,489	6,509
Texas	1,710,624	515,462	77,550	26,965	100,123	223,335	13,402	143	48,108	514,630	6,897	156,266	27,741
Utah	183,397	28,066	7,820	5,934	12,736	30,149	850	592	7,109	67,321	1,023	19,294	2,502
Vermont	68,681	13,469	4,974	10	5,106	8,194	274	82	4,259	22,633	552	7,878	1,250
Virginia	457,917	84,425	19,420	29,334	30,343	73,577	628	10	23,651	143,359	3,014	50,156	0
Washington	400,936	94,508	17,813	21,761	22,930	57,742	2,514	2,597	15,319	120,064	2,176	37,335	6,177
West Virginia	179,339	57,100	7,753	16	11,636	23,449	45	0	8,275	42,450	1,237	21,738	5,641
Wisconsin	409,962	101,937	18,972	6,474	25,106	57,479	981	1,435	16,147	127,609	2,306	44,808	6,707
Wyoming	61,614	13,287	4,974	5,460	4,977	7,562	595	287	3,046	13,002	532	6,605	1,287
Indian tribe setaside	70,234	0	6,763	0	12,311	35,848	0	0	0	0	2,540	10,572	2,200
Undistributed	389,922	22,843	1,120	67,549	2,812	0	0	0	2,138	292,717	7	735	0
Outlying areas													
American Samoa	7,670	0	1,328	0	349	3,096	194	0	614	822	89	819	358
Federated States of Micronesia	852	0	0	0	100	0	450	0	0	0	0	0	302
Guam	16,300	0	3,092	0	720	7,415	510	0	1,577	1,316	124	1,352	195
Marshall Islands	203	0	0	0	100	0	0	0	0	0	0	0	103
North Mariana Islands	4,899	0	756	0	344	2,254	107	0	79	489	87	680	103
Palau	1,204	0	2	0	100	662	0	0	0	0	57	202	182
Puerto Rico	652,497	213,443	24,209	1,181	25,864	49,534	490	0	18,104	258,262	1,516	50,104	9,791
Trust Territory of the Pacific	798	0	0	0	0	0	0	0	798	0	0	0	0
Virgin Islands	14,954	0	2,552	137	847	6,045	352	0	1,618	1,194	87	1,742	380

[1] Title I, formerly called Chapter 1, Education Consolidation and Improvement Act of 1981, includes Grants to Local Education Agencies, Migrant Education—Basic State Grants, Program for Neglected and Delinquent Children, Capital Expenses, and Even Start—State Educational Agencies.

[2] Title VI, formerly called Chapter 2 Education Consolidation and Improvement Act of 1981, includes Eisenhower Professional Development Grants, Drug-Free Schools and Communities—State Grants, Education for Homeless Children and Youth, and Innovative Education Program Strategies.

[3] Impact Aid—Basic Support Payments and Impact Aid—Payments for Children with Disabilities.

[4] Includes Vocational Education—Basic Grants to States, Tech-Prep Education, and Adult Education-State Grant Program.

[5] Includes Special Education—Grants to States, Preschool Grants, Special Education—Grants for Infants and Families with Disabilities, and Education of Children with Disabilities.

[6] Includes Emergency Immigrant Education Program and Bilingual Education State Grants.

[7] Includes Institutional Aid to Strengthen Higher Education Institutions serving significant numbers of low-income students, Other Special Programs for the Disadvantaged, Cooperative Education, Fund for the Improvement of Postsecondary Education, Fellowships and Scholarships, and annual interest subsidy grants for facilities construction.

[8] Includes Pell Grants, State Student Incentive Grants, and Guaranteed Student Loan interest subsidies.

[9] Includes Public Library Services, Public Library Construction and Technology Enhancement, and Interlibrary Cooperation and Resource Sharing.

[10] Includes Rehabilitation Services—Vocational Rehabilitation Grants to States, Supported Employment Services for Individuals with Severe Disabilities, Rehabilitation Services—Client Assistance Program, Independent Living—State Grants, and Program of Protection and Advocacy of Individual Rights.

[11] Includes State and Local Education Systemic Improvement Grants.

NOTE.—Data reflect revisions to figures in the *Budget of the United States Government, Fiscal Year 1998*. To the extent possible, data represent obligations rather than outlays. Because of the exclusion of certain programs, totals in this table are lower than those reported in other tables. Because of rounding, details may not add to totals.

SOURCE: U.S. Department of Education, National Center for Education Statistics, based on unpublished tabulations from the Office of Management and Budget; and U.S. Department of Commerce, Bureau of the Census, *Federal Expenditures by State for Fiscal Year 1996*. (This table was prepared April 1997.)

Table 364.—U.S. Department of Education obligations for major programs, by state or other area: Fiscal year 1995

[In thousands]

State or other area	Total	Grants for the disadvantaged[1]	Block grants to states for school improvement[2]	School assistance in federally affected areas[3]	Vocational and adult education[4]	Education for the handicapped[5]	Bilingual education[6]	Indian education	Higher and continuing education[7]	Student financial assistance[8]	Public library programs[9]	Rehabilitation services[10]	Goals 2000[11]
1	2	3	4	5	6	7	8	9	10	11	12	13	14
Total	$24,713,604	$7,172,237	$1,062,672	$671,707	$1,362,074	$3,116,710	$204,058	$75,027	$1,215,321	$7,358,439	$130,711	$2,129,820	$214,829
Alabama	440,213	128,941	17,236	4,167	26,241	51,327	214	1,215	43,017	118,587	2,001	45,666	1,602
Alaska	136,832	25,363	5,266	64,392	5,144	10,115	1,151	6,965	2,723	5,843	552	7,662	1,656
Arizona	431,724	106,516	16,015	65,399	20,871	39,638	7,167	8,232	11,457	122,077	2,118	32,205	30
Arkansas	245,492	79,036	10,373	1,621	15,463	28,857	254	118	15,478	61,533	1,517	27,569	3,672
California	2,580,239	832,630	118,812	58,102	140,624	301,648	71,297	4,917	97,023	745,262	12,763	196,899	262
Colorado	278,419	69,808	13,115	7,281	16,207	33,217	4,076	432	14,142	88,070	2,097	25,661	4,312
Connecticut	199,189	55,722	10,410	5,015	12,482	40,331	2,011	24	8,350	42,712	1,898	16,753	3,481
Delaware	64,864	16,655	5,256	68	5,464	9,118	275	0	5,105	12,934	1,018	7,672	1,299
District of Columbia	335,327	21,109	5,159	1,056	5,415	1,330	1,476	0	222,847	64,399	570	11,489	477
Florida	1,022,864	304,566	46,195	11,809	61,216	154,221	7,528	60	30,629	283,523	6,774	100,382	15,961
Georgia	561,323	173,817	26,991	6,481	38,459	69,390	589	0	38,434	140,799	3,234	60,768	2,361
Hawaii	89,852	19,809	5,257	18,868	6,479	7,293	1,153	0	6,950	13,973	652	8,028	1,390
Idaho	110,494	27,062	5,248	4,425	6,954	11,622	1,540	255	3,983	37,252	627	11,068	458
Illinois	965,142	327,916	46,011	9,550	53,115	135,154	7,795	80	39,175	244,871	5,641	79,739	16,096
Indiana	460,156	113,142	20,109	1,675	31,514	66,853	212	9	15,897	162,579	2,979	43,452	1,734
Iowa	241,169	52,324	10,067	185	15,088	32,946	576	115	14,235	90,425	1,518	22,804	887
Kansas	311,494	59,694	9,523	8,556	12,766	27,861	903	319	12,305	153,983	1,347	21,025	3,212
Kentucky	373,196	133,099	16,237	1,117	24,168	46,576	100	0	16,947	86,490	2,124	40,531	5,808
Louisiana	533,405	194,266	22,239	5,945	27,481	47,914	2,055	455	27,037	149,527	1,751	46,716	8,019
Maine	129,461	29,510	5,257	2,656	12,082	30,542	998	124	6,003	27,369	676	12,586	1,658
Maryland	328,453	88,597	16,605	8,649	19,908	46,805	1,234	154	20,508	87,229	2,316	31,037	5,412
Massachusetts	516,746	126,138	18,469	4,301	24,277	76,366	3,282	255	22,872	196,776	2,733	40,925	42
Michigan	941,097	319,510	40,675	6,735	48,009	183,716	1,186	3,071	29,237	213,820	4,112	76,565	14,462
Minnesota	353,501	85,678	16,789	5,040	20,889	51,016	1,672	4,115	15,825	114,525	1,829	36,094	30
Mississippi	352,855	127,060	14,085	3,462	18,012	34,601	100	1,123	19,084	98,657	1,630	33,681	1,360
Missouri	415,170	115,526	19,802	6,504	27,348	58,853	920	42	16,577	120,096	2,423	47,041	37
Montana	123,053	26,427	5,253	21,760	5,924	10,070	2,587	3,843	7,704	29,828	812	8,398	450
Nebraska	154,745	31,051	6,060	6,869	8,359	19,565	709	348	5,527	60,267	1,041	14,382	567
Nevada	73,313	19,564	5,319	3,324	6,702	13,163	486	863	2,222	10,486	903	8,854	1,427
New Hampshire	75,824	16,727	5,254	875	6,414	12,689	280	0	3,219	20,992	788	8,586	0
New Jersey	519,558	145,617	26,526	11,323	30,819	109,368	2,816	104	17,080	128,009	4,373	41,075	2,448
New Mexico	242,779	61,206	8,014	38,213	9,889	23,468	6,288	6,180	9,998	58,342	1,157	17,226	2,798
New York	1,948,936	632,977	75,419	15,686	75,221	204,539	29,144	1,461	50,559	711,394	7,583	117,662	27,290
North Carolina	540,594	135,690	23,770	8,401	39,470	75,365	429	2,314	38,817	138,961	3,675	65,906	7,796
North Dakota	90,895	17,890	5,245	11,702	5,466	7,108	1,511	1,185	5,120	27,457	593	7,610	8
Ohio	1,097,689	307,509	43,793	3,814	57,482	218,237	224	29	26,912	332,456	4,938	98,579	3,715
Oklahoma	347,533	85,716	13,175	19,883	19,283	33,075	7,323	13,544	18,623	102,420	1,747	32,719	25
Oregon	244,631	79,138	11,191	2,982	15,163	34,740	2,706	1,331	10,173	55,901	1,590	25,681	4,035
Pennsylvania	1,261,464	316,544	44,636	3,033	56,340	110,176	2,214	0	30,738	575,703	5,799	100,650	15,631
Rhode Island	98,344	22,023	5,258	2,514	6,626	12,759	972	34	3,802	36,040	738	7,567	0
South Carolina	333,527	93,744	14,066	6,233	22,839	45,008	100	26	20,259	90,327	1,596	38,055	1,275
South Dakota	137,342	20,077	5,244	14,699	5,570	9,473	1,699	2,757	4,342	64,497	600	7,937	427
Tennessee	420,616	123,584	19,166	3,097	29,685	62,924	228	0	26,220	103,435	2,370	49,869	37
Texas	1,826,529	627,229	82,176	26,903	99,930	217,848	16,177	162	57,469	502,530	7,517	151,966	36,522
Utah	198,606	34,190	8,379	6,631	12,614	26,755	1,191	996	8,610	76,055	1,080	18,808	3,296
Vermont	70,495	16,338	5,255	12	5,290	6,661	267	97	4,650	22,505	455	7,685	1,281
Virginia	467,012	101,656	20,899	30,568	30,919	71,441	1,147	11	26,823	132,986	2,921	47,642	0
Washington	418,884	113,253	18,808	23,873	22,989	57,305	2,551	4,952	19,987	109,407	2,761	36,634	6,364
West Virginia	190,207	70,712	7,913	79	12,048	23,486	0	0	9,162	43,799	917	21,314	778
Wisconsin	433,263	125,832	19,876	6,747	25,729	56,409	510	2,118	19,507	128,606	2,345	43,901	1,683
Wyoming	66,456	16,283	5,150	7,126	5,146	7,358	349	591	2,803	14,240	532	6,508	370
Indian tribe setaside	43,338	0	1,256	0	0	28,767	0	0	0	0	2,508	10,271	536
Undistributed	100,493	15,291	328	80,948	400	0	314	0	2,494	0	0	719	0
Outlying areas													
American Samoa	14,478	4,998	2,111	0	376	3,127	100	0	659	2,174	89	800	45
Federated States of Micronesia	204	0	0	0	100	0	0	0	30	0	0	0	74
Guam	22,389	4,866	3,422	0	789	7,488	552	0	1,816	1,439	254	1,763	0
Marshall Islands	155	0	0	0	100	0	0	0	30	0	0	0	25
North Mariana Islands	6,766	2,372	822	0	375	1,632	0	0	153	638	87	662	25
Palau	1,204	0	13	0	100	746	0	0	31	1	76	212	25
Puerto Rico	700,733	261,631	25,253	1,179	47,317	3,706	945	0	21,356	292,973	1,854	44,461	59
Trust Territory of the Pacific	958	0	0	0	0	0	100	0	858	0	0	0	0
Virgin Islands	22,245	8,510	2,423	173	920	4,948	373	0	1,730	1,261	111	1,704	93

[1] Title I, formerly called Chapter 1, Education Consolidation and Improvement Act of 1981, includes Grants to Local Education Agencies, Migrant Education—Basic State Grants, Program for Neglected and Delinquent Children, Capital Expenses, State Improvement Grants, and Even Start—State Educational Agencies.

[2] Title VI, formerly called Chapter 2 Education Consolidation and Improvement Act of 1981, includes Dwight D. Eisenhower Professional Development Grants, Drug-Free Schools and Communities—State Grants, Education for Homeless Children and Youth, Christa McAuliffe Fellowships, and Innovative Education Program Strategies.

[3] Impact Aid—Basic Support Payments and Impact Aid—Payments for Children with Disabilities.

[4] Includes Vocational Education—Basic Grants to States, State Councils, Tech-Prep Education, Adult Education-State Administered Basic Grant Program, and State Literacy Resource Centers.

[5] Includes Special Education—Grants to States (Part B, Individuals with Disabilities Education Act), Preschool Incentive Grants to States, Special Education—Grants for Infants and Families with Disabilities, and Education of Children with Disabilities in State Operated or Supported Schools.

[6] Includes Emergency Immigrant Education Program and Bilingual Education State Grants.

[7] Includes Institutional Aid to Strengthen Higher Education Institutions serving significant numbers of low-income students, Other Special Programs for the Disadvantaged, Cooperative Education, Fund for the Improvement of Postsecondary Education, Fellowships and Scholarships, and annual interest subsidy grants for facilities construction.

[8] Includes Pell Grants, State Student Incentive Grants, Guaranteed Student Loan interest subsidies, and Postsecondary Review Program.

[9] Includes Public Library Services, Public Library Construction and Technology Enhancement, and Interlibrary Cooperation and Resource Sharing.

[10] Includes Rehabilitation Services—Vocational Rehabilitation Grants to States, Supported Employment Services for Individuals with Severe Disabilities, Rehabilitation Services—Client Assistance Program, Independent Living—State Grants, and Program of Protection and Advocacy of Individual Rights.

[11] Includes State and Local Systemic Improvement.

NOTE.—Data reflect revisions to figures in the *Budget of the United States Government, Fiscal Year 1997*. To the extent possible, data represent obligations rather than outlays. Because of the exclusion of certain programs, totals in this table are lower than those reported in other tables. Because of rounding, details may not add to totals.

SOURCE: U.S. Department of Education, National Center for Education Statistics, based on unpublished tabulations from the Office of Management and Budget; and U.S. Department of Commerce, Bureau of the Census, *Federal Expenditures by State for Fiscal Year 1995*. (This table was prepared April 1996.)

Table 365.—Appropriations for Title I and Title VI, Elementary and Secondary Education Act (ESEA)[1] of 1994, by state or other area: 1995–96 and 1996–97

[In thousands]

State or other area	Title I total, school year 1995–96[2]	Title I,[3] school year 1996–97[4]							Title VI[5]	
		Total	Total local education grants	Basic grants	Concentration grants	Neglected and delinquent children	Migrant children	Other[6]	1995 appropriations for 1995–96	1996 appropriations for 1996–97
1	2	3	4	5	6	7	8	9	10	11
Total[7]	$7,214,160	$7,215,249	$6,730,348	$5,985,839	$677,241	$39,311	$305,474	$140,116	$347,250	$273,075
Alabama	128,941	128,784	123,588	109,394	14,194	765	2,558	1,872	5,329	4,220
Alaska	25,363	25,348	14,768	13,670	1,098	161	9,935	484	1,724	1,365
Arizona	106,404	105,959	96,885	85,076	11,808	735	6,774	1,566	5,445	4,312
Arkansas	78,984	78,937	73,881	65,500	8,380	404	3,491	1,161	3,208	2,541
California	832,630	830,700	718,895	636,279	82,616	4,016	91,622	16,166	40,033	31,703
Colorado	69,756	69,894	65,437	59,862	5,575	159	3,276	1,023	4,794	3,797
Connecticut	55,664	55,932	51,796	48,447	3,348	859	2,163	1,114	3,813	3,020
Delaware	16,551	17,074	15,782	14,235	1,546	198	412	682	1,724	1,365
District of Columbia	21,109	21,703	19,946	17,571	2,375	892	193	672	1,724	1,365
Florida	304,566	306,097	276,157	247,458	28,699	1,498	24,005	4,437	15,759	12,480
Georgia	173,817	175,799	167,492	150,082	17,410	1,150	4,765	2,393	9,204	7,289
Hawaii	19,809	19,751	19,148	17,446	1,702	108	0	495	1,724	1,365
Idaho	27,062	27,055	21,593	19,900	1,693	115	4,817	530	1,725	1,366
Illinois	327,812	327,388	318,070	285,475	32,595	1,768	1,716	5,835	14,853	11,763
Indiana	113,142	113,324	107,837	100,226	7,611	795	2,835	1,856	7,303	5,784
Iowa	52,168	52,283	50,647	47,861	2,786	271	299	1,066	3,709	2,937
Kansas	59,694	59,938	51,974	48,392	3,582	614	6,466	884	3,469	2,748
Kentucky	133,099	132,963	123,216	109,224	13,992	668	7,000	2,079	4,855	3,845
Louisiana	194,266	192,972	186,947	164,131	22,816	677	1,908	3,440	6,150	4,870
Maine	29,510	29,334	25,261	23,586	1,675	158	3,359	557	1,724	1,365
Maryland	88,441	88,763	85,552	78,783	6,769	1,220	266	1,724	6,055	4,795
Massachusetts	125,630	125,917	119,706	109,564	10,141	769	2,728	2,714	6,858	5,431
Michigan	319,510	319,186	301,328	271,510	29,818	1,034	11,873	4,952	12,492	9,893
Minnesota	85,678	85,557	81,130	75,273	5,857	235	2,326	1,867	6,259	4,957
Mississippi	127,060	126,428	122,733	108,047	14,686	297	1,344	2,054	3,760	2,978
Missouri	117,658	117,408	113,470	102,300	11,169	687	825	2,426	6,872	5,442
Montana	26,271	26,226	24,891	22,243	2,648	116	703	516	1,724	1,365
Nebraska	30,947	34,365	30,504	28,535	1,969	246	2,667	947	2,233	1,768
Nevada	19,502	19,543	18,392	16,698	1,693	171	485	495	1,789	1,417
New Hampshire	16,629	16,648	15,774	14,758	1,017	257	96	521	1,724	1,365
New Jersey	145,617	145,386	138,216	127,101	11,114	2,418	949	3,803	9,260	7,333
New Mexico	61,206	61,052	58,411	51,299	7,112	349	1,244	1,049	2,451	1,941
New York	629,845	627,760	605,122	541,515	63,607	2,532	5,707	14,399	21,432	16,973
North Carolina	135,690	136,057	129,098	118,883	10,215	885	4,222	1,852	8,535	6,759
North Dakota	17,786	17,773	16,649	14,956	1,693	51	516	557	1,724	1,365
Ohio	307,509	307,328	297,225	266,368	30,857	2,156	1,814	6,134	14,183	11,232
Oklahoma	85,716	85,198	82,401	73,140	9,261	293	1,288	1,216	4,402	3,486
Oregon	79,138	79,527	66,217	60,750	5,467	985	11,274	1,050	3,930	3,112
Pennsylvania	316,544	315,880	301,176	273,857	27,319	725	5,532	8,447	14,376	11,385
Rhode Island	22,023	21,939	20,774	18,736	2,038	307	153	706	1,724	1,365
South Carolina	93,744	93,480	90,762	81,526	9,236	866	568	1,284	4,647	3,680
South Dakota	19,973	19,921	18,688	16,964	1,724	98	605	531	1,724	1,365
Tennessee	123,584	123,385	120,850	106,841	14,009	640	99	1,796	6,375	5,049
Texas	627,277	625,538	571,097	504,863	66,234	1,497	43,794	9,150	25,634	20,300
Utah	34,138	34,293	32,272	30,208	2,064	385	1,132	504	3,361	2,661
Vermont	16,338	16,327	14,806	13,789	1,017	107	910	503	1,724	1,365
Virginia	102,077	102,822	99,659	91,983	7,676	838	777	1,548	7,768	6,151
Washington	113,253	113,398	97,894	90,095	7,799	812	13,142	1,550	6,944	5,499
West Virginia	70,712	70,426	69,048	60,868	8,180	270	100	1,008	2,200	1,742
Wisconsin	125,832	125,368	121,420	113,634	7,785	1,032	646	2,270	6,827	5,406
Wyoming	16,283	16,270	15,455	14,355	1,100	155	171	489	1,724	1,365
Other activities										
Bureau of Indian Affairs	41,324	41,609	41,609	0	0	0	0	0	0	0
Migrant coordination activities	6,000	5,999	0	0	0	0	5,999	0	0	0
Even Start Migrant, Indian, and Territory setaside	5,101	8,600	3,500	3,500	0	0	0	5,100	0	0
Even Start Evaluation/Technical Assistance	1,400	1,374	0	0	0	0	0	1,374	0	0
Even Start/State Literacy Initiative	1,000	0	0	0	0	0	0	0	0	0
Competitive grants	5,000	5,000	5,000	0	0	0	0	0	0	0
Outlying areas										
American Samoa	4,998	4,978	4,978	0	0	0	0	0	417	330
Guam	4,866	4,846	4,846	0	0	0	0	0	974	771
Northern Marianas	2,372	2,362	2,362	0	0	0	0	0	238	188
Puerto Rico	261,631	261,604	249,546	219,080	30,465	868	3,924	7,266	5,839	4,624
Virgin Islands	8,510	8,474	8,474	0	0	0	0	0	802	635

[1] Elementary and Secondary Education Act was most recently revised through the Improving America's Schools Act (IASA) of 1994.
[2] Data are based on fiscal year 1996 budget authorizations. Excludes $3,664,000 for evaluation and studies.
[3] Formerly Chapter 1.
[4] Data are based on fiscal year 1997 budget authorizations. Excludes $3,359,000 for evaluation and studies.
[5] Formerly Chapter 2.
[6] Includes capital expenses, and Even Start grants.
[7] Total includes other activities and outlying areas.

NOTE.—Column 3 total includes columns 4, 7, 8, and 9. Columns 5 and 6 are subset totals of column 4. Because of rounding, details may not add to totals.

SOURCE: U.S. Department of Education, Budget Service, Elementary, Secondary, and Vocational Education Analysis Division; and unpublished data. (This table was prepared February 1997.)

Table 366.—Federal science and engineering obligations to colleges and universities, by agency and state: Fiscal year 1995 [1]

[In thousands]

State or other area	Total	Department of Agriculture	Department of Defense	Department of Education	Department of Energy	Environmental Protection Agency	Department of Health and Human Services	National Aeronautics and Space Administration	National Science Foundation	Other [2]
1	2	3	4	5	6	7	8	9	10	11
United States	$18,536,982	$943,630	$2,197,104	$187,934	$3,238,361	$164,464	$7,036,182	$1,878,496	$2,397,153	$493,658
Alabama	237,819	25,747	14,852	4,006	3,059	2,097	124,659	41,208	17,206	4,985
Alaska	33,093	3,709	1,230	341	49	128	1,885	11,457	8,985	5,309
Arizona	273,616	10,080	20,915	4,117	6,194	4,729	69,946	40,053	112,973	4,609
Arkansas	55,215	23,112	3,542	3,540	60	305	18,009	1,588	3,855	1,204
California	3,918,612	36,462	216,956	22,010	994,525	15,439	959,125	1,224,557	411,462	38,076
Colorado	359,221	14,876	22,523	4,679	9,804	3,076	130,445	23,301	129,580	20,937
Connecticut	257,255	6,794	9,693	880	11,203	287	199,312	2,237	22,588	4,261
Delaware	39,375	7,255	10,323	2,529	846	623	4,387	751	8,143	4,518
District of Columbia	190,663	1,764	32,931	4,499	3,092	746	83,648	9,511	11,370	43,102
Florida	300,639	22,162	35,986	5,239	12,346	2,862	127,713	21,819	56,266	16,246
Georgia	338,027	29,775	87,057	3,680	15,464	5,537	124,514	21,080	34,736	16,184
Hawaii	65,870	7,156	6,328	1,115	3,164	200	18,010	8,810	14,368	6,719
Idaho	20,487	9,050	245	984	0	802	3,143	603	2,898	2,762
Illinois	1,122,329	28,224	53,192	8,744	620,509	2,114	258,619	13,206	127,546	10,175
Indiana	213,025	23,434	20,573	1,998	15,830	533	91,941	5,334	50,164	3,218
Iowa	188,579	26,273	4,948	1,697	31,836	3,500	92,068	6,518	15,466	6,273
Kansas	78,346	13,978	1,707	5,346	3,659	5,247	33,067	2,837	11,254	1,251
Kentucky	86,452	23,591	1,120	2,088	5,249	1,312	39,233	1,550	11,568	741
Louisiana	140,148	18,395	11,774	1,334	19,225	5,997	54,452	5,767	12,238	10,966
Maine	19,184	8,661	493	1,156	220	284	2,735	295	3,467	1,873
Maryland	934,277	16,519	420,387	3,482	16,121	4,725	337,742	47,268	41,337	46,696
Massachusetts	1,214,730	15,164	453,517	4,133	90,617	9,098	386,153	63,414	172,166	20,468
Michigan	454,417	26,384	29,777	4,381	12,710	16,734	241,400	28,929	79,453	14,649
Minnesota	237,093	21,671	13,922	2,594	5,588	2,334	138,156	3,617	40,735	8,476
Mississippi	76,768	31,027	5,971	1,718	8,265	1,011	14,635	2,052	8,892	3,197
Missouri	275,337	26,369	8,605	3,851	4,929	695	202,697	5,875	20,934	1,382
Montana	36,546	11,933	1,143	1,406	1,598	706	4,706	1,998	11,357	1,699
Nebraska	60,153	17,218	1,845	706	669	103	21,970	1,999	12,109	3,534
Nevada	28,140	4,598	174	373	4,229	1,437	5,507	1,177	7,910	2,735
New Hampshire	70,103	4,422	2,802	488	1,260	695	36,076	10,912	9,994	3,454
New Jersey	357,376	14,720	31,521	2,537	132,831	8,844	92,433	7,658	55,205	11,627
New Mexico	681,628	8,661	53,249	3,462	542,141	663	27,181	26,488	18,641	1,142
New York	1,444,689	30,349	70,397	9,980	370,375	5,052	699,480	25,790	220,955	12,311
North Carolina	539,050	37,937	30,346	5,336	11,522	12,989	338,884	10,137	55,046	36,853
North Dakota	40,871	14,169	320	634	11,027	1,098	4,949	709	6,579	1,386
Ohio	399,785	23,185	55,135	6,678	6,951	6,755	222,176	21,922	43,556	13,427
Oklahoma	77,956	17,880	6,730	1,886	3,692	1,158	20,000	7,111	14,939	4,560
Oregon	189,259	24,069	21,350	5,973	9,686	6,725	73,661	5,855	29,809	12,131
Pennsylvania	863,724	33,151	168,002	12,408	22,859	4,808	483,956	19,038	110,855	8,647
Rhode Island	82,196	9,432	11,476	0	2,743	766	23,744	3,457	21,108	9,470
South Carolina	104,214	16,378	8,129	1,580	16,954	550	32,165	2,537	14,745	11,176
South Dakota	17,614	7,657	0	318	0	0	1,884	1,397	5,991	367
Tennessee	237,484	26,281	14,958	2,656	30,633	1,746	131,091	7,792	20,113	2,214
Texas	759,487	40,574	107,466	7,802	25,697	9,412	421,628	41,796	93,668	11,444
Utah	160,674	9,302	34,587	2,753	5,845	1,048	71,827	10,030	23,665	1,617
Vermont	39,893	7,652	776	1,587	534	410	25,187	324	3,374	49
Virginia	342,053	22,282	27,340	6,020	98,838	1,305	110,745	24,892	34,583	16,048
Washington	400,270	25,562	43,299	2,718	21,071	1,039	225,007	12,961	52,141	16,472
West Virginia	78,699	8,672	2,142	755	3,945	3,910	8,276	19,204	30,234	1,561
Wisconsin	308,406	24,059	13,306	7,593	17,452	2,164	167,911	14,704	51,721	9,496
Wyoming	16,988	5,480	734	237	1,213	477	1,144	975	5,798	930
Outlying areas	69,147	20,375	1,310	1,907	32	189	26,900	3,996	13,407	1,031
American Samoa	1,311	1,305	0	6	0	0	0	0	0	0
Guam	4,256	2,326	356	102	0	0	779	0	536	157
Puerto Rico	57,796	12,325	898	1,782	32	189	24,916	3,996	12,871	787
Trust Territory of the Pacific	2,584	2,445	0	17	0	0	122	0	0	0
Virgin Islands	3,200	1,974	56	0	0	0	1,083	0	0	87

[1] Dollars reflect actual obligations during the fiscal year regardless of when the funds were actually spent by a recipient institution. Data include obligations to federally funded research and development centers administered by colleges and universities.

[2] Includes U.S. Department of Commerce, U.S. Department of Housing and Urban Development, U.S. Department of the Interior, Agency for International Development, U.S. Department of Labor, U.S. Department of Transportation, and Nuclear Regulatory Commission.

NOTE.—Totals exclude loans to individuals, such as the Federal Family Education Loan Program sponsored by the U.S. Department of Education, and federal training and development activities, as well as funds allocated to state agencies, even though the final recipient of such funds is known to be an academic institution. Tuition support programs such as Pell Grants are included in these figures.

SOURCE: National Science Foundation, *Federal Support to Universities, Colleges, and Nonprofit Institutions, Fiscal Year 1995*. (This table was prepared May 1997.)

Table 367.—Summary of federal funds for research, development, and R & D plant: Fiscal years 1989 to 1997

[In millions]

Item	Actual							Estimate		Percent change, 1996 to 1997
	1989	1990	1991	1992	1993	1994	1995	1996	1997	
1	2	3	4	5	6	7	8	9	10	11
Total outlays for research, development, and R & D plant	$61,476.4	$64,276.5	$64,292.3	$65,719.0	$68,385.8	$68,335.9	$68,410.0	$69,180.0	$70,118.4	1.4
Research and development	59,450.4	62,246.8	61,130.4	62,934.5	65,241.3	66,158.8	66,374.6	66,876.9	67,691.5	1.2
R & D plant	2,026.1	2,029.7	3,162.0	2,784.5	3,144.5	2,177.1	2,035.4	2,303.1	2,426.9	5.4
Total obligations for research, development, and R & D plant	63,570.9	65,950.9	64,990.5	68,577.2	70,414.7	69,427.0	71,011.8	71,047.5	70,148.6	−1.3
Research and development obligations	61,405.8	63,667.3	61,295.2	65,592.6	67,314.0	67,255.8	68,754.9	69,076.7	68,063.7	−1.5
Performers										
Federal intramural [1]	13,184.5	16,002.5	15,238.1	15,690.1	16,556.2	16,139.1	17,342.7	16,897.0	16,403.7	−2.9
Industrial firms	30,484.4	29,378.3	26,420.6	29,744.8	30,326.1	30,454.4	30,468.7	31,267.6	30,712.6	−1.8
FFRDCs [2] administered by industrial firms	1,960.0	2,237.6	2,068.3	2,009.8	1,451.3	1,293.5	1,203.9	1,231.3	1,339.5	8.8
Universities and colleges	8,672.0	9,142.2	10,168.5	10,271.2	11,156.1	11,828.7	11,933.0	12,251.2	12,362.2	0.9
FFRDCs [2] administered by universities and colleges	3,497.1	3,466.4	3,603.8	3,855.5	3,666.5	3,292.9	3,574.3	3,302.2	3,230.6	−2.2
Other nonprofit institutions	1,999.1	2,249.6	2,637.4	2,803.6	2,811.9	2,929.6	2,805.5	2,866.4	2,883.6	0.6
FFRDCs [2] administered by nonprofit institutions	522.0	632.3	679.4	745.6	753.4	735.5	831.4	721.2	644.1	−10.7
State and local governments	167.4	213.9	215.1	184.1	320.3	325.4	316.5	273.8	281.6	2.8
Foreign	919.4	344.7	263.9	287.9	272.2	256.6	277.8	266.0	205.9	−22.6
Research obligations	20,765.4	21,738.9	23,968.4	24,490.6	26,890.5	27,440.4	28,573.4	28,577.8	29,173.5	2.1
Performers										
Federal intramural [1]	5,981.5	5,953.3	6,539.3	6,615.7	7,360.1	7,488.2	7,787.8	7,404.3	7,696.1	3.9
Industrial firms	2,875.1	3,199.9	3,406.5	3,451.2	4,018.9	4,063.5	4,727.9	4,672.8	4,799.7	2.7
FFRDCs [2] administered by industrial firms	519.8	542.7	624.6	592.4	795.8	737.2	818.0	877.7	1,005.5	14.6
Universities and colleges	7,793.2	8,141.5	8,867.5	9,060.7	9,844.1	10,323.5	10,371.6	10,919.9	10,823.3	−0.9
FFRDCs [2] administered by universities and colleges	1,703.4	1,808.1	2,160.9	2,351.8	2,347.6	2,181.1	2,235.6	2,085.7	2,131.1	2.2
Other nonprofit institutions	1,519.7	1,662.2	1,925.9	2,049.6	2,041.3	2,094.9	2,056.1	2,101.0	2,199.9	4.7
FFRDCs [2] administered by nonprofit institutions	109.5	148.2	170.9	139.9	173.4	178.0	210.1	183.7	191.6	4.3
State and local governments	121.2	126.4	129.3	109.3	211.8	230.8	221.4	198.9	207.0	4.1
Foreign	142.1	156.5	143.4	120.0	97.4	143.3	144.8	133.9	119.3	−10.9
Fields of science										
Life sciences	8,495.1	8,837.8	9,622.0	9,910.5	10,772.1	11,078.8	11,979.0	12,266.4	12,415.0	1.2
Psychology	421.7	448.6	482.4	298.1	550.7	550.2	653.6	677.4	687.7	1.5
Physical sciences	3,705.2	3,808.7	4,235.3	4,439.2	4,427.0	6,792.7	4,851.2	4,928.7	5,002.9	1.5
Environmental sciences	1,773.3	2,174.1	2,149.8	2,207.6	2,608.5	2,032.0	2,722.9	2,669.5	2,681.5	0.4
Mathematics and computer sciences	735.5	840.7	903.7	1,150.3	1,225.4	1,242.3	1,667.9	1,654.1	1,691.3	2.2
Engineering	4,442.0	4,335.2	4,944.5	4,977.0	5,499.4	4,023.3	4,952.7	4,686.8	4,908.2	4.7
Social sciences	551.1	630.0	727.3	689.7	674.9	655.0	682.9	670.7	728.9	8.7
Other sciences	641.6	663.7	903.4	806.3	1,132.5	1,066.1	1,063.2	1,024.1	1,058.0	3.3
Basic research obligations	10,602.0	11,285.6	12,170.8	12,489.9	13,399.1	13,552.9	13,895.5	14,482.1	14,732.4	1.7
Performers										
Federal intramural [1]	2,370.7	2,366.0	2,446.5	2,397.0	2,605.1	2,505.0	2,712.9	2,413.9	2,667.8	10.5
Industrial firms	773.2	887.5	949.9	920.3	959.2	1,109.1	1,221.2	1,225.7	1,279.1	4.4
FFRDCs [2] administered by industrial firms	166.7	175.4	209.1	187.8	237.3	237.6	239.1	339.9	368.3	8.3
Universities and colleges	5,221.4	5,548.2	6,064.5	6,331.8	6,798.5	7,024.2	6,951.3	7,753.6	7,405.5	−4.5
FFRDCs [2] administered by universities and colleges	1,098.1	1,227.3	1,306.2	1,394.1	1,437.8	1,336.0	1,438.3	1,503.5	1,519.7	1.1
Other nonprofit institutions	838.9	924.1	1,015.5	1,097.2	1,164.9	1,125.7	1,134.2	1,062.1	1,270.2	19.6
FFRDCs [2] administered by nonprofit institutions	42.2	59.2	80.8	65.5	71.3	73.9	75.2	71.6	82.9	15.8
State and local governments	43.6	50.4	49.1	42.4	71.7	75.2	78.7	70.4	92.3	31.2
Foreign	47.4	47.6	49.1	53.8	53.3	66.1	44.5	41.3	46.5	12.6
Fields of science										
Life sciences	4,915.7	5,177.5	5,433.6	5,841.7	6,288.8	6,429.8	6,746.7	6,999.2	7,140.0	2.0
Psychology	187.1	215.1	225.5	122.6	246.8	247.4	279.8	292.9	298.4	1.9
Physical sciences	2,506.5	2,661.5	2,881.5	2,951.4	2,907.1	3,649.2	2,709.3	3,004.5	3,039.1	1.2
Environmental sciences	1,016.9	1,274.8	1,263.5	1,303.6	1,533.5	997.2	1,410.7	1,449.2	1,436.4	−0.9
Mathematics and computer sciences	349.8	406.9	426.1	481.4	511.3	503.6	626.1	671.2	673.1	0.3
Engineering	1,183.7	1,101.5	1,233.7	1,249.8	1,207.4	1,061.7	1,432.2	1,356.1	1,419.1	4.6
Social sciences	154.6	146.0	161.4	139.9	194.1	191.7	210.8	215.9	228.0	5.6
Other sciences	291.7	302.3	545.6	399.4	510.1	472.4	479.9	493.2	498.1	1.0
Applied research obligations	10,163.3	10,453.3	11,797.6	12,000.7	13,491.4	13,887.5	14,677.9	14,095.7	14,441.3	2.5
Performers										
Federal intramural [1]	3,610.8	3,587.3	4,092.8	4,218.7	4,755.0	4,983.2	5,074.9	4,990.4	5,028.3	0.8
Industrial firms	2,101.8	2,312.4	2,456.6	2,530.9	3,059.7	2,954.4	3,506.7	3,447.1	3,520.6	2.1
FFRDCs [2] administered by industrial firms	353.2	367.3	415.5	404.6	558.6	499.6	578.9	537.7	637.2	18.5
Universities and colleges	2,571.8	2,593.4	2,803.0	2,728.9	3,045.5	3,299.3	3,420.3	3,166.3	3,417.8	7.9
FFRDCs [2] administered by universities and colleges	605.4	580.8	854.7	957.6	909.8	845.1	797.3	582.2	611.4	5.0
Other nonprofit institutions	680.8	738.1	910.4	952.5	876.4	969.2	921.9	1,038.9	929.7	−10.5
FFRDCs [2] administered by nonprofit institutions	67.3	89.0	90.1	74.5	102.2	104.0	134.9	112.1	108.7	−3.0
State and local governments	77.6	76.1	80.2	66.9	140.1	155.5	142.7	128.5	114.7	−10.8
Foreign	94.6	109.0	94.3	66.2	44.1	77.2	100.3	92.6	72.8	−21.3
Fields of science										
Life sciences	3,579.4	3,660.3	4,188.4	4,068.8	4,483.3	4,649.0	5,232.3	5,267.2	5,275.0	0.1
Psychology	234.5	233.5	258.9	175.6	303.9	302.9	373.9	384.5	389.2	1.2
Physical sciences	1,198.8	1,147.2	1,353.9	1,467.7	1,519.8	3,143.5	2,141.9	1,924.2	1,963.8	2.1
Environmental sciences	756.3	899.3	886.3	904.0	1,075.0	1,034.8	1,312.3	1,220.3	1,245.1	2.0
Mathematics and computer sciences	389.7	433.9	477.6	678.9	714.1	738.7	1,041.7	983.0	1,018.2	3.6
Engineering	3,258.3	3,233.7	3,710.8	3,727.1	4,292.0	2,961.6	3,520.5	3,330.8	3,489.1	4.8
Social sciences	396.4	484.0	566.0	549.8	480.8	463.3	472.0	454.8	500.9	10.1
Other sciences	350.0	361.5	357.8	406.8	622.4	593.8	583.3	531.0	559.9	5.5

Table 367.—Summary of federal funds for research, development, and R & D plant: Fiscal years 1989 to 1997—Continued

[In millions]

Item	Actual							Estimate		Percent change, 1996 to 1997
	1989	1990	1991	1992	1993	1994	1995	1996	1997	
1	2	3	4	5	6	7	8	9	10	11
Development obligations	40,640.4	41,928.4	37,326.8	41,102.0	40,423.5	39,815.4	40,181.4	40,499.2	38,890.2	−3.7
Performers										
Federal intramural [1]	7,203.0	10,049.2	8,698.8	9,074.4	9,196.2	8,650.9	9,554.9	9,492.8	8,707.6	−8.3
Industrial firms	27,609.3	26,178.4	23,014.1	26,293.6	26,307.2	26,390.9	25,740.7	26,594.8	25,912.9	−2.6
FFRDCs [2] administered by industrial firms	1,440.2	1,694.9	1,443.7	1,417.4	655.5	556.3	385.9	353.6	334.0	−5.5
Universities and colleges	878.8	1,000.5	1,301.0	1,210.6	1,312.0	1,505.2	1,561.4	1,331.3	1,538.9	15.6
FFRDCs [2] administered by universities and colleges	1,793.6	1,658.3	1,442.9	1,503.7	1,318.9	1,111.8	1,338.7	1,216.5	1,099.5	−9.6
Other nonprofit institutions	479.5	587.4	711.5	753.9	770.6	834.8	750.4	765.6	683.7	−10.7
FFRDCs [2] administered by nonprofit institutions	412.4	484.0	508.5	605.7	580.0	557.6	621.3	537.5	452.5	−15.8
State and local governments	46.3	87.5	85.8	74.8	108.5	94.7	95.1	74.9	74.6	−0.4
Foreign	777.3	188.1	120.5	167.9	174.8	113.3	133.0	132.2	86.5	−34.6
R & D plant obligations	2,165.1	2,283.6	3,695.4	2,984.6	3,100.7	2,171.2	2,256.9	1,970.8	2,084.9	5.8
Performers										
Federal intramural [1]	329.5	359.9	461.1	506.2	432.0	392.6	482.6	571.1	723.7	26.7
Industrial firms	900.4	884.0	1,889.2	1,014.4	1,048.2	746.8	696.6	415.0	407.5	−1.8
FFRDCs [2] administered by industrial firms	212.3	231.0	279.6	202.2	124.4	119.4	95.1	77.1	83.3	8.0
Universities and colleges	204.9	155.8	253.3	241.5	361.4	209.0	323.8	279.6	157.4	−43.7
FFRDCs [2] administered by universities and colleges	489.9	495.8	624.6	579.5	619.5	608.8	543.9	536.2	642.1	19.7
Other nonprofit institutions	14.2	121.3	154.6	393.9	415.6	20.9	25.6	21.7	12.2	−43.7
FFRDCs [2] administered by nonprofit institutions	8.4	31.4	19.7	46.3	65.5	72.9	62.6	69.7	58.2	−16.5
State and local governments	1.4	0.5	0.6	0.5	0.5	0.8	0.5	0.5	0.5	0.0
Foreign	4.2	3.9	12.8	0.0	33.4	0.2	26.1	0.0	0.0	0.0

[1] Includes costs associated with the administration of intramural and extramural programs by federal personnel as well as actual intramural performance.
[2] Federally funded research and development centers.

NOTE.—Some data have been revised from previously published figures. Because of rounding, details may not add to totals.

SOURCE: National Science Foundation, *Federal Funds for Research and Development,* various years. (This table was prepared May 1997.)

Table 368.—Federal obligations to colleges and universities for research and development, by field: United States and outlying areas, 1980 to 1994

Field of science or engineering	1980	1981	1986	1988	1989	1990[1]	1991[1]	1992[1]	1993[1]	1994[1]
1	2	3	4	5	6	7	8	9	10	11
Total, all fields	$4,160,543	$4,410,931	$6,456,743	$7,719,237	$8,523,190	$9,008,083	$10,031,058	$10,844,500	$10,923,070	$11,768,416
Engineering, total	612,456	792,223	998,312	1,129,303	1,157,047	474,709	543,530	587,404	683,676	702,397
Aeronautical	28,044	31,056	42,257	47,946	66,096	45,965	44,207	48,539	50,114	82,826
Astronautical	4,634	4,875	24,147	32,516	42,276	11,803	20,977	21,407	13,402	16,071
Chemical	22,210	27,667	50,379	67,647	45,829	56,845	67,968	63,900	67,234	58,293
Civil	48,130	58,300	35,402	30,947	43,026	37,306	34,064	30,756	44,252	55,969
Electrical	86,916	115,011	212,175	251,336	240,638	53,162	60,299	68,416	69,045	74,686
Mechanical	42,593	37,954	56,416	60,551	71,137	52,652	54,674	60,748	67,471	52,118
Metallurgy and materials	63,057	52,815	101,457	121,228	146,253	81,678	91,686	76,926	180,553	164,272
Engineering, other	316,872	464,545	476,079	517,132	501,792	135,298	169,655	216,712	191,605	198,162
All sciences, total	3,548,087	3,618,708	5,458,431	6,589,934	7,366,143	8,533,374	9,487,528	10,257,166	10,239,360	11,065,982
Physical sciences	507,884	500,657	770,254	859,764	979,037	890,444	1,022,807	1,134,579	1,022,880	1,135,704
Astronomy	52,736	54,835	78,435	89,791	103,271	98,804	115,212	149,417	139,579	214,549
Chemistry	170,048	165,189	255,593	281,573	299,417	272,929	295,576	325,224	321,105	324,213
Physics	249,661	250,342	379,289	426,005	505,723	453,538	518,840	544,200	511,036	539,758
Physical sciences, other	35,439	30,291	56,937	62,395	70,626	65,173	93,179	115,738	51,160	57,184
Mathematical sciences	53,987	53,668	96,405	119,217	134,998	109,587	125,893	140,544	131,875	76,793
Computer sciences	37,585	37,493	82,691	84,424	123,197	99,214	113,545	124,962	137,893	162,286
Environmental sciences	379,453	330,079	468,882	474,695	554,917	522,767	572,584	622,748	632,792	744,996
Atmospheric sciences	86,486	95,112	124,657	132,379	131,959	139,914	149,426	171,557	162,385	236,503
Geological sciences	109,523	101,207	118,401	131,913	152,449	147,517	173,492	172,185	181,384	186,542
Oceanography	92,079	91,863	121,855	129,473	163,035	117,636	94,448	107,897	103,472	116,229
Environmental sciences, other	91,365	41,897	103,969	80,930	107,474	117,700	155,218	171,109	185,551	205,722
Life sciences	2,137,751	2,290,587	3,463,114	4,349,268	4,730,663	4,773,434	5,319,947	5,629,395	5,566,756	6,310,555
Agricultural sciences	111,739	134,660	143,249	155,772	180,908	181,453	193,763	207,817	184,308	180,718
Biological sciences	1,085,602	1,192,756	1,849,516	2,345,433	2,558,987	2,578,470	2,820,183	2,950,701	2,931,726	3,191,832
Environmental biology	13,137	14,636	86,088	97,126	108,584	104,053	124,218	130,633	109,351	171,381
Medical sciences	885,898	904,963	1,325,157	1,689,606	1,829,888	1,853,979	2,102,127	2,252,375	2,253,419	2,689,314
Life sciences, other	41,375	43,572	59,104	61,331	52,296	55,479	79,656	87,869	87,952	77,310
Psychological sciences	86,459	87,734	138,338	186,924	209,344	225,987	258,886	254,311	277,667	318,832
Biological aspects	28,269	26,273	39,049	53,287	66,959	71,705	80,438	75,307	8,542	3,792
Social aspects	31,129	28,846	38,589	52,113	59,502	66,960	82,257	75,285	4,754	7,357
Psychological sciences, other	27,061	32,615	60,700	81,524	82,883	87,322	96,191	103,719	264,371	307,683
Social sciences	203,948	197,695	172,148	184,539	218,404	250,366	303,798	301,056	267,080	279,575
Anthropology	7,757	5,543	6,455	5,972	7,054	7,061	8,768	9,015	8,474	8,115
Economics	51,414	56,704	43,764	48,039	51,806	58,441	60,142	70,582	68,102	60,478
History	1,688	1,069	1,508	1,527	1,665	1,890	2,116	2,166	2,014	0
Linguistics	2,997	2,745	2,481	3,248	3,402	3,055	3,383	3,684	3,554	0
Political science	5,890	5,122	5,003	5,926	6,988	7,415	8,287	8,894	7,687	6,625
Sociology	34,903	38,136	34,580	55,204	75,404	96,240	113,829	104,430	35,666	30,602
Social sciences, other	99,299	88,376	78,357	64,623	72,085	76,264	107,273	102,285	141,583	173,755
Other sciences	141,020	120,795	266,599	331,103	415,583	1,661,575	1,770,068	2,049,571	2,202,417	2,037,241
Residual amounts	0	0	0	0	0	0	0	−70	34	37

[1] All U.S. Department of Defense data are reported as other sciences.

NOTE.—Some data have been revised from previously published figures.

SOURCE: National Science Foundation, Science Resources Studies Division, unpublished data. (This table was prepared May 1996.)

Table 369.—U.S. Department of Agriculture obligations for child nutrition programs, by state or other area: Fiscal years 1995 and 1996

[In thousands]

State or other area	Total, fiscal year 1995	Fiscal year 1996								
		Total	Special milk	School lunch[1]	School breakfast	State administrative expenses	Commodities and cash in lieu of commodities[2]	Child and adult care	Summer food service	Nutrition education and training
1	2	3	4	5	6	7	8	9	10	11
Total	$8,362,921	$8,527,590	$18,918	$4,761,006	$1,122,062	$99,900	$704,826	$1,552,637	$258,245	$9,995
Alabama	161,661	162,114	38	94,864	20,661	1,953	14,187	26,420	3,837	153
Alaska	21,225	22,384	6	13,267	1,896	405	1,306	5,428	14	63
Arizona	141,671	152,469	182	82,327	21,683	1,755	10,263	31,541	4,563	155
Arkansas	97,920	100,111	29	54,953	16,877	1,475	9,374	15,177	2,139	87
California	996,563	1,069,307	842	622,015	159,967	11,678	73,076	178,151	22,471	1,106
Colorado	86,904	89,243	130	45,177	7,416	1,296	7,924	25,522	1,647	130
Connecticut	62,948	65,571	497	36,008	7,891	857	6,537	11,314	2,359	108
Delaware	22,619	23,224	45	9,847	2,557	424	1,476	8,012	802	63
District of Columbia	21,964	23,245	13	14,144	3,174	349	1,270	2,523	1,710	63
Florida	414,622	433,007	140	263,025	65,564	4,412	30,200	46,118	23,104	443
Georgia	273,973	289,944	41	167,320	52,136	2,836	26,364	32,408	8,582	258
Hawaii	33,551	35,625	8	21,879	4,778	483	3,715	4,386	313	63
Idaho	32,162	32,386	216	20,213	3,165	531	2,871	4,637	690	63
Illinois	299,757	313,903	2,673	183,187	27,305	3,529	25,704	57,048	14,036	422
Indiana	124,866	126,965	319	72,251	14,890	1,561	14,494	21,720	1,532	199
Iowa	74,481	77,341	172	41,414	6,723	1,007	10,977	16,104	842	102
Kansas	91,398	91,049	140	40,296	9,030	931	7,650	32,046	863	92
Kentucky	136,412	143,730	113	82,423	25,780	1,642	15,352	15,079	3,209	133
Louisiana	234,257	239,544	58	127,668	38,045	3,061	18,814	44,965	6,760	173
Maine	32,865	34,389	129	16,211	3,018	494	2,881	10,788	805	63
Maryland	116,514	120,036	385	62,026	12,532	1,542	10,338	30,119	2,925	169
Massachusetts	133,231	145,662	512	71,609	16,301	1,823	13,696	37,404	4,121	196
Michigan	211,255	223,117	947	117,182	26,108	2,593	20,334	51,251	4,367	334
Minnesota	150,547	153,856	1,072	59,204	10,252	2,423	12,650	65,298	2,788	169
Mississippi	150,102	152,096	10	88,614	27,609	1,831	11,596	18,826	3,502	109
Missouri	148,563	148,921	438	79,777	20,501	1,871	12,951	29,389	3,810	183
Montana	25,591	27,096	46	13,054	2,327	742	2,658	7,783	424	63
Nebraska	58,413	60,179	224	24,393	3,531	993	6,545	23,780	649	63
Nevada	27,796	31,112	134	18,211	4,737	471	2,932	3,368	1,195	63
New Hampshire	18,296	19,190	235	10,288	1,914	476	2,941	2,947	326	63
New Jersey	152,008	159,973	960	96,525	13,216	1,745	15,870	24,751	6,649	258
New Mexico	91,372	94,822	6	42,136	11,354	1,780	4,461	29,554	5,469	63
New York	583,279	599,469	1,162	341,610	77,361	6,331	44,110	88,827	39,457	610
North Carolina	225,646	231,740	132	126,905	37,136	2,613	22,031	39,170	3,519	234
North Dakota	25,104	25,613	67	9,724	1,399	531	2,628	10,843	359	63
Ohio	244,491	246,381	932	138,759	28,519	2,909	25,889	44,535	4,452	386
Oklahoma	118,610	122,854	79	64,997	18,270	1,687	10,830	24,714	2,156	121
Oregon	83,270	88,585	214	40,246	10,356	1,194	7,256	27,876	1,338	106
Pennsylvania	245,960	251,751	834	149,758	27,261	2,724	23,282	33,162	14,334	396
Rhode Island	19,677	21,961	128	13,186	1,693	404	2,129	3,079	1,280	63
South Carolina	144,621	148,417	33	82,795	25,896	1,569	12,623	17,780	7,589	131
South Dakota	28,021	29,023	47	14,603	2,617	470	3,143	7,117	964	63
Tennessee	160,606	164,136	39	92,083	25,089	1,916	15,921	24,367	4,541	179
Texas	742,563	776,792	106	452,187	125,733	8,795	62,203	108,988	18,046	735
Utah	73,008	73,697	74	32,496	4,095	1,158	6,385	27,430	1,969	89
Vermont	14,196	15,150	101	6,841	1,578	344	1,422	4,538	263	63
Virginia	151,544	152,677	237	89,199	21,586	1,152	14,121	23,014	3,155	213
Washington	135,961	140,536	262	73,030	16,914	1,830	11,374	34,205	2,733	188
West Virginia	60,502	59,791	47	32,626	11,357	774	4,694	8,664	1,567	63
Wisconsin	108,580	115,045	1,575	62,239	6,316	1,418	17,100	24,001	2,211	185
Wyoming	14,831	15,382	12	7,310	1,227	339	1,606	4,742	83	63
Administrative costs	6,755	6,396	0	0	0	0	6,396	0	0	0
Department of Defense dependents schools	5,942	5,566	0	4,759	0	0	807	0	0	0
Outlying areas										
American Samoa	63	63	0	0	0	0	0	0	0	63
Guam	4,483	4,769	0	2,808	856	223	531	291	0	60
Northern Marianas	72	63	0	0	0	0	0	0	0	63
Puerto Rico	159,370	165,018	0	108,313	25,182	1,671	10,006	14,980	4,735	132
Trust Territory of the Pacific	152	57	0	0	0	0	54	0	0	3
Virgin Islands	6,617	5,583	3	3,629	209	241	563	525	350	63
Undistributed[3]	353,492	199,464	2,074	119,394	8,474	638	−3,685	65,934	6,641	−5

[1] Special Meal Assistance program is combined with "School Lunch" program.
[2] Commodities are based on preliminary food orders for fiscal year 1996.
[3] Undistributed amount reflects the difference between preliminary state earnings reports and federal obligations as of September 30, 1996.

NOTE.—Data are based on obligations as reported September 30, 1996. Negative amounts occur when program receipts exceed the obligations. Because of rounding, details may not add to totals.

SOURCE: U.S. Department of Agriculture, Food and Nutrition Service, Budget Division, unpublished data. (This table was prepared February 1997.)

Table 370.—U.S. Department of Health and Human Services allocations for Head Start and enrollment in Head Start, by state or other area: Fiscal years 1993 to 1996

State or other area	1993		1994		1995		1996	
	Head Start allocations (in thousands)	Head Start enrollment [1]	Head Start allocations (in thousands)	Head Start enrollment [2]	Head Start allocations (in thousands)	Head Start enrollment [3]	Head Start allocations (in thousands)	Head Start enrollment [4]
1	2	3	4	5	6	7	8	9
Total	$2,683,158	713,943	$3,215,946	740,493	$3,402,946	750,696	$3,438,268	752,077
Alabama	46,937	14,106	54,282	14,525	57,542	14,552	58,265	14,429
Alaska	5,316	1,143	6,295	1,209	6,534	1,209	6,748	1,299
Arizona	35,503	9,189	44,416	9,846	47,208	10,029	47,617	9,818
Arkansas	26,337	8,792	30,719	9,065	32,681	9,244	33,153	9,193
California	305,180	67,684	371,227	70,995	392,331	72,650	392,965	72,606
Colorado	25,505	7,672	31,787	8,118	35,757	8,576	36,364	8,647
Connecticut	22,066	5,561	26,061	5,660	27,022	5,625	27,382	5,567
Delaware	5,265	1,455	5,815	1,455	6,027	1,574	6,239	1,455
District of Columbia	11,631	2,841	12,854	2,841	14,329	2,913	14,530	3,339
Florida	92,741	25,333	118,976	27,398	125,508	27,623	127,325	27,535
Georgia	66,499	18,594	81,974	19,445	85,792	19,523	86,596	19,563
Hawaii	8,882	2,183	9,939	2,260	10,312	2,226	10,981	2,517
Idaho	8,329	1,850	9,574	1,912	10,009	1,841	10,043	1,869
Illinois	117,770	30,268	139,137	30,537	148,120	31,579	148,915	31,817
Indiana	37,979	11,107	46,558	11,730	48,871	11,739	49,804	11,847
Iowa	20,111	5,758	23,430	5,946	25,539	6,199	25,968	6,178
Kansas	17,885	5,389	22,095	5,793	24,772	6,158	25,129	6,074
Kentucky	45,318	13,791	54,364	14,071	58,383	14,267	58,935	14,447
Louisiana	62,996	18,677	75,876	19,344	78,691	19,344	79,596	19,344
Maine	11,011	3,361	12,610	3,439	13,118	3,439	13,734	10,816
Maryland	32,073	8,338	38,810	8,509	42,023	8,874	42,461	8,915
Massachusetts	49,615	10,929	57,264	10,794	61,129	10,990	61,742	3,466
Michigan	107,451	29,960	126,686	30,701	132,990	30,936	135,349	31,198
Minnesota	30,823	8,167	36,930	8,576	38,281	8,576	38,812	8,641
Mississippi	83,560	24,036	92,012	24,110	95,493	24,150	97,001	24,081
Missouri	45,641	13,592	55,979	14,063	58,752	14,064	59,241	14,035
Montana	8,211	2,226	9,563	2,304	9,772	2,304	10,048	2,304
Nebraska	12,322	3,465	14,342	3,644	15,456	3,764	15,890	3,800
Nevada	6,341	1,593	8,017	1,793	8,315	1,793	8,213	1,823
New Hampshire	4,895	1,131	5,699	1,156	6,379	1,232	6,558	1,235
New Jersey	63,902	12,773	71,189	12,898	74,610	13,016	75,151	13,085
New Mexico	18,954	6,055	24,241	6,397	27,269	6,821	27,731	6,587
New York	181,968	37,829	215,678	39,062	226,840	39,491	228,243	40,365
North Carolina	54,263	15,296	66,643	15,695	71,603	16,161	72,594	16,002
North Dakota	5,666	1,653	6,723	1,738	6,966	1,738	7,206	1,874
Ohio	110,420	32,567	133,913	33,919	139,497	34,215	141,607	33,919
Oklahoma	32,274	10,625	39,073	11,165	40,705	11,165	41,397	11,165
Oregon	21,782	4,431	27,080	4,638	29,086	4,698	29,460	4,695
Pennsylvania	99,688	24,866	119,354	25,672	126,251	26,149	127,086	26,198
Rhode Island	8,328	2,380	10,060	2,476	10,453	2,434	10,549	2,567
South Carolina	33,063	9,709	40,772	10,142	44,021	10,415	44,540	10,164
South Dakota	6,629	1,894	7,985	2,025	8,258	2,025	8,480	2,258
Tennessee	47,993	13,859	58,610	14,380	61,630	14,213	62,163	14,291
Texas	172,536	49,110	213,394	51,521	223,309	51,925	224,923	52,107
Utah	13,208	3,822	15,832	4,028	18,145	4,334	18,219	4,201
Vermont	5,339	1,260	5,957	1,271	7,636	1,486	7,811	1,531
Virginia	39,440	10,650	46,411	10,993	48,896	11,147	49,706	11,028
Washington	37,558	7,799	45,968	8,260	53,385	8,803	52,311	8,878
West Virginia	22,303	6,317	26,014	6,402	27,626	6,522	28,125	6,515
Wisconsin	40,956	11,247	49,461	11,953	52,633	12,171	54,013	12,283
Wyoming	4,149	1,245	4,925	1,323	5,099	1,313	5,195	1,279
Migrant programs	108,011	33,886	130,409	35,063	138,802	35,243	139,438	35,117
American Indian/Alaskan Native programs	74,800	17,973	90,793	18,738	95,130	18,821	96,836	19,071
Special projects	—	—	76	—	—	—	—	—
Outlying areas								
Puerto Rico	113,047	31,306	127,066	32,145	132,423	32,118	134,072	31,744
Pacific Territories	7,613	5,779	9,019	5,849	9,309	5,849	9,541	5,849
Virgin Islands	5,074	1,421	6,009	1,501	6,228	1,430	6,267	1,446

[1] The distribution of enrollment by age was: 6 percent were 5 years old and over; 64 percent were 4-year-olds; 27 percent were 3-year-olds; and 3 percent were under 3 years of age. Handicapped children accounted for 13.2 percent in Head Start programs. The racial/ethnic composition was: American Indian/Alaskan Native, 4 percent; Hispanic, 24 percent; black, 36 percent; white, 33 percent; and Asian, 3 percent.

[2] The distribution of enrollment by age was: 6 percent were 5 years old and over; 64 percent were 4-year-olds; 27 percent were 3-year-olds; and 3 percent were under 3 years of age. Handicapped children accounted for 13.0 percent in Head Start programs. The racial/ethnic composition was: American Indian/Alaskan Native, 4 percent; Hispanic, 24 percent; black, 36 percent; white, 33 percent; and Asian, 3 percent.

[3] The distribution of enrollment by age was: 7 percent were 5 years old and over; 61 percent were 4-year-olds; 28 percent were 3-year-olds; and 4 percent were under 3 years of age. Handicapped children accounted for 13.1 percent in Head Start programs. The racial/ethnic composition was: American Indian/Alaskan Native, 4 percent; Hispanic, 25 percent; black, 36 percent; white, 33 percent; and Asian, 3 percent.

[4] The distribution of enrollment by age was: 6 percent were 5 years old and over; 62 percent were 4-year-olds; 29 percent were 3-year-olds; and 4 percent were under 3 years of age. Handicapped children accounted for 12.8 percent in Head Start programs. The racial/ethnic composition was: American Indian/Alaskan Native, 3.5 percent; Hispanic, 25.2 percent; black, 36 percent; white, 32.3 percent; and Asian, 3 percent.

—Not applicable.

NOTE.—Because of rounding, details may not add to totals.

SOURCE: U.S. Department of Health and Human Services, Office of Human Development Services. (This table was prepared March 1997.)

Table 371.—Public school students receiving federally funded free or reduced price lunches, by selected school characteristics: School year 1993–94

School characteristics	Percent of students participating in program			
	Total	Elementary	Secondary	Combined[1]
1	2	3	4	5
Total	**33.2**	**38.8**	**22.0**	**39.1**
Community type				
Central city	44.9	52.1	29.0	52.2
Urban fringe/large town	24.0	28.6	15.4	24.0
Rural/small town	32.2	36.6	22.9	40.1
School size (students)				
Less than 150	38.6	38.4	35.8	50.3
150–299	38.1	39.5	28.4	51.8
300–499	37.0	38.8	26.2	37.3
500–749	33.5	36.0	22.3	34.7
750 or more	29.7	42.5	20.6	34.3
Minority students				
Less than 5%	22.0	22.4	17.0	28.6
5 to 19%	18.9	22.2	11.7	30.8
20 to 49%	32.0	38.1	20.1	38.5
50% or more	57.3	65.5	38.9	60.6

[1] Includes schools beginning with grade 6 or below and ending with grade 9 or above.

NOTE.—Some data have been revised from previously published figures.

SOURCE: U.S. Department of Education, National Center for Education Statistics, "Schools and Staffing Survey, 1993–94." (This table was prepared September 1996.)

Table 372.—Public and private school students receiving federally funded Chapter 1[1] services, by selected school characteristics: School year 1993–94

School characteristics	Percent of students participating in program								
	All schools	Public				Private			
		Total	Elementary	Secondary	Combined[2]	Total	Elementary	Secondary	Combined[2]
1	2	3	4	5	6	7	8	9	10
Total	**13.1**	**14.3**	**18.5**	**6.1**	**13.6**	**3.3**	**4.6**	**1.9**	**1.4**
Community type									
Central city	17.0	19.4	24.2	9.2	14.3	4.4	6.7	2.5	0.8
Urban fringe/large town	9.3	10.2	13.2	4.7	8.3	2.2	2.7	0.9	1.9
Rural/small town	13.2	13.9	18.4	5.2	15.0	2.7	3.5	2.5	1.8
School size (students)									
Less than 150	9.8	16.7	20.0	11.1	15.7	3.8	3.3	8.1	3.8
150–299	13.1	16.7	19.2	7.6	11.6	5.1	6.2	4.1	1.4
300–499	14.7	16.3	18.0	7.0	13.0	2.6	3.7	0.9	0.8
500–749	14.7	15.5	17.6	6.0	18.3	2.0	3.8	1.1	0.3
750 or more	11.3	11.7	20.1	5.8	11.4	1.3	4.5	0.8	0.4
Minority students									
Less than 5%	7.8	8.8	11.7	3.7	9.7	1.7	2.4	0.6	0.8
5 to 19%	6.0	6.6	8.6	2.3	14.3	2.1	3.0	1.6	0.9
20 to 49%	10.2	10.8	14.6	3.3	13.6	2.7	2.7	3.7	1.7
50% or more	27.8	29.0	35.8	14.9	18.0	10.0	12.4	2.5	5.2

[1] Chapter 1 was reauthorized under the Improving America's Schools Act (IASA) of 1994 and is now called Title I.
[2] Includes schools beginning with grade 6 or below and ending with grade 9 or above.

NOTE.—Some data have been revised from previously published figures.

SOURCE: U.S. Department of Education, National Center for Education Statistics, "Schools and Staffing Survey, 1993–94." (This table was prepared September 1996.)

CHAPTER 5
Outcomes of Education

This chapter contains tables comparing educational attainment and work force characteristics. The data show labor force participation and income levels of high school dropouts and high school and college graduates. Population characteristics are provided for many of the measures to help evaluate disparities among various demographic groups. The first set of tables contains data from the Bureau of the Census on educational attainment and income of the labor force, and data from the Bureau of Labor Statistics on employment and unemployment. These tables provide information on the educational attainment of the labor force, by occupation, sex, and race/ethnicity; income, by level of education attained; and unemployment rates, by levels of education attained, sex, and race/ethnicity.

The second group of tables was compiled from Bureau of Labor Statistics reports on high school dropouts and graduates. These data show the labor force participation and college enrollment of high school students within the year after they leave school. The tabulations also provide comparative labor force participation and unemployment rates for graduates and dropouts. Additional information on college enrollment rates by race/ethnicity and sex have been included to help form a more complete picture of high school outcomes.

The third set of tables has been prepared from the Recent College Graduates and Baccalaureate and Beyond surveys from the National Center for Education Statistics, and from a Bureau of the Census survey on earnings and education. These tables provide data on employment outcomes for high school and college graduates. A table provides a salary comparison by field of college degree for the entire population. Trends in salaries received by college graduates also are featured in this section.

Statistics on educational attainment of the entire population are in Chapter 1. More detailed data on the number of high school and college graduates are contained in Chapters 2 and 3. Chapter 3 contains trend data on the proportion of high school graduates going to college. Additional data on the income of persons by educational attainment may be obtained from the Bureau of the Census in the *Current Population Reports,* Series P–60. The Bureau of Labor Statistics has a series of publications dealing with the educational characteristics of the labor force. Further information on survey methodologies is in the "Guide to Sources" in the appendix and in the publications cited in the source notes.

Opinions

One life goal consistently rated "very important" by young men and women was "being successful in work." A survey of 1992 high school seniors found that 89 percent of the men and 90 percent of the women rated "being successful in work" as a "very important goal." Two of the other most highly rated goals in the 1992 survey were "finding steady work" ("very important" for 87 percent of men and 89 percent of women) and "having strong friendships" ("very important" for 80 percent of both men and women). Two years later in 1994, these values continued to be highly rated by the former high school seniors. Another value that was highly rated two years after high school was "Providing better opportunities for my children" which was cited by 91 percent of the young adults as "very important" (table 374).

Labor Force

Adults with higher levels of education were more likely to participate in the labor force than those with less education. About 81 percent of adults, 25 years and over, with a bachelor's degree participated in the labor force in 1996 compared with 66 percent of persons who were high school graduates and 41 percent of those who were not high school graduates. The labor force participation rates for blacks, age 25 and older, with bachelor's degrees and high school diplomas were higher than the average for all people with similar levels of education (table 375).

Persons with lower levels of educational attainment were more likely to be unemployed than those who had higher levels of educational attainment. The 1996 unemployment rate for adults (25 years old and over) who had not completed high school was 8.7 percent compared with 4.7 percent for those with 4 years of high school and 2.2 percent for those with a bachelor's degree or higher. Among persons with at least a high school diploma, young people had higher unemployment rates than persons 25 and over (table 377).

One year after graduating from college in 1992–93, 87 percent of those receiving bachelor's degrees were employed (73 percent full time and 14 percent part time), 4.5 percent were unemployed, and 8.5 percent were not in the labor force (table 384).

Income

Between 1990 and 1995, median annual income of male full-time workers, when adjusted for inflation, declined 4 percent. However, there was no change for female full-time workers overall. Income of men who were year-round full-time workers with 4 or more years of college increased by 1 percent, compared with a 9 percent drop for men with 1 to 3 years of high school. Income for men who had completed high school dropped by 5 percent (table 378).

Women's incomes are much lower than men's incomes, even after adjusting for level of education. The average 1995 incomes for full-time year-round workers with a bachelor's degree were $45,266 for men and $32,051 for women.

Dropouts and Graduates

The difficulties in entering the job market for dropouts, and youth in general, are highlighted by comparing their labor force and unemployment status. Only 58 percent of 1995–96 dropouts were in the labor force (employed or looking for work), and 28 percent of the labor force were unemployed. Of the 1996 high school graduates who were not in college, 78 percent were in the labor force, and 24 percent of those in the labor force were unemployed (tables 380 and 381).

About two-thirds of the college graduates of the class of 1992–93 had jobs in professional, managerial, and technical areas in 1994. The remainder were employed in nonprofessional, nonmanagerial, and nontechnical areas. Overall, about 56 percent of the employees reported that their bachelor's degree was necessary to obtain their current job (table 384).

A 1992 assessment of literacy skills for adults found that about 22 percent of the adult population lacked the ability to perform simple arithmetic operations, and 21 percent could not locate a simple piece of information in a short text excerpt. Only about one-fifth of the population could solve mathematical problems requiring 2 or more steps or integrate information from complex passages (table 388).

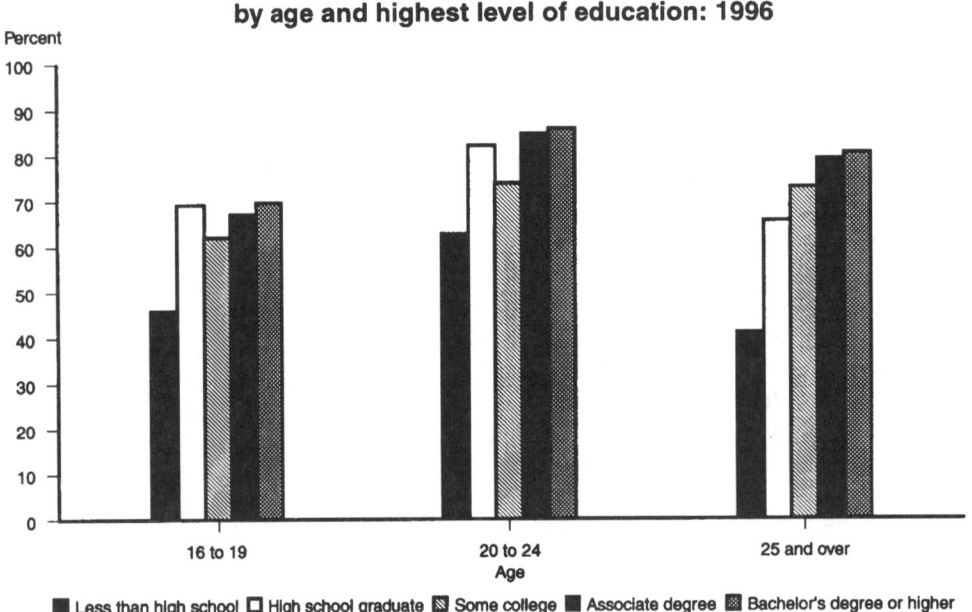

Figure 23.-Labor force participation of persons 16 years old and over, by age and highest level of education: 1996

SOURCE: U.S. Department of Labor, Bureau of Labor Statistics, Office of Employment and Unemployment Statistics, Current Population Survey, 1996.

OUTCOMES OF EDUCATION 417

Figure 24.-Unemployment rates of persons 25 years old and over, by highest degree attained: 1996

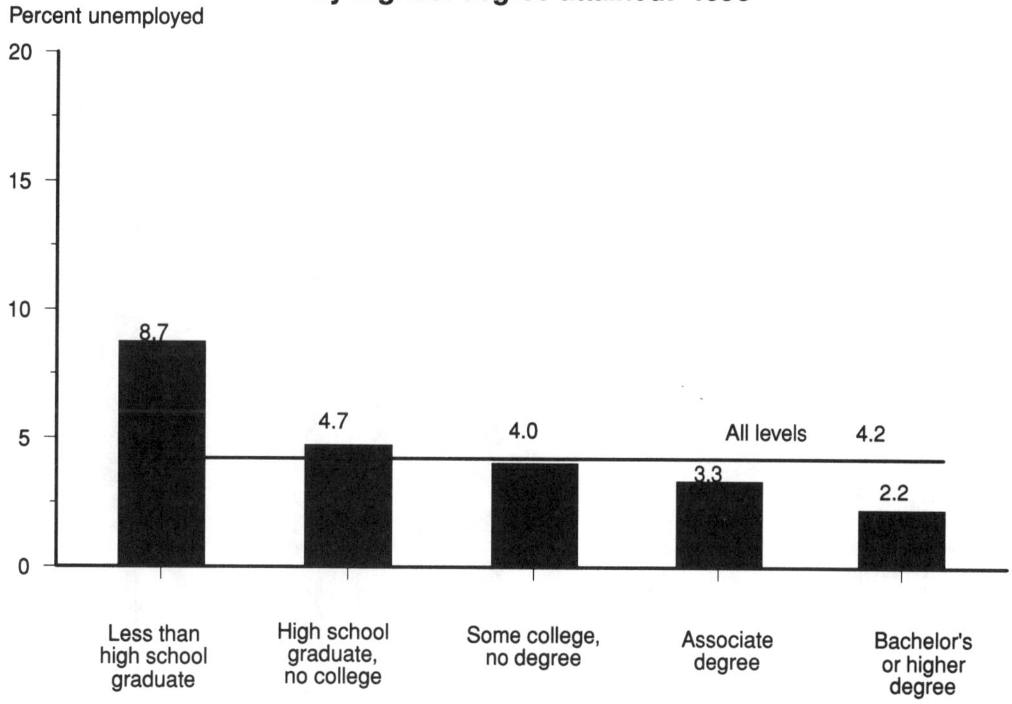

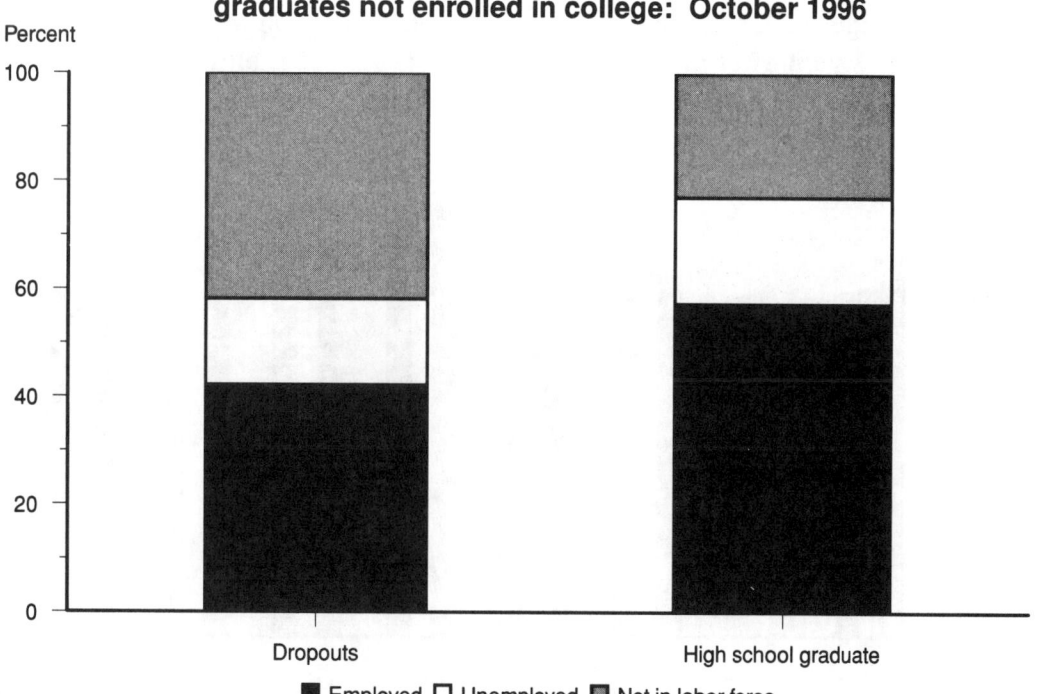

SOURCE: U.S. Department of Labor, Bureau of Labor Statistics, Office of Employment and Unemployment Statistics, Current Population Survey, 1996.

Figure 25.-Labor force status of 1995–96 high school dropouts and graduates not enrolled in college: October 1996

SOURCE: U.S. Department of Labor, Bureau of Labor Statistics, "Employment Status of School Age Youth, High School Graduates and Dropouts, 1996."

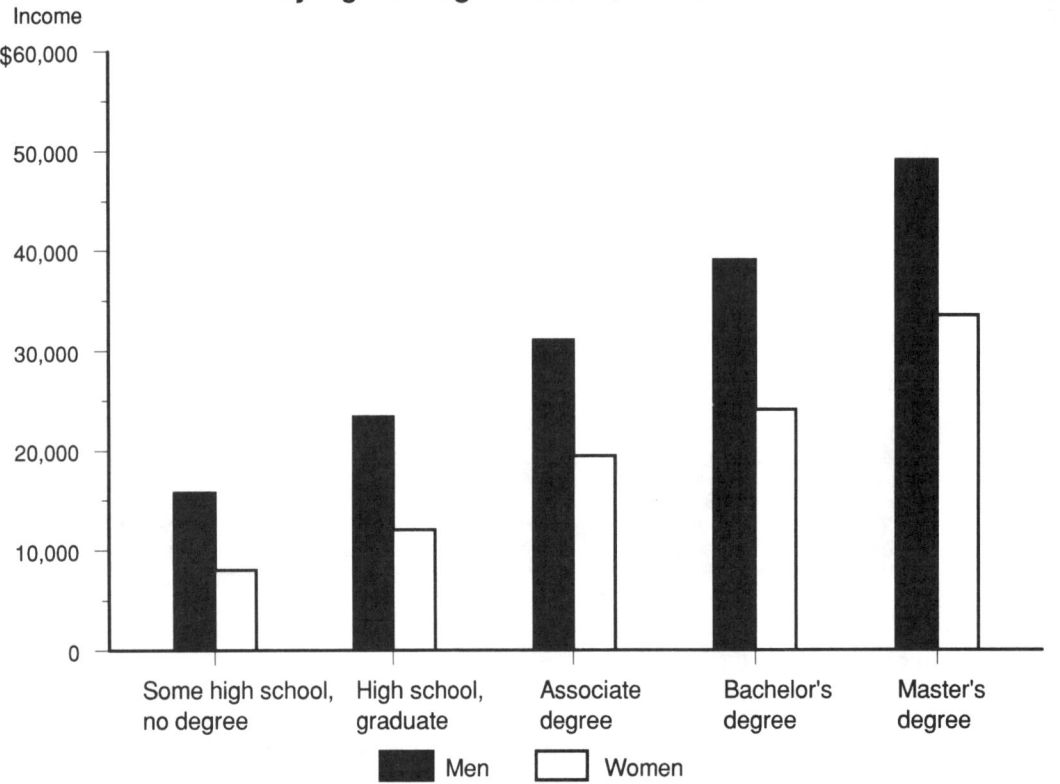

Figure 26.-Median annual income of persons with income 25 years old and over, by highest degree attained and sex: 1995

SOURCE: U.S. Department of Commerce, Bureau of the Census, *Current Population Reports*, Series P-60, "Money Income in the United States: 1995."

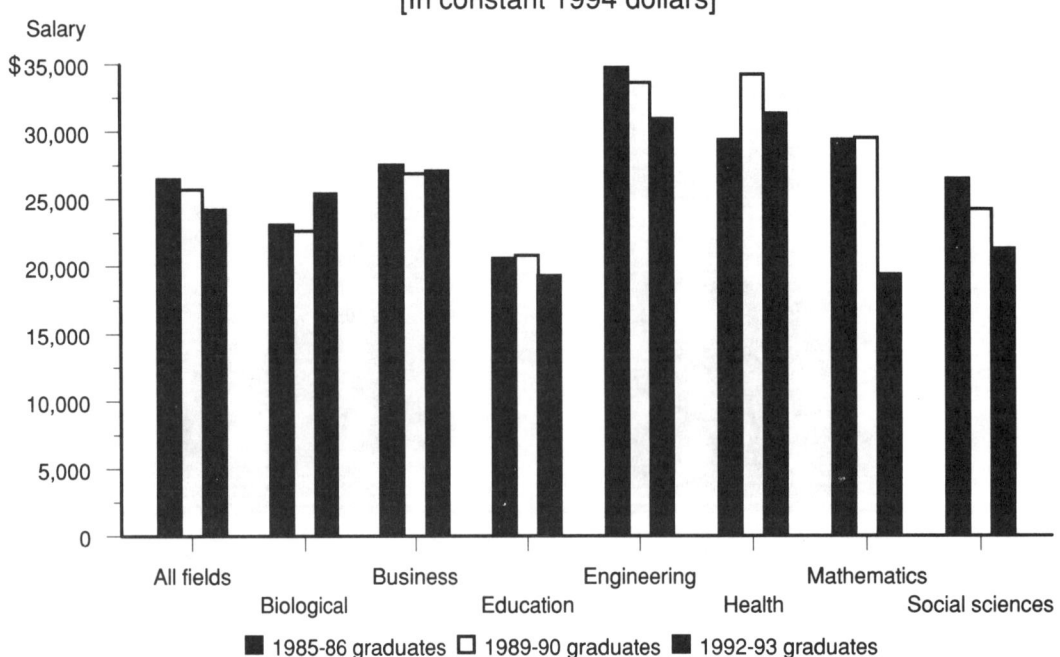

Figure 27.-Salaries of recent bachelor's degree recipients 1 year after graduation, by field: 1987, 1991, and 1994
[In constant 1994 dollars]

SOURCE: U.S. Department of Education, National Center for Education Statistics, "Recent College Graduates" surveys, 1987 and 1991 and "Baccalaureate and Beyond Longitudinal Study, First Follow-up" survey.

Table 373.—Percent of 18- to 25-year-olds reporting drug use during the past 30 days and the past year: 1979 to 1995

Drug	1979	1982	1985	1988	1990	1991	1992	1993	1994	1995
1	2	3	4	5	6	7	8	9	10	11
	Percent reporting drug use during past 30 days									
Any illicit use	38.0	—	25.3	17.9	15.0	15.4	13.1	13.6	13.3	14.2
Marijuana	35.6	27.2	21.7	15.3	12.7	12.9	10.9	11.1	12.1	12.0
Cocaine	9.9	7.0	8.1	4.8	2.3	2.2	2.0	1.6	1.2	1.3
Alcohol	75.1	66.6	70.1	64.7	62.8	63.1	58.6	58.7	63.1	61.3
Cigarettes	—	—	47.4	45.6	40.9	41.7	41.5	37.9	34.6	35.3
	Percent reporting drug use during past year									
Any illicit use	45.5	—	37.4	29.1	26.1	26.6	24.1	24.2	24.6	25.5
Marijuana	44.2	37.4	34.0	26.1	23.0	22.9	21.2	21.4	21.8	21.8
Cocaine	17.0	15.9	13.6	10.5	6.5	6.7	5.5	4.4	3.6	4.3
Alcohol	84.6	80.6	84.2	79.6	78.1	80.7	75.6	76.9	78.5	76.5
Cigarettes	—	—	49.9	50.9	45.1	46.9	46.8	43.7	41.1	42.5

—Data not available or low precision; no estimate reported.

NOTE.—Due to changes in the survey instrument and administration and to improve comparability with new data, estimates for 1979 through 1983 have been adjusted and may differ from those reported in previous years.

SOURCE: U.S. Department of Health and Human Services, Substance Abuse and Mental Health Services Administration, "Preliminary Estimates from the 1995 National Household Survey on Drug Abuse," 1996. (This table was prepared April 1997.)

Table 374.—Percent of 1972, 1982, and 1992 high school seniors who felt that certain life values were "very important," by sex: 1972 to 1994

Value	Percent of 1972 seniors						Percent of 1982 seniors						Percent of 1992 seniors				
	1972		1974 (2 years after high school)		1976 (4 years after high school)		1982		1984 (2 years after high school)		1986 (4 years after high school)		1992		1994 (2 years after high school)		
	Male	Female	Male	Female	Male	Female	Male	Female	Male	Female	Male	Female	Male	Female	Total	Male	Female
1	2	3	4	5	6	7	8	9	10	11	12	13	14	15	16	17	18
Being successful in work	86.5	83.0	81.2	74.9	80.3	69.7	88.2	85.5	88.7	84.2	84.0	77.2	89.0	89.6	90.1	89.9	90.3
Finding steady work	82.3	73.7	74.7	59.9	79.3	62.1	88.0	84.4	87.4	83.3	84.2	76.3	87.1	88.6	89.7	88.7	90.7
Having lots of money	26.0	9.8	17.8	9.1	17.7	9.4	41.3	24.1	35.8	20.9	27.8	16.9	45.3	29.4	35.2	39.5	30.9
Being a leader in the community	14.9	8.0	8.5	4.4	9.2	4.2	11.3	5.9	13.7	6.4	9.5	4.5	—	—	—	—	—
Correcting inequalities	22.5	31.1	16.6	18.2	16.2	17.1	11.8	11.7	13.3	13.9	10.7	10.9	17.0	23.6	—	—	—
Having children	—	—	—	—	—	—	37.0	47.0	42.7	56.3	41.4	56.2	39.0	49.2	—	—	—
Having a happy family life	78.6	85.7	83.1	86.7	84.2	86.4	81.6	86.3	86.1	90.2	86.8	87.8	—	—	—	—	—
Providing better opportunities for my children	66.6	66.2	59.5	61.6	59.8	58.8	71.0	68.7	72.1	69.9	68.4	67.4	74.5	76.5	90.5	90.3	90.8
Living closer to parents or relatives	6.8	8.2	8.3	12.4	7.7	11.9	15.0	15.7	15.6	20.1	12.9	19.8	15.2	18.7	—	—	—
Moving from area	14.3	14.6	8.3	7.4	6.7	6.4	14.4	12.8	10.5	9.1	9.0	7.4	20.7	20.1	—	—	—
Having strong friendships	81.2	78.7	76.5	74.7	76.1	72.1	80.4	79.1	80.1	79.7	76.5	75.0	79.8	80.0	87.6	88.1	87.0
Having leisure time	—	—	60.9	55.1	65.4	60.1	70.2	68.8	74.5	72.0	70.1	68.9	65.3	62.0	—	—	—

—Question not asked.

SOURCE: U.S. Department of Education, National Center for Education Statistics, "National Longitudinal Study," "High School and Beyond" surveys, and "National Education Longitudinal Study," second and third followup surveys. (This table was prepared June 1995.)

420 OUTCOMES OF EDUCATION

Table 375.—Labor force participation of persons 16 years old and over, by age, sex, race/ethnicity, and highest level of education: 1996

Age, sex, and race/ethnicity	Labor force participation rate [1]						Employment/population ratio [2]					
	Total	Less than high school graduate [3]	High school graduate	College			Total	Less than high school graduate [3]	High school graduate	College		
				Some college, no degree	Associate degree	Bachelor's degree or higher				Some college, no degree	Associate degree	Bachelor's degree or higher
1	2	3	4	5	6	7	8	9	10	11	12	13
16 to 19 years old [4]	52.3	45.8	69.2	62.1	67.1	69.7	43.5	36.7	58.9	57.0	57.8	67.9
Men	53.2	46.9	73.1	61.2	63.7	69.7	43.6	37.0	62.0	55.4	59.3	67.0
Women	51.3	44.4	65.6	62.7	68.8	69.7	43.5	36.4	55.9	58.2	57.1	69.7
White [5]	55.9	49.5	71.7	65.5	70.5	73.5	47.9	41.1	62.9	60.9	60.4	71.4
Black [5]	39.2	32.9	59.8	([6])	([6])	([6])	26.0	20.5	40.9	([6])	([6])	([6])
Hispanic [7]	43.4	37.2	64.6	([6])	([6])	([6])	33.1	27.5	51.3	([6])	([6])	([6])
20 to 24 years old [4]	76.8	62.8	82.2	73.9	84.8	85.9	69.7	50.7	73.3	68.9	81.0	81.5
Men	82.5	81.0	89.9	75.0	88.2	85.0	74.7	67.8	80.3	69.7	84.4	79.8
Women	71.3	43.5	73.7	72.8	82.2	86.5	64.9	32.5	65.6	68.2	78.2	82.4
White [5]	79.1	65.8	84.1	76.1	86.5	87.4	73.0	55.3	76.6	71.7	83.0	82.9
Black [5]	69.0	51.0	75.9	68.1	76.4	84.5	56.0	31.6	60.8	59.2	68.8	79.4
Hispanic [7]	73.1	62.7	80.9	76.9	81.8	81.3	64.5	53.6	71.7	69.3	75.7	74.8
25 and older	67.0	41.1	65.6	72.9	79.2	80.5	64.2	37.5	62.6	70.0	76.6	78.7
Men	76.2	54.0	76.6	80.5	86.7	85.1	73.1	49.8	73.0	77.4	84.0	83.3
Women	58.7	29.6	56.6	66.1	73.6	75.3	56.2	26.6	54.0	63.4	71.1	73.5
White [5]	67.0	41.6	65.0	71.9	78.8	80.3	64.5	38.3	62.4	69.3	76.5	78.6
Black [5]	66.6	37.6	70.2	79.2	83.0	84.0	61.5	32.8	63.8	73.9	78.4	81.4
Hispanic [7]	68.4	56.8	74.6	80.5	82.5	82.9	63.6	51.3	69.6	76.5	78.4	79.7

[1] Percent of the civilian population who are employed or seeking employment.
[2] Number of persons employed as a percent of civilian population.
[3] Includes persons reporting no school years completed.
[4] Excludes persons enrolled in school.
[5] Includes persons of Hispanic origin.
[6] Sample size too small for stable estimates.
[7] Hispanics may be of any race.

SOURCE: U.S. Department of Labor, Bureau of Labor Statistics, Office of Employment and Unemployment Statistics, unpublished tabulations from the Current Population Survey. (This table was prepared April 1997.)

Table 376.—Occupation of employed persons 25 years old and over, by educational attainment and sex: 1996

Sex and occupation	Total employed, in thousands	Percentage distribution, by years of school completed							
		Total	Less than one year of high school	High school		College			
				1–4 years of high school, no diploma	High school graduate	Some college, no degree	Associate degree	Bachelor's degree	More than a bachelor's degree
1	2	3	4	5	6	7	8	9	10
All persons									
All occupational groups	108,070	100.0	3.7	6.8	32.7	19.1	8.7	19.2	9.9
Managerial and professional specialty	34,413	100.0	0.5	1.4	12.9	14.2	8.8	35.6	26.7
Executive, administrative, and managerial	16,892	100.0	0.7	2.3	20.5	20.1	8.4	33.1	14.9
Professional specialty occupations	17,521	100.0	0.2	0.5	5.6	8.4	9.1	38.0	38.1
Teachers, except college and university	4,365	100.0	0.1	0.5	5.0	6.2	3.1	48.1	37.0
Teachers, college and university	806	100.0	0.0	0.0	0.6	2.6	1.6	15.3	79.8
Technical, sales, and administrative support	31,138	100.0	0.9	3.6	35.6	26.0	11.1	19.3	3.5
Technicians and related support	3,478	100.0	0.2	1.4	19.4	25.1	23.1	24.8	6.0
Sales occupations	12,096	100.0	1.4	5.0	32.8	23.0	7.9	25.3	4.6
Administrative support, including clerical	15,564	100.0	0.6	3.0	41.5	28.5	10.9	13.4	2.1
Service occupations	12,656	100.0	8.1	13.2	43.0	19.6	7.4	7.4	1.2
Precision production, craft, and repair	12,186	100.0	5.4	11.3	47.3	20.1	9.2	5.6	1.0
Operators, fabricators, and laborers	14,745	100.0	8.8	15.7	50.4	15.6	4.8	4.1	0.7
Farming, forestry, and fishing	2,932	100.0	19.1	12.8	37.9	13.5	5.4	9.1	2.3
Men									
All occupational groups	58,468	100.0	4.5	7.5	31.9	18.4	7.6	19.3	10.8
Managerial and professional specialty	17,855	100.0	0.7	1.5	11.6	14.0	6.7	35.5	30.0
Executive, administrative, and managerial	9,593	100.0	1.0	2.4	17.5	18.5	7.3	35.9	17.4
Professional specialty occupations	8,261	100.0	0.3	0.5	4.8	8.8	6.1	34.9	44.6
Teachers, except college and university	1,123	100.0	0.1	0.3	3.4	6.4	2.7	44.7	42.5
Teachers, college and university	460	100.0	0.0	0.0	0.4	2.6	2.0	13.3	82.0
Technical, sales, and administrative support	11,326	100.0	1.3	3.4	27.3	24.8	9.7	27.8	5.7
Technicians and related support	1,635	100.0	0.1	1.4	17.6	25.3	19.5	28.7	7.4
Sales occupations	6,566	100.0	1.5	3.5	26.0	23.5	7.7	31.4	6.4
Administrative support, including clerical	3,125	100.0	1.4	4.1	35.0	27.1	8.8	19.9	3.6
Service occupations	4,947	100.0	8.8	10.8	37.7	22.3	8.5	10.3	1.7
Precision production, craft, and repair	11,084	100.0	5.3	11.2	47.4	20.3	9.4	5.3	1.0
Operators, fabricators, and laborers	10,913	100.0	8.1	15.1	50.2	16.5	5.0	4.4	0.7
Farming, forestry, and fishing	2,343	100.0	20.9	13.2	37.8	12.6	4.7	8.5	2.2
Women									
All occupational groups	49,602	100.0	2.7	5.9	33.6	19.8	10.1	19.1	8.8
Managerial and professional specialty	16,558	100.0	0.3	1.2	14.4	14.3	11.0	35.7	23.1
Executive, administrative, and managerial	7,299	100.0	0.4	2.0	24.5	22.3	9.8	29.4	11.6
Professional specialty occupations	9,259	100.0	0.2	0.6	6.4	8.0	11.9	40.7	32.2
Teachers, except college and university	3,242	100.0	0.2	0.6	5.5	6.2	3.2	49.3	35.1
Teachers, college and university	346	100.0	0.0	0.0	0.9	2.6	1.2	17.9	77.2
Technical, sales, and administrative support	19,812	100.0	0.7	3.7	40.4	26.7	11.9	14.4	2.2
Technicians and related support	1,843	100.0	0.3	1.5	21.0	25.0	26.2	21.3	4.7
Sales occupations	5,530	100.0	1.4	6.8	40.8	22.3	8.3	18.1	2.4
Administrative support, including clerical	12,439	100.0	0.4	2.7	43.1	28.9	11.5	11.7	1.7
Service occupations	7,708	100.0	7.6	14.8	46.5	17.9	6.8	5.5	1.0
Precision production, craft, and repair	1,103	100.0	7.3	12.1	46.4	18.1	6.6	8.5	1.1
Operators, fabricators, and laborers	3,832	100.0	10.7	17.2	50.9	13.0	4.4	3.2	0.5
Farming, forestry, and fishing	589	100.0	12.1	10.9	38.2	16.8	8.0	11.5	2.7

NOTE.—Because of rounding, details may not add to totals.

SOURCE: U.S. Department of Labor, Bureau of Labor Statistics, Office of Employment and Unemployment Statistics, unpublished tabulations from the Current Population Survey. (This table was prepared April 1997.)

Table 377.—Unemployment rate of persons 16 years old and over, by age, sex, race/ethnicity, and highest degree attained: 1994, 1995, and 1996

Sex, race/ethnicity, and highest degree attained	Percent unemployed, 1994[1]				Percent unemployed, 1995[1]				Percent unemployed, 1996[1]			
	16- to 24-year-olds[2]			25 years old and over	16- to 24-year-olds[2]			25 years old and over	16- to 24-year-olds[2]			25 years old and over
	Total	16 to 19 years	20 to 24 years		Total	16 to 19 years	20 to 24 years		Total	16 to 19 years	20 to 24 years	
1	2	3	4	5	6	7	8	9	10	11	12	13
All persons												
All education levels	12.5	17.6	9.7	4.8	12.1	17.3	9.1	4.3	12.0	16.7	9.3	4.2
Less than a high school graduate	21.0	21.5	19.9	9.8	20.2	20.8	18.6	9.0	19.7	19.7	19.4	8.7
High school graduate, no college	11.9	14.5	10.9	5.4	12.0	14.7	10.8	4.8	12.0	14.9	10.8	4.7
Some college, no degree	7.9	9.2	7.5	4.7	6.7	8.4	6.3	4.3	7.0	8.1	6.7	4.0
Associate degree	5.4	—	5.5	3.8	5.3	11.2	5.1	3.3	4.8	13.8	4.5	3.3
Bachelor's degree or higher	5.2	—	5.2	2.6	5.5	6.5	5.5	2.4	5.3	2.6	5.3	2.2
Men												
All education levels	13.2	19.0	10.2	4.8	12.5	18.4	9.2	4.3	12.6	18.1	9.5	4.1
Less than a high school graduate	20.8	22.5	17.5	9.3	19.9	21.6	15.9	8.8	19.8	21.2	16.4	7.8
High school graduate, no college	12.0	15.3	10.9	5.5	11.7	15.3	10.4	4.8	11.9	15.1	10.6	4.7
Some college, no degree	8.4	10.1	8.0	4.5	6.8	9.3	6.3	4.0	7.5	9.4	7.1	3.9
Associate degree	5.7	—	5.7	3.8	4.9	25.8	4.8	3.3	4.1	7.0	4.2	3.2
Bachelor's degree or higher	6.1	—	6.1	2.5	6.3	11.8	6.3	2.3	6.1	3.9	6.1	2.1
Women												
All education levels	11.6	16.2	9.2	4.9	11.7	16.1	9.0	4.4	11.3	15.2	9.0	4.3
Less than a high school graduate	21.3	20.2	25.2	10.5	20.8	19.9	24.4	9.2	19.5	18.1	25.3	10.1
High school graduate, no college	11.9	13.7	11.0	5.2	12.3	14.2	11.4	4.7	12.2	14.7	10.9	4.6
Some college, no degree	7.4	8.5	7.1	5.0	6.6	7.7	6.3	4.6	6.6	7.2	6.4	4.1
Associate degree	5.2	—	5.3	3.8	5.5	5.7	5.5	3.3	5.2	17.0	4.8	3.3
Bachelor's degree or higher	4.5	—	4.5	2.7	5.0	—	4.9	2.7	4.8	—	4.8	2.4
White[3]												
All education levels	10.6	15.1	8.1	4.3	10.2	14.5	7.7	3.9	10.2	14.2	7.8	3.7
Less than a high school graduate	18.1	18.7	16.8	8.9	17.2	17.7	15.9	8.3	16.7	17.0	16.0	8.0
High school graduate, no college	9.9	11.8	9.1	4.7	10.0	11.9	9.2	4.2	9.9	12.2	8.9	4.0
Some college, no degree	6.6	7.9	6.2	4.2	5.8	7.3	5.3	3.7	6.0	7.0	5.8	3.5
Associate degree	4.8	—	4.8	3.4	4.8	8.5	4.7	3.1	4.2	14.5	3.9	3.0
Bachelor's degree or higher	5.2	—	5.2	2.4	5.1	—	5.1	2.3	5.1	2.9	5.1	2.1
Black[3]												
All education levels	24.5	35.2	19.5	8.6	23.9	35.7	17.7	7.4	23.9	33.6	18.8	7.7
Less than a high school graduate	39.8	39.6	40.3	13.5	39.1	40.4	35.8	12.4	37.8	37.6	38.2	12.6
High school graduate, no college	23.1	31.4	20.6	9.9	22.5	31.8	19.3	8.2	23.0	31.5	20.0	9.1
Some college, no degree	15.8	21.4	14.9	8.1	13.0	18.7	12.2	7.5	13.7	17.1	13.1	6.7
Associate degree	12.0	—	12.1	5.8	10.7	66.4	8.5	4.6	9.7	—	10.0	5.5
Bachelor's degree or higher	5.0	—	5.1	3.5	8.7	—	8.6	3.2	6.1	—	6.0	3.1
Hispanic origin[4]												
All education levels	15.7	24.5	11.8	8.3	15.5	24.1	11.5	7.6	15.5	23.6	11.8	7.1
Less than a high school graduate	20.5	27.9	14.5	11.1	20.2	28.2	13.7	10.4	20.1	26.1	14.6	9.7
High school graduate, no college	13.8	20.5	12.0	7.6	14.1	18.7	12.3	6.8	13.6	20.7	11.5	6.6
Some college, no degree	10.2	14.3	9.2	6.9	10.4	14.1	9.4	6.1	10.5	13.2	9.8	4.9
Associate degree	9.2	—	9.3	5.9	4.3	15.6	3.0	5.5	8.2	—	7.5	4.9
Bachelor's degree or higher	4.9	—	4.9	4.2	7.4	19.4	7.8	3.5	8.1	—	8.0	3.8

[1] The unemployment rate is the percent of individuals in the labor force who are not working and who made specific efforts to find employment sometime during the prior 4 weeks. The labor force includes both employed and unemployed persons.
[2] Excludes persons enrolled in school.
[3] Includes persons of Hispanic origin.
[4] Persons of Hispanic origin may be of any race.

—Data not available.

SOURCE: U.S. Department of Labor, Bureau of Labor Statistics, Office of Employment and Unemployment Statistics, unpublished tabulations from the Current Population Survey. (This table was prepared April 1997.)

Table 378.—Median annual income of year-round full-time workers 25 years old and over, by level of education completed and sex: 1989 to 1995

Sex and year	Total	Elementary/secondary			College						
		Less than 9th grade [1]	9th to 12th grade, no diploma [2]	High school graduate [3]	Some college, no degree [4]	Associate degree [5]	Bachelor's degree or higher [6]				
							Total [6]	Bachelor's [7]	Master's [8]	Professional [8]	Doctorate [8]
1	2	3	4	5	6	7	8	9	10	11	12
Current dollars											
Men											
1989	$30,465	$17,555	$21,065	$26,609	$31,308	—	$41,892	$38,565	—	—	—
1990	30,733	17,394	20,902	26,653	31,734	—	42,671	39,238	—	—	—
1991	31,613	17,623	21,402	26,779	31,663	$33,817	45,138	40,906	$49,734	$73,996	$57,187
1992 [9]	32,057	17,294	21,274	27,280	32,103	33,433	45,802	41,355	49,973	76,220	57,418
1993	32,359	16,863	21,752	27,370	32,077	33,690	47,740	42,757	51,867	80,549	63,149
1994	33,440	17,532	22,048	28,037	32,279	35,794	49,228	43,663	53,500	75,009	61,921
1995	34,551	18,354	22,185	29,510	33,883	35,201	50,481	45,266	55,216	79,667	65,336
Women											
1989	20,570	12,188	13,923	17,528	21,631	—	28,799	26,709	—	—	—
1990	21,372	12,251	14,429	18,319	22,227	—	30,377	28,017	—	—	—
1991	22,043	12,066	14,455	18,836	22,143	25,000	31,310	29,079	34,949	46,742	43,303
1992 [9]	23,139	12,958	14,559	19,427	23,157	25,624	32,304	30,326	36,037	46,257	45,790
1993	23,629	12,415	15,386	19,963	23,056	25,883	34,307	31,197	38,612	50,211	47,248
1994	24,399	12,430	15,133	20,373	23,514	25,940	35,378	31,741	39,457	50,615	51,119
1995	24,875	13,577	15,825	20,463	23,997	27,311	35,259	32,051	40,263	50,000	48,141
Constant 1995 dollars											
Men											
1989	$37,442	$21,576	$25,890	$32,703	$38,479	—	$51,487	$47,398	—	—	—
1990	35,836	20,282	24,372	31,078	37,003	—	49,756	45,753	—	—	—
1991	35,373	19,719	23,948	29,964	35,429	$37,839	50,507	45,771	$55,649	$82,797	$63,989
1992 [9]	34,822	18,785	23,109	29,633	34,872	36,316	49,752	44,922	54,283	82,793	62,370
1993	34,128	17,785	22,941	28,866	33,831	35,532	50,350	45,095	54,703	84,953	66,601
1994	34,388	18,029	22,673	28,832	33,194	36,808	50,623	44,900	55,016	77,135	63,676
1995	34,551	18,354	22,185	29,510	33,883	35,201	50,481	45,266	55,216	79,667	65,336
Women											
1989	25,281	14,979	17,112	21,542	26,585	—	35,395	32,826	—	—	—
1990	24,920	14,285	16,825	21,360	25,917	—	35,420	32,669	—	—	—
1991	24,665	13,501	16,174	21,076	24,777	27,974	35,034	32,538	39,106	52,302	48,454
1992 [9]	25,135	14,076	15,815	21,102	25,154	27,834	35,090	32,941	39,145	50,246	49,739
1993	24,921	13,094	16,227	21,054	24,317	27,298	36,183	32,903	40,723	52,956	49,831
1994	25,090	12,782	15,562	20,950	24,180	26,675	36,381	32,641	40,575	52,049	52,568
1995	24,875	13,577	15,825	20,463	23,997	27,311	35,259	32,051	40,263	50,000	48,141
Number with income (in thousands)											
Men											
1989	44,596	2,425	3,312	16,392	9,028	—	13,439	7,473	—	—	—
1990	44,406	2,250	3,315	16,394	9,113	—	13,334	7,569	—	—	—
1991	44,199	1,807	3,083	15,025	8,034	2,899	13,350	8,456	3,073	1,147	674
1992 [9]	44,752	1,815	3,009	14,722	8,067	3,203	13,937	8,719	3,178	1,295	745
1993	45,873	1,790	3,083	14,604	8,493	3,557	14,346	9,178	3,131	1,231	808
1994	47,566	1,895	3,057	15,109	8,783	3,735	14,987	9,636	3,225	1,258	868
1995	48,500	1,946	3,335	15,331	8,908	3,926	15,054	9,597	3,395	1,208	853
Women											
1989	28,056	906	1,830	11,785	6,217	—	7,318	4,465	—	—	—
1990	28,636	847	1,861	11,810	6,462	—	7,655	4,704	—	—	—
1991	29,474	733	1,819	10,959	5,633	2,523	7,807	5,263	2,025	312	206
1992 [9]	30,346	734	1,659	11,039	5,904	2,655	8,355	5,604	2,192	334	225
1993	30,683	765	1,576	10,513	6,279	3,067	8,483	5,735	2,166	323	260
1994	31,379	696	1,675	10,785	6,256	3,210	8,756	5,901	2,174	398	283
1995	32,673	774	1,763	11,064	6,329	3,336	9,406	6,434	2,268	421	283

[1] Includes fewer than 9 years education for 1989 and 1990.
[2] Includes 1 to 3 years high school for 1989 and 1990.
[3] Includes 4 years of high school for 1989 and 1990, and equivalency certificates for the other years.
[4] Includes 1 to 3 years of college and associate degrees for 1989 and 1990.
[5] Not reported separately for 1989 and 1990.
[6] Includes 4 or more years of college for 1989 and 1990.
[7] Includes 4 years of college for 1989 and 1990.
[8] Data not collected in 1989 and 1990.
[9] Data are based on 1990 census controls.

—Data not available or not applicable.

NOTE.—Due to rounding, numbers may not add to totals.

SOURCE: U.S. Department of Commerce, Bureau of the Census, *Current Population Reports,* Series P-60, "Money Income of Households, Families, and Persons in the United States," "Income, Poverty, and Valuation of Noncash Benefits," various years, and "Money Income in the United States: 1995," P60–193. (This table was prepared April 1997.)

Table 379.—Total annual money income and median income of persons 25 years old and over, by educational attainment and sex: 1995

Sex, earnings, and age	Total	Less than 9th grade	Some high school (no diploma)	High school graduate (includes equivalency)	College						
					Some college, no degree	Associate degree	Bachelor's degree or more				
							Total	Bachelor's degree	Master's degree	Professional degree	Doctor's degree
1	2	3	4	5	6	7	8	9	10	11	12
	Number, in thousands										
Men, 25 years old and over											
Total	80,339	6,604	7,931	25,649	13,998	5,303	20,855	13,219	4,812	1,671	1,152
With income	78,264	6,277	7,490	24,909	13,715	5,230	20,644	13,065	4,774	1,657	1,149
	Percentage distribution of men with income										
Total	100.0	100.0	100.0	100.0	100.0	100.0	100.0	100.0	100.0	100.0	100.0
$1 to $4,999 or loss	5.0	10.1	9.1	5.0	4.3	3.5	2.8	3.4	1.8	1.6	2.3
$5,000 to $9,999	9.5	30.5	18.9	8.8	6.6	5.2	3.4	3.8	3.0	1.8	1.6
$10,000 to $14,999	11.2	22.4	19.1	12.4	10.4	6.2	5.2	6.1	3.9	3.7	3.2
$15,000 to $24,999	21.4	24.2	28.0	27.0	21.4	22.4	11.1	13.3	7.6	6.6	7.0
$25,000 to $34,999	17.2	7.1	13.9	20.2	20.4	20.6	14.9	17.0	12.2	9.6	9.1
$35,000 to $49,999	16.5	3.8	7.2	15.9	20.3	23.1	20.2	20.8	22.5	11.6	15.3
$50,000 to $74,999	11.9	1.5	2.6	8.3	11.6	14.5	22.3	21.0	25.5	20.0	26.9
$75,000 and over	7.4	0.4	1.2	2.4	4.9	4.6	20.1	14.5	23.6	45.0	34.6
Median income	$26,346	$11,723	$15,791	$23,365	$28,004	$31,027	$43,322	$39,040	$49,076	$66,257	$57,356
	Number, in thousands										
Women, 25 years old and over											
Total	87,984	7,019	9,171	30,911	15,203	6,868	18,813	13,321	4,288	745	459
With income	82,457	6,020	8,122	28,785	14,619	6,642	18,269	12,875	4,205	732	457
	Percentage distribution of women with income										
Total	100.0	100.0	100.0	100.0	100.0	100.0	100.0	100.0	100.0	100.0	100.0
$1 to $4,999 or loss	17.7	26.0	25.2	18.9	16.2	13.5	12.5	14.1	9.4	6.1	4.8
$5,000 to $9,999	20.5	44.6	35.4	23.0	16.7	12.8	7.9	8.9	5.0	9.3	5.9
$10,000 to $14,999	14.7	17.7	19.1	17.4	15.5	12.3	7.9	9.0	5.2	6.1	5.9
$15,000 to $24,999	20.9	9.2	14.6	24.1	25.1	24.9	17.5	19.8	13.1	10.2	6.6
$25,000 to $34,999	12.4	1.4	3.4	9.9	14.8	18.4	19.8	20.4	19.8	12.2	16.2
$35,000 to $49,999	8.5	0.6	1.6	4.7	8.0	12.4	19.3	16.7	26.6	19.9	28.0
$50,000 to $74,999	3.8	0.4	0.4	1.5	2.7	4.6	10.5	8.2	15.4	16.4	19.5
$75,000 and over	1.5	0.2	0.2	0.5	1.0	1.2	4.6	3.0	5.5	19.9	13.3
Median income	$13,821	$7,096	$8,057	$12,046	$15,552	$19,450	$26,843	$24,065	$33,509	$38,588	$39,821

NOTE.—Because of rounding, details may not add to totals.

SOURCE: U.S. Department of Commerce, Bureau of the Census, *Current Population Reports*, Series P-60, No. 189, "Income, Poverty, and Valuation of Noncash Benefits: 1994 and "Money Income in the United States: 1995, P60 -193. (This table was prepared April 1997.)

Table 380.—College enrollment and labor force status of 1995 and 1996 high school graduates 16 to 24 years old, by sex and race/ethnicity: October 1995 and October 1996

[Numbers in thousands]

Item	Civilian noninstitutional population			Civilian labor force [1]					Not in labor force
	Number	Percent	Percent of high school graduates	Number	Labor force participation rate	Employed	Unemployed		
							Number	Unemployment rate	
1	2	3	4	5	6	7	8	9	10
1995 high school graduates [2]									
Total	2,599	100.0	100.0	1,546	59.5	1,284	262	16.9	1,053
Men	1,238	47.6	47.6	749	60.5	602	147	19.6	489
Women	1,361	52.4	52.4	797	58.6	682	115	14.4	564
White [3]	2,088	80.3	80.3	1,278	61.2	1,096	182	14.2	810
Black [3]	356	13.7	13.7	202	56.9	144	59	29.1	153
Hispanic origin [4]	288	11.1	11.1	161	55.9	96	65	40.5	127
Enrolled in college, October 1995	1,610	100.0	61.9	756	47.0	659	97	12.8	853
Men	775	48.1	29.8	358	46.1	305	52	14.7	417
Women	835	51.9	32.1	398	47.7	354	45	11.2	436
2-year	559	34.7	21.5	359	64.1	299	60	16.7	201
4-year	1,050	65.2	40.4	397	37.8	360	37	9.4	653
Full-time students	1,450	90.0	55.8	626	43.2	541	85	13.5	824
Part-time students	159	9.9	6.1	130	81.7	118	12	9.6	29
White [3]	1,308	81.2	50.3	636	48.6	569	67	10.6	672
Black [3]	183	11.4	7.0	77	41.9	56	21	27.0	106
Hispanic origin [4]	155	9.6	6.0	69	44.6	40	29	([5])	86
Not enrolled in college, October 1995	990	100.0	38.1	790	79.8	625	165	20.9	200
Men	463	46.8	17.8	391	84.5	297	94	24.1	72
Women	527	53.2	20.3	399	75.7	328	70	17.7	128
White [3]	780	78.8	30.0	642	82.4	528	115	17.9	137
Black [3]	173	17.5	6.7	126	72.9	88	38	30.3	47
Hispanic origin [4]	133	13.4	5.1	92	68.9	56	36	39.0	41
1996 high school graduates [6]									
Total	2,660	100.0	100.0	1,528	57.4	1,225	303	19.8	1,132
Men	1,297	48.8	48.8	772	59.5	605	167	21.6	526
Women	1,363	51.2	51.2	756	55.5	620	136	18.0	606
White [3]	2,092	78.6	78.6	1,253	59.9	1,047	206	16.4	839
Black [3]	416	15.6	15.6	232	55.6	150	82	35.4	185
Hispanic origin [4]	227	8.5	8.5	138	60.6	100	37	27.1	89
Enrolled in college, October 1996	1,729	100.0	65.0	801	46.3	676	126	15.7	928
Men	779	45.0	29.3	348	44.7	286	63	18.0	431
Women	950	54.9	35.7	453	47.7	390	63	14.0	497
2-year	615	35.6	23.1	379	61.7	310	69	18.3	235
4-year	1,115	64.5	41.9	422	37.9	366	57	13.4	692
Full-time students	1,589	91.9	59.7	681	42.8	562	119	17.5	908
Part-time students	140	8.1	5.3	120	86.1	113	7	5.8	19
White [3]	1,377	79.6	51.8	679	49.4	584	96	14.1	697
Black [3]	230	13.3	8.6	94	40.9	74	21	21.8	136
Hispanic origin [4]	115	6.6	4.3	66	57.4	55	12	([5])	49
Not enrolled in college, October 1996	931	100.0	35.0	726	78.1	549	177	24.4	204
Men	518	55.6	19.5	423	81.7	319	104	24.6	95
Women	413	44.4	15.5	303	73.5	231	73	23.9	109
White [3]	716	76.9	26.9	574	80.2	463	111	19.3	142
Black [3]	186	20.0	7.0	137	73.8	76	61	44.8	49
Hispanic origin [4]	112	12.0	4.2	71	63.9	46	26	([5])	40

[1] The labor force includes all employed persons plus those seeking employment. The labor force participation rate is the percentage of persons either employed or seeking employment.
[2] Includes persons who graduated from high school between January and October 1995.
[3] Includes persons of Hispanic origin.
[4] Persons of Hispanic origin may be of any race.
[5] Data not shown where base is less than 75,000.
[6] Includes persons who graduated from high school between January and October 1996.

NOTE.—Data are based upon sample surveys of the civilian noninstitutional population. Percents are only shown when the base is 75,000 or greater. Even though the standard errors are large, smaller estimates are shown to permit users to combine categories in various ways. Because of rounding, details may not add to totals.

SOURCE.—U.S. Department of Labor, Bureau of Labor Statistics, "College Enrollment and Work Activity of 1995 High School Graduates" and "College Enrollment and Work Activity of 1996 High School Graduates. (This table was prepared July 1997.)

Table 381.—Labor force status of 1979–80 to 1995–96 high school dropouts 16 to 24 years old, by sex and race/ethnicity: October 1980 to October 1996

[Numbers in thousands]

Year, sex, and race [1]	Dropouts [1]		Dropouts in civilian labor force [2]						Not in labor force
	Number	Percent of total	Number	Labor force participation rate	Employed		Unemployed		
					Number	Percent of dropouts	Number	Unemployment rate	
1	2	3	4	5	6	7	8	9	10
All dropouts									
1979–80 dropouts in October	739	100.0	471	63.7	322	43.6	149	31.6	268
1984–85 dropouts in October	612	100.0	413	67.5	266	43.5	147	35.6	199
1985–86 dropouts in October	562	100.0	359	63.9	259	46.1	100	27.9	203
1986–87 dropouts in October	502	100.0	333	66.4	207	41.2	126	37.8	169
1987–88 dropouts in October	552	100.0	327	59.2	240	43.5	87	26.7	225
1988–89 dropouts in October	446	100.0	292	65.4	210	47.1	82	28.0	154
1989–90 dropouts in October	405	100.0	280	69.0	189	46.7	90	32.3	125
1990–91 dropouts in October	380	100.0	235	61.8	140	36.9	95	40.3	145
1991–92 dropouts in October	406	100.0	242	59.6	147	36.3	95	39.1	164
1992–93 dropouts in October	399	100.0	254	63.8	187	47.0	67	26.3	145
1993–94 dropouts in October	510	100.0	311	61.1	219	42.9	93	29.8	198
1994–95 dropouts in October	604	100.0	409	67.7	288	47.7	121	29.6	195
1995–96 dropouts in October	496	100.0	289	58.4	210	42.3	80	27.6	206
Men									
1979–80 dropouts in October	422	57.1	305	72.3	212	50.2	93	30.5	117
1984–85 dropouts in October	321	52.5	261	81.3	163	50.8	98	37.5	60
1989–90 dropouts in October	215	53.1	173	80.2	110	51.2	63	36.2	42
1990–91 dropouts in October	189	49.7	142	75.0	92	48.8	50	35.0	47
1992–93 dropouts in October	213	53.4	156	73.5	132	61.8	25	15.9	57
1993–94 dropouts in October	259	50.8	198	76.5	151	58.2	47	23.9	61
1994–95 dropouts in October	339	56.1	251	74.0	179	52.8	72	28.7	88
1995–96 dropouts in October	241	48.6	178	74.0	123	51.0	56	31.1	63
Women									
1979–80 dropouts in October	317	42.9	166	52.4	110	34.7	56	33.7	151
1984–85 dropouts in October	291	47.5	152	52.2	103	35.4	49	32.2	139
1989–90 dropouts in October	190	46.9	107	56.3	79	41.6	28	26.1	83
1990–91 dropouts in October	191	50.3	93	48.8	48	25.2	45	48.4	98
1992–93 dropouts in October	186	46.6	98	52.6	56	30.1	42	42.9	88
1993–94 dropouts in October	251	49.2	113	45.2	68	27.1	45	40.0	137
1994–95 dropouts in October	265	43.9	157	59.5	109	41.1	49	30.9	107
1995–96 dropouts in October	255	51.4	111	43.6	87	34.1	24	21.8	144
White [3]									
1979–80 dropouts in October	580	78.5	392	67.6	286	49.3	106	27.0	188
1984–85 dropouts in October	458	74.8	330	72.1	214	46.7	116	35.2	128
1989–90 dropouts in October	303	74.8	211	69.8	156	51.4	56	26.3	92
1990–91 dropouts in October	273	71.8	177	65.1	109	40.0	68	38.5	96
1992–93 dropouts in October	304	76.2	209	68.8	159	52.2	50	24.1	95
1993–94 dropouts in October	382	74.9	252	66.0	177	46.3	75	29.8	130
1994–95 dropouts in October	448	74.2	312	69.8	227	50.8	85	27.2	135
1995–96 dropouts in October	365	73.6	238	65.1	178	48.6	60	25.3	127
Black [3]									
1979–80 dropouts in October	146	19.8	73	50.0	33	22.6	40	(4)	73
1984–85 dropouts in October	132	21.6	69	52.3	39	29.5	30	(4)	63
1989–90 dropouts in October	86	21.2	56	65.3	26	29.9	30	(4)	30
1990–91 dropouts in October	98	25.8	54	55.0	28	28.4	26	(4)	44
1992–93 dropouts in October	80	20.1	34	42.9	21	26.2	13	(4)	46
1993–94 dropouts in October	100	19.6	48	47.9	34	34.1	14	(4)	52
1994–95 dropouts in October	109	18.0	66	61.0	40	36.4	27	(4)	42
1995–96 dropouts in October	111	22.4	40	35.7	23	20.7	17	(4)	71
Hispanic [5]									
1979–80 dropouts in October	91	12.3	60	65.9	43	47.3	17	(4)	31
1984–85 dropouts in October	106	17.3	73	68.9	40	37.7	33	(4)	33
1989–90 dropouts in October	67	16.5	32	(4)	22	(4)	10	(4)	35
1990–91 dropouts in October	61	16.1	48	(4)	30	(4)	18	(4)	13
1992–93 dropouts in October	60	15.0	43	(4)	28	(4)	15	(4)	17
1993–94 dropouts in October	108	21.2	51	47.5	31	28.6	20	(4)	57
1994–95 dropouts in October	174	28.8	119	68.6	84	48.5	35	29.3	55
1995–96 dropouts in October	105	21.2	71	67.7	57	54.5	14	(4)	34

[1] Persons who dropped out of school between October of the earlier year and October of the later year.
[2] The labor force includes all employed persons plus those seeking employment. The labor force participation rate is the percentage of persons either employed or seeking employment. The unemployment rate is the percent of persons in the labor force who are seeking employment.
[3] Includes persons of Hispanic origin.
[4] Data not shown where base is less than 75,000.
[5] Persons of Hispanic origin may be of any race.

NOTE.—Data are based upon sample surveys of the civilian noninstitutional population. Includes dropouts from any grade, including a small number from elementary and middle schools. Percents are only shown when the base is 75,000 or greater. Even though the standard errors are large, smaller estimates are shown to permit users to combine categories in various ways. Detail for the above race and Hispanic-origin groups will not sum to totals because data for the "other races" group are not presented and Hispanics are included in both the white and black population groups. Because of rounding, details may not add to totals.

SOURCE: U.S. Department of Labor, Bureau of Labor Statistics, *College Enrollment of High School Graduates*, various years. (This table was prepared July 1997.)

Table 382.—Employment of 12th graders, by selected student characteristics: 1992

Employment characteristics	Total	Sex		Race/ethnicity					Socioeconomic status[1]				Location of school attended		
		Male	Female	White	Black	Hispanic	Asian	American Indian	Low	Middle low	Middle high	High	Urban	Suburban	Rural
1	2	3	4	5	6	7	8	9	10	11	12	13	14	15	16
Average hours worked per week during senior year									Percentage distribution						
Total	100.0	100.0	100.0	100.0	100.0	100.0	100.0	100.0	100.0	100.0	100.0	100.0	100.0	100.0	100.0
Did not work during year	31.8	33.0	30.7	27.6	47.4	38.9	43.3	45.0	38.2	29.8	28.2	32.5	35.6	29.4	31.6
1 to 5 hours	6.8	6.0	7.6	7.0	4.9	6.0	9.5	8.5	5.5	5.5	5.8	10.1	6.7	6.6	7.2
6 to 10 hours	9.8	8.9	10.7	11.2	6.5	5.3	6.7	5.6	6.7	8.3	10.6	12.6	9.4	9.6	10.6
11 to 15 hours	12.7	11.1	14.4	14.1	7.2	11.3	9.3	6.2	9.5	11.9	13.7	15.0	12.2	13.6	12.1
16 to 20 hours	16.1	15.0	17.2	17.3	11.9	13.3	13.5	12.5	13.4	18.6	18.4	14.0	14.3	18.3	14.9
More than 20 hours	22.7	26.0	19.5	22.8	22.1	25.2	17.7	22.3	27.1	25.9	23.3	15.8	21.7	22.5	23.7
21 to 25 hours	9.8	10.2	9.5	10.0	8.8	10.7	8.1	12.0	10.2	10.9	10.8	8.0	9.5	10.6	9.1
26 to 30 hours	5.6	6.5	4.8	5.5	6.4	6.6	4.4	3.8	6.8	6.4	5.9	3.4	5.3	5.7	5.8
31 to 35 hours	2.5	3.1	1.9	2.6	2.4	2.4	0.8	5.0	3.6	3.2	2.4	1.3	2.3	2.5	2.7
36 to 40 hours	3.3	4.2	2.4	3.3	2.9	4.1	3.7	0.9	4.3	4.2	2.7	2.1	3.3	2.4	4.3
More than 40 hours	1.5	2.0	1.0	1.5	1.7	1.4	0.8	0.7	2.2	1.4	1.6	1.0	1.3	1.4	1.8
Most recent type of work for employed students															
Total	100.0	100.0	100.0	100.0	100.0	100.0	100.0	100.0	100.0	100.0	100.0	100.0	100.0	100.0	100.0
Lawn work or odd jobs	2.2	4.2	0.3	2.5	0.8	0.9	1.7	5.3	2.3	2.0	2.1	2.5	1.3	2.2	2.9
Food service	24.0	22.2	25.7	22.8	34.8	24.8	22.9	24.6	28.0	26.6	25.1	18.6	23.6	23.1	25.4
Delivery person	1.6	2.5	0.6	1.5	1.9	1.1	3.2	1.3	0.8	1.7	1.3	2.1	1.5	1.7	1.5
Babysitter or child care	4.3	0.6	7.9	4.8	2.4	2.2	5.0	1.1	3.2	3.9	4.5	5.4	4.9	4.4	3.9
Camp counselor/life guard	0.7	0.8	0.7	0.9	0.0	0.5	0.6	0.0	0.2	0.3	0.9	1.3	0.8	0.9	0.5
Farm worker	2.2	4.4	0.1	2.7	0.0	1.1	0.0	0.0	3.7	3.3	1.6	1.1	0.2	1.1	5.5
Mechanic	1.4	2.8	0.0	1.5	0.7	1.5	1.0	1.4	2.0	1.8	1.5	0.6	1.0	1.3	1.9
Grocery clerk or cashier	14.5	12.5	16.4	14.8	15.9	11.6	8.5	25.7	15.5	16.6	14.5	12.3	14.2	13.4	16.4
Beautician	0.2	0.1	0.3	0.1	1.1	0.3	0.0	0.0	0.6	0.2	0.2	0.1	0.2	0.2	0.3
House cleaning	0.9	0.7	1.1	0.8	0.8	2.0	0.6	0.0	1.5	0.6	1.2	0.6	0.7	0.6	1.4
Construction	2.0	4.0	0.1	2.1	1.0	1.9	0.9	2.0	2.6	2.3	1.9	1.4	1.4	1.8	2.7
Office or clerical	6.9	2.9	10.7	6.3	9.2	8.7	12.1	5.8	6.3	6.0	7.2	8.0	9.0	6.8	5.4
Health services	1.6	0.9	2.3	1.6	2.1	1.1	1.0	4.5	2.5	2.0	1.4	0.9	1.5	1.6	1.7
Salesperson	11.8	9.8	13.7	12.0	8.7	11.9	15.0	7.9	7.2	8.8	12.5	15.8	13.4	14.1	7.3
Warehouse worker	2.1	3.9	0.4	2.2	1.3	1.7	2.0	2.3	1.7	2.5	1.9	2.1	2.0	2.3	1.9
Other	23.5	27.7	19.6	23.5	19.3	28.8	25.4	18.3	22.0	21.4	22.3	27.4	24.4	24.6	21.3
Most recent hourly wage for employed students															
Total	100.0	100.0	100.0	100.0	100.0	100.0	100.0	100.0	100.0	100.0	100.0	100.0	100.0	100.0	100.0
Less than $4.25 per hour	9.9	7.2	12.4	10.3	8.3	8.8	7.9	5.8	12.2	11.4	9.0	8.0	7.9	7.5	14.8
$4.25 to $6.00 per hour	77.5	75.6	79.2	76.7	80.9	81.1	77.0	79.3	79.0	76.8	80.0	74.8	80.1	77.0	75.8
$6.01 to $8.00 per hour	7.7	10.3	5.3	8.0	5.8	6.1	10.7	6.7	5.3	8.3	6.8	9.3	7.3	9.2	6.1
$8.01 or more per hour	5.0	6.9	3.2	5.1	5.0	4.0	4.5	8.3	3.5	3.5	4.1	7.9	4.8	6.3	3.4

[1] Socioeconomic status was measured by a composite score on parental education and occupations, and family income. The "Low" SES group is the lowest quartile.

SOURCE: U.S. Department of Education, National Center for Education Statistics, "National Education Longitudinal Study of 1988," Second Followup survey. (This table was prepared August 1995.)

Table 383.—Full-time employment status of bachelor's degree recipients 1 year after graduation, by field of study: 1976 to 1991

Field of study	Percent employed full-time						Percent employed full-time in a job closely related to field of study						Percent employed full-time in nonprofessional job[1]					
	1974–75 graduates in May 1976	1979–80 graduates in May 1981	1983–84 graduates in June 1985	1985–86 graduates in June 1987	1989–90 graduates in April 1991	1974–75 graduates in May 1976	1979–80 graduates in May 1981	1983–84 graduates in June 1985	1985–86 graduates in June 1987	1989–90 graduates in April 1991	1974–75 graduates in May 1976	1979–80 graduates in May 1981	1983–84 graduates in June 1985	1985–86 graduates in June 1987	1989–90 graduates in April 1991
1	2	3	4	5	6	7	8	9	10	11	12	13	14	15	16
Total	67	71	73	74	74	35	38	38	38	39	10	12	13	14	13
Professional/technical fields	77	80	82	81	80	51	51	47	47	48	9	10	13	11	11
Arts and sciences fields	56	56	56	62	64	18	17	15	25	26	12	14	15	15	14
Other	65	74	75	74	73	36	43	47	36	38	9	19	12	17	13
Newly qualified to teach	66	75	73	68	74	43	56	54	47	58	7	8	9	9	6
Not newly qualified to teach	67	71	73	74	73	33	36	36	37	36	12	13	13	14	14
Professional/technical fields	80	81	82	82	83	52	49	47	47	48	10	10	13	11	12
Engineering	79	84	84	83	84	57	55	53	46	50	4	2	3	5	3
Business and management	84	83	85	85	83	49	44	41	40	42	15	14	19	17	16
Health	75	77	75	76	86	71	66	70	65	83	2	4	2	3	1
Education[2]	66	67	63	73	67	22	29	24	57	39	12	18	16	9	11
Public affairs and services	—	77	74	72	66	—	46	31	37	49	—	10	15	20	9
Arts and sciences fields	57	56	56	63	64	17	16	15	25	23	13	15	15	15	15
Biological sciences	56	45	43	42	50	26	18	17	15	26	6	8	11	11	8
Physical sciences and mathematics[3]	50	58	51	76	72	19	29	20	48	48	6	2	7	9	7
Psychology	61	56	57	66	59	22	17	12	22	22	18	17	16	19	14
Social sciences	59	61	61	61	68	12	10	13	12	16	15	21	14	17	20
Humanities	56	55	59	59	59	12	14	17	19	11	17	18	19	19	21
Other	68	71	77	75	73	36	43	42	36	37	10	20	14	21	14
Communications	—	71	76	77	75	—	31	31	33	29	—	24	16	18	17
Miscellaneous	66	76	77	74	73	35	46	46	38	38	11	19	13	23	13

[1] Includes those not working in technical, managerial, or administrative types of jobs who reported that they did not need a college degree to obtain their job.
[2] Includes those who have not finished all requirements for teaching certification or were previously qualified to teach.
[3] Includes computer sciences.
—Data not available.

NOTE.—Data are from sample surveys of recent college graduates. Notes on methodology are included in the Guide to Sources. Data exclude bachelor's recipients from U.S. Service Schools. Deceased graduates and graduates living at foreign addresses at the time of the survey are not included.

SOURCE: U.S. Department of Education, National Center for Education Statistics, "Recent College Graduates" surveys. (This table was prepared August 1993.)

428 OUTCOMES OF EDUCATION

Table 384.—Employment status of 1992–93 bachelor's degree recipients 1 year after graduation, by field of study and occupational area: 1994
[Percentage distribution]

Status in April 1994	All fields of study	Professional/technical fields					Arts and sciences						Other fields
		Business and management	Education	Engineering	Health professions	Public affairs and social services	Biological sciences	Mathematics, computer, and physical sciences	Social sciences	History	Humanities	Psychology	
1	2	3	4	5	6	7	8	9	10	11	12	13	14
Total 1992–93 graduates	100.0	100.0	100.0	100.0	100.0	100.0	100.0	100.0	100.0	100.0	100.0	100.0	100.0
Time between high school graduation and degree completion													
4 years or less	31.1	27.5	28.0	21.4	18.0	24.3	47.7	35.0	45.1	43.2	34.3	36.6	29.9
More than 4, up to 5 years	27.6	27.2	30.9	35.2	26.2	28.3	22.7	22.8	24.7	19.3	26.0	26.5	30.3
More than 5, up to 6 years	11.2	9.4	10.5	16.2	12.7	11.9	11.7	10.1	10.1	16.8	11.0	7.2	13.3
More than 6, up to 10 years	12.7	13.3	12.1	13.4	15.1	14.5	6.8	16.1	12.7	6.5	14.1	9.8	11.7
More than 10 years	17.4	22.6	18.5	13.8	28.1	21.0	11.1	15.9	7.4	14.3	14.6	20.0	14.7
Enrollment status in April 1994													
Enrolled full-time	12.0	5.0	10.9	14.6	10.5	8.7	26.6	20.5	14.4	18.2	14.2	18.4	10.5
Enrolled part-time	5.8	4.7	8.2	6.6	6.8	5.4	8.6	4.5	4.9	5.3	5.1	9.9	4.5
Not enrolled	82.2	90.3	80.9	78.8	82.7	85.9	64.9	75.1	80.7	76.6	80.7	71.7	85.0
Employed	87.0	92.4	89.4	85.0	88.7	87.8	68.8	81.6	85.5	86.1	84.3	81.4	88.3
Full time	73.1	84.7	68.3	75.8	73.4	74.6	51.6	67.8	72.5	71.7	64.1	66.9	74.6
Part time	13.9	7.7	21.1	9.2	15.3	13.2	17.3	13.9	12.9	14.4	20.2	14.5	13.8
Unemployed [1]	4.5	3.6	3.4	6.2	4.5	4.6	7.4	4.9	4.8	5.4	4.9	5.1	4.5
Not in labor force [2]	8.5	3.9	7.3	8.8	6.7	7.6	23.8	13.5	9.8	8.5	10.8	13.6	7.2
Unemployment experiences since graduation													
Experienced any unemployment	28.7	27.2	34.0	33.1	19.1	26.8	28.3	25.7	31.3	34.8	30.0	23.8	28.8
Average number of consecutive months unemployed	5.1	5.4	4.6	5.7	5.1	5.1	5.7	5.8	5.1	5.0	4.8	5.8	4.6
April 1994 unemployment rate [3]	4.9	3.8	3.6	6.8	4.9	4.9	9.7	5.7	5.3	5.9	5.5	5.8	4.8
Total employed	100.0	100.0	100.0	100.0	100.0	100.0	100.0	100.0	100.0	100.0	100.0	100.0	100.0
Occupation													
Business management	20.1	31.4	9.2	12.2	7.2	16.3	9.3	8.0	26.4	23.9	16.7	25.6	26.9
School teacher	11.7	1.2	57.1	1.5	2.0	1.2	7.7	11.9	3.2	15.1	11.3	6.9	6.0
Engineering	4.4	0.5	(⁴)	54.3	1.5	(⁴)	0.7	6.9	(⁴)	(⁴)	1.0	(⁴)	1.7
Health professions	5.8	(⁴)	1.5	(⁴)	60.2	1.4	6.6	1.3	1.0	0.5	1.3	5.0	1.9
Other profession [5]	15.5	19.6	7.0	2.7	5.3	27.5	14.5	11.3	15.5	12.6	24.5	19.5	20.2
Computer science/programming	3.9	3.9	0.8	7.9	0.7	0.6	3.4	25.9	2.3	1.4	3.4	1.5	1.7
Non-computer technician	3.0	1.1	0.7	5.4	7.9	1.7	15.9	4.7	1.7	1.4	1.1	2.9	3.4
Administrative/clerical/support	17.9	23.6	13.3	5.1	7.4	15.4	16.8	16.6	26.7	18.0	21.3	22.2	16.2
Mechanic operator/laborer	4.1	3.2	2.4	5.9	1.2	4.1	8.1	4.8	3.4	3.8	5.1	2.2	6.7
Sales	7.1	11.7	2.5	2.1	2.3	4.4	9.0	4.6	10.0	7.7	7.8	4.4	7.9
Service	4.2	2.4	4.5	1.3	3.7	5.4	6.2	3.0	5.5	6.8	5.4	8.7	5.4
Military/protective service	2.3	1.1	0.7	1.5	0.6	21.9	2.1	1.1	4.3	8.9	1.2	0.7	2.1
Job characteristics in April 1994													
Definite/possible career potential	72.0	77.2	75.4	81.5	80.0	67.8	57.4	75.1	68.0	66.5	65.5	52.6	67.6
Bachelor's degree required to obtain job	55.9	51.4	65.7	78.6	73.0	49.4	48.8	67.7	46.5	41.2	44.6	45.3	51.5
Job related to bachelor's degree	75.1	85.1	78.5	87.4	90.5	71.6	64.3	82.3	57.2	41.6	58.2	57.3	73.6
Annual salaries [6]													
Less than $5,000	1.0	0.4	1.3	0.6	1.0	0.6	1.5	0.2	0.7	5.9	1.5	1.5	1.6
$5,000 to $9,999	3.5	1.7	5.8	0.8	3.1	1.8	3.7	3.5	4.8	6.8	5.7	7.4	3.4
$10,000 to $14,999	17.8	12.5	29.8	3.4	6.3	24.7	26.3	14.5	19.3	21.1	24.3	25.4	19.5
$15,000 to $19,999	17.3	14.9	21.3	4.5	5.5	24.6	17.6	12.8	20.2	19.2	17.9	22.4	26.1
$20,000 to $24,999	22.7	22.5	27.5	12.6	13.6	21.4	24.2	20.2	28.1	16.9	27.5	23.4	23.1
$25,000 to $34,999	24.5	31.1	10.9	46.2	38.1	16.9	19.9	32.1	20.1	22.8	14.4	14.7	19.1
$35,000 to $49,000	9.9	11.8	2.0	30.4	24.1	7.6	3.9	14.2	4.2	2.5	7.3	4.8	4.4
$49,999 to $74,999	2.5	3.9	0.9	1.2	7.8	2.0	1.8	2.1	1.7	4.8	0.8	0.4	1.8
$75,000 or more	0.7	1.1	0.4	0.4	0.6	0.4	1.1	0.4	0.9	0.0	0.5	0.0	0.8
Average annual salary [7]	$24,195	$27,069	$19,280	$30,948	$31,302	$22,042	$22,763	$25,414	$22,082	$21,047	$21,307	$19,463	$21,619

[1] Percent not working, but looking for work.
[2] Percent not working and not looking for work.
[3] Excluding those not in the labor force.
[4] Less than 0.5 percent.
[5] All other professional occupations excluding business, teaching, engineering, and health.
[6] Salaries for those employed full-time in April 1994.
[7] Respondents reporting salaries less than $1,000 or more than $500,000 were excluded.

NOTE.—Because of rounding, details may not add to totals.
SOURCE: U.S. Department of Education, National Center for Education Statistics, "Baccalaureate and Beyond Longitudinal Study, First Follow-up" survey. (This table was prepared August 1997.)

Table 385.—Percentage of 1992–93 bachelor's degree recipients pursuing further education within one year after graduation, by type of enrollment and undergraduate major: April 1994

Undergraduate major field of study	Ever enrolled since graduation	Enrolled full-time	Enrolled part-time	Enrolled and employed	Enrolled and not employed	Enrolled in degree program beyond bachelor's
1	2	3	4	5	6	7
All graduates	27.3	12.0	5.8	—	—	17.0
Professional fields	23.5	8.6	6.1	—	—	14.2
Engineering	28.3	14.6	6.6	7.0	8.1	20.8
Business and management	15.7	5.0	4.7	13.9	8.9	8.8
Health professions	23.9	10.5	6.8	7.8	6.1	14.7
Education	33.9	10.9	8.2	15.2	11.3	19.9
Public affairs and social services	24.7	8.7	5.4	2.7	2.9	13.8
Arts and sciences fields	34.5	17.5	5.9	—	—	22.5
Biological sciences	50.0	26.6	8.6	6.4	13.2	32.6
Mathematics and other sciences	36.0	20.5	4.5	6.7	10.3	25.0
Psychology	38.0	18.4	9.9	5.8	5.7	24.0
Social sciences	31.2	14.4	4.9	10.0	10.4	19.6
History	38.4	18.2	5.3	2.1	2.7	28.8
Humanities	27.5	14.2	5.1	10.1	10.1	17.5
Other	23.6	10.5	4.5	12.2	10.4	14.0
Highest degree graduate expects to obtain						
Bachelor's degree	8.5	1.1	2.0	—	—	0.5
Postbaccalaureate certificate	31.7	5.3	0.8	—	—	11.5
Master's degree	22.9	7.4	6.0	—	—	12.8
Doctor's degree	50.5	29.5	8.6	—	—	38.6
First-professional degree	52.3	34.8	6.3	—	—	41.7
Other degree	31.0	11.9	8.7	—	—	15.1

—Data not available.

NOTE.—Data are from a sample survey of recent college graduates. Notes on methodology are included in the Guide to Sources.

SOURCE: U.S. Department of Education, National Center for Education Statistics, "Baccalaureate and Beyond Longitudinal Study, First Follow-up" survey. (This table was prepared July 1997.)

Table 386.—Average annual salary of bachelor's degree recipients employed full-time 1 year after graduation, by field of study: 1976 to 1994

Field of study	Average salary[1] of 1974–75 degree recipients in February 1976		Average salary[1] of 1979–80 degree recipients in May 1981		Average salary[1] of 1983–84 degree recipients in June 1985		Average salary of 1985–86 degree recipients in June 1987		Average salary of 1989–90 degree recipients in June 1991		Average salary of 1992–93 degree recipients in April 1994	Percent change in constant dollars, 1976 to 1994	Percent change in constant dollars, 1991 to 1994
	Current dollars	Constant 1994 dollars	Current dollars	Constant 1994 dollars	Current dollars	Constant 1994 dollars	Current dollars	Constant 1994 dollars	Current dollars	Constant 1994 dollars			
1	2	3	4	5	6	7	8	9	10	11	12	13	14
Total	$7,600	$19,800	$15,200	$24,800	$17,700	$24,400	$20,400	$26,500	$23,600	$25,700	$24,200	22.2	−5.8
Engineering	12,200	31,800	22,400	36,500	24,100	33,200	26,600	34,700	30,900	33,600	30,900	−2.8	−8.0
Business and management	10,200	26,600	16,300	26,600	18,700	25,800	21,100	27,500	24,700	26,900	27,100	1.9	0.7
Health professions	8,600	22,400	17,300	28,200	20,800	28,600	22,600	29,400	31,500	34,200	31,300	39.7	−8.5
Education[2]	6,300	16,400	11,500	18,700	13,800	19,000	15,800	20,600	19,100	20,800	19,300	17.7	−7.2
Public affairs and social services	—	—	13,700	22,300	15,100	20,800	17,700	23,100	20,800	22,600	22,700	—	0.4
Biological sciences	6,500	16,900	14,500	23,600	15,100	20,800	16,400	21,400	21,100	22,900	25,400	50.3	10.9
Mathematics and other sciences	7,000	18,200	16,300	26,600	17,500	24,100	22,500	29,400	27,200	29,500	19,400	6.6	−34.2
Psychology	—	—	12,500	20,400	14,600	20,100	17,300	22,600	19,200	20,800	22,100	—	6.3
Social sciences	6,700	17,500	14,000	22,800	15,800	21,800	20,300	26,500	22,200	24,200	21,300	21.7	−12.0
History	—	—	—	—	—	—	—	—	—	—	21,000	—	—
Humanities	5,800	15,100	12,600	20,500	14,000	19,300	16,200	21,200	19,100	20,700	21,300	41.1	2.9
Communications[3]	—	—	—	—	16,200	22,300	—	—	—	—	—	—	—
Miscellaneous	6,800	17,700	15,100	24,600	18,600	25,600	17,600	23,000	20,800	22,600	21,600	22.0	−4.4

[1] Reported salaries of full-time workers under $2,600 in 1976, $4,200 in 1981, and $5,000 in 1985 were excluded from the tabulations.
[2] Most educators work 9- to 10-month contracts.
[3] In 1994, data was not collected in Communications as a separate field of study.
—Data not available.

NOTE.—Data exclude bachelor's recipients from U.S. Service Schools and graduates living at foreign addresses at the time of the survey. Constant dollar adjustments based on the Consumer Price Index.

SOURCE: U.S. Department of Education, National Center for Education Statistics, "Recent College Graduates" surveys and "Baccalaureate and Beyond Longitudinal Study, First Follow-up" survey. (This table was prepared July 1997).

Table 387.—Participation of young adults in voluntary or community service activities, by selected characteristics: 1992 to 1994

Young adult characteristics	Any activity	Percent participating in voluntary or community service activity								Percentage distribution of volunteer hours per week				
		Sports teams or clubs	Church activities	Union, farm, trade, or professional associations	Educational organizations	Youth organizations	Political clubs	Organized volunteer work[1]	Other voluntary group	None[2]	Less than 2 hours	2 to 4 hours	4 to 6 hours	6 hours or more
1	2	3	4	5	6	7	8	9	10	11	12	13	14	15
							1992 to 1994[3]							
Total	37.2	7.2	11.8	1.8	6.0	10.3	3.0	10.4	7.3	62.7	15.2	7.9	5.8	8.3
Sex														
Male	36.8	9.5	11.1	1.9	4.6	11.2	2.9	8.3	7.3	63.2	14.7	7.7	5.6	8.8
Female	37.9	4.9	12.7	1.6	7.1	9.4	3.2	12.6	7.3	62.2	15.8	8.2	6.1	7.9
Race/ethnicity														
White, non-Hispanic	38.5	7.5	11.3	2.0	5.8	10.3	3.1	11.6	7.8	61.5	17.1	8.0	5.5	7.9
Black, non-Hispanic	35.9	6.3	15.8	1.1	6.4	11.5	3.1	5.8	6.2	64.1	9.6	8.1	7.7	10.6
Hispanic	31.7	6.3	11.2	0.8	6.5	9.6	2.3	6.7	5.4	68.4	9.8	7.3	6.0	8.5
Asian	35.8	5.7	10.5	1.4	7.1	8.1	3.4	13.0	8.4	64.2	14.9	8.7	4.3	8.0
American Indian	34.1	12.1	14.6	3.6	6.1	11.9	3.8	5.1	3.9	65.9	8.7	6.3	8.1	11.1
Socioeconomic status														
Low	26.4	5.0	10.4	0.9	4.0	7.4	1.5	5.9	5.0	73.6	8.2	5.8	4.5	7.9
Low-middle	30.4	6.3	10.8	1.3	3.9	8.3	2.1	7.1	6.3	69.6	11.0	6.0	5.9	7.5
High-middle	38.6	7.0	13.0	2.0	5.8	10.9	3.3	9.2	7.5	61.4	16.9	7.9	6.1	7.8
High	51.1	9.2	14.7	2.7	9.7	14.2	4.9	18.0	10.3	48.9	24.6	11.4	5.9	9.2

[1] E.g., hospital volunteer.
[2] Not a volunteer.
[3] Sample survey in 1994 based on people who were high school seniors in spring 1992. Respondents to the survey were asked about their voluntary participation in selected organizations over the previous 24-month period.

NOTE.—Some persons participated in more than one organization.

SOURCE: U.S. Department of Education, National Center for Education Statistics, "National Education Longitudinal Study, Third Followup." (This table was prepared July 1995.)

OUTCOMES OF EDUCATION 431

Table 388.—Literacy skills of adults, 16 years old and over, by selected characteristics: 1992

Selected characteristics	Prose literacy[1]							Document literacy[2]							Quantitative literacy[3]						
	Average score	Percent of adults with proficiency at level						Average score	Percent of adults with proficiency at level						Average score	Percent of adults with proficiency at level					
		1	2	3	4	5			1	2	3	4	5			1	2	3	4	5	
1	2	3	4	5	6	7		8	9	10	11	12	13		14	15	16	17	18	19	
Total	272	21	27	32	17	3		267	23	28	31	15	3		271	22	25	31	17	4	
Sex																					
Male	272	22	26	31	18	4		269	23	27	31	17	3		277	21	23	31	20	5	
Female	273	20	28	33	17	3		265	23	30	31	14	2		266	23	28	31	15	3	
Age																					
16 to 18 years old	271	16	35	38	11	1		274	15	34	38	12	1		268	20	35	33	12	1	
19 to 24 years old	280	14	29	37	18	2		280	14	29	37	18	2		277	16	28	37	16	2	
25 to 39 years old	284	15	24	34	22	5		282	16	25	35	21	4		283	17	23	33	21	5	
40 to 54 years old	286	15	23	34	22	5		278	17	27	33	19	3		286	16	22	33	23	6	
55 to 64 years old	260	26	31	30	12	1		249	30	34	26	8	1		261	25	30	30	13	2	
65 years old and older	230	44	32	19	5	1		217	53	32	13	2	0		227	45	26	20	7	2	
Race/ethnicity																					
White	286	14	25	36	21	4		280	16	27	34	19	3		287	14	24	35	21	5	
Black	237	38	37	21	4	0		230	43	36	18	3	0		224	46	34	17	3	0	
Asian or Pacific Islander	242	36	25	25	12	2		245	34	25	28	12	2		256	30	23	27	16	4	
American Indian	254	25	39	28	7	1		254	27	37	29	7	0		250	33	32	28	7	1	
Hispanic, Mexican	206	54	25	16	5	0		205	54	25	16	4	0		205	54	25	17	4	0	
Hispanic, Cuban	211	53	24	17	6	1		212	48	30	18	4	0		223	46	20	25	6	3	
Hispanic, Puerto Rican	218	47	32	17	3	0		215	49	29	18	3	0		212	51	28	17	3	1	
Hispanic, Central/South American	207	56	22	17	4	1		206	53	25	16	4	0		203	53	25	18	4	0	
Hispanic, other	260	25	27	33	13	2		254	28	26	32	12	2		246	31	25	31	11	1	
Highest level of education																					
Still in high school	271	16	36	37	11	0		274	15	35	38	12	1		269	19	35	32	12	1	
0 to 8 years	177	75	20	4	0	0		170	79	18	3	0	0		169	76	18	5	1	0	
9 to 12 years	231	42	38	17	2	0		227	46	37	15	2	0		227	45	34	17	3	0	
GED	268	14	39	39	7	0		264	17	42	34	7	0		268	16	38	35	10	1	
High school diploma	270	16	36	37	10	1		264	20	38	33	9	1		270	18	33	37	12	1	
Some college	294	8	23	45	22	3		290	9	27	42	20	2		295	8	23	42	23	4	
Associate degree	308	4	19	41	32	4		299	6	23	43	25	3		307	4	19	43	29	5	
Bachelor's degree	322	4	11	35	40	10		314	4	15	37	36	8		322	4	12	35	38	12	
Graduate studies/degree	336	2	7	28	47	16		326	3	10	34	41	12		334	2	9	30	42	17	
Region																					
Northeast	270	22	28	31	16	3		264	24	29	30	14	2		267	24	25	31	16	4	
Midwest	279	16	28	35	18	3		274	19	30	33	16	2		280	17	26	34	19	4	
South	267	23	28	30	15	3		262	26	29	29	14	2		265	25	27	29	15	4	
West	276	20	23	33	21	4		271	22	24	32	18	3		276	20	22	32	20	5	
Prison population	246	31	37	26	6	0		240	33	38	25	4	0		236	40	32	22	6	1	

[1] Prose literacy is the ability to understand and use information contained in various kinds of textual material. A level 1 score of 0 to 225 requires the reader to locate a single piece of information in a short text. A level 2 score of 226 to 275 requires the reader to locate a single piece of information in the text with several distractors or to make low-level inferences. A level 3 score of 276 to 325 requires the reader to make literal or synonymous matches between the text and information given in the task, or to make low-level inferences. A level 4 score of 326 to 375 requires the reader to perform multiple-feature matches and to integrate or synthesize information from complex passages. A level 5 score of 376 to 500 requires the reader to search for information in dense text which contains a number of distractors.

[2] Document literacy reflects the knowledge and skills used to process information from documents. A level 1 score of 0 to 225 requires the reader to locate pieces of information based on a literal match. A level 2 score of 226 to 275 requires the reader to match a single piece of information among several distractors. A level 3 score of 276 to 325 requires the reader to integrate multiple pieces of information from one or more documents. A level 4 score of 326 to 375 requires the performance of multiple-feature matches, cycling through documents, and integrating information. A level 5 score of 376 to 500 requires the reader to search through complex displays that contain multiple distractors, to make high-level text-based inferences.

[3] Quantitative literacy is the ability to perform numerical operations in everyday life. A level 1 score of 0 to 225 requires the reader to perform a single, relatively simple, arithmetic operation. A level 2 score of 226 to 275 requires the reader to perform a single operation using numbers that are either stated in the task or easily located in the material. A level 3 score of 276 to 325 requires the reader to use two or more numbers to solve the problem. A level 4 score of 326 to 375 requires the reader to perform two or more sequential operations or a single operation in which the quantities are found in different types of displays. A level 5 score of 376 to 500 requires the reader to perform multiple operations sequentially. They must extract the features of the problem from text or rely on background knowledge to determine the quantities or operations needed.

SOURCE: U.S. Department of Education, National Center for Education Statistics, National Adult Literacy Survey, *Adult Literacy in America, 1992*, prepared by Educational Testing Service. (This table was prepared February 1994.)

CHAPTER 6
International Comparisons of Education

This chapter offers a broad perspective on education across the nations of the world. It also provides an international context for examining the condition of education in the United States. In the early 1990s, the National Center for Education Statistics (NCES) expanded its role in collecting international data by serving as the national research center for the International Association for the Evaluation of Educational Achievement (IEA) Reading Literacy Study. In addition, NCES has provided funding for international research studies comparing mathematics and science education, including the Third International Mathematics and Science Study (TIMSS) and the Second International Assessment of Educational Progress. NCES is also cooperating with international agencies in the compilation of statistics and the development of education indicators.

Some of the data in this chapter were drawn from materials prepared by the United Nations Educational, Scientific, and Cultural Organization (UNESCO), the Institute of International Education, the Organization for Economic Cooperation and Development (OECD), and the International Assessment of Educational Progress (IAEP). The basic summary data on enrollments, teachers, enrollment ratios, and finances were synthesized from information appearing in Education at a Glance published by OECD. Even though OECD tabulations are very carefully prepared, international data users should be cautioned about the many problems of definition and reporting involved in the collection of data about the educational systems in the world. This chapter provides information from the Third International Mathematics and Science Study (TIMSS), carried out by the International Association for the Evaluation of Educational Achievement (IEA). The mathematics and science performance of 8th grade students in 41 countries, and 4th grade students in 26 countries, was studied through assessments administered during 1994–95. The mathematics and science performance of students at the end of secondary schooling (12th grade in the U.S.) was also assessed at the same time, but the results were not available in time for presentation in this edition of the Digest.

A different perspective is provided by data on foreign students enrolled in U.S. institutions of higher education. These data from the Institute of International Education provide information on the number of foreign students and their countries of origin.

Further information on survey methodologies is in the "Guide to Sources" in the appendix and in the publications cited in the source notes.

Population

The percent of young people in a population can influence the proportion of national income spent per student. Countries with a greater proportion of young people must set aside larger proportions of domestic product for their education. Among the OECD countries, Turkey had the largest percentage of young people ages 5 to 13 at 19.7 percent in 1995. The closest followers were Ireland at 15.2 percent, and Korea at 14.5 percent. Countries with relatively small numbers of persons in this age group included Italy at 9.1 percent, and Denmark at 9.7 percent. The proportion of 5- to 13-year-olds in the U.S was 13.0 percent, which was higher than most other OECD countries (table 386).

Enrollments

In 1994, over 1 billion students were enrolled in schools around the world. Of these students, 639 million were in elementary-level programs, 351 million were in secondary programs, and 77 million were in higher education programs (table 388).

Between 1980 and 1994, enrollment changes varied from region to region. Elementary enrollment changes ranged from increases of 44 percent in Africa and 23 percent in Central and South America to a 2 percent decrease in Europe. Enrollment increases at the secondary level generally outpaced increases at the primary (elementary) level, especially in Africa (105 percent), Central and South America (46 percent), and Asia (42 percent). Secondary-level enrollment decreased in Europe by 1 percent, and in Northern America (U.S., Canada, and Greenland) by 3 percent (table 391).

Pupil/teacher ratios in elementary and secondary schools vary from country to country. Developed countries with relatively low pupil/teacher ratios at the elementary level in 1994 were Italy (10.2) and Denmark (11.0). Countries with relatively high ratios included Turkey (27.4) and Ireland (24.3) (table 393).

At the postsecondary level, developing areas of the world had substantial increases in enrollment between 1980 and 1994. Postsecondary enrollment rose by 135 percent in Africa and by 105 percent in Asia. Postsecondary enrollment in Oceania and Central and South America increased by 85 percent and 60 percent, respectively, followed by Europe at 23 percent and Northern America at 22 percent. These increases are due to growth in the postsecondary attendance rates and increased population (table 391).

Postsecondary enrollment varied among countries partially due to differing definitions of postsecondary education and at what age it begins. In 1994, among the OECD countries, Canada reported the largest proportion of 18- to 21-year-olds enrolled in postsecondary education at 40 percent, followed by the United States (35 percent), France (33 percent), New Zealand (31 percent), and Ireland (31 percent). In 1994, for the 22 to 25 age group, Finland's enrollment rate was highest at 27 percent, with Norway following at 24 percent, Canada at 23 percent, Denmark at 22, and the U.S. at 21 (table 387).

In 1995–96, there were 454,000 foreign students studying at U.S. colleges and universities. This was about the same as the year before. Approximately 57 percent of the students were from South and East Asian countries (table 408).

Achievement

TIMSS is the largest, most comprehensive comparative study of education that has ever been undertaken, testing a half million students. The study was designed to focus on students at different stages in school: midway through elementary school, midway through lower secondary school, and at the end of upper secondary school. Results from the fourth and eighth grade levels were released in late 1996 and 1997, respectively. Findings for twelfth grade are scheduled for release in early 1998.

The results of the 1994–95 TIMSS show U.S. fourth graders performing above the international average in both mathematics and science, and showing a stronger standing than eighth graders in both subjects. In addition, U.S. students perform better in science overall than in mathematics compared to their international counterparts at both grade levels.

Mathematics

In the 1994–95 TIMSS assessment in mathematics, U.S. fourth graders scored above the international average of 26 countries that participated. U.S. fourth graders performed below students in 7 countries, not significantly different from students in 6 countries, and above students in 12 countries. U.S. fourth graders scored below Japan, not significantly different from Canada, and above England (table 401). U.S. eighth graders scored below the international average of the 41 countries that were tested. In mathematics, U.S. eighth graders scored below their counterparts in 20 countries, including top performer Singapore, but not significantly different from England and Germany (table 395).

U.S. fourth graders' scores were above the international average in five out of six mathematics content areas tested: whole numbers; fractions and proportionality, data representation, analysis and probability; geometry; and patterns, relations and functions. The only area in which U.S. fourth graders did less well compared to other nations was measurement, estimation, and number sense. U.S. eighth graders' performance fell at about the international average in three areas (algebra; data representation, analysis, and probability; and fractions and number) out of the 6 content areas assessed. U.S. eighth grade students performed less well compared to other nations in the other three areas: geometry; measurement; and proportionality.

Science

U.S. fourth graders performed above the international average of the 26 countries testing fourth grade students in science. Only Korea scored above the U.S., with U.S. fourth graders outperforming 19 other countries, including England and Canada. The remaining countries' scores, including Japan's, were not significantly different from those of U.S. fourth grade students (table 402). U.S. eighth graders compared more favorably with other countries in science than mathematics, scoring above the international average of 41 countries. U.S. eighth students scored below their peers in nine countries, not significantly different from 16 countries, including Canada, England, and Germany, and outperformed students in 15 nations (table 397).

U.S. fourth grade students were above the international average in all four science content areas studied by TIMSS. Among the five science content areas studied at the 8th grade level in TIMSS, U.S. students performed above the international average in earth science, life science, and environmental issues, and no different from the international average in chemistry and physics.

Degrees

Ratios of bachelor's degrees conferred per hundred 22- or 23-year-olds in 1994 ranged from 1 in Italy and 2 in Portugal to 32 in the United States and Australia. In 1994, women had higher bachelor's degree ratios than men in 13 out of 16 countries reporting data (table 405).

Countries pay careful attention to the percent of graduates in the math and science fields. For undergraduate degrees awarded in science fields (including natural sciences, mathematics, and computer science, and engineering), OECD countries reported rates from 18 to 41 percent for 1994. Germany, Finland, Belgium, Switzerland, Japan, and Austria were over 30 percent, while the United States, Canada, and New Zealand were under 20 percent (table 406). The proportion of graduate degrees awarded in science fields also ranged widely across countries. Among the countries with the highest proportions were Japan (54 percent), Sweden (44 percent), and Austria (37 percent). Among the countries with the lowest proportions were the United States (14 percent), Australia (14 percent), and New Zealand (19 percent) (table 407).

Finances

In general, higher income countries spend more per student than lower income countries. At the primary level of education, Sweden, the United States, and Switzerland ranked at the upper end of per pupil expenditures in 1993. For primary education per student, Sweden spent about $4,900 per student, the U.S. spent $5,500, and Switzerland spent about $5,800. At the secondary level, Switzerland, Austria, United States, Germany and Denmark had expenditures over $6,000 per student. Switzerland, the U.S., and Sweden spent relatively large amounts per student in higher education, with each having expenditures per student over $12,000 (table 408).

A comparison of public expenditures on education as a percent of gross domestic product (GDP) in OECD countries shows that national investment in education in 1993 ranged from 3.3 percent of GDP in Turkey to 7.6 percent in Norway (table 409).

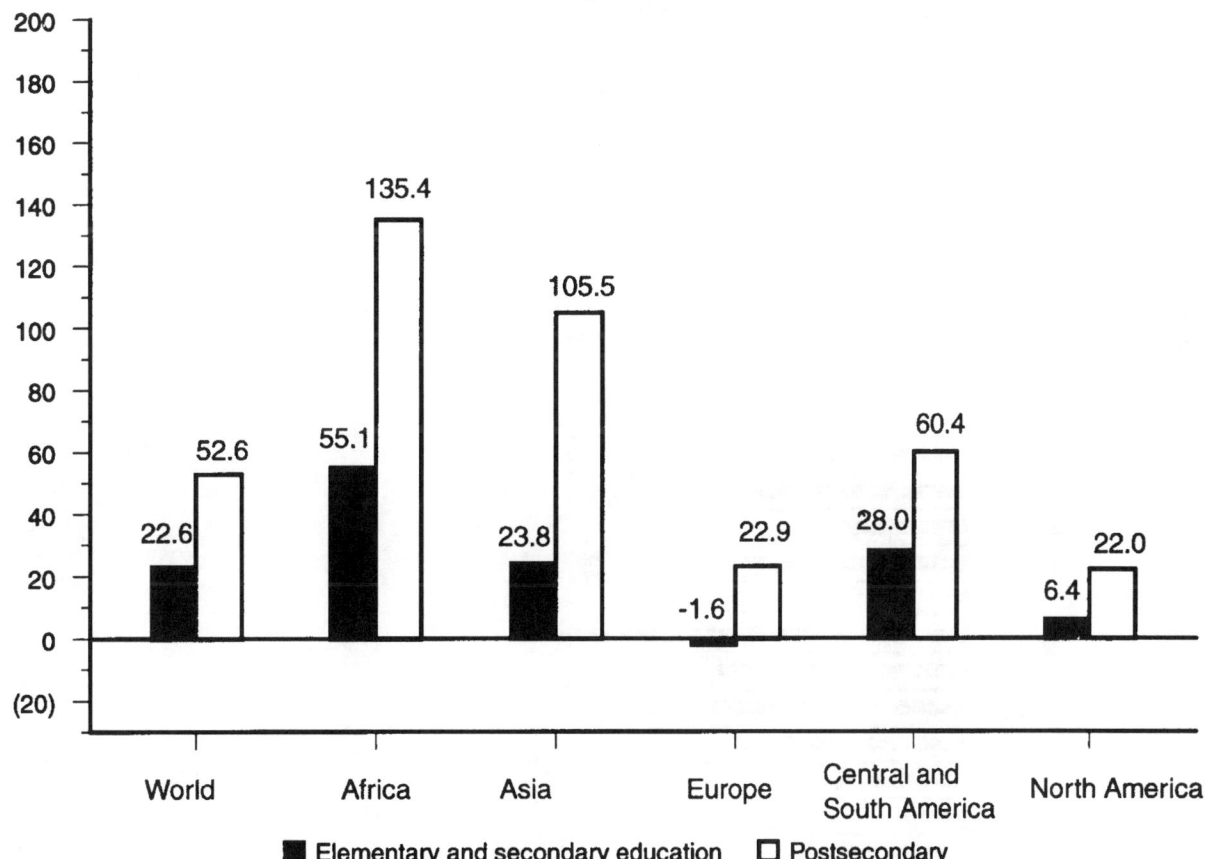

Figure 28.-Percentage change in enrollment, by area of the world and level of education: 1980 to 1994

SOURCE: United Nations Educational, Scientific, and Cultural Organization, Paris, *Statistical Yearbook*, various years.

Figure 29.-Public expenditures for education as a percentage of gross national product: Selected countries, 1993

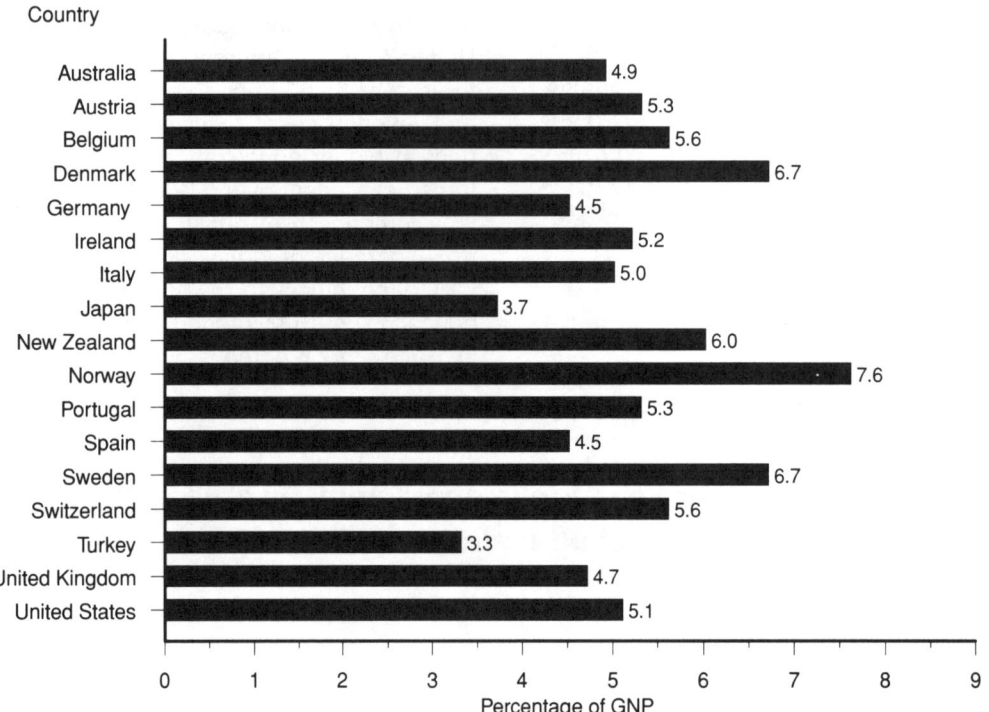

SOURCE: Organization for Economic Cooperation and Development, *Education at a Glance*, 1996; and unpublished data.

Figure 30.-Bachelor's degree recipients as a percent of population for selected countries, by sex: 1994

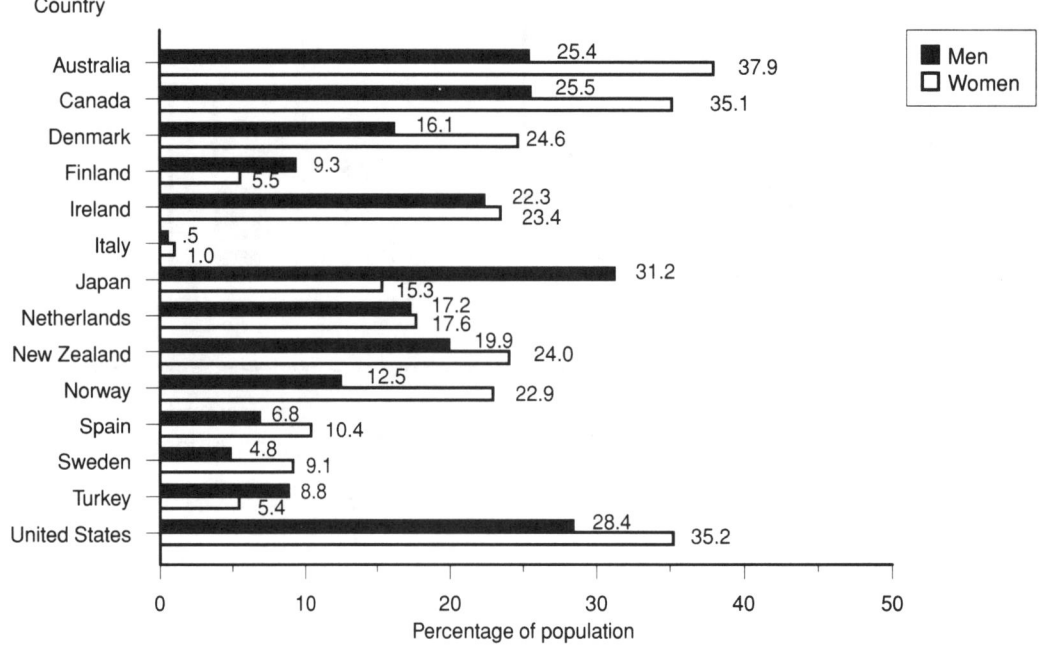

SOURCE: Organization for Economic Cooperation and Development, *Education at a Glance*, 1996.

Figure 31.-Nations' average mathematics performance compared to the United States: 1995

Fourth grade

Average scores significantly higher than the United States

Singapore
Korea
Japan
Hong Kong
(Netherlands)
Czech Republic
(Austria)

Average scores not significantly different from the United States

(Slovenia)   Canada
Ireland   (Israel)
(Hungary)
(Australia)

Average scores significantly lower than the United States

(Latvia)   Norway   Portugal
Scotland   New Zealand   Iceland
England   Greece   Iran, Islamic Republic
Cyprus   (Thailand)   (Kuwait)

Eighth grade

Average scores significantly higher than the United States

Singapore   Swtizerland   Russian Federation
Korea   (Netherlands)   (Australia)
Japan   (Slovenia)   Ireland
Hong Kong   (Bulgaria)   Canada
Belgium- Flemish   (Austria)   (Belgium-French)
Czech Republic   France   Sweden
Slovak Republic   Hungary

Average scores not significantly different from the United States

(Thailand)   Norway   Spain
(Israel)   (Denmark)   Iceland
(Germany)   (Scotland)   (Greece)
New Zealand   Latvia   (Romania)
England

Average scores significantly lower than the United States

Lithuania   (Kuwait)
Cyprus   (Colombia)
Portugal   (South Africa)
Iran, Islamic Republic

NOTE: Nations not meeting international guidelines are shown in parentheses.

SOURCE: U.S. Department of Education, National Center for Education Statistics, *Pursuing Excellence: A Study of U.S. Fourth-Grade Mathematics and Science Achievement in International Context*, 1997 and *Pursuing Excellence: A Study of U.S. Eighth-Grade Mathematics and Science Achievement in International Context*, 1996.

Figure 32.-Nations' average science performance compared to the United States: 1995

Fourth grade

Average scores significantly higher than the United States

Korea

Average scores not significantly different from the United States

Japan
(Austria)
(Australia)
(Netherlands)
Czech Republic

Average scores significantly lower than the United States

England   Hong Kong   Iceland
Canada   (Hungary)   Greece
Singapore   New Zealand   Portugal
(Slovenia)   Norway   Cyprus
Ireland   (Latvia)   (Thailand)
Scotland   (Israel)   Iran, Islamic Republic
                               (Kuwait)

Eighth grade

Average scores significantly higher than the United States

Singapore   (Bulgaria)   Hungary
Czech Republic   (Netherlands)
Japan   (Slovenia)
Korea   (Austria)

Average scores not significantly different from the United States

England   Sweden   (Thailand)
Belgium-Flemish   (Germany)   (Israel)
(Australia)   Canada   Hong Kong
Slovak Republic   Norway   Switzerland
Russian Federation New Zealand   (Scotland)
Ireland

Average scores significantly lower than the United States

Spain   Portugal   Kuwait
France   (Denmark)   Colombia
(Greece)   Lithuania   (South Africa)
Iceland   (Belgium-French)
(Romania)   Iran, Islamic Republic
Latvia   Cyprus

NOTE: Nations not meeting international guidelines are shown in partentheses.

SOURCE: U.S. Department of Education, National Center for Education Statistics, *Pursuing Excellence: A Study of U.S. Fourth-Grade Mathematics and Science Achievement in International Context*, 1997 and *Pursuing Excellence: A Study of U.S. Eighth-Grade Mathematics and Science Achievement in International Context*, 1996.

Table 389.—School-age populations as a percent of total population: Selected countries, 1985, 1990, and 1995

Country	5- to 13-year-olds as a percent of total population			14- to 17-year-olds as a percent of total population		
	1985	1990	1995	1985	1990	1995
1	2	3	4	5	6	7
Australia	14.5	13.1	12.9	6.6	6.4	5.6
Belgium	11.4	10.9	10.7	5.8	5.1	4.9
Canada	12.8	12.4	12.2	6.1	5.5	5.4
Czech Republic	—	—	11.6	—	—	6.5
Denmark	12.0	10.1	9.7	5.8	5.7	4.7
Finland	11.5	11.8	11.4	5.6	4.9	5.1
France	12.8	12.1	12.0	6.2	5.8	5.3
Germany [1]	9.1	8.7	10.0	6.1	4.1	4.3
Greece	—	—	10.7	—	5.5	5.8
Iceland	15.7	15.0	14.3	6.7	6.8	6.4
Ireland	17.9	17.5	15.2	7.7	8.0	7.8
Italy	12.7	10.3	9.1	6.5	6.0	4.8
Japan	14.0	11.8	10.2	6.2	6.5	5.4
Korea	—	—	14.5	—	—	7.1
Luxembourg	10.2	10.1	10.5	5.5	4.4	4.4
Netherlands	12.0	10.7	10.8	6.8	5.4	4.8
New Zealand	15.3	13.5	13.5	7.5	6.7	5.7
Norway	12.5	11.0	11.2	6.4	5.8	4.9
Portugal	15.3	14.3	10.9	6.9	6.8	6.1
Russian Federation	—	—	14.3	—	—	5.8
Spain	15.0	12.9	10.2	6.8	6.8	6.2
Sweden	11.3	10.2	10.8	5.4	5.2	4.6
Switzerland	10.6	10.1	10.4	5.8	4.8	4.5
Turkey	20.6	20.6	19.7	8.7	8.9	8.8
United Kingdom	11.4	11.1	11.6	6.3	5.2	4.8
United States	12.6	12.8	13.0	6.2	5.4	5.5

[1] Data for 1985 are for the former West Germany.
—Data not available.

SOURCE: Organization for Economic Cooperation and Development, *Education at a Glance*, 1996; and unpublished data. (This table was prepared July 1997.)

Table 390.—Percent of population enrolled in secondary and postsecondary institutions, by age group: Selected countries, 1985, 1990, and 1994

Country	Secondary schools, 14 to 17 years old			Postsecondary institutions								
				18 to 21 years old			22 to 25 years old			26 to 29 years old		
	1985	1990	1994	1985	1990	1994	1985	1990	1994	1985	1990	1994
1	2	3	4	5	6	7	8	9	10	11	12	13
Belgium	91.7	—	—	24.5	—	—	7.2	—	—	1.5	—	—
Canada	92.5	95.8	—	25.5	28.9	40.3	9.5	11.4	22.8	3.0	3.4	9.6
Denmark	89.9	90.0	—	7.4	7.4	9.1	16.3	17.9	22.1	8.2	9.3	10.9
Finland	89.8	98.2	—	9.3	13.6	16.6	17.3	20.7	27.3	7.9	10.2	12.2
France	93.0	95.1	—	19.4	24.6	33.2	10.0	11.8	17.0	4.3	3.9	4.6
Germany [1]	94.7	94.2	—	8.8	8.5	11.2	15.5	15.9	17.2	8.9	10.4	10.3
Ireland	83.6	87.2	—	15.2	20.3	30.5	2.8	4.3	7.9	—	—	2.4
Japan	95.7	95.7	—	—	—	—	—	—	—	—	—	—
Netherlands	93.0	92.5	—	14.4	17.9	22.1	11.9	13.4	18.4	5.7	4.7	6.2
New Zealand	74.4	84.2	—	14.9	20.8	30.9	9.6	13.8	13.9	—	—	7.2
Norway	90.0	93.2	—	8.8	14.4	17.1	13.2	18.9	23.6	5.7	8.2	10.4
Portugal	—	—	—	5.8	—	19.3	5.4	—	13.4	2.3	—	4.8
Spain	67.3	79.1	—	14.9	21.2	25.4	10.6	13.5	17.5	4.0	4.5	6.2
Sweden	91.3	91.4	—	7.9	8.7	12.3	11.3	11.4	15.3	6.5	6.1	7.2
Switzerland	88.9	89.8	—	5.7	6.4	7.6	10.6	12.1	14.2	5.2	6.4	7.1
Turkey	—	32.6	—	—	7.4	10.5	—	4.6	7.2	—	2.3	3.2
United Kingdom	77.7	83.3	—	—	16.1	23.6	—	4.7	8.4	—	—	4.4
United States [2]	92.1	92.9	—	33.0	36.2	34.9	14.5	17.1	20.9	8.2	8.5	10.4

[1] Data for 1985 are for the former West Germany.
[2] Postsecondary includes higher education only.
—Data not available.

NOTE.—Some increases in enrollment rates may be due to more complete reporting by countries.

SOURCE: Organization for Economic Cooperation and Development, *Education at a Glance*, 1996; and unpublished data. (This table was prepared May 1997.)

Table 391.—Estimated population, school enrollment, teachers, and public expenditures for education in major areas of the world: 1980, 1990, 1993, and 1994

Item	World total [1]	Major areas of the world					
		Africa [2]	Asia [3]	Europe [4]	Central and South America [5]	Northern America [5]	Oceania [6]
1	2	3	4	5	6	7	8
1980							
Population, all ages,[7] in thousands	4,444,361	475,666	2,642,110	692,997	358,440	252,461	22,687
Enrollment, all levels,[8] in thousands	858,235	80,146	494,052	132,101	87,216	59,904	4,815
First (primary) level	539,471	64,249	335,871	48,669	65,319	22,611	2,752
Second level[9]	268,187	14,355	144,495	66,810	16,967	23,914	1,647
Third level[10]	50,578	1,543	13,687	16,623	4,930	13,379	416
Teachers, all levels,[8] in thousands	38,124	2,406	19,466	8,233	3,732	4,015	272
First (primary) level	18,854	1,712	10,830	2,343	2,261	1,579	129
Second level[9]	15,525	600	7,477	4,573	1,083	1,679	112
Third level[10]	3,745	94	1,159	1,317	388	757	31
Public expenditures on education, in millions of U.S. dollars	$526,700	$22,900	$103,500	$200,600	$34,200	$155,100	$10,400
As a percent of gross national product	4.9	5.3	4.4	[11] 5.1	3.9	5.2	5.6
1990							
Population, all ages,[7] in thousands	5,284,843	632,672	3,186,447	721,739	439,719	277,838	26,428
Enrollment, all levels,[8] in thousands	977,149	108,274	564,914	131,805	104,974	61,971	5,211
First (primary) level	593,177	80,815	361,881	47,504	75,479	24,774	2,724
Second level[9]	315,412	24,509	179,989	65,408	22,079	21,569	1,859
Third level[10]	68,560	2,950	23,045	18,893	7,416	15,627	628
Teachers, all levels,[8] in thousands	46,793	3,809	24,069	9,399	5,154	4,031	331
First (primary) level	22,614	2,411	12,670	2,697	3,006	1,686	144
Second level[9]	19,216	1,241	9,680	5,180	1,520	1,450	146
Third level[10]	4,964	157	1,719	1,522	628	896	42
Public expenditures on education, in millions of U.S. dollars	$1,017,000	$26,000	$227,100	$368,000	$47,100	$330,200	$18,600
As a percent of gross national product	4.9	5.7	4.2	[11] 5.0	4.1	5.4	5.6
1993							
Population, all ages,[7] in thousands	5,543,608	688,786	3,349,520	725,679	465,065	286,867	27,691
Enrollment, all levels,[8] in thousands	1,043,315	120,300	609,095	132,564	110,291	65,478	5,586
First (primary) level	626,422	88,821	382,302	47,312	79,018	26,103	2,865
Second level[9]	341,345	27,987	199,642	65,221	23,495	23,057	1,942
Third level[10]	75,547	3,492	27,151	20,031	7,778	16,317	779
Teachers, all levels,[8] in thousands	49,613	4,196	25,563	9,817	5,459	4,231	346
First (primary) level	23,920	2,681	13,216	2,839	3,216	1,819	149
Second level[9]	20,336	1,332	10,354	5,413	1,581	1,502	154
Third level[10]	5,356	183	1,993	1,565	662	911	43
Public expenditures on education, in millions of U.S. dollars	$1,176,000	$26,200	$289,800	$391,100	$66,600	$382,100	$20,200
As a percent of gross national product	5.1	6.2	4.3	5.2	4.6	5.6	6.0
1994							
Population, all ages,[7] in thousands	5,629,635	708,288	3,403,427	726,355	473,544	289,899	28,122
Enrollment, all levels,[8] in thousands	1,067,192	125,572	622,850	134,008	113,251	65,848	5,662
First (primary) level	638,908	92,473	389,032	47,583	80,485	26,415	2,920
Second level[9]	351,098	29,466	205,694	66,003	24,856	23,107	1,972
Third level[10]	77,185	3,632	28,125	20,422	7,910	16,326	770
Teachers, all levels,[8] in thousands	50,494	4,360	25,947	10,000	5,594	4,245	348
First (primary) level	24,324	2,789	13,381	2,881	3,295	1,828	151
Second level[9]	20,681	1,378	10,517	5,504	1,623	1,505	155
Third level[10]	5,488	194	2,049	1,616	676	912	42
Public expenditures on education, in millions of U.S. dollars	$1,275,700	$26,300	$315,700	$432,700	$72,100	$405,400	$23,500
As a percent of gross national product	5.2	6.1	4.4	5.4	4.5	5.4	6.1

[1] Enrollment and teacher data exclude the Democratic People's Republic of Korea. Expenditure data exclude Albania, Cambodia, Democratic People's Republic of Korea, Lao People's Democratic Republic, Lebanon, Mongolia, Mozambique, South Africa, and Viet Nam.
[2] Excludes Rodrigues and other small islands.
[3] Excludes the former U.S.S.R., the Democratic People's Republic of Korea, and Arab states, but includes both the Asian and the European portions of Turkey.
[4] Includes the former U.S.S.R.
[5] Northern America includes Bermuda, Canada, Greenland, St. Pierre, Miquelon and the United States of America. Hawaii is included in Northern America rather than Oceania. Central and South America includes the rest of America.
[6] Includes American Samoa, Australia, Guam and New Zealand.
[7] Estimate of midyear population.
[8] Excludes special and adult education provided outside regular schools. Data prior to 1992 exclude preprimary.
[9] Includes general, teacher training and vocational education.
[10] Includes universities and other institutions of higher education.
[11] This figure is for Europe, not including the former U.S.S.R.

SOURCE: United Nations Educational, Scientific, and Cultural Organization, Paris, 1996 Statistical Yearbook, "Facts on Education, Technology, and Culture Worldwide," various years. (This table was prepared May 1997.)

Table 392.—Selected statistics for countries[1] with populations over 10 million, by continent: 1980, 1990, and 1994

Country	Population in millions			Persons per square kilometer in 1993	First level[2]					
					Enrollment in thousands			Enrollment ratio[6]		
	1980	1990	1994		1980	1990	1994	1980	1990	1994
1	2	3	4	5	6	7	8	9	10	11
World total[7]	4,444.4	5,284.8	5,629.6	42	541,484	596,697	638,908	96.1	99.6	99.5
Africa										
Algeria[8]	18.7	24.9	27.3	11	3,119	4,189	4,549	94	100	105
Angola	7.0	9.2	10.7	9	1,301	990	—	175	91	—
Cameroon	8.7	11.5	12.9	27	1,379	1,964	1,897	98	101	89
Cote D'Ivoire	8.2	12.0	13.8	43	1,025	1,415	1,612	79	71	68
Egypt[8]	43.7	56.3	61.6	62	4,663	6,964	[15]7,313	73	94	98
Ethiopia	36.4	47.4	53.4	[17]45	2,131	2,466	[9]2,284	34	31	[9]27
Ghana	10.7	15.0	16.9	71	[19]1,378	1,945	—	80	77	—
Kenya[8]	16.6	23.6	27.3	47	3,927	5,392	[9]5,643	115	95	[9]91
Madagascar[8]	9.1	12.6	14.3	24	1,724	1,571	[9]1,505	136	87	[9]73
Morocco	19.4	24.3	26.5	59	2,172	2,484	3,007	83	67	80
Mozambique[8]	12.1	14.2	15.5	19	1,387	1,260	1,302	99	66	62
Nigeria[8]	72.0	96.2	108.5	117	[21]12,117	13,607	16,191	105	85	89
South Africa	29.2	37.1	40.6	33	4,353	6,952	7,972	85	109	117
Sudan[8]	18.7	24.6	27.4	11	1,464	2,043	[9]2,377	50	50	[9]55
Uganda	13.1	17.9	20.6	86	1,292	2,470	[9]2,456	[24]50	[24]70	[9,24]67
United Republic of Tanzania	18.6	25.6	28.8	33	[25]3,368	[25]3,379	[9,25]3,737	93	70	[9]70
Zaire	27.0	37.4	42.6	18	4,196	4,562	[9]4,939	92	70	[9]68
Zimbabwe	7.1	9.9	11.0	28	1,235	2,116	[9]2,376	85	116	[9]115
Asia										
Afghanistan[8]	16.1	15.0	18.9	29	1,116	623	1,161	34	27	44
Bangladesh	88.2	108.1	117.8	818	8,240	11,940	—	61	79	—
China[8]	998.9	1,155.3	1,208.8	126	146,270	122,414	[9]124,212	113	127	[9]118
India	688.9	850.6	918.6	279	73,873	99,118	[9]108,201	83	98	[9]102
Indonesia	151.0	182.8	194.6	102	25,537	29,754	[9]29,876	107	115	[9]115
Iran, Islamic Republic of[8]	39.3	58.9	65.8	40	4,799	9,370	9,746	87	110	[9]101
Iraq	13.0	18.1	19.9	45	2,616	3,328	—	113	111	—
Japan	116.8	123.5	124.8	330	11,827	9,373	8,583	101	100	102
Kazakhstan	14.9	16.7	17.0	6	1,064	1,197	1,252	85	88	87
Korea, North (DPR)	18.3	21.8	23.5	195	—	[28]1,543	—	—	—	—
Korea, South (Republic of)	38.1	42.9	44.6	449	5,658	4,869	4,099	110	105	98
Malaysia	13.8	17.9	19.7	60	2,009	[20]2,456	[9]2,803	93	93	93
Myanmar (former Burma)	33.8	41.8	45.6	67	4,148	5,385	5,711	91	105	100
Nepal[8]	14.9	19.3	21.4	152	1,068	2,789	[9]3,092	84	103	[9]109
Pakistan	85.3	121.9	136.6	172	5,474	11,451	[9]15,532	39	56	[9]69
Philippines	48.3	60.8	66.2	221	[19]8,034	10,427	10,904	112	113	111
Saudi Arabia	9.6	16.0	17.5	8	927	1,877	[9]2,111	61	73	[9]77
Sri Lanka[8]	14.8	17.2	18.1	276	2,081	2,112	1,960	103	105	105
Syrian Arab Republic	8.7	12.3	14.2	77	1,556	2,452	2,651	100	109	103
Thailand[8]	46.7	55.6	58.2	113	7,393	6,957	5,986	99	99	87
Turkey	44.4	56.1	60.8	78	5,656	6,862	[9]6,526	96	110	[9]97
Uzbekistan	15.9	20.4	22.3	50	1,391	1,778	1,906	82	82	77
Vietnam[8]	53.7	66.7	72.9	220	7,887	8,862	10,048	109	103	114
Yemen	8.2	11.3	13.9	26	703	[30]1,671	[9]2,679	—	—	[9]83
Europe										
Belarus	9.6	10.2	10.2	49	750	615	636	104	95	97
Czechoslovakia (former)[8]	15.3	15.6	15.6	122	1,904	1,924	[33]861	92	94	—
Czech Republic	10.3	10.3	10.3	131	—	546	523	—	96	100
Slovakia	5.0	5.3	5.3	109	—	—	338	—	—	101
France	53.9	56.7	57.7	105	4,610	4,149	4,011	111	108	105
Germany[34]	78.3	79.4	81.3	228	3,636	3,431	[9]3,524	—	101	[9]97
Greece	9.6	10.2	10.4	79	901	813	[9]724	103	98	[9]95
Hungary	10.7	10.4	10.2	109	1,162	1,131	985	96	95	97
Italy	56.4	57.0	57.2	190	4,423	3,056	[9]2,863	100	97	[9]98
Netherlands[8]	14.1	15.0	15.4	377	1,333	1,082	[9]1,057	100	102	[9]97
Poland	35.6	38.1	38.3	119	4,167	5,189	5,205	100	98	99
Romania	22.2	23.2	22.9	96	3,237	1,253	1,336	102	91	94
Russian Federation	138.5	147.9	147.4	9	6,009	7,596	7,849	102	109	109
Spain	37.5	39.3	39.6	78	3,610	2,820	[9]2,448	109	107	[9]104
Ukrainian S.S.R.	50.0	51.6	51.5	85	3,592	3,991	[9,37]2,659	102	89	[9]87
United Kingdom	56.3	57.4	58.1	238	[19]4,911	[19]4,533	[9,19]5,143	103	104	[9,39]114
Yugoslavia, Federal Republic	9.5	10.2	10.8	105	—	467	[9]460	—	72	[9]70
North America										
Canada	24.6	27.8	29.1	3	2,185	2,376	[9]2,404	99	103	[9]103
Cuba[8]	9.7	10.6	11.0	99	1,469	888	1,008	106	99	104
Mexico	67.1	84.5	91.9	47	14,666	14,402	14,574	122	115	111
United States[41]	227.8	249.9	260.6	28	20,420	22,429	[9]23,694	100	105	[9]107
South America										
Argentina	28.1	32.5	34.2	12	3,917	4,965	5,126	106	106	111
Brazil[8]	121.3	148.5	159.1	19	22,598	28,944	31,220	99	109	114
Chile	11.1	13.2	14.0	19	2,185	[26]2,034	2,120	109	[26]100	99
Colombia	26.5	32.3	34.5	30	4,168	4,247	4,648	124	110	121
Ecuador	8.0	10.3	11.2	40	1,534	1,846	[17]1,987	117	116	[17]123
Peru	17.3	21.6	23.3	18	3,161	3,855	4,031	114	118	123
Venezuela	15.1	19.5	21.4	23	[44]3,158	[44]4,053	[9,44]4,217	93	96	[9]94
Oceania										
Australia	[46]14.6	[46]16.9	[46]17.9	2	1,718	1,583	1,640	112	108	107

[1] Selection based on total population for midyear 1993.
[2] First level enrollment generally consists of elementary school, grades 1–6.
[3] Second level enrollment includes general education, teacher training (at the second level), and technical and vocational education. This level generally corresponds to secondary education in the United States, grades 7–12.
[4] Third level enrollment includes college and university enrollment, and technical and vocational education beyond the high school level. There is considerable variation in reporting from country to country.
[5] In many countries, a child may be exempt from school attendance if there is no suitable school within a reasonable distance of his/her home.
[6] Data are the total enrollment of all ages in the school level divided by the population of the specific age groups which correspond to the school level. The year shown in this column is the one in which the school or academic year starts. Adjustments have been made for the varying lengths of first and second level programs. Because some countries have many students from outside the normal age range, ratios may exceed 100.
[7] Enrollment totals and ratios exclude Democratic People's Republic of Korea. Data do not include adult education or special education provided outside regular schools.
[8] Classification of first and/or second levels have been revised. Data by level may not be comparable over time.
[9] Data for 1993–94.
[10] Data exclude Ecole Nationale d'Administration et de Magistrature (ENAM).
[11] Eastern Cameroon.
[12] Data for 1986–87.
[13] Data for 1988–89.
[14] The educational system allows for other alternatives.
[15] Data do not include Al Azhar.
[16] Excludes all private institutions.
[17] Data for 1992.
[18] Data for 1985–86.
[19] Data refer to public education only.
[20] Data for 1989–90.
[21] Data for 1979.
[22] Data for 1984.
[23] Data for 1981.
[24] Data refer to government maintained and aided schools only.

Table 392.—Selected statistics for countries[1] with populations over 10 million, by continent: 1980, 1990, and 1994—Continued

Second level[3]						Third level[4]						Age for compulsory attendance[5]
Enrollment in thousands			Enrollment ratio[6]			Enrollment in thousands			Enrollment ratio[6]			
1980	1990	1994	1980	1990	1994	1980	1990	1994	1980	1990	1994	
12	13	14	15	16	17	18	19	20	21	22	23	24
264,371	314,150	351,098	46.3	51.2	55.4	51,038	68,820	77,185	12.2	13.7	15.3	—
1,028	2,176	2,473	33	61	62	79	286	—	5.9	11.4	—	6–15
191	186	—	20	12	—	2	7	—	0.4	0.8	—	7–15
234	500	[9]550	18	28	27	[10]12	33	—	1.6	3.2	—	[11]6–12
222	—	—	19	23	25	20	[12]24	—	2.9	[13]3.1	—	[14]7–13
2,929	[15]5,507	[15]6,138	50	76	77	716	[16]708	—	16.1	17.5	[9]16.9	6–11
[18]666	866	[17]721	8	13	11	14	34	—	0.4	0.8	—	7–13
693	[20]830	—	41	37	—	8	10	—	1.6	1.4	—	[14]6–14
428	[18]458	—	20	[18]21	25	13	[20]31	—	0.9	1.6	—	6–14
[21]234	—	—	[22]30	17	[9]14	23	36	—	2.6	3.1	[17]3.5	6–13
797	1,124	1,299	26	35	38	112	221	251	5.9	10.1	10.0	7–13
[23]108	160	171	5	8	7	1	[17]5	[9]5	0.1	[18]0.1	[9]0.4	[14]7–13
[21]1,865	2,908	4,451	16	23	30	150	[20]336	—	2.2	[18]3.3	—	6–12
—	2,743	3,571	[12]55	68	82	—	439	618	—	12.8	15.9	7–16
384	732	—	16	23	—	29	[20]60	—	1.7	3.0	—	7–12
87	268	[9]261	[24]5	[24]12	[24]11	6	18	[9]24	[24]0.5	[24]1.1	[13,24]1.3	
[25]79	[25]167	[9]197	3	5	5	—	[20]5	—	—	[18]0.3	—	7–13
862	[26]1,097	[9]1,341	24	[18]26	[9]24	28	[13]61	—	1.2	[13]1.9	—	6–12
75	661	[9]640	8	49	44	8	49	—	1.3	5.2	—	7–15
137	182	498	10	9	22	[12]22	24	—	—	1.7	—	7–13
2,659	3,593	—	18	19	—	240	434	—	2.8	3.9	—	6–10
56,778	51,054	[9]53,837	46	48	[9]55	[27]1,161	[27]2,147	[9]4,505	1.7	2.9	[9]3.8	[14]7–16
32,748	[18]44,485	[9]64,116	30	44	[9]49	3,545	4,951	—	5.2	6.0	—	6–14
5,722	10,965	[9]11,360	29	44	[9]45	[22]980	[26]1,773	[17]1,795	—	8.5	—	7–13
2,718	5,085	7,653	42	54	69	[18]184	[19]312	478	0.0	9.1	12.7	6–10
1,033	[18]1,191	[17]1,145	57	47	—	107	[13]210	—	8.7	12.6	—	6–12
9,558	11,026	[9]10,203	93	97	[9]98	2,412	[26]2,899	—	30.5	29.1	—	[14]6–15
1,996	2144	[9]2,020	93	98	[9]91	525	537	483	34.1	40.2	33.6	6–18
—	[28]2,468	—	—	—	—	—	[28]390	—	—	—	—	5–15
4,286	4,560	4,569	78	90	96	[29]648	1,691	2,197	14.7	38.6	50.8	6–15
1,084	[20]1,456	[26]1,567	48	58	61	58	121	[9]170	4.1	7.2	[9]9.6	[14]6–16
1,066	[18]1,284	—	22	23	30	163	[26]196	[9]235	4.7	4.3	[9]5.1	5–10
512	709	[9]910	21	31	[9]36	[19]34	94	[9]102	2.7	4.9	[9]4.8	6–11
2,166	4,345	—	14	23	—	[18]268	[20]337	—	[18]2.5	2.9	—	
2,929	4,034	4,763	64	73	80	1,276	1,709	—	24.4	27.4	[9]26.8	7–13
349	893	[9]1,199	29	44	52	62	154	[9]201	7.1	11.6	[9]13.9	
1,267	2,082	2,316	55	74	75	43	[26]55	60	2.7	5.2	6.1	5–15
604	914	929	46	52	45	140	222	[17]194	16.9	18.3	[17]17.6	6–11
1,920	2,230	3,432	29	30	49	[18]1,027	[20]952	[17]1,156	14.7	15.7	20.6	6–11
2,218	3,808	[9]4,523	35	54	[9]64	246	750	1,174	5.4	12.9	[9]19.6	6–14
2,879	3,195	3,319	106	100	93	516	603	—	28.5	30.6	[17]31.8	
—	—	—	—	—	—	115	[20]186	—	2.1	2.8	[9]3.2	6–11
73	[31]421	[9]212	—	42	33	8	[26]53	—	—	[26]4.4	—	6–15
760	968	1,025	98	93	94	340	322	[9]300	39.0	45.9	[9]42.4	[14,32]6–15
781	864	—	89	83	—	197	190	—	17.4	17.0	—	6–16
—	—	1,147	—	—	92	120	118	165	17.5	16.0	19.2	6–15
—	—	664	—	—	90	—	—	82	—	—	18.7	6–15
5,014	5,522	[9]5,737	85	99	[9]106	1,077	1,699	[9]2,083	25.3	39.6	[9]49.7	6–16
[35]8,457	7,398	[9]7,796	—	98	[9]101	1,624	2,049	[9]1,875	27.2	33.9	[9]35.6	6–18
740	851	[9]851	81	99	[9]98	121	283	[9]314	17.1	25.5	[9]42.5	[14]6–16
357	514	523	70	79	81	101	102	[9]134	14.1	14.0	[9]16.9	6–16
5,308	5,118	[9]4,716	72	79	[9]81	1,118	1,452	[9]1,682	27.0	30.8	[9]37.3	6–13
[36]1,391	1,402	[9]1,352	93	120	[9]123	360	479	[9]512	29.3	39.8	[9]47.1	[14]5–16
1,674	1,888	2,443	77	81	96	589	545	[9]748	18.1	21.7	[9]27.5	7–14
871	2,838	2,252	71	92	78	193	[20]165	[9]250	12.1	[20]8.5	[9]12.9	7–14
12,991	13,956	[9]13,732	96	94	[9]88	5,700	5,100	4,458	46.1	52.2	43.3	[14]7–17
3,977	4,755	[9]4,734	87	105	[9]113	698	1,222	[9]1,469	23.2	36.7	[9]44.1	6–15
3,406	3,408	[9]4,731	94	93	92	[38]880	[38]895	—	41.6	46.5	—	[14,32]7–15
5,342	4,336	[17]4,537	83	86	[9]94	827	1,258	[9]1,615	19.1	29.1	[9]40.6	5–16
—	788	[9]812	—	—	[9]62	—	[26]133	144	—	[26]18.0	[26]18.3	7–15
2,323	2,292	[9]2,472	88	101	[9]106	[40]1,173	1,917	[9]2,011	57.1	94.7	[9]102.9	[14]6–16
1,146	1,002	674	81	89	75	152	242	141	17.3	20.9	13.9	6–11
4,742	6,704	7,265	48	55	60	930	1,311	—	14.2	14.1	[9]13.8	6–14
[42]21,585	[42]19,270	[9,42]20,578	91	92	[9]97	12,097	13,710	[9]14,473	55.6	74.1	[9]79.7	[14]7–16
[23]1,366	2,160	2,238	56	68	67	491	[26]1,077	1,052	21.8	[26]40.7	35.8	[14]6–14
2,819	3,499	4,510	34	39	46	1,409	1,540	1,661	11.1	11.3	11.4	7–14
538	720	664	52	72	68	145	255	[43]343	12.3	[26]23.2	[9]26.7	6–13
1,733	[26]2,378	2,936	41	[17]61	64	272	[26]511	588	9.1	[17]15.5	17.5	6–12
592	[18]730	[17]814	53	55	[17]55	270	207	—	34.9	20.0	—	6–14
1,203	1,698	1,996	59	67	74	306	682	756	17.3	30.4	30.9	6–16
[45]222	[45]281	[9,45]311	21	35	[9]35	307	550	—	20.6	29.0	—	5–15
1,100	1,278	1,274	71	82	84	324	485	933	25.4	35.5	40.9	[14]6–16

[25] Data refer to Tanzania mainland only.
[26] Data for 1991–92.
[27] Includes full time students only.
[28] Data for 1987–88.
[29] Data do not include Air & Correspondence courses.
[30] Data for Former Democratic Yemen do not include schools for nomads.
[31] Former Yemen Arab Republic only.
[32] Grade levels changed for compatibility with ISCED.
[33] Data are a combination of data for the Czech Republic and Slovakia.
[34] Data include both former East and West Germany.
[35] Excludes technical education, consisting of both on the job training and school education.
[36] Data do not include apprenticeships and health care training.
[37] Enrollment data refer to grades 1–4 only since 1992–93.
[38] Excludes students enrolled in third level programs in secondary specialized schools.
[39] Includes infant classes in primary schools, previously considered as preprimary education.
[40] Excludes trade and vocational programs.

[41] Population data are from the U.S. Bureau of the Census, *Current Population Reports*, "Population Estimates." Enrollment totals and ratios are based on data compiled by the National Center for Education Statistics and the U.S. Bureau of the Census. First level includes grades 1 through 6 (ages 5–10), second level includes grades 7 through 12 (ages 11–16), and third level includes ages 20–24.
[42] Revised data series corresponding to grades 7–12.
[43] Data for 1995.
[44] Data refer to grades 1 to 9 (basic education).
[45] Data refer to grades 10 and 11.
[46] Includes Norfolk Island.
—Data not available.

NOTE.—Some data have been revised from previously published figures.

SOURCE: United Nations Educational, Scientific, and Cultural Organization (UNESCO), Paris, *Statistical Yearbook*, various years; U.S. Department of Commerce, Bureau of the Census, *Current Population Reports*, Series P-20; and U.S. Department of Education, National Center for Education Statistics, Common Core of Data and "Fall Enrollment in Institutions of Higher Education" surveys, and Integrated Postsecondary Education Data System (IPEDS), "Fall Enrollment" survey. (This table was prepared May 1997.)

Table 393.—Pupils per teacher in public and private elementary and secondary schools, by level of education: Selected countries, 1985 to 1994

Country	Elementary					Junior high schools					Senior high schools				
	1985	1990	1991	1992	1994	1985	1990	1991	1992	1994	1985	1990	1991	1992	1994
1	2	3	4	5	6	7	8	9	10	11	12	13	14	15	16
Australia[1]	[1]13.8	—	18.0	[2]18.4	18.5	—	—	—	—	—	3.2	—	—	—	—
Austria	11.3	11.6	11.6	12.2	11.9	9.2	7.7	7.6	7.7	8.3	15.2	12.4	11.9	11.6	7.8
Belgium	—	—	9.3	13.7	13.3	—	—	—	—	—	—	—	4.6	—	—
Canada	18.1	17.1	—	—	16.5	16.0	15.5	—	—	19.1	16.0	15.3	—	—	19.1
Denmark	12.7	11.2	11.1	[3]10.9	11.0	10.2	9.3	9.2	[3]9.1	9.0	14.8	13.3	12.6	[3]10.4	9.1
France	—	—	22.7	[4]20.4	19.6	—	—	—	—	—	—	—	5.6	—	—
Germany[5]	20.7	20.3	21.4	[6]19.6	20.5	16.9	14.6	14.8	[6]14.6	15.7	23.7	21.0	20.4	[6]19.0	12.0
Ireland	—	—	—	25.6	24.3	—	—	—	—	—	7.2	8.3	8.6	—	—
Italy	12.8	10.7	10.9	10.9	10.2	9.6	8.5	8.3	9.0	8.0	10.8	10.7	10.5	8.8	8.9
Japan	—	[1]20.8	[1]20.3	[7]19.8	19.2	—	18.6	17.7	[7]16.8	16.2	—	16.2	16.2	[7]16.4	15.8
Netherlands	20.2	19.2	19.0	[8]23.6	22.4	12.7	12.4	10.2	—	16.9	—	—	—	—	16.5
New Zealand	20.1	19.1	18.4	18.5	20.2	—	—	—	—	16.7	—	—	—	—	13.2
Norway	—	—	10.7	—	—	—	—	8.7	—	—	—	—	8.1	—	—
Portugal	—	—	13.3	—	12.2	—	—	0.1	—	—	—	—	5.2	—	—
Spain	26.8	21.2	19.7	21.2	19.2	21.4	18.8	17.8	17.6	18.2	15.3	14.8	14.7	15.9	14.8
Sweden	11.6	10.6	10.4	11.9	12.5	10.8	10.2	9.7	10.6	10.9	13.1	11.9	11.9	16.0	14.6
Turkey	31.1	30.6	30.5	29.3	27.4	41.3	48.4	49.7	47.5	45.6	11.0	12.1	13.1	13.2	14.1
United Kingdom	19.7	22.0	22.2	20.8	20.7	—	18.5	18.6	15.9	16.9	11.1	13.9	13.7	[9]14.8	15.1
United States	17.0	15.6	15.5	—	—	16.5	15.9	16.1	16.8	—	16.2	15.8	15.6	15.0	—

[1] Public schools only.
[2] Teachers include principals, deputy principals and senior teachers mainly involved in administrative tasks.
[3] Full-time and part-time teachers are estimates. Distribution by school level (primary and lower secondary levels) is also an estimate. Kindergartens are classified as public institutions.
[4] The number of full-time equivalent teachers does not take into account the additional hours given by teachers. In public secondary education institutions, an increase of 6.6 per cent of total full-time equivalents would be observed if the additional hours were taken into account. The number of teachers in independent private secondary education institutions are entirely estimates. About 18 per cent of all the pedagogical and support staff, and about 7 per cent of all the staff employed in education have been estimated.
[5] Data for 1985 are for the former West Germany.
[6] Most components are estimates.
[7] Principals and vice-principals are included in "Teachers" while other staff is included in "Support staff." Full-time equivalents of part-time teachers are not calculated, since there are no valid and reliable data available on the basis of which such calculations can be made.
[8] Teaching staff do not include direction staff.
[9] Figures on teachers at lower secondary education are included in upper secondary education.
—Data not available.

SOURCE: Organization for Economic Cooperation and Development, *Education at a Glance*, various years; and unpublished data. (This table was prepared April 1997.)

Table 394.—Geography proficiency of 13-year-olds in educational systems participating in the International Assessment of Educational Progress: 1991

Country	Average percent correct			
	All geography items [1]	Geographic skills and tools [2]	Physical geography items [3]	Cultural geography items [4]
1	2	3	4	5
Hungary	69.8 (0.6)	76.3 (0.5)	67.8 (0.7)	65.0 (0.7)
Slovenia	65.3 (0.6)	67.9 (0.5)	63.6 (0.7)	64.3 (0.9)
Canada [5]	63.0 (0.5)	69.5 (0.4)	61.0 (0.6)	58.2 (0.6)
Soviet Union (former) [6]	62.6 (1.1)	72.2 (0.9)	61.2 (1.0)	53.4 (1.8)
United States	61.9 (0.8)	69.4 (0.6)	58.3 (1.0)	58.1 (1.0)
Spain [7]	60.1 (0.7)	62.4 (0.9)	58.9 (0.7)	58.9 (1.1)
Korea	59.7 (0.5)	67.8 (0.5)	52.1 (0.7)	60.3 (0.6)
Ireland	58.5 (0.6)	62.7 (0.6)	59.5 (0.8)	52.3 (0.8)
Scotland	58.3 (0.6)	66.2 (0.5)	57.1 (0.8)	50.6 (0.8)

[1] All 24 geographic items.
[2] Eight items testing ability to use maps, charts, and globes.
[3] Nine items testing knowledge of location of physical features and concepts of climate.
[4] Seven items testing knowledge of cultural entities and interactions between people and their environment.
[5] Eight provinces.
[6] Schools in 14 republics where instruction is in Russian.
[7] Schools where instruction is in Spanish, in all regions except Cataluna.

NOTE.—Standard errors appear in parentheses.

SOURCE: U.S. Department of Education, National Center for Education Statistics, International Assessment of Educational Progress, *Learning About The World*, 1992. (This table was prepared May 1993.)

INTERNATIONAL COMPARISONS OF EDUCATION 443

Table 395.—Average eighth grade mathematics scores by content areas, and average time spent studying out of school, by country: 1994–95

Country	Mathematics overall	Average percent correct by content area						Distribution of daily out-of-school study time in all subjects, with mean mathematics scores							
		Fractions and number sense	Geometry	Algebra	Data representation, analysis and probability	Measurement	Proportionality	Less than 1 hour		At least 1, but less than 2 hours		At least 2, but less than 3 hours		More than 3 hours	
								Percent	Mean score	Percent	Mean score	Percent	Mean score	Percent	Mean score
1	2	3	4	5	6	7	8	9	10	11	12	13	14	15	16
International average percent correct	55 (0.1)	58 (0.1)	56 (0.1)	52 (0.2)	62 (0.1)	51 (0.1)	45 (0.2)	—	—	—	—	—	—	—	—
Australia[1]	58 (0.9)	61 (0.9)	57 (1.0)	55 (1.0)	67 (0.8)	54 (1.0)	47 (0.9)	15 (0.9)	486 (5.7)	46 (1.0)	541 (4.4)	22 (0.6)	543 (5.2)	17 (0.7)	532 (4.8)
Austria[1]	62 (0.8)	66 (0.8)	57 (1.0)	59 (0.8)	68 (0.8)	62 (1.0)	49 (0.9)	9 (0.8)	524 (6.7)	46 (1.3)	551 (4.1)	21 (0.9)	544 (4.5)	24 (1.2)	528 (5.3)
Belgium (Flemish)	66 (1.4)	71 (1.2)	64 (1.5)	63 (1.7)	73 (1.3)	60 (1.3)	53 (1.8)	2 (0.4)	[2]	25 (1.3)	552 (8.9)	28 (1.1)	592 (5.9)	45 (1.6)	560 (4.6)
Belgium (French)[1]	59 (0.9)	62 (1.0)	58 (1.0)	53 (1.1)	68 (1.0)	56 (1.0)	48 (0.9)	7 (0.8)	466 (7.4)	32 (1.0)	543 (4.6)	21 (1.3)	544 (5.5)	40 (1.5)	519 (4.5)
Bulgaria[1]	60 (1.2)	60 (1.4)	65 (1.0)	62 (1.5)	62 (1.0)	54 (1.6)	47 (1.5)	—	—	—	—	—	—	—	—
Canada	59 (0.5)	64 (0.6)	58 (0.6)	54 (0.7)	69 (0.5)	51 (0.7)	48 (0.7)	14 (1.2)	514 (5.6)	47 (1.1)	538 (2.8)	18 (0.7)	534 (3.7)	21 (1.1)	511 (3.6)
Colombia[1]	29 (0.8)	31 (0.9)	29 (0.9)	28 (0.9)	37 (1.0)	25 (1.5)	23 (0.9)	2 (0.4)	[2]	17 (1.1)	394 (5.2)	20 (1.2)	389 (3.6)	61 (1.9)	390 (3.5)
Cyprus	48 (0.5)	50 (0.6)	47 (0.6)	48 (0.7)	53 (0.6)	44 (0.7)	40 (0.7)	9 (0.5)	442 (5.8)	19 (0.7)	475 (3.9)	26 (0.8)	491 (4.0)	46 (0.9)	475 (2.9)
Czech Republic	66 (1.1)	69 (1.1)	66 (1.1)	65 (1.3)	68 (0.9)	62 (1.2)	52 (1.3)	13 (1.1)	551 (7.1)	57 (1.1)	571 (5.1)	17 (0.9)	568 (8.2)	13 (0.8)	542 (7.6)
Denmark[1]	52 (0.7)	53 (0.9)	54 (0.9)	45 (0.7)	67 (0.9)	49 (1.0)	41 (0.8)	39 (1.6)	517 (4.4)	39 (1.4)	508 (3.8)	13 (0.8)	479 (4.1)	9 (0.7)	468 (6.9)
England[1]	53 (0.7)	54 (0.8)	54 (1.0)	49 (0.9)	66 (0.7)	50 (0.9)	41 (1.1)	—	—	—	—	—	—	—	—
France	61 (0.8)	64 (0.8)	66 (0.8)	54 (1.0)	71 (0.8)	57 (0.9)	49 (0.9)	8 (0.7)	505 (8.0)	33 (1.2)	545 (3.6)	28 (1.0)	547 (4.5)	31 (1.2)	537 (3.7)
Germany[1]	54 (1.1)	58 (1.1)	51 (1.4)	48 (1.3)	64 (1.2)	51 (1.1)	42 (1.3)	14 (1.1)	476 (6.7)	51 (1.2)	521 (4.3)	18 (1.1)	524 (7.0)	17 (0.9)	498 (5.0)
Greece[1]	49 (0.5)	53 (0.8)	51 (0.7)	46 (0.8)	56 (0.8)	43 (0.9)	39 (1.1)	6 (0.6)	450 (7.4)	14 (0.7)	483 (5.2)	26 (1.2)	485 (3.9)	59 (1.2)	491 (3.3)
Hong Kong	70 (1.4)	72 (1.4)	73 (1.5)	70 (1.5)	72 (1.3)	65 (1.7)	62 (1.4)	13 (1.0)	539 (9.3)	32 (0.9)	586 (6.6)	25 (0.9)	607 (6.1)	30 (1.1)	604 (7.2)
Hungary	62 (0.7)	65 (0.8)	60 (0.8)	63 (0.9)	66 (0.7)	56 (0.8)	47 (0.9)	4 (0.4)	483 (11.3)	33 (1.1)	536 (5.0)	22 (0.9)	541 (5.2)	41 (1.3)	545 (3.7)
Iceland	50 (1.1)	54 (1.2)	51 (1.4)	40 (1.3)	63 (1.1)	45 (1.4)	38 (1.4)	5 (1.0)	450 (12.0)	46 (1.7)	501 (5.1)	25 (1.3)	489 (5.4)	23 (1.4)	477 (7.3)
Iran, Islamic Republic	38 (0.6)	39 (0.6)	43 (0.8)	37 (0.8)	41 (0.6)	29 (1.2)	36 (0.8)	1 (0.2)	[2]	5 (0.5)	428 (5.6)	12 (1.0)	436 (4.8)	82 (1.3)	431 (2.4)
Ireland	59 (1.2)	65 (1.2)	51 (1.3)	53 (1.3)	69 (1.1)	53 (1.3)	51 (1.2)	5 (0.6)	465 (8.8)	29 (1.0)	517 (5.3)	40 (1.1)	547 (5.5)	26 (1.2)	533 (5.7)
Israel[1]	57 (1.3)	60 (1.4)	57 (1.4)	61 (1.6)	63 (1.3)	48 (1.6)	43 (1.6)	5 (0.6)	539 (10.9)	36 (2.2)	546 (6.3)	26 (1.5)	521 (6.8)	33 (2.1)	502 (6.3)
Japan	73 (0.4)	75 (0.4)	80 (0.4)	72 (0.6)	78 (0.4)	67 (0.5)	61 (0.5)	13 (0.8)	578 (5.3)	39 (0.8)	607 (2.6)	20 (0.6)	609 (4.0)	28 (1.0)	612 (2.7)
Korea	72 (0.5)	74 (0.5)	75 (0.6)	69 (0.6)	78 (0.6)	66 (0.7)	62 (0.6)	15 (0.9)	582 (4.9)	32 (1.1)	604 (3.5)	25 (0.8)	607 (4.0)	29 (1.2)	628 (4.3)
Kuwait[1]	30 (0.7)	27 (0.8)	38 (1.0)	30 (1.0)	38 (1.0)	23 (1.0)	21 (0.7)	3 (0.5)	358 (10.3)	13 (1.5)	401 (5.5)	19 (1.3)	397 (5.1)	65 (1.8)	392 (2.0)
Latvia (Latvian-speaking schools)[1]	51 (0.8)	53 (0.9)	57 (0.8)	51 (0.9)	56 (0.8)	47 (0.9)	39 (0.9)	4 (0.5)	467 (9.4)	35 (1.1)	507 (4.4)	32 (1.2)	497 (4.9)	29 (1.2)	487 (3.4)
Lithuania[1]	48 (0.9)	51 (1.0)	53 (1.1)	47 (1.2)	52 (1.0)	43 (0.9)	35 (0.9)	5 (0.6)	453 (9.4)	39 (1.4)	487 (3.9)	28 (1.0)	481 (4.6)	28 (1.4)	474 (5.4)
Netherlands[1]	60 (1.6)	62 (1.6)	59 (1.8)	53 (1.6)	72 (1.7)	57 (1.6)	51 (1.9)	3 (0.9)	492 (16.2)	54 (1.7)	539 (9.0)	27 (1.0)	562 (7.0)	16 (0.8)	524 (6.0)
New Zealand	54 (1.0)	57 (1.1)	54 (1.1)	49 (1.1)	66 (1.0)	48 (1.2)	42 (1.0)	12 (0.6)	472 (5.6)	51 (1.2)	519 (4.7)	21 (1.0)	518 (6.1)	17 (0.9)	495 (5.6)
Norway	54 (0.5)	58 (0.6)	51 (0.6)	45 (0.7)	66 (0.6)	51 (0.6)	40 (0.6)	6 (0.5)	481 (6.8)	50 (1.2)	514 (2.9)	24 (0.9)	510 (3.6)	21 (0.9)	483 (3.6)
Portugal	43 (0.7)	44 (0.7)	44 (0.8)	40 (0.8)	54 (0.7)	39 (0.7)	32 (0.8)	3 (0.3)	458 (8.1)	41 (1.1)	463 (3.1)	18 (0.7)	455 (3.3)	38 (1.2)	448 (3.0)
Romania[1]	49 (1.0)	48 (1.0)	52 (0.9)	52 (1.3)	49 (1.0)	48 (1.1)	42 (1.2)	9 (0.7)	459 (10.4)	16 (1.0)	464 (7.0)	15 (0.7)	481 (5.4)	60 (1.6)	494 (4.2)
Russian Federation	60 (1.3)	62 (1.2)	63 (1.4)	63 (1.5)	60 (1.2)	56 (1.5)	48 (1.5)	4 (0.5)	493 (10.3)	33 (1.1)	538 (5.3)	25 (1.0)	538 (5.2)	38 (1.4)	544 (6.9)
Scotland[1]	52 (1.3)	53 (1.3)	52 (1.4)	46 (1.5)	65 (1.3)	48 (1.6)	40 (1.4)	17 (1.4)	461 (4.8)	54 (1.2)	506 (5.7)	17 (1.0)	517 (8.6)	12 (0.8)	503 (7.4)
Singapore	79 (0.9)	84 (0.8)	76 (1.0)	76 (1.1)	79 (0.8)	77 (1.0)	75 (1.0)	2 (0.3)	[2]	7 (0.4)	642 (8.0)	13 (0.6)	652 (6.6)	78 (0.9)	643 (4.9)
Slovak Republic	62 (0.8)	66 (0.8)	63 (0.8)	62 (0.9)	62 (0.7)	60 (0.9)	49 (1.0)	6 (0.5)	549 (8.3)	46 (0.9)	556 (3.9)	25 (0.7)	548 (4.4)	23 (1.0)	532 (4.1)
Slovenia[1]	61 (0.7)	63 (0.7)	60 (0.9)	61 (0.8)	66 (0.7)	59 (0.9)	49 (0.9)	5 (0.5)	551 (9.8)	36 (1.0)	561 (4.1)	21 (0.8)	537 (4.8)	37 (1.1)	523 (3.4)
South Africa[1]	24 (1.1)	26 (1.4)	24 (1.0)	23 (1.1)	26 (1.2)	18 (1.1)	21 (0.9)	—	—	—	—	—	—	—	—
Spain	51 (0.5)	52 (0.5)	49 (0.6)	54 (0.8)	60 (0.7)	44 (0.7)	40 (0.8)	3 (0.4)	443 (5.5)	26 (1.0)	490 (3.1)	18 (0.9)	495 (3.3)	53 (1.3)	487 (2.4)
Sweden	56 (0.7)	62 (0.8)	48 (0.7)	44 (0.9)	70 (0.7)	56 (0.9)	44 (0.9)	7 (0.6)	496 (6.9)	55 (1.2)	528 (3.1)	17 (0.8)	525 (4.3)	21 (0.9)	503 (4.2)
Switzerland[1]	62 (0.6)	67 (0.7)	60 (0.8)	53 (0.7)	72 (0.7)	61 (0.8)	52 (0.7)	4 (0.3)	523 (7.9)	44 (1.2)	556 (3.4)	19 (0.8)	548 (5.1)	33 (1.1)	536 (4.0)
Thailand[1]	57 (1.4)	60 (1.5)	62 (1.3)	53 (1.7)	63 (1.1)	50 (1.4)	51 (1.5)	3 (0.3)	495 (11.9)	26 (1.0)	514 (5.4)	18 (0.7)	515 (5.7)	54 (1.5)	531 (6.6)
United States	53 (1.4)	59 (1.1)	48 (1.2)	51 (1.2)	65 (1.1)	40 (1.1)	42 (1.1)	17 (1.1)	471 (7.20)	42 (0.9)	514 (4.2)	17 (0.7)	507 (5.5)	24 (0.8)	498 (5.9)

[1] Countries not meeting all International Association for the Evaluation of Educational Achievement's sampling specifications.
[2] Insufficient data.
—Data not available or not applicable.

NOTE.—Standard errors appear in parentheses.
SOURCE: International Association for the Evaluation of Educational Achievement, *Mathematics Achievement in the Middle School Years: IEA's Third International Mathematics and Science Study*, 1997. (This table was prepared June 1997.)

Table 396.—Instructional practices and time spent teaching mathematics in eighth grade, by country: 1994–95

Country	Percent of students whose teachers report using each organizational approach "most of every lesson"						Average number of hours mathematics is taught weekly to mathematics classes							
	Work together as a class and students respond to one another	Work together as a class and teacher teaches whole class	Work individually with assistance from teacher	Work individually without assistance from teacher	Work in pairs or groups with assistance from teacher	Work in pairs or groups without assistance from teacher	Less than 2 hours		At least 2, but less than 3.5 hours		At least 3.5, but less than 5 hours		5 hours or more	
							Percent	Mean score	Percent	Mean score	Percent	Mean score	Percent	Mean score
1	2	3	4	5	6	7	8	9	10	11	12	13	14	15
Australia[1]	[2]14	[2]46	[2]64	[2]27	[2]25	[2]9	[2]5 (1.7)	528 (19.5)	50 (3.7)	518 (6.2)	44 (3.7)	552 (7.6)	1 (0.7)	[3] —
Austria[1]	26	252	251	223	219	27	20 (0.0)	[3] —	99 (0.1)	549 (4.1)	1 (0.1)	[3] —	0 (0.0)	[3] —
Belgium (Flemish)	10	59	57	36	6	5	40 (0.0)	[3] —	50 (4.4)	572 (5.6)	50 (4.4)	603 (5.4)	0 (0.0)	[3] —
Belgium (French)[1]	47	438	455	429	411	45	40 (0.0)	[3] —	83 (4.2)	486 (12.9)	83 (4.2)	544 (4.7)	14 (3.8)	564 (10.0)
Canada	[2]12	37	57	225	[2]28	214	3 (1.2)	528 (11.8)	31 (3.8)	521 (5.0)	50 (3.6)	537 (4.3)	17 (3.1)	520 (10.2)
Colombia	25	41	55	219	44	[2]22	24 (2.0)	389 (8.2)	25 (5.5)	367 (8.8)	58 (5.4)	397 (3.9)	13 (3.3)	390 (8.2)
Cyprus	213	261	273	223	226	29	[3] —	[3] —	[3] —	[3] —	[3] —	[3] —	[3] —	[3] —
Czech Republic	5	47	72	42	13	8	1 (0.9)	[3] —	6 (2.0)	587 (17.2)	90 (2.7)	561 (5.1)	3 (1.6)	535 (10.2)
Denmark[1]	5	41	74	16	18	4	—	—	—	—	—	—	—	—
England[1]	419	446	457	425	414	48	—	—	—	—	—	—	—	—
France	11	48	56	26	17	4	22 (1.4)	[3] —	10 (3.2)	532 (13.4)	87 (3.3)	539 (3.9)	2 (1.3)	[3] —
Germany[1]	423	470	454	415	420	49	42 (1.5)	[3] —	85 (3.1)	523 (5.3)	12 (2.9)	463 (13.3)	1 (0.9)	[3] —
Greece[1]	4	58	60	18	14	3	4 (1.7)	459 (10.8)	88 (2.8)	486 (3.5)	3 (1.6)	544 (4.7)	4 (1.6)	480 (8.9)
Hong Kong	11	37	62	17	9	4	45 (2.4)	612 (47.4)	26 (5.2)	590 (19.5)	63 (5.8)	590 (7.6)	6 (2.9)	567 (30.1)
Hungary	11	60	65	22	7	1	0 (0.0)	[3] —	75 (3.6)	538 (3.9)	23 (3.6)	536 (7.0)	1 (1.0)	[3] —
Iceland	22	239	282	238	232	217	20 (0.0)	[3] —	90 (2.9)	492 (5.3)	8 (2.9)	467 (3.5)	1 (0.2)	—
Iran, Islamic Republic	33	66	55	8	42	10	26 (4.1)	523 (13.7)	41 (8.0)	520 (12.7)	47 (8.1)	514 (9.2)	6 (3.7)	579 (22.6)
Israel[1]	270	265	235	268	251	262	4 (1.8)	607 (24.3)	91 (2.3)	602 (2.7)	4 (1.4)	649 (18.5)	0 (0.5)	[3] —
Japan	22	78	27	15	7	1	1 (0.7)	[3] —	90 (3.0)	610 (2.8)	5 (1.8)	608 (13.8)	5 (2.3)	604 (19.5)
Korea	39	89	41	30	12	11	—	—	—	—	—	—	—	—
Kuwait[1]	3	34	48	14	7	5	2 (1.6)	[3] —	21 (6.5)	396 (6.8)	76 (6.6)	391 (2.3)	1 (1.0)	[3] —
Latvia (Latvian-speaking schools)	24	86	90	255	28	211	1 (0.5)	[3] —	30 (4.8)	491 (5.8)	62 (5.3)	492 (4.3)	8 (2.6)	489 (15.0)
Lithuania	10	55	72	25	32	10	1 (0.8)	[3] —	61 (4.1)	482 (5.0)	29 (3.9)	481 (7.5)	9 (2.3)	448 (13.8)
Netherlands[1]	7	56	65	38	49	34	3 (1.9)	529 (54.2)	97 (1.9)	542 (8.1)	0 (0.0)	[3] —	0 (0.0)	[3] —
New Zealand	19	52	63	28	25	14	5 (1.8)	484 (11.6)	42 (4.3)	514 (7.1)	50 (4.3)	507 (6.4)	3 (1.5)	503 (27.3)
Norway	217	258	271	44	236	46	27 (2.6)	502 (5.0)	80 (3.9)	508 (3.1)	8 (2.8)	502 (7.7)	5 (2.1)	513 (7.7)
Portugal	10	67	69	5	50	4	1 (0.8)	[3] —	89 (2.9)	455 (2.7)	10 (2.8)	452 (7.8)	0 (0.0)	[3] —
Romania[1]	12	86	56	19	18	3	8 (2.6)	497 (17.6)	80 (3.4)	481 (5.0)	9 (2.5)	482 (12.4)	2 (0.6)	[3] —
Russian Federation	6	66	65	37	22	13	0 (0.0)	[3] —	17 (3.6)	519 (8.6)	70 (5.6)	533 (5.1)	14 (4.8)	567 (18.0)
Scotland[1]	25	234	262	228	27	23	5 (2.0)	473 (14.7)	35 (4.4)	500 (11.6)	60 (4.6)	494 (7.1)	0 (0.0)	[3] —
Singapore	15	61	48	27	20	6	0 (0.0)	[3] —	52 (4.7)	654 (6.9)	48 (4.7)	633 (7.6)	0 (0.0)	[3] —
Slovak Republic	35	47	50	31	8	7	0 (0.0)	[3] —	2 (1.3)	[3] —	86 (3.0)	544 (3.2)	11 (2.9)	561 (11.0)
Slovenia[1]	211	260	287	234	240	211	20 (0.0)	[3] —	87 (3.4)	542 (4.0)	12 (3.3)	525 (9.5)	1 (0.8)	[3] —
Spain	215	268	258	224	215	210	22 (1.1)	[3] —	28 (4.0)	480 (5.5)	62 (4.7)	490 (3.6)	8 (2.6)	494 (9.2)
Sweden	224	250	272	21	243	25	23 (1.2)	506 (24.2)	97 (1.3)	520 (3.2)	0 (0.4)	[3] —	0 (0.3)	[3] —
Switzerland	44	448	461	425	435	420	42 (1.4)	[3] —	14 (3.4)	520 (17.8)	71 (3.5)	557 (6.5)	13 (3.0)	566 (12.4)
Thailand[1]	219	458	241	218	222	25	[3] —	[3] —	[3] —	[3] —	[3] —	[3] —	[3] —	[3] —
United States	222	249	250	219	226	212	48 (1.4)	492 (26.2)	24 (3.4)	501 (9.9)	58 (4.4)	507 (5.4)	11 (2.8)	498 (10.0)

[1] Countries not meeting all International Association for the Evaluation of Educational Achievement's sampling specifications.
[2] Teacher response data available for 70 to 84 percent of students.
[3] Insufficient data.
[4] Teacher response data available for 50 to 69 percent of students.

—Data not available or not applicable.

NOTE.—Standard errors appear in parentheses.

SOURCE: International Association for the Evaluation of Educational Achievement, *Mathematics Achievement in the Middle School Years: IEA's Third International Mathematics and Science Study*, 1997. (This table was prepared June 1997.)

Table 397.—Average eighth grade science scores by content areas, and average time spent studying out of school, by country: 1994–95

Country	Average percent correct by content area							Distribution of daily out-of-school study time in all subjects, with mean science scores							
	Overall science scores	Earth science	Life science	Physics	Chemistry	Environmental issues and the nature of science		Less than 1 hour		At least 1, but less than 2 hours		At least 2, but less than 3 hours		More than 3 hours	
								Percent	Mean score	Percent	Mean score	Percent	Mean score	Percent	Mean score
1	2	3	4	5	6	7		8	9	10	11	12	13	14	15
International average percent correct	56 (0.1)	55 (0.1)	59 (0.1)	55 (0.1)	51 (0.2)	53 (0.2)		—	—	—	—	—	—	—	—
Australia [1]	60 (0.7)	57 (0.8)	63 (0.8)	60 (0.7)	54 (0.9)	62 (1.0)		15 (0.9)	505 (6.9)	46 (1.0)	556 (4.1)	22 (0.6)	557 (4.9)	17 (0.7)	546 (5.0)
Austria [1]	61 (0.7)	62 (0.8)	65 (0.7)	62 (0.7)	58 (1.1)	55 (0.9)		9 (0.8)	551 (9.9)	46 (1.3)	563 (4.8)	21 (0.9)	561 (5.0)	24 (1.2)	553 (4.8)
Belgium (Flemish)	60 (1.1)	62 (1.2)	64 (1.1)	61 (1.1)	51 (1.3)	58 (1.5)		2 (0.4)	[2]	25 (1.3)	545 (5.0)	28 (1.1)	562 (5.9)	45 (1.6)	547 (3.6)
Belgium (French) [1]	50 (0.7)	50 (0.9)	55 (0.9)	51 (0.7)	41 (0.8)	46 (1.0)		7 (0.8)	428 (6.9)	32 (1.0)	481 (4.7)	21 (1.3)	481 (4.5)	40 (1.5)	467 (4.0)
Bulgaria [1]	62 (1.0)	58 (1.2)	64 (1.0)	60 (1.0)	65 (1.7)	59 (1.5)		—	—	—	—	—	—	—	—
Canada	59 (0.5)	58 (0.6)	62 (0.6)	59 (0.4)	52 (0.7)	61 (0.7)		14 (1.2)	524 (6.1)	47 (1.1)	541 (2.8)	18 (0.7)	531 (3.9)	21 (1.1)	517 (3.6)
Colombia [1]	39 (0.8)	37 (0.8)	44 (0.9)	37 (0.8)	32 (1.0)	40 (1.1)		2 (0.4)	[2]	17 (1.1)	421 (5.3)	20 (1.2)	422 (4.9)	61 (1.9)	413 (5.8)
Cyprus	47 (0.4)	46 (0.6)	49 (0.5)	46 (0.4)	45 (0.6)	46 (0.8)		9 (0.5)	430 (7.0)	19 (0.7)	468 (4.4)	26 (0.8)	475 (3.4)	46 (0.9)	466 (2.9)
Czech Republic	64 (0.8)	63 (1.2)	69 (0.8)	64 (0.5)	60 (1.2)	59 (1.1)		13 (1.1)	558 (9.0)	57 (1.1)	579 (3.9)	17 (0.9)	582 (7.2)	13 (0.8)	560 (6.4)
Denmark [1]	51 (0.6)	49 (0.7)	56 (0.7)	53 (0.7)	41 (0.8)	47 (1.0)		39 (1.6)	494 (4.4)	39 (1.4)	479 (4.1)	13 (0.8)	459 (5.5)	9 (0.7)	457 (6.8)
England [1]	61 (0.6)	59 (0.8)	64 (0.8)	62 (0.6)	55 (0.8)	65 (1.0)		—	—	—	—	—	—	—	—
France	54 (0.6)	55 (0.8)	56 (0.8)	54 (0.5)	47 (0.9)	53 (0.9)		8 (0.7)	481 (6.8)	33 (1.2)	497 (3.3)	28 (1.0)	506 (4.0)	31 (1.2)	499 (3.4)
Germany [1]	58 (1.0)	57 (1.0)	63 (1.1)	57 (1.0)	54 (1.3)	51 (1.3)		14 (1.1)	505 (8.2)	51 (1.2)	541 (4.6)	18 (1.0)	544 (7.0)	17 (0.9)	525 (6.5)
Greece [1]	52 (0.5)	49 (0.6)	54 (0.6)	53 (0.5)	51 (0.6)	51 (0.6)		6 (0.6)	473 (4.8)	14 (0.7)	497 (5.0)	21 (0.7)	500 (3.1)	59 (1.2)	502 (2.5)
Hong Kong	58 (1.0)	54 (1.0)	61 (1.0)	58 (0.9)	55 (1.0)	55 (1.3)		13 (1.0)	489 (7.3)	32 (0.9)	519 (4.7)	25 (0.9)	534 (4.8)	30 (1.1)	534 (5.2)
Hungary	61 (0.6)	60 (0.8)	65 (0.7)	60 (0.6)	60 (0.8)	53 (0.8)		4 (0.4)	519 (10.0)	33 (1.1)	553 (4.4)	22 (0.9)	557 (5.6)	41 (1.3)	557 (3.0)
Iceland	52 (0.9)	50 (1.2)	58 (1.0)	53 (0.9)	42 (0.8)	49 (1.0)		5 (1.0)	470 (8.7)	46 (1.7)	505 (5.6)	25 (1.3)	493 (4.5)	23 (1.4)	488 (7.5)
Iran, Islamic Republic	47 (0.6)	45 (0.6)	49 (0.6)	48 (0.7)	52 (0.8)	39 (0.7)		1 (0.2)	[2]	5 (0.5)	476 (6.0)	12 (1.0)	479 (5.2)	82 (1.3)	471 (2.7)
Ireland	58 (0.9)	61 (1.0)	60 (1.1)	56 (0.8)	54 (1.0)	60 (1.1)		5 (0.6)	475 (9.0)	29 (1.0)	529 (5.4)	40 (1.1)	550 (4.7)	26 (1.2)	550 (4.9)
Israel [1]	57 (1.1)	55 (1.1)	61 (1.1)	57 (1.1)	53 (1.5)	52 (1.6)		5 (0.6)	532 (13.5)	36 (2.2)	555 (7.7)	26 (1.5)	523 (6.9)	33 (2.1)	505 (5.2)
Japan	65 (0.3)	61 (0.4)	71 (0.4)	67 (0.3)	61 (0.5)	60 (0.7)		13 (0.8)	551 (4.4)	39 (0.8)	573 (2.2)	20 (0.6)	572 (3.0)	28 (1.0)	577 (2.4)
Korea	66 (0.3)	63 (0.5)	70 (0.4)	65 (0.5)	63 (0.6)	64 (0.8)		15 (0.9)	544 (5.0)	32 (1.1)	564 (2.9)	25 (0.8)	562 (3.1)	29 (1.2)	581 (3.7)
Kuwait [1]	43 (0.9)	43 (1.0)	45 (1.1)	43 (0.7)	40 (1.5)	39 (1.3)		3 (0.6)	400 (10.4)	13 (1.5)	436 (7.8)	19 (1.3)	432 (7.1)	65 (1.8)	431 (3.4)
Latvia (Latvian-speaking schools)	50 (0.6)	48 (0.8)	53 (0.7)	51 (0.7)	48 (0.8)	47 (1.0)		4 (0.5)	468 (8.5)	35 (1.1)	492 (4.1)	32 (1.2)	490 (4.1)	29 (1.2)	481 (3.0)
Lithuania [1]	49 (0.7)	46 (0.9)	52 (0.9)	49 (0.8)	48 (0.9)	40 (1.0)		5 (0.6)	457 (9.1)	39 (1.4)	484 (4.5)	28 (1.0)	483 (3.8)	28 (1.4)	472 (4.7)
Netherlands [1]	62 (1.0)	61 (1.4)	67 (1.4)	63 (0.9)	52 (0.9)	65 (1.6)		3 (0.9)	519 (17.1)	54 (1.7)	559 (6.1)	27 (1.7)	578 (5.4)	16 (0.8)	545 (5.7)
New Zealand	58 (0.8)	56 (0.9)	60 (1.0)	58 (0.7)	53 (1.1)	59 (1.2)		12 (0.9)	488 (7.6)	51 (1.2)	536 (4.6)	21 (1.0)	537 (5.7)	17 (0.9)	516 (5.7)
Norway	58 (0.4)	61 (0.6)	61 (0.6)	57 (0.4)	49 (0.6)	55 (0.6)		6 (0.5)	501 (7.3)	50 (1.2)	533 (2.5)	24 (0.9)	536 (3.4)	21 (0.9)	516 (3.7)
Portugal	50 (0.6)	50 (0.7)	53 (0.6)	48 (0.5)	50 (0.9)	45 (0.8)		3 (0.3)	465 (8.8)	41 (1.1)	488 (2.9)	18 (0.7)	478 (4.1)	38 (1.2)	474 (2.8)
Romania [1]	50 (0.8)	49 (1.0)	55 (1.0)	49 (0.8)	46 (1.0)	42 (1.0)		9 (0.7)	460 (11.7)	16 (1.0)	468 (7.0)	15 (0.7)	487 (5.7)	60 (1.6)	499 (5.2)
Russian Federation	58 (0.8)	58 (0.8)	62 (0.7)	57 (0.9)	57 (1.3)	50 (0.8)		4 (0.5)	511 (10.1)	33 (1.1)	542 (4.4)	25 (1.0)	538 (4.4)	38 (1.4)	543 (4.6)
Scotland [1]	55 (1.0)	52 (1.0)	57 (1.1)	55 (0.4)	51 (1.3)	57 (1.4)		17 (1.4)	470 (5.3)	54 (1.2)	526 (5.1)	17 (1.0)	537 (8.5)	12 (0.8)	532 (6.5)
Singapore	70 (1.0)	65 (1.1)	72 (1.0)	69 (0.8)	69 (1.2)	74 (1.1)		2 (0.3)	[2]	7 (0.4)	604 (8.4)	13 (0.6)	617 (5.3)	78 (0.9)	607 (5.4)
Slovak Republic	59 (0.6)	60 (0.7)	60 (0.6)	61 (0.6)	57 (0.8)	53 (0.9)		6 (0.5)	551 (7.1)	46 (0.9)	552 (3.7)	25 (0.7)	541 (3.8)	23 (1.0)	536 (4.7)
Slovenia [1]	62 (0.5)	64 (0.7)	65 (0.6)	61 (0.6)	56 (0.9)	59 (0.9)		5 (0.5)	559 (9.2)	36 (1.0)	580 (3.5)	21 (0.8)	557 (3.2)	37 (1.1)	544 (3.3)
South Africa [1]	27 (1.3)	26 (1.1)	27 (1.3)	27 (1.4)	26 (1.4)	26 (1.3)		—	—	—	—	—	—	—	—
Spain	56 (0.4)	57 (0.5)	58 (0.5)	55 (0.4)	51 (0.7)	53 (0.6)		3 (0.4)	482 (7.9)	26 (1.0)	522 (2.8)	18 (0.9)	522 (3.5)	53 (1.3)	516 (2.2)
Sweden	59 (0.6)	62 (0.7)	63 (0.7)	57 (0.8)	56 (0.7)	52 (0.8)		7 (0.6)	520 (6.0)	55 (1.2)	544 (3.2)	17 (0.8)	539 (4.9)	21 (0.9)	523 (4.9)
Switzerland [1]	56 (0.5)	56 (1.0)	58 (0.6)	58 (0.5)	50 (0.7)	51 (0.8)		4 (0.3)	500 (8.3)	44 (1.2)	530 (3.1)	19 (0.8)	526 (6.2)	33 (1.1)	514 (3.5)
Thailand [1]	57 (0.9)	56 (1.0)	66 (0.9)	54 (0.7)	43 (1.2)	62 (1.1)		3 (0.3)	510 (8.8)	26 (1.0)	520 (4.0)	18 (0.7)	519 (4.3)	54 (1.5)	532 (4.1)
United States	58 (1.0)	58 (1.0)	63 (1.1)	56 (0.8)	53 (1.2)	61 (1.0)		17 (1.1)	507 (9.5)	42 (0.9)	548 (4.1)	17 (0.7)	541 (5.2)	24 (0.8)	533 (5.7)

[1] Countries not meeting all International Association for the Evaluation of Educational Achievement's sampling specifications.
[2] Insufficient data.
—Data not available or not applicable.

NOTE.—Standard errors appear in parentheses.
SOURCE: International Association for the Evaluation of Educational Achievement, *Science Achievement in the Middle School Years: IEA's Third International Mathematics and Science Study*, 1997. (This table was prepared June 1997.)

Table 398.—Instructional practices and time spent teaching science in eighth grade, by country: 1994–95

Country	Percent of students whose teachers report using each organizational approach "most of every lesson"							Average number of hours science is taught weekly to science classes							
	Work together as a class and students respond to one another	Work together as a class and teacher teaches whole class	Work individually with assistance from teacher	Work individually without assistance from teacher	Work in pairs or groups with assistance from teacher	Work in pairs or groups without assistance from teacher		Less than 2 hours		At least 2, but less than 3.5 hours		At least 3.5, but less than 5 hours		5 hours or more	
								Percent	Mean score	Percent	Mean score	Percent	Mean score	Percent	Mean score
1	2	3	4	5	6		7	8	9	10	11	12	13	14	15
Austria[1]	2 3	2 65	2 13	2 3	2 18		2 12	—	—	—	—	—	—	—	—
Belgium (Flemish)	2 11	2 62	2 19	2 6	2 13		2 7	—	—	—	—	—	—	—	—
Belgium (French)[1]	3 11	3 53	3 24	3 8	3 8		3 4	—	—	—	—	—	—	—	—
Canada	3 17	2 28	2 26	2 23	2 33		3 24	2 11 (2.1)	512 (8.9)	69 (3.9)	540 (3.8)	11 (2.5)	528 (5.5)	8 (2.1)	517 (10.3)
Colombia[1]	2 33	2 48	2 55	2 10	2 43		2 13	2 6 (2.3)	416 (4.5)	75 (4.2)	415 (5.6)	13 (3.2)	404 (5.5)	6 (2.4)	403 (18.6)
Cyprus	3 3	3 74	3 35	3 3	3 17		3 6	[4]	[4]	[4]	[4]	[4]	[4]	[4]	[4]
Czech Republic	1 1	70	2 46	15	2 13		4	—	—	—	—	—	—	—	—
Denmark[1]	3 2	3 22	3 25	3 3	3 46		3 13	—	—	—	—	—	—	—	—
France	16	57	34	16	27		12	—	—	—	—	—	—	—	—
Germany[1]	3 30	3 69	3 28	3 7	3 19		3 5	—	—	—	—	—	—	—	—
Greece[1]	3	67	45	10	13		1	—	—	—	—	—	—	—	—
Hong Kong	12	45	35	2	44		13	7 (2.3)	492 (29.9)	82 (3.9)	526 (5.3)	9 (3.3)	518 (8.6)	2 (1.6)	([4])
Hungary	7	80	54	13	11		2	—	—	—	—	—	—	—	—
Iceland	3 1	2 35	2 30	2 16	2 16		2 6	—	—	—	—	—	—	—	—
Iran, Islamic Republic	25	57	36	2	25		11	—	—	—	—	—	—	—	—
Ireland	37	3 62	3 25	3 6	3 20		3 6	3 4 (1.9)	578 (16.5)	94 (2.1)	540 (6.2)	2 (0.8)	[4]	0 (0.0)	[4]
Israel[1]	3 17	2 41	2 30	2 15	2 32		2 18	3 19 (7.9)	547 (19.6)	77 (7.2)	520 (9.1)	4 (3.5)	529 (0.0)	0 (0.0)	[4]
Japan	19	79	12	8	12		6	5 (1.6)	618 (15.2)	94 (1.7)	569 (1.5)	0 (0.0)	[4]	1 (0.6)	[4]
Korea	34	83	28	8	15		3	43 (2.9)	569 (3.3)	51 (3.2)	561 (3.1)	1 (0.8)	[4]	5 (2.3)	568 (12.7)
Kuwait[1]	29	2 46	2 45	2 0	2 36		2 2	23 (2.6)	409 (1.9)	97 (2.6)	426 (4.4)	1 (0.5)	[4]	0 (0.0)	[4]
Latvia (Latvian-speaking schools)	3 25	3 84	3 59	3 32	3 24		3 8	—	—	—	—	—	—	—	—
Lithuania	2 16	2 60	2 57	2 22	2 26		2 8	—	—	—	—	—	—	—	—
Netherlands[1]	25	2 63	2 36	2 23	2 25		2 18	—	—	—	—	—	—	—	—
New Zealand	15	41	33	26	44		20	1 (0.9)	[4]	52 (4.1)	527 (6.3)	47 (4.2)	525 (6.6)	0 (0.0)	[4]
Norway	3 24	3 62	3 23	3 1	3 23		3 4	3 27 (4.9)	526 (3.0)	73 (4.9)	524 (2.6)	1 (0.6)	[4]	0 (0.0)	[4]
Portugal	14	66	54	3	54		5	—	—	—	—	—	—	—	—
Romania[1]	15	86	47	8	27		2	—	—	—	—	—	—	—	—
Russian Federation	9	68	43	21	13		7	—	—	—	—	—	—	—	—
Scotland[1]	37	3 22	3 27	3 11	3 56		3 19	3 14 (3.1)	538 (23.4)	83 (3.6)	519 (4.8)	3 (1.7)	488 (22.5)	0 (0.0)	[4]
Singapore	12	59	41	17	40		19	0 (0.0)	[4]	24 (4.4)	618 (14.6)	76 (4.4)	603 (6.0)	0 (0.0)	[4]
Slovak Republic	2 48	2 64	2 45	2 15	2 3		2 1	—	—	—	—	—	—	—	—
Slovenia[1]	27	2 65	2 57	2 19	2 34		2 13	—	—	—	—	—	—	—	—
Spain	2 14	2 65	2 46	2 14	2 18		2 7	2 5 (2.6)	532 (2.5)	84 (3.9)	518 (2.1)	11 (3.0)	502 (9.4)	1 (0.7)	[4]
Switzerland	33	3 56	3 21	36	3 30		8	3 41 (4.7)	532 (6.6)	37 (4.4)	524 (8.4)	9 (3.1)	486 (13.7)	13 (3.5)	519 (15.6)
Thailand[1]	2 16	2 38	2 33	2 10	2 32		2 11	[4]	[4]	[4]	[4]	[4]	[4]	[4]	[4]
United States	—	—	—	—	—		—	—	—	—	—	—	—	—	—

[1] Countries not meeting all International Association for the Evaluation of Educational Achievement's sampling specifications.
[2] Insufficient data.
[3] Teacher response data available for 70 to 84 percent of students.
[4] Teacher response available for 50 to 69 percent of students.

—Data not available or not applicable.

NOTE.—Standard errors appear in parentheses.

SOURCE: International Association for the Evaluation of Educational Achievement, *Science Achievement in the Middle School Years: IEA's Third International Mathematics and Science Study*, 1997. (This table was prepared June 1997.)

Table 399.—Average size of eighth grade mathematics class, and frequency teachers assign mathematics homework, by country: 1994–95

Country	Average size of mathematics class				Percent of students taught mathematics by teachers, by frequency and average length of assignment							
	1 to 20 students	21 to 30 students	31 to 40 students	41 or more students	Never assigning homework	Assigning homework less than once a week		Assigning homework once or twice a week		Assigning homework 3 or more times a week	
						30 minutes or less	More than 30 minutes	30 minutes or less	More than 30 minutes	30 minutes or less	More than 30 minutes
1	2	3	4	5	6	7	8	9	10	11	12
Australia[1]	[2]13 (2.4)	71 (3.3)	16 (2.6)	1 (0.5)	[2]1 (0.8)	6 (1.6)	0 (0.2)	21 (2.6)	4 (1.9)	62 (3.4)	5 (1.7)
Austria[1]	—	—	—	—	[2]0 (0.0)	1 (0.5)	0 (0.0)	24 (4.4)	3 (1.4)	63 (5.0)	10 (2.1)
Belgium (Flemish)	49 (3.6)	51 (3.6)	0 (0.0)	0 (0.0)	0 (0.0)	17 (3.5)	2 (1.1)	52 (4.8)	10 (2.6)	15 (2.9)	5 (2.1)
Belgium (French)[1]	[3]43 (5.3)	57 (5.3)	0 (0.0)	0 (0.0)	1 (1.2)	2 (1.4)	0 (0.0)	30 (5.1)	5 (2.2)	55 (5.5)	7 (2.8)
Canada	[2]11 (2.1)	65 (4.0)	23 (3.6)	1 (0.5)	[2]2 (1.1)	2 (0.9)	1 (0.7)	22 (3.4)	2 (0.9)	59 (3.7)	13 (2.7)
Colombia[1]	[2]16 (4.2)	6 (2.2)	29 (4.0)	48 (4.6)	0 (0.0)	1 (0.9)	1 (0.8)	17 (4.7)	13 (2.9)	29 (4.2)	39 (4.2)
Cyprus	1 (0.0)	37 (3.9)	62 (3.9)	0 (0.0)	[2]0 (0.0)	0 (0.0)	0 (0.0)	0 (0.0)	0 (0.0)	50 (5.3)	50 (5.3)
Czech Republic	13 (3.3)	77 (5.3)	11 (4.5)	0 (0.0)	0 (0.4)	14 (4.5)	0 (0.0)	62 (5.2)	0 (0.3)	23 (3.5)	1 (0.6)
Denmark[1]	[2]49 (4.8)	51 (4.8)	0 (0.0)	0 (0.0)	0 (0.0)	4 (1.8)	0 (0.0)	42 (4.7)	3 (1.6)	49 (5.2)	2 (1.0)
England[1]	[3]18 (3.1)	62 (3.7)	20 (3.4)	0 (0.0)	0 (0.0)	3 (1.0)	1 (0.6)	44 (3.8)	47 (3.7)	3 (1.4)	2 (1.1)
France	11 (2.6)	86 (2.9)	3 (1.8)	0 (0.0)	0 (0.0)	0 (0.0)	2 (0.9)	7 (2.5)	4 (1.2)	77 (3.9)	10 (2.8)
Germany[1]	[3]25 (4.4)	72 (4.5)	3 (1.8)	0 (0.0)	1 (1.4)	1 (1.4)	0 (0.0)	22 (4.4)	0 (0.0)	73 (5.0)	3 (1.8)
Greece[1]	9 (2.3)	64 (4.4)	27 (3.9)	0 (0.0)	0 (0.0)	1 (0.9)	0 (0.0)	0 (0.0)	0 (0.2)	31 (3.4)	67 (3.5)
Hong Kong	3 (1.9)	4 (2.2)	56 (5.7)	37 (5.9)	1 (1.4)	4 (2.2)	3 (1.8)	25 (4.7)	15 (4.1)	38 (6.0)	14 (4.1)
Hungary	37 (4.0)	57 (4.1)	6 (2.2)	0 (0.0)	0 (0.0)	1 (0.7)	0 (0.0)	2 (1.3)	0 (0.0)	82 (3.0)	15 (3.1)
Iceland	[2]36 (5.9)	64 (5.9)	0 (0.0)	0 (0.0)	0 (0.0)	0 (0.0)	0 (0.0)	5 (2.0)	1 (1.0)	75 (5.5)	19 (5.5)
Iran, Islamic Republic	[2]1 (0.9)	26 (4.5)	54 (5.3)	19 (4.4)	0 (0.0)	1 (0.5)	3 (1.4)	10 (3.0)	59 (4.4)	2 (1.1)	26 (4.3)
Ireland	[2]12 (2.7)	68 (4.5)	20 (3.9)	0 (0.0)	0 (0.0)	0 (0.0)	0 (0.0)	1 (0.9)	0 (0.0)	94 (2.2)	5 (2.0)
Israel[1]	[2]14 (5.1)	36 (7.4)	49 (9.1)	2 (1.6)	[2]0 (0.0)	1 (1.2)	0 (0.0)	3 (2.2)	0 (0.0)	48 (7.1)	48 (6.8)
Japan	0 (0.2)	4 (1.4)	88 (2.0)	8 (1.5)	0 (0.0)	27 (4.0)	4 (1.7)	37 (3.7)	10 (2.3)	16 (2.9)	6 (1.5)
Korea	2 (1.2)	1 (1.0)	4 (1.5)	93 (2.0)	0 (0.0)	5 (1.6)	8 (2.2)	27 (3.7)	21 (3.3)	21 (3.2)	18 (3.4)
Kuwait[1]	0 (0.0)	49 (6.5)	49 (6.3)	2 (1.9)	0 (0.0)	0 (0.0)	0 (0.0)	19 (6.1)	2 (2.0)	60 (8.3)	18 (6.0)
Latvia (Latvian-speaking schools)	[2]41 (4.0)	51 (3.8)	4 (2.1)	4 (2.0)	0 (0.0)	0 (0.0)	0 (0.0)	8 (2.8)	1 (0.9)	83 (3.9)	9 (2.4)
Lithuania	[2]43 (3.8)	54 (3.7)	3 (1.6)	0 (0.0)	0 (0.0)	0 (0.0)	0 (0.0)	2 (1.3)	0 (0.0)	76 (3.9)	22 (3.9)
Netherlands[1]	16 (4.7)	77 (5.6)	7 (3.6)	0 (0.0)	1 (1.2)	1 (0.9)	0 (0.0)	12 (3.5)	2 (1.4)	81 (4.2)	4 (2.2)
New Zealand	11 (2.2)	68 (3.8)	21 (3.1)	0 (0.0)	0 (0.0)	5 (1.9)	2 (0.1)	34 (4.3)	4 (1.5)	54 (4.2)	2 (1.2)
Norway	[2]20 (3.5)	79 (3.7)	1 (0.5)	1 (0.8)	[2]0 (0.0)	0 (0.0)	0 (0.0)	7 (2.7)	8 (2.7)	67 (4.3)	18 (4.0)
Portugal	12 (2.8)	80 (3.7)	7 (2.6)	0 (0.0)	0 (0.0)	1 (0.9)	1 (0.5)	30 (4.0)	2 (1.1)	57 (4.1)	9 (2.4)
Romania[1]	23 (2.7)	51 (4.3)	24 (4.1)	2 (1.2)	0 (0.0)	0 (0.0)	0 (0.0)	1 (0.8)	1 (0.6)	11 (2.8)	87 (2.8)
Russian Federation	15 (2.7)	75 (3.6)	9 (2.3)	0 (0.0)	0 (0.0)	0 (0.0)	0 (0.0)	2 (0.9)	1 (0.8)	42 (3.5)	55 (3.4)
Scotland[1]	[2]12 (2.8)	80 (3.8)	8 (2.7)	0 (0.0)	[2]0 (0.4)	20 (4.3)	4 (2.0)	46 (5.1)	6 (2.3)	24 (4.1)	0 (0.0)
Singapore	1 (0.7)	10 (2.5)	72 (4.3)	18 (4.0)	0 (0.0)	1 (0.9)	0 (0.0)	3 (1.5)	11 (3.1)	26 (4.1)	58 (4.5)
Slovak Republic	15 (2.8)	67 (4.2)	19 (3.6)	0 (0.0)	0 (0.0)	1 (0.9)	0 (0.0)	12 (2.8)	1 (0.7)	83 (3.4)	4 (1.7)
Slovenia[1]	[2]15 (3.1)	80 (3.6)	5 (1.8)	0 (0.0)	[2]0 (0.0)	0 (0.0)	0 (0.0)	2 (1.4)	0 (0.0)	74 (4.0)	24 (4.2)
Spain	[2]13 (2.8)	48 (4.0)	36 (4.2)	4 (1.7)	[2]0 (0.0)	4 (1.6)	0 (0.0)	18 (3.3)	9 (2.7)	47 (4.4)	22 (3.7)
Sweden	[2]36 (3.9)	61 (4.0)	2 (1.2)	0 (0.0)	[2]0 (0.4)	19 (3.0)	7 (1.9)	45 (4.0)	26 (3.3)	2 (1.2)	1 (1.2)
Switzerland	[3]56 (4.5)	44 (4.5)	0 (0.0)	0 (0.0)	0 (0.0)	1 (0.4)	1 (0.3)	26 (4.2)	4 (1.5)	61 (4.4)	6 (2.3)
Thailand[1]	—	—	—	—	[2]0 (0.0)	0 (0.0)	0 (0.0)	6 (3.5)	20 (4.8)	16 (4.7)	58 (6.6)
United States	[3]24 (3.0)	59 (3.9)	12 (2.2)	4 (1.8)	[2]0 (0.1)	3 (1.3)	0 (0.0)	7 (1.8)	3 (0.9)	64 (2.9)	23 (3.1)

[1] Countries not meeting all International Association for the Evaluation of Educational Achievement's sampling specifications.
[2] Teacher response data available for 70 to 84 percent of students.
[3] Teacher response data available for 50 to 69 percent of students.
—Data not available or not applicable.

NOTE.—Standard errors appear in parentheses.

SOURCE: International Association for the Evaluation of Educational Achievement, *Mathematics Achievement in the Middle School Years: IEA's Third International Mathematics and Science Study*, 1997. (This table was prepared June 1997.)

448 INTERNATIONAL COMPARISONS OF EDUCATION

Table 400.—Eighth grade students' perceptions about mathematics achievement and hours spent on leisure activities, by country: 1994–95

Country	Students' self-perceptions about usually doing well in mathematics									Average hours each day					
	Strongly disagree		Disagree		Agree		Strongly agree		Watching TV or videos	Playing or talking with friends	Doing jobs at home	Playing sports	Reading for enjoyment	Playing computer games
	Percent	Mean score	Percent	Mean score	Percent	Mean score	Percent	Mean score						
1	2	3	4	5	6	7	8	9	10	11	12	13	14	15
Australia[1]	3 (0.3)	457 (7.9)	17 (0.7)	487 (5.6)	60 (0.8)	530 (3.9)	20 (0.9)	586 (4.7)	2.4 (0.05)	1.4 (0.03)	0.9 (0.02)	1.6 (0.03)	0.6 (0.02)	0.6 (0.02)
Austria[1]	3 (0.4)	512 (10.1)	21 (1.1)	508 (5.4)	45 (1.2)	535 (4.0)	31 (1.4)	572 (4.3)	1.9 (0.06)	2.9 (0.08)	0.8 (0.03)	1.9 (0.07)	0.8 (0.03)	0.6 (0.03)
Belgium (Flemish)	5 (0.4)	512 (6.7)	29 (1.0)	548 (5.9)	48 (1.1)	567 (6.4)	17 (0.9)	609 (7.2)	2.0 (0.05)	1.6 (0.05)	1.1 (0.03)	1.8 (0.07)	0.7 (0.03)	0.5 (0.06)
Belgium (French)[1]	3 (0.4)	467 (7.8)	19 (1.3)	505 (5.4)	48 (1.3)	528 (3.8)	29 (1.5)	550 (5.0)	1.9 (0.08)	1.7 (0.10)	0.8 (0.03)	1.8 (0.04)	0.8 (0.03)	0.7 (0.03)
Canada	3 (0.3)	480 (9.0)	13 (0.6)	480 (4.9)	49 (1.1)	514 (2.3)	35 (1.1)	570 (3.4)	2.3 (0.04)	2.2 (0.05)	1.0 (0.02)	1.9 (0.03)	0.8 (0.02)	0.5 (0.02)
Colombia[1]	2 (0.4)	—	17 (1.3)	373 (3.7)	51 (1.9)	385 (4.6)	30 (1.4)	398 (5.3)	2.2 (0.07)	1.9 (0.06)	2.3 (0.07)	1.9 (0.06)	0.9 (0.05)	2 0.4 (0.06)
Cyprus	5 (0.4)	411 (7.6)	18 (0.8)	432 (3.7)	46 (1.0)	469 (2.6)	31 (1.0)	521 (4.4)	2.3 (0.04)	1.7 (0.04)	1.0 (0.03)	1.4 (0.04)	0.8 (0.02)	0.8 (0.03)
Czech Republic	2 (0.3)	—	37 (1.4)	516 (4.2)	48 (1.4)	584 (5.2)	13 (1.0)	640 (8.0)	2.6 (0.05)	2.9 (0.09)	1.3 (0.04)	1.9 (0.06)	1.0 (0.03)	0.6 (0.03)
Denmark[1]	1 (0.2)	—	8 (0.6)	431 (7.0)	53 (1.4)	492 (3.0)	38 (1.3)	537 (4.0)	2.2 (0.06)	2.8 (0.07)	1.1 (0.04)	1.7 (0.06)	0.7 (0.03)	0.7 (0.03)
England[1]	1 (0.2)	—	6 (0.6)	475 (8.3)	69 (1.0)	500 (3.0)	24 (1.0)	538 (5.8)	2.7 (0.07)	2.5 (0.06)	0.8 (0.03)	1.5 (0.05)	0.7 (0.03)	0.9 (0.05)
France	6 (0.7)	495 (6.1)	26 (1.1)	513 (4.0)	46 (1.0)	548 (3.4)	22 (0.8)	564 (5.1)	1.5 (0.04)	1.5 (0.05)	0.9 (0.03)	1.7 (0.04)	0.8 (0.03)	0.5 (0.02)
Germany[1]	7 (0.5)	474 (7.1)	24 (1.0)	491 (5.2)	33 (1.1)	511 (5.1)	36 (1.1)	529 (5.3)	1.9 (0.04)	3.5 (0.07)	0.9 (0.02)	1.7 (0.04)	0.7 (0.02)	0.8 (0.04)
Greece[3]	2 (0.3)	—	16 (0.7)	454 (3.6)	55 (0.8)	481 (3.2)	27 (0.8)	515 (4.2)	2.1 (0.04)	1.5 (0.04)	0.9 (0.03)	1.8 (0.04)	1.0 (0.03)	0.7 (0.03)
Hong Kong	11 (0.9)	536 (9.5)	51 (1.2)	577 (6.7)	33 (1.2)	620 (6.7)	5 (0.5)	643 (8.2)	2.6 (0.05)	1.2 (0.04)	0.7 (0.02)	0.9 (0.03)	0.9 (0.02)	0.8 (0.03)
Hungary	3 (0.3)	469 (11.7)	25 (0.9)	490 (4.2)	57 (1.0)	545 (3.4)	15 (0.8)	608 (4.8)	3.0 (0.06)	2.3 (0.05)	2.0 (0.04)	1.7 (0.04)	1.2 (0.04)	0.7 (0.03)
Iceland	3 (0.6)	421 (10.1)	14 (1.4)	447 (4.9)	55 (1.6)	486 (4.5)	28 (1.8)	519 (9.5)	2.2 (0.05)	3.1 (0.06)	0.8 (0.03)	1.8 (0.06)	0.9 (0.06)	0.7 (0.06)
Iran, Islamic Republic	1 (0.4)	—	8 (0.7)	403 (4.3)	62 (1.4)	423 (2.6)	29 (1.4)	450 (3.7)	1.8 (0.06)	1.2 (0.04)	1.8 (0.06)	1.2 (0.09)	1.1 (0.04)	2 0.2 (0.02)
Ireland	3 (0.3)	475 (7.7)	18 (1.0)	492 (5.5)	61 (0.9)	530 (5.2)	18 (1.0)	572 (7.6)	2.1 (0.03)	1.5 (0.06)	0.9 (0.03)	1.4 (0.05)	0.6 (0.02)	0.5 (0.03)
Israel[1]	2 (0.4)	—	12 (1.3)	494 (10.1)	45 (1.9)	513 (6.2)	41 (1.9)	549 (8.3)	3.3 (0.10)	2.4 (0.08)	1.2 (0.05)	1.9 (0.09)	1.0 (0.04)	0.9 (0.04)
Japan	10 (0.5)	523 (3.7)	45 (0.7)	577 (2.3)	40 (0.7)	650 (2.5)	4 (0.3)	669 (7.8)	2.6 (0.04)	1.9 (0.04)	0.6 (0.01)	1.3 (0.03)	0.9 (0.02)	0.6 (0.02)
Korea	9 (0.5)	535 (5.7)	53 (1.0)	572 (3.0)	32 (0.9)	669 (3.0)	6 (0.6)	702 (5.7)	2.0 (0.04)	0.9 (0.03)	0.5 (0.02)	0.5 (0.03)	0.8 (0.03)	0.3 (0.02)
Kuwait[3]	3 (0.7)	364 (11.3)	9 (0.9)	382 (3.6)	49 (1.7)	386 (2.4)	39 (2.1)	405 (3.9)	1.9 (0.07)	1.5 (0.11)	1.2 (0.08)	1.5 (0.10)	1.0 (0.04)	0.7 (0.05)
Latvia (Latvian-speaking schools)	2 (0.3)	—	43 (1.2)	471 (3.5)	43 (1.2)	505 (3.7)	12 (0.8)	542 (5.5)	2.6 (0.05)	2.1 (0.06)	1.5 (0.04)	1.2 (0.04)	1.1 (0.03)	0.7 (0.04)
Lithuania	5 (0.5)	446 (7.5)	46 (1.2)	454 (3.4)	38 (1.2)	492 (4.3)	11 (0.8)	544 (6.0)	2.8 (0.05)	2.7 (0.06)	1.2 (0.03)	1.2 (0.04)	1.0 (0.03)	0.9 (0.04)
Netherlands[1]	4 (0.5)	487 (12.4)	21 (1.4)	504 (7.1)	43 (1.3)	537 (8.4)	32 (1.6)	580 (7.3)	2.5 (0.09)	2.8 (0.08)	0.9 (0.04)	1.8 (0.06)	0.6 (0.03)	0.7 (0.04)
New Zealand	2 (0.3)	—	13 (0.8)	466 (6.1)	62 (0.9)	501 (4.5)	22 (0.8)	559 (5.5)	2.5 (0.05)	1.5 (0.04)	0.9 (0.02)	1.5 (0.04)	0.8 (0.02)	0.7 (0.03)
Norway	3 (0.3)	434 (7.4)	18 (0.9)	455 (3.2)	58 (1.0)	504 (2.2)	21 (0.8)	555 (4.4)	2.5 (0.04)	3.2 (0.06)	1.1 (0.03)	1.9 (0.05)	0.7 (0.02)	0.8 (0.03)
Portugal	7 (0.5)	419 (3.6)	37 (1.1)	435 (2.3)	42 (1.1)	463 (2.5)	14 (0.8)	502 (5.2)	2.0 (0.04)	1.7 (0.05)	1.0 (0.04)	1.7 (0.04)	0.7 (0.02)	0.7 (0.03)
Romania[1]	6 (0.6)	455 (12.0)	25 (1.0)	459 (4.6)	49 (0.9)	488 (4.3)	20 (1.0)	505 (6.3)	1.9 (0.06)	1.5 (0.06)	1.9 (0.08)	1.3 (0.05)	1.3 (0.07)	0.6 (0.05)
Russian Federation	2 (0.3)	—	37 (1.4)	501 (7.1)	43 (1.1)	547 (5.1)	18 (0.8)	590 (4.9)	2.9 (0.05)	2.9 (0.05)	1.5 (0.03)	1.0 (0.03)	1.3 (0.04)	1.0 (0.04)
Scotland[1]	2 (0.3)	—	10 (0.8)	455 (5.5)	66 (1.3)	491 (4.8)	22 (1.3)	553 (9.3)	2.7 (0.05)	2.8 (0.08)	0.7 (0.02)	1.9 (0.05)	0.7 (0.02)	1.0 (0.04)
Singapore	6 (0.4)	587 (9.0)	38 (1.2)	624 (5.2)	46 (1.1)	659 (4.9)	11 (0.6)	677 (6.2)	2.7 (0.05)	1.5 (0.04)	1.0 (0.03)	0.7 (0.03)	1.1 (0.02)	0.6 (0.03)
Slovak Republic	1 (0.2)	—	28 (1.1)	496 (3.8)	55 (1.1)	555 (3.8)	15 (0.7)	619 (5.2)	2.7 (0.05)	2.9 (0.07)	1.5 (0.05)	1.8 (0.04)	1.0 (0.03)	0.6 (0.03)
Slovenia[1]	2 (0.3)	—	24 (1.1)	497 (4.0)	53 (1.0)	538 (3.6)	21 (0.9)	602 (4.2)	2.0 (0.04)	1.7 (0.05)	1.6 (0.05)	1.6 (0.04)	0.9 (0.03)	0.6 (0.02)
Spain	5 (0.5)	441 (4.6)	23 (1.0)	456 (2.6)	45 (1.1)	488 (2.6)	27 (1.0)	522 (3.4)	1.8 (0.05)	1.8 (0.06)	1.1 (0.03)	1.7 (0.04)	0.6 (0.02)	0.3 (0.02)
Sweden	2 (0.3)	—	16 (0.7)	475 (3.4)	61 (0.9)	517 (3.0)	21 (0.8)	565 (3.8)	2.3 (0.04)	2.3 (0.05)	0.9 (0.02)	1.6 (0.04)	0.7 (0.02)	0.6 (0.02)
Switzerland	3 (0.4)	497 (10.1)	21 (0.9)	528 (4.0)	47 (0.9)	541 (3.0)	28 (1.1)	575 (3.3)	1.3 (0.03)	2.4 (0.05)	1.0 (0.03)	1.8 (0.03)	0.8 (0.02)	0.4 (0.02)
Thailand[1]	2 (0.3)	—	38 (1.5)	510 (5.1)	45 (1.1)	529 (6.6)	15 (0.9)	537 (7.4)	2.1 (0.07)	1.2 (0.03)	1.6 (0.03)	1.1 (0.02)	1.0 (0.02)	0.3 (0.02)
United States	3 (0.3)	430 (5.1)	11 (0.6)	462 (4.8)	52 (0.9)	491 (4.3)	34 (1.0)	534 (5.9)	2.6 (0.07)	2.5 (0.06)	1.2 (0.04)	2.2 (0.05)	0.7 (0.02)	0.7 (0.03)

[1] Countries not meeting all International Association for the Evaluation of Educational Achievement's sampling specifications.
[2] Student response data available for 70 to 84 percent of students.
—Data not available or not applicable.

NOTE.—Standard errors appear in parentheses.
SOURCE: International Association for the Evaluation of Educational Achievement, *Mathematics Achievement in the Middle School Years: IEA's Third International Mathematics and Science Study*, 1997. (This table was prepared June 1997.)

INTERNATIONAL COMPARISONS OF EDUCATION 449

Table 401.—Average fourth grade mathematics scores,[1] by content areas, and average time spent studying mathematics out of school, by country: 1994–95

Country	Overall mathematics scores	Average percent correct by content area						Amount of daily out-of-school study time in mathematics						
		Whole numbers	Fractions and proportionality	Measurement, estimation, and number sense	Data representation, analysis, and probability	Geometry	Patterns, relations, and functions	No time		Less than 1 hour		1 hour or more		Average hours[2]
								Percent	Mean score	Percent	Mean score	Percent	Mean score	
1	2	3	4	5	6	7	8	9	10	11	12	13	14	15
Australia[3]	63 (0.6)	67 (0.6)	51 (0.7)	60 (0.7)	67 (0.8)	74 (0.7)	64 (0.9)	15 (0.9)	526 (5.6)	61 (1.2)	559 (3.2)	24 (1.0)	530 (4.4)	0.8 (0.02)
Austria[3]	65 (0.7)	74 (0.8)	51 (0.8)	69 (0.8)	66 (1.1)	67 (0.8)	64 (1.1)	4 (0.7)	555 (8.6)	58 (1.8)	571 (3.8)	38 (1.6)	546 (4.1)	1.0 (0.03)
Canada	60 (1.0)	68 (0.9)	48 (1.0)	54 (1.1)	68 (1.4)	72 (1.4)	62 (1.5)	14 (1.1)	526 (4.4)	60 (1.1)	544 (4.0)	26 (1.2)	522 (5.0)	0.8 (0.02)
Cyprus	54 (0.6)	65 (0.7)	48 (0.7)	48 (0.8)	52 (0.9)	53 (0.9)	55 (1.1)	9 (0.7)	473 (6.1)	51 (1.9)	519 (3.6)	40 (1.6)	495 (3.8)	1.1 (0.03)
Czech Republic	66 (0.6)	75 (0.6)	53 (0.8)	68 (0.7)	67 (0.9)	71 (0.7)	67 (0.9)	9 (0.9)	547 (6.6)	69 (1.2)	576 (3.6)	22 (1.1)	560 (4.3)	0.7 (0.02)
England[4,5]	57 (0.7)	58 (0.7)	45 (0.8)	52 (0.7)	64 (0.9)	74 (0.8)	55 (1.0)	—	—	—	—	—	—	—
Greece	51 (0.9)	62 (1.0)	42 (1.1)	48 (1.0)	50 (1.2)	53 (1.2)	47 (1.2)	6 (0.5)	453 (6.8)	38 (1.6)	512 (4.1)	56 (1.7)	493 (4.0)	1.6 (0.04)
Hong Kong	73 (0.9)	79 (0.9)	66 (1.0)	69 (0.9)	76 (1.0)	74 (0.8)	73 (1.2)	6 (0.7)	550 (7.9)	44 (1.2)	595 (4.2)	50 (1.2)	586 (4.5)	1.3 (0.03)
Hungary[3]	64 (0.8)	76 (0.7)	49 (0.9)	64 (0.9)	60 (1.0)	66 (0.8)	69 (1.1)	5 (0.7)	543 (10.8)	58 (1.3)	563 (3.9)	37 (1.4)	533 (4.2)	1.0 (0.03)
Iceland	50 (0.8)	56 (0.9)	36 (1.0)	44 (0.9)	58 (1.2)	63 (1.0)	48 (1.4)	10 (0.8)	457 (4.3)	63 (1.4)	483 (3.5)	27 (1.4)	472 (3.2)	0.8 (0.02)
Iran, Islamic Republic[6]	38 (0.9)	51 (1.2)	32 (1.0)	36 (0.9)	23 (0.9)	42 (0.9)	40 (1.4)	5 (0.7)	402 (6.6)	17 (1.3)	433 (6.0)	78 (1.5)	443 (4.5)	2.3 (0.07)
Ireland	63 (0.8)	70 (0.8)	58 (1.0)	56 (0.9)	69 (0.9)	66 (0.8)	64 (1.0)	7 (0.6)	516 (7.1)	70 (1.3)	565 (3.6)	23 (1.2)	530 (4.9)	0.8 (0.02)
Israel[3,6,7]	59 (1.0)	71 (1.0)	48 (1.1)	54 (1.0)	64 (1.2)	62 (1.0)	60 (1.5)	14 (1.3)	525 (6.4)	46 (2.2)	535 (4.7)	40 (1.9)	528 (4.1)	1.1 (0.05)
Japan	74 (0.4)	82 (0.4)	65 (0.6)	72 (0.5)	79 (0.5)	72 (0.6)	76 (0.6)	10 (0.7)	558 (4.3)	60 (1.1)	598 (2.3)	31 (1.2)	610 (3.0)	0.9 (0.02)
Korea	76 (0.4)	88 (0.3)	65 (0.5)	72 (0.5)	80 (0.6)	72 (0.6)	83 (0.7)	14 (0.8)	593 (4.2)	44 (1.1)	610 (2.5)	42 (1.2)	621 (2.3)	1.0 (0.02)
Kuwait[3]	32 (0.5)	36 (0.5)	25 (0.5)	35 (0.6)	26 (0.6)	36 (0.6)	33 (1.0)	5 (0.7)	372 (5.7)	34 (1.4)	410 (3.0)	60 (1.5)	401 (2.8)	1.9 (0.05)
Latvia (Latvian-speaking schools)[3]	59 (1.0)	68 (0.9)	44 (1.3)	60 (1.0)	54 (1.3)	67 (1.0)	65 (1.2)	7 (0.7)	476 (7.5)	61 (1.9)	542 (6.3)	33 (1.7)	518 (5.1)	1.0 (0.03)
Netherlands[3]	69 (0.7)	75 (0.8)	60 (0.9)	70 (0.8)	75 (0.9)	71 (0.8)	65 (1.1)	47 (2.7)	593 (4.3)	39 (2.3)	578 (3.6)	14 (1.5)	541 (6.1)	0.5 (0.03)
New Zealand	53 (1.0)	57 (1.0)	41 (1.1)	49 (1.1)	61 (1.3)	66 (1.1)	52 (1.2)	21 (1.6)	488 (9.7)	54 (1.7)	512 (4.4)	25 (1.4)	493 (5.2)	0.8 (0.03)
Norway	53 (0.7)	61 (0.8)	38 (0.7)	56 (0.7)	59 (0.9)	58 (0.9)	50 (1.2)	23 (1.3)	503 (4.1)	58 (1.2)	512 (3.3)	19 (1.1)	497 (5.3)	0.6 (0.02)
Portugal	48 (0.7)	57 (0.8)	38 (0.7)	49 (0.8)	43 (1.1)	52 (1.0)	47 (1.1)	3 (0.5)	420 (9.1)	55 (1.7)	489 (3.9)	42 (1.6)	470 (3.9)	1.3 (0.03)
Scotland[4]	58 (0.8)	61 (0.8)	46 (1.0)	53 (0.9)	66 (1.0)	72 (0.8)	57 (1.0)	26 (1.8)	519 (7.2)	63 (2.0)	528 (3.8)	11 (1.0)	501 (8.9)	0.5 (0.02)
Singapore	76 (0.8)	83 (0.7)	74 (1.0)	67 (1.0)	81 (0.8)	72 (0.8)	76 (0.9)	—	—	—	—	—	—	—
Slovenia[3]	64 (0.6)	74 (0.6)	50 (0.9)	64 (0.9)	64 (1.0)	72 (0.8)	68 (0.8)	3 (0.4)	502 (11.4)	57 (1.5)	563 (3.7)	40 (1.4)	548 (3.7)	1.0 (0.03)
Thailand[3]	50 (1.1)	58 (1.3)	44 (1.0)	44 (1.0)	56 (1.5)	53 (1.2)	50 (1.3)	17 (1.3)	470 (4.3)	44 (1.6)	496 (4.5)	39 (1.8)	489 (6.1)	1.0 (0.03)
United States	63 (0.6)	71 (0.7)	51 (0.8)	53 (0.6)	73 (0.9)	71 (0.7)	66 (0.9)	8 (0.5)	516 (4.4)	60 (1.1)	561 (3.1)	32 (1.1)	528 (2.9)	1.0 (0.03)

[1] Fourth grade students or equivalent in most countries.
[2] Average hours based on: No time = 0; Less than 1 hour = .5; 1–2 hours = 1.5; 3–4 hours = 3.5; More than 4 hours = 5.
[3] Did not satisfy one or more guidelines for sample participation rates, age/grade specifications, or classroom sampling procedures.
[4] Met guidelines for sample participation only after replacement schools were included for question about mathematics content areas.
[5] National defined population covers less than 90 percent of international desired population.
[6] Indicates a 70 to 84 percent student response rate on question about time spent studying mathematics.
[7] National defined population does not cover all of international desired population.
—Data not available or not applicable.

NOTE.—Standard errors appear in parentheses.

SOURCE: International Association for the Evaluation of Educational Achievement, *Mathematics Achievement in the Primary School Years*, and *Science Achievement in the Primary School Years: IEA's Third International Mathematics and Science Study*, 1997. (This table was prepared July 1997.)

450 INTERNATIONAL COMPARISONS OF EDUCATION

Table 402.—Average fourth grade science scores,[1] by content areas, and average time spent teaching science in school, by country: 1994–95

Country	Overall science scores	Science content areas					Average number of hours science is taught weekly to science classes							
		Earth science	Life science	Physical science	Environmental issues and the nature of science		Less than 1 hour		1 to 2 hours		2 to 3 hours		More than 3 hours	
							Percent	Mean score	Percent	Mean score	Percent	Mean score	Percent	Mean score
1	2	3	4	5	6		7	8	9	10	11	12	13	14
Australia[2,3]	66 (0.5)	61 (0.6)	72 (0.5)	63 (0.7)	63 (0.8)		35 (3.9)	556 (5.0)	55 (4.0)	568 (5.9)	5 (1.5)	562 (18.1)	5 (2.1)	562 (8.4)
Austria[2]	66 (0.7)	62 (0.8)	72 (0.7)	64 (0.8)	54 (1.0)		0 (0.0)	—	0 (0.0)	—	97 (1.8)	566 (3.6)	3 (1.8)	540 (30.3)
Canada	64 (0.6)	62 (0.6)	68 (0.6)	61 (0.7)	56 (0.7)		8 (2.0)	536 (10.1)	42 (3.8)	542 (5.1)	27 (3.3)	567 (5.4)	23 (3.2)	550 (4.6)
Cyprus	51 (0.5)	48 (0.7)	55 (0.5)	50 (0.7)	42 (1.0)		—	—	—	—	—	—	—	—
Czech Republic	65 (0.5)	64 (0.6)	71 (0.5)	62 (0.7)	56 (0.9)		2 (1.1)	—	79 (3.6)	557 (3.9)	3 (1.4)	572 (6.8)	16 (3.2)	563 (7.3)
England[4,5]	63 (0.6)	61 (0.6)	68 (0.6)	60 (0.8)	56 (1.0)		6 (1.7)	540 (8.7)	27 (4.1)	548 (7.5)	44 (4.8)	556 (5.9)	23 (3.8)	550 (8.2)
Greece	54 (0.8)	52 (0.9)	61 (0.9)	49 (0.9)	43 (1.2)		—	—	—	—	—	—	—	—
Hong Kong	62 (0.7)	61 (0.6)	68 (0.7)	60 (0.8)	50 (1.1)		13 (3.4)	530 (13.3)	84 (3.7)	534 (4.3)	2 (1.5)	—	1 (0.8)	—
Hungary[2]	62 (0.6)	62 (0.7)	66 (0.6)	59 (0.8)	50 (0.9)		6 (2.2)	556 (13.3)	72 (4.1)	529 (3.7)	8 (3.0)	521 (8.4)	14 (3.1)	549 (10.5)
Iceland[3]	55 (0.7)	55 (0.7)	60 (0.8)	52 (0.7)	47 (1.2)		17 (4.1)	513 (7.3)	41 (5.6)	504 (7.7)	30 (5.1)	499 (6.5)	12 (4.3)	523 (6.8)
Iran, Islamic Republic	40 (0.7)	38 (0.7)	44 (0.7)	40 (0.9)	26 (0.9)		—	—	—	—	—	—	—	—
Ireland	61 (0.6)	60 (0.8)	66 (0.6)	57 (0.7)	55 (0.9)		47 (5.0)	536 (5.6)	40 (4.4)	540 (5.8)	11 (3.1)	550 (7.1)	2 (0.9)	—
Israel[2,3,6]	57 (0.8)	51 (0.8)	61 (0.9)	55 (0.9)	51 (1.3)		0 (0.0)	—	53 (5.6)	508 (5.5)	32 (5.8)	494 (6.9)	15 (4.3)	493 (10.6)
Japan	70 (0.3)	66 (0.4)	73 (0.3)	70 (0.4)	62 (0.6)		2 (1.3)	542 (8.3)	1 (0.6)	—	95 (1.8)	575 (1.8)	2 (1.2)	—
Korea	74 (0.4)	72 (0.5)	76 (0.4)	75 (0.5)	70 (0.8)		0 (0.0)	527 (5.4)	1 (0.6)	—	95 (1.8)	597 (1.9)	5 (1.7)	588 (10.3)
Kuwait[2,3]	39 (0.5)	36 (0.6)	45 (0.6)	37 (0.5)	25 (0.7)		0 (0.0)	—	1 (0.7)	—	96 (2.0)	402 (3.9)	4 (1.8)	416 (42.2)
Latvia (Latvian-speaking schools)[2]	56 (0.8)	57 (1.0)	60 (0.8)	54 (0.9)	46 (1.2)		89 (2.9)	505 (5.7)	5 (2.2)	538 (47.2)	5 (2.2)	532 (11.9)	1 (0.8)	—
Netherlands[2]	67 (0.5)	61 (0.6)	73 (0.5)	65 (0.6)	61 (0.9)		38 (5.1)	559 (4.0)	44 (4.8)	556 (4.5)	9 (2.6)	556 (7.2)	9 (2.7)	549 (20.1)
New Zealand[3]	60 (0.9)	57 (0.9)	66 (0.9)	57 (1.1)	54 (1.2)		29 (4.2)	542 (8.3)	48 (4.4)	536 (6.1)	14 (3.1)	537 (17.2)	9 (2.6)	509 (21.2)
Norway[3]	60 (0.6)	60 (0.6)	67 (0.7)	55 (0.7)	53 (0.9)		73 (5.0)	527 (5.4)	27 (5.0)	535 (7.6)	0 (0.0)	—	0 (0.0)	—
Portugal	50 (0.7)	50 (0.8)	54 (0.8)	49 (0.8)	39 (1.0)		2 (1.1)	—	3 (1.4)	486 (28.2)	12 (3.1)	474 (8.8)	84 (3.6)	481 (4.8)
Scotland[3,4]	60 (0.8)	58 (0.9)	65 (0.8)	57 (0.8)	53 (1.2)		35 (4.7)	543 (5.9)	44 (4.7)	534 (6.4)	14 (3.3)	531 (13.2)	7 (2.5)	529 (12.5)
Singapore	64 (0.8)	58 (0.8)	70 (0.8)	64 (0.8)	53 (1.1)		0 (0.0)	—	4 (1.5)	548 (18.9)	96 (1.5)	547 (5.1)	0 (0.0)	—
Slovenia[2]	64 (0.7)	64 (0.7)	68 (0.7)	61 (0.8)	54 (0.8)		3 (1.9)	544 (18.9)	60 (5.3)	541 (4.6)	18 (4.0)	550 (9.5)	19 (3.4)	548 (6.8)
Thailand[2,3]	49 (0.9)	48 (0.9)	52 (0.8)	46 (1.0)	48 (1.4)		2 (1.2)	—	9 (3.5)	463 (21.5)	17 (6.1)	469 (16.5)	73 (6.6)	477 (6.5)
United States[3]	66 (0.5)	64 (0.7)	71 (0.6)	60 (0.6)	65 (0.8)		9 (2.1)	562 (11.5)	16 (2.9)	550 (10.2)	33 (3.8)	578 (5.9)	42 (4.1)	565 (5.1)

—Data not available or not applicable.

NOTE.—Standard errors appear in parentheses.

[1] Fourth grade or equivalent in most countries.
[2] Did not satisfy one or more guidelines for sample participation rates, age/grade specification, or classroom sampling procedures.
[3] Teacher response data on amount of time science is taught is 84 percent or less.
[4] Met guidelines for sample participation rates only after replacement schools were included.
[5] National defined population covers less than 90 percent of international desired population.
[6] National defined population does not cover all of international desired population.

SOURCE: International Association for the Evaluation of Educational Achievement, *Science Achievement in the Primary School Years: IEA's Third International Mathematics and Science Study*, 1997. (This table was prepared July 1997.)

Table 403.—Reading literacy test scores of 9-year-olds: Selected countries, 1992

Country	Grade tested	Mean age	Overall mean score (s.e.)[1]	Narrative[2] 1st quartile	Narrative[2] mean score (s.e.)[1]	Narrative[2] 3rd quartile	Expository[3] mean score (s.e.)[1]	Documents[4] mean score (s.e.)[1]
1	2	3	4	5	6	7	8	9
Finland	3	9.7	569 (3.4)	508	568 (3.0)	602	569 (3.1)	569 (4.0)
United States	4	10.0	547 (2.8)	476	553 (3.1)	619	538 (2.6)	550 (2.7)
Sweden	3	9.8	539 (2.8)	467	536 (2.6)	592	542 (2.7)	539 (3.2)
France	4	10.1	531 (4.0)	467	532 (4.1)	580	533 (4.1)	527 (3.9)
Italy	4	9.9	529 (4.3)	468	533 (4.0)	576	538 (4.0)	517 (4.9)
New Zealand	5	10.0	528 (3.3)	452	534 (3.5)	594	531 (3.1)	521 (3.3)
Norway	3	9.8	524 (2.6)	455	525 (2.8)	576	528 (2.3)	519 (2.8)
Iceland[5]	3	9.8	518 (0.0)	448	518 (0.0)	571	517 (0.0)	519 (0.0)
Hong Kong	4	10.0	517 (3.9)	431	494 (4.1)	548	503 (3.4)	554 (4.2)
Singapore	3	9.3	515 (1.0)	450	521 (1.1)	567	519 (1.0)	504 (1.0)
Switzerland	3	9.7	511 (2.7)	438	506 (2.6)	566	507 (2.7)	522 (2.8)
Ireland	4	9.3	509 (3.6)	445	518 (3.7)	571	514 (3.2)	495 (3.8)
Belgium[6]	4	9.8	507 (3.2)	439	510 (3.3)	558	505 (2.8)	506 (3.5)
Greece	4	9.3	504 (3.7)	447	514 (3.8)	567	511 (3.6)	488 (3.8)
Spain	4	10.0	504 (2.5)	429	497 (2.4)	543	505 (2.3)	509 (2.7)
Germany (former West)	3	9.4	503 (3.0)	421	491 (2.8)	543	497 (2.9)	520 (3.2)
Canada[7]	3	8.9	500 (3.0)	437	502 (3.5)	566	499 (2.7)	500 (2.8)
Germany (former East)	3	9.5	499 (4.3)	414	482 (4.2)	531	493 (3.6)	522 (5.0)
Hungary	3	9.3	499 (3.1)	437	496 (2.9)	541	493 (3.1)	509 (3.5)
Slovenia	3	9.7	498 (2.6)	435	502 (2.7)	570	489 (2.5)	503 (2.5)
Netherlands	3	9.2	485 (3.6)	425	494 (3.3)	539	480 (3.4)	481 (3.9)
Cyprus	4	9.8	481 (2.3)	421	492 (2.4)	548	475 (2.3)	476 (2.1)
Portugal	4	10.4	478 (3.6)	419	483 (3.3)	531	480 (3.0)	471 (4.5)
Denmark	3	9.8	475 (3.5)	386	463 (3.4)	539	467 (3.5)	496 (3.6)
Trinidad/Tobago	4	9.6	451 (3.4)	383	455 (3.6)	502	458 (3.4)	440 (3.3)
Indonesia	4	10.8	394 (3.0)	351	402 (2.8)	436	411 (3.2)	369 (3.0)
Venezuela	4	10.1	383 (3.4)	322	378 (3.2)	426	396 (3.3)	374 (3.7)

[1] s.e.=standard error.
[2] Narrative prose is continuous text in which the writer's aim is to tell a story.
[3] Expository prose is continuous text designed to describe factual information to the reader.
[4] Documents are structured information presented in the form of charts, tables, maps, graphs, lists, or sets of instructions.
[5] Iceland tested all students, therefore standard errors are not applicable.
[6] Only French-speaking students were tested.
[7] British Columbia only.

SOURCE: International Association for the Evaluation of Educational Achievement, *How in the World Do Students Read?*, 1992. (This table was prepared April 1993.)

Table 404.—Reading literacy test scores of 14-year-olds: Selected countries, 1992

Country	Grade tested	Mean age	Overall mean score (s.e.)[1]	Narrative[2] mean score (s.e.)[1]	Expository[3] 1st quartile	Expository[3] mean score (s.e.)[1]	Expository[3] 3rd quartile	Documents[4] mean score (s.e.)[1]
1	2	3	4	5	6	7	8	9
Finland	8	14.7	560 (2.5)	559 (2.8)	493	541 (2.2)	575	580 (2.5)
France	9	15.4	549 (4.3)	556 (4.2)	484	546 (4.3)	580	544 (4.2)
Sweden	8	14.8	546 (2.5)	556 (2.6)	469	533 (2.4)	576	550 (2.4)
New Zealand	10	15.0	545 (5.6)	547 (5.7)	457	535 (5.7)	597	552 (5.3)
Hungary	8	14.1	536 (3.3)	530 (3.1)	469	536 (3.6)	577	542 (3.2)
Iceland[5]	8	14.8	536 (0.0)	550 (0.0)	472	548 (0.0)	617	509 (0.0)
Switzerland	8	14.9	536 (3.2)	534 (3.4)	466	525 (3.2)	572	549 (3.0)
Hong Kong	9	15.2	535 (3.7)	509 (3.7)	480	540 (3.8)	576	557 (3.8)
United States	9	15.0	535 (4.8)	539 (4.9)	456	539 (5.6)	599	528 (4.0)
Singapore	8	14.4	534 (1.1)	530 (1.1)	476	539 (1.2)	574	533 (1.1)
Slovenia	8	14.7	532 (2.3)	534 (2.6)	471	525 (2.2)	576	537 (2.2)
Germany (former East)	8	14.4	526 (3.5)	512 (3.9)	464	523 (3.5)	566	543 (2.9)
Denmark	8	14.8	525 (2.1)	517 (2.0)	458	524 (2.2)	573	532 (2.1)
Portugal	9	15.6	523 (3.1)	523 (2.5)	469	523 (3.4)	556	523 (3.4)
Canada[6]	8	13.9	522 (3.0)	526 (3.1)	449	516 (3.1)	569	522 (2.7)
Germany (former West)	8	14.6	522 (4.4)	514 (4.9)	453	521 (4.5)	573	532 (3.9)
Norway	8	14.8	516 (2.3)	515 (2.1)	464	520 (2.4)	569	512 (2.4)
Italy	8	14.1	515 (3.4)	520 (3.6)	459	524 (3.2)	565	501 (3.3)
Netherlands	8	14.3	514 (4.9)	506 (4.8)	442	503 (4.7)	546	533 (5.3)
Ireland	9	14.5	511 (5.2)	510 (5.3)	439	505 (5.3)	555	518 (4.9)
Greece	9	14.4	509 (2.9)	526 (2.9)	450	508 (3.1)	548	493 (2.6)
Cyprus	9	14.8	497 (2.2)	516 (2.2)	427	492 (2.4)	536	482 (2.0)
Spain	8	14.2	490 (2.5)	500 (3.0)	435	495 (2.6)	536	475 (2.0)
Belgium[7]	8	14.3	481 (4.9)	484 (5.1)	415	477 (4.8)	522	483 (4.7)
Trinidad/Tobago	9	14.4	479 (1.7)	482 (1.7)	408	485 (1.8)	537	472 (1.7)
Thailand	9	15.2	477 (6.2)	468 (6.6)	429	486 (5.9)	533	478 (6.2)
Philippines	8	14.5	430 (3.9)	421 (3.6)	378	439 (4.1)	472	430 (3.9)
Venezuela	9	15.5	417 (3.1)	407 (2.9)	381	433 (3.3)	482	412 (3.0)
Nigeria[8,9]	9	15.3	401 (—)	402 (—)	351	406 (—)	441	394 (—)
Zimbabwe[9]	9	15.5	372 (3.8)	367 (3.3)	326	374 (3.6)	411	373 (4.6)
Botswana	9	14.7	330 (2.0)	340 (1.6)	294	339 (1.9)	371	312 (2.4)

[1] s.e.=standard error.
[2] Narrative prose is continuous text in which the writer's aim is to tell a story.
[3] Expository prose is continuous text designed to describe factual information to the reader.
[4] Documents are structured information presented in the form of charts, tables, maps, graphs, lists, or sets of instructions.
[5] Iceland tested all students, therefore standard errors are not applicable.
[6] British Columbia only.
[7] Only French-speaking students were tested.
[8] Insufficient data to calculate the standard error.
[9] Sampling response rate of schools was below 80 percent.
—Data not available.

SOURCE: International Association for the Evaluation of Educational Achievement, *How in the World Do Students Read?*, 1992. (This table was prepared April 1993.)

INTERNATIONAL COMPARISONS OF EDUCATION 453

Table 405.—Number of bachelor's degree recipients per 100 persons of the theoretical age of graduation,[1] by sex: Selected countries, 1989 to 1994

Country	Men and women					Men					Women				
	1989	1990	1991	1992	1994	1989	1990	1991	1992	1994	1989	1990	1991	1992	1994
1	2	3	4	5	6	7	8	9	10	11	12	13	14	15	16
Australia	20.8	—	24.4	26.3	31.5	19.3	—	21.6	22.0	25.4	22.3	—	27.3	30.8	37.9
Austria	6.7	7.8	7.8	—	—	7.7	8.7	8.5	7.8	—	5.6	7.0	7.0	5.2	—
Belgium	—	—	13.3	—	—	—	—	15.0	—	—	—	—	11.5	—	—
Canada	30.2	31.8	33.3	32.2	30.2	26.9	27.6	28.2	26.9	25.5	33.5	36.0	38.7	37.7	35.1
Denmark	12.9	15.0	16.5	22.1	[2]20.2	11.5	13.2	14.4	17.6	[2]16.1	14.4	16.8	18.7	26.9	[2]24.6
Finland	—	—	—	6.5	7.5	—	—	—	—	9.3	—	—	—	—	5.5
France	13.9	14.9	16.3	—	—	13.8	14.7	14.9	—	—	14.0	15.1	17.7	—	—
Germany[3]	13.2	12.9	13.3	—	—	16.1	15.7	15.9	—	—	10.1	10.0	10.6	—	—
Ireland	16.3	17.5	16.0	17.4	[2]22.8	—	16.9	15.8	17.7	[2]22.3	—	18.2	16.2	17.1	[2]23.4
Italy	—	—	—	—	.8	—	—	—	—	0.5	—	—	—	—	1.0
Japan	—	21.8	23.7	23.4	23.4	—	30.9	33.5	32.3	31.2	—	12.3	13.7	14.1	15.3
Netherlands	10.2	8.0	8.3	17.8	[2]17.4	12.3	9.4	9.6	17.6	[2]17.2	7.9	6.5	6.9	18.0	[2]17.6
New Zealand	15.7	15.1	16.1	18.0	[2]21.9	16.4	15.7	16.5	17.7	[2]19.9	15.0	14.6	15.8	18.3	[2]24.0
Norway	—	—	—	19.4	17.6	—	—	—	14.8	12.5	—	—	—	24.2	22.9
Portugal	—	—	—	—	1.8	—	—	—	—	1.2	—	—	—	—	2.4
Spain	—	—	—	8.0	[2]8.6	—	—	—	5.8	[2]6.8	—	—	—	10.4	[2]10.4
Sweden	13.1	12.2	12.5	11.4	6.9	11.1	10.5	11.0	9.6	4.8	15.1	14.0	14.2	13.3	9.1
Switzerland	7.7	7.8	7.6	—	—	10.1	10.3	9.8	—	—	5.3	5.1	5.4	—	—
Turkey	6.3	6.5	6.5	6.0	[2]7.1	7.9	8.2	8.2	7.4	[2]8.8	4.7	4.7	4.7	4.4	[2]5.4
United Kingdom	—	—	—	20.4	27.0	—	—	—	21.1	26.5	—	—	—	19.7	27.5
United States	27.8	28.1	28.1	27.4	31.8	26.1	25.9	25.3	24.7	28.4	29.6	30.5	31.0	30.3	35.2

[1] In most countries the theoretical age of graduation was 22 or 23. The range was from 21 to 25. The number of bachelor's degree recipients may be of any age.
[2] Data for 1993.
[3] Data for 1989 are for the former West Germany.

—Data not available.

SOURCE: Organization for Economic Cooperation and Development, Education at a Glance, 1996. (This table was prepared April 1997.)

Table 406.—Percent of bachelor's degrees awarded in science: Selected countries, 1985 to 1994

Country	All science degrees				Natural sciences				Mathematics and computer science				Engineering			
	1985	1990	1991	1994	1985	1990	1991	1994	1985	1990	1991	1994	1985	1990	1991	1994
1	2	3	4	5	6	7	8	9	10	11	12	13	14	15	16	17
Australia	—	—	21.6	21.5	—	—	15.9	10.6	—	—	—	3.8	—	—	5.7	7.1
Austria	16.8	19.6	20.1	30.2	5.0	5.3	5.9	11.5	4.1	5.2	4.8	5.4	7.7	9.0	9.5	13.3
Belgium	14.7	—	32.2	[1]32.0	4.6	—	4.3	[1]9.3	1.7	—	1.7	[1]2.1	8.4	—	26.3	[1]20.6
Canada	17.1	16.4	15.5	19.3	4.9	6.0	5.7	8.2	4.5	4.2	3.7	3.7	7.7	6.2	6.1	7.4
Denmark	22.5	26.1	27.6	[1]23.4	6.3	4.4	6.1	[1]6.6	—	—	0.1	[1]1.3	16.2	21.7	21.4	[1]15.5
Finland	39.3	33.5	34.5	40.2	7.7	4.1	4.2	8.8	6.3	5.9	6.6	7.1	25.3	23.4	23.7	24.3
Germany[2]	23.8	31.3	31.5	[1]41.3	5.0	7.2	7.3	[1]12.6	2.3	3.5	3.9	[1]5.5	16.5	20.5	20.2	[1]23.2
Ireland	28.8	34.1	28.5	[1]30.0	12.8	14.1	12.4	[1]13.5	4.0	6.3	4.4	[1]5.0	12.0	13.7	11.6	[1]11.5
Italy	19.5	19.7	19.8	23.6	8.1	7.6	7.5	8.8	3.1	3.9	3.8	2.9	8.3	8.3	8.5	11.9
Japan	22.7	23.5	23.5	31.1	2.4	2.4	2.4	9.6	—	—	—	—	20.3	21.0	21.1	21.5
Netherlands	21.8	21.1	21.4	[1]22.5	8.5	7.1	6.5	[1]6.6	1.2	1.6	1.6	[1]2.5	12.1	12.4	13.3	13.4
New Zealand	20.5	19.5	16.3	[1]19.0	11.7	8.2	7.1	[1]8.5	5.5	5.5	4.0	[1]4.3	3.3	5.8	5.2	[1]6.2
Norway	6.1	12.9	12.3	26.9	2.5	2.1	1.8	7.2	1.8	0.6	0.6	0.9	1.8	10.2	9.9	[1]18.8
Portugal	—	24.3	—	21.7	6.5	6.7	—	5.9	—	7.0	—	2.5	—	10.5	—	13.3
Spain	13.9	15.0	15.4	[1]20.0	5.5	5.7	5.3	[1]6.8	1.3	2.6	2.9	[1]3.7	7.0	6.7	7.1	9.5
Sweden	15.4	24.0	24.3	27.9	2.6	4.1	4.2	6.8	1.6	4.7	4.9	5.2	11.3	15.2	15.2	15.9
Switzerland	20.2	23.0	22.7	31.3	10.3	11.2	11.0	16.3	2.1	3.7	3.8	3.4	7.9	8.1	7.9	11.6
Turkey	23.0	20.6	21.3	[1]29.6	3.6	4.6	4.9	[1]10.5	1.6	2.1	2.3	[1]2.8	17.8	13.8	14.1	16.3
United States	21.7	16.9	15.9	18.2	6.3	5.1	5.1	7.3	5.5	4.0	3.6	3.3	9.8	7.8	7.2	[1]7.6

[1] Data for 1993.
[2] Data for 1985 are for the former West Germany.
—Data not available.

SOURCE: Organization for Economic Cooperation and Development, Education at a Glance, 1996. (This table was prepared April 1997.)

Table 407.—Percent of graduate degrees awarded in science: Selected countries, 1985, 1990, and 1991

Country	All science degrees			Natural sciences			Mathematics and computer science			Engineering		
	1985	1990	1991	1985	1990	1991	1985	1990	1991	1985	1990	1991
1	2	3	4	5	6	7	8	9	10	11	12	13
Australia	—	—	13.9	—	—	9.6	—	—	—	—	—	4.3
Austria	43.3	37.7	37.4	14.2	12.3	13.4	7.3	4.6	6.1	21.7	20.8	17.9
Canada	19.7	20.0	19.7	7.5	7.8	7.7	2.8	3.4	3.4	9.4	8.8	8.7
Denmark	16.0	22.2	22.9	4.1	5.8	5.4	2.7	4.8	4.5	9.2	11.6	13.0
Finland	47.6	30.6	29.2	24.0	14.7	12.4	6.3	5.4	4.6	17.2	10.5	12.2
Germany[1]	27.7	33.2	33.9	18.7	23.5	23.3	1.8	2.3	2.2	7.2	7.4	8.4
Ireland	31.4	34.5	28.4	18.9	19.5	15.7	2.6	5.8	4.1	9.9	9.3	8.6
Japan	50.1	54.6	54.2	9.5	9.5	9.5	—	—	—	40.5	45.1	44.7
Netherlands	—	28.9	29.9	20.6	17.7	16.7	—	1.5	1.6	7.5	9.7	11.6
New Zealand	45.1	22.6	19.3	24.6	13.8	11.5	5.4	4.7	3.6	15.1	4.0	4.2
Norway	40.1	33.4	33.8	17.9	8.0	7.9	3.5	2.1	2.5	18.7	23.3	23.4
Spain	35.6	26.9	26.6	28.6	19.7	19.1	1.8	1.4	2.5	5.1	5.7	5.0
Sweden	48.0	48.5	44.4	21.2	19.4	15.1	6.8	9.2	8.2	20.0	19.9	21.1
Switzerland	30.7	30.2	32.6	20.3	22.0	23.1	2.8	1.7	1.8	7.6	6.5	7.6
Turkey	35.8	24.0	21.7	6.6	7.6	6.4	2.8	3.3	2.8	26.3	13.2	12.4
United States	13.5	14.5	13.8	4.5	4.2	3.8	2.8	3.4	3.2	6.3	6.9	6.7

[1] Data for 1985 are for the former West Germany.
—Data not available.

SOURCE: Organization for Economic Cooperation and Development, unpublished data. (This table was prepared May 1995.)

Table 408.—Public education expenditures per student, by level of student: Selected countries, 1985 to 1993

[In constant 1993 dollars]

Country	Primary					Secondary					Higher education				
	1985	1990	1991	1992	1993[1]	1985	1990	1991	1992	1993[1]	1985	1990	1991	1992	1993[1]
1	2	3	4	5	6	7	8	9	10	11	12	13	14	15	16
Austria	$3,554	$3,632	$3,791	$4,130	$4,291	$4,061	$4,771	$4,965	$6,612	$6,721	$6,753	$6,560	$6,834	$5,994	$8,642
Belgium	2,299	2,195	2,273	2,462	2,953	5,437	4,949	5,305	5,304	5,373	7,310	6,363	6,615	6,787	6,380
Denmark	3,677	4,579	4,665	4,346	4,745	5,196	5,459	5,706	5,088	6,175	8,826	8,582	8,153	6,911	8,045
France	—	—	2,749	2,987	3,154	—	—	4,923	5,593	5,685	—	—	5,050	6,200	6,033
Germany[2]	—	—	—	3,069	2,815	—	—	—	4,388	6,481	—	—	—	—	7,902
Japan	—	—	—	3,636	3,960	—	—	—	4,017	4,356	—	—	—	12,205	7,556
Ireland	1,363	1,472	1,636	1,823	1,882	2,346	2,475	2,640	2,853	3,031	5,327	5,693	5,927	7,488	7,076
Norway	3,505	3,995	4,122	4,614	—	4,961	5,307	5,704	6,386	—	8,092	8,887	8,917	8,981	8,343
Portugal	1,369	1,989	2,239	—	2,581	1,811	—	2,508	—	2,491	3,844	—	6,536	—	5,667
Spain	1,482	1,854	1,974	2,091	2,293	2,058	2,787	2,896	3,234	3,033	1,964	3,250	3,440	3,883	3,835
Sweden[1]	—	5,429	5,803	4,985	4,917	—	6,480	7,039	6,231	5,651	—	8,929	9,083	7,333	12,693
Switzerland[1]	—	—	5,779	3,667	5,835	—	—	6,963	—	7,024	—	—	15,577	13,286	15,731
Turkey	—	—	599	—	832	—	—	535	—	587	—	—	2,965	—	2,696
United Kingdom	2,406	2,984	2,964	3,213	3,295	3,979	5,664	4,514	4,521	4,494	—	—	10,207	10,680	8,241
United States	4,495	5,380	5,492	5,768	5,492	5,440	6,742	6,866	6,664	6,541	10,527	12,373	12,521	12,236	14,607

[1] Change in definition in 1992.
[2] Data for 1985 are for the former West Germany.
—Data not available.

NOTE.—Data adjusted to U.S. dollars using the purchasing-power-parity (PPP) index. The data used per student include only the expenditure for educational institutions. Public subsidies for students' living expenses are excluded. The figures include public expenditures per student in public and private institutions.

SOURCE: Organization for Economic Cooperation and Development, *Education at a Glance,* 1996; and unpublished data. (This table was prepared September 1997.)

Table 409.—Public expenditures for education as a percentage of gross domestic product, by level of education: Selected countries, 1985 to 1993

Country	All levels [1]								Primary education							Secondary education							Higher education						
	1985	1988	1989	1990	1991	1992	1993		1985	1988	1989	1990	1991	1993		1985	1988	1989	1990	1991	1993		1985	1988	1989	1990	1991	1992	1993
1	2	3	4	5	6	7	8		9	10	11	12	13	14		15	16	17	18	19	20		21	22	23	24	25	26	27
Australia	6.0	5.5	—	—	4.6	4.5	4.9		1.8	1.6	—	—	1.5	1.6		2.1	1.9	—	—	1.5	2.1		1.8	1.8	—	—	1.5	1.8	1.1
Austria	5.7	5.5	5.3	5.2	5.4	—	5.3		1.0	1.0	0.9	0.9	1.0	1.0		2.8	2.7	2.6	2.5	2.6	2.5		1.1	1.1	1.1	1.1	1.1	—	1.1
Belgium	6.4	5.6	5.7	5.2	—	—	5.6		1.1	1.0	0.9	0.9	—	1.1		3.0	2.5	2.5	2.3	—	2.6		1.0	0.9	0.9	0.9	—	—	1.0
Denmark	6.2	6.4	6.4	6.2	6.1	6.2	6.7		1.7	1.7	—	—	1.7	1.5		2.8	2.9	2.9	2.7	2.7	2.9		1.2	1.3	1.3	1.3	1.3	1.3	1.3
Germany[2]	4.6	4.3	—	—	4.1	3.7	4.5		0.6	0.6	—	1.7	0.5	0.7		2.2	2.0	—	2.7	1.9	2.3		1.0	1.0	—	1.3	0.9	1.0	0.9
Ireland	5.9	5.6	5.3	5.2	5.4	5.7	5.2		1.7	1.6	1.6	1.5	1.6	1.5		2.4	2.3	2.2	2.1	2.2	2.2		0.9	1.0	1.0	1.0	1.1	1.4	1.0
Italy	4.7	4.9	5.0	5.2	—	—	5.0		1.2	1.1	1.2	1.1	—	1.1		2.0	2.2	2.3	2.2	—	2.4		0.6	0.8	0.7	1.0	—	—	0.8
Japan	—	—	—	—	—	3.6	3.7		—	—	—	—	—	1.4		—	—	—	—	—	1.6		—	—	—	—	—	0.3	0.4
Luxembourg	—	6.0	5.8	—	—	—	—		—	2.1	2.0	—	—	—		—	2.5	2.4	—	—	—		—	0.2	0.2	—	—	—	—
New Zealand	—	5.2	6.3	—	5.8	—	6.0		—	1.4	1.7	—	1.5	1.7		—	1.2	1.5	—	1.3	2.7		—	1.6	1.8	—	2.0	—	1.2
Norway	5.6	6.4	6.5	6.4	6.8	—	7.6		1.7	1.9	1.8	1.6	1.7	1.7		2.7	2.9	2.8	2.7	2.8	2.7		0.8	1.0	1.1	1.2	1.3	—	1.5
Portugal	—	—	4.8	4.8	5.5	5.2	5.3		2.1	2.3	2.1	2.1	2.2	1.9		1.2	1.4	1.6	1.6	2.0	1.9		0.6	0.8	0.9	0.9	0.9	0.9	0.8
Spain	3.6	3.9	4.2	4.4	4.5	4.2	4.5		1.2	1.1	1.1	1.0	1.0	1.0		1.8	2.1	2.2	2.3	2.4	2.4		0.4	0.6	0.6	0.7	0.8	0.9	0.8
Sweden	—	5.9	5.5	5.7	6.1	6.2	6.7		—	2.2	2.0	2.0	2.2	2.0		0.0	2.5	2.4	2.5	2.7	2.6		—	1.0	0.9	1.1	1.1	1.0	1.5
Switzerland	5.1	5.1	—	—	5.4	6.7	5.6		2.9	2.8	—	—	1.4	1.6		1.3	1.3	—	—	2.4	2.5		1.0	1.0	—	—	1.2	—	1.2
Turkey	—	5.0	—	—	4.0	—	3.3		—	—	—	—	1.9	1.7		—	—	—	—	1.0	0.8		—	—	—	—	1.0	—	0.8
United Kingdom	5.3	5.0	4.9	5.1	4.9	4.1	4.7		1.2	1.3	1.3	1.3	1.3	1.6		2.2	2.3	2.2	2.3	2.2	2.3		1.1	0.9	0.9	0.9	1.0	0.1	0.7
United States	5.0	5.2	5.1	5.6	5.7	5.7	5.1		1.5	1.7	1.8	1.8	1.8	1.8		1.9	1.9	1.9	2.0	2.0	1.9		1.3	1.4	1.2	1.5	1.5	1.6	1.2

[1] Includes primary, secondary, and higher education not classified by level of education.
[2] Data before 1990 are for the former West Germany.
—Data not available.

SOURCE: Organization for Economic Cooperation and Development, *Education at a Glance*, 1996; and unpublished data. (This table was prepared April 1997.)

Table 410.—Foreign students enrolled in institutions of higher education in the United States and outlying areas, by continent, region, and selected countries of origin: 1980–81 to 1995–96

Continent, region, and country	1980–81		1985–86		1990–91		1991–92		1992–93		1993–94		1994–95		1995–96	
	Number	Percent	Number	Percent	Number	Percent	Number	Percent	Number	Percent	Number	Percent	Number	Percent	Number	Percent
1	2	3	4	5	6	7	8	9	10	11	12	13	14	15	16	17
Total	311,880	100.0	343,780	100.0	407,530	100.0	419,590	100.0	438,620	100.0	449,704	100.0	452,635	100.0	453,787	100.0
Africa	38,180	12.2	34,190	9.9	23,800	5.8	21,900	5.2	20,520	4.7	20,569	4.6	20,724	4.6	20,844	4.6
Eastern Africa	6,260	2.0	6,730	2.0	7,590	1.9	7,040	1.7	6,950	1.6	7,093	1.6	7,139	1.6	7,596	1.7
Central Africa	1,130	0.4	1,540	0.4	1,650	0.4	1,690	0.4	1,470	0.3	1,472	0.3	1,430	0.3	1,346	0.3
North Africa	7,310	2.3	5,980	1.7	4,540	1.1	4,090	1.0	3,730	0.9	3,614	0.8	3,522	0.8	3,422	0.8
Southern Africa	1,480	0.5	2,360	0.7	2,840	0.7	2,660	0.6	2,560	0.6	2,563	0.6	2,672	0.6	2,657	0.6
West Africa	22,000	7.1	17,580	5.1	7,180	1.8	6,400	1.5	5,800	1.3	5,804	1.3	5,943	1.3	5,818	1.3
Nigeria	17,350	5.6	13,710	4.0	3,710	0.9	3,160	0.8	2,490	0.6	2,285	0.5	2,147	0.5	2,093	0.5
Europe	25,330	8.1	34,310	10.0	49,640	12.2	53,710	12.8	58,010	13.2	62,442	13.9	64,811	14.3	67,353	14.8
Eastern Europe	1,670	0.5	1,770	0.5	4,780	1.2	6,890	1.6	9,800	2.2	12,929	2.9	15,906	3.5	18,032	4.0
Western Europe	23,660	7.6	32,540	9.5	44,860	11.0	46,820	11.2	48,210	11.0	49,496	11.0	48,905	10.8	49,326	10.9
France	—	—	3,680	1.1	5,630	1.4	5,580	1.3	5,660	1.3	5,976	1.3	5,843	1.3	5,710	1.3
Germany, Federal Republic of[1]	3,310	1.1	4,730	1.4	7,000	1.7	7,570	1.8	7,880	1.8	8,508	1.9	8,592	1.9	9,017	2.0
Greece	3,750	1.2	4,440	1.3	4,360	1.1	4,490	1.1	4,350	1.0	4,144	0.9	3,699	0.8	3,365	0.7
Spain	—	—	1,740	0.5	4,300	1.1	4,590	1.1	5,160	1.2	5,246	1.2	5,126	1.1	4,809	1.1
United Kingdom	4,440	1.4	5,940	1.7	7,300	1.8	7,470	1.8	7,630	1.7	7,828	1.7	7,786	1.7	7,799	1.7
Latin America	49,810	16.0	45,480	13.2	47,580	11.7	43,200	10.3	43,250	9.9	45,246	10.1	47,239	10.4	47,253	10.4
Caribbean	10,650	3.4	11,100	3.2	12,610	3.1	11,120	2.7	10,270	2.3	10,672	2.4	11,286	2.5	10,737	2.4
Central America	12,970	4.2	12,740	3.7	15,950	3.9	12,820	3.1	13,460	3.1	13,886	3.1	14,923	3.3	14,220	3.1
Mexico	6,730	2.2	5,460	1.6	6,740	1.7	6,650	1.6	7,580	1.7	8,021	1.8	9,003	2.0	8,687	1.9
South America	26,190	8.4	21,640	6.3	19,020	4.7	19,250	4.6	19,530	4.5	20,708	4.6	21,030	4.6	22,296	4.9
Brazil	—	—	2,840	0.8	3,900	1.0	4,260	1.0	4,540	1.0	4,977	1.1	5,017	1.1	5,497	1.2
Colombia	—	—	4,010	1.2	3,180	0.8	2,930	0.7	2,850	0.6	3,077	0.7	3,208	0.7	3,462	0.8
Venezuela	11,750	3.8	7,040	2.0	2,890	0.7	3,130	0.7	3,440	0.8	3,742	0.8	4,092	0.9	4,456	1.0
Middle East	84,710	27.2	52,720	15.3	33,420	8.2	31,210	7.4	30,240	6.9	29,509	6.6	30,246	6.7	30,563	6.7
Iran	47,550	15.2	14,210	4.1	6,260	1.5	4,930	1.2	4,090	0.9	3,621	0.8	2,896	0.6	2,628	0.6
Jordan	6,140	2.0	6,590	1.9	4,320	1.1	3,700	0.9	3,260	0.7	2,826	0.6	2,431	0.5	2,222	0.5
Lebanon	6,770	2.2	7,090	2.1	3,900	1.0	3,080	0.7	2,540	0.6	2,165	0.5	1,835	0.4	1,554	0.3
Saudi Arabia	10,440	3.3	6,900	2.0	3,590	0.9	3,550	0.8	3,750	0.9	3,721	0.8	4,075	0.9	4,191	0.9
Turkey	—	—	2,460	0.7	4,080	1.0	4,560	1.1	4,980	1.1	5,474	1.2	6,716	1.5	7,678	1.7
North America[2]	14,790	4.7	16,030	4.7	18,950	4.6	19,780	4.7	21,550	4.9	23,288	5.2	23,394	5.2	23,644	5.2
Canada	14,320	4.6	15,410	4.5	18,350	4.5	19,190	4.6	20,970	4.8	22,655	5.0	22,747	5.0	23,005	5.1
Oceania	4,180	1.3	4,030	1.2	4,230	1.0	3,870	0.9	4,300	1.0	3,857	0.9	4,327	1.0	4,202	0.9
South and East Asia	94,640	30.3	156,830	45.6	229,830	56.4	245,810	58.6	260,670	59.4	264,693	58.9	261,789	57.8	259,893	57.3
East Asia	51,650	16.6	80,720	23.5	146,020	35.8	158,490	37.8	168,410	38.4	171,279	38.1	168,190	37.2	166,717	36.7
China	2,770	0.9	13,980	4.1	39,600	9.7	42,940	10.2	45,130	10.3	44,381	9.9	39,403	8.7	39,613	8.7
Hong Kong	9,660	3.1	10,710	3.1	12,630	3.1	13,190	3.1	14,020	3.2	13,752	3.1	12,935	2.9	12,018	2.6
Japan	13,500	4.3	13,360	3.9	36,610	9.0	40,700	9.7	42,840	9.8	43,770	9.7	45,276	10.0	45,531	10.0
Korea, Republic of	6,150	2.0	18,660	5.4	23,360	5.7	25,720	6.1	28,520	6.5	31,076	6.9	33,599	7.4	36,231	8.0
Taiwan	19,460	6.2	23,770	6.9	33,530	8.2	35,550	8.5	37,430	8.5	37,581	8.4	36,407	8.0	32,702	7.2
South Central Asia	14,540	4.7	25,800	7.5	42,370	10.4	46,810	11.2	50,430	11.5	48,941	10.9	47,836	10.6	45,401	10.0
India	9,250	3.0	16,070	4.7	28,860	7.1	32,530	7.8	35,950	8.2	34,796	7.7	33,537	7.4	31,743	7.0
Pakistan	2,990	1.0	5,440	1.6	7,730	1.9	8,120	1.9	8,020	1.8	7,299	1.6	6,989	1.5	6,427	1.4
South East Asia	28,450	9.1	50,310	14.6	41,440	10.2	40,510	9.7	41,830	9.5	44,461	9.9	45,763	10.1	47,774	10.5
Indonesia	3,250	1.0	8,210	2.4	9,520	2.3	10,250	2.4	10,920	2.5	11,744	2.6	11,872	2.6	12,820	2.8
Malaysia	6,010	1.9	23,020	6.7	13,610	3.3	12,650	3.0	12,660	2.9	13,718	3.1	13,617	3.0	14,015	3.1
Philippines	—	—	3,920	1.1	4,270	1.0	3,950	0.9	3,700	0.8	3,528	0.8	3,472	0.8	3,127	0.7
Singapore	—	—	3,930	1.1	4,500	1.1	4,760	1.1	4,860	1.1	4,823	1.1	4,473	1.0	4,098	0.9
Thailand	6,550	2.1	6,940	2.0	7,090	1.7	7,690	1.8	8,630	2.0	9,537	2.1	10,889	2.4	12,165	2.7
Stateless[3]	240	0.1	190	0.1	80	(4)	120	(4)	80	(4)	100	(4)	105	(4)	30	(4)

[1] 1990–91 and later years data are for Germany, which includes the former Federal Republic of Germany and the former Democratic Republic of Germany.
[2] Excludes Mexico and Central America, which are included with Latin America.
[3] Home country unknown or undeclared.
[4] Less than .05 percent.
—Data not available.

NOTE.—Data are for "nonimmigrants," i.e., students who have not migrated to this country. Because of rounding, details may not add to totals.

SOURCE: Institute of International Education, *Open Doors*, various years; and unpublished data. (Latest edition copyright © 1996 by the Institute of International Education. All rights reserved.) (This table was prepared April 1997.)

CHAPTER 7
Learning Resources and Technology

This chapter contains statistics on libraries and on the use of information technologies. These data show the extent of America's access to information technologies outside of formal classroom activities. The data also provide a capsule description of the magnitude and availability of library resources. Access to information has been widely cited as the key to success in a growing number of endeavors. Thus, how information is made available and to whom become matters of concern.

The first section of the chapter deals with public libraries, public and private school libraries, school Internet access, and college and university libraries. It contains data on collections, population served, staff, and expenditures. Two tables provide institutional-level information for the largest public libraries and the largest college libraries in the country.

The second half of the chapter provides information on the availability and use of technology. For example, the proportion of children using computers at school compared over time. Also included are data on the use of home computers by adults and school children, with comparisons among various demographic groups.

Related data may be found in various sections of this report. For example, statistics on the number of degrees conferred in computer and information sciences and library sciences are in chapter 3. Further information on survey methodologies are in the "Guide to Sources" and in the publications cited in the source notes.

Resources

In 1993–94, there were 83 school library visits each week per 100 public school students. Elementary school students were more likely to visit their school libraries (89 visits per 100 students each week) than secondary school students (69 per 100). Private school students were slightly less likely to visit their libraries (77 per 100). The average number of library staff per school was 1.8 at public schools, and 1.2 at private schools. Public school libraries generally had smaller numbers of books on a per student basis than private school libraries. In 1994–94, public school libraries held an average of 2,585 books per 100 students compared to an average of 3,716 per 100 students at private schools. Although public elementary school libraries had slightly smaller holdings than public secondary schools on a per student basis, the elementary school students checked out twice as many books on a per student basis (1.5 per week compared to .7 per week) (table 411).

In 1994, there were 8,921 public libraries in the United States with 672 million books and serial volumes. The annual attendance per capita was 4.1 and the reference transactions per capita was 1.1 (table 419).

The increase in college library resources maintained pace with increases in enrollment between 1984–85 and 1994–95. The library staff to student ratio decreased slightly from 153 students per staff member to 150 students per staff member. The college library operating expenditure per student average rose 9 percent in constant dollars to $417 in 1994–95. However, other college expenditures rose faster than library expenditures and the proportion of college education budgets spent on libraries fell from 3.4 percent in 1984–85 to 2.9 percent in 1994–95 (table 416).

Technology

There has been widespread introduction of computers into the schools in recent years. In 1995, the average public school contained 72 computers. One important technological advance that has come to schools following the introduction of computers has been connections to the Internet. The number of schools with Internet access has increased rapidly from 35 percent in 1994, to 50 percent in 1995, to 65 percent in 1996. Although some access is now widespread, most schools are not extensively connected. Only about 14 percent of instructional rooms had access to the Internet in 1996. Of the schools which had Internet access in 1995, more than one-third had access at only one computer, and another one-third had access at 2 to 5 computers (table 415).

The total computer usage rate of students at school increased from 27 percent in 1984, to 43 percent in 1989, to 59 percent in October 1993. The rate for grades 1 to 8 increased from 52 percent in 1989 to 69 percent in 1993. The computer usage rate in 1993 was 58 percent for students in high school and 55 percent for students in college. Sizable percentages of students used computers at home, though fewer actually used them for schoolwork. About 25 percent of elementary school children used computers at home and about 11 percent used them for schoolwork. Students at the high school and undergraduate level were about twice as likely as the elementary school children to use home computers for schoolwork. In general, students in higher income families were more likely to use computers at home and use them for schoolwork than students from lower income families. About 13 percent of the high school students in the $25,000 to $29,999 household income group used computers at home for school work compared to 45 percent in the $75,000 and over income group (table 422).

The use of computers has become widespread in the workplace. In October 1993, 46 percent of all workers used computers on the job. More frequent use of computers was associated with higher levels of education and higher incomes. Only 34 percent of the high school graduates and 10 percent of the high school dropouts used computers compared to 71 percent of those with master's degrees. Among those who did use computers, the master's degree recipients were more likely to use the computers for a wider variety of applications than high school graduates. The most common uses of computers on the job were: bookkeeping/invoicing (45 percent), word processing (44 percent), communications (39 percent), analysis/spreadsheets (36 percent), and data bases (35 percent). Workers in the 25- to 49-year-old age range were more likely to use computers than younger or older workers. Elementary and secondary teachers were less likely to use computers than persons employed in other managerial or professional fields (table 420).

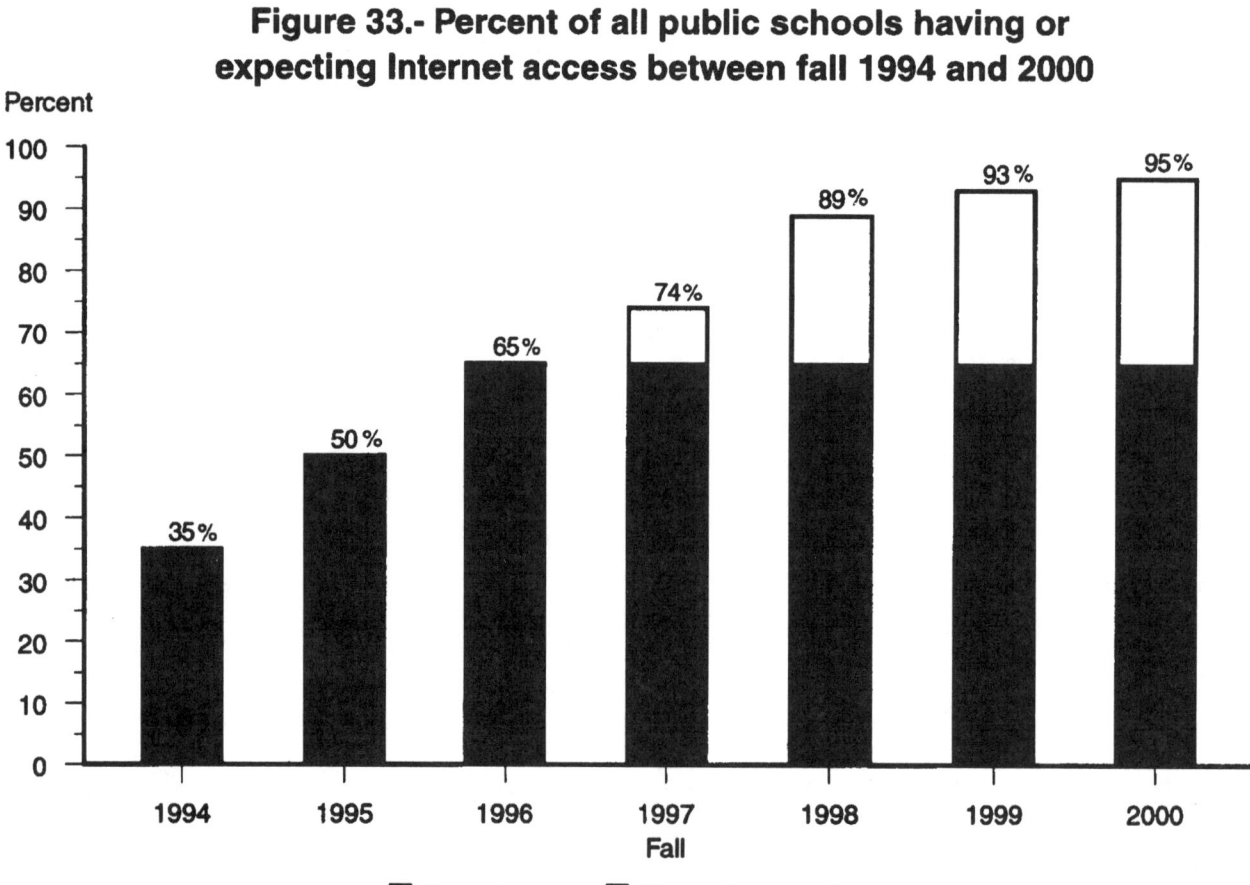

Figure 33.- Percent of all public schools having or expecting Internet access between fall 1994 and 2000

SOURCE: U.S. Department of Education, National Center for Education Statistics, Fast Response Survey System, *Survey on Advanced Telecommunications in U.S. Public Schools*, Fall 1996.

LIBRARY RESOURCES AND TECHNOLOGY: LIBRARIES 459

Table 411.—Percentage of school library/media centers that offered selected services and equipment, and library/media center expenditures, by control and level of school: 1993–94

Selected statistics	Public				Private			
	Total	Elementary	Secondary	Combined	Total	Elementary	Secondary	Combined
1	2	3	4	5	6	7	8	9
Number of schools with libraries	72,286 —	53,059 —	17,356 —	1,871 —	19,301 —	10,880 —	4,178 —	4,243 —
Average number of staff per library								
Total	1.81 (0.02)	1.69 (0.03)	2.12 (0.03)	1.71 (0.07)	1.23 (0.03)	1.09 (0.03)	1.58 (0.06)	1.25 (0.07)
Certified library/media specialists	0.86 (0.01)	0.79 (0.02)	1.03 (0.02)	0.79 (0.05)	0.28 (0.01)	0.20 (0.02)	0.47 (0.03)	0.30 (0.02)
Full-time	0.61 (0.01)	0.51 (0.01)	0.84 (0.02)	0.51 (0.04)	0.17 (0.01)	0.07 (0.01)	0.35 (0.03)	0.21 (0.02)
Part-time	0.25 (0.01)	0.28 (0.02)	0.19 (0.01)	0.28 (0.04)	0.11 (0.01)	0.12 (0.02)	0.11 (0.01)	0.09 (0.02)
Other professional staff	0.27 (0.01)	0.27 (0.01)	0.26 (0.02)	0.29 (0.03)	0.66 (0.02)	0.65 (0.02)	0.65 (0.04)	0.70 (0.06)
Full-time	0.13 (0.01)	0.13 (0.01)	0.14 (0.01)	0.13 (0.03)	0.23 (0.02)	0.19 (0.01)	0.26 (0.03)	0.32 (0.04)
Part-time	0.13 (0.01)	0.14 (0.01)	0.13 (0.01)	0.16 (0.02)	0.43 (0.01)	0.47 (0.02)	0.39 (0.03)	0.39 (0.04)
Other paid employees	0.68 (0.02)	0.63 (0.02)	0.83 (0.02)	0.62 (0.04)	0.29 (0.02)	0.24 (0.02)	0.46 (0.03)	0.25 (0.03)
Full-time	0.34 (0.01)	0.28 (0.01)	0.49 (0.02)	0.29 (0.03)	0.07 (0.01)	0.05 (0.01)	0.12 (0.02)	0.07 (0.01)
Part-time	0.34 (0.01)	0.34 (0.02)	0.34 (0.02)	0.33 (0.03)	0.22 (0.01)	0.19 (0.02)	0.34 (0.02)	0.18 (0.03)
Percentage of schools' library media centers with the following equipment								
Telephone	61.2 (1.3)	55.8 (1.8)	74.7 (1.6)	51.6 (3.3)	40.8 (1.3)	30.7 (1.6)	52.8 (2.5)	54.6 (4.2)
Fax machine	7.8 (0.5)	4.7 (0.6)	15.1 (0.8)	8.8 (1.4)	5.1 (0.5)	3.1 (0.6)	7.9 (1.1)	7.4 (1.2)
Computer with modem	34.3 (1.0)	28.3 (1.2)	48.2 (1.5)	38.1 (3.0)	19.5 (1.0)	12.2 (1.5)	30.2 (1.9)	27.9 (2.7)
Automated catalog	24.0 (0.9)	20.3 (1.1)	32.8 (1.1)	20.5 (1.9)	9.7 (0.7)	5.5 (0.5)	15.8 (1.9)	14.4 (2.3)
Automated circulation system	37.9 (1.1)	34.1 (1.6)	47.7 (1.3)	27.8 (2.6)	9.5 (0.7)	5.4 (0.6)	16.0 (1.8)	13.8 (1.8)
Database searching with CD-ROM	31.2 (0.8)	23.9 (1.2)	48.1 (1.3)	31.4 (3.1)	13.9 (0.8)	6.3 (0.8)	25.7 (1.6)	21.6 (2.2)
On-line database searching	9.4 (0.5)	5.4 (0.5)	18.9 (0.9)	8.8 (1.5)	5.5 (0.5)	0.7 (0.3)	12.2 (1.2)	11.0 (1.7)
Compact disc for periodical indices, etc.	46.7 (1.1)	39.6 (1.5)	63.5 (1.3)	46.6 (3.7)	19.6 (1.0)	12.3 (1.1)	33.5 (2.2)	24.6 (2.2)
Video laser disc	31.9 (1.0)	30.3 (1.3)	36.1 (1.3)	26.1 (2.8)	6.3 (0.6)	4.8 (0.7)	9.9 (1.2)	6.9 (1.1)
Connection to Internet	12.0 (0.6)	9.5 (0.8)	17.5 (0.8)	15.0 (1.9)	5.3 (0.5)	2.8 (0.8)	9.2 (1.1)	7.5 (1.2)
Cable television	76.2 (0.8)	75.0 (1.1)	80.6 (0.9)	57.7 (3.6)	39.9 (1.3)	42.6 (2.0)	43.1 (2.8)	30.1 (2.7)
Broadcast television	48.6 (1.0)	48.0 (1.4)	49.9 (1.3)	48.1 (3.1)	39.9 (1.6)	42.9 (1.9)	39.7 (2.5)	32.2 (3.9)
Closed circuit television	25.5 (0.7)	22.0 (1.0)	34.0 (1.0)	20.9 (2.2)	8.8 (0.7)	5.7 (1.0)	19.2 (1.6)	6.3 (1.5)
Satellite dish	22.9 (0.6)	14.4 (0.7)	41.1 (1.1)	45.2 (3.0)	8.7 (0.9)	5.6 (0.9)	15.6 (1.2)	9.8 (2.5)
Total students using library per 100 students each week [1]	83.4 (0.4)	88.9 (0.5)	68.6 (0.9)	66.4 (1.8)	76.5 (0.9)	84.9 (1.0)	64.6 (1.7)	60.0 (2.6)
Books checked out per 100 students each week [1]	128 (2)	150 (3)	67 (4)	85 (8)	116 (18)	146 (28)	47 (8)	68 (5)
Percentage of schools offering—								
Microcomputers	90.1 (0.7)	88.5 (1.0)	94.0 (1.0)	87.4 (1.5)	75.8 (1.6)	72.8 (2.1)	80.6 (2.9)	78.5 (3.5)
Long distance learning	19.0 (0.8)	15.9 (1.1)	24.8 (1.0)	36.4 (2.6)	8.8 (0.9)	8.3 (0.9)	8.2 (1.6)	10.9 (2.9)
Average holdings per 100 students at the end of the 1992–93 school year								
Books (number of volumes)	2,585 (57)	2,467 (81)	2,891 (101)	3,085 (262)	3,716 (252)	3,455 (349)	5,383 (726)	3,677 (286)
Current serial subscriptions (print/microfilm)	9 ([2])	7 ([2])	14 (1)	15 (3)	8 (1)	7 (1)	16 (1)	8 (1)
Video materials (tape and disc)	38 (2)	35 (2)	46 (2)	70 (11)	47 (5)	44 (5)	50 (6)	54 (10)
Other audio-visual materials	116 (4)	114 (6)	117 (7)	187 (24)	76 (6)	74 (5)	120 (16)	63 (16)
Microcomputer software	18 (1)	20 (1)	12 (1)	21 (2)	26 (4)	28 (5)	11 (4)	26 (9)
CD-ROM titles	1 ([2])	1 ([2])	2 ([2])	3 ([2])	1 ([2])	— ([2])	2 (1)	2 (1)
Locally budgeted expenditures [3] per student, 1992–93								
Books	$8.52 (0.23)	$7.80 (0.25)	$10.06 (0.42)	$14.40 (2.06)	$7.86 (0.45)	$6.94 (0.52)	$12.86 (1.26)	$8.09 (0.97)
Current serial subscriptions (print/microfilm)	2.18 (0.05)	1.49 (0.06)	4.15 (0.14)	3.33 (0.30)	1.57 (0.09)	0.95 (0.10)	4.83 (0.36)	1.78 (0.20)
Video materials (tape and disc)	1.24 (0.04)	1.04 (0.05)	1.77 (0.10)	1.74 (0.35)	1.07 (0.09)	0.87 (0.08)	1.49 (0.15)	1.40 (0.27)
Other audio-visual materials	0.82 (0.04)	0.77 (0.06)	0.87 (0.07)	1.54 (0.30)	0.55 (0.05)	0.55 (0.06)	0.72 (0.10)	0.45 (0.11)
Microcomputer software	1.09 (0.09)	0.89 (0.07)	1.50 (0.35)	2.84 (0.90)	1.41 (0.19)	1.25 (0.20)	1.86 (0.59)	1.63 (0.36)
CD-ROM titles	0.63 (0.05)	0.38 (0.06)	1.24 (0.09)	2.09 (0.53)	0.69 (0.17)	0.59 (0.25)	1.69 (0.18)	0.53 (0.11)
Expenditures (all sources) per student, 1992–93								
Total, library/media materials	17.18 (0.35)	14.86 (0.45)	22.71 (0.82)	31.11 (3.02)	15.96 (0.80)	13.68 (0.92)	27.29 (2.29)	16.99 (1.53)
Microcomputer hardware	3.84 (0.25)	3.43 (0.33)	4.73 (0.46)	7.15 (1.42)	3.60 (0.59)	2.62 (0.55)	8.68 (1.87)	3.98 (1.27)
Audiovisual equipment	2.24 (0.15)	2.00 (0.17)	2.98 (0.46)	2.25 (0.30)	1.57 (0.19)	1.39 (0.25)	3.12 (0.60)	1.37 (0.32)
On-line database searching/electronic communications	0.30 (0.04)	0.25 (0.06)	0.43 (0.05)	0.55 (0.26)	0.31 (0.13)	0.29 (0.19)	0.60 (0.16)	0.24 (0.06)

[1] During the most recent full week of school.
[2] Data less than 0.5 are rounded to 0.
[3] Locally budgeted expenditures exclude federal gifts and grants.
—Data not available.

NOTE.—Percentages are based on schools that have library/media centers. In school year 1990–91, 96 percent of public and 87 percent of private schools had library/media centers. Standard errors appear in paranthesis.

SOURCE: U.S. Department of Education, National Center for Education Statistics, *Schools and Staffing Survey, 1993–94*, unpublished data. (This table was prepared August 1997.)

Table 412.—Selected statistics on public school library/media centers, by level and enrollment size of school: 1993–94

Selected statisics	Public elementary, secondary, and combined	Elementary libraries, by enrollment size of school					Secondary libraries, by enrollment size of school				
		Total	Less than 150	150 to 499	500 to 749	750 or more	Total	Less than 150	150 to 499	500 to 749	750 or more
1	2	3	4	5	6	7	8	9	10	11	12
Number of schools with libraries	84,415 —	53,059 —	4,068 —	27,288 —	15,587 —	6,116 —	17,536 —	1,991 —	5,431 —	3,610 —	6,503 —
Average number of staff per library											
Total	1.81 (0.02)	1.69 (0.03)	1.39 (0.09)	1.61 (0.04)	1.76 (0.05)	2.03 (0.07)	2.12 (0.03)	1.66 (0.09)	1.73 (0.04)	1.80 (0.05)	2.90 (0.04)
Certified library/media specialists	0.86 (0.01)	0.79 (0.02)	0.65 (0.07)	0.75 (0.03)	0.85 (0.04)	0.90 (0.04)	1.03 (0.02)	0.80 (0.06)	0.93 (0.03)	0.98 (0.03)	1.36 (0.03)
Full-time	0.61 (0.01)	0.51 (0.01)	0.13 (0.04)	0.42 (0.02)	0.66 (0.02)	0.82 (0.04)	0.84 (0.02)	0.28 (0.04)	0.68 (0.02)	0.92 (0.02)	1.27 (0.04)
Part-time	0.25 (0.01)	0.28 (0.02)	0.52 (0.06)	0.33 (0.02)	0.19 (0.02)	0.08 (0.02)	0.19 (0.01)	0.52 (0.06)	0.24 (0.02)	0.06 (0.01)	0.09 (0.01)
Other professional staff	0.27 (0.01)	0.27 (0.01)	0.30 (0.05)	0.27 (0.02)	0.25 (0.02)	0.31 (0.04)	0.26 (0.02)	0.33 (0.05)	0.23 (0.03)	0.17 (0.02)	0.25 (0.02)
Full-time	0.13 (0.01)	0.13 (0.01)	0.09 (0.02)	0.13 (0.01)	0.12 (0.02)	0.22 (0.03)	0.14 (0.01)	0.13 (0.04)	0.11 (0.02)	0.08 (0.02)	0.17 (0.02)
Part-time	0.13 (0.01)	0.14 (0.01)	0.21 (0.04)	0.14 (0.02)	0.13 (0.02)	0.09 (0.03)	0.13 (0.01)	0.19 (0.03)	0.11 (0.02)	0.09 (0.02)	0.08 (0.01)
Other paid employees	0.68 (0.02)	0.63 (0.02)	0.44 (0.06)	0.59 (0.03)	0.66 (0.04)	0.82 (0.06)	0.83 (0.02)	0.54 (0.06)	0.57 (0.04)	0.66 (0.05)	1.29 (0.04)
Full-time	0.34 (0.01)	0.28 (0.01)	0.10 (0.03)	0.22 (0.02)	0.34 (0.03)	0.51 (0.04)	0.49 (0.02)	0.28 (0.04)	0.27 (0.03)	0.39 (0.03)	0.86 (0.03)
Part-time	0.34 (0.01)	0.34 (0.02)	0.34 (0.05)	0.37 (0.03)	0.32 (0.03)	0.31 (0.04)	0.34 (0.02)	0.26 (0.04)	0.31 (0.02)	0.27 (0.04)	0.43 (0.02)
Percentage of schools' library media centers with the following equipment											
Telephone	61.2 (1.3)	55.8 (1.8)	40.1 (5.0)	49.4 (2.3)	64.0 (2.8)	73.8 (4.0)	74.7 (1.6)	42.7 (4.9)	68.0 (2.6)	85.5 (1.9)	92.9 (1.0)
Fax machine	7.8 (0.5)	4.7 (0.6)	8.2 (2.6)	3.4 (0.7)	5.7 (1.3)	5.1 (1.4)	15.1 (0.8)	11.5 (2.3)	16.4 (1.5)	18.7 (2.3)	18.5 (1.3)
Computer with modem	34.3 (1.0)	28.3 (1.2)	21.9 (4.5)	24.9 (1.7)	33.4 (2.8)	34.6 (3.1)	48.2 (1.5)	46.4 (4.1)	47.3 (2.6)	51.3 (2.9)	59.0 (2.0)
Automated catalog	24.0 (0.9)	20.3 (1.1)	14.2 (3.8)	17.5 (1.4)	24.9 (2.1)	25.4 (2.2)	32.8 (1.1)	21.6 (3.5)	25.9 (2.1)	32.2 (2.7)	43.6 (1.7)
Automated circulation system	37.9 (1.1)	34.1 (1.6)	16.0 (3.8)	28.5 (1.9)	40.4 (2.7)	55.0 (3.3)	47.7 (1.3)	22.4 (3.9)	41.6 (2.5)	48.0 (3.1)	64.7 (1.8)
Database searching with CD-ROM	31.2 (0.8)	23.9 (1.2)	23.3 (3.3)	21.9 (1.7)	25.3 (2.6)	30.1 (2.8)	48.1 (1.3)	35.5 (4.1)	48.6 (2.3)	53.1 (3.1)	63.0 (2.1)
On-line database searching	9.4 (0.5)	5.4 (0.5)	6.0 (1.3)	4.1 (0.7)	7.1 (1.3)	6.8 (1.3)	18.9 (0.9)	14.6 (2.2)	19.9 (2.0)	20.5 (2.6)	26.3 (1.4)
Compact disc for periodical indices, etc.	46.7 (1.1)	39.6 (1.5)	27.0 (3.5)	37.5 (2.1)	42.6 (2.7)	49.5 (3.4)	63.5 (1.3)	50.4 (3.9)	62.4 (2.3)	69.8 (2.7)	76.9 (1.5)
Video laser disc	31.9 (1.0)	30.3 (1.3)	19.6 (4.8)	24.8 (1.7)	37.2 (2.3)	44.3 (3.1)	36.1 (1.3)	20.0 (4.3)	27.5 (2.1)	41.1 (2.1)	43.5 (1.7)
Connection to Internet	12.0 (0.6)	9.5 (0.8)	5.0 (1.3)	8.7 (1.4)	11.9 (1.8)	10.0 (1.5)	17.5 (0.8)	12.3 (2.8)	18.5 (1.7)	18.9 (2.5)	23.8 (1.6)
Cable television	76.2 (0.8)	75.0 (1.1)	59.8 (4.9)	78.0 (1.6)	74.7 (2.3)	73.0 (3.0)	80.6 (0.9)	65.5 (4.5)	80.3 (1.9)	81.9 (2.5)	83.9 (1.1)
Broadcast television	48.6 (1.0)	48.0 (1.4)	47.0 (4.8)	45.2 (1.6)	51.5 (2.5)	52.3 (4.1)	49.9 (1.3)	36.4 (4.3)	46.0 (2.7)	52.0 (3.1)	59.4 (1.5)
Closed circuit television	25.5 (0.7)	22.0 (1.0)	7.0 (2.1)	19.2 (1.4)	23.1 (2.0)	41.4 (2.9)	34.0 (1.0)	14.3 (3.4)	26.8 (2.0)	46.1 (3.1)	44.5 (1.5)
Satellite dish	22.9 (0.6)	14.4 (0.7)	15.4 (2.8)	13.6 (1.2)	12.7 (1.4)	21.3 (3.1)	41.1 (1.1)	48.1 (4.9)	53.3 (2.2)	54.5 (2.7)	42.4 (1.8)
Total students using library per 100 students each week[1]	83.4 (0.4)	88.9 (0.5)	93.6 (1.0)	91.7 (0.7)	88.0 (1.0)	75.1 (2.0)	68.6 (0.9)	87.9 (2.5)	74.2 (1.4)	67.0 (1.8)	58.9 (1.1)
Books checked out per 100 students each week[1]	128 (2)	150 (3)	222 (11.5)	161 (5.2)	134 (4.6)	93 (4.7)	67 (4.0)	227 (21.3)	66 (4.2)	46 (3.6)	31 (1.1)
Percentage of schools offering—											
Microcomputers	90.1 (0.7)	88.5 (1.0)	79.2 (3.4)	89.1 (1.6)	88.4 (2.0)	92.1 (2.2)	94.0 (1.0)	88.4 (2.7)	96.4 (1.1)	96.4 (0.9)	96.5 (0.8)
Long distance learning	19.0 (0.8)	15.9 (1.1)	16.7 (2.7)	16.3 (1.6)	14.4 (1.7)	17.5 (2.6)	24.8 (1.0)	33.0 (3.0)	26.6 (1.6)	25.6 (2.0)	25.3 (1.4)
Average holdings per 100 students at the end of the 1992–93 school year											
Books (number of volumes)	2,585 (57)	2,467 (81)	5,774 (355)	2,721 (124)	1,600 (46)	1,340 (37)	2,891 (101)	10,071 (815)	2,809 (79)	1,822 (50)	1,354 (22)
Current serial subscriptions (print/microfilm)	9 ([2])	7 ([2])	25 (3)	7 ([2])	4 ([2])	3 ([2])	14 (1)	55 (4)	14 ([2])	8 ([2])	5 (0)
Video materials (tape and disc)	38 (2)	35 (2)	91 (12)	36 (4)	24 (2)	20 (2)	46 (2)	129 (15)	49 (3)	35 (2)	23 (1)
Other audio-visual materials	116 (4)	114 (6)	183 (37)	122 (8)	96 (9)	73 (8)	117 (7)	267 (34)	123 (17)	102 (10)	74 (4)
Microcomputer software	18 (1)	20 (1)	60 (13)	22 (2)	11 (1)	10 (1)	12 (1)	47 (11)	8 (1)	8 (1)	6 (0)
CD-ROM titles	1 ([2])	1 ([2])	2 ([2])	1 ([2])	1 ([2])	0 ([2])	2 ([2])	9 (1)	1 ([2])	1 ([2])	1 ([2])
Locally budgeted expenditures[3] per student, 1992–93											
Books	$8.52 (0.23)	$7.80 (0.25)	$17.30 (1.3)	$7.95 (0.3)	$6.36 (0.4)	$4.49 (0.3)	$10.06 (0.4)	$28.34 (2.3)	$11.20 (0.7)	$6.84 (0.4)	$5.30 (0.2)
Current serial subscriptions (print/microfilm)	2.18 (0.05)	1.49 (0.06)	4.66 (0.47)	1.53 (0.08)	0.89 (0.05)	0.76 (0.06)	4.15 (0.14)	13.59 (1.05)	4.11 (0.22)	2.84 (0.15)	2.02 (0.06)
Video materials (tape and disc)	1.24 (0.04)	1.04 (0.05)	2.58 (0.37)	0.97 (0.05)	0.91 (0.07)	0.67 (0.07)	1.77 (0.10)	5.67 (0.67)	1.75 (0.15)	1.26 (0.11)	0.89 (0.05)
Other audio-visual materials	0.82 (0.04)	0.77 (0.06)	1.30 (0.49)	0.79 (0.07)	0.70 (0.06)	0.53 (0.07)	0.87 (0.07)	2.63 (0.53)	0.89 (0.09)	0.64 (0.08)	0.45 (0.03)
Microcomputer software	1.09 (0.09)	0.89 (0.07)	1.95 (0.47)	0.92 (0.09)	0.77 (0.13)	0.41 (0.06)	1.48 (0.35)	7.52 (3.10)	1.07 (0.13)	0.69 (0.10)	0.46 (0.03)
CD-ROM titles	0.63 (0.05)	0.38 (0.06)	0.92 (0.28)	0.33 (0.04)	0.42 (0.16)	0.16 (0.02)	1.24 (0.09)	3.76 (0.55)	1.24 (0.13)	0.84 (0.10)	0.69 (0.04)
Expenditures (all sources) per student, 1992–93											
Total, library/media materials	17.18 (0.35)	14.88 (0.45)	35.43 (2.38)	15.31 (0.58)	11.19 (0.55)	8.51 (0.43)	22.71 (0.82)	69.98 (5.56)	23.74 (0.98)	14.91 (0.71)	11.72 (0.35)
Microcomputer hardware	3.84 (0.25)	3.43 (0.33)	10.82 (3.37)	2.91 (0.30)	3.10 (0.49)	1.72 (0.26)	4.73 (0.46)	7.81 (2.43)	5.68 (1.15)	4.06 (0.71)	3.36 (0.39)
Audiovisual equipment	2.24 (0.15)	2.00 (0.17)	5.21 (1.73)	1.71 (0.13)	1.88 (0.24)	1.45 (0.26)	2.98 (0.46)	10.44 (4.10)	2.75 (0.24)	1.70 (0.15)	1.59 (0.10)
On-line database searching/ searching electronic communications	0.30 (0.04)	0.25 (0.06)	0.30 (0.13)	0.27 (0.08)	0.26 (0.15)	0.11 (0.03)	0.43 (0.05)	0.79 (0.31)	0.62 (0.14)	0.27 (0.05)	0.26 (0.04)

[1] During the most recent full week of school.
[2] Data less than 0.5 are rounded to 0.
[3] Locally budgeted expenditures exclude federal gifts and grants.
—Data not available.

NOTE.—Percentages are based on schools that have library/media centers. In school year 1990–91, 96 percent of public and 87 percent of private schools had library/media centers. Standard errors appear in paranstheses.

SOURCE: U.S. Department of Education, National Center for Education Statistics, Schools and Staffing Survey, 1993–94, unpublished data. (This table was prepared August 1997.)

Table 413.—Selected statistics on public school library/media centers, by state: 1993–94

State or other area	Percent of centers offering selected services/equipment						Books held per 100 students	Total students using library per 100 students each week [1]	Total expenditures for materials per student [2]	Expenditure for microcomputers for library per student [2]	Expenditure for audiovisual materials for library per student [2]
	Computer with modem	Automated catalog	Database searching with CD-ROM	On-line database searching	Compact disc for indices, etc.	Connection to the Internet					
1	2	3	4	5	6	7	8	9	10	11	12
United States	**34.3 (1.0)**	**24.0 (0.9)**	**31.2 (0.8)**	**9.4 (0.5)**	**46.7 (1.1)**	**12.0 (0.6)**	**2,585 (57)**	**83.4 (0.4)**	**$17.18 (0.35)**	**$3.84 (0.25)**	**$2.24 (0.15)**
Alabama	33.0 (4.2)	37.6 (5.9)	29.3 (4.0)	5.7 (2.0)	44.1 (4.6)	3.2 (1.5)	1,510 (61)	76.3 (2.2)	11.22 (0.62)	1.91 (0.39)	0.91 (0.22)
Alaska	34.7 (3.6)	34.3 (4.0)	39.7 (4.7)	6.8 (1.9)	44.6 (4.5)	15.1 (2.3)	4,167 (260)	85.0 (2.0)	47.38 (5.86)	9.76 (2.55)	1.94 (0.30)
Arizona	28.1 (3.5)	38.3 (5.3)	28.0 (4.0)	5.6 (2.2)	43.0 (4.4)	6.0 (1.9)	2,552 (211)	81.0 (3.3)	17.55 (3.05)	4.66 (1.37)	1.56 (0.31)
Arkansas	19.0 (4.0)	18.7 (4.0)	20.5 (4.1)	5.6 (2.4)	29.7 (4.6)	8.5 (2.5)	2,377 (355)	78.3 (2.8)	15.03 (1.45)	1.92 (0.53)	1.56 (0.29)
California	19.9 (4.3)	14.0 (3.4)	23.4 (3.7)	3.1 (1.0)	38.0 (5.7)	6.2 (2.3)	1,751 (193)	77.9 (2.7)	7.26 (1.00)	3.13 (0.87)	0.59 (0.17)
Colorado	47.0 (4.7)	43.6 (5.7)	43.3 (5.5)	30.7 (4.7)	60.7 (5.5)	16.3 (3.5)	2,190 (177)	80.6 (2.5)	16.42 (1.81)	3.01 (0.57)	1.63 (0.25)
Connecticut	43.8 (6.5)	12.8 (2.7)	45.4 (5.3)	17.9 (3.8)	54.4 (6.0)	6.5 (2.6)	2,289 (129)	88.0 (2.2)	15.71 (2.06)	2.84 (1.01)	1.21 (0.21)
Delaware	41.8 (3.6)	22.5 (3.0)	34.7 (3.5)	14.4 (2.5)	48.2 (3.5)	5.7 (2.0)	1,587 (84)	80.5 (2.3)	8.68 (0.87)	1.63 (0.24)	0.64 (0.23)
District of Columbia	23.5 (4.0)	4.4 (2.2)	25.4 (2.8)	10.4 (3.3)	31.2 (3.2)	1.7 (1.1)	1,578 (74)	65.6 (2.9)	8.06 (0.69)	0.49 (0.13)	1.46 (0.30)
Florida	45.3 (3.8)	29.8 (3.3)	39.9 (3.6)	11.8 (2.8)	71.0 (4.0)	21.1 (3.4)	1,855 430	76.6 (2.6)	13.61 (1.98)	1.85 (0.29)	2.30 (0.33)
Georgia	29.8 (4.7)	48.2 (4.4)	34.5 (4.6)	13.6 (2.6)	46.6 (4.7)	10.8 (2.7)	1,535 (72)	83.9 (1.6)	13.02 (0.65)	2.99 (0.71)	2.21 (0.38)
Hawaii	75.3 (5.3)	27.1 (4.4)	47.7 (5.7)	24.3 (4.9)	64.8 (4.9)	29.4 (5.0)	1,592 (100)	83.3 (2.6)	10.90 (1.01)	2.77 (0.46)	1.59 (0.42)
Idaho	29.9 (4.2)	15.4 (4.0)	21.6 (4.4)	6.2 (2.3)	32.1 (5.1)	8.6 (3.1)	2,457 (289)	86.6 (1.9)	12.20 (1.24)	2.50 (0.63)	1.12 (0.24)
Illinois	32.2 (3.5)	17.7 (3.8)	23.0 (3.4)	7.9 (1.7)	36.6 (4.2)	7.1 (2.2)	2,517 (264)	85.7 (1.8)	13.40 (1.34)	4.09 (1.48)	1.59 (0.19)
Indiana	29.9 (6.7)	31.0 (4.9)	32.0 (5.9)	2.4 (0.7)	66.1 (6.3)	5.5 (1.2)	2,518 (387)	86.2 (2.4)	14.40 (1.12)	12.45 (3.24)	2.20 (0.45)
Iowa	38.8 (6.4)	17.4 (5.0)	44.2 (5.7)	14.6 (3.6)	71.2 (5.7)	8.6 (3.1)	4,549 (698)	91.0 (1.8)	23.04 (2.23)	5.14 (2.03)	2.78 (0.61)
Kansas	24.9 (3.0)	31.5 (4.9)	20.9 (3.1)	9.7 (2.0)	46.6 (4.5)	10.6 (2.5)	3,797 (218)	89.1 (1.8)	30.85 (2.76)	11.16 (2.26)	2.93 (0.49)
Kentucky	30.1 (6.2)	33.1 (7.0)	32.3 (5.5)	4.3 (2.2)	60.3 (6.3)	5.3 (2.4)	1,732 (110)	84.8 (2.3)	15.16 (1.08)	2.32 (0.51)	2.40 (0.31)
Louisiana	24.2 (3.9)	13.9 (3.5)	21.9 (3.4)	2.3 (0.8)	28.1 (3.8)	6.2 (2.4)	1,784 (74)	64.8 (3.9)	16.18 (3.82)	1.43 (0.42)	0.50 (0.08)
Maine	33.3 (5.4)	18.9 (4.4)	25.5 (3.8)	5.4 (2.0)	38.9 (6.7)	5.4 (1.6)	2,331 (169)	89.4 (2.7)	17.83 (2.74)	2.21 (0.58)	0.64 (0.16)
Maryland	41.0 (3.9)	15.4 (3.4)	31.8 (4.5)	22.3 (3.1)	46.2 (4.7)	32.6 (3.5)	1,510 (70)	87.0 (1.8)	11.70 (0.73)	0.25 (0.06)	1.65 (0.45)
Massachusetts	38.2 (4.9)	9.1 (1.6)	45.3 (4.8)	8.9 (1.6)	46.3 (4.8)	24.1 (3.8)	2,523 (224)	74.8 (3.9)	10.14 (1.22)	1.50 (0.29)	1.77 (0.52)
Michigan	42.2 (7.6)	12.1 (3.9)	38.1 (6.3)	10.2 (3.8)	57.9 (6.1)	15.1 (5.3)	1,820 (100)	83.5 (4.1)	13.36 (2.13)	1.62 (0.55)	1.35 (0.39)
Minnesota	35.6 (4.8)	53.4 (6.1)	52.9 (6.1)	13.8 (3.0)	69.0 (5.6)	17.3 (3.6)	3,114 (253)	86.5 (2.8)	22.39 (3.60)	6.01 (0.96)	4.93 (1.70)
Mississippi	9.4 (2.0)	5.2 (2.1)	14.2 (3.9)	3.0 (1.4)	23.2 (3.6)	3.1 (1.3)	1,593 (69)	74.6 (2.5)	16.26 (4.13)	1.58 (0.62)	1.30 (0.30)
Missouri	31.3 (4.3)	39.4 (6.7)	31.4 (5.0)	17.8 (3.9)	46.0 (5.9)	15.7 (4.2)	2,681 (232)	81.4 (2.6)	16.95 (1.64)	2.80 (0.90)	1.23 (0.20)
Montana	50.8 (4.3)	20.6 (3.1)	43.7 (4.1)	17.4 (3.3)	58.2 (3.6)	6.2 (2.0)	9,562 (1,005)	89.5 (2.3)	67.92 (8.98)	15.79 (6.03)	5.61 (1.22)
Nebraska	31.6 (5.0)	29.0 (4.9)	36.3 (5.7)	12.1 (2.5)	58.8 (6.0)	15.8 (3.0)	7,103 (817)	90.3 (2.7)	41.70 (4.30)	23.16 (10.55)	13.52 (6.68)
Nevada	18.4 (4.0)	48.2 (5.5)	32.2 (4.5)	3.0 (1.3)	37.1 (4.2)	9.4 (2.9)	1,827 (168)	87.0 (1.7)	11.15 (1.00)	1.46 (0.38)	0.77 (0.14)
New Hampshire	43.9 (6.6)	21.4 (4.8)	39.8 (6.6)	8.2 (2.6)	51.2 (5.9)	17.4 (4.4)	2,221 (182)	87.1 (1.8)	18.97 (1.75)	2.83 (0.86)	1.41 (0.24)
New Jersey	39.1 (6.6)	28.5 (6.5)	30.2 (6.4)	7.2 (1.4)	46.2 (7.2)	5.2 (1.3)	2,954 (400)	84.2 (3.0)	22.91 (3.96)	3.52 (1.37)	2.05 (0.88)
New Mexico	32.8 (6.1)	21.9 (5.3)	32.0 (4.3)	3.9 (1.5)	43.1 (5.5)	7.8 (2.4)	2,533 (223)	82.9 (2.8)	16.80 (3.05)	1.55 (0.44)	1.73 (0.32)
New York	39.5 (5.5)	14.3 (3.9)	25.2 (3.4)	12.5 (2.4)	44.8 (5.1)	16.0 (3.6)	2,207 (213)	82.0 (3.4)	13.67 (1.21)	1.56 (0.46)	1.15 (0.35)
North Carolina	40.4 (4.6)	29.4 (4.0)	42.0 (4.3)	10.8 (1.7)	65.0 (4.1)	7.9 (2.3)	1,630 (50)	80.8 (2.4)	14.19 (0.94)	4.39 (0.53)	2.10 (0.28)
North Dakota	65.8 (5.3)	18.0 (3.6)	27.3 (5.1)	39.1 (5.7)	41.1 (6.5)	36.8 (5.5)	6,607 (689)	93.0 (1.3)	29.45 (2.25)	3.77 (0.84)	5.02 (1.77)
Ohio	33.1 (7.1)	12.9 (5.0)	16.9 (3.9)	3.3 (1.1)	31.9 (6.7)	7.1 (2.3)	3,796 (762)	86.5 (3.2)	11.03 (1.48)	0.75 (0.25)	1.53 (0.75)
Oklahoma	20.1 (2.7)	32.7 (3.8)	32.5 (3.5)	6.7 (1.7)	44.1 (4.2)	4.0 (1.7)	2,851 (163)	84.2 (1.5)	36.26 (4.69)	3.46 (0.60)	7.51 (4.23)
Oregon	38.6 (5.8)	39.2 (5.2)	51.5 (6.7)	18.9 (4.7)	49.5 (6.5)	11.7 (4.2)	3,154 (362)	84.3 (3.2)	21.32 (2.14)	7.59 (2.49)	2.75 (0.86)
Pennsylvania	33.9 (6.9)	17.3 (4.0)	32.6 (5.5)	2.5 (1.1)	39.2 (6.4)	6.4 (3.1)	2,562 (203)	89.6 (2.6)	15.33 (2.09)	2.23 (0.60)	1.97 (0.67)
Rhode Island	25.0 (4.9)	11.8 (3.2)	13.0 (3.5)	1.0 (0.6)	21.7 (4.8)	18.6 (4.2)	1,835 (232)	84.0 (2.5)	8.58 (1.51)	0.23 (0.10)	0.34 (0.14)
South Carolina	44.0 (5.4)	46.4 (5.0)	39.4 (5.7)	6.9 (1.7)	55.4 (7.1)	13.5 (4.1)	1,655 (133)	80.3 (3.2)	11.01 (0.71)	2.39 (0.55)	1.03 (0.19)
South Dakota	56.2 (6.8)	12.6 (3.4)	37.7 (6.2)	23.1 (4.2)	60.2 (5.5)	9.0 (2.7)	5,049 (542)	89.8 (2.0)	45.53 (5.37)	8.26 (1.61)	3.73 (1.41)
Tennessee	15.1 (4.3)	18.9 (5.1)	16.6 (4.5)	2.5 (2.3)	34.9 (6.5)	3.6 (1.9)	1,677 (102)	85.4 (2.2)	8.60 (0.68)	2.65 (1.04)	0.91 (0.20)
Texas	39.4 (4.6)	20.5 (4.2)	27.2 (3.1)	9.9 (2.8)	33.9 (3.8)	24.7 (4.2)	1,885 (123)	83.3 (2.0)	18.94 (1.79)	3.75 (1.18)	2.95 (0.40)
Utah	22.2 (3.6)	37.4 (4.1)	28.6 (3.6)	5.1 (2.3)	39.1 (3.6)	6.7 (1.9)	1,557 (105)	79.5 (2.2)	9.08 (0.95)	1.62 (0.26)	1.82 (0.32)
Vermont	47.0 (4.9)	27.2 (5.6)	35.3 (4.2)	14.5 (3.3)	51.9 (4.8)	32.2 (3.4)	3,155 179	87.5 (1.8)	34.53 (4.95)	6.18 (1.57)	2.90 (0.52)
Virginia	61.7 (8.3)	35.5 (6.1)	38.6 (5.8)	10.6 (2.9)	72.4 (7.0)	31.4 (5.6)	1,974 (108)	88.2 (2.2)	15.20 (1.09)	3.48 (0.66)	3.71 (1.01)
Washington	40.2 (5.2)	35.7 (5.6)	43.1 (3.6)	11.7 (2.9)	53.1 (4.9)	13.0 (2.6)	2,004 (84)	89.7 (1.3)	14.70 (1.27)	3.34 (0.69)	1.52 (0.29)
West Virginia	24.7 (6.0)	16.7 (4.2)	18.0 (4.0)	8.3 (3.5)	31.0 (5.5)	6.4 (3.2)	2,039 (201)	76.0 (4.7)	7.37 (1.41)	0.77 (0.25)	0.17 ([2])
Wisconsin	34.2 (6.5)	27.2 (4.7)	36.1 (5.0)	14.8 (3.8)	57.1 (6.1)	9.0 (2.6)	2,895 (157)	86.5 (2.8)	23.99 (1.18)	5.40 (1.55)	4.10 (0.74)
Wyoming	39.0 (3.4)	28.0 (4.2)	32.1 (5.7)	8.1 (2.5)	41.7 (4.5)	6.6 (2.3)	10,729 (1,185)	83.5 (3.4)	46.04 (5.36)	3.23 (0.59)	3.92 (0.85)

[1] During the most recent full week of school.
[2] Locally budgeted expenditures exclude federal gifts and grants.

NOTE.—Percentages are based on schools that have library/media centers. In school year 1990–91, 96 percent of public and 87 percent of private schools had library media centers. Standard errors appear in parentheses.

SOURCE: U.S. Department of Education, National Center for Education Statistics, *Schools and Staffing Survey, 1993–94,* unpublished data. (This table was prepared August 1997.)

Table 414.—Percent of public and private schools having access to selected telecommunication capabilities, by location of access site and control of school: 1995

Telecommunications capabilities	Percent of schools having access	Percent of schools with telecommunications access, by location[1]				
		Administrative offices	Teacher workrooms	Classrooms	Computer labs	Library/media centers
1	2	3	4	5	6	7
All public schools						
Computer with any telecommunication capabilities via local area network	77	73	20	45	71	64
Computer with any telecommunication capabilities via modem	76	61	10	30	41	64
Computer with any telecommunication capabilities via wide area network	61	58	14	35	41	68
Broadcast television	71	35	28	82	47	88
Cable television	76	33	25	72	42	91
Closed circuit television	28	50	32	91	60	89
Two-way video with 2–way audio	13	24	17	57	37	69
One-way video with two-way audio or computer link	7	26	15	63	41	54
All private schools						
Computer with any telecommunication capabilities via local area network	43	71	18	33	58	35
Computer with any telecommunication capabilities via modem	48	70	14	24	38	33
Computer with any telecommunication capabilities via wide area network	29	59	15	26	41	40
Broadcast television	52	24	23	81	27	59
Cable television	37	21	21	75	29	60
Closed circuit television	5	32	29	99	51	71
Two-way video with 2–way audio	5	9	13	50	54	44
One-way video with two-way audio or computer link	2	32	21	66	39	46

[1] Location estimates are based on those schools having access to each type of telecommunication capability. Percents of schools reporting telecommunication locations do not sum to 100 because many schools have access in more than one location.

NOTE.—Data are derived from a sample survey and are subject to sampling error.

SOURCE: U.S. Department of Education, National Center for Education Statistics, Fast Response Survey System, *Advanced Telecommunications in U.S. Public Elementary and Secondary Schools, 1995*; and *Advanced Telecommunications in U.S. Private Schools, K–12, Fall 1995*. (This table was prepared September 1997.)

Table 415.—Percent of public schools and school classrooms having access to the Internet, by school characteristics: 1994, 1995, and 1996

School characteristics	Estimated number of schools, 1995	Percent of schools having access to Internet			Percent of instructional rooms[1] having access to Internet			Mean number of all computers,[2] per school 1995	Percent of computers[2] with Internet access, 1995	Number of computers[2] with Internet access in schools with Internet access, 1995				
										Mean number of computers, 1995	Percent distribution of computers			
		1994	1995	1996	1994	1995	1996				1 computer	2 to 5 computers	6 to 9 computers	10 or more computers
1	2	3	4	5	6	7	8	9	10	11	12	13	14	15
All public schools	77,853	35	50	65	3	8	14	72	14	12	35	38	6	21
Instructional level[3]														
Elementary	57,705	30	46	61	3	8	13	60	13	9	40	37	5	18
Secondary	18,083	49	65	77	4	8	16	112	13	16	25	39	9	27
Size of enrollment														
Less than 300	20,673	30	39	57	3	9	15	41	15	7	34	42	8	16
300 to 999	50,044	35	52	66	3	8	13	71	15	12	38	35	6	21
1,000 or more	7,136	58	69	80	3	4	16	164	8	15	19	45	5	31
Metropolitan status														
City	17,906	40	47	64	4	6	12	84	11	11	29	39	6	26
Urban fringe	18,464	38	59	75	4	8	16	83	13	12	38	34	6	22
Town	19,539	29	47	61	3	8	14	72	16	14	36	35	6	22
Rural	21,944	35	48	60	3	8	14	54	14	9	36	42	6	16
Percent of students eligible for free or reduced-price lunch														
Less than 11 percent	13,192	—	62	78	—	9	18	77	15	14	29	38	6	26
11 to 30 percent	21,876	—	59	72	—	10	16	78	15	13	35	33	7	25
31 to 70 percent	28,017	—	47	58	—	7	14	68	12	9	40	40	5	15
71 percent or more	14,651	—	31	53	—	3	7	65	10	9	32	43	4	21

[1] Includes all classrooms, computer labs, and library/media centers.
[2] Includes computers used for instructional or administrative purposes.
[3] Excludes combined elementary/secondary schools because of small sample size.
—Data not available.

NOTE.—Data are derived from a sample survey and are subject to sampling error. Details may not add to totals because of rounding of weighted estimates.

SOURCE: U.S. Department of Education, National Center for Education Statistics, Fast Response Survey System, *Advanced Telecommunications in U.S. Public Elementary and Secondary Schools, Fall 1996*; and *Advanced Telecommunications in U.S. Public Elementary and Secondary Schools, 1995*. (This table was prepared August 1997.)

Table 416.—General statistics of college and university libraries: 1974–75 to 1994–95

Item	1974–75[1]	1975–76[1]	1976–77[1]	1978–79[1]	1981–82	1984–85	1987–88	1991–92	1994–95
1	2	3	4	5	6	7	8	9	10
Number of libraries	2,972	2,987	3,058	3,122	3,104	3,322	3,438	3,274	3,639
Transactions, general collection	—	—	—	—	—	—	—	—	186,092
Transactions, reserve collection	—	—	—	—	—	—	—	—	49,567
Total enrollment, in thousands[2]	10,322	11,291	11,121	11,392	12,372	12,242	12,767	14,359	14,279
Full-time-equivalent enrollment, in thousands[2]	7,805	8,480	8,313	8,348	9,015	8,952	9,230	10,361	10,348
Collections, thousands of units									
Number of volumes at end of year	447,059	468,033	481,442	519,895	567,826	631,727	718,504	749,429	792,707
Number of volumes added during year	23,242	22,977	22,367	21,608	19,507	20,658	21,907	20,982	22,460
Number of serial subscriptions[3]	4,434	4,618	4,670	4,775	4,890	6,317	6,416	6,966	6,780
Microform titles at end of year	—	—	—	—	—	—	—	—	160,188
Computer files at end of year	—	—	—	—	—	—	—	—	480
Library staff, in full-time equivalents									
Total staff in regular positions[3]	56,836	56,852	57,087	58,416	58,476	58,476	67,251	67,166	68,920
FTE enrollment per FTE staff	137.3	149.2	145.6	142.9	154.2	153.1	137.2	154.3	150.1
Librarians and professional staff	23,530	23,104	23,308	23,676	23,816	21,822	25,115	26,341	27,376
Other paid staff	33,306	33,748	33,779	34,740	34,660	38,026	40,733	40,421	41,227
Contributed services	—	—	—	—	—	—	1,403	404	317
Student assistants	—	—	—	—	—	—	33,821	29,075	29,077
Hours of student and other assistance, in thousands	34,687	36,725	39,950	39,552	40,068	28,360	—	—	—
Library operating expenditures (excluding capital outlay)									
Operating expenditures, total, in thousands	$1,091,784	$1,180,128	$1,259,637	$1,502,158	$1,943,769	$2,404,524	$2,770,075	$3,648,654	$4,317,847
Salaries[4]	592,568	649,374	698,090	824,438	1,081,894	1,156,138	1,451,551	1,889,368	2,058,375
Hourly wages	61,474	66,175	68,683	79,535	100,847	—	—	—	—
Fringe benefits	—	—	—	—	—	231,209	—	—	238,984
Preservation	22,206	22,375	22,521	25,274	30,351	32,939	34,144	43,126	47,296
Furniture/equipment	—	—	—	—	—	—	—	—	56,432
Computer hardware/software	—	—	—	—	—	—	—	—	126,936
Utilities/networks/consortia	—	—	—	—	—	—	—	—	81,686
Collections	327,904	357,544	373,699	450,180	561,199	750,282	891,281	1,197,293	1,374,407
Print materials	—	—	—	—	—	—	—	420,930	451,988
Serial subscriptions	—	—	—	—	—	—	—	639,128	703,463
Microforms	—	—	—	—	—	—	—	43,666	61,702
Audiovisual materials	—	—	—	—	—	—	—	23,879	29,375
Machine readable materials	—	—	—	—	—	—	—	29,093	72,735
Collections, loans	—	—	—	—	—	—	—	—	12,440
Other collection expenditures	—	—	—	—	—	—	—	40,596	42,704
Other library operating expenditures	87,632	84,660	96,643	122,731	169,478	233,957	393,099	518,867	333,732
Operating expenditures per FTE student	140	139	152	180	216	269	300	352	417
Operating expenditures per FTE student in constant 1994–95 dollars	406	377	388	395	345	382	390	383	417
Operating expenditures, total, in percents	100.0	100.0	100.0	100.0	100.0	100.0	100.0	100.0	100.0
Salaries[4]	54.3	55.0	55.4	54.9	55.7	48.1	52.4	51.8	47.7
Hourly wages	5.6	5.6	5.5	5.3	5.2	—	—	—	—
Fringe benefits	—	—	—	—	—	9.6	—	—	5.5
Preservation	2.0	1.9	1.8	1.7	1.6	1.4	1.2	1.2	1.1
Collections	30.0	30.3	29.7	30.0	28.9	31.2	32.2	32.8	31.8
Other library operating expenditures	8.0	7.2	7.7	8.2	8.7	9.7	14.2	14.2	13.9
Library operating expenditures as percent of total institutional expenditures for educational and general purposes	3.9	3.8	3.8	3.7	3.5	3.4	3.2	3.0	2.9

[1] Includes data for U.S. territories.
[2] Fall enrollment for the academic year specified.
[3] Data are for end of year. Excludes student assistants.
[4] Includes expenditures for fringe benefits (except for 1984–85 and 1987–88) and salary equivalents of contributed services staff.
—Data not available.

NOTE.—Because of rounding, details may not add to totals.

SOURCE: U.S. Department of Education, National Center for Education Statistics, *Library Statistics of Colleges and Universities*, various years; and Integrated Postsecondary Education Data System, "Academic Library Survey." (This table was prepared July 1997.)

Table 417.—Selected statistics on the collections, staff, and operating expenditures of 60 large college and university libraries: 1994

Institution	Rank order, by number of volumes	Number of volumes at end of year, in thousands	Full-time-equivalent staff		Operating expenditures, in thousands		Public service hours per week	Gate count per week	Reference transactions per week
			Total	Professional	Total	Salaries and wages			
1	2	3	4	5	6	7	8	9	10
Harvard University (Mass.)[1]	1	12,395	1,096	363	$54,451	$29,467	95	([2])	([2])
Yale University (Conn.)	2	10,503	623	191	38,333	16,254	90	([2])	([2])
University of Illinois, Urbana Campus	3	8,475	513	152	21,535	10,704	94	([2])	13,516
University of Texas, Austin	4	7,020	643	144	22,387	12,517	107	170,346	13,664
University of Michigan, Ann Arbor	5	6,664	590	140	30,521	13,424	99	([2])	([2])
University of California, Berkeley	6	6,654	543	132	32,954	16,696	82	([2])	([2])
Columbia University, Main Division (N.Y.)	7	6,532	568	170	27,916	14,768	103	([2])	([2])
Stanford University (Calif.)	8	6,409	555	162	36,203	18,658	49	([2])	([2])
University of California, Los Angeles	9	6,306	560	126	27,313	13,141	87	79,871	12,996
University of Chicago (Ill.)	10	5,710	362	75	18,124	8,781	109	24,370	1,407
Indiana University, Bloomington	11	5,554	471	142	22,761	11,400	101	([2])	15,644
University of Wisconsin, Madison	12	5,536	533	150	25,320	13,245	131	129,254	10,314
University of Washington	13	5,355	485	130	23,846	12,704	104	([2])	([2])
Princeton University (N.J.)	14	5,186	400	121	23,608	11,556	120	([2])	([2])
University of Minnesota, Twin Cities	15	5,101	446	104	23,870	11,883	122	([2])	6,450
Ohio State University, Main Campus	16	4,786	409	103	19,772	9,304	168	50,616	18,926
Cornell University (N.Y.)	17	4,705	458	134	20,415	9,768	79	([2])	4,818
Duke University (N.C.)	18	4,330	330	104	20,929	8,619	113	([2])	3,734
University of Pennsylvania	19	4,210	376	108	21,498	10,200	137	51,923	8,433
University of North Carolina, Chapel Hill	20	4,155	430	122	20,668	10,006	110	([2])	6,401
University of Arizona	21	4,126	361	84	17,171	7,272	158	55,783	4,068
University of Virginia, Main Campus	22	4,059	353	92	17,011	8,157	111	([2])	3,400
Michigan State University	23	3,904	290	64	13,369	6,871	109	([2])	([2])
University of Iowa	24	3,567	304	94	15,095	7,250	107	([2])	([2])
New York University	25	3,335	440	140	24,418	11,889	115	50,000	6,000
University of Southern California	26	3,248	346	107	17,794	9,061	168	6,433	5,731
University of Georgia	27	3,216	317	83	14,455	6,534	114	26,398	2,775
University of Pittsburgh, Main Campus (Penn.)	28	3,201	379	95	18,671	7,689	121	42,017	6,203
University of Kansas, Main Campus	29	3,117	282	88	11,760	5,420	100	([2])	([2])
University of Florida	30	3,092	400	110	15,780	8,553	74	187,737	15,000
University of Hawaii, Manoa	31	2,942	258	74	13,203	7,277	106	55,620	3,165
Northwestern University (Ill.)	32	2,932	315	84	12,663	6,422	119	22,401	2,727
Johns Hopkins University (Md.)	33	2,874	281	81	16,853	6,771	123	15,219	1,579
State U of New York, Buffalo, Main Campus	34	2,864	257	91	12,681	6,554	90	69,700	6,215
University of Rochester (N.Y.)	35	2,843	218	69	9,841	4,377	97	17,385	635
Wayne State University (Mich.)	36	2,834	261	79	12,938	6,023	97	46,709	9,649
Syracuse University, Main Campus (N.Y.)	37	2,779	251	70	9,435	4,910	105	23,318	2,193
Louisiana State U. & A&M & Hebert Laws Center	38	2,778	201	48	9,444	4,466	99	([2])	3,400
Arizona State University	39	2,777	314	86	14,053	6,892	97	6,000	5,260
Brown University (R.I.)	40	2,710	264	79	13,028	5,746	111	25,329	2,019
University of Missouri, Columbia	41	2,684	248	58	10,166	4,444	105	42,000	2,503
Southern Illinois University, Carbondale	42	2,648	215	42	9,508	4,453	92	22,974	2,660
University of South Carolina at Columbia	43	2,639	236	69	10,549	5,008	111	39,392	5,110
University of Massachusetts at Amherst	44	2,604	189	51	10,432	5,493	95	28,892	3,137
University of Kentucky	45	2,557	325	78	11,652	5,950	146	47,034	8,876
Pennsylvania State University, Main Campus	46	2,541	419	84	18,067	9,558	168	65,231	8,426
University of Colorado, Boulder	47	2,504	249	62	13,512	5,841	107	74,629	5,029
Washington University (Missouri)	48	2,476	188	52	10,355	4,039	102	16,811	5,292
University of Maryland, College Park Campus	49	2,454	464	104	14,473	7,538	126	72,844	12,636
North Carolina State University at Raleigh	50	2,399	244	63	11,937	4,943	107	39,954	3,109
University of California, Davis	51	2,391	306	65	13,132	7,066	87	20,167	4,939
Massachusetts Institute of Technology	52	2,366	226	85	11,771	6,072	100	30,000	3,000
University of Utah	53	2,350	319	65	12,856	5,713	100	32,672	1,307
Brigham Young University	54	2,326	291	100	12,421	5,877	101	73,668	13,231
University of Nebraska at Lincoln	55	2,324	221	56	9,445	4,339	108	18,556	1,243
University of California, San Diego	56	2,297	335	81	15,078	8,166	100	43,753	3,333
Southern Methodist University	57	2,240	159	50	7,752	3,737	116	([2])	2,500
Indiana University of Pennsylvania[1]	58	2,236	232	60	10,707	5,111	104	([2])	([2])
Auburn University, Main Campus	59	2,234	191	51	8,911	3,733	99	24,714	3,999
University of Oklahoma, Norman Campus	60	2,225	149	42	6,957	2,862	97	30,402	4,017

[1] Data estimated based on previous year's report.
[2] Data not available.

SOURCE: U.S. Department of Education, National Center for Education Statistics, Integrated Postsecondary Education Data System, *1994 Academic Library Survey*. (This table was prepared July 1997.)

LIBRARY RESOURCES AND TECHNOLOGY: LIBRARIES 465

Table 418.—General statistics of public libraries, by population of legal service area: 1994

Item	Population of legal service area						
	Total	Under 10,000	10,000 to 49,999	50,000 to 99,999	100,000 to 249,999	250,000 to 499,999	500,000 and over
1	2	3	4	5	6	7	8
Number of public library service outlets	16,896	5,762	4,128	1,785	2,086	1,108	2,027
Central libraries	8,876	5,420	2,496	493	321	76	70
Branch libraries	7,024	264	1,282	1,087	1,581	957	1,853
Bookmobiles	996	78	350	205	184	75	104
Collections, in thousands							
Books and serial volumes [1]	671,742	92,889	165,318	81,072	96,947	69,508	166,008
Audio and video materials and films	32,835	3,125	7,752	4,038	5,004	2,950	9,966
Serial subscriptions	1,772	265	462	209	232	154	450
Paid staff, in full-time equivalents							
Librarians	38,045	5,514	9,655	4,606	5,405	3,763	9,104
Librarians with ALA-MLS [2]	25,878	1,048	5,848	3,304	4,223	3,120	8,335
Other staff	74,739	4,909	17,961	10,015	12,800	8,300	20,753
Income, in thousands							
Total operating income	$5,260,086	$354,252	$1,202,080	$658,202	$843,131	$605,998	$1,596,423
	Percentage distribution						
Source of operating income							
Total	100.0	100.0	100.0	100.0	100.0	100.0	100.0
Federal [3]	1.1	1.4	0.8	0.9	1.1	1.1	1.3
State	12.3	9.4	10.9	14.0	9.7	10.7	15.3
Local	78.2	74.3	79.7	77.9	82.3	82.6	74.2
Other	8.4	14.9	8.6	7.3	6.9	5.6	9.2

[1] Some data are different from other tables due to a different population base.
[2] ALA-MLS=A master's degree from a graduate library education program accredited by the American Library Association (ALA).
[3] Excludes some federal funds received through state library agencies.

NOTE.—Because of rounding, details may not add to totals. Totals may be underestimated due to nonresponse on item or legal service area.

SOURCE: U.S. Department of Education, National Center for Education Statistics, *Public Libraries in the United States: 1994*. (This table was prepared March 1997.)

Table 419.—Public libraries, books and serial volumes, library visits, and reference transactions, by state: 1994

State	Number of public libraries	Number of books and serial volumes [1] (in thousands)	Number of books and serial volumes per capita	Library visits per capita [2]	Circulation per capita	Public library reference transactions per capita [3]	State	Number of public libraries	Number of books and serial volumes [1] (in thousands)	Number of books and serial volumes per capita	Library visits per capita [2]	Circulation per capita	Public library reference transactions per capita [3]
1	2	3	4	5	6	7	1	2	3	4	5	6	7
United States	8,921	671,815	2.7	4.1	6.4	1.1							
Alabama	207	7,372	2.0	3.3	3.9	0.7	Missouri	147	19,475	4.0	4.3	7.8	0.9
Alaska	87	1,867	3.1	3.8	6.3	0.7	Montana	82	2,541	3.1	3.5	6.0	0.7
Arizona	39	7,311	2.0	4.7	6.8	1.3	Nebraska	269	4,705	3.8	—	7.8	—
Arkansas	35	4,714	2.1	2.3	4.0	0.4	Nevada	23	293	2.0	3.1	4.8	0.7
California	170	59,072	1.9	4.0	4.6	1.3	New Hampshire	229	4,825	4.4	4.8	7.5	0.7
Colorado	120	9,522	2.6	4.3	7.8	1.2	New Jersey	309	29,234	3.8	4.7	5.8	0.9
Connecticut	194	12,854	4.3	6.3	8.1	1.1	New Mexico	73	3,765	3.3	—	6.5	0.8
Delaware	29	1,255	1.9	3.3	4.3	0.6	New York	741	69,875	4.2	4.9	7.1	1.6
District of Columbia	1	2,165	3.6	3.5	3.1	1.6	North Carolina	74	13,468	2.0	3.3	5.9	0.8
Florida	97	21,961	1.7	—	5.1	—	North Dakota	78	1,890	3.5	5.4	7.3	—
Georgia	54	12,724	1.8	2.8	4.4	0.6	Ohio	250	40,400	3.6	5.0	11.8	1.6
Hawaii	1	2,875	2.3	2.9	5.7	1.3	Oklahoma	112	5,635	2.2	3.9	6.4	0.7
Idaho	107	2,997	3.3	4.9	7.9	0.9	Oregon	124	6,479	2.4	—	9.6	0.8
Illinois	606	35,416	3.4	5.3	7.5	1.3	Pennsylvania	445	24,661	2.1	3.0	4.7	0.7
Indiana	238	19,653	3.7	5.7	9.6	1.1	Rhode Island	51	3,873	4.1	5.4	6.2	1.0
Iowa	518	10,904	3.9	5.2	8.9	0.6	South Carolina	40	6,337	1.7	2.9	4.3	1.1
Kansas	324	9,016	4.4	5.1	9.2	1.3	South Dakota	113	2,277	3.4	3.7	7.0	—
Kentucky	116	7,160	2.0	2.6	5.1	0.3	Tennessee	140	8,358	1.7	2.5	3.9	1.0
Louisiana	65	9,659	2.2	2.3	4.4	0.6	Texas	496	32,360	2.0	3.0	4.3	1.1
Maine	232	4,874	4.9	—	7.6	—	Utah	69	4,899	2.7	—	8.9	—
Maryland	24	13,086	2.7	4.5	9.1	1.1	Vermont	200	2,335	4.8	—	7.1	—
Massachusetts	373	28,015	4.7	—	6.9	0.7	Virginia	90	15,576	2.5	4.4	7.0	1.0
Michigan	380	26,297	2.9	3.8	5.4	0.9	Washington	69	14,297	2.8	—	10.1	1.0
Minnesota	132	12,513	2.8	4.6	9.4	1.4	West Virginia	97	4,608	2.5	3.4	4.6	1.0
Mississippi	47	5,079	2.0	2.5	3.1	0.4	Wisconsin	381	16,363	3.2	5.2	8.7	1.2
							Wyoming	23	2,225	4.7	4.7	8.1	0.7

[1] Some data are different from other tables due to a different population base.
[2] The total number of persons entering the library for whatever purpose during the year.
[3] A reference transaction is an information contact which involves the knowledge, use, recommendations, interpretation or instructions in the use of one or more information sources by a member of the library staff.

—Response rate less than 70 percent.

NOTE.—Totals may be underestimated due to nonresponse.

SOURCE: U.S. Department of Education, National Center for Education Statistics, *Public Libraries in the United States: 1994*. (This table was prepared March 1997.)

Table 420.—Percent of workers, 18 years old and over, using computers on the job, by selected characteristics and computer activities: October 1993

Selected characteristics	Percent using computers at work	Number using computers at work, in thousands	Analysis/ spreadsheets	Book-keeping, invoicing, and inventory	Communications[2]	CAD[3]	Data bases	Desktop publishing/ graphics	Education	Programming	Sales and telemarketing	Word processing	Using 4 or more categories
1	2	3	4	5	6	7	8	9	10	11	12	13	14
Total	45.8	51,106	36.1	45.0	38.7	7.6	34.5	22.3	15.7	13.1	16.2	44.4	40.7
Age													
18 to 24	34.4	4,965	25.0	45.3	27.1	6.0	27.1	15.9	10.4	11.2	19.9	34.7	29.8
25 to 29	48.3	8,424	37.2	45.2	38.7	7.7	35.0	22.8	14.3	13.9	17.0	45.7	41.8
30 to 39	50.7	14,969	38.8	45.4	40.4	8.7	36.0	25.0	15.8	14.9	16.4	45.0	42.9
40 to 49	51.3	13,854	38.6	45.1	42.0	7.9	36.8	23.4	18.5	12.9	14.5	47.5	43.4
50 to 59	43.9	6,881	34.5	44.3	38.8	6.4	33.3	20.4	15.8	11.2	15.0	43.9	39.2
60 or older	27.2	2,014	28.0	42.7	31.6	4.5	27.4	15.0	14.0	9.3	16.9	40.0	33.9
Educational attainment and sex													
Not high school graduate	10.0	1,190	19.1	54.4	20.4	3.8	22.2	9.9	9.6	8.8	20.6	16.0	21.8
High school graduate	34.2	13,307	23.7	52.5	29.4	4.4	25.8	13.3	9.5	8.9	17.6	30.8	29.9
Some college	50.4	11,548	33.5	49.5	38.5	7.3	33.9	20.6	13.0	11.3	18.0	40.9	40.0
Associate degree	58.2	5,274	37.5	47.0	39.7	7.9	34.7	21.7	13.8	14.2	14.9	41.6	40.7
Bachelor's degree	68.8	13,162	46.9	40.0	45.1	10.4	41.5	28.8	19.4	16.7	17.0	54.8	49.2
Master's degree	71.2	4,628	47.9	29.3	48.5	10.0	41.9	35.3	31.0	18.1	10.4	63.8	52.1
Doctor's or professional degree	66.9	1,999	42.8	27.9	45.9	7.6	39.2	28.3	21.3	15.2	5.2	66.5	46.2
Male	40.3	24,414	41.1	45.2	39.4	11.1	35.2	25.3	14.8	17.0	18.1	40.7	43.0
Not high school graduate	8.5	642	20.2	56.0	20.9	5.6	19.8	10.9	9.1	9.6	16.2	12.2	21.1
High school graduate	24.2	4,942	23.4	52.0	24.6	7.2	19.6	12.9	7.7	9.6	17.7	17.3	25.4
Some college	42.8	5,086	35.8	50.4	37.1	10.4	33.4	22.0	12.8	15.6	20.9	32.1	40.0
Associate degree	52.6	2,358	41.8	46.8	39.3	13.3	36.0	26.2	14.7	19.1	16.8	36.6	41.9
Bachelor's degree	69.8	7,324	52.3	42.6	47.1	13.8	43.4	31.6	16.6	21.0	20.9	53.8	53.2
Master's degree	75.4	2,601	56.0	34.1	51.7	13.0	46.8	37.8	25.2	22.5	13.8	63.3	57.2
Doctor's or professional degree	66.5	1,461	45.0	29.2	46.0	8.6	38.7	29.9	20.9	17.9	5.2	67.7	47.9
Female	52.4	26,692	31.6	44.8	38.1	4.4	33.8	19.6	16.5	9.5	14.5	47.8	38.6
Not high school graduate	12.5	547	17.8	52.5	19.9	1.7	25.1	8.7	10.3	7.9	25.8	20.5	22.6
High school graduate	45.2	8,365	23.8	52.8	32.2	2.8	29.4	13.6	10.5	8.6	17.5	38.8	32.5
Some college	58.6	6,461	31.6	48.7	39.7	4.8	34.3	19.4	13.1	8.0	15.7	47.9	40.0
Associate degree	63.7	2,916	34.0	47.1	40.0	3.5	33.6	18.1	13.1	10.2	13.5	45.7	39.6
Bachelor's degree	67.6	5,838	40.2	36.8	42.5	6.1	39.2	25.3	22.9	11.5	12.0	56.1	44.1
Master's degree	66.5	2,027	37.4	23.2	44.3	6.0	35.6	32.1	38.5	12.4	6.0	64.4	45.5
Doctor's or professional degree	68.2	538	36.8	24.1	45.4	4.8	40.8	24.1	22.3	7.7	5.2	74.3	41.5
Race/ethnicity													
White, non-Hispanic	48.7	43,020	37.2	45.8	39.3	7.8	35.2	23.0	15.9	13.4	16.7	45.9	41.8
Black, non-Hispanic	36.2	4,016	27.5	38.3	37.3	5.8	31.2	16.8	15.7	10.9	12.9	35.5	34.1
Hispanic	29.3	2,492	29.1	45.6	32.1	6.5	27.6	18.7	13.3	10.8	16.0	33.6	32.9
Other	43.9	1,578	39.7	39.4	37.2	8.9	33.5	22.6	12.9	15.2	10.2	44.5	39.0
Occupational group													
Managerial and professional specialty	67.7	21,044	46.5	39.3	45.7	10.6	40.3	31.1	22.2	16.7	11.6	56.7	49.7
Executive, administrative, and managerial	72.3	10,645	54.5	54.3	49.0	8.1	44.3	29.6	15.9	14.9	18.4	58.3	55.6
Professional specialty occupations	68.3	7,712	43.2	26.6	45.8	15.4	40.7	33.2	16.1	20.0	5.4	54.2	45.2
Teachers, except college and university	49.1	2,091	18.9	16.4	28.0	5.5	20.1	30.0	69.6	11.2	2.3	52.0	36.2
Teachers, college and university	72.5	597	44.0	15.8	48.9	11.2	33.4	34.9	47.0	23.8	2.2	77.4	51.1
Technical, sales, and administrative support	65.5	22,316	31.2	50.7	36.5	5.1	33.4	17.3	11.9	10.9	22.6	42.0	38.7
Technicians and related support	69.9	2,592	41.5	29.0	38.1	13.1	37.9	21.2	11.0	28.8	4.7	37.4	37.9
Sales occupations	48.8	6,220	34.1	59.9	33.6	4.7	31.5	18.5	11.0	8.2	53.7	34.8	43.5
Administrative support, including clerical	76.7	13,505	27.9	50.6	37.5	3.7	33.3	16.0	12.4	8.7	11.7	46.2	36.6
Service occupations	14.7	2,126	15.2	31.3	31.5	2.7	20.9	7.5	9.1	6.6	11.6	20.5	18.7
Precision production, craft, and repair	23.2	2,976	32.0	45.3	29.2	9.9	26.1	16.4	11.0	14.4	9.6	20.6	28.2
Operators, fabricators, and laborers	14.9	2,382	15.3	51.8	18.3	6.1	17.0	12.5	6.5	7.1	9.6	11.4	16.4
Farming, forestry, and fishing	8.5	262	27.5	65.3	16.4	1.8	27.3	16.2	8.6	7.6	10.4	28.2	31.7
Family income[4]													
Less than $20,000	25.1	5,224	24.4	46.6	28.8	5.1	27.4	15.5	12.1	9.4	18.7	33.1	30.6
$20,000 to $29,999	38.4	7,337	29.3	48.9	35.3	6.1	31.1	19.2	13.8	11.2	17.8	38.6	36.7
$30,000 to $39,999	45.7	8,911	32.3	47.1	35.7	6.9	31.5	20.6	15.1	11.8	15.0	40.7	37.1
$40,000 to $49,999	51.9	7,027	34.2	45.4	37.3	7.3	33.0	20.6	15.6	12.9	13.4	42.2	38.2
$50,000 to $74,999	60.6	12,643	40.4	43.4	42.2	8.9	37.5	24.4	17.8	14.6	15.2	47.6	43.7
$75,000 or more	65.9	8,994	49.3	40.6	47.8	9.5	42.1	29.5	17.0	16.3	17.5	57.9	52.2

[1] Individuals may be counted in more than one computer activity.
[2] Includes bulletin boards and electronic mail.
[3] Computer assisted design.
[4] Excludes persons whose income data were not available.

NOTE.—Data are based on a sample survey of households and are subject to sampling and nonsampling error.

SOURCE: U.S. Department of Commerce, Bureau of the Census, Current Population Survey, October 1993, unpublished data. (This table was prepared March 1994.)

Table 421.—Access to and use of home computers, by selected characteristics of students and other users: October 1993

Selected characteristics	Percent with computers at home	Percent using computers at home	Distribution of frequency of use per week for persons using computers in home				Percent of persons whose home computer has specific components [1]				Percent of computer users using specific applications [2]					
			6 or 7 days	4 or 5 days	2 or 3 days	1 day or less	Hard disk	Printer	Color monitor	Fax or modem	Communications [3]	School assignments	Education programs	Games	Job-related	Word processing
1	2	3	4	5	6	7	8	9	10	11	12	13	14	15	16	17
Total, all persons	27.1	17.6	14.7	17.1	33.3	34.9	80.7	75.8	68.2	38.5	33.5	28.3	34.6	34.9	23.8	53.2
Age																
Less than 25	30.8	21.0	11.1	15.5	36.2	37.3	79.5	75.2	69.1	36.2	8.4	48.9	38.1	57.2	3.1	37.7
25 to 29	23.4	16.6	16.8	18.4	33.4	31.3	83.5	68.5	66.3	44.2	48.0	22.6	30.0	21.1	35.2	63.4
30 to 39	30.7	21.0	16.2	17.9	33.2	32.7	82.3	74.0	70.3	42.3	51.2	15.6	34.2	22.2	38.6	61.9
40 to 49	36.4	23.0	16.9	17.9	30.9	34.3	80.9	79.4	69.6	39.0	48.6	15.7	33.5	19.1	39.1	65.1
50 to 59	27.1	15.8	17.7	19.8	27.9	34.7	80.2	79.2	65.0	37.1	50.9	9.5	30.8	19.5	37.2	64.7
60 or older	10.5	4.6	20.7	16.7	28.7	33.9	80.2	77.5	60.0	33.2	51.4	3.3	27.4	19.7	26.5	59.4
Family income																
Less than $20,000	9.2	5.6	19.2	15.7	31.3	33.8	72.4	64.6	57.8	28.6	32.3	34.7	33.0	33.7	16.2	50.2
$20,000 to $29,999	18.5	11.3	16.6	16.6	33.9	32.9	74.6	73.0	62.8	32.1	33.8	28.4	37.8	36.8	21.2	50.2
$30,000 to $39,999	26.5	16.9	14.0	16.8	34.2	35.0	76.8	72.7	66.7	33.7	33.6	27.5	35.3	35.4	22.2	49.2
$40,000 to $49,999	35.2	22.9	13.9	16.6	33.8	35.7	81.6	77.2	71.4	37.5	31.4	26.0	32.8	35.4	21.0	48.9
$50,000 to $74,999	47.3	31.6	13.5	17.6	33.2	35.7	82.5	78.6	70.4	41.7	33.3	28.5	34.2	35.4	25.2	53.8
$75,000 or more	62.8	42.4	14.3	17.9	33.0	34.8	87.6	80.1	72.2	46.1	35.3	26.9	35.0	33.6	29.1	60.2
Total, all students	36.1	26.5	12.4	16.3	36.3	35.1	80.6	76.3	69.9	37.5	11.8	55.1	39.1	55.1	5.7	41.8
Preprimary	29.6	15.3	4.7	10.7	39.5	45.0	82.3	72.0	69.6	40.9	0.7	4.1	62.0	86.6	0.0	5.1
1st to 8th grade	31.9	24.3	9.9	14.1	37.9	38.1	79.9	75.2	72.1	36.9	2.6	43.6	48.2	86.4	0.0	28.0
9th to 12th grade	37.2	28.1	11.6	17.7	37.3	33.3	77.7	78.0	69.7	34.6	7.1	73.0	26.6	32.9	2.3	47.6
Undergraduate	44.7	32.4	16.2	19.2	31.8	32.8	81.5	78.1	66.8	36.3	26.5	70.6	26.8	16.3	12.1	62.0
Graduate	60.4	51.8	25.5	21.4	33.2	20.0	89.4	77.9	67.8	50.3	47.8	69.5	39.2	21.9	37.0	80.1
Sex																
Male	36.2	26.9	15.1	17.0	34.1	33.7	81.0	76.1	70.5	38.7	12.7	54.1	39.4	57.8	6.1	40.1
Preprimary	28.5	14.8	6.0	13.1	37.3	43.6	82.7	71.1	71.0	41.3	0.4	5.8	61.3	90.7	0.0	4.4
1st to 8th grade	31.8	24.5	11.6	14.3	36.6	37.5	80.6	75.1	72.1	36.2	2.2	40.5	47.4	88.8	0.0	26.0
9th to 12th grade	36.6	27.6	15.0	19.7	33.4	31.9	77.5	77.8	69.7	36.5	8.5	72.5	27.4	34.3	2.3	45.1
Undergraduate	48.7	36.1	20.2	19.8	30.0	30.0	82.1	78.8	68.2	40.7	29.4	72.1	27.8	18.3	12.5	61.9
Graduate	62.6	55.2	31.0	20.7	30.2	18.1	89.7	75.0	69.2	51.8	53.6	71.6	42.1	25.1	42.4	80.6
Female	36.0	26.2	9.6	15.5	38.5	36.5	80.2	76.5	69.4	36.3	10.8	56.2	38.8	52.3	5.4	43.6
Preprimary	30.9	15.8	3.4	8.2	41.9	46.5	82.0	73.0	68.2	40.6	1.0	2.2	62.7	82.3	0.0	5.8
1st to 8th grade	32.1	24.2	8.0	13.8	39.4	38.7	79.2	75.2	72.1	37.6	3.1	46.9	49.1	83.9	0.0	30.2
9th to 12th grade	37.9	28.6	8.1	15.6	41.4	34.9	77.9	78.2	69.7	32.6	5.7	73.5	25.8	31.5	2.3	50.1
Undergraduate	41.5	29.4	12.3	18.6	33.5	35.6	80.9	77.5	65.6	32.0	23.7	69.0	25.8	14.3	11.8	62.1
Graduate	58.4	48.8	19.9	22.1	36.1	21.8	89.2	80.7	66.4	48.9	41.8	67.5	36.2	18.7	31.6	79.7
Race/ethnicity																
White, non-Hispanic	43.3	32.2	11.9	16.0	35.8	36.3	81.1	77.6	70.1	38.0	11.4	55.2	38.4	55.6	5.7	42.6
Preprimary	35.8	19.0	4.4	11.8	37.4	46.4	83.7	72.7	70.2	41.7	0.7	4.3	62.0	87.1	0.0	5.7
1st to 8th grade	39.6	30.8	9.7	13.8	37.1	39.5	80.5	76.8	72.3	37.5	2.7	43.8	47.2	87.0	0.0	28.9
9th to 12th grade	46.2	35.1	10.9	16.6	38.1	34.4	78.2	79.5	69.8	35.5	7.1	73.5	25.5	31.8	2.1	48.7
Undergraduate	49.4	35.5	15.8	19.3	31.2	33.7	81.9	79.2	67.0	36.4	26.1	71.2	25.5	15.5	13.2	64.0
Graduate	61.4	52.8	25.1	22.1	32.5	20.3	89.3	78.1	67.3	50.1	47.3	70.8	39.3	21.0	36.2	82.1
Black, non-Hispanic	16.1	10.8	13.8	16.8	37.0	32.4	73.8	64.8	68.4	34.5	14.2	53.0	50.8	56.3	7.4	33.9
Preprimary	12.3	4.1	5.9	2.9	53.6	37.7	67.9	59.2	66.9	39.3	0.0	0.0	76.7	85.7	0.0	0.0
1st to 8th grade	13.1	8.9	10.6	16.9	42.8	29.7	73.6	60.7	70.6	33.8	3.2	44.8	64.9	84.5	0.0	22.6
9th to 12th grade	14.6	10.3	12.6	22.0	29.0	36.4	71.4	59.7	61.5	21.2	3.7	67.9	36.1	40.4	5.6	27.2
Undergraduate	27.0	19.1	18.7	13.9	33.0	34.4	76.1	75.2	70.7	41.3	37.2	60.6	40.3	27.5	9.3	56.7
Graduate	56.7	47.6	21.7	18.8	32.2	27.3	82.3	75.3	69.5	48.6	37.4	60.3	35.8	24.9	47.9	60.2
Hispanic	15.2	10.3	13.9	21.1	39.6	25.5	74.7	73.0	63.0	32.7	17.2	54.9	34.7	51.2	5.2	35.3
Preprimary	11.7	5.6	7.9	6.8	36.7	48.6	70.5	75.5	53.8	29.7	0.0	0.0	39.6	71.1	0.0	0.0
1st to 8th grade	12.1	7.4	11.2	16.1	42.8	29.9	72.3	70.4	65.3	31.2	0.8	38.9	40.4	84.7	0.0	17.6
9th to 12th grade	14.4	9.6	13.7	33.2	29.6	23.5	71.5	76.9	67.4	31.2	15.8	68.7	27.7	41.3	2.4	47.1
Undergraduate	27.3	21.9	15.0	22.4	42.1	20.5	78.2	70.5	55.5	31.4	30.8	73.1	30.3	12.7	5.8	47.5
Graduate	56.3	52.2	28.5	16.5	44.4	10.6	95.1	84.9	77.9	58.8	69.8	71.8	39.6	37.7	43.5	75.4
Family income																
Less than $20,000	15.2	10.9	18.5	16.0	34.1	31.3	74.9	65.9	57.9	29.2	20.4	62.0	35.3	44.0	8.4	47.6
$20,000 to $29,999	25.5	18.6	13.4	16.8	38.6	31.2	72.7	71.8	63.7	31.1	13.0	53.3	41.2	51.5	7.0	38.6
$30,000 to $39,999	34.3	25.1	11.9	15.4	38.2	34.6	76.3	73.2	67.5	32.8	11.5	55.3	41.0	54.1	6.9	36.9
$40,000 to $49,999	42.6	31.5	10.9	16.7	37.0	35.3	80.4	78.8	74.0	36.0	8.9	53.2	38.1	61.3	4.8	35.7
$50,000 to $74,999	55.9	42.0	10.5	17.3	34.1	38.1	82.8	79.9	73.4	41.8	10.1	54.1	38.1	56.9	4.4	41.9
$75,000 or more	73.7	54.1	12.1	15.2	37.2	35.5	87.8	80.5	74.6	43.6	10.4	54.5	40.8	57.9	4.9	46.7

[1] Data are for the most recently purchased computer for families with more than one computer. Percent based on persons who have a computer in their home.
[2] Individuals may be counted in more than one computer activity.
[3] Includes bulletin boards and electronic mail.

NOTE.—Data are based on a sample survey of households and are subject to sampling and nonsampling error.

SOURCE: U.S. Department of Commerce, Bureau of the Census, Current Population Survey, October 1993, unpublished data. (This table was prepared May 1994.)

Table 422.—Student use of computers, by level of instruction and selected characteristics: October 1984, 1989, and 1993

Student and school characteristics	October 1984 Total	October 1989						October 1993					
		Total	Prekindergarten and kindergarten	Grades 1 to 8	Grades 9 to 12	1st to 4th year of college	5th or later year of college	Total	Prekindergarten and kindergarten	Grades 1 to 8	Grades 9 to 12	1st to 4th year of college	5th or later year of college
1	2	3	4	5	6	7	8	9	10	11	12	13	14
Percent of students using computers at school													
Total	27.3	42.7	14.7	52.3	39.2	39.2	40.7	59.0	26.2	68.9	58.2	55.2	52.1
Sex													
Male	29.0	43.5	13.9	52.9	38.7	42.1	47.0	59.4	25.9	69.5	56.5	57.5	56.7
Female	25.5	41.9	15.6	51.7	39.8	36.8	34.9	58.7	26.5	68.4	60.0	53.3	47.8
Race/ethnicity													
White, non-Hispanic	30.0	45.7	17.0	58.4	40.6	40.0	39.6	61.6	29.4	73.7	59.9	54.9	49.8
Black, non-Hispanic	16.8	32.6	7.4	35.7	36.0	35.1	35.2	51.5	16.5	56.5	54.5	56.9	57.9
Hispanic	18.6	34.9	10.1	40.2	33.6	32.4	37.8	52.3	19.2	58.4	54.1	51.9	53.7
Other	28.6	42.7	8.5	47.0	41.4	43.9	58.0	59.0	23.5	65.7	57.3	60.9	69.4
Household income													
Less than $5,000	18.7	36.7	8.5	40.4	35.6	40.1	53.5	51.2	19.6	55.0	50.6	61.7	66.7
$5,000 to 9,999	21.0	36.1	9.2	40.3	32.7	40.5	60.2	53.3	24.4	60.3	51.9	53.9	56.2
$10,000 to 14,999	22.4	38.4	14.6	44.4	39.1	30.8	55.2	56.4	20.1	64.7	56.7	50.7	76.1
$15,000 to 19,999	25.9	41.5	11.9	50.9	34.8	39.6	44.0	58.1	23.8	67.5	57.4	51.2	58.5
$20,000 to 24,999	26.7	42.4	14.6	51.8	40.1	32.5	44.4	56.4	23.7	64.3	53.0	57.4	52.4
$25,000 to 29,999	30.5	46.1	16.1	56.4	43.8	40.4	42.1	60.0	28.0	70.1	60.3	51.5	58.0
$30,000 to 34,999	30.5	44.2	17.4	56.8	37.8	37.1	33.3	59.1	23.7	69.6	59.7	51.7	45.3
$35,000 to 39,999	32.3	45.2	16.1	58.3	41.5	34.5	45.3	60.7	27.1	72.1	61.7	49.2	47.9
$40,000 to 49,999	32.8	44.7	15.4	59.7	36.7	38.1	35.4	59.3	28.5	70.3	57.2	53.9	48.6
$50,000 to 74,999	35.5	47.0	16.2	61.2	44.6	43.4	31.8	62.6	28.6	75.6	61.5	57.4	44.2
$75,000 or more	36.0	51.2	21.2	67.0	45.8	49.6	31.0	64.6	33.5	78.7	62.5	60.9	47.7
Control of school													
Public	27.4	43.3	16.4	51.9	39.0	37.5	41.3	60.2	30.1	68.6	58.1	53.9	54.1
Private	26.5	38.9	11.8	56.6	42.6	46.3	39.7	52.1	18.7	72.5	60.7	60.7	48.0
Percent of students using computers at home													
Total	11.5	18.8	10.2	17.8	20.7	21.3	33.4	27.0	15.6	24.7	28.7	32.8	52.6
Sex													
Male	14.0	20.7	11.0	18.7	23.9	25.4	36.0	27.4	15.1	24.8	28.2	36.6	56.1
Female	9.0	17.0	9.3	16.9	17.4	18.0	31.1	26.6	16.1	24.6	29.2	29.7	49.5
Race/ethnicity													
White, non-Hispanic	13.7	22.7	12.2	22.3	25.3	23.6	35.6	32.8	19.4	31.4	35.9	36.0	53.6
Black, non-Hispanic	4.9	7.3	3.7	6.8	8.5	9.1	18.6	10.9	4.2	9.0	10.4	19.4	48.1
Hispanic	3.6	7.5	3.4	6.6	8.2	11.5	27.1	10.4	5.7	7.5	9.8	22.0	52.2
Other	9.0	18.8	9.9	16.6	21.6	23.7	24.7	28.7	17.0	23.2	37.0	33.0	47.1
Household income													
Less than $5,000	2.9	8.4	4.5	4.1	6.6	17.7	29.4	9.7	1.1	4.1	6.8	25.6	45.2
$5,000 to 9,999	3.2	5.4	1.0	2.7	4.4	14.2	28.4	8.0	0.9	4.5	5.3	21.3	45.6
$10,000 to 14,999	5.0	7.2	1.9	6.2	6.5	11.8	26.5	11.4	4.6	6.4	8.7	29.8	50.0
$15,000 to 19,999	7.5	11.3	3.2	9.2	13.6	15.8	33.6	15.1	6.9	10.9	14.1	28.9	43.0
$20,000 to 24,999	9.9	12.9	6.8	11.6	13.6	16.9	32.2	16.8	7.4	13.1	17.9	27.7	49.6
$25,000 to 29,999	12.8	17.0	11.9	16.5	17.1	19.2	29.6	21.1	12.3	19.3	22.0	26.1	47.0
$30,000 to 34,999	15.8	17.7	8.0	17.6	20.2	19.4	30.7	24.1	18.7	20.5	29.1	26.4	44.4
$35,000 to 39,999	19.4	21.4	8.7	22.2	25.1	22.1	26.5	27.1	13.0	26.3	28.1	32.7	52.7
$40,000 to 49,999	20.4	25.7	14.8	27.5	27.7	21.7	40.7	32.2	21.6	32.9	33.9	32.5	45.9
$50,000 to 74,999	24.2	31.6	20.6	33.8	34.3	27.6	41.1	43.0	25.5	45.3	46.4	40.1	58.2
$75,000 or more	22.1	43.8	25.2	50.9	53.4	33.9	41.4	56.1	38.2	62.3	61.0	47.0	64.7
Control of school													
Public	11.2	17.9	8.3	16.8	19.7	20.7	32.2	25.3	12.1	23.0	27.2	31.9	50.0
Private	13.8	24.4	13.4	27.7	35.9	23.8	35.9	37.4	22.4	41.5	47.2	36.9	57.7
Percent of students using computers at home for school work													
Total	4.6	8.9	0.6	6.3	12.2	13.7	23.9	14.9	0.6	10.8	20.9	23.1	36.6
Sex													
Male	5.9	9.5	0.6	6.3	13.6	16.0	25.9	14.8	0.9	10.1	20.5	26.3	40.3
Female	3.3	8.3	0.6	6.2	10.8	11.7	22.0	15.0	0.4	11.5	21.4	20.5	33.2
Race													
White, non-Hispanic	5.4	10.7	0.6	7.7	15.2	15.1	25.5	18.2	0.8	13.8	26.5	25.7	37.8
Black, non-Hispanic	2.3	3.4	0.9	2.7	4.0	6.2	12.6	5.7	—	4.0	6.9	11.5	30.1
Hispanic	1.4	3.6	—	2.8	4.4	6.4	24.8	5.6	—	2.9	6.7	15.9	36.8
Other	3.8	9.1	—	5.8	13.4	15.5	14.8	16.0	1.1	9.3	27.0	23.7	29.2
Household income													
Less than $5,000	1.0	5.0	—	1.5	4.1	12.6	23.8	6.7	—	2.5	4.0	18.7	36.0
$5,000 to 9,999	1.5	3.2	—	0.6	2.6	10.3	26.5	4.8	—	1.1	3.6	16.1	35.5
$10,000 to 14,999	1.9	3.5	0.7	1.8	3.6	8.1	19.3	7.3	—	2.6	5.6	25.9	34.6
$15,000 to 19,999	3.0	4.5	—	2.1	5.2	9.3	30.2	8.6	0.4	4.7	10.8	18.7	31.0
$20,000 to 24,999	3.1	5.7	0.3	3.8	7.6	10.5	23.8	9.8	0.7	5.1	12.6	22.9	35.0
$25,000 to 29,999	5.1	6.4	0.3	4.1	8.2	12.3	19.7	10.4	1.1	6.3	13.4	19.5	34.9
$30,000 to 34,999	4.9	8.0	0.1	5.7	12.0	12.8	19.8	13.0	0.8	8.1	21.9	18.0	35.1
$35,000 to 39,999	7.1	10.5	1.2	7.9	15.0	15.9	18.7	15.4	0.8	12.4	21.0	22.6	37.2
$40,000 to 49,999	9.2	11.9	0.7	9.7	17.1	14.3	29.4	17.1	1.1	14.7	24.2	22.2	32.1
$50,000 to 74,999	11.5	15.2	0.8	12.7	21.2	17.5	28.5	23.2	1.0	19.7	35.0	27.0	38.2
$75,000 or more	9.8	22.0	2.4	21.9	34.2	21.2	22.2	30.4	0.8	29.4	45.2	30.6	41.5
Control of school													
Public	4.5	8.5	0.6	5.9	11.5	13.1	22.2	14.2	0.5	10.1	19.8	22.7	34.7
Private	5.4	11.4	0.5	9.4	23.6	15.8	27.1	18.8	1.0	17.8	35.4	24.8	40.1

—Data not available.

NOTE.—Data are based on a sample survey of households and are subject to sampling and nonsampling error.

SOURCE: U.S. Department of Commerce, Bureau of the Census, Current Population Survey, October 1984, 1989, and 1993, unpublished data. (This table was prepared April 1994.)

Guide to Tabular Presentation

This section is intended to assist the reader in following the basic structure of the *Digest* tables and to provide a legend for some of the common symbols and indexes used throughout the book. Unless otherwise noted, all data are for the 50 states and the District of Columbia.

Table Components

Title Describes the table content concisely.

Unit Indicator Informs the reader of the measurement united in the table—"In thousands," "In millions of dollars," etc. Noted below the title unless several units are used, in which case the unit indicators are generally given in the spanner or individual column heads.

Spanner Describes a group of two or more columns.

Column head Describes specific column.

Stub Describes a row or a group of rows. Each stub is followed by a number of dots (leaders) or by a semicolon if no data appears in the data fields.

Field The area of the table which contains the data elements.

Rules in the field

Single horizontal rules indicate
— that the data below the line add to the figure immediately above the line, or
— in the case of derived figures (e.g., percents, medians) that the datum above the line represents a cumulative figure.

Double horizontal rules demarcate groups of related rows.

Single vertical rules delineate columns.

Double vertical rules divide the table into sections with unique stubs.

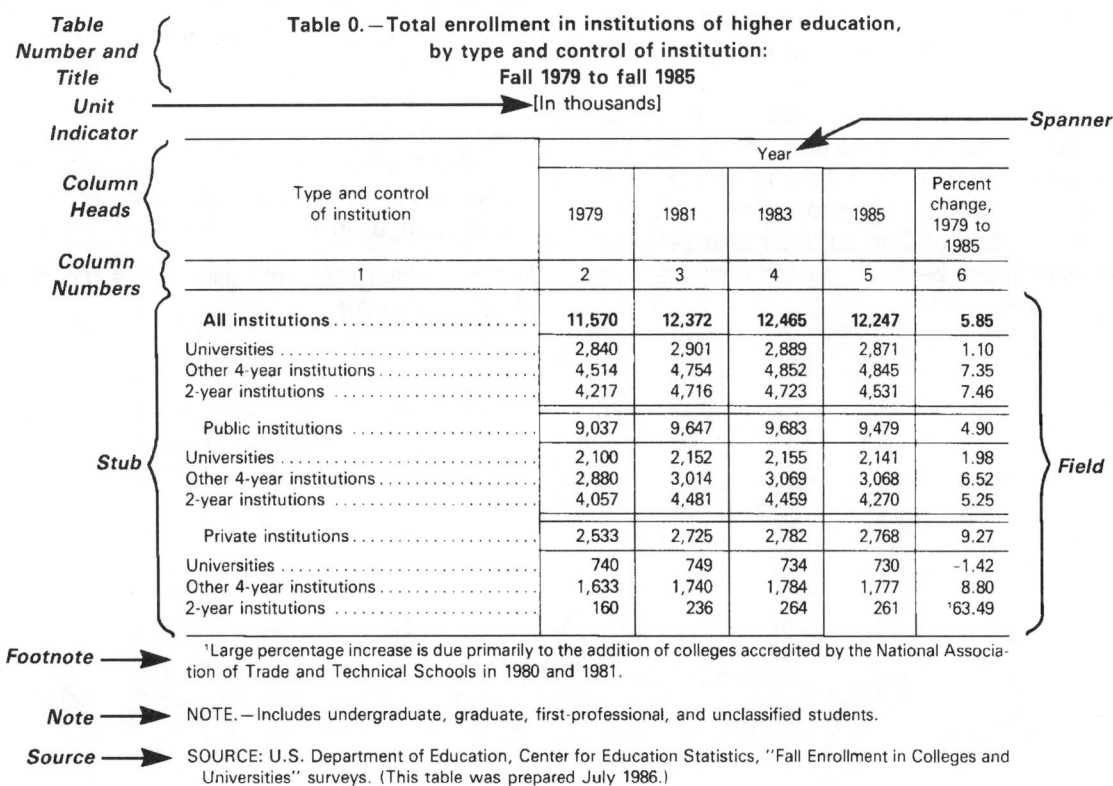

Example of Table Structure

Table 0.—Total enrollment in institutions of higher education, by type and control of institution: Fall 1979 to fall 1985

[In thousands]

| Type and control of institution | \multicolumn{5}{c}{Year} |
	1979	1981	1983	1985	Percent change, 1979 to 1985
1	2	3	4	5	6
All institutions	11,570	12,372	12,465	12,247	5.85
Universities	2,840	2,901	2,889	2,871	1.10
Other 4-year institutions	4,514	4,754	4,852	4,845	7.35
2-year institutions	4,217	4,716	4,723	4,531	7.46
Public institutions	9,037	9,647	9,683	9,479	4.90
Universities	2,100	2,152	2,155	2,141	1.98
Other 4-year institutions	2,880	3,014	3,069	3,068	6.52
2-year institutions	4,057	4,481	4,459	4,270	5.25
Private institutions	2,533	2,725	2,782	2,768	9.27
Universities	740	749	734	730	-1.42
Other 4-year institutions	1,633	1,740	1,784	1,777	8.80
2-year institutions	160	236	264	261	[1]63.49

[1]Large percentage increase is due primarily to the addition of colleges accredited by the National Association of Trade and Technical Schools in 1980 and 1981.

NOTE.—Includes undergraduate, graduate, first-professional, and unclassified students.

SOURCE: U.S. Department of Education, Center for Education Statistics, "Fall Enrollment in Colleges and Universities" surveys. (This table was prepared July 1986.)

Footnote Describes a unique circumstance relating to a specific item within the table. Usually listed below the bottom rule of the table.

Note Furnishes general information that relates to the entire table.

Source The document or reference from which the data are drawn. This note may also include the organizational unit responsible for preparing the data.

Descriptive Terms

Average A number that is used to represent the "typical value" of a group of numbers. It is regarded as a measure of "location" or "central tendency" of a group of numbers.

Arithmetic mean is the most commonly used average. It is derived by summing the individual item values of a particular group and dividing that sum by the number of items. This value is often referred to simply as the "mean" or "average."

Median is the measure of central tendency that occupies the middle position in a rank order of values. It generally has the same number of items above it as below it. If there is an even number of items in the group, the median is the average of the middle two items.

Per capita, or per person, figure represents an average computed for every person in a specified group, or population. It is derived by dividing the total for an item (such as income or expenditures) by the number of persons in the specified population.

Index number A value that provides a means of measuring, summarizing, and communicating the nature of changes that occur from time to time or from place to place. An index is used to express changes in prices over periods of time but may also be used to express differences between related subjects at a single point in time.

The *Digest* most often uses the Consumer Price Index to compare purchasing power over time.

To compute a price index, a base year or period is selected. The base year price is then designated as the base or reference price to which the prices for other years or periods are related.

A method of expressing the price relationship is:

$$\text{Index number} = \frac{\text{Price of a set of one or more items for related year}}{\text{Price of the same set of items for base year}} \times 100$$

When 100 is subtracted from the index number, the result equals the percent change in price from the base year.

Current and constant dollars are used in a number of tables to express finance data. Unless otherwise noted, all figures are in current dollars, not adjusted for inflation. Constant dollars provide a measure of the impact of inflation on the current dollars.

Current dollar figures reflect actual prices or costs prevailing during the specified year(s).

Constant dollar figures attempt to remove the effects of price changes (inflation) from statistical series reported in dollar terms.

The constant dollar value for an item is derived by dividing the base year price index (for example, the Consumer Price Index for 1986) by the price index for the year of data to be adjusted and multiplying by the item to be adjusted. The result is an adjusted dollar value as it would presumably exist if prices were the same as the base year—in other words, as if the dollar had constant purchasing power. Any changes in the constant dollar amounts would reflect only changes in the real values.

NOTE: Tables may not include data for all years implied in table titles.

Guide to Sources
Sources and Comparability of Data

The information presented in this report was obtained from many sources, including federal and state agencies, private research organizations, and professional associations. The data were collected using many research methods, including surveys of a universe (such as all colleges) or of a sample, compilations of administrative records, and statistical projections. *Digest* users should take particular care when comparing data from different sources. Differences in procedures, timing, phrasing of questions, interviewer training, and so forth mean that the results from the different sources may not be strictly comparable. Following the general discussion of data accuracy below, descriptions of the information sources and data collection methods are presented, grouped by sponsoring organization. More extensive documentation of a particular survey's procedures does not imply more problems with the data, only that more information is available.

Accuracy of Data

The accuracy of any statistic is determined by the joint effects of "sampling" and "nonsampling" errors. Estimates based on a sample will differ somewhat from the figures that would have been obtained if a complete census had been taken using the same survey instruments, instructions, and procedures. In addition to such sampling errors, all surveys, both universe and sample, are subject to design, reporting, and processing errors and errors due to nonresponse. To the extent possible, these nonsampling errors are kept to a minimum by methods built into the survey procedures. In general, however, the effects of nonsampling errors are more difficult to gauge than those produced by sampling variability.

Sampling Errors

The samples used in surveys are selected from a large number of possible samples of the same size that could have been selected using the same sample design. Estimates derived from the different samples would differ from each other. The difference between a sample estimate and the average of all possible samples is called the sampling deviation. The standard or sampling error of a survey estimate is a measure of the variation among the estimates from all possible samples and, thus, is a measure of the precision with which an estimate from a particular sample approximates the average result of all possible samples.

The sample estimate and an estimate of its standard error permit us to construct interval estimates with prescribed confidence that the interval includes the average result of all possible samples. If all possible samples were selected under essentially the same conditions and an estimate and its estimated standard error were calculated from each sample, then: (1) approximately 2/3 of the intervals from one standard error below the estimate to one standard error above the estimate would include the average value of all possible samples; and (2) approximately 19/20 of the intervals from two standard errors below the estimate to two standard errors above the estimate would include the average value of all possible samples. We call an interval from two standard errors below the estimate to two standard errors above the estimate a 95 percent confidence interval.

To illustrate this concept, consider the table of standard errors and 95 percent confidence intervals for estimates from the 1989–90 Beginning Postsecondary Students Survey (table A1). For the estimate that 28.1 percent of all female students in a vocational certificate program completed the program in 9 months or less, the table shows that the standard error is 3 percent. Therefore, we can create a 95 percent confidence interval which is approximately 22.1 to 34.1 (28.1 percent ± 2 times 3 percent).

Analysis of standard errors can help assess how valid a comparison between two estimates might be. The **standard error of a difference** between two independent sample estimates is equal to the square root of the sum of the squared standard errors of the estimates. The standard error (se) of the difference between independent sample estimates "a" and "b" is:

$$se_{a,b} = (se_a^2 + se_b^2)^{1/2}$$

It should be noted that most of the standard error estimates presented in subsequent sections and in the original documents are approximations. That is, to derive estimates of standard errors that would be applicable to a wide variety of items and could be prepared at a moderate cost, a number of approximations were required. As a result, the standard error estimates provide a general order of magnitude rather than the exact standard error for any specific item. The preceding discussion on sampling variability was directed toward a situation concerning one or two estimates. Determining the accuracy of statistical projections is more difficult. In general, the further away the projection date is from the date of the actual data being used for the projection, the greater the probable error in the projections. If, for instance, annual data from 1970 to 1995 are being used to project enrollment in institutions of higher education, the further beyond 1995 one projects, the more variability in the projection. One will be less sure of the 2005 enrollment projection than of the 2000 projection. A detailed discussion of the projections methodology is contained in *Projections of Education Statistics to 2007* (National Center for Education Statistics, 1997).

Nonsampling Errors

Universe and sample surveys are subject to nonsampling errors. Nonsampling errors may arise when respondents or interviewers interpret questions differently, when respondents must estimate values, or when coders, keyers, and other processors handle answers differently, when persons who should be included in the universe are not, or when persons fail to respond (completely or partially). Nonsampling errors usually, but not always, result in an understatement of total survey error and thus an overstatement of the precision of survey estimates. Since estimating the magnitude of nonsampling errors often would require special experiments or access to independent data, these nonsampling errors are seldom available.

To compensate for nonresponse, adjustments of the sample estimates are often made. An adjustment made for either type of nonresponse, total or partial, is often referred to as an imputation, which is often a substitution of the "average" questionnaire response for the nonresponse. Imputations are usually made separately within various groups of sample members which have similar survey characteristics. Imputation for item nonresponse is usually made by substituting for a missing item the response to that item of a respondent having characteristics that are similar to those of the nonrespondent.

Although the magnitude of nonsampling error in the data compiled in this *Digest* is frequently unknown, idiosyncrasies that have been identified are noted on the appropriate tables.

Department of Education

National Center for Education Statistics (NCES)

Beginning Postsecondary Student Longitudinal Study

The Beginning Postsecondary Student Longitudinal Study (BPS) provides information concerning persistence, progress, and attainment from initial time of entry into postsecondary education through leaving and entering the workforce. BPS includes traditional and nontraditional (e.g., older) students and is representative of all beginning students in postsecondary education. BPS follows first-time, beginning students for at least 6 years at 2-year intervals, collecting student data, postsecondary transcripts, and financial aid reports. By starting with a cohort that has already entered postsecondary education, and following it for 6 years, BPS will be able to determine to what extent, if any, students who start postsecondary education later differ in their progress, persistence, and attainment.

Further information on the Beginning Postsecondary Student Longitudinal Survey may be obtained from:

Paula R. Knepper
Data Development and Longitudinal Studies Group
National Center for Education Statistics
555 New Jersey Avenue NW
Washington, DC 20208–5652
Paula_Knepper@ed.gov

Common Core of Data

NCES uses the Common Core of Data (CCD) survey to acquire and maintain statistical data from each of the 50 states, the District of Columbia, and the outlying areas. Information about staff and students is collected annually at the school, LEA (local education agency or school district), and state levels. Information about revenues and expenditures is also collected at the state level.

Data are collected for a particular school year (July 1 through June 30) via survey instruments sent to the state education agencies during the subsequent school year. States have one year in which to modify the data originally submitted.

Since the CCD is a universe survey, the CCD information presented in this edition of the *Digest* is not subject to sampling errors. However, nonsampling errors could come from two sources—nonreturn and inaccurate reporting. Almost all of the states submit the six CCD survey instruments each year, but submissions are sometimes incomplete or too late for publication.

Understandably, when 57 education agencies compile and submit data for approximately 85,000 public schools and 15,000 local school districts, misreporting can occur. Typically, this results from varying interpretation of NCES definitions and differing recordkeeping systems. NCES attempts to minimize these errors by working closely with the Council of Chief State School Officers (CCSSO) and its Committee on Evaluation and Information Systems (CEIS).

The state education agencies report data to NCES from data collected and edited in their regular reporting cycles. NCES encourages the agencies to incorporate into their own survey systems the NCES items they do not already collect so that those items will also be available for the subsequent CCD survey. Over time, this has meant fewer missing data cells in each state's response, reducing the need to impute data.

NCES subjects data from the education agencies to a comprehensive edit. Where data are determined to be inconsistent, missing, or out of range, NCES contacts the education agencies for verification. NCES-prepared state summary forms are returned to the state education agencies for verification. States are also given an opportunity to revise their state-level aggregates from the previous survey cycle.

Questions concerning the Common Core of Data can be directed to:

John Sietsema
Surveys and Cooperative Systems Group
National Center for Education Statistics
555 New Jersey Avenue NW
Washington, DC 20208–5651
John_Sietsema@ed.gov

Federal Support for Education

NCES prepares an annual compilation of federal funds for education. Data for U.S. Department of Education programs come from the *Budget of the U.S. Government*. Budget offices of other federal agencies provide information for all other federal program support except for research funds, which are obligations reported by the National Science Foundation in *Federal Funds for Research and Development*. Some data are estimated, based on reports from the federal agencies contacted and the *Budget of the U.S. Government*.

Except for money spent on research, outlays were used to report program funds to the extent possible. Some tables are obligations as noted in the title of the table. Some federal program funds not commonly recognized as education assistance are also included in the totals reported. For example, portions of federal funds paid to some states and counties as shared revenues resulting from the sale of timber and minerals from public lands have been estimated as funds used for education purposes. Parts of the funds received by states (in 1980) and localities (throughout the period) under the General Revenue Sharing Program are also included, as are portions of federal funds received by the District of Columbia. The share of these funds allocated to education was assumed equal to the share of general funds expended for elementary and secondary education by states and localities in the same year as reported by the U.S. Bureau of the Census in its annual publication, *Governmental Finances*.

All state intergovernmental expenditures for education were assumed earmarked for elementary/secondary education. Contributions of parent governments of dependent school systems to their public schools amounted to approximately 9 percent of local government revenues and local government revenue sharing in each year. Therefore, 9 percent of local government revenue-sharing funds were assumed allocated each fiscal year to elementary and secondary education. Parent government contributions to public school systems were obtained from the U.S. Bureau of the Census, *Finances of Public School Systems*. The amount of state revenue-sharing funds allocated for postsecondary education in 1980 was assumed to be 13 percent, the proportion of direct state expenditures for institutions of higher education reported in *Governmental Finances* for that year.

The share of federal funds for the District of Columbia assigned to education was assumed equal to the share of the city's general fund expenditures for each level of education.

For the job training programs conducted by the Department of Labor, only estimated sums spent on classroom training have been reported as educational program support.

During the 1970s, the Office of Management and Budget (OMB) prepared annual reports on federal education program support. These were published in *Budget of the United States Government [Special Analyses]*. The information presented in this report is not, however, a continuation of the OMB series. A number of differences in the two series should be noted. OMB required all federal agencies to report outlays for education-related programs using a standardized form, thereby assuring agency compliance in reporting. The scope of education programs reported here differs from OMB. Off-budget items such as the annual volume of guaranteed student loans were not included in OMB's reports. Finally, while some mention is made of an annual estimate of federal tax expenditures, OMB did not include them in its annual analysis of federal education support. Estimated federal tax expenditures for education are the difference between current federal tax receipts and what these receipts would be without existing education deductions to income allowed by federal tax provisions.

Recipients' data are estimated based on *Estimating Federal Funds for Education: A New Approach Applied to Fiscal Year 1980*, U.S. Department of Education, "Federal Support for Education, Fiscal Years 1980 to 1984," and *Catalog of Federal Domestic Assistance*. The recipients' data are estimated and tend to undercount institutions of higher education (IHEs), students, and local education agencies (LEAs). This is because some of the federal programs have more than one recipient receiving funds. In these cases, the recipients were put into a "mixed recipients" category, because there was no way to disaggregate the amount each recipient received.

Charlene Hoffman
Data Development and Longitudinal Studies Group
National Center for Education Statistics
555 New Jersey Ave NW
Washington, DC 20208–5652
Charlene_Hoffman@ed.gov

High School and Beyond

High School and Beyond (HS&B) is a national longitudinal survey of 1980 high school sophomores and seniors. The base-year survey was a probability sample of 1,015 high schools with a target number of 36 sophomores and 36 seniors in each of the schools. A total of 58,270 students participated in the base-year survey. Substitutions were made for noncooperating schools—but not for students—in those strata where it was possible. Overall, 1,122 schools were selected in the original sample and 811 of these schools participated in the survey. An additional 204 schools were drawn in a replacement sample. Student refusals and absences resulted in an 82 percent completion rate for the survey.

Several small groups in the population were oversampled to allow for special study of certain types of schools and students. Students completed questionnaires and took a battery of cognitive tests. In addition, a sample of parents of sophomores and seniors (about 3,600 for each cohort) was surveyed.

HS&B first follow-up activities took place in the spring of 1982. The sample design of the first follow-up survey called for the selection of approximately 30,000 persons who were sophomores in 1980. The completion rate for sophomores eligible for on-campus survey administration was about 96 percent. About 89 percent of the students who left school between the base year and first follow-up surveys (dropouts, transfer students, and early graduates) completed the first follow-up sophomore questionnaire.

As part of the first follow-up survey of HS&B, transcripts were requested in fall 1982 for an 18,152 member subsample of the sophomore cohort. Of the 15,941 transcripts actually obtained, 1,969 were excluded because the students had dropped out of school before graduation, 799 were excluded because they were incomplete, and 1,057 were excluded because the student graduated before 1982 or the transcript indicated neither a dropout status nor graduation. Thus, 12,116 transcripts were utilized for the overall curriculum analysis presented in this publication. All courses in each transcript were assigned a six-digit code based on *A Classification of Secondary School Courses* (developed by Evaluation Technologies, Inc. under contract with NCES). Credits earned in each course were expressed in Carnegie units. (The Carnegie unit is a standard of measurement that represents one credit for the completion of a 1-year course. To receive credit for a course, the student must have received a passing grade— "pass," "D," or higher.) Students who transferred from public to private schools or from private to public schools between their sophomore and senior years were eliminated from public/private analyses.

In designing the senior cohort first follow-up survey, one of the goals was to reduce the size of the retained sample, while still keeping sufficient numbers of minorities to allow important policy analyses. A total of 11,227 (94 percent) of the 11,995 persons subsampled completed the questionnaire. Information was obtained about the respondents' school and employment experiences, family status, and attitudes and plans.

The sample for the second follow-up, which took place in spring 1984, consisted of about 12,000 members of the senior cohort and about 15,000 members of the sophomore cohort. The completion rate for the senior cohort was 91 percent, and the completion rate for the sophomore cohort was 92 percent.

HS&B third follow-up data collection activities were performed in spring of 1986. Both the sophomore and senior cohort samples for this round of data collection were the same as those used for the second follow-up survey. The completion rates for the sophomore and senior cohort samples were 91 percent and 88 percent, respectively.

Table A2 contains the maximum number of cases that are available for the tabulations of the specific classification variables used throughout this publication.

The standard error (se) of an individual percentage (p) based on HS&B data can be approximated by the formula

$$se_p = DEFT\,[p(100-p)/n]^{1/2}$$

where n is the sample size and DEFT, the square root of the design effect, is a factor used to adjust for the particular sample design used in HS&B. Table A3 provides the DEFT factors for different HS&B samples and subsamples.

In evaluating a difference between two independent percentages, the standard error of the difference may be conservatively approximated by taking the square root of the sum of the squared standard errors of the two percentages. For example, in the 1986 follow-up of 1980 sophomores, 84.0 percent of the men and 77.2 percent of the women felt that being successful in work was "very important," a difference of 6.8 percentage points. Using the formula and the sample sizes from table A2 and the DEFT factors from table A3, the standard errors of the two percentages being compared are calculated to be:

$$1.43[(84.0)(16.0)/(5,391)]^{1/2} = .714$$
$$1.43[(77.2)(22.8)/(5,857)]^{1/2} = .784$$

The standard error of the difference is therefore

$$(.714^2 + .784^2)^{1/2} = (.510 + .615)^{1/2} = 1.06$$

The sampling error (95 chances in 100) of the difference is approximately double the standard error, or approximately 2.1 percentage points, and the 95 percent confidence interval for the difference is 6.8 ± 2.1, or 4.7 to 8.9 percentage points.

The standard error estimation procedure outlined above does not compensate for survey item nonresponse, which is a source of nonsampling error. (Table A2 reflects the maximum number of responses that could be tabulated by demographic characteristics.) For example, of the 10,925 respondents in the 1984 follow-up survey of 1980 high school graduates, 372, or 3.4 percent, did not respond to the particular question on whether they had ever used a pocket calculator. Item nonresponse varied considerably. A very low nonresponse rate of 0.1 percent was obtained for a question asking whether the respondent had attended a postsecondary institution. A much higher item nonresponse rate of 12.2 percent was obtained for a question asking if the respondent had used a micro or minicomputer in high school. Typical item nonresponse rates ranged from 3 to 4 percent.

The Hispanic analyses presented in this report relied on students' self-identification as members of one of four Hispanic subgroups: Mexican, Mexican-American, Chicano; Cuban; Puerto-Rican, Puertorriqueno, or Boricua; or other Latin American, Latino, Hispanic, or Spanish descent.

An NCES series of technical reports and data file users manuals provides additional information on the survey methodology.

Further information on the High School and Beyond survey may be obtained from:

Aurora M. D'Amico
Data Development and Longitudinal Studies Group
National Center for Education Statistics
555 New Jersey Avenue NW
Washington, DC 20208-5652
Aurora__D'Amico@ed.gov

1990 High School Transcript Study Tabulations

This study involved analysis of transcripts of 1990 high school graduates from 330 schools. The analyses were based on approximately 21,500 1990 graduates selected for the National Assessment of Educational Progress (NAEP) in 1990. The study collected information such as course lists, graduation requirements, and the definition of units of credit and grades, on a school-level basis.

Similar studies were conducted of course taking patterns of 1987 and 1982 graduates. The 1987 data are based on approximately 22,799 transcripts from 433 schools obtained as part of the 1987 High School Transcript Study. The 1982 data are based on approximately 12,000 transcripts collected by the High School and Beyond Project.

Because the 1982 High School and Beyond study used a different method for identifying handicapped students than did the 1987 and 1990 transcript studies, and in order to make the statistical summaries as comparable as possible, all the counts and percentages in this report are restricted to students whose records indicate that they had not participated in a special education program. This restriction lowers the number of 1990 graduates represented in the tables to 20,866.

Further information can be obtained from:

Steve Gorman
Assessment Group
National Center for Education Statistics
555 New Jersey Avenue NW
Washington, DC 20208-5653
Steve__Gorman@ed.gov

Integrated Postsecondary Education Data System

The Integrated Postsecondary Education Data System (IPEDS) surveys approximately 11,000 postsecondary institutions, including universities and colleges, as well as institutions offering technical and vocational education beyond the high school level. This survey, which began in 1986, replaced the Higher Education General Information Survey (HEGIS).

IPEDS consists of eight integrated components that obtain information on who provides postsecondary education (institutions), who participates in it and completes it (students), what programs are offered and what programs are completed, and both the human and financial resources involved in the provision of institutionally based postsecondary education. Specifically, these components include: Institutional Characteristics, including instructional activity; Fall Enrollment, including age and residence; Enrollment in Occupationally Specific Programs; Completions; Finance; Staff; Salaries of Full-Time Instructional Faculty; and Academic Libraries.

The higher education portion of this survey is a census of accredited 2- and 4-year colleges. Prior to 1993, data from the technical and vocational institutions were collected through a sample survey. Beginning in 1993, all data are gathered in a census of all postsecondary institutions. The tabulations on "Institutional Characteristics" developed for this edition of the *Digest* are based on lists of all institutions and are not subject to sampling errors.

Prior to the establishment of IPEDS in 1986, HEGIS acquired and maintained statistical data on the characteristics and operations of institutions of higher education. Implemented in 1966, HEGIS was an annual universe survey of institutions accredited at the college level by an agency recognized by the Secretary of the U.S. Department of Education. These institutions were listed in NCES's *Education Directory, Colleges and Universities.*

The trend tables presented in this report draw on HEGIS surveys which solicited information concerning institutional characteristics, faculty salaries, finances, enrollment, and degrees. Since these surveys were distributed to all higher education institutions, the data presented are not subject to sampling error. However, they are subject to nonsampling error, the sources of which varied with the survey instrument. Information concerning the nonsampling error of the enrollment and degrees surveys draws extensively on the "HEGIS Post-Survey Validation Study" conducted in 1979.

Further information on IPEDS may be obtained from:

Roslyn A. Korb
Surveys and Cooperative Systems Group
National Center for Education Statistics
555 New Jersey Avenue NW
Washington, DC 20208–5652
Roslyn_Korb@ed.gov

Institutional Characteristics

This survey provides the basis for the universe of institutions presented in the *Directory of Postsecondary Institutions.* The universe comprises institutions that met certain accreditation criteria and offered at least a 1-year program of college-level studies leading toward a degree. All of these institutions were certified as eligible by the U.S. Department of Education's Division of Eligibility and Agency Evaluation. The survey collects basic information necessary to classify the institutions including control, level, and kinds of programs; information on tuition, fees, and room and board charges; and unduplicated full-year enrollment counts and instructional activity.

Fall Enrollment

This survey has been part of the HEGIS and IPEDS series since 1966. The enrollment survey response rate is relatively high; the 1995 response rate was 97 percent for higher education institutions, or 89 percent overall. Major sources of nonsampling error for this survey as identified in the 1979 report, were classification problems, the unavailability of needed data, interpretation of definitions, the survey due date, and operational errors. Of these, the classification of students appears to have been the main source of error. Institutions had problems in correctly classifying first-time freshmen and other first-time students for both full-time and part-time categories. These problems occurred most often at 2-year institutions (private and public) and private 4-year institutions. In the 1977–78 HEGIS validation studies, the classification problem led to an estimated overcount of 11,000 full-time students and an undercount of 19,000 part-time students. Although the ratio of error to the grand total was quite small (less than 1 percent), the percentage of errors was as high as 5 percent for detailed student levels and even higher at certain aggregation levels.

Beginning with fall 1986, the survey system was redesigned with the introduction of the Integrated Postsecondary Education Data System (IPEDS) (see above). The IPEDS system comprises all postsecondary institutions, but also maintains comparability with earlier surveys by allowing HEGIS institutions to be tabulated separately. The survey allows (in alternating years) for the collection of age and residence data.

Salaries, Tenure, and Fringe Benefits of Full-Time Instructional Faculty

This institutional survey has been conducted for most years from 1966–67 to 1987–88, and annually since 1989–90. Although the survey form changed a number of times during those years, only comparable data are presented in this report.

Between 1966–67 and 1985–86 this survey differed from other HEGIS surveys in that imputations were not made for nonrespondents. Thus, there is some possibility that the salary averages presented in this report may differ from the results of a complete enumeration of all colleges and universities. Beginning with the surveys for 1987–88, the IPEDS data tabulation procedures included imputations for survey nonrespondents. The response rate for the 1995–96 survey was 95 percent for higher education institutions, or 83 percent overall. Because of the higher response rate for public colleges, it is probable that the public colleges' salary data are more accurate than the data for private colleges. Although data from these surveys are not subject to sampling error, sources of nonsampling error may include computational errors and misclassification in reporting and processing. NCES reviews individual colleges' data for internal and longitudinal consistency and contacts the colleges to check inconsistent data.

Completions

This survey was part of the HEGIS series throughout its existence. However, the degree classification taxonomy was revised in 1970–71, 1982–83, and 1991–92. Collection of degree data has been maintained through the IPEDS system.

Though information from survey years 1970–71 through 1981–82 is directly comparable, care must be taken if information before or after that period is included in any comparison. Degrees-conferred trend tables arranged by the 1991–92 classification are included in the *Digest* to provide consistent data from 1970–71 to 1994–95. Data in this edition on associate and other formal awards below the baccalaureate, by field of study, cannot be made comparable with figures prior to 1982–83. The nonresponse rate did not appear to be a significant source of nonsampling error for this survey. The return rate over the years has been high, with the higher education response rate for the 1994–95 survey at 97 percent. The overall response rate including the noncollegiate institutions is 88 percent. Because of the high return rate for the institutions of higher education, nonsampling error caused by imputation is also minimal.

The major sources of nonsampling error for this survey were differences between the NCES program taxonomy and taxonomies used by the colleges, classification of double majors, operational problems, and survey timing. In the 1979 HEGIS validation study, these sources of nonsampling contributed to an error rate of 0.3 percent overreporting of bachelor's degrees and 1.3 percent overreporting of master's degrees. The differences, however, varied greatly among fields. Over 50 percent of the fields selected for the validation study had no errors identified. Categories of fields that had large differences were business and management, education, engineering, letters, and psychology. It was also shown that differences in proportion to the published figures were less than 1 percent for most of the selected fields that had some errors. Exceptions to these were: master's and Ph.D. programs in labor and industrial relations (20 percent and 8 percent); bachelor's and master's programs in art education (3 percent and 4 percent); bachelor's and Ph.D. programs in business and commerce, and in distributive education (5 percent and 9 percent); master's programs in philosophy (8 percent); and Ph.D. programs in psychology (11 percent).

Financial Statistics

This survey was part of the HEGIS series and has been continued under the IPEDS system. Changes were made in the financial survey instruments in fiscal years (FY) 1976, 1982, and 1987. The FY 76 survey instrument contained numerous revisions to earlier survey forms and made direct comparisons of line items very difficult. Beginning in FY 82, Pell Grant data were collected in the categories of federal restricted grants and contracts revenues and restricted scholarships and fellowships expenditures. The introduction of IPEDS in the FY 87 survey included several important changes to the survey instrument and data processing procedures. While these changes were significant, considerable effort has been made to present only comparable information on trends in this report and to note inconsistencies. Finance tables for this publication have been adjusted by subtracting the largely duplicative Pell Grant amounts from the later data to maintain comparability with pre-FY 82 data.

Possible sources of nonsampling error in the financial statistics include nonresponse, imputation, and misclassification. The response rate has been about 85 to 90 percent for most of the years reported. The response rate for the FY 1995 survey was 94 percent for higher education institutions, or 83 percent overall.

Two general methods of imputation were used in HEGIS. If the prior year's data were available for a nonresponding institution, these data were inflated using the Higher Education Price Index and adjusted according to changes in enrollments. If no previous year's data were available, current data were used from peer institutions selected for location (state or region), control, level, and enrollment size of institution. In most cases estimates for nonreporting institutions in IPEDS were made using data from peer institutions.

Beginning with FY 87, the IPEDS survey system included all postsecondary institutions, but maintained comparability with earlier surveys by allowing 2- and 4-year HEGIS institutions to be tabulated separately. The finance data tabulated for this publication reflect totals for the HEGIS or higher education institutions only. For FY 87 through FY 91, in order to maintain comparability with the historical time series of HEGIS institutions, data were combined from two of the three different survey forms that make up the IPEDS survey system. The vast majority of the data were tabulated from Form 1, which was used to collect information from public and private nonprofit 2- and 4-year colleges. Form 2, a condensed form, was used to gather data for the 2-year proprietary institutions. Because of the differences in the data requested on the two forms, several assumptions were made about the Form 2 reports so that their figures could be included in the institutions of higher education totals.

In IPEDS, the Form 2 institutions were not asked to separate appropriations from grants and contracts, nor state from local sources of funding. For the Form 2 institutions, all the federal revenues were assumed to be federal grants and contracts and all of the state and local revenues were assumed to be restricted state grants and contracts. All other Form 2 sources of revenue, except for tuition and fees and sales and services of educational activities, were included under "other." Similar adjustments were made to the expenditure accounts. The Form 2 institutions reported instruction and scholarship and fellowship expenditures only. All other educational and general expenditures were allocated to academic support.

To reduce reporting error, NCES uses national standards for reporting finance statistics. These standards are contained in *College and University Business Administration: Administrative Services (1974 Edition)*, and the *Financial Accounting and Reporting Manual for Higher Education (1990 Education)*, published by the National Association of College and University Business Officers; *Audits of Colleges and Universities* (as amended August 31, 1974), by the American Institute of Certified Public Accountants; and *HEGIS Financial Reporting Guide (1980)*, by NCES. Wherever possible, definitions and formats in the survey form are consistent with those in these four accounting texts.

Staff

The fall staff data presented in this publication were collected by NCES, through the IPEDS system, which collected data from postsecondary institutions, including all 2- and 4-year higher education institutions. The NCES collects staff data biennially in odd numbered years in institutions of postsecondary education.

The "Fall Staff" questionnaires were mailed out by NCES between October and November 1993; the respondents reported the employment statistics in their institution that cover the payroll period closest to October 1 of the survey year.

The "Fall Staff" survey had an overall response rate of 87 percent. The response rate for higher education institutions was 92 percent.

The Third International Mathematics and Science Study

The Third International Mathematics and Science Study (TIMSS) is the largest, most comprehensive, and most rigorous international comparison of education ever undertaken. During the 1995 school year, the study tested the mathematics and science knowledge of half a million students from 41 nations at five different grade levels. At the same time, the students, their teachers, and the principals of their schools were asked to respond to questionnaires about their backgrounds and their attitudes, experiences, and practices in the teaching and learning of mathematics and science.

TIMSS is a collaborative research project sponsored by the International Association for the Evaluation of Educational Achievement (IEA). The TIMSS International Study Center is housed in the Center for the Study of Testing, Evaluation, and Educational Policy (CSTEEP) at Boston College. The TIMSS International Study Director, Albert E. Beaton, directs the international activities of the study, together with his staff at the International Study Center. To contact the TIMSS International Study Center:

Dr. Albert Beaton
TIMSS International Study Director
CSTEEP, Campion Hall 323
Boston College
Chestnut Hill, MA 02167

National Adult Literacy Survey

The National Adult Literacy Survey was created as a new measure of literacy and funded by the Department of Education and by 12 states. It is the third and largest assessment of adult literacy funded by the federal government. The aim of the survey is to profile the English literacy of adults in the United States based on their performance across a wide array of tasks that reflect the types of materials and demands they encounter in their daily lives.

To gather the information on adults' literacy skills, trained staff interviewed nearly 13,600 individuals aged 16 and older during the first eight months of 1992. These participants had been randomly selected to represent the adult population in the country as a whole. Black and Hispanic households were oversampled to ensure reliable estimates of literacy proficiencies and to permit analyses of the performance of these subpopulations. In addition, some 1,100 inmates from 80 federal and state prisons were interviewed to gather information on the proficiencies of the prison population. In total, over 26,000 adults were surveyed.

Each survey participant was asked to spend approximately an hour responding to a series of diverse literacy tasks as well as questions about his or her demographic characteristics, educational background, reading practices, and other areas related to literacy. Based on their responses to the survey tasks, adults received proficiency scores along three scales which reflect varying degrees of skill in prose, document and quantitative literacy. The results of the survey were published in a report, *Adult Literacy in America* in September 1993.

Further information on the National Adult Literacy Survey may be obtained from:

Andrew Kolstad
Assessment Group
National Center for Education Statistics
555 New Jersey Avenue NW
Washington, DC 20208–5653
Andrew_Kolstad@ed.gov

National Assessment of Educational Progress

The National Assessment of Educational Progress (NAEP) is a series of cross-sectional studies designed and initially implemented in 1969. NAEP has gathered information about selected levels of educational achievement across the country. NAEP has surveyed the educational attainments by age and grade (9-, 13-, and 17-year-olds, and 4th-, 8th-, and 12th-graders), and young adults (ages 25–35) in 10 learning areas. Long-term trends are assessed by age and measure changes in educational achievement, while specific subject areas are assessed periodically by grade level. Different learning areas have been assessed periodically, and all areas have been reassessed in order to measure possible changes in educational achievement.

The assessment data presented in this publication were derived from tests designed and conducted by the Education Commission of the States (1969–1983) and by the Educational Testing Service (1983 to present). Three-stage probability samples have been used. The primary sampling units have been stratified by region and, within region, by state, size of community, and, for the two smaller sizes of community strata, by socioeconomic level. The first stage of sampling entails defining and selecting primary sampling units (PSUs). For each age/grade level (4, 8, and 12) the second stage entails enumerating, stratifying, and randomly selecting schools, both public and private, within each PSU selected at the first stage. The third stage involves randomly selecting students within a school for participation in NAEP. Assessment exercises have been administered either to individuals or to small groups of students by specially trained personnel.

Sample sizes for the reading proficiency portion of the 1995–96 NAEP long-term trends study were 5,019 for the 9-year-olds, 5,493 for the 13-year-olds, and 4,669 for the 17-year-olds. Response rates were 96 percent, 92 percent, and 84 percent, respectively. Response rates for earlier years (1970–71, 1974–75, 1979–80) were generally lower. For example, the lowest response rate for the 9-year-olds was 88 percent in 1974–75, and the lowest response rate overall was 70 percent for the 17-year-olds in 1974–75.

Sample sizes in math and science portions of the long-term trends were: 5,414 9-year-olds, 5,658 13-year-olds, and 3,539 17-year-olds. Response rates were 95, 93, and 84 percent, respectively.

Assessments focusing on particular subject areas are conducted separately from long-term assessments. The 1993–94 U.S. history data in this report are based on a nationally representative sample of 5,499 4th-graders, 8,767 8th-graders, and 7,818 12th-graders. The response rates were: 90 percent for 4th-graders, 90 percent for 8th-graders, and 89 percent for 12th-graders.

The 1991–92 writing assessment was administered to 7,166 4th-graders, 11,112 8th-graders, and 11,532 12th-graders. Student response rates for the 1992–93 writing assessment were 93 percent for the 4th-graders, 89 percent for the 8th-graders, and 81 percent for the 12th-graders. Sample sizes varied depending on the test items and the scoring method used.

In 1995–96, a science assessment was administered to 7,305 4th-graders, 7,774 8th-graders, and 7,537 12th-graders. The response rates were 94 percent for the 4th-graders, 94 percent for the 8th-graders, and 93 percent for the 12th-graders.

The 1993–94 geography assessment was administered to 5,507 4th-graders, 6,878 8th-graders, and 6,234 12th-graders. The response rates for the assessment were 93 percent for the 4th-graders, 93 percent for the 8th-graders, and 90 percent for the 12th-graders.

In 1990, representative state-level data were produced for mathematics at the 8th-grade level. This was the first time NAEP had produced data on a state-by-state level. In 1996, state-level assessments were conducted in 4th- and 8th-grade mathematics and 8th-grade science.

Information from NAEP is subject to both nonsampling and sampling error. Two possible sources of nonsampling error are nonparticipation and instrumentation. Certain populations have been oversampled to assure samples of sufficient size for analysis. Instrumentation nonsampling error could result from failure of the test instruments to measure what is being taught and, in turn, what is being learned by the students.

For further information on NAEP, contact:

Gary W. Phillips
Assessment Group
National Center for Education Statistics
555 New Jersey Avenue NW
Washington, DC 20208–5653
Gary_Phillips@ed.gov

National Education Longitudinal Study of 1988

The National Education Longitudinal Study of 1988 (NELS:88) is the third major longitudinal study sponsored by the National Center for Education Statistics. The two studies that preceded NELS:88, the National Longitudinal Study of the High School Class of 1972 (NLS–72) and High School and Beyond (HS&B) in 1980, surveyed high school seniors (and sophomores in HS&B) through high school, postsecondary education, and work and family formation experiences. Unlike its predecessors, NELS:88 begins with a cohort of 8th-grade students. In 1988, some 25,000 eighth graders, their parents, their teachers, and their school principals were surveyed. Follow-ups were conducted in 1990, 1992, and 1994, when a majority of these students were in 10th and 12th grades, and then 2 years after their scheduled high school graduation. A similar follow-up will be conducted in 2000.

NELS:88 is designed to provide trend data about critical transitions experienced by young people as they develop, attend school, and embark on their careers. It will complement and strengthen state and local efforts by furnishing new information on how school policies, teacher practices, and family involvement affect student educational outcomes (i.e., academic achievement, persistence in school, and participation in postsecondary education). For the base year, NELS:88 includes a multifaceted student questionnaire, four cognitive tests, a parent questionnaire, a teacher questionnaire, and a school questionnaire.

In 1990, when the students were in 10th grade, the students, school dropouts, their teachers, and their school principals were surveyed. The 1988 survey of parents was not a part of the 1990 follow-up. In 1992, when the students were in 12th grade, the second follow-up conducted surveys of students, dropouts, parents, teachers, and school principals. Also, information on the students' transcripts, the schools' course offerings, and enrollments were collected, and there was a school effects survey. Tables A4 and A5 present the respondent counts and design effects of NELS:88 and the 1990 and 1992 follow-ups.

Further information about the NELS:88 survey can be obtained from:

Jeffrey A. Owings
Data Development and Longitudinal Studies Group
National Center for Education Statistics
555 New Jersey Avenue NW
Washington, DC 20208–5651
Jeffrey_Owings@ed.gov

National Household Education Survey

The National Household Education Survey (NHES) is a data collection system that is designed to address a wide range of education-related issues. Surveys were conducted in 1991, 1993, 1995, and 1996.

The NHES targets specific populations for detailed data collection. It is intended to provide more detailed data on the topics and populations of interest than are collected through supplements to other household surveys.

The topics addressed by the NHES:91 were early childhood education and adult education. About 60,000 households were screened for the NHES:91. In the Early Childhood Education component, about 14,000 parents/guardians of 3- to 8-year olds completed interviews about their children's early educational experiences. Included in this component were participation in nonparental care/education, care/education arrangements and school, and family, household, and child characteristics. In the NHES:91 Adult Education component, about 9,800 persons 16 years of age and older, identified as having participated in an adult education activity in the previous 12 months, were questioned about their activities. Data were collected on programs and up to four courses, including the subject matter duration, sponsorship, purpose, and cost. Information on the household and the adult's background and current employment also was collected. In the NHES:95 survey, of the 23,969 adults sampled for the adult education component, 80 percent (19,722) completed the interview.

In the NHES:93, nearly 64,000 households were screened. Approximately 11,000 parents of 3- to 7-year olds completed interviews for the School Readiness component. Topics included were the developmental characteristics of preschoolers, school adjustment and teacher feedback to parents for kindergartners and primary students, center-based program participation, early school experiences, home activities with family members, and health status. In the School Safety and Discipline component, about 12,700 parents of children in grades 3 through 12, and about 6,500 youth in grades 6 through 12, were interviewed about their school experiences. Topics included the school learning environment, discipline policy, safety at school, victimization, the availability and use of alcohol/drugs, and alcohol/drug education. Peer norms for behavior in school and substance use were also included in this topical component. Extensive family and household background information was collected, as well as characteristics of the school attended by the child.

In the NHES:95 survey, the Early Childhood Program participation component and the Adult Education component were similar to those in 1991. In the Early Childhood component, about 14,000 parents of children from birth to third grade were interviewed. For the Adult Education component, about 19,500 civilian adults were interviewed.

In the spring of 1996, Parent and Family Involvement in Education and Civic Involvement were covered. For the Parent and Family Involvement component, nearly 21,000 parents of children grades 3 to 12 were interviewed. For the Civic Involvement component, about 8,000 youth grades 6 to 12, about 9,000 parents, and about 2,000 adults were interviewed. The 1996 survey also addressed public library use. Adults in almost 55,000 households were interviewed to support state-level estimates of household public library use.

For more information contact:

Kathryn Chandler
Surveys and Cooperative Systems Group
National Center for Education Statistics
555 New Jersey Avenue NW
Washington, DC 20208–5651
Kathryn__Chandler@ed.gov

National Longitudinal Study

The National Longitudinal Study (NLS) of the high school class of 1972 began with the collection of base-year survey data from a sample of about 19,000 high school seniors in spring of 1972. Five more follow-up surveys of these students were conducted in 1973, 1974, 1976, 1979, and 1986. The NLS was designed to provide the education community with information on the transitions of young adults from high school through postsecondary education and the workplace.

The sample design for the NLS is a stratified, two-stage probability sample of students from all schools, public and private, in the 50 states and the District of Columbia with a 12th-grade enrollment during the 1971–72 school year. During the first stage of sampling, about 1,070 schools were selected for participation in the base-year survey. As many as 18 students were selected at random from each of the sample schools. Both the size of the school and student samples were increased during the first follow-up survey. Beginning with the first follow-up and continuing through the fourth follow-up, about 1,300 schools participated in the survey and slightly under 23,500 students were sampled. The response rates for each of the different rounds of data collection have been 80 percent or higher.

Sample retention rates across the survey years have been quite high. For example, of the individuals responding to the base-year questionnaire, the percentages who responded to the first, second, third, and fourth follow-up questionnaires were about 94, 93, 89, and 83 percent, respectively.

Further information may be obtained from:

Aurora M. D'Amico
Data Development and Longitudinal Studies Group
National Center for Education Statistics
555 New Jersey Avenue NW
Washington, DC 20208–5652
Aurora __D'Amico@ed.gov

National Postsecondary Student Aid Study

The National Postsecondary Student Aid Study (NPSAS) is a comprehensive nationwide study of how students and their families pay for postsecondary education. It covers national representative samples of undergraduates, graduates, and first-professional students; students attending less than 2-year institutions, 2- to 3-year schools, 4-year colleges, and major universities. Participants include students who do not receive aid and their parents as well as students who do receive financial aid and their parents. Study results are used to help determine future federal policy regarding student financial aid. The study is conducted every three years.

The first NPSAS was conducted during the 1986–87 school year. Data were gathered from about 1,074 colleges, universities, and other postsecondary institutions; 60,000 students; and 14,000 parents. These data provided information on the cost of postsecondary education, the distribution of financial aid, and the characteristics of both aided and nonaided students and their families.

As a part of the 1992–93 NPSAS, information on 77,000 undergraduates and graduate students enrolled during the school year was collected at 1,000 postsecondary institutions. The sample included students enrolled at any time between July 1, 1992 and June 30, 1993. About 66,000 students and a subsample of their parents were interviewed by telephone.

The 1996 NPSAS contains information on more than 48,000 undergraduate and graduate students from 973 postsecondary institutions. Students were enrolled at any time during the 1995–96 school year.

Further information may be obtained from:

Andrew G. Malizio
Data Development and Longitudinal Studies Group
National Center for Education Statistics
555 New Jersey Avenue NW
Washington, DC 20208–5652
Andrew__Malizio@ed.gov

National Study of Postsecondary Faculty

This study is in response to a continuing need for data on faculty and instructors—persons who directly affect the quality of education in postsecondary institutions. Faculty are the pivotal resource around which the process and outcomes of postsecondary education revolve. They often determine curriculum content, student performance standards, and the quality of students' preparation for careers. Faculty members perform research and development work upon which this nation's technological and economic advancement depend. Through their public service activities, they make valuable contributions to society. For these reasons, it is essential to understand who they are; what they do; and whether, how, and why they are changing. The National Study of Postsecondary Faculty (NSOPF) was designed to provide data about faculty to postsecondary researchers, planners, and policymakers. NSOPF is the most comprehensive study of faculty in postsecondary educational institutions ever undertaken.

The first cycle of NSOPF was conducted by the National Center for Education Statistics (NCES) with support from the National Endowment for the Humanities (NEH) in 1987–88 (NSOPF:88) with a sample of 480 colleges and universities, over 3,000 department chairpersons, and over 11,000 instructional faculty. The second cycle of NSOPF was conducted by NCES with support from NEH and the National Science Foundation (NSF) in 1992–93 (NSOPF:93). NSOPF:93 was limited to surveys of institutions and faculty, but with a substantially expanded sample of 974 colleges and universities, and 31,354 faculty and instructional staff.

Linda J. Zimbler
Surveys and Cooperative Systems Group
National Center for Education Statistics
555 New Jersey Avenue NW
Washington, DC 20208–5652
Linda __Zimbler@ed.gov

Projections of Education Statistics

Since 1964, NCES has published projections of key statistics for elementary and secondary schools and institutions of higher education. These projections include statistics such as enrollments, instructional staff, graduates, earned degrees, and expenditures. The *Projections* reports include several alternative projection series and a methodology section describing the techniques and assumptions used to prepare them. Data in this edition of the *Digest* reflect the middle alternative projection series.

Differences between the reported and projected values are, of course, almost inevitable. An evaluation of past projections revealed that, at the elementary and secondary level, projections of enrollments have been quite accurate: mean absolute percentage differences for enrollment were less than 1 percent for projections from 1 to 5 years in the future, while those for teachers were less than 4 percent. At the higher education level, projections of enrollment have been fairly accurate: mean absolute percentage differences were 5 percent or less for projections from 1 to 5 years into the future.

For further information about projection methodology and accuracy, contact:

Debra E. Gerald
Data Development and Longitudinal Studies Group
National Center for Education Statistics
555 New Jersey Avenue NW
Washington, DC 20208–5654
Debra__Gerald@ed.gov

Library Statistics Program

Nationwide, public library statistics are collected using the Public Libraries Survey and disseminated annually through the Federal-State Cooperative System for public library data (FSCS). Descriptive statistics are produced for nearly 9,000 public libraries. The Public Libraries Survey includes information about staffing; operating income and expenditures; type of governance; type of administrative structure; size of collection; and service measures such as reference transactions, public service hours, interlibrary loans, circulation, and library visits. In FSCS, respondents supply the information electronically, and data are edited and tabulated in machine-readable form.

The respondents are 8,921 public libraries identified in the 50 states and the District of Columbia by state library agencies. At the state level, FSCS is administered by State Data Coordinators, appointed by the Chief Officer of each State Library Agency. The State Data Coordinator collects the requested data from local public libraries and submits these data to NCES. An annual training conference sponsored by NCES is provided for the State Data Coordinators. A steering committee representing State Data Coordinators and other public library constituents is active in the development of FSCS data elements and software. Technical assistance to states is provided by phone and in person by the FSCS steering committee and by NCES staff and contractors. All 50 states and the District of Columbia have submitted data which are available for individual public libraries and are also aggregated to state and national levels.

Since 1990, data collections have been collected electronically. The most recent software is called DECPLUS. It includes identifying information on all known public libraries and their outlets, some state libraries, and some library systems and cooperatives. Beginning in 1994, this resource was available for drawing samples for special surveys on such topics as literacy, access for the disabled, and library construction.

Under the Academic Libraries Survey (ALS), NCES surveyed academic libraries on a 3-year cycle between 1966 and 1988. Since 1988, ALS has been a component of the Integrated Postsecondary Education Data System and is on a 2-year cycle. ALS provides data on about 3,500 academic libraries. In aggregate, these data provide an overview of the status of academic libraries nationally and statewide. The survey collects data on the libraries in the entire universe of accredited higher education institutions and on the libraries in nonaccredited institutions with a program of 4 years or more. ALS produces descriptive statistics on academic libraries in postsecondary institutions in the 50 states, the District of Columbia and the outlying areas.

The School Library Statistics Survey collected data on school libraries/media centers in 1990–91. This survey asked questions on libraries in public and private schools as part of the Schools and Staffing Survey (SASS). These questionnaires were revised and a sample survey of about 7,600 schools was conducted during school year 1993–94. The library components of the 1990–91 SASS include: number of students served and number of professional staff and aides; at the district level, number of full-time equivalent librarians/media specialists, vacant positions, positions abolished, and approved positions; and amount of librarian input in establishing curriculum. The 1993–94 survey was much more extensive and added questions concerning media centers and collections of libraries.

Additional information on these academic and school library studies is available from:

Jeff Williams
Surveys and Cooperative Systems Group
National Center for Education Statistics
555 New Jersey Avenue NW
Washington, DC 20208–5652
Jeff_Williams@ed.gov

Survey of Recent College Graduates

Since 1976, NCES has conducted six surveys of baccalaureate and master's degree recipients 1 year after graduation. The Recent College Graduates surveys have concentrated on those graduates entering the teaching profession. The surveys link major field of study with outcomes such as whether the respondent entered the labor force or was seeking additional education. Data on labor force includes employment status (unemployed, part-time or full-time employed), occupation, salary, career potential, relation to major field of study, and need for a college degree. To obtain accurate results on teachers, graduates with a major in education are oversampled. The latest 2 surveys continued to oversample education majors, but increased the sampling of graduates with majors in other fields.

The survey involves a two-stage sampling procedure. First, the universe of institutions awarding bachelor's and master's degrees is stratified by number or percentage of degrees awarded to education graduates and by control of institution (public or private). A sample of institutions within each strata is then selected. Second, for each of the selected institutions, a list of their graduates by major field of study is obtained and a sample of graduates is drawn by major field of study. Graduates in certain major fields of study (e.g., education, mathematics, physical sciences) are sampled at higher rates than graduates in other fields. Roughly one year after graduation the sample of graduates is located, contacted by mail or telephone, and asked to respond to the questionnaire.

The locating process is more detailed than in most surveys. Nonresponse rates are directly related to the time, effort, and resources used in locating graduates rather than to graduates' refusals to participate. Despite the difficulties in locating graduates, response rates for recent studies are comparable to studies without locating problems. The data presented in this report provide valuable information not available elsewhere about college outcomes.

The 1976 survey of 1974–75 college graduates was the first and smallest of the series. The sample consisted of 211 schools, of which 200 (96 percent) responded. Of the 5,854 graduates in the sample, 4,350 responded, for a response rate of 79 percent.

The 1981 survey was somewhat larger, with a coverage of 297 institutions and 15,852 graduates. Responses were obtained from 283 institutions, for an institutional response rate of 95 percent, and from 9,312 graduates (716 others were determined to be out of scope), for a response rate of 74 percent.

The 1985 survey sampled 404 colleges and 18,738 graduates of whom 17,853 were found to be in scope. Responses were obtained from 13,200 students, for a response rate of 78 percent. The response rate for the colleges was 98 percent. The 1987 survey form was sent to 21,957 graduates. Responses were received from 16,878, for a response rate of 79.7 percent.

The 1991 RCG study involved a sample of 18,135 graduates of 400 bachelor's and master's degree-granting institutions. The 18,135 graduates consisted of 16,172 bachelor's degrees recipients and 1,963 master's degree recipients between July 1, 1989 and June 30, 1990. Random samples of graduates were selected from lists stratified by field of study. Graduates in education, mathematics, and the physical sciences were sampled at a higher rate, as were minority graduates to provide a sufficient number of these graduates for analysis purposes. The graduates included in the sample were selected in proportion to the institution's number of graduates. The institutional response rate was 95 percent and the graduate response rate was 83 percent.

Table A10 contains sample sizes for number of graduates, by field, for the 1976, 1981, 1985, 1987, and 1991 surveys.

Further information on this survey may be obtained from:

Peter Stowe
Surveys and Cooperative Systems Group
National Center for Education Statistics
555 New Jersey Avenue NW
Washington, DC 20208–5652
Peter__Stowe@ed.gov

Baccalaureate and Beyond Longitudinal Study

The Baccalaureate and Beyond Longitudinal Study (B&B) is based on the National Postsecondary Student Aid Study (NPSAS) and provides information concerning education and work experience after completing the bachelor's degree. B&B provides cross-sectional information 1 year after bachelor's degree completion (comparable to the Recent College Graduate Study), while at the same time providing longitudinal data concerning entry into and progress through graduate level education and the work force. It also provides information on entry into, persistence and progress through, and completion of graduate level education—information not available through follow-ups involving high school cohorts or even college entry cohorts, both of which are restricted in the number who actually complete a bachelor's degree and continue their education.

B&B will follow NPSAS baccalaureate degree completers for a 12-year period after completion, beginning with NPSAS:93. About 11,000 students who completed their degrees in the 1992–93 academic year were included in the first B&B (B&B:93/94). In addition to the student data, B&B collected postsecondary transcripts covering the undergraduate period, providing complete information on progress and persistence at both the undergraduate and graduate levels. New B&B cohorts will alternate with BPS in using NPSAS as their base.

For additional information about B&B contact:

Paula R. Knepper
Data Development and Longitudinal Studies Group
National Center for Education Statistics
555 New Jersey Avenue NW
Washington, DC 20208–5652
Paula__Knepper@ed.gov

Public School Principal Survey on Safe, Disciplined, and Drug-Free Schools

This sample survey used the NCES Fast Response Survey System (FRSS), which is designed to gather timely information for policy makers. The survey was conducted in 1991 by Westat, Inc. A national sample of 830 public school principals, represented by a response rate of 94 percent, answered questions regarding the extent of discipline problems within their schools. They were also questioned about the nature and effectiveness of their schools' current policies and drug education programs.

This survey categorized principals by instructional level (elementary, secondary), type of school location (city, urban fringe, town, rural), enrollment size (less than 300, 300 to 999, 1,000 or more), region (Northeast, Central, Southeast, and West), and percentage of students receiving free or reduced-price lunches (10 percent or less, 11 to 40 percent, 41 percent or more).

For more information about this survey contact:

Bernie Greene
Data Development and Longitudinal Studies Group
National Center for Education Statistics
555 New Jersey Avenue NW
Washington, DC 20208–5651
Bernard__Greene@ed.gov

Public School Kindergarten Teachers' Views on Children's Readiness for School

This sample survey of 1,448 public school kindergarten teachers was conducted as part of a national early childhood assessment system for National Education Goal One: "By the year 2000, all American children will start school ready to learn." The survey obtained data on kindergarten teachers' views of children's readiness and on the teacher's classroom practices.

For more information about this survey contact:

Bernie Greene
Data Development and Longitudinal Studies Group
National Center for Education Statistics
555 New Jersey Avenue NW
Washington, DC 20208–5651
Bernard__Greene@ed.gov

Advanced Telecommunications in U.S. Public Elementary and Secondary Schools, 1996

Current information regarding the availability and use of telecommunications, and in particular, access to the Internet, was requested by this sample survey. The data were gathered from a nationally representative sample of public elementary and secondary schools in fall 1996. The survey was commissioned in response to the National Information Infrastructure (NII) set forth by the President to encourage an acceleration of the goal to connect all of the nation's school classrooms, as well as libraries, hospitals, and law enforcement agencies, to the "Information Superhighway."

For more information about this survey contact:

Bernie Greene
Data Development and Longitudinal Studies Group
National Center for Education Statistics
555 New Jersey Avenue NW
Washington, DC 20208–5651
Bernard_Greene@ed.gov

Schools and Staffing Survey

The Schools and Staffing Survey (SASS) is a set of linked questionnaires that covers public school districts, public and private schools, principals, and teachers, as its core components. SASS was first conducted for the National Center for Education Statistics by the Bureau of the Census during the 1987–88 school year. SASS subsequently was conducted in 1990–91 and in 1993–94. The next SASS is scheduled for school year 1999–2000. SASS is a mailed questionnaire with telephone follow-up that collects data on the nation's public and private elementary and secondary teaching force, characteristics of schools and school principals, demand for teachers, and school/school district policies. The 1990–91 and 1993–94 SASS also collected data on Bureau of Indian Affairs (BIA) schools. The SASS data are collected through a sample survey of schools, the school districts associated with sampled schools, school principals, and teachers. The 1993–94 SASS expanded as well to cover school libraries and librarians, and field tested an administrative student records questionnaire.

The 1993–94 SASS estimates are based upon a sample consisting of approximately 9,900 public schools, 3,300 private schools, and 5,500 public school districts associated with the public schools in the sample. From these schools, about 57,000 public school teachers and 11,500 private school teachers were selected for the 1993–94 SASS teacher survey.

The public school sample for the 1993–94 SASS was based upon the 1991–92 school year Common Core of Data (CCD), the compilation of all the nation's public school districts and public schools. CCD is collected annually from state education agencies. The frame includes regular public schools, Department of Defense-operated military base schools in the United States, and nonregular schools such as special education, vocational, and alternative schools. SASS is designed to provide national estimates for public and private school characteristics and state estimates for school districts, public schools, principals, and teachers. The teacher survey is designed as well to allow comparisons between new and experienced teachers, and between bilingual/ESL teachers and other teachers.

The private school sample for the 1993–94 SASS was selected from the 1991–92 Private School Universe Survey (PSS), supplemented with list updates from states and some associations available in time for sample selection. PSS collects basic data on all of the nation's private schools from two sources: the list frame and the area search frame. The list frame was compiled from a set of private school associations that provide NCES with their membership lists and states that gather lists of private schools. The area search frame consisted of schools not included on the list frame that were compiled from local sources in a sample of counties around the United States. Private school estimates are available at the national level and by type of private school.

The Teacher Demand and Shortage (school district) and School Principal Questionnaires were mailed out first in October 1993, along with School Library/Media Center and Library Media Specialist/Librarian Questionnaires. The weighted response rate for the Teacher Demand and Shortage Questionnaire was 93.9 percent. Weighted response rates for the Public School Principal Questionnaire and the Private School Questionnaire were 96.6 percent and 87.6 percent, respectively.

In December 1993, public, private, and BIA school questionnaires were mailed out. The public, private, and BIA teacher questionnaires were sent out in several batches, between mid-December 1993 and early February 1994. Weighted response rates for the Public School Questionnaire and the Private School Questionnaire were 92.3 percent and 83.2 percent, respectively. Five percent of public schools and 9 percent of private schools did not provide a list of teachers in their schools and were thus ineligible for sampling. Weighted response rates were 88.2 percent for public school teachers and 80.2 percent for private school teachers.

Item response rates were varied, but generally high, ranging from 67 to 100 percent for the TDS, 65 to 100 percent for public school principal questions, 55 to 100 percent for private school principal items, 83 to 100 percent for public school items, 61 to 100 percent for private school survey items, 71 to 100 percent for public school teacher items, and 69 to 100 percent for private school teacher items.

Public-use and restricted-use microdata files are available on CD-ROM or 9-track tape. Summary data from the 1993–94 SASS can be found in *Schools and Staffing in the United States: Selected Data for Public and Private Schools, 1993–94* (NCES 95–191). More detailed results from the 1993–94 SASS are published in *Schools and Staffing in the United States: A Statistical Profile, 1993–94* (NCES 96–124). Data by state are available in *SASS by State—1993–94 Schools and Staffing Survey Selected State Results* (NCES 96–312). Further information about the sample may be obtained from *1993–94 Schools and Staffing Survey: Sample Design and Estimation* (NCES 96–086). Data from previous SASS collections are published in the 1987–88 and 1990–91 *Profile* (NCES 92–127 and 93–146, respectively), as well as the 1987–88 and 1990–91 versions of the sample design report (NCES 91–127 and 93–449, respectively).

For more information about this survey or to order reports, contact:

Kerry Gruber
Surveys and Cooperative Systems Group
National Center for Education Statistics
555 New Jersey Avenue NW
Washington, DC 20208–5651
Kerry_Gruber@ed.gov

Office for Civil Rights

Civil Rights Survey of Elementary and Secondary Schools

The Office for Civil Rights (OCR), U.S. Department of Education, conducts biennial surveys of public school districts and of schools within those districts. Data are obtained on the characteristics of pupils enrolled in public schools throughout the Nation. Such information is required under Title VI of the Civil Rights Act of 1964, Title IX of the Education Amendments of 1972, and Section 504 of the Rehabilitation Act of 1973 to enable OCR to carry out its compliance responsibilities. The 1990 survey included the 100 largest public school districts, those of special interest (i.e., court order, compliance review), and a stratified random sample of approximately 3,500 districts representing approximately 40,000 schools. School, district, and national data are currently available.

Further information is available from:

Peter McCabe
Office for Civil Rights
U.S. Department of Education
330 C Street SW
Washington, DC 20202

Office of Special Education and Rehabilitative Services

Annual Report to Congress on the Implementation of the Education of the Handicapped Act

The Individuals with Disabilities Education Act (IDEA), formerly the Education of the Handicapped Act (EHA), requires the Secretary of Education to transmit to Congress annually a report describing the progress in serving the nation's handicapped children. The annual report contains information on children served by the public schools under the provisions of Part B of the IDEA and for children served in state-operated programs (SOP) for the handicapped under Chapter I of the Elementary and Secondary Education Act (ESEA). Statistics on children receiving special education and related services in various settings and school personnel providing such services are reported in an annual submission of data to the Office of Special Education and Rehabilitative Services (OSERS), by the 50 states, the District of Columbia, and the outlying areas. The child count information is based on the number of handicapped children receiving special education and related services on December 1st of each year.

Since each participant in programs for the handicapped is reported to OSERS, the data are not subject to sampling error. However, nonsampling error can occur from a variety of sources. Some states follow a noncategorical approach to the delivery of special education services, but produce counts by handicapping condition because EHA–B requires it. In those states that do categorize their handicapped students, definitions and labeling practices vary.

Further information on the Annual Report to Congress may be obtained from:

Office of Special Education Programs
Office of Special Education and Rehabilitative Services
330 C Street SW
Washington, DC 20202

National Longitudinal Transition Study of Special Education Students

As part of the 1983 amendments to the Education of the Handicapped Act (EHA), Congress requested that the U.S. Department of Education conduct a national longitudinal study of the transition of secondary special education students to determine how they fare in terms of education, employment, and independent living. A 5-year study was mandated, which was to include youth from ages 13 to 21 who were in special education at the time they were selected and who represented all 11 federal disability categories. Data were drawn from extensive telephone interviews with parents, from school records, and from a survey of educators in secondary schools attended by youth in the study.

The study was conducted by SRI International and began in April, 1987. The National Transition Study involves a nationally representative sample of more than 8,000 secondary-age youth with disabilities. A sample of 450 school districts was randomly selected from the universe of approximately 14,000 school districts serving secondary special education students. An additional replacement sample of 176 additional districts was selected due to a low rate of agreement to participate from the initial group of districts. Participation in the study was invited from the approximately 80 special schools serving secondary-age deaf, blind, and deaf-blind schools. A total of approximately 300 school districts and 25 special schools agreed to have youth selected for the study.

For further information about this study, contact:

Office of Special Education and Rehabilitative Services
Office of Special Education Programs
330 C Street SW
Washington, DC 20202

Other Governmental Agencies

Bureau of the Census

Current Population Survey

Current estimates of school enrollment, as well as social and economic characteristics of students, are based on data collected in the Census Bureau's monthly household survey of about 60,000 households. The monthly Current Population Survey (CPS) sample consists of 729 areas comprising 1,973 counties, independent cities, and minor civil divisions throughout the 50 states and the District of Columbia. The sample was initially selected from the 1980 census files and is periodically updated to reflect new housing construction.

The monthly CPS deals primarily with labor force data for the civilian noninstitutional population (i.e., excluding military personnel and their families living on post and inmates of institutions). In addition, in October of each year, supplemental questions are asked about highest grade completed, level and grade of current enrollment, attendance status, number and type of courses, degree or certificate objective, and type of organization offering instruction for each member of the household. In March of each year, supplemental questions on income are asked. The responses to these questions are combined with answers to two questions on educational attainment: highest grade of school ever attended, and whether that grade was completed.

The estimation procedure employed for the monthly CPS data involves inflating weighted sample results to independent estimates of characteristics of the civilian noninstitutional population in the United States by age, sex, and race. These independent estimates are based on statistics from decennial censuses; statistics on births, deaths, immigration, and emigration; and statistics on the population in the armed services. Generalized standard error tables are provided in the *Current Population Reports*. The data are subject to both nonsampling and sampling errors.

Further information is available in the *Current Population Reports,* Series P–20, or by contacting:

Education Branch
Population Division
Bureau of the Census
U.S. Department of Commerce
Washington, DC 20233

School Enrollment

Each October, the Current Population Survey (CPS) includes supplemental questions on the enrollment status of the population 3 years old and over. The main sources of nonsampling variability in the responses to the supplement are those inherent in the survey instrument. The question of current enrollment may not be answered accurately for various reasons. Some respondents may not know current grade information for every student in the household, a problem especially prevalent for households with members in college or in nursery school. Confusion over college credits or hours taken by a student may make it difficult to determine the year in which the student is enrolled. Problems may occur with the definition of nursery school (a group or class organized to provide educational experiences for children), where respondents' interpretations of "educational experiences" vary.

Examples of sampling variability in the estimates of school enrollment rates are given in Table A7. Questions concerning the CPS "School Enrollment" survey may be directed to:

Education Branch
Bureau of the Census
U.S. Department of Commerce
Washington, DC 20233

Educational Attainment

Data on years of school completed are derived from questions on the Current Population Survey (CPS) instrument. Formal reports documenting educational attainment are produced by the Bureau of the Census using March CPS results. The latest report is *Educational Attainment in the United States,*

March 1994 and 1993, Series P–20, No. 476, which is available from the Government Printing Office.

In addition to the general constraints of the CPS, some data indicate that the respondents have a tendency to overestimate the educational level of members of their household. Some inaccuracy is due to a lack of the respondent's knowledge of the exact educational attainment of each household member and the hesitancy to acknowledge anything less than a high school education. Another cause of nonsampling variability is the change in the numbers in the armed services over the years. In 1970, 25 percent of all males 20 and 21 years old were in the armed services. By 1974, this had decreased to less than 10 percent. The exclusion of members of the armed services appears to increase the proportion of the CPS population with some college and decrease the proportion of those who finished high school but went no further. After 1974, there was more stability in the proportion of young men in the military.

Beginning with the data for March 1980, tabulations have been controlled to the 1980 census. Examples of the sampling variability in the estimates of educational attainment are given in Table A8. The figures shown in the table hold for total or white population estimates only. The variability in estimates for subgroups (region, household relationships, etc.) can be estimated using the tables presented in *Current Population Reports.*

Questions concerning "Educational Attainment in the United States" may be directed to:

Education Branch
Population Division
Bureau of the Census
U.S. Department of Commerce
Washington, DC 20233

Government Finances

The Census Bureau conducts an annual survey of *Government Finances* as authorized by law under Title 13, United States Code, Section 182. This survey covers the entire range of government finance activities: revenue, expenditure, debt, and assets. Revenues and expenditures comprise actual receipts and payments of a government and its agencies, including government-operated enterprises, utilities, and public trust funds. The expenditure reporting categories comprise all amounts of money paid out by a government and its agencies with the exception of amounts for debt retirement and for loan, investment, agency, and private trust transactions.

Most of the federal government statistics for 1994 are based on figures that appear in *The Budget of the United States Government for the Fiscal Year 1995.* Since the classification used by the Census Bureau for reporting state and local government finance statistics differs in a number of important respects from the classification used in the United States Budget, it was necessary to adjust the federal data. For this report, federal budget expenditures include interest accrued, but not paid, during the fiscal year; Census data on interest are on a disbursement basis.

The state government finances for 1994 are based primarily on the annual Census Bureau survey of state finances for fiscal year 1994. Census staff compiled figures from official records and reports of the various states for most of the state financial data.

The sample of local governments is drawn from the 1987 Census of Governments and consists of certain local governments taken with certainty plus a sample below the certainty level.

The statistics in this Census report, *Governmental Finances,* that are based wholly or partly on data from the sample are subject to sampling error. State government finance data are not subject to sampling error. Estimates of major United States totals for local governments are subject to a computed sampling variability of less than one-half of I percent. The estimates are also subject to the inaccuracies in classification, response, and processing which would occur if a complete census had been conducted under the same conditions as the sample.

Further information can be obtained from:

Governments Division
Bureau of the Census
U.S. Department of Commerce
Washington, DC 20233

1990 Census of Population—Education in the United States

This report is based on a part of the decennial census which consists of questions asked of a 1-in-6 sample of persons and housing units in the United States. This sample was asked more detailed questions about income, occupation and housing costs in addition to general demographic information.

School Enrollment

Persons classified as enrolled in school reported attending a "regular" public or private school or college at any time between February 1, 1990 and the time listed. Questions asked were whether the institution attended was public or private, and level of school in which the student was enrolled.

Educational Attainment

Data for educational attainment were tabulated for persons 15 years and over, and classified according to the highest grade completed or the highest degree received. Instructions were also given to include the level of the previous grade attended or the highest degree received for persons currently enrolled in school.

Poverty status

To determine poverty status, answers to income questions were used and compared to the appropriate poverty threshold. All persons except institutionalized persons, persons in military group quarters and in college dormitories, and unrelated persons under 15 years old were considered. If total income of each family or unrelated individual in the sample was less than the corresponding cutoff, that family or individual was classified as "below the poverty level."

Further information can be obtained from:

Population Division
Bureau of the Census
U.S. Department of Commerce
Washington, DC 20233

National Institute on Drug Abuse

The National Institute on Drug Abuse of the U.S. Department of Health and Human Services is the primary supporter of the long-term study entitled "Monitoring the Future: A Continuing Study of the Lifestyles and Values of Youth," conducted at the University of Michigan, Institute for Social Research. One component of the study deals with student drug abuse. Results of a national sample survey have been published annually since 1975. Approximately 125 to 135 schools have participated each year. With the exception of 1975 when about 9,400 students participated in the survey, the annual senior samples are comprised of roughly 17,000 students. They complete self-administered questionnaires given to them in their classrooms by University of Michigan personnel. Beginning in 1991, similar surveys of nationally representative samples of 8th and 10th grade samples have been conducted annually. The 10th grade samples involve about 15,000 students in 125 schools each year, while the 8th grade samples have approximately 18,000 students in 160 schools. Over the years, the response rate has varied from 77 to 84 percent. Table A9 provides examples of the survey's sampling error.

Understandably, there will be some reluctance to admit illegal activities. Also, students who were out of school on the day of the survey were nonrespondents. The survey did not include high school dropouts. The inclusion of these two groups would tend to increase the proportion of individuals who had used drugs. A 1983 study found that the inclusion of the absentees could increase some of the drug usage estimates by as much as 2.7 percent. (Details on that study and its methodology were published in *Drug Use Among American High School Students, College Students, and Other Young Adults,* by Lloyd D. Johnston, Patrick M. O'Malley, and Jerald G. Bachman, available from the National Clearinghouse on Drug Abuse Information, 5600 Fishers Lane, Rockville, MD 20857.)

Further information on this survey may be obtained from:

National Institute of Drug Abuse
Division of Epidemiology and Statistical Analysis
5600 Fishers Lane
Rockville, MD 20857

National Science Foundation

Survey of Earned Doctorates Awarded in the United States

The Survey of Earned Doctorates Awarded in the United States has collected basic statistics from the universe of doctoral recipients in the United States each year since 1958. It has been supported by five federal agencies: the National Science Foundation, in conjunction with the U.S. Department of Education; the National Endowment for the Humanities; the U.S. Department of Agriculture; and the National Institute of Health.

A survey form is distributed, with the assistance of graduate deans, to each person completing the requirements for a doctorate. Of the approximately 40,000 persons eligible for the survey, approximately 95 percent respond. The questionnaire obtains information on sex, race/ethnicity, marital status, citizenship, handicaps, dependents, specialty field of doctorate, educational institutions attended, time spent in completion of doctorate, financial support, educational debt, postgraduation plans, and educational attainment of parents. The data were collected, edited, and published by the National Academy of Sciences.

For further information contact:

Science and Engineering Education and Human
  Resources Program
Division of Science Resources Studies
National Science Foundation
4201 Wilson Boulevard
Arlington, Virginia 22230

Federal Obligations to Universities, Colleges and Nonprofit Institutions

Each year, the National Science Foundation collects data on obligations to colleges and universities from federal agencies. Obligations differ from expenditures in that funds obligated during one fiscal year may be spent by the recipient in later years. Obligation amounts include direct federal support, so that amounts subcontracted to other institutions are included. Those funds received through subcontracts from prime contractors are excluded. Also excluded from the data are certain types of financial assistance, such as the Department of Education's Guaranteed Student Loan Program and obligations to the U.S. service academies. For purposes of tabulations in this publication, university-administered federally funded research and development centers (FFRDCs) have been included in appropriate state totals.

The universe of academic institutions for this survey is based on the Integrated Postsecondary Education Data Survey conducted by the National Center for Education Statistics (see above). Institutions without federal support were excluded and some systems were combined into single reporting units.

Further information on this survey may be obtained from *Federal Support to Universities, Colleges, and Nonprofit Institutions,* published by the National Science Foundation, or by contacting:

Science and Engineering Activities Program
Division of Science Resources Studies
National Science Foundation
4201 Wilson Boulevard
Arlington, Virginia 22230

Survey of Scientific and Engineering Expenditures at Universities and Colleges

The National Science Foundation's annual academic survey collects data on research and development expenditures in the sciences and engineering from a sample of 459 institutions in the United States and outlying areas. Those institutions were selected from the universe of 595 schools that grant a graduate science or engineering degree and/or perform activities for which at least $50,000 has been funded from separately budgeted R&D expenditures. In addition, the survey includes 19 university-affiliated, federally funded research and development centers (FFRDCs).

The 459 institutions sampled for FY 1991 include all doctorate-granting institutions, all historically black colleges and universities with any R&D expenditures, and a random sample of all other institutions. The response rate was 97 percent. Data presented are assembled from the most recently completed survey.

Further information on this survey may be obtained from *Academic Science/Engineering, R&D Funds,* published by the National Science Foundation, or by contacting:

Science and Engineering Activities Program
Division of Science Resources Studies
National Science Foundation
4201 Wilson Boulevard
Arlington, Virginia 22230

Other Organization Sources

American College Testing Program

The American College Testing (ACT) Assessment is designed to measure educational development in the areas of English, mathematics, social studies, and natural sciences. The ACT Assessment is taken by college-bound high school students and the test results are used to predict how well students might perform in college.

Prior to the 1984–85 school year, national norms were based on a 10 percent sample of the students taking the test. Since then, national norms are based on the test scores of all students taking the test. Moreover, beginning with 1984–85, these norms have been based on the most recent ACT scores available from students scheduled to graduate in the spring of the year. Duplicate test records are no longer used to produce national figures.

Separate ACT standard scores are computed for English, mathematics, social studies, science reasoning, and, as of October 1989, reading. ACT standard scores are reported for each subject area on a scale from 1 to 36. The four ACT standard scores have a mean (average) of about 19 and a standard deviation of about 6 for college-bound students nationally. A composite score is obtained by taking the simple average of the four standard scores and is an indication of student's overall academic development across these subject areas. Beginning with the October 1989 test date, a new version of the ACT was introduced.

It should be noted that college-bound students who take the ACT Assessment are not representative of college-bound students nationally. First, students who live in the Midwest, Rocky Mountains and Plains, and the South are overrepresented among ACT-tested students as compared with college-bound students nationally. Second, ACT-tested students tend to enroll in public colleges and universities more frequently than do college-bound students nationally.

For further information, contact:

The American College Testing Program
2201 North Dodge Street
P.O. Box 168
Iowa City, IA 52243

American Federation of Teachers

The American Federation of Teachers (AFT) has reported national and state average salaries and earnings for teachers, other school employees, government workers, and professional employees over the past 25 years. The AFT's survey of state departments of education obtains information on minimum salaries, experienced teachers reentering the classroom, and teacher age and experience. Most data from the survey are reported as received, although some data are confirmed by telephone. These data are available in the AFT's annual report *Survey and Analysis of Salary Trends.* While this serves as the primary vehicle for reporting the results of the AFT's annual survey of state departments of education, several other data sources are also used in the report.

Further information on this survey can be obtained from:

American Federation of Teachers
555 New Jersey Avenue NW
Washington, DC 20001

College Entrance Examination Board

The Admissions Testing Program of the College Board comprises a number of college admissions tests, including the Preliminary Scholastic Assessment Test (PSAT) and the Scholastic Assessment Test (SAT). High school students participate in the testing program as sophomores, juniors, or seniors—some more than once during these 3 years. If they have taken the tests more than once, only the most recent scores are tabulated. The PSAT and SAT report subscores in the areas of mathematics and verbal ability.

The SAT results are not representative of high school students or college-bound students nationally since the sample is self-selected. Generally, tests are taken by students who need the results to attend a particular college or university. The state totals are greatly affected by the requirements of its state colleges. Public colleges in a number of states require ACT scores rather than SAT scores. Thus, the proportion of students taking the SAT in these states is very low and is inappropriate for any comparison. In recent years, more than 1 million high school students have taken the examination annually.

Further information on the SAT can be obtained from:

College Entrance Examination Board
Educational Testing Service
Princeton, NJ 08541

Council for Aid to Education

The Council for Aid to Education, Inc., (CFAE) is a not-for-profit corporation funded by contributions from business. CFAE largely provides consulting and research services on voluntary support to corporations and information services to education institutions. Each year CFAE conducts a survey of colleges and universities and private elementary and secondary schools to obtain information on the amounts, sources, and purposes of private gifts, grants, and bequests received during the academic year.

In the 1991–92 study, survey forms were sent to approximately 2,900 colleges and universities and 1,280 responded. The response rates were much higher for the 4-year colleges than for the 2-year colleges. For example, 89 percent of the doctoral-level institutions and 55 percent of the comprehensive and general baccalaureate colleges participated in the survey, but only 12 percent of the 2-year colleges responded. CFAE estimates that about 84 percent of all voluntary support is reported in the survey because of the high participation of institutions receiving large amounts of funding.

Survey forms are reviewed by CFAE for internal consistency before preparing a computerized database. Institutional reports of voluntary support data from the CFAE "Survey of Voluntary Support of Education" are more comprehensive and detailed than the related data in the "Financial Statistics of Institutions of Higher Education" survey conducted by NCES. The results from the "Survey of Voluntary Support of Education" are published in the annual *Voluntary Support of Education,* which may be purchased from CFAE.

Further information is available from:

Director of Research
Council for Aid to Education, Inc.
51 Madison Avenue
Suite 2200
New York, NY 10010

Council of Chief State School Officers

The Council of Chief State School Officers (CCSSO) is a nonprofit organization of the 57 public officials who head departments of public education in every state, the outlying areas, the District of Columbia, and the Department of Defense Dependents Schools. In 1985, the CCSSO founded the State Education Assessment Center to provide a locus of leadership by the states to improve the monitoring and assessment of education. *State Education Indicators, 1993* is the principal report of the Assessment Center's program of indicators on education. Most of the data are obtained from a member questionnaire; the remainder of the data are obtained from federal government agencies. Information on mathematics education was taken from *CCSSO, State Policies on Science and Mathematics Evaluation, 1992.*

For additional information, contact:

Edward Roeber
State Education Assessment Center
Council of Chief State School Officers
One Massachusetts Avenue NW
7th Floor
Washington, DC 20001

Council of State Directors of Programs for the Gifted

The Council of State Directors of Programs for the Gifted is composed of the director or individual in the leadership position for gifted education in each of the 50 states, the District of Columbia, and the outlying areas. The Council has conducted many surveys in the past and most recently conducted two comprehensive state surveys in order to produce a profile of gifted education throughout the Nation. These data are reported in the 1985, 1987, 1990 and 1994 "State of the States Gifted and Talented Education" reports. This edition of the *Digest* uses data from the 1995–96 school year.

Further information is available from:

Michael Hall, Executive Director
Council of State Directors of Programs for the Gifted
c/o Office of Public Instruction
P.O Box 202501
Helena, MT 59620–2501

Education Commission of the States

The Education Commission of the States (ECS) Clearinghouse collects information on laws and standards in the field of education and reports them periodically in "Clearinghouse Notes." The Commission collects information about administrators, principals, and teachers. It also examines policy areas, such as assessment and testing, collective bargaining, early childhood issues, quality education, and school schedules. The information is collected by reading state newsletters, tracking state legislation, and surveying state education agencies. Data are verified by the individual states when necessary. Even though ECS monitors state activity on a continuous basis, it updates the reports only when there is significant change in state activity.

Further information is available from:

Shawni Arora
Education Commission of the States
707 17th Street, Suite 2700
Denver, CO 80202–3427

Gallup Poll

Each year the Gallup Poll conducts the "Public Attitudes Toward the Public Schools" survey, funded by Phi Delta Kappa. The survey includes interviews with adults representing the civilian noninstitutional population 18 years old and over.

The sample used in the 27th annual survey was made up of a total of 1,311 respondents and is described as a modified probability sample of the nation. Personal, in-home interviewing was conducted in representative communities.

The survey is a sample survey and is subject to sampling error. The size of error depends largely on the number of respondents providing data. Table A10 shows the approximate sampling errors associated with different percentages and sample sizes for the survey. Table A11 provides approximate sampling errors for comparisons of two sample percentages.

For example, an estimated percentage of about 10 percent based on the responses of 1,000 sample members has an approximate sampling error of 2 percent at the 95 percent confidence level. The sampling error for the difference in two percentages (50 percent versus 41 percent) based on two samples of 750 members and 400 members, respectively, is about 8 percent at the 95 percent confidence level.

Further information on this survey can be obtained from:

Neville Robertson
Phi Delta Kappa
P.O. Box 789
Bloomington, IN 47402–0789

Independent Sector

In 1992, Independent Sector commissioned the Gallup Poll to conduct a national survey on the giving and volunteering behavior of Americans. This survey is part of a series of surveys that will be conducted every 2 years. The information was obtained from in-home personal interviews conducted from April 3 to May 17, 1992, with a representative national sample of 2,671 adult Americans 18 or more years old. The sampling procedure did not include those with incomes above $200,000 because they constitute such a small percentage of the population.

The results from this survey are published in Giving and Volunteering in the United States and may be purchased from:

Independent Sector
1828 L Street NW
Washington, DC 20036

International Association for the Evaluation of Educational Achievement (IEA)

The International Association for the Evaluation of Educational Achievement, known as the IEA, is comprised of research centers and scholars from around the world whose aim is to investigate education problems common among countries. In 1988, the IEA General Assembly, composed of the research institutes participating in IEA projects, decided to undertake a study of reading literacy. The study held its first National Research Coordinator (NRC) meeting in November 1988. The construction and pilot testing of instruments was conducted in the period from November 1988 to July 1990. The main testing took place in the period October 1990 to April 1991 depending on the school year in each country. Thirty-two school systems were involved in the IEA Reading Literacy Study. Data were collected from 210,059 students, 10,518 teachers, and 9,073 schools. All students took reading tests for two sessions totaling 75 minutes at the 9-year-old level and two sessions totaling 85 minutes at the 14-year-old population. All students responded to a background questionnaire about their reading at home and at school. Teachers and school principals responded to questionnaires about themselves, their teaching and the school organization. Each national center (NCES was the center for the United States) completed a National Case Study Questionnaire.

For more information, contact:

Marilyn Binkley, NRC USA
National Center for Education Statistics
555 New Jersey Avenue NW
Washington, DC 20208–5650

Institute of International Education

Each year the Institute of International Education (IIE) conducts a survey of the number of foreign students studying in American colleges and universities and reports these data in *Open Doors,* an annual publication. All of the regionally accredited institutions in the *Education Directory, Colleges and Universities* published by NCES are surveyed by IIE. The data presented in the *Digest* are drawn from the IIE survey which requests the total enrollment of foreign students in an institution and information on student characteristics, such as country of origin. For the 1994–95 survey, 2,684 out of 2,758 (97.3 percent) institutions reported data for the survey.

Additional information can be obtained from the publication *Open Doors* or by contacting:

Todd M. Davis
Institute of International Education
809 United Nations Plaza
New York, NY 10017–3580

Metropolitan Life Insurance Company

The Metropolitan Life Survey of the American Teacher for the Metropolitan Life Insurance Company was conducted by Louis Harris and Associates. This survey was designed to measure the experiences of new public school teachers who began their first year of teaching in the 1990–91 school year. It includes questions on their experiences with students, administrators, other teachers, and parents. There were three surveys of this cohort of new teachers. The first survey was conducted during the summer of 1990 to measure the expectations of new graduates from teaching schools immediately prior to their first year of teaching in public schools. The second survey compared how these new teachers' experiences in their first year of teaching affected their attitudes, and how the actual experience of teaching compared with their prior expectations. The current survey focuses on these teachers' experience two years into their teaching career. It includes questions which allow comparisons on their attitudes toward teaching now versus one and two years ago.

A total of 1,000 teachers who began their first year of teaching in the public schools in the 1990–91 school year were surveyed. The sample was designed to be representative of all new teachers in the public schools who graduated from teaching colleges in 1990 and taught for the first time in a public school in the 1990–91 school year.

The sample was drawn from lists of 1990 graduates from a probability sample of colleges listed by the *American Association of Colleges for Teacher Education.* Graduates who did not teach full-time in public schools in 1990–91 were excluded from the sample.

The priority for fielding the sample was as follows: first, any respondents from the second phase of the study (after the first year of teaching); second, any respondents from the first phase (before teaching) who were not also included in the second phase; finally, any remaining teachers from the original sample group who were not used in the first phase.

All interviews were conducted by telephone in May and June 1992.

For more information contact:

Metropolitan Life Survey of the American Teacher
Louis Harris and Associates
111 Fifth Avenue
New York, NY 10003

National Association of State Scholarship and Grant Programs

The National Association of State Scholarship and Grant Programs (NASSGP) is an association of states with general programs of scholarship or grant assistance for undergraduate study. Executive officers responsible for grant program administration represent each state in the Association. The *26th Annual Survey Report: 1994–95 Academic Year* is produced the by the New York State Higher Education

Services Corporation, and data are reported for all 50 states, the District of Columbia, and Puerto Rico.

For more information on this survey, contact:

Charles Treadwell
New York State Higher Education Services
 Corporation
99 Washington Avenue, Room 1438
Albany, NY 12255
Attention: NASSGAP

National Education Association

The National Education Association (NEA) reports enrollment, expenditure, revenue, graduate, teacher, and instructional staff salary data in its annual publication, *Estimates of School Statistics*. Each year NEA prepares regression-based estimates of financial and other education statistics and submits them to the states for verification. Generally about 30 states adjust these estimates based on their own data. These preliminary data are published by NEA along with revised data from previous years. States are asked to revise previously submitted data as final figures become available. The most recent publication contains all changes reported to the NEA.

Status of the American Public School Teacher

The "Status of the American Public School Teacher" survey is conducted every 5 years by the National Education Association (NEA). The survey was designed by the NEA Research Division and initially administered in 1956. The intent of the survey is to solicit information covering various aspects of public school teachers' professional, family, and civic lives.

Participants for the survey are selected using a two-stage sample design, with the first-stage stratum determined by the number of students enrolled in the districts. Selection probabilities are determined so that the resulting sample is self-weighting. In 1990–91, questionnaires were sent to a sample of 1,981 of the nation's approximately 2,400,000 public school teachers. With an initial and four follow-up mailings, 1,499 questionnaires were returned, of which 145 were not usable. The sample was adjusted to 1,836 to reflect the 145 unusable responses. The response rate was 73.7 percent.

Possible sources of nonsampling errors are nonresponses, misinterpretation, and—when comparing data over years—changes in the sampling method and instrument. Misinterpretation of the survey items should be minimal, as the sample responding is not from the general population but one knowledgeable about the area of concern. Also, the sampling procedure changed after 1956 and some wording of items has changed over the different administrations.

Since sampling is used, sampling variability is inherent in the data. An approximation to the maximum standard error for estimating the population percentages is 1.4 percent (Table A12). To estimate the 90 percent confidence interval for population percentages, the maximum standard error of 1.4 percent is multiplied by 1.65 (1.4 x 1.65). The resulting percentage (2.3) is added and subtracted from the population estimate to establish upper and lower bounds for the confidence interval. For example, if a sample percentage is 60 percent, there is a 90 percent chance that the population percentage lies between 57.7 percent and 62.3 percent (60 percent ± 2.3 percent).

Questions concerning the "Status of the American Public School Teacher" survey may be directed to:

Brooke E. Whiting
National Education Association–Research
1201 16th Street NW
Washington, DC 20036

Organization for Economic Cooperation and Development

The Organization for Economic Cooperation and Development (OECD) publishes analyses of national policies in education, training, and economics in more than 20 countries. The countries surveyed are: Australia, Austria, Belgium, Canada, Czech and Slovak Federal Republics, Denmark, Finland, France, Germany, Hungary, Ireland, Italy, Japan, Luxembourg, Netherlands, New Zealand, Norway, Portugal, Spain, Sweden, Switzerland, Turkey, United Kingdom, United States, and the former Yugoslavia.

Since only developed nations, mostly European, are included in these studies, the range of analysis is limited. However, OECD data allow for some detailed international comparison of financial resources or other education variables to be made for this selected group of countries.

In the past several years, OECD has revised its data collection procedures to highlight current education issues. The Centre for Educational Research and Innovation (CERI) has developed an Indicators of Education Systems (INES) project involving representatives of the OECD countries and the OECD Secretariat to improve international education statistics. Large improvements in data quality and comparability among OECD countries have resulted from the country to country interaction sponsored through the INES project. The most recent publication in this series is *Education at a Glance* (1996).

More complete information on INES may be obtained from:

Andreas Schleicher
INES/OECD
2, rue Andre-Pascal
75775 Paris CEDEX 16
France

Research Associates of Washington

Research Associates annually compiles the Higher Education Price Index (HEPI) which measures average changes in prices of goods and services purchased by colleges and universities through current-fund educational and general expenditures. Sponsored research and auxiliary enterprises are not priced by the HEPI.

The HEPI is based on the prices (or salaries) of faculty and of administrators and other professional service personnel; clerical, technical, service, and other nonprofessional personnel; and contracted services, such as data processing, communication, transportation, supplies and materials, equipment, books and periodicals, and utilities. These represent the items purchased for current operations by colleges and universities. Prices for these items are obtained from salary surveys conducted by various national higher education associations, the American Association of University Professors, the Bureau of Labor Statistics, and the National Center for Education Statistics; and from components of the Consumer Price Index (CPI) and the Producer Price Index (PPI) published by the U.S. Department of Labor, Bureau of Labor Statistics.

The quantities of these goods and services have been kept constant based on the 1971–72 buying pattern of colleges and universities. The weights assigned the various items priced, which represent their relative importance in the current-fund educational and general budget, are estimated national averages. Variance in spending patterns of individual institutions from these national averages reduces only slightly the applicability of the HEPI to any given institutional situation. Modest differences in the weights attached to expenditure categories have little effect on overall index values. This is because the HEPI is dominated by the trend in faculty salaries and similar salary trends for other personnel hired by institutions, which absorbs or diminishes the effects of price changes in other items purchased in small quantities.

For more information, contact:

Kent Halstead
Research Associates of Washington
1200 North Nash St.
#225
Arlington, VA 22209

United Nations Educational, Scientific, and Cultural Organization

The United Nations Educational, Scientific, and Cultural Organization (UNESCO) conducts annual surveys of education statistics of its member countries. Besides official surveys, data are supplemented by information obtained by UNESCO through other publications and sources. Each year more than 200 countries reply to the UNESCO surveys. In some cases, estimates are made by UNESCO for particular items such as world and continent totals. While great efforts are made to make them as comparable as possible, the data still reflect the vast differences among the countries of the world in the structure of education. While there is some agreement about the reporting of first- and second-level data, the third level (postsecondary education) presents numerous substantial problems. Some countries report only university enrollment while other countries report all postsecondary, including vocational and technical schools and correspondence programs. A very high proportion of some countries' third-level students attend institutions in other countries. While definition problems are many in this sort of study, other survey problems should not be overlooked. The member countries that provide data to UNESCO are responsible for their validity. Thus, data for particular countries are subject to nonsampling error and perhaps sampling error as well. Some countries may furnish only rough estimates, while data from other countries may be very accurate. Other difficulties are caused by the varying periodicity of data collection among the countries of the world. In spite of such problems, many researchers use UNESCO data because they are the best available for such a large group of countries. Users should examine footnotes carefully to recognize some of the data limitations.

More complete information may be obtained from the Statistical Yearbook published by UNESCO or from:

Office of Statistics
UNESCO
7, Place de Fontenoy
75700 Paris
France

Table A1.—Standard errors for enrollment and completion status of first-time postsecondary students starting during the 1989–90 academic year, by degree objective and other student characteristics: 1994

Student characteristics	2-year college students starting in 1989–90						Students seeking bachelor's degrees in 1989–90					
	Attained by 1994[1]				No degree by 1994		Highest degree completed, not enrolled for bachelor's degree[2]				Still enrolled for bachelor's[3]	No degree, not enrolled[4]
	Total	Certificate	Associate	Bachelor's	Enrolled	Not enrolled	Total, degree	Certificate	Associate	Bachelor's		
Total	1.9	1.3	1.7	1.0	1.5	2.0	1.3	0.5	0.9	1.4	1.0	1.2
Male	2.6	1.8	1.9	1.4	2.4	2.9	1.9	0.7	1.0	1.7	1.5	1.7
Female	2.8	1.9	2.6	1.3	1.8	2.9	1.7	0.8	1.3	1.9	1.2	1.6
Race												
White, non-Hispanic	2.2	1.6	1.9	1.1	1.5	2.2	1.5	0.6	1.0	1.6	1.0	1.3
Black, non-Hispanic	6.6	4.9	4.3	2.2	4.8	7.5	4.1	1.2	3.1	3.3	2.8	4.1
Hispanic	6.2	4.9	4.4	3.0	6.7	7.0	5.5	3.3	2.2	4.8	4.6	5.5
Asian/Pacific Islander	—	—	—	—	—	—	5.9	0.6	3.1	6.0	4.8	6.4
Socioeconomic status in 1989–90												
Low (25 percent)	4.7	3.6	2.6	1.0	3.0	4.9	4.7	3.2	2.9	3.7	3.6	4.9
Middle (50 percent)	2.7	1.8	2.0	1.3	2.3	2.9	1.9	0.8	1.1	2.0	1.6	1.9
High (25 percent)	3.3	2.1	3.3	2.3	2.5	3.0	1.8	0.7	1.1	1.8	1.3	1.4
Dependent student family income in 1989–90												
Less than $20,000	4.4	3.3	3.9	2.1	3.7	4.4	2.8	0.5	1.6	2.6	2.3	3.0
$20,000 to $39,999	4.2	2.9	3.3	2.5	3.2	4.0	2.3	1.1	1.3	2.1	1.9	2.2
$40,000 to $59,999	4.8	3.0	4.3	2.6	3.2	4.7	2.6	1.3	1.2	2.4	1.7	2.5
$60,000 or more	6.2	2.9	6.7	3.8	5.6	5.9	2.5	0.6	2.0	3.0	2.2	1.7
Diploma/delayed entry status[5]												
Diploma, did not delay	2.3	1.6	2.3	1.7	2.0	2.2	1.4	0.5	0.8	1.5	1.0	1.2
Diploma, delayed entry	2.9	2.4	1.9	0.8	2.2	3.1	3.8	2.3	2.7	2.7	3.7	4.3
No diploma	5.7	4.8	3.1	1.3	2.9	6.3	6.1	2.0	1.4	5.1	6.8	9.1
Age (as of 12/31/89)												
18 years or younger	2.6	1.7	2.6	2.0	2.1	2.7	1.5	0.6	0.9	1.5	1.1	1.3
19 years	4.5	3.4	3.8	1.2	3.9	4.8	3.1	1.1	1.3	2.9	2.9	3.1
20 to 29 years	3.8	3.1	2.3	1.1	3.1	4.3	4.9	3.4	3.9	3.6	4.5	5.8
30 years or over	4.5	3.5	2.5	0.6	2.9	4.4	5.9	1.8	4.5	3.3	7.0	8.6
Marital status												
Never married	2.2	1.5	1.9	1.4	1.9	2.4	1.4	0.6	1.0	1.5	1.0	1.2
Married	4.6	3.6	2.5	1.3	2.7	5.1	5.8	1.6	1.2	5.3	6.2	7.5
Divorced, widowed, separated	6.8	6.7	2.5	1.0	4.6	7.8	9.0	0.6	7.8	5.3	10.5	11.8
Expected degree level for 2-year students												
Less than 2 years	6.7	6.4	2.5	0.0	5.8	7.4	—	—	—	—	—	—
2 to 4 years	4.5	3.7	2.6	1.0	3.1	4.4	—	—	—	—	—	—
Bachelor's or higher	2.3	1.5	2.1	1.4	1.8	2.5	—	—	—	—	—	—
Average hours worked per week while enrolled												
None	4.7	4.2	3.1	2.0	2.9	5.0	2.5	0.8	1.3	2.5	1.8	2.5
1 to 20 hours	4.8	2.9	4.0	2.5	2.9	4.3	2.2	0.6	1.2	2.2	1.6	1.9
More than 20 hours	2.2	1.6	1.8	1.2	1.9	2.5	1.9	0.9	1.0	1.9	1.4	—
Received financial aid during 1989–90												
Yes	3.1	2.2	2.3	1.9	2.3	3.2	1.5	0.4	0.6	1.6	0.9	1.4
No	2.3	1.6	2.1	1.0	1.7	2.5	2.1	0.9	1.6	2.0	1.6	1.8

[1] Highest degree attained at any institution. Students who have attained may also be enrolled.

[2] Status as of 1994. Includes those students who are no longer working towards a bachelor's degree, but who had completed another type of degree or award.

[3] Status as of 1994. Includes students who had completed another type of degree or award (associate degree: 11.8 percent, certificate: 2.7 percent) but are still working toward a bachelor's degree.

[4] Status as of 1994. Enrollment can be full-time or part-time. Includes students who are still enrolled, but are no longer working toward a bachelor's degree.

[5] Students were considered to have a diploma only if they had a regular high school diploma. Students with a GED or other high school credentials were considered to have no diploma.

—Data not available or not applicable.

NOTE.—Data reflect completion and enrollment status by spring 1994 of first-time postsecondary students starting in academic year 1989–90.

SOURCE: U.S. Department of Education, National Center for Education Statistics, Beginning Postsecondary Student Longitudinal Survey, 1994. (This table was prepared September 1996.)

Table A2.—Respondent counts for selected High School and Beyond surveys

Classification variable and subgroup	Followup survey of 1980 sophomores in 1982	Followup survey of 1980 seniors in 1982	Followup survey of 1980 sophomores in 1984	Followup survey of 1980 seniors in 1984	Followup survey of 1980 sophomores in 1986	Followup survey of 1980 seniors in 1986
Total respondents (unweighted)	25,830	11,227	11,463	10,925	11,248	10,536
Sex						
Male	12,717	5,213	5,514	5,058	5,391	4,832
Female	13,113	6,014	5,949	5,867	5,857	5,704
Race/ethnicity						
White, non-Hispanic	17,295	5,180	7,285	5,057	7,194	5,246
Black, non-Hispanic	3,338	2,724	1,651	2,625	1,585	2,726
Hispanic	4,439	2,749	1,795	2,654	1,745	1,950
Asian or Pacific Islander	413	367	425	355	413	356
American Indian or Alaskan Native	248	191	253	185	246	200
Other or unclassified	97	16	54	49	65	58
Socioeconomic status composite (SES)[1]						
Low	6,752	3,940	2,831	3,857	2,751	3,668
Low-middle	6,234	2,390	2,624	2,314	2,559	2,289
High-middle	6,134	2,168	2,849	2,107	2,817	1,995
High	6,341	1,988	3,086	1,936	3,044	1,900
Unclassified	369	741	73	711	77	684
Father's highest level of education						
Less than high school	5,179	—	—	—	—	—
High school graduate[2]	11,961	—	—	—	—	—
College graduate[3]	5,169	—	—	—	—	—
Don't know/missing	3,521	—	—	—	—	—
High school program (self-reported)						
Academic	10,152	4,145	6,547	4,007	—	3,899
General	8,789	3,829	3,468	3,764	—	3,602
Vocational	6,664	2,660	3,611	2,581	—	2,481
Unclassified	225	593	56	573	—	554
High school type						
Public	—	9,969	8,647	9,727	—	9,385
Catholic	—	964	2,479	911	—	876
Other private	—	294	337	287	—	275
Postsecondary education status[4]						
Full-time	—	—	4,466	—	—	—
Part-time	—	—	3,275	—	—	—
Never enrolled	—	—	3,678	—	—	—
Missing/unclassified	—	—	44	—	—	—
October 1980 postsecondary education attendance status						
Part-time 2-year public institution	—	—	—	—	—	352
Part-time 4-year public institution	—	—	—	—	—	152
Full-time 2-year public institution	—	—	—	—	—	1,312
Full-time 4-year public institution	—	—	—	—	—	1,986
Full-time 4-year private institution	—	—	—	—	—	1,015
Not a student	—	—	—	—	—	4,523
Other and missing	—	—	—	—	—	1,196
Postsecondary education plans						
No plans	—	—	—	—	—	1,623
Attend vocational/technical school	—	—	—	—	—	1,835
Attend college less than four years	—	—	—	—	—	1,528
Earn bachelor's degree	—	—	—	—	—	2,631
Earn advanced degree	—	—	—	—	—	2,265
Missing	—	—	—	—	—	654
Participation in high school extracurricular activities[5]						
Never participated	—	—	—	—	—	1,024
Participated as a member	—	—	—	—	—	4,104
Participated as a leader	—	—	—	—	—	4,457

[1] The SES index is a composite of five equally weighted measures: father's education, mother's education, family income, father's occupation, and presence of certain items in the respondent's household.
[2] Includes attendance at a vocational, trade, or business school, or 2-year college; or attendance at a 4-year college resulting in less than a bachelor's degree.
[3] Includes those with a bachelor's or higher level degree.
[4] Postsecondary education status was determined by students' enrollment in academic or vocational study during the four semesters—fall 1982, spring 1983, fall 1983, and spring 1984—following their scheduled high school graduation. Students who enrolled in full-time study in each of the four semesters were classified as full time. Students who were enrolled in part-time study in any of the four semesters and those who were enrolled in full-time study in fewer than four semesters were classified as part time. Students who had enrolled on neither a full-time nor part-time basis in each of the four semesters were classified as never enrolled.
[5] Responses to questions concerning participation in each of 15 different extracurricular activity areas (i.e., varsity sports, debate, band, subject-matter clubs, etc.) were used to classify students' overall level of participation in extracurricular activities. The difference between the sum of the three category respondent counts and the total sample size is due to missing data.

—Data not applicable.

NOTE.—Data from students who dropped out of school between the 10th and 12th grades were not used in analyses of sophomore samples.

Table A3.—Design effects (DEFF) and root design effects (DEFT) for selected High School and Beyond surveys and subsamples

Subsample characteristic	Followup survey of 1980 sophomores in 1984	Followup survey of 1980 seniors in 1984	Followup survey of 1980 sophomores in 1986	Followup survey of 1980 seniors in 1986
Total sample	**2.40 (1.54)**	**2.87 (1.69)**	**2.19 (1.47)**	**2.28 (1.50)**
Sex				
Male	—	—	2.07 (1.43)	2.13 (1.45)
Female	—	—	2.06 (1.43)	2.26 (1.50)
Race/ethnicity				
White and other	2.06 (1.42)	2.09 (1.44)	1.92 (1.38)	1.70 (1.30)
Black	2.22 (1.47)	2.26 (1.50)	2.19 (1.47)	2.40 (1.54)
Hispanic	3.15 (1.73)	3.72 (1.92)	3.11 (1.76)	4.06 (2.01)
Socioeconomic status composite (SES)				
Low	1.91 (1.37)	2.28 (1.50)	1.83 (1.35)	2.31 (1.51)
Middle	1.95 (1.39)	1.81 (1.34)	2.06 (1.42)	2.02 (1.42)
High	2.05 (1.42)	1.93 (1.38)	1.92 (1.38)	1.71 (1.30)

—Not available

NOTE.—The average design effect for the 1980 sophomore cohort first followup (1982) survey is 3.59(1.89) and the average design effect for the 1980 senior first followup (1982) survey is 2.64(1.62).

Table A4.—Respondent counts for the National Educational Longitudinal Study: 1988, 1990, and 1992

Classification variable and subgroup	Base year, 1988	First followup 1990	Second followup 1992
Total respondents (unweighted)	**24,599**	**20,706**	**21,188**
Sex			
Male	12,241	10,462	10,713
Female	12,358	10,244	10,475
Race/ethnicity			
White, non-Hispanic	16,317	13,837	14,024
Black, non-Hispanic	3,009	2,218	2,260
Hispanic	3,171	2,751	2,922
Asian or Pacific Islander	1,527	1,302	1,406
American Indian or Alaskan Native	299	259	266
Other or unclassified	276	399	310
Socioeconomic status composite (SES)			
Low	5,934	4,556	4,395
Low-middle	5,788	4,472	4,501
High-middle	5,836	4,378	4,516
High	7,030	5,262	5,437
Unclassified	11	2,038	2,339
High school program (self-reported)			
Academic	7,298	6,420	7,567
General	3,369	7,990	6,125
Vocational	4,161	1,806	1,911
Unclassified	9,771	4,490	5,585
High school type			
Public	19,396	16,813	15,145
Catholic	2,602	1,012	934
Other private	2,601	1,602	1,530
Not enrolled	—	1,043	2,725
Missing	—	236	854
Postsecondary education plans			
No plans	2,685	2,483	2,646
Attend vocational/technical school	2,102	2,323	2,072
Attend college less than 4 years	3,078	3,074	2,457
Earn bachelor's degree	10,251	5,874	5,631
Earn advanced degree	6,268	5,269	5,580
Missing	215	1,683	2,802
School academic clubs and extracurricular activities			
Never participated	21,516	15,292	17,117
Participated as a member	2,798	5,144	3,355
Participated as a leader	285	270	716

—Not applicable.

Table A5.—Design effects (DEFF) and root design effects (DEFT) for selected National Educational Longitudinal Survey samples

Subsample characteristic	Base year 1988		First follow-up 1990		Second follow-up 1992	
	Mean DEFF	Mean DEFT	Mean DEFF	Mean DEFT	Mean DEFF	Mean DEFT
All students	2.54	1.56	3.802	1.912	3.668	1.881
Dropouts	—	—	4.705	1.997	2.919	1.686
Sex						
Male	1.98	1.39	3.456	1.817	3.094	1.729
Female	1.93	1.38	3.324	1.783	3.238	1.785
Race/ethnicity						
White and other	2.25	1.48	3.101	1.729	3.084	1.737
Black	1.65	1.27	3.804	1.867	2.938	1.654
Hispanic	2.06	1.41	2.643	1.591	2.772	1.626
Asian/Pacific Islander	2.00	1.40	2.758	1.609	2.511	1.562
American Indian/Alaskan Native	—	—	2.066	1.362	3.292	1.687
Socioeconomic status composite (SES)						
Low	1.58	1.25	2.797	1.644	2.931	1.680
Middle	1.66	1.28	3.138	1.732	2.516	1.569
High	1.84	1.34	3.576	1.817	3.849	1.921
High school type						
Public	2.27	1.48	3.147	1.736	3.116	1.733
Catholic	2.70	1.59	2.619	1.513	2.545	1.564
Other private	8.80	1.83	6.529	2.391	6.049	2.334
Community type						
Urban	—	—	3.463	1.842	3.742	1.897
Suburban	—	—	3.412	1.788	2.998	1.705
Rural	—	—	2.634	1.571	3.311	1.687

—Data not available.

Table A6.—Respondent counts of full-time workers from the Recent College Graduate survey: 1976 to 1991

Field of study	Number employed full time				
	1974–75 graduates in May 1976	1979–80 graduates in May 1981	1983–84 graduates in April 1985	1985–86 graduates in April 1987	1989–90 graduates in April 1991
Total respondents (unweighted)	**2,464**	**5,521**	**6,799**	**15,024**	**9,451**
Professions	1,840	4,260	3,730	8,987	3,825
Arts and sciences	514	811	2,586	4,869	2,256
Other	110	450	483	1,168	3,370
Newly qualified to teach	1,337	2,469	1,109	2,546	1,966
Not newly qualified to teach	1,127	3,052	5,690	12,478	7,485
Professions	601	1,841	2,809	7,043	2,549
Engineering	80	270	601	915	411
Business and management	290	749	1,532	2,407	1,598
Health	72	252	387	3,106	281
Education[1]	141	464	146	521	188
Public affairs and services	18	106	143	94	71
Arts and sciences	433	770	2,430	4,369	2,006
Biological sciences	83	116	243	380	179
Physical sciences and mathematics	40	103	1,062	1,782	466
Psychology	64	105	189	366	316
Social sciences	107	252	449	780	813
Humanities	139	194	487	1,061	232
Other	93	441	451	1,066	2,930
Communications	7	73	240	392	217
Miscellaneous	86	368	211	674	2,713

[1] Includes those who had not finished all requirements for teaching certification or were previously qualified to teach.

Table A7.—Estimated enrollment rates and standard errors in the October Current Population Survey

Base of percentage, in thousands	Estimated percentage				
	2 or 98	5 or 95	10 or 90	25 or 75	50
Total or white persons					
100	2.1	3.3	4.6	6.6	7.6
250	1.3	2.1	2.9	4.2	4.8
500	1.0	1.5	2.0	2.9	3.4
1,000	0.7	1.0	1.4	2.1	2.4
2,500	0.4	0.7	0.9	1.3	1.5
5,000	0.3	0.5	0.6	0.9	1.1
10,000	0.2	0.3	0.5	0.7	0.8
25,000	0.13	0.2	0.3	0.4	0.5
50,000	0.09	0.15	0.2	0.3	0.3
100,000	0.07	0.10	0.05	0.2	0.2
150,000	0.05	0.12	0.12	0.2	0.2
Black or Hispanic persons					
75	2.6	4.1	5.6	8.1	9.3
100	2.3	3.5	4.8	7.0	8.1
250	1.4	2.2	3.1	4.4	5.1
500	1.0	1.6	2.2	3.1	3.6
1,000	0.7	1.1	1.5	2.2	2.5
2,500	0.5	0.7	1.0	1.4	1.6
5,000	0.3	0.5	0.7	1.0	1.1
10,000	0.2	0.4	0.5	0.7	0.8
15,000	0.2	0.3	0.4	0.6	0.7
20,000	0.2	0.2	0.3	0.5	0.6

Table A8.—Estimated educational attainment rates and standard errors in the March Current Population Survey

Estimate	Base of percentage in thousands	Standard error	90 percent confidence interval [1]		90 percent confidence interval [1]	
			Lower bound	Upper bound	Lower bound	Upper bound
2 or 98	100	2.00	0.0	5.3	0.0	5.9
	100,000	0.06	1.9	2.1	1.9	2.10
10 or 90	100	4.30	2.9	17.1	1.6	18.4
	100,000	0.14	9.8	10.2	9.7	10.3
50	100	7.20	38.1	61.9	35.9	64.1
	100,000	0.20	49.7	50.3	49.6	50.4

[1] The confidence interval for the larger values can be found by taking the complement of that shown, e.g., for 98 it would be 94.1 to 100 for 95 percent confidence.

Table A9.—Percent of seniors who had ever used selected drugs and 95 percent confidence limits: 1986 [1]

Drug	Lower limit	Observed estimate	Upper limit
Alcohol	89.7	91.3	92.7
Marijuana/hashish	48.7	50.9	53.1
LSD	6.3	7.2	8.2
PCP	3.8	4.8	6.0
Cocaine	15.5	16.9	18.4
Heroin	0.8	1.1	1.4

[1] Approximate sample size = 15,200.

Table A10.—Sampling errors (95 percent confidence level) for percentages estimated from the Gallup Poll: 1992 and 1993

Percent	Size of sample						
	1,500	1,000	750	600	400	200	100
	Recommended allowance for sampling error of a percentage						
Percentages near 10 or 90	2	2	3	3	4	5	8
Percentages near 20 or 80	3	3	4	4	5	7	10
Percentages near 30 or 70	3	4	4	5	6	8	12
Percentages near 40 or 60	3	4	5	5	6	9	12
Percentages near 50	3	4	5	5	6	9	13
Percentages near 60	3	4	5	5	6	9	12
Percentages near 70	3	4	5	5	6	8	12
Percentages near 80	3	3	4	4	5	7	10
Percentages near 90	2	2	3	3	4	5	8

Table A11.—Sampling errors (95 percent confidence level) for the difference in two percentages estimated from the Gallup Poll: 1992 and 1993

Size of sample	Size of sample					
	1,500	1000	750	600	400	200
	Recommended allowance for sampling error of a difference in percentages (percentages near 80 or 20)					
1,500	4					
1,000	4	5				
750	5	5	5			
600	5	5	6	6		
400	6	6	6	7	7	
200	8	8	8	8	9	10
	Recommended allowance for sampling error of a difference in percentages (percentages near 50)					
1,500	5					
1,000	5	6				
750	6	6	7			
600	6	7	7	7		
400	7	8	8	8	9	
200	10	10	10	10	11	13

Table A12.—Maximum differences required for significance (90 percent confidence level) between sample subgroups of the "Status of the American Public School Teacher" survey

Size of one subgroup	Size of other subgroup						
	100	200	300	400	500	600	700
100	11.6	10.1	9.5	9.2	9.0	8.9	8.8
200	10.1	8.2	7.5	7.1	6.9	6.7	6.6
300	9.5	7.5	6.7	6.3	6.0	5.8	5.7
400	9.2	7.1	6.3	5.8	5.5	5.3	5.2
500	9.0	6.9	6.0	5.5	5.2	5.0	4.8
600	8.9	6.7	5.8	5.3	5.0	4.7	4.6
700	8.8	6.6	5.7	5.2	4.8	4.6	4.4

Definitions

Academic support This category of college expenditures includes expenditures for support services that are an integral part of the institution's primary missions of instruction, research, or public service. Includes expenditures for libraries, galleries, audio/visual services, academic computing support, ancillary support, academic administration, personnel development, and course and curriculum development.

Achievement test An examination that measures the extent to which a person has acquired certain information or mastered certain skills, usually as a result of specific instruction.

Administrative support staff Includes personnel dealing with salary, benefits, supplies, and contractual fees for the office of the principal, full-time department chairpersons, and graduation expenses.

Agriculture Courses designed to improve competencies in agricultural occupations. Included is the study of agricultural production, supplies, mechanization and products, agricultural science, forestry, and related services.

American College Testing Program (ACT) The ACT assessment program measures educational development and readiness to pursue college-level coursework in English, mathematics, natural science, and social studies. Student performance on the tests does not reflect innate ability and is influenced by a student's educational preparedness.

Appropriation (federal funds) Budget authority provided through the congressional appropriation process that permits federal agencies to incur obligations and to make payments.

Appropriation (institutional revenues) An amount (other than a grant or contract) received from or made available to an institution through an act of a legislative body.

Associate degree A degree granted for the successful completion of a sub-baccalaureate program of studies, usually requiring at least 2 years (or equivalent) of full-time college-level study. This includes degrees granted in a cooperative or work-study program.

Auxiliary enterprises This category includes those essentially self-supporting operations which exist to furnish a service to students, faculty, or staff, and which charge a fee that is directly related to, although not necessarily equal to, the cost of the service. Examples are residence halls, food services, college stores, and intercollegiate athletics.

Average daily attendance (ADA) The aggregate attendance of a school during a reporting period (normally a school year) divided by the number of days school is in session during this period. Only days on which the pupils are under the guidance and direction of teachers should be considered days in session.

Average daily membership (ADM) The aggregate membership of a school during a reporting period (normally a school year) divided by the number of days school is in session during this period. Only days on which the pupils are under the guidance and direction of teachers should be considered as days in session. The average daily membership for groups of schools having varying lengths of terms is the average of the average daily memberships obtained for the individual schools.

Bachelor's degree A degree granted for the successful completion of a baccalaureate program of studies, usually requiring at least 4 years (or equivalent) of full-time college-level study. This includes degrees granted in a cooperative or work-study program.

Books Non-periodical printed publications bound in hard or soft covers, or in loose-leaf format, of at least 49 pages, exclusive of the cover pages; juvenile nonperiodical publications of any length found in hard or soft covers.

Budget authority (BA) Authority provided by law to enter into obligations that will result in immediate or future outlays. It may be classified by the period of availability (1-year, multiple-year, no-year), by the timing of congressional action (current or permanent), or by the manner of determining the amount available (definite or indefinite).

Business Program of instruction that prepares individuals for a variety of activities in planning, organizing, directing, and controlling business office systems and procedures.

Carnegie unit A standard of measurement that represents one credit for the completion of a 1-year course.

Catholic school A private school over which a Roman Catholic church group exercises some control or provides some form of subsidy. Catholic schools for the most part include those operated or supported by: a parish, a group of parishes, a diocese, or a Catholic religious order.

Central cities The largest cities, with 50,000 or more inhabitants, in a Metropolitan Statistical Area (MSA). A smaller city within a MSA may also qualify if it has at least 25,000 inhabitants or has a population of one-third or more of that of the largest city and a minimum population of 25,000. An exception occurs where two cities have contiguous boundaries and constitute, for economic and social purposes, a single community of at least 50,000, the smaller of which must have a population of at least 15,000.

Class size The membership of a class at a given date.

Classroom teacher A staff member assigned the professional activities of instructing pupils in self-contained classes or courses, or in classroom situations. Usually expressed in full-time equivalents.

Cohort A group of individuals that have a statistical factor in common, for example, year of birth.

College A postsecondary school which offers general or liberal arts education, usually leading to an associate, bachelor's, master's, doctor's, or first-professional degree. Junior colleges and community colleges are included under this terminology.

Combined elementary and secondary school A school which encompasses instruction at both the elementary and the secondary levels. Includes schools starting with grade 6 or below and ending with grade 9 or above.

Computer science A group of instructional programs that describes computer and information sciences, including computer programming, data processing, and information systems.

Constant dollars Dollar amounts that have been adjusted by means of price and cost indexes to eliminate inflationary factors and allow direct comparison across years.

Consumer, personal, and miscellaneous services A group of instructional programs that describes the fundamental skills a person is normally thought to need in order to function productively in society. Some examples are child development, consumer education, and family relations.

Consumer Price Index (CPI) This price index measures the average change in the cost of a fixed market basket of goods and services purchased by consumers.

Consumption That portion of income which is spent on the purchase of goods and services rather than being saved.

Control of institutions A classification of institutions of elementary/secondary or higher education by whether the institution is operated by publicly elected or appointed officials (public control) or by privately elected or appointed officials and derives its major source of funds from private sources (private control).

Credit The unit of value, awarded for the successful completion of certain courses, intended to indicate the quantity of course instruction in relation to the total requirements for a diploma, certificate, or degree. Credits are frequently expressed in terms such as "Carnegie units," "semester credit hours," and "quarter credit hours."

Current dollars Dollar amounts that have not been adjusted to compensate for inflation.

Current expenditures (elementary/secondary) The expenditures for operating local public schools, excluding capital outlay and interest on school debt. These expenditures include such items as salaries for school personnel, fixed charges, student transportation, school books and materials, and energy costs. Beginning in 1980–81, expenditures for State administration are excluded.

Current expenditures per pupil in average daily attendance Current expenditures for the regular school term divided by the average daily attendance of full-time pupils (or full-time equivalency of pupils) during the term. See also Current expenditures and Average daily attendance.

Current-fund expenditures (higher education) Money spent to meet current operating costs, including salaries, wages, utilities, student services, public services, research libraries, scholarships and fellowships, auxiliary enterprises, hospitals, and independent operations. Excludes loans, capital expenditures, and investments.

Current-fund revenues (higher education) Money received during the current fiscal year from revenue which can be used to pay obligations currently due, and surpluses reappropriated for the current fiscal year.

Current Population Survey See Guide to Sources.

Disposable personal income Current income received by persons less their contributions for social insurance, personal tax, and nontax payments. It is the income available to persons for spending and saving. Nontax payments include passport fees, fines and penalties, donations, and tuitions and fees paid to schools and hospitals operated mainly by the government. See also Personal income.

Doctor's degree An earned degree carrying the title of Doctor. The Doctor of Philosophy degree (Ph.D.) is the highest academic degree and requires mastery within a field of knowledge and demonstrated ability to perform scholarly research. Other doctorates are awarded for fulfilling specialized requirements in professional fields, such as education (Ed.D.), musical arts (D.M.A.), business administration (D.B.A.), and engineering (D.Eng. or D.E.S.). Many doctor's degrees in academic and professional fields require an earned master's degree as a prerequisite. First-professional degrees, such as M.D. and D.D.S., are not included under this heading.

Educational and general expenditures The sum of current funds expenditures on instruction, research, public service, academic support, student services, institutional support, operation and maintenance of plant, and awards from restricted and unrestricted funds.

Educational attainment The highest grade of regular school attended and completed.

Elementary education/programs Learning experiences concerned with the knowledge, skills, appreciations, attitudes, and behavioral characteristics which are considered to be needed by all pupils in terms of their awareness of life within our culture and the world of work, and which normally may be achieved during the elementary school years (usually kindergarten through grade 8 or kindergarten through grade 6), as defined by applicable state laws and regulations.

Elementary school A school classified as elementary by state and local practice and composed of any span of grades not above grade 8. A preschool or kindergarten school is included under this heading only if it is an integral part of an elementary school or a regularly established school system.

Elementary/secondary school As reported in this publication, includes only regular schools (i.e., schools that are part of State and local school systems, and also most not-for-profit private elementary/secondary schools, both religiously affiliated and nonsectarian). Schools not reported include subcollegiate departments of institutions of higher education, residential schools for exceptional children, Federal schools for American Indians, and Federal schools on military posts and other Federal installations.

Employment Includes civilian, noninstitutional persons who: 1) worked during any part of the survey week as paid employees; worked in their own business, profession, or farm; or worked 15 hours or more as unpaid workers in a family-owned enterprise; or 2) were not working but had jobs or businesses from which they were temporarily absent due to illness, bad weather, vacation, labor-management dispute, or personal reasons whether or not they were seeking another job.

Endowment A trust fund set aside to provide a perpetual source of revenue from the proceeds of the endowment investments. Endowment funds are often created by donations from benefactors of an institution, who may designate the use of the endowment revenue. Normally, institutions or their representatives manage the investments, but they are not permitted to spend the endowment fund itself, only the proceeds from the investments. Typical uses of endowments would be an endowed chair for a particular department or for a scholarship fund. Endowment totals tabulated in this book also include funds functioning as endowments, such as funds left over from the previous year and placed with the endowment investments by the institution. These funds may be withdrawn by the institution and spent as current funds at any time. Endowments are evaluated by two different measures, book value and market value. Book value is the purchase price of the endowment investment. Market value is the current worth of the endowment investment. Thus, the book value of a stock held in an endowment fund would be the purchase price of the stock. The market value of the stock would be its selling price as of a given day.

Engineering Instructional programs that describe the mathematical and natural science knowledge gained by study, experience, and practice and applied with judgment to develop ways to utilize the materials and forces of nature economically for the benefit of mankind. Include programs that prepare individuals to support and assist engineers and similar professionals.

English A group of instructional programs that describes the English language arts, including composition, creative writing, and the study of literature.

Enrollment The total number of students registered in a given school unit at a given time, generally in the fall of a year.

Expenditures Charges incurred, whether paid or unpaid, which are presumed to benefit the current fiscal year. For elementary/secondary schools, these include all charges for current outlays plus capital outlays and interest on school debt. For institutions of higher education, these include current outlays plus capital outlays. For government, these include charges net of recoveries and other correcting transactions other than for retirement of debt, investment in securities, extension of credit, or as agency transaction. Government expenditures include only external transactions, such as the provision of perquisites or other payments in kind. Aggregates for groups of governments exclude intergovernmental transactions among the governments.

Expenditures per pupil Charges incurred for a particular period of time divided by a student unit of measure, such as average daily attendance or average daily membership.

Extracurricular activities Activities that are not part of the required curriculum and that take place outside of the regular course of study. As used here, they include both school-sponsored (e.g., varsity athletics, drama and debate clubs) and community-sponsored (e.g., hobby clubs and youth organizations like the Junior Chamber of Commerce or Boy Scouts) activities.

Family A group of two persons or more (one of whom is the householder) related by birth, marriage, or adoption and residing together. All such persons (including related subfamily members) are considered as members of one family.

Federal funds Amounts collected and used by the federal government for the general purposes of the government. There are four types of federal fund accounts: the general fund, special funds, public enterprise funds, and intragovernmental funds. The major federal fund is the general fund, which is derived from general taxes and borrowing. Federal funds also include certain earmarked collections, such as those generated by and used to finance a continuing cycle of business-type operations.

Federal sources Includes federal appropriations, grants, and contracts, and federally-funded research and development centers (FFRDCs). Federally subsidized student loans and Pell Grants are not included.

First-professional degree A degree that signifies both completion of the academic requirements for beginning practice in a given profession and a level of professional skill beyond that normally required for a bachelor's degree. This degree usually is based on a program requiring at least 2 academic years of work prior to entrance and a total of at least 6 academic years of work to complete the degree program, including both prior-required college work and the professional program itself. By NCES definition, first-professional degrees are awarded in the fields of dentistry (D.D.S. or D.M.D.), medicine (M.D.), optometry (O.D.), osteopathic medicine (D.O.), pharmacy (D.Phar.), podiatric medicine (D.P.M.), veterinary medicine (D.V.M.), chiropractic (D.C. or D.C.M.), law (J.D.), and theological professions (M.Div. or M.H.L.).

First-professional enrollment The number of students enrolled in a professional school or program which requires at least 2 years of academic college work for entrance and a total of at least 6 years for a degree. By NCES definition, first-professional enrollment includes only students in certain programs. (See First-professional degree for a list of programs.)

Fiscal year The yearly accounting period for the Federal Government, which begins on October 1 and ends on the following September 30. The fiscal year is designated by the calendar year in which it ends; e.g., fiscal year 1988 begins on October 1, 1987, and ends on September 30, 1988. (From fiscal year 1844 to fiscal year 1976, the fiscal year began on July 1 and ended on the following June 30.)

Foreign languages A group of instructional programs that describes the structure and use of language that is common or indigenous to people of the same community or nation, the same geographical area, or the same cultural traditions. Programs cover such features as sound, literature, syntax, phonology, semantics, sentences, prose, and verse, as well as the development of skills and attitudes used in communicating and evaluating thoughts and feelings through oral and written language.

Full-time enrollment The number of students enrolled in higher education courses with total credit load equal to at least 75 percent of the normal full-time course load.

Full-time-equivalent (FTE) enrollment For institutions of higher education, enrollment of full-time students, plus the full-time equivalent of part-time students. The full-time equivalent of the part-time students is estimated using different factors depending on the type and control of institution and level of student.

Full-time instructional faculty Those members of the instruction/research staff who are employed full time as defined by the institution, including faculty with released time for research and faculty on sabbatical leave. Full-time counts exclude faculty who are employed to teach less than two semesters, three quarters, two trimesters, or two 4-month sessions; replacements for faculty on sabbatical leave or those on leave without pay; faculty for preclinical and clinical medicine; faculty who are donating their services; faculty who are members of military organizations and paid on a different pay scale from civilian employees; academic officers, whose primary duties are administrative; and graduate students who assist in the instruction of courses.

Full-time worker In educational institutions, an employee whose position requires being on the job on school days throughout the school year at least the number of hours the schools are in session. For higher education, a member of an educational institution's staff who is employed full time.

General administration support services Includes salary, benefits, supplies, and contractual fees for boards of education staff and executive administration. Excludes state administration.

General Educational Development (GED) program Academic instruction to prepare persons to take the high school equivalency examination. See GED recipient.

GED recipient A person who has obtained certification of high school equivalency by meeting State requirements and passing an approved exam, which is intended to provide an appraisal of the person's achievement or performance in the broad subject matter areas usually required for high school graduation.

General program A program of studies designed to prepare students for the common activities of a citizen, family member, and worker. A general program of studies may include instruction in both academic and vocational areas.

Geographic region 1) One of four regions used by the Bureau of Economic Analysis of the U.S. Department of Commerce, the National Assessment of Educational Progress, and the National Education Association, as follows: (The National Education Association designated the Central region as Middle region in its classification.)

Northeast	**Southeast**
Connecticut	Alabama
Delaware	Arkansas
District of Columbia	Florida
Maine	Georgia
Maryland	Kentucky
Massachusetts	Louisiana
New Hampshire	Mississippi
New Jersey	North Carolina
New York	South Carolina
Pennsylvania	Tennessee
Rhode Island	Virginia
Vermont	West Virginia

Central (Middle)	**West**
Illinois	Alaska
Indiana	Arizona
Iowa	California
Kansas	Colorado
Michigan	Hawaii
Minnesota	Idaho
Missouri	Montana
Nebraska	Nevada
North Dakota	New Mexico
Ohio	Oklahoma
South Dakota	Oregon
Wisconsin	Texas
	Utah
	Washington
	Wyoming

2) One of the regions or divisions used by the U.S. Bureau of the Census in Current Population Survey tabulations, as follows:

Northeast	**Midwest**
(New England)	*(East North Central)*
Maine	Ohio
New Hampshire	Indiana
Vermont	Illinois
Massachusetts	Michigan
Rhode Island	Wisconsin
Connecticut	
(Middle Atlantic)	*(West North Central)*
New York	Minnesota
New Jersey	Iowa
Pennsylvania	Missouri
	North Dakota
	South Dakota
	Nebraska
	Kansas

South	**West**
(South Atlantic)	*(Mountain)*
Delaware	Montana
Maryland	Idaho
District of Columbia	Wyoming
Virginia	Colorado
West Virginia	New Mexico
North Carolina	Arizona
South Carolina	Utah
Georgia	Nevada
Florida	
(East South Central)	*(Pacific)*
Kentucky	Washington

Tennessee
Alabama
Mississippi

Oregon
California
Alaska
Hawaii

(West South Central)
Arkansas
Louisiana
Oklahoma
Texas

Government appropriation An amount (other than a grant or contract) received from or made available to an institution through an act of a legislative body.

Government grant or contract Revenues from a government agency for a specific research project or other program.

Graduate An individual who has received formal recognition for the successful completion of a prescribed program of studies.

Graduate enrollment The number of students who hold the bachelor's or first-professional degree, or the equivalent, and who are working towards a master's or doctor's degree. First-professional students are counted separately. These enrollment data measure those students who are registered at a particular time during the fall. At some institutions, graduate enrollment also includes students who are in postbaccalaureate classes but not in degree programs. In specified tables, graduate enrollment includes all students in regular graduate programs and all students in postbaccalaureate classes but not in degree programs (unclassified postbaccalaureate students).

Graduate Record Examination (GRE) Multiple-choice examinations administered by the Educational Testing Service and taken by college students who are intending to attend certain graduate schools. The tests are offered in a variety of subject areas. Ordinarily, a student will take only the exam that applies to the intended field of study.

Graduation Formal recognition given an individual for the successful completion of a prescribed program of studies.

Gross domestic product (GDP) The total national output of goods and services valued at market prices. GDP can be viewed in terms of expenditure categories which include purchases of goods and services by consumers and government, gross private domestic investment, and net exports of goods and services. The goods and services included are largely those bought for final use (excluding illegal transactions) in the market economy. A number of inclusions, however, represent imputed values, the most important of which is rental value of owner-occupied housing. GDP, in this broad context, measures the output attributable to the factors of production—labor and property—supplied by U.S. residents.

Handicapped Those children evaluated as having any of the following impairments, who because of these impairments need special education and related services. (These definitions apply specifically to data from the U.S. Office of Special Education and Rehabilitative Services presented in this publication.)

Deaf Having a hearing impairment which is so severe that the student is impaired in processing linguistic information through hearing (with or without amplification) and which adversely affects educational performance.

Deaf-blind Having concomitant hearing and visual impairments which cause such severe communication and other developmental and educational problems that the student cannot be accommodated in special education programs solely for deaf or blind students.

Hard of hearing Having a hearing impairment, whether permanent or fluctuating, which adversely affects the student's educational performance, but which is not included under the definition of "deaf" in this section.

Mentally retarded Having significantly subaverage general intellectual functioning, existing concurrently with defects in adaptive behavior and manifested during the developmental period, which adversely affects the child's educational performance.

Multihandicapped Having concomitant impairments (such as mentally retarded-blind, mentally retarded-orthopedically impaired, etc.), the combination of which causes such severe educational problems that the student cannot be accommodated in special education programs solely for one of the impairments. Term does not include deaf-blind students but does include those students who are severely or profoundly mentally retarded.

Orthopedically impaired Having a severe orthopedic impairment which adversely affects a student's educational performance. The term includes impairment resulting from congenital anomaly, disease, or other causes.

Other health impaired Having limited strength, vitality, or alertness due to chronic or acute health problems such as a heart condition, tuberculosis, rheumatic fever, nephritis, asthma, sickle cell anemia, hemophilia, epilepsy, lead poisoning, leukemia, or diabetes which adversely affects the student's educational performance.

Seriously emotionally disturbed Exhibiting one or more of the following characteristics over a long period of time, to a marked degree, and adversely affecting educational performance: an inability to learn which cannot be explained by intellectual, sensory, or health factors; an inability to build or maintain satisfactory interpersonal relationships with peers and teachers; inappropriate types of behavior or feelings under normal circumstances; a general pervasive mood of unhappiness or depression; or a tendency to develop physical symptoms or fears associated with personal or school problems. This term does not include children who are socially maladjusted, unless they also display one or more of the listed characteristics.

Specific learning disabled Having a disorder in one or more of the basic psychological processes involved in understanding or in using spoken or written language, which may manifest itself in an imperfect ability to listen, think, speak, read, write, spell, or do mathematical calculations. The term includes such conditions as perceptual handicaps, brain injury, minimal brain dysfunction, dyslexia, and developmental aphasia. The term does not include children who have learning problems which are primarily the result of visual, hearing, or environmental, cultural, or economic disadvantage.

Speech impaired Having a communication disorder, such as stuttering, impaired articulation, language impairment, or voice impairment, which adversely affects the student's educational performance.

Visually handicapped Having a visual impairment which, even with correction, adversely affects the student's educational performance. The term includes partially seeing and blind children.

Higher education Study beyond secondary school at an institution that offers programs terminating in an associate, baccalaureate, or higher degree.

Higher education institutions (alternative classification)

Doctoral-granting Characterized by a significant level and breadth of activity in commitment to doctoral-level education as measured by the number of doctorate recipients and the diversity in doctoral-level program offerings.

Comprehensive Characterized by diverse postbaccalaureate programs (including first-professional) but not engaged in significant doctoral-level education.

General baccalaureate Characterized by primary emphasis on general undergraduate, baccalaureate-level education. Not significantly engaged in postbaccalaureate education.

Specialized Baccalaureate or postbaccalaureate institution emphasizing one area (plus closely related specialties), such as business or engineering. The programmatic emphasis is measured by the percentage of degrees granted in the program area.

2-year Conferring at least 75 percent of its degrees and awards for work below the bachelor's level.

New These institutions, though not necessarily newly organized, are new additions to the Higher Education General Information Survey universe. When degree and award data become available, they will be reclassified.

Non-degree-granting Offering undergraduate or graduate study but not conferring degrees or awards. In this volume, these institutions are included under Specialized.

Higher education institutions (traditional classification)

4-year institution An institution legally authorized to offer and offering at least a 4-year program of college-level studies wholly or principally creditable toward a baccalaureate degree. In some tables, a further division between universities and other 4-year institutions is made. A "university" is a postsecondary institution which typically comprises one or more graduate professional schools (also see University). For purposes of trend comparisons in this volume, the selection of universities has been held constant for all tabulations after 1982. "Other 4-year institutions" would include the rest of the nonuniversity 4-year institutions.

2-year institution An institution legally authorized to offer and offering at least a 2-year program of college-level studies which terminates in an associate degree or is principally creditable toward a baccalaureate degree. Also includes some institutions that have a less than 2-year program, but were designated as institutions of higher education in the Higher Education General Information Survey.

Higher Education Price Index A price index which measures average changes in the prices of goods and services purchased by colleges and universities through current-fund education and general expenditures (excluding expenditures for sponsored research and auxiliary enterprises).

High school A secondary school offering the final years of high school work necessary for graduation, usually including grades 10, 11, 12 (in a 6–3–3 plan) or grades 9, 10, 11, and 12 (in a 6–2–4 plan).

High school program A program of studies designed to prepare students for their postsecondary education and occupation. Three types of programs are usually distinguished—academic, vocational, and general. An academic program is designed to prepare students for continued study at a college or university. A vocational program is designed to prepare students for employment in one or more semiskilled, skilled, or technical occupations. A general program is designed to provide students with the understanding and competence to function effectively in a free society and usually represents a mixture of academic and vocational components.

Historically black colleges and universities Accredited institutions of higher education established prior to 1964 with the principal mission of educating black Americans. Federal regulations (20 USC 1061 (2)) allow for certain exceptions of the founding date.

Household All the persons who occupy a housing unit. A house, apartment, or other group of rooms, or a single room, is regarded as a housing unit when it is occupied or intended for occupancy as separate living quarters, that is, when the occupants do not live and eat with any other persons in the structure, and there is direct access from the outside or through a common hall.

Housing unit A house, an apartment, a mobile home, a group of rooms, or a single room that is occupied as separate living quarters.

Imaginative writing This type of writing can take a variety of forms, such as stories, poems, plays, or lyrics. It represents a special approach to sharing experiences and understanding the world and ourselves. In this form of writing, special attention is given to rhythm and tone; the use of anecdote; the presence of metaphor and simile; shifts in plots; and the unexpected use of words, phrases, or punctuation.

Income tax Taxes levied on net income, that is, on gross income less certain deductions permitted by law. These taxes can be levied on individuals or on corporations or unincorporated businesses where the income is taxed distinctly from individual income.

Independent operations A group of self-supporting activities under control of a college or university. For purposes of financial surveys conducted by the National Center for Education Statistics, this category is composed principally of Federally Funded Research and Development Centers (FFRDC).

Informative writing This type of writing is used to share information and to convey messages, directions, and ideas. It often involves reporting or retelling events or experiences that have already occurred.

Institutional support The category of higher education expenditures that includes day-to-day operational support for colleges, excluding expenditures for physical plant operations. Examples of institutional support include general administrative services, executive direction and planning, legal and fiscal operations, and community relations.

Instruction That category including expenditures of the colleges, schools, departments, and other instructional divisions of higher education institutions and expenditures for departmental research and public service which are not separately budgeted. Includes expenditures for both credit and noncredit activities. Excludes expenditures for academic administration where the primary function is administration (e.g., academic deans).

Instruction (elementary and secondary) Instruction encompasses all activities dealing directly with the interaction between teachers and students. Teaching may be provided for students in a school classroom, in another location such as a home or hospital, and in other learning situations such as those involving co-curricular activities. Instruction may be provided through some other approved medium such as television, radio, telephone, and correspondence. Instruction expenditures include: salaries, employee benefits, purchased services, supplies, and tuition to private schools.

Instructional staff Full-time-equivalent number of positions, not the number of different individuals occupying the positions during the school year. In local schools, includes all public elementary and secondary (junior and senior high) day-school positions that are in the nature of teaching or in the improvement of the teaching-learning situation. Includes consultants or supervisors of instruction, principals, teachers, guidance personnel, librarians, psychological personnel, and other instructional staff. Excludes administrative staff, attendance personnel, clerical personnel, and junior college staff.

Instructional support services Includes salary, benefits, supplies, and contractual fees for staff providing instructional improvement, educational media (library and audiovisual), and other instructional support services.

Junior high school A separately organized and administered secondary school intermediate between the elementary and senior high schools, usually including grades 7, 8, and 9 (in a 6–3–3 plan) or grades 7 and 8 (in a 6–2–4 plan).

Labor force Persons employed as civilians, unemployed (but looking for work), or in the armed services during the survey week. The "civilian labor force" comprises all civilians classified as employed or unemployed.

Land-grant colleges The First Morrill Act of 1862 facilitated the establishment of colleges through grants of land or funds in lieu of land. The Second Morrill Act in 1890 provided for money grants and for the establishment of black land-grant colleges and universities in those states with dual systems of higher education.

Local education agency See School district.

Mandatory transfer A transfer of current funds that must be made in order to fulfill a binding legal obligation of the institution. Included under mandatory transfers are debt service provisions relating to academic and administrative buildings, including (1) amounts set aside for debt retirement and interest and (2) required provisions for renewal and replacement of buildings to the extent these are not financed from other funds.

Master's degree A degree awarded for successful completion of a program generally requiring 1 or 2 years of full-time college-level study beyond the bachelor's degree. One type of master's degree, including the Master of Arts degree, or M.A., and the Master of Science degree, or M.S., is awarded in the liberal arts and sciences for advanced scholarship in a subject field or discipline and demonstrated ability to perform scholarly research. A second type of master's degree is awarded for the completion of a professionally oriented program, for example, an M.Ed. in education, an M.B.A. in business administration, an M.F.A. in fine arts, an M.M. in music, an M.S.W. in social work, and an M.P.A. in public administration. A third type of master's degree is awarded in professional fields for study beyond the first-professional degree, for example, the Master of Laws (L.L.M.) and Master of Science in various medical specializations.

Mathematics A group of instructional programs that describes the science of numbers and their operations, interrelations, combinations, generalizations, and abstractions and of space configurations and their structure, measurement, transformations, and generalizations.

Mean test score The score obtained by dividing the sum of the scores of all individuals in a group by the number of individuals in that group.

Metropolitan population The population residing in Metropolitan Statistical Areas (MSAs). See Metropolitan Statistical Area.

Metropolitan Statistical Area (MSA) A large population nucleus and the nearby communities which have a high degree of economic and social integration with that nucleus. Each MSA consists of one or more entire counties (or county equivalents) that meet specified standards pertaining to population, commuting ties, and metropolitan character. In New England, towns and cities, rather than counties, are the basic units. MSAs are designated by the Office of Management and Budget. An MSA includes a city and, generally, its entire urban area and the remainder of the county or counties in which the urban area is located. An MSA also includes such additional outlying counties which meet specified criteria relating to metropolitan character and level of commuting of workers into the central city or counties. Specified criteria governing the definition of MSAs recognized before 1980 are published in Standard Metropolitan Statistical Areas: 1975, issued by the Office of Management and Budget. New MSAs were designated when 1980 counts showed that they met one or both of the following criteria:

1. Included a city with a population of at least 50,000 within their corporate limits, or

2. Included a Census Bureau-defined urbanized area (which must have a population of at least 50,000) and a total MSA population of at least 100,000 (or, in New England, 75,000).

Migration Geographic mobility involving a change of usual residence between clearly defined geographic units, that is, between counties, States, or regions.

Minimum-competency testing Measuring the acquisition of competence or skills to or beyond a certain specified standard.

National Assessment of Educational Progress (NAEP) See Guide to Sources.

Newly qualified teacher Persons who: 1) first became eligible for a teaching license during the period of the study referenced or who were teaching at the time of survey but were not certified or eligible for a teaching license; and 2) had never held full-time, regular teaching positions (as opposed to substitute) prior to completing the requirements for the degree which brought them into the survey.

Nonmetropolitan residence group The population residing outside Metropolitan Statistical Areas. See Metropolitan Statistical Area.

Nonresident alien A person who is not a citizen of the United States and who is in this country on a temporary basis and does not have the right to remain indefinitely.

Nonsupervisory instructional staff Persons such as curriculum specialists, counselors, librarians, remedial specialists, and others possessing education certification but not responsible for day-to-day teaching of the same group of pupils.

Normal school A normal school was an institution which was engaged primarily in the preparation of teachers for positions in elementary and secondary schools. Prior to 1900, normal schools were often secondary schools with teacher training programs. During the early 20th century, normal schools gradually developed into higher education institutions.

Obligations Amounts of orders placed, contracts awarded, services received, or similar legally binding commitments made by Federal agencies during a given period that will require outlays during the same or some future period.

Occupational home economics Courses of instruction emphasizing the acquisition of competencies needed for getting and holding a job or preparing for advancement in an occupational area using home economics knowledge and skills.

Occupied housing unit Separate living quarters with occupants currently inhabiting the unit.

Off-Budget Federal entities Organizational entities, federally owned in whole or in part, whose transactions belong in the budget under current budget accounting concepts but that have been excluded from the budget totals under provisions of law.

Operation and maintenance services Includes salary, benefits, supplies, and contractual fees for supervision of operations and maintenance, operating buildings (heating, lighting, ventilating, repair, and replacement), care and upkeep of grounds and equipment, vehicle operations and maintenance (other than student transportation), security, and other operations and maintenance services.

Other foreign languages and literatures Any instructional program in foreign languages and literatures not described in tables 239 and 240, including language groups and individual languages such as the non-Semitic African languages, Native American languages, the Celtic languages, Pacific language groups, the Ural-Altaic languages, Basque, and others.

Other support services Includes salary, benefits, supplies, and contractual fees for business support services, central support services, other support services not otherwise classified.

Other support services staff All staff not reported in other categories. This group includes media personnel, social workers, bus drivers, security, cafeteria workers, and other staff.

Outlays The value of checks issued, interest accrued on the public debt, or other payments made, net of refunds and reimbursements.

Part-time enrollment The number of students enrolled in higher education courses with a total credit load less than 75 percent of the normal full-time credit load.

Per capita income The mean income computed for every man, woman, and child in a particular group. It is derived by dividing the total income of a particular group by the total population in that group.

Personal income Current income received by persons from all sources minus their personal contributions for social insurance. Classified as "persons" are individuals (including owners of unincorporated firms), nonprofit institutions serving individuals, private trust funds, and private noninsured welfare funds. Personal income includes transfers (payments not resulting from current production) from government and business such as social security benefits and military pensions but excludes transfers among persons.

Persuasive writing This type of writing attempts to bring about some action or change. Its primary purpose is to influence others. It is concerned with the positions, beliefs, and attitudes of the readers.

Physical plant assets Includes the values of land, buildings, and equipment owned, rented, or utilized by colleges. Does not include those plant values which are a part of endowment or other capital fund investments in real estate. Excludes construction in progress.

Postbaccalaureate enrollment The number of graduate and first-professional students working towards advanced degrees and of students enrolled in graduate-level classes but not enrolled in degree programs. See also Graduate enrollment and First-professional enrollment.

Postsecondary education The provision of formal instructional programs with a curriculum designed primarily for students who have completed the requirements for a high school diploma or equivalent. This includes programs of an academic, vocational, and continuing professional education purpose, and excludes avocational and adult basic education programs.

Private school or institution A school or institution which is controlled by an individual or agency other than a State, a subdivision of a State, or the Federal Government, which is usually supported primarily by other than public funds, and the operation of whose program rests with other than publicly elected or appointed officials.

Property tax The sum of money collected from a tax levied against the value of property.

Proprietary institution An educational institution that is under private control but whose profits derive from revenues subject to taxation.

Public school or institution A school or institution controlled and operated by publicly elected or appointed officials and deriving its primary support from public funds.

Pupil-teacher ratio The enrollment of pupils at a given period of time, divided by the full-time-equivalent number of classroom teachers serving these pupils during the same period.

Racial/ethnic group Classification indicating general racial or ethnic heritage based on self-identification, as in data collected by the Bureau of the Census or on observer identification, as in data collected by the Office for Civil Rights. These categories are in accordance with the Office of Management and Budget standard classification scheme presented below:

White A person having origins in any of the original peoples of Europe, North Africa, or the Middle East. Normally excludes persons of Hispanic origin except for tabulations produced by the Bureau of the Census, which are noted accordingly in this volume.

Black A person having origins in any of the black racial groups in Africa. Normally excludes persons of Hispanic origin except for tabulations produced by the Bureau of the Census, which are noted accordingly in this volume.

Hispanic A person of Mexican, Puerto Rican, Cuban, Central or South American, or other Spanish culture or origin, regardless of race.

Asian or Pacific Islander A person having origins in any of the original peoples of the Far East, Southeast Asia, the Indian subcontinent, or the Pacific Islands. This area includes, for example, China, India, Japan, Korea, the Philippine Islands, and Samoa.

American Indian or Alaskan Native A person having origins in any of the original peoples of North America and maintaining cultural identification through tribal affiliation or community recognition.

Remedial education Instruction for a student lacking those reading, writing, or math skills necessary to perform college-level work at the level required by the attended institution.

Resident population Includes civilian population and armed forces personnel residing within the United States. Excludes armed forces personnel residing overseas.

Revenue All funds received from external sources, net of refunds, and correcting transactions. Noncash transactions such as receipt of services, commodities, or other receipts "in kind" are excluded as are funds received from the issuance of debt, liquidation of investments, and nonroutine sale of property.

Salary The total amount regularly paid or stipulated to be paid to an individual, before deductions, for personal services rendered while on the payroll of a business or organization.

Sales and services Revenues derived from the sales of goods or services that are incidental to the conduct of instruction, research, or public service. Examples include film rentals, scientific and literary publications, testing services, university presses, and dairy products.

Sales tax Tax imposed upon the sale and consumption of goods and services. It can be imposed either as a general tax on the retail price of all goods and services sold or as a tax on the sale of selected goods and services.

Scholarships and fellowships This category of college expenditures applies only to money given in the form of outright grants and trainee stipends to individuals enrolled in formal coursework, either for credit or not. Aid to students in the form of tuition or fee remissions is included. College Work-Study funds are excluded and are reported under the program in which the student is working. In the tabulations in this volume, Pell Grants are not included in this expenditure category.

Scholastic Aptitude Test (SAT) An examination administered by the Educational Testing Service and used to predict the facility with which an individual will progress in learning college-level academic subjects.

School A division of the school system consisting of students in one or more grades or other identifiable groups and organized to give instruction of a defined type. One school may share a building with another school or one school may be housed in several buildings.

School administration support services Includes salary, benefits, supplies, and contractual fees for the office of the principal, full-time department chairpersons, and graduation expenses.

School climate The social system and culture of the school, including the organizational structure of the school and values and expectations within it.

School district An education agency at the local level that exists primarily to operate public schools or to contract for public school services. Synonyms are "local basic administrative unit" and "local education agency."

Science The body of related courses concerned with knowledge of the physical and biological world and with the processes of discovering and validating this knowledge.

Secondary instructional level The general level of instruction provided for pupils in secondary schools (generally covering grades 7 through 12 or 9 through 12) and any instruction of a comparable nature and difficulty provided for adults and youth beyond the age of compulsory school attendance.

Secondary school A school comprising any span of grades beginning with the next grade following an elementary or middle-school (usually 7, 8, or 9) and ending with or below grade 12. Both junior high schools and senior high schools are included.

Secondary enrollment The total number of students registered in a school beginning with the next grade following an elementary or midde-school (usually 7, 8, or 9) and ending with or below grade 12 at a given time.

Senior high school A secondary school offering the final years of high school work necessary for graduation.

Serial volumes Publications issued in successive parts, usually at regular intervals, and as a rule, intended to be continued indefinitely. Serials include periodicals, newspapers, annuals, memoirs, proceedings, and transactions of societies.

Social studies A group of instructional programs that describes the substantive portions of behavior, past and present activities, interactions, and organizations of people associated together for religious, benevolent, cultural, scientific, political, patriotic, or other purposes.

Socioeconomic status (SES) For the High School and Beyond study and the National Longitudinal Study of the High School Class of 1972, the SES index is a composite of five equally weighted, standardized components: father's education, mother's education, family income, father's occupation, and household items. The terms high, middle, and low SES refer to the upper, middle two, and lower quartiles of the weighted SES composite index distribution.

Special education Direct instructional activities or special learning experiences designed primarily for students identified as having exceptionalities in one or more aspects of the cognitive process or as being underachievers in relation to general level or model of their overall abilities. Such services usually are directed at students with the following conditions: (1) physically handicapped; (2) emotionally handicapped; (3) culturally different, including compensatory education; (4) mentally retarded; and (5) students with learning disabilities. Programs for the mentally gifted and talented are also included in some special education programs. See also Handicapped.

Standardized test A test composed of a systematic sampling of behavior, administered and scored according to specific instructions, capable of being interpreted in terms of adequate norms, and for which there are data on reliability and validity.

Standardized test performance The weighted distributions of composite scores from standardized tests used to group students according to performance.

Standard Metropolitan Statistical Area (SMSA) See Metropolitan Statistical Area (MSA).

Student An individual for whom instruction is provided in an educational program under the jurisdiction of a school, school system, or other education institution. No distinction is made between the terms "student" and "pupil," though "student" may refer to one receiving instruction at any level while "pupil" refers only to one attending school at the elementary or secondary level. A student may receive instruction in a school facility or in another location, such as at home or in a hospital. Instruction may be provided by direct student-teacher interaction or by some other approved medium such as television, radio, telephone, and correspondence.

Student support services Includes salary, benefits, supplies, and contractual fees for staff providing attendance and social work, guidance, health, psychological services, speech pathology, audiology, and other support to students.

Subject-matter club Organizations that are formed around a shared interest in a particular area of study and whose primary activities promote that interest. Examples of such organizations are math, science, business, and history clubs.

Supervisory staff Principals, assistant principals, and supervisors of instruction. Does not include superintendents or assistant superintendents.

Tax base The collective value of objects, assets, and income components against which a tax is levied.

Tax expenditures Losses of tax revenue attributable to provisions of the Federal income tax laws that allow a special exclusion, exemption, or deduction from gross income or provide a special credit, preferential rate of tax, or a deferral of tax liability affecting individual or corporate income tax liabilities.

Technical education A program of vocational instruction that ordinarily includes the study of the sciences and mathematics underlying a technology, as well as the methods, skills, and materials commonly used and the services performed in the technology. Technical education prepares individuals for positions—such as draftsman or lab technician—in the occupational area between the skilled craftsman and the professional person.

Total expenditure per pupil in average daily attendance Includes all expenditures allocable to per pupil costs divided by average daily attendance. These allocable expenditures include current expenditures for regular school programs, interest on school debt, and capital outlay. Beginning in 1980–81, expenditures for State administration are excluded and expenditures for other programs (summer schools, community colleges, and private schools) are included.

Trade and industrial occupations The branch of vocational education which is concerned with preparing persons for initial employment or with updating or retraining workers in a wide range of trade and industrial occupations. Such occupations are skilled or semiskilled and are concerned with layout designing, producing, processing, assembling, testing, maintaining, servicing, or repairing any product or commodity.

Transcript An official list of all courses taken by a student at a school or college showing the final grade received for each course, with definitions of the various grades given at the institution.

Trust funds Amounts collected and used by the Federal Government for carrying out specific purposes and programs according to terms of a trust agreement or statute, such as the social security and unemployment trust funds. Trust fund receipts that are not anticipated to be used in the immediate future are generally invested in interest-bearing Government securities and earn interest for the trust fund.

Tuition and fees A payment or charge for instruction or compensation for services, privileges, or the use of equipment, books, or other goods.

Unclassified students Students who are not candidates for a degree or other formal award, although they are taking higher education courses for credit in regular classes with other students.

Unadjusted dollars See **current dollars.**

Undergraduate students Students registered at an institution of higher education who are working in a program leading to a baccalaureate degree or other formal award below the baccalaureate, such as an associate degree.

Unemployed Civilians who had no employment but were available for work and: 1) had engaged in any specific jobseeking activity within the past 4 weeks; 2) were waiting to be called back to a job from which they had been laid off; or 3) were waiting to report to a new wage or salary job within 30 days.

U.S. Service Schools These institutions of higher education are controlled by the U.S. Department of Defense and the U.S. Department of Transportation. The ten institutions counted in the NCES surveys of higher education institutions include: the Air Force Institute of Technology, Community College of the Air Force, Naval Postgraduate School, Uniformed Services University of the Health Sciences, U.S. Air Force Academy, U.S Army Command And General Staff College, U.S. Coast Guard Academy, U.S. Merchant Marine Academy, U.S. Military Academy, and the U.S. Naval Academy.

University An institution of higher education consisting of a liberal arts college, a diverse graduate program, and usually two or more professional schools or faculties and empowered to confer degrees in various fields of study. For purposes of maintaining trend data in this publication, the selection of university institutions has not been revised since 1982.

Visual and performing arts A group of instructional programs that generally describes the historic development, aesthetic qualities, and creative processes of the visual and performing arts.

Vocational education Organized educational programs, services, and activities which are directly related to the preparation of individuals for paid or unpaid employment, or for additional preparation for a career, requiring other than a baccalaureate or advanced degree.

Vocational home economics Vocational courses of instruction emphasizing the acquisition of competencies needed for getting and holding a job or preparing for advancement in an occupational area using home economics knowledge or skills.

Index of Table Numbers

A

Academic programs in high school, 135–139, 136, 147
Accounting, degrees conferred, 247–249, 253, 254
Achievement tests. See Assessment
Activities
    elementary school, 143
    college faculty, 228, 229
    high school, 144, 146, 147
    kindergarten, 50, 143
    young adults, 387
Additions to plant value, higher education, 350
Administration expenditures
    elementary and secondary schools, 161–163, 166, 167
    institutions of higher education, 334, 335, 337–339, 341–345, 349
Administrative units (school districts), 89–93
Adult basic education, 355
Adult education participants in, 353, 354
Adult and vocational education, 213, 247–249, 353, 354, 356
    Federal funds for, 359, 361, 363, 364
Affiliation, religious
    elementary and secondary schools, 59–62, 140–142, 144–146
    institutions of higher education, 179
Age
    enrollment, 6, 7
    for compulsory school attendance, 152
    of college students, 174–176, 186, 211–213
Agriculture
    degrees conferred, 10, 247–254, 256–259, 263, 264, 266, 267, 269, 270, 272, 273, 277
    enrollment, higher education, 213, 214
    faculty in higher education, 231–233
    formal awards, organized occupational curricula, 247–249
    units earned by high school graduates, 137
Alcohol use by students or adults, 148–151, 373
All levels of education, 1–38
American Indians
    activities, 144–146
    attendance patterns, 153
    attitudes about schools, 142, 154
    courses taken by high school students, 136–140
    degrees conferred, 262–276, 299–305, 307
    educational attainment, 12
    enrolled in colleges and universities, 206–211, 315
    enrolled in public schools, 45
    expected occupations, 141
    financial aid, 315
    high school program, 135
    testing, 111, 115, 127, 128
Annual expenditure per pupil, public schools, 39, 88, 92, 168, 169, 408
Annual salary. See Salaries.
Applications, college, 185
Applied research funds, 334, 335, 337–339, 341–345, 349, 357, 367, 368
Architecture
    degrees conferred, 247–252, 256–259, 263, 264, 266, 267, 269, 270, 272, 273, 278
    enrollment, higher education, 213
Area studies,
    degrees conferred, 247–254, 256–259, 263, 264, 266, 267, 269, 270, 272, 273
Art, degrees conferred, 247–254, 256–259, 263, 264, 266, 267, 269, 270, 272, 273, 298
Asian or Pacific Islander
    activities, 144–147
    attendance patterns, 153
    attitudes about schools, 142, 154
    courses taken by high school students, 136–140
    degrees conferred, 262–276, 299–305, 307
    educational attainment, 12
    enrolled in colleges and universities, 206–211, 315
    enrolled in public schools, 45
    expected occupations, 141
    financial aid, 315
    high school program, 135
    testing, 111, 115, 116, 127, 128
Assessment
    American College Testing, 134
    Graduate Record Examination, 311
    international, 394–404
    minimum-competency, 156, 157
    National Assessment of Educational Progress, 107–124, 126
    National Education Longitudinal Study, 127
    Scholastic Assessment Test, 128–133
Associate degrees, 9, 11, 170, 171, 217–219, 244, 246–249, 255–259, 262–264
Athletics, participation in school activities, 144, 146, 147
Attendance patterns, 153
Attitudes about

education, 22–29, 69, 74–76
  life values, 374
  selected classes, 140
  school climate, 142
Attrition, college student, 307, 310
Auxiliary enterprises, higher education, 324–328, 330, 331, 334, 335, 337–339 Aver
age daily attendance, 39, 44, 51
Average daily membership, 39
Average length of school year, 39, 122

B

Bachelor's degrees, 9–14, 170, 171, 216, 244–246, 250, 253, 254, , 255–259, 265–267, 277–298
Basic administrative units, 89–93
Basic student charges, higher education, 312–314
Behavior, student, 27, 28, 140–151, 153, 154
Benefits expenditure, 163, 164
Biological sciences
  credits earned by college graduates, 308
  credits earned by high school graduates, 136, 138
  degrees conferred, 10, 247–254, 256–259, 263, 264, 266, 267, 269, 270, 272, 273, 279, 280, 299, 303
  enrollment, higher education, 213
  faculty, 232
  Graduate Record Examination, 311
Blacks
  activities, 144, 146, 147
  adult education, 353, 354
  attendance patterns, 153
  attitudes about schools, 142, 154
  courses taken by high school students, 136–140
  degrees conferred, 9, 10, 12, 219, 262–276, 299–305, 307
  dropouts, 103, 104, 381
  drug use, 148
  educational attainment, 8–10, 12
  enrolled in colleges and universities, 183, 186, 206–212, 218, 219, 310, 315, 380
  enrolled in public schools, 45
  enrolled in school, 7
  expected occupations, 141
  family characteristics, 19
  financial aid, 315
  high school program 135
  historically black colleges and universities, 218–220
  labor force participation, 375, 380, 381
  literacy, 388
  parental involvement in school activities, 25
  persistence in higher education, 307, 310
  population, 16
  poverty status, 21
  testing, 107, 110–113, 116–119, 123, 124, 126–128
  unemployment rate, 377, 380, 381
  years of school completed, 8–10, 12
Black colleges, 218–220
Board rates, 312, 313
Business and management
  credits earned by college graduates, 308
  credits earned by high school graduates, 137
  degrees conferred, 10, 247–254, 256–259, 263, 264, 266, 267, 269, 270, 272, 273, 281, 299
  enrollment, higher education, 213
  faculty in higher education, 232, 233
  vocational programs, 247–249

C

Cable television, 414
Capital outlay
  higher education, 35, 350
  public elementary and secondary schools, 35, 39, 162, 163, 166, 167
Carnegie classification of colleges, 328, 335
Catholic schools
  achievement test scores, 127
  elementary and secondary, 59–62
  expected occupations of students, 141
  institutions of higher education, 179
  participation in extracurricular activities, 144, 146
  student attitudes about classes, 140, 154
  student attitudes about school climate, 142
  student attendance patterns, 153
Center-based programs for preschool, 41, 42, 46, 47, 49, 143
Chapter 1 (Title 1), 88, 359, 361, 363–365, 372
Cheerleading, participation in school activities, 144, 147
Chemical engineering, 253, 254, 286
Chemistry, degrees conferred, 253, 254, 293
Chemistry, Graduate Record Examination, 311
Child care, 47, 49
Church affiliation
  elementary and secondary schools, 59–62, 127, 140, 144–147, 153, 154
  institutions of higher education, 179
City school systems, 88, 92, 93, 145, 151, 371, 372
Civil engineering, 253, 254, 286
Class rank, 132
Class size, 69, 228, 229
Classroom teachers
  attitudes about schools, 26–28, 74–76, 151
  characteristics of private school teachers, 67
  characteristics of public school teachers, 67–69, 71
  mobility, 72
  new teachers' experiences, 74–76
  opinions about teaching, 26–28, 74–76
  private schools, 4, 60, 62–64, 67, 72, 73
  public schools, 4, 39, 64–79, 82–85, 88, 92
  salaries of private school teachers, 73
  salaries of public school teachers, 73, 77–79
  satisfaction with teaching, 26–28, 69, 74–76

INDEX OF TABLE NUMBERS 519

teaching assignments, 70, 71
Climate in schools, 27, 28, 142
Closing of institutions of higher education, 243
Clubs, participation in school activities, 144, 147
College faculty. See Faculty, higher education.
College and university education, 170–352
College plans and applications, 145, 185
Communications
    degrees conferred, 247–254, 256–259, 263, 264, 266, 267, 269, 270, 272, 273, 282
    enrollment, 213
    faculty, 232
Competency testing
    students, 122, 156
    teachers, 157
Compulsory attendance, age for, 152
Computer and information sciences
    courses taken by high school graduates, 136, 142
    credits earned by college graduates, 308
    degrees conferred, 247–254, 256–259, 263, 264, 266, 267, 269, 270, 272, 273, 283
    enrollment in college, 213, 214
    faculty, 232
Computers, use of, 414, 415, 420–422
Consumer Price Index, 38
Courses completed by college graduates, 308
Courses completed by high school graduates, 136–139
Current expenditures
    higher education, 171, 217–219, 334–339, 346, 348, 349
    public schools, 39, 88, 92, 162, 163, 165–169
Current-fund revenues in higher education, 171, 217, 219, 322, 324–333

D

Daily attendance as a percent of enrollment, 39
Day care, 47, 49
Degrees, earned
    associate, 9, 11, 170, 171, 217–219, 244, 246–249, 255–259, 262–264
    bachelor's and higher, 9–12, 170, 171, 217–219, 244, 246, 250–306
    by race, 9, 10, 12, 219, 262–276, 299–305
    by sex, 9, 10, 170, 171, 219, 244, 247–249, 253, 254, 260–279, 281–285, 287, 288, 290–292, 294–296, 298–305
    first-professional, 9, 170, 171, 217–219, 244, 246, 255, 260, 261, 274–276
    historical summary, 171, 244
    historically black colleges, 218, 219
    international comparison, 405–407
    large institutions of higher education, 217
    major field of study, 10, 247–254, 256–261, 263, 264, 266, 267, 269, 270, 272, 273, 275–305
    number of institutions, by field, 258–260
Denominational affiliation

elementary and secondary schools, 59–62, 127, 140, 144–147, 153, 154
institutions of higher education, 179
Dentistry
    degrees conferred, 260, 261, 275, 276
    dental assisting, awards in, 247–249
    enrollment, higher education, 213
Department of Education outlays, 358–366
    For other Departments, see Federal funds.
Disabled, 52–55, 58, 105, 106, 211
Discipline problems, 23, 27, 28, 142, 148, 151
Disposable personal income, 37
Districts, school, 89–93
Doctor's degrees, 9, 11, 170, 171, 217–219, 244, 246, 253, 254, 252, 255, 256, 257–259, 271–273, 277–306
Dormitory rooms, charges for, 312, 313
Dramatic arts, degrees conferred, 253, 254
Dropouts (high school)
    employment and unemployment, 375, 377, 379, 381
    income of, 378, 379
    number, 381
    percent, by age group, 8, 9, 11–14, 103, 104
Dropouts (college), 307, 310
Drug abuse, 23, 27, 148–151, 373

E

Earned degrees. See Degrees, earned.
Earnings by years of school completed, 378–379, 386
Earnings of recent college graduates, 386
Economics,
    degrees conferred, 253, 254, 297
    faculty, 232
Education
    adult, 353–355
    all levels, 1–38
    bilingual, 58, 359, 361, 363, 364
    credits earned by college graduates, 308
    degrees conferred, 170, 171, 217–219, 244–306
    degrees conferred in education, 10, 247–254, 256–259, 263, 266, 267, 269, 270, 272, 273, 284, 299, 300
    elementary and secondary, 39–169
    enrollment, higher education, 1–3, 170–220
    faculty in higher education, 221–233
    Federal programs, 357–372
    Graduate Record Examination, 311
    handicapped students, 52–55, 58, 105, 106, 211
    higher, 170–356
    international, 389–410
    outcomes, 8–14, 99–139, 244–311, 373–388, 394–407
    price indexes, 38
    statistics related to, 373–388
    structure, (figure 1)

520 INDEX OF TABLE NUMBERS

vocational, 58, 70, 71, 135–137, 247–249, 353, 355, 359, 361, 363, 364
Education in the U.S., structure of, (figure 1)
Educational administration and supervision, degrees conferred, 253, 254
Educational attainment, 8–14
Educational attainment in the work force, 375–379
Electrical engineering, 253, 254, 286
Elementary and secondary education, 1–5, 31–33, 35, 36, 39–169
Elementary and Secondary Price Index, 38
Elementary education, degrees conferred, 253, 254
Elementary schools, number
  private, 5, 59, 61–63, 89
  public, 5, 88, 89, 92, 94–98
Employees
  colleges, 221–224
  private elementary and secondary schools, 60
  public elementary and secondary schools, 82–86
Employment
  college graduates, 375–377, 379, 383–385
  handicapped students, 106
  high school dropouts, 375–377, 379, 381
  high school graduates, 375–377, 379, 380
  high school seniors, 382
Endowment funds, 171, 351, 352
Endowment funds, revenue from, 324–328, 330, 331
Engineering
  credits earned by college graduates, 308
  degrees conferred, 10, 247–254, 256–259, 263, 264, 266, 267, 269, 270, 272, 273, 285, 286, 299, 301
  enrollment, higher education, 213, 214
  faculty in higher education, 231–233
  Graduate Record Examination, 311
  graduates, organized occupational curricula, 247–249, 263, 264
English
  credits earned by high school graduates, 136, 139
  enrollment in higher education, 213
  faculty, 232
  degrees conferred, 247–254, 256–259, 263, 264, 266, 267, 269, 270, 287
  requirements for graduation, 155
  teachers, public high schools, 70
Enrollment
  adult basic education, 355
  adult education, 353–355
  affiliation,
    elementary and secondary schools, 59, 61, 62
    institutions of higher education, 179
  ages, 6, 7, 174–176, 186, 212, 213, 315, 354, 353
  all levels of education, 1–3, 6, 7
  by grade, 41–43
  by grade span of school, 95
  by race, 7, 45, 59, 179, 183, 206–210, 212, 219, 353, 354, 380
  by sex, 6, 7, 170–172, 174, 175, 177–179, 181.182, 184, 187–189, 193–195, 207, 211, 212, 217, 219, 353, 354, 380
  elementary and secondary
    private, 1–3, 46, 56, 58, 59, 61–63
    public, 1–3, 39–46, 51, 56–58, 66, 86, 88, 90, 92, 93, 95
    total, 1–3
  elementary schools
    private, 2, 3, 58, 61, 62
    public, 2, 3, 39–43, 58, 95
    total, 1–3
  engineering, 213, 214
  exceptional children, 52–55, 58, 105, 106, 211
  foreign languages, public secondary schools, 57
  foreign students in American colleges, 206–210, 410
  handicapped, 52–54, 58, 105, 106, 211
  higher education
    affiliation, 179
    age, 174–176, 186, 212, 213, 353, 354
    disabled, 106, 211
    engineering, 213, 214
    first-professional, 2, 175, 177, 189, 197–199, 207
    four-year colleges, 170, 173, 176–178, 181, 196, 198–201, 205, 206, 209, 213–220, 310
    freshmen, 181–184, 203–205, 212
    full-time, 172, 174–182, 187–189, 193–195, 217, 219
    full-time-equivalent, 200–202, 217
    graduate, 2, 175, 177, 188, 197–199, 207, 213, 214, 217, 319, 320
    historically black colleges and universities, 218–220
    large institutions of higher education, 215–217
    major field of study, 213, 214
    minority, 183, 185, 186, 206–212, 219
    part-time, 172, 174–182, 187–189, 193–195, 217, 219
    private institutions, 2, 3, 170, 172, 173, 176–182, 187– 189, 192, 195, 196, 198–202, 206, 209, 215–220
    public institutions, 2, 3, 170, 172, 173, 176–182, 187– 189, 191, 194, 196, 198–202, 206, 209, 215–220
    race, 183, 186, 206–213, 219
    rate, 6, 7, 179–182, 301, 307, 380, 389, 390
    sex, 170–172, 174, 175, 177–182, 184, 187–189, 193– 195, 207, 211, 212, 217, 219
    total, 1–3, 170–179, 190–199, 206–210, 212, 213, 215–220
    traditionally black colleges, 218–220
    two-year colleges, 170, 173, 176–178, 181, 196, 198–201, 205, 206, 209, 213, 215–219, 310
    type of institution, 170, 173, 176–178, 181, 196, 198–201, 205, 206, 209, 213–220, 310

INDEX OF TABLE NUMBERS 521

undergraduate, 2, 175, 177, 187, 197–199, 207, 211–213, 217, 315–318
high schools. See Secondary schools.
international, 389–391
kindergarten, 41, 43, 46, 47, 50, 52, 53, 55
large school districts, 88, 90, 92, 93
mathematics, higher education, 136, 138, 213, 214
preprimary programs, 41–43, 46, 47, 49, 52, 53, 55
race, elementary and secondary schools, 45
science, 136, 138, 213, 214
secondary schools
    private, 2, 3, 56, 58, 61, 62
    public, 2, 3, 39–43, 56, 58, 95
    total, 1–3, 56, 58
school districts, 90, 92, 93
social sciences, higher education, 213, 214
special education for exceptional children, 52–55, 58, 211
two-year colleges, 170, 173, 176–178, 181, 196, 198–201, 205, 206, 213, 215–219, 310
Ethnicity. See Spanish origin and race.
Exceptional children, enrollment, 52–55, 58, 105, 106, 211
Expenditures
    all schools, 31–33
    administration, 161–163, 166, 167, 334, 335, 337, 341–345, 349
    by other countries, 391, 408, 409
    Federal Government, 33, 34, 357–372
    governmental, 33–37
    higher education, 31–36, 171, 217–219, 333–349
    instruction, 88, 92, 162–164, 166, 167, 334,335, 337, 338, 341–345, 349
    libraries, 334, 335, 337–339, 341–345, 349, 416–418
    per pupil, public schools, 39, 88, 92, 168, 169
    per pupil, by country, 408
    per student, higher education, 334, 336, 341–345, 349
    public elementary and secondary schools, 31–33, 35, 36, 39, 88, 92, 161–169
    private elementary and secondary schools, 31–33
    pupil transportation, 51, 163, 166, 167
    research, 334, 335, 337–339, 341–345, 349, 367, 368
    State and local expenditures, 34–37. Also see Revenues.
Extracurricular activities participation, 50, 143, 144, 146, 147

F

Faculty, higher education
    academic rank, 226, 227, 230, 231, 234, 235, 238–240
    age, 227, 230, 231
    classes taught, 228, 229
    control of institution, 1, 4, 221, 225, 227–230, 233–240
    employment status, 222, 225, 227–232
    field, 231–233
    productivity, 228, 229
    race/ethnicity, 222, 225–227, 230–232
    salary, 227, 230, 233–239
    sex, 171, 222, 223, 226, 227, 230–232, 234, 235, 240
    tenure, 240
Faculty salaries, 227, 230, 233–239
Families
    income, 37
    number, 18, 19
    parental involvement with school activities, 25
    poverty status, 21
    with children, 18, 19
Federally affected areas, aid to, 359, 361, 363, 364
Federal funds for education, 354–372
Federal sources, receipts from
    higher education, 33, 324–328, 330, 331, 333
    public elementary and secondary schools, 33, 39, 88, 92, 158–161
Fees, higher education students, 312–314
Fellowships and scholarships, 315–321, 335–339, 341–345, 349
Field of study
    achievement scores. See Tests.
    characteristics of the population, 10
    earned degrees, 10, 247–261, 263, 264, 266, 267, 269, 270, 272, 273, 275–305
    enrollment in higher education, 213, 214
    employment, 383, 384, 386
    faculty in higher education, 231–233
    Federal funds for colleges, 368
    salaries, 386
Finances. See Capital outlay, Current expenditures, Expenditures, Income, Property, Revenues, Salaries.
Financial aid to college students, 315–323
Fine and applied arts
    degrees conferred, 247–254, 256–259, 263, 264, 266, 267, 269, 270, 272, 273, 298
    faculty in higher education, 231–232
First-professional degrees, 9, 170, 171, 217–219, 244, 246, 255, 260, 261, 274–276
First-professional enrollment, 2, 175, 177, 189, 197–199, 207
Freshmen, 180–184, 203–205, 207, 212
Foreign languages
    degrees conferred, 247–254, 256–259, 263, 264, 266, 267, 269, 270, 272, 273, 288, 289
    courses taken by high school students, 136, 139
    enrollment, public high schools, 57
Foreign students in American colleges, 206–210, 410
Forestry, degrees conferred, 253, 254
Four-year institutions

enrollment, 170, 173, 176–178, 180, 181, 196, 198–201, 205, 206, 209, 213–220, 307, 316–320
faculty, 223–225, 227–229, 230, 233–240
finance, 217–219, 321, 328, 334, 337, 341, 342, 344, 345, 349
number, 5, 210, 236–238
staff, 223, 224
French
degrees conferred, 253, 254, 289
enrollment, public secondary schools, 57
Full-time college students, 172, 174–182, 187–189, 193–195, 217, 219
Full-time-equivalent enrollment, 200–202, 217
Funds, Federal, for education, 34, 39, 88, 92, 158–161, 324–328, 330, 331, 333, 357–372

G

GED, 102
General programs in high school, 135
Geography assessment, 116, 117, 394
Geography, degrees conferred, 253, 254
Geology, degrees conferred, 253, 254, 293
German
degrees conferred, 253, 254, 289
enrollment, public secondary schools, 57
Gifted and talented, state legislation, 54
Gifts and grants, higher education, 324–328, 330, 340
Goals for education, 26
Governmental finances, 33–37
Government and political science, degrees conferred, 253, 254, 297
Grade enrollment, 41–43
Graduate enrollment, 2, 175, 177, 188, 197–199, 207, 211, 213, 214, 217, 319, 320
Graduates
high school
attainment, 8–14
attainment in the work force, 375–379
college attendance of, 183–185, 380
employment, 380
GED, 102
number, 39, 63, 92, 99, 100, 183, 184, 380
institutions of higher education. See Degrees.
organized occupational curricula, 247–250
Graduate Record Examination, 311
Graduation rate, college, 307, 310
Graduation requirements, 155
Greek, degrees conferred, 253, 254
Gross domestic product, 31, 37
Gross domestic product price deflator, 38
Guidance personnel, public elementary and secondary schools, 82–84
Guidance personnel, private elementary and secondary schools, 60

H

Health and physical education, activities of high school students, 144, 146, 147
Handicapped, special education for the, 52–55, 58, 105, 106, 211
Head Start, 48, 359, 370
Health professions
degrees conferred, 247–254, 256–259, 263, 264, 266, 267, 269, 270, 272, 273, 290
enrollment, higher education, 213, 214
faculty in higher education, 231–233
High school graduates
attainment, 8–14
attainment in the work force, 375–379
college attendance of, 183–185, 380
employment, 380
GED, 102
number, 39, 63, 99, 100, 183, 184, 380
private, 63, 99
public, 39, 92, 99, 100
total, 99, 183, 184, 380
High school seniors
activities, 144, 146, 147
attitudes, 140, 142
attendance patterns, 153
college applications, 185
college plans, 145
drug use, 150
employment, 382
enrollment, 41–43
expected occupations, 141
reasons for taking math and science courses, 140
High school students' extracurricular activities, 144, 146, 147
High schools. See Secondary schools.
Higher education, 1–5, 170–356
Higher Education Price Index, 38
Hispanics
activities, 144, 146, 147
adult education, 353, 354
attendance patterns, 153
attitudes about school climate, 142
courses completed by high school students, 136–139
degrees conferred, 8, 9, 12, 262–276, 299–305, 307
dropouts, 103, 104, 381
drug use, 148
educational attainment, 8, 9, 12
enrolled in colleges and universities, 183, 186, 206–212, 310, 315, 380
enrolled in public schools, 45
enrolled in school, 7
expected occupations, 141
family characteristics, 19
financial aid, 315
high school program, 135

labor force participation, 375, 380, 381
literacy, 388
parental involvement in school activities, 25
persistence in higher education, 307, 310
population, 16
poverty, 21
testing, 107, 110, 111, 113, 116–119, 123–128
unemployment rate, 377, 380, 381
years of school completed, 8, 9, 12
Historically black colleges and universities, 218–220
Historical summary statistics
enrollment, all levels, 3
higher education, 170
public schools, 39
History,
degrees conferred, 253, 254, 297
faculty, 232
testing, 115, 116, 127
Home activities, 50, 109, 112, 118, 122, 143, 144, 146, 147, 400, 421, 422
Home computers, 421, 422
Home economics
courses taken by high school students, 137
degrees conferred, 247–254, 256–259, 263, 264, 266, 267, 269, 270, 272, 273
graduates, organized occupational curricula, 247–249
Homework, 109, 122, 395, 397, 399, 401, 402
Hospitals, university, 324–328, 330, 331, 335–339
Household income, 20
Humanities
degrees conferred, 247–254, 256–259, 263, 264, 266, 267, 269, 270, 272, 273, 287–289, 296–298, 299, 302, 305
faculty in higher education, 231–233

I

Illiteracy, 388. Also see Educational attainment.
Income
by years of school completed, 378–379
graduates, 378–379, 386
higher education institutions, 171, 217–219, 321, 324–333
personal, 37
public schools, 39, 88, 92, 158–161
Institutions of higher education
by control, 5, 171, 179, 215, 241–243, 258–260
by denominational affiliation, 179
by size of enrollment, 215, 216
by type, 5, 215, 241–243
closing, 243
conferring most doctor's degrees, 306
enrolling largest numbers of students, 216, 217
historically black, 218–220
offering remedial instruction, 309
receiving most Federal funds, 333
traditionally black, 218–220

with large endowments, 352
with large libraries, 417
Instruction practices, higher education, 228, 229
Instruction expenditures, 88, 92, 162–164, 166, 167, 335–339, 341–345, 349
Instructional staff, elementary and secondary schools
private, 60, 62
public, 39, 80–84
Interest on school debt, 39, 162, 163, 166, 167
International educational comparisons, 389–410
Italian
degrees conferred, 253, 254
enrollment, public secondary schools, 57

J

Journalism, degrees conferred, 253, 254
Junior colleges
faculty, 223–225, 227–229, 230, 233–237, 240
finance, 217–219, 321, 328, 334, 337, 343, 349
number, 5, 210, 236–238
staff, 223, 224
enrollment, 167, 170, 173–175, 177, 192, 194–197, 201, 202, 204, 208, 210–214, 307, 316–318
number, 5, 210, 236–238
Junior high schools, 94, 98
Junior-senior high schools, 5, 94–96, 98

K

Kindergarten
activities, 50, 143
enrollment, 41–43, 46–48, 54, 143
readiness, 49

L

Labor force status
by educational attainment, 375–377, 380–385
disabled persons exiting the education system, 105, 106
recent college graduates, 383–385
recent high school dropouts, 381
recent high school graduates, 380
Latin
degrees conferred, 253, 254
enrollment, public secondary schools, 57
Law
first-professional degrees conferred, 260, 261, 275, 276
enrollment, 206
other degrees conferred, 247–254, 256–259, 263, 264, 266, 267, 269, 270, 272, 273
Letters, degrees conferred, 247–254, 256–259, 263, 264, 266, 267, 269, 270, 272, 273, 287
Level of school completed, 8–14
Librarians
higher education institutions, 416, 417

public, 418
private schools, 60, 411
public schools, 82–84, 411–413
Libraries
college and university, 416, 417
large university, 417
private school, 411
public, 418, 419
public school, 411–413
technology use, 411–413, 414
Library expenditures
college and university, 335–339, 341–345, 349, 416, 417
public, 418, 419
Library science, degrees conferred, 247–254, 256–259, 263, 264, 266, 267, 269, 270, 272, 273
Life sciences
courses completed by high school graduates, 136, 138
credits earned by college graduates, 308
degrees conferred, 247–254, 256–259, 263, 264, 266, 267, 269, 270, 272, 273, 279, 280, 299, 303
enrollment, higher education, 213, 214
faculty, 232
Graduate Record Examination, 311
Life values, 374
Literacy, 388, 403, 404
Literature, degrees conferred, 247–254, 256–259, 263, 264, 266, 267, 269, 270, 272, 273, 287
Literature, Graduate Record Examination, 311
Local basic administrative units, 89–93
Local public school systems with largest enrollments, 92, 93
Local sources, receipts from
higher education, 33–36, 324–328, 330–342
public schools, 33–36, 39, 88, 92, 158–160
Lunch, school program, 163, 166, 167, 359, 369, 371

M

Major field of study
earned degrees, 247–254, 256–259, 263, 264, 266, 267, 269, 270, 272, 275–305
enrollment in higher education, 213, 214
Federal obligations to colleges, 368
Master's degrees, 9, 11, 170, 171, 217–219, 244, 246, 251, 253–259, 268–270, 277–298
Mathematics
attitudes about classes, 140
courses taken by high school students, 123, 136, 138
credits earned by college graduates, 308
degrees conferred, 241–248, 250–253, 257, 258, 263, 264, 266, 267, 269, 270, 272, 273, 291
enrollment, higher education, 213, 214
faculty, 232

testing, 118–123, 127–134, 311, 395, 396, 399–401
Medical laboratory technologies, degrees conferred, 247–249
Medicine
degrees conferred, 253, 254
first-professional degrees, 260, 261, 275, 276
enrollment, 213, 214
Membership, public schools, 39. Also see Enrollment.
Mentally retarded, special education, 52, 53, 105, 106
Metropolitan area,
internet access, 415
participation in federal programs, 371, 372
public school statistics, 88
testing, 107, 113, 126
years of school completed, 14
Microcomputers, use of, 411–413, 420–422
Middle schools, number, 94, 97
Migration of college students, 203–205
Military sciences, degrees conferred, 247–254, 256–259, 263, 264, 266, 267, 269, 270, 272, 273
Minimum-competency testing for students, 122, 156
Minimum-competency testing for teachers, 157
Minorities
college graduation rates, 307, 310
degrees conferred, 219, 262–276, 299–305, 307
educational attainment, 8–10, 12
enrolled in colleges, 183, 184, 186, 206–212, 216
enrolled in elementary and secondary schools, 45
enrolled in school, 7
high school courses taken, 136–139
high school dropouts, 103, 104, 381
high school graduates, 183, 380
testing, 107, 110, 113, 115–119, 123–128
Mobility of teachers, 72, 76
Music, degrees conferred, 253, 254
Music education, degrees conferred, 253, 254
Music, participation in high school activities, 144, 146, 147

N

National Assessment of Educational Progress
geography, 116, 117
history, 115, 116, 127
international geography, 394
international reading literacy, 403, 404
mathematics, 118–121, 123, 127
reading, 107–112, 127
science, 125–127
writing, 113, 114
Natural science
courses taken by high school students, 136, 138, 139
faculty in higher education, 231–233
Nonpublic schools. See Private schools.

Nursery school, 41, 42, 46–48, 143
Nursing, degrees conferred, 247–249, 253, 254

O

Occupational programs (higher education)
  awards, 247–249
  enrollment, 213
  schools offering, 5
Occupational programs (secondary), 137
Occupation and employment
  college graduates, 375–379, 383–386
  expected occupations of 8th, 10th and 12th graders, 141
  high school graduates, 105, 106, 375–380
  high school seniors, 382
  school dropouts, 375–379, 381
Office occupations (vocational) credits, 137
One-teacher schools, public, 89, 94
Operation and maintenance expenditures
  elementary and secondary, 88, 162, 163, 166, 167
  higher education, 335–339, 341–345, 349
Opinions on education
  attitudes about classes, 140
  average grade for schools, 22
  opinions about school climate, 28, 142
  opinions about schools, 22–29, 69, 74–76
  perception about student behavior, 27, 142, 151
  problems in schools, 23, 27, 28, 142, 148, 151
  reasons why 10th graders go to school, 154
  school choice, 24
  teachers' attitudes, 26–28, 69
Organized occupational curricula, formal awards based on, 247–249
Outcomes of education, 373–388. Also see Degrees and Graduates.

P

Parental involvement, 23, 25, 27, 140, 143
Part-time college students, 172, 174–182, 187–189, 193–195, 216, 219
Pell grants, finance, 322, 359, 361, 363, 364
Pell grants, received by students, 319
Per capita personal income, 37
Per pupil cost of transportation, 51
Per pupil expenditures, 39, 88, 92, 168, 169, 409
Per student expenditures (higher education), 334, 335, 341–345, 349
Persistence in higher education, 307, 310
Personal income, 37
Pharmacy, degrees conferred, 253, 254, 261, 275, 276
Philosophy and religion, degrees conferred, 241–248, 250–253, 257, 258, 261, 263, 264, 266, 267, 269, 270, 272, 273, 275, 276
Physical education, degrees conferred, 253, 254
Physical plant additions, 350

Physical plant, higher education, value of, 171, 351
Physical sciences
  courses taken by high school students, 136, 138, 139
  credits earned by college graduates, 308
  degrees conferred, 241–248, 250–253, 257, 258, 261, 263, 264, 266, 267, 269, 270, 272, 273, 292, 293, 299, 304
  enrollment in higher education, 213, 214
  faculty, 232
Physics, degrees conferred, 253, 254, 293
Plant value, higher education, 171, 351
Preschool education, 41, 42, 46–48, 143
Political science
  degrees conferred, 253, 254, 297
  faculty, 232
Population
  by continent, 391
  by country, 392
  by years of school completed, 8–14
  percent enrolled in school, 6, 7
  poverty, 20, 21
  school-age, 15–17
  total, 15, 17, 37, 39
Postsecondary education, 5, 170–356. Also see Higher education.
Poverty, 20, 21
Preprimary programs, enrollment in, 41–43, 46–48, 52, 53, 55
Price indexes, 38
Principals, private schools, 60, 87
Principals, public schools, 82–84, 87
Private elementary and secondary schools
  college application rates, 185
  enrollment, 1–3, 46, 56, 58, 59, 61–63
  expenditures, 32, 33
  graduates, 63, 99
  libraries, 411
  mobility of teachers, 72
  number, 5, 59, 61, 63, 89
  opinions of teachers, 26–28
  principals, 60, 87
  pupils per teacher, 60, 64
  salaries of teachers, 73
  staff, 1, 60
  teachers, 1, 4, 60, 62–64, 67, 72, 73
Private gifts and grants, higher education, 324–328, 330, 331, 340
Private institutions of higher education
  degrees conferred, 170, 245, 255–260
  endowment, 352
  enrollment, 2, 3, 170, 172, 173, 176–182, 187–189, 192, 195, 196, 198–202, 206, 209, 215–220, 317–320
  expenditures, 32, 33, 334, 336, 339, 344, 345, 348, 349
  faculty number, 4, 221–225, 227–230, 233

faculty salaries, 227, 230, 233–239
faculty tenure, 240
financial aid, 316–322
number, 5, 179, 209, 215, 241–243, 258–260
opinions, 29
physical plant additions, 350
revenues, 33, 322, 326, 328, 332
student charges, 312–314
Professional degrees. See Degrees and First-professional degrees.
Property, higher education, value of, 171, 351, 352
Protective services, degrees conferred, 241–248, 250–253, 257, 258, 261, 263, 264, 266, 267, 269, 270, 272, 273
Protestant institutions of higher education, 179
Psychology
degrees conferred, 241–248, 250–253, 257, 258, 261, 263, 264, 266, 267, 269, 270, 272, 273, 294
enrollment, 213, 214
faculty, 232
Public affairs, degrees conferred, 241–248, 250–253, 257, 258, 261, 263, 264, 266, 267, 269, 270, 272, 273
Public elementary and secondary schools
districts, 89–93
college application rates, 185
enrollment, 1–3, 39–46, 51, 56, 58, 66, 86, 88, 90, 92, 93, 95
expenditures, 32, 33, 35, 36, 39, 88, 92, 162–169
finance, 34–36
graduates, 92, 99, 100
graduation requirements, 155
instructional staff, 39, 82–84
librarians, 82–84
libraries, 411–413
minimum-competency testing, 122, 156, 157
number, 5, 88, 89, 92, 94–98
principals, 82–84, 87
revenue receipts, 39, 88, 92, 158–161
teachers, 1, 4, 39, 64–79, 82–85, 88, 92
telecommunications use, 411–415
Public institutions of higher education
degrees conferred, 170, 245, 255–260
endowment, 352
enrollment, 2, 3, 170, 172, 173, 176–182, 187–189, 192, 195, 196, 198–202, 206, 209, 215–220, 317–320
expenditures, 32, 33, 334, 336, 338, 341–343, 346, 347
faculty number, 4, 221–225, 227–230, 233
faculty salaries, 227, 230, 233–239
faculty tenure, 240
financial aid, 316–322
number, 5, 179, 209, 215, 241–243, 258–260
opinions, 29
physical plant additions, 350

revenues, 33, 322, 325, 328–332
student charges, 312–314
Public opinions on schools, 22–29, 69, 73–76
Public school systems, 89–93
Pupils. See Enrollment.
Pupil-staff ratio, 60, 82, 86
Pupil-teacher ratio, 60, 64, 66, 82, 88, 91
Pupil, expenditure per, 39, 88, 92, 168, 169, 408
Pupils transported at public expense, 51

R

Race
adult education, 353, 354
college faculty, 222, 226, 227, 230–232
college graduation rates, 307, 310
courses completed by high school students, 136–139
degrees conferred, 9, 10, 12, 219, 262–276, 299–305, 307, 310, 315
enrolled in college, 183, 186, 206–212, 219
enrolled in preprimary education, 46, 48
enrolled in public elementary and secondary schools, 45
enrolled in school, 7
going to college, 145, 183, 185, 186, 380
high school dropouts, 8–10, 12, 104–105, 381
high school graduates, 8–10, 12, 183, 380
high school program, 135
labor force participation, 375, 380, 381
literacy, 388
parental involvement in education, 25
persistence in higher education, 307, 310
population, 16
poverty, 21
testing, 107, 110, 111, 113, 116–119, 123–127, 129
unemployment, 377, 380, 381
years of school completed, 8–10, 12
Readiness for school, 49
Reading tests, 107–112, 127–134, 403, 404
Receipts. See Revenue.
Regular 4-year high schools, 94, 98
Religion degrees conferred, 253, 254. Also see Philosophy and religion.
Religious affiliation
elementary and secondary schools, 59–62, 140–142, 144–146
institutions of higher education, 179
Remedial instruction, 58, 309
Research funds, 335–339, 341–345, 349, 357, 359, 367, 368
Residence and migration of college students, 203–205
Resident population, 15–17, 39
Retention rates in higher education, 307, 310
Revenues, institutions of higher education, 33, 171, 322, 324–333

INDEX OF TABLE NUMBERS 527

Revenues, receipts, public schools, 33, 39, 88, 92, 158–161
Room charges, 312, 313
Russian
  degrees conferred, 253, 254
  enrollment, public secondary schools, 57

S

Salaries
  higher education
    bachelor's degree recipients, 378, 379, 386
    faculty, 227, 230, 233–239
    library expenditures for, 416, 417
  private school teachers, 73
  public schools
    outlays, 163, 164
    teachers, 73, 77–81
    total instructional staff, 39, 80, 81
Scholarships and fellowships, 320–323, 337–339, 335–339, 341–345, 349
Scholastic Aptitude Test, 128–133
School-age population, 16, 17, 39
School assistance in federally affected areas, 88, 359, 361, 363, 364
School districts, 89–92
School lunch program, 359, 369, 371, 414
School readiness, 64
School systems, 89–93
School year, length, 39, 122, 152, 395
School years completed, 8–14
Schools
  climate, 27, 28, 142
  elementary and secondary
    private, 5, 59, 61, 63, 89
    public, 5, 88, 89, 92, 94–98
  higher education, 5, 171, 179, 209, 215, 241–243, 258–260
  noncollegiate postsecondary, 356
Science
  attitudes about classes, 140
  courses taken by college graduates, 308
  courses taken by high school students, 136, 138, 139
  degrees conferred, 241–248, 250–253, 257, 258, 261, 263, 264, 266, 267, 269, 270, 272, 273, 277, 279, 280, 292, 293, 299, 303, 304
  enrollment in higher education, 213, 214
  faculty in higher education, 231–233
  testing, 124–127, 134, 311, 397, 398, 402
Secondary schools
  private, 5, 59, 61, 62, 89
  public
    junior high, 94, 98
    total, 5, 89, 94–96, 98
Secondary school teachers, public, by field, 70, 71
Senior high schools, 94, 98
Size of enrollment

institutions of higher education, 215
  largest colleges, 216, 217
  largest school districts, 92, 93
  school districts, 90
  schools, 95, 412
Social sciences
  credits earned by college graduates, 308
  degrees conferred, 241–248, 250–253, 257, 258, 261, 263, 264, 266, 267, 269, 270, 272, 273, 296, 297, 299, 305
  enrollment, higher education, 213, 214
  faculty in higher education, 231, 233
Social work, degrees conferred, 253, 254
Sociology
  degrees conferred, 253, 254, 297
  faculty, 232
Spanish
  degrees conferred, 253, 254, 289
  enrollment, public high schools, 57
Spanish origin. See Hispanic.
Special education
  completions, 105, 106
  degrees conferred, 253, 254
  enrollment, 52–55, 58, 211
Speech, degrees conferred, 253, 254
Sports, participation in school activities, 144, 146, 147
Staff. See Faculty, Classroom teachers, Instructional.
Staff,
  private elementary and secondary schools, 1, 60
  public elementary and secondary schools, 1, 39, 82–86, 161
  all schools, 1
  pupil-staff ratio, 60, 82, 86
State
  adult basic education, 355
  assessment, 111, 112, 120, 121
  compulsory school attendance, 152
  degrees conferred, 245, 246
  Department of Agriculture obligations, 369
  Department of Education obligations, 363–365
  Department of Health and Human Services allocations, 370
  educational attainment, 11–14
  enrollment in higher education, 182, 190–199, 201–205, 210
  enrollment in private schools, 63
  enrollment in public schools, 40–42, 44, 45, 66, 86
  expenditure per pupil, 168
  expenditures for public higher education, 346–348
  expenditures for public schools, 161, 165–168
  Federal obligations to colleges, 363, 364, 367
  governmental expenditures, 35, 36
  graduation requirements, 155
  Head Start allocations, 370
  high school graduates, private, 63
  high school graduates, public, 100

homework, 122
household income, 20
instruction expenditures, 164, 166, 167
mathematics, 120-122
minimum-competency testing, 122, 156, 157
number of institutions of higher education, 242
number of noncollegiate institutions, 356
number of public schools, 96-98
number of school districts, 91
population, 17
poverty, 20
proficiency in mathematics, 120, 121
proficiency in reading, 111, 112
pupil-teacher ratio, 66
residence and migration of college students, 203-205
revenues for higher education, 329-332
revenues for public schools, 159-161
salaries, public instructional staff, 80
salaries, public school teachers, 78, 79
salaries, higher education faculty, 236-239
Scholastic Assessment Test, 133
staff, public schools, 83-86, 161
state education agencies, 161
state regulations, 54, 152, 155-157
state student financial aid, 323
teachers, private schools, 63
teachers, public schools, 65, 66, 83-85
teachers, characteristics of public school, 68
television watching, 112, 122
testing, 111, 112, 120, 121, 133
tuition and fees in higher education, 313
years of school completed, 11-14
State governments, receipts from
　higher education, 324-328, 328-332
　public schools, 158-160
Statistics, degrees conferred, 253, 254
Statistics related to American education, 373-388
Structure of education in the U.S., figure 1
Student fees,
　higher education, 312-314
　private elementary and secondary, 61
Student loan (Federal) program, 315-320, 357, 359, 361
Students. See Enrollment.
Students receiving financial aid, 315-320
Supplies expenditure, 163, 164

T

Teachers
　all levels of education, 1, 4
　elementary and secondary schools
　　by field, 70
　　by sex, 39, 67, 69
　　characteristics, 67-72
　　large districts, 92
　　opinions, 26-28, 49, 69, 74-76, 151

　　private, 1, 4, 60, 62-64, 67, 72, 73
　　pupil-teacher ratio, 60, 64, 66, 82, 88, 92
　　public, 1, 4, 39, 64-79, 82-85, 88, 92
　　salaries, 73, 77-79
　higher education instructional staff
　　number, 4, 221-225, 227, 230, 232
　　salaries, 227, 230, 232-239
　　tenure, 240
Technology, use of, 411-415, 420-422
Technical education, enrollment, 213, 353, 354
Technical programs, degrees, 247-249
Telecommunications, 411-415, 420, 421
Television, 112, 118, 122, 143, 146, 400, 411, 413
Tenure of higher education faculty, 240
Tests
　American College Testing, 134
　Graduate Record Examination, 311
　international, 394-404
　minimum-competency, 122, 156, 157
　National Assessment of Educational Progress, 107-126
　National Education Longitudinal Study, 127
　Scholastic Aptitude Test, 128-133
Theology, degrees conferred, 247-254, 256-259, 261, 263, 264, 266, 267, 269, 270, 272, 273, 275, 276
Total expenditures. See Expenditures.
Trade and industry courses taken by high school students, 135, 137
Traditionally black colleges, 218-220
Transportation of public school pupils, 51, 163, 166, 167
Tuition and fees, higher education, 312-314
Tuition, private elementary and secondary schools, 61
Tuition revenues, higher education, 322, 324-328, 330, 331
Two-year institutions
　enrollment, 170, 173, 176-178, 181, 196, 198-201, 205, 206, 209, 213, 215-219, 310
　faculty, 223, 224, 227, 226, 227-230, 233-237, 240
　finance, 217-219, 322, 328, 336, 335, 343, 349
　number, 5, 215, 241-243
　staff, 223

U

Undergraduate enrollment, 2, 175, 177, 187, 197-199, 207, 2011213, 217, 315-318
Unemployment, 377, 380, 381
U.S. education, structure of, (figure 1)
Universities
　enrollment, 173, 209, 215
　finances, 328, 335, 341, 344, 349
　number, 209, 215, 242

V

Value of physical plant, higher education, 171, 350, 351
Value of endowment funds, higher education, 171, 351, 352
Value of property, higher education, 171, 351
Values, life, 374
Veterinary medicine
  degrees conferred, 261, 275, 276
  enrollment for professional degrees, 214
Violence, student exposure to, 148, 151
Visual and performing arts, degrees conferred, 247–254, 256–259, 263, 264, 266, 269, 270, 272, 273, 298
Vocational education
  awards, 170, 247–249
  credits earned by high school students, 136, 137
  enrollment, 170, 354, 353
  Federal funds, 359, 361, 363, 364
  high school program, 135
  institutions offering, 356
  teachers, 71
Volumes
  college and university libraries, 416, 417
  public libraries, 418, 419
  private school libraries, 411
  public school libraries, 411
Voluntary support for education, 30, 340

W

Wages. See Income.
Whites
  activities, 144–147
  adult education, 353, 354
  attendance patterns, 153
  attitudes about school climate, 142
  courses completed by high school students, 136–139
  degrees conferred, 9, 10, 12, 262–276, 299–305, 307
  dropouts, 103, 104, 381
  drug use, 148
  educational attainment, 8–10, 12
  enrolled in colleges and universities, 183, 186, 206–212, 310, 315, 380
  enrolled in public schools, 45
  enrolled in school, 7
  expected occupations, 141
  family characteristics, 19
  financial aid, 315
  high school program, 135
  parental involvement in school activities, 25
  labor force participation, 375, 380, 381
  literacy, 388
  persistence in higher education, 307, 310
  population, 16
  poverty status, 21
  testing, 107, 110, 111, 113, 116–119, 123–127, 128
  unemployment rate, 377, 380, 381
  years of school completed, 8–10, 12
Writing tests, 113, 114

Y

Years of school completed
  income, 378, 379, 386
  occupations, 376
  adults, 8–14
  persons 25 to 29 years old, 8, 9, 11–14
  unemployment, 377

Z

Zoology, degrees conferred, 253, 254

Welcome to NCES on the Internet
http://nces.ed.gov

NATIONAL CENTER FOR EDUCATION STATISTICS

The purpose of the Center is to collect and report "...statistics and information showing the condition and progress of education in the United States and other nations in order to promote and accelerate the improvement of American education."

- Welcome
- What's New?
- Education at a Glance
- Frequently Asked Questions
- Other Education Sites
- Search
- Publications
- Data and Surveys
- Projects with Partners
- Locate Education Expertise

Dept. of Education   Help   Education Gopher

The National Center for Education Statistics (NCES) is the Nation's principal education statistics agency. Our Web site provides access to a wide range of statistical information about education in the United States and other nations.

The NCES Home Page includes:

A *Welcome* section describing the NCES and its statistical programs.

What's New offers a description of recently released reports, databases and upcoming conferences.

Education at a Glance provides direct links to NCES materials which describe or analyze education topics such as crime in public schools, access, and costs of higher education.

Frequently Asked Questions provides responses to questions about NCES data.

Other Education Sites includes links to other education related sites including federal and state education agencies.

Search provides a link to NCES information via a keyword and concept index.

Publications gives you the capability to find publications by subject or survey. Data products are also listed here by release date.

Data and Surveys provides detailed information on all NCES surveys and provides direct links to publications and data bases that can be freely downloaded.

Projects with Partners provides descriptions and links of NCES collaborative projects with state education agencies, education associations, task forces, and other groups.

Locate Education Expertise provides a search mechanism that allows you to locate NCES and other Department of Education staff by topic, survey, or name.

How to access the NCES Home Page:
The home page may be accessed directly at:

http://nces.ed.gov

Addresses for some of our more interesting or popular information include:

http://nces.ed.gov/pubs/ce/ (*The Condition of Education*)
http://nces.ed.gov/pubs/digest97/ (*Digest of Education Statistics 1997*)
http://nces.ed.gov/NAEP/ (for information on educational assessment)
http://nces.ed.gov/timss (The *T*hird *I*nternational *M*athematics and *S*cience *S*tudy)
http://nces.ed.gov/ipeds (for information on the nation's colleges and universities)
http://nces.ed.gov/ccd (for information on the nation's public elementary and secondary schools and school districts)

NCES publications can be found at:

http://nces.ed.gov/ncespub1.html

Future plans include improving our search capabilities and allowing customers to retrieve portions of our databases by user-defined selection criteria.

Selected Publications of the National Center for Education Statistics

Advanced Telecommunications in U.S. Private Schools: K–12
  GPO #065-000-01036-4, $7

America's Teachers: Profile of a Profession
  GPO #065-000-01046-1, $25

Approaching Kindergarten: A Look at Preschoolers in the United States
  GPO #065-000-00807-6, $3

Arts in Public Elementary and Secondary Schools
  GPO #065-000-00811-4, $5.50

Campus Crime and Security at Postsecondary Education Institutions
  GPO #065-000-00973-1, $11

Characteristics of American Indian and Alaska Native Education
  GPO #065-000-00982-0, $20

The Condition of Education 1997
  GPO #065-000-00997-8, $25

The Condition of Education 1996
  GPO #065-000-00871-8, $25

Findings from the Condition of Education series:

  High School Students Ten Years After "A Nation At Risk": Findings from the Condition of Education 1994
    GPO #065-000-00761-4, $2

  The Educational Progress of Black Students: Findings from the Condition of Education 1994
    GPO #065-000-00762-2, $2

  America's Teachers Ten Years After "A Nation At Risk": Findings from the Condition of Education 1994
    GPO #065-000-00763-1, $2

  The Educational Progress of Women: Findings from the Condition of Education 1995
    GPO #065-000-00831-9, $1.25

  The Educational Progress of Hispanic Students: Findings from the Condition of Education 1995
    GPO #065-000-00799-1, $2.25

  The Cost of Higher Education: Findings from the Condition of Education 1995
    GPO #065-000-00861-1, $2

  Teachers' Working Conditions: Findings from the Condition of Education 1996
    GPO #065-000-00971-4, $4.50

  Preparation for Work: Findings from the Condition of Education 1996
    GPO #065-000-00972-2, $3.75

  Minorities in Higher Education: Findings from the Condition of Education 1996
    GPO #065-000-00978-1, $4.50

Developments in School Finance, 1996
  GPO #065-000-01042-9, $17

Digest of Education Statistics, 1997
  GPO #065-000-01098-4, $44

Directory of Federal Libraries and Information Centers, 1994
  GPO #065-000-01056-9, $9.50

Dropout Rates in the United States, 1995
  GPO #065-000-01034-8, $13

Education in the States and Nations
  GPO #065-000-00873-4, $22

Education Indicators: An International Perspective
  GPO #065-000-00901-3, $20

Enrollment in Higher Education: Fall 1995
  GPO #065-000-01039-9, $15

Federal Support for Education, Fiscal Years 1980 to 1997
  GPO #065-000-01081-0, $7

Historically Black Colleges and Universities, 1976-94
  GPO #065-000-00903-0, $9

Institutional Policies and Practices Regarding Faculty in Higher Education
  GPO #065-000-00950-1, $12

Literacy of Older Adults in America: Results From the National Adult Literacy Survey
  GPO #065-000-00939-1, $17

NAEP 1996 Trends in Academic Progress: Report in Brief
  GPO #065-000-01063-1, $4

NAEP 1996 Mathematics Report Card for the Nation and the States
  GPO #065-000-00984-6, $12

NAEP 1996 Science Report Card for the Nation and the States
  GPO #065-000-01004-6, $12

NAEP 1994 Geography Report Card
  GPO #065-000-00872-6, $10

NAEP 1994 U.S. History Report Card
  GPO #065-000-00865-3, $10

Nontraditional Undergraduates
  GPO #065-000-00951-0, $8

Private Schools in the U.S.: A Statistical Profile, 1993-94
  GPO #065-7000-01045-3, $20

Profile of Policies and Practices for Limited English Proficient Students
  GPO #065-000-00976-5, $4.50

Profiles of Students with Disabilities as Identified in NELS:88
  GPO #065-000-01031-3, $13

Programs at Higher Education Institutions for Disadvantaged Precollege Students
  GPO #065-000-00833-5, $6.50

Projections of Education Statistics to 2007
  GPO #065-000-01030-5, $19

Pursuing Excellence: A Study of United States Eighth-Grade Mathematics and Science Teaching, Learning, Curriculum, and Achievement in International Context
  GPO #065-000-00959-5, $9.50

Pursuing Excellence: A Study of United States Fourth Grade Mathematics and Science Achievement in International Context
  GPO #065-000-01018-6, $4.75

Reading Literacy in the United States
  GPO #065-000-00875-1, $9

Reading Literacy in an International Perspective
  GPO #065-000-00966-8, $20

Some publications are produced annually: *The Condition of Education* in June; *Dropout Rates in the United States* in November; *Digest of Education Statistics* in November; and *Projections of Education Statistics* in December. Please check with the **Order Desk** at the **U.S. Government Printing Office** for information on the latest edition. The telephone number is **202-512-1800**. The U.S. Government Printing Office (GPO) order blank is on a later page. Most publications are available at: *http://nces.ed.gov/ncespub1.html*

Remedial Education at Higher Education Institutions in Fall 1995
GPO #065-000-00953-6, $9.50

Schools and Staffing in the United States: A Statistical Profile, 1993–94 Survey (SASS)—SASS by State
GPO #065-000-00889-1, $15

State Indicators in Education 1997
GPO #065-000-01079-8, $17

Students Selecting Stories: The Effects of Choice in Reading Assessment
GPO #065-000-01050-0, $8.50

Teacher Professionalism and Teacher Commitment: A Multilevel Analysis
GPO #065-000-00975-7, $4.50

Time Spent Teaching Core Academic Subjects in Elementary Schools
GPO #065-000-00980-3, $9.50

Urban Schools: The Challenge of Location and Poverty
GPO #065-000-00869-6, $14

Urban Schools: The Challenge of Location and Poverty Executive Summary
GPO #065-000-00870-0, $1

Vocational Education in the United States: The Early 1990s, Findings from
GPO #065-000-00963-3, $3.75

Youth Indicators: 1996
GPO #065-000-00898-0, $12

—Available from OERI—

Advanced Telecommunications in the U.S. Public Elementary and Secondary Schools, Fall 1996
NCES 97-944

Adult Civic Involvement in the United States
NCES 97-906

Are Limited English Proficient (LEP) Students Being Taught by Teachers with LEP Training?
NCES 97-907

"At-Risk" Eighth-Graders Four Years Later
NCES 95-736

Changes in Math Proficiency Between 8th and 10th Grades
NCES 93-455

Credentials and Tests in Teacher Hiring: What Do Districts Require?
NCES 97-592

Do Districts Enrolling High Percentages of Minority Students Spend Less?
NCES 97-917

Do Rich and Poor Districts Spend Alike?
NCES 97-916

Education Statistics on Disk, 1996 Edition
NCES 97-076

Findings From Vocational Education in the United States: The Early 1990s
NCES 97-391

How Much Time Do Public and Private School Teachers Spend in Their Work?
NCES 94-709

How Widespread is Site-Based Decisionmaking in the Public Schools?
NCES 97-908

Learning About Education Through Statistics
NCES 96-871

Mini-Digest of Education Statistics, 1996
NCES 97-379

Programs and Plans of the National Center for Education Statistics
NCES 95-133

Programs for Aspiring Principals: Which Principals Participated?
NCES 97-591

Public Attitudes Toward Secondary Education
NCES 97-595

Public Libraries in the United States, FY 1994
NCES 97-418

Public School Choice Programs, 1993-94
NCES 97-909

Schools Serving Family Needs: Extended-Day Programs in Public and Private Schools
NCES 97-590

Student Strategies To Avoid Harm at School
NCES 95-203

Student Victimization at School
NCES 95-204

Teachers' Sense of Community: How Do Public and Private Schools Compare?
NCES 97-910

Use of Public Library Services by Households in the United States: 1996
NCES 97-446

Who Reports Participation in Varsity Intercollegiate Sports at 4-Year Colleges?
NCES 97-911

Findings from the Condition of Education series:

The Social Context of Education: Findings from the Condition of Education 1997
NCES 97-981

Women in Mathematics and Science: Findings from the Condition of Education 1997
NCES 97-982

Public and Private Schools: How Do They Differ? Findings from the Condition of Education 1997
NCES 97-983

Postsecondary Persistence and Attainment: Findings from the Condition of Education 1997
NCES 97-984

Most publications are available on the U.S. Department of Education Web site: *http://nces.ed.gov/ncespub1.html*

Publications with GPO stock numbers and prices are available from the Government Printing Office. An order form follows these pages for your convenience.

For single copies of NCES publications that are available from OERI, contact the National Library of Education at **1–800–424–1616**.

ISBN 0-16-049343-9

 **United States Government INFORMATION**
PUBLICATIONS ★ PERIODICALS ★ ELECTRONIC PRODUCTS

Order Processing Code:
* 8138

*Charge your order.
It's easy!*

Please type or print.

Fax your orders to: (202) 512-2250
Phone your orders to: (202) 512-1800
Mail to: Superintendent of Documents
P.O. Box 371954
Pittsburgh, PA 15250-7954

Qty.	Stock Number	Title	Price Each	Total Price
				Total

The total cost of my order is $ _____. Price includes regular shipping and handling and is subject to change. International customers please add 25%.

_____ (Please type or print)
Company or personal name

_____
Additional address/attention line

_____
Street address

_____
City, State, Zip code

_____
Daytime phone including area code

_____
Purchase order number (optional)

Check method of payment:
❏ Check payable to Superintendent of Documents
❏ GPO Deposit Account ☐☐☐☐☐☐☐–☐
❏ VISA   ❏ MasterCard
☐☐☐☐☐☐☐☐☐☐☐☐☐☐☐☐
☐☐☐☐ (expiration date)   *Thank you for your order!*

_____
Authorizing signature   8/96

Important: Please include this completed order form with your payment. Photocopies of form are acceptable.